Pocket Oxford Italian Dictionary

Third Edition

Italian ---> English
English ---> Italian

Editors
Pat Bulhosen
Francesca Logi
Loredana Riu

W9-AQI-903

OXFORD
UNIVERSITY PRESS

OXFORD
UNIVERSITY PRESS

Great Clarendon Street, Oxford ox2 6DP

Oxford University Press is a department of the University of Oxford.
It furthers the University's objective of excellence in research, scholarship,
and education by publishing worldwide in

Oxford New York

Auckland CapeTown DaresSalaam HongKong Karachi
KualaLumpur Madrid Melbourne MexicoCity Nairobi
New Delhi Shanghai Taipei Toronto

With offices in

Argentina Austria Brazil Chile Czech Republic France Greece
Guatemala Hungary Italy Japan Poland Portugal Singapore
South Korea Switzerland Thailand Turkey Ukraine Vietnam

Oxford is a registered trade mark of Oxford University Press
in the UK and in certain other countries

Published in the United States
by Oxford University Press Inc., New York

© Oxford University Press 1997, 2000, 2004, 2006

The moral rights of the author have been asserted
Database right Oxford University Press (maker)

First published 1997
Reissued with new cover 2000
Second edition 2004
Third edition 2006

All rights reserved. No part of this publication may be reproduced,
stored in a retrieval system, or transmitted, in any form or by any means,
without the prior permission in writing of Oxford University Press,
or as expressly permitted by law, or under terms agreed with the appropriate
reprographics rights organization. Enquiries concerning reproduction
outside the scope of the above should be sent to the Rights Department,
Oxford University Press, at the address above

You must not circulate this book in any other binding or cover
and you must impose this same condition on any acquirer

British Library Cataloguing in Publication Data

Data available

Library of Congress Cataloging in Publication Data

Data available

Typeset in Nimrod, Arial and Meta by Morton Word Processing Ltd
Printed in Great Britain by Clays Ltd, Bungay, Suffolk

ISBN 0–19–861436–5
ISBN 978–0–19861436–4

10 9 8 7 6 5 4 3 2 1

Preface / Prefazione

This dictionary has been designed to meet the needs of students, tourists and all those who require quick and reliable answers to their translation questions. It provides clear guidance on selecting the most appropriate translation, illustrative examples to help with construction and usage, and precise information on grammar and style.

Focussing on everyday, idiomatic Italian and English, both spoken and written, this easy-to-use dictionary also offers generous treatment of business and computing vocabulary. Its up-to-the-minute coverage and wealth of accurate translations make it an ideal reference tool and study aid.

This third edition also offers a wide range of supplementary materials such as an extensively revised and updated A–Z of Italian life and culture, a calendar of festive days in Italy, a correspondence section containing model letters to help with personal and business letter-writing in Italian, a new section on text messaging, and a grammar summary.

Questo dizionario è stato creato per soddisfare le esigenze degli studenti, dei turisti e di tutti coloro che hanno bisogno di risposte rapide e sicure ai problemi di traduzione. Il lettore è guidato con chiarezza nella scelta del termine più appropriato, con esempi di uso della lingua e con indicazioni precise di grammatica e di stile.

Basandosi sull'uso contemporaneo dell'inglese e dell'italiano, scritto e parlato, questo dizionario di facile consultazione dedica particolare attenzione al lessico dell'informatica e degli affari. Attuale e aggiornato, con abbondante e precisa terminologia, rappresenta uno strumento di consultazione ideale e un valido sussidio didattico.

Questa terza edizione contiene anche un vasto repertorio di materiali aggiuntivi: un supplemento aggiornato su aspetti della civiltà britannica e statunitense, un calendario di giorni festivi nel Regno Unito e negli Stati Uniti, una sezione di corrispondenza che propone lettere-modello in inglese, una nuova sezione dedicata ai messaggi SMS, e note di grammatica.

List of contributors / Hanno collaborato

First edition/Prima edizione

Editors/Redazione
Debora Mazza
Jane Goldie
Donatella Boi
Francesca Logi
Peter Terrell
Sonia Tinagli-Baxter
Carla Zipoli

Allan Cameron
Michela Masci
Ilaria Panuccio

Copy editors/Segreteria di redazione
Alice Grandison
Mary Rigby
Daphne Trotter

Project management by/A cura di
LEXUS

Second edition/Seconda edizione

Pat Bulhosen
Francesca Logi
Loredana Riu

Third edition/Terza edizione

Joanna Brough
Stephen Curtis
Penelope Isaac
Francesca Logi

Contents / Indice

Introduction / Introduzione

Here is some basic information on the way the entries in this dictionary are organized.

A swung dash ~ is used to replace the headword within the entry.

Compounds are listed in alphabetical order. Remember this when looking for a word. The entry 'password', for example, is entered alphabetically – at some distance from the entry 'pass'. Likewise 'paintbrush' and 'paintpot' will have 'painter', 'pain threshold' and 'painting' entered in between.

Indicators are provided to guide the user to the best translation for a specific sense of a word. Types of indicator are:

field labels (see the list on p x), which indicate a general area of usage (commercial, computing, photography etc);

sense indicators, eg: **bore** *n* (*of gun*) calibro *m*; (*person*) seccatore, -trice *mf*;

typical subjects of verbs, eg: **bond** *vt* ‹*glue*› attaccare;

typical objects of verbs, placed after the translation of the verb, eg: **boost** *vt* stimolare ‹*sales*›; sollevare ‹*morale*›;

nouns that typically go together with certain adjectives, eg: **rich** *a* ricco; ‹*food*› pesante.

1, **2**, etc mean that the same word is being translated as a different part of speech, eg. **partition** **1** *n* ... **2** *vt* ...

A solid black square is used to

Ecco le informazioni essenziali su come sono organizzate le voci nel dizionario.

Un trattino ondulato ~ è utilizzato al posto del lemma all'interno della voce.

I vocaboli composti sono in ordine alfabetico. È importante ricordarlo quando si cerca la parola che interessa. La voce 'password', ad esempio, essendo in ordine alfabetico, compare a una certa distanza dopo la voce 'pass'. Per la stessa ragione fra 'paintbrush' and 'paintpot' compaiono 'painter', 'pain threshold' e 'painting'.

Degli indicatori vengono forniti per indirizzare l'utente verso la traduzione corrispondente al senso voluto di una parola. I tipi di indicatori sono:

etichette semantiche (vedi la lista a p x), indicanti l'ambito specifico in cui la parola viene generalmente usata in quel senso (commercio, informatica, fotografia ecc);

indicatori di significato, es.: **redazione** *nf* (*ufficio*) editorial office; (*di testi*) editing;

soggetti tipici di verbi, es.: **trovarsi** *vr* ‹*luogo*› be;

complementi oggetti tipici di verbi, collocati dopo la traduzione dello stesso verbo, es: **superare** *vt* overtake ‹*veicolo*›; pass ‹*esame*›;

sostantivi che ricorrono tipicamente con certi aggettivi, es.: **solare** *a* ‹*energia, raggi*› solar; ‹*crema*› sun.

1, **2**, ecc indicano che la stessa

• •

identify phrasal verbs, eg ■ **strip down** *vt* ... Phrasal verbs are listed in alphabetical order directly after the main verb. So 'strip down' comes after 'strip' and before 'strip cartoon'.

English pronunciation is given for the Italian user in the International Phonetic Alphabet (see p ix).

Italian stress is shown by a ' placed in front of the stressed syllable in a word.

Square brackets are used around parts of an expression which can be omitted without altering the sense.

parola viene tradotta come una diversa parte del discorso, es. **calcolatore** ① *a* ... ② *nm* ...

Un quadratino nero viene utilizzato per indicare i phrasal verbs, ad esempio: ■ **strip down** *vt* ... I phrasal verbs si trovano in ordine alfabetico immediatamente dopo il verbo principale. Così 'strip down' viene subito dopo 'strip' e subito prima di 'strip cartoon'.

La pronuncia inglese è data usando l'Alfabetico Fonetico Internazionale (vedi p ix).

L'accento tonico nelle parole italiane è indicato dal segno ' collocato davanti alla sillaba accentata.

Delle parentesi quadre racchiudono parti di espressioni che possono essere omesse senza alterazioni di senso.

• •

Proprietary terms / Marche depositate

• •

This dictionary includes some words which are, or are asserted to be, proprietary names or trademarks. Their inclusion does not imply that they have acquired for legal purposes a non-proprietary or general significance, nor is any other judgment implied concerning their legal status. In cases where the editor has some evidence that a word is used as a proprietary name or trademark this is indicated by the symbol ®, but no judgment concerning the legal status of such words is made or implied thereby.

Questo dizionario include alcune parole che sono o vengono considerate nomi di marche depositate. La loro presenza non implica che abbiano acquisito legalmente un significato generale, né si suggerisce alcun altro giudizio riguardo il loro stato giuridico. Qualora il redattore abbia trovato testimonianza dell'uso di una parola come marca depositata, questa è stata contrassegnata dal simbolo ®, ma nessun giudizio riguardo lo stato giuridico di tale parola viene espresso o suggerito in tal modo.

Pronunciation of Italian

Vowels

a	is broad like *a* in *father*: **casa**.
e	has two sounds: closed like *ey* in *they*: **sera**; open like *e* in *egg*: **sette**.
i	is like *ee* in *feet*: **venire**.
o	has two sounds: closed like *o* in *show*: **croma**; open like *o* in *dog*: **bocca**.
u	is like *oo* in *moon*: **luna**.

When two or more vowels come together each vowel is pronounced separately: **buono**; **baia**.

Consonants

b, **d**, **f**, **l**, **m**, **n**, **p**, **t**, **v** are pronounced as in English. When these are double they are sounded distinctly: **bello**.

c	before **a**, **o**, or **u** and before consonants is like *k* in *king*: **cane**.
	before **e** or **i** is like *ch* in *church*: **cena**.
ch	is also like *k* in *king*: **chiesa**.
g	before **a**, **o**, or **u** is hard like *g* in *got*: **gufo**.
	before **e** or **i** is like *j* in *jelly*: **gentile**.
gh	is like *g* in *gun*: **ghiaccio**.
gl	when followed by **a**, **e**, **o**, or **u** is like *gl* in *glass*: **gloria**.
gli	is like *lli* in *million*: **figlio**.
gn	is like *ni* in *onion*: **bagno**.
h	is silent.
ng	is like *ng* in *finger* (not *singer*): **ringraziare**.
r	is pronounced distinctly.
s	between two vowels is like *s* in *rose*: **riso**.
	at the beginning of a word it is like *s* in *soap*: **sapone**.
sc	before **e** or **i** is like *sh* in *shell*: **scienza**.
z	sounds like *ts* within a word: **fazione**; like *dz* at the beginning: **zoo**.

The stress is shown by the sign ˈ printed before the stressed syllable.

Pronuncia inglese

Simboli fonetici

Vocali e dittonghi

æ	bad	ʊ	put	aʊ	now
ɑ:	*ah*	u:	too	aʊə	flour
e	wet	ə	ago	ɔɪ	coin
ɪ	sit	ɜ:	work	ɪə	here
i:	see	eɪ	made	eə	hair
ɒ	got	əʊ	home	ʊə	poor
ɔ:	door	aɪ	five		
ʌ	cup	aɪə	fire		

Consonanti

b	boy	l	leg	t	ten
d	day	m	man	tʃ	chip
dʒ	page	n	new	θ	three
f	foot	ŋ	sing	ð	this
g	go	p	pen	v	verb
h	he	r	run	w	wet
j	yes	s	speak	z	his
k	coat	ʃ	ship	ʒ	pleasure

Note:
ˈ precede la sillaba accentata.
La vocale nasale in parole quali *nuance* è indicata nella trascrizione fonetica
come ɒ̃: njuːɒ̃s.

Abbreviations / Abbreviazioni

adjective	adj	aggettivo
abbreviation	abbr	abbreviazione
administration	Admin	amministrazione
adverb	adv	avverbio
aeronautics	Aeron	aeronautica
American	Am	americano
anatomy	Anat	anatomia
archaeology	Archaeol	archeologia
architecture	Archit	architettura
astrology,	Astr	astrologia,
astronomy		astronomia
attributive	attrib	attributo
automobiles	Auto	automobile
auxiliary	aux	ausiliario
biology	Biol	biologia
botany	Bot	botanica
British English	Br	inglese britannico
Chemistry	Chem	chimica
commerce	Comm	commercio
computers	Comput	informatica
conjunction	conj	congiunzione
cooking	Culin	cucina
definite article	def art	articolo
		determinativo
	ecc	eccetera
economics	Econ	economia
electricity	Electr	elettricità
et cetera	etc	
feminine	f	femminile
familiar	fam	familiare
figurative	fig	figurato
finance	Fin	finanza
formal	fml	formale
geography	Geog	geografia
geology	Geol	geologia
grammar	Gram	grammatica
humorous	hum	umoristico
indefinite article	indef art	articolo
		indeterminativo
interjection	int	interiezione
interrogative	inter	interrogativo
invariable	inv	invariabile
(no plural form)		
journalism	Journ	giornalismo
law	Jur	legge/giuridico
literary	liter	letterario
masculine	m	maschile
mathematics	Math	matematica
mechanics	Mech	meccanica
medicine	Med	medicina
meteorology	Metereol	meteorologia

masculine or feminine	mf	maschile o femminile
military	Mil	militare
music	Mus	musica
noun	n	sostantivo
nautical	Naut	nautica
old use	old	antiquato
pejorative	pej	peggiorativo
personal	pers	personale
photography	Phot	fotografia
physics	Phys	fisica
plural	pl	plurale
politics	Pol	politica
possessive	poss	possessivo
past participle	pp	participio passato
prefix	pref	prefisso
preposition	prep	preposizione
present tense	pres	presente
pronoun	pron	pronome
psychology	Psych	psicologia
past tense	pt	tempo passato
	qcno	qualcuno
	qcsa	qualcosa
proprietary term	®	marca depositata
rail	Rail	ferrovia
reflexive	refl	riflessivo
religion	Relig	religione
relative pronoun	rel pron	pronome relativo
somebody	sb	
school	Sch	scuola
singular	sg	singolare
slang	sl	gergo
something	sth	
suffix	suff	suffisso
technical	Techn	tecnico
telephone	Teleph	telefono
theatrical	Theat	teatrale
television	TV	televisione
typography	Typ	tipografia
university	Univ	università
auxiliary verb	v aux	verbo ausiliare
intransitive verb	vi	verbo intransitivo
reflexive verb	vr	verbo riflessivo
transitive verb	vt	verbo transitivo
transitive and intransitive	vt/i	verbo transitivo e intransitivo
vulgar	vulg	volgare
cultural equivalent	≈	equivalenza culturale

a (**ad** *before vowel*) *prep* to; (stato in luogo, tempo, età) at; (con mese, città) in; (mezzo, modo) by; **dire qualcosa a qualcuno** tell somebody something; **alle tre** at three o'clock; **a vent'anni** at the age of twenty; **a Natale** at Christmas; **a dicembre** in December; **ero al cinema** I was at the cinema; **vivo a Londra** I live in London; **a due a due** two by two; **a piedi** on *or* by foot; **maglia a maniche lunghe** long-sleeved sweater; **casa a tre piani** house with three floors; **giocare a tennis** play tennis; **50 km all'ora** 50 km an hour; **2 euro al chilo** 2 euros a kilo; **al mattino/alla sera** in the morning/evening; **a venti chilometri/due ore da qui** twenty kilometres/two hours away

'abaco *nm* abacus

a'bate *nm* abbot

abbacchia'mento *nm* fam dejection

abbacchi'ato *adj* fam dejected, downhearted

ab'bacchio *nm* [young] lamb. **abbacchio alla romana** spring lamb

abbaci'nare *vt* dazzle, blind; fig deceive

abbagli'ante ① *adj* dazzling ② *nm* headlight, high-beam Am; **mettere gli abbaglianti** put the headlights on full beam

abbagli'are *vt* dazzle

ab'baglio *nm* blunder; **prendere un** ∼ make a blunder

abbaia'mento *nm* barking

abbai'are *vi* bark

abba'ino *nm* dormer window; (mansarda) loft

abbando'nare *vt* abandon; leave ⟨luogo⟩; give up ⟨piani ecc⟩; ∼ **il campo** Mil desert in the face of the enemy

abbando'narsi *vr* let oneself go; ∼ **a** give oneself up to ⟨ricordi ecc⟩

abbando'nato *adj* abandoned

abban'dono *nm* abandoning; fig abandon; (stato) neglect

abbarbi'carsi *vr* ∼ **a** cling to

abbassa'mento *nm* (di temperatura, acqua, prezzi) drop

abbas'sare *vt* lower; turn down ⟨radio, TV⟩; ∼ **i fari** dip the headlights

abbas'sarsi *vr* stoop; ⟨sole ecc⟩ sink; fig demean oneself

ab'basso ① *adv* below ② *int* down with

abba'stanza *adv* enough; (alquanto) quite; ∼ **nuovo** newish; **ne ho** ∼! I've had enough!, I'm fed up!

ab'battere *vt* demolish; shoot down ⟨aereo⟩; put down ⟨animale⟩; topple ⟨regime⟩; (fig: demoralizzare) dishearten

ab'battersi *vr* (cadere) fall; fig be discouraged; ∼ **a terra/al suolo** fall down

abbatti'mento *nm* (morale) despondency

abbat'tuto *adj* despondent, down-in-the-mouth

abba'zia *nf* abbey

abbelli'mento *nm* embellishment

abbel'lire *vt* embellish

abbel'lirsi *vr* adorn oneself

abbeve'rare *vt* water

abbevera'toio *nm* drinking trough

abbiccì *nm inv* fig rudiments *pl*; **l'**∼ **di** the ABC of

abbi'ente *adj* well-to-do

abbi'etto *adj* despicable, abject

abbiglia'mento *nm* clothes *pl*; (industria) clothing industry, fam rag trade. **abbigliamento da bambino** children's wear. **abbigliamento da donna** ladies' wear. **abbigliamento per uomo** menswear. **abbigliamento sportivo** sportswear

abbigli'are *vt* dress

abbigli'arsi *vr* dress up

abbina'mento *nm* combining

abbi'nare *vt* combine; match ⟨colori⟩

abbindo'lare *vt* cheat

abbocca'mento *nm* interview; (conversazione) talk

abboc'care *vi* bite; ⟨tubi⟩ join; fig swallow the bait

abboc'cato *adj* ⟨vino⟩ fairly sweet

abbof'farsi = ABBUFFARSI

abbona'mento *nm* subscription; (ferroviario ecc) season-ticket; **fare l'**∼ take out a subscription. **abbonamento all'autobus** bus pass. **abbonamento mensile** monthly ticket. **abbonamento alla televisione** television licence

abbo'nare *vt* make a subscriber

abbo'narsi *vr* subscribe (**a** to); take out a season-ticket (**a** for) ⟨teatro, stadio⟩

abbo'nato, -a *nmf* subscriber

abbon'dante *adj* abundant; ⟨quantità⟩ copious; ⟨nevicata⟩ heavy; ⟨vestiario⟩ roomy; ∼ **di** abounding in

abbondante'mente *adv* ⟨*mangiare*⟩ copiously

abbon'danza *nf* abundance

abbon'dare *vi* abound

abbor'dabile *adj* ⟨*persona*⟩ approachable; ⟨*prezzo*⟩ reasonable

abbor'daggio *nm* Mil boarding

abbor'dare *vt* board ⟨*nave*⟩; approach ⟨*persona*⟩; (fam: attaccar bottone a) chat up; tackle ⟨*compito ecc*⟩

abbotto'nare *vt* button up

abbotto'nato *adj* fig tight-lipped

abbottona'tura *nf* [row of] buttons; con ∼ da donna/uomo ⟨*giacca*⟩ that buttons on the left/right

abboz'zare ① *vt* sketch [out] ⟨*disegno*⟩; draft ⟨*documento*⟩; ∼ un sorriso give a little smile
② *vi* fam (rassegnarsi) resign oneself

ab'bozzo *nm* (di disegno) sketch; (di documento) draft

abbracci'are *vt* embrace; hug, embrace ⟨*persona*⟩; take up ⟨*professione*⟩; fig include

ab'braccio *nm* hug

abbrevi'are *vt* shorten; (ridurre) curtail; abbreviate ⟨*parola*⟩

abbreviazi'one *nf* abbreviation

abbron'zante *nm* suntan lotion

abbron'zare *vt* bronze; tan ⟨*pelle*⟩

abbron'zarsi *vr* get a tan

abbron'zato *adj* tanned

abbronza'tura *nf* [sun]tan

abbrusto'lire *vt* toast; roast ⟨*caffè ecc*⟩

abbruti'mento *nm* brutalization

abbru'tire *vt* brutalize; ⟨*lavoro*⟩ stultify

abbru'tirsi *vr* become brutalized

abbuf'farsi *vr* fam stuff oneself

abbuf'fata *nf* fam blowout

abbuo'nare *vt* reduce; fig overlook ⟨*mancanza, errore*⟩

abbu'ono *nm* allowance; Sport handicap

abdi'care *vi* abdicate

abdicazi'one *nf* abdication

aber'rante *adj* aberrant

aberrazi'one *nf* aberration

abe'taia *nf* wood of fir trees

a'bete *nm* fir

abi'etto *adj* despicable

abiezi'one *nf* degradation

abige'ato *nm* Jur cattle-stealing, rustling

'abile *adj* able; (idoneo) fit; (astuto) clever

abilità *nf inv* ability; (idoneità) fitness; (astuzia) cleverness

abili'tante *adj* corso abilitante [officially recognized] training course

abili'tare *vt* qualify

abili'tato *adj* qualified

abilitazi'one *nf* qualification; (titolo) diploma

abil'mente *adv* ably; (con astuzia) cleverly

abis'sale *adj* abysmal

a'bisso *nm* abyss

abi'tabile *adj* inhabitable

abitabilità *nf* fitness for human habitation; licenza di ∼ document certifying that a building is fit for human habitation

abi'tacolo *nm* Auto passenger compartment

abi'tante *nmf* inhabitant

abi'tare *vi* live

abi'tato ① *adj* inhabited
② *nm* built-up area

abitazi'one *nf* house; crisi delle abitazioni housing problem

abi'tino *nm* Relig scapular

'abito *nm* (da donna) dress; (da uomo) suit; abiti *pl* clothes. **abito da ballo** ball dress. **abito da cerimonia** formal dress. **abito da cocktail** cocktail dress. **abito mentale** mentality. **'abito scuro'** (su inviti) 'black tie'. **abito da sera** evening dress. **abito talare** cassock. **abito da uomo** suit

abitu'ale *adj* usual, habitual

abitual'mente *adv* usually

abitu'are *vt* accustom

abitu'arsi *vr* ∼ a get used to

abitu'ato *adj* ∼ a used to

abitudi'nario, -a ① *adj* of fixed habits
② *nmf* person of fixed habits

abi'tudine *nf* habit; d'∼ usually; per ∼ out of habit; avere l'∼ di fare qualcosa be in the habit of doing something; abitudini *pl* customs

abiu'rare *vt* renounce

abla'tivo *nm* ablative

abluzi'oni *nfpl* fare le ∼ wash

abnegazi'one *nf* self-sacrifice

ab'norme *adj* abnormal

abo'lire *vt* abolish; repeal ⟨*legge*⟩

abolizi'one *nf* abolition; (di legge) repeal

abolizio'nismo *nm* abolitionism

abolizio'nista *adj & nmf* abolitionist

abomi'nevole *adj* abominable

abo'rigeno, -a *adj & nmf* aboriginal

abor'rire *vt* abhor

abor'tire *vi* miscarry; (volontariamente) have an abortion; fig fail

abor'tista *adj* pro-choice

abor'tivo *adj* abortive

a'borto *nm* miscarriage; (volontario) abortion

abrasi'one *nf* abrasion

abra'sivo *adj & nm* abrasive

abro'gare *vt* repeal

abroga'tivo *adj* **referendum abrogativo** referendum to repeal a law

abrogazi'one *nf* repeal

abruz'zese ① *adj* Abruzzi *attrib* ② *nmf* person from the Abruzzi ③ *nm* Abruzzi dialect

'abside *nf* apse

abu'lia *nf* apathy

a'bulico *adj* apathetic

abu'sare *vi* ~ di abuse; over-indulge in ⟨*alcol*⟩; (approfittare di) take advantage of; (violentare) rape

abusi'vismo *nm* large-scale abuse. **abusivismo edilizio** building without planning permission

abu'sivo *adj* illegal

a'buso *nm* abuse; 'ogni ~ sarà punito' 'penalty for misuse'. **abuso di confidenza** breach of confidence. **abusi** *pl* **sessuali** sexual abuse

a.C. *abbr* (**avanti Cristo**) BC

a'cacia *nf* acacia

'acaro *nm* Zool mite

'acca *nf* fam **non ho capito un'**~ I understood damn all

acca'demia *nf* academy. **Accademia di Belle Arti** Academy of Fine Arts. **accademia militare** military academy

acca'demico, -a ① *adj* academic ② *nmf* academician

acca'dere *vi* happen; **accada quel che accada** come what may

acca'duto *nm* event

accalappia'cani *nm inv* dog-catcher

accalappi'are *vt* catch; fig allure

accal'care *vt* cram together

accal'carsi *vr* crowd

accal'darsi *vr* get overheated; (per fatica) get hot; fig get excited

accal'dato *adj* overheated; (per fatica) hot; fig excited

accalo'rarsi *vr* get excited

accampa'mento *nm* camp

accam'pare *vt* fig put forth

accam'parsi *vr* camp

accani'mento *nm* tenacity; (odio) rage

acca'nirsi *vr* persist; (infierire) rage

accanita'mente *adv* ⟨*odiare*⟩ fiercely; ⟨*insistere*⟩ persistently; ⟨*lavorare*⟩ assiduously

acca'nito *adj* persistent; ⟨*odio*⟩ fierce; ⟨*fumatore*⟩ inveterate; ⟨*lavoratore*⟩ assiduous

ac'canto *adv* near; ~ a *prep* next to; **la ragazza della porta** ~ the girl next door

accanto'nare *vt* set aside; Mil billet

accaparra'mento *nm* hoarding; Comm cornering

accapar'rare *vt* hoard

accapar'rarsi *vr* grab; corner ⟨*mercato*⟩

accaparra|'tore, -trice *nmf* hoarder

accapigli'arsi *vr* scuffle; (litigare) squabble

accappa'toio *nm* bathrobe; (per spiaggia) beachrobe

accappo'nare *vt* **fare** ~ **la pelle a qualcuno** make somebody's flesh creep

accarez'zare *vt* caress, stroke; fig cherish

accartocci'are *vt* scrunch up

accartocci'arsi *vr* curl up

acca'sarsi *vr* get married

accasci'arsi *vr* flop down; fig lose heart

accata'stare *vt* pile up

accatti'vante *adj* beguiling

accatti'varsi *vr* ~ **le simpatie/la stima/l'affetto di qualcuno** gain somebody's sympathy/respect/affection

accatto'naggio *nm* begging

accat'tone, -a *nmf* beggar

accaval'lare *vt* cross ⟨*gambe*⟩

accaval'larsi *vr* pile up; fig overlap

acce'cante *adj* ⟨*luce*⟩ blinding

acce'care ① *vt* blind ② *vi* go blind

ac'cedere *vi* access; ~ a enter; (acconsentire) comply with; Comput access

accele'rare ① *vi* accelerate ② *vt* speed up, accelerate; ~ **il passo** quicken one's pace

accele'rata *nf* sudden acceleration

accele'rato *adj* rapid

accelera'tore *nm* accelerator. **acceleratore grafico** Comput graphics accelerator

accelerazi'one *nf* acceleration

ac'cendere *vt* light; turn on, switch on ⟨*luce, TV ecc*⟩; fig inflame; **ha da** ~? have you got a light?

ac'cendersi *vr* catch fire; (illuminarsi) light up; fig become inflamed; ⟨*TV, computer*⟩ turn on, switch on

accendi'gas *nm inv* gas lighter; (su cucina) automatic ignition

accen'dino *nm* lighter

accendi'sigari *nm inv* cigar-lighter

accen'nare ① *vt* indicate; hum ⟨*melodia*⟩; give a hint of ⟨*sorriso*⟩ ② *vi* ~ **a** beckon to; fig hint at; (far l'atto di) make as if to; **accenna a piovere** it looks like rain

ac'cenno *nm* gesture; (con il capo) nod; fig hint

accensi'one *nf* lighting; (di motore) ignition

accen'tare *vt* accent; (con accento tonico) stress

accentazi'one *nf* accentuation

ac'cento *nm* accent; (tonico) stress. **accento acuto** acute [accent]. **accento circonflesso** circumflex [accent]. **accento grave** grave [accent]

accentra'mento *nm* centralizing

accen'trare *vt* centralize

accentra'tore *adj* ⟨*persona*⟩ who refuses to delegate; ⟨*politica*⟩ of centralization

accentu'are *vt* accentuate

accentu'arsi *vr* become more noticeable

accentu'ato *adj* marked

accerchia'mento *nm* surrounding

accerchi'are *vt* surround

accerchi'ato *adj* surrounded

accer'tabile *adj* ascertainable

accerta'mento *nm* check; **accertamenti** *pl* [medici] tests

accer'tare *vt* ascertain; (controllare) check; assess ⟨*reddito*⟩

ac'ceso *adj* lighted; ⟨*radio, TV ecc*⟩ on; ⟨*colore*⟩ bright

acces'sibile *adj* accessible; ⟨*persona*⟩ approachable; ⟨*spesa*⟩ reasonable

ac'cesso *nm* access; (Med: di rabbia) fit; 'vietato l'∼' 'no entry'; '∼ riservato a ...' 'access restricted to ...'. **accesso diretto** Comput direct access. **accesso disabili** wheelchair access. **accesso a Internet** Comput Internet access. **accesso multiplo** Comput multi-access. **accesso remoto** Comput remote access

accessori'ato *adj* accessorized

acces'sorio ①*adj* accessory; (secondario) of secondary importance ②*nm* accessory; **accessori** *pl* (rifiniture) fittings. **accessori** *pl* **per il bagno** bathroom fittings. **accessori** *pl* **moda** fashion accessories

ac'cetta *nf* hatchet

accet'tabile *adj* acceptable

accet'tare *vt* accept; (aderire a) agree to

accettazi'one *nf* acceptance; (luogo) reception; [banco] **accettazione** check-in [desk]; **accettazione** [bagagli] check-in

ac'cetto *adj* agreeable; **essere bene** ∼ be very welcome

accezi'one *nf* meaning

acchiap'pare *vt* catch

+acchiotto *suff* **lupacchiotto** *nm* wolf cub; (affettuoso) baby wolf; **orsacchiotto** *nm* teddy bear; **fessacchiotto** *nm* nitwit

ac'chito *nm* **di primo** ∼ at first

acciac'care *vt* crush; fig prostrate

acciac'cato, -a *adj* **essere** ∼ ache all over

acci'acco *nm* infirmity; **acciacchi** (*pl*: afflizioni) aches and pains

acciaie'ria *nf* steelworks

acci'aio *nm* steel. **acciaio inossidabile** stainless steel

acciambel'larsi *vr* curl up

acciden'tale *adj* accidental

accidental'mente *adv* accidentally

acciden'tato *adj* ⟨*terreno*⟩ uneven

acci'dente *nm* accident; Med stroke; **non capisce/non vede un** ∼ fam he doesn't understand/can't see a damn thing; **mandare un** ∼ **a qualcuno** fam tell somebody to go to hell

acci'denti *int* fam damn!; ∼ **a te!** damn you!, blast you!

ac'cidia *nf* sloth

accigli'arsi *vr* frown

accigli'ato *adj* frowning

ac'cingersi *vr* ∼ **a** be about to

+accio *suff* **erbaccia** *nf* weed; **donnaccia** *nf* tart; **faticaccia** *nf* hard slog; **lavoraccio** *nm* (lavoro faticoso) helluva job fam; (lavoro malfatto) botched job; **fattaccio** *nm* hum foul deed; **parolaccia** *nf* swear word; **avaraccio** *nm* skinflint

acciotto'lato *nm* cobbled paving, cobblestones *pl*

acci'picchia *int* good Lord!

acciuf'fare *vt* catch

acci'uga *nf* anchovy

accla'mare *vt* applaud; (eleggere) acclaim

acclamazi'one *nf* applause

acclima'tare *vt* acclimatize

acclima'tarsi *vr* get acclimatized

acclimatazi'one *nf* acclimatization

ac'cludere *vt* enclose

ac'cluso *adj* enclosed

accocco'larsi *vr* squat

acco'darsi *vr* tag along

accogli'ente *adj* welcoming; (confortevole) cosy

accogli'enza *nf* welcome

ac'cogliere *vt* receive; (con piacere) welcome; (contenere) hold

accol'lare *vt* ∼ **qualcosa a qualcuno** fig saddle somebody with something

accol'larsi *vr* take on ⟨*responsabilità, debiti, doveri*⟩

accol'lato *adj* ⟨*maglia*⟩ high-necked

accoltel'lare *vt* knife

accoman'dante *nmf* Jur sleeping partner

accomanda'tario, -a *nmf* Jur general partner

accoman'dita *nf* Jur limited partnership. **accomandita per azioni** limited partnership based on shares

accomia'tare *vt* dismiss

accomia'tarsi *vr* take one's leave (**da** of)

accomoda'mento *nm* arrangement

accomo'dante *adj* accommodating

accomo'dare *vt* (riparare) mend; (disporre) arrange

accomo'darsi *vr* make oneself at home; **si accomodi!** come in!; (si sieda) take a seat!

accompagna'mento *nm* accompaniment; (seguito) retinue

accompa'gnare *vt* accompany; ∼ qualcuno a casa see somebody home; ∼ qualcuno alla porta show somebody to the door; ∼ qualcuno con lo sguardo follow somebody with one's eyes

accompa'gnarsi *vr* ⟨cibi, colori ecc⟩ go [well] together; ∼ con *o* a qualcuno accompany somebody

accompagna|'tore, -trice *nmf* companion; (di comitiva) escort; Mus accompanist. ∼ turistico tour guide

accomu'nare *vt* pool

acconci'are *vt* arrange

acconci'arsi *vr* do one's hair

acconcia'tura *nf* hairstyle; (ornamento) headdress; 'acconciature' 'ladies' hairdresser'

accondiscen'dente *adj* too obliging

accondiscen'denza *nf* excessive desire to please

accondi'scendere *vi* ∼ a condescend to; comply with ⟨desiderio⟩; (acconsentire) consent to

acconsen'tire *vi* consent

acconten'tare *vt* satisfy

acconten'tarsi *vr* be content (**di** with)

ac'conto *nm* deposit; **in** ∼ on account; **lasciare un** ∼ leave a deposit. **acconto di dividendo** interim dividend

accop'pare *vt* fam bump off

accoppia'mento *nm* coupling; (di animali) mating

accoppi'are *vt* couple; mate ⟨animali⟩

accoppi'arsi *vr* pair off; ⟨animali⟩ mate

accoppi'ata *nf* (scommessa) bet placed on two horses for first and second place; **sono una strana** ∼ they make strange bedfellows; **accoppiata vincente** fig winning combination

accoppia'tore *nm* **accoppiatore acustico** Comput acoustic coupler

acco'rato *adj* sorrowful

accorci'are *vt* shorten

accorci'arsi *vr* get shorter

accor'dare *vt* concede; match ⟨colori ecc⟩; Mus tune

accor'darsi *vr* agree

accorda|'tore, -trice *nmf* Mus tuner

ac'cordo *nm* agreement; Mus chord; (armonia) harmony; **andare d'**∼ get on well; **d'**∼**!** agreed!; **essere d'**∼ agree; **in** ∼ **con** in collusion with; **prendere accordi con qualcuno** make arrangements with somebody. **accordo collettivo** joint agreement

ac'corgersi *vr* ∼ **di** notice; (capire) realize

accorgi'mento *nm* shrewdness; (espediente) device

accorpa'mento *nm* amalgamation

accor'pare *vt* amalgamate

ac'correre *vi* hasten

accorta'mente *adv* astutely

accor'tezza *nf* (previdenza) forethought

ac'corto *adj* shrewd; **mal** ∼ incautious

accosta'mento *nm* (di colori) combination

acco'stare *vt* draw close to; approach ⟨persona⟩; put ajar ⟨porta ecc⟩

acco'starsi *vr* ∼ **a** come near to

accovacci'arsi *vr* crouch, squat down

accovacci'ato *adj* squatting

accoz'zaglia *nf* jumble; (di persone) mob

accoz'zare *vt* ∼ **colori** mix colours that clash

accredi'tabile *adj* reliable

accredita'mento *nm* credit. **accreditamento tramite bancogiro** Bank Giro Credit

accredi'tare *vt* confirm ⟨notizia⟩; Comm credit

accredi'tato *adj* accredited; ⟨notizia⟩ reliable

ac'crescere *vt* increase

ac'crescersi *vr* grow larger

accresci'mento *nm* increase

accresci'tivo *adj* augmentative

accucci'arsi *vr* ⟨cane⟩ lie down; ⟨persona⟩ crouch

accu'dire *vi* ∼ **a** attend to

accumu'lare *vt* accumulate

accumu'larsi *vr* pile up, accumulate

accumula'tore *nm* accumulator; Auto, Comput battery

accumulazi'one *nf* accumulation

ac'cumulo *nm* (di merce) build-up

accurata'mente *adv* carefully

accura'tezza *nf* care

accu'rato *adj* careful

ac'cusa *nf* accusation; Jur charge; **essere in stato di** ∼ Jur have been charged; **mettere qualcuno sotto** ∼ Jur charge somebody; **la Pubblica Accusa** Jur the public prosecutor

accu'sare *vt* accuse; Jur charge; complain of ⟨dolore⟩; ∼ **ricevuta di** Comm acknowledge receipt of

accusa'tivo nm Gram accusative

accu'sato, -a nmf accused

accusa'tore ⟨1⟩ adj accusing ⟨2⟩ nm Jur prosecutor

a'cerbo adj sharp; (non maturo) unripe

'acero nm maple

a'cerrimo adj implacable

ace'tato nm acetate

a'ceto nm vinegar.**aceto di vino** wine vinegar

ace'tone nm nail polish remover

ace'tosa nf Culin [edible] sorrel

aceto'sella nf Bot sorrel

A.C.I. nf abbr (**Automobile Club d'Italia**) Italian Automobile Association, ≈ AAA Am, ≈ RAC Br

acidità nf acidity. **acidità di stomaco** acid stomach

'acido ⟨1⟩ adj acid; (persona) sour ⟨2⟩ nm acid. ~ **cloridrico** hydrochloric acid

a'cidulo adj slightly sour

'acino nm berry; (chicco) grape

'acme nf acme

'acne nf acne

'acqua nf water; fare ~ Naut leak; ~ **in bocca!** fig mum's the word!; **avere l'~ alla gola, essere con l'~ alla gola** fig be pushed for time; **ho fatto un buco nell'~** fig I had no luck whatsoever; **in cattive acque** in deep water; **navigare in cattive acque** be in financial difficulties. **acqua calda** hot water. **acqua di Colonia** eau de Cologne. **acqua corrente** running water. **acqua dolce** fresh water. **acqua minerale** mineral water. **acqua minerale gassata** fizzy mineral water. **acqua naturale** still mineral water. **acqua potabile** drinking water. **acqua del rubinetto** tap water. **acqua salata** salt water. **acqua saponata** suds. **acqua tonica** tonic water

acqua'forte nf etching

acqua'gym nf aquarobics

ac'quaio nm sink

acquama'rina adj aquamarine

acquapark nm inv waterpark

acqua'plano nm hydroplane

acqua'ragia nf white spirit

acqua'rello nm watercolour

a'cquario nm aquarium, fish tank; Astr Aquarius

acquartie'rare vt Mil billet

acqua'santa nf holy water

acquasanti'era nf font

acqua'scivolo nm water slide

acqua'scooter nm inv water-scooter

a'cquata nf fam downpour

a'cquatico adj aquatic; **sport acquatico** water sport

acquat'tarsi vr crouch

acqua'vite nf brandy

acquaz'zone nm downpour

acque'dotto nm aqueduct

'acqueo adj vapore ~ steam, water vapour

acque'rello nm watercolour

acquicol'tura nf aquaculture

acquie'scente adj acquiescent

acquie'tare vt appease; calm ⟨dolore⟩

acquie'tarsi vr calm down

acqui'rente nmf purchaser

acqui'sire vt acquire

acqui'sito adj acquired

acquisizi'one nf attainment

acqui'stare vt purchase; (ottenere) acquire; ~ **in** ⟨prestigio, bellezza⟩ gain in

a'cquisto nm purchase; **uscire per acquisti** go shopping; **fare acquisti** shop; **ufficio acquisti** purchasing department. **acquisto rateale** hire purchase, HP, installment plan Am; **acquisto d'impulso** impulse buy. **acquisto a termine** Fin forward buying

acqui'trino nm marsh

acquo'lina nf far venire l'~ **in bocca a qualcuno** make somebody's mouth water; **ho l'~ in bocca** my mouth is watering

a'cquoso adj watery

'acre adj acrid; (al gusto) sour; fig harsh

a'credine nf acridness; (al gusto) sourness; fig harshness

acre'mente adv acridly

a'crilico nm acrylic

a'critico adj acritical

a'crobata nmf acrobat

acro'batico adj acrobatic

acroba'zia nf acrobatics pl

acroba'zie nfpl acrobatics; **fare** ~ fig do acrobatics

a'cronimo nm acronym

a'cropoli nf acropolis

acu'ire vt sharpen

acu'irsi vr become more intense

a'culeo nm sting; Bot prickle

a'cume nm acumen

acumi'nato adj pointed

a'custica nf acoustics pl

acustica'mente adv acoustically

a'custico adj acoustic

acuta'mente adv shrewdly

acu'tezza nf acuteness; fig shrewdness; (di suoni) shrillness

acutiz'zare vt aggravate (dolore)

acutiz'zarsi vr become worse

a'cuto ⟨1⟩ adj sharp; ⟨suono⟩ shrill; ⟨freddo⟩ intense; Gram, Math, Med acute ⟨2⟩ nm Mus high note

ad (*before vowel*) *prep* = A

A.D. *abbr* Pol (**Alleanza Democratica**) Democratic Alliance

adagi'are *vt* lay down

adagi'arsi *vr* lie down

a'dagio [1] *adv* slowly

[2] *nm* Mus adagio; (proverbio) adage

ada'mitico *adj* in costume ∼ in one's birthday suit, stark naked

adat'tabile *adj* adaptable

adattabilità *nf* adaptability

adatta'mento *nm* adaptation; **avere spirito di ∼** be adaptable. **adattamento cinematografico** film adaptation, adaptation for the cinema

adat'tare *vt* adapt; (aggiustare) fit

adat'tarsi *vr* adapt

adatta'tore *nm* adaptor

a'datto *adj* suitable (**a** for); (giusto) right

addì *adv* ∼ **15 settembre 1995** on 15th September 1995

addebita'mento *nm* debit. **addebitamento diretto** direct debit

addebi'tare *vt* debit; fig ascribe ‹colpa›

ad'debito *nm* charge

addensa'mento *nm* thickening; (di persone) gathering

adden'sare *vt* thicken

adden'sarsi *vr* thicken; (affollarsi) gather

adden'tare *vt* bite

adden'trarsi *vr* penetrate

ad'dentro *adv* deeply; **essere ∼ in** be in on

addestra'mento *nm* training. **addestramento iniziale** basic training

adde'strare *vt* train

adde'strarsi *vr* train

addestra|'tore, -trice *nmf* trainer

ad'detto, -a [1] *adj* assigned

[2] *nmf* employee; (diplomatico) attaché. **adetti** *pl* **ai lavori** persons involved in the work; 'vietato l'ingresso ai non addetti ai lavori' 'staff only'. **addetto commerciale** salesman. **addetto culturale** cultural attaché. **addetto stampa** information officer, press officer. **addetto ai traslochi** removal man

addi'accio *nm* **dormire all'∼** sleep in the open

addi'etro *adv* (indietro) back; (nel passato) before

ad'dio *nm* & *int* goodbye. **addio al celibato** stag night, stag party. **addio al nubilato** hen night. **cena d'addio** farewell dinner

addirit'tura *adv* (perfino) even; (assolutamente) absolutely; ∼! really!

ad'dirsi *vr* ∼ **a** suit

addi'tare *vt* point at; (per identificare) point out; fig point to

addi'tivo *adj* & *nm* additive

addizio'nale [1] *adj* additional

[2] *nf* (imposta) surtax

addizional'mente *adv* additionally

addizio'nare *vt* add [up]

addiziona'trice *nf* adding machine

addizi'one *nf* addition

addob'bare *vt* decorate

ad'dobbo *nm* decoration

addol'cire *vt* sweeten; tone down ‹colore›; fig soften

addol'cirsi *vr* fig mellow

addolo'rare *vt* grieve

addolo'rarsi *vr* be upset (**per** by)

addolo'rato *adj* pained, distressed

ad'dome *nm* abdomen

addomesti'care *vt* tame

addomestica|tore, -trice *nmf* tamer

addomi'nale [1] *adj* abdominal

[2] *nmpl* addominali abdominals

addormen'tare *vt* put to sleep

addormen'tarsi *vr* go to sleep

addormen'tato *adj* asleep; fig slow

addos'sare *vt* ∼ **a** (appoggiare) lean against; (attribuire) lay on

addos'sarsi *vr* (ammassarsi) crowd; shoulder ‹responsabilità ecc›

ad'dosso *adv* on; ∼ **a** *prep* on; (molto vicino) right next to; **andare/venire ∼ a** qualcuno run into somebody; **mettere gli occhi ∼ a qualcuno/qualcosa** hanker after somebody/something; **non mettermi le mani ∼!** keep your hands off me!; **stare ∼ a qualcuno** fig be on somebody's back; **farsela ∼** (fam: bisogni corporali) dirty oneself; (pipì) wet oneself

ad'durre *vt* produce ‹prova, documento›; give ‹pretesto, esempio›

adegua'mento *nm* adjustment

adegu'are *vt* adjust

adegu'arsi *vr* conform

adeguata'mente *adv* suitably

adegua'tezza *nf* suitability

adegu'ato *adj* suitable; ∼ **a** suited to, suitable for

a'dempiere *vt* fulfil

adempi'mento *nm* fulfilment

adem'pire *vt* fulfil

ade'noidi *nfpl* adenoids

a'depto, -a *nmf* adherent

ade'rente [1] *adj* adhesive; ‹vestito› tight

[2] *nmf* follower

ade'renza *nf* adhesion; **aderenze** *pl* connections

ade'rire *vi* ∼ **a** stick to, adhere to; support ‹sciopero, petizione›; agree to ‹richiesta›

adesca'mento *nm* Jur soliciting
ade'scare *vt* bait; fig entice
adesca'trice *nf* fille de joie
adesi'one *nf* adhesion; fig agreement
ade'sivo ① *adj* adhesive
　② *nm* sticker; Auto bumper sticker
a'desso *adv* now; (poco fa) just now; (tra poco) any moment now; **da ~ in poi** from now on; **per ~** for the moment; **fino ~** up till now
adia'cente *adj* adjacent; **~ a** next to
adia'cenze *nfpl* adjacent areas
adi'bire *vt* **~ a** put to use as
'adipe *nm* adipose tissue
adi'poso *adj* adipose
adi'rarsi *vr* get irate
adi'rato *adj* irate
a'dire *vt* resort to; **~ le vie legali** take legal proceedings; **~ la successione** Jur take possession of an inheritance
'adito *nm* dare **~ a** give rise to
ADM *nfpl abbr* (**Armi di Distruzione di Massa**) WMD
adocchi'are *vt* eye; (con desiderio) covet
adole'scente *adj & nmf* adolescent *attrib*
adole'scenza *nf* adolescence
adolescenzi'ale *adj* adolescent
adombra'mento *nm* darkening
adom'brare *vt* darken; fig veil
adom'brarsi *vr* (offendersi) take offence
adope'rare *vt* use
adope'rarsi *vr* take trouble
ado'rabile *adj* adorable
ado'rare *vt* adore
adorazi'one *nf* adoration; **in ~** adoring
ador'nare *vt* adorn
a'dorno *adj* adorned (**di** with)
adot'tare *vt* adopt
adot'tivo *adj* adoptive
adozi'one *nf* adoption
adrena'lina *nf* adrenalin
adri'atico ① *adj* Adriatic
　② *nm* **l'Adriatico** the Adriatic
adu'lare *vt* flatter
adula|'tore, -trice *nmf* flatterer
adula'torio *adj* sycophantic
adulazi'one *nf* flattery
a'dultera *nf* adulteress
adulte'rare *vt* adulterate
adulte'rato *adj* adulterated
adulte'rino *adj* adulterous
adul'terio *nm* adultery
a'dultero ① *adj* adulterous
　② *nm* adulterer
a'dulto, -a *adj & nmf* adult; (maturo) mature

adu'nanza *nf* assembly
adu'nare *vt* gather
adu'nata *nf* Mil parade
a'dunco *adj* hooked
adunghi'are *vt* claw
ae'rare *vt* air ⟨*stanza*⟩
aera'tore *nm* ventilator
aerazi'one *nf* ventilation
a'ereo ① *adj* aerial; (dell'aviazione) air *attrib*
　② *nm* aeroplane, plane; **andare in ~** fly. **aereo da carico** cargo plane. **aereo da guerra** warplane. **aereo di linea** airliner. **aereo navetta** shuttle. **aereo a reazione** jet [plane]
ae'robica *nf* aerobics
ae'robico *adj* aerobic
aerodi'namica *nf* aerodynamics *sg*
aerodi'namico *adj* aerodynamic
aero'grafo *nm* airbrush
aero'gramma *nm* aerogram[me]
aero'linea *nf* airline
aero'mobile *nm* aircraft
aeromo'dello *nm* model aircraft
aero'nautica *nf* aeronautics; Mil Air Force
aero'nautico *adj* aeronautical
aerona'vale *adj* air and sea *attrib*
aero'plano *nm* aeroplane
aero'porto *nm* airport
aeroportu'ale *adj* airport *attrib*
aero'scalo *nm* cargo and servicing area
aero'sol *nm inv* aerosol. **apparecchio per aerosol** vaporizer
aerospazi'ale *adj* aerospace *attrib*
aero'statico *adj* **pallone aerostatico** aerostat
ae'rostato *nm* aerostat
aerostazi'one *nf* air terminal
aerosti'ere *nm* balloonist
aero'via *nf* air corridor
A.F. *abbr* (**alta frequenza**) HF
'afa *nf* sultriness
af'fabile *adj* affable
affabilità *nf* affability
affaccen'darsi *vr* busy oneself (**a** with)
affacci'arsi *vr* show oneself; **~ alla finestra** appear at the window
affacen'dato *adj* busy
affa'mare *vt* starve [out]
affa'mato *adj* starving
affan'nare *vt* leave breathless
affan'narsi *vr* busy oneself; (agitarsi) get worked up
affan'nato *adj* breathless; **dal respiro ~** wheezy
af'fanno *nm* breathlessness; fig worry; **essere in ~ per** be anxious about

affannosa'mente *adv* breathlessly

affan'noso *adj* exhausting; **respiro** ∼ heavy breathing

af'fare *nm* matter; (occasione) bargain; Comm transaction, deal; **pensa agli affari tuoi** mind your own business; **non sono affari tuoi** fam it's none of your business; **fare affari d'oro** have a field day; **affari** *pl* business; **d'affari** ⟨uomo, cena, viaggio⟩ business; **affari** *pl* **esteri** foreign affairs; **ministro degli affari esteri** Foreign Secretary Br, Secretary of State Am

affa'rismo *nm* pej wheeling and dealing

affa'rista *nmf* wheeler-dealer

affasci'nante *adj* fascinating; ⟨persona, sorriso⟩ bewitching

affasci'nare *vt* bewitch; fig charm

affastel'lare *vt* tie up in bundles

affatica'mento *nm* fatigue

affati'care *vt* tire; (sfinire) exhaust

affati'carsi *vr* tire oneself out; (affannarsi) strive

affati'cato *adj* fatigued, suffering from fatigue; ∼ **dal troppo lavoro** overworked

af'fatto *adv* completely; **non ... ∼** not ... at all; **niente ∼!** not at all!

affer'mare *vt* affirm; (sostenere) assert

affer'marsi *vr* establish oneself

affermativa'mente *adv* in the affirmative

afferma'tivo *adj* affirmative

affer'mato *adj* established

affermazi'one *nf* assertion; (successo) achievement

affer'rare *vt* seize; catch ⟨oggetto⟩; (capire) grasp; ∼ **al volo** fig be quick on the uptake

affer'rarsi *vr* ∼ **a** a grasp at, clutch at

affet'tare *vt* slice; (ostentare) affect

affet'tato ① *adj* sliced; ⟨sorriso, maniere⟩ affected
② *nm* cold meat, sliced meat

affetta'trice *nf* bacon-slicer

affettazi'one *nf* affectation

affet'tivo *adj* affective; **rapporto affettivo** emotional tie

af'fetto[1] *nm* affection; **con ∼** affectionately; **gli affetti familiari** family ties

af'fetto[2] *adj* ∼ **da** suffering from

affettuosa'mente *adv* affectionately

affettuosi'tà *nf inv* (gesto) affectionate gesture

affettu'oso *adj* affectionate

affezio'narsi *vr* ∼ **a** grow fond of

affezio'nato *adj* devoted, attached (**a** to)

affezi'one *nf* affection; Med ailment

affian'care *vt* put side by side; Mil flank; fig support

affian'carsi *vr* come side by side; fig stand together, stand shoulder to shoulder; ∼ **a qualcuno** fig help somebody out

affiata'mento *nm* harmony

affia'tarsi *vr* get on well together

affia'tato *adj* close-knit; **una coppia affiatata** a very close couple

affibbi'are *vt* ∼ **qualcosa a qualcuno** saddle somebody with something; ∼ **un pugno a qualcuno** let fly at somebody

affi'dabile *adj* reliable, dependable

affidabilità *nf* reliability, dependability

affida'mento *nm* (Jur: dei minori) custody; **fare ∼ su qualcuno** rely on somebody; **non dare ∼ (a qualcuno)** not inspire confidence (in somebody)

affi'dare *vt* entrust

affi'darsi *vr* ∼ **a** rely on

affida'tario *adj* (famiglia) foster

af'fido *nm* **un bambino in ∼** a foster child

affievoli'mento *nm* weakening

affievo'lirsi *vr* grow weak

af'figgere *vt* affix

affilacol'telli *nm inv* knife sharpener

affi'lare *vt* sharpen

affili'are *vt* affiliate

affili'arsi *vt* become affiliated

affiliazi'one *nf* affiliation

affi'nare *vt* sharpen; (perfezionare) refine

affinché *conj* so that, in order that

af'fine *adj* similar

affinità *nf inv* affinity

affiora'mento *nm* emergence; Naut surfacing

affio'rare *vi* emerge; fig come to light

affissi'one *nf* bill-posting; **'divieto di ∼'** 'stick no bills'

af'fisso *nm* bill; Gram affix

affitta'camere ① *nm inv* landlord
② *nf inv* landlady

affit'tare *vt* (dare in affitto) let; (prendere in affitto) rent. **affittasi** to let, for rent

af'fitto *nm* rent; **contratto d'∼** lease; **dare in ∼** let; **prendere in ∼** rent

affittu'ario, -a *nmf* Jur lessee

af'fliggere *vt* torment

af'fliggersi *vr* distress oneself

af'flitto *adj* distressed

afflizi'one *nf* distress; fig affliction

afflosci'are *vt* **la pioggia ha afflosciato le foglie** the rain has made the leaves go all limp

afflosci'arsi *vr* become floppy; (accasciarsi) flop down

afflu'ente *adj* & *nm* tributary

afflu'enza *nf* flow; (di gente) crowd

afflu'ire *vi* flow; fig pour in

af'flusso nm influx

affoga'mento nm drowning

affo'gare vt/i drown; Culin poach; ~ **in** fig be swamped with

affo'garsi vr (suicidarsi) drown oneself

affo'gato ① adj ⟨persona⟩ drowned; ⟨uova⟩ poached
② nm **affogato al caffè** ice cream with hot espresso poured over it

affolla'mento nm crowd

affol'lare vt crowd

affol'larsi vr crowd

affol'lato adj crowded

affonda'mento nm sinking

affon'dare vt/i sink

affon'darsi vr sink

affossa'mento nm (avvallamento) pothole; fig burial

affran'care vt redeem ⟨bene⟩; stamp ⟨lettera⟩; free ⟨schiavo⟩

affran'carsi vr free oneself

affran'cato adj ⟨lettera⟩ stamped; ⟨schiavo⟩ freed; già ~ ⟨busta⟩ prepaid

affranca'trice nf franking machine, franker

affranca'tura nf stamping; (di spedizione) postage. **affrancatura a carico del destinatario** freepost. **affrancatura per l'estero** postage abroad

af'franto adj prostrate with grief, grief-stricken; (esausto) worn out

affre'scare vt paint a fresco on

af'fresco nm fresco

affret'tare vt speed up

affret'tarsi vr hurry

affretta'mente adv hastily

affret'tato adj ⟨passo⟩ fast; ⟨decisione⟩ hasty; ⟨lavoro⟩ rushed

affron'tare vt face; confront ⟨nemico⟩; meet ⟨spese⟩

affron'tarsi vr clash

af'fronto nm affront, insult; **fare un ~ a qualcuno** insult somebody

affumi'care vt fill with smoke; Culin smoke

affumi'cato adj ⟨prosciutto, formaggio⟩ smoked; ⟨lenti, vetro⟩ tinted

affuso'lare vt taper [off]

affuso'lato adj tapering

Af'ganistan nm Afghanistan

af'gano adj & nmf Afghani, Afghan

AFI nm abbr (**Alfabeto Fonetico Internazionale**) IPA

aficio'nado, -**a** nmf aficionado

'afide nm aphid

'afono adj (rauco) hoarse

afo'risma nm aphorism

a'foso adj sultry

'Africa nf Africa. **Africa orientale** East Africa. **Africa nera** Black Africa. **Africa del Nord** North Africa

afri'cano, -**a** adj & nmf African

afri'kaans nm Afrikaans

afroameri'cano, -**a** adj & nmf Afro-American

afroasi'atico adj Afro-Asian

afroca'ribico adj Afro-Caribbean

afrocu'bano adj Afro-Cuban

afrodi'siaco adj & nm aphrodisiac

a'genda nf diary. **agenda elettronica** personal organizer, electronic organizer; **agenda da tavolo** desk diary

agen'dina nf pocket-diary

a'gente nm agent; **agenti** pl **atmosferici** atmospheric agents. **agente di cambio** stockbroker. **agente di custodia** prison warder. **agente del fisco** assessor. **agente immobiliare** estate agent, realtor Am. **agente marittimo** shipping agent. **agente di polizia** police officer. **agente segreto** secret agent. **agente teatrale** theatrical agent; (di compagnia) impresario. **agente di viaggio** travel agent

agen'zia nf agency; (filiale) branch office; (di banca) branch. **agenzia di collocamento** employment exchange. **agenzia immobiliare** estate agency, realtor Am. **agenzia matrimoniale** dating agency. **agenzia pubblicitaria** advertising agency. **agenzia di recupero crediti** debt collection agency. **agenzia di stampa** news agency, press agency. **agenzia di viaggi** travel agency

agevo'lare vt facilitate

agevolazi'one nf facilitation. **agevolazioni** pl **fiscali** tax breaks

a'gevole adj easy; ⟨strada⟩ smooth

agevol'mente adv easily

agganci'are vt hook up; Rail couple

agganci'arsi vr ⟨vestito⟩ hook up; ~ **a** ⟨maglia⟩ catch on; ⟨rimorchio⟩ hook onto

ag'gancio nm Aeron docking

ag'geggio nm gadget

agget'tivo nm adjective

agghiacci'ante adj terrifying

agghiacci'are vt fig ~ **qualcuno** make somebody's blood run cold

agghiacci'arsi vr freeze

agghin'dare vt fam dress up

agghin'darsi vr fam doll oneself up

agghin'dato adj dressed up; ⟨sala⟩ decorated; ⟨fig: stile⟩ stilted

aggiornabilità nf Comput upgradability

aggiorna'mento nm update; (azione) updating; **corso di ~** refresher course

aggior'nare vt (rinviare) postpone; (mettere a giorno) bring up to date, update

aggior'narsi vr get up to date

aggior'nato adj up-to-date; ⟨versione⟩ updated

aggio'taggio nm Jur manipulation of the market

aggira'mento nm Mil outflanking

aggi'rare vt surround; (fig: ingannare) trick

aggi'rarsi vr hang about; ~ su ⟨discorso ecc⟩ be about; ⟨somma⟩ be around

aggiudi'care vt award; (all'asta) knock down

aggiudi'carsi vr win

aggi'ungere vt add

aggi'unta nf addition; in ~ in addition

aggiun'tare vt splice

aggiun'tivo adj supplementary

aggi'unto ① adj added ② adj & nm (assistente) assistant

aggiu'stare vt mend; (sistemare) settle; (fam: mettere a posto) fix; **ora l'aggiusto io** fig I'll sort him out

aggiu'starsi vr adapt; (mettersi in ordine) tidy oneself up; (decidere) sort things out; ⟨tempo⟩ clear up

aggiusta'tina nf dare un'~ a neaten

agglomera'mento nm conglomeration

agglome'rante nm binder

agglome'rato nm built-up area

aggrap'pare vt grasp

aggrap'parsi vr ~ a cling to

aggrava'mento nm worsening; (di pena) increase

aggra'vante Jur ① nf aggravation ② adj aggravating; **circostanza aggravante** aggravation

aggra'vare vt (peggiorare) make worse; increase ⟨pena⟩; (appesantire) weigh down

aggra'varsi vr worsen

ag'gravio nm **aggravio fiscale** tax burden

aggrazi'ato adj graceful

aggre'dire vt attack

aggre'gare vt add; (associare a un gruppo ecc) admit

aggre'garsi vr ~ a join

aggre'gato ① adj associated ② nm aggregate; (di case) block

aggregazi'one nf (di persone) gathering

aggressi'one nf aggression; (atto) attack. **aggressione a mano armata** armed assault

aggressività nf aggressiveness

aggres'sivo adj aggressive

aggres'sore nm aggressor

aggrin'zare, aggrin'zire vt wrinkle

aggrin'zirsi vr wrinkle

aggrot'tare vt ~ **le ciglia/la fronte** frown

aggrovigli'are vt tangle

aggrovigli'arsi vr get entangled; fig get complicated

aggrovigli'ato adj entangled; fig confused

agguan'tare vt catch

agguan'tarsi vr ~ a grasp

aggu'ato nm ambush; (tranello) trap; **stare in ~** lie in wait; **tendere un ~ a qualcuno** set an ambush for somebody

agguer'rito adj fierce

agiata'mente adv comfortably

agia'tezza nf comfort

agi'ato adj ⟨persona⟩ well off; ⟨vita⟩ comfortable

a'gibile adj ⟨palazzo⟩ fit for human habitation

agibilità nf fitness for human habitation

'agile adj agile

agilità nf agility

agil'mente adv agilely

'agio nm ease; **mettersi a proprio ~** make oneself at home

a'gire vi act; ⟨comportarsi⟩ behave; (funzionare) work; ~ **su** affect

agi'tare vt shake; wave ⟨mano⟩; (fig: turbare) trouble; '~ **prima dell'uso**' 'shake before using'

agi'tarsi vr toss about; (essere inquieto) be restless; ⟨mare⟩ get rough

agi'tato adj restless; ⟨mare⟩ rough

agita|'tore, -trice nmf (persona) agitator

agitazi'one nf agitation; **mettere in ~ qualcuno** send somebody into a flat spin

'agli = A + GLI

'aglio nm garlic

a'gnello nm lamb

agno'lotti nmpl ravioli sg

a'gnostico, -a adj & nmf agnostic

'ago nm needle; **a 9 aghi** ⟨stampante⟩ 9-pin. **ago di pino** pine-needle

ago'gnare vt liter yearn for, thirst for

ago'nia nf agony

ago'nismo nm competitiveness

ago'nistica nf competition

ago'nistico adj competitive

agoniz'zante adj in one's death throes

agoniz'zare vi be on one's deathbed

agopun|'tore, -trice nmf acupuncturist

agopun'tura nf acupuncture

agorafo'bia nf agoraphobia

ago'rafobo, -a nmf agoraphobic

agostini'ano, -a adj & nmf Augustinian

a'gosto nm August

a'graria nf agriculture

a'grario ① adj agricultural ② nm landowner

a'greste adj rustic

a'gricolo *adj* agricultural

agricol'tore *nm* farmer

agricol'tura *nf* agriculture. **agricoltura biologica** organic farming

agri'foglio *nm* holly

agrimen'sore *nm* land-surveyor

agritu'rismo *nm* farm holidays, agrotourism

'agro[1] *adj* sour; **all'~** Culin pickled

'agro[2] *nm* countryside around a town

agroalimen'tare *adj* food *attrib*

agro'dolce *adj* bitter-sweet; Culin sweet-and-sour; **in ~** sweet and sour

agrono'mia *nf* agronomy

a'gronomo, -a *nmf* agriculturalist

agropasto'rale *adj* based on farming

a'grume *nm* citrus fruit; (pianta) citrus tree

agru'meto *nm* citrus plantation

aguz'zare *vt* sharpen; **~ le orecchie** prick up one's ears; **~ la vista** look hard

aguz'zino *nm* slave-driver; (carceriere) jailer

a'guzzo *adj* pointed

ah *int* ah!; **ah, davvero?** oh really?

ahi *int* ow!

ahimè *int* alas!

'ai = A + I

'aia *nf* threshing-floor

'Aia *nf* **L'~** The Hague

Aids *nm* Aids

AIE *abbr* (**Associazione Italiana degli Editori**) association of Italian publishers

air bag *nm inv* Auto air bag

ai'rone *nm* heron

air terminal *nm inv* air terminal

ai'tante *adj* sturdy

aiu'ola *nf* flowerbed

aiu'tante [1] *nmf* assistant [2] *nm* Mil adjutant. **aiutante di campo** aide-de-camp

aiu'tare *vt* help

ai'uto *nm* help, aid; (assistente) assistant; **dare un ~** lend a hand; **venire in ~ a qualcuno** come to somebody's rescue; **~!** help!; **aiuti** *pl* **alimentari** food aid. **aiuti** *pl* **umanitari** relief supplies. **aiuto chirurgo** assistant surgeon. **aiuto domestico** mother's help. **aiuto infermiere** nursing auxiliary. **aiuto in linea** Comput on-line help

aiz'zare *vt* incite; **~ contro** set on

al = A + IL

'ala *nf* wing; **fare ~** make way; **avere le ali ai piedi** fig run like the wind; **tarpare le ali a qualcuno** fig clip somebody's wings. **ala destra/sinistra** (in calcio) right/left wing

ala'bastro *nm* alabaster

'alacre *adj* brisk

alam'bicco *nm* alembic

a'lano *nm* Great Dane

a'lare *nm* firedog; **apertura alare** wingspan

A'laska *nf* Alaska

'alba *nf* dawn

alba'nese *adj* & *nmf* Albanian

Alba'nia *nf* Albania

'albatro *nm* albatross

albeggi'are *vi* dawn

albe'rare *vi* line with trees ‹strada›

albe'rato *adj* wooded; ‹viale› tree-lined

albera'tura *nf* Naut masts *pl*

albe'rello *nm* sapling

alber'gare [1] *vt* ‹edificio› accommodate [2] *vi* liter lodge

alberga|'tore, -trice *nmf* hotel-keeper

alberghi'ero *adj* hotel *attrib*

al'bergo *nm* hotel. **albergo diurno** hotel where rooms are rented during the daytime. **albergo a 3 stelle** 3-star hotel

'albero *nm* tree; Naut mast; Mech shaft. **albero a camme** camshaft. **albero a foglie caduche** deciduous tree. **albero da frutto** fruit tree. **albero genealogico** family tree. **albero a gomiti** crankshaft. **albero della gomma** rubber tree. **albero maestro** Naut mainmast. **albero di Natale** Christmas tree. **albero di trasmissione** Mech transmission shaft, prop shaft

albi'cocca *nf* apricot

albi'cocco *nm* apricot (tree)

al'bino *nm* albino

'albo *nm* register; (libro ecc) album; (per avvisi) notice board

album *nm inv* album. **album da colorare** colouring book. **album da disegno** sketch-book

al'bume *nm* albumen

albu'mina *nf* albumin

alca'lino *adj* alkaline

'alce *nm* elk

alchi'mia *nf* alchemy

alchi'mista *nm* alchemist

'alcol *nm* alcohol; Med spirit; (liquori forti) spirits *pl*; **darsi all'~** take to drink. **alcol denaturato** meths, surgical spirit. **alcol etilico** ethyl alcohol

alcolicità *nf* alcohol content

al'colico [1] *adj* alcoholic [2] *nm* alcoholic drink

alco'lismo *nm* alcoholism

alco'lista *nmf* alcoholic

alcoliz'zato, -a *adj* & *nmf* alcoholic

alco'test® *nm inv* breathalyser® Br, breathalyzer®

al'cova *nf* alcove

al'cun, alcuno *adj & pron* any; **non ha** ∼ **amico** he hasn't any friends, he has no friends; **alcuni** *pl* some, a few; **alcuni suoi amici** some of his friends

aldilà *nm* next world, hereafter

alea'torio *adj* unpredictable; Jur aleatory

aleggi'are *vi* ⟨*brezza*⟩ blow gently; ⟨*profumo*⟩ waft

a'letta *nf* Mech fin

alet'tone *nm* Aeron aileron; Auto stabilizer

'alfa *nf inv* alpha

alfa'betico *adj* alphabetical

alfabetizzazi'one *nf* **alfabetizzazione della popolazione** teaching people to read and write; **tasso di alfabetizzazione** literacy rate

alfa'beto *nm* alphabet. **Alfabeto Fonetico Internazionale** International Phonetic Alphabet. **alfabeto Morse** Morse code

alfanu'merico *adj* alphanumeric

alfi'ere *nm* (negli scacchi) bishop

al'fine *adv* eventually, in the end

'alga *nf* weed; **alghe** *pl* marine seaweed

'algebra *nf* algebra

Al'geri *nf* Algiers

Alge'ria *nf* Algeria

alge'rino, -a *adj & nmf* Algerian

algocol'tura *nf* seaweed farming

algo'ritmo *nm* algorithm

ali'ante *nm* glider

'alibi *nm inv* alibi

a'lice *nf* anchovy

alie'nabile *adj* Jur alienable

alie'nare *vt* alienate

alie'narsi *vr* become estranged; ∼ **le simpatie di qualcuno** lose somebody's good will

ali'enato, -a ① *adj* alienated ② *nmf* lunatic

alienazi'one *nf* alienation

a'lieno, -a ① *nmf* alien ② *adj* **è** ∼ **da invidia** envy is foreign *or* alien to him

alimen'tare ① *vt* feed; fig foment ② *adj* food *attrib*; ⟨*abitudine*⟩ dietary ③ *nmpl* **alimentari** foodstuffs

alimenta'tore *nm* power unit. **alimentatore automatico di documenti** automatic paper feed

alimentazi'one *nf* feeding; (cibo) food; (elettrica, a gas ecc) supply

ali'mento *nm* food; **alimenti** *pl* food; Jur alimony

a'liquota *nf* share; (di imposta) rate. **aliquota minima** basic rate; **ad** ∼ **zero** zero-rated

ali'scafo *nm* hydrofoil

'alito *nm* breath; **alito cattivo** bad breath

ali'tosi *nf inv* halitosis

all. *abbr* (**allegato**) encl

'alla = A + LA

allaccia'mento *nm* connection

allacci'are *vt* fasten ⟨*cintura*⟩; lace up ⟨*scarpe*⟩; do up ⟨*vestito*⟩; (collegare) connect; form ⟨*amicizia*⟩

allacci'arsi *vr* do up, fasten ⟨*vestito, cintura*⟩

allaga'mento *nm* flooding

alla'gare *vt* flood

alla'garsi *vr* to become flooded

allampa'nato *adj* lanky

allarga'mento *nm* (di strada, ricerche) widening

allar'gare *vt* widen; open ⟨*braccia, gambe*⟩; let out ⟨*vestito ecc*⟩; fig extend

allar'garsi *vr* to widen

allar'mante *adj* alarming

allar'mare *vt* alarm

allar'mato *adj* panicky, alarmed

al'larme *nm* alarm; **dare l'**∼ raise the alarm; **mettere in** ∼ **qualcuno** alarm somebody; **far scattare il campanello d'**∼ set the alarm bells ringing; **falso allarme** fig false alarm. **allarme aereo** air-raid siren; (suono) air-raid warning. **allarme antifumo** smoke alarm. **allarme antincendio** fire alarm. **allarme rosso** red alert

allar'mismo *nm* alarmism

allar'mista *nmf* alarmist

allatta'mento *nm* (di animale) suckling; (di neonato) feeding

allat'tare *vt* suckle ⟨*animale*⟩; feed ⟨*neonato*⟩; ∼ **artificialmente** bottle feed

'alle = A + LE

alle'anza *nf* alliance. **Alleanza Democratica** Pol Democratic Alliance. **Alleanza Nazionale** Pol National Alliance

alle'are *vt* unite

alle'arsi *vr* form an alliance

alle'ato, -a ① *adj* allied ② *nmf* ally

alle'gare[1] *vt* Jur allege

alle'gare[2] *vt* (accludere) enclose; set on edge ⟨*denti*⟩

alle'gato ① *adj* enclosed; Comput attached ② *nm* enclosure; Comput attachment; **in** ∼ attached, appended

allegazi'one *nf* Jur allegation

alleggeri'mento *nm* alleviation

allegge'rire *vt* lighten; fig alleviate

allegge'rirsi *vr* become lighter; (vestirsi leggero) put on lighter clothes

allego'ria *nf* allegory

alle'gorico *adj* allegorical

allegra'mente *adv* breezily

alle'gria *nf* gaiety

al'legro ① *adj* cheerful; ⟨*colore*⟩ bright; (brillo) tipsy
② *nm* Mus allegro

alle'luia *int* hallelujah

allena'mento *nm* training

alle'nare *vt* train

alle'narsi *vr* train

allena|'**tore**, **-trice** *nmf* trainer, coach

allen'tare *vt* loosen; fig relax

allen'tarsi *vr* become loose; Mech work loose

aller'gia *nf* allergy

al'lergico *adj* allergic

aller'gologo, **-a** *nmf* allergist

al'lerta *nf* stare ∼ be alert, be on the alert; **essere in stato di** ∼ Mil be in a state of alert; **mettere in stato di** ∼ put on the alert

allesti'mento *nm* preparation; **in** ∼ preparation. **allestimento scenico** Theat set

alle'stire *vt* prepare; stage ⟨*spettacolo*⟩; Naut fit out

allet'tante *adj* alluring; **poco** ∼ unattractive

allet'tare *vt* entice

allet'tato *adj* bed-bound, laid up

alleva'mento *nm* breeding; (processo) bringing up; (luogo) farm; (per piante) nursery; **pollo di allevamento** battery chicken. **allevamento in batteria** battery farming. **allevamento a terra** free-range farming; **pollo/uova di allevamento a terra** free-range chicken/eggs

alle'vare *vt* bring up ⟨*bambini*⟩; breed ⟨*animali*⟩; grow ⟨*piante*⟩

alleva|'**tore**, **-trice** *nmf* breeder

allevia'mento *nm* alleviation

allevi'are *vt* alleviate; fig lighten

alli'bito *adj* astounded; **rimanere** ∼ be astounded

allibra'tore *nm* bookmaker

allie'tare *vt* gladden

allie'tarsi *vr* rejoice

alli'evo, **-a** ① *nmf* pupil
② *nm* Mil cadet

alliga'tore *nm* alligator

allinea'mento *nm* alignment

alline'are *vt* line up; Typ align; Fin adjust

alline'arsi *vr* line up; fig fall into line; ∼ **con qualcuno** fig align oneself with somebody

alline'ato *adj* lined up; **i paesi non allineati** the non-aligned states

'allo = A + LO

allo'care *vt* allocate

al'locco[1] *nm* tawny owl

al'locco[2], **-a** *nmf* fig idiot

allocuzi'one *nf* speech

al'lodola *nf* [sky]lark

alloggi'are ① *vt* ⟨*persona*⟩ put up; ⟨*casa*⟩ provide accommodation for; Mil billet
② *vi* put up, stay; Mil be billeted

al'loggio *nm* (appartamento) flat, apartment Am; Mil billet. **alloggio popolare** council flat

allontana'mento *nm* removal

allonta'nare *vt* move away; (licenziare) dismiss; avert ⟨*pericolo*⟩

allonta'narsi *vr* go away

allopa'tia *nf* Med allopathy

al'lora *adv* then; (a quel tempo) at that time; (in tal caso) in that case; ∼ ∼ just then; **d'**∼ **in poi** from then on; **e** ∼**?** what now?; (e con ciò?) so what?; **fino** ∼ until then

allorché *conj* when, as soon as

al'loro *nm* laurel; Culin bay; **dormire sugli allori** rest on one's laurels

'alluce *nm* big toe

alluci'nante *adj* fam incredible; **sostanza allucinante** hallucinogen

alluci'nato, **-a** *nmf* person who suffers from hallucinations; fam space cadet

allucina'torio *adj* hallucinatory

allucinazi'one *nf* hallucination

allucino'geno *adj* ⟨*sostanza*⟩ hallucinatory

al'ludere *vi* ∼ **a** allude to

allu'minio *nm* aluminium

allu'naggio *nm* moon-landing

allu'nare *vi* land on the moon

allun'gabile *adj* ⟨*tavolo*⟩ extending

allun'gare *vt* lengthen; stretch out ⟨*mano*⟩; stretch ⟨*gamba*⟩; extend ⟨*tavolo*⟩; (diluire) dilute; ∼ **il collo** crane one's neck; ∼ **il muso** pull a long face; ∼ **il passo** quicken one's step; ∼ **le mani su qualcuno** touch somebody up; (picchiare) start fighting with somebody; ∼ **uno schiaffo a qualcuno** slap somebody

allun'garsi *vr* grow longer; (crescere) grow taller; (sdraiarsi) lie down, stretch out

allun'gato *adj* ⟨*forma*⟩ elongated

al'lungo *nm* (nel calcio) pass; (nella corsa) spurt; (nel pugilato) lunge

allusi'one *nf* allusion

allu'sivo *adj* allusive

alluvio'nale *adj* alluvial

alluvio'nato *adj* ⟨*popolazione*⟩ flooded out; ⟨*territorio*⟩ flooded

alluvi'one *nf* flood

alma'nacco *nm* almanac. **almanacco nobiliare** peerage

al'meno *adv* at least; **[se]** ~ **venisse il sole!** if only the sun would come out!

a'logena *nf* halogen lamp

a'logeno ① *nm* halogen
② *adj* **lampada alogena** halogen lamp

a'lone *nm* halo

alo'pecia *nf* Med alopecia

al'paca *nm inv* alpaca

al'pestre *adj* Alpine

'Alpi *nfpl* **le** ~ the Alps

alpi'nismo *nm* mountaineering

alpi'nista *nmf* mountaineer

alpi'nistico *adj* mountaineering *attrib*

al'pino ① *adj* Alpine
② *nm* Mil **gli alpini** the Alpine troops

al'quanto ① *adj* a certain amount of
② *adv* rather

Al'sazia *nf* Alsace

alt *int* stop; **intimare l'**~ give the order to halt

alta'lena *nf* swing; (tavola in bilico) see-saw

altale'nare *vi* fig vacillate

alta'mente *adv* highly

al'tare *nm* altar

alta'rino *nm* **scoprire gli altarini di qualcuno** reveal somebody's guilty secrets

alte'rabile *adj* which can be changed, alterable

alte'rare *vt* alter; adulterate ‹*vino*›; (falsificare) falsify

alte'rarsi *vr* be altered; ‹*cibo*› go bad; ‹*merci*› deteriorate; (arrabbiarsi) get angry

alte'rato *adj* ‹*suono*› distorted; ‹*viso*› careworn; ‹*cibo*› spoilt; ‹*vino*› adulterated; (arrabbiato) angry

alterazi'one *nf* alteration; (di vino) adulteration

al'terco *nm* altercation

alte'rigia *nf* haughtiness

alter'nanza *nf* alternation; (in agricoltura) rotation; Pol regular change in government

alter'nare *vt* alternate

alter'narsi *vr* alternate

alterna'tiva *nf* alternative

alterna'tivo *adj* alternate; **medicina alternativa** alternative medicine

alter'nato *adj* alternating

alterna'tore *nm* Electr alternator

al'terno *adj* alternate; **a giorni alterni** every other day

al'tero *adj* haughty

al'tezza *nf* height; (profondità) depth; (suono) pitch; (di tessuto) width; (titolo) Highness; **essere all'**~ **di** be on a level with; fig be up to. **altezza libera di passaggio** headroom

altezzosa'mente *adv* haughtily

altezzosità *nf* haughtiness

altez'zoso *adj* haughty

al'ticcio *adj* tipsy, merry

al'timetro *nm* altimeter

altipi'ano *nm* plateau

altiso'nante *adj* high-sounding

alti'tudine *nf* altitude

'alto ① *adj* high; (di statura) tall; (profondo) deep; ‹*suono*› high-pitched; ‹*tessuto*› wide; Geog northern; **a notte alta** in the middle of the night; **avere degli alti e bassi** have some ups and downs; **di** ~ **bordo** high-class; **di** ~ **rango** high-ranking; **ad alta definizione** high-definition; **ad alta fedeltà** high-fidelity; **ad** ~ **livello** high-level; **a voce alta, ad alta voce** in a loud voice; ‹*leggere*› aloud; **essere in** ~ **mare** be on the high seas; fig be all at sea. **alta borghesia** *nf* gentry. **alta finanza** *nf* high finance. **alta frequenza** *nf* high frequency. **alta moda** *nf* high fashion. **alta pressione** *nf* (meteorologica) high pressure. **alta società** *nf* high society. **alta tensione** *nf* high voltage. **alto commissariato** *nm* High Commission. **alto medioevo** *nm* Dark Ages. **alto tradimento** *nm* high treason
② *adv* high; **in** ~ ‹*essere*› at the top; ‹*guardare*› up; **mani in** ~**!** hands up!; **dall'**~ from above; **guardare qualcuno dall'**~ **in basso** look down on somebody

altoate'sino *adj* South Tyrolean

alto'forno *nm* blast furnace

altolà *int* halt there!

altolo'cato *adj* highly placed

altopar'lante *nm* loudspeaker

altopi'ano *nm* plateau

altret'tanto ① *adj & pron* as much; (*pl*) as many
② *adv* likewise; **buona fortuna! –grazie,** ~ good luck! –thank you, the same to you

altri'menti *adv* otherwise

'altro ① *adj* other; **un** ~, **un'altra** another; **l'altr'anno** last year; **l'**~ **ieri** the day before yesterday; **domani l'**~ the day after tomorrow; **l'ho visto l'**~ **giorno** I saw him the other day
② *pron* other [one]; **un** ~, **un'altra** another [one]; **ne vuoi dell'**~**?** would you like some more?; **l'un l'**~ one another; **nessun** ~ nobody else; **gli altri** (la gente) other people
③ *nm* something else; **non fa** ~ **che lavorare** he does nothing but work; **desidera** ~**?** (in negozio) anything else?; **più che** ~**, sono stanco** I'm tired more than anything; **se non** ~ at least; **senz'**~ certainly; **tra l'**~ what's more; ~ **che!** absolutely!

altroché *adv* absolutely!

altroi'eri *nm* **l'**~ the day before yesterday

al'tronde: d'∼ adv on the other hand

al'trove adv elsewhere

al'trui ① adj other people's
② nm other people's belongings pl

altru'ismo nm altruism

altruista nmf altruist

al'tura nf high ground; Naut deep sea

a'lunno, -a nmf pupil

alve'are nm hive

'alveo nm bed

alzabandi'era nm inv flag-raising

alzacri'stallo nm Auto window winder

al'zare vt lift, raise; (costruire) build; Naut hoist; ∼ **le spalle** shrug one's shoulders; ∼ **i tacchi** fig take to one's heels; ∼ **la voce** raise one's voice; ∼ **il volume** turn up the volume

al'zarsi vr (in piedi) stand up; (da letto) get up; ⟨vento, temperatura⟩ rise

al'zata nf lifting; (aumento) rise; (da letto) getting up; Archit elevation. **alzata di spalle** shrug of the shoulders

alza'taccia nf fam **fare un'**∼ get up at the crack of dawn

al'zato adj up

A.M. abbr (**aeronautica militare**) Air Force

a'mabile adj lovable; ⟨vino⟩ sweet

amabilità nf kindness

amabil'mente adv kindly

a'maca nf hammock

a'malgama nm amalgam

amalga'mare vt amalgamate

amalga'marsi vr amalgamate

ama'nita nf Bot amanita

a'mante ① adj ∼ **di** fond of
② nmf fig lover. **amante degli animali** animal lover. **amante della lettura** book lover
③ nm lover
④ nf mistress

amara'mente adv bitterly

ama'ranto ① nm Bot amarant[h]us; (colore) rich purple
② adj rich purple

a'mare vt love; be fond of ⟨musica, sport ecc⟩

amareggia'mento nm bitterness

amareggi'are vt embitter

amareggi'arsi vr become embittered

amareggi'ato adj embittered

ama'rena nf sour black cherry

ama'retto nm macaroon

ama'rezza nf bitterness; (dolore) sorrow

a'maro ① adj bitter
② nm bitterness; (liquore) bitters pl

ama'rognolo adj rather bitter

a'mato, -a ① adj loved
② nmf beloved

ama|'tore, -trice nmf lover

a'mazzone nf (in mitologia) Amazon; **all'**∼ side saddle

Amaz'zonia nf Amazonia

amaz'zonico adj Amazonian

ambasce'ria nf diplomatic mission

ambasci'ata nf embassy; (messaggio) message

ambascia|'tore, -trice ① nm ambassador
② nf ambassadress

ambe'due adj & pron both

ambi'destro adj ambidextrous

ambien'tale adj environmental

ambienta'lismo nm environmentalism

ambienta'lista adj & nmf environmentalist

ambienta'mento nm acclimatization

ambien'tare vt acclimatize; set ⟨storia, film ecc⟩

ambien'tarsi vr get acclimatized

ambi'ente nm environment; (stanza) room

ambiguità nf inv ambiguity; (di persona) shadiness

am'biguo adj ambiguous; ⟨persona⟩ shady

am'bire vi ∼ **a** aspire to

am'bito¹ adj ⟨lavoro, incarico⟩ much sought-after

'ambito² nm sphere

ambiva'lente adj ambivalent

ambiva'lenza nf ambivalence

ambizi'one nf ambition

ambizi'oso adj ambitious

amblio'pia nf lazy eye

'ambo ① adj inv both
② nm (in tombola, lotto) double

'ambra nf amber

am'brato adj amber

ambu'lante adj wandering; **venditore ambulante** hawker

ambu'lanza nf ambulance

ambulatori'ale adj **essere trattato con intervento** ∼ have day surgery

ambula'torio nm (di medico) surgery; (di ospedale) out-patients' [department]. **ambulatorio dentistico** dental clinic

Am'burgo nf Hamburg

a'meba nf amoeba

a'mebico adj amoebic

'amen int amen; **e allora** ∼! well, so be it!

amenità nf inv (facezia) pleasantry

a'meno adj pleasant

amenor'rea nf Med amenorrhoea

A'merica nf America. **America centrale** Central America. **America**

Latina Latin America. **America del Nord/Sud** North/South America

america'nata nf (pej: film) American rubbish

america'nismo nm Americanism; (patriottismo) flag-waving

americaniz'zarsi vr become Americanized

ameri'cano, -a adj & nmf American

ame'rindio adj Native American

ame'tista nf amethyst

ami'anto nm asbestos

ami'chevole adj friendly

ami'cizia nf friendship; **fare ∼ con qualcuno** make friends with somebody; **amicizie** pl (amici) friends

a'mico, -a ① adj ⟨parola, persona⟩ friendly ② nmf friend. **amico del cuore** bosom friend. **amico d'infanzia** childhood friend. **amico intimo** close friend. **amico di penna** penfriend, penpal

'amido nm starch

ammac'care vt dent ⟨metallo⟩; bruise ⟨frutto⟩

ammac'carsi vr ⟨metallo⟩ get dented; ⟨frutto⟩ bruise

ammac'cato adj ⟨metallo⟩ dented; ⟨frutto⟩ bruised

ammacca'tura nf dent; (livido) bruise

ammaestra'mento nm training

ammae'strare vt (istruire) teach; train ⟨animale⟩

ammae'strato adj trained

ammaestra|'tore, -trice nmf trainer

ammainabandi'era nm inv flag-lowering

ammai'nare vt lower ⟨bandiera⟩; furl ⟨vele⟩

amma'larsi vr fall ill

amma'lato, -a adj ill nmf sick person; (paziente) patient

ammali'are vt bewitch

ammali'ato adj bewitched

ammalia|'tore, -trice ① adj bewitching ② nm enchanter ③ nf enchantress

am'manco nm deficit

ammanet'tare vt handcuff

ammani'carsi vr fig acquire connections

ammani'cato adj **essere ∼** have connections

ammanigli'arsi vr fig = AMMANICARSI

ammanigli'ato adj fig = AMMANICATO

amman'sire vt tame, domesticate ⟨animali⟩; fig pacify, placate

amman'sirsi vr ⟨animali⟩ become tame; fig calm down

amman'tarsi vr ⟨persona⟩ wrap oneself up in a cloak; **∼ di** fig feign ⟨virtù⟩

amma'raggio nm splashdown

amma'rare vi put down on the sea; ⟨navicella spaziale⟩ splash down

ammassa'mento nm Mil build-up

ammas'sare vt amass

ammas'sarsi vr crowd together

am'masso nm mass; (mucchio) pile

ammat'tire vi go mad

ammazzacaffè nm inv liqueur

ammazza'fame nm inv stodge

ammaz'zare vt kill

ammaz'zarsi vr (suicidarsi, fig) kill oneself; (rimanere ucciso) be killed

am'menda nf amends pl; (multa) fine; **fare ∼ di qualcosa** make amends for something

am'messo ① pp di AMMETTERE ② conj **∼ che** supposing that

am'mettere vt admit; (riconoscere) acknowledge; (supporre) suppose; **ammettiamo che ...** let's suppose [that]...

ammez'zato nm (piano ammezzato) mezzanine

ammic'care vi wink

ammini'strare vt administer; (gestire) run

ammini'strarsi vr fig manage one's finances

amministra'tivo adj administrative

amministra|'tore, -trice nmf administrator; (di azienda) manager; (di società) director. **amministratore aggiunto** associate director. **amministratore del condominio** property manager. **amministratore delegato** managing director. **amministratore unico** sole director

amministrazi'one nf administration; **fatti di ordinaria ∼** fig routine matters. **amministrazione aziendale** (studi) business studies. **amministrazione comunale** local council. **amministrazione controllata** receivership. **amministrazione pubblica** civil service. **amministrazione regionale** regional council

ammino'acido nm amino acid

ammi'rabile adj admirable

ammi'raglia nf flag-ship

ammiragli'ato nm admiralty

ammi'raglio nm admiral

ammi'rare vt admire

ammi'rato adj restare/essere **∼** be full of admiration

ammira|'tore, -trice nmf admirer

ammirazi'one nf admiration

ammis'sibile adj admissible

ammissibilità *nf* acceptability

ammissi'one *nf* admission; (approvazione) acknowledgement

ammobili'are *vt* furnish

ammobili'ato *adj* furnished; **stanza ammobiliata** furnished room

ammoderna'mento *nm* modernization

ammoder'nare *vt* modernize

ammoder'narsi *vr* move with the times

am'modo ① *adj* proper ② *adv* properly

ammogli'are *vt* marry off

ammogli'arsi *vr* get married

ammogli'ato ① *adj* married ② *nm* married man

am'mollo *nm* in ∼ soaking; **mettere in** ∼ pre-soak

ammo'niaca *nf* ammonia

ammoni'mento *nm* warning; (di rimprovero) admonishment

ammo'nire *vt* warn; (rimproverare) admonish

ammoni'tore *adj* admonishing

ammonizi'one *nf* Sport warning; (rimprovero) admonishment

ammon'tare ① *vi* ∼ a amount to ② *nm* amount

ammonticchi'are *vt* heap up, pile up

ammonticchi'arsi *vr* pile up

ammor'bare *vt* (con odore) pollute; (con malattie) infect

ammorbi'dente *nm* (per panni) softener

ammorbi'dire *vt* soften

ammorbi'dirsi *vr* soften

ammorta'mento *nm* Comm amortization

ammor'tare *vt* pay off ⟨spesa⟩; Comm amortize ⟨debito⟩

ammortiz'zare *vt* Comm = AMMORTARE; Mech damp

ammortizza'tore *nm* shock-absorber

ammosci'are *vt* make flabby

ammosci'arsi *vt* get flabby

ammucchi'are *vt* pile up

ammucchi'arsi *vr* pile up

ammucchi'ata *nf* (sl: orgia) orgy; **un'**∼ **di** (fam: ammasso) loads of

ammuf'fire *vi* go mouldy

ammuf'firsi *vr* go mouldy

ammuf'fito *adj* mouldy; fig stuffy

ammutina'mento *nm* mutiny

ammuti'narsi *vr* mutiny

ammuti'nato ① *adj* mutinous ② *nm* mutineer

ammuto'lire *vi* be struck dumb

ammuto'lirsi *vr* fall silent

amne'sia *nf* amnesia

amni'stia *nf* amnesty

amnisti'are *vt* amnesty

'amo *nm* hook; fig bait

amo'rale *adj* amoral

amoralità *nf* amorality

a'more *nm* love; d'∼ ⟨canzone, film⟩ love; **fare l'**∼ make love; **per l'amor di Dio/del cielo!** for heaven's sake!; **andare d'**∼ **e d'accordo** get on like a house on fire; **amor proprio** self-respect; **amor cortese** courtly love; **è un** ∼ ⟨persona⟩ he's/she's a darling; **per** ∼ **di** for the sake of; **amori** *pl* love affairs

amoreggi'are *vi* flirt

amo'revole *adj* loving

amorevol'mente *adv* lovingly

a'morfo *adj* shapeless; ⟨persona⟩ colourless, grey

amo'rino *nm* cherub

amorosa'mente *adv* lovingly

amo'roso *adj* loving; ⟨sguardo ecc⟩ amorous; ⟨lettera, relazione⟩ love *attrib*

am'pere *nm inv* ampere; **da 15** ∼ 15-amp

ampe'rometro *nm* ammeter

ampia'mente *adv* widely

ampi'ezza *nf* (di esperienza) breadth; (di stanza) spaciousness; (di gonna) fullness; (importanza) scale. **ampiezza di vedute** broadmindedness

'ampio *adj* ample; ⟨esperienza⟩ wide; ⟨stanza⟩ spacious; ⟨vestito⟩ loose; ⟨gonna, descrizione⟩ full; ⟨pantaloni⟩ baggy; **di ampie vedute** broadminded

am'plesso *nm* embrace

amplia'mento *nm* (di cosa, porto) enlargement; (di strada, conoscenze) broadening

ampli'are *vt* broaden, widen ⟨strada, conoscenze⟩; enlarge ⟨casa⟩

ampli'arsi *vr* broaden, grow wider

amplifi'care *vt* amplify; fig magnify

amplifica'tore *nm* amplifier

amplificazi'one *nf* amplification

am'polla *nf* cruet

ampol'loso *adj* pompous

ampu'tare *vt* amputate

amputazi'one *nf* amputation

amu'leto *nm* amulet

A.N. *abbr* Pol (**Alleanza Nazionale**) National Alliance (right-wing party)

anabbagli'ante ① *adj* Auto dipped ② *nm* **anabbaglianti** *pl* dipped headlights

anaboliz'zante *nm* anabolic steroid

ana'cardi *nmpl* cashew nuts

ana'cardio *nm* cashew

ana'conda *nf* Zool anaconda

anacro'nismo *nm* anachronism

19

anacro'nistico *adj* anachronistic; essere ∼ be an anachronism
anae'robico *adj* anaerobic
anafi'lassi *nf* anaphylaxis
anafi'lattico *adj* **shock anafilattico** Med anaphylactic shock
a'nagrafe *nf* (ufficio) registry office; (registro) register of births, marriages and deaths
ana'grafico *adj* **dati** *pl* **anagrafici** personal data
ana'gramma *nm* anagram
anal'colico ① *adj* non-alcoholic ② *nm* soft drink, non-alcoholic drink
a'nale *adj* anal
analfa'beta *adj & nmf* illiterate
analfabe'tismo *nm* illiteracy
anal'gesico *nm* painkiller
a'nalisi *nf inv* analysis; Med test; **in ultima** ∼ in the final analysis. **analisi grammaticale/del periodo/logica** parsing. **analisi di mercato** market research. **analisi del percorso critico** critical path analysis. **analisi del sangue** blood test
ana'lista *nmf* analyst. **analista economico** economic analyst. **analista finanziario** business analyst
ana'litico *adj* analytical
analiz'zabile *adj* analysable
analiz'zare *vt* analyse; Med test, analyse
anal'lergico *adj* hypoallergenic
analoga'mente *adv* analogously
analo'gia *nf* analogy
ana'logico *adj* analogue
analo'gismo *nm* reasoning by analogy
a'nalogo *adj* analogous
anam'nesi *nf inv* medical history
'ananas *nm inv* pineapple
anar'chia *nf* anarchy
a'narchico, -a ① *adj* anarchic ② *nmf* anarchist
anar'chismo *nm* anarchism
A.N.A.S. *nf abbr* (**Azienda Nazionale Autonoma delle Strade**) national road maintenance authority
ana'tema *nm* anathema
anato'mia *nf* anatomy
ana'tomico *adj* anatomical; ⟨sedia⟩ contoured, ergonomic
'anatra *nf* duck. **anatra selvatica** mallard
ana'troccolo *nm* duckling
'anca *nf* hip; (di animale) flank
ance'strale *adj* ancestral
'anche *conj* also, too, as well; (persino) even; **parla** ∼ **francese** he also speaks French, he speaks French too, he speaks French as well; ∼ **se** even if

ancheggi'are *vi* wiggle one's hips
anchilo'sarsi *vr* fig stiffen up
anchilo'sato *adj* fig stiff
an'cora¹ *adv* still; (con negazione) yet; (di nuovo) again; (di più) some more; ∼ **una volta** once more; **non** ∼ not yet; ∼ **esistente** extant; ∼ **più bello** even more beautiful; ∼ **una birra** another beer, one more beer
'ancora² *nf* anchor; **gettare l'**∼ drop anchor. **ancora di salvezza** fig last hope
anco'raggio *nm* anchorage
anco'rare *vt* anchor
anco'rarsi *vr* anchor; drop anchor; ∼ **a** fig cling to
Andalu'sia *nf* Andalusia
anda'luso, -a *adj & nmf* Andalusian
anda'mento *nm* (del mercato, degli affari) trend
an'dante ① *adj* (corrente) current; (di poco valore) cheap ② *nm* Mus andante
an'dare ① *vi* go; (funzionare) work; (essere di moda) be in; ∼ **via** (partire) leave; ⟨macchia⟩ come out; ∼ **a piedi** walk; ∼ **a sciare** go skiing; ∼ **[bene]** (confarsi) suit; ⟨taglia⟩ fit; **ti va bene alle tre?** does three o'clock suit you?; **non mi va di mangiare** I don't feel like eating; ∼ **di fretta** be in a hurry; ∼ **fiero di** be proud of; ∼ **di moda** be in fashion; **va per i 40 anni** he's nearly 40; **ma va' [là]!** come on!; **come va?** how are things?; ∼ **a male** go off; ∼ **a fuoco** go up in flames; ∼ **perduto** be lost; **va spedito [entro] stamattina** it must be sent this morning; **ne va del mio lavoro** my job is at stake; **come è andata a finire?** how did it turn out?; **cosa vai dicendo?** what are you talking about?; **andarsene** go away; (morire) pass away ② *nm* going; ∼ **e venire** (andirivieni) comings and goings pl; **a lungo** ∼ eventually; **a tutto** ∼ at full speed; **con l'**∼ **del tempo** with the passing of time
an'data *nf* going; (viaggio) outward journey; **biglietto di sola andata/di andata e ritorno** single/return [ticket]
anda'tura *nf* walk; (portamento) bearing; Naut tack; Sport pace
an'dazzo *nm* fam turn of events; **prendere un brutto** ∼ turn nasty
'Ande *nfpl* **le** ∼ the Andes
an'dino *adj* Andean
andirivi'eni *nm inv* comings and goings pl
'andito *nm* passage
An'dorra *nf* Andorra
an'drone *nm* entrance
andro'pausa *nf* male menopause
a'neddoto *nm* anecdote
ane'lare *vt* ∼ **a** long for

a'nelito *nm* longing

a'nello *nm* ring; (di catena) link. **anello di fidanzamento** engagement ring. **anello d'oro** gold ring

ane'mia *nf* anaemia

a'nemico *adj* anaemic

a'nemone *nm* anemone

aneste'sia *nf* anaesthesia; (sostanza) anaesthetic. **anestesia peridurale** epidural

aneste'sista *nmf* anaesthetist

ane'stetico *adj & nm* anaesthetic

anestetiz'zare *vt* anaesthetize

a'neto *nm* dill

anfeta'mina *nf* amphetamine

an'fibi *nmpl* (scarponi) army boots

an'fibio ① *nm* amphibian ② *adj* amphibious

anfite'atro *nm* amphitheatre

'anfora *nf* amphora

an'fratto *nm* ravine

an'gelico *adj* angelic

'angelo *nm* angel. **angelo custode** guardian angel

anghe'ria *nf* harassment

an'gina *nf inv* **angina [pectoris]** angina [pectoris]

angi'ologo, **-a** *nmf* Med angiologist

anglica'nesimo *nm* Relig Anglicanism

angli'cano, **-a** *adj & nmf* Relig Anglican

angli'cismo *nm* Anglicism

angliciz'zare *vt* anglicize

anglo+ *pref* Anglo+

angloameri'cano, **-a** *nmf* Anglo-American

an'glofilo, **-a** *adj & nmf* Anglophile

an'glofono, **-a** *nmf* English-speaker

anglofran'cese *adj* Anglo-French

anglo'sassone *adj & nmf* Anglo-Saxon

An'gola *nf* Angola

ango'lano, **-a** *adj & nmf* Angolan

ango'lare *adj* angular

angolazi'one *nf* angle shot; fig point of view

angoli'era *nf* (mobile) corner cupboard

'angolo *nm* corner; Math angle; **dietro l'~** round the corner; **fare ~ con** ‹negozio, casa› be on the corner of. **angolo acuto** acute angle. **angolo [di] cottura** kitchenette. **angolo retto** right angle

ango'loso *adj* angular; ‹carattere› difficult to get on with

'angora *nf* **[lana d']angora** angora

an'goscia *nf* anguish

angosci'are *vt* torment

angosci'arsi *vr* (preoccuparsi) worry oneself sick, torment oneself

angosci'ato *adj* agonized

angosci'oso *adj* (disperato) anguished; (che dà angoscia) distressing

angu'illa *nf* eel

an'guria *nf* water-melon

an'gustia *nf* (ansia) anxiety; (penuria) poverty

angusti'are *vt* distress

angusti'arsi *vr* be distressed (**per** about)

angusti'ato *adj* distressed

an'gusto *adj* narrow

'anice *nm* anise; Culin aniseed; (liquore) anisette

ani'cino *nm* (biscotto) aniseed biscuit

ani'dride *nf* **anidride carbonica** carbon dioxide. **anidride solforosa** sulphur dioxide

'anima *nf* soul; **non c'era ~ viva** there was not a soul about; **all'~ !** good grief!; **mi fa dannare l'~ !** he'll be the death of me!; **l' ~ della festa** the life and soul of the party; **un'~ in pena** a soul in torment; **volere un bene dell'~ a qualcuno** love somebody to death; **la buon'~ della zia** my late aunt, God rest her soul. **anima gemella** soul mate

ani'male *adj & nm* animal. **animali** *pl* **domestici** pets. **animali** *pl* **selvatici** wild animals

anima'lesco *adj* animal

anima'lista *nmf* animal rights activist

ani'mare *vt* give life to; (ravvivare) enliven; (incoraggiare) encourage

ani'marsi *vr* come to life; (accalorarsi) become animated

ani'mato *adj* animate; ‹discussione› animated; ‹strada, paese› lively

anima|'tore, **-trice** *nmf* leading spirit; Cinema animator

animazi'one *nf* animation; **con ~** animatedly. **animazione elettronica** animatronics

ani'melle *nfpl* (di agnello, vitello) sweetbread

'animo *nm* (mente) mind; (indole) disposition; (cuore) heart; **perdersi d'~** lose heart; **farsi ~** take heart

animosa'mente *adv* with animosity

animosità *nf* animosity

ani'moso *adj* brave; (ostile) hostile

ani'setta *nf* anisette

'anitra *nf* duck

annacqua'mento *nm* fig watering down, dilution

annac'quare *vt* anche fig water down

annac'quato *adj* watered down; ‹colore, resoconto› insipid

annaffi'are *vt* water

annaffia'toio *nm* watering-can

an'nali *nmpl* annals; **restare negli ~** go down in history

anna'spare *vi* flounder

an'nata *nf* year; (importo annuale) annual amount; ⟨di vino⟩ vintage. **vino d'annata** vintage wine

annebbia'mento *nm* fog build-up; fig clouding

annebbi'are *vt* cloud ⟨vista, mente⟩

annebbi'arsi *vr* get misty; (in città, su autostrada) get foggy; ⟨vista, mente⟩ grow dim

annega'mento *nm* drowning

anne'gare *vt/i* drown

anne'rire *vt/i* blacken

anne'rirsi *vr* become black

an'nessi *nmpl* (costruzioni) outbuildings; **tutti gli ~ e i connessi** all the appurtenances

annessi'one *nf* (di nazione) annexation

an'nesso 1 pp di ANNETTERE 2 *adj* attached; ⟨Stato⟩ annexed

an'nettere *vt* add; (accludere) enclose; annex ⟨Stato⟩

annichi'lire *vt* annihilate

anni'darsi *vr* nest

annienta'mento *nm* annihilation

annien'tare *vt* annihilate

annien'tarsi *vr* abase oneself

anniver'sario *adj & nm* anniversary. **anniversario di matrimonio o di nozze** wedding anniversary

'anno *nm* year; **Buon Anno!** Happy New Year!; **quanti anni ha?** how old are you?; **Tommaso ha dieci anni** Thomas is ten [years old]; **gli anni '30** the '30s. **anno accademico** academic year. **anno bisestile** leap year. **anno civile** calendar year. **anno giudiziario** law year. **anno luce** light year. **anno nuovo** New Year. **anno sabbatico** Univ sabbatical. **anni verdi** *pl* salad days

anno'dare *vt* knot; do up ⟨cintura⟩; fig form

anno'darsi *vr* become knotted

annoi'are *vt* bore; (recare fastidio) annoy

annoi'arsi *vr* get bored; (condizione) be bored

annoi'ato *adj* bored

an'noso *adj* ⟨questione⟩ age-old

anno'tare *vt* note down; annotate ⟨testo⟩

annotazi'one *nf* note

annove'rare *vt* number

annu'ale *adj* annual, yearly

annual'mente *adv* annually

annu'ario *nm* year-book

annu'ire *vi* nod; (acconsentire) agree

annulla'mento *nm* annulment; (di appuntamento) cancellation

annul'lare *vt* annul; cancel ⟨appuntamento⟩; (togliere efficacia a) undo; disallow ⟨gol⟩; (distruggere) destroy

annul'larsi *vr* cancel each other out

an'nullo *nm* (timbro) franking

annunci'are *vt* announce; (preannunciare) foretell

annuncia|'tore, -trice *nmf* announcer

annunciazi'one *nf* Annunciation

an'nuncio *nm* announcement; (pubblicitario) advertisement, ad; (notizia) news. **annunci** *pl* **economici** classified advertisements. **annunci** *pl* **mortuari** obituaries, death notices. **annuncio personale** personal ad. **annuncio pubblicitario** advertisement

'annuo *adj* annual, yearly

annu'sare *vt* sniff

annu'sata *nf* **dare un'~** a have a sniff at

annuvola'mento *nm* clouding over

annuvo'lare *vt* cloud

annuvo'larsi *vr* cloud over

'ano *nm* anus

a'nodino *adj* anodyne

'anodo *nm* anode

anoma'lia *nf* anomaly

a'nomalo *adj* anomalous

a'nonima *nf* **Anonima Alcolisti** Alcoholics Anonymous. **anonima sequestri** Italian criminal organization specializing in kidnapping

anoni'mato *nm* **mantenere l'~** remain anonymous

anonimità *nf* anonymity

a'nonimo, -a 1 *adj* anonymous 2 *nmf* unknown person; (pittore, scrittore) anonymous painter/writer

anores'sia *nf* Med anorexia

ano'ressico, -a *nmf* anorexic

anor'male 1 *adj* abnormal 2 *nmf* deviant, abnormal person

anormalità *nf inv* abnormality

ANSA *nf abbr* (**Agenzia Nazionale Stampa Associata**) Italian press agency

'ansa *nf* handle; (di fiume) bend

an'sante *adj* panting

an'sare *vi* pant

'ansia, ansietà *nf* anxiety; **stare/essere in ~ per** be anxious about

ansi'mante *adj* breathless

ansi'mare *vi* gasp for breath

ansio'litico *nm* tranquillizer

ansi'oso *adj* anxious

'anta *nf* (di finestra) shutter; (di armadio) door

antago'nismo *nm* antagonism

antago'nista *nmf* antagonist

antago'nistico *adj* antagonistic

an'tartico *adj & nm* Antarctic

An'tartide *nf* Antarctica

ante'bellico *adj* pre-war

antece'dente ① *adj* preceding
② *nm* precedent

ante'fatto *nm* prior event

ante'guerra ① *adj* pre-war
② *nm* pre-war period

ante'nato, -a *nmf* ancestor

an'tenna *nf* Radio, TV aerial; (di animale) antenna; Naut yard; **rizzare le antenne** fig prick up one's ears. **antenna parabolica** satellite dish. **antenna radar** radar scanner

ante'porre *vt* put before

ante'prima *nf* preview; **vedere qualcosa in ~** have a sneak preview of something. **anteprima di stampa** Comput print preview

anteri'ore *adj* front *attrib*; (nel tempo) previous

anterior'mente *adv* (nel tempo) previously; (nello spazio) in front

antesi'gnano, -a *nmf* fig forerunner

anti+ *pref* anti+

antiabor'tista ① *nmf* antiabortionist
② *adj* antiabortion *attrib*

anti'acido *nm* antacid

antiade'rente *adj* ⟨padella⟩ nonstick

antia'ereo *adj* anti-aircraft *attrib*

antial'lergico *adj* hypoallergenic

antia'partheid *adj inv* antiapartheid

antia'tomico *adj* anti-nuclear; **rifugio antiatomico** fallout shelter

antibat'terico *adj* antibacterial

antibi'otico *adj & nm* antibiotic

antibloc'caggio *adj inv* antilock *attrib*

anti'caglia *nf* (oggetto) piece of old junk

antical'care *nm* softener

antica'mente *adv* in ancient times, long ago

anti'camera *nf* ante-room; **fare ~** be kept waiting

antichità *nf inv* antiquity; (oggetto) antique

antici'clone *nm* anticyclone

antici'clonico *adj* ⟨area⟩ anti-cyclonic

antici'pare ① *vt* advance; Comm pay in advance; (prevedere) anticipate; (prevenire) forestall
② *vi* be early

anticipata'mente *adv* in advance

antici'pato *adj* upfront; **pagamento anticipato** advance payment

anticipazi'one *nf* anticipation; (notizia) advance news

an'ticipo *nm* advance; (caparra) deposit; **in ~** early; (nel lavoro) ahead of schedule; **giocare d'~** Sport, fig anticipate the next move

an'tico ① *adj* ancient; ⟨mobile ecc⟩ antique; (vecchio) old; **all'antica** old-fashioned
② *nm* **gli antichi** the ancients

anticomu'nista *adj & nmf* anti-communist

anticoncezio'nale *adj & nm* contraceptive

anticonfor'mismo *nm* unconventionality

anticonfor'mista *nmf* nonconformist

anticonfor'mistico *adj* unconventional, nonconformist

anticonge'lante *adj & nm* anti-freeze

anticonsu'mismo *nm* anti-consumerism

anti'corpo *nm* antibody

anticostituzio'nale *adj* unconstitutional

anti'crimine *adj inv* ⟨squadra⟩ crime *attrib*

antidemo'cratico *adj* undemocratic

antidepres'sivo *nm* antidepressant

antidiluvi'ano *adj* fig antediluvian

antidolo'rifico *nm* painkiller

anti'doping *nm inv* Sport dope test

an'tidoto *nm* antidote

anti'droga *adj inv* ⟨campagna⟩ anti-drugs; ⟨squadra⟩ drug *attrib*

antie'stetico *adj* ugly

antifa'scismo *nm* anti-fascism

antifa'scista *adj & nmf* anti-fascist

an'tifona *nf* fig dull and repetitive speech; **capire l'~** take the hint; **sempre la stessa ~** always the same old story

anti'forfora *adj inv* dandruff *attrib*

anti'fumo *adj inv* anti-smoking

anti'furto ① *nm* anti-theft device; (allarme) alarm. **antifurto della macchina** car alarm
② *adj inv* ⟨sistema⟩ anti-theft

anti'gelo ① *adj inv* anti-freeze
② *nm* antifreeze; (parabrezza) defroster

anti'gene *nm* antigen

antigi'enico *adj* unhygienic

anti-inflazi'one *adj inv* anti-inflation

An'tille *nfpl* **le ~** the West Indies

an'tilope *nf* antelope

anti'mafia *adj inv* anti-Mafia

antimilita'rista ① *adj inv* anti-militaristic, anti-war
② *nmf* anti-militarist

antin'cendio *adj inv* **allarme antincendio** fire alarm; **porta antincendio** fire door

anti'nebbia *adj inv* [faro] **antinebbia** Auto foglamp, foglight

antine'vralgico ① *adj* pain-killing
② *nm* pain-killer

antinfiamma'torio *adj & nm* anti-inflammatory

antinflazio'nistico *adj* anti-inflationary

antinquina'mento *adj inv* anti-pollution

antinucle'are *adj* anti-nuclear

antio'rario *adj* anti-clockwise, counter-clockwise Am

antiparassi'tario *nm* insecticide

antiparlamen'tare *adj* unparliamentary

antipasti'era *nf* hors d'oeuvre dish

anti'pasto *nm* hors d'oeuvre, starter. **antipasti** *pl* **caldi** hot starters. **antipasti** *pl* **freddi** cold starters. **antipasti** *pl* **misti** variety of starters

antipa'tia *nf* antipathy

anti'patico *adj* unpleasant

an'tipodi *nmpl* Antipodes; **essere agli ∼** *fig* be poles apart

anti'polio ① *nf inv* (vaccino) polio vaccine; **fare l'∼** have a polio injection ② *adj* ⟨siero, vaccino⟩ polio *attrib*

antipopo'lare *adj* anti-working-class

antiproibizio'nismo *nm* anti-prohibitionism

antiproibizio'nista *adj & nmf* anti-prohibitionist

antiproi'ettile *adj inv* bullet-proof

antiquari'ato *nm* antique trade; **pezzo d'antiquariato** antique

anti'quario, -a *nmf* antique dealer

anti'quato *adj* antiquated

antiraz'zismo *nm* antiracism

antiraz'zista *adj* anti-racist

antiretrovi'rale *adj* antiretroviral

antireu'matico *adj & nm* anti-rheumatic

antiri'flesso *adj inv* antiglare

anti'ruggine ① *nm inv* rust-inhibitor ② *adj* anti-rust

anti'rughe *adj inv* anti-wrinkle *attrib*

anti'scasso *adj inv* ⟨porta⟩ burglar-proof

antisci'opero *adj inv* anti-strike

anti'scippo *adj inv* theft-proof

anti'scivolo *adj inv* nonskid

antise'mita *adj* anti-Semitic

antisemi'tismo *nm* anti-Semitism

anti'settico *adj & nm* antiseptic

antisinda'cale *adj* ⟨comportamento⟩ anti-trade-union

anti'sismico *adj* earthquake-proof

antisoci'ale *adj* anti-social

antiso'lare *adj & nm* suntan

antisommer'gibile ① *adj inv* anti-submarine ② *nm* submarine hunter

antista'minico *nm* antihistamine

anti'stante *prep* ∼ **a** in front of

anti'tarlo *nm inv* woodworm treatment

anti'tarmico *adj* mothproof

antiterro'rismo *nm* counter-terrorism

antiterro'rista *adj* antiterrorist

antiterro'ristico *adj* antiterrorist

an'titesi *nf inv* antithesis

antite'tanica *nf* tetanus injection

antite'tanico *adj* tetanus *attrib*

anti'tetico *adj* antithetical

anti'trust *adj* antitrust

antitumo'rale *adj* which stops the growth of tumours

anti'urto *adj* shockproof

antivaio'losa *nf* smallpox injection

anti'vipera *adj* **siero antivipera** snakebite antidote

antivi'rale *adj* anti-viral

anti'virus *nm inv* Comput antivirus software

antolo'gia *nf* anthology

an'tonimo *nm* antonym

antono'masia: per ∼ a ⟨poeta⟩ quintessential

antra'cite *nf* anthracite; (colore) charcoal [grey]

'antro *nm* cavern

antro'pofago *adj* man-eating, cannibalistic

antropolo'gia *nf* anthropology

antropo'logico *adj* anthropological

antro'pologo, -a *nmf* anthropologist

anu'lare *nm* ring-finger

An'versa *nf* Antwerp

'anzi *conj* in fact; (o meglio) or better still; (al contrario) on the contrary

anzianità *nf* old age; (di servizio) seniority

anzi'ano, -a ① *adj* old, elderly; (di grado ecc) senior ② *nmf* elderly person

anziché *conj* rather than

anzi'tempo *adv* prematurely

anzi'tutto *adv* first of all

a'orta *nf* aorta

A'pache *mf inv* Apache

apar'theid *nf* apartheid

apar'titico *adj* unaligned

apa'tia *nf* apathy

a'patico *adj* apathetic

'ape *nf* bee. **ape regina** queen bee

aperi'tivo *nm* aperitif

aperta'mente *adv* openly

a'perto *adj* open; **all'aria aperta** in the open air; **all'∼** ⟨piscina, teatro⟩ open-air; **∼ a tutti** open to all comers; **rimanere a bocca aperta** be dumbfounded

aper'tura *nf* opening; (inizio) beginning; (ampiezza) spread; (di arco) span; Pol overtures *pl*; Phot aperture. **apertura alare** wing span. **apertura di credito** loan agreement. **apertura di credito presso un negozio** charge account. **apertura domenicale [dei negozi]** Sunday trading. **apertura mentale** openness

api'ario *nm* apiary

'apice *nm* apex; **l'~ di** the acme of

apicol'tore, -trice *nmf* beekeeper

apicol'tura *nf* beekeeping

a'plomb *nm inv* (di un abito) hang; fig aplomb, self-assuredness

ap'nea *nf* **immersione in apnea** free diving

Apoca'lisse *nf* **l'~** the Apocalypse

apoca'littico *adj* apocalyptic

a'pocrifo *adj* apocryphal

apo'geo *nm* apogee

a'polide ① *adj* stateless ② *nmf* stateless person

apo'litico *adj* apolitical

A'pollo *nm* Apollo

apolo'geta *nmf* apologist (**di** for)

apolo'gia *nf* apologia; (celebrazione) eulogy. **apologia di reato** condoning of a criminal act

apoples'sia *nf* apoplexy

apo'plettico *adj* apoplectic

a'postolo *nm* apostle

apostro'fare *vt* (mettere un apostrofo a) write with an apostrophe; reprimand ⟨*persona*⟩

a'postrofo *nm* apostrophe

apote'osi *nf* apotheosis

appaga'mento *nm* fulfilment

appa'gare *vt* satisfy

appa'garsi *vr* **~ di** be satisfied with

appa'gato *adj* sated

appai'are *vt* pair; mate ⟨*animali*⟩

appallotto'lare *vt* roll into a ball

appallotto'larsi *vr* ⟨*gatto*⟩ curl up in a ball; ⟨*farina*⟩ become lumpy

appal'tare *vt* contract out; **~ a imprese esterne** outsource

appalta'tore *nm* contractor

ap'palto *nm* contract; **dare in ~** contract out; **appalto a imprese esterne** outsourcing; **gara di appalto** call for tenders

appan'naggio *nm* (in denaro) annuity; fig prerogative

appan'nare *vt* mist ⟨*vetro*⟩; dim ⟨*vista*⟩

appan'narsi *vr* mist over; ⟨*vista*⟩ grow dim

appa'rato *nm* apparatus; (apparecchiamento) array; (pompa) display.

apparato digerente digestive system.

apparato scenico set

apparecchi'are ① *vt* prepare ② *vi* lay the table Br, set the table

apparecchia'tura *nf* (impianti) equipment

appa'recchio *nm* apparatus; (congegno) device; (radio, TV ecc) set; (aeroplano) aircraft; (telefono) phone. **apparecchio acustico** hearing aid

appa'rente *adj* apparent

apparente'mente *adv* apparently

appa'renza *nf* appearance; **in ~** apparently

appa'rire *vi* appear; (sembrare) look

appari'scente *adj* striking; pej gaudy

apparizi'one *nf* apparition

apparta'mento *nm* flat, apartment Am. **appartamento ammobiliato** furnished flat. **appartamento in multiproprietà** timeshare

appar'tarsi *vr* withdraw

appar'tato *adj* secluded

apparte'nente *adj* **~ a** belonging to

apparte'nenza *nf* membership

apparte'nere *vi* belong

appassio'nante *adj* (storia, argomento) exciting

appassio'nare *vt* excite; (commuovere) move

appassio'narsi *vr* **~ a** become excited by

appassio'nato *adj* passionate; **~ di** (entusiastico) fond of

appas'sire *vi* wither

appas'sirsi *vr* fade

appas'sito *adj* faded

appel'larsi *vr* **~ a** appeal to

ap'pello *nm* appeal; (chiamata per nome) rollcall; (esami) exam session; **fare l'~** call the roll

ap'pena ① *adv* just; (a fatica) hardly ② *conj* [non] **~** as soon as, no sooner ... than; **~ prima di** just before

ap'pendere *vt* hang [up]

appendi'abiti *nm inv* hat-stand, hallstand

appen'dice *nf* appendix; **romanzo d'appendice** novel serialized in a magazine or newspaper

appendi'cite *nf* appendicitis

Appen'nini *nmpl* **gli ~** the Apennines

appen'ninico *adj* Apennine

appesan'tire *vt* weigh down

appesan'tirsi *vr* become heavy

ap'peso ① pp di APPENDERE ② *adj* hanging; (impiccato) hanged

appe'tito *nm* appetite; **aver ~** be hungry; **buon ~!** enjoy your meal!

appetitoso ⋯⋟ approvare

appeti'toso *adj* appetizing; fig tempting

appezza'mento *nm* plot of land

appia'nare *vt* level; fig smooth over

appia'narsi *vr* improve

appiat'tire *vt* flatten

appiat'tirsi *vr* flatten oneself; fig level out

appic'care *vt* ∼ **il fuoco a** set fire to

appicci'care ① *vt* stick; ∼ **a** (fig: appioppare) palm off on ② *vi* be sticky

appicci'carsi *vr* stick; ⟨*cose*⟩ stick together; ∼ **a qualcuno** fig stick to somebody like glue

appiccica'ticcio *adj* sticky; fig clingy

appicci'cato *adj* **stare** ∼ **a qualcuno** be all over somebody

appicci'coso *adj* sticky; fig clingy

appie'dato *adj* **sono** ∼ I don't have the car; **sono rimasto** ∼ I was stranded

appi'eno *adv* fully

appigli'arsi *vr* ∼ **a** get hold of; fig stick to

ap'piglio *nm* fingerhold; (per piedi) foothold; fig pretext

appiop'pare *vt* ∼ **a** palm off on; (fam: dare) give; ∼ **un ceffone a qualcuno** slap somebody

appiso'larsi *vr* doze off

applau'dire *vt/i* applaud

ap'plauso *nm* applause

appli'cabile *adj* applicable

appli'care *vt* apply; enforce ⟨*legge ecc*⟩

appli'carsi *vr* apply oneself

appli'cato ① *nmf* (impiegato) senior clerk ② *adj* (nel ricamo) appliqué; **matematica applicata** applied mathematics

applica'tore *nm* applicator

applicazi'one *nf* application; (di legge) enforcement. **applicazioni** *pl* **tecniche** handicrafts

appoggi'are *vt* lean (**a** against); (mettere) put; (sostenere) back

appoggi'arsi *vr* ∼ **a** lean against; fig rely on

appoggi'ato *adj* leaning (**su** on; **contro**, **a** against)

ap'poggio *nm* support; **appoggi** *pl* fig influential contacts

appollai'arsi *vr* fig perch

ap'porre *vt* affix

appor'tare *vt* bring; (causare) cause; ∼ **delle modifiche a qualcosa** modify something

ap'porto *nm* contribution

apposita'mente *adv* (specialmente) especially; **fatto** ∼ purpose-made

ap'posito *adj* proper

apposizi'one *nf* apposition

ap'posta *adv* on purpose; (espressamente) specially; **neanche a farlo** ∼! what a coincidence!

apposta'mento *nm* ambush; (caccia) lying in wait

appo'stare *vt* post ⟨*soldati*⟩

appo'starsi *vr* lie in wait

ap'prendere *vt* understand; (imparare) learn

apprendi'mento *nm* learning. **apprendimento assistito dal computer** computer-aided learning

appren'dista *nmf* apprentice

apprendi'stato *nm* apprenticeship

apprensi'one *nf* apprehension; **essere in** ∼ **per** be anxious about

appren'sivo *adj* apprehensive

ap'presso *adv & prep* (vicino) near; (dietro) behind; **come** ∼ as follows

appre'stare *vt* prepare

appre'starsi *vr* get ready

apprez'zabile *adj* appreciable

apprezza'mento *nm* appreciation; (giudizio) opinion

apprez'zare *vt* appreciate

apprez'zato *adj* appreciated

ap'proccio *nm* approach

appro'dare *vi* land; ∼ **a** fig come to; **non** ∼ **a nulla** come to nothing

ap'prodo *nm* landing; (luogo) landing-stage

approfit'tare *vi* take advantage (**di** of), profit (**di** by)

approfitta|'tore, -trice *nmf* chancer

approfondi'mento *nm* deepening; **di** ∼ ⟨*corso*⟩ advanced

approfon'dire *vt* broaden, widen ⟨*indagine, conoscenze*⟩

approfon'dirsi *vr* ⟨*divario*⟩ widen

approfon'dito *adj* ⟨*studio, ricerca*⟩ in-depth

appron'tare *vt* get ready, prepare

appropri'arsi *vr* ∼ **a** (essere adatto a) suit; ∼ **di** take possession of; ∼ **indebitamente di** embezzle, misappropriate

appropri'ato *adj* appropriate

appropriazi'one *nf* Jur appropriation. **appropriazione indebita** Jur embezzlement

approssi'mare *vt* ∼ **per eccesso/difetto** round up/down

approssi'marsi *vr* draw near

approssimativa'mente *adv* approximately

approssima'tivo *adj* approximate

approssimazi'one *nf* approximation

appro'vare *vt* approve of; approve ⟨*legge*⟩

a

approvazi'one *nf* approval

approvvigiona'mento *nm* supplying; **approvvigionamenti** *pl* provisions

approvvigio'nare *vt* supply

approvvigio'narsi *vr* stock up

appunta'mento *nm* appointment; fam date; **fissare un** ∼, **prendere un** ∼ make an appointment; **darsi** ∼ decide to meet

appun'tare *vt* (annotare) take notes; (fissare) fix; (con spillo) pin; (appuntire) sharpen

appun'tarsi *vr* ∼ **su** ⟨*teoria*⟩ be based on

appun'tato *nm* (carabiniere) lowest rank in the Carabinieri

ap'puntel'larsi *vr* (sostenersi) support oneself

ap'pun'tino *adv* meticulously

appun'tire *vt* sharpen

appun'tito *adj* ⟨*matita*⟩ sharp; ⟨*mento*⟩ pointed

ap'punto¹ *nm* note; (piccola critica) niggle

ap'punto² *adv* exactly; **per l'**∼! exactly!; **stavo** ∼ **dicendo ...** I was just saying ...

appura'mento *nm* verification

appu'rare *vt* verify

a'pribile *adj* that can be opened; **tettuccio apribile** Auto sun roof

apribot'tiglie *nm inv* bottle-opener

a'prile *nm* April; **primo d'aprile** April Fool's Day

aprio'ristico *adj* a priori

a'prire *vt* open; turn on ⟨*luce, acqua ecc*⟩; (con chiave) unlock; open up ⟨*ferita ecc*⟩; ∼ **le ostilità** Mil commence hostilities; **apriti cielo!** heavens above!

a'prirsi *vr* open; (spaccarsi) split; (confidarsi) confide (**con** in)

apri'scatole *nm inv* tin opener, Br, can opener

APT *abbr* (**Azienda di Promozione Turistica**) Tourist Board

aqua'planing *nm* **andare in** ∼ aquaplane

'aquila *nf* eagle; **non è un'**∼! fig he's no genius!

aqui'lino *adj* aquiline

aqui'lone *nm* (giocattolo) kite

aqui'lotto *nm* (piccolo dell'aquila) eaglet

AR *abbr* (**andata e ritorno**) return [ticket]; *abbr* (**avviso di ricevimento**) return receipt for registered letters

ara'besco *nm* arabesque; hum scribble

A'rabia *nf* Arabia. **l'Arabia Saudita** Saudi Arabia

'arabo, -a ① *adj* Arab; ⟨*lingua*⟩ Arabic ② *nmf* Arab ③ *nm* (lingua) Arabic

arabo-israeli'ano *adj* Arab-Israeli

a'rachide *nf* peanut

arago'nese *adj* Aragonese

ara'gosta *nf* lobster

a'raldica *nf* heraldry

a'raldico *adj* heraldic

a'raldo *nm* herald

aran'ceto *nm* orange grove

a'rancia *nf* orange; **succo d'arancia** orange juice

aranci'ata *nf* orangeade

a'rancio *nm* orange (tree); (colore) orange

aranci'one *adj & nm* orange

a'rare *vt* plough

ara'tore *nm* ploughman

a'ratro *nm* plough

ara'tura *nf* ploughing

a'razzo *nm* tapestry

arbi'traggio *nm* Comm arbitrage; Sport refereeing; Jur arbitration

arbi'trare *vt* arbitrate in; Sport referee

arbitrarietà *nf* arbitrariness

arbi'trario *adj* arbitrary

arbi'trato *nm* arbitration

ar'bitrio *nm* will; **è un** ∼ it's very high-handed

'arbitro *nm* arbiter; (Sport: nel calcio, boxe) referee, ref fam; (nel baseball, tennis, cricket) umpire

arboricol'tura *nf* arboriculture

ar'busto *nm* shrub

'arca *nf* ark; (cassa) chest. **l'**∼ **di Noè** Noah's Ark

ar'caico *adj* archaic

arca'ismo *nm* archaism

ar'cangelo *nm* archangel

ar'cano ① *adj* mysterious ② *nm* mystery

ar'cata *nf* arch; (serie di archi) arcade

archeolo'gia *nf* archaeology

archeo'logico *adj* archaeological

arche'ologo, -a *nmf* archaeologist

ar'chetipo *nm* archetype

ar'chetto *nm* Mus bow

architet'tare *vt* fig devise; **cosa state architettando?** fig what are you plotting?

archi'tetto *nm* architect. **architetto d'interni** interior designer

architet'tonico *adj* architectural

architet'tura *nf* anche Comput architecture

archi'trave *nm* lintel

archivi'abile *adj* that can be filed

archivi'are *vt* file, archive; Jur close

archiviazi'one *nf* filing; (Jur: di caso) closing. **archiviazione dati** data storage

ar'chivio *nm* archives *pl*; Comput file

archi'vista *nmf* filing clerk

archi'vistica *nf* rules governing the keeping of archives and records

ARCI *nf abbr* (**Associazione Ricreativa Culturale Italiana**) Italian cultural and leisure association

arci'duca *nm* archduke

arcidu'chessa *nf* archduchess

arci'ere *nm* archer

ar'cigno *adj* grim

arci'one *nm* saddle

arci'pelago *nm* archipelago

arci'vescovo *nm* archbishop

'arco *nm* arch; Math arc; (arma, Mus) bow; **nell'∼ di una giornata/due mesi** in the space of a day/two months. **arco rampante** flying buttress. **arco temporale** time-frame

arcoba'leno *nm* rainbow

arcu'are *vt* bend; **∼ la schiena** ‹gatto› arch its back

arcu'arsi *vr* bend

arcu'ato *adj* bent; ‹schiena di gatto› arched

ar'dente *adj* burning; fig ardent. **camera ardente** chapel of rest

ardente'mente *adv* ardently

'ardere *vt/i* burn. **legna da ardere** firewood

ar'desia *nf* slate

ardi'mento *nm* boldness

ar'dire ① *vi* dare ② *nm* (coraggio) daring, boldness; (sfrontatezza) impudence

ar'dito *adj* daring; (coraggioso) bold; (sfacciato) impudent

ar'dore *nm* (calore) heat; fig ardour

'arduo *adj* arduous; (ripido) steep

'area *nf* area; (superficie) surface. **area fabbricabile** building land. **area di rigore** (in calcio) penalty area, penalty box. **area di servizio** service area. **area soggetta a vincoli ambientali** conservation area. **area [di sosta] per roulotte** trailer park Am, caravan site. **area di sviluppo** growth area

a'rena *nf* arena

are'naria *nf* sandstone

are'narsi *vr* run aground; ‹fig: trattative› reach deadlock; **mi sono arenato** I'm stuck

are'nile *nm* stretch of sand

areo'plano *nm* aeroplane

'argano *nm* winch

argen'tato *adj* silver-plated

ar'genteo *adj* silvery

argente'ria *nf* silver[ware]

argenti'ere *nm* silversmith

Argen'tina *nf* Argentina

argen'tina *nf* (maglia) round-necked pullover

argen'tino[1] *adj* silvery

argen'tino[2], **-a** *adj & nmf* Argentinian

ar'gento *nm* silver; **d'∼** silver. **argento vivo** Chem quicksilver

ar'gilla *nf* clay

argil'loso *adj* ‹terreno› clayey; (simile all'argilla) clay-like

argi'nare *vt* embank; fig hold in check, contain

'argine *nm* embankment; (diga) dike; **fare ∼ a** fig hold in check, contain

argomen'tare *vi* argue

argo'mento *nm* argument; (motivo) reason; (soggetto) subject

argu'ire *vt* deduce

arguta'mente *adv* (con astuzia) shrewdly; (con facezia) wittily

ar'guto *adj* witty; (astuto) shrewd

ar'guzia *nf* wit; (battuta) witticism; (astuzia) shrewdness

'aria *nf* air; (aspetto) appearance; Mus tune; Auto choke; **avere l'∼...** look ...; **mandare all'∼ qualcosa** fig ruin something; **andare all'∼** fig fall through; **a tenuta d'∼** draughtproof; **avere la testa per ∼** fig be absent-minded, have one's head in the clouds; **che ∼ tirava?** fig what was the atmosphere like?; **cambiare ∼** fig have a change of scene; **cambia ∼!** hum get out of here!. **corrente d'aria** draught; **aria-aria** *adj inv* Mil air-to-air. **aria condizionata** air-conditioning. **aria-terra** *adj inv* air-to-ground

ari'ano *adj* Aryan

arida'mente *adv* without emotion

aridità *nf* aridity

'arido *adj* arid

arieggi'are *vt* air; **∼ una stanza** give a room an airing

arieggi'ato *adj* airy

ari'ete *nm* ram; (strumento) battering-ram; Ariete Astr Aries

ari'etta *nf* (brezza) breeze

a'ringa *nf* herring

ari'oso *adj* ‹locale› light and airy

'arista *nf* chine of pork

aristo'cratico, **-a** ① *adj* aristocratic ② *nmf* aristocrat

aristo'crazia *nf* aristocracy

arit'metica *nf* arithmetic

arit'metico *adj* arithmetical

arlec'chino *nm* Harlequin; fig buffoon

'arma *nf* weapon; (forze armate) [armed] forces; **armi** *pl* arms; **chiamare alle armi** call up; **sotto le armi** in the army; **alle prime armi** fig inexperienced, fledg[e]ling; **prendere/deporre le armi** take up arms/ put down one's arms; **passare qualcuno** ⋯⟶

per le armi execute somebody;
confrontarsi ad armi pari compete on an
equal footing. **arma bianca** knife.
arma a doppio taglio fig double-edged
sword. **arma da fuoco** firearm. **arma
di distruzione di massa** weapon of
mass destruction. **arma impropria**
makeshift weapon. **arma segreta** fig
secret weapon. **armi** pl **nucleari** nuclear
weapons

armadi'etto nm locker, cupboard; (in
aereo) overhead locker. **armadietto del
bagno** bathroom cabinet. **armadietto
dei medicinali** medicine cabinet

arma'dillo nm armadillo

ar'madio nm cupboard; (guardaroba)
wardrobe. **armadio a muro** fitted
cupboard

armamen'tario nm tools pl; fig
paraphernalia

arma'mento nm armament, weaponry;
Naut fitting out

ar'mare vt arm; (equipaggiare) fit out; Archit
reinforce

ar'marsi vr arm oneself (**di** with)

ar'mata nf army; (flotta) fleet

ar'mato adj armed; **rapina a mano
armata** armed robbery

arma'tore nm shipowner

arma'tura nf framework; (impalcatura)
scaffolding; (di guerriero) armour

armeggi'are vi fig manoeuvre

Ar'menia nf Armenia

ar'meno, -a adj & nmf Armenian

arme'ria nf Mil armoury

armi'stizio nm armistice

armo'nia nf harmony

ar'monica nf armonica [**a bocca**]
mouth-organ

ar'monico adj harmonic

armoniosa'mente adv harmoniously

armoni'oso adj harmonious

armoniz'zare ① vt harmonize
② vi match

armoniz'zarsi vr ⟨colori⟩ go together,
match

ar'nese nm tool; (oggetto) thing; (congegno)
gadget; **male in ~** in bad condition

'arnia nf beehive

a'roma nm aroma; aromi pl herbs; aromi
pl **naturali/artificiali** natural/artificial
flavourings

aromatera'pia nf aromatherapy

aro'matico adj aromatic

aromatiz'zare vt flavour

'arpa nf harp

ar'peggio nm arpeggio

ar'pia nf harpy

arpi'one nm hook; (pesca) harpoon

ar'pista nmf harpist

arrabat'tarsi vr do all one can

arrabbi'arsi vr get angry

arrabbi'ato adj angry

arrabbia'tura nf rage; **prendersi un'~**
fly into a rage

arraf'fare vt grab

arraf'fone nm fam thief

arrampi'carsi vr climb [up]; **~ sugli
specchi** fig clutch at straws

arrampi'cata nf climb

arrampica|'tore, -trice nmf climber.
arrampicatore sociale social climber

arran'care vi limp, hobble; fig struggle,
limp along

arrangia'mento nm arrangement

arrangi'are vt arrange

arrangi'arsi vr manage; **~ alla meglio**
get by; **arrangiati!** get on with it!

arrangia|'tore, -trice nmf Mus arranger

arra'parsi vr vulg get randy

arre'care vt bring; (causare) cause

arreda'mento nm interior decoration;
(l'arredare) furnishing; (mobili ecc)
furnishings pl

arre'dare vt furnish

arreda|'tore, -trice nmf interior
designer

ar'redo nm furnishings pl

arrem'baggio nm lanciarsi all'**~** fig
stampede

ar'rendersi vr surrender; **~ all'evidenza
dei fatti** face facts

arren'devole adj ⟨persona⟩ yielding

arrendevo'lezza nf softness

arre'stare vt arrest; (fermare) stop

arre'starsi vr halt

ar'resto nm stop; Jur arrest; **la dichiaro in
[stato d'] ~** you are under arrest;
mandato di arresto warrant. **arresto
cardiaco** heart failure, cardiac arrest.
arresti pl **domiciliari** Jur house arrest

arretra'mento nm withdrawal

arre'trare ① vt withdraw; pull back
⟨giocatore⟩
② vi withdraw

arre'trato ① adj (paese ecc) backward;
(Mil: posizione) rear; **numero arretrato** (di
rivista) back number **del lavoro ~** a backlog
of work
② nm (di stipendio) back pay; **essere in ~**
be behind schedule; **arretrati** pl arrears.
arretrati pl **di paga** back pay

arricchi'mento nm enrichment

arric'chire vt enrich

arric'chirsi vr get rich

arric'chito, -a nmf nouveau riche

arricciaca'pelli nm inv tongs

arricci'are vt curl; **~ il naso** turn up
one's nose

ar'ridere *vi* ∼ a qualcuno ⟨*sorte*⟩ smile on somebody

ar'ringa *nf* Jur closing address

arrin'gare *vt* harangue

arrischi'arsi *vr* dare

arrischi'ato *adj* risky; (imprudente) rash

arri'vare *vi* arrive; ∼ a (raggiungere) reach; (ridursi) be reduced to

arri'vato, -a ① *adj* successful; **ben** ∼! welcome!
② *nmf* successful person; **il primo/secondo** ∼ (in gare) the first/second to finish

arrive'derci *int* goodbye; ∼ **a domani** see you tomorrow

arri'vismo *nm* social climbing; (nel lavoro) careerism

arri'vista *nmf* social climber; (nel lavoro) careerist

ar'rivo *nm* arrival; Sport finish; ∼ **previsto per le ore ...** expected time of arrival ...

arro'gante *adj* arrogant

arro'ganza *nf* arrogance

arro'garsi *vr* ∼ **il diritto di fare qualcosa** take it upon oneself to do something; ∼ **il merito** take the credit

arrossa'mento *nm* reddening

arros'sare *vt* make red, redden ⟨*occhi*⟩

arros'sarsi *vr* go red

arros'sire *vi* blush, go red

arro'stire *vt* roast; toast ⟨*pane*⟩; (ai ferri) grill

arro'stirsi *vr* fig broil

ar'rosto *adj & nm* roast; **molto fumo e niente** ∼ fig all show and no substance. **arrosto d'agnello** roast lamb

arro'tare *vt* sharpen; (fam: investire) run over

arro'tino *nm* knife-sharpener

arroto'lare *vt* roll up

arroton'dare *vt* round; Math ecc round off; ∼ **lo stipendio** supplement one's income

arroton'darsi *vr* become round; ⟨*persona*⟩ get plump

arrovel'larsi *vr* ∼ **il cervello** rack one's brains

arroven'tare *vt* make red-hot

arroven'tarsi *vr* become red-hot

arroven'tato *adj* red-hot; ⟨*fig: discorso*⟩ fiery

arruf'fare *vt* ruffle; fig confuse

arruf'farsi *vr* become ruffled

arruf'fato *adj* ⟨*capelli*⟩ dishevelled, tousled

arruffia'narsi *vr* ∼ **[con]** qualcuno fig butter somebody up

arruggi'nire *vt* rust

arruggi'nirsi *vr* go rusty; fig (fisicamente) stiffen up; ⟨*conoscenze*⟩ go rusty

arruggi'nito *adj* rusty

arruola'mento *nm* enlistment

arruo'lare *vt/i* enlist

arruo'larsi *vr* enlist

arse'nale *nm* arsenal; (cantiere) [naval] dockyard

ar'senico *nm* arsenic

'arso ① *pp di* ARDERE
② *adj* burnt; (arido) dry

ar'sura *nf* burning heat; (sete) parching thirst

art déco *nf* art deco

'arte *nf* art; (abilità) craftsmanship; **senza** ∼ **né parte** incapable; **nome d'arte** professional name. **arte drammatica** dramatics; **le belle arti** *pl* the fine arts. **arti** *pl* **figurative** figurative arts. **arti** *pl* **dello spettacolo** performing arts

arte'fare *vt* adulterate ⟨*vino*⟩; disguise ⟨*voce*⟩

arte'fatto *adj* fake; ⟨*vino*⟩ adulterated

ar'tefice ① *nm* craftsman; fig author
② *nf* craftswoman

ar'teria *nf* artery. **arteria [stradale]** arterial road

arterio'sclerosi *nf* arteriosclerosis, hardening of the arteries

arterioscle'rotico *adj* senile

arteri'oso *adj* Anat arterial

'Artico *nm* l'∼ the Arctic

'artico *adj* Arctic

artico'lare ① *adj* articular
② *vt* articulate; (suddividere) divide

artico'larsi *vr* fig ∼ **in** consist of

artico'lato *adj* Auto articulated; fig well-constructed

articolazi'one *nf* Anat articulation

ar'ticolo *nm* article; **articoli** *pl* **per la casa** household goods; **articoli** *pl* **per la cucina** kitchenware; **articoli** *pl* **di marca** brand name goods; **articoli** *pl* **da regalo** gifts; **articoli** *pl* **da spiaggia** beach gear; **articoli** *pl* **sportivi** sports gear; **negozio di articoli sportivi** sports shop; **articoli** *pl* **vari** sundries. **articolo civetta** Comm loss leader. **articolo determinativo** Gram definite article. **articolo di fondo** leader, leading article. **articolo indeterminativo** Gram indefinite article. **articolo di prima pagina** Journ cover story. **articolo principale** Journ lead story

'Artide *nf* l'∼ the Arctic [region]

artifici'ale *adj* artificial

artifici'ere *nm* Mil explosives expert, bomb disposal expert

arti'ficio *nm* artifice; (affettazione) affectation

artificiosità *nf* artificiality

artifici'oso *adj* artful; (affettato) affected

artigi'ana *nf* craftswoman

artigia'nale *adj* made by hand; hum amateurish

artigianal'mente *adv* with craftsmanship; hum amateurishly

artigia'nato *nm* craftsmanship; (ceto) craftsmen *pl*

artigi'ano *nm* craftsman

artigli'ato *adj* with claws

artigli'ere *nm* artilleryman

artiglie'ria *nf* artillery. **artiglieria antiaerea** flak

ar'tiglio *nm* claw; fig clutch; **sfoderare gli artigli** fig show one's claws

ar'tista *nmf* artist

artistica'mente *adv* artistically

ar'tistico *adj* artistic

arti'stoide *adj* arty

art nouveau *nf* art nouveau

'arto *nm* limb

ar'trite *nf* arthritis

ar'tritico, -a *nmf* arthritic

ar'trosi *nf* rheumatism

arzigogo'lato *adj* fantastic, bizarre

ar'zillo *adj* sprightly

a'scella *nf* armpit

ascen'dente ① *adj* ascending ② *nm* (antenato) ancestor; (influenza) ascendancy; Astr ascendant

ascen'denza *nf* ancestry

a'scendere *vi* ascend

ascensi'one *nf* ascent; **l'Ascensione** the Ascension

ascen'sore *nm* lift, elevator Am

a'scesa *nf* ascent; (al trono) accession; (al potere) rise

a'scesi *nf* asceticism

a'scesso *nm* abscess

a'sceta *nmf* ascetic

a'scetico *adj* ascetic

'ascia *nf* axe

asciugabianche'ria *nm inv* (stenditoio) clothes horse; (macchina) tumble-drier

asciugaca'pelli *nm inv* hair dryer, hairdrier

asciuga'mano *nm* towel. **asciugamano di carta** paper towel

asciu'gare *vt* dry; ~ **le stoviglie** do the drying-up

asciu'garsi *vr* dry oneself; (diventare asciutto) dry up; ~ **le mani** dry one's hands

asciuga'trice *nf* tumble dryer

asci'utto *adj* dry; (magro) wiry; ⟨risposta⟩ curt; **essere all'**~ fig be hard up

ascol'tare ① *vt* listen to ② *vi* listen

ascolta|'tore, -trice *nmf* listener

a'scolto *nm* listening; **dare** ~ **a** listen to; **essere in** ~ Radio be listening; **mettersi in** ~ Radio tune in; **prestare** ~ listen

a'scrivere *vt* (attribuire) ascribe; ~ **a** (annoverare) number among

asessu'ato *adj* asexual

a'settico *adj* aseptic

asfal'tare *vt* asphalt

asfal'tato *adj* tarmac

a'sfalto *nm* asphalt

asfis'sia *nf* asphyxia

asfissi'ante *adj* ⟨caldo⟩ oppressive; ⟨fig: persona⟩ annoying

asfissi'are *vt* asphyxiate; fig annoy

'Asia *nf* Asia. **Asia Minore** Asia Minor

asi'ago *nm* full-fat white cheese

asi'atico, -a *adj & nmf* Asian

a'silo *nm* shelter; (d'infanzia) nursery school. **asilo infantile** day nursery. **asilo nido** day nursery. **asilo politico** political asylum

asim'metrico *adj* asymmetric[al]

a'sincrono *adj* asynchronous

a'sino *nm* donkey; (fig: persona stupida) ass; Sch dunce; **qui casca l'**~**!** fig that's where it falls down!

'asma *nf* asthma

a'smatico *adj* asthmatic

asoci'ale *adj* asocial

'asola *nf* buttonhole

a'sparagi *nmpl* asparagus *sg*

aspara'gina *nf* Bot asparagus fern

a'sparago *nm* asparagus

a'spergere *vt* ~ **con/di** sprinkle with

asperità *nf inv* harshness; (di terreno) roughness

asper'sorio *nm* aspergillum, holy-water sprinkler

aspet'tare ① *vt* wait for; (prevedere) expect; ~ **un bambino** be expecting [a baby]; **fare** ~ **qualcuno** keep somebody waiting ② *vi* wait

aspet'tarsi *vr* expect

aspetta'tiva *nf* expectation; (nel lavoro) leave of absence; **all'altezza delle aspettative** up to expectations; **inferiore alle aspettative** not up to expectations. **aspettativa per malattia** sick leave. **aspettativa per maternità** maternity leave

a'spetto¹ *nm* look; (di problema) aspect; **di bell'**~ good-looking

a'spetto² *nm* **sala d'aspetto** waiting room

'aspic *nm* aspic

aspi'rante ① *adj* aspiring; ⟨pompa⟩ suction *attrib*

2 *nmf* (a un posto) applicant; (al trono) aspirant; **gli aspiranti al titolo** the contenders for the title

aspira'polvere *nm inv* vacuum cleaner; **passare l'~** vacuum, hoover

aspi'rare **1** *vt* inhale; Mech suck in; (con elettrodomestici) vacuum, hoover **2** *vi* ~ **a** aspire to

aspi'rato *adj* aspirate

aspira'tore *nm* extractor fan

aspirazi'one *nf* inhalation; Mech suction; (ambizione) ambition

aspi'rina® *nf* aspirin

aspor'tare *vt* take away

a'sporto **da ~** take-away

aspra'mente *adv* (duramente) severely

a'sprezza *nf* (al gusto) sourness; (di clima) severity; (di carattere, parole, suono) harshness; (di odore) pungency; (di litigio) bitterness

a'sprigno *adj* slightly sour

'aspro *adj* ‹al gusto› sour; ‹clima› severe; ‹suono, parole› harsh; ‹odore› pungent; ‹litigio› bitter

assaggi'are *vt* taste

assaggia|'tore, **-trice** *nmf* taster

assag'gini *nmpl* Culin samples

as'saggio *nm* tasting; (piccola quantità) taste; (fig: campione) sample

as'sai *adv* very; (moltissimo) very much; (abbastanza) enough

assa'lire *vt* attack

assali|'tore, **-trice** *nmf* assailant

assal'tare *vt* Mil attack, charge; hold up (banca, treno)

assalta'tore *nm* hold-up man

as'salto *nm* attack; **d'~** ‹giornalismo› aggressive; **prendere d'~** storm ‹città›; fig mob ‹persona›; hold up ‹banca›

assapo'rare *vt* savour

assas'sina *nf* murderess

assassi'nare *vt* murder, assassinate; fig murder

assas'sinio *nm* murder, assassination

assas'sino **1** *adj* murderous **2** *nm* murderer

'asse **1** *nf* board. **asse da stiro** ironing board. **2** *nm* Techn axle; Math axis

assecon'dare *vt* satisfy; (favorire) support; **~ i capricci di qualcuno** indulge somebody's every whim; **~ i desideri di qualcuno** comply with somebody's wishes

assedi'are *vt* besiege

assedi'ato *adj* besieged

as'sedio *nm* siege

assegna'mento *nm* allotment; **fare ~ su** rely on

asse'gnare *vt* allot; award ‹premio›

assegna'tario, **-a** *nmf* recipient

assegnazi'one *nf* (di alloggio, denaro, borsa di studio) allocation; (di premio) award

as'segno *nm* allowance; (bancario) cheque; **contro ~** cash on delivery; **pagare con un ~** pay by cheque. **assegno circolare** bank draft. **assegni familiari** *pl* family allowance. **assegno post-datato** post-dated cheque. **assegno sbarrato** crossed cheque. **assegno non trasferibile** cheque made out to "account payee only". **assegno turistico** traveller's cheque. **assegno a vuoto** bad cheque, dud cheque

assem'blaggio *nm* assemblage

assem'blare *vt* assemble

assem'blea *nf* assembly; (adunanza) gathering. **assemblea generale annuale** Annual General Meeting, AGM

assembra'mento *nm* gathering

assem'brare *vt* gather

assen'nato *adj* sensible

as'senso *nm* assent

assen'tarsi *vr* go away; (da stanza) leave the room

as'sente **1** *adj* absent; (distratto) absent-minded **2** *nmf* absentee

assente'ismo *nm* absenteeism

assente'ista *nmf* frequent absentee

assen'tire *vi* acquiesce (**a** in)

as'senza *nf* absence; (mancanza) lack. **assenza di gravità** zero gravity. **assenze** *pl* **ingiustificate** (a scuola) truancy

asse'rire *vi* assert

asser|'tore, **-trice** *nmf* supporter

asserragli'arsi *vr* barricade oneself

asser'tivo *adj* assertive

asservi'mento *nm* subservience

asser'vire *vt* fig enslave

asser'virsi *vr* fig be subservient

asserzi'one *nf* assertion

assesso'rato *nm* [council] department

asses'sore *nm* councillor

assesta'mento *nm* settlement

asse'stare *vt* arrange; **~ un colpo** deal a blow

asse'starsi *vr* settle oneself

asse'stato *adj* **ben ~** well-judged

asse'tato *adj* parched

as'setto *nm* order; Naut, Aeron trim; **in ~ di guerra** on a war footing; **cambiare l'~ territoriale dell'Europa** change the map of Europe

assi'cella *nf* lath

assicu'rabile *adj* insurable

assicu'rare vt assure; Comm insure; register ⟨posta⟩; (fissare) secure; (accertare) ensure

assicu'rarsi vr (con contratto) insure oneself; (legarsi) fasten oneself; ~ **che** make sure that

assicu'rata nf registered letter

assicura'tivo adj insurance attrib

assicu'rato adj insured; **lettera assicurata** registered letter

assicura|'tore, -trice ① nmf insurance agent
② adj insurance; **società assicuratrice** insurance company

assicurazi'one nf assurance; (contratto) insurance; **fare un'~** take out insurance. **assicurazione multirischi** blanket cover. **assicurazione sanitaria** medical insurance. **assicurazione di viaggio** travel insurance

assidera'mento nm exposure

asside'rarsi vr fam be frozen; Med be suffering from exposure

asside'rato adj Med suffering from exposure; fam frozen

assidua'mente adv assiduously

assiduità nf assiduity

as'siduo adj assiduous; ⟨cliente⟩ regular

assi'eme adj [together] with

assil'lante adj ⟨persona, pensiero⟩ nagging

assil'lare vt pester

assil'larsi vr torment oneself

as'sillo nm worry

assimi'lare vt assimilate

assimilazi'one nf assimilation

assi'oma nm axiom

assio'matico adj axiomatic

As'siria nf Assyria

as'sise nfpl assizes; **Corte d'Assise** Court of Assize[s]

assi'stente nmf assistant. **assistente sociale** social worker. **assistente sociosanitario** care worker. **assistente universitario** assistant lecturer. **assistente di volo** flight attendant

assi'stenza nf assistance; (presenza) presence. **assistenza alla clientela** customer care. **assistenza medica** medical care. **assistenza ospedaliera** hospital treatment. **assistenza sanitaria** health care. **assistenza sociale** social work

assistenzi'ale adj welfare

assistenzia'lismo nm abuse of the welfare state

as'sistere ① vt assist; (curare) nurse
② vi ~ **a** (essere presente) be present at; watch (spettacolo ecc)

assi'stito adj ~ **da computer** computer-aided

'asso nm ace; **piantare in** ~ leave in the lurch. **asso nella manica** trump card

associ'are vt join; (collegare) associate

associ'arsi vr join forces; Comm enter into partnership; ~ **a** join; subscribe to (giornale ecc)

associ'ato, -a ① adj associate
② nmf partner

associazi'one nf association. **associazione di categoria** trade-union. **associazione per delinquere** criminal organization. **Associazione Europea di Libero Scambio** European Free Trade Association. **associazione in partecipazione** Comm joint venture

associazio'nismo nm Pol excessive tendency to form associations; Psych associationism

asso'dare vt ascertain ⟨verità⟩

assogget'tare vt subject

assogget'tarsi vr submit

asso'lato adj sunny

assol'dare vt recruit

as'solo nm Mus solo

as'solto pp di ASSOLVERE

assoluta'mente adv absolutely

assolu'tismo nm absolutism

assolu'tista nmf absolutist

assolu'tistico adj absolutist

asso'luto adj absolute

assolu'torio adj **formula assolutoria** acquittal

assoluzi'one nf acquittal; Relig absolution

as'solvere vt perform ⟨compito⟩; Jur acquit; Relig absolve

assolvi'mento nm performance

assomigli'are vi ~ **a** be like, resemble

assomigli'arsi vr resemble each other

assom'marsi vr combine; ~ **a qualcosa** add to something

asso'nanza nf assonance

asson'nato adj drowsy

asso'pirsi vr doze off

assor'bente adj & nm absorbent. **assorbente igienico** sanitary towel

assor'bire vt absorb

assor'dante adj deafening

assor'dare vt deafen

assorti'mento nm assortment

assor'tire vt match ⟨colori⟩

assor'tito adj assorted; ⟨colori, persone⟩ matched

as'sorto adj engrossed

assottiglia'mento nm thinning; (aguzzamento) sharpening

assottigli'are *vt* make thin; (aguzzare) sharpen; (ridurre) reduce

assottigli'arsi *vr* grow thin; ⟨finanze⟩ be whittled away

assue'fare *vt* accustom

assue'farsi *vr* ∼ **a** get used to

assue'fatto *adj* (a caffè, aspirina) immune to the effects; (a droga) addicted

assuefazi'one *nf* (a caffè, aspirina) immunity to the effects; (a droga) addiction

as'sumere *vt* assume; take on ⟨impiegato⟩ ∼ **informazioni** make inquiries

as'sunto ① *pp di* ASSUMERE ② *nm* task

assunzi'one *nf* (di impiegato) employment; **l'Assunzione** Relig Assumption

assurdità *nf inv* absurdity; **dire delle** ∼ talk nonsense

as'surdo *adj* absurd

'asta *nf* pole; Mech bar; Comm auction; **a mezz'**∼ at half-mast. **asta di livello [dell'olio]** Auto dip-stick

a'stemio *adj* abstemious

aste'nersi *vr* abstain (**da** from)

astensi'one *nf* abstention

astensio'nismo *nm* persistent abstention

astensio'nista *nmf* persistent abstainer

astensio'nistico *adj* **tendenza astensionistica** tendency to abstain

aste'nuto, -a *nmf* abstainer

aste'risco *nm* asterisk

aste'roide *nm* asteroid

'astice *nm* crayfish

asti'cella *nf* stick; (in salto in alto) bar

astig'matico *adj* astigmatic

astigma'tismo *nm* astigmatism

asti'nenza *nf* abstinence; **crisi di astinenza** withdrawal symptoms

'astio *nm* rancour; **avere** ∼ **contro qualcuno** bear somebody a grudge

asti'oso *adj* resentful

a'stragalo *nm* anklebone

'astrakan *nm* astrakhan

astrat'tezza *nf* abstractness

astrat'tismo *nm* abstractionism

a'stratto *adj* abstract

astrin'gente *adj & nm* astringent

'astro *nm* star

+astro *suff* **giovinastro** *nm* lout; **giallastro** *adj* yellowish; **dolciastro** *adj* sweetish

astro'fisica *nf* astrophysics

astro'fisico, -a ① *adj* astrophysical ② *nmf* astrophysicist

astrolo'gia *nf* astrology

astro'logico *adj* astrological

a'strologo, -a *nmf* astrologer

astro'nauta *nmf* astronaut

astro'nautica *nf* astronautics

astro'nave *nf* spaceship

astrono'mia *nf* astronomy

astro'nomico *adj* (anche fig) astronomic, astronomical

a'stronomo, -a *nmf* astronomer

astrusità *nf* abstruseness

a'struso *adj* abstruse

a'stuccio *nm* case

a'stuto *adj* shrewd; (furbo) cunning

a'stuzia *nf* shrewdness; (azione) trick

a'tavico *adj* atavistic

ate'ismo *nm* atheism

ate'lier *nm inv* (di alta moda) atelier; (di artista) [artist's] studio

A'tene *nf* Athens

ate'neo *nm* university

ateni'ese *adj & nmf* Athenian

'ateo, -a *adj & nmf* atheist

a'tipico *adj* atypical

at'lante *nm* atlas; **i monti dell'Atlante** the Atlas Mountains

at'lantico *adj* Atlantic; **l'[Oceano] Atlantico** the Atlantic [Ocean]

at'leta *nmf* athlete

a'tletica *nf* athletics *sg.* **atletica leggera** track and field events. **atletica pesante** weight-lifting, boxing, wrestling, etc

a'tletico *adj* athletic

atle'tismo *nm* athleticism

atmo'sfera *nf* atmosphere

atmo'sferico *adj* atmospheric

a'tollo *nm* atoll

a'tomica *nf* atom bomb

a'tomico *adj* atomic

atomiz'zare *vt* atomize

atomizza'tore *nm* atomizer

'atomo *nm* atom

'atono *adj* unstressed

'atrio *nm* entrance hall, lobby

a'troce *adj* atrocious; ⟨terrible⟩ dreadful

atroce'mente *adv* atrociously

atrocità *nf inv* atrocity

atro'fia *nf* atrophy

atrofiz'zare *vt* atrophy

atrofiz'zarsi *vr* Med, fig atrophy

attac'cabile *adj* attachable

attaccabot'toni *nmf inv* [crashing] bore

attacca'brighe *nmf inv* troublemaker

attacca'mento *nm* attachment

attac'cante ① *adj* attacking ② *nm* Sport forward

34

attacca'panni *nm inv* [coat-]hanger; (a muro) [clothes-]hook

attac'care ① *vt* attach; (legare) tie; (appendere) hang; (cucire) sew on; (contagiare) pass on; (assalire) attack; (iniziare) start ② *vi* stick; (diffondersi) catch on

attac'carsi *vr* cling; (affezionarsi) become attached; (litigare) quarrel

attacca'ticcio *adj* sticky; fig clinging and tiresome

attac'cato *adj* stuck

attacca'tura *nf* junction.
attaccatura dei capelli hairline

attac'chino *nm* billposter

at'tacco *nm* attack; (punto d'unione) junction; (accesso) fit. **attacco aereo** air attack. **attacco cardiaco** heart attack. **attacco epilettico** epileptic fit

attanagli'are *vt* (fig: tormentare) haunt

attar'darsi *vr* stay late; (indugiare) linger

attec'chire *vi* take; (moda ecc) catch on

atteggia'mento *nm* attitude

atteggi'are *vt* assume

atteggi'arsi *vr* ∼ a pose as

attem'pato *adj* elderly

atten'darsi *vr* camp, pitch camp

atten'dente *nm* Mil batman

at'tendere ① *vt* wait for ② *vi* ∼ a attend to

at'tendersi *vr* expect

atten'dibile *adj* reliable

attendibilità *nf* reliability

atte'nersi *vr* ∼ a stick to

attenta'mente *adv* attentively

atten'tare *vi* ∼ a make an attempt on

atten'tato *nm* act of violence; (politico) assassination attempt; ∼ alla vita di attempted murder of. **attentato dinamitardo** bombing

attenta|'tore, -trice *nmf* attacker; (a scopo politico) terrorist

at'tento *adj* attentive; (accurato) careful; ∼! look out!; stare ∼ pay attention; 'attenti al cane' 'beware of the dog'

attenu'ante *nf* extenuating circumstance

attenu'are *vt* attenuate; (minimizzare) minimize; subdue (colori ecc); calm (dolore); soften ⟨colpo⟩

attenu'arsi *vr* diminish

attenuazi'one *nf* lessening

attenzi'one *nf* attention; (cura) care; **fare** ∼ be careful; ∼! watch out!; ∼, **prego** your attention, please; **coprire di attenzioni** lavish attention on

atter'raggio *nm* landing. **atterraggio di fortuna** emergency landing

atter'rare ① *vt* knock down ② *vi* land

atter'rire *vt* terrorize

atter'rirsi *vr* be terrified

at'tesa *nf* waiting; (aspettativa) expectation; in ∼ di waiting for

at'teso *pp di* ATTENDERE

atte'stabile *adj* certifiable

atte'stare *vt* state; (certificare) certify

atte'stato *nm* certificate

attestazi'one *nf* certificate; (dichiarazione) declaration

'Attica *nf* Attica

'attico¹ *nm* (lingua) Attic

'attico² *nm* (appartamento) penthouse

at'tiguo *adj* adjacent

attil'lato *adj* ⟨vestito⟩ close-fitting

'attimo *nm* second; un ∼! just a sec!; in un ∼ in double-quick time; non ho avuto un ∼ di respiro I haven't had time to draw breath

atti'nente *adj* ∼ a pertaining to

at'tingere *vt* draw; fig obtain

atti'rare *vt* attract

atti'rarsi *vr* draw ⟨attenzione⟩; incur ⟨odio⟩

attitudi'nale *nm* test attitudinale aptitude test

atti'tudine *nf* (disposizione) aptitude; (atteggiamento) attitude

atti'vare *vt* activate

attivazi'one *nf* setting in motion, turning on; Phys, Chem activation

atti'vismo *nm* activism

atti'vista *nmf* activist

attività *nf inv* activity; Comm assets *pl*. **attività fisse** *pl* fixed assets. **attività liquide** *pl* Comm liquid assets

at'tivo ① *adj* active; Comm productive ② *nm* assets *pl*

attiz'zare *vt* poke; fig stir up

attizza'toio *nm* poker

'atto *nm* act; (azione) action; Comm, Jur deed; (certificato) certificate; **fare** ∼ **di presenza** put in an appearance; **mettere in** ∼ put into action; atti *pl* (di società ecc) proceedings. **atti** *pl* **di libidine violenta** indecent assault. **atti** *pl* **osceni** gross indecency. **atto di vendita** bill of sale

+attolo *suff* vermiciattolo *nm* slimy individual

at'tonito *adj* astonished

attorcigli'are *vt* twist

attorcigli'arsi *vr* get twisted

at'tore *nm* actor

attorni'are *vt* surround

attorni'arsi *vr* ∼ di surround oneself with

at'torno ① *adv* around, about ② *prep* ∼ a around, about

attrac'care *vt/i* dock

attra'ente *adj* attractive

at'trarre *vt* attract

at'trarsi *vr* be attracted to each other

attrat'tiva *nf* charm, attraction

attraversa'mento *nm* (di strada) crossing. **attraversamento pedonale** pedestrian crossing, crosswalk Am

attraver'sare *vt* cross; (passare) go through

attra'verso *prep* through; (obliquamente) across

attrazi'one *nf* attraction. **attrazioni** *pl* **turistiche** tourist attractions

attrez'zare *vt* equip; Naut rig

attrez'zarsi *vr* kit oneself out

attrezza'tura *nf* equipment; Naut rigging. **attrezzatura da campeggio** camping equipment

at'trezzo *nm* tool; **attrezzi** *pl* equipment; Sport appliances *pl*

attribu'ibile *adj* attributable

attribu'ire *vt* attribute

attribu'irsi *vr* ascribe to oneself; ～ **il merito di** claim credit for

attri'buto *nm* attribute

attribuzi'one *nf* attribution

at'trice *nf* actress

at'trito *nm* friction

attrup'pare *vt* assemble

attrup'parsi *vr* gather

attu'abile *adj* feasible

attuabilità *nf* viability

attu'ale *adj* present; (di attualità) topical; (effettivo) actual

attualità *nf* topicality; (avvenimento) news; **programma di attualità** current affairs programme

attualiz'zare *vt* update

attual'mente *adv* at present

attu'are *vt* carry out

attu'ario, -a *nmf* actuary

attu'arsi *vr* be realized

attua'tore *nm* Techn actuator

attuazi'one *nf* carrying out

attuti'mento *nm* (di colpo) softening; (di suoni) muffling

attu'tire *vt* deaden; ～ **il colpo** soften the blow

au'dace *adj* daring, bold; (insolente) audacious

au'dacia *nf* daring, boldness; (insolenza) audacity

audiapprendi'mento *nm* audio-based learning

'audience *nf inv* (telespettatori) audience

'audio *nm* audio

audiocas'setta *nf* audio cassette

audio'leso *adj* hearing-impaired

audio'libro *nm* audiobook, talking book

audio'metrico *adj* Med aural

audiovi'sivo *adj* audiovisual

'auditing *nm* auditing

audi'torio *nm* auditorium

audizi'one *nf* audition; Jur hearing

'auge *nm* height; **essere in** ～ be popular

augu'rare *vt* wish

augu'rarsi *vr* hope

au'gurio *nm* wish; (presagio) omen; **auguri!** all the best!; (a Natale) Happy Christmas!; **tanti auguri** best wishes

au'gusto *adj* august

'aula *nf* classroom; Univ lecture-hall; (sala) hall; **silenzio in** ～**!** silence in court!. **aula bunker** (in tribunale) secure courtroom. **aula magna** Univ great hall. **aula del tribunale** courtroom

aumen'tare *vt/i* increase; ～ **di peso** gain weight

au'mento *nm* increase; (di stipendio) [pay] rise. **aumento di prezzo** price increase

'aureo *adj* golden

au'reola *nf* halo

au'rora *nf* dawn. **aurora boreale** aurora borealis, Northern Lights

auscul'tare *vt* Med auscultate

ausili'are *adj & nmf* auxiliary

auspi'cabile *adj* è ～ **che ...** it is to be hoped that ...

auspi'care *vt* hope for

au'spicio *nm* omen; **auspici** *pl* (protezione) auspices; **è di buon** ～ it is a good omen

austerità *nf* austerity

au'stero *adj* austere

Austra'lasia *nf* Australasia

au'strale *adj* southern

Au'stralia *nf* Australia

australi'ano, -a *adj & nmf* Australian

'Austria *nf* Austria

au'striaco, -a *adj & nmf* Austrian

austroun'garico *adj* Austro-Hungarian

autar'chia *nf* autarchy

au'tarchico *adj* autarchic

aut aut *nm inv* either-or [choice]

autenti'care *vt* authenticate

autenti'cato *adj* certified

autenticità *nf* authenticity

au'tentico *adj* authentic; (vero) true

au'tismo *nm* autism

au'tista *nm* driver

au'tistico *adj* autistic

'auto *nf inv* car; **viaggiare in** ～ travel by car. **auto blindata** armour-plated car. **auto a quattro ruote motrici** four-wheel drive car. **auto sportiva** sports car. **auto a trazione anteriore** front- ⋯⟶

wheel drive car. **auto usata** second-hand car

auto+ *pref* self+

autoabbron'zante ① *nm* self-tan ② *adj* self-tanning

autoaccesso'rista *nmf* car accessory supplier

autoade'sivo ① *adj* self-adhesive ② *nm* sticker

autoaffermazi'one *nf* self-assertion

autoambu'lanza *nf* ambulance

autoa'nalisi *nf* self-analysis

autoartico'lato *nm* articulated lorry

autobiogra'fia *nf* autobiography

autobio'grafico *adj* autobiographical

auto'blinda *nf* armoured car

auto'bomba *nf* car-bomb

auto'botte *nf* tanker

'autobus *nm inv* bus

auto'carro *nm* lorry

autocertificazi'one *nf* self-certification

autoci'sterna *nf* tanker

auto'clave *nf* (contenitore ad alta pressione) autoclave; (idraulica) surge tank

autocombusti'one *nf* spontaneous combustion

autocommiserazi'one *nf* self-pity

autocompiaci'mento *nm* smugness, self-satisfaction

autocompiaci'uto *adj* smug, self-satisfied

autoconcessio'nario *nm* car dealer

autocon'trollo *nm* self-control

au'tocrate *nm* autocrat

auto'cratico *adj* autocratic

auto'critica *nf* self-criticism

au'toctono *adj* native, aboriginal

autode'nuncia *nf* spontaneous confession

autodeterminazi'one *nf* self-determination

autodi'datta ① *adj* self-taught ② *nmf* self-educated person, autodidact

autodi'fesa *nf* self-defence

autodisci'plina *nf* self-discipline

autodi'struggersi *vr* self-destruct, auto-distruct

autodistrut'tivo *adj* self-destructive

autodistruzi'one *nf* self-destruction

autoferrotranvi'ario *adj* public transport *attrib*

autoferrotranvi'eri *nmpl* public transport workers

autoffi'cina *nf* garage

autofinanzia'mento *nm* self-financing

autofinanzi'arsi *vr* be self-financing; ⟨*persona*⟩ use one's own finance

autogesti'one *nf* self-management

autoge'stirsi *vr* ⟨operai, studenti⟩ be self-managing

autoge'stito *adj* self-managed

auto'gol *nm inv* Sport own goal

autogo'verno *nm* home rule, self-rule

au'tografo *adj & nm* autograph

auto'grill *nm inv* motorway café

autogrù *nf inv* breakdown truck, recovery vehicle

autogui'dato *adj* homing *attrib*

autoim'mune *adj* autoimmune

autoiro'nia *nf* self-mockery

autola'vaggio *nm* car wash

autolesi'one *nf* self-inflicted wound

autolesio'nismo *nm* self-harm; fig self-destruction

autolesio'nistico *adj* self-destructive

auto'linea *nf* bus line

au'toma *nm* robot

automatica'mente *adv* automatically

auto'matico ① *adj* automatic; **auto con cambio ~** automatic ② *nm* (bottone) press-stud; (fucile) automatic

automatiz'zare *vt* automate

automatizzazi'one *nf* automation

automazi'one *nf* automation

auto'mezzo *nm* motor vehicle; **uscita automezzi** motor vehicles exit

auto'mobile *nf* [motor] car. **automobile da corsa** racing car

automobi'lina *nf* toy car

automobi'lismo *nm* motoring

automobi'lista *nmf* motorist

automobi'listico *adj* ⟨industria⟩ automobile *attrib*

automodel'lismo *nm* model car making; (collezione) model car collecting

autono'leggio *nm* car rental

autonoma'mente *adv* autonomously

autono'mia *nf* autonomy; Auto range; (di laptop, cellulare) battery life

au'tonomo *adj* autonomous

auto'parco *nm* (insieme di auto) fleet of cars

autopat'tuglia *nf* patrol car

auto'pista *nf* [fairground] race track

auto'pompa *nf* fire engine

auto'psia *nf* autopsy

autopunizi'one *nf* self-punishment

auto'radio *nf inv* car radio; (veicolo) radio car

au|'tore, -trice *nmf* author; (di pitture) painter; (di furto ecc) perpetrator; **quadro d'~** genuine master

autoregolamentazi'one *nf* self-regulation

autore'parto *nm* Mil mechanized unit

auto'revole *adj* authoritative; (che ha influenza) influential

autorevo'lezza *nf* authority

autoriduzi'one *nf* protest which takes the form of paying less than the requisite amount

autori'messa *nf* garage

autoriparazi'oni *nfpl* '∼' 'car repairs', 'auto repairs'

autorità *nf inv* authority

autori'tario *adj* autocratic

autorita'rismo *nm* authoritarianism

autori'tratto *nm* self-portrait

autoriz'zare *vt* authorize

autorizzazi'one *nf* authorization

auto'scatto *nm* Phot automatic shutter release

auto'scontro *nm inv* bumper car

autoscu'ola *nf* driving school

autosno'dato *nm* articulated bus

autosoc'corso *nm* breakdown service; (veicolo) breakdown van, breakdown truck

auto'starter *nm inv* Auto self-starter

auto'stop *nm* hitch-hiking, hitching; **fare l'∼** hitch-hike, hitch

autostop'pista *nmf* hitch-hiker

auto'strada *nf* motorway, highway Am. **autostrada dell'informazione** information superhighway. **autostrada a pedaggio** toll motorway. **Autostrada del Sole** Highway of the Sun (connecting Milan and Reggio Calabria)

autostra'dale *adj* motorway *attrib*, highway *attrib* Am

autosuffici'ente *adj* self-sufficient

autosuffici'enza *nf* self-sufficiency

autosuggesti'one *nf* autosuggestion

autotrasporta|'tore, -trice *nmf* haulier, carrier

autotra'sporto *nm* road haulage

auto'treno *nm* articulated lorry, roadtrain

autove'icolo *nm* motor vehicle

auto'velox *nm inv* speed camera

autovet'tura *nf* motor vehicle

autun'nale *adj* autumnal; ⟨giornata, vestiti⟩ autumn *attrib*

au'tunno *nm* autumn

aval'lare *vt* endorse, back ⟨cambiale⟩: fig endorse

a'vallo *nm* endorsement

avam'braccio *nm* forearm

avam'posto *nm* Mil forward position

A'vana *nf* Havana

a'vana ① *nm inv* (sigaro) Havana [cigar]; (colore) tobacco, dark brown
② *adj inv* ⟨colore⟩ tobacco-coloured, dark brown

avangu'ardia *nf* vanguard; fig avant-garde; **essere all'∼** be in the forefront; Techn be at the leading edge; **d'∼** avant-garde

avansco'perta *nf* reconnaissance; **andare in ∼** reconnoitre

avanspet'tacolo *nm* **da ∼** in poor taste

a'vanti ① *adv* (in avanti) forward; (davanti) in front; (prima) before; **∼!** (entrate) come in!; (suvvia) come on!; '**∼**' (su semaforo) 'cross now', 'walk' Am; **∼ diritto** straight ahead; **più ∼** further on; **va' ∼!** go ahead!; **andare ∼** (precedere) go ahead; ⟨orologio⟩ be fast; **∼ e indietro** backwards and forwards
② *adj* (precedente) before
③ *prep* **∼ a** before; (in presenza di) in the presence of

avanti'eri *adv* the day before yesterday

avan'treno *nm* front axle assembly

avanza'mento *nm* progress; (promozione) promotion

avan'zare ① *vi* advance; (progredire) progress; (essere d'avanzo) be left [over]
② *vt* advance; (superare) surpass; (promuovere) promote

avan'zarsi *vr* advance; (avvicinarsi) approach

avan'zata *nf* advance

avan'zato *adj* advanced; (nella notte) late; **in età avanzata** elderly

a'vanzo *nm* remainder; Comm surplus; **avanzi** *pl* (rovine) remains; (di cibo) leftovers. **avanzo di galera** jailbird

ava'raccio *nm* Scrooge

ava'ria *nf* (di motore) engine failure

avari'arsi *vr* spoil

avari'ato *adj* ⟨frutta, verdura⟩ rotten; ⟨carne⟩ tainted

ava'rizia *nf* avarice

a'varo, -a ① *adj* stingy
② *nmf* miser

a'vena *nf* oats *pl*

a'vere ① *vt* have; (ottenere) get; (indossare) wear; (provare) feel; **ho trent'anni** I'm thirty; **ha avuto il posto** he got the job; **∼ fame/freddo** be hungry/cold; **ho mal di denti** I've got toothache; **cos'ha a che fare con lui?** what has it got to do with him?; **∼ da fare** be busy; **∼ luogo** take place; **che hai?** what's the matter with you?; **nei hai per molto?** will you be long?; **quanti ne abbiamo oggi?** what date is it today?; **avercela con qualcuno** have it in for somebody
② *v aux* have; **non l'ho visto** I haven't seen him; **lo hai visto?** have you seen him?; **l'ho visto ieri** I saw him yesterday
③ *nm* **averi** *pl* wealth *sg*

avia|'tore, -trice *nmf* aviator

aviazi'one *nf* aviation; Mil Air Force

a

avicol'tura *nm* poultry farming
avida'mente *adv* avidly
avidità *nf* avidness
'avido *adj* avid
avi'ere *nm* aircraft[s]man
avio'getto *nm* jet [plane]
avio'linea *nf* airline
aviotraspor'tato *adj* airborne
avitami'nosi *nf* vitamin deficiency
a'vito *adj* ancestral
'avo, -a *nmf* ancestor
avo'cado *nm inv* avocado
a'vorio *nm* ivory
a'vulso *adj* ∼ **dal contesto** fig taken out of context
Avv. *abbr* (**avvocato**) lawyer
avva'lersi *vr* avail oneself (**di** of)
avvalla'mento *nm* depression
avvalo'rare *vt* bear out ⟨*tesi*⟩; endorse ⟨*documento*⟩; (accrescere) enhance
avvam'pare *vi* flare up; (arrossire) blush
avvantaggi'are *vt* favour
avvantaggi'arsi *vr* ∼ **di** benefit from; (approfittare) take advantage of
avve'dersi *vr* (accorgersi) notice; (capire) realize
avve'duto *adj* shrewd
avvelena'mento *nm* poisoning
avvele'nare *vt* poison
avvele'narsi *vr* poison oneself
avvele'nato *adj* poisoned
avve'nente *adj* attractive
avve'nenza *nf* attraction, charm
avveni'mento *nm* event
avve'nire ① *vi* happen; (aver luogo) take place ② *nm* future
avveni'rismo *nm* excessive confidence in the future
avveni'ristico *adj* futuristic
avven'tarsi *vr* fling oneself
avventata'mente *adv* recklessly
avven'tato *adj* ⟨*decisione*⟩ rash
avven'tizio *adj* (personale) temporary; (guadagno) casual
av'vento *nm* advent; Relig Advent
avven'tore *nm* regular customer
avven'tura *nf* adventure; (amorosa) affair; **d'**∼ ⟨*film*⟩ adventure *attrib*
avventu'rarsi *vr* venture
avventuri'ero, -a ① *nm* adventurer ② *nf* adventuress
avventu'rismo *nm* adventurism
avventu'ristico *adj* adventurist
avventu'roso *adj* adventurous
avve'rabile *adj* ⟨*previsione*⟩ that may come true

avve'rarsi *vr* come true
av'verbio *nm* adverb
avver'sare *vt* oppose
avver'sario, -a ① *adj* opposing ② *nmf* opponent
avversi'one *nf* aversion
avversità *nf inv* adversity
av'verso *adj* (sfavorevole) adverse; (contrario) averse
avver'tenza *nf* (cura) care; (avvertimento) warning; (avviso) notice; (premessa) foreword; **avvertenze** *pl* (istruzioni) instructions
avver'tibile *adj* (disagio) perceptible
avverti'mento *nm* warning
avver'tire *vt* warn; (informare) inform; (sentire) feel
avvertita'mente *adv* deliberately
avvez'zare *vt* accustom
avvez'zarsi *vr* accustom oneself
av'vezzo *adj* ∼ **a** used to
avvia'mento *nm* starting; Comm goodwill
avvi'are *vt* start
avvi'arsi *vr* set out
avvi'ato *adj* under way; **bene** ∼ thriving
avvicenda'mento *nm* (in agricoltura) rotation; (nel lavoro) replacement; (delle stagioni) change
avvicen'dare *vt* rotate
avvicen'darsi *vr* take turns, alternate
avvicina'mento *nm* approach
avvici'nare *vt* bring near; approach ⟨*persona*⟩
avvici'narsi *vr* come nearer, approach; **avvicinarsi a** come nearer to, approach
avvi'lente *adj* demoralizing; (umiliante) humiliating
avvili'mento *nm* despondency; (degradazione) degradation
avvi'lire *vt* dishearten; (degradare) degrade
avvi'lirsi *vr* lose heart; (degradarsi) degrade oneself
avvi'lito *adj* disheartened; (degradato) degraded
avvilup'pare *vt* envelop
avvilup'parsi *vr* wrap oneself up; (aggrovigliarsi) get entangled
avvinaz'zato *adj* drunk
avvin'cente *adj* ⟨*libro ecc*⟩ enthralling
av'vincere *vt* enthral
avvinghi'are *vt* clutch
avvinghi'arsi *vr* cling
av'vio *nm* start-up; **dare l'**∼ **a qualcosa** get something under way; **prendere l'**∼ get under way
avvi'saglia *nf* (di malattia) first sign
avvi'sare *vt* inform; (mettere in guardia) warn

av'viso *nm* notice; (annuncio) announcement; (avvertimento) warning; (pubblicitario) advertisement; **a mio ~** in my opinion. **avviso di accreditamento** advice slip. **avviso a cura del ministero della salute** government health warning. **avviso di chiamata in linea** call waiting. **avviso di garanzia** Jur notification that one is to be the subject of a legal enquiry

avvista'mento *nm* sighting

avvi'stare *vt* catch sight of; **~ terra** make landfall

avvi'tare *vt* screw in; screw down ‹coperchio›

avvi'tarsi *vr* ‹aereo› go into a spin

avvi'tata *nf* (di aereo) spin

avviz'zire *vi* wither

avviz'zito *adj* withered

avvo'cato *nm* lawyer; fig advocate. **avvocato del diavolo** devil's advocate

avvoca'tura *nf* legal profession; (insieme di avvocati) lawyers

av'volgere *vt* wrap [up]

av'volgersi *vr* wrap oneself up

avvol'gibile *nm* roller blind

avvolgi'mento *nm* winding

av'volto *adj* **~ in** wrapped in

avvol'toio *nm* vulture

aza'lea *nf* azalea

Azerbaigi'an *nm* Azerbaijan

azerbaigi'ano, **-a** *adj* & *nmf* Azerbaijani

azi'enda *nf* business, firm. **azienda agricola** farm. **azienda elettrica** electricity board. **azienda a partecipazioni statali** enterprise in which the government has a shareholding. **azienda di soggiorno** tourist bureau

azien'dale *adj* ‹politica, dirigente› company *attrib*; ‹giornale› in-house

azienda'listico *adj* company *attrib*

azio'nabile *adj* which can be operated

aziona'mento *nm* operation

azio'nare *vt* operate

azio'nario *adj* share *attrib*; **mercato azionario** share market

azi'one *nf* action; Fin share; **d'~** ‹romanzo, film› action[-packed]; **ad ~** ritardata delayed action. **azione sindacale** industrial action

azio'nista *nmf* shareholder

a'zoto *nm* nitrogen

az'teco, **-a** *adj* & *nmf* Aztec

azzan'nare *vt* seize with its teeth; sink its teeth into ‹gamba›

azzar'dare *vt* risk

azzar'darsi *vr* dare

azzar'dato *adj* risky; (precipitoso) rash

az'zardo *nm* hazard; **gioco d'azzardo** game of chance

azzec'care *vt* hit; (fig: indovinare) guess

azzera'mento *nm* setting to zero; fig **corso di azzeramento** remedial classes *pl*

azze'rare *vt* reset

azzi'mato *adj* dapper

'azzimo *adj* unleavened

azzit'tire *vt* silence, hush

azzit'tirsi *vr* go quiet, fall silent

azzop'pare *vt* lame

Az'zorre *nfpl* **le ~** the Azores

azzuf'farsi *vr* come to blows

azzur'rato *adj* ‹lenti› blue-tinted

az'zurro *adj* & *nm* blue; **principe azzurro** Prince Charming; **gli azzurri** the Italian national team

azzur'rognolo *adj* bluish

Bb

babà *nm inv* **~ al rum** rum baba

bab'beo [1] *adj* foolish [2] *nm* idiot

'babbo *nm* fam dad, daddy. **Babbo Natale** Father Christmas

bab'buccia *nf* slipper

babbu'ino *nm* baboon

ba'bordo *nm* Naut port side

baby boom *nm* baby boom

baby'sitter *nmf inv* baby-sitter; **fare il/la ~** babysit, do baby-sitting

ba'cato *adj* worm-eaten; **avere il cervello ~** have a slate loose

'bacca *nf* berry

baccalà *nm inv* dried salted cod

bac'cano *nm* din

bac'cello *nm* pod

bac'chetta *nf* rod; (magica) wand; (di direttore d'orchestra) baton; (di tamburo) drumstick

ba'checa *nf* showcase; (in ufficio) notice board. **bacheca elettronica** Comput bulletin board

bacia'mano *nm* kiss on the hand; **fare il ∼ a qualcuno** kiss somebody's hand

baci'are *vt* kiss

baci'arsi *vr* kiss [each other]

ba'cillo *nm* bacillus

baci'nella *nf* basin; (contenuto) basinful

ba'cino *nm* basin; Anat pelvis; (di porto) dock; (di minerali) field. **bacino carbonifero** coalfield. **bacino d'utenza** catchment area

'bacio *nm* kiss; **bacio sulla bocca** kiss on the lips

backgammon *nm* backgammon

'baco *nm* worm. **baco da seta** silkworm

'bacon *nm* bacon

ba'cucco *adj* **un vecchio ∼** a senile old man

'bada *nf* **tenere qualcuno a ∼** keep somebody at bay

ba'dare *vi* take care (**a** of); (fare attenzione) look out; **bada ai fatti tuoi!** mind your own business!

ba'dia *nf* abbey

ba'dile *nm* shovel

'badminton *nm* badminton

'baffi *nmpl* moustache *sg*; (di animale) whiskers; **mi fa un baffo** I don't give a damn; **ridere sotto i ∼** laugh up one's sleeve

baf'futo *adj* moustached

ba'gagli *nmpl* luggage, baggage; **ritiro bagagli** baggage claim

bagagli'aio *nm* Rail luggage van, baggage car Am; Auto boot

ba'gaglio *nm* luggage, baggage; Mil kit; **un ∼** a piece of luggage. **bagaglio a mano** hand-luggage, hand-baggage. **bagaglio in eccesso, bagaglio eccedente** excess baggage

baga'rino *nm* ticket tout

baga'tella *nf* trifle; Mus bagatelle

baggia'nata *nf* piece of nonsense; **non dire baggianate** don't talk nonsense

Bagh'dad *nf* Baghdad

bagli'ore *nm* glare; (improvviso) flash; (fig: di speranza) glimmer

bagna'cauda *nf* vegetables (especially raw) in an oil, garlic and anchovy sauce typical of Piedmont

ba'gnante *nmf* bather

ba'gnare *vt* wet; (inzuppare) soak; (immergere) dip; (innaffiare) water; ⟨mare, lago⟩ wash; ⟨fiume⟩ flow through

ba'gnarsi *vr* get wet; (al mare ecc) swim, bathe; **'vietato ∼'** 'no bathing'

bagnasci'uga *nm inv* edge of the water, waterline

ba'gnato *adj* wet; **bagnato fradicio** soaked

ba'gnino, -a *nmf* life guard

'bagno *nm* bath; (stanza) bathroom; (gabinetto) toilet; (al mare) swim, bathe; **bagni** *pl* (stabilimento) lido; **fare il ∼** have a bath; (nel mare ecc) [have a] swim, bathe; **andare in ∼** go to the bathroom, go to the toilet; **mettere a ∼** soak; **con ∼** ⟨camera⟩ en suite. **bagno oculare** eyebath. **bagno rivelatore** Phot developing bath. **bagno di sangue** bloodbath. **bagno di sviluppo** Phot developing bath. **bagno turco** Turkish bath

bagnoma'ria *nm* **cuocere a ∼** cook in a double saucepan

bagnoschi'uma *nm inv* bubble bath, foam bath

ba'guette *nf inv* French loaf, baguette

Ba'hamas *nfpl* **le ∼** the Bahamas

Bah'rain *nm* Bahrain, Bahrein

'baia *nf* bay

baio'netta *nf* bayonet

'baita *nf* mountain chalet

bala'ustra, balau'strata *nf* balustrade

balbet'tare *vt/i* stammer; ⟨bambino⟩ babble

balbet'tio *nm* stammering; (di bambino) babble

bal'buzie *nf* stutter

balbuzi'ente ① *adj* stuttering ② *nmf* stutterer

Bal'cani *nmpl* Balkans

bal'canico *adj* Balkan

balco'nata *nf* Theat balcony, dress circle

balcon'cino *nm* **reggiseno a balconcino** underwired bra

bal'cone *nm* balcony

baldac'chino *nm* canopy; **letto a baldacchino** four-poster bed

bal'danza *nf* boldness

baldan'zoso *adj* bold

bal'doria *nf* revelry; **far ∼** have a riotous time

Bale'ari *nfpl* **le [isole] ∼** the Balearics, the Balearic Islands

ba'lena *nf* whale

bale'nare *vi* lighten; fig flash; **mi è balenata un'idea** I've just had an idea

bale'niera *nf* whaler

ba'leno *nm* **in un ∼** in a flash

balenot'tera *nf* **balenottera azzurra** blue whale

ba'lera *nf* dance hall

ba'lestra *nf* crossbow

'balia¹ *nf* wetnurse

ba'lia² *nf* **in ∼ di** at the mercy of

ba'listico *adj* ballistic; **perito balistico** ballistics expert

'balla *nf* bale; (fam: frottola) tall story

bal'labile *adj* **essere** ∼ be good for dancing to

bal'lare *vi* dance; **andare a** ∼ go dancing

bal'lata *nf* ballad

balla'toio *nm* (nelle scale) landing

balle'rino, -a ① *nmf* dancer; (classico) ballet dancer ② *nf* (classica) ballet dancer, ballerina

bal'letto *nm* ballet

bal'lista *nmf* fam bullshitter

'ballo *nm* dance; (il ballare) dancing; **sala da ballo** ballroom; **essere in** ∼ ⟨lavoro, vita⟩ be at stake; ⟨persona⟩ be committed; **tirare qualcuno in** ∼ involve somebody. **ballo liscio** ballroom dancing. **ballo in maschera** masked ball

ballonzo'lare *vi* skip about

ballot'taggio *nm* second count [of votes]

balne'are *adj* bathing *attrib*; **stagione balneare** swimming season; **stazione balneare** seaside resort

balneazi'one *nf* 'divieto di balneazione' 'no bathing'

ba'lordo *adj* foolish; (stordito) stunned; **tempo** ∼ nasty weather

bal'samico *adj* ⟨aria⟩ balmy

'balsamo *nm* balsam; (per capelli) conditioner; (lenimento) remedy

'baltico *adj* Baltic; **il [mar] Baltico** The Baltic [Sea]

balu'ardo *nm* bulwark

'balza *nf* crag; (di abito) flounce

bal'zano *adj* (idea) weird

bal'zare *vi* bounce; (saltare) jump; ∼ **in piedi** leap to one's feet

'balzo *nm* bounce; (salto) jump; **prendere la palla al** ∼ fig seize an opportunity

bam'bagia *nf* cotton wool; **vivere nella** ∼ fig be in clover

bam'bina *nf* little girl; (piccola) baby; **ha avuto una** ∼ she had a [baby] girl

bambi'naia *nf* nursemaid, nanny

bambi'nata *nf* childish thing to do/say

bam'bino *nm* child; (appena nato) baby; **avere un** ∼ have a baby; (maschio) have a [baby] boy; **bambini** *pl* children, kids; (piccoli) babies. **bambino prodigio** child prodigy

bambi'none, -a *nmf* pej big *or* overgrown child

bam'boccio *nm* chubby child; (sciocco) simpleton; (fantoccio) rag doll

'bambola *nf* doll

bambo'lotto *nm* male doll

bambù *nm* bamboo

ba'nale *adj* banal

banalità *nf inv* banality

banaliz'zare *vt* trivialize

ba'nana *nf* banana

ba'nano *nm* banana (tree)

'banca *nf* bank. **banca d'affari** merchant bank, investment bank. **banca [di] dati** databank. **banca etica** ethical bank. **Banca Europea per la Ricostruzione e lo Sviluppo** European Bank for Reconstruction and Development. **banca degli occhi** eye bank. **banca del sangue** blood bank. **banca dello sperma** sperm bank

banca'rella *nf* stall

bancarel'lista *nmf* stallholder

ban'cario, -a ① *adj* banking *attrib*; **trasferimento bancario** bank transfer ② *nmf* bank employee

banca'rotta *nf* bankruptcy; **fare** ∼ go bankrupt

banchet'tare *vi* banquet

ban'chetto *nm* banquet

banchi'ere *nm* banker

ban'china *nf* Naut quay; (in stazione) platform; (di strada) path. **banchina spartitraffico** central reservation, median strip Am. **banchina non transitabile** soft verge

ban'chisa *nf* floe

'banco *nm* (di scuola) desk; (di negozio) counter; (di officina) bench; (di gioco, banca) bank; (di mercato) stall; (degli imputati) dock; **sotto** ∼ under the counter; **medicinale da banco** over the counter medicines. **banco dei formaggi** (in supermercato) cheese counter; (in mercato) cheese stall. **banco di ghiaccio** ice floe. **banco informazioni** information desk. **banco di nebbia** fog bank. **banco di sabbia** sandbank

'bancomat® *nm inv* (sportello) cashpoint, cash dispenser, cash machine; (carta) bank card, cash card

ban'cone *nm* counter; (in bar) bar

banco'nota *nf* banknote, bill Am; **banconote** *pl* paper currency

'banda *nf* band; (di delinquenti) gang. **banda d'atterraggio** Aeron landing strip. **banda larga** Comput broadband. **banda passante** bandwidth. **banda rumorosa** rumble strip

ban'dana *nf* bandanna

banderu'ola *nf* weathercock; Naut pennant

bandi'era *nf* flag; **cambiare** ∼ change sides, switch allegiances

bandie'rina *nf* (nel calcio) corner flag

bandie'rine *nfpl* bunting

ban'dire *vt* banish; (pubblicare) publish; fig dispense with ⟨formalità, complimenti⟩

ban'dista *nmf* bandsman

bandi'tismo *nm* banditry

ban'dito *nm* bandit

bandi'tore *nm* (di aste) auctioneer

'bando *nm* proclamation. **bando di concorso** job advertisement (published in an official gazette for a job for which a competitive examination has to be sat)

bang *nm inv* wham. **bang sonico** sonic boom

Bangla'desh *nm* Bangladesh

bar *nm inv* bar

'bara *nf* coffin

ba'racca *nf* hut; (catapecchia) hovel; **mandare avanti la ∼** keep the ship afloat

barac'cato, -a ① *adj* living in a shanty town
② *nmf* shanty town dweller

barac'chino *nm* (di gelati, giornali) kiosk; Radio CB radio

barac'cone *nm* (roulotte) circus caravan; (in luna park) booth; (fig: organizzazione) lumbering great dinosaur of an organization

barac'copoli *nf inv* shanty town

bara'onda *nf* chaos; **non fare ∼** don't make a mess

ba'rare *vi* cheat

'baratro *nm* chasm

barat'tare *vt* barter

ba'ratto *nm* barter

ba'rattolo *nm* jar; (di latta) tin

'barba *nf* beard; (fam: noia) bore; **farsi la ∼** shave; **in ∼ a** in spite of; **è una ∼** (noia) it's boring

barbabi'etola *nf* beetroot; **barbabietole** *pl* beetroot. **barbabietola da zucchero** sugar beet

Bar'bados *nfpl* **le ∼** Barbados

barbagi'anni *nm inv* barn owl

bar'barico *adj* barbaric

bar'barie *nf inv* barbarity

barba'rismo *nm* barbarism

'barbaro ① *adj* barbarous
② *nm* barbarian

'barbecue *nm inv* barbecue, BBQ

bar'betta *nf* Naut painter

barbi'ere *nm* barber; (negozio) barber's

bar'biglio *nm* barb

barbi'turico *nm* barbiturate

bar'bone, -a ① *nm* (vagabondo) vagrant; (cane) poodle
② *nf* bag lady

bar'boso *adj* fam boring

barbu'gliare *vi* mumble

bar'buto *adj* bearded

'barca *nf* boat; **una ∼ di** fig a lot of. **barca a motore** motorboat. **barca da pesca** fishing boat. **barca a remi** rowing boat, rowboat Am. **barca di salvataggio** lifeboat. **barca a vela** sailing boat, sailboat Am

barcai'olo *nm* boatman

barcame'narsi *vr* manage

barca'rola *nf* Mus barcarole

Barcel'lona *nf* Barcelona

barcol'lare *vi* stagger

barcol'loni *adv* camminare **∼** stagger

bar'cone *nm* barge; (di ponte) pontoon

bar'dare *vt* harness

bar'darsi *vr* hum dress up

barda'tura *nf* (per cavallo) harness

ba'rella *nf* stretcher

barelli'ere *nm* stretcher-bearer

'Barents *nm* **mare di Barents** Barents Sea

ba'rese *adj* from Bari

bari'centro *nm* centre of gravity

ba'rile *nm* barrel

bari'lotto *nm* fig tub of lard

ba'rista ① *nm* barman
② *nf* barmaid

ba'ritono *nm* baritone

bar'lume *nm* glimmer; **un ∼ di speranza** a glimmer of hope

'barman *nm inv* barman

'baro *nm* cardsharp

ba'rocco *adj & nm* baroque

ba'rometro *nm* barometer

baro'nale *adj* baronial

ba'rone *nm* baron; **i baroni** fig the top brass

baro'nessa *nf* baroness

'barra *nf* bar; (lineetta) oblique; Naut tiller. **barra delle applicazioni** Comput task bar. **barra dei menu** Comput menu bar. **barra di navigazione** navigation bar. **barra retroversa** backslash. **barra di rimorchio** tow bar. **barra di scorrimento** Comput scroll bar. **barra spaziatrice** space bar. **barra di stato** Comput status bar. **barra degli strumenti** Comput tool bar. **barra di titolo** Comput title bar; **barre** *pl* **laterali antintrusione** Auto side impact bars

bar'rage *nm inv* Sport jump-off

bar'rare *vt* block off ‹strada›

barri'care *vt* barricade

barri'cata *nf* barricade

barri'era *nf* barrier; (stradale) road-block; Geol reef. **barriera corallina** coral reef. **barriera linguistica** language barrier. **barriera razziale** colour bar. **barriera del suono** sound barrier

bar'rire *vi* trumpet

bar'rito *nm* trumpeting

ba'ruffa *nf* scuffle; **far ∼** quarrel

barzel'letta *nf* joke; **∼ sporca** o **spinta** dirty joke

basa'mento *nm* base; Geol bedrock

ba'sare *vt* base

ba'sarsi *vr* ∼ **su** be based on; **mi baso su ciò che ho visto** I'm going on [the basis of] what I saw

'**basco, -a** ① *adj & nmf* Basque ② *nm* (copricapo) beret

'**base** *nf* basis; (fondamento) foundation; Mil base; Pol rank and file; **a** ∼ **di** containing; **in** ∼ **a** on the basis of. **base di controllo** ground control. **base [di] dati** database. **base d'intesa** common ground. **base logica** logical basis. **base navale** naval base

'**baseball** *nm* baseball

ba'setta *nf* sideburn

basi'lare *adj* basic

ba'silica *nf* basilica

Basili'cata *nf* Basilicata

ba'silico *nm* basil

ba'sista *nm* grass roots politician; (di un crimine) mastermind

'**basket** *nm* basketball

bas'sezza *nf* lowness; (di statura) shortness; (viltà) vileness

bas'sista *nmf* bassist

'**basso** ① *adj* low; (di statura) short; ⟨acqua⟩ shallow; ⟨televisione⟩ quiet; (vile) despicable; **parlare a bassa voce** speak quietly, speak in a low voice, **la bassa Italia** southern Italy ② *nm* lower part; Mus bass [guitar]; **guardare in** ∼ look down

basso'fondo *nm* (pl **bassifondi**) shallows; **bassifondi** *pl* (quartieri poveri) slums

bassorili'evo *nm* bas-relief

bas'sotto *nm* dachshund

ba'stardo, -a ① *adj* bastard; (di animale) mongrel ② *nmf* bastard; (animale) mongrel

ba'stare *vi* be enough; (durare) last; **basta!** that's enough!, that'll do!; **basta che** (purché) provided that; **basta così** that's enough; **basta così?** is that enough?, will that do?; (in negozio) will there be anything else?; **basta andare alla posta** you only have to go to the post office; **basta che tu lo faccia bene** make sure you do it well

Basti'an con'trario *nm* contrary old so-and-so

basti'mento *nm* ship; (carico) cargo

basti'one *nm* bastion

basto'nare *vt* beat

basto'nata *nf* **dare una** ∼ **a** beat with a stick

baston'cino *nm* (da sci) ski pole. **bastoncino di pesce** fish finger, fish stick Am

ba'stone *nm* stick; (da golf) club; (da passeggio) walking stick. **bastone da hockey** hockey stick

ba'tosta *nf* blow

bat'tage *nm inv* **battage pubblicitario** media hype

bat'taglia *nf* battle; (lotta) fight

battagli'are *vi* battle; fig fight

bat'taglio *nm* (di campana) clapper; (di porta) knocker

battagli'one *nm* battalion

bat'tello *nm* boat; (motonave) steamer

bat'tente *nm* (di porta) wing; (di finestra) shutter; (battaglio) knocker

'**battere** ① *vt* beat; hit, knock ⟨testa, spalla⟩; (percorrere) scour; thresh ⟨grano⟩; break ⟨record⟩ ② *vi* (bussare, urtare) knock; ⟨cuore⟩ beat; ⟨ali ecc⟩ flap; Tennis serve; ∼ **a macchina** type; ∼ **gli occhi** blink; ∼ **il piede** tap one's foot; ∼ **le mani** clap [one's hands]; ∼ **le ore** strike the hours

bat'teri *nmpl* bacteria

batte'ria *nf* battery; Mus drums *pl*; (Sport: eliminatoria) heat. **batteria a bottone** button battery

bat'terico *adj* bacterial

bat'terio *nm* bacterium

batteriolo'gia *nf* bacteriology

batterio'logico *adj* bacteriological

batte'rista *nmf* drummer

'**battersi** *vr* fight

bat'tesimo *nm* baptism, christening

battez'zare *vt* baptize, christen

battiba'leno *nm* **in un** ∼ in a flash

batti'becco *nm* squabble

batticu'ore *nm* palpitation; **mi venne il** ∼ I was scared

bat'tigia *nf* water's edge

batti'mano *nm* applause

batti'panni *nm inv* carpetbeater

batti'scopa *nm inv* skirting board

batti'stero *nm* baptistery

batti'strada *nm inv* outrider; (di pneumatico) tread; Sport pacesetter

battitap'peto *nm inv* carpet sweeper

'**battito** *nm* (alle tempie) throbbing; (di orologio) ticking; (della pioggia) beating. **battito cardiaco** heartbeat

batti|'tore, -trice *nmf* Sport batsman

bat'tuta *nf* beat; (colpo) knock; (spiritosaggine) wisecrack; (osservazione) remark; Mus bar; Tennis service; Theat cue; (dattilografia) stroke. **battuta d'arresto** setback

ba'tuffolo *nm* flock

ba'ule *nm* trunk

bau'xite *nf* bauxite

'**bava** *nf* dribble; (di cane ecc) slobber; **aver la** ∼ **alla bocca** foam at the mouth

bava'glino *nm* bib

ba'vaglio *nm* gag

bava'rese *nf* ice-cream cake with milk, eggs and cream

'**bavero** *nm* collar

ba'zar *nm inv* bazaar

ba'zooka *nm inv* bazooka

baz'zecola *nf* trifle

bazzi'care *vt/i* haunt

baz'zotto *adj* soft-boiled

be'arsi *vr* delight (**di** in)

beata'mente *adv* blissfully

beatifi'care *vt* beatify

beati'tudine *nf* bliss

be'ato *adj* blissful; Relig blessed; ∼ **te!** lucky you!

beauty-'case *nm inv* toilet bag

bebè *nm inv* baby

bec'caccia *nf* woodcock

bec'care *vt* peck; fig catch

bec'carsi *vr* (litigare) quarrel

bec'cata *nf* beakful; (colpo) peck

beccheggi'are *vi* pitch

bec'chime *nm* birdseed

bec'chino *nm* gravedigger

'**becco** *nm* beak; (di caffettiera ecc) spout; **chiudi il** ∼ fam shut your trap; **non ha il** ∼ **di un quattrino** fam he's skint; **restare a** ∼ **asciutto** fam end up with nothing. **becco Bunsen** Bunsen [burner]. **becco a gas** gas burner

bec'cuccio *nm* spout

'**beeper** *nm inv* beeper

be'fana *nf* legendary old woman who brings presents to children on Twelfth Night; (giorno) Twelfth Night; (donna brutta) old witch

'**beffa** *nf* hoax; **farsi beffe di qualcuno** mock somebody

bef'fardo *adj* derisory; ⟨persona⟩ mocking

bef'fare *vt* mock

bef'farsi *vr* ∼ **di** make fun of

beffeggi'are *vt* taunt

'**bega** *nf* quarrel; **è una bella** ∼ it's really annoying

be'gonia *nf* begonia

beh *int* well

'**beige** *adj inv & nm* beige

Bei'rut *nf* Beirut

be'lare *vi* bleat

be'lato *nm* bleating

'**belga** *adj & nmf* Belgian

'**Belgio** *nm* Belgium

Bel'grado *nf* Belgrade

Be'lize *nm* Belize

'**bella** *nf* (in carte, Sport) decider; (innamorata) sweetheart. **bella di giorno** Bot morning glory. **bella di notte** fig lady of the night

bel'lezza *nf* beauty; **che** ∼! how lovely!; **per** ∼ (per decorazione) for decoration; **chiudere/finire in** ∼ end on a high note; **la** ∼ **di tre mesi/500 euro** all of three months/500 euros

belli'cismo *nm* warmongering

belli'cistico *adj* warmongering

'**bellico** *adj* war *attrib*; **periodo bellico** wartime

bellicosità *nf* belligerence

belli'coso *adj* warlike

bellige'rante *adj & nmf* belligerent

bellige'ranza *nf* belligerence

bellim'busto *nm* dandy

'**bello** ①*adj* nice; (di aspetto) beautiful; ⟨uomo⟩ handsome; (moralmente) good; **cosa fai di** ∼ **stasera?** what are you up to tonight?; **oggi fa** ∼ it's a nice day today; **una bella cifra** a lot; **un bel piatto di pasta** a big plate of pasta; **nel bel mezzo** right in the middle; **un bel niente** absolutely nothing; **bell'e fatto** over and done with; **bell'amico sei!** fine friend you are!; **questa è bella!** that's a good one!; **bel voto** good mark; **il bel mondo** the beautiful people; **le belle arti** the fine arts ② *nm* (bellezza) beauty; (innamorato) sweetheart; **sul più** ∼ at the crucial moment; **il** ∼ **è che** ... the funny thing is that ...

beltà *nf liter* beauty

'**belva** *nf* wild beast

be'molle *nm* Mus flat

ben ▶ BENE

benché *conj* though, although

'**benda** *nf* bandage; (per occhi) blindfold

ben'dare *vt* bandage; blindfold ⟨occhi⟩

bendi'sposto *adj* **essere** ∼ **verso** be well-disposed towards

'**bene** ① *adv* well; **ben** ∼ thoroughly; ∼! good!; **star** ∼ (di salute) be well; ⟨vestito, stile⟩ suit; (finanziariamente) be well off; **non sta** ∼ (non è educato) it's not nice; **sta/va** ∼! all right!; **ti sta** ∼! [it] serves you right!; **voler** ∼ **a** love; **di** ∼ **in meglio** better and better; **fare** ∼ (aver ragione) do the right thing; **fare** ∼ **a** ⟨cibo⟩ be good for; **una persona per** ∼ a good person; **per** ∼ ⟨fare⟩ properly; **è ben difficile** it's very difficult; **ben cotto** well done; **come tu ben sai** as you well know; **lo credo** ∼! I can well believe it! ② *nm* good; **per il tuo** ∼ for your own good; **beni** *pl* (averi) property *sg*; **un** ∼ **di famiglia** a family heirloom. **beni ambientali** *pl* environment. **beni di consumo** *pl* consumer products, consumer goods. **beni culturali** *pl* cultural heritage. **beni immobili** *pl* real estate, realty Am. **beni mobili** *pl* movables

benedet'tino *adj & nm* Benedictine

bene'detto *adj* blessed

bene'dire *vt* bless; **mandare qualcuno a farsi** ∼ fam tell somebody to get lost.

benedizi'one *nf* blessing

benedu'cato *adj* well-mannered

benefat'|tore, -trice *nmf* benefactor; benefactress

benefi'care *vt* help

benefi'cenza *nf* charity

benefici'are *vi* ∼ **di** profit by

benefici'ario, -a *adj & nmf* beneficiary

bene'ficio *nm* benefit; **con** ∼ **di inventario** with reservations. **beneficio accessorio** perquisite

be'nefico *adj* beneficial; (di beneficenza) charitable

'Benelux *nm* Benelux

beneme'renza *nf* benevolence

bene'merito *adj* worthy

bene'placito *nm* consent, approval

be'nessere *nm* well-being

bene'stante ① *adj* well off ② *nmf* well-off person

bene'stare *nm* consent

benevo'lenza *nf* benevolence

be'nevolo *adj* benevolent

ben'fatto *adj* well-made

Ben'gala *nm* Bengal

ben'godi *nm* **il paese di** ∼ a land of plenty

benia'mino *nm* favourite

be'nigno *adj* kindly; Med benign

Be'nin *nm* Benin

beninfor'mato ① *adj* well-informed ② *npl* **i beninformati** those in the know

benintenzio'nato, -a ① *adj* well-meaning ② *nmf* well-meaning person

benin'teso *adv* needless to say, of course; ∼ **che ...** of course, ...

be'nissimo *int* fine

benpen'sante *adj & nmf* self-righteous

bensì *conj* but rather

benser'vito *nm* **dare il** ∼ **a qualcuno** give somebody the sack

benve'nuto *adj & nm* welcome; **benvenuta!** welcome!

ben'visto *adj* **essere** ∼ **(da qualcuno)** go down well (with somebody)

benvo'lere *vt* **farsi** ∼ **da qualcuno** win somebody's affection; **prendere a** ∼ **qualcuno** take a liking to somebody; **essere benvoluto da tutti** be well-liked by everyone

benvo'luto *adj* well-liked

ben'zene *nm* benzene

ben'zina *nf* petrol, gas Am; **far** ∼ get petrol. **benzina avio** aviation fuel. **benzina con piombo** leaded petrol.

benzina senza piombo o **verde** leadfree petrol, unleaded petrol. **benzina super** four-star petrol, premium gas Am

benzi'naio, -a *nmf* petrol station attendant, gas station attendant Am

be'one, -a *nmf* fam boozer

'berbero, -a *adj & nmf* Berber

'bere ① *vt* drink; (assorbire) absorb; fig swallow; ∼ **una tazza di tè** have a cup of tea ② *nm* drinking; **da** ∼ **e da mangiare** food and drink

berga'motto *nm* bergamot

'Bering *nm* **il mare di** ∼ the Bering Sea; **lo stretto di** ∼ the Bering Straits

ber'lina *nf* Auto saloon; **mettere alla** ∼ **qualcuno** ridicule somebody

berli'nese ① *nmf* Berliner ② *adj* Berlin *attrib*

Ber'lino *nm* Berlin. **Berlino Est** East Berlin

Ber'muda *nfpl* **le** ∼ the Bermudas

ber'muda *nmpl* (pantaloni) Bermuda shorts

'Berna *nf* Berne

ber'noccolo *nm* bump; (disposizione) flair

ber'retto *nm* beret, cap. **berretto a pompon** bobble hat

bersagli'are *vt* fig bombard

ber'saglio *nm* target

bescia'mella *nf* béchamel, white sauce

be'stemmia *nf* swearword; (maledizione) oath; (sproposito) blasphemy

bestemmi'are *vi* swear

'bestia *nf* animal; (persona brutale) beast; (persona sciocca) fool; **andare in** ∼ fam blow one's top; **lavorare come una** ∼ slave away. **bestia nera** fig pet hate

besti'ale *adj* bestial; ⟨espressione, violenza⟩ brutal; fam: ⟨freddo, fame⟩ terrible; **fa un caldo/freddo** ∼ it's dreadfully hot/cold

bestialità *nf inv* bestiality; fig nonsense

besti'ame *nm* livestock

betabloc'cante *nm* betablocker

Be'tlemme *nf* Bethlehem

betoni'era *nf* concrete mixer

'bettola *nf* fig dive

be'tulla *nf* birch. **betulla bianca** silver birch

be'vanda *nf* drink. **bevanda alcolica** alcoholic drink

bevi'|tore, -trice *nmf* drinker

be'vuta *nf* drink

be'vuto pp di BERE

Bhu'tan *nm* Bhutan

bi+ *pref* bi+

bi'ada *nf* fodder

bianche'ria *nf* linen. **biancheria per la casa** household linen. **biancheria** ⋯⟩

intima underwear; (da donna) lingerie.
biancheria da letto bed linen

bian'chetto *nm* whitener

bi'anco, -a ① *adj* white; ⟨foglio⟩ blank;
voce bianca treble voice
② *nmf* white
③ *nm* white; **mangiare in** ∼ eat bland
food; **andare in** ∼ fam not score; **in** ∼ **e
nero** ⟨film, fotografia⟩ black and white,
monochrome; **passare una notte in** ∼
have a sleepless night. **bianco sporco**
off white. **bianco d'uovo** egg white

biancomangi'are *nm* blancmange

bian'core *nm* (bianchezza) whiteness

bianco'segno *nm* Jur blank document
bearing a signature

bianco'spino *nm* hawthorn

biasci'care *vt* (mangiare) eat noisily;
(parlare) mumble

biasi'mare *vt* blame

biasi'mevole *adj* blameworthy

bi'asimo *nm* blame

'Bibbia *nf* Bible

bibe'ron *nm inv* [baby's] bottle

'bibita *nf* [soft] drink. **bibita alcolica**
alcopop. **bibita gasata** fizzy drink

'biblico *adj* biblical

bibliogra'fia *nf* bibliography

biblio'grafico *adj* bibliographical

biblio'teca *nf* library; (mobile) bookcase

bibliote'cario, -a *nmf* librarian

bicame'rale *adj* two-chamber *attrib*,
bicameral

bicarbo'nato *nm* bicarbonate.
bicarbonato di sodio bicarbonate of
soda

bicchie'rata *nf* glassful

bicchi'ere *nm* glass

bicchie'rino *nm* fam tipple

bicente'nario *nm* bicentenary

'bici *nf* fam bike

bici'cletta *nf* bicycle, bike; **andare in** ∼
cycle, go by bike; (saper portare la bicicletta)
ride a bicycle. **bicicletta da corsa**
racer

bi'cipite *nm* biceps

bi'cocca *nf* hovel

bico'lore *adj* two-coloured

bidè *nm inv* bidet

bi'dello, -a *nmf* janitor, [school]
caretaker

bidirezio'nale *adj* bidirectional

bido'nare *vt* con, swindle; **farsi** ∼ be
conned

bido'nata *nf* fam swindle

bi'done *nm* bin; (fam: truffa) swindle; **fare
un** ∼ **a qualcuno** fam stand somebody up.
bidone dell'immondizia, bidone

della spazzatura rubbish bin, trash
can Am

bidon'ville *nf inv* shantytown

bi'eco *adj* callous

bi'ella *nf* connecting rod

Bielo'russia *nf* Belarus

bielo'russo, -a *adj & nmf* Belorussian

bien'nale *adj* biennial

bi'ennio *nm* two-year period

bi'erre *nfpl* (Brigate Rosse) Red Brigades

bi'etola *nf* beet

bifo'cale *adj* bifocal

bi'folco, -a *nmf* fig boor

bifor'carsi *vr* fork

biforcazi'one *nf* fork

bifor'cuto *adj* forked

biga'mia *nf* bigamy

'bigamo, -a ① *adj* bigamous
② *nmf* bigamist

big bang *nm* big bang

bighello'nare *vi* loaf around

bighel'lone *nm* loafer

bigiotte'ria *nf* costume jewellery;
(negozio) jeweller's

bigliet'taio *nm* booking clerk; (sui treni)
ticket-collector

bigliette'ria *nf* ticket-office; Theat box-
office. **biglietteria automatica** ticket
vending machine

bigli'etto *nm* ticket; (lettera breve) note;
(cartoncino) card; (di banca) banknote.
biglietto di sola andata single
[ticket]. **biglietto di andata e ritorno**
return [ticket]. **biglietto di auguri** card.
biglietto chilometrico ticket allowing
travel up to a maximum specified
distance. **biglietto collettivo** group
ticket. **biglietto elettronico** e-ticket.
biglietto giornaliero day pass.
biglietto d'ingresso entrance ticket.
biglietto d'invito invitation card.
biglietto della lotteria lottery ticket.
biglietto da visita business card

bigliet'tone *nm* (fam: soldi) big one

bignè *nm inv* puff. **bignè alla crema**
cream puff

bigo'dino *nm* roller

bi'gotto *nm* bigot

bi'kini *nm inv* bikini

bi'lancia *nf* scales *pl*; (di orologio, Comm)
balance; **Bilancia** Astr Libra. **bilancia
commerciale** balance of trade.
bilancia da cucina kitchen scales
bilancia dei pagamenti balance of
payments. **bilancia pesapersone**
scales

bilanci'are *vt* balance; fig weigh

bilancia'tura *nf* **bilanciatura
gomme** wheel-balancing

bilanci'ere *nm* (in sollevamento pesi) barbell; (di orologio) balance wheel

bi'lancio *nm* budget; Comm balance [sheet]; **fare il ~** balance the books; fig take stock; **chiudere il ~ in attivo/passivo** to end the financial year in profit/with a loss. **bilancio patrimoniale** balance sheet. **bilancio preventivo** budget

bilate'rale *adj* bilateral

'bile *nf* bile; fig rage

bili'ardo *nm* billiards *sg*

'bilico *nm* equilibrium; **in ~** in the balance

bi'lingue *adj* bilingual

bilingu'ismo *nm* bilingualism

bili'one *nm* billion

bili'oso *adj* bilious

bilo'cale ① *adj* two-room ② *nm* two-room flat

'bimbo, -a *nmf* child. **~ in fasce** babe in arms

bimen'sile *adj* fortnightly Br, twice-monthly

bime'strale *adj* bimonthly

bi'mestre *nm* two months

bi'nario *nm* track; (piattaforma) platform

bi'nocolo *nm* binoculars *pl.*

bi'nomio *nm* binomial

bio+ *pref* bio+

bioagricol'tore *nm* organic farmer

bioagricol'tura *nf* organic farming

bio'chimica *nf* biochemistry

bio'chimico, -a ① *nmf* biochemist ② *adj* biochemical

biodegra'dabile *adj* biodegradable

biodiversità *nf* biodiversity

bio'etica *nf* bioethics

bio'fisica *nf* biophysics

biogra'fia *nf* biography

bio'grafico *adj* biographical

bi'ografo, -a *nmf* biographer

bioingegne'ria *nf* bioengineering

biolo'gia *nf* biology

biologica'mente *adv* biologically

bio'logico *adj* biological; ‹agricoltura› organic

bi'ologo, -a *nmf* biologist

bi'onda *nf* blonde. **bionda ossigenata** peroxide blonde. **bionda platinata** platinum blonde

bi'ondo ① *adj* blond ② *nm* fair colour; (uomo) fair-haired man. **biondo cenere** ash blond. **biondo platino** platinum blonde

bi'onico *adj* bionic

bio'psia *nf* biopsy

bio'ritmo *nm* biorhythm

bio'sfera *nf* biosphere

bi'ossido *nm* dioxide. **biossido di carbonio** carbon dioxide

biotecnolo'gia *nf* biotechnology

bioterro'rismo *nm* bioterrorism

bip *nm inv* blip

bipar'titico *adj* bipartisan

biparti'tismo *nm* two-party system

bipar'tito ① *adj* bipartite, two-party *attrib* ② *nm* two-party coalition

bipartizi'one *nf* division into two parts

bipo'lare *adj* Electr bipolar; Pol dominated by two large parties

bipola'rismo *nm* Pol system in which the numerous parties line up behind two main parties

bipolarizzazzi'one *nf* Pol tendency towards 'bipolarism'

bi'posto *adj inv & nm inv* two-seater

'birba *nf*, **birbante** *nm* rascal, rogue

birbo'nata *nf* trick

bir'bone *adj* wicked

birdie *nm inv* (golf) birdie

biri'chino, -a ① *adj* naughty ② *nmf* little devil

bi'rillo *nm* skittle; (di segnaletica stradale) traffic cone

Bir'mania *nf* Burma

bir'mano, -a *adj & nmf* Burmese

'birra *nf* beer; **a tutta ~** fig flat out. **birra chiara** lager; **birra grande** ≈ pint. **birra piccola** ≈ half-pint. **birra scura** dark beer, brown ale Br

birre'ria *nf* beer-house; (fabbrica) brewery

bis *nm inv* encore

bi'saccia *nf* haversack

bi'sbetica *nf* shrew

bi'sbetico *adj* bad-tempered

bisbigli'are *vt/i* whisper

bi'sboccia *nf* **fare ~** make merry

'bisca *nf* gambling-house

Bi'scaglia *nf* **il golfo di ~** the Bay of Biscay

'biscia *nf* snake

biscotti'era *nf* biscuit barrel, biscuit tin

bi'scotto *nm* biscuit. **biscotto per cani** dog-biscuit

bisessu'ale *adj & nmf* bisexual

bise'stile *adj* **anno ~** leap year

bisettima'nale *adj* twice-weekly

biset'trice *nf* bisector

bisezi'one *nf* bisection

bisil'labico *adj* two-syllable *attrib*, bisyllabic

bi'slacco *adj* peculiar

bi'slungo *adj* oblong

bi'snonno, -a ① *nm* great-grandfather

2 *nf* great-grandmother

biso'gnare *vi* **bisogna agire subito** we must act at once; **bisogna farlo** it is necessary to do it; **non bisogna scongelarlo** you don't need to defrost it

bi'sogno *nm* need; (povertà) poverty; **aver** ~ **di** need

biso'gnoso *adj* needy; (povero) poor; ~ **di** in need of

bi'sonte *nm* bison

bi'stecca *nf* steak. **bistecca di cavallo** horsemeat steak. **bistecca ai ferri** grilled steak. **bistecca alla fiorentina** large grilled beef steak

bi'sticci *nmpl* bickering

bisticci'are *vi* quarrel

bi'sticcio *nm* quarrel; (gioco di parole) pun

bistrat'tare *vt* mistreat

bistrò *nm inv* bistro

'bisturi *nm inv* scalpel

bi'sunto *adj* very greasy

bit *nm inv* bit

bito'nale *adj* two-tone

bi'torzolo *nm* lump

'bitter *nm inv* bitter aperitif

bi'tume *nm* bitumen

bivac'care *vi* bivouac

bi'vacco *nm* bivouac

'bivio *nm* crossroads; (di strada) fork

bizan'tino *adj* Byzantine

'bizza *nf* tantrum; **fare le bizze** ⟨*bambini*⟩ play up

bizzar'ria *nf* eccentricity

biz'zarro *adj* bizarre

biz'zeffe *adv* **a** ~ galore

'blackjack *nm inv* blackjack

blan'dire *vt* soothe; (allettare) flatter

'blando *adj* mild

bla'sfemo *adj* blasphemous

bla'sone *nm* coat of arms

blate'rare *vi* blather; ~ **di qualcosa** burble on about something

'blatta *nf* cockroach

'bleso *adj* lisping

blin'dare *vt* armour-plate

blin'dato *adj* armoured

'blinker *nm inv* blinker

'blister *nm inv* blister pack

blitz *nm inv* blitz

bloc'care *vt* block; (isolare) cut off; Mil blockade; Comm freeze; stop ⟨*assegno*⟩; ~ **l'accesso a** seal off

bloc'carsi *vr* Mech jam

blocca'sterzo *nm* steering lock

bloc'cato *adj* blocked

bloc'chetto *nm* **blocchetto per appunti** memo pad **blocchetto di biglietti** book of tickets

'blocco *nm* block; Mil blockade; (dei fitti) restriction; (di carta) pad; (unione) coalition; **in** ~ Comm in bulk. **blocco chiamate** Teleph call barring. **blocco per appunti** notepad. **blocco psicologico** mental block. **blocco stradale** road-block

block-notes *nm inv* memo pad

blu *adj inv* & *nm* blue

blu'astro *adj* bluish

blue chip *nf inv* Fin blue chip

blue-'jeans *nmpl* jeans

bluff *nm inv* (carte, fig) bluff

bluf'fare *vi* (carte, fig) bluff

'blusa *nf* blouse

'boa **1** *nm* boa [constrictor]; (sciarpa) [feather] boa
2 *nf* Naut buoy

bo'ato *nm* rumbling

bo'bina *nf* spool; (di film) reel; Electr coil

bobi'nare *vt* spool

'bocca *nf* mouth; **a** ~ **aperta** fig dumbfounded; **in** ~ **al lupo!** fam break a leg!; **fare la respirazione** ~ **a** ~ **a qualcuno** give somebody mouth to mouth resuscitation, give somebody the kiss of life; **essere di** ~ **buona** eat anything; fig be easily satisfied; **essere sulla** ~ **di tutti** be the talk of the town. **bocca del camino** chimneybreast. **bocca di leone** snapdragon

boccac'cesco *adj* licentious

boc'caccia *nf* grimace; **far boccacce** make faces

boc'caglio *nm* nozzle

boc'cale *nm* jug; (da birra) mug

bocca'porto *nm* Naut hatch

bocca'scena *nm inv* proscenium

boc'cata *nf* (di fumo) puff; **prendere una** ~ **d'aria** get a breath of fresh air

boc'cetta *nf* small bottle

boccheggi'are *vi* gasp

boc'chino *nm* cigarette holder; (di pipa, Mus) mouthpiece

'boccia *nf* (palla) bowl; **bocce** *pl* (gioco) bowls *sg*; **giocare a bocce** play bowls

bocci'are *vt* (agli esami) fail; (respingere) reject; (alle bocce) hit; **essere bocciato** fail; (ripetere) repeat a year

boccia'tura *nf* failure

bocci'olo *nm* bud

'boccolo *nm* ringlet

boccon'cino *nm* morsel

boc'cone *nm* mouthful; (piccolo pasto) snack

boc'coni *adv* face down[wards]

Bo'emia *nf* Bohemia

bo'emo, -a *adj* & *nmf* Bohemian

bo'ero, -a *nmf* Afrikaner

bofonchi'are *vi* grumble

boh *int* dunno

'boia *nm* executioner; **fa un freddo** ∼ **fam** it's brass-monkey weather; **ho un sonno** ∼ fam I can't keep my eyes open

boi'ata *nf* fam rubbish

boicot'taggio *nm* boycotting

boicot'tare *vt* boycott

bo'lero *nm* bolero

'bolgia *nf* (caos) bedlam

'bolide *nm* meteor; **passare come un** ∼ shoot past [like a rocket]

Bo'livia *nf* Bolivia

bolivi'ano, -a *adj & nmf* Bolivian

'bolla *nf* bubble; (vescica, in tappezzeria) blister; **finire in una** ∼ **di sapone** go up in smoke. **bolla di accompagnamento** packing list. **bolla d'aria** (in acqua) air bubble. **bolla di consegna** packing list

bol'lare *vt* stamp; fig brand

bol'lato *adj* fig branded; **carta bollata** paper with stamp showing payment of duty

bol'lente *adj* boiling [hot]

bol'letta *nf* bill; **essere in** ∼ be hard up

bollet'tino *nm* bulletin; Comm list. **bollettino d'informazione** fact sheet. **bollettino meteorologico** weather report. **bollettino ufficiale** gazette

bolli'latte *nm inv* milk pan

bol'lino *nm* coupon

bol'lire *vt/i* boil

bol'lito *nm* boiled meat

bolli'tore *nm* boiler; (per l'acqua) kettle

bolli'tura *nf* boiling

'bollo *nm* stamp; Auto tax disc

bol'lore *nm* boil; (caldo) intense heat; fig ardour

Bo'logna *nf* Bologna

bolo'gnese *nmf* person from Bologna; **spaghetti alla bolognese** spaghetti bolognese

'bomba *nf* bomb; **a prova di** ∼ bomb-proof; **tornare a** ∼ get back to the point. **bomba atomica** nuclear bomb. **bomba intelligente** smart bomb. **bomba a mano** hand grenade. **bomba molotov** petrol bomb. **bomba ad orologeria** time bomb. **bomba sporca** dirty bomb

bombarda'mento *nm* shelling; (con aerei) bombing; fig bombardment. **bombardamento aereo** air raid

bombar'dare *vt* shell; (con aerei) bomb; fig bombard; ∼ **a tappeto** carpet-bomb

bombardi'ere *nm* bomber

bom'bato *adj* domed

'bomber *nm inv* bomber jacket

bom'betta *nf* bowler [hat]

'bombo *nm* bumblebee

'bombola *nf* cylinder. **bombola di gas** gas bottle, gas cylinder

bombo'letta *nf* spray can

bombo'lone *nm* doughnut

bomboni'era *nf* wedding keep-sake

bo'naccia *nf* Naut calm

bonacci'one, -a ①️ *nmf* good-natured person
②️ *adj* good-natured

bo'nario *adj* kindly

bo'nifica *nf* land reclamation

bonifi'care *vt* reclaim

bo'nifico *nm* Comm discount. **bonifico [bancario]** [credit] transfer

bontà *nf* goodness; (gentilezza) kindness

'bonus-'malus *nm inv* Auto car-insurance policy with no claims bonus clause

'boogie *nm* boogie

'bookmaker *nm inv* bookmaker

'boomerang *nm inv* boomerang

boot *nm* Comput boot-up; **eseguire il** ∼ boot up

'bora *nf* cold north-east wind in the upper Adriatic

borbot'tare *vi* mumble; (stomaco) rumble

borbot'tio *nm* mumbling; (di stomaco) rumbling

'borchia *nf* stud

borchi'ato *adj* studded

bor'dare *vt* border

bor'data *nf* Naut broadside

borda'tura *nf* border

bor'deaux ①️ *nm inv* (vino) claret, Bordeaux
②️ *adj inv* (colore) claret

bor'dello *nm* brothel; fig bedlam; (disordine) mess

bor'dino *nm* narrow border

'bordo *nm* border; (estremità) edge; **a** ∼ Aeron, Naut on board; **d'alto** ∼ ⟨prostituta⟩ high-class. **bordo d'attacco** Aeron leading edge

bor'dura *nf* border

bor'gata *nf* hamlet

bor'ghese *adj* bourgeois; ⟨abito⟩ civilian; **in** ∼ in civilian dress; ⟨poliziotto⟩ in plain clothes

borghe'sia *nf* middle classes *pl*

'borgo *nm* village; (quartiere) district

'boria *nf* conceit

bori'oso *adj* conceited

bor'lotto *nm* **[fagiolo] borlotto** pinto bean

'Borneo *nm* Borneo

boro'talco *nm* talcum powder

bor'raccia *nf* flask

'Borsa *nf* **Borsa [valori]** Stock Exchange

'borsa *nf* bag; (borsetta) handbag. **borsa dell'acqua calda** hot-water bottle. ····⫸

borsa frigo cool-box. **borsa della spesa** shopping bag. **borsa di studio** scholarship. **borsa termica** cool bag. **borsa da viaggio** travel bag

borsai'olo *nm* pickpocket

bor'seggio *nm* pickpocketing

borsel'lino *nm* purse

bor'sello *nm* (portamonete) purse; (borsetto) man's handbag

bor'setta *nf* handbag

bor'setto *nm* man's handbag

bor'sino *nm* Fin dealing room

bor'sista *nmf* Fin speculator; Sch scholarship holder

bor'sone *nm* carryall

bo'scaglia *nf* woodlands *pl*

boscai'olo *nm* woodman; (guardaboschi) forester

bo'schetto *nm* grove

'bosco *nm* wood

bo'scoso *adj* wooded

'Bosnia *nf* Bosnia

bos'niaco, -a *adj & nmf* Bosnian

Bosnia-Erzego'vina *nf* Bosnia-Herzegovina

boss *nm inv* **boss mafioso** Mafia boss

'bosso *nm* boxwood

'bossolo *nm* cartridge case

Bot *nm abbr* (**Buoni Ordinari Del Tesoro**) T-bills

bo'tanica *nf* botany

bo'tanico ① *adj* botanical ② *nm* botanist

'botola *nf* trapdoor

Bot'swana *nm* Botswana

'botta *nf* blow; (rumore) bang; **fare a botte** come to blows. **botta e risposta** fig thrust and counter-thrust

botta'trice *nf* monkfish

'botte *nf* barrel

bot'tega *nf* shop; (di artigiano) workshop

botte'gaio, -a *nmf* shopkeeper

botte'ghino *nm* Theatr box-office; (del lotto) lottery-shop

bot'tiglia *nf* bottle; **in ~** bottled

bottiglie'ria *nf* wine shop

bot'tino *nm* loot; Mil booty

'botto *nm* bang; **di ~** all of a sudden

bot'tone *nm* button; Bot bud. **bottone di carica** winder

botu'lismo *nm* botulism

'bourbon *nm* bourbon

bo'vini *nmpl* cattle

bo'vino *adj* bovine; **carne bovina** beef

'bowling *nm* bowling, tenpin bowling Br

box *nm inv* (per cavalli) loosebox; (recinto per bambini) play-pen

'boxe *nf* boxing

'boxer *nmpl* jockey shorts

'bozza *nf* draft; Typ proof; (bernoccolo) bump. **bozza in colonna** galley [proof]. **bozza definitiva** page proof. **bozza impaginata** page proof. **bozza di stampa** page proof

boz'zetto *nm* sketch

'bozzolo *nm* cocoon

BR *nfpl abbr* (**Brigate Rosse**) Red Brigades

brac'care *vt* hunt

brac'cetto *nm* **a ~** arm in arm

bracci'ale *nm* bracelet; (fascia) armband

braccia'letto *nm* bracelet; (di orologio) watch-strap. **braccialetto identificativo** identity bracelet

bracci'ante *nm* day labourer

bracci'ata *nf* (nel nuoto) stroke

'braccio *nm* (pl *nf* **braccia**) arm; (di fiume, pl **bracci**) arm. **braccio di ferro** arm wrestling

bracci'olo *nm* (di sedia) arm[rest]; (da nuoto) armband

'bracco *nm* hound

bracconi'ere *nm* poacher

'brace *nf* embers *pl*; **alla ~** char-grilled

'brache *nfpl* (fam: pantaloni) britches; **calare le ~** fig chicken out

braci'ere *nm* brazier

braci'ola *nf* chop. **braciola di maiale** pork chop

'brado *adj* **allo stato ~** in the wild

braille *nm* Braille

brain-'storming *nm inv* brainstorming

'brama *nf* longing

bra'mare *vt* long for

bra'mino *nm* Brahmin

bramo'sia *nf* yearning

'branca *nf* branch

'branchia *nf* gill

'branco *nm* (di cani) pack; (pej: di persone) gang

branco'lare *vi* grope

'branda *nf* camp-bed

bran'dello *nm* scrap; **a brandelli** in tatters

bran'dina *nf* cot

bran'dire *vt* brandish

'brandy *nm* brandy

'brano *nm* piece; (di libro) passage

bran'zino *nm* sea bass

bra'sare *vt* braise

bra'sato *nm* braised beef with herbs

Bra'sile *nm* Brazil

brasili'ano, -a *adj & nmf* Brazilian

bra'vata *nf* bragging

'bravo *adj* good; (abile) clever; (coraggioso) brave; **~!** well done!

bra'vura nf skill

'breccia nf breach; **sulla** ∼ fig very successful, at the top

brecci'ame nm loose chipping pl

bre'saola nf dried, salted beef sliced thinly and eaten cold

Bre'tagna nf Brittany

bre'tella nf shoulder-strap; (strada) link road; Mech brace; **bretelle** pl (di calzoni) braces, suspenders Am

'bretone adj & nmf Breton

'breve adj brief, short; **in** ∼ briefly; **tra** ∼ shortly

brevet'tare vt patent

bre'vetto nm patent; (attestato) licence

brevità nf shortness

'brezza nf breeze

bricco'nata nf dirty trick

bric'cone nm blackguard; hum rascal

'briciola nf crumb; fig grain

'briciolo nm fragment; **non hai un** ∼ **di cervello!** you don't have an ounce of common sense!

bridge nm (carte) bridge

'briga nf (fastidio) trouble; (lite) quarrel; **attaccar** ∼ pick a quarrel; **prendersi la** ∼ **di fare qualcosa** go to the trouble of doing something

brigadi'ere nm (dei Carabinieri) sergeant

brigan'taggio nm highway robbery

bri'gante nm bandit; hum rogue

bri'gare vi to intrigue

bri'gata nf brigade; (gruppo) group

briga'tista nmf Pol member of the Red Brigades

'briglia nf rein; **a** ∼ **sciolta** at full gallop; fig at breakneck speed

bril'lante ① adj brilliant; (scintillante) sparkling ② nm diamond

brillan'tina nf brilliantine

bril'lare vi shine; ⟨metallo⟩ glitter; (scintillare) sparkle

'brillo adj tipsy

'brina nf hoar-frost

brin'dare vi toast; ∼ **a qualcuno** drink a toast to somebody

'brindisi nm inv toast

'brio nm vivacity

bri'oche nf inv croissant

bri'oso adj vivacious

'briscola nf (seme) trumps

bri'tannico adj British

'brivido nm shiver; (di paura ecc) shudder; (di emozione) thrill; **avere i brividi** have the shivers; **dare i brividi a qualcuno** give somebody the shivers

brizzo'lato adj ⟨capelli, barba⟩ greying

'brocca nf jug

broc'cato nm brocade

'broccoli nmpl broccoli sg

bro'daglia nf pej dishwater

'brodo nm broth; (per cucinare) stock. **brodo di manzo** beef tea. **brodo di pollo** chicken broth; (per cucinare) chicken stock. **brodo ristretto** consommé. **brodo vegetale** clear broth; (per cucinare) vegetable stock

'broglio nm **broglio elettorale** gerrymandering

'broker nmf inv broker. **broker d'assicurazioni** insurance broker

'bromo nm Chem bromine

bro'muro nm bromide

bronchi'ale adj bronchial

bron'chite nf bronchitis

bron'chitico adj chesty

'broncio nm sulk; **fare il** ∼ sulk

bronto'lare vi grumble; ⟨tuono ecc⟩ rumble; ∼ **contro qualcuno/qualcosa** grumble or grouch about somebody/ something

bronto'lio nm grumbling; (di tuono, stomaco) rumbling

bronto'lone, -a nmf grumbler

'bronzo nm bronze; **una faccia di** ∼ fam a brass neck

bros'sura nf **edizione in brossura** paperback

bru'care vt ⟨pecora⟩ graze

bruciacchi'are vt scorch

bruci'ante adj burning

brucia'pelo adv **a** ∼ point-blank

bruci'are ① vt burn; (scottare) scald; (incendiare) set fire to ② vi burn; (scottare) scald

bruci'arsi vr burn oneself

bruci'ato adj burnt; fig burnt-out

brucia'tore nm burner

brucia'tura nf burn

bruci'ore nm burning sensation

'bruco nm grub

'brufolo nm spot, pimple

brufo'loso adj spotty, pimply

brughi'era nf heath

bruli'care vi swarm

bruli'chio nm swarming

'brullo adj bare

'bruma nf mist

Bru'nei nm Brunei

'bruno adj brown; ⟨occhi, capelli⟩ dark

brusca'mente adv (di colpo) suddenly; (in tono brusco) sharply

bru'schetta nf toasted bread rubbed with garlic and sprinkled with olive oil

'brusco adj sharp; (persona) brusque, abrupt; (improvviso) sudden

bru'sio nm buzzing

bru'tale adj brutal

brutalità nf inv brutality

brutaliz'zare vt brutalize

'bruto adj & nm brute

brut'tezza nf ugliness

'brutto adj ugly; ⟨tempo, tipo, situazione, affare⟩ nasty; (cattivo) bad. **brutta copia** nf rough copy. ~ **tiro** nm dirty trick

brut'tura nf ugly thing

bub'bone nm Med swelling

'buca nf hole; (avvallamento) hollow. **buca delle lettere** letter-box

buca'neve nm inv snowdrop

bucani'ere nm buccaneer

bu'care ① vt make a hole in; (pungere) prick; punch ⟨biglietti⟩ ② vi have a puncture

'Bucarest nf Bucharest

bu'carsi vr prick oneself; (con droga) shoot up

buca'tini nmpl pasta similar to spaghetti but thicker and hollow

bu'cato nm washing; **fare il** ~ do the washing

'buccia nf peel, skin; **bucce** pl (di frutta) parings. **buccia di banana** banana skin

bucherel'lare vt riddle

bucherel'lato adj pitted

'buco nm hole. **buco della serratura** keyhole

bu'colica nf bucolic

bu'colico nm bucolic

'Budda nm Buddha

bud'dista nmf Buddhist

bu'dello nm (pl nf **budella**) bowel

'budget nm inv budget. **budget provvisorio** minibudget

budge'tario adj budgetary

bu'dino nm pudding

'bue nm (pl **buoi**) ox

'bufalo nm buffalo

bu'fera nf storm; (di neve) blizzard

bufferiz'zato adj Comput buffered

buf'fet nm inv snack bar; (mobile) sideboard; (pasto) buffet

buf'fetto nm cuff

'buffo ① adj funny; Theat comic ② nm funny thing

buffo'nata nf (scherzo) joke

buf'fone nm buffoon; **fare il** ~ play the fool

bu'gia nf lie; ~ **pietosa** white lie

bugi'ardo, -a ① adj lying ② nmf liar

bugi'gattolo nm cubby-hole

'buio ① adj dark

② nm darkness; **al** ~ in the dark; ~ **pesto** pitch dark

'bulbo nm bulb; (dell'occhio) eyeball

Bulga'ria nf Bulgaria

'bulgaro, -a adj & nmf Bulgarian

buli'mia nf bulimia

bu'limico nmf bulimic

'bullo nm bully

bul'lone nm bolt

'bunker nm inv bunker

buona'fede nf good faith

buo'nanima nf **la** ~ **di mio zio** my late uncle, God rest his soul

buona'notte int good night

buona'sera int good evening

buonco'stume nf Vice Squad

buondì int good day

buon'giorno int good morning; (di pomeriggio) good afternoon

buon'grado nm **di** ~ willingly

buongu'staio, -a nmf gourmet, foodie fam

buon'gusto nm good taste

bu'ono ① adj good; ⟨momento⟩ right; **dar** ~ (convalidare) accept; **alla buona** easy-going; ⟨cena⟩ informal; **buona fortuna!** good luck!; **buona notte/sera** good night/evening; **buon compleanno/Natale!** happy birthday/merry Christmas!; **buon viaggio!** have a good trip!; **buon appetito!** enjoy your meal!; ~ **senso** common sense; **di buon'ora** early; **a buon mercato** cheap; **una buona volta** once and for all; **una buona parte di** the best part of; **tre ore buone** three good hours

② nm good; (in film) goody; (tagliando) voucher; (titolo) bond; **con le buone** gently. **buono acquisto** gift token. **buono sconto** money-off-coupon

③ nmf buono, -a **a nulla** dead loss

buontem'pone, -a nmf happy-go-lucky person

buonu'more nm good temper

buonu'scita nf retirement bonus; (di dirigente) golden handshake

buratti'naio nm puppeteer

burat'tino nm puppet

'burbero adj surly; (nei modi) rough

bu'rino, -a nmf hick

Bur'kina 'Faso nm Burkina (Faso)

'burla nf joke; **fare una** ~ **a** play a trick on; **per** ~ for fun

bur'lare vt make a fool of

bur'larsi vr ~ **di** make fun of

bu'rocrate nm bureaucrat

burocra'tese nm gobbledygook

buro'cratico adj bureaucratic

burocra'zia nf bureaucracy

bu'rotica nf office automation

bur'rasca *nf* storm

burra'scoso *adj* stormy

'burro *nm* butter. **burro di arachidi** peanut butter

bur'rone *nm* ravine

Bu'rundi *nm* Burundi

bus *nm inv* Comput bus. **bus locale** local bus

bu'scare *vt* catch; **buscarle** fam get a hiding

bu'scarsi *vr* catch

bus'sare *vt* knock

'bussola *nf* compass; **perdere la ∼** lose ones bearings

'busta *nf* envelope; (astuccio) case. **busta affrancata** business reply envelope. **busta a finestra** window envelope.

busta imbottita Jiffy bag®, padded envelope. **busta paga** pay-packet

busta'rella *nf* bribe

bu'stina *nf* (di tè) tea bag; (per medicine) sachet

'busto *nm* bust; (indumento) girdle; **a mezzo ∼** half-length

bu'tano *nm* Calor gas®

buttafu'ori *nm inv* bouncer

but'tare *vt* throw; **∼ giù** (demolire) knock down; (inghiottire) gulp down; scribble down ⟨scritto⟩; fam put on ⟨pasta⟩; (scoraggiare) dishearten; **∼ via** throw away

but'tarsi *vr* throw oneself; (saltare) jump

butte'rato *adj* pitted

buz'zurro *nm* fam yokel

byte *nm inv* Comput byte

• •

Cc

• •

c.a. *abbr* (**cortese attenzione**) attn.

caba'ret *nm inv* cabaret

cabaret'tistico *adj* cabaret *attrib*

ca'bina *nf* Naut, Aeron cabin; (al mare) beach hut; (di funivia) [cable] car. **cabina elettorale** polling booth. **cabina di pilotaggio** cockpit; (di aereo di linea) flight deck. **cabina di prova** fitting room. **cabina telefonica** telephone box Br, phone booth

cabi'nato *nm* cabin cruiser

ca'blaggio *nm* Electr wiring

ca'blato *adj* ⟨messaggio⟩ cable *attrib*

cablo'gramma *nm* cablegram

cabo'taggio *nm* Naut coastal navigation

cabrio'let *nm inv* Auto convertible

ca'cao *nm* cocoa

ca'care *vi* vulg have a crap

caca'toa *nm inv* cockatoo

'cacca *nf* fam poo, number two

'cacchio *nm* fam hell; **ma che ∼ fai/dici?** fam what the hell are you doing/saying?

'caccia ① *nf* hunt; (con fucile) shooting; (inseguimento) chase; (selvaggina) game ② *nm inv* Aeron fighter; Naut destroyer; **andare a ∼** go hunting. **caccia alla balena** whaling. **caccia grossa** big game. **caccia all'uomo** man-hunt. **caccia alla volpe** fox hunting

cacciabombardi'ere *nm* Aeron fighter-bomber

cacciagi'one *nf* game

cacci'are ① *vt* hunt; (mandar via) chase away; (scacciare) drive out; (ficcare) shove;

caccia [fuori] i soldi! fam out with the money!; **∼ un urlo** fam let out a yell ② *vi* go hunting

cacci'arsi *vr* (nascondersi) hide; (andare a finire) get to; **∼ nei guai** get into trouble

caccia'tora *nf* **alla ∼ a** Culin chasseur

caccia|'tore, -trice *nmf* hunter. **cacciatore di dote** gold digger. **cacciatore di frodo** poacher. **cacciatore di taglie** bounty hunter. **cacciatore di teste** Comm head-hunter

cacciatorpedini'ere *nm inv* destroyer

caccia'vite *nm inv* screwdriver

cacci'ucco *nm* **cacciucco alla livornese** soup of seafood, tomato and wine served with bread

cache-'sexe *nm inv* thong

ca'chet *nm inv* Med capsule; (colorante) colour rinse; (stile) cachet

'cachi ① *nm inv* persimmon ② *adj inv* (colore) khaki

'cacio *nm* (formaggio) cheese

caci'otta *nf* creamy, fairly soft cheese

'caco *nm* fam persimmon

cacofo'nia *nf* cacophony

'cactus *nm inv* cactus

cada'uno *adj* each

ca'davere *nm* corpse

cada'verico *adj* fig deathly pale

ca'dente *adj* falling; ⟨casa⟩ crumbling

ca'denza *nf* cadence; (ritmo) rhythm; Mus cadenza

caden'zare *vt* give rhythm to

caden'zato *adj* measured

ca'dere *vi* fall; ⟨*capelli ecc*⟩ fall out; (capitombolare) tumble; ⟨*vestito ecc*⟩ hang; **far ~** (di mano) drop; **~ dal sonno** feel very sleepy; **lasciar ~** drop; **~ dalle nuvole** fig be taken aback; **~ dalla finestra** fall out of the window

ca'detto *nm* cadet

ca'duta *nf* fall; fig downfall. **caduta dei capelli** hair loss. **caduta libera** freefall. **caduta massi** rockfall; (avviso) falling rocks

ca'duto *nm* **i caduti** the dead; **monumento ai caduti** war memorial

caffè *nm inv* coffee; (locale) café. **caffè corretto** espresso with a dash of liqueur. **caffè Internet** cybercafe, Internet café. **caffè lungo** weak black coffee. **caffè macchiato** coffee with a dash of milk. **caffè ristretto** extra-strong espresso coffee. **caffè solubile** instant coffee

caffe'ina *nf* caffeine

caffel'latte *nm inv* white coffee

caffette'ria *nf* coffee bar

caffetti'era *nf* coffee-pot. **caffettiera a stantuffo** cafetière

cafo'naggine *nf* boorishness

cafo'nata *nf* boorishness

ca'fone, -a *nmf* boor

cafone'ria *nf* (comportamento) boorishness; **è stata una ~** it was boorish

ca'gare *vi* vulg crap; **va' a ~!** go and get stuffed!

cagio'nare *vt* cause

cagio'nevole *adj* delicate

cagli'are *vi* curdle

cagli'arsi *vr* curdle

cagli'ata *nf* curd cheese

caglia'tura *nf* curdling

'cagna *nf* bitch

ca'gnara *nf* fam din

ca'gnesco *adj* **guardare qualcuno in ~** scowl at somebody

ca'gnetto *nm* lapdog

C.A.I. *nm abbr* (**Club Alpino Italiano**) Italian mountain sports association

cai'mano *nm* cayman

'caio *nm* so-and-so

'Cairo *nm* **il ~** Cairo

'cala *nf* creek

cala'brese *adj & nmf* Calabrian

Ca'labria *nf* Calabria

cala'brone *nm* hornet

cala'maio *nm* inkpot

calama'retto *nm* small squid

cala'mari *nmpl* squid *sg*

cala'maro *nm* squid

cala'mita *nf* magnet

calamità *nf inv* calamity; **~ pl naturali** natural disasters

calami'tare *vt* draw ⟨*attenzione*⟩

ca'lante *adj* waning

ca'lare ① *vi* come down; ⟨*vento*⟩ drop; (diminuire) fall; (tramontare) set; **~ di peso** lose weight; **~ di tono** fig drag ② *vt* (abbassare) lower; (nei lavori a maglia) decrease ③ *nm* (di luna) waning

ca'larsi *vr* lower oneself

ca'lata *nf* (invasione) invasion

'calca *nf* throng

cal'cagno *nm* (pl f **calcagna**) heel; **stare alle calcagna di qualcuno** fig follow somebody around

cal'care[1] *nm* limestone

cal'care[2] *vt* tread; (premere) press [down]; **~ la mano** fig exaggerate; **~ le orme di qualcuno** fig follow in somebody's footsteps; **~ le scene** fig tread the boards

'calce[1] *nf* lime. **calce viva** quicklime

'calce[2] *nm* **in ~** at the foot of the page

calce'struzzo *nm* concrete

cal'cetto *nm* Sport five-a-side [football]; (da tavolo) table football

calci'are *vt* kick

calcia'tore *nm* footballer

calcifi'carsi *vr* calcify

calcificazi'one *nf* calcification

cal'cina *nf* mortar

calci'naccio *nm* (pezzo di intonaco) flake of plaster; (pezzo di muro) piece of rubble

'calcio[1] *nm* kick; Sport football; (di arma da fuoco) butt; **dare un ~ a** kick; **giocare a ~** play football. **calcio d'angolo** corner [kick]. **calcio di punizione** free kick. **calcio di rigore** penalty [kick]

'calcio[2] *nm* Chem calcium

calcio-mer'cato *nm inv* transfer market

'calco *nm* (con carta) tracing; (arte) cast

calco'lare *vt* calculate; (considerare) consider

calco'lato *adj* calculated

calcola'tore ① *adj* calculating ② *nm* calculator; (macchina elettronica) computer. **calcolatore digitale** (calcolatrice) calculator

calcola'trice *nf* calculating machine

'calcolo *nm* calculation; Med stone; **per ~** fig out of self-interest; **mi sono fatto i calcoli** fig I've weighed up the pros and cons. **calcolo approssimativo** guesstimate. **calcolo biliare** gallstone. **calcolo renale** kidney stone

cal'daia *nf* boiler. **caldaia ad accumulo** storage heater

caldar'rosta *nf* roast chestnut

caldeggi'are *vt* support

'caldo 1 *adj* warm; (molto caldo) hot; ⟨*situazione, zona*⟩ dangerous; ⟨*notizie*⟩ latest; **non gli fa né ∼ né freddo** fig he doesn't give a damn; **ondata di caldo** heatwave; **tavola calda** snack bar
2 *nm* heat; **avere ∼** be warm, be hot; **fa ∼** it's warm, it's hot

caleido'scopio *nm* kaleidoscope

calen'dario *nm* calendar. **calendario sportivo** sporting calendar

ca'lesse *nm* gig

cali'brare *vt* calibrate

cali'brato *adj* calibrated; fig balanced; **taglie** *pl* **calibrate** clothes for non-standard sizes

'calibro *nm* calibre; (strumento) callipers *pl*; **di grosso ∼** ⟨*persona*⟩ top *attrib*

'calice *nm* goblet; Relig chalice

californi'ano, -a *adj & nmf* Californian

ca'ligine *nm* fog; (industriale) smog

call-girl *nf inv* call girl

calligra'fia *nf* handwriting; (cinese) calligraphy

calli'grafico *adj* **perizia calligrafica** handwriting analysis

cal'ligrafo, -a *nmf* calligrapher

cal'lista *nmf* chiropodist

'callo *nm* corn; **fare il ∼ a** become hardened to

cal'loso *adj* callous

'calma *nf* calm; **mantenere la ∼** keep calm; **prendersela con ∼** fig take it easy; **fare qualcosa con ∼** take one's time doing something

cal'mante 1 *adj* calming
2 *nm* sedative

cal'mare *vt* calm [down]; (lenire) soothe

cal'marsi *vr* calm down; ⟨*vento*⟩ drop; ⟨*dolore*⟩ die down

calmie'rare *vt* control the prices of

calmi'ere *nm* price control

'calmo *adj* calm

'calo *nm* Comm fall; (di volume) shrinkage; (di peso) loss; **in ∼** dwindling

ca'lore *nm* heat; (moderato) warmth; **in ∼** (di animale) on heat

calo'ria *nf* calorie

ca'lorico *adj* calorific

calo'rifero *nm* radiator

calorosa'mente *adv* warmly

calorosità *nf* fig warmth

calo'roso *adj* warm

ca'lotta *nf* **calotta cranica** skullcap. **calotta glaciale** icecap. **calotta polare** polar icecap

calpe'stare *vt* trample [down]; fig trample on ⟨*diritti, sentimenti*⟩; **'vietato ∼ l'erba'** 'keep off the grass'

calpe'stio *nm* (passi) footsteps *pl*; (rumore) stamping

ca'lunnia *nf* slander

calunni'are *vt* slander

calunni'oso *adj* slanderous

ca'lura *nf* heat

cal'vario *nm* Calvary; fig trial

calvi'nismo *nm* Calvinism

calvi'nista *nmf* Calvinist

cal'vizie *nf* baldness

'calvo *adj* bald

'calza *nf* (da reggicalze) stocking; (da uomo) sock. **calza della befana** ≈ Christmas stocking

calza'maglia *nf* tights *pl*; (per danza) leotard

cal'zante *adj* fig fitting

cal'zare 1 *vt* (indossare) wear; (mettersi) put on
2 *vi* fit; **∼ a pennello** ⟨*indumenti*⟩ fit like a glove

calza'scarpe *nm inv* shoehorn

calza'tura *nf* footwear; **calzature** *pl* footwear *sg*

calzaturi'ficio *nm* shoe factory

cal'zetta *nf* ankle sock; **è una mezza ∼** fig he's no use

calzet'tone *nm* knee-length woollen sock

cal'zino *nm* sock

calzo'laio *nm* shoe mender

calzole'ria *nf* (negozio) shoe shop

calzon'cini *nmpl* shorts. **calzoncini da bagno** swimming trunks

cal'zone *nm* Culin folded pizza with tomato, mozzarella etc inside

cal'zoni *nmpl* trousers, pants Am. **calzoni alla cavallerizza** jodhpurs

camale'onte *nm* chameleon

cambi'ale *nf* Comm bill of exchange

cambia'mento *nm* change

cambi'are 1 *vt* change; move ⟨*casa*⟩; (fare cambio di) exchange; **∼ canale** TV switch over; **∼ rotta** Naut alter course; **∼ l'aria in una stanza** air a room; **∼ sesso** have a sex change
2 *vi* change; (fare cambio) exchange

cambi'arsi *vr* change

cambiava'lute *nm* bureau de change

'cambio *nm* change; (Comm, scambio) exchange; Mech gear; **dare il ∼ a qualcuno** relieve somebody; **in ∼ di** in exchange for. **cambio della guardia** changeover. **cambio dell'olio** oil change

Cam'bogia *nf* Cambodia

cambogi'ano, -a *adj & nmf* Cambodian

cam'busa *nf* pantry

ca'melia *nf* camellia

'camera *nf* room; (mobili) [bedroom] suite; **Camera** Pol, Comm Chamber. **camera ammobiliata** bedsit. **camera** ⋯⃗

ardente chapel of rest. **camera d'aria** inner tube. **camera blindata** strong room. **Camera di Commercio** Chamber of Commerce. **Camera dei Comuni** House of Commons. **Camera dei Deputati** ≈ House of Commons. **Camera dei Lord** House of Lords. **Camera dei Rappresentanti** House of Representatives. **camera doppia** double room. **camera a gas** gas chamber. **camera da letto** bedroom. **camera a due letti** twin room. **camera matrimoniale** double room. **camera oscura** darkroom. **camera degli ospiti** guest room. **camera singola** single room

came'rata¹ *nf* (dormitorio) dormitory; Mil barrack room

came'rata² *nmf* mate

camera'tesco *adj* comradely

camera'tismo *nm* comradeship

cameri'era *nf* maid; (di ristorante) waitress; (in albergo) chamber-maid

cameri'ere *nm* manservant; (di ristorante) waiter

came'rino *nm* dressing-room

came'ristico *adj* Mus chamber

'Camerun *nm* il ∼ Cameroon

'camice *nm* overall

camice'ria *nf* shirt shop

cami'cetta *nf* blouse

ca'micia *nf* shirt; **essere nato con la** ∼ fig be born lucky. **uovo in camicia** poached egg. **camicia di forza** strait-jacket. **camicia nera** Blackshirt. **camicia da notte** nightdress; (da uomo) nightshirt

camici'aio *nm* (venditore) shirtseller; (sarto) shirtmaker

camici'ola *nf* vest

cami'netto *nm* fireplace. **caminetto alimentato a carbone** coalfire

ca'mino *nm* chimney; (focolare) fireplace, hearth

'camion *nm inv* lorry Br, truck. **camion della nettezza urbana** dust-cart Br, garbage truck Am

camion'cino *nm* van

camio'netta *nf* jeep

camio'nista *nmf* lorry driver Br, truck driver

'camma *nf* cam; **albero a camme** Auto camshaft

cam'mello ① *nm* camel; (tessuto) camel-hair ② *adj inv* (colore) camel

cam'meo *nm* cameo

cammi'nare *vi* walk; ⟨auto, orologio⟩ go; ∼ **avanti e indietro** pace up and down

cammi'nata *nf* walk; **fare una** ∼ go for a walk

cam'mino *nm* way; **essere in** ∼ be on the way; **mettersi in** ∼ set out; **cammin facendo** on the way

camo'milla *nf* camomile; (bevanda) camomile tea

camo'millarsi *vr sl* **camomillati!** don't get your knickers in a twist!, cool it!

Ca'morra *nf* local mafia

camor'rista *nmf* member of the 'Camorra'

ca'moscio *nm* chamois; (pelle) suede

cam'pagna *nf* country; (paesaggio) countryside; Comm, Mil campaign; **in** ∼ in the country. **campagna elettorale** election campaign. **campagna promozionale** promotional campaign, marketing campaign. **campagna pubblicitaria** publicity campaign

campa'gnola *nf* Auto cross-country vehicle

campa'gnolo, -a ① *adj* rustic ② *nm* countryman ③ *nf* countrywoman

cam'pale *adj* field *attrib*; **giornata campale** fig strenuous day

cam'pana *nf* bell; (di vetro) belljar; **a** ∼ bellshaped; **essere sordo come una** ∼ be as deaf as a doorpost; **sentire anche l'altra** ∼ fig hear the other side of the story; **vivere sotto una** ∼ **di vetro** fig be mollycoddled; **campane** *pl* **eoliche** wind chimes; **campane** *pl* **a morto** death knell

campa'naccio *nm* cowbell

campa'naro *nm* bell-ringer

campa'nella *nf* (di tenda) curtain ring

campa'nello *nm* door-bell; (cicalino) buzzer

Cam'pania *nf* Campania

campa'nile *nm* bell tower

campani'lismo *nm* parochialism

campani'lista *nmf* person with a parochial outlook

campani'listico *adj* parochial

cam'panula *nf* Bot campanula

cam'pare *vi* live; (a stento) get by; **tirare a** ∼ fig live from day to day

cam'pato *adj* ∼ **in aria** unfounded

campeggi'are *vi* camp; (spiccare) stand out

campeggia'tore, -trice *nmf* camper

cam'peggio *nm* camping; (terreno) campsite; **andare in** ∼ go camping; **fare** ∼ **libero** camp in the wild. **campeggio per roulotte** caravan site

'camper *nm inv* camper (van)

cam'pestre *adj* rural

Campi'doglio *nm* Capitol

'camping *nm inv* campsite

campiona'mento *nm* sampling

campio'nario ① *nm* [set of] samples

2 *adj* fiera campionaria trade fair

campio'nato *nm* championship. **Campionato Mondiale di Calcio** World Cup

campiona'tura *nf* (di merce) range of samples; (in statistica) sampling. **campionatura casuale** random sample

campi'one *nm* champion; Comm sample; (esemplare) specimen; **indagine campione** (in statistica) sample. **campione gratuito** free sample; '∼ senza valore' 'sample, no commercial value'

campio'nessa *nf* ladies' champion

'campo *nm* field; (accampamento) camp; Mil encampment; **abbandonare il** ∼ Mil desert in the face of the enemy; fig throw in the towel; **a tutto** ∼ fig wide-ranging; **avere** ∼ **libero** fig have a free hand; **non avere** ∼ ⟨cellulare⟩ to be out of range; **giocare a tutto** ∼ Sport cover the entire pitch. **campo d'aviazione** airfield. **campo base** base camp. **campo di battaglia** battlefield. **campo da calcio** football pitch. **campo di concentramento** concentration camp. **campo in erba** grass court. **campo da golf** golf course. **campo di grano** cornfield. **campo da hockey** hockey field. **campo di mais** cornfield. **campo di prigionia** prison camp. **campo profughi** refugee camp. **campo sportivo** sports ground. **campo di sterminio** death camp. **campo in superficie dura** hard court. **campo da tennis** tennis court

campo'santo *nm* cemetery

'campus *nm inv* (di università) campus

camuf'fare *vt* disguise

camuf'farsi *vr* disguise oneself

ca'muso *adj* naso ∼ snub nose

'Canada *nm* Canada

cana'dese *adj & nmf* Canadian

ca'naglia *nf* scoundrel; (plebaglia) rabble

ca'nale *nm* channel; (artificiale) canal. **Canal Grande** Gran Canal. **canale della Manica** English Channel. **canale di scolo** dyke

canaliz'zare *vt* channel ⟨acque, energie⟩

canalizzazi'one *nf* channelling; (rete) pipes *pl*

'canapa *nf* hemp. **canapa indiana** (droga) cannabis

Ca'narie *nfpl* le ∼ the Canaries

cana'rino *nm* canary

cancel'labile *adj* erasable; ⟨impegno, incontro⟩ which can be cancelled

cancel'lare *vt* cross out; (con la gomma) rub out; fig wipe out; (annullare) cancel; Comput delete, erase

cancel'larsi *vr* be erased, be wiped out

cancel'lata *nf* railings *pl*

cancel'lato *adj* cancelled

cancella'tura *nf* erasure

cancellazi'one *nf* cancellation; Comput deletion; ∼ **del debito** (ai paesi poveri) debt relief

cancelle'ria *nf* chancellery; (articoli per scrivere) stationery

cancel'letto *nm* hash sign

cancelli'ere *nm* chancellor; (di tribunale) clerk

cancel'lino *nm* duster

can'cello *nm* gate

cance'rogeno **1** *nm* carcinogen **2** *adj* carcinogenic

cance'roso *adj* cancerous

can'crena *nf* gangrene; **andare in** ∼ become gangrenous

cancre'noso *adj* gangrenous

'cancro *nm* cancer; **Cancro** Astr Cancer; **tropico del Cancro** Tropic of Cancer

candeggi'are *vt* bleach

candeg'gina *nf* bleach

can'deggio *nm* bleaching

can'dela *nf* candle; Auto spark plug; **a lume di** ∼ by candle-light; ⟨cena⟩ candlelit; **tenere la** ∼ fig play gooseberry; **il gioco non vale la** ∼ the game is not worth the candle. **candela magica** sparkler

cande'labro *nm* candelabra

cande'letta *nf* Med pessary

candeli'ere *nm* candlestick

cande'line *nfpl* candles

cande'lotto *nm* (di dinamite) stick. **candelotto lacrimogeno** tear gas grenade

candida'mente *adv* innocently

candi'dare *vt* put forward as a candidate

candi'darsi *vr* stand as a candidate

candi'dato, -a *nmf* candidate

candida'tura *nf* Pol candidacy; (per lavoro) application

'candido *adj* snow-white; (sincero) candid; (puro) pure

can'dito **1** *adj* candied **2** *nm* piece of candied fruit

can'dore *nm* whiteness; fig innocence

'cane *nm* dog; (di arma da fuoco) cock; **un tempo da cani** foul weather; **fa un freddo** ∼ it's bitterly cold; **non c'era un** ∼ fig there wasn't a soul about; **solo come un** ∼ fig all on one's own; **essere come** ∼ **e gatto** fig fight like cat and dog; **essere un** ∼ ⟨attore, cantante⟩ be appalling, be a dog sl; **fatto da cani** fig ⟨lavoro⟩ botched; **mangiare da cani** fig eat very badly; **figlio di un** ∼ fam son of a bitch. **cane da caccia** hunting dog. **cane per ciechi** guide-dog. **cane da corsa** greyhound. ⋯⋗

cane da guardia guard-dog. **cane lupo** alsatian. **cane poliziotto** police dog. **cane da salotto** lapdog. **cane sciolto** fig maverick

ca'nestro nm basket; **fare ~ score a** basket

'canfora nf camphor

cangi'ante adj iridescent; **seta cangiante** shot silk

can'guro nm kangaroo

ca'nicola nf scorching heat

ca'nile nm kennel; (di allevamento) kennels pl. **canile municipale** dog pound

ca'nino adj & nm canine

ca'nizie nm white hair

'canna nf reed; (da zucchero) cane; (di fucile) barrel; (bastone) stick; (di bicicletta) crossbar; (asta) rod; (fam: hashish) joint; **povero in ~** destitute. **canna fumaria** flue. **canna da pesca** fishing-rod. **canna da zucchero** sugar cane

cannabis nf cannabis

can'nella nf cinnamon

cannel'loni nmpl **cannelloni al forno** rolls of pasta stuffed with meat and baked in the oven

can'neto nm bed of reeds

can'nibale nm cannibal

canniba'lismo nm cannibalism

cannocchi'ale nm telescope

can'noli nmpl **cannoli alla siciliana** cylindrical pastries filled with ricotta and candied fruit

canno'nata nf cannon shot; **è una ~** fig it's brilliant

cannon'cino nm (dolce) cream horn

can'none nm cannon; fig ace

cannoneggia'mento nm cannonade

cannoni'era nf gunboat

cannoni'ere nm (soldato) gunner; (calciatore) top goal scorer

can'nuccia nf [drinking] straw; (di pipa) stem

ca'noa nf canoe

cano'ismo nm canoeing

'canone nm canon; (del telefono) standing charge; (affitto) rent; **equo canone** rent set by law

ca'nonica nf manse

ca'nonico nm canon

canoniz'zare vt canonize

canonizzazi'one nf canonization

ca'noro adj melodious

ca'notta nf (estiva) vest top

canot'taggio nm canoeing; (voga) rowing

canotti'era nf vest, singlet

canotti'ere nm oarsman

ca'notto nm [rubber] dinghy

cano'vaccio nm (trama) plot; (straccio) duster; (per ricamo) canvas

can'tante nmf singer. **cantante lirico** opera-singer

can'tare vt/i sing; **~ vittoria** fig crow; **fare ~ qualcuno** sl make somebody talk; **me le ha cantate** fam he told me off

canta'storie nmf inv story-teller

can'tata nf Mus cantata

can'tato adj sung

cantau|'tore, -trice nmf singer-song-writer

canticchi'are vt sing softly; (a bocca chiusa) hum

'cantico nm hymn

canti'ere nm yard; Naut shipyard; (di edificio) construction site. **cantiere navale** naval dockyard; (per piccole imbarcazioni) boatyard

cantie'ristica nf construction

canti'lena nf singsong; (ninna-nanna) lullaby

can'tina nf cellar; (per vini) wine cellar; (osteria) wine shop

'canto[1] nm singing; (canzone) song; Relig chant; (poesia) poem. **canto di Natale o natalizio** Christmas carol. **canto degli uccelli** birdsong

'canto[2] nm (angolo) corner; (lato) side; **dal ~ mio** for my part; **d'altro ~** on the other hand

canto'nale adj cantonal

canto'nata nf **prendere una ~** fig be sadly mistaken

can'tone nm canton; (angolo) corner

can'tore nm chorister

can'tuccio nm nook; **stare in un ~** fig hold oneself aloof

ca'nuto adj liter whitehaired

canzo'nare vt tease

canzona'torio adj teasing

canzona'tura nf teasing

can'zone nf song. **canzone d'amore** love song

canzo'netta nf fam pop song

canzoni'ere nm songbook

'caos nm chaos

ca'otico adj chaotic

C.A.P. nm abbr (**Codice di Avviamento Postale**) post code, zip code Am

cap. abbr (**capitolo**) chap., chapter

ca'pace adj able; (esperto) skilled; ⟨stadio, contenitore⟩ big; **~ di** (disposto a) capable of; **è ~ a cantare?** can he sing?

capacità nf inv ability; (attitudine) skill; (capienza) capacity. **capacità d'assorbimento** absorbency. **capacità di credito** creditworthiness. **capacità di memorizzazione** retentiveness.

capacità produttiva production capacity. **capacità di resistenza** staying power

capaci'tarsi *vr* ∼ **di** (rendersi conto) understand; (accorgersi) realize

ca'panna *nf* hut

capan'nello *nm* knot of people; **fare** ∼ **intorno a qualcuno/qualcosa** gather round somebody/something

ca'panno *nm* **capanno degli attrezzi** garden shed. **capanno da spiaggia** beach hut, cabana

capan'none *nm* shed; Aeron hangar

caparbietà *nf* obstinacy

ca'parbio *adj* obstinate

ca'parra *nf* deposit

capa'tina *nf* short visit; **fare una** ∼ **in città/da qualcuno** pop into town/in on somebody

ca'pello *nm* hair; **non torcere un** ∼ **a qualcuno** fig not lay a finger on somebody; **capelli** *pl* (capigliatura) hair *sg*; **lavarsi/asciugarsi i capelli** wash/dry one's hair; **avere i capelli a spazzola** have a crew-cut; **spaccare il** ∼ **in quattro** split hairs; **averne fin sopra i capelli** fig be fed up to the back teeth; **mettersi le mani nei capelli** fig tear one's hair out; **capelli** *pl* **d'angelo** vermicelli

capel'lone *nm* long-haired type, hippie

capel'luto *adj* hairy; **cuoio capelluto** scalp

ca'pestro *nm* noose; **contratto capestro** strait-jacket of a contract

capez'zale *nm* bolster; fig bedside

ca'pezzolo *nm* nipple

capi'ente *adj* capacious

capi'enza *nf* capacity

capiglia'tura *nf* hair

capil'lare *adj* capillary

ca'pire *vt* understand; **non capisco** I don't understand; ∼ **male** misunderstand; **si capisce!** naturally!; **sì, ho capito** yes, I see

capi'tale ① *adj* Jur capital; (principale) main
② *nf* (città) capital
③ *nm* Comm capital. **capitale di avviamento** start-up capital. **capitale azionario** Fin equity capital, share capital. **capitale di investimento** investment capital. **capitale di rischio** venture capital. **capitale sociale** Fin share capital

capita'lismo *nm* capitalism

capita'lista *nmf* capitalist

capita'listico *adj* capitalist

capitaliz'zare *vt* capitalize

capitalizzazi'one *nf* capitalization

capita'nare *vt* lead (rivolta); Sport captain

capitane'ria *nf* **capitaneria di porto** port authorities *pl*

capi'tano *nm* captain. **capitano di lungo corso** Naut captain

capi'tare *vi* (giungere per caso) come; (accadere) happen

'capite: pro ∼ *adv* per capita

capi'tello *nm* Archit capital

capito'lare *vi* capitulate

capitolazi'one *nf* capitulation

ca'pitolo *nm* chapter

capi'tombolo *nm* headlong fall; **fare un** ∼ tumble down

'capo *nm* head; (chi comanda) boss fam; (di vestiario) item; Geog cape; (in tribù) chief; (parte estrema) top; **a** ∼ (in dettato) new paragraph; **da** ∼ over again; **giramento di** ∼ dizziness; **mal di** ∼ headache; **in** ∼ **a un mese** within a month; **non ha né** ∼ **né coda** ⟨discorso, ragionamento⟩ I can't make head nor tail of it. **capo d'abbigliamento** item of clothing. **capo d'accusa** Jur charge, count. **capo di bestiame** head of cattle. **Capo di Buona Speranza**. Cape of Good Hope. **capo reparto** head of department. **il Capo Verde** Cape Verde

capo'banda *nm* Mus band-master; (di delinquenti) ringleader

capocameri'ere, **-a** ① *nm* head waiter
② *nf* head waitress

ca'pocchia *nf* **capocchia di spillo** pinhead

ca'poccia *nm* (fam: testa) nut

capocci'one, **-a** *nmf* fam brainbox

capo'classe *nmf* ≈ form captain

capocor'data *nmf* (alpinista) leader

capocu'oco, **-a** *nmf* head cook

Capo'danno *nm* New Year's Day

capofa'miglia *nm* head of the family

capoffi'cina *nm* head mechanic

capo'fitto *nm* **a** ∼ headlong

capo'giro *nm* giddiness

capo'gruppo *nm* group leader

capola'voro *nm* masterpiece

capo'linea *nm* terminus

capo'lino *nm* **fare** ∼ peep in

capo'lista *nmf* Sport league leaders *pl*; Pol candidate whose name appears first on the list

capolu'ogo *nm* main town

capo'mafia *nm* Mafia boss

capo'mastro *nm* master builder

capo'rale *nm* lance-corporal

capore'parto *nmf* department head, head of department

capo'sala *nf inv* Med ward sister

capo'saldo *nm* stronghold

capo'scalo *nm* airline manager

capo'squadra *nm inv* foreman; Sport team captain

capostazi'one *nm inv* stationmaster

capo'stipite *nmf* (di famiglia) progenitor; (di esemplare) archetype

capo'tavola *nmf* (persona) head of the table; **sedere a ~** sit at the head of the table

capo'treno *nm* guard

ca'potta *nf* top

capot'tare *vi* somersault

capouf'ficio *nmf* department head

capo'verso *nm* first line; Jur paragraph

capo'volgere *vt* overturn; fig reverse

capo'volgersi *vr* overturn; ⟨barca⟩ capsize; fig be reversed

capovolgi'mento *nm* turnaround

capo'volto ① *pp di* CAPOVOLGERE ② *adj* upside down

'cappa *nf* cloak; (di camino) cowl; (di cucina) hood

cappa'santa *nf* Culin scallop

cap'pella *nf* chapel. **la Cappella Sistina** the Sistine Chapel

cappel'lano *nm* chaplain

cappel'letti *nmpl* small filled pasta parcels

cappelli'era *nf* hatbox

cappel'lino *nm* **cappellino di carta** party hat

cap'pello *nm* hat; **tanto di ~!** I take my hat off to you! **cappello a cilindro** top hat. **cappello da cow boy** stetson, cowboy hat **cappello di feltro** homburg. **cappello di paglia** straw hat. **cappello da sole** sun hat

'cappero *nm* caper; **capperi!** fam gosh!

'cappio *nm* noose; **avere il ~ al collo** fig have a millstone round one's neck; ⟨marito⟩ be henpecked

cap'pone *nm* capon

cap'potto *nm* [over] coat

cappuc'cino *nm* (frate) Capuchin [friar]; (bevanda) white coffee

cap'puccio *nm* hood; (di penna stilografica) cap

'capra *nf* goat; **salvare ~ e cavoli** fig run with the hare and hunt with the hounds

ca'pretto *nm* kid

ca'priccio *nm* whim; (bizzarria) freak; **fare i capricci** have tantrums

capricci'oso *adj* capricious; ⟨bambino⟩ naughty

Capri'corno *nm* Astr Capricorn

capri'foglio *nm* honeysuckle

ca'prino *nm* goat's cheese

capri'ola *nf* somersault

capriolo *nm* roe (deer)

'capro *nm* [billy-]goat. **capro espiatorio** scapegoat

ca'prone *nm* [billy-] goat

'capsula *nf* capsule; (di proiettile) cap; (di dente) crown

cap'tare *vt* Radio, TV pick up; catch ⟨attenzione⟩

C.A.R. *nm abbr* (**Centro Addestramento Reclute**) basic training camp

cara'bina *nf* carbine

carabini'ere *nm* carabiniere; **Carabinieri** *pl* Italian police force (which is a branch of the army)

ca'raffa *nf* carafe

Ca'raibi *nmpl* (zona) Caribbean *sg*; (isole) Caribbean Islands; **il mar dei ~** the Caribbean [Sea]

cara'ibico *adj* Caribbean

cara'mella *nf* sweet. **caramella alla menta** mint

cara'mello *nm* caramel

ca'rato *nm* carat

ca'rattere *nm* character; (caratteristica) characteristic; **di buon ~** good-natured; **in ~ con** (intonato) in keeping with; **è una persona di ~** (deciso) he's got character. **carattere jolly** Comput wild card. **carattere tipografico** typeface

caratte'rino *nm* difficult nature

caratte'rista ① *nm* character actor ② *nf* character actress

caratte'ristico, -a ① *adj* characteristic; (pittoresco) quaint ② *nf* characteristic

caratteriz'zare *vt* characterize

caratterizzazi'one *nf* characterization

cara'tura *nf* carats; Comm part-ownership

'caravan *nm inv* caravan

carboi'drato *nm* carbohydrate

car'bonchio *nm* anthrax

carbon'cino *nm* (per disegno) charcoal

car'bone *nm* coal; **stare sui carboni ardenti** fig be on tenterhooks. **carbone fossile** anthracite

carbo'nifero *adj* carboniferous

car'bonio *nm* carbon. **carbonio 14** carbon-14

carboniz'zare *vt* burn to a cinder, burn to a crisp; **è morto carbonizzato** he was burned to death

carboniz'zato *adj* charred

carbu'rante *nm* fuel

carbu'rare ① *vt* carburize ② *vi* fig be firing on all four cylinders; **il motore carbura male** the mixture is wrong

carbura'tore *nm* carburettor

carburazi'one *nf* carburation

car'cassa *nf* carcass; *fig* old wreck

carce'rario *adj* prison *attrib*

carce'rato, -a *nmf* prisoner

carcerazione *nf* imprisonment

'carcere *nm* prison; (punizione) imprisonment. **carcere di massima sicurezza** maximum security prison

carceri'ere, -a *nmf* gaoler

carci'noma *nm* carcinoma

carcio'fino *nm* baby artichoke

carci'ofo *nm* artichoke

cardel'lino *nm* goldfinch

car'diaco *adj* cardiac; **disturbo cardiaco** heart disease

'cardigan *nm inv* cardigan

cardi'nale *adj & nm* cardinal

'cardine *nm* hinge

cardiochi'rurgo *nm* heart surgeon

cardiolo'gia *nf* cardiology

cardi'ologo *nm* heart specialist

cardio'patico, -a *nmf* person suffering from a heart complaint

cardio'tonico *nm* heart stimulant

cardiovasco'lare *adj* cardiovascular

'cardo *nm* thistle

ca'rena *nf* Naut bottom

care'naggio *nm* **bacino di carenaggio** dry dock

ca'rente *adj* ∼ **di** lacking in

ca'renza *nf* lack; (scarsità) scarcity

care'stia *nf* famine; (mancanza) dearth

ca'rezza *nf* stroke; (di madre, amante) caress; **fare una** ∼ **a** stroke; (madre, amante) caress

carez'zare *vt* stroke; ⟨madre, amante⟩ caress

carez'zevole *adj fig* sweet

'cargo *nm inv* (nave) cargo boat, freighter; (aereo) cargo plane, freight plane

cari'are *vt* decay

cari'arsi *vi* decay

cari'ato *adj* decayed

'carica *nf* office; Mil, Electr charge; *fig* drive; **dotato di una forte** ∼ **di simpatia** really likeable. **carica esplosiva** payload

caricabatte'ria *nm inv* battery charger

cari'care *vt* load ⟨camion, software⟩; Mil, Electr charge; wind up ⟨orologio⟩

cari'carsi *vr* Electr charge [up]; ∼ **di lavoro** take on too much work

cari'cato *adj fig* affected

carica'tore *nm* (per proiettile) magazine; (per diapositive) carousel

carica'tura *nf* caricature

caricatu'rale *adj* grotesque

caricatu'rista *nmf* caricaturist

'carico ① *adj* loaded (**di** with); ⟨colore⟩ strong; ⟨orologio⟩ wound [up]; ⟨batteria⟩ charged

② *nm* load; (di nave) cargo; (il caricare) loading; **avere un** ∼ **di lavoro** have a heavy workload; **testimone a** ∼ Jur witness for the prosecution; **a** ∼ **di** Comm to be charged to; ⟨persona⟩ dependent on. **carico utile** payload

'carie *nf* [tooth] decay

caril'lon *nm inv* musical box

carino *adj* pretty, nice-looking; (piacevole) agreeable

ca'risma *nm* charisma

cari'smatico *adj* charismatic

carità *nf* charity; **per** ∼**!** (come rifiuto) God forbid!

carita'tevole *adj* charitable

car'linga *nf* fuselage

car'lino *nm* pug

carnagi'one *nf* complexion

car'naio *nm fig* shambles

car'nale *adj* carnal; **cugino carnale** first cousin

'carne *nf* flesh; (alimento) meat; **di** ∼ meaty. **carne macinata** mince, ground beef Am. **carne di maiale** pork. **carne di manzo** beef. **carne di vitella** veal

car'nefice *nm* executioner

carnefi'cina *nf* slaughter

carne'vale *nm* carnival

carneva'lesco *adj* carnival

car'nivoro ① *nm* carnivore ② *adj* carnivorous

car'noso *adj* fleshy

'caro, -a ① *adj* dear; **cari saluti** kind regards

② *nmf* fam darling, dear; **i miei cari** my nearest and dearest

ca'rogna *nf* carcass; *fig* bastard

caro'sello *nm* merry-go-round

ca'rota *nf* carrot

caro'vana *nf* caravan; (di veicoli) convoy

caro'vita *nm* high cost of living

'carpa *nf* carp

car'paccio *nm* finely sliced raw beef with oil, lemon and slivers of Parmesan

Car'pazi *nmpl* **i** ∼ the Carpathians

carpenti'ere *nm* carpenter

car'pire *vt* seize; (con difficoltà) extort

car'pone, carponi *adv* on all fours; **camminare** ∼ crawl

car'rabile *adj* suitable for vehicles; **passo** ∼ = **passo carraio**

car'raio *adj* **passo** ∼ entrance to driveway, garage etc where parking is forbidden

carreggi'ata *nf* roadway; **doppia carreggiata** dual carriageway, divided ···⋗

highway Am; **rimettersi in** ~ fig straighten oneself out

carrel'lata *nf* TV pan; (fig: di notizie) round-up

car'rello *nm* trolley; (di macchina da scrivere) carriage; Aeron undercarriage; Cinema, TV dolly. **carrello d'atterraggio** Aeron landing gear. **carrello dei dolci** dessert trolley. **carrello portabagagli** luggage trolley, baggage cart Am. **carrello della spesa** shopping trolley

car'retta *nf* (veicolo vecchio) old banger; **tirare la** ~ fig plod along

car'retto *nm* cart

carri'era *nf* career; **di gran** ~ at full speed; **fare** ~ get on

carrie'rismo *nm* careerism

carrie'rista *nmf* **è un** ~ his career is all that matters

carri'ola *nf* wheelbarrow

'carro *nm* cart. **carro armato** tank. **carro attrezzi** breakdown vehicle, tow truck, wrecker Am. **carro funebre** hearse. **carro merci** truck

car'rozza *nf* carriage; Rail coach, car. **carrozza bagagliaio** Rail guard's van. **carrozza belvedere** Rail observation car. **carrozza cuccette** sleeping car. **carrozza fumatori** Rail smoker. **carrozza letti** Rail sleeping car. **carrozza ristorante** Rail restaurant car, buffet car

carroz'zella *nf* (per bambini) pram; (per invalidi) wheelchair

carrozze'ria *nf* bodywork; (officina) bodyshop

carrozzi'ere *nm* panel beater

carroz'zina *nf* pram; (pieghevole) push-chair, stroller Am

carroz'zone *nm* (di circo) caravan; (fig: organizzazione) slow-moving great monster of an organization

car'ruba *nf* carob

car'rubo *nm* carob

car'rucola *nf* pulley

carta *nf* paper; (da gioco) card; (statuto) charter; Geog map. **carta di addebito** charge card. **carta d'argento** senior citizens' railcard. **carta assegni** cheque card. **carta assorbente** blotting-paper. **carta carbone** carbon paper. **carta di credito** credit card. **carta crespata** crepe paper. **carta di debito** debit card. **carta fedeltà** loyalty card. **carta geografica** map. **carta d'identità** identity card. **carta igienica** toilet-paper. **carta d'imbarco** boarding card. **carta intelligente** smart card. **carta da lettere** writing-paper. **carta millimetrata** graph paper. **carta da pacchi** wrapping paper. **carta da parati** wallpaper. **carta da regali** giftwrap. **carta di riso** rice paper. **carta**

SIM SIM card. **carta smerigliata** emery paper. **carta stagnola** silver foil; Culin aluminium foil. **carta straccia** waste paper. **carta stradale** road map. **carta termica** thermal paper. **carta topografica** ≈ Ordnance Survey Map. **carta velina** tissue-paper. **carta verde** Auto green card. **carta vetrata** sandpaper. **carta dei vini** wine-list

cartacar'bone *nf* carbon paper

car'taccia *nf* waste paper

car'taceo *adj* paper

carta'modello *nm* pattern

cartamo'neta *nf* paper money

carta'pecora *nf* vellum

carta'pesta *nf* papier mâché

carta'straccia *nf* waste paper

cartave'trare *vt* sand [down]

car'teggio *nm* correspondence

car'tella *nf* (per documenti ecc) briefcase; (di cartoncino) folder; (di scolaro) satchel, schoolbag. **cartella clinica** medical record

cartel'lina *nf* document wallet, folder

cartel'lino *nm* (etichetta) label; (dei prezzi) price-tag; (di presenza) time-card; **timbrare il** ~ clock in; (all'uscita) clock out

car'tello *nm* sign; (pubblicitario) poster; (stradale) road sign; (di protesta) placard; (Comm, di droga) cartel

cartel'lone *nm* poster; Theat bill. **cartellone pubblicitario** billboard

cartello'nista *nmf* poster designer

cartello'nistica *nf* poster designing

carti'era *nf* paper-mill

carti'lagine *nf* cartilage

car'tina *nf* (geografica) map; (per sigarette) cigarette paper. **cartina di tornasole** litmus paper

car'toccio *nm* paper bag; **al** ~ Culin baked in foil

cartogra'fia *nf* cartography

car'tografo *nm* cartographer

carto'laio, -a *nmf* stationer

cartole'ria *nf* stationer's [shop]

cartolibre'ria *nf* stationer's and book shop

carto'lina *nf* postcard. **cartolina postale** postcard. **cartolina [precetto]** call-up papers

carto'mante *nmf* fortune-teller

carton'cino *nm* (materiale) card; (biglietto) card

car'tone *nm* cardboard; (arte) cartoon. **cartone animato** [animated] cartoon. **cartone ondulato** corrugated cardboard. **cartone di uova** egg box

car'tuccia *nf* cartridge; **mezza** ~ fig weakling. **cartuccia d'inchiostro** ink cartridge

'casa *nf* house; (abitazione propria) home; (ditta) firm; **amico di** ∼ family friend; **andare a** ∼ go home; **uscire di** ∼ leave the house; **essere di** ∼ be like one of the family; **fatto in** ∼ home-made; ∼ **per** ∼ house-to-house. **casa d'aste** auction house. **casa di correzione** ≈ reform school. **casa di cura** nursing home. **casa del custode** gatehouse. **casa famiglia** care home. **casa madre** Comm parent company. **casa di mode** fashion house. **casa in multiproprietà** timeshare. **casa popolare** council house. **casa rifugio** women's refuge. **casa di riposo** old people's home, retirement home. **casa dello studente** hall of residence. **casa per le vacanze** holiday home

ca'sacca *nf* military coat; (giacca) jacket

ca'saccio: **a** ∼ *adv* at random; **sparare a** ∼ **su qualcuno/qualcosa** take a potshot at somebody/something

ca'sale *nm* (gruppo di case) hamlet; (casolare) farmhouse

casa'linga *nf* housewife

casa'lingo 1 *adj* domestic; (fatto in casa) home-made; (amante della casa) home-loving; (semplice) homely
2 *nm* **casalinghi** *pl* household goods

casa'nova *nm inv* (donnaiolo) Casanova

ca'sata *nf* family

ca'sato *nm* family name

ca'scante *adj* falling; (floscio) flabby

ca'scare *vi* fall [down]

ca'scata *nf* (di acqua) waterfall

casca|'tore, -trice 1 *nm* stuntman 2 *nf* stuntwoman

cas'chetto *nm* **[capelli a] caschetto** bob

ca'scina *nf* farm building

casci'nale *nm* farmhouse

'casco *nm* crash-helmet; (asciugacapelli) [hair-]drier. **casco di banane** bunch of bananas. **Caschi blu** *pl* Mil Blue Helmets, Blue Berets

caseggi'ato *nm* block of flats Br, apartment block

casei'ficio *nm* dairy

ca'sella *nf* pigeon-hole. **casella postale** post office box, PO box; (elettronica) mailbox

casel'lante *nmf* (per treni) signalman; (in autostrada) toll collector

casel'lario *nm* (mobile) filing cabinet; (di documenti) file. **casellario giudiziario** record of convictions; **avere il** ∼ **giudiziario vuoto** have no criminal record

ca'sello *nm* (di autostrada) [motorway] toll booth

case'reccio *adj* home-made

ca'serma *nf* barracks *pl*; **da** ∼ ⟨linguaggio⟩ barrack room *attrib*.

caserma dei Carabinieri military police station. **caserma dei pompieri**, **caserma dei vigili del fuoco** fire station

caser'mone *nm* pej barracks *pl*

cash and carry *nm inv* cash-and-carry

casi'nista *nmf* fam muddler

ca'sino *nm* fam (bordello) brothel; (fig *sl:* confusione) racket; (disordine) mess; **un** ∼ **di** loads of; **è un** ∼ (complicato) it's too complicated

casinò *nm inv* casino

ca'sistica *nf* (classificazione) record of occurrences

'caso *nm* chance; (fatto, circostanza, Med, Gram) case; **a** ∼ at random; ∼ **mai** if need be; **far** ∼ **a** pay attention to; **non far** ∼ **a** take no account of; **per** ∼ by chance. **caso [giudiziario]** [legal] case, court case. **caso urgente** Med emergency case

caso'lare *nm* farmhouse

'caspita *int* good gracious

'cassa *nf* till; (di legno) crate; Comm cash; (luogo di pagamento) cash desk; (mobile) chest; (istituto bancario) bank. **cassa automatica prelievi** cash dispenser, automatic teller. **cassa comune** kitty **cassa continua** cash machine. **cassa da morto** coffin. **cassa di risparmio** savings bank. **cassa toracica** ribcage

cassa'forte *nf* safe

cassa'panca *nf* linen chest

cas'sata *nf* ice-cream cake

cas'sero *nm* Naut quarterdeck

casseru'ola *nf* saucepan

cas'setta *nf* case; (per registratore) cassette; **far buona** ∼ Theatr be good box-office. **cassetta degli attrezzi** toolbox. **cassetta delle lettere** postbox, letterbox. **cassetta delle offerte** charity box. **cassetta portapane** breadbin. **cassetta portavalori** cash box. **cassetta del pronto soccorso** first-aid kit. **cassetta di sicurezza** strong-box, safe-deposit box

cas'setto *nm* drawer; (di fotocopiatrice ecc) tray. **cassetto di inserimento [dei] fogli** paper feed tray

casset'tone *nm* chest of drawers

cassi'ere, -a *nmf* cashier; (di supermercato) checkout assistant, checkout operator; (di banca) teller

cassinte'grato, -a *nmf* person who has been laid off

cas'sone *nm* (cassa) chest; (per acqua) cofferdam

casso'netto *nm* rubbish bin, wheelie bin, trash can Am

'casta *nf* caste

ca'stagna *nf* chestnut; **prendere qualcuno in** ∼ fig catch somebody in the act. **castagna d'India** horse chestnut

casta'gnaccio nm tart from Tuscany made with chestnut flour

casta'gneto nm chestnut grove

ca'stagno nm chestnut[-tree]

casta'gnola nf (petardo) firecracker

ca'stano adj chestnut; ⟨occhi, capelli⟩ brown

ca'stello nm castle; (impalcatura) scaffold. **castello incantato** enchanted castle. **castello di sabbia** sandcastle

casti'gare vt punish

casti'gato adj (casto) chaste; ⟨abito, atteggiamento⟩ prim and proper

ca'stigo nm punishment

castità nf chastity

'casto adj chaste

ca'storo nm beaver

ca'strante adj fig frustrating

ca'strare vt castrate

ca'strato adj castrated; (inibito) inhibited; (cantante) castrato

castrazi'one nf gelding

ca'strone nm gelding

castrone'ria nf fam rubbish

'casual nm inv casual wear

casu'ale adj chance attrib

casual'mente adv by chance

ca'supola nf little house

cata'clisma nm fig upheaval

cata'comba nf catacomb

cata'falco nm catafalque

cata'fascio nm andare a ∼ go to rack and ruin

cata'litico adj **marmitta catalitica** Auto catalytic converter

cataliz'zare vt fig heighten

cataliz'zato adj Auto fitted with a catalytic converter

catalizza'tore ① adj Phys catalysing; **centro ∼** fig catalyst ② nm Auto catalytic converter; fig catalyst

catalo'gabile adj which can be listed

catalo'gare vt catalogue

catalogazi'one nf cataloguing

cata'logna nf type of chicory with large leaves

ca'talogo nm catalogue

catama'rano nm (da diporto) catamaran

cata'pecchia nf hovel; fam dump

cata'pulta nf catapult

catapul'tare vt (scaraventare fuori) eject

catapul'tarsi vr (precipitarsi) dive

catarifran'gente nm reflector

ca'tarro nm catarrh

catar'roso adj ⟨voce⟩ catarrhal

ca'tarsi nf inv catharsis

ca'tartico adj cathartic

ca'tasta nf pile

cata'stale adj **registro catastale** land registry; **rendita catastale** revenue from landed property

ca'tasto nm land register

cata'strofe nf catastrophe

cata'strofico adj catastrophic

catastro'fismo nm catastrophe theory

catch nm all-in wrestling

cate'chismo nm catechism

catego'ria nf category

cate'gorico adj categorical

categoriz'zare vt categorize

ca'tena nf chain. **catena montuosa** mountain range. **catene da neve** pl [snow] chains

cate'naccio nm bolt

cate'nella nf (collana) chain; (di orologio) watch chain; **tirare la ∼** (del gabinetto) flush, pull the plug

cate'nina nf chain

cate'ratta nf cataract

ca'terva nf **una ∼ di** heaps of, loads of

ca'tetere nm catheter

'catgut nm inv catgut

cati'nella nf basin; **piovere a catinelle** bucket down

ca'tino nm basin

ca'todico adj cathode; **raggi catodici** cathode rays

ca'torcio nm fam old wreck

catra'mare vt tar

ca'trame nm tar

'cattedra nf (tavolo di insegnante) desk; (di università) chair

catte'drale nf cathedral

catte'dratico, -a ① nmf professor ② adj ⟨pedante⟩ pedantic; ⟨insegnamento⟩ university attrib

catti'veria nf wickedness; (azione) wicked action; **fare una ∼ a qualcuno** be nasty to somebody

cattività nf captivity

cat'tivo adj bad; ⟨bambino⟩ naughty

cattocomu'nista nmf Catholic-communist

cattoli'cesimo nm Catholicism

cat'tolico, -a adj & nmf [Roman] Catholic

cat'tura nf capture

cattu'rare vt capture

cau'casico, -a nmf Caucasian

'Caucaso nm **il ∼** the Caucasus

caucciù nm rubber

'causa nf cause; Jur lawsuit; **far ∼ a qualcuno** sue somebody. **causa di forza maggiore** circumstances beyond one's control; (in assicurazione) act of God

cau'sale *adj* causal
cau'sare *vt* cause
'caustico *adj* caustic
cauta'mente *adv* cautiously
cau'tela *nf* caution
caute'lare *vt* protect
caute'larsi *vr* take precautions
cauteriz'zare *vt* cauterize
cauterizzazi'one *nf* cauterization
'cauto *adj* cautious
cauzi'one *nf* security; (per libertà provvisoria) bail; (deposito) deposit
cav. *abbr* (**cavaliere**) Kt, Knight
'cava *nf* quarry; fig mine
caval'care *vt* ride; (stare a cavalcioni) sit astride
caval'cata *nf* ride; (corteo) cavalcade
cavalca'via *nm* flyover
cavalci'oni: a ~ *adv* astride
cavali'ere *nm* rider; (titolo) knight; (accompagnatore) escort; (al ballo) partner
cavalle'resco *adj* chivalrous
cavalle'ria *nf* chivalry; Mil cavalry
cavalle'rizzo, -a ① *nm* horseman ② *nf* horsewoman
caval'letta *nf* grasshopper
caval'letto *nm* trestle; (di macchina fotografica) tripod; (di pittore) easel
caval'lina *nf* (ginnastica) horse; (gioco) leapfrog; **correre la** ~ fig pursue a life of pleasure
caval'lino *adj* equine
ca'vallo *nm* horse; (misura di potenza) horsepower; (scacchi) knight; (dei pantaloni) crotch; **a** ~ on horseback; **andare a** ~ go horse-riding. **cavallo di battaglia** war horse. **cavallo a dondolo** rocking-horse. **cavallo da tiro** carthorse. **cavallo di Troia** Trojan horse
caval'lona *nf* pej ungainly female
caval'lone *nm* (ondata) roller
caval'luccio *nm* **cavalluccio marino** sea horse
ca'vare *vt* take out; (di dosso) take off; **cavarsela** get away with it; **se la cava bene** he's/she's doing all right
cavasti'vali *nm inv* bootjack
cava'tappi *nm inv* corkscrew
ca'veau *nm inv* (di banca) vault
ca'verna *nf* cave
caver'nicolo, -a *nmf* cave dweller
caver'noso *adj* ⟨voce⟩ deep
ca'vetto *nm* Electr lead
ca'vezza *nf* halter; **mettere la** ~ **al collo a qualcuno** put somebody on a tight rein
'cavia *nf* guinea-pig
cavi'ale *nm* caviar
ca'viglia *nf* ankle

cavil'lare *vi* quibble
ca'villo *nm* quibble
cavil'loso *adj* pettifogging
cavità *nf inv* cavity
'cavo ① *adj* hollow ② *nm* cavity; (di metallo) cable; Naut rope. **televisione via cavo** cable TV. **cavo di collegamento** [connecting] cable. **cavo seriale** serial cable. **cavo di spiegamento** ripcord
cavo'lata *nf* fam rubbish; **non dire cavolate** fam don't talk rubbish; **non fare cavolate** fam don't act like an idiot
cavo'letto *nm* **cavoletto di Bruxelles** Brussels sprout
cavolfi'ore *nm* cauliflower
'cavolo *nm* cabbage; ~! fam sugar!; **non ho capito un** ~ fam I understood bugger-all; **che** ~ **succede?** what the heck is going on?. **cavolo cappuccio** spring cabbage
caz'zata *nf* vulg shit; **non dire cazzate** don't talk shit; **non fare cazzate** don't fuck things up
'cazzo *vulg* ① *nm* prick ② *int* fuck!; **non capisce un** ~ he doesn't understand a fucking thing; **non me ne importa un** ~! I don't give a fuck!; **sono cazzi miei!** it's my fucking business!
caz'zotto *nm* punch; **prendere qualcuno a cazzotti** beat somebody up
cazzu'ola *nf* trowel
CB *nf abbr* (**banda cittadina**) CB
cc *abbr* (**centimetri cubi**) cc
c/c *abbr* (**conto corrente**) c/a
ccn *nf abbr* (**copia carbone nascosta**) bcc
CCT *nm abbr* (**Certificato di Credito del Tesoro**) T-bill
CD *nm inv* CD
CD-ROM *nm inv* CD-Rom
ce ① *pers pron* (a noi) us; **ce lo ha dato** he gave it to us ② *adv* there; **ce ne sono molti** there are many; **ce ne vuole!** it takes some doing!
cec'chino *nm* sniper; Pol MP who votes against his own party
'cece *nm* chickpea
Ce'cenia *nf* Chechnya
cecità *nf* blindness
'ceco, -a *adj & nmf* Czech; **la Repubblica Ceca** the Czech Republic
Cecoslo'vacchia *nf* Czechoslovakia
'cedere ① *vi* (arrendersi) surrender; (concedere) yield; (sprofondare) subside ② *vt* give up; make over ⟨proprietà ecc⟩
ce'devole *adj* ⟨terreno ecc⟩ soft; fig yielding
ce'diglia *nf* cedilla
cedi'mento *nm* (di terreno) subsidence

'cedola *nf* coupon

cedo'lino *nm* (dello stipendio) wage slip

'cedro *nm* (albero) cedar; (frutto) citron

C.E.E. *nf abbr* (**Comunità Economica Europea**) E[E]C

cefa'lea *nf* headache

ce'falo *nm* mullet

'ceffo *nm* (muso) snout; (pej: persona) mug

cef'fone *nm* slap

ce'lare *vt* conceal

ce'larsi *vr* conceal oneself

ce'lato *adj* concealed

cele'brare *vt* celebrate, observe ⟨festività⟩

celebra'tivo *adj* celebratory

celebrazi'one *nf* celebration

'celebre *adj* famous

celebrità *nf inv* celebrity

'celere ① *adj* swift; **corso celere** crash course
② *nf* (polizia) flying squad

celerità *nf* speed; **con ~** speedily

ce'leste ① *adj* (divino) heavenly
② *adj & nm* (colore) pale blue

celesti'ale *adj* celestial

celi'bato *nm* celibacy

'celibe ① *adj* single
② *nm* bachelor

'cella *nf* cell. **cella frigorifera** cold store. **cella di isolamento** solitary confinement

+cello *suff* **monticello** *nm* mound; **praticello** *nm* small meadow

'cellofan *nm inv* cellophane; Culin cling film

cellofa'nare *vt* wrap in cling film

'cellula *nf* cell. **cellula fotoelettrica** electronic eye

cellu'lare ① *nm* (telefono) mobile (phone), cell phone
② *adj* **furgone cellulare** police van; **telefono cellulare** mobile (phone)

cellu'lite *nf* cellulite

cellu'litico *adj* full of cellulite

cellu'loide *adj* celluloid; **il mondo della ~** fig the celluloid world

cellu'losa *nf* cellulose

'Celsius *adj inv* Celsius

'celta *nm* Celt

'celtico *adj* Celtic

'cembalo *nm* Mus cembalo, harpsichord

cemen'tare *vt* cement

cementifi'care *vt* turn into a cement jungle

cementificazi'one *nf* turning into a cement jungle

cementi'ficio *nm* cement factory

ce'mento *nm* cement. **cemento armato** reinforced concrete

'cena *nf* dinner; (leggera) supper; (festa) dinner party

ce'nacolo *nm* circle

ce'nare *vi* have dinner; **~ fuori** eat out

'cencio *nm* rag; (per spolverare) duster; **bianco come un ~** white as a sheet

cenci'oso *adj* in rags

'cenere *nf* ash; (di carbone ecc) cinders *pl*; **le Ceneri** *pl* Ash Wednesday

Cene'rentola *nf* Cinderella

ce'netta *nf* (cena semplice) informal dinner; (cena intima) romantic dinner

'cenno *nm* sign; (col capo) nod; (con la mano) wave; (allusione) hint; (breve resoconto) mention; **far ~ di sì** nod

ce'none *nm* **il ~ di Capodanno/Natale** special New Year's Eve/Christmas Eve dinner

ceno'tafio *nm* cenotaph

censi'mento *nm* census

cen'sire *vt* take a census of

CENSIS *nm abbr* (**Centro Studi Investimenti Sociali**) national opinion research institute

cen'sore *nm* censor

cen'sura *nf* censorship

censu'rare *vt* censor

centelli'nare *vt* sip; fig measure out carefully

cente'nario, -a ① *adj & nmf* centenarian
② *nm* (commemorazione) centenary

centen'nale *adj* centennial

cen'tesimo ① *adj* hundredth
② *nm* hundredth; (di dollaro, euro) cent; **non avere un ~** be penniless

cen'tigrado *adj* centigrade

cen'tilitro *nm* centilitre

cen'timetro *nm* centimetre

centi'naia *nfpl* hundreds

centi'naio *nm* hundred

'cento *adj & nm* a or one hundred; **per ~** percent

centodi'eci *nm* a or one hundred and ten; **~ e lode** Univ ≈ first class honours

centome'trista *nmf* Sport one hundred metres runner

cento'mila *nm* a or one hundred thousand

cen'trale ① *adj* central
② *nf* (di azienda ecc) head office. **centrale atomica** atomic power station. **centrale elettrica** power station, power plant. **centrale idroelettrica** hydroelectric power station. **centrale nucleare** nuclear power station. **centrale operativa** (di polizia)

operations room. **centrale telefonica**
[telephone] exchange

centra'lina *nf* Teleph switchboard;
(apparecchiatura) junction box

centralinista *nmf* (switchboard/
telephone) operator

centra'lino *nm* Teleph exchange; (di
albergo ecc) switchboard

centra'lismo *nm* centralism

centraliz'zare *vt* centralize

cen'trare *vt* ~ qualcosa hit something
in the centre; (fissare nel centro) centre; fig
hit on the head (idea)

cen'trato *adj* (tiro, colpo) well-aimed; fig
(osservazione) right on target

centrat'tacco *nm* Sport centre forward

cen'trifuga *nf* spin-drier. **centrifuga**
[asciugaverdure] shaker. **centrifuga**
elettrica juice extractor

centrifu'gare *vt* Techn centrifuge;
(lavatrice) spin

cen'trino *nm* doily

cen'trismo *nm* Pol centrism

cen'trista *adj* Pol centrist

'centro *nm* centre; in ~ (essere) in town;
(andare) into town. **centro di**
accoglienza detention centre. **centro**
di attrazione focal point. **centro**
benessere wellness centre. **centro**
città city centre, midtown Am. **centro**
commerciale shopping centre, mall.
centro di costi Comm cost centre.
centro culturale arts centre. **centro**
di gravità centre of gravity. **centro di**
informazioni turistiche tourist
information office. **centro operativo** Mil
operations room. **centro polisportivo**
sports centre. **centro di riabilitazione**
halfway house. **centro sociale**
community centre. **centro sportivo**
leisure centre. **centro storico** old town

centrocam'pista *nm* Sport midfielder

centro'campo *nm* midfield

centro'destra *nm inv* Pol centre right

centromedi'ano *nm* Sport centre half

centrosi'nistra *nm inv* Pol centre left

centro'tavola *nm inv* centre-piece

centupli'care *vt* fig multiply

'ceppo *nm* (di albero) stump; (da ardere) log;
(fig: gruppo) stock

'cera *nf* wax; (aspetto) look. **cera d'api**
beeswax. **cera per auto** car wax. **cera**
per il pavimento floor-polish

cera'lacca *nf* sealing-wax

ce'ramica *nf* (arte) ceramics; (materia)
pottery; (oggetto) piece of pottery

cera'mista *nmf* ceramicist

ce'rata *nf* (giacca) waxed jacket

ce'rato *adj* (tela) waxed

cerbi'atto *nm* fawn

cerbot'tana *nf* blowpipe

'cerca *nf* andare in ~ di look for

cercaper'sone *nm inv* beeper;
chiamare con il ~ beep

cer'care ① *vt* look for
② *vi* ~ di try to

cerca|'tore, -trice *nmf* **cercatore**
d'oro gold seeker

'cerchia *nf* circle. **cerchia familiare**
family circle

cerchi'are *vt* circle, draw a circle
around (parola)

cerchi'ato *adj* (occhi) black-ringed

cerchi'etto *nm* (per capelli) hairband

'cerchio *nm* circle; (giocattolo) hoop

cerchi'one *nm* alloy wheel

cere'ale *nm* cereal

cerea'licolo *adj* grain *attrib*, cereal
attrib

cere'brale *adj* cerebral

'cereo *adj* waxen

ce'retta *nf* depilatory wax; fare la ~
wax

cer'foglio *nm* chervil

ceri'monia *nf* ceremony. **cerimonia**
inaugurale induction ceremony.
cerimonia nuziale marriage ceremony.
cerimonia di premiazione awards
ceremony

cerimoni'ale *nm* ceremonial

cerimoni'ere *nm* master of ceremonies

cerimoni'oso *adj* ceremonious

ce'rino *nm* [wax] match

cerni'era *nf* hinge; (di borsa) clasp.
cerniera lampo zip[-fastener], zipper
Am

'cernita *nf* selection

'cero *nm* candle

ce'rone *nm* greasepaint

ce'rotto *nm* [sticking] plaster. **cerotto**
callifugo corn plaster. **cerotto**
[transdermico] alla nicotina nicotine
patch

certa'mente *adv* certainly

cer'tezza *nf* certainty

certifi'care *vt* certify

certifi'cato *nm* certificate. **certificato**
medico doctor's note, sick note.
certificato di morte death certificate

certificazi'one *nf* certification.
certificazione di bilancio Fin auditors'
report

'certo ① *adj* certain; (notizia) definite;
(indeterminativo) some; sono ~ di riuscire I
am certain to succeed; a una certa età at a
certain age; certi giorni some days; un ~
signor Giardini a Mr Giardini; una certa
Anna somebody called Anna; certa gente
pej some people; ho certi dolori! I'm in   ···>

such pain!; **certi** *pron pl* some; (alcune persone) some people

2 *adv* of course; **sapere per** ∼ know for sure; **di** ∼ surely; ∼ **che ...** surely ...

cer'tosa *nf* Carthusian monastery

certo'sino *nm* Carthusian [monk]; **pazienza certosina** exceptional patience

cer'tuni *pron* some

ce'rume *nm* earwax

cer'vello *nm* brain; **avere un** ∼ **da gallina** be a bird-brain

cervel'lone, -a *nmf* hum brainbox

cervel'lotico *adj* (macchinoso) over-elaborate

cervi'cale *adj* cervical

'cervice *nf* cervix

'cervo *nm* deer

ce'sareo *adj* Med Caesarean; **parto cesareo** Caesarean

cesel'lare *vt* chisel

cesel'lato *adj* chiselled

cesella'tura *nf* chiselling

ce'sello *nm* chisel

ce'soie *nfpl* shears

'cespite *nm* source of income

ce'spuglio *nm* bush

cespugli'oso *adj* ⟨terreno⟩ bushy

ces'sare **1** *vi* stop, cease

2 *vt* stop

ces'sate *nm* **cessate il fuoco** ceasefire

ces'sato *adj* ∼ **allarme/pericolo** all clear

cessazi'one *nf* cessation. **cessazione d'esercizio** closing down

cessi'one *nf* handover

'cesso *nm sl* (gabinetto) bog, john Am; (fig: locale, luogo) dump

'cesta *nf* [large] basket

ce'stello *nm* (di lavatrice) drum

cesti'nare *vt* throw away; bin ⟨lettera⟩ turn down ⟨proposta⟩

ce'stino *nm* [small] basket; (per la carta straccia) waste-paper basket

'cesto *nm* basket. **cesto della biancheria** linen basket

ce'sura *nf* caesura

ce'taceo *nm* cetacean

'ceto *nm* [social] class

'cetra *nf* lyre

cetrio'lino *nm* gherkin

cetri'olo *nm* cucumber

cfr *abbr* (**confronta**) cf

C.G.I.L. *nf abbr* (**Confederazione Generale Italiana del Lavoro**) trades union organization

'Chad *nm* Chad

cha'let *nm inv* chalet

cham'pagne *nm inv* champagne

'chance *nf inv* chance

chape'ron *nm inv* chaperone

char'lotte *nf inv* ice-cream cake with fresh cream, biscuits and fruit

'charter *nm inv* charter plane; **volo charter** charter flight

chat'tare *vi* chat

che **1** *rel pron* (persona: soggetto) who; (persona: oggetto) whom; (cosa, animale) which; **questa è la casa** ∼ **ho comprato** this is the house [that] I've bought; **il** ∼ **mi sorprende** which surprises me; **dal** ∼ **deduco che ...** from which I gather that ...; **avere di** ∼ **vivere** have enough to live on; **grazie! –non c'è di che!** thank you –don't mention it; **il giorno** ∼ **ti ho visto** fam the day I saw you

2 *inter adj* what; (esclamativo: con aggettivo) how; (con nome) what a; ∼ **macchina prendiamo, la tua o la mia?** which car are we taking, yours or mine?; ∼ **bello!** how nice!; ∼ **idea!** what an idea!; ∼ **bella giornata!** what a lovely day!

3 *inter pron* what; **a** ∼ **pensi?** what are you thinking about?

4 *conj* that; (con comparazioni) than; **credo** ∼ **abbia ragione** I think [that] he is right; **era così commosso** ∼ **non riusciva a parlare** he was so moved, [that] he couldn't speak; **aspetto** ∼ **telefoni** I'm waiting for him to phone; **è da un po'** ∼ **non lo vedo** it's been a while since I saw him; **mi piace più Roma** ∼ **Milano** I like Rome better than Milan; ∼ **ti piaccia o no** whether you like it or not; ∼ **io sappia** as far as I know

'checca *nf* fam queen

checché *pron* whatever

check-'in *nm inv* check-in; **fare il** ∼ check in

check-'up *nm inv* Med check-up; **fare un** ∼ have a check-up

cheese'burger *nm inv* cheeseburger

'chef *nm inv* chef

'chela *nf* nipper

chemiotera'pia *nf* chemotherapy, chemo fam

chemisi'er *nm inv* chemise

chero'sene *nm* paraffin

cheru'bino *nm* cherub

che'tare *vt* quieten

che'tarsi *vr* quieten down

cheti'chella: alla ∼ *adv* silently

'cheto *adj* quiet

chi **1** *rel pron* whoever; (coloro che) people who; **ho trovato** ∼ **ti può aiutare** I found somebody who can help you; **c'è** ∼ **dice che ...** some people say that ...; **senti** ∼ **parla!** look who's talking!

2 *inter pron* (soggetto) who; (oggetto, con preposizione) whom; (possessivo) **di** ∼ whose; ∼ **sei?** who are you?; ∼ **hai incontrato?**

who did you meet?, whom did you meet?
fml; **di** ~ **sono questi libri?** whose books
are these?; **con** ~ **parli?** who are you
talking to?, to whom are you talking? fml;
a ~ **lo dici!** tell me about it!

chi'acchiera *nf* chat; (pettegolezzo)
gossip; **chiacchiere** *pl* chitchat; **far quattro
chiacchiere** have a chat

chiacchie'rare *vi* chat; (far pettegolezzi)
gossip

chiacchie'rato *adj* **essere** ~ ⟨persona⟩
be the subject of gossip

chi'acchiere *nfpl* (dolci) sweet pastries
fried and sprinkled with icing sugar

chiacchie'rone, **-a** ① *adj* talkative
② *nmf* chatterbox

chia'mare *vt* call; (far venire) send for;
come ti chiami? what's your name?; **mi
chiamo Roberto** my name is Robert; ~
alle armi call up; **mandare a** ~ send for; ~
a rapporto debrief

chia'marsi *vr* be called

chia'mata *nf* call; Mil call-up. **chiamata
a carico del destinatario** reverse
charge call, transferred charge call.
chiamata interurbana long-distance
call. **chiamata in teleselezione** direct
dialling, toll call Am. **chiamata urbana**
local call

chi'appa *nf* fam cheek

chiara'mente *adv* clearly

chia'rezza *nf* clarity; (limpidezza)
clearness

chiarifi'care *vt* clarify

chiarifica'tore *adj* clarificatory

chiarificazi'one *nf* clarification

chiari'mento *nm* clarification

chia'rire *vt* make clear; (spiegare) clear up

chia'rirsi *vr* become clear

chi'aro *adj* clear; (luminoso) bright;
⟨colore⟩ light; ⟨capelli⟩ fair

chia'rore *nm* glimmer

chiaro'scuro *nm* (tecnica) chiaroscuro

chiaroveg'gente ① *adj* clear-sighted
② *nmf* clairvoyant

chi'asso *nm* din

chiassosa'mente *adv* (rumorosamente)
rowdily; (vistosamente) gaudily

chias'soso *adj* (rumoroso) rowdy; (vistoso)
gaudy

chi'atta *nf* canal boat, canal barge

chi'ave *nf* key; **chiudere a** ~ lock.
chiave dell'accensione ignition key.
chiave di basso Mus bass clef. **chiave
inglese** monkey-wrench. **chiave
[inglese] a rullino** adjustable spanner

chia'vetta *nf* (in tubi) key

chiavi'stello *nm* latch

chi'azza *nf* stain. **chiazza di petrolio**
oil-slick

chiaz'zare *vt* stain

chiaz'zato *adj* dappled

chic *adj inv* chic

chicches'sia *pron* anybody

chicchirichi *nm inv* cock-a-doodle-doo

'chicco *nm* grain; (di caffè) bean; (d'uva)
grape. **chicco di caffè** coffee bean.
chicco di grandine hailstone. **chicco
d'orzo** barleycorn

chi'edere *vt* ask; (per avere) ask for;
(esigere) demand; ~ **notizie di** ask after

chi'edersi *vr* wonder

chieri'chetto *nm* altar boy

chi'erico *nm* cleric

chi'esa *nf* church. **Chiesa anglicana**
Church of England

chi'esto *pp di* CHIEDERE

chif'fon *nm* chiffon

'chiglia *nf* keel

chi'gnon *nm inv* bun

'chilo *nm* kilo

chilo'grammo *nm* kilogram[me]

chilo'hertz *nm inv* kilohertz

chilome'traggio *nm* Auto ≈ mileage

chilo'metrico *adj* in kilometres; fig
endless

chi'lometro *nm* kilometre

'chilowatt *nm inv* kilowatt

chilowat'tora *nm inv* kilowatt hour

chi'mera *nf* fig illusion

'chimica *nf* chemistry. **chimica
organica** organic chemistry

'chimico, **-a** ① *adj* chemical
② *nmf* chemist

chi'mono *nm* kimono

'china *nf* (declivio) slope; **inchiostro di
china** Indian ink

chi'nare *vt* lower

chi'narsi *vr* stoop

chincaglie'rie *nfpl* knick-knacks

chinesitera'pia *nf* physiotherapy

chi'nino *nm* quinine

'chino *adj* bent

chi'notto *nm* sparkling soft drink

chintz *nm* chintz

chi'occia *nf* sitting hen

chi'occiola *nf* snail; Comput at sign, @.
scala a chiocciola spiral staircase

chio'dato *adj* **pneumatici chiodati** snow
tyres; **scarpe chiodate** shoes with
crampons

chi'odo *nm* nail; (idea fissa) obsession.
chiodo di garofano clove

chi'oma *nf* [head of] hair; (fogliame)
foliage

chi'osco *nm* kiosk; (per giornali) newsstand

chi'ostro *nm* cloister

chip nm inv chip **[di silicio]** chip

'chipset nm inv chipset

chiro'mante nmf fortune teller, palmist

chiroman'zia nf palmistry

chiro'pratico, -a nmf chiropractor

chirur'gia nf surgery. **chirurgia endoscopica** keyhole surgery. **chirurgia estetica** cosmetic surgery

chirurgica'mente adv surgically

chi'rurgico adj surgical

chi'rurgo nm surgeon

chissà adv who knows; ~ **quando arriverà** I wonder when he will arrive

chi'tarra nf guitar. **chitarra acustica** acoustic guitar. **chitarra basso** bass guitar

chitar'rista nmf guitarist

chi'udere ① vt shut, close; (con chiave) lock; turn off, switch off ‹luce ecc›; turn off ‹acqua›; (per sempre) close down ‹negozio, fabbrica ecc›; (recingere) enclose; **chiudi il becco!** shut up!
② vi shut, close; (con chiave) lock up

chi'udersi vr shut; ‹tempo› cloud over; ‹ferita› heal over; fig withdraw into oneself

chi'unque ① pron anyone, anybody
② rel pron whoever

chi'usa nf enclosure; (di canale) lock; (conclusione) close

chi'uso ① pp di CHIUDERE
② adj closed, shut; ‹tempo› overcast; ‹persona› reserved; '~ **per turno**' 'closing day'

chiu'sura nf closing; (sistema) lock; (allacciatura) fastener; '~ **settimanale il lunedì**' 'closed on Mondays'. **chiusura centralizzata** Auto central locking. **chiusura lampo** zip, zipper Am

ci ① pron (personale) us; (riflessivo) ourselves; (reciproco) each other; (a ciò, di ciò ecc) about it; **non ci disturbare** don't disturb us; **aspettateci** wait for us; **ci ha detto tutto** he told us everything; **ci consideriamo ...** we consider ourselves ...; **ci laviamo le mani** we wash our hands; **ci odiamo** we hate each other; **non ci penso mai** I never think about it; **pensaci!** think about it!
② adv (qui) here; (lì) there; (moto per luogo) through it; **ci siamo** here we are; **ci siete?** are you there?; **ci siamo passati tutti** we all went through it; **c'è** there is; **ci vuole pazienza** it takes patience; **non ci vedo/ sento** I can't see/hear

C.ia abbr (**compagnia**) Co.

cia'batta nf slipper

ciabat'tare vi shuffle

ciabat'tino nm cobbler

ci'ac nm inv Cinema ~ **si gira!** action!

ci'alda nf wafer

cial'trone nm (mascalzone) scoundrel; (fannullone) wastrel

ciam'bella nf Culin ring-shaped cake; (salvagente) lifebelt; (gonfiabile) rubber ring

ci'ance nfpl yapping

cianci'are vi gossip

cianfru'saglie nfpl knick-knacks

cia'notico adj ‹viso› puce

cia'nuro nm cyanide

ci'ao int fam (all'arrivo) hello!, hi!; (alla partenza) bye-bye!, cheerio!

ciar'lare vi chat

ciarla'tano nm charlatan

ciarli'ero adj (loquace) talkative

cia'scuno ① adj each
② pron everyone, everybody; (distributivo) each [one]; **per** ~ each

ci'bare vt feed

ci'barie nfpl provisions

ci'barsi vr eat; ~ **di** live on

ciber'netica nf cybernetics

ciber'netico adj cybernetic

ciber'spazio nm cyberspace

'cibo nm food; **non toccare** ~ leave one's food untouched; **non ha toccato** ~ **da ieri** he hasn't had a bite to eat since yesterday. **cibo per animali** pet food; **cibi** pl **precotti** ready meals

ci'cala nf cicada

cica'lino nm buzzer

cica'trice nf scar

cicatriz'zante nm ointment

cicatriz'zare vi heal [up]

cicatriz'zarsi vr heal [up]

cicatrizzazi'one nf healing

'cicca nf cigarette end; (fam: sigaretta) fag; (fam: gomma) [chewing] gum

cic'chetto nm fam (bicchierino) nip; (rimprovero) telling-off

'ciccia nf fam fat, flab

cicci'one, -a nmf fam fatty, fatso

cice'rone nm guide

cicla'mino nm cyclamen

ciclica'mente adv cyclically

'ciclico adj cyclical

ci'clismo nm cycling

ci'clista nmf cyclist

'ciclo nm cycle; (di malattia) course. **ciclo economico** business cycle

ciclo'cross nm cyclo-cross

ciclomo'tore nm moped

ci'clone nm cyclone

ci'clonico adj cyclonic

ciclosti'lare vt duplicate

ciclosti'lato ① nm duplicate [copy]
② adj duplicate

ci'cogna nf stork

ci'coria nf chicory

ci'cuta *nf* hemlock

ci'eco, -a ① *adj* blind ② *nmf* blind man; blind woman; **i parzialmente ciechi** the partially sighted

ciel'lino *nmf* Pol member of the Comunione e Liberazione movement

ci'elo *nm* sky; Relig heaven; **al settimo ∼** in seventh heaven; **santo ∼!** good heavens!

'cifra *nf* figure; (somma) sum; (monogramma) monogram; (codice) code; **una ∼** sl like crazy

ci'frare *vt* embroider with a monogram; (codificare) code

ci'frato *adj* monogrammed; (codificato) coded

'ciglio *nm* (bordo) edge; (degli occhi) eyelash; **ciglia** *pl* eyelashes

'cigno *nm* swan

cigo'lante *adj* squeaky

cigo'lare *vt* squeak

cigo'lio *nm* squeak

'Cile *nm* Chile

ci'lecca *nf* far ∼ miss

ci'leno, -a *adj & nmf* Chilean

cili'egia *nf* cherry

cili'egio *nm* cherry[-tree]

cilin'drata *nf* cubic capacity, c.c.; **macchina di grossa ∼** highpowered car .

ci'lindro *nm* cylinder; (cappello) top hat, topper

'cima *nf* top; (fig: persona) genius; **in ∼ a** at the top of; **da ∼ a fondo** from top to bottom. **cima alla genovese** *baked veal stuffed with chicken and chopped vegetables, served cold*. **cime di rapa** *pl* turnip greens

ci'melio *nm* relic; **cimeli** *pl* memorabilia

cimen'tare *vt* put to the test

cimen'tarsi *vr* (provare) try one's hand; **∼ in** (arrischiarsi) venture into

'cimice *nf* bug; (puntina) drawing pin, thumbtack Am

cimini'era *nf* chimney; Naut funnel

cimi'tero *nm* cemetery. **cimitero delle macchine** breaker's yard

ci'mosa *nf* selvage, selvedge

ci'murro *nm* distemper

'Cina *nf* China

cincial'legra *nf* great tit

cincia'rella *nf* blue tit

cincillà *nm inv* chinchilla

cin cin *int* cheers!

cincischi'are *vi* fiddle

cincischi'arsi *vr* mess around

'cine *nm* fam cinema

cine'asta *nmf* film maker

Cinecittà *nf* (stabilimento) film complex in the suburbs of Rome

cine'club *nm inv* film club

ci'nefilo, -a *nmf* cinemagoer, film buff

cinegior'nale *nm* newsreel

cinema *nm inv* cinema, movie theater Am. **cinema d'essai** arts cinema

cine'matica *nf* kinematics

cinematogra'fare *vt* film

cinematogra'fia *nf* cinematography

cinemato'grafico *adj* film *attrib*

cinema'tografo *nm* cinema

cine'presa *nf* cine-camera

ci'nereo *adj* ashen

ci'nese *adj & nmf* Chinese

cinese'rie *nfpl* chinoiserie

cine'teca *nf* (raccolta) film collection

ci'netica *nf* kinetics

ci'netico *adj* kinetic

'cingere *vt* (circondare) surround

'cinghia *nf* strap; (cintura) belt. **cinghia del ventilatore** fanbelt. **cinghia della ventola** fanbelt

cinghi'ale *nm* wild boar; **pelle di cinghiale** pigskin

cinghi'ata *nf* lash

cingo'lato ① *adj* (mezzi) caterpillar *attrib* ② *nm* caterpillar

'cingolo *nm* Mech belt

cinguet'tare *vi* twitter

cinguet'tio *nm* twittering

cinica'mente *adv* cynically

'cinico *adj* cynical

ci'niglia *nf* (tessuto) chenille

ci'nismo *nm* cynicism

ci'nofilo *adj* ⟨unità⟩ dog-loving

cin'quanta *adj & nm* fifty

cinquanten'nale *nm* fiftieth anniversary

cinquan'tenne *adj & nmf* fifty-year-old

cinquan'tesimo *adj & nm* fiftieth

cinquan'tina *nf* una ∼ di about fifty

'cinque *adj & nm* five

cinquecen'tesco *adj* sixteenth-century

cinque'cento ① *adj* five hundred ② *nm* il Cinquecento the sixteenth century

cinque'mila *adj & nm* five thousand

cin'quina *nf* (in tombola) five in a row

'cinta *nf* (di pantaloni) belt; **muro di cinta** [boundary] wall

cin'tare *vt* enclose

'cintola *nf* (di pantaloni) belt

cin'tura *nf* belt. **cintura nera** black belt. **cintura di salvataggio** lifebelt. **cintura di sicurezza** Aeron, Auto seat belt

cintu'rato *nm* Auto radial tyre

cintu'rino *nm* **cinturino**
[dell'orologio] watch-strap; (di metallo)
bracelet

ciò *pron* this; that; ~ **che** what; ~
nondimeno nevertheless

ci'occa *nf* lock

ciocco'lata *nf* chocolate; (bevanda) [hot]
chocolate. **cioccolata in polvere**
drinking chocolate

ciocco'latino *nm* chocolate

ciocco'lato *nm* chocolate. **cioccolato
fondente** plain chocolate, dark
chocolate. **cioccolato al latte** milk
chocolate. **cioccolato da pasticceria**
cooking chocolate

cioè *adv* that is

ciondo'lare *vi* dangle

ciondo'lio *nm* dangling

ci'ondolo *nm* pendant

ciondo'loni *adv* fig hanging about

cionono'stante *adv* nonetheless

ci'otola *nf* bowl

ci'ottolo *nm* pebble; **ciottoli** *pl* (in spiaggia)
shingle

ci'piglio *nm* frown; **con** ~ with a frown

ci'polla *nf* onion; (bulbo) bulb

cipol'lotto *nm* green onion

ci'presso *nm* cypress

'cipria *nf* [face] powder

cipri'ota *adj* & *nmf* Cypriot

'Cipro *nm* Cyprus

'circa *adv* & *prep* about

cir'cense *adj* circus *attrib*

'circo *nm* circus

circo'lare ①*adj* circular
②*nf* circular; (di metropolitana) circle line
③*vi* circulate

circola'torio *adj* Med circulatory

circolazi'one *nf* circulation; (traffico)
traffic

'circolo *nm* circle; (società) club. **circolo
del golf** golf-club. **Circolo polare
antartico** Antarctic Circle. **Circolo
polare artico** Arctic Circle. **circolo
sociale** social club

circon'cidere *vt* circumcise

circoncisi'one *nf* circumcision

circon'dare *vt* surround

circon'dario *nm* (amministrativo)
administrative district; (vicinato)
neighbourhood

circon'darsi *vr* ~ **di** surround oneself
with

circonfe'renza *nf* circumference.
circonferenza del collo collar size.
circonferenza dei fianchi hip
measurement. **circonferenza [della]
vita** waist measurement

circon'flesso *adj* **e con l'accento** ~
circumflex e

circonvallazi'one *nf* ring road

circo'scritto ① pp di CIRCOSCRIVERE
② *adj* limited

circo'scrivere *vt* circumscribe

circoscrizio'nale *adj* area

circoscrizi'one *nf* area.
circoscrizione elettorale
constituency

circo'spetto *adj* wary

circospezi'one *nf* **con** ~ warily

circo'stante *adj* surrounding

circo'stanza *nf* circumstance;
(occasione) occasion

circostanzi'ato *adj* circumstantial

circu'ire *vt* (ingannare) trick

circuite'ria *nf* circuitry

cir'cuito *nm* circuit

circumnavi'gare *vt* circumnavigate

circumnavigazi'one *nf*
circumnavigation

ci'rillico *adj* Cyrillic

cir'ripede *nm* barnacle

cir'rosi *nf* cirrhosis

Cisgior'dania *nf* West Bank

C.I.S.L. *nf abbr* (**Confederazione
Italiana Sindacati Lavoratori**) trades
union organization

C.I.S.N.A.L. *nf abbr* (**Confederazione
Italiana Sindacati Nazionali dei
Lavoratori**) trades union organization

'cispa *nf* (nell'occhio) sleep

ci'sposo *adj* bleary-eyed

ci'sterna *nf* cistern; (serbatoio) tank

'cisti *nf inv* cyst

cisti'fellea *nf* gall bladder

ci'stite *nf* cystitis

C.I.T. *nm abbr* (**Compagnia Italiana
Turismo**) Italian tourist organization

ci'tare *vt* (riportare brani ecc) quote; (come
esempio) cite; Jur summons

citazi'one *nf* quotation; Jur summons *sg*

citofo'nare *vt* buzz

ci'tofono *nm* entry phone; (in ufficio, su
aereo ecc) intercom

cito'logico *adj* cytological

'citrico *adj* citric

ci'trullo, -a *nmf* fam dimwit

città *nf inv* town; (grande) city. **Città del
Capo** Cape Town. **città dormitorio**
dormitory town. **città fantasma** ghost
town. **città giardino** garden city. **Città
del Vaticano** Vatican City

citta'della *nf* citadel

citta'dina *nf* town

cittadi'nanza *nf* citizenship;
(popolazione) citizens *pl*

citta'dino, -a *nmf* citizen; (abitante di città)
city dweller

ciucci'are *vt* fam suck

ci'uccio *nm* fam dummy

ci'uco *nm* ass

ci'uffo *nm* tuft

ci'urma *nf* Naut crew

ciur'maglia *nf* (gentaglia) rabble

ci'vetta *nf* owl; (fig: donna) flirt; **[auto]** civetta unmarked police car

civet'tare *vi* flirt

civette'ria *nf* flirtatiousness, coquettishness

civettu'olo *adj* flirtatious, coquettish

'civico *adj* civic

ci'vile ⟦1⟧ *adj* civil ⟦2⟧ *nm* civilian

civi'lista *nmf* (avvocato) specialist in civil law

civiliz'zare *vt* civilize

civiliz'zarsi *vr* become civilized

civiliz'zato *adj* ⟨paese⟩ civilized

civilizzazi'one *nf* civilization

civil'mente *adv* civilly

civiltà *nf inv* civilization; (cortesia) civility

ci'vismo *nm* public spirit

CL *nf abbr* (**Comunione e Liberazione**) young Catholics association

cl *abbr* (**centilitro**) centilitre(s)

'clacson *nm inv* horn

clacso'nare *vi* beep the horn, hoot

cla'more *nm* clamour; **fare ∼** cause a sensation

clamorosa'mente *adv* ⟨sbagliare⟩ sensationally

clamo'roso *adj* noisy; ⟨sbaglio⟩ sensational

clan *nm inv* clan; fig clique

clandestina'mente *adv* secretly

clandestinità *nf* secrecy; **vivere nella ∼** live underground

clande'stino *adj* clandestine; **movimento ∼** underground movement; **passeggero ∼** stowaway

'claque *nf inv* claque

clarinet'tista *nmf* clarinettist

clari'netto *nm* clarinet

'classe *nf* class; (aula) classroom; **di prima ∼** first-class. **classe economica** economy class. **classe operaia** working class. **classe turistica** tourist class

classicheggi'ante *adj* classical

classi'cismo *nm* classicism

classi'cista *nmf* classicist

'classico ⟦1⟧ *adj* classical; (tipico) classic ⟦2⟧ *nm* classic

classifica *nf* classification; Sport league. **classifica dei singoli** singles charts

classifi'cabile *adj* classifiable

classifi'care *vt* classify

classifi'carsi *vr* be placed

classifica'tore *nm* (cartella) folder; (mobile) filing cabinet

classificazi'one *nf* classification

clas'sista ⟦1⟧ *adj* class-conscious ⟦2⟧ *nmf* class-conscious person

claudi'cante *adj* lame

'clausola *nf* clause. **clausola penale** Jur, Comm penalty clause. **clausola di recesso** Jur, Comm escape clause

claustrofo'bia *nf* claustrophobia

claustro'fobico *adj* claustrophobic

clau'sura *nf* Relig cloistered life; **di ∼** ⟨suora⟩ cloistered; **essere in ∼** fig shut oneself up; **vivere in ∼** fig live like a hermit

'clava *nf* club

clavicemba'lista *nmf* harpsichord player

clavi'cembalo *nm* harpsichord

cla'vicola *nf* collar-bone

clavi'cordo *nm* clavichord

cle'mente *adj* merciful; ⟨tempo⟩ mild

cle'menza *nf* mercy, clemency

clep'tomane *nmf* kleptomaniac

cleptoma'nia *nf* kleptomania

cleri'cale *adj* clerical

'clero *nm* clergy

cles'sidra *nf* hourglass

clic *nm inv* Comput click; **fare ∼ su** click on; **fare doppio ∼** double-click

clic'care *vi* Comput click; **∼ su** click on

cliché *nm inv* cliché

click ≈ CLIC

cli'ente *nmf* client; (di negozio) customer

clien'tela *nf* customers *pl*, clientele; (di avvocato) clientele

cliente'lare *adj* Pol nepotistic

cliente'lismo *nm* nepotism

'clima *nm* climate

clima'terio *nm* climacteric

climatica'mente *adv* climatically

cli'matico *adj* climatic; **stazione climatica** health resort

climatizza'tore *nm* air conditioner

climatizzazi'one *nf* air conditioning

'clinica *nf* clinic. **clinica di allergologia** allergy clinic. **clinica odontoiatrica** dental clinic. **clinica ostetrica** maternity hospital. **clinica psichiatrica** mental hospital

'clinico ⟦1⟧ *adj* clinical ⟦2⟧ *nm* clinician

clip *nf inv* paper-clip; (di orecchino) clip

cli'stere *nm* Med enema

clo'aca *nf* sewer

'cloche nf inv cloche hat
clo'nare vt clone
clonazi'one nf cloning
'clone nm clone
clo'rato adj chlorate
'cloro nm chlorine
cloro'filla nf chlorophyll
clorofluorocar'buro nm chlorofluorocarbon, CFC
cloro'formio nm chloroform
clou adj inv momenti ∼ highlights
club nm inv club. **club per i giovani** youth club. **club sportivo** sports club
club-'sandwich nm inv club sandwich
cm abbr (**centimetro**) cm
CNR nm abbr (**Consiglio Nazionale delle Ricerche**) national research council
Co. abbr (**compagnia**) Co
coabi'tare vi live together
coabitazi'one nf (di razze) coexistence
coadiu'tore, **-trice** nmf (in ufficio) assistant
coadiu'vare vt cooperate with
coagu'lante nm coagulant
coagu'lare vt coagulate
coagu'larsi vr coagulate
coagulazi'one nf coagulation
coalizi'one nf coalition
coaliz'zare vt fig unite
coaliz'zarsi vr unite
co'atto adj Jur compulsory
co'balto nm cobalt; (colore) cobalt blue
COBAS nmpl abbr (**Comitati di Base**) independent trade unions
'cobra nm inv cobra
'Coca® nf Coke®
Coca 'cola® nf Coca Cola
coca'ina nf cocaine
cocai'nomane nmf cocaine addict
coc'carda nf rosette
cocchi'ere nm coachman
coc'chio nm coach
coc'cige nm coccyx
cocci'nella nf ladybird
'coccio nm earthenware; (frammento) fragment
cocciu'taggine nf stubbornness
cocciuta'mente adv stubbornly
cocci'uto adj stubborn
'cocco nm coconut palm; fam love; **noce di cocco** coconut
coccodè nm inv cluck
cocco'drillo nm crocodile
cocco'lare vt cuddle
co'cente adj ⟨sole⟩ burning; ⟨lacrime, delusione⟩ bitter

'cocker nm inv **cocker [spaniel]** cocker spaniel
'cocktail nm inv (ricevimento) cocktail party
co'comero nm watermelon
co'cuzzolo nm top; (di testa, cappello) crown
'coda nf tail; (di abito) train; (fila) queue; (di traffico) tailback; **fare la** ∼ queue [up], stand in line Am. **coda di cavallo** (acconciatura) pony tail. **coda dell'occhio** corner of one's eye. **coda di paglia** guilty conscience
co'dardo, **-a** ① adj cowardly ② nmf coward
co'dazzo nm train
code'ina nf codeine
co'desto adj that
codice nm code; **in** ∼ ⟨messaggio⟩ coded, in code; **mettere in** ∼ encode. **codice di avviamento postale** postal code, zip code Am. **codice a barre** bar-code. **codice civile** civil code. **codice fiscale** National Insurance number Br, tax code. **codice penale** penal code. **codice PIN** PIN. **codice della strada** highway code
codi'cillo nm codicil
co'difica nf coding
codifi'care vt encode; codify ⟨legge⟩
codifica|'tore, **-trice** nmf Comput encoder
codificazi'one nf encoding; (di legge) codification
co'dini nmpl bunches
coeffici'ente nm coefficient
coercizi'one nf coercion
coe'rente adj consistent
coe'renza nf consistency
coesi'one nf cohesion
coe'sistere vi coexist
coe'sivo adj cohesive
coe'taneo, **-a** adj & nmf contemporary
cofa'netto nm casket
'cofano nm (forziere) chest; Auto bonnet, hood Am
cofirma'tario, **-a** nmf cosignatory
coge'stire vt co-manage
cogi'tare vi ponder
'cogliere vt pick; (sorprendere) catch; (afferrare) seize; (colpire) hit; ∼ **la palla al balzo** seize the opportunity; ∼ **di sorpresa** take by surprise
co'glione nm vulg ball; (sciocco) dickhead; **rompere i coglioni a qualcuno** get on somebody's tits
'Cognac nm cognac
co'gnato, **-a** ① nm brother-in-law ② nf sister-in-law

cognizi'one *nf* knowledge; **con ∼ di causa** on an informed basis

cognome *nm* surname, second name. **cognome da ragazza/da nubile** maiden name

cogu'aro *nm* cougar

'coi = CON + I

coi'bente *adj* insulating

coinci'denza *nf* coincidence; (di treno ecc) connection

coin'cidere *vi* coincide

coinqui'lino *nm* flatmate

coin'volgere *vt* involve

coinvolgi'mento *nm* involvement

coin'volto *adj* involved

'coito *nm* coitus

col = CON + IL

colà *adv* there

cola'brodo *nm inv* strainer; **ridotto a un ∼** fam full of holes

cola'pasta *nm inv* colander

co'lare ① *vt* strain; (versare lentamente) drip
② *vi* (gocciolare) drip; (perdere) leak; **∼ a picco** Naut sink

co'lata *nf* (di metallo) casting; (di lava) flow

colazi'one *nf* (del mattino) breakfast; (di mezzogiorno) lunch; **far ∼** have breakfast/ lunch. **prima colazione** breakfast. **colazione di lavoro** working lunch. **colazione al sacco** packed lunch

col'bacco *nm* fur hat

co'lei *pron f* the one

co'lera *nm* cholera

coleste'rolo *nm* cholesterol

colf *nf inv abbr* (**collaboratrice familiare**) home help

colibrì *nm inv* humming-bird

'colica *nf* colic

co'lino *nm* [tea] strainer

'colla *nf* glue; (di farina) paste. **colla di pesce** gelatine

collabo'rare *vi* collaborate; **∼ con** ⟨polizia⟩ co-operate with; **∼ a** ⟨rivista⟩ contribute to

collabora|'tore, -trice *nmf* collaborator; (di rivista) contributor. **collaboratrice familiare** domestic help

collaborazi'one *nf* collaboration; (con polizia) co-operation

collaborazio'nista *nmf* collaborator

col'lage *nm inv* collage

col'lana *nf* necklace; (serie) series. **collana di perle** pearl necklace

col'lant *nmpl* tights. **collant velati** sheer tights

col'lante *adj* adhesive

col'lare *nm* collar

colla'rino *nm* dog collar

col'lasso *nm* collapse. **collasso cardiaco** syncope. **collasso renale** kidney failure

collate'rale *adj* collateral

collau'dare *vt* test

collauda|'tore, -trice *nmf* tester

col'laudo *nm* test

collazio'nare *vt* collate

'colle *nm* hill; (passo) pass

col'lega *nmf* colleague

colle'gabile *adj* compatible (**a** with)

collega'mento *nm* connection; Mil liaison; Radio ecc link. **collegamento dati** data link. **collegamento ipertestuale** hyperlink. **collegamento in rete** networking

colle'gare *vt* connect

colle'garsi *vr* TV, Radio link up (**a** with); (Comput: a una rete ecc) go on line (**a** to)

collegi'ale ① *nmf* boarder
② *adj* ⟨responsabilità, decisione⟩ collective

col'legio *nm* (convitto) boarding-school. **collegio elettorale** constituency

'collera *nf* anger; **andare in ∼** get angry

col'lerico *adj* irascible

col'letta *nf* collection

collettività *nf inv* community

collet'tivo ① *adj* collective; ⟨interesse⟩ general; **biglietto collettivo** group ticket
② *nm* (studentesco, femminista) collective

col'letto *nm* collar

collet'tore *nm* (di fognatura) main sewer

collezio'nare *vt* collect

collezi'one *nf* collection. **collezione invernale** winter collection

collezio'nismo *nm* collecting

collezio'nista *nmf* collector. **collezionista di francobolli** stamp collector

colli'mare *vi* coincide

col'lina *nf* hill

colli'nare *adj* hill *attrib*

colli'netta *nf* knoll

colli'noso *adj* ⟨terreno⟩ hilly

col'lirio *nm* eyewash

collisi'one *nf* collision

'collo *nm* neck; (pacco) package; **a ∼ alto** high-necked; **a rotta di ∼** breakneck. **collo del piede** instep

colloca'mento *nm* placing; (impiego) employment

collo'care *vt* place

collo'carsi *vr* take one's place

collocazi'one *nf* placing

colloqui'ale *adj* ⟨termine⟩ colloquial; ⟨tono⟩ informal

col'loquio *nm* conversation; (udienza ecc) interview; (esame) oral [exam]

col'loso *adj* glutinous

col'lottola *nf* nape

collusi'one *nf* collusion

colluttazi'one *nf* scuffle

col'mare *vt* fill; bridge ⟨*divario*⟩; ~ qualcuno di gentilezze overwhelm somebody with kindness

'**colmo** ① *adj* full; un cucchiaio ~ a heaped spoonful
② *nm* top; fig height; al ~ della disperazione in the depths of despair; questo è il ~! (con indignazione) this is the last straw!; (con stupore) I don't believe it!; per ~ di sfortuna to crown it all

+**colo** *suff* poetucolo second rate poet

co'lomba *nf* dove. **colomba pasquale** dove-shaped cake with candied fruit eaten at Easter

colom'baccio *nm* wood pigeon

colom'baia *nf* dovecote

Co'lombia *nf* Colombia

colombi'ano *adj & nmf* Colombian

co'lombo *nm* pigeon; colombi *pl* (innamorati) lovebirds

Co'lonia *nf* Cologne; [acqua di] colonia [eau de] Cologne

colonia *nf* colony; (per bambini) holiday camp, summer camp

coloni'ale *adj* colonial

colonia'lista *nmf* colonialist

co'lonico *adj* ⟨*terreno, casa*⟩ farm *attrib*

coloniz'zare *vt* colonize

colonizza'|tore, -trice *nmf* colonizer

colonizzazi'one *nf* colonization

co'lonna *nf* column; (di auto) tailback. **colonna sonora** sound-track. **colonna vertebrale** spine

colon'nato *nm* colonnade

colon'nello *nm* colonel

colon'nina *nf* (distributore) petrol pump, gas pump Am

co'lono *nm* tenant farmer

colo'rante *nm* colouring. **colorante alimentare** food colouring

colo'rare *vt* colour; colour in ⟨*disegno*⟩

co'lore *nm* colour; (carte) suit; a colori in colour; di ~ coloured; farne di tutti i colori get up to all sorts of mischief; passarne di tutti i colori go through hell; diventare di tutti i colori fig turn scarlet. **colore a olio** oil paint. **colore primario** primary colour

colori'ficio *nm* paint and dyes shop

colo'rito ① *adj* coloured; ⟨*viso*⟩ rosy; ⟨*racconto, linguaggio*⟩ colourful
② *nm* complexion

co'loro *pron pl* the ones

colos'sale *adj* colossal

Colos'seo *nm* Coliseum

co'losso *nm* colossus

'**colpa** *nf* fault; (biasimo) blame; (colpevolezza) guilt; (peccato) sin; dare la ~ a blame; essere in ~ be at fault; per ~ di because of; è ~ mia it's my fault

col'pevole ① *adj* guilty
② *nmf* culprit

col'pire *vt* hit, strike; fig strike; ~ nel segno hit the nail on the head

'**colpo** *nm* blow; (di arma da fuoco) shot; (urto) knock; (emozione) shock; Med, Sport stroke; (furto) robbery; di ~ suddenly; far ~ make a strong impression; far venire un ~ a qualcuno fig give somebody a fright; perdere colpi ⟨*motore*⟩ keep missing; a ~ d'occhio at a glance; a ~ sicuro for certain. **colpo d'aria** chill. **colpo basso** blow below the belt. **colpo di frusta** Med whiplash injury. **colpo di grazia** kiss of death. **colpo da maestro** masterstroke. **colpo di scena** sensational development. **colpo di sole** sunstroke. **colpi di sole** *pl* (su capelli) highlights. **colpo di Stato** coup [d'état]. **colpo di telefono** ring, call; dare un ~ di telefono a qn give somebody a ring *or* call. **colpo di testa** [sudden] impulse. **colpo di vento** gust of wind

col'poso *adj* omicidio ~ manslaughter

coltel'lata *nf* stab

coltelle'ria *nf* cutlery shop

col'tello *nm* knife; avere il ~ dalla parte del manico have the upper hand. **coltello per il pane** breadknife. **coltello a serramanico** jackknife

colti'vare *vt* cultivate

coltiva'|tore, -trice *nmf* farmer

coltivazi'one *nf* farming; (di piante) growing. **coltivazione intensiva** intensive farming

'**colto** ① *pp di* COGLIERE
② *adj* cultured

'**coltre** *nf* blanket

col'tura *nf* cultivation. **coltura alternata** crop rotation

co'lui *pron m* the one

'**colza** *nf* Bot (oilseed) rape

'**coma** *nm inv* coma; in ~ in a coma; in ~ irreversibile brain dead

comanda'mento *nm* commandment

coman'dante *nm* commander; Naut, Aeron captain

coman'dare ① *vt* command; Mech control; ~ a qualcuno di fare qualcosa order somebody to do something
② *vi* be in charge

co'mando *nm* command; (di macchina) control

co'mare *nf* (pettegola) gossip

coma'toso *adj* Med comatose

combaci'are *vi* fit together; ⟨*testimonianze*⟩ concur

combattente ① *adj* fighting ② *nm* combatant. **ex combattente** ex-serviceman. **combattente per la libertà** freedom fighter

com'battere *vt/i* fight

combatti'mento *nm* fight; Mil battle; **fuori ∼** (pugilato) knocked out

combat'tuto *adj* ⟨*gara*⟩ hard fought; (tormentato) torn; ⟨*discussione*⟩ heated

combi'nare *vt/i* arrange; (mettere insieme) combine; (fam: fare) do; **cosa stai combinando?** what are you doing?

combi'narsi *vr* combine; (mettersi d'accordo) come to an agreement

combinazi'one *nf* combination; (caso) coincidence; **per ∼** by chance

com'briccola *nf* gang

combu'stibile ① *adj* combustible ② *nm* fuel

combusti'one *nf* combustion

com'butta *nf* gang; **in ∼** in league

'come ① *adv* like; (in qualità di) as; (interrogativo, esclamativo) how; **questo vestito è ∼ il tuo** this dress is like yours; **∼?** pardon?; **∼ stai?** how are you?; **∼ va?** how are things?; **∼ mai?** how come?; **∼?** what?; **non sa ∼ fare** he doesn't know what to do; **∼ sta bene!** how well he looks!; **∼ no!** that will be right!; **∼ tu sai** as you know; **fa' ∼ vuoi** do as you like; **∼ se** as if ② *conj* (non appena) as soon as

come'done *nm* blackhead

co'meta *nf* comet

'comfort *nm inv* comfort; **con tutti i ∼** with all mod cons

'comico ① *adj* comical; ⟨*teatro, attore*⟩ comic ② *nm* funny side; (attore) comic actor, comedian ③ *nf* comedienne; (attrice) comic actress, comedienne; (a torte in faccia) slapstick sketch

co'mignolo *nm* chimney-pot

cominci'are *vt/i* begin, start; **a ∼ da oggi** from today; **per ∼** to begin with; **cominciamo bene!** we're off to a fine start!

comi'tato *nm* committee. **comitato consultivo** advisory committee. **comitato direttivo** steering committee. **comitato esecutivo** executive committee. **comitato di gestione** management committee

comi'tiva *nf* party, group

co'mizio *nm* meeting. **comizio elettorale** election rally

'comma *nm* (capoverso) paragraph

com'mando *nm inv* commando

com'media *nf* comedy; (opera teatrale) play; fig sham. **commedia musicale** musical

commedi'ante ① *nm* comic actor; fig pej phoney ② *nf* comic actress; fig pej phoney

commedi'ografo, -a *nmf* playwright

commemo'rare *vt* commemorate

commemorazi'one *nf* commemoration. **commemorazione dei defunti** (2 novembre) All Soul's Day

commenda'tore *nm* commander

commen'sale *nmf* fellow diner

commen'tare *vt* comment on; (annotare) annotate

commen'tario *nm* commentary

commenta|'tore, -trice *nmf* commentator

com'mento *nm* comment; TV, Radio commentary. **commento musicale** music

commerci'ale *adj* commercial; ⟨*relazioni, trattative*⟩ trade; ⟨*attività*⟩; business; **centro commerciale** shopping centre

commerci'alista *nmf* business consultant; (contabile) accountant, certified public accountant Am

commercializ'zare *vt* market; pej commercialize

commercializzazi'one *nf* marketing; pej commercialization. **commercializzazione di massa** mass-marketing

commerci'ante *nmf* trader, merchant; (negoziante) shopkeeper. **commerciante all'ingrosso** wholesaler. **commerciante di oggetti d'arte** art dealer

commerci'are *vi* **∼ in** deal in

com'mercio *nm* commerce; (internazionale) trade; (affari) business; **in ∼** (prodotto) on sale. **commercio al dettaglio** *o* **al minuto** retail trade. **commercio all'ingrosso** wholesale trade.

com'messo, -a ① *pp di* COMMETTERE ② *nmf* shop assistant; **commessi** *pl* counter staff. **commesso viaggiatore** commercial traveller ③ *nf* (ordine) order

comme'stibile ① *adj* edible ② *nm* **commestibili** *pl* groceries

com'mettere *vt* commit; make ⟨*sbaglio*⟩; **∼ un reato** commit an offence

commi'ato *nm* leave; **prendere ∼ da** take leave of

commise'rare *vt* commiserate

commise'rarsi *vr* feel sorry for oneself

commissari'ato *nm* (di polizia) police station

commis'sario *nm* ≈ [police] superintendent; (membro di commissione) commissioner; Sport steward; Comm commission agent. **commissario di bordo** purser; **commissario capo** chief superintendent. **commissario d'esame** examiner. **commissario di gara** race official, steward. **commissario tecnico** (della nazionale) national team manager

commissi'one *nf* (incarico) errand; (comitato, percentuale) commission; (Comm: di merce) order; **commissioni** *pl* (acquisti) **fare commissioni** go shopping. **commissione d'esame** board of examiners. **Commissione Europea** European Commission. **commissione d'inchiesta** court of inquiry

commit'tente *nmf* purchaser

com'mosso ① pp di COMMUOVERE ② *adj* moved

commo'vente *adj* moving

commozi'one *nf* emotion. **commozione cerebrale** concussion

commu'overe *vt* touch, move

commu'oversi *vr* be touched

commu'tare *vt* change; Jur commute

commuta'tore *nm* Electr commutator

commutazi'one *nf* (di pena) commutation

comò *nm inv* chest of drawers

comoda'mente *adv* comfortably

como'dino *nm* bedside table

comodità *nf inv* comfort; (convenienza) convenience

'comodo ① *adj* comfortable; (conveniente) convenient; (spazioso) roomy; (facile) easy; **stia comodo!** don't get up!; **far ∼** be useful ② *nm* comfort; **fare il proprio ∼** do as one pleases; **prendila con ∼!** take it easy!

Co'more *nfpl* **le (isole) ∼** Comoros

'compact disc *nm inv* compact disc

compae'sano, -a ① *nm* fellow countryman ② *nf* fellow countrywoman

com'pagine *nf* (squadra) team

compa'gnia *nf* company; (gruppo) party; **fare ∼ a qualcuno** keep somebody company; **essere di ∼** be sociable. **compagnia aerea** airline. **compagnia di bandiera** (aerea) national airline. **compagnia low cost** budget airline, no frills airline

com'pagno, -a *nmf* companion; (Comm, Sport, in coppia) partner; Pol comrade. **compagno di classe** classmate. **compagno di scuola** schoolmate, schoolfriend. **compagno di squadra** team-mate. **compagno di viaggio** fellow traveller

compa'rabile *adj* comparable

compa'rare *vt* compare

compara'tivo *adj & nm* comparative

comparazi'one *nf* comparison

com'pare *nm* sidekick

compa'rire *vi* appear; (spiccare) stand out; **∼ in giudizio** appear in court

com'parso, -a ① pp di COMPARIRE ② *nf* appearance; Cinema extra; Theat walk-on

compartecipazi'one *nf* sharing; (quota) share

comparti'mento *nm* compartment; (amministrativo) department

compas'sato *adj* calm and collected

compassi'one *nf* compassion; **aver ∼ per** feel pity for; **far ∼** arouse pity

compassio'nevole *adj* compassionate

com'passo *nm* [pair of] compasses *pl*

compa'tibile *adj* (conciliabile) compatible; (scusabile) excusable

compatibilità *nf* compatibility

compatibil'mente *adv* **∼ con i miei impegni** if my commitments allow

compati'mento *nm* **un'aria di ∼** air of condescension

compa'tire *vt* pity; (scusare) make allowances for

compatri'ota *nmf* compatriot

compat'tezza *nf* (di materia) compactness; (fig: di partito) solidarity

com'patto *adj* compact; (denso) dense; (solido) solid; fig united

compendi'are *vt* (fare un sunto) summarize

com'pendio *nm* outline; (sunto) synopsis; (libro) compendium

compene'trare *vt* pervade

compen'sare *vt* compensate; (supplire) make up for

compen'sarsi *vr* balance each other out

compen'sato *nm* (legno) plywood

compensazi'one *nf* compensation

com'penso *nm* compensation; (retribuzione) remuneration; **in compenso** (in cambio) in return; (d'altra parte) on the other hand; (invece) instead

'compera *nf* purchase; **far compere** do some shopping

compe'rare *vt* buy

compe'tente *adj* competent; ⟨ufficio⟩ appropriate

compe'tenza *nf* competence; (responsabilità) responsibility; **competenze** *pl* (onorari) fees

com'petere *vi* compete; **∼ a** ⟨compito⟩ be the responsibility of

competitività *nf* competitiveness

competi'tivo *adj* ⟨prezzo, carattere⟩ competitive

competi'tore, -trice *nmf* competitor

competizi'one *nf* competition

compia'cente *adj* obliging

compia'cenza *nf* obligingness; **avere la ∼ di** ... be so obliging as to ...

compia'cere *vt/i* please

compia'cersi *vr* (congratularsi) congratulate; **∼ di** (degnarsi) condescend to

compiaci'mento *nm* satisfaction; pej smugness

compiaci'uto *adj* satisfied; ⟨*aria, sorriso*⟩ smug

compi'angere *vt* pity; (per lutto ecc) sympathize with

'compiere *vt* (concludere) complete; commit ⟨*delitto*⟩; **∼ gli anni** have one's birthday

'compiersi *vr* end; (avverarsi) come true

compi'lare *vt* compile; fill in ⟨*modulo*⟩

compila|'tore, -trice *nmf* compiler

compilazi'one *nf* compilation

compi'mento *nm* completion; **portare a ∼ qualcosa** conclude something

com'pire *vt* = COMPIERE

compi'tare *vt* spell

'compito[1] *nm* task; (dovere) duty; Sch homework; **fare i compiti** do one's homework

com'pito[2] *adj* polite

compiu'tezza *nf* completeness

compi'uto *adj* **avere 30 anni compiuti** be over 30

comple'anno *nm* birthday

complemen'tare *adj* complementary; (secondario) subsidiary

comple'mento *nm* complement; Mil draft. **complemento oggetto** Gram direct object

comples'sato *adj* hung-up

complessità *nf* complexity

complessiva'mente *adv* on the whole; (in totale) altogether

comples'sivo *adj* comprehensive; (totale) total

com'plesso[1] *adj* complex; (difficile) complicated
[2] *nm* complex, hang up fam; Psych complex; (di cantanti ecc) group; (di circostanze, fattori) combination; **in ∼** on the whole; (in totale) altogether. **complesso di inferiorità** inferiority complex

completa'mente *adv* completely

completa'mento *nm* completion

comple'tare *vt* complete

comple'tezza *nf* completeness

com'pleto[1] *adj* complete; (pieno) full [up]; **al ∼** ⟨*teatro*⟩ sold out; ⟨*albergo*⟩ full; '**∼** ' 'no vacancies'; **la famiglia al ∼** the whole family
[2] *nm* (vestito) suit; (insieme di cose) set

compli'care *vt* complicate

compli'carsi *vr* become complicated

compli'cato complicated

complicazi'one *nf* complication; **salvo complicazioni** all being well

'complice [1] *nmf* accomplice
[2] *adj* ⟨*sguardo*⟩ knowing

complicità *nf* complicity

complimen'tare *vt* compliment

complimen'tarsi *vr* **∼ con** congratulate

compli'mento *nm* compliment; **complimenti** *pl* (ossequi) regards; (congratulazioni) congratulations; **fare complimenti** stand on ceremony

complot'tare *vi* plot

com'plotto *nm* plot

compo'nente [1] *adj & nm* component
[2] *nmf* member

componen'tistica *nf* (per auto, elettronica) accessories *pl*

compo'nibile *adj* ⟨*cucina*⟩ fitted; ⟨*mobili*⟩ modular

componi'mento *nm* composition; (letterario) work

com'porre *vt* compose; (sistemare) put in order; Typ set; lay out ⟨*salma*⟩; settle (lite)

com'porsi *vr* **∼ di** be made up of

comportamen'tale *adj* behavioural

comporta'mento *nm* behaviour

compor'tare *vt* (implicare) involve

compor'tarsi *vr* behave

com'posito *adj* Chem, Phot composite

composi|'tore, -trice *nmf* composer; Typ compositor

composizi'one *nf* composition. **composizione floreale** flower arrangement

com'posta *nf* stewed fruit; (concime) compost

compo'stezza *nf* composure

com'posto [1] pp di COMPORRE
[2] *adj* ⟨*parola*⟩ compound; **essere ∼ da** consist of, comprise; **stai ∼**! sit properly!
[3] *nm* Chem compound; Culin mixture

com'prare *vt* buy; (fig: corrompere) buy off, bribe

compra|'tore, -trice *nmf* buyer

compra'vendita *nf* buying and selling; **atto di compravendita** deed of sale

com'prendere *vt* understand; (includere) comprise

compren'donio *nm* **essere duro di ∼** be slow on the uptake

compren'sibile *adj* understandable

comprensibil'mente *adv* understandably

comprensi'one *nf* understanding

compren'sivo *adj* understanding; (che include) inclusive

com'preso ① pp di COMPRENDERE
② adj included; **tutto compreso** ⟨prezzo⟩
all-in; **da lunedì a venerdì** ∼ Monday to
Friday inclusive

com'pressa nf compress; (pastiglia)
tablet

compressi'one nf compression.
compressione dati Comput data
compression

com'presso ① pp di COMPRIMERE
② adj compressed

compres'sore nm (rullo) steamroller

compri'mario, -a ① nm Theat
supporting actor
② nf supporting actress

com'primere vt press; (reprimere)
repress; Comput compress

compro'messo ① pp di
COMPROMETTERE
② nm compromise; (contratto) preliminary
but binding agreement

compromet'tente adj compromising

compro'mettere vt compromise

comproprietà nf multiple ownership

comproprie'tario, -a nmf joint owner

compro'vare vt prove

com'punto adj contrite

compunzi'one nf compunction

compu'tare vt calculate; (addebitare)
estimate

com'puter nm inv computer.
computer da casa home computer

computeriz'zare vt computerize

computeriz'zato adj computerized

computerizzazi'one nf
computerization

computiste'ria nf book-keeping

'computo nm calculation

comu'nale adj municipal

co'mune ① adj common; ⟨parti⟩
communal, common; ⟨amico⟩ mutual;
(ordinario) ordinary
② nm municipality; **in** ∼ shared; **fuori del**
∼ out of the ordinary; **avere qualcosa in**
∼ have something in common
③ nf collective farm; commune

comu'nella nf **fare** ∼ form a clique

comune'mente adv commonly

comuni'cante adj interconnecting

comuni'care vt communicate; pass on
⟨malattia⟩; Relig administer Communion
to

comuni'carsi vr receive Communion

comunica'tiva nf communicativeness

comunica'tivo adj communicative

comuni'cato nm communiqué.
comunicato commerciale Radio
commercial. **comunicato stampa**
press release

comunicazi'one nf communication;
Teleph [phone] call; **avere la** ∼ get through;
dare la ∼ a qualcuno put somebody
through. **comunicazione dati** Comput
data communications

comuni'one nf communion; Relig [Holy]
Communion

comu'nismo nm communism

comu'nista adj & nmf communist

comunità nf inv community.
Comunità [Economica] Europea
European [Economic] Community.
Comunità degli Stati Indipendenti
Commonwealth of Independent States.
comunità terapeutica rehabilitation
centre

co'munque ① conj however
② adv anyhow

con prep with; (mezzo) by; ∼ **facilità**
easily; ∼ **mia grande gioia** to my great
delight; **è gentile** ∼ **tutti** he is kind to
everyone; **col treno** by train; ∼ **questo**
tempo in this weather

co'nato nm **conato di vomito**
retching

'conca nf basin; (valle) dell

concate'nare vt link together

concate'narsi vr ⟨idee⟩ be connected

concatenazi'one nf connection

'concavo adj concave

con'cedere vt grant; award ⟨premio⟩;
(ammettere) admit

con'cedersi vr allow oneself ⟨pausa⟩;
treat oneself to ⟨lusso, vacanza⟩

concentra'mento nm concentration

concen'trare vt concentrate

concen'trarsi vr concentrate

concen'trato ① adj concentrated
② nm concentrate. **concentrato di**
pomodoro tomato pureé

concentrazi'one nf concentration

con'centrico adj concentric

concepi'mento nm conception

conce'pire vt conceive ⟨bambino⟩;
(capire) understand; (figurarsi) conceive of;
devise ⟨piano ecc⟩

con'cernere vt concern

concer'tare vt Mus harmonize;
(organizzare) arrange

concer'tarsi vr agree

concer'tista nmf concert performer

con'certo nm concert; (composizione)
concerto. **concerto rock** rock concert

concessio'nario nm agent

concessi'one nf concession

con'cesso pp di CONCEDERE

con'cetto nm concept; (opinione) opinion

concet'toso adj cerebral

concezi'one nf conception; (idea)
concept

con'chiglia *nf* [sea] shell. **conchiglia del pellegrino** scallop shell, **conchiglia di san Giacomo** scallop shell

'concia *nf* tanning; (di tabacco) curing

conci'are *vt* tan; cure ⟨*tabacco*⟩; ~ qualcuno per le feste give somebody a good hiding

conci'arsi *vr* (sporcarsi) get dirty; (vestirsi male) dress badly

conci'ato *adj* ⟨*pelle, cuoio*⟩ tanned; essere ~ come un barbone look like something the cat dragged in

concili'abile *adj* compatible

concili'abolo *nm* private meeting

concili'ante *adj* conciliatory

concili'are *vt* reconcile; pay ⟨*contravvenzione*⟩; (favorire) induce

concili'arsi *vr* go together; (mettersi d'accordo) become reconciled

conciliazi'one *nf* reconciliation; Jur settlement

con'cilio *nm* Relig council; (riunione) assembly

conci'maia *nf* dunghill

conci'mare *vt* feed ⟨*pianta*⟩

con'cime *nm* manure; (chimico) fertilizer

concisi'one *nf* conciseness

con'ciso *adj* concise

conci'tato *adj* excited

concitta'dino, -a *nmf* fellow citizen

concla'mato *adj* Med full blown

con'clave *nm* conclave

con'cludere *vt* conclude; (finire con successo) successfully complete

con'cludersi *vr* come to an end

conclusi'one *nf* conclusion; in ~ (insomma) in short

conclu'sivo *adj* conclusive

con'cluso pp di CONCLUDERE

concomi'tante *adj* contributory

concomi'tanza *nf* (di circostanze, fatti) combination; in ~ con combined with, in conjunction with

concor'danza *nf* agreement

concor'dare ① *vt* agree [on]; Gram make agree
② *vi* (sul prezzo) agree

concor'dato *nm* agreement; Jur, Comm composition

con'corde *adj* in agreement; (unanime) unanimous

con'cordia *nf* concord

concor'rente ① *adj* concurrent; (rivale) competing
② *nmf* Comm, Sport competitor; (candidato) candidate; (a quiz, concorso di bellezza) contestant

concor'renza *nf* competition. **concorrenza sleale** unfair competition

concorrenzi'ale *adj* competitive

con'correre *vi* (contribuire) combine; (andare insieme) go together; (competere) compete

con'corso ① pp di CONCORRERE
② *nm* competition; fuori ~ not in the official competition. **concorso di bellezza** beauty contest. **concorso di circostanze** combination of circumstances. **concorso di colpa** contributory negligence. **concorso ippico** showjumping event. **concorso a premi** prize-winning competition. **concorso in reato** Jur complicity. **concorso per titoli** competition in which exam results are not the sole criterion

concreta'mente *adv* concretely

concre'tare, concretizzare *vt* put into concrete form

con'creto *adj* concrete; in ~ in concrete terms

concu'bina *nf* concubine

concussi'one *nf* acceptance of a bribe

con'danna *nf* sentence; pronunziare una ~ hand down a sentence. **condanna a morte** death sentence. **condanna penale** prison sentence

condan'nare *vt* (disapprovare) condemn; Jur sentence

condan'nato, -a ① *adj* (destinato) forced
② *nmf* prisoner

con'densa *nf* condensation

conden'sare *vt* condense

conden'sarsi *vr* condense

condensa'tore *nm* Electr condenser

condensazi'one *nf* condensation

condi'mento *nm* seasoning; (salsa) dressing. **condimento per insalata** salad dressing

con'dire *vt* flavour; dress ⟨*insalata*⟩

condiscen'dente *adj* indulgent; pej condescending; (arrendevole) compliant

condiscen'denza *nf* indulgence; pej condescension; (arrendevolezza) compliance

con'dito *adj* Culin seasoned

condi'videre *vt* share

condizio'nale ① *adj* & *nm* conditional
② *nf* Jur suspended sentence

condiziona'mento *nm* Psych conditioning

condizio'nare *vt* condition

condizionata'mente *adv* conditionally

condizio'nato *adj* conditional (da on); aria condizionata air-conditioning

condiziona'tore *nm* air conditioner

condizi'one *nf* condition; a ~ che on condition that; condizioni *pl* di credito credit terms. **condizione imprescindibile** precondition

condogli'anze *nfpl* condolences; **fare le** ∼ **a** offer one's condolences to

'condom *nm inv* condom

condomini'ale *adj* ⟨spese⟩ common; ⟨riunione⟩ tenants' *attrib*

condo'minio *nm* joint ownership; (edificio) condominium

condo'mino, -a *nmf* joint owner

condo'nare *vt* remit

con'dono *nm* remission

con'dotta *nf* conduct, (circoscrizione di medico) country practice; (di gara ecc) management; (tubazione) pipe

con'dotto 1 pp di CONDURRE 2 *adj* **medico condotto** country doctor 3 *nm* pipe; Anat duct. **condotto dell'aria** air duct. **condotto sotterraneo** culvert

condu'cente *nmf* driver. **conducente di autobus** bus driver

con'durre *vt* lead; drive ⟨veicoli⟩ (accompagnare) take; conduct ⟨gas, elettricità ecc⟩; (gestire) run; ∼ **a termine** complete; ∼ **delle indagini** carry out an investigation

con'dursi *vr* behave

condut|'tore, -trice 1 *nmf* TV presenter; (di veicolo) driver 2 *nm* Electr conductor

condut'tore *adj* **filo conduttore** leitmotif

condut'tura *nf* duct. **conduttura del gas** gas main

conduzi'one *nf* conduction

confabu'lare *vi* have a confab

confa'cente *adj* suitable

con'farsi *vr* confarsi a suit

confederazi'one *nf* confederation. **Confederazione elvetica** Swiss Confederation

confe'renza *nf* (discorso) lecture; (congresso) conference. **conferenza stampa** press conference, news conference

conferenzi'ere, -a *nmf* lecturer, speaker

confe'rire 1 *vt* (donare) confer 2 *vi* (consultarsi) confer

con'ferma *nf* confirmation; **dare** ∼ confirm

confer'mare *vt* confirm

confes'sare *vt* confess

confes'sarsi *vr* confess

confessio'nale 1 *adj* ⟨segreto⟩ of the confession 2 *nm* confessional

confessi'one *nf* confession

confes'sore *nm* confessor

con'fetto *nm* (di mandorla) sugared almond

confet'tura *nf* jam

confezionare *vt* manufacture; make ⟨abiti⟩ package ⟨merci⟩; ∼ **sottovuoto** vacuum-pack

confezio'nato *adj* ⟨vestiti⟩ off-the-peg; ⟨gelato⟩ wrapped

confezi'one *nf* manufacture; (di abiti) making; (di pacchi) packaging; **di** ∼ ⟨abiti⟩ off-the-peg; **confezioni** *pl* clothes. **confezione economica** economy pack, economy size. **confezione famiglia** family size. **confezione multipla** multipack. **confezione regalo** gift set. **confezione da sei** (di bottiglie, lattine) six-pack

confic'care *vt* thrust

confic'carsi *vr* lodge

confic'cato *adj* ∼ **in** lodged in, embedded in

confi'dare 1 *vt* confide 2 *vi* ∼ **in** trust

confi'darsi *vr* ∼ **con** confide in

confi'dente 1 *adj* confident 2 *nmf* confidant; (informatore) informer

confi'denza *nf* confidence; (familiarità) familiarity; **prendersi delle confidenze** take liberties

confidenzi'ale *adj* confidential; ⟨tono⟩ familiar; **in via** ∼ confidentially

configu'rare *vt* Comput configure

configurazi'one *nf* configuration

confi'nante *adj* neighbouring

confi'nare 1 *vt* (relegare) confine 2 *vi* ∼ **con** border on

confi'narsi *vr* (ritirarsi) withdraw

confi'nato 1 *adj* confined 2 *nm* prisoner

CONFIN'DUSTRIA *nf abbr* (**Confederazione generale dell'Industria italiana**) ≈ CBI

con'fine *nm* border; (tra terreni) boundary

con'fino *nm* political exile

con'fisca *nf* (di proprietà) confiscation

confi'scare *vt* confiscate

conflagrazi'one *nf* conflagration

con'flitto *nm* conflict. **conflitto aereo** air war

conflittu'ale *adj* adversarial

conflittualità *nf* adversarial nature

conflu'enza *nf* confluence; (di strade) junction

conflu'ire *vi* ⟨fiumi⟩ flow together; ⟨strade⟩ meet

con'fondere *vt* confuse; (imbarazzare) embarrass

con'fondersi *vr* (mescolarsi) mingle; (sbagliarsi) be mistaken

confor'mare *vt* standardize (**a** in line with)

confor'marsi *vr* conform

conformazi'one *nf* conformity (**a** with); (del terreno) nature

con'forme *adj* standard

conforme'mente *adv* accordingly

confor'mismo *nm* conformity

confor'mista *nmf* conformist

conformità *nf* (a norma) conformity (**a** with); **in ∼ a** in accordance with, in conformity with

confor'tante *adj* comforting

confor'tare *vt* comfort

confor'tevole *adj* (comodo) comfortable

con'forto *nm* comfort; **a ∼ di** (una tesi) in support of; **conforti** *pl* **religiosi** last rites

confra'telli *nmpl* brethren

confra'ternita *nf* brotherhood

confron'tare *vt* compare

con'fronto *nm* comparison; **in ∼ a** by comparison with; **nei tuoi confronti** towards you; **senza ∼** far and away, by far. **confronto diretto** head to head

confusio'nario *adj* (persona) muddle-headed

confusi'one *nf* confusion; (baccano) racket; (disordine) mess; (imbarazzo) embarrassment

con'fuso ① pp di CONFONDERE ② *adj* confused; (indistinto) indistinct; (imbarazzato) embarrassed

confu'tare *vt* confute

conge'dare *vt* dismiss; Mil discharge

conge'darsi *vr* take one's leave

con'gedo *nm* leave; **essere in ∼** be on leave. **congedo malattia** sick leave. **congedo [di] maternità** maternity leave. **congedo [di] paternità** paternity leave

conge'gnare *vt* devise; (mettere insieme) assemble

con'gegno *nm* device

congelamento *nm* freezing; Med frostbite. **congelamento dei prezzi** price freeze

conge'lare *vt* freeze

conge'lato *adj* (cibo) deep-frozen

congela'tore *nm* freezer

congeni'ale *adj* congenial

con'genito *adj* congenital

congestio'nare *vt* congest

congestio'nato *adj* (traffico) congested; (viso) flushed

congesti'one *nf* congestion

conget'tura *nf* conjecture

congi'ungere *vt* join, connect; join (mani); combine (sforzi)

congi'ungersi *vr* join, connect

congiunti'vite *nf* conjunctivitis

congiun'tivo *nm* subjunctive

congi'unto ① pp di CONGIUNGERE ② *adj* joined; (azione) joint; (forze, sforzo) combined ③ *nm* relative

congiun'tura *nf* junction; (situazione) situation

congiuntu'rale *adj* economic

congiunzi'one *nf* Gram conjunction

congi'ura *nf* conspiracy

congiu'rare *vi* conspire

conglome'rato *nm* conglomerate; fig conglomeration; (da costruzione) concrete

'Congo *nm* Congo

congo'lese *adj & nmf* Congolese

congratu'larsi *vr* **∼ con qualcuno per** congratulate somebody on

congratulazi'oni *nfpl* congratulations

con'grega *nf* band

congre'gare *vt* gather

congre'garsi *vr* congregate

congregazi'one *nf* congregation

congres'sista *nmf* convention participant

con'gresso *nm* congress, convention; (americano) Congress. **Congresso Nazionale Africano** African National Congress

'congrua *nf* stipend

'congruo *adj* proper; (giusto) fair

conguagli'are *vt* balance

congu'aglio *nm* balance

coni'are *vt* coin

conia'tura *nf* coinage

coniazi'one *nf* coinage

'conico *adj* conical

co'nifera *nf* conifer

co'niglia *nf* female rabbit, doe

conigli'era *nf* rabbit hutch

conigli'etta *nf* bunny girl

conigli'etto *nm* bunny

co'niglio *nm* rabbit

coniu'gale *adj* marital; (vita) married

coniu'gare *vt* conjugate

coniu'garsi *vr* get married; Gram conjugate

coniu'gato *adj* (sposato) married

coniugazi'one *nf* conjugation

'coniuge *nmf* spouse

connazio'nale *nmf* compatriot

connessi'one *nf* connection. **connessione a banda larga** broadband connection

con'nesso pp di CONNETTERE

con'nettere ① *vt* connect ② *vi* think rationally

con'nettersi vr (Comput: a Internet) log on (a to)

connet'tore nm connector

conni'vente adj conniving

conno'tare vt connote

conno'tato nm distinguishing feature; **connotati** pl description; **rispondere ai connotati** fit the description; **cambiare i connotati a qualcuno** hum re-arrange somebody's face

con'nubio nm fig union

'cono nm cone

cono'scente nmf acquaintance

cono'scenza nf knowledge; (persona) acquaintance; (sensi) consciousness; **perdere ~** lose consciousness; **riprendere ~** regain consciousness, come to. **conoscenza di lavoro** business contact

co'noscere vt know; (essere a conoscenza di) be acquainted with; (fare la conoscenza di) meet; **~ qualcosa a fondo** know something inside out

conosci|'tore, **-trice** nmf connoisseur

conosci'uto ① pp di CONOSCERE ② adj well-known

con'quista nf conquest

conqui'stare vt conquer; fig win

conquista'tore nm conqueror; fig ladykiller

consa'crare vt consecrate; ordain ⟨sacerdote⟩; (dedicare) dedicate

consa'crarsi vr devote oneself

consa'crato adj ⟨suolo⟩ hallowed

consacrazi'one nf consecration

consangu'ineo, **-a** nmf blood relation

consa'pevole adj conscious

consapevo'lezza nf consciousness

consapevol'mente adv consciously

conscia'mente adv consciously

'conscio adj conscious

consecu'tivo adj consecutive; (seguente) next

con'segna nf delivery; (merce) consignment; (custodia) care; (di prigioniero) handover; (Mil: ordine) orders pl; (Mil: punizione) confinement to barracks; **pagamento alla consegna** cash on delivery. **consegna della posta** mail delivery

conse'gnare vt deliver; Mil confine to barracks; hand over ⟨prigioniero, chiavi⟩

consegna'tario nm consignee

consegu'ente adj consequent

consegu'enza nf consequence; **di ~** (perciò) consequently; ⟨agire, comportarsi⟩ accordingly

consegui'mento nm achievement

consegu'ire ① vt achieve ② vi follow

con'senso nm consent; (della popolazione) consensus

consensu'ale adj consensus-based

consen'tire ① vi consent ② vt allow

consenzi'ente adj consenting

con'serto adj **a braccia conserte** with one's arms folded

con'serva nf preserve; (di frutta) jam; (di agrumi) marmalade. **conserva di pomodoro** tomato sauce

conser'vare vt preserve; (mantenere) keep; **~ in frigo** keep refrigerated; **~ in luogo asciutto** keep dry

conser'varsi vr keep; **~ in salute** keep well

conserva|'tore, **-trice** adj & nmf Pol conservative; **partito conservatore** Conservative Party, Tory Party Br

conserva'torio nm conservatory, school of music

conservato'rismo nm conservatism

conservazi'one nf preservation; **a lunga ~** long-life

con'sesso nm assembly

conside'rare vt consider; (stimare) regard

conside'rato adj (stimato) esteemed

considerazi'one nf consideration; (osservazione, riflessione) remark; (stima) respect

conside'revole adj considerable

consigli'abile adj advisable

consigli'are vt advise; (raccomandare) recommend

consigli'arsi vr **~ con qualcuno** ask somebody's advice

consigli'ere, **-a** nmf adviser; (membro di un consiglio) councillor. **consigliere d'amministrazione** board member. **consigliere delegato** managing director

con'siglio nm advice; (ente) council; **un ~** a piece of advice. **consiglio d'amministrazione** board of directors. **consiglio di guerra** war cabinet. **consiglio d'istituto** parent-teacher association. **consiglio dei ministri** Cabinet. **consiglio scolastico** education committee. **Consiglio di Sicurezza** (dell'ONU) Security Council. **Consiglio Superiore della Magistratura** body responsible for ensuring the independence of the judiciary

con'simile adj similar

consi'stente adj substantial; (spesso) thick; fig ⟨argomento⟩ solid

consi'stenza nf consistency; (spessore) thickness; (fig: di argomento) solidity

con'sistere vi **~ in** consist of

consoci'arsi *vr* go into partnership

consoci'ata *nf* (azienda) subsidiary

consociati'vismo *nm* excessive tendency to form associations

consoci'ato *nm* associate

con'socio, -a *nmf* fellow-member

conso'lante *adj* consoling

conso'lare¹ *adj* consular

conso'lare² *vt* console

conso'larsi *vr* console oneself

conso'lato *nm* consulate

consolazi'one *nf* consolation

'console¹ *nm* consul

con'sole² *nf inv* (tastiera) console. **console per videogiochi** games console

consolida'mento *nm* consolidation

consoli'dare *vt* consolidate

consoli'darsi *vr* consolidate

consommé *nm inv* consommé

conso'nante *nf* consonant

conso'nanza *nf* consonance

'consono *adj* appropriate (**a** to), suitable (**a** for)

con'sorte *nmf* consort

con'sorzio *nm* consortium

con'stare *vi* ∼ **di** consist of; (risultare) appear; **a quanto mi consta** as far as I know; **mi consta che ...** seemingly ...;

consta'tare *vt* ascertain

constatazi'one *nf* statement of fact

consu'eto ① *adj* usual ② *nm* **più del** ∼ more than usual

consuetudi'nario *adj* ⟨diritto⟩ common; ⟨persona⟩ set in one's ways

consue'tudine *nf* habit; (usanza) custom

consu'lente *nmf* consultant. **consulente aziendale** management consultant; (azienda) management consultancy. **consulente matrimoniale** marriage guidance counsellor

consu'lenza *nf* consultancy

consul'tare *vt* consult

consul'tarsi *vr* ∼ **con** consult with

consultazi'one *nf* consultation

consul'tivo *adj* consultative

con'sulto *nm* consultation

consul'torio *nm* free clinic providing treatment for sexual problems and advice

consu'mare *vt* (usare) consume; wear out ⟨abito, scarpe⟩; consummate ⟨matrimonio⟩; commit ⟨delitto⟩

consu'marsi *vr* consume; ⟨abito, scarpe⟩ wear out; (struggersi) pine; **'da** ∼ **preferibilmente entro il ...'** 'best before ...'

consu'mato *adj* ⟨politico⟩ consummate; ⟨scarpe, tappeto⟩ worn [out]

consuma|'tore, -trice *nmf* consumer

consumazi'one *nf* consumption; (bibita) drink; (spuntino) snack; (di matrimonio) consummation; (di delitto) commission

consu'mismo *nm* consumerism

consu'mista *nmf* consumerist

con'sumo *nm* consumption; (uso) use; **generi di consumo** consumer goods. **consumo [di carburante]** [fuel] consumption

consun'tivo *nm* **bilancio consuntivo** balance sheet; **fare il** ∼ **di** fig take stock of

con'sunto *adj* well-worn

conta'balle *nmf* fam storyteller

con'tabile ① *adj* book-keeping ② *nmf* accountant

contabilità *nf inv* accounting; (ufficio) accounts department; **tenere la** ∼ keep the accounts. **contabilità di gestione** management accounts. **contabilità in partita doppia** double entry book-keeping

contachi'lometri *nm inv* mileometer, odometer Am

conta'dino, -a *nmf* farm-worker, agricultural labourer; (proprietario) farmer; (medievale) peasant

contagi'are *vt* infect; **la sua allegria contagia tutti** his cheerfulness is very contagious

contagi'ato *adj* infected

con'tagio *nm* contagion

contagi'oso *adj* contagious

conta'giri *nm inv* rev counter

conta'gocce *nm inv* dropper; **dare qualcosa col** ∼ fig dole something out in dribs and drabs

contami'nare *vt* contaminate

contaminazi'one *nf* contamination. **contaminazione incrociata** cross-contamination

contami'nuti *nm inv* timer

con'tante *nm* cash; **pagare in contanti** pay cash

con'tare ① *vt* count; (tenere conto di) take into account; **devi** ∼ **un'ora per il viaggio** you have to allow an hour for the journey ② *vi* count; ∼ **di fare qualcosa** plan to do something

conta'scatti *nm inv* Teleph time-unit counter

con'tato *adj* ⟨giorni, ore⟩ numbered

conta'tore *nm* meter. **contatore del gas** gas meter

contat'tare *vt* contact

con'tatto *nm* contact; **essere in** ∼ **con** be in touch or contact with; **mettersi in** ∼ **con** contact, get in touch with

'conte *nm* count, earl Br

con'tea *nf* county

conteggi'are ① *vt* include ② *vi* calculate

con'teggio nm calculation. **conteggio alla rovescia** countdown

con'tegno nm behaviour; (atteggiamento) attitude; **darsi un ~** pull oneself together

conte'gnoso adj dignified

contem'plare vt contemplate; (fissare) gaze at

contempla'tivo adj contemplative

contemplazi'one nf contemplation

con'tempo nm **nel ~** in the meantime

contemporanea'mente adv at the same time

contempo'raneo, -a adj & nmf contemporary

conten'dente nmf competitor

con'tendere ① vi compete; (litigare) quarrel
② vt dispute

con'tendersi vr **~ qualcosa** compete for something

conte'nere vt contain; (reprimere) repress

conte'nersi vr contain oneself

conteni'tore nm container

conten'tabile adj **facilmente ~** easy to please

conten'tare vt please

conten'tarsi vr **~ di** be content with

conten'tezza nf happiness

conten'tino nm placebo

con'tento adj glad; (soddisfatto) happy

conte'nuto nm contents pl; (di libro, testo) content

contenzi'oso ① adj contentious
② nm dispute; (ufficio) legal department

con'tesa nf disagreement; Sport contest

con'teso ① pp di CONTENDERE
② adj contested

con'tessa nf countess

conte'stare vt contest; Jur give notification of ⟨contravvenzione⟩; **~ un reato a qualcuno** charge somebody with an offence

contesta|'tore, -trice ① nmf person who is anti-authority
② adj anti-authority

contestazi'one nf (disputa) dispute; (protesta) protest; (di contravvenzione) notification

con'testo nm context

con'tiguo adj adjacent

continen'tale adj continental

conti'nente nm continent

conti'nenza nf continence

contin'gente nm contingent; (quota) quota

contin'genza nf contingency

continua'mente adv (senza interruzione) continuously; (frequentemente) continually

continu'are vt/i continue; (riprendere) resume; **~ gli studi** stay on at school

continua'tivo adj on-going, continuous

continuazi'one nf continuation

continuità nf continuity

con'tinuo adj continuous; (molto frequente) continual; **di ~** continuously; (frequentemente) continually; **corrente continua** direct current

con'tinuum nm inv continuum

'conto nm calculation; (in banca, negozio) account; (di ristorante ecc) bill, check Am; (stima) consideration; **a conti fatti** all things considered; **ad ogni buon ~** in any case; **di poco/nessun ~** of little/no importance; **in fin dei conti** when all's said and done; **per ~ di** on behalf of; **per ~ mio** (a mio parere) in my opinion; (da solo) on my own; **per ~ terzi** for a third party; **sul ~ di qualcuno** ⟨voci, informazioni⟩ about somebody; **far ~ di** (supporre) suppose; (proporsi) intend; **far ~ su** rely on; **fare i propri conti** do one's accounts; **fare i conti con qualcuno** fig sort somebody out; **fare i conti in tasca a qualcuno** estimate how much somebody is worth; **fare i conti senza l'oste** forget the most important thing; **render ~ a qualcuno di qualcosa** be accountable to somebody for something; **rendersi ~ di qualcosa** realize something; **starsene per ~ proprio** be on one's own; **tener ~ di qualcosa** take something into account; **tenere da ~ qualcosa** look after something. **conto in banca** bank account. **conto congiunto** joint account. **conto corrente** current account, checking account Am. **conto [corrente] comune** joint account. **conto corrente postale** Giro account. **conto profitti e perdite** profit and loss account. **conto alla rovescia** countdown. **conto spese** expense account

con'torcere vt twist

con'torcersi vr twist about

contor'nare vt surround

con'torno nm contour; Culin vegetables pl

contorsi'one nf contortion

contorsio'nista nmf contortionist

con'torto ① pp di CONTORCERE
② adj twisted

contrabban'dare vt smuggle

contrabbandi'ere, -a nmf smuggler

contrab'bando nm contraband

contrabbas'sista nmf double bass player

contrab'basso nm double bass

contraccambi'are vt return

contrac'cambio nm return

contraccet'tivo nm contraceptive

contraccezi'one nf contraception

contrac'colpo nm rebound; (di arma da fuoco) recoil; fig repercussion

con'trada nf (rione) district

contrad'detto pp di CONTRADDIRE

contrad'dire vt contradict

contraddi'stinguere vt differentiate, distinguish

contraddi'stinto ① pp di CONTRADDISTINGUERE
② adj ～ da distinguished by

contraddit'torio adj contradictory

contraddizi'one nf contradiction

contra'ente nmf contracting party

contra'ereo adj anti-aircraft

contraf'fare vt disguise

contraf'fatto ① pp di CONTRAFFARE
② adj disguised

contraffazi'one nf disguising

contraf'forte nm buttress

con'tralto ① nm counter-tenor
② nf contralto

contrap'peso nm counterbalance

contrap'porre vt (confrontare) compare; ～ A a B counter B with A

contrap'porsi vr be in opposition; ～ a contrast with; (opporsi a) be opposed to

contrap'punto nm Mus counterpoint

contraria'mente adv ～ a contrary to; ～ a me unlike me

contrari'are vt oppose; (infastidire) annoy

contrari'arsi vr get annoyed

contrarietà nf inv adversity; (ostacolo) set-back

con'trario ① adj contrary, opposite; (direzione) opposite; (esito, vento) unfavourable
② nm contrary, opposite; al ～ on the contrary

con'trarre vt contract

contrasse'gnare vt mark

contras'segno nm mark; [in] ～ (spedizione) cash on delivery, COD. **contrassegno IVA** VAT receipt

contra'stante adj contrasting

contra'stare ① vt oppose; (contestare) contest
② vi contrast; (colori) clash

con'trasto nm contrast; (di colori) clash; (litigio) dispute

contrattac'care vt counter-attack

contrat'tacco nm counter-attack

contrat'tare vt/i negotiate; (mercanteggiare) bargain

contrattazi'one nf contravention; (salariale) bargaining. **contrattazione di azioni** share dealing

contrat'tempo nm hitch

con'tratto ① pp di CONTRARRE
② nm contract. **contratto di lavoro** employment contract. **contratto a termine** fixed-term contract. **contratti a termine** pl Fin futures

contrattu'ale adj contractual

contravve'nire vi contravene a law

contravvenzi'one nf (multa) fine

contrazi'one nf contraction; (di prezzi) reduction

contribu'ente nmf contributor; (del fisco) taxpayer

contribu'ire vi contribute

contribu'tivo adj contributory

contri'buto nm contribution; **contributi** pl pensionistici pension contributions

con'trito adj contrite

'contro ① prep against; ～ di me against me
② nm il pro e il ～ the pros and cons pl

contro'battere vt counter

controbilanci'are vt counterbalance

controcor'rente ① adj (idee, persona) nonconformist
② adv upriver; fig upstream; andare ～ fig swim against the tide

controcul'tura nf counterculture

contro'curva nf second bend

contro'esodo nm massive return from holiday

controfa'gotto nm double bassoon

controffen'siva nf counter-offensive

controfi'gura nf stand-in

controfi'letto nm sirloin

contro'firma nf countersignature

controfir'mare vt countersign

controindicazi'one nf Med contraindication

controinterroga'torio nm cross-examination

control'labile adj (emozione) controllable; Tech which can be monitored

control'lare vt control; (verificare) check

control'larsi vr control oneself

control'lato adj controlled

con'troller nm inv Fin controller

con'trollo nm control; (verifica) check; Med check-up; perdere il ～ di lose control of. **controllo degli armamenti** arms control. **controllo automatico della velocità** automatic speed check. **controllo bagagli** baggage control. **controllo biglietti** ticket inspection. **controllo dei cambi** exchange control. **controllo del credito** credit control. **controllo delle nascite** birth control. **controllo ortografico** Comput spellchecker; fare il ～ ortografico spellcheck. **controllo passaporti** passport control. **controllo [di] qualità** ···⟶

quality control. **controllo radar della velocità** radar speed check

control'lore *nm* controller; (sui treni ecc) [ticket] inspector. **controllore di volo** air-traffic controller

contro'luce *nf* in ∼ against the light

contro'mano *adv* in the wrong direction

contromi'sura *nf* countermeasure

contropar'tita *nf* compensation; **in** ∼ in return

contropi'ede *nm* Sport breakaway; **prendere in** ∼ fig catch off guard

controprodu'cente *adj* counter-productive

contro'prova *nf* cross-check; **fare la** ∼ **di qualcosa** cross-check something

con'trordine *nm* counter order; **salvo contrordini** unless I/you hear to the contrary

contro'senso *nm* contradiction in terms

controspio'naggio *nm* counterespionage

controten'denza *nf* countertrend

controva'lore *nm* equivalent

contro'vento *adv* against the wind

contro'versia *nf* controversy; Jur dispute

contro'verso *adj* controversial

contro'voglia *adv* unwillingly

contu'mace *adj* Jur in default, absent

contu'macia *nf* default; **in** ∼ in one's absence

contun'dente *adj* ⟨corpo, arma⟩ blunt

contur'bante *adj* perturbing

contur'bare *vt* perturb

contusi'one *nf* bruise

con'tuso *nm* person with cuts and bruises

convale'scente *adj & nmf* convalescent

convale'scenza *nf* convalescence; **essere in** ∼ be convalescing

con'valida *nf* ratification; (di nomina) confirmation; (di biglietto) validation

convali'dare *vt* ratify; confirm ⟨nomina⟩; validate ⟨atto, biglietto⟩

con'vegno *nm* meeting; (congresso) convention, congress

conve'nevole *adj* suitable

conve'nevoli *nmpl* pleasantries

conveni'ente *adj* convenient; (vantaggioso) advantageous; ⟨prezzo⟩ attractive

conveni'enza *nf* convenience; (interesse) advantage; (di prezzo) attractiveness

conve'nire ① *vi* agree; (riunirsi) gather; (essere opportuno) be convenient; **ci conviene andare** it's better to go; **non mi**

conviene stancarmi I'd better not tire myself out
② *vt* agree [on]

conven'ticola *nf* clique

con'vento *nm* (di suore) convent; (di frati) monastery

conve'nuto *adj* agreed

convenzio'nale *adj* conventional

convenzio'nato *adj* ⟨prezzo⟩ controlled

convenzi'one *nf* convention

conver'gente *adj* converging

conver'genza *nf* convergence

con'vergere *vi* converge

con'versa *nf* lay sister

conver'sare *vi* converse

conversa|'tore, -trice *nmf* conversationalist

conversazi'one *nf* conversation

conversi'one *nf* conversion

con'verso *pp di* CONVERGERE

conver'tibile *nf* Auto convertible

conver'tire *vt* convert

conver'tirsi *vr* convert

conver'tito, -a ① *adj* converted
② *nmf* convert

converti'tore *nm* converter

con'vesso *adj* convex

convezi'one *nf* convection

convin'cente *adj* convincing

con'vincere *vt* convince

con'vinto *adj* convinced

convinzi'one *nf* conviction

convi'tato *nm* guest

con'vitto *nm* boarding school

convi'vente ① *nm* common-law husband
② *nf* common-law wife

convi'venza *nf* cohabitation

con'vivere *vi* live together

convivi'ale *adj* convivial

convo'care *vt* summon; Jur summons; convene ⟨riunione⟩

convocazi'one *nf* summoning; Jur summoning; (atto) summons; (riunione) meeting

convogli'are *vt* convey; ⟨navi⟩ convoy

con'voglio *nm* convoy; (ferroviario) train

convolare *vi* ∼ **a giuste nozze** hum tie the knot

convulsa'mente *adv* convulsively

convulsi'one *nf* convulsion; fig fit

convul'sivo *adj* Med convulsive; ⟨riso⟩ hysterical

coope'rante *nmf* aid worker

coope'rare *vi* co-operate

coopera'tiva *nf* co-operative

cooperazi'one *nf* co-operation

coordina'mento *nm* co-ordination

coordi'nare *vt* co-ordinate

coordi'nata *nf* Math co-ordinate; **coordinate** *pl* (su mappa) grid reference; **coordinate** *pl* **bancarie** bank details

coordi'nato ① *adj* co-ordinated ② *nm* (intimo) lingerie set

coordina|'tore, -trice *nmf* co-ordinator

coordinazi'one *nf* co-ordination. **coordinazione occhio-mano** hand-eye coordination

co'perchio *nm* lid; (copertura) cover

co'perta *nf* blanket; (copertura) cover; Naut deck. **coperta elettrica** electric blanket

coper'tina *nf* cover; (di libro) dust-jacket

co'perto ① *pp di* COPRIRE ② *adj* covered; (vestito) wrapped up; ‹cielo› overcast; ‹piscina› indoor ③ *nm* (a tavola) place; (prezzo del coperto) cover charge; **al ∼** under cover

coper'tone *nm* tarpaulin; (gomma) tyre

coper'tura *nf* cover; (azione) covering; (di strada) surfacing; (di malefatta) cover-up. **copertura globale** blanket coverage

'copia *nf* copy; **bella/brutta ∼** fair/rough copy; **essere la ∼ spiccicata di qualcuno** be the spitting image of somebody. **copia su carta** hard copy. **copia pirata** pirate copy. **copia di riserva** Comput backup copy.

'copia e in'colla *nm inv* Comput copy and paste; **fare un ∼** copy and paste

copi'are *vt* copy

copia'trice *nf* copier

copi'lota *nmf* co-pilot; (di auto) co-driver

copi'one *nm* Cinema, TV script

copi'oso *adj* copious

'coppa *nf* (calice) goblet; (bicchiere) glass; (per gelato ecc) dish; Sport cup. **coppa [di] gelato** ice-cream (served in a dish). **coppa del mondo** World Cup

cop'petta *nf* (di ceramica, vetro) bowl; (di gelato) small tub

'coppia *nf* couple; **∼ di fatto** de facto couple; (in carte, voga) pair

co'prente *adj* ‹cipria, vernice› thick; ‹collant› opaque

copri'capo *nm* head covering

coprifu'oco *nm* curfew

copri'letto *nm* bedspread

copri'mozzo *nm* hub-cap

copriobiet'tivo *nm* lens cap

copripiu'mino *nm* duvet cover

co'prire *vt* cover; drown [out] ‹suono›; hold ‹carica›

co'prirsi *vr* (vestirsi) cover oneself up; (vestirsi pesante) dress warmly; fig cover up; (proteggersi) cover oneself; ‹cielo› become overcast

copritei'era *nm* tea cosy

co-protago'nista *nmf* Cinema co-star

'coque: alla ∼ *adj* ‹uovo› soft-boiled

co'raggio *nm* bravery, courage; (sfacciataggine) nerve; **∼!** chin up!

coraggiosa'mente *adv* bravely, courageously

coraggi'oso *adj* brave, courageous

co'rale *adj* choral

co'rallo *nm* coral

co'rano *nm* Koran

co'razza *nf* armour; (di animali) shell

coraz'zata *nf* battleship

coraz'zato *adj* ‹nave› armour-plated

corazza'tura *nf* armour plating

corazzi'ere *nm* cuirassier

corbelle'ria *nf* piece of nonsense; **dire corbellerie** talk nonsense

'corda *nf* cord; (spago, Mus) string; (fune) rope; (cavo) cable; **essere giù di ∼** be down; **dare ∼ a qualcuno** encourage somebody; **tagliare la ∼** cut and run; **tenere qualcuno sulla ∼** keep somebody on tenterhooks; **corde** *pl* **vocali** vocal cords. **corda per il bucato** washing line

cor'data *nf* roped party

cordi'ale ① *adj* cordial; **cordiali saluti** best wishes ② *nm* (bevanda) cordial

cordialità *nf inv* cordiality; **∼ pl** (saluti) best wishes

'cordless *nm inv* Teleph cordless (phone)

cor'doglio *nm* grief; (lutto) mourning

cor'done *nm* cord; (schieramento) cordon. **cordone ombelicale** umbilical cord. **cordone sanitario** cordon sanitaire

Corea *nf* Korea. **Corea del Nord** North Korea. **Corea del Sud** South Korea

core'ano, -a *adj & nmf* Korean

coreogra'fare *vt* choreograph

coreogra'fia *nf* choreography; **fare la ∼ di** choreograph

core'ografo, -a *nmf* choreographer

Corfù *nf* Corfu

cori'aceo *adj* tough

cori'andoli *nmpl* (di carta) confetti *sg*

cori'andolo *nm* (spezia) coriander

cori'care *vt* put to bed

cori'carsi *vr* go to bed

Co'rinto *nf* Corinth

co'rista *nmf* choir member

'corna ▸ CORNO

cor'nacchia *nf* crow

corna'musa *nf* bagpipes *pl*

'cornea *nf* cornea

'corner *nm inv* corner; **salvarsi in ∼** fig have a lucky escape

cor'netta *nf* Mus cornet; (del telefono) receiver

cor'netto nm (brioche) croissant. ~ **acustico** ear trumpet

cor'nice nf frame. **cornice a giorno** clip frame

cornici'one nm cornice

cornifi'care vt fam cheat on

'**corno** nm (pl f **corna**) horn; **fare le corna a qualcuno** fam cheat on somebody; **fare le corna** (per scongiuro) ≈ touch wood; **un ~!** you must be joking!; (per niente) nonsense!. **corno da caccia** French horn

Corno'vaglia nf Cornwall

cornu'copia nf cornucopia

cor'nuto ① adj horned
② nm (fam: marito tradito) cuckold; (insulto) bastard

'**coro** nm chorus; Relig choir

co'rolla nf corolla

corol'lario nm corollary

co'rona nf crown; (di fiori) wreath; (rosario) rosary

corona'mento nm (di sogno) fulfilment; (di carriera) crowning achievement

coro'nare vt fulfil ⟨sogno⟩

coro'nario adj ⟨arteria⟩ coronary

cor'petto nm bodice

'**corpo** nm body; (Mil, diplomatico) corps inv; [a] ~ a ~ Mil hand to hand; **lottare [a] ~ a ~** have a punch-up, slug it out; **dare ~ a qualcosa** give substance to something; **buttarsi a ~ morto in qualcosa** throw oneself desperately into something; **andare di ~** move one's bowels. **corpo di ballo** corps de ballet. **corpo estraneo** foreign body. **corpo insegnante** teaching staff. **corpo del reato** murder weapon

corpo'rale adj corporal

corporati'vismo nm corporatism

corpora'tura nf build

corporazi'one nf corporation

cor'poreo adj bodily

cor'poso adj full-bodied

corpu'lento adj stout

'**corpus** nm inv corpus

cor'puscolo nm corpuscle

corre'dare vt (di note) supply (**di** with); **corredato di curriculum** accompanied by a CV

corre'dino nm (per neonato) layette

cor'redo nm (nuziale) trousseau; (di informazioni ecc) set

correggere vt correct; lace ⟨bevanda⟩; **~ le bozze** proof-read

corre'lare vt correlate

cor'rente ① adj running; (in vigore) current; (frequente) everyday; ⟨inglese ecc⟩ fluent
② nf current; (d'aria) draught; **essere al ~ di qualcosa** be aware of something; **tenersi al ~** keep up to date (**di** with). **corrente continua** direct current. **corrente trasversale** cross current

corrente'mente adv ⟨parlare⟩ fluently; (comunemente) commonly

'**correre** ① vi run; (affrettarsi) hurry; Sport race; ⟨notizie⟩ circulate; **lascia ~!** let it go!; **~ dietro a** run after; **tra loro non corre buon sangue** there is bad blood between them
② vt run; **~ un pericolo** run a risk; **corre voce che ...** there's a rumour that ...

correspon'sabile nmf person jointly responsible

corresponsi'one nf payment

corretta'mente adv correctly; ⟨sedersi, mangiare⟩ properly; ⟨trattare, fare qualcosa⟩ right

corret'tivo nm corrective

cor'retto ① pp di CORREGGERE
② adj correct; ⟨caffè⟩ with a drop of alcohol

corret|'tore, -trice ① nmf **correttore di bozze** proof-reader
② nm **correttore grammaticale** Comput grammar checker. **correttore ortografico** Comput spellchecker

correzi'one nf correction. **correzione di bozze** proof-reading. **correzione errori** Comput error correction

cor'rida nf bullfight

corri'doio nm corridor; Aeron aisle

corri|'dore, -trice nmf (automobilistico) driver; (ciclista) cyclist; (a piedi) runner

corri'era nf coach, bus

corri'ere nm courier; (posta) mail; (spedizioniere) carrier. **corriere della droga** drug mule

corri'mano nm banister

corrispet'tivo nm amount due

corrispon'dente ① adj corresponding
② nmf correspondent. **corrispondente estero** foreign correspondent

corrispon'denza nf correspondence; **tenersi in ~ con** correspond with; **per ~** ⟨fare un corso⟩ by correspondence; **corso per corrispondenza** correspondence course; **vendite per corrispondenza** mail-order [shopping]

corri'spondere vi correspond; ⟨stanza⟩ communicate; **~ a** (contraccambiare) return

corri'sposto adj ⟨amore⟩ reciprocated

corrobo'rare vt strengthen; fig corroborate

cor'rodere vt corrode

cor'rodersi vr corrode

cor'rompere vt corrupt; (con denaro) bribe

corrosi'one nf corrosion

corro'sivo *adj* corrosive

cor'roso *pp di* CORRODERE

cor'rotto ① *pp di* CORROMPERE ② *adj* corrupt

corrucci'arsi *vr* be vexed

corrucci'ato *adj* vexed

corru'gare *vt* wrinkle; ∼ **la fronte** knit one's brows

corrut'tela *nf* depravity

corruzi'one *nf* corruption; (con denaro) bribery

'corsa *nf* running; (rapida) dash; Sport race; (di treno ecc) journey; **di** ∼ at a run; **di gran** ∼ in a great hurry; **fare una** ∼ (sbrigarsi) run, hurry. **corsa agli armamenti** arms race. **corsa ciclistica** cycle race. **corsa ippica** horse race. **corsa all'oro** gold rush. **corsa a ostacoli** obstacle race. **corsa piana** flat racing. **corsa semplice** one way [ticket]

cor'sia *nf* gangway; (di ospedale) ward; Aut lane; (di supermercato) aisle. **corsia autobus** bus lane. **corsia d'emergenza** Aut hard shoulder. **corsia di sorpasso** fast lane, outside lane

'Corsica *nf* Corsica

cor'sivo *nm* italics *pl*; **in** ∼ in italics

'corso ① *pp di* CORRERE ② *nm* course; (strada) main street; Comm circulation; (in borsa) price, quotation; **essere in** ∼ be underway; **lavori in** ∼ work in progress; **nel** ∼ **di** during; **avere** ∼ **legale** be legal tender. **corso d'acqua** waterway. **corso per corrispondenza** correspondence course; **corso di formazione** training course. **corso di formazione professionale** vocational course. **corso full immersion** immersion course. **corso del giorno** current daily price. **corso di laurea** degree course. **corso serale** evening class; **corsi** *pl* **di studio a distanza** distance learning

'corte *nf* [court] yard; (Jur, regale) court; **fare la** ∼ **a qualcuno** court somebody. **corte d'appello** court of appeal. **Corte d'assise** crown court. **Corte di cassazione** supreme court of appeal. **Corte dei conti** National Audit Office. **Corte europea per i diritti dell'uomo** European Court of Human Rights. **Corte europea di giustizia** European Court of Justice. **corte di giustizia** court of law

cor'teccia *nf* bark

corteggia'mento *nm* courtship

corteggi'are *vt* court

corteggia'tore *nm* admirer

cor'teo *nm* procession. **corteo di auto** motorcade. **corteo funebre** funeral cortège. **corteo nuziale** bridal party

cor'tese *adj* courteous

corte'sia *nf* courtesy; **per** ∼ please

cortigi'ano, -a ① *nmf* courtier ② *nf* courtesan

cor'tile *nm* courtyard

cor'tina *nf* curtain; (schermo) screen

'corto *adj* short; **per farla corta** to cut a long story short; **a** ∼ **di** short of, hard up for. **corto circuito** *nm* short [circuit]

cortome'traggio *nm* Cinema short

cor'vino *adj* jet-black

'corvo *nm* raven

'cosa ① *nf* thing; (faccenda) matter ② *inter, rel pron* what; [che] ∼ what; **nessuna** ∼ nothing; **ogni** ∼ everything; **per prima** ∼ first of all; **tante cose** [so] many things; (augurio) all the best; ∼**?** what?; ∼ **hai detto?** what did you say?; **le cose le vanno bene** she's doing all right

'cosca *nf* clan

'coscia *nf* thigh; Culin leg; **cosce** *pl* **di rana** frogs' legs

cosci'ente *adj* conscious

cosci'enza *nf* conscience; (consapevolezza) consciousness; **mettersi la** ∼ **a posto** salve one's conscience

coscienziosa'mente *adv* conscientiously

coscienzi'oso *adj* conscientious

cosci'otto *nm* leg

co'scritto *nm* conscript

coscrizi'one *nf* conscription

così ① *adv* so; (in questo modo) like this, like that; (perciò) therefore; **le cose stanno** ∼ that's how things stand; **fermo** ∼**!** hold it!; **proprio** ∼**!** exactly!; **basta** ∼**!** that will do!; **ah, è** ∼**?** it's like that, is it?; ∼ ∼ so-so; **e** ∼ **via** and so on; **per** ∼ **dire** so to speak; **più di** ∼ any more; **una** ∼ **cara ragazza!** such a nice girl!; **è stato** ∼ **generoso da aiutarti** he was kind enough to help you ② *conj* (allora) so ③ *adj inv* (tale) like that, such; **una ragazza** ∼ a girl like that, such a girl

cosicché *conj* and so

cosid'detto *adj* so-called

co'smesi *nf* beauty treatment

co'smetico ① *adj* cosmetic ② *nm* **cosmetici** *pl* cosmetics; (trucchi) make-up

'cosmico *adj* cosmic

'cosmo *nm* cosmos

cosmo'nauta *nmf* cosmonaut

cosmopo'lita *adj* cosmopolitan

co'spargere *vt* sprinkle; (disseminare) scatter; ∼ **il pavimento di cera** spread wax on the floor

co'spetto *nm* **al** ∼ **di** in the presence of

co'spicuo *adj* conspicuous; ⟨somma ecc⟩ considerable

cospi'rare *vi* conspire, plot

cospira|'tore, -trice *nmf* conspirator, plotter

cospirazi'one *nf* conspiracy, plot

'**costa** *nf* coast, coastline; Anat rib; **sotto** ~ inshore. **Costa d'Avorio** Ivory Coast. **Costa Azzurra** Côte d'Azur. **Costa Smeralda** Emerald coast (in Sardinia)

costà *adv* there

co'stante *adj & nf* constant

co'stanza *nf* constancy

co'stare *vi* cost; **quanto costa?** how much is it?; **costi quel che costi** whatever the cost

'**Costa 'Rica** *nm* Costa Rica

co'stata *nf* chop. **costata [di manzo]** rib steak

co'stato *nm* ribs *pl*

costeggi'are *vt* (per mare) coast; (per terra) skirt

co'stei *pers pron* (soggetto) she; (complemento) her

costellazi'one *nf* constellation

coster'nato *adj* dismayed

costernazi'one *nf* consternation

costi'era *nf* stretch of coast

costi'ero *adj* coastal

co'stine *nfpl* (di maiale) spare ribs

'**costing** *nm* costing

costi'pato *adj* constipated; **essere** ~ (raffreddato) have a bad cold

costipazi'one *nf* constipation; (raffreddore) bad cold

costitu'ire *vt* constitute; (essere) be; (formare) form; (nominare) appoint

costitu'irsi *vr* ⟨criminale⟩ give oneself up

costituzio'nale *adj* constitutional

costituzional'mente *adv* Pol constitutionally

costituzi'one *nf* constitution; (formazione) formation

'**costo** *nm* cost; **a nessun** ~ on no account; **a** ~ **di perdere la salute** at the cost of one's health; **sotto** ~ at less than cost price; **costi** *pl* **di gestione** administration costs; **costi** *pl* **di spedizione** freight charges. **costo del denaro** Fin cost of money. **costo unitario** unit cost. **costo della vita** cost of living

'**costola** *nf* rib; (di libro) spine; **stare alle costole di qualcuno** follow somebody around

costo'letta *nf* cutlet

co'storo *pron* (soggetto) they; (complemento) them

co'stoso *adj* costly

co'stretto *pp di* COSTRINGERE

co'stringere *vt* force, compel

costrit'tivo *adj* coercive

costrizi'one *nf* compulsion

costru'ire *vt* build, construct

costrut'tivo *adj* constructive

costruzi'one *nf* building, construction; (edificio) building

co'stui *pers pron* (soggetto) he; (complemento) him

co'stume *nm* (usanza) custom; (indumento) costume; **costumi** *pl* (morale) morals. **costume da bagno** swim-suit; (da uomo) swimming trunks. **costume intero** one-piece. **costume tradizionale** traditional costume

costu'mista *nmf* wardrobe assistant

cote'chino *nm* spiced pork sausage

co'tenna *nf* pigskin; (della pancetta) rind. ~ **arrostita** crackling

co'togna *nf* quince

coto'letta *nf* cutlet. **cotoletta alla milanese** veal cutlet in breadcrumbs

coto'nato *adj* ⟨capelli⟩ back-combed

co'tone *nm* cotton. **cotone idrofilo** cotton wool, absorbent cotton Am

cotoni'ficio *nm* cotton mill

'**cotta** *nf* Relig surplice; (fam: innamoramento) crush; **prendere una** ~ **per qualcuno** fam have a crush on somebody

'**cottimo** *nm* piece-work

'**cotto** ① *pp di* CUOCERE ② *adj* done; (fam: innamorato) in love; (sbronzo) drunk; **ben** ~ well cooked; ⟨carne⟩ underdone; **troppo** ~ overcooked; ⟨carne⟩ overdone

cotton fi'oc® *nm inv* cotton bud

cot'tura *nf* cooking

'**country** *nm* country and western

cou'pon *nm inv* coupon

cou'scous *nm inv* couscous

co'vare *vt* hatch; sicken for ⟨malattia⟩; harbour ⟨rancore⟩

co'vata *nf* brood

'**covo** *nm* den

co'vone *nm* sheaf

cow-'boy *nm inv* cowboy

'**cozza** *nf* mussel. **cozze alla marinara** *pl* moules marinière

coz'zare *vi* ~ **contro** bump into

'**cozzo** *nm* fig clash

C.P. *abbr* (**Casella Postale**) PO Box

crac *nm inv* crack; (di tessuto) rip

crack *nm* (droga) crack

Cra'covia *nf* Cracow

'**crafen** *nm inv* cream doughnut

'**crampo** *nm* cramp

'**cranio** *nm* skull

cra'tere *nm* crater

cra'vatta *nf* tie; (a farfalla) bow-tie

cre'anza *nf* manners *pl*; **mala** ∼ bad manners

cre'are *vt* create; ∼ **assuefazione** be habit-forming

creatività *nf* creativity

crea'tivo *adj* creative

cre'ato *nm* creation

crea'|'tore, -trice *nmf* creator; **andare al** ∼ go to meet one's maker

crea'tura *nf* creature; (bambino) baby; **povera** ∼! poor thing!

creazi'one *nf* creation

cre'dente *nmf* believer

cre'denza *nf* belief; Comm credit; (mobile) sideboard

credenzi'ali *nfpl* credentials

'credere ① *vt* believe; (pensare) think ② *vi* ∼ **in** believe in; **credo di sì** I think so; **non ti credo** I don't believe you; **non posso crederci!** I can't believe it!

'credersi *vr* think oneself to be; **si crede uno scrittore** he flatters himself he is a writer

cre'dibile *adj* credible, believable

credibilità *nf* credibility

credi'tizio *adj* credit attrib

'credito *nm* credit; (stima) esteem; **comprare a** ∼ buy on credit; **dare** ∼ **a qualcosa** give credence to something; **fare** ∼ give credit. **credito all'esportazione** export credit. **credito inesigibile** bad debt

credi'|'tore, -trice *nmf* creditor

'credo *nm inv* credo

credulità *nf* credulity

'credulo *adj* credulous

credu'lone, -a *nmf* simpleton

'crema *nf* cream; (di uova e latte) custard. **crema base per il trucco** vanishing cream. **crema depilatoria** depilatory [cream]. **crema detergente** cleansing cream. **crema idratante** moisturizer. **crema per le mani** hand cream. **crema pasticciera** confectioner's custard. **crema per la pelle** skin cream. **crema protettiva** barrier cream. **crema solare** suntan lotion. **crema per il viso** face cream

cremagli'era *nf* ratchet

cre'mare *vt* cremate

crema'torio *nm* crematorium

cremazi'one *nf* cremation

crème cara'mel *nf* crème caramel

creme'ria *nf* dairy (also selling ice cream and cakes)

Crem'lino *nm* Kremlin

cre'moso *adj* creamy

cren *nm* horseradish

'crepa *nf* crack

cre'paccio *nm* cleft; (di ghiacciaio) crevasse

crepacu'ore *nm* heart-break

crepa'pelle: **a** ∼ *adv* fit to burst

cre'pare *vi* crack; (fam: morire) kick the bucket; ∼ **dal ridere** laugh fit to burst

crepa'tura *nf* crevice

crêpe *nf inv* pancake

crepi'tare *vi* crackle

crepi'tio *nm* crackling

cre'puscolo *nm* twilight

cre'scendo *nm* crescendo

cre'scenza *nf* creamy white cheese

'crescere ① *vi* grow; (aumentare) increase, grow ② *vt* (allevare) bring up; (aumentare) increase

cresci'one *nm* watercress

'crescita *nf* growth; (aumento) increase, growth

cresci'uto *pp di* CRESCERE

'cresima *nf* confirmation

cresi'mare *vt* confirm

cre'spato *adj* crinkly

cre'spella *nf* pancake

'crespo ① *adj* ⟨capelli⟩ frizzy ② *nm* crêpe

'cresta *nf* crest; (cima) peak; **abbassare la** ∼ become less cocky; **alzare la** ∼ become cocky; **sulla** ∼ **dell'onda** on the crest of a wave

'creta *nf* clay

'Creta *nf* Crete

cre'tese *adj & nmf* Cretan

creti'nata *nf* something stupid; **dire cretinate** talk nonsense

cre'tino, -a ① *adj* stupid ② *nmf* idiot

C.R.I. *abbr* (**Croce Rossa Italiana**) Italian Red Cross

'cribbio *int* gosh!, golly!

cric *nm inv* jack

'cricca *nf* gang

'cricco *nm* jack

cri'ceto *nm* hamster

'cricket *nm* cricket

crimi'nale *adj & nmf* criminal

criminalità *nf* crime. **criminalità organizzata** organized crime

'crimine *nm* crime

criminolo'gia *nf* criminology

crimi'nologo, -a *nmf* criminologist

crimi'noso *adj* criminal

'crine *nm* horsehair

crini'era *nf* mane

crino'lina *nf* crinoline

crioge'nia *nf* cryogenics

'cripta *nf* crypt

crip'tare vt encrypt

crisan'temo nm chrysanthemum

'crisi nf inv crisis; Med fit; essere in ∼ di astinenza be having withdrawal symptoms, be cold turkey fam. crisi di nervi hysterics. crisi del settimo anno seven-year itch

cristal'lino ① adj crystal clear ② nm crystalline lens

cristalliz'zare vt crystallize

cristalliz'zarsi vr crystallize; fig ⟨parola, espressione⟩ become part of the language

cri'stallo nm crystal

Cristia'nesimo nm Christianity

cristianità nf Christendom

cristi'ano, -a adj & nmf Christian

'Cristo nm Christ; avanti ∼ BC; dopo ∼ AD; un povero c∼ a poor beggar

cri'terio nm criterion; ⟨buon senso⟩ [common] sense

'critica nf criticism; ⟨recensione⟩ review; fare la ∼ di review ⟨film, libro⟩. critica letteraria literary criticism

criti'care vt criticize

'critico ① adj critical ② nm critic. critico letterario literary critic

criti'cone, -a nmf fault finder

crittazi'one nf crittazione [dei] dati Comput data encryption

crivel'lare vt riddle (di with)

cri'vello nm sieve

cro'ato, -a adj & nmf Croatian, Croat

Cro'azia nf Croatia

croc'cante ① adj crisp ② nm type of crunchy nut biscuit

croc'chetta nf croquette

'crocchia nf bun

'crocchio nm cluster

'croce nf cross; a occhio e ∼ roughly; fare testa e ∼ toss a coin; fare o mettere una ∼ sopra qualcosa fig forget about something; mettere in ∼ ⟨criticare⟩ crucify; ⟨tormentare⟩ nag nonstop. Croce Rossa Red Cross

croceros'sina nf Red Cross nurse

croce'via nm inv crossroads sg

croci'ata nf crusade

croci'ato ① adj cruciform ② nm crusader

cro'cicchio nm crossroads sg

croci'era nf cruise; velocità di crociera cruising speed

croci'figgere vt crucify

crocifissi'one nf crucifixion

croci'fisso ① pp di CROCIFIGGERE ② adj crucified ③ nm crucifix

crogio'larsi vr bask

crogi'olo nm crucible; fig melting pot

crogiu'olo nm = CROGIOLO

crois'sant nm inv croissant

crol'lare vi collapse; ⟨prezzi⟩ slump

'crollo nm collapse; ⟨dei prezzi⟩ slump

'croma nf quaver

cro'mato adj chromium-plated

'cromo nm chrome

cromo'soma nm chromosome

'cronaca nf chronicle; ⟨di giornale⟩ news; TV, Radio commentary; fatto di ∼ news item. cronaca mondana gossip column. cronaca nera crime news

'cronico adj chronic

cro'nista nmf reporter; ⟨di partita⟩ commentator

croni'storia nf chronicle

cro'nografo nm chronograph

cronolo'gia nf chronology

cronologica'mente adv chronologically

crono'logico adj chronological

cronome'traggio nm timing

cronome'trare vt time

cronome'trista nmf Sport timekeeper

cro'nometro nm chronometer; Sport stopwatch

cross nm ⟨corsa campestre⟩ cross-country; ⟨motocross⟩ motocross

cros'sista nmf scrambler; ⟨a piedi⟩ cross-country runner

'crosta nf crust; ⟨di formaggio⟩ rind; ⟨di ferita⟩ scab; ⟨quadro⟩ daub

cro'staceo nm shellfish

cro'stata nf tart. crostata di frutta fruit tart. crostata di mele apple pie

cro'stino nm croûton; crostini pl pieces of toasted bread served as a starter

croupi'er nmf inv croupier

crucci'are vt torment

crucci'arsi vr torment oneself

'cruccio nm torment

cruci'ale adj crucial

cruci'verba nm inv crossword [puzzle]

cru'dele adj cruel

crudel'mente adv cruelly

crudeltà nf inv cruelty

'crudo adj raw; ⟨linguaggio⟩ crude

cru'ento adj bloody

crumi'raggio nm strike-breaking

cru'miro nm blackleg, scab

'crusca nf bran

cru'scotto nm dashboard

C.S.I. nf abbr (Comunità degli Stati Indipendenti) CIS

'Cuba nf Cuba

cu'bano, **-a** *adj* & *nmf* Cuban

cu'betto *nm* **cubetto di ghiaccio** ice cube

'cubico *adj* cubic

cu'bismo *nm* cubism

cu'bista *adj* & *nmf* cubist

cubi'tale *adj* **a caratteri cubitali** in enormous letters

'cubo *nm* cube

cuc'cagna *nf* abundance; (baldoria) merry-making; **paese della ~** land of plenty

cuc'cetta *nf* (su un treno) couchette; Naut berth

cucchiai'ata *nf* spoonful

cucchia'ino *nm* teaspoon; (contenuto) teaspoon[ful]

cucchi'aio *nm* spoon; **un ~** a spoon[ful] (di of); **al ~** ⟨dolce⟩ creamy. **cucchiaio di legno** wooden spoon. **cucchiaio da minestra** soup-spoon. **cucchiaio da tavola** tablespoon; (contenuto) tablespoon[ful]

cucchiai'one *nm* serving spoon

'cuccia *nf* basket; (in giardino) kennel; **[fa' la] ~!** down!

cuccio'lata *nf* litter

'cucciolo *nm* puppy

cu'cina *nf* kitchen; (il cucinare) cooking; (cibo) food; (apparecchio) cooker; **far da ~** cook; **libro di cucina** cook[ery] book. **cucina casalinga** home cooking. **cucina componibile** fitted kitchen. **cucina a gas** gas cooker

cuci'nare *vt* cook

cuci'nino *nm* kitchenette

cu'cire *vt* sew; **macchina da cucire** sewing-machine; **cucilo a macchina** do it on the machine

cu'cito *nm* sewing

cuci'tura *nf* seam

cucù *nm inv* cuckoo; **~!** peekaboo!

'cuculo *nm* cuckoo

cuffia *nf* bonnet; (ricevitore) headphones *pl.* **cuffia da bagno** bathing cap. **cuffia con microfono** (per telefonino) headset

cu'gino, **-a** *nmf* cousin

'cui *pron* rel (persona: con prep) who[m]; (cose, animali: con prep) which; (tra articolo e nome) whose; **la persona con ~ ho parlato** the person I spoke to, the person to whom I spoke fml; **la ditta per ~ lavoro** the company I work for, the company for which I work; **l'amico il ~ libro è stato pubblicato** the friend whose book was published; **in ~** (dove) where; (quando) that; **per ~** (perciò) so; **la città in ~ vivo** the city I live in, the city where I live; **il giorno in ~ l'ho visto** the day [that] I saw him

cu'latta *nf* breech

culi'naria *nf* cookery

culi'nario *adj* culinary

'culla *nf* cradle

cul'lare *vt* rock; fig cherish ⟨sogno, speranza⟩

cul'larsi *vr* **~ nella speranza di** liter cherish the fond hope that

culmi'nante *adj* culminating

culmi'nare *vi* culminate

'culmine *nm* peak

'culo *nm* vulg arse; (fortuna) luck; **prendere qualcuno per il ~** take the piss out of somebody

'culto *nm* cult; Relig religion; (adorazione) worship

cul'tura *nf* culture. **cultura generale** general knowledge. **cultura di massa** mass culture

cultu'rale *adj* cultural

cultu'rismo *nm* body-building

cultu'rista *nmf* body-builder

cu'mino *nm* **cumino nero** cumin

cumula'tivo *adj* cumulative; ⟨prezzo⟩ all-in, all-inclusive; **biglietto cumulativo** group ticket

'cumulo *nm* pile; (mucchio) heap; (nuvola) cumulus

'cuneo *nm* wedge

cu'netta *nf* gutter

cu'nicolo *nm* tunnel

cu'ocere ① *vt* cook; fire ⟨ceramica⟩ ② *vi* cook; ⟨ceramica⟩ fire

cu'oco, **-a** *nmf* cook

cu'oia *nfpl* **tirare le ~** fam kick the bucket

cu'oio *nm* leather. **cuoio capelluto** scalp

cu'ore *nm* heart; **cuori** *pl* (carte) hearts; **di [buon] ~** ⟨persona⟩ kind-hearted; **di tutto ~** wholeheartedly; **ti ringrazio di tutto ~** many thanks; **nel profondo del ~** in one's heart of hearts; **nel ~ della notte** in the middle of the night; **senza ~** heartless; **mettersi il ~ in pace** come to terms with it; **parlare a ~ aperto** have a heart-to-heart (con with); **stare a ~ a qualcuno** be very important to somebody. **~ tenero** (persona) softy

cupa'mente *adv* darkly

cupi'digia *nf* greed

Cu'pido *nm* Cupid

'cupo *adj* gloomy; ⟨voce⟩ deep

'cupola *nf* dome; **a ~** domed

'cura *nf* care; (amministrazione) management; Med treatment; **aver ~ di** look after; **a ~ di** ⟨libro⟩ edited by; **in ~** under treatment; **fare delle cure termali** take the waters. **cura dimagrante** diet. **cura della fertilità** fertility treatment

cu'rabile *adj* curable

cu'rante *adj* **medico curante** GP, doctor

cu'rare *vt* take care of, look after; Med treat; (guarire) cure; edit ⟨*testo*⟩

cu'rarsi *vr* take care of oneself, look after oneself; ∼ **dei fatti propri** mind one's own business

cu'rato *nm* parish priest

cura|'tore, -trice *nmf* trustee; (di testo) editor. **curatore fallimentare** official receiver

'curcuma *nf* turmeric

curcu'mina *nf* turmeric

'curdo, -a ① *nmf* Kurd ② *adj* Kurdish

'curia *nf* curia

curio'saggine *nf* nosiness

curio'sare *vi* be curious; (mettere il naso) pry (in into); (nei negozi) look around

curiosità *nf inv* curiosity

curi'oso ① *adj* curious; (strano) odd, curious ② *nm* busybody

'curling *nm* Sport curling

cur'ricolo *nm* curriculum

cur'riculum *nm inv* curriculum

'curry *nm inv* curry. **curry in polvere** curry powder

cur'sore *nm* Comput cursor

'curva *nf* curve; (stradale) bend. **curva a gomito** dogleg. **curva di**

apprendimento learning curve

cur'vare *vt/i* bend, curve

cur'varsi *vr* bend, curve

'curvo *adj* curved; (piegato) bent

cusci'netto *nm* pad; Mech bearing. **cuscinetto puntaspilli** pincushion. **cuscinetto a sfere** ball bearing

cu'scino *nm* cushion; (guanciale) pillow. **cuscino gonfiabile** air cushion

cu'scus *nm inv* couscous

'cuspide *nf* spire

cu'stode *nm* caretaker; (di abitazione) concierge; (di fabbrica) guard; (di museo) custodian. ∼ **giudiziario** official receiver

cu'stodia *nf* care; Jur custody; (astuccio) case; **ottenere la** ∼ **di** get custody of. **custodia cautelare** remand

custo'dire *vt* keep; (badare) look after

cu'taneo *adj* skin *attrib*

'cute *nf* skin

cu'ticola *nf* cuticle

'cutter *nm inv* cutter

CV *abbr* (**cavallo vapore**) hp

cyber'spazio *nm* cyberspace

cyberterro'rismo *nm* cyberterrorism

cy'clette® *nf inv* exercise bicycle

Dd

da *prep* from; (con verbo passivo) by; (moto a luogo) to; (moto per luogo) through; (stato in luogo) at; (temporale) since; (continuativo) for; (causale) with; (in qualità di) as; (con caratteristica) with; (come) like; **da Roma a Milano** from Rome to Milan; **staccare un quadro dalla parete** take a picture off the wall; **i bambini dai 5 ai 10 anni** children between 5 and 10; **vedere qualcosa da vicino/lontano** see something from up close/from a distance; **amato da tutti** loved by everybody; **scritto da** written by; **andare dal panettiere** go to the baker's; **passo da te più tardi** I'll come over to your place later; **passiamo da qui** let's go this way; **un appuntamento dal dentista** an appointment at the dentist's; **il treno passa da Venezia** the train goes through Venice; **dall'anno scorso** since last year; **vivo qui da due anni** I've been living here for two years; **da domani** from tomorrow; **piangere dal dolore** cry with pain; **ho molto da fare** I have a lot to do; **occhiali da sole** sunglasses; **qualcosa da mangiare** something to eat; **un uomo dai**

capelli scuri a man with dark hair; **è un oggetto da poco** it's not worth much; **da solo** alone; **l'ho fatto da solo** I did it by myself; **si è fatto da sé** he is a self-made man; **vive da re** he lives like a king; **non è da lui** it's not like him

dab'bene *adj* honest

dac'capo *adv* again; (dall'inizio) from the beginning

dacché *conj* since

dada'ismo *nm* (arte) Dadaism

dada'ista *adj & nmf* Dadaist

'dado *nm* dice; Culin stock cube; Techn nut. **dado ad alette** wing nut

daf'fare *nm* work

'dagli = DA + GLI

dai¹ = DA + I

dai² *int* come on!; ∼, **non fare così!** come on, don't be like that!; ∼, **sbrigati!** come on, get a move on!

'daino *nm* deer; (pelle) buckskin

dal = DA + IL

'**dalia** *nf* dahlia

'**dalla** = DA + LA

'**dalle** = DA + LE

'**dallo** = DA + LO

'**dalmata** *nm* (cane) Dalmatian

Dal'mazia *nf* Dalmatia

dal'tonico *adj* colour-blind

'**dama** *nf* lady; (nei balli) partner; (gioco) draughts. **dama di compagnia** lady's companion. **dama di corte** lady-in-waiting

dama'scato *adj* damask

da'masco *nm* (tessuto) damask

dame'rino *nm* (bellimbusto) dandy

dami'gella *nf* (di sposa) bridesmaid

damigi'ana *nf* demijohn

dam'meno *adv* non essere ~ be no less good (di than)

DAMS *nm abbr* (**Discipline delle Arti, della Musica e dello Spettacolo**) (corso di laurea) degree in fine art, music and drama

da'naro *nm* = DENARO

dana'roso *adj* loaded

da'nese ① *adj* Danish
② *nmf* Dane
③ *nm* (lingua) Danish

Dani'marca *nf* Denmark

dan'nare *vt* damn; **far** ~ **qualcuno** drive somebody mad

dan'narsi *vr* fig wear oneself out; ~ l'anima (a fare qualcosa) wear oneself out (doing something)

dan'nato, -a ① *adj* damned, damn fam
② *nmf* damned person; **lavorare/studiare come un** ~ fig work/study like mad

dannazi'one *nf* damnation

danneggia'mento *nm* damage

danneggi'are *vt* damage; (nuocere) harm

danneggi'ato *adj* Jur injured

'**danno** *nm* damage; (a persona) harm; **danni** *pl* damage; **danni collaterali** collateral damage; **danni** *pl* **alla struttura portante** structural damage

dan'noso *adj* harmful

dan'tesco *adj* Dantean, Dantesque

danubi'ano *adj* Danubian

Da'nubio *nm* Danube

'**danza** *nf* dance; (il danzare) dancing. ~ **folcloristica** country dancing

dan'zante *adj* **serata danzante** dance

dan'zare *vi* dance

danza|'tore, -trice *nmf* dancer. **danzatrice del ventre** belly dancer

dapper'tutto *adv* everywhere

dap'poco *adj* worthless

dap'prima *adv* at first

Darda'nelli *nmpl* i ~ the Dardanelles

'**dardo** *nm* dart

'**dare** ① *vt* give; sit (esame); have (festa); ~ **qualcosa a qualcuno** give somebody something; ~ **da mangiare a qualcuno** give somebody something to eat; ~ **fuoco a qualcosa** set fire to something; ~ **il benvenuto a qualcuno** welcome somebody; ~ **la buonanotte a qualcuno** say good night to somebody; ~ **del tu/del lei a qualcuno** address somebody as "tu/lei"; ~ **del cretino a qualcuno** call somebody an idiot; ~ **qualcosa per scontato** take something for granted; ~ **fastidio a** annoy; **cosa danno alla TV stasera?** what's on TV tonight?; **darle a qualcuno** (picchiare) give somebody a walloping
② *vi* ~ **nell'occhio** be conspicuous; ~ **alla testa** go to one's head; ~ **su** (finestra, casa) look on to; ~ **sui** o **ai nervi a qualcuno** get on somebody's nerves
③ *nm* Comm debit

'**darsena** *nf* dock

'**darsi** *vr* (scambiarsi) give each other; ~ **da fare** get down to it; **si è dato tanto da fare!** he went to so much trouble!; ~ **a** (cominciare) take up; ~ **al bere** take to drink; ~ **per** (malato) pretend to be; ~ **per vinto** give up; **può** ~ maybe

darvini'ano *adj* Darwinian

darvi'nista *nmf* Darwinist

'**data** *nf* date; **di lunga** ~ old established. **data di emissione** date of issue. **data di nascita** date of birth. **data di scadenza** expiry date; (su alimenti) best before date

data'base *nm inv* database. **database relazionale** relational database

da'tabile *adj* datable

da'tare *vt* date; **a** ~ **da** as from

da'tario *nm* (su orologio) calendar

da'tato *adj* dated

da'tivo *nm* dative

'**dato** ① *adj* given; (dedito) addicted; ~ **che** seeing that, given that
② *nm* datum; **dati** *pl* data. **dato di fatto** well established fact; **dati sensibili** sensitive data

da'tore *nm* giver. **datore di lavoro** employer

'**dattero** *nm* date

dattilogra'fare *vt/i* type; ~ **a tastiera cieca** touch-type

dattilogra'fia *nf* typing. **dattilografia a tastiera cieca** touch-typing

datti'lografo, -a *nmf* typist

dattilo'scritto *adj* (copia) typewritten

dat'torno *adv* togliersi ~ clear off

da'vanti ① *adv* before; (dirimpetto) opposite; (di fronte) in front
② *adj inv* front
③ *nm* front; ~ **di dietro** (maglia) back-to-front; ~ **a** *prep* before, in front of; **passare** ~ **a** pass, go past

davan'zale *nm* window sill

da'vanzo *adv* **ce n'è** ∼ there is more than enough

dav'vero *adv* really; **per** ∼ in earnest; **dici** ∼? honestly?

dazi'ario *adj* excise

'dazio *nm* duty; (ufficio) customs *pl*. **dazi doganali** *pl* customs duties. **dazio d'importazione** import duty

D.C. *nf abbr* (**Democrazia Cristiana**) Christian Democratic Party

d.C. *abbr* (**dopo Cristo**) AD

D.D.T. *nm* (insetticida) DDT

'dea *nf* goddess

deambula'torio *adj* ambulatory

debel'lare *vt* defeat

debili'tante *adj* weakening

debili'tare *vt* weaken

debili'tarsi *vr* become debilitated

debilitazi'one *nf* debilitation

debita'mente *adv* duly

'debito ① *adj* due; **a tempo** ∼ in due course
② *nm* debt. **debito pubblico** national debt

debi'tore, -trice *nmf* debtor

'debole ① *adj* weak; (luce) dim; (suono) faint
② *nm* weak point; **avere un** ∼ **per qualcuno** have a soft spot for somebody; **avere un** ∼ **per qualcosa** have a weakness for something

debo'lezza *nf* weakness

debor'dare *vi* overflow

debosci'ato *adj* debauched

debrai'ata *nf* Auto declutching

debut'tante ① *adj* beginner
② *nmf* beginner; (attore) actor/actress making his/her début

debut'tare *vi* make one's début

de'butto *nm* début

'decade *nf* period of ten days

deca'dente *adj* decadent

decaden'tismo *nm* decadence

deca'denza *nf* decline; Jur loss

deca'dere *vi* lapse

decadi'mento *nm* (delle arti) decline

deca'duto *adj* (persona) impoverished; (decreto, norma) no longer in force

decaffei'nato ① *adj* decaffeinated
② *nm* decaffeinated coffee, decaf *fam*

deca'grammo *nm* decagram

decal'care *vt* trace

decalcifi'carsi *vr* become brittle

decalcificazi'one *nf* (condizione) brittle bones

decalcoma'nia *nf* transfer

de'calitro *nm* decalitre

de'calogo *nm* fig rule book

de'cametro *nm* decametre

de'cano *nm* dean

decan'tare *vt* (lodare) praise

decapi'tare *vt* decapitate; behead (condannato)

decapitazi'one *nf* decapitation; beheading

decappot'tabile *adj* convertible

decappot'tare *vt* take down the hood of

'decathlon *nm* decathlon

de'cedere *vi* (morire) die

dece'duto *adj* deceased

decele'rare *vt/i* slow down, decelerate

decelerazi'one *nf* deceleration

decen'nale ① *adj* ten-yearly
② *nm* (anniversario) tenth anniversary

de'cenne *adj* (bambino) ten-year-old

de'cennio *nm* decade

de'cente *adj* decent

decente'mente *adv* decently

decentraliz'zare *vt* decentralize

decentra'mento *nm* decentralization

decen'trare *vt* decentralize

de'cenza *nf* decency

de'cesso *nm* death, decease fml; **atto di decesso** death certificate

'decibel *nm inv* decibel

de'cidere *vt* decide; settle (questione)

de'cidersi *vr* make up one's mind

deci'frabile *adj* decipherable

deci'frare *vt* decipher; (documenti cifrati) decode

decifrazi'one *nf* deciphering

de'cigrado *nm* tenth of a degree

deci'grammo *nm* decigram

de'cilitro *nm* decilitre

deci'male *adj* decimal

deci'mare *vt* decimate

de'cimetro *nm* decimetre

'decimo *adj & nm* tenth

de'cina *nf* Math ten; **una** ∼ **di** (circa dieci) about ten

decisa'mente *adv* definitely, decidedly

decisio'nale *adj* decision-making

decisi'one *nf* decision; **prendere una** ∼ make *or* take a decision; **con** ∼ decisively

decisio'nismo *nm* tendency to make decisions without consulting others

decisio'nista *nmf* person who does not consult others before making decisions

deci'sivo *adj* decisive

de'ciso ① *pp di* DECIDERE
② *adj* decided

decla'mare *vt/i* declaim

declama'torio *adj* (stile) declamatory

declas'sare *vt* downgrade

decli'nabile *adj* Gram declinable; ⟨*offerta*⟩ that can be refused

decli'nare 1 *vt* decline; turn down, refuse ⟨*invito*⟩; ∼ **ogni responsabilità** disclaim all responsibility
2 *vi* go down; (tramontare) set

declinazi'one *nf* Gram declension

de'clino *nm* decline; **in** ∼ ⟨*popolarità*⟩ on the decline

de'clivio *nm* downward slope

dé'co *adj inv* Art Deco

de'coder *nm inv* TV set-top box

deco'difica *nf* decoding

decodifi'care *vt* decode

decodifica'tore *nm* TV descrambler

decodificazi'one *nf* decoding

decol'lare *vi* take off

décolle'té 1 *adj inv* low cut
2 *nm inv* low neckline

de'collo *nm* take-off

decolonizzazi'one *nf* decolonization

decolo'rante *nm* bleach

decolo'rare *vt* bleach

decolorazi'one *nf* bleaching

decom'porre *vt* decompose

decom'porsi *vr* decompose

decomposizi'one *nf* decomposition

decompressi'one *nf* decompression

decom'primere *vt* decompress

deconcen'trarsi *vr* become distracted

deconge'lare *vt* defrost

decongestio'nare *vt* Med, fig relieve congestion in

decontami'nare *vt* Techn decontaminate

decontaminazi'one *nf* decontamination

decontrazi'one *nf* relaxation

deco'rare *vt* decorate

decora'tivo *adj* decorative

deco'rato *adj* (ornato) decorated

decora|'tore, -trice *nmf* decorator

decorazi'one *nf* decoration.
  decorazione floreale flower arranging

de'coro *nm* decorum

decorosa'mente *adv* decorously

deco'roso *adj* dignified

decor'renza *nf* ∼ **dal …** with effect from …, effective from…

de'correre *vi* pass; **a** ∼ **da** with effect from

de'corso 1 pp di DECORRERE
2 *nm* passing; Med course

decre'mento *nm* decrease

de'crepito *adj* decrepit

decre'scente *adj* decreasing

de'crescere *vi* decrease; ⟨*prezzi*⟩ go down; ⟨*acque*⟩ subside

decre'tare *vt* decree; ∼ **lo stato d'emergenza** declare a state of emergency

de'creto *nm* decree. **decreto ingiuntivo** decree. **decreto legge** decree which has the force of law. **decreto legislativo** decree requiring the approval of Parliament

decre'tone *nm* Pol portmanteau bill

de'cubito *nm* **piaghe da decubito** bedsores

decur'tare *vt* reduce

decurtazi'one *nf* reduction

'dedalo *nm* maze

'dedica *nf* dedication

dedi'care *vt* dedicate

dedi'carsi *vr* dedicate oneself

'dedito *adj* ∼ **a** given to; (assorto) engrossed in; addicted to ⟨*vizi*⟩

dedizi'one *nf* dedication

de'dotto 1 pp di DEDURRE
2 *adj* deduced

dedu'cibile *adj* ⟨*tassa*⟩ allowable

de'durre *vt* deduce; (sottrarre) deduct

dedut'tivo *adj* deductive

deduzi'one *nf* deduction

défail'lance *nf inv* (cedimento) collapse

defal'care *vt* deduct

defalcazi'one *nf* deduction

defe'care *vi* defecate

defecazi'one *nf* defecation

defene'strare *vt* fig remove from office

defe'rente *adj* deferential

defe'renza *nf* deference

deferi'mento *nm* referral

defe'rire *vt* Jur remit

defezio'nare *vi* (abbandonare) defect

defezi'one *nf* defection

defezio'nista *nmf* defector

defici'ente 1 *adj* (mancante) deficient; Med mentally deficient
2 *nmf* mental defective; pej half-wit

defici'enza *nf* deficiency; (lacuna) gap; Med mental deficiency

'deficit *nm inv* deficit, shortfall; **essere in** ∼ be in deficit

defici'tario *adj* ⟨*bilancio*⟩ deficit *attrib*; ⟨*sviluppo*⟩ insufficient

defi'larsi *vr* (scomparire) slip away; ∼ **da qualcosa** sneak away from something

défi'lé *nm inv* fashion show

defi'nibile *adj* definable; ∼ **dall'utente** Comput user-definable

defi'nire *vt* define; (risolvere) settle

definitiva'mente *adv* for good

defini'tivo *adj* definitive

defi'nito *adj* definite

definizi'one *nf* definition; (soluzione) settlement

defiscaliz'zare *vt* abolish the tax on

defiscalizzazi'one *nf* abolition of tax

defla'grare *vt* (esplodere) explode

deflagrazi'one *nf* (esplosione) explosion

deflazio'nare *vt* deflate

deflazi'one *nf* deflation

deflazio'nistico *adj* deflationary

deflet'tore *nm* Auto quarterlight

deflu'ire *vi* ‹liquidi› flow away; ‹persone› stream out

de'flusso *nm* (di marea) ebb

defogli'ante ① *adj* defoliating ② *nm* defoliant

deforestazi'one *nf* deforestation

defor'mante *adj* artrite ∼ acute arthritis

defor'mare *vt* deform ‹arto›; fig distort

defor'marsi *vr* lose its shape

defor'mato *adj* warped

deformazi'one *nf* (di fatti) distortion; è una ∼ **professionale** put it down to the job

de'forme *adj* deformed

deformità *nf inv* deformity

deframmen'tare *vt* defragment, fam defrag

defrau'dare *vt* defraud

de'funto, -a *adj & nmf* deceased

degene'rare *vi* degenerate

degenera'tivo *adj* ‹processo› degenerative

degene'rato *adj* degenerate

degenerazi'one *nf* degeneration

de'genere *adj* degenerate

de'gente ① *adj* bedridden ② *nmf* patient

de'genza *nf* confinement. **degenza ospedaliera** stay in hospital

'degli = DI + GLI

deglu'tire *vt* swallow

deglutizi'one *nf* swallowing

de'gnare *vt* ∼ qualcuno/qualcosa di uno sguardo deign or condescend to look at somebody/something

de'gnarsi *vr* deign, condescend

'degno *adj* worthy; (meritevole) deserving. **degno di lode** praiseworthy. **degno di nota** noteworthy

degrada'mento *nm* degradation

degra'dante *adj* demeaning

degra'dare *vt* degrade

degra'darsi *vr* lower oneself; ‹città› fall into a state of disrepair

degradazi'one *nf* degradation

de'grado *nm* deterioration. **degrado ambientale** environmental damage. **degrado urbano** urban blight, urban decay

degu'stare *vt* taste

degustazi'one *nf* tasting. **degustazione di vini** wine tasting

'dei = DI + I

deindiciz'zare *vt* deindex

déjà vu *nm inv* déjà vu

del = DI + IL

dela'|tore, -trice *nmf* [police] informer

delazi'one *nf* informing

'delega *nf* proxy; legge ∼ law that does not require Parliamentary approval

dele'gante *nmf* Jur representative

dele'gare *vt* delegate

dele'gato *nm* delegate

delegazi'one *nf* delegation

delegitti'mare *vt* delegitimize

dele'terio *adj* harmful

del'fino *nm* dolphin; (stile di nuoto) butterfly [stroke]; **nuotare a** ∼ do the butterfly

de'libera *nf* bylaw

delibe'rante *adj* ‹organo› decision making

delibe'rare *vt/i* deliberate; ∼ **su/in** rule on/in

deliberata'mente *adv* deliberately

delibe'rato *adj* (intenzionale) deliberate

delicata'mente *adv* delicately

delica'tezza *nf* delicacy; (fragilità) frailty; (tatto) tact

deli'cato *adj* delicate; ‹salute› frail; ‹suono, colore› soft

delimi'tare *vt* define

delimita'tivo *adj* defining

delimitazi'one *nf* definition

deline'are *vt* outline

deline'arsi *vr* be outlined; fig take shape

deline'ato *adj* outlined

delineazi'one *nf* outline

delinqu'ente *nmf* delinquent. **delinquente minorile** young offender. **delinquente recidivo** habitual offender

delinqu'enza *nf* delinquency. **delinquenza minorile** juvenile crime

delinquenzi'ale *adj* criminal

de'linquere *vi* commit a criminal act; **associazione per delinquere** conspiracy [to commit a crime]; **istigazione a delinquere** incitement to crime

de'liquio *nm* cadere in ∼ swoon

deli'rante *adj* Med delirious; (assurdo) insane; (sfrenato) frenzied

deli'rare *vi* be delirious

de'lirio *nm* delirium; fig frenzy; mandare/andare in ∼ fig send/go into a frenzy

de'litto *nm* crime. **delitto passionale** crime of passion

delittu'oso *adj* criminal

de'lizia *nf* delight

delizi'are *vt* delight

delizi'arsi *vr* ~ **di** delight in

delizi'oso *adj* delightful; (cibo) delicious

'della = DI + LA

'delle = DI + LE

'dello = DI + LO

'delta *nm inv* delta

delta'plano *nm* hang-glider; **fare** ~ go hang-gliding

deluci'dare *vt* fig clarify

delucidazi'one *nf* clarification

delu'dente *adj* disappointing

de'ludere *vt* disappoint

delusi'one *nf* disappointment

de'luso *adj* disappointed; **essere** ~ **di qualcosa/qualcuno** be disillusioned with something/somebody

dema'gogico *adj* popularity-seeking, demagogic

dema'gogo *nm* demagogue

deman'dare *vt* entrust

demani'ale *adj* ⟨proprietà⟩ government *attrib*

de'manio *nm* government property

demar'care *vt* demarcate

demarcazi'one *nf* demarcation; **linea di demarcazione** demarcation line

de'mente *adj* demented

de'menza *nf* dementia. **demenza senile** senile dementia

demenzi'ale *adj* (assurdo) zany

de'merito *nm* **nota di** ~ demerit mark

demilitariz'zare *vt* demilitarize

demilitarizzazi'one *nf* demilitarization

demistifi'care *vt* debunk

demistifica|'tore, -trice *nmf* debunker

demistifica'torio *adj* debunking

demistificazi'one *nf* debunking

demitiz'zare *vt* demythologize

demitizzazi'one *nf* demythologization

democratica'mente *adv* democratically

demo'cratico *adj* democratic

democratiz'zare *vt* democratize

democra'zia *nf* democracy

democristi'ano, -a *adj & nmf* Christian Democrat

'demodisk *nm inv* Comput demo disk

demogra'fia *nf* demography

demo'grafico *adj* demographic; **incremento demografico** increase in population

demo'lire *vt* demolish

demo'lito *adj* demolished

demolizi'one *nf* demolition

'demone *nm* demon

demo'niaco *adj* demonic

de'monio *nm* demon

demoniz'zare *vt* demonize

demonizzazi'one *nf* demonization

demoraliz'zante *adj* demoralizing

demoraliz'zare *vt* demoralize

demoraliz'zarsi *vr* become demoralized

demoraliz'zato *adj* demoralized

de'mordere *vi* give up

demoti'vare *vt* demotivate

demoti'varsi *vr* become demotivated

demoti'vato *adj* demotivated

demotivazi'one *nf* demotivation

de'nari *nmpl* (nelle carte) diamonds

de'naro *nm* money. **denaro virtuale** e-cash

denatu'rato *adj* **alcol denaturato** methylated spirits

denazionaliz'zare *vt* denationalize

deni'grare *vt* denigrate

denigra|'tore, -trice ➀ *adj* denigrating ➁ *nmf* denigrator

denigra'torio *adj* denigratory

denigrazi'one *nf* denigration

denomi'nare *vt* name

denomi'narsi *vr* be named

denomina'tivo *adj* denominative

denomina'tore *nm* denominator

denominazi'one *nf* denomination. **denominazione di origine controllata** mark guaranteeing the quality of a wine

deno'tare *vt* denote

denotazi'one *nf* denotation

densa'mente *adv* densely

densità *nf* density. **ad alta/bassa densità di popolazione** densely/sparsely populated

'denso *adj* thick, dense

den'tale *adj* dental

den'tario *adj* dental

den'tata *nf* bite

den'tato *adj* ⟨lama⟩ serrated

denta'tura *nf* teeth *pl*; Techn serration

'dente *nm* tooth; (di forchetta) prong; (di montagna) jagged peak; **al** ~ Culin just slightly firm; **lavarsi i denti** brush one's teeth. **dente del giudizio** wisdom tooth. **dente di latte** milk tooth. **dente di leone** Bot dandelion

'dentice *nm* dentex (type of sea bream)

denti'era *nf* dentures *pl*, false teeth *pl*; **mettersi la** ~ put one's false teeth in

denti'fricio *nm* toothpaste

den'tista *nmf* dentist

'dentro ① *adv* in, inside; (in casa) indoors; **da ∼** from within; **qui ∼** in here; **metter ∼** (fam: in prigione) lock up, put inside
② *prep* in, inside; (di tempo) within, by
③ *nm* inside

denucleariz'zare *vt* denuclearize

denucleariz'zato *adj* nuclear-free, denuclearized

denuclearizzazi'one *nf* denuclearization

denu'dare *vt* bare

denu'darsi *vr* strip

de'nuncia *nf* denunciation; (alla polizia) reporting; **fare una ∼** draw up a report. **denuncia dei redditi** income tax return

denunci'are *vt* denounce; (accusare) report

de'nunzia = DENUNCIA

denu'trito *adj* underfed

denutrizi'one *nf* malnutrition

deodo'rante *adj & nm* deodorant. **deodorante antitraspirante** antiperspirant. **deodorante per ambienti** air-freshener. **deodorante a sfera** roll-on

deodo'rare *vt* deodorize

deontolo'gia *nf* (etica professionale) code of conduct

depenaliz'zare *vt* decriminalize

depenalizzazi'one *nf* decriminalization

dépen'dance *nf inv* outbuilding

depe'ribile *adj* perishable

deperi'mento *nm* wasting away; (di merci) deterioration

depe'rire *vi* waste away

depe'rito *adj* wasted

depi'lare *vt* depilate

depi'larsi *vr* shave ⟨gambe⟩; pluck ⟨sopracciglia⟩

depila'tore ① *adj* depilatory
② *nm* (apparecchio) hair remover

depila'torio *adj* depilatory

depilazi'one *nf* hair removal. **depilazione diatermica** electrolysis

depi'staggio *nm* fig diversionary manoeuvre

depi'stare *vt* fig throw off the track

dépli'ant *nm inv* brochure, leaflet

deplo'rabile *adj* deplorable

deplo'rare *vt* deplore; (dolersi di) grieve over

deplo'revole *adj* deplorable

depoliticiz'zare *vt* depoliticize

de'porre *vt* put down; lay down ⟨armi⟩; lay ⟨uova⟩; (togliere da una carica) depose; (testimoniare) testify

depor'tare *vt* deport

depor'tato, **-a** *nmf* deportee

deportazi'one *nf* deportation

deposi'tante *nmf* Fin depositor

deposi'tare *vt* Fin deposit; (lasciare in custodia) leave; (in magazzino) store

deposi'tario, **-a** *nmf* (di segreto) repository

deposi'tarsi *vr* settle

de'posito *nm* deposit; (luogo) warehouse; Mil depot. **deposito d'armi** arms dump. **deposito bagagli** left-luggage office, baggage checkroom Am. **deposito bagagli automatico** left-luggage lockers. **deposito bancario** deposit account. **deposito bancario vincolato** fixed term deposit account

deposizi'one *nf* deposition; (da una carica) removal

de'posto *adj* deposed

depotenzi'are *vt* weaken

depra'vare *vt* deprave

depra'vato *adj* depraved

depravazi'one *nf* depravity

depre'cabile *adj* appalling

depre'care *vt* deprecate

depre'dare *vt* plunder

depressio'nario *adj* area depressionaria Meteorol area of low pressure

depressi'one *nf* depression; **area di depressione** Meteorol area of low pressure; Econ depressed area

depres'sivo *adj* depressive

de'presso ① *pp di* DEPRIMERE
② *adj* depressed

depressuriz'zare *vt* depressurize

depressurizzazi'one *nf* depressurization

deprezza'mento *nm* depreciation

deprez'zare *vt* depreciate

deprez'zarsi *vr* depreciate

depri'mente *adj* depressing

de'primere *vt* depress

de'primersi *vr* get depressed

deprivazi'one *nf* deprivation

depu'rare *vt* purify

depu'rarsi *vr* be purified

depura'tore *nm* purifier

depurazi'one *nf* purification; (di detriti) effluent

depu'tare *vt* delegate

depu'tato, **-a** *nmf* ≈ Member of Parliament, MP

deputazi'one *nf* deputation

dequalifi'care *vt* disqualify

dequalifi'carsi *vr* disqualify oneself

dequalificazi'one *nf* disqualification

deraglia'mento *nm* derailment

deragli'are *vi* go off the lines; **far ∼** derail

deraglia'tore *nm* derailleur gears *pl*

dera'pare *vi* Auto skid; ⟨*sciatore*⟩ sideslip

derattiz'zare *vt* clear of rats

derattizzazi'one *nf* rodent control

'derby *nm inv* Sport local derby

deregolamen'tare *vt* Comm deregulate

deregolamentazi'one *nf* deregulation

dere'litto *adj* derelict

deresponsabiliz'zare *vt* deprive of responsibility

deresponsabiliz'zarsi *vr* abdicate responsibility

deresponsabilizzazi'one *nf* depriving of responsibility

dere'tano *nm* backside, bottom

de'ridere *vt* deride

derisi'one *nf* derision

deri'sorio *adj* derisory

de'riva *nf* drift; andare alla ∼ drift

deri'vabile *adj* derivable

deri'vare ① *vi* ∼ da (provenire) derive from
② *vt* derive; (sviare) divert

deri'vata *nf* Math derivative

deri'vato ① *adj* derived
② *nm* by-product

derivazi'one *nf* derivation; (di fiume) diversion

derma'tite *nf* dermatitis

dermatolo'gia *nf* dermatology

dermato'logico *adj* dermatological

derma'tologo, -a *nmf* dermatologist

derma'tosi *nf* dermatosis

dermoprotet'tivo *adj* ⟨*crema*⟩ skin *attrib*; ⟨*azione*⟩ protective

'deroga *nf* dispensation

dero'gare *vi* ∼ a depart from

deroga'torio *adj* derogatory

der'rata *nf* merchandise. **derrate alimentari** *pl* foodstuffs

deru'bare *vt* rob

deru'bato *adj* robbed

desaliniz'zare *vt* desalinate

desalinizzazi'one *nf* desalination

desapare'cido *nmf* (pl ∼**s**) disappeared man/woman, desaparecido

descolarizzazi'one *nf* deschooling

descrit'tivo *adj* descriptive

de'scritto *pp di* DESCRIVERE

de'scrivere *vt* describe

descri'vibile *adj* describable

descrizi'one *nf* description

desensibiliz'zare *vt* desensitize

desensibilizzazi'one *nf* desensitization

de'sertico *adj* desert

de'serto ① *adj* uninhabited
② *nm* desert

deside'rabile *adj* desirable

deside'rare *vt* wish; (volere) want; (intensamente) long for; (bramare) desire; desidera? what would you like?, can I help you?; lasciare a ∼ leave a lot to be desired

deside'rato *adj* intended

desi'derio *nm* wish; (brama) desire; (intenso) longing

deside'roso *adj* desirous; (bramoso) longing

desi'gnare *vt* appoint, designate; (fissare) fix

desi'gnato *adj* designate *attrib*

designazi'one *nf* appointment

de'signer *nmf inv* designer

desi'nare ① *vi* dine
② *nm* dinner

desi'nenza *nf* ending

de'sistere *vi* ∼ da desist from

'desktop 'publishing *nm* desktop publishing, DTP

deso'lante *adj* distressing

deso'lare *vt* distress

deso'lato *adj* desolate; (spiacente) sorry; siamo desolati di dovervi comunicare che ... (in lettere) we are sorry to have to inform you that ...

desolazi'one *nf* desolation

'despota *nm* despot

desqua'marsi *vr* flake off

desquamazi'one *nf* flaking off

destabiliz'zante *adj* destabilizing

destabiliz'zare *vt* destabilize

destabilizzazi'one *nf* destabilization

de'stare *vt* waken; fig awaken

de'starsi *vr* waken; fig awaken

desti'nare *vt* destine; (nominare) appoint; (assegnare) assign; (indirizzare) address

destina'tario *nm* (di lettera, pacco) addressee

desti'nato *adj* essere ∼ a fare qualcosa be destined *or* fated to do something

destinazi'one *nf* destination; fig purpose; con ∼ Parigi ⟨*aereo, treno*⟩ destined for Paris

de'stino *nm* destiny; (fato) fate

destitu'ire *vt* dismiss

destitu'ito *adj* ∼ di devoid of

destituzi'one *nf* dismissal

'desto *adj* liter awake

'destra *nf* (parte) right; (mano) right hand; prendere a ∼ turn right; a ∼ ⟨*essere*⟩ on the right; ⟨*andare*⟩ to the right; la prima a ∼ the first on the right; sulla ∼ on the ⋯⋗

right-hand side; **di** ∼ Pol right wing; **la** ∼ Pol the Right

destreggi'are *vi* manoeuvre

destreggi'arsi *vr* manoeuvre

de'strezza *nf* dexterity; (abilità) skill

'**destro** *adj* right; (abile) skilful

de'stroide *adj* Pol right-wing

destruttu'rato *adj* (incoerente) unstructured

desu'eto *adj* obsolete

de'sumere *vt* (congetturare) infer; (ricavare) obtain

desu'mibile *adj* inferable

detas'sare *vt* abolish the tax on

detassazi'one *nf* abolition of tax

detei'nato *adj* tannin free

dete'nere *vt* hold; ⟨polizia⟩ detain

deten'tivo *adj* **pena detentiva** custodial sentence

deten|'tore, **-trice** *nmf* holder. **detentore del titolo** titleholder

dete'nuto, **-a** *nmf* prisoner

detenzi'one *nf* detention

deter'gente ① *adj* cleaning; ⟨latte, crema⟩ cleansing ② *nm* detergent; (per la pelle) cleanser

deteriora'mento *nm* deterioration

deterio'rare *vt* cause to deteriorate ⟨cibo, relazione⟩

deterio'rarsi *vr* deteriorate

determi'nabile *adj* determinable

determinabi'lità *nf* determinability

determi'nante *adj* decisive

determi'nare *vt* determine

determi'narsi *vr* ∼ **a** resolve to

determina'tezza *nf* determination

determina'tivo *adj* ⟨articolo⟩ definite; **pronome** ∼ determiner

determi'nato *adj* (risoluto) determined; (particolare) specific; (stabilito) certain

determinazi'one *nf* determination; (decisione) decision

determi'nismo *nm* determinism

deter'rente *adj* & *nm* deterrent

deter'sivo *nm* detergent. **detersivo biologico** biological powder. **detersivo per bucato** washing powder. **detersivo per i piatti** washing-up liquid, dishwashing liquid Am

dete'stare *vt* detest, hate

dete'starsi *vr* hate oneself

deto'nare *vi* detonate

detona'tore *nm* detonator

detonazi'one *nf* detonation

detra'ibile *adj* deductible

de'trarre *vt* deduct (**da** from)

de'tratto ① pp di DETRARRE ② *adj* deducted

detrat|'tore, **-trice** *nmf* detractor

detrazi'one *nf* deduction; (da tasse) tax allowance

detri'mento *nm* detriment; **a** ∼ **di** to the detriment of

de'trito *nm* debris; **detriti** *pl* (di fiume) detritus. **detrito di falda** scree

detroniz'zare *vt* dethrone

'**detta** *nf* **a** ∼ **di** according to

dettagli'ante *nmf* Comm retailer

dettagli'are *vt* detail

dettagliata'mente *adv* in detail

det'taglio *nm* detail; **al** ∼ Comm retail

det'tame *nm* dictate; **i dettami della moda** the dictates of fashion

det'tare *vt* dictate; ∼ **legge** fig lay down the law

det'tato *nm* Sch dictation

detta'tura *nf* dictation

'**detto** ① pp di DIRE ② *adj* said; (chiamato) called; (soprannominato) nicknamed; ∼ **fatto** no sooner said than done ③ *nm* ∼ [popolare] saying

detur'pare *vt* disfigure

deturpazi'one *nf* disfigurement

deumidifi'care *vt* dehumidify

deumidifica'tore *nm* dehumidifier

deumidificazi'one *nf* dehumidification

devalutazi'one *nf* devaluation

deva'stante *adj* devastating

deva'stare *vt* devastate

deva'stato *adj* devastated

devasta|'tore, **-trice** ① *adj* destructive; fig devastating ② *nmf* destroyer

devastazi'one *nf* devastation; fig ravages *pl*

devi'ante *adj* deviant

devi'anza *nf* deviance

devi'are ① *vi* deviate ② *vt* divert

devi'ato *adj* ⟨mente⟩ warped

deviazi'one *nf* deviation; (stradale) diversion; **fare una** ∼ Auto make a detour

devitaliz'zare *vt* kill the nerve of, devitalize fml

devitalizzazi'one *nf* killing of the nerve, devitalization fml

devo'luto ① pp di DEVOLVERE ② *adj* devolved

devoluzi'one *nf* devolution

de'volvere *vt* devolve; ∼ **qualcosa in beneficenza** give something to charity

devota'mente *adv* devoutly

de'voto *adj* devout; (affezionato) devoted

devozi'one *nf* devotion

dg *abbr* (**decigrammi**) decigrams

di *prep* of; (partitivo) some; (scritto da) by; ⟨*parlare, pensare ecc*⟩ about; (con causa, mezzo) with; (con provenienza) from; (in comparazioni) than; (con infinito) to; **la casa di mio padre/dei miei genitori** my father's/my parents' house; **compra del pane** buy some bread; **hai del pane?** do you have any bread?; **un film di guerra** a war film; **piangere di dolore** cry with pain; **coperto di neve** covered with snow; **sono di Genova** I'm from Genoa; **uscire di casa** leave one's house; **mi è uscito di mente** it slipped my mind; **più alto di te** taller than you; **è ora di partire** it's time to go; **crede di aver ragione** he thinks he's right; **dire di sì** say yes; **di domenica** on Sundays; **di sera** in the evening; **una pausa di un'ora** an hour's break; **un corso di due mesi** a two-month course

dia'bete *nm* diabetes

dia'betico, -a *adj & nmf* diabetic

diabolica'mente *adv* devilishly

dia'bolico *adj* diabolic[al]

di'acono *nm* deacon

dia'critico *adj* diacritic

dia'dema *nm* diadem; (di donna) tiara

di'afano *adj* diaphanous

dia'framma *nm* diaphragm; (divisione) screen

di'agnosi *nf inv* diagnosis

dia'gnostica *nf* Med diagnostics

diagnosti'care *vt* diagnose

dia'gnostici *nmpl* Comput diagnostics

dia'gnostico *adj* diagnostic

diago'nale *adj & nf* diagonal

diagonal'mente *adv* diagonally

dia'gramma *nm* diagram. **diagramma a barre** bar chart. **diagramma di flusso** flowchart

dialet'tale *adj* dialect *attrib*; **poesia dialettale** poetry in dialect

dialettaleggi'ante *adj* dialect *attrib*

dia'lettica *nf* dialectics

dia'lettico *adj* dialectic

dia'letto *nm* dialect

di'alisi *nf* dialysis

dialo'gante *adj* **unità dialogante** Comput interactive terminal

dialo'gare ① *vt* write the dialogue for ⟨*scena*⟩ ② *vi* ~ **con** converse with

dialo'gato *adj* in dialogue

dialo'ghista *nmf* (scrittore) dialogue writer

di'alogo *nm* dialogue

dia'mante *nm* diamond

diaman'tifero *adj* diamond bearing

diametral'mente *adv* diametrically

di'ametro *nm* diameter

di'amine *int* **che** ~ ... what on earth ...

di'apason *nm inv* (per accordatura) tuning fork

diaposi'tiva *nf* slide

di'aria *nf* daily allowance

di'ario *nm* diary. **diario di bordo** logbook. **diario di classe** class register

dia'rista *nmf* (scrittore) diarist

diar'rea *nf* diarrhoea

di'aspora *nf* Diaspora

dia'triba *nf* diatribe

diavole'ria *nf* (azione) devilment; (marchingegno) weird contraption

diavo'letto *nm* imp; (hum: bambino) little devil

di'avolo *nm* devil; **va' al** ~**!** fam go to hell!; **che** ~ **fai?** fam what the hell are you doing?

di'battere *vt* debate

di'battersi *vr* struggle

dibattimen'tale *adj* Jur of the hearing

dibatti'mento *nm* (discussione) debate; Jur hearing

di'battito *nm* debate; (meno formale) discussion

dica'stero *nm* office

di'cembre *nm* December

dice'ria *nf* rumour

dichia'rare *vt* state; (ufficialmente) declare; ~ **colpevole** Jur convict; **niente da** ~**?** anything to declare?

dichia'rarsi *vr* (in amore) declare one's love; ~ **soddisfatto** declare oneself satisfied; **si dichiara innocente** he says he's innocent; ~ **a favore di qualcosa** declare oneself in favour of something; **si dichiara che ...** (in documenti) it is hereby declared that ...; ~ **vinto** acknowledge defeat

dichia'rato *adj* avowed

dichiarazi'one *nf* statement; (documento, di guerra, d'amore) declaration; **fare una** ~ (ufficialmente) make a statement. **dichiarazione dei diritti** Pol bill of rights. **dichiarazione doganale** customs declaration. **dichiarazione dei redditi** [income] tax return

dician'nove *adj & nm* nineteen

dicianno'venne *adj & nmf* nineteen-year-old

dicianno'vesimo *adj & nm* nineteenth

dicias'sette *adj & nm* seventeen

diciasset'tenne *adj & nmf* seventeen-year-old

diciasset'tesimo *adj & nm* seventeenth

diciot'tenne *adj & nmf* eighteen-year-old

diciot'tesimo *adj & nm* eighteenth

dici'otto *adj & nm* eighteen; Univ pass mark

dici'tura *nf* wording

dicoto'mia *nf* dichotomy

didasca'lia *nf* (di film) subtitle; (di illustrazione) caption; Theat stage direction

dida'scalico *adj* ⟨letteratura⟩ didactic

di'dattica *nf* didactics

didattica'mente *adv* didactically

di'dattico *adj* didactic; ⟨televisione⟩ educational

di'dentro *adv* inside

didi'etro ① *adv* behind
② *nm* hum hindquarters *pl*

di'eci *adj & nm* ten

dieci'mila *adj & nm* ten thousand

die'cina = DECINA

di'eresi *nf* diaeresis

'diesel *adj & nm inv* diesel

di'esis *nm inv* sharp

di'eta *nf* diet; **a ∼** on a diet

die'tetica *nf* dietetics

die'tetico *adj* diet

die'tista *nmf* dietician

die'tologo *nmf* dietician

di'etro ① *adv* behind
② *prep* behind; (dopo) after
③ *adj* back; ⟨zampe⟩ hind
④ *nm* back; **le stanze di ∼** the back rooms; **le zampe di ∼** the hind legs

dietro'front *nm inv* about-turn; fig U-turn; **∼!** about turn!

dietrolo'gia *nf* investigative journalism

di'fatti *adv* in fact

di'fendere *vt* defend

di'fendersi *vr* defend oneself; (fam: cavarsela) get by

difen'dibile *adj* defendable, defensible

difen'siva *nf* **stare sulla ∼** be on the defensive

difen'sivo *adj* defensive

difen'sore ① *adj* **avvocato difensore** defence counsel
② *nm* defender. **difensore civico** ombudsman

di'fesa *nf* defence; **prendere le difese di qualcuno** come to somebody's defence. **difesa civile** Civil Defence

di'feso ① pp di DIFENDERE
② *adj* defended; (luogo) sheltered

difet'tare *vi* be defective; **∼ di** lack

difet'tivo *adj* defective

di'fetto *nm* defect; (morale) fault, flaw; (mancanza) lack; (in tessuto, abito) flaw; **essere in ∼** be at fault; **far ∼** be lacking. **difetto di pronuncia** speech impediment

difet'toso *adj* defective; ⟨abito⟩ flawed

diffa'mare *vt* (con parole) slander; (per iscritto) libel

diffama|'tore, -trice *nmf* slanderer; (per iscritto) libeller

diffama'torio *adj* slanderous; (per iscritto) libellous

diffamazi'one *nf* slander; (scritta) libel

diffe'rente *adj* different

differente'mente *adv* differently

diffe'renza *nf* difference; **a ∼ di** unlike; **non fare ∼** make no distinction (**fra** between). **differenza di fuso orario** time difference

differenzi'abile *adj* differentiable

differenzi'ale *adj & nm* differential

differenzi'are *vt* differentiate

differenzi'arsi *vr* **∼ da** differ from

differenzi'ato *adj* differentiated

differenziazi'one *nf* differentiation

diffe'ribile *adj* postponable

diffe'rire ① *vt* postpone
② *vi* be different

diffe'rita *nf* **in ∼** TV prerecorded

dif'ficile ① *adj* difficult; (duro) hard; (improbabile) unlikely
② *nm* difficulty

difficil'mente *adv* with difficulty

difficoltà *nf inv* difficulty; **trovarsi in ∼** be in trouble; **mettere qualcuno in ∼** put somebody on the spot. **difficoltà d'apprendimento** special needs; **bambini con ∼ d'apprendimento** children with special needs

dif'fida *nf* warning

diffi'dare ① *vi* **∼ di** distrust
② *vt* warn

diffi'dente *adj* mistrustful

diffi'denza *nf* mistrust

dif'fondere *vt* spread; diffuse ⟨calore, luce ecc⟩

dif'fondersi *vr* spread

difformità *nf inv* deformation; (di opinioni) difference of opinion

diffusa'mente *adv* at length

diffusi'one *nf* diffusion; (di giornale) circulation

dif'fuso ① pp di DIFFONDERE
② *adj* common; ⟨malattia⟩ widespread; ⟨luce⟩ diffuse

diffu'sore *nm* (per asciugacapelli) diffuser

difi'lato *adv* straight; (subito) straightaway

di'fronte *adj inv & adv* opposite; **∼ all'ingresso** in front of the entrance; (dall'altro lato della strada) opposite the entrance

difte'rite *nf* diphtheria

'diga *nf* dam; (argine) dike

dige'rente *adj* alimentary

dige'ribile *adj* digestible

digeribilità *nf* digestibility

dige'rire *vt* digest; fam stomach

digesti'one *nf* digestion

dige'stivo ① *adj* digestive
② *nm* digestive; (dopo cena) liqueur

Digi'one *nf* Dijon

digi'tale ① *adj* digital; (delle dita) finger *attrib*
② *nf* (fiore) foxglove

digitaliz'zare *vt* digitalize

digitalizzazi'one *nf* digitalizing

digi'tare *vt* key in ⟨dati⟩

digiu'nare *vi* fast

digi'uno ① *adj* essere ∼ have an empty stomach
② *nm* fast; a ∼ ⟨bere ecc⟩ on an empty stomach

dignità *nf* dignity

digni'tario *nm* dignitary

dignitosa'mente *adv* with dignity

digni'toso *adj* dignified

DIGOS *nf abbr* (**Divisione Investigazioni Generali e Operazioni Speciali**) ≈ riot police

digressi'one *nf* digression

digri'gnare *vi* ∼ i denti grind one's teeth

digros'sare *vt* fig impart basic concepts to

dik'tat *nm inv* (trattato) diktat

dila'gare *vi* flood; fig spread

dilani'are *vt* tear to pieces

dilapi'dare *vt* squander

dilapidazi'one *nf* squandering

dila'tare *vt* dilate

dila'tarsi *vr* dilate; ⟨legno⟩ swell; ⟨metallo, gas⟩ expand

dila'tato *adj* dilated; ⟨legno⟩ swollen; ⟨metallo, gas⟩ expanded

dilatazi'one *nf* dilation; (di legno) swelling; (di metallo, gas) expansion

dilazio'nabile *adj* postponable

dilazio'nare *vt* delay

dilazi'one *nf* delay

dileggi'are *vt* mock

dilegu'are *vt* disperse

dilegu'arsi *vr* disappear

di'lemma *nm* dilemma

dilet'tante *nmf* amateur

dilettan'tesco *adj* amateurish

dilettan'tismo *nm* amateurism

dilettan'tistico *adj* amateurish

dilet'tare *vt* delight

dilet'tarsi *vr* ∼ di delight in

dilet'tevole *adj* delightful

di'letto, -a ① *adj* beloved
② *nm* (piacere) delight
③ *nmf* (persona) beloved

dili'gente *adj* diligent; ⟨lavoro⟩ accurate

dili'genza *nf* diligence

dilu'ente *nm* Techn diluent; (per vernici) thinner

diluire *vt* dilute

diluizione *nf* dilution

dilun'gare *vt* prolong

dilun'garsi *vr* ∼ su dwell on ⟨argomento⟩

diluvi'are *vi* pour [down]

di'luvio *nm* downpour; fig flood. il ∼ universale the Flood

dima'grante *adj* slimming, diet

dimagri'mento *nm* loss of weight

dima'grire *vi* lose weight

dima'grirsi *vr* lose weight

dime'nare *vt* wave; wag ⟨coda⟩

dime'narsi *vr* be agitated

dimensio'nare *vt* fig get into proportion

dimensi'one *nf* dimension; (misura) size

dimenti'canza *nf* forgetfulness; (svista) oversight; per ∼ accidentally

dimenti'care *vt* forget; l'ho dimenticato a casa I left it at home

dimenti'carsi *vr* ∼ [di] forget

dimentica'toio *nm* andare/finire nel ∼ hum fall into oblivion

di'mentico *adj* ∼ di (che non ricorda) forgetful of; (non curante) oblivious of

dimessa'mente *adv* modestly

di'messo ① *pp di* DIMETTERE
② *adj* humble; (trasandato) shabby; ⟨voce⟩ low

dimesti'chezza *nf* familiarity

di'mettere *vt* dismiss; (da ospedale ecc) discharge

di'mettersi *vr* resign

dimez'zare *vt* halve

diminu'ire *vt/i* diminish; (in maglia) decrease

diminu'ito *adj* Mus diminished

diminu'tivo *adj & nm* diminutive

diminuzi'one *nf* decrease; (riduzione) reduction; in ∼ dwindling

dimissio'nario ① *adj* outgoing
② *nmf* outgoing chairman/president etc

dimissi'oni *nfpl* resignation *sg*; dare le ∼ resign

di'mora *nf* residence

dimo'rare *vi* reside

dimo'strabile *adj* demonstrable

dimostrabilità *nf* demonstrability

dimo'strante *nmf* demonstrator

dimo'strare *vt* demonstrate; (provare) prove; (mostrare) show

dimo'strarsi *vr* prove [to be]

dimostra'tivo *adj* demonstrative

dimostrazi'one *nf* demonstration; Math proof

di'namica *nf* dynamics; ∼ **dei fatti** sequence of events

di'namico *adj* dynamic

dina'mismo *nm* dynamism

dinami'tardo, -a ① *adj* **attentato dinamitardo** bomb attack ② *nmf* bomber

dina'mite *nf* dynamite

'dinamo *nf inv* dynamo

di'nanzi ① *adv* in front ② *prep* ∼ **a** in front of

'dinaro *nm* (moneta) dinar

dina'stia *nf* dynasty

di'nastico *adj* dynastic

din'don *nm inv* dingdong

'dingo *nm inv* (cane) dingo

dini'ego *nm* denial

dinocco'lato *adj* lanky

dino'sauro *nm* dinosaur

din'torni *nmpl* outskirts; **nei ∼ di** in the vicinity of

din'torno *adv* around

'dio *nm* (pl **dei**) god; **Dio** God; **Dio mio!** my God!

dioce'sano *adj* diocesan

di'ocesi *nf inv* diocese

dioni'siaco *adj* Dionysian

dios'sina *nf* dioxin

diot'tria *nf* dioptre

dipa'nare *vt* wind into a ball; fig unravel

diparti'mento *nm* department

dipen'dente ① *adj* depending ② *nmf* employee

dipen'denza *nf* dependence; (edificio) annexe

di'pendere *vi* ∼ **da** depend on; (provenire) derive from; **dipende** it depends

di'pingere *vt* paint; (descrivere) describe

di'pinto ① *pp di* DIPINGERE ② *adj* painted ③ *nm* painting

di'ploma *nm* diploma

diplo'mare *vt* graduate

diplo'marsi *vr* graduate

diplomatica'mente *adv* diplomatically

diplo'matico ① *adj* diplomatic ② *nm* diplomat; (pasticcino) millefeuille (with alcohol)

diplo'mato ① *nmf* person with school qualification ② *adj* qualified

diploma'zia *nf* diplomacy

di'porto *nm* **imbarcazione da** ∼ pleasure craft

dirada'mento *nf* thinning out

dira'dare *vt* thin out; make less frequent ⟨visite⟩

dira'darsi *vr* thin out; ⟨nebbia⟩ clear

dira'mare *vt* issue

dira'marsi *vr* branch out

diramazi'one *nf* (di strada, fiume) fork; (di albero, impresa) branch; (di ordine) issuing

'dire ① *vt* say; (raccontare, riferire) tell; ∼ **quello che si pensa** speak one's mind; **voler** ∼ mean; **volevo ben** ∼! I wondered!; ∼ **di sì/no** say yes/no; **si dice che ...** rumour has it that ...; **come si dice "casa" in inglese?** what's the English for "casa"?; **questo nome mi dice qualcosa** the name rings a bell; **che ne dici di ...?** how about ...?; **non c'è che** ∼ there's no disputing that; **e** ∼ **che ...** to think that ...; **a dir poco/tanto** at least/most ② *vi* ∼ **bene/male di** speak highly/ill of somebody; **dica pure** (in negozio) how can I help you?; **dici sul serio?** are you serious?; **per modo di** ∼ as it were

di'retta *nf* TV live broadcast; **in** ∼ live

diretta'mente *adv* directly

diret'tissima *nf* (strada) main route; **per** ∼ ⟨processare⟩ without going through the normal procedures

diret'tissimo *nm* fast train

diret'tiva *nf* directive; **direttive** *pl* (indicazioni) guidelines

diret'tivo ① *adj* (dirigente) management *attrib*, managerial ② *nm* Pol executive

di'retto ① *pp di* DIRIGERE ② *adj* direct; **il mio** ∼ **superiore** my immediate superior; ∼ **a** (inteso) meant for; **essere** ∼ **a** be heading for; **in diretta** ⟨trasmissione⟩ live ③ *nm* (treno) through train

diret'tore *nm* manager; (più in alto nella gerarchia) director; (di scuola) headmaster. **direttore amministrativo** company secretary. **direttore artistico** artistic director. **direttore del carcere** prison governor. **direttore di filiale** branch manager. **direttore di gara** referee. **direttore generale** managing director, chief executive officer. **direttore di giornale** newspaper editor. **direttore d'istituto** Univ department head. **direttore d'orchestra** conductor. **direttore del personale** personnel manager/director. **direttore di produzione** production manager/ director. **direttore spirituale** spiritual advisor. **direttore sportivo** team manager. **direttore tecnico** Sport manager. **direttore di zona** area manager, regional director

diret'trice *nf* manageress; (di scuola) headmistress; (indirizzo) guiding principle

direzio'nale *adj* directional

direzio'nare *vt* direct

direzi'one *nf* direction; (di società) management; Sch headmaster's/

headmistress's office (*primary school*); **in ~ nord** (traffico) northbound; **'tutte le direzioni'** Auto 'all routes'

diri'gente ① *adj* ruling ② *nmf* executive. **dirigente d'azienda** company director. **dirigente di partito** Pol party leader

diri'genza *nf* (gestione) management; (i dirigenti) top management; Pol leadership. **dirigenza aziendale** business management

dirigenzi'ale *adj* management *attrib*, managerial

di'rigere *vt* direct; conduct ⟨*orchestra*⟩; run ⟨*impresa*⟩

di'rigersi *vr* **~ verso** head for

diri'gibile *nm* airship

dirim'petto ① *adv* opposite ② *prep* **~ a** facing

di'ritto[1] ① *adj* straight; (destro) right ② *adv* straight; **andare ~** go straight on; **sempre ~** straight ahead, straight on ③ *nm* right side; Tennis forehand; **fare un ~** (a maglia) knit one

di'ritto[2] *nm* right; Jur law. **diritti degli animali** *pl* animal rights. **diritti d'autore** *pl* royalties. **diritti civili** *pl* civil rights. **diritti di prelievo** *pl* Fin drawing rights. **diritti umani** *pl* human rights. **diritto civile** civil law. **diritto commerciale** commercial law. **diritto penale** criminal law. **diritto di voto** right to vote, suffrage

dirit'tura *nf* straight line; fig honesty. **~ d'arrivo** Sport, fig home straight

diroc'cato *adj* tumbledown

dirom'pente *adj* anche fig explosive

dirotta'mento *nm* hijacking

dirot'tare ① *vt* reroute ⟨*treno, aereo*⟩; (illegalmente) hijack; divert ⟨*traffico*⟩ ② *vi* alter course

dirotta|'tore, -trice *nmf* hijacker, (solo di aereo) skyjacker

di'rotto *adj* ⟨*pioggia*⟩ pouring; ⟨*pianto*⟩ uncontrollable; **piovere a ~** rain heavily

di'rupo *nm* precipice

di'sabile ① *adj* disabled ② *nmf* disabled person

disabili'tare *vt* disable

disabi'tato *adj* uninhabited

disabitu'arsi *vr* **~ a** get out of the habit of

disac'cordo *nm* disagreement

disadatta'mento *nm* maladjustment

disadat'tato, -a ① *adj* maladjusted ② *nmf* misfit

disa'dorno *adj* unadorned

disaffezi'one *nf* disaffection

disa'gevole *adj* (scomodo) uncomfortable; (difficile) inconvenient

disagi'ato *adj* poor; ⟨*vita*⟩ hard; (scomodo) uncomfortable

di'sagio *nm* discomfort; (difficoltà) inconvenience; (imbarazzo) embarrassment, uneasiness; **sentirsi a ~** feel uncomfortable; **disagi** *pl* (privazioni) hardships

di'samina *nf* close examination

disamora'mento *nm* estrangement

disanco'rare *vt* Fin de-link

disappro'vare *vt* disapprove of

disapprovazi'one *nf* disapproval

disap'punto *nm* disappointment; **con suo grande ~** [much] to his chagrin

disarcio'nare *vt* unseat

disar'mante *adj* fig disarming

disar'mare *vt/i* disarm

disar'mato *adj* disarmed; fig defenceless

di'sarmo *nm* disarmament

disartico'lato *adj* fig disjointed

disa'strato, -a ① *adj* devastated ② *nmf* victim (of flood, earthquake ecc)

di'sastro *nm* disaster; (fam: grande confusione) mess; (fam: persona) disaster area. **disastro aereo** air crash

disastrosa'mente *adv* disastrously

disa'stroso *adj* disastrous

disat'tento *adj* inattentive

disattenzi'one *nf* inattention; (svista) oversight

disatti'vare *vt* de-activate

disa'vanzo *nm* deficit

disavve'duto *adj* thoughtless

disavven'tura *nf* misadventure

disavver'tenza *nf* inadvertence

di'sbrigo *nm* dispatch

di'scapito *nm* **a ~ di** to the detriment of

di'scarica *nf* scrap-yard

di'scarico *nm* (di merce) unloading; **prova a discarico** evidence for the defence; **testimone a discarico** witness for the defence

discen'dente ① *adj* descending ② *nmf* descendant

discen'denza *nf* descent; (discendenti) descendants *pl*

di'scendere ① *vi* (dal treno) get off; (da cavallo) dismount; (sbarcare) land; **~ da** (trarre origine da) be a descendant of ② *vt* descend

discen'sore *nm* (attrezzo) karabiner

di'scepolo, -a *nmf* disciple

di'scernere *vt* discern

discerni'mento *nm* discernment

di'scesa *nf* descent; (pendio) slope; **~ in picchiata** (di aereo) nosedive; **essere in ~** ⟨*strada*⟩ go downhill. **discesa libera** (in sci) downhill race

disce'sista *nmf* (sciatore) downhill skier

di'sceso pp di DISCENDERE

di'schetto nm Comput diskette

dischi'udere vt open; (svelare) disclose

dischi'udersi vr open up

di'scinto adj scantily dressed

disci'ogliere vt dissolve; thaw ⟨neve⟩; (fondersi) melt

disci'olto pp di DISCIOGLIERE

disci'plina nf discipline

discipli'nare ① adj disciplinary ② vt discipline

discipli'nato adj disciplined

disc-'jockey nm inv disc jockey, DJ

'disco nm disc; Sport discus; Mus record; **ernia del disco** slipped disc. **disco a 33 giri** LP. **disco a 45 giri** single. **disco fisso** Comput fixed disk, hard disk. **disco dei freni** brake disc. **disco master** Comput master disk. **disco rigido** Comput hard disk. **disco volante** flying saucer

discogra'fia nf (insieme di incisioni) discography; (industria) record industry

disco'grafico ① adj ⟨industria⟩ record attrib, recording; ⟨mercato, raccolta⟩ record attrib; **casa discografica** record company, recording company ② nmf record producer

'discolo ① nmf rascal ② adj unruly

di'scolpa nf clearing; **a sua ∼ si deve dire che ...** in his defence it must be said that ...

discol'pare vt clear

discol'parsi vr clear oneself

discon'nettere vt disconnect

disco'noscere vt deny; disown ⟨figlio⟩

discontinuità nf (nel lavoro) irregularity; (di stile) unevenness

discon'tinuo adj intermittent; fig ⟨impegno, rendimento⟩ uneven

discopa'tia nf disc problems pl

discor'dante adj discordant

discor'danza nf discordance; **essere in ∼** clash

discor'dare vi ⟨opinioni⟩ conflict

di'scorde adj clashing

di'scordia nf discord; (dissenso) dissension

di'scorrere vi talk (**di** about)

discor'sivo adj colloquial

di'scorso ① pp di DISCORRERE ② nm speech; (conversazione) talk. **discorso indiretto** indirect speech. **discorso di ringraziamento** vote of thanks

di'scosto ① adj distant ② adv far away; **stare ∼** stand apart

disco'teca nf disco; (raccolta) record library

discote'caro, -a nmf pej disco freak

di'scount nm inv discount store

discredi'tare vt discredit

di'scredito nm discredit

discre'pante adj contradictory

discre'panza nf discrepancy

di'screto adj discreet; (moderato) moderate; (abbastanza buono) fairly good

discrezionalità nf discretion

discrezi'one nf discretion; (giudizio) judgement; **a ∼ di** at the discretion of

discrimi'nante ① adj extenuating ② nf Jur extenuating circumstances pl

discrimi'nare vt discriminate

discrimina'tivo adj ⟨provvedimento⟩ discriminatory

discrimina'torio adj ⟨atteggiamento⟩ discriminatory

discriminazi'one nf discrimination. **discriminazione in base all'età** age discrimination. **discriminazione sessuale** sexual discrimination

discussi'one nf discussion; (alterco) argument; **messa in ∼** questioning

di'scusso ① pp di DISCUTERE ② adj controversial

di'scutere ① vt discuss; (formale) debate; (litigare) argue ② vi **∼ su qualcosa** discuss something

discu'tibile adj debatable; ⟨gusto⟩ questionable

disde'gnare vt disdain

di'sdegno nm disdain

disde'gnoso adj disdainful

di'sdetta nf retraction; (sfortuna) bad luck; Comm cancellation

di'sdetto pp di DISDIRE

disdi'cevole adj unbecoming

di'sdire vt retract; (annullare) cancel

disedu'care vt have a bad effect on

diseduca'tivo adj bad for children

dise'gnare vt draw; (progettare) design

disegna|'tore, -trice nmf designer. **disegnatore di moda** fashion designer

di'segno nm drawing; (progetto, linea) design. **disegno di legge** bill. **disegno in scala** scale drawing. **disegno tecnico** technical drawing. **disegno dal vero** life drawing

diser'bante ① nm weed-killer ② adj weed-killing

diser'bare vt weed

disere'dare vt disinherit

disere'dato ① adj dispossessed ② nmf **i diseredati** the dispossessed

diser'tare vt/i desert; **∼ la scuola** stay away from school

diser'tore nm deserter

diserzi'one nf desertion

disfaci'mento *nm* decay; fig decline; **in ~ decaying**; fig in decline

di'sfare *vt* undo; strip ⟨*letto*⟩; (smantellare) take down; (annientare) defeat; **~ le valigie** unpack [one's bags]

di'sfarsi *vr* fall to pieces; (sciogliersi) melt; **~ di** (liberarsi di) get rid of

di'sfatta *nf* defeat

disfat'tismo *nm* defeatism

disfat'tista *adj & nmf* defeatist

di'sfatto *adj* fig worn out

disfunzio'nale *adj* dysfunctional

disfunzi'one *nf* disorder

disge'lare *vt/i* thaw

disge'larsi *vr* thaw

di'sgelo *nm* thaw

disgi'ungere *vt* disconnect

disgi'unto *adj* ⟨*firme*⟩ separate

di'sgrazia *nf* misfortune; (incidente) accident; (sfavore) disgrace

disgraziata'mente *adv* unfortunately

disgrazi'ato, -a 1 *adj* unfortunate 2 *nmf* wretch

disgrega'mento *nm* disintegration

disgre'gare *vt* break up

disgre'garsi *vr* disintegrate

disgrega'tivo *adj* disintegrating

disgrega'tore *adj* disintegrating

disgregazi'one *nf* (di società) break-up

disgu'ido *nm* **disguido postale** mistake in delivery

disgu'stare *vt* disgust

disgu'starsi *vr* **~ di** be disgusted by

di'sgusto *nm* disgust

disgustosa'mente *adv* disgustingly; **~ dolce** nauseatingly sweet

disgu'stoso *adj* disgusting

disidra'tante *adj* dehydrating

disidra'tare *vt* dehydrate

disidra'tarsi *vr* become dehydrated

disidra'tato *adj* dehydrated

disidratazi'one *nf* dehydration

disil'ludere *vt* disenchant, disillusion

disil'ludersi *vr* become disenchanted, become disillusioned

disillusi'one *nf* disenchantment, disillusionment

disil'luso *adj* disenchanted, disillusioned

disimbal'laggio *nm* unpacking

disimbal'lare *vt* unpack

disimpa'rare *vt* forget

disimpe'gnare *vt* release; (compiere) fulfil; redeem ⟨*oggetto dato in pegno*⟩

disimpe'gnarsi *vr* disengage oneself; (cavarsela) manage

disim'pegno *nm* (locale) vestibule; (disinteresse) lack of interest

disimpi'ego *nm* re-allocation; (di truppe) reassignment

disincagli'are *vt* Naut refloat

disincagli'arsi *vr* Naut float off

disincan'tato *adj* (disilluso) disillusioned, disenchanted

disincar'nato *adj* disembodied

disincenti'vante *adj* demotivating

disincenti'vare *vt* demotivate

disincen'tivo *nm* disincentive

disincroci'are *vt* uncross

disinfe'stare *vt* disinfest

disinfestazi'one *nf* disinfestation

disinfet'tante *adj & nm* disinfectant

disinfet'tare *vt* disinfect

disinfezi'one *nf* disinfection

disinfiam'marsi *vr* become less inflamed

disinflazio'nare *vt* disinflate

disinflazi'one *nf* disinflation

disinflazio'nistico *adj* disinflationary

disinfor'mato *adj* uninformed

disinformazi'one *nf* lack of information; (informazione erronea) misinformation

disingan'nare *vt* disabuse

disin'ganno *nm* disillusion

disini'birsi *vr* lose one's inhibitions

disini'bito *adj* uninhibited

disinne'scare *vt* defuse

disin'nesco *nm* (di bomba) bomb disposal

disinne'stare *vt* disengage

disinne'starsi *vr* disengage

disin'nesto *nm* disengagement

disinquina'mento *nm* cleaning up

disinqui'nare *vt* clean up

disinse'rire *vt* disconnect

disinse'rito *adj* disconnected

disinte'grare *vt* disintegrate

disinte'grarsi *vr* disintegrate

disintegrazi'one *nf* disintegration

disinteressa'mento *nm* lack of interest

disinteres'sarsi *vr* **~ di** take no interest in

disinteressata'mente *adv* without interest; (senza secondo fine) disinterestedly

disinteres'sato *adj* uninterested; (senza secondo fine) disinterested

disinte'resse *nm* indifference; (oggettività) disinterestedness

disintossi'care *vt* detoxify

disintossi'carsi *vr* come off drugs; ⟨*alcolizzato*⟩ dry out, detox

disintossicazi'one *nf* giving up alcohol/drugs, detox; **programma di ~** detox programme

disinvolta'mente *adv* in a relaxed way

disin'volto *adj* relaxed

disinvol'tura *nf* confidence

disi'stima *nf* lack of respect

disles'sia *nf* dyslexia

di'slessico *adj* dyslexic

disli'vello *nm* difference in height; fig inequality

disloca'mento *nm* Mil posting

dislo'care *vt* Mil post

dismenor'rea *nf* dysmenorrhoea

dismi'sura *nf* excess; **a ~** excessively

disobbedi'ente *adj* disobedient

disobbe'dire *vt* disobey

disoccu'pato, -a ① *adj* unemployed ② *nmf* unemployed person

disoccupazi'one *nf* unemployment

disonestà *nf* dishonesty

diso'nesto *adj* dishonest

disono'rare *vt* dishonour

disono'rato *adj* dishonoured

diso'nore *nm* dishonour

di'sopra ① *adv* above ② *adj* upper ③ *nm* top

disordi'nare *vt* disarrange

disordinata'mente *adv* untidily

disordi'nato *adj* untidy; (sregolato) immoderate

di'sordine *nm* disorder, untidiness; (sregolatezza) debauchery

disores'sia *nf* eating disorder

disor'ganico *adj* inconsistent

disorganiz'zare *vt* disorganize

disorganiz'zato *adj* disorganized

disorganizzazi'one *nf* disorganization

disorienta'mento *nm* disorientation

disorien'tare *vt* disorientate

disorien'tarsi *vr* lose one's bearings

disorien'tato *adj* fig bewildered

disos'sare *vt* bone

disos'sato *adj* boned

di'sotto ① *adv* below ② *adj* lower ③ *nm* bottom

di'spaccio *nm* dispatch

dispa'rato *adj* disparate

'dispari *adj* odd, uneven

dispa'rire *vi* disappear

disparità *nf inv* disparity

di'sparte *adv* **in ~** apart; **stare in ~** stand aside

di'spendio *nm* expenditure; pej waste

dispendiosa'mente *adv* extravagantly

dispendi'oso *adj* expensive

di'spensa *nf* pantry; (distribuzione) distribution; (mobile) cupboard; Jur exemption; Relig dispensation; (pubblicazione periodica) number

dispen'sare *vt* distribute; (esentare) exonerate

dispen'sario *nm* dispensary

di'spenser *nm inv* display rack; (confezione) dispenser

dispe'rare *vi* despair (**di** of)

dispe'rarsi *vr* despair

disperata'mente *adv* ⟨piangere⟩ desperately; ⟨studiare⟩ like mad

dispe'rato *adj* desperate; ⟨tentativo⟩ last-ditch

disperazi'one *nf* despair

di'sperdere *vt* scatter, disperse

di'sperdersi *vr* scatter, disperse

dispersi'one *nf* dispersion; (di truppe) dispersal

disper'sivo *adj* disorganized

di'sperso ① pp di DISPERDERE ② *adj* scattered; (smarrito) lost ③ *nm* missing soldier

di'spetto *nm* spite; **a ~ di** in spite of; **fare un ~ a qualcuno** spite somebody

dispet'toso *adj* spiteful

dispia'cere ① *nm* upset; (rammarico) regret; (dolore) sorrow; (preoccupazione) worry ② *vi* **mi dispiace** I'm sorry; **non mi dispiace** I don't dislike it; **se non ti dispiace** if you don't mind

dispiaci'uto *adj* sorry

dispie'gare *vt* unfold

dispie'garsi *vr* unfurl

dispo'nibile *adj* available; (gentile) helpful

disponibilità *nf* availability; (gentilezza) helpfulness. **disponibilità correnti** *pl* Fin current assets

di'sporre ① *vt* arrange ② *vi* dispose; (stabilire) order; **~ di** have at one's disposal

di'sporsi *vr* (in fila) line up

disposi'tivo *nm* device. **dispositivo di emergenza** emergency button/handle. **dispositivo di puntamento** Comput pointing device

disposizi'one *nf* disposition; (ordine) order; (libera disponibilità) disposal

di'sposto ① pp di DISPORRE ② *adj* ready; (incline) disposed; **essere ben disposto verso** be favourably disposed towards

dispotica'mente *adv* despotically

di'spotico *adj* despotic

dispo'tismo *nm* despotism

dispregia'tivo *adj* disparaging

disprez'zabile *adj* despicable

disprez'zare *vt* despise

di'sprezzo *nm* contempt

'disputa *nf* dispute

dispu'tare *vi* dispute; (gareggiare) compete

dispu'tarsi *vr* ~ **qualcosa** contend for something

disqui'sire *vi* discourse

disquisizi'one *nf* disquisition

dissa'crante *adj* debunking

dissa'crare *vt* debunk

dissacra|'tore, -trice *nmf* debunker

dissacra'torio *adj* debunking

dissacrazi'one *nf* debunking

dissangua'mento *nm* loss of blood; fig impoverishment

dissangu'are *vt* bleed; fig bleed dry

dissangu'arsi *vr* bleed; fig become impoverished

dissangu'ato *adj* bloodless; fig impoverished

dissa'pore *nm* disagreement

dissec'care *vt* dry up

dissec'carsi *vr* dry up

dissemi'nare *vt* disseminate; (notizie) spread

dissen'nato *adj* ⟨politica⟩ senseless

dis'senso *nm* dissent; (disaccordo) disagreement

dissente'ria *nf* dysentery

dissen'tire *vi* disagree (da with)

disseppelli'mento *nm* exhumation

disseppel'lire *vt* exhume ⟨cadavere⟩; disinter ⟨rovine⟩; fig unearth

dissertazi'one *nf* dissertation

disser'vizio *nm* poor service

disse'stare *vt* upset; Comm damage

disse'stato *adj* ⟨strada⟩ uneven; ⟨azienda⟩ shaky

dis'sesto *nm* ruin

disse'tante *adj* thirst-quenching

disse'tare *vt* ~ **qualcuno** quench somebody's thirst

disse'tarsi *vr* quench one's thirst

dissezio'nare *vr* dissect

dissezi'one *nf* dissection

dissi'dente *adj* & *nmf* dissident

dissi'denza *nf* dissidence

dis'sidio *nm* disagreement

dis'simile *adj* unlike, dissimilar

dissimu'lare *vt* conceal

dissimu'lato *adj* concealed

dissimula|'tore, -trice *nmf* dissembler

dissimulazi'one *nf* concealment

dissi'pare *vt* dissipate; (sperperare) squander

dissi'parsi *vr* ⟨nebbia⟩ clear; ⟨dubbio⟩ disappear

dissipa'tezza *nf* dissipation

dissi'pato *adj* dissipated

dissipa'tore *nm* **dissipatore termico** heat sink

dissipazi'one *nf* squandering

dissoci'abile *adj* separable

dissoci'are *vt* dissociate

dissoci'arsi *vr* dissociate oneself

dissoci'ato, -a ① *adj* Pol dissenting ② *nmf* Pol dissenter

dissociazi'one *nf* Pol dissociation

dissoda'mento *nm* tillage

disso'dare *vt* till

dis'solto *pp di* DISSOLVERE

disso'lubile *adj* dissoluble

dissolu'tezza *nf* dissoluteness

dissolu'tivo *adj* divisive

disso'luto *adj* dissolute

dissol'venza *nf* (di immagine) fade-out, dissolve

dis'solvere *vt* dissolve; (disperdere) dispel

dis'solversi *vr* dissolve; (disperdersi) clear

disso'nante *adj* dissonant

disso'nanza *nf* dissonance

dissotterra'mento *nm* disinterment

dissotter'rare *vt* disinter ⟨bara⟩; fig resurrect ⟨rancore⟩

dissua'dere *vt* dissuade

dissuasi'one *nf* dissuasion

dissua'sivo *adj* dissuasive

distacca'mento *nm* Mil detachment

distac'care *vt* detach; Sport leave behind

distac'carsi *vr* be detached

distac'cato *adj* ⟨tono, voce⟩ expressionless

di'stacco *nm* detachment; (separazione) separation; Sport lead

di'stante ① *adj* far away; fig ⟨person⟩ detached ② *adv* far away

di'stanza *nf* distance

distanzia'mento *nm* spacing [out]; Sport outdistancing

distanzi'are *vt* space out; Sport outdistance

di'stare *vi* be distant; **quanto dista?** how far is it?; **Roma dista 20 chilometri da qui** Rome is 20 kilometres away, Rome is 20 kilometres from here

di'stendere *vt* stretch out ⟨parte del corpo⟩; (spiegare) spread; (deporre) lay

di'stendersi *vr* stretch; (sdraiarsi) lie down; (rilassarsi) relax

distensi'one *nf* stretching; (rilassamento) relaxation; Pol dètente

disten'sivo *adj* relaxing

di'stesa *nf* expanse

di'steso *pp di* DISTENDERE

distil'lare *vt/i* distil

distil'lato ① *adj* distilled
② *nm* distillate

distillazi'one *nf* distillation

distille'ria *nf* distillery

di'stinguersi *vr* (per bravura ecc)
distinguish oneself; **si distingue dagli altri
per ...** it is distinguished from the others
by ...

distin'guibile *adj* distinguishable

di'stinguo *nm inv* distinction

di'stinta *nf* Comm. list. **distinta di
pagamento** receipt. **distinta di
versamento** paying-in slip

distinta'mente *adv* (separatamente)
individually, separately; (chiaramente)
clearly; (in modo elegante) in a distinguished
way; **vi saluto ~** Yours truly

distin'tivo ① *adj* distinctive
② *nm* badge

di'stinto ① *pp di* DISTINGUERSI
② *adj* distinct; (signorile) distinguished;
distinti saluti Yours faithfully

distinzi'one *nf* distinction

di'stogliere *vt* **~ da** (allontanare) remove
from; (dissuadere) dissuade from

di'stolto *pp di* DISTOGLIERE

di'storcere *vt* twist; distort (suono)

di'storcersi *vr* sprain (caviglia)

distorsi'one *nf* Med sprain; (alterazione)
distortion

di'storto *adj* warped; (suono) distorted

di'strarre *vt* distract; (divertire) amuse

di'strarsi *vr* (deconcentrarsi) be distracted;
(svagarsi) amuse oneself; **non ti distrarre!**
pay attention!

distratta'mente *adv* absently

di'stratto ① *pp di* DISTRARRE
② *adj* absentminded; (disattento)
inattentive

distrazi'one *nf* absent-mindedness;
(errore) inattention; (svago) amusement;
errore di distrazione absent-minded
mistake

di'stretto *nm* district

distrettu'ale *adj* district *attrib*

distribu'ire *vt* distribute; (disporre)
arrange; deal (carte)

distribu'tore *nm* distributor; (di benzina)
petrol pump, gas pump Am; (automatico) slot
machine. **distributore automatico di
biglietti** ticket machine. **distributore
di bevande** drinks dispenser.
distributore di monete change
machine

distribuzi'one *nf* distribution

distri'care *vt* disentangle

distri'carsi *vr* fig get out of it

distro'fia *nf* **distrofia muscolare**
muscular dystrophy

di'strofico *adj* dystrophic

di'struggere *vt* destroy

di'struggersi *vr* **si distrugge col bere**
he is destroying himself with drink; **la
macchina si è distrutta** the car has been
written off

distruttività *nf* destructiveness

distrut'tivo *adj* destructive; (critica)
negative

di'strutto ① *pp di* DISTRUGGERE
② *adj* destroyed; **un uomo ~** a broken
man

distrut'tore *nm* **distruttore di
documenti** paper shredder

distruzi'one *nf* destruction

distur'bare *vt* disturb; (sconvolgere) upset

distur'barsi *vr* trouble oneself; **non si
disturbi** please don't trouble yourself

distur'bato *adj* Med (mente) disordered;
(intestino) upset

di'sturbo *nm* bother; (indisposizione)
trouble; Med problem; Radio, TV
interference; **disturbi** *pl* Radio, TV static.
disturbo da deficit dell'attenzione
attention deficit disorder. **disturbi di
stomaco** *pl* stomach trouble

disubbidi'ente *adj* disobedient

disubbidi'enza *nf* disobedience

disubbi'dire *vi* **~ a** disobey

disuguagli'anza *nf* disparity;
(eterogeneità) irregularity

disugu'ale *adj* unequal; (eterogeneo)
irregular

disumanità *nf* inhumanity

disu'mano *adj* inhuman

disuni'one *nf* disunity

disu'nire *vt* divide

di'suso *nm* cadere in **~** fall into disuse

di'tale *nm* thimble

di'tata *nf* poke; (impronta) finger-mark

'dito *nm* (pl nf **dita**) finger; (di vino, acqua)
finger. **dito del piede** toe

'ditta *nf* firm. **ditta di vendita per
corrispondenza** mail order firm

dit'tafono *nm* dictaphone

ditta'tore *nm* dictator

dittatori'ale *adj* dictatorial

ditta'tura *nf* dictatorship

dit'tongo *nm* diphthong

diu'retico *adj* diuretic

di'urno *adj* daytime; **spettacolo diurno**
matinée

'diva *nf* diva

diva'gare *vi* digress

divagazi'one *nf* digression.
divagazione sul tema digression

divam'pare *vi* burst into flames; fig spread like wildfire

di'vano *nm* settee, sofa. **divano letto** sofa bed

divari'care *vt* open

divari'carsi *vr* splay

divari'cata *nf* splits *pl*

divari'cato *adj* ⟨gambe, braccia⟩ splayed

di'vario *nm* discrepancy; **un ∼ di opinioni** a difference of opinion

di'vellere *vt* ⟨sradicare⟩ uproot

di'velto pp di DIVELLERE

dive'nire *vi* = DIVENTARE

diven'tare *vi* become; ⟨lentamente⟩ grow; ⟨rapidamente⟩ turn

dive'nuto pp di DIVENIRE

di'verbio *nm* squabble

diver'gente *adj* divergent

diver'genza *nf* divergence. **divergenza di opinioni** difference of opinion

di'vergere *vi* diverge

diversa'mente *adv* ⟨altrimenti⟩ otherwise; ⟨in modo diverso⟩ differently. **diversamente abile** differently abled

di'versi *adj & pron* ⟨parecchi⟩ several

diversifi'care *vt* diversify

diversifi'carsi *vr* differ; be different

diversifi'cato *adj* broad-based

diversificazi'one *nf* diversification

diversi'one *nf* diversion

diversità *nf inv* diversity; **ci sono molte ∼** there are many differences

diver'sivo ① *adj* diversionary ② *nm* diversion

di'verso *adj* different

diver'tente *adj* amusing

diver'ticolo *nm* digression

diverti'mento *nm* fun, amusement; **buon ∼!** enjoy yourself!, have fun!

diver'tire *vt* amuse

diver'tirsi *vr* enjoy oneself, have fun

diver'tito *adj* amused

divi'dendo *nm* dividend

di'videre *vt* divide; ⟨condividere⟩ share

di'vidersi *vr* ⟨separarsi⟩ separate

divi'eto *nm* prohibition. **'divieto di pesca'** 'fishing prohibited'; **'divieto di sosta'** 'no parking'

divina'mente *adv* divinely

divinco'larsi *vr* wriggle

divinità *nf inv* divinity

di'vino *adj* divine

di'visa *nf* uniform; Fin currency

divi'sibile *adj* divisible

divisi'one *nf* division

divisio'nismo *nm* ⟨in arte⟩ pointillism

di'vismo *nm* worship; ⟨atteggiamento⟩ superstar mentality

di'viso ① pp di DIVIDERE ② *adj* divided

divi'sore *nm* divisor

divi'sorio *adj* dividing; **muro divisorio** partition wall

'divo, -a *nmf* star

divo'rare *vt* devour

divo'rarsi *vr* **∼ da** be consumed with

divorzi'are *vi* divorce

divorzi'ato, -a *nmf* divorcee

di'vorzio *nm* divorce

divul'gare *vt* divulge; ⟨rendere popolare⟩ popularize

divul'garsi *vr* spread

divulga'tivo *adj* popular

divulgazi'one *nf* spread; ⟨di cultura, scienza⟩ popularization

dizio'nario *nm* dictionary. **dizionario dei sinonimi** thesaurus

dizi'one *nf* diction

DJ *nm inv* DJ

DNA *nm inv* DNA

do *nm* Mus ⟨chiave, nota⟩ C

D.O.C. *abbr* (**Denominazione di Origine Controllata**) mark guaranteeing the quality of a wine

'doccia *nf* shower; ⟨grondaia⟩ gutter; **fare la ∼** have a shower, shower

doccia'tura *nf* Med douche

do'cente ① *adj* teaching ② *nmf* teacher; ⟨di università⟩ lecturer

do'cenza *nf* university teacher's qualification

D.O.C.G. *abbr* (**Denominazione di Origine Controllata e Garantita**) mark guaranteeing the high quality of a wine

'docile *adj* docile

docilità *nf* docility

documen'tare *vt* document

documen'tario *adj & nm* documentary

documen'tarsi *vr* gather information ⟨su about⟩

documen'tato *adj* well-documented; ⟨persona⟩ well-informed

documentazi'one *nf* documentation

docu'mento *nm* document; **documenti** *pl* papers. **documento d'identità** ID

Dodecan'neso *nm* **il ∼** the Dodecanese

dodi'cenne *adj & nmf* twelve-year-old

dodi'cesimo *adj & nm* twelfth

'dodici *adj & nm* twelve

do'gana *nf* customs *pl*; ⟨dazio⟩ duty. **dogana merci** customs for freight. **dogana passeggeri** passenger customs

doga'nale *adj* customs *attrib*

dogani'ere *nm* customs officer

'doglie *nfpl* labour pains

'dogma *nm* dogma

dog'matico *adj* dogmatic

dogma'tismo *nm* dogmatism

'dolce ① *adj* sweet; ⟨*clima*⟩ mild; ⟨*voce, consonante*⟩ soft; ⟨*acqua*⟩ fresh ② *nm* (portata) dessert; (torta) cake; **non mangio dolci** I don't eat sweet things; **dolci** *pl* **della casa** (in menu) home-made cakes

dolce'mente *adv* sweetly

dolce'vita *adj inv* (maglione) rollneck

dol'cezza *nf* sweetness; (di clima) mildness

dolci'ario *adj* confectionery

dolci'astro *adj* sweetish

dolcifi'cante ① *nm* sweetener ② *adj* sweetening

dolcifica'tore *nm* (per acqua) softener

dolci'umi *nmpl* sweets

do'lente *adj* painful; (spiacente) sorry; **punto** ~ sore point

do'lere *vi* ache, hurt; (dispiacere) regret

do'lersi *vr* regret; (protestare) complain; ~ **di** be sorry for

'dollaro *nm* dollar

'dolly *nm inv* Cinema, TV dolly

'dolmen *nm inv* dolmen

'dolo *nm* Jur malice; (truffa) fraud

Dolo'miti *nfpl* **le** ~ the Dolomites

dolo'mitico *adj* Dolomite, of the Dolomites

dolo'rante *adj* aching

do'lore *nm* pain; (morale) sorrow; **avere dei dolori** be in pain. **dolori post-partum** *pl* after-pains

dolorosa'mente *adv* painfully

dolo'roso *adj* painful

do'loso *adj* malicious

do'manda *nf* question; (richiesta) request; (scritta) application; Comm demand; ~ **e offerta** supply and demand; **fare una** ~ (a qualcuno) ask (somebody) a question. **domanda di impiego** job application. **domanda riconvenzionale** counterclaim. **domanda trabocchetto** trick question

doman'dare *vt* ask; (esigere) demand; ~ **qualcosa a qualcuno** ask somebody for something

doman'darsi *vr* wonder

do'mani ① *adv* tomorrow; ~ **sera** tomorrow evening; **a** ~ see you tomorrow ② *nm* **il** ~ the future

do'mare *vt* tame; fig control ⟨*emozioni*⟩

doma'tore, -trice *nmf* tamer. **domatore di cavalli** horsebreaker

domat'tina *adv* tomorrow morning

doma'tura *nf* (di cavallo) breaking

do'menica *nf* Sunday; **di** ~ on Sundays. **Domenica delle Palme** Palm Sunday

domeni'cale *adj* Sunday *attrib*

domeni'cano *adj* Dominican

do'mestico, -a ① *adj* domestic; **le pareti domestiche** one's own four walls ② *nm* servant ③ *nf* maid

domicili'are *adj* **arresti domiciliari** Jur house arrest; **perquisizione domiciliare** Jur house search

domicili'arsi *vr* settle

domi'cilio *nm* domicile; (abitazione) home; **recapitiamo a** ~ we do home deliveries

domi'nante *adj* ⟨*nazione, colore*⟩ dominant; ⟨*caratteri*⟩ chief; ⟨*opinione*⟩ prevailing; ⟨*motivo*⟩ main

domi'nanza *nf* Biol, Zool dominance

domi'nare ① *vt* dominate; (controllare) control ② *vi* rule; (prevalere) be dominant

domi'narsi *vr* control oneself

domina'tore, -trice ① *adj* domineering ② *nmf* ruler

dominazi'one *nf* domination

Domi'nica *nf* Dominica

domini'cano *adj* **la Repubblica Dominicana** the Dominican Republic

do'minio *nm* control; Pol dominion; (ambito) field; **di** ~ **pubblico** common knowledge

'domino *nm* (gioco) dominoes

don *nm* (ecclesiastico) Father

do'nare ① *vt* give; donate ⟨*sangue, organo*⟩ ② *vi* ~ **a** (giovare esteticamente) suit

do'narsi *vr* dedicate oneself

dona'tore, -trice *nmf* donor. **donatore di organi** organ donor. **donatore del seme** sperm donor

donazi'one *nf* donation

dondo'lare ① *vt* swing; (cullare) rock ② *vi* sway

dondo'larsi *vr* swing

dondo'lio *nm* rocking

'dondolo *nm* swing; **cavallo/sedia a** ~ rocking-horse/chair

dongio'vanni *nm inv* Romeo, Don Juan

'donna *nf* woman; **fare la prima** ~ act like a prima donna; **'donne'** 'ladies'. **donna d'affari** businesswoman. **donna delle pulizie** cleaner. **donna di servizio** domestic help. **donna di vita** (prostituta) lady of the night

don'naccia *nf* pej hussy

donnai'olo *nm* womanizer

donnicci'ola *nf* fig old woman

'donnola *nf* weasel

'dono *nm* gift

'doping *nm* Sport drug-taking; **fa uso di ~** he takes drugs

'dopo ① *prep* after; (a partire da) since ② *adv* after; afterwards; (più tardi) later; (in seguito) later on; **~ di me** after me

dopo'barba *nm inv* aftershave

dopo'cena *nm inv* evening

dopodiché *adv* after which

dopodo'mani *adv* the day after tomorrow

dopogu'erra *nm inv* post-war period

dopola'voro *nm inv* working man's club

dopo'pranzo *nm inv* afternoon

dopo'sci *adj & nm inv* après-ski

doposcu'ola *nm inv* after-school activities *pl*

dopo-'shampoo ① *nm inv* conditioner ② *adj inv* conditioning

dopo'sole ① *nm inv* aftersun cream ② *adj inv* aftersun

dopo'tutto *adv* after all

doppi'aggio *nm* dubbing

doppia'mente *adv* (in misura doppia) doubly

doppi'are *vt* Naut double; Sport lap; Cinema dub

doppia|'tore, -trice *nmf* dubber

doppi'etta *nf* (fucile) double-barrelled shotgun; Auto double-declutch; (in calcio) two goals; (in pugilato) one-two

doppi'ezza *nf* duplicity

'doppio ① *adj & adv* double. **doppia nazionalità** dual nationality. **doppi vetri** double glazing. **doppio clic** Comput double click; **fare un ~ su** double-click on. **doppio fallo** Tennis double fault. **doppio gioco** double-dealing. **doppio mento** double chin. **doppio senso** double entendre ② *nm* double, twice the quantity; Tennis doubles *pl*. **doppio misto** Tennis mixed doubles

doppio'fondo *nm* Naut double hull; (in valigia) false bottom

doppiogio'chista *nmf* double-dealer

doppi'one *nm* duplicate

doppio'petto *adj* double-breasted

dop'pista *nmf* Tennis doubles player

do'rare *vt* gild; Culin brown

do'rato *adj* gilt; (color oro) golden

dora'tura *nf* gilding

'dorico *adj* Archit Doric

do'rifora *nf* Colorado beetle

dormicchi'are *vi* doze

dormigli'one, -a *nmf* sleepyhead; fig lazybones

dor'mire *vi* sleep; (essere addormentato) be asleep; fig be asleep; **andare a ~** go to bed; **~ come un ghiro** sleep like a log; **~ in**

piedi fig be half asleep; (essere stanco) be dead tired; **dormirci sopra** sleep on it

dor'mita *nf* good sleep; **fare una bella ~** have a good sleep

dormi'tina *nf* nap

dormi'torio *nm* dormitory. **dormitorio pubblico** night shelter

dormi'veglia *nm* **essere nel ~** be half asleep

dor'sale ① *adj* dorsal ② *nf* (di monte) ridge

dor'sista *nmf* backstroke swimmer

'dorso *nm* back; (di libro) spine; (di monte) crest; (nel nuoto) backstroke; **a ~ di cavallo** on horseback

do'saggio *nm* dosage; fig weighing; **sbagliare il ~** get the amount wrong

do'sare *vt* dose; fig measure; **~ le parole** weigh one's words

do'sato *adj* measured

dosa'tore *nm* measuring jug

'dose *nf* dose; **~ eccessiva** overdose; **in buona ~** fig in good measure

dos'sier *nm inv* (raccolta di dati, fascicolo) file

'dosso *nm* (dorso) back; (su strada) bump **levarsi di ~ gli abiti** take off one's clothes. **dosso di rallentamento** road hump, speed hump

do'tare *vt* endow; (di accessori) equip

do'tato *adj* ⟨persona⟩ gifted; (fornito) equipped

dotazi'one *nf* (attrezzatura) equipment; (mezzi finanziari) endowment; **avere qualcosa in ~** be equipped with something

'dote *nf* dowry; (qualità) gift

dott. *abbr* (**dottore**) Dr.

'dotto ① *adj* learned ② *nm* scholar; Anat duct

dotto'rale *adj* doctoral; pej pedantic

dotto'rando, -a *nmf* postgraduate student

dotto'rato *nm* doctorate

dot'tor|e, ~'essa *nmf* doctor

dot'trina *nf* doctrine

dott.ssa *abbr* (**dottoressa**) Dr.

double-'face *adj inv* reversible

'dove *adv* where; **di ~ sei?** where do you come from; **fin ~?** how far?; **per ~?** which way?

do'vere ① *vi* (obbligo) have to, must; **devo andare** I have to go, I must go; **devo venire anch'io?** do I have to come too?; **avresti dovuto dirmelo** you should have told me, you ought to have told me; **devo sedermi un attimo** I must sit down for a minute, I need to sit down for a minute; **dev'essere successo qualcosa** something must have happened; **come si deve** properly

2 vt (essere debitore di, derivare) owe; **essere dovuto a** be due to

3 nm duty; **per ~** out of duty; **rivolgersi a chi di ~** apply to the appropriate authorities

dove'roso adj right and proper

do'vizia nf **con ~ di particolari** in great detail

do'vunque **1** adv (dappertutto) everywhere; (in qualsiasi luogo) anywhere **2** conj wherever

dovuta'mente adv duly

do'vuto adj due; (debito) proper; **essere ~ a** be attributable to; **ha fatto più del ~** he did more than he had to

Down: **sindrome di ~** nf Med Down's syndrome

doz'zina nf **una ~ di uova** a dozen eggs; **mezza ~ di uova** half a dozen eggs

dozzi'nale adj cheap

'draga nf (scavatrice) dredger

draga'mine nf inv minesweeper

dra'gare vt dredge

'drago nm dragon

'dramma nm drama; **fare un ~ di qualcosa** fig make a drama out of something

drammatica'mente adv dramatically

drammaticità nf dramatic force

dram'matico adj dramatic

drammatiz'zare vt dramatize

drammatizzazi'one nf dramatization

drammatur'gia nf (genere) drama

dramma'turgo nm playwright

dram'mone nm (film) tear-jerker, weepy

drappeggi'are vt drape

drap'peggio nm drapery

drap'pello nm Mil squad; (gruppo) band

'drappo nm (tessuto) cloth

drastica'mente adv drastically

'drastico adj drastic

dre'naggio nm drainage. **drenaggio di capitali** transfer of capital. **drenaggio fiscale** fiscal drag

dre'nare vt drain

'Dresda nf Dresden

dres'sage nm inv (gara) dressage

drib'blare vt (in calcio) dribble; fig dodge

'dribbling nm inv (in calcio) dribble

'dritta nf (mano destra) right hand; Naut starboard; (informazione) pointer, tip; **a ~ e a manca** (dappertutto) left, right and centre

dritta'mente adv (furbescamente) craftily

'dritto, -a **1** adj = DIRITTO[1] **2** nmf fam crafty so-and-so

'drive nm inv Comput drive

drive-'in nm inv drive-in

driz'zare vt straighten; (rizzare) prick up

driz'zarsi vr straighten [up]; (alzarsi) raise; **mi si sono drizzati i capelli** fig my hair stood on end

'droga nf drug. **droga leggera** soft drug. **droga di passaggio** gateway drug. **droga pesante** hard drug

dro'gare vt drug

dro'garsi vr take drugs

drogato, -a **1** adj drugged **2** nmf drug addict

droghe'ria nf grocery

droghi'ere, -a nmf grocer

drome'dario nm dromedary

'druso nmf Druse

dua'lismo nm dualism; (contrasto) conflict

'dubbio **1** adj doubtful; (ambiguo) dubious **2** nm doubt; (sospetto) suspicion; **mettere in ~** doubt; **essere fuori ~** be beyond doubt; **essere in ~** be doubtful

dubbiosa'mente adv doubtfully

dubbi'oso, dubitante adj doubtful

dubi'tare vi doubt; **~ di** doubt; (diffidare) mistrust; **dubito che venga** I doubt whether he'll come

dubita'tivo adj (ambiguo) ambiguous

Du'blino nf Dublin

'duca nm duke

du'cale adj ducal

'duce nm (nel fascismo) Duce

du'chessa nf duchess

'due adj & nm two

duecen'tesco adj thirteenth-century

duecen'tesimo two hundredth

duecento adj & nm two hundred

duel'lante nmf dueller

duel'lare vi duel

du'ello nm duel

due'mila adj & nm two thousand

due'pezzi nm inv (bikini) bikini; (vestito) two-piece suit

du'etto nm duo; Mus duet

'dumping nm Fin dumping

'duna nf dune

dune 'buggy nm inv beach buggy

'dunque conj therefore; (allora) well [then]; **arrivare al ~** get down to the nitty-gritty

'duo nm inv duo; Mus duet

duodeci'male adj duodecimal

duode'nale adj **ulcera ~** duodenal ulcer

duo'deno nm duodenum

du'omo nm cathedral

'duplex nm Teleph party line

dupli'care vt duplicate

dupli'cato nm duplicate

duplicazi'one nf duplication

'duplice adj double; **in ~** in duplicate

duplicità nf duplicity

dura'mente *adv* ⟨*lavorare*⟩ hard; ⟨*rimproverare*⟩ harshly

du'rante *prep* during

du'rare ① *vi* last; ⟨*cibo*⟩ keep; ⟨resistere⟩ hold out; **così non può ~** this can't go on any longer; **~ in carica** remain in office; **finché dura** as long as it lasts ② *vt* **~ fatica** sweat blood

du'rata *nf* duration. **durata del collegamento** on-line time. **durata di conservazione** shelf-life. **durata della vita** life span

dura'turo *adj* lasting

du'revole *adj* ⟨*pace*⟩ lasting, enduring

du'rezza *nf* hardness; (di carne)

toughness; (di voce, padre) harshness

'duro, -a ① *adj* hard; ⟨*persona, carne*⟩ tough; ⟨*voce*⟩ harsh; ⟨*pane*⟩ stale; **tieni ~!** (resistere) hang in there!; **~ d'orecchio** hard of hearing ② *nmf* (persona) tough person, toughie *fam*

du'rone *nm* hardened skin

'duttile *adj* ⟨*materiale*⟩ ductile; ⟨*carattere, persona*⟩ malleable

duttilità *nf* (di materiale) ductility; (di individuo) malleability

'duty free *nm inv* duty-free shop

DVD ① *nm inv* (disco) DVD ② *nm inv* (lettore) DVD player

Ee

e *conj* and

eba'nista *nmf* cabinet-maker

'ebano *nm* ebony

eb'bene *conj* well [then]

eb'brezza *nf* inebriation; (euforia) elation; **guida in stato di ~** drink-driving; **l'~ della velocità** the thrill of speed

'ebbro *adj* inebriated; **~ di gioia** delirious with joy

'ebete *adj* stupid

ebollizi'one *nf* boiling

e'braico *adj & nm* Hebrew

ebra'ismo *nm* Judaism

e'breo, -a ① *adj* Jewish ② *nm* Jew ③ *nf* Jewess

'Ebridi *nfpl* **le ~** the Hebrides

eca'tombe *nf* **fare un'~** wreak havoc

ecc *abbr* (**eccetera**) etc

eccì *int* atishoo

ecce'dente *adj* ⟨*peso, bagaglio*⟩ excess

ecce'denza *nf* excess; (d'avanzo) surplus; **avere qualcosa in ~** have an excess of something; **bagagli in ~** excess baggage. **eccedenza di cassa** surplus. **eccedenza di peso** excess weight

ec'cedere ① *vt* exceed ② *vi* go too far; **~ nel bere** drink to excess; **~ nel mangiare** overeat

eccel'lente *adj* excellent

eccel'lenza *nf* excellence; (titolo) Excellency; **per ~** par excellence

ec'cellere *vi* excel (**in** at)

eccentricità *nf inv* eccentricity

ec'centrico, -a *adj & nmf* eccentric

ecce'pire *vt* object to

eccessiva'mente *adv* excessively

ecces'sivo *adj* excessive

ec'cesso *nm* excess; **andare agli eccessi** go to extremes; **dare in eccessi** fly into a temper; **all'~** to excess. **eccesso di personale** over-manning. **eccesso di peso** excess weight. **eccesso di velocità** speeding

ec'cetera *adv* et cetera

ec'cetto *prep* except; **~ che** (a meno che) unless

eccettu'are *vt* except

eccezio'nale *adj* exceptional; **in via [del tutto] ~** as an exception

eccezional'mente *adv* exceptionally; (contrariamente alla regola) as an exception

eccezi'one *nf* exception; Jur objection; **a ~ di** with the exception of; **d'~** exceptional

ec'chimosi *nf inv* bruising

ec'cidio *nm* massacre

ecci'tabile *adj* ⟨*persona, carattere*⟩ excitable

eccita'mento *nm* excitement

ecci'tante ① *adj* exciting; ⟨*sostanza*⟩ stimulant ② *nm* stimulant

ecci'tare *vt* excite; (sessualmente) excite, arouse

ecci'tarsi *vr* get excited; (sessualmente) become aroused *or* excited

ecci'tato *adj* excited; (sessualmente) excited, aroused; **~ da** flushed with

eccitazi'one *nf* excitement; (sessuale) arousal, excitement

ecclesi'astico ① *adj* ecclesiastical ② *nm* priest

'ecco *adv* (qui) here; (là) there; ~! (con approvazione) that's right!; ~ **qua!** (dando qualcosa) here you are!; ~ **la tua borsa** here is your bag; ~ **mio figlio** there is my son; **eccomi** here I am; ~ **fatto** there we are; ~ **perché** this is why; ~ **tutto** that is all

ec'come *adv & int* and how!

ECG *abbr* (**elettrocardiogramma**) ECG

echeggi'are *vi* echo

e'clettico *adj* eclectic

eclet'tismo *nm* eclecticism

eclis'sare *vt* fig eclipse

eclis'sarsi *vr* (sparire) disappear

e'clissi *nf inv* eclipse. **eclissi di sole** solar eclipse

'eco *nmf* (pl m **echi**) echo; **ha suscitato una vasta ~** it caused a great stir

eco+ *pref* eco+; **eco-guerrigliero** eco-warrier

ecogra'fia *nf* scan

ecolo'gia *nf* ecology

eco'logico *adj* ecological; ⟨prodotto⟩ environmentally friendly, eco-friendly

e'cologo, -a *nmf* ecologist

e commerci'ale *nf* ampersand

econo'mia *nf* economy; (scienza) economics; **fare ~** economize (**di** on); [**fatto**] **in ~** [done] on the cheap; **senza ~** unstintingly; **fare qualcosa senza ~** spare no expense doing something. **economia aziendale** business administration. **economia domestica** Sch home economics. **economia di mercato** market economy. **economia di libero mercato** free market. **economia mista** mixed economy. **economia sommersa** black economy

economicità *nf* economy

eco'nomico *adj* economic; (a buon prezzo) cheap; (con pochi costi) economical; **difficoltà economiche** financial difficulties; **classe economica** economy class; **edizione economica** paperback

econo'mie *nfpl* (risparmi) savings

econo'mista *nmf* economist

economiz'zare ① *vt* save ⟨denaro⟩ ② *vi* economize (**su** on)

economizza'tore *nm* Auto fuel economizer

e'conomo, -a ① *adj* thrifty ② *nmf* (di collegio) bursar

ecosi'stema *nm* ecosystem

eco'tassa *nf* carbon tax

ecoterro'rismo *nm* ecoterrorism

e'cru *adj inv* fawn

Ecua'dor *nm* Ecuador

ecuadori'ano, -a *adj & nmf* Ecuadorian

ecu'menico *adj* ecumenical

ec'zema *nm* eczema

ed *conj* ▶ **E**

e'dema *nm* oedema

'Eden *nm* Eden

'edera *nf* ivy

e'dicola *nf* [newspaper] kiosk

edifi'cabile *adj* ⟨area, terreno⟩ classified as suitable for development

edifi'cante *adj* edifying

edifi'care *vt* build; (indurre al bene) edify

edi'ficio *nm* building; fig structure

e'dile ① *adj* building *attrib* ② *nm* **edili** *pl* construction workers

edi'lizia *nf* building trade

edi'lizio *adj* building *attrib*

Edim'burgo *nf* Edinburgh

E'dipo *nm* Oedipus; **complesso di Edipo** Oedipus complex

edi'tare *vt* edit

'editing *nm* editing

'edito *adj* published

edi|'tore, -trice ① *adj* publishing ② *nmf* publisher; (curatore) editor

edito'ria *nf* publishing. **editoria elettronica** desktop publishing, electronic publishing. **editoria telematica** online publishing

editori'ale ① *adj* publishing ② *nm* (articolo) editorial, leader

e'ditto *nm* edict

edizi'one *nf* edition; (di manifestazione) performance; **in ~ italiana** ⟨film⟩ dubbed into Italian. **edizione ridotta** abridgement, abridged version. **edizione della sera** (di telegiornale) evening news.

edo'nismo *nm* hedonism

edo'nistico *adj* hedonistic

educagi'oco *nm* edutainment

edu'canda *nf* [convent school] boarder; fig prim and proper girl

edu'care *vt* educate; (allevare) bring up

educa'tivo *adj* educational

edu'cato *adj* polite

educa|'tore, -trice *nmf* educator

educazi'one *nf* education; (di bambini) upbringing; (buone maniere) [good] manners *pl*; **bella ~!** what manners! **educazione fisica** physical education. **educazione sessuale** sex education

edulco'rare *vt* ~ **la pillola** sweeten the pill

EED *abbr* (**elaborazione elettronica [dei] dati**) EDP

e'felide *nf* freckle

effemi'nato *adj* effeminate

effe'rato *adj* brutal

efferve'scente *adj* effervescent; (frizzante) fizzy; ⟨aspirina®⟩ soluble

effettiva'mente *adv* **è troppo tardi –~** it's too late –so it is

effet'tivo [1] *adj* actual; (efficace) effective; ⟨*personale*⟩ permanent; Mil regular [2] *nm* (somma totale) sum total

ef'fetto *nm* effect; (impressione) impression; (cambiale) bill; **fare ∼** ⟨*medicina*⟩ take effect; **fare ∼ su** have an effect on, affect; **in effetti** in fact; **a tutti gli effetti** to all intents and purposes; **ad effetto** ⟨*frase*⟩ catchy; **la vista del sangue mi fa ∼** I can't stand the sight of blood; **tiro con ∼** spin. **effetto boomerang** boomerang effect. **effetto di luce** trick of the light. **effetti personali** *pl* personal belongings, personal effects fml. **effetto ritardato** delayed effect. **effetto serra** greenhouse effect. **effetto sonoro** sound effect. **effetto speciale** Cinema, TV special effect

effettu'are *vt* effect; carry out ⟨*controllo, sondaggio*⟩

effettu'arsi *vr* take place; **'si effettua dal ... al ...'** 'this service is available from ... till ...'

effi'cace *adj* effective

effi'cacia *nf* effectiveness

effici'ente *adj* efficient

effici'enza *nf* efficiency; **in piena ∼** in full swing

ef'figie *nf* effigy

ef'fimero *adj* ephemeral

ef'flusso *nm* outflow

ef'fluvio *nm* stink

ef'fondersi *vr* **∼ in ringraziamenti** be profuse in one's thanks

effrazi'one *nf* **effrazione con scasso** Jur breaking and entering

effusi'one *nf* effusion

'Egadi *nfpl* **le [isole] ∼** the Egadi Islands

egemo'nia *nf* hegemony

E'geo *nm* **l'∼** the Aegean [Sea]

e'gida *nf* **sotto l'∼ di** under the aegis of

E'gitto *nm* Egypt

egizi'ano, **-a** *adj* & *nmf* Egyptian

e'gizio, **-a** *adj* & *nmf* Ancient Egyptian

'egli *pers pron* he; **∼ stesso** he himself

ego'centrico, **-a** [1] *adj* egocentric [2] *nmf* egocentric person

egocen'trismo *nm* egocentricity

ego'ismo *nm* selfishness

ego'ista [1] *adj* selfish [2] *nmf* selfish person

egoistica'mente *adv* selfishly

ego'istico *adj* selfish

Egr. *abbr* (egregio) **∼ Sig.** (su busta) Mr.

e'gregio *adj* distinguished; **Egregio Signore** Dear Sir

eguali'tario *adj* & *nm* egalitarian

eh *int* huh!

'ehi *int* hey!

ehilà *int* hi!

ehm *int* um

eiacu'lare *vi* ejaculate

eiaculazi'one *nf* ejaculation

eiet'tabile *adj* ⟨*sedile*⟩ ejector

eiezi'one *nf* Aeron ejection

'Eire *nf* Eire

elabo'rare *vt* elaborate; process ⟨*dati*⟩

elabo'rato [1] *adj* elaborate [2] *nm* (tabulato) preprinted form

elabora'tore *nm* **elaboratore [di testi]** word processor

elaborazi'one *nf* elaboration; (di dati) processing. **elaborazione elettronica [dei] dati** electronic data processing. **elaborazione sequenziale** Comput batch processing. **elaborazione [di] testi** word processing

elar'gire *vt* lavish

elasti'cità *nf* elasticity. **elasticità mentale** mental agility. **elasticità di movimento** litheness

elastici'zzato *adj* ⟨*stoffa*⟩ elasticated

e'lastico [1] *adj* elastic; ⟨*tessuto*⟩ stretch; ⟨*passo*⟩ springy; ⟨*orario, mente*⟩ flexible; ⟨*persona*⟩ easy-going; ⟨*morale*⟩ lax; **collant** *pl* **elastici** support tights [2] *nm* elastic; (fascia) rubber band

'Elba *nf* Elba

eldo'rado *nm* eldorado

ele'fante *nm* elephant; **avere una memoria da ∼** have a memory like an elephant; **fare passi da ∼** thump about. **∼ marino** sea-elephant

elefan'tesco *adj* elephantine

elefan'tessa *nf* cow[-elephant]

elefan'tiaco *adj* (enorme) elephantine

ele'gante *adj* elegant

elegante'mente *adv* elegantly

ele'ganza *nf* elegance

e'leggere *vt* elect

eleg'gibile *adj* eligible

ele'gia *nf* elegy

elemen'tare *adj* elementary; **scuola elementare** primary school

ele'mento *nm* element; (componente) part; **trovarsi nel proprio ∼** be in one's element; **elementi** *pl* (fatti) data; (rudimenti) elements

ele'mosina *nf* charity; **chiedere l'∼** beg; **vivere d'∼** live on charity; **fare l'∼** give money to beggars

elemosi'nare *vt/i* beg

elen'care *vt* list

e'lenco *nm* list. **elenco [degli] abbonati** Teleph telephone directory. **elenco telefonico** telephone directory

elet'tivo *adj* ⟨*carica*⟩ elective

e'letto, **-a** [1] *pp di* ELEGGERE [2] *adj* chosen

3 *nmf* (nominato) elected member; **per pochi eletti** fig for the chosen few

eletto'rale *adj* electoral

elettora'lismo *nm* electioneering

eletto'rato *nm* electorate

elet|'tore, -trice *nmf* voter

elet'trauto *nm inv* electrics garage

elettri'cista *nm* electrician

elettricità *nf* electricity; **togliere l'~** cut the electricity off; **è mancata l'~** there was a power cut

e'lettrico *adj* electric

elettriz'zante *adj* ⟨notizia, gara⟩ electrifying

elettriz'zare *vt* fig electrify

elettriz'zato *adj* fig electrified

elettro+ *pref* electro+

elettrocardio'gramma *nm* electrocardiogram, ECG

elettrocuzi'one *nf* electrocution

e'lettrodo *nm* electrode

elettrodo'mestico *nm* [electrical] household appliance

elettroencefalo'gramma *nm* electroencephalogram

elettroesecuzi'one *nf* electrocution

elet'trogeno *adj* **gruppo elettrogeno** generator

elet'trolisi *nf* electrolysis

elettromo'tore *nm* electric motor

elettromo'trice *nf* electric train

elet'trone *nm* electron

elet'tronico, -a **1** *adj* electronic **2** *nf* electronics

elettroshocktera'pia *nf* electroshock therapy, electroshock treatment, EST

elettro'tecnica *nf* electrical engineering

elettro'tecnico *nm* electrical engineer

elettro'treno *nm* electric train

ele'vare *vt* raise; (promuovere) promote; (erigere) erect; (fig: migliorare) better; **~ al quadrato/cubo** square/cube

ele'varsi *vr* rise; ⟨edificio⟩ stand

ele'vato *adj* high; (fig: sentimento) lofty; **~ al cubo/al quadrato** cubed/squared; **~ a dieci** raised to the power of ten

eleva'tore *nm* fork-lift truck

elevazi'one *nf* elevation

elezi'one *nf* election; **elezioni** *pl* **amministrative** local council elections; **elezioni** *pl* **politiche** general election

eliambu'lanza *nf* air ambulance

'elica *nf* Naut screw, propeller; Aeron propeller; (del ventilatore) blade

eli'cottero *nm* helicopter

elimi'nabile *adj* which can be eliminated

elimi'nare *vt* eliminate

elimina'toria *nf* Sport [preliminary] heat

eliminazi'one *nf* elimination

'elio *nm* (gas) helium

eli'porto *nm* heliport

elisabetti'ano *adj & nmf* Elizabethan

é'lite *nf inv* élite

eli'tista *adj* élitist

'ella *pers pron* liter she; **~ stessa** she herself

el'lenico *adj* Hellenic

elle'nistico *adj* Hellenistic

ellepì *nm inv* LP

+ellino *suff* **campanellino** *nm* [small] bell; **fiorellino** *nm* [little] flower; **gonnellina** *nf* short skirt

el'lisse *nf* ellipse

el'lissi *nf inv* ellipsis

el'littico *adj* elliptical

+ello *suff* **finestrella** *nf* little window; **pecorella** *nf* woolly sheep; **saltello** *nm* skip

el'metto *nm* helmet

elogi'are *vt* praise

elogia'tivo *adj* laudatory

e'logio *nm* praise; (discorso, scritto) eulogy; **degno di ~** laudable, praiseworthy; **ti faccio i miei elogi per** congratulations on. **~ funebre** funeral oration

elo'quente *adj* eloquent; fig tell-tale

elo'quenza *nf* eloquence

El Salva'dor *nm* El Salvador; **nel Salvador** in El Salvador

e'ludere *vt* elude; evade ⟨sorveglianza, controllo⟩

elusi'one *nf* **elusione fiscale** tax avoidance

elu'sivo *adj* elusive

el'vetico *adj* Swiss; **Confederazione Elvetica** Swiss Confederation

emaci'ato *adj* emaciated

e-mail *nf inv* e-mail; **mandare per ~** e-mail, send by e-mail; **indirizzo ~** e-mail address

ema'nare **1** *vt* give off; pass ⟨legge⟩ **2** *vi* emanate

emanazi'one *nf* giving off; (di legge) enactment

emanci'pare *vt* emancipate

emanci'parsi *vr* become emancipated

emanci'pato *adj* emancipated

emancipazi'one *nf* emancipation

emargi'nato *nm* marginalized person

emarginazi'one *nf* marginalization

ema'toma *nm* haematoma

em'bargo *nm* embargo. **embargo sulle armi** arms embargo

em'blema *nm* emblem

emble'matico *adj* emblematic

embo'lia *nf* embolism

'**embolo** *nm* embolus
embrio'nale *adj* Biol, fig embryonic; **allo stato ∼** ⟨*progetto, idea*⟩ embryonic
embri'one *nm* embryo
emenda'mento *nm* amendment
emen'dare *vt* amend
emen'darsi *vr* reform
emer'gente *adj* emergent
emer'genza *nf* emergency; **in caso di ∼** in an emergency; **di ∼** ⟨di riserva⟩ stand-by; **uscita d'emergenza** emergency exit. **emergenza sanitaria** ambulance
e'mergere *vi* emerge; ⟨sottomarino⟩ surface; (distinguersi) stand out
e'merito *adj* ⟨professore⟩ emeritus; **un ∼ imbecille** a prize idiot
e'merso *pp di* EMERGERE
e'messo *pp di* EMETTERE
e'metico *adj* emetic
e'mettere *vt* emit; give out ⟨luce, suono⟩; let out ⟨grido⟩; (mettere in circolazione) issue
emi'crania *nf* migraine
emi'grare *vi* emigrate
emi'grato, -a *nmf* immigrant
emigrazi'one *nf* emigration
emi'nente *adj* eminent
emi'nenza *nf* eminence; **Sua Eminenza** His/Your Eminence. **eminenza grigia** éminence grise
emi'rato *nm* emirate; **Emirati** *pl* **Arabi Uniti** United Arab Emirates
e'miro *nm* emir
emi'sfero *nm* hemisphere
emis'sario *nm* emissary; (fiume) effluent
emissi'one *nf* emission; (di denaro, francobolli) issue; (trasmissione) broadcast; '**∼ del biglietto**' 'take your ticket here'
emit'tente ① *adj* issuing; (trasmittente) broadcasting ② *nf* Radio transmitter
'**emmental** *nm* Emmenthal
emofi'lia *nf* haemophilia
emofi'liaco, -a *nmf* haemophiliac
emoglo'bina *nf* haemoglobin
emorra'gia *nf* haemorrhage; **avere un'∼** haemorrhage
emor'roidi *nfpl* haemorrhoids, piles
emo'statico *adj* haemostatic
emotiva'mente *adv* emotionally
emotività *nf* emotional make-up
emotivo *adj* emotional; **con turbe emotive** emotionally disturbed
emozio'nante *adj* exciting; (commovente) moving
emozio'nare *vt* excite; (commuovere) move
emozio'narsi *vr* become excited; (commuoversi) be moved

emozio'nato *adj* excited; (commosso) moved
emozi'one *nf* emotion; (agitazione) excitement
empietà *nf inv* impiety
'**empio** *adj* impious; (spietato) pitiless; (malvagio) wicked
em'pirico *adj* empirical
empi'rismo *nm* empiricism
empi'rista *nmf* empiricist
em'porio *nm* emporium; (negozio) general store
emù *nm inv* emu
emu'lare *vt* emulate
emulazi'one *nf* emulation. **emulazione di terminale** terminal emulation
emulsio'nare *vt* emulsify
emulsio'narsi *vr* emulsify
emulsi'one *nf* emulsion
ena'lotto *nm* weekly lottery
encefa'lite *nf* encefalite **spongiforme bovina** Bovine Spongiform Encephalopathy, BSE
encefalo'gramma *nm* encephalogram
en'ciclica *nf* encyclical
enciclope'dia *nf* encyclopaedia
enciclo'pedico *adj* ⟨mente, cultura, dizionario⟩ encyclopaedic
encomi'are *vt* commend
en'comio *nm* commendation
ende'mia *nf* (situazione) endemic
en'demico *adj* endemic
endocrinolo'gia *nf* endocrinology
endo'vena ① *nf inv* intravenous injection ② *adv* intravenously
endove'noso *adj* intravenous; **per via endovenosa** intravenously
ener'getico *adj* ⟨risorse, crisi⟩ energy *attrib*; ⟨alimento⟩ energy-giving
ener'gia *nf* energy; **pieno di ∼** full of energy. **energia alternativa** alternative energy. **energia atomica** atomic energy. **energia elettrica** electricity. **energia eolica** windpower. **energia idroelettrica** hydroelectricity. **energia nucleare** nuclear energy, nuclear power. **energia solare** solar energy, solar power
energica'mente *adv* energetically
e'nergico *adj* energetic; (efficace) strong
ener'gumeno *nm* Neanderthal
'**enfasi** *nf* emphasis
en'fatico *adj* emphatic
enfatiz'zare *vt* emphasize
enfi'sema *nm* emphysema
e'nigma *nm* enigma
enig'matico *adj* enigmatic

enig'mistica *nf* puzzles *pl*

E.N.I.T. *nm abbr* (**Ente Nazionale Italiano per il Turismo**) Italian State Tourist Office

en'nesimo *adj* Math nth; fam umpteenth; **all'ennesima potenza** Math, fig to the nth power/degree

eno'logico *adj* wine attrib

e'norme *adj* enormous, great big fam; **è un'ingiustizia** ~ it's enormously unfair

enorme'mente *adv* massively

enormità *nf inv* enormity; (assurdità) absurdity

eno'teca *nf* wine-tasting shop

eno'tera *nf* evening primrose

en pas'sant *adv* in passing

'ente *nm* board; (società) company; (in filosofia) being

ente'rite *nf* enteritis

entero'clisma *nm* Med enema

entità *nf inv* (filosofia) entity; (gravità) seriousness; (dimensione) extent

entomolo'gia *nf* entomology

entou'rage *nm inv* entourage

en'trambi *adj & pron* both

en'trare *vi* go in, enter; ~ **in** go into; (stare in, trovar posto in) fit into; (arruolarsi) join; **entrarci** (avere a che fare) have to do with; **tu che c'entri?** what has it got to do with you?; **da che parte si entra?** how do you get in?; **fallo** ~ (in ufficio, dal medico ecc) show him in; **'vietato** ~' 'no entry'

en'trata *nf* entry, entrance. **entrata libera** admission free. **entrata di servizio** tradesman's entrance; **entrate** *pl* Comm takings; (reddito) income *sg*

'entro *prep* (tempo) within; ~ **oggi** by the end of today

entro'bordo *nm* (motore) inboard motor; (motoscafo) speedboat

entro'terra *nm inv* hinterland

entusia'smante *adj* fascinating, exciting

entusia'smare *vt* arouse enthusiasm in

entusia'smarsi *vr* be enthusiastic (**per** about)

entusi'asmo *nm* enthusiasm

entusi'asta ① *adj* enthusiastic ② *nmf* enthusiast

entusi'astico *adj* enthusiastic

enucle'are *vt* define

enume'rare *vt* enumerate

enumerazi'one *nf* enumeration

enunci'are *vt* enunciate

enunciazi'one *nf* enunciation

E'olie *nfpl* **le** ~ the Aeolian Islands

epa'tite *nf* hepatitis

epi'centro *nm* epicentre

'epico *adj* epic

epide'mia *nf* epidemic

epi'dermide *nf* epidermis

epidu'rale *adj* (Med: anestesia) epidural

Epifa'nia *nf* Epiphany

epi'gramma *nm* epigram

epiles'sia *nf* epilepsy

epi'lettico, -a *adj & nmf* epileptic

e'pilogo *nm* epilogue

episco'pato *nm* episcopacy

epi'sodico *adj* episodic; **caso** ~ one-off case

epi'sodio *nm* episode

e'pistola *nf* epistle

episto'lare *adj* epistolary

episto'lario *nm* correspondence, letters *pl*

epi'taffio *nm* epitaph

e'piteto *nm* epithet

'epoca *nf* age; (periodo) period; **a quell'**~ in those days; **un avvenimento che ha fatto** ~ an epoch-making event; **auto d'epoca** vintage car; **mobile d'epoca** period furniture

e'ponimo *adj* eponymous

epo'pea *nf* epic

ep'pure *conj* [and] yet

E.P.T. *abbr* (**Ente Provinciale per il Turismo**) Italian local tourist board

epu'rare *vt* purge; purify ⟨acqua⟩

epura'tore *nm* water purifier

epurazi'one *nf* purging; (di acqua) purification. **epurazione etnica** ethnic cleansing

equalizza'tore *nm* equalizer

e'quanime *adj* level-headed; (imparziale) impartial

equa'tore *nm* equator

equatori'ale *adj* equatorial

equazi'one *nf* equation

e'questre *adj* equestrian; **circo equestre** circus

equidi'stante *adj* equidistant

equi'latero *adj* equilateral

equili'brare *vt* balance

equili'brato *adj* (persona) well-balanced

equi'librio *nm* balance; (buon senso) common sense; (di bilancia) equilibrium

equili'brismo *nm* **fare** ~ do a balancing act

equili'brista *nmf* tightrope walker

e'quino *adj* horse *attrib*

equi'nozio *nm* equinox

equipaggia'mento *nm* equipment

equipaggi'are *vt* equip; (di persone) man

equi'paggio *nm* crew; Aeron cabin crew. **equipaggio di volo** aircrew

equipa'rare *vt* make equal
equipa'rato *adj* equal
é'quipe *nf inv* team
equità *nf* equity
equitazione *nf* riding, horseriding, horseback riding *Am*
equiva'lente *adj & nm* equivalent
equiva'lenza *nf* equivalence
equiva'lere *vi* ∼ a be equivalent to
equivo'care *vi* misunderstand
e'quivoco ① *adj* equivocal; (sospetto) suspicious; **un tipo** ∼ a shady character ② *nm* misunderstanding; **a scanso di equivoci** to avoid any misunderstandings; **giocare sull'**∼ equivocate
'equo *adj* fair, just
equosoli'dale *adj* fair trade
'era *nf* era. **era glaciale** Ice Age
'erba *nf* grass; (medicinale) herb; **in** ∼ ⟨attore⟩ budding. **erba cipollina** chives
er'baccia *nf* weed
er'baceo *adj* herbaceous
erbi'cida *nm* weedkiller
erbi'voro ① *adj* herbivorous ② *nm* herbivore
erbo'rista *nmf* herbalist
erboriste'ria *nf* herbalist's shop
er'boso *adj* grassy
Erco'lano *nf* Herculaneum
'Ercole *nm* Hercules
er'culeo *adj* ⟨forza⟩ herculean
e'rede ① *nm* heir ② *nf* heiress
eredità *nf inv* inheritance; Biol heredity
eredi'tare *vt* inherit
ereditarietà *nf* heredity
eredi'tario *adj* hereditary
erediti'era *nf* heiress
+erello *suff* **furterello** *nm* petty theft; **pioggerella** *nf* drizzle
ere'mita *nm* hermit
'eremo *nm* isolated place; fig retreat
ere'sia *nf* heresy
e'retico, -a ① *adj* heretical ② *nmf* heretic
e'retto ① *pp di* ERIGERE ② *adj* erect
erezi'one *nf* erection; (costruzione) building
ergasto'lano, -a *nmf* prisoner serving a life sentence, lifer *fam*
er'gastolo *nm* life sentence; (luogo) prison
ergono'mia *nf* ergonomics
ergo'nomico *adj* ergonomic
ergotera'pia *nf* occupational therapy
ergotera'pista *nmf* occupational therapist

'erica *nf* heather
e'rigere *vt* erect; (fig: fondare) found
eri'tema *nm* (cutaneo) inflammation; (solare) sunburn. **eritema da pannolini** nappy rash
Eri'trea *nf* Eritrea
eri'treo, -a *adj & nmf* Eritrean
ermafro'dito *adj & nm* hermaphrodite
ermel'lino *nm* ermine
ermetica'mente *adv* hermetically
er'metico *adj* hermetic; (a tenuta d'aria) airtight
'ernia *nf* hernia
e'rodere *vi* erode
e'roe *nm* hero
ero'gare *vt* distribute; (fornire) supply
erogazi'one *nf* supply
e'rogeno *adj* erogenous
eroica'mente *adv* heroically
e'roico *adj* heroic
ero'ina *nf* heroine; (droga) heroin
eroi'nomane *nmf* heroin addict
ero'ismo *nm* heroism
'eros *nm* Eros
erosi'one *nf* erosion
e'rotico *adj* erotic
ero'tismo *nm* eroticism
'erpice *nm* harrow
er'rante *adj* wandering
er'rare *vi* (vagare) wander; (sbagliare) be mistaken
er'rato *adj* (sbagliato) mistaken; **se non vado** ∼ if I'm not mistaken
'erre *nf* **erre moscia** burr
erronea'mente *adv* mistakenly
er'rore *nm* error, mistake; (di stampa) misprint; **essere in** ∼ be wrong. **errore giudiziario** miscarriage of justice. **errore di stampa** printing error, typo
'erta *nf* **stare all'**∼ be on the alert
eru'dirsi *vr* get educated
eru'dito *adj* learned
erut'tare ① *vt* ⟨vulcano⟩ erupt ② *vi* (ruttare) belch
eruzi'one *nf* eruption; Med rash
Es *nm* Psych l'∼ the id
es. *abbr* (**esempio**) eg.
esacer'bare *vt* exacerbate
esage'rare ① *vt* exaggerate; ∼ **le cose** exaggerate things, go over the top ② *vi* exaggerate; (nel comportamento) go over the top; ∼ **nel mangiare** eat too much
esagerata'mente *adv* excessively
esage'rato ① *adj* exaggerated; ⟨prezzo⟩ exorbitant ② *nm* **è un** ∼ he exaggerates

esagerazi'one nf exaggeration; è costato un'∼ it cost the earth; senza ∼ with no exaggeration

esago'nale adj hexagonal

e'sagono nm hexagon

esa'lare [1] vt give off; ∼ l'ultimo respiro breathe one's last [2] vi emanate

esalazi'one nf emission; esalazioni pl fumes

esal'tare vt exalt; (entusiasmare) elate

esal'tarsi vr (entusiasmarsi) get excited (per about)

esal'tato [1] adj (fanatico) fanatical [2] nm fanatic

esaltazi'one nf exaltation; (in discorso) fervour

e'same nm examination, exam; dare un ∼ take or sit an exam; prendere in ∼ examine. **esame di ammissione** Sch entrance examination. **esame di coscienza** soul-searching. **esame di guida** driving test. **esami di maturità** ≈ A-levels. **esame orale** Sch, Univ viva. **esame del sangue** blood test. **esame della vista** eye test

esami'nando, -a nmf examinee

esami'nare vt examine

esamina|'tore, -trice nmf examiner

e'sangue adj bloodless

e'sanime adj lifeless

esaspe'rante adj exasperating

esaspe'rare vt exasperate

esaspe'rarsi vr get exasperated

esasperazi'one nf exasperation

esatta'mente adv exactly

esat'tezza nf exactness; (precisione) precision; (di risposta, risultato) accuracy

e'satto adj exact; (risposta, risultato) correct; (orologio) right; hai l'ora esatta? do you have the right time?; sono le due esatte it's two o'clock exactly

esat'tore nm collector. **esattore dei crediti** Fin debt collector. **esattore delle imposte** tax collector, tax man

esau'dire vt grant; fulfil (speranze)

esauri'ente adj exhaustive

esauri'mento nm exhaustion; 'fino ad ∼ delle scorte' 'subject to availability'. **esaurimento nervoso** nervous breakdown

esau'rire vt exhaust

esau'rirsi vr exhaust oneself; (merci ecc) run out

esau'rito adj exhausted; (merci) sold out; (libro) out of print; fare il tutto ∼ (spettacolo) play to a full house; 'tutto ∼' 'sold out'

esazi'one nf collection. **esazione crediti** debt collection

'**esca** nf bait

escande'scenza nf outburst; dare in escandescenze lose one's temper

escava'tore nm excavator

escava'trice nf excavator

escla'mare vi exclaim

esclama'tivo adj exclamatory

esclamazi'one nf exclamation

e'scludere vt exclude; rule out (possibilità, ipotesi)

esclusi'one nf exclusion; senza ∼ di colpi (attacco) all-out

esclu'siva nf exclusive right, sole right; in ∼ exclusive

esclusiva'mente adv exclusively

esclusi'vista nmf exclusive agent

esclu'sivo adj exclusive

e'scluso [1] pp di ESCLUDERE [2] adj non è ∼ che ci sia it's not out of the question that he'll be there; **esclusi i presenti** with the exception of those present; **esclusi sabati e festivi** except Saturdays and Sundays/holidays [3] nm outcast

escogi'tare vt contrive

escoriazi'one nf graze

escre'mento nm excrement; escrementi pl excrement

escursi'one nf (gita) excursion; (camminata) hike; (scorreria) raid. **escursione termica** difference between the lowest and the highest temperature in a 24 hours period

escursio'nismo nm hiking

ese'crabile adj abominable

ese'crare vt abhor

esecu'tivo adj & nm executive

esecu|'tore, -trice nmf executor; Mus performer

esecuzi'one nf execution; Mus performance. **esecuzione capitale** capital punishment

esegu'ibile nm Comput executable file

esegu'ire vt carry out; Jur execute; Mus perform

e'sempio nm example; ad o per ∼ for example; dare l'∼ a qualcuno set somebody an example; fare un ∼ give an example

esem'plare [1] adj examplary [2] nm specimen; (di libro) copy

esemplifi'care vt exemplify

esen'tare vt exempt

esen'tarsi vr free oneself

esen'tasse adj tax-free

e'sente adj exempt. **esente da imposta** duty-free. **esente da IVA** VAT exempt

e'sequie nfpl funeral rites

eser'cente nmf shopkeeper

eserci'tare *vt* exercise; (addestrare) train; (fare uso di) exert; (professione) practise

eserci'tarsi *vr* practise; **~ nella danza** practise dancing

eserci'tato *adj* ‹occhio› practised; **tenere la memoria esercitata** give one's memory some exercise

esercitazi'one *nf* exercise; Mil drill; (di musica, chimica) practical class

e'sercito *nm* army. **Esercito della Salvezza** Salvation Army

eser'cizio *nm* exercise; (pratica) practice; Comm financial year; (azienda) business; **essere fuori ~** be out of practice; **nell'~ delle proprie funzioni** in the line of duty. **esercizio finanziario** financial year. **esercizio fiscale** tax year. **esercizi a terra** *pl* floor exercises. **esercizio tributario** tax year

esi'bire *vt* show off; produce ‹documenti›

esi'birsi *vr* Theat perform; fig show off

esibizi'one *nf* Theat performance; (di documenti) production. **esibizione in volo** Aeron air display

esibizio'nismo *nm* showing off

esibizio'nista *nmf* exhibitionist

esi'gente *adj* exacting; (pignolo) fastidious

esi'genza *nf* demand; (bisogno) need

e'sigere *vt* demand; (riscuotere) collect

e'siguo *adj* meagre

esila'rante *adj* exhilarating

esila'rare *vt* exhilarate

'esile *adj* slender; ‹voce› thin

esili'are *vt* exile

esili'arsi *vr* go into exile

esili'ato, -a ① *adj* exiled ② *nmf* exile

e'silio *nm* exile

e'simere *vt* release

e'simersi *vr* **~ da** get out of

e'simio *adj* distinguished

esi'stente *adj* existing

esi'stenza *nf* existence

esistenzi'ale *adj* existential

esistenzi'alismo *nm* existentialism

e'sistere *vi* exist

esi'tante *adj* hesitating; ‹voce› faltering

esi'tare *vi* hesitate

esitazi'one *nf* hesitation

'esito *nm* result; **avere buon ~** be a success

'esodo *nm* exodus; **l'~ estivo, il grande ~** (per le vacanze) the summer *or* holiday exodus

e'sofago *nm* oesophagus

esone'rare *vt* exempt

e'sonero *nm* exemption

esorbi'tante *adj* exorbitant

esorbi'tare *vi* **~ da** exceed

esor'cismo *nm* exorcism

esor'cista *nmf* exorcist

esorciz'zare *vt* exorcize

esordi'ente *nmf* person making his/her début

e'sordio *nm* opening; (di attore) début

esor'dire *vi* début

esor'tare *vt* (pregare) beg; (incitare) urge

eso'terico *adj* esoteric

e'sotico *adj* exotic

espa'drillas *nfpl* espadrilles

e'spandere *vt* expand

e'spandersi *vr* expand; (diffondersi) extend

espan'dibile *adj* Comput upgradeable

espandibilità *nf* Comput upgradeability

espansi'one *nf* expansion; **in ~** expanding

espansio'nista *nmf* expansionist

espansio'nistico *adj* expansionist

espan'sivo *adj* expansive; ‹persona› friendly

espatri'are *vi* leave one's country

espatri'ato, -a *nmf* expatriate, expat fam

e'spatrio *nm* expatriation

espedi'ente *nm* expedient; **vivere di espedienti** live by one's wits

e'spellere *vt* expel; send off ‹calciatore›

esperi'enza *nf* experience; **per ~** ‹sapere, parlare› from experience; **non ha ~** he doesn't have any experience

esperi'mento *nm* experiment

e'sperto, -a *adj & nmf* expert. **esperto di computer** computer expert

espi'are *vt* atone for

espia'torio *adj* expiatory

espi'rare *vt/i* breathe out

espirazi'one *nf* exhalation; (scadenza) expiry

espli'care *vt* carry on

esplicita'mente *adv* explicitly

e'splicito *adj* explicit

e'splodere ① *vi* explode ② *vt* ‹arma› fire

esplo'rare *vt* explore

esplora|'tore, -trice *nmf* explorer; **giovane esploratore** boy scout; **giovane esploratrice** girl guide

esplorazi'one *nf* exploration

esplosi'one *nf* explosion

esplo'sivo *adj & nm* explosive

espo'nente *nm* exponent; **2 all'~** superscript 2

esponenzi'ale *adj* exponential

e'sporre *vt* expose; display ‹merci›; (spiegare) expound; exhibit ‹quadri ecc›

e'sporsi *vr* (compromettersi) compromise oneself; (al sole) expose oneself; (alle critiche) lay oneself open

espor'tare *vt* Comm, Comput export

esporta|'tore, -trice *nmf* exporter

esportazi'one *nf* export

espo'simetro *nm* light meter

esposi|'tore, -trice [1] *nmf* exhibitor; [2] *nm* display rack

esposizi'one *nf* (mostra) exhibition; (in vetrina) display; (spiegazione ecc) exposition; (posizione, fotografia) exposure; **con ∼ a nord/sud** north-/south-facing. **esposizione a radiazioni** radiation exposure

e'sposto [1] *pp di* ESPORRE [2] *adj* exposed; ⟨merce⟩ on show; ⟨spiegato⟩ set out; **∼ a nord/sud** north-/south-facing [3] *nm* submission

espressa'mente *adv* expressly; **non l'ha detto ∼** he didn't put it in so many words

espressi'one *nf* expression

espressio'nismo *nm* expressionism

espressio'nista *adj & nmf* expressionist

espressio'nistico *adj* expressionistic

espres'sivo *adj* expressive

e'spresso [1] *pp di* ESPRIMERE [2] *adj* express [3] *nm* (lettera) special delivery; (treno) express train; (caffè) espresso; **per ∼** ⟨spedire⟩ [by] express [post]; **piatto ∼** meal made to order

e'sprimere *vt* express

e'sprimersi *vr* express oneself

espropri'are *vt* dispossess

espropriazi'one *nf* Jur expropriation

e'sproprio *nm* expropriation

espulsi'one *nf* expulsion

e'spulso *pp di* ESPELLERE

esqui'mese *adj & nmf* Eskimo

es'senza *nf* essence

essenzi'ale [1] *adj* essential [2] *nm* important thing; **l'∼** (di teoria ecc) the bare bones; **l'∼ è ...** (la cosa più importante) the main thing is ...

essenzial'mente *adv* essentially

'essere [1] *vi* be; **c'è** there is; **ci sono** there are; **ci sono!** (ho capito) I've got it!; **ci siamo!** (siamo arrivati) here we are at last!; **non ce n'è più** there's none left; **c'è di che essere contenti** there's a lot to be happy about; **che ora è?** –**sono le dieci** what time is it? –it's ten o'clock; **chi è?** –**sono io** who is it? –it's me; **è stato detto che** it has been said that; **siamo in due** there are two of us; **questa camicia è da lavare** this shirt is to be washed; **non è da te** it's not like you; **∼ di** belong to; (provenire da) be

from; **∼ per** (favorevole) be in favour of; **se fossi in te, ...** if I were you, ...; **sarà!** if you say so!; **come sarebbe a dire?** what are you getting at?

[2] *v aux* have; (in passivi) be; **siamo arrivati** we have arrived; **ci sono stato ieri** I was there yesterday; **sono nato a Torino** I was born in Turin; **è riconosciuto come...** he is recognized as ...

[3] *nm* being; **∼ umano** human being; **∼ vivente** living creature

essic'care *vt* dry

essic'cato *adj* dried; ⟨noce di cocco⟩ desiccated

'esso, -a *pers pron* he, she; (cosa, animale) it

est *nm* east; **l'Est europeo** Eastern Europe

'estasi *nf* ecstasy; **andare in ∼ per** go into raptures over

estasi'are *vt* enrapture

estasi'arsi *vr* go into raptures

e'state *nf* summer

e'statico *adj* ecstatic

estempo'raneo *adj* impromptu

e'stendere *vt* extend

e'stendersi *vr* spread; (allungarsi) stretch

estensione *nf* extension; (ampiezza) expanse; Mus range. **estensione del file** Comput file extension

esten'sivo *adj* extensive

estenu'ante *adj* exhausting

estenu'are *vt* exhaust

estenu'arsi *vr* exhaust oneself

'estere *nm* ester

esteri'ore *adj & nm* exterior

esteriorità *nf* outward appearance; **badare all'∼** judge by appearances

esterioriz'zare *vt* externalize

esterior'mente *adv* externally; (di persone) outwardly

esterna'mente *adv* on the outside

ester'nare *vt* express, show

e'sterno, -a [1] *adj* external; (scala) outside; **per uso ∼** for external use only [2] *nm* Archit exterior; (in film) location shot [3] *nmf* day-pupil

'estero [1] *adj* foreign [2] *nm* foreign countries *pl*; **all'∼** abroad; **ministero degli esteri** ≈ Foreign Office Br, State Department Am

esterofi'lia *nf* xenophilia

este'rofilo *adj* xenophile

esterre'fatto *adj* horrified

e'steso [1] *pp di* ESTENDERE [2] *adj* extensive; (diffuso) widespread; **per ∼** ⟨scrivere⟩ in full

e'steta *nmf* aesthete

e'stetica *nf* aesthetics

estetica'mente *adv* aesthetically

esteticità *nf* aestheticism

e'stetico *adj* aesthetic; ‹*chirurgia, chirurgo*› plastic

este'tismo *nm* (dottrina, carattere) aestheticism

este'tista *nmf* beautician

estima'tore, -trice *nmf* fan

'estimo *nm* estimate

e'stinguere *vt* extinguish; close ‹*conto*›

e'stinguersi *vr* die out

e'stinto, -a ① *pp di* ESTINGUERE ② *nmf* deceased

estin'tore *nm* [fire] extinguisher

estinzi'one *nf* extinction; (di incendio) putting out

estir'pare *vt* uproot; extract ‹*dente*›; fig eradicate ‹*crimine, malattia*›

estirpazi'one *nf* eradication; (di dente) extraction

e'stivo *adj* summer *attrib*

'estone *adj & nm* Estonian

E'stonia *nf* Estonia

e'storcere *vt* extort

estorsi'one *nf* extortion

e'storto *pp di* ESTORCERE

estradizi'one *nf* extradition

estra'gone *nm* tarragon

estra'ibile *adj* removable

e'straneo, -a ① *adj* extraneous; (straniero) foreign ② *nmf* stranger

estrani'are *vt* estrange

estrani'arsi *vr* become estranged

estrapo'lare *vt* extrapolate

e'strarre *vt* extract; (sorteggiare) draw

e'stratto ① *pp di* ESTRARRE ② *nm* extract; (brano) excerpt; (documento) abstract. **estratto conto** statement [of account], bank statement

estrazi'one *nf* extraction; (a sorte) draw. **estrazione a premi** prize draw

estrema'mente *adv* extremely

estre'mismo *nm* extremism

estre'mista *nmf* extremist

estremità ① *nf inv* extremity; (di una corda) end; ② *pl* Anat extremities

e'stremo ① *adj* extreme; (ultimo) last; **misure estreme** drastic measures; **fare un ~ tentativo** make one last try; **l'Estremo Oriente** the Far East; **~ saluto** Mil military funeral; **l'estrema unzione** last rites ② *nm* (limite) extreme; **all'~** in the extreme; **passare da un ~ all'altro** go from one extreme to the other; **estremi** *pl* (di documento) main points; (di reato) essential elements; **essere agli estremi** be at the end of one's tether; **andare agli estremi** go to extremes; **essere all'~ delle forze** have no strength left

'estro *nm* (disposizione artistica) talent; (ispirazione) inspiration; (capriccio) whim

e'strogeno *nm* oestrogen

estro'mettere *vt* expel

estromissi'one *nf* ejection

e'stroso *adj* talented; (capriccioso) unpredictable

estro'verso ① *adj* extroverted ② *nm* extrovert

estu'ario *nm* estuary

esube'rante *adj* exuberant

esube'ranza *nf* exuberance

e'subero *nm* **esubero cassa integrazione** voluntary redundancy

esu'lare *vi* **~ da** be beyond the scope of

'esule *nmf* exile

esul'tante *adj* exultant

esul'tanza *nf* exultation

esul'tare *vi* rejoice

esu'mare *vt* exhume

età *nf* age; **raggiungere la maggiore ~** come of age; **un uomo di mezz'~ a** middle-aged man; **avere la stessa ~** be the same age; **che ~ gli daresti?** how old would you say he was?; **fin dalla più tenera ~** from his/her etc earliest years; **in ~ avanzata** of advanced years; **è senza ~** it's hard to tell his age. **età del bronzo** Bronze Age. **età della pensione** retirement age

e'tano *nm* ethane

eta'nolo *nm* ethanol

'etere *nm* ether. **etere etilico** ether

e'tereo *adj* ethereal

eterna'mente *adv* eternally

eternità *nf* eternity; **è un'~ che non la vedo** I haven't seen her for ages

e'terno *adj* eternal; ‹*questione, problema*› age-old; fig ‹*discorso, conferenza*› never-ending; **in ~** *fam* for ever; **giurare amore ~** swear undying love; **un ~ bambino** a child

etero'geneo *adj* diverse, heterogeneous

eterosessu'ale *adj & nmf* heterosexual

eterosessualità *nf* heterosexuality

'etica *nf* ethics

eti'chetta¹ *nf* label; (con il prezzo) price-tag

eti'chetta² *nf* (cerimoniale) etiquette

etichet'tare *vt* label

etichetta'trice *nf* labelling machine

etichetta'tura *nf* (operazione) labelling

'etico *adj* ethical

eti'lometro *nm* Breathalyzer®

etimolo'gia *nf* etymology

e'tiope *adj & nmf* Ethiopian

Eti'opia *nf* Ethiopia

eti'opico *adj* Ethiopian

'Etna nm Etna

et'nia nf ethnic group

'etnico adj ethnic

etnolo'gia nf ethnology

e'trusco adj & nmf Etruscan

'ettaro nm hectare

+ettino suff **cosettina** nf small thing; **è una cosettina da niente** it's nothing

'etto, **etto'grammo** nm hundred grams, quarter pound

+etto suff **cameretta** nf little bedroom; **scherzetto** nf prank; **piccoletto** nm pej shorty

et'tolitro nm hectolitre

euca'lipto nm eucalyptus

eucari'stia nf Eucharist

eufe'mismo nm euphemism

eufe'mistico adj euphemistic

eufo'ria nf elation; Med euphoria

eu'forico adj elated; Med euphoric

euge'netica nf eugenics

eu'nuco nm eunuch

EUR abbr (**euro**) e

Eur'asia nf Eurasia

eurasi'atico adj Eurasian

'EURATOM nf abbr (**Comunità Europea dell'Energia Atomica**) EURATOM

euro+ pref Euro+

'euro nm inv Fin euro

eurobbligazi'one nf Eurobond

euro'cheque nm inv Eurocheque

Euro'city nm inv Rail international intercity

eurodepu'tato nm Euro MP, MEP

eurodi'visa nf Eurocurrency

euro'dollaro nm Eurodollar

Eu'ropa nf Europe

europe'ismo nm Europeanism

euro'peo, -a adj & nmf European

euro'scettico nm Euro-sceptic

eutana'sia nf euthanasia

evacu'are vt evacuate

evacuazi'one nf evacuation

e'vadere ① vt evade; (sbrigare) deal with ② vi ∼ **da** escape from

evane'scente adj vanishing

evan'gelico adj evangelical

evange'lista nm evangelist

evan'gelo nm = VANGELO

evapo'rare vi evaporate

evaporazi'one nf evaporation

evasi'one nf escape; (fiscale) evasion; fig escapism

evasiva'mente adv evasively

eva'sivo adj evasive

e'vaso, -a ① pp di EVADERE

② nmf fugitive

eva'sore nm **evasore fiscale** tax evader

eveni'enza nf eventuality; **in ogni** ∼ if need be

e'vento nm event

eventu'ale adj possible

eventualità nf inv eventuality; **in ogni** ∼ at all events; **nell'**∼ **che** in the event that

eventual'mente adv if necessary

ever'sivo adj subversive

evi'dente adj evident

evidente'mente adv evidently

evi'denza nf evidence; **mettere in** ∼ emphasize; **mettersi in** ∼ make oneself conspicuous; **arrendersi all'**∼ face the facts

evidenzi'are vt highlight

evidenzia'tore nm (penna) highlighter

evi'rare vt emasculate

evi'tare vt avoid; (risparmiare) spare

'evo nm age

evo'care vt evoke

evolu'tivo adj evolutionary

evo'luto ① pp di EVOLVERE ② adj evolved; (progredito) progressive; ‹civiltà, nazione› advanced; **una donna evoluta** a modern woman

evoluzi'one nf evolution; (di ginnasta, aereo) circle

e'volvere vt develop

e'volversi vr evolve

ev'viva int hurray; ∼ **il Papa!** long live the Pope!; **gridare** ∼ cheer; ∼ **la modestia!** what modesty!

ex prep ex, former; **ex moglie** ex-wife

ex 'aequo adv **arrivare** ∼ come in joint first

ex-Jugo'slavia nf ex-Yugoslavia

ex-jugo'slavo adj & nmf ex-Yugoslav

ex 'libris nm inv bookplate

ex'ploit nm inv feat, exploit

'extra ① adj inv extra; ‹qualità› first-class ② nm inv extra

extracomuni'tario, -a ① adj non-EC, non-EU ② nmf immigrant from outside the EU

extraconiu'gale adj extramarital

extraeuro'peo adj non-European

extraparlamen'tare adj extraparliamentary

extrasco'lastico adj extra-curricular

extrasensori'ale adj extrasensory

extrater'restre nmf extra-terrestrial

extrauniversi'tario adj extramural

ex 'voto nm inv ex voto

Ff

fa¹ *nm inv* Mus (chiave, nota) F

fa² *adv* ago; **due mesi ~** two months ago

fabbi'sogno *nm* requirements *pl*, needs *pl*. **fabbisogno dello Stato** government spending estimates

'fabbrica *nf* factory

fabbri'cabile *adj* ‹area, terreno› that can be built on

fabbri'cante *nm* manufacturer. **fabbricante d'armi** arms manufacturer

fabbri'care *vt* build; (produrre) manufacture; (fig: inventare) fabricate

fabbri'cato *nm* building

fabbricazi'one *nf* manufacturing; (costruzione) building

'fabbro *nm* blacksmith

fac'cenda *nf* matter; **faccende** *pl* **domestiche** housework *sg*

faccendi'ere *nm* wheeler-dealer

fac'chino *nm* porter

'faccia *nf* face; (di foglio) side; **~ a ~** face to face; **~ tosta** cheek; **voltar ~** change sides; **di ~** (palazzo) opposite; **alla ~ di** (fam: a dispetto di) in spite of; **alla ~!** (stupore) bloody hell!

facci'ata *nf* façade; (di foglio) side; (fig: esteriorità) outward appearance

fa'cente *nmf* **facente funzioni** deputy

fa'ceto *adj* facetious; **tra il serio e il ~** half joking

fa'cezia *nf* (battuta) witticism

fa'chiro *nm* fakir

'facile *adj* easy; (affabile) easy-going; **essere ~ alle critiche** be quick to criticize; **essere ~ al riso** laugh a lot; **~ a farsi** easy to do; **è ~ che piova** it's likely to rain

facilità *nf* ease; (disposizione) aptitude; **avere ~ di parola** express oneself well. **facilità d'uso** ease of use, user-friendliness

facili'tare *vt* facilitate

facilitazi'one *nf* facility; **facilitazioni** *pl* Fin special terms; **facilitazioni** *pl* **di pagamento** easy terms; **facilitazioni** *pl* **creditizie** credit facilities

facil'mente *adv* (con facilità) easily; (probabilmente) probably

faci'lone *adj* slapdash

facilone'ria *nf* slapdash attitude

facino'roso *adj* violent

facoltà *nf inv* faculty; (potere) power; **essere nel pieno possesso delle proprie ~** be compos mentis

facolta'tivo *adj* optional; **fermata facoltativa** request stop

facol'toso *adj* wealthy

fac'simile *nm inv* facsimile

fac'totum ① *nm inv* man Friday ② *nf inv* girl Friday

'faggio *nm* beech

fagi'ano *nm* pheasant

fagio'lino *nm* French bean

fagi'olo *nm* bean; **a ~** ‹arrivare, capitare› at the right time. **fagiolo borlotto** borlotti bean. **fagiolo bianco di Spagna** runner bean, haricot bean

fagoci'tare *vt* gobble up ‹società›

fa'gotto *nm* bundle; Mus bassoon

Fahren'heit *adj* Fahrenheit

'faida *nf* feud

fai da te *nm* do-it-yourself, DIY

fa'ina *nf* weasel

fa'lange *nf* (dito, Mil) phalanx

fal'cata *nf* stride

'falce *nf* scythe. **falce e martello** (simbolo) the hammer and sickle

fal'cetto *nm* sickle

falci'are *vt* cut; fig mow down

falci'ata *nf* (quantità d'erba) swathe

falcia'trice *nf* [lawn]mower

'falco *nm* hawk

fal'cone *nm* falcon

'falda *nf* stratum; (di neve) flake; (di cappello) brim; (di cappotto, frac) coat-tails; (pendio) slope. **falda freatica** water table

fale'gname *nm* carpenter

falegname'ria *nf* carpentry

fa'lena *nf* moth

'Falkland *nfpl* **le [isole] ~** the Falklands

'falla *nf* leak

fal'lace *adj* deceptive

'fallico *adj* phallic

fallimen'tare *adj* disastrous; Jur bankruptcy

falli'mento *nm* Comm bankruptcy; fig failure

fal'lire ① *vi* Comm go bankrupt; fig fail ② *vt* miss ‹colpo›

fal'lito ① *adj* unsuccessful ② *adj & nm* bankrupt

'fallo *nm* fault; (errore) mistake; Sport foul; (imperfezione) flaw; **senza ~** without fail; ┄┄>

cogliere in ∼ catch red-handed; **mettere un piede in** ∼ slip. **fallo di mano** (in calcio) handball

falò nm inv bonfire

fal'sare vt alter; (falsificare) falsify

falsa'riga nf **sulla** ∼ **di** along the same lines as

fal'sario, -a nmf forger; (di documenti) counterfeiter

fal'setto nm falsetto

falsifi'care vt fake; (contraffare) forge

falsificazi'one nf (di documenti) falsification

falsità nf falseness

'falso ① adj false; (sbagliato) wrong; ⟨opera d'arte ecc⟩ fake; ⟨gioielli, oro⟩ imitation; **essere un** ∼ **magro** be fatter than one looks
② nm forgery; **giurare il** ∼ commit perjury. **falso in atto pubblico** forgery of a legal document

'fama nf fame; (reputazione) reputation

'fame nf hunger; **aver** ∼ be hungry; **fare la** ∼ barely scrape a living; **da** ∼ ⟨stipendio⟩ miserly; **avere una** ∼ **da lupo** be ravenous

fa'melico adj ravenous

famige'rato adj infamous

fa'miglia nf family. **famiglia affidataria** foster family, foster home

famili'are ① adj family attrib; (ben noto) familiar; (senza cerimonie) informal
② nm relative, relation

familiarità nf familiarity; (informalità) informality

familiariz'zarsi vr familiarize oneself

fa'moso adj famous

fa'nale nm lamp; Auto ecc light. **fanali posteriori** pl Auto rear lights

fana'lino nm **fanalino di coda** Auto tail light; **essere il** ∼ **di coda** fig bring up the rear, be the back marker

fa'natico, -a ① adj fanatical; **essere** ∼ **di calcio/cinema** be a football/cinema fanatic
② nmf fanatic

fana'tismo nm fanaticism

fanciul'lezza nf childhood

fanci'ullo, -a nmf liter young boy; young girl

fan'donia nf lie; **fandonie!** nonsense!

fan'fara nf fanfare; (complesso) brass band

fanfaro'nata nf brag; **fanfaronate** pl bragging

fanfa'rone, -a nmf braggart

fan'ghiglia nf mud

'fango nm mud

fan'goso adj muddy

fannul'lone, -a nmf idler

fantasci'enza nf science fiction

fanta'sia nf fantasy; (immaginazione) imagination; (capriccio) fancy; (di tessuto) pattern; **fantasie** pl (sciocchezze) moonshine

fantasi'oso adj ⟨stilista, ragazzo⟩ imaginative; ⟨resoconto⟩ improbable, fanciful

fan'tasma nm ghost; **essere il** ∼ **di se stesso** be a shadow of one's former self; **città fantasma** ghost town; **governo fantasma** shadow cabinet

fantasti'care vi day-dream, fantasize

fantasti che'ria nf day-dream, fantasy

fan'tastico adj fantastic; ⟨racconto⟩ fantasy attrib

'fante nm infantryman; (nelle carte) jack

fante'ria nm infantry

fan'tino nm jockey

fan'toccio nm puppet

fanto'matico adj (inafferrabile) phantom attrib; (immaginario) mythical

fara'butto nm trickster

fara'ona nf (uccello) guinea-fowl

'farcia nf stuffing; (di torta) filling

far'cire vt stuff; fill ⟨torta⟩

far'cito adj stuffed; ⟨dolce⟩ filled

fard nm inv blusher

far'dello nm bundle; fig burden

'fare ① vt do; make ⟨dolce, letto, ecc⟩; (recitare la parte di) play; (trascorrere) spend; ∼ **una pausa/un sogno** have a break/a dream; ∼ **colpo su** impress; ∼ **paura a** frighten; ∼ **piacere a** please; **farla finita** put an end to it; ∼ **l'insegnante** be a teacher; ∼ **lo scemo** play the idiot; ∼ **una settimana al mare** spend a week at the seaside; **3 più 3 fa 6** 3 and 3 makes 6; **quanto fa?** –**fanno 50 euro** how much is it? –it's 50 euros; **far** ∼ **qualcosa a qualcuno** get somebody to do something; (costringere) make somebody do something; ∼ **vedere** show; **fammi parlare** let me speak; **niente a che** ∼ **con** nothing to do with; **non c'è niente da** ∼ (per problema) there is nothing we/you etc can do; **fa caldo/buio** it's warm/dark; **non fa niente** it doesn't matter; **strada facendo** on the way; **farcela** (riuscire) manage
② vi **fai in modo di venire** try and come; ∼ **da** act as; ∼ **per** make as if to; ∼ **presto** be quick; **non fa per me** it's not for me
③ nm (comportamento) manner; **sul far del giorno** at daybreak

fa'retto nm spot[light]

far'falla nf butterfly

farfal'lino nm (cravatta) bow tie

farfugli'are vt mutter

fa'rina nf flour. **farina di ceci** chickpea flour, gram flour. **farina gialla** maize flour. **farina integrale** wholemeal flour. **farina lattea** powdered milk for babies. **farina d'ossa** bonemeal

fari'nacei nmpl starchy food sg

fa'ringe *nf* pharynx

farin'gite *nf* pharyngitis

fari'noso *adj* ⟨neve⟩ powdery; ⟨mela⟩ soft; ⟨patata⟩ floury

farma'ceutico *adj* pharmaceutical; **industria farmaceutica** pharmaceuticals industry

farma'cia *nf* pharmacy; (negozio) chemist's [shop]. **farmacia di turno** duty pharmacy

farma'cista *nmf* chemist, pharmacist

'farmaco *nm* drug; **essere sotto farmaci** be on medication

'faro *nm* Auto headlight; Aeron beacon; (costruzione) lighthouse; **abbassare i fari** dip one's headlights; **accendere i fari** switch on one's lights. **fari antinebbia** *pl* fog lamps. **fari posteriori** *pl* rear lights

farragi'noso *adj* confused

'farsa *nf* farce

far'sesco *adj* farcical

'farsi *vr* (diventare) get; (sl: drogarsi) shoot up; ∼ **avanti** come forward; ∼ **i fatti propri** mind one's own business; ∼ **la barba** shave; ∼ **la villa** fam buy a villa; ∼ **il ragazzo** fam find a boyfriend; ∼ **due risate** have a laugh; ∼ **male** hurt oneself; ∼ **un nome** make a name for oneself; **farsela sotto** fam wet oneself

Far 'west *nm* Wild West

fa'scetta *nf* strip; (per capelli) hair band; (di giornale) wrapper

'fascia *nf* band; (zona) area; (ufficiale) sash; (benda) bandage; (di smoking) cummerbund; (in statistica) bracket. **fascia per capelli** hair band. **fascia elastica** crepe bandage; (ventriera) girdle. **fascia d'età** age bracket, age group. **fascia d'ozono** ozone layer. **fascia di reddito** income bracket

fasci'are *vt* bandage; cling to ⟨fianchi⟩

fasci'arsi *vr* bandage; ∼ **la testa prima di rompersela** worry about something that might never happen

fascia'tura *nf* dressing; (azione) bandaging

fascicola|'tore, -trice *nmf* sorter

fa'scicolo *nm* file; (di rivista) issue; (libretto) booklet

fa'scina *nf* faggot

'fascino *nm* fascination

fasci'noso *adj* charming

'fascio *nm* bundle; (di fiori) bunch. **fascio di luce** beam of light

fa'scismo *nm* fascism

fa'scista *adj & nmf* fascist

'fase *nf* phase; **il motore è fuori** ∼ the timing is wrong; **sono fuori** ∼ I'm not firing on all four cylinders; **essere in** ∼ **di miglioramento** be on the mend, be

recovering; **essere in** ∼ **di espansione** be expanding

fast 'food *nm inv* fast food; (ristorante) fast food restaurant

fa'stidio *nm* nuisance; (scomodo) inconvenience; **fastidi** *pl* (preoccupazioni) worries; (disturbi) troubles; **dar** ∼ **a qualcuno** bother somebody

fastidi'oso *adj* tiresome

'fasto *nm* pomp

fa'stoso *adj* sumptuous

fa'sullo *adj* bogus

'fata *nf* fairy

fa'tale *adj* fatal; (inevitabile) fated; **donna fatale** femme fatale

fata'lismo *nm* fatalism

fata'lista ① *nmf* fatalist ② *adj* fatalistic

fatalità *nf inv* fate; (caso sfortunato) misfortune

fatal'mente *adv* inevitably

fa'tato *adj* ⟨anello, bacchetta⟩ magic

fa'tica *nf* effort; (lavoro faticoso) hard work; (stanchezza, di metalli) fatigue; **a** ∼ with great difficulty; **è** ∼ **sprecata** it's a waste of time; **fare** ∼ **a fare qualcosa** find it difficult to do something; **senza [nessuna]** ∼ without [any] effort; **fare** ∼ **a finire qualcosa** struggle to finish something; **uomo di fatica** odd-job man

fati'caccia *nf* pain

fati'care *vi* toil; ∼ **a** (stentare) find it difficult to

fati'cata *nf* effort; (sfacchinata) grind

fati'coso *adj* tiring; (difficile) difficult

fati'scente *adj* crumbling

'fato *nm* fate

fat'taccio *nm hum* foul deed

fat'tezze *nfpl* features

fat'tibile *adj* feasible

fatti'specie *nf* **nella** ∼ in this case

'fatto ① *pp di* FARE; **ormai è fatta!** what's done is done ② *adj* made; ∼ **a mano/in casa** handmade/home-made; **essere ben** ∼ ⟨persona⟩ have a nice figure; **un uomo** ∼ a grown man ③ *nm* fact; (azione) action; (avvenimento) event; (faccenda) business, matter; **sa il** ∼ **suo** he knows his business; **le ho detto il** ∼ **suo** I told her what I thought of her; **di** ∼ in fact; **in** ∼ **di** as regards; ∼ **sta che** the fact remains that; **mettere di fronte al** ∼ **compiuto** present with a fait accompli

fat'tore *nm* (causa, Math) factor; (di fattoria) farm manager. **fattore di protezione solare** protection factor

fatto'ria *nf* farm; (casa) farmhouse

fatto'rino *nm* messenger [boy]. **fattorino d'albergo** bellboy

fattucchi'era *nf* witch

fat'tura *nf* (stile) cut; (lavorazione) workmanship; Comm invoice. **fattura di acquisto** purchase invoice. **fattura pro-forma** pro forma [invoice]. **fattura di vendita** sales invoice

fattu'rare *vt* invoice; (adulterare) adulterate

fattu'rato *nm* turnover, sales *pl*

fatturazi'one *nf* invoicing, billing

'fatuo *adj* fatuous

'fauci *nfpl* (di leone) maw *sg*, jaws *pl*

'fauna *nf* fauna

'fausto *adj* propitious

fau'tore *nm* supporter

'fava *nf* broad bean

fa'vella *nf* speech

fa'villa *nf* spark

'favo *nm* honeycomb

'favola *nf* fable; (fiaba) story; (oggetto di pettegolezzi) laughing-stock; **è una ∼!** (meraviglia) it's divine!

favo'loso *adj* fabulous

fa'vore *nm* favour; **essere a ∼ di** be in favour of; **per ∼** please; **di ∼** ‹condizioni, trattamento› preferential; **col ∼ delle tenebre** under cover of darkness

favoreggia'mento *nm* Jur aiding and abetting

favo'revole *adj* favourable

favorevol'mente *adv* favourably

favo'rire *vt* favour; (promuovere) promote; **vuol ∼?** (a cena, pranzo) will you have some?; (entrare) will you come in?; **favorisca alla cassa** please pay at the cash-desk; **favorisca i documenti** your papers please

favo'rito, -a *adj & nmf* favourite

fax *nm inv* fax; **inviare via ∼** fax, send by fax. **fax a carta comune** plain paper fax

fa'xare *vt* fax

fazi'one *nf* faction

faziosità *nf* bias

fazi'oso *nm* sectarian

fazzolet'tino *nm* **fazzolettino [di carta]** [paper] tissue

fazzo'letto *nm* handkerchief, hanky; (da testa) headscarf

feb'braio *nm* February

'febbre *nf* fever; **avere la ∼** have *o* run a temperature. **febbre da fieno** hay fever

febbrici'tante *adj* fevered

feb'brile *adj* feverish

febbril'mente *adv* feverishly

'feccia *nf* dregs *pl*

'fecola *nf* potato flour

fecon'dare *vt* fertilize

feconda'tore *nm* fertilizer

fecondazi'one *nf* fertilization. **fecondazione artificiale** artificial insemination. **fecondazione in vitro** in vitro fertilization, IVF

fe'condo *adj* fertile

'fede *nf* faith; (fiducia) trust; (anello) wedding ring; **in buona/mala ∼** in good/ bad faith; **prestar ∼ a** believe; **tener ∼ alla parola** keep one's word; **aver ∼ in qualcuno** have faith in somebody, believe in somebody; **degno di ∼** reliable; **in ∼** Yours faithfully

fe'dele ① *adj* faithful ② *nmf* believer, worshipper; (seguace) follower; **i fedeli** the faithful

fedel'mente *adv* faithfully

fedeltà *nf* faithfulness; **alta fedeltà** high fidelity

'federa *nf* pillowcase

fede'rale *adj* federal

federa'lismo *nm* federalism

federa'lista *adj* federalist

fede'rato *adj* federate

federazi'one *nf* federation

fe'difrago, -a ① *adj* faithless; *hum* two-timing ② *nm* faithless wretch; *hum* two-timer

fe'dina *nf* **avere la ∼ penale sporca/ pulita** have a/no criminal record

fega'telli *nmpl* (di maiale) pork liver

fega'tino *nm* **fegatini** *pl* **di pollo** chicken livers

'fegato *nm* liver; fig guts *pl*; **mangiarsi il ∼, rodersi il ∼** be consumed with rage

'felce *nf* fern

fe'lice *adj* happy; (fortunato) lucky; **∼ come una Pasqua** blissfully happy

felice'mente *adv* happily; (con successo) successfully

felicità *nf* happiness

felici'tarsi *vr* **∼ con** congratulate

felicitazi'oni *nfpl* congratulations

fe'lino *adj* feline

'felpa *nf* (indumento) sweatshirt; (stoffa) felt

fel'pato *adj* brushed; ‹passo› stealthy

'feltro *nm* felt; (cappello) felt hat

'femmina *nf* female

femmi'nile ① *adj* feminine; ‹rivista, abbigliamento› women's; ‹sesso› female ② *nm* feminine

femminilità *nf* femininity

femmi'nismo *nm* feminism

'femore *nm* femur

'fendere *vt* split

fendi'nebbia *nm inv* fog lamp

fendi'tura *nf* split; (in roccia) crack

fe'nice *nf* phoenix

feni'cottero *nm* flamingo

fenome'nale *adj* phenomenal

fe'nomeno *nm* phenomenon

'feretro *nm* coffin

feri'ale *adj* weekday; **giorno feriale** weekday

'ferie *nfpl* holidays; **andare in ∼** go on holiday; **prendere le ∼** go on holiday; **prendere delle ∼** take time off; **prendere un giorno di ∼** take a day off

feri'mento *nm* wounding

fe'rire *vt* wound; (in incidente) injure; fig hurt

fe'rirsi *vr* injure oneself

fe'rita *nf* wound. **ferita d'arma da fuoco** gunshot wound

fe'rito ① *adj* wounded ② *nm* wounded person; Mil casualty; **∼ grave** seriously injured person; **i feriti** the injured

feri'toia *nf* loophole; **feritoie** *pl* **per le schede di espansione** Comput expansion slots

'ferma *nf* Mil period of service

fermacal'zoni *nm inv* cycle clip

fermaca'pelli *nm inv* hair slide

ferma'carte *nm inv* paperweight

ferma'coda *nm inv* (di stoffa) scrunchie

fermacra'vatta *nm inv* tiepin

ferma'fogli *nm inv* bulldog clip

fer'maglio *nm* clasp; (spilla) brooch; (per capelli) hair slide

ferma'mente *adv* firmly

ferma'porta *nm inv* doorstop

fer'mare ① *vt* stop; (fissare) fix; Jur detain ② *vi* stop

fer'marsi *vr* stop

fer'mata *nf* stop; **'∼ prenotata'** 'bus stopping'; **senza fermate** (tragitto) non-stop. **fermata dell'autobus** bus stop. **fermata obbligatoria** compulsory stop. **fermata a richiesta** request stop

fermen'tare *vi* ferment

fermentazi'one *nf* fermentation

fer'mento *nm* ferment; (lievito) yeast; **essere in ∼** be in/get into a tizzy

fer'mezza *nf* firmness

'fermo ① *adj* still; (veicolo) stationary; (stabile) steady; (orologio) not working; **∼!** don't move!; **∼ restando che ...** it being understood that ...; **'∼ per manutenzione'** 'closed for repairs' ② *nm* Jur detention; Mech catch; **in stato di fermo** in custody. **fermo immagine** TV freeze frame. **fermo posta** poste restante, general delivery Am

fer'net® *nm inv* bitter digestive liqueur

fe'roce *adj* fierce, ferocious; (bestia) wild; (freddo, dolore) unbearable

feroce'mente *adv* fiercely, ferociously

fe'rocia *nf* ferocity

fer'raglia *nf* scrap iron

ferra'gosto *nm* 15 August (bank holiday in Italy); (periodo) August holidays *pl*

ferra'menta *nfpl* ironmongery *sg*; **negozio di ferramenta** ironmonger's

fer'rare *vt* shoe (cavallo)

fer'rato *adj* **∼ in** (preparato in) well up in

'ferreo *adj* iron

'ferro *nm* iron; (attrezzo) tool; (di chirurgo) instrument; **di ∼** (memoria) excellent; (alibi) cast-iron; **salute di ∼** iron constitution; **ai ferri** (bistecca) grilled; **essere ai ferri corti** be at daggers drawn; **mettere il paese a ∼ e fuoco** put a country to the sword; **i ferri del mestiere** the tools of the trade. **ferro battuto** wrought iron. **ferro da calza** knitting needle. **ferro di cavallo** horseshoe. **ferro da stiro** iron. **ferro a vapore** steam iron

fer'roso *adj* ferrous

ferro'vecchio *nm* scrap merchant

ferro'via *nf* railway, railroad Am; **Ferrovie** *pl* **dello Stato** Italian State Railways

ferrovi'ario *adj* railway *attrib*, railroad Am *attrib*

ferrovi'ere *nm* railwayman, railroad worker Am

'fertile *adj* fertile

fertilità *nf* fertility

fertiliz'zante *nm* fertilizer

fertilizzazi'one *nf* fertilization

fer'vente *adj* blazing; fig fervent

fervente'mente *adv* fervently

'fervere *vi* (preparativi); be well under way

fervida'mente *adv* fervently

'fervido *adj* fervent; **fervidi auguri** best wishes

fer'vore *nm* fervour; (di discussione) heat

'fesa *nf* (carne) rump

fesse'ria *nf* **dire/fare una ∼** fam say/do something stupid

'fesso ① pp di FENDERE ② *adj* cracked; (fam: sciocco) foolish ③ *nm* (fam: idiota) fool; **far ∼ qualcuno** fam con somebody

fes'sura *nf* crack; (per gettone ecc) slot. **fessura [per la scheda] di espansione** Comput expansion slot

'festa *nf* feast; (giorno festivo) holiday; (compleanno) birthday; (ricevimento) party; fig joy; **fare ∼ a qualcuno** welcome somebody; **essere in ∼** be on holiday; **far ∼** celebrate; **della ∼** (vestito, tovaglia) best; **conciare qualcuno per le feste** give somebody a sound thrashing; **le feste** (Natale, Capodanno ecc) the holidays. **festa di addio al celibato** stag night, stag party. **festa di addio al nubilato** hen party. **festa di compleanno** birthday ⋯⫶

party. **festa della mamma** Mother's
Day, Mothering Sunday. **festa
mascherata** fancy dress party. **festa
nazionale** public holiday, legal holiday
Am. **festa del papà** Father's Day

festai'olo-a ⓵ *adj* festive
⓶ *nmf* party animal

festeggia'mento *nm* celebration;
(manifestazione) festivity; **festeggiamenti** *pl*
celebrations

festeggi'are *vt* celebrate; (accogliere
festosamente) give a hearty welcome to

fe'stino *nm* party

'festival *nm inv* festival. **festival
cinematografico** film festival

festività *nfpl* festivities

fe'stivo *adj* holiday; (lieto) festive; **festivi**
pl public holidays

fe'stone *nm* (nel cucito) scallop, scollop; (di
carta) paper chain

fe'stoso *adj* merry

fe'tente ⓵ *adj* evil smelling; fig
revolting
⓶ *nmf fam* bastard

fe'ticcio *nm* fetish

'feto *nm* foetus

fe'tore *nm* stench

'fetta *nf* slice; **a fette** sliced. **fetta
biscottata** slices of crispy toast-like
bread

fet'tina *nf* thin slice

fet'tuccia *nf* tape; (con nome) name tape

fettuc'cine *nfpl* ribbon-shaped pasta

feu'dale *adj* feudal

'feudo *nm* feud

fez *nm inv* fez

FFSS *abbr* (**Ferrovie dello Stato**)
Italian State Railways

fi'aba *nf* fairy-tale

fia'besco *adj* fairy-tale *attrib*

fi'acca *nf* weariness; (indolenza) laziness;
battere la ~ be sluggish

fiac'care *vt* weaken

fi'acco *adj* weak; (indolente) slack; (stanco)
weary; 〈partita〉 dull

fi'accola *nf* torch

fiacco'lata *nf* torchlight procession

fi'ala *nf* phial

fia'letta *nf* phial. **fialetta puzzolente**
stink bomb

fi'amma *nf* flame; Naut pennant; **in
fiamme** in flames; **andare in fiamme** go up
in flames; **dare alle fiamme** commit to the
flames; **alla ~** Culin flambé; **le Fiamme
Gialle** body responsible for border control
and investigating fraud. **fiamma
ossidrica** blowtorch

fiam'mante *adj* flaming; **nuovo ~**
brand new

fiam'mata *nf* blaze

fiammeggi'are ⓵ *vi* blaze
⓶ *vt* singe 〈pollo〉

fiam'mifero *nm* match

fiam'mingo, -a ⓵ *adj & nm* Flemish
⓶ *nmf* Fleming

fian'cata *nf* wing

fiancheggi'are *vt* border; fig support

fi'anco *nm* side; (di persona) hip; (di animale)
flank; Mil wing; **al mio ~** by my side; **~ a
~** 〈lavorare〉 side by side

Fi'andre *nfpl* **le ~** Flanders

fia'schetta *nf* hip flask

fiaschette'ria *nf* wine shop

fi'asco *nm* flask; fig fiasco; **fare ~** be a
fiasco

fia'tare *vi* breathe; (parlare) breathe a
word

fi'ato *nm* breath; (vigore) stamina;
strumenti a ~ wind instruments; **avere il
~ corto** be short of breath; **senza ~**
breathlessly; **tutto d'un ~** 〈bere, leggere〉
all in one go

'fibbia *nf* buckle

'fibra *nf* fibre; **fibre** *pl* (alimentari) roughage.
fibre artificiali *pl* man-made fibres.
fibra ottica optical fibre; **a fibre ottiche**
〈cavo〉 fibre optic. **fibra sintetica** man-
made fibre, synthetic. **fibra di vetro**
fibreglass

fi'broma *nm* fibroid

fi'broso *adj* fibrous

ficca'naso *nmf inv* nosey parker

fic'care *vt* thrust; drive 〈chiodo ecc〉; (fam:
mettere) shove

fic'carsi *vr* thrust oneself; (nascondersi)
hide; **~ nei guai** get oneself into trouble

'fiche *nf inv* (gettone) chip

'fico¹ *nm* (albero) fig-tree; (frutto) fig. **fico
d'India** prickly pear; **non me ne importa
un ~ [secco]** *fam* I don't give a damn; **non
capisce un ~ [secco]** *fam* he doesn't
understand a bloody thing; **non vale un ~
[secco]** *fam* it's totally worthless

'fico², -a ⓵ *nmf fam* cool sort
⓶ *adj* cool

fidanza'mento *nm* engagement;
rompere il ~ break off one's engagement,
break it off

fidan'zarsi *vr* get engaged

fidan'zata *nf* (ufficiale) fiancée; (innamorata)
girlfriend

fidan'zato *nm* (ufficiale) fiancé; (innamorato)
boyfriend

fi'darsi *vr* **~ di** trust

fi'dato *adj* trustworthy

'fido ⓵ *adj* 〈compagno〉 loyal
⓶ *nm* devoted follower; Comm credit

fi'ducia *nf* confidence; **degno di ~**
trustworthy; **persona di ~** reliable
person; **di ~** 〈fornitore, banca〉 regular,

usual; **avere ∼ in se stessi** believe in oneself; **incarico di ∼** important job

fiduci'ario, -a ① *adj* ⟨*rapporto, transazione*⟩ based on trust ② *nmf* trustee

fiduci'oso *adj* hopeful

fi'ele *nm* bile; *fig* bitterness; **amaro come il ∼** bitter

fienagi'one *nf* haymaking

fie'nile *nm* barn

fi'eno *nm* hay

fi'era *nf* fair. **fiera commerciale** trade fair. **fiera del libro** book fair

fie'rezza *nf* (dignità) pride

fi'ero *adj* proud

fi'evole *adj* faint; ⟨*luce*⟩ dim

'fifa *nf* fam jitters; **aver ∼** have the jitters

fi'fone, -a *nmf* fam chicken, yellowbelly

FIGC *nf abbr* **(Federazione Italiana Gioco Calcio)** Italian Football Association

Figi *nfpl* **le isole ∼** Fiji

'figli *nmpl* children

'figlia *nf* daughter. **figlia unica** only child

figli'are *vi* ⟨*animale*⟩; calve

figli'astra *nf* stepdaughter

figli'astro *nm* stepson

'figlio *nm* son; (generico) child; **è ∼ d'arte** he was born in a trunk. **figlio adottivo** adopted child. **figlio di papà** spoilt brat. **figlio di puttana** vulg son of a bitch. **figlio unico** only child

figli'occia *nf* goddaughter

figli'occio *nm* godson

figli'ola *nf* girl

figlio'lanza *nf* offspring

figli'olo *nm* boy; **figlioli** *pl* children

'figo, -a *adj* ▶ FICO

fi'gura *nf* figure; (aspetto esteriore) shape; (illustrazione) illustration; (in carte da gioco) picture [card]; **far bella/brutta ∼** make a good/bad impression; **mi hai fatto fare una brutta ∼** you made me look a fool; **che ∼!** how embarrassing! **figura paterna** father figure. **figura retorica** figure of speech

figu'raccia *nf* bad impression

figu'rare ① *vt* represent; (simboleggiare) symbolize; (immaginare) imagine ② *vi* (far figura) cut a fine figure; (in lista) appear, figure; **∼ in testa al cartellone** Theat get top billing

figu'rarsi *vr* (immaginarsi) imagine; **figurati!** imagine that!; **posso? –[ma] figurati!** may I? –of course!

figura'tivo *adj* figurative

figu'rina *nf* (da raccolta) cigarette card; (statuetta) figurine

figuri'nista *nmf* dress designer

figu'rino *nm* fashion sketch

fi'guro *nm* **un losco ∼** a shady character

figu'rone *nm* **fare un ∼** make an excellent impression

fil *nm* **fil di ferro** wire

'fila *nf* line; (di soldati ecc) file; (di oggetti) row; (coda) queue; **di ∼** in succession; **fare la ∼** queue [up], stand in line Am; **in ∼ indiana** single file

fila'mento *nm* filament

fi'lanca® *nf* type of synthetic stretch fabric

fi'lante *adj* ⟨*formaggio*⟩ stringy; **stella filante** (di carta) streamer

filantro'pia *nf* philanthropy

filan'tropico *adj* philanthropic

fi'lantropo, -a *nmf* philanthropist

fi'lare ① *vt* spin; Naut pay out ② *vi* (andarsene) run away; ⟨*liquido*⟩ trickle; ⟨*ragionamento*⟩ hang together; **fila!** fam scram!; **∼ con** (fam: amoreggiare) go out with; **∼ dritto** toe the line ③ *nm* (di viti, alberi) row

filar'monica *nf* (orchestra) orchestra

filar'monico *adj* philharmonic

fila'strocca *nf* rigmarole; (per bambini) nursery rhyme

filate'lia *nf* philately, stamp collecting

fila'telico, -a *nmf* philatelist

fi'lato ① *adj* spun; (ininterrotto) running; (continuato) uninterrupted; **di ∼** (subito) immediately; **andare dritto ∼ a** go straight to ② *nm* yarn

fila|'tore, -'trice *nmf* spinner

fila'tura *nf* spinning; (filanda) spinning mill

'file *nm inv* Comput file

filetta'tura *nf* (di vite) thread

fi'letto *nm* (bordo) border; ⟨*di vite*⟩ thread; Culin fillet. **filetto ai ferri** grilled fillet of beef

fili'ale ① *adj* filial ② *nf* Comm branch

filibusti'ere *nm* rascal

fili'forme *adj* stringy

fili'grana *nf* filigree; (su carta) watermark

fi'lippica *nf* invective

filip'pino, -a *adj & nmf* Filipino

film *nm inv* film. **film catastrofico** disaster movie. **film comico** comedy. **film drammatico** drama. **film di fantascienza** science fiction film. **film giallo** thriller. **film a lungometraggio** feature film. **film dell'orrore** horror film. **film poliziesco** detective film. **film verità** docudrama

fil'mare *vt* film

fil'mato ① *adj* filmed ② *nm* short film

fil'mina nf film strip

fil'mino nm cine film

'**filo** nm thread; (tessile) yarn; (metallico) wire; (di lama) edge; (venatura) grain; (di perle) string; (d'erba) blade; (di luce) ray; un ~ di (poco) a drop of; con un ~ di voce in a whisper; per ~ e per segno in detail; fare il ~ a qualcuno fancy somebody; perdere il ~ lose the thread; essere appeso a un ~ be hanging by a thread; essere sul ~ del rasoio be on a knife-edge; un ~ d'aria a breath of air; un ~ di speranza a glimmer of hope. **filo interdentale** dental floss. **filo a piombo** plumb-line. **filo spinato** barbed wire

filo+ pref philo+

filoameri'cano adj pro-American

'**filobus** nm inv trolleybus

filocomu'nista adj pro-communist

filodiffusi'one nf rediffusion

filodram'matica nf amateur dramatic society

filolo'gia nf philology

filo'logico adj philological

fi'lologo, -a nmf philologist

filon'cino nm ≈ French stick

fi'lone nm vein; (di pane) long loaf, Vienna loaf

fi'loso adj stringy

filoso'fia nf philosophy

fi'losofo, -a nmf philosopher

fil'traggio nm filtering

fil'trare vt filter

'**filtro** nm filter. **filtro chiamate** Teleph call screening. **filtro dell'olio** oil filter

'**filza** nf string

fin ▸ FINO[1]

fi'nale [1] adj final
[2] nm end
[3] nf Sport final

fina'lista nmf finalist

finalità nf inv finality; (scopo) aim

final'mente adv at last; (in ultimo) finally

fi'nanza nf finance; **Guardia di** ~ body of police officers responsible for border control and for investigating fraud; **intendenza di** ~ inland revenue office

finanzia'mento nm funding

finanzi'are vt fund, finance

finanzi'aria nf investment company; (holding) holding company; Jur finance bill

finanzi'ario adj financial

finanzia|'tore, -trice nmf backer

finanzi'ere nm financier; (guardia di finanza) customs officer

finché conj until; (per tutto il tempo che) as long as

'**fine** [1] adj fine; (sottile) thin; ⟨udito, vista⟩ keen; (raffinato) refined

[2] nf end; alla ~ in the end; alla fin ~ after all; in fin dei conti when all's said and done; che ~ ha fatto Anna? what became of Anna?; che ~ hanno fatto le chiavi? where have the keys got to?; senza ~ endless. **fine settimana** weekend

[3] nm aim; andare a buon ~ be successful; to lo dico a fin di bene I'm telling you for your own good

fi'nestra nf window. **finestra a battenti** casement window

fine'strella nf Comput box. **finestrella di aiuto** help window. **finestrella di dialogo** dialog box, dialogue box Br. **finestrella di messaggio** message box

fine'strino nm Rail, Auto window

fi'nezza nf fineness; (sottigliezza) thinness; (raffinatezza) refinement

'**fingere** vt pretend; feign ⟨affetto ecc⟩

'**fingersi** vr pretend to be

fini'menti nmpl finishing touches; (per cavallo) harness sg

fini'mondo nm end of the world; fig pandemonium

fi'nire vt finish, end; (smettere) stop; (diventare, andare a finire) end up; **finiscila!** stop it!

fi'nito adj finished; (abile) accomplished

fini'tura nf finish

finlan'dese [1] adj Finnish
[2] nmf Finn
[3] nm (lingua) Finnish

Fin'landia nf Finland

'**fino**[1] prep ~ a till, until; (spazio) as far as; ~ all'ultimo to the last; ~ alla nausea ⟨ripetere, leggere⟩ ad nauseam; fin da (tempo) since; (spazio) from; fin dall'inizio from the beginning; fin qui as far as here; fin troppo too much; ~ a che punto how far

'**fino**[2] adj fine; (acuto) subtle; (puro) pure

fi'nocchio nm fennel; (fam: omosessuale) poof

fi'nora adv so far, up till now

'**finta** nf pretence, sham; Sport feint; far ~ di pretend to; far ~ di niente act as if nothing had happened; per ~ (per scherzo) for a laugh

'**finto, -a** [1] pp di FINGERE
[2] adj false; (artificiale) artificial; finta pelle fake leather; fare il ~ tonto act dumb

finzi'one nf pretence

fi'occo nm bow; (di neve) flake; (nappa) tassel; Naut jib; **coi fiocchi** fig excellent; **fiocchi** pl di avena oatmeal; (cotti) porridge; **fiocchi** pl di granoturco cornflakes; **fiocchi** pl di latte cottage cheese. **fiocco di neve** snowflake

fi'ocina nf harpoon

fi'oco adj weak; ⟨luce⟩ dim

fi'onda nf catapult

fio'raio, **-a** *nmf* florist

fiorda'liso *nm* cornflower

fi'ordo *nm* fiord

fi'ore *nm* flower; **a fior d'acqua** on the surface of the water; **a fiori** flowery; **in ~** flowering; **fior di** (abbondanza) a lot of; **il fior ~ di** the cream of; **ha i nervi a fior di pelle** his nerves are on edge; **nel ~ degli anni** in one's prime; **è il suo ~ all'occhiello** that's feather in his cap; **suo figlio è il suo ~ all'occhiello** his son is his pride and joy. **fiori d'arancio** *pl* orange blossom. **fiore di campo** wild flower. **fior di latte** (formaggio) soft cheese. **fiore selvatico** wild flower. **fiori di zucca fritti** *pl* fried pumpkin flowers

fio'rente *adj* ⟨industria⟩ booming

fioren'tina *nf* (bistecca) T-bone steak

fioren'tino *adj* Florentine

fio'retto *nm* (scherma) foil; Relig act of mortification

fi'ori *nmpl* (nelle carte) clubs

fiori'era *nf* container

fio'rino *nm* **fiorino olandese** guilder

fio'rire *vi* flower; ⟨albero⟩ blossom; fig flourish

fio'rista *nmf* florist; (negozio) florist's

fiori'tura *nf* flowering; (di albero) blossoming; (insieme di fiori) flowers *pl*

fio'rone *nm* (fico) early fig

fi'otto *nm* (di sangue) spurt; **scorrere a fiotti** pour out; **piove a fiotti** the rain is pouring down

Fi'renze *nf* Florence

'firma *nf* signature; (nome) name

firma'mento *nm* firmament

fir'mare *vt* sign

firma'tario, **-a** *nmf* signatory

fir'mato *adj* ⟨quadro, lettera⟩ signed; ⟨abito, borsa⟩ designer *attrib*

fisar'monica *nf* accordion

fi'scale *adj* fiscal

fisca'lista *nmf* tax consultant

fiscaliz'zare *vt* finance with government funds

fischi'are **①** *vi* whistle; **mi fischiano le orecchie** I've got a ringing noise in my ears; fig my ears are burning **②** *vt* whistle; (in segno di disapprovazione) boo

fischi'ata *nf* whistle

fischiet'tare *vt* whistle

fischiet'tio *nm* whistling

fischi'etto *nm* whistle

'fischio *nm* whistle; **fischi** *pl* Theat booing; **prendere fischi per fiaschi** get hold of the wrong end of the stick

'fisco *nm* Inland Revenue Br, IRS Am; (tasse) taxation; **il ~** the taxman

'fisica *nf* physics. **fisica atomica** atomic physics. **fisica nucleare** nuclear physics

fisica'mente *adv* physically

'fisico, **-a** **①** *adj* physical **②** *nmf* physicist. **fisico nucleare** atomic scientist **③** *nm* physique

'fisima *nf* whim

fisiolo'gia *nf* physiology

fisio'logico *adj* physiological

fisi'ologo, **-a** *nmf* physiologist

fisiono'mia *nf* features *pl*, face; (di paesaggio) appearance

fisiotera'pia *nf* physiotherapy

fisiotera'pista *nmf* physiotherapist, physio fam

fissa'mente *adv* fixedly; (permanentemente) steadily

fis'sare *vt* fix, fasten; (guardare fissamente) stare at; arrange ⟨appuntamento, ora⟩

fis'sarsi *vr* (stabilirsi) settle; (fissare lo sguardo) stare; **~ su** (ostinarsi) set one's mind on; **~ di fare qualcosa** become obsessed with doing something

fissa'tivo *nm* Phot fixative

fis'sato, **-a** **①** *adj* (al muro) fixed; ⟨prezzo⟩ agreed **②** *nm* (persona) person with an obsession

fissa'tore *nm* hair spray

fissazi'one *nf* fixation; (ossessione) obsession

'fisso **①** *adj* fixed; **un lavoro ~** a regular job; **senza fissa dimora** of no fixed abode; **avere una ragazza fissa** have a steady girlfriend **②** *adv* fixedly; **guardare ~ negli occhi qualcuno** stare at somebody; ⟨innamorato⟩ gaze into somebody's eyes

fitotera'pia *nf* herbalism; (per piante) plant health

'fitta *nf* sharp pain

fit'tavolo *nm* tenant

fit'tizio *adj* fictitious

'fitto¹ **①** *adj* thick; **~ di** full of **②** *nm* depth

'fitto² *nm* (affitto) rent; **dare a ~** let; **prendere a ~** rent; (noleggiare) hire

fiu'mana *nf* swollen river; fig stream

fi'ume **①** *nm* river; fig stream **②** *adj inv* ⟨discussione⟩ endless, never-ending; **romanzo fiume** roman-fleuve

fiu'tare *vt* smell; ⟨animale⟩ scent; snort ⟨cocaina⟩

fi'uto *nm* [sense of] smell; fig nose

'flaccido *adj* flabby

fla'cone *nm* bottle

flagel'lare *vt* flog

flagellazi'one *nf* flagellation

fla'gello *nm* scourge

fla'grante *adj* flagrant; **in** ~ in the act
fla'menco *nm* flamenco
flan *nm inv* baked custard
fla'nella *nf* flannel
'flangia *nf* (su ruota) flange
flash *nm inv* Journ newsflash
flau'tista *nfm* flautist
'flauto *nm* flute **flauto diritto** recorder. **flauto traverso** flute
'flebile *adj* feeble
fle'bite *nf* phlebitis
flebo'clisi *nf inv* drip
'flemma *nf* calm; Med phelgm
flem'matico *adj* phlegmatic
fles'sibile *adj* flexible
flessibilità *nf* flexibility
flessi'one *nf* (del busto in avanti) forward bend; (a terra) sit-up; (delle ginocchia) kneebend; (di vendite, produzione) drop, fall
fles'sivo *adj* Gram inflected
'flesso ① *pp di* FLETTERE ② *adj* Gram inflected
flessu'oso *adj* supple
'flettere *vt* bend
flip-'flop *nm inv* flip flop
flir'tare *vi* flirt
F.lli *abbr* (**fratelli**) Bros.
'floppy disk *nm inv* floppy disk
'flora *nf* flora
'florido *adj* flourishing
florovival'istica *nf* ⟨attività⟩ growing under glass
'floscio *adj* limp; (flaccido) flabby
'flotta *nf* fleet
flot'tiglia *nf* flotilla
flu'ente *adj* fluent
fluidità *nf* fluidity; (nel parlare) fluency
flu'ido *nm* fluid
flu'ire *vi* flow
fluore'scente *adj* fluorescent
fluore'scenza *nf* fluorescence
flu'oro *nm* fluorine
fluo'ruro *nm* fluoride
'flusso *nm* flow; Med flux; (del mare) flood-tide. **flusso e riflusso** ebb and flow. **flusso di cassa** cash flow
'flutti *nmpl* billows
fluttu'ante *adj* fluctuating
fluttu'are *vi* ⟨prezzi⟩ fluctuate; ⟨moneta⟩ float
fluttuazi'one *nf* fluctuation; (di moneta) floating
fluvi'ale *adj* river
fo'bia *nf* phobia
'fobico *adj* phobic
'foca *nf* seal

fo'caccia *nf* (pane) flat bread; (dolce) ≈ raisin bread
fo'cale *adj* ⟨distanza, punto⟩ focal
focaliz'zare *vt* get into focus ⟨fotografia⟩; focus ⟨attenzione⟩; define ⟨problema⟩
'foce *nf* mouth
fo'chista *nm* stoker
foco'laio *nm* Med focus; fig centre
foco'lare *nm* hearth; (caminetto) fireplace; Techn furnace
fo'coso *adj* fiery
'fodera *nf* lining; (di libro) dust-jacket; (di poltrona ecc) loose cover
fode'rare *vt* line; cover ⟨libro⟩
fode'rato *adj* lined; ⟨libro⟩ covered
'foga *nf* impetuosity
'foggia *nf* fashion; ⟨maniera⟩ manner; (forma) shape
foggi'are *vt* mould
'foglia *nf* leaf; (di metallo) foil; **mangiare la** ~ catch on. **foglia di alloro** bay leaf
fogli'ame *nm* foliage
fogliet'tino *nm* **fogliettino igienico** (per pannolini) nappy liner
fogli'etto *nm* (pezzetto di carta) piece of paper
'foglio *nm* sheet; (pagina) leaf; (di domanda, iscrizione) form. **foglio di carta** sheet of paper. **foglio elettronico** Comput spreadsheet. **foglio illustrativo** instruction leaflet. **foglio protocollo** foolscap. **foglio rosa** provisional driving licence. **foglio di via** expulsion order
'fogna *nf* sewer
fogna'tura *nf* sewerage
fohn *nm inv* hair dryer
fo'lata *nf* gust
fol'clore *nm* folklore
folclo'ristico *adj* folk; (bizzarro) weird
folgo'rante *adj* ⟨idea⟩ brilliant
folgo'rare ① *vi* (splendere) shine ② *vt* (con un fulmine) strike
folgo'rato *adj* fig thunderstruck
folgorazi'one *nf* (da fulmine, elettrica) electrocution; (fig: idea) brainwave
'folgore *nf* thunderbolt
'folio: in ~ *adj* folio
'folla *nf* crowd
'folle *adj* mad; ⟨velocità⟩ breakneck; **in** ~ Auto in neutral; **andare in** ~ Auto coast
folleggi'are *vi* paint the town red
folle'mente *adv* madly
fol'letto *nm* elf
fol'lia *nf* madness; **alla** ~ ⟨amare⟩ to distraction; **costare una** ~ cost the earth; **fare una** ~ go mad; **farei follie per lei** I'd do anything for her
'folto *adj* thick

fomen'tare *vt* stir up

fond'ale *nm* Theat backcloth. **fondale marino** sea bed

fonda'menta *nfpl* foundations

fondamen'tale *adj* fundamental

fondamenta'lismo *nm* fundamentalism

fondamenta'lista *nmf* fundamentalist

fonda'mento *nm* (di principio, teoria) foundation; **privo di ~** groundless, without foundation

fon'dant *nm inv* fondant

fon'dare *vt* establish; base ⟨ragionamento, accusa⟩

fon'darsi *vr* be based (**su** on)

fon'dato *adj* ⟨ragionamento⟩ well-founded; **~ su** based on

fondazi'one *nf* establishment; **fondazioni** *pl* (di edificio) foundations

fon'delli *nmpl* **prendere qualcuno per i ~** fam pull somebody's leg

fon'dente *adj* ⟨cioccolato⟩ dark

'fondere ①*vt* melt; fuse ⟨metallo⟩ ②*vi* melt; ⟨metallo⟩ fuse; ⟨colori⟩ blend

fonde'ria *nf* foundry

'fondersi *vr* melt; Comm merge

'fondo ①*adj* deep; **è notte fonda** it's the middle of the night ②*nm* bottom; (fine) end; (sfondo) background; (indole) nature; (somma di denaro) fund; (feccia) dregs *pl*; (terreno) land; [sci pl] **~** cross-country skiing; **andare a ~** ⟨nave⟩ sink; **in ~** after all; **in ~ a** at the end/bottom of; **in ~ in ~** deep down; **fino in ~** right to the end; ⟨capire⟩ thoroughly; **andare fino in ~ a qualcosa** get to the bottom of something; **dar ~ a** use up; **a doppio ~** false bottomed; **toccare il ~** touch bottom; fig hit rock bottom; **senza ~** bottomless; **fondi** *pl* (denaro) funds; (di caffè) grounds; **fondi** *pl* **di magazzino** old stock; **fondi** *pl* **neri** slush fund. **articolo di fondo** (in giornale) editorial; **fondo fiduciario** trust fund. **fondo [comune] di investimento** investment trust. **Fondo Monetario Internazionale** International Monetary Fund. **fondo pensione** pension fund. **fondo per la ricostruzione** disaster fund. **fondo sopravvenienze passive** contigency fund. **fondo stradale** road surface

fondo'tinta *nm inv* foundation [cream]

fon'due *nf* (di formaggio) fondue

fon'duta *nf* fondue

fo'nema *nm* phoneme

fo'netica *nf* phonetics

fo'netico *adj* phonetic

fonolo'gia *nf* phonology

fon'tana *nf* fountain; (di farina) well

fonta'nella *nf* drinking fountain; Anat fontanelle

'fonte ①*nf* spring; fig source ②*nm* font

fon'tina *nf* soft mature cheese often used in cooking

'football *nm* **football americano** American football

foraggi'are *vt* fodder

fo'raggio *nm* forage

fo'rare ①*vt* pierce; punch ⟨biglietto⟩ ②*vi* puncture

fo'rarsi *vr* ⟨gomma, pallone⟩ go soft

fora'tura *nf* puncture

'forbici *nfpl* scissors; **un paio di ~** a pair of scissors. **forbici da siepe** garden shears. **forbici a zigzag** pinking shears, pinking scissors

forbi'cina *nf* earwig; **forbicine** *pl* (per le unghie) nail scissors

for'bito *adj* erudite

'forca *nf* fork; (patibolo) gallows *pl*

for'cella *nf* fork; (per capelli) hairpin

for'chetta *nf* fork; **essere una buona ~** enjoy one's food

forchet'tata *nf* (quantità) forkful

forchet'tone *nm* carving fork

for'cina *nf* hairpin

'forcipe *nm* forceps *pl*

for'cone *nm* pitchfork

for'ense *adj* forensic

fo'resta *nf* forest. **foresta equatoriale** rain forest. **Foresta Nera** Black Forest

fore'stale *adj* forest *attrib*; **la Forestale** branch of the police with responsibility for national forests

foreste'ria *nf* guest rooms *pl*

foresti'ero, **-a** ①*adj* foreign ②*nmf* foreigner

for'fait *nm inv* fixed price; **dare ~** (abbandonare) give up; **prezzo [a] forfait** all-in price; **contratto [a] forfait** lump-sum contract

forfe'tario *adj* flat rate

'forfora *nf* dandruff

'forgia *nf* forge

forgi'are *vt* forge

'forma *nf* form; (sagoma) shape; Culin mould; (per scarpe) shoe tree; (di calzolaio) last; **essere in ~** be in good form; **in (gran) ~** (very) fit, on (top) form; **a ~ di** in the shape of; **sotto ~ di** in the form of; **forme** *pl* (del corpo) curves; (convenzioni) appearances

formag'giera *nf* [covered] cheese board

formag'gino *nm* processed cheese

for'maggio *nm* cheese. **formaggio erborinato** blue cheese

for'male *adj* formal

forma'lina *nf* formalin

forma'lismo *nm* formalism

forma'lista *nmf* formalist

formalità *nf inv* formality

formaliz'zare *vt* formalize

formaliz'zarsi *vr* stand on ceremony, be formal

formal'mente *adv* formally

'forma 'mentis *nf inv* way of thinking, mindset

for'mare *vt* form; dial ⟨*numero di telefono*⟩

for'marsi *vr* form; (sviluparsi) develop

for'mato *nm* size; (di libro, dischetto) format. **formato famiglia** economy pack, economy size. **formato tessera** ⟨*fotografia*⟩ passport-size

format'tare *vt* format

formattazi'one *nf* formatting

formazi'one *nf* formation; Sport line-up; **in ∼** in the process of being formed. **formazione professionale** vocational training. **formazione professionale postlaurea** graduate training scheme

for'mella *nf* tile

for'mica[1] *nf* ant

'formica[2]® *nf* Formica

formi'caio *nm* anthill

formichi'ere *nm* anteater

formico'lare *vi* ⟨*braccio ecc*⟩ tingle; **∼ di** be swarming with; **mi formicola la mano** I have pins and needles in my hand

formico'lio *nm* swarming; (di braccio ecc) pins and needles *pl*

formi'dabile *adj* (tremendo) formidable; (eccezionale) tremendous

for'mina *nf* mould

for'moso *adj* curvy

'formula *nf* formula; **assolvere con ∼ piena** acquit. **formula di cortesia** polite form of address

formu'lare *vt* formulate; (esprimere) express

formulazi'one *nf* formulation

for'nace *nf* furnace; (per laterizi) kiln

for'naio, -a *nmf* baker; (negozio) bakery

fornel'letto *nm* **fornelletto a gas** gas stove

for'nello *nm* stove; (di pipa) bowl. **fornello da campeggio** camping stove

fornicazi'one *nf* fornication

for'nire *vt* supply (di with); **∼ qualcosa a qualcuno** supply somebody with something

for'nirsi *vr* **∼ di** provide oneself with

forni'tore *nm* supplier. **fornitore di servizi [Internet]** [Internet] service provider

forni'tura *nf* supply; **forniture** *pl* per ufficio office supplies

'forno *nm* oven; (panetteria) bakery; **al ∼** roast; **da ∼** ⟨*stoviglie*⟩ ovenproof. **forno autopulente** self-cleaning oven. **forno crematorio** cremator. **forno elettrico** electric oven. **forno a gas** oven. **forno a microonde** microwave [oven]

'foro *nm* hole; (romano) forum; (tribunale) [law] court

'forse *adv* perhaps, maybe; **essere in ∼** be in doubt

forsen'nato, -a [1] *adj* mad [2] *nmf* madman; madwoman

'forte [1] *adj* strong; ⟨*colore*⟩ bright; ⟨*suono*⟩ loud; (resistente) tough; ⟨*spesa*⟩ considerable; ⟨*dolore*⟩ severe; ⟨*pioggia*⟩ heavy; (fam: simpatico) great; ⟨*taglia*⟩ large; **essere ∼ in qualcosa** be good at something [2] *adv* strongly; ⟨*parlare*⟩ loudly; (velocemente) fast; ⟨*piovere*⟩ heavily [3] *nm* (fortezza) fort; (specialità) strong point

for'tezza *nf* fortress; (forza morale) fortitude

fortifi'care *vt* fortify

fortifi'cato *adj* ⟨*città*⟩ walled

for'tino *nm* Mil blockhouse

for'tissimo *adj* ⟨*caffè, liquore*⟩ extra-strong

for'tuito *adj* fortuitous; **incontro fortuito** chance encounter

for'tuna *nf* fortune; (successo) success; (buona sorte) luck; **atterraggio di ∼** forced landing; **aver ∼** be lucky; **buona ∼!** good luck!; **di ∼** makeshift; **per ∼** luckily; **hai una ∼ sfacciata!** fam you lucky blighter!

fortu'nale *nm* storm

fortunata'mente *adv* fortunately

fortu'nato *adj* lucky, fortunate; ⟨*impresa*⟩ successful

fortu'noso *adj* ⟨*giornata*⟩ eventful

fo'runcolo *nm* pimple; (grosso) boil

forunco'loso *adj* spotty

'forza *nf* strength; (potenza) power; (fisica) force; **di ∼** by force; **a ∼ di** by dint of; **con ∼** hard; **∼!** come on!; **in ∼ di** under, in accordance with; **∼ maggiore** circumstances beyond one's control; **la ∼ pubblica** the police; **le forze armate** the armed forces; **per ∼** against one's will; (naturalmente) of course; **farsi ∼** bear up; **mare ∼ 8** force 8 gale; **bella ∼!** fam big deal!; **che ∼!** (che simpatico, divertente) cool eh?. **forza di gravità** [force of] gravity. **forza lavoro** workforce; **forze** *pl* **di mercato** market forces. **forza di volontà** will-power

for'zare *vt* force; (scassare) break open; (sforzare) strain

for'zato [1] *adj* forced; ⟨*sorriso*⟩ strained [2] *nm* convict

forza'tura *nf* (di cassaforte) forcing; **sostenere che ... è una ∼** to maintain that ... is forcing things

forzi'ere *nm* coffer

for'zuto *adj* strong

fo'schia *nf* haze, mist

'fosco *adj* dark

fo'sfato *nm* phosphate

'fosforo *nm* phosphorus

'fossa *nf* pit; (tomba) grave. **fossa biologica** cesspool. **fossa comune** mass grave. **fossa dell'orchestra** orchestra pit

fos'sato *nm* (di fortificazione) moat

fos'setta *nf* (di guancia) dimple

'fossile *nm* fossil

'fosso *nm* ditch; Mil trench

'foto *nf inv* fam photo; **fare delle ~** take some photos

foto'camera *nf* camera. **fotocamera digitale** digital camera, fam digicam

foto'cellula *nf* photocell

fotocomposi'|tore, -trice *nmf* filmsetter

fotocomposizi'one *nf* filmsetting, photo-composition

foto'copia *nf* photocopy

fotocopi'are *vt* photocopy

fotocopia'trice *nf* photocopier

foto'finish *nm inv* photo finish

foto'genico *adj* photogenic

fotogiorna'lista *nmf* photojournalist

fotogra'fare *vt* photograph

fotogra'fia *nf* (arte) photography; (immagine) photograph; **fare fotografie** take photographs. **fotografia aerea** aerial photography

foto'grafico *adj* photographic; **macchina fotografica** camera

fo'tografo, -a *nmf* photographer; (negozio) photographer's

foto'gramma *nm* frame

fotoincisi'one *nf* photoengraving

fotomo'dello, -a *nmf* [photographer's] model

fotomon'taggio *nm* photomontage

foto'ottica *nf* camera shop and optician's

fotorepor'tage *nm inv* photo essay

fotore'porter *nmf inv* newspaper photographer; (di rivista) magazine photographer

fotori'tocco *nm* retouching

fotoro'manzo *nm* photo story

foto'sintesi *nf* photosynthesis

'fottere *vt* (sl: rubare) nick; (sl: imbrogliare) screw; vulg fuck, screw

'fottersene *vr* vulg not give a fuck; **va' a farti ~!** vulg fuck off!

fot'tuto *adj* (sl: maledetto) bloody

fou'lard *nm inv* scarf

foxhound *nm inv* foxhound

fox-'terrier *nm inv* fox terrier

fo'yer *nm inv* foyer

fra *prep* (in mezzo a due) between; (in un insieme) among; (tempo, distanza) in; **detto ~ noi** between you and me; **~ sé e sé** to oneself; **~ l'altro** what's more; **~ breve** soon; **~ quindici giorni** in two weeks' time; **~ tutti, siamo in venti** there are twenty of us altogether

fracas'sare *vt* smash

fracas'sarsi *vr* shatter

fracas'sato *adj* smashed

fra'casso *nm* din; (di cose che cadono) crash

fracas'sone, -a *nmf* clumsy person

'fradicio *adj* (bagnato) soaked; **ubriaco ~** blind drunk

'fragile *adj* fragile; fig frail

fragilità *nf* fragility; fig frailty

'fragola *nf* strawberry

fra'gore *nm* uproar; (di cose rotte) clatter; (di tuono) rumble

frago'roso *adj* uproarious; ⟨tuono⟩ rumbling; ⟨suono⟩ clanging

fra'grante *adj* fragrant

fra'granza *nf* fragrance

frain'tendere *vt* misunderstand

frain'tendersi *vr* be at cross-purposes

frain'teso *pp di* FRAINTENDERE

frammen'tario *adj* fragmentary

fram'mento *nm* fragment

fram'misto *adj* **~ di** interspersed with

'frana *nf* landslide; (fam: persona) walking disaster area

fra'nare *vi* slide down

franca'mente *adv* frankly

france'scano *adj & nm* Franciscan

fran'cese ① *adj* French ② *nm* Frenchman; (lingua) French ③ *nf* Frenchwoman

france'sina *nf* (scarpa) brogue

fran'chezza *nf* frankness; **in tutta ~** in all honesty

fran'chigia *nf* **franchigia bagaglio** (per aereo) baggage allowance

'Francia *nf* France

'franco¹ *adj* frank; Comm free; **farla franca** get away with something; **parlare ~** speak frankly. **franco a bordo** free on board. **franco domicilio** delivered free of charge. **franco fabbrica** ex-works; **franco di porto** carriage free, carriage paid

'franco² *nm* (moneta) franc

franco'bollo *nm* stamp

franco-cana'dese *adj & nmf* French Canadian

fran'cofono *adj* Francophone, French-speaking.

Franco'forte nf Frankfurt

fran'gente nm (onda) breaker; (scoglio) reef; (fig: momento difficile) crisis; **in quel ~** in the circumstances

fran'getta nf fringe

'frangia nf fringe

frangi'flutti nm inv bulwark

frangi'vento nm windbreak

fra'noso adj subject to landslides

fran'toio nm olive-press

frantu'mare vt shatter

frantu'marsi vr shatter

fran'tumi nmpl splinters; **in ~** smashed; **andare in ~** be smashed to smithereens

frappè nm inv milkshake

frap'porre vt interpose

frap'porsi vr intervene

fra'sario nm vocabulary; (libro) phrase book

'frasca nf [leafy] branch; **saltare di palo in ~** jump from subject to subject

'frase nf sentence; (espressione) phrase. **frase fatta** cliché

fraseolo'gia nf phrases pl

'frassino nm ash [tree]

frastagli'are vt make jagged

frastagl'iato adj jagged

frastor'nare vt daze

frastor'nato adj dazed

frastu'ono nm racket

'frate nm friar; (monaco) monk

fratel'lanza nf brotherhood

fratellastro nm step brother, half-brother

fratel'lino nm little brother

fra'tello nm brother; **fratelli** pl (fratello e sorella) brother and sister; Relig brethren. **fratello gemello** twin brother. **fratello di sangue** blood brother

fraternità nf brotherhood

fraterniz'zare vi fraternize

fra'terno adj brotherly

fratri'cida ① adj fratricidal ② nm fratricide

frat'taglie nfpl (di pollo ecc) giblets

frat'tanto adv in the meantime

frat'tura nf fracture

frattu'rare vt break

frattu'rarsi vr break

fraudo'lento adj fraudulent

frazi'one nf fraction; (borgata) hamlet; (paese) administrative division of a municipality

'freccia nf arrow; Auto indicator

frecci'ata nf (osservazione pungente) cutting remark

fredda'mente adv coldly

fred'dare vt cool; (fig: con sguardo, battuta) cut down; (uccidere) kill

fred'dezza nf coldness

'freddo adj & nm cold; **aver ~** be cold; **fa ~** it's cold; **a ~** (sparare) in cold blood; (lavare) in cold water

freddo'loso adj sensitive to cold, chilly

fred'dura nf pun

fre'gare vt rub; (fam: truffare) cheat; (fam: rubare) swipe; **fregarsene** fam not give a damn; **me ne frego!** I don't give a damn!; **chi se ne frega!** what the heck!

fre'garsi vr (occhi, mani)

fre'gata nf rub; (nave) frigate

frega'tura nf fam (truffa) swindle; (delusione) letdown

'fregio nm Archit frieze; (ornamento) decoration

'fregola nf rutting; **avere la ~ di fare qualcosa** fam have a craze for doing something

fre'mente adj quivering

'fremere vi quiver

'fremito nm quiver

fre'nare ① vt brake; fig restrain; hold back (lacrime, impazienza) ② vi brake

fre'narsi vr check oneself

fre'nata nf **fare una ~ brusca** hit the brakes

frene'sia nf frenzy; (desiderio smodato) craze

frenetica'mente adv frantically

fre'netico adj frantic

'freno nm brake; fig check; **togliere il ~** release the brake; **usare il ~** apply the brake; **tenere a ~** restrain; **tenere a ~ la lingua** hold one's tongue; **porre un ~ a** fig rein in; **freni** pl **a disco** disc brakes. **freno a mano** handbrake. **freno a pedale** footbrake

frequen'tare vt frequent; attend (scuola ecc); mix with (persone); **non ci frequentiamo più** we don't see each other any more

fre'quente adj frequent; **di ~** frequently

fre'quenza nf frequency; (assiduità) attendance

'fresa nf mill

fre'sare vt mill

fre'schezza nf freshness; (di temperatura) coolness

'fresco ① adj fresh; (temperatura) cool; **~ di studi** fresh out of school; **stai ~!** fam you're for it!; **se ti vede stai ~** fam you're done for if he sees you ② nm coolness; **far ~** be cool; **mettere/tenere in ~** put/keep in a cool place; **al ~** (fam: in prigione) inside

fre'scura nf cool

'fresia nf freesia

'fretta *nf* hurry, haste; **aver ∼** be in a hurry; **far ∼ a qualcuno** hurry somebody; **in ∼ e furia** in a great hurry; **andarsene in ∼** rush away; **senza [nessuna] ∼** at your/his etc leisure

frettolosa'mente *adv* hurriedly

fretto'loso *adj* ⟨*persona*⟩ hasty; ⟨*lavoro*⟩ rushed, hurried

fri'abile *adj* crumbly

fricas'sea *nf* stewed meat served with an egg and lemon sauce

'friggere ❶ *vt* fry; **vai a farti ∼!** get lost! ❷ *vi* sizzle; **∼ di impazienza** be on tenterhooks

friggi'trice *nf* electric chip pan

frigidità *nf* frigidity

'frigido *adj* frigid

fri'gnare *vi* whine

fri'gnone, **-a** *nmf* whiner

'frigo *nm inv* fridge

frigo'bar *nm inv* minibar

frigocongela'tore *nm* fridge-freezer

frigo'rifero ❶ *adj* refrigerating; ⟨*camion*⟩ refrigerated ❷ *nm* refrigerator

fringu'ello *nm* chaffinch

'frisbee® *nm inv* frisbee

frit'tata *nf* omelette

frit'tella *nf* fritter; (fam: macchia d'unto) grease stain

'fritto ❶ *pp di* FRIGGERE ❷ *adj* fried; **essere ∼** be done for ❸ *nm* fried food. **fritto misto** mixed fried fish/vegetables

frit'tura *nf* (pietanza) fried dish. **frittura di pesce** variety of fried fish

frivo'lezza *nf* frivolity

'frivolo *adj* frivolous

frizio'nare *vt* rub

frizi'one *nf* friction; Mech clutch; (di pelle) rub

friz'zante *adj* fizzy; ⟨*vino*⟩ sparkling; ⟨*aria*⟩ bracing

'frizzo *nm* gibe

fro'dare *vt* defraud

'frode *nf* fraud. **frode fiscale** tax evasion; **con la ∼** Jur under false pretences

frol'lino *nm* (biscotto) ≈ shortbread biscuit

'frollo *adj* tender; ⟨*selvaggina*⟩ high; ⟨*persona*⟩ spineless; **pasta frolla** short[crust] pastry

'fronda *nf* [leafy] branch; fig rebellion

fron'doso *adj* leafy

fron'tale *adj* frontal; ⟨*scontro*⟩ head-on

'fronte ❶ *nf* forehead; (di edificio) front; **di ∼** opposite; **di ∼ a** opposite, facing; (a paragone) compared with ❷ *nm* Mil, Pol front; **far ∼ a** face

fronteggi'are *vt* face

fronte'spizio *nm* title page

fronti'era *nf* frontier, border

fron'tone *nm* pediment

'fronzolo *nm* frill

'frotta *nf* swarm; (di animali) flock

'frottola *nf* fib; **frottole** *pl* nonsense *sg*

fru'gale *adj* frugal

fru'gare ❶ *vi* rummage ❷ *vt* search

fru'ire *vi* **∼ di** make use of, take advantage of

frul'lare ❶ *vt* Culin whisk ❷ *vi* ⟨*ali*⟩ whirr

frul'lato *nm* **frullato di frutta** fruit drink with milk and crushed ice

frulla'tore *nm* [electric] mixer

frul'lino *nm* whisk

fru'mento *nm* wheat

frusci'are *vi* rustle

fru'scio *nm* rustle; (radio, giradischi) ground noise; (di acque) murmur

'frusta *nf* whip; (frullino) whisk

fru'stare *vt* whip

fru'stata *nf* lash

fru'stino *nm* riding crop

fru'strare *vt* frustrate

fru'strato *adj* frustrated

frustrazi'one *nf* frustration

'frutta *nf* fruit; **negozio di ∼ e verdura** greengrocer's. **frutta esotica** exotic fruit, tropical fruit. **frutta fresca di stagione** seasonal fruit. **frutta secca** nuts *pl*

frut'tare ❶ *vi* bear fruit; Comm give a return ❷ *vt* yield

frut'teto *nm* orchard

frutticol'tore *nm* fruit farmer

frutticol'tura *nf* fruit farming, fruit growing

frutti'era *nf* fruit bowl

frut'tifero *adj* ⟨*albero*⟩ fruit-bearing; Fin ⟨*deposito*⟩ interest-bearing

frutti'vendolo, **-a** *nmf* greengrocer

'frutto *nm* anche fig fruit; Fin yield; **frutti di bosco** *pl* fruits of the forest; **frutti di mare** *pl* seafood *sg*. **frutto della passione** passion fruit

fruttu'oso *adj* profitable

FS *abbr* (**Ferrovie dello Stato**) Italian State Railways

f.to *abbr* (**firmato**) signed

fu *adj* (defunto) late; **il fu signor Rossi** the late Mr Rossi

fuci'lare *vt* shoot, execute by firing squad

fucilazi'one *nf* execution [by firing squad]

fu'cile nm rifle. **fucile ad aria compressa** air rifle. **fucile a canne mozze** sawn-off shotgun

fuci'lata nf shot

fu'cina nf forge

'fuco nm kelp

'fucsia nf fuchsia

'fuga nf escape; (perdita) leak; (di ciclisti) breakaway; Mus fugue; **darsi alla** ∼ take to flight; **mettere qualcuno in** ∼ put somebody to flight. **fuga di cervelli** brain drain. **fuga di gradini** flight of steps. **fuga di notizie** leak. **fuga romantica** elopement

fu'gace adj fleeting

fug'gevole adj short-lived

fuggi'asco, -a nmf fugitive

fuggi'fuggi nm stampede

fug'gire vi flee; ⟨innamorati⟩ elope; fig fly

fuggi'tivo, -a nmf fugitive

'fulcro nm fulcrum

ful'gore nm splendour

fu'liggine nf soot

fuliggi'noso adj sooty

full nm inv (nel poker) full house

fulmi'nante adj (sguardo) withering; **è morto di leucemia** ∼ he died very soon after contracting leukaemia

fulmi'nare vt strike by lightning; (con sguardo) look daggers at; (con scarica elettrica) electrocute

fulmi'narsi vr burn out

fulmi'nato adj **rimanere** ∼ electrocute oneself

'fulmine nm lightning; **colpo di fulmine** fig love at first sight; **un** ∼ **a ciel sereno** a bolt from the blue

ful'mineo adj rapid; ⟨sguardo⟩ withering

'fulvo adj tawny

fumai'olo nm funnel; (di casa) chimney

fu'mante adj ⟨minestra, tazza⟩ steaming

fu'mare vt/i smoke; (in ebollizione) steam; 'vietato ∼' 'no smoking'

fu'mario adj (canna) flue

fu'mata nf (segnale) smoke signal

fuma|'tore, -trice nmf smoker; **non fumatori** ⟨scompartimento⟩ non-smoker, non-smoking

fu'metto nm comic strip; **fumetti** pl comics

'fumo nm smoke; (vapore) steam; fig hot air; **andare in** ∼ vanish; **vendere** ∼ put on an act; **cercava di vendere** ∼ it was all hot air; **fumi** pl (industriali) fumes; **sotto i fumi dell'alcol** under the influence of alcohol. **fumo passivo** passive smoking

fu'mogeno adj **cortina fumogena** smoke screen

fu'moso adj ⟨ambiente⟩ smoky; ⟨discorso⟩ vague

funambo'lesco adj acrobatic

fu'nambolo, -a nmf tightrope walker

'fune nf rope; (cavo) cable

'funebre adj funeral; (cupo) gloomy

fune'rale nm funeral

fu'nereo adj ⟨aria⟩ funereal

fu'nesto adj sad

'fungere vi ∼ **da** act as

'fungo nm mushroom; Bot, Med fungus; **funghi** pl Bot fungi. **fungo atomico** mushroom cloud. **fungo commestibile** edible mushroom

funico'lare nf funicular [railway]

funi'via nf cableway

funzio'nale adj functional

funzionalità nf functionality

funziona'mento nm functioning

funzio'nare vi work, function; ∼ **da** (fungere da) act as

funzio'nario nm official. **funzionario statale** civil servant

funzi'one nf function; (carica) office; Relig service; **entrare in** ∼ take up office; **mettere in** ∼ ⟨motore⟩ start up; **vivere in** ∼ **di** live for

fu'oco nm fire; (fisica, fotografia) focus; **far** ∼ fire; **dar** ∼ **a** set fire to; **andare a** ∼ go up in flames; **prendere** ∼ catch fire; **a** ∼ **vivo** ⟨cuocere⟩ on a high heat; **a** ∼ **lento** ⟨cuocere⟩ on a low heat; **'vietato accendere fuochi'** 'no campfires'; **fuochi** pl **d'artificio** fireworks. **fuoco amico** friendly fire. **fuoco di paglia** nine-days' wonder; **fuochi** pl **pirotecnici** pyrotechnics

fuorché prep except

fu'ori ① adv out; (all'esterno) outside; (all'aperto) outdoors; ∼**!** fam get out!; ∼ **i soldi!** fork up!; **andare di** ∼ (traboccare) spill over; **essere** ∼ **di sé** be beside oneself; **essere in** ∼ (sporgere) stick out; **far** ∼ fam get rid of; **fuori commercio** not for sale; ∼ **luogo** (inopportuno) out of place; ∼ **mano** out of the way; ∼ **moda** old-fashioned; ∼ **pasto** between meals; ∼ **pericolo** out of danger; ∼ **programma** unscheduled; ∼ **questione** out of the question; **fuori uso** out of use ② nm outside

fuori'bordo nm speedboat (with outboard motor), powerboat

fuori'campo adj inv Cinema ⟨voce⟩ off-screen

fuori'classe nmf inv champion

fuoricombatti'mento nm knockout

fuorigi'oco nm & adv offside

fuori'legge nmf inv outlaw

fuori'pista nm (sci) off-piste skiing

fuori'serie ① adj custom-made ② nf inv Auto custom-built model

fuori'strada nm inv off-road vehicle, off-roader

fuoriu'scita *nf* (perdita) leak
fuoriu'scito, -a *nmf* exile
fuorvi'are ① *vt* lead astray
　② *vi* go astray
furbacchi'one *nm* crafty old devil
fur'bastro, -a *nmf* crafty devil
furbe'ria *nf* cunning
fur'besco *adj* sly, cunning
fur'bizia *nf* cunning
'furbo *adj* sly, cunning; (intelligente) clever;
　(astuto) shrewd; **bravo** ∼! nice one!; **fare il**
　∼ try to be clever
fu'rente *adj* furious
fu'retto *nm* ferret
fur'fante *nm* scoundrel
furgon'cino *nm* delivery van
fur'gone *nm* van. **furgone postale**
　mail van
'furia *nf* fury; (fretta) haste; **a** ∼ **di** by dint
　of; **andare su tutte le furie** fly into a rage
furi'bondo *adj* furious
furi'ere *nm* Mil quartermaster
furiosa'mente *adv* furiously
furi'oso *adj* furious; ⟨litigio⟩ violent
fu'rore *nm* fury; (veemenza) frenzy; **far** ∼
　be all the rage
furoreggi'are *vi* be a great success
furtiva'mente *adv* covertly, stealthily
fur'tivo *adj* furtive, stealthy
'furto *nm* theft; **commettere un** ∼ steal; **è**
　un ∼! fig it's daylight robbery!. **furto**

d'auto car theft. **furto di minore**
　entità petty theft. **furto con scasso**
　burglary
'fusa *nfpl* fare le ∼ purr
fu'scello *nm* (di legno) twig; (di paglia)
　straw; **sei un** ∼ you're as light as a
　feather
fu'seaux *nmpl* leggings
fu'sibile *nm* fuse
fu'silli *nmpl* pasta twirls
fusi'one *nf* fusion; Comm merger
'fuso ① *pp di* FONDERE
　② *adj* melted
　③ *nm* spindle; **a** ∼ spindle-shaped. **fuso**
　orario time zone
fusoli'era *nf* fuselage
fu'stagno *nm* corduroy
fu'stella *nf* (talloncino) part of packaging
　on prescribed medicine returned by the
　pharmacist to claim a refund
fusti'gare *vt* flog; fig castigate
fu'stino *nm* (di detersivo) box
'fusto *nm* stem; (tronco) trunk; (recipiente di
　metallo) drum; (di legno) barrel. **fusto del**
　letto bedstead
'futile *adj* futile
futilità *nf* futility
futu'rismo *nm* futurism
futu'rista *nmf* futurist
fu'turo *adj & nm* future; **predire il** ∼ tell
　fortunes, foretell. **futuro anteriore** Gram
　future perfect

Gg

gabardine *nf* (tessuto) gabardine
gab'bare *vt* cheat
gab'barsi *vr* ∼ **di** make fun of
'gabbia *nf* cage; (da imballaggio) crate.
　gabbia dell'ascensore lift cage.
　gabbia degli imputati dock. **gabbia**
　toracica rib cage
gabbi'ano *nm* [sea]gull. **gabbiano**
　comune common gull
gabi'netto *nm* (di medico) consulting
　room; Pol cabinet; (toilette) toilet; (laboratorio)
　laboratory; **andare al** ∼ go to the toilet;
　gabinetti *pl* **pubblici** public convenience
'Gabon *nm* Gabon
ga'elico *nm* Gaelic
'gaffa *nf* boathook
'gaffe *nf inv* blunder
gagli'ardo *adj* vigorous
gai'ezza *nf* gaiety

'gaio *adj* cheerful
'gala *nf* gala
ga'lante *adj* gallant
galante'ria *nf* gallantry
galantu'omo *nm* (pl **galantuomini**)
　gentleman
ga'lassia *nf* galaxy
gala'teo *nm* [good] manners *pl*; (trattato)
　book of etiquette
gale'otto *nm* (rematore) galley-slave;
　(condannato) convict
ga'lera *nf* (nave) galley; fam slammer
'galla *nf* Bot gall; **a** ∼ afloat; **venire a** ∼
　surface
galleggi'ante ① *adj* floating
　② *nm* craft; (boa) float
galleggi'are *vi* float
galle'ria *nf* (traforo) tunnel; (d'arte) gallery;
　Theat circle; (arcata) arcade; **prima galleria** ⋯⋗

dress circle. **galleria aerodinamica**
wind tunnel

'Galles *nm* Wales

gal'lese ① *adj* Welsh
② *nm* Welshman; (lingua) Welsh
③ *nf* Welshwoman

gal'letta *nf* cracker

gal'letto *nm* cockerel; **fare il ~** show off,
impress the girls

'gallico *adj* Gallic

gal'lina *nf* hen

galli'nella *nf* **gallinella d'acqua**
moorhen

gal'lismo *nm* machismo

'gallo *nm* cock. **gallo cedrone**
capercaillie

gal'lone *nm* stripe; (misura) gallon

galop'pante *adj* galloping

galop'pare *vi* gallop

galop'pino *nm* **fare da ~ a qualcuno** fam
be somebody's gopher

ga'loppo *nm* gallop; **al ~** at a gallop

galvaniz'zare *vt* galvanize

'gamba *nf* leg; (di lettera) stem; **darsela a
gambe** take to one's heels; **essere in ~**
(essere forte) be strong; (capace) be smart

gam'bale *nm* (di stivale) bootleg

gamba'letto *nm* pop sock

gambe'retti *nmpl* shrimps.
gamberetti in salsa rosa prawn
cocktail

'gambero *nm* prawn; (di fiume) crayfish

gambe'roni *nmpl* king prawns

'Gambia *nf* the Gambia

gambiz'zare *vt* kneecap

'gambo *nm* stem; (di pianta) stalk

ga'mella *nf* billy

game 'point *nm inv* game point

ga'mete *nm* gamete

'gamma *nf* Mus scale; fig range. **gamma
d'onda** waveband. **gamma di prezzi**
price range. **gamma di prodotti**
product range

ga'nascia *nf* jaw; **ganasce** *pl* **del freno**
brake shoes

'gancio *nm* hook

'Gange *nm* Ganges

'ganghero *nm* **uscire dai gangheri** fig get
into a temper

'gangster *nm inv* gangster

'gara *nf* competition; (di velocità) race; **fare
a ~** compete. **gara d'appalto** call for
tenders. **gara a cronometro** time trial

ga'rage *nm inv* garage

gara'gista *nmf* garage owner

ga'rante *nmf* guarantor

garan'tire *vt* guarantee; (rendersi garante)
vouch for; (assicurare) assure

garan'tirsi *vr* **~ contro, ~ da** guard
against, insure against

garan'tismo *nm* protection of civil
liberties

garan'tito *adj* guaranteed

garan'zia *nf* guarantee; **in ~** under
guarantee. **garanzia collaterale**
collateral. **garanzia di rimborso**
money-back guarantee. **garanzia a vita**
lifetime guarantee

gar'bare *vi* like; **non mi garba** I don't
like it

gar'bato *adj* courteous

'garbo *nm* courtesy; (grazia) grace; **con ~**
graciously

gar'buglio *nm* muddle

gar'denia *nf* gardenia

gareggi'are *vi* compete

garga'nella *nf* **a ~** from the bottle

garga'rismo *nm* gargle; **fare i
gargarismi** gargle

ga'ritta *nf* sentry box

ga'rofano *nm* carnation; **chiodo di
garofano** clove

gar'retto *nm* shank

gar'rire *vi* chirp

gar'rotta *nf* garrotte

'garrulo *adj* garrulous

'garza *nf* gauze

gar'zone *nm* boy. **garzone di stalla**
stable-boy

gas *nm inv* gas; **dare ~** Auto accelerate; **a
~** gas-fired; **a tutto ~** flat out. **gas
asfissiante** poisonous gas. **gas
esilarante** laughing gas. **gas
lacrimogeno** tear gas. **gas nobile**
inert gas. **gas propellente** propellant.
gas di scarico *pl* exhaust fumes

gas'dotto *nm* natural gas pipeline

ga'solio *nm* diesel oil. **gasolio
invernale** diesel containing anti-freeze

ga'sometro *nm* gasometer

gas'sare *vt* aerate; (uccidere col gas) gas

gas'sato ① *adj* gassy; ⟨bevanda⟩ fizzy
② *nf* lemonade

gas'soso, -a *adj* gassy

'gastrico *adj* gastric

ga'strite *nf* gastritis

gastroente'rite *nf* gastro-enteritis

gastrono'mia *nf* gastronomy

gastro'nomico *adj* gastronomic[al]

ga'stronomo, -a *nmf* gourmet

'gatta *nf* **una ~ da pelare** a headache

gatta'buia *nf hum* clink

gatta'iola *nf* catflap

gat'tino, -a *nmf* kitten

'gatto, -a *nmf* cat; **c'erano solo quattro
gatti** there were only a few people. **gatto
delle nevi** snowmobile. **gatto a nove**

code cat-o'-nine-tails. **gatto selvatico** wildcat

gat'toni *adv* on all fours

gat'tuccio *nm* dogfish

gau'dente *adj* pleasure-loving

'gaudio *nm* joy

ga'vetta *nf* mess tin; **fare la ∼** rise through the ranks

gay *adj inv* gay

Gaza *nf* **la striscia di ∼** Gaza strip

ga'zebo *nm inv* gazebo

'gazza *nf* magpie

gaz'zarra *nf* racket; **fare ∼** make a racket

gaz'zella *nf* gazelle; Auto police car

gaz'zetta *nf* gazette. **Gazzetta Ufficiale** official journal

gazzet'tino *nm* (titolo) title page; (rubrica) page

gaz'zosa *nf* clear lemonade

GB *abbr* (**Gran Bretagna**) GB

'geco *nm* gecko

ge'lare *vt/i* freeze; **far ∼ il sangue** make somebody's blood run cold

ge'lata *nf* frost

gela'taio, -a 1 *nmf* ice-cream seller 2 *nm* (negozio) ice-cream shop

gelate'ria *nf* ice-cream parlour

gelati'era *nf* ice-cream maker

gela'tina *nf* gelatine; (dolce) jelly. **gelatina di frutta** fruit jelly

gelati'noso *adj* gelatinous

ge'lato 1 *adj* frozen 2 *nm* ice-cream. **gelato alla vaniglia** vanilla ice-cream

'gelido *adj* freezing

'gelo *nm* (freddo intenso) freezing cold; (brina) frost; fig chill

ge'lone *nm* chilblain

gelosa'mente *adv* jealously

gelo'sia *nf* jealousy

ge'loso *adj* jealous

'gelso *nm* mulberry[-tree]

gelso'mino *nm* jasmine

gemel'laggio *nm* twinning

gemel'lare 1 *vt* twin 2 *adj* twin

ge'mello, -a *adj & nmf* twin; **gemelli** *pl* (di polsino) cuff-link. **gemelli** *pl* **monozigoti** identical twins; **Gemelli** *pl* Astr Gemini *sg*

'gemere *vi* groan

'gemito *nm* groan

'gemma *nf* gem; Bot bud

gemmolo'gia *nf* gemmology

gen'darme *nm* gendarme

'gene *nm* gene

genealo'gia *nf* genealogy

genea'logico *adj* genealogical

gene'rale[1] *adj* general; **in ∼** (tutto sommato) in general, on the whole; **parlando in ∼** generally speaking

gene'rale[2] *nm* Mil general. **generale di divisione** major-general

generalità *nf inv* (qualità) generality, general nature; (maggior parte) majority; **∼** *pl* (dati) particulars *pl*

generaliz'zare *vt* generalize

generalizzazi'one *nf* generalization

general'mente *adv* generally

gene'rare *vt* give birth to; (causare) breed; Techn generate

genera'tore *nm* Techn generator

generazio'nale *adj* generation *attrib*

generazi'one *nf* generation; **di ∼ in ∼** from generation to generation

'genere *nm* kind; Biol genus; Gram gender; (letterario, artistico) genre; (prodotto) product; **cose del ∼** such things; **il ∼ umano** mankind; **in ∼** generally; **generi** *pl* **alimentari** provisions; **generi** *pl* **di prima necessità** essentials

generica'mente *adv* generically

ge'nerico *adj* generic; **medico generico** general practitioner

'genero *nm* son-in-law

generosa'mente *adv* generously

generosità *nf* generosity

gene'roso *adj* generous

'genesi *nf* genesis

genetica'mente *adv* genetically; **∼ modificato** genetically modified

ge'netico, -a 1 *adj* genetic 2 *nf* genetics

gene'tista *nmf* geneticist

gen'giva *nf* gum

geni'ale *adj* ingenious; liter (congeniale) congenial

geni'ere *nm* Mil sapper

'genio *nm* genius; **andare a ∼** be to one's taste. **genio civile** civil engineering. **genio incompreso** misunderstood genius. **genio [militare]** Engineers

geni'tale 1 *adj* genital 2 *nm* **genitali** *pl* genitals

geni'tore *nm* parent

gen'naio *nm* January

geno'cidio *nm* genocide

ge'noma *nm* genome

geno'teca *nf* gene library

'Genova *nf* Genoa

geno'vese *adj* Genoese

gen'taglia *nf* rabble

'gente *nf* people *pl*

gen'tile *adj* kind; **Gentile Signore** (in lettere) Dear Sir

genti'lezza nf kindness; **per** ∼ (per favore) please

gentil'mente adv kindly

gentilu'omo (pl **gentiluomini**) nm gentleman

genu'flettersi vr kneel down

genuina'mente adv genuinely

genu'ino adj genuine; ⟨cibo, prodotto⟩ natural

genzi'ana nf gentian

geo'fisica nf geophysics

geo'fisico, **-a** nmf geophysician

geogra'fia nf geography

geo'grafico adj geographical

ge'ografo, **-a** nmf geographer

geolo'gia nf geology

geo'logico adj geological

ge'ologo, **-a** nmf geologist

ge'ometra nmf surveyor

geome'tria nf geometry

geometrica'mente adv geometrically

geo'metrico adj geometric[al]

geopo'litico adj geopolitical

Ge'orgia nf Georgia

geo'termico adj geothermal, geothermic

ge'ranio nm geranium

gerar'chia nf hierarchy

gerarchica'mente adv hierarchically

ge'rarchico adj hierarchic[al]

ger'billo nm gerbil

ge'rente ① nm manager ② nf manageress

'gergo nm jargon; (dei giovani) slang. **gergo burocratico** bureaucratic jargon

geri'atra nmf geriatrician

geria'tria nf geriatrics

geri'atrico adj geriatric

'gerla nf wicker basket

Ger'mania nf Germany. **Germania [dell']Est** East Germany. **Germania [dell']Ovest** West Germany

ger'manico adj Germanic

'germe nm germ; (fig: principio) seed. **germe di grano** wheat germ

germogli'are vi sprout

ger'moglio nm sprout; **in** ∼ Bot sprouting; **germogli** pl **di soia** beansprouts

gero'glifico nm hieroglyph; **geroglifici** pl hieroglyphics

geron'tologo, **-a** nmf gerontologist

ge'rundio nm gerund

Gerusa'lemme nf Jerusalem

ges'setto nm chalk

'gesso nm chalk; (Med, scultura) plaster

ge'staccio nm ≈ V-sign

gestazi'one nf gestation

gestico'lare vi gesticulate

gestio'nale adj management attrib

gesti'one nf management. **gestione aziendale** business management. **gestione dei dati** Comput data management. **gestione disco** Comput disk management. **gestione dell'energia** energy resource management. **gestione del flusso di cassa** cashflow management. **gestione patrimoniale** financial management

ge'stire vi manage; ∼ **male** mishandle

ge'stirsi vr budget one's time and money

'gesto nm gesture; (azione: pl f **gesta**) deed

ge'store nm manager

Gesù nm Jesus. **Gesù bambino** baby Jesus

gesu'ita nm Jesuit

gesu'itico adj Jesuit attrib

get'tare vt throw; (scagliare) fling; (emettere) spout; Techn, fig cast; ∼ **via** throw away

get'tarsi vr throw oneself; ∼ **in** ⟨fiume⟩ flow into

get'tata nf throw; Techn casting

'gettito nm **gettito fiscale** tax revenue

'getto nm throw; (di liquidi, gas) jet; **a** ∼ **continuo** in a continuous stream; **di** ∼ straight off

getto'nato adj ⟨canzone⟩ popular

get'tone nm token; (per giochi) counter; **a** ∼ coin operated

gettoni'era nf coin box

'geyser nm inv geyser

'Ghana nm Ghana

ghe'pardo nm cheetah

'gheppio nm kestrel

gher'mire vt grasp

'ghette nfpl (per neonato) leggings

ghettiz'zare vt ghettoize

'ghetto nm ghetto

ghiacci'aia nf glacier

ghiacci'aio nm glacier

ghiacci'are vt/i freeze

ghiacci'ato adj frozen; (freddissimo) ice-cold

ghi'accio nm ice; Auto black ice. **ghiaccio secco** dry ice

ghiacci'olo nm icicle; (gelato) ice lolly

ghi'aia nf gravel

ghiai'oso adj gritty

ghi'anda nf acorn

ghian'daia nf jay

ghi'andola nf gland. **ghiandola pituitaria** pituitary gland. **ghiandola sudoripara** sweat gland. **ghiandola surrenale** adrenal gland

ghigliot'tina *nf* guillotine

ghi'gnare *vi* sneer

'ghigno *nm* sneer

ghi'otto *adj* greedy, gluttonous; (appetitoso) appetizing

ghiot'tone, **-a** *nmf* glutton

ghiottone'ria *nf* (caratteristica) gluttony; (cibo) tasty morsel

ghiri'goro *nm* flourish

ghir'landa *nf* (corona) wreath; (di fiori) garland

'ghiro *nm* dormouse; **dormire come un ~** sleep like a log

'ghisa *nf* cast iron

già *adv* already; (un tempo) formerly; **~!** indeed!; **~ da ieri** since yesterday

gi'acca *nf* jacket. **giacca a vento** windcheater

giacché *conj* since

giac'cone *nm* jacket

gia'cenza *nf* **giacenze** *pl* **di magazzino** unsold stock

gia'cere *vi* lie

giaci'mento *nm* deposit. **giacimento di petrolio** oil deposit

gia'cinto *nm* hyacinth

gi'ada *nf* jade

giaggi'olo *nm* iris

giagu'aro *nm* jaguar

gial'lastro *adj* yellowish

gi'allo *adj* & *nm* yellow; [libro] giallo crime novel; [film] giallo thriller. **giallo dell'uovo** egg yolk

Gia'maica *nf* Jamaica

giamai'cano, **-a** *adj* & *nmf* Jamaican

gian'duia *nm* *inv* soft hazelnut chocolate typical of Piedmont

Giap'pone *nm* Japan

giappo'nese *adj* & *nmf* Japanese

gi'ara *nf* jar

giardi'naggio *nm* gardening

giardi'niere, **-a** ① *nmf* gardener. **giardiniera di verdure** diced, mixed vegetables, cooked and pickled ② *nf* Auto estate car

giar'dino *nm* garden. **giardino d'infanzia** kindergarten. **giardino pensile** roof-garden; **giardini** *pl* **pubblici** park. **giardino zoologico** zoo

giarretti'era *nf* garter

Gi'ava *nf* Java

giavel'lotto *nm* javelin

Gi'buti *nf* Djibouti

gi'gante *nm* giant

gigan'tesco *adj* gigantic

gigantogra'fia *nf* blow-up

'giglio *nm* lily

gilè *nm* *inv* waistcoat

gin *nm* *inv* gin

gin'cana *nf* gymkhana

ginecolo'gia *nf* gynaecology

gineco'logico *adj* gynaecological

gine'cologo, **-a** *nmf* gynaecologist

gi'nepro *nm* juniper

gi'nestra *nf* broom

Gi'nevra *nf* Geneva

gingil'larsi *vr* fiddle; (perder tempo) potter

gin'gillo *nm* plaything; (ninnolo) knick-knack

gin'nasio *nm* (scuola) grammar school

gin'nasta *nmf* gymnast

gin'nastica *nf* gymnastics; (esercizi) exercises *pl*. **ginnastica ritmica** eurhythmics

ginocchi'ata *nf* **prendere una ~** bang one's knee

ginocchi'era *nf* knee-pad

gi'nocchio *nm* (*pl m* **ginocchi** *o f* **ginocchia**) knee; **in ~** on one's knees, kneeling; **mettersi in ~** kneel down; (per supplicare) go down on one's knees; **al ~** (gonna) knee-length

ginocchi'oni *adv* kneeling

gio'care *vt/i* play; (giocherellare) toy; (puntare) stake; (ingannare) trick; **~ a calcio/a pallavolo** play football/volleyball; **~ d'astuzia** be crafty; **~ d'azzardo** gamble; **~ in Borsa** speculate on the Stock Exchange; **~ in casa** Sport, fig play at home

gio'carsi *vr* **~ la carriera** throw one's career away

gioca'tore, **-trice** *nmf* player; (d'azzardo) gambler

gio'cattolo *nm* toy

giocherel'lare *vi* toy; (nervosamente) fiddle

giocherel'lone *adj* skittish

gi'oco *nm* game; (di bambini, Techn) play; (d'azzardo) gambling; (scherzo) joke; (insieme di pezzi ecc) set; **essere in ~** be at stake; **fare il doppio ~ con qualcuno** double-cross somebody; **è un ~ da ragazzi** fam it's a cinch. **gioco elettronico** computer game; **giochi** *pl* **della gioventù** nation-wide sports tournament for children. **gioco dell'oca** snakes and ladders; **Giochi** *pl* **Olimpici** Olympic Games; **giochi** *pl* **online** on-line gaming. **gioco di parole** play on words. **gioco di pazienza** game of manual skill. **gioco di prestigio** conjuring trick. **gioco di società** board game

giocoli'ere *nm* juggler

gio'coso *adj* playful

gi'ogo *nm* yoke

gi'oia *nf* joy; (gioiello) jewel; (appellativo) sweetie

gioielle'ria *nf* jeweller's [shop]

gioi'elli *nmpl* jewellery

gioielli'ere, **-a** *nmf* jeweller; (negozio) jeweller's

gioi'ello *nm* jewel

gioiosa'mente *adv* joyfully

gioi'oso *adj* joyful

gio'ire *vi* ~ per rejoice at

Gior'dania *nf* Jordan

gior'dano, **-a** *adj & nmf* Jordanian

giorna'laio, **-a** *nmf* newsagent, newsdealer

gior'nale *nm* [news]paper; (diario) journal. **giornale di bordo** logbook. **giornale gratuito** freebie. **giornale del mattino** morning paper. **giornale radio** radio news. **giornale della sera** evening paper

giornali'ero ① *adj* daily ② *nm* (per sciare) day pass

giorna'lino *nm* comic

giorna'lismo *nm* journalism

giorna'lista *nmf* journalist

giornal'mente *adv* daily

gior'nata *nf* day; **buona** ~! have a good day!; **in** ~ today; **a** ~ ⟨essere pagato⟩ on a day-to-day basis; **vivere alla** ~ live from day to day. **giornata lavorativa** working day

gi'orno *nm* day; **al** ~ per day; **al** ~ **d'oggi** nowadays; **di** ~ by day; **in pieno** ~ in broad daylight; **un** ~ **sì, un** ~ **no** every other day; ~ **per** ~ day by day. **giorno di chiusura** closing day. **giorno delle elezioni** polling day. **giorno fatidico** (importante) D-day. **giorno feriale** weekday. **giorno festivo** public holiday. **giorno del giudizio** Judgement Day. **giorno dei morti** All Souls' day. **giorno di paga** payday

gi'ostra *nf* merry-go-round

gio'strarsi *vr* manage

giova'mento *nm* **trarre** ~ **da** derive benefit from

gi'ovane ① *adj* young; (giovanile) youthful ② *nm* youth; young man; **giovani** *pl* young people ③ *nf* girl, young woman

giova'nile *adj* youthful; ⟨scritto⟩ early

giova'notto *nm* young man

gio'vare *vi* ~ **a** be useful to; (far bene a) be good for

gio'varsi *vr* ~ **di** avail oneself of

Gi'ove *nm* Jupiter, Jove

giovedì *nm inv* Thursday; **di** ~ on Thursdays. **giovedì grasso** last Thursday before Lent. **giovedì santo** Maundy Thursday

gioventù *nf* youth; (i giovani) young people *pl*; ~ **bruciata** young drop-outs *pl*

giovi'ale *adj* jovial

giovi'nezza *nf* youth

gi'rabile *adj* ⟨assegno⟩ endorsable

gira'dischi *nm inv* record-player

gi'raffa *nf* giraffe; Cinema boom

gira'mondo *nmf inv* globetrotter; **da** ~ globetrotting

gi'randola *nf* (fuoco d'artificio) Catherine wheel; (giocattolo) windmill; (banderuola) weathercock

gi'rare ① *vt* turn; (andare intorno, visitare) go round; Comm endorse; Cinema shoot ② *vi* turn; ⟨aerei, uccelli⟩ circle; (andare in giro) wander; ~ **sotto** ... Comput run under ...; **mi gira la testa** I feel dizzy; **far** ~ **la testa a qualcuno** make somebody's head spin; **far** ~ **le scatole a qualcuno** fam drive somebody round the twist; ~ **al largo** steer clear

girar'rosto *nm* spit

gi'rarsi *vr* turn [round]

gira'sole *nm* sunflower

gi'rata *nf* turn; Comm endorsement; (in macchina ecc) ride; **fare una** ~ (a piedi) go for a walk; (in macchina) go for a ride

gira'volta *nf* spin; fig U-turn

gi'rello *nm* (per bambini) babywalker; Culin topside

gi'revole *adj* revolving; **ponte girevole** swing bridge

gi'rino *nm* tadpole

'giro *nm* turn; (circolo) circle; (percorso) round; (viaggio) tour; (passeggiata) short walk; (in macchina) drive; (in bicicletta) ride; (circolazione di denaro) circulation; **andare a fare un** ~ (a piedi) go for a stroll; (in macchina) go for a drive; (in bicicletta) go for a cycle ride; **fare il** ~ **di** go round; **nel** ~ **di un mese/anno** within a month/year; **prendere in** ~ **qualcuno** pull somebody's leg; **sentir dire in** ~ **qualcosa** hear something on the grapevine; **a** ~ **di posta** by return mail. **giro d'affari** Comm turnover. **giro in barca** boat trip. **giro guidato** guided tour. **giro [della] manica** armhole; **giri** *pl* **al minuto** revs per minute, rpm. **giro d'onore** lap of honour; **giri** *pl* **di parole** beating about the bush. **giro di pista** lap. **giro di prova** trial lap. **giro turistico** sightseeing tour. **giro vita** waist measurement. **giro di vite** fig clampdown

giro'collo *nm* choker; **a** ~ roundneck

gi'rone *nm* round. **girone di andata** first half of the season. **girone di ritorno** second half of the season

gironzo'lare *vi* wander about

giro'tondo *nm* ring-a-ring-o'-roses

girova'gare *vi* wander about

gi'rovago *nm* wanderer

'gita *nf* trip; **andare in** ~ go on a trip. **gita didattica** field trip. **gita organizzata** package tour. **gita in**

pullman coach trip. **gita scolastica** school trip

gi'tano, -a *nmf* gipsy

gi'tante *nmf* tripper

giù *adv* down; (sotto) below; (dabbasso) downstairs; **a testa in ∼** (a capofitto) headlong; **essere ∼** (di morale) be down, be depressed; (di salute) be run down; **∼ di corda** down; **∼ di lì, su per ∼** more or less; **non andare ∼ a qualcuno** stick in somebody's craw

gi'ubba *nf* jacket; Mil tunic

giub'botto *nm* bomber jacket, jerkin. **giubbotto antiproiettile** bulletproof vest. **giubbotto di pelle** leather jacket. **giubbotto di salvataggio** lifejacket

gi'ubilo *nm* rejoicing

giudi'care *vt* judge; (ritenere) consider

gi'udice *nm* judge. **giudice conciliatore** justice of the peace. **giudice di gara** umpire. **giudice di linea** linesman. **giudice di pace** Justice of the Peace, JP

giudizi'ario *adj* legal, judicial

giu'dizio *nm* judg[e]ment; (opinione) opinion; (senno) wisdom; (processo) trial; (sentenza) sentence; **mettere ∼** become wise. **giudizio universale** Last Judgement

giudizi'oso *adj* sensible

gi'ugno *nm* June

giugu'lare *nf* jugular

giul'lare *nm* jester

giu'menta *nf* mare

giun'chiglia *nf* jonquil

gi'unco *nm* reed

gi'ungere ① *vi* arrive; **∼ a** (riuscire) succeed in; **mi giunge nuovo** it's news to me
② *vt* (unire) join

gi'ungla *nf* jungle. **giungla d'asfalto** concrete jungle

gi'unta *nf* addition; **per ∼** in addition. **giunta comunale** district council. **giunta [militare]** [military] junta

gi'unto ① *pp di* GIUNGERE
② *nm* Mech joint. **giunto sferico** ball-and-socket joint

giun'tura *nf* joint

giuo'care, giu'oco = GIOCARE, GIOCO

giura'mento *nm* oath; **sotto ∼** under oath; **prestare ∼** take the oath. **giuramento d'Ippocrate** Hippocratic oath

giu'rare *vt/i* swear

giu'rato, -a ① *adj* sworn
② *nmf* juror

giu'ria *nf* jury

giu'ridico *adj* legal

giurisdizi'one *nf* jurisdiction

giurispru'denza *nf* jurisprudence

giu'rista *nmf* jurist

giu'stezza *nf* justness

giustifi'care *vt* justify

giustifi'carsi *vr* justify oneself; **∼ di** *o* **per qualcosa** give an explanation for something

giustificazi'one *nf* justification

giu'stizia *nf* justice; **farsi ∼ da sé** take the law into one's own hands

giustizi'are *vt* execute

giustizi'ere *nm* executioner

gi'usto ① *adj* just, fair; (adatto) right; (esatto) exact
② *nm* (uomo retto) just man; (cosa giusta) right
③ *adv* exactly; **∼ ora** just now

glaci'ale *adj* glacial

gladia'tore *nm* gladiator

gla'diolo *nm* gladiolus

'glassa *nf* Culin icing

glau'coma *nm* glaucoma

gli ① *def art m pl* the; ▶ IL
② *pers pron* (a lui) [to] him; (a esso) [to] it; (a loro) [to] them; **non ∼ credo** I don't believe him/them

glice'mia *nf* glycaemia

glice'rina *nf* glycerine

'glicine *nm* wisteria

gli'elo *pron* (a lui) to him; (a lei) to her; (a loro) to them; (a Lei, forma di cortesia) to you; **∼ prestai** I lent it to him/her etc; **gliel'ho chiesto** I've asked him/her etc

glie'ne *pron* (di ciò) of it; **∼ ho dato un po'** I gave him/her/them/you some [of it]; **∼ ho parlato** I've talked to him/her etc about it

glis'sare *vi* avoid the issue; **∼ su qualcosa** skate over something

glo'bale *adj* global; fig overall

globalizzazi'one *nf* globalization

global'mente *adv* globally

'globo *nm* globe. **globo oculare** eyeball. **globo terrestre** globe

'globulo *nm* globule; Med corpuscle. **globulo bianco** white cell, white corpuscle. **globulo rosso** red cell, red corpuscle

'gloria *nf* glory

glori'arsi *vr* **∼ di** be proud of

glorifi'care *vt* glorify

gloriosa'mente *adv* gloriously

glori'oso *adj* glorious

'glossa *nf* gloss

glos'sario *nm* glossary

glottolo'gia *nf* linguistics

glu'cosio *nm* glucose

glutam'mato *nm* **glutammato di sodio** monosodium glutamate

'gluteo nm buttock

'gnocchi nmpl (di patate) small flour and potato dumplings

'gnomo nm gnome

'gnorri nm fare lo ~ play dumb

goal nm inv goal; **fare un** ~ score or get a goal

'gobba nf hump

'gobbo, -a [1] adj hunchbacked [2] nmf hunchback

goc'cetto nm pick-me-up

'goccia nf drop; (di sudore) bead; **è stata l'ultima** ~ it was the last straw. **goccia di pioggia** raindrop. **goccia di rugiada** dewdrop

goccio'lare vi drip

goccio'lio nm dripping

go'dere vi (sl: sessualmente) come; ~ **di qualcosa** enjoy something, make the most of something

go'dersi vr ~ **qualcosa** enjoy something; **godersela** have a good time

godi'mento nm enjoyment

gof'faggine nf awkwardness

goffa'mente adv awkwardly

'goffo adj awkward

go-'kart nm inv go-kart

'gola nf throat; (ingordigia) gluttony; Geog gorge; (di camino) flue; **avere mal di** ~ have a sore throat; **far** ~ **a qualcuno** tempt somebody

go'letta nf schooner

golf nm inv jersey; Sport golf

gol'fino nm jumper

'golfo nm gulf

goli'ardico adj student attrib

golosità nf inv greediness; (cibo) tasty morsel

go'loso adj greedy

'golpe nm inv coup

go'mena nf painter

gomi'tata nf nudge; **dare una** ~ **a qualcuno** elbow somebody

'gomito nm elbow; **alzare il** ~ (fam: bere) raise one's elbow; ~ **a** ~ (lavorare) side by side

go'mitolo nm ball

'gomma nf rubber; (colla) gum; (pneumatico) tyre; **avere una** ~ **a terra** have a flat. **gomma arabica** gum arabic. **gomma da masticare** chewing gum. **gomma di scorta** spare tyre

gommapi'uma® nf foam rubber

gom'mino nm rubber tip

gom'mista nm tyre specialist

gom'mone nm [rubber] dinghy

gom'moso adj chewy

'gondola nf gondola

gondoli'ere nm gondolier

gonfa'lone nm banner

gonfi'abile adj inflatable

gonfi'are [1] vi swell [2] vt blow up; pump up (pneumatico); (esagerare) exaggerate

gonfi'arsi vr swell; (acque) rise

'gonfio adj swollen; (pneumatico) inflated

gonfi'ore nm swelling

gongo'lante adj overjoyed

gongo'lare vi be overjoyed

goni'ometro nm protractor

'gonna nf skirt. **gonna pantalone** culottes pl. **gonna a pieghe** pleated skirt. **gonna a portafoglio** wrapover skirt

gonor'rea nf gonorrh[o]ea

'gonzo nm simpleton

gorgheggi'are vi warble

gor'gheggio nm warble

'gorgo nm whirlpool

gorgogli'ante adj burbling, gurgling

gorgogli'are vi gurgle

gor'goglio nm burble

gorgon'zola nm strong, soft blue cheese

go'rilla nm inv gorilla; (guardia del corpo) bodyguard, minder

'gota nf cheek

'gotico adj & nm Gothic

'gotta nf gout

gover'nante nf housekeeper

gover'nare vt govern; (dominare) rule; (dirigere) manage; (curare) look after

governa'tivo adj government

governa'tore nm governor

go'verno nm government; (dominio) rule; **al** ~ in power. **governo ombra** shadow government

'gozzo nm (di animale) crop; Med goitre; fam throat

gozzovigli'are vi eat, drink and be merry

gracchi'are vi caw; fig (persona) screech

'gracchio nm caw

graci'dare vi croak

'gracile adj delicate

gra'dasso nm braggart

gradata'mente adv gradually

gradazi'one nf gradation. **gradazione alcolica** alcohol[lic]content. **a bassa gradazione alcolica** (birra) low-alcohol

gra'devole adj agreeable

gradevol'mente adv pleasantly, agreeably

gradi'ente nm gradient

gradi'mento *nm* liking; **indice di gradimento** Radio, TV popularity rating; **non è di mio ∼** it's not to my liking

gradi'nata *nf* flight of steps; (di stadio, teatro) tiers *pl*

gra'dino *nm* step

gra'dire *vt* like; (desiderare) wish

gra'dito *adj* pleasant; (bene accetto) welcome

'grado *nm* degree; (rango) rank; **di buon ∼** willingly; **essere in ∼ di fare qualcosa** be in a position to do something; (essere capace a) be able to do something; **per gradi** ⟨*procedere*⟩ by degrees

gradu'ale *adj* gradual

gradual'mente *adv* gradually

gradu'are *vt* graduate

gradu'ato ① *adj* graded; (provvisto di scala graduata) graduated ② *nm* Mil noncommissioned officer

gradua'toria *nf* list

graduazi'one *nf* graduation

'graffa *nf* clip; (segno grafico) brace

graf'fetta *nf* staple

graffi'are *vt* scratch

graffia'tura *nf* scratch

'graffio *nm* scratch

gra'fia *nf* [hand]writing; (ortografia) spelling

'grafica *nf* graphics; (disciplina) graphics, graphic design. **grafica pubblicitaria** commercial art

grafica'mente *adv* in graphics, graphically

'grafico ① *adj* graphic ② *nm* graph; (persona) graphic designer. **grafico a torta** pie chart

gra'fite *nf* graphite

gra'fologo, -a *nmf* graphologist

gra'migna *nf* weed

gram'matica *nf* grammar

grammati'cale *adj* grammatical

grammatical'mente *adv* grammatically

gram'matico *nm* grammarian

'grammo *nm* gram[me]

gram'mofono *nm* gramophone

gran ▶ GRANDE

'grana *nf* grain; (formaggio) parmesan; (fam: seccatura) trouble; (fam: soldi) readies *pl*

gra'naio *nm* barn

gra'nata *nf* Mil grenade; (frutto) pomegranate

granati'ere *nm* Mil grenadier

gra'nato *nm* garnet

Gran Bre'tagna *nf* Great Britain

gran'cassa *nf* bass drum

gran'cevola *nf* spiny spider crab

'granchio *nm* crab; (fig: errore) blunder; **prendere un ∼** make a blunder

grandango'lare *nm* wide-angle lens

gran'dangolo *nm* wide-angle lens

'grande ① (a volte **gran**) *adj* (ampio) large; (grosso) big; (alto) tall; (largo) wide; (fig: senso morale) great; (grandioso) grand; (adulto) grown-up; **∼ e grosso** beefy; **ho una gran fame** I'm very hungry; **fa un gran caldo** it's very hot; **in ∼** on a large scale; **in gran parte** to a great extent; **non è un gran che** it is nothing much; **di gran carriera** hotfoot; **un gran ballo** a grand ball; **alla ∼** sl in a big way ② *nmf* (persona adulta) grown-up; (persona eminente) great man/woman

grandeggi'are *vi* **∼ su** tower over; (darsi arie) show off

gran'dezza *nf* greatness; (ampiezza) largeness; (larghezza) width, breadth; (dimensione) size; (fasto) grandeur; (prodigalità) lavishness; **a ∼ naturale** life-size

grandi'nare *vi* hail; **grandina** it's hailing

'grandine *nf* hail

grandiosità *nf* grandeur

grandi'oso *adj* grand

gran'duca *nm* grand duke

grandu'cato *nm* grand duchy

grandu'chessa *nf* grand duchess

gra'nello *nm* grain; (di frutta) pip

gra'nita *nf* crushed ice drink

gra'nito *nm* granite

'grano *nm* grain; (frumento) wheat. **grano di pepe** peppercorn. **grano saraceno** buckwheat

gran[o]'turco *nm* corn

'granulo *nm* granule

'grappa *nf* very strong, clear spirit distilled from grapes; (morsa) cramp

'grappolo *nm* bunch. **grappolo d'uva** bunch of grapes

gras'setto *nm* bold [type]

gras'sezza *nf* fatness; (untuosità) greasiness

'grasso ① *adj* fat; ⟨*cibo*⟩ fatty; (unto) greasy; ⟨*terreno*⟩ rich; (grossolano) coarse ② *nm* fat; (sostanza) grease; **a basso contenuto di grassi** low-fat; **senza grassi** nonfat, fat-free

gras'soccio *adj* plump

gras'sone, -a *nmf* dumpling

'grata *nf* grating

gra'tella *nf* Culin grill

gra'ticcio *nm* (per piante) trellis; (stuoia) rush matting

gra'ticola *nf* Culin grill

gra'tifica *nf* bonus

gratificazi'one *nf* satisfaction

gra'tin *nm inv* gratin. **gratin di patate** potatoes with grated cheese

grati'nare *vt* cook au gratin

grati'nato *adj* au gratin

'gratis *adv* free

grati'tudine *nf* gratitude

'grato *adj* grateful; (gradito) pleasant

gratta'capo *nm* trouble

grattaci'elo *nm* skyscraper

'gratta e 'vinci *nm inv* scratch card

grat'tare ① *vt* scratch; (raschiare) scrape; (grattugiare) grate; (fam: rubare) pinch ② *vi* grate

grat'tarsi *vr* scratch oneself

grat'tugia *nf* grater

grattugi'are *vt* grate

gratuita'mente *adv* free [of charge]

gra'tuito *adj* free [of charge]; (ingiustificato) gratuitous

gra'vare ① *vt* burden ② *vi* ~ **su** weigh on

'grave *adj* (pesante) heavy; (serio) serious; (difficile) hard; ⟨voce, suono⟩ low; (fonetica) grave; **essere** ~ (gravemente ammalato) be seriously ill

grave'mente *adv* seriously, gravely

gravi'danza *nf* pregnancy. **gravidanza extrauterina** ectopic pregnancy. **gravidanza indesiderata** unwanted pregnancy

'gravido *adj* pregnant

gravità *nf* seriousness; Phys gravity

gravi'tare *vi* gravitate

gra'voso *adj* onerous

'grazia *nf* grace; (favore) favour; Jur pardon; **entrare nelle grazie di qualcuno** get into somebody's good books; **ministero di grazia e giustizia** Ministry of Justice

grazi'are *vt* pardon

'grazie *int* thank you!, thanks!; ~ **mille!** many thanks!, thanks a lot!; ~ **a Dio/al cielo!** thank God/goodness!; ~ **a** thanks to

grazi'oso *adj* charming; (carino) pretty

'Grecia *nf* Greece

greco, -a *adj & nmf* Greek. **greco antico** (lingua) classical Greek

gre'gario ① *adj* gregarious ② *nm* (ciclismo) supporting rider

'gregge *nm* flock

'greggio ① *adj* raw ② *nm* (petrolio) crude [oil]

grembi'ale, **grembi'ule** *nm* apron

'grembo *nm* lap; (utero) womb; fig bosom

gre'mire *vt* pack

gre'mirsi *vr* become crowded (**di** with)

gre'mito *adj* packed

'gretto *adj* stingy; (di vedute ristrette) narrow minded

'greve *adj* heavy

'grezzo *adj* = GREGGIO

gri'dare ① *vi* shout; (di dolore) scream; ⟨animale⟩ cry ② *vt* shout; ~ **qualcosa ai quattro venti** shout something from the rooftops

'grido *nm* (pl m **gridi** o pl f **grida**) shout, cry; (di animale) cry; **all'ultimo** ~ the latest fashion; **scrittore di** ~ celebrated writer. **grido d'aiuto** cry for help. **grido di battaglia** battle cry

'grigio *adj & nm* grey. **grigio perla** pearl grey

'griglia *nf* grill; **alla** ~ grilled; **cuocere alla** ~ grill

grigli'ata *nf* barbecue. **grigliata mista** mixed grill. **grigliata di pesce** grilled fish

gril'letto *nm* trigger

'grillo *nm* cricket; (fig: capriccio) whim

grimal'dello *nm* picklock

'grinfia *nf* fig clutch

'grinta *nf* grit

grin'toso *adj* determined

'grinza *nf* wrinkle; (di stoffa) crease; **non fare una** ~ fig ⟨ragionamento⟩ be flawless

grip'pare *vi* Mech seize up

gri'sou *nm* firedamp

gris'sino *nm* bread-stick

'grizzly *nm inv* grizzly

groenlan'dese ① *adj* of Greenland ② *nmf* Greenlander

Groen'landia *nf* Greenland

'groggy *adj inv* punch-drunk

'gronda *nf* eaves *pl*

gron'daia *nf* gutter

gron'dare *vi* pour; (essere bagnato fradicio) be dripping wet

'groppa *nf* back

'groppo *nm* knot; **avere un** ~ **alla gola** have a lump in one's throat

gros'sezza *nf* size; (spessore) thickness

gros'sista *nmf* wholesaler

'grosso ① *adj* big, large; (spesso) thick; (grossolano) coarse; (grave) serious ② *nm* big part; (massa) bulk; **farla grossa** do a stupid thing

grossolanità *nf inv* (qualità) coarseness; (di errore) grossness; (gesto) boorishness

grosso'lano *adj* coarse; ⟨errore⟩ gross; ⟨comportamento⟩ boorish

grosso'modo *adv* roughly

'grotta *nf* cave, grotto

grot'tesco *adj & nm* grotesque

grovi'era *nmf* Gruyère

gro'viglio *nm* tangle; fig muddle

gru *nf inv* (uccello, edilizia) crane

'gruccia *nf* (stampella) crutch; (per vestito) hanger. **gruccia appendiabiti** clotheshanger

grufo'lare *vi* root

gru'gnire *vi* grunt

gru'gnito *nm* grunt

'grugno *nm* snout

'grullo *adj* silly

'grumo *nm* clot; (di farina ecc) lump

gru'moso *adj* lumpy

'grunge *nm* grunge

'gruppo *nm* group; (comitiva) party. **gruppo d'azione** action group. **gruppo pop** pop group. **gruppo sanguigno** blood group. **gruppo di sostegno** support group. **gruppo di utenti** user group

gruvi'era *nmf* = GROVIERA

'gruzzolo *nm* nest-egg

guada'gnare *vt* earn; gain ⟨tempo, forza ecc⟩

guada'gnarsi *vr* ∼ **da vivere** earn a living

gua'dagno *nm* gain; (profitto) profit; (entrate) earnings *pl*; **guadagni** *pl* **illeciti** ill-gotten gains

gu'ado *nm* ford; **passare a** ∼ ford

gua'ina *nf* sheath; (busto) girdle

gu'aio *nm* trouble; **che** ∼**!** that's just brilliant!; **essere nei guai** be in a fix; **guai a te se lo tocchi!** don't you dare touch it!

gua'ire *vi* yelp

gua'ito *nm* yelp; **guaiti** *pl* yelping

gu'ancia *nf* cheek

guanci'ale *nm* pillow

gu'anto *nm* glove. **guanto da forno** oven glove. **guanto di spugna** face cloth

guan'tone *nm* mitt; **guantoni** *pl* [da boxe] boxing gloves

guarda'boschi *nm inv* forester

guarda'caccia *nm inv* gamekeeper

guarda'coste *nm inv* coastguard

guarda'linee *nm inv* Sport linesman

guarda'macchine *nmf* car-park attendant

guarda'parco *nm inv* park ranger

guar'dare ① *vt* look at; (osservare) watch; (badare a) look after; ⟨finestra⟩ look out on; ∼ **la televisione** watch television ② *vi* look; (essere orientato verso) face; ∼ **in su** look up

guarda'roba *nm inv* wardrobe; (di locale pubblico) cloakroom

guardarobi'ere, -a *nmf* cloakroom attendant

guar'darsi *vr* look at oneself; ∼ **da** beware of; (astenersi) refrain from

gu'ardia *nf* guard; (poliziotto) policeman; (vigilanza) watch; ⟨medico⟩ be on duty; **fare la** ∼ **a** keep guard over; **mettere in** ∼ **qualcuno** warn somebody; **stare in** ∼ be on one's guard.

guardia carceraria prison warder, prison officer. **guardia del corpo** bodyguard, minder. **Guardia di finanza** body of police officers responsible for border control and for investigating fraud. **guardia forestale** forest ranger. **guardia medica** duty doctor

guardi'ano, -a *nmf* caretaker. **guardiano notturno** night watchman. **guardiano dello zoo** zoo keeper

guar'dingo *adj* cautious

guardi'ola *nf* gatekeeper's lodge

guarigi'one *nf* recovery

gua'rire ① *vt* cure ② *vi* recover; ⟨ferita⟩ heal [up]

gua'rito *adj* cured

guari'|tore, -trice *nmf* healer

guarnigi'one *nf* garrison

guar'nire *vt* trim; Culin garnish

guarnizi'one *nf* trimming; Culin garnish; Mech gasket. **guarnizione del freno** brake lining

guasta'feste *nmf inv* spoilsport

gua'stare *vt* spoil; (rovinare) ruin; break ⟨meccanismo⟩

gua'starsi *vr* spoil; (andare a male) go bad; ⟨tempo⟩ change for the worse; ⟨meccanismo⟩ break down

gu'asto ① *adj* broken; ⟨ascensore, telefono⟩ out of order; ⟨auto⟩ broken down; ⟨cibo, dente⟩ bad ② *nm* breakdown; (danno) damage; **ho un** ∼ **alla macchina** my car's not working. **guasto al motore** engine failure

Guate'mala *nm* Guatemala

guazza'buglio *nm* muddle

guaz'zare *vi* wallow

gu'ercio *adj* cross-eyed

gu'erra *nf* war; (tecnica bellica) warfare; **la grande** ∼ the Great War, World War I. **guerra batteriologica** germ warfare. **guerra biologica** biological warfare. **guerra civile** civil war. **guerra fredda** Cold War. **guerra del Golfo** Gulf War. **guerra lampo** blitzkrieg. **guerra mondiale** world war. **prima guerra mondiale** World War I, WW1. **seconda guerra mondiale** World War II, WW2. **guerra dei prezzi** price war. **guerra di secessione** American Civil War

guerrafon'daio, -a *nmf* warmonger

guerreggi'are *vi* wage war

guer'resco *adj* (di guerra) war; (bellicoso) warlike

guerri'ero *nm* warrior

guer'riglia *nf* guerrilla warfare

guerrigli'ero, -a *nmf* guerrilla

'gufo *nm* owl

'guglia *nf* spire

gu'ida *nf* guide; (direzione) guidance; (comando) leadership; (elenco) directory; Auto ⋯❖

driving; (tappeto) runner; **chi era alla ∼?** who was driving?; **essere alla ∼ di** fig be the head of; **fare da ∼** be a guide (**a** to). **guida commerciale** trade directory. **guida a destra** right-hand drive. **guida a sinistra** left-hand drive. **guida telefonica** phone book, telephone directory. **guida turistica** tourist guide

gui'dare *vt* guide; Auto drive; steer ⟨*nave*⟩; **∼ a passo d'uomo** drive at walking speed

guida|'tore, -trice *nmf* driver. **guidatore della domenica** Sunday driver

Gui'nea *nf* Guinea

Gui'nea-Bis'sau *nf* Guinea-Bissau

Gui'nea Equato'riale *nf* Equatorial Guinea

guin'zaglio *nm* leash

gu'isa *nf* **a ∼ di** like

guiz'zare *vi* dart; ⟨*luce*⟩ flash

gu'izzo *nm* dart; (di luce) flash

'gulag *nm inv* Gulag

'gulasch *nm inv* goulash

'guru *nm inv* high priest

'guscio *nm* shell; (di cellulare) fascia

gu'stare ① *vt* taste
② *vi* like

'gusto *nm* taste; (piacere) liking; **mangiare di ∼** eat heartily; **prenderci ∼** come to enjoy it, develop a taste for it; **al ∼ di pistacchio** pistachio flavoured; **buon ∼** good taste

gu'stoso *adj* tasty; fig delightful

guttu'rale *adj* guttural

Gu'yana *nf* Guyana

Hh

'habitat *nm inv* habitat

habitué *nmf inv* regular [customer]

'hacker *nmf inv* Comput hacker

Ha'iti *nf* Haiti

haiti'ano, -a *adj & nmf* Haitian

'halal *adj* halal

hall *nf inv* foyer; (di stazione) concourse

ham'burger *nm inv* hamburger. **hamburger vegetariano** veggie burger

'handicap *nm inv* handicap

handicap'pare *vt* handicap

handicap'pato, -a ① *adj* disabled ② *nmf* disabled person. **handicappato mentale** mentally handicapped person

'hangar *nm inv* hangar

'hard[-core] *adj* hard core

hard 'disk *nm inv* hard disk

hard 'rock *nm* hard rock

'hardware *nm inv* Comput hardware

'harem *nm inv* harem

'hashish *nm* hashish

hawa'iano, -a *adj & nmf* Hawaiian

'Hawaii *nfpl* **le ∼** Hawaii

'heavy metal *nm* Mus heavy metal

henné *nm* henna

'herpes *nm inv* herpes; (su labbra) cold sore. **herpes zoster** shingles

'hi-fi *nm inv* hi-fi

high 'tech *nf* high tech

'Himalaia *nm* Himalayas *pl*

'hinterland *nm inv* hinterland

'hippy *adj & nmf inv* hippy

'hit parade *nf inv* hit parade, charts *pl*

HIV *nm* HIV

'hockey *nm* hockey. **hockey su ghiaccio** ice hockey. **hockey su prato** field hockey

'holding *nf inv* holding company

hollywoo'diano *adj* Hollywood

Hong 'Kong *nf* Hong Kong

'hostess *nf inv* (air) stewardess

hot 'dog *nm inv* hot dog

'hotel *nm inv* hotel

'humus *nm* humus

Ii

i *def art mpl* the; ▸ IL

i'ato *nm* hiatus

i'berico *adj* Iberian

iber'nare *vi* hibernate

ibernazi'one *nf* hibernation

i'bisco *nm* hibiscus

ibri'dare *vt* interbreed

ibridazi'one *nf* interbreeding

'ibrido *adj & nm* hybrid

'iceberg *nm inv* iceberg; **la punta dell'~** fig the tip of the iceberg

i'cona *nf* icon

iconiz'zare *vt* iconize

icono'clasta *adj & nmf* iconoclast

icono'clastico *adj* iconoclastic

id'dio *nm* God

i'dea *nf* idea; (opinione) opinion; (ideale) ideal; (indizio) inkling; (piccola quantità) hint; (intenzione) intention; **cambiare ~** change one's mind; **neanche per ~!** not on your life!; **chiarirsi le idee** get one's ideas straight; **dare l'~ di ...** give the impression that ...; **essere dell'~ che ...** be of the opinion that ...; **non ne ho ~!** I've no idea!. **idea fissa** obsession

ide'ale *adj & nm* ideal

idea'lista *nmf* idealist

idealiz'zare *vt* idealize

ide'are *vt* conceive

idea|'tore, -trice *nmf* originator

'idem *adv* the same

identica'mente *adv* identically

i'dentico *adj* identical

identifi'cabile *adj* identifiable

identifi'care *vt* identify

identifica'tivo *nm* **identificativo del chiamante** caller identification

identificazi'one *nf* identification

identi'kit® *nm inv* identikit. **identikit elettronico** e-fit

identità *nf inv* identity

ideo'gramma *nm* ideogram

ideolo'gia *nf* ideology

ideologica'mente *adv* ideologically

ideo'logico *adj* ideological

idillica'mente *adv* idyllically

i'dillico *adj* idyllic

i'dillio *nm* idyll

idi'oma *nm* language

idio'matico *adj* idiomatic; **espressione idiomatica** idiom, idiomatic expression

idiosincra'sia *nf* fig aversion; Med allergy

idi'ota [1] *adj* idiotic [2] *nmf* idiot

idio'zia *nf* idiocy; **dire/fare un'~** do/say something stupid; **dire idiozie** talk nonsense; **non fare idiozie!** don't act daft!

idola'trare *vt* worship

idoleggi'are *vt* idolize

'idolo *nm* idol

idoneità *nf* suitability; Mil fitness; **esame di idoneità** qualifying examination

i'doneo *adj* **~ a** suitable for; Mil fit for

i'drante *nm* hydrant; (tubo) hose; (usato dalla polizia) water cannon

idra'tante *adj* ‹crema› moisturizing

idra'tare *vt* hydrate; ‹cosmetico› moisturize

idratazi'one *nf* moisturizing

i'draulico [1] *adj* hydraulic [2] *nm* plumber

'idrico *adj* water *attrib*

idrocar'buro *nm* hydrocarbon

idroelettricità *nf* hydroelectricity

idroe'lettrico *adj* hydroelectric

i'drofilo *adj* **cotone ~** cotton wool, absorbent cotton Am

idrofo'bia *nf* rabies *sg*

i'drofobo *adj* rabid; fig furious

i'drofugo *adj* water-repellent

i'drogeno *nm* hydrogen

idrogra'fia *nf* hydrography

i'drolisi *nf* hydrolysis

idromas'saggio *nm* (sistema) whirlpool bath; **vasca con ~** jacuzzi®

idro'mele *nm* mead

idrorepel'lente *adj & nm* water-repellent

idroso'lubile *adj* water-soluble

idrotera'pia *nf* hydrotherapy

idrovo'lante *nm* seaplane

i'druro *nm* hydride

i'ella *nf* fam bad luck; **portare ~** be bad luck

iel'lato *adj* fam jinxed, plagued by bad luck

i'ena *nf* hyena

i'eri *adv* yesterday; **~ l'altro, l'altro ~** the day before yesterday; **il giornale di ~** yesterday's paper; **~ mattina** yesterday evening

ietta|'tore, -trice *nmf* jinx

ietta'tura *nf* (sfortuna) bad luck

igi'ene *nf* hygiene; **ufficio d'igiene** ≈ Public Health Service. **igiene mentale** mental health. **igiene personale** personal hygiene. **igiene pubblica** public health

igienica'mente *adv* hygienically

igi'enico *adj* hygienic

igie'nista *nmf* hygienist

ig'loo *nm inv* igloo

i'gname *nm* yam

i'gnaro *adj* unaware

i'gnifugo *adj* flame-retardant, fire-retardant

i'gnobile *adj* despicable

ignobil'mente *adv* despicably
igno'minia *nf* disgrace
igno'rante ① *adj* ignorant
② *nmf* ignoramus
igno'ranza *nf* ignorance; **ignoranza crassa** crass ignorance
igno'rare *vt* (non sapere) be unaware of; (trascurare) ignore; **essere ignorato** go unheeded
i'gnoto *adj* unknown
i'guana *nf* iguana
il *def art m* the; **il latte fa bene** milk is good for you; **il signor Magnetti** Mr Magnetti; **il dottor Piazza** Doctor Piazza; **ha il naso grosso** he's got a big nose; **ha gli occhi azzurri** he's got blue eyes; **mettiti il cappello** put your hat on; **il lunedì** on Mondays; **il 2004** 2004; **costa 5 euro il chilo** it costs 5 euros a kilo
'ilare *adj* merry
ilarità *nf* hilarity
i'leo *nm* hipbone
illangui'dire *vi* grow weak
illazi'one *nf* inference
illecita'mente *adv* illicitly
il'lecito *adj* illicit
ille'gale *adj* illegal
illegalità *nf* illegality
illegal'mente *adv* illegally
illeg'gibile *adj* illegible; ⟨libro⟩ unreadable
illegittimità *nf* illegitimacy
ille'gittimo *adj* illegitimate
il'leso *adj* unhurt, uninjured
illette'rato, -a *adj & nmf* illiterate
illi'bato *adj* chaste
illimitata'mente *adv* indefinitely
illimi'tato *adj* unlimited
illivi'dire ① *vt* bruise
② *vi* (per rabbia) turn livid
illogica'mente *adv* illogically
il'logico *adj* illogical
il'ludere *vt* deceive
il'ludersi *vr* deceive oneself
illumi'nare *vt* light up; fig enlighten; ⁓ **a giorno** floodlight
illumi'narsi *vr* light up
illuminazi'one *nf* lighting; fig enlightenment. **illuminazione a gas** gas lighting. **illuminazione al neon** strip lighting
Illumi'nismo *nm* Enlightenment
illusi'one *nf* illusion; **farsi illusioni** delude oneself. **illusione ottica** optical illusion
illusio'nismo *nm* conjuring
illusio'nista *nmf* conjurer
il'luso, -a ① *pp di* ILLUDERE
② *adj* deluded

③ *nmf* day-dreamer
illu'sorio *adj* illusory
illu'strare *vt* illustrate
illustra'tivo *adj* illustrative
illustra|'tore, -trice *nmf* illustrator
illustrazi'one *nf* illustration. **illustrazione a colori/in bianco e nero** colour/black and white illustration
il'lustre *adj* distinguished
imbacuc'care *vt* wrap up
imbacuc'carsi *vr* wrap up
imbacuc'cato *adj* wrapped up
imbal'laggio *nm* packing
imbal'lare *vt* pack; Auto race
imballa|'tore, -trice *nmf* packer
imbalsa'mare *vt* embalm; stuff ⟨animale⟩
imbalsa'mato *adj* embalmed; ⟨animale⟩ stuffed
imbambo'lato *adj* vacant
imban'dito *adj* ⟨tavola⟩ covered with food
imbaraz'zante *adj* embarrassing
imbaraz'zare *vt* embarrass; (ostacolare) encumber
imbaraz'zato *adj* embarrassed
imba'razzo *nm* embarrassment; (ostacolo) hindrance; **trarre qualcuno d'** ⁓ help somebody out of a difficulty; **avere l'**⁓ **della scelta** be spoilt for choice. **imbarazzo di stomaco** indigestion.
imbarba'rire *vt* barbarize
imbarba'rirsi *vr* become barbarized
imbarca'dero *nm inv* landing-stage
imbar'care *vt* embark; (fam: rimorchiare) score; ⁓ **acqua** ship water
imbar'carsi *vr* go on board; fig embark (in on)
imbarcazi'one *nf* boat. **imbarcazione da pesca** fishing boat. **imbarcazione di salvataggio** lifeboat
im'barco *nm* boarding; (banchina) landing-stage; '⁓ **immediato**' 'now boarding'
imbastar'dire *vt* debase
imbastar'dirsi *vr* become debased
imba'stire *vt* tack, baste; fig sketch
imbasti'tura *nf* tacking, basting
im'battersi *vr* ⁓ **in** run into
imbat'tibile *adj* unbeatable
imbat'tuto *adj* unbeaten
imbavagli'are *vt* gag
imbec'cata *nf* Theat prompt
imbe'cille ① *adj* stupid
② *nmf* Med imbecile
imbellet'tarsi *vr* hum doll oneself up
imbel'lire *vt* embellish
im'berbe *adj* beardless; fig inexperienced

imbestia'lire *vi* fly into a rage; **far ∼ qualcuno** drive somebody crazy

imbestia'lirsi *vr* fly into a rage

imbestia'lito *adj* enraged

im'bevere *vt* imbue (**di** with)

im'beversi *vr* absorb

imbe'vibile *adj* undrinkable

imbe'vuto *adj* ∼ **di** ⟨*acqua*⟩ soaked in; ⟨*nozioni*⟩ imbued with

imbian'care ① *vt* whiten ② *vi* turn white

imbian'chino *nm* [house] painter

imbion'dire ① *vt* bleach ② *vi* become bleached

imbion'dirsi *vr* become bleached

imbizzar'rire *vr* become restless; (arrabbiarsi) become angry

imbizzar'rirsi *vi* become restless; (arrabbiarsi) become angry

imboc'care *vt* feed; (entrare) enter; fig prompt

imbocca'tura *nf* opening; (ingresso) entrance; (Mus: di strumento) mouthpiece

im'bocco *nm* entrance

imboni'mento *nm* spiel

imboni'tore *nm* clever talker

imborghe'sire *vi* become middle class

imborghe'sirsi *vr* become middle class

imbo'scare *vt* hide

imbo'scarsi *vr* Mil shirk military service

imbo'scata *nf* ambush

imbo'scato *nm* draft dodger

imbottiglia'mento *nm* traffic jam

imbottigli'are *vt* bottle

imbottigli'arsi *vr* get snarled up in a traffic jam

imbottigli'ato *adj* ⟨*vino, acqua*⟩ bottled; ⟨*auto*⟩ stuck in a traffic jam, snarled up; **nave imbottigliata** ship in a bottle

imbot'tire *vt* stuff; pad (giacca); Culin fill

imbot'tirsi *vr* ∼ **di** (fig, di pasticche) stuff oneself with

imbot'tita *nf* quilt

imbot'tito *adj* ⟨*spalle*⟩ padded; ⟨*cuscino*⟩ stuffed; ⟨*panino*⟩ filled

imbotti'tura *nf* stuffing; (di giacca) padding; Culin filling

imbraca'tura *nf* harness

imbracci'are *vt* shoulder ⟨*fucile*⟩; grasp ⟨*scudo*⟩

imbra'nato *adj* clumsy

imbrat'tare *vt* mark

imbrat'tarsi *vr* dirty oneself

imbrigli'are *vt* bridle ⟨*cavallo*⟩; dam ⟨*acque*⟩

imbroc'care *vt* hit; **imbroccarla giusta** hit the nail on the head

imbrogli'are *vt* muddle; (raggirare) cheat; ∼ **le carte** fig confuse the issue

imbrogli'arsi *vr* get tangle; (confondersi) get confused

im'broglio *nm* tangled; (pasticcio) mess; (inganno) trick

imbrogli'one, -a *nmf* cheat

imbronci'are *vi* sulk

imbronci'arsi *vr* sulk

imbronci'ato *adj* sulky

imbru'nire *vi* get dark; **all'∼** at dusk

imbrut'tire ① *vt* make ugly ② *vi* become ugly

imbu'care *vt* post, mail; (nel biliardo) pot

imbu'cato *adj* fam **è ∼** he only got the job because of who he knows

imbufa'lirsi *vr* hit the roof

imbur'rare *vt* butter

im'buto *nm* funnel

i'mene *nm* hymen

imi'tare *vt* imitate

imita|'tore, -trice *nmf* imitator, impersonator

imitazi'one *nf* imitation; **'diffidare delle imitazioni'** 'beware of imitations'

immaco'lato *adj* spotless, immaculate; **l'immacolata Concezione** the Immaculate Conception

immagazzi'nare *vt* store

immagi'nare *vt* imagine; (supporre) suppose; **s'immagini!** don't mention it!

immagi'nario *adj* imaginary

immaginazi'one *nf* imagination; **è frutto della tua ∼** it's a figment of your imagination

im'magine *nf* image; (rappresentazione, idea) picture. **immagine aziendale** corporate image. **immagine della marca** brand image. **immagine speculare** mirror image

immagi'noso *adj* full of imagery

immalinco'nire *vt* sadden

immalinco'nirsi *vr* grow melancholy

imman'cabile *adj* unfailing

immancabil'mente *adv* without fail

im'mane *adj* huge; (orribile) terrible

imma'nente *adj* immanent

immangi'abile *adj* inedible

immatrico'lare *vt* register

immatrico'larsi *vr* ⟨*studente*⟩ matriculate

immatrico'lato *adj* registered

immatricolazi'one *nf* registration; (di studente) matriculation

immaturità *nf* immaturity

imma'turo *adj* unripe; ⟨*persona*⟩ immature; (precoce) premature

immedesi'marsi *vr* ∼ **in** identify oneself with

immedesimazi'one *nf* identification

immediata'mente *adv* immediately

immedia'tezza *nf* immediacy

immedi'ato *adj* immediate; nell'∼ futuro in the immediate future

immemo'rabile *adj* immemorial

im'memore *adj* oblivious

immensa'mente *adv* enormously

immensità *nf* immensity

im'menso *adj* immense

immensu'rabile *adj* immeasurable

im'mergere *vt* immerse

im'mergersi *vr* plunge; ‹sommergibile› dive; ∼ in immerse oneself in

immeritata'mente *adv* undeservedly

immeri'tato *adj* undeserved

immeri'tevole *adj* undeserving

immersi'one *nf* immersion; (di sommergibile, palombaro) dive. **immersione [subacquea]** skin diving, scuba diving

im'merso *pp di* IMMERGERE

im'mettere *vt* introduce

im'mettersi *vr* introduce oneself

immi'grante *adj & nmf* immigrant

immi'grare *vi* immigrate

immi'grato, -a *nmf* immigrant

immigrazi'one *nf* immigration. **immigrazione interna** migration

immi'nente *adj* imminent

immi'nenza *nf* imminence

immischi'are *vt* involve

immischi'arsi *vr* ∼ in meddle in

immi'scibile *adj* immiscible

immis'sario *nm* tributary

immissi'one *nf* insertion; Techn intake; (introduzione) introduction. **immissione [di] dati** data entry

im'mobile *adj* motionless

im'mobili *nmpl* real estate

immobili'are *adj* **società immobiliare** building society, savings and loan Am

immobilità *nf* immobility

immobiliz'zare *vt* immobilize; Comm tie up

immobiliz'zato *adj* immobilized. **immobilizzato a letto** confined to bed

immobilizza'tore *nm* **immobilizzatore elettronico** Auto immobilizer

immobilizzazi'one *nf* immobilization; Fin fixed asset; **spese d'**∼ capital expenditure

immoderata'mente *adv* immoderately

immode'rato *adj* immoderate

immo'destia *nf* immodesty

immo'desto *adj* immodest

immo'lare *vt* sacrifice

immo'larsi *vr* sacrifice oneself

immondez'zaio *nm* rubbish tip

immon'dizia *nf* filth; (spazzatura) rubbish

im'mondo *adj* filthy

immo'rale *adj* immoral

immoral'mente *adv* immorally

immorta'lare *vt* immortalize

immor'tale *adj* immortal

immortalità *nf* immortality

immoti'vato *adj* unjustified, unmotivated

im'moto *adj* motionless

im'mune *adj* exempt; Med immune

immunità *nf* immunity. **immunità diplomatica** diplomatic immunity. **immunità parlamentare** parliamentary privilege

immuniz'zare *vt* immunize

immunizzazi'one *nf* immunization

immunodefici'enza *nf* immunodeficiency

immunodepres'sivo *adj & nm* immunodepressant

immunolo'gia *nf* immunology

immuno'logico *adj* immunological

immuso'nirsi *vr* sulk

immuso'nito *adj* sulky

immu'tabile *adj* unchangeable

immu'tato *adj* unchanging

impacchet'tare *vt* wrap up

impacci'are *vt* hamper; (disturbare) inconvenience; (imbarazzare) embarrass

impacciata'mente *adv* awkwardly

impacci'ato *adj* embarrassed; (goffo) awkward

im'paccio *nm* embarrassment; (ostacolo) hindrance; (situazione difficile) awkward situation; **trarsi d'**∼ get out of an awkward situation

im'pacco *nm* compress

impadro'nirsi *vr* ∼ **di** take possession of; (fig: imparare) master

impa'gabile *adj* priceless

impagi'nare *vt* paginate

impaginazi'one *nf* pagination

impagli'are *vt* stuff ‹animale›

impa'lare *vt* impale

impa'lato *adj* fig stiff

impalca'tura *nf* scaffolding; fig structure

impal'lare *vt* snooker

impalli'dire *vi* turn pale; (fig: perdere d'importanza) pale into insignificance

impalli'nare *vt* riddle with bullets

impal'pabile *adj* impalpable; ‹tessuto› gossamer-like

impa'nare *vt* Culin bread

impa'nato *adj* breaded

impanta'narsi *vr* get bogged down

impape'rarsi *vr* falter, stammer

impappi'narsi *vr* falter, stammer

impa'rare *vt* learn; ∼ **a proprie spese** learn to one's cost

impara'ticcio *nm* half-baked

impareggi'abile *adj* incomparable

imparen'tarsi *vr* ∼ **con** become related to

imparen'tato *adj* related

'impari *adj* unequal; (dispari) odd

impar'tire *vt* impart

imparzi'ale *adj* impartial

imparzialità *nf* impartiality

im'passe *nf inv* impasse

impas'sibile *adj* impassive; **con aria** ∼ impassively

impa'stare *vt* Culin knead; blend ⟨colori⟩

impasta'tura *nf* kneading

impastic'carsi *vr* pop pills

impasticci'are *vt* make a mess of

im'pasto *nm* Culin dough; (miscuglio) mixture

im'patto *nm* impact. **impatto ambientale** environmental impact

impau'rire *vt* frighten

impau'rirsi *vr* get frightened

im'pavido *adj* fearless

impazi'ente *adj* impatient; ∼ **di fare qualcosa** eager to do something

impazien'tirsi *vr* lose patience

impazi'enza *nf* impatience

impaz'zata *nf* all'∼ at breakneck speed

impaz'zire *vi* go mad; ⟨maionese⟩ separate; **far** ∼ **qualcuno** drive somebody mad; ∼ **per** be crazy about; **da** ∼ ⟨mal di testa⟩ blinding

impaz'zito *adj* crazed

impec'cabile *adj* impeccable

impeccabil'mente *adv* impeccably

impedi'mento *nm* hindrance; (ostacolo) obstacle

impe'dire *vt* (impacciare) hinder; (ostruire) obstruct; ∼ **di** prevent from; ∼ **a qualcuno di fare qualcosa** prevent somebody [from] doing something

impe'gnare *vt* (dare in pegno) pawn; (vincolare) bind; (prenotare) reserve; (assorbire) take up

impe'gnarsi *vr* apply oneself; ∼ **a fare qualcosa** commit oneself to doing something

impegna'tiva *nf* referral

impegna'tivo *adj* binding; ⟨lavoro⟩ demanding

impe'gnato *adj* politically committed

im'pegno *nm* engagement; Comm commitment; (zelo) care; **con** ∼ with dedication; **ho un** ∼ I'm doing something

impego'larsi *vr* ∼ **in** become enmeshed in

impel'lente *adj* pressing

impene'trabile *adj* impenetrable

impen'narsi *vr* ⟨cavallo⟩ rear; fig bristle

impen'nata *nf* (di prezzi) sharp rise; (di cavallo) rearing; (di moto) wheelie; (di aereo) climb

impen'sabile *adj* unthinkable

impen'sato *adj* unexpected

impensie'rire *vt* worry

impensie'rirsi *vr* worry

impe'rante *adj* prevailing

impe'rare *vi* reign

impera'tivo *adj & nm* imperative

impera'|tore, -trice ① *nm* emperor ② *nf* empress

impercet'tibile *adj* imperceptible

impercettibil'mente *adv* imperceptibly

imperdo'nabile *adj* unforgivable

imperfetta'mente *adv* imperfectly

imper'fetto *adj & nm* imperfect

imperfezi'one *nf* imperfection

imperi'ale *adj* imperial

imperia'lismo *nm* imperialism

imperia'lista *adj & nmf* imperialist

imperia'listico *adj* imperialistic

imperi'oso *adj* imperious; (impellente) urgent

imperi'turo *adj* immortal

impe'rizia *nf* lack of skill

imper'lare *vt* bead

imperma'lire *vt* offend

imperma'lirsi *vr* take offence

imperme'abile ① *adj* ⟨orologio⟩ waterproof; ⟨terreno⟩ impermeable ② *nm* raincoat

imperni'are *vt* pivot; (fondare) base

imperni'arsi *vr* ∼ **su** be based on

im'pero *nm* empire; (potere) rule; **stile impero** empire style

imperscru'tabile *adj* inscrutable

imperso'nale *adj* impersonal

imperso'nare *vt* personify; (interpretare) act [the part of]

imper'territo *adj* undaunted, undeterred

imperti'nente *adj* impertinent

imperti'nenza *nf* impertinence

impertur'babile *adj* imperturbable

impertur'bato *adj* unperturbed

imperver'sare *vi* rage

im'pervio *adj* inaccessible

'impeto *nm* impetus; (impulso) impulse; (slancio) transport

impet'tito *adj* stiff

impetuosa'mente *adv* impetuously

impetu'oso *adj* impetuous; ‹vento› blustering

impiallacci'are *vt* veneer

impiallacci'ato *adj* veneered

impian'tare *vt* install; set up ‹azienda›

impi'anto *nm* plant; (sistema) system; (operazione) installation. **impianto di amplificazione** public address system, PA system. **impianto audio** sound system. **impianto elettrico** electrical system; **impianti** *pl* **fissi** fixtures and fittings. **impianto radio** Auto car stereo system. **impianto di rilavorazione [di scorie nucleari]** reprocessing plant. **impianto di riscaldamento** heating system. **impianto stereo** hi-fi

impia'strare *vt* plaster; (sporcare) dirty

impia'strarsi *vr* get dirty; ~ **le mani** get one's hands dirty

impi'astro *nm* poultice; ‹persona noiosa› bore; (pasticcione) cack-handed person

impiccagi'one *nf* hanging

impic'care *vt* hang

impic'carsi *vr* hang oneself

impic'cato, -a ① *nm* hanged man ② *nf* hanged woman

impicci'arsi *vr* meddle

im'piccio *nm* hindrance; (seccatura) bother

impicci'one, -a *nmf* nosey parker

impie'gare *vt* employ; (usare) use; spend ‹tempo, denaro›; Fin invest; **l'autobus ha impiegato un'ora** it took the bus an hour

impie'garsi *vr* get [oneself] a job

impiega'tizio *adj* clerical

impie'gato, -a *nmf* employee; (di ufficio) office worker. **impiegato di banca** bank clerk. **impiegato di concetto** administrative employee. **impiegato in prova** probationer. **impiegato statale** civil servant

impi'ego *nm* employment; (posto) job; Fin investment; **pubblico impiego** public sector. **impiego fisso** permanent job. **impieghi** *pl* **saltuari** odd jobs, casual employment. **impiego temporaneo** temporary job

impieto'sire *vt* move to pity

impieto'sirsi *vr* be moved to pity

impie'toso *adj* pitiless

impie'trito *adj* petrified

impigli'are *vt* entangle

impigli'arsi *vr* get entangled

impi'grire *vt* make lazy

impi'grirsi *vr* get lazy

impi'lare *vt* stack

impingu'are *vt* fig fill

impiom'bare *vt* seal ‹cassa, porta›

impla'cabile *adj* implacable

implemen'tare *vt* implement

impli'care *vt* implicate; (sottintendere) imply

impli'carsi *vr* become involved

implicazi'one *nf* implication

implicita'mente *adv* implicitly

im'plicito *adj* implicit

implo'rante *adj* imploring

implo'rare *vt* implore

implorazi'one *nf* entreaty

implosi'one *nf* implosion

impolli'nare *vt* pollinate

impollinazi'one *nf* pollination

impoltro'nire *vt* make lazy

impoltro'nirsi *vr* become lazy

impolve'rare *vt* cover with dust

impolve'rarsi *vr* get covered with dust

impolve'rato *adj* dusty

impoma'tare *vt* put brilliantine on

impoma'tarsi *vr* put brilliantine on ‹capelli›

imponde'rabile *adj* imponderable; ‹causa, evento› unpredictable

impo'nente *adj* imposing

impo'nenza *nf* impressiveness

impo'nibile ① *adj* taxable ② *nm* taxable income

impopo'lare *adj* unpopular

impopolarità *nf* unpopularity

imporpo'rarsi *vr* turn red

im'porre *vt* impose; (ordinare) order

im'porsi *vr* assert oneself; (aver successo) be successful; ~ **di** (prefiggersi di) set oneself the task of

impor'tante ① *adj* important ② *nm* important thing

impor'tanza *nf* importance; **di vitale ~** crucially important

impor'tare ① *vt* Comm, Comput import; (comportare) cause ② *vi* matter; (essere necessario) be necessary; **non importa!** it doesn't matter!; **non me ne importa niente!** I couldn't care less!

importa|'tore, -trice ① *adj* importing ② *nmf* importer

importazi'one *nf* importation; (merce importata) import

import-'export *nm inv* import-export

im'porto *nm* amount

importu'nare *vt* pester; ~ **qualcuno per qualcosa** pester somebody for something

impor'tuno *adj* troublesome; (inopportuno) untimely

imposizi'one *nf* imposition; (imposta) tax

imposses'sarsi *vr* ~ **di** seize
impos'sibile ① *adj* impossible
  ② *nm* **fare l'**~ do absolutely all one can
impossibilità *nf* impossibility
im'posta[1] *nf* tax. **imposta fondiaria** land tax. **imposta patrimoniale** property tax. **imposta sul reddito** income tax. **imposta sui redditi di capitale** capital gains tax. **imposta sulle società** corporation tax. **imposta supplementare** surtax. **imposta sul valore aggiunto** value added tax
im'posta[2] *nf* (di finestra) shutter
impo'stare *vt* (progettare) plan; (basare) base; Mus pitch; (imbucare) post, mail; set out ⟨*domanda, problema*⟩
impostazi'one *nf* planning; (di voce) pitching; **impostazioni** *pl* Comput, Teleph settings
im'posto pp di IMPORRE
impo'store, -a *nmf* impostor
impo'stura *nf* imposture
impo'tente *adj* powerless; Med impotent
impo'tenza *nf* powerlessness; Med impotence
impoveri'mento *nm* impoverishment
impove'rire *vt* impoverish
impove'rirsi *vr* become poor; ⟨*risorse*⟩ become depleted; ⟨*linguaggio*⟩ become impoverished
imprati'cabile *adj* impracticable; ⟨*strada*⟩ impassable
impraticabilità *nf* **per** ~ **del terreno/delle strade** because of the state of the pitch/roads
imprati'chire *vt* train
imprati'chirsi *vr* ~ **in,** ~ **a** get practice in
impre'care *vi* curse
imprecazi'one *nf* curse
impreci'sabile *adj* indeterminable
impreci'sato *adj* indeterminate
imprecisi'one *nf* inaccuracy
impre'ciso *adj* inaccurate
impre'gnare *vt* impregnate; (imbevere) soak; fig imbue
impre'gnarsi *vr* become impregnated with
imprendi|'tore, -trice *nmf* entrepreneur
imprenditori'ale *adj* entrepreneurial
imprepa'rato *adj* unprepared
im'presa *nf* undertaking; (gesta) exploit; ⟨*azienda*⟩ firm. **impresa edile** property developer. **impresa familiare** family business. **impresa di pompe funebri** undertakers, funeral directors. **impresa pubblica** state-owned company. **impresa di traslochi** removals firm Br

impre'sario *nm* impresario; (appaltatore) contractor. **impresario di pompe funebri** undertaker, funeral director, mortician Am. **impresario teatrale** theatre manager
imprescin'dibile *adj* inescapable
impressio'nabile *adj* impressionable
impressio'nante *adj* impressive; (spaventoso) frightening
impressio'nare *vt* impress; (spaventare) frighten; expose ⟨*foto*⟩
impressio'narsi *vr* be affected; (spaventarsi) be frightened
impressi'one *nf* impression; (sensazione) sensation; (impronta) mark; **far** ~ **a qualcuno** upset somebody; **dare l'**~ **di essere …** give the impression of being …
impressio'nismo *nm* impressionism
impressio'nista *adj* & *nmf* impressionist
impressio'nistico *adj* impressionistic
im'presso ① pp di IMPRIMERE
  ② *adj* printed
impre'stare *vt* lend
impreve'dibile *adj* unforeseeable; ⟨*persona*⟩ unpredictable
imprevedibil'mente *adv* unexpectedly
imprevi'dente *adj* improvident
impre'visto ① *adj* unforeseen
  ② *nm* unforeseen event; **salvo imprevisti** all being well
imprigiona'mento *nm* imprisonment
imprigio'nare *vt* imprison
im'primere *vt* impress; (stampare) print; (comunicare) impart; **rimanere impresso a qualcuno** stick in somebody's mind
impro'babile *adj* unlikely, improbable; **è** ~ **che ci sia** he is unlikely to be there
improbabilità *nf* improbability
improdut'tivo *adj* unproductive
im'pronta *nf* impression; (di dito) print; fig mark. **impronta digitale** fingerprint; **impronte** *pl* **genetiche** genetic fingerprinting. **impronta del piede** footprint
impron'tato *adj* ~ **all'ironia** tinged with irony
impronunci'abile *adj* unpronounceable
impro'perio *nm* insult; **improperi** *pl* abuse *sg*
impropo'nibile *adj* unrealistic
im'proprio *adj* improper
improro'gabile *adj* which cannot be extended
improvvisa'mente *adv* suddenly
improvvi'sare *vt/i* improvise
improvvi'sarsi *vr* turn oneself into a
improvvi'sata *nf* surprise

improvvi'sato adj ⟨discorso⟩ unrehearsed

improvvisazi'one nf improvisation

improv'viso adj unexpected, sudden; **all'**∼ unexpectedly, suddenly

impru'dente adj imprudent

imprudente'mente adv imprudently

impru'denza nf imprudence

impu'dente adj impudent

impudente'mente adv impudently

impu'denza nf impudence

impu'dico adj immodest

impu'gnare vt grasp; Jur contest

impugna'tura nf grip; (manico) handle. **impugnatura a due mani** two-handed grip

impulsiva'mente adv impulsively

impulsività nf impulsiveness

impul'sivo adj impulsive

im'pulso nm impulse; **agire d'**∼ act on impulse

impune'mente adv with impunity

impunità nf impunity

impu'nito adj unpunished

impun'tarsi vr fig dig one's heels in

impun'tura nf stitching

impuntu'rare vt backstitch

impurità nf inv impurity

im'puro adj impure

impu'tabile adj attributable (**a** to); Jur indictable

impu'tare vt attribute; Jur charge

impu'tato, -a nmf accused

imputazi'one nf charge. **imputazione di omicidio** murder charge

imputri'dire vi putrefy

imputri'dito adj putrefied

in prep in; (moto a luogo) to; (su) on; (dentro) within; (mezzo) by; (con materiale) made of; **essere in casa/ufficio** be at home/at the office; **in mano/tasca** in one's hand/pocket; **in fondo alla strada/borsa** at the bottom of the street/bag; **andare in Francia/campagna** go to France/the country; **salire in treno** get on the train; **versa la birra nel bicchiere** pour the beer into the glass; **in alto** up there; **in giornata** within the day; **nel 1997** in 1997; **una borsa in pelle** a bag made of leather, a leather bag; **alzarsi in piedi** stand up; **in macchina** ⟨viaggiare, venire⟩ by car; **in contanti** [in] cash; **in vacanza** on holiday; **di giorno in giorno** from day to day; **se fossi in te** if I were you; **siamo in sette** there are seven of us

inabbor'dabile adj unapproachable

i'nabile adj incapable; (fisicamente) unfit

inabilità nf incapacity

inabi'tabile adj uninhabitable

inacces'sibile adj inaccessible; ⟨persona⟩ unapproachable

inaccet'tabile adj unacceptable

inaccettabilità nf unacceptability

inacer'barsi vr grow bitter

inacer'bire vt embitter; exacerbate ⟨rapporto⟩

inaci'dire vt turn sour

inaci'dirsi vr go sour; ⟨persona⟩ become embittered

ina'datto adj unsuitable

inadegua'tezza nf inadequacy

inadegu'ato adj inadequate

inadempi'ente nmf defaulter

inadempi'enza nf nonfulfilment (**a** of). **inadempienza contrattuale** breach of contract

inadempi'mento nm nonfulfilment

inaffer'rabile adj elusive

inaffi'dabile adj untrustworthy

inaffon'dabile adj unsinkable

ina'lare vt inhale

inala'tore nm inhaler

inalazi'one nf inhalation

inalbe'rare vt hoist

inalbe'rarsi vr ⟨cavallo⟩ rear [up]; (adirarsi) lose one's temper

inalie'nabile adj inalienable

inalte'rabile adj unchanging; ⟨colore⟩ fast

inalte'rato adj unchanged

inami'dare vt starch

inami'dato adj starched

inammis'sibile adj inadmissible

inamovi'bile adj ⟨disco ecc⟩ non-removable

inanel'lato adj bejewelled

inani'mato adj inanimate; (senza vita) lifeless

inappa'gabile adj unsatisfiable

inappaga'mento nm nonfulfilment

inappa'gato adj unfulfilled

inappel'labile adj final

inappe'tenza nf lack of appetite

inappli'cabile adj inapplicable

inappropri'ato adj inapt

inappun'tabile adj faultless

inar'care vt arch; raise ⟨sopracciglia⟩

inar'carsi vr ⟨legno⟩ warp; ⟨ripiano⟩ sag; ⟨linea⟩ curve

inari'dire vt parch; empty of feelings ⟨persona⟩

inari'dirsi vr dry up; ⟨persona⟩ become empty of feelings

inarre'stabile adj unstoppable

inartico'lato adj inarticulate

inascol'tato adj unheard

inaspettata'mente *adv* unexpectedly

inaspet'tato *adj* unexpected

inaspri'mento *nm* (di carattere) embitterment; (di conflitto) worsening

ina'sprire *vt* embitter

ina'sprirsi *vr* become embittered

inattac'cabile *adj* unassailable; (irreprensibile) irreproachable

inatten'dibile *adj* unreliable

inat'teso *adj* unexpected

inattività *nf* inactivity

inat'tivo *adj* inactive

inattu'abile *adj* impracticable

inau'dito *adj* unheard of

inaugu'rale *adj* inaugural; **cerimonia inaugurale** official opening; **viaggio inaugurale** maiden voyage

inaugu'rare *vt* inaugurate; open ‹*mostra*›; unveil ‹*statua*›; christen ‹*lavastoviglie ecc*›

inaugurazi'one *nf* inauguration; (di mostra) opening; (di statua) unveiling

inavve'duto *adj* inadvertent; (sbadato) careless

inavver'tenza *nf* inadvertence

inavvertita'mente *adv* inadvertently

inavvici'nabile *adj* unapproachable

in'breeding *nm inv* inbreeding

'inca *adj & nmf* (pl **inca** o **incas**) Inca

incagli'are ① *vi* ground ② *vt* hinder

incagli'arsi *vr* run aground

in'caglio *nm* running aground; fig obstacle

incalco'labile *adj* incalculable

incal'lirsi *vr* grow callous; (abituarsi) become hardened

incal'lito *adj* callous; (abituato) hardened

incal'zante *adj* ‹*ritmo*› driving; ‹*richiesta*› urgent; ‹*crisi*› imminent

incal'zare *vt* pursue; fig press

incame'rare *vt* appropriate

incammi'nare *vt* get going; (fig: guidare) set off

incammi'narsi *vr* set out

incanala'mento *nm* canalization; fig channelling

incana'lare *vt* canalize; fig channel

incana'larsi *vr* converge on

incancel'labile *adj* indelible

incande'scente *adj* incandescent; ‹*discussione*› burning

incande'scenza *nf* incandescence

incan'tare *vt* enchant

incan'tarsi *vr* stand spellbound; (incepparsi) jam

incanta|'tore, -trice *nmf* enchanter; enchantress. **incantatore di serpenti** snake charmer

incan'tesimo *nm* spell

incan'tevole *adj* enchanting

in'canto *nm* spell; fig delight; (asta) auction; **come per ~** as if by magic

incanu'tire *vt* turn white

incanu'tito *adj* white

inca'pace *adj* incapable; **incapace d'intendere e di volere** Jur unfit to plead

incapacità *nf* incapability

incapo'nirsi *vr* be set

incap'pare *vi* ~ **in** run into

incappucci'arsi *vr* wrap up

incapretta'mento *nm* method of trussing up a victim by the ankles

incapricci'arsi *vr* ~ **di** take a fancy to

incapsu'lare *vt* seal; crown ‹*dente*›

incarce'rare *vt* imprison

incarcerazi'one *nf* imprisonment

incari'care *vt* charge

incari'carsi *vr* take upon oneself; **me ne incarico io** I will see to it

incari'cato, -a ① *adj* in charge ② *nmf* representative. **incaricato d'affari** chargé d'affaires

in'carico *nm* charge; **per ~ di** on behalf of

incar'nare *vt* embody

incar'narsi *vr* become incarnate

incarnazi'one *nf* incarnation

incarta'mento *nm* documents *pl*

incartapeco'rito *adj* shrivelled up

incar'tare *vt* wrap [in paper]

incasel'lare *vt* pigeonhole

incasi'nato *adj* fam ‹*vita*› screwed up; ‹*stanza*› messed up

incas'sare *vt* pack; Mech embed; (incastonare) set; (riscuotere) cash; take ‹*colpo*›

incas'sato *adj* set; ‹*fiume*› deeply embanked

in'casso *nm* collection; (introito) takings *pl*

incasto'nare *vt* set

incasto'nato *adj* embedded; ‹*anello*› inset (**di** with)

incastona'tura *nf* setting

inca'strare *vt* fit in; (fam: in situazione) corner

inca'strarsi *vr* fit, interlock

in'castro *nm* joint; **a ~** ‹*pezzi*› interlocking. **incastro a coda di rondine** dovetail joint

incate'nare *vt* chain

incatra'mare *vt* tar

incatti'vire *vt* turn nasty

incauta'mente *adv* imprudently

in'cauto *adj* imprudent

inca'vare *vt* hollow out

inca'vato *adj* hollow

incava'tura *nf* hollow

in'cavo *nm* hollow; (scanalatura) groove

incavo'larsi *vr* fam get shirty

incavo'lato *adj* fam shirty

in'cedere fml ① *vi* advance solemnly
② *nm* solemn gait

incendi'are *vt* set fire to; fig inflame

incendi'ario, -a ① *adj* incendiary; fig ⟨*discorso*⟩ inflammatory; fig ⟨*bellezza*⟩ sultry
② *nmf* arsonist

incendi'arsi *vr* catch fire

in'cendio *nm* fire. **incendio doloso** arson; **incendi** *pl* **dolosi** cases of arson

inceneri'mento *nm* incineration; (cremazione) cremation

incene'rire *vt* burn to ashes; (cremare) cremate

incene'rirsi *vr* be burnt to ashes

inceneri'tore *nm* incinerator

in'censo *nm* incense

incensu'rabile *adj* irreproachable

incensu'rato *adj* blameless; **essere** ∼ Jur have a clean record

incenti'vare *vt* motivate

incen'tivo *nm* incentive. **incentivo fiscale** tax incentive

incen'trarsi *vr* ∼ **su** centre on

incep'pare *vt* block; fig hamper

incep'parsi *vr* jam

ince'rata *nf* oilcloth

incerot'tato *adj* with a plaster on

incer'tezza *nf* uncertainty

in'certo ① *adj* uncertain, unsure
② *nm* uncertainty; **sono gli incerti del mestiere** that's the way it goes in this business

incespi'care *vi* (inciampare) stumble

inces'sante *adj* unceasing

incessante'mente *adv* incessantly

in'cesto *nm* incest

incestu'oso *adj* incestuous

in'cetta *nf* buying up; **fare** ∼ **di** stockpile

inchi'esta *nf* investigation; **fare un'**∼ conduct an inquiry. **inchiesta giudiziaria** criminal investigation. **inchiesta parlamentare** parliamentary inquiry

inchi'nare *vt* bow

inchi'narsi *vr* bow

in'chino *nm* bow; (di donna) curtsy

inchio'dare *vt* nail; nail down ⟨*coperchio*⟩; ∼ **a letto** ⟨*malattia*⟩ confine to bed

inchi'ostro *nm* ink. **inchiostro di china** Indian ink. **inchiostro simpatico** invisible ink. **inchiostro di stampa** newsprint

inciam'pare *vi* stumble; ∼ **in** trip over; (imbattersi) run into

inci'ampo *nm* hindrance

inciden'tale *adj* incidental

inci'dente *nm* (episodio) incident; (infortunio) accident. **incidente aereo** plane crash. **incidente d'auto** car accident. **incidente sul lavoro** industrial accident. **incidente stradale** road accident

inci'denza *nf* incidence

in'cidere ① *vt* cut; (arte) engrave; (registrare) record
② *vi* ∼ **su** (gravare) weigh upon

in'cinta *adj* pregnant

incipi'ente *adj* incipient

incipri'are *vt* powder

incipri'arsi *vr* powder one's face

in'circa *adv* **all'**∼ more or less

incisi'one *nf* incision; (arte) engraving; (acquaforte) etching; (registrazione) recording

inci'sivo ① *adj* incisive
② *nm* (dente) incisor

in'ciso *nm* **per** ∼ incidentally

inci'sore *nm* engraver

incita'mento *nm* incitement

inci'tare *vt* incite

inci'vile *adj* uncivilized; (maleducato) impolite

inciviltà *nf* barbarism; (maleducazione) rudeness

inclassifi'cabile *adj* unclassifiable

incle'mente *adj* harsh

incle'menza *nf* harshness

incli'nabile *adj* reclining

incli'nare ① *vt* tilt
② *vi* ∼ **a** be inclined to

incli'narsi *vr* ⟨*torre*⟩ lean; ⟨*aereo*⟩ tilt

incli'nato *adj* tilted; ⟨*terreno*⟩ sloping

inclinazi'one *nf* slope, inclination

in'cline *adj* inclined

in'cludere *vt* include; (allegare) enclose

inclusi'one *nf* inclusion

inclu'sivo *adj* inclusive

in'cluso ① pp di INCLUDERE
② *adj* included; (compreso) inclusive; (allegato) enclosed

incoe'rente *adj* (contraddittorio) inconsistent

incoerente'mente *adv* inconsistently

incoe'renza *nf* inconsistency

in'cognita *nf* unknown quantity

in'cognito ① *adj* unknown
② *nm* **in** ∼ incognito

incol'lare *vt* stick; (con colla liquida) glue; Comput paste

incol'larsi *vr* stick to; ∼ **a qualcuno** stick close to somebody

incolla'tura *nf* (nell'ippica) neck

incolle'rirsi *vr* lose one's temper

incolle'rito *adj* enraged

incol'mabile *adj* ⟨differenza⟩ unbridgeable; ⟨vuoto⟩ unfillable

incolon'nare *vt* line up

inco'lore *adj* colourless

incol'pare *vt* blame

in'colto *adj* uncultivated; ⟨persona⟩ uneducated

in'colume *adj* unhurt

incom'bente *adj* impending

incom'benza *nf* task

in'combere *vi* ∼ **su** hang over; ∼ **a** (spettare) be incumbent on

incombu'stibile *adj* noncombustible

incominci'are *vt/i* begin, start

incommensu'rabile *adj* immeasurable

incomo'dare *vt* inconvenience

incomo'darsi *vr* trouble

in'comodo ① *adj* uncomfortable; (inopportuno) inconvenient ② *nm* inconvenience; **fare il terzo** ∼ play gooseberry

incompa'rabile *adj* incomparable

incompa'tibile *adj* incompatible

incompatibilità *nf inv* incompatibility. **incompatibilità di carattere** incompatibility

incompe'tente *adj* incompetent

incompe'tenza *nf* incompetence

incompi'uto *adj* unfinished

incom'pleto *adj* incomplete

incompren'sibile *adj* incomprehensible, unintelligible

incomprensibil'mente *adv* incomprehensibly

incomprensi'one *nf* lack of understanding; (malinteso) misunderstanding

incom'preso *adj* misunderstood

inconce'pibile *adj* inconceivable

inconcili'abile *adj* irreconcilable

inconclu'dente *adj* inconclusive; ⟨persona⟩ ineffectual

incondizionata'mente *adv* unconditionally

incondizio'nato *adj* unconditional

inconfes'sabile *adj* unmentionable

inconfon'dibile *adj* unmistakable

inconfondibil'mente *adv* unmistakably

inconfu'tabile *adj* irrefutable

inconfutabil'mente *adv* irrefutably

incongru'ente *adj* inconsistent

incongru'enza *nf* incongruity

in'congruo *adj* inadequate

inconsa'pevole *adj* unaware; (inconscio) unconscious

inconsapevol'mente *adv* unwittingly

inconscia'mente *adv* unconsciously

in'conscio *adj & nm* Psych unconscious

inconsegu'ente *adj* **essere** ∼ be a non sequitur

inconside'rabile *adj* negligible

inconside'rato *adj* inconsiderate

inconsi'stente *adj* insubstantial; ⟨notizia ecc⟩ unfounded

inconsi'stenza *nf* (di ragionamento, prove) flimsiness

inconso'labile *adj* inconsolable

inconsu'eto *adj* unusual

incon'sulto *adj* rash

incontami'nato *adj* uncontaminated

inconte'nibile *adj* irrepressible

inconten'tabile *adj* insatiable; (esigente) hard to please

inconte'stabile *adj* indisputable

inconte'stato *adj* unchallenged

inconti'nente *adj* incontinent

inconti'nenza *nf* incontinence

incon'trare *vt* meet; encounter, meet with ⟨difficoltà⟩

incon'trario: **all'**∼ *adv* the other way around; (in modo sbagliato) the wrong way around

incon'trarsi *vr* meet; ∼ **con qualcuno** meet somebody

incontra'stabile *adj* incontrovertible

incontra'stato *adj* undisputed

in'contro ① *nm* meeting; (casuale) encounter; (di calcio, rugby) match; (di tennis) game; (di pugilato) fight. **incontro al vertice** summit meeting ② *prep* ∼ **a** towards; **andare** ∼ **a qualcuno** go to meet somebody; fig meet somebody half way

incontrol'labile *adj* uncontrollable

incontrollata'mente *adv* uncontrollably

inconveni'ente *nm* drawback

incoraggia'mento *nm* encouragement

incoraggi'ante *adj* encouraging

incoraggi'are *vt* encourage

incor'nare *vt* gore

incornici'are *vt* frame

incornicia'tura *nf* framing

incoro'nare *vt* crown

incoronazi'one *nf* coronation

incorpo'rare *vt* incorporate; (mescolare) blend

incorpo'rarsi *vr* blend; ⟨*territori*⟩ merge

incorreg'gibile *adj* incorrigible

in'correre *vt* ∼ in incur; ∼ **nel pericolo di** ... run the risk of ...

incorrut'tibile *adj* incorruptible

incosci'ente ① *adj* unconscious; (irresponsabile) reckless ② *nmf* irresponsible person

incosci'enza *nf* unconsciousness; (irresponsabilità) recklessness

inco'stante *adj* changeable; ⟨*persona*⟩ fickle

inco'stanza *nf* changeableness; (di persona) fickleness

incostituzio'nale *adj* unconstitutional

incostituzionalità *nf* unconstitutionality

incre'dibile *adj* incredible, unbelievable

incredibil'mente *adv* incredibly, unbelievably

incredulità *nf* incredulity

in'credulo *adj* incredulous

incremen'tale *adj* Comput, Math incremental

incremen'tare *vt* increase; (intensificare) step up

incre'mento *nm* increase. **incremento demografico** population growth. **incremento produttivo** increase in production

incresci'oso *adj* regrettable

incre'spare *vt* ruffle; wrinkle ⟨*tessuto*⟩; make frizzy ⟨*capelli*⟩; ∼ **la fronte** frown

incre'sparsi *vr* ⟨*acqua*⟩ ripple; ⟨*tessuto*⟩ wrinkle; ⟨*capelli*⟩ go frizzy

incrimi'nabile *adj* indictable

incrimi'nante *adj* incriminating

incrimi'nare *vt* indict; fig incriminate

incriminazi'one *nf* indictment

incri'nare *vt* crack; fig affect ⟨*amicizia*⟩

incri'narsi *vr* crack; ⟨*amicizia*⟩ be affected

incrina'tura *nf* crack

incroci'are ① *vt* cross ② *vi* Naut, Aeron cruise

incroci'arsi *vr* cross; ⟨*razze*⟩ interbreed

incroci'ato *adj* crossover

incrocia'tore *nm* cruiser

in'crocio *nm* crossing; (di strade) crossroads *sg*

incrol'labile *adj* indestructible

incro'stare *vt* encrust

incrostazi'one *nf* encrustation

incuba'trice *nf* incubator

incubazi'one *nf* incubation

'incubo *nm* nightmare; **da** ∼ nightmarish

in'cudine *nf* anvil

incul'care *vt* inculcate

incune'are *vt* wedge

incune'arsi *vr* slot in

incune'ato *adj* Med impacted

incu'pirsi *vr* fig darken

incu'rabile *adj* incurable

incu'rante *adj* careless

in'curia *nf* negligence

incurio'sire *vt* make curious

incurio'sirsi *vr* become curious

incursi'one *nf* raid. **incursione aerea** air raid, airstrike

incurva'mento *nm* bending

incur'vare *vt* bend

incur'varsi *vr* bend

incurva'tura *nf* bending

in'cusso *pp di* INCUTERE

incusto'dito *adj* unguarded

in'cutere *vt* arouse; ∼ **spavento a qualcuno** strike fear into somebody

'indaco *nm* indigo

indaffa'rato *adj* busy

inda'gare *vt/i* investigate

indaga'tore *adj* ⟨*sguardo*⟩ enquiring

in'dagine *nf* research; (giudiziaria) investigation. **indagine demoscopica** public opinion poll. **indagine di mercato** market survey

indebi'tare *vt* get into debt

indebi'tarsi *vr* get into debt

in'debito *adj* undue

indeboli'mento *nm* weakening

indebo'lire *vt* weaken

indebo'lirsi *vr* weaken

inde'cente *adj* indecent

indecente'mente *adv* indecently

inde'cenza *nf* indecency; (vergogna) disgrace

indeci'frabile *adj* indecipherable

indecisi'one *nf* indecision

inde'ciso *adj* undecided

indecli'nabile *adj* indeclinable

indeco'roso *adj* indecorous

inde'fesso *adj* tireless

indefi'nibile *adj* indefinable

indefi'nito *adj* indefinite

indefor'mabile *adj* crushproof

in'degno *adj* unworthy

inde'lebile *adj* indelible

indelebil'mente *adv* indelibly

indelicata'mente *adv* indiscreetly

indelica'tezza *nf* indelicacy; (azione) tactless act

indeli'cato *adj* indiscreet; (grossolano) indelicate

indemagli'abile *adj* ladderproof

indemoni'ato *adj* possessed

in'denne *adj* uninjured; (da malattia) unaffected

inden'nità *nf inv* allowance; (per danni) compensation. **indennità di accompagnamento** mobility allowance. **indennità di contingenza** cost-of-living allowance. **indennità di disoccupazione** job seeker's allowance. **indennità di fine rapporto** severance payment. **indennità di malattia** sickpay. **indennità parlamentare** MP's salary. **indennità di trasferimento** relocation allowance. **indennità di trasferta** travel allowance

indenniz'zare *vt* compensate

inden'nizzo *nm* compensation

indero'gabile *adj* binding

indescri'vibile *adj* indescribable

indescrivibil'mente *adv* indescribably

indeside'rabile *adj* undesirable

indeside'rato *adj* ⟨figlio, ospite⟩ unwanted

indetermi'nabile *adj* indeterminable

indetermina'tezza *nf* vagueness

indetermina'tivo *adj* indefinite

indetermi'nato *adj* indeterminate

'India *nf* India

indi'ano, **-a** *adj & nmf* Indian; **in fila indiana** in single file. **indiano d'America** American Indian

indiavo'lato *adj* possessed; (vivace) wild

indi'care *vt* show, indicate; (col dito) point at; (far notare) point out; (consigliare) advise

indicativa'mente *adv* as an idea; **può dirmi quanto costa ~?** can you give me an idea of the price?

indica'tivo ① *adj* indicative; ⟨prezzo, cifra⟩ rough
② *nm* Gram indicative

indica'tore *nm* indicator; Techn gauge; (prontuario) directory. **indicatore di direzione** indicator light. **indicatore economico** economic indicator. **indicatore [del livello] dell'olio** oil gauge. **indicatore di velocità** speedometer

indicazi'one *nf* indication; (istruzione) direction. **indicazione stradale** road sign

'indice *nm* (dito) forefinger; (lancetta) pointer; (di libro, statistica) index; (fig: segno) sign. **indice di ascolto** audience rating. **indice azionario** share index. **indice di gradimento** popularity rating. **indice di mortalità** death rate. **indice di natalità** birth rate

indi'cibile *adj* inexpressible

indiciz'zare *vt* index-link

indiciz'zato *adj* index-linked

indicizzazi'one *nf* indexing

indietreggi'are *vi* draw back; Mil withdraw

indi'etro *adv* back, behind; **all' ~** backwards; **essere ~** be behind; (mentalmente) be backward; (con pagamenti) be in arrears; (di orologio) be slow; **fare marcia ~** reverse; **rimandare ~** send back; **rimanere ~** be left behind; **torna ~!** come back!

indifen'dibile *adj* indefensible

indi'feso *adj* undefended; (inerme) helpless

indiffe'rente *adj* indifferent; **mi è ~** it's all the same to me

indifferente'mente *adv* (senza fare distinzioni) without distinction; (con indifferenza) indifferently; **funziona ~ con i due programmi** it works equally well with either program

indiffe'renza *nf* indifference

in'digeno, **-a** ① *adj* indigenous ② *nmf* native

indi'gente *adj* needy, poverty-stricken

indi'genza *nf* poverty

indigesti'one *nf* indigestion

indi'gesto *adj* indigestible

indi'gnare *vt* make indignant

indi'gnarsi *vr* be indignant

indi'gnato *adj* indignant

indignazi'one *nf* indignation

indimenti'cabile *adj* unforgettable

'indio, **-a** ① *adj* Indian ② *nmf* (mpl **indii** o **indios**) Indian

indipen'dente *adj* independent; ⟨economicamente⟩ self-supporting

indipendente'mente *adv* independently; **~ da** regardless of

indipen'denza *nf* independence

in'dire *vt* announce

indiretta'mente *adv* indirectly

indi'retto *adj* indirect

indiriz'zare *vt* address; (mandare) send; (dirigere) direct

indiriz'zario *nm* mailing list

indiriz'zarsi *vr* direct one's steps

indi'rizzo *nm* address; (direzione) direction. **indirizzo di consegna** delivery address. **'indirizzo del destinatario'** 'addressee'. **indirizzo di memoria** Comput memory address. **'indirizzo del mittente'** 'sender's address'. **indirizzo di posta elettronica** e-mail address

indisci'plina *nf* lack of discipline

indiscipli'nato *adj* undisciplined

indi'screto *adj* indiscreet; **in modo ~** indiscreetly

indiscrezi'one *nf* indiscretion

indiscriminata'mente *adv* indiscriminately

indiscrimi'nato *adj* indiscriminate

indi'scusso *adj* unquestioned

indiscu'tibile *adj* unquestionable

indiscutibil'mente *adv* unquestionably

indispen'sabile *adj* essential; ⟨*persona*⟩ indispensable

indispet'tire *vt* irritate

indispet'tirsi *vr* get irritated

indi'sporre *vt* anger

indisposizi'one *nf* indisposition

indi'sposto ⓵ pp di INDISPORRE ⓶ *adj* indisposed

indisso'lubile *adj* indissoluble

indissolubil'mente *adv* indissolubly

indistin'guibile *adj* indiscernible

indistinta'mente *adv* without exception

indi'stinto *adj* indistinct

indistrut'tibile *adj* indestructible

indistur'bato *adj* undisturbed

in'divia *nf* endive

individu'abile *adj* detectable

individu'ale *adj* individual

individua'lista *nmf* individualist

individua'listico *adj* individualistic

individualità *nf* individuality

individu'are *vt* individualize; (localizzare) locate; (riconoscere) single out

indi'viduo *nm* individual

indivi'sibile *adj* indivisible

indivisibilità *nf* indivisibility

indi'viso *adj* undivided

indizi'are *vt* throw suspicion on

indizi'ario *adj* circumstantial

indizi'ato, -a ⓵ *adj* suspected ⓶ *nmf* suspect

in'dizio *nm* sign; Jur circumstantial evidence

Indo'cina *nf* Indochina

indoeuro'peo *adj* Indo-European

'indole *nf* nature

indo'lente *adj* indolent

indo'lenza *nf* indolence

indolenzi'mento *nm* stiffness, ache

indolen'zire *vt* stiffen up

indolen'zirsi *vr* stiffen up, go stiff

indolen'zito *adj* stiff

indo'lore *adj* painless

indo'mabile *adj* untameable

indo'mani *nm* l'∼ the following day

in'domito *adj* untamed

Indo'nesia *nf* Indonesia

indonesi'ano, -a *adj & nmf* Indonesian

indo'rare *vt* gild; ∼ **la pillola** sugar the pill

indos'sare *vt* wear; (mettere addosso) put on

indossa'tore, -trice ⓵ *nm* [male] model ⓶ *nf* model

in'dotto pp di INDURRE

indottri'nare *vt* indoctrinate

indovi'nare *vt* guess; (predire) foretell

indovi'nato *adj* successful; (scelta) well-chosen

indovi'nello *nm* riddle

indo'vino, -a *nmf* fortune-teller

indù *adj inv & nmf inv* Hindu

indubbia'mente *adv* undoubtedly

in'dubbio *adj* undoubted

indubi'tabile *adj* indubitable

indubitabil'mente *adv* indubitably

indugi'are *vi* linger

indugi'arsi *vr* linger

in'dugio *nm* delay

indu'ismo *nm* Hinduism

indul'gente *adj* indulgent

indul'genza *nf* indulgence

in'dulgere *vi* ∼ **a** indulge in

in'dulto ⓵ pp di INDULGERE ⓶ *nm* Jur pardon

indu'mento *nm* garment; **indumenti** *pl* clothes. **indumenti intimi** *pl* underwear

induri'mento *nm* hardening

indu'rire *vt* harden

indu'rirsi *vr* harden

in'durre *vt* induce; ∼ **qualcuno a fare** induce somebody to do; ∼ **in tentazione** lead into temptation

in'dustria *nf* industry. **industria dell'abbigliamento** clothing industry, fam rag trade. **industria leggera** light industry. **industria pesante** heavy industry. **industria dello spettacolo** show business, entertainment industry, fam showbiz. **industria terziaria** service industry. **industria tessile** textile industry, textiles

industri'ale ⓵ *adj* industrial; **zona industriale** industrial estate ⓶ *nmf* industrialist

industrializ'zare *vt* industrialize

industrializ'zato *adj* industrialized

industrializzazi'one *nf* industrialization

industrial'mente *adv* industrially

industri'arsi *vr* ∼ **per guadagnare qualcosa** set to and earn some money

industriosa'mente *adv* industriously

industri'oso *adj* industrious

indut'tivo *adj* inductive

indut'tore *nm* inductor

induzi'one *nf* induction
inebe'tire *vt* daze
inebe'tito *adj* stunned
inebri'ante *adj* intoxicating, exciting
inebri'are *vt* intoxicate
inebri'arsi *vr* become inebriated
inecce'pibile *adj* unexceptionable
i'nedia *nf* starvation
i'nedito *adj* unpublished
inedu'cato *adj* impolite
inef'fabile *adj* inexpressible
ineffi'cace *adj* ineffective
ineffici'ente *adj* inefficient
ineffici'enza *nf* inefficiency
ineguagli'abile *adj* incomparable
ineguaglianza *nf* inequality
ineguagli'ato *adj* unequalled
inegu'ale *adj* unequal; ⟨superficie⟩ uneven
inelut'tabile *adj* inescapable
inenar'rabile *adj* indescribable
inequivo'cabile *adj* unequivocal
inequivocabil'mente *adv* unequivocally
ine'rente *adj* ∼ a inherent in
inerente'mente *adv* ∼ a concerning
i'nerme *adj* defenceless
inerpi'carsi *vr* ∼ su clamber up
i'nerte *adj* inactive; Phys inert
i'nerzia *nf* inactivity; Phys inertia
inesat'tezza *nf* inaccuracy
ine'satto *adj* inaccurate; (erroneo) incorrect; (non riscosso) uncollected
inesau'ribile *adj* inexhaustible
inesi'stente *adj* non-existent
inesi'stenza *nf* non-existence
ineso'rabile *adj* inexorable
inesorabil'mente *adv* inexorably
inesperi'enza *nf* inexperience
ine'sperto *adj* inexperienced
inespli'cabile *adj* inexplicable
inesplicabil'mente *adv* inexplicably
inesplo'rato *adj* undiscovered
ine'sploso *adj* unexploded
inespres'sivo *adj* expressionless
inespri'mibile *adj* inexpressible
inespu'gnabile *adj* impregnable
ineste'tismo *nm* blemish
inesti'mabile *adj* inestimable
inestin'guibile *adj* ⟨sete⟩ insatiable; ⟨odio⟩ undying
inestir'pabile *adj* impossible to eradicate
inestri'cabile *adj* inextricable
inestricabil'mente *adv* inextricably
inetti'tudine *nf* ineptitude

i'netto *adj* inept; ∼ a unsuited to
ine'vaso *adj* ⟨pratiche, corrispondenza⟩ pending
inevi'tabile *adj* inevitable
inevitabil'mente *adv* inevitably
in ex'tremis *adv* ⟨segnare un gol⟩ in the nick of time; (prima di morire) in extremis
i'nezia *nf* trifle
infagot'tare *vt* wrap up
infagot'tarsi *vr* wrap [oneself] up
infal'libile *adj* infallible
infa'mante *adj* defamatory
infa'mare *vt* defame
infama'torio *adj* defamatory
in'fame *adj* infamous; (fam: orrendo) awful, shocking
in'famia *nf* infamy
infan'gare *vt* cover with mud; fig sully
infan'garsi *vr* get muddy
infanti'cida *nmf* infanticide
infanti'cidio *nm* infanticide
infan'tile *adj* ⟨letteratura, abbigliamento⟩ children's *attrib*; ⟨ingenuità⟩ childlike; pej childish
in'fanzia *nf* childhood; (bambini) children *pl*; prima infanzia infancy
infar'cire *vt* stuff (di with)
infari'nare *vt* flour; ∼ di sprinkle with
infarina'tura *nf* fig smattering
in'farto *nm* heart attack
infasti'dire *vt* irritate
infasti'dirsi *vr* get irritated
infati'cabile *adj* untiring
infaticabil'mente *adv* tirelessly
in'fatti *conj* as a matter of fact; (veramente) indeed
infatu'arsi *vr* ∼ di become infatuated with
infatu'ato *adj* infatuated
infatuazi'one *nf* infatuation
in'fausto *adj* ill-omened
infecondità *nf* infertility
infe'condo *adj* infertile
infe'dele *adj* unfaithful
infedeltà *nf* unfaithfulness
infe'lice *adj* unhappy; (inappropriato) unfortunate; (cattivo) bad
infelicità *nf* unhappiness
infel'trire *vi* matt
infel'trirsi *vr* matt
infel'trito *adj* matted
inferi'ore ① *adj* (più basso) lower; ⟨qualità⟩ inferior ② *nmf* inferior
inferiorità *nf* inferiority
infe'rire *vt* infer; strike ⟨colpo⟩

inferme'ria *nf* infirmary; (di nave, scuola) sickbay

infermi'ere, -a ① *nm* [male] nurse ② *nf* nurse

infermità *nf* sickness. **infermità mentale** mental illness

in'fermo, -a ① *adj* sick ② *nmf* invalid

infer'nale *adj* infernal; (spaventoso) hellish

in'ferno *nm* hell; **va' all'∼!** go to hell!

infero'cirsi *vr* become fierce

inferri'ata *nf* grating

infervo'rare *vt* arouse enthusiasm in

infervo'rarsi *vr* get excited

infe'stare *vt* infest

infestato *adj* infested; **∼ dai fantasmi** haunted

infestazi'one *nf* infestation

infet'tare *vt* infect

infet'tarsi *vr* become infected

infet'tivo *adj* infectious

in'fetto *adj* infected

infezi'one *nf* infection

infiac'chire *vt/i* weaken

infiac'chirsi *vr* weaken

infiam'mabile *adj* [in]flammable

infiam'mare *vt* set on fire; Med, fig inflame

infiam'marsi *vr* catch fire; Med become inflamed

infiammazi'one *nf* Med inflammation

infia'scare *vt* bottle

infici'are *vt* Jur invalidate

in'fido *adj* treacherous

infie'rire *vi* (imperversare) rage; **∼ su** attack furiously

in'figgere *vt* drive

in'figgersi *vr* **∼ in** penetrate

infi'lare *vt* thread; (mettere) insert; (indossare) put on

infi'larsi *vr* slip on ⟨vestito⟩ **∼ in** (introdursi) slip into

infil'trarsi *vr* infiltrate

infil'trato, -a *nmf* infiltrator

infiltrazi'one *nf* infiltration; (d'acqua) seepage; (Med: iniezione) injection

infil'zare *vt* pierce; (infilare) string; (conficcare) stick

'infimo *adj* lowest

in'fine *adv* finally; (insomma) in short

infin'gardo *adj* slothful

infinità *nf* infinity; **un'∼ di** masses of

infinita'mente *adv* infinitely

infinitesi'male *adj* infinitesimal

infi'nito ① *adj* infinite; Gram infinitive ② *nm* infinite; Gram infinitive; Math infinity; **all'∼** endlessly

infinocchi'are *vt* fam hoodwink

infiocchet'tare *vt* tie up with ribbons

infiore'scenza *nf* inflorescence

infischi'arsi *vr* **∼ di** not care about; **me ne infischio** fam I couldn't care less

in'fisso ① pp di INFIGGERE ② *nm* fixture; (di porta, finestra) frame

infit'tire *vt/i* thicken

infit'tirsi *vr* thicken

inflazi'one *nf* inflation. **inflazione galoppante** galloping inflation. **inflazione strisciante** creeping inflation

inflazio'nistico *adj* inflationary

infles'sibile *adj* inflexible

inflessibilità *nf* inflexibility

inflessi'one *nf* inflection, inflexion

in'fliggere *vt* inflict

in'flitto pp di INFLIGGERE

influ'ente *adj* influential

influ'enza *nf* influence; Med influenza; **prendere l'∼** catch the flu. **influenza aviaria** o **dei polli** bird flu; **influenza gastrointestinale** gastric flu

influen'zabile *adj* ⟨mente, opinione⟩ impressionable

influen'zare *vt* influence

influen'zato *adj* **essere ∼** (con febbre) have the flu

influ'ire *vi* **∼ su** influence

in'flusso *nm* influence

info'carsi *vr* catch fire; ⟨viso⟩ go red; ⟨discussione⟩ become heated

info'gnarsi *vr* fam get into a mess

infol'tire *vt/i* thicken

infon'dato *adj* unfounded

in'fondere *vt* instil

infor'care *vt* fork ⟨fieno⟩; get on ⟨bici⟩; put on ⟨occhiali⟩

inforca'tura *nf* crotch

infor'male *adj* informal

infor'mare *vt* inform

infor'marsi *vr* inquire (**di** about)

infor'matica *nf* information technology

infor'matico *adj* computer *attrib*

informa'tivo *adj* informative

infor'mato *adj* informed; **male ∼** ill-informed

inform'tore, -trice *nmf* (di polizia) informer. **informatore medico scientifico** representative of a pharmaceutical company

informazi'one *nf* information; **un'∼** a piece of information; **informazioni** *pl* information; **servizio informazioni** enquiries. **informazione genetica** genetic code. **informazione riservata** confidential information; **informazioni** *pl* sbagliate misinformation; **informazioni** *pl* **sulla viabilità** travel news

in'forme *adj* shapeless

infor'nare *vt* put into the oven

infortu'narsi *vr* have an accident

infortu'nato, -a ① *adj* injured ② *nmf* injured person; **gli infortunati** the injured

infor'tunio *nm* accident. **infortunio sul lavoro** industrial accident

infortu'nistica *nf* study of industrial accidents

infos'sarsi *vr* sink; ⟨*guance, occhi*⟩ become hollow

infos'sato *adj* sunken, hollow

infradici'are *vt* drench

infradici'arsi *vr* get drenched; (diventare marcio) rot

infra'dito *nmpl* (scarpe) flip-flops

in'frangere *vt* break; (in mille pezzi) shatter

in'frangersi *vr* break; (in mille pezzi) shatter

infran'gibile *adj* unbreakable

in'franto ① pp di INFRANGERE ② *adj* shattered; fig ⟨*cuore*⟩ broken

infra'rosso *adj* infra-red

infrasettima'nale *adj* midweek

infrastrut'tura *nf* infrastructure

infrazi'one *nf* offence. **infrazione al codice della strada** traffic offence

infredda'tura *nf* cold

infreddo'lirsi *vr* feel cold

infreddo'lito *adj* cold

infre'quente *adj* infrequent

infruttu'oso *adj* fruitless

infuo'care *vt* make red-hot

infuo'cato *adj* burning

infu'ori *adv* all'∼ outwards; all'∼ di except; denti ∼ buck teeth

infuri'are *vi* rage

infuri'arsi *vr* fly into a rage

infuri'ato *adj* blustering

infusi'one *nf* infusion

in'fuso ① pp di INFONDERE ② *nm* infusion

Ing. *abbr* **ingegnere**

ingabbi'are *vt* cage; (fig: mettere in prigione) jail

ingaggi'are *vt* engage; sign up ⟨*calciatori ecc*⟩; begin ⟨*lotta, battaglia*⟩

in'gaggio *nm* engagement; (di calciatore) signing [up]

ingan'nare *vt* deceive; (essere infedele a) be unfaithful to; ∼ **l'attesa** kill time

ingan'narsi *vr* deceive oneself; **se non m'inganno** if I am not mistaken

ingan'nevole *adj* deceptive

in'ganno *nm* deceit; (frode) fraud; **trarre in** ∼ deceive

ingarbugli'are *vt* entangle; (confondere) confuse

ingarbugli'arsi *vr* get entangled; (confondersi) become confused

ingarbu'gliato *adj* confused

inge'gnarsi *vr* do one's best; ∼ **per vivere** try to scrape a living

inge'gnere *nm* engineer. **ingegnere aeronautico** aeronautical engineer. **ingegnere civile** civil engineer. **ingegnere edile** structural engineer. **ingegnere meccanico** mechanical engineer. **ingegnere minerario** mining engineer. **ingegnere navale** marine engineer

ingegne'ria *nf* engineering. **ingegneria aeronautica** aeronautical engineering. **ingegneria civile** civil engineering. **ingegneria edile** structural engineering. **ingegneria genetica** genetic engineering. **ingegneria meccanica** mechanical engineering

in'gegno *nm* brains *pl*; (genio) genius; (abilità) ingenuity

ingegnosa'mente *adv* ingeniously

ingegnosità *nf* ingenuity

inge'gnoso *adj* ingenious

ingelo'sire *vt* make jealous

ingelo'sirsi *vr* become jealous

in'gente *adj* huge

ingenua'mente *adv* artlessly

ingenuità *nf* ingenuousness

in'genuo *adj* ingenuous; (credulone) naïve

inge'renza *nf* interference

inge'rire *vt* swallow

inges'sare *vt* put in plaster

ingessa'tura *nf* plaster, plaster cast

Inghil'terra *nf* England

inghiot'tire *vt* swallow

in'ghippo *nm* trick

ingial'lire *vi* turn yellow

ingial'lirsi *vr* turn yellow

ingial'lito *adj* yellowed

ingigan'tire ① *vt* magnify; blow up out of proportion ⟨*problema*⟩ ② *vi* take on gigantic proportions

ingigan'tirsi *vr* take on gigantic proportions

inginocchi'arsi *vr* kneel [down]

inginocchi'ato *adj* kneeling

inginocchia'toio *nm* prie-dieu

ingioiel'larsi *vr* put on one's jewels

ingioiel'lato *adj* bejewelled

ingiù *adv* down; all'∼ downwards; **a testa** ∼ head downwards

ingi'ungere *vt* order

ingiunzi'one *nf* injunction, court order. ~ **di pagamento** final demand

ingi'uria *nf* insult; (torto) wrong; (danno) damage

ingiuri'are *vt* insult; (fare un torto a) wrong

ingiuri'oso *adj* insulting

ingiusta'mente *adv* unjustly

ingiustifi'cabile *adj* unjustifiable; ⟨comportamento⟩ indefensible

ingiustifi'cato *adj* unjustified

ingiu'stizia *nf* injustice

ingi'usto *adj* unjust

in'glese 1 *adj* English
2 *nm* Englishman; (lingua) English; **gli inglesi** the English
3 *nf* Englishwoman

inglori'oso *adj* inglorious

ingob'bire *vi* become stooped

ingoi'are *vt* swallow

ingol'fare *vt* flood ⟨motore⟩

ingol'farsi *vr* fig get involved; ⟨motore⟩ flood

ingol'lare *vt* gulp down

ingom'brante *adj* cumbersome

ingom'brare *vt* clutter up; fig cram ⟨mente⟩

in'gombro *nm* encumbrance; **essere d'**~ be in the way

ingor'digia *nf* greed

in'gordo *adj* greedy

ingor'gare *vt* block

ingor'garsi *vr* be blocked [up]

in'gorgo *nm* blockage; (del traffico) jam

ingoz'zare *vt* gobble up; (nutrire eccessivamente) stuff; fatten ⟨animali⟩

ingoz'zarsi *vr* stuff oneself (**di** with)

ingra'naggio *nm* gear; fig mechanism

ingra'nare 1 *vt* engage
2 *vi* be in gear

ingrandi'mento *nm* enlargement

ingran'dire *vt* enlarge; (esagerare) magnify

ingran'dirsi *vr* become larger; (aumentare) increase

ingrandi'tore *nm* Phot enlarger

ingras'saggio *nm* greasing, lubrication

ingras'sare 1 *vt* fatten [up]; Mech lubricate, grease
2 *vi* put on weight

ingras'sarsi *vr* put on weight

in'grasso *nm* **mettere all'**~ force-feed

ingrati'tudine *nf* ingratitude

in'grato *adj* ungrateful; (sgradevole) thankless

ingrazi'arsi *vr* ingratiate oneself with

ingredi'ente *nm* ingredient

in'gresso *nm* entrance; (accesso) admittance; (sala) hall; Comput input
ingresso gratuito *o* **libero** admission free; '**vietato l'**~' 'no entry'; 'no admittance'. **ingresso degli artisti** stage door. **ingresso principale** main entrance. **ingresso di servizio** tradesmen's entrance. **ingresso/uscita** Comput input/output. **ingresso video** Techn video input

ingros'sare 1 *vt* make big; (gonfiare) swell
2 *vi* grow big; (gonfiare) swell

ingros'sarsi *vr* grow big; (gonfiare) swell

in'grosso: **all'**~ *adv* wholesale

inguai'arsi *vr* get into trouble

inguai'nare *vt* sheathe

ingual'cibile *adj* crease-resistant

ingua'ribile *adj* incurable

inguaribil'mente *adv* incurably

'inguine *nm* groin

ingurgi'tare *vt* gulp down

ini'bire *vt* inhibit; (vietare) forbid

ini'bito *adj* inhibited

inibi'tore *nm* suppressant

inibizi'one *nf* inhibition; (divieto) prohibition

iniet'tare *vt* inject

iniet'tarsi *vr* ~ **di sangue** ⟨occhi⟩ become bloodshot

iniezi'one *nf* injection. **iniezione endovenosa** intravenous injection. **iniezione intramuscolare** intramuscular injection

inimic'arsi *vr* ~ **qualcuno** make an enemy of somebody

inimi'cizia *nf* enmity

inimi'tabile *adj* inimitable

inimmagi'nabile *adj* unimaginable

ininfiam'mabile *adj* nonflammable

intelli'gibile *adj* unintelligible

ininterrotta'mente *adv* continuously

ininter'rotto *adj* continuous

iniquità *nf inv* iniquity

i'niquo *adj* iniquitous

inizi'ale *adj & nf* initial

inizial'mente *adv* initially

inizi'are 1 *vt* begin; (avviare) open; ~ **a fare qualcosa** begin doing something; ~ **qualcuno a qualcosa** initiate somebody in something
2 *vi* begin

inizia'tiva *nf* initiative; **prendere l'**~ take the initiative. **iniziativa privata** private enterprise

inizi'ato, -a *nmf* initiated

inizia|'tore, -trice *nmf* initiator

iniziazi'one *nf* initiation

i'nizio *nm* beginning, start; **dare ~ a** start; **avere ~** get under way

innaffi'are *vt* water

innaffia'toio *nm* watering-can

innal'zare *vt* raise; (erigere) erect

innal'zarsi *vr* rise

innamo'rarsi *vr* fall in love (**di** with)

innamo'rato, -a ① *adj* in love ② *nm* boyfriend ③ *nf* girlfriend

in'nanzi ① *adv* (stato in luogo) in front; (di tempo) ahead; (avanti) forward; (prima) before; **d'ora ~** from now on ② *prep* (prima) before; **~ a** in front of; **~ tutto = innanzitutto**

innanzi'tutto *adv* (soprattutto) above all; (per prima cosa) first of all

in'nato *adj* innate

innatu'rale *adj* unnatural

inne'gabile *adj* undeniable

innegabil'mente *adv* undeniably

inneggi'are *vi* praise

innervo'sire *vt* make nervous

innervo'sirsi *vr* get irritated

inne'scare *vt* prime

in'nesco *nm* primer

inne'stare *vt* graft; Mech engage; (inserire) insert

in'nesto *nm* graft; Mech clutch; Electr connection

inneva'mento *nm* snowfall. **innevamento artificiale** snow-making

inne'vato *adj* covered in snow

'inno *nm* hymn. **inno nazionale** national anthem

inno'cente *adj* innocent; Jur not guilty

innocente'mente *adv* innocently

inno'cenza *nf* innocence

in'nocuo *adj* innocuous

inno'vare *vt* update

innova'tivo *adj* innovative

innova'tore *adj* trail-blazing

innovazi'one *nf* innovation

innume'revole *adj* innumerable

+ino *suff* fratellino *nm* little brother; sorellina *nf* little sister; freddino *adj* (piuttosto freddo) chilly; bellino *adj* (abbastanza bello) pretty; benino *adv* (così così) not bad; pochino *adv* (troppo poco) not enough; un pochino a little bit

inocu'lare *vt* inoculate

ino'doro *adj* odourless

inoffen'sivo *adj* inoffensive, harmless; ⟨animale⟩ harmless

inol'trare *vt* forward

inol'trarsi *vr* advance

inol'trato *adj* late

i'noltre *adv* besides

i'noltro *nm* forwarding

inon'dare *vt* flood

inondazi'one *nf* flood

inope'roso *adj* idle

inopi'nabile *adj* unimaginable

inoppor'tuno *adj* untimely

inor'ganico *adj* inorganic

inorgo'glire *vt* make proud

inorgo'glirsi *vr* become proud

inorri'dire ① *vt* horrify ② *vi* be horrified

inospi'tale *adj* inhospitable

inosser'vato *adj* unobserved; (non rispettato) disregarded; **passare ~** go unnoticed

inossi'dabile *adj* stainless

'inox *adj inv* ⟨acciaio⟩ stainless; ⟨pentole⟩ stainless steel

'input *nm inv* **input dati** data input

inqua'drare *vt* frame; fig set

inqua'drarsi *vr* **~ in** fit into

inquadra'tura *nf* framing

inqualifi'cabile *adj* unspeakable

inquie'tante *adj* unnerving

inquie'tare *vt* worry

inquie'tarsi *vr* get worried; (impazientirsi) get cross

inqui'eto *adj* restless; (preoccupato) worried

inquie'tudine *nf* anxiety

inqui'lino, -a *nmf* tenant

inquina'mento *nm* pollution. **inquinamento acustico** noise pollution. **inquinamento atmosferico** air pollution. **inquinamento delle prove** Jur tampering with the evidence

inqui'nare *vt* pollute

inqui'nato *adj* polluted

inqui'rente *adj* Jur ⟨magistrato⟩ examining; ⟨commissione⟩ of investigation

inqui'sire *vt/i* investigate

inqui'sito ① *adj* under investigation ② *nm* person under investigation

inquisi|'tore, -trice ① *adj* inquiring ② *nmf* inquisitor

inquisi'torio *adj* questioning

inquisizi'one *nf* inquisition

insabbi'are *vt* bury

insabbi'arsi *vr* run aground

insa'lata *nf* salad. **insalata belga** Belgian endive. **insalata di mare** seafood salad. **insalata mista** mixed salad. **insalata di riso** rice salad. **insalata russa** Russian salad

insalati'era *nf* salad bowl

insa'lubre *adj* unhealthy

insa'nabile *adj* incurable

insangui'nare *vt* stain with blood

insangui'nato *adj* blood-stained
insapo'nare *vt* soap
insapo'narsi *vr* soap oneself
insapo'nata *nf* soaping
insa'pore *adj* tasteless
insapo'rire *vt* flavour
insa'puta *nf* all'∼ **di** unknown to
in'saturo *adj* unsaturated
insazi'abile *adj* insatiable
inscato'lare *vt* can
inscatola'trice *nf* canning machine
insce'nare *vt* stage
inscin'dibile *adj* inseparable
in'scrivere *vt* Math inscribe
insec'chire *vt/i* wither
insedia'mento *nm* installation
insedi'are *vt* install
insedi'arsi *vr* install oneself
in'segna *nf* sign; (bandiera) flag; (decorazione) decoration; (emblema) insignia *pl*; (stemma) symbol. **insegna luminosa** neon sign
insegna'mento *nm* teaching
inse'gnante ① *adj* teaching ② *nmf* teacher. **insegnante di matematica** maths teacher. **insegnante di sostegno** tutor. **insegnante tirocinante** student teacher
inse'gnare *vt/i* teach; ∼ **qualcosa a qualcuno** teach somebody something
insegui'mento *nm* pursuit
insegu'ire *vt* pursue
insegui|'tore, -trice *nmf* pursuer
inselvati'chire ① *vt* make wild ② *vi* grow wild
inselvati'chirsi *vr* grow wild
insemi'nare *vt* inseminate
inseminazi'one *nf* insemination. **inseminazione artificiale** artificial insemination
insena'tura *nf* inlet
insensata'mente *adv* senselessly
insen'sato *adj* senseless; (folle) crazy
insen'sibile *adj* fig insensitive; **avere le gambe insensibili** have no feeling in one's legs
insensibilità *nf* lack of feeling; fig insensitivity
insepa'rabile *adj* inseparable
inseri'mento *nm* insertion
inse'rire *vt* insert, place ⟨annuncio⟩; Electr connect
inse'rirsi *vr* ∼ **in** get into
inseri'tore *nm* **inseritore fogli (singoli)** (single) sheetfeed
in'serto *nm* file; (in un giornale) supplement; (in un film ecc) insert

inservi'ente *nmf* attendant
inserzi'one *nf* insertion; (avviso) advertisement; **inserzioni** *pl* classified ads
inserzio'nista *nmf* advertiser
insetti'cida *nm* insecticide
insetti'fugo *nm* insect repellent
in'setto *nm* insect
insicu'rezza *nf* insecurity
insi'curo *adj* insecure
in'sidia *nf* trick; (tranello) snare
insidi'are *vt/i* lay a trap for
insidi'oso *adj* insidious
insi'eme ① *adv* together; (contemporaneamente) at the same time ② *prep* ∼ **a** [together] with ③ *nm* whole; (completo) outfit; Theat ensemble; Math set; **nell'**∼ as a whole; **tutto** ∼ (in una volta) at one go
insie'mistica *nf* set theory
in'signe *adj* renowned
insignifi'cante *adj* insignificant
insi'gnire *vt* decorate
insin'cero *adj* insincere
insinda'cabile *adj* final
insinu'ante *adj* insinuating
insinu'are *vt* insinuate
insinu'arsi *vr* penetrate; ∼ **in** fig creep into
insinuazi'one *nf* insinuation
in'sipido *adj* insipid
insi'stente *adj* insistent
insistente'mente *adv* repeatedly
insi'stenza *nf* insistence
in'sistere *vi* insist; (perseverare) persevere
'insito *adj* inherent
insoddisfa'cente *adj* unsatisfactory
insoddi'sfatto *adj* unsatisfied; (scontento) dissatisfied
insoddisfazi'one *nf* dissatisfaction
insoffe'rente *adj* intolerant
insoffe'renza *nf* intolerance
insolazi'one *nf* sunstroke
inso'lente *adj* rude, insolent
insolente'mente *adv* insolently
inso'lenza *nf* rudeness, insolence; (commento) insolent remark
insolita'mente *adv* unusually
in'solito *adj* unusual
inso'lubile *adj* insoluble
inso'luto *adj* unsolved; (non pagato) unpaid
insol'vente *adj* Jur insolvent
insol'venza *nf* insolvency
insol'vibile *adj* insolvent
in'somma *adv* in short; ∼! well!
inson'dabile *adj* unfathomable
in'sonne *adj* sleepless

in'sonnia *nf* insomnia
insonno'lito *adj* sleepy
insonoriz'zare *vt* soundproof
insonoriz'zato *adj* soundproofed
insoppor'tabile *adj* unbearable
insoppri'mibile *adj* unsuppressible
insor'genza *nf* onset
in'sorgere *vi* revolt, rise up; ⟨*problema*⟩ arise
insormon'tabile *adj* ⟨*ostacolo, difficoltà*⟩ insurmountable
in'sorto ① pp di INSORGERE ② *adj* rebellious ③ *nm* rebel
insospet'tabile *adj* unsuspected
insospet'tire ① *vt* make suspicious ② *vi* become suspicious
insospet'tirsi *vr* becomes suspicious
insoste'nibile *adj* untenable; (insopportabile) unbearable
insostitu'ibile *adj* irreplaceable
insoz'zare *vt* dirty
inspe'rabile *adj* hopeless; (insperato) unhoped-for
inspe'rato *adj* unhoped-for
inspie'gabile *adj* inexplicable
inspiegabil'mente *adv* inexplicably
inspi'rare *vt* breathe in
in'stabile *adj* unstable; (variabile) unsettled
instabilità *nf* instability; (di tempo) changeability
instal'lare *vt* install
instal'larsi *vr* (in casa, lavoro) settle in
installa|'tore, -trice *nmf* fitter
installazi'one *nf* installation; installazioni *pl* di bordo on-board equipment
instan'cabile *adj* untiring
instancabil'mente *adv* tirelessly
instau'rare *vt* found
instau'rarsi *vr* become established
instaurazi'one *nf* foundation
instra'dare *vt* direct
insù: all'∼ *adv* upwards; naso all'∼ turned-up nose
insubordi'nato *adj* insubordinate
insubordinazi'one *nf* insubordination
insuc'cesso *nm* failure
insudici'are *vt* dirty
insudici'arsi *vr* get dirty
insuffici'ente ① *adj* insufficient; (inadeguato) inadequate ② *nf* Sch fail
insufficiente'mente *adv* insufficiently
insuffici'enza *nf* insufficiency; (inadeguatezza) inadequacy; Sch fail.

insufficienza cardiaca cardiac insufficiency. insufficienza di prove lack of evidence
insu'lare *adj* insular
insu'lina *nf* insulin
in'sulso *adj* insipid; (sciocco) silly
insul'tare *vt* insult
in'sulto *nm* insult; coprire qualcuno di insulti heap abuse on somebody
insupe'rabile *adj* insuperable; (eccezionale) incomparable
insurrezi'one *nf* insurrection
insussi'stente *adj* groundless
intac'cabile *adj* subject to corrosion; fig open to criticism
intac'care *vt* nick; (corrodere) corrode; draw on ⟨*capitale*⟩; (danneggiare) damage
intagli'are *vt* carve
in'taglio *nm* carving
intan'gibile *adj* untouchable
in'tanto *adv* meanwhile; (per ora) for the moment; (avversativo) but; ∼ che while
intarsi'are *vt* inlay
intarsi'ato *adj* ∼ di inset with
in'tarsio *nm* inlay
intasa'mento *nm* (ostruzione) blockage; (ingorgo) traffic jam
inta'sare *vt* block, clog
inta'sarsi *vr* become blocked
inta'sato *adj* blocked
inta'scare *vt* pocket
in'tatto *adj* intact
intavo'lare *vt* start
inte'gerrimo *adj* of integrity
inte'grale *adj* whole; edizione integrale unabridged edition; pane integrale wholemeal bread; versione integrale (di film) uncut version; (di romanzo) unabridged version
integra'lista *nmf* fundamentalist
integral'mente *adv* fully
inte'grante *adj* integral
inte'grare *vt* integrate; (aggiungere) supplement
inte'grarsi *vr* integrate
integra'tivo *adj* supplementary, additional; esame integrativo test taken by pupil wishing to transfer from arts to a scientific stream etc
integra'tore *nm* integratore alimentare dietary supplement
integrazi'one *nf* integration
integrità *nf* integrity
'integro *adj* complete; (retto) upright
intelaia'tura *nf* framework
intellet'tivo *adj* intellectual
intel'letto *nm* intellect
intellettu'ale *adj* & *nmf* intellectual

intellettual'mente *adv* intellectually

intelli'gente *adj* intelligent

intelligente'mente *adv* intelligently

intelli'genza *nf* intelligence. **intelligenza artificiale** artificial intelligence

intelli'ghenzia *nf* intelligentsia

intelli'gibile *adj* intelligible

intelligibil'mente *adv* intelligibly

intelligi'oco *nm* computer game

intempe'rante *adj* intemperate

intempe'ranza *nf* intemperance; **intemperanze** *pl* excesses

intem'perie *nfpl* bad weather

intempe'stivo *adj* untimely

inten'dente *nm* superintendent

inten'denza *nf* **intendenza di finanza** inland revenue office

in'tendere *vt* (comprendere) understand; (udire) hear; (avere intenzione) intend; (significare) mean; **[siamo] intesi?** is that clear?

in'tendersi *vr* (capirsi) understand each other; ∼ **di** (essere esperto in) have a good knowledge of; **intendersela con** (fam: avere una relazione con) have it off with

intendi'mento *nm* understanding; (intenzione) intention

intendi|'tore, -trice *nmf* connoisseur; **intenditori** *pl* cognoscenti

intene'rire *vt* soften; (commuovere) touch

intene'rirsi *vr* be touched

intensa'mente *adv* intensely

intensifi'care *vt* intensify

intensifi'carsi *vr* intensify

intensità *nf* intensity

intensiva'mente *adv* intensively

inten'sivo *adj* intensive; **terapia intensiva** intensive care

in'tenso *adj* intense

inten'tare *vt* start up; ∼ **causa contro qualcuno** bring *or* institute proceedings against somebody

inten'tato *adj* **non lasciare nulla di** ∼ try everything

in'tento ① *adj* engrossed (**a** in) ② *nm* purpose

intenzio'nale *adj* intentional

intenzio'nato *adj* **essere** ∼ **a fare qualcosa** have the intention of doing something

intenzi'one *nf* intention; **senza** ∼ unintentionally; **avere** ∼ **di fare qualcosa** intend to do something, have the intention of doing something

intera'gire *vi* interact

intera'mente *adv* completely, entirely

interat'tivo *adj* interactive

interazi'one *nf* interaction

interca'lare ① *nm* stock phrase ② *vt* insert ⟨*esclamazione*⟩

intercambi'abile *adj* interchangeable

interca'pedine *nf* cavity

inter'cedere *vi* intercede

intercessi'one *nf* intercession

intercet'tare *vt* intercept; tap ⟨*telefono*⟩

intercettazi'one *nf* interception. ∼ **telefonica** telephone tapping

inter'city *nm inv* inter-city

intercomuni'cante *adj* [inter]communicating

interconfessio'nale *adj* interdenominational

intercon'nettere *vt* interconnect

intercontinen'tale *adj* intercontinental

inter'correre *vi* ⟨*tempo*⟩ elapse; (esistere) exist

interco'stale *adj* intercostal

interden'tale *adj* between the teeth; **filo interdentale** dental floss

inter'detto ① *pp di* INTERDIRE ② *adj* astonished; (proibito) forbidden; **rimanere** ∼ be taken aback; **lasciare qualcuno** ∼ astonish somebody, dumbfound somebody ③ *nm* Relig interdict

interdipartimen'tale *adj* interdepartmental

interdipen'dente *adj* interdependent

interdipen'denza *nf* interdependence

inter'dire *vt* ban; (nel calcio) intercept; Jur deprive of civil rights; Relig interdict; ∼ **a qualcuno di fare qualcosa** forbid somebody to do something

interdiscipli'nare *adj* interdisciplinary

interdizi'one *nf* ban; (nel calcio) interception; Relig interdict. **interdizione giudiziale** appointment of a legal guardian to a person of unsound mind. **interdizione legale** legally imposed ban. **interdizione dai pubblici uffici** ban on taking public office

interessa'mento *nm* interest

interes'sante *adj* interesting; **essere in stato** ∼ be pregnant

interes'sare ① *vt* interest; (riguardare) concern ② *vi* ∼ **a** interest; **non mi interessa** I'm not interested; (non mi importa) I don't care, it doesn't matter to me

interes'sarsi *vr* ∼ **a** take an interest in; ∼ **di** take care of

interes'sato *adj* (attento) interested; pej self-interested; **diretto** ∼ person concerned

inte'resse *nm* interest; **fare qualcosa per** ∼ do something out of self-interest; **essere nell'**∼ **di qualcuno** be in somebody's interest; **un ~ del 4%** 4% interest. **interesse attivo** interest charge. **interesse maturato** accrued interest. **interesse privato in atti di ufficio** abuse of public office. **interesse a tasso variabile** floating rate interest

interes'senza *nf* Econ profit-sharing

inter'faccia *nf* interface. **interfaccia grafica** graphics interface. **interfaccia uomo/macchina** man/machine interface. **interfaccia utente** user interface

interfacci'are *vt* interface

interfacci'arsi *vr* interface

interfe'renza *nf* interference

interfe'rire *vi* interfere

inter'fono *nm* intercom

interga'lattico *adj* intergalactic

interiet'tivo *adj* interjectory

interiezi'one *nf* interjection

'interim *nm inv* (incarico) temporary appointment; (periodo) interim; **ad ~ on a** temporary basis; ⟨*presidente*⟩ acting

interi'ora *nfpl* entrails

interi'ore *adj* inner

interioriz'zare *vt* internalize

interior'mente *adv* (nella parte interiore) internally; (emotivamente) inwardly

inter'linea *nf* line spacing; Typ leading. **interlinea doppia** double spacing

interline'are ①*vt* space out ②*adj* line *attrib*

interlocu'tore, -trice *nmf* speaker, interlocutor *fml*; **il mio ~** the person I am/was speaking to

inter'ludio *nm* interlude

intermedi'ario, -a *adj & nmf* intermediary; Econ middleman

intermediazi'one *nf* (intervento) mediation

inter'medio *adj* in-between

inter'mezzo *nm* Theat, Mus intermezzo

intermi'nabile *adj* interminable

interministeri'ale *adj* interdepartmental

intermissi'one *nf* intermission

intermit'tente *adj* intermittent; ⟨*vulcano*⟩ dormant

intermit'tenza *nf* **a ~** intermittent

interna'mente *adv* internally

interna'mento *nm* internment; (in manicomio) committal

inter'nare *vt* intern; (in manicomio) commit [to a mental institution]

inter'nato, -a ①*adj* interned ②*nmf* internee ③*nm* boarding school

internazio'nale *adj* international

internazional'mente *adv* internationally

'Internet *nf* Internet; **in ~** on the Internet; **via ~** through the Internet. **~ point** Internet kiosk

inter'nista *nmf* internist

in'terno ①*adj* internal; Geog inland; (interiore) inner; ⟨*politica*⟩ national; **alunno ~** boarder ②*nm* interior; (di condominio) flat; Teleph extension; Cinema interior shot; **all'~** inside; **ministero degli interni** Ministry of the Interior, ≈ Home Office

in'tero ①*adj* whole, entire; Math whole; (intatto) intact; (completo) complete; **per ~** in full ②*nm* (totalità) whole

interparlamen'tare *adj* interparliamentary

interpar'titico *adj* cross-party

interpel'lanza *nf* parliamentary question

interpel'lare *vt* consult

interpel'lato, -a *nmf* person being questioned

interperso'nale *adj* interpersonal

interplane'tario *adj* interplanetary

interpo'lare *vt* interpolate

inter'porre *vt* interpose; use ⟨*influenza*⟩; **~ ostacoli a** put obstacles in the way of

inter'porsi *vr* intervene; **~ tra** come between

inter'posto *adj* **per interposta persona** through a third party

interpre'tare *vt* interpret; Mus perform; **~ male** misinterpret

interpretari'ato *nm* interpreting

interpretazi'one *nf* interpretation; Mus performance

in'terprete *nmf* interpreter; Mus performer

interpunzi'one *nf* punctuation

inter'rare *vt* (seppellire) bury; (riempire) fill in; lay underground ⟨*cavo, tubo*⟩; plant ⟨*pianta, seme*⟩

inter'rato *nm* basement

interregio'nale *nm* long-distance train, stopping at most stations

interro'gante *nmf* questioner

interro'gare *vt* question; Sch examine

interrogativa'mente *adv* ⟨*guardare*⟩ inquiringly

interroga'tivo ①*adj* interrogative; (sguardo) questioning; **punto interrogativo** question mark ②*nm* question

interro'gato *adj* ⟨*studente*⟩ examinee; Jur person questioned

interroga'torio *adj & nm* questioning

interrogazi'one *nf* question; Sch oral [test]. **interrogazione ciclica** polling. **interrogazione parlamentare** parliamentary question

inter'rompere *vt* interrupt; (sospendere) stop; cut off ⟨collegamento⟩

inter'rompersi *vr* break off

interrut'tore *nm* switch. **interruttore a reostato** dimmer

interruzi'one *nf* interruption; **senza ~** non-stop. **interruzione della corrente** power cut. **interruzione di gravidanza** termination of pregnancy

interscambi'abile *adj* interchangeable

inter'scambio *nm* import-export trade

interse'care *vt* intersect

interse'carsi *vr* intersect

intersezi'one *nf* intersection

inter'stizio *nm* interstice

interur'bana *nf* long-distance call

interur'bano *adj* inter-city; **telefonata interurbana** long-distance call

interval'lare *vt* space out

inter'vallo *nm* interval; (spazio) space; (in ufficio) tea/coffee break; TV, Sch break; **fare un ~** have a break; **a intervalli regolari** at regular intervals. **intervallo del pranzo** lunch hour, lunch break. **intervallo pubblicitario** commercial break

interve'nire *vi* intervene; (Med: operare) operate; **~ a** take part in

inter'vento *nm* intervention; (presenza) presence; (chirurgico) operation; **pronto intervento** emergency services; **un ~ a cuore aperto** open-heart surgery

inter'vista *nf* interview. **intervista esclusiva** exclusive interview

intervi'stare *vt* interview

intervi'stato, -a *nmf* interviewee

intervista|'tore, -trice *nmf* interviewer

in'tesa *nf* understanding; **d'~** ⟨cenno⟩ of acknowledgement

in'teso, -a [1] *pp di* INTENDERE [2] *adj* **resta ~ che ...** needless to say, ...; **~ a** meant to; **[siamo] intesi!** agreed! [3] *nf* understanding

in'tessere *vt* weave together

inte'stare *vt* head; write one's name and address at the top of ⟨lettera⟩; Comm register

inte'starsi *vr* **~ a fare qualcosa** take it into one's head to do something

intesta'tario, -a *nmf* holder

intestazi'one *nf* heading; (su carta da lettere) letterhead

intesti'nale *adj* intestinal

inte'stino [1] *adj* ⟨lotte⟩ internal [2] *nm* intestine. **intestino crasso** large intestine. **intestino tenue** small intestine

intiepi'dire *vt* (scaldare) warm; cool ⟨passione, desiderio⟩

intiepi'dirsi *vr* cool [down]; (scaldarsi) warm [up]; ⟨fede⟩ wane

intima'mente *adv* ⟨conoscere⟩ intimately

inti'mare *vt* order; **~ l'alt** give the order to halt; **~ l'alt a qualcuno** order somebody to stop

intimazi'one *nf* order. **intimazione di sfratto** eviction notice

intimida'torio *adj* threatening, intimidating

intimidazi'one *nf* intimidation

intimi'dire *vt* intimidate

intimi'dirsi *vr* be overwhelmed with shyness

intimità *nf* intimacy, togetherness

'intimo [1] *adj* intimate; (interno) innermost; ⟨amico⟩ close [2] *nm* (amico) close friend; (dell'animo) heart

intimo'rire *vt* frighten

intimo'rirsi *vr* get frightened

intimo'rito *adj* frightened

in'tingere *vt* dip

in'tingolo *nm* sauce; (pietanza) stew

intiriz'zire *vt* numb

intiriz'zirsi *vr* grow numb

intiriz'zito *adj* **essere ~** (dal freddo) be perished

intito'lare *vt* entitle; (dedicare) dedicate

intito'larsi *vr* be called

intolle'rabile *adj* intolerable

intolle'rante *adj* intolerant

intona'care *vt* plaster

intonaca'tore *nm* plasterer

in'tonaco *nm* plaster. **intonaco a pinocchino** pebbledash

into'nare *vt* start to sing; tune ⟨strumento⟩; match ⟨colori⟩

into'narsi *vr* match

into'nato *adj* ⟨persona⟩ able to sing in tune; ⟨voce, strumento⟩ in tune; ⟨colore⟩ matching

intonazi'one *nf* (inflessione) intonation; ⟨ironica⟩ tone; (cantando) ability to sing in tune

in'tonso *adj* ⟨libro⟩ untouched

inton'tire [1] *vt* ⟨botta⟩ stun, daze; ⟨gas⟩ make dizzy; fig stun [2] *vi* go ga-ga

inton'tito *adj* dazed; fig stunned; ⟨con l'età⟩ ga-ga

intop'pare *vi* **~ in** run into

in'toppo *nm* **c'è un ~** something's come up

in'torno [1] *adv* around [2] *prep* **~ a** around; (circa) about; **~ al mondo** round-the-world

intorpi'dire *vt* numb

intorpi'dirsi *vr* become numb

intorpi'dito *adj* torpid

intossi'care *vt* poison

intossi'carsi *vr* be poisoned

intossicazi'one *nf* poisoning.
intossicazione alimentare food
poisoning

intra-azien'dale *adj* in-house

intradu'cibile *adj* untranslatable

intralci'are *vt* hamper

in'tralcio *nm* hitch; **essere d'~ (a
qualcuno/qualcosa)** be a hindrance (to
somebody/something)

intrallaz'zare *vi* intrigue

intral'lazzo *nm* racket

intramon'tabile *adj* timeless

intramusco'lare *adj* intramuscular

intra'net *nf inv* intranet

intransi'gente *adj* intransigent,
uncompromising

intransi'genza *nf* intransigence

intransi'tivo *adj* intransitive

intrappolato *adj* **rimanere ~** be
trapped

intrapren'dente *adj* enterprising

intrapren'denza *nf* initiative

intra'prendere *vt* undertake

intrat'tabile *adj* very difficult

intratte'nere *vt* entertain

intratte'nersi *vr* linger

intratteni'mento *nm* entertainment

intrave'dere *vt* catch a glimpse of;
(presagire) foresee

intrecci'are *vt* interweave; plait
⟨*capelli, corda*⟩; **~ le mani** clasp one's
hands

intrecci'arsi *vr* intertwine; (aggrovigliarsi)
become tangled

in'treccio *nm* (trama) plot; (di nastri, strade)
tangle

in'trepido *adj* intrepid

intri'cato *adj* tangled

intri'gante ① *adj* intriguing
② *nmf* schemer

intri'gare ① *vt* entangle; (incuriosire)
intrigue
② *vi* be intriguing

intri'garsi *vr* become entangled;
(immischiarsi) meddle

in'trigo *nm* plot; **intrighi** *pl* plotting; (di
corte) intrigues

intrinseca'mente *adv* intrinsically

in'trinseco *adj* intrinsic

in'triso *adj* **~ di** soaked with; fig imbued
with

intri'stire *vt* sadden

intri'stirsi *vr* grow sad

intro'durre *vt* introduce; (inserire) insert;
~ a (iniziare a) introduce to

intro'dursi *vr* get in; **~ in** get into

introdut'tivo *adj* ⟨*pagine, discorso*⟩
introductory

introduzi'one *nf* introduction

in'troito *nm* income, revenue; (incasso)
takings *pl*

intro'mettere *vt* introduce

intro'mettersi *vr* interfere; (interporsi)
intervene

intromissi'one *nf* intervention

introspet'tivo *adj* introspective

intro'vabile *adj* unobtainable

intro'verso, -a ① *adj* introverted
② *nmf* introvert

intrufo'larsi *vr* sneak in

in'truglio *nm* concoction

intrusi'one *nf* intrusion

in'truso, -a *nmf* intruder

intu'ibile *adj* deducible

intu'ire *vt* perceive

intuitiva'mente *adv* intuitively

intui'tivo *adj* intuitive

in'tuito *nm* intuition

intuizi'one *nf* intuition

inu'mano *adj* inhuman

inu'mare *vt* inter

inumi'dire *vt* dampen; moisten ⟨*labbra*⟩

inumi'dirsi *vr* become damp

i'nutile *adj* useless; (superfluo)
unnecessary

inutilità *nf* uselessness

inutiliz'zabile *adj* unusable

inutiliz'zato *adj* unused

inutil'mente *adv* fruitlessly

inva'dente *adj* intrusive

in'vadere *vt* invade; (affollare) overrun

inva'ghirsi *vr* **~ di** take a fancy to

invali'cabile *adj* impassable; **'limite ~'**
Mil 'no access beyond this point'

invali'dare *vt* invalidate

invalidità *nf* disability; Jur invalidity

in'valido, -a ① *adj* invalid; (handicappato)
disabled
② *nmf* disabled person; **gli invalidi** the
handicapped. **invalido di guerra**
disabled ex-serviceman. **invalido del
lavoro** industrial accident victim

in'vano *adv* in vain

invari'abile *adj* invariable

invariabil'mente *adv* invariably

invari'ato *adj* unchanged

invasi'one *nf* invasion

in'vaso pp di INVADERE

inva'sore ① *adj* invading
② *nm* invader

invecchia'mento *nm* (di vino)
maturation

invecchi'are *vt/i* age

in'vece *adv* instead; (anzi) but; ~ **di** instead of

inve'ire *vi* ~ **contro** inveigh against

invele'nito *adj* embittered

inven'dibile *adj* unsaleable

inven'duto *adj* unsold

inven'tare *vt* invent

inventari'are *vt* make an inventory of

inven'tario *nm* inventory

inven'tato *adj* made-up

inven'tiva *nf* inventiveness

inven'tivo *adj* inventive

inven|'tore, -trice *nmf* inventor

invenzi'one *nf* invention

inver'nale *adj* wintry; **sport** *pl* **invernali** winter sports

in'verno *nm* winter

invero'simile *adj* improbable

inverosimil'mente *adv* incredibly

inversa'mente *adv* inversely; ~ **proporzionale** in inverse proportion

inversi'one *nf* inversion; Mech reversal; **fare un'**~ **a U** do a U-turn. **inversione di fondo** Comput reverse video. **inversione di tendenza** turnaround

in'verso ① *adj* inverse; (opposto) opposite ② *nm* opposite

inverte'brato *adj* & *nm* invertebrate

inver'tire *vt* reverse; (capovolgere) turn upside-down

investi'gare *vt* investigate

investiga|'tore, -trice *nmf* investigator. **investigatore privato** private investigator, private eye

investigazi'one *nf* investigation

investi'mento *nm* investment; (incidente) crash

inve'stire *vt* invest; (urtare) collide with; (travolgere) run over; ~ **qualcuno di** invest somebody with

investi'tura *nf* investiture

invete'rato *adj* inveterate

invet'tiva *nf* invective

invi'are *vt* send

invi'ato, -a *nmf* envoy; (di giornale) correspondent. **inviato di pace** peace envoy

in'vidia *nf* envy

invidi'are *vt* envy

invidi'oso *adj* envious

invigo'rire *vt* invigorate

invigo'rirsi *vr* become strong

invin'cibile *adj* invincible

in'vio *nm* dispatch; Comput enter

invio'labile *adj* inviolable

invipe'rirsi *vr* get nasty

invipe'rito *adj* furious

invischi'arsi *vr* get involved (in in)

invi'sibile *adj* invisible

invisibilità *nf* invisibility

invi'tante *adj* ⟨piatto, profumo⟩ enticing

invi'tare *vt* invite

invi'tato, -a *nmf* guest

in'vito *nm* invitation

invo'care *vt* invoke; (implorare) beg

invocazi'one *nf* invocation

invogli'are *vt* tempt; (indurre) induce

invogli'arsi *vr* ~ **di** take a fancy to

involga'rire *vt* vulgarize

involontaria'mente *adv* involuntarily

involon'tario *adj* involuntary

invol'tini *nmpl* stuffed rolls (of meat, pastry)

in'volto *nm* parcel; (fagotto) bundle

in'volucro *nm* wrapping

invo'luto *adj* involved

invulne'rabile *adj* invulnerable

inzacche'rare *vt* splash with mud

inzup'pare *vt* soak; (intingere) dip

inzup'parsi *vr* get soaked

'io ① *pers pron* I; **sono io** it's me; **l'ho fatto io [stesso]** I did it myself ② *nm* **l'io** the ego

i'odio *nm* iodine

i'one *nm* ion

i'onico *adj* Ionic

l'onio *nm* **lo** ~ the Ionian [Sea]

iono'sfera *nf* ionosphere

i'osa: **a** ~ *adv* in abundance

iperattività *nf* hyperactivity

iperat'tivo *adj* hyperactive

i'perbole *nf* hyperbole

iper'critico *adj* hypercritical

ipermer'cato *nm* hypermarket

iper'metrope *adj* long-sighted

ipersen'sibile *adj* hypersensitive

ipertensi'one *nf* high blood pressure

iper'testo *nm* Comput hypertext

iperte'stuale *adj* **collegamento ipertestuale** hyperlink

iperventi'lare *vi* hyperventilate

ip'nosi *nf* hypnosis

ipnotera'pia *nf* hypnotherapy

ip'notico *adj* hypnotic

ipno'tismo *nm* hypnotism

ipnotiz'zare *vt* hypnotize

ipoaller'genico *adj* hypoallergenic

ipoca'lorico *adj* low-calorie

ipo'centro *nm* focus

ipocon'dria *nf* hypochondria

ipocon'driaco, -a *adj* & *nmf* hypochondriac

ipocri'sia *nf* hypocrisy

i'pocrita ① *adj* hypocritical

2 *nmf* hypocrite
ipocrita'mente *adv* hypocritically
ipo'dermico *adj* hypodermic
i'pofisi *nf* pituitary gland
ipo'teca *nf* mortgage
ipote'cabile *adj* mortgageable
ipote'care *vt* mortgage
ipote'cario *adj* mortgage *attrib*
ipote'nusa *nf* hypotenuse
ipo'termia *nf* hypothermia
i'potesi *nf inv* hypothesis; (caso, eventualità) eventuality; **nella migliore delle** ∼ at best; **nella peggiore delle** ∼ if the worst comes to the worst
ipo'tetico *adj* hypothetical
ipotiz'zare *vt* hypothesize
'ippico, -a 1 *adj* horse *attrib* **2** *nf* riding
ippoca'stano *nm* horse-chestnut
ip'podromo *nm* racecourse
ippo'potamo *nm* hippopotamus
'ipsilon *nf inv* [the letter] y
'ira *nf* anger
ira'scibile *adj* irascible
i'rato *adj* irate
'iride *nf* Anat iris; (arcobaleno) rainbow
'iris *nm inv* Bot iris
Ir'landa *nf* Ireland. **Irlanda del Nord** Northern Ireland
irlan'dese 1 *adj* Irish **2** *nm* Irishman; (lingua) Irish **3** *nf* Irishwoman
iro'nia *nf* irony
i'ronico *adj* ironic[al]
irradi'are *vt/i* radiate
irradiazi'one *nf* radiation
irraggiun'gibile *adj* unattainable
irragio'nevole *adj* unreasonable; ⟨speranza, timore⟩ irrational; (assurdo) absurd
irranci'dire *vi* go rancid
irrazio'nale *adj* irrational
irrazionalità *adj* irrationality
irrazional'mente *adv* irrationally
irre'ale *adj* unreal
irrea'listico *adj* unrealistic
irrealiz'zabile *adj* unattainable
irrealtà *nf* unreality
irrecupe'rabile *adj* irrecoverable
irrecu'sabile *adj* incontrovertible
irredi'mibile *adj* irredeemable
irrefre'nabile *adj* uncontrollable
irrefu'tabile *adj* irrefutable
irrego'lare *adj* irregular
irregolarità *nf inv* irregularity; (di terreno) unevenness; Sport foul

irregolar'mente *adv* ⟨frequentare⟩ irregularly; ⟨comportarsi⟩ erratically; ⟨disporre⟩ unevenly
irremo'vibile *adj* fig adamant
irrepa'rabile *adj* irreparable
irrepe'ribile *adj* ⟨persona⟩ not to be found; **sarò irreperibile** I'm not going to be contactable
irrepren'sibile *adj* irreproachable
irrepri'mibile *adj* irrepressible
irrequi'eto *adj* restless
irresi'stibile *adj* irresistible
irresistibil'mente *adv* irresistibly
irreso'luto *adj* irresolute
irrespon'sabile *adj* irresponsible
irresponsabilità *nf* irresponsibility
irrestrin'gibile *adj* preshrunk
irre'tire *vt* seduce
irrever'sibile *adj* irreversible
irreversibil'mente *adv* irrevocably
irrevo'cabile *adj* irrevocable
irrevocabil'mente *adv* irreversibly
irricono'scibile *adj* unrecognizable
irridu'cibile *adj* irreducible
irri'gare *vt* irrigate; ⟨fiume⟩ flow through
irrigazi'one *nf* irrigation
irrigidi'mento *nm* (di muscoli) stiffening; (di disciplina) tightening
irrigi'dire *vt* stiffen up
irrigi'dirsi *vr* stiffen up
irrile'vante *adj* unimportant
irrimedi'abile *adj* irreparable
irrimediabil'mente *adv* irreparably
irripe'tibile *adj* unrepeatable
irri'solto *adj* unresolved
irri'sorio *adj* derisive; (insignificante) derisory
irri'tabile *adj* irritable
irri'tante *adj* aggravating, annoying
irri'tare *vt* irritate, annoy
irri'tarsi *vr* get annoyed
irri'tato *adj* irritated, annoyed; ⟨gola⟩ sore
irritazi'one *nf* irritation
irrive'renza *nf* (qualità) irreverence; (azione) irreverent action
irrobu'stire *vt* fortify
irrobu'stirsi *vr* get stronger
ir'rompere *vi* burst (in into)
irro'rare *vt* sprinkle
irrorazi'one *nf* (di piante) crop spraying
irru'ente *adj* impetuous
irruvi'dire *vt* roughen
irruvi'dirsi *vr* become rough
irruzi'one *nf* raid; fig eruption; **fare** ∼ **in** burst into
ir'suto *adj* shaggy

'irto *adj* bristly

i'scritto, -a ① pp di ISCRIVERE
② *adj* registered
③ *nmf* member; **per ~** in writing

i'scrivere *vt* register

i'scriversi *vr* **~ a** register at, enrol at ‹*scuola*›; join ‹*circolo ecc*›

iscrizi'one *nf* registration; (epigrafe) inscription

i'slamico *adj* Islamic

isla'mismo *nm* Islam

isla'mista *nmf* Islamist

I'slanda *nf* Iceland

islan'dese ① *adj* Icelandic
② *nmf* Icelander

i'sobara *nf* isobar

'isola *nf* island; **le isole britanniche** the British Isles; **l'~ di Man** Isle of Man. **isola deserta** desert island. **isola pedonale** traffic island. **isola spartitraffico** traffic island

iso'lano, -a ① *adj* insular
② *nmf* islander

iso'lante ① *adj* insulating
② *nm* insulator

iso'lare *vt* isolate; Mech, Electr insulate; (acusticamente) soundproof

iso'lato ① *adj* isolated
② *nm* (di appartamenti) block

isolazio'nismo *nm* isolationism

iso'metrico *adj* isometric

i'soscele *adj* isosceles

is'panico *adj* Hispanic

ispessi'mento *nm* thickening

ispes'sire *vt* thicken

ispes'sirsi *vr* thicken

ispetto'rato *nm* inspectorate

ispet'tore *nm* inspector. **ispettore capo** chief inspector. **ispettore di polizia** police inspector. **ispettore scolastico** inspector of schools. **ispettore delle tasse** tax inspector. **ispettore di zona** Comm area manager

ispezio'nare *vt* inspect

ispezi'one *nf* inspection; (di nave) boarding

'ispido *adj* bristly

ispi'rare *vt* inspire; suggest ‹*idea, soluzione*›

ispi'rarsi *vr* **~ a** be based on

ispi'rato *adj* inspired

ispirazi'one *nf* inspiration; (idea) idea

Isra'ele *nm* Israel

israeli'ano, -a *adj & nmf* Israeli

is'sare *vt* hoist

ist. *abbr* (**istituto**) dept

istan'taneo, -a ① *adj* instantaneous
② *nf* snapshot

i'stante *nm* instant; **all'~** instantly

i'stanza *nf* petition. **istanza di divorzio** petition for divorce

isterecto'mia *nf* hysterectomy

i'sterico *adj* hysterical; **attacco isterico** hysterics *pl*

iste'rismo *nm* hysteria. **isterismo di massa** mass hysteria

isti'gare *vt* instigate; **~ qualcuno al male** incite somebody to evil

istiga|'tore, -trice *nmf* instigator

istigazi'one *nf* instigation; **~ a delinquere** incitement to crime

istintiva'mente *adv* instinctively

istin'tivo *adj* instinctive

i'stinto *nm* instinct; **d'~** instinctively. **istinto di conservazione** instinct of self-preservation. **istinto materno** maternal instinct

istitu'ire *vt* institute; (fondare) found; initiate ‹*manifestazione*›

isti'tuto *nm* institute; Sch secondary school; Univ department. **istituto di bellezza** beauty salon. **istituto commerciale** business college. **istituto di credito** bank. **istituto per l'infanzia** children's home. **istituto tecnico professionale** technical college

istitu|'tore, -trice *nmf* (insegnante) tutor; (fondatore) founder

istituzio'nale *adj* institutional

istituzionaliz'zare *vt* institutionalize

istituzionaliz'zarsi *vr* become an institution

istituzionalizzazi'one *nf* institutionalization

istituzi'one *nf* institution; **le istituzioni** state institutions

'istmo *nm* isthmus

isto'gramma *nm* bar chart

istolo'gia *nf* histology

istra'dare *vt* divert; fig guide (**a** towards)

'istrice *nm* porcupine

istri'one *nm* clown; Theat sl ham

istru'ire *vt* instruct; (addestrare) train; (informare) inform; Jur prepare

istru'ito *adj* well-educated

istrut'tivo *adj* instructive, enlightening

istrut|'tore, -trice *nmf* instructor, **giudice istruttore** examining magistrate. **istruttore di guida** driving instructor. **istruttore di nuoto** swimming instructor

istrut'toria *nf* Jur investigation

istruzi'one *nf* instruction; Sch education; **ministero della pubblica istruzione** Department of Education. **istruzioni** *pl* **per l'uso** instructions for use

istupi'dire *vt* stupefy

I'talia *nf* Italy
itali'ano, **-a** *adj & nmf* Italian
itine'rante *adj* wandering; ⟨*mostra*⟩ touring; ⟨*spettacolo*⟩ travelling
itine'rario *nm* route, itinerary. **itinerario turistico** tourist route
itte'rizia *nf* jaundice

'ittico *adj* fishing *attrib*

i'uta *nf* jute

I.V.A. *nf abbr* (**imposta sul valore aggiunto**) VAT; **I.V.A. compresa** inclusive of VAT, VAT inclusive

'ivi *adv* (linguaggio burocratico) therein

Jj

ja'bot *nm inv* jabot
jack *nm inv* jack
ja'cquard *adj inv* (nella maglia) jacquard
'jais *nm* jet
'jam-session *nf inv* jam-session
jazz *nm* jazz
jaz'zista *nmf* jazz player
jeep *nf inv* jeep
'jersey *nm* jersey
jet *nm inv* jet. **jet privato** private jet
jet-'set *nm* jet set
'jingle *nm inv* jingle
'jodel *nm inv* yodel
'jogging *nm* jogging
joint 'venture *nf inv* Comm joint

venture
'jolly ① *nm inv* (carta da gioco) joker ② *adj* Comput **carattere jolly** wildcard [character]
'joystick *nm inv* joystick
Jugo'slavia *nf* Yugoslavia
jugo'slavo, **-a** *adj & nmf* Yugoslav[ian]
ju'jitsu *nm* ju-jitsu
juke'box *nm inv* juke box
jumbo-jet *nm inv* jumbo jet
junghi'ano, **-a** *adj & nmf* Jungian
'junior ① *adj inv* junior ② *nm* (pl **juniores**) junior
'juta *nf* jute

Kk

kafki'ano *adj* Kafkan, Kafkaesque
ka'jal *nm inv* kohl
'kaki ① *adj inv* khaki ② *nm inv* persimmon
Kala'hari *nm* il ~ the Kalahari [Desert]
ka'pok *nm* kapok
ka'putt *adj inv* kaput
kara'kiri *nm* fare ~ commit hara-kiri
kara'oke *nm inv* karaoke; **apparecchio per** ~ karaoke machine
kara'te *nm* karate
kart *nm inv* go-kart
kar'tismo *nm* go-karting; **fare del** ~ go go-karting
'kasher *adj inv* kosher
'Kashmir *nm* Kashmir
ka'yak *nm inv* kayak
Ka'zakistan *nm* Kazakhstan

KB Comput *abbr* (**kilobyte**) K, KB
Kbyte Comput *abbr* (**kilobyte**) kbyte
'Kenya *nm* Kenya
ker'messe *nf inv* fair; fig rowdy celebration
kero'sene *nm* paraffin
'ketchup *nm* ketchup
kg *abbr* (**chilogrammo**) kg
kib'butz *nm inv* kibbutz
'killer *nmf inv* assassin, hit man
'kilo *nm* kilo
kilt *nm inv* kilt
ki'mono *nm inv* kimono
kinesitera'pia *nf* physiotherapy
Kir'ghizistan *nm* Kyrgyzstan
kit *nm inv* **kit di aggiornamento** upgrade kit. **kit multimediale** multimedia kit

kitsch *adj inv* kitschy
'kiwi *nm inv* kiwi
'kleenex® *nm inv* Kleenex
km *abbr* (**chilometro**) km
km/h *abbr* (**chilometro**) kph
kmq *abbr* (**chilometro quadrato**) km²
ko'ala *nm inv* koala
koso'varo -a *adj & nmf* Kosovan

'Kosovo *nm* Kosovo
'krapfen *nm inv* doughnut
'kripton *nm* krypton
'Kurdistan *nm* Kurdistan
kuwaiti'ano *nm* Kuwaiti
kW *abbr* (**kilowatt**) kW
K-'way® *nm inv* cagoule
kWh *abbr* (**kilowatt all'ora**) kWh

Ll

l' *def art mf* (*before vowel*) the; ▷ IL
lì *adv* there; **fin lì** as far as there; **giù di lì**
thereabouts; **lì per lì** there and then; **la
cosa è finita lì** that was the end of it
la ① *def art f* the; ▷ IL
② *pron* (oggetto, riferito a persona) her; (riferito
a cosa, animale) it; (forma di cortesia) you
③ *nm inv* Mus (chiave, nota) A
là *adv* there; **di là** (in quel luogo) in there; (da
quella parte) that way; **eccolo là!** there he
is!; **farsi più in là** (far largo) make way; **là
dentro** in there; **là fuori** out there; **[ma] va'
là!** come off it!; **più in là** (nel tempo) later
on; (nello spazio) further on
'labbro *nm* (pl nf **labbra**) lip; **pendere
dalle labbra di qualcuno** hang on
somebody's every word. **labbro
leporino** harelip
labi'ale *adj & nf* labial
'labile *adj* fleeting
labiolet'tura *nf* lip-reading
labi'rinto *nm* labyrinth; (di sentieri ecc)
maze
labora'torio *nm* laboratory; (di negozio,
officina ecc) workshop. **laboratorio
linguistico** language lab
laboriosa'mente *adv* laboriously
labori'oso *adj* (operoso) industrious;
(faticoso) laborious
labra'dor *nm inv* labrador
labu'rista ① *adj* Labour
② *nmf* member of the Labour Party
'lacca *nf* lacquer; (per capelli) hairspray
lac'care *vt* lacquer
lacchè *nm inv* lackey
'laccio *nm* noose; (lazo) lasso; (trappola)
snare; (stringa) lace. **laccio emostatico**
tourniquet
lace'rante *adj* (grido) earsplitting
lace'rare *vt* tear; lacerate (carne)
lace'rarsi *vr* tear
lacerazi'one *nf* laceration
'lacero *adj* torn; (cencioso) ragged

la'conico *adj* laconic
'lacrima *nf* tear; (goccia) drop
lacri'male *adj* (condotto, ghiandola) tear
attrib
lacri'mare *vi* weep
lacri'mevole *adj* tear-jerking
lacri'mogeno *adj* **gas lacrimogeno**
tear gas
lacri'moso *adj* tearful
la'cuna *nf* gap
lacu'noso *adj* (preparazione, resoconto)
incomplete
la'custre *adj* lake *attrib*
lad'dove *conj* whereas
'ladro, -a ① *adj* thieving
② *nmf* thief; **al ~!** stop thief!
ladro'cinio *nm* theft
la'druncolo *nm* petty thief
'lager *nm inv* concentration camp
laggiù *adv* down there; (lontano) over
there
'lagna *nf* (fam: persona) moaning Minnie;
(film) bore
la'gnanza *nf* complaint
la'gnarsi *vr* moan, whinge; (protestare)
complain (di about)
la'gnoso *adj* (persona) moaning,
whining; (film) weepy
'lago *nm* lake. **lago di Garda** Lake
Garda. **lago di sangue** pool of blood
la'guna *nf* lagoon
lagu'nare *adj* lagoon *attrib*
laiciz'zare *vt* laicize
'laico, -a ① *adj* lay; (vita) secular
② *nm* layman
③ *nf* laywoman
'lama ① *nf* blade; **a doppia ~** (rasoio)
twin-blade
② *nm inv* (animale) llama
lambic'carsi *vr* **~ il cervello** rack one's
brains
lam'bire *vt* lap

lamé *nm* lamé

la'mella *nf* (di fungo) lamella; (di metallo, plastica) sheet

lamen'tare *vt* lament

lamen'tarsi *vr* moan; ~ **di** (lagnarsi) complain about

lamen'tela *nf* complaint

lamen'tevole *adj* mournful; (pietoso) pitiful

la'mento *nm* moan

la'metta *nf* **lametta [da barba]** razor blade

lami'era *nf* sheet metal. **lamiera ondulata** corrugated iron

'lamina *nf* foil. **lamina d'oro** gold leaf

lami'nare *vt* laminate

lami'naria *nf* kelp

lami'nato ① *adj* laminated ② *nm* laminate; (tessuto) lamé

'lampada *nf* lamp. **lampada abbronzante** sunlamp. **lampada alogena** halogen lamp. **lampada da comodino** beside lamp. **lampada a gas** gas lamp. **lampada a olio** oil lamp. **lampada a pila** torch. **lampada da soffitto** overhead light. **lampada da tavolo** table lamp

lampa'dario *nm* chandelier

lampa'dato *nm* sl sun-bed freak

lampa'dina *nf* light bulb

lam'pante *adj* clear

lam'para *nf* light used when fishing at night

lampeg'giante *adj* flashing

lampeggi'are *vi* flash

lampeggia'tore *nm* Auto indicator

lampi'one *nm* street lamp

'lampo *nm* flash of lightning; (luce) flash; **lampi** *pl* lightning *sg*; **cerniera lampo** zip [fastener], zipper Am. **lampo di genio** stroke of genius. **lampo al magnesio** magnesium flash

lam'pone *nm* raspberry

'lana *nf* wool; **di** ~ woollen. **lana d'acciaio** steel wool. **lana grossa** double knitting [wool]. **lana merino** botany wool. **lana vergine** new wool. **lana di vetro** glass wool

lan'cetta *nf* pointer; (di orologio) hand. **lancetta dei minuti** minute hand. **lancetta delle ore** hour hand. **lancetta dei secondi** second hand

'lancia *nf* (arma) spear, lance; Naut launch. **lancia di salvataggio** lifeboat

lanciafi'amme *nm inv* flamethrower

lancia'missili *nm inv* missile launcher

lancia'palle *adj inv* **macchina lanciapalle** ball launcher for tennis practice

lancia'razzi ① *adj inv* **pistola lanciarazzi** Very pistol ② *nm inv* rocket launcher

lanci'are *vt* throw; (da un aereo) drop; launch ⟨missile, prodotto, attacco⟩; give ⟨grido⟩; Comput run ⟨file⟩; ~ **uno sguardo a** glance at; ~ **in alto** throw up

lanci'arsi *vr* fling oneself; (intraprendere) launch out

lanci'nante *adj* piercing

'lancio *nm* throwing; (da aereo) drop; (di missile, prodotto) launch; (Comput: di file) running. **lancio del disco** discus [throwing]. **lancio del giavellotto** javelin [throwing]. **lancio col paracadute** (di persona) parachute jump; (di pacco) airdrop, parachute drop. **lancio del peso** putting the shot, shot put

'landa *nf* moor

languida'mente *adv* languidly

'languido *adj* languid; (debole) feeble

langu'ore *nm* languor; (spossatezza) listlessness. **languore di stomaco** hunger pangs *pl*

lani'ero *adj* wool; **industria laniera** wool industry

lani'ficio *nm* woollen mill

lano'lina *nf* lanolin

la'noso *adj* woolly

lan'terna *nf* lantern; (faro) lighthouse

la'nugine *nf* down

'Laos *nm* Laos

lapalissi'ano *adj* obvious

laparosco'pia *nf* laparoscopy

lapi'dare *vt* stone; fig demolish

lapi'dario *adj* (conciso) terse; **arte lapidaria** stone carving

'lapide *nf* tombstone; (commemorativa) memorial tablet

'lapis *nm inv* pencil

lapi'slazzuli *nm inv* lapis lazuli

'lappa *nf* Bot burr

Lap'ponia *nf* Lapland

'lapsus *nm inv* lapse, error. **lapsus freudiano** Freudian slip

'laptop *nm inv* laptop

lardel'lare *vt* Culin lard

'lardo *nm* lard

larga'mente *adv* (ampiamente) widely

largheggi'are *vi* ~ **in** be free with

lar'ghezza *nf* width; (di spalle) breadth; fig liberality. **larghezza di vedute** broad-mindedness

'largo ① *adj* wide; (ampio) broad; ⟨abito⟩ loose; (liberale) liberal; (abbondante) generous; **stare alla larga** keep away; ~ **di manica** fig generous; ~ **di spalle** broad-shouldered; **a gambe larghe** with one's legs wide apart; **di larghe vedute** broad-minded

2) *nm* width; **andare al** ∼ Naut go out to sea; **fare** ∼ make room; **farsi** ∼ make one's way; **al** ∼ **di** off the coast of

'**larice** *nm* larch

la'ringe *nf* larynx

larin'gite *nf* laryngitis

'**larva** *nf* larva; (persona emaciata) shadow. **larva di pidocchio** nit

la'sagne *nfpl* lasagne *sg*

'**lasca** *nf* roach

lasciapas'sare *nm inv* pass

lasci'are *vt* leave; (rinunciare) give up; (rimetterci) lose; (smettere di tenere) let go [of]; (concedere) let; ∼ **a desiderare** leave a lot to be desired; ∼ **di fare qualcosa** (smettere) stop doing something; **lascia perdere!** forget it!; **lascialo venire, lascia che venga** let him come

lasci'arsi *vr* (reciproco) leave each other, split up; ∼ **andare** let oneself go

'**lascito** *nm* legacy

la'scivo *adj* lascivious

'**laser** *adj & nm inv* [**raggio**] **laser** laser [beam]

lasertera'pia *nf* laser treatment

lassa'tivo *adj & nm* laxative

las'sismo *nm* laxity

'**lasso** *nm* **lasso di tempo** period of time

lassù *adv* up there

'**lastra** *nf* slab; (di ghiaccio) sheet; (di metallo, Phot) plate; (radiografia) X-ray [plate]. **lastra di pietra** paving slab, paving stone. **lastra di vetro** plate glass

lastri'care *vt* pave

lastri'cato *nm* pavement

'**lastrico** *nm* paving; **sul** ∼ on one's beam-ends

la'tente *adj* latent

late'rale *adj* side *attrib*; Med, Techn ecc lateral; **via** ∼ side street

lateral'mente *adv* sideways

late'rizi *nmpl* bricks

'**latice** *nm* latex

latifon'dista *nmf* big landowner

lati'fondo *nm* large estate

lati'nismo *nm* Latinism

la'tino *adj & nm* Latin

latino-ameri'cano, -**a** *adj & nmf* Latin American

lati'tante **1)** *adj* in hiding   **2)** *nmf* fugitive [from justice]

lati'tanza *nf* **darsi alla** ∼ go into hiding

lati'tudine *nf* latitude

'**lato** **1)** *adj* **in senso** ∼ broadly speaking   **2)** *nm* side; (aspetto) aspect; **a** ∼ **di** beside; **dal** ∼ **mio** (punto di vista) for my part;

d'altro ∼ fig on the other hand. **lato B** B side

la'tore, -**trice** *nmf* Comm bearer

la'trare *vi* bark

la'trato *nm* barking

la'trina *nf* latrine

'**latta** *nf* (materiale) tin; (recipiente) tin, can

lat'taio, -**a** **1)** *nm* milkman   **2)** *nf* milkwoman

lat'tante **1)** *adj* breast-fed   **2)** *nmf* suckling

'**latte** *nm* milk. **latte acido** sour milk. **latte condensato** condensed milk, evaporated milk. **latte detergente** cleansing milk. **latte di gallina** eggnog. **latte intero** whole milk, full-cream milk. **latte a lunga conservazione** long-life milk. **latte materno** mother's milk, breast milk. **latte parzialmente scremato** semi-skimmed milk. **latte in polvere** powdered milk. **latte scremato** skimmed milk. **latte di soia** soya milk

lat'teo *adj* milky; **dieta lattea** milk diet; **la Via Lattea** the Milky Way

latte'ria *nf* dairy

'**lattice** *nm* latex

latti'cello *nm* buttermilk

latti'cini *nmpl* dairy products

latti'era *nf* milk jug

lattigi'noso *adj* milky

lat'tina *nf* can, tin can

lat'tosio *nm* lactose

lat'tuga *nf* lettuce. **lattuga romana** cos lettuce

'**laudano** *nm* laudanum

'**laurea** *nf* degree; **prendere la** ∼ graduate. **laurea breve** degree that takes less than the standard period of time. **laurea in Lettere** arts degree

laure'ando, -**a** *nmf* final-year student

laure'are *vt* confer a degree on

laure'arsi *vr* graduate

laure'ato, -**a** *adj & nmf* graduate

'**lauro** *nm* laurel

'**lauto** *adj* lavish; ∼ **guadagno** handsome profit

'**lava** *nf* lava

la'vabile *adj* washable. **lavabile in lavastoviglie** dishwasher-safe

la'vabo *nm* wash-basin

lavacri'stallo *nm* windscreen wiper

la'vaggio *nm* washing. **lavaggio automatico** (per auto) carwash. **lavaggio del cervello** brainwashing. **lavaggio a secco** dry-cleaning

la'vagna *nf* slate; Sch blackboard. **lavagna a fogli mobili** flipchart. **lavagna luminosa** overhead projector, OHP

lava'macchine *nmf inv* car washer

la'vanda *nf* wash; Bot lavender; **gli hanno fatto la ∼ gastrica** he had his stomach pumped

lavande'ria *nf* laundry. **lavanderia automatica** launderette

lavan'dino *nm* sink; (hum: persona) bottomless pit

lavapi'atti *nmf inv* dishwasher

la'vare *vt* wash; **∼ i piatti** wash up; **∼ a secco** dry-clean; **∼ a mano** wash by hand; **∼ i panni** do the washing

la'varsi *vr* wash; **∼ i denti** brush one's teeth; **∼ la testa** o **i capelli** wash one's hair

lava'secco *nmf inv* dry-cleaner's

lavasto'viglie *nf inv* dishwasher

la'vata *nf* wash; **darsi una ∼** have a wash. **lavata di capo** fig scolding

lava'tivo, -a *nmf* idler

lava'trice *nf* washing-machine

lava'vetri *nm inv* squeegee

la'vello *nm* kitchen sink

'lavico *adj* formed by lava

la'vina *nf* snowslide

lavo'rante *nmf* worker

lavo'rare ① *vi* work; **∼ di fantasia** (sognare) day-dream
② *vt* work; knead ⟨*pasta ecc*⟩; till ⟨*la terra*⟩; **∼ a maglia** knit; **∼ troppo** overwork

lavora'tivo *adj* working; **giorno lavorativo** workday; **settimana lavorativa** working week

lavo'rato *adj* ⟨*legno*⟩ carved; ⟨*cuoio*⟩ tooled; ⟨*metallo*⟩ wrought; ⟨*terra*⟩ cultivated

lavora|'tore, -trice ① *nmf* worker. **lavora|tore a domicilio** homeworker
② *adj* working

lavorazi'one *nf* manufacture; (di terra) working; (del terreno) cultivation. **lavorazione [artigianale]** workmanship. **lavorazione del metallo** metalwork. **lavorazione in serie** mass production

lavo'rio *nm* intense activity

la'voro *nm* work; (faticoso, sociale) labour; (impiego) job; **andare al ∼** go to work; **essere senza ∼** be out of work; **mettersi al ∼ (su qualcosa)** set to work (on something); **ministero dei lavori pubblici** Department of Public Works; **lavori** *pl* **di casa** housework; **lavori** *pl* **in corso** roadworks **lavori** *pl* **forzati** hard labour *sg*; **lavori** *pl* **stradali** roadworks. **ministero del lavoro** Department of Employment. **lavoro atipico** employment relationship not conforming to the usual model of full-time, continuous employment with a single employer over a long time span. **lavoro a domicilio** homeworking. **lavoro di gruppo** Sch group work.

lavoro interinale temping. **lavoro a maglia** knitting. **lavoro nero** moonlighting. **lavoro part time** part-time job. **lavoro straordinario** overtime. **lavoro teatrale** play. **lavoro a tempo pieno** full-time job

lazza'rone *nm* rascal

le ① *def art fpl* the; ▶ IL
② *pers pron* (oggetto) them; (a lei) her; **le hai parlato?** did you talk to her? (forma di cortesia) you

'leader ① *nm inv* leader
② *adj inv* leading; **prodotto leader** market leader

le'ale *adj* loyal

leal'mente *adv* loyally

lealtà *nf* loyalty

'leasing *nm inv* lease-purchase, leasing

'lebbra *nf* leprosy

lecca 'lecca *nm inv* lollipop

leccapi'edi *nmf inv* pej bootlicker

lec'care *vt* lick; fig suck up to

lec'carsi *vr* lick; (fig: agghindarsi) doll oneself up; **da ∼ i baffi** mouth-watering

lec'cata *nf* lick

lec'cato *adj* ⟨persona⟩ dressed to kill

'leccio *nm* holm oak

leccor'nia *nf* delicacy

lecita'mente *adv* lawfully

'lecito *adj* lawful; (permesso) permissible

'ledere *vt* damage; Med injure

'lega *nf* league; (di metalli) alloy; **far ∼ con qualcuno** take up with somebody. **lega doganale** customs union

le'gaccio *nm* string; (delle scarpe) shoelace

le'gale ① *adj* legal
② *nm* lawyer

legalità *nf* legality

legaliz'zare *vt* authenticate; (rendere legale) legalize

legalizzazi'one *nf* legalization

legal'mente *adv* legally

Legam'biente *nf* Italian association for environmental protection

le'game *nm* tie; (amoroso) liaison; (connessione) link. **legame di parentela** family relationship. **legame di sangue** blood relationship. **legame sentimentale** emotional relationship

lega'mento *nm* Med ligament

le'gare ① *vt* tie; tie up ⟨persona⟩; tie together ⟨due cose⟩; (unire, rilegare) bind; alloy ⟨metalli⟩; (connettere) connect; **legarsela al dito** fig bear a grudge
② *vi* (far lega) get on well

le'garsi *vr* bind oneself; **∼ a qualcuno** become attached to somebody

lega'tario, -a *nmf* legatee

le'gato *nm* legacy; Relig legate

lega'tura *nf* tying; (di libro) binding

legazi'one *nf* legation

le'genda *nf* legend, key

'legge *nf* law; (parlamentare) act; **a norma di ~** by law. **legge marziale** martial law

leg'genda *nf* legend; (didascalia) key

leggen'dario *adj* legendary

'leggere *vt/i* read; **~ male** (sbagliato) misread

legge'rezza *nf* lightness; (frivolezza) frivolity; (incostanza) fickleness

legger'mente *adv* slightly

leg'gero *adj* light; (bevanda) weak; (lieve) slight; (frivolo) frivolous; (incostante) fickle; **~ come una piuma** [as] light as a feather; **alla leggera** lightly

leggi'adro *adj* liter graceful

leg'gibile *adj* (scrittura) legible; (stile) readable

leg'gio *nm* lectern; Mus music stand

legife'rare *vi* legislate

legio'nario *nm* legionary

legi'one *nf* legion

legisla'tivo *adj* legislative

legisla'tore *nm* legislator

legisla'tura *nf* legislature

legislazi'one *nf* legislation

legittima'mente *adv* legitimately

legittimità *nf* legitimacy

le'gittimo *adj* legitimate; (giusto) proper; **legittima difesa** self-defence

'legna *nf* firewood

le'gnaia *nf* woodshed

le'gname *nm* timber

le'gnata *nf* blow with a stick

'legno *nm* wood; **di ~** wooden; **legni** *pl* Mus woodwind. **legno compensato** plywood

le'gnoso *adj* woody; (di legno) wooden; (gambe) stiff; (movimento) wooden

le'gume *nm* pod

'lei *pers pron* (soggetto) she; (oggetto, con prep) her; (forma di cortesia) you; **lo ha fatto ~ stessa** she did it herself

'lembo *nm* edge; (di terra) strip

'lemma *nm* headword

'lemming *nm inv* lemming

'lena *nf* vigour

'lendine *nm* nit

le'nire *vt* soothe

lenta'mente *adv* slowly

'lente *nf* lens. **lente a contatto** contact lens; **mettersi le lenti a contatto** put in one's contact lenses. **lente a contatto morbida** soft lens. **lente a contatto rigida** hard lens. **lente d'ingrandimento** magnifying glass. **lente semi-rigida** gas-permeable lens

len'tezza *nf* slowness

len'ticchia *nf* lentil

len'tiggine *nf* freckle

'lento *adj* slow; (allentato) slack; (abito) loose

'lenza *nf* fishing-line

len'zuolo *nm* sheet; **le lenzuola** the sheets. **lenzuolo con gli angoli** fitted sheet. **lenzuolo funebre** shroud

leon'cino *nm* lion cub

le'one *nm* lion; Astr Leo. **leone marino** sea lion

leo'nessa *nf* lioness

leo'pardo *nm* leopard

lepo'rino *adj* **labbro leporino** harelip

'lepre *nf* hare

le'protto *nm* leveret

'lercio *adj* filthy

lerci'ume *nm* filth

'lesbica *nf* lesbian

'lesbico *adj* lesbian

lesi'nare [1] *vt* grudge [2] *vi* be stingy

lesio'nare *vt* damage

lesi'one *nf* lesion; (danno) damage. **lesione cerebrale** brain damage. **lesione interna** internal injury. **lesioni** *pl* **personali** grievous bodily harm, GBH

'leso [1] *pp di* LEDERE [2] *adj* injured; **lesa maestà** high treason

les'sare *vt* boil

lessi'cale *adj* lexical

'lessico *nm* vocabulary

lessicogra'fia *nf* lexicography

lessi'cografo, -a *nmf* lexicographer

'lesso [1] *adj* boiled [2] *nm* boiled meat

'lesto *adj* quick; (mente) sharp. **lesto di mano** light-fingered

le'tale *adj* lethal

leta'maio *nm* dunghill; fig pigsty

le'tame *nm* dung

le'targico *adj* lethargic

le'targo *nm* lethargy; (di animali) hibernation

le'tizia *nf* joy

'lettera *nf* letter; **alla ~** literally; **eseguire qualcosa alla ~** carry out something to the letter; **lettere** *pl* (letteratura) literature *sg*; Univ Arts; **dottore in lettere** BA, Bachelor of Arts. **lettera d'accompagnamento** covering letter. **lettera d'amore** love letter. **lettera assicurata** registered letter. **lettera di cambio** bill of exchange. **lettera di credito** letter of credit. **lettera maiuscola** capital [letter]. **lettera minuscola** small letter. **lettera di presentazione** letter of introduction. **lettera raccomandata** recorded delivery letter. **lettera di scuse** letter

of apology. **lettera di trasporto aereo**
air waybill

lette'rale *adj* literal

letteral'mente *adv* literally

lette'rario *adj* literary

lette'rato ① *adj* well-read
② *nm* scholar; **letterati** *pl* literati

lettera'tura *nf* literature. **letteratura pulp** pulp fiction

letti'era *nf* (per gatto) litter

let'tiga *nf* stretcher

let'tino *nm* cot; Med couch. **lettino [pieghevole]** camp bed

'letto *nm* bed; **andare a** ∼ go to bed; **[ri]fare il** ∼ make the bed. **letto a castello** bunkbed. **letto di fiume** river bed. **letti** *pl* **gemelli** twin beds. **letto matrimoniale** double bed. **letto a una piazza** single bed. **letto a due piazze** double bed. **letto singolo** single bed

Let'tonia *nf* Latvia

letto'rato *nm* (corso) tutorial

let|'tore, -trice ① *nmf* reader; Univ language assistant
② *nm* Comput disk drive. **lettore di CD** CD player, CD system. **lettore [di] CD-ROM** CD-Rom drive. **lettore di codice a barre** barcode reader, scanner. **lettore di compact disc** compact disc player. **lettore di disco** disk drive. **lettore di floppy** floppy [disk] drive. **lettore di minidisc** minidisc player. **lettore di MP3** MP3 player

let'tura *nf* reading

leuce'mia *nf* leukaemia

'leva *nf* lever; Mil call-up; **nuove leve** *pl* new blood, young blood; **far** ∼ lever. **leva del cambio** gear lever. **leva di comando** control lever

le'vante *nm* East; (vento) east wind

leva'punti *nm inv* staple remover

le'vare *vt* (alzare) raise; (togliere) take away; (rimuovere) take off; (estrarre) pull out, lift, abolish ⟨divieto, tassa⟩; ∼ **di mezzo qualcosa** get something out of the way

le'varsi *vr* move (da away from); ⟨vento⟩ get up; ⟨sole⟩ rise; ∼ **di mezzo** get out of the way

le'vata *nf* rising; (di posta) collection

leva'taccia *nf* **fare una** ∼ get up at the crack of dawn

leva'toio *adj* **ponte levatoio** drawbridge

leva'trice *nf* midwife

leva'tura *nf* intelligence

levi'gare *vt* smooth; (con carta vetro) rub down

levi'gato *adj* ⟨superficie⟩ polished; ⟨pelle⟩ smooth

leviga'trice *nf* sander

levi'tare *vi* levitate

levitazi'one *nf* levitation

Le'vitico *nm* Leviticus

levri'ero *nm* greyhound. **levriero afgano** Afghan hound

lezi'one *nf* lesson; Univ lecture; (rimprovero) rebuke. **lezione di guida** driving lesson. **lezione di italiano** Italian lesson, Italian class

lezi'oso *adj* ⟨stile, modi⟩ affected

'lezzo *nm* stench

li *pers pron mpl* them

li'ana *nf* liana

liba'nese *adj* & *nmf* Lebanese

Li'bano *nm* Lebanon

'libbra *nf* (peso) pound

li'beccio *nm* south-west wind

li'bello *nm* libel

li'bellula *nf* dragon-fly

libe'rale ① *adj* liberal; (generoso) generous
② *nmf* liberal

libera'lismo *nm* **liberalismo [economico]** economic liberalism

liberalità *nf* generosity

liberal'mente *adv* liberally

libe'rare *vt* free; release ⟨prigioniero⟩ vacate ⟨stanza⟩; (salvare) rescue

libe'rarsi *vr* ⟨stanza⟩ become vacant; Teleph become free; (da impegno) get out of it; ∼ **di** get rid of

libera|'tore, -trice ① *adj* liberating
② *nmf* liberator

libera'torio *adj* liberating. **pagamento liberatorio** full and final payment

liberazi'one *nf* liberation; **la Liberazione** (ricorrenza) Liberation Day. **liberazione della donna** women's liberation, women's lib

Li'beria *nf* Liberia

libe'rismo *nm* free trade

'libero *adj* free; ⟨strada⟩ clear; ∼ **come l'aria** free as a bird. **libero arbitrio** *nm* free will. **libero docente** *nm* qualified university lecturer. **libero professionista** *nm* self-employed person

libertà *nf* freedom; (di prigioniero) release; ∼ *pl* (confidenze) liberties; **prendersi la** ∼ **di fare qualcosa** take the liberty of doing something. **libertà di espressione** freedom of speech. **libertà di parola** free speech. **libertà di pensiero** freedom of thought. **libertà provvisoria** Jur bail. **libertà di stampa** freedom of the press. **libertà vigilata** probation

liber'tino, -a ① *adj* dissolute, libertine
② *nmf* libertine

'liberty *nm* & *adj inv* Art Nouveau

'Libia *nf* Libya

'**libico**, **-a** *adj* & *nmf* Libyan

li'**bidine** *nf* lust

libidi'noso *adj* lustful

li'**bido** *nf* libido

libra'io *nm* bookseller

libre'ria *nf* (negozio) bookshop; (mobile) bookcase

li'**bretto** *nm* booklet; Mus libretto. **libretto degli assegni** cheque book. **libretto di circolazione** logbook. **libretto d'istruzioni** instruction booklet. **libretto di risparmio** savings account; (documento) passbook, savings book. **libretto universitario** book held by students which records details of their exam performances

'**libro** *nm* book. **libro bianco** White Paper. **libro dei canti** hymn-book. **libro contabile** account book. **libro degli esercizi** workbook. **libro giallo** crime novel. **libro mastro** Comm ledger. **libro paga** payroll. **libro di ricette** cookbook, recipe book; **libri** *pl* **sociali** company's books. **libro tascabile** paperback. **libro di testo** course book

li'**cantropo** *nm* werewolf

lice'ale ① *nmf* secondary-school student ② *adj* secondary-school *attrib*

li'**cenza** *nf* licence; (permesso) permission; Mil leave; Sch school-leaving certificate; **essere in ~** be on leave. **licenza di caccia** hunting licence. **licenza di esportazione** export licence. **licenza matrimoniale** marriage licence. **licenza di pesca** fishing licence. **licenza poetica** poetic licence. **licenza di porto d'armi** gun licence

licenzia'mento *nm* dismissal, lay-off

licenzi'are *vt* dismiss, sack *fam*; (conferire un diploma) grant a school-leaving certificate to

licenzi'arsi *vr* (da un impiego) resign; (accomiatarsi) take one's leave

licenzi'oso *adj* licentious

li'**ceo** *nm* secondary school, high school. **liceo classico** secondary school with an emphasis on humanities. **liceo scientifico** secondary school with an emphasis on sciences

li'**chene** *nm* lichen

'**lido** *nm* beach

'**Liechtenstein** *nm* Liechtenstein

lieta'mente *adv* happily

li'**eto** *adj* glad; ⟨evento⟩ happy; **molto ~!** pleased to meet you!. **lieto fine** happy ending

li'**eve** *adj* light; (debole) faint; (trascurabile) slight

lievi'tare ① *vi* rise ② *vt* leaven

li'**evito** *nm* yeast. **lievito in polvere** baking powder

lift *nm inv* liftboy

'**lifting** *nm inv* face-lift

'**ligio** *adj* essere **~ al dovere** have a sense of duty

li'**gnaggio** *nm* lineage

'**ligneo** *adj* wooden

'**lilla** *nm* (colore) lilac

lillà *nm* Bot lilac

'**lima** *nf* file

limacci'oso *adj* slimy

li'**manda** *nf* dab

li'**mare** *vt* file

lima'tura *nf* (atto) filing; (residui) filings *pl*

'**limbo** *nm* limbo

li'**metta** *nf* **limetta [da unghie]** nail file; (di carta) emery board

limi'tare ① *nm* threshold ② *vt* limit

limi'tarsi *vr* **~ a fare qualcosa** restrict oneself to doing something; **~ in qualcosa** cut down on something

limitata'mente *adv* to a limited extent

limita'tivo *adj* limiting

limi'tato *adj* limited

limitazi'one *nf* limitation

'**limite** ① *adj* ⟨caso⟩ extreme ② *nm* limit; (confine) boundary; **entro certi limiti** within certain limits. **limite di credito** credit limit, credit ceiling. **limite di sopportazione** breaking point. '**limite di sosta**' 'restricted parking'. **limite di tempo** time limit. **limite di velocità** speed limit; **rispettare il ~ di velocità** keep to the speed limit

li'**mitrofo** *adj* neighbouring

'**limo** *nm* slime

limo'nata *nf* (bibita) lemonade; (succo) lemon juice. **limonata amara** bitter lemon

li'**mone** *nm* lemon; (albero) lemon tree

'**limpido** *adj* clear; ⟨occhi⟩ limpid

'**lince** *nf* lynx

linci'are *vt* lynch

'**lindo** *adj* neat; (pulito) clean}

'**linea** *nf* line; (di autobus, aereo) route; (di metropolitana) line; (di abito) cut; (di auto, mobile) design; (fisico) figure; **in ~ d'aria** as the crow flies; **è caduta la ~** I've been cut off; **in ~ di massima** as a rule; **a grandi linee** in outline; **mantenere la ~** keep one's figure; **in ~** Comput on-line; **in prima ~** in the front line; **mettersi in ~** line up. **nave di linea** liner; **volo di linea** scheduled flight. **linea aerea** airline. **linea d'arrivo** Sport finishing line. **linea commutata** Teleph switched line. **linea di confine** boundary. **linea continua** unbroken line. **linea dedicata** dedicated line. **linea di demarcazione** border line. **linea ferroviaria** railway line. **linea di fondo** baseline. **linea d'immersione** water line. **linea laterale** Sport touch line. **linee** *pl* **della mano** lines of the hand. **linea di marea** tidemark. **linea mediana** Sport halfway line. **linea di partenza** Sport starting line. **linea principale** Rail main line. **linea punteggiata** dotted line. **linea secondaria** Rail branch line. **linea di tiro** line of fire. **linea tratteggiata** broken line

linea'menti *nmpl* features

line'are *adj* linear; ‹*discorso*› to the point; ‹*ragionamento*› consistent

line'etta *nf* (tratto lungo) dash; (d'unione) hyphen

'linfa *nf* Anat lymph; Bot sap. **linfa vitale** fig life blood

lin'fatico *adj* Anat lymphatic

linfoghi'andola *nf* lymph gland

linfo'nodo *nm* lymph node

linge'rie *nf* lingerie

lin'gotto *nm* ingot

'lingua *nf* tongue; (linguaggio) language; **avere la ~ lunga** fig have a big mouth. **lingua d'arrivo** target language. **lingua moderna** modern language. **lingua morta** dead language. **lingua di partenza** source language. **lingua straniera** foreign language

lingu'accia *nf* (persona) backbiter; **fare le linguacce** put one's tongue out (**a** at)

lingu'aggio *nm* language. **linguaggio infantile** baby-talk. **linguaggio per la marcatura di ipertesti** Comput hypertext markup language. **linguaggio dei segni** sign language

lingu'etta *nf* (di scarpa) tongue; (di busta) flap; Mus reed; (da tirare) tab

lingu'ista *nmf* linguist

lingu'istica *nf* linguistics

lingu'istico *adj* linguistic

lin'kare *vt* Comput link ‹*siti Web*›

'lino *nm* Bot flax; (tessuto) linen

li'noleum *nm* linoleum

liofiliz'zare *vt* freeze-dry

liofiliz'zato *adj* freeze dried

li'pide *nm* lipid

liposuzi'one *nf* liposuction

li'quame *nm* slurry

lique'fare *vt* liquefy; (sciogliere) melt

lique'farsi *vr* liquefy; (sciogliersi) melt

liqui'dare *vt* liquidate; settle ‹*conto*›; pay off ‹*debiti*›; clear ‹*merce*›; (fam: uccidere) get rid of

liquida'tore *nm* liquidator

liquidazi'one *nf* liquidation; (di conti) settling; (di merce) clearance sale. **liquidazione totale [per cessata attività]** closing-down sale

'liquido *adj & nm* liquid. **liquido dei freni** brake fluid. **liquido scongelante**

Auto de-icer. **liquido tergicristallo** screen wash

liqui'gas® *nm* Calor gas®

liqui'rizia *nf* liquorice

li'quore *nm* liqueur; **liquori** *pl* (superalcolici) liquors

'lira *nf* (ex moneta italiana) lira; (moneta di vari paesi) pound; Mus lyre. **lira sterlina** pound sterling

'lirico, -a ① *adj* lyrical; ‹*poesia*› lyric; ‹*cantante, musica*› opera *attrib* ② *nf* lyric poetry; Mus opera

li'rismo *nm* lyricism

'lisca *nf* fishbone; **avere la ~** (fam: nel parlare) have a lisp

lisci'are *vt* smooth; (accarezzare) stroke

'liscio *adj* smooth; ‹*capelli*› straight; ‹*liquore*› neat, straight; ‹*acqua minerale*› still; **passarla liscia** get away with it

li'seuse *nf inv* bed jacket

'liso *adj* worn [out]

'lista *nf* list; (striscia) strip; **fare una ~** make out a list. **lista di attesa** waiting list; **in ~ di attesa** on the waiting list; Aeron on stand-by. **lista elettorale** list of candidates. **lista degli invitati** guest list. **lista nera** blacklist. **lista di nozze** wedding list. **lista della spesa** shopping list. **lista dei vini** wine list

li'stare *vt* edge; Comput list

li'stino *nm* list. **listino di borsa** Stock-Exchange list. **listino dei cambi** exchange rates *pl*. **listino [dei] prezzi** price list

Lit. *abbr* (lire italiane) Italian lire

lita'nia *nf* litany

'litchi *nm inv* lychee

'lite *nf* quarrel; (baruffa) row; Jur lawsuit

liti'gante *nmf* Jur litigant

liti'gare *vi* quarrel; Jur litigate

li'tigio *nm* quarrel

litigi'oso *adj* quarrelsome

'litio *nm* lithium

litogra'fia *nf* (procedimento) lithography; (stampa) lithograph

li'tografo, -a *nmf* lithographer

lito'rale ① *adj* coastal ② *nm* coast

lito'raneo *adj* coastal

'litro *nm* litre

Litu'ania *nf* Lithuania

litu'ano, -a *adj & nmf* Lithuanian

litur'gia *nf* liturgy

li'turgico *adj* liturgical

li'uto *nm* lute

li'vella *nf* level. **livella a bolla d'aria** spirit level

livella'mento *nm* levelling out, levelling off

livel'lare *vt* level

livel'larsi *vr* level out

livella'tore *adj* levelling

livella'trice *nf* bulldozer

li'vello *nm* level; **passaggio a livello** level crossing; **sotto/sul ∼ del mare** below/above sea level; **ad alto ∼** ⟨*conferenza, trattative*⟩ top-level, high-level; **a più livelli** multilevel. **livello di guardia** danger level. **livello di magazzino** stock level. **livello occupazionale** level of employment

'livido ① *adj* livid; (per il freddo) blue; (per una botta) black and blue. **livido di rabbia** livid ② *nm* bruise

li'vore *nm* spite

Li'vorno *nf* Leghorn

li'vrea *nf* livery

'lizza *nf* lists *pl*; **essere in ∼ per qualcosa** be in the running for something

lo ① *def art m* (before s + consonant, gn, ps, z) the; ▶ IL ② *pron* (riferito a persona) him; (riferito a cosa) it; **non lo so** I don't know

'lobbia *nf* Homburg [hat]

lob'bismo *nm* lobbying

lob'bista *nmf* lobbyist

'lobby *nf inv* lobby

lo'belia *nf* lobelia

'lobo *nm* lobe

loboto'mia *nf* lobotomy

lo'cale ① *adj* local ② *nm* (stanza) room; (treno) local train; **locali** *pl* (edifici) premises. **locale notturno** nightclub

località *nf* locality. **località balneare** seaside resort. **località turistica** tourist resort. **località di villeggiatura** holiday resort

localiz'zare *vt* localize; (reperire) locate

localiz'zarsi *vr* ∼ **in** be located in

localiz'zato *adj* localized

localizzazi'one *nf* localization; (reperimento) location

local'mente *adv* locally

lo'canda *nf* inn

locandi'ere, -a *nmf* innkeeper

locan'dina *nf* bill, poster

loca'tario, -a *nmf* tenant. **locatario residente** sitting tenant

loca'tivo *adj* Gram locative; Jur rental

loca'tore, -trice ① *nm* landlord ② *nf* landlady

locazi'one *nf* tenancy

locomo'tiva *nf* locomotive. **locomotiva a vapore** steam engine

locomo'tore *nm* locomotive, engine

locomozi'one *nf* locomotion; **mezzi di locomozione** means of transport

'loculo *nm* burial niche

lo'custa *nf* locust

locuzi'one *nf* expression

lo'dare *vt* praise

'lode *nf* praise; **degno di lode** praiseworthy; **laurea con lode** first-class degree

'loden *nm inv* (cappotto) loden [coat]; (stoffa) loden

lo'devole *adj* praiseworthy

'lodola *nf* lark

loga'ritmo *nm* logarithm

'loggia *nf* loggia; (massonica) lodge

loggi'one *nm* gallery, gods *pl*

'logica *nf* logic

logica'mente *adv* (in modo logico) logically; (ovviamente) of course

logicità *nf* logic

'logico *adj* logical

lo'gistica *nf* logistics

lo'gistico *adj* logistic[al]

'logo *nm inv* logo

logope'dia *nf* speech therapy

logope'dista *nmf* speech therapist

logo'rante *adj* ⟨*attesa, esperienza*⟩ wearing

logo'rare *vt* wear out; (sciupare) waste

logo'rarsi *vr* wear out; ⟨*persona*⟩ wear oneself out

logo'rio *nm* wear and tear; (stress) stress

'logoro *adj* worn-out

logor'roico *adj* loquacious

lom'baggine *nf* lumbago

Lombar'dia *nf* Lombardy

lom'bardo *adj* Lombardy *attrib*

lom'bare *adj* lumbar

lom'bata *nf* loin. **lombata di manzo** sirloin

'lombo *nm* Anat loin

lom'brico *nm* earthworm

londi'nese ① *adj* London *attrib* ② *nmf* Londoner

'Londra *nf* London

long-'drink *nm inv* long drink

longevità *nf* longevity

lon'gevo *adj* long-lived

longhe'rone *nm* strut

longi'lineo *adj* rangy

longitudi'nale *adj* lengthwise

longitudinal'mente *adv* lengthwise

longi'tudine *nf* longitude

long 'playing *nm inv* LP, long-playing record

lontana'mente *adv* distantly; (vagamente) vaguely; **neanche ∼** not for a moment

lonta'nanza *nf* distance; (separazione) separation; **in ~** in the distance

lon'tano ① *adj* far; (distante) distant; (nel tempo) far-off, distant; ⟨parente⟩ distant; (vago) vague; (assente) absent; **più ~** further; **è ~ un paio di chilometri** it is a couple of kilometres away
② *adv* far [away]; **da ~** from a distance; **tenersi ~ da** keep away from; **andare ~** (allontanarsi) go away; (avere successo) go far

'lontra *nf* otter

'lonza *nf* (lombata) loin

lo'quace *adj* talkative

'lordo *adj* dirty; ⟨somma, peso⟩ gross; **al ~ di imposte** pre-tax

'loro[1] *pers pron pl* (soggetto) they; (oggetto) them; (forma di cortesia) you; **sta a ~** it is up to them

'loro[2] ① (**il ~** *m*, **la ~** *f*, **i ~** *mpl*, **le ~** *fpl*) *poss adj* their; (forma di cortesia) your; **un ~ amico** a friend of theirs; (forma di cortesia) a friend of yours
② *poss pron* theirs; (forma di cortesia) yours; **i ~** (famiglia) their folk

lo'sanga *nf* lozenge; **a losanghe** diamond-shaped

losca'mente *adv* suspiciously

'losco *adj* suspicious

'loto *nm* lotus

'lotta *nf* fight, struggle; (contrasto) conflict; Sport wrestling. **lotta di classe** class struggle. **lotta libera** all-in wrestling

lot'tare *vi* fight, struggle; Sport, fig wrestle

lotta|'tore, -trice *nmf* wrestler

lotte'ria *nf* lottery. **Lotteria di Stato** National Lottery

lottiz'zare *vt* divide up ⟨terreno⟩; fig parcel out

lottizzazi'one *nf* (di terreno) division into lots; fig parcelling out

'lotto *nm* [state] lottery; (porzione) lot; (di terreno) plot

lozi'one *nf* lotion. **lozione idratante** moisturizer. **lozione solare** suntan lotion

lubrifi'cante ① *adj* lubricating
② *nm* lubricant

lubrifi'care *vt* lubricate

luc'chetto *nm* padlock

lucci'cante *adj* sparkling

lucci'care *vi* sparkle

lucci'chio *nm* sparkle

lucci'cone *nm* **far venire i lucciconi** bring tears to the eyes

'luccio *nm* pike

'lucciola *nf* glow-worm; (fam: prostituta) lady of the night

'luce *nf* light; Auto highlight; **accendere/ spegnere la ~** switch the light on/off; **far ~ su** fig shed light on; **dare alla ~** give birth to; **venire alla ~** come to light; **luci**

pl **di arresto** Auto stop lights; **luci** *pl* **d'atterraggio** landing lights; **luci** *pl* **d'emergenza** Auto hazard [warning] lights, hazards. **luce della luna** moonlight; **luci** *pl* **di posizione** Auto sidelights; **luci** *pl* **posteriori** Auto rear-lights; **luci** *pl* **di retromarcia** Auto reversing lights. **luce del sole** sunlight. **luce stroboscopica** strobe

lu'cente *adj* shining

lucen'tezza *nf* shine

lucer'nario *nm* skylight

lu'certola *nf* lizard

lucida'labbra *nm inv* lip gloss

luci'dare *vt* polish

lucida'trice *nf* [floor-]polisher

'lucido ① *adj* shiny; ⟨pavimento, scarpe⟩ polished; (chiaro) clear; ⟨persona, mente⟩ lucid; ⟨occhi⟩ watery
② *nm* shine. **lucido [da scarpe]** [shoe] polish

lucra'tivo *adj* lucrative

'lucro *nm* lucre; **senza fini di ~** non-profit-making, not-for-profit Am

luculli'ano *adj* ⟨pranzo⟩ lavish

ludo'teca *nf* playroom

'luglio *nm* July

'lugubre *adj* gloomy

'lui *pers pron* (soggetto) he; (oggetto, con prep) him; **lo ha fatto ~ stesso** he did it himself

lu'maca *nf* (mollusco) snail; fig slowcoach

'lume *nm* lamp; (luce) light; **a ~ di candela** by candlelight; **perdere il ~ della ragione** be beside oneself with rage

lumi'nare *nmf* luminary

lumi'narie *nfpl* illuminations

lumine'scente *adj* luminescent

lumine'scenza *nf* luminescence

lu'mino *nm* **lumino da notte** nightlight

luminosa'mente *adv* luminously

luminosità *nf* brightness

lumi'noso *adj* luminous; ⟨stanza, cielo ecc⟩ bright; **idea luminosa** brain wave

'luna *nf* moon; **chiaro di luna** moonlight; **avere la ~ storta** be in a bad mood. **luna di miele** honeymoon. **luna piena** full moon

'luna park *nm inv* fairground

lu'nare *adj* lunar

lu'naria *nf* moonstone

lu'nario *nm* almanac; **sbarcare il ~** make [both] ends meet

lu'natico *adj* moody

lunedì *nm inv* Monday; **di ~** on Mondays

lu'netta *nf* half-moon [shape]

lun'gaggine *nf* slowness

lunga'mente *adv* at great length

lun'ghezza nf length; **di ~ media** medium-length. **lunghezza d'onda** wavelength

'**lungi** adv ero [ben] **~ dall'immaginare che...** I never dreamt for a moment that...

lungimi'rante adj far-seeing

lungimi'ranza nf far-sightedness

'**lungo** ① adj long; (diluito) weak; (lento) slow; **a ~ andare** in the long run; **saperla lunga** be shrewd; **andare per le lunghe** drag on; **di gran lunga** by far; **di lunga data** long-term
② nm length
③ prep (durante) throughout; (per la lunghezza di) along

lungofi'ume nm riverside

lungo'lago nm lakeside

lungo'mare nm seafront

lungome'traggio nm feature film

lu'notto nm rear window. **lunotto termico** heated rear window

'**lunula** nf half-moon

lu'ogo nm place; (punto preciso) spot; (passo d'autore) passage; **aver ~** take place; **dar ~ a** give rise to; **fuori ~** out of place; **del ~** ⟨usanze⟩ local. **luogo comune** cliché. **luogo di nascita** birthplace. **luogo natale** birthplace. **luogo pubblico** public place. **luogo di villeggiatura** holiday resort

luogote'nente nm Mil lieutenant

'**lupa** nf she-wolf

lu'para nf sawn-off shotgun

lu'petto nm Cub [Scout]

'**lupo** nm wolf. **lupo mannaro** werewolf

'**luppolo** nm hop

'**lurido** adj filthy

luri'dume nm filth

lu'singa nf flattery

lusin'gare vt flatter

lusin'garsi vr flatter oneself; (illudersi) fool oneself

lusinghi'ero adj flattering

lus'sare vt dislocate

lus'sarsi vr dislocate

lussazi'one nf dislocation

Lussem'burgo nm Luxembourg

'**lusso** nm luxury; **di ~** luxury attrib

lussuosa'mente adv luxuriously

lussu'oso adj luxurious

lussureggi'ante adj luxuriant

lus'suria nf lust

lussuri'oso adj dissolute

lu'strare vt polish

lu'strino nm sequin

'**lustro** ① adj shiny
② nm sheen; fig prestige; (quinquennio) five-year period

lute'rano adj & nmf Lutheran

'**lutto** nm mourning; **parato a ~** draped in black. **lutto stretto** deep mourning

luttu'oso adj mournful

Mm

m abbr (**metro**) m

ma conj but; (eppure) yet; **ma!** (dubbio) I don't know; (indignazione) really!; **ma davvero?** really?; **ma va'?** really?; **ma sì!** why not!; (certo che sì) of course!

'**macabro** adj macabre

macché int of course not!

macche'roni nmpl macaroni sg

macche'ronico adj ⟨italiano⟩ broken

'**macchia**[1] nf stain; (di diverso colore) spot; (piccola) speck; **senza ~** spotless; **spargersi a ~ d'olio** spread rapidly. **macchia di colore** splash of colour. **macchia d'inchiostro** ink stain. **macchia di sangue** bloodstain

'**macchia**[2] nf (boscaglia) scrub; **darsi alla ~** take to the woods

macchi'are vt stain

macchi'arsi vr stain

macchi'ato ① adj ⟨caffè⟩ with a dash of milk; ⟨pelo⟩ spotted; **~ di** (sporco) stained with; **~ d'inchiostro** ink-stained, inky.
② nm (caffè) espresso with a dash of milk

macchi'etta nf spot

'**macchina** nf machine; (motore) engine; (automobile) car; **in ~** by car; **giro in ~** drive; **cimitero delle macchine** scrapyard. **macchina del caffè** coffee-maker. **macchina da cucire** sewing machine. **macchina per l'espresso** coffee machine. **macchina fotografica** camera. **macchina fototessere** photo booth. **macchina obliteratrice** ticket-stamping machine. **macchina da presa** cine camera. **macchina da scrivere** typewriter. **macchina sverniciante** paint stripper. **macchina utensile** machine tool. **macchina della verità** lie detector

macchinal'mente *adv* mechanically

macchi'nare *vt* plot

macchi'nario *nm* machinery

macchinazi'oni *nfpl* machinations, scheming

macchi'netta *nf* (per i denti) brace; (per il caffè) espresso coffee maker; (accendino) lighter

macchi'nista *nm* Rail engine driver; Naut engineer; Theat stagehand

macchi'noso *adj* complicated

Mace'donia *nf* Macedonia

mace'donia *nf* fruit salad

macel'laio, -a *nmf* butcher

macel'lare *vt* slaughter

macellazi'one *nf* slaughtering

macelle'ria *nf* butcher's [shop]

ma'cello *nm* (mattatoio) slaughterhouse; fig shambles *sg*; **andare al ∼** fig go to the slaughter; **mandare al ∼** fig send to his/her death

mace'rare *vt* macerate; fig distress

mace'rarsi *vr* be consumed

macerazi'one *nf* maceration

ma'cerie *nfpl* rubble *sg*; (rottami) debris *sg*

'macero *nm* pulping; (stabilimento) pulping mill

mach *nm inv* Mach

ma'chete *nm inv* machete

machia'vellico *adj* Machiavellian

ma'chismo *nm* machismo

'macho *adj inv* macho

ma'cigno *nm* boulder

maci'lento *adj* emaciated

'macina *nf* millstone

macinacaffè *nm inv* coffee mill

macina'pepe *nm inv* pepper mill

maci'nare *vt* mill

maci'nato ① *adj* ground ② *nm* (carne) mince

maci'nino *nm* mill; (hum: macchina) old banger

maciul'lare *vt* (stritolare) crush

'macro *nf inv* Comput macro

macrobi'otica *nf* **negozio di macrobiotica** health-food shop

macrobi'otico *adj* macrobiotic

macro'clima *nm* macroclimate

macro'cosmo *nm* macrocosm

macrofotogra'fia *nf* macrophotography

macro'scopico *adj* macroscopic

macu'lato *adj* spotted

Madaga'scar *nm* Madagascar

madami'gella *nf* young lady

'madia *nf* cupboard with a covered trough on top for making bread

'madido *adj* **∼ di** damp with ⟨sudore⟩

Ma'donna *nf* Our Lady

mador'nale *adj* gross

'madre *nf* mother. **madre biologica** birth mother. **madre single** single mother

madre'lingua *adj inv* **inglese madrelingua** English native speaker

madre'patria *nf* native land

madre'perla *nf* mother-of-pearl

ma'drepora *nf* madrepore

madri'gale *nm* madrigal

ma'drina *nf* godmother

maestà *nf* majesty

maestosa'mente *adv* majestically

maestosità *nf* majesty

mae'stoso *adj* majestic

ma'estra *nf* teacher; Sch primary school teacher. **maestra d'asilo** kindergarten teacher. **maestra di canto** singing teacher. **maestra di piano** piano teacher. **maestra di sci** ski instructor

mae'strale *nm* northwest wind

mae'stranza *nf* workers *pl*

mae'stria *nf* mastery

ma'estro ① *nm* teacher; Sch primary school teacher; Mus maestro; (esperto) master; **colpo da maestro** masterstroke. **maestro d'asilo** kindergarten teacher. **maestro di canto** singing teacher. **maestro di cerimonie** master of ceremonies. **maestro di piano** piano teacher. **maestro di sci** ski instructor ② *adj* (principale) main; (di grande abilità) skilful

'mafia *nf* Mafia

mafi'oso ① *adj* of the Mafia ② *nm* member of the Mafia, Mafioso

'maga *nf* sorceress, magician

ma'gagna *nf* fault

ma'gari ① *adv* (forse) maybe ② *int* I wish! ③ *conj* (per esprimere desiderio) if only; (anche se) even if

magazzini'ere *nm* storeman, warehouseman

magaz'zino *nm* (deposito) warehouse; (in negozio) stockroom; (emporio) shop; **grande magazzino** department store. **magazzini** *pl* **portuali** naval stores

Magg. *abbr* (**maggiore**) Maj

mag'gese *nm* field lying fallow

'maggio *nm* May

maggio'lino *nm* May bug

maggio'rana *nf* marjoram

maggio'ranza *nf* majority

maggio'rare *vt* increase

maggior'domo *nm* butler

maggi'ore ① *adj* (di dimensioni, numero) bigger, larger; (superlativo) biggest, largest; ⋯⟶

(di età) older; (superlativo) oldest; (di importanza, Mus) major; (superlativo) greatest; **la maggior parte di** most; **la maggior parte del tempo** most of the time

2️⃣ *pron* (di dimensioni) the bigger, the larger; (superlativo) the biggest, the largest; (di età) the older; (superlativo) the oldest; (di importanza) the major; (superlativo) the greatest

3️⃣ *nm* Mil major; Aeron squadron leader

maggio'renne 1️⃣ *adj* of age
2️⃣ *nmf* adult

maggiori'tario *adj* (della maggioranza) majority; ⟨sistema⟩ first-past-the-post *attrib*

maggior'mente *adv* [all] the more; (più di tutto) most

'**Magi** *nmpl* **i re** ~ the Magi

ma'gia *nf* magic; (trucco) magic trick

magica'mente *adv* magically

'**magico** *adj* magic

magi'stero *nm* (insegnamento) teaching; (maestria) skill; **facoltà di magistero** arts faculty

magi'strale *adj* masterly; **istituto magistrale** teacher-training college

magistral'mente *adv* in a masterly fashion

magi'strato *nm* magistrate

magistra'tura *nf* magistrature; **la** ~ the Bench

'**maglia** *nf* stitch; (lavoro ai ferri) knitting; (tessuto) jersey; (di rete) mesh; (indumento intimo) vest; (esterno) top; (di calciatore) shirt; **fare la** ~ knit. **maglia con cappuccio** *fam* hoody. **maglia diritta** knit. **maglia rosa** (ciclismo) ≈ yellow jersey. **maglia rovescia** purl

magli'aia *nf* knitter

maglie'ria *nf* knitwear

magli'etta *nf* **maglietta [a maniche corte]** tee-shirt

magli'ficio *nm* knitwear factory

ma'glina *nf* (tessuto) jersey

'**maglio** *nm* mallet

magli'one *nm* sweater, jumper. **maglione dolcevita** polo neck [jumper]. **maglione a girocollo** crew neck [sweater]. **maglione a V** V-neck [sweater]

'**magma** *nm* magma

ma'gnaccia *nm inv fam* pimp

ma'gnanimo *adj* magnanimous

ma'gnate *nm* magnate

ma'gnesia *nf* magnesia

ma'gnesio *nm* magnesium

ma'gnete *nm* magnet

magnetica'mente *adv* magnetically

ma'gnetico *adj* magnetic

magne'tismo *nm* magnetism

magne'tofono *nm* tape recorder

magnifica'mente *adv* magnificently

magnifi'cenza *nf* magnificence; (generosità) munificence

ma'gnifico *adj* magnificent; (generoso) munificent

magni'tudine *nf* Astr magnitude

'**magno** *adj* **aula magna** main hall

ma'gnolia *nf* magnolia

'**magnum** *nf inv* (bottiglia, pistola) magnum

'**mago** *nm* magician

ma'gone *nm* **avere il** ~ be down; **mi è venuto il** ~ I've got a lump in my throat

'**magra** *nf* low water

ma'grezza *nf* thinness

'**magro** *adj* thin; ⟨carne⟩ lean; (scarso) meagre; **magra consolazione** cold comfort

'**mai** *adv* never; (interrogativo, talvolta) ever; **caso** ~ if anything; **caso** ~ **tornasse** in case he comes back; **come** ~? why?; **cosa** ~? what on earth?; ~ **più** never again; **più che** ~ more than ever; **quando** ~? whenever?; **quasi** ~ hardly ever

mai'ale *nm* pig; (carne) pork. **maiale arrosto** roast pork

maia'lino *nm* piglet

'**mailing** *nm* direct mail, mailing

mai'olica *nf* majolica

maio'nese *nf* mayonnaise

'**mais** *nm* maize

mai'uscola *nf* capital [letter]; **bloc maiusc** (tasto) caps lock

mai'uscolo *adj* capital

mai'zena® *nf* cornflour

mal ▶ MALE

'**mala** *nf sl* **la** ~ the underworld

malac'corto *adj* unwise

mala'fede *nf* bad faith

malaf'fare *nm* **gente di malaffare** shady characters *pl*

mala'lingua *nf* backbiter

mala'mente *adv* ⟨ridotto⟩ badly; ⟨rispondere⟩ rudely

malan'dato *adj* in bad shape; (di salute) in poor health

ma'lanimo *nm* ill will

ma'lanno *nm* misfortune; (malattia) illness; **prendersi un** ~ catch something

mala'pena *adv* **a** ~ hardly

ma'laria *nf* malaria

mala'ticcio *adj* sickly

ma'lato, -a 1️⃣ *adj* ill, sick; ⟨pianta⟩ diseased
2️⃣ *nmf* sick person. **malato di Aids** AIDS sufferer. **malato di cancro** cancer patient. **malato di mente** mentally ill person

malat'tia *nf* disease, illness; **ho preso due giorni di** ~ I had two days off sick;

essere in ~ be on sick leave. **malattia nervosa** nervous disease. **malattia venerea** venereal disease, VD

malaugurataʼmente *adv* unfortunately

malauguʼrato *adj* ill-omened

malauʼgurio *nm* bad *or* ill omen

malaʼvita *nf* underworld

malaviʼtoso, **-a** *nmf* gangster

malaʼvoglia *nf* unwillingness; **di** ~ unwillingly

Maʼlawi *nm* Malawi

malcapiʼtato *adj* wretched

malceʼlato *adj* ill-concealed

malʼconcio *adj* battered

malconʼtento *nm* discontent

malcoʼstume *nm* immorality

malʼdestro *adj* awkward; (inesperto) inexperienced

maldiʼcente *adj* slanderous

maldiʼcenza *nf* slander

maldiʼsposto *adj* ill-disposed

Malʼdive *nfpl* Maldives

'male ① *adv* badly; **funzionare** ~ not work properly; **star** ~ be ill; **star** ~ **a qualcuno** ⟨vestito ecc⟩ not suit somebody; **rimanerci** ~ be hurt; **ho dormito** ~ I didn't sleep well; **non c'è** ~! not bad at all!
② *nm* evil; (dolore) pain, ache; (malattia) illness; (danno) harm; **distinguere il bene dal** ~ know right from wrong; **andare a** ~ go off; **aver** ~ **a** have a pain in; **dove hai** ~? where does it hurt?, where is the pain?; **far** ~ **a qualcuno** (provocare dolore) hurt somebody; ⟨cibo⟩ be bad for somebody; **le cipolle mi fanno** ~ onions don't agree with me; **mi fa** ~ **la schiena** my back is hurting; **farsi** ~ **alla schiena** hurt one's back. **mal d'aereo** airsickness. **mal d'aria** airsickness; **soffrire il mal d'aria** be airsick. **mal d'auto** carsickness. **mal di denti** toothache. **mal di gola** sore throat. **mal di mare** seasickness; **avere il mal di mare** be seasick. **mal d'orecchi** earache. **mal di pancia** stomach-ache. **mal di schiena** backache. **mal di testa** headache

maledettaʼmente *adv* flipping

maleʼdetto *adj* cursed; (orribile) awful

maleʼdire *vt* curse

malediziʼone *nf* curse; ~! damn!

maleducataʼmente *adv* rudely

maleduʼcato *adj* ill-mannered

maleducaziʼone *nf* rudeness

maleʼfatta *nf* misdeed

maleʼficio *nm* witchcraft

maʼlefico *adj* ⟨azione⟩ evil; (nocivo) harmful

maleodoʼrante *adj* foul-smelling

maʼlese *adj* & *nmf* Malaysian

Maʼlesia *nf* Malaysia

maʼlessere *nm* indisposition; fig uneasiness

maʼlevolo *adj* malevolent

malfaʼmato *adj* of ill repute

malʼfatto *adj* badly done; (malformato) ill-shaped

malfatʼtore *nm* wrongdoer

malʼfermo *adj* unsteady; ⟨salute⟩ poor

malforʼmato *adj* misshapen

malformaziʼone *nf* malformation

malʼgascio, **-a** *adj* & *nmf* Malagasy

malgoʼverno *nm* misgovernment

malʼgrado ① *prep* in spite of ② *conj* although

'Mali *nm* Mali

maʼlia *nf* spell

malignaʼmente *adv* maliciously

maliʼgnare *vi* malign

malignità *nf inv* malice; Med malignancy

maʼligno *adj* malicious; (perfido) evil; Med malignant

malincoʼnia *nf* melancholy

malinconicaʼmente *adv* melancholically

malinʼconico *adj* melancholy

malincuʼore: **a** ~ *adv* unwillingly, reluctantly

malinforʼmato *adj* misinformed

malintenzioʼnato, **-a** *nmf* miscreant

malinʼteso ① *adj* mistaken ② *nm* misunderstanding

maʼlizia *nf* malice; (astuzia) cunning; (espediente) trick

maliziosaʼmente *adv* mischievously, naughtily

maliziosità *nf* naughtiness

maliziʼoso *adj* (birichino) mischievous, naughty

malleʼabile *adj* malleable

malʼleolo *nm* Anat malleolus

mallevaʼdore *nm* guarantor

'mallo *nm* husk

malʼloppo *nm* fam loot

malmeʼnare *vt* ill-treat

malʼmesso *adj* (vestito male) shabbily dressed; ⟨casa⟩ poorly furnished; (fig: senza soldi) hard up

malnuʼtrito *adj* undernourished

malnutriziʼone *nf* malnutrition

'malo *adj* **in** ~ **modo** badly

maʼlocchio *nm* evil eye

maʼlora *nf* ruin; **della** ~ awful; **andare in** ~ go to ruin

maʼlore *nm* illness; **essere colto da** ~ be suddenly taken ill

m

malri'dotto adj ⟨persona⟩ in a sorry state; ⟨auto, casa⟩ dilapidated, in a sorry state

mal'sano adj unhealthy

malsi'curo adj unsafe; (incerto) uncertain

'malta nf mortar

mal'tempo nm bad weather

mal'tese adj & nmf Maltese

'malto nm malt

mal'tosio nm maltose

maltratta'mento nm ill-treatment

maltrat'tare vt ill-treat

malu'more nm bad mood; **di** ~ in a bad mood

'malva adj inv mauve

mal'vagio adj wicked

malvagità nf inv wickedness

malva'sia nf type of dessert wine

malversazi'one nf embezzlement

mal'visto adj unpopular (**da** with)

malvi'vente nm criminal

malvolenti'eri adv unwillingly

malvo'lere vt farsi ~ make oneself unpopular; **prendere qualcuno a** ~ take a dislike to somebody

'mamma nf mummy, mum; ~ **mia!** good gracious!

mam'mario adj mammary

mam'mella nf breast

mam'mifero nm mammal

mam'mismo nm (del figlio) dependency on the mother figure; (della madre) excessive motherliness

mammogra'fia nf mammograph

'mammola nf violet

mammo'letta nf shrinking violet

mam'mone nm mummy's boy

mam'mut nm inv mammoth

ma'nata nf handful; (colpo) slap

'manca nf ▶ MANCO

manca'mento nm avere un ~ faint

man'cante adj missing

man'canza nf lack; (assenza) absence; (insufficienza) shortage; (fallo) fault; (imperfezione) defect; **in** ~ **d'altro** failing all else; **sento la sua** ~ I miss him. **mancanza di tatto** lack of tact, indelicacy

man'care ① vi be lacking; (essere assente) be missing; (venir meno) fail; (morire) pass away; ~ **di** be lacking in; ~ **a** fail to keep ⟨promessa⟩; **mi manca casa** I miss home; **mi manchi** I miss you; **mi è mancato il tempo** I didn't have [the] time; **mi mancano 10 euro** I'm 10 euros short; **quanto manca alla partenza?** how long before we leave?; **è mancata la corrente** there was a power failure; **sentirsi** ~ feel faint; **sentirsi** ~ **il respiro** be unable to breathe [properly]

② vt miss ⟨bersaglio⟩; **è mancato poco che cadesse** he nearly fell

man'cato adj ⟨appuntamento⟩ missed; ⟨tentativo⟩ unsuccessful; ⟨occasione⟩ wasted

'manche nf inv heat

man'chevole adj defective

'mancia nf tip. ~ **competente** reward

manci'ata nf handful

man'cino adj left-handed

'manco, -a ① adj left
② nf left hand
③ adv (nemmeno) not even

man'dante nmf (di delitto) instigator; Jur principal

manda'rancio nm clementine

man'dare vt send; (emettere) give off; utter ⟨suono⟩; ~ **a chiamare** send for; ~ **avanti la casa** run the house; ~ **giù** (ingoiare) swallow

manda'rino nm Bot mandarin

man'data nf consignment; (di serratura) turn; **chiudere a doppia** ~ double lock

manda'tario nm Jur agent

man'dato nm (incarico) mandate; Jur warrant. **mandato di comparizione [in giudizio]** subpoena. **mandato di pagamento** money order; **mandato di perquisizione** search warrant

man'dibola nf jaw

mando'lino nm mandolin

'mandorla nf almond; **a** ~ ⟨occhi⟩ almond-shaped. **mandorla amara** bitter almond

mandor'lato nm nut brittle (type of nougat)

'mandorlo nm almond [tree]

man'dragola nf mandrake

'mandria nf herd

mandri'ano nm cowherd

man'drillo nm (scimmia) mandrill; (attrezzo) mandrel; fig fam goat

maneg'gevole adj easy to handle

maneggi'are vt handle

ma'neggio nm handling; (intrigo) plot; (scuola di equitazione) riding school

ma'nesco adj quick to hit out

ma'netta nf lever; **a tutta** ~ flat out; **manette** pl handcuffs

man'forte nm dare ~ **a qualcuno** support somebody

manga'nello nm truncheon

manga'nese nm manganese

mange'reccio adj edible

mangiacas'sette nm inv cassette player

mangia'dischi® nm inv portable record player

mangia'fumo *adj inv* **candela ∼** air-purifying candle

mangia'nastri *nm inv* cassette player

mangi'are ① *vt/i* eat; (consumare) eat up; (corrodere) eat away; take ⟨scacchi, carte ecc⟩; **dar da ∼ al gatto/cane** feed the cat/dog
② *nm* eating; (cibo) food; (pasto) meal

mangi'arsi *vr* **∼ le parole** mumble; **∼ le unghie** bite one's nails

mangia'soldi *adj inv* **macchinetta mangiasoldi** one-armed bandit

mangi'ata *nf* big meal; **farsi una bella ∼ di...** feast on...

mangia'toia *nf* manger

mangia|'tore, -trice *nmf* eater. **mangiatore di fuoco** fire-eater; **mangiatrice di uomini** maneater

man'gime *nm* fodder. **mangime per i polli** chicken feed

mangi'one, -a *nmf fam* glutton

mangiucchi'are *vt* nibble

'mango *nm* mango

man'grovia *nf* mangrove

man'gusta *nf* mongoose

ma'nia *nf* mania. **mania di grandezza** delusions of grandeur. **mania di persecuzione** persecution complex

mania'cale *adj* manic

ma'niaco, -a ① *adj* maniacal
② *nmf* maniac. **maniaco sessuale** sex maniac

ma'niaco-depres'sivo *adj & nmf* manic-depressive

'Manica *nf* **la ∼** the [English] Channel

'manica *nf* sleeve; (fam: gruppo) band; **a maniche lunghe** long-sleeved; **senza maniche** sleeveless; **essere in maniche di camicia** be in shirt sleeves; **essere di ∼ larga** be generous; **essere di ∼ stretta** be strict. **manica a vento** wind sock

manica'retto *nm* tasty dish

maniche'ismo *nm* Manicheism

mani'chetta *nf* hose

mani'chino *nm* (da sarto, vetrina) dummy

'manico *nm* handle; Mus neck. **manico di scopa** broom handle

mani'comio *nm* mental home; (fam: confusione) tip

mani'cotto *nm* muff; Mech sleeve

mani'cure ① *nf* manicure
② *nmf inv* (persona) manicurist

mani'era *nf* manner; **in ∼ che** so that

manie'rato *adj* affected; ⟨stile⟩ mannered

manie'rismo *nm* mannerism

mani'ero *nm* manor

manifat'tura *nf* manufacture; (fabbrica) factory

manifatturi'ero *adj* manufacturing

manifesta'mente *adv* demonstrably, manifestly

manife'stante *nmf* demonstrator

manife'stare ① *vt* show; (esprimere) express
② *vi* demonstrate

manifes'tarsi *vr* show oneself

manifestazi'one *nf* show; (espressione) expression; (sintomo) manifestation; (dimostrazione pubblica) demonstration

mani'festo ① *adj* evident
② *nm* poster; (dichiarazione pubblica) manifesto

ma'niglia *nf* handle; (sostegno, in autobus ecc) strap

manipo'lare *vt* handle; (massaggiare) massage; (alterare) adulterate; fig manipulate

manipola|'tore, -trice ① *nmf* manipulator
② *adj* manipulative

manipolazi'one *nf* handling; (massaggio) massage; (alterazione) adulteration; fig manipulation

mani'scalco *nm* smith

'manna *nf* **manna dal cielo** manna from heaven

man'naia *nf* (scure) axe; (da macellaio) cleaver

man'naro *adj* **lupo ∼** werewolf

'mano *nf* hand; (strato di vernice ecc) coat; **alla ∼** informal; **fuori ∼** out of the way; **man ∼** little by little; **man ∼ che** as; **sotto ∼** to hand; **di seconda ∼** secondhand; **a mani vuote** empty-handed; **a ∼** ⟨scritto, ricamato, fatto⟩ by hand; ⟨trapano ecc⟩ hand[-held]; **dare una ∼ a qualcuno** give *or* lend somebody a hand; **ha le mani di pasta frolla** he is a butterfingers

mano'dopera *nf* labour

ma'nometro *nm* manometer, pressure gauge

mano'mettere *vt* tamper with; (violare) violate

ma'nopola *nf* (di apparecchio) knob; (guanto) mitten; (su autobus) handle

mano'scritto ① *adj* handwritten
② *nm* manuscript

mano'vale *nm* labourer

mano'vella *nf* handle; Techn crank. **manovella alzacristalli** winder

ma'novra *nf* manoeuvre; Rail shunting; **fare le manovre** Auto manoeuvre; **manovre** *pl* **di corridoio** lobbying

mano'vrabile *adj* manoeuvrable; fig ⟨persona⟩ easy to manipulate

mano'vrare ① *vt* (azionare) operate; fig manipulate ⟨persona⟩
② *vi* manoeuvre

manro'vescio *nm* slap

man'sarda *nf* attic

mansio'nario *nm* job description

mansi'one *nf* task; (dovere) duty

mansu'eto *adj* meek; ‹*animale*› docile

'manta *nf* Zool manta

mante'cato ① *nm* soft ice cream
② *adj* creamy

man'tella *nf* cape

man'tello *nm* cloak; (soprabito, di animale) coat; (di neve) mantle

mante'nere *vt* (conservare) keep; (in buono stato, sostentare) maintain

mante'nersi *vr* ~ **in forma** keep fit

manteni'mento *nm* maintenance.
mantenimento dell'ordine pubblico policing. **mantenimento della pace** Mil, Pol peacekeeping

mante'nuta *nf* kept woman

'mantice *nm* bellows *pl*; (di automobile) hood, top

'mantide *nf* mantis

man'tiglia *nf* mantilla

'manto *nm* cloak; (coltre) mantle

'Mantova *nf* Mantua

manto'vana *nf* (di tende) pelmet

manu'ale *adj & nm* manual. **manuale di conversazione** phrasebook. **manuale d'uso** user manual

manual'mente *adv* manually

ma'nubrio *nm* handle; (di bicicletta) handlebars *pl*; (per ginnastica) dumb-bell

manu'fatto *adj* manufactured

manutenzi'one *nf* maintenance; **un giardino che richiede poca** ~ a low-maintenance garden

'manzo *nm* steer; (carne) beef

maomet'tano *adj & nm* Muslim

Mao'metto *nm* Mohammed, Muhammad

ma'ori *adj inv & nmf inv* Maori

'mappa *nf* map

mappa'mondo *nm* globe

mar ▸ MARE

mara'chella *nf* prank

maragià *nm inv* maharajah

maran'tacea *nf* Bot arrowroot

mara'schino *nm* maraschino, sweet liqueur

ma'rasma *nm* fig decline

mara'tona *nf* marathon

marato'neta *nmf* marathon runner

'marca *nf* mark; Comm brand; (fabbricazione) make; (scontrino) ticket; **di** ~ branded. **marca da bollo** stamp showing that the necessary duties have been paid

mar'care *vt* mark; Sport score

marcata'mente *adv* markedly

mar'cato *adj* ‹tratto, accento› strong, marked

marca'tore *nm* (chi segna un gol) scorer; (chi marca un avversario) marker; (pennarello) marker pen

'Marche *nfpl* Marches

mar'chese, -a ① *nm* marquis
② *nf* marchioness

mar'chetta *nf* (assicurativa) National Insurance stamp; **fare marchette** fam be on the game

marchi'are *vt* brand

'marchio *nm* brand; (caratteristica) mark. **marchio depositato** registered trademark. **marchio di fabbrica** trademark, TM. **marchio registrato** registered trademark

'marcia *nf* march; Auto gear; Sport walk; **mettere in** ~ put into gear; **mettersi in** ~ start off; **cambiare** ~ change gear. **marcia a senso unico alternato** temporary one way system in operation. **marcia forzata** forced march. **marcia funebre** funeral march. **marcia indietro** reverse gear; **fare** ~ **indietro** reverse; fig back-pedal. **marcia nuziale** wedding march

marcia'longa *nf* (di sci) cross-country skiing race; (a piedi) long-distance race

marciapi'ede *nm* pavement, sidewalk Am; (di stazione) platform

marci'are *vi* march; (funzionare) go, work

marcia|'tore, -trice *nmf* walker

'marcio ① *adj* rotten
② *nm* rotten part; fig corruption

mar'cire *vi* go bad, rot

mar'cita *nf* water meadow

'marco *nm* (moneta) mark

marco'nista *nmf* radio operator

'mare *nm* sea; (luogo di mare) seaside; **sul** ~ ‹casa› at the seaside; ‹città› on the sea; **andare al** ~ go to the sea; **in alto** ~ on the high seas; **d'alto** ~ ocean-going; **essere in alto** ~ fig not know which way to turn. **mare Adriatico** Adriatic Sea; **mar Cinese** China Sea; **mar Ionio** Ionian Sea. **mare d'Irlanda** Irish Sea; **mar Mediterraneo** Mediterranean; **mar Morto** Dead Sea; **mar Nero** Black Sea. **mare del Nord** North Sea; **mar Tirreno** Tyrrhenian Sea

ma'rea *nf* tide; **una** ~ **di** hundreds of; **alta/bassa marea** high/low tide. **marea montante** flood tide

mareggi'ata *nf* [sea] storm

mare'moto *nm* tidal wave, seaquake

maresci'allo *nm* (ufficiale) marshal; (sottufficiale) warrant officer

ma'retta *nf* choppiness; fig tension

marga'rina *nf* margarine

marghe'rita *nf* marguerite. **margherita settembrina** Michaelmas daisy

margheri'tina *nf* daisy

margi'nale *adj* marginal

marginaliz'zare *vt* marginalize

marginal'mente *adv* marginally

'margine *nm* margin; (orlo) brink; (bordo) border. **margine di errore** margin of error. **margine di sicurezza** safety margin. **margine di vendita** mark-up

mari'ano *adj* Relig Marian

ma'rina *nf* navy; (costa) seashore; (quadro) seascape. **marina mercantile** merchant navy. **marina militare** navy

mari'naio *nm* sailor. **marinaio d'acqua dolce** landlubber

mari'nare *vt* marinate; ∼ **la scuola** play truant

mari'naro *adj* seafaring

mari'nata *nf* marinade

mari'nato *adj* Culin marinated

ma'rino *adj* sea *attrib*, marine

mario'netta *nf* puppet

mari'tare *vt* marry

mari'tarsi *vr* get married

ma'rito *nm* husband

mari'tozzo *nm* currant bun

ma'rittimo *adj* maritime

mar'maglia *nf* rabble

marmel'lata *nf* jam; (di agrumi) marmalade

mar'mitta *nf* pot; Auto silencer. **marmitta catalitica** catalytic converter

'marmo *nm* marble

mar'mocchio *nm* fam brat

mar'moreo *adj* marble

marmoriz'zato *adj* marbled

mar'motta *nf* marmot

maroc'chino, -a *adj & nmf* Moroccan

Ma'rocco *nm* Morocco

ma'roso *nm* breaker

mar'rone ① *adj* brown
② *nm* brown; (castagna) chestnut; **marroni** *pl* **canditi** marrons glacés

'Marshall *nfpl* **le isole** ∼ Marshall Islands

mar'sina *nf* tails *pl*

marsupi'ale *nm* marsupial

mar'supio *nm* (borsa) bumbag

'Marte *nm* Mars

martedì *nm* Tuesday; **di** ∼ on Tuesdays. **martedì grasso** Shrove Tuesday

martel'lante *adj* ⟨mal di testa⟩ pounding, throbbing; **hanno fatto una pubblicità** ∼ they hyped the product, they bombarded the market with publicity

martel'lare ① *vt* hammer
② *vi* throb

martel'lata *nf* hammer blow

martel'letto *nm* (di giudice) gavel; (di pianoforte) hammer; (di medico) percussion hammer

martel'lio *nm* hammering

mar'tello *nm* hammer; (di battente) knocker. ∼ **pneumatico** pneumatic drill

marti'netto *nm* Mech jack

mar'tin pesca'tore *nm inv* kingfisher

'martire *nmf* martyr

mar'tirio *nm* martyrdom

'martora *nf* marten

martori'are *vt* torment

mar'xismo *nm* Marxism

mar'xista *adj & nmf* Marxist

marza'pane *nm* marzipan

marzi'ale *adj* martial

marzi'ano, -a *adj & nmf* Martian

'marzo *nm* March

mascal'zone *nm* rascal

ma'scara *nm inv* mascara

mascar'pone *nm* full-fat cream cheese often used for desserts

ma'scella *nf* jaw

'maschera *nf* mask; (costume) fancy dress; Cinema, Theat usher *m*, usherette *f*; (nella commedia dell'arte) stock character. **maschera antigas** gas mask. **maschera di bellezza** face pack. **maschera mortuaria** death mask. **maschera ad ossigeno** oxygen mask

maschera'mento *nm* masking; Mil camouflage

masche'rare *vt* mask; fig camouflage

masche'rarsi *vr* put on a mask; ∼ **da** dress up as

masche'rata *nf* masquerade

maschi'accio *nm* (ragazza) tomboy

ma'schile ① *adj* masculine; ⟨sesso⟩ male
② *nm* masculine [gender]

maschi'lismo *nm* male chauvinism

maschi'lista ① *adj* sexist
② *nm* male chauvinist

'maschio ① *adj* male; (virile) manly
② *nm* male; (figlio) son. **maschio dominante** alpha male

masco'lino *adj* masculine

ma'scotte *nf inv* mascot

maso'chismo *nm* masochism

maso'chista *adj & nmf* masochist

'massa *nf* mass; Electr earth, ground Am; **una** ∼ **[di gente]** a crowd [of people]

massa'crante *adj* gruelling

massa'crare *vt* massacre

mas'sacro *nm* massacre; fig mess

massaggi'are *vt* massage

massaggia|'tore, -trice ① *nm* masseur

2 *nf* masseuse

mas'saggio *nm* massage. **massaggio cardiaco** heart massage

mas'saia *nf* housewife

mas'sello **1** *nm* (metallo) ingot **2** *adj* ⟨legno⟩ solid

masse'rizie *nfpl* household effects

massiccia'mente *adv* on a big scale

massicci'ata *nf* hard core

mas'siccio **1** *adj* massive; ⟨oro ecc⟩ solid; ⟨corporatura⟩ heavy **2** *nm* massif

massifi'care *vt* de-individualize ⟨società⟩

massificazi'one *nf* de-individualization

'massima *nf* maxim; (temperatura) maximum

massi'male *nm* (assicurazione) limit of indemnity

massimiz'zare *vt* maximize

massimizzazi'one *nf* maximization

'massimo **1** *adj* greatest; ⟨quantità⟩ maximum, greatest **2** *nm* il ∼ the maximum; **al** ∼ at [the] most, as a maximum. **massimo storico** all-time high

'masso *nm* rock

mas'sone *nm* [Free]mason

massone'ria *nf* Freemasonry

mastecto'mia *nf* mastectomy

ma'stello *nm* wooden box for the grape or olive harvest

masteriz'zare *vt* ⟨CD, DVD⟩ burn

masterizza'tore *nm* **masterizzatore di CD** CD burner

masti'care *vt* chew; (borbottare) mumble

'mastice *nm* mastic, filler; (per vetri) putty

ma'stino *nm* mastiff

masto'dontico *adj* gigantic

ma'stoide *nm* mastoid

'mastro *nm* master; **libro mastro** ledger

mastur'barsi *vr* masturbate

masturbazi'one *nf* masturbation

ma'tassa *nf* skein

match 'point *nm inv* Tennis match point

matelassé *nm* quilting

mate'matica *nf* mathematics, maths, math *Am*. **matematica pura** pure mathematics

mate'matico, -a **1** *adj* mathematical **2** *nmf* mathematician

materas'sino *nm* small mattress. **materassino gonfiabile** air bed, lilo®

mate'rasso *nm* mattress. **materasso ad acqua** water bed. **materasso di gommapiuma** foam mattress. **materasso a molle** spring mattress

ma'teria *nf* matter; (materiale) material; (di studio) subject. **materia grigia** grey matter. **materia oscura** dark matter. **materia prima** raw material

materi'ale **1** *adj* material; (grossolano) coarse **2** *nm* material. **materiale da costruzione** building material. **materiale pubblicitario** publicity material. **materiale di scarto** waste material

materia'lismo *nm* materialism

materia'lista **1** *adj* materialistic; **non** ∼ unworldly **2** *nmf* materialist

materializ'zarsi *vr* materialize

material'mente *adv* physically

materna'mente *adv* maternally

maternità *nf* motherhood; **è alla prima** ∼ it's her first baby; **ospedale di maternità** maternity hospital

ma'terno *adj* maternal; **lingua materna** mother tongue

ma'tita *nf* pencil; **matite** *pl* **colorate** colour[ed] pencils. **matita emostatica** styptic pencil. **matita per gli occhi** eyeliner pencil

matriar'cale *adj* matriarchal

ma'trice *nf* matrix; (origini) roots *pl*; Comm counterfoil. **matrice attiva** Comput active matrix. **matrice passiva** Comput passive matrix

ma'tricola *nf* (registro) register; Univ fresher; **numero di matricola** (di studente) matriculation number

ma'trigna *nf* stepmother

matrimoni'ale *adj* matrimonial; **vita matrimoniale** married life

matri'monio *nm* marriage; (cerimonia) wedding. **matrimonio in bianco** unconsummated marriage; white wedding. **matrimonio civile** civil wedding. **matrimonio di convenienza** marriage of convenience. **matrimonio di fatto** common-law marriage

ma'trona *nf* matron

'matta *nf* (nelle carte) joker

mattacchi'one, -a *nmf* rascal

mat'tanza *nf* (di tonni) tuna fishing; fig killings *pl*

matta'toio *nm* slaughterhouse

matta'tore *nm* (artista) star performer

matte'rello *nm* rolling-pin

mat'tina *nf* morning; **la** ∼, **alla** ∼ in the morning; **domani** ∼ tomorrow morning; **ieri** ∼ yesterday morning

matti'nata *nf* morning; Theat matinée

mattini'ero *adj* **essere** ∼ be an early riser

mat'tino *nm* morning

'**matto**, **-a** ① *adj* mad, crazy; Med insane; (falso) false; (opaco) matt. **matto da legare** barking mad; **avere una voglia matta di...** be dying for... ② *nm* madman ③ *nf* madwoman

mat'tone *nm* brick; (libro) bore

matto'nella *nf* tile. **mattonella grezza** quarry tile

mattu'tino *adj* morning *attrib*

matu'rare *vt* ripen; Fin mature

maturazi'one *nf* ripening; Fin maturity; (fig: di idea ecc) gestation; **arrivare a** ∼ ⟨frutta⟩ ripen; ⟨polizza⟩ mature

maturità *nf* maturity; Sch school-leaving certificate

ma'turo *adj* mature; ⟨frutto⟩ ripe

ma'tusa *nm* fam old fogey

Mauri'tania *sf* Mauritania

Mau'rizio *nf* [isola di] ∼ Mauritius

mauso'leo *nm* mausoleum

maxis'chermo *nm* wide screen

'**mayday** *nm inv* Radio Mayday

'**mazza** *nf* club; (martello) hammer; (da baseball, cricket) bat. **mazza da golf** golf-club

maz'zata *nf* blow

maz'zetta *nf* (di banconote) bundle; (tangente) bribe

'**mazzo** *nm* bunch; (carte da gioco) pack

Mb *nm abbr* (**megabyte**) Comput Mb

me *pers pron* me; **me lo ha dato** he gave it to me; **secondo me** in my opinion; **fai come me** do as I do; **è più veloce di me** he is faster than me *or* faster than I am

me'andro *nm* meander

'**Mecca** *nf* **la** ∼ Mecca

mec'canica *nf* mechanics. **meccanica quantistica** quantum mechanics

meccanica'mente *adv* mechanically

mec'canico ① *adj* mechanical ② *nm* mechanic

mecca'nismo *nm* mechanism

meccanizza'zione *nf* mechanization

meccanogra'fia *nf* data processing

meccano'grafico *adj* data processing *attrib*

mece'nate *nmf* patron

mèche *nfpl* highlights; **farsi [fare] le** ∼ have highlights put in, have one's hair streaked

me'daglia *nf* medal. **medaglia d'oro** (premio) gold medal; (atleta) gold medallist. **medaglia al valore** medal for valour

medagli'ere *nm* medal collection

medagli'one *nm* medallion; (gioiello) locket; **medaglioni** *pl* **di vitello** Culin medallions of veal

me'desimo *adj* same

'**media** *nf* average; Sch average mark; Math mean; **essere nella** ∼ be in the mid-range

medi'ano ① *adj* middle ② *nm* (calcio) half-back. **mediano di mischia** scrum half

medi'ante *prep* by

medi'are *vt* act as intermediary in

media|'tore, **-trice** *nmf* mediator; Comm middleman. **mediatore d'affari** business agent. **mediatore culturale** voluntary or professional worker who helps immigrants integrate into Italian daily life

mediazi'one *nf* mediation

medica'mento *nm* medicine

medi'care *vt* treat; dress ⟨ferita⟩

medi'cato *adj* ⟨shampoo⟩ medicated

medicazi'one *nf* medication; (di ferita) dressing

me'diceo *adj* from the period of the Medici, Medicean

medi'cina *nf* medicine. **medicina alternativa** alternative medicine, complementary medicine. **medicina del lavoro** occupational health. **medicina legale** forensic medicine, forensic science. **medicina popolare** folk medicine

medici'nale ① *adj* medicinal ② *nm* medicine

'**medico** ① *adj* medical ② *nm* doctor. **medico di base** general practitioner, GP. **medico di famiglia** family doctor. **medico generico** general practitioner, GP. **medico legale** forensic scientist. **medico di turno** duty doctor

medie'vale *adj* medieval

'**medio** ① *adj* average; ⟨punto⟩ middle; ⟨statura⟩ medium; **scuola media** secondary school ② *nm* (dito) middle finger. **Medio Oriente** Middle East

medi'ocre *adj* mediocre; (scadente) poor

mediocre'mente *adv* indifferently

medio'evo *nm* Middle Ages *pl*

mediorien'tale *adj* middle-eastern

medita'bondo *adj* meditative

medi'tare ① *vt* meditate; (progettare) plan; (considerare attentamente) think over ② *vi* meditate

medita'tivo meditative

meditazi'one *nf* meditation

mediter'raneo *adj* Mediterranean; **il** [mar] **Mediterraneo** the Mediterranean [Sea]

me'dusa *nf* jellyfish

'**megabyte** *nm inv* Comput megabyte

me'gafono *nm* megaphone

m

megaga'lattico *adj* gigantic

mega'lite *nm* megalith

mega'lomane *nmf* megalomaniac

me'gera *nf* hag

'meglio ① *adv* better; **tanto** ~, ~ **così** so much the better
② *adj* better; (superlativo) best
③ *nmf* best
④ *nf* **avere la** ~ **su** have the better of; **fare qualcosa alla [bell'e]** ~ do something as best one can
⑤ *nm* **fare del proprio** ~ do one's best; **fare qualcosa il** ~ **possibile** make an excellent job of something; **al** ~ to the best of one's ability; **per il** ~ for the best

'mela *nf* apple; **succo di mela** apple juice. **mela cotogna** quince

mela'grana *nf* pomegranate

mé'lange ① *nm* flecked wool
② *adj inv* ‹lana› flecked

mela'nina *nf* melanin

melan'zana *nf* aubergine, eggplant Am; **melanzane** *pl* **alla parmigiana** baked layers of aubergine, tomato and cheese

me'lassa *nf* molasses *sg*

me'lenso *adj* ‹persona, film› dull

me'leto *nm* apple orchard

mel'lifluo *adj* ‹parole› honeyed; ‹voce› sugary

'melma *nf* slime

mel'moso *adj* slimy

'melo *nm* apple [tree]

melo'dia *nf* melody

me'lodico *adj* melodic

melodi'oso *adj* melodious

melo'dramma *nm* melodrama

melodrammatica'mente *adv* melodramatically

melodram'matico *adj* melodramatic

melo'grano *nm* pomegranate tree

me'lone *nm* melon

mem'brana *nf* membrane

'membro *nm* member; (pl nf **membra** Anat) limb

memo'rabile *adj* memorable

'memore *adj* mindful; (riconoscente) grateful

me'moria *nf* memory; (oggetto ricordo) souvenir; **imparare a** ~ learn by heart; **memorie** *pl* (biografiche) memoirs. **memoria cache** Comput cache memory. **memoria collettiva** folk memory. **memoria dinamica** Comput RAM. **memoria di massa** Comput mass storage. **memoria permanente** Comput non-volatile memory. **memoria di sola lettura** Comput read-only memory, ROM. **memoria a tampone** Comput buffer [memory]. **memoria volatile** Comput volatile memory

memori'ale *nm* memorial

memoriz'zare *vt* memorize; Comput save, store

mena'dito: **a** ~ *adv* perfectly

me'nare *vt* lead; (fam: picchiare) hit; ~ **la coda** ‹cane› wag its tail; ~ **qualcuno per il naso** pull somebody's leg

mendi'cante *nmf* beggar, panhandler Am

mendi'care *vt/i* beg

menefre'ghista *adj* devil-may-care

mene'strello *nm* minstrel

me'ningi *nfpl* **spremersi le** ~ rack one's brains

menin'gite *nf* meningitis

me'nisco *nm* meniscus

'meno ① *adv* less; (superlativo) least; (in operazioni, con temperatura) minus; ~ **di** less than; **di** ~ less; ~ **moderno** less modern; **il** ~ **moderno di tutti** the least modern of all; **far qualcosa alla** ~ **peggio** do something as best one can; **fare a** ~ **di qualcosa** do without something; **non posso fare a** ~ **di ridere** I can't help laughing; ~ **male!** thank goodness!; **sempre** ~ less and less; **venir** ~ (svenire) faint; **venir** ~ **a qualcuno** ‹coraggio› fail somebody; **sono le tre** ~ **un quarto** it's a quarter to three; **che tu venga o** ~ whether you're coming or not; **quanto** ~ at least
② *adj inv* less; (con nomi plurali) fewer
③ *nm* least; Math minus sign; **il** ~ **possibile** as little as possible; **per lo** ~ at least
④ *prep* except [for]
⑤ *conj* **a** ~ **che** unless

meno'mare *vt* ‹incidente› maim

meno'mato, -a ① *adj* disabled
② *nmf* disabled person

meno'pausa *nf* menopause

'mensa *nf* table; Mil mess; (di azienda, scuola) canteen

men'sile ① *adj* monthly
② *nm* (stipendio) [monthly] salary; (rivista) monthly

mensilità *nf inv* monthly salary

mensil'mente *adv* monthly

'mensola *nf* bracket; (scaffale) shelf

'menta *nf* mint; **al gusto di** ~ mint-flavoured. **menta piperita** peppermint. **menta verde** spearmint

men'tale *adj* mental

mentalità *nf inv* mentality. **mentalità ristretta** bigotry

'mente *nf* mind; **a** ~ **fredda** in cold blood; **cosa ti è saltato in** ~**?** what possessed you?; **venire in** ~ **a qualcuno** occur to somebody

men'tina *nf* mint

men'tire *vi* lie

'**mento** *nm* chin

men'tolo *nm* menthol; **al ∼** mentholated

'**mentre** *conj* (temporale) while; (invece) whereas

me'nu *nm inv* menu. **menu a discesa** Comput pull-down menu. **menu fisso** set menu. **menu a tendina** Comput pull-down menu, drop-down menu. **menu turistico** tourist menu

menzio'nare *vt* mention

menzi'one *nf* mention. **menzione speciale** special mention

men'zogna *nf* lie

mera'viglia *nf* wonder; **a ∼** marvellously; **che ∼!** how wonderful!; **con mia grande ∼** much to my amazement; **mi fa ∼ che...** I am surprised that...

meravigli'are *vt* surprise

meravigli'arsi *vr* **∼ di** be surprised at

meravigliosa'mente *adv* marvellously

meravigli'oso *adj* marvellous, wonderful

mer'cante *nm* merchant. **mercante d'arte** art dealer. **mercante di schiavi** slave trader

mercanteggi'are *vi* trade; (sul prezzo) bargain

mercan'tile ① *adj* mercantile ② *nm* merchant ship

mercan'zia *nf* merchandise, goods *pl*

merca'tino *nm* (di quartiere) local street market; Fin unlisted securities market

mer'cato *nm* market; Fin market[place]; **a buon ∼** ⟨comprare⟩ cheap[ly]; ⟨articolo⟩ cheap. **mercato all'aperto** street market. **mercato aperto** Econ open market. **mercato azionario** Fin equity market, share market. **mercato dei cambi** foreign exchange market. **Mercato Comune [Europeo]** [European] Common Market. **mercato coperto** covered market, indoor market. **mercato dell'eurovaluta** eurocurrency market. **mercato immobiliare** property market. **mercato libero** free market. **mercato di massa** mass market. **mercato nero** black market. **mercato del pesce** fish market. **mercato di prova** test market. **mercato al rialzo** Fin bull market. **mercato al ribasso** Fin bear market. **mercato specializzato** niche market. **mercato unico** Single Market

'**merce** *nf* goods *pl*, merchandise; **la ∼ venduta non si cambia senza lo scontrino** goods will not be exchanged without a receipt. **merce in conto vendita** sale or return goods. **merce deperibile** perishable goods

mercé *nf* **alla ∼ di** at the mercy of

merce'nario *adj* & *nm* mercenary

merceolo'gia *nf* study of commodities

merce'ria *nf* haberdashery; (negozio) haberdasher's

mercifi'care *vt* commercialize

mercificazi'one *nf* commercialization

mercoledì *nm inv* Wednesday; **di ∼** on Wednesdays. **mercoledì delle Ceneri** Ash Wednesday

mer'curio *nm* mercury

me'renda *nf* afternoon snack; **far ∼** have an afternoon snack

meridi'ana *nf* sundial

meridi'ano ① *adj* midday ② *nm* meridian

meridio'nale ① *adj* southern ② *nmf* southerner

meridi'one *nm* south

me'ringa *nf* meringue

merin'gata *nf* meringue pie

meri'tare *vt* deserve

meri'tato *adj* deserved

meri'tevole *adj* deserving

'**merito** *nm* merit; (valore) worth; **in ∼ a** as to; **per ∼ di** thanks to

merito'cratico *adj* meritocratic

meri'torio *adj* meritorious

merla'tura *nf* battlements *pl*

merlet'taia *nf* lacemaker

mer'letto *nm* lace

'**merlo** *nm* blackbird; **bravo ∼!** you fool!

mer'luzzo *nm* cod

'**mero** *adj* mere

mesca'lina *nf* mescaline

'**mescere** *vt* pour out

meschine'ria *nf* meanness

me'schino ① *adj* wretched; (gretto) mean ② *nm* wretch

'**mescita** *nf* wine shop

mescola'mento *nm* mixing

mesco'lanza *nf* mixture

mesco'lare *vt* mix; shuffle ⟨carte⟩; (confondere) mix up; blend ⟨tè, tabacco ecc⟩

mesco'larsi *vr* mix; (immischiarsi) meddle

mesco'lata *nf* (a carte) shuffle; Culin stir

'**mese** *nm* month. **mese civile** calendar month

me'setto *nm* **un ∼** about a month, a month or so

'**messa**[1] *nf* Mass. **messa nera** black mass. **messa da requiem** requiem mass. **messa solenne** High Mass

'**messa**[2] *nf* (il mettere) putting. **messa in moto** Auto starting. **messa in piega** (di capelli) set; **farsi fare la ∼ in piega** have one's hair set. **messa a punto** adjustment. **messa in scena** production; fig production number. **messa a terra** earthing, grounding Am

messagge'ria *nf* **messaggeria elettronica** Comput messaging

messag'gero *nm* messenger

messa'ggiare *vi* Teleph text

messa'ggino *nm* text message

mes'saggio *nm* message. **messaggio di errore** Comput error message. **messaggio di testo** Teleph text message

mes'sale *nm* missal

'messe *nf* harvest

Mes'sia *nm* Messiah

messi'cano, -a *adj & nmf* Mexican

'Messico *nm* Mexico

messin'scena *nf* staging; fig act

'messo 1 pp di METTERE 2 *nm* messenger

mesti'ere *nm* trade; ⟨*lavoro*⟩ job; **essere del** ∼ be an expert, know one's trade

'mesto *adj* sad

'mestola *nf* (di cuoco) ladle; (di muratore) trowel

mestru'ale *adj* menstrual

mestruazi'one *nf* menstruation; **mestruazioni** *pl* period

'meta *nf* destination; fig aim

metà *nf inv* half; (centro) middle; **a** ∼ **prezzo** half price; **a** ∼ **strada** halfway; **a** ∼ **serata** halfway through the evening; **fare a** ∼ **con qualcuno** go halves with somebody; **fare [a]** ∼ **e** ∼ go halves

metabo'lismo *nm* metabolism

meta'carpo *nm* metacarpus

meta'done *nm* methadone

meta'fisica *nf* metaphysics

meta'fisico *adj* metaphysical

me'tafora *nf* metaphor

metaforica'mente *adv* metaphorically

meta'forico *adj* metaphorical

me'tallico *adj* metallic

metalliz'zato *adj* ⟨*grigio*⟩ metallic

me'tallo *nm* metal. **metallo vile** base metal

metal'loide *nm* metalloid

metallur'gia *nf* metallurgy

metal'lurgico *adj* metallurgical

metalmec'canico 1 *adj* engineering 2 *nm* engineering worker

meta'morfosi *nf inv* metamorphosis

me'tano *nm* methane

metano'dotto *nm* methane pipeline

meta'nolo *nm* methanol

me'tastasi *nf inv* metastasis

meta'tarso *nm* metatarsus

me'teora *nf* meteor

meteo'rite *nm* meteorite

meteorolo'gia *nf* meteorology

meteoro'logico *adj* meteorological

meteo'rologo *nm* meteorologist

me'ticcio, -a *nmf* half-caste

meticolosa'mente *adv* meticulously

metico'loso *adj* meticulous

me'tile *nm* methyl

me'todico *adj* methodical

meto'dista *adj & nmf* Methodist

'metodo *nm* method

metodolo'gia *nf* methodology

metodo'logico *adj* methodological

me'traggio *nm* length (in metres); **vendere a** ∼ sell by the metre

'metrico, -a 1 *adj* metric; (in poesia) metrical 2 *nf* metrics

'metro[1] *nm* metre; (nastro) tape measure. **metro cubo** cubic metre. **metro quadrato** square metre

'metro[2] *nf inv* fam underground, subway Am

me'tronomo *nm* metronome

metro'notte *nmf inv* night security guard

me'tropoli *nf inv* metropolis

metropoli'tana *nf* underground, subway Am

metropoli'tano *adj* metropolitan

'mettere *vt* put; (indossare) put on; (fam: installare) put in; ∼ **al mondo** bring into the world; ∼ **da parte** set aside; ∼ **fiducia** inspire trust; ∼ **qualcosa in chiaro** make something clear; ∼ **in mostra** display; ∼ **a posto** tidy up; ∼ **in vendita** put up for sale; ∼ **su** set up ⟨*casa, azienda*⟩; **metter su famiglia** start a family; **ci ho messo un'ora** it took me an hour; **mettiamo che…** let's suppose that…

'mettersi *vr* (indossare) put on; (diventare) turn out; ∼ **a** start to; ∼ **con qualcuno** (fam: formare una coppia) start to go out with somebody; ∼ **a letto** go to bed; ∼ **a sedere** sit down; ∼ **in viaggio** set out

metti'foglio *nm* feeder

'mezza *nf* **è la** ∼ it's half past twelve; **sono le quattro e** ∼ it's half past four

mezza'dria *nf* sharecropping

mezza'luna *nf* half moon; (simbolo islamico) crescent; (coltello) two-handled chopping knife; **a** ∼ half-moon

mezza'manica *nf* **a** ∼ ⟨*maglia*⟩ short-sleeved; **mezzemaniche** *pl* pej pen-pushers

mezza'nino *nm* mezzanine

mez'zano, -a *adj* middle

mezza'notte *nf* midnight; **aspettare la** ∼ see in the New Year

mezz'asta: **a** ∼ *adv* at half mast

mezze'ria *nf* centre line

'mezzo 1 *adj* half; **di mezza età** middle aged; ∼ **bicchiere** half a glass; **una mezza idea** a vague idea; **siamo mezzi morti**

we're half dead; **sono le quattro e** ∼ it's half past four. **mezza cartuccia** *nf* runt. **mezza dozzina** *nf* half-dozen. **mezza età** *nf* middle age, midlife. **mezza giornata** *nf* half day. **mezzo guanto** *nm* mitt. **mezzo litro** *nm* half a litre. **mezz'ora** *nf* half an hour. **mezza pensione** *nf* half board. **mezza stagione** *nf* demi-season; **una giacca di** ∼ **stagione** a spring/autumn jacket. **mezza verità** *nf* half-truth.

2 *adv* (a metà) half; ∼ **addormentato** half asleep; ∼ **morto** half-dead; ∼ **morto di paura** petrified; ∼ **e** ∼ (così così) so so **3** *nm* (metà) half; (centro) middle; (per raggiungere un fine) means *sg*; **uno e** ∼ one and a half; **tre anni e** ∼ three and a half years; **in** ∼ **a** in the middle of; **il giusto** ∼ the happy medium; **levare di** ∼ clear away; **per** ∼ **di** by means of; **a** ∼ **posta** by mail; **via di** ∼ *fig* halfway house; (soluzione) middle way; **mezzi** *pl* (denaro) means *pl*; **mezzi** *pl* **di comunicazione di massa** mass media; **mezzi** *pl* **pubblici** public transport; **mezzi** *pl* **di trasporto** [means of] transport

mezzo'busto *nm* (statua) bust; TV talking head; **a** ∼ ⟨*foto, ritratto*⟩ half-length

mezzo'fondo *nm* middle-distance running

mezzogi'orno *nm* midday, noon; (sud) South; **il Mezzogiorno** Southern Italy. **mezzogiorno in punto** high noon

mezzo'sangue *nmf* crossbreed

mezzo'servizio *nm* **lavorare a** ∼ do part-time cleaning work

mi **1** *pers pron* me; (refl) myself; **mi ha dato un libro** he gave me a book; **non mi parla** he doesn't talk to me; **mi lavo le mani** I wash my hands; **eccomi** here I am **2** *nm* Mus (chiave, nota) E

'mia ▸ MIO

miago'lare *vi* miaow

miago'lio *nm* miaowing

mi'ao *nm* miaow

'mica¹ *nf* mica

'mica² *adv* fam (per caso) by any chance; **hai** ∼ **visto Paolo?** have you seen Paul, by any chance?; **non è** ∼ **bello** it is not at all nice; ∼ **male** not bad

'miccia *nf* fuse

micidi'ale *adj* deadly

'micio *nm* pussy cat

mi'cosi *nf inv* athlete's foot

mi'cotico *adj* fungal

microbiolo'gia *nf* microbiology

'microbo *nm* microbe

microchirur'gia *nf* microsurgery

micro'clima *nm* microclimate

microcom'puter *nm inv* microcomputer

micro'cosmo *nm* microcosm

micro'fiche *nf inv* microfiche

micro'film *nm inv* microfilm

micro'fisica *nf* microphysics

mi'crofono *nm* microphone. **microfono con la clip** clip-on microphone. **microfono spia** bugging device, bug. **microfono a stelo** boom microphone

microfotogra'fia *nf* Phot micrograph; (tecnica) micrography

microinfor'matica *nf* microcomputing

micro'onda *nf* microwave

microorga'nismo *nm* microorganism

microproces'sore *nm* microprocessor

micro'scheda *nf* microfiche

micro'scopico *adj* microscopic

micro'scopio *nm* microscope; **passare qualcosa al** ∼ fig examine something in microscopic detail

microse'condo *nm* microsecond

micro'solco *nm* (disco) long-playing record

micro'spia *nf* bug

mi'dollo *nm* (pl *nf* **midolla**, Anat) marrow; **fino al** ∼ ⟨*bagnato*⟩ through and through; ⟨*corrotto*⟩ to the core. **midollo osseo** bone marrow. **midollo spinale** spinal cord

'mie ▸ MIO

mi'ei ▸ MIO

mi'ele *nm* honey. **miele d'acacia** acacia honey

mi'etere *vt* reap

mietitrebbia'trice *nf* combine harvester

mieti'trice *nf* harvester

mieti'tura *nf* harvest

migli'aia *nfpl* thousands

migli'aio *nm* (pl *nf* **migliaia**) thousand; **a migliaia** in thousands

'miglio *nm* Bot millet; (misura: pl f **miglia**) mile. **miglia aeree** *pl* Br Air Miles, Am frequent-flyer miles. **miglio nautico** nautical mile. **miglia** *pl* **all'ora** miles per hour, mph. **miglio terrestre** mile

migliora'mento *nm* improvement

miglio'rare *vt/i* improve

migli'ore **1** *adj* better; (superlativo) the best; ∼ **amico** best friend; **i migliori auguri** best wishes **2** *nmf* **il/la** ∼ the best

miglio'ria *nf* improvement

mi'gnatta *nf* leech

'mignolo *nm* little finger, pinkie fam; (del piede) little toe

mi'gnon *adj inv* (bottiglie) miniature

mi'grare *vi* migrate

migra'tore *adj* migratory

migra'torio *adj* migratory

migrazi'one *nf* migration

'mila ▶ MILLE

mila'nese *adj & nmf* Milanese

Mi'lano *nf* Milan

miliar'dario, -a ① *nm* millionaire; (pluri-miliardario) billionaire ② *nf* millionairess; billionairess

mili'ardo *nm* billion

mili'are *adj* **pietra miliare** milestone

milio'nario ① *nm* millionaire ② *nf* millionairess

mili'one *nm* million

milio'nesimo *adj & nm* millionth

mili'tante *adj & nmf* militant

mili'tanza *nf* militancy

mili'tare ① *vi* ∼ **in** be a member of ⟨un partito ecc⟩ ② *adj* military ③ *nm* soldier; **fare il** ∼ do one's military service. **militare di carriera** regular [soldier]. **militare di leva** National Serviceman

milita'rismo *nm* militarism

milita'rista *adj* militaristic

militariz'zare *vt* militarize

militas'solto *adj* having done National Service

'milite *nm* soldier

milite'sente *adj* exempt from National Service

mil'izia *nf* militia

millanta|'tore, -trice *nmf* boaster

'mille *adj & nm* (pl **mila**) a *or* one thousand; **due/tre mila** two/three thousand; ∼ **grazie!** thanks a lot!; **millenovecentonovantaquattro** *nm* nineteen ninety-four

mille'foglie *nm inv* Culin vanilla slice

mil'lennio *nm* millennium

millepi'edi *nm inv* centipede

mil'lesimo *adj & nm* thousandth

milli'bar *nm inv* millibar

milli'grammo *nm* milligram

mil'lilitro *nm* millilitre

mil'limetro *nm* millimetre

'milza *nf* spleen

mi'mare ① *vt* mimic ⟨persona⟩ ② *vi* mime

mi'metico *adj* **tuta mimetica** camouflage; **animale mimetico** animal which has the ability to camouflage itself; **vernice mimetica** camouflage paint

mime'tismo *nm* ability to camouflage itself. **mimetismo politico** chameleon-like political traits

mimetiz'zare *vt* camouflage

mimetiz'zarsi *vr* camouflage oneself

'mimica *nf* mime. **mimica facciale** facial expressions *pl*

'mimico *adj* mimic

'mimo *nm* mime

mi'mosa *nf* mimosa

'mina *nf* mine; (di matita) lead

mi'naccia *nf* threat; **avere una** ∼ **di aborto** come close to having a miscarriage. **minaccia di morte** death threat

minacci'are *vt* threaten

minacciosa'mente *adv* threateningly, menacingly

minacci'oso *adj* threatening; ⟨onde⟩ menacing

mi'nare *vt* mine; fig undermine

mina'reto *nm* minaret

mina'tore *nm* miner

mina'torio *adj* threatening

mine'rale *adj & nm* mineral

mineralo'gia *nf* mineralogy

mine'rario *adj* mining *attrib*

mi'nestra *nf* soup. **minestra in brodo** noodle soup. **minestra di verdure** vegetable soup

mine'strone *nm* minestrone (vegetable soup); (fam: insieme confuso) hotchpotch

mingher'lino *adj* skinny

'mini ① *nf inv* (gonna) mini ② *adj inv* mini

mini+ *pref* mini+

miniapparta'mento *nm* studio flat Br, studio apartment

minia'tura *nf* miniature

miniaturiz'zato *adj* miniaturized

mini'bus *nm inv* minibus

mini'disc *nm inv* minidisc

mini'disco *nm* minidisc

mini'era *nf* mine; **una** ∼ **di notizie** a mine of information; **è una** ∼ **di idee** he's full of ideas. **miniera a cielo aperto** opencast mine. **miniera d'oro** gold mine

mini'golf *nm* minigolf, miniature golf

mini'gonna *nf* miniskirt, mini

'minima *nf* (atmosferica) minimum temperature; Med minimum blood-pressure level; Mus minim

minima'lista *nmf* minimalist

minima'mente *adv* minimally

mini'market *nm inv* minimarket

minimiz'zare *vt* minimize, downplay

'minimo ① *adj* least, slightest; (il più basso) lowest; ⟨salario⟩ minimum ② *nm* minimum; **girare al** ∼ Auto idle; **toccare il** ∼ **storico** be at an all-time low; **come** ∼ at least, as a minimum

mini'moto *nf inv* pocket bike

'minio *nm* red lead

ministeri'ale *adj* (di ministero) ministerial; (di governo) government

mini'stero *nm* ministry; (governo) government. **ministero dell'Ambiente e della Tutela del Territorio** ≈ Department of Natural Resources Am, ≈ Department of the Environment Br. **ministero degli [affari] Esteri** Foreign Office Br, State Department Am. **ministero della Difesa** Ministry of Defence Br, Department of Defense Am. **ministero di Grazia e Giustizia** Justice Department Am. **ministero degli Interni** Ministry of the Interior, ≈ Home Office. **ministero dell'Istruzione** Department for Education and Skills Br. **ministero del Lavoro e delle Politiche Sociali** ≈ Department for Work and Pensions. **ministero per le Politiche Agricole e Forestali** ≈ Department for Environment, Food, and Rural Affairs Br. **ministero della Salute** Department of Health

mi'nistro *nm* minister. **ministro della Difesa** Defence Minister Br, Defense Secretary Am. **ministro degli Esteri** Foreign Secretary Br, Secretary of State Am, foreign minister. **ministro di Grazia e Giustizia** Attorney General. **ministro dell'Interno** Home Secretary Br, Secretary of the Interior Am. **ministro del Lavoro** Employment Minister, Employment Secretary Br. **ministro del Tesoro** Chancellor of the Exchequer Br, Secretary of the Treasury Am

mini'tower *nm inv* Comput minitower

mino'ranza *nf* minority. **minoranza etnica** ethnic minority

mino'rato, -a ① *adj* disabled ② *nmf* disabled person

Mi'norca *nf* Menorca

mi'nore ① *adj* ⟨gruppo, numero⟩ smaller; (superlativo) smallest; ⟨distanza⟩ shorter; (superlativo) shortest; ⟨prezzo⟩ lower; (superlativo) lowest; (di età) younger; (superlativo) youngest; (di importanza) minor; (superlativo) least important ② *nmf* younger; (superlativo) youngest; Jur minor; **il ∼ dei mali** the lesser of two evils; **i minori di 14 anni** children under 14

mino'renne ① *adj* under age ② *nmf* minor

minori'tario *adj* minority *attrib*

minu'etto *nm* minuet

mi'nuscolo, -a ① *adj* tiny, minuscule ② *nf* small letter

mi'nuta *nf* rough copy

minuta'mente *adv* ⟨esaminato⟩ in minute detail, minutely; ⟨lavorato, tritato⟩ finely

mi'nuto¹ *adj* minute; ⟨persona⟩ delicate; ⟨ricerca⟩ detailed; ⟨pioggia, neve⟩ fine; **al ∼** Comm retail

mi'nuto² *nm* ⟨di tempo⟩ minute; **spaccare il ∼** be dead on time; **minuti** *pl* di recupero Sport injury time

mi'nuzia *nf* trifle; **minuzie** *pl* minutiae

minuziosa'mente *adv* minutely

minuzi'oso *adj* minute, detailed; ⟨persona⟩ meticulous

'mio ① (il mio *m*, la mia *f*, i miei *mpl*, le mie *fpl*) *poss adj* my; **questa macchina è mia** this car is mine; **∼ padre** my father; **un ∼ amico** a friend of mine ② *poss pron* mine; **i miei** (genitori ecc) my folks

'miope *adj* short-sighted

mio'pia *nf* short-sightedness

'mira *nf* aim; (bersaglio) target; **prendere la ∼** take aim; **prendere di ∼ qualcuno** fig have it in for somebody

mi'rabile *adj* admirable

miraco'lato *adj* ⟨malato⟩ miraculously cured

mi'racolo *nm* miracle

miracolosa'mente *adv* miraculously

miraco'loso *adj* miraculous

mi'raggio *nm* mirage

mi'rare *vi* [take] aim; **∼ alto** aim high

mi'rarsi *vr* (guardarsi) look at oneself

mi'riade *nf* myriad

mi'rino *nm* sight; Phot view-finder

'mirra *nf* myrrh

mir'tillo *nm* blueberry

'mirto *nm* myrtle

mi'santropo, -a *nmf* misanthropist

mi'scela *nf* mixture; ⟨di caffè, tabacco ecc⟩ blend

misce'lare *vt* mix

miscela'tore *nm* ⟨apparecchio⟩ blender; (di acqua) mixer tap

miscel'lanea *nf* miscellany

'mischia *nf* scuffle; (nel rugby) scrum

mischi'are *vt* mix; shuffle ⟨carte da gioco⟩

mischi'arsi *vr* mix; (immischiarsi) interfere

misco'noscere *vt* not appreciate

miscre'dente *nmf* heretic

mi'scuglio *nm* mixture; fig medley

mise'rabile *adj* wretched

misera'mente *adv* ⟨finire⟩ miserably; ⟨vivere⟩ in abject poverty; ⟨vestirsi⟩ shabbily

mi'seria *nf* poverty; (infelicità) misery; **guadagnare una ∼** earn a pittance; **miserie** *pl* (disgrazie) misfortunes; **porca ∼!** fam hell!

miseri'cordia *nf* mercy

misericordi'oso *adj* merciful

'misero *adj* (miserabile) wretched; (povero) poor; (scarso) paltry

mi'sfatto *nm* misdeed

mi'sogino *nm* misogynist

mis'saggio *nm* vision mixer

'**missile** *nm* missile. **missile cruise** cruise missile. **missile terra-aria** surface-to-air missile

missi'**listico** *adj* missile *attrib*

missio'**nario, -a** *nmf* missionary

missi'**one** *nf* mission. **missione di pace** peace mission

misteriosa'**mente** *adv* mysteriously

misteri'**oso** *adj* mysterious

mi'**stero** *nm* mystery

'**mistica** *nf* mysticism

misti'**cismo** *nm* mysticism

'**mistico** ① *adj* mystic[al] ② *nm* mystic

mistifi'**care** *vt* distort ⟨*verità*⟩

mistificazi'**one** *nf* (della verità) distortion

'**misto** ① *a* mixed; **scuola mista** mixed *or* co-educational school ② *nm* mixture; (di oggetti) miscellany. **misto lana** wool mixture; **misto lana/cotone** wool/cotton mix

mi'**sura** *nf* measure; (dimensione) measurement; (taglia) size; (limite) limit; **su ∼** ⟨*abiti*⟩ made to measure; ⟨*mobile*⟩ custom-made; **a ∼** ⟨*andare, calzare*⟩ perfectly; **nella ∼ in cui** insofar as. **misura di sicurezza** safety measure. **misura di capacità** unit of capacity. **misura di lunghezza** unit of length. **misura profilattica** prophylactic. **misure** *pl* **antidiscriminatorie** positive discrimination

misu'**rare** *vt* measure; try on ⟨*indumenti*⟩; (limitare) limit

misu'**rarsi** *vr* **∼ con** (gareggiare) compete with

misu'**rato** *adj* measured

misu'**rino** *nm* measuring spoon

'**mite** *adj* mild; ⟨*prezzo*⟩ moderate

'**mitico** *adj* mythical

miti'**gare** *vt* mitigate

miti'**garsi** *vr* calm down; ⟨*clima*⟩ become mild

'**mitilo** *nm* mussel

mitiz'**zare** *vt* mythicize

'**mito** *nm* myth

mitolo'**gia** *nf* mythology

mito'**logico** *adj* mythological

mi'**tomane** *nmf* compulsive liar

'**mitra** ① *nf* Relig mitre ② *nm inv* Mil machine-gun

mitragli'**are** *vt* machine-gun; **∼ di domande** fire questions at

mitraglia'**trice** *nf* machine-gun

mitt. *abbr* (**mittente**) sender

mitteleuro'**peo** *adj* Central European

mit'**tente** *nmf* sender

'**mixer** *nm inv* mixer

mne'**monico** *adj* mnemonic; **frase mnemonica** mnemonic

mo' *nm* **a mo' di** by way of ⟨*esempio, consolazione*⟩

'**mobile**[1] *adj* mobile; ⟨*volubile*⟩ fickle; (che si può muovere) movable; **beni** *pl* **mobili** movable personal estate; **squadra mobile** flying squad

'**mobile**[2] *nm* piece of furniture; **mobili** *pl* furniture *sg*. **mobile bar** drinks cabinet; **mobili** *pl* **da giardino** garden furniture; **mobili** *pl* **in stile** reproduction furniture

mo'**bilia** *nf* furniture

mobili'**are** *adj* ⟨*capitale*⟩ movable; ⟨*credito*⟩ medium-term; ⟨*mercato*⟩ share *attrib*; **patrimonio mobiliare** non-property assets

mobili'**ere** *nm* furniture dealer

mobili'**ficio** *nm* furniture factory

mo'**bilio** *nm* furniture

mobilità *nf* mobility. **mobilità del lavoro** labour mobility. **mobilità sociale** social mobility

mobili'**tare** *vt* mobilize

mobilitazi'**one** *nf* mobilization

'**moca** *nm inv* mocha

mocas'**sino** *nm* moccasin

mocci'**coso, -a** ① *adj* snotty ② *nmf* snottynosed kid; brat

'**moccolo** *nm* (di candela) candle-end; (moccio) snot

'**moda** *nf* fashion; **di ∼** in fashion; **andare di ∼** be in fashion; **alla ∼** ⟨*musica, vestiti*⟩ up to-date; **fuori ∼** unfashionable

mo'**dale** *adj* ⟨*verbo*⟩ modal

modalità *nf inv* formality. **modalità d'uso** instruction

modana'**tura** *nf* moulding

mo'**della** *nf* model

model'**lante** *adj* ⟨*gel per capelli*⟩ styling

model'**lare** *vt* model

model'**lino** *nm* model

model'**lismo** *nm* model-making; (collezionismo) collecting models

model'**lista** *nmf* model-maker; (moda) [fashion] designer

mo'**dello** *nm* model; ⟨*stampo*⟩ mould; (di carta) pattern; (modulo) form; (moda) male model. **modello CUD** ≈ P45. **modello in scala** scale model

'**modem** *nm inv* modem; **mandare per ∼** modem, send by modem

'**modem-fax** *nm inv* fax-modem

mode'**rare** *vt* moderate; (diminuire) reduce

mode'**rarsi** *vr* control oneself

moderata'**mente** *adv* moderately

mode'**rato** *adj* moderate

modera'**tore, -trice** ① *nmf* (in tavola rotonda) moderator ② *adj* moderating

moderazi'one *nf* moderation

moderna'mente *adv* (in modo moderno) in a modern style

modernari'ato *nm* collecting 20th-century art and products

moder'nismo *nm* modernism

modernità *nf* modernity

moderniz'zare *vt* modernize

modernizzazi'one *nf* modernization

mo'derno *adj* modern

mo'destia *nf* modesty

mo'desto *adj* modest

'modico *adj* reasonable

mo'difica *nf* modification

modifi'care *vt* modify

modifi'cato *adj* modified. **modificato geneticamente** genetically modified

modifica'tore *nm* modifier

modificazi'one *nf* modification

mo'dista *nf* milliner

'modo *nm* way; (garbo) manners *pl*; (occasione) chance; (Gram mood; ad ogni ∼ anyhow; di ∼ che so that; fare in ∼ di try to; in che ∼ (interrogativa) how; in qualche ∼ somehow; in questo ∼ like this. **modo di dire** idiom; **per ∼ di dire** so to speak; **in ∼ ottimistico/pessimistico/anormale** optimistically/pessimistically/abnormally

modu'lare *vt* modulate

modula'tore *nm* modulator. **modulatore di frequenza** frequency modulator

modulazi'one *nf* modulation **modulazione di frequenza** frequency modulation

'modulo *nm* form; (lunare, di comando) module. **modulo continuo** continuous paper. **modulo di domanda** application form. **modulo di iscrizione** enrolment form. **modulo di ordinazione** order form. **modulo di richiesta** claim form

'modus ope'randi *nm inv* modus operandi

'modus vi'vendi *nm inv* modus vivendi

mof'fetta *nf* skunk

'mogano *nm* mahogany

'mogio *adj* dejected

'moglie *nf* wife

moi'cano *adj* taglio [di capelli] alla moicana mohican [haircut]

mo'ine *nfpl* fare le ∼ behave in an affected way

'mola *nf* millstone; Mech grindstone

mo'lare *nm* molar

mo'lato *adj* (vetro) cut

mola'trice *nf* Mech grinder

Mol'davia *nf* Moldavia

'mole *nf* mass; (dimensione) size

mo'lecola *nf* molecule

moleco'lare *adj* molecular

mole'stare *vt* bother; (più forte) molest

molesta'tore, -trice *nmf* molester

mo'lestia *nf* nuisance; **molestie** *pl* **sessuali** sexual harassment *sg*

mo'lesto *adj* bothersome

Mo'lise *nm* Molise

'molla *nf* spring; **molle** *pl* tongs; **prendere qualcuno con le molle** handle somebody with kid gloves

mol'lare ① *vt* let go; (fam: lasciare) leave; fam give (ceffone); Naut cast off ② *vi* cease; **mollala!** fam stop that!

'molle *adj* soft; (bagnato) wet

molleggi'are ① *vi* be springy ② *vt* spring

molleggi'arsi *vr* bend at the knees

molleggi'ato *adj* bouncy, springy

mol'leggio *nm* (di auto) suspension; (di letto) springs *pl*; (esercizio) knee-bends *pl*

mol'letta *nf* (per capelli) hairgrip, barrette Am; (per bucato) clothes-peg; **mollette** *pl* (per ghiaccio ecc) tongs

mollet'tone *nm* (per tavolo) padded table cloth

mol'lezza *nf* softness; **mollezze** *pl* fig luxury

mol'lica *nf* crumb

mol'liccio *adj* squidgy

mol'lusco *nm* mollusc

'molo *nm* pier; (banchina) dock

'molotov *adj inv* **bottiglia molotov** Molotov cocktail

mol'teplice *adj* manifold; (numeroso) numerous

molteplicità *nf* multiplicity

mol'tiplica *nf* (di bicicletta) gear ratio, gear wheel

moltipli'care *vt* multiply

moltipli'carsi *vr* multiply

moltiplica'tore *nm* multiplier

moltiplica'trice *nf* calculating machine

moltiplicazi'one *nf* multiplication

molti'tudine *nf* multitude

'molto ① *adj* a lot of; (con negazione e interrogazione) much, a lot of; (con nomi plurali) many, a lot of; **non ∼ tempo** not much time, not a lot of time; **molte grazie** thank you very much ② *adv* very; (con verbi) a lot; (con avverbi) much; ∼ **stupido** very stupid; ∼ **bene, grazie** very well, thank you; **mangiare** ∼ eat a lot; ∼ **più veloce** much faster; **non mangiare** ∼ not eat a lot, not eat much ③ *pron* a lot; (molto tempo) a lot of time; (con negazione e interrogazione) much, a lot; (plurale) many; **non ne ho** ∼ I don't have much, I don't have a lot; **non ne ho molti** I don't have many, I don't have a lot; **non ci** ⋯➤

metterò ∼ I won't be long; fra non ∼ before long; **molti** (persone) a lot of people; **eravamo in molti** there were a lot of us

momentanea'mente *adv* momentarily; **è** ∼ **assente** he's not here at the moment

momen'taneo *adj* momentary

mo'mento *nm* moment; **a momenti** (a volte) sometimes; (fra un momento) in a moment; **dal** ∼ **che** since; **per il** ∼ for the time being; **al** ∼ at the moment; **da un** ∼ **all'altro** ⟨cambiare idea ecc⟩ from one moment to the next; ⟨aspettare l'arrivo di qualcuno ecc⟩ at any moment

'monaca *nf* nun

'Monaco *nf* (di Baviera) Munich; **Principato di Monaco** Monaco

'monaco *nm* monk

mo'narca *nm* monarch

monar'chia *nf* monarchy

mo'narchico, -a ① *adj* monarchic ② *nmf* monarchist

mona'stero *nm* (di monaci) monastery; (di monache) convent

mo'nastico *adj* monastic

monche'rino *nm* stump

'monco *adj* maimed; (fig: troncato) truncated; ∼ **di un braccio** one-armed

mon'dana *nf* lady of the night

mondanità *nf* (gente) beau monde; ∼ *pl* pleasures of the world

mon'dano *adj* worldly; **vita mondana** social life

mon'dare *vt* (sbucciare) peel; shell ⟨piselli⟩; (pulire) clean

mondi'ale *adj* world *attrib*; ⟨scala⟩ worldwide; (fam: fantastico) fantastic; **di fama** ∼ world-famous

mondi'ali *nmpl* World Cup

mondial'mente *adv* ⟨operare⟩ worldwide; ∼ **noto** world-famous

mon'dina *nf* seasonal worker in the rice fields

'mondo *nm* world; **il bel** ∼ fashionable society; **un** ∼ (molto) a lot; **non è la fine del** ∼ it's not the end of the world; **è la fine del** ∼ (fam: fantastico) it's out the world; ∼ **cane!** fam damn!. **mondo accademico** academia. **mondo del lavoro** world of work. **mondo dei sogni** never-never land. **mondo dello spettacolo** show biz

mondovisi'one *nf* **in** ∼ transmitted worldwide

monelle'ria *nf* prank

mo'nello, -a *nmf* urchin

mo'neta *nf* coin; (denaro) money; (denaro spicciolo) [small] change. **moneta estera** foreign currency. **moneta [a corso] legale** legal tender. **moneta unica** single currency

mone'tario *adj* monetary

mongolfi'era *nf* hot air balloon

Mon'golia *nf* Mongolia

'mongolo *adj* Mongol

mo'nile *nm* jewel

'monito *nm* warning

'monitor *nm inv* monitor

monito'raggio *nm* monitoring

moni'tore *nm* monitor

mono'albero *adj inv* single-camshaft *attrib*

mono'blocco ① *nm* Auto cylinder block ② *adj inv* ⟨cucina⟩ fitted

mo'nocolo *nm* monocle

monoco'lore *adj* Pol one-party

monocro'matico *adj* monochrome

mono'dose *adj inv* individually packaged

monoga'mia *nf* monogamy

mo'nogamo *adj* monogamous

monogra'fia *nf* monograph

mono'gramma *nm* monogram

mono'kini *nm inv* monokini

mono'lingue *adj* monolingual

mono'lito *nm* monolith

monolo'cale *nm* studio flat Br, studio apartment

mo'nologo *nm* monologue

monoma'nia *nf* monomania

mononucle'osi *nf inv* **mononucleosi infettiva** glandular fever

monoparen'tale *adj* single-parent *attrib*

mono'pattino *nm* [child's] scooter

mono'petto *adj* single-breasted

mono'plano *nm* monoplane

mono'polio *nm* monopoly. **monopolio di Stato** state monopoly

monopoliz'zare *vt* monopolize

mono'posto *nm* single-seater

mono'reddito *adj* single-income *attrib*

monosac'caride *nm* monosaccharide

mono'sci *nm inv* monoski

monosil'labico *adj* monosyllabic

mono'sillabo ① *nm* monosyllable ② *adj* monosyllabic

mo'nossido *nm* **monossido di carbonio** carbon monoxide

monote'istico *adj* monotheistic

monotona'mente *adv* monotonously

monoto'nia *nf* monotony

mo'notono *adj* monotonous

mono'uso *adj* disposable

monou'tente *adj inv* single-user *attrib*

monovo'lume *nf* people carrier, multi-purpose vehicle

monsi'gnore *nm* monsignor

mon'sone *nm* monsoon

'monta *nf* Zool covering; (modo di cavalcare) riding style; **stallone da monta** stud horse

monta'carichi *nm inv* hoist

mon'taggio *nm* Mech assembly; Cinema editing; **scatola di montaggio** assembly kit; **catena di montaggio** production line

mon'tagna *nf* mountain; (zona) mountains *pl*. **Montagne** *pl* **Rocciose** Rocky Mountains. **montagne** *pl* **russe** roller coaster, big dipper

monta'gnoso *adj* mountainous

monta'naro, -a *nmf* highlander

mon'tano *adj* mountain *attrib*

mon'tante *nm* (di finestra, porta) upright; Fin total amount; (nel pugilato) upper cut

mon'tare *vt/i* mount; get on ⟨veicolo⟩; (aumentare) rise; Mech assemble; frame ⟨quadro⟩; Culin whip; edit ⟨film⟩; (a cavallo) ride; fig blow up

mon'tarsi *vr* ~ **la testa** get big-headed

monta'scale *nm inv* stairlift

mon'tato, -a *nmf* fam poser

monta‖'tore, -trice *nmf* assembler

monta'tura *nf* Mech assembling; (di occhiali) frame; (di gioiello) mounting; fig exaggeration

'monte *nm* anche fig mountain; **a** ~ up stream; **andare a** ~ be ruined; **mandare a** ~ **qualcosa** ruin something. **Monte Bianco** Mont Blanc. **monte di pietà** pawnshop

Monte'negro *nm* Montenegro

monte'premi *nm inv* jackpot

mont'gomery *nm inv* duffel coat

mon'tone *nm* ram; **carne di montone** mutton

montu'oso *adj* mountainous

monumen'tale *adj* monumental

monu'mento *nm* monument. **monumento ai caduti** war memorial. **monumento commemorativo** memorial. **monumento nazionale** national monument

mo'plen® *nm* moulded plastic

mo'quette *nf* (tappeto) fitted carpet

'mora *nf* (di gelso) mulberry; (di rovo) blackberry

mo'rale ① *adj* moral
② *nf* morals *pl*; (di storia) moral
③ *nm* morale

mora'lista *nmf* moralist

mora'listico *adj* moralistic

moralità *nf inv* morality; (condotta) morals *pl*

moraliz'zare *vt/i* moralize

moral'mente *adv* morally

mora'toria *nf* moratorium

morbida'mente *adv* softly

morbi'dezza *nf* softness

'morbido *adj* soft

mor'billo *nm* measles *sg*

'morbo *nm* disease. **morbo di Alzheimer** Alzheimer's disease. **morbo di Creutzfeldt Jakob** Creutzfeldt-Jakob disease, CJD. **morbo della mucca pazza** mad cow disease

morbosa'mente *adv* morbidly

morbosità *nf* (qualità) morbidity

mor'boso *adj* morbid

'morchia *nf* sludge

mor'dace *adj* cutting

mor'dente *adj* biting

'mordere *vt* bite; (corrodere) bite into

mordi e fuggi *adj* ⟨vacanza⟩ very short

mordicchi'are *vt* gnaw

mo'rello ① *nm* black horse
② *adj* blackish

mo'rena *nf* moraine

mo'rente *adj* dying

mo'resco *adj* Moorish

mor'fina *nf* morphine

morfi'nomane *nmf* morphine addict

morfolo'gia *nf* morphology

morfo'logico *adj* morphological

mori'bondo *adj* dying

morige'rato *adj* moderate

mo'rire *vi* die; fig die out; **fa un freddo da** ~ it's freezing cold, it's perishing; ~ **di noia** be bored to death; **c'era da** ~ **dal ridere** it was hilariously funny; **morir di fame** starve to death; fig starve

mor'mone *nmf* Mormon

mormo'rare *vt/i* murmur; ⟨brontolare⟩ mutter

mormo'rio *nm* murmuring; (lamentela) grumbling

'moro ① *adj* dark
② *nm* Moor

morosità *nf* default

mo'roso *adj* in arrears

'morra *nf* game for two players where each shouts a number at the same time as showing a number of fingers

'morsa *nf* vice; fig grip

'morse *adj* **alfabeto morse** Morse code

mor'setto *nm* clamp; (stringinaso) nose clip. **morsetto per batteria** battery lead connection

morsi'care *vt* bite

morsica'tura *nf* [snake] bite

'morso *nm* bite; (di cibo, briglia) bit; **i morsi della fame** hunger pangs

morta'della *nf* mortadella (type of salted pork)

mor'taio *nm* mortar

mor'tale *adj* mortal; (simile a morte) deadly; **di una noia** ~ deadly

mortalità *nf* mortality

mortal'mente *adv* ⟨ferito⟩ fatally; ⟨offeso⟩ mortally; ⟨annoiato⟩ to death; ∼ **stanco** fam dead tired

morta'retto *nm* firecracker

'morte *nf* death; **non è la** ∼ **di nessuno** it's not the end of the world; **lo odia a** ∼ fam she can't stand the sight of him; **annoiarsi a** ∼ fam be bored to death. ∼ **cerebrale** brain death

mortifi'cante *adj* mortifying

mortifi'care *vt* mortify

mortifi'carsi *vr* be mortified

mortifi'cato *adj* mortified

mortificazi'one *nf* mortification

'morto, -a ① pp di MORIRE
② *adj* dead; ∼ **di freddo** frozen to death; **stanco** ∼ dead tired
③ *nm* dead man
④ *nf* dead woman

mor'torio *nm* funeral

mo'saico *nm* mosaic

'Mosca *nf* Moscow

'mosca *nf* fly; ⟨barba⟩ goatee; **cadere come le mosche** be dropping like flies; **essere una** ∼ **bianca** be a rarity; **non si sentiva volare una** ∼ you could have heard a pin drop. **mosca cieca** blindman's buff

mo'scato ① *adj* muscat; **noce moscata** nutmeg
② *nm* muscatel

mosce'rino *nm* midge; (fam: persona) midget

mo'schea *nf* mosque

moschetti'ere *nm* musketeer

mo'schetto *nm* musket

moschet'tone *nm* (in alpinismo) snaplink; (gancio) spring clip

moschi'cida ① *adj inv* **carta** ∼ fly paper
② *nm* fly spray

'moscio *adj* limp; **avere l'erre moscia** not be able to say one's rs properly

mo'scone *nm* bluebottle; (barca) pedalo

Mosè *nm* Moses

'mossa *nf* movement; (passo) move

'mosso ① pp di MUOVERE
② *adj* ⟨mare⟩ rough; ⟨capelli⟩ wavy; ⟨fotografia⟩ blurred

mo'starda *nf* mustard. **mostarda di Cremona** preserve made from candied fruit in grape must or sugar with mustard

'mostra *nf* show; (d'arte) exhibition; **far** ∼ **di** pretend; **in** ∼ on show; **mettersi in** ∼ make oneself conspicuous; **far bella** ∼ **di sé** show off; **far bella** ∼ **di sé** look impressive. **mostra dell'artigianato** craft fair

'mostra-mer'cato *nf* trade fair

mo'strare *vt* show; (indicare) point out; (spiegare) explain; ∼ **di** (sembrare) seem; (fingere) pretend

mos'trarsi *vr* show oneself; (apparire) appear

mo'strina *nf* flash

'mostro *nm* monster; (fig: persona) genius. **mostro sacro** fig sacred cow

mostruosa'mente *adv* tremendously

mostru'oso *adj* monstrous; (incredibile) enormous

mo'tel *nm inv* motel

moti'vare *vt* cause; Jur justify

moti'vato *adj* ⟨persona⟩ motivated; ⟨azione⟩ justified

motivazi'one *nf* motivation; (giustificazione) justification

mo'tivo *nm* reason; (movente) motive; (in musica, letteratura) theme; (disegno) pattern, motif; **senza** ∼ for no reason; (senza giustificazione) unjustifiably. **motivo cachemire** paisley. **motivo a scacchi** chequered pattern

'moto ① *nm* motion; (esercizio) exercise; (gesto) movement; (sommossa) rising; **mettere in** ∼ start ⟨motore⟩. **moto ondoso** swell. **moto perpetuo** perpetual motion
② *nf inv* (motocicletta) motor bike

moto'carro *nm* three-wheeler

motoci'cletta *nf* motorcycle, motorbike. **motocicletta da corsa** racing motorbike, racer

motoci'clismo *nm* motorcycling

motoci'clista *nmf* motorcyclist, biker

moto'cross *nm* motocross, scrambling

motocros'sista *nmf* scrambler

moto'lancia *nf* motor launch

moto'nautica *nf* speedboat racing

moto'nave *nf* motor vessel

mo'tore ① *adj* motor *attrib*
② *nm* motor, engine; **con** ∼ **turbo** turbocharged. **motore diesel** diesel engine. **motore a iniezione** fuel injection engine. **motore raffreddato ad aria** air-cooled engine. **motore a reazione** jet [engine]. **motore di ricerca** Comput search engine. **motore a scoppio** internal combustion engine

moto'retta *nf* motor scooter

moto'rino *nm* moped. **motorino d'avviamento** starter motor

mo'torio *adj* motor *attrib*

moto'rista *nmf* **motorista di bordo** flight engineer

motoriz'zare *vt* motorize

motoriz'zato *adj* Mil motorized

motorizzazi'one *nf* (ufficio) vehicle licensing office

moto'scafo *nm* motorboat

moto'sega *nf* chain saw

motove'detta *nf* patrol vessel, patrol boat

mo'trice *nf* engine

'motto *nm* motto; (facezia) witticism; (massima) saying

'mountain bike *nf inv* mountain bike

mouse *nm inv* Comput mouse

mousse *nf inv* Culin mousse. **mousse al cioccolato** chocolate mousse

mo'vente *nm* motive

mo'venze *nfpl* movements

movimen'tare *vt* enliven

movimen'tato *adj* lively

movi'mento *nm* movement; **essere sempre in ∼** be always on the go. **movimento passeggeri e merci** passenger and freight traffic

Mozam'bico *nm* Mozambique

mozi'one *nf* motion. **mozione d'ordine** point of order

mozzafi'ato *adj inv* nail-biting

moz'zare *vt* cut off; dock ⟨coda⟩; **∼ il fiato a qualcuno** take somebody's breath away

mozza'rella *nf* mozzarella (mild, white cheese)

mozzi'cone *nm* (di sigaretta) stub

'mozzo ① *nm* Mech hub; Naut ship's boy ② *adj* ⟨coda⟩ truncated; ⟨testa⟩ severed

ms *abbr* (**manoscritto**) MS

'mucca *nf* cow; **morbo della mucca pazza** mad cow disease

'mucchio *nm* heap, pile; **un ∼ di** fig lots of

mucil'lagine *nf* Bot mucilage

'muco *nm* mucus

'muffa *nf* mould; **fare la ∼** go mouldy

muf'fire *vi* go mouldy

muf'fola *nf* mitt

mu'flone *nm* Zool mouflon

mugghi'are *vi* ⟨vento, mare⟩ roar

mug'gire *vi* ⟨mucca⟩ moo, low; ⟨toro⟩ bellow

mug'gito *nm* moo; (di toro) bellow; (azione) mooing; bellowing

mu'ghetto *nm* lily of the valley

mugo'lare *vi* whine; ⟨persona⟩ moan

mugo'lio *nm* whining

mugu'gnare *vt* fam mumble

mulatti'era *nf* mule track

mu'latto, -a *nmf* mulatto

mu'leta *nf inv* muleta

muli'ebre *adj* liter feminine

muli'nare *vi* spin

muli'nello *nm* (d'acqua) whirlpool; (di vento) eddy; (giocattolo) windmill

mu'lino *nm* mill. **mulino a vento** windmill

'mulo *nm* mule

'multa *nf* fine. **multa per divieto di sosta** parking ticket

mul'tare *vt* fine

multico'lore *adj* multicoloured

multicultu'rale *adj* multicultural

multi'etnico *adj* multi-ethnic

multifo'cale *adj* ⟨lente⟩ varifocal. **occhiali multifocali** varifocals

multifunzio'nale *adj* multifunction[al]

multilate'rale *adj* multilateral

multi'lingue *adj inv* multilingual

multi'media *nmpl* multimedia

multimedi'ale *adj* multimedia *attrib*

multimedialità *nf* multimedia

multimiliar'dario, -a *nmf* multi-millionaire

multinazio'nale *adj & nf* multinational

'multiplo *adj & nm* multiple

multiproprietà *nf inv* time-share; **una casa in ∼** a time-share

multiraz'ziale *adj* multi-racial

multi'sale *adj inv* **cinema multisale** multiplex [cinema]

multi'tasking *nm* Comput multitasking

multi'uso *adj inv* ⟨utensile⟩ all-purpose

'mummia *nf* mummy; (fig: persona) old fogey

mummifi'care *vt* mummify

'mungere *vt* milk

mungi'tura *nf* milking

munici'pale *adj* municipal

municipalità *nf inv* town council

muni'cipio *nm* town hall

munifi'cenza *nf* munificence, bounty

mu'nifico *adj* munificent

mu'nire *vt* fortify; **∼ di** (provvedere) supply with; **munitevi di un carrello/cestino** please take a trolley/basket

munizi'oni *nfpl* ammunition *sg*

'munto *pp di* MUNGERE

mu'overe *vt* move; (suscitare) arouse

mu'oversi *vr* move; **muoviti!** hurry up!, come on!

'mura *nfpl* (di città) walls

mu'raglia *nf* wall

mu'rale *adj* mural; ⟨pittura⟩ wall *attrib*

mur'are *vt* wall up

mu'rario *adj* masonry *attrib*; **cinta muraria** walls *pl*; **opera muraria** masonry

mura'tore *nm* bricklayer; (con pietre) mason; (operaio edile) builder

mura'tura *nf* (di pietra) masonry, stonework; (di mattoni) brickwork

mu'rena *nf* moray eel

'muro *nm* wall; (di nebbia) bank; **a ~** ⟨*armadio*⟩ built-in. **muro divisorio** partition wall. **muro di gomma** fig wall of indifference; **fare ~ di gomma** stonewall. **muro a intercapedine** cavity wall. **Muro del pianto** Wailing Wall. **muro portante** load-bearing wall. **muro del suono** sound barrier

'musa *nf* anche fig muse

muschi'ato *adj* musky

'muschio *nm* musk; Bot moss

musco'lare *adj* muscular

muscola'tura *nf* muscles *pl*

'muscolo *nm* muscle

musco'loso *adj* muscular

mu'seo *nm* museum

museru'ola *nf* muzzle

'musica *nf* music. **musica gospel** gospel music. **musica folk** folk [music]

'musical *nm inv* musical

musi'cale *adj* musical

musi'care *vt* set to music

musicas'setta *nf* cassette

musi'cista *nmf* musician

musicolo'gia *nf* musicology

'muso *nm* muzzle; (pej: di persona) mug; (di aeroplano) nose; **fare il ~** sulk

mu'sone, -a *adj & nmf* sulker

'mussola *nf* muslin

mussul'mano, -a *adj & nmf* Muslim, Moslem

'muta *nf* (cambio) change; (di penne) moult; (di cani) pack; (per immersione subacquea) wetsuit

muta'mento *nm* change

mu'tande *nfpl* pants

mutan'dine *nfpl* panties. **mutandine da bagno** bathing trunks; (da donna) bikini bottom

mutan'doni *nmpl* (da uomo) long johns; (da donna) bloomers

mu'tante *nmf* mutant

mu'tare *vt* change

mutazi'one *nf* mutation

mu'tevole *adj* changeable

muti'lare *vt* mutilate

muti'lato, -a ① *adj* crippled ② *nmf* disabled person. **mutilato di guerra** disabled ex-serviceman. **mutilato del lavoro** person disabled at work

mutilazi'one *nf* mutilation

mu'tismo *nm* dumbness; fig obstinate silence

'muto *adj* dumb; (silenzioso) silent; (fonetica) mute

'mutua *nf* **[cassa] mutua** sickness benefit fund

mutu'abile *adj* ⟨*farmaco*⟩ prescribable on the NHS

mutu'are *vt* borrow ⟨*teoria, parola*⟩

mutua'tario, -a *nmf* Fin borrower

mutu'ato, -a *nmf* ≈ NHS patient

'mutuo¹ *adj* mutual

'mutuo² *nm* loan; (per la casa) mortgage; **fare un ~** take out a mortgage; **società di mutuo soccorso** friendly society **mutuo ipotecario** mortgage

Nn

N° *abbr* (**numero**) No.

na'babbo *nm* nabob; **vivere da ~** live in the lap of luxury

'nacchera *nf* castanet

na'dir *nm* nadir

'nafta *nf* naphtha; (per motori) diesel oil; **a ~** ⟨*bruciatore*⟩ oil-burning

'naia *nf* cobra; (sl: servizio militare) national service

'nailon *nm* nylon

Na'mibia *nf* Namibia

na'nismo *nm* dwarfism

'nanna *nf* (sl: infantile) bye-byes; **andare a ~** go bye-byes; **fare la ~** sleep

'nano, -a *adj & nmf* dwarf

nanose'condo *nm* nanosecond

'napalm *nm* napalm

napole'tana *nf* (caffettiera) Neapolitan coffee maker

napole'tano, -a *adj & nmf* Neapolitan

'Napoli *nf* Naples

'nappa *nf* tassel; (pelle) soft leather

narci'sismo *nm* narcissism

narci'sista *adj & nmf* narcissist

nar'ciso *nm* narcissus

nar'cosi *nf* general anaesthesia

nar'cotici *nf* Drug Squad

nar'cotico *adj & nm* narcotic

na'rice *nf* nostril

nar'rare *vt* tell

narra'tivo, -a ① *adj* narrative ② *nf* fiction

narra|'tore, -trice *nmf* narrator

narrazi'one *nf* narration; (racconto) story

na'sale *adj* nasal

na'scente *adj* budding

'nascere *vi* (venire al mondo) be born; (germogliare) sprout; (sorgere) rise; ∼ **da** fig arise from

'nascita *nf* birth

nasci'turo *nm* unborn child

na'scondere *vt* hide

na'scondersi *vr* hide

nascon'diglio *nm* hiding place

nascon'dino *nm* hide-and-seek

na'scosto ① pp di NASCONDERE ② *adj* hidden; **di** ∼ secretly; **ascoltare di** ∼ ‹*conversazione*› listen in on ‹*conversazione*›

na'sello *nm* (pesce) hake

'naso *nm* nose

na'sone *nm* big nose, hooter fam

'nassa *nf* lobster pot

'nastro *nm* ribbon; (di registratore ecc) tape. **nastro adesivo** adhesive tape, sticky tape. **nastro isolante** insulating tape. **nastro magnetico** magnetic tape, magtape fam. **nastro trasportatore** conveyor belt

Na'tale *nm* Christmas

na'tale *adj* ‹giorno, paese› of one's birth

na'tali *nmpl* parentage

natalità *nf* [number of] births, birthrate

nata'lizio *adj* (del Natale) Christmas *attrib*

na'tante ① *adj* floating ② *nm* craft

'natica *nf* buttock

na'tio *adj* native

Natività *nf* Nativity

na'tivo, -a *adj & nmf* native

'NATO *nf* Nato, NATO

'nato ① pp di NASCERE ② *adj* born; **uno scrittore** ∼ a born writer; **nata Rossi** née Rossi

na'tura *nf* nature; **pagare in** ∼ pay in kind; **di** ∼ **politica** of a political nature. **natura morta** still life

natu'rale *adj* natural; **al** ∼ ‹alimento› plain, natural; ∼**!** naturally, of course

natura'lezza *nf* naturalness

naturaliz'zare *vt* naturalize

natural'mente *adv* (ovviamente) naturally, of course

natu'rista *nmf* naturalist

natu'ristico *adj* naturist

naufra'gare *vi* be wrecked; ‹*persona*› be shipwrecked

nau'fragio *nm* shipwreck; fig wreck

'naufrago, -a *nmf* survivor

'nausea *nf* nausea; **avere la** ∼ feel sick

nausea'bondo *adj* nauseating

nause'are *vt* nauseate

'nautica *nf* navigation

'nautico *adj* nautical

na'vale *adj* naval

na'vata *nf* (centrale) nave; (laterale) aisle

'nave *nf* ship. **nave ammiraglia** flagship. **nave da carico** cargo boat. **nave cisterna** tanker. **nave da crociera** cruise liner. **nave fattoria** factory ship. **nave da guerra** warship. **nave di linea** liner. **nave passeggeri** passenger ship. **nave portacontainer** container ship. **nave spaziale** spaceship. **nave traghetto** ferry

na'vetta *nf* shuttle

navi'cella *nf* **navicella spaziale** nose cone

navi'gabile *adj* navigable

navi'gare *vi* sail; ∼ **in Internet** surf the Net, browse

naviga|'tore, -trice *nmf* navigator; (in Internet) surfer. **navigatore solitario** lone yachtsman. **navigatore spaziale** spaceman

navigazi'one *nf* navigation; **della** ∼ navigational

na'viglio *nm* fleet; (canale) canal

nazifa'scismo *nm* Nazi fascism

nazifa'scista *nmf* Nazi fascist

nazio'nale ① *adj* national ② *nf* Sport national team

naziona'lismo *nm* nationalism

naziona'lista *nmf* nationalist

nazionalità *nf inv* nationality

nazionaliz'zare *vt* nationalize

nazi'one *nf* nation; **Nazioni** *pl* **Unite** United Nations

na'zista *adj & nmf* Nazi

N.B. *abbr* (**nota bene**) NB

n.d.r. *abbr* (**nota del redattore**) editor's note

'n 'drangheta *nf* Calabrian Mafia

n.d.t. *abbr* (**nota del traduttore**) translator's note

NE *abbr* (**nord-est**) NE

ne ① *pron* (di lui) about him; (di lei) about her; (di loro) about them; (di ciò) about it; (da ciò) from that; (di un insieme) of it; (di un gruppo) of them; **ne sono contento** I'm happy about it; **non ne conosco nessuno** I don't know any of them; **ne ho** I have some; **non ne ho più** I don't have any left ② *adv* from there; **ne vengo ora** I've just come from there; **me ne vado** I'm off; **ne va della mia reputazione** my reputation is at stake

né *conj* né... né... neither... nor...; **non ne ho il tempo né la voglia** I don't have either the time or the inclination; **né tu né io vogliamo andare** neither you nor I want ⋯⋗

to go; **né l'uno né l'altro** neither [of them/ us]

ne'anche [1] *adv* (neppure) not even; (senza neppure) without even [2] *conj* (e neppure) neither...nor; **io non parlo inglese e lui** ~ I don't speak English, neither does he *or* and he doesn't either

'nebbia *nf* mist; (in città, autostrada) fog

nebbi'oso *adj* misty; ⟨città, autostrada⟩ foggy

nebuliz'zare *vt* atomize

nebulizza'tore *nm* atomizer; (per il naso) nasal spray

nebulizzazi'one *nf* atomizing; **fare delle nebulizzazioni** take nasal sprays

nebulosità *nf* vagueness

nebu'loso *adj* hazy; ⟨teoria⟩ nebulous; ⟨discorso⟩ woolly

necessaria'mente *adv* necessarily

neces'sario [1] *adj* necessary [2] *nm* **fare il** ~ do the necessary, do the needful

necessità *nf inv* necessity; (bisogno) need

necessi'tare *vi* ~ **di** need; (essere necessario) be necessary

necro'logio *nm* obituary

ne'cropoli *nf inv* necropolis

ne'crosi *nf* necrosis

ne'fando *adj* wicked

ne'fasto *adj* ill-omened

ne'frite *nf* nephritis

nefrolo'gia *nf* nephrology

ne'frologo, -a *nmf* nephrologist

ne'gabile *adj* deniable

ne'gare *vt* deny; (rifiutare) refuse; **essere negato per qualcosa** be no good at something

nega'tiva *nf* negative

nega'tivo *adj* negative

negazi'one *nf* negation; (diniego) denial; Gram negative

ne'gletto *adj* neglected

'negli = IN + GLI

negli'gente *adj* negligent

negli'genza *nf* negligence

negozi'abile *adj* negotiable

negozi'ante *nmf* dealer; (bottegaio) shopkeeper

negozi'are [1] *vt* negotiate [2] *vi* ~ **in** trade in, deal in

negozi'ati *nmpl* negotiations

ne'gozio *nm* shop. **negozio di abbigliamento** clothes shop. **negozio di alimentari** grocer's. **negozio di antiquariato** antique shop. **negozio duty free** duty-free shop. **negozio di ferramenta** hardware shop. **negozio**

giuridico legal transaction. **negozio di souvenir** gift shop

'negro, -a [1] *adj* Negro, black [2] *nmf* Negro, black; (scrittore) ghost writer; **come un** ~ ⟨lavorare⟩ like a slave

negro'mante *nmf* necromancer

'nei = IN + I

nel = IN + IL

'nella = IN + LA

'nelle = IN + LE

'nello = IN + LO

'nembo *nm* nimbus

ne'mesi *nf* nemesis

ne'mico, -a [1] *adj* hostile [2] *nmf* enemy

nem'meno *conj* not even

'nenia *nf* dirge; (per bambini) lullaby; (piagnucolio) wail

'neo *nm* mole; (applicato) beauty spot

neo+ *pref* neo+

neo'classico *adj* neoclassical

neocolonia'lismo *nm* neocolonialism

neofa'scismo *nm* neofascism

neola'tino *adj* Romance

neolaure'ato, -a *nmf* recent graduate

neo'litico *adj* Neolithic

neolo'gismo *nm* neologism

'neon *nm* neon

neo'nato, -a [1] *adj* new born [2] *nmf* newborn baby

neona'zismo *nm* Neonazism

neona'zista *adj & nmf* Neonazi

neozelan'dese [1] *adj* New Zealand *attrib* [2] *nmf* New Zealander

'Nepal *nm* Nepal

nep'pure *conj* not even

ne'rastro *adj* blackish

'nerbo *nm* (forza) strength; fig backbone; **senza** ~ effete

nerbo'ruto *adj* brawny

ne'retto *nm* Typ bold [type]

'nero [1] *adj* black; (fam: arrabbiato) fuming [2] *nm* black; **l'ho visto** ~ **su bianco** I've seen it in black and white; **mettere** ~ **su bianco** put in writing. **nero pieno** Typ solid. **nero di seppia** sepia

nerva'tura *nf* nerves *pl*; Bot veining; (di libro) band

ner'vetti *nmpl* chopped beef and veal with onions

ner'vino *adj* ⟨gas⟩ nerve *attrib*

'nervo *nm* nerve; Bot vein; **avere i nervi** be bad-tempered; **dare ai** *o* **sui nervi a qualcuno** get on somebody's nerves

nervo'sismo *nm* nerviness

ner'voso *adj* nervous, edgy; (irritabile) bad-tempered; **avere il** ~ be irritable; **esaurimento nervoso** nervous breakdown '**nespola** *nf* medlar

'**nespolo** *nm* medlar[-tree]

'**nesso** *nm* link, connection

nes'suno ① *adj* no, not... any; (qualche) any; **non ho nessun problema** I don't have any problems, I have no problems; **non ha nessun valore** it hasn't any value, it has no value; **da nessuna parte** nowhere; **non lo trovo da nessuna parte** I can't find it anywhere; **in nessun modo** on no account; **per nessun motivo** for no reason; **nessuna notizia?** any news?
② *pron* nobody, no one, not... anybody, not... anyone; (qualcuno) anybody, anyone; **hai delle domande?** –**nessuna** do you have any questions? - none; ∼ **di voi** none of you; ∼ **dei due** (di voi due) neither of you; **non ho visto** ∼ **dei tuoi amici** I haven't seen any of your friends; **c'è** ∼**?** is anybody there?

'**nesting** *nm inv* Comput nesting

net *nm inv* Tennis net cord

'**nettare**[1] *nm* nectar

net'tare[2] *vt* clean

netta'rina *nf* nectarine

net'tezza *nf* cleanliness. **nettezza urbana** cleansing department

'**netto** *adj* clean; (chiaro) clear; Comm net; **di** ∼ just like that

Net'tuno *nm* Neptune

nettur'bino *nm* dustman

'**network** *nm inv* network. **network televisivo** network television

'**neuro** *nf* neurological clinic

neuro+ *pref* neuro+

neurochirur'gia *nf* brain surgery

neurochi'rurgo *nm* brain surgeon

neurolo'gia *nf* neurology

neurologico *adj* neurological

neuropsichi'atra *nmf* neuropsychiatrist

neuropsichia'tria *nf* neuropsychiatry

neu'trale *adj & nm* neutral

neutralità *nf* neutrality

neutraliz'zare *vt* neutralize

'**neutro** ① *adj* neutral; Gram neuter
② *nm* Gram neuter

neu'trone *nm* neutron

ne'vaio *nm* snow-field

'**neve** *nf* snow

nevi'care *vi* snow; **nevica** it is snowing

nevi'cata *nf* snowfall

ne'vischio *nm* sleet

ne'voso *adj* snowy

nevral'gia *nf* neuralgia

ne'vralgico *adj* neuralgic; **punto nevralgico** nerve centre; (di questione ecc) crucial point

nevraste'nia *nf* neurasthenia

nevra'stenico *adj* neurasthenic; (irritabile) hot tempered

ne'vrite *nf* neuritis

ne'vrosi *nf inv* neurosis

ne'vrotico *adj* neurotic

'**nibbio** *nm* kite

Nica'ragua *nm* Nicaragua

nicara'guense *adj & nmf* Nicaraguan

'**nicchia** *nf* niche

nicchi'are *vi* shilly-shally

'**nichel** *nm* nickel

nichi'lista ① *nmf* nihilist
② *adj* nihilistic

nico'tina *nf* nicotine

nidi'ace *nm* nestling

nidi'ata *nf* brood

nidifi'care *vi* nest

nidifi'cato *adj* Comput nested

nidificazi'one *nf* Zool nesting

'**nido** *nm* nest; (giardino d'infanzia) crèche; **a** ∼ **d'ape** ⟨tessuto⟩ honeycomb. **nido di uccello** bird's nest. **nido di vipere** fig nest of vipers

ni'ente ① *pron* nothing, not... anything; (qualcosa) anything; **non ho fatto** ∼ **di male** I didn't do anything wrong, I did nothing wrong; **nient'altro?** anything else?; **grazie!** –**di** ∼**!** thank you! –don't mention it!; **non serve a** ∼ it is no use; **vuoi** ∼**?** do you want anything?; **dal** ∼ ⟨venire su⟩ from nothing; **da** ∼ (poco importante) minor; (di poco valore) worthless
② *adj inv* fam ∼ **pesci oggi** no fish today; **non ho** ∼ **fame** I'm not the slightest bit hungry
③ *adv* **non fa** ∼ (non importa) it doesn't matter; **per** ∼ at all; ⟨litigare⟩ over nothing; ∼ **affatto!** no way!
④ *nm* **un bel** ∼ absolutely nothing, damn-all fam; **basta un** ∼ **per spaventarlo** it doesn't take much to scare him

nientedi'meno, nientemeno ① *adv* ∼ **che** no less than
② *int* fancy that!

'**Niger** *nm* Niger

Ni'geria *nf* Nigeria

neurochi'rurgo *nm* brain surgeon

night *nm inv* night club

'**Nilo** *nm* Nile

'**ninfa** *nf* nymph

nin'fea *nf* water lily

nin'fomane *nf* nymphomaniac; **da** ∼ nymphomaniac

ninna'nanna *nf* lullaby

'**ninnolo** *nm* plaything; (fronzolo) knick-knack

ni'pote ① *nm* (di zii) nephew; (di nonni) grandson, grandchild; **nipoti** *pl* (collettivo) grandchildren, nephews and nieces

2 *nf* (di zii) niece; (di nonni) granddaughter, grandchild

nip'ponico *adj* Japanese

'**nisba** *pron* (sl: niente) zilch

'**nitido** *adj* neat; (chiaro) clear

ni'trato *nm* nitrate

'**nitrico** *adj* nitric

ni'trire *vi* neigh

ni'trito *nm* (di cavallo) neigh; Chem nitrite

nitro+ *pref* nitro+

nitroglice'rina *nf* nitroglycerine

'**niveo** *adj* snow-white

N.N. *abbr* (**numeri**) Nos

NO abbr (**nord-ovest**) NW

no 1 *adv* no; **credo di no** I don't think so; **perché no?** why not?; **io no** not me; **sì o no?** yes or no?; **ha detto così, no?** he said so, didn't he?; **fa freddo, no?** it's cold, isn't it?; **se no** otherwise
2 *nm* no; (nelle votazioni) nay

nobil'donna *nf* noblewoman

'**nobile 1** *adj* noble; **metallo ~** noble metal; **di animo ~** noble-minded
2 *nm* noble, nobleman
3 *nf* noble, noblewoman

nobili'are *adj* noble

nobiltà *nf* nobility

nobilu'omo *nm* (*pl* **nobiluomini**) nobleman

'**nocca** *nf* knuckle

nocci'ola *nf* hazelnut

noccio'line [americane] *nfpl* peanuts

nocci'olo[1] *nm* (albero) hazel

'**nocciolo**[2] *nm* stone; Phys core; fig heart; **il ~ della questione** the heart of the matter

'**noce 1** *nf* walnut. **noce moscata** nutmeg. **noce pecan** pecan. **noce di vitello** veal with mushrooms
2 *nm* (legno) walnut; (albero) walnut [tree]

noce'pesca *nf* nectarine

no'cino *nm* walnut liqueur

no'civo *adj* harmful

no'dino *nm* veal chop

'**nodo** *nm* knot; fig lump; Comput node; **fare il ~ della cravatta** do up one's tie. **nodo alla gola** lump in the throat; **nodo della questione** crux of the matter. **nodo ferroviario** railway junction. **nodo piano** reef knot. **nodo scorsoio** slipknot

no'doso *adj* knotty

'**nodulo** *nm* nodule

Noè *nm* Noah

no-'global *adj* anti-globalization

'**noi** *pers pron* (soggetto) we; (oggetto, con prep) us; **chi è? –siamo ~** who is it? –it's us; **~ due** the two of us

'**noia** *nf* boredom; (fastidio) bother; (persona) bore; **dar ~** annoy

noi'altri *pers pron* we

noi'oso *adj* boring; (fastidioso) tiresome

noleggi'are *vt* hire; (dare a noleggio) hire out; charter ⟨*nave, aereo*⟩

no'leggio *nm* hire; (di nave, aereo) charter. **noleggio barche/biciclette/ sci** boat/cycle/ski hire

'**nolo** *nm* hire; Naut freight; **a ~** for hire

'**nomade 1** *adj* nomadic
2 *nmf* nomad

'**nome** *nm* name; Gram noun; **a ~ di** ⟨*da parte di*⟩ on behalf of; **di ~** by name; **farsi un ~** make a name for oneself; **nel ~ di...** in the name of.... **nome d'arte** professional name. **nome di battaglia** nom de guerre. **nome di battesimo** first name. **nome in codice** code name. **nome depositato** trade-name. **nome di dominio** Comput domain name. **nome per esteso** full name. **nome del file** filename. **nome proprio** proper noun. **nome da ragazza** maiden name. **nome da sposata** married name. **nome utente** username

no'mea *nf* reputation

nomencla'tura *nf* nomenclature

no'mignolo *nm* nickname

'**nomina** *nf* appointment; **di prima ~** newly appointed

nomi'nale *adj* nominal; Gram noun *attrib*

nomi'nare *vt* name; (menzionare) mention; (eleggere) appoint

nomina'tivo 1 *adj* nominative; Comm registered
2 *nm* nominative; (nome) name; **caso nominativo** nominative case

non *adv* not; **~ ti amo** I do not *or* don't love you; **~ c'è di che** not at all; **~ più** no longer

nonché *conj* (tanto meno) let alone; (e anche) as well as

nonconfor'mista *adj & nmf* nonconformist

nonconformità *nf* noncompliance

noncu'rante *adj* nonchalant; (negligente) indifferent

noncu'ranza *nf* nonchalance; (negligenza) indifference

nondi'meno *conj* nevertheless

'**nonna** *nf* grandmother, grandma fam, gran fam

'**nonno** *nm* grandfather, grandpa fam; **nonni** *pl* grandparents

non'nulla *nm inv* trifle

'**nono** *adj & nm* ninth

nono'stante 1 *prep* in spite of
2 *conj* although

non stop *adj inv & adv* nonstop

nontiscordardimé *nm inv* forget-me-not

nonvio'lento *adj* nonviolent

nonvio'lenza *nf* nonviolence

no 'profit *adj inv* non profit

nor'cino *nm* pig butcher

nord *nm* north; **del** ~ northern

nord-'est *nm* northeast; **a** ~ northeasterly; **del** ~ northeastern; **vento di nord-est** northeasterly [wind]

'nordico *adj* northern

nor'dista *adj & nmf* Yankee

nordocciden'tale *adj* northwestern

nordorien'tale *adj* northeastern

nord-'ovest *nm* northwest; **a** ~ northwesterly; **del** ~ northwestern **vento di nord-ovest** northwesterly [wind]

'norma *nf* norm; (regola) rule; (per l'uso) instruction; **a** ~ **di legge** according to law; **è buona** ~ it's advisable; **di** ~ as a rule, normally

nor'male ① *adj* normal ② *nm* **fuori del** ~ out of the ordinary; **superiore al** ~ above average

normalità *nf* normality; **rientrare nella** ~ be quite normal

normaliz'zare *vt* normalize

normal'mente *adv* normally

Norman'dia *nf* Normandy

nor'manno *adj* from Normandy; (storico) Norman

normativa *nf* regulations *pl*, laws *pl*

norma'tivo *adj* normative, prescriptive

nor'mografo *nm* stencil

nor'reno *adj* Norse

norve'gese *adj & nmf* Norwegian

Nor'vegia *nf* Norway

noso'comio *nm fml* hospital

nossi'gnore *adv* (assolutamente no) no way

nostal'gia *nf* (di casa, patria) homesickness; (del passato) nostalgia; **aver** ~ be homesick; **aver** ~ **di qualcuno** miss somebody

no'stalgico, -a ① *adj* nostalgic ② *nmf* reactionary

nostra ▸ NOSTRO

no'strale *adj* local

no'strano *adj* local; (fatto in casa) home-made

'nostre ▸ NOSTRO

'nostri ▸ NOSTRO

'nostro ① (**il nostro** *m*, **la nostra** *f*, **i nostri** *mpl*; **le nostre** *fpl*) *poss adj* our; **quella macchina è nostra** that car is ours; ~ **padre** our father; **un** ~ **amico** a friend of ours ② *poss pron* ours

no'stromo *nm* bo's'n, boatswain

'nota *nf* (segno) sign; (comunicazione, commento, Mus) note; (conto) bill; (lista) list; **degno di** ~ noteworthy; **prendere** ~ take note; **una** ~ **di colore** a touch of colour; **mettere in** ~ **qualcosa** add something to the list. **nota di accredito** Comm credit note; **note** *pl* **caratteristiche** distinguishing marks. **nota spese** expense account

no'tabile *adj & nm* notable

no'taio *nm* notary

no'tare *vt* (segnare) mark; (annotare) note down; (osservare) notice; **far** ~ **qualcosa** point something out; **farsi** ~ get oneself noticed; **nota bene che...** please note that...

notazi'one *nf* marking; (annotazione) notation

'notebook *nm inv* Comput notebook (PC)

'notes *nm inv* notepad

no'tevole *adj* (degno di nota) remarkable; (grande) considerable

no'tifica *nf* notification

notifi'care *vt* notify; Comm advise; ~ **un ordine di comparizione [in giudizio]** subpoena

notificazi'one *nf* notification

no'tizia *nf* **una** ~ a piece of news, some news; (informazione) a piece of information, some information; **le notizie** the news *sg*; **per avere** ~ **di** ⟨telefonare⟩ for news of; **non ha più dato notizie di sé** he hasn't been in touch since. **notizia di attualità** news item

notizi'ario *nm* news *sg*

'noto *adj* [well-]known; **rendere** ~ (far sapere) announce

notorietà *nf* fame; **raggiungere la** ~ become famous

no'torio *adj* well-known; *pej* notorious

not'tambulo *nm* night-bird

not'tata *nf* night; **far** ~ stay up all night

'notte *nf* night; **di** ~ at night; **a** ~ **fatta** when night had fallen; **la** ~ (durante la notte) at night; **buona** ~ good night; **fermarsi per la** ~ stay overnight; **peggio che andar di** ~ worse than ever; **prima** ~ **di nozze** wedding night. **notte in bianco** sleepless night

notte'tempo *adv* at night[-time]

not'turno *adj* nocturnal; ⟨servizio ecc⟩ night *attrib*; **in notturna** ⟨partita⟩ under flood-lights

'notula *nf* (conto) fee note

no'vanta *adj & nm* ninety

novan'tenne *adj & nmf* ninety year old

novan'tesimo *adj & nm* ninetieth

novan'tina *nf* about ninety

'nove *adj & nm* nine; **prova del** ~ Math casting out nines

nove'cento adj & nm nine hundred; il Novecento the twentieth century; **stile novecento** twentieth-century

no'vella nf short story

novelli'ere nm short-story writer

novel'lino, -a ① adj inexperienced ② nmf novice, beginner

no'vello adj new. **patate novelle** new potatoes

no'vembre nm November

nove'mila adj & nm nine thousand

no'vena nf novena

novi'lunio nm new moon

novità nf inv novelty; (notizie) news sg; **l'ultima ~** (moda) the latest fashion

novizi'ato nm Relig novitiate; (tirocinio) apprenticeship

nozi'one nf notion; **perdere la ~ del tempo** lose track of time; **non avere la ~ del tempo** have no sense of time; **nozioni** pl rudiments; **poche nozioni di inglese** very basic English

nozio'nismo nm accumulation of facts

'nozze nfpl marriage sg; (cerimonia) wedding sg; **andare a ~** (godersela) have a field day. **nozze d'argento** silver wedding [anniversary]. **nozze di diamante** diamond wedding [anniversary]. **nozze d'oro** golden wedding [anniversary]

'nube nf cloud. **nube di mistero** shroud of mystery. **nube tossica** toxic cloud

nubi'fragio nm cloudburst

'nubile ① adj unmarried ② nf unmarried woman

'nuca nf nape

nucle'are adj nuclear

'nucleo nm nucleus; (unità) unit. **nucleo familiare** family unit

nu'dismo nm nudism

nu'dista nmf nudist

nudità nf nudity, nakedness

'nudo adj naked; (spoglio, terra) bare; **a occhio ~** to the naked eye; **verità nuda e cruda** naked truth; **a piedi nudi** barefoot

'nugolo nm large number

'nulla = NIENTE

nulla'osta nm inv permit

nullate'nente nm i nullatenenti the have-nots

nullità nf inv (persona) nonentity

'nullo adj Jur null and void

'nume nm numen

nume'rabile adj countable

nume'rale adj & nm numeral

nume'rare vt number

numera'tore nm Math numerator

numerazi'one nf numbering

nu'merico adj numerical

'numero nm number; (romano, arabo) numeral; (di scarpe) size; **fare** o **comporre il ~** dial [the number]; **dare i numeri** fam be off one's head; **avere tutti i numeri per** have what it takes to. **numero arretrato** back issue. **numero cardinale** cardinal [number]. **numero di conto** account number. **numero decimale** decimal. **numero di fax** fax number. **numero intero** whole number. **numero ordinale** ordinal [number]. **numero d'ordine** Comm order number. **numero di previdenza sociale** ≈ National Insurance number. **numero di protocollo** reference number. **numero di telefono** phone number. **numero uno** number one. **numero verde** ≈ Freephone® number, toll-free number Am. **numero di volo** flight number

nume'roso adj numerous

numi'smatico adj numismatic

'nunzio nm nuncio

nu'ocere vi ~ a harm

nu'ora nf daughter-in-law

nuo'tare vi swim; fig wallow; **~ come un pesce** swim like a fish; **~ nell'oro** be stinking rich, be rolling in it

nuo'tata nf swim; **fare una ~** have a swim

nuota'tore, -trice nmf swimmer

nu'oto nm swimming; **stili** mpl **di ~** swimming strokes

nu'ova nf piece of news; **buone nuove** good news; **nessuna ~, buona ~** no news is good news

Nu'ova Cale'donia nf New Caledonia

Nu'ova Gui'nea nf New Guinea

nuova'mente adv again

Nu'ova Ze'landa nf New Zealand

nu'ovo adj new; **di ~** again; **uscire di ~** go/come back out, go/come out again; **mi risulta ~** that's news to me; **~ di pacca** o **zecca** brand new; **rimettere a ~** give a new lease of life to; **~ del mestiere** new to the job; **il ~ anno** [the] New Year. **nuova linfa** nf new blood. **nuovo stile** new look. **Nuovo Testamento** New Testament

'nursery nf nursery

nutri'ente adj nourishing

nutri'mento nm nourishment

nu'trire ① vt feed (animale, malato, pianta); harbour (sentimenti); cherish (sogno) ② vi (essere nutriente) be nourishing

nu'trirsi vr eat; **~ di** fig live on

nutri'tivo adj nourishing, nutritional

nutrizi'one nf nutrition

'nuvola nf cloud; **avere la testa fra le nuvole** have one's head in the clouds;

vivere fra le nuvole live in cloud cuckoo land; **cadere dalle nuvole** be astounded
nuvo'loso *adj* cloudy

nuzi'ale *adj* nuptial; ⟨*vestito, anello ecc*⟩ wedding *attrib*; **pranzo nuziale** wedding breakfast

O *abbr* (**ovest**) W

o *conj* or; **o l'uno o l'altro** one or the other; either; **o... o...** either...or...

'oasi *nf inv* oasis

obbedi'ente = UBBIDIENTE

obbedi'enza = UBBIDIENZA

obbe'dire = UBBIDIRE

obbli'gare *vt* force, oblige

obbli'garsi *vr* ~ **a** undertake to

obbli'gato *adj* obliged

obbligatoria'mente *adv* **fare qualcosa** ~ be obliged to do something; **bisogna** ~ **farlo** you absolutely have to do it

obbliga'torio *adj* compulsory

obbligazi'one *nf* obligation; Comm bond. **obbligazione a premio** premium bond

'obbligo *nm* obligation; (dovere) duty; **avere obblighi verso** be under an obligation to; **d'**~ obligatory

ob'brobrio *nm* disgrace

obbrobri'oso *adj* disgraceful

obe'lisco *nm* obelisk

obe'rare *vt* overburden

obesità *nf* obesity

o'beso *adj* obese

obiet'tare *vt/i* object; ~ **su** object to

obiettiva'mente *adv* objectively

obiettività *nf* objectivity

obiet'tivo ① *adj* objective
② *nm* objective; (scopo) object

obiet'tore *nm* objector. **obiettore di coscienza** conscientious objector

obiezi'one *nf* objection; **fare** ~ **di coscienza** be a conscientious objector

obi'torio *nm* mortuary

o'blio *nm* oblivion

o'bliquo *adj* oblique; fig underhand

oblite'rare *vt* obliterate

oblò *nm inv* porthole

ob'lungo *adj* oblong

'oboe *nm* oboe

obsole'scenza *nf* obsolescence

obso'leto *adj* obsolete

'oca *nf* (pl **oche**) goose; (donna) silly girl

occasio'nale *adj* occasional

occasional'mente *adv* occasionally

occasi'one *nf* occasion; (buon affare) bargain; (motivo) cause; (opportunità) chance; **d'**~ secondhand

occhi'aia *nf* eye socket; **occhiaie** *pl* shadows under the eyes

occhi'ali *nmpl* glasses, spectacles. **occhiali multifocali** varifocals. **occhiali scuri** dark glasses. **occhiali da sole** sunglasses. **occhiali da sole avvolgenti** wraparound sunglasses. **occhiali da vista** glasses, spectacles

occhia'luto *adj* wearing glasses

occhi'ata *nf* look; **dare un'**~ **a** have a look at

occhieggi'are ① *vt* ogle
② *vi* (far capolino) peep

occhi'ello *nm* buttonhole; (asola) eyelet

'occhio *nm* eye; ~**!** watch out!; ~ **ai falsi** beware of imitations; **a quattr'occhi** in private; **abbassare gli occhi** look down, lower one's eyes; **sollevare gli occhi** look up, raise one's eyes; **tenere d'**~ **qualcuno** keep an eye on somebody; **perdere d'**~ lose sight of; **a** ~ **[e croce]** roughly; **chiudere un** ~ **(su qualcosa)** turn a blind eye (to something); **dare nell'**~ attract attention; **pagare o spendere un** ~ **[della testa]** pay an arm and a leg; **saltare agli occhi** be blindingly obvious. **occhio di falco** eagle eye. **occhio nero** (pesto) black eye. **occhio di pernice** (callo) corn

occhio'lino *nm* **fare l'**~ **a qualcuno** wink at somebody, give somebody a wink

occiden'tale ① *adj* western
② *nmf* westerner

occidentaliz'zare *vt* westernize

occidentaliz'zarsi *vr* become westernized

occi'dente *nm* west; (paesi capitalisti) West

oc'cludere *vt* obstruct

occlusi'one *nf* occlusion

occor'rente ① *adj* necessary
② *nm* **l'occorrente** the necessary

occor'renza *nf* need; **all'**~ if need be

oc'correre *vi* be necessary; **non occorre farlo** there is no need to do it

occulta'mento *nm* **occultamento di prove** concealment of evidence

occul'tare *vt* hide

occul'tismo *nm* occult

oc'culto *adj* hidden; (magico) occult

occu'pante *nmf* occupier; (abusivo) squatter

occu'pare *vt* occupy; spend ⟨tempo⟩; take up ⟨spazio⟩; (dar lavoro a) employ

occu'parsi *vr* occupy oneself; (trovare lavoro) find a job; ~ **di** (badare) look after; **occupati dei fatti tuoi!** mind your own business!

occu'pato *adj* engaged; ⟨persona⟩ busy; ⟨posto⟩ taken; **casa occupata** (alloggio abusivo) squat

occupazi'one *nf* occupation; Comm employment; (passatempo) pastime; **trovarsi un'~** (interesse) find oneself something to do

o'ceano *nm* ocean. **oceano Atlantico** Atlantic [Ocean]. **oceano Indiano** Indian Ocean. **oceano Pacifico** Pacific [Ocean]

'ocra *nf* ochre

'OCSE *nf abbr* (**Organizzazione per la Cooperazione e lo Sviluppo Economico**) OECD

ocu'lare *adj* ocular; ⟨testimone, bagno⟩ eye *attrib*

ocula'tezza *nf* care

ocu'lato *adj* ⟨scelta, persona⟩ prudent

ocu'lista *nmf* optician; (per malattie) ophthalmologist

od *conj* (davanti alla vocale o) or

'ode *nf* ode

odi'are *vt* hate; ~ **a morte** not be able to stand

odi'erno *adj* of today; (attuale) present

'odio *nm* hatred; **avere in ~** hate

odi'oso *adj* hateful

odis'sea *nf* odyssey

o'dometro *nm* Auto milometer, odometer Am

odo'rare ① *vt* smell; (profumare) perfume ② *vi* ~ **di** smell of

odo'rato *nm* sense of smell

o'dore *nm* smell; (profumo) scent; **c'è ~ di...** there's a smell of...; **avere un buon/cattivo ~** smell nice/awful; **sentire ~ di** smell; **odori** *pl* Culin herbs

odo'roso *adj* fragrant

of'fendere *vt* offend; (ferire) injure

of'fendersi *vr* take offence

offen'siva *nf* Mil, fig offensive

offen'sivo *adj* offensive

offen'sore *nm* offender

offe'rente *nmf* offerer; (in aste) bidder; **il miglior ~** the highest bidder

of'ferta *nf* offer; (donazione) donation; Comm supply; (nelle aste) bid; (di appalto) tender; **in ~ speciale** on special offer;

"offerte d'impiego" "situations vacant". **offerta pubblica di acquisto** takeover bid

of'ferto *pp di* OFFRIRE

offer'torio *nm* offertory

of'fesa *nf* offence

of'feso ① *pp di* OFFENDERE ② *adj* offended

offi'ciare *vt* officiate

offi'cina *nf* workshop. **officina [meccanica]** garage

officinale *adj* ⟨pianta⟩ medicinal

of'frire *vt* offer

of'frirsi *vr* offer oneself; ⟨occasione⟩ present itself; ~ **di fare qualcosa** offer to do something

off'set *nm inv* offset printing

off'shore *nm inv* (motoscafo) speedboat

offu'scare *vt* darken; fig dull ⟨memoria, bellezza⟩; blur ⟨vista⟩

offu'scarsi *vr* darken; fig ⟨memoria, bellezza⟩ fade away; ⟨vista⟩ become blurred

of'talmico *adj* ophthalmic

ogget'tistica *nf* manufacture and selling of household and gift items; (oggetti) household and gift items; **negozio di oggettistica** gift shop

oggettività *nf* objectivity

ogget'tivo *adj* objective

og'getto *nm* object; (argomento) subject. **oggetto sessuale** sex object. **oggetti smarriti** *pl* lost property, lost and found Am

'oggi *adv & nm* today; (al giorno d'oggi) nowadays; **da ~ in poi** from today on; ~ **[a] otto** a week today; **dall'~ al domani** overnight; **il giornale di ~** today's paper; **al giorno d'~** these days, nowadays

oggigi'orno *adv* nowadays

o'giva *nf* Mil warhead

'ogni *adj inv* every; (qualsiasi) any; ~ **tre giorni** every three days; **ad ~ costo** at any cost; **ad ~ modo** anyway; ~ **ben di Dio** all sorts of good things; ~ **cosa** everything; ~ **tanto** now and then; ~ **volta che** every time, whenever

o'gnuno *pron* everyone, everybody; ~ **di voi** each of you

ohibò *int* oh dear!

ohimè *int* oh dear!

o'kay *nm* **dare l'~ a qualcuno/qualcosa** give somebody/something the OK

'ola *nf inv* Mexican wave

O'landa *nf* Holland

olan'dese ① *adj* Dutch ② *nm* Dutchman; (lingua) Dutch; (formaggio) Edam ③ *nf* Dutchwoman

ole'andro *nm* oleander

ole'ato *adj* oiled; **carta oleata** greaseproof paper

oleo'dotto *nm* oil pipeline

ole'oso *adj* oily

ol'fatto *nm* sense of smell

oli'are *vt* oil

olia'tore *nm* oilcan

oli'era *nf* cruet

Olim'piadi *nfpl* Olympic games, Olympics

o'limpico *adj* Olympic

olim'pionico *adj* ⟨primato, squadra⟩ Olympic; **costume** ~ Olympic swimming costume

+olino *suff* **bestiolina** *nf* (affettuoso) little creature; **macchiolina** *nf* spot; **pesciolino** *nm* little fish; **risolino** *nm* giggle; **sassolino** *nm* pebble; **strisciolina** *nf* thin strip; **magrolino** *adj* skinny

'olio *nm* oil; **sott'**~ in oil; **colori a** ~ oils; **quadro a** ~ oil painting. **olio [di semi] di arachidi** groundnut oil. **olio essenziale** essential oil. **olio extravergine di oliva** extra-virgin olive oil. **olio di fegato di merluzzo** cod-liver oil. **olio di gomito** elbow grease. **olio lubrificante** lubricating oil. **olio di mais** corn oil. **olio minerale** mineral oil. **olio [del] motore** engine oil. **olio d'oliva** olive oil. **olio di semi** vegetable oil. **olio [di semi] di lino** linseed oil. **olio solare** suntan oil. **olio [di semi] di vinaccioli** grapeseed oil

o'liva *nf* olive

oli'vastro *adj* olive

oli'veto *nm* olive grove

oli'vetta *nf* toggle

o'livo *nm* olive tree

'olmo *nm* elm

olo'causto *nm* holocaust; **l'Olocausto** the Holocaust

o'lografo *adj* holograph

olo'gramma *nm* hologram

oltraggi'are *vt* offend

ol'traggio *nm* offence. **oltraggio al pudore** Jur gross indecency

oltraggi'oso *adj* offensive

ol'tranza *nf* **ad** ~ to the bitter end

'oltre ① *adv* (di luogo) further; (di tempo) longer

② *prep* (nello spazio) beyond; (di tempo) later than; (più di) more than; (in aggiunta) besides; ~ **a** (eccetto) except, apart from; **per** ~ **due settimane** for more than two weeks; **una settimana e** ~ a week and more

oltrecon'fine *adj* cross-border

oltre'mare *adv* overseas

oltre'modo *adv* extremely

oltrepas'sare *vt* go beyond; (eccedere) exceed; **oltrepassi il semaforo** go past the traffic lights; ~ **il limite di velocità** break the speed limit; **'non** ~**'** 'no trespassing'

OM *abbr* Radio (**onde medie**) MW

omacci'one *nm* bruiser

o'maggio *nm* homage; (dono) gift; **in** ~ **con** free with. **omaggi** *pl* (saluti) respects

'Oman *nm* Oman

ombeli'cale *adj* umbilical; **cordone ombelicale** umbilical cord

ombe'lico *nm* navel

'ombra *nf* (zona) shade; (immagine oscura) shadow; **all'**~ in the shade

ombreggi'are *vt* shade

ombreggia'ture *nfpl* shading

om'brello *nm* umbrella

ombrel'lone *nm* beach umbrella

om'bretto *nm* eye-shadow

om'broso *adj* shady; ⟨cavallo⟩ skittish; ⟨persona⟩ touchy

ome'lette *nf inv* omelette

ome'lia *nf* Relig sermon

omeopa'tia *nf* homeopathy

omeo'patico ① *adj* homeopathic ② *nm* homeopath

omertà *nf* conspiracy of silence

o'messo pp di OMETTERE

o'mettere *vt* omit

'OMG *nm abbr* (**Organismo Modificato Geneticamente**) GMO

omi'cida ① *adj* murderous, homicidal ② *nmf* murderer

omi'cidio *nm* murder. **omicidio colposo** manslaughter. **omicidio di massa** mass murder. **omicidio volontario** Jur culpable homicide

omissi'one *nf* omission

'omnibus *nm inv* omnibus

omofo'bia *nf* homophobia

omogeneiz'zare *vt* homogenize

omogeneiz'zato *adj* homogenized

omo'geneo *adj* homogeneous

o'mografo *nm* homograph

omolo'gare *vt* approve; **fare** ~ **un testamento** prove a will

omologazi'one *nf* probate

o'monimo, -a ① *nmf* namesake ② *nm* (parola) homonym ③ *adj* of the same name

omosessu'ale *adj & nmf* homosexual

omosessualità *nf* homosexuality

'OMS *nf abbr* (**Organizzazione Mondiale della Sanità**) WHO

On. *abbr* (**onorevole**) MP, Hon.

'oncia *nf* ounce. **oncia fluida** fluid ounce

'onda *nf* wave; **andare in** ~ TV, Radio go on the air; **seguire l'**~ go with the crowd; **onde** *pl* **corte** short wave; **onde** *pl* **lunghe** long wave. **onda di maremoto** tidal ⋯⟶

wave; **onde** *pl* **medie** medium wave; **onde**
pl **radio** radio waves. **onda d'urto** shock
wave

on'data *nf* wave; **a ondate** in waves.
ondata di freddo cold snap

'onde *conj* fml so that

ondeggi'are *vi* wave; ⟨*barca*⟩ roll

ondu'lato *adj* wavy

ondula'torio *adj* undulating

ondulazi'one *nf* undulation; (di capelli)
wave

+one *suff* **cucchiaione** *nm* big spoon;
gattone *nm* fat cat; **bacione** *nm* smacker;
bacioni *pl* (in lettera) love and kisses;
omone *nm* big guy; **nasone** *nm* big nose;
nebbione *nm* dense fog, peasouper *fam*;
simpaticone *nm* very friendly person;
lumacone *nm* slowcoach; **testone** *nm*
mule; **facilone** *nm* pej over-casual sort of
person; **grassone** *nm* pej fat slob; **pigrone**
nm lazy-bones *sg*; **chiacchierone** *nm*
chatterbox; **criticone** *nm* nit-picker;
pasticcione *nm* bungler

'onere *nm* burden

oner'oso *adj* onerous

onestà *nf* honesty; (rettitudine) integrity,
honesty

o'nesto *adj* honest; (giusto) just

'ONG *nf abbr* (**organizzazione non
governativa**) non-governmental
organization

'onice *nf* onyx

o'nirico *adj* dream *attrib*

o'nisco *nm* slater

ONLUS *nf abbr* (**organizzazione non
lucrativa di utilità sociale**) non-profit
organization

onnipo'tente *adj* omnipotent

onnipre'sente *adj* ubiquitous; Rel
omnipresent

onnisci'ente *adj* omniscient

ono'mastico *nm* name day

onomato'pea *nf* onomatopoeia

onomato'peico *adj* onomatopoeic

ono'rabile *adj* honourable

ono'rare *vt* (fare onore a) be a credit to;
honour ⟨*promessa*⟩

ono'rario ① *adj* honorary
② *nm* fee

ono'rarsi *vr* ~ **di** be proud of

ono'rato *adj* ⟨*famiglia, professione*⟩
respectable; **considerarsi** ~ **da qualcosa**
consider oneself honoured by something;
l'onorata società *nf* the Mafia

o'nore *nm* honour; **in** ~ **di** ⟨*festa,
ricevimento*⟩ in honour of; **fare** ~ **a** do
justice to ⟨*pranzo*⟩; **farsi** ~ in excel in; **a
onor del vero** to tell the truth; **fare gli
onori di casa** do the honours

ono'revole ① *adj* honourable
② *nmf* Member of Parliament

onorifi'cenza *nf* honour; (decorazione)
decoration

ono'rifico *adj* honorary

'onta *nf* shame

on'tano *nm* alder

'O.N.U. *nf abbr* (**Organizzazione delle
Nazioni Unite**) UN

opacità *nf* opaqueness, opacity

o'paco *adj* opaque; ⟨*colori ecc*⟩ dull;
⟨*fotografia, rossetto*⟩ matt

o'pale *nf* opal

'OPEC *nf* Opec, OPEC

'opera *nf* (lavoro) work; (azione) deed; Mus
opera; (teatro) opera house; (ente)
institution; **mettere in** ~ put into effect;
mettersi all'~ get to work. **opera d'arte**
work of art. **opera lirica** opera; **opere** *pl*
pubbliche public works

ope'rabile *adj* operable

ope'raio, -a ① *adj* working
② *nmf* worker. **operaio edile** building
worker. **operaio specializzato** skilled
worker

ope'rare ① *vt* Med operate on; ~
qualcuno al cuore operate on somebody's
heart; **farsi** ~ have an operation
② *vi* operate; (agire) work

opera'tivo, **operatorio** *adj* operating
attrib

opera|'tore, -trice *nmf* operator; TV
cameraman. **operatore ecologico**
refuse collector. **operatore sanitario**
health worker. **operatore turistico**
tour operator

operazi'one *nf* operation; Comm
transaction. **operazione antidroga**
anti-drug operation; **operazioni** *pl* **di
soccorso** rescue operations. **operazione
d'urgenza** emergency operation

ope'retta *nf* operetta

ope'roso *adj* industrious

opini'one *nf* opinion; **rimanere della
propria** ~ still feel the same way.
opinione pubblica public opinion, vox
pop

oplà *int* oops

o'possum *nm inv* possum

'oppio *nm* opium

oppo'nente ① *adj* opposing
② *nmf* opponent

op'porre *vt* oppose; (obiettare) object; ~
resistenza offer resistance

op'porsi *vr* ~ **a** oppose

opportu'nismo *nm* expediency

opportu'nista *nmf* opportunist

opportunità *nf inv* opportunity; (l'essere
opportuno) timeliness; **avere il senso dell'**~
have a sense of what is appropriate

oppor'tuno *adj* opportune; (adeguato)
appropriate; **ritenere** ~ **fare qualcosa**

think it appropriate to do something; **il momento** $\sim$ the right moment

opposi'tore *nm* opposer

opposizi'one *nf* opposition; **d'**$\sim$ ⟨*giornale, partito*⟩ opposition *attrib*; **in** $\sim$ in opposition

op'posto ① *pp di* OPPORRE
② *adj* opposite; ⟨*opinioni*⟩ opposing
③ *nm* opposite; **all'**$\sim$ on the contrary

oppressi'one *nf* oppression

oppres'sivo *adj* oppressive

op'presso ① *pp di* OPPRIMERE
② *adj* oppressed

oppres'sore *nm* oppressor

oppri'mente *adj* oppressive

op'primere *vt* oppress; (gravare) weigh down

op'pure *conj* otherwise, or [else]; **lunedì** $\sim$ **martedì** Monday or Tuesday

ops *int* oops

op'tare *vi* $\sim$ **per** opt for

'optional *nm inv* optional extra

opu'lento *adj* opulent

opu'lenza *nf* opulence

o'puscolo *nm* booklet; (pubblicitario) brochure

opzio'nale *adj* optional

opzi'one *nf* option

'ora[1] *nf* time; (unità) hour; **di buon'**$\sim$ early; **che** $\sim$ **è?, che ore sono?** what time is it?; **a che** $\sim$**?** at what time?; **mezz'**$\sim$ half an hour; **a ore** ⟨*lavorare, pagare*⟩ by the hour; **50 km all'**$\sim$ 50 km an hour; **è** $\sim$ **di finirla!** that's enough now!; **a un'**$\sim$ **di macchina** one hour by car; **non vedo l'**$\sim$ **di vederti** I can't wait to see you; **fare le ore piccole** stay up until the small hours. $\sim$ **d'arrivo** arrival time. **ora di cena** dinnertime. **l'ora esatta** Teleph speaking clock. **ora legale** daylight saving time. **ora locale** local time. **ora di pranzo** lunchtime. **ora di punta, ore** *pl* **di punta** peak time; (per il traffico) rush hour. **ora solare** Greenwich Mean Time, GMT. **ora zero** Mil, fig zero hour

ora[2] ① *adv* now; (tra poco) presently; $\sim$ **come** $\sim$ just now, at the moment; **d'**$\sim$ **in poi** from now on; **per** $\sim$ for the time being, for now;
② *conj* (dunque) now [then]; $\sim$ **che ci penso,...** now that I [come to] think about it...

o'racolo *nm* oracle

'orafo *nm* goldsmith

o'rale *adj & nm* oral; **per via** $\sim$ by mouth

ora'mai *adv* = ORMAI

o'rario ① *adj* ⟨*tariffa*⟩ hourly; ⟨*segnale*⟩ time *attrib*; ⟨*velocità*⟩ per hour; **in senso** $\sim$ clockwise
② *nm* time; (tabella dell'orario) timetable, schedule Am; **essere in** $\sim$ be on time;

partire in $\sim$ leave on time; **lavorare fuori** $\sim$ work outside normal hours. **orario di apertura** opening hours *pl*. **orario di chiusura** closing time. **orario estivo** summer timetable. **orario ferroviario** railway timetable, railroad schedule Am. **orario flessibile** flexitime. **orario invernale** winter timetable. **orario di lavoro** working hours *pl*. **orario degli spettacoli** performance times *pl*. **orario di sportello** banking hours *pl*. **orario d'ufficio** business hours *pl*. **orario di visita** visiting hours *pl*, visiting time; (del medico) consulting hours *pl*. **orario di volo** flight time

o'rata *nf* gilthead

ora||'tore, -trice *nmf* orator; (conferenziere) speaker

ora'torio, -a ① *adj* oratorical
② *nm* Mus oratorio
③ *nmf* oratory

orazi'one *nf* Relig prayer

'orbita *nf* orbit; Anat [eye-]socket

'Orcadi *nfpl* Orkneys

or'chestra *nf* orchestra; (parte del teatro) pit. **orchestra da camera** chamber orchestra. **orchestra sinfonica** symphony orchestra

orche'strale ① *adj* orchestral
② *nmf* member of an/the orchestra

orche'strare *vt* orchestrate

orchi'dea *nf* orchid

'orco *nm* ogre

'orda *nf* horde

or'digno *nm* device; (arnese) tool. **ordigno esplosivo** explosive device. **ordigno incendiario** incendiary device, firebomb

ordi'nale *adj & nm* ordinal

ordina'mento *nm* order; (leggi) rules *pl*

ordi'nanza *nf* (del sindaco) bylaw; **d'**$\sim$ ⟨*soldato*⟩ on duty

ordi'nare *vt* (sistemare) arrange; (comandare) order; (prescrivere) prescribe; Relig ordain

ordi'nario ① *adj* ordinary; (grossolano) common; ⟨*professore*⟩ with a permanent position; **di ordinaria amministrazione** routine
② *nm* ordinary; Univ professor; **fuori dell'**$\sim$ out of the ordinary

ordi'nato *adj* (in ordine) tidy

ordinazi'one *nf* order; **fare un'**$\sim$ place an order

'ordine *nm* order; (di avvocati, medici) association; **mettere in** $\sim$ put in order; tidy up ⟨*appartamento ecc*⟩; **di prim'**$\sim$ first-class; **di terz'**$\sim$ ⟨*film, albergo*⟩ third-rate; **di** $\sim$ **pratico/economico** ⟨*problema*⟩ of a practical/economic nature; **fino a nuovo** $\sim$ until further notice; **parola d'ordine** password. **ordine di acquisto** ···>

Comm purchase order. **ordine del giorno** agenda. **ordine di pagamento** banker's order. **ordine permanente** Fin standing order. **ordine pubblico** law and order. **ordini** *pl* **sacri** Holy Orders

or'dire *vt* (tramare) plot

orecchi'ette *nfpl* small pasta shells

orec'chino *nm* ear-ring; **orecchini** *pl* **con le clip** clip-ons

o'recchio *nm* (pl nf **orecchie**) ear; **avere** ∼ have a good ear; **esser duro d'**∼ be hard of hearing; **mi è giunto all'**∼ **che...** I've heard that...; **parlare all'**∼ **a qualcuno** whisper in somebody's ear; **suonare a** ∼ play by ear

orecchi'oni *nmpl* Med mumps *sg*

o'refice *nm* jeweller

orefice'ria *nf* (arte) goldsmith's art; (negozio) goldsmith's [shop]

'orfano, -a ① *adj* orphan ② *nmf* orphan

orfano'trofio *nm* orphanage

orga'netto *nm* barrel-organ; (a bocca) mouth-organ; (fisarmonica) accordion

or'ganico ① *adj* organic ② *nm* personnel

orga'nino *nm* hurdy-gurdy

orga'nismo *nm* organism; (corpo umano) body

orga'nista *nmf* organist

organizza'|tore, -trice *nmf* organizer

organiz'zare *vt* organize

organiz'zarsi *vr* get organized

organizza'tivo *adj* organizational

organizzazi'one *nf* organization. **organizzazione del servizio d'ordine** policing. **organizzazione studentesca** student union. **organizzazione umanitaria** relief agency, aid agency

'organo *nm* organ

or'gasmo *nm* orgasm; fig agitation

'orgia *nf* orgy

or'goglio *nm* pride

orgogli'oso *adj* proud

orien'tale *adj* eastern; (cinese ecc) oriental

orienta'mento *nm* orientation; **perdere l'**∼ lose one's bearings; **senso dell'**∼ sense of direction. **orientamento professionale** careers guidance. **orientamento scolastico** educational guidance

orien'tare *vt* orientate

orien'tarsi *vr* find one's bearings; (tendere) tend

ori'ente *nm* east. **l'Estremo Oriente** the Far East. **il Medio Oriente** the Middle East

orien'teering *nm* orienteering

o'rigano *nm* oregano

origi'nale ① *adj* original; (eccentrico) odd ② *nm* original

originalità *nf* originality

origi'nare *vt/i* originate

origi'nario *adj* (nativo) native

o'rigine *nf* origin; **in** ∼ originally; **aver** ∼ **da** originate from; **dare** ∼ **a** give rise to

origli'are *vi* eavesdrop

o'rina *nf* urine

ori'nale *nm* chamber-pot

ori'nare *vi* urinate

ori'undo *adj* native

orizzon'tale *adj* horizontal

orizzon'tare *vt* = ORIENTARE

oriz'zonte *nm* horizon

or'lare *vt* hem

orla'tura *nf* hem

'orlo *nm* edge; (di vestito ecc) hem

'orma *nf* track; (di piede) footprint; (impronta) mark

or'mai *adv* by now; (passato) by then; (quasi) almost

ormegg'iare *vt* moor

or'meggio *nm* mooring

ormo'nale *adj* hormonal

or'mone *nm* hormone

ornamen'tale *adj* ornamental

orna'mento *nm* ornament; **d'**∼ ⟨oggetto⟩ ornamental

or'nare *vt* decorate

or'narsi *vr* deck oneself

or'nato *adj* ⟨stile⟩ ornate

ornitolo'gia *nf* ornithology

orni'tologo, -a *nmf* ornithologist

ornito'rinco *nm* platypus

'oro *nm* gold; **d'**∼ gold; fig golden; **una persona d'**∼ a wonderful person. **oro nero** black gold

orologe'ria *nf* watchmaker

orologi'aio, -a *nmf* clockmaker, watchmaker

oro'logio *nm* (da polso, tasca) watch; (da tavolo, muro ecc) clock. **orologio biologico** biological clock. **orologio a carica automatica** self-winding watch. **orologio a cucù** cuckoo clock. **orologio digitale** digital clock. **orologio a pendolo** grandfather clock. **orologio da polso** wristwatch. **orologio al quarzo** quartz watch. **orologio a sveglia** alarm clock

o'roscopo *nm* horoscope

or'rendo *adj* awful, dreadful

or'ribile *adj* horrible

orribil'mente *adv* horribly

orripi'lante *adj* horrifying

or'rore *nm* horror; **avere qualcosa in** ∼ hate something; ∼**!** heck!; **film/romanzo dell'orrore** horror film/story

orsacchi'otto *nm* teddy bear

or'setto *nm* **orsetto lavatore** raccoon

'orso *nm* bear; (persona scontrosa) hermit. **orso bianco** polar bear. **orso bruno** brown bear

orsù *int* come now!

or'taggio *nm* vegetable

or'tensia *nf* hydrangea

or'tica *nf* nettle; **buttare qualcosa alle ortiche** fig fam chuck in

orti'caria *nf* nettle rash

orticol'tura *nf* horticulture

'orto *nm* vegetable plot

orto'dontico *adj* orthodontic

ortodon'zia *nf* orthodontics

ortodos'sia *nf* conformity

orto'dosso *adj* orthodox

ortofrut'ticolo *adj* **mercato ortofrutticolo** fruit and vegetable market

ortofrutticol'tore *nm* market gardener, truck farmer *Am*

ortofrutticol'tura *nf* market gardening

ortogo'nale *adj* perpendicular

ortogra'fia *nf* spelling

orto'grafico *adj* spelling *attrib*

orto'lano *nm* market gardener, truck farmer *Am*; (negozio) greengrocer's

ortope'dia *nf* orthopaedics

orto'pedico ① *adj* orthopaedic ② *nm* orthopaedic specialist

orzai'olo *nm* sty

or'zata *nf* barley-water

'orzo *nm* barley. **orzo perlato** pearl barley

osan'nato *adj* (esaltato) praised to the skies

o'sare *vt/i* dare; (avere audacia) be daring

oscenità *nf inv* obscenity

o'sceno *adj* obscene

oscil'lare *vi* swing; (prezzi ecc) fluctuate; Tech oscillate; (fig: essere indeciso) vacillate

oscillazi'one *nf* swinging; (di prezzi) fluctuation; Tech oscillation

oscura'mento *nm* darkening; (fig: di vista, mente) dimming; (totale) black-out

oscu'rare *vt* darken; fig obscure

oscu'rarsi *vr* get dark

oscurità *nf* darkness; (incomprensibilità) obscurity; **uscire dall'**∼ fig emerge from obscurity; **morire nell'**∼ fig die in obscurity

o'scuro *adj* dark; (triste) gloomy; (incomprensibile) obscure

o'smosi *nf* osmosis

ospe'dale *nm* hospital. **ospedale universitario** teaching hospital

ospedali'ero *adj* hospital *attrib*

ospi'tale *adj* hospitable

ospitalità *nf* hospitality; **non voglio abusare della tua** ∼ I don't want to outstay my welcome

ospi'tare *vt* give hospitality to

'ospite ① *nm* (chi ospita) host; (chi viene ospitato) guest ② *nf* hostess; guest

o'spizio *nm* (per anziani) [old people's] home

ossa'tura *nf* bone structure; (di romanzo) structure, framework

'osseo *adj* bone *attrib*

osse'quente *adj* deferential; ∼ **alla legge** law-abiding

ossequi'are *vt* pay one's respects to

os'sequio *nm* homage; **ossequi** *pl* respects

ossequi'oso *adj* obsequious

osser'vabile *adj* observable

osser'vante *adj* (cattolico) practising

osser'vanza *nf* observance

osser'vare *vt* observe; (notare) notice; keep (ordine, silenzio)

osserva|'tore, -trice *nmf* observer

osserva'torio *nm* Astr observatory; Mil observation post

osservazi'one *nf* observation; (rimprovero) reproach

ossessio'nante *adj* haunting; (persona) nagging

ossessio'nare *vt* obsess; (infastidire) nag

ossessi'one *nf* obsession; (assillo) pain in the neck

osses'sivo *adj* obsessive; (paura) neurotic

os'sesso *adj* obsessed

os'sia *conj* that is

ossi'dabile *adj* liable to tarnish

ossi'dante *adj* tarnishing

ossi'dare *vt* oxidize

ossi'darsi *vr* oxidize

'ossido *nm* oxide. **ossido di carbonio** carbon monoxide. **ossido di zinco** zinc oxide

os'sidrico *adj* **fiamma ossidrica** blowlamp

ossige'nare *vt* oxygenate; (decolorare) bleach

ossige'narsi *vr* put back on its feet (azienda); ∼ **i capelli** dye one's hair blonde

os'sigeno *nm* oxygen

'osso *nm* (Anat pl *nf* ossa) bone; **senz'**∼ boneless. **osso mascellare** jawbone

osso'buco *nm* marrowbone

os'suto *adj* bony

ostaco'lare *vt* hinder, obstruct

ostaco'lista *nmf* hurdler

o'stacolo *nm* obstacle; Sport hurdle

o'staggio *nm* hostage; **prendere in** ∼ take hostage

o'stello *nm* **ostello della gioventù** youth hostel

osten'tare *vt* show off; ∼ **indifferenza** pretend to be indifferent

ostentata'mente *adv* ostentatiously

ostentazi'one *nf* ostentation

osteopo'rosi *nf inv* osteoporosis

oste'ria *nf* inn

oste'tricia *nf* obstetrics

o'stetrico, -a ① *adj* obstetric ② *nmf* obstetrician

'ostia *nf* host; (cialda) wafer

'ostico *adj* tough

o'stile *adj* hostile

ostilità *nf inv* hostility

osti'narsi *vr* ∼ persist (**a** in)

osti'nato *adj* obstinate

ostinazi'one *nf* obstinacy

ostra'cismo *nm* ostracism

'ostrica *nf* oyster

ostro'goto *nm* **parlare** ∼ talk double Dutch

ostru'ire *vt* obstruct

ostruzi'one *nf* obstruction

ostruzio'nismo *nm* obstructionism; Sport obstruction. **ostruzionismo sindacale** work-to-rule

oto'rino *nm* ear, nose and throat *attrib*

otorinolaringoi'atra *nmf* ear, nose and throat specialist

'otre *nm* leather bottle

ottago'nale *adj* octagonal

ot'tagono *nm* octagon

ot'tanta *adj & nm* eighty

ottan'tenne *adj & nmf* eighty-year-old

ottan'tesimo *adj & nm* eightieth

ottan'tina *nf* about eighty

ot'tava *nf* octave

ot'tavo *adj & nm* eighth

otte'nere *vt* obtain; (più comune) get; (conseguire) achieve

ot'tetto *nm* Mus octet

'ottico, -a ① *adj* optic[al] ② *nmf* optician ③ *nf* (scienza) optics *sg*; (di lenti ecc) optics *pl*

otti'male *adj* optimum

ottima'mente *adv* very well

otti'mismo *nm* optimism

otti'mista *nmf* optimist

otti'mistico *adj* optimistic

ottimiz'zare *vt* optimize

'ottimo ① *adj* very good ② *nm* optimum; **essere all'**∼ **della forma** be on top form

'otto *adj & nm* eight

+otto *suff* **bassotto** *adj* (piuttosto basso) quite short; **contadinotto** *nm* pej (semplicotto) country bumpkin; **paesotto** *nm* hamlet; **leprotto** *nm* leveret; (affettuoso) baby hare; **pienotto** *adj* ⟨viso⟩ chubby

ot'tobre *nm* October

otto'cento *adj & nm* eight hundred; **l'Ottocento** the nineteenth century

ot'tone *nm* brass; **gli ottoni** Mus the brass

ottuage'nario, -a *adj & nmf* octogenarian

ot'tundere *vt* blunt

ottu'rare *vt* block; fill ⟨dente⟩

ottu'rarsi *vr* clog

ottura'tore *nm* Phot shutter

otturazi'one *nf* stopping; (di dente) filling

ot'tuso ① *pp di* OTTUNDERE ② *adj* obtuse

ouver'ture *nf inv* overture

o'vaia *nf* ovary

o'vale *adj & nm* oval

o'vatta *nf* cotton wool, absorbent cotton Am

ovat'tato *adj* ⟨suono, passi⟩ muffled

ovazi'one *nf* ovation

'ove *adv* liter where

over'dose *nf inv* overdose

'overdrive *nm inv* Auto overdrive

'ovest *nm* west

o'vile *nm* sheep-fold, pen

o'vino *adj* sheep *attrib*

ovoi'dale *adj* egg-shaped

ovo'via *nf* two-seater cable car

ovulazi'one *nf* ovulation

o'vunque *adv* = DOVUNQUE

ov'vero *conj* or; (cioè) that is

ovvia'mente *adv* obviously

ovvi'are *vi* ∼ **a qualcosa** counter something

'ovvio *adj* obvious

ozi'are *vi* laze around

'ozio *nm* idleness; **stare in** ∼ idle about

ozi'oso *adj* idle; ⟨questione⟩ pointless

o'zono *nm* ozone; **buco nell'ozono** hole in the ozone layer

Pp

pacare *vt* calm

paca'tezza *nf* calm[ness]

pa'cato *adj* calm

'pacca *nf* slap

pac'chetto *nm* packet; (postale) parcel, package; (di sigarette) pack, packet. **pacchetto informativo** information pack. **pacchetto integrato** Comput integrated package. **pacchetto software** software package

'pacchia *nf* (fam: situazione) bed of roses

pacchia'nata *nf* è una ∼ it's so garish

pacchi'ano *adj* garish

'pacco *nm* parcel; (involto) bundle; **disfare un** ∼ unwrap a parcel; **fare un** ∼ make up a parcel; **pacchi** *pl* **postali** parcels, packages. **pacco bomba** parcel bomb. **pacco regalo** gift-wrapped package; **le faccio un** ∼ **regalo?** would you like it gift-wrapped?. **pacco umanitario** aid package

paccot'tiglia *nf* (roba scadente) junk, rubbish

'pace *nf* peace; **darsi** ∼ forget it; **fare** ∼ **con qualcuno** make it up with somebody; **lasciare in** ∼ **qualcuno** leave somebody in peace; **mettere** ∼ **fra** pacify, make [the] peace between; **andate in** ∼ Relig peace be with you; **in tempo di** ∼ in peacetime; **del tempo di** ∼ peacetime; **di** ∼ ⟨milizia⟩ peacekeeping; **firmare la** ∼ sign a peace treaty; **per amor di** ∼ for a quiet life

pace-'maker *nm inv* (apparecchio) pacemaker

pachi'derma *nm* (animale) pachyderm; fig thick-skinned person

pachi'stano, -a *nmf & adj* Pakistani

paci'ere *nm* peacemaker

pacifi'care *vt* reconcile; (mettere pace) pacify

pacificazi'one *nf* reconciliation

pa'cifico ① *adj* pacific; (calmo) peaceful; **è** ∼ **che...** (comunemente accettato) it is clear that...
② *nm* **il Pacifico** the Pacific

paci'fismo *nm* pacifism

paci'fista *adj & nmf* pacifist

pacioc'cone, -a *nmf* fam chubby-chops

paci'ugo *nm* (poltiglia) mush

pa'dano *adj* **pianura padana** Po Valley

pa'della *nf* frying-pan; (per malati) bedpan; **cuocere in** ∼ fry; **dalla** ∼ **alla brace** out of the frying pan into the fire

padel'lata *nf* **una** ∼ **di** a frying-panful of

padigli'one *nm* pavilion. **padiglione auricolare** auricle

'Padova *nf* Padua

'padre *nm* father; **padri** *pl* (antenati) forefathers; **i padri della chiesa** the Church Fathers; **di** ∼ **in figlio** from father to son. **padre adottivo** (marito della madre) stepfather. **padre di famiglia** father, paterfamilias; **sono** ∼ **di famiglia** I have a family to look after. **padre spirituale** spiritual father

padre'nostro *nm* **il** ∼ the Lord's Prayer

padre'terno *nm* God Almighty

pa'drino *nm* godfather; ∼ **e madrina** godparents

padro'nale *adj* principal

padro'nanza *nf* mastery. **padronanza di sé** self-control

pa'drone, -a *nmf* master; mistress; (datore di lavoro) boss; (proprietario) owner. **padrone di casa** (di inquilini) landlord; landlady; (in ricevimento) master of the house; lady of the house

padroneggi'are *vt* master

padro'nesco *adj* domineering

padro'nissimo *adj* **essere** ∼ **di fare qualcosa** be quite at liberty to do something

pae'saggio *nm* scenery; (pittura) landscape. **paesaggio marino** seascape. **paesaggio montano** mountain landscape

paesag'gista *nmf* landscape architect

paesag'gistico *adj* landscape *attrib*

pae'sano, -a ① *adj* country *attrib* ② *nmf* villager

pa'ese *nm* (nazione) country; (territorio) land; (villaggio) village; **il Bel Paese** Italy; **va' a quel** ∼**!** get lost!; **il mio** ∼ **natio** where I was born; **Paesi** *pl* **Bassi** Netherlands; **paesi** *pl* **dell'est** Eastern Bloc countries

paf'futo *adj* plump

pag. *abbr* (**pagina**) p.

'paga *nf* pay, wages *pl*

pa'gabile *adj* payable

pa'gaia *nf* paddle

paga'mento *nm* payment; **a** ∼ ⟨parcheggio⟩ which you have to pay to use. **pagamento anticipato** Comm advance payment. **pagamento alla consegna** cash on delivery, COD. **pagamento pedaggio** toll

paga'nesimo *nm* paganism

pa'gano, -a *adj & nmf* pagan

pa'gante *nmf* payer

pa'gare *vt/i* pay; ~ **da bere a qualcuno** buy somebody a drink; **pagato in anticipo** prepaid, paid in advance; **te la faccio ~** you'll pay for this; **quanto pagherei per poter venire!** what I wouldn't give to be able to come!

pa'gella *nf* [school] report

pagg. *abbr* (**pagine**) pp.

pag'gio *nm* pageboy

'pagina *nf* page; **prima ~** *Journ* front page; ~ **economica** financial news, financial pages; **Pagine** *pl* **gialle®** Yellow Pages®. **pagina mastra** master page. **pagina web** *Comput* web page

pagi'none *nm* centrefold

'paglia *nf* straw. **paglia e fieno** *Culin* mixture of ordinary and green tagliatelle

pagliac'cesco *adj* farcical

pagliac'cetto *nm* (per bambini) rompers *pl*; (da donna) camiknickers

pagliac'ciata *nf* farce

pagli'accio *nm* clown; **fare il ~** act *or* play the clown

pagli'aio *nm* haystack

paglie'riccio *nm* straw mattress

pagli'etta *nf* (cappello) boater; (per pentole) steel wool

pagli'uzza *nf* wisp of straw; (di metallo) particle

pa'gnotta *nf* [round] loaf

'pago *adj* satisfied

pa'goda *nf* pagoda

pa'guro *nm* hermit crab

pail'lard *nf inv* slice of grilled veal

pail'lette *nf inv* sequin

'paio *nm* (pl *nf* **paia**) pair; **un ~** (circa due) a couple; **un ~ di** ‹*scarpe, forbici*› a pair of; **è un altro ~ di maniche** *fig* that's a different kettle of fish

pai'olo *nm* copper pot

'Pakistan *nm* Pakistan

paki'stano, -a *adj & nmf* Pakistani

'pala *nf* shovel; (di remo, elica) blade; (di ruota) paddle; (di mulino) blade, vane. **pala d'altare** altar piece. **pala da fornaio** shovel. **pala meccanica** mechanical digger

pala'dino *nm* paladin; *fig* champion

pala'fitta *nf* pile-dwelling

palan'drana *nf* (abito largo) big long coat

pala'sport *nm inv* indoor sports arena

pa'late *nfpl* **a ~** ‹*fare soldi*› hand over fist

pa'lato *nm* palate

palaz'zetto *nm* **palazzetto dello sport** indoor sports arena

palaz'zina *nf* villa

pa'lazzo *nm* palace; (edificio) building. ~ **comunale** town hall. **Palazzo Ducale** Doge's Palace. **palazzo delle esposizioni** exhibition centre. **palazzo di giustizia** law courts *pl*, courthouse. **palazzo dello sport** indoor sports arena

'palco *nm* (pedana) platform; *Theat* box; (palcoscenico) stage

palco'scenico *nm* stage

paleogra'fia *nf* palaeography

paleo'grafico *adj* palaeographical

pale'ografo, -a *nmf* palaeographer

paleo'litico *adj* palaeolithic

pale'sare *vt* disclose

pale'sarsi *vr* reveal oneself

pa'lese *adj* evident

Pale'stina *nf* Palestine

palesti'nese *adj & nmf* Palestinian

pa'lestra *nf* gymnasium, gym; (ginnastica) gymnastics *pl*

pa'letta *nf* spade; (per focolare) shovel. **paletta [della spazzatura]** dustpan

palet'tata *nf* shovelful

pa'letto *nm* peg

palin'sesto *nm* (documento) palimpsest; *TV* programme schedule

'palio *nm* (premio) prize; **il Palio** horse-race held at Siena

palis'sandro *nm* rosewood

paliz'zata *nf* fence

'palla *nf* ball; (proiettile) bullet; (fam: bugia) porkie; **prendere la ~ al balzo** seize an opportunity; **essere una ~** *sl* be a drag; **che palle!** *vulg* this is a pain in the arse!, what a drag!. **palla da biliardo** billiard ball. **palla medica** medicine ball. **palla di neve** snowball. **palla al piede** *fig* millstone round one's neck

pallaca'nestro *nf* basketball

palla-'goal *nf* **hanno avuto molte palle-goal** they had a lot of goal-scoring opportunities

palla'mano *nf* handball

pallanuo'tista *nmf* water polo player

pallanu'oto *nf* water polo

pallavo'lista *nmf* volleyball player

palla'volo *nf* volleyball

palleggi'are *vi* (calcio) practise ball control; *Tennis* knock up

pal'leggio *nm* *Sport* warm-up

'pallet *nm inv* pallet

pallet'toni *nmpl* buckshot

pallia'tivo *nm* palliative

'pallido *adj* pale; **non ne ho la più pallida idea** I don't have the faintest *or* foggiest idea

pal'lina *nf* (di vetro) marble

pal'lino *nm* avere il ∼ del calcio be crazy about football, be football crazy

pallon'cino *nm* balloon; (lanterna) Chinese lantern; (fam: etilometro) Breathalyzer®

pal'lone *nm* ball; (calcio) football; (aerostato) balloon; **essere/andare nel** ∼ be/become confused. **pallone da calcio** football. **pallone gonfiato: è un** ∼ **gonfiato** he's so puffed-up. **pallone sonda** weather balloon

pallo'netto *nm* lob

pal'lore *nm* pallor

pal'loso *adj* sl boring

pal'lottola *nf* pellet; (proiettile) bullet. **pallottola dum-dum** dumdum bullet

pallottoli'ere *nm* abacus

'palma *nf* Bot palm. **palma da cocco** coconut palm. **palma da datteri** date palm

palmarès *nm inv* (di festival) award winners *pl*; (fig: i migliori) top names *pl*

pal'mato *adj* ⟨piede⟩ webbed

pal'mento *nm* mangiava a quattro palmenti he was really tucking in

pal'meto *nm* palm grove

palmi'pede *nm* web-footed animal

'palmo *nm* Anat palm; (misura) hand's breadth; **restare con un** ∼ **di naso** feel disappointed

'palo *nm* pole; (di sostegno) stake; (in calcio) goalpost; **fare il** ∼ ⟨ladro⟩ keep a lookout. **palo d'arrivo** (in ippica) finishing post **palo della luce** lamppost. **palo di partenza** (in ippica) starting post

palom'baro *nm* diver

pa'lombo *nm* dogfish

pal'pare *vt* feel

pal'pata *nf* **dare una** ∼ **a qualcosa** give something a feel

'palpebra *nf* eyelid

palpeggi'are *vt* feel

palpi'tare *vi* throb; (fremere) quiver

palpitazi'one *nf* palpitation; **avere le palpitazioni** have palpitations

'palpito *nm* throb; (del cuore) beat

paltò *nm inv* overcoat

pa'lude *nf* marsh, swamp

palu'doso *adj* marshy

pa'lustre *adj* marshy; ⟨piante, uccelli⟩ marsh *attrib*

'pampas *nfpl* pampas

'pamphlet *nm inv* pamphlet

pamphlet'tista *nmf* pamphleteer

'pampino *nm* vine leaf

pan *nm* ▶ PANE

pana'cea *nf* panacea

pa'nache *nm inv* far ∼ (in ippica) fall

'Panama *nm* Panama; **il canale di** ∼ the Panama Canal

'panca *nf* bench; (in chiesa) pew

pancarré *nm* sliced bread

pan'cetta *nf* Culin bacon; (ciccia) paunch. **pancetta affumicata** smoked bacon

pan'chetto *nm* [foot]stool

pan'china *nf* garden seat; (in calcio) bench

'pancia *nf* belly, tummy fam; (di bottiglia, vaso) body; **mal di pancia** stomach-ache; **a** ∼ **piena/vuota** on a full/empty stomach; **metter su** ∼ develop a paunch; **a** ∼ **in giù** lying face down

panci'ata *nf* **prendere una** ∼ (in tuffo) do a belly flop

panci'era *nf* corset

panci'olle: stare in ∼ lounge about

panci'one *nm* (persona) pot belly

panci'otto *nm* waistcoat

panci'uto *adj* potbellied

'pancreas *nm inv* pancreas

pancre'atico *adj* pancreatic

'panda *nm inv* panda

pande'monio *nm* pandemonium

pan'dolce *nm* Christmas cake similar to panettone

pan'doro *nm* kind of sponge cake traditionally eaten at Christmas time

'pane *nm* bread; (pagnotta) loaf; (di burro) block. **pane casereccio** home-made bread. **pane a cassetta** sliced bread; **pan grattato** breadcrumbs *pl*. **pane integrale** wholemeal bread, granary bread. **pane nero** blackbread. **pane di segale** rye bread; **pan di Spagna** sponge cake. **pane tostato** toast

'panel *nm inv* (gruppo) panel

panette'ria *nf* bakery; (negozio) baker's [shop]

panetti'ere, -a *nmf* baker

panet'tone *nm* dome-shaped cake with sultanas and candied fruit eaten at Christmas

'panfilo *nm* yacht

pan'forte *nm* nougat-like spicy delicacy from Siena

'panico *nm* panic; **farsi prendere dal** ∼ panic

pani'ere *nm* basket; (cesta) hamper

pani'ficio *nm* bakery; (negozio) baker's [shop]

pani'naro, -a *nmf* preppie

pa'nino *nm* [bread] roll. **panino imbottito** filled roll. **panino al prosciutto** ham roll

panino'teca *nf* sandwich bar

'panna *nf* cream. **panna cotta** kind of creme caramel. **panna da cucina** ⋯⟫

[single] cream. **panna montata** whipped cream

'panne *nf* Mech **in** ∼ broken down; **restare in** ∼ break down

panneggi'ato *adj* draped

pan'neggio *nm* drapery

pan'nello *nm* panel. **pannello di controllo** control panel. **pannello solare** solar panel

'panno *nm* cloth; (di tavolo da gioco) baize; **panni** *pl* (abiti) clothes; **mettersi nei panni di qualcuno** fig put oneself in somebody's shoes

pan'nocchia *nf* (di granturco) cob

panno'lenci® *nm* brightly coloured felt

panno'lino *nm* (per bambini) nappy; (da donna) sanitary towel

pano'rama *nm* panorama; fig overview

pano'ramica *nf* (rassegna) overview

pano'ramico *adj* panoramic

panpe'pato *nm* type of gingerbread

pantacol'lant *nmpl* leggings

pantagru'elico *adj* ⟨pranzo⟩ gargantuan

pantalon'cini *nmpl* shorts. **pantaloncini da ciclista** cycling shorts. **pantaloncini corti** shorts

panta'loni *nmpl* trousers, pants Am. **pantaloni da sci** ski pants. **pantaloni della tuta** sweat pants. **pantaloni a tubo** drain-pipe trousers. **pantaloni a zampa d'elefante** bell-bottoms, flares

pan'tano *nm* bog

panta'noso *adj* marshy

pan'tera *nf* panther; (auto della polizia) high-speed police car. **pantera nera** black panther

pan'tofola *nf* slipper

pantofo'laio, -a *nmf* fig stay-at-home

panto'mima *nf* pantomime; fig act

pan'zana *nf* fib

'panzer *nm inv* Mil tank

pao'nazzo *adj* purple

'papa *nm* Pope; **a ogni morte di** ∼ fig once in a blue moon

papà *nm inv* dad[dy]

pa'paia *nf* pawpaw, papaya

pa'pale *adj* papal

papa'lina *nf* skull-cap

papa'razzo *nm* paparazzo

pa'pato *nm* papacy

pa'pavero *nm* poppy

'papera *nf* (errore) slip of the tongue

'papero *nm* gosling

pa'pilla *nf* **papilla gustativa** taste bud

papil'lon *nm inv* bow tie

pa'piro *nm* papyrus

'pappa *nf* (per bambini) baby food; **trovare la** ∼ **pronta** fig have everything ready and waiting

pappagal'lino *nm* budgerigar, budgie

pappa'gallo *nm* parrot

pappa'gorgia *nf* double chin

pappa'molle *nmf* wimp

pappar'delle *nfpl* strips of pasta usually served with a meat sauce

pap'parsi *vr* fam tuck away

pap'pone *nm* sl (mangione) pig; (sfruttatore) pimp

'paprica *nf* paprika

Pap test *nm inv* smear test

'Papua 'Nuova Gui'nea *nf* Papua New Guinea

'para *nf* **suole di** ∼ crepe soles

parà *nm inv* para

pa'rabola *nf* parable; (curva) parabola

para'bolico *adj* parabolic

para'brezza *nm inv* windscreen, windshield Am

paracadu'tare *vt* parachute

paracadu'tarsi *vr* parachute

paraca'dute *nm inv* parachute

paracadu'tismo *nm* parachuting. **paracadutismo ascensionale** parascending

paracadu'tista *nmf* parachutist

para'carro *nm* roadside post

para'digma *nm* Gram paradigm

paradi'siaco *adj* heavenly

para'diso *nm* paradise. **paradiso fiscale** tax haven. **paradiso terrestre** Eden, earthly paradise

parados'sale *adj* paradoxical

para'dosso *nm* paradox

para'fango *nm* mudguard

parafarma'cia *nf* over-the-counter products

paraf'fina *nf* paraffin

parafra'sare *vt* paraphrase

pa'rafrasi *nf inv* paraphrase

para'fulmine *nm* lightning conductor

para'fuoco *nm inv* fireguard

pa'raggi *nmpl* neighbourhood *sg*

parago'nabile *adj* comparable (**a** to)

parago'nare *vt* compare

parago'narsi *vr* compare oneself

para'gone *nm* comparison; **a** ∼ **di** in comparison with; **non c'è** ∼! there's no comparison!

paragra'fare *vt* paragraph

pa'ragrafo *nm* paragraph

paraguai'ano, -a *adj & nmf* Paraguyan

Paragu'ay *nm* Paraguay

pa'ralisi *nf inv* paralysis

para'litico, -a *adj & nmf* paralytic

paraliz'zante *adj* crippling

paraliz'zare *vt* paralyse

paraliz'zato *adj* (dalla paura) transfixed

paral'lela *nf* parallel line; è una ∼ di... ⟨*strada*⟩ it runs parallel to...; **parallele** *pl* parallel bars

parallela'mente *adv* in parallel

paralle'lismo *nm* parallelism

paral'lelo *adj & nm* parallel; **fare un** ∼ **tra** draw a parallel between

parallelo'gramma *nm* parallelogram

para'lume *nm* lampshade

para'medico *nm* paramedic

para'mento *nm* hangings *pl*

pa'rametro *nm* parameter

paramili'tare *adj* paramilitary

pa'ranco *nm* block and tackle

para'noia *nf* paranoia

para'noico, -a *adj & nmf* paranoid

paranor'male *adj & nm* paranormal

para'occhi *nmpl* blinkers

parao'recchie *nm inv* earmuffs

parapen'dio *nm* paragliding

para'petto *nm* parapet

para'piglia *nm* turmoil

para'plegico, -a *adj & nmf* paraplegic

pa'rare ① *vt* (addobbare) adorn; (riparare) shield; save ⟨*tiro, pallone*⟩; ward off, parry ⟨*schiaffo, pugno*⟩
② *vi* (mirare) lead up to

pa'rarsi *vr* (abbigliarsi) dress up; (da pioggia, pugni) protect oneself; ∼ **dinanzi a qualcuno** appear in front of somebody

parasco'lastico *adj* ⟨*attività*⟩ extracurricular

para'sole *nm inv* parasol

paras'sita ① *adj* parasitic
② *nm* parasite

parassi'tario *adj* anche fig parasitic

parassi'tismo *nm* parasitism

parasta'tale *adj* government-controlled

para'stinchi *nm inv* shinpad, shinguard

pa'rata *nf* parade; (in calcio) save; (in scherma, pugilato) parry. **parata aerea** flypast

para'tia *nf* bulkhead

parauniversi'tario *adj* at university level

para'urti *nm inv* Auto bumper, fender Am. **paraurti** *pl* **tubolari rigidi** bull bars

para'vento *nm inv* screen

par'boiled *adj* **riso parboiled** parboiled rice

par'cella *nf* bill

parcheggi'are *vt* anche fig park; ∼ **in doppia fila** double-park

parcheggia|'tore, -trice *nmf* parking attendant. **parcheggiatore abusivo** person who illegally earns money by looking after parked cars

par'cheggio *nm* parking; (posteggio) car park, parking lot Am. **parcheggio carta** Comput paper park. **parcheggio custodito** car park with attendant. **parcheggio incustodito** unattended car park. **parcheggio a pagamento** paying car park. **parcheggio sotterraneo** underground car park, underground parking garage Am

par'chimetro *nm* parking meter

'parco[1] *adj* sparing; (moderato) moderate; **essere** ∼ **nel mangiare** eat sparingly

'parco[2] *nm* park. **parco di divertimenti** fun fair. **parco giochi** playground. **parco macchine** Auto fleet of cars. **parco naturale** wildlife park. **parco nazionale** national park. **parco regionale** [regional] wildlife park

pa'recchio ① *adj* quite a lot of; **parecchi** *pl* several, quite a lot of
② *pron* quite a lot; **parecchi** *pl* several, quite a lot
③ *adv* rather; (parecchio tempo) quite a time

pareggi'are ① *vt* level; (eguagliare) equal; Comm balance; ∼ **il bilancio** balance the budget
② *vi* draw; **hanno pareggiato nel secondo tempo** they equalized in the second half

pa'reggio *nm* Comm balance; Sport draw; **il gol del** ∼ the equalizer

paren'tado *nm* relatives *pl*; (vincolo di sangue) relationship

pa'rente *nmf* relative, relation. **parente acquisito** relation by marriage. **parente alla lontana** distant relation. **parente stretto** close relation

paren'tela *nf* relatives *pl*; (vincolo di sangue) relationship; **grado di parentela** degree of kinship

pa'rentesi *nf inv* parenthesis; (segno grafico) bracket; (fig: pausa) break; **aprire una** ∼ fig digress; ∼ *pl* **graffe** curly brackets; ∼ *pl* **quadre** square brackets; **tra** ∼ **quadre** in square brackets; ∼ *pl* **tonde** round brackets; **fra** ∼,... (a proposito) by the way,...

pa'reo *nm* (copricostume) sarong; **a** ∼ ⟨*gonna*⟩ wrap-around

pa'rere[1] *nm* opinion; **a mio** ∼ **in my opinion; essere del** ∼ **che** be of the opinion that

pa'rere[2] *vi* seem; (pensare) think; **che te ne pare?** what do you think of it?; **pare di sì** it seems so; **mi pare che...** I think that...; **non mi par vero** I can't believe it; **mi pareva bene!** I thought as much!

pa'rete *nf* wall; (in alpinismo) face. **parete divisoria** partition wall

'pargolo *nf* liter child

'pari[1] *adj inv* equal; ⟨*numero*⟩ even; **andare di** ∼ **passo** keep pace; **essere** ∼ be even *or* quits; **arrivare** ∼ draw; ∼ ∼ ···÷

⟨*copiare, ripetere*⟩ word for word; **fare ∼ o dispari** toss a coin

2 *nmf inv* equal, peer; **ragazza alla ∼** au pair [girl]; **lavorare alla ∼** work [as an] au pair; **mettersi in ∼ con qualcosa** catch up with something

3 *nm* (titolo nobiliare) peer

'**paria** *nm inv* pariah

parifi'cato *adj* ⟨*scuola*⟩ state-recognized

Pa'rigi *nf* Paris

pari'gino, -a *adj & nmf* Parisian

pa'riglia *nf* pair; **rendere la ∼ a qualcuno** give somebody tit for tat

parità *nf* equality; Tennis deuce; **a ∼ di condizioni/voti** if all circumstances/the votes are equal; **finire in ∼** ⟨*partita*⟩ end in a draw. **parità dei diritti** equal rights. **parità monetaria** monetary parity. **parità dei sessi** sexual equality, equality of the sexes

pari'tario *adj* parity *attrib*

'**parka** *nm inv* parka

parlamen'tare 1 *adj* parliamentary
2 *nmf* Member of Parliament
3 *vi* negotiate

parla'mento *nm* Parliament; **il Parlamento europeo** the European Parliament

par'lante *adj* ⟨*bambola, pappagallo*⟩ talking

parlan'tina *nf* **avere la ∼** be a chatterbox

par'lare *vt/i* speak, talk; speak ⟨*inglese, italiano*⟩; (confessare) talk; **∼ bene/male di qualcuno** speak well/ill of somebody; **∼ da solo** speak to oneself; **chi parla?** Teleph who's speaking?; **senti chi parla!** look who's talking!; **non parliamone più** let's forget about it!; **non se ne parla nemmeno!** don't even mention it!; **∼ a braccio** speak off the top of one's head; **far ∼ qualcuno** make somebody talk

par'lato *adj* ⟨*lingua*⟩ spoken

parla|'tore, -trice *nmf* speaker

parla'torio *nm* parlour; (in prigione) visiting room

parlot'tare *vi* mutter

parlot'tio *nm* muttering

parlucchi'are *vt* speak a little, have a smattering of ⟨*lingua*⟩

parmigi'ano *nm* Parmesan

paro'dia *nf* parody, send-up; **fare la ∼ di qualcuno** take somebody off

parodi'are *vt* parody, mimic

paro'distico *adj* ⟨*tono*⟩ parodying; **programma parodistico** take-off show

pa'rola *nf* word; (facoltà) speech; **è una ∼!** it is easier said than done!; **parole** *pl* (di canzone) words, lyrics; **rivolgere la ∼ a** address; **passare ∼** spread the word; **non fare ∼ di qualcosa con nessuno** not breathe a word of something to anybody;

ti credo sulla ∼ I'll take your word for it; **togliere la ∼ di bocca a qualcuno** take the words [right] out of somebody's mouth; **voler sempre l'ultima ∼** always want to have the last word; **dire due parole a qualcuno** have a word *or* chat with somebody; **di poche parole** ⟨*persona*⟩ of few words; **dare a qualcuno la propria ∼** give somebody one's word; **∼ per ∼** word for word; **in parole povere** crudely speaking. **parola chiave** keyword; **parole** *pl* **incrociate** crossword [puzzle]. **parola di moda** buzzword. **parola d'onore** word of honour. **parola d'ordine** password

paro'laccia *nf* swearword

paro'liere *nm* lyricist

paro'lina *nf* **dire due paroline a qualcuno** have a word *or* chat with somebody

paro'loni *nmpl* mumbo jumbo

paros'sismo *nm* paroxysm

paros'sistico *adj* Med paroxysmal

par'quet *nm inv* (pavimento) parquet flooring

parri'cida *nmf* parricide

parri'cidio *nm* parricide

par'rocchia *nf* parish

parrocchi'ale *adj* parish *attrib*

parrocchi'ano, -a *nmf* parishioner

'**parroco** *nm* parish priest

par'rucca *nf* wig

parrucchi'ere, -a *nmf* hairdresser

parruc'chino *nm* toupée, hairpiece

parsi'monia *nf* thrift

parsimoni'oso *adj* thrifty

'**parso** *pp di* PARERE[2]

'**parte** *nf* part; (lato) side; (partito) party; (porzione) share; (fazione) group; **a ∼** apart from; **in ∼** in part; **la maggior ∼ di** the majority of; **d'altra ∼** on the other hand; **da ∼** aside; (in disparte) to one side; **farsi da ∼** stand aside; **da ∼ di** from; (per conto di) on behalf of; **è gentile da ∼ tua** it is kind of you; **fare una brutta ∼ a qualcuno** behave badly towards somebody; **da che ∼ è...?** whereabouts is...?; **da una parte..., dall'altra...** on the one hand..., on the other hand...; **dall'altra ∼ di** on the other side of; **da nessuna ∼** nowhere; **da qualche ∼** somewhere; **da qualche altra ∼** somewhere else, elsewhere; **da tutte le parti** (essere) everywhere; **da questa ∼** (in questa direzione) this way; **da queste parti** hereabouts; **da un anno a questa ∼** for about a year now; **mettere qualcosa da ∼** put something aside; **essere dalla ∼ di qualcuno** be on somebody's side; **prendere le parti di qualcuno** take somebody's side; **dalla ∼ della ragione/del torto** in the right/the wrong; **essere ∼ in causa** be involved; **fare ∼ di** (appartenere a) be a member of; **fare la propria ∼** do one's share *or* bit; **mettere qualcuno a ~ di qualcosa** inform somebody of something; **prendere ~ a qualcosa** take part in something. **parte civile** plaintiff. **parte del discorso** part of speech

parteci'pante *nmf* participant

parteci'pare *vi* **~ a** participate in, take part in; (condividere) share in

partecipazi'one *nf* participation; (annuncio) announcement; Fin shareholding; (presenza) presence; **con la ~ [straordinaria] di...** featuring.... **partecipazione statale** (quota) state interest

par'tecipe *adj* participating

parteggi'are *vi* **~ per** side with

par'tenza *nf* departure; Sport start; **in ~ per** leaving for; **falsa partenza** false start

parti'cella *nf* particle

parti'cina *nf* bit part

parti'cipio *nm* participle. **participio passato** past participle. **participio presente** present participle

partico'lare ⓵ *adj* particular; (privato) private; (speciale) special, particular ⓶ *nm* detail, particular; **fin nei minimi particolari** down to the smallest detail; **in ~** (particolarmente) in particular

particolareggi'ato *adj* detailed

particolarità *nf inv* particularity; (dettaglio) detail

particolar'mente *adv* particularly

partigi'ano, -a *adj & nmf* partisan

par'tire *vi* leave; (aver inizio) start; (fam: rompersi) break; **a ~ da** [beginning] from; **~ molto bene** get off to a flying start; **~ in quarta** go off at half cock; **è partito** (fam: ubriaco) he's away

par'tita *nf* game; (incontro) match; Comm lot; (contabilità) entry; **dare ~ vinta a qualcuno** fig give in to somebody. **partita amichevole** friendly [match]. **partita di calcio** football match. **partita a carte** game of cards. **partita doppia** Comm double-entry book keeping. **partita di ritorno** Sport return match, rematch. **partita semplice** Comm single-entry book keeping

parti'tario *nm* Comm ledger. **partitario vendite** sales ledger

par'tito *nm* party; (scelta) choice; (occasione di matrimonio) match; **per ~ preso** out of sheer pig-headedness. **partito di governo** governing party. **partito di maggioranza** majority party. **partito politico** political party

partitocra'zia *nf* concentration of power in the hands of political parties to the detriment of parliamentary democracy

partizi'one *nf* (divisione) division; (Comput: di disco) partition

'**partner** *nmf inv* (in affari, coppia) partner

'**parto** *nm* childbirth; **un ~ facile** an easy birth *or* labour; **dolori** *pl* **del ~** labour pains; **morire di ~** die in childbirth. **parto cesareo** Caesarean. **parto in acqua** water birth. **parto indolore** natural childbirth. **parto pilotato** induction, induced labour. **parto prematuro** premature birth

partori'ente *nf* woman in labour

parto'rire *vt* anche fig give birth to

part-'time ⓵ *adj* part-time ⓶ *nm* **chiedere il ~** ask to work part-time

pa'rure *nf inv* (di gioielli) set of jewellery; (di biancheria intima) set of matching lingerie

par'venza *nf* appearance

parzi'ale *adj* partial

parzialità *nf* partiality; **fare ~ per qualcuno** be biased towards somebody

parzial'mente *adv* partially; (con parzialità) with bias; **parzialmente cieco** partially sighted; **parzialmente scremato** semi-skimmed

'**pascere** ⓵ *vi* ‹mucche› graze ⓶ *vt* graze on (erba)

pasci'uto *adj* **ben ~** plump

pasco'lare *vt* graze

'**pascolo** *nm* pasture

'**Pasqua** *nf* Easter; **l'isola di Pasqua** Easter Island

pa'squale *adj* Easter *attrib*

pa'squetta *nf* (lunedì di Pasqua) Easter Monday

'**passa**: **e ~** *adv* (e oltre) plus

pas'sabile *adj* passable

pas'saggio *nm* passage; (traversata) crossing; Sport pass; (su veicolo) lift, ride; **essere di ~** be passing through; **è stato un ~ obbligato** fig it was something essential, it had to be done. **passaggio a livello** level crossing, grade crossing Am. **passaggio pedonale** pedestrian crossing, crosswalk Am. **passaggio di proprietà** transfer of ownership, conveyancy

passamane'ria *nf* braid

passamon'tagna *nm inv* balaclava

pas'sante ⓵ *nmf* passer-by ⓶ *nm* (di cintura) loop ⓷ *adj* Tennis passing

passa'porto *nm* anche fig passport. **passaporto europeo** European passport, Europassport

pas'sare ⓵ *vi* pass; (attraversare) pass through; (far visita) call; (andare) go; (essere approvato) be passed; **~ davanti a qualcuno** go in front of somebody; **~ alla storia** go down in history; **~ di moda** go out of fashion; **mi è passato di mente** it slipped my mind; **~ sopra a qualcosa** pass over something; **~ per un genio/idiota** be taken for a genius/an idiot; **farsi ~ per qualcuno** ⋯⊱

pass oneself off as somebody; **passo!** (nelle carte) pass!; (per radio) over!

2 *vt* (far scorrere) pass over; (sopportare) go through; (al telefono) put through; Culin strain; pass ⟨*esame, visita*⟩; ∼ **in rivista** review; ∼ **qualcosa a qualcuno** pass something to somebody; **le passo il signor Rossi** Teleph I'll put you through to Mr Rossi; ∼ **qualcosa su qualcosa** ⟨*crema, cera ecc*⟩ give something a coat of something; ∼ **il limite** go over the limit; **passarsela bene** be well off; **come te la passi?** how are you doing?

3 *nm* **col** ∼ **del tempo** with the passing *or* passage of time

pas'sata *nf* (di vernice) coat; (spolverata) dusting; (occhiata) look

passa'tempo *nm* pastime

pas'sato **1** *adj* past; **l'anno** ∼ last year; **sono le tre passate** it's past *or* after three o'clock

2 *nm* past; Culin purée; Gram past tense; **in** ∼ in the past; **la musica del** ∼ the music of yesteryear. **passato di moda** old-fashioned. **passato prossimo** present perfect. **passato remoto** [simple] past. **passato di verdure** cream of vegetable soup

passaver'dure *nm inv* food mill

passavi'vande *nm inv* serving hatch

passeg'gero, -a **1** *adj* passing **2** *nmf* passenger. **passeggero in transito** transit passenger

passeggi'are *vi* walk, stroll

passeg'giata *nf* walk, stroll; (luogo) public walk; (in bicicletta) ride; **fare una** ∼ go for a walk

passeggia'trice *nf* streetwalker

passeg'gino *nm* pushchair, stroller Am

pas'seggio *nm* walk; (luogo) promenade; **andare a** ∼ go for a walk; **scarpe da passeggio** walking shoes

passe-par'tout *nm inv* master-key

passe'rella *nf* gangway; Aeron boarding bridge; (per sfilate) catwalk

'passero *nm* sparrow

passe'rotto *nm* (passero) sparrow

pas'sibile *adj* ∼ **di** liable to

passio'nale *adj* passionate; **delitto passionale** crime of passion

passi'one *nf* passion; **avere la** ∼ **del gioco** have a passion for gambling

passiva'mente *adv* passively

passivi'tà *nf inv* (inerzia) passiveness, passivity; Fin liabilities *pl*; ∼ *pl* **correnti** current liabilities

pas'sivo **1** *adj* passive **2** *nm* passive; Fin liabilities *pl*; **in** ∼ ⟨*azienda*⟩ in deficit; ⟨*bilancio*⟩ debit, in deficit

'passo *nm* step; (orma) footprint; (andatura) pace, step; (di libro) passage; (valico) pass; **a**

due passi da qui a stone's throw away; **a** ∼ **d'uomo** at walking pace; **di buon** ∼ at a spanking pace, at a cracking pace; **a passi felpati** stealthily; **di questo** ∼ at this rate; ∼ ∼ step by step; **fare due passi** go for a stroll; **allungare il** ∼ quicken one's pace, step out; **tornare sui propri passi** retrace one's steps; **fare un** ∼ **avanti** anche fig take a step forward; **fare un** ∼ **falso** fig make a wrong move; **di pari** ∼ fig hand in hand; **stare al** ∼ **con i tempi** keep up with the times, keep abreast of the times; **tenere il** ∼ keep up. **passo carrabile**, **passo carraio** driveway. **passo dell'oca** goose-step

'pasta *nf* (impasto per pane ecc) dough; (per dolci, pasticcino) pastry; (pastasciutta) pasta; (massa molle) paste; fig nature; **sono fatti della stessa** ∼ they're birds of a feather. **pasta e fagioli** very thick soup with blended borlotti beans and small pasta. **pasta al forno** pasta baked in white sauce with grated cheese. **pasta frolla** shortcrust pastry. **pasta al ragù** pasta with Bolognese sauce

pastasci'utta *nf* pasta

pa'stella *nf* batter

pa'stello *nm* pastel

pa'sticca *nf* pastille; (fam: pastiglia) pill

pasticce'ria *nf* cake shop, patisserie; (pasticcini) pastries *pl*; (arte) confectionery

pasticci'are **1** *vi* make a mess **2** *vt* make a mess of

pasticci'ere, -a *nmf* confectioner

pastic'cino *nm* little cake

pa'sticcio *nm* Culin pie; (lavoro disordinato) mess; **mettersi nei pasticci** get into trouble

pasticci'one, -a **1** *nmf* bungler **2** *adj* bungling

pasti'ficio *nm* pasta factory

pa'stiglia *nf* Med pill, tablet; (di menta) sweet. **pastiglia dei freni** Auto brake pad. **pastiglia per la gola** throat pastille. **pastiglia per la tosse** cough sweet

pa'stina *nf* small pasta shape. **pastina in brodo** noodle soup

'pasto *nm* meal; **fuori** ∼ between meals; **dare qualcosa in** ∼ **a** fig serve something up on a platter to ⟨*pubblico, stampa*⟩. **pasto pronto** TV dinner

pa'stora *nf* shepherdess

pasto'rale *adj* pastoral

pa'store *nm* shepherd; Relig pastor, vicar. **pastore scozzese** collie. **pastore tedesco** German shepherd, Alsatian

pasto'rizio *adj* sheep farming *attrib*

pastoriz'zare *vt* pasteurize

pastoriz'zato *adj* pasteurized

pastorizzazi'one *nf* pasteurization

pa'stoso *adj* doughy; fig mellow

pa'strocchio *nm* mess

pa'stura *nf* pasture; (per pesci) bait

pa'tacca *nf* (macchia) stain; (fig: oggetto senza valore) piece of junk

pa'tata *nf* potato. **patata americana** sweet potato; **patate** *pl* **arrosto** roast potatoes; **patate** *pl* **al cartoccio** jacket potatoes; **patate** *pl* **fritte** chips Br, French fries; **patate** *pl* **in insalata** potato salad; **patate** *pl* **lesse** boiled potatoes

pata'tine *nfpl* [potato] crisps, [potato] chips Am

pata'trac *nm inv* (crollo) crash

patch'work *nm inv* patchwork

pâté *nm inv* pâté. **pâté di fegato** liver pâté

pa'tella *nf* limpet

pa'tema *nm* anxiety

pa'tente *nf* licence; **prendere la** ∼ get one's driving licence. **patente di guida** driving licence, driver's license Am

pater'nale *nf* scolding

paterna'lismo *nm* paternalism

paterna'lista *nm* paternalist

paterna'listico *adj* paternalistic

paternità *nf* paternity

pa'terno *adj* paternal; ⟨affetto ecc⟩ fatherly

pa'tetico *adj* pathetic; **cadere nel** ∼ become over-sentimental

'pathos *nm* pathos

pa'tibolo *nm* gallows *sg*

pati'mento *nm* suffering

'patina *nf* patina; (sulla lingua) coating

'patio *nm* patio garden

pa'tire *vt/i* suffer

pa'tito, -a ① *adj* suffering ② *nmf* fanatic. **patito della musica** music lover

patolo'gia *nf* pathology. **patologia da radiazioni** radiation sickness. **patologia da sforzo ripetuto** repetitive strain injury, RSI

pato'logico *adj* pathological

pa'tologo, -a *nmf* pathologist

'patria *nf* native land; **amor di** ∼ love of one's country

patri'arca *nm* patriarch

patriar'cale *adj* patriarchal

patriar'cato *nm* patriarchy

pa'trigno *nm* stepfather

patrimoni'ale *adj* property *attrib*

patri'monio *nm* estate

patri'ota *nmf* patriot

patri'ottico *adj* patriotic

patriot'tismo *nm* patriotism

pa'trizio, -a *adj & nmf* patrician

patroci'nante *adj* sponsoring

patroci'nare *vt* support

patro'cinio *nm* support; **sotto il** ∼ **di** under the sponsorship of; Jur defended by. **patrocinio gratuito** legal aid

patro'nato *nm* patronage

pa'trono *nm* Relig patron saint; Jur counsel

'patta¹ *nf* (di tasca) flap

'patta² *nf* (pareggio) draw

patteggia'mento *nm* bargaining

patteggi'are *vt/i* negotiate

patti'naggio *nm* skating. **pattinaggio artistico** figure skating. **pattinaggio su ghiaccio** ice skating. **pattinaggio a rotelle** roller-skating

patti'nare *vi* skate; (auto) skid

pattina|'tore, -'trice *nmf* skater

'pattino *nm* skate; Aeron skid. **pattino da ghiaccio** ice skate. **pattino a rotelle** roller skate

'patto *nm* deal; Pol pact; **a** ∼ **che** on condition that; **scendere a patti, venire a patti** reach a compromise

pat'tuglia *nf* patrol; **essere di** ∼ be on patrol. **pattuglia stradale** highway patrol Am, ≈ patrol car; police motorbike

pattu'ire *vt* negotiate

pat'tume *nm* rubbish

pattumi'era *nf* dustbin, trashcan Am

pa'ura *nf* fear; (spavento) fright; **aver** ∼ be afraid; **mettere** ∼ **a** frighten; **per** ∼ **di** for fear of; **da** ∼ (sl: libro, film) brilliant

pau'roso *adj* (che fa paura) frightening; (che ha paura) fearful; (fam: enorme) awesome

'pausa *nf* pause; (nel lavoro) break; **fare una** ∼ pause; (nel lavoro) have a break. **pausa [per il] caffè** coffee break. **pausa [per il] pranzo** lunchbreak, lunch hour

pavida'mente *adv* timidly

'pavido ① *adj* cowardly ② *nm* coward

pavimen'tare *vt* pave ⟨strada⟩

pavimentazi'one *nf* paving

pavi'mento *nm* floor

pa'vone *nm* peacock

pavoneggi'arsi *vr* strut

pay tv *nf inv* pay TV

pazien'tare *vi* be patient

pazi'ente *adj & nmf* patient

paziente'mente *adv* patiently

pazi'enza *nf* patience; ∼! never mind!; **perdere la** ∼ lose one's patience

'pazza *nf* madwoman

pazza'mente *adv* madly

pazzerel'lone, -a *nmf* madcap

paz'zesco *adj* foolish; (esagerato) crazy

paz'zia *nf* madness; (azione) [act of] folly

'pazzo ① *adj* mad; *fig* crazy; **sei ~?** you must be crazy!, are you crazy?
② *nm* madman; **essere ~ di/per** be crazy about; **~ di gioia** mad with joy; **da pazzi** *fam* crackpot; **darsi alla pazza gioia** live it up

paz'zoide *adj fam* whacky

P.C.I. *nm abbr* (**Partito Comunista Italiano**) Italian Communist Party

'pecan *nm inv* pecan

'pecca *nf* fault; **senza ~** flawless

peccami'noso *adj* sinful

pec'care *vi* sin; **~ di** be guilty of (ingratitudine)

pec'cato *nm* sin; **~ che...** it's a pity that...; **[che] ~!** [what a] pity!. **peccato di gioventù** youthful folly

pecca|'tore, -trice *nmf* sinner

'pece *nf* pitch; **nero come la ~** black as pitch

pechi'nese *nm* Pekin[g]ese

Pe'chino *nf* Beijing, Peking

'pecora *nf* sheep. **pecora nera** black sheep

peco'raio *nm* shepherd

peco'rella *nf* **cielo a pecorelle** sky full of fluffy white clouds. **pecorella smarrita** lost sheep

peco'rino *nm* (formaggio) sheep's milk cheese

peculi'are *adj* **~ di** peculiar to

peculiarità *nf inv* peculiarity

pecuni'ario *adj* money *attrib*

pe'daggio *nm* toll

pedago'gia *nf* pedagogy

peda'gogico *adj* pedagogical

peda'gogo, -a *nmf* pedagogue

peda'lare *vi* pedal

peda'lata *nf* push on the pedals

pe'dale *nm* pedal. **pedale dell'acceleratore** gas pedal. **pedale del freno** brake pedal

pedalò *nm inv* pedalo

pe'dana *nf* footrest; *Sport* springboard

pe'dante *adj* pedantic

pedante'ria *nf* pedantry

pedan'tesco *adj* pedantic

pe'data *nf* (calcio) kick; (impronta) footprint

pede'rasta *nm* pederast

pe'destre *adj* pedestrian

pedi'atra *nmf* paediatrician

pedia'tria *nf* paediatrics

pedi'atrico *adj* paediatric

pedi'cure ① *nmf inv* chiropodist, podiatrist *Am*
② *nm* (cura dei piedi) pedicure

pedi'gree *nm inv* pedigree

pedi'luvio *nm* footbath

pe'dina *nf* (alla dama) piece; *fig* pawn

pedina'mento *nm* shadowing

pedi'nare *vt* shadow

pedofi'lia *nf* paedophilia

pe'dofilo, -a *nmf* paedophile

pedo'nale *adj* pedestrian

pe'done *nm* pedestrian

'pedule *nfpl* hiking boots

'peeling *nm inv* exfoliation treatment

'peggio ① *adv* worse; **~ per te!** too bad!, tough!; **tanto ~** too bad; **~ di così** any worse; **la persona ~ vestita** the worst dressed person
② *adj* worse; **niente di ~** nothing worse; **stare ~** di be worse off than
③ *nm* **il ~ è che...** the worst of it is that...; **pensare al ~** think the worst
④ *nf* **alla ~** at worst; **avere la ~** get the worst of it; **alla meno ~** as best I can

peggiora'mento *nm* worsening

peggio'rare ① *vt* make worse, worsen
② *vi* get worse, worsen

peggiora'tivo *adj* pejorative

peggi'ore ① *adj* worse; (superlativo) worst; **nella ~ delle ipotesi** if the worst comes to the worst;
② *nmf* **il/la ~** the worst

'pegno *nm* pledge; (nei giochi di società) forfeit; *fig* token; **dare qualcosa in ~** pawn something; **in ~ d'amicizia** as a token of friendship

pelan'drone *nm* slob

pe'lare *vt* (spennare) pluck; (spellare) skin; (sbucciare) peel; (fam: spillare denaro) fleece

pe'larsi *vr fam* lose one's hair

pe'lati *nmpl* (pomodori) peeled tomatoes

pe'lato *adj* (calvo) bald

pel'lame *nm* skins *pl*

'pelle *nf* skin; (cuoio) leather; (buccia) peel; **avere la ~ d'oca** have goose-flesh; **non stare più nella ~** be beside oneself; **salvare la ~** save one's skin; **lasciarci la ~** buy it; **essere ~ e ossa** be all skin and bones; **avere la ~ dura** be tough; **borsa di pelle** leather bag. **pelle scamosciata** suede

pellegri'naggio *nm* pilgrimage

pelle'grino, -a *nmf* pilgrim

pelle'rossa *nmf* Red Indian, Redskin

pellette'ria *nf* leather goods *pl*

pelli'cano *nm* pelican

pellicce'ria *nf* furrier's [shop]

pel'liccia *nf* fur; (indumento) fur [coat]

pellicci'aio, -a *nmf* furrier

pel'licola *nf* *Phot, Cinema* film. **pellicola a colori** colour film. **pellicola trasparente** *Culin* cling film

'pelo *nm* hair; (di animale) coat; (di lana) pile; **per un ~** by the skin of one's teeth;

cavarsela per un ∼ have a narrow escape; **cercare il** ∼ **nell'uovo** nitpick
pe'loso *adj* hairy
'peltro *nm* pewter
pe'luche *nm* **giocattolo di peluche** soft toy; **orsetto di peluche** teddy bear
pe'luria *nf* down
'pelvico *adj* pelvic
'pena *nf* (punizione) punishment; (sofferenza) pain; (dispiacere) sorrow; (disturbo) trouble; **a mala** ∼ hardly; **mi fa** ∼ I pity him; **vale la** ∼ **andare** it is worth [while] going; **pene** *pl* **dell'inferno** hellfire. **pena di morte** death sentence
pe'nale *adj* criminal; **diritto penale** criminal law
pena'lista *nmf* criminal lawyer
penalità *nf inv* penalty
penaliz'zare *vt* penalize
penalizzazi'one *nf* (penalità) penalty
pe'nare *vi* suffer; (faticare) find it difficult
pen'daglio *nm* pendant
pen'dant *nm inv* **fare** ∼ **[con]** match
pen'dente ① *adj* hanging; Comm outstanding
② *nm* (ciondolo) pendant; **pendenti** *pl* drop earrings
pen'denza *nf* slope; Comm outstanding account
'pendere *vi* hang; (superficie) slope; (essere inclinato) lean
pen'dio *nm* slope; **in** ∼ sloping
'pendola *nf* grandfather clock
pendo'lare ① *adj* pendulum
② *nmf* commuter
pendo'lino *nm* (treno) special, first class only, fast train
'pendolo *nm* pendulum; **orologio a pendolo** grandfather clock
'pene *nm* penis
pene'trante *adj* penetrating; (freddo) biting
pene'trare ① *vt/i* penetrate; (trafiggere) pierce
② *vt* (odore) get into
③ *vi* (entrare furtivamente) steal in
penetrazi'one *nf* penetration
penicil'lina *nf* penicillin
pe'nisola *nf* peninsula
peni'tente *adj & nmf* penitent
peni'tenza *nf* penitence; (punizione) penance; (in gioco) forfeit
penitenzi'ario *nm* penitentiary
'penna *nf* (per scrivere) pen; (di uccello) feather. **penna a feltro** felt-tip[ped pen]. **penna ottica** light pen. **penna a sfera** ball-point [pen]. **penna stilografica** fountain-pen
pen'nacchio *nm* plume
penna'rello *nm* felt-tip[ped pen]

'penne *nfpl* pasta quills
pennel'lare *vt* paint
pennel'lata *nf* brushstroke
pen'nello *nm* brush; **a** ∼ (a perfezione) perfectly. ∼ **da barba** shaving brush
pen'nino *nm* nib
pen'none *nm* (di bandiera) flagpole
pen'nuto *adj* feathered
pe'nombra *nf* half-light
pe'noso *adj* (fam: pessimo) painful
pen'sabile *adj* **non è** ∼ it's unthinkable
pen'sare ① *vi* think; **penso di sì** I think so; ∼ **a** think of; remember to (chiudere il gas ecc); **pensa ai fatti tuoi!** mind your own business!; **ci penso io** I'll take care of it; ∼ **di fare qualcosa** think of doing something; **a pensarci bene** on second thoughts; ∼ **tra sé e sé** think to oneself; **pensarci su** think it over
② *vt* think
pen'sata *nf* idea
pensa'tore, -trice *nmf* thinker
pensi'ero *nm* thought; (mente) mind; (preoccupazione) worry; **stare in** ∼ **per** be anxious about; **levarsi il** ∼ to get something out of the way
pensie'roso *adj* pensive
'pensile ① *adj* hanging; **giardino pensile** roof-garden
② *nm* (mobile) wall unit
pensi'lina *nf* (di fermata d'autobus) bus shelter
pensio'nante *nmf* boarder; (ospite pagante) lodger
pensio'nato, -a ① *nmf* pensioner
② *nm* (per anziani) [old folks'] home; (per studenti) hostel
pensi'one *nf* pension; (albergo) boarding house; (vitto e alloggio) board and lodging; (da lavoro) retirement **andare in** ∼ retire; **essere in** ∼ be retired; **mezza pensione** half board. **pensione di anzianità** old-age pension. **pensione completa** full board. **pensione di invalidità** disability pension
pen'soso *adj* pensive
pen'tagono *nm* pentagon; **il Pentagono** the Pentagon
pen'tathlon *nm* pentathlon
Pente'coste *nf* Whitsun, Whit Sunday
penti'mento *nm* repentance
pen'tirsi *vr* ∼ **di** repent of; (rammaricarsi) regret
penti'tismo *nm* turning informant
pen'tito *nm* terrorist *or* Mafioso turned informant
'pentola *nf* saucepan; (contenuto) potful. **pentola a pressione** pressure cooker
pento'lino *nm* saucepan

pe'nultimo *adj* last but one, penultimate

pe'nuria *nf* shortage

penzo'lare *vi* dangle

penzo'loni *adv* dangling

pe'onia *nf* peony

pepai'ola *nf* pepper pot

pe'pare *vt* pepper

pe'pato *adj* peppery

'pepe *nm* pepper; **grano di pepe** peppercorn. **pepe di Caienna** cayenne pepper. **pepe in grani** whole peppercorns. **pepe macinato** ground pepper; **pepe nero** black pepper

pepero'nata *nf* dish of peppers and tomatoes

peperon'cino *nm* chilli pepper

pepe'rone *nm* [sweet] pepper; **rosso come un ~** red as a beetroot; **peperoni** *pl* **ripieni** stuffed peppers. **peperone rosso** red pepper. **peperone verde** green pepper

pepi'era *nf* pepper pot; (macinino) pepper mill

pe'pita *nf* nugget

'peptico *adj* peptic

'per *prep* for; (attraverso) through; (stato in luogo) in, on; (distributivo) per; (mezzo, entro) by; (causa) with; (in qualità di) as; **mi è passato per la mente** it crossed my mind; **~ strada** on the street; **~ la fine del mese** by the end of the month; **in fila ~ due** in double file; **l'ho sentito ~ telefono** I spoke to him on the phone; **~ iscritto** in writing; **~ caso** by chance; **~ esempio** for example; **ho aspettato ~ ore** I've been waiting for hours; **~ tutta la durata del viaggio** for the entire journey; **~ tempo** in time; **~ sempre** forever; **~ scherzo** as a joke; **gridare ~ il dolore** scream with pain; **vendere ~ diecimila euro** sell for ten thousand euros; **uno ~ volta** one at a time; **uno ~ uno** one by one; **venti ~ cento** twenty per cent; **~ fare qualcosa** [in order to] do something; **stare ~** be about to; **è troppo bello ~ essere vero** it's too good to be true

'pera *nf* pear; **farsi una ~** (sl: di eroina) shoot up

perbe'nismo *nm* prissiness

perbe'nista *adj inv* prissy

per'calle *nm* gingham

per'cento *adv* per cent

percentu'ale *nf* percentage

perce'pibile *adj* perceivable; (somma) payable

perce'pire *vt* perceive; (riscuotere) cash

percet'tibile *adj* perceptible

percettibil'mente *adv* perceptibly

percezi'one *nf* perception

perché ① *conj* (in interrogative) why; (per il fatto che) because; (affinché) so that; **~ non vieni?** why don't you come?; **dimmi ~** tell me why; **~ no/sì!** because!; **è troppo difficile ~ lo possa capire** it's too difficult for him to understand
② *nm inv* reason [why]; **senza un ~** without any reason

perciò *conj* so

per'correre *vt* cover ⟨distanza⟩; (viaggiare) travel

percor'ribile *adj* ⟨strada⟩ drivable, passable

percorribilità *nf* **percorribilità delle strade** road conditions *pl*

per'corso ① *pp di* PERCORRERE
② *nm* (tragitto) course, route; (distanza) distance; (viaggio) journey. **percorso ecologico** nature trail. **percorso di guerra** assault course. **percorso a ostacoli** obstacle course. **percorso vascolare** cardiovascular circuit

per'cossa *nf* blow; **percosse** *pl* Jur assault and battery

per'cosso *pp di* PERCUOTERE

percu'otere *vt* strike

percussi'one *nf* percussion; **strumenti a ~** percussion instruments

percussio'nista *nmf* percussionist

per'dente *nmf* loser

'perdere ① *vt* lose; (sprecare) waste; (non prendere) miss; (fig: vizio) ruin; **~ tempo** waste time; **lascia ~!** forget it!; **~ di vista** lose touch with
② *vi* lose; (recipiente) leak; **a ~** ⟨vuoto⟩ nonreturnable; **non avere niente da ~** have nothing to lose

'perdersi *vr* get lost; (reciproco) lose touch [with each other]

perdifi'ato: **a ~** *adv* ⟨gridare⟩ at the top of one's voice

perdigi'orno *nmf inv* idler

'perdita *nf* loss; (spreco) waste; (falla) leak; **a ~ d'occhio** as far as the eye can see; **chiudere in ~** (azienda) show a loss. **perdita di gas** gas leak. **perdita di sangue** loss of blood, bleeding. **perdita di tempo** waste of time

perdi'tempo *nm* waste of time

perdizi'one *nf* perdition

perdo'nare ① *vt* forgive; (scusare) excuse; **mi perdoni se interrompo** sorry to interrupt, excuse me for interrupting; **per farsi ~** as an apology
② *vi* **~ a qualcuno** forgive somebody; **un male che non perdona** an incurable disease

per'dono *nm* forgiveness; Jur pardon; **chiedere ~** ask for forgiveness; (scusarsi) apologize

perdu'rare *vi* last; (perseverare) persist

perduta'mente *adv* hopelessly

per'duto ① pp di PERDERE
② *adj* lost; (rovinato) ruined

pe'renne *adj* everlasting; Bot perennial; **nevi perenni** perpetual snow

perenne'mente *adv* perpetually

peren'torio *adj* peremptory

per'fetto ① *adj* perfect
② *nm* Gram perfect [tense]

perfezio'nare *vt* perfect; (migliorare) improve

perfezio'narsi *vr* improve oneself; (specializzarsi) specialize

perfezi'one *nf* perfection; **alla ~** to perfection

perfezio'nismo *nm* perfectionism

perfezio'nista *nmf* perfectionist

per'fidia *nf* wickedness; (atto) wicked act

'perfido *adj* treacherous; (malvagio) perverse

per'fino *adv* even

perfo'rare *vt* pierce; punch ‹schede›; Mech drill

perfora'tore, -trice ① *nmf* punch-card operator
② *nm* (apparecchio) punch. **perforatore di schede** card punch

perforazi'one *nf* perforation; (di schede) punching

per'formance *nf inv* Theat performance

perga'mena *nf* parchment

'pergola *nf* pergola

pergo'lato *nm* bower

periar'trite *nf* rheumatoid arthritis

perico'lante *adj* precarious; ‹azienda› shaky

pe'ricolo *nm* danger; (rischio) risk; **mettere in ~** endanger; **essere fuori ~** be out of danger. **pericolo pubblico** danger to society. **pericolo di valanghe** danger of avalanches

pericolosa'mente *adv* dangerously

pericolosità *nf* danger

perico'loso *adj* dangerous

peridu'rale *nf* epidural

perife'ria *nf* periphery; (di città) outskirts *pl*; fig fringes *pl*

peri'ferica *nf* peripheral; ‹strada› ring road. **periferica di input** Comput input device

peri'ferico *adj* peripheral; ‹quartiere› outlying

pe'rifrasi *nf inv* circumlocution

perime'trale *adj* ‹muro› perimeter *attrib*

pe'rimetro *nm* perimeter

peri'odico ① *nm* periodical
② *adj* periodical; ‹vento, mal di testa, numero› recurring

pe'riodo *nm* period; Gram sentence. **periodo nero** bad patch. **periodo di**

prova trial period. **periodo di ripensamento** cooling-off period. **periodo di riposo** breathing space. **periodo di transizione** transitional period, interim. **periodo di validità** period of validity

peripe'zie *nfpl* misadventures

pe'rire *vi* perish

peri'scopio *nm* periscope

pe'rito, -a ① *adj* skilled
② *nmf* expert. **perito agrario** agriculturalist. **perito di assicurazione** Comm loss adjuster. **perito edile** chartered surveyor. **perito elettronico** electronics engineer

perito'nite *nf* peritonitis

pe'rizia *nf* skill; (valutazione) survey. **perizia medico-legale** forensic tests

peri'zoma *nm inv* loincloth

'perla *nf* pearl. **perla coltivata** cultured pearl

per'lina *nf* bead

perli'nato *nm* matchboard

perlo'meno *adv* at least

perlu'strare *vt* patrol

perlustrazi'one *nf* patrol; **andare in ~** go on patrol

perma'loso *adj* touchy

perma'nente ① *adj* permanent
② *nf* perm; **farsi [fare] la ~** have a perm

perma'nenza *nf* permanence; (soggiorno) stay; **in ~** permanently. **permanenza in carica** tenure

perma'nere *vi* remain

perme'are *vt* permeate

perme'ato *adj* **~ di** fig permeated with

per'messo ① pp di PERMETTERE
② *nm* permission; (autorizzazione) permit, licence; Mil leave; **[è] ~?, con ~** (posso entrare?) may I come in?; (posso passare?) excuse me. **permesso di lavoro** work permit. **permesso di soggiorno** residence permit

per'mettere *vt* allow, permit; **potersi ~ qualcosa** (finanziariamente) be able to afford something

per'mettersi *vr* **~ di fare qualcosa** allow oneself to do something; **come si permette?** how dare you?

permis'sivo *adj* permissive

permutazi'one *nf* exchange; Math permutation

per'nacchia *nf* fam raspberry fam

per'nice *nf* partridge

pernici'oso *adj* pernicious

'perno *nm* pivot

pernot'tare *vi* stay overnight

'pero *nm* pear-tree

però *conj* but; (tuttavia) however

pe'rone *nm* Anat fibula

pero'rare *vt* plead

perpendico'lare *adj & nf* perpendicular

perpe'trare *vt* perpetrate

per'petua *nf* (di prete) priest's housekeeper

perpetu'are *vt* perpetuate

per'petuo *adj* perpetual

perplessità *nf inv* perplexity; (dubbio) doubt

per'plesso *adj* perplexed, puzzled

perqui'sire *vt* search

perquisizi'one *nf* search. **perquisizione domiciliare** search of the premises

persecu|'tore, -trice *nmf* persecutor

persecuzi'one *nf* persecution

persegu'ire *vt* pursue

persegui'tare *vt* persecute

persegui'tato, -a *nmf* victim of persecution

perseve'rante *adj* persevering

perseve'ranza *nf* perseverance

perseve'rare *vi* persevere

'Persia *nf* Persia

persi'ana *nf* shutter. **persiana avvolgibile** roller shutter

persi'ano, -a *adj & nmf* Persian

'persico *adj* Persian

per'sino *adv* = PERFINO

persi'stente *adj* persistent; ⟨dubbio⟩ nagging

persi'stenza *nf* persistence

per'sistere *vi* persist; ∼ **nel fare qualcosa** persist in doing something

'perso ① *pp di* PERDERE
② *adj* lost; **a tempo** ∼ in one's spare time

per'sona *nf* person; (un tale) somebody; **di** ∼, **in** ∼ in person, personally; **per** ∼ per person, a head; **per interposta** ∼ through an intermediary; **curare la propria** ∼ look after oneself, look after number one; **persone** *pl* people. **persona a carico** dependant. **persona di colore** black person. **persona giuridica** legal person. **persona di servizio** domestic

perso'naggio *nm* (persona di riguardo) personality; Theat ecc character

perso'nale ① *adj* personal
② *nm* staff; (aspetto) build. **personale di terra** ground crew

personalità *nf inv* personality

personaliz'zare *vt* customize ⟨auto ecc⟩; personalize ⟨penna ecc⟩

personifi'care *vt* personify

personificazi'one *nf* personification

perspi'cace *adj* shrewd

perspi'cacia *nf* shrewdness

persua'dere *vt* convince; impress ⟨critici⟩; ∼ **qualcuno a fare qualcosa** persuade somebody to do something

persuasi'one *nf* persuasion; **fare opera di** ∼ **su qualcuno** try to persuade somebody

persuasività *nf* persuasiveness

persua'sivo *adj* persuasive

persu'aso *pp di* PERSUADERE

persua'sore *nm* persuader

per'tanto *conj* therefore

'pertica *nf* pole

perti'nace *adj* pertinacious

perti'nente *adj* relevant

per'tosse *nf* whooping cough

per'tugio *nm* opening

pertur'bare *vt* perturb

perturbazi'one *nf* disturbance. **perturbazione atmosferica** atmospheric disturbance

Perù *nm* Peru

peruvi'ano, -a *adj & nmf* Peruvian

per'vadere *vt* pervade

perva'sivo *adj* pervasive

per'vaso *pp di* PERVADERE

perven'ire *vi* reach; **far** ∼ **qualcosa a qualcuno** send something to somebody

perversa'mente *adv* perversely

perversi'one *nf* perversion

perversità *nf inv* perversity

per'verso *adj* perverse

perver'tire *vt* pervert

perver'tirsi *vr* ⟨gusti, costumi⟩ become debased

perver'tito ① *adj* perverted
② *nm* pervert

pervi'cace *adj* obstinate

pervicace'mente *adv* obstinately

pervi'cacia *nf* obstinacy

per'vinca¹ *nm* (colore) blue with a touch of purple

per'vinca² *nf* Bot periwinkle

p.es. *abbr* (**per esempio**) e.g.

'pesa *nf* weighing; (bilancia) weighing machine; (per veicoli) weighbridge

pe'sante ① *adj* heavy; ⟨stomaco⟩ overfull; ⟨accusa, ingiuria⟩ serious; (noioso) boring; **andarci** ∼ **con qualcuno** be heavy-handed with somebody
② *adv* ⟨vestirsi⟩ warmly

pesante'mente *adv* ⟨cadere⟩ heavily; ⟨insultare⟩ seriously

pesan'tezza *nf* heaviness

pesaper'sone *nm inv* scales

pe'sare ① *vt* weigh; ∼ **le parole** weigh one's words
② *vi* weigh; (essere pesante) be heavy; ∼ **su** fig lie heavy on

pe'sarsi *vr* weigh oneself

'**pesca**¹*nf* (frutto) peach

'**pesca**²*nf* fishing; **andare a ~** go fishing. **pesca di beneficenza** lucky dip. **pesca con la lenza** angling. **pesca subacquea** underwater fishing

pe'scare *vt* (andare a pesca di) fish for; (prendere) catch; (fam: trovare) dig up, find; **guai se ti pesco!** there will be trouble if I catch you!

pesca'tore *nm* fisherman. **pescatore di frodo** poacher. **pescatore di perle** pearl diver

'**pesce** *nm* fish; **non sapere che pesci pigliare** fig not know which way to turn; **prendere qualcuno a pesci in faccia** fig treat somebody like dirt; **sentirsi un ~ fuor d'acqua** feel like a fish out of water. **pesce d'aprile!** April Fool!. **pesce in carpione** soused fish. **pesce al cartoccio** fish baked in foil. **pesce gatto** catfish. **pesce grosso** fig big fish. **pesce persico** perch. **pesce piccolo** fig small fry. **pesce rosso** goldfish. **pesce spada** swordfish

pesce'cane *nm* shark

pesche'reccio *nm* fishing boat

pesche'ria *nf* fishmonger's [shop]

peschi'era *nf* fish-pond

'**Pesci** *nmpl* Astr Pisces

pescio'lino *nm* **pesciolino d'acqua dolce** minnow

pesci'vendolo *nm* fishmonger

'**pesco** *nm* peach tree

pe'scoso *adj* teeming with fish

pe'seta *nf* peseta

pe'sista *nm* (in sollevamento pesi) weight-lifter; (in lancio del peso) shot-putter

'**peso** *nm* weight; **essere di ~ per qualcuno** be a burden to somebody; **alzare di ~** lift up in one go; **avere un ~ sullo stomaco** have a lead weight on one's stomach; **di poco ~** (senza importanza) not very important; **non dare ~ a qualcosa** not attach any importance to something. **peso massimo** (nel pugilato) heavy weight. **peso medio** (nel pugilato) middleweight. **peso morto** dead weight. **peso netto** net weight. **peso piuma** (nel pugilato) featherweight **peso specifico** specific gravity. **peso welter** (nel pugilato) welterweight

pessi'mismo *nm* pessimism

pessi'mista ① *nmf* pessimist ② *adj* pessimistic

pessimistica'mente *adv* pessimistically

'**pessimo** *adj* very bad

pe'staggio *nm* beating-up

pe'stare *vt* tread on; (picchiare) beat; crush ⟨aglio, prezzemolo, uva⟩; **~ i piedi** [per terra] stamp one's feet [on the ground]; **~ un piede a qualcuno** tread on somebody's foot

pe'stata *nf* bash; **dare una ~ a un piede a qualcuno** tread on somebody's foot

'**peste** *nf* plague; (persona) pest; **dire ~ e corna di qualcuno** tear somebody to bits. **peste bubbonica** bubonic plague

pe'stello *nm* pestle

pesti'cida *nm* pesticide

pe'stifero *adj* (fastidioso) pestilential

pesti'lenza *nf* pestilence; (fetore) stench, stink

pestilenzi'ale *adj* ⟨odore, aria⟩ noxious

'**pesto** ① *adj* ground; **occhio pesto** black eye ② *nm* basil and garlic sauce

'**petalo** *nm* petal

pe'tardo *nm* banger

petizi'one *nf* petition; **fare una ~** draw up a petition

petro'dollaro *nm* petrodollar

petrol'chimico *adj* petrochemical

petroli'era *nf* [oil] tanker

petroli'ere *nm* oilman

petro'lifero *adj* oil-bearing

pe'trolio *nm* oil

pettego'lare *vi* gossip

pettego'lezzo *nm* piece of gossip; **pettegolezzi** *pl* gossip *sg*; **far pettegolezzi** gossip

pet'tegolo, -a ① *adj* gossipy ② *nmf* gossip

petti'nare *vt* comb

petti'narsi *vr* comb one's hair

pettina'tura *nf* combing; (acconciatura) hairstyle; **~ a caschetto** bob

'**pettine** *nm* comb

'**petting** *nm* petting

petti'nino *nm* (fermaglio) comb

petti'rosso *nm* robin [redbreast]

'**petto** *nm* chest; (seno) breast; **a doppio ~** double-breasted; **prendere qualcosa/qualcuno di ~** face up to something/somebody; **petti** *pl* **di pollo** chicken breasts

petto'rale ① *nm* Sport number; **pettorali** pecs ② *adj* pectoral

petto'rina *nf* (di salopette) bib

petto'ruto *adj* ⟨donna⟩ full-breasted; ⟨uomo⟩ broad-chested

petu'lante *adj* impertinent

petu'lanza *nf* impertinence

pe'tunia *nf* petunia

'**pezza** *nf* cloth; (toppa) patch; (rotolo di tessuto) roll; **trattare qualcuno come una ~ da piedi** walk all over somebody. **pezza d'appoggio** voucher. **pezza giustificativa** voucher

pez'zato *adj* ⟨cavallo, mucca⟩ piebald

pez'zente *nmf* tramp; (avaro) miser

'**pezzo** *nm* piece; (parte) part; Mus piece; un bel ∼ d'uomo a fine figure of a man; un ∼ (di tempo) some time; (di spazio) a long way; al ∼ ⟨costare⟩ each; essere a pezzi (stanco) be shattered; fare a pezzi tear to shreds; andare in mille pezzi break into a thousand pieces; cadere a pezzi fall to pieces, fall to bits. **pezzo forte** centre-piece; **pezzi** *pl* **grossi** top brass. **pezzo grosso** bigwig, big shot. **pezzo di imbecille** stupid idiot. **pezzo di ricambio** spare [part]

pezzu'ola *nf* scrap of material

photo'fit® *nm inv* Photofit

pia'cente *adj* attractive

pia'cere ① *nm* pleasure; (favore) favour; a ∼ as much as one likes; per ∼! please!; ∼ [di conoscerla]! (nelle presentazioni) pleased to meet you!; con ∼ with pleasure; fare un ∼ a qualcuno do somebody a favour

② *vi* la Scozia mi piace I like Scotland; mi piacciono i dolci I like sweets; mi piacerebbe venire I'd like to come; faccio come mi pare e piace I do as I please; ti piace? do you like it?; lo spettacolo è piaciuto the show was a success

pia'cevole *adj* pleasant

piacevol'mente *adv* agreeably

piaci'mento *nm* a ∼ as much as you like

pia'dina *nf* unleavened focaccia bread

pi'aga *nf* sore; fig scourge; (fig: persona noiosa) pain; (fig: ricordo doloroso) wound

pia'gato *adj* covered with sores

piagni'steo *nm* whining

piagnuco'lare *vi* whimper

piagnuco'lio *nm* whimpering

piagnuco'loso *adj* maudlin

pi'alla *nf* plane

pial'lare *vt* plane

pialla'tura *nf* planing

pi'ana *nf* (pianura) plane

pianeggi'ante *adj* level

piane'rottolo *nm* landing

pia'neta *nm* planet

pi'angere ① *vi* cry; (disperatamente) weep; mi piange il cuore my heart bleeds; mettersi a ∼ come una fontana turn the waterworks on; ∼ sul latte versato cry over split milk

② *vt* (lamentare) lament; (per un lutto) mourn; ∼ la morte di qualcuno mourn somebody's death

pianifi'care *vt* plan

pianificazi'one *nf* planning. **pianificazione aziendale** corporate planning. **pianificazione familiare** family planning. **pianificazione territoriale** town-and-country planning

pia'nista *nmf* Mus pianist

pi'ano ① *adj* flat; (a livello) flush; (regolare) smooth; (facile) easy; i 400 metri piani the 400 metres flat race

② *adv* slowly; (con cautela) gently; (sottovoce) quietly; andarci ∼ go carefully

③ *nm* plain; (di edificio) floor, storey; (livello) plane; (progetto) plan; Mus piano; di primo ∼ first-rate; primo piano Phot close-up; in primo ∼ in the foreground; essere/mettersi in primo ∼ fig take/occupy centre-stage; secondo piano middle distance. **piano d'azione** action plan. **piano bar** piano bar. **piano d'emergenza** contingency plan. **piano di incentivi** incentive scheme. **piano di lavoro** work surface; (programma) work schedule. **piano di pensionamento** pension plan, pension scheme. **piano regolatore** town plan. **piano di sopra** upstairs. **piano di sotto** downstairs. **piano di studi** syllabus. **piano superiore** upper floor

piano'forte *nm* piano. **pianoforte a coda** grand [piano]. **pianoforte verticale** upright [piano]

pia'nola *nf* pianola

piano'terra *nm inv* ground floor, first floor Am

pi'anta *nf* plant; (del piede) sole; (disegno) plan; (di città) map; di sana ∼ (totalmente) entirely; in ∼ stabile permanently. **pianta da appartamento** house-plant. **pianta stradale** road map

piantagi'one *nf* plantation

pianta'grane *nmf inv* fam è un/una ∼ he's/she's bolshy

pian'tare *vt* plant; (conficcare) drive; pitch ⟨tenda⟩; (fam; abbandonare) dump; **piantala!** fam stop it!; **piantato in** ⟨spina, chiodo⟩ embedded in; ∼ baracca e burattini drop everything; (per sempre) chuck everything in

pian'tarsi *vr* plant oneself; (fam; lasciarsi) leave each other

pianta|'tore, -'trice *nmf* planter

pianter'reno *nm* ground floor, first floor Am

pi'anto ① *pp di* PIANGERE

② *nm* crying; (disperato) weeping; (lacrime) tears *pl*

pianto'nare *vt* guard

pian'tone *nm* guard; stare di ∼ stand guard; mettere di ∼ put on guard. **piantone dello sterzo** Auto steering column

pia'nura *nf* plain. **pianura padana** Po valley

pi'astra *nf* plate; (lastra) slab; Culin griddle. **piastra elettronica** circuit board. **piastra madre** Comput motherboard. **piastra di registrazione** cassette deck

pia'strella *nf* tile

pia'strina *nf* Mil identity disc; Med platelet; Comput chip. **piastrina di riconoscimento** identity tag. **piastrina di silicio** silicon chip

piatta'forma *nf* platform. **piattaforma di lancio** launch pad. **piattaforma petrolifera** oil platform, offshore rig. **piattaforma rivendicativa** *o* **sindacale** union claims *pl*

piat'tino *nm* (di tazzina) saucer; (piatto piccolo) side plate

pi'atto ① *adj* flat; (monotono) dull ② *nm* plate; (da portata, vivanda) dish; (portata) course; (parte piatta) flat; (di giradischi) turntable; (di bilancia) pan; **piatti** *pl* Mus cymbals; **lavare i piatti** do the dishes, do the washing-up; **piatti** *pl* **da asporto** takeaway Br, carryout Am; **piatti** *pl* **caldi** hot dishes; **piatti** *pl* **di carne** meat dishes. **piatto fondo** soup plate. **piatto del giorno** dish of the day. **piatto piano** [ordinary] plate. **piatto di portata** serving dish, server. **piatto pronto** ready meal. **piatto unico** complete meal

pi'azza *nf* square; Comm market; **letto a una piazza** single bed; **letto a due piazze** double bed; **far** ∼ **pulita** make a clean sweep; **mettere qualcosa in** ∼ fig make something public; **scendere in** ∼ fig take to the streets. **piazza d'armi** parade ground. **piazza del mercato** market square. **Piazza San Pietro** St Peter's Square

piazza'forte *nf* stronghold

piaz'zale *nm* large square

piazza'mento *nm* (in classifica) placing

piaz'zare *vt* place

piaz'zarsi *vr* Sport be placed; ∼ **secondo** come second, be placed second

piaz'zato *adj* (cavallo) placed; **ben** ∼ (robusto) well-built

piaz'zista ① *nm* salesman ② *nf* saleswoman

piaz'z[u]ola *nf* **piazz[u]ola di partenza** (nel golf) tee. **piazz[u]ola di sosta** pull-in

pic'cante *adj* hot; (pungente) sharp; (salace) spicy

pic'carsi *vr* (risentirsi) take offence; ∼ **di** (vantarsi di) claim to

pic'cata *nf* veal in sour lemon sauce

'picche *nfpl* (in carte) spades

picchet'taggio *nm* picketing

picchet'tare *vt* stake; (scioperanti) picket

pic'chetto *nm* picket

picchi'are ① *vt* hit; ∼ **la testa (contro qualcosa)** bang *or* hit one's head (against something) ② *vi* (bussare) knock; Aeron nosedive; ∼ **in testa** (motore) knock

picchi'arsi *vr* ∼ **il petto** beat one's breast

picchi'ata *nf* beating; Aeron nosedive; **scendere in** ∼ nosedive

picchi'ato *adj* (matto) touched

picchia'tore *nm* goon

picchiet'tare *vt* tap; (punteggiare) spot

picchiet'tato *adj* spotted

picchiet'tio *nm* tapping

'picchio *nm* woodpecker

pic'cino ① *adj* tiny; (gretto) mean; (di poca importanza) petty ② *nm* little one, child

piccion'cini *nmpl* fam lovebirds; **fare** ∼ get all lovey-dovey

picci'one *nm* pigeon; **prendere due piccioni con una fava** kill two birds with one stone. **piccione viaggiatore** carrier pigeon

'picco *nm* peak; **a** ∼ vertically; **colare a** ∼ sink

picco'lezza *nf* (di persona, ambiente) smallness; (grettezza) meanness; (inezia) trifle

'piccolo, -a ① *adj* small, little; (vacanza, pausa) little, short; (di statura) short; (gretto) petty ② *nmf* child, little one; **da** ∼ as a child; **in** ∼ in miniature; **nel mio** ∼ in my own small way

pic'cone *nm* pickaxe. **piccone da ghiaccio** ice pick

pic'cozza *nf* ice axe

pic'nic *nm inv* picnic

pi'docchio *nm* louse

pidocchi'oso ① *adj* flea-bitten; (fam: avaro) stingy ② *nm* fam miser

piè *nm inv* **a** ∼ **di pagina** at the foot of the page; **saltare a** ∼ **pari** skip; **ad ogni** ∼ **sospinto** all the time, endlessly

pi'ede *nm* foot; (di armadio, letto) leg; **a piedi** on foot; **andare a piedi** walk; **a piedi nudi** barefoot; **avere i piedi piatti** have flat feet, be flat-footed; **a** ∼ **libero** free; **in piedi** standing; **alzarsi in piedi** stand up; **in punta di piedi** on tiptoe; **ai piedi di** (montagna) at the foot of; **avere qualcuno ai propri piedi** have somebody at one's feet; **essere sul** ∼ **di guerra** be ready for action; (nazione) be on war footing; **prendere** ∼ fig gain ground; (moda) catch on; **partire col** ∼ **sbagliato** get off on the wrong foot; **mettere in piedi** (allestire) set up; **togliti dai piedi!** get out of the way!. **piede di insalata** head of lettuce. **piede di porco** (strumento) jemmy

pie'dino *nm* **fare ∼ a qualcuno** fam play footsie with somebody

piedi'stallo *nm* pedestal

pi'ega *nf* (piegatura) fold; (di gonna) pleat; (di pantaloni) crease; (grinza) wrinkle; (andamento) turn; **a pieghe** with pleats, pleated; **non fare una ∼** (ragionamento) be flawless; (persona) not bat an eyelid; **prendere una brutta ∼** get into bad ways

pie'gare ① *vt* fold; (flettere) bend ② *vi* bend

pie'garsi *vr* bend; **∼ a** fig yield to

piega'tura *nf* folding; (piega) fold

pieghet'tare *vt* pleat

pieghet'tato *adj* pleated

pie'ghevole ① *adj* pliable; (tavolo) folding ② *nm* leaflet

Pie'monte *nm* Piedmont

piemon'tese *adj* & *nmf* Piedmontese

pi'ena *nf* (di fiume) flood; (folla) crowd

pi'eno ① *adj* full; (massiccio) solid; **in piena estate** in the middle of summer; **a pieni voti** (diplomarsi) ≈ with A-grades, with first class honours ② *nm* (colmo) height; (carico) full load; **in ∼** (completamente) fully; **fare il ∼** (di benzina) fill up; **nel ∼ delle forze** in top physical form

pie'none *nm* **c'era il ∼** the place was packed

'piercing *nm inv* body piercing. **piercing all'ombelico** navel ring. **piercing nella lingua** tongue stud

pietà *nf* pity; (misericordia) mercy; **senza ∼** (persona) pitiless; (spietatamente) pitilessly; **avere ∼ di qualcuno** take pity on somebody; **far ∼** (far pena) be pitiful; (fam: essere orrendo) be useless

pie'tanza *nf* dish

pie'toso *adj* pitiful, merciful; (fam: pessimo) terrible

pi'etra *nf* stone. **pietra dura** semiprecious stone. **pietra preziosa** precious stone. **pietra dello scandalo** cause of the scandal

pie'traia *nf* scree

pie'trame *nm* stones *pl*

pietrifi'care *vt* petrify

pie'trina *nf* (di accendino) flint

pie'troso *adj* stony

'piffero *nm* fife

pigi'ama *nm* pyjamas *pl*, pajamas Am

'pigia 'pigia *nm inv* crowd, crush

pigi'are *vt* press

pigia'trice *nf* winepress

pigi'one *nf* rent; **dare a ∼** let, rent out; **prendere a ∼** rent

pigli'are *vt* (fam: afferrare) catch

'piglio *nm* air

pig'mento *nm* pigment

pig'meo, -a *adj* & *nmf* pygmy

'pigna *nf* cone. **pigna di abete** fir cone

pi'gnolo *adj* pedantic

pignora'mento *nm* Jur distraint

pigno'rare *vt* Jur distrain upon

pigo'lare *vi* chirp

pigo'lio *nm* chirping

pigra'mente *adv* lazily

pi'grizia *nf* laziness

'pigro *adj* lazy; (d'intelletto) slow

PIL *abbr* (**prodotto interno lordo**) GDP

'pila *nf* pile; Electr battery; (fam: lampadina tascabile) torch; (vasca) basin; **a pile** battery operated, battery powered

pi'lastro *nm* pillar

'pillola *nf* pill; **prendere la ∼** be on the pill. **pillola del giorno dopo** morning-after pill

pi'lone *nm* pylon; (di ponte) pier

pi'lota ① *nmf* pilot; Auto driver. **pilota automatico** automatic pilot. **pilota di caccia** fighter pilot ② *adj inv* **progetto pilota** pilot project

pilo'taggio *nm* flying; **cabina di pilotaggio** flight deck

pilo'tare *vt* pilot; drive (auto)

pinaco'teca *nf* art gallery

'Pinco Pal'lino *nm* so-and-so

pi'neta *nf* pine-wood

ping-'pong *nm* table tennis, ping-pong fam

'pingue *adj* fat

pingu'edine *nf* fatness

pingu'ino *nm* penguin; (gelato) choc ice on a stick

'pinna *nf* fin; (per nuotare) flipper

pin'nacolo *nm* pinnacle

'pino *nm* pine[-tree]. **pino marittimo** cluster pine, maritime pine

pi'nolo *nm* pine kernel

'pinta *nf* pint

pin-'up *nf inv* pin-up [girl]

'pinza *nf* pliers *pl*; Med forceps *pl*; **prendere qualcosa con le pinze** fig treat something cautiously

pin'zare *vt* (con pinzatrice) staple

pinza'trice *nf* stapler

pin'zette *nfpl* tweezers

pinzi'monio *nm* sauce for crudités

'pio *adj* pious; (benefico) charitable

piogge'rella *nf* drizzle

pi'oggia *nf* rain; (fig: di pietre, insulti) hail, shower; **sotto la ∼** in the rain. **pioggia acida** acid rain. **pioggia radioattiva** radioactive fallout

pi'olo *nm* (di scala) rung

piom'bare ① *vi* fall heavily; ∼ **su** fall upon; ∼ **all'improvviso nella stanza** suddenly burst into the room
② *vt* ∼ **qualcuno nella disperazione** plunge somebody into despair

piom'bino *nm* (sigillo) [lead] seal; (da pesca) sinker; (in tende) weight

pi'ombo *nm* lead; (sigillo) [lead] seal; **a** ∼ plumb; **senza** ∼ ⟨*benzina*⟩ unleaded; **avere un sonno di** ∼ be a very heavy sleeper; **andare con i piedi di** ∼ tread carefully; **anni di** ∼ years when terrorism was at its height

pioni'ere, **-a** *nmf* pioneer

pi'oppo *nm* poplar

pior'rea *nf* pyorrhoea

pio'vano *adj* **acqua piovana** rainwater

pi'overe *vi* rain; ∼ it's raining; ∼ **addosso a qualcuno** ⟨*guai, debiti*⟩ rain down on somebody; [**su questo**] **non ci piove** fam that's for sure

pioviggi'nare *vi* drizzle

pio'voso *adj* rainy

pi'ovra *nf* octopus

pio'vuto *adj* ∼ **dal cielo** fallen into one's lap

pipì *nf* **fare** [**la**] ∼ pee, piddle; **andare a fare** [**la**] ∼ go for a pee

'pipa *nf* pipe

pipe'rito *adj* **menta piperita** peppermint

pipi'strello *nm* bat

piqué *nm* piqué

'pira *nf* pyre

pi'ramide *nf* pyramid

pi'ranha *nm inv* piranha

pi'rata ① *nm* pirate. **pirata dell'aria** skyjacker. **pirata della strada** hit-and-run driver; (prepotente) road-hog
② *adj inv* pirate

pirate'ria *nf* piracy. **pirateria informatica** software piracy

pi'rite *nf* pyrite

piro'etta *nf* pirouette

pi'rofila *nf* (tegame) oven-proof dish

pi'rofilo *adj* heat-resistant

pi'romane *nmf* pyromaniac

piroma'nia *nf* pyromania

pi'roscafo *nm* steamer. **piroscafo di linea** liner

'piscia *nf* vulg piss

pisci'are *vi* vulg piss

pisci'ata *nf* vulg piss

pi'scina *nf* [swimming] pool. **piscina coperta** indoor [swimming] pool. **piscina gonfiabile** [inflatable] paddling pool. **piscina olimpionica** Olympic [swimming] pool. **piscina per il parto** birthing pool. **piscina scoperta** outdoor [swimming] pool, lido

pi'sello *nm* pea; (fam: pene) willie; **piselli** *pl* **odorosi** sweetpeas

piso'lino *nm* nap; **fare un** ∼ have a nap

'pista *nf* track; Aeron runway, tarmac; (orma) footprint; (sci) slope, piste. **pista d'atterraggio** runway. **pista da ballo** dance floor. **pista ciclabile** cycle track. **pista da fondo** cross-country ski track. **pista di pattinaggio** ice rink. **pista per principianti** nursery slope. **pista di sci** ski slope, ski run, piste. **pista per slitte** toboggan run

pi'stacchio *nm* pistachio

pi'stola *nf* gun, pistol; (per spruzzare) spray-gun. **pistola a capsule** cap gun. **pistola a spruzzo** paint spray. **pistola a tamburo** revolver

pisto'lero *nm* gunslinger

pi'stone *nm* piston

'pitbull *nm inv* pitbull (terrier)

pi'tocco *nm* miser

pi'tone *nm* python

pitto'gramma *nm* pictogram

pit|'tore, **-trice** *nmf* painter

pitto'resco *adj* picturesque

pit'torico *adj* pictorial

pit'tura *nf* painting; **pitture** *pl* **di guerra** warpaint. **pittura a guazzo** poster paint. **pittura rupestre** cave painting

pittu'rare *vt* paint

pitui'tario *adj* pituitary

più ① *adv* more; (superlativo) most; Math plus; ∼ **importante** more important; **il** ∼ **importante** the most important; ∼ **caro/grande** dearer/bigger; **il** ∼ **caro/grande** the dearest/biggest; **di** ∼ more; **una coperta in** ∼ an extra blanket; **non ho** ∼ **soldi** I don't have any more money; **non vive** ∼ **a Milano** he no longer lives in Milan; ∼ **o meno** more or less; **il** ∼ **lentamente possibile** as slow as possible; **al** ∼ **presto** as soon as possible; **per di** ∼ what's more; **mai** ∼! never again!; ∼ **di** more than; **sempre** ∼ more and more
② *adj* more; (superlativo) most; ∼ **tempo** more time; **la classe con** ∼ **alunni** the class with most pupils; ∼ **volte** several times
③ *nm* most; Math plus sign; **il** ∼ **è fatto** the worst is over; **parlare del** ∼ **e del meno** make small talk; **i** ∼ the majority

piuccheper'fetto *nm* pluperfect

pi'uma *nf* feather

piu'maggio *nm* plumage

piu'mato *adj* plumed

piu'mino *nm* (di cigni) down; (copriletto) eiderdown; (per cipria) powder-puff; (per spolverare) feather duster; (giacca) down jacket

piu'mone® *nm* duvet, continental quilt

piut'tosto *adv* rather; (invece) instead

'**piva** *nf* con le pive nel sacco emptyhanded

pi'**vello** *nm* fam greenhorn

'**pivot** *nm inv* (in pallacanestro) centre

'**pizza** *nf* pizza; Cinema reel; (fam: noia) bore. **pizza margherita** tomato and mozzarella pizza. **pizza marinara** pizza with tomato, oregano, garlic and anchovies. **pizza napoletana** pizza with tomato, mozzarella and anchovies. **pizza quattro stagioni** pizza with tomato, mozzarella, ham, mushrooms and artichokes

pizzai'ola: alla ∼ *adj* with tomatoes, garlic, and oregano

pizze'ria *nf* pizza restaurant, pizzeria

piz'zetta *nf* small pizza

piz'zetto *nm* (barba) goatee

pizzi'care ① *vt* pinch; (pungere) sting; (di sapore) taste sharp; (fam: sorprendere) catch; Mus pluck
② *vi* scratch; ⟨cibo⟩ be spicy

'**pizzico**, **pizzi'cotto** *nm* pinch

'**pizzo** *nm* lace; (di montagna) peak

pla'**care** *vt* placate; assuage ⟨fame, dolore⟩

pla'**carsi** *vr* calm down

'**placca** *nf* plate; (commemorativa, dentale) plaque; Med patch. **placca batterica** plaque

plac'**care** *vt* plate

plac'**cato** *adj* **placcato d'argento** silver-plated. **placcato d'oro** gold-plated

placca'tura *nf* plating

pla'**cebo** *nm inv* placebo; **effetto placebo** placebo effect

pla'**centa** *nf* placenta, afterbirth

'**placido** *adj* placid

pla'**fond** *nm inv* Comm ceiling

plafoni'**era** *nf* ceiling light

plagi'**are** *vt* plagiarize; pressure ⟨persona⟩

'**plagio** *nm* plagiarism

plaid *nm inv* tartan rug

pla'**nare** *vi* glide

'**plancia** *nf* Naut bridge; (passerella) gangplank

'**plancton** *nm* plankton

plane'**tario** ① *adj* planetary
② *nm* planetarium

pla'**smare** *vt* mould

'**plastica** *nf* (materia) plastic; Med plastic surgery; (arte) plastic art; **sacchetto di plastica** plastic bag

'**plastico** ① *adj* plastic; (rappresentazione) three-dimensional
② *nm* plastic model

'**platano** *nm* plane tree

pla'**tea** *nf* stalls *pl*; (pubblico) audience

'**platino** *nm* platinum

pla'**tonico** *adj* platonic

plau'**sibile** *adj* plausible; **poco** ∼ implausible

plausibilità *nf* plausibility

'**plauso** *nm* (consenso) approval

play'**back** *nm* **cantare in** ∼ mime

play'**boy** *nm inv* playboy

play'**maker** *nm inv* Sport playmaker

p.le *abbr* (**piazzale**) Sq.

ple'**baglia** *nf* pej mob

'**plebe** *nf* common people

ple'**beo, -a** *adj & nmf* plebeian

plebi'**scito** *nm* plebiscite

ple'**nario** *adj* plenary

pleni'**lunio** *nm* full moon

'**plettro** *nm* plectrum

pleu'**rite** *nf* pleurisy

'**plico** *nm* packet; **in** ∼ **a parte** under separate cover

plissé *adj inv* plissé; (gonna) accordeon pleated

plop *nm inv* plop; **fare** ∼ plop

plo'**tone** *nm* platoon; (di ciclisti) group. **plotone d'esecuzione** firing squad

'**plotter** *nm inv* Comput plotter. **plotter da tavolo** flatbed plotter

'**plumbeo** *adj* leaden

plum-'cake *nm inv* fruit cake

plu'**rale** *adj & nm* plural; **al** ∼ in the plural

pluralità *nf* (maggioranza) majority

pluridiscipli'**nare** *adj* multidisciplinary

plurien'**nale** *adj* ∼ **esperienza** many years' experience

plurigemel'**lare** *adj* ⟨parto⟩ multiple

pluripar'**titico** *adj* Pol multi-party

Plu'**tone** *nm* Pluto

plu'**tonio** *nm* plutonium

pluvi'**ale** *adj* rain *attrib*

pluvi'**ometro** *nm* rain gauge

pneu'**matico** ① *adj* pneumatic
② *nm* tyre. **pneumatico radiale** radial [tyre]

pneu'**monia** *nf* pneumonia

PNL *abbr* (**prodotto nazionale lordo**) GNP

Po *nm* Po

po' ▶ POCO

po'**chette** *nf inv* clutch bag

po'**chino** *nm* **un** ∼ a little bit

'**poco** ① *adj* little; ⟨tempo⟩ short; (con nomi plurali) few
② *pron* little; (poco tempo) a short time; (plurale) few
③ *nm* little; **un po'** a little [bit]; **un po' di** a little, some; (con nomi plurali) a few; **a** ∼ **a** ∼ little by little; **fra** ∼ soon; **per** ∼ (a poco

prezzo) cheap; (quasi) nearly; ∼ **fa** a little while ago; **sono arrivato da** ∼ I have just arrived; **un bel po'** quite a lot; **un bel po' di più/meno** quite a lot more/less; **un** ∼ **di buono** a shady character

4 *adv* (con verbi) not much; (con avverbi, aggettivi) not very; **parla** ∼ he doesn't speak much; **lo conosco** ∼ I don't know him very well; ∼ **spesso** not very often

po'dere *nm* farm

pode'roso *adj* powerful

'podio *nm* dais; Mus podium

po'dismo *nm* walking

po'dista *nmf* walker

po'ema *nm* poem. **poema epico** epic [poem]. **poema sinfonico** symphonic poem

poe'sia *nf* poetry; (componimento) poem

po'eta *nm* poet

poe'tessa *nf* poetess

po'etico *adj* poetic

poggiapi'edi *nm inv* footrest

poggi'are **1** *vt* lean; (posare) place **2** *vi* ∼ **su** be based on

poggia'testa *nm inv* head-rest

'poggio *nm* hillock

poggi'olo *nm* balcony

'poi **1** *adv* (dopo) then; (più tardi) later [on]; (finalmente) finally; **d'ora in** ∼ from now on; **questa** ∼**!** well! **2** *nm* **pensare al** ∼ think of the future

poiché *conj* since

pois *nm inv* **a** ∼ polka-dot

'poker *nm* poker

po'lacco, -a **1** *adj* Polish **2** *nmf* Pole **3** *nm* (lingua) Polish

po'lare *adj* polar

polarità *nf inv* polarity

polariz'zare *vt* polarize

pola'roid® *nf inv* instant camera

'polca *nf* polka

po'lemica *nf* controversy

polemica'mente *adv* controversially

polemiciz'zare *vi* engage in controversy

po'lemico *adj* controversial

po'lenta *nf* cornmeal porridge

poli'clinico *nm* general hospital

policro'mia *nf* polychromy

po'licromo *adj* polychrome

poli'estere *nm* polyester

polieti'lene *nm* polyethylene

poliga'mia *nf* polygamy

poli'gamico *adj* polygamous

po'ligamo *adj* polygamous

poli'glotta *nmf* polyglot

po'ligono *nm* polygon; (di tiro) rifle range

po'limero *nm* polymer

Poli'nesia *nf* Polynesia

polinesi'ano *adj & nmf* Polynesian

'polio[mie'lite] *nf* polio[myelitis]

'polipo *nm* polyp

polisti'rolo *nm* polystyrene

poli'tecnico *nm* polytechnic

po'litica *nf* politics *sg*; (linea di condotta) policy; **fare** ∼ be in politics; **darsi alla** ∼ go into politics. **politica energetica** energy policy. **politica estera** foreign policy. **politica monetaria** monetary policy

politica'mente *adv* politically; ∼ **corretto** politically correct, pc

politi'chese *nm* political jargon

politiciz'zare *vt* politicize

po'litico, -a **1** *adj* political **2** *nmf* politician

poliva'lente *adj* all-purpose

poli'zia *nf* police, police force. **polizia giudiziaria** Criminal Investigation Department, CID. **polizia scientifica** forensics. **polizia stradale** traffic police

polizi'esco *adj* police *attrib*; ⟨romanzo, film⟩ detective *attrib*

polizi'otto **1** *nm* policeman. **poliziotto in borghese** plain clothes policeman. **poliziotto privato** private detective **2** *adj* police *attrib*

'polizza *nf* policy. **polizza di assicurazione** insurance policy

pol'laio *nm* chicken run; (fam: luogo chiassoso) mad house

pol'lame *nm* poultry

polla'strella *nf* spring chicken; fig fam bird

polla'strello *nm* spring chicken

pol'lastro *nm* cockerel

polle'ria *nf* poultry butcher, poulterer

'pollice *nm* thumb, (unità di misura) inch

'polline *nm* pollen; **allergia al polline** hay fever

polli'vendolo, -a *nmf* poulterer

'pollo *nm* chicken; (fam: semplicione) simpleton; **far ridere i polli** be ridiculous. **pollo allevato a terra** free-range chicken. **pollo arrosto** roast chicken. **pollo di batteria** battery chicken. **pollo alla cacciatora** chicken chasseur

polmo'nare *adj* pulmonary

pol'mone *nm* lung. **polmone d'acciaio** iron lung

polmo'nite *nf* pneumonia

'polo *nm* pole; Sport polo; (maglietta) polo top; Pol party; (conservatori) Italian Conservatives. **polo magnetico** magnetic pole. **polo nord** North Pole. **polo sud** South Pole

Po'lonia *nf* Poland

'polpa *nf* pulp

pol'paccio *nm* calf

polpa'strello *nm* fingertip

pol'petta *nf* meatball

polpet'tone *nm* meatloaf. **polpettone sentimentale** *fam* hokum

'polpo *nm* octopus

pol'poso *adj* fleshy

pol'sino *nm* cuff

'polso *nm* pulse; Anat wrist; fig authority; **avere** ∼ be strict; **essere privo di** ∼ be soft

pol'tiglia *nf* mush

pol'trire *vi* lie around

pol'trona *nf* armchair; Theat seat in the stalls

pol'trone *adj* lazy

'polvere *nf* dust; (sostanza polverizzata) powder; **in** ∼ powdered; **sapone in polvere** soap powder. **polvere da sparo** gun powder

polveri'era *nf* gunpowder magazine; fig tinderbox

polve'rina *nf* (medicina) powder

polveriz'zare *vt* pulverize; (nebulizzare) atomize; smash, shatter ⟨record⟩; ∼ **qualcuno** pulverize somebody

polve'rone *nm* cloud of dust

polve'roso *adj* dusty

po'mata *nf* ointment, cream. **pomata cicatrizzante** healing cream for cuts

pomel'lato *adj* dappled

po'mello *nm* knob; (guancia) cheek

pomeridi'ano *adj* afternoon *attrib*; **alle tre pomeridiane** at three in the afternoon, at three p.m.

pome'riggio *nm* afternoon; **buon** ∼! have a good afternoon!; **oggi** ∼ this afternoon; **questo** ∼ this afternoon

'pomice *nf* pumice

pomici'are *vi* fam snog, neck

pomici'ata *nf* fam snogging, necking

'pomo *nm* (oggetto) knob. **pomo d'Adamo** Adam's apple

pomo'doro *nm* tomato

'pompa *nf* pump; (sfarzo) pomp. **pompa della benzina** petrol pump, gas pump Am; **pompe** *pl* **funebri** (funzione) funeral

pom'pare *vt* pump; (gonfiare d'aria) pump up; (fig: esagerare) exaggerate; ∼ **fuori** pump out

pompei'ano, **-a** *adj & nmf* Pompeian

pom'pelmo *nm* grapefruit

pompi'ere *nm* fireman; **i pompieri** the fire brigade

pom'pon *nm inv* pompom

pom'poso *adj* pompous

'poncho *nm inv* poncho

ponde'rare *vt* ponder

ponde'roso *adj* ponderous

po'nente *nm* west

'ponte *nm* bridge; Naut deck; (impalcatura) scaffolding; **fare il** ∼ fig make a long weekend of it. **legge ponte** interim *or* bridging law; **governo ponte** interim government. **ponte aereo** airlift. **ponte auto** car deck. **ponte di coperta** main deck. **ponte levatoio** drawbridge. **ponte radio** radio link. **ponte dei Sospiri** Bridge of Sighs. **ponte di volo** flight deck

pon'tefice *nm* pontiff

pontifi'care *vi* pontificate

pontifi'cato *nm* pontificate

ponti'ficio *adj* papal

pon'tile *nm* jetty

'pony *nm inv* pony. **pony express** express delivery service

pool *nm inv* Comm consortium; (di giornalisti) team; (di esperti) pool, team. ∼ **genico** gene pool

pop'corn *nm* popcorn

'popelin *nm* poplin

popò ① *nf* fam pooh
② *nm inv* fam bottie, bum

popo'lano *adj* of the [common] people

popo'lare ① *adj* popular; (comune) common
② *vt* populate; **essere popolato da** (pieno di) be full by

popolarità *nf* popularity

popo'larsi *vr* get crowded

popolazi'one *nf* population

'popolo *nm* people

popo'loso *adj* populous

'poppa *nf* Naut stern; (mammella) breast; **a** ∼ astern

pop'pare *vt* suck

pop'pata *nf* (pasto) feed

poppa'toio *nm* [feeding-]bottle

popu'lista *nmf* populist

por'caio *nm* anche fig pigsty; **fare un** ∼ fam make a mess

por'cata *nf* load of rubbish; **porcate** *pl* (fam: cibo) junk food; **fare una** ∼ **a qualcuno** play a dirty trick on somebody

porcel'lana *nf* porcelain, china. **porcellana fine** bone china

porcel'lino *nm* piglet. **porcellino d'India** guinea-pig

porche'ria *nf* dirt; (fig: cosa orrenda) piece of filth; (fam: robaccia) rubbish

por'chetta *nf* roast sucking pig

por'cile *nm* pigsty

por'cino ① *adj* pig *attrib*
② *nm* (fungo) cep (edible mushroom)

'porco *nm* pig; (carne) pork

porco'spino *nm* porcupine

'porfido *nm* porphyry

'porgere *vt* give; (offrire) offer; ∼ **orecchio** lend an ear; **porgo distinti saluti** (in lettera) I remain, yours sincerely

'porno *adj inv* porn

pornogra'fia *nf* pornography

porno'grafico *adj* pornographic

'poro *nm* pore

po'roso *adj* porous

'porpora *nf* purple

'porre *vt* put; (collocare) place; (supporre) suppose; ask ⟨*domanda*⟩; present ⟨*candidatura*⟩; ∼ **una domanda a qualcuno** ask somebody a question; **poniamo [il caso] che…** let us suppose that…; ∼ **fine** o **termine a** put an end to

'porro *nm* Bot leek; (verruca) wart

'porsi *vr* put oneself; ∼ **a sedere** sit down; ∼ **in cammino** set out

'porta *nf* door; Sport goal; (di città) gate; Comput port; ∼ **a** ∼ door-to-door; **mettere alla** ∼ show somebody the door; **a porte chiuse** ⟨riunione, processo⟩ behind closed doors, in camera; **essere alle porte** (vicino) be on the doorstep. **porta a due battenti** double door[s]. **porta d'ingresso** front door. **porta parallela** Comput parallel port. **porta seriale** Comput serial port. **porta di servizio** tradesman's entrance. **porta di sicurezza** emergency exit. **porta per la stampante** Comput printer port. **porta a vento** swing-door

portaba'gagli *nm inv* (facchino) porter; (su treno ecc) luggage-rack; Auto boot, trunk Am; (sul tetto di un'auto) roof-rack

portabandi'era *nmf inv* standard-bearer

portabici'clette *nm inv* cycle rack

portabot'tiglie *nm inv* bottle rack, wine rack

porta'burro *nm inv* butter dish

porta'cenere *nm inv* ashtray

portachi'avi *nm inv* keyring

porta'cipria *nm inv* compact

portacon'tainer *nm inv* container truck

portadocu'menti *nm inv* document wallet

porta'erei *nf inv* aircraft carrier

portafi'nestra *nf* French window

porta'foglio *nm* wallet; (per documenti) portfolio; (ministero) ministry; **a** ∼ ⟨gonna⟩ wrap-over

portafor'tuna ① *nm inv* lucky charm ② *adj inv* lucky

portagi'oie *nm inv* jewellery box

por'tale *nm* door; Comput portal

portama'tite *nm inv* pencil case

porta'mento *nm* deportment; (condotta) behaviour

porta'mina *nm inv* propelling pencil

portamo'nete *nm inv* purse

por'tante *adj* bearing *attrib*

portan'tina *nf* sedan-chair

portaom'brelli *nm inv* umbrella stand

porta'pacchi *nm inv* roof rack; (su bicicletta) luggage rack

porta'penne *nm inv* pencil case

por'tare *vt* (verso chi parla) bring; (lontano da chi parla) take; (sorreggere, Math) carry; (condurre) lead; (indossare) wear; (avere) bear; ∼ **a spasso il cane** take the dog for a walk; ∼ **a termine** bring to a close; ∼ **avanti** carry on; ∼ **bene/male** bring good/bad luck; ∼ **bene/male gli anni** look young/old for one's age; ∼ **fortuna** be lucky; ∼ **rancore** bear a grudge; ∼ **via** take away

portari'viste *nm inv* magazine rack

por'tarsi *vr* (trasferirsi) move; (comportarsi) behave

porta'sci *nm inv* ski rack

portasciuga'mano *nm* towel rail

portasiga'rette *nm inv* cigarette-case

porta'spilli *nm inv* pin-cushion

por'tata *nf* (di pranzo) course; Auto carrying capacity; (di arma) range; (fig: abilità) capability; **a** ∼ **di mano** within reach; **alla** ∼ **di tutti** accessible to all; (finanziariamente) within everybody's reach; **di grande** ∼ (scoperta) with far-reaching consequences

por'tatile ① *adj* portable ② *nm* Comput laptop

por'tato *adj* ⟨indumento⟩ worn; (dotato) gifted; **essere** ∼ **per qualcosa** have a gift for something; **essere** ∼ **a** (tendere a) be inclined to

porta|'tore, -trice *nmf* bearer; **al** ∼ to the bearer. **portatore di handicap** disabled person

portatovagli'olo *nm* napkin ring

portau'ovo *nm inv* egg-cup

porta'voce *nmf inv* spokesperson

por'tello *nm* hatch. **portello di sicurezza** escape hatch

por'tento *nm* marvel; (persona dotata) prodigy

porten'toso *adj* wonderful

port'folio *nm inv* (di fotografie ecc) portfolio

porti'cato *nm* portico

'portico *nm* portico

porti'era *nf* (di auto) door; (tendaggio) door curtain

porti'ere *nm* porter, doorman; Sport goalkeeper. **portiere di notte** night porter

P

porti'naio, **-a** *nmf* caretaker, concierge

portine'ria *nf* concierge's room; (di ospedale) porter's lodge

'**porto** ① *pp di* PORGERE
② *nm* harbour; (complesso) port; (vino) port [wine]; (spesa di trasporto) carriage; **andare in ~** succeed. **porto d'armi** gun licence. **porto container** container port. **porto fluviale** river port. **porto franco** free port. **porto marittimo** seaport

Porto'gallo *nm* Portugal

porto'ghese *adj & nmf* Portuguese

por'tone *nm* main door

portori'cano, **-a** *adj & nmf* Puerto Rican

Porto'rico *nm* Puerto Rico

portu'ale *nm* dock worker, docker

porzi'one *nf* portion

'**posa** *nf* laying; (riposo) rest; Phot exposure; (atteggiamento) pose; **mettersi in ~** pose; **senza ~** without rest

po'sare ① *vt* put; (giù) put [down]
② *vi* (poggiare) rest; (per un ritratto) pose

po'sarsi *vr* alight; (sostare) rest; Aeron land

po'sata *nf* piece of cutlery; **posate** *pl* cutlery *sg*, flatware *sg* Am

po'sato *adj* sedate

po'scritto *nm* postscript

posi'tivo *adj* positive

posizio'nare *vt* position

posizi'one *nf* position; **farsi una ~** get ahead; **prendere ~** fig take a stand

posolo'gia *nf* dosage

po'sporre *vt* place after; (posticipare) postpone

po'sposto *pp di* POSPORRE

posse'dere *vt* possess, own

possedi'mento *nm* possession

posses'sivo *adj* possessive

pos'sesso *nm* possession, ownership; (bene) possession; **entrare in ~ di** come into possession of; **essere in ~ di** be in possession of; **prendere ~ di** take possession of

posses'sore *nm* owner

pos'sibile ① *adj* possible; **il più presto ~** as soon as possible
② *nm* **fare [tutto] il ~** do one's best

possibilità ① *nf inv* possibility; (occasione) chance; **avere la ~ di fare qualcosa** have the chance *or* opportunity to do something
② *nfpl* (mezzi) means

possi'dente *nmf* land-owner

'**posso** ▶ POTERE

'**posta** *nf* post, mail; (ufficio postale) post office; (al gioco) stake; **spese di ~** postage; **per ~** by post, by mail; **la ~ in gioco è...** fig what's at stake is...; **a bella ~** on

purpose; **Poste e Telecomunicazioni** [Italian] Post Office. **posta aerea** airmail. **posta centrale** main post office, central post office. **posta del cuore** agony column. **posta elettronica** electronic mail, e-mail; **spedire per ~ elettronica** e-mail. **posta elettronica vocale** voicemail. **posta in arrivo** inbox. **posta prioritaria** ≈ first-class mail

posta'giro *nm* postal giro

po'stale *adj* postal

postazi'one *nf* position; Mil emplacement

post'bellico *adj* postwar

postda'tare *vt* postdate ⟨assegno⟩

posteggi'are *vt/i* park

posteggia|'tore, **-trice** *nmf* parking attendant

po'steggio *nm* car-park, parking lot Am; (di taxi) taxi-rank

'**posteri** *nmpl* descendants

posteri'ore ① *adj* back *attrib*, rear *attrib*; (nel tempo) later
② *nm* fam posterior; behind

posterità *nf* posterity

po'sticcio ① *adj* artificial; (barba) false
② *nm* hair-piece

postici'pare *vt* postpone

po'stilla *nf* note; Jur rider

po'stino *nm* postman, mailman Am

postmo'derno *adj* postmodern

'**posto** ① *pp di* PORRE
② *nm* place; (spazio) room; (impiego) job; Mil post; (sedile) seat; **a/fuori ~** in/out of place; **prendere ~** take up room; **sul ~** on-site; **essere a ~** ⟨casa, libri⟩ be tidy; **no grazie, sono a ~** no thanks, I'm all right; **mettere a ~** tidy ⟨stanza⟩; **fare ~** a make room for; **al ~ di** (invece di) in place of, instead of. **posto di blocco** checkpoint. **posto di guardia** guard post. **posto di guida** driving seat. **posto di lavoro** job; Comput workstation; **posti** *pl* in piedi standing room. **posto di polizia** police station; **posti** *pl* a sedere seating, seats

post-'partum *adj* post-natal

'**postumo** ① *adj* posthumous
② *nm* after-effect; **postumi** *pl* della sbornia hangover

po'tabile *adj* drinkable; **acqua potabile** drinking water; **non ~** undrinkable

po'tare *vt* prune

po'tassa *nf* potash

po'tassio *nm* potassium

po'tente *adj* powerful; (efficace) potent

po'tenza *nf* power; (efficacia) potency. **potenza mondiale** world power. **potenza nucleare** nuclear power

potenzi'ale *adj & nm* potential

po'tere ① *nm* power; **al ~** in power.
potere d'acquisto purchasing power, spending power. **il quarto potere** the fourth estate
② *vi* can, be able to; **posso entrare?** can I come in?; (formale) may I come in?; **mi spiace, non posso venire alla festa** I'm sorry, I can't come to the party *or* I won't be able to come to the party; **posso fare qualche cosa?** can I do something?; **che tu possa essere felice!** may you be happy!; **non ne posso più** (sono stanco) I can't go on; (sono stufo) I can't take any more; **può darsi** perhaps; **può darsi che sia vero** perhaps it's true; **potrebbe aver ragione** he could be right, he might be right; **avresti potuto telefonare** you could have phoned, you might have phoned; **spero di poter venire** I hope to be able to come; **senza poter telefonare** without being able to phone; **spero che potremo incontrarci presto** I hope we can meet soon

potestà *nf* power

pot-pour'ri *nm inv* medley

'povero, -a ① *adj* poor; (semplice) plain; **~ di** (paese, terreno) lacking in; **in parole povere** in a few words
② *nf* poor woman
③ *nm* poor man; **i poveri** the poor

povertà *nf* poverty

pozi'one *nf* potion

'pozza *nf* pool

poz'zanghera *nf* puddle

'pozzo *nm* well; (minerario) pit. **pozzo petrolifero** oil well. **pozzo di petrolio** oil well. **pozzo di ventilazione** air shaft

pp. *abbr* (**pagine**) pp

PP.TT. *abbr* (**Poste e Telecomunicazioni**) [Italian] Post Office

PR *nfpl abbr* PR

prêt-à-por'ter *nm* ready-to-wear clothing

'Praga *nf* Prague

prag'matico *adj* pragmatic

prali'nato *adj* (mandorla, gelato) praline-coated

pram'matica *nf* **essere di ~** be customary

pranotera'pia *nf* laying on of hands

pran'zare *vi* lunch.

'pranzo *nm* lunch. **pranzo di lavoro** business lunch, working lunch. **pranzo della mensa scolastica** school lunch. **pranzo di nozze** wedding breakfast

'prassi *nf* standard procedure

prate'ria *nf* grassland, prairie

'pratica *nf* practice; (esperienza) experience; (documentazione) file; **avere ~ di qualcosa** be familiar with something, have experience of something; **mettere**

qualcosa **in ~** put something into practice; **far ~** gain experience; **fare le pratiche per** gather the necessary papers for

prati'cabile *adj* practicable; (strada) passable

pratica'mente *adv* practically

prati'cante *nmf* apprentice; Relig [regular] churchgoer

prati'care *vt* practise; (frequentare) associate with; (fare) make

praticità *nf* practicality

'pratico *adj* practical; (esperto) experienced, knowledgeable; (comodo) convenient; **essere ~ di qualcosa** know about something; **all'atto ~** in practice

'prato *nm* meadow; (di giardino) lawn. **prato all'inglese** lawn

preaccensi'one *nf* Auto pre-ignition

pre'ambolo *nm* preamble

preannunci'are *vt* give advance notice of

prean'nuncio *nm* advance notice

preavvi'sare *vt* forewarn

preav'viso *nm* warning

precari'cato *adj* preloaded

precarietà *nf* frailty

pre'cario *adj* precarious

precauzi'one *nf* precaution; (cautela) care

prece'dente ① *adj* previous
② *nm* precedent; **avere dei precedenti penali** have a criminal record; **senza precedenti** (successo) unprecedented

precedente'mente *adv* previously

prece'denza *nf* precedence; (di veicoli) right of way; **dare la ~ a** give priority to; Auto give way to; **avere la ~** have priority; Auto have right of way; **~ assoluta** top priority

pre'cedere *vt* precede

pre'cetto *nm* precept

precet'tore, -trice *nmf* tutor

precipi'tare ① *vt* **~ le cose** precipitate events; **~ qualcuno nella disperazione** cast somebody into a state of despair
② *vi* fall headlong; (situazione, eventi) come to a head

precipi'tarsi *vr* (gettarsi) throw oneself; (affrettarsi) rush; **~ a fare qualcosa** rush to do something

precipitazi'one *nf* (fretta) haste; (atmosferica) precipitation

precipi'toso *adj* hasty; (avventato) reckless; (caduta) headlong

preci'pizio *nm* precipice; **a ~** headlong

preci'sabile *adj* specifiable

precisa'mente *adv* precisely

preci'sare vt specify; (spiegare) clarify; **ci tengo a ∼ che...** I want to make the point that...

precisazi'one nf clarification

precisi'one nf precision

pre'ciso adj precise; ⟨calcolo, risposta⟩ accurate; ⟨ore⟩ sharp; (identico) identical

pre'cludere vt preclude

pre'cludersi vr ∼ **ogni possibilità** preclude every possibility

pre'cluso pp di PRECLUDERE

pre'coce adj precocious; (prematuro) premature

precocità nf precociousness

precon'cetto ① adj preconceived ② nm prejudice

preconfezio'nato adj pre-packed

preconfigu'rato adj preconfigured

pre'correre vt (anticipare) anticipate; ∼ **i tempi** be ahead of one's time

precorri'|tore, -trice nmf precursor, forerunner

pre'cotto adj ready-cooked. **precotto e surgelato** cook-chill

precur'sore nm forerunner, precursor

'preda nf prey; (bottino) booty; **essere in ∼ al panico** be panic-stricken; **in ∼ alle fiamme** engulfed in flames

pre'dare vt plunder

preda'tore nm predator

predeces'sore nmf predecessor

pre'della nf platform

predel'lino nm step

predesti'nare vt predestine

predesti'nato adj predestined, preordained

predestinazi'one nf predestination

predetermi'nare vt predetermine

predetermi'nato adj predetermined, preordained

pre'detto pp di PREDIRE

'predica nf sermon; fig lecture

predi'care vt preach

predi'cato nm predicate

predige'rito adj predigested

predi'|letto, -a ① pp di PREDILIGERE ② adj favourite ③ nmf pet fam

predilezi'one nf predilection; **avere una ∼ per** have a predilection for, be partial to

predi'ligere vt prefer

prediposizi'one nf predisposition; (al disegno ecc) bent (a for)

pre'dire vt foretell

predi'sporre vt arrange; ∼ **qualcuno a qualcosa** Med predispose somebody to something; (preparare) prepare somebody for something

predi'sporsi vr ∼ **a** prepare oneself for

predi'sposto, -a ① pp di PREDISPORRE ② adj arranged. **predisposto per la TV via cavo** cable-ready

predizi'one nf prediction

predomi'nante adj predominant

predomi'nare vi predominate

predo'minio nm predominance

pre'done nm robber

prefabbri'cato ① adj prefabricated ② nm prefabricated building

prefazi'one nf preface

prefe'renza nf preference; **di ∼** preferably

preferenzi'ale adj preferential; **corsia preferenziale** bus and taxi lane

prefe'ribile adj preferable

preferibil'mente adv preferably

prefe'rire vt prefer

prefe'rito, -a adj & nmf favourite

pre'fetto nm prefect

prefet'tura nf prefecture

pre'figgere vt decide in advance, pre-arrange ⟨termine⟩

pre'figgersi vr ∼ **uno scopo** set oneself an objective

prefigu'rare vt (anticipare) foreshadow

prefinanzia'mento nm bridging loan

prefis'sare vt pre-arrange ⟨data, appuntamento⟩

pre'fisso ① pp di PREFIGGERE ② nm prefix; Teleph [dialling] code

pre'gare ① vi Relig pray ② vt Relig pray to; (supplicare) beg; **farsi ∼** need persuading; ∼ **qualcuno di fare qualcosa** ask somebody to do something; **si prega di...** please...; **si prega di non...** please do not...; **si prega di non fumare** please refrain from smoking

pre'gevole adj valuable

preghi'era nf prayer; (richiesta) request

pregi'arsi vr **si pregia di non essere mai in ritardo** he prides himself on never being late

pre'giato adj esteemed; (prezioso) valuable

'pregio nm esteem; (valore) value; (di persona) good point; **di ∼** valuable

pregiudi'care vt prejudice; (danneggiare) harm

pregiudi'cato ① adj prejudiced ② nm Jur previous offender

pregiu'dizio nm prejudice; (danno) detriment

pre'gnante adj (parola) pregnant, pregnant with meaning

'pregno adj (parola) pregnant; (pieno) full; ∼ **di** ⟨umidità⟩ saturated with; ⟨significato⟩ pregnant with

'prego *int* (non c'è di che) don't mention it!; (per favore) please; ~? I beg your pardon?; **posso? –~** may I? –please do

pregu'stare *vt* look forward to

preinstal'lato *adj* preinstalled

prei'storia *nf* prehistory

prei'storico *adj* prehistoric

pre'lato *nm* prelate

prela'vaggio *nm* prewash

preleva'mento *nm* withdrawal

prele'vare *vt* withdraw ⟨*soldi*⟩; collect ⟨*merci*⟩; Med take

preli'evo *nm* (di soldi) withdrawal. **prelievo di sangue** blood sample

prelimi'nare ① *adj* preliminary ② *nm* **preliminari** *pl* preliminaries

pre'ludere *vi* ~ **a** herald

pre'ludio *nm* prelude

prema'man ① *nm inv* maternity dress ② *adj inv* maternity *attrib*

prematrimoni'ale *adj* premarital

prematura'mente *adv* prematurely

prema'turo, -a ① *adj* premature ② *nmf* premature baby

premedi'tare *vt* premeditate

premeditazi'one *nf* premeditation; **con ~** ⟨*omicidio*⟩ premeditated

'premere ① *vt* press; Comput hit ⟨*tasto*⟩ ② *vi* ~ **a** (importare) matter to; **mi preme sapere** I need to know; ~ **su** press on; push ⟨*pulsante*⟩; (fig: fare pressione su) put pressure on, pressure; ~ **per ottenere qualcosa** push for something

pre'messa *nf* introduction; **senza tante premesse** without further ado

pre'messo *pp di* PREMETTERE; ~ **che** bearing in mind that

pre'mettere *vt* (mettere prima) put before; **premetto che...** I want to make it clear first that...; ~ **un'introduzione a un libro** put an introduction at the beginning of a book

premi'are *vt* give a prize to; (ricompensare) reward

premi'ato *adj* award-winning

premiazi'one *nf* prize giving

premi'nente *adj* pre-eminent

premi'nenza *nf* pre-eminence

'premio *nm* prize; (ricompensa) reward; (di produzione ecc) bonus; Fin premium. **premio di assicurazione** insurance premium. **premio di consolazione** consolation prize; (ridicolo) booby prize. **premio di ingaggio** Sport signing fee. **premio di produzione** productivity bonus

premoni'tore *adj* ⟨*sogno, segno*⟩ premonitory

premonizi'one *nf* premonition

premu'nire *vt* fortify

premu'nirsi *vr* take protective measures; ~ **di** provide oneself with; ~ **contro** protect oneself against

pre'mura *nf* (fretta) hurry; (cura) care; **far ~ a qualcuno** hurry somebody up

premu'roso *adj* thoughtful

prena'tale *adj* antenatal

'prendere ① *vt* take; (afferrare) seize; catch ⟨*treno, malattia, ladro, pesce*⟩; have ⟨*cibo, bevanda*⟩; (far pagare) charge; (assumere) take on; (ottenere) get; (occupare) take up; (guadagnare) earn; ~ **informazioni** make inquiries; ~ **in giro qualcuno** pull somebody's leg; ~ **a calci/pugni** kick/punch; **che ti prende?** what's got into you?; **quanto prende?** what do you charge?; ~ **una persona per un'altra** mistake a person for somebody else; **passare a ~ qualcuno** collect somebody, pick somebody up ② *vi* (voltare) turn; (attecchire) take root; (rapprendersi) set; ⟨*fuoco*⟩ catch, take; ~ **a destra/sinistra** turn right/left; ~ **a fare qualcosa** start doing something; **la colla non ha preso** the glue didn't take

'prendersi *vr* ~ **a pugni** come to blows; ~ **cura di** take care of ⟨*ammalato*⟩; **prendersela** take it to heart; **si prende troppo sul serio** he takes himself too seriously

prendi'sole *nm inv* sundress

preno'tare *vt* book, reserve

preno'tarsi *vr* ~ **per** put one's name down for

preno'tato *adj* booked, reserved

prenotazi'one *nf* booking, reservation. **prenotazione di gruppo** group booking

'prensile *adj* prehensile

preoccu'pante *adj* alarming

preoccu'pare *vt* worry

preoccu'parsi *vr* ~ worry (di about); ~ **di fare qualcosa** take the trouble to do something

preoccu'pato *adj* worried; (apprensivo) concerned

preoccupazi'one *nf* worry; (apprensione) concern

preopera'torio *adj* preoperative

prepa'gato-a ① *adj* prepaid ② *nm* Teleph pay-as-you-go

prepa'rare *vt* prepare; study for ⟨*esame*⟩; ~ **da mangiare** prepare a meal

prepa'rarsi *vr* get ready

prepara'tivi *nmpl* preparations

prepa'rato *nm* (prodotto) preparation

prepara'torio *adj* preparatory

preparazi'one *nf* preparation; (competenza) knowledge

prepensiona'mento *nm* early retirement

prepondeʹrante *adj* predominant, preponderant

prepondeʹranza *nf* preponderance, prevalence

preʹporre *vt* place before

preposiziʹone *nf* preposition

preʹposto ① pp di PREPORRE
② *adj* ~ **a** (addetto a) in charge of

prepoʹtente ① *adj* overbearing
② *nmf* bully; **fare il/la** ~ **con qualcuno** bully somebody

prepoʹtenza *nf* high-handedness

preprogramʹmato *adj* Comput preprogrammed

preʹpuzio *nm* foreskin, prepuce

prerogaʹtiva *nf* prerogative

ʹpresa *nf* taking; (conquista) capture; (stretta) hold; (di cemento ecc) setting; Electr socket; (di gas, acqua) inlet, connection; (pizzico) pinch; **essere alle prese con** be struggling *or* grappling with; **a** ~ **rapida** ⟨cemento, colla⟩ quick-setting; **fare** ~ **su qualcuno** influence somebody.
macchina da presa cine camera.
presa d'aria air vent.**presa in giro** leg-pull. **presa multipla** adaptor. **presa scart** scart connector

preʹsagio *nm* omen

presaʹgire *vt* foretell

presaʹlario *nm* maintenance grant

ʹpresbite *adj* long-sighted

presbiteriʹano, -a *adj & nmf* Presbyterian

presbiʹterio *nm* presbytery

preʹscelto *adj* selected

preʹscindere *vi* ~ **da** leave aside; **a** ~ **da** apart from

prescoʹlare *adj* pre-school; **in età** ~ pre-school

preʹscritto pp di PRESCRIVERE

preʹscrivere *vt* prescribe

prescriziʹone *nf* prescription; (norma) rule; **cadere in** ~ cease to be valid as a result of the statute of limitations

preseleziʹone *nf* preliminary selection; (per il traffico) advance lane markings; Sport [qualifying] heats *pl*

presenʹtare *vt* present; (far conoscere) introduce; show ⟨documento⟩; (inoltrare) submit

presenʹtarsi *vr* present oneself; (farsi conoscere) introduce oneself; (a ufficio) attend; (alla polizia ecc) report; (come candidato) stand, run (**a** for); ⟨occasione⟩ occur; ~ **bene/male** ⟨persona⟩ make a good/ bad impression; ⟨situazione⟩ look good/ bad

presentaʹtore, -trice *nmf* presenter; (di notiziario) announcer. **presentatore di talk show** chatshow host

presentaziʹone *nf* presentation; (per conoscersi) introduction; **fare le presentazioni** do the introductions; **dietro** ~ **di ricetta medica** on doctor's prescription only

preʹsente ① *adj* present; (attuale) current; (questo) this; **aver** ~ remember ② *nm* present; **i presenti** those present ③ *nf* **allegato alla** ~ (in lettera) enclosed

presentiʹmento *nm* foreboding

preʹsenza *nf* presence; (aspetto) appearance; **in** ~ **di, alla** ~ **di** in the presence of; **di bella** ~ personable.
presenza di spirito presence of mind

presenziʹare *vi* ~ **a** attend

preʹsepe, preʹsepio *nm* crib

preserʹvare *vt* preserve; (proteggere) protect (**da** from)

preservaʹtivo *nm* condom

preservaziʹone *nf* preservation

ʹpreside ① *nm* headmaster
② *nf* headmistress

presiʹdente ① *nm* chairman; Pol president
② *nf* chairwoman; Pol president.
presidente del consiglio [dei ministri] Prime Minister. **presidente della repubblica** President of the Republic

presidenʹtessa *nf* chairwoman

presiʹdenza *nf* presidency; (di assemblea) chairmanship

presidenziʹale *adj* presidential

presidiʹare *vt* garrison

preʹsidio *nm* garrison

presiʹedere *vt* preside over

ʹpreso pp di PRENDERE

ʹpressa *nf* Mech press

press-ʹagent *mf inv* publicist, press agent

presʹsante *adj* urgent

pressapʹpoco *adv* about

presʹsare *vt* press

pressiʹone *nf* pressure; **far** ~ **su** put pressure on; **essere sotto** ~ fig be under pressure; **esercitare pressioni su qualcuno** put pressure on somebody; **a/di alta** ~ high pressure. **pressione fiscale** tax burden. **pressione delle gomme** tyre pressure. **pressione del sangue** blood pressure

ʹpresso ① *prep* near; (a casa di) with; (negli indirizzi) care of, c/o; ⟨lavorare⟩ for; **richiedere qualcosa** ~ **una società** request something from a company
② *nmpl* **pressi**: **nei pressi di...** in the neighbourhood *or* vicinity of...

pressoché *adv* almost

pressurizʹzare *vt* pressurize

pressurizʹzato *adj* pressurized

prestabiʹlire *vt* arrange in advance

prestabi'lito *adj* agreed, predetermined

prestam'pato ① *adj* printed
② *nm* (modulo) form

pre'stante *adj* good-looking

pre'stanza *nf* good looks *pl*

pre'stare *vt* lend; ~ **attenzione** pay attention; ~ **aiuto** lend a hand; ~ **ascolto** lend an ear; ~ **fede** a give credence to; ~ **giuramento** take the oath; **farsi** ~ borrow (da from)

pre'starsi *vr* ⟨frase⟩ lend itself; ⟨persona⟩ offer

prestazi'one *nf* performance; **prestazioni** *pl* (servizi) services

prestigia|'tore, -trice *nmf* conjuror, conjurer

pre'stigio *nm* prestige; **gioco di prestigio** conjuring trick

prestigi'oso *nm* prestigious

'prestito *nm* loan; **dare in** ~ lend; **prendere in** ~ borrow. **prestito bancario** bank loan. **prestito con garanzia collaterale** collateral loan

'presto *adv* soon; (di buon'ora) early; (in fretta) quickly; **a** ~ see you soon; **al più** ~ as soon as possible; ~ **o tardi** sooner or later; **far** ~ be quick

pre'sumere *vt* presume; (credere) think

presu'mibile *adj* **è** ~ **che...** presumably, ...

pre'sunto *adj* ⟨colpevole⟩ presumed

presuntu'oso ① *adj* presumptuous
② *nmf* presumptuous person

presunzi'one *nf* presumption

presup'porre *vt* suppose; (richiedere) presuppose

presupposizi'one *nf* presupposition

presup'posto *nm* essential requirement

'prete *nm* priest

preten'dente ① *nmf* pretender
② *nm* (corteggiatore) suitor

pre'tendere ① *vt* (sostenere) claim; (esigere) demand
② *vi* ~ **a** claim to; ~ **di** (esigere) demand to

pretensi'one *nf* pretension

pretenzi'oso *adj* pretentious

preterintenzio'nale *adj* **omicidio preterintenzionale** manslaughter

pre'terito *nm* preterite

pre'tesa *nf* pretension; (esigenza) claim; **senza pretese** unpretentious

pre'teso pp di PRETENDERE

pre'testo *nm* pretext

pre'tore *nm* magistrate

pretta'mente *adv* decidedly

'pretto *adj* pure

pre'tura *nf* magistrate's court

preva'lente *adj* prevalent

prevalente'mente *adv* primarily, predominantly

preva'lenza *nf* prevalence

preva'lere *vi* prevail

pre'valso pp di PREVALERE

preve'dere *vt* foresee; forecast ⟨tempo⟩; ⟨legge ecc⟩ provide for

preve'nire *vt* precede; (evitare) prevent; (avvertire) forewarn

preventi'vare *vt* estimate; (aspettarsi) budget for

preven'tivo ① *adj* preventive; **bilancio preventivo** budget
② *nm* Comm estimate

preve'nuto *adj* forewarned; (maldisposto) prejudiced

prevenzi'one *nf* prevention; (preconcetto) prejudice

previ'dente *adj* provident

previ'denza *nf* foresight. **previdenza integrativa** supplementary social security, supplementary welfare Am. **previdenza sociale** social security, welfare Am

previdenzi'ale *adj* provident

'previo *adj* ~ **pagamento** on payment

previsi'one *nf* forecast; **in** ~ **di** in anticipation of; **previsioni** *pl* **del tempo** weather forecast

pre'visto ① pp di PREVEDERE
② *adj* foreseen
③ *nm* **più/meno/prima del** ~ more/less/earlier than expected

prezi'oso *adj* precious

prez'zemolo *nm* parsley

'prezzo *nm* price; **[a] metà** ~ half price; **a** ~ **ribassato** at a reduced price; **non aver** ~ fig be priceless. **prezzo d'acquisto** purchase price. **prezzo di costo** cost price. **prezzo al dettaglio** o **prezzo al minuto** retail price. **prezzo di fabbrica** factory price. **prezzo di favore** special price. **prezzo all'ingrosso** wholesale price. **prezzo intero** full price. **prezzo di listino** list price. **prezzo di mercato** market price. **prezzo d'offerta** offer price. **prezzo politico** subsidized price. **prezzo di riferimento** benchmark price. **prezzo scontato** sale price. **prezzo sorvegliato** controlled price. **prezzo stracciato** slashed price, drastically reduced price. **prezzo trattabile** price negotiable. **prezzo unitario** unit price. **prezzo di vendita** selling price

prigi'one *nf* prison; (pena) imprisonment; **mettere in** ~ imprison, put in prison

prigio'nia *nf* imprisonment

prigioni'ero, -a ① *adj* imprisoned
② *nmf* prisoner; **tenere** ~ **qualcuno** keep somebody prisoner. **prigioniero di** ⋯▷

guerra prisoner of war, POW.
prigioniero politico political prisoner

'**prima** ① *adv* before; (più presto) earlier; (in anticipo) beforeheand; (in primo luogo) first; **finiamo questo,** ∼ let's finish this first; **puoi venire** ∼? (di giorni) can't you come any sooner?; (di ore) can't you come any earlier?; ∼ **o poi** sooner or later; **quanto** ∼ as soon as possible
② *prep* ∼ **di** before; ∼ **di mangiare** before eating; ∼ **d'ora** before now
③ *conj* ∼ **che** before; ∼ **che posso** as soon as I can; ∼ **possibile** asap
④ *nf* first class; Theat first night; Auto first [gear]. **prima elementare** first grade

pri'mario *adj* primary; (principale) principal

pri'mate *nm* primate

prima'tista *nmf* record-holder

pri'mato *nm* supremacy; Sport record

prima'vera *nf* spring

primave'rile *adj* spring *attrib*

primeggi'are *vi* excel

primi'tivo *adj* primitive; (originario) original

pri'mizie *nfpl* early produce *sg*

'**primo** ① *adj* first; (fondamentale) principal; (in importanza) main; (precedente tra due) former; (iniziale) early; (migliore) best
② *nm* first; **il** ∼ **d'aprile** April the first, April Fools' Day; **primi** *pl* **tempi** (i primi giorni) the beginning; **in un** ∼ **tempo** at first. **prima colazione** *nf* breakfast. **prima copia** *nf* master copy. **prima linea** *nf* Mil front line. **prima serata** *nf* prime time; **in prima serata trasmetteremo...** in the early evening slot we are bringing you...

primo'genito, -a *adj & nmf* first-born

primogeni'tura *nf* primogeniture; **vendere la** ∼ sell one's birthright

primordi'ale *adj* primordial

'**primula** *nf* primrose

princi'pale ① *adj* main
② *nm* head, boss fam

princi'pato *nm* principality. **il Principato di Monaco** Monaco

'**principe** *nm* prince; **da** ∼ princely. **principe ereditario** crown prince. **principe del foro** famous lawyer

princi'pesco *adj* princely

princi'pessa *nf* princess

principi'ante *nmf* beginner

principi'are *vt/i* begin, start

prin'cipio *nm* beginning; (concetto) principle; (causa) cause; **per** ∼ on principle; **una questione di** ∼ a matter of principle. **principio attivo** active ingredient

pri'ore *nm* prior

pri'ori: **a** ∼ ① *adv* ⟨decidere⟩ a priori; **farsi a** ∼ **un'opinione di** prejudge
② *adj* a priori

priorità *nf inv* priority

priori'tario *adj* having priority; ⟨obiettivo⟩ priority *attrib*; **la nostra scelta prioritaria** our decision, which must take priority

'**prisma** *nm* prism

'**privacy** *nf* privacy

pri'vare *vt* deprive

pri'varsi *vr* deprive oneself

privatiz'zare *vt* privatize

privatizzazi'one *nf* privatization

pri'vato, -a ① *adj* private
② *nmf* private citizen; **in** ∼ in private; **ritirarsi a vita privata** withdraw from public life

privazi'one *nf* deprivation

privilegi'are *vt* privilege; (considerare più importante) favour

privi'legio *nm* privilege; **avere il** ∼ **di** have the privilege of; **questo saggio ha il** ∼ **della chiarezza** this essay has the merit of clarity

'**privo** *adj* ∼ **di** devoid of; (mancante) lacking in

pro ① *prep* for
② *nm* advantage; **a che** ∼? what's the point?; **il** ∼ **e il contro** the pros and cons

pro'babile *adj* probable

probabilità *nf inv* probability; **avere buone** ∼ have a fighting chance; ∼ **di riuscita** chances of success

probabil'mente *adv* probably

pro'bante *adj* convincing

probità *nf* probity

pro'blema *nm* problem; **non c'è** ∼ no problem

proble'matico *adj* problematic

pro'boscide *nf* trunk

procacci'are *vt* obtain

procacci'arsi *vr* obtain

pro'cace *adj* ⟨ragazza⟩ provocative

pro'cedere *vi* (in percorso, discorso) go on, proceed *fml*; (iniziare) start; **il lavoro procede bene** the work is going well; ∼ **contro** Jur start legal proceedings against

procedi'mento *nm* process; Jur proceedings *pl*. **procedimento giudiziario** legal proceedings

proce'dura *nf* procedure. **procedura civile** civil proceedings *pl*. **procedura fallimentare** bankruptcy proceedings *pl*

procedu'rale *adj* procedural

proces'sare *vt* Jur try

processi'one *nf* procession

pro'cesso *nm* process; Jur trial; **essere sotto** ∼ be on trial; **mettere sotto** ∼ put

on trial. **processo di pace** peace
process

proces'sore *nm* Comput processor

processu'ale *adj* trial *attrib*

pro'cinto *nm* essere in ∼ **di** be about to

proci'one *nm* raccoon

pro'clama *nm* proclamation

procla'mare *vt* proclaim

proclamazi'one *nf* proclamation

procrasti'nare *vt* liter postpone

procre'are *vt* procreate

procreazi'one *nf* procreation

pro'cura *nf* power of attorney; **per** ∼ by
proxy. **Procura [della Repubblica]**
Public Prosecutor's office

procu'rare *vt/i* procure; (causare) cause;
(cercare) try

procura'tore *nm* attorney.
Procuratore Generale Attorney
General. **procuratore legale** lawyer.
procuratore della repubblica public
prosecutor

'prode *adj* brave

pro'dezza *nf* bravery

prodi'gare *vt* lavish

prodi'garsi *vr* do one's best

pro'digio *nm* prodigy

prodigi'oso *adj* prodigious

'prodigo *adj* prodigal

prodi'torio *adj* treasonable

pro'dotto ① pp di PRODURRE
② *nm* product; **prodotti** *pl* **agricoli** farm
produce *sg*; ∼ **artigianalmente** *adj* made
by craftsmen; **prodotti** *pl* **di bellezza**
cosmetics. **prodotto derivato** by-
product; ∼ **in fabbrica** *adj* factory-made.
prodotto finito end product, finished
product. **prodotto interno lordo** gross
domestic product. **prodotto nazionale
lordo** gross national product

pro'durre *vt* produce

pro'dursi *vr* ⟨attore⟩ play; (accadere)
happen, occur

produt'|tore, -trice ① *adj* producing.
produttore di petrolio oil-producing
② *nmf* producer

produttività *nf* productivity

produt'tivo *adj* productive; **poco** ∼
unproductive

produzi'one *nf* production.
produzione in serie mass production

Prof. *abbr* (**professore**) Prof.

profa'nare *vt* desecrate

profanazi'one *nf* desecration

pro'fano ① *adj* profane
② *nm* **i profani** *pl* the uninitiated

profe'rire *vt* utter

Prof.essa *abbr* (**Professoressa**) Prof.

profes'sare *vt* profess; practise
⟨professione⟩

professio'nale *adj* professional; **istituto
professionale** training college

professionalità *nf* professionalism

professi'one *nf* profession; **libera
professione** profession

professio'nismo *nm* professionalism

professio'nista *nmf* professional

professo'rale *adj* professorial

profes'sor|e, -essa *nmf* Sch teacher;
Univ lecturer; (titolare di cattedra) professor

pro'feta *nm* prophet

pro'fetico *adj* prophetic

profetiz'zare *vt* prophesy

profe'zia *nf* prophecy

pro'ficuo *adj* profitable

profi'lare *vt* outline; (ornare) border; Aeron
streamline

profi'larsi *vr* stand out

profi'lattico ① *adj* prophylactic
② *nm* condom

pro'filo *nm* profile; (breve studio) outline; **di**
∼ in profile. **profilo genetico** genetic
profiling

profite'roles *nmpl* profiteroles

profit'tare *vi* ∼ **di** (avvantaggiarsi) profit
by; (approfittare) take advantage of

pro'fitto *nm* profit; (vantaggio) advantage;
mettere qualcosa a ∼ turn something to
one's advantage; **trarre** ∼ **da** (vantaggio)
derive benefit from

profonda'mente *adv* deeply,
profoundly

profondità *nf inv* depth; (del pensiero ecc)
depth, profundity; **in** ∼ in depth;
passaggio in ∼ Sport deep pass [down the
field]. **profondità di campo** Phot depth
of field

pro'fondo *adj* deep; ⟨pensiero ecc⟩
profound; ⟨cultura⟩ great

pro 'forma ① *adj* routine; **fattura pro
forma** pro forma [invoice]
② *adv* as a formality
③ *nm inv* formality

'profugo, -a *nmf* refugee

profu'mare ① *vi* smell good; ∼ **di** smell
of
② *vt* perfume

profu'marsi *vr* put on perfume

profumata'mente *adv* **pagare** ∼ pay
through the nose

profu'mato *adj* ⟨fiore⟩ fragrant;
⟨fazzoletto ecc⟩ scented

profume'ria *nf* perfumery

pro'fumo *nm* perfume, scent

profusi'one *nf* profusion; **a** ∼ in
profusion

pro'fuso *adj* profuse

pro'genie *nf* progeny

progeni|'tore, **-trice** nmf ancestor

proget'tare vt plan; plan, design ⟨costruzione⟩

progettazione nf planning, design. **progettazione assistita da computer** computer-aided design, CAD

proget'tista nmf designer

pro'getto nm plan; (di lavoro importante) project. **progetto di legge** bill. **progetto pilota** pilot scheme

prog'nosi nf inv prognosis; **in ~ riservata** on the danger list

pro'gramma nm programme; Comput program; **avere qualcosa in ~** have something planned, have something on; **programmi** pl **televisivi del mattino** breakfast TV. **programma antivirus** Comput antivirus program, antivirus software. **programma assemblatore** Comput assembler. **programma aziendale** business plan. **programma per la gestione dei file** Comput file manager. **programma di grafica** Comput graphics program. **programma politico** manifesto. **programma scolastico** syllabus. **programma di setup** Comput setup program. **programma di utilità** Comput utility

program'mare vt programme; Comput program

program'mato adj ⟨sviluppo⟩ planned

programma|'tore, **-trice** nmf [computer] programmer

programmazi'one nf programming

progre'dire vi [make] progress

progres'sione nf progression

progres'sista nmf progressive

progres'sivo adj progressive

pro'gresso nm progress; **fare progressi** make progress

proi'bire vt forbid

proibi'tivo adj prohibitive

proi'bito adj forbidden; **è ~ fumare qui** it's no smoking here

proibizi'one nf prohibition

proibizio'nismo nm prohibition

proiet'tare vt project; show ⟨film⟩

proi'ettile nm bullet

proiet'tore nm projector; Auto headlight. **proiettore per diapositive** slide projector

proiezi'one nf projection. **proiezione di diapositive** slide show

'prole nf offspring

proletari'ato nm proletariat

prole'tario adj & nm proletarian

prolife'rare vi proliferate

pro'lifico adj prolific

prolissità nf prolixity, diffuseness

pro'lisso adj verbose, prolix

pro 'loco nf tourist office (in small towns)

'prologo nm prologue

pro'lunga nf extension

prolunga'mento nm extension

prolun'gare vt extend ⟨contratto, scadenza, strada⟩; prolong ⟨vita⟩; lengthen ⟨vita, strada⟩

prolun'garsi vr continue, go on; **~ su** (dilungarsi) dwell upon

prome'moria nm memo; (per se stessi) reminder, note; (formale) memorandum

pro'messa nf promise; **era già una ~ del...** he was already a promising new talent in...

pro'messo ① pp di PROMETTERE ② adj ⟨terra⟩ promised; **promessa sposa** nf betrothed. **promesso sposo** nm betrothed

promet'tente adj promising

pro'mettere vt/i promise

promi'nente adj prominent

promi'nenza nf prominence

promiscuità nf promiscuity

pro'miscuo adj promiscuous

promon'torio nm promontory

pro'mosso ① pp di PROMUOVERE ② adj Sch who has gone up a year; Univ who has passed an exam

promo|'tore, **-trice** nmf promoter

promozio'nale adj promotional; **vendita promozionale** special offer

promozi'one nf promotion

promul'gare vt promulgate

promulgazi'one nf promulgation

promu'overe vt promote; Sch move up a class; **essere promosso** Sch, Univ pass one's exams

proni'pote ① nm (di bisnonno) great-grandson; (di prozio) great-nephew; **pronipoti** pl great-grandchildren ② nf (di bisnonno) great-granddaughter; (di prozio) great-niece

pro'nome nm pronoun

pronomi'nale adj pronominal

pronosti'care vt forecast, predict

pronostica|'tore, **-trice** nmf forecaster

pro'nostico nm forecast

pron'tezza nf readiness; (rapidità) quickness. **prontezza di riflessi** quick reflexes pl; **con ~ di spirito** quick-wittedly

'pronto adj ready; (rapido) quick; **~!** Teleph hello!; **tenersi ~ (per qualcosa)** be ready (for something); **pronti, attenti, via!** (in gare) ready! steady! go!; **a pronta cassa** cash on delivery. **pronto intervento** nm emergency service. **pronto soccorso** nm first aid; (in ospedale) accident and emergency, A&E

prontu'ario nm handbook

pro'nuncia *nf* pronunciation

pronunci'are *vt* pronounce; (dire) utter; deliver ⟨*discorso*⟩

pronunci'arsi *vr* (su un argomento) give one's opinion; ~ **a favore/contro qualcosa** pronounce oneself in favour of/against something

pronunci'ato *adj* pronounced; (prominente) prominent

pro'nunzia = PRONUNCIA

pronunzi'are = PRONUNCIARE

propa'ganda *nf* propaganda. **propaganda elettorale** electioneering. **propaganda di partito** party political propaganda

propa'gare *vt* propagate

propa'garsi *vr* spread

propagazi'one *nf* propagation

prope'deutico *adj* introductory

propel'lente *nm* propellant

pro'pendere *vi* ~ **per** be in favour of

propensi'one *nf* inclination, propensity

pro'penso ① pp di PROPENDERE ② *adj* essere ~ **a fare qualcosa** be inclined to do something

propi'nare *vt* administer

pro'pizio *adj* favourable

proponi'mento *nm* resolution

pro'porre *vt* propose; (suggerire) suggest

pro'porsi *vr* set oneself ⟨*obiettivo, meta*⟩; ~ **di** intend to

proporzio'nale *adj* proportional

proporzio'nare *vt* proportion

proporzio'nato *adj* proportioned

proporzi'one *nf* proportion

pro'posito *nm* intention; **ho fatto il** ~ **di...** I have made the decision to...; **a** ~ by the way; **a** ~ **di** with regard to; **di** ~ (apposta) on purpose; **capitare a** ~, **giungere a** ~ come at just the right time; **propositi** *pl* **per l'anno nuovo** New Year's resolutions

proposizi'one *nf* clause; (frase) sentence

pro'posta *nf* proposal, suggestion. **proposta di legge** bill. **proposta di matrimonio** [marriage] proposal

pro'posto pp di PROPORRE

propria'mente *adv* ~ **detto** in the strict sense of the word

proprietà *nf inv* property; (diritto) ownership; (correttezza) propriety; **essere di** ~ **di qualcuno** be somebody's property. **proprietà collettiva** collective ownership. **proprietà immobiliare** property. **proprietà di linguaggio** correct use of language. **proprietà privata** private property

proprie'taria *nf* owner; (di casa affittata) landlady

proprie'tario *nm* owner; (di casa affittata) landlord

'proprio ① *adj* one's [own]; (caratteristico) typical; (appropriato) proper ② *adv* just; (veramente) really; **non** ~ not really, not exactly; (affatto) not... at all ③ *pron* one's own ④ *nm* one's own; **lavorare in** ~ be one's own boss; **mettersi in** ~ set up on one's own

propu'gnare *vt* support

propulsi'one *nf* propulsion; **a** ~ **atomica** atomic[-powered]. **propulsione a getto** jet propulsion

propul'sore *nm* propeller

'prora *nf* Naut prow

'proroga *nf* extension

proro'gabile *adj* extendable

proro'gare *vt* extend

pro'rompere *vi* burst out

'prosa *nf* prose

pro'saico *adj* prosaic

pro'sciogliere *vt* release; Jur acquit

prosciogli'mento *nm* release

pro'sciolto pp di PROSCIOGLIERE

prosciu'gare *vt* dry up; (bonificare) reclaim

prosciu'garsi *vr* dry up

prosci'utto *nm* ham. **prosciutto cotto** cooked ham. **prosciutto crudo** type of dry-cured ham, Parma ham

pro'scritto, -a ① pp di PROSCRIVERE ② *nmf* exile

pro'scrivere *vt* exile, banish

proscrizi'one *nf* exile, banishment

prosecuzi'one *nf* continuation

prosegui'mento *nm* continuation; **buon** ~! (viaggio) have a good journey!; (festa) enjoy the rest of the party!

prosegu'ire ① *vt* continue ② *vi* go on, continue

pro'selito *nm* convert

prospe'rare *vi* prosper

prosperità *nf* prosperity

'prospero *adj* prosperous; (favorevole) favourable

prospe'roso *adj* flourishing; (ragazza) buxom

prospet'tare *vt* show

prospet'tarsi *vr* seem

prospet'tiva *nf* perspective; (panorama) view; fig prospect

pro'spetto *nm* (vista) view; (facciata) façade; (tabella) table

prospici'ente *adj* facing

prossima'mente *adv* soon

prossimità *nf* proximity; **in** ~ **di** near

'prossimo, -a ① *adj* near; (seguente) next; (molto vicino) close; **l'anno** ~ next ⋯⟶

year; **∼ venturo** next; **essere ∼ a fare qualcosa** be about to do something ② *nmf* neighbour

'prostata *nf* prostate

prostitu'irsi *vr* prostitute oneself

prosti'tuta *nf* prostitute

prostituzi'one *nf* prostitution

pro'strare *vt* prostrate

pro'strarsi *vr* prostrate oneself

pro'strato *adj* prostrate

protago'nista *nmf* protagonist; **ruolo/ attore non ∼** supporting role/actor

pro'teggere *vt* protect; (favorire) favour; **∼ da sovrascrittura** write-protect

pro'teico *adj* protein *attrib*; **molto ∼** rich in protein

prote'ina *nf* protein

pro'tendere *vt* stretch out

pro'tendersi *vr* (in avanti) lean out

pro'teso pp di PROTENDERE

pro'testa *nf* protest; (dichiarazione) protestation

prote'stante *adj & nmf* Protestant

prote'stare *vt/i* protest

prote'starsi *vr* **∼ innocente** protest one's innocence

protet'tivo *adj* protective

pro'tetto, -a ① pp di PROTEGGERE ② *adj* protected; **non ∼** unprotected. **protetto da password** password-protected

protetto'rato *nm* protectorate

protet'|tore, -trice ① *nmf* protector; (sostenitore) patron ② *nm* (di prostituta) pimp

protezi'one *nf* protection. **protezione aerea** air cover. **protezione dell'ambiente** environmental protection. **protezione antivirus** virus protection. **protezione civile** civil defence

protocol'lare ① *adj* (visita) protocol ② *vt* register

proto'collo *nm* protocol; (registro) register; **carta protocollo** official stamped paper. **protocollo di gestione remota della posta elettronica** IMAP. **protocollo Internet** Internet protocol. **protocollo per il trasferimento di file** file transfer protocol. **protocollo per il trasferimento di ipertesti** hypertext transfer protocol

pro'totipo *nm* prototype

pro'trarre *vt* protract; (differire) postpone

pro'trarsi *vr* go on, continue

pro'tratto pp di PROTRARRE

protube'rante *adj* protuberant

protube'ranza *nf* protuberance

'prova *nf* test; (dimostrazione) proof; (tentativo) try, attempt; (di abito) fitting; Sport heat; Theat rehearsal; (bozza) proof; **prove** *pl* evidence; **fino a ∼ contraria** until I'm told otherwise; **in ∼** (assumere) for a trial period; **mettere alla ∼** put to the test; **a ∼ di bomba** bombproof; **a ∼ di ladro** burglarproof. **prova del fuoco** fig acid test. **prova generale** dress rehearsal. **prova medico-legale** forensic evidence

pro'vare *vt* test; (dimostrare) prove; (tentare) try; try on ⟨abiti ecc⟩; (sentire) feel; Theat rehearse; **prova!** just try!

pro'varsi *vr* try

proveni'enza *nf* origin

prove'nire *vi* **∼ da** come from

pro'vento *nm* proceeds *pl*

prove'nuto pp di PROVENIRE

pro'verbio *nm* proverb

pro'vetta *nf* test-tube; **bambino in provetta** test-tube baby

pro'vetto *adj* skilled

pro'vincia *nf* province

provinci'ale *adj* provincial; **strada provinciale** B road, secondary road

pro'vino *nm* specimen; Cinema screen test

provo'cante *adj* provocative

provo'care *vt* provoke; (causare) cause

provoca'|tore, -trice *nmf* trouble-maker

provoca'torio *adj* provocative, confrontational

provocazi'one *nf* provocation

provo'lone *nm* type of cheese with a slightly smoked flavour

provve'dere *vi* **∼ a** provide for

provvedi'mento *nm* measure; (previdenza) precaution. **provvedimento disciplinare** disciplinary measure

provvedito'rato *nm* **provveditorato agli studi** education department

provvedi'tore *nm* **provveditore agli studi** director of education

provvi'denza *nf* providence

provvidenzi'ale *adj* providential

provvigi'one *nf* Comm commission; **lavorare a ∼** work on commission

provvi'sorio *adj* provisional; **in via provvisoria** provisionally, for the time being

prov'vista *nf* supply

pro'zia *nf* great-aunt

pro'zio *nm* great-uncle

'prua *nf* Naut prow

pru'dente *adj* prudent

pru'denza *nf* prudence; **per ∼** as a precaution

prudenzi'ale *adj* prudential

'prudere *vi* itch

'**prugna** *nf* plum. **prugna secca** prune. **prugna selvatica** damson

'**prugno** *nm* plum[-tree]

'**prugnolo** *nm* sloe

prurigi'noso *adj* itchy

pru'rito *nm* itch

P.S. *abbr* (**Pubblica Sicurezza**) police

pseu'donimo *nm* pseudonym

psica'nalisi *nf* psychoanalysis

psicana'lista *nmf* psychoanalyst

psicanaliz'zare *vt* psychoanalyse

'**psiche** *nf* psyche

psiche'delico *adj* psychedelic

psichi'atra *nmf* psychiatrist

psichia'tria *nf* psychiatry

psichi'atrico *adj* psychiatric

'**psichico** *adj* mental

psico'farmaco *nm* drug that affects the mind

psicolo'gia *nf* psychology

psico'logico *adj* psychological

psi'cologo, -a *nmf* psychologist

psico'patico, -a ① *adj* psychopathic ② *nmf* psychopath

psicopedago'gia *nf* educational psychology

psi'cosi *nf inv* psychosis

psicoso'matico *adj* psychosomatic

psicotera'peuta *nmf* psychotherapist

psicotera'pista *nmf* psychotherapist

psi'cotico, -a *adj & nmf* psychotic

PT *abbr* (**Posta e Telegrafi**) PO

puàh *int* yuck!

pub *nm inv* pub

pubbli'care *vt* publish

pubblicazi'one *nf* publication; **pubblicazioni** *pl* (di matrimonio) banns. **pubblicazione periodica** periodical

pubbli'cista *nmf* Journ correspondent

pubblicità *nf inv* publicity, advertising; (annuncio) advertisement, advert; **fare ~ a qualcosa** advertise something; **piccola pubblicità** small advertisements

pubblici'tario *adj* advertising

'**pubblico** ① *adj* public; **scuola pubblica** state school ② *nm* public; (spettatori) audience; **in ~** in public; **grande ~** general public; **Pubblica Sicurezza** police. **pubblico ministero** public prosecutor. **pubblico ufficiale** civil servant

'**pube** *nm* pubis

pubertà *nf* puberty

pu'dico *adj* modest

pu'dore *nm* modesty

pue'rile *adj* children's; pej childish

'**puerpera** *nf* new mother

puerpe'rale *adj* of childbirth, puerperal *fml*; (depressione) postnatal

puer'perio *nm* postnatal period

pugi'lato *nm* boxing

'**pugile** *nm* boxer

'**Puglia** *nf* Apulia

pugli'ese *adj & nmf* Apulian

pugna'lare *vt* stab

pugna'lata *nf* stab

pu'gnale *nm* dagger

'**pugno** *nm* fist; (colpo) punch; (manciata) fistful; (fig: numero limitato) handful; **dare un ~ a** punch; **di proprio ~** (scrivere) in one's own hand; **fare a pugni** (colori) clash; **tenere in ~** (situazione) have under control; have in the palm of one's hand (persona); **un ~ in un occhio** fig an eyesore. **pugno di ferro** iron fist

'**pula** *nf* sl **la ~** the fuzz

'**pulce** *nf* flea; (microfono) bug; **mettere la ~ nell'orecchio a qualcuno** sow a doubt in somebody's mind

pul'cino *nm* chick; (nel calcio) junior

pu'ledra *nf* filly

pu'ledro *nm* foal, colt

pu'leggia *nf* pulley

pu'lire *vt* clean; **~ a secco** dry-clean; **far ~ qualcosa** have something cleaned

puliscipi'edi *nm inv* boot scraper

pu'lito *adj* clean

puli'tura *nf* cleaning

puli'zia *nf* (il pulire) cleaning; (l'essere pulito) cleanliness; **pulizie** *pl* housework; **fare le pulizie** do the cleaning. **pulizia personale** personal hygiene

'**pullman** *nm inv* coach; (urbano) bus; **gita in ~** coach trip

pull'over *nm inv* pullover

pul'mino *nm* minibus

'**pulpito** *nm* pulpit

pul'sante *nm* button; Electr [push-]button. **pulsante di accensione** on/off switch. **pulsante di alimentazione** power switch

pul'sare *vi* pulsate

pulsazi'one *nf* pulsation

pul'viscolo *nm* dust

'**puma** *nm inv* puma

'**punching 'bag** *nf inv* punchbag

pun'gente *adj* prickly; (insetto) stinging; (odore ecc) sharp

'**pungere** *vt* prick; (insetto) sting; **~ qualcuno sul vivo** cut somebody to the quick

pungersi *vr* prick oneself; **~ un dito** prick one's finger

pungigli'one *nm* sting

pungo'lare *vt* goad

pu'nire *vt* punish

puni'tivo adj punitive

punizi'one nf punishment; Sport penalty; (in calcio) free kick. **punizione corporale** corporal punishment

'punta nf point; (estremità) tip; (di monte) peak, top; (un po') pinch; Sport forward; **doppie punte** (di capelli) split ends; **di ~** ‹ore› peak; ‹personaggio› leading

pun'tare ① vt point; (spingere con forza) push; (scommettere) bet; (fam: appuntare) fasten

② vi **~ su** fig rely on; (scommettere) bet on; **~ verso** (dirigersi) head for; **~ a** aspire to; **punta e clicca** Comput point and click

punta'spilli nm inv pincushion

pun'tata nf (di una storia) instalment; (televisiva) episode; (al gioco) stake, bet; (breve visita) flying visit; **a puntate** serialized, in instalments; **fare una ~ a/in** pop over to ‹luogo›

punteggia'tura nf punctuation

pun'teggio nm score

puntel'lare vt prop

pun'tello nm prop

punteru'olo nm awl

pun'tiglio nm spite; (ostinazione) obstinacy

puntigli'oso adj punctilious, pernickety pej

pun'tina nf (di giradischi) stylus. **puntina da disegno** drawing pin, thumb tack Am

pun'tine nfpl Aut **puntine** [platinate] points

pun'tino nm dot; **a ~** perfectly; ‹cotto› to a T; **puntini** pl [di sospensione] suspension points

'punto nm point; (in cucito, Med) stitch; (in punteggiatura) full stop; **in che ~?** where, exactly?; **di ~ in bianco** all of a sudden; **essere sul ~ di fare qualcosa** be on the point of doing something, be about to do something; **in ~** sharp; **mettere a ~** put right; fig fine-tune; tune up ‹motore›; **messa a ~** fine tuning; **due punti** colon; **punti** pl **cardinali** points of the compass. **punto cieco** blind spot. **punto di congelamento** freezing point. **punto croce** cross-stitch. **punto debole** weak spot. **punto di domanda** question mark. **punto di ebollizione** boiling point. **punto esclamativo** exclamation mark. **punto di fuga** vanishing point. **punto di fusione** melting point. **punto d'incontro** meeting-point. **punto di infiammabilità** flashpoint. **punto interrogativo** question mark. **punto morto** fig stand-off. **punto nero** (comedone) blackhead. **punto di pareggio** Fin breakeven point. **punto di partenza** starting point. **punto di riferimento** landmark; (per la qualità) benchmark. **punto di rottura** breaking point. **punto a smerlo** blanket stitch. **punto [di] vendita** point of sale, outlet;

pubblicità al ~ [di] vendita point-of-sale publicity. **punto e virgola** semicolon. **punto di vista** point of view

puntu'ale adj punctual; **essere ~** be punctual, be on time

puntualità nf punctuality

puntualiz'zare vt make clear, clarify

puntual'mente adv punctually, on time; (come al solito) as usual

pun'tura nf (di ago ecc) prick; Med puncture; (iniezione) injection; (fitta) stabbing pain. **puntura d'ape** bee sting. **puntura d'insetto** insect bite. **puntura di spillo** pinprick. **puntura di zanzara** mosquito bite

punzecchi'are vt prick; fig tease

punzo'nare vt Techn punch, stamp

pun'zone nm punch

può ▶ POTERE; **~ darsi** maybe, perhaps

'pupa nf doll

pu'pazzo nm puppet. **pupazzo di neve** snowman

pup'illa nf Anat pupil

pu'pillo, -a nmf Jur ward; (di professore) favourite

purché conj provided

'pure ① adv too, also; (concessivo) **fate ~!** please do!; **io ~** me too; **è venuto ~ lui** he came too, he also came

② conj (tuttavia) yet; (anche se) even if; **pur di** just to

purè nm purée. **purè di patate** mashed potatoes, creamed potatoes

pu'rezza nf purity

'purga nf purge

pur'gante nm laxative

pur'gare vt purge

purga'torio nm purgatory

purifi'care vt purify

purificazi'one nf purification

pu'rista nmf purist

puri'tano, -a adj & nmf Puritan

'puro adj pure; ‹vino ecc› undiluted; **per ~ caso** by sheer chance, purely by chance. **puro cotone** nm pure cotton, 100% cotton; **pura lana vergine** nf pure new wool; **pura seta** nf pure silk

puro'sangue adj & nm thoroughbred

pur'troppo adv unfortunately

pus nm pus

'pustola nf pimple

puti'ferio nm uproar

putre'fare vi putrefy

putre'farsi vr putrefy

putre'fatto adj rotten

putrefazi'one nf putrefaction

'putrido adj putrid

putt nm inv putt

put'tana nf vulg whore

'puzza *nf* stink; **avere la** ∼ **sotto il naso** be sniffy

puz'zare *vi* anche fig stink; ∼ **di bruciato** fig smell fishy; ∼ **d'imbroglio** stink; ∼ **di corruzione** stink of corruption; **questa storia mi puzza** the story stinks

'puzzo *nm* stink
'puzzola *nf* polecat
puzzo'lente *adj* stinking
puz'zone *nm* fam bastard
p.zza *abbr* (**piazza**) Sq.

Qq

Qatar *nm* Qatar

QI *abbr* (**quoziente di intelligenza**) IQ

qua *adv* here; **da un anno in** ∼ for the last year; **da quando in** ∼? since when?; **di** ∼ this way; **di** ∼ **di** on this side of; ∼ **dentro** in here; ∼ **sotto** under here; ∼ **vicino** near here; ∼ **e là** here and there

'quacchero, -a *nmf* Quaker

qua'derno *nm* exercise book; (per appunti) notebook. **quaderno a quadretti** maths exercise book. **quaderno a righe** lined exercise book

quadrango'lare *adj* ⟨forma⟩ quadrangular; **incontro quadrangolare** Sport four-sided tournament

qua'drangolo *nm* quadrangle

qua'drante *nm* quadrant; (di orologio) dial

qua'drare ① *vt* square; ⟨contabilità⟩ balance
② *vi* fit in

qua'drato ① *adj* square; (equilibrato) level-headed
② *nm* square; (nel pugilato) ring; **al** ∼ squared

quadra'tura *nf* Math squaring; (di bilancio) balancing

quadret'tare *vt* divide into small squares

quadret'tato *adj* squared; ⟨carta⟩ graph attrib; ⟨tessuto⟩ check, checked

qua'dretto *nm* square; (piccolo quadro) small picture; **a quadretti** ⟨tessuto⟩ check

quadricro'mia *nf* four-colour printing

quadrien'nale *adj* (che dura quattro anni) four-year; (ogni quattro anni) four-yearly

quadri'foglio *nm* four-leaf clover

qua'driglia *nf* square dance

quadri'latero *nm* quadrilateral

quadri'mestre *nm* (periodo) four-month period; Sch term

quadrimo'tore *nm* four-engined plane

quadri'nomio *nm* Math quadrinomial

quadripar'tito ① *adj* four-party
② *nm* (politica) four-party government

quadri'plegico *adj* quadriplegic

'quadro *nm* picture, painting; (quadrato) square; (fig: scena) sight; (tabella) table; Theat scene; (dirigente) executive; **fare il** ∼ **della situazione** outline the situation; **fuori** ∼ Cinema, TV out of shot; **quadri** *pl* (carte) diamonds; **a quadri** ⟨tessuto, giacca, motivo⟩ check, checked. **quadro clinico** case history. **quadro di comando** control panel; **quadri** *pl* **direttivi** senior management. **quadro di distribuzione** Electr switchboard; **quadri** *pl* **intermedi** middle management. **quadro degli interruttori** switch panel. **quadro degli strumenti** instrument panel

qua'drupede *nm* quadruped

quadrupli'care *vt* quadruple

quadrupli'carsi *vr* quadruple

qua'druplice *adj* quadruple

'quadruplo *adj* & *nm* quadruple

quaggiù *adv* down here

'quaglia *nf* quail

'qualche *adj* (alcuni) a few, some; (un certo) some; (in interrogative) any; **ho** ∼ **problema** I have a few problems, I have some problems; ∼ **tempo fa** some time ago; **hai** ∼ **libro italiano?** have you any Italian books?; **posso prendere** ∼ **libro?** can I take some books?; **in** ∼ **modo** somehow; **in** ∼ **posto** somewhere; ∼ **volta** sometimes; ∼ **cosa** = **qualcosa**

qualche'duno *pron* somebody, someone

qual'cosa *pron* something; (in interrogative) anything; **qualcos'altro** something else; **vuoi qualcos'altro?** would you like anything else?; ∼ **di strano** something strange; **vuoi** ∼ **da mangiare?** would you like something to eat?; **vuoi** ∼ **da bere?** would you like a drink?, would you like something to drink?

qual'cuno *pron* someone, somebody; (in interrogative) anyone, anybody; (alcuni) some; (in interrogative) any; **qualcun altro** someone else, somebody else; **c'è qualcun altro che aspetta?** is anybody else waiting?; **ho letto** ∼ **dei suoi libri** I've read some of his books; **conosci** ∼ **dei suoi amici?** do you know any of his friends?

p
q

'quale ❶ *adj* which; (indeterminato) what; (come) as, like; ∼ **macchina è la tua?** which car is yours?; ∼ **motivo avrà di parlare così?** what reason would he have to speak like that?; ∼ **onore!** what an honour!; **città quali Venezia** towns like Venice; ∼ **che sia la tua opinione** whatever you may think
❷ *pron inter* which [one]; ∼ **preferisci?** which [one] do you prefer?
❸ *pron rel* il/la ∼ (persona) who; (animale, cosa) that, which; (oggetto: con prep) whom; (oggetto: animale, cosa) which; **ho incontrato tua madre, la ∼ mi ha detto...** I met your mother who told me...; **l'ufficio nel ∼ lavoro** the office in which I work; **l'uomo con il ∼ parlavo** the man to whom I was speaking
❹ *adv* (come) as

qua'lifica *nf* qualification; (titolo) title

qualifi'cabile *adj* qualifiable

qualifi'care *vt* qualify; (definire) define

qualifi'carsi *vr* be placed

qualifica'tivo *adj* qualifying

qualifi'cato *adj* ⟨operaio⟩ semi-skilled

qualificazi'one *nf* qualification

qualità *nf inv* quality; (specie) kind; **in ∼ di** in one's capacity as; **di prima ∼** high quality; **di ottima/cattiva ∼** top/poor quality

qualitativa'mente *adv* qualitatively

qualita'tivo *adj* qualitative

qua'lora *conj* in case

qualsiasi, qualunque *adj* any; (non importa quale) whatever; (ordinario) ordinary; **dammi una penna ∼** give me any pen [whatsoever]; **farei ∼ cosa** I would do anything; ∼ **cosa io faccia** whatever I do; ∼ **persona** anyone, anybody; **in ∼ caso** in any case; **uno ∼** any one, whichever; **l'uomo qualunque** the man in the street; **vivo in una casa ∼** I live in an ordinary house

qualunqu'ismo *nm* lack of political views

qualunqu'ista *nmf* (menefreghista) person with no political views

'quando *conj & adv* when; **da ∼ ti ho visto** since I saw you; **da ∼ esci con lui?** how long have you been going out with him?; **da ∼ in qua?** since when?; ∼... ∼... sometimes..., sometimes...; **continua ad insistere ∼ sa di avere torto** he keeps on insisting even when he knows he's wrong

quantifi'cabile *adj* quantifiable

quantifi'care *vt* quantify

quantità *nf inv* quantity, amount; **una ∼ di** (gran numero) a great deal of

quantitativa'mente *adv* quantitatively

quantita'tivo ❶ *nm* amount
❷ *adj* quantitative

'quanto ❶ *adj inter* how much; (con nomi plurali) how many; (in esclamazione) what a lot of; (tempo) how long; **quanti anni hai?** how old are you?
❷ *adj rel* as much...as; (tempo) as long as; (con nomi plurali) as many... as; **prendi ∼ denaro ti serve** take as much money as you need; **prendi quanti libri vuoi** take as many books as you like
❸ *pron inter* how much; (quanto tempo) how long; (plurale) how many; **quanti ne abbiamo oggi?** what date is it today?
❹ *pron rel* as much as; (quanto tempo) as long as; (plurale) as many as; **prendine ∼/ quanti ne vuoi** take as much/as many as you like; **stai ∼ vuoi** stay as long as you like; **questo è ∼** that's it
❺ *adv inter* how much; (quanto tempo) how long; ∼ **sei alto?** how tall are you?; ∼ **hai aspettato?** how long did you wait for?; ∼ **costa?** how much is it?; ∼ **mi dispiace!** I'm so sorry!; **quant'è bello!** how nice!
❻ *adv rel* as much as; **lavoro ∼ posso** I work as much as I can; **è tanto intelligente ∼ bello** he's as intelligent as he's good-looking; **in ∼** (in qualità di) as; (poiché) since; ∼ **a** as for; **in ∼ a me** as far as I'm concerned; **per ∼** however; **per ∼ ne sappia** as far as I know; **per ∼ mi riguarda** as far as I'm concerned; **per ∼ mi sia simpatico** much as I like him; ∼ **prima** (al più presto) as soon as possible

quan'tunque *conj* although

qua'ranta *adj & nm* forty

quaran'tena *nf* quarantine

quaran'tenne ❶ *adj* forty-year-old; (sulla quarantina) in his/her forties
❷ *nmf* forty-year-old; (sulla quarantina) person in his/her forties

quaran'tennio *nm* period of forty years

quaran'tesimo *adj & nm* fortieth

quaran'tina *nf* una ∼ about forty

qua'resima *nf* Lent

quar'tetto *nm* quartet

quarti'ere *nm* district, area; Mil quarters *pl*; **quartieri** *pl* **alti** smart districts; **quartieri** *pl* **bassi** poor areas. **quartiere cinese** China-town. **quartiere dormitorio** dormitory town. **quartiere generale** headquarters. **quartiere a luci rosse** red light area. **quartiere residenziale** residential area

quar'tino *nm* (strumento musicale) instrument similar to a clarinet; Typ quarto; (di vino) quarter litre

'quarto ❶ *adj* fourth
❷ *nm* fourth; (quarta parte) quarter; **le sette e un ∼** [a] quarter past seven, [a] quarter after seven Am; **a tre quarti** (giacca, maniche) three-quarter length; **quarti** *pl* **di finale** quarter-finals. **quarto d'ora** quarter of an hour
❸ *nf* (marcia) fourth [gear]

quarto'genito, -a *nmf* fourth child

quar'tultimo, -a *adj* & *nmf* fourth last

'quarzo *nm* quartz; **al ~** quartz. **quarzo rosa** rose quartz

'quasi ① *adv* almost, nearly; **~ mai** hardly ever
② *conj* (come se) as if; **~ ~ sto a casa** I'm tempted to stay home

quassù *adv* up here

qua'terna *nf* (lotto, tombola) set of four winning numbers

quater'nario *nm* (era) Quaternary

'quatto *adj* crouching; (silenzioso) silent; **starsene ~ ~** keep very quiet

quattordi'cenne *adj* & *nmf* fourteen-year-old

quattordi'cesimo *adj* & *nm* fourteenth

quat'tordici *adj* & *nm* fourteen

quat'trini *nmpl* money *sg*, dosh *sg fam*

'quattro *adj* & *nm* four; **dirne ~ a qualcuno** give somebody a piece of one's mind; **farsi in ~** (per qualcuno/per fare qualcosa) go to a lot of trouble (for somebody/to do something); **in ~ e quattr'otto** in a flash. **~ per ~** *nf inv* Auto four-wheel drive [vehicle], four-by-four; **a ~ tempi** Auto four-stroke

quat'trocchi *adv* **a ~** in private

quattrocen'tesco *adj* fifteenth-century

quattro'cento *adj* & *nm* four hundred; **il Quattrocento** the fifteenth century

quattro'mila *adj* & *nm* four thousand

Qué'bec *nm* Quebec

'quello ① *adj* that (*pl* those); **quell'albero** that tree; **quegli alberi** those trees; **quel cane** that dog; **quei cani** those dogs
② *pron* that [one] (*pl* those [ones]); **~ lì** that one over there; **~ che** the one that; (ciò che) what; **quelli che** the ones that, those that; **~ a destra** the one on the right

'quercia *nf* oak; **di ~** oak

que'rela *nf* [legal] action

quere'lante *nmf* plaintiff

quere'lare *vt* bring an action against

quere'lato, -a *nmf* defendant

que'sito *nm* question

questio'nare *vi* dispute

questio'nario *nm* questionnaire

quest'ione *nf* question; (faccenda) matter; (litigio) quarrel; **in ~** in doubt; **è fuori ~** it's out of the question; **è ~ di vita o di morte** it's a matter of life and death; **mettere qualcosa in ~** cast doubt on something; **una ~ personale** a personal matter

'questo ① *adj* this (*pl* these)
② *pron* this [one] (*pl* these [ones]); **~ qui, ~ qua** this one here; **~ è quello che ha detto** that's what he said; **per ~** for this *or* that reason; **quest'oggi** today

que'store *nm* chief of police

'questua *nf* collection

que'stura *nf* police headquarters

qui ① *adv* here; **da ~ in poi, da ~ in avanti** from now on; **di ~ a una settimana** in a week's time; **fin ~** (nel tempo) up till now, until now; **~ dentro** in here; **~ sotto** under here; **~ vicino** near here
② *nm* **~ pro quo** misunderstanding

quie'scenza *nf* (di vulcano) dormancy; (pensione) retirement; **trattamento di quiescenza** retirement package

quie'tanza *nf* receipt

quie'tare *vt* calm

quie'tarsi *vr* calm down

qui'ete *nf* quiet; **disturbo della quiete pubblica** breach of the peace; **stato di quiete** Phys state of rest

qui'eto *adj* quiet

'quindi ① *adv* then
② *conj* therefore

quindi'cenne *adj* & *nmf* fifteen-year-old

quindi'cesimo *adj* & *nm* fifteenth

'quindici *adj* & *nm* fifteen; **~ giorni** a fortnight Br, two weeks *pl*

quindi'cina *nf* **una ~** about fifteen; **una ~ di giorni** a fortnight Br, two weeks *pl*

quindici'nale ① *adj* fortnightly Br, twice-monthly
② *nm* fortnightly magazine Br, twice-monthly magazine

quinquen'nale *adj* (che dura cinque anni) five-year; (ogni cinque anni) five-yearly

quin'quennio *nm* [period of] five years

'quinta *nf* Auto fifth [gear], overdrive

quin'tale *nm* a hundred kilograms

'quinte *nfpl* Theat wings

quintes'senza *nf* quintessence

quin'tetto *nm* quintet

'quinto *adj* & *nm* fifth

quintupli'care *vt* quintuple

quin'tuplo *adj* quintuple

qui'squilia *nf* trifle; **perdersi in quisquilie** get bogged down in details

quiz *nm inv* **[gioco a] quiz** quiz game. **quiz radiofonico** radio quiz

'quota *nf* quota; (rata) instalment; (altitudine) height; Aeron altitude, height; (ippica) odds *pl*; **perdere/prendere ~** lose/ gain altitude *or* height; **da alta ~** high-flying. **quota fissa** fixed amount. **quota non imponibile** personal allowance. **quota di iscrizione** entry fee; (di club) membership fee. **quota di mercato** market share. **quota zero** sea level

quo'tare *vt* Comm quote

quo'tato *adj* quoted; **essere ~ in Borsa** be quoted on the Stock Exchange

quotazi'one *nf* quotation. **quotazione d'acquisto** buying rate. **quotazione ⟶**

q

ufficiale (in Borsa) official quotation.
quotazione di vendita selling rate
quotidiana'mente *adv* daily
quotidi'ano ① *adj* daily; (ordinario)
everyday

② *nm* daily [paper]
'quoto *nm* Math quotient
quozi'ente *nm* quotient. **quoziente
d'intelligenza** intelligence quotient, IQ.
quoziente di purezza purity

Rr

ra'barbaro *nm* rhubarb
'rabbia *nf* rage; (ira) anger; Med rabies *sg*;
che ∼! what a nuisance!; **mi fa ∼** it
makes me angry
'rabbico *adj* ⟨virus⟩ rabies *attrib*
rab'bino *nm* rabbi
rabbiosa'mente *adv* furiously
rabbi'oso *adj* hot-tempered; Med rabid;
(violento) violent
rabboc'care *vt* top up ⟨fiasco⟩
rabbo'nire *vt* pacify
rabbo'nirsi *vr* calm down
rabbrivi'dire *vi* shudder; (di freddo)
shiver
rabbuf'fare *vt* reprimand; ruffle
⟨capelli⟩
rab'buffo *nm* reprimand
rabbui'arsi *vr* get dark; ⟨viso⟩ darken
rabdo'mante *nmf* water diviner
rabdoman'zia *nf* water divining
raccapez'zare *vt* put together
raccapez'zarsi *vr* see one's way ahead
raccapricci'ante *adj* horrifying
raccatta'palle ① *nm inv* ball boy
② *nf inv* ball girl
raccat'tare *vt* pick up
rac'chetta *nf* racket. **racchetta da
neve** snowshoe. **racchetta da ping
pong** table-tennis bat. **racchetta da
sci** ski stick, ski pole. **racchetta da
tennis** tennis racket
'racchio *adj* fam ugly
racchi'udere *vt* contain
rac'cogliere *vt* pick; (da terra) pick up;
(mietere) harvest; (collezionare) collect;
(radunare) gather; win ⟨voti ecc⟩; (dare asilo a)
take in
rac'cogliersi *vr* gather; (concentrarsi)
collect one's thoughts
raccogli'mento *nm* concentration
raccogli'tore, -trice ① *nmf* collector
② *nm* **raccoglitore a fogli mobili**
ring-binder
rac'colta *nf* collection; (di scritti)
compilation; (del grano ecc) harvesting;
(adunata) gathering; **chiamare a ∼** call or

gather together. **raccolta
differenziata** collection of items for
recycling. **raccolta di fondi** fund-
raising
rac'colto, -a ① *pp di* RACCOGLIERE
② *adj* (rannicchiato) hunched; (intimo) cosy;
(concentrato) engrossed
③ *nm* (mietitura) harvest
raccoman'dabile *adj* advisable; **poco
∼** ⟨persona⟩ shady
raccoman'dare *vt* recommend; (affidare)
entrust
raccoman'darsi *vr* (implorare) beg
raccoman'data *nf* letter sent by
recorded delivery, certified mail Am; **per
∼** by recorded delivery. **raccomandata
con ricevuta di ritorno** letter sent by
recorded delivery with acknowledgement
of receipt
raccoman'data-e'spresso *nf*
express recorded delivery service
raccomandazi'one *nf*
recommendation
raccomo'dare *vt* repair
raccon'tare *vt* tell
rac'conto *nm* story. **racconto
dell'orrore** horror story
raccorci'are *vt* shorten
raccorci'arsi *vr* become shorter;
⟨giorni⟩ draw in
raccor'dare *vt* join
rac'cordo *nm* connection; ⟨stradale⟩
feeder. **raccordo anulare** ring road.
raccordo autostradale motorway
junction Br, intersection. **raccordo
ferroviario** siding. **raccordo a
gomito** elbow
ra'chitico *adj* rickety; (poco sviluppato)
stunted
racimo'lare *vt* scrape together
'racket *nm inv* racket
'rada *nf* Naut roads *pl*
'radar *nm inv* radar; **uomo radar** air
traffic controller
radden'sare *vt* thicken
radden'sarsi *vr* thicken
raddob'bare *vt* refit

rad'dobbo *nm* refit

raddol'cire *vt* sweeten; fig soften

raddol'cirsi *vr* become milder; ‹*carattere*› mellow

raddoppia'mento *nm* doubling

raddoppi'are *vt* double; increase twofold

rad'doppio *nm* doubling, twofold increase; (equitazione) gallop; (biliardo) double

raddriz'zabile *adj* which can be straightened

raddriz'zare *vt* straighten

raddrizza'tore *nm* (di corrente) rectifier

ra'dente *adj* grazing, shaving; **tiro radente** Mil grazing fire; Sport low shot just skimming the surface; **volo radente** Aeron hedge-hopping

'radere *vt* shave; graze ‹*muro*›; ~ **al suolo** raze [to the ground]

'radersi *vr* shave

radi'ale *adj* radial

radi'ante ① *adj* radiant ② *nm* Math radian

radi'are *vt* strike off; ~ **dall'albo** strike off ‹*medico*›; debar ‹*avvocato*›

radia'tore *nm* radiator

radiazi'one *nf* radiation. **radiazione nucleare** nuclear radiation

'radica *nf* briar

radi'cale ① *adj* radical ② *nm* Gram root; Pol radical

radical'mente *adv* radically

radi'carsi *vr* ~ **in** be rooted in

radi'cato *adj* deep-seated

ra'dicchio *nm* chicory

ra'dice *nf* root; **mettere [le] radici** ‹*pianta*› take root; fig put down roots. **radice quadrata** square root

'radio ① *nf inv* radio; **via** ~ by radio; **contatto radio** radio contact; **ponte radio** radio link. **radio pirata** pirate radio. **radio portatile** portable radio. **radio ricevente** receiver. **radio [a] transistor** transistor radio. **radio trasmittente** transmitter ② *nm* Chem radium

radioama|'tore, **-trice** *nmf* radio ham

radioascolta|'tore, **-trice** *nmf* listener

radioassi'stito *adj* radio-assisted

radioattività *nf* radioactivity

radioat'tivo *adj* radioactive

radiobiolo'gia *nf* radiobiology

radio'bussola *nf* radio compass

radiocoman'dare *vt* operate by remote control

radiocoman'dato *adj* remote-controlled, radio-controlled

radio'cronaca *nf* radio commentary; **fare la** ~ **di** commentate on

radiocro'nista *nmf* radio reporter

radiodiffusi'one *nf* broadcasting

radio'faro *nm* radio beacon

radio'fonico *adj* radio *attrib*

radiofre'quenza *nf* radio frequency

radiogo'niometro *nm* direction finder, radiogoniometer

radiogra'fare *vt* X-ray

radiogra'fia *nf* X-ray [photograph]; (radiologia) radiography; **fare una** ~ ‹*paziente*› have an X-ray; ‹*dottore*› take an X-ray

radio'lina *nf* transistor

radiolocaliz'zare *vt* locate by radar

radiolo'gia *nf* radiology

radi'ologo, **-a** *nmf* radiologist

radio'onda *nf* radio wave

radioregistra'tore *nm* **radioregistratore portatile** portable radio cassette recorder

radiosco'pia *nf* Med radioscopy

radio'scopico *adj* radioscopic

radi'oso *adj* radiant

radio'spia *nf* bug

radio'sveglia *nf* radio alarm, clock radio

radio'taxi *nm inv* radio taxi

radiote'lefono *nm* radio-telephone; (privato) cordless [phone]

radiotelevi'sivo *adj* broadcasting *attrib*

radiotera'pia *nf* radiotherapy

radiotra'smettere *vt* radio

radiotrasmetti'tore *nm* radio

radiotrasmit'tente *nf* radio station

'rado *adj* sparse; (non frequente) rare; **di** ~ seldom

radu'nare *vt* gather [together]

radu'narsi *vr* gather [together]

radu'nata *nf* gathering. **radunata sediziosa** seditious assembly

ra'duno *nm* meeting; Sport rally

ra'dura *nf* clearing

'rafano *nm* horseradish

raffazzo'nato *adj* ‹*discorso, lavoro*› botched

raf'fermo *adj* stale

'raffica *nf* gust; (di armi da fuoco) burst; (di domande, insulti) barrage

raffigu'rare *vt* represent

raffigurazi'one *nf* representation

raffi'nare *vt* refine

raffinata'mente *adv* elegantly

raffina'tezza *nf* refinement

raffi'nato *adj* refined

raffine'ria *nf* refinery. **raffineria di petrolio** oil refinery

rafforza'mento *nm* reinforcement; (di muscolatura, carattere) strengthening

raffor'zare *vt* reinforce

rafforza'tivo ① *adj* Gram intensifying ② *nm* Gram intensifier

raffredda'mento *nm* (processo) cooling; di ∼ cooling. **raffreddamento ad acqua** water-cooling. **raffreddamento ad aria** air-cooling

raffred'dare *vt* cool

raffred'darsi *vr* get cold; (prendere un raffreddore) catch a cold; ⟨sentimento, passione⟩ cool [off]

raffred'dato *adj* essere ∼ ⟨persona⟩ have a cold

raffred'dore *nm* cold; avere il ∼ have a cold. **raffreddore da fieno** hay fever

raf'fronto *nm* comparison

'rafia *nf* raffia

Rag. *abbr* ragioniere

ra'gazza *nf* girl; (fidanzata) girlfriend; nome da ragazza maiden name. **ragazza copertina** cover girl. **ragazza madre** unmarried mother. **ragazza alla pari** au pair [girl]. **ragazza squillo** call girl

ragaz'zata *nf* prank

ra'gazzo *nm* boy; (fidanzato) boyfriend; da ∼ (da giovane) as a boy. **ragazzo padre** unmarried father. **ragazzo di strada** guttersnipe. **ragazzo di vita** rent boy

ragge'lare *vt* fig freeze

ragge'larsi *vr* fig turn to ice

raggi'ante *adj* radiant

raggi'era *nf* (di ruota) spokes *pl*; a ∼ with a pattern like spokes radiating from a centre

'raggio *nm* ray; Math radius; (di ruota) spoke; a raggi infrarossi infrared. **raggio d'azione** range. **raggio laser** laser beam. **raggio di luna** moonbeam. **raggio di sole** ray of sunshine, sunbeam. **raggio di speranza** ray of hope. **raggio ultravioletto** ultraviolet ray; raggi *pl* X X-rays

raggi'rare *vt* trick, deceive

rag'giro *nm* trick, con trick

raggi'ungere *vt* reach; (conseguire) achieve

raggiun'gibile *adj* ⟨luogo⟩ within reach

raggiungi'mento *nm* attainment

raggomito'lare *vt* wind

raggomito'larsi *vr* curl up

raggranel'lare *vt* scrape together

raggrin'zire *vt* wrinkle

raggrin'zirsi *vr* wrinkle

raggru'mare *vt* curdle ⟨latte⟩

raggru'marsi *vr* ⟨latte⟩ curdle

raggruppa'mento *nm* (gruppo) group; (azione) grouping; Comm groupage

raggrup'pare *vt* group together

ragguagli'are *vt* compare; (informare) inform

raggu'aglio *nm* comparison; (informazione) information

ragguar'devole *adj* considerable

'ragia *nf* resin; acqua ∼ turpentine

ragià *nm inv* rajah

ragiona'mento *nm* reasoning; (discussione) discussion. **ragionamento per assurdo** reductio ad absurdum

ragio'nare *vi* reason; (discutere) discuss

ragio'nato *adj* ⟨argomento⟩ reasoned; ⟨cruciverba⟩ cryptic

ragi'one *nf* reason; (ciò che è giusto) right; a ∼ o a torto rightly or wrongly; aver ∼ be right; perdere la ∼ go out of one's mind; a ragion veduta after due consideration; prenderle/darle di santa ∼ get/give a good walloping; ragion d'essere raison d'être. **ragione di scambio** terms of trade. **ragione sociale** company name; ragion di Stato reasons *pl* of State

ragione'ria *nf* accountancy; (scuola) secondary school which provides training in accountancy

ragio'nevole *adj* reasonable

ragionevol'mente *adv* reasonably

ragioni'ere, -a *nmf* accountant

ra'glan *adj inv* ⟨manica⟩ raglan

ragli'are *vi* bray

'raglio *nm* bray

ragna'tela *nf* cobweb, web, spider web

'ragno *nm* spider

ragù *nm inv* meat sauce

RAI *nf abbr* (**Radio Audizioni Italiane**) Italian public broadcasting company

'raid *nm inv* raid

'raion® *nm* rayon®

ra'lenti *nm* al ∼ in slow motion

rallegra'menti *nmpl* congratulations

ralle'grare *vt* gladden

ralle'grarsi *vr* rejoice; ∼ con qualcuno congratulate somebody

rallenta'mento *nm* slowing down

rallen'tare *vt/i* slow down; (allentare) slacken

rallen'tarsi *vr* slow down

rallenta'tore *nm* (su strada) speed bump; al ∼ in slow motion

'rally *nm inv* rally

RAM *nf* RAM

ramai'olo *nm* ladle

raman'zina *nf* reprimand

ra'mare *vt* stake ⟨pianta⟩

ra'marro *nm* (animale) type of lizard

ra'mato *adj* ⟨capelli⟩ copper[-coloured], coppery

'rame nm copper; **color** ∼ copper-coloured

ramifi'care vi ⟨pianta⟩ put out branches

ramifi'carsi vr ⟨pianta⟩ put out branches; ⟨strada, fiume ecc⟩ branch; ⟨teoria⟩ ramify, branch

ramificazi'one nf ramification

ra'mino nm rummy

rammari'carsi vr ∼ **di** regret; (lamentarsi) complain (**di** about)

ram'marico nm regret

rammen'dare vt darn

ram'mendo nm darning

rammen'tare vt remember; ∼ **qualcosa a qualcuno** (richiamare alla memoria) remind somebody of something

rammen'tarsi vr remember

rammol'lire vt soften

rammol'lirsi vr go soft

rammol'lito, -a nmf wimp

'ramo nm branch

ramo'scello nm twig

'rampa nf (di scale) flight. **rampa d'accesso** slip road. **rampa di carico** loading ramp. **rampa di lancio** launch[ing] pad

ram'pante adj ⟨leone, cavallo⟩ rampant; **giovane** ∼ yuppie

rampi'cante 1 adj climbing 2 nm Bot creeper

ram'pino nm hook; fig pretext

ram'pollo nm hum brat; (discendente) descendant

ram'pone nm harpoon; (per scarpe) crampon

'rana nf frog; (nel nuoto) breaststroke; **uomo rana** frogman

ranch nm inv ranch

'rancido adj rancid

'rancio nm rations pl

ran'core nm rancour, resentment; **serbare** ∼ **verso qualcuno** bear somebody a grudge

'randa nf mainsail

ran'dagio adj stray

randel'lata nf blow with a club

ran'dello nm club

'rango nm rank

rannicchi'arsi vr huddle up

rannuvola'mento nm clouding over

rannuvo'larsi vr cloud over

ra'nocchio nm frog

ranto'lare vi wheeze

'rantolo nm wheeze; (di moribondo) death rattle

ra'nuncolo nm buttercup

'rapa nf turnip

ra'pace adj rapacious; ⟨uccello⟩ predatory

rapa'nello nm radish

ra'pare vt crop

ra'parsi vr fam have one's head shaved

'rapida nf rapids pl

rapida'mente adv quickly, rapidly

rapidità nf speed

'rapido 1 adj fast, quick; ⟨guarigione, sviluppo⟩ rapid 2 nm (treno) express [train]

rapi'mento nm (crimine) kidnapping

ra'pina nf robbery, hold-up fam. **rapina a mano armata** armed robbery. **rapina in banca** bank robbery

rapi'nare vt rob

rapina'tore nm robber. **rapinatore di banca** bank robber

ra'pire vt abduct; (per riscatto) kidnap; (fig: estasiare) ravish

ra'pito, -a 1 adj abducted; (per riscatto) kidnapped; (estasiato) rapt 2 nmf kidnap victim

rapi|'tore, -trice nmf kidnapper

rappacifi'care vt pacify

rappacifi'carsi vr be reconciled, make it up

rappacificazi'one nf reconciliation

'rapper nmf inv Mus rapper

rappez'zare vt patch up

rappor'tare vt reproduce ⟨disegno⟩; (confrontare) compare

rap'porto nm report; (connessione) relation; (legame) relationship; Math, Techn ratio; **rapporti** pl relations, relationship; **essere in buoni rapporti** be on good terms; **rapporti** pl **d'affari** business relations. **rapporto di amicizia** friendship; **avere un** ∼ **di amicizia con qualcuno** be friends with somebody. **rapporto di lavoro** working relationship. **rapporto di parentela** family relationship; **avere un** ∼ **di parentela con qualcuno** be related to somebody; **rapporti** pl **prematrimoniali** premarital sex. **rapporto prezzo-prestazioni** price/performance ratio. **rapporto prezzo-qualità** value for money; **rapporti** pl **sessuali** sexual intercourse. **rapporto di trasmissione** Auto gear

rap'prendersi vr set; ⟨latte⟩ curdle

rappre'saglia nf reprisal

rappresen'tante nmf representative. **rappresentante di classe** class representative. **rappresentante di commercio** sales representative, [sales] rep fam. **rappresentante sindacale** trade union representative

rappresen'tanza nf delegation; Comm agency; **spese di rappresentanza** entertainment expenses; **di** ∼ ····⟩

⟨*appartamento, macchina*⟩ company *attrib.* **rappresentanza esclusiva** sole agency. **rappresentanza legale** legal representation. **rappresentanza proporzionale** proportional representation, PR

rappresen'tare *vt* represent; Theat perform

rappresenta'tiva *nf* representatives *pl*

rappresenta'tivo *adj* representative

rappresentazi'one *nf* representation; (spettacolo) performance

rap'preso *pp di* RAPPRENDERSI

rapso'dia *nf* rhapsody

'raptus *nm inv* fit of madness

rara'mente *adv* rarely, seldom

rare'fare *vt* rarefy

rare'farsi *vr* rarefy

rare'fatto *adj* rarefied

rarità *nf inv* rarity

'raro *adj* rare

ra'sare *vt* shave; trim ⟨*siepe ecc*⟩

ra'sarsi *vr* shave

ra'sato *adj* shaved

rasa'tura *nf* shaving

raschia'mento *nm* Med curettage

raschi'are *vt* scrape; (togliere) scrape off

raschi'arsi *vr* ~ **la gola** clear one's throat

rasen'tare *vt* go close to

ra'sente *prep* very close to

'raso ① *pp di* RADERE
② *adj* smooth; (colmo) full to the brim; ⟨*barba*⟩ close-cropped; ~ **terra** close to the ground; **un cucchiaio** ~ a level spoonful
③ *nm* satin

ra'soio *nm* razor. **rasoio elettrico** electric shaver. **rasoio a mano libera** cut-throat razor

'raspa *nf* rasp

'raspo *nm* (di uva) small bunch

ras'segna *nf* review; (mostra) exhibition; (musicale, cinematografica) festival; **passare in** ~ review; Mil inspect

rasse'gnare *vt* present

rasse'gnarsi *vr* resign oneself

rassegnata'mente *adv* with resignation

rasse'gnato *adj* ⟨*persona, aria, tono*⟩ resigned

rassegnazi'one *nf* resignation

rassere'nare *vt* clear; fig cheer up

rassere'narsi *vr* become clear; fig cheer up

rasset'tare *vt* tidy up; (riparare) mend

rassicu'rante *adj* ⟨*persona, parole, presenza*⟩ reassuring

rassicu'rare *vt* reassure

rassicurazi'one *nf* reassurance

rasso'dare *vt* harden; fig strengthen

rassomigli'ante *adj* similar

rassomigli'anza *nf* resemblance

rassomigli'are *vi* ~ **a** resemble

rastrella'mento *nm* (di fieno) raking; (perlustrazione) combing

rastrel'lare *vt* rake; (perlustrare) comb

rastrelli'era *nf* rack; (per biciclette) bicycle rack; (scolapiatti) [plate] rack

ra'strello *nm* rake

'rata *nf* instalment; (di mutuo) mortgage repayment; **pagare a rate** pay by instalments; **comprare qualcosa a rate** buy something on hire purchase, buy something on the installment plan Am

rate'ale *adj* by instalments; **pagamento rateale** payment by instalments; **vendita rateale** hire purchase

rate'are, **rateizzare** *vt* divide into instalments

ra'tifica *nf* Jur ratification

ratifi'care *vt* Jur ratify

'ratto[1] *nm* liter (rapimento) abduction

'ratto[2] *nm* (roditore) rat. **ratto comune** black rat

rattop'pare *vt* patch

rat'toppo *nm* patch

rattrap'pire *vt* make stiff

rattrap'pirsi *vr* become stiff

rattri'stare *vt* sadden

rattri'starsi *vr* become sad

rau'cedine *nf* hoarseness

'rauco *adj* hoarse

rava'nello *nm* radish

ravi'oli *nmpl* ravioli *sg*

ravve'dersi *vr* mend one's ways

ravvi'are *vt* tidy ⟨*capelli, stanza*⟩

ravvicina'mento *nm* (tra persone) reconciliation; Pol rapprochement

ravvici'nare *vt* bring closer; (riconciliare) reconcile

ravvici'narsi *vr* be reconciled

ravvi'sare *vt* recognize

ravvi'vare *vt* revive; fig brighten up

ravvi'varsi *vr* revive

rav'volgere *vt* roll up

rav'volgersi *vr* wrap oneself up

'rayon® *nm* rayon

razio'cinio *nm* rational thought; (buon senso) common sense

razio'nale *adj* rational

razionalità *nf* (raziocinio) rationality; (di ambiente) functional nature

razionaliz'zare *vt* rationalize ⟨*programmi, metodi, spazio*⟩

razional'mente *adv* (con raziocinio) rationally

raziona'mento *nm* rationing

razio'nare *vt* ration

razi'one *nf* ration

'razza *nf* race; (di cani ecc) breed; (genere) kind; **che ~ di idiota!** fam what an idiot!

raz'zia *nf* raid

razzi'ale *adj* racial

raz'zismo *nm* racism

raz'zista *adj & nmf* racist

'razzo *nm* rocket. **razzo da segnalazione** flare

razzo'lare *vi* ⟨polli⟩ scratch about

re *nm inv* king; (Mus: chiave, nota) D; **Re** *pl* **Magi** Wise Men

rea'gente *adj & nm* reactant

rea'gire *vi* react

re'ale *adj* real; (di re) royal

rea'lismo *nm* realism

rea'lista *nmf* realist; (fautore del re) royalist

realistica'mente *adv* realistically

rea'listico *adj* realistic

realiz'zabile *adj* feasible

realiz'zare *vt* (attuare) carry out, realize; Comm make; score ⟨gol, canestro⟩; (rendersi conto di) realize

realiz'zarsi *vr* come true; (nel lavoro ecc) fulfil oneself

realiz'zato *adj* ⟨persona⟩ fulfilled

realizzazi'one *nf* realization; (di sogno, persona) fulfilment. **realizzazione scenica** production

rea'lizzo *nm* (vendita) proceeds *pl*; (riscossione) yield

real'mente *adv* really

realtà *nf inv* reality; **in ~** in reality; (a dire il vero) actually. **realtà virtuale** virtual reality

re'ame *nm* realm

re'ato *nm* crime, criminal offence; **reati** *pl* **informatici** computer crime. **reato minore** minor offence

reattività *nf* reactivity; (a farmaco) reaction

reat'tivo *adj* reactive

reat'tore *nm* reactor; Aeron jet [aircraft]. **reattore nucleare** atomic reactor

reazio'nario, -a *adj & nmf* reactionary

reazi'one *nf* reaction; **a ~** ⟨motore, aereo⟩ jet. **reazione a catena** chain reaction. **reazione chimica** chemical reaction

'rebus *nm inv* rebus; (enigma) puzzle

recapi'tare *vt* deliver

re'capito *nm* address; (consegna) delivery; **in caso di mancato ~...** if undelivered... **recapito a domicilio** home delivery. **recapito telefonico** contact telephone number

re'care *vt* bear; (produrre) cause

re'carsi *vr* go

re'cedere *vi* recede; fig give up

recensi'one *nf* review

recen'sire *vt* review

recen'sore *nm* reviewer

re'cente *adj* recent; **di ~** recently

recente'mente *adv* recently

re'ception *nf inv* reception [desk]

re'ceptionist *nmf* receptionist

recessi'one *nf* recession

reces'sivo *adj* Biol recessive; Econ recessionary

re'cesso *nm* recess

re'cidere *vt* cut off

reci'diva *nf* Jur recidivism; Med relapse; **furto con ~** repeat offence of theft

recidività *nf* recidivism

reci'divo, -a ① *adj* Med recurrent ② *nmf* repeat offender, persistent offender, recidivist *fml*; **è ~** fig he's lapsed back into his old ways

recin'tare *vt* close off

re'cinto *nm* enclosure; (per animali) pen; (per bambini) playpen. **recinto delle grida** Fin [trading] floor. **recinto del peso** (ippica) weigh-in room

recinzi'one *nf* (azione) enclosure; (muro) wall; (rete) wire fence; (cancellata) railings *pl*

recipi'ente *nm* container

re'ciproco *adj* reciprocal

re'ciso ① *pp di* RECIDERE ② *adj* (risoluto) definite

'recita *nf* performance. **recita scolastica** school play

re'cital *nm inv* recital

reci'tare ① *vt* recite; Theat act; play ⟨ruolo⟩ ② *vi* act; **~ a soggetto** improvise

recitazi'one *nf* recitation; Theat acting; **scuola di ~** drama school

recla'mare ① *vi* protest ② *vt* claim

ré'clame *nf inv* advertising; (avviso pubblicitario) advertisement

reclamiz'zare *vt* advertise

re'clamo *nm* complaint; **ufficio reclami** complaints department

recli'nabile *adj* reclining; **sedile reclinabile** reclining seat

recli'nare *vt* tilt ⟨sedile⟩; lean ⟨capo⟩

reclusi'one *nf* imprisonment

re'cluso, -a ① *adj* secluded ② *nmf* prisoner

'recluta *nf* recruit

recluta'mento *nm* recruitment

reclu'tare *vt* recruit

re'condito *adj* secluded; (intimo) secret

'record ① *nm inv* record; **a tempo di** ∼ in record time
② *adj inv* ⟨*cifra*⟩ record *attrib*

recrimi'nare *vi* recriminate

recriminazi'one *nf* recrimination

recrude'scenza *nf* Med fresh outbreak; fig (di violenza) renewed outbreak; (di criminalità) upsurge

recupe'rare ① *vt* recover; rehabilitate ⟨*tossicodipendente*⟩; make up ⟨*ore di assenza*⟩; ∼ **il tempo perduto** make up for lost time
② *vi* catch up

re'cupero *nm* recovery; (di tossicodipendenti) rehabilitation; (salvataggio) rescue; **corso di recupero** additional classes *pl*; **materiali di recupero** recycled material; (che possono essere recuperati) recyclable material; **[minuti di] recupero** Sport injury time; **partita di recupero** rematch. **recupero crediti** debt collection. **recupero [dei] dati** data recovery

redargu'ire *vt* rebuke

re'datto *pp di* REDIGERE

redat|'tore, -trice *nmf* editor; (di testo) writer. **redattore capo** editor in chief

redazi'one *nf* (ufficio) editorial office; (di testi) editing

redditività *nf* earning power

reddi'tizio *adj* profitable

'reddito *nm* income; **a basso** ∼ ⟨*famiglia*⟩ low income. **imposta sul reddito** income tax. **reddito complessivo** gross income. **reddito imponibile** taxable income. **reddito non imponibile** non-taxable income. **reddito da lavoro** earned income; **redditi** *pl* **occasionali** casual earnings. **reddito pubblico** government revenue

re'dento *pp di* REDIMERE

reden'tore *nm* redeemer

redenzi'one *nf* redemption

re'digere *vt* write; draw up ⟨*documento*⟩

re'dimere *vt* redeem

re'dimersi *vr* redeem oneself

redi'mibile *adj* ⟨*titoli*⟩ redeemable

redin'gote *nf inv* frock-coat; **abito a redingote** fitted button-through dress

'redini *nfpl* reins

redi'vivo *adj* restored to life

'reduce ① *adj* ∼ **da** back from
② *nmf* survivor

refe'rendum *nm inv* referendum

refe'renza *nf* reference

referenzi'ato *adj* with references

re'ferto *nm* report. **referto medico** medical report

refet'torio *nm* refectory

reflazio'nare *vt* Econ reflate

reflazi'one *nf* Econ reflation

'reflex *nm inv* reflex camera

'refluo *nm* effluent

refrat'tario *adj* refractory; **essere** ∼ **a** fig be insensitive to ⟨*sentimenti*⟩; **sono** ∼ **alla matematica** maths are a closed book to me

refrige'rante *adj* cooling *attrib*

refrige'rare *vt* refrigerate

refrigerazi'one *nf* refrigeration

refur'tiva *nf* stolen goods *pl*

re'fuso *nm* Typ literal, typo

rega'lare *vt* give

re'gale *adj* regal

re'galo ① *nm* present, gift; **articoli da regalo** gifts
② *adj* **confezione regalo** gift set

re'gata *nf* regatta

'reggae *nm* Mus reggae

reg'gente *nmf* regent

reg'genza *nf* regency

'reggere ① *vt* (sorreggere) bear; (tenere in mano) hold; (dirigere) run; (governare) govern; Gram take
② *vi* (resistere) hold out; (durare) last; fig stand

'reggersi *vr* stand

'reggia *nf* royal palace

reggi'calze *nm inv* suspender belt

reggi'mento *nm* regiment; (fig: molte persone) army

reggi'petto, reggiseno *nm* bra

re'gia *nf* Cinema direction; Theat production

re'gime *nm* regime; (dieta) diet; (di fiume) rate of flow; **a** ∼ **torrentizio** in spate; **a pieno** ∼ ⟨*funzionare*⟩ at full speed. **regime alimentare** diet. **regime fiscale** tax system. **regime di giri** (di motore) revs per minute, rpm. **regime militare** military regime. **regime monetario aureo** gold standard. **regime di vita** lifestyle

re'gina *nf* queen; **ape regina** queen bee. **regina madre** queen mother

'regio *adj* royal

regio'nale *adj* regional

regiona'lismo *nm* (parola) regionalism

regional'mente *adv* regionally

regi'one *nf* region

re'gista *nmf* Cinema, TV director; Theat producer

regi'strare *vt* register; Comm enter; (incidere su nastro) tape, record; (su disco) record

registra'tore *nm* recorder; (magnetofono) tape-recorder. **registratore di cassa** cash register. **registratore a cassette** tape recorder, cassette recorder. **registratore di volo** flight recorder

registrazi'one *nf* registration; Comm entry; (di programma) recording; **sala di registrazione** recording studio.
registrazione [dei] dati data capture
re'gistro *nm* register; (ufficio) registry. **registro di bordo** log. **registro di cassa** ledger. **registro di classe** class register; **registro linguistico** register
re'gnare *vi* reign
'**regno** *nm* kingdom; (sovranità) reign. **regno animale** animal kingdom. **Regno Unito** United Kingdom. **regno vegetale** plant kingdom
'**regola** *nf* rule; **essere in** ∼ be in order; ⟨persona⟩ have one's papers in order; **a** ∼ **d'arte** in a workmanlike fashion
rego'labile *adj* ⟨velocità, luminosità⟩ adjustable
regola'mento *nm* regulation; Comm settlement. **regolamento di conti** settling of scores
rego'lare ① *adj* regular ② *vt* regulate; (ridurre, moderare) limit; (sistemare) settle
regolarità *nf* regularity
regolariz'zare *vt* settle ⟨debito⟩; regularize ⟨situazione⟩
rego'larsi *vr* (agire) act; (moderarsi) control oneself
rego'lata *nf* **darsi una** ∼ pull oneself together
regola'tore, -trice ① *adj* **piano regolatore** urban development plan ② *nmf* regulator
'**regolo** *nm* ruler. **regolo calcolatore** slide-rule
regre'dire *vi* Biol, Psych regress
regressi'one *nf* regression
regres'sivo *adj* regressive
re'gresso *nm* decline
reincar'narsi *vr* ∼ **in...** be reincarnated as...
reincarnazi'one *nf* reincarnation
reinseri'mento *nm* (di persona) reintegration
reinser'irsi *vr* (in ambiente) reintegrate
reinstal'lare *vt* reinstall
reinte'grare *vt* restore
reinven'tare *vt* reinvent
reinvesti'mento *nm* reinvestment
reinve'stire *vt* reinvest ⟨soldi⟩
reite'rare *vt* reiterate
reiterazi'one *nf* reiteration
re'lais *nm inv* relay
relativa'mente *adv* relatively; ∼ **a** as regards
relatività *nf* relativity
rela'tivo *adj* relative
rela'tore, -trice *nmf* (in una conferenza) speaker; (di tesi) supervisor

re'lax *nm* relaxation
relazi'one *nf* relation; (di lavoro ecc) relationship; (rapporto amoroso) [love] affair; (resoconto) report; **pubbliche relazioni** *pl* public relations. **relazione extraconiugale** extramarital relationship; **relazioni** *pl* **industriali** industrial relations
rele'gare *vt* relegate
relegazi'one *nf* relegation
religi'one *nf* religion
religi'oso, -a ① *adj* religious ② *nm* monk ③ *nf* nun
re'liquia *nf* relic
reliqui'ario *nm* reliquary
re'litto *nm* wreck
re'mainder *nm inv* (libro) remainder
re'make *nm inv* remake
re'mare *vi* row
rema|'tore, -trice *nmf* rower
remini'scenza *nf* reminiscence
remissi'one *nf* remission; (sottomissione) submissiveness. **remissione del debito** remission of debt. **remissione di querela** withdrawal of an action
remissiva'mente *adv* submissively
remis'sivo *adj* submissive
re'mix *nm inv* Mus remix
'**remo** *nm* oar
'**remora** *nf* **senza remore** without hesitation
re'moto *adj* remote
remo'vibile *adj* removable
remune'rare *vt* remunerate
remunera'tivo *adj* remunerative
remunerazi'one *nf* remuneration
re'nale *adj* renal, kidney *attrib*
'**rendere** *vt* (restituire) return; (esprimere) render; (fruttare) yield; (far diventare) make
'**rendersi** *vr* become; ∼ **conto di qualcosa** realize something; ∼ **utile** make oneself useful
rendi'conto *nm* report
rendi'mento *nm* rendering; (produzione) yield
'**rendita** *nf* income; (dello Stato) revenue; **vivere di** ∼ fig rest on one's laurels. **rendita vitalizia** life annuity
'**rene** *nm* kidney. **rene artificiale** kidney machine
'**reni** *nfpl* (schiena) back
reni'tente ① *adj* **essere** ∼ **a** ⟨consigli di qualcuno⟩ be loath to accept; refuse to obey ⟨legge⟩ ② *nm* **renitente alla leva** person who fails to report for military service after being called up, draft dodger Am
'**renna** *nf* reindeer (pl inv); (pelle) buckskin

r

'Reno nm Rhine

'reo, -a ① adj guilty
② nmf criminal. **reo confesso** self-confessed criminal

Rep. abbr (**repubblica**) Rep.

re'parto nm department; Mil unit; **reparti**
pl **d'assalto** Mil assault troops. **reparto
d'attacco** Sport attack. **reparto
difensivo** Sport defence. **reparto grandi
ustionati** Med burns unit. **reparto di
massima sicurezza** secure unit.
reparto maternità maternity ward.
reparto radiologia X-ray unit

repel'lente adj repulsive

repen'taglio nm **mettere a ∼** risk

repentina'mente adv suddenly

repen'tino adj sudden

reper'ibile adj available; **non è ∼**
(perduto) it's not to be found

reperibilità nf availability

repe'rire vt trace ⟨fondi⟩

re'perto nm **reperto archeologico**
find. **reperto giudiziario** exhibit

reper'torio nm repertory; (elenco) index;
immagini pl **di repertorio** archive footage

re'play nm inv [instant] replay

'replica nf reply; (obiezione) objection;
(copia) replica; Theat repeat performance

repli'care vt reply; Theat repeat

repor'tage nm inv report

repressi'one nf repression

repres'sivo adj repressive

re'presso pp di REPRIMERE

re'primere vt repress

re'pubblica nf republic. **Repubblica
Ceca** Czech Republic. **Repubblica
Centrafricana** Central African Repblic.
Repubblica Dominicana Dominican
Republic. **Repubblica d'Irlanda**
Republic of Ireland, Irish Republic.
repubblica parlamentare
parliamentary republic. **Repubblica
Popolare cinese** People's Republic of
China. **repubblica presidenziale**
presidential-style republic. **Repubblica
Slovacca** Slovakia

repubbli'cano, -a adj & nmf
republican

repu'tare vt consider

repu'tarsi vr consider oneself

reputazi'one nf reputation

'requiem nm inv requiem

requi'sire vt requisition

requi'sito nm requirement

requisi'toria nf (arringa) closing speech

requisizi'one nf requisition

'resa nf surrender; Comm rendering. **resa
dei conti** rendering of accounts. **resa
incondizionata** unconditional
surrender

re'scindere vt cancel

'residence nm inv residential hotel

resi'dente adj & nmf resident

resi'denza nf residence; (soggiorno) stay.
residenza protetta sheltered
accomodation

residenzi'ale adj residential; **zona
residenziale** residential district

re'siduo ① adj residual
② nm remainder; **residui** pl **industriali**
industrial waste

'resina nf resin

resi'stente adj resistant. **resistente
all'acqua** water resistant

resi'stenza nf resistance; (fisica)
stamina; Electr resistor; **la Resistenza** the
Resistance. **resistenza passiva** passive
resistance. **resistenza a pubblico
ufficiale** resisting arrest

re'sistere vi **∼ [a]** resist; (a colpi, scosse)
stand up to; **∼ alla pioggia/al vento** be
rain/wind-resistant

'reso pp di RENDERE

reso'conto nm report. **resoconto
annuale** annual report

respin'gente nm Rail buffer

re'spingere vt repel; (rifiutare) reject;
(bocciare) fail

re'spinto pp di RESPINGERE

respi'rare vt/i breathe

respira'tore nm respirator.
respiratore artificiale life support
machine. **respiratore [a tubo]** snorkel

respira'torio adj respiratory

respirazi'one nf breathing; Med
respiration. **respirazione artificiale**
artificial respiration. **respirazione
assistita** life support. **respirazione
bocca a bocca** mouth-to-mouth
resuscitation, kiss of life

re'spiro nm breath; (il respirare) breathing;
fig respite. **respiro di sollievo** sigh of
relief

respon'sabile ① adj responsible (**di**
for); Jur liable
② nmf person responsible.
**responsabile della gestione del
portafoglio fondi di investimento**
investment manager. **responsabile
della produzione** production manager.
responsabile delle risorse umane
human resources manager

responsabilità nf inv responsibility;
Jur liability. **responsabilità civile** Jur
civil liability. **responsabilità limitata**
limited liability. **responsabilità
penale** criminal liability

responsabiliz'zare vt give
responsibility to ⟨dipendente⟩; give a
sense of responsibility to ⟨gente⟩

responsabil'mente adv responsibly

re'sponso nm response

283

ressa ⋯∶ revisione ⋯

'ressa *nf* crowd

re'stante ① *adj* remaining ② *nm* remainder

re'stare *vi* = RIMANERE

restau'rare *vt* restore

restaura|'tore, -trice *nmf* restorer

restaurazi'one *nf* restoration

re'stauro *nm* (riparazione) repair; (arte) restoration

re'stio *adj* restive; ∼ **a** reluctant to

restitu'ibile *adj* returnable

restitu'ire *vt* return; (reintegrare) restore

restituzi'one *nf* return; Jur restitution

'resto *nm* rest, remainder; (saldo) balance; (denaro) change; **resti** *pl* (avanzi) remains; **del** ∼ besides

re'stringere *vt* contract; take in ⟨vestiti⟩; (limitare) restrict; shrink ⟨stoffa⟩

re'stringersi *vr* contract; (farsi più vicini) close up; ⟨stoffa⟩ shrink

restringi'mento *nm* (di tessuto) shrinkage. **restringimento del campo visivo** Med tunnel vision

restrit'tivo *adj* restrictive

restrizi'one *nf* restriction

resurrezi'one *nf* resurrection

resusci'tare ① *vt* revive; resuscitate ⟨moribondo⟩ ② *vi* ⟨Cristo⟩ rise again; fig revive

re'taggio *nm* legacy

re'tata *nf* round-up

'rete *nf* net; (sistema) network; ⟨televisiva⟩ channel; (in calcio, hockey) goal; fig trap; (per la spesa) string bag; **la Rete** (Internet) the net, the web. **rete commutata pubblica** Teleph switched public network. **rete di distribuzione** Comm distribution network. **rete locale** Comput local [area] network, LAN. **rete di protezione** (per acrobata) safety net. **rete stradale** road network. **rete telematica** communications network. **rete televisiva satellitare** satellite channel. **rete televisiva via cavo** cable company

reti'cente *adj* reticent

reti'cenza *nf* reticence

retico'lato *nm* grid; (rete metallica) wire netting

re'ticolo *nm* network. **reticolo geografico** grid

re'tina¹ *nf* (per capelli) hair net

'retina² *nf* Anat retina

re'tino *nm* net

retorica'mente *adv* rhetorically

re'torico, -a ① *adj* rhetorical; **domanda retorica** rhetorical question; **figura retorica** figure of speech ② *nf* rhetoric

re'trattile *adj* ⟨punta⟩ retractable

retribu'ire *vt* remunerate

retribu'tivo *adj* salary *attrib*

retribuzi'one *nf* remuneration

'retro ① *adv* behind; **vedi** ∼ see over ② *nm inv* back. **retro di copertina** outside back cover

retroat'tivo *adj* retroactive

retrobot'tega *nm inv* back shop

retro'cedere ① *vi* retreat ② *vt* Mil demote; Sport relegate

retrocessi'one *nf* Sport relegation

retroda'tare *vt* backdate, predate

retro'fit *nm inv* Auto retrofitted catalytic converter

re'trogrado *adj* retrograde; fig old-fashioned; Pol reactionary

retrogu'ardia *nf* Mil reaguard

retro'gusto *nm* after-taste

retro'marcia *nf* reverse [gear]

retro'scena *nm inv* Theat backstage; **i** ∼ fig the real story

retrospettiva'mente *adv* retrospectively

retrospet'tivo *adj* retrospective

retro'stante *adj* **il palazzo** ∼ the building behind

retro'via *nf* Mil area behind the front lines

retro'virus *nm inv* retrovirus

retrovi'sore *nm* rear-view mirror

'retta¹ *nf* Math straight line; (di collegio, pensionato) fee

'retta² *nf* **dar** ∼ **a qualcuno** take somebody's advice

rettango'lare *adj* rectangular

ret'tangolo ① *adj* right-angled ② *nm* rectangle

ret'tifica *nf* rectification

rettifi'care *vt* rectify

'rettile *nm* reptile

retti'lineo ① *adj* rectilinear; (retto) upright ② *nm* Sport back straight

retti'tudine *nf* rectitude

'retto ① *pp di* REGGERE ② *adj* straight; fig upright; (giusto) correct; **angolo retto** right angle ③ *nm* rectum

ret'tore *nm* Relig rector; Univ chancellor

reu'matico *adj* rheumatic

reuma'tismi *nmpl* rheumatism

reve'rendo *adj* reverend

rever'sibile *adj* reversible

revisio'nare *vt* revise; Comm audit; Auto overhaul

revisi'one *nf* revision; Comm audit; Auto overhaul. **revisione di bilancio** audit. **revisione di bozze** proof-reading. ⋯∶

revisione dello stipendio salary review

revisio'nismo nm Pol revisionism

revisio'nista adj ⟨politica⟩ revisionist

revi'sore nm (di conti) auditor; (di bozze) proofreader; (di traduzioni) reviser

re'vival nm inv revival

'revoca nf repeal

revo'care vt repeal

revolve'rata nf revolver shot

rhythm and blues nm rhythm and blues, R & B

riabbas'sare vt lower again

riabbas'sarsi vr ⟨acque⟩ recede; ⟨temperatura⟩ fall again

riabotto'nare vt button up again

riabbracci'are vt (abbracciare di nuovo) embrace again; (fig: rivedere) see again

riabili'tare vt rehabilitate

riabilitazi'one nf rehabilitation; **centro di riabilitazione** rehabilitation centre

riabitu'are vt ∼ qualcuno a qualcosa reaccustom somebody to something, get somebody used to something again

riabitu'arsi vr ∼ a qualcosa get used to something again, reaccustom oneself to something

riac'cendere vt switch on again ⟨luce, TV⟩; rekindle, revive ⟨interesse, passione⟩; rekindle ⟨fuoco⟩

riac'cendersi vr ⟨luce⟩ come back on; ⟨interesse, passione⟩ rekindle, revive

riaccensi'one nf la continua ∼ continual switching on and off

riaccer'tare vt reassess

riacqui'stare vt buy back; regain ⟨libertà, prestigio⟩; recover ⟨vista, udito⟩

riacutiz'zarsi vr get worse again

riadatta'mento nm readjustment

riadat'tare vt convert ⟨stanza⟩; alter ⟨indumento⟩

riadat'tarsi vr readjust

riaddormen'tare vt get [back] to sleep again

riaddormen'tarsi vr fall asleep again

riadope'rare vt reuse

riaffacci'arsi vr (alla finestra) appear again; ⟨idea⟩ surface again

riaffermare vt reaffirm, reassert

riaffon'dare vi sink again

riaffron'tare vt deal with again ⟨situazione⟩; take up again ⟨argomento⟩

riagganci'are ① vt replace ⟨ricevitore⟩; ∼ la cornetta hang up
② vi hang up

riaggre'garsi vr regroup

riallac'ciare vt refasten; reconnect ⟨corrente⟩; renew ⟨amicizia⟩

riallar'gare vt widen again ⟨tunnel, strada⟩

riallinea'mento nm realignment

rialline'are vt realign

rialloggi'are vt rehouse

rial'zare ① vt raise
② vi rise

rial'zarsi vr get up again

rial'zato adj **piano rialzato** mezzanine

ri'alzo nm rise; **al** ∼ Fin bullish. **rialzo dei prezzi** price rise

ria'mare vt ∼ qualcuno reciprocate somebody's love, love somebody back

riamma'larsi vr fall ill again

riam'mettere vt readmit ⟨socio, studente⟩

rian'dare vi return

riani'mare vt Med resuscitate; (ridare forza a) revive; (ridare coraggio a) cheer up

riani'marsi vr regain consciousness; (riprendere forza) revive; (riprendere coraggio) cheer up

rianimazi'one nf intensive care [unit]; **sala di rianimazione** intensive care unit

rianno'dare vt retie ⟨filo⟩; renew ⟨rapporti⟩

riaper'tura nf reopening

riappa'rire vi reappear

riap'pendere vt replace ⟨cornetta⟩; ∼ [il telefono] hung up

riappiso'larsi vr doze off again

riappropri'arsi vr ∼ di take back

ria'prire vt reopen

ria'prirsi vr reopen

ri'armo nm rearmament

ri'arso adj parched

riascol'tare vt listen to again

riasse'gnare vt reallocate

riassicu'rare vt reinsure

riassicurazi'one nf reinsurance

riassorbi'mento nm reabsorption

riassor'bire vt reabsorb

rias'sumere vt re-employ, take on again ⟨impiegato⟩; (ricapitolare) resume

riassu'mibile adj (riepilogabile) which can be summarized, summarizable

riassun'tivo adj summarizing

rias'sunto ① pp di RIASSUMERE
② nm summary

riattac'care ① vt ∼ il telefono hang up
② vi (al telefono) hang up

riatti'vare vt reactivate ⟨processo⟩; reintroduce, bring back ⟨servizio⟩; start up again, restart ⟨congegno⟩; stimulate ⟨circolazione sanguigna⟩

ria'vere vt get back; regain ⟨salute, vista⟩

ria'versi vr recover

riavvicina'mento nm (tra persone) reconciliation; (tra paesi) rapprochement

riavvici'nare *vt* fig reconcile ⟨*paesi, persone*⟩

riavvici'narsi *vr* (riconciliarsi) be reconciled, make it up fam

riav'volgere *vt* rewind

riba'dire *vt* (confermare) reaffirm

ri'balta *nf* flap; Theat footlights *pl*; fig limelight

ribal'tabile *adj* tip-up

ribal'tare *vt/i* tip over; Naut capsize

ribal'tarsi *vr* tip over; Naut capsize

ribas'sare ① *vt* lower
② *vi* fall

ribas'sato *adj* reduced

ri'basso *nm* fall; (sconto) discount

ri'battere ① *vt* (a macchina) retype; (controbattere) deny
② *vi* answer back

ribattez'zare *vt* rename

ribel'larsi *vr* rebel

ri'belle ① *adj* rebellious
② *nmf* rebel

ribelli'one *nf* rebellion

'ribes *nm* (rosso) redcurrant; (nero) blackcurrant

ribol'lire *vi* (fermentare) ferment; fig seethe

ri'brezzo *nm* disgust; **far ~ a** disgust

ribut'tante *adj* repugnant

ribut'tare *vt* (buttare di nuovo) throw back

rica'dere *vi* fall back; (nel peccato ecc) lapse; (pendere) hang [down]; **~ su** (riversarsi) fall on

rica'duta *nf* relapse; **avere una ~** to have a relapse

rical'care *vt* trace

ricalci'trante *adj* recalcitrant

ricalco'lare *vt* recalculate

rica'mare *vt* embroider

rica'mato *adj* embroidered

ri'cambi *nmpl* spare parts

ricambi'are *vt* return; reciprocate ⟨*sentimento*⟩; **~ qualcosa a qualcuno** repay somebody for something

ri'cambio *nm* replacement; Biol metabolism; **pezzo di ricambio** spare [part]

ri'camo *nm* embroidery

ricandi'dare *vt* (a elezioni) put forward as a candidate again

ricandi'darsi *vr* (a elezioni) stand again

ricapito'lare *vt* sum up; **ricapitoliamo** let's recap

ricapitolazi'one *nf* summary, recap fam

ri'carica *nf* (di sveglia) winder; (di batteria) recharging; (di penna) refill; (di fucile) reloading; Teleph top-up card

ricari'cabile *adj* rechargeable

ricari'care *vt* reload ⟨*macchina fotografica, fucile, camion*⟩; recharge ⟨*batteria*⟩; Comput reboot; rewind ⟨*orologio*⟩; top up ⟨*cellulare*⟩

ricat'tare *vt* blackmail

ricatta|'tore, -trice *nmf* blackmailer

ricatta'torio *adj* blackmail *attrib*

ri'catto *nm* blackmail. **ricatto morale** moral blackmail, emotional blackmail

rica'vare *vt* get; (ottenere) obtain; (dedurre) draw

rica'vato *nm* proceeds *pl*

ri'cavo *nm* proceeds *pl*

ricca'mente *adv* lavishly

ric'chezza *nf* wealth; fig richness; **ricchezze** *pl* riches

'riccio ① *adj* curly
② *nm* curl; (animale) hedgehog. **riccio di mare** sea-urchin

'ricciolo *nm* curl

riccio'luto *adj* curly

ricci'uto *adj* ⟨*barba*⟩ curly; ⟨*persona*⟩ curly-haired

'ricco, -a ① *adj* rich. **ricco sfondato** fam filthy rich
② *nmf* rich person; **i ricchi** the rich

ri'cerca *nf* search; (indagine) investigation; (scientifica) research; Sch project. **ricerca avanzata** Comput advanced search. **ricerca sul campo** field work. **ricerca di mercato** market research. **ricerca operativa** operational research

ricer'care *vt* search for; (fare ricerche su) research

ricer'cata *nf* wanted woman

ricercata'mente *adv* ⟨*vestire*⟩ with refinement; ⟨*parlare*⟩ in a refined way

ricerca'tezza *nf* refinement

ricer'cato ① *adj* sought-after; (raffinato) refined
② *nm* (dalla polizia) wanted man

ricerca|'tore, -trice *nmf* researcher

ricetrasmit'tente *nf* transceiver, two-way radio

ri'cetta *nf* Culin recipe; Med prescription

ricet'tacolo *nm* receptacle

ricet'tario *nm* (di cucina) recipe book; (di medico) prescription pad

ricetta|'tore, -trice *nmf* receiver of stolen goods, fence fam

ricettazi'one *nf* receiving [stolen goods]

rice'vente ① *adj* ⟨*apparecchio, stazione*⟩ receiving
② *nmf* receiver

ri'cevere *vt* receive; (dare il benvenuto) welcome; (di albergo) accommodate

ricevi'mento *nm* receiving; (accoglienza) welcome; (trattenimento) reception

ricevi'tore *nm* receiver. **ricevitore delle imposte** tax man. **ricevitore del lotto** lottery ticket agent

ricevito'ria *nf* **ricevitoria delle imposte** ≈ Inland Revenue. **ricevitoria del lotto** agency authorized to sell lottery tickets

rice'vuta *nf* receipt. **ricevuta d'acquisto** proof of purchase. **ricevuta doganale** docket. **ricevuta fiscale** tax receipt. **ricevuta di ritorno** acknowledgement of receipt. **ricevuta di versamento** receipt (given for bills etc paid at the Post Office)

rice'vuto *int* roger

ricezi'one *nf* Radio, TV reception

richia'mare *vt* (al telefono) call back; (far tornare) recall; (rimproverare) rebuke; (attirare) draw; ∼ **alla mente** call to mind

richi'amo *nm* recall; (attrazione) call

richie'dente *nmf* applicant

richi'edere *vt* ask for; (di nuovo) ask again for; ∼ **a qualcuno di fare qualcosa** ask *or* request somebody to do something

richi'esta *nf* request; Comm demand. **richiesta di indennizzo** claim for damages

richi'esto *adj* sought-after

ri'chiudere *vt* shut again, close again

ri'chiudersi *vr* ⟨ferita⟩ heal; ⟨porta⟩ shut again, close again

rici'clabile *adj* recyclable

rici'claggio *nm* recycling; (di denaro) laundering

rici'clare *vt* recycle ⟨carta, vetro⟩; launder ⟨denaro sporco⟩

rici'clarsi *vr* retrain; (cambiare lavoro) change one's line of work

rici'clato *adj* recycled

'ricino *nm* **olio di ricino** castor oil

ricogni'tore *nm* reconnaissance plane

ricognizi'one *nf* Mil reconnaissance

ricolle'gare *vt* (collegare di nuovo) reconnect

ricolle'garsi *vr* ∼ **a** ⟨evento, fatto⟩ relate to, tie up with

ricol'mare *vt* fill to the brim

ri'colmo *adj* full

ricominci'are *vt/i* start again; ∼ **da capo** start all over again

ricompa'rire *vi* reappear

ricom'parsa *nf* reappearance

ricom'pensa *nf* reward

ricompen'sare *vt* reward

ricom'porre *vt* (riscrivere) rewrite; (ricostruire) reform; Teleph redial; Typ reset

ricom'porsi *vr* regain one's composure

ricomposizi'one *nf* Teleph **ricomposizione automatica dell'ultimo numero** redial facility

riconcili'are *vt* reconcile

riconcili'arsi *vr* be reconciled

riconciliazi'one *nf* reconciliation

riconfer'mare *vt* reappoint

ricongi'ungere *vt* reunite

ricongi'ungersi *vr* become reunited

ricono'scente *adj* grateful

ricono'scenza *nf* gratitude

rico'noscere *vt* recognize; (ammettere) acknowledge

ricono'scibile *adj* recognizable

riconosci'mento *nm* recognition; (ammissione) acknowledgement; (per la polizia) identification. **riconoscimento vocale** Comput voice recognition

riconosci'uto *adj* recognized

ricon'quista *nf* reconquest

riconqui'stare *vt* Mil reconquer

ricon'segna *nf* return

riconse'gnare *vt* return

riconside'rare *vt* rethink

ricontrol'lare *vt* double-check

riconversi'one *nf* Econ restructuring

ricopi'are *vt* recopy

rico'prire *vt* re-cover; (rivestire) coat; (di insulti) shower (di with); hold ⟨carica⟩; ∼ **qualcuno di attenzioni** lavish attention on somebody

ricor'dare *vt* remember; (richiamare alla memoria) recall; (far ricordare) remind; (rassomigliare) look like

ricor'darsi *vr* ∼ [di] remember; ∼ **di fare qualcosa** remember to do something

ri'cordo *nm* memory; (oggetto) memento; (di viaggio) souvenir; **ricordi** *pl* (memorie) memoirs. ∼ **di famiglia** family heirloom

ricor'reggere *vt* correct again

ricor'rente *adj* recurrent

ricor'renza *nf* recurrence; (anniversario) anniversary

ri'correre *vi* recur; (accadere) occur; ⟨data⟩ fall; ∼ **a** have recourse to; (rivolgersi a) turn to

ri'corso ⓵ *pp di* RICORRERE ⓶ *nm* recourse; Jur appeal

ricostitu'ente *nm* tonic

ricostitu'ire *vt* re-establish

ricostru'ire *vt* reconstruct

ricostruzi'one *nf* reconstruction

ricove'rare *vt* give shelter to; ∼ **in ospedale** admit to hospital, hospitalize

ricove'rato, -a *nmf* hospital patient

ri'covero *nm* shelter; (ospizio) home

ricreare *vt* recreate; (ristorare) restore

ricre'arsi *vr* amuse oneself

ricrea'tivo *adj* recreational

ricreazi'one *nf* recreation; Sch break, playtime

ri'credersi *vr* change one's mind

ri'crescere *vi* grow again

ricu'cire *vt* sew up; stitch up ⟨*ferita*⟩

ricupe'rare, ricupero = RECUPERARE, RECUPERO

ri'curvo *adj* bent

ricu'sare *vt* refuse

ridacchi'are *vi* giggle

ri'dare *vt* give back, return

rida'rella *nf* giggles *pl*

ridefi'nire *vt* redefine

ri'dente *adj* ⟨piacevole⟩ pleasant

'ridere *vi* laugh; ~ **di** ⟨deridere⟩ laugh at

ride'stare *vt* reawaken ⟨*ricordo*⟩

ri'detto pp di RIDIRE

ridicoliz'zare *vt* ridicule

ri'dicolo *adj* ridiculous

ridimensiona'mento *nm* restructuring

ridimensio'nare *vt* restructure ⟨*azienda*⟩; fig get into perspective

ridi'pingere *vt* repaint

ri'dire *vt* repeat; **trova sempre da** ~ he's always finding fault; **hai qualcosa da** ~? do you have something to say?; **se non hai niente da** ~,... if you've no objection...

ridi'scendere *vi* go back down

ridistribu'ire *vt* redistribute

ridistribuzi'one *nf* redistribution

ridon'dante *adj* redundant

ri'dosso: **a** ~ **di** *adv* behind

ri'dotto ① pp di RIDURRE ② *nm* Theat foyer ③ *adj* reduced **essere** ~ **male** be worn out

ri'durre *vt* reduce

ri'dursi *vr* diminish; ~ **a fare qualcosa** be reduced to doing something; ~ **a** ⟨*problema*⟩ come down to

ridut'tivo *adj* reductive

ridut'tore *nm* Electr adaptor

riduzi'one *nf* reduction. **riduzione cinematografica** film adaptation. **riduzione della pena** reduced sentence. **riduzione di prezzo** price cut. **riduzione teatrale** adaptation for the theatre

riedifi'care *vt* rebuild

rieducazi'one *nf* ⟨di malato⟩ rehabilitation

rie'leggere *vt* re-elect

rielezi'one *nf* re-election

rie'mergere *vi* resurface

riem'pire *vt* fill [up]; fill in ⟨*moduli ecc*⟩

riem'pirsi *vr* fill [up]

riempi'tivo ① *adj* filling ② *nm* filler

rien'tranza *nf* recess

rien'trare *vi* go/come back in; ⟨tornare⟩ return; ⟨piegare indentro⟩ recede; ~ **in** ⟨far parte⟩ fall within

ri'entro *nm* return; ⟨di astronave⟩ re-entry; **grande** ~ mass return home after the holidays

riepilo'gare *vt* recapitulate

rie'pilogo *nm* summing-up

rie'same *nm* reassessment

riesami'nare *vt* reappraise

ri'essere *vi* **ci risiamo!** here we go again!

riesu'mare *vt* exhume

rievo'care *vt* ⟨commemorare⟩ commemorate; recall ⟨*passato*⟩

rievocazi'one *nf* ⟨commemorazione⟩ commemoration; ⟨ricordo⟩ recollection

rifaci'mento *nm* remake

ri'fare *vt* do again; ⟨creare⟩ make again; ⟨riparare⟩ repair; ⟨imitare⟩ imitate; make ⟨*letto*⟩

ri'farsi *vr* ⟨rimettersi⟩ recover; ⟨vendicarsi⟩ get even; ~ **una vita/carriera** make a new life/career for oneself; ~ **il trucco** touch up one's makeup; ~ **di** make up for

ri'fatto pp di RIFARE

riferi'mento *nm* reference

rife'rire ① *vt* report; ~ **a** attribute to ② *vi* make a report

rife'rirsi *vr* ~ **a** refer to

rifi'lare *vt* ⟨tagliare a filo⟩ trim; ⟨fam; affibbiare⟩ saddle

rifi'nire *vt* finish off

rifini'tura *nf* finish

rifio'rire *vi* blossom again

rifiu'tare *vt* refuse; ~ **di fare qualcosa** refuse to do something

rifi'uto *nm* refusal; **acque** *pl* **di** ~ waste water; **rifiuti** *pl* ⟨immondizie⟩ rubbish; **rifiuti** *pl* **industriali** industrial waste; **rifiuti** *pl* **urbani** urban waste

riflessi'one *nf* reflection; ⟨osservazione⟩ remark

rifles'sivo *adj* thoughtful; Gram reflexive

ri'flesso ① pp di RIFLETTERE ② *nm* ⟨luce⟩ reflection; Med reflex; **per** ~ indirectly

ri'flettere ① *vt* reflect ② *vi* think ⟨su about⟩

ri'flettersi *vr* be reflected

riflet'tore *nm* reflector; ⟨proiettore⟩ search-light

ri'flusso *nm* ebb

rifocil'lare *vt* restore

rifocil'larsi *vr* liter, hum take some refreshment

rifondazi'one *nf* refounding. **Rifondazione Comunista** diehard Communist party

ri'fondere *vt* ⟨rimborsare⟩ refund

ri'forma *nf* reform; Relig reformation; Mil exemption on medical grounds

r

rifor'mare *vt* re-form; (migliorare) reform; Mil declare unfit for military service

riforma|'tore, **-trice** *nmf* reformer

rifor'mato *adj* ‹chiesa› Reformed; ‹recluta, soldato› unfit for military service

riforma'torio *nm* reformatory

riformat'tare *vt* Comput reformat

rifor'mista *adj & nmf* reformist

riformu'lare *vt* recast

riforni'mento *nm* supply; (scorta) stock; (di combustibile) refuelling; **stazione di rifornimento** petrol station

rifor'nire *vt* restock; ∼ **di** provide with

rifor'nirsi *vr* restock, stock up (**di** with)

ri'frangere *vt* refract

ri'fratto *pp di* RIFRANGERE

rifrazi'one *nf* refraction

rifug'gire ① *vt* shun ‹gloria, celebrità› ② *vi* escape again; ∼ **da** fig shun

rifugi'arsi *vr* take refuge

rifugi'ato, **-a** *nmf* refugee

ri'fugio *nm* shelter; (nascondiglio) hideaway, safe house. **rifugio antiaereo** bomb shelter. **rifugio antiatomico** fallout shelter

'riga *nf* line; (fila) row; (striscia) stripe; (scriminatura) parting; (regolo) rule; **a righe** (stoffa) striped; ‹quaderno› ruled; **mettersi in** ∼ line up

ri'gaglie *nfpl* (interiora) giblets

ri'gagnolo *nm* rivulet

ri'gare ① *vt* rule ‹foglio› ② *vi* ∼ **dritto** behave well

riga'toni *nmpl* small ridged pasta tubes

rigatti'ere *nm* junk dealer

rigene'rante *adj* regenerative

rigene'rare *vt* regenerate

riget'tare *vt* (gettare indietro) throw back; (respingere) reject; (vomitare) throw up

ri'getto *nm* rejection

ri'ghello *nm* ruler

rigida'mente *adv* rigidly

rigidità *nf* rigidity; (di clima) severity; (severità) strictness. **rigidità cadaverica** rigor mortis

'rigido *adj* rigid; (freddo) severe; (severo) strict

rigi'rare ① *vt* turn again; (ripercorrere) go round; fig twist ‹argomentazione› ② *vi* walk about

rigi'rarsi *vr* turn round; (nel letto) turn over

ri'giro *nm* (imbroglio) trick

'rigo *nm* line; Mus staff

ri'goglio *nm* bloom

rigogliosa'mente *adv* luxuriantly

rigogli'oso *adj* luxuriant

rigonfia'mento *nm* swelling

rigonfi'are *vt* reinflate

ri'gonfio *adj* swollen

ri'gore *nm* rigours *pl*; **a rigor di logica** strictly speaking; **calcio di rigore** penalty [kick]; **area di rigore** penalty area; **essere di** ∼ be compulsory

rigorosa'mente *adv* ‹giudicare› severely; ‹seguire istruzioni› exactly; **vestito** ∼ **in giacca e cravatta** wearing the obligatory jacket and tie

rigo'roso *adj* (severo) strict; (scrupoloso) rigorous

rigover'nare *vt* wash up

riguada'gnare *vt* regain, win back ‹stima›; win more ‹tempo, punti›

riguar'dare *vt* look at again; (considerare) regard; (concernere) concern; **per quanto riguarda...** with regard to...

riguar'darsi *vr* take care of oneself

rigu'ardo *nm* care; (considerazione) consideration; **nei riguardi di** towards; ∼ **a** with regard to

rigurgi'tante *adj* ∼ **di** swarming with

rigurgi'tare ① *vt* regurgitate ② *vi* ∼ **di** fig be swarming with

ri'gurgito *nm* regurgitation; (fig: di xenofobia, nazionalismo ecc) resurgence

rilanci'are ① *vt* throw back ‹palla›; (di nuovo) throw again; increase ‹offerta›; revive ‹moda›; relaunch ‹prodotto› ② *vi* (a carte) raise the stakes; **rilancio di dieci** I'll raise you ten

ri'lancio *nm* (di offerta) increase; (di prodotto) re-launch

rilasci'are *vt* (concedere) grant; (liberare) release; issue ‹documento›

rilasci'arsi *vr* relax

ri'lascio *nm* release; (di documento) issue

rilassa'mento *nm* relaxation. **rilassamento cutaneo** sagging of the skin

rilas'sare *vt* relax

rilas'sarsi *vr* relax

rilas'sato *adj* relaxed

rile'gare *vt* bind ‹libro›

rile'gato *adj* bound

rilega|'tore, **-trice** *nmf* bookbinder

rilega'tura *nf* binding

ri'leggere *vt* reread

ri'lento: **a** ∼ *adv* slowly

rileva'mento *nm* survey; Comm buyout. **rilevamento dirigenti** management buyout, MBO

rile'vante *adj* considerable

rile'vanza *nf* significance

rile'vare *vt* (trarre) get; (mettere in evidenza) point out; (notare) notice; (in topografia) survey; Comm take over; Mil relieve

rilevazi'one *nf* (statistica) survey

rili'evo *nm* relief; Geog elevation; (in topografia) survey; (importanza) importance;

(osservazione) remark; **mettere in ∼ qualcosa** point something out

rilut'tante *adj* reluctant

rilut'tanza *nf* reluctance, unwillingness

'**rima** *nf* rhyme; **far ∼ con qualcosa** rhyme with something; **rispondere a qualcuno per le rime** give somebody as good as one gets. **rima alternata** alternate rhyme. **rima baciata** rhyming couplet

riman'dare *vt* (posporre) postpone; (mandare indietro) send back; (mandare di nuovo) send again; (far ridare un esame) make resit an examination

ri'mando *nm* return; (in un libro) cross-reference

rimaneggia'mento *nm* rejig

rimaneggi'are *vt* rejig, recast

rima'nente ① *adj* remaining ② *nm* remainder

rima'nenza *nf* remainder; **rimanenze** *pl* remnants; **rimanenze** *pl* **di magazzino** unsold stock

rima'nere *vi* stay remain; (essere d'avanzo) be left; (venirsi a trovare) be; (restare stupito) be astonished; (restare d'accordo) agree; **∼ senza parole** be speechless

rimangi'are *vt* (mangiare di nuovo) have again, eat again

rimangi'arsi *vr* **∼ la parola** break one's promise

rimar'care *vt* remark

rimar'chevole *adj* remarkable

ri'mare *vt/i* rhyme

rimargi'nare *vt* heal

rimargi'narsi *vr* heal

ri'masto *pp di* RIMANERE

rima'sugli *nmpl* (di cibo) leftovers

rimbal'zare *vi* rebound; (proiettile) ricochet; **far ∼** bounce

rim'balzo *nm* rebound; (di proiettile) ricochet

rimbam'bire ① *vi* be in one's dotage ② *vt* stun

rimbam'bito *adj* in one's dotage

rimbec'care *vi* retort

rimbecil'lire *vt* make brain-dead

rimbecil'lito *adj* (stupido) brain-dead; (frastornato) stunned

rimboc'care *vt* turn up; roll up (maniche); tuck in (coperte); **∼ le coperte a qualcuno** tuck somebody into bed

rimboc'carsi *vr* **∼ le maniche** roll up one's sleeves

rimbom'bare *vi* boom, resound

rim'bombo *nm* boom

rimbor'sabile *adj* reclaimable

rimbor'sare *vt* reimburse, repay

rim'borso *nm* reimbursement, repayment. **rimborso d'imposta** tax

rebate. **rimborso spese** reimbursement of expenses

rimboschi'mento *nm* reafforestation Br, reforestation

rim'brotto *nm* reproach

rimedi'abile *adj* (errore) which can be remedied

rimedi'are *vi* **∼ a** remedy; make up for (errore); (procurare) scrape up

ri'medio *nm* remedy

rimesco'lare *vt* mix [up]; shuffle (carte); (rivangare) rake up; **mi fa ∼ il sangue** it makes my blood boil

rimesco'lio *nm* (turbamento) shock

ri'messa *nf* (per veicoli) garage; (per aerei) hangar; (per autobus) depot; (di denaro) remittance; (di merci) consignment. **rimessa laterale** Sport throw-in

ri'messo *pp di* RIMETTERE

rime'stare *vt* stir well

ri'mettere *vt* (a posto) put back; (restituire) return; (affidare) entrust; (perdonare) remit; (rimandare) put off; (vomitare) bring up; **∼ in gioco** (nel calcio) throw in; **∼ in moto** restart; **rimetterci** (fam: perdere) lose [out]

ri'mettersi *vr* (ristabilirsi) recover; (tempo) clear up; **∼ a** start again

'**rimmel**® *nm inv* mascara

rimoder'nare *vt* modernize

ri'monta *nf* Sport recovery

rimon'tare ① *vt* (risalire) go up; Mech reassemble ② *vi* remount; **∼ a** (risalire) go back to

rimorchi'are *vt* tow; fam pick up (ragazza)

rimorchia'tore *nm* tug[boat]

ri'morchio *nm* tow; (veicolo) trailer

ri'mordere *vt* **mi rimorde la coscienza** fig it's preying on my conscience

ri'morso *nm* remorse

rimo'stranza *nf* complaint

rimo'vibile *adj* removable

rimozi'one *nf* removal; (da un incarico) dismissal. **rimozione forzata** illegally parked vehicles removed at owner's expense

rimpagi'nare *vt* regret

rim'pallo *nm* bounce

rim'pasto *nm* Pol reshuffle

rimpatri'are ① *vt* repatriate ② *vi* return home

rimpatri'ata *nf* reunion

rim'patrio *nm* repatriation

rim'piangere *vt* regret

rimpi'anto ① *pp di* RIMPIANGERE ② *nm* regret

rimpiat'tino *nm* hide-and-seek

rimpiaz'zare *vt* replace

rimpi'azzo *nm* replacement

rimpiccioli'mento *nm* shrinkage
rimpiccio'lire ① *vt* make smaller ② *vi* become smaller
rimpinz'are *vt* ∼ di stuff with
rimpin'zarsi *vr* stuff oneself
rimpol'pare *vt* (ingrassare) fatten up; fig pad out ‹scritto›
rimprove'rare *vt* reproach; ∼ qualcosa a qualcuno reproach somebody for something
rim'provero *nm* reproach
rimugi'nare *vt* liter rummage; fig ∼ su brood over
rimune'rare *vt* remunerate
rimunera'tivo *adj* remunerative
rimunerazi'one *nf* remuneration
ri'muovere *vt* remove
ri'nascere *vi* be reborn, be born again
rinascimen'tale *adj* Renaissance
Rinasci'mento *nm* Renaissance
ri'nascita *nf* rebirth
rincal'zare *vt* (sostenere) support; (rimboccare) tuck in
rin'calzo *nm* support; rincalzi *pl* Mil reserves
rincantucci'arsi *vr* hide oneself away in a corner
rinca'rare ① *vt* increase the price of ② *vi* become more expensive
rin'caro *nm* price increase
rincar'tare *vt* rewrap
rinca'sare *vi* return home
rinchi'udere *vt* shut up
rinchi'udersi *vr* shut oneself up
rincon'trare *vt* meet again
rincon'trarsi *vr* meet [each other] again
rin'correre *vt* run after
rin'corsa *nf* run-up
rin'corso *pp* di RINCORRERE
rin'crescere *vi* mi rincresce di non... I'm sorry *or* I regret that I can't...; se non ti rincresce if you don't mind; rincresce vedere... it's sad to see...
rincresci'mento *nm* regret
rincresci'uto *pp* di RINCRESCERE
rincreti'nire ① *vt* make brain-dead ② *vi* go brain-dead
rincu'lare *vi* ‹arma› recoil; ‹cavallo› shy
rin'culo *nm* recoil
rincuo'rare *vt* encourage
rincuo'rarsi *vr* take heart
rinfacci'are *vt* ∼ qualcosa a qualcuno throw something in somebody's face
rinfode'rare *vt* sheathe
rinfor'zare *vt* strengthen; (rendere più saldo) reinforce
rinfor'zarsi *vr* become stronger

rin'forzo *nm* reinforcement; fig support; rinforzi *pl* Mil reinforcements
rinfran'care *vt* reassure
rinfre'scante *adj* cooling
rinfre'scare ① *vt* cool; (rinnovare) freshen up ② *vi* get cooler
rinfre'scarsi *vr* freshen [oneself] up
rin'fresco *nm* light refreshment; (ricevimento) party
rin'fusa *nf* alla ∼ at random
ringalluz'zire ① *vt* make cocky ② *vi* get cocky
ringhi'are *vi* snarl
ringhi'era *nf* railing; (di scala) banisters *pl*
ringhi'oso *adj* snarling
ringiova'nire ① *vt* rejuvenate ‹pelle, persona, vestito› make look younger ② *vi* become young again; (sembrare) look young again
ringrazia'mento *nm* thanks *pl*
ringrazi'are *vt* thank
rinne'gare *vt* disown
rinne'gato, -a *nmf* renegade
rinno'vabile *adj* renewable; ‹risorsa, foresta› sustainable
rinnova'mento *nm* renewal; (di edifici) renovation
rinno'vare *vt* renew; renovate ‹edifici›
rinno'varsi *vr* be renewed; (ripetersi) recur, happen again
rin'novo *nm* renewal
rinoce'ronte *nm* rhinoceros
rino'mato *adj* renowned
rinsal'dare *vt* consolidate
rinsa'vire *vi* come to one's senses
rinsec'chire *vi* shrivel up
rinsec'chito *adj* shrivelled up
rinta'narsi *vr* hide oneself away; ‹animale› retreat into its den
rintoc'care *vi* ‹compana› toll; ‹orologio› strike
rin'tocco *nm* toll; (di orologio) stroke
rinton'tire *vt* anche fig stun
rinton'tito *adj* (stordito) dazed
rintracci'are *vt* trace
rintro'nare ① *vt* stun ② *vi* boom
rintuz'zare *vt* blunt; (ribattere) retort; (reprimere) repress
ri'nuncia *nf* renunciation
rinunci'are *vi* ∼ a renounce, give up
rinuncia'tario *adj* defeatist
ri'nunzia, rinunziare = RINUNCIA, RINUNCIARE
rinveni'mento *nm* (di reperti) discovery; (di refurtiva) recovery

rinve'nire ① *vt* find
 ② *vi* (riprendere i sensi) come round; (ridiventare fresco) revive

rinvi'are *vt* put off; (mandare indietro) return; (in libro) refer; ~ **a giudizio** indict

rinvigo'rire *vt* strengthen

rin'vio *nm* Sport goal kick; (in libro) cross-reference; (di appuntamento) postponement; (di merce) return. **rinvio a giudizio** indictment

rioccu'pare *vt* reoccupy

rio'nale *adj* local

ri'one *nm* district

riordina'mento *nm* reorganization

riordi'nare *vt* tidy [up]; (ordinare di nuovo) reorder

riorganiz'zare *vt* reorganize

riorganizzazi'one *nf* reorganization

R.I.P. *abbr* (**riposi in pace**) RIP

ripa'gare *vt* repay

ripa'rare ① *vt* (proteggere) shelter, protect; (aggiustare) repair; (porre rimedio) remedy
 ② *vi* ~ **a** make up for

ripa'rarsi *vr* take shelter

ripa'rato *adj* ⟨luogo⟩ sheltered

riparazi'one *nf* repair; fig reparation

ripar'lare *vi* **ne riparliamo stasera** we'll talk about it again tonight

ri'paro *nm* shelter; (rimedio) remedy

ripar'tire ① *vt* (dividere) divide
 ② *vi* leave again

ripartizi'one *nf* division

ripas'sare ① *vt* recross; (rivedere) revise
 ② *vi* pass again

ripas'sata *nf* (spolverata) quick dust; (stirata) quick iron; (di vernice) second coat; (fam: rimprovero) telling-off; **dar una ~ a** ⟨lezione⟩ revise

ri'passo *nm* (di lezione) revision

ripensa'mento *nm* second thoughts *pl*

ripen'sare *vi* ~ **a** a think back to; **ripensarci** (cambiare idea) change one's mind; **ripensaci!** think again!

riper'correre *vt* (con la memoria) go back over; trace ⟨storia⟩; ~ **la strada fatta** go back the way one came

riper'cosso *pp di* RIPERCUOTERE

ripercu'otere *vt* strike again

ripercu'otersi *vr* ⟨suono⟩ reverberate; ~ **su qualcosa** (fig: avere conseguenze) impact on something

ripercussi'one *nf* repercussion

ripe'scare *vt* (recuperare) fish out; (ritrovare) find again

ripe'tente *nmf* student who is repeating a year

ri'petere *vt* repeat

ri'petersi *vr* ⟨evento⟩ recur; ⟨persona⟩ repeat oneself

ripeti'tore *nm* TV relay

ripetizi'one *nf* repetition; (di lezione) revision; (lezione privata) private lesson

ripetuta'mente *adv* repeatedly

ri'piano *nm* (di scaffale) shelf; (terreno pianeggiante) terrace

ri'picca, ri'picco *nf* spite; **fare qualcosa per ~** do something out of spite

ripida'mente *adv* steeply

'ripido *adj* steep

ripie'gare ① *vt* refold; (abbassare) lower
 ② *vi* (indietreggiare) retreat

ripie'garsi *vr* bend; ⟨sedile⟩ fold

ripi'ego *nm* expedient; (via d'uscita) way out

ripi'eno ① *adj* full; Culin stuffed
 ② *nm* filling; Culin stuffing

ripiom'bare *vi* (per terra) fall down again; ~ **nella disperazione** sink back into despair

ripopo'lare *vt* repopulate

ripopo'larsi *vr* be repopulated

ri'porre *vt* put back; (mettere da parte) put away; (collocare) place; repeat ⟨domanda⟩

ripor'tare *vt* (restituire) bring/take back; (riferire) report; (subire) suffer; Math carry; win ⟨vittoria⟩; transfer ⟨disegno⟩

ripor'tarsi *vr* go back; (riferirsi) refer

ri'porto *nm* (su abito, scarpa) appliqué; ~ **di 4** Math carry 4; **cane da riporto** gun dog, retriever; **nascondere la calvizie con un ~** comb one's hair over a bald spot

ripo'sante *adj* restful

ripo'sare ① *vi* rest
 ② *vt* put back

ripo'sarsi *vr* rest

ripo'sato *adj* ⟨mente⟩ fresh; ⟨viso⟩ rested

ri'poso *nm* rest; **andare a ~** retire; **~! Mil** at ease!; **giorno di riposo** day off

ripo'stiglio *nm* cupboard

ri'posto *pp di* RIPORRE

ri'prendere *vt* take again; (prendere indietro) take back; (riconquistare) recapture; (recuperare) recover; (ricominciare) resume; (rimproverare) reprimand; take in ⟨cucitura⟩; Cinema shoot

ri'prendersi *vr* recover; (correggersi) correct oneself

ri'presa *nf* resumption; (ricupero) recovery; Theat revival; Cinema shot; Auto acceleration; Mus repeat. **ripresa aerea** bird's-eye view; **riprese** *pl* Cinema filming

ripresen'tare *vt* resubmit ⟨domanda, certificato⟩; reintroduce ⟨problema, persona⟩

ripresen'tarsi *vr* (a ufficio) go/come back again; (come candidato) stand again, run again; ⟨occasione⟩ arise again; ⟨problema⟩ come up again, reappear; (a esame) resit

ri'preso *pp di* RIPRENDERE

r

ripristi'nare vt restore

ripro'dotto pp di RIPRODURRE

ripro'durre vt reproduce

ripro'dursi vr Biol reproduce; ⟨fenomeno⟩ happen again, recur

riprodut'tivo adj reproductive

riproduzi'one nf reproduction. **'riproduzione vietata'** 'copyright'

ripro'mettersi vr (intendere) intend

ripro'porre vt put forward again

ripro'porsi vr ∼ **di fare qualcosa** intend to do something; (come candidato) stand again; ⟨problema⟩ come up again, reappear

ri'prova nf confirmation; **a** ∼ **di** as confirmation of

ripro'vare vt/i retry

riprovazi'one nf **riprovazione generale** outcry

riprove'vole adj reprehensible

ripubbli'care vt republish

ripudi'are vt repudiate

ripu'gnante adj repugnant

ripu'gnanza nf disgust

ripu'gnare vi ∼ **a** disgust

ripu'lire vt clean [up]; fig polish

ripu'lita nf quick clean; **darsi una** ∼ have a wash and brushup

ripulsi'one nf repulsion

ripul'sivo adj repulsive

ri'quadro nm square; (pannello) panel

riqualifi'care vt reskill ⟨lavoratori⟩

riqualifica'zione nf retraining

ri'sacca nf undertow

ri'saia nf rice field, paddy field

risa'lire ① vt go back up ② vi ∼ **a** (nel tempo) date back to; (individuare) trace ⟨colpevole⟩

risa'lita nf ascent; **impianto di risalita** ski lift

risal'tare vi (emergere) stand out

ri'salto nm prominence; (rilievo) relief

risana'mento nm reclamation, redevelopment

risa'nare vt heal; (bonificare) reclaim; redevelop ⟨area, quartiere⟩

risa'puto adj well-known

risar'cibile adj refundable

risarci'mento nm compensation

risar'cire vt indemnify; **mi hanno risarcito i danni** they compensated me for the damage

ri'sata nf laugh

riscalda'mento nm heating. **riscaldamento autonomo** central heating (for one flat). **riscaldamento centralizzato** central heating system for whole block of flats

riscal'dare vt heat; warm ⟨persona⟩

riscal'darsi vr warm up

riscat'tabile adj redeemable

riscat'tare vt ransom

riscat'tarsi vr redeem oneself

ri'scatto nm ransom; (morale) redemption

rischia'rare vt light up; brighten ⟨colore⟩

rischia'rarsi vr light up; ⟨cielo⟩ clear up

rischi'are ① vt risk ② vi run the risk; ∼ **inutilmente** take needless risks

'rischio nm risk; **a** ∼ ⟨soggetti⟩ at-risk; **a basso** ∼ low-risk

rischi'oso adj risky

risciac'quare vt rinse

risci'acquo nm rinse

risciò nm inv rickshaw

riscon'trare vt (confrontare) compare; (verificare) verify; (rilevare) find

ri'scontro nm comparison; (verifica) verification; (Comm: risposta) reply

risco'prire vt rediscover

ri'scossa nf revolt; (riconquista) recovery

riscossi'one nf collection

ri'scosso pp di RISCUOTERE

ri'scrivere vt (scrivere di nuovo) rewrite; (rispondere) write back

riscri'vibile adj rewritable

riscu'otere vt shake; (percepire) draw; (ottenere) gain; cash ⟨assegno⟩

riscu'otersi vr rouse oneself

risen'tire ① vt hear again; (provare) feel ② vi ∼ **di** feel the effect of

risen'tirsi vr (offendersi) take offence

risentita'mente adv resentfully

risen'tito adj resentful

ri'serbo nm reserve; **mantenere il** ∼ remain tight-lipped

ri'serva nf reserve; (di caccia, pesca) reserve; Sport substitute, reserve; **di** ∼ spare; **senza riserve** wholeheartedly ⟨accettare, appoggiare⟩. **riserva di caccia** game reserve. **riserva indiana** Indian reservation. **riserva naturale** wildlife reserve

riser'vare vt reserve; (prenotare) book; (per occasione) keep

riser'varsi vr (ripromettersi) plan for oneself ⟨cambiamento⟩; **mi riservo la sorpresa** I want it to be a surprise

riserva'tezza nf reserve

riser'vato adj reserved; (confidenziale) classified; '∼ **ai clienti dell'albergo**' 'for hotel guests only'; '∼ **carico**' 'loading only'

ri'sguardo nm endpaper

ri'siedere vi ∼ **a** reside in

'risma nf ream; fig kind

'riso¹ ① pp di RIDERE
② *nm* (pl *nf* **risa**) laughter; (singolo) laugh
'riso² *nm* (cereale) rice. **riso integrale** brown rice

riso'lino *nm* giggle

risolle'vare *vt* raise again; raise ⟨*morale*⟩; raise again, bring up again ⟨*problema, questione*⟩; increase, improve ⟨*sorti*⟩

risolle'varsi *vr* (da terra) rise again; fig pick up

ri'solto pp di RISOLVERE

risoluta'mente *adv* energetically

risolu'tezza *nf* determination

risolu'tivo *adj* (determinante) decisive; **scelta risolutiva** solution

riso'luto *adj* resolute, determined

risoluzi'one *nf* resolution

ri'solvere *vt* resolve; Math solve

ri'solversi *vr* (decidersi) decide; ∼ **in** turn into

riso'nanza *nf* resonance; **aver** ∼ fig arouse great interest. **risonanza magnetica** magnetic resonance, magnetic resonance imaging

riso'nare *vi* resound; (rimbombare) echo

ri'sorgere *vi* rise again

risorgi'mento *nm* revival; **il Risorgimento** the Risorgimento

ri'sorsa *nf* resource; (espediente) resort; **risorse** *pl* **energetiche** energy resources; **risorse** *pl* **naturali** natural resources; **risorse** *pl* **umane** human resources

ri'sorto pp di RISORGERE

ri'sotto *nm* risotto. **risotto alla marinara** sea-food risotto. **risotto alla milanese** risotto with saffron

ri'sparmi *nmpl* (soldi) savings

risparmi'are *vt* save; (salvare) spare

risparmia'tore, -trice *nmf* saver

ri'sparmio *nm* saving. **risparmio energetico** energy saving

rispecchi'are *vt* reflect

rispe'dire *vr* send back, return

rispet'tabile *adj* respectable

rispettabilità *nf* respectability

rispet'tare *vt* respect; **farsi** ∼ command respect

rispet'tivo *adj* respective

ri'spetto *nm* respect; ∼ **a** as regards; (a paragone di) compared to

rispettosa'mente *adv* respectfully

rispet'toso *adj* respectful

risplen'dente *adj* shining

ri'splendere *vi* shine

rispon'dente *adj* ∼ **a** in keeping with

rispon'denza *nf* correspondence

ri'spondere *vi* answer; (rimbeccare) answer back; (obbedire) respond; ∼ **a** a reply to; ∼ **di** (rendersi responsabile) answer for

rispo'sare *vt* remarry

rispo'sarsi *vr* remarry

ri'sposta *nf* answer, reply; (reazione) response; **senza risposta** unanswered ⟨*domanda, lettera*⟩

ri'sposto pp di RISPONDERE

rispun'tare *vi* ⟨*persona, sole*⟩ reappear

'rissa *nf* brawl

ris'soso *adj* pugnacious

ristabi'lire *vt* re-establish

ristabi'lirsi *vr* (in salute) recover

rista'gnare *vi* stagnate; (sangue) coagulate

ri'stagno *nm* stagnation

ri'stampa *nf* reprint; (azione) reprinting

ristam'pare *vt* reprint

risto'rante *nm* restaurant

risto'rare *vt* refresh

risto'rarsi *vr* liter take some refreshment; (riposarsi) take a rest

ristora|'tore, -trice ① *nmf* (proprietario di ristorante) restaurateur; (fornitore) caterer ② *adj* refreshing

ri'storo *nm* refreshment; (sollievo) relief; **servizio di ristoro** refreshments *pl*

ristret'tezza *nf* narrowness; (povertà) poverty; **vivere in ristrettezze** live in straitened circumstances

ri'stretto ① pp di RESTRINGERE ② *adj* narrow; (condensato) condensed; (limitato) restricted; **di idee ristrette** narrow-minded

ristruttu'rante *adj* ⟨*cosmetico*⟩ conditioning

ristruttu'rare *vt* Comm restructure; renovate ⟨*casa*⟩; repair ⟨*capelli*⟩

ristrutturazi'one *nf* Comm restructuring; (di casa) renovation

risucchi'are *vt* suck in

ri'succhio *nm* whirlpool; (di corrente) undertow

risul'tare *vi* result; (riuscire) turn out

risul'tato *nm* result; **risultati** *pl* **parziali** (di elezioni) preliminary results; (di partite) half-time results

risuo'nare ① *vt* play again ⟨*pezzo musicale*⟩; ring again ⟨*campanello*⟩ ② *vi* ⟨*grida, parola*⟩ echo; Phys resonate

risurrezi'one, risuscitare = RESURREZIONE, RESUSCITARE

risvegli'are *vt* reawaken ⟨*interesse*⟩

risvegli'arsi *vr* wake up; ⟨*natura*⟩ awake; ⟨*desiderio*⟩ be aroused

ri'sveglio *nm* waking up; (dell'interesse) revival; (del desiderio) arousal

r

ri'svolto *nm* (di giacca) lapel; (di pantaloni) turn-up, cuff Am; (di manica) cuff; (di tasca) flap; (di libro) inside flap

ritagli'are *vt* cut out

ri'taglio *nm* cutting; (di stoffa) scrap

ritar'dare ① *vi* be late; ‹orologio› be slow
② *vt* delay; slow down ‹progresso›; (differire) postpone

ritarda'tario, -a *nmf* latecomer

ritar'dato ① pp di RITARDARE
② *adj* delayed; **a scoppio ~** delayed action *attrib*; Psych retarded

ri'tardo *nm* delay; **essere in ~** be late; ‹volo› be delayed

ri'tegno *nm* reserve

ritem'prare *vt* restore

rite'nere *vt* retain; deduct ‹somma›; (credere) believe

riten'tare *vt* try again

rite'nuta *nf* (sul salario) deduction.
ritenuta d'acconto tax deducted in advance from payments made to self-employed people. **ritenuta diretta** taxation at source. **ritenuta alla fonte** taxation at source, deduction at source

ritenzi'one *nf* Med retention

riti'rare *vt* throw back ‹palla›; (prelevare) withdraw; (riscuotere) draw; collect ‹pacco›

riti'rarsi *vr* withdraw; ‹stoffa› shrink; (da attività) retire; ‹marea› recede

riti'rata *nf* retreat; (WC) toilet

ri'tiro *nm* withdrawal; Relig retreat; (da attività) retirement. **ritiro bagagli** baggage reclaim

'ritmica *nf* rhythmic gymnastics

ritmica'mente *adv* rhythmically

'ritmico *adj* rhythmic[al]

'ritmo *nm* rhythm; **a ~ serrato** at a cracking pace

'rito *nm* rite; **di ~** customary. **rito funebre** funeral service

ritoc'care *vt* (correggere) touch up

ri'tocco *nm* alteration; **ritocchi** *pl* Phot retouching

ri'torcersi *vr* **~ contro qualcuno** boomerang on somebody

ritor'nare *vi* return; (andare/venire indietro) go/come back; (ricorrere) recur; (ridiventare) become again

ritor'nello *nm* refrain

ri'torno *nm* return

ritorsi'one *nf* retaliation

ri'torto *adj* ‹filo, cavo› twisted

ritra'durre *vt* (tradurre di nuovo) retranslate

ri'trarre *vt* (ritirare) withdraw; (distogliere) turn away; (rappresentare) portray

ritra'smettere *vt* TV show again, re-broadcast

ritrat'tabile *adj* ‹accusa› which can be withdrawn

ritrat'tare *vt* retract, withdraw ‹dichiarazione›

ritrattazi'one *nf* withdrawal, retraction

ritrat'tista *nmf* portrait painter

ri'tratto ① pp di RITRARRE
② *nm* portrait

ritrazi'one *nf* retraction

ritrosa'mente *adv* shyly

ritro'sia *nf* shyness

ri'troso *adj* (timido) shy; **a ~** backwards; **~ a** reluctant to

ritrova'mento *nm* (azione) finding; (cosa) find

ritro'vare *vt* find [again]; regain ‹salute›

ritro'varsi *vr* meet; (di nuovo) meet again; (capitare) find oneself; (raccapezzarsi) see one's way

ritro'vato *nm* discovery

ri'trovo *nm* meeting-place. **ritrovo notturno** night club

'ritto *adj* upright; (diritto) straight

ritu'ale *adj & nm* ritual

ritual'mente *adv* ritually

riunifi'care *vt* reunify

riunifi'carsi *vr* be reunited

riunificazi'one *nf* reunification

riuni'one *nf* meeting; (dopo separazione) reunion. **riunione del corpo insegnante** staff meeting. **riunione dei genitori (degli alunni)** parents' evening

riu'nire *vt* (unire) join together; (radunare) gather

riu'nirsi *vr* be reunited; (adunarsi) meet

riu'sare *vt* reuse

riusc'ire *vi* (aver successo) succeed; (in matematica ecc) be good (**in** at); (aver esito) turn out; **le è riuscito simpatico** she found him likeable

riu'scita *nf* (esito) result; (successo) success

ri'uso *nm* reuse

riutiliz'zare *vt* reuse

'riva *nf* (di mare, lago) shore; (di fiume) bank; **in ~ al mare** on the seashore

rivacci'nare *vt* revaccinate

ri'vale *nmf* rival

rivaleggi'are *vi* compete (**con** with)

rivalità *nf inv* rivalry

ri'valsa *nf* revenge; **prendersi una ~ su qualcuno** take revenge on somebody

rivalu'tare *vt* reappraise

rivalutazi'one *nf* revaluation

rivan'gare *vt* dig up again

rive'dere *vt* see again; revise ‹lezione›; review ‹accordo›; (verificare) check

rive'dibile adj ‹accordo› reviewable; ‹recluta› temporarily unfit

rive'lare vt reveal

rive'larsi vr (dimostrarsi) turn out

rivela'tore ① adj revealing ② nm Techn detector. **rivelatore di mine** mine detector

rivelazi'one nf revelation

ri'vendere vt resell

rivendi'care vt claim

rivendicazi'one nf claim

ri'vendita nf (negozio) shop. **rivendita autorizzata** authorized retailer

rivendi‖'tore, -trice nmf retailer. **rivenditore autorizzato** authorized retailer

riverbe'rare vt reflect ‹luce›

ri'verbero nm reverberation; (bagliore) glare

rive'renza nf reverence; (inchino) curtsy; (di uomo) bow

rive'rire vt respect; (ossequiare) pay one's respects to

rivernici'are vt repaint; (con smalto) revarnish

river'sare vt pour

river'sarsi vr ‹fiume› flow

river'sibile adj = REVERSIBLE

rivesti'mento nm covering

rive'stire vt (rifornire di abiti) clothe; (ricoprire) cover; (internamente) line; hold ‹carica›

rive'stirsi vr get dressed again

rive'stito adj ∼ di covered with

rivi'era nf coast; (in corsa a ostacoli) water jump; **la ∼ ligure** the Italian Riviera

ri'vincita nf Sport return match; (vendetta) revenge

rivis'suto pp di RIVIVERE

ri'vista nf review; (pubblicazione) magazine; Theat revue; **passare in ∼** review. **rivista patinata** glossy magazine

rivitaliz'zare vt revitalize

rivitalizzazi'one nf revitalization

ri'vivere ① vi come to life again; (riprendere le forze) revive ② vt relive

'rivo nm stream

rivo'lere vt (volere di nuovo) want again; (volere indietro) want back

ri'volgere vt turn; (indirizzare) address

ri'volgersi vr turn round; **∼ a** (indirizzarsi) turn to

rivolgi'mento nm upheaval

ri'volta nf revolt

rivol'tante adj revolting, disgusting

rivol'tare vt turn [over]; (mettendo l'interno verso l'esterno) turn inside out; (sconvolgere) upset

rivol'tarsi vr (ribellarsi) revolt

rivol'tella nf revolver

ri'volto pp di RIVOLGERE

rivol'toso, -a nmf rebel, insurgent

rivoluzio'nare vt revolutionize

rivoluzio'nario, -a adj & nmf revolutionary

rivoluzi'one nf revolution; (fig: disordine) chaos. **rivoluzione francese** French Revolution. **rivoluzione industriale** Industrial Revolution

riz'zare vt raise; (innalzare) erect; prick up ‹orecchie›

riz'zarsi vr stand up; ‹capelli› stand on end; ‹orecchie› prick up

'roaming nm Teleph **roaming internazionale** roaming

'roast-beef nm inv roast beef

'roba nf stuff; (personale) belongings pl, stuff; (faccenda) thing; (sl: droga) drugs pl; **∼ da matti!** absolute madness!. **roba da bere** drink. **roba da lavare** washing. **roba da mangiare** food, things to eat. **roba da stirare** ironing

ro'baccia nf rubbish

robi'vecchi nm inv second-hand dealer

ro'bot nm inv robot; (da cucina) food processor

ro'botica nf robotics

ro'botico adj robotic

robotiz'zato adj robotic, robotized

robu'stezza nf sturdiness, robustness; (forza) strength

ro'busto adj sturdy, robust; (forte) strong

rocambo'lesco adj incredible

'rocca nf fortress

rocca'forte nf stronghold

rocchetti'era nf winder

roc'chetto nm reel

'roccia nf rock; (sport) rock-climbing

rock nm rock [music]. **rock acrobatico** rock 'n' roll

'roco adj throaty

ro'daggio nm running in

'Rodano nm Rhone

ro'dare vt run in

ro'deo nm rodeo

'rodere vt gnaw; (corrodere) corrode

'rodersi vr **∼ da** (logorarsi) be consumed with

rodi'tore nm rodent

rodo'dendro nm rhododendron

'rogito nm Jur deed

'rogna nf scabies sg; fig nuisance

ro'gnone nm Culin kidney

ro'gnoso adj scabby

'rogo nm (supplizio) stake; (per cadaveri) pyre

rol'lare ① vt roll ‹sigaretta›

2 *vi* ⟨*aereo, nave*⟩ roll

ROM *nf* Comput ROM

rom *adj inv & nmf inv* (zingaro) Roma, Romany

'Roma *nf* Rome

Roma'nia *nf* Romania

ro'manico *adj* Romanesque

ro'mano, -a *adj & nmf* Roman

romantica'mente *adv* romantically

romanti'cismo *nm* romanticism

ro'mantico *adj* romantic

ro'manza *nf* romance

roman'zare *vt* fictionalize

roman'zato *adj* romanticized, fictionalized

roman'zesco *adj* fictional; (stravagante) wild, unrealistic

roman'zetto *nm* **romanzetto rosa** novelette

romanzi'ere *nm* novelist

ro'manzo **1** *adj* Romance

2 *nm* novel; (storia incredibile romantica) romance. **romanzo d'appendice** serial story. **romanzo giallo** thriller. **romanzo sceneggiato** novel adapted for television/radio

rom'bare *vi* rumble

'rombo *nm* rumble; Math rhombus; (pesce) turbot

romboi'dale *adj* rhomboid, diamond-shaped

'rompere *vt* break; break off ⟨*relazione*⟩; non ~ **[le scatole]!** (fam: seccare) don't be a pain [in the neck]!

'rompersi *vr* break; ~ **una gamba** break one's leg

rompi'capo *nm* nuisance; (indovinello) puzzle

rompi'collo *nm* daredevil; **a ~** at breakneck speed

rompighi'accio *nm inv* ice-breaker

rompi'mento *nm* fam pain

rompi'scatole *nmf inv* fam pain

'ronda *nf* rounds *pl*

ron'della *nf* Mech washer

'rondine *nf* swallow

ron'done *nm* swift

ron'fare *vi* (russare) snore; (fare le fusa) purr

ron'zare *vi* buzz; ~ **attorno a qualcuno** fig hang about somebody

ron'zino *nm* jade

ron'zio *nm* buzz

'rosa **1** *nf* rose. **rosa rampicante** rambler, rambling rose. **rosa selvatica** wild rose. **rosa dei venti** wind rose **2** *adj & nm inv* (colore) pink

ro'saio *nm* rosebush

ro'sario *nm* rosary

ro'sato **1** *adj* rosy **2** *nm* (vino) rosé

'rosbif = ROAST-BEEF

rosé *nm inv* rosé

'roseo *adj* pink

ro'seto *nm* rose garden

ro'setta *nf* (coccarda) rosette; Mech washer

rosicchi'are *vt* nibble; (rodere) gnaw

rosma'rino *nm* rosemary

'roso *pp di* RODERE

roso'lare *vt* brown

roso'lato *adj* sauté

roso'lia *nf* German measles *sg*

ro'sone *nm* rosette; (apertura) rose window

'rospo *nm* toad

ros'setto *nm* lipstick

'rosso *adj & nm* red; **diventare ~** go red; **ha i capelli rossi** she's a redhead; **passare col ~** go through a red light, jump a red light. **rosso mattone** *adj* brick red. **rosso sangue** *adj* blood red. **rosso scarlatto** *adj* scarlet. **rosso d'uovo** [egg] yolk. **rosso vermiglio** *adj* vermilion

ros'sore *nm* redness; (della pelle) flush

rosticce'ria *nf* shop selling cooked meat and other prepared food

'rostro *nm* rostrum; (becco) bill

ro'tabile *adj* **strada rotabile** carriageway

ro'taia *nf* rail; (solco) rut

ro'tante *adj* rotating

ro'tare *vt/i* rotate

rota'tiva *nf* rotary press

rota'torio *adj* rotary

rotazi'one *nf* rotation; (di personale) turnover. **rotazione delle colture** crop rotation

rote'are *vt/i* roll

ro'tella *nf* small wheel; (di mobile) castor

roto'calco *nm* (sistema) rotogravure; ⟨*rivista*⟩ illustrated magazine

roto'lare *vt/i* roll

roto'larsi *vr* roll [about]

roto'lio *nm* rolling

'rotolo *nm* roll; (di pergamena) scroll; **andare a rotoli** go to rack and ruin. **rotolo di carta igienica** toilet roll

roto'loni *adv* **cadere ~** tumble

ro'tonda *nf* roundabout, traffic circle Am

rotondità *nf inv* (qualità) roundness; ~ *pl* (curve femminili) curves *pl*, curvaceousness

ro'tondo, -a **1** *adj* round **2** *nf* (spiazzo) terrace

ro'tore *nm* rotor

'rotta[1] *nf* Naut, Aeron course; **far ~ per** set a course for; **fuori ~** off course; **in ~ di collisione** on a collision course '**rotta**[2] *nf* a ~ di collo at breakneck speed; **essere in** ~ **con** be on bad terms with

rotta'maio *nm* junkyard

rot'tame *nm* scrap; fig wreck

'**rotto** [1] pp di ROMPERE [2] *adj* broken; (stracciato) torn

rot'tura *nf* break; **che** ~ **di scatole!** fam what a pain!

'**rotula** *nf* kneecap

rou'lette *nf inv* roulette. **roulette russa** Russian roulette

rou'lotte *nf inv* caravan, trailer Am

rou'tine *nf inv* routine; **di** ~ ⟨operazioni, controlli⟩ routine

ro'vente *adj* scorching

'**rovere** *nm* (legno) oak

rovescia'mento *nm* overthrow

rovesci'are *vt* (buttare a terra) knock over; (sottosopra) turn upside down; (rivoltare) turn inside out; spill ⟨liquido⟩ overthrow ⟨governo⟩; reverse ⟨situazione⟩

rovesci'arsi *vr* (capovolgersi) overturn; (riversarsi) pour

ro'vescio [1] *adj* (contrario) reverse; **alla rovescia** (capovolto) upside down; (con l'interno all'esterno) inside out [2] *nm* reverse; (nella maglia) purl; (di pioggia) downpour; Tennis backhand

ro'vina *nf* ruin; (crollo) collapse; **in** ~ in ruins

rovi'nare [1] *vt* ruin; (guastare) spoil [2] *vi* crash

rovi'narsi *vr* be ruined; ⟨persona⟩ ruin oneself

rovi'nato *adj* ruined

ro'vine *nfpl* ruins

rovi'noso *adj* ruinous

rovi'stare *vt* ransack

'**rovo** *nm* bramble

rozza'mente *adv* crudely

roz'zezza *nf* indelicacy

'**rozzo** *adj* rough

R.R. *abbr* (**ricevuta di ritorno**) acknowledgement of receipt

R.U. *abbr* (**Regno Unito**) UK

'**ruba** *nf* **andare a** ~ sell like hot cakes

rubacchi'are *vt* pilfer

rubacu'ori *nm inv* heart-throb

ru'bare *vt* steal

rubi'condo *adj* ruddy

rubi'netto *nm* tap, faucet Am

ru'bino *nm* ruby

ru'bizzo *adj* spry

'**rublo** *nm* rouble

ru'brica *nf* (in giornale) column; (in programma televisivo) TV report; (quaderno con indice) address book. **rubrica degli annunci personali** personal column.

rubrica dei cuori solitari lonely hearts' column. **rubrica sportiva** sports column. **rubrica degli spettacoli** listings. **rubrica telefonica** telephone and address book.

'**rucola** *nf* rocket

'**rude** *adj* rough

'**rudere** *nm* ruin

ru'dezza *nf* bluntness

rudimen'tale *adj* rudimentary

rudi'menti *nmpl* rudiments

ruffi'ana *nf* procuress

ruffi'ano *nm* pimp; (adulatore) bootlicker

'**ruga** *nf* wrinkle

'**ruggine** *nf* rust; **fare la** ~ go rusty

ruggi'noso *adj* rusty

rug'gire *vi* roar

rug'gito *nm* roar

rugi'ada *nf* dew

ru'goso *adj* wrinkled

rul'lare *vi* roll; Aeron taxi

rul'lino *nm* film

rul'lio *nm* rolling; Aeron taxiing

'**rullo** *nm* roll; Techn roller

rum *nm* rum

ru'meno, -a *adj & nmf* Romanian

rumi'nante *nm* ruminant

rumi'nare *vt* ruminate

ru'more *nm* noise; fig rumour

rumoreggi'are *vi* rumble

rumorosa'mente *adv* noisily

rumo'roso *adj* noisy; (sonoro) loud

ru'olo *nm* Theat role; **di** ~ on the staff. **ruolo delle imposte** tax notice. **ruolo primario/secondario** major/minor role

ru'ota *nf* wheel; **andare a** ~ **libera** free-wheel; **fare la** ~ do a cartwheel. **ruota dentata** cogwheel. **ruota di scorta** spare wheel. **ruota di stampa** (di stampante) print wheel. **ruota del timone** helm

'**rupe** *nf* cliff

ru'pestre *adj* ⟨pittura⟩ rock *attrib*

ru'pia *nf* rupee

ru'rale *adj* rural

ru'scello *nm* stream

'**ruspa** *nf* bulldozer

ru'spante *adj* free-range

rus'sare *vi* snore

'**Russia** *nf* Russia

'**russo, -a** [1] *adj & nmf* Russian [2] *nm* (lingua) Russian

'**rustico** *adj* rural; ⟨carattere⟩ rough

'**ruta** *nf* Bot rue

rut'tare *vi* belch, burp

rut'tino *nm* (di bambino) burp

'**rutto** *nm* belch, burp

'ruvido *adj* coarse
ruzzo'lare *vi* tumble down
ruzzo'lone *nm* tumble; **cadere ruzzoloni**

tumble down, tumble [helter-skelter]

'Rwanda *nm* Rwanda

Ss

S. *abbr* (**santo, santa**) St.; *abbr* (**sud**) south
'sabato *nm* Saturday; **di ~** on Saturdays
sab'batico *adj* sabbatical; **anno sabbatico** sabbatical [year]
'sabbia *nf* sand; **sabbie** *pl* **mobili** quicksand
sabbi'are *vt* sandblast
sabbia'tura *nf* (di vetro, metallo) sandblasting; (terapeutica) sand-bath
sabbi'oso *adj* sandy
sabo'taggio *nm* sabotage
sabo'tare *vt* sabotage
sabota|'tore, -trice *nmf* saboteur
'sacca *nf* bag. **sacca di resistenza** pocket of resistance. **sacca da viaggio** travel[ling]-bag, duffel bag
sacca'rina *nf* saccharin
sac'cente ① *adj* conceited
② *nmf* know-all, know-it-all Am
saccente'ria *nf* conceit
saccheggi'are *vt* sack; hum plunder ⟨frigo⟩
saccheggia|'tore, -trice *nmf* plunderer
sac'cheggio *nm* sack
sac'chetto *nm* bag. **sacchetto di plastica** plastic bag. **sacchetto per la spazzatura** bin liner, bin bag
'sacco *nm* sack; Anat sac; (contenuto) sack[ful]; **mettere nel ~** fig swindle; **un ~** (moltissimo) a lot; **un ~ di** (gran quantità) lots of; **un ~ di soldi** shedloads of money fam. **sacco a pelo** sleeping-bag. **sacco postale** mail-bag
saccope'lista *nmf* backpacker
sacer'dote *nm* priest
sacer'dozio *nm* priesthood
sacra'mento *nm* sacrament
sacrifi'cale *adj* sacrificial
sacrifi'care *vt* sacrifice
sacrifi'carsi *vr* sacrifice oneself
sacrifi'cato *adj* sacrificed; (non valorizzato) wasted
sacri'ficio *nm* sacrifice
sacri'legio *nm* sacrilege
sa'crilego *adj* sacrilegious

'sacro ① *adj* sacred; **la Sacra Bibbia** the Holy Bible
② *nm* Anat sacrum
sacro'santo *adj* sacrosanct; (verità) gospel; (diritto) sacred
'sadico, -a ① *adj* sadistic
② *nmf* sadist
sa'dismo *nm* sadism
sa'etta *nf* arrow; (fulmine) thunderbolt; **correre come una ~** run like the wind
sa'fari *nm inv* safari
'saga *nf* saga
sa'gace *adj* shrewd
sa'gacia *nf* sagacity
sag'gezza *nf* wisdom
saggia'mente *adv* sagely
saggi'are *vt* test
'saggio¹ *nm* (scritto) essay; (prova) proof; (di metallo) assay; (campione) sample; (esempio) example
'saggio² ① *adj* wise
② *nm* (persona) sage
sag'gista *nmf* essayist
sag'gistica *nf* non-fiction
Sagit'tario *nm* Astr Sagittarius
'sago = SAGÙ
'sagoma *nf* shape; (profilo) outline; (in falegnameria) template; **che ~!** fam what a character!
sago'mare *vt* make according to a template
'sagra *nf* festival
sa'grato *nm* churchyard
sagre'stano *nm* sacristan
sagre'stia *nf* sacristy
sagù *nm* sago
Sa'hara *nm* Sahara
'sala *nf* hall; (salotto) living room; (per riunioni ecc) room; (di cinema) cinema. **sala arrivi** arrivals lounge. **sala d'aspetto** waiting room. **sala d'attesa** waiting room. **sala da ballo** ballroom. **sala di comando** control room. **sala conferenze** conference hall. **sala giochi** amusement arcade, games room. **sala d'imbarco** departure lounge. **sala di lettura** reading room. **sala macchine** engine room. **sala**

operatoria operating theatre Br, operating room Am. **sala parto** delivery room. **sala da pranzo** dining room. **sala professori** staff room, common room. **sala di regia** Radio, TV control room. **sala di ricevimento** function room. **sala riunioni** conference room. **sala da tè** tea shop

sa'lace *adj* salacious

sa'lame *nm* salami *sg*

salame'lecchi *nmpl* fare ∼ bow and scrape; **prendi quello che vuoi senza tanti** ∼ don't stand on ceremony, take what you want

sala'moia *nf* brine

sa'lare *vt* salt

salari'ato *nm* wage earner

sa'lario *nm* wages *pl*

salas'sare *vt* Med bleed; fig bleed dry

sa'lasso *nm* bleeding; **essere un** ∼ fig cost a fortune

sala'tini *nmpl* savouries (eaten with aperitifs)

sa'lato *adj* salty; (costoso) dear; **acqua salata** salt water

sal'ciccia *nf* = SALSICCIA

sal'dare *vt* weld; set ⟨osso⟩; pay off ⟨debito⟩; settle ⟨conto⟩; ∼ **a stagno** solder

sal'darsi *vr* ⟨osso⟩ knit; ⟨ferita⟩ heal

saldat'rice *nf* soldering iron

salda'tura *nf* soldering; (giunzione) join

'saldo ① *adj* firm, unshaken; (resistente) strong; ∼ **come una roccia** solid as a rock; **essere** ∼ **nei propri principi** stick to one's principles

② *nm* (pagamento) settlement; Comm balance; (di conto corrente) bank balance; **saldi** *pl* sale; **i** ∼ **di fine stagione** the end of season sales; **in** ∼ ⟨essere⟩ on sale; ⟨comprato⟩ in a sale. **saldo iniziale** opening balance

'sale *nm* salt; **non ha** ∼ **in zucca** fam he hasn't got an ounce of common sense; **restare di** ∼ be struck dumb [with astonishment]; **sali** *pl* Med smelling salts; **sali** *pl* **da bagno** bath salts. **sale da cucina** cooking salt. **sale fino** table salt. **sale grosso** cooking salt. **sale marino** sea salt. **sali e tabacchi** *pl* (negozio) tobacconist's shop

'salice *nm* willow. **salice piangente** weeping willow

sali'ente *adj* outstanding; **i punti salienti** the main points, the highlights

sali'era *nf* salt-cellar

sa'lina *nf* salt-works *sg*

salinità *nf* saltiness

sa'lino *adj* saline

sa'lire ① *vi* go/come up; (levarsi) rise; (su treno ecc) get on; (in macchina) get in ② *vt* go/come up ⟨scale⟩

sa'lita *nf* climb; (aumento) rise; **in** ∼ uphill

sa'liva *nf* saliva

sali'vare ① *vt* salivate ② *adj* ⟨ghiandola⟩ salivary

salmì *nm* **in** ∼ marinated and slowly cooked in the marinade

'salma *nf* corpse

sal'mastro ① *adj* brackish ② *nm* salt air

salmi'strare *vt* Culin cure

'salmo *nm* psalm

sal'mone *nm & adj inv* salmon. **salmone affumicato** smoked salmon

salmo'nella *nf* salmonella

sa'lone *nm* (salotto) living room; (di parrucchiere) salon. **salone dell'automobile** motor show. **salone di bellezza** beauty parlour. **salone del libro** book fair

salo'pette *nf inv* dungarees *pl*

salotti'ero *adj* pej mundane; **discorso salottiero** small talk

salot'tino *nm* bower

sa'lotto *nm* drawing room; (soggiorno) sitting room; (mobili) [three-piece] suite; **fare** ∼ chat. **salotto letterario** literary salon

sal'pare ① *vi* sail ② *vt* ∼ **l'ancora** weigh anchor

'salsa *nf* sauce; Mus salsa. **salsa di pomodoro** tomato sauce. **salsa di rafano** horseradish sauce. **salsa di soia** soy sauce. **salsa tartara** tartar sauce

sal'sedine *nf* saltiness

sal'siccia *nf* sausage

salsi'era *nf* sauce-boat, gravy boat

sal'tare ① *vi* jump; (venir via) come off; (balzare) leap; (esplodere) blow up; **saltar fuori** spring from nowhere; ⟨oggetto cercato⟩ turn up; **è saltato fuori che …** it emerged that …; ∼ **fuori con …** come out with …; **salta agli occhi** (è evidente) it hits you; ∼ **in aria** blow up; ∼ **in mente** spring to mind ② *vt* jump [over]; skip ⟨pasti, lezioni⟩; Culin sauté

sal'tato *adj* Culin sautéed

saltel'lare *vi* hop; (di gioia) skip

saltim'banco *nm* acrobat

saltim'bocca *nm inv* slice of veal rolled with ham and sage and shallow-fried

'salto *nm* jump; (balzo) leap; (dislivello) drop; (fig: omissione, lacuna) gap; **fare un** ∼ **da** (visitare) drop in on; **in un** ∼ fig in a jiffy; **fare i salti mortali** fig go to great lengths; **fare quattro salti** fam go dancing; **fare un** ∼ **nel buio** fig take a leap in the dark. **salto in alto** high jump. **salto con l'asta** pole-vault. **salto con** ⋯⟶

S

l'elastico bungee jump. **salto con la corda** skipping. **salto in lungo** long jump. **salto pagina** Comput page down. **salto di qualità** quality leap

saltuaria'mente *adv* occasionally, from time to time

saltu'ario *adj* desultory. **lavoro saltuario** casual work

sa'lubre *adj* healthy

salume'ria *nf* delicatessen

sa'lumi *nmpl* cold cuts

salumi'ere *nm* person who sells cold meat

salu'tare ① *vt* greet; (congedandosi) say goodbye to; (portare i saluti a) give one's regards to; Mil salute; **ti saluto!** fam cheerio!
② *adj* healthy

salu'tarsi *vr* (all'arrivo) greet each other; (alla partenza) say goodbye to each other

sa'lute *nf* health; **godere di ottima ~** be in the best of health, enjoy excellent health; **in ~** in good health; **~!** (dopo uno starnuto) bless you!; (a un brindisi) cheers!. **salute di ferro** iron constitution

salu'tista *nmf* health fanatic; (dell'Esercito della Salvezza) Salvationist

sa'luto *nm* greeting; (di addio) goodbye; Mil salute; **saluti** *pl* (ossequi) regards

'salva *nf* salvo; **sparare a salve** shoot blanks; **a salve** ⟨*pistola*⟩ loaded with blank cartridges

salvacon'dotto *nm* safe-conduct

salvada'naio *nm* money box

salva'gente *nm* lifebelt; (a giubbotto) lifejacket; (ciambella) rubber ring; (spartitraffico) traffic island

salvaguar'dare *vt* protect, safeguard

salvaguar'darsi *vr* protect oneself

salvagu'ardia *nf* safeguard

sal'vare *vt* save; (proteggere) protect; **~ la faccia** save face; **~ la pelle** save one's skin

sal'varsi *vr* save oneself

salva'schermo *nm inv* Comput screen saver

salva'slip *nm inv* panty-liner

salva'taggio *nm* rescue; Naut salvage; Comput saving; **battello di salvataggio** lifeboat

salva'vita *nm inv* Electr circuit breaker

'salve ▶ SALVA

salva|'tore, -trice *nmf* saviour

sal'vezza *nf* safety; Relig salvation. **ancora di salvezza** fig salvation

'salvia *nf* sage

salvi'etta *nf* serviette

'salvo ① *adj* safe
② *nm* **trarre in ~** rescue
③ *prep* except [for]

④ *conj* **~ che** (a meno che) unless; (eccetto che) except that

samari'tano, -a *adj & nmf* Samaritan; **un buon ~** a good Samaritan

'samba *nf* samba

sam'buca *nf* sambuca

sam'buco *nm* elder

Sa'moa *nfpl* **Samoa Occidentali** Western Samoa

san *nm* (before proper names starting with a consonant) saint; ▶ SANTO

sa'nabile *adj* curable

sa'nare *vt* heal; (bonificare) reclaim; **~ il bilancio** balance the books

sana'toria *nf* decree legitimizing a situation which is in principle illegal

sana'torio *nm* sanatorium

san'cire *vt* sanction

'sandalo *nm* sandal; Bot sandalwood

sandi'nista *adj & nmf* Sandinista

'sandwich *nm inv* sandwich. **uomo sandwich** sandwich-man

san'gallo *nm* (tessuto) broderie anglaise

san'gria *nf* sangria

'sangue *nm* blood; **a ~ freddo** in cold blood; **al ~** Culin rare; **appena al ~** Culin medium-rare; **farsi cattivo ~ per** worry about; **iniettato di ~** ⟨*occhio*⟩ bloodshot; **all'ultimo ~** ⟨*lotta*⟩ to the death; **di ~ blu** blue-blooded; **perdere ~ dal naso** have a nose bleed; **sudare ~** sweat blood. **sangue freddo** composure

sangue'misto *nm* half-caste

sangu'igno *adj* blood *attrib*

sangui'naccio *nm* Culin black pudding

sangui'nante *adj* bleeding

sangui'nare *vi* bleed

sangui'nario *adj* bloodthirsty

sangui'noso *adj* bloody

sangui'suga *nf* leech

sanità *nf* soundness; (salute) health; **ministero della sanità** Department of Health. **sanità di costumi** morality. **sanità mentale** sanity, mental health

sani'tario ① *adj* sanitary; **servizio sanitario** health service
② *nm* doctor

San Ma'rino *nm* San Marino

'sano *adj* sound; (salutare) healthy; **~ come un pesce** as fit as a fiddle. **sano di mente** sane

'sansa *nf* husk

San Sil'vestro *nm* New Year's Eve

santifi'care *vt* sanctify

santità *nf* sainthood

'santo, -a ① *adj* holy; (con nome proprio) saint; **Sant'Antonio** St Anthony; **San Francesco d'Assisi** St Francis of Assisi; **di santa ragione** in no uncertain terms

2 *nmf* saint. **santo patrono**, **santa patrona** patron saint

san'tone *nm* guru

santo'reggia *nf* Bot savory

santu'ario *nm* sanctuary

san Valen'tino *nm* St Valentine's Day; **giorno di san Valentino** Valentine's Day

sanzio'nare *vt* sanction

sanzi'one *nf* sanction. **sanzione amministrativa** administrative sanction. **sanzione penale** legal sanction

sa'pere 1 *vt* know; (essere capace di) be able to; (venire a sapere) hear; **saperla lunga** know a thing or two; **non lo so** I don't know; **non so che farci** there's nothing I can do about it; ∼ **a memoria** know by heart; ∼ **il fatto proprio** know what one is talking about; **per quanto ne sappia** insofar as I know

2 *vi* ∼ **di** know about; (aver sapore di) taste of; (aver odore di) smell of; **saperci fare** know how to go about it; **saperci fare con i bambini** be good with children

3 *nm* knowledge

sapi'ente 1 *adj* wise; (esperto) expert

2 *nm* sage

sapiente'mente *adv* wisely; (abilmente) skilfully

sapien'tone *nm* smart alec[k]

sapi'enza *nf* wisdom

sa'pone *nm* soap; **bolla di** ∼ soap bubble; **finire in una bolla di** ∼ fig come to nothing. **sapone da barba** shaving soap. **sapone da bucato** washing soap

sapo'netta *nf* bar of soap

sapo'noso *adj* soapy

sa'pore *nm* taste; **sentire** ∼ **di** detect a hint of

saporita'mente *adv* ⟨condire⟩ skilfully; ⟨mangiare⟩ appreciatively; ⟨dormire⟩ soundly

sapo'rito *adj* tasty

sapu'tello, **-a** *adj & nm* sl know-all, know-it-all Am

sara'banda *nf* fig uproar

sara'ceno, **-a** *adj & nmf* Saracen; **grano saraceno** buckwheat

saraci'nesca *nf* roller shutter; (di chiusa) sluice gate

'sarago *nm* white bream

sar'casmo *nm* sarcasm

sarcastica'mente *adv* sarcastically

sar'castico *adj* sarcastic

sar'cofago *nm* sarcophagus

Sar'degna *nf* Sardinia

sar'dina *nf* sardine

'sardo, **-a** *adj & nmf* Sardinian

sar'donico *adj* sardonic

SARS *nf* SARS

sarti'ame *nm* rigging

'sarto, **-a** 1 *nm* tailor

2 *nf* dressmaker

sarto'ria *nf* (da uomo) tailor's; (da donna) dressmaker's; (arte) couture

s.a.s. *abbr* **società in accomandita semplice**

sas'saia *nf* stony ground

sassai'ola *nf* hail of stones

sas'sata *nf* blow with a stone; **una** ∼ **ha rotto il vetro** a stone broke the window; **prendere a sassate** throw stones at, stone

'sasso *nm* stone; (ciottolo) pebble; **sono rimasto di** ∼ I was struck dumb [with astonishment]

sassofo'nista *nmf* saxophonist

sas'sofono *nm* saxophone

'sassone *nmf* Saxon; **genitivo sassone** Saxon genitive

sas'soso *adj* stony

'Satana *nm* Satan

sa'tanico *adj* satanic

sa'tellite *adj inv & nm* satellite; **città satellite** satellite town

sati'nare *vt* glaze; polish ⟨metallo⟩

sati'nato *adj* glazed; ⟨metallo⟩ polished

'satira *nf* satire

sa'tirico *adj* satirical

satol'lare *vt* hum stuff

sa'tollo *adj* hum replete, full

satu'rare *vt* saturate

saturazi'one *nf* saturation

satur'nismo *nm* lead poisoning

Sa'turno *nm* Saturn

'saturo *adj* saturated; (pieno) full

'S.A.U.B. *nf abbr* (**Struttura Amministrativa Unificata di Base**) Italian national health service

'sauna *nf* sauna

sa'vana *nf* savannah

savoi'ardo *nm* (biscotto) sponge finger

savoir-'faire *nm* expertise, know-how

sazi'are *vt* satiate

sazi'arsi *vr* ∼ **di** fig grow tired of

sazietà *nf* **mangiare a** ∼ eat one's fill

'sazio *adj* satiated

sbaciucchi'are *vt* smother with kisses

sbaciucchi'arsi *vr* kiss and cuddle

sbada'taggine *nf* carelessness; **è stata una** ∼ it was careless

sbadata'mente *adv* carelessly

sba'dato *adj* careless

sbadigli'are *vi* yawn

sba'diglio *nm* yawn

sba'fare *vt* sponge

sba'fata *nf* fam nosh; **farsi una** ∼ fam have a nosh-up

'sbaffo *nm* smear

'**sbafo** *nm* sponging; **a** ~ (gratis) without paying

sbagli'are ① *vi* make a mistake; (aver torto) be wrong
② *vt* make a mistake in; ~ **strada** go the wrong way; ~ **numero** get the number wrong; Teleph dial a wrong number; **sbagliando s'impara** practice makes perfect

sbagli'arsi *vr* make a mistake; **ti sbagli** you're mistaken, you're wrong; ~ **di grosso** be totally wrong

sbagli'ato *adj* wrong

'**sbaglio** *nm* mistake; **per** ~ by mistake

sbale'strare *vt* fig disconcert

sbale'strato *adj* disconcerted

sbal'lare ① *vt* unpack; fam screw up ⟨conti⟩
② *vi* fam go crazy

sbal'lato *adj* (squilibrato) unbalanced

'**sballo** *nm* fam scream; (per droga) trip; **da** ~ sl terrific

sballot'tare *vt* toss about

sbalordi'mento *nm* amazement

sbalor'dire ① *vt* stun
② *vi* be stunned

sbalordi'tivo *adj* amazing

sbalor'dito *adj* stunned; **restare** ~ be stunned

sbal'zare ① *vt* throw; (da una carica) dismiss
② *vi* bounce; (saltare) leap

'**sbalzo** *nm* bounce; (sussulto) jolt; (di temperatura) sudden change; **a sbalzi** in spurts; **a** ~ (a rilievo) embossed

sban'care *vt* bankrupt; excavate ⟨terreno⟩; ~ **il banco** break the bank

sbanda'mento *nm* Auto skid; Naut list; fig going off the rails

sban'dare *vi* Auto skid; Naut list

sban'darsi *vr* (disperdersi) disperse

sban'data *nf* skid; Naut list; **prendere una** ~ **per** develop a crush on

sban'dato, -a ① *adj* mixed-up
② *nmf* mixed-up person

sbandie'rare *vt* wave; fig display

sbarac'care *vt/i* clear up

sbaragli'are *vt* rout

sba'raglio *nm* rout; **mettere allo** ~ rout

sbaraz'zare *vt* clear

sbaraz'zarsi *vr* ~ **di** get rid of

sbaraz'zino, -a ① *adj* mischievous
② *nmf* scamp

sbar'bare *vt* shave

sbar'barsi *vr* shave

sbarba'tello, -a *adj & nmf* novice

sbar'care *vt/i* disembark; ~ **il lunario** make ends meet

'**sbarco** *nm* landing; (di merci) unloading

'**sbarra** *nf* bar; (di passaggio a livello) barrier. **sbarra spaziatrice** space bar

sbarra'mento *nm* barricade

sbar'rare *vt* bar; (ostruire) block; cross ⟨assegno⟩; (spalancare) open wide

sbar'retta *nf* oblique

sbatacchi'are *vt/i* bang, slam

'**sbattere** ① *vt* bang; slam, bang ⟨porta⟩; (urtare) knock; Culin beat; flap ⟨ali⟩; shake ⟨tappeto⟩; ~ **le palpebre** blink
② *vi* bang; ⟨porta⟩ slam, bang; ~ **contro** knock against; **andare a** ~ **contro** run into

sbat'tersi *vr* sl rush around; **sbattersene di qualcosa** not give a toss about something

sbat'tuto *adj* tossed; Culin beaten; fig run down

sba'vare *vi* dribble; ⟨colore⟩ smear

sbava'tura *nf* smear; **senza sbavature** fig faultless

sbec'care *vt* chip

sbec'cato *adj* chipped

sbeffeggi'are *vt* mock

sbelli'carsi *vr* ~ **dalle risa** split one's sides [with laughter]

sben'dare *vt* unbandage

'**sberla** *nf* slap

sbevaz'zare *vi* fam tipple

sbia'dire *vt/i* fade

sbia'dirsi *vr* fade

sbia'dito *adj* faded; fig colourless

sbian'cante *nm* whitener

sbian'care *vt/i* whiten

sbian'carsi *vr* whiten

sbi'eco *adj* slanting; **di** ~ on the slant; ⟨guardare⟩ sidelong; **guardare qualcuno di** ~ look askance at somebody; **tagliare di** ~ cut on the bias

sbigot'tire ① *vt* dismay
② *vi* be dismayed

sbigot'tirsi *vr* be dismayed

sbigot'tito *adj* dismayed

sbilanci'are ① *vt* unbalance
② *vi* (perdere l'equilibrio) overbalance

sbilanci'arsi *vr* lose one's balance

sbi'lancio *nm* lack of balance; Comm deficit

sbirci'are *vt* cast sidelong glances at

sbirci'ata *nf* furtive glance

sbircia'tina *nf* **dare una** ~ **a** sneak a glance at

'**sbirro** *nm* pej cop

sbizzar'rirsi *vr* satisfy one's whims

sbloc'care *vt* unblock; Mech release; decontrol ⟨prezzi⟩

'**sbobba** *nf* fam pigswill

sboc'care *vi* ~ **in** ⟨fiume⟩ flow into; ⟨strada⟩ lead to; ⟨folla⟩ pour into

sboc'cato *adj* foul-mouthed

sbocci'are *vi* blossom

'sbocco *nm* flowing; (foce) mouth; Comm outlet

sbolo'gnare *vt* fam get rid of

'sbornia *nf* **prendere una ~** get drunk; **smaltire la ~** sober up

sbor'sare *vt* pay out

sbot'tare *vi* burst out

sbotto'nare *vt* unbutton

sbotto'narsi *vr* (fam: confidarsi) open up; **~ la camicia** unbutton one's shirt

sboz'zare *vt* draft; sketch out ⟨*dipinto*⟩

sbra'carsi *vr* put on something more comfortable; **~ dalle risate** fam kill oneself laughing

sbracci'arsi *vr* wave one's arms

sbracci'ato *adj* bare-armed; ⟨*abito*⟩ sleeveless

sbrai'tare *vi* bawl

sbra'nare *vt* tear to shreds *or* pieces

sbra'narsi *vr* tear each other to shreds

sbrat'tare *vt* clean up

sbrec'cato *adj* chipped

sbricio'lare *vt* crumble

sbricio'larsi *vr* crumble

sbri'gare *vt* deal with; (occuparsi di) attend to

sbri'garsi *vr* hurry up, be quick

sbriga'tivo *adj* hurried, quick

sbrigli'ato *adj* ⟨*fantasia*⟩ unbridled

sbri'nare *vt* defrost; Auto de-ice

sbrina'tore *nm* Auto de-icer; (di frigo) defrost button

sbrindel'lare *vt* tear to shreds

sbrindel'lato *adj* in rags

sbrodo'lare *vt* stain

sbrodo'lone, **-a** *nmf* messy eater

sbrogli'are *vt* disentangle

'sbronza *nf* fam **prendersi una ~** get drunk, get hammered fam

sbron'zarsi *vr* get drunk, get hammered fam

'sbronzo *adj* (ubriaco) drunk, hammered fam

sbruffo'nata *nf* boast

sbruf'fone, **-a** *nmf* boaster

sbu'care *vi* come out

sbucci'are *vt* peel; shell ⟨*piselli*⟩

sbucci'arsi *vr* graze oneself

sbuccia'tore *nm* parer

sbuccia'tura *nf* graze

sbudel'lare *vt* gut ⟨*pesce*⟩; draw ⟨*pollo*⟩; disembowel ⟨*persona*⟩

sbudel'larsi *vr* **~ dal ridere** die laughing

sbuf'fare *vi* snort; (per impazienza) fume

'sbuffo *nm* puff; **a ~** ⟨*maniche*⟩ puff *attrib*

sbugiar'dare *vt* show to be a liar

sbuz'zare *vt* fam gut ⟨*pesce*⟩; draw ⟨*pollo*⟩; disembowel ⟨*persona*⟩

'scabbia *nf* scabies *sg*

'scabro *adj* rough; ⟨*terreno*⟩ uneven; ⟨*stile*⟩ bald

sca'broso *adj* rough; ⟨*terreno*⟩ uneven; ⟨*fig: questione*⟩ difficult; ⟨*scena*⟩ offensive

scacchi'era *nf* chessboard

scacciapensi'eri *nm inv* Mus Jew's harp

scacci'are *vt* chase away

'scacco *nm* check; **scacchi** *pl* (gioco) chess; (pezzi) chessmen; **dare ~ matto a** checkmate; **a scacchi** ⟨*tessuto*⟩ checked; **subire uno ~** fig suffer a humiliating defeat

sca'dente *adj* shoddy, low-quality

sca'denza *nf* (di contratto) expiry; (di progetto) deadline; Comm maturity; **a breve/ lunga ~** short-/long-term

scaden'zario *nm* schedule

sca'dere *vi* expire; ⟨*valore*⟩ decline; ⟨*debito*⟩ be due

sca'duto *adj* ⟨*biglietto*⟩ out-of-date

sca'fandro *nm* diving suit

scaffala'tura *nf* shelves *pl*, shelving

scaf'fale *nm* shelf; (libreria) bookshelf

sca'fista *nmf* person who ferries illegal immigrants to Italy by boat for a high fee

'scafo *nm* hull

scagion'are *vt* exonerate

'scaglia *nf* scale; (di sapone) flake; (scheggia) chip

scagli'are *vt* fling

scagli'arsi *vr* fling oneself; **~ contro** fig rail against

scaglio'nare *vt* space out

scagli'one *nm* group; **a scaglioni** in groups. **scaglione di reddito** tax bracket

sca'gnozzo *nm* henchman

'scala *nf* staircase; (portatile) ladder; (Mus, misura) scale; **scale** *pl* stairs; **in ~** to scale; **su larga ~** large-scale *attrib*. **scala allungabile** extension ladder. **scala antincendio** fire escape. **scala Beaufort** Beaufort scale. **scala a chiocciola** spiral staircase. **scala mobile** escalator; (dei salari) cost of living index. **scala Richter** Richter scale. **scala di servizio** backstairs. **scala di sicurezza** fire escape

sca'lare ① *adj* scalar ② *vt* climb; layer ⟨*capelli*⟩; (detrarre) deduct

sca'lata *nf* climb; (dell'Everest ecc) ascent; **fare delle scalate** go climbing

scala|'tore, **-trice** *nmf* climber

scalci'agnato *adj* down at heel

scalci'are *vi* kick

S

scalci'nato *adj* shabby

scalda'acqua *nm inv* water-heater

scalda'bagno *nm* water-heater

scalda'muscoli *nm inv* legwarmer

scal'dare *vt* heat

scal'darsi *vr* warm up; (eccitarsi) get excited

sca'leno *adj* scalene

sca'leo *nm* step-ladder

scal'fire *vt* scratch

scalfit'tura *nf* scratch

scali'nata *nf* flight of steps. **scalinata di piazza di Spagna** Spanish Steps

sca'lino *nm* step; (di scala a pioli) rung

scalma'narsi *vr* rush about; (nel parlare) get worked up

scalma'nato *adj* worked up; è ∼ (vivace) he can't sit still

'scalmo *nm* rowlock

'scalo *nm* slipway; Naut port of call; **fare ∼ a** call at; Aeron land at; **senza scalo** nonstop. **scalo merci** freight depot, goods yard. **scalo passeggeri** stopover

sca'logna *nf* fam bad luck

scalo'gnato *adj* fam unlucky

sca'logno *nm* Bot scallion

scalop'pina *nf* escalope

scal'pare *vt* scalp

scalpel'lare *vt* chisel

scalpel'lino *nm* stone-cutter

scal'pello *nm* chisel

scalpi'tare *vi* paw the ground; fig champ at the bit

scalpi'tio *nm* pawing of the ground

'scalpo *nm* scalp

scal'pore *nm* noise; **fare ∼** fig cause a sensation

scal'trezza *nf* shrewdness

scal'trirsi *vr* get shrewder

'scaltro *adj* shrewd

scal'zare *vt* bare the roots of ‹*albero*›; fig undermine; (da una carica) oust

'scalzo *adj & adv* barefoot

scambi'are *vt* exchange; ∼ **qualcuno per qualcun altro** mistake somebody for somebody else

scambi'arsi *vr* exchange; ∼ **i saluti** exchange greetings

scambi'evole *adj* reciprocal

'scambio *nm* exchange; Comm trade. **libero scambio** free trade. **scambio di persona** mistaken identity

scamici'ato *nf* pinafore [dress]

sca'morza *nf* soft cheese

scamosci'ato *adj* suede *attrib*

scampa'gnata *nf* trip to the country

scampa'nato *adj* ‹*gonna*› flared

scampanel'lata *nf* [loud] ring

scampanel'lio *nm* ringing

scampan'io *nm* peal[ing]

scam'pare *vt* save; (evitare) escape; **scamparla bella** have a lucky escape

scam'pato ① *adj* **lo ∼ pericolo** the escape from danger ② *nmf* survivor

'scampi *nmpl* (crostaceo) scampi

'scampo *nm* escape; **non c'è ∼** there's no way out

'scampolo *nm* remnant

scanala'tura *nf* groove

scandagli'are *vt* sound

scanda'lismo *nm* muckraking

scanda'listico *adj* sensational; ‹*giornale*› sensationalist

scandaliz'zare *vt* scandalize

scandaliz'zarsi *vr* be scandalized

'scandalo *nm* scandal

scanda'loso *adj* scandalous; ‹*somma ecc*› scandalous; ‹*fortuna*› outrageous

Scandi'navia *nf* Scandinavia

scan'dinavo, -a *adj & nmf* Scandinavian

scan'dire *vt* scan ‹*verso*›; pronounce clearly ‹*parole*›; ∼ **il tempo** beat time

scandi'tore *nm* **scanditore ottico** Comput optical scanner

scan'nare *vt* slaughter

scan'nello *nm* lectern

'scanner *nm inv* scanner. **scanner manuale** Comput handheld scanner. **scanner piatto** flatbed scanner

scanneriz'zare *vt* Comput scan

scansafa'tiche *nmf inv* lazybones *sg*

scan'sare *vt* shift; (evitare) avoid

scan'sarsi *vr* get out of the way

scan'sia *nf* shelves *pl*

scansi'one *nf* Comput scanning

'scanso *nm* **a ∼ di** in order to avoid; **a ∼ di equivoci** to avoid any misunderstanding

scanti'nato *nm* basement

scanto'nare *vi* turn the corner; (svignarsela) sneak off

scanzo'nato *adj* easy-going

scapacci'one *nm* smack

scape'strato *adj* dissolute

scapigli'ato *adj* dishevelled

scapito *nm* loss; **a ∼ di** to the detriment of

'scapola *nf* shoulder-blade

'scapolo *nm* bachelor

scappa'mento *nm* Auto exhaust

scap'pare *vi* escape; (andarsene) dash [off]; (sfuggire) slip; **mi scappa da ridere!** I want to burst out laughing; **mi scappa la pipì** I'm bursting, I need a pee; **mi ha fatto ∼ la pazienza** he tried my patience a bit too far; **lasciarsi** ∼ **l'occasione** let the opportunity slip; **scappar via** run off *or* away

scap'pata *nf* fam short visit

scappa'tella *nf* escapade; (infedeltà) fling

scappa'toia *nf* way out

scappel'lotto *nm* cuff

scarabeo¹ *nm* scarab beetle

scarabeo² *nm* Scrabble®

scarabocchi'are *vt* scribble

scara'bocchio *nm* scribble

scara'faggio *nm* cockroach

scara'mantico *adj* ⟨gesto⟩ to ward off the evil eye

scaraman'zia *nf* superstition

scara'mazzo *adj* ⟨perla⟩ baroque

scara'muccia *nf* skirmish

scaraven'tare *vt* hurl

scarcas'sato *adj* fam: ⟨macchina⟩ beat-up

scarce'rare *vt* release [from prison]

scardi'nare *vt* unhinge

'scarica *nf* discharge; (di arma da fuoco) volley; fig shower; **una** ∼ **di botte** a hail of blows

scaricaba'rili *nm* **fare a** ∼ blame each other

scari'care *vt* discharge; Comput download; unload ⟨arma, merci, auto⟩; fig unburden

scari'carsi *vr* ⟨fiume⟩ flow; ⟨orologio, batteria⟩ run down; fig unwind

scarica'tore *nm* loader; (di porto) docker

'scarico ① *adj* unloaded; (vuoto) empty; ⟨orologio⟩ run-down; ⟨batteria⟩ flat; fig untroubled
② *nm* unloading; (di rifiuti) dumping; (di acqua) draining; (di sostanze inquinanti) discharge; (luogo) [rubbish] dump; Auto exhaust; (idraulico) drain; (tubo) waste pipe. **'divieto di scarico'** 'no dumping'; **tubo di scarico** waste pipe.

scarlat'tina *nf* scarlet fever

scar'latto *adj* scarlet

scarmigli'ato *adj* ruffled

sca'rnire *vt* fig simplify

'scarno *adj* thin; ⟨fig: stile⟩ bare

sca'rogna, scarognato = SCALOGNA, ▶SCALOGNATO

sca'rola *nf* curly endive

'scarpa *nf* shoe; (fam: persona) dead loss; **fare le scarpe a qualcuno** fig double-cross somebody; **scarpe** *pl* **basse** flat shoes, flats; **scarpe** *pl* **da danza** ballet shoes; **scarpe** *pl* **da ginnastica** trainers, gym shoes; **scarpe** *pl* **col tacco** high heels; **scarpe** *pl* **col tacco a spillo** stilettos; **scarpe** *pl* **con la zeppa** platform shoes

scar'pata *nf* slope; (burrone) escarpment

scarpi'era *nf* shoe rack

scarpi'nare *vi* hike

scarpon'cino *nm* ankle boot. **scarponcino Clark®** desert boot

scar'pone *nm* boot. **scarpone da alpinismo** climbing boot. **scarponi** *pl* **da sci** ski boots. **scarponi** *pl* **da trekking** walking boots

scarroz'zare *vt/i* drive around

scarroz'zata *nf* fam trip

scarruf'fato *adj* ruffled

scarseggi'are *vi* be scarce; ∼ **di** (mancare) be short of

scar'sezza *nf* scarcity, shortage

scarsità *nf* shortage

'scarso *adj* scarce; (manchevole) short

scartabel'lare *vt* skim through

scarta'mento *nm* Rail gauge. **scartamento ridotto** narrow gauge

scar'tare ① *vt* discard; unwrap ⟨pacco⟩; (respingere) reject ② *vi* (deviare) swerve

scartave'trare *vt* sand

'scarto *nm* scrap; (in carte) discard; (deviazione) swerve; (distacco) gap

scartocci'are *vt* unwrap

scar'toffie *nfpl* bumf, bumph

scas'sare *vt* break

scas'sato *adj* fam clapped out

scassi'nare *vt* force open; pick ⟨serratura⟩

scassina|'tore, -trice *nmf* burglar

'scasso *nm* (furto) house-breaking

scata'fascio = CATAFASCIO

scate'nare *vt* fig stir up ⟨folla⟩; arouse ⟨sentimenti⟩

scate'narsi *vr* break out; ⟨fig: temporale⟩ break; (fam: darsi alla pazza gioia) go crazy, go wild; (fam: infiammarsi) get excited

scate'nato *adj* crazy, wild; **pazzo** ∼ fam off his head

'scatola *nf* box; (di latta) can, tin Br; **in** ∼ ⟨cibo⟩ canned, tinned Br; **rompere le scatole a qualcuno** fam get on somebody's nerves; **a** ∼ **chiusa** ⟨comprare⟩ sight unseen. **scatola del cambio** gearbox. **scatola nera** Aeron black box

scato'lame *nm* (cibo) canned food

scato'letta *nf* small box; (di cibo) tin

scato'logico *adj* scatological

scat'tante *adj* zippy

scat'tare *vi* go off; (balzare) spring up; (adirarsi) lose one's temper; take ⟨foto⟩

'scatto *nm* (balzo) spring; (d'ira) outburst; (di telefono) unit; (dispositivo) release; **a scatti** jerkily; **di** ∼ suddenly

scatu'rire *vi* spring

scaval'care *vt* jump over ⟨muretto⟩; climb over ⟨muro⟩; (fig: superare) overtake

sca'vare *vt* dig ⟨*buca*⟩; dig up ⟨*tesoro*⟩; excavate ⟨*città sepolta*⟩

scava'trice *nf* excavator

scavezza'collo *nm* daredevil

'scavo *nm* excavation

scazzot'tare *vt* fam beat up

scazzot'tata *nf* fam punch-up; **prendersi una** ∼ get beaten up

'scegliere *vt* choose, select

sce'icco *nm* sheikh

scelle'rato *adj* wicked

'scelta *nf* choice; (di articoli) range; **... a** ∼ (in menu) choice of ...; **prendine uno a** ∼ take your choice *or* pick; **di prima** ∼ top-grade, choice; ⟨*albergo*⟩ first-rate; **di seconda** ∼ second grade, pej second-rate. **scelta multipla** multiple choice

'scelto ① pp di SCEGLIERE ② *adj* select; ⟨*merce ecc*⟩ choice. **tiratore scelto** marksman

sce'mare *vt/i* diminish

sce'menza *nf* silliness; (azione) silly thing to do/say; **non diciamo scemenze!** let's not be silly!

'scemo ① *adj* idiotic ② *nm* idiot

scempi'aggine *nf* foolish thing to do/ say

'scempio *nm* havoc; (fig: di paesaggio) ruination; **fare** ∼ **di** play havoc with

'scena *nf* scene; (palcoscenico) stage; **entrare in** ∼ Theat go/come on [stage]; fig come on the scene; **fare** ∼ put on an act; **fare una** ∼ make a scene; **fare scene** make a fuss; **andare in** ∼ Theat: ⟨*spettacolo*⟩ be staged, be put on; **fare** ∼ **muta** not open one's mouth; **scomparire dalla** ∼ fig vanish from the scene; **mettere in** ∼ produce, stage; **messa in** ∼ production, staging; fig set-up

sce'nario *nm* scenery

sce'nata *nf* row, scene

'scendere ① *vi* go/come down; (da treno, autobus) get off; (da macchina) get out; ⟨*strada*⟩ slope; ⟨*notte, prezzi*⟩ fall ② *vt* go/come down ⟨*scale*⟩

scendi'letto *nm* bedside rug

sceneggi'are *vt* dramatize

sceneggi'ato *nm* television serial

sceneggia'tura *nf* screenplay

'scenico *adj* scenic

scenogra'fia *nf* set design

sce'nografo, -a *nmf* set designer

sce'riffo *nm* sheriff

scervel'larsi *vr* rack one's brains

scervel'lato *adj* brainless

'sceso pp di SCENDERE

scetti'cismo *nm* scepticism

'scettico, -a ① *adj* sceptical ② *nmf* sceptic

'scettro *nm* sceptre

'scheda *nf* card. **scheda audio** Comput sound card. **scheda elettorale** ballot-paper. **scheda di espansione** Comput expansion card. **scheda grafica** Comput graphics card. **scheda madre** Comput motherboard. **scheda magnetica** card key. **scheda perforata** punch card. **scheda di rete** Comput network card. **scheda sonora** Comput sound card. **scheda telefonica** phonecard. **scheda di valutazione scolastica** report card, school report. **scheda video** Comput video card

sche'dare *vt* file

sche'dario *nm* file; (mobile) filing cabinet

sche'dato, -a ① *adj* with a police record ② *nmf* person with a police record

sche'dina *nf* ≈ pools coupon; **giocare la** ∼ ≈ do the pools

'scheggia *nf* fragment; (di legno) splinter

scheggi'are *vt* splinter

scheggi'arsi *vr* chip; ⟨*legno*⟩ splinter

sche'letrico *adj* skeletal

'scheletro *nm* skeleton; **essere ridotto ad uno** ∼ be all skin and bones

'schema *nm* diagram; (abbozzo) outline; **uscire dagli schemi** break with tradition

schematica'mente *adv* schematically

sche'matico *adj* schematic

schematiz'zare *vt* present schematically

'scherma *nf* fencing

scher'maglia *nf* skirmish

scher'mirsi *vr* protect oneself

'schermo *nm* screen; **sul grande** ∼ on the big screen; **farsi** ∼ **con** shield oneself with. **schermo panoramico** wide screen. **schermo al plasma** plasma screen. **schermo a sfioramento** Comput touch screen

scher'nire *vt* mock

'scherno *nm* mockery

scher'zare *vi* joke; (giocare) play; **c'è poco da** ∼! it's nothing to laugh about!

'scherzo *nm* joke; (trucco) trick; (effetto) play; Mus scherzo; **fare uno** ∼ **a qualcuno** play a joke on somebody; **giocare brutti scherzi (a qualcuno)** ⟨*memoria, vista*⟩ play tricks (on somebody); **per** ∼ for fun; **scherzi a parte** joking apart, seriously; **stare allo** ∼ take a joke. **scherzo di natura** freak of nature

scher'zoso *adj* playful

schiaccia'noci *nm inv* nutcrackers *pl*

schiacci'ante *adj* damning; ⟨*vittoria*⟩ crushing

schiacci'are *vt* crush; (in tennis ecc) smash; press ⟨*pulsante*⟩; crack ⟨*noce*⟩; ∼ **un pisolino** grab forty winks

schiacci'arsi *vr* get crushed

schiaccia'sassi *nf inv* steamroller

schiaf'fare *vt fam* shove

schiaffeggi'are *vt* slap

schi'affo *nm* slap; **dare uno ~ a** a slap; **avere una faccia da schiaffi** have the kind of face you'd love to take a swipe at. **schiaffo morale** slap in the face

schiamaz'zare *vi* make a racket; ⟨galline⟩ cackle

schia'mazzo *nm* din; **schiamazzi** *pl* **notturni** disturbing the peace

schian'tare 1 *vt* break 2 *vi* **schianto dalla fatica** I'm wiped out

schian'tarsi *vr* crash

'schianto *nm* crash; *fam* knock-out; ⟨divertente⟩ scream

schia'rire 1 *vt* clear; (sbiadire) fade 2 *vi* brighten up

schia'rirsi *vr* brighten up; **~ la gola** clear one's throat; **~ le idee** get things clear in one's head; (dopo aver bevuto) clear one's head

schia'rita *nf* sunny interval

schiat'tare *vi* burst; **~ di invidia** be green with envy

schia'vista *nmf* slave-driver

schiavitù *nf* slavery

schi'avo, **-a** *nmf* slave

schi'ena *nf* back. **mal di schiena** backache

schie'nale *nm* (di sedia) back

schi'era *nf* *Mil* rank; (moltitudine) crowd

schiera'mento *nm* lining up; *Mil* battle line. **schieramento di forze** rallying of the troops

schie'rare *vt* draw up; rally ⟨forze⟩

schie'rarsi *vr* draw up; ⟨forze⟩ rally; **~ dalla parte di qualcuno**, **~ con qualcuno** rally [in support] to somebody; **~ contro qualcuno** rally in opposition to somebody

schiet'tezza *nf* frankness

schi'etto *adj* frank; (puro) pure

schi'fezza *nf* **è una ~** it's disgusting; ⟨film, libro⟩ it's rubbish

schifil'toso *adj* fussy

'schifo *nm* disgust; **fare ~** be disgusting; **è uno ~!** it's disgusting!

schi'foso *adj* disgusting, yucky *fam*; (di cattiva qualità) rubbishy

schioc'care 1 *vt* crack ⟨frusta⟩; snap, click ⟨dita⟩; click ⟨lingua⟩ 2 *vi* crack

schi'occo *nm* (di frusta) crack; (di bacio) smack; (di dita, lingua) click

schioppet'tata *nf* shot

schi'oppo *nm* *fam* rifle; **a un tiro di ~** *fig* a stone's throw away

schiri'bizzo *nm* *fam* fancy; **se mi salta lo ~** ... if it takes my fancy ...

schi'udere *vt* open

schi'udersi *vr* open

schi'uma *nf* foam; (di sapone) lather; (di bucato) suds; (feccia) scum. **schiuma da barba** shaving foam

schiu'mare 1 *vt* skim 2 *vi* foam

schiuma'rola *nf* *Culin* skimmer

schiu'mogeno *adj* foaming

schiu'moso *adj* ⟨birra, crema⟩ frothy, foamy; ⟨liquido⟩ scummy

schi'uso *pp di* SCHIUDERE

schi'vare *vt* avoid

'schivo *adj* bashful

schizofre'nia *nf* schizophrenia

schizo'frenico, **-a** *adj & nmf* schizophrenic

schiz'zare 1 *vt* squirt; (inzaccherare) splash; (abbozzare) sketch; **~ qualcuno/ qualcosa di qualcosa** splatter somebody/ something with something 2 *vi* spurt; **~ via** *fig* scurry away

schiz'zato, **-a** *adj & nmf fam* loony

schizzi'noso *adj* squeamish

'schizzo *nm* squirt; (di fango) splash; (abbozzo) sketch

sci *nm inv* ski; (sport) skiing. **sci d'acqua**, **sci acquatico** water-skiing. **sci acrobatico** hot dogging. **sci di fondo** cross-country skiing

'scia *nf* wake; (di fumo ecc) trail; **sulla ~ di qualcuno** following in somebody's footsteps

sci'abola *nf* sabre

sciabor'dare *vt/i* lap

sciabor'dio *nm* lapping

sciacal'laggio *nm* profiteering

scia'callo *nm* jackal; *fig* profiteer

sciac'quare *vt* rinse

sciac'quarsi *vr* rinse oneself

sci'acquo *nm* mouthwash

scia'gura *nf* disaster

sciagu'rato *adj* unfortunate; (scellerato) wicked

scialac'quare *vt* squander

scialacqua|**'tore**, **-trice** *nmf* squanderer

scia'lare *vi* spend money like water

sci'albo *adj* pale; *fig* dull

sci'alle *nm* shawl

scia'luppa *nf* dinghy. **scialuppa di salvataggio** lifeboat

sciaman'nato *adj* good-for-nothing

scia'mano *nm* shaman

scia'mare *vi* swarm

sci'ame *nm* swarm; **a sciami** in swarms

sci'ampo *nm* shampoo

scian'cato *adj* lame

sci'are *vi* ski; **andare a ~** go skiing

sci'arpa nf scarf

sci'atica nf Med sciatica

scia|'tore, -trice nmf skier

sciatte'ria nf slovenliness

sci'atto adj slovenly; ⟨stile⟩ careless

sciat'tone, -a nmf slovenly person

'scibile nm knowledge; **lo ~ umano** the sum of human knowledge

scic'coso adj fam snazzy

scienti'fico adj scientific

sci'enza nf science; ⟨sapere⟩ knowledge; **avere la ~ infusa** be naturally talented; **scienze** pl **sociali** social science

scienzi'ato, -a nmf scientist

sci'ita adj & nmf Shiite

scilin'guagnolo nm fig **avere lo ~** be a chatterbox

'scimmia nf monkey

scimmiot'tare vt ape

scimpanzé nm inv chimpanzee, chimp

scimu'nito adj idiotic

'scindere vt separate; **~ in** break down into

'scindersi vr divide; **~ in** divide into

scin'tilla nf spark

scintil'lante adj sparkling

scintil'lare vi sparkle

scintil'lio nm sparkle

sciò int shoo!

scioc'cante adj shocking

scioc'care vt shock

scioc'chezza nf foolishness; ⟨assurdità⟩ foolish thing; **sciocchezze!** nonsense!

sci'occo adj foolish

sci'ogliere vt untie; undo, untie ⟨nodo⟩; ⟨liberare⟩ release; ⟨liquefare⟩ melt; dissolve ⟨contratto, qualcosa nell'acqua⟩; loosen up ⟨muscoli⟩

sci'ogliersi vr ⟨nodo⟩ come undone; ⟨liquefarsi⟩ melt; ⟨contratto⟩ be dissolved; ⟨pastiglia⟩ dissolve

sciogli'lingua nm inv tongue-twister

scio'lina nf ski wax

sciol'tezza nf agility; ⟨disinvoltura⟩ ease

sci'olto ➀ pp di SCIOGLIERE ➁ adj loose; ⟨agile⟩ agile; ⟨disinvolto⟩ easy; **versi** pl **sciolti** blank verse

sciope'rante nmf striker

sciope'rare vi go on strike, strike

sci'opero nm strike, industrial action; **in ~** on strike. **sciopero bianco** work-to-rule. **sciopero generale** general strike. **sciopero a singhiozzo** on-off strike

sciori'nare vt fig show off

sciovi'nismo nm chauvinism

sciovi'nista nmf Pol chauvinist

sciovi'nistico adj Pol chauvinistic

sci'pito adj insipid

scip'pare vt fam snatch; **~ qualcuno** snatch somebody's bag/bracelet etc

scippa|'tore, -trice nmf bag-snatcher

'scippo nm bag-snatching

sci'rocco nm sirocco

scirop'pato adj ⟨frutta⟩ in syrup

sci'roppo nm syrup

scirop'poso adj syrupy

'scisma nm schism

scissi'one nf division

scissio'nista adj breakaway attrib

'scisso pp di SCINDERE

sciupacchi'are vt spoil

sciupacchi'ato adj spoilt

sciu'pare vt spoil; ⟨sperperare⟩ waste

sciu'parsi vr get spoiled; ⟨deperire⟩ wear oneself out

sciu'pio nm waste

scivo'lare vi slide; ⟨involontariamente⟩ slip

'scivolo nm slide; Techn chute

scivo'lone nm fall; ⟨fig: errore⟩ blunder

scivo'loso adj slippery

scle'rosi nf sclerosis. **sclerosi multipla, sclerosi a placche** multiple sclerosis, MS

scoc'care ➀ vt fire ⟨freccia⟩; strike ⟨ore⟩ ➁ vi ⟨scintilla⟩ shoot out; **sono scoccate le cinque** five o'clock has just struck

scocci'are vt fam ⟨dare noia a⟩ bother

scocci'arsi vr fam be bored; **mi sono scocciato di aspettare** I'm fed up with waiting

scocci'ato adj fam fed up

scoccia|'tore, -trice nmf nuisance

scoccia'tura nf fam nuisance

sco'della nf bowl

scodel'lare vt dish out, dish up

scodinzo'lare vi wag its tail

scogli'era nf cliff; ⟨a fior d'acqua⟩ reef

'scoglio nm rock; ⟨fig: ostacolo⟩ stumbling block

scoglio'nato adj vulg pissed off

scoi'attolo nm squirrel

scola'pasta nm inv colander

scolapi'atti nm inv dish drainer

sco'lara nf schoolgirl

sco'lare¹ ➀ vt drain; strain ⟨pasta, verdura⟩ ➁ vi drip

sco'lare² adj school attrib; **in età ~** ⟨bambino⟩ school-age

scola'resca nf pupils pl

sco'laro nm schoolboy

sco'lastico adj school attrib; **gita scolastica** school trip

scoli'osi nf curvature of the spine

scollacci'ato *adj* low-cut

scol'lare *vt* cut away the neck of ⟨*abito*⟩; (staccare) unstick

scol'lato *adj* ⟨*abito*⟩ low-necked

scolla'tura *nf* neckline; ~ **profonda** plunging neckline

scolle'gare *vt* disconnect

'scollo *nm* neckline. **scollo a V** V-neck

'scolo *nm* drainage

scolo'rare *vt* fade

scolori'mento *nm* fading

scolo'rire *vt* fade

scolo'rirsi *vr* fade

scolo'rito *adj* faded

scol'pire *vt* carve; (imprimere) engrave

scombi'nare *vt* upset

scombusso'lare *vt* muddle up

scom'messa *nf* bet

scom'messo *pp di* SCOMMETTERE

scom'mettere *vt* bet; **ci puoi ~!** you bet!

scomo'dare *vt* trouble

scomo'darsi *vr* trouble

scomodità *nf inv* discomfort

'scomodo ① *adj* uncomfortable ② *nm* **essere di ~ a qualcuno** be a trouble to somebody

scompagin'are *vt* mess up

scompa'gnare *vt* split

scompa'gnato *adj* odd

scompa'rire *vi* disappear; (morire) pass away

scom'parsa *nf* disappearance; (morte) death, passing

scom'parso, -a ① *pp di* SCOMPARIRE ② *adj* missing; (morto) departed ③ *nmf* missing person; (morto) departed

scomparti'mento *nm* compartment

scom'parto *nf* compartment. **scomparto freezer** freezer compartment

scompen'sare *vt* throw off balance

scom'penso *nm* imbalance. **scompenso cardiaco** cardiac insufficiency

scompigli'are *vt* disarrange

scom'piglio *nm* confusion

scompisci'arsi *vr* fam ~ **[dalle risa]** wet oneself, split one's sides laughing

scom'porre *vt* break down; ruffle ⟨*capelli*⟩; (fig: turbare) upset

scom'porsi *vr* lose one's composure

scomposizi'one *nf* breaking down

scom'posto ① *pp di* SCOMPORRE ② *adj* (sguaiato) unseemly; (disordinato) untidy

sco'munica *nf* excommunication

scomuni'care *vt* excommunicate

sconcer'tante *adj* disconcerting; (che rende perplesso) bewildering, baffling

sconcer'tare *vt* disconcert; (rendere perplesso) bewilder, baffle

sconcer'tato *adj* disconcerted; (perplesso) bewildered, baffled

scon'cezza *nf* indecency

'sconcio ① *adj* indecent ② *nm* **è uno ~ che ...** it's a disgrace that ...

sconclusio'nato *adj* incoherent

scon'dito *adj* unseasoned; (insalata) with no dressing

sconfes'sare *vt* disown

scon'figgere *vt* defeat

sconfi'nare *vi* cross the border; (in proprietà privata) trespass

sconfi'nato *adj* unlimited

scon'fitta *nf* defeat; **subire una ~** be defeated, suffer defeat

scon'fitto *pp di* SCONFIGGERE

sconfor'tante *adj* disheartening, discouraging

scon'forto *nm* discouragement; **farsi prendere dallo ~** get discouraged, get disheartened

sconge'lare *vt* thaw out ⟨*cibo*⟩; defrost ⟨*frigo*⟩

scongiu'rare *vt* beseech; (evitare) avert

scongi'uro *nm* **fare gli scongiuri** ≈ touch wood, knock on wood Am

scon'nesso ① *pp di* SCONNETTERE ② *adj* fig incoherent

scon'nettere *vt* disconnect

sconosci'uto, -a ① *adj* unknown ② *nmf* stranger

sconquas'sare *vt* smash; (sconvolgere) upset

sconsa'crare *vt* deconsecrate

sconsiderata'mente *adv* inconsiderately

sconsidera'tezza *nf* lack of consideration, thoughtlessness

sconside'rato *adj* inconsiderate, thoughtless

sconsigli'abile *adj* not advisable

sconsigli'are *vt* advise against

sconso'lato *adj* disconsolate

scon'tare *vt* discount; (dedurre) deduct; (pagare) pay off; serve ⟨*pena*⟩; ~ **la propria colpa** pay for one's sins

scon'tato *adj* discounted; (ovvio) expected; ~ **del 10%** with 10% discount; **era ~** it was to be expected; **dare qualcosa per ~** take something for granted

scon'tento ① *adj* displeased ② *nm* discontent

'sconto *nm* discount; **fare uno ~** give a discount. **sconto commerciale** trade discount

scon'trarsi vr clash; (urtare) collide

scon'trino nm ticket; (di cassa) receipt; '**munirsi dello ~ alla cassa**' sign reminding customers that payment must be made at the cash desk beforehand

'**scontro** nm clash; (urto) collision. **scontro automobilistico** car crash. **scontro frontale** head-on collision. **scontro a fuoco** shootout

scontrosità nf surliness

scon'troso adj surly

sconveni'ente adj unprofitable; (scorretto) unseemly

sconvol'gente adj (sorprendente) mind-blowing; (inquietante) upsetting

scon'volgere vt upset; (mettere in disordine) disarrange

sconvolgi'mento nm upheaval

scon'volto ① pp di SCONVOLGERE ② adj distraught, upset

'**scooter** nm inv scooter

'**scopa** nf broom; (gioco di carte) type of card game

sco'pare vt sweep; vulg shag

sco'pata nf sweep; vulg shag; **dare una ~ per terra** give the floor a sweep

scoperchi'are vt take the lid off ⟨pentola⟩; take the roof off ⟨casa⟩

sco'perta nf discovery

sco'perto ① pp di SCOPRIRE ② adj uncovered; (senza riparo) exposed; (conto) overdrawn; (spoglio) bare

'**scopo** nm aim; **a ~ di** for the sake of; **allo ~ di** in order to

sco'pone nm (gioco di carte) type of card game

scoppi'are vi burst; fig break out

scoppiet'tare vi crackle

'**scoppio** nm burst; (di guerra) outbreak; (esplosione) explosion; **a ~ ritardato** ⟨bomba⟩ delayed action; **ha reagito a ~ ritardato** he did a double take

sco'prire vt discover; (togliere la copertura a) uncover; unveil ⟨statua⟩; **~ gli altarini** fam reveal his/her etc guilty secrets

scoraggia'mento nm discouragement

scoraggi'ante adj discouraging

scoraggi'are vt discourage

scoraggi'arsi vr lose heart

scor'butico adj Med suffering from scurvy; (fig: scontroso) disagreeable

scor'buto nm Med scurvy

scorci'are vt shorten

scorcia'toia nf short cut

'**scorcio** nm (di cielo) patch; (in arte) foreshortening; **di ~** (vedere) from an angle. **scorcio panoramico** panoramic view. **scorcio del secolo** end of the century

scor'dare vt forget; **~ qualcosa a casa** leave something at home

scor'darsi vr forget; **~ di qualcosa** forget something

scor'dato adj Mus out of tune

scorda'tura nf Mus going out of tune

sco'reggia nf fam fart

scoreggi'are vi fam fart

'**scorfano** nm scorpion fish

'**scorgere** vt make out; (notare) notice

'**scoria** nf waste; (di carbone) slag; **scorie** pl **nucleari** nuclear waste

scor'nare vt fig humiliate

scor'narsi vr fig come a cropper

scor'nato adj fig hangdog

'**scorno** nm humiliation

scorpacci'ata nf bellyful; **fare una ~ di** stuff oneself with

scorpi'one nm scorpion; Astr Scorpio

scorraz'zare vi run about

'**scorrere** ① vt (dare un'occhiata) glance through ② vi run; (scivolare) slide; (fluire) flow; Comput scroll; (attorno a un oggetto) wrap

scorre'ria nf raid

scorret'tezza nf (mancanza di educazione) bad manners pl

scor'retto adj incorrect; (sconveniente) improper

scor'revole adj **porta scorrevole** sliding door

scorri'banda nf raid; fig excursion

scorri'mento nm Comput scrolling; (attorno a un oggetto) wrapping

'**scorsa** nf glance; **dare una ~ a** glance through

'**scorso** ① pp di SCORRERE ② adj last; **l'anno ~** last year

scor'soio adj **nodo scorsoio** noose

scor'ta nf escort; (provvista) supply

scor'tare vt escort

scortecci'are vt debark ⟨albero⟩; strip ⟨muro⟩

scor'tese adj rude

scorte'sia nf rudeness

scorti'care vt skin

scortica'tura nf graze

'**scorto** pp di SCORGERE

'**scorza** nf peel; (crosta) crust; (corteccia) bark; fig exterior. **scorza d'arancia** orange peel

scorzo'nera nf salsify

sco'sceso adj steep

'**scossa** nf shake; Electr, fig shock; **prendere la ~** get an electric shock. **scossa elettrica** electric shock. **scossa sismica** earth tremor

'**scosso** ① pp di SCUOTERE ② adj shaken; (sconvolto) upset

scos'sone *nm* jolt
sco'stante *adj* off-putting
sco'stare *vt* push away
sco'starsi *vr* stand aside
scostu'mato *adj* dissolute; (maleducato) ill-mannered
Scotch® *nm* Scotch tape®
scoten'nare *vt* skin ‹maiale›; scalp ‹persona›
scot'tante *adj* ‹argomento› burning; ‹fig: notizia› sensational
scot'tare ① *vt* burn; (con liquido, vapore) scald; Culin blanch
② *vi* ‹bevanda, cibo› be too hot; ‹sole, pentola› be very hot
scot'tarsi *vr* burn oneself; (con liquido, vapore) scald oneself; (al sole) get sunburnt; fig get one's fingers burnt
scot'tato *adj* Culin blanched
scotta'tura *nf* burn; (da liquido) scald; fig painful experience. **scottatura solare** sunburn
'Scottex® *nm* paper towel
'scotto¹ *adj* overcooked
'scotto² *nm* score; **pagare lo ∼ di qualcosa** pay for something
scout ① *adj inv* scout *attrib*
② *nmf inv* scout
scou'tismo *nm* scout movement
sco'vare *vt* (scoprire) discover
scovo'lino *nm* bottle brush; (per pipa) pipe cleaner
'Scozia *nf* Scotland
scoz'zese ① *adj* Scottish
② *nmf* Scot
'scrambler *nm* Radio, Teleph scrambler
screan'zato *adj* rude
scredi'tare *vt* discredit
scre'mare *vt* skim
screpo'lare *vt* chap
screpo'larsi *vr* get chapped; ‹intonaco› crack
screpo'lato *adj* chapped; ‹intonaco› cracked
screpola'tura *nf* crack
screzi'ato *adj* speckled
'screzio *nm* disagreement
scribacchi'are *vt* scribble
scribac'chino, -a *nmf* scribbler; ‹impiegato› penpusher
scricchio'lante *adj* creaky
scricchio'lare *vi* creak
scricchio'lio *nm* creaking
'scricciolo *nm* wren; fig delicate-looking creature
'scrigno *nm* casket
scrimina'tura *nf* parting
scriteri'ato *adj* empty-headed

'scritta *nf* writing; (su muro) graffiti
'scritto ① *pp di* SCRIVERE
② *adj* written; **∼ col computer** word-processed; **∼ a macchina** typed; **∼ a mano** handwritten
③ *nm* writing; (lettera) letter
scrit'toio *nm* writing-desk
scrit'tore, -trice *nmf* writer
scrit'tura *nf* writing; Relig scripture; (calligrafia) handwriting; **scritture** *pl* **contabili** account books. **scrittura privata** Jur legal document drawn up by an individual
scrittu'rare *vt* engage
scriva'nia *nf* desk
scri'vente *nmf* writer
'scrivere *vt* write; (descrivere) write about; **∼ a macchina** type
scroc'care *vt* fam **∼ a** sponge off
scrocchi'are *vi* crack
'scrocco¹ *nm* fam **a ∼** without paying; **vivere a ∼** sponge off other people
'scrocco² *nm* **coltello a scrocco** pocket knife; **serratura a scrocco** spring lock
scroc'cone, -a *nmf* fam sponger
'scrofa *nf* sow
scrol'lare *vt* shake; **∼ le spalle** shrug one's shoulders; **∼ la testa** shake one's head
scrol'larsi *vr* shake oneself; **∼ qualcosa di dosso** shake something off
'scrolling *nm* Comput scrolling
scrosci'ante *adj* pouring; ‹applausi› thunderous
scrosci'are *vi* roar; ‹pioggia›; pelt down
'scroscio *nm* roar; (di pioggia) pelting; **uno ∼ di applausi** thunderous applause; **piovere a ∼** lash down
scro'stare *vt* scrape
scro'starsi *vr* flake
scro'stato *adj* flaky
'scroto *nm* scrotum
'scrupolo *nm* scruple; (diligenza) care; **senza scrupoli** unscrupulous, without scruples; **farsi scrupoli per qualcosa** have scruples about something
scrupo'loso *adj* scrupulous
scru'tare *vt* scan; (indagare) search
scruta'tore *nm* (di voti) returning officer
scruti'nare *vt* scrutinize
scru'tinio *nm* (di voti) poll; Sch assessment of progress; **scrutini** *pl* Sch meeting of teachers to discuss pupils' work and assign marks. **scrutinio segreto** secret ballot
scu'cire *vt* unstitch; **scuci i soldi!** fig fam cough up [the money]!

scu'cirsi vr come unstitched; (fig: parlare) talk; **non si scuce** he won't talk

scuci'tura nf unstitching

scude'ria nf stable; **scuderie** pl mews

scu'detto nm Sport championship shield; (campionato) national championship

scudi'ero nm squire

scudisci'ata nf whipping

'scudo nm shield; **farsi ~ con qualcosa** shield oneself with something

scuffi'are vi capsize

scu'gnizzo nm street urchin

sculacci'are vt spank

sculacci'ata nf spanking; **prendere a sculacciate** spank

sculacci'one nm spanking

sculet'tare vi wiggle one's hips

scul'tore, -trice ① nm sculptor ② nf sculptress

scul'tura nf sculpture

scu'ola nf school. **scuola allievi ufficiali** cadet school. **scuola per bambini con difficoltà d'apprendimento** special school. **scuola elementare** primary school, grade school Am. **scuola guida** driving school. **scuola materna** day nursery. **scuola media** secondary school. **scuola media inferiore** secondary school (10-13), junior high school Am. **scuola media superiore** secondary school (13-18). **scuola dell'obbligo** compulsory education. **scuola privata** private school, public school Br. **scuola di sci** ski school. **scuola serale** evening school. **scuola statale** state school. **scuola superiore** secondary school

scu'otere vt shake

scu'otersi vr (destarsi) rouse oneself; **~ qualcosa di dosso** fig shake something off

'scure nf axe

scu'rire vt/i darken

'scuro ① adj dark ② nm darkness; (imposta) shutter

scur'rile adj scurrilous

'scusa nf apology; (giustificazione) excuse; (pretesto) pretext; **chiedere ~** apologize; **[chiedo] ~!** [I'm] sorry!

scu'sare vt excuse

scu'sarsi vr apologize (di for); **[mi] scusi!** excuse me!; (chiedendo perdono) [I'm] sorry!

sdebi'tarsi vr repay the kindness

sde'gnare vt despise; (fare arrabbiare) enrage

sde'gnarsi vr become angry

sde'gnato adj indignant

'sdegno nm disdain; (ira) indignation

sde'gnoso adj disdainful

sden'tato adj toothless

sdipa'nare vt wind

sdogana'mento nm customs clearance

sdoga'nare vt clear through customs

sdolci'nato adj sentimental, schmaltzy

sdoppia'mento nm splitting. **sdoppiamento della personalità** split personality

sdoppi'are vt halve

sdrai'arsi vr lie down

'sdraio nf [sedia a] ~ deckchair

sdrammatiz'zare ① vt take the heat out of ② vi take the heat out of the situation

sdruccio'lare vi slither

sdruccio'levole adj slippery

sdruccio'lone nm slip

SE abbr (**sud-est**) SE

se ① conj if; (interrogativo) whether, if; **se mai** (caso mai) if need be; **se mai telefonasse,...** should he call,..., if he calls,...; **se no** otherwise, or else; **se non altro** at least, if nothing else; **se pure** (sebbene) even though; (anche se) even if; **non so se sia vero** I don't know whether it's true, I don't know if it's true; **come se** as if; **se lo avessi saputo prima!** if only I had known before!; **e se andassimo fuori a cena?** how about going out for dinner? ② nm inv if; **non voglio né se né ma** I don't want any ifs or buts

sé pers pron oneself; (lui) himself; (lei) herself; (esso, essa) itself; (loro) themselves; **l'ha fatto da sé** he did it himself; **ha preso i soldi con sé** he took the money with him; **si sono tenuti le notizie per sé** they kept the news to themselves

se'baceo adj sebaceous

seb'bene conj although

'sebo nm sebum

sec. abbr (**secolo**) c.

'secca nf shallows pl; **in ~** (nave) grounded

sec'cante adj annoying

sec'care ① vt dry; (importunare) annoy ② vi dry up

sec'carsi vr dry up; (irritarsi) get annoyed

secca|'tore, -trice nmf nuisance

secca'tura nf bother; **dare una ~ a qualcuno** trouble somebody, bother somebody; **non voglio seccature!** I don't want the bother!

secchi'ata nf bucketful

secchi'ello nm bucket. **secchiello del ghiaccio** ice bucket

'secchio nm bucket. **secchio della spazzatura** rubbish bin, trash can Am

sec'chione, -a nmf fam dweeb

'secco, -a ① adj dry; (disseccato) dried; (magro) thin; (brusco) curt; (preciso) sharp;

restare a ∼ be left penniless; **restarci** ∼
(fam: morire di colpo) be killed on the spot;
frutta secca nuts pl

[2] nm (siccità) drought; **lavare a** ∼ dry-
clean

secessi'one nf secession. **guerra di
secessione** War of Secession

seco'lare adj age-old; (laico) secular

'**secolo** nm century; (epoca) age; **è un** ∼
che non lo vedo fam I haven't seen him for
ages or yonks

se'conda [1] nf Sch, Rail second class; Auto
second [gear]

[2] prep **a** ∼ **di** according to

secon'dario adj Jur collateral; **effetto** ∼
side effect

se'condo [1] adj second

[2] nm second, sec fam; (secondo piatto) main
course; **un** ∼! just a sec[ond]!

[3] prep according to; ∼ **me** in my opinion

secondo'genito, -a adj & nm second-
born

secrezi'one nf secretion

'**sedano** nm celery. **sedano rapa**
celeriac

se'dare vt put down, suppress ⟨rivolta⟩;
fig soothe

seda'tivo adj & nm sedative;
somministrare sedativi a sedate

'**sede** nf seat; (centro) centre; Relig see;
Comm head office; **in** ∼ **di esami** during
the exams; **in separata** ∼ in private.
sede centrale head office. **sede
sociale** registered office

seden'tario adj sedentary

se'dere [1] vi sit

[2] nm (deretano) bottom

se'dersi vr sit down

'**sedia** nf chair. **sedia a dondolo**
rocking chair. **sedia elettrica** electric
chair. **sedia da giardino** garden seat.
sedia girevole swivel chair. **sedia a
rotelle** wheelchair. **sedia a sdraio**
deckchair

sedi'cenne adj & nmf sixteen-year-old

sedi'cente adj self-styled

sedi'cesimo, -a adj & nm sixteenth

'**sedici** adj & nm sixteen

se'dile nm seat

sedimen'tare vi leave a sediment

sedi'mento nm sediment

sedizi'one nf sedition

sedizi'oso adj seditious

se'dotto pp di SEDURRE

sedu'cente adj seductive; (allettante)
enticing

se'durre vt seduce

se'duta nf session; (di posa) sitting; ∼
stante adv here and now

se'duto adj sitting

sedut|'tore, -trice [1] nm charmer
[2] nf temptress

seduzi'one nf seduction

seg. abbr (**seguente**) foll.

'**sega** nf saw; vulg wank; **mezza** ∼ vulg
tosser; **non capire una** ∼ vulg understand
damn all. **sega circolare** circular saw.
sega a mano handsaw. **sega a nastro**
band saw

'**segale** nf rye. **pane di segale** rye
bread

sega'ligno adj wiry

se'gare vt saw

sega'trice nf saw. **segatrice a
nastro** band saw

sega'tura nf sawdust

'**seggio** nm seat. **seggio elettorale**
polling station

seg'giola nf chair

seggio'lino nm seat; (da bambino) child
seat. **seggiolino per auto** car seat.
seggiolino regolabile adjustable seat

seggio'lone nm (per bambini) high chair

seggio'via nf chair lift

seghe'ria nf sawmill

se'ghetto nm hacksaw

segmen'tare vt segment

seg'mento nm segment

segna'carte nm bookmark

segna'lare vt signal; (annunciare)
announce; (indicare) point out

segna'larsi vr distinguish oneself

segnalazi'one nf signals pl; (di candidato)
recommendation. **segnalazione
stradale** road signs pl

se'gnale nm signal; (stradale) sign.
segnale acustico beep. **segnale
d'allarme** alarm; (in treno)
communication cord Br, emergency brake;
fig warning sign . **segnale digitale**
Comput digital signal. **segnale di libero**
Teleph dialling tone. **segnale orario**
Teleph time signal, speaking clock

segna'letica nf signals pl; '∼ **in
rifacimento**' 'road signs being repainted'.
segnaletica orizzontale painted road
markings pl. **segnaletica stradale**
road signs pl

segna'letico adj dati segnaletici
description; **foto segnaletica** photograph
used for identification purposes

segna'libro nm bookmark

segna'punti nm inv pegboard

se'gnare vt mark; (prendere nota) note;
(indicare) indicate; Sport score; ∼ **la fine di
qualcosa** sound the death knell for
something; ∼ **il passo** mark time

se'gnarsi vr cross oneself

se'gnato adj marked

'segno *nm* sign; (traccia, limite) mark; (bersaglio) target; **far** ~ (col capo) nod; (con la mano) beckon; **fare** ~ **di no** (con la testa) shake one's head; **fare** ~ **di sì** (con la testa) nod [one's head]; **lasciare il** ~ leave a mark; **non dare segni di vita** give no sign of life; **oltrepassare il** ~ fig overstep the mark. **segno della croce** sign of the cross. **segno premonitore** early warning. **segno di sottolineatura** underscore. **segno più** plus sign. **segno zodiacale** sign of the Zodiac, birth sign, star sign

segre'gare *vt* segregate

segre'garsi *vr* cut oneself off

segre'gato *adj* in isolation

segregazi'one *nf* segregation

segregazio'nistico *adj* segregated

segretari'ato *nm* secretariat

segre'tario, **-a** *nmf* secretary; **fare da** ~ **a qualcuno** be somebody's secretary; **segretaria tuttofare** girl Friday. **segretario bilingue** bilingual secretary. **segretario comunale** town clerk. **segretario di direzione** executive secretary. **segretario personale** personal assistant, PA. **Segretario di Stato** Secretary of State

segrete'ria *nf* (ufficio) administrative office; (segretariato) secretariat. **segreteria studenti** Univ admissions office. **segreteria telefonica** answering machine, answerphone

segre'tezza *nf* secrecy

se'greto *adj & nm* secret; **in** ~ in secret

segu'ace *nmf* follower; **avere molti seguaci** have a large following

segu'ente *adj* following, next

se'gugio *nm* bloodhound

segu'ire *vt/i* follow; (continuare) continue; ~ **con lo sguardo** follow with one's eyes; ~ **le orme di qualcuno** follow in somebody's footsteps; ~ **un corso** take a course

segui'tare *vt/i* continue

'seguito *nm* retinue; (sequela) series; (continuazione) continuation; **di** ~ in succession; **in** ~ later on; **in** ~ **a** following; (a causa di) owing to; **al** ~ **in** his/her wake; **fare** ~ **a** Comm follow up

'sei *adj & nm* six

sei'cento *adj & nm* six hundred; **il Seicento** the seventeenth century

sei'mila *adj & nm* six thousand

'selce *nf* flint

sel'ciato *nm* paving

se'lenio *nm* selenium

selettività *nf* selectivity

selet'tivo *adj* selective; **memoria selettiva** selective memory

selet'tore *nm* selector

selezio'nare *vt* select; '~ **il numero'** 'dial [the number]'

selezi'one *nf* selection. **selezione naturale** natural selection

self-con'trol *nm* self-control

self-'service *adj & nm inv* self-service

'sella *nf* saddle

sel'lare *vt* saddle

seltz *nm* soda water

'selva *nf* forest; (fig: di errori, capelli) mass; (di ammiratori) horde

selvag'gina *nf* game

sel'vaggio, **-a** ① *adj* wild; (primitivo) savage ② *nmf* savage

sel'vatico *adj* wild

selvicol'tura *nf* forestry

se'maforo *nm* traffic lights *pl*

se'mantica *nf* semantics

se'mantico *adj* semantic

sembi'anza *nf* semblance; **sembianze** *pl* (di persona) appearance

sem'brare *vi* seem; (assomigliare) look like; **che te ne sembra?** what do you think?; **mi sembra che ...** I think ...; **sembra che vada bene** it's fine, seemingly or apparently

'seme *nm* seed; (di mela) pip; (di carte) suit; (sperma) semen. **seme della discordia** seeds *pl* of discord

se'mente *nf* seed

seme'strale *adj* ⟨corso⟩ six-month; ⟨pagamento⟩ six-monthly, half-yearly

se'mestre *nm* six months; Univ term, semester Am

semia'perto *adj* half-open

semi'asse *nm* axle

semiauto'matico *adj* semiautomatic

semi'breve *nf* Mus semibreve

semi'cerchio *nm* semicircle

semicirco'lare *adj* semicircular

semicirconfe'renza *nf* semicircle

semicondut'tore *adj & nm* semiconductor

semicon'vitto *nm* **scuola a semiconvitto** school for dayboarders

semicosci'ente *adj* semi-conscious; half-conscious

semi'croma *nf* Mus semiquaver

semifi'nale *nf* semifinal

semifina'lista *nmf* semifinalist

semi'freddo *nm* cold dessert resembling ice cream

semilavo'rato ① *adj* semi-finished ② *nm* **semilavorati** *pl* semi-finished goods

semi'minima *nf* Mus crotchet

'semina *nf* sowing

semi'nare *vt* sow; fam shake off ⟨inseguitori⟩; ~ **zizzania** cause trouble

semi'nario *nm* seminar; Relig seminary

semina'rista *nm* seminarist

seminfermità *nf* partial disability. **seminfermità mentale** diminished responsibility

seminter'rato *nm* basement

semi'nudo *adj* half-naked

semioscurità *nf* semi-darkness

semiprezi'oso *adj* semiprecious

semi'secco *adj* medium-dry

semi'serio *adj* semi-serious

se'mitico *adj* Semitic

semi'tono *nm* Mus semitone

sem'mai ① *conj* in case
② *adv* è lui, ~, che ... if anyone, it's him who...

'semola *nf* bran

semo'lato *adj* ⟨zucchero⟩ caster *attrib*

semo'lino *nm* semolina

'semplice *adj* simple; **in parole semplici** in plain words

semplice'mente *adv* simply

semplici'otto, -a *nmf* simpleton

sempli'cistico *adj* simplistic

semplicità *nf* simplicity

semplifi'care *vt* simplify

'sempre *adv* always; (ancora) still; **per ~** for ever; **~ più** more and more; **pur ~** still, nevertheless

sempre'verde *adj & nm* evergreen

'senape *nf* mustard

se'nato *nm* senate

sena|'tore, -trice*nmf* senator

'Senegal *nm* Senegal

se'nile *adj* senile

senilità *nf* senility

'senior ① *adj inv* senior
② *nmf* (pl **seniores**) Sport senior

'senno *nm* sense; **giudicare col ~ del poi** use hindsight

sennò *adv* otherwise, or else

sennonché *conj* but, except that; (fuorché) but, except

'seno *nm* (petto) breast; Math sine; **in ~ a** in the bosom of

sen'sale *nm* broker

sen'sato *adj* sensible

sensazio'nale *adj* sensational

sensaziona'listico *adj* sensationalist

sensazi'one *nf* sensation; **fare ~** ⟨notizia, scoperta⟩ cause a sensation

sen'sibile *adj* sensitive; (percepibile) perceptible; (notevole) considerable; **mondo ~** tangible world

sensibilità *nf* sensitivity

sensibiliz'zare *vt* make more aware (**a** of)

sensibil'mente *adv* appreciably

sensi'tivo ① *adj* sensory
② *nmf* sensitive person; (medium) medium

'senso *nm* sense; (significato) meaning; (direzione) direction; **far ~ a qualcuno** make somebody shudder; **in ~ orario/antiorario** clockwise/anticlockwise; **ai sensi della legge** in accordance with the law; **non ha ~** it doesn't make sense; **avere il ~ degli affari** have good business sense; **di buon ~** ⟨persona⟩ sensible; **senza ~** meaningless; **in un certo ~** ... in a sense *or* way ...; **perdere i sensi** lose consciousness; **a ~** ⟨ripetere, tradurre⟩ in general terms; **in ~ opposto** in the opposite direction; **a ~ unico** ⟨strada⟩ one-way; **a doppio ~ [di marcia]** ⟨strada⟩ two-way; **a doppio ~** ⟨parola, espressione⟩ with a double meaning. **senso dell'umorismo** sense of humour; **'senso vietato'** 'no entry'

sen'sore *nm* sensor

sensu'ale *adj* sensual

sensualità *nf* sensuality

sen'tenza *nf* sentence; (proverbio) saying; **pronunciare una ~** hand down a sentence; **pronunciare la ~** pronounce sentence

sentenzi'are *vi* pass judgment

senti'ero *nm* path. **sentiero luminoso di avvicinamento** Aeron approach lights

sentimen'tale *adj* sentimental

sentimenta'lista *nmf* sentimentalist

sentimental'mente *adv* sentimentally

senti'mento *nm* feeling; **essere fuori di ~** be out of one's mind

sen'tina *nf* Naut bilge

senti'nella *nf* sentry; **essere di ~** be on guard

sen'tire ① *vt* feel; (udire) hear; (ascoltare) listen to; (gustare) taste; (odorare) smell
② *vi* feel; (udire) hear; **~ caldo/freddo** feel hot/cold

sen'tirsi *vr* feel; **~ di fare qualcosa** feel like doing something; **~ bene/male** feel well/ill; **sentirsela di fare qualcosa** feel up to doing something

sen'tito *adj* (sincero) sincere; **per ~ dire** by hearsay

sen'tore *nm* inkling

'senza *prep* without; **~ ombrello** without an umbrella; **~ correre** without running; **senz'altro** certainly; **~ un soldo** penniless; **'~ conservanti'** 'no preservatives'; **fare ~** do without

senza'tetto *nm inv* **i ~** the homeless

'sepalo *nm* sepal

sepa'rare *vt* separate

sepa'rarsi *vr* separate; (prendere commiato) part; **~ da** be separated from

separata'mente *adv* separately

separa'tista *nmf* separatist

sepa'rato *adj* separate

separazi'one *nf* separation. **separazione consensuale** separation by mutual consent. **separazione legale** legal separation

sepol'crale *adj liter* sepulchral

se'polcro *nm* sepulchre

se'polto [1] pp di SEPPELLIRE [2] *adj* buried; **morto e** ~ *fig* dead and buried

sepol'tura *nf* burial; **dare** ~ **a qualcuno** bury somebody

seppel'lire *vt* bury

seppel'lirsi *vr fig* cut oneself off

'seppia [1] *nf* cuttle fish [2] *adj inv* sepia

sep'pure *conj* even if

se'quela *nf* series, succession; (di insulti) string

se'quenza *nf* sequence

sequenzi'ale *adj* sequential

seque'strare *vt* (rapire) kidnap; (confiscare) confiscate; Jur impound

sequestra|'tore, -trice *nmf* kidnapper

se'questro *nm* Jur impounding; (di persona) kidnap[ping]

se'quoia *nf* sequoia

'sera *nf* evening, night; **di** ~, **la** ~ in the evening; **da** ~ ⟨abito⟩ evening *attrib*; **alle 8 di** ~ at 8 o'clock in the evening, at 8 o'clock at night; **buona** ~! good evening!; **dalla mattina alla** ~ from morning to night; **ieri** ~ yesterday evening, last night; **questa** ~ this evening, tonight

se'rale *adj* evening *attrib*

seral'mente *adv* every evening, every night

se'rata *nf* evening; (ricevimento) party. **serata danzante** dance. **serata di gala** gala night

ser'bare *vt* keep; harbour ⟨odio⟩; cherish ⟨speranza⟩

serba'toio *nm* tank. **serbatoio d'acqua** water tank. **serbatoio della benzina** petrol tank, gas tank Am

'Serbia *nf* Serbia

'serbo¹, -a [1] *adj & nmf* Serbian [2] *nm* (lingua) Serbian

'serbo² *nm* **mettere in** ~ put aside

serbo-cro'ato *nmf* Serbo-Croat[ian]

sere'nata *nf* serenade

serenità *nf* serenity

se'reno *adj* serene; ⟨cielo⟩ clear; **un fulmine a ciel** ~ *fam* bolt from the blue

ser'gente *nm* sergeant

'serial *nm inv* serial [televisivo] television serial

seri'ale *adj* serial

seria'mente *adv* seriously

'serico *adj* silk

'serie *nf inv* series; (complesso) set; Sport division; **fuori** ~ custom-built; **produzione in** ~ mass production. **serie A** (di calcio) ≈ Premier League. **serie B** (di calcio) ≈ First Division; **di** ~ **B** *fig* second-rate. **serie numerica** numerical series

serietà *nf* seriousness

'serio *adj* serious; (degno di fiducia) reliable; **sul** ~ seriously; (davvero) really

ser'mone *nm* sermon

seroto'nina *nf* serotonin

'serpe *nf liter* viper

serpeggi'ante *adj* ⟨strada⟩ twisting, winding

serpeggi'are *vi* ⟨strada⟩ twist, wind; (fig: diffondersi) spread

ser'pente *nm* snake. **serpente a sonagli** rattlesnake. **serpente velenoso** poisonous snake

serpen'tina *nf* **a** ~ twisting and turning, winding; **fare una** ~ weave

'serra *nf* greenhouse. **effetto serra** greenhouse effect

ser'raglio *nm* harem

ser'randa *nf* shutter

ser'rare *vt* shut; (stringere) tighten; (incalzare) press on

ser'rata *nf* lockout

serra'tura *nf* lock

'server *nm inv* server. **server di posta** mail server. **server web** web server

ser'vibile *adj* usable

ser'vile *adj* servile

servi'lismo *nm* servility

ser'vire [1] *vt* serve; (al ristorante) wait on [2] *vi* serve; (essere utile) be of use; **non serve** it's no good; '~ **freddo**' 'serve chilled'

ser'virsi *vr* (di cibo) help oneself; ~ **da** buy from; ~ **di** use

servi|'tore *nm* retainer

servitù *nf* servitude; (personale di servizio) servants *pl*

servizi'evole *adj* obliging

ser'vizio *nm* service; (da caffè ecc) set; (di cronaca, sportivo) report; (in tennis) serve; **servizi** *pl* bathroom; **essere di** ~ be on duty; **fare** ~ ⟨autobus ecc⟩ run; **servizi** *pl* (terziario) services; **servizi** *pl* **bancari a domicilio** home banking; **servizi** *pl* **bancari via telefono** telephone banking; **servizi** *pl* **igienici** toilet block; **servizi** *pl* **di pronto intervento** emergency services; **servizi** *pl* **pubblici** (bagni) public toilets; **servizi** *pl* **sociali** welfare services. **donna di servizio** maid. **fuori servizio** ⟨bus⟩ not in service; ⟨ascensore⟩ out of order. **servizio bus navetta** courtesy bus. **servizio compreso** service charge included. **servizio escluso** not including service charge. **area di**

servizio service station. **servizio in camera** room service. **servizio civile** civilian duties done instead of national service. **servizio filmato** film report. **servizio di linea** passenger service. **servizio militare** military service. **servizio pubblico** utility company. **servizio al tavolo** waiter service. **servizio da tavola** dinnerware. **servizio traghetto** passenger ferry

'**servo**, **-a** *nmf* servant

servo'freno *nm* servo brake

servo'sterzo *nm* power steering

'**sesamo** *nm* sesame

ses'santa *adj & nm* sixty

sessan'tenne *adj & nmf* sixty-year-old

sessan'tesimo *adj & nm* sixtieth

sessan'tina *nf* una ~ di about sixty

Sessan'totto *nm* protest movement of 1968

sessi'one *nf* session

ses'sista *adj* sexist

'**sesso** *nm* sex; **fare** ~ sl have sex. **sesso forte** stronger sex. **gentil sesso** fair sex. **sesso sicuro** safe sex

sessu'ale *adj* sexual

sessualità *nf* sexuality

'**sesto**[1] *adj & nm* sixth

sesto[2] *nm* rimettere in ~ put back on its feet ⟨azienda⟩; restore ⟨vestito⟩; recondition ⟨motore, auto⟩

set *nm inv* set

'**seta** *nf* silk; di ~ silk *attrib*

setacci'are *vt* sieve

se'taccio *nm* sieve; **passare qualcosa al** ~ fig go through something with a fine-tooth comb

'**sete** *nf* thirst; **avere** ~ be thirsty. **sete di sangue** blood lust

'**setola** *nf* bristle

'**setta** *nf* sect

set'tanta *adj & nm* seventy

settan'tenne *adj & nmf* seventy-year-old

settan'tesimo *adj & nm* seventieth

settan'tina *nf* una ~ di about seventy

set'tario *adj* sectarian

'**sette** *adj & nm* seven

sette'cento *adj & nm* seven hundred; **il Settecento** the eighteenth century

set'tembre *nm* September

settentrio'nale [1] *adj* northern [2] *nmf* northerner

settentri'one *nm* north

'**setter** *nm inv* setter

'**settico** *adj* septic

setti'mana *nf* week; **alla** ~ per week; **a metà** ~ midweek, half-way through the week. **settimana corta** five-day week. **settimana lavorativa** working week

settima'nale *adj & nm* weekly

setti'mino, **-a** [1] *adj* born two months premature [2] *nmf* baby born two months premature

'**settimo** *adj & nm* seventh

set'tore *nm* sector

settori'ale *adj* sector-based

severità *nf* severity

se'vero *adj* severe; (rigoroso) strict

se'vizia *nf* torture; **sevizie** *pl* torture *sg*

sevizi'are *vt* torture

Sey'chelles *nfpl* Seychelles

sezio'nare *vt* divide; Med dissect

sezi'one *nf* section; (reparto) department; Med dissection

sfaccen'dare *vi* bustle about

sfaccen'dato *adj* idle

sfaccet'tare *vt* cut

sfaccet'tato *adj* cut; fig many-sided, multifaceted

sfaccetta'tura *nf* cutting; fig facet

sfacchi'nare *vi* toil

sfacchi'nata *nf* drudgery

sfaccia'taggine *nf* cheek

sfacciata'mente *adv* cheekily

sfacci'ato *adj* cheeky, fresh Am

sfa'celo *nm* ruin; **in** ~ in ruins

sfagio'lare *vi* fam **non mi sfagiola** it's/he's/she's not my cup of tea

sfal'darsi *vr* flake off

sfal'sare *vt* stagger; ~ **il tiro** shoot wide

sfa'mare *vt* feed

sfa'marsi *vt* satisfy one's hunger, eat one's fill

sfarfal'lio *nm* (di schermo, luce) flicker

'**sfarzo** *nm* pomp

sfar'zoso *adj* sumptuous

sfa'sato *adj* fam confused; ⟨motore⟩ which needs tuning; **sentirsi** ~ fam be out of sync[h]

sfasci'are *vt* unbandage; (fracassare) smash

sfasci'arsi *vr* fall to pieces

sfasci'ato *adj* beat-up

'**sfascio** *nm* ruin; **andare allo** ~ go to rack and ruin

sfa'tare *vt* explode

sfati'cato *adj* lazy

'**sfatto** *adj* unmade

sfavil'lante *adj* sparkling

sfavil'lare *vi* sparkle

sfavo'revole *adj* unfavourable

sfavo'rire *vt* disadvantage, put at a disadvantage

sfeb'brare *vi* **comincia a** ~ his temperature is starting to come down

S

'sfera nf sphere. **sfera affettiva** area of feelings and emotions. **sfera celeste** celestial sphere. **sfera di cristallo** crystal ball. **sfera di influenza** sphere of influence

'sferico adj spherical

sfer'rare vt unshoe ⟨cavallo⟩; give ⟨calcio, pugno⟩

sferruz'zare vi knit

sfer'zare vt whip

sfer'zata nf whip; fig telling-off

sfian'cante adj wearing

sfian'care vt wear out

sfian'carsi vr wear oneself out

sfiata'toio nm blowhole

sfi'brare vt exhaust

sfi'brato adj exhausted

'sfida nf challenge

sfi'dare vt challenge

sfi'ducia nf mistrust

sfiduci'ato adj discouraged

'sfiga nf sl bloody bad luck; **avere** ∼ be bloody unlucky

sfi'gato, -a sl ① adj bloody unlucky
② nmf unlucky beggar

sfigu'rare ① vt disfigure
② vi (far brutta figura) look out of place

sfilacci'are vt fray

sfilacci'arsi vr fray

sfi'lare ① vt unthread; (togliere di dosso) take off
② vi ⟨truppe⟩ march past; (in parata) parade

sfi'larsi vr come unthreaded; ⟨collant⟩ ladder; take off ⟨pantaloni⟩

sfi'lata nf parade; (sfilza) series. **sfilata di moda** fashion show

sfila'tino nm long, thin loaf

'sfilza nf string

'sfinge nf sphinx

sfi'nire vt wear out

sfi'nito adj worn out

sfio'rare vt skim; touch on ⟨argomento⟩

sfio'rire vi wither; ⟨bellezza⟩ fade

sfis'sare vt cancel

'sfitto adj vacant

'sfizio nm whim, fancy; **togliersi uno** ∼ satisfy a whim

sfizi'oso adj nifty

sfo'cato adj out of focus

sfoci'are vi ∼ **in** flow into

sfode'rare vt draw ⟨pistola, spada⟩; fig show off ⟨cultura⟩; ∼ **un sorriso** smile insincerely

sfode'rato adj ⟨giacca⟩ unlined

sfo'gare vt vent

sfo'garsi vr give vent to one's feelings

sfoggi'are vt/i show off

'sfoggio nm show, display; **fare** ∼ **di** show off

'sfoglia nf sheet of pastry. **pasta sfoglia** puff pastry

sfogli'are vt leaf through

sfogli'ata¹ nf flaky pastry with filling

sfogli'ata² nf dare una ∼ a ⟨libro, giornale⟩ flick through

'sfogo nm outlet; fig outburst; Med rash; **dare** ∼ **a** give vent to

sfolgo'rante adj blazing

sfolgo'rare vi blaze

sfolla'gente nm inv truncheon, billy Am

sfol'lare ① vt clear
② vi Mil be evacuated

sfol'lato, -a nmf evacuee

sfol'tire vt thin [out]; **farsi** ∼ **i capelli** have one's hair thinned

sfon'dare ① vt break down
② vi (aver successo) make a name for oneself

'sfondo nm background; **un'aggressione a** ∼ **politico/razziale** a politically/racially motivated attack

sfon'done nm fam blunder

sfor'mare vt pull out of shape ⟨tasche⟩

sfor'marsi vi lose its shape; ⟨persona⟩ lose one's figure

sfor'mato nm Culin flan

sfor'nito adj ∼ **di** ⟨negozio⟩ out of

sfor'tuna nf bad luck

sfortunata'mente adv unfortunately, unluckily

sfortu'nato adj unlucky

sfor'zare vt force

sfor'zarsi vr try hard

sfor'zato adj forced

'sforzo nm effort; (tensione) stress

'sfottere vt sl tease

sfracel'larsi vr smash; ∼ **al suolo** crash to the ground

sfrangi'ato adj fringed

sfrat'tare vt evict

'sfratto nm eviction

sfrecci'are vi flash past

sfrega'mento nm fricton, rubbing

sfre'gare vt rub

sfregi'are vt slash

sfregi'ato, -a ① adj scarred
② nmf scarface

'sfregio nm slash

sfre'narsi vr run wild

sfre'nato adj wild

sfrigo'lio nm crackling

sfron'dare vt prune

sfron'tato adj shameless, brazen

sfrutta'mento nm exploitation

sfrut'tare *vt* exploit; take advantage of, make the most of ‹*occasione*›

sfug'gente *adj* elusive; ‹*mento*› receding

sfug'gire ⓵ *vi* escape; ∼ **a** escape [from]; **mi sfugge** it escapes me; **mi è sfuggito [di mente]** it [completely] slipped my mind; **mi è sfuggito di mano** I lost hold of it; **lasciarsi** ∼ **un'occasione** let an opportunity slip; **mi è sfuggito un rutto** I just came out with a belch; **gli è sfuggito un colpo dal fucile** the rifle just went off in his hands ⓶ *vt* avoid

sfug'gita *nf* **di** ∼ in passing

sfu'mare ⓵ *vi* (svanire) vanish; ‹*colore*› shade off ⓶ *vt* soften ‹*colore*›

sfuma'tura *nf* shade

sfuri'ata *nf* outburst [of anger]

sga'bello *nm* stool

sgabuz'zino *nm* cupboard

sgam'bato *adj* ‹*costume da bagno*› high-cut

sgambet'tare *vi* kick one's legs; (camminare) trot

sgam'betto *nm* **fare lo** ∼ **a qualcuno** trip somebody up

sganasci'arsi *vr* ∼ **dalle risa** roar with laughter

sganci'are *vt* unhook; Rail uncouple; drop ‹*bombe*›; fam cough up ‹*denaro*›

sganci'arsi *vr* become unhooked; fig get away

sganghe'rato *adj* ramshackle

sgar'bato *adj* rude

'sgarbo *nm* discourtesy; **fare uno** ∼ **a qualcuno** be rude to somebody; **ricevere uno** ∼ be treated rudely

sgargi'ante *adj* garish

sgar'rare *vi* be wrong; (da regola) stray from the straight and narrow

'sgarro *nm* mistake, slip

sga'sato *adj* flat

sgattaio'lare *vi* sneak away; ∼ **via** decamp

sge'lare *vt/i* thaw

'sghembo *adj* slanting; **a** ∼ obliquely

sghiacci'are *vt* defrost; thaw out ‹*carne*›

sghignaz'zare *vi* laugh scornfully

sghiri'bizzo *nm* whim, fancy

sgob'bare *vi* slog; fam: ‹*studente*› swot

sgob'bone, -a *nmf* slogger; (fam: studente) swot

sgoccio'lare *vi* drip

sgoccio'lio *nm* dripping

sgo'larsi *vr* shout oneself hoarse

sgomb[e]'rare *vt* clear [out]

'sgombro ⓵ *adj* clear

⓶ *nm* (trasloco) removal; (pesce) mackerel

sgomen'tare *vt* dismay

sgomen'tarsi *vr* be dismayed

sgo'mento *nm* dismay

sgomi'nare *vt* defeat

sgom'mare *vi* make the tyres screech

sgom'mata *nf* screech of tyres

sgonfi'are *vt* deflate

sgonfi'arsi *vr* go down

'sgonfio *adj* flat

'sgorbio *nm* scrawl; (fig: vista sgradevole) sight

sgor'gare ⓵ *vi* gush [out] ⓶ *vt* flush out, unblock ‹*lavandino*›

sgoz'zare *vt* ∼ **qualcuno** cut somebody's throat

sgra'devole *adj* disagreeable

sgra'dito *adj* unwelcome

sgraffi'are *vt* scratch

'sgraffio *nm* scratch

sgrammaticata'mente *adv* ungrammatically

sgrammati'cato *adj* ungrammatical

sgra'nare *vt* shell ‹*piselli*›; open wide ‹*occhi*›

sgra'nato *adj* grainy; ‹*fagioli*› shelled; ‹*occhi*› wide-open

sgran'chire *vt* stretch

sgran'chirsi *vr* stretch

sgranocchi'are *vt* munch

sgras'sare *vt* remove the grease from

'sgravio *nm* relief. **sgravio fiscale** tax relief

sgrazi'ato *adj* ungainly

sgreto'lare *vt* crumble

sgreto'larsi *vr* crumble

sgri'dare *vt* scold

sgri'data *nf* scolding

sgron'dare *vt* drain

sgros'sare *vt* rough-hew ‹*marmo*›; fig polish

sguai'ato *adj* coarse

sgual'cire *vt* crumple

sgual'drina *nf* slut

sgu'ardo *nm* look; (breve) glance; **dare uno** ∼ **a** glance at ‹*giornale, testo*›. **sguardo di insieme** overview

sguar'nito *adj* unadorned; (privo di difesa) undefended

'sguattero, -a *nmf* skivvy

sguaz'zare *vi* splash; (nel fango) wallow

'sguincio *nm* sidelong glance

sguinzagli'are *vt* unleash

sgusci'are ⓵ *vt* shell ⓶ *vi* (sfuggire) slip away; ∼ **fuori** slip out

'shaker *nm inv* shaker

shake'rare *vt* shake

'shampoo nm inv shampoo; ∼ **e messa in piega** shampoo and set

'shopper nm inv carrier bag

'shuttle nm inv [space] shuttle

si¹ pers pron (riflessivo) oneself; (lui) himself; (lei) herself; (esso, essa) itself; (loro) themselves; (reciproco) each other; (tra più di due) one another; (impersonale) you, one fml; **lavarsi** wash [oneself]; **si è lavata** she washed [herself]; **lavarsi le mani** wash one's hands; **si è lavata le mani** she washed her hands; **si è mangiato un pollo intero** he ate an entire chicken by himself; **incontrarsi** meet each other; **la gente si aiuta a vicenda** people help one another; **si potrebbe pensare che ...** you might think that ..., one might think that ... fml; **non si sa mai** you never know, one never knows; **queste cose si dimenticano facilmente** these things are easily forgotten

si² nm Mus (chiave, nota) B

sì adv yes; **credo di sì** I believe so; **penso di sì** I think so; **ha detto di sì** she said yes; **sì?** really?; **sì che mi piace!** yes I do like it!

sia¹ ▶ ESSERE

sia² conj ∼... ∼... (entrambi) both... and...; (o l'uno o l'altro) either... or...; ∼ **che venga**, ∼ **che non venga** whether he comes or not; **voglio** ∼ **questo che quello** I want both this one and that one; **verranno** ∼ **Giuseppe** ∼ **Giacomo** both Giuseppe and Giacomo are coming

sia'mese adj Siamese

Si'beria nf Siberia

sibi'lare vi hiss

sibil'lino adj sibylline

'sibilo nm hiss

si'cario nm hired killer

sicché conj (perciò) so [that]; (allora) then

siccità nf drought

sic'come conj as

Si'cilia nf Sicily

sicili'ano, **-a** adj & nmf Sicilian

sico'moro nm sycamore

si'cura nf safety catch; (di portiera) childproof lock

sicura'mente adv definitely; ∼ **sarà arrivato** he must have arrived by now

sicu'rezza nf (certezza) certainty; (salvezza) safety; **di** ∼ ⟨dispositivo⟩ safety attrib; **di massima** ∼ top security. **uscita di sicurezza** emergency exit

si'curo ① adj (non pericoloso) safe; (certo) sure; ⟨saldo⟩ steady; Comm sound ② adv certainly ③ nm safety; **al** ∼ safe; **andare sul** ∼ play [it] safe; **di** ∼ definitely; **di** ∼ **sarà arrivato** he must have arrived; ∼! sure!

'sidecar nm inv sidecar

siderur'gia nf iron and steel industry

side'rurgico adj iron and steel attrib

'sidro nm cider

si'epe nf hedge

si'ero nm serum

sieronega'tivo, **-a** ① adj HIV negative ② nmf person who is HIV negative

sieroposi'tivo, **-a** ① adj HIV positive ② nmf person who is HIV positive

Si'erra Le'one nf Sierra Leone

si'esta nf afternoon nap, siesta; **fare la** ∼ have an afternoon nap

si'fone nm siphon

Sig. abbr (**signore**) Mr

Sig.a abbr (**signora**) Mrs, Ms

siga'retta nf cigarette; **pantaloni** pl a ∼ drainpipes

'sigaro nm cigar

Sigg. abbr (**signori**) Messrs

sigil'lare vt seal

si'gillo nm seal

'sigla nf acronym; (iniziali) initials pl. **sigla musicale** signature tune

si'glare vt initial

Sig.na abbr (**signorina**) Miss, Ms

signifi'care vt mean

significa'tivo adj significant

signifi'cato nm meaning

si'gnora nf lady; (davanti a nome proprio) Mrs; (non sposata) Miss; (in lettere ufficiali) Dear Madam; **la** ∼ **Rossi** Mrs Rossi; **il signor Vené e** ∼ **Vené** Mr and Mrs Vené

si'gnore nm gentleman; Relig lord; (davanti a nome proprio) Mr; **il signor Rossi** Mr Rossi

signo'rile adj gentlemanly; (di lusso) luxury

signo'rina nf young lady; (seguito da nome proprio) Miss; **la** ∼ **Rossi** Miss Rossi

silenzia'tore nm silencer

si'lenzio nm silence. **silenzio di tomba** deathly hush

silenzi'oso adj silent

'silfide nf sylph

silhou'ette nf inv silhouette, outline; **che** ∼! you're so slim!

si'licio nm **piastrina di silicio** silicon chip

sili'cone nm silicone

'sillaba nf syllable

silla'bario nm primer

sillaba'tore nm Comput hyphenation program

sillo'gismo nm syllogism

silu'rare vt torpedo

si'luro nm torpedo

simbi'osi nf symbiosis; **vivere in** ∼ need each other, have a symbiotic relationship

simboleggi'are vt symbolize

sim'bolico *adj* symbolic[al]

simbo'lismo *nm* symbolism

simbo'lista *nmf* symbolist

'simbolo *nm* symbol

similarità *nf inv* similarity

'simile ① *adj* similar; (tale) such; **è ∼ a...** it's like..., it's similar to..., **qualcosa di ∼** something similar
② *nm* (il prossimo) fellow human being, fellow man

simili'tudine *nf* Gram simile

simil'mente *adv* similarly

simil'pelle *nf* Leatherette®

simme'tria *nf* symmetry

sim'metrico *adj* symmetric[al]

simpa'tia *nf* liking; (compenetrazione) sympathy; **prendere qualcuno in ∼** take a liking to somebody; **provare ∼ per** like

sim'patico *adj* nice. **inchiostro simpatico** invisible ink

simpatiz'zante *nmf* well-wisher

simpatiz'zare *vt* **∼ con** take a liking to; **∼ per qualcosa/qualcuno** lean towards something/somebody

sim'posio *nm* symposium

simu'lare *vt* simulate; feign ⟨amicizia, interesse⟩

simula'tore *nm* simulator

simulazi'one *nf* simulation. **simulazione di reato** Jut making of false accusations

simul'tanea *nf* **in ∼** simultaneously

simul'taneo *adj* simultaneous

sina'goga *nf* synagogue

sincera'mente *adv* sincerely; (a dire il vero) honestly

since'rarsi *vr* make sure

sincerità *nf* sincerity

sin'cero *adj* sincere

'sincope *nf* syncopation; Med fainting fit

sincron'ia *nf* sync[h]

sincro'nismo *nm* synchronism

sincroniz'zare *vt* synchronize

sincroniz'zato *adj* synchronized; **essere ben ∼ con** be in sync[h] with

sincronizzazi'one *nf* synchronization

'sincrono *adj* synchronous

sinda'cabile *adj* arguable

sinda'cale *adj* [trade] union *attrib*, [labor] union Am

sindaca'lista *nmf* trade unionist, labor union member Am

sinda'care *vt* inspect

sinda'cato *nm* [trade] union, [labor] union Am; (associazione) syndicate. **sindacato di categoria** trade union

'sindaco *nm* mayor

'sindrome *nf* syndrome. **sindrome da colon irritabile** irritable bowel

syndrome. **sindrome di Down** Down's syndrome. **sindrome da edifici malsani** sick building syndrome. **sindrome premestruale** premenstrual syndrome, PMS. **sindrome respiratoria acuta severa** severe acute respiratory syndrome, SARS

sinfo'nia *nf* symphony

sin'fonico *adj* symphonic

Singa'pore *nf* Singapore

singhioz'zare *vi* (di pianto) sob

singhi'ozzo *nm* hiccup; (di pianto) sob; **avere il ∼** have the hiccups

'single *nmf inv* single

singo'lare ① *adj* singular; (strano) peculiar
② *nm* Gram singular

singolar'mente *adv* individually; (stranamente) peculiarly

'singolo ① *adj* single
② *nm* individual; Mus single; Tennis singles *pl*; **un ∼ di successo** a hit single

si'nistra *nf* left; **a ∼** on the left; **girare a ∼** turn to the left; **la seconda a ∼** the second on the left; **con la guida a ∼** ⟨auto⟩ with left-hand drive; **la ∼** Pol the left; **di ∼** Pol left wing

sini'strare *vt* injure; damage ⟨casa⟩

sini'strato *adj* injured; ⟨casa⟩ damaged

si'nistro ① *adj* left[-hand]; (avverso) sinister
② *nm* accident

sini'strorso, **-a** *nmf* pej leftie

'sino *prep* = FINO¹

si'nonimo ① *adj* synonymous
② *nm* synonym

sin'tassi *nf* syntax

sin'tattico *adj* syntactic[al]

'sintesi *nf* synthesis; (riassunto) summary

sin'tetico *adj* synthetic; (conciso) summary

sintetiz'zare *vt* summarize

sintetizza'tore *nm* synthesizer

sinto'matico *adj* symptomatic

'sintomo *nm* symptom

sinto'nia *nf* tuning; **in ∼** on the same wavelength; **in ∼ con** in harmony with, in tune with

sintonizza'tore *nm* tuner

sinu'oso *adj* ⟨strada⟩ winding

sinu'site *nf* sinusitis

sio'nismo *nm* Zionism

sio'nista *adj & nmf* Zionist

si'pario *nm* curtain

si'rena *nf* siren; (di nave) hooter

'Siria *nf* Syria

siri'ano, **-a** *adj & nmf* Syrian

si'ringa *nf* syringe

'sismico *adj* seismic

S

si'smografo *nm* seismograph
sismolo'gia *nf* seismology
si'stema *nm* system; non è ∼! that's no
way to behave!. **sistema di
amplificazione sonora** induction loop.
sistema di gestione banca dati
database management system, DBMS.
sistema immunitario immune system.
Sistema Monetario Europeo
European Monetary System. **sistema
nervoso** nervous system. **sistema
operativo** Comput operating system.
sistema solare solar system. **sistema
di vita** way of life
siste'mare *vt* (mettere) put; tidy up ‹*casa,
camera*›; (risolvere) sort out; (procurare lavoro
a) fix up with a job; (trovare alloggio a) find
accommodation for; (sposare) marry off;
(fam: punire) sort out
siste'marsi *vr* settle down; (trovare un
lavoro) find a job; (trovare alloggio) find
accommodation; (sposarsi) marry
sistematica'mente *adv*
systematically
siste'matico *adj* systematic
sistemazi'one *nf* arrangement; (di
questione) settlement; (lavoro) job; (alloggio)
accommodation; (matrimonio) marriage
siste'mista *nmf* Comput systems
engineer
'sistole *nf* systole
'sit-in *nm inv* sit-in
'sito *nm* site. **sito web** Comput web site
sitografia *nf* webliography
situ'are *vt* place
situazi'one *nf* situation; essere
all'altezza della ∼ be equal to the
situation, be up to the situation
'skai *nm* Leatherette®
'skateboard *nm inv* skateboard
sketch *nm inv* sketch
ski-'lift *nm inv* ski tow
'skipper *nmf inv* skipper
slab'brare *vt* stretch out of shape
‹*maglia, tasca*›
slab'brato *adj* ‹*maglia, tasca*› shapeless
slacci'are *vt* unfasten; unlace ‹*scarpe*›
'slalom *nm inv* slalom; a ∼ slalom *attrib*
slanci'arsi *vr* hurl oneself
slanci'ato *adj* slender
'slancio *nm* impetus; (impulso) impulse;
agire di ∼ act on impulse
sla'vato *adj* ‹*carnagione*› fair
'slavo *adj* Slav[onic]
sle'ale *adj* disloyal; concorrenza sleale
unfair competition
slealtà *nf* disloyalty
sle'gare *vt* untie
sle'garsi *vr* untie oneself
slip *nmpl* underpants

'slitta *nf* sledge; (trainata) sleigh
slitta'mento *nm* (di macchina) skid; (fig: di
riunione) postponement
slit'tare *vi* Auto skid; ‹*riunione*› be put off
slit'tata *nf* skid
slit'tino *nm* toboggan
'slogan *nm inv* slogan, rallying cry
slo'gare *vt* dislocate
slo'garsi *vr* ∼ una caviglia sprain one's
ankle
slo'gato *adj* sprained
sloga'tura *nf* sprain
sloggi'are ① *vt* dislodge
② *vi* move out
slot *nm* **slot di espansione** Comput
expansion slot
slot-ma'chine *nf inv* slot-machine
Slo'vacchia *nf* Slovakia
slo'vacco, -a *adj & nmf* Slovak
Slo'venia *nf* Slovenia
smacchi'are *vt* clean
smacchia'tore *nm* stain remover
'smacco *nm* humiliating defeat
smagli'ante *adj* dazzling
smagli'arsi *vr* ‹*calza*› ladder *Br*, run
smaglia'tura *nf* ladder *Br*, run
smagnetiz'zare *vt* demagnetize
smagnetiz'zatore *nm* demagnetizer
sma'grito *adj* thinner
smalizi'ato *adj* cunning
smal'tare *vt* enamel; glaze ‹*ceramica*›;
varnish ‹*unghie*›
smal'tato *adj* enamelled; ‹*ceramica*›
glazed; ‹*unghie*› varnished
smalta'tura *nf* enamelling; (di ceramica)
glazing
smalti'mento *nm* disposal; (di merce)
selling off; (di grassi) burning off.
smaltimento [dei] rifiuti waste
disposal
smal'tire *vt* burn off; (merce) sell off; fig
get through ‹*corrispondenza*›; ∼ la
sbornia sober up
'smalto *nm* enamel; (di ceramica) glaze;
(per le unghie) nail varnish, nail polish
smance'ria *nf* fare smancerie be
overpolite
smance'roso *adj* simpering
'smania *nf* fidgets *pl*; (desiderio) longing;
avere la ∼ di have a craving for
smani'are *vi* have the fidgets; ∼ per
long for
smani'oso *adj* restless
smantella'mento *nm* dismantling
smantel'lare *vt* dismantle
smarri'mento *nm* loss; (psicologico)
bewilderment
smar'rire *vt* lose; (temporaneamente) mislay

smar'rirsi *vr* get lost; (turbarsi) be bewildered

smar'rito *adj* lost; ⟨sguardo⟩ bewildered, lost

smasche'rare *vt* unmask

smasche'rarsi *vr* fig reveal oneself

SME *nm abbr* (**Sistema Monetario Europeo**) EMS

smem'brare *vt* dismember

smemo'rato, -a ① *adj* forgetful ② *nmf* scatterbrain

smen'tire *vt* deny

smen'tita *nf* denial

sme'raldo *nm & adj inv* emerald

smerci'are *vt* sell off

'smercio *nm* sale

smerigli'ato *adj* emery. **vetro smerigliato** frosted glass

sme'riglio *nm* emery

smer'lare *vt* scallop

'smerlo *nm* scallop

'smesso ① pp di SMETTERE ② *adj* ⟨abiti⟩ cast-off

'smettere *vt* stop; stop wearing ⟨abiti⟩; **smettila!** stop it!

smidol'lato *adj* spineless

smilitariz'zare *vt* demilitarize

'smilzo *adj* thin

sminu'ire *vt* diminish

sminu'irsi *vr* fig belittle oneself

sminuz'zare *vt* crumble; (fig: analizzare) analyse in detail

smista'mento *nm* clearing; (postale) sorting; **stazione di ∼** shunting yard, marshalling yard. **smistamento rifiuti** sorting of waste

smi'stare *vt* sort; Mil post; Rail marshall

smisu'rato *adj* boundless; (esorbitante) excessive

smitiz'zare *vt* demythologize

smobili'tare *vt* demobilize

smobilitazi'one *nf* demobilization

smo'dato *adj* immoderate

smog *nm* smog

'smoking *nm inv* dinner jacket, tuxedo Am

smon'tabile *adj* jointed

smon'taggio *nm* disassembly

smon'tare ① *vt* take to pieces; (scoraggiare) dishearten; take down ⟨tenda⟩ ② *vi* (da veicolo) get off; (da cavallo) dismount; (dal servizio) go off duty

smon'tarsi *vr* lose heart

'smorfia *nf* grimace; (moina) simper; **fare smorfie** make faces

smorfi'oso *adj* affected

'smorto *adj* pale; ⟨colore⟩ dull

smor'zare *vt* dim ⟨luce⟩; tone down ⟨colori⟩; deaden ⟨suoni⟩; quench ⟨sete⟩

smor'zata *nf* Sport drop shot

'smosso pp di SMUOVERE

smotta'mento *nm* landslide

SMS *nm abbr* SMS message, text message; **mandare un ∼ a qualcuno** text somebody

'smunto *adj* emaciated

smu'overe *vt* shift; (commuovere) move

smu'oversi *vr* move; (commuoversi) be moved

smus'sare *vt* round off; (fig: attenuare) tone down

smus'sarsi *vr* go blunt

smussa'tura *nf* bevel

snack bar *nm inv* snack bar

snatu'rato *adj* inhuman

snazionaliz'zare *vt* denationalize

S.N.C. *abbr* **società in nome collettivo**

snel'lire *vt* slim down

snel'lirsi *vr* slim [down]

'snello *adj* slim

sner'vante *adj* enervating

sner'vare *vt* enervate

sner'varsi *vr* get exhausted

sni'dare *vt* drive out

snif'fare *vt* snort

snob'bare *vt* snub

sno'bismo *nm* snobbery

snoccio'lare *vt* stone; fig blurt out

snoccio'lato *adj* ⟨olive⟩ pitted, with the stones removed

sno'dabile *adj* jointed

sno'dare *vt* untie; (sciogliere) loosen

sno'darsi *vr* come untied; ⟨strada⟩ wind

sno'dato *adj* ⟨persona⟩ double-jointed; ⟨dita⟩ flexible

'snodo *nm* coupling. **snodo ferroviario** coupling

'snowboard *nm inv* snowboard; **fare ∼** snowboard

SO *abbr* (**sud-ovest**) SW

soap 'opera *nf inv* soap [opera]

so'ave *adj* gentle

sobbal'zare *vi* jerk; (trasalire) start

sob'balzo *nm* jerk; (trasalimento) start

sobbar'carsi *vr* ∼ **a** undertake

sobbol'lire *vi* simmer

sob'borgo *nm* suburb

sobil'lare *vt* stir up

sobilla|'tore, -trice *nm* instigator

sobrietà *nf* sobriety

'sobrio *adj* sober

soc'chiudere *vt* half-close

socchi'uso ① pp di SOCCHIUDERE

2 *adj* ‹occhi› half-closed; ‹porta› ajar

soc'combere *vi* succumb

soc'correre *vt* assist

soccorri'tore, -trice *nmf* rescue worker

soc'corso **1** pp di SOCCORRERE **2** *nm* assistance, help; **venire in ~** come to help, come to the rescue; **venire in ~ a qualcuno** come to somebody's rescue; **soccorsi** *pl* help; (persone) rescuers; (dopo disastro) relief workers. **soccorso alpino** mountain rescue. **soccorso disastri** disaster relief. **soccorso stradale** breakdown service, wrecking service Am

socialdemo'cratico, -a **1** *adj* Social Democratic **2** *nmf* Social Democrat

socialdemocra'zia *nf* Social Democracy

soci'ale *adj* social

socia'lismo *nm* Socialism

socia'lista *adj & nmf* Socialist

socializ'zare *vi* socialize

società *nf inv* society; Comm company. **società in accomandita semplice** limited partnership. **società per azioni** public limited company, plc. **società dei consumi** consumer society. **società in nome collettivo** commercial partnership. **società fiduciaria** trust company. **società a responsabilità limitata** limited liability company. **società di telecomunicazioni** communications company

soci'evole *adj* sociable

'socio, -a *nmf* member; Comm partner

socioeco'nomico *adj* socio-economic

sociolo'gia *nf* sociology

socio'logico *adj* sociological

soci'ologo, -a *nmf* sociologist

'soda *nf* soda. **soda da bucato** washing soda

soda'lizio *nm* association, society

soddisfa'cente *adj* satisfactory

soddi'sfare *vt/i* satisfy; meet ‹richiesta›; make amends for ‹offesa›

soddi'sfatto **1** pp di SODDISFARE **2** *adj* satisfied

soddisfazi'one *nf* satisfaction

'sodo **1** *adj* hard; fig firm; ‹uovo› hard-boiled **2** *adv* hard; **dormire ~** sleep soundly **3** *nm* **venire al ~** get to the point

sofà *nm inv* sofa

soffe'rente *adj* (malato) ill

soffe'renza *nf* suffering

soffer'marsi *vr* pause; **~ su** dwell on

sof'ferto pp di SOFFRIRE

soffi'are **1** *vt* blow; reveal ‹segreto›; (rubare) pinch fam **2** *vi* blow

soffi'ata *nf* **datti una ~ al naso** blow your nose; **fare una ~ a qualcuno** fig sl tip somebody off, give somebody a tip-off

'soffice *adj* soft

soffi'etto *nm* bellows; **a ~** ‹borsa› expanding. **soffietto editoriale** blurb

'soffio *nm* puff; Med murmur

sof'fitta *nf* attic

sof'fitto *nm* ceiling

soffoca'mento *nm* suffocation

soffo'cante *adj* suffocating

soffo'care *vt/i* choke; fig stifle

sof'friggere *vt* fry lightly

sof'frire *vt/i* suffer; (sopportare) bear; **~ di** suffer from; **~ di [mal di] cuore** suffer from or have a heart condition; **~ la fame/il freddo** be hungry/cold

sof'fritto **1** pp di SOFFRIGGERE **2** *nm* fried ingredients *pl*

sof'fuso *adj* ‹luce› soft, suffused

sofisti'care **1** *vt* (adulterare) adulterate **2** *vi* (sottilizzare) quibble

sofisti'cato *adj* sophisticated

soft *adj inv* soft

'softcopy *nf* Comput soft copy

'soft-core **1** *nm* soft-core, soft porn **2** *adj inv* **pornografia soft-core** soft porn

'software *nm inv* software; **dei ~** software packages. **software di accesso** access software. **software applicativo** application software. **software di autoapprendimento** tutorial package, tutorial software. **software di comunicazione** communications software, comms software. **software didattico** educational software. **software di gestione errori** error correction software. **software di OCR** OCR software. **software di sistema** system software

softwa'rista *nmf* Comput software engineer

soggettiva'mente *adv* subjectively

sogget'tivo *adj* subjective

sog'getto **1** *nm* subject; **cattivo ~** bad sort **2** *adj* subject; **essere ~ a** be subject to

soggezi'one *nf* subjection; (rispetto) awe

sogghi'gnare *vi* sneer

sog'ghigno *nm* sneer

soggio'gare *vt* subdue

soggior'nare *vi* stay

soggi'orno *nm* stay; (stanza) living room. **permesso di soggiorno** residence permit

soggi'ungere *vt* add

'soglia *nf* threshold; **alle soglie di qualcosa** on the threshold of something. **soglia del dolore** pain threshold. **soglia di povertà** poverty line

'sogliola *nf* sole. **sogliola limanda** lemon sole

so'gnare *vt/i* dream; ∼ **a occhi aperti** daydream

so'gnarsi *vr* dream; **non te lo sogni neppure!** forget it!, don't even think of it!

sogna'tore, -trice *nmf* dreamer

'sogno *nm* dream; **fare un** ∼ have a dream; **neanche per** ∼**!** not on your life!; **essere un** ∼ (bellissimo) be a dream; **una casa da** ∼ a dream house; **il mio** ∼ **nel cassetto** my secret dream

'soia *nf* soya

sol *nm* Mus (chiave, nota) G

so'laio *nm* attic

sola'mente *adv* only

so'lare *adj* ⟨energia, raggi⟩ solar; ⟨crema⟩ sun *attrib*

so'larium *nm inv* solarium

sol'care *vt* plough

'solco *nm* furrow; (di ruota) track; (di nave) wake; (di disco) groove

solda'tessa *nf* servicewoman

sol'dato *nm* soldier. **soldato semplice** private

'soldo *nm* **non ha un** ∼ he hasn't got a penny to his name; **senza un** ∼ penniless; **al** ∼ **di** in the pay of; **soldi** *pl* (denaro) money *sg*; **fare [i] soldi** make money; **prelevare dei soldi** withdraw money; **da quattro soldi** cheapo, nickel-and-dime Am

'sole *nm* sun; (luce del sole) sun[light]; **al** ∼ in the sun; **prendere il** ∼ sunbathe

sole'cismo *nm* solecism

soleggi'ato *adj* sunny

so'lenne *adj* solemn

solen'nità *nf* solemnity

so'lere *vi* be in the habit of; **come si suol dire** as they say

so'letta *nf* insole

sol'fato *nm* sulphate

sol'feggio *nm* sol-fa

'solfuro *nm* sulphur

soli'dale *adj* in agreement

solidarietà *nf* solidarity

solidifi'care *vt/i* solidify

solidifi'carsi *vr* solidify

solidità *nf* solidity; (di colori) fastness

'solido ① *adj* solid; (robusto) sturdy; ⟨colore⟩ fast; **in** ∼ Jur jointly and severally ② *nm* solid

soli'loquio *nm* soliloquy

so'lista ① *adj* solo ② *nmf* soloist

solita'mente *adv* usually

soli'tario ① *adj* solitary; (isolato) lonely ② *nm* (brillante) solitaire; (gioco di carte) patience, solitaire

'solito ① *adj* usual; **essere** ∼ **fare qualcosa** be in the habit of doing something ② *nm* the usual; **di** ∼ usually

soli'tudine *nf* solitude

solleci'tare *vt* speed up; urge ⟨persona⟩

sollecitazi'one *nf* (richiesta) request; (preghiera) entreaty

sol'lecito ① *adj* prompt ② *nm* reminder

solleci'tudine *nf* promptness; (interessamento) concern; **con la massima** ∼ Comm as soon as possible

solle'one *nm* noonday sun; (periodo) dog days of summer

solleti'care *vt* tickle

sol'letico *nm* tickling; **fare il** ∼ **a qualcuno** tickle somebody; **soffrire il** ∼ be ticklish

solleva'mento *nm* **sollevamento pesi** weightlifting

solle'vare *vt* lift; (elevare) raise; (confortare) comfort; ∼ **una questione** raise a question; ∼ **qualcuno da un incarico** relieve somebody of a responsibility

solle'varsi *vr* rise; (riaversi) recover

solle'vato *adj* relieved

solli'evo *nm* relief; **che** ∼**!** what a relief!

'solo, -a ① *adj* alone; (isolato) lonely; (unico) only; Mus solo; **da** ∼ by myself/yourself/himself etc ② *nmf* **il** ∼**, la sola** the only one ③ *nm* Mus solo ④ *adv* only; ∼ **il sabato/la domenica** Saturdays/Sundays only, only on Saturdays/Sundays

sol'stizio *nm* solstice

sol'tanto *adv* only

so'lubile *adj* soluble; ⟨caffè⟩ instant

soluzi'one *nf* solution; Comm payment; **senza** ∼ **di continuità** without interruption; **in unica** ∼ Comm as a lump sum. **soluzione salina per lenti** soaking solution

sol'vente ① *nm* solvent. **solvente per lo smalto** nail varnish remover. **solvente per unghie** nail polish remover ② *adj* solvent. **reparto solvente** pay ward

solvi'bilità *nf* Fin solvency

'soma *nf* load. **bestia da soma** beast of burden

'somalo, -a *adj* & *nmf* Somali

so'maro *nm* ass, donkey; Sch dunce

so'matico *adj* somatic; **tratti somatici** physical features

S

somatiz'zare *vt* react psychosomatically to

som'brero *nm* sombrero

somigli'ante *adj* similar

somigli'anza *nf* resemblance

somigli'are *vi* ~ **a** look like, resemble

somigli'arsi *vr* be alike; **chi si somiglia si piglia** birds of a feather flock together

'somma *nf* sum; Math addition

som'mare *vt* add; (totalizzare) add up

sommaria'mente *adv* summarily

som'mario *adj & nm* summary

som'mato *adj* **tutto** ~ all things considered

somme'lier *nm inv* wine waiter

som'mergere *vt* submerge

sommer'gibile *nm* submarine

som'merso ① *pp di* SOMMERGERE ② *nm* Econ black economy

som'messo *adj* soft

sommini'strare *vt* administer

somministrazi'one *nf* administration; ~ **per via orale** to be taken orally

sommità *nf inv* summit

'sommo ① *adj* highest; fig supreme ② *nm* summit

som'mossa *nf* rising

sommozza'tore *nm* frogman

so'naglio *nm* bell

'sonar *nm inv* sonar

so'nata *nf* sonata; fig fam beating

'sonda *nf* Mech drill; (spaziale, Med) probe

son'daggio *nm* drilling; (spaziale, Med) probe; (indagine) survey. **sondaggio d'opinione** opinion poll

son'dare *vt* sound; (investigare) probe

so'netto *nm* sonnet

sonnambu'lismo *nm* sleepwalking

son'nambulo, -a *nmf* sleepwalker

sonnecchi'are *vi* doze

son'nifero *nm* sleeping-pill

'sonno *nm* sleep; **aver** ~ be sleepy; **morire di** ~ be dead tired, be dead on one's feet; **morto di** ~ (fam: stupido) zombie; **perdere il** ~ anche fig lose sleep. **sonno eterno** Relig eternal rest

sonno'lenza *nf* sleepiness

'sono ▸ ESSERE

sonoriz'zare *vt* add a soundtrack to

so'noro ① *adj* resonant; (rumoroso) loud; ⟨onde, scheda⟩ sound *attrib* ② *nm* (Tech: di film) soundtrack

sontu'oso *adj* sumptuous

sopo'rifero *adj* soporific

sop'palco *nm* platform. **soppalco abitabile** loft conversion

soppe'rire *vi* ~ **a qualcosa** provide for something

soppe'sare *vt* weigh up ⟨situazione⟩

soppi'atto: **di** ~ *adv* furtively

soppor'tare *vt* support; (tollerare) stand; bear ⟨dolore⟩

sopportazi'one *nf* patience

soppressi'one *nf* removal; (di legge) abolition; (di diritti, pubblicazione) suppression; (annullamento) cancellation

sop'presso *pp di* SOPPRIMERE

sop'primere *vt* get rid of; abolish ⟨legge⟩; suppress ⟨diritti, pubblicazione⟩; (annullare) cancel

'sopra ① *adv* on top; (più in alto) higher [up]; (al piano superiore) upstairs; (in testo) above; **mettilo lì** ~ put it up there; **di** ~ upstairs; **dormirci** ~ fig sleep on it; **pensarci** ~ think about it; **vedi** ~ see above
② *prep* [a] on; (senza contatto, oltre) over; (riguardo a) about; **è** ~ **al tavolo, è** ~ **il tavolo** it's on the table; **il quadro è appeso** ~ **al camino** the picture is hanging over the fireplace; **il ponte passa** ~ **all'autostrada** the bridge crosses over the motorway; **è caduto** ~ **il tetto** it fell on the roof; **l'uno** ~ **l'altro** on top of the other; (senza contatto) one above the other; **abita** ~ **di me** he lives upstairs from me; **i bambini** ~ **i dieci anni** children over ten; **20°** ~ **lo zero** 20 above zero; ~ **il livello del mare** above sea level; **rifletti** ~ **quello che è successo** think about what happened; **prendere** ~ **di sé la responsabilità di qualcosa** assume responsibility for something; **scaricare la colpa** ~ **qualcuno** put the blame on somebody; **non ha nessuno** ~ **di sé** he has nobody above him; **al di** ~ **di** over; **al di** ~ **di ogni sospetto** beyond suspicion
③ *nm* **il [di]** ~ the top

so'prabito *nm* overcoat

soprac'ciglio *nm* (pl nf **sopracciglia**) eyebrow

sopracco'perta *nf* (di letto) bedspread

sopraccoper'tina *nf* book jacket, dust jacket

soprad'detto *adj* above-mentioned

sopraele'vare *vt* raise

sopraele'vata *nf* elevated railway

sopraele'vato *adj* raised

sopraf'fare *vt* overwhelm

sopraf'fatto *pp di* SOPRAFFARE

sopraffazi'one *nf* abuse of power

sopraf'fino *adj* excellent; ⟨gusto, udito⟩ highly refined

sopraggi'ungere *vi* ⟨persona⟩ turn up; (accadere) happen; **è sopraggiunta la pioggia** and then it started to rain

soprallu'ogo *nm* inspection

sopram'mobile *nm* ornament

soprannatu'rale *adj & nm* supernatural

sopran'nome *nm* nickname

soprannomi'nare *vt* nickname

sopran'numero *adv* sono in ∼ there are too many of them; **ce ne sono 15 in** ∼ there are 15 too many of them, there are 15 of them too many

so'prano *nm* or *nf inv* soprano

soprappensi'ero *adv* lost in thought

sopras'salto *nm* di ∼ with a start

soprasse'dere *vi* ∼ a postpone

soprat'tassa *nf* surtax. **soprattassa postale** excess postage

soprat'tetto *nm* fly sheet

soprat'tutto *adv* above all

sopravvalu'tare *vt* overvalue; overestimate ⟨forze⟩

sopravvalutazi'one *nf* overvaluation; (di forze) overestimation

sopravve'nire *vi* turn up; (accadere) happen

soprav'vento *nm* fig upper hand; **prendere il** ∼ take the upper hand

sopravvis'suto, -a ① pp di SOPRAVVIVERE
② *adj* surviving
③ *nmf* survivor

sopravvi'venza *nf* survival

soprav'vivere *vi* survive; ∼ a outlive ⟨persona⟩

soprinten'dente *nmf* supervisor; (di museo ecc) keeper

soprinten'denza *nf* supervision; (ente) board

so'pruso *nm* abuse of power

soq'quadro *nm* mettere a ∼ turn upside down

sor'betto *nm* sorbet

sor'bire *vt* sip; fig put up with

'sorcio *nm* mouse; **far vedere i sorci verdi a qualcuno** give somebody a rough time

'sordido *adj* sordid; (avaro) stingy

sor'dina *nf* mute; **in** ∼ fig on the quiet

sordità *nf* deafness

'sordo, -a ① *adj* deaf; ⟨rumore, dolore⟩ dull
② *nmf* deaf person

sordo'muto, -a ① *adj* deaf-and-dumb, deaf without speech
② *nmf* deaf mute

so'rella *nf* sister. **sorella gemella** twin sister

sorel'lastra *nf* stepsister, half-sister

sor'gente *nf* spring; (fonte) source. **programma sorgente** Comput source program

'sorgere *vi* rise; fig arise

sormon'tare *vt* surmount

sorni'one *adj* sly

sorpas'sare *vt* surpass; (eccedere) exceed; overtake, pass Am ⟨veicolo⟩

sorpas'sato *adj* old-fashioned

sor'passo *nm* overtaking, passing Am

sorpren'dente *adj* surprising; (straordinario) remarkable

sorprendente'mente *adv* surprisingly

sor'prendere *vt* surprise; (cogliere in flagrante) catch

sor'prendersi *vr* be surprised; ∼ a fare qualcosa catch oneself doing something; **non c'è da** ∼ it's hardly surprising

sor'presa *nf* surprise; di ∼ by surprise; **provare** ∼ feel surprised

sor'preso pp di SORPRENDERE

sor'reggere *vt* support; (tenere) hold up

sor'reggersi *vr* support oneself

sor'retto pp di SORREGGERE

sorri'dente *adj* smiling

sor'ridere *vi* smile; **la fortuna mi ha sorriso** fortune smiled on me

sor'riso ① pp di SORRIDERE
② *nm* smile

sorseggi'are *vt* sip

'sorso *nm* sip; (piccola quantità) drop

'sorta *nf* sort; di ∼ whatever; ogni ∼ di all sorts of

'sorte *nf* fate; (caso imprevisto) chance; **tirare a** ∼ draw lots; **per buona** ∼ liter by good fortune

sorteggi'are *vt* draw lots for

sor'teggio *nm* draw

sorti'legio *nm* witchcraft

sor'tire ① *vi* come out
② *vt* bring about ⟨effetto⟩

sor'tita *nf* Mil sortie; (battuta) witticism

'sorto pp di SORGERE

sorvegli'ante *nmf* keeper; (controllore) overseer

sorvegli'anza *nf* watch; Mil ecc surveillance. **sorveglianza tramite braccialetto elettronico** electronic tagging

sorvegli'are *vt* watch over; (controllare) oversee; ⟨polizia⟩ watch, keep under surveillance

sorvegli'ato, -a ① *adj* under surveillance
② *nmf* **sorvegliato speciale** person kept under special surveillance

sorvo'lare *vt* fly over; fig skip

SOS *nm inv* SOS

'sosia *nm inv* double

so'spendere *vt* hang; (interrompere) stop; (privare di una carica) suspend

sospensi'one *nf* suspension. **sospensione condizionale [della pena]** suspended sentence

sospen'sorio *nm* Sport jockstrap

so'speso ① pp di SOSPENDERE
② adj ⟨impiegato, alunno⟩ suspended; ~ a hanging from; ~ **a un filo** fig hanging by a thread
③ nm **in** ~ pending; (emozionato) in suspense

sospet'tare vt suspect

so'spetto ① adj suspicious
② nm suspicion; (persona) suspect; **al di sopra di ogni** ~ above suspicion

sospet'toso adj suspicious

so'spingere vt drive

so'spinto pp di SOSPINGERE

sospi'rare ① vi sigh
② vt long for

so'spiro nm sigh

'sosta nf stop, stop-off; (pausa) pause; **senza** ~ nonstop; '~ **autorizzata ...'** 'parking permitted for ...'. **'divieto di sosta'** 'no parking'

sostan'tivo nm noun

so'stanza nf substance; **sostanze** pl (patrimonio) property sg; **in** ~ to sum up; **la** ~ **della questione** the nub of the matter

sostanzi'oso adj substantial; ⟨cibo⟩ nourishing; **poco** ~ insubstantial

so'stare vi stop; (fare una pausa) pause

so'stegno nm support. **sostegno morale** moral support

soste'nere vt support; (sopportare) bear; (resistere) withstand; (affermare) maintain; (nutrire) sustain; sit ⟨esame⟩; ~ **le spese** meet the costs; ~ **delle spese** incur expenditure; ~ **una carica** hold a position; ~ **una parte** play a role

soste'nersi vr support oneself

soste'nibile adj ⟨sviluppo, crescita⟩ sustainable

sosteni|'tore, -trice nmf supporter

sostenta'mento nm maintenance

soste'nuto ① adj ⟨stile⟩ formal; ⟨velocità⟩ high; ⟨mercato, prezzi⟩ steady
② nm **fare il** ~ be stand-offish

sostitu'ire vt substitute (**a** for), replace (**con** with)

sostitu'irsi vr ~ **a** replace

sosti'tuto, -a ① nmf replacement, stand-in
② nm (surrogato) substitute.

sostituzi'one nf substitution

sotta'ceto adj pickled; **sottaceti** pl pickles

sot'tacqua adv underwater

sot'tana nf petticoat; (di prete) cassock

sotter'fugio nm subterfuge; **di** ~ secretly

sotter'raneo ① adj underground
② nm cellar

sotter'rare vt bury

sottigli'ezza nf slimness; fig subtlety

sot'tile adj thin; ⟨udito, odorato⟩ keen; ⟨osservazione, distinzione⟩ subtle

sotti'letta® nf cheese slice

sottiliz'zare vi split hairs

sottin'tendere vt imply

sottin'teso ① pp di SOTTINTENDERE
② nm allusion; **senza sottintesi** openly
③ adj implied

'sotto ① adv below; (più in basso) lower [down]; (al di sotto) underneath; (al piano di sotto) downstairs; **è lì** ~ it's underneath; ~ ~ deep down; (di nascosto) on the quiet; **di** ~ downstairs; **mettersi** ~ fig get down to it; **mettere** ~ (fam: investire) knock down; **fatti** ~! fam get stuck in!
② prep ~ **[a]** under; (al di sotto di) under[neath]; **il fiume passa** ~ **un ponte** the river passes under[neath] a bridge; **è** ~ **il tavolo, è** ~ **al tavolo** it's under[neath] the table; **abita** ~ **di me** he lives downstairs from me; **i bambini** ~ **i dieci anni** children under ten; **20°** ~ **zero** 20 below zero; ~ **il livello del mare** below sea level; ~ **la pioggia** in the rain; ~ **Elisabetta I** under Elizabeth I; ~ **calmante** under sedation; ~ **chiave** under lock and key; ~ **condizione che ...** on condition that ...; ~ **giuramento** under oath; ~ **sorveglianza** under surveillance; ~ **Natale/gli esami** around Christmas/exam time; **al di** ~ **di** under; **andare** ~ **i 50 all'ora** do less than 50km an hour
③ nm **il [di]** ~ the bottom

sotto'banco adv ⟨vendere, comprare⟩ under the counter

sottobicchi'ere nm coaster

sotto'bosco nm undergrowth

sotto'braccio adv arm in arm

sottoccu'pato adj underemployed

sottochi'ave adv under lock and key

sotto'costo adj & adv at less than cost price

sottodi'rectory nf inv Comput subdirectory

sottoe'sporre vt underexpose

sotto'fondo nm background

sotto'gamba adv **prendere qualcosa** ~ take something lightly

sotto'gonna nf underskirt

sottoindi'cato adj undermentioned

sottoinsi'eme nm Math subset

sottoline'are vt underline; fig underline ⟨importanza⟩; emphasize ⟨forma degli occhi ecc⟩

sot'tolio adv in oil

sotto'mano adv within reach

sottoma'rino adj & nm submarine

sotto'messo ① pp di SOTTOMETTERE
② adj (remissivo) submissive

sotto'mettere vt submit; subdue ⟨popolo⟩

sotto'mettersi vr submit

sottomissi'one nf submission

sottopa'gare vt underpay

sottopas'saggio nm underpass; (pedonale) subway

sottopi'atto nm place mat, table mat

sotto'porre vt submit; (costringere) subject

sotto'porsi vr submit oneself; ∼ a undergo

sotto'posto pp di SOTTOPORRE

sottoproletari'ato nm underclass

sotto'scala nm cupboard under the stairs

sotto'scritto ① pp di SOTTOSCRIVERE ② nm undersigned

sotto'scrivere vt sign; (approvare) sanction, subscribe to

sottoscrizi'one nf (petizione) petition; (approvazione) sanction; (raccolta di denaro) appeal

sottosegre'tario nm undersecretary

sotto'sopra adv upside-down

sotto'stante adj la strada ∼ the road below

sottosu'olo nm subsoil

sottosvilup'pato adj underdeveloped

sottosvi'luppo nm underdevelopment

sottote'nente nm second lieutenant; Naut sub-lieutenant

sotto'terra adv underground

sottotito'lato adj subtitled

sotto'titolo nm (di film, programma) subtitle; (in libro, giornale) subheading

sottovalu'tare vt underestimate

sotto'vento adv downwind

sotto'veste nf slip

sotto'voce adv in a low voice

sottovu'oto adj vacuum-packed

sotto'zero adj inv subzero

sot'trarre vt remove; embezzle (fondi); Math subtract

sot'trarsi vr ∼ a escape from; avoid (responsabilità)

sot'tratto pp di SOTTRARRE

sottrazi'one nf removal; (di fondi) embezzlement; Math subtraction

sottuffici'ale nm non-commissioned officer; Naut petty officer

sou'brette nf inv showgirl

souf'flé nm inv soufflé

souve'nir nm inv souvenir. **negozio di souvenir** souvenir shop

so'vente adv liter often

soverchie'ria nf bullying; **fare soverchierie a** bully

so'vietico, -a adj & nmf Soviet

sovrabbon'danza nf overabundance

sovraccari'care vt overload

sovrac'carico ① adj overloaded (di with) ② nm overload

sovraffati'carsi vr overexert oneself

sovraffolla'mento nm overcrowding

sovralimen'tare vt overfeed

sovrannatu'rale adj & nm = SOPRANNATURALE

sovrannazio'nale adj supranational

so'vrano, -a ① adj sovereign; fig supreme ② nmf sovereign

sovrappopo'lato adj overpopulated

sovrap'porre vt superimpose

sovrap'porsi vr overlap

sovrapposizi'one nf superimposition

sovrapro'fitto nm excess profits

sovra'stare vt dominate; fig: (pericolo) hang over

sovrastrut'tura nf superstructre

sovratensi'one nf Electr overload, overvoltage

sovrecci'tarsi vr get overexcited

sovrecci'tato adj overexcited

sovresposizi'one nf Phot overexposure

sovrimpressi'one nf Phot double exposure

sovrinten'dente, sovrintendenza = SOPRINTENDENTE, SOPRINTENDENZA

sovru'mano adj superhuman

sovvenzio'nare vt subsidize

sovvenzio'nato ① pp di SOVVENZIONARE ② adj subsidized; ∼ **dallo Stato** state-funded

sovvenzi'one nf subsidy

sovver'sivo, -a adj & nmf subversive

sovver'tire vt subvert

'sozzo adj filthy

SP nf abbr (**strada provinciale**) secondary road

S.p.A. abbr (**società per azioni**) plc

spac'care vt split; chop (legna); ∼ **il minuto** keep perfect time; ∼ **il muso a qualcuno** sl smash somebody's face in; **o la va o la spacca** it's all or nothing; **un sole che spacca le pietre** a sun hot enough to fry an egg

spac'carsi vr split

spacca'tura nf split

spacci'are vt deal in, push (droga); ∼ **qualcosa per qualcosa** pass something off as something; **essere spacciato** be done for, be a goner

spacci'arsi vr ∼ **per** pass oneself off as

spaccia|'tore, -trice nmf (di droga) dealer, pusher; (di denaro falso) distributor

'spaccio nm (di droga) dealing; (negozio) shop

'**spacco** *nm* split

spacco'nate *nfpl* blustering

spac'cone, -a *nmf* boaster

'**spada** *nf* sword

spadac'cino *nm* swordsman

spadroneggi'are *vi* act the boss

spae'sato *adj* disorientated

spa'ghetti *nmpl* spaghetti *sg*. **spaghetti in bianco** spaghetti with butter, oil and cheese. **spaghetti alla carbonara** spaghetti with egg, cheese and diced bacon. **spaghetti al sugo** spaghetti with a sauce

spa'ghetto *nm* (fam: spavento) fright

'**Spagna** *nf* Spain

spagno'letta *nf* spool

spa'gnolo, -a ① *adj* Spanish ② *nmf* Spaniard ③ *nm* (lingua) Spanish

'**spago** *nm* string; (fam: spavento) fright; **dare ~ a qualcuno** encourage somebody

spai'ato *adj* odd

spalan'care *vt* open wide

spalan'carsi *vr* open wide

spalan'cato *adj* wide open

spa'lare *vt* shovel

'**spalla** *nf* shoulder; (di comico) straight man; **spalle** *pl* (schiena) back; **alzata di spalle** shrug [of the shoulders]; **alle spalle di** behind; **alle spalle di qualcuno** ⟨ridere⟩ behind somebody's back; **avere qualcuno/ qualcosa alle spalle** have somebody/ something behind one; **di ~** ⟨violino ecc⟩ second; **vivere alle spalle di qualcuno** live off somebody; **con le spalle al muro** anche fig with one's back to the wall; **voltare le spalle** turn one's back

spal'lata *nf* push with the shoulder; (alzata di spalle) shrug [of the shoulders]

spalleggi'are *vt* back up

spal'letta *nf* parapet

spalli'era *nf* back; (di letto) headboard; (ginnastica) wall bars *pl*

spal'lina *nf* strap; (imbottitura) shoulder pad; **senza spalline** strapless

spal'mare *vt* spread

spal'marsi *vr* cover oneself

spa'nato *adj* ⟨vite⟩ threadless

spanci'ata *nf* belly flop

'**spandere** *vt* spread; (versare) spill; **spendere e ~** spend and spend

'**spandersi** *vr* spread

spandighi'aia *nm inv* gritter

'**spaniel** *nm inv* spaniel

spappo'lare *vt* crush

spa'rare *vt/i* shoot; **spararle grosse** talk big; **~ fandonie** talk nonsense

spa'rarsi *vr* shoot oneself; **si è sparato un colpo alla tempia** he shot himself in the temple

spa'rata *nf* fam tall story

spa'rato *nm* (della camicia) dicky

spara'toria *nf* shooting. **sparatoria da auto in corsa** drive-by shooting

sparecchi'are *vt* clear

spa'reggio *nm* Comm deficit; Sport play-off

'**spargere** *vt* scatter; (diffondere) spread; shed ⟨lacrime, sangue⟩

'**spargersi** *vr* spread

spargi'mento *nm* scattering; (di lacrime, sangue) shedding. **spargimento di sangue** bloodshed

spa'rire *vi* disappear; **sparisci!** get lost!, scram!

sparizi'one *nf* disappearance

spar'lare *vi* **~ di** run down

'**sparo** *nm* shot. **sparo d'avvertimento** warning shot

sparpagli'are *vt* scatter

sparpagli'arsi *vr* scatter

sparpagli'ato *adj* far-flung

'**sparso** ① *pp di* SPARGERE ② *adj* scattered; (sciolto) loose

sparti'neve *nm inv* snowplough

spar'tire *vt* share out; (separare) separate

spar'tirsi *vr* share

spar'tito *nm* Mus score

sparti'traffico *nm inv* traffic island; (di autostrada) central reservation, median strip Am

spartizi'one *nf* division

spa'ruto *adj* gaunt; ⟨gruppo⟩ small; ⟨peli, capelli⟩ sparse

sparvi'ero *nm* sparrow-hawk

spasi'mante *nm* hum admirer

spasi'mare *vi* suffer agonies; **~ per** be madly in love with

'**spasimo** *nm* spasm

spa'smodico *adj* spasmodic

spas'sarsi *vr* amuse oneself; **spassarsela** have a good time

spassio'nato *adj* ⟨osservatore⟩ dispassionate, impartial

'**spasso** *nm* fun; **essere uno ~** be hilarious; **andare a ~** go for a walk; **essere a ~** be out of work

spas'soso *adj* hilarious

'**spastico** *adj* spastic

'**spatola** *nf* spatula

spau'racchio *nm* scarecrow; fig bugbear

spau'rire *vt* frighten

spa'valdo *adj* defiant

spaventa'passeri *nm inv* scarecrow

spaven'tare *vt* frighten, scare

spaven'tarsi *vr* be frightened, be scared

spa'vento *nm* fright; **brutto da fare** ∼ incredibly ugly

spaven'toso *adj* frightening; (fam: enorme) incredible

spazi'ale *adj* spatial; (cosmico) space *attrib*

spazi'are ① *vt* space out ② *vi* range

spazien'tirsi *vr* lose [one's] patience

'spazio *nm* space. **spazio aereo** airspace. **spazio indietro** Comput backspace. **spazio di tempo** period of time. **spazio vitale** elbowroom. **spazio web** web space

spazi'oso *adj* spacious

spazio-tempo'rale *adj* spatiotemporal

spazzaca'mino *nm* chimney sweep

spazza'neve *nm inv* (anche sci) snowplough

spaz'zare *vt* sweep; ∼ **via** sweep away; (fam: mangiare) devour

spazza'trice *nf* sweeper

spazza'tura *nf* (immondizia) rubbish

spaz'zino *nm* road sweeper; (netturbino) dustman, refuse collector

'spazzola *nf* brush; (di tergicristallo) blade; **capelli a** ∼ crew cut

spazzo'lare *vt* brush

spazzo'larsi *vr* ∼ **i capelli** brush one's hair

spazzo'lino *nm* small brush. **spazzolino da denti** toothbrush. **spazzolino per le unghie** nailbrush

spazzo'lone *nm* scrubbing brush

'speaker *nm inv* Radio, TV announcer

specchi'arsi *vr* look at oneself in a/the mirror; (riflettersi) be mirrored; ∼ **in qualcuno** model oneself on somebody

specchi'ato *adj* **di specchiata onestà** of spotless integrity

specchi'etto *nm* small mirror. **specchietto laterale** wing mirror. **specchietto retrovisore** driving mirror, rear-view mirror

'specchio *nm* mirror. **specchio unilaterale** two-way mirror

speci'ale ① *adj* special ② *nm* TV special [programme]

specia'lista *nmf* specialist

specialità *nf inv* speciality, specialty

specializ'zare *vt* specialize

specializ'zarsi *vr* specialize

specializ'zato *adj* (operaio) skilled; **siamo specializzati in ...** we specialize in ...

special'mente *adv* especially

'specie *nf inv* (scientifico) species; (tipo) kind; **fare** ∼ **a** a surprise; **in** ∼ especially. **specie a rischio** endangered species

specifi'care *vt* specify

specificata'mente *adv* specifically

spe'cifico *adj* specific

speci'oso *adj* specious

specu'lare¹ *vi* speculate; ∼ **su** (indagare) speculate on; Fin speculate in

specu'lare² *adj* mirror *attrib*

specula'tivo *adj* speculative

specula'tore *nm* speculator

speculazi'one *nf* speculation

spe'dire *vt* send; ∼ **per posta** mail, post Br; ∼ **qualcuno all'altro mondo** send somebody to meet his/her maker

spe'dito ① *pp di* SPEDIRE ② *adj* quick; (parlata) fluent

spedizi'one *nf* (di lettere ecc) dispatch; Comm consignment, shipment; (scientifica) expedition

spedizioni'ere *nm* Comm freight forwarder

'spegnere *vt* put out; turn off, switch off (motore, luce, televisione); turn off (gas); quench, slake (sete)

'spegnersi *vr* go out; (morire) pass away

spegni'mento *nm* standby

spelacchi'ato *adj* (tappeto) threadbare; (cane) mangy

spe'lare *vt* remove the fur of (coniglio)

spe'larsi *vr* (cane, tappeto) moult

speleolo'gia *nf* potholing, speleology

spel'lare *vt* skin; fig fleece

spel'larsi *vr* (serpente) shed its skin; (per il sole) peel; **mi sono spellato un ginocchio** I grazed *or* skinned my knee

spe'lonca *nf* cave; fig dingy hole

spendacci'one, -a *nmf* spendthrift

'spendere *vt* spend; ∼ **fiato** waste one's breath

spen'nare *vt* pluck; fam fleece (cliente)

spennel'lare ① *vt* brush ② *vi* paint

spensierata'mente *adv* blithely

spensiera'tezza *nf* lightheartedness

spensie'rato *adj* lighthearted, carefree

'spento ① *pp di* SPEGNERE ② *adj* off; (gas) out; (smorto) dull; (vulcano) extinct

spenzo'lare *vt* dangle

spe'ranza *nf* hope; **pieno di** ∼ hopeful; **senza** ∼ hopeless

spe'rare ① *vt* hope for; (aspettarsi) expect ② *vi* ∼ **in** trust in; **spero di sì** I hope so

'sperdersi *vr* get lost

sper'duto *adj* lost; (isolato) secluded

spergiu'rare *vi* commit perjury

spergi'uro, -a ① *nmf* perjurer ② *nm* perjury

sperico'lato *adj* swashbuckling

sperimen'tale *adj* experimental

sperimen'tare *vt* experiment with; test (resistenza, capacità, teoria)

S

sperimen'tato *adj* ⟨*metodo*⟩ tried and tested

sperimentazi'one *nf* experimentation; **~ sugli animali** animal testing

'sperma *nm* sperm

spermi'cida ① *adj* spermicidal ② *nm* spermicide

spero'nare *vt* ram

spe'rone *nm* spur

sperpe'rare *vt* squander

'sperpero *nm* waste, squandering

spersonaliz'zare *vt* depersonalize

spersonaliz'zarsi *vr* become depersonalized

spersonalizzazi'one *nf* depersonalization

'spesa *nf* expense; (acquisto) purchase; **andare a far spese** go shopping; **darsi a spese folli** go on a shopping spree; **fare la ~** do the shopping; **fare le spese di** pay for; **a proprie spese** at one's own expense; **spese** *pl* **di amministrazione** handling charge; **spese** *pl* **bancarie** bank charges; **spese** *pl* **di capitale** capital expenditure; **spese** *pl* **a carico del destinatario** carriage forward; **spese** *pl* **di esercizio** business expenses; **spese** *pl* **extra** out-of-pocket expenses; **spese** *pl* **di gestione** operating costs; **spese** *pl* **di movimentazione** handling charge; **spese** *pl* **di spedizione** shipping costs; **spese** *pl* **di viaggio** travel expenses

spe'sare *vt* pay expenses for; **spesato dalla ditta** paid for by the company, on the company

spe'sato *adj* all-expenses-paid

'speso *pp di* SPENDERE

'spesso¹ *adj* thick

'spesso² *adv* often

spes'sore *nm* thickness; (fig: consistenza) substance

spet'tabile *adj* (Comm *abbr* **Spett.**) **Spettabile ditta Rossi** Messrs Rossi

spettaco'lare *adj* spectacular

spet'tacolo *nm* spectacle; (rappresentazione) show; **dare ~ di sé** make a spectacle *or* an exhibition of oneself; **il mondo dello ~** show business. **spettacolo di burattini** Punch-and-Judy show. **spettacolo di varietà** variety show

spettaco'loso *adj* spectacular

spet'tanza *nf* concern

spet'tare *vi* **~ a** be up to; ⟨*diritto*⟩ be due to

spetta|'tore, -trice *nmf* spectator; **spettatori** *pl* (di cinema ecc) audience *sg*

spettego'lare *vi* gossip

spetti'nare *vt* **~ qualcuno** ruffle somebody's hair

spetti'narsi *vr* ruffle one's hair

spet'trale *adj* ghostly

'spettro *nm* ghost; (fig: della fame) spectre; Phys spectrum; **ad ampio ~** ⟨*medicina*⟩ broad-spectrum

spezi'are *vt* add spices to, spice

spezi'ato *adj* spicy

'spezie *nfpl* spices

spez'zare *vt* break

spez'zarsi *vr* break

spezza'tino *nm* stew

spez'zato ① *adj* broken ② *nm* coordinated jacket and trousers

spezzet'tare *vt* break into small pieces

spez'zone *nm* Cinema clip, footage *no pl*; (bomba) cluster bomb

'spia *nf* spy; (della polizia) informer; (di porta) peep-hole; **fare la ~** sneak. **spia di accensione** power-on light. **spia di attività dell'hard disk** Comput hard disk activity light. **spia della benzina** petrol gauge. **spia luminosa** warning light. **spia dell'olio** oil [warning] light

spiacci'care *vt* squash

spia'cente *adj* sorry

spia'cevole *adj* unpleasant

spi'aggia *nf* beach

spia'nare *vt* level; (rendere liscio) smooth; roll out ⟨*pasta*⟩; raze to the ground ⟨*edificio*⟩

spia'nata *nf* flat ground

spi'ano *nm* **a tutto ~** flat out

spian'tato *adj* fig penniless

spi'are *vt* spy on; wait for ⟨*occasione ecc*⟩

spiattel'lare *vt* blurt out; shove ⟨*oggetto*⟩

spiaz'zare *vt* wrong-foot

spi'azzo *nm* (radura) clearing

spic'care ① *vt* **~ un salto** jump; **~ il volo** take flight ② *vi* stand out

spic'cato *adj* marked

'spicchio *nm* (di agrumi) segment; (di aglio) clove

spicci'arsi *vr* hurry up

spiccia'tivo *adj* speedy

'spiccio *adj* no-nonsense

'spiccioli *nmpl* change

spicci'olo *adj* (comune) banal; ⟨*denaro*⟩ in change

'spicco *nm* relief; **fare ~** stand out; **di ~** high-profile

'spider *nmf inv* open-top sports car

spie'dino *nm* kebab

spi'edo *nm* spit; **allo ~** on a spit, spitroasted

spiega'mento *nm* deployment

spie'gare *vt* explain; open out ⟨*cartina*⟩; unfurl ⟨*vele*⟩

spie'garsi *vr* explain oneself; ⟨*vele, bandiere*⟩ unfurl; **non so se mi spiego** need I say more?; **mi sono spiegato?** (minaccia) do I make myself clear?; **non riesco a spiegarmi come ...** I can't understand how ...

spie'gato *adj* ⟨*ali*⟩ outspread; **a sirene spiegate** with sirens blaring; **a voce spiegata** at the top of one's voice; **a vele spiegate** under full sail, with all sails in the wind

spiegazi'one *nf* explanation; **venire a una ∼ con qualcuno** sort things out with somebody

spiegaz'zare *vt* crumple

spiegaz'zato *adj* crumpled

spieta'tezza *nf* ruthlessness

spie'tato *adj* ruthless

spiffe'rare ① *vt* blurt out
② *vi* ⟨*vento*⟩ whistle

'**spiffero** *nm* (corrente d'aria) draught

'**spiga** *nf* spike; Bot ear

spi'gato *adj* herringbone

spigli'ato *adj* self-possessed

'**spigola** *nf* sea bass

spigo'lare *vt* glean

'**spigolo** *nm* edge; (angolo) corner

'**spilla** *nf* (gioiello) brooch. **spilla da balia** safety pin. **spilla di sicurezza** safety pin

spil'lare *vt* tap

'**spillo** *nm* pin. **spillo di sicurezza** safety pin

spil'lone *nm* hatpin

spilluzzi'care *vt* pick at

spi'lorcio, -a ① *adj* stingy
② *nm* miser, skinflint

spilun'gone, -a *nmf* beanpole

'**spina** *nf* thorn; (di pesce) bone; Electr plug; **a ∼ di pesce** ⟨*tessuto, disegno*⟩ herringbone; ⟨*parcheggio*⟩ in two angled rows; **stare sulle spine** be on tenterhooks; **una ∼ nel fianco** a thorn in one's side. **spina dorsale** spine

spi'naci *nmpl* spinach

spi'nale *adj* spinal

spi'nato ① *adj* ⟨*filo*⟩ barbed
② *nm* (tessuto) herringbone

spi'nello *nm* (fam: droga) joint

'**spingere** *vt* push; fig drive

'**spingersi** *vr* (andare) proceed

'**spinnaker** *nm inv* spinnaker

spi'noso *adj* thorny

spi'notto *nm* Electr plug

'**spinta** *nf* push; (violenta) thrust; fig spur; **dare una ∼ a qualcuno/qualcosa** give somebody/something a push; **farsi largo a spinte** push one's way through

spinta'rella *nf* (fam: raccomandazione) **ha ottenuto il lavoro grazie alla ∼ dello zio**

his uncle got him the job by pulling a few strings

'**spinto** ① *pp di* SPINGERE
② *adj* ⟨*barzelletta, spettacolo*⟩ risqué

spin'tone *nm* shove

spio'naggio *nm* espionage, spying

spi'one, -a *nmf* tell-tale

spio'vente ① *adj* ⟨*tetto*⟩ sloping
② *nm* slope

spi'overe *vi* liter stop raining; (ricadere) fall; (scorrere) flow down

'**spira** *nf* coil

spi'raglio *nm* small opening; (soffio d'aria) breath of air; (raggio di luce) gleam of light

spi'rale ① *adj* spiral
② *nm* spiral; (negli orologi) hairspring; (anticoncezionale) coil; **a ∼** spiral-shaped

spi'rare *vi* (soffiare) blow; (morire) pass away

spiri'tato *adj* possessed; ⟨*espressione*⟩ wild

spiri'tismo *nm* spiritualism

spiri'tista *nmf* spiritualist

spiri'tistico *adj* spiritualist

'**spirito** *nm* spirit; (arguzia) wit; (intelletto) mind; **fare dello ∼** be witty; **persona di ∼** witty person; **sotto ∼** in brandy. **spirito civico** community spirit. **spirito di contraddizione** contrariness. **Spirito Santo** Holy Spirit, Holy Ghost

spirito'saggine *nf* witticism

spiri'toso *adj* witty

spiritu'ale *adj* spiritual

spiritual'mente *adv* spiritually

splen'dente *adj* shining; **denti bianchi splendenti** gleaming white teeth

'**splendere** *vi* shine

'**splendido** *adj* splendid

splen'dore *nm* splendour

'**spocchia** *nf* conceit

spocchi'oso *adj* conceited

spode'stare *vt* dispossess; depose ⟨*re*⟩

spoetiz'zare *vt* disenchant

'**spoglia** *nf* (di animale) skin; **spoglie** *pl* (salma) mortal remains; (bottino) spoils; **sotto false spoglie** under false pretences

spogli'are *vt* strip; (svestire) undress; (fare lo spoglio di) go through; **∼ qualcuno di un diritto** divest somebody of a right

spogliarel'lista *nmf* strip-tease artist, stripper

spoglia'rello *nm* strip-tease

spogli'arsi *vr* strip, undress

spoglia'toio *nm* (in piscina, palestra) locker room; Sport changing room; (guardaroba) cloakroom, checkroom Am

'**spoglio** ① *adj* undressed; ⟨*albero, muro*⟩ bare; **∼ di** (privo) stripped of
② *nm* (scrutinio) perusal

'**spoiler** *nm inv* Auto spoiler

'**spola** *nf* shuttle; **fare la** ∼ shuttle

spo'letta *nf* spool

spolmo'narsi *vr* shout oneself hoarse

spol'pare *vt* take the flesh off; fig fleece

spolve'rare *vt* dust; fam devour ⟨*cibo*⟩

'**sponda** *nf* (di mare, lago) shore; (di fiume) bank; (bordo) edge. **sponda posteriore ribaltabile** Auto tailgate

sponsoriz'zare *vt* sponsor

sponsorizzazi'one *nf* sponsorship

spontaneità *nf* spontaneity

spon'taneo *adj* spontaneous

'**spooling** *nm* Comput spooling

spopola'mento *nm* depopulation

spopo'lare ① *vt* depopulate ② *vi* (avere successo) draw the crowds

spopo'larsi *vr* become depopulated

'**spora** *nf* spore

sporadica'mente *adv* sporadically

spo'radico *adj* sporadic

sporcacci'one, -**a** *nmf* dirty pig

spor'care *vt* dirty; (macchiare) soil

spor'carsi *vr* get dirty

spor'cizia *nf* dirt

'**sporco** ① *adj* dirty; (macchiato) soiled **avere la coscienza sporca** have a guilty conscience ② *nm* dirt

spor'gente *adj* jutting, protruding; **ha i denti sporgenti** fam she has goofy teeth

spor'genza *nf* projection

'**sporgere** ① *vt* stretch out; ∼ **querela contro** take legal action against ② *vi* jut out

'**sporgersi** *vr* lean out

sport *nm inv* sport; **fare qualcosa per** ∼ do something for fun. **sport** *pl* **estremi** extreme sports. **sport** *pl* **invernali** winter sports

'**sporta** *nf* shopping basket

spor'tello *nm* door; (di banca ecc) window. **sportello automatico** cash dispenser, cash point, cash machine, hole-in-the-wall. **sportello della biglietteria** ticket window. **sportello pacchi** parcels counter

spor'tivo, -**a** ① *adj* sports *attrib*; ⟨*persona*⟩ sporty ② *nm* sportsman ③ *nf* sportswoman

'**sporto** *pp di* SPORGERE

'**sposa** *nf* bride; **dare in** ∼ give in marriage, give away; **prendere in** ∼ marry

sposa'lizio *nm* wedding

spo'sare *vt* marry; fig espouse

spo'sarsi *vr* get married; ⟨*vino*⟩ go ⟨con with⟩

spo'sato *adj* married

spo'sini *nmpl* newly-weds

'**sposo** *nm* bridegroom; **sposi** *pl* [**novelli**] newlyweds

spossa'tezza *nf* exhaustion

spos'sato *adj* exhausted, worn out

sposses'sato *adj* dispossessed

sposta'mento *nm* displacement. **spostamento d'aria** airflow

spo'stare *vt* move; (differire) postpone; (cambiare) change

spo'starsi *vr* move

spo'stato, -**a** ① *adj* ill-adjusted ② *nmf* (disadattato) misfit

spot *nm inv* **spot** [**pubblicitario**] commercial

S.P.R. *abbr* (**si prega rispondere**) RSVP

'**spranga** *nf* bar

spran'gare *vt* bar

'**sprazzo** *nm* (di colore) splash; (di luce) flash; fig glimmer

spre'care *vt* waste

'**spreco** *nm* waste

spre'cone *adj* spendthrift

spre'gevole *adj* despicable

spregia'tivo *adj* pejorative

'**spregio** *nm* contempt; **fare uno** ∼ **a qualcuno** offend somebody

spregiudi'cato *adj* unprejudiced; pej unscrupulous

'**spremere** *vt* squeeze

'**spremersi** *vr* ∼ **le meningi** rack one's brains

spremi'aglio *nm inv* garlic press

spremia'grumi *nm inv* lemon squeezer

spremili'moni *nm inv* lemon squeezer

spre'muta *nf* juice. **spremuta d'arancia** fresh orange juice, freshly squeezed orange juice

spre'tato *nm* former priest

sprez'zante *adj* contemptuous

sprigio'nare *vt* emit

sprigio'narsi *vr* burst out

sprint *nm inv* sprint; **fare uno** ∼ put on a spurt

spriz'zare *vt/i* spurt; be bursting with ⟨*salute, gioia*⟩

sprofon'dare *vi* sink; (crollare) collapse

sprofon'darsi *vr* ∼ **in** sink into; fig be engrossed in

spron *nm* ▶ SPRONE

spro'nare *vt* spur on

'**sprone** *nm* spur; (sartoria) yoke; **a spron battuto** instantly; **andare a spron battuto** go hell-for-leather

sproporzio'nato *adj* disproportionate

sproporzi'one *nf* disproportion

sproposi'tato *adj* full of blunders; (enorme) huge

spro'posito *nm* blunder; (eccesso) excessive amount; **a ~** inopportunely

sprovve'duto *adj* unprepared; **~ di** lacking in

sprov'visto *adj* **~ di** out of; lacking in ⟨*fantasia, pazienza*⟩; **alla sprovvista** unexpectedly

spruz'zare *vt* sprinkle; (vaporizzare) spray; (inzaccherare) spatter

spruzza'tore *nm* spray

'spruzzo *nm* spray; (di fango) splash

spudorata'mente *adv* shamelessly

spudora'tezza *nf* shamelessness

spudo'rato *adj* shameless

'spugna *nf* sponge; (tessuto) towelling

spu'gnoso *adj* spongy

'spuma *nf* foam; (schiuma) froth; Culin mousse

spu'mante *nm* sparkling wine, spumante

spumeggi'ante *adj* bubbly; ⟨*mare*⟩ foaming

spumeggi'are *vi* ⟨*champagne*⟩ bubble; ⟨*birra*⟩ foam

'spunta *nf* **segno di spunta** tick

spun'tare ① *vt* (rompere la punta di) break the point of; trim ⟨*capelli*⟩; check off ⟨*lista, elenco*⟩; **spuntarla** fig win ② *vi* ⟨*pianta*⟩ sprout; ⟨*capelli*⟩ begin to grow; (sorgere) rise; (apparire) appear

spun'tarsi *vr* get blunt

spun'tata *nf* trim

spun'tino *nm* snack

'spunto *nm* cue; fig starting point; **dare ~ a** give rise to

spur'gare *vt* purge

spur'garsi *vr* Med expectorate

'spurio *adj* spurious

spu'tacchio *nm* spittle

spu'tare *vt/i* spit; spit out ⟨*cibo*⟩; **~ sentenze** pass judgement; **~ l'osso** sl spit it out

'sputo *nm* spit

'squadra *nf* (gruppo) team, squad; (di polizia ecc) squad; (da disegno) square; **lavoro di squadra** teamwork. **squadra del buoncostume** Vice Squad. **squadra mobile** Flying Squad. **squadra narcotici** Drug Squad. **squadra di soccorso** rescue team

squa'drare *vt* square; (guardare) look up and down

squa'driglia *nf*, **squadrigli'one** *nm* squadron

squa'drone *nm* squadron

squagli'are *vt* melt

squagli'arsi *vr* melt; **squagliarsela** (fam: svignarsela) steal out

squa'lifica *nf* disqualification

squalifi'care *vt* disqualify

'squallido *adj* squalid

squal'lore *nm* squalor

'squalo *nm* shark

'squama *nf* scale; (di pelle) flake

squa'mare *vt* scale

squa'marsi *vr* ⟨*pelle*⟩ flake off

squa'moso *adj* scaly; ⟨*pelle*⟩ flaky

squarcia'gola: **a ~** *adv* at the top of one's voice

squarci'are *vt* rip

'squarcio *nm* rip; (di ferita, in nave) gash; (di cielo) patch

squar'tare *vt* quarter; dismember ⟨*animale*⟩

squarta'tore *nm* **Jack lo ~** Jack the Ripper

squash *nm* squash

squas'sare *vt* shake

squattri'nato *adj* penniless

squaw *nf inv* squaw

squilib'rare *vt* unbalance

squili'brato, -a ① *adj* unbalanced ② *nmf* lunatic

squi'librio *nm* imbalance

squil'lante *adj* shrill

squil'lare *vi* ⟨*campana*⟩ peal; ⟨*tromba*⟩ blare; ⟨*telefono*⟩ ring

'squillo *nm* blare; Teleph ring

squinter'nato *adj* anche fig crazy

squisi'tezza *nf* refinement

squi'sito *adj* exquisite; (fam: pietanza) yummy

squit'tire *vi* ⟨*pappagallo*⟩, fig squawk; ⟨*topo*⟩ squeak

sradi'care *vt* uproot; eradicate ⟨*vizio, male*⟩

sragio'nare *vi* rave

sregola'tezza *nf* dissipation

srego'lato *adj* inordinate; (dissoluto) dissolute

s.r.l. *abbr* (**società a responsabilità limitata**) Ltd

sroto'lare *vt* uncoil

SS *abbr* (**strada statale**) national road; *abbr* (**Santissimo**) Most Holy

ss *abbr* (**seguenti**) following

sst *int* sh!

'stabile ① *adj* stable; (permanente) lasting; ⟨*saldo*⟩ steady. **compagnia stabile** Theat repertory company ② *nm* (edificio) building

stabili'mento *nm* factory; (industriale) plant; (edificio) establishment. **stabilimento balneare** lido

stabi'lire *vt* establish; (decidere) decide

stabi'lirsi *vr* settle

stabilità nf stability
stabi'lito adj established
stabiliz'zare vt stabilize
stabiliz'zarsi vr stabilize
stabilizza'tore nm stabilizer
stacano'vista nmf workaholic
stac'care ① vt detach; pronounce clearly ⟨parole⟩; (separare) separate; turn off ⟨corrente⟩; ~ **gli occhi da** take one's eyes off
② vi (fam: finire di lavorare) knock off
stac'carsi vr come off; ~ **da** break away from ⟨partito, famiglia⟩; **si stacca alle cinque** knocking off time is five o'clock
staccata'mente adv staccato
stac'cato adj Mus staccato
staccio'nata nf fence
'stacco nm gap
'stadio nm stadium, sports ground
'staffa nf stirrup; **perdere le staffe** fig fly off the handle
staf'fetta nf Sport relay [race]; Mil dispatch rider
staffet'tista nmf Sport relay runner
stagio'nale adj seasonal
stagio'nare vt season ⟨legno⟩; mature ⟨formaggio⟩
stagio'nato adj ⟨legno⟩ seasoned; ⟨formaggio⟩ matured
stagiona'tura nf (di legno) seasoning; (di formaggio) maturation, maturing
stagi'one nf season; **di** ~ in season; **fuori** ~ out of season. **alta/bassa stagione** high/low season. **stagione lirica** opera season. **stagione delle piogge** rainy season
stagli'arsi vr stand out
sta'gnante adj stagnant
sta'gnare ① vt (saldare) solder; (chiudere ermeticamente) seal
② vi ⟨acqua⟩ stagnate
'stagno ① adj (a tenuta d'acqua) watertight
② nm (acqua ferma) pond; (metallo) tin
sta'gnola nf tinfoil
stalag'mite nf stalagmite
stalat'tite nf stalactite
'stalla nf stable; (per buoi) cowshed
stalli'ere nm groom
stal'lone nm stallion
sta'mani, **stamat'tina** adv this morning
stam'becco nm ibex
stam'berga nf hovel
'stampa nf Typ printing; (giornali, giornalisti) press; (riproduzione) print; **stampe** (postale) printed matter. **stampa fronte retro** two-sided printing, duplex printing. **stampa scandalistica** gutter press, tabloid press

stam'pante nf printer. **stampante ad aghi** dot matrix [printer]. **stampante a getto d'inchiostro** inkjet [printer]. **stampante laser** laser [printer]. **stampante a matrice di punti** dot matrix [printer]. **stampante seriale** serial printer. **stampante termica** thermal printer
stam'pare vt print
stampa'tello nm block letters pl, block capitals pl
stam'pato ① adj printed
② nm leaflet; Comput hard copy, printout; (modulo) print; **stampati** pl (pubblicità) promotional literature
stam'pella nf crutch
stampigli'are vt stamp
stampiglia'tura nf stamping; (dicitura) stamp
stam'pino nm stencil
'stampo nm mould; **di vecchio** ~ ⟨persona⟩ of the old school
sta'nare vt drive out
stan'care vt tire; (annoiare) bore
stan'carsi vr get tired
stan'chezza nf tiredness
'stanco adj tired; ~ **di** (stufo) fed up with; ~ **morto** dead tired, knackered fam
stand nm inv stand
'standard adj & nm inv standard
standardiz'zare vt standardize
standardizzazi'one nf standardization
'stand-by adj inv stand-by
'stanga nf bar; (persona) beanpole
stan'gare vt fam fail ⟨studente⟩; (con le tasse ecc) clobber
stan'gata nf fig blow; (fam: nel calcio) big kick; **prendere una** ~ (fam: agli esami, economica) come a cropper
stan'ghetta nf (di occhiali) leg
sta'notte nf tonight; (la notte scorsa) last night
'stante prep on account of; **a sé** ~ separate
stan'tio adj stale
stan'tuffo nm piston
'stanza nf room; (metrica) stanza. **stanza dei giochi** games room. **stanza da pranzo** dining room
stanzia'mento nm allocation
stanzi'are vt allocate
stan'zino nm walk-in cupboard
stap'pare vt uncork
star nf inv (del cinema, dello sport) star
'stare vi (rimanere) stay; (abitare) live; (con gerundio) be; **sto solo cinque minuti** I'll stay only five minutes; **sto in piazza Peyron** I live in Peyron Square; **sta dormendo** he's sleeping; ~ **a** (attenersi) keep to; (spettare) be

up to; ~ **bene** (economicamente) be well off; (di salute) be well; (addirsi) suit; **sta bene!** that's fine!; ~ **dietro a** (seguire) follow; (sorvegliare) keep an eye on; (corteggiare) run after; ~ **in piedi** stand; ~ **per** be about to; ~ **sempre a fare qualcosa** be always doing something; **ben ti sta!** it serves you right!; **come stai/sta?** how are you?; **lasciar** ~ leave alone; **starci** (essere contenuto) go into; (essere d'accordo) agree; **il 3 nel 12 ci sta 4 volte** 3 into 12 goes 4; **non sa** ~ **agli scherzi** he can't take a joke; ~ **su** (con la schiena) sit up straight; ~ **sulle proprie** keep oneself to oneself

'**starna** *nf* partridge

starnaz'zare *vi* quack; fig shriek

starnu'tire *vi* sneeze

star'nuto *nm* sneeze

'**starsene** *vr* (rimanere) stay

'**starter** *nm inv* choke

sta'sera *adv* this evening, tonight

'**stasi** *nf* stasis

sta'tale [1] *adj* state *attrib*
[2] *nmf* state employee, civil servant
[3] *nf* (strada) main road, trunk road

'**statico** *adj* static

sta'tista *nm* statesman

sta'tistica *nf* statistics *sg*

sta'tistico *adj* statistical

'**Stati 'Uniti [d'America]** *nmpl* gli ~ ~ the United States [of America]

'**stato** [1] pp di ESSERE, STARE
[2] *nm* state; (posizione sociale) position; Jur status; **lo Stato** Pol the state. **stato d'animo** frame of mind. **stato di attesa** Comput wait state. **stato canaglia** rogue state. **stato civile** marital status. **stato cuscinetto** buffer state. **Stato Maggiore** Mil General Staff. **stato di salute** state of health

stato-nazi'one *nm* nation-state

'**statua** *nf* statue. **statua di cera** waxwork

statu'ario *adj* statuesque

statuni'tense [1] *adj* United States *attrib*, US *attrib*
[2] *nmf* US citizen

sta'tura *nf* height; **di alta** ~ tall; **di bassa** ~ short; **di media** ~ of average height. **statura morale** moral stature

sta'tuto *nm* statute

stazio'nario *adj* stationary

stazi'one *nf* station; (città) resort. **stazione degli autobus** bus station. **stazione balneare** seaside resort. **stazione climatica** health resort. **stazione ferroviaria** railway station *Br*, train station. **stazione marittima** ferry terminal. **stazione master** Comput master station. **stazione multimediale** Comput multimedia station. **stazione dei pullman** coach station *Br*, bus station.

stazione radiofonica radio station. **stazione di servizio** petrol station *Br*, service station. **stazione slave** Comput slave station. **stazione spaziale** space station. **stazione termale** spa, health resort

'**stecca** *nf* stick; (di ombrello) rib; (da biliardo) cue; Med splint; (di sigarette) carton; (di reggiseno) stiffener; **fare una** ~ Mus fluff a note

stec'cato *nm* fence

stec'chino *nm* cocktail stick

stec'chito *adj* skinny; (rigido) stiff; (morto) stone cold dead

'**stele** *nf* stele

'**stella** *nf* star; **salire alle stelle** ⟨prezzi⟩ rise sky-high, rocket. **stella alpina** edelweiss. **stella cadente** shooting star. **stella del cinema** movie star. **stella cometa** comet. **stella filante** streamer. **stella di mare** starfish. **stella polare** Pole Star, North Star

stel'lare *adj* star *attrib*; ⟨grandezza⟩ stellar

stel'lato *adj* starry

stel'lina *nf* starlet

'**stelo** *nm* stem. **lampada a stelo** standard lamp *Br*, floor lamp

'**stemma** *nm* coat of arms

stempe'rare *vt* dilute

stempi'ato *adj* bald at the temples

sten'dardo *nm* standard

'**stendere** *vt* spread out; (appendere) hang out; (distendere) stretch [out]; (scrivere) write down

'**stendersi** *vr* stretch out

stendibianche'ria *nm inv* clothes horse

stendi'toio *nm* clothes horse

stenodattilogra'fia *nf* shorthand typing

stenodatti'lografo, -a *nmf* shorthand typist

stenogra'fare *vt* take down in shorthand

stenogra'fia *nf* shorthand

sten'tare *vi* ~ **a** find it hard to

sten'tato *adj* laboured

'**stento** *nm* (fatica) effort; **a** ~ with difficulty; **stenti** *pl* hardships, privations

'**step** *nm* step aerobics

'**steppa** *nf* steppe

'**sterco** *nm* dung

stereo[fonico] *adj* stereo[phonic]

stereo'scopico *adj* stereoscopic

stereoti'pato *adj* stereotyped; ⟨sorriso⟩ insincere

stere'otipo *nm* stereotype

'**sterile** *adj* sterile; ⟨terreno⟩ barren

sterilità *nf* sterility

sterriliz'zare vt sterilize
sterilizzazi'one nf sterilization
ster'lina nf pound. **lira sterlina** [pound] sterling
stermi'nare vt exterminate
stermi'nato adj immense
ster'minio nm extermination
'sterno nm breastbone
ste'roide nm steroid
ster'paglia nf brushwood
ster'rare vt excavate; dig up ⟨strada⟩
ster'rato ① adj ⟨strada⟩ dug up ② nm excavation; (di strada) digging up
ster'zare vi steer
'sterzo nm steering; (volante) steering wheel
'steso pp di STENDERE
'stesso ① adj same; **io ~** myself; **tu ~** yourself; **me ~** myself; **se ~** himself; **in quel momento ~** at that very moment; **è stato ricevuto dalla stessa regina** (in persona) he was received by the Queen herself; **tuo fratello ~ dice che hai torto** even your brother says you're wrong; **l'ho visto coi miei stessi occhi** I saw it with my own eyes; **con le mie stesse mani** with my own hands; **è venuto il giorno ~** he came the same day, he came that very day; **lo farò oggi ~** I'll do it straight away today
② pron **lo ~** the same one; (la stessa cosa) the same; **fa lo ~** it's all the same; **ci vado lo ~** I'll go just the same
ste'sura nf drawing up; (documento) draft
steto'scopio nm stethoscope
'steward nm inv steward, air steward
stick nm inv **colla a stick** glue stick; **deodorante in stick** stick deodorant
stiepi'dire vt warm
'stigma nm inv stigma
'stigmate nfpl stigmata
sti'lare vt draw up
'stile nm style; **in grande ~** in style; **essere nello ~ di qualcuno** be typical of somebody, be just like somebody. **stile libero** (nel nuoto) freestyle, crawl. **stile di vita** life style
sti'lista nmf [fashion] designer; (parrucchiere) stylist
stiliz'zato adj stylized
'stilla nf drop
stil'lare vi ooze
stilo'grafica nf fountain pen
stilo'grafico adj **penna stilografica** fountain pen
'stima nf esteem; (valutazione) estimate
sti'mare vt esteem; (valutare) estimate; (ritenere) consider
sti'marsi vr consider oneself
sti'mato adj well-thought-of

stimo'lante ① adj stimulating ② nm stimulant
stimo'lare vt stimulate; (incitare) incite
'stimolo nm stimulus; (fitta) pang
'stinco nm shin; **non è uno ~ di santo** fam he's no saint
'stingere vt/i fade
'stingersi vr fade
'stinto pp di STINGERE
sti'pare vt cram
sti'parsi vr crowd together
stipendi'are vt pay a salary to
stipendi'ato ① adj salaried ② nm salaried worker
sti'pendio nm salary. **stipendio base** basic salary. **stipendio iniziale** starting salary
'stipite nm doorpost
stipu'lare vt stipulate
stipulazi'one nf stipulation; (accordo) agreement
stira'mento nm sprain
sti'rare vt iron; (distendere) stretch
sti'rarsi vr (distendersi) stretch; pull ⟨muscolo⟩
stira'tura nf ironing
'stiro nm **ferro da stiro** iron
'stirpe nf stock
stiti'chezza nf constipation
'stitico adj constipated
'stiva nf Naut hold
sti'vale nm boot; **lo Stivale** (Italia) Italy; **stivali** pl **di gomma** Wellington boots, Wellingtons; **poeta dei miei stivali!** fam poet my eye!, poet my foot!
stiva'letto nm ankle boot
stiva'lone nm high boot; **stivaloni** pl **da caccia** hunting boots; **stivaloni** pl **di gomma** waders
sti'vare vt load
'stizza nf anger
stiz'zire vt irritate
stiz'zirsi vr become irritated
stiz'zito adj irritated
stiz'zoso adj peevish
stocca'fisso nm stockfish
stoc'cata nf stab; (battuta pungente) gibe
Stoc'colma nf Stockholm
stock nm Comm stock
'stock-car nm inv stock car
'stoffa nf material; fig stuff; **avere ~** have what it takes
stoi'cismo nm stoicism
'stoico adj & nm stoic
sto'ino nm doormat
'stola nf stole
'stolido adj stolid
'stolto adj foolish

stoma'chevole *adj* revolting

'stomaco *nm* stomach. **mal di stomaco** stomachache

stoma'tite *nf* stomatitis

sto'nare ① *vt/i* sing/play out of tune ② *vi* (non intonarsi) clash

sto'nato *adj* out of tune; (discordante) clashing; (confuso) bewildered

stona'tura *nf* false note; (discordanza) clash

stop *nm inv* (segnale stradale) stop sign; (in telegramma) stop

stop'pare *vt* stop

'stopper *nm inv* Sport fullback

'stoppia *nf* stubble

stop'pino *nm* wick

stop'poso *adj* tough

'storcere *vt* twist

'storcersi *vr* twist

stor'dire *vt* stun; (intontire) daze

stor'dirsi *vr* dull one's senses

stor'dito *adj* stunned; (intontito) dazed; (sventato) heedless

'storia *nf* history; (racconto, bugia) story; (pretesto) excuse; **senza storie!** no fuss!; **fare [delle] storie** make a fuss. **storia d'amore** love story. **storia di vita vissuta** human interest story

'storico ① *adj* historical; (di importanza storica) historic ② *nm* historian

stori'ella *nf* fam little story

storiogra'fia *nf* historiography

stori'ografo *nm* historiographer

stori'one *nm* sturgeon

'stormo *nm* flock

stor'nare *vt* avert; transfer ⟨somma⟩

'storno *nm* starling

storpi'are *vt* cripple; mangle ⟨parole⟩

storpia'tura *nf* deformation

'storpio, -a ① *adj* crippled ② *nmf* cripple

'storta *nf* (distorsione) sprain; **prendere una ~ alla caviglia** sprain one's ankle

'storto ① *pp di* STORCERE ② *adj* crooked; (ritorto) twisted; ⟨gambe⟩ bandy; fig wrong

stor'tura *nf* deformity; **~ mentale** twisted way of thinking

sto'viglie *nfpl* crockery *sg*, flatware Am

'strabico *adj* cross-eyed; **essere ~** be cross-eyed, [have a] squint

strabili'ante *adj* astonishing

strabili'are *vt* astonish

stra'bismo *nm* squint

straboc'care *vi* overflow

strabuz'zare *vt* **~ gli occhi** goggle; **ha strabuzzato gli occhi** his eyes popped out of his head

straca'narsi *vr* fam work like a slave, slave away

stra'carico *adj* overloaded

strac'chino *nm* soft cheese from Lombardy

stracci'are *vt* tear; (fam: vincere) thrash

straccia'tella *nf* vanilla ice cream with chocolate chips

stracci'ato *adj* torn; ⟨persona⟩ in rags; ⟨prezzi⟩ slashed; **a un prezzo ~** at a knock-down price, dirt cheap

'straccio ① *adj* torn ② *nm* rag; (strofinaccio) cloth; **essere ridotto ad uno ~** feel like a wet rag

stracci'one *nm* tramp

stracci'vendolo *nm* ragman

stracol'larsi *vr* sprain

stra'cotto ① *adj* overdone; (fam: innamorato) head over heels ② *nm* stew

'strada *nf* road; (di città) street; (fig: cammino) way; **essere fuori ~** be on the wrong track; **fare ~** lead the way; **tener la macchina in ~** keep the car on the road; (parcheggiare) keep the car on the street; **su ~** ⟨trasportare⟩ by road; **farsi ~** (aver successo) make one's way [in the world]. **strada d'accesso** approach road. **strada camionabile** road for heavy vehicles. **strada maestra** main road. **strada pedonale** pedestrianized street. **strada principale** main road. **strada privata** private road. **strada secondaria** secondary road. **strada a senso unico** one-way street. **strada senza uscita** dead end, cul-de-sac. **strada di terra battuta** dirt track

stra'dale ① *adj* road *attrib* ② *nf* **la Stradale** fam traffic police

stra'dario *nm* street plan

stra'dina *nf* little street; (in campagna) little road

strafalci'one *nm* blunder

stra'fare *vi* overdo it, overdo things

stra'foro: di ~ *adv* on the sly

strafot'tente *adj* arrogant

strafot'tenza *nf* arrogance

'strage *nf* slaughter

stra'grande *adj* vast

stralci'are *vt* remove

'stralcio *nm* removal; (parte) extract

stralu'nare *vt* **~ gli occhi** open one's eyes wide

stralu'nato *adj* ⟨occhi⟩ staring; ⟨persona⟩ distraught

stramaz'zare *vi* fall heavily; **~ al suolo** crash to the ground

strambe'ria *nf* oddity

'strambo *adj* strange

strampa'lato *adj* odd

stra'nezza nf strangeness
strango'lare vt strangle
strani'ero, -a ① adj foreign
② nmf foreigner
'strano adj strange; ~ ma vero surprisingly enough, funnily enough
straordinaria'mente adv extraordinarily
straordi'nario adj extraordinary; (notevole) remarkable; ⟨edizione⟩ special. **lavoro straordinario** overtime; **treno straordinario** special [train]
strapaz'zare vt ill-treat; scramble ⟨uova⟩
strapaz'zarsi vr tire oneself out
stra'pazzo nm strain; **da ~** fig worthless
strapi'eno adj overflowing
strapi'ombo nm projection; **a ~** sheer
strapo'tere nm overwhelming power
strappa'lacrime adj inv weepy
strap'pare vt tear; (per distruggere) tear up; pull out ⟨dente, capelli⟩; (sradicare) pull up; (estorcere) wring
strap'parsi vr get torn; (allontanarsi) tear oneself away; **~ i capelli** fig be tearing one's hair out
'strappo nm tear; (strattone) jerk; (fam: passaggio) lift; **fare uno ~ alla regola** make an exception to the rule. **strappo muscolare** muscle strain
strapun'tino nm folding seat
strari'pare vi flood
strasci'care vt trail; shuffle ⟨piedi⟩; drawl ⟨parole⟩
'strascico nm train; fig after-effect
strasci'coni: **a ~** adv dragging one's feet
straseco'lare vi be amazed
strass nm inv rhinestone
strata'gemma nm stratagem
stra'tega nmf strategist
strate'gia nf strategy
stra'tegico adj strategic; **mossa strategica** strategic move
stratifi'care vt stratify
stratigra'fia nf Geol stratigraphy
'strato nm layer; (di vernice ecc) coat, layer; (roccioso, sociale) stratum. **strato di nuvole** cloud layer
strato'sfera nf stratosphere
strato'sferico adj stratospheric; fig sky-high
stravac'carsi vr fam slouch
stravac'cato adj fam slouching
strava'gante adj extravagant; (eccentrico) eccentric
strava'ganza nf extravagance; (eccentricità) eccentricity
stra'vecchio adj ancient

strave'dere vt **~ per** worship
stravizi'are vi indulge oneself
stra'vizio nm excess
stra'volgere vt twist; (turbare) upset
stravolgi'mento nm twisting
stra'volto adj distraught; (fam: stanco) done in
strazi'ante adj heartrending; ⟨dolore⟩ agonizing
strazi'are vt grate on ⟨orecchie⟩; break ⟨cuore⟩
'strazio nm agony; **essere uno ~** be agony; **che ~!** fam it's awful!; **fare ~ di qualcosa** fam: ⟨attore, cantante⟩ murder something
'streamer nm inv Comput streamer
'strega nf witch
stre'gare vt bewitch
stre'gone nm wizard
stregone'ria nf witchcraft
'stregua nf **alla ~ di** in the same way as; **alla stessa ~** ⟨giudicare⟩ by the same yardstick; **a questa ~** at this rate
stre'mare vt exhaust
stre'mato adj exhausted
'stremo ① adj extreme ② nm **ridotto allo ~** at the end of one's tether
'strenna nf present
'strenuo adj strenuous
strepi'tare vi make a din
strepi'tio nm din, uproar
strepi'toso adj noisy; fig resounding
strepto'cocco nm Med streptococcus
streptomi'cina nf Med streptomycin
stress nm stress
stres'sante adj ⟨lavoro, situazione⟩ stressful
stres'sare vt put under stress, be stressful for
stres'sarsi vr get stressed
stres'sato adj stressed [out]
'stretta nf grasp, squeeze; (dolore) pang; **essere alle strette** be in dire straits; **mettere alle strette qualcuno** have somebody's back up against the wall; **provare una ~ al cuore** feel a pang. **stretta di mano** handshake
stret'tezza nf narrowness; **strettezze** pl (difficoltà finanziarie) financial difficulties
'stretto ① pp di STRINGERE ② adj narrow; (serrato) tight; (vicino) close; ⟨dialetto⟩ broad; (rigoroso) strict; **lo ~ necessario** the bare minimum ③ nm Geog strait. **stretto di Messina** Straits of Messina
stret'toia nf bottleneck; (fam: difficoltà) tight spot
stri'ato adj striped

stria'tura *nf* streak

stri'dente *adj* strident

'stridere *vi* squeak; fig clash

stri'dore *nm* screech

'stridulo *adj* shrill

strigli'are *vt* groom

strigli'ata *nf* grooming; fig dressing down

stril'lare *vi/t* scream

'strillo *nm* scream

stril'lone *nm* newspaper seller

strimin'zito *adj* skimpy; (magro) skinny

strimpel'lare *vt* strum

stri'nare *vt* singe, scorch

'stringa *nf* lace; Comput string

strin'gato *adj* fig terse

'stringere ① *vt* press; (serrare) squeeze; (tenere stretto) hold tight; take in ⟨abito⟩; (comprimere) be tight; (restringere) tighten; ∼ la mano a shake hands with ② *vi* (premere) press

'stringersi *vr* (accostarsi) draw close (a to); (avvicinarsi) squeeze up

strip'pata *nf* fam nosh-up; farsi una ∼ have a nosh-up

strip-'tease *nm inv* striptease

'striscia *nf* strip; (riga) stripe; a strisce striped; strisce *pl* di mezzeria Auto lane markings; strisce *pl* [pedonali] zebra crossing *sg*, crosswalk Am

strisci'are ① *vi* crawl; (sfiorare) graze ② *vt* drag ⟨piedi⟩

strisci'arsi *vr* ∼ a rub against

strisci'ata *nf* scratch

'striscio *nm* graze; Med smear; colpire di ∼ graze

strisci'one *nm* banner

strito'lare *vt* grind

strizzacer'velli *nmf inv* sl shrink

striz'zare *vt* squeeze; (torcere) wring [out]; ∼ l'occhio wink

'strofa *nf* strophe

strofi'naccio *nm* cloth; (per spolverare) duster. **strofinaccio da cucina** tea towel. **strofinaccio per i piatti** dishtowel

strofi'nare *vt* rub

strofi'nio *nm* rubbing

strom'bare *vt* splay

strombaz'zare ① *vt* boast about ② *vi* hoot

strombaz'zata *nf* (di clacson) hoot

stron'care *vt* cut off; (reprimere) crush; (criticare) tear to shreds

stron'zate *nfpl* vulg crap

'stronzo *nm* vulg shit

stropicci'are *vt* rub; crumple ⟨vestito⟩

stropicci'ata *nf* rub

stro'piccio *nm* rubbing

stroppi'are *vt* il troppo stroppia enough is as good as a feast

stroz'zare *vt* strangle

strozza'tura *nf* strangling; (di strada) narrowing

strozzi'naggio *nm* loan-sharking

stroz'zino *nm* pej usurer; (truffatore) shark

struc'cante *nm* make-up remover

struc'carsi *vr* remove one's make-up

strug'gente *adj* all-consuming

'struggersi *vr* liter pine [away]; ∼ di invidia/desiderio be consumed with envy/desire

struggi'mento *nm* yearning

strumen'tale *adj* instrumental

strumentaliz'zare *vt* make use of

strumen'tario *nm* instruments *pl*

strumentazi'one *nf* instrumentation

strumen'tista *nm* instrumentalist

stru'mento *nm* instrument; (arnese) tool. **strumento a corda/fiato** string/wind instrument. **strumento musicale** musical instrument. **strumento a percussione** percussion instrument

strusci'are *vt* rub

strusci'arsi *vr* ⟨gatto⟩ rub itself; ⟨due innamorati⟩ caress each other; ∼ intorno a qualcuno fam suck up to somebody

'strutto *nm* lard

strut'tura *nf* structure

struttu'rale *adj* structural

struttura'lismo *nm* structuralism

struttural'mente *adv* structurally

struttu'rare *vt* structure

strutturazi'one *nf* structuring

'struzzo *nm* ostrich

stuc'care *vt* plaster; (per decorazione) stucco; put putty in ⟨vetri⟩

stucca'tore *nm* plasterer; (decorativo) stucco worker

stucca'tura *nf* plastering; (decorativo) stucco work

stuc'chevole *adj* nauseating

'stucco *nm* plaster; (decorativo) stucco; (per vetro) putty; rimanere di ∼ be thunder-struck

stu'dente, **-essa** *nmf* student; (di scuola) schoolboy; schoolgirl

studen'tesco *adj* student; (di scolaro) school *attrib*

studi'are *vt* study

studi'arsi *vr* ∼ di try to

'studio *nm* studying; (stanza, ricerca) study; (di artista, TV ecc) studio; (di professionista) office. **studio cinematografico** film studio. **studio dentistico** dental surgery

studi'oso, **-a** ① *adj* studious

2 *nmf* scholar

'**stufa** *nf* stove. **stufa elettrica** electric fire. **stufa a gas** gas fire. **stufa a legna** wood-[burning] stove

stu'fare *vt* Culin stew; (dare fastidio) bore

stu'farsi *vr* get bored

stu'fato *nm* stew

'**stufo** *adj* bored; **essere ~ di** be bored with, be fed up with

stu'oia *nf* mat

stu'olo *nm* crowd

stupefa'cente 1 *adj* amazing
2 *nm* drug

stupe'fare *vt* stun

stu'pendo *adj* stupendous; **~ !** brilliant!

stupi'daggine *nf* (azione) stupid thing; (cosa da poco) nothing; **non dire stupidaggini!** don't talk stupid!

stupi'data *nf* stupid thing

stupidità *nf* stupidity

'**stupido** *adj* stupid

stu'pire 1 *vt* astonish
2 *vi* be astonished

stu'pirsi *vr* be astonished

stu'pore *nm* amazement

stu'prare *vt* rape

stupra'tore *nm* rapist

'**stupro** *nm* rape

sturabot'tiglie *nm inv* corkscrew

sturalavan'dini *nm inv* plunger

stu'rare *vt* uncork; unblock ⟨*lavandino*⟩

stuzzica'denti *nm inv* toothpick

stuzzi'care *vt* prod [at]; pick ⟨*denti*⟩; poke ⟨*fuoco*⟩; (molestare) tease; whet ⟨*appetito*⟩

stuzzi'chino *nm* Culin appetizer

su 1 *prep* on; (senza contatto) over; (riguardo a) about; (circa, intorno a) about, around; **le chiavi sono sul tavolo** the keys are on the table; **il quadro è appeso sul camino** the picture is hanging over the fireplace; **un libro sull'antico Egitto** a book on or about Ancient Egypt; **sarò lì sulle cinque** I'll be there about five, I'll be there around five; **è durato sulle tre ore** it lasted for about three hours; **costa sui 75 euro** it costs about 75 euros; **decidere sul momento** decide at the time; **su commissione** on commission; **su due piedi** on the spot; **su misura** made to measure; **uno su dieci** one out of ten; **stare sulle proprie** keep oneself to oneself; **sul mare** ⟨*casa*⟩ by the sea
2 *adv* (sopra) up; (al piano di sopra) upstairs; (addosso) on; **andare su** go up; (al piano di sopra) go upstairs; **ho su il cappotto** I've got my coat on; **in su** ⟨*guardare*⟩ up; **dalla vita in su** from the waist up; **su!** come on!

sua'dente *adj* persuasive

sub *nmf inv* skin-diver

sub+ *pref* sub+

su'bacqueo, **-a** 1 *adj* underwater
2 *nmf* skin-diver

subaffit'tare *vt* sublet

subaf'fitto *nm* sublet; **in ~** sublet

suba'gente *nm* subagent

subal'terno *adj & nm* subordinate

subappal'tare *vt* subcontract

subappalta|'**tore**, **-trice** *nmf* subcontractor

subap'palto *nm* subcontract; **in ~** subcontracted; **dare in ~** subcontract; **prendere in ~** take on a subcontract basis

sub'buglio *nm* turmoil

sub'conscio *adj & nm* subconscious

subconti'nente *nm* subcontinent

subcosci'ente *adj & nm* subconscious

subdi'rectory *nf inv* Comput subdirectory

subdola'mente *adv* deviously

'**subdolo** *adj* devious, underhand

suben'trare *vi* ⟨*circostanze*⟩ come up; **~ a** take the place of

su'bentro *nm* changeover

subequatori'ale *adj* subequatorial

su'bire *vt* undergo; (patire) suffer

subis'sare *vt* fig **~ di** overwhelm with

subi'taneo *adj* sudden

'**subito** *adv* at once, immediately, right away; **~ dopo** straight after; **vengo ~** I'll be right there

subli'mare *vt* sublimate

su'blime *adj* sublime

sublimi'nale *adj* subliminal

sublingu'ale *adj* sublingual

sublo'care *vt* sublease

subloca'tario *nm* sublessor

sublocazi'one *nf* sublease

subnor'male *adj* subnormal

subodo'rare *vt* suspect

subordi'nare *vt* subordinate

subordi'nato, **-a** *adj & nmf* subordinate

su'bordine *nm* **in ~** second in order of importance

subrou'tine *nf* Comput subroutine

subsi'denza *nf* Geol subsidence

sub'strato *nm* substratum, substrate

subto'tale *nm* subtotal

subtropi'cale *adj* subtropical

subu'mano *adj* subhuman

subur'bano *adj* suburban

suc'cedere *vi* (accadere) happen; **~ a** (in carica) succeed; (venire dopo) follow; **~ al trono** succeed to the throne

suc'cedersi *vr* happen one after the other; **si sono succeduti molti ...** there was a series of ...

successi'one *nf* succession; **in ~** in succession

successiva'mente *adv* subsequently

succes'sivo *adj* successive; ⟨*mese, giorno*⟩ following

suc'cesso ① *pp di* SUCCEDERE ② *nm* success; (esito) outcome; (disco ecc) hit

succes'sone *nm* huge success

succes'sore *nm* successor

succhi'are *vt* suck [up]; ∼ **il sangue a qualcuno** *fig* bleed somebody dry

succhi'ello *nm* gimlet

succinta'mente *adv* succinctly

suc'cinto *adj* (conciso) concise; ⟨*abito*⟩ scanty

'succo *nm* juice; *fig* essence. **succo d'arancia** orange juice. **succo di frutta** fruit juice. **succo di limone** lemon juice

suc'coso *adj* juicy

'succube *nm* **essere ∼ di qualcuno** be totally dominated by somebody

succu'lento *adj* succulent

succur'sale *nf* branch [office]

sud *nm* south; **del ∼** southern; **a ∼ di** [to the] south of

Su'dafrica *nm* South Africa

sudafri'cano *adj & nmf* South African

Suda'merica *nf* South America

sudameri'cano, **-a** *adj & nmf* South American

Su'dan *nm* **il ∼** the Sudan

suda'nese *adj & nmf* Sudanese

su'dare *vi* sweat, perspire; (faticare) sweat blood; ∼ **freddo** be in a cold sweat; ∼ **sangue** sweat blood; **mi fa ∼ freddo** it brings me out in a cold sweat; ∼ **sette camicie** sweat blood

su'data *nf anche fig* sweat

suda'ticcio *adj* sweaty

su'dato *adj* sweaty; ⟨*vittoria*⟩ hard-won; ⟨*pane*⟩ hard-earned

sud'detto *adj* above-mentioned

'suddito, **-a** *nmf* subject

suddi'videre *vt* subdivide

suddivisi'one *nf* subdivision

su'd-est *nm* southeast

'sudicio *adj* dirty, filthy

sudici'ume *nm* dirt, filth

sudocciden'tale *adj* southwestern

sudorazi'one *nf* perspiring

su'dore *nm* sweat, perspiration; *fig* sweat; **in un bagno di ∼** bathed in sweat; **con il ∼ della fronte** *fig* by the sweat of one's brow. **sudore freddo** cold sweat

sudo'riparo *adj* sweat *attrib*

su'd-ovest *nm* southwest

'sue ▶ SUO

suffici'ente ① *adj* sufficient; (presuntuoso) conceited

② *nm* bare essentials *pl*; Sch pass mark

suffici'enza *nf* sufficiency; (presunzione) conceit; Sch pass; **a ∼** enough; **prendere la ∼** get the pass-mark

suf'fisso *nm* suffix

sufflè *nm inv* Culin soufflé

suffra'getta *nf* suffragette

suf'fragio *nm* (voto) vote; **in ∼ di qualcuno** in homage to somebody. **suffragio universale** universal suffrage

suffu'migio *nm* inhalation

suggel'lare *vt* seal

suggeri'mento *nm* suggestion

sugge'rire *vt* suggest; Theat prompt

suggeri|'tore, **-trice** *nmf* Theat prompter

suggestio'nabile *adj* suggestible

suggestio'nare *vt* influence

suggestio'nato *adj* influenced

suggesti'one *nf* influence

sugge'stivo *adj* suggestive; ⟨*musica ecc*⟩ evocative

'sughero *nm* cork

'sugli = SU + GLI

'sugo *nm* (di frutta) juice; (di carne) gravy; (salsa) sauce; (sostanza) substance

'sui = SU + I

sui'cida ① *adj* suicidal ② *nmf* suicide

suici'darsi *vr* commit suicide

sui'cidio *nm anche fig* suicide; **tentato ∼** attempted suicide

su'ino ① *adj* **carne suina** pork ② *nm* swine

suite *nf inv* suite

sul = SU + IL

sulfa'midico *nm* sulphonamide/sulpha drug

sul'fureo *adj* sulphuric

'sulla = SU + LA

'sulle = SU + LE

'sullo = SU + LO

sul'tana *nf* (persona) sultana

sulta'nina *adj* **uva ∼** sultana

sul'tano *nm* sultan

'sunto *nm* summary

'suo, **-a** ① *poss adj* **il ∼**, **i suoi** his; (di cosa, animale) its; (forma di cortesia) your; **la sua**, **le sue** her; (di cosa, animale) its; (forma di cortesia) your; **questa macchina è sua** this car is his/hers; ∼ **padre** his/her/your father; **un ∼ amico** a friend of his/hers/ yours

② *poss pron* **il ∼**, **i suoi** his; (di cosa, animale) its; (forma di cortesia) yours; **la sua**, **le sue** hers; (di cosa animale) its; (forma di cortesia) yours; **i suoi** his/her folk[s]

su'ocera *nf* mother-in-law

su'ocero *nm* father-in-law

su'oi ▶ SUO

su'ola *nf* sole; **suole** *pl* **di para** crepe soles

su'olo *nm* ground; (terreno) soil. **suolo pubblico** public land

suo'nare ① *vt* Mus play; ring ⟨*campanello*⟩; sound ⟨*allarme, clacson*⟩; ⟨*orologio*⟩ strike ⟨*ore*⟩; ~ **il clacson** sound the horn, hoot the horn; (fam: imbrogliare) do ② *vi* ⟨*campanello, telefono, sveglia*⟩ ring; ⟨*clacson*⟩ hoot; ⟨*sirena*⟩ go [off]; ⟨*giradischi*⟩ play

suo'nato *adj* fam bonkers

suona|'tore, -trice *nmf* player

suone'ria *nf* alarm; (di cellulare) ringtone

su'ono *nm* sound

su'ora *nf* nun; **Suor Maria** Sister Maria

'super *nf* 4-star [petrol], premium [gas] Am

super+ *pref* super+

supe'rabile *adj* surmountable

superal'colico ① *nm* spirit ② *adj* **bevande superalcoliche** spirits

supera'mento *nm* (di timidezza) overcoming; (di esame) success (**di** in)

supe'rare *vt* surpass; (eccedere) exceed; (vincere) overcome; overtake, pass Am ⟨*veicolo*⟩; pass ⟨*esame*⟩; ~ **la barriera del suono** break the sound barrier; ~ **se stessi** surpass oneself; **ha superato la trentina** he's over thirty

su'perbia *nf* haughtiness

su'perbo *adj* haughty; (magnifico) superb

super'donna *nf* superwoman

superdo'tato *adj* highly gifted, super-talented

superfici'ale ① *adj* superficial ② *nmf* superficial person

superficialità *nf* superficiality

super'ficie *nf* surface; (area) area; **in** ~ on the surface; fig: ⟨*esaminare*⟩ superficially

su'perfluo *adj* superfluous

Super-'Io *nm* Psych superego

superi'ora *nf* superior; Relig mother superior

superi'ore ① *adj* superior; (di grado) senior; (più elevato) higher; (sovrastante) upper; (al di sopra) above ② *nm* superior

superiorità *nf* superiority

superla'tivo *adj & nm* superlative

supermer'cato *nm* supermarket

supermo'della *nf* supermodel

super'nova *nf* Astr supernova

superpetroli'era *nf* Naut supertanker

superpo'tenza *nf* superpower

super'sonico *adj* supersonic

su'perstite ① *adj* surviving

② *nmf* survivor

superstizi'one *nf* superstition

superstizi'oso *adj* superstitious

super'strada *nf* toll-free motorway. **superstrada informatica** information superhighway

superu'omo *nm* superman

supervalu'tare *vt* overvalue

supervalutazi'one *nf* overvaluation

supervisi'one *nf* supervision

supervi'sore *nm* supervisor

su'pino *adj* supine

suppel'lettili *nfpl* furnishings

suppergiù *adv* about

supplemen'tare *adj* additional, supplementary

supple'mento *nm* supplement. **supplemento illustrato** colour supplement. **supplemento rapido** express train supplement

sup'plente ① *adj* temporary ② *nmf* Sch supply teacher

sup'plenza *nf* temporary post

'supplica *nf* plea; (domanda) petition

suppli'care *vt* beg

suppli'chevole *adj* imploring

sup'plire ① *vt* replace ② *vi* ~ **a** (compensare) make up for

sup'plizio *nm* torture

sup'porre *vt* suppose

suppor'tare *vt* Comput support

sup'porto *nm* support. **supporto di sistema** Comput system support

supposizi'one *nf* supposition

sup'posta *nf* suppository

sup'posto *pp* di SUPPORRE

suppu'rare *vi* fester

suppurazi'one *nf* suppuration; **andare in** ~ fester

suprema'zia *nf* supremacy

su'premo *adj* supreme

surclas'sare *vt* outclass

surf *nm inv* surfboard; (sport) surfboarding

sur'fista *nmf* surfer

surge'lare *vt* deep-freeze

surge'lato ① *adj* frozen ② *nm* **surgelati** *pl* frozen food *sg*

Suri'name *nm* Surinam

'surplus *nm* surplus

surre'ale *adj* surreal

surrea'lismo *nm* surrealism

surrea'lista *nmf* surrealist

surrea'listico *adj* surrealist

surre'nale *adj* adrenal

surriscal'dare *vt* overheat

surriscal'darsi *vr* overheat

surro'gato *nm* substitute

suscet'tibile *adj* touchy

suscettibilità *nf* touchiness

susci'tare *vt* stir up; arouse ‹*ammirazione ecc*›

su'sina *nf* plum. **susina selvatica** damson

su'sino *nm* plumtree

su'spense *nf* suspense

sussegu'ente *adj* subsequent

sussegu'irsi *vr* follow one after the other

sussidi'are *vt* subsidize

sussidi'ario *adj* subsidiary

sus'sidio *nm* subsidy; (aiuto) aid. **sussidio didattico** study aid. **sussidio di disoccupazione** unemployment benefit. **sussidio di malattia** sickness benefit

sussi'ego *nm* haughtiness; **con ∼** haughtily

sussi'stenza *nf* subsistence

sus'sistere *vi* subsist; (essere valido) hold good

sussul'tare *vi* start; **far ∼ qualcuno** give somebody a start

sus'sulto *nm* start

sussur'rare *vt/i* whisper; **si sussurra che ...** it is rumoured that ...

sussur'rio *nm* murmur

sus'surro *nm* whisper

su'tura *nf* suture

sutu'rare *vt* suture

suv'via *int* come on!

sva'gare *vt* amuse

sva'garsi *vr* amuse oneself

'svago *nm* relaxation; (divertimento) amusement; **prendersi un po' di ∼** have a break

svaligi'are *vt* rob; burgle ‹*casa*›

svalu'tare *vt* devalue; fig underestimate

svalu'tarsi *vr* lose value

svalutazi'one *nf* devaluation

svam'pito, -a *nmf* airhead

sva'nire *vi* vanish

sva'nito, -a ① *adj* ‹*persona*› absent-minded; ‹*sapore, sogno*› faded ② *nmf* absent-minded person

svantaggi'ato *adj* at a disadvantage; ‹*bambino, paese*› disadvantaged

svan'taggio *nm* disadvantage; **essere in ∼** Sport be losing; **in ∼ di tre punti** three points down; **in ∼ rispetto a qualcuno** at a disadvantage compared with somebody

svantaggi'oso *adj* disadvantageous

svapo'rare *vi* evaporate

svari'ato *adj* varied

svari'one *nm* blunder

sva'sare *vt* splay; flare ‹*gonna*›

sva'sato *adj* ‹*gonna*› flared

svasa'tura *nf* flare

'svastica *nf* swastika

sve'dese ① *adj & nm* (lingua) Swedish ② *nmf* Swede

'sveglia *nf* (orologio) alarm [clock]; **∼!** get up!; **mettere la ∼** set the alarm [clock]. **sveglia automatica** alarm call. **sveglia telefonica** wake-up call

svegli'are *vt* wake up; fig awaken; **∼ l'appetito a qualcuno** whet somebody's appetite

svegli'arsi *vr* wake up

'sveglio *adj* awake; (di mente) alert, sharp

sve'lare *vt* reveal

svel'tezza *nf* speed; fig quick-wittedness

svel'tire *vt* quicken

svel'tirsi *vr* ‹*persona*› liven up

'svelto *adj* quick; (slanciato) svelte; **alla svelta** quickly; **a passo ∼** quickly

sve'narsi *vr* slash one's wrists; fig reduce oneself to poverty

'svendere *vt* undersell

'svendita *nf* [clearance] sale

sve'nevole *adj* sentimental

sveni'mento *nm* fainting fit

sve'nire *vi* faint; **da ∼** incredibly

sven'tare *vt* foil

sven'tato ① *adj* thoughtless ② *nmf* thoughtless person

'sventola *nf* slap. **orecchie a sventola** protruding ears, jug-handle ears fam

svento'lare *vt/i* wave

svento'larsi *vr* fan oneself

svento'lio *nm* flutter

sventra'mento *nm* disembowelment; (di pollo) gutting; (fig: di edificio) demolition ‹*edificio*›

sven'trare *vt* disembowel; gut ‹*pollo*›; fig demolish ‹*edificio*›

sven'tura *nf* misfortune

sventu'rato *adj* unfortunate

sve'nuto *pp di* SVENIRE

svergi'nare *vt* deflower

svergo'gnato *adj* shameless

sver'nare *vi* winter

svernici'ante *nm* paint stripper

svernici'are *vt* strip

sve'stire *vt* undress

sve'stirsi *vr* undress, get undressed

svet'tare *vi* ‹*albero, torre*› stand out; **∼ verso il cielo** stretch skywards

'Svezia *nf* Sweden

svezza'mento *nm* weaning

svez'zare *vt* wean

svi'are *vt* divert; (corrompere) lead astray

svi'arsi *vr* fig go astray

S

svico'lare *vi* turn down a side street;
(fig: dalla questione ecc) evade the issue; (fig:
da una persona) dodge out of the way

svi'gnarsela *vr* slip away

svigo'rire *vt* emasculate

svili'mento *nm* debasement

svi'lire *vt* debase

svilup'pare *vt* develop

svilup'parsi *vr* develop

sviluppa|'**tore**, **-trice** *nmf* developer.
sviluppatore web web developer

svi'luppo *nm* development. **paese in
via di sviluppo** developing country

svinco'lare *vt* release; clear ⟨*merce*⟩;
redeem ⟨*deposito*⟩

svinco'larsi *vr* free oneself

'**svincolo** *nm* clearance; (di autostrada)
exit; ∼ **di un deposito cauzionale**
redemption of a deposit

svioli'nata *nf* fawning

svisce'rare *vt* gut; fig dissect

svisce'rato *adj* ⟨*amore*⟩ passionate;
(ossequioso) obsequious

'**svista** *nf* oversight

svi'tare *vt* unscrew

svi'tato *adj* (fam: matto) cracked, nutty

'**Svizzera** *nf* Switzerland

'**svizzera** *nf* (carne) hamburger

'**svizzero**, **-a** *adj & nmf* Swiss

svoglia'taggine *nf* laziness; (riluttanza)
unwillingness

svogli'atamente *adv* half-heartedly;
(senza energia) listlessly

svoglia'tezza *nf* half-heartedness;
(mancanza di energia) listlessness

svogli'ato *adj* half-hearted; (senza energia)
listless

svolaz'zante *adj* ⟨*capelli*⟩ wind-swept

svolaz'zare *vi* flutter

svolaz'zio *nm* flutter

'**svolgere** *vt* unwind; unwrap ⟨*pacco*⟩;
(risolvere) solve; (portare a termine) carry out;
(sviluppare) develop

'**svolgersi** *vr* (accadere) take place

svolgi'mento *nm* course; (sviluppo)
development

'**svolta** *nf* turning; fig turning-point

svol'tare *vi* turn

'**svolto** *pp di* SVOLGERE

svuo'tare *vt* empty [out]; (fig: di significato)
deprive

'**Swaziland** *nm* Swaziland

swing *nm* Mus swing

switch *nm* Comput switch

Tt

T *abbr* (**tabaccheria**) tobacconist

tabac'caio, **-a** *nmf* tobacconist

tabacche'ria *nf* tobacconist's (which
also sells stamps, postcards etc)

ta'bacco *nm* tobacco; **tabacchi** *pl*
cigarettes and tobacco

taba'gismo *nm* nicotine addiction

ta'bella *nf* table; (lista) list. **tabella di
conversione** conversion table. **tabella
di marcia** fig schedule. **tabella dei
prezzi** price list. **tabella retributiva**
salary scale

tabel'lina *nf* Math multiplication table

tabel'lone *nm* wall chart. **tabellone
degli arrivi** arrivals board. **tabellone
del canestro** backboard. **tabellone
delle partenze** departures board.
tabellone segnapunti scoreboard

taber'nacolo *nm* tabernacle

tabù *adj & nm inv* taboo

tabu'lare *vt* tabulate

tabu'lato *nm* Comput [data] printout

tabula'tore *nm* tabulator

tabulazi'one *nf* tabulation

TAC *nf inv abbr* (**tomografia assiale
computerizzata**) CAT scan

'**tacca** *nf* notch; **di mezza** ∼ ⟨*attore,
giornalista*⟩ second-rate

taccagne'ria *nf* penny-pinching

tac'cagno *adj* fam stingy

taccheggia|'**tore**, **-trice** *nmf*
shoplifter

tac'cheggio *nm* shoplifting

tac'chetto *nm* Sport stud

tac'chino *nm* turkey

tacci'are *vt* ∼ **qualcuno di qualcosa**
accuse somebody of something

'**tacco** *nm* heel; **alzare i tacchi** take to
one's heels; **scarpe senza** ∼ flat shoes,
flats; **colpo di tacco** backheel. **tacchi** *pl*
a spillo stiletto heels, stilettos

taccu'ino *nm* notebook

ta'cere ① *vi* be silent
② *vt* say nothing about; **mettere a** ∼
qualcosa ⟨*scandalo*⟩ hush something up;
mettere a ∼ **qualcuno** silence somebody

tachicar'dia *nf* tachycardia

ta'chigrafo *nm* tachograph

ta'chimetro *nm* speedometer

tacita'mente *adv* tacitly; (in silenzio) silently

'**tacito** *adj* tacit, unspoken; (silenzioso) silent

taci'turno *adj* taciturn

ta'fano *nm* horsefly

taffe'ruglio *nm* scuffle

taffettà *nm* taffeta

'**taglia** *nf* (riscatto) ransom; (ricompensa) reward; (statura) height; (di abiti) size; **per taglie forti** outsize, OS. **taglia unica** one size

taglia'carte *nm inv* paperknife

'**taglia e in'colla** *nm inv* cut and paste; **fare un ∼** cut and paste

taglia'erba *nm inv* lawnmower

tagliafu'oco 1 *adj inv* **porta tagliafuoco** fire door; **striscia tagliafuoco** fire break
2 *nm inv* (in bosco) fire break

tagli'ando *nm* coupon; **fare il ∼** ≈ put one's car in for its MOT. **tagliando di controllo** manufacturer's sticker; (da raccogliere) token. **tagliando controllo bagaglio** baggage claim sticker. **tagliando di garanzia** warranty

taglia'pasta 1 *adj inv* **rotella ∼** pastry cutter
2 *nm inv* pastry cutter

tagliapa'tate *nm inv* potato peeler

tagli'are 1 *vt* cut; (attraversare) cut across; cut off ⟨telefono, elettricità⟩; carve ⟨carne⟩; mow ⟨erba⟩; **farsi ∼ i capelli** have a haircut, have one's hair cut; **∼ i viveri a qualcuno** stop somebody's allowance
2 *vi* cut

tagli'arsi *vr* cut oneself; **∼ il dito** cut one's finger; **∼ i capelli** have a haircut, have one's hair cut

taglia'sigari *nm inv* cigar cutter

tagli'ata *nf* finely-cut beef fillet; **dare una ∼ a qualcosa** give something a cut, cut something

tagli'ato *adj* (a pezzi) jointed; **essere ∼ per qualcosa** fig be cut out for something

taglia'unghie *nm inv* nail clippers *pl*

taglieggi'are *vt* extort money from

tagli'ente 1 *adj* sharp
2 *nm* cutting edge

tagli'ere *nm* chopping board. **∼ per il pane** breadboard

taglie'rina *nf* (per carta) guillotine; (per foto) trimmer; (per metallo, vetro) cutter

'**taglio** *nm* cut; (di stoffa) length; (di capelli) [hair-]cut; (parte tagliente) cutting edge; **di ∼** edgeways; **a doppio ∼** fig double-edged. **taglio e cucito** dressmaking; **dacci un ∼!** fam put a sock in it!. **taglio di carne** cut of meat. **taglio cesareo** Caesarean section. **taglio di personale** personnel cut. **taglio dei prezzi** price cutting. **taglio alla spesa** spending cut

tagli'ola *nf* trap

taglio'lini *nmpl* thin soup noodles

tagli'one *nm* **legge del taglione** an eye for an eye and a tooth for a tooth

tagliuz'zare *vt* cut into small pieces

tail'leur *nm inv* [lady's] suit

Tai'wan *nf* Taiwan

ta'lare *adj* **prendere la veste ∼** take holy orders

talassotera'pia *nf* therapy based on seawater

'**talco** *nm* talcum powder, talc

'**tale** 1 *adj* such a; (con nomi plurali) such; **c'è un ∼ disordine** there is such a mess; **non accetto tali scuse** I won't accept such excuses; **è un ∼ bugiardo!** he's such a liar!; **il rumore era ∼ che non si sentiva nulla** there was so much noise you couldn't hear yourself think; **il ∼ giorno** on such and such a day; **vai il tal giorno alla tal ora** go on such a day at such a time; **quel tal signore** that gentleman; **∼ padre ∼ figlio** like father like son; **∼ quale** just like
2 *pron* **un ∼** someone; **quel ∼** that man; **il tal dei tali** such and such a person

ta'lea *nf* cutting

tale'bano *adj & nm* Taliban

ta'lento *nm* talent

'**talent scout** *nmf inv* talent scout

tali'smano *nm* talisman

tallo'nare *vt* be hot on the heels of

tallon'cino *nm* coupon. **talloncino del prezzo** price tag

tal'lone *nm* heel. **tallone di Achille** fig Achilles' heel. **tallone aureo** Econ gold standard

tal'mente *adv* so

ta'lora *adv* = TALVOLTA

'**talpa** *nf* mole

tal'volta *adv* sometimes

tamburel'lare *vi* (con le dita) drum; (pioggia) beat, drum

tambu'rello *nm* tambourine

tambu'rino *nm* drummer

tam'buro *nm* drum. **tamburo del freno** brake drum

tame'rice *nf* tamarisk

'**tamia** *nm inv* chipmunk

Ta'migi *nm* Thames

tampona'mento *nm* Auto collision; (di ferita) dressing; (di falla) plugging. **tamponamento a catena** pile-up

tampo'nare *vt* (urtare) crash into; plug (falla); dress (ferita)

tam'pone *nm* swab; (per timbri) pad; (per mestruazioni) tampon; (per treni, Comput) buffer

tam'tam *nm inv* bush telegraph

TAN *abbr* (**tasso annuale nominale**) Fin AER

'**tana** *nf* den

'**tandem** *nm inv* tandem; **in** ∼ ⟨*lavorare*⟩ in tandem

'**tanfo** *nm* stench

'**tanga** *nm inv* tanga

tan'gente ① *adj* tangent
② *nf* tangent; (somma) bribe

tangen'topoli *nf* widespread corruption in Italy in the early 90s

tangenzi'ale *nf* orbital road

tan'gibile *adj* tangible

tangibil'mente *adv* tangibly

'**tango** *nm* tango

'**tanica** *nf* (contenitore) jerry can; (serbatoio di nave) tank. **tanica di benzina** petrol can

tan'nino *nm* tannin

tan'tino: **un** ∼ *adv* a little [bit]

'**tanto** ① *adj* [so] much; (con nomi plurali) [so] many, [such] a lot of; ∼ **tempo** [such] a long time; **non ha tanta pazienza** he doesn't have much patience; ∼ **tempo quanto ti serve** as much time as you need; **tanti amici quanti parenti** as many friends as relatives
② *pron* much; (plurale) many; (tanto tempo) much time; **è un uomo come tanti** he's just an ordinary man; **tanti** (molte persone) many people; **non ci vuole così** ∼ it doesn't take that long; ∼ **quanto** as much as; **tanti quanti** as many as
③ *conj* (comunque) anyway, in any case
④ *adv* (così) so; (con verbi) so much; **è** ∼ **debole che non sta in piedi** he's so weak that he can't stand; **è** ∼ **ingenuo da crederle** he's naive enough to believe her; **di** ∼ **in** ∼ every now and then; ∼ **l'uno come l'altro** both; ∼ **quanto** as much as; **tre volte** ∼ three times as much; **una volta** ∼ once in a while; ∼ **meglio così!** so much the better!; **tant'è** so much so; ∼ **vale che andiamo a casa** we might as well go home; ∼ **per cambiare** for a change

Tan'zania *nf* Tanzania

tapi'oca *nf* tapioca

ta'piro *nm* tapir

ta'pis rou'lant *nm inv* conveyor belt

'**tappa** *nf* (parte di viaggio) stage; **fare** ∼ **a** break one's journey in

tappa'buchi *nm inv* stopgap

tap'pare *vt* plug; cork ⟨*bottiglia*⟩; ∼ **la bocca a qualcuno** fam shut somebody up

tappa'rella *nf* fam roller blind; **tirar su la** ∼ pull the blind up

tap'parsi *vr* ∼ **gli occhi** cover one's eyes; ∼ **il naso** hold one's nose; ∼ **le orecchie** put one's fingers in one's ears

tappe'tino *nm* mat; Comput mouse mat. **tappetino antiscivolo** [anti-slip] safety bathmat. **tappetino da bagno** bathmat

tap'peto *nm* carpet; (piccolo) rug; **andare al** ∼ (pugilato) hit the canvas; **mandare qualcuno al** ∼ knock somebody down; **bombardamento a tappeto** carpet bombing. **tappeto erboso** lawn. **tappeto persiano** Persian carpet. **tappeto stradale** road surface. **tappeto verde** (tavolo) card table. **tappeto volante** magic carpet

tappez'zare *vt* paper ⟨*pareti*⟩; (con manifesti) cover

tappezze'ria *nf* tapestry; (di carta) wallpaper; (arte) upholstery; **fare da** ∼ fig be a wallflower

tappezzi'ere *nm* upholsterer; (imbianchino) decorator

'**tappo** *nm* plug; (di sughero) cork; (di metallo, per penna) top; (fam pej: persona piccola) dwarf. **tappo di bottiglia** bottle top. **tappo a corona** crown cap. **tappi** *pl* **per le orecchie** earplugs. **tappo salvagocce** anti-drip top. **tappo di scarico [della coppa]** sump drain plug. **tappo a strappo** ring-pull. **tappo a vite** screw top

'**tara** *nf* (difetto) flaw; (ereditaria) hereditary defect; (peso) tare

taran'tella *nf* tarantula

ta'rantola *nf* tarantula

ta'rare *vt* Techn calibrate; Comm discount

ta'rato *adj* Comm discounted; Techn calibrated; Med with a hereditary defect; fam crazy

tarchi'ato *adj* stocky

tar'dare ① *vi* be late
② *vt* delay

'**tardi** *adv* late; **al più** ∼ at the latest; **più** ∼ later [on]; **sul** ∼ late in the day; **far** ∼ (essere in ritardo) be late; (con gli amici) stay up late; **a più** ∼ see you later; **svegliarsi troppo** ∼ oversleep

tardiva'mente *adv* late

tar'divo *adj* late; ⟨*bambino*⟩ retarded

'**tardo** *adj* slow; ⟨*pomeriggio, mattinata*⟩ late

'**targa** *nf* plate; Auto numberplate

tar'gato *adj* **un'auto targata…** a car with the registration number…

targ'hetta *nf* (su porta) nameplate; (sulla valigia) name tag. **targhetta di circolazione** numberplate. **targhetta commemorativa** memorial plaque. **targhetta stradale** street sign

ta'riffa *nf* rate, tariff; **a** ∼ **ridotta** Teleph offpeak. **tariffa aerea** airfare. **tariffa doganale** customs tariff. **tariffa**

ferroviaria [rail] fares. **tariffa interna** inland postage. **tariffa ore di punta** peak rate. **tariffa professionale** [professional] fee. **tariffa telefonica** telephone charges. **tariffa unica** flat rate

tarif'fario ① adj tariff adv ② nm price list

tar'larsi vr get worm-eaten

tar'lato adj worm-eaten

'tarlo nm woodworm

'tarma nf moth

tar'marsi vr get moth-eaten

tarmi'cida nm ≈ moth-repellent

ta'rocco nm tarot; **tarocchi** pl tarot

tar'pare vt clip

tartagli'are vi stutter

'tartaro adj & nm tartar; **salsa tartara** tartar[e] sauce

tarta'ruga nf tortoise; (di mare) turtle; (per pettine ecc) tortoiseshell

tartas'sare vt (angariare) harass

tar'tina nf canapé

tar'tufo nm truffle

'tasca nf pocket; (in borsa) compartment; **da ~** pocket attrib; **avere le tasche piene di qualcosa** fam have had a bellyful of something; **se ne è stato con le mani in ~** fig he didn't lift a finger [to help]. **tasca a battente** flap pocket. **tasca del nero** (di polpo, seppia) ink sac. **tasca da pasticciere** icing bag. **tasca tagliata** slit pocket. **tasca a toppa** patchpocket

ta'scabile ① adj pocket attrib ② nm paperback

tasca'pane nm inv haversack

ta'schino nm breast pocket

tassì nm inv taxi

'tassa nf tax; (d'iscrizione ecc) fee; (doganale) duty. **tassa di circolazione** road tax. **tassa di esportazione** export duty. **tassa d'iscrizione** registration fee. **tassa di soggiorno** tourist tax, visitors' tax; **tasse** pl **scolastiche** school fees; **tasse** pl **universitarie** tuition fees

tas'sabile adj taxable

tas'sametro nm meter

tas'sare vt tax

tassativa'mente adv without fail

tassa'tivo adj strict

tassazi'one nf taxation

tas'sello nm wedge; (di stoffa) gusset; (per legno, parete) rawlplug

tas'sista nmf taxi driver

'tasso[1] nm Bot yew; (animale) badger

'tasso[2] Comm rate. **tasso agevolato** cut rate; **prestito a ~ agevolato** soft loan. **tasso base** base rate. **tasso base di interesse** base lending rate. **tasso di cambio** exchange rate. **tasso di**

crescita growth rate. **tasso di disoccupazione** unemployment rate. **tasso d'inquinamento** pollution level. **tasso di interesse** interest rate. **tasso di mortalità** death rate. **tasso di sconto** discount rate

ta'stare vt feel; **~ il terreno** fig test the water or ground

tasti'era nf keyboard. **tastiera numerica** Comput numeric keypad. **telefono a tastiera** touch-tone telephone

tastie'rino nm **tastierino numerico** numeric keypad

tastie'rista nmf keyboarder

'tasto nm key; (tatto) touch. **tasto Alt** Alt key. **tasto di cancellazione** delete key. **tasto control** Comput control key. **tasto cursore** Comput cursor key. **tasto delicato** fig touchy subject. **tasto eject** eject button. **tasto escape** escape key. **tasto funzione** Comput function key. **tasto numerico** Comput numeric[al] key. **tasto di ritorno a margine** return key. **tasto tabulatore** tab [key]

ta'stoni: a ~ adv gropingly; **camminare a ~** grope around; **cercare qualcosa a ~** grope for something

'tattica nf tactics pl

'tattico adj tactical

'tattile adj tactile

'tatto nm (senso) touch; (accortezza) tact; **aver ~** be tactful

tatu'aggio nm tattoo

tatu'are vt tattoo

tautolo'gia nf tautology

tauto'logico adj tautological

'tavola nf table; (illustrazione) plate; (asse) plank; **saper stare a ~** have good table manners; **calmo come una ~ (mare)** like a mill pond. **tavola calda** snackbar. **tavola fredda** salad bar. **tavola periodica degli elementi** periodic table. **tavola pitagorica** multiplication table. **tavola rotonda** fig round table. **tavola a vela** sailboard; **fare ~ a vela** sailboard, windsurf

tavo'lato nm (pavimento) wooden flooring

tavo'letta nf bar; (medicinale) tablet; **andare a ~** Auto drive flat out. **tavoletta di cioccolata** chocolate bar. **tavoletta grafica** Comput digitizing tablet

tavo'lino nm [small] table; (da salotto) coffee table

'tavolo nm table. **tavolo anatomico** mortuary table, slab fam. **tavolo da biliardo** pool table. **tavolo da cucina** kitchen table. **tavolo da gioco** card table. **tavolo operatorio** Med operating table. **tavolo da pranzo** dining-table

tavo'lozza nf palette

taxi nm inv taxi

t

'tazza *nf* cup; (del water) bowl. **tazza da caffè/tè** coffee-cup/teacup

taz'zina *nf* **tazzina da caffè** espresso coffee cup

TBC *nf abbr* (**tuberculosi**) TB

T.C.I. *abbr* (**Touring Club Italiano**) association promoting tourism nationally and internationally

te *pers pron* you; **te l'ho dato** I gave it to you

tè *nm inv* tea. **tè al latte** tea with milk. **tè al limone** lemon tea

tea'trale *adj* theatre *attrib*; (affettato) theatrical

te'atro *nm* theatre. **teatro all'aperto** open-air theatre. **teatro lirico** opera [house]. **teatro neorealista** kitchen sink drama. **teatro di posa** Cinema set. **teatro tenda** marquee for fashions shows, concerts etc.

'techno *nf* techno (music)

'tecnico, -a ① *adj* technical ② *nmf* technician. **tecnico elettronico** electronics engineer. **tecnico informatico** computer engineer. **tecnico delle luci** Cinema, TV gaffer. **tecnico delle riparazioni** repairman. **tecnico del suono** sound technician ③ *nf* technique

tec'nigrafo *nm* drawing board

tec'nocrate *nmf* technocrat

tec'nofobo *adj* technophobe

tecnolo'gia *nf* technology

tecno'logico *adj* technological

te'desco, -a *adj & nmf* German

'tedio *nm* tedium

tedi'oso *adj* tedious

'TEE *nm abbr* (**treno espresso transeuropeo**) Trans-Europe-Express [train]

te'game *nm* saucepan; **uova al tegame** fried eggs

'teglia *nf* baking tin

'tegola *nf* tile; fig blow

tei'era *nf* teapot

te'ina *nf* theine

tek *nm* teak

tel. *abbr* (**telefono**) tel.

'tela *nf* cloth; (per quadri, vele) canvas; Theat curtain. **tela cerata** oilcloth. **tela indiana** cheesecloth. **tela di iuta** hessian. **tela di lino** linen. **tela rigida** buckram

te'laio *nm* (di bicicletta, finestra) frame; Auto chassis; (per tessere) loom

'tele *nf* fam telly, TV

tele'camera *nf* television camera

telecoman'dato *adj* remote-controlled, remote control *attrib*

teleco'mando *nm* remote control

'Telecom I'talia *nf* Italian State telephone company

telecomunicazi'oni *nfpl* telecommunications, telecomms

teleconfe'renza *nf* teleconference

tele'cronaca *nf* [television] commentary; **fare la ~ di** commentate on. **telecronaca diretta** live [television] coverage. **telecronaca registrata** recording

telecro'nista *nmf* television commentator

tele'ferica *nf* cableway

tele'film *nm inv* film [made] for television. **telefilm a episodi** series

telefo'nare *vt/i* [tele]phone, ring

telefo'nata *nf* call, [tele]phone call; **fare una ~** make a phone call. **telefonata anonima** nuisance call. **telefonata a carico del destinatario** reverse charge [phone] call; **fare una ~ a carico [del destinatario]** reverse the charges. **telefonata interurbana** long-distance call. **telefonata di lavoro** business call. **telefonata in teleselezione** ≈ STD call. **telefonata urbana** local call

telefonica'mente *adv* by [tele]phone

tele'fonico *adj* [tele]phone *attrib*

telefo'nino *nm* mobile [phone]

telefo'nista *nmf* operator

te'lefono *nm* [tele]phone; **numero di telefono** [tele]phone number. **telefono amico** the Samaritans. **telefono azzurro** children in need help line. **telefono cellulare** cell[ular] [tele]phone, mobile. **telefono cordless** cordless [phone]. **telefono interno** intercom. **telefono a monete** pay phone. **telefono pubblico** public telephone. **telefono rosso** Mil, Pol hotline. **telefono a scatti** telephone with call charges based on time-units. **telefono a scheda** cardphone. **telefono a tastiera** push-button phone

tele'genico *adj* telegenic

telegior'nale *nm* television news

telegra'fare *vt* telegraph

telegra'fia *nf* telegraphy

telegrafica'mente *adv* (con telegrafo) by telegram

tele'grafico *adj* telegraphic; (risposta) monosyllabic; **sii ~** keep it brief

te'legrafo *nm* telegraph

tele'gramma *nm* telegram

telela'voro *nm* teleworking

tele'matica *nf* data communications, telematics

teleno'vela *nf* soap opera

teleobiet'tivo *nm* telephoto lens

telepa'tia *nf* telepathy

tele'patico *adj* telepathic

tele'quiz *nm inv* TV quiz programme

teleradiotra'smettere *vt* simulcast

telero'manzo *nm* television serial

tele'schermo *nm* television screen

tele'scopio *nm* telescope

telescri'vente *nf* telex [machine]

teleselet'tivo *adj* direct dialling

teleselezi'one *nf* subscriber trunk dialling, STD; **chiamare in ~** call direct, dial direct. **teleselezione internazionale** international direct dialling

telespetta|'tore, -trice *nmf* viewer; **i telespettatori** the viewing public

tele'text *nm* Teletext

'telethon *nm* telethon

Tele'video *nm* Teletext, Ceefax

televisi'one *nf* television; **guardare la ~** watch television; **alla ~** on television. **televisione ad alta definizione** high-definition television. **televisione in bianco e nero** black and white television. **televisione via cavo** cable TV. **televisione a circuito chiuso** closed-circuit television, CCTV. **televisione a colori** colour television. **televisione satellitare** satellite television

televi'sivo *adj* television, TV *attrib*; **apparecchio televisivo** television set; **operatore televisivo** television cameraman

televi'sore *nm* television [set], TV [set]. **televisore portatile** portable [TV], portable [television set]. **televisore con schermo panoramico** wide-screen TV

'telex ① *nm inv* telex
② *adj inv* telex *attrib*

tel'lurico *adj* telluric

'telo *nm* [piece of] cloth. **telo da bagno** beach towel. **telo di salvataggio** rescue blanket

'tema *nm* theme; Sch essay

te'matica *nf* main theme

teme'rario *adj* reckless

te'mere ① *vt* be afraid of
② *vi* be afraid

tem'paccio *nm* filthy weather

'tempera *nf* tempera; (pittura) painting in tempera

temperama'tite *nm inv* pencil-sharpener

tempera'mento *nm* temperament

tempe'rare *vt* temper; sharpen (matita)

tempe'rato *adj* temperate

tempera'tura *nf* temperature. **temperatura ambiente** room temperature

tempe'rino *nm* penknife

tem'pesta *nf* storm. **tempesta magnetica** magnetic storm. **tempesta**

di neve snowstorm. **tempesta di sabbia** sandstorm

tempe'stare *vt* **~ qualcuno di colpi** rain blows on somebody; **~ qualcuno di domande** bombard somebody with questions

tempe'stato *adj* (anello, diadema) encrusted (**di** with)

tempestiva'mente *adv* quickly, in a short space of time

tempe'stivo *adj* timely, well-timed

tempe'stoso *adj* stormy

'tempia *nf* Anat temple

'tempio *nm* Relig temple

tem'pismo *nm* timing

'tempo *nm* time; (atmosferico) weather; Mus tempo; Gram tense; (di film) part; (di partita) half; **a suo ~** in due course; **~ fa** some time ago; **per molto ~, per tanto ~** for a long time; **tanto ~ fa** a long time ago; **un ~** once; **ha fatto il suo ~** it's out of date; **a ~ indeterminato** ⟨*contratto*⟩ permanent; **primo tempo** (di film, partita) first half. **tempo di accesso** Comput access time. **tempo di cottura** cooking time. **tempo di esposizione** Phot exposure time. **tempo libero** free time, leisure time. **tempo limite di accettazione** latest check-in time. **tempo di pace** peacetime. **tempo reale** Comput real time; **in tempo reale** real-time *attrib*. **tempo supplementare** extra time; Sport extra time, overtime Am; **andare ai tempi supplementari** Sport go into extra time

tempo'rale ① *adj* temporal
② *nm* [thunder]storm

temporanea'mente *adv* temporarily

tempo'raneo *adj* temporary

temporeggi'are *vi* play for time

tem'prare *vt* form

te'nace *adj* tenacious, strong-willed

tenace'mente *adv* tenaciously

te'nacia *nf* tenacity

te'naglia *nf* pincers *pl*

'tenda *nf* curtain; (per campeggio) tent; (tendone) awning; **tirare le tende** draw the curtains. **tenda della doccia** shower curtain. **tenda a ossigeno** oxygen tent

ten'denza *nf* tendency. **tendenza al rialzo/ribasso** Fin bull/bear market

tendenzial'mente *adv* by nature

tendenzi'oso *adj* tendentious

'tendere ① *vt* (allargare) stretch [out]; (tirare) tighten; (porgere) hold out; fig lay ⟨trappola⟩
② *vi* **~ a** aim at; (essere portato a) tend to

'tendersi *vr* tauten

'tendine *nm* tendon. **tendine d'Achille** Achille's tendon. **tendine del** ⋯⟩

garretto hamstring. **tendine del ginocchio** hamstring

ten'done *nm* awning. **tendone del circo** big top

ten'dopoli *nf inv* tent city

'tenebre *nfpl* darkness

tene'broso ① *adj* gloomy ② *nm* bel ∼ dark and handsome man

te'nente *nm* lieutenant. **tenente colonnello** wing commander

tenera'mente *adv* tenderly

te'nere ① *vt* hold; (mantenere) keep; (gestire) run; (prendere) take; (seguire) follow; (considerare) consider ② *vi* hold; ∼ **stretto** hold tight; ∼ **a qualcosa** ⟨oggetto⟩ be fond of something; **tengo alla sua presenza** I very much want him to be there; ∼ **per** ⟨squadra⟩ support

tene'rezza *nf* tenderness

'tenero *adj* tender

tene'rone, -a *nmf* softie

te'nersi *vr* hold on to (a to); (in una condizione) keep oneself; ∼ **indietro** stand back

'tenia *nf* tapeworm

'tennis *nm* tennis. **tennis da tavolo** table tennis

ten'nista *nmf* tennis player

te'nore *nm* standard; Mus tenor; **a** ∼ **di legge** by law. **tenore di vita** standard of living

tensi'one *nf* tension; Electr voltage; **mettere sotto** ∼ energize; **in** ∼ under stress. **alta tensione** high voltage. **tensione premestruale** premenstrual tension, PMT

ten'tacolo *nm* tentacle

ten'tare *vt* attempt; (sperimentare) try; (indurre in tentazione) tempt; ∼ **la strada di** make a foray *or* venture into

tenta'tivo *nm* attempt

ten'tato *adj* **tentato suicidio** suicide attempt

tentazi'one *nf* temptation

tentenna'mento *nm* wavering; **ha avuto dei tentennamenti** he wavered a bit

tenten'nare *vi* waver

ten'toni *adv* **cercare qualcosa a** ∼ grope for something

'tenue *adj* fine; (debole) weak; (esiguo) small; (leggero) slight

te'nuta *nf* (capacità) capacity; (Sport, resistenza) stamina; (possedimento) estate; (divisa) uniform; (abbigliamento) clothes *pl*; **a** ∼ **d'aria** airtight. **tenuta di strada** road holding

teolo'gia *nf* theology

teo'logico *adj* theological

te'ologo *nm* theologian

teo'rema *nm* theorem

teo'ria *nf* theory

teorica'mente *adv* theoretically

te'orico *adj* theoretical

te'pore *nm* warmth

'teppa *nf* mob

tep'pismo *nm* hooliganism

tep'pista *nm* hooligan, yob *fam*

te'quila *nf* tequila

tera'peutico *adj* therapeutic

tera'pia *nf* therapy; **in** ∼ in therapy. **terapia genica** gene therapy. **terapia di gruppo** group therapy. **terapia ormonale sostitutiva** hormone replacement therapy, HRT. **terapia d'urto** shock treatment

tergicri'stallo *nm* windscreen wiper, windshield wiper *Am*

tergilu'notto *nm* rear windscreen wiper

tergiver'sante *adj* equivocating, pussyfooting *fam*

tergiver'sare *vi* equivocate, pussyfoot around *fam*

'tergo *nm* **a** ∼ behind; **segue a** ∼ please turn over, PTO

teri'lene® *nm* Terylene®

'terital® *nm* Terylene®

ter'male *adj* thermal; **stazione termale** spa

'terme *nfpl* thermal baths

'termico *adj* thermal; **borsa termica** cool bag

'terminal *nm inv* air terminal

termi'nale *adj & nm* terminal; **malato terminale** terminally ill person

termina'lista *nmf* computer operator

termi'nare *vt/i* end, finish

terminazi'one *nf* (fine) termination; Gram ending. **terminazione nervosa** nerve ending

'termine *nm* (limite) limit; (fine) end; (condizione, parola) term; (scadenza) deadline; **ai termini della legge...** under the terms of act...; **contratto a termine** fixed-term contract. **termine di paragone** Gram term of comparison. **termine ultimo** final deadline

terminolo'gia *nf* terminology

'termite *nf* termite

termoco'perta *nf* electric blanket

termogra'fia *nf* thermal imaging

ter'mometro *nm* thermometer

'termos *nm inv* thermos®

termosi'fone *nm* radiator; (sistema) central heating

ter'mostato *nm* thermostat

termotera'pia *nf* Med heat treatment

termoventila'tore *nm* fan heater

'**terra** *nf* earth; (regione) land; (terreno) ground; (argilla) clay; (cosmetico) bronzing powder; **a ∼** (sulla costa) ashore; (installazioni) onshore; **essere a ∼** (gomma) be flat; fig be at rock bottom; **per ∼** on the ground; (su pavimento) on the floor; **sotto ∼** underground; **far ∼ bruciata** carry out a scorched earth policy. **terra promessa** Promised Land. **Terra Santa** Holy Land. **terra di Siena** sienna

terra'cotta *nf* terracotta; **vasellame di ∼** earthenware

terra'ferma *nf* dry land

Terra'nova *nf* Newfoundland

terrapi'eno *nm* embankment

ter'razza *nf*, **ter'razzo** *nm* balcony

terremo'tato, -a ① *adj* (zona) affected by an earthquake
② *nmf* earthquake victim

terre'moto *nm* earthquake

ter'reno ① *adj* earthly
② *nm* ground; (suolo) soil; (proprietà terriera) land; **perdere/guadagnare ∼** lose/gain ground. **terreno alluvionale** alluvial soil. **terreno di bonifica** reclaimed land. **terreno boschivo** woodland. **terreno edificabile** building land. **terreno di gioco** playing field. **terreno di scontro** battlefield

ter'restre *adj* terrestrial; ⟨diametro⟩ of the earth; **esercito terrestre** land forces *pl*

ter'ribile *adj* terrible

terribil'mente *adv* terribly

ter'riccio *nm* potting compost

'**terrier** *nm inv* terrier

terri'ero *adj* ⟨proprietario⟩ land *attrib*; ⟨aristocrazia⟩ landed; **proprietà** *pl* **terriere** landed property

terrifi'cante *adj* terrifying

territori'ale *adj* territorial; **acque territoriali** territorial waters

terri'torio *nm* territory

ter'rone, -a *nmf* pej bloody Southerner

ter'rore *nm* terror

terro'rismo *nm* terrorism

terro'rista *nmf* terrorist

terroriz'zare *vt* terrorize

'**terso** *adj* clear

'**terza** *nf* (marcia) third [gear]

ter'zetto *nm* trio

terzi'ario ① *adj* tertiary
② *nm* service sector. **terziario avanzato** hi-tech sector

'**terzo** ① *adj* third; **di terz'ordine** ⟨locale, servizio⟩ third-rate; **fare il ∼ grado a qualcuno** give somebody the third degree; **la terza età** the third age; **il ∼ mondo** the Third World. **terzo settore** voluntary sector.
② *nm* third; **terzi** *pl* Jur third party

terzo'genito, -a *nmf* third-born

ter'zultimo, -a *adj & nmf* third from last

'**tesa** *nf* brim

'**teschio** *nm* skull

'**tesi** *nf inv* thesis

'**teso** ① pp di TENDERE
② *adj* taut; fig tense

tesore'ria *nf* treasury

tesori'ere *nm* treasurer

te'soro *nm* treasure; (tesoreria) treasury; **ministro del Tesoro** Finance Minister; ≈ Chancellor of the Exchequer Br

'**tessera** *nf* card; (abbonamento all'autobus) season ticket; (di club) membership card. **tessera magnetica** swipe card. **tessera dei trasporti pubblici** travel card. **tessera di sconto** discount card

'**tessere** *vt* weave; hatch (complotto); **∼ le lodi di qualcosa** sing the praises of something

tesse'rino *nm* travel card

tessile ① *adj* textile
② *nm* **tessili** *pl* textiles; (operai) textile workers

tessi'tore, -trice *nmf* weaver

tessi'tura *nf* weaving

tes'suto ① pp di TESSERE
② *adj* woven; **∼ a mano** hand-woven
③ *nm* fabric, material; Anat tissue. **tessuto sintetico** synthetic material. **tessuto di spugna** terry towelling

'**test** *nm inv* test; **test** *pl* **genetici** genetic testing

'**testa** *nf* head; (cervello) brain; **essere in ∼ a** be ahead of; **in ∼** Sport in the lead; **∼ o croce?** heads or tails?; **fare a ∼ o croce** spin a coin, toss a coin; **andare a ∼ alta** hold one's head up. **testa di rapa** fam pinhead. **testa di sbarco** beachhead. **testa di serie** (squadra) seeded team. **testa del treno** front of the train

testa-'coda *nm inv* **fare un ∼** spin right round

testa'mento *nm* will. **testamento biologico** living will. **Antico Testamento** Relig Old Testament. **Nuovo Testamento** Relig New Testament

testar'daggine *nf* stubbornness

testarda'mente *adv* stubbornly

te'stardo *adj* stubborn

te'stare *vt* test

te'stata *nf* head; (intestazione) heading; (colpo) [head]butt. **testata nucleare** nuclear warhead

'**teste** *nmf* witness

'**tester** *nm inv* tester

te'sticolo *nm* testicle

testi'mone *nmf* witness; **essere ∼ di qualcosa** witness something. **testimone** ⋯⋙

di Geova Jehovah's Witness.
testimone oculare eye witness
testi'monial *nmf inv* celebrity who endorses a product
testimoni'anza *nf* testimony; **falsa testimonianza** Jur perjury
testimoni'are ① *vt* testify to ② *vi* testify, give evidence
te'stina *nf* head; (di stampante) printhead. **testina di cancellazione** Comput erase head. **testina di lettura** Comput read head. **testina rotante** (di macchina da scrivere) golf-ball. **testina di vitello** Culin calf's head
'testo *nm* text; **far ~** be authoritative; **con ~ a fronte** ‹*traduzione*› with the original text on the opposite page
te'stone, -a *nmf* blockhead
testoste'rone *nm* testosterone
testu'ale *adj* textual
'tetano *nm* tetanus
te'traggine *nf* bleakness
tetra'pak® *nm* tetrapak
'tetro *adj* bleak
tetta'rella *nf* teat
'tetto *nm* roof; **abbandono del ~ coniugale** Jur desertion. **tetto apribile** (di auto) sun[shine] roof. **tetto a terrazza** flat roof
tet'toia *nf* roofing
tet'tuccio *nm* **tettuccio apribile** sun-roof
teu'tonico *adj* Teutonic
'Tevere *nm* Tiber
ti *pers pron* you; (riflessivo) yourself; **ti ha dato un libro** he gave you a book; **lavati le mani** wash your hands; **eccoti!** here you are!; **sbrigati!** hurry up!
ti'ara *nf* tiara
'Tibet *nm* Tibet
tic *nm inv* tic
ticchet'tare *vi* tick
ticchet'tio *nm* ticking
'ticchio *nm* tic; (ghiribizzo) whim
'ticket *nm inv* (per farmaco, analisi) prescription charges, amount paid by National Health patients
tie-break *nm inv* tie break[er]
tiepida'mente *adv* half-heartedly
ti'epido *adj* lukewarm; fig half-hearted
ti'fare *vi* **~ per** be a fan of
'tifo *nm* Med typhus; **fare il ~ per** (appoggiare) be a fan of
tifoi'dea *nf* typhoid
ti'fone *nm* typhoon
ti'foso, -a *nmf* fan
tight *nm inv* morning dress
'tiglio *nm* lime
'tigna *nf* ringworm

ti'grato *adj* **gatto tigrato** tabby [cat]
'tigre *nf* tiger
'tilde *nf* tilde
tim'ballo *nm* Culin pie
tim'brare *vt* stamp; **~ il cartellino** (all'entrata) clock in; (all'uscita) clock out
'timbro *nm* stamp; (di voce) tone. **timbro a secco** embossing stamp
time out *nm inv* Sport time-out
'timer *nm inv* timer
timida'mente *adv* timidly, shyly
timi'dezza *nf* timidity, shyness
'timido *adj* timid, shy
'timo *nm* thyme
ti'mone *nm* helm, rudder. **timone di direzione** (di aereo) rudder. **timone di quota** (di aereo) elevator
timoni'ere *nm* helmsman
timo'rato *adj* **~ di Dio** God-fearing
ti'more *nm* fear; (soggezione) awe
'Timor 'Est *nm* East Timor
timo'roso *adj* timorous
'timpano *nm* eardrum; Mus kettledrum; **timpani** *pl* Mus timpani, kettledrums; **rompere i timpani a qualcuno** fig shatter somebody's eardrums
ti'nello *nm* dining-room
'tingere *vt* dye; (macchiare) stain
'tingersi *vr* (viso, cielo) be tinged (**di** with); **~ i capelli** have one's hair dyed; (da solo) dye one's hair
'tino *nm*, **'tinozza** *nf* tub
'tinta *nf* dye; (colore) colour; **in ~ unita** plain, self-coloured
tinta'rella *nf* fam suntan
tintin'nare *vi* tinkle
'tinto *pp di* TINGERE
tinto'ria *nf* (negozio) cleaner's
tin'tura *nf* dyeing; (colorante) dye. **tintura di iodio** iodine
tipica'mente *adv* typically
'tipico *adj* typical
'tipo *nm* type; (fam: individuo) chap, guy
tipogra'fia *nf* printer's; (arte) typography
tipo'grafico *adj* typographic[al]
ti'pografo *nm* printer
tip tap *nm* tap dancing
ti'raggio *nm* draught
tiranneggi'are *vt* tyrannize
tiran'nia *nf* tyranny
ti'ranno, -a ① *adj* tyrannical ② *nmf* tyrant
tiranno'sauro *nm* tyrannosaurus
ti'rante *nm* rope
tirapi'edi *nm inv* pej hanger-on
tira'pugni *nm inv* knuckle-duster

ti'rare ⟦1⟧ *vt* pull; (gettare) throw; (nel calcio) kick; (tracciare) draw; (stampare) print; fam land ⟨*calci, pugni*⟩

⟦2⟧ *vi* pull; ⟨*vento*⟩ blow; ⟨*abito*⟩ be tight; ⟨*sparare*⟩ fire; ∼ **avanti** fig get by; ∼ **su** bring up ⟨*figli*⟩; (da terra) pick up; **tirar su [col naso]** sniffle

ti'rarsi *vr* ∼ **indietro** fig back out, pull out

tiras'segno *nm* target shooting; (alla fiera) rifle range

ti'rata *nf* (strattone) pull, tug; **in una** ∼ in one go; **dare a qualcuno una** ∼ **d'orecchi** fig give somebody a telling off

tira'tore *nm* shot. **tiratore scelto** marksman

tira'tura *nf* printing; (di giornali) circulation; (di libri) [print] run

tirchie'ria *nf* meanness

'tirchio *adj* mean

tiri'tera *nf* spiel

'tiro *nm* (lancio) throw; (azione) throwing; (sparo) shot; (azione) shooting; (scherzo) trick; **cavallo da tiro** draught horse. **tiro con l'arco** archery. **tiro al bersaglio** target practice. **tiro alla fune** tug-of-war. **tiro al piattello** clay pigeon shooting. **tiro in porta** shot at goal. **tiro a segno** rifle-range

tiroci'nante *nmf* trainee

tiro'cinio *nm* training

ti'roide *nf* thyroid

Tir'reno *nm* il [mar] ∼ the Tyrrhenian Sea

ti'sana *nf* herb[al] tea

'tisi *nf* consumption

ti'tanio *nm* titanium

tito'lare ⟦1⟧ *adj* permanent

⟦2⟧ *nmf* (proprietario) owner; (nel calcio) regular player; (Jur: di diritto) holder

'titolo *nm* title; ⟨*accademico*⟩ qualification; Comm security; **a** ∼ **di** as; **a** ∼ **di favore** as a favour; **titoli** *pl* (di giornale, telegiornale) headlines. **titoli** *pl* **di coda** closing credits. **titolo di credito** credit instrument. **titolo mondiale** world title. **titolo obbligazionario** bond. **titoli** *pl* **delle principali notizie** news headlines. **titolo in sovrimpressione** superimposed title. **titolo di Stato** government security. **titoli** *pl* **di studio** qualifications. **titoli** *pl* **di testa** Cinema, TV opening credits. **titolo a tutta pagina** banner headline

titu'bante *adj* hesitant

titu'banza *nf* hesitation

titu'bare *vi* hesitate

tivù *nf inv* fam TV, telly

'tizio, -a ⟦1⟧ *nm* so-and-so; **un** ∼ some man

⟦2⟧ *nf* **una tizia** some woman

tiz'zone *nm* brand

toc'cante *adj* touching

toc'care ⟦1⟧ *vt* touch; touch on ⟨*argomento*⟩; (tastare) feel; (riguardare) concern

⟦2⟧ *vi* ∼ **a** (capitare) happen to; **mi tocca aspettare** I'll have to wait; **tocca a te** it's your turn; (a pagare da bere) it's your round; **'non** ∼**'** 'please do not touch'

tocca'sana *nm inv* panacea

toc'cato *adj* (fam: matto) touched

'tocco ⟦1⟧ *nm* touch; (di pennello, orologio) stroke; (di pane ecc) chunk; **il** ∼ **finale** the finishing touches

⟦2⟧ *adj* fam crazy, touched

toc toc *nm inv* knock, knock

'toga *nf* toga; (accademica, di magistrato) gown

'togliere *vt* take off ⟨*coperta*⟩; (Math, da scuola) take away; quench ⟨*sete*⟩; take out, remove ⟨*tonsille, dente ecc*⟩; ∼ **qualcosa di mano a qualcuno** take something away from somebody; ∼ **qualcuno dai guai** get somebody out of trouble; **ciò non toglie che...** nevertheless..., the fact remains that...; **farsi** ∼ **le tonsille** have one's tonsils [taken] out

'togliersi *vr* take off ⟨*abito*⟩; ∼ **la vita** take one's [own] life; ∼ **di mezzo** get out of the way; **togliti dai piedi** get out of the way!

'Togo *nm* Togo

toi'lette *nf inv* toilet; (mobile) dressing table

to'letta *nf* toilet; (mobile) dressing table

tolle'rante *adj* tolerant

tolle'ranza *nf* tolerance; **casa di tolleranza** brothel

tolle'rare *vt* tolerate

'tolto pp di TOGLIERE

to'maia *nf* upper

'tomba *nf* grave

tom'bino *nm* manhole cover

'tombola *nf* bingo; (caduta) tumble

to'mino *nm* goat-cheese

'tomo *nm* tome

tomogra'fia *nf* Med tomography. **tomografia assiale computerizzata** computerized axial tomography, CAT

'tonaca *nf* habit

to'nale *adj* tonal

tonalità *nf inv* Mus tonality

to'nante *adj* booming

'tondo ⟦1⟧ *adj* (cifra) round

⟦2⟧ *nm* circle

'toner *nm inv* toner

'tonfo *nm* thud; (in acqua) splash

'Tonga *nf* Tonga

'tonica *nf* Mus keynote

'tonico ⟦1⟧ *adj* ⟨*sillaba*⟩ stressed; ⟨*muscoli*⟩ well toned

2 *nm* tonic
tonifi'care *vt* tone up ⟨*muscoli*⟩
ton'nara *nf* tuna-fishing net
ton'nato *adj* **vitello tonnato** veal with a tuna and mayonnaise sauce
tonnel'laggio *nm* tonnage
tonnel'lata *nf* ton. **tonnellata corta americana** short ton, net ton
'tonno *nm* tuna [fish]
'tono *nm* tone
ton'sille *nfpl* tonsils
tonsil'lite *nf* tonsillitis
'tonto *adj* fam thick
top *nm inv* (indumento) sun-top
to'pazio *nm* topaz
'topless *nm inv* in ~ topless
top 'model *nf inv* supermodel
'topo *nm* mouse. **topo di albergo/appartamento** thief in a hotel/block of flats. **topo di biblioteca** bookworm. **topo domestico** domestic mouse
topogra'fia *nf* topography
topo'grafico *adj* topographic[al]
to'ponimo *nm* place name
topo'ragno *nm* shrew
'toppa *nf* (rattoppo) patch; (serratura) keyhole
to'race *nm* chest
to'racico *adj* thoracic; **gabbia toracica** rib cage
'torba *nf* peat
'torbido *adj* cloudy; fig troubled
'torcere *vt* twist; wring ⟨*biancheria*⟩
'torcersi *vr* twist
'torchio *nm* press
'torcia *nf* torch. **torcia elettrica** torch
torci'collo *nm* stiff neck
'tordo *nm* thrush
to'rero *nm* bullfighter
To'rino *nf* Turin
tor'menta *nf* snowstorm
tormen'tare *vt* torment
tormen'tato *adj* tormented
tor'mento *nm* torment
tormen'tone *nm* (frase) catchphrase; (argomento) constantly repeated topic; (canzone) catchy song that is constantly played on the radio
torna'conto *nm* benefit
tor'nado *nm inv* tornado
tor'nante *nm* hairpin bend
tor'nare *vi* return, go/come back; (ridiventare) become again; ⟨*conto*⟩ add up; ~ **a sorridere** smile again; ~ **su** go back up
tor'neo *nm* tournament
'tornio *nm* lathe
'torno *nm* **togliersi di** ~ get out of the way

'toro *nm* bull; Astr Taurus
tor'pedine *nf* torpedo
torpedini'era *nf* torpedo boat
tor'pore *nm* torpor
'torre *nf* tower; (scacchi) castle. **torre d'avorio** ivory tower. **torre di controllo** control tower. **torre di osservazione** observation tower. **torre pendente, torre di Pisa** Leaning Tower of Pisa
torrefazi'one *nf* roasting; (negozio) coffee retailer
tor'rente *nm* torrent, mountain stream; (fig: di lacrime) flood; (fig: di parole) torrent
torrenzi'ale *adj* torrential; **in regime** ~ in spate
tor'retta *nf* turret
'torrido *adj* torrid, sweltering
torri'one *nm* keep
tor'rone *nm* nougat
torsi'one *nf* twisting; (in ginnastica) twist
'torso *nm* torso; (di mela, pera) core; **a** ~ **nudo** bare-chested
'torsolo *nm* core
'torta *nf* cake; (crostata) tart. **torta di compleanno** birthday cake. **torta di mele** apple tart. **torta nuziale** wedding cake. **torta pasqualina** spinach pie
torti'era *nf* cake tin
tor'tino *nm* pie
'torto **1** pp di TORCERE
2 *adj* twisted
3 *nm* wrong; (colpa) fault; **aver** ~ be wrong; **a** ~ wrongly; **far** ~ **a qualcuno** wrong somebody; fig not do somebody justice; **non hai tutti i torti** you're not altogether wrong
'tortora *nf* turtle-dove
tortuosa'mente *adv* tortuously
tortu'oso *adj* winding; (ambiguo) tortuous
tor'tura *nf* torture
tortu'rare *vt* torture
'torvo *adj* ⟨*sguardo*⟩ menacing
tosa'erba *nm inv* lawnmower
to'sare *vt* shear
tosasi'epi *nm inv* hedge trimmer
tosa'tura *nf* shearing
To'scana *nf* Tuscany
to'scano, -a *adj & nmf* Tuscan
'tosse *nf* cough
'tossico **1** *adj* toxic
2 *nm* poison
tossicodipen'denza *nf* drug habit
tossi'comane *nmf* drug addict, drug user
tos'sire *vi* cough
tosta'pane *nm inv* toaster. **tostapane a espulsione automatica** pop-up toaster

to'stare *vt* toast ⟨*pane*⟩; roast ⟨*caffè*⟩

'tosto ① *adv* (subito) soon
② *adj* fam cool; **faccia tosta** cheek

tot ① *adj inv* **una cifra** ∼ such and such a figure
② *nm* **un** ∼ so much

to'tale *adj* & *nm* total. **totale complessivo** grand total. **totale parziale** subtotal

totalità *nf* entirety; **la** ∼ **dei presenti** all those present

totali'tario *adj* totalitarian

totaliz'zare *vt* total; score ⟨*punti*⟩

totalizza'tore *nm* (per scommesse) totalizer, tote

total'mente *adv* totally

'totano *nm* squid

'totem *nm inv* totem pole

toto'calcio *nm* ≈ [football] pools *pl*

'touche *nf inv* touch line

tou'pet *nm inv* toupee

tournée *nf inv* tour

to'vaglia *nf* tablecloth

tovagli'etta *nf* **tovaglietta [all'americana]** place mat

tovagli'olo *nm* napkin. **tovagliolo di carta** paper napkin

'tozzo ① *adj* squat
② *nm* **tozzo di pane** stale piece of bread

tra = FRA

trabal'lante *adj* staggering; ⟨*sedia*⟩ rickety, wonky

trabal'lare *vi* stagger; ⟨*veicolo*⟩ jolt

tra'biccolo *nm* fam contraption; (auto) jalopy

traboc'care *vi* overflow

traboc'chetto *nm* trap

traca'gnotto *adj* dumpy

tracan'nare *vt* gulp down

'traccia *nf* track; (orma) footstep; (striscia) trail; (residuo) trace; fig sign

tracci'are *vt* trace; sketch out ⟨*schema*⟩; draw ⟨*linea*⟩

tracci'ato *nm* (schema) layout. **tracciato di gara** circuit

tra'chea *nf* windpipe, trachea

tra'colla *nf* shoulder-strap; **borsa a tracolla** shoulder-bag

tra'collo *nm* collapse

tradi'mento *nm* betrayal; Pol treason; **alto tradimento** high treason

tra'dire *vt* betray; be unfaithful to ⟨*moglie, marito*⟩

tradi'tore, **-trice** *nmf* traitor

tradizio'nale *adj* traditional

tradiziona'lista *nmf* traditionalist

tradizional'mente *adv* traditionally

tradizi'one *nf* tradition

tra'dotto *pp* di TRADURRE

tra'durre *vt* translate

tradut'tore, **-trice** *nmf* translator. **traduttore elettronico** electronic phrasebook

traduzi'one *nf* translation. **traduzione consecutiva** consecutive interpreting. **traduzione simultanea** simultaneous interpreting

tra'ente *nmf* Comm drawer

trafe'lato *adj* breathless

traffi'cante *nmf* dealer, trafficker. **trafficante d'armi** arms dealer. **trafficante di droga** drug dealer

traffi'care *vi* (affaccendarsi) busy oneself; ∼ **in** pej traffic in

'traffico *nm* traffic; Comm trade. **traffico aereo** air traffic. **traffico della droga** drug trafficking. **traffico ferroviario** rail traffic. **traffico di stupefacenti** drug trafficking

traffi'cone, **-a** *nmf* fam wheeler dealer

tra'figgere *vt* penetrate, pierce; fig pierce

tra'fila *nf* fig rigmarole

trafi'letto *nm* minor news item

trafo'rare *vt* bore, drill

tra'foro *nm* boring, drilling; (galleria) tunnel; **lavoro di traforo** fretwork

trafu'gare *vt* steal

tra'gedia *nf* tragedy

traghet'tare *vt* ferry

tra'ghetto *nm* ferrying; (nave) ferry

tragica'mente *adv* tragically

'tragico ① *adj* tragic
② *nm* (autore) tragedian

tra'gitto *nm* journey; (per mare) crossing

tragu'ardo *nm* finishing post; (meta) goal

traiet'toria *nf* trajectory

trai'nare *vt* drag; (rimorchiare) tow

tralasci'are *vt* interrupt; (omettere) leave out; ∼ **di fare qualcosa** fail to do something, omit to do something

'tralcio *nm* Bot shoot

tra'liccio *nm* (tela) ticking; (graticcio) trellis

tra'lice: **in** ∼ *adv* (tagliare) on the slant; (guardare) sideways

tralu'cente *adj* shining

tram *nm inv* tram, streetcar Am

'trama *nf* weft; (di film ecc) plot

traman'dare *vt* hand down

tra'mare *vt* weave; (macchinare) plot

tram'busto *nm* turmoil

trame'stio *nm* bustle

tramez'zino *nm* sandwich

tra'mezzo *nm* partition

'tramite ① *prep* through

2 *nm* link; **con il ~ di** by means of; **fare da ~** act as go-between

tramon'tana *nf* north wind

tramon'tare *vi* set; (declinare) decline

tra'monto *nm* sunset; (declino) decline

tramor'tire **1** *vt* stun **2** *vi* faint

trampoli'ere *nm* wader

trampo'lino *nm* springboard; (per lo sci) ski-jump. **trampolino di lancio** fig launch pad

'trampolo *nm* stilt

tramu'tare *vt* transform

trance *nf* trance; **essere in ~** be in a trance

'trancia *nf* shears *pl*; (fetta) slice

tra'nello *nm* trap

trangugi'are *vt* gulp down

'tranne *prep* except

tranquilla'mente *adv* peacefully

tranquil'lante *nm* tranquillizer

tranquillità *nf* calm; (di spirito) tranquillity

tranquilliz'zare *vt* reassure

tran'quillo *adj* quiet; (pacifico) peaceful; (coscienza) easy; **stai ~ !** (non preoccuparti) don't worry!

transa'tlantico **1** *adj* transatlantic **2** *nm* ocean liner

tran'satto pp di TRANSIGERE

transazi'one *nf* Comm transaction; Jur settlement

tran'senna *nf* (barriera) barrier

transessu'ale *nmf* transsexual

tran'setto *nm* transept

'transfert *nm inv* Psych transference

tran'sigere *vi* Jur reach a settlement; (cedere) compromise

tran'sistor *nm inv* fam transistor [radio]

transi'tabile *adj* passable

transi'tare *vi* pass

transi'tivo *adj* transitive

'transito *nm* transit; **'divieto di ~'** 'no thoroughfare'; **diritto di transito** right of way. **'transito alterno'** 'temporary one-way system'

transi'torio *adj* transitory

transizi'one *nf* transition; **di ~** transitional

tran'tran *nm* fam routine

tranvi'ere *nm* tram driver, streetcar driver Am

'trapano *nm* drill. **trapano elettrico** electric drill

trapas'sare **1** *vt* pierce, penetrate **2** *vi* (morire) pass away

trapas'sato *nm* pluperfect

tra'passo *nm* passage

trape'lare *vi* anche fig leak out

tra'pezio *nm* trapeze; Math trapezium

trapian'tare *vt* transplant

trapi'anto *nm* transplant. **trapianto di cuore** heart transplant

'trappola *nf* trap

tra'punta *nf* quilt

'trarre *vt* draw; (ricavare) obtain; **~ in inganno** deceive

trasa'lire *vi* start

trasan'dato *adj* shabby

trasbor'dare **1** *vt* transfer; Naut tran[s]ship **2** *vi* change

tra'sbordo *nm* trans[s]hipment

trascenden'tale *adj* transcendental

tra'scendere **1** *vt* transcend **2** *vi* (eccedere) go too far

trasci'nare *vt* drag; (fig: entusiasmo) carry away; **~ e rilasciare** Comput drag and drop

trasci'narsi *vr* drag oneself; (camminare piano) dawdle

tra'scorrere **1** *vt* spend **2** *vi* pass

tra'scritto pp di TRASCRIVERE

tra'scrivere *vt* transcribe

trascrizi'one *nf* transcription

trascu'rabile *adj* negligible

trascu'rare *vt* neglect; (non tenere conto di) disregard

trascurata'mente *adv* carelessly

trascura'tezza *nf* negligence

trascu'rato *adj* negligent; (curato male) neglected; (nel vestire) slovenly

traseco'lato *adj* amazed

trasferi'mento *nm* transfer; (trasloco) move. **trasferimento automatico** direct debit. **trasferimento bancario** bank transfer

trasfe'rire *vt* transfer

trasfe'rirsi *vr* move

tra'sferta *nf* transfer; (indennità) subsistence allowance; Sport away match; **in ~** ⟨impiegato⟩ on secondment; **giocare in ~** play away

trasfigu'rare *vt* transfigure

trasfor'mare *vt* transform; (in rugby) convert

trasfor'marsi *vr* be transformed; **~ in** turn into

trasforma'tore *nm* transformer

trasformazi'one *nf* transformation; (in rugby) conversion

trasfor'mista *nmf* (artista) quick-change artist

trasfusi'one *nf* transfusion

trasgre'dire *vt* disobey; Jur infringe

trasgredi'trice *nf* transgressor

trasgressi'one nf infringement; (di ordine) failure to obey

trasgres'sivo adj intended to shock

trasgres'sore nm transgressor

tra'slato adj metaphorical

traslitte'rare vt transliterate

traslo'care ① vt move ② vi move [house]

traslo'carsi vr move [house]

tra'sloco nm move; **compagnia di trasloco** removal company

tra'smesso pp di TRASMETTERE

tra'smettere vt pass on; TV, Radio broadcast; Techn, Med transmit

trasmetti'tore nm transmitter

trasmis'sibile adj transmissible

trasmissi'one nf transmission; TV, Radio programme. **trasmissione dati** data transmission. **trasmissione via fax** fax transmission. **trasmissione radiofonica** radio programme. **trasmissione remota** remote transmission. **trasmissione televisiva** television programme

trasmit'tente ① nm transmitter ② nf broadcasting station

traso'gnare vi day-dream

traso'gnato adj dreamy

traspa'rente adj transparent

traspa'renza nf transparency; **in ∼** against the light

traspa'rire vi show [through]

traspi'rare vi perspire; fig transpire

traspirazi'one nf perspiration

tra'sporre vt transpose

traspor'tare vt transport; **lasciarsi ∼ da** get carried away by; **∼ con ponte aereo** airlift

traspor'tato adj transported; **∼ dall'aria** airborne

trasporta'tore nm conveyor; (società) transport company, road haulier

tra'sporto nm transport; (fig: passione) passion; **ministro dei trasporti** Ministry of Transport. **trasporto aereo** air freight. **trasporto ferroviario** rail transport. **trasporto pesante** heavy goods transport. **trasporti** pl **pubblici** public transport. **trasporto stradale** road transport, road haulage

trastul'lare vt amuse

trastul'larsi vr amuse oneself; (perdere tempo) fool around

trasu'dare ① vt ooze [with] ② vi ooze

trasver'sale adj transverse; **strada trasversale** cross street

trasversal'mente adv widthways

trasvo'lare ① vt fly over ② vi **∼ su** fig skim over

trasvo'lata nf crossing [by air]

'tratta nf (traffico illegale) trade; Comm draft. **tratta bancaria** Fin banker's draft. **tratta delle bianche** white slave trade. **tratta documentaria** documentary bill

trat'tabile adj or nearest offer, o.n.o.

tratta'mento nm treatment. **trattamento automatico delle informazioni** electronic data processing, EDP. **trattamento di bellezza** beauty treatment. **trattamento di fine rapporto** severance pay. **trattamento dell'immagine** image processing **trattamento di riguardo** special treatment

trat'tante adj conditioning

trat'tare ① vt treat; (commerciare in) deal in; (negoziare) negotiate ② vi **∼ di** deal with

trat'tario nm Comm drawee

trat'tarsi vr **di che si tratta?** what's it about?; **si tratta di...** it's about...

tratta'tive nfpl negotiations; **il tavolo delle ∼** the negotiating table

trat'tato nm treaty; (opera scritta) treatise. **trattato di pace** peace treaty

tratteggi'are vt outline; (descrivere) sketch

tratte'nere vt (far restare) keep; hold (respiro, in questura); hold back ⟨lacrime, riso⟩; (frenare) restrain; (da paga) withhold; **sono stato trattenuto** (ritardato) I got held up

tratte'nersi vr restrain oneself; (fermarsi) stay; **∼ su** (indugiare) dwell on

tratteni'mento nm entertainment; (ricevimento) party

tratte'nuta nf deduction

trat'tino nm dash; (in parole composte) hyphen

'tratto ① pp di TRARRE ② nm (di spazio, tempo) stretch; (di penna) stroke; (linea) line; (brano) passage; **tratti** pl (lineamenti) features; **a tratti** at intervals; **ad un ∼** suddenly

trat'tore nm tractor

tratto'ria nf restaurant

'trauma nm trauma

trau'matico adj traumatic

traumatiz'zante adj traumatic

traumatiz'zare vt traumatize

tra'vaglio nm labour; (angoscia) anguish

trava'sare vt decant

tra'vaso nm decanting

trava'tura nf beams pl

'trave nf beam. **trave a sbalzo** cantilever

tra'veggole nfpl **avere le ∼** be seeing things

'travellers cheque nm inv traveller's cheque

t

tra'versa *nf* (nel calcio) crossbar; **è una ~ di via Roma** it's off via Roma, it crosses via Roma

traver'sare *vt* cross

traver'sata *nf* crossing

traver'sie *nfpl* misfortunes

traver'sina *nf* Rail sleeper

tra'verso ① *adj* crosswise ② *adv* **di ~** crossways; **andare di ~** ‹*cibo*› go down the wrong way; **camminare di ~** not walk in a straight line; **guardare qualcuno di ~** look askance at somebody; **sapere per vie traverse** *fam* find out indirectly

traver'sone *nm* (in calcio) cross

travesti'mento *nm* disguise

trave'stire *vt* disguise

trave'stirsi *vr* disguise oneself

travesti'tismo *nm* transvestism, crossdressing

trave'stito ① *adj* disguised ② *nm* transvestite

travi'are *vt* lead astray

travisa'mento *nm* distortion

travi'sare *vt* distort

travol'gente *adj* overwhelming

tra'volgere *vt* sweep away; (sopraffare) overwhelm

tra'volto *pp di* TRAVOLGERE

trazi'one *nf* traction. **trazione anteriore/posteriore** front-/rear-wheel drive

tre *adj & nm* three

tre'alberi *nm inv* three-masted ship, three-master

trebbi'are *vt* thresh

trebbia'trice *nf* threshing machine.

'treccia *nf* plait, braid; (in maglia) cable; **a trecce** cable *attrib*

tre'cento *adj & nm* three hundred; **il Trecento** the fourteenth century

tredi'cesima *nf* extra month's salary paid as a Christmas bonus

tredi'cesimo, -a *adj & nm* thirteenth

'tredici *adj & nm* thirteen

'tregua *nf* truce; *fig* respite

'trekking *nm* trekking

tre'mante *adj* trembling, quivering; (per il freddo) shivering

tre'mare *vi* tremble, quiver; (di freddo) shiver

trema'rella *nf fam* jitters *pl*

tremenda'mente *adv* terribly, tremendously

tre'mendo *adj* terrible, tremendous; **ho una fame tremenda** I'm terribly hungry

tremen'tina *nf* turpentine

tre'mila *adj & nm* three thousand

'tremito *nm* tremble, quiver; (per il freddo) shiver

tremo'lare *vi* shake; (luce) flicker

tre'more *nm* trembling

'tremulo *adj* tremulous

tre'nino *nm* miniature railway

'treno *nm* train. **treno merci** freight train, goods train. **treno navetta** shuttle. **treno passeggeri** passenger train. **treno postale** mail train. **treno straordinario** special train

'trenta *adj & nm* thirty. **trenta e lode** Univ ≈ first-class honours

trentatré 'giri *nm inv* LP

tren'tenne *adj & nmf* thirty-year-old

tren'tesimo *adj & nm* thirtieth

tren'tina *nf* **una ~ di** about thirty

trepi'dare *vi* be anxious

'trepido *adj* anxious

treppi'ede *nm* tripod

'tresca *nf* intrigue; ‹*amorosa*› affair

'trespolo *nm* perch

triango'lare *adj* triangular

tri'angolo *nm* triangle. **triangolo delle Bermude** Bermuda Triangle. **triangolo equilatero** equilateral triangle. **triangolo isoscele** isosceles triangle. **triangolo rettangolo** right-angled triangle. **triangolo di segnalazione** warning triangle

tri'bale *adj* tribal

tribo'lare *vi* (soffrire) suffer; (fare fatica) go to a lot of trouble

tribolazi'one *nf* suffering

tri'bordo *nm* starboard

tribù *nf inv* tribe

tri'buna *nf* podium, dais; (per uditori) gallery; Sport stand. **tribuna coperta** stand. **tribuna riservata al pubblico** public gallery. **tribuna della stampa** press gallery

tribu'nale *nm* court. **tribunale fallimentare** bankruptcy court. **tribunale minorile** juvenile court. **tribunale penale internazionale** international criminal court, ICC

tribu'tare *vt* bestow, confer

tribu'tario *adj* tax *attrib*

tri'buto *nm* tribute; (tassa) tax

tri'checo *nm* walrus

tri'ciclo *nm* tricycle

trico'lore ① *adj* three-coloured ② *nm* (bandiera) Italian flag

tri'dente *nm* trident

tridimensio'nale *adj* three-dimensional

trien'nale *adj* (ogni tre anni) three-yearly; (lungo tre anni) three-year

tri'ennio *nm* three-year period

tri'fase *adj* three-phase

tri'foglio *nm* clover

trifo'lato *adj* sliced thinly and cooked with olive oil, parsley and garlic

tri'gemino *adj* **parto trigemino** birth of triplets

'triglia *nf* mullet

trigonome'tria *nf* trigonometry, trig *fam*

tri'lingue *adj* trilingual

tril'lare *vi* trill

'trillo *nm* trill

trilo'gia *nf* trilogy

trime'strale *adj* quarterly

tri'mestre *nm* quarter

'trina *nf* lace

trin'cea *nf* trench

trince'rare *vt* entrench

trincia'pollo *nm inv* poultry shears *pl*

trinci'are *vt* cut up

trincia'trice *nf* **trinciatrice di documenti** document shredder

Trini'dad e To'bago *nm* Trinidad and Tobago

Trinità *nf* Trinity

'trio *nm* trio

trion'fale *adj* triumphal

trionfal'mente *adv* triumphantly

trion'fante *adj* triumphant

trion'fare *vi* triumph (**su** over)

tri'onfo *nm* triumph

tri'pletta *nf* Sport hat trick

tripli'care *vt* triple

'triplice *adj* triple; **in ∼ [copia]** in triplicate

'triplo ① *adj* treble, triple; **una somma tripla del previsto** an amount three times as much as forecast
② *nm* **il ∼ (di)** three times as much (as)

'trippa *nf* tripe; (fam: pancia) belly

tripudi'are *vi* rejoice

tri'pudio *nm* jubilation

tris *nm* (gioco) noughts and crosses, tick-tack-toe Am

'triste *adj* sad; ‹luogo› gloomy

tri'stezza *nf* sadness; (di luogo) gloominess

'tristo *adj* nasty

trita'carne *nm inv* mincer

tritaghi'accio *nm inv* ice-crusher

tri'tare *vt* mince

trita'tutto *nm inv* (elettrico) [food] processor

'trito *adj* ∼ **e ritrito** well-worn, trite

tri'tolo *nm* TNT

tri'tone *nm* (mitologia) Triton; Zool newt

trit'tico *nm* triptych

trit'tongo *nm* triphthong

tritu'rare *vt* chop finely

triumvi'rato *nm* triumvirate

tri'vella *nf* drill

trivel'lare *vt* drill

trivi'ale *adj* vulgar

tro'feo *nm* trophy

troglo'dita *nmf* (preistoria) cave-dweller; fig Neanderthal

'trogolo *nm* (per maiali) trough

'troia *nf* sow; vulg bitch; (sessuale) whore

'tromba *nf* trumpet; Auto horn; **partire in ∼** dive in head first. **tromba d'aria** whirlwind. **tromba di Eustachio** Eustachian tube. **tromba di Falloppio** Fallopian tube. **tromba delle scale** stairwell

trom'bare ① *vt* vulg bonk; (fam: in esame) fail
② *vi* vulg bonk

trom'betta *nm* toy trumpet

trombetti'ere *nm* bugler

trombet'tista *nmf* trumpet-player

trom'bone *nm* trombone

trom'bosi *nf inv* thrombosis. **trombosi coronarica** coronary thrombosis. **trombosi venosa profonda** deep-vein thrombosis, DVT

tron'care *vt* sever; truncate ‹parola›

tron'chese *nm* wire cutters *pl*

tronche'sino *nm* (per le unghie) nail clippers *pl*

tron'chetto *nm* **tronchetto natalizio** Yule log

'tronco ① *adj* truncated; **licenziare in ∼** fire on the spot
② *nm* trunk; (di strada) section. **tronco d'albero** tree trunk. **tronco di cono** truncated cone

tron'cone *nm* stump

troneggi'are *vi* ∼ **su** tower over

'trono *nm* throne

tropi'cale *adj* tropical

'tropico *nm* tropic. **tropico del Cancro** Tropic of Cancer. **tropico del Capricorno** Tropic of Capricorn. **tropici** *pl* Tropics

'troppo ① *adj* too much; (con nomi plurali) too many
② *pron* too much; (plurale) too many; (troppo tempo) too long; **troppi** (troppa gente) too many people; **me ne hai dato ∼** you gave me too much
③ *adv* too; (con verbi) too much; ∼ **stanco** too tired; **ho mangiato ∼** I ate too much; **hai fame? –non ∼** are you hungry? –not very; **sentirsi di ∼** feel unwanted

'trota *nf* trout. **trota di mare** sea trout. **trota salmonata** salmon trout

trot'tare *vi* trot

t

trotterel'lare *vi* trot along; ⟨*bambino*⟩ toddle

'trotto *nm* trot; **andare al** ∼ trot

'trottola *nf* [spinning] top; (movimento) spin

troupe *nf inv* **troupe televisiva** camera crew

trousse *nf inv* (per trucco) make-up bag

tro'vare *vt* find; (scoprire) find out; (incontrare) meet; (ritenere) think; **andare a** ∼ go to see

trova'robe *nmf* (persona) props *sg*

tro'varsi *vr* find oneself; (luogo) be; (sentirsi) feel

tro'vata *nf* bright idea. **trovata pubblicitaria** advertising gimmick, publicity stunt

trova'tello, -a *nmf* foundling

truc'care *vt* make up; cook ⟨*libri contabili*⟩; soup up ⟨*motore*⟩; rig ⟨*elezioni*⟩

truc'carsi *vr* put one's make-up on

truc'cato *adj* made-up; ⟨*libri contabili*⟩ cooked; ⟨*partita, elezioni*⟩ rigged; ⟨*motore*⟩ souped up

trucca'tore, -trice *nmf* make-up artist

'trucco *nm* (cosmetici) make-up; (imbroglio) trick; **trucchi** *pl* **del mestiere** tricks of the trade

'truce *adj* fierce; ⟨*delitto*⟩ savage

truci'dare *vt* slay

trucio'lato *nm* chipboard

'trucolo *nm* shaving

trucu'lento *adj* ⟨*delitto*⟩ savage; ⟨*film*⟩ violent

'truffa *nf* fraud

truf'fare *vt* defraud

truffa'tore, -trice *nmf* fraudster

'trullo *nm* traditional house with a conical roof found in Apulia

'truppa *nf* troops *pl*: (gruppo) group; **truppe** *pl* **d'assalto** assault troops; **truppe** *pl* **di terra** ground troops

T-shirt *nf inv* tee-shirt, T-shirt

tsu'nami *nm* tsunami

tu *pers pron* you; **sei tu?** is that you?; **l'hai fatto tu?** did you do it yourself?; **a tu per tu** in private; **darsi del tu** use the familiar tu to each other

'tua ▶ TUO

'tuba *nf* Mus tuba; (cappello) top hat

tu'bare *vi* coo; ⟨*innamorati*⟩ bill and coo

tuba'tura *nf* piping

tubazi'one *nf* piping; **tubazioni** *pl* piping *sg*, pipes

tuberco'lina *nf* tuberculin

tuberco'losi *nf* tuberculosis

'tubero *nm* tuber

tube'rosa *nf* tuberose

tu'betto *nm* tube. **tubetto di colore** tube of paint

tu'bino *nm* (vestito) shift; (cappello) bowler; derby Am

'tubo *nm* pipe; Anat canal; **non ho capito un** ∼ fam I understood zilch. **tubo digerente** alimentary canal. **tubo a raggi catodici** cathode-ray tube. **tubo di scappamento** exhaust [pipe]. **tubo di scarico** waste pipe

tubo'lare *adj* tubular

'tue ▶ TUO

tuf'fare *vt* plunge

tuf'farsi *vr* dive; **'vietato** ∼**'** 'no diving'

tuffa'tore, -trice *nmf* diver

'tuffo *nm* dive; (bagno) dip; **ho avuto un** ∼ **al cuore** my heart leapt into my mouth. **tuffo di testa** dive

'tufo *nm* tufa

tu'gurio *nm* hovel

tuli'pano *nm* tulip

'tulle *nm* tulle

tume'fatto *adj* swollen

tumefazi'one *nf* swelling

'tumido *adj* swollen

tu'more *nm* tumour. **tumore benigno** benign tumour. **tumore del collo dell'utero** cervical cancer. **tumore maligno** malignant tumour

tumulazi'one *nf* burial

'tumulo *nm* (di pietre) cairn

tu'multo *nm* turmoil; (sommossa) riot

tumultu'oso *adj* tumultuous

tung'steno *nm* tungsten

'tunica *nf* tunic

Tuni'sia *nf* Tunisia

tuni'sino *adj & nmf* Tunisian

'tunnel *nm inv* tunnel. **tunnel sotto la Manica** Channel Tunnel

'tuo ① (il ∼ *m*, la tua *f*, i tuoi *mpl*, le tue *fpl*) *poss adj* your; **è tua questa macchina?** is this car yours?; **un** ∼ **amico** a friend of yours; ∼ **padre** your father ② *poss pron* yours; **i tuoi** your folk

tu'oi ▶ TUO

tuo'nare *vi* thunder

tu'ono *nm* thunder

tu'orlo *nm* yolk

tu'racciolo *nm* stopper; (di sughero) cork

tu'rare *vt* block; cork ⟨*bottiglia*⟩

tu'rarsi *vr* become blocked; ∼ **le orecchie** stick one's fingers in one's ears; ∼ **il naso** hold one's nose

'turba *nf* (folla) rabble. **turba psichica** mental illness

turba'mento *nm* disturbance; (sconvolgimento) upsetting. **turbamento della quiete pubblica** breach of the peace

tur'bante *nm* turban
tur'bare *vt* upset
tur'barsi *vr* get upset
tur'bato *adj* upset
tur'bina *nf* turbine
turbi'nare *vi* whirl
'turbine *nm* whirl. **turbine di polvere** dust storm. **turbine di vento** whirlwind
'turbo *nm inv* turbo
turbocompres'sore *nm* Tech turbocharger
turbo'lento *adj* turbulent
turbo'lenza *nf* turbulence
turboreat'tore *nm* turbo-jet
tur'chese *adj & nmf* turquoise
Tur'chia *nf* Turkey
tur'chino *adj & nm* deep blue
'turco, -a ① *adj* Turkish ② *nmf* Turk; **fumare come un ~** smoke like a chimney; **bestemmiare come un ~** swear like a trooper ③ *nm* (lingua) Turkish; fig double Dutch
'turgido *adj* turgid
tu'rismo *nm* tourism
tu'rista *nmf* tourist
tu'ristico *adj* tourist *attrib*
tur'nista *nmf* shift-worker
'turno *nm* turn; **a ~** in turn; **fare a ~** take turns; **fare i turni** work shifts; **di ~** on duty. **turno eliminatorio** heat. **turno di giorno** day shift. **turno di guardia** guard duty. **turno di lavoro** shift. **turno di notte** night shift; **del turno di notte** night shift *attrib*; **fare il turno di notte** be on night shift
'turpe *adj* base
turpi'loquio *nm* foul language
'tuta *nf* overalls *pl*. **tuta da ginnastica** tracksuit. **tuta da lavoro** overalls *pl*. **tuta mimetica** camouflage. **tuta da sci** ski suit. **tuta spaziale** spacesuit. **tuta subacquea** wetsuit
tu'tela *nf* Jur guardianship; (protezione)

protection. **tutela dell'ambiente** environmental protection
tute'lare *vt* protect
tu'tina *nf* sleepsuit; (da danza) leotard
tu|'tore, -trice *nmf* guardian
'tutta *nf* **mettercela ~ per fare qualcosa** go flat out for something
tutta'via *conj* nevertheless, still
'tutto ① *adj* whole; (con nomi plurali) all; (ogni) every; **tutta la classe** the whole class, all the class; **tutti gli alunni** all the pupils; **a tutta velocità** at full speed; **ho aspettato ~ il giorno** I waited all day [long]; **vestito di ~ punto** all kitted out; **in ~ il mondo** all over the world; **noi tutti** all of us; **era tutta contenta** she was delighted; **tutti e due** both; **tutti e tre** all three ② *pron* all; (tutte le cose) everything; (qualunque cosa) anything; **c'è ancora del dolce? –no, l'ho mangiato ~** is there still some cake? –no, I ate it all; **le finestre sono pulite, le ho lavate tutte** the windows are clean, I washed them all; **raccontami ~** tell me everything; **tutti** (tutta la gente) everybody; **lo sanno tutti** everybody knows; **è capace di ~** he's capable of anything; **~ compreso** all in; **del ~** quite; **in ~** altogether ③ *adv* completely; **tutt'a un tratto** all at once; **tutt'altro** not at all; **tutt'altro che...** anything but... ④ *nm* whole; **tentare il ~ per ~** go for broke; **~ compreso** all-inclusive; **~ esaurito** Theat full house
tutto'fare *adj inv & nmf inv* [impiegato] **tuttofare** general handyman
tut'tora *adv* still
tutù *nm inv* tutu; (lungo) ballet dress
tv *nf inv* TV. **tv via cavo** cable TV. **tv digitale** digital (television) **tv interattiva** interactive TV
tweed *nm* tweed

Uu

ubbidi'ente *adj* obedient
ubbidiente'mente *adv* obediently
ubbidi'enza *nf* obedience
ubbi'dire *vi* **~ (a)** obey
ubi'cato *adj* located
ubicazi'one *nf* location

ubiquità *nf* **non ho il dono dell'~** I can't be in two places at once
ubria'care *vt* get drunk
ubria'carsi *vr* get drunk; **~ di** fig become intoxicated with
ubria'chezza *nf* drunkenness; **in stato di ~** inebriated; **in stato di ~ molesta** drunk and disorderly

ubri'aco, **-a** ① *adj* drunk. **ubriaco fradicio** dead *or* blind drunk ② *nmf* drunk

ubria'cone ① *nm* drunkard ② *adj* **un marito ~** a drunkard of a husband

uccelli'era *nf* aviary

uccel'lino *nm* baby bird

uc'cello *nm* bird; (vulg: pene) cock. **uccello acquatico** water fowl. **uccello da cacciagione** game bird. **uccello del malaugurio** bird of ill omen. **uccello notturno** night *or* nocturnal bird. **uccello del paradiso** bird of paradise. **uccello di passo** bird of passage. **uccello rapace** bird of prey

uc'cidere *vt* kill

uc'cidersi *vr* kill oneself; (morire) be killed

+uccio *suff* **boccuccia** *nf* pretty little mouth; **calduccio** *nm* cosy warmth; **c'è un bel calduccio** it's nice and cosy; **tesoruccio** *nm* sweetie; **avvocatuccio** *nm* pej small town lawyer; **cosuccia** *nf* trifle; **è una cosuccia da niente** it's nothing; **doloruccio** *nm* twinge; **vestituccio** *nm* pej skimpy little dress

uccisi'one *nf* killing

uc'ciso pp di UCCIDERE

ucci'sore *nm* killer

U'craina *nf* l' ~ the Ukraine

u'craino, **-a** *adj & nmf* Ukrainian

u'dente *adj* **i non udenti** the hearing-impaired

u'dibile *adj* audible

udi'enza *nf* audience; (colloquio) interview; Jur hearing. **udienza a porte chiuse** hearing in camera

u'dire *vt* hear

udi'tivo *adj* auditory

u'dito *nm* hearing

udi'|tore, **-trice** *nmf* listener; Sch unregistered student (allowed to sit in on lectures)

udi'torio *nm* audience

UE *abbr* (**Unione Europea**) EU

uff *int* phew!

'uffa *int* (con impazienza) come on!; (con tono seccato) damn!

uffici'ale ① *adj* official ② *nm* officer; (funzionario) official; **pubblico ufficiale** public official. **ufficiale dell'esercito** army officer. **ufficiale giudiziario** clerk of the court. **ufficiale sanitario** health officer. **ufficiale dello Stato civile** registrar

ufficialità *nf* official status

ufficializ'zare *vt* make official, officialize

uffici'al'mente *adv* officially

uf'ficio *nm* office; (dovere) duty; (reparto) department; **andare in ~** go to the office. **ufficio acquisti** purchasing department. **ufficio cambi** bureau de change, exchange bureau. **ufficio di collocamento** employment office, jobcentre Br. **Ufficio Dazi e Dogana** Customs and Excise. **ufficio funebre** Relig funeral service. **ufficio delle imposte** tax office. **ufficio informazioni** information office. **ufficio di informazioni turistiche** tourist information office *or* centre. **ufficio oggetti smarriti** lost property office, lost and found Am. **ufficio del personale** personnel department. **ufficio postale** post office. **ufficio prenotazioni** advance booking office. **ufficio della redazione** newspaper office. **ufficio del turismo** tourist office. **ufficio turistico** tourist office

ufficiosa'mente *adv* unofficially

uffici'oso *adj* unofficial, off-the-record

'ufo¹ *nm inv* UFO

'ufo² **a ~** *adv* without paying

ufolo'gia *nf* ufology

U'ganda *nf* Uganda

ugan'dese *adj & nmf* Ugandan

uggiosità *nf* dullness

uggi'oso *adj* boring

uguagli'anza *nf* equality

uguagli'are *vt* make equal; (essere uguale) equal; (livellare) level

uguagli'arsi *vr* ~ **a** compare oneself to

ugu'ale ① *adj* equal; (lo stesso) the same; (simile) like; **due più due è ~ a quattro** two plus two equals four ② *nm* Math equals sign; **che non ha ~** unequalled

ugual'mente *adv* equally; (malgrado tutto) all the same

'ulcera *nf* ulcer. **ulcera gastrica** gastric ulcer. **ulcera peptica** peptic ulcer

u'liva *nf* ▶ OLIVA

uli'veto *nm* olive grove

u'livo *nm* olive[-tree]

'ulna *nf* Anat ulna

ulteri'ore *adj* further

ulterior'mente *adv* further

ultima'mente *adv* lately

ulti'mare *vt* complete

ulti'matum *nm inv* ultimatum

ulti'missime *nfpl* Journ stop press, latest news *sg*

'ultimo ① *adj* last; ‹notizie ecc› latest; (più lontano) farthest; fig ultimate; ‹prezzo› rockbottom; **l' ~ piano** the top floor ② *nm* last; **fino all' ~** to the last; **per ~** at the end

ultimo'genito, **-a** *nmf* last-born

ultrà *nmf inv* Sport fanatical supporter

ultraleg'gero *nm* (aereo) microlight

ultrapi'atto *adj* ultra-thin

ultrapo'tente *adj* extra-strong

ultra'rapido *adj* extra-fast

ultraresi'stente *adj* extra-strong

ultrasen'sibile *adj* ultrasensitive

ultra'sonico *adj* ultrasonic

ultrasu'ono *nm* ultrasound

ultrater'reno *adj* ⟨vita⟩ after death

ultravio'letto *adj* ultraviolét

ulu'lare *vi* howl

ulu'lato *nm* howling; **gli ululati** the howls, the howling

umana'mente *adv* ⟨trattare⟩ humanely; ~ **impossibile** not humanly possible

uma'nesimo *nm* humanism

uma'nista *nmf* humanist

umanità *nf* humanity

umani'tario *adj* humanitarian

u'mano *adj* human; (benevolo) humane

'Umbria *nf* Umbria

'umbro, -a *adj & nmf* Umbrian

umet'tare *vt* moisten

umidifica'tore *nm* humidifier

umidità *nf* dampness; (di clima) humidity

'umido ① *adj* damp; ⟨clima⟩ humid; ⟨mani, occhi⟩ moist ② *nm* dampness; **in** ~ Culin stewed

'umile *adj* humble

umili'ante *adj* humiliating

umili'are *vt* humiliate

umili'arsi *vr* humble oneself

umiliazi'one *nf* humiliation

umil'mente *adv* humbly

umiltà *nf* humility

u'more *nm* humour; (stato d'animo) mood; **di cattivo/buon** ~ in a bad/good mood

umo'rismo *nm* humour

umo'rista *nmf* humorist

umoristica'mente *adv* humorously

umo'ristico *adj* humorous

un ▶ UNO

un' ▶ UNO

'una ▶ UNO

u'nanime *adj* unanimous

unanime'mente *adv* unanimously

unanimità *nf* unanimity; **all'** ~ unanimously

unci'nare *vt* hook

unci'nato *adj* hooked; ⟨parentesi⟩ angle *attrib*

unci'netto *nm* crochet hook

un'cino *nm* hook

undi'cenne *adj & nmf* eleven-year-old

undi'cesimo *adj & nm* eleventh

'undici *adj & nm* eleven

'ungere *vt* grease; (sporcare) get greasy; Relig anoint; (blandire) flatter

'ungersi *vr* (con olio solare) oil oneself; ~ **le mani** get one's hands greasy

unghe'rese ① *adj & nmf* Hungarian ② *nm* (lingua) Hungarian

Unghe'ria *nf* Hungary

'unghia *nf* nail; (di animale) claw; **cadere sotto le unghie di qualcuno** fall into somebody's clutches. **unghia fessa** cloven hoof

unghi'ata *nf* (graffio) scratch

ungu'ento *nm* ointment

unica'mente *adv* only

unicellu'lare *adj* single-cell, unicellular

unicità *nf* uniqueness

'unico *adj* only; (singolo) single; (incomparabile) unique

uni'corno *nm* unicorn

unidimensio'nale *adj* one-dimensional

unidirezio'nale *adj* unidirectional

unifamili'are *adj* one-family

unifi'care *vt* unify

unificazi'one *nf* unification

unifor'mare *vt* level

unifor'marsi *vr* conform (a to)

uni'forme ① *adj* uniform ② *nf* uniform. **uniforme di gala** Mil mess dress

uniformità *nf* uniformity

unilate'rale *adj* unilateral

unilateral'mente *adv* unilaterally

uninomi'nale *adj* Pol single-candidate

uni'one *nf* union; (armonia) unity; **Unione economica e monetaria** Economic and Monetary Union. **unione di fatto** registered partnership. **Unione Europea** European Union. **Unione Monetaria Europea** European Monetary Union. **unione sindacale** trade union, labor union Am. **Unione Sovietica** Soviet Union

unio'nista *nmf* Pol Unionist

u'nire *vt* unite; (collegare) join; blend ⟨colori ecc⟩

u'nirsi *vr* unite; (collegarsi) join

'unisex *adj inv* unisex

u'nisono *nm* **all'** ~ in unison

unità *nf inv* unity; (Math, Mil, reparto ecc) unit; Comput drive. **unità di archivio dati** data storage device. **unità di backup a nastro** Comput tape backup drive. **unità centrale di elaborazione** Comput central processing unit, CPU. **unità floppy disk** Comput floppy disk drive. **unità di inizializzazione** Comput boot drive. **unità di memoria di massa** Comput mass storage device. **unità di misura** unit of measurement. ···⟩

u

unità a nastro magnetico Comput tapedrive. **unità periferica** Comput peripheral. **unità di produzione** factory unit. **unità socio-sanitaria locale** local health centre. **unità di visualizzazione** Comput visual display unit, VDU

uni'tario *adj* unitary; **prezzo unitario** unit price

u'nito *adj* united; ⟨*tinta*⟩ plain; ⟨*comunità*⟩ tight-knit

univer'sale *adj* universal

universaliz'zare *vt* universalize

universal'mente *adv* universally

università *nf inv* university

universi'tario, -a ① *adj* university *attrib*
② *nmf* (docente) university lecturer; (studente) undergraduate

uni'verso *nm* universe

u'nivoco *adj* unambiguous

uno, -a ① *art indef* a; (davanti a vocale o h muta) an; **un esempio** an example;
② *pron* one; **a ∼ a ∼** one by one; **∼ alla volta** one at a time; **l'∼ e l'altro** both [of them]; **né l'∼ né l'altro** neither [of them]; **∼ di noi** one of us; **∼ fa quello che può** you do what you can
③ *adj* a, one
④ *nm* (numerale) one; (un tale) some man
⑤ *nf* some woman

'unto ① *pp* ▶ di UNGERE
② *adj* greasy
③ *nm* grease

untu'oso *adj* greasy

unzi'one *nf* **l'Estrema Unzione** Extreme Unction, last rites

u'omo *nm* (pl **uomini**) man; **'uomini'** (bagni) 'gents', 'men's room'. **uomo d'affari** business man. **uomo di colore** black man. **uomo di fiducia** right-hand man. **uomo di mondo** man of the world. **uomo-oggetto** toy boy. **uomo delle pulizie** cleaner; **uomo sandwich** sandwich-man. **uomo di Stato** statesman. **uomo della strada** man on the street

u'ovo *nm* (pl f **uova**) egg; **uova** *pl* **al bacon** bacon and eggs. **uovo barzotto** o **bazzotto** soft-boiled egg. **uovo in camicia** poached egg. **uovo di Colombo** obvious simple solution. **uovo all'occhio di bue** fried egg. **uovo all'ostrica** raw egg. **uovo di Pasqua** Easter egg. **uova** *pl* **al prosciutto** ham and eggs. **uovo sodo** hard-boiled egg. **uovo strapazzato** scrambled egg. **uovo al tegamino** fried egg

upgra'dabile *adj* upgradeable

'upupa *nf inv* hoopoe

ura'gano *nm* hurricane

u'ranio *nm* uranium

U'rano *nm* Uranus

urba'nesimo *nm* urbanization

urba'nista *nmf* town planner

urba'nistica *nf* town planning

urba'nistico *adj* urban

urbaniz'zare *vt* urbanize

urbanizzazi'one *nf* urbanization

ur'bano *adj* urban; (cortese) urbane

u'rea *nf* urea

u'retra *nf* Anat urethra

ur'gente *adj* urgent

urgente'mente *adv* urgently

ur'genza *nf* urgency; **in caso d'∼** in an emergency; **d'∼** ⟨*misura, chiamata*⟩ emergency *attrib*; **operare d'∼** perform an emergency operation on

'urgere *vi* be urgent

u'rina *nf* urine

uri'nare *vi* urinate

ur'lare *vi* shout, yell; ⟨*cane, vento*⟩ howl

'urlo *nm* (pl m **urli**, pl f **urla**) shout; (di cane, vento) howling

'urna *nf* urn; (elettorale) ballot box; **andare alle urne** go to the polls

urrà *int* hurrah!

URSS *nf abbr* (**Unione delle Repubbliche Socialiste Sovietiche**) USSR

ur'tare *vt* knock against; (scontrarsi) bump into; fig irritate

ur'tarsi *vr* collide; fig clash

'urto *nm* knock; (scontro) crash; (contrasto) conflict; fig clash; **d'∼** ⟨*misure, terapia*⟩ shock

Uru'guay *nm* Uruguay

U.S.A. *nmpl* US[A] *sg*

usa e getta *adj inv* ⟨*rasoio, siringa*⟩ throw-away, disposable

u'sanza *nf* custom; (moda) fashion

u'sare ① *vt* use; (impiegare) employ; (esercitare) exercise; **∼ fare qualcosa** be in the habit of doing something
② *vi* (essere di moda) be fashionable; **non si usa più** it is out of fashion; ⟨*attrezzatura, espressione*⟩ it's not used any more

u'sato ① *adj* used; (non nuovo) second-hand
② *nm* second-hand goods *pl*; **dell'∼** second-hand

u'sbeco, -a *adj* & *nmf* Uzbekistani

u'scente *adj* ⟨*presidente*⟩ outgoing

usci'ere *nm* usher

'uscio *nm* door

u'scire *vi* come out; (andare fuori) go out; (sfuggire) get out; (essere sorteggiato) come up; ⟨*giornale*⟩ come out; **∼ da** Comput exit from, quit; **∼ di strada** leave the road

u'scita *nf* exit, way out; (spesa) outlay; (di autostrada) junction; (battuta) witty remark;

(in ginnastica artistica) dismount; **uscite** pl Fin outgoings; **essere in libera** ∼ be off duty. **uscita di servizio** back door. **uscita di sicurezza** emergency exit, fire exit

usi'gnolo nm nightingale

'**uso** nm use; (abitudine) custom; (usanza) usage; **fuori** ∼ out of use; **per** ∼ **esterno** ⟨medicina⟩ for external use only. **uso e dosi** use and dosage

us'saro nm hussar

U.S.S.L. nf abbr (**Unità Socio-Sanitaria Locale**) local health centre

ustio'narsi vr burn oneself

ustio'nato, -a ① nmf burns case ② adj burnt

usti'one nf burn; **ustioni di primo grado** first-degree burns

usu'ale adj usual

usual'mente adv usually

usucapi'one nf Jur usucaption

usufru'ire vi ∼ **di** take advantage of, make use of

usu'frutto nm Jur use, usufruct fml

usufruttu'ario, -a nmf user, usufructuary fml

u'sura nf usury

usu'raio nm usurer

usur'pare vt usurp

usurpa'tore, -trice nmf usurper

u'tensile nm tool; Culin utensil; **cassetta degli utensili** tool box; **utensili** pl **da cucina** kitchen utensils

u'tente nmf user. **utente finale** end user. **utenti** pl **della strada** road users

u'tenza nf use; (utenti) users pl. **utenza finale** end users pl

ute'rino adj uterine

'**utero** nm womb

'**utile** ① adj useful ② nm Comm profit; **unire l'**∼ **al dilettevole** combine business with pleasure. **utile su cambi** foreign exchange gain. **utile sul capitale investito** return on investment

utilità nf usefulness, utility; Comput utility

utili'tario, -a ① adj utilitarian ② nf Auto small car

utilita'ristico adj utilitarian

u'tility nm inv utility

utiliz'zare vt utilize

utilizzazi'one nf utilization

uti'lizzo nm use

util'mente adv usefully

Uto'pia nf Utopia

uto'pista nmf Utopian

uto'pistico adj Utopian

UVA nmpl abbr (**ultravioletto prossimo**) UV

'**uva** nf grapes pl; **chicco d'uva** grape. **uva bianca** white grapes. **uva nera** black grapes. **uva passa** raisins pl. **uva sultanina** currants pl. **uva da tavola** [eating] grapes. **uva da vino** wine grapes

u'vetta nf raisins pl

uxori'cida ① nm wife-killer, uxoricide fml ② nf husband-killer

Uzbeki'stan nm Uzbekistan

Vv

va' ▸ ANDARE

va'cante adj vacant

va'canza nf holiday, vacation Am; **[giorno di]** ∼ holiday; (posto vacante) vacancy; **vacanze** pl holidays, vacation Am; Univ vacation, vac fam; **essere in** ∼ be on holiday/vacation; **prendersi una** ∼ take a holiday/vacation; **andare in** ∼ go on holiday/vacation; **è** ∼ it's a holiday. **vacanza avventura** adventure holiday **vacanze** pl **estive** summer holidays/vacation; **vacanze** pl **di Natale** Christmas holidays/vacation; **vacanze** pl **di Pasqua** Easter holidays/vacation; **vacanze** pl **scolastiche** school holidays/vacation

vacan'ziere, -a nmf vacationer Am, holidaymaker Br

'**vacca** nf cow. **vacca da latte** dairy cow

vac'caro, -a nf cowherd

vacci'nare vt vaccinate; **farsi** ∼ get vaccinated

vaccinazi'one nf vaccination

vac'cino nm vaccine

vacil'lante adj tottering; ⟨oggetto⟩ wobbly; ⟨luce⟩ flickering; fig wavering, faltering

vacil'lare vi totter; ⟨oggetto⟩ wobble; ⟨luce⟩ flicker; fig waver

'**vacuo** ① adj (vano) vain; fig empty ② nm vacuum

'**vado** ▸ ANDARE

vaffan'culo int vulg fuck off!

vagabon'daggio *nm* Jur vagrancy

vagabon'dare *vi* wander

vaga'bondo ① *adj* ‹cane› stray ② *nmf* tramp

vaga'mente *adv* vaguely

va'gante *adj* wandering; **mina vagante** floating mine; **proiettile vagante** stray bullet

va'gare *vi* wander

vagheggi'are *vt* long for

va'ghezza *nf* vagueness

va'gina *nf* vagina

vagi'nale *adj* vaginal

va'gire *vi* whimper

va'gito *nm* whimper

'vaglia *nm inv* money order. **vaglia bancario** bank draft. **vaglia cambiario** promissory note. **vaglia internazionale** international money order. **vaglia postale** postal order

vagli'are *vt* sift; fig weigh

'vaglio *nm* sieve

'vago *adj* vague

vagon'cino *nm* (di funivia) car. **vagoncino a piattaforma** flat[bed] wagon

va'gone *nm* (per passeggeri) carriage, car; (per merci) truck, wagon. **vagone bagagliaio** luggage van, baggage car Am. **vagone ferroviario** railway carriage Br, railroad car Am **vagone frigorifero** refrigerator van. **vagone letto** sleeper. **vagone postale** mail coach. **vagone ristorante** restaurant car, dining car

vai'olo *nm* smallpox

va'langa *nf* avalanche

val'chiria *nf* Valkyrie

val'dese *adj & nmf* Waldensian

va'lente *adj* skilful

va'lenza *nf* Chem valency; (fig: valore) value

va'lere ① *vi* be worth; (contare) count; ‹regola› apply (**per** to); (essere valido) be valid; **far ~ i propri diritti** assert one's rights; **farsi ~** assert oneself; **non vale!** that's not fair!; **tanto vale che me ne vada** I might as well go ② *vt* **~ qualcosa a qualcuno** (procurare) earn somebody something; **valerne la pena** be worth it; **vale la pena di vederlo** it's worth seeing; **valersi di** avail oneself of

valeri'ana *nf* valerian

va'lersi *vr* **valersi di** avail oneself of

va'levole *adj* valid

'valgo *adj* **alluce valgo** hallux valgus; **ginocchia** *pl* **valghe** knock knees

vali'care *vt* cross

'valico *nm* pass

valida'mente *adv* validly; (efficacemente) efficiently; ‹contribuire› effectively

validità *nf* validity; **con ~ illimitata** valid indefinitely

'valido *adj* valid; (efficace) efficient; ‹contributo› valuable

valige'ria *nf* (fabbrica) leather factory; (negozio) leather goods shop

vali'getta *nf* small case; (per attrezzi) box. **valigetta del pronto soccorso** first aid kit. **valigetta ventiquattrore** overnight bag

va'ligia *nf* suitcase; **fare le valigie** pack; fig pack one's bags. **valigia diplomatica** diplomatic bag

val'lata *nf* valley

'valle *nf* valley; **a ~** downstream

val'letta *nf* TV assistant

val'letto *nm* valet; TV assistant

'vallo *nm* wall; **il ~ di Adriano** Hadrian's Wall

val'lone¹ *nm* (valle) deep valley

val'lone², **-a** *adj & nmf* Walloon

va'lore *nm* value, worth; (merito) merit; (coraggio) valour; **valori** *pl* Comm securities; **di ~** (oggetto) valuable; **oggetti di valore** valuables; **di grande ~** of great value; ‹medico, scienziato› top *attrib*; **senza ~** worthless; **a ~ aggiunto** value-added. **valore bollato** revenue stamp. **valore contabile** book value. **valore effettivo** real value. **valore di mercato** market value, street value. **valore mobiliare** security. **valore nominale** nominal value. **valore di realizzo** break-up value. **valore di riscatto** surrender value

valoriz'zare *vt* (mettere in valore) use to advantage; (aumentare di valore) increase the value of; (migliorare l'aspetto di) enhance

valoriz'zarsi *vr* **il paese ha bisogno di ~ migliorando...** the country needs to enhance the value of its assets by improving...

valorosa'mente *adv* courageously

valo'roso *adj* courageous

'valso *pp di* VALERE

va'luta *nf* currency. **valuta a corso legale** legal tender. **valuta estera** foreign currency

valu'tare *vt* value; weigh up ‹situazione›

valu'tario *adj* ‹mercato, norme› currency *attrib*

valuta'tivo *adj* for evaluation, evaluative

valutazi'one *nf* valuation

'valva *nf* valve

'valvola *nf* valve; Electr fuse. **valvola a farfalla** butterfly valve. **valvola pneumatica** air valve. **valvola di sicurezza** anche fig safety valve

'valzer *nm inv* waltz

vamp *nf inv* vamp

vam'pata *nf* blaze; (di calore) blast; (al viso) flush

vam'piro *nm* vampire; fig bloodsucker

va'nadio *nm* vanadium

vanaglori'oso *adj* vainglorious

vana'mente *adv* (inutilmente) in vain; (con vanità) vainly

van'dalico *adj* atto ∼ act of vandalism

vanda'lismo *nm* vandalism

vandalizzare *vt* vandalize

vandalizzazione *nf* vandalizing

'vandalo, -a *nmf* vandal

vaneggia'mento *nm* delirium

vaneggi'are *vi* rave

va'nesio *adj* conceited

'vanga *nf* spade

van'gare *vt* dig

van'gata *nf* (quantità) spadeful; (azione) blow with a spade

van'gelo *nm* Gospel; (fam; verità) gospel [truth]

vanifi'care *vt* nullify

va'niglia *nf* vanilla

vanigli'ato *adj* ⟨zucchero⟩ vanilla

vanil'lina *nf* vanillin

vanità *nf* vanity

vanitosa'mente *adv* vainly

vani'toso *adj* vain

'vano ⓵ *adj* vain
⓶ *nm* (stanza) room; (spazio vuoto) hollow. **vano doccia** shower room. **vano portabagagli** Auto boot, trunk Am

van'taggio *nm* advantage; Sport lead; Tennis advantage; **trarre ∼ da qualcosa** derive benefit from something

vantaggiosa'mente *adv* advantageously

vantaggi'oso *adj* advantageous

van'tare *vt* praise; (possedere) boast

van'tarsi *vr* boast

vante'ria *nf* boasting; **vanterie** *pl* boasting

'vanto *nm* boast

'vanvera *nf* a ∼ at random; **parlare a ∼** talk nonsense

va'pore *nm* steam; (di benzina, cascata) vapour; **a ∼** steam *attrib*; **al ∼** Culin steamed; **battello a vapore** steamboat. **vapore acqueo** steam, water vapour

vapo'retto *nm* ferry

vapori'era *nf* steam engine

vaporiz'zare *vt* vaporize

vaporizza'tore *nm* spray

vapo'roso *adj* ⟨vestito⟩ filmy; **capelli** *pl* **vaporosi** big hair

va'rano *nm* monitor [lizard]

va'rare *vt* launch

var'care *vt* cross

'varco *nm* passage; **aspettare al ∼** lie in wait

vare'china *nf* bleach

vari'abile ⓵ *adj* changeable, variable
⓶ *nf* Math variable

variabilità *nf* changeableness, variability

varia'mente *adv* variously

vari'ante *nf* variant

vari'are *vt/i* vary; **∼ di umore** change one's mood

vari'ato *adj* varied

variazi'one *nf* variation

va'rice *nf* varicose vein

vari'cella *nf* chickenpox

vari'coso *adj* varicose

varie'gato *adj* variegated

varietà ⓵ *nf inv* variety
⓶ *nm inv* variety show

'vario *adj* varied; **vari** (parecchi) various, several; **varie ed eventuali** any other business

vario'pinto *adj* multicoloured

'varo *nm* launch

Var'savia Warsaw

vasaio *nm* potter

'vasca *nf* tub; (piscina) pool; (lunghezza) length. **vasca da bagno** bath. **vasca con idromassaggio** whirlpool bath. **vasca di sviluppo** Phot developing tank

va'scello *nm* vessel; **capitano di vascello** captain

va'schetta *nf* tub; Phot tray. **vaschetta per il ghiaccio** ice-tray

vasco'lare *adj* Anat, Bot vascular

vasecto'mia *nf* vasectomy

vase'lina *nf* Vaseline®

vasel'lame *nm* china. **vasellame d'oro/d'argento** gold/silver plate

va'setto *nm* small pot; (per marmellata) [jam] jar

'vaso *nm* pot; (da fiori) vase; Anat vessel; (per cibi) jar. **vaso da notte** chamberpot. **vaso sanguigno** blood vessel

vasocostrit'tore *adj* vasoconstrictor

vasodilata'tore *adj* vasodilator

vas'sallo *nm* vassal

vas'soio *nm* tray

vastità *nf* vastness

'vasto *adj* vast; **di vaste vedute** broadminded

Vati'cano *nm* Vatican

vati'cinio *nm* prophecy

vattela'pesca *adv* fam God knows

'vattene! go away!; ▸ ANDARE

VCR *abbr* (**videoregistratore**) VCR

ve *pers pron* you; **ve l'ho dato** I gave it to you

'**vecchia** *nf* old woman

vecchi'aia *nf* old age

'**vecchio, -a** ① *adj* old
② *nmf* old man; old woman; **i vecchi** old people; ∼ **mio** old man

'**veccia** *nf* vetch

'**vece** *nf* **in** ∼ **di** in place of; **fare le veci di qualcuno** take somebody's place

ve'dente *adj* **i non** ∼ the visually handicapped

ve'dere ① *vt* see; see, watch ⟨*film, partita*⟩; **far** ∼ show; **farsi** ∼ show one's face; **non si vede** ⟨*macchia, imperfezione*⟩ it doesn't show; **non veder l'ora di fare qualcosa** be raring to go; **non poter** ∼ **qualcuno** not be able to stand the sight of somebody; **vederci doppio** have double vision; **ne ho viste di tutti i colori** *fig* I've really seen life; **da** ∼ ⟨*film, spettacolo*⟩ not to be missed; **questo è da** ∼! that remains to be seen!; **chi si vede!** *fam* look who it is!
② *vi* see

ve'dersi *vr* see oneself; (reciproco) see each other; **vedersela brutta** have a narrow escape

ve'detta *nf* (luogo) lookout; *Naut* patrol vessel

'**vedova** *nf* widow. **vedova nera** Zool black widow [spider]

'**vedovo** *nm* widower

ve'duta *nf* view

vee'mente *adj* vehement

vege'tale *adj* & *nm* vegetable

vegetali'ano *adj* & *nmf* vegan

vegeta'lismo *nm* veganism

vege'tare *vi* vegetate

vegetaria'nismo *nm* vegetarianism

vegetari'ano, -a *adj* & *nmf* vegetarian

vegeta'tivo *adj* vegetative

vegetazi'one *nf* vegetation

'**vegeto** *adj* ▶ **vivo**

veg'gente *nmf* clairvoyant

'**veglia** *nf* watch; **fare la** ∼ keep watch. **veglia funebre** vigil

vegli'are *vi* be awake; ∼ **su** watch over

vegli'one *nm* **veglione di Capodanno** New Year's Eve celebration

veico'lare ① *vt* carry ⟨*malattia*⟩
② *adj* ⟨*traffico*⟩ vehicular

ve'icolo *nm* vehicle. **veicolo pesante** heavy goods vehicle, HGV. **veicolo spaziale** spacecraft

'**vela** *nf* sail; Sport sailing; **andare a gonfie vele** *fig* go beautifully; ⟨*affari*⟩ be booming; **far** ∼ set sail. **vela di taglio** mainsail

ve'lare *vt* veil; (fig: nascondere) hide

ve'larsi *vr* ⟨*vista*⟩ mist over; ⟨*voce*⟩ go husky

velata'mente *adv* indirectly

ve'lato *adj* veiled; ⟨*occhi*⟩ misty; ⟨*collant*⟩ sheer

vela'tura *nf* sails *pl*

'**velcro**® *nm* velcro®

veleggi'are *vi* sail

ve'leno *nm* poison

velenosa'mente *adv* ⟨*rispondere*⟩ venomously

vele'noso *adj* poisonous; ⟨*frase*⟩ venomous

ve'letta *nf* (di cappello) veil

'**velico** *adj* ⟨*circolo*⟩ sailing *attrib*; **superficie velica** sail area

veli'ero *nm* sailing ship

ve'lina *nf* **(carta) velina** tissue paper; (copia) carbon copy

ve'lista ① *nm* yachtsman
② *nf* yachtswoman

ve'livolo *nm* aircraft

velleità *nf inv* foolish ambition

vellei'tario *adj* unrealistic

'**vello** *nm* fleece

vellu'tato *adj* velvety

vel'luto *nm* velvet. **velluto a coste** corduroy

'**velo** *nm* veil; (di zucchero, cipria) dusting; (tessuto) voile

ve'loce *adj* fast

veloce'mente *adv* quickly

velo'cipede *nm* penny-farthing

velo'cista *nmf* Sport sprinter

velocità *nf inv* speed; (Auto: marcia) gear; **a due** ∼ *fig* two-tier. **velocità di clock** Comput clock speed. **velocità di crociera** cruising speed. **velocità di stampa** print speed

velociz'zare *vt* speed up

ve'lodromo *nm* cycle track

'**vena** *nf* vein; **essere in** ∼ **di** be in the mood for. **vena poetica** poetic mood

ve'nale *adj* venal; ⟨*persona*⟩ mercenary, venal

ve'nato *adj* grainy

vena'torio *adj* hunting *attrib*

vena'tura *nf* (di legno) grain; (di foglia, marmo) vein

ven'demmia *nf* grape harvest

vendemmi'are *vt* harvest

vendemmia|'tore, -trice *nmf* grapepicker

'**vendere** *vt* sell

'**vendersi** *vr* sell oneself; '**vendesi** 'for sale'

ven'detta *nf* revenge. **vendetta trasversale** vendetta

vendi'care *vt* avenge

vendi'carsi *vr* take revenge, get one's revenge; ∼ **di qualcuno** take one's vengeance on somebody; ∼ **di qualcosa** take revenge for something

vendicativa'mente *adv* vindictively

vendica'tivo *adj* vindictive

vendica|'tore, -trice *nmf* avenger

'**vendita** *nf* sale; in ∼ on sale. **vendita all'asta** sale by auction. **vendita di beneficenza** bring and buy sale. **vendita per corrispondenza** mail-order; **azienda di** ∼ **per corrispondenza** mail-order company; **catalogo di** ∼ **per corrispondenza** mail-order catalogue. **vendita al dettaglio** retailing. **vendita all'ingrosso** wholesaling. **vendita al minuto** retailing. **vendita porta a porta** door-to-door selling. **vendita a rate** hire purchase, installment plan Am; **vendite** *pl* **al dettaglio** retail sales

vendi|'tore, -trice *nmf* seller. **venditore ambulante** hawker, pedlar. **venditore al dettaglio** retailer. **venditore all'ingrosso** wholesaler. **venditore al mercato** market trader. **venditore al minuto** retailer

ven'duto *adj* ⟨*merce*⟩ sold; fig: ⟨*arbitro*⟩ bent; **arbitro** ∼**!** whose side are you on, ref!

vene'rabile, vene'rando *adj* venerable

vene'rare *vt* revere

venerazi'one *nf* reverence

venerdì *nm inv* Friday; **di** ∼ on Fridays. **Venerdì Santo** Good Friday

'**Venere** *nf* Venus

ve'nereo *adj* venereal

'**Veneto** *nm* Veneto

'**veneto** *adj* from the Veneto

Ve'nezia *nf* Venice

venezi'ano, -a ① *adj & nmf* Venetian ② *nf* (*persiana*) Venetian blind; Culin sweet bun

Vene'zuela *nm* Venezuela

venezue'lano, -a *adj & nmf* Venezuelan

'**vengo** ▶ VENIRE

veni'ale *adj* venial

ve'nire *vi* come; (riuscire) turn out; (costare) cost; (in passivi) be; **quanto viene?** how much is it?; **viene prodotto in serie** it's mass-produced; ∼ **a sapere** learn; ∼ **in mente** occur; **mi è venuto un dubbio** I've just had a doubt; **gli è venuta la febbre** he's got a temperature; ∼ **meno** (svenire) faint; ∼ **meno a un contratto** go back on a contract, renege on a contract; ∼ **via** come away; (staccarsi) come off; **mi viene da piangere** I feel like crying; **vieni a prendermi** come and pick me up; **vieni a trovarmi** come and see me; **nei giorni a** ∼ in [the] days to come

ve'noso *adj* venous

ven'taglio *nm* fan

ven'tata *nf* gust [of wind]; fig breath

ven'tenne *adj & nmf* twenty-year-old

ven'tesimo *adj & nm* twentieth

'**venti** *adj & nm* twenty

venti'lare *vt* ventilate, air; ∼ **un'idea** give an idea an airing; **poco ventilato** ⟨*stanza*⟩ airless

ventila'tore *nm* fan

ventilazi'one *nf* ventilation

ven'tina *nf* **una** ∼ (circa venti) about twenty

ventiquat'trore ① *nf inv* (valigetta) overnight bag ② *adv* ∼ **su ventiquattro** ⟨*lavorare*⟩ round-the-clock; ⟨*aperto*⟩ 24 hours

'**vento** *nm* wind; **c'è molto** ∼ it's very windy; **farsi** ∼ fan oneself. **vento contrario** headwind. **vento di prua** headwind. **vento di traverso** crosswind

'**ventola** *nf* fan

vento'lina *nf* fan. **ventolina di raffreddamento** Comput cooling fan

ven'tosa *nf* sucker, suction pad

ven'toso *adj* windy

'**ventre** *nm* stomach; (fig: della Terra) bowels *pl*; **basso** ∼ lower abdomen

ventrico'lare *adj* Med ventricular

ven'tricolo *nm* ventricle

ven'triloquo *nm* ventriloquist

ventu'nesimo *adj & nm* twenty-first

ven'tuno *adj & nm* twenty-one

ven'tura *nf* fortune; **andare alla** ∼ trust to luck

ven'turo *adj* next

ve'nuta *nf* coming; ∼ **meno a** breaking

'**vera** *nf* (anello) wedding ring

vera'mente *adv* really

ve'randa *nf* veranda

ver'bale ① *adj* verbal ② *nm* (di riunione) minutes *pl*. ∼ **di contravvenzione** fine

verbal'mente *adv* verbally

ver'bena *nf* verbena

'**verbo** *nm* verb; **il Verbo** Relig the Word. **verbo ausiliare** auxiliary [verb]. **verbo modale** modal auxiliary. **verbo riflessivo** reflexive verb

ver'boso *adj* verbose

ver'dastro *adj* greenish

'**verde** ① *adj* green; ∼ **d'invidia** green with envy ② *nm* green; (vegetazione) greenery; (semaforo) green light; **essere al** ∼ be broke. **verde bottiglia** bottle green. **verde oliva** olive green. **verde pisello** pea green. **verde pubblico** public parks *pl*

verdeggi'ante *adj* liter verdant

V

verde'mare *adj & nm inv* sea-green
verde'rame *nm* verdigris
ver'detto *nm* verdict. **verdetto di assoluzione** not guilty verdict. **verdetto di condanna** guilty verdict
ver'done *nm* greenfinch
ver'dura *nf* vegetables *pl*; **una ~** a vegetable; **verdure** *pl* **miste** mixed vegetables
'verga *nf* rod
ver'gato *adj* lined
vergi'nale *adj* virginal
'vergine ① *nf* virgin; Astr Virgo ② *adj* virgin; ⟨*cassetta*⟩ blank
vergini'tà *nf* virginity
ver'gogna *nf* shame; (timidezza) shyness
vergo'gnarsi *vr* feel ashamed; (essere timido) feel shy
vergognosa'mente *adv* shamefully
vergo'gnoso *adj* ashamed; (timido) shy; (disonorevole) shameful
veridi'cità *nf* veracity
ve'rifica *nf* check. **verifica dei bilanci** audit. **verifica di cassa** cash check
verifi'cabile *adj* verifiable
verifi'care *vt* check; verify ⟨*teoria*⟩
verifi'carsi *vr* come true
verifica|'tore, -trice *nmf* checker
ve'rismo *nm* realism
veri'tà *nf inv* truth
veriti'ero *adj* truthful
'verme *nm* worm. **verme solitario** tapeworm
vermi'celli *nmpl* vermicelli *sg* (pasta thinner than spaghetti)
ver'mifugo ① *adj* vermifugal ② *nm* vermifuge
ver'miglio *adj & nm* vermilion
'vermut *nm* vermouth
ver'nacolo *nm* vernacular
ver'nice *nf* paint; (trasparente) varnish; (pelle) patent leather; fig veneer; '**~ fresca**' 'wet paint'. **vernice a spirito** spirit varnish
vernici'are *vt* paint; (con vernice trasparente) varnish
vernicia'tura *nf* painting; (con vernice trasparente) varnishing; (strato) paintwork; fig veneer
vernis'sage *nm inv* vernissage
'vero ① *adj* true; (autentico) real; (perfetto) perfect; **è ~?** is that so?; **~ e proprio** full-blown; **sei stanca, ~?** you're tired, aren't you; **non ti piace, ~?** you don't like it, do you?. **vero cuoio** real leather ② *nm* truth; (realtà) life
verosimigli'anza *nf* plausibility
vero'simile *adj* probable, likely
verosimil'mente *adv* probably

ver'ruca *nf* wart; (sotto la pianta del piede) verruca
versa'mento *nm* (pagamento) payment; (in banca) deposit
ver'sante *nm* slope
ver'sare ① *vt* pour; (spargere) shed; (rovesciare) spill; pay ⟨*denaro*⟩ (in banca) pay in ② *vi* (trovarsi) be
ver'sarsi *vr* spill; (sfociare) flow
ver'satile *adj* versatile
versatili'tà *nf* versatility
ver'sato *adj* (pratico) versed
ver'setto *nm* verse
versifica|'tore, -trice *nmf* versifier
versi'one *nf* version; (traduzione) translation. '**versione integrale**' (libro) 'unabridged version'; (film) 'uncut'. **versione originale** original version. '**versione ridotta**' 'abridged version'. **versione teatrale** dramatization
'verso[1] *nm* verse; (grido) cry; (gesto) gesture; (senso) direction; (modo) manner; **fare il ~ a qualcuno** ape somebody; **non c'è ~ di** there is no way of; **versi** *pl* **sciolti** blank verse
'verso[2] *prep* towards; (nei pressi di) round about; **~ dove?** which way?
'vertebra *nf* vertebra
verte'brale *adj* vertebral
verte'brato *nm* vertebrate
ver'tenza *nf* dispute. **vertenza sindacale** industrial dispute
'vertere *vi* **~ su** focus on
verti'cale ① *adj* vertical; (in parole crociate) down ② *nf* handstand; **fare la ~** do a handstand
vertical'mente *adv* vertically
'vertice *nm* summit; Math vertex; **conferenza al vertice** summit conference; **incontro al vertice** summit meeting
ver'tigine *nf* dizziness; Med vertigo; **vertigini** *pl* giddy spells; **avere le vertigini** feel dizzy
vertiginosa'mente *adv* dizzily
vertigi'noso *adj* dizzy; ⟨*velocità*⟩ breakneck; ⟨*prezzi*⟩ sky-high; ⟨*scollatura*⟩ plunging
'vescia *nf* puffball
ve'scica *nf* bladder; (sulla pelle) blister
'vescovo *nm* bishop
'vespa *nf* wasp
'Vespa® *nf* scooter, Vespa®
vespasi'ano *nm* urinal
'vespro *nm* vespers *pl*
ves'sare *vt* fml oppress
ves'sillo *nm* standard
ve'staglia *nf* dressing gown, robe Am
'veste *nf* dress; (rivestimento) covering; **in ~ di** in the capacity of; **in ~ ufficiale** in

an official capacity. **veste da camera** dressing gown, robe Am. **veste editoriale** layout. **veste tipografica** typographical design

vesti'ario *nm* clothing

ve'stibolo *nm* hall

ve'stigio *nm* (pl m **vestigi**, pl f **vestigia**) trace

ve'stire *vt* dress

ve'stirsi *vr* get dressed; ~ **da** dress up as a

ve'stito ① *adj* dressed
② *nm* (da uomo) suit; (da donna) dress; vestiti *pl* clothes. **vestito da sposa** wedding dress

vete'rano, **-a** *adj & nmf* veteran

veteri'nario, **-a** ① *adj* veterinary
② *nm* veterinary surgeon
③ *nf* veterinary science

'veto *nm* veto

ve'traio *nm* glazier

ve'trato, **-a** ① *adj* glazed
② *nf* big window; (in chiesa) stained-glass window; (porta) glass door

vetre'ria *nf* glass works

ve'trina *nf* [shop-]window; (mobile) display cabinet

vetri'nista *nmf* window dresser

ve'trino *nm* (di microscopio) slide

vetri'olo *nm* vitriol

'vetro *nm* glass; (di finestra, porta) pane. ~ **di sicurezza** safety glass

vetro'resina *nf* fibreglass

ve'troso *adj* vitreous

'vetta *nf* peak

vet'tore *nm* vector

vetto'vaglie *nfpl* provisions

vet'tura *nf* coach; ⟨ferroviaria⟩ coach, carriage; Auto car. **vettura di cortesia** courtesy car. **vettura d'epoca** vintage car

vettu'rino *nm* coachman

vezzeggi'are *vt* fondle

vezzeggia'tivo *nm* pet name

'vezzo *nm* habit; (attrattiva) charm; vezzi *pl* (moine) affectation

vez'zoso *adj* charming; pej affected

VF *abbr* (**Vigili del Fuoco**) fire brigade, fire department Am

vi ① *pers pron* you; (riflessivo) yourselves; (reciproco) each other; (tra più persone) one another; vi ho dato un libro I gave you a book; lavatevi le mani wash your hands; eccovi! here you are!
② *adv* = ci

'via¹ *nf* street, road; fig way; Anat tract; in ~ **di** in the course of; per ~ **di** on account of; per ~ **aerea** by airmail. **Via Lattea** Astr Milky Way. **via di mezzo** halfway

house. **via respiratoria** Anat airway. **via d'uscita** let-out

'via² ① *adv* away; (fuori) out; **andar** ~ go away; ⟨macchia⟩ come off, come out; **e così** ~ and so on; **e** ~ **dicendo** and whatnot; ~ ~ **che** as
② *int* ~! go away!; Sport go!; (andiamo) come on!; ~, **non ci credo** come off it *or* come on, I don't believe it
③ *nm* starting signal

viabilità *nf* road conditions *pl*; (rete) road network; (norme) road and traffic laws *pl*

via'card *nf inv* motorway card

vi'ado *nm* (pl **viados**) rent boy

via'dotto *nm* viaduct

viaggi'are *vi* travel; **il treno viaggia con 20 minuti di ritardo** the train is 20 minutes late

viaggia|'tore, **trice** *nmf* traveller

vi'aggio *nm* journey; (breve) trip; **buon** ~! safe journey!, have a good trip!; **fare un** ~ go on a journey; **essere in** ~ be underway; **mettersi in** ~ get underway. **viaggio d'affari** business trip. **viaggio di lavoro** working trip **viaggio di nozze** honeymoon. **viaggio organizzato** package tour

vi'ale *nm* avenue; (privato) drive

via'letto *nm* path

via'vai *nm* coming and going

vi'brante *adj* vibrant

vi'brare *vi* vibrate; (fremere) quiver

vibra'tore *nm* vibrator

vibra'torio *adj* vibratory

vibrazi'one *nf* vibration

vi'cario *nm* vicar

'vice *nmf inv* deputy

vice+ *pref* vice+

vicecoman'dante *nm* Mil second in command

vicediret|'tore, **-trice** ① *nm* assistant manager
② *nf* assistant manageress

vi'cenda *nf* event; a ~ (fra due) each other; (a turno) in turn[s]

vicendevol'mente *adv* each other

vice'preside *nmf* vice-principal

vicepresi'dente *nmf* vice-president; Comm vice-chairman, vice-president Am

vicepresi'denza *nf* vice-presidency; Sch deputy head's office

viceré *nm inv* viceroy

viceret'tore *nm* vice-chancellor

vice'versa *adv* vice versa

vi'chingo, **-a** *adj & nmf* Viking

vici'nanza *nf* nearness; vicinanze (*pl*: paraggi) neighbourhood

vici'nato *nm* neighbourhood; (vicini) neighbours *pl*

vi'cino, **-a** ① *adj* near; (accanto) next

2 adv near, close
3 prep ～ a near [to]
4 nmf neighbour. **vicino di casa** nextdoor neighbour

vicissi'tudine nf vicissitude

'vicolo nm alley. **vicolo cieco** anche fig blind alley

'video nm inv (musicale) video; (schermo) screen. **video interattivo** interactive video

video'camera nf camcorder

videocas'setta nf video, video cassette

videoci'tofono nm video entry phone, videophone

video'clip nm inv video clip

videoconfe'renza nf videoconference

video'disco nm videodisc

videofo'nino® n videophone, camera phone

videogi'oco nm video game

video'leso, -a **1** adj visually handicapped, visually impaired **2** nmf visually handicapped person

videoregistra'tore nm videorecorder

videoscrit'tura nf word processing

videosorvegli'anza nf video surveillance

video'teca nf video library

video'tel® nm ≈ Videotex®

videote'lefono nm view phone

videotermi'nale nm visual display unit, VDU

vidi'mare vt authenticate

vi'eni ▶ VENIRE

Vi'enna nf Vienna

vien'nese adj & nmf Viennese

vie'tare vt forbid; ～ qualcosa a qualcuno forbid somebody something

vie'tato adj forbidden; **sosta vietata** no parking; ～ **fumare** no smoking; ～ **ai minori di 18 anni** ⟨film⟩ for over 18-year-olds only, X-rated

Vi'etnam nm Vietnam

vietna'mita adj & nmf Vietnamese

vi'gente adj in force

'vigere vi be in force

vigi'lante adj vigilant

vigi'lanza nf vigilance; (a scuola) supervision; (di polizia) surveillance. **vigilanza notturna** night security guards pl. **vigilanza urbana** traffic police (in towns)

vigi'lare **1** vt keep an eye on **2** vi keep watch

vigi'lato, -a **1** adj under surveillance **2** nmf person under police surveillance. **vigilato speciale** person under special police surveillance

'vigile **1** adj watchful

2 nm ～ [urbano] traffic policeman. **vigile del fuoco** firefighter. **vigili** pl **del fuoco** firemen, fire brigade, fire service. **vigili** pl **urbani** traffic police (in towns)

vi'gilia nf eve; Relig fast. **vigilia di Natale** Christmas Eve

vigliacca'mente adv in a cowardly way

vigliacche'ria nf cowardice

vigli'acco, -a **1** adj cowardly **2** nmf coward

'vigna nf, **vi'gneto** nm vineyard

vi'gnetta nf cartoon

vignet'tista nm cartoonist

vi'gogna nf (tessuto) vicuña

vi'gore nm vigour; **entrare in** ～ come into force; **essere in** ～ be in force

vigorosa'mente adv energetically

vigo'roso adj vigorous

'vile adj cowardly; (abietto) vile

vili'pendio nm scorn, contempt

'villa nf villa

vil'laggio nm village. **villaggio olimpico** Olympic village. **villaggio residenziale** commuter town. **villaggio satellite** satellite village. **villaggio turistico** holiday village

villa'nia nf rudeness

vil'lano **1** adj rude **2** nm boor; (contadino) peasant

villeggi'ante nmf holidaymaker

villeggi'are vi spend one's holidays

villeggia'tura nf holiday[s] [pl]. vacation Am

vil'letta nf small detached house. **villetta bifamiliare** semi-detached house. **villette** pl **a schiera** terraced houses

vil'lino nm detached house

vil'loso adj hairy

vil'mente adv in a cowardly way; (in modo spregevole) contemptibly

viltà nf cowardice

'vimine nm wicker; **sedia di vimini** wicker chair

vi'naio, -a nmf wine merchant

'vincere vt win; (sconfiggere) beat; (superare) overcome

'vincita nf win; (somma vinta) winnings pl

vinci'|tore, -trice **1** nmf winner; (di battaglia) victor, winner **2** adj winning, victorious

vinco'lante adj binding

vinco'lare vt bind; Comm tie up

vinco'lato adj Fin nonredeemable; **deposito vincolato** fixed deposit, term deposit

'vincolo nm bond

vi'nicolo adj wine attrib

vi'nile nm vinyl

vi'nilico *adj* vinyl

vinil'pelle® *nm* Leatherette®

'vino *nm* wine. **vino d'annata** vintage wine. **vino bianco** white wine; **vin brûlé** mulled wine. **vino della casa** house wine. **vino da dessert** dessert wine. **vino nuovo** new wine. **vino rosato** rosé [wine]. **vino rosé** rosé [wine]. **vino rosso** red wine. **vino spumante** sparkling wine. **vino da taglio** blending wine. **vino da tavola** table wine

vin'santo *nm* dessert wine from Tuscany

'vinto *pp di* VINCERE

vi'ola *nf* Bot violet; Mus viola. **viola del pensiero** Bot pansy

vio'laceo *adj* purplish; ⟨labbra⟩ blue

vio'lare *vt* violate

violazi'one *nf* violation. **violazione di contratto** breach of contract. **violazione di domicilio** breaking and entering

violen'tare *vt* rape

violente'mente *adv* violently

vio'lento *adj* violent

vio'lenza *nf* violence. **violenza carnale** rape

vio'letto, -a ① *adj & nm* (colore) violet ② *nf* violet

violi'nista *nmf* violinist

vio'lino *nm* violin

violon'cello *nm* cello

vi'ottolo *nm* path

'vipera *nf* viper

vi'raggio *nm* Phot toning; Naut, Aeron turn

vi'rale *adj* viral

vi'rare *vi* turn; ⟨nave⟩ put about; **virare di bordo** change course

vi'rata *nf* (di aereo) turning; (di nave) coming about; (nel nuoto) turn; fig change of direction

'virgola *nf* comma; Math [decimal] point; **punto e virgola** semicolon; **quattro ∼ due (4,2)** four point two (4.2)

virgo'lette *nfpl* inverted commas, quotation marks

vi'rile *adj* virile; (da uomo) manly

virilità *nf* virility; manliness

viril'mente *adv* in a manly way

vi'rologo *nm* virologist

virtù *nf inv* virtue; **in ∼ di** ⟨legge⟩ under

virtu'ale *adj* virtual

virtual'mente *adv* virtually

virtuo'sismo *nm* bravura

virtu'oso ① *adj* virtuous ② *nm* virtuoso

viru'lento *adj* virulent

'virus *nm inv* virus

visa'gista *nmf* beautician

visce'rale *adj* visceral; ⟨odio⟩ deep-seated; ⟨reazione⟩ gut

'viscere *nfpl* guts

'vischio *nm* mistletoe

vischi'oso *adj* viscous; (appiccicoso) sticky

'viscido *adj* slimy

vi'sconte *nm* viscount

viscon'tessa *nf* viscountess

vi'scoso *adj* viscous

vi'sibile *adj* visible

visi'bilio *nm* profusion; **andare in ∼** go into ecstasies

visibilità *nf* visibility; **scarsa visibilità** poor visibility

visi'era *nf* (di elmo) visor; (di berretto) peak

visio'nare *vt* examine; Cinema screen

visio'nario, -a *adj & nmf* visionary

visi'one *nf* vision; **prima visione** Cinema first showing; **seconda visione** re-release, second showing. **visione notturna** night vision

'visita *nf* visit; (breve) call; Med examination; **fare ∼ a qualcuno** pay somebody a visit. **visita di controllo** Med checkup. **visita di cortesia** courtesy visit. **visita doganale** customs inspection. **visita a domicilio** home visit, call-out, house call. **visita fiscale** tax inspection. **visita guidata** guided tour. **visita lampo** flying visit. **visita di leva** medical examination for military service

visi'tare *vt* visit; (brevemente) call on; Med examine

visita|'tore, -trice *nmf* visitor

visiva'mente *adv* visually

vi'sivo *adj* visual

'viso *nm* face. **viso pallido** paleface

vi'sone *nm* mink

'vispo *adj* lively

vis'suto ① *pp di* VIVERE ② *adj* experienced

'vista *nf* sight; (veduta) view; **a ∼ d'occhio** ⟨crescere⟩ visibly; ⟨estendersi⟩ as far as the eye can see; **in ∼ di** in view of; **perdere di ∼ qualcuno** lose sight of somebody; fig lose touch with somebody; **a prima ∼** at first sight. **vista sul mare** sea view

'visto ① *pp di* VEDERE ② *nm* visa. **visto di entrata** *o* **di ingresso** entry visa, entry permit. **visto d'uscita** exit visa. ③ *conj* **∼ che...** seeing that...

vistosa'mente *adv* conspicuously

vi'stoso *adj* showy; (notevole) considerable

visu'ale *adj* visual

visualiz'zare *vt* visualize; Comput display

visualizza'tore *nm* Comput display, VDU. **visualizzatore a cristalli liquidi** Comput liquid crystal display

visualizzazi'one *nf* Comput display

'**vita** *nf* life; (durata della vita) lifetime; Anat waist; **a** ∼ for life; **essere in fin di** ∼ be at death's door; **essere in** ∼ be alive; **fare la bella** ∼ lead the good life; **costo della vita** cost of living. **vita eterna** eternal life. **vita media** Biol life expectancy. **vita mondana** high life; **fare** ∼ **mondana** lead the high life. **vita notturna** night life. **vita terrena** Relig life on earth

vi'taccia *nf* slog

vi'tale *adj* vital

vitalità *nf* vitality

vita'lizio ① *adj* life *attrib* ② *nm* [life] annuity

vita'mina *nf* vitamin

vita'minico *adj* vitamin-enriched

vitaminiz'zato *adj* vitamin-enriched

'**vite** *nf* Mech screw; Bot vine; **giro di vite** fig clampdown. **vite canadese** Virginia creeper. **vite di coda** Aeron tailspin. **vite perpetua** endless screw

vi'tella *nf* (animale) calf; (carne) veal

vi'tello *nm* calf; (carne) veal; (pelle) calfskin. **vitello di latte** milk-fed veal. **vitello tonnato** sliced veal with tuna, anchovy, oil and lemon sauce

vi'ticcio *nm* tendril

viticol'tore *nm* wine grower

viticol'tura *nf* wine growing

vi'tino *nm* narrow waist. **vitino di vespa** slender little waist

'**vitreo** *adj* vitreous; (sguardo) glassy

'**vittima** *nf* victim

'**vitto** *nm* food; (pasti) board. **vitto e alloggio** board and lodging

vit'toria *nf* victory

vittori'ano *adj* Victorian

vittoriosa'mente *adv* victoriously, triumphantly

vittori'oso *adj* victorious

vitupe'rare *vt* vituperate

vitu'perio *nm* insult

vi'uzza *nf* narrow lane

'**viva** *int* hurrah!; ∼ **la Regina!** long live the Queen!

vi'vace *adj* vivacious; (mente) lively; (colore) bright

vivace'mente *adv* vivaciously

vivacità *nf* vivacity; (di mente) liveliness; (di colore) brightness

vivaciz'zare *vt* liven up

vi'vaio *nm* nursery; (per pesci) pond; fig breeding ground

viva'mente *adv* (ringraziare) warmly

vi'vanda *nf* food; (piatto) dish

vi'vente ① *adj* living ② *nmpl* **i viventi** the living

'**vivere** ① *vi* live; ∼ **di** live on; **vive** Typ stet ② *vt* (passare) go through ③ *nm* life; **modo di vivere** way of life

'**viveri** *nmpl* provisions

vivida'mente *adv* vividly

'**vivido** *adj* vivid

vivi'paro *adj* viviparous

vivisezio'nare *vt* vivisect

vivisezi'one *nf* vivisection

'**vivo** ① *adj* alive; (vivente) living; (vivace) lively; (colore) bright. **vivo e vegeto** alive and kicking; **farsi** ∼ keep in touch; (arrivare) turn up ② *nm* **colpire qualcuno sul** ∼ cut somebody to the quick; **dal** ∼ (trasmissione) live; (disegnare) from life; **i vivi** the living

vizi'are *vt* spoil (bambino ecc); (guastare) vitiate

vizi'ato *adj* spoilt; (aria) stale

'**vizio** *nm* vice; (cattiva abitudine) bad habit; (difetto) flaw. **vizio capitale** deadly sin. **vizio di forma** legal technicality. **vizio procedurale** procedural error

vizi'oso *adj* dissolute; (difettoso) faulty; **circolo vizioso** vicious circle

'**vizzo** *adj* (pelle) wrinkled; (pianta) withered

V.le *abbr* (**viale**) Ave

vocabo'lario *nm* dictionary; (lessico) vocabulary

vo'cabolo *nm* word

vo'cale ① *adj* vocal ② *nf* vowel

vo'calico *adj* (corde) vocal; (suono) vowel *attrib*

vocazi'one *nf* vocation

'**voce** *nf* voice; (diceria) rumour; (di bilancio, dizionario) entry. **voce bianca** Mus treble voice. **voce fuori campo** voiceover

voci'are ① *vi* (spettegolare) gossip ② *nm* buzz of conversation

vocife'rare *vi* shout; **si vocifera che...** it is rumoured that...

'**vodka** *nf inv* vodka

'**voga** *nf* rowing; (lena) enthusiasm; (moda) vogue; **essere in** ∼ be in vogue

vo'gare *vi* row; ∼ **a bratto** scull; ∼ **di coppia** scull

voga'tore *nm* oarsman; (attrezzo) rowing machine

'**voglia** *nf* desire; (volontà) will; (sulla pelle) birthmark; **aver** ∼ **di fare qualcosa** feel like doing something; **morire dalla** ∼ **di qualcosa** be dying for something; **di buona** ∼ willingly

'**voglio** ▶ VOLERE

vogli'oso *adj* (occhi, persona) covetous; **essere** ∼ **di qualcosa** want something

'voi *pers pron* you; **siete ~?** is that you?; **l'avete fatto ~?** did you do it yourselves?

voia'ltri *pers pron* you

vo'lano *nm* shuttlecock; Mech flywheel

vo'lant *nm inv* valance

vo'lante ① *adj* flying; ⟨*foglio*⟩ loose ② *nm* steering-wheel

volanti'nare *vi* hand out leaflets

volan'tino *nm* leaflet

vo'lare *vi* fly

vo'lata *nf* Sport final sprint; **di ~** in a rush

vo'latile ① *adj* ⟨*liquido*⟩ volatile ② *nm* bird

volatiliz'zarsi *vr* vanish

vol-au-'vent *nm inv* vol-au-vent

vo'lée *nf inv* Tennis volley

vo'lente *adj* **~ o nolente** whether you like it or not

volente'roso *adj* willing

volenti'eri *adv* willingly; **~!** with pleasure!

vo'lere ① *vt* want; (chiedere di) ask for; (aver bisogno di) need; **non voglio** I don't want to; **vuole che lo faccia io** he wants me to do it; **fai come vuoi** do as you like; **se tuo padre vuole, ti porto al cinema** if your father agrees, I'll take you to the cinema; **questa pianta vuole molte cure** this plant needs a lot of care; **vorrei un caffè** I'd like a coffee; **la leggenda vuole che...** legend has it that...; **la vuoi smettere?** will you stop that!; **senza ~** without meaning to; **voler bene/male a qualcuno** love/have something against somebody; **voler dire** mean; **ci vuole il latte** we need milk; **ci vuole tempo/pazienza** it takes time/patience; **volerne a** have a grudge against; **vuoi... vuoi...** either... or... ② *nm* will; **voleri** *pl* wishes

vol'gare *adj* vulgar; (popolare) common

volgarità *nf inv* vulgarity; **dire ~** use vulgar language; be vulgar

volgariz'zare *vt* popularize

volgarizzazi'one *nf* popularization

volgar'mente *adv* (grossolanamente) vulgarly; (comunemente) commonly, popularly

'volgere *vt/i* turn

'volgersi *vr* turn [round]; **~ a** (dedicarsi) take up

'volgo *nm* common people

voli'era *nf* aviary

voli'tivo *adj* strong-minded

'volo *nm* flight; **al ~** ⟨*fare qualcosa*⟩ quickly; ⟨*prendere qualcosa*⟩ in mid-air; **alzarsi in ~** ⟨*uccello*⟩ take off; **in ~** airborne. **volo di andata** outward flight. **volo charter** charter flight. **volo diretto** direct flight. **volo di linea** scheduled flight. **volo nazionale**
domestic flight. **volo di ritorno** return flight. **volo strumentale** flying on instruments. **volo a vela** gliding

volontà *nf inv* will; (desiderio) wish; **a ~** ⟨*mangiare*⟩ as much as you like

volontaria'mente *adv* voluntarily

volon'tario ① *adj* voluntary ② *nm* volunteer

volonte'roso *adj* willing

'volpe *nf* fox

vol'pino ① *adj* ⟨*astuzia*⟩ fox-like ② *nm* (cane) Pomeranian

volt *nm inv* volt

'volta *nf* time; (turno) turn; (curva) bend; Archit vault; **4 volte 4** 4 times 4; **a volte, qualche ~** sometimes; **c'era una ~...** once upon a time there was...; **una ~** once; **due volte** twice; **tre/quattro volte** three/four times; **una ~ per tutte** once and for all; **una ~ ogni tanto** every so often; **uno alla ~** one at a time; **alla ~ di** in the direction of. **volta a botte** barrel vault. **volta celeste** vault of heaven. **volta cranica** cranial vault. **volta a crociera** groin vault. **volta a vela** ribbed vault. **volta a ventaglio** fan vault

volta'faccia *nm inv* volte-face

voltagab'bana *nmf inv* turncoat

vol'taggio *nm* voltage

vol'tare *vt/i* turn; (rigirare) turn round; (rivoltare) turn over; **~ pagina** fig turn over a new leaf

vol'tarsi *vr* turn [round]

volta'stomaco *nm* nausea; fig disgust

volteggi'are *vi* circle; (ginnastica) vault

'volto ① *pp di* VOLGERE ② *nm* face; **ha mostrato il suo vero ~** he revealed his true colours

vol'tura *nf* (catastale) transfer of property. **~ di contratto** transfer of contract

vo'lubile *adj* fickle

volubil'mente *adv* in a fickle way, inconstantly

vo'lume *nm* volume. **volume di gioco** Sport possession

volumi'noso *adj* voluminous

vo'luta *nf* (spirale) spiral; (di capitello) volute

voluta'mente *adv* deliberately

vo'luto *adj* deliberate, intended

voluttà *nf* voluptuousness

voluttu'ario *adj* non-essential; **beni** *pl* **voluttuari** non-essentials

voluttu'oso *adj* voluptuous

vomi'tare *vi* vomit, be sick

vomi'tevole *adj* nauseating

'vomito *nm* vomit

'vongola *nf* clam

vo'race *adj* voracious

vorace'mente *adv* voraciously

vo'ragine *nf* abyss

vor'rei ▸ VOLERE

'**vortice** *nm* whirl; (gorgo) whirlpool; (di vento) whirlwind

vorticosa'mente *adv* in whirls

'**vostro** ① (il ∼ *m*, la vostra *f*, i vostri *mpl*, le vostre *fpl*) *poss adj* your; è vostra questa macchina? is this car yours?; un ∼ amico a friend of yours; ∼ **padre** your father

② *poss pron* yours; **i vostri** your folks

vo'tante *nmf* voter

vo'tare *vi* vote

votazi'one *nf* voting; Sch marks *pl*. **votazione di fiducia** Pol, fig vote of confidence. **votazione per alzata di mano** show of hands. **votazione a scrutinio segreto** secret ballot

'**voto** *nm* vote; Sch mark; Relig vow. **voto decisivo** casting vote. **voto per alzata di mano** show of hands

vs. *abbr* Comm (**vostro**) yours

'**vudu** *nm inv* voodoo

vul'canico *adj* volcanic

vul'cano *nm* volcano. **vulcano intermittente** dormant volcano. **vulcano spento** extinct volcano

vulne'rabile *adj* vulnerable

vulnerabilità *nf* vulnerability

'**vulva** *nf* vulva

vuo'tare *vt* empty

vuo'tarsi *vr* empty

vu'oto ① *adj* empty; (non occupato) vacant; ∼ **di** (sprovvisto) devoid of

② *nm* empty space; Phys vacuum; fig void; **assegno a** ∼ dud cheque; **sotto** ∼ ⟨*prodotto*⟩ vacuum-packed. **vuoto d'aria** air pocket. **vuoto a perdere** no deposit. **vuoto a rendere** ⟨*bottiglia*⟩ returnable

Ww

W *abbr* (**viva**) long live

'**wafer** *nm inv* (biscotto) wafer

wagon-'lit *nm inv* sleeping car

walkie-'talkie *nm inv* walkie-talkie

'**water** *nm inv* toilet, loo fam

watt *nm inv* watt

wat'tora *nm inv* Phys watt-hour

WC *nm inv* WC

'**web** *nm inv* Web

web'cam *nf inv* web cam

web'master *nm inv* webmster

wee'kend *nm inv* weekend

'**welter** *adj & nm inv* (in pugilato) welterweight

'**western** ① *adj inv* cowboy *attrib* ② *nm inv* Cinema western

'**whisky** *nm inv* whisky. **whisky di malto** malt [whisky]

wind'surf *nm inv* (tavola) windsurf; (sport) windsurfing; **fare** ∼ windsurf

windsur'fista *nmf* sailboarder, windsurfer

'**würstel** *nm inv* frankfurter

Xx

xenofo'bia *nf* xenophobia

xe'nofobo, -a ① *adj* xenophobic ② *nmf* xenophobe

'**xeres** *nm inv* sherry

xero'copia *nf* xerox

xeroco'piare *vt* photocopy

xerocopia'trice *nf* photocopier

xilofo'nista *nmf* xylophone player

'**xilofono** *nm* xylophone

Yy

yacht *nm inv* yacht
yak *nm inv* Zool yak
'yankee *nmf inv* Yank
'Yemen *nm* Yemen
yeme'nita *nmf* Yemeni
yen *nm inv* yen
'yeti *nm* yeti
'yiddish *adj & nm inv* Yiddish

'yoga *nm* yoga
adj inv yoga *attrib*
'yogurt *nm inv* yoghurt
yogurti'era *nf* yoghurt-maker
'yorkshire *nm inv* (cane) Yorkshire terrier
yo-'yo® *nm inv* yo-yo®
yup'pismo *nm* yuppiedom

Zz

zaba[gl]ione *nm* zabaglione (dessert made from eggs, wine and marsala and sugar)
'zacchera *nf* (schizzo) splash of mud
zaf'fata *nf* whiff; (di fumo) cloud
zaffe'rano *nm* saffron
zaf'firo *nm* sapphire
'zagara *nf* orange-blossom
'zaino *nm* rucksack
Za'ire *nm* Zaire
'Zambia *nm* Zambia
'zampa *nf* leg; **a quattro zampe** (animale) four-legged; (carponi) on all fours; **zampe** *pl* **di gallina** fig crow's feet; **zampe** *pl* **posteriori** hind legs
zam'pata *nf* paw; **dare una ∼ a** hit with its paw
zampet'tare *vi* scamper
zam'petto *nm* Culin knuckle
zampil'lante *adj* spurting
zampil'lare *vi* spurt
zam'pillo *nm* spurt
zam'pino *nm* paw; **mettere lo ∼ in** fig have a hand in
zam'pogna *nf* bagpipe
zampo'gnaro *nm* piper
zam'pone *nfpl* stuffed pigs trotter usually served with lentils
'zangola *nf* churn
'zanna *nf* fang; (di elefante) tusk
zan'zara *nf* mosquito
zanzari'era *nf* (velo) mosquito net; (su finestra) insect screen
'zappa *nf* hoe; **darsi la ∼ sui piedi** fig shoot oneself in the foot
zap'pare *vt* hoe

zap'pata *nf* **dare una ∼ a** hit with a hoe
zappet'tare *vt* hoe
'zapping *nm* channel-hopping Br, channel-surfing Am; **fare lo ∼** channel-hop Br, channel-surf Am
zar *nm inv* tzar
za'rina *nf* tzarina
za'rista *adj & nmf* tzarist
zatte'roni *nmpl* (scarpe) wedge shoes
za'vorra *nf* ballast; fig dead wood
zavor'rare *vt* load with ballast
'zazzera *nf* mop of hair
'zebra *nf* zebra; **zebre** *pl* (passaggio pedonale) zebra crossing, crosswalk Am
ze'brato *adj* ⟨tessuto⟩ with black and white stripes
'zecca¹ *nf* mint; **nuovo di ∼** brand-new
'zecca² *nf* (parassita) tick
zec'chino *nm* sequin; **oro zecchino** pure gold
ze'lante *adj* zealous
'zelo *nm* zeal
'zenit *nm* zenith
'zenzero *nm* ginger
'zeppa *nf* wedge
'zeppo *adj* packed full; **pieno ∼ di** crammed *or* packed with
zer'bino *nm* doormat
'zero *nm* zero, nought; (in calcio) nil; Tennis love; **due a ∼** (in partite) two nil; **ricominciare da ∼** fig start again from scratch; **sparare a ∼ su qualcuno** fig lay into somebody; **avere il morale sotto ∼** fig be down in the dumps

'zeta nf zed, zee Am

'zia nf aunt

zibel'lino nm sable

zi'gano, **-a** adj & nmf gypsy

'zigolo nm Zool bunting

'zigomo nm cheekbone

zigri'nato adj ⟨pelle⟩ grained; ⟨metallo⟩ milled

zig'zag nm inv zigzag; **andare a** ∼ zigzag

Zim'babwe nm Zimbabwe

zim'bello nm decoy; (oggetto di scherno) laughing-stock

'zinco nm zinc

zinga'resco adj gypsy attrib

'zingaro, **-a** nmf gypsy

'zio nm uncle

'zippo nm sl lighter

zi'tella nf spinster; pej old maid

zitel'lona nf pej old maid

zit'tire ① vi fall silent ② vt silence

'zitto adj silent; **sta'** ∼! keep quiet!

ziz'zania nf (discordia) discord; **seminare** ∼ cause trouble

'zoccola nf vulg whore

'zoccolo nm clog; (di cavallo) hoof; (di terra) clump; (di parete) skirting board, baseboard Am; (di colonna) base. **zoccolo duro** Pol hard core. **zoccolo fesso** cloven foot, cloven hoof

zodia'cale adj of the zodiac; **segno zodiacale** sign of the zodiac, birth sign

zo'diaco nm zodiac

zolfa'nello nm match

'zolfo nm sulphur

'zolla nf clod

zol'letta nf sugar cube, sugar lump

'zombi nmf inv fig zombie

zom'pare vi sl bonk

'zona nf zone; (area) area. **zona calda** fig hot spot. **zona denuclearizzata** nuclear-free zone. **zona di depressione** area of low pressure. **zona disastrata** disaster area. **zona disco** area for parking discs only. **zona erogena** erogenous zone. **zona di esclusione aerea** air exclusion zone. **zona giorno** living area. **zona industriale** industrial estate. **zona notte** sleeping area. **zona d'ombra** fig twilight zone. **zona pedonale** pedestrian precinct. **zona a traffico limitato** restricted traffic area. **zona verde** green belt

zonizzazi'one nf zoning

'zonzo: **a zonzo** adv **andare a** ∼ stroll about

'zoo nm inv zoo

zoolo'gia nf zoology

zoo'logico adj zoological

zo'ologo, **-a** nmf zoologist

zoosa'fari nm inv safari park

zootec'nia nf animal husbandry

zoo'tecnico adj ⟨progresso⟩ in animal husbandry; **patrimonio zootecnico** livestock

zoppi'cante adj limping; fig shaky

zoppi'care vi limp; (essere debole) be shaky

'zoppo, **-a** ① adj lame ② nmf cripple

'zotico adj uncouth

zoti'cone nm boor

zu'ava nf **calzoni** pl **alla** ∼ plus-fours

'zucca nf marrow; (fam: testa) head; (fam: persona) thickie; **cos'hai in quella** ∼? haven't you got anything between your ears?

zuc'cata nf **prendere una** ∼ fam hit one's head

zucche'rare vt sugar

zucche'rato adj sugared; **non** ∼ ⟨succo d'arancia ecc⟩ unsweetened

zuccheri'era nf sugar bowl

zuccheri'ficio nm sugar refinery

zucche'rino ① adj sugary ② nm sugar cube, sugar lump; fig sweetener; **essere uno** ∼ ⟨persona⟩ be a softy; ⟨cosa⟩ be a cinch

'zucchero nm sugar. **zucchero di canna** cane sugar. **zucchero filato** candyfloss **zucchero greggio** brown sugar. **zucchero vanigliato** vanilla sugar. **zucchero a velo** icing sugar, confectioners' sugar Am

zucche'roso adj fig honeyed

zuc'chetto nm (cappello) beanie

zuc'china nf courgette, zucchini Am

zuc'chino nm courgette, zucchini Am

zuc'cone nm fam blockhead

zuc'cotto nm dessert made with sponge, cream, chocolate and candied fruit

'zuffa nf scuffle

zufo'lare vt/i whistle

'zufolo nm penny whistle

zu'mare vi zoom

zu'mata nf zoom

'zuppa nf soup. **zuppa inglese** trifle

zup'petta nf **fare** ∼ [con] dunk

zuppi'era nf soup tureen

'zuppo adj soaked

Contents

Calendar
Culture / Cultura
Letters / Lettere

Italian traditions, festivals, and holidays

1 January
Capodanno (New Year's Day).
A public holiday often spent getting over the excesses of New Year's Eve.

6 January
Epifania (Twelfth Night).
A public holiday and religious festival celebrating the adoration of Jesus by the three kings. By popular tradition it is also the day when Befana, a legendary old woman on a broomstick, brings children gifts: they are supposed to hang up their stockings the night before and in the morning should find them full of sweets, cakes, and little presents or, if they have been naughty, coal (though nowadays it is usually a sugary substitute).

14 February
San Valentino (St Valentine's Day).
As in other countries, this day is for lovers, marked by flowers, chocolates, and candlelit dinners.

8 March
Festa delle donne (Women's Day).
Since the 1970s, Women's Day has been celebrated with sprays of mimosa and discussions on women's issues.

19 March
Festa del papà (Father's Day).
St Joseph's Day is the day on which Italian fathers are celebrated.

1 April
Pesce d'aprile.
This is April Fool's Day, when it is traditional to play jokes and tricks on people. Children have fun trying to stick a little paper fish (*pesciolino*) onto people's backs without their noticing, and then calling, '*Il pesce d'aprile!*' (literally, 'April fish').

25 April
Anniversario della Liberazione (Anniversary of the Liberation).
A public holiday, this is a day of official ceremonies. It commemorates the day in 1945 when Italy was liberated from Nazi German occupation by invading Allied forces.

1 May
Festa del lavoro (International Labour Day) is a public holiday. This is a civil festival celebrating the workers of the world.

2 June
Festa della Repubblica is a public holiday, a civil festival to commemorate the referendum of 2 June 1946 which led to the proclamation of the Italian Republic.

15 August
L'Assunzione (Feast of the Assumption) is a public holiday – a religious festival that celebrates the Assumption of the Virgin Mary to heaven. Also known as *ferragosto*, it marks the peak of the summer holidays. The factories in the north are closed, as are many shops, except for those in tourist areas.

1 November
I Santi/Ognissanti (All Saints' Day).
Public holiday and religious festival celebrating all the saints. Typically, cakes made with nuts and raisins, which vary from region to region, are eaten during this festival. People go to the cemetery to take flowers for their dead loved ones, although the Festival of the Dead (I Morti) is the following day, 2 November, which is not a public holiday.

8 December
L'immacolata Concezione (Feast of the Immaculate Conception).
Public holiday and religious festival that celebrates the purity of the Virgin Mary.

24 December
La vigilia di Natale (Christmas Eve) is not a public holiday, although the schools are usually closed. Families get together, and often a large dinner is prepared. Afterwards people open their Christmas presents from under the tree. The faithful go to midnight Mass.

25 December
Natale (Christmas Day) is a public holiday and one of the most important religious festivals for Italians. Families

who did not open their presents the night before do so on Christmas morning. Children who believe in Father Christmas think that he has come down the chimney to bring their presents during the night. Families get together to eat a big dinner, typically including a capon and ending with *panettone* (a dome-shaped cake with sultanas and candied fruit) and a glass of spumante, Italian sparkling wine.

26 December
Santo Stefano (St Stephen's Day). A public and religious holiday during which Christmas celebrations continue.

31 December
San Silvestro (New Year's Eve). The celebration of the end of the old year and beginning of the new. It is a working day for many people, although students are on holiday, but in the evening there is usually a big meal and a party, either at home or in a restaurant. Typical dishes are lentils (which are said to bring wealth) and *cotechino* (a large pork sausage), and a great deal of champagne and spumante is drunk. On the stroke of midnight, fireworks are set off. In days gone by, it was traditional to throw crockery and other belongings out of the window to mark the rejection of the old in readiness for the New Year, but this no longer happens, to avoid damage to cars and injury to passers-by.

Movable holidays

Giovedì grasso (the Thursday before Lent). Fancy dress parties are held and people traditionally eat pancakes and fried pastries.

Martedì grasso (Shrove Tuesday). In some regions schools are closed.

Mercoledì delle ceneri (Ash Wednesday) is a religious occasion that marks the beginning of Lent. Some people fast on this day.

Venerdì santo (Good Friday). A religious occasion. It is not a public holiday, though some schools are closed.

Pasqua (Easter) is the most important Catholic festival, celebrating the resurrection of Christ. A popular saying goes: *'Natale con i tuoi, Pasqua con chi vuoi'* (Christmas with your family, Easter with whoever you want), and in fact Italians often take the opportunity of the holiday period to go away on holiday. Those who stay at home cook a big meal, usually of lamb because of its symbolic meaning. A *colomba* (dove-shaped cake) is the traditional Easter cake.

Pasquetta (Easter Monday) is a public holiday when people often go out for the day, to the sea, the mountains, or the countryside.

L'Ascensione (Ascension). A religious festival celebrating the ascension of Christ to heaven. It falls on the Thursday forty days after Easter.

Pentecoste (Whitsun) is a religious festival celebrating the descent of the holy spirit to the apostles. It falls fifty days after Easter.

Festa della Mamma (Mothers' Day) is on the second Sunday in May. Cards are sent and sometimes a present: perfume, chocolates, or flowers, especially roses.

Festival dei Due Mondi or Festival di Spoleto (in the province of Perugia) takes place each year from late June to mid-July. It hosts dance, theatre, opera, and music events, to which the biggest world names are invited.

Festival di Sanremo This Ligurian tourist resort has hosted the festival of Italian music every year since 1951. After a period of decline in the 1970s, the festival has recently regained its popularity. Established singers take part, but it is also often the launch pad for new talent.

Calendar

Giorni festivi nei paesi anglofoni

1 gennaio
New Year's Day (Capodanno).
Giorno festivo, generalmente trascorso a riprendersi dai festeggiamenti della notte precedente.

2 gennaio
Giorno festivo in Scozia.

6 gennaio
Epiphany o Twelfth Night (Epifania).
Non ci sono particolari tradizioni legate a questa giornata, ma molti in questo giorno disfano l'albero di Natale e mettono via le decorazioni natalizie.

25 gennaio
Burns Night.
Ricorrenza della nascita del poeta scozzese Robert Burns (XVIII secolo). Gli scozzesi festeggiano con una cena detta *Burns Supper* il cui piatto forte si chiama *haggis* (intestino di pecora farcito con una miscela di avena, frattaglie, cipolle e spezie). Tradizionalmente, durante la cena accompagnata dal suono delle cornamuse, si beve whisky e si leggono ad alta voce brani delle poesie di Robert Burns.

2 febbraio
Groundhog Day.
Giorno in cui, secondo la tradizione statunitense, la marmotta (*groundhog*) esce dalla sua tana sotterranea alla fine del letargo. Se c'è il sole e la marmotta vede la propria ombra si nasconderà nella tana e ci saranno altre sei settimane di cattivo tempo. Se non vede la propria ombra, si crede che la primavera comincerà presto.

14 febbraio
St Valentine's Day (San Valentino).
Nel giorno di San Valentino gli innamorati si scambiano fiori e regali. Esiste inoltre la tradizione di inviare un biglietto anonimo alla persona per cui si prova una tenera simpatia.

1 marzo
St David's Day.
Giorno di festa nazionale in Galles, di cui San Davide è il santo protettore.

17 marzo
St Patrick's Day.
La festa di San Patrizio, patrono d'Irlanda, viene celebrata dagli irlandesi in tutto il mondo con musica, canti e grandi bevute.

1 aprile
April Fools' Day (Pesce d'Aprile).
Giornata in cui si fanno numerosi scherzi: le vittime di tali scherzi sono dette *April Fools*.

23 aprile
St George's Day.
San Giorgio è il patrono d'Inghilterra.

1 luglio
Canada Day.
Festa nazionale che commemora l'unificazione delle colonie britanniche nordamericane del 1° luglio 1867.

4 luglio
Independence Day.
In questo giorno di festa nazionale negli Stati Uniti si celebra l'approvazione della Dichiarazione d'Indipendenza (1776) con parate, spettacoli di fuochi artificiali e picnic. In moltissime case viene esposta la bandiera americana.

12 ottobre
Columbus Day.
Giorno festivo negli Stati Uniti, ricorrenza della scoperta dell'America da parte di Cristoforo Colombo nel 1492.

31 ottobre
Hallowe'en (vigilia d'Ognissanti).
La notte della vigilia d'Ognissanti in cui, secondo un'antica credenza anglosassone, è possibile vedere i fantasmi. Oggi è festeggiata per lo più dai bambini, che ricavano lanterne dalle

zucche svuotate, si mascherano e fanno il giro del vicinato per chiedere dolci e regalini con il *trick or treat* ('dolcetto o scherzetto').

5 novembre
Bonfire Night/Guy Fawkes Night.
In Gran Bretagna si festeggia il fallimento della Congiura delle Polveri per far saltare in aria il Parlamento nel 1605. Ovunque si organizzano spettacoli di fuochi d'artificio e falò in cui viene bruciato un pupazzo rudimentale detto *guy* che rappresenta Guy Fawkes, uno dei cospiratori.

11 novembre
Remembrance Day,
Veteran's Day negli USA.
Giornata in cui si commemorano i caduti di tutte le guerre e la firma dell'armistizio (1918) che mise fine alla prima guerra mondiale.
   In Gran Bretagna la ricorrenza è anche nota come Poppy Day (giorno del papavero), per l'usanza di portare un papavero rosso di stoffa o carta sul petto (dai campi di papaveri in cui morirono migliaia di soldati sui fronti francese e belga).

30 novembre
St Andrew's Day.
Sant'Andrea è il patrono della Scozia.

25 dicembre
Christmas Day (giorno di Natale).
Giorno festivo. Per tradizione i familiari si scambiano i doni intorno all'albero la mattina di Natale e i bambini spesso trovano, al risveglio, una calza (*Christmas stocking*) piena di dolci e regalini lasciata da Father Christmas, anche chiamato Santa Claus.

26 dicembre
Boxing Day in Gran Bretagna,
St Stephen's Day in Irlanda.
Giorno festivo.

31 dicembre
New Year's Eve (la notte di San Silvestro).
In Scozia si chiama **Hogmanay** ed è tradizione andare a trovare amici e vicini di casa per augurare loro pace e prosperità portando in dono un pezzo di carbone o del whisky o qualcosa da mangiare.

Calendar

A–Z of Italian life and culture

Accademia della Crusca An academy for the study of the Italian language, founded in Florence in 1583, with the original aim of establishing the supremacy of the literary dialect in Florence – or of separating the 'flour' of pure language from the 'bran' (*crusca* – hence its name) of vulgarity. From 1612 it published the *Vocabolario degli accademici della Crusca* (Dictionary of the Members of the Accademia della Crusca), which became a model for similar works on the major European languages, and was printed in various editions until 1923. With only one interruption, from 1783 to 1811, the Academy has continued its work down to the present day. Currently based in the Villa di Castello near Florence, it is a centre for linguistic, philological, and lexicographical research. Unlike the French Académie Française or the Spanish Real Academia, however, it does not have the last word on what is correct or incorrect in Italian.

acqua alta An exceptionally high tide that sometimes affects the lagoon of Venice during the winter months. It is caused by particular wind conditions, but exacerbated by human interference with the environment. When the level of the lagoon rises, peaking sometimes at 1.4 metres (4.6 feet) and over, many of the streets and piazzas of Venice disappear under centimetres of water. Sirens are sounded three or four hours before the *acqua alta* reaches full height, and footbridges are put up to allow pedestrians to continue to use the busiest routes.

agriturismo A holiday based on a farm. It was originally intended that the holiday-makers would help with work on the farm in some capacity, but nowadays this virtually never happens. The word *agriturismo* is also used for the venue – the farmhouse, often renovated and refurbished specially for tourists. This type of holiday offers activities such as walking, horse-riding, etc. Good food and the open-air lifestyle are the main attractions. It is becoming much more popular and more expensive than it was at first.

Alto Adige The northern part of the Trentino-Alto Adige region, consisting of the province of Bolzano (called Südtirol [South Tirol] in German), ceded to Italy after the First World War. The majority of the population are German-speaking and of German descent. Since 1948 it has had a degree of autonomy, reinforced in 1972; place names are shown in Italian and German and holders of public offices have to pass an exam to show they are bilingual. Teaching in schools, however, is in German only for those of German descent, or Italian only for those of Italian descent. In future, this system is to be replaced by genuine bilingualism.

anno scolastico The Italian school year usually begins in mid-September and ends at the beginning of June (except for students who are taking exams). As well as a few days' holiday for the various civil and religious festivals, there are about ten days' holiday over Christmas, New Year, and Twelfth Night, plus a few days at Easter. *See also* SCUOLA.

aperitivo It is an Italian tradition to have an aperitif, which may or may not be alcoholic and is served with a few peanuts, olives, or other appetizers, before lunch or dinner. Many bars have their own, homemade *aperitivo*, based on liqueurs and fruit juices. Taking time for a pre-meal drink also provides a chance to catch up with friends.

ASL – Azienda Sanitaria Locale The Servizio Nazionale di Assistenza Sanitaria (or National Health Service) provides care for citizens through these local health authorities.

autostrade Italy has a network of motorways – toll roads with two or more lanes on each carriageway. The tolls paid for using motorways finance their construction, management, and maintenance. The tariff depends on the vehicle in which you are travelling and the stretch of motorway concerned, the relative costs of construction and maintenance being taken into account (e.g. mountain stretches can be more expensive). Usually you take a ticket from the booth when joining the motorway and hand it in for payment at the other end. The maximum speed limit for cars is 130 km/h (80 mph), or up to 150 km/h (94 mph) on some stretches.

Azzurri A popular name for the Italian national team in sports such as football, rugby, and hockey, from the blue shirts worn by the players.

Banca d'Italia The Italian central bank, founded in 1893. Since 1926 it has had a monopoly on the issue of currency, and supervisory jurisdiction over the Italian banking system. It also acts as the state treasury. Its central offices are located in the Via Nazionale in Rome. In the media, Via Nazionale is often used to mean the Bank of Italy.

Bancomat This is the name of the system of automatic cash withdrawal, of the actual cash machine, and of the card itself. The same card is often used as both a credit card and a bancomat card, so when you pay with the card in a shop you can use it as a credit card, or – by keying in your PIN on a special keypad – as a debit card.

bandiera arancione The orange flag is the mark of environmental quality awarded by the Italian Touring Club in inland areas. The criteria for the awarding of the orange flag are the development of cultural heritage, protection of the environment, standards of hospitality, and quality both of restoration and of local products.

Culture

bandiera blu The blue flag is an award given to beaches and ports in the member countries of the FEE (Federation for Environmental Education). The criteria that have to be met are, for beaches, the quality of the water and the coast, safety measures and services, and the promotion of environmental education. For ports, it is the quality of the water in the harbour, safety and disposal services, and environmental information.

bar A real institution of Italian life and culture, the bar is the place where you can have snacks, sandwiches, coffees, soft and alcoholic drinks, etc. Usually drinks are taken standing at the bar. In many bars there are also tables where you can sit and read the newspapers. Bars also play an important role in the lives of sports fans, as they meet there to watch football matches or other events on the television.

bel canto A style of singing, still practised today, that combines a light, bright quality of voice with the ability to sustain a beautifully clear and even tone through complicated passages. It emerged in Italy in the 15th and 16th centuries and was at its height in the early 19th century, when the composers Rossini, Bellini, and Donizetti exploited it to the full in their operas.

Biennale di Venezia An international show for the visual arts, cinema, architecture, dance, music, and theatre. The visual arts section still takes place every two years and often welcomes avant-garde artists. *See also* MOSTRA INTERNAZIONALE D'ARTE CINEMATOGRAFICA.

Bocconi With its headquarters in Milan, the Bocconi commercial university is an extremely prestigious private university, with only one faculty – economics.

caffè Coffee is a favourite Italian drink. Outside the home it can be drunk quickly standing at a bar counter, or in a more leisurely fashion while chatting at a table. In bars or restaurants you can order *un caffè* (normal), *ristretto* or *lungo* (weaker or stronger), *macchiato* (hot or cold, with a drop of milk), or *corretto* (with a drop of spirits). Also on offer are decaff and hot malt drinks (*caffè d'orzo*).

calcio Football is the sport that Italians love most, and of course it is a sport in which Italian teams have always excelled. The national league is divided into Serie A, Serie B, and Serie C. Some of the most famous Italian teams are Juventus, Milan, Inter (also in Milan), Roma, and Lazio. *See also* AZZURRI.

Camera dei Deputati The legislative assembly that, along with the SENATO, makes up the Italian Parliament. It is composed of 630 deputies, elected by universal direct suffrage by citizens over 18 years of age.

Camicie rosse ▶ I MILLE

Camorra An organized-crime network operating in Naples and the Campania. The Camorra is not a single organization but made up of groups (families) who often fight for control of criminal activities. Emerging in the 1500s, it has for centuries practised blackmail and extortion on small businesses in Naples. After the Second World War, and particularly from the 1980s, it began to control drugs and arms trafficking, prostitution, and the allocation of public contracts, developing political links and assuming ever greater control of the Naples area.

Canton Ticino This is the only canton of the Swiss Confederation which has Italian as its official language. It is also the only Swiss region located south of the Alps. The history, culture, and language of this area are intermingled with those of the neighbouring Italian regions.

Capitoline One of the SEVEN HILLS OF ROME, the Capitoline was the acropolis and religious centre of the ancient city, and is now the headquarters of the City of Rome. The Piazza del Campidoglio at its top was designed by Michelangelo; the square is flanked by three palazzi now housing the Capitoline Museums. In the centre of the piazza stands a statue of Roman emperor, Marcus Aurelius, on horseback.

Caporetto A First World War battle in which Italian troops were heavily defeated. On 24 October 1917, Austrian and German troops launched a major offensive on the Italian front, breaking through near the small town of Caporetto (now Kobarid in Slovenia). The Italians retreated in disorder with very heavy losses. The name Caporetto entered the language as a byword for a total defeat or failure.

Capri An island close to the southern entrance to the Bay of Naples, and favourite tourist destination. Capri is chiefly famous for its romantic setting, for the Blue Grotto – a sea cave with a low entrance, which gets its name from the colour of the light filtered through the water, and for the remains of Roman villas built by the Emperor Tiberius, who made Capri his headquarters from AD 27–37.

carabinieri A corps of the Italian army that has the task of guaranteeing the safety of citizens and their property and ensuring that state laws are observed. As well as being a military police force and responsible for public safety, the *carabinieri* also function as judiciary police. *See also* POLIZIA DI STATO.

Carnevale This is the period before Lent running from Twelfth Night to Ash Wednesday. It is celebrated with fancy dress parties, confetti, and streamers, especially during the weekend running from '*giovedì grasso*' (the last Thursday) to '*martedì grasso*' (Shrove Tuesday), which is the final day. The Venice Carnival is one of the most famous, with its open-air shows and fancy-dress balls, and the Viareggio Carnival is also well known.

carta d'identità An identity document issued to all citizens aged 15 and over. It is valid for foreign travel within the countries of the European Union, and for trips to some other countries with which there is an agreement. It is renewed every five years at the town hall. An electronic card, the same size as a credit card, can be requested.

Cassa integrazione or **Cassa integrazione guadagni** The benefit system for employees who are temporarily laid off because of a crisis in the company they work for. It is run by the INPS, which undertakes to pay 80 per cent of normal salary for a period of one or two years.

Cattolica The 'Catholic university' is a prestigious private institute with humanities and science faculties, spread over five different campuses throughout Italy.

Cavaliere – short for *Cavaliere al merito del lavoro* (Knight for services to industry) – is an official title, conferred since 1901 on those who make a major contribution to economic development. However, it is not uncommon for successful entrepreneurs to give their surnames the prefix *cavaliere* unofficially. Another frequently encountered title is that of *commendatore*, in common use over the past few decades as an honorific for any wealthy person.

Cavallino rampante The 'prancing horse' symbol of Ferrari. Enzo Ferrari adopted the symbol from a coat of arms belonging to a First World War flying ace. He first used it on the Alfa Romeo cars in his racing stable, then on the cars he began to produce himself in 1947 in Maranello (near Modena). Today it is synonymous with Ferrari both as a car-maker and as a Formula 1 team.

Cinecittà A complex of all of the different cinematographic studios set up on the outskirts of Rome in 1937. It includes a large number of film studios as well as studios for soundtracking.

CNR The Consiglio Nazionale delle Ricerche (National Research Council) is a national public body which carries out and promotes research activities for the scientific, technological, economic, and social development of the country.

codice civile e penale The civil and penal codes. The Italian codes, like those of other continental European countries, were modelled on the Code Napoléon, the French civil code first introduced in 1804. These superseded the common law, restructuring it on the enlightened principles of the French Revolution. The unified Italian state, founded in 1861, brought together the codes of the various states that made it up to constitute the civil code, the code of civil procedure, and the code of criminal procedure (on the French model) in 1865, and the criminal code in 1889. The new codes drawn up in the 20th century followed the same lines, with some modifications.

codice fiscale A combination of letters and numbers, based on the holder's particulars, which identifies every citizen or resident of Italy for tax purposes and other dealings with the authorities. It is indispensable if a person wishes to work, open a bank account, use the health service, etc. In current usage the term *codice fiscale* (tax code) also refers to the plastic card, similar in size to a credit card, issued to everybody by the Ministry of the Economy and Finance and bearing the holder's code and personal details.

Colosseo The name given in the Middle Ages to the 'colossal' Flavian Amphitheatre, the most famous monument of Ancient Rome, which was begun by Vespasian in about 75 AD and inaugurated by Titus in 80 AD. It is oval in shape and up to 50,000 spectators could attend the bloody battles between gladiators and beasts that were staged there.

comuni Each province is subdivided into municipalities (*comuni*), each of which is run by a council and municipal committee headed by a SINDACO (mayor). The functions of the *comuni* are mainly administrative.

Confederazioni sindacali The three large Italian trade union organizations that represent workers in all categories and sectors: the formerly Communist-oriented CGIL (Confederazione generale italiana del lavoro); the Christian-oriented CISL (Confederazione italiana sindacati lavoratori) and the social-democrat-oriented UIL (Unione italiana del lavoro). During the 1970s and 1980s they formed an alliance and collaborated to play a central role in politics and in the Italian economy. However, recent transformations in the economy and the labour market have reduced their unity of action, and their role has been partly reshaped by the rise of autonomous sectoral unions.

consiglio dei ministri A body composed of ministers and headed by the PRESIDENTE DEL CONSIGLIO: it forms the government.

consultorio familiare Social-health service set up in the mid-1970s. It provides health education (including preventive medicine) in the fields of gynaecology and paediatrics, as well as advice and support for people with mental health or legal problems.

Corte Costituzionale The constitutional court, in operation since 1955, which has the duty of ensuring that laws passed by parliament do not conflict with the COSTITUZIONE and of ruling on conflicts between the powers of the state and those of the regions. It is made up partly of magistrates and partly of jurists chosen by the parliament and the PRESIDENTE DELLA REPUBBLICA. It is based in Rome, in the Palazzo della

Consulta (the Consulta being a former papal institution) next door to the QUIRINALE, and is often referred to as La Consulta.

costituzione The constitution of the Italian Republic, which came into force on 1 January 1948. It was drawn up by a constituent assembly, elected by the people, and based on the principles of liberty, equality, and democracy. A constitutional court (CORTE COSTITUZIONALE) ensures that any individual laws passed by parliament conform to the constitution.

denominazione di origine controllata (*DOC*) The state-certified mark of quality awarded to Italian wines that possess certain verified characteristics, such as origin within a defined zone of production, derivation from particular types of vines and soils, ratio between the quantity of grapes used and quantity of wine obtained, and methods used in production. *DOC* wines that have become particularly famous for their special qualities are now certified as *DOCG* (*denominazione di origine controllata e garantita*), a mark based on even stricter standards of verification. *See also* VINO.

Divina Commedia The most celebrated and important work in Italian literature, written by Dante Alighieri between 1306 and 1321. *The Divine Comedy* is divided into three parts, *Inferno* (Hell), *Purgatorio* (Purgatory), and *Paradiso* (Heaven), each containing thirty-three cantos (plus one introductory canto to make 100). It describes a journey through the Christian afterlife and is probably best known and loved for its retelling of the stories of the characters Dante discovers in the three realms. Part of Dante's purpose was to prove that the Italian language could be used for serious works of literature. In his writing, he blended the language of court with the most expressive elements of his native Tuscan and other dialects, helping to lay the foundations of modern Italian.

Dolce Vita, La A film, whose title literally means 'The Sweet Life', made by the director Federico Fellini and released in 1960. It depicted the emptiness and squalor of high society in Rome. Its title very quickly became a cliché for a worldly Italian lifestyle that perhaps never even existed, and it ended up as banal slogan for mass tourism.

dottore The legally recognized title in Italy for a person who receives a degree after completing a university course lasting at least four years. It is widely used both in writing (on letters or on business cards) or as a form of address to refer formally to all graduates, not simply graduates in medicine. There is a saying in Italy that 'no one ever denies being doctor', meaning that anyone – with or without a degree – is happy to accept *dottore* as a term of deference from waiters, parking attendants, and so on. *See also* LAUREA.

enoteca A place where good local wines are offered for sale and often for tasting. In many *enoteche* you can also eat while tasting the wines.

Extracomunitari The Italian term used to refer to immigrants from Third World countries (black Africa, the Arab countries of North Africa, the Philippines, Sri Lanka, and China) or European countries that are not yet members of the European Union (Albania, Romania). Though the term may seem purely bureaucratic, *extracomunitario* (literally, 'outside the community') is a discriminatory word in common speech reflecting deep-seated prejudices; it is used with mistrust or fear, sometimes with scorn or hostility, as a label for poor immigrants, exploited as underpaid labour, often staying illegally without a residence permit, and involved in illegal trafficking or criminal activities.

FAI The Fondo per l'Ambiente Italiano (Fund for the Italian Environment), set up in 1975 with the aim of contributing to the protection, conservation, and use of Italy's artistic and environmental heritage. It has acquired, mostly through donations, many important buildings and sites (villas, palaces, castles, parks, and gardens) that it has subsequently restored and opened to the public.

Farnesina A term used in the media to refer to the Italian Ministry of Foreign Affairs which, since 1959, has been housed in the Palazzo della Farnesina, a vast building constructed in a functional style between 1938 and the 1950s outside the historic centre of Rome.

Fascism A movement, based on an ultra-conservative, anti-socialist, nationalist, racist, and authoritarian ideology, which controlled Italy from 1922 to 1943. The name comes from the *fasces*, an axe with its handle encased in a bundle of rods, which was a symbol of power and unity in Roman times. The Fascists, led by Benito Mussolini (known as *il duce*, the leader), were both a political party and a paramilitary organization. They ruled dictatorially, intimidating, imprisoning, and sometimes murdering, their political opponents. Under the Fascist regime Italian armies conquered Abyssinia and Albania, but military failures during World War II, in which Italy was initially allied with Germany and Japan, led to the Fascists' downfall.

Fiamme Gialle The nickname (literally meaning 'Yellow Flames') for the *guardia di finanza*, an Italian police force organized along military lines, which specializes in combating economic, financial, and fiscal crime (fraud, tax evasion, and money laundering) and guarding Italy's land and sea borders (against smuggling, drug trafficking, and illegal immigration). It was set up in 1881 and its members wear uniforms with yellow insignia, hence the nickname.

foglio rosa This is the provisional driving licence, which can be applied for at the minimum age (18 years old for driving cars) and is valid for six months.

Fratelli d'Italia The name by which Italy's national anthem is commonly known. Its official name is the *Inno di Mameli* (Mameli's hymn), after its author, the poet and patriot Goffredo Mameli, who died in 1849, aged 22, fighting with Garibaldi for the defence of the Roman Republic (*see* I MILLE). It was adopted as the national anthem in 1946. The common name comes from the opening lines of the first verse: *Fratelli d'Italia, l'Italia s'è desta, / dell'elmo di Scipio s'è cinta la testa* (Brothers of Italy, Italy has awoken / It has circled its head with the helmet of Scipio). All Italians know the tune (composed by Mameli's friend, the choirmaster Michele Novaro), but very few know the rest of the words (it has five verses) by heart.

Gazzetta dello Sport This is the sports daily, printed on its characteristic pink paper. It was founded in Milan in 1896 and is the most widely read sports newspaper in Italy. It organizes the GIRO D'ITALIA.

Gazzetta Ufficiale The official newspaper of the Italian state, which publishes approved laws, decrees, and various official announcements.

gelato Made with milk, sugar, eggs, and various other ingredients, this is an Italian speciality. The hand-made variety, bought in *gelaterie*, can be served in a dish or in a cone. There are dozens of flavours to choose from.

giornali Among the main Italian dailies are *Repubblica* and *Corriere della Sera*. The daily financial paper is *il Sole 24 ore*. The weekly magazines *L'Espresso* and *Panorama* deal with current affairs, politics, and culture. As well as Italian versions of international titles, the weekly magazines *Grazia*, *Anna*, and *Donna Moderna* cater for women. *Famiglia Cristiana* is the Catholic weekly. Of the gossip magazines, *Novella 2000* is the most popular.

giro d'Italia Like the Tour de France, one of the most famous cycling races in the world. It takes place from mid-May to the beginning of June. The route changes every year, but the last stage always ends in Milan. The winner is awarded the pink jersey. *See also* GAZZETTA DELLO SPORT.

gondola A low narrow boat with a raised curved prow, used on the canals of Venice. The gondola is propelled by a *gondoliere* (gondolier) using a single oar that pivots on a small post attached to the starboard side. The gondoliers usually dress in traditional striped tops and a straw hat. A 17th-century *doge* (*see* VENETIAN REPUBLIC) ordered that all gondolas should be painted black, so as not to glorify worldly wealth. They remain black, but are now used almost exclusively for tourists.

Culture

Herculaneum ▶ VESUVIUS

Informagiovani As the name suggests, this is a service of information and guidance for young people. Promoted by local bodies, the various centres (and their web sites) provide information about all areas of interest to young people: courses and training, jobs, culture, politics, voluntary work, travel, etc. The first centres opened in Turin and Milan in the early 1980s; now there are about 600 centres throughout Italy. In addition to supplying information, they carry out a role of 'listening' to young people and also promote projects created by young people for young people.

INPS – Istituto Nazionale per la Previdenza Sociale (National Institute of Social Security). This is the major public body in Italy that pays workers' old-age pensions after receiving contributions from them during their working lives. It also manages the various kinds of assistance provided by the welfare state, such as the CASSA INTEGRAZIONE, sickness, maternity, unemployment, and invalidity benefit.

Internet The World Wide Web is much used in Italy, as elsewhere. All major Italian newspapers and television stations have their own websites, as do councils, museums, etc. The suffix for Italian sites is '.it'.

laghi The north of Italy is the area with the highest concentration of lakes, which includes the three largest and most famous: Lake Garda (the largest of all), Lake Maggiore, and Lake Como. The area's mild climate and abundant greenery have always held a great attraction for both Italians and foreigners. Some lakes are equipped for water sports; others offer luxurious hotels and health farms.

laurea The title, meaning 'graduate', that is traditionally awarded in Italy to people who complete a course of study at a university, usually lasting four years. Recently a *laurea triennale* (or *breve*) was introduced; this 'three-year' or 'short degree' gives immediate access to the labour market. In contrast the *laurea specialistica*, 'specialist degree', requires a further two years of study and entitles the holder to be known as DOTTORE.

Leaning Tower of Pisa The eight-storey bell tower of the cathedral of Pisa. Building work began in 1183, but the tower started to lean noticeably to the north, as the ground beneath it was unstable. Work continued on and off on the tower for the next 200 years, and by 1360 it was complete – it was now leaning to the south, however. Over the centuries, the problem worsened. Finally, in the late 1990s, engineers removed rock and soil from under the north side of the tower and succeeded in reducing the angle of tilt from 10 per cent to 5 per cent. The tower is now said to be safe for the next 300 years.

Liberazione, La The effective end of the Second World War in Italy in late

April 1945, when a general uprising staged by the RESISTENZA in the northern cities (Turin, Milan, and Genoa) led to the surrender or retreat of German troops before the arrival of the victorious Anglo-American forces. It is celebrated by the Festa della Liberazione (Liberation Day holiday) on 25 April each year.

liceo A type of secondary school, similar to a grammar school, which aims to form students' characters, pass on theoretical rather than applied knowledge, and develop the capacity for independent judgement and criticism. These aims are fully embodied in the more traditional type of *liceo*, the *liceo classico*, focused on the study of ancient languages (Latin and Greek). In the *liceo scientifico*, a more recent type, mathematics and the sciences are strongly represented in the curriculum along with Latin and philosophy, the latter being trademark subjects of *liceo* teaching whatever the school's specialism, whether science, modern languages, or art, etc. The evolution of the Italian school system is leading to the term *liceo* also being applied to schools that specialize in technical or business subjects.

Lotto The lottery game first appeared in Italy in Genoa during the 16th century, and during the following century spread to the other Italian states. From the 19th century it has been run directly by the state, and since 1871 there have been weekly Saturday draws in ten cities (known as *ruote*). Over the centuries a popular myth has grown up that the interpretation of dreams can help in the selection of winning numbers. The principles, a mixture of esotericism and cabbalism, are set out in the book of *Smorfia* (a corruption of Morpheus, the name of the Greek and Roman god of sleep and dreams). This ancient game still has great potential, as the development of recent variants such as the hugely popular Superenalotto has shown.

Mafia Since the Second World War, the Sicilian Mafia (also called Cosa Nostra) has expanded and developed substantially, creating an alternative power that is partly complementary to that of the state. Starting from illegal activities such as extortion and usury, it then assumed control of the building trade and the award of public contracts, and finally took over the traffic in illegal drugs, which brought in enormous profits. The Mafia has a vertical structure (a strict hierarchy of 'families'), but it is distinguished from other criminal organizations above all by its close relationships and complicity with political authorities.

Mani pulite The name (meaning 'clean hands') given to the landmark judicial inquiry, which, beginning in 1992 in Milan, brought to light the system of *tangenti* (payments on the side) and corruption in which the governing parties were involved. It resulted in their dissolution and the end of the so-called 'first republic' (PRIMA REPUBBLICA).

Culture

Manifesti funebri Small posters printed by the family of someone who has died, announcing the death, saying a few words about the deceased, and giving the date and time of the funeral. These are put up on special boards – or indeed on any available surface – to inform local people of what has happened and to ensure a large attendance at the funeral.

matrimoni Traditionally, marriages in Italy were arranged by the couple's families, and it is still not uncommon for a male relative of the groom to visit the bride's father or uncle to ask formally for the girl's hand on the groom's behalf. Traditionally, too, the bride would be given a dowry – nowadays her family and friends will usually arrange bridal showers before the wedding to provide her with household goods, and she carries a satin bag at the reception into which guests put money. Weddings in Italy do not usually take place during the solemn church seasons of Advent and Lent, or during the months of May and August. Other customs include the throwing of confetti (not scraps of paper, but small bags of sugared almonds) and the breaking of a glass or vase at the end of the wedding feast, which is usually sumptuous. The number of pieces into which the object breaks is supposed to represent the number of years the couple will live together.

maturità This is the exam that students take at the end of the five years of secondary school, between the ages of 18 and 19. It consists of two written tests (one of which is Italian language) and two orals. Marks (the maximum is 60 out of 60) depend on both the result of the tests and the average marks achieved over the previous three years. The diploma is a requirement for university entrance and, depending on the type of secondary school attended, it can be in science, classics, arts, or technology, etc.

mercati Every Italian town and city has its own market, either open-air or covered, where fruit, vegetables, cheeses, cooked meats, and a range of other produce is sold. There is also a weekly market where it is possible to buy clothes, bags, household goods, and other items. The prices are cheaper than in the shops, and people often haggle over the goods displayed on the stalls.

Mezzogiorno A term referring to southern Italy, including Sicily and Sardinia, which is less economically developed than the north. The name literally means 'midday', i.e. siesta time, indicating that – though it has a wealth of artistic treasures and beautiful countryside – the pace of life here is markedly less frenetic than in northern Italy.

I Mille In 1860, soldier Giuseppe Garibaldi (1807–82) set sail from Genoa with two ships and just over 1,000 volunteers (*i mille*), known as the *Camicie rosse* (Red Shirts). Garibaldi and his followers managed to wrest Sicily and Naples from Bourbon hands, territory which he then handed over to King Victor Emmanuel II of Sardinia. In the following year, Victor Emmanuel was declared king of the newly unified Italy. The original 1,000 volunteers remained a symbol of the most notable event of the Italian RISORGIMENTO, and are commemorated in street names in many Italian cities.

Mole Antonelliana The Mole Antonelliana, an extremely unusual monument (167 m – 548 ft – high), is the symbol of Turin. Destined to be a synagogue, the building was begun in 1863 but, following financial problems and arguments about its stability, it was not finished until 1889. Subsequently acquired by the city, it is now the home of the New Museum of the Cinema. A glass lift provides access to the steeple.

Montecitorio A palace, built between 1650 and 1697, to house papal courts. It is situated in a piazza of the same name in the centre of Rome. Since 1871 it has been home to the lower house of the Italian parliament, the CAMERA DEI DEPUTATI (Chamber of Deputies). The term Montecitorio is used in the media to refer to the Chamber itself.

Monza A small city north of Milan, best known as the site of Autodromo nazionale, the motor-racing circuit where the Italian Grand Prix is held.

Mostra Internazionale d'Arte Cinematografica Also known as the Venice Film Festival, this is the film section of the BIENNALE DI VENEZIA. It was started in the 1930s and takes place every year at the end of August at the Palazzo del Cinema on the Venice Lido. One of the largest film festivals in Europe (and indeed the world), it attracts films, actors, directors, and other technicians from around the world. The festival winners are awarded the Golden Lion.

negozi The hours of opening for shops vary according to the type of shop and where it is located. In general, food shops open at about 8 a.m. and close at 7.30 p.m. with a lunch break from 12.30 to 3.30 p.m. Clothes shops, bookshops, etc. open from 9 a.m. until 12.30 or 1 p.m. and then again from 3.30 to 7.30 p.m. In summer the lunch break is longer and shops stay open until 8.00 p.m. Some supermarkets and department stores in the big cities are open all day. Weekly closing also varies according to the type of shop. Some shops close for two to three weeks in August, after the summer sales, then reopen with the new autumn-season stock.

Nordest The northeast, the area comprising the regions Veneto, Trentino, and Friuli, where a highly successful model of industrial development was applied during the 1990s. This led to the rapid emergence of many small and medium-sized companies, producing mainly textiles, footwear, and mechanical goods, and to strong export growth. Since then, however, the 'northeastern model' has been discussed mainly in terms of its downsides (damage to the environment, absence of general social development, lack of professional training for workers). Today it is in difficulties because of globalized competition; it no longer appears to be a more successful alternative to the traditional industrial area of the northwest, the TRIANGOLO INDUSTRIALE.

Normale The Scuola Normale Superiore di Pisa was set up in the early 1800s as a branch of the Paris Ecole Normale. Today, it is an extremely prestigious institute offering first degree courses and research doctorates in science and the humanities.

onomastico This is the feast day of the saint whose name a person bears. Although less important than his or her birthday, a saint's day is always celebrated with cards and sometimes with a small gift.

oratorio In Italy there are thousand of *oratorios* (usually buildings with courtyards and playing fields attached to Catholic parishes), which are used by pupils – on afternoons when they are not in school – as meeting places and for recreation (typically for ball games, but also for many other sporting or theatrical activities, etc.) and educational purposes. They are supervised by priests or their lay assistants. Created in the 19th century to rescue poor boys from immorality and crime, they have become a typical feature of young people's lives at all social levels in Italy.

Padania A term used by the political party Lega Nord (the Northern League) to refer to the whole of northern Italy, roughly the area falling within the basin of the River Po and the Venetian regions, supposed to be inhabited by a population of Celtic rather than Latin origin. According to its more extreme proponents, Padania should aim to secede from the rest of Italy (dominated by a 'corrupt' Rome), and especially from the uncivilized and backward south. But, for critics and opponents of the League, Padania is a meaningless term, because it does not correspond to a unified area that can be defined geographically, historically, or linguistically – and because the idea that the Padanians are direct descendants of the ancient Celts is mythical nonsense.

Palazzo Chigi The seat of the Italian government since 1961. The Palazzo Chigi, built in the 16th and 17th centuries, is situated in Piazza Colonna in the heart of Rome near the MONTECITORIO palace. In the media, the term Palazzo Chigi means the Italian government or PRESIDENTE DELLA REPUBBLICA.

Palio di Siena A popular event that takes place every year in Siena on 2 July and 16 August. The *contrade*, or districts of the city, fight for the *palio*, a banner, in a frantic race on horseback around the medieval Piazza del Campo. It has deep historical roots but is still passionately followed by the Sienese and is a huge attraction for tourists from all over the world. There

Culture

is a spectacular historical procession in brightly coloured Renaissance costumes before the race.

Papal States Areas of central Italy owned and governed by the Pope from the early Middle Ages until the 19th century, including Latium, Umbria, Marche, and the city of Rome itself. The process of transferring these areas to secular government began with the conquest of Italy by Napoleon Bonaparte, but was not completed until 1870, when the Pope was forced to relinquish control of Rome, enabling it to become the capital of a united Italy.

parchi nazionali In Italy there are about twenty national parks covering 5 per cent of the territory. Controlled by the Ministry of the Environment, their objective is the protection and development of large areas that are of particular importance in terms of environment and landscape. The best-known are 'Gran Paradiso', the national parks in Abruzzi, Lazio, and Molise, and the National Park of the Maddalena Archipelago. The marine parks, which aim to protect stretches of sea, coast, and sometimes whole islands and archipelagos, are becoming increasingly important.

partiti politici Even today Italy has problems in reuniting various political tendencies in a small number of major political parties. So there are still many political parties, which can still be roughly classified as belonging to the left, right, or centre. Under the so-called PRIMA REPUBBLICA, the centre ruled supreme, but it is now divided. Of the minor Catholic parties (La Margherita, UDC, Udeur), some are aligned with the left (in an alliance called L'Ulivo [the Olive Tree], then L'Unione), others with the right (in an alliance called Casa delle Libertà [House of Freedoms]). On the left there are the Democratici di Sinistra (DS) or Democrats of the Left, former Communists who have abandoned Marxism, the more radical Partito della Rifondazione Comunista (PRC) (Party of Communist Refoundation) and the Verdi (Greens). On the right there are the Alleanza Nazionale (AN) (National Alliance), an ex-neofascist group, and the Lega Nord (Northern League), which has separatist and xenophobic tendencies. Forza Italia (FI) (literally 'Go on, Italy'), the large centre-right party, which first came to power under Silvio Berlusconi in 1994 and returned to power in 2001, draws its support from former Christian Democrats, Socialists, and Liberals.

passeggiata This typical Italian custom involves walking with family or friends in the square or main street, or along the promenade. It usually takes place before eating, on Saturday afternoon or Sunday morning, and in the summer it can also take place in the evening after dinner. Depending on the time and the weather, people might have an aperitif or an ice cream. The purpose is to stretch one's legs, chat, see who is around, and be seen.

pasta The basic ingredient of many Italian dishes, which is made by mixing flour from durum (hard) wheat with water, and sometimes adding other ingredients such as beaten egg or cooked spinach. Fresh pasta is soft and can be moulded into a variety of different forms, such as flat sheets (lasagne), long thin sticks (spaghetti), tubes (macaroni, cannelloni), or small square pillow shapes (ravioli). Commercially made pasta is dried after shaping until hard. In this form it will keep for a long time. Pasta is also a healthy food as it contains very little fat.

patente a punti Following reform of the Italian highway code, each driving licence is now given an initial value of twenty points, which are reduced if traffic offences are committed. For example, for the more serious offences (overtaking on a bend, drink driving, or driving while under the effect of drugs), ten points are deducted; passing a red light costs you six points, while parking in an area reserved for public transport costs two points. Once the number of infringements committed has reduced the initial number of points to zero, the licence is withdrawn and the driving test has to be retaken. Drivers with the worst records are required to undergo courses of 're-education'. The points system is also applied to foreign citizens who are passing though Italy: the penalties are totted up and filed in a special register.

permesso di soggiorno Foreigners who enter Italy with a passport and visa, especially for work or study, have to apply for this residence permit from the state police – that is from a QUESTURA or a *commissariato* (police headquarters or local police station) – within eight days of arrival. The permit is valid for between three months and two years, depending on the circumstances, and is renewable. It entitles the holder to be issued with an identity card (CARTA D'IDENTITÀ) and a tax code (CODICE FISCALE). *See also* POLIZIA DI STATO.

Piazza Affari A term commonly used in the media to refer to the Milan stock exchange, the most important in Italy. The stock exchange came into existence in 1808 and is now housed in the Palazzo della Borsa (built between 1928 and 1931), situated in the centre of the city in the Piazza degli Affari.

Pinocchio The hero of the children's book, *Le Avventure di Pinocchio* (The Adventures of Pinocchio) by Carlo Collodi (1826–90), Pinocchio is a wooden puppet whose nose grows whenever he tells a lie. After various tribulations, accompanied by such famous characters as Geppetto (the puppetmaker), the Blue Fairy, the Fire-Eater, Lucignolo, and the whale, etc., Pinocchio is turned into a real boy. Adapted for television and as a cartoon, the story has also been reinterpreted from a sociological and psychoanalytical point of view.

pizza Now a 'global food', pizza was for centuries a speciality of the city of

Culture

Naples, and many people still think that it cannot be properly appreciated elsewhere. Pizze (flattened pieces of bread dough) were eaten in Naples in the late Middle Ages with garlic and lard, cheese and basil, or small fish. The modern pizza, with tomato, appeared in the late 1700s. The first pizzeria was opened in Naples in 1830 (before that, pizza was sold and eaten in the street). In 1889 the *pizzaolo* (pizza-maker) Raffaele Esposito made a pizza topped with tomato, ricotta, and some leaves of basil (thus red, white, and green, the colours of the Italian flag) for Queen Margherita, the wife of Umberto I. Since then, this, the most widespread type of pizza, has been known as pizza margherita.

politecnico A scientific and technological university that includes faculties of engineering and architecture among its specializations. There are three in Italy. The oldest and most famous are those of Turin (1859) and Milan (1863); the latest is in Bari.

polizia di stato The name, meaning 'state police', of the Italian civil police force. The force was organized along military lines from 1919 to 1981 and called the Corpo delle Guardie di Pubblica Sicurezza (PS), Guards of Public Safety. It had headquarters (QUESTURE) in the capital city of each province, and police stations (*commissariati*) in city districts and minor centres. The reform of 1981 demilitarized and democratized it, and many of its officers and staff are now women. It continues to assist the CARABINIERI (who cover a wider area) in the task of maintaining law and order.

Pompeii ▶ VESUVIUS

Ponte Vecchio The ancient bridge in Florence that spans the River Arno. It carries a roadway lined with goldsmiths' and jewellers' shops.

popular music In Italy the popular and classical traditions of vocal music tend to merge. The repertoires of star singers such as Luciano Pavarotti and Andrea Boccelli include popular Italian, especially Neapolitan songs, alongside operatic arias. Italian pop singers are less well known abroad. Singers such as Mina, Lucio Battista, and Eros Ramazzetti tend to specialize in romantic ballads or songs exploiting Mediterranean folk rhythms. Italy does, however, have its share of rock, hip-hop, etc, artists and groups, of whom the most famous is perhaps the singer Zucchero.

Premio Strega The most famous literary prize in Italy, instituted in 1947 and sponsored by a wealthy liquor manufacturer (producer of the Strega liqueur). Previous winners have included Edoardo De Filippo, Pierpaolo Pasolini, and Umberto Eco. The prize is awarded annually, in July, in the 16th-century Ninfeo (a garden with monumental fountain) of the Villa Giulia in Rome.

presepio (or *presepe*) A 'crib', a representation of the Nativity and the Adoration of the Magi in the form of wood or terracotta statues against a painted landscape. Cribs first appeared in Tuscany in the 13th and 14th centuries, but it was in Naples in the 17th and 18th centuries, during the baroque and rococo periods, that churches began to display magnificent examples. Scenes of everyday life were reproduced down to the smallest detail. During the 19th century, families began to build their own cribs for the Christmas season, with terracotta, plaster, or papier-mâché figurines. In recent years this custom has become a little less common with the introduction of the Christmas tree from northern Europe.

presidente del consiglio This is the title of the Italian prime minister, the head of the government and of the CONSIGLIO DEI MINISTRI. Nominated by the PRESIDENTE DELLA REPUBBLICA, he proposes the ministers. He controls and is responsible for government policy.

Culture

presidente della repubblica The head of state who represents the nation. He/she is elected by parliament and remains in office for seven years. As Italy is a parliamentary republic, the duties of the president are: to enact laws, to dissolve parliament and call new elections when necessary, to nominate the prime minister and ratify his choice of the ministers, and to grant pardons. He/she also chairs the body which oversees the appointment of judges.

Prima repubblica The name (meaning 'first republic') given to the political system that collapsed in 1992–93 in the wake of scandals revealed by the MANI PULITE (Clean Hands) inquiry and the weakening of the opposing ideological positions associated with the Cold War. The big governing parties of those days – especially the Christian Democrats and the Socialist Party – disbanded, and new parties emerged; these are still active today (*see also* PARTITI POLITICI).

provincia In Italy's system of local government, each province is made up of neighbouring municipalities, the most important of which acts as the provincial capital. Each province is served by a provincial council, a committee, and a president.

quadrilatero della moda The 'fashion quadrilateral' is an area in the centre of Milan defined by the Via Montenapoleone, Via della Spiga, Via Manzoni, and Via Sant'Andrea, where the biggest names in Italian fashion, such as Armani, Trussardi, Valentino, Versace, Prada, Missoni, and Dolce & Gabbana, have their boutiques and showrooms.

questure Provincial headquarters of the police force. Thefts are reported to the *questura* and passports renewed there.

Quirinale A 16th-century building on the hill of the same name in Rome, now the residence of the PRESIDENTE DELLA REPPUBLICA. It was formerly the summer residence of the popes and then of the kings of Italy.

RAI The state radio and television company. There are three television channels, RAI 1, RAI 2, and RAI 3, and three radio stations, Radio 1, Radio 2, and Radio 3, which tend to be supportive of the government.

Reality TV Reality television has become as popular in Italy as in other countries. Most Italian shows follow the same formats used elsewhere. Italy has its own version of 'Big Brother' (*Grande fratello*), of 'Survivor' (*Isola dei Famosi*) and various 'life-swap' programmes, such as *Una giornata particolare*, in which Italian sports and media stars spend a day doing a very ordinary job, like being a cleaner or mechanic. Italy has, however, contributed at least one reality show of its own. The popular Sunday programme, *Domenica In*, features *A Spasso con Mamma*, which is similar to 'Blind Date', except that it sends single young men out on dates with the mothers of single girls, and only if the mother gives a favourable report does the young man get to meet the girl.

regione Italy is subdivided into twenty regions, five of which have a certain amount of political autonomy. Each region is subdivided in its turn into provinces (*see* PROVINCIA) and municipalities. The regions can issue legislative standards. They also have administrative duties which can be delegated to the provinces and the municipalities. Each region is served by a council, a committee, and a regional president.

repubblica The Italian republic was founded after the Second World War, based on the results of the referendum of 2 June 1946, which abolished the monarchy in favour of a republican form of government. The COSTITUZIONE published in 1948 established its parliamentary character.

Resistenza On 8 September 1943, Italy, which had been allied to Hitler's Germany, surrendered to British and US forces. The Germans reacted immediately by invading the greater part of the peninsula, which was not yet occupied by allied forces, and by imposing a harshly oppressive regime on their former ally. Soldiers from the disbanded army and antifascist civilians organized themselves into groups of partisans to fight the Germans and their Fascist collaborators behind the lines, leading to the Liberation in 1945. The ideals of liberty and democracy that inspired the partisans and their unity of action in spite of differing political views were the foundation of the new post-war Italian republic. For this reason, the Resistance still carries considerable political weight in present-day Italy.

Risorgimento The name, meaning 'the Resurgence', given to the historical period marked by the struggles for Italian independence and unification. After its beginnings in 1820–21 and 1831 and the uprisings of

Culture

1848–49, its principal events were the three wars of independence against Austria-Hungary (1848–49, 1859, and 1866) and the expedition of Garibaldi and I MILLE (the 1,000) in 1860. The moderate monarchical movement prevailed against the republican and revolutionary tendency of Guiseppe Mazzini, so that the House of Savoy (under Victor Emmanuel II) obtained the Italian crown in 1861. Rome became the capital city in 1871 (*see also* PAPAL STATES).

riviera The Italian word *riviera* means a 'coastal region'. It has been borrowed by many other languages and come to mean an area with a warm climate, fashionable resorts, and beaches for holidaymakers. The Italian, or Ligurian, Riviera is the stretch of coastline that begins at the French border and extends as far as Tuscany. The main city and port in the region is Genoa – popular holiday towns include Portofino, San Remo, and Rapallo.

rugby Both rugby union and rugby league are played in Italy, mainly in northern regions. There has been a national championship in rugby union since 1929, and in 2000 Italy joined England, Wales, Scotland, Ireland, and France to make up the Six Nations competition.

sagra A popular festival with a fair and market, which takes place in many villages once a year, sometimes more frequently. *Sagre* usually have a theme such as wine, sausages, fish, or truffles – depending on what the local speciality is.

St Peter's The largest Christian church in the world, situated in the VATICANO in Rome. The Basilica of St Peter's is not a cathedral; its importance lies in its closeness to the papal residence and its use for most papal ceremonies, as well as in its size and architectural magnificence. The present building was designed by Bramante – various other famous artists participated, including Michelangelo, who designed the dome – and it was constructed between 1506 and 1615.

San Marino The republic of San Marino forms an enclave within Italian territory, but is an independent sovereign state completely surrounded by Italian soil, lying between Emilia-Romagna and the Marche, not far from the Adriatic coast. At just over 60 sq. km (23 sq. miles) in area, it is one of the smallest states in the world.

santo patrono In Italy the worship of saints is widespread. The patron saint of a town or community is considered to be its protector. His or her saint's day is a religious holiday on which schools, offices, and most shops are closed. It is celebrated with a special mass and processions. In towns and cities, illuminations are put up and there are stalls and sometimes a fair, in a mixture of the sacred and the secular.

Scala, La The Teatro alla Scala, the Milan opera house, is one of the most famous opera houses in the world. Built in 1776–78, it has recently undergone a programme of restoration, during which the Teatro degli Arcimboldi, outside the city, staged its productions.

scuola The Italian system provides for primary schools, middle schools, and secondary schools. Primary school lasts for five years from the age of six, middle school lasts for three years, and secondary school for five. Primary and middle schools all follow the same curriculum but there are a number of different types of secondary schools: scientific, classical, linguistic, and artistic grammar schools, various technical and commercial institutes, and schools for training nursery school teachers (*see also* LICEO).

Senato The upper house of the Italian Parliament. Three hundred and fifteen senators are elected by universal suffrage by citizens over 25 years of age. Senators must be at least 40 years old. These 315 seats are elected on a

regional basis, i.e. they are split between the regions in proportion to population. The elected senators are joined by ex-heads of state and life senators. These are nominated by the PRESIDENTE DELLA REPUBBLICA from people who have given exceptional service to the country in the scientific, social, artistic, or literary fields.

settimana bianca A winter holiday spent with family or schoolfriends in a ski resort.

Seven Hills of Rome A group of seven small hills lying east of the River Tiber. According to tradition, the ancient city of Rome was founded by Romulus on the Palatine hill. The city gradually spread to cover the other six, the CAPITOLINE, Quirinal (QUIRINALE), Viminal (VIMINALE), Esquiline, Caelian, and Aventine hills. The hills are no longer a prominent geographical feature in modern Rome, but some are still associated with districts that have a distinctive character. The Capitoline hill, for instance, remains a seat of government, just as it was in Roman times.

sindaco The mayor is the head of local government and holds power for four years. He chairs and represents the council and municipal committee.

Sistine Chapel A chapel in the Vatican, built by Pope Sixtus IV. In 1505, Pope Julius II commissioned Michelangelo to decorate the ceiling with a series of scenes from the book of Genesis. Michelangelo also painted his vision of the *Last Judgement* on the east wall.

spaghetti western A low-budget western made in Europe by an Italian director or production company, often in English and with an American star, usually featuring lots of explicit violence. The best and most famous of these films are *A Fistful of Dollars*, *For a Few Dollars More*, and *The Good, the Bad and the Ugly*, directed by Sergio Leone.

spumante A sparkling white wine, sometimes seen as the poor relation of French champagne but also often greatly prized. It can be dry or sweet and always features on Italian Christmas, New Year, and party menus.

stabilimento balneare A stretch of beach equipped with parasols, loungers, showers, huts, perhaps a swimming-pool, and a bar. There is a charge for using it. These beach clubs vary from large and crowded to very chic and exclusive, and from fairly basic to luxurious. Many of them organize sports tournaments, card games, beauty contests, and dances.

stellone A big star, *stellone d'Italia* or *stellone italico* (star of Italy) which, since the RISORGIMENTO, has been associated with the personification of Italy (a woman with a star on her forehead or in her crown). Representing a beacon of hope in times of difficulty, it became part of the coat of arms of the unified kingdom and was then incorporated into the emblem of the Republic. Today it is mainly used ironically or polemically to criticize the tendency of Italians – a sign both of their vitality and of their happy-go-lucky attitude and fatalism – to trust to good luck rather than to hard work to get them through times of national crisis.

tabaccaio The tobacconist sells cigarettes and tobacco and is also the only shop apart from the post office where you can buy revenue stamps and postage stamps. It also sells bus tickets and other products. Sometimes there is also a bar. Its sign features a white 'T' on a black background.

Tangentopoli A name ('kick-back city') widely used in the Italian media to refer first to Milan, where the judiciary investigated a series of episodes of corruption, and then extended to mean the whole system of illicit financing used by the governing parties, unmasked by the famous MANI PULITE inquiry in 1992–93.

Telecom Italia One of the largest telephone companies supplying both land lines and mobile phones.

terrone A pejorative, racist term typically applied by northern Italians to southern Italians, and usually accompanied by equally disparaging adjectives such as 'ignorant', 'filthy', and 'uncivilized'. The word derives from *terra* (earth, land), depicting the typical southerner as an argicultural labourer. It became widespread in the 1960s and 1970s when large-scale immigration from the south to the industrial northwest took place. In present-day Italy, racist insults are mainly reserved for despised foreign immigrants (EXTRACOMUNITARI), while the term *terrone* is less widely used and has even acquired a jocular tone (the more so since it is used by southerners themselves). The pejorative sense has, however, been given a new lease of life in the anti-southern polemics of the Northern League (*see* PARTITI POLITICI).

Culture

trattoria A trattoria used to be distinguishable from a restaurant because it was simpler, often family-run, and less expensive. Nowadays it is merely a 'typical' local restaurant, serving traditional local dishes in a country-style setting. It can also be very sophisticated, and sometimes quite expensive.

triangolo industriale A name for the industrial zone of northwestern Italy, a triangle with the cities of Milan, Turin, and Genoa at its corners, where modern industry began to develop at the end of the 19th century. It has been the major productive centre in Italy, attracting large-scale internal immigration from the south, especially between the 1950s and 1970s. The subsequent decline of heavy industry has transformed the industrial triangle into an area where small and medium-sized enterprises and the tertiary sector now predominate. Other models of strong development have emerged elsewhere, particularly in the areas around Venice (*see* NORDEST).

Tricolore The Italian national flag: green, white, and red in vertical bands of equal width. It was designed at the end of 1700s and adopted as the flag of the republic after the Second World War.

Uffizi A vast art gallery in Florence, famous for its collection of works by Italian Renaissance painters such as Botticelli, Piero della Francesca, Leonardo, and Raphael. The building containing the gallery was built in the late 15th century to house government administration – hence its name, which means 'offices'.

Ultima cena *The Last Supper*, one of Leonardo da Vinci's most famous works, painted on the wall of the refectory of the monastery of St Maria della Grazia in Milan. Leonardo was experimenting with a new technique for fresco (painting directly onto fresh plaster), which was not altogether successful. As a result, the painting has deteriorated badly over the centuries and been restored several times.

Valle dei Templi An archaeological zone in the province of Agrigento that provides the most glorious evidence of Ancient Greek civilization in Sicily. The remains of many temples are to be found on a ridge (not a valley as the name suggests), among the almond trees. Built in the Doric style in the 5th century BC, the temples were burnt down by the Carthaginians, restored by the Romans in the 1st century AD, then half-destroyed by earthquakes and plundered over the following centuries, so that the only one that now remains intact is the magnificent Tempio della Concordia.

Vaticano The Vatican (also called Vatican City) has been an independent state within the city of Rome and the seat of the Pope since 1929. The Vatican Palace, which surrounds ST PETER'S, is the Pope's residence and houses artistic treasures such as the SISTINE CHAPEL and Raphael's frescos, as well as museums.

Venetian Republic For over a thousand years, from 697 to 1797, the island city of Venice and the mainland territory surrounding it formed an independent republic ruled by an elected chief magistrate (the *doge*) and a council of ten (the *dieci*). From the time of the Crusades to the late 15th century, Venice was the major power in the eastern Mediterranean and became enormously wealthy thanks to its trade with the Muslim world and Asia. From the 16th century, however, its power began to wane. It lost its independence when conquered by Napoleon, and eventually became part of Italy in 1866.

Vespa A motor scooter designed by aeronautical engineer, Corradino D'Ascanio, for the Piaggio company just after World War II. D'Ascanio's brief was to design a vehicle that would be affordable, easy to drive, carry a passenger, and not get the driver's clothes dirty – hence the trademark upswept mudguard behind the handlebars. The Vespa is particularly associated with the 1950s and 1960s in Italy, but it remains a popular means of transport to this day.

Vesuvius An active volcano, near Naples, that has erupted many times, most notably in AD 79, when it overwhelmed the ancient Roman cities of Pompeii and Herculaneum. The explosion buried the area under volcanic ash, preserving many of the buildings, as well as the bodies of those who did not flee, virtually intact. The towns were only rediscovered in the 18th century; excavations have revealed a stunning record of daily life in Roman times.

vigile urbano This policeman is responsible for controlling traffic and levying fines for traffic offences, for environmental protection, and for ensuring that municipal regulations and town laws are observed. He also deals with social problems, such as abandoned children, and the monitoring of refugees' and travellers' camps.

Viminale A media name for the Italian Ministry of Internal Affairs (or Home Office), which since 1961 has been housed in the Palazzo del Viminale, a vast Renaissance-style building erected in the early 20th century on the Viminal hill in Rome (*see* SEVEN HILLS OF ROME).

vino Wine is produced in every region of Italy, and the Italian wine-making tradition dates back 4,000 years to prehistoric times. Italy produces some white wine, but is mainly renowned for its red wines. The most internationally famous of these is Chianti, produced in Tuscany. Other famous varieties include Valpolicella, Barolo, Marsala, and Soave. High-quality Italian wines are labelled *DOC* (DENOMINAZIONE DI ORIGINE CONTROLLATA) or *DOCG* (*denominazione di origine controllata e garantita*).

Vita e cultura nel mondo anglofono dalla A alla Z

ABC 1. American Broadcasting Company Una delle principali reti televisive statunitensi, attualmente di proprietà della Walt Disney.
2. Australian Broadcasting Corporation Rete radiotelevisiva statale australiana.

ACT – American College Test Esame che gli studenti nordamericani devono superare per l'ammissione all'università. Generalmente ha luogo al termine della HIGH SCHOOL e copre alcune delle principali materie, come ad es. inglese e matematica.

Advance Australia Fair Inno nazionale australiano.

A level ▶ EXAMINATIONS

Alliance Party ▶ NORTHERN IRELAND

American Dream Il sogno americano è la convinzione che negli Stati Uniti chiunque sia disposto a lavorare sodo possa migliorare la propria posizione economica e sociale. Per gli immigrati e le minoranze il concetto significa anche libertà e uguaglianza di diritti.

American Football Il football americano è un gioco simile al rugby. Si gioca con una palla ovale e le due squadre in campo sono composte da undici giocatori ciascuna. È uno sport spettacolare ma molto violento e i giocatori indossano pertanto caschi e imbottiture protettive. L'evento principale della stagione è il Super Bowl, la finale di campionato della National Football League.

American Indian ▶ NATIVE AMERICAN

Anglican Church ▶ CHURCH OF ENGLAND

Anzac Soldato dell'Australian and New Zealand Army Corps. Questo contingente partecipò alla prima e alla seconda guerra mondiale e viene ricordato in particolare per l'eroismo con cui si distinse durante la disastrosa campagna di Gallipoli (in Turchia), nel 1915–16. Il valore degli *Anzacs* giocò un ruolo importante nel consolidare il sentimento di coscienza nazionale in Australia e Nuova Zelanda; viene commemorato annualmente il 25 aprile, l'Anzac Day.

April Fool's Day ▶ GIORNI FESTIVI NEI PAESI ANGLOFONI

Armistice Day ▶ POPPY DAY

A/S Level ▶ EXAMINATIONS

Australia Day Festa nazionale australiana celebrata il primo lunedì dopo il 26 gennaio. Commemora l'arrivo dei primi coloni britannici nell'allora Port Jackson, oggi la baia di Sydney, nel 1788.

Australian Rules Gioco australiano simile al rugby, giocato in un campo ovale da squadre di 18 giocatori che si disputano un pallone ovale. È lo sport invernale più popolare in gran parte dell'Australia.

Authorized Version Traduzione inglese della Bibbia pubblicata per la prima volta nel 1611. Realizzata da un gruppo di eruditi e commissionata da Giacomo I d'Inghilterra, per cui è anche chiamata la Bibbia di re Giacomo (*King James Bible*). Dal XVII al XX secolo è stata l'unica versione della Bibbia autorizzata per l'uso nell'ambito della Chiesa Anglicana (CHURCH OF ENGLAND). Il testo ha profondamente influenzato la letteratura e la lingua inglese.

bank holiday Termine che nel Regno Unito indica alcuni giorni festivi, nei quali si ha la chiusura di banche, poste, uffici e scuole. Cade sempre di lunedì.

barrister ▶ LAWYER

baseball È lo sport nazionale degli Stati Uniti. Il torneo annuale più importante è la *World Series*.

B & B ▶ BED AND BREAKFAST

BBC – British Broadcasting Corporation Uno dei principali enti radiotelevisivi britannici. Non è finanziato dalla pubblicità commerciale ma attraverso un canone di abbonamento che chiunque abbia la televisione deve pagare. Ha l'obbligo di fornire un servizio di informazione imparziale.

bed and breakfast I *bed & breakfast* o *B&B* sono piccole pensioni o case di privati che offrono camera e colazione a prezzi generalmente abbastanza convenienti.

Big Apple Significa letteralmente 'la grande mela' ed è l'appellativo di New York.

Bill of Rights I primi dieci emendamenti alla Costituzione degli Stati Uniti d'America. Tra i diritti che essi garantiscono ai cittadini statunitensi ci sono la libertà di culto, di parola, di stampa e vari diritti nel caso una persona venga accusata di un qualche reato. Il celebre Quinto Emendamento (*Fifth Amendment*) stabilisce tra l'altro che nessuno è obbligato a deporre contro se stesso. Il Secondo Emendamento tutela invece il diritto di portare armi.

Bonfire Night ▶ GIORNI FESTIVI NEI PAESI ANGLOFONI

Cultura

Boxing Day ▶ GIORNI FESTIVI NEI PAESI ANGLOFONI

British Isles Le Isole Britanniche comprendono la Gran Bretagna (GREAT BRITAIN), l'Irlanda – sia l'Irlanda del Nord (NORTHERN IRELAND) che la Repubblica d'Irlanda (Republic of Ireland) – e le isole più piccole quali le Shetlands, l'Isola di Man (Isle of Man), e le Isole Anglo-Normanne o del Canale (CHANNEL ISLANDS).

Broadway Strada nel quartiere newyorkese di Manhattan, celebre per i numerosi teatri. Il termine Broadway si usa infatti anche per indicare il teatro e il mondo dello spettacolo americano in generale. Prima della nascita dell'industria cinematografica era il luogo principale dove attori e artisti potevano esibirsi e diventare famosi.

Buckingham Palace Residenza ufficiale del sovrano britannico a Londra. Il cambio della guardia, accompagnato dalla banda del reggimento, ha luogo quasi tutte le mattine davanti al palazzo reale.

Burns Night ▶ GIORNI FESTIVI NEI PAESI ANGLOFONI

Cabinet È il Gabinetto del governo britannico, equivalente al nostro Consiglio dei Ministri. Formato da una ventina di ministri nominati dal Primo Ministro, ciascuno dei quali è responsabile di un settore specifico. Il Cabinet al completo si riunisce regolarmente per discutere e decidere la politica del governo. Il leader del principale partito all'opposizione nomina lo Shadow Cabinet, un Gabinetto ombra omologo al governo.

Canada Situato a nord degli Stati Uniti e secondo al mondo per superficie, il Canada è uno stato federale costituito da dieci province e tre territori. Storicamente legato alla Gran Bretagna ed appartenente al Commonwealth, è una monarchia costituzionale (il capo dello stato è la regina Elisabetta II) e democrazia parlamentare, con Parlamento a Ottawa, la capitale. Le lingue ufficiali sono l'inglese e il francese; quanto alla religione circa il 42% della popolazione canadese è cattolica, mentre il 23% è protestante. Florida nazione industriale, il Canada è molto ricco di risorse naturali; possiede oltre il 60% dei laghi mondiali: i Grandi Laghi (Superiore, Michigan, Huron, Erie e Ontario) si trovano al confine con gli Stati Uniti, come pure le spettacolari Cascate del Niagara; vanta inoltre ampie foreste da legname e catene montuose (tra cui le Montagne Rocciose canadesi). Una istituzione tipica del paese è infine la Royal Canadian Mounted Police, le leggendarie Giubbe Rosse che vantano la reputazione di acciuffare immancabilmente il loro uomo.

Capitol Il Campidoglio è la sede del Congresso degli Stati Uniti d'America (CONGRESS) situata sul Capitol Hill, nella città di Washington. The Capitol indica anche il Congresso stesso.

CBS – Columbia Broadcasting System Uno dei tre principali enti radiotelevisivi nazionali degli Stati Uniti.

Central Park Vasto parco nel quartiere di Manhattan a New York, caro ai newyorkesi in quanto costituisce un'oasi di verde in una zona fortemente urbanizzata.

Channel Islands Le Isole Anglo-Normanne (o Isole del Canale) sono un arcipelago situato nella Manica, vicino alla costa francese. Non fanno parte del Regno Unito ma sono dipendenze autonome della corona britannica. Jersey e Guernsey sono le isole più grandi.

Christmas Day ▶ GIORNI FESTIVI NEI PAESI ANGLOFONI

Church of England Il termine Chiesa d'Inghilterra indica la Chiesa Anglicana, chiesa protestante ufficiale in Inghilterra. Fu creata nel 1534 da Enrico VIII, il quale con l'Atto di supremazia (Act of Supremacy) si sostituì al Papa come capo della chiesa in Inghilterra. Ancora oggi il sovrano è il governatore supremo della Chiesa Anglicana; i vescovi e gli arcivescovi sono nominati dalla Corona su proposta del Primo Ministro. Il capo spirituale è invece l'Arcivescovo di Canterbury. L'Inghilterra è suddivisa in 44 diocesi e da 13.000 parrocchie (*parishes*), ciascuna con a capo un parroco (*vicar*). Nel 1992, il Sinodo Generale (General Synod) ha approvato l'ordinazione di sacerdoti donna. Fuori dall'Inghilterra si hanno altre comunioni anglicane: la Chiesa Episcopale in Scozia e negli Stati Uniti (Episcopalian Church), la Chiesa d'Irlanda (Church of Ireland), la Chiesa gallese (Church of Wales).

City Zona nel centro di Londra dove un tempo si trovava l'antica città. Oggi la City è il centro finanziario della capitale britannica e qui hanno la propria sede centrale banche e istituti finanziari; molto spesso il termine indica proprio tali istituzioni finanziarie.

Civil War **1. (negli Stati Uniti)** La Guerra di Secessione (1861–65), combattuta tra gli stati del nord e quelli del sud, scoppiata principalmente per la questione della schiavitù. Gli stati del sud, la cui economia agricola dipendeva dalla manodopera fornita dagli schiavi neri, nel 1861 costituirono la Confederazione degli Stati d'America separandosi così dall'Unione. Il conflitto tra sudisti e nordisti ebbe inizio il 12 aprile 1861 e il 9 aprile 1865 gli stati della Confederazione si arresero. La conclusione della guerra segnò l'abolizione della schiavitù; il 13° emendamento della Costituzione e successivamente il 14° (del 1868) e il 15° (del 1870) garantirono ai neri gli stessi diritti dei cittadini bianchi, almeno sulla carta. **2. (in Inghilterra)** Conflitto tra la Corona e il Parlamento (1642–51). Da un lato erano schierati i Royalists o Cavaliers (i monarchici sostenitori di Carlo I Stuart) e dall'altro le forze parlamentari, le cosiddette Teste rotonde

(Roundheads) per il taglio corto dei capelli, capeggiate da Oliver Cromwell. Molti dei fattori all'origine della guerra civile avevano a che vedere con i problemi religiosi ed economici dell'epoca. Il Parlamento si opponeva a concedere fondi a Carlo I per finanziare il suo assolutismo; il tentativo del sovrano di arrestare alcuni parlamentari portò infine allo scoppio della guerra. Sconfitto nelle battaglie di Marston Moor (1644) e di Naseby (1645), il re si arrese all'esercito scozzese un anno più tardi. Processato e condannato a morte da una commissione parlamentare sotto Cromwell, fu decapitato nel 1649. L'Inghilterra si dette un ordinamento repubblicano e Cromwell la governò per anni con pieni poteri, sciogliendo in varie occasioni il Parlamento. La monarchia fu restaurata nel 1660, due anni dopo la morte di Cromwell, quando il figlio di Carlo I, Carlo II, salì al trono.

CNN – Cable News Network Emittente televisiva statunitense che trasmette programmi di informazione via satellite 24 ore su 24.

Cockney Una persona nata e cresciuta nei quartieri popolari della zona est (EAST END) londinese. È anche il nome del dialetto tipico della zona, caratterizzato dalla sostituzione di parole con altre che vi fanno rima, ad esempio '*apples and pears*' significa '*stairs*' e '*trouble and strife*' sta per '*wife*'.

common law Sistema giuridico anglosassone basato sulla consuetudine e sulle sentenze delle corti di giustizia (rispettivamente diritto consuetudinario e giurisprudenza) e non sulle leggi create dal Parlamento e quindi sulla codificazione del diritto. Si ricorre alla *common law* soltanto per quelle questioni su cui il diritto scritto (*statute law*) non si pronuncia.

Commonwealth Il Commonwealth, fondato nel 1931, è l'insieme delle ex colonie e possedimenti dell'ex impero britannico. I paesi membri, oggi per lo più stati indipendenti (a parte alcuni quali Gibilterra, Bermuda e le Isole Falkland o Malvine), sono legati da rapporti economici e culturali. I vari capi di stato si incontrano con scadenza biennale (the Commonwealth Conference) e progetti educativi internazionali vengono promossi regolarmente. Ogni quattro anni, inoltre, si tengono i Commonwealth Games, manifestazioni sportive cui partecipano atleti dei vari paesi.

community college Istituto statunitense che offre corsi biennali indirizzati alla comunità locale, per lo più di carattere pratico.

comprehensive school Tipo di scuola secondaria britannica per studenti dagli 11 ai 18 anni, di tutti i livelli di rendimento. Le *comprehensive schools* vennero istituite negli anni Sessanta allo scopo di creare un sistema educativo più ugualitario, contrapposto al sistema selettivo operante all'epoca. *Vedi anche* GRAMMAR SCHOOL.

Cultura

Congress L'organo legislativo nazionale degli Stati Uniti. Si riunisce al Campidoglio (CAPITOL) ed è formato da due Camere: il Senato (SENATE) e la Camera dei Rappresentanti (HOUSE OF REPRESENTATIVES). Si rinnova ogni due anni e ha il compito di redigere e approvare le leggi. Ogni nuova legge deve essere approvata prima dalle due Camere e poi dal Presidente (PRESIDENT).

Conservative Party Uno dei maggiori partiti politici britannici. È un partito di centrodestra che appoggia il sistema capitalista, la libera impresa e la privatizzazione dell'industria e dei servizi pubblici. Il Partito Conservatore nacque intorno al 1830–40 dall'evoluzione del Partito Tory, nome col quale ancora oggi viene spesso indicato.

constituency Una delle ripartizioni in cui sono suddivisi Regno Unito, Canada, e Australia a fini elettorali.

Constitution La Costituzione americana, redatta dopo l'indipendenza dalla Gran Bretagna e ratificata nel 1789 dai rappresentanti di ciascuna delle tredici ex colonie che formavano gli Stati Uniti d'America, inclusi alcuni dei padri fondatori della nazione (FOUNDING FATHERS). La Costituzione stabiliva la suddivisione dei tre poteri dello stato: quello legislativo affidato al Congresso (CONGRESS), quello esecutivo al Presidente (PRESIDENT) e quello giudiziario alle Corti federali con al vertice la Corte Suprema di giustizia (SUPREME COURT). La spartizione dei poteri tra diversi organi dello Stato si ispirava alle idee degli Illuministi francesi e aveva lo scopo di garantire maggiore democrazia. Il testo della Costituzione resta essenzialmente in vigore ancora oggi. Dal 1789 ci sono stati tuttavia 27 emendamenti, di cui i primi dieci prendono il nome di BILL OF RIGHTS.

council Ai fini amministrativi la Gran Bretagna è suddivisa in varie aree. Le più grandi sono le COUNTIES, e in Scozia le *regions*, ripartite a loro volta in *districts*. I *parish councils*, e i *community councils* in Scozia e Galles, rappresentano le ripartizioni amministrative più piccole. A capo delle varie unità vi sono i consigli (*councils*). Tali autorità locali hanno poteri conferiti dal governo centrale e sono formate da consiglieri (*councillors*) eletti dai cittadini nelle elezioni amministrative (*local elections*). I *councils* sono responsabili dell'educazione, dei servizi sociali, di polizia e vigili del fuoco, degli alloggi popolari, delle biblioteche, e di altri servizi a livello locale.

county Principale unità amministrativa in Inghilterra, suddivisa a sua volta in *districts*. I confini delle contee hanno spesso radici storiche e risalgono a molti anni fa. Tuttavia, negli ultimi decenni sia l'estensione che i nomi delle *counties* sono cambiati, e il termine stesso è meno usato. Anche negli Stati Uniti la maggior parte degli stati è suddivisa in contee, per un totale di circa 3.000.

Cultura

courts Negli Stati Uniti la giustizia è amministrata nei vari stati tramite organi giudiziari indipendenti, ma esistono anche tribunali federali che si occupano tra le altre cose di controversie tra stati e tra cittadini di stati diversi. La Corte Suprema (SUPREME COURT) è un tribunale federale. Nella maggior parte degli stati esistono sia tribunali civili che penali e anche una sorta di corti d'appello. Un tipico procedimento penale viene giudicato in un tribunale distrettuale, dove il procuratore distrettuale (*district attorney*) sostiene l'accusa. Il giudice indossa la toga nera mentre gli avvocati (*counsels*) indossano abbigliamento normale. In Inghilterra e in Galles i tribunali locali sono detti *magistrates' courts* e si occupano di cause civili e reati minori. I reati più gravi competono alle *crown courts*, dove i *barristers* (avvocati abilitati ad esercitare in corti di livello superiore) sostengono l'accusa e la difesa. Il tribunale di ultima istanza è la Camera dei Lords (HOUSE OF LORDS). In Scozia, dove esiste un sistema giuridico diverso, le cause per reati minori sono giudicate dalle *magistrates' courts* o da tribunali di polizia. I reati più gravi

vengono giudicati dallo *sheriff* (il giudice di grado più alto in un distretto). I tribunali di massimo livello sono la High Court of Justiciary e la Court of Session, rispettivamente per le cause penali e civili. Nelle aule dei tribunali d'Inghilterra, Galles e Scozia sia giudici che avvocati portano toga e parrucca.

Cup final ▶ FOOTBALL

degree Diploma di laurea assegnato alla fine di un corso universitario. Esistono due livelli di laurea e due qualifiche corrispondenti: *bachelor's degree* e *master's degree*; il livello ancora superiore è il *doctorate*, che equivale al dottorato di ricerca. Una laurea di primo livello in lettere e filosofia o altre discipline umanistiche si chiama *Bachelor of Arts* (*BA* e negli Stati Uniti anche *AB*); una laurea di secondo livello in discipline scientifiche è un *Master of Sciences* (*MSc*, in America detto anche *ScM*); il *doctorate* è il *PhD*. *BA*, *MSc*, ecc. indicano il titolo ma anche il titolare della qualifica, ad es. Patricia Ramsay, *MA* (*Master of Arts*).

Democratic Party Fondato nel 1792, è uno dei due principali partiti politici statunitensi. L'altro è il Partito Repubblicano (REPUBLICAN PARTY). Il Partito Democratico è considerato fautore di una politica più liberale, particolarmente rispetto alle questioni sociali. Per questo motivo ha l'appoggio dei sindacati e delle minoranze.

devolution Nel Regno Unito il termine *devolution* indica il trasferimento di alcune competenze del governo centrale a enti regionali della Scozia, del Galles, dell'Irlanda del Nord e di altre regioni periferiche dello stato britannico. Dopo la vittoria del partito laburista nelle elezioni del 1997, il processo di decentramento fu attuato con il riconoscimento del Parlamento Scozzese, dell'Assemblea dell'Irlanda del Nord e di quella gallese. *Vedi anche* SCOTLAND, NORTHERN IRELAND, WALES.

District Attorney ▶ COURTS

Dow Jones Averages Detto anche Dow Jones Index (indice Dow Jones), indica il prezzo medio espresso in punti delle trenta azioni industriali principali quotate alla Borsa di New York ogni giorno di transazioni. Viene utilizzato per prevedere le tendenze generali del mercato azionario statunitense.

Downing Street Strada nel centro di Londra, nel quartiere di Westminster. Al numero 10 si trova la residenza ufficiale del Primo Ministro (Prime Minister) britannico e al numero 11 quella del Chancellor of the Exchequer (il Cancelliere dello Scacchiere, equivalente del Ministro delle Finanze e del Tesoro). Le espressioni 'Downing Street' e 'Number 10' sono spesso usate dalla stampa per indicare il Primo Ministro.

driving Nel Regno Unito, in Australia, in Nuova Zelanda e in Sudafrica si ha la guida a sinistra, ossia i veicoli procedono sul lato sinistro della strada. Negli Stati Uniti e in Canada si ha invece la guida a destra, come in Italia e nel resto d'Europa.

East End Quartieri nella zona est di Londra, tradizionalmente abitati dalla classe operaia e sede della zona del porto londinese (Docklands), oggi quasi completamente chiuso alle navi. La zona portuale dei Docklands negli ultimi anni è stata profondamente riurbanizzata e adesso ospita complessi residenziali di lusso e numerose strutture commerciali, quali l'imponente grattacielo di Canary Wharf, sedi di quotidiani e istituti finanziari. La zona è collegata al resto di Londra tramite il servizio ferroviario dei DLR (Docklands Light Railway).

East Side A New York, è la zona a est di Central Park, tradizionalmente più ricca e moderna del West Side, la parte ovest della città.

Edinburgh Festival La più importante manifestazione culturale britannica, istituita nel 1947. Si tiene annualmente nella capitale scozzese ad agosto, per tre settimane. Il festival offre spettacoli di musica, teatro, danza, cabaret e attira ogni anno moltissimi visitatori. Un settore sempre molto interessante è quello del cosiddetto the Edinburgh Fringe, ossia degli eventi fuori dal programma ufficiale.

education Negli Stati Uniti l'insegnamento primario e secondario è fornito gratuitamente dal governo federale. A cinque anni i bambini iniziano a frequentare il *kindergarten* che insieme ai successivi cinque o sei anni di scuola costituisce le elementari (ELEMENTARY SCHOOL). Seguono poi due anni di *junior high school* o tre anni di *middle school* e infine gli ultimi anni di educazione superiore nella HIGH SCHOOL che termina intorno ai 18 anni. Dopodiché l'educazione non è più gratuita, ma i vari stati in qualche modo la sussidiano. Circa il 45% degli americani continua gli studi dopo le superiori e oltre il 20% consegue un diploma presso istituti o università.

Nel Regno Unito la scuola obbligatoria va dai cinque ai 16 anni. I bambini iniziano frequentando l'*infant school* e poi la *primary school* (educazione elementare). A partire dagli 11 anni ha inizio la scuola secondaria, che si tratta nella maggioranza dei casi di una COMPREHENSIVE SCHOOL. Un numero ridotto di ragazzi frequenta le più selettive GRAMMAR SCHOOLS. Dopo i 16 anni alcuni alunni lasciano la scuola, mentre altri proseguono gli studi in istituti a carattere più professionale quali i *colleges of further education* o per preparare gli *A levels*. Se desiderano accedere all'università gli studenti devono pagarsi sia le tasse universitarie che le spese di vitto e alloggio, per cui molti devono chiedere prestiti in banca. Nel complesso la maggioranza dei ragazzi frequenta la scuola pubblica e soltanto una minoranza è iscritta alle INDEPENDENT SCHOOLS che sono a pagamento.

elections Negli Stati Uniti si indicono elezioni per la carica di Presidente (PRESIDENT), per i seggi nelle due Camere del Congresso (CONGRESS) e per cariche a livello statale e locale. I candidati si presentano per il Partito

Repubblicano (REPUBLICAN PARTY) o per il Partito Democratico (DEMOCRATIC PARTY). I candidati indipendenti possono presentarsi avendo fatto una petizione con le firme dei propri sostenitori. Le elezioni presidenziali hanno luogo ogni quattro anni. I partiti selezionano i propri candidati nelle elezioni primarie (PRIMARY) indette nei singoli stati. La selezione finale dei candidati alla presidenza e vicepresidenza si effettua in occasione della *party convention*, il congresso che ciascun partito tiene nei mesi di luglio e agosto. Il presidente viene eletto a novembre col sistema dell'ELECTORAL COLLEGES. Nel Regno Unito, le elezioni politiche (*general elections*) vengono indette per legge ogni cinque anni.

Tuttavia il Primo Ministro può indire elezioni anticipate se ritiene di avere buone probabilità di vittoria. Nel Regno Unito ci sono 659 CONSTITUENCIES, ciascuna delle quali elegge un rappresentante in Parlamento (MP). Il sistema elettorale è il *first-past-the-post system*, sta a dire quello della maggioranza relativa. Il leader del partito che ottiene il maggior numero di seggi diventa Primo Ministro e forma il nuovo governo.

electoral college Sistema adottato negli Stati Uniti per l'elezione del Presidente e del Vicepresidente. In ciascuno stato gli elettori eleggono dei delegati (*electors*), i quali formano l'assemblea dell'*electoral college* e a loro volta si impegnano a votare per un determinato candidato. Tutti i voti di uno stato vanno a un candidato. Bastano 270 voti (*electoral college votes*) per vincere le elezioni, il che significa che il Presidente può essere eletto anche senza ottenere la maggioranza del voto popolare.

elementary school Negli Stati Uniti è una scuola elementare per bambini tra i 6 e i 12 anni. Detta anche *grade school*.

England L'Inghilterra è il più esteso e popolato dei paesi che costituiscono il

Regno Unito. Nel corso dei secoli affermò il predominio militare, politico ed economico sulla Scozia, il Galles e gli altri paesi che formano le Isole Britanniche (BRITISH ISLES). Tale processo è oggi parzialmente invertito (*vedi* DEVOLUTION) e Scozia, Galles e Irlanda del Nord hanno organi legislativi distinti con poteri più o meno autonomi. L'Inghilterra è invece governata esclusivamente dal Parlamento Britannico.

examinations In Inghilterra, Galles e Irlanda del Nord al termine del quinto anno di scuola secondaria si sostengono gli esami del *General Certificate of Secondary Education* (*GCSE*), in varie combinazioni di materie. I ragazzi che proseguono gli studi sostengono, in un numero minore di materie, gli esami dell'*Advanced Supplementary* (*A/S*) *Level* alla fine del sesto anno, e poi gli esami dell'*Advanced Level* (*A Level*) l'ultimo anno delle superiori. Per l'accesso all'università è necessario passare almeno due *A levels*. I ragazzi che invece preferiscono compiere studi presso scuole professionali e istituti tecnici sostengono gli esami per le *General National Vocational Qualifications* (*GNVQs*). In Scozia, invece, si sostengono gli esami dello *Standard Grade* al termine del quarto anno di superiori e gli *Higher* e *Advanced Higher* per accedere all'università. Negli Stati Uniti il sistema scolastico non prevede esami ufficiali. Gli alunni conseguono un diploma di scuola secondaria al termine della HIGH SCHOOL, per cui ci si basa principalmente sui voti assegnati dai professori delle varie materie. Per l'accesso ad alcuni istituti universitari è richiesto il *College Test* (*vedi* ACT), un esame in inglese, matematica o scienze. *Vedi anche* EDUCATION.

Fifth Amendment ▶ BILL OF RIGHTS

Flower of Scotland Inno nazionale scozzese.

football Il calcio è lo sport più popolare del Regno Unito. Molte delle squadre più celebri sono a Londra (Arsenal, Chelsea, Tottenham Hotspur) e in città dell'Inghilterra centrale e del nord (Manchester United, Newcastle United, Aston Villa). Le squadre scozzesi giocano in campionati separati; le squadre principali (Celtic e Rangers) hanno sede a Glasgow. Negli Stati Uniti il calcio si chiama *soccer* in quanto per football si intende football americano.

Founding Fathers I padri fondatori che nel 1787 contribuirono a fondare gli Stati Uniti d'America in occasione nella *Federal Constitution Convention*, durante la quale venne redatta la costituzione americana (CONSTITUTION). I più noti sono George Washington, Thomas Jefferson e Benjamin Franklin.

fraternity Associazione studentesca maschile presso molte università americane. Il nome delle varie *fraternities* è formato da due o tre lettere dell'alfabeto greco, ad es. '*Lambda Delta Chi*'. Di solito i soci di una *fraternity* dividono gli alloggi della *fraternity house*. Alcune confraternite si occupano di opere di beneficenza, mentre altre approfondiscono argomenti di carattere accademico. Le *fraternities* sono state spesso criticate perché considerate istituzioni elitarie e discriminatorie, ma attualmente sono più accettate: oggi che l'educazione è sempre più cara, la loro essenza comunitaria aiuta a ridurre il costo della vita degli studenti. *Vedi anche* SORORITY.

FTSE-100 (pronunciato *Footsie one hundred*) La media del valore dei 100 principali titoli che compaiono nel listino della Borsa di Londra, pubblicato giornalmente sul quotidiano finanziario, *the Financial Times*. Fornisce importanti indicazioni sulla situazione economica in Gran Bretagna.

further education In Gran Bretagna il termine indica qualunque tipo di educazione per studenti oltre i 16 anni di età (la fine della scuola dell'obbligo) ad esclusione dell'educazione universitaria, nel qual caso si parla di *higher education*. Negli Stati Uniti, invece, *further education* si usa spesso anche per riferirsi all'educazione universitaria.

gap year In Gran Bretagna il *gap year* è l'anno di intervallo che molti studenti si prendono tra la fine delle superiori e l'università. Molti studenti utilizzano questo periodo sabbatico per fare esperienza nel mondo del lavoro e mettere da parte qualche risparmio, altri invece ne approfittano per viaggiare all'estero e conoscere il mondo.

GCSE ▶ EXAMINATIONS

Gettysburg Address Il discorso tenuto da Abraham Lincoln nel 1863, per l'inaugurazione del cimitero per i caduti nella battaglia di Gettysburg durante la Guerra di Secessione (CIVIL WAR). Contiene la storica definizione di democrazia come 'governo di popolo, dal popolo e per il popolo'.

GNVQ ▶ EXAMINATIONS

God Save the Queen Inno nazionale britannico. Non si sa chi ne compose il testo o la musica, ma si cantava già nel XVIII secolo.

grade school ▶ ELEMENTARY SCHOOL

grammar school In alcune zone dell'Inghilterra e del Galles è un tipo di scuola secondaria (*secondary school*) cui accedono alunni che hanno superato una prova d'ammissione. Dal 1965 le *grammar schools* sono state sostituite per la maggioranza dalle COMPREHENSIVE SCHOOLS.

Grand National In Gran Bretagna, la corsa di cavalli a ostacoli più importante, tenuta annualmente a Aintree, presso Liverpool. È un evento di portata nazionale che attira puntualmente un forte interesse. Sono molte le persone che puntano sui cavalli solo in occasione di questa corsa.

Great Britain La Gran Bretagna è la più grande delle Isole Britanniche (BRITISH ISLES). Include l'Inghilterra, la Scozia e il Galles. Spesso si usa erroneamente il termine '*Britain*' per indicare il Regno Unito (UNITED KINGDOM) o l'Inghilterra.

green card Negli Stati Uniti è un documento ufficiale che concede a qualsiasi persona priva della cittadinanza americana il permesso di risiedere e lavorare indefinitivamente negli Stati Uniti. Nel Regno Unito, invece, è un documento che i conducenti o proprietari di autoveicoli devono richiedere alla propria compagnia di assicurazione per convalidare la polizza in occasione di viaggi all'estero.

Greyhound bus Veicolo della più grande compagnia di pulmann statunitense (The Greyhound Lines Company) che collegando le maggiori città copre tutto il paese. È il mezzo di trasporto più usato dai giovani e dai turisti con budget limitato per percorrere grandi distanze.

Groundhog Day ▶ GIORNI FESTIVI NEI PAESI ANGLOFONI

gun control Il controllo sulle armi da fuoco è al momento un tema molto controverso negli Stati Uniti. Molti ritengono che il porto d'armi dovrebbe essere vietato ai comuni cittadini, dato il gran numero di omicidi e altri reati commessi. Altri sostengono invece che l'abolizione del porto d'armi contravverrebbe alla Costituzione (CONSTITUTION), la quale con il '*right to bear arms*' ne sancisce il diritto. La NATIONAL RIflE ASSOCIATION si oppone a ogni legge al riguardo. Nel 1993 il congresso ha tuttavia approvato la Brady Bill che limita la vendita e l'uso di alcuni tipi di arma.

Gunpowder Plot ▶ BONFIRE NIGHT

Guy Fawkes' Night ▶ BONFIRE NIGHT

haka Il rituale urlo di guerra dei Maori neozelandesi, cantato battendo energicamente i piedi per terra e muovendo le braccia. La nazionale neozelandese di rugby esegue l'*haka* prima di ogni partita.

Halloween ▶ GIORNI FESTIVI NEI PAESI ANGLOFONI

high school Negli Stati Uniti indica la scuola secondaria, generalmente per alunni di età compresa tra i 14 e i 18 anni. In Gran Bretagna, il termine si ritrova solo nel nome di alcune scuole.

holidays ▶ GIORNI FESTIVI NEI PAESI ANGLOFONI

homecoming Incontro annuale degli ex studenti di istituti universitari o HIGH SCHOOLS statunitensi. In genere ha luogo in autunno quando i vecchi studenti fanno una rimpatriata e partecipano a varie attività, tra cui una partita di football americano, la *homecoming parade* e la *homecoming dance*. In questa occasione viene anche eletta la *homecoming queen*.

House of Commons La Camera dei Comuni è la camera bassa del Parlamento britannico HOUSES OF PARLIAMENT. I deputati eletti si chiamano MPS (*members of Parliament*). La Camera dei Comuni è anche la camera bassa del Parlamento canadese, con 308 membri, eletti per cinque anni a suffragio diretto.

House of Lords La Camera dei Lord è la camera alta del Parlamento britannico (HOUSES OF PARLIAMENT). La sua funzione è discutere e poi approvare alcuni disegni di legge della HOUSE OF COMMONS o suggerire dei cambiamenti. La Camera dei Lord ha anche la funzione nel sistema giudiziario come corte di ultima istanza. I Lord sono per la maggioranza nominati (non eletti), e fino al 1999 un certo numero di cariche erano ereditarie. Sono state proposte alcune riforme per far sì che una percentuale di loro siano eletti direttamente dal popolo.

House of Representatives La camera bassa del Congresso degli Stati Uniti (CONGRESS). È costituita da 435 rappresentanti (REPRESENTATIVES) eletti ogni due anni; a ciascuno stato spetta un numero di rappresentanti proporzionale alla propria popolazione. La House of Representatives è incaricata dell'approvazione di ogni nuova legge.

Houses of Parliament Sono le due camere del Parlamento britannico, la Camera dei Comuni (HOUSE OF COMMONS) e la Camera dei Lord (HOUSE OF LORDS). Il termine indica anche la sede del Parlamento, il Palazzo di Westminster situato in riva al Tamigi nel centro di Londra.

Inauguration Day Negli Stati Uniti è il giorno in cui il neoeletto Presidente assume ufficialmente il potere. La cerimonia di insediamento ha sempre luogo il 20 gennaio, a Washington DC.

Independence Day ▶ GIORNI FESTIVI NEI PAESI ANGLOFONI

independent school Tipo di scuola britannica privata che si autofinanzia tramite il pagamento di quote da parte dei genitori degli alunni, anziché ricevere finanziamenti statali. Le PUBLIC SCHOOLS e le PREPARATORY SCHOOLS rientrano in questa categoria.

infant school ▶ EDUCATION

IRA (Irish Republican Army) L'IRA (Esercito Repubblicano Irlandese) è un'organizzazione paramilitare clandestina il cui obiettivo è l'unificazione della Repubblica d'Irlanda e dell'Irlanda del Nord. Nel 1970, come reazione a una politica considerata repressiva nei confronti delle minoranze cattoliche dell'Irlanda del Nord, una fazione dell'IRA (Provisional IRA) portò avanti atti terroristici in Irlanda del Nord e in Inghilterra. Nel 1998, l'accordo del Venerdì Santo (Good Friday Agreement) ha dato inizio a un periodo di relativa pace tra le comunità contrapposte dell'Irlanda del Nord. *Vedi anche* SINN FEIN.

ITV – Independent Television Gruppo di enti televisivi privati che offrono una programmazione diversificata in 15 diverse zone del Regno Unito.

Ivy League Il gruppo delle più antiche e rinomate università statunitensi, situate nel nordest del paese: Harvard, Yale, Columbia University, Cornell University, Dartmouth College, Brown University, Princeton University e la University of Pennsylvania. Il nome deriva dall'edera che cresce sugli antichi edifici universitari.

junior high school ▶ EDUCATION

junior school Scuola statale britannica per alunni di età compresa tra i 7 e gli 11 anni.

King James Bible ▶ AUTHORIZED VERSION

kirk In scozzese significa chiesa. 'The Kirk' indica the Church of Scotland (la Chiesa Episcopale scozzese).

kiwi Uccello privo di ali e coda originario della Nuova Zelanda. Il termine Kiwis viene anche usato per indicare i neozelandesi e le squadre sportive di questo paese.

Labor Day Festa del Lavoro. Negli Stati Uniti questa festività in onore dei lavoratori viene celebrata a livello nazionale il primo lunedì di settembre.

Labor Party In Australia è uno dei principali partiti politici. Rappresenta il centro-sinistra moderato.

Labour Party In Gran Bretagna il Partito Laburista è uno dei maggiori partiti politici. Andò per la prima volta al potere nel 1924, con l'obiettivo di farsi portavoce degli interessi dei lavoratori e dei sindacati. Negli ultimi anni il partito ha abbandonato alcune posizioni della sinistra storica, ad es. riguardo alla privatizzazione dell'industria e dei servizi pubblici. I suoi leader preferiscono oggi il termine 'New Labour'.

lawyer Termine generico per avvocato. Nel Regno Unito si ha il *solicitor* e il *barrister*. Il primo offre consulenza legale ai cittadini riguardo a questioni minori (è una figura tra l'avvocato e il notaio). Il secondo rappresenta i clienti davanti a corti di livello più alto; quando un *barrister* è ammesso ad esercitare l'avvocatura si dice che '*has been called to the Bar*'. Negli Stati Uniti non si ha questa distinzione. Sia nel Regno Unito che negli Stati Uniti si usa il termine *counsel* per indicare un avvocato o un gruppo di avvocati che presentano una causa in tribunale.

Cultura

Liberal Democratic Party Il Partito Liberaldemocratico, familiarmente abbreviato in 'Lib Dems'. È per importanza il terzo partito della Gran Bretagna. Si è costituito nel 1988 dalla fusione del Partito Liberale (Liberal Party) e del Partito Socialdemocratico (Social Democratic Party).

Liberal Party Importante partito australiano, fautore di una politica essenzialmente conservatrice.

L-plates Nel Regno Unito è un cartello di plastica bianco, con la lettera 'L' in rosso. Va applicato sul davanti e sul retro di un veicolo per segnalare che il conducente si sta preparando all'esame di guida.

mayor Negli Stati Uniti il sindaco di una città viene eletto dagli abitanti. In Inghilterra e Galles è il capo del consiglio comunale (*council*), tradizionalmente eletto dagli altri consiglieri (*councillors*), ma ha prevalentemente incarichi di rappresentanza nelle cerimonie ufficiali, senza reale autorità politica. Talvolta ha il titolo di *lord mayor* (in Scozia *provost* o

lord provost). Recentemente in alcune grandi città è stata creata la figura di un *mayor* eletto dal popolo.

member of Parliament ▶ MP

Memorial Day Festività statunitense che commemora gli americani caduti in guerra. Generalmente ricorre l'ultimo lunedì di maggio.

middle school ▶ EDUCATION

midterms (*midterm elections*) Negli Stati Uniti sono le elezioni per la Camera dei Rappresentanti (HOUSE OF REPRESENTATIVES) indette a metà del mandato presidenziale.

Mormon La Chiesa di Gesù Cristo dei Santi dell'Ultimo Giorno (Church of Jesus Christ of Latter-Day Saints) conta oggi circa 10 milioni di fedeli, meglio conosciuti come Mormoni. Fu fondata negli Stati Uniti nel 1830 da Joseph Smith. Successivamente, sotto la guida di Brigham Young, i membri si spostarono nella parte ovest del paese, dove fondarono Salt Lake City nello stato dello Utah, i cui abitanti sono ancora oggi Mormoni. Hanno regole morali molto rigide e non bevono né alcolici né caffè.

Morris dancing Una danza folkloristica originaria del Regno Unito, eseguita solitamente da gruppi di soli uomini (*Morris men*) disposti in file. I danzatori, che indossano una camicia bianca, un cappello di paglia e pantaloni con applicati campanelli, agitano bastoni o fazzoletti.

Mother's Day (Mothering Sunday) ▶ GIORNI FESTIVI NEI PAESI ANGLOFONI

motorways La Gran Bretagna ha un'ampia rete di autostrade a tre corsie, segnalate dalla lettera 'M' seguita da un numero. Il limite di velocità sulla motorway è di 70 miglia all'ora, che equivale a 112 km/h. A differenza dell'Italia non si deve in genere pagare il pedaggio. Attualmente una sola *motorway* è a pagamento.

MP (*member of Parliament*) Un membro della Camera dei Comuni che rappresenta una delle 659 'CONSTITUENCIES' in cui è suddiviso il Regno Unito. *Vedi anche* HOUSE OF COMMONS.

National Guard Un corpo militare statunitense la cui origine risale all'epoca coloniale, composto di volontari reclutati in ciascuno stato. In caso di catastrofi naturali o di emergenze civili può passare sotto il comando federale. Oggi la National Guard è considerata parte dell'esercito nazionale.

National Health Service (NHS) È il servizio di assistenza sanitaria britannico, finanziato in gran parte dal governo, per cui l'assistenza è per lo più gratuita. I medicinali prescritti e le cure dentistiche sono a pagamento, eccetto per alcune categorie di persone, quali i bambini e i pensionati.

National Insurance È il servizio di previdenza sociale in Gran Bretagna. Lavoratori e datori di lavoro versano dei contributi fiscali (*National Insurance contributions*) da cui dipendono i diversi servizi che offre lo stato, quali la pensione, l'assistenza sanitaria, i sussidi di disoccupazione. Chiunque lavori o faccia domanda per i sussidi deve richiedere un numero di identificazione (*National Insurance number*).

National Lottery La lotteria nazionale britannica. Parte dei proventi viene destinata a iniziative culturali e sportive, alla conservazione del patrimonio del paese e a organizzazioni no-profit.

National Party Importante partito politico neozelandese, fautore di una politica fondamentalmente conservatrice.

National Rifle Association (NRA) Una organizzazione statunitense favorevole al possesso di armi da fuoco da usare nella caccia, gli sport e la legittima difesa. Secondo i suoi 3,4 milioni di iscritti il diritto di ogni cittadino a possedere armi è garantito dalla Costituzione americana (CONSTITUTION).

National Trust Una fondazione britannica senza scopo di lucro finalizzata alla conservazione dei luoghi di interesse storico e del patrimonio ambientale. Finanziato da donazioni e sovvenzioni private, il National Trust è il maggiore proprietario terriero del Regno Unito. Nel corso degli anni ha acquisito enormi estensioni di terreni (circa 248.000 ettari) e di litorali (circa 960 km), come pure edifici, borghi e giardini, molti dei quali vengono aperti al pubblico in certi periodi dell'anno. In Scozia esiste una fondazione analoga ma indipendente, il National Trust for Scotland.

Native American È il termine più ampiamente accettato per indicare i

Cultura

popoli indigeni di tutto il continente americano. Negli Stati Uniti si sta sostituendo all'espressione American Indian (Indiano d'America). Qui secondo il Bureau of Indian Affairs, l'organizzazione governativa statunitense che si occupa delle questioni indiane, esistono circa 550 tribù per un totale di 1,2 milioni di persone. Circa un milione di indiani vive nelle riserve e di questi il 37% è disoccupato. Molte riserve aprono case da gioco, sulla base che sono libere di stabilire le proprie regole.

NBC – National Broadcasting Company Il primo ente radiofonico istituito negli Stati Uniti (1926). Il primo canale televisivo della NBC cominciò a trasmettere nel 1940.

Newspapers Negli Stati Uniti il 95% della popolazione legge la stampa locale. Esiste un unico quotidiano nazionale, *USA Today*, gli altri sono locali. I quotidiani di alcune grandi città, quali il *New York Times*, il *Los Angeles Times*, e il *Washington Post*, sono comunque diffusi in tutto il paese. Anche

l'*International Herald Tribune*, pubblicato fuori dagli Stati Uniti, viene letto da molti americani all'estero. Il *Wall Street Journal*, che pubblica il DOW JONES AVERAGE, è il quotidiano di economia e finanza più importante degli Stati Uniti. La stampa americana è nel complesso piuttosto conservatrice, in modo da garantirsi una più alta distribuzione. Nel Regno Unito i quotidiani escono in due formati: quello grande dei *broadsheets* e quello più piccolo e compatto dei *tabloids*. Fino a poco tempo fa i quotidiani nazionali più seri erano tutti *broadsheets*. Il *Daily Telegraph* e il *Financial Times* (stampato sull'inconfondibile carta color salmone) hanno conservato questo formato, ma recentemente il *Times*, l'*Independent* e il *Guardian* hanno ridotto il formato. Del gruppo dei popolarissimi quotidiani più sensazionalistici (tutti in formato tabloid), fanno parte il *Sun*, il *Mirror*, l'*Express* e il *Mail*. Questi giornali sono rinomati per enfatizzare l'aspetto umano e spesso puramente scandalistico delle notizie. Sia negli Stati Uniti che nel Regno Unito i quotidiani che escono il sabato o la domenica hanno un gran numero di supplementi di sport, viaggi, cultura ecc.

Northern Ireland È una provincia del Regno Unito, situata nella parte nordorientale dell'Irlanda. Rimase a far parte del Regno Unito, con autonomia limitata, quando, nel 1920, il resto dell'isola divenne indipendente. La vita in Irlanda del Nord è stata a lungo dominata dal conflitto tra la maggioranza protestante che vuole restare vincolata al Regno Unito e la minoranza cattolica che vorrebbe unirsi alla Repubblica d'Irlanda. Gli anni dal 1969 al 1998 sono stati anni di sanguinosa violenza, sia in Irlanda nel Nord sia nei territori della Gran Bretagna; mentre i cattolici erano impegnati nella campagna per i diritti civili, organizzazioni paramilitari di ambo le parti hanno portato avanti assassinii, rapresaglie e atti terroristici. Durante gran parte di questo periodo la provincia è tornata sotto il diretto governo britannico e truppe britanniche vi erano stanziate stabilmente. L'accordo del Venerdì Santo (Good Friday Agreement) del 1998 ha messo fine alla violenza e la semiautonomia è stata restaurata sulla base di un accordo sulla spartizione del potere. Il Parlamento dell'Irlanda del Nord è stato tuttavia sospeso più volte, in quanto la cooperazione tra i partiti non è sempre attuabile. I singoli partiti sono spesso divisi in fazioni. Il Partito Democratico Unionista (Democratic Unionist Party) e il più moderato Partito Unionista dell'Ulster (Ulster Unionist Party) rappresentano la comunità protestante, mentre SINN FEIN e i più moderati Partito Social Democratico (Social Democratic) e Partito Laburista (Labour Party) rappresentano i cattolici. Il piccolo Partito dell'Alleanza (Alliance Party) si oppone invece alla divisione religiosa. *Vedi anche* IRA.

Number Ten ▶ DOWNING STREET

NVQ ▶ EXAMINATIONS

Old Glory ▶ STARS AND STRIPES

Open University (OU) Università a distanza britannica fondata nel 1969.

Oxbridge Termine che indica nel loro insieme le università più antiche e prestigiose del Regno Unito: Oxford e Cambridge.

Pancake Day ▶ SHROVE TUESDAY

Parliament Il Parlamento britannico è l'organo legislativo del Regno Unito ed è suddiviso in due Camere: la Camera dei Comuni (HOUSE OF COMMONS) e la Camera dei Lord (HOUSE OF LORDS). Il Parlamento canadese è costituito dal Senato (SENATE) e dalla Camera dei Comuni. *Vedi anche* MP.

PBS – Public Broadcasting Service Servizio radiotelevisivo statunitense, finanziato dal governo e rinomato per i programmi di qualità. È costituito dall'associazione di emittenti locali che trasmettono senza scopo di lucro e senza pubblicità.

Peace Corps Agenzia federale statunitense fondata nel 1961. I Corpi di Pace, composti da volontari, operano principalmente nei paesi in via di sviluppo in settori quali l'insegnamento, la sanità, l'agricoltura e l'ambiente.

Pentagon L'edificio a pianta ottagonale situato a Washington dove hanno sede gli uffici centrali del ministero della Difesa e delle forze armate americani. Talvolta la stampa utilizza il termine per riferirsi allo Stato Maggiore.

Pledge of Allegiance Giuramento di fedeltà che i cittadini degli Stati Uniti prestano alla bandiera e alla patria. In molte scuole gli studenti lo ripetono tutte le mattine davanti alla bandiera tenendo una mano sul petto.

Cultura

Poppy Day ▶ GIORNI FESTIVI NEI PAESI ANGLOFONI

preparatory school Negli Stati Uniti è un tipo di scuola secondaria in cui viene offerta una speciale preparazione preuniversitaria. In Gran Bretagna, dov'è anche detta *prep school*, è una scuola privata per alunni dai 7 ai 13 anni. Generalmente non è un istituto misto e in molte *preparatory schools* parte degli alunni stanno a convitto. La maggioranza degli alunni prosegue poi gli studi in una scuola privata (PUBLIC SCHOOL).

President Negli Stati Uniti il Presidente può restare in carica per un massimo di due mandati (*terms*) ciascuno di durata quadriennale. Poiché il paese è una repubblica federale di tipo presidenziale, egli è il capo dello stato e allo stesso tempo il capo del governo. È responsabile della politica estera e il comandante in capo delle forze armate.

President's Day ▶ GIORNI FESTIVI NEI PAESI ANGLOFONI

primary (primary election) Negli Stati Uniti le elezioni primarie (*primaries*) vengono indette per selezionare i candidati prima delle elezioni principali, specialmente nel caso delle presidenziali. I candidati alla carica di presidente (PRESIDENT) vengono eletti dopo una serie di primarie a livello statale. *Vedi anche* ELECTIONS.

primary school ▶ EDUCATION

Provost ▶ MAYOR

pub (*public house*) Letteralmente 'casa aperta al pubblico', il *pub* è il tipico locale dove in Gran Bretagna e Irlanda si va per bere birra e altre bevande, alcoliche e non. Le origini dei *pub* risalgono all'epoca dei Romani. Alla fine del XIV secolo chiunque producesse e vendesse birra (*ale*) doveva esporre un cartello e le caratteristiche insegne colorate contraddistinguono i *pub* ancora oggi. Il *pub* è spesso al centro della vita sociale e culturale del quartiere o del paese.

public access channel Negli Stati Uniti è un canale televisivo riservato a programmi di persone e organizzazioni che operano senza fini di lucro.

public house ▶ PUB

public school In Gran Bretagna sono, al contrario di quanto farebbe pensare il nome, scuole private a pagamento, per alunni tra i 13 e i 18 anni. Spesso si tratta di scuole miste e nella maggior parte di esse gli allievi sono a convitto. In Scozia e negli Stati Uniti il termine *public school* indica invece una scuola statale. *Vedi anche* PREPARATORY SCHOOL.

Remembrance Sunday ▶ POPPY DAY

Representative Un membro della Camera dei Rappresentanti (HOUSE OF REPRESENTATIVES) americana.

Cultura

Republican Party Uno dei maggiori partiti politici statunitensi. Sebbene sia stato fondato nel 1854 da chi appoggiava l'abolizione della schiavitù, viene considerato più conservatore del Partito Democratico (DEMOCRATIC PARTY), l'altro principale partito americano.

rugby Il gioco della palla ovale, originario della Gran Bretagna. Esistono due varianti di questo sport, il rugby a 13 (*rugby league*) con squadre composte di 13 giocatori e il rugby a 15 (*rugby union*) con 15 giocatori. Il *rugby league* è stato fin dagli inizi giocato a livello professionale, mentre il *rugby union* lo è divenuto nel 1995.

SAT Negli Stati Uniti indica lo *Scholastic Aptitude Test*, una prova attitudinale sostenuta generalmente l'ultimo anno della HIGH SCHOOL. È necessario superare il *SAT* per accedere alla maggior parte delle università. In Inghilterra e Galles indica invece lo *Standard Assessment Test* o *Task*, una prova sostenuta a 7, 11 e 14 anni dagli alunni di tutte le scuole allo scopo di valutarne i progressi.

Cultura

Scotland La parte più settentrionale del Regno Unito, la cui popolazione è concentrata in una cintura centrale intorno alle due città principali, Glasgow e Edimburgo, la capitale. La Scozia è particolarmente rinomata per la bellezza delle montagne, dei laghi (in scozzese '*loch*') e delle Highlands, la zona a nordest di Edimburgo. Fino al secolo XVI la Scozia era frequentemente in guerra con l'Inghilterra. Nel 1603, re Giacomo IV (James) di Scozia diventò anche re d'Inghilterra (regnandovi come James I) e l'unione dei due paesi venne finalizzata nel 1707 quando il Parlamento scozzese si sciolse. La Scozia tuttavia conserva molte delle proprie istituzioni. Il sistema scolastico, ad esempio, è diverso dal resto del Regno Unito. Tra gli scozzesi ci sono sempre stati coloro che pensano che la Scozia dovrebbe essere completamente indipendente. Reistaurato nel 1999 (*vedi* DEVOLUTION), lo Scottish Parliament ha sede a Edimburgo. A differenza dell'Assemblea gallese, esso ha pieni poteri sul piano legislativo e esecutivo riguardo alle questioni scozzesi, mentre ha autorità limitata relativamente al sistema fiscale. *Vedi anche* WALES.

SDLP ▶ NORTHERN IRELAND

Senate Negli Stati Uniti il Senato è la camera alta del Congresso (CONGRESS). È formato da 100 senatori (*senators*), due per ciascuno stato, eletti con mandato di sei anni. Le nuove leggi devono essere approvate sia dal Senato che dalla Camera dei Rappresentanti (HOUSE OF REPRESENTATIVES). Il Parlamento canadese è costituito dal Senato e dalla Camera dei Comuni (HOUSE OF COMMONS).

Shadow Cabinet ▶ CABINET

Shrove Tuesday ▶ GIORNI FESTIVI NEI PAESI ANGLOFONI

Sinn Fein Partito politico irlandese fondato nel 1905 con l'obiettivo di unificare le 32 contee dell'Irlanda nella Repubblica d'Irlanda creata nel 1949. Viene considerato l'ala politica dell'IRA, anche se nega qualunque legame con l'organizzazione paramilitare.

Smithsonian Institution Rinomato istituto statunitense che raccoglie vari musei e centri di ricerca. Situato a Washington DC, è familiarmente soprannominato '*the nation's attic*', la soffitta della nazione.

social security number Un numero di identificazione che negli Stati Uniti tutti devono avere. Inizialmente veniva richiesto per poter lavorare ed essere coperti dalla sicurezza sociale. Tuttavia nel 1987 il governo ha deciso di assegnarlo anche ai bambini. Attualmente viene usato in molte occasioni diverse: compare sugli assegni, sulla patente, ed è il numero con cui vengono identificati gli alunni degli istituti superiori.

sorority Una delle associazioni studentesche femminili presenti in molti istituti universitari. *Vedi anche* FRATERNITY.

Speaker La persona che presiede i dibattiti nella Camera dei Comuni (HOUSE OF COMMONS), eletta dai deputati (MPS) dei vari partiti.

Speaker of the House Negli Stati Uniti è la persona incaricata di presiedere la maggior parte delle attività della Camera dei Rappresentanti (HOUSE OF REPRESENTATIVES). È responsabile di mantenere l'ordine durante i dibattiti, di nominare i comitati e di presentar loro le proposte di legge. È un rappresentante del partito di maggioranza alla Camera dal quale viene eletto. È la persona che segue al vicepresidente nella successione per la presidenza.

Stars and Stripes La bandiera degli Stati Uniti. Le cinquanta stelle (*stars*) rappresentano i cinquanta stati e le tredici strisce (*stripes*) orizzontali rappresentano le prime tredici colonie che formarono gli Stati Uniti all'epoca dell'indipendenza. Viene anche chiamata Old Glory o STAR-SPANGLED BANNER.

Star-Spangled Banner Uno dei nomi con cui si indica la bandiera degli Stati Uniti. È anche il titolo dell'inno nazionale statunitense, composto nel 1814 ma adottato come tale soltanto nel 1931.

state school In Gran Bretagna indica una scuola statale che è finanziata direttamente o indirettamente dallo stato e offre educazione gratuita. La maggior parte dei ragazzi frequenta questo tipo di scuole.

State of the Union Address Tradizionale discorso che il Presidente degli Stati Uniti (PRESIDENT) tiene annualmente al Congresso (CONGRESS) per

Cultura

metterlo al corrente della 'situazione dell'Unione', come previsto dalla Costituzione (CONSTITUTION). Il discorso è l'occasione per parlare dei progressi del governo, dei suoi progetti e della politica per il futuro. Viene trasmesso in diretta alla televisione.

Statue of Liberty La celebre statua situata sulla Liberty Island nella baia di New York. Donata dal popolo francese come omaggio al popolo americano, raffigura una donna che innalza la fiaccola della libertà. È ormai l'inconfondibile simbolo di New York e dell'America.

summer camp Negli Stati Uniti indica il campeggio estivo cui moltissimi ragazzi si recano per socializzare e praticare attività ricreative e sportive all'aria aperta; tra queste il nuoto, il canottaggio, l'arrampicata e i corsi di sopravvivenza.

Super Bowl ▸ AMERICAN FOOTBALL

Supreme Court È l'organo più importante del sistema giudiziario statunitense, composto da nove giudici, nominati a vita dal Presidente (PRESIDENT) con l'approvazione del Congresso (CONGRESS). La Corte Suprema decide riguardo alla costituzionalità delle leggi e ha inoltre la facoltà di impedire l'approvazione delle leggi, tanto federali quanto statali o locali. È anche la corte di ultima istanza, che riesamina i casi già passati davanti ai tribunali di grado inferiore. Le sentenze della Corte Suprema costituiscono giurisprudenza, vale a dire possono essere usate come precedenti in altri processi.

tabloid ▸ NEWSPAPERS

Teamsters Teamsters Union è il più grosso sindacato degli Stati Uniti, con circa 1 milione e mezzo di iscritti. Sebbene inizialmente rappresentasse i camionisti (*teamsters*), oggi ne fanno parte lavoratori di molti altri settori.

Thanksgiving ▸ GIORNI FESTIVI NEI PAESI ANGLOFONI

TOEFL (*Test of English as a Foreign Language*) Un esame che valuta il livello di conoscenza dell'inglese degli studenti che fanno domanda d'iscrizione in un'università americana ma non sono di madrelingua inglese.

Tory ▸ CONSERVATIVE PARTY

trick or treat ▸ HALLOWEEN

Uncle Sam Personaggio immaginario che rappresenta gli Stati Uniti, il suo governo e i suoi cittadini. Nell'iconografia è tradizionalmente rappresentato con la barba bianca, vestito dei colori nazionali bianco, rosso e azzurro, con un gran cappello a cilindro con le stelle della bandiera statunitense. Spesso utilizzato quando si fa appello al patriottismo americano.

Cultura

Union Jack o **Union Flag** Il nome della bandiera del Regno Unito. È formata da tre croci: quella di San Giorgio (St George), patrono d'Inghilterra, quella di Sant'Andrea (St Andrew), patrono di Scozia, e quella di San Patrizio (St Patrick), patrono d'Irlanda. Il Galles e San David suo patrono non vi sono rappresentati.

United Kingdom Il Regno Unito di Gran Bretagna e Irlanda del Nord (United Kingdom of Great Britain and Northern Ireland) comprende l'Inghilterra, la Scozia, il Galles e l'Irlanda del Nord. Fa parte del COMMONWEALTH e dell'Unione Europea.

Veterans Day ▶ **GIORNI FESTIVI NEI PAESI ANGLOFONI**

Wales Parte del Regno Unito confinante con l'Inghilterra centro-occidentale. La maggior parte dei centri abitati sono situati sulla costa (l'interno del paese è montuoso e poco popolato), in particolare lungo la costa meridionale, intorno alle due maggiori città, Cardiff, la capitale, e Swansea.

Nel nord del Galles il sentimento nazionalistico è più sentito e la lingua gallese (WELSH) è maggiormente diffusa. L'occupazione inglese del Galles ebbe inizio poco dopo la conquista normanna del 1066. Nel XVI secolo il Galles fu integrato all'Inghilterra ai fini legali, amministrativi e parlamentari. Nel 1999, in seguito al processo di decentramento (DEVOLUTION) è stata istituita l'Assemblea Nazionale del Galles, anche detta Assemblea Gallese (Welsh Assembly). Relativamente agli affari gallesi ha poteri legislativi secondari limitati.

Wall Street Via di Manhattan, a New York, dove hanno sede la Borsa e molti altri istituti finanziari. Quando si parla di Wall Street ci si riferisce spesso a tali istituti.

Weddings Nei paesi anglosassoni il matrimonio tradizionale si svolge in chiesa. La sposa (*bride*) indossa l'abito bianco ed ha al seguito una o più damigelle d'onore (*bridesmaids*). Il padre accompagna la sposa all'altare, mentre lo sposo (*bridegroom*) è affiancato dal *best man*, un parente o amico. Gli sposi si scambiano gli anelli (*wedding rings* o *bands*). Nel caso di matrimonio civile la cerimonia si svolge in comune. Dopo la cerimonia ha luogo il rinfresco nuziale (*wedding reception*) durante il quale il padre della sposa e il *best man* tengono un discorso. Alla fine del rinfresco gli sposi vanno in luna di miele (*honeymoon*). La sera prima del matrimonio, religioso o civile, è tradizione che il promesso sposo esca con gli amici per dare l'addio al celibato (la serata è detta *stag night* o negli Stati Uniti *bachelor party*). Oggi anche la sposa festeggia con le amiche l'addio al nubilato (*hen night*, e negli Stati Uniti *bachelorette party*). Negli Stati Uniti un'amica o una parente della sposa (di solito la damigella d'onore) organizza anche la cosiddetta *shower*, una festicciola in occasione della quale si danno alla sposa dei regali.

Welfare Negli Stati Uniti il termine *welfare* e *welfare programs* indicano le diverse misure di sicurezza sociale prese dal governo per garantire il benessere dei cittadini, in particolare in caso di povertà, malattia, disoccupazione. Fanno parte di questo sistema Medicare, Medicaid e i buoni per l'acquisto di viveri (*food stamps*).

Welsh È il gallese (*Cymraeg*), lingua di origine celtica, come il bretone e il cornico. È la lingua madre del 20% della popolazione gallese e negli ultimi quarant'anni ha vissuto una certa rinascita. In Galles oggi è usata insieme all'inglese in certi contesti ufficiali ed è materia obbligatoria nella maggior parte delle scuole.

Westminster Un quartiere del centro di Londra dove sono situati alcuni dei principali edifici governativi, quali il Parlamento (HOUSES OF PARLIAMENT) e la residenza del Primo Ministro in DOWNING STREET, ed anche l'Abbazia di Westminster (Westminster Abbey). Oggi la stampa usa il termine 'Westminster' per indicare il Parlamento britannico.

West Side ▶ EAST SIDE

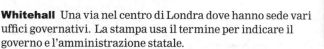

whip Nella Camera dei Comuni britannica (HOUSE OF COMMONS), *whips* sono i deputati (MPS) incaricati di far rispettare la disciplina parlamentare ai colleghi del proprio partito, di assicurarsi che siano presenti alle sessioni e che votino. Negli Stati Uniti sono membri del Congresso (CONGRESS) con simili responsabilità.

Whitehall Una via nel centro di Londra dove hanno sede vari uffici governativi. La stampa usa il termine per indicare il governo e l'amministrazione statale.

White House La Casa Bianca, situata a Washington, è la residenza ufficiale del Presidente degli Stati Uniti. La stampa usa il termine per indicare il Presidente e i suoi collaboratori.

World Series ▶ BASEBALL

Yankee Termine spregiativo con cui durante la Guerra di Secessione i sudisti chiamavano i nordisti. Oggi è usato in tutto il mondo per indicare gli americani in generale. Negli Stati Uniti del sud ha ancora il significato originario, mentre in quelli del nord è utilizzato per indicare gli oriundi del New England.

yearbook Negli Stati Uniti è l'album che annualmente viene pubblicato per gli studenti dell'ultimo anno della HIGH SCHOOL. Contiene un profilo di ciascun studente con notizie sulle sue attività accademiche, sportive e ricreative, accompagnato da una fotografie e da una dedica.

Cultura

Letter-writing / Redazione di lettere

Christmas and New Year wishes (informal)

Natale 2004

Cari Teresa e Federico,

Buon Natale e Felice Anno Nuovo

Vi auguro con tutto il cuore un anno pieno di belle sorprese e spero che ci sia al più presto l'occasione di rivederci.

Un abbraccio a tutti e due,

Paola

■ *You write the date like this on greetings cards. For Easter you write Pasqua and the year. For other occasions (birthdays, etc.) you can write the date in full: 6 febbraio 2004 with the number, the month without a capital letter, then the year, or as a number: 6/2/04.*

■ *Standard greeting for Christmas and New Year cards.*

Christmas and New Year wishes (formal)

On the envelope:

Gentile Dott. Bossi e famiglia

■ *In Italy fewer people send Christmas cards than in Great Britain. Young people don't send them; it's considered slightly formal. If you send a present to someone you might attach a card, but if you exchange presents in person you don't normally give them a card, just wish them Buon Natale. The same goes for birthdays.*

Monza, Natale 2004

BUON NATALE E FELICE ANNO NUOVO

I miei più sentiti auguri a Lei ① e alla famiglia

Fausto Mameli

■ *Inside greetings cards you can write the place you are writing from in front of the date.*

① *Lei is written with a capital letter in more formal letters.*

Auguri di Buon Natale e Buon Anno

Su un biglietto:

[Best wishes for a] Happy ① Christmas and
a Prosperous New Year

Best wishes for Christmas and the New Year

Wishing you every happiness this Christmas
and in the New Year

① *Oppure:* Merry.

In una lettera:

44 Louis Gardens
London NW6 4GM

December 20th 2003

Dear Peter and Claire,

First of all, a very happy Christmas and all the best for the New Year to you
and the children. ② We hope you're all well ③ and that we'll see you again.
It seems ages since we last met up.

We've had a very eventful year. Last summer Gavin came off his bike and
broke his arm and collarbone. Kathy scraped through her A Levels and is
now at Sussex doing European Studies. Poor Tony was made redundant in
October and is still looking for a job.

Do come and see us next time you are over this way. Just give us a ring a
couple of days before so we can fix something.

All best wishes

Tony and Ann

② *Oppure (se i figli sono adulti):* to you and your family.

③ *Oppure (informale):* flourishing.

. . . .

Invitation to a wedding and wedding reception

Filippo Bartolini   *Cristiana Tedeschi*

Annunciano il loro matrimonio

Chiesa di S. Jacopo – Siena

Sabato 22 maggio 2005 – ore 16.30

Siena –   *Volterra –*
Via della Salute, 50   *Via A. Diaz, 6*

- Invitations to weddings are called 'partecipazioni' and are written or printed.

- Very formal invitations are sent out by the parents who are announcing their son's or daughter's wedding.

Filippo e Cristiana

dopo la cerimonia saranno lieti di salutare
parenti ed amici presso la
Villa 'Il Poggio'
Via Marradi 45 – Siena

R.S.V.P.

Invitation to a christening

Invitations to parties are usually by word of mouth, while for weddings announcements are usually sent out.

Fabrizio Castelli e Katherine Ferguson
partecipano la nascita di Luigi

Vi invitano al suo battesimo nel Duomo di Barga
il 15 febbraio 2005 alle ore 12.00
e al rinfresco che seguirà alla Locanda da Gabriele
in località la Mocchia di Barga

RSVP *tel. 0583 – 861042*

- When a phone number is given after RSVP you reply to the invitation by phone.

. . . .

Invito (informale)

- *La data si può anche scrivere nei modi seguenti: April 10, 10 April, 10th April. Il nome del mese è in maiuscolo.*

- *In alto a destra si indica il nome e l'indirizzo del mittente, e sotto si scrive la data.*

35 Winchester Drive
Stoke Gifford
Bristol
BS34 8PD

April 22nd 2003

Dear Luca,

Is there any chance of your coming to stay with us in the summer holidays? Roy and Debbie would be delighted if you could (as well as David and me, of course). We hope to go to North Wales at the end of July/beginning of August, and you'd be very welcome to come too. It's really beautiful up there. We'll probably take tents - I hope that's OK by you.

Let me know as soon as possible if you can manage it.

All best wishes

Rachel Hemmings

Invito (formale)

Invito a un matrimonio e al rinfresco

Mr and Mrs Peter Thompson

request the pleasure of your company

at the marriage of their daughter

Hannah Louise

to

Steven David Warner

at St Mary's Church, Little Bourton

on Saturday 22nd July 2001 at 2 p.m.

And afterwards at the Golden Cross Hotel, Billing

R.S.V.P

23 Santers Lane
Little Bourton
Northampton
NN6 1AZ

Accepting an invitation (formal)

CARLO E BEATRICE BUOZZI

*ringraziano calorosamente per il gentile invito
e sono lieti di poter partecipare.*

Invitation (informal)

Cara Claudia

*È un po' che non ci sentiamo ma spero che tutto vada bene,
sia con Andrea che con l'università. Il 7 agosto è il mio
compleanno e pensavo di fare una festa. Che ne dici ① di
venire qui a Napoli? Naturalmente sei invitata a casa mia
per qualche giorno e ne approfitteremo per fare un po' di
chiacchiere e un po' di mare. Fammi sapere al più presto!
Spero tanto che tu venga, da sola o accompagnata, se tu e
Andrea state ancora insieme. Il mio indirizzo email è
grazia@hotmail.com.*

Un bacione ② e a prestissimo,

Grazia

■ *Invitations to parties are usually made in person or on the phone, unless it's a really formal occasion.*

① *For a letter to a friend you use the 'tu' form.*

② *This affectionate ending is used with close friends or relatives. Other informal endings are Baci or Un abbraccio.*

Accepting an invitation (informal)

24 aprile 2005

Cara Grazia

*Quanto tempo! Scusa se non mi sono fatta più viva ma tra
gli esami e altre storie il tempo è volato. Certo che vengo giù
a Napoli. L'ultimo esame lo dovrei avere a fine luglio e non
ho ancora programmato niente per le vacanze, tanto più
che adesso sono sola (mollata da Andrea due mesi fa, ma
senza troppi drammi). Ora che ci siamo rimesse in
contatto prometto di non sparire e non vedo l'ora di
rivederti di persona. Torno a studiare.*

Un abbraccio,

Claudia

■ *In informal letters you write the date at the top but not your address.*

■ *In replies to informal invitations you also use only the Christian name, the 'tu' form and an affectionate ending.*

. . . .

Per accettare un invito (informale)

> *Luca Vallerini*
> *viale Italia 78*
> *20162 Milano*
>
> *2 May 2003*
>
> Dear Mrs Hemmings ①,
>
> Many thanks for your letter and kind invitation. Since I don't have anything fixed yet for the summer holidays, I'd be delighted to come. However I mustn't be away for more than four or five days since my mother hasn't been very well.
>
> You must let me know what I should bring. How warm is it in North Wales? Can you swim in the sea? Camping is fine as far as I'm concerned, we take our tents everywhere.
>
> Looking forward to seeing you soon,
>
> Yours ②,
>
> Luca

Letters / Lettere

① *Questa è la lettera che un ragazzo scrive alla madre di un amico e quindi, anche se il tono generale è informale, si apre in modo piuttosto formale.*

② *Altre formule per questo tipo di lettera:* With best wishes, Yours sincerely, Kind/Kindest regards.

Risposta a un invito (formale)

> **Per accettare:** Richard Willis has great pleasure in accepting Mr and Mrs Peter Thompson's kind invitation to the marriage of their daughter Hannah Louise to Steven Warner at St Mary's Church, Little Bourton, on Saturday 22nd July.
>
> **Per declinare:** Richard Willis regrets that he is unable to accept Mr and Mrs Peter Thompson's kind invitation to . . . ., owing to a prior engagement.

- *Si ripetono i particolari dell'invito, ma in modo meno dettagliato.*
- *Nel caso non si possa accettare l'invito è consigliabile scrivere una lettera ai genitori della sposa, specialmente se si conoscono di persona.*

Letters / Lettere

Replying to a job advertisement

- *When you don't know the name of the person use this style. If you are writing to a company you can also use* Spett.le Ditta.

- *In letters written in reply to an advertisement you should make specific reference to the advert: under* oggetto *you put the position you are applying for with the reference number or abbreviation, as well as the newspaper and date that the advert appeared.*

Bristol, 25 settembre 2005

Grifoni S.p.a.
viale Marconi, 67
20100 Milano

Oggetto: ricerca programmatore
Rif. AB 067
Corriere della Sera 12.09.2005

Gentili Signori

Ho letto con molto interesse il Vostro annuncio apparso sul Corriere della Sera del 12 settembre scorso e Vi sarei grato se poteste inviarmi ulteriori informazioni riguardo la posizione in oggetto.

Attualmente sono impiegato presso un'azienda di Bristol ma il mio contratto termina alla fine del mese e vorrei approfittare di questa opportunità per lavorare a Milano. Come risulta dal curriculum vitae che allego alla presente, oltre a possedere i titoli e l'esperienza richiesti, ho vissuto per qualche tempo in Italia ed ho un'ottima conoscenza della lingua italiana.

Resto a disposizione per un eventuale colloquio nel momento che riterrete più opportuno e faccio presente che dal 6 ottobre prossimo sarò raggiungibile a Milano al seguente indirizzo:

via Indipendenza 7
20100 Milano
tel. 02 429.96.67

In attesa di un Vostro cortese riscontro porgo cordiali saluti

David Baker
67 Whiteley Avenue
Bristol, BS5 6TW
UK

- *When you are writing you should always include your own address after the signature either on the right or on the left.*

• •

Risposta a un annuncio di lavoro

---

via Giolitti 32
00100 Rome

26 September 2005

The Personnel Manager ①
Patterson Software plc
Milton State
Bath BA6 8YZ

Dear Sir or Madam ①,

I am interested in the post of programmer advertised in The Guardian of 12 September and would be very grateful if you could send me further particulars. ②

I am currently working for the Sempo Corporation, but my contract finishes at the end of the month, and I would like ③ to come and work in England. As you can see from my CV (enclosed), I have an excellent command of English and also the required qualifications and experience.

I will be available for interview any time after 6th October, from which date I can be contacted at the following address in the UK:

c/o Lewis
51 Dexter Road
London N7 6BW
Tel. 0208 607 5512

I look forward to hearing from you. ④

Yours sincerely

Maria Luisa Bianchi

Encl.

---

① *Oppure:* Ms Angela Summers, … *se nell'inserzione compare* Reply to Angela Summers; *oppure* Dear Ms Summers, Dear Mrs Wright *se compare solo il cognome.*

② *Oppure:* and would like to apply for this position, *se l'annuncio è ben dettagliato.*

③ *Se al momento si è disoccupati si scrive invece:* I am currently looking for work and I would like…

④ *Oppure:* Thanking you in anticipation/advance.

Curriculum Vitae

CURRICULUM VITAE

Nome e cognome	Gina Allen
Luogo e data di nascita	Birmingham, 21 settembre 1981
Residenza	127 Chatterton Terrace
	Londra W10 4RT, Gran Bretagna
Telefono abitazione	+44 (0)20 8741390
Telefono cellulare	+44 776 63294031
Indirizzo di posta elettronica	gina.allen@aol.com
Stato civile	Nubile ①
Nazionalità	Britannica ②

FORMAZIONE

1996–1998	'A Levels' (equivalente al diploma di scuola secondaria superiore) in italiano, storia e storia dell'arte, presso il Fulham Sixth Form College
1998–1999	Soggiorno in Italia durante il quale ho seguito un corso di italiano per stranieri a Bologna.
1999–2002	Laurea in storia dell'arte, University of Westminster di Londra, con tesi sul Mantegna.
	Durante l'ultimo anno di corso ho fatto uno stage presso la casa d'aste Sotheby's.
autunno 2002	Corso trimestrale di ricerca fotografica.

ESPERIENZE LAVORATIVE

dal luglio 2004	Ricercatrice fotografica presso la casa editrice Zoom. Mi occupo della ricerca iconografica per le pubblicazioni d'arte.
2003–2004	Assistente presso l'archivio fotografico 'PhotoArt' di Londra, specializzato in immagini di Belle Arti.
1998–1999	Impiego part-time presso un'agenzia di viaggi di Bologna.
Conoscenze linguistiche	Inglese madrelingua - Italiano buono parlato e scritto
Conoscenze informatiche	Buone conoscenze. Esperienza di ISDN/Photoshop
Interessi	Fotografia, cinema, yoga, ciclismo

① *A single man would put* celibe. *Otherwise you could put* coniugato/a *(you can add, if it is relevant,* senza figli *or* un figlio *etc.),* divorziato/a, vedovo/a.

② *Italian men also have to add whether they have completed their military service.*

CURRICULUM VITAE ①

Name:	Maria Luisa Bianchi
Address:	via Giolitti 32
	00100 Rome
	Italy
Telephone:	(+39) 06 243 53 94
Nationality:	Italian
Date of Birth:	11/3/73

EDUCATION:

1990–95	Degree Course in Information Technology and English at Università degli Studi of Rome.
1987–1991	Diploma di Maturità Scientifica (equivalent to A levels) at the Liceo Scientifico in Rome.

EMPLOYMENT:

1996–present	Program development engineer with Sempo Informatica, Rome, specializing in computer graphics.
1995–1996	Trainee programmer with Oregon-Italia, Rome.

FURTHER SKILLS:

Languages:	Italian (mother tongue),
	English (fluent, spoken and written),
	French (good).
Interests:	Travel, fashion, tennis.

① Oppure: Resumé *(inglese americano)*

Inquiry to a tourist office

9 febbraio 2005

Azienda di promozione turistica
Piazza Duomo 2
07100 Sassari

Gentili Signori

Sto programmando di trascorrere le vacanze in Sardegna con la famiglia
e sarei grato se volessero inviarmi un elenco delle case vacanza e dei
campeggi nella zona di San Teodoro.

Grazie per l'attenzione.

> Distinti saluti
> Brian McGregor
> 16 Victoria Road
> London
> SW2 5HU
> UK

■ *Standard formula for closing a formal letter.*

Lettera all'ufficio del turismo

■ *Formula standard nella corrispondenza commerciale quando non si conosce il nome del destinatario e non si sa se sia uomo o donna. Nel caso di una ditta o un ente si può anche scrivere* Dear Sirs *(come in questo caso, se la lettera fosse indirizzata a* The Regional Tourist Office, *anziché a* The Manager*).*

---

via Manzoni 9
16100 Genoa
Italy

4th May 2005

The Manager
Regional Tourist Office
3 Virgin Road
Canterbury
CT1 3AA

Dear Sir or Madam,

Please send me a list of hotels and guesthouses in Canterbury in the medium price range.

I would also like details of coach trips to local sights in the second half of August.

Yours faithfully

Antonio Brizzi

■ *Formula di saluto che si usa nelle lettere formali, quando non si conosce il nome del destinatario. Si chiudono così le lettere che si aprono con* Dear Sir or Madam, Dear Sirs, Dear Sir *o* Dear Madam.

Booking a hotel room

18 giugno 2004

Hotel La rosa
Corso del Partigiano, 56
22100 Como

Gentile Signora Pacini ①
In seguito alla conversazione telefonica di stamattina, le scrivo
per confermare la prenotazione di una camera doppia con bagno
② dall'8 al 12 luglio. Mia moglie ed io arriveremo nel tardo
pomeriggio di giovedì 8. Per ogni comunicazione urgente il mio
numero di telefono è +44 031 5790 3352.

Cordiali saluti
P. Bromfield
Cardross Gardens
Edinburgh
EH2 5EG
Gran Bretagna

① *Alternatively you can write* Gentili Signori *if you don't know the name of the person you are writing to.*

② *Or:* una camera singola/con doccia

Booking a place in a campsite

Campeggio `Il Gabbiano'
Via del Parco
14100 Asti

5 maggio 2005

Egregi signori,

il Vostro campeggio mi è stato segnalato dall'Ufficio del
turismo di Asti. Vorrei prenotare una piazzola per la nostra
tenda dal 5 al 15 agosto. Preferirei un posto tranquillo,
possibilmente non troppo vicino al mini-market.

Resto in attesa di una Vostra conferma.

Cordiali saluti,

Mary J Stevens
55 Old Road
Wallingford OX10 5DH
Gran Bretagna

. . . .

Prenotazione di una camera d'albergo

The Manager
Torbay Hotel
Dawlish
Devon
EX37 2LR

35 Prince Edward Road
Oxford OX7 3AA

Tel. 01865 322435

23rd April 2003

Dear Sir or Madam,

I saw your hotel listed in the Inns of Devon guide for last year, and wish to reserve a double (or twin-bedded) room with shower ① in a quiet position from August 2nd-11th (nine nights), also a single room for my son.

If you have anything suitable for this period please let me know the price and whether you require a deposit.

Yours faithfully,

Charles Fairhurst

① *Oppure:*
with bath/with
ensuite.

Prenotazione in un campeggio

22 Daniel Avenue
Caldwood
Leeds LS8 7RR

Tel. 01132 998767

25th April 2003

Mr Joseph Vale
Lakeside Park
Rydal
Cumbria
LA22 9RZ

Dear Mr Vale,

Your campsite was recommended to me by James Dallas, who knows it from several visits ① . I and two friends would like to come for a week from July 18th to 25th. Could you please reserve us a pitch for one tent ②, preferably close to the shore ③.

Please confirm the booking and let me know if you require a deposit. Would you also be good enough to send me instructions on how to reach you from the motorway.

Yours sincerely,

Frances Good

① *O se si è trovato
il nome del
campeggio in una
guida, un depliant
o su Internet:*
I found your site
in the Good
Camper's Guide/
the Tourist
Board's list/on a
website ecc.

② *Oppure:*
a pitch for one
caravan.

③ *Per una posizione
alternativa:*
in a shady/
sheltered spot.

Letters / Lettere

Cancelling a reservation

16 maggio 2005

Pensione La Torre
via Don Bosco 61
Chiusdino
Grosseto

Gentili Signori,
la settimana scorsa ho prenotato telefonicamente una camera
singola dal 6 al 12 giugno. Sono molto spiacente ma, per motivi
familiari, mi trovo costretta a rimandare il soggiorno in
Toscana e perciò a disdire la prenotazione.
Sperando di non aver arrecato troppo disturbo, porgo distinti
saluti.

Sally Lewis
56 Nelson Rd
Farnborough
GU14 9RK
Hants
UK

Per disdire una prenotazione

via Giotto 2
90100 Palermo
Italy

July 20th 2002

Mrs J. Warrington
Downlands
Steyning
West Sussex
BN44 6LZ

Dear Mrs Warrington,
Unfortunately I have to cancel my/our reservation for the week of
August 7th ①. Due to unforeseen circumstances ②, I/we have had
to abandon my/our holiday plans.
I very much regret having to cancel (at such a late stage) and hope
it does not cause you undue inconvenience.
Yours sincerely,

Carlo Rubini

① *Oppure:*
for the period
from August 7th
to 14th.

② *Altri possibili
motivi:*
Owing to my
father's sudden
death/my wife's
ilness/son's
hospitalization
ecc.

Letters / Lettere

Sending an e-mail

The illustration shows a typical interface for sending e-mail.

File Modifica Visualizza Messagio Inserisci Formato ?

A: anna.rossi@hotmail.com
Da: gaia@yahoo.it
Oggetto: foto

Ciao Anna ①

ora che sono anch'io collegato ② a Internet sarà più facile comunicare! Allego ③ alcune foto delle vacanze in montagna. Ci siamo divertiti un sacco questa volta.

Un bacione ④

Gaia

Letters / Lettere

① *The beginning changes according to how formal it is. You can use caro/cara or leave it out.*

② Collegata *if the person writing is a girl or woman.*

③ Allegare *means to enclose and also to attach in e-mails.*

④ *In more formal e-mails you can end with* 'Distinti saluti' *like in letters.*

E-mail

File Edit View Mail Insert Format Help

Subject: < click here to enter the subject >

Dear Katie,

Just a quick note to let you know that I received your test e-mail. I'm glad that we can communicate over the Internet and I look forward to receiving that attachment you promised me.

All the best,

Clare

SMS (electronic text-messaging)

The basic principles governing Italian SMS abbreviations are similar to those governing English SMS. Certain words or syllables can be represented by letters or numbers that sound the same but take up less space. The word 'sei', for example, can be replaced by '6', and the word 'che' shortened to 'ke'. Another way of shortening words and phrases is simply to omit certain letters, especially vowels. For example, 'comunque' becomes 'cmq' and 'ci vediamo dopo' becomes 'cvd'.

As in English, 'faccine' (emoticons) are very popular, and some of the more established ones are included in the table below.

Glossary of Italian SMS abbreviations

Abbreviation	Full word
"xxx"	tanti baci
+o-	più o meno
6 la +	sei la migliore
6 sxme	sei speciale per me
amò	amore
ap	a presto
axitivo	aperitivo
ba	bacio
cel	cellulare
cmq	comunque
cvd	ci vediamo dopo
dom	domani
dx	destra
ke	che
-male	meno male
midi	mi dispiace
MMT+	mi manchi tantissimo
msg	messaggio
Nm	numero
Nn	non
qlc	qualcuno
qls	qualcosa
risp	rispondimi
sx	sinistra
t tel + trd	ti telefono + tardi
tat	ti amo tanto
tel	telefono
tipe	ti penso
to	ti odio
ttp	torno tra un pò
tu6	tu sei

Abbreviation	Full word
tvb	ti voglio bene
tvtb	ti voglio tanto bene
vng dp	vengo dopo
x	per
x fv	per favore
x me	per me
xdere	perdere
xh	per ora
xké	perché

*Emoticons**

:-)	sorriso
:-(	tristezza
:-D	risata
;-)	strizzare l'occhio
:-*	baciare
!(	occhio nero
:-/	scettico
:'(	piangere
#:-o	traumatizzato
:-i	penso
:-o	sorpreso
:-q	nauseato
:-P	linguaccia
$)	felice di aver vinto la lotteria
:*)	pagliaccio
*<:-)	Babbo Natale

*NB: the '-' which depicts the nose is often omitted or replaced by an 'o' e.g. :) or :o)

SMS (messaggi elettronici)

Poiché lo spazio per gli SMS è limitato (solitamente 160 caratteri al massimo), anche in inglese quando si scrive un messaggino si ricorre a molte abbreviazioni. Spesso si accorciano le parole eliminando alcune lettere, ad esempio 'please' è in genere abbreviato con 'pls'. Un altro metodo consiste nel sostituire alcune parole o suoni con numeri o lettere. Un tipico esempio è l'uso di '2' invece della parola 'to' e della lettera 'U' al posto di 'you'.

Anche gli 'emoticons' (le faccine) sono popolari e alcuni dei più usati si trovano nel glossario qui sotto.

Glossario di abbreviazioni SMS inglesi

Abbreviazione	Senso
afaik	as far as I know
atb	all the best
b4	before
bbl	be back late(r)
brb	be right back
btw	by the way
cu	see you
cul8r	see you later
f2f	face to face
fwiw	for what it's worth
fyi	for your information
gr8	great
h8	hate
hand	have a nice day
hth	hope this helps
ic	I see
imho	in my humble opinion
imo	in my opinion
iow	in other words
jk	just kidding
lol	laughing out loud/lots of luck
msg	message
myob	mind your own business
ne1	anyone
no1	no one
oic	oh I see
otoh	on the other hand
pls	please
ppl	people
r	are
rofl	rolling on the floor, laughing

Abbreviazione	Senso
ruok	are you OK?
som1	someone
thkq	thank you
tx	thanks
ur	you are
wan2	want to
wot	what
xlnt	excellent
2moro	tomorrow

Faccina*	
:-)	happy face
:-(	sad face
:-D	laughing
;-)	winking
:-*	big kiss!
!(	black eye
:-/	sceptical
:'(	crying
#:-o	traumatized
:-i	I'm thinking
:-o	surprised
:-q	feeling sick
:-P	tongue sticking out
$)	I've just won the lottery
:*)	clown
@}-,-'--	a rose

*NB: il '-' che rappresenta il naso è spesso sostituito con 'o' ad es. :) o :o)

SMS

a¹, **A** /eɪ/ (letter) a, A *f inv*; Mus la *m inv*

a² /ə/ **①** stressed /eɪ/ (before a vowel **an**) *indef art* un *m*, una *f*; (before s + consonant, *gn*, *ps*, *z*) uno; (before *nf* starting with vowel) un'; (each) a; **I am a lawyer** sono avvocato; **a tiger is a feline** la tigre è un felino; **a knife and fork** un coltello e una forchetta; **a Mr Smith is looking for you** un certo signor Smith ti sta cercando; **£2 a kilo/a head** due sterline al chilo/a testa
② *n* Mus la *m inv*

A & E *n* Br *abbr* (**Accident and Emergency**) pronto soccorso *m*

A2 *n* ⟨*exam/course*⟩ esame *m* sostenuto al termine del secondo anno del biennio di preparazione agli A-Level

A4 *adj* A4

AA *n* Br *abbr* (**Automobile Association**) ≈ A.C.I. *m*; *abbr* **Alcoholics Anonymous**

AAA *n* Am *abbr* (**American Automobile Association**) ≈ A.C.I. *m*

aback /ə'bæk/ *adv* **be taken** ~ essere preso in contropiede

abacus /'æbəkəs/ *n* (pl **-cuses**) abaco *m*

abandon /ə'bændən/ **①** *vt* abbandonare; (give up) rinunciare a
② *n* abbandono *m*

abandoned /ə'bændnd/ *adj* abbandonato; ⟨*behaviour*⟩ dissoluto

abandonment /ə'bændnmənt/ *n* (of strike, plan etc) rinuncia *f*

abashed /ə'bæʃt/ *adj* imbarazzato

abate /ə'beɪt/ *vi* calmarsi

abattoir /'æbətwɑː(r)/ *n* mattatoio *m*

abbess /'æbes/ *n* badessa *f*

abbey /'æbɪ/ *n* abbazia *f*

abbot /'æbət/ *n* abate *m*

abbreviate /ə'briːvɪeɪt/ *vt* abbreviare

abbreviation /əbriːvɪ'eɪʃn/ *n* abbreviazione *f*

ABC **①** *n* (alphabet) alfabeto *m*; **the** ~ **of** (basics) l'ABC *m inv* di
② *n abbr* (**American Broadcasting Company**) rete *f* televisiva americana

abdicate /'æbdɪkeɪt/ **①** *vi* abdicare
② *vt* rinunciare a

abdication /æbdɪ'keɪʃn/ *n* abdicazione *f*

abdomen /'æbdəmən/ *n* addome *m*

abdominal /əb'dɒmɪnl/ *adj* addominale

abduct /əb'dʌkt/ *vt* rapire

abduction /əb'dʌkʃn/ *n* rapimento *m*

abductor /əb'dʌktə(r)/ *n* rapitore, -trice *mf*

aberrant /ə'berənt/ *adj* ⟨*behaviour, nature*⟩ aberrante

aberration /æbə'reɪʃn/ *n* aberrazione *f*

abet /ə'bet/ *vt* (pt/pp **abetted**) **aid and** ~ Jur essere complice di

abeyance /ə'beɪəns/ *n* **in** ~ in sospeso; **fall into** ~ cadere in disuso

abhor /əb'hɔː(r)/ *vt* (pt/pp **abhorred**) aborrire

abhorrence /əb'hɒrəns/ *n* orrore *m*

abhorrent /əb'hɒrənt/ *adj* ripugnante

abide /ə'baɪd/ **①** *vt* (pt/pp **abided**) (tolerate) sopportare
② **abide by** *vi* rispettare

abiding /ə'baɪdɪŋ/ *adj* perpetuo

ability /ə'bɪlətɪ/ *n* capacità *f inv*

abject /'æbdʒekt/ *adj* ⟨*poverty*⟩ degradante; ⟨*apology*⟩ umile; ⟨*coward*⟩ abietto

ablative /'æblətɪv/ *n* ablativo *m*

ablaze /ə'bleɪz/ *adj* in fiamme; **be** ~ **with light** risplendere di luci

able /'eɪbl/ *adj* capace, abile; **be** ~ **to do something** poter fare qualcosa; **were you** ~ **to...?** sei riuscito a...?

able-bodied /-'bɒdɪd/ *adj* robusto; Mil abile

able seaman *n* marinaio *m* scelto

ably /'eɪblɪ/ *adv* abilmente

abnegation /æbnɪ'geɪʃn/ *n* (of rights, privileges) rinuncia *f*; (self-abnegation) abnegazione *f*

abnormal /æb'nɔːml/ *adj* anormale

abnormality /æbnɔː'mælətɪ/ *n* anormalità *f inv*

abnormally /æb'nɔːməlɪ/ *adv* in modo anormale

aboard /ə'bɔːd/ *adv & prep* a bordo

abode /ə'bəʊd/ *n* dimora *f*

abolish /ə'bɒlɪʃ/ *vt* abolire

abolition /æbə'lɪʃn/ *n* abolizione *f*

abominable /ə'bɒmɪnəbl/ *adj* abominevole

abominably /ə'bɒmɪnəblɪ/ *adv* disgustosamente

abominate /ə'bɒmɪneɪt/ *vt* abominare

aboriginal /æbə'rɪdʒɪnl/ *adj & n* (native) aborigeno, -a *mf*, indigeno, -a *mf*

Aborigine /æbə'rɪdʒəniː/ *n* aborigeno, -a *mf* d'Australia

abort /ə'bɔːt/ *vt* fare abortire; fig annullare

abortion /əˈbɔːʃn/ n aborto m; **have an** ~ abortire

abortionist /əˈbɔːʃnɪst/ n persona f che pratica aborti, specialmente clandestini

abortive /əˈbɔːtɪv/ adj ‹attempt› infruttuoso

abound /əˈbaʊnd/ vi abbondare (**in** di)

about /əˈbaʊt/ **1** adv (here and there) [di] qua e [di] là; (approximately) circa; **be** ~ ‹illness, tourists› essere in giro; **be up and** ~ essere alzato; **leave something lying** ~ lasciare in giro qualcosa
2 prep (concerning) su; (in the region of) intorno a; (here and there in) per; **what is the book/the film** ~? di cosa parla il libro/il film?; **he wants to see you –what** ~? ti vuole vedere –a che proposito?; **talk/know** ~ parlare/sapere di; **I know nothing** ~ it non ne so niente; ~ **5 o'clock** intorno alle 5; **travel** ~ **the world** viaggiare per il mondo; **be** ~ **to do something** stare per fare qualcosa; **how** ~ **going to the cinema?** e se andassimo al cinema?

about-face n, **about-turn** n dietro front m inv

above /əˈbʌv/ adv & prep sopra; ~ **all** soprattutto

above-board adj onesto

above-ground adv in superficie

above-mentioned /-menʃnd/ adj suddetto

above-named /-neɪmd/ adj suddetto

abrasion /əˈbreɪʒn/ n (injury) abrasione f

abrasive /əˈbreɪsɪv/ **1** adj abrasivo; (remark) caustico
2 n abrasivo m

abreast /əˈbrest/ adv fianco a fianco; **come** ~ **of** allinearsi con; **keep** ~ **of** tenersi al corrente di

abridged /əˈbrɪdʒd/ adj ridotto

abridg[e]ment /əˈbrɪdʒmnt/ n (version) edizione f ridotta

abroad /əˈbrɔːd/ adv all'estero

abrupt /əˈbrʌpt/ adj brusco

abruptly /əˈbrʌptlɪ/ adv bruscamente

ABS n abbr (**anti-lock braking system**) ABS m inv

abscess /ˈæbsɪs/ n ascesso m

abscond /əbˈskɒnd/ vi fuggire

abseiling /ˈæbseɪlɪŋ/ n Br discesa f a corda doppia; **to go** ~ fare discesa a corda doppia

absence /ˈæbsəns/ n assenza f, (lack) mancanza f

absent[1] /ˈæbsənt/ adj assente

absent[2] /æbˈsent/ vt ~ **oneself** essere assente

absentee /æbsənˈtiː/ n assente mf

absenteeism /æbsənˈtiːɪzm/ n assenteismo m

absentee landlord n proprietario m che affitta una casa in cui non abita

absently /ˈæbsntlɪ/ adv ‹say, look› distrattamente

absent-minded /-ˈmaɪndɪd/ adj distratto

absent-mindedly /-ˈmaɪndɪdlɪ/ adv distrattamente

absent-mindedness /-ˈmaɪndɪdnɪs/ n distrazione f

absolute /ˈæbsəluːt/ adj assoluto; **an** ~ **idiot** un perfetto idiota

absolutely /ˈæbsəluːtlɪ/ adv assolutamente; (fam: indicating agreement) esattamente; ~ **not** assolutamente no

absolution /æbsəˈluːʃn/ n assoluzione f

absolve /əbˈzɒlv/ vt assolvere

absorb /əbˈsɔːb/ vt assorbire; ~**ed in** assorto in

absorbency /əbˈsɔːbənsɪ/ n capacità f d'assorbimento

absorbent /əbˈsɔːbənt/ adj assorbente

absorbent cotton n Am cotone m idrofilo, ovatta f

absorbing /əbˈsɔːbɪŋ/ adj avvincente

absorption /əbˈsɔːpʃn/ n assorbimento m; (in activity) concentrazione f

abstain /əbˈsteɪn/ vi astenersi (**from** da)

abstemious /əbˈstiːmɪəs/ adj moderato

abstention /əbˈstenʃn/ n Pol astensione f

abstinence /ˈæbstɪnəns/ n astinenza f

abstract /ˈæbstrækt/ **1** adj astratto
2 n astratto m; (summary) estratto m

abstraction /əbˈstrækʃn/ n **an air of** ~ un'aria distratta

absurd /əbˈsɜːd/ adj assurdo

absurdity /əbˈsɜːdətɪ/ n assurdità f inv

absurdly /əbˈsɜːdlɪ/ adv assurdamente

abundance /əˈbʌndəns/ n abbondanza f

abundant /əˈbʌndənt/ adj abbondante

abundantly /əˈbʌndəntlɪ/ adv ~ **clear** più che chiaro

abuse[1] /əˈbjuːz/ vt (misuse) abusare di; (insult) insultare; (ill-treat) maltrattare

abuse[2] /əˈbjuːs/ n abuso m; (verbal) insulti mpl; (ill-treatment) maltrattamento m; ~ **of power** sopraffazione f

abusive /əˈbjuːsɪv/ adj offensivo

abut /əˈbʌt/ vi (pt/pp **abutted**) confinare (**onto** con)

abysmal /əˈbɪzml/ adj fam pessimo; ‹ignorance› abissale

abyss /əˈbɪs/ n abisso m

a/c abbr (**account**) c/c

academia /ækəˈdiːmɪə/ n mondo m accademico

academic /ækə'demɪk/ **1** *adj* teorico; ⟨*qualifications, system*⟩ scolastico; **be ~** ⟨*person*⟩ avere predisposizione allo studio **2** *n* docente *mf* universitario, -a

academically /ækə'demɪklɪ/ *adv* ⟨*gifted*⟩ accademicamente

academician /əkædə'mɪʃn/ *n* accademico, -a *mf*

academy /ə'kædəmɪ/ *n* accademia *f*; (of music) conservatorio *m*

ACAS /'eɪkæs/ *n* Br *abbr* (**Advisory Conciliation and Arbitration Service**) organismo *m* pubblico di mediazione tra i lavoratori e i datori di lavoro

accede /ək'siːd/ *vi* **~ to** accedere a ⟨*request*⟩; salire a ⟨*throne*⟩

accelerate /ək'seləreɪt/ *vt/i* accelerare

acceleration /əksələ'reɪʃn/ *n* accelerazione *f*

accelerator /ək'seləreɪtə(r)/ *n* Auto, Comput acceleratore *m*

accent¹ /'æksənt/ *n* accento *m*

accent² /æk'sent/ *vt* accentare

accented /'æksəntɪd/ *adj* ⟨*speech*⟩ con accento marcato

accentuate /ək'sentjʊeɪt/ *vt* accentuare

accept /ək'sept/ *vt* accettare

acceptability /ækseptə'bɪlɪtɪ/ *n* ammissibilità *f*

acceptable /ək'septəbl/ *adj* accettabile

acceptance /ək'septəns/ *n* accettazione *f*

access /'ækses/ **1** *n* accesso *m* **2** *vt* Comput accedere a

accessible /ək'sesəbl/ *adj* accessibile

accession /ək'seʃn/ *n* ⟨*to throne*⟩ ascesa *f* al trono

accessory /ək'sesərɪ/ *n* accessorio *m*; Jur complice *mf*

accident /'æksɪdənt/ *n* incidente *m*; (chance) caso *m*; **by ~** per caso; (unintentionally) senza volere; **I'm sorry, it was an ~** mi dispiace, non l'ho fatto apposta

accidental /æksɪ'dentl/ *adj* ⟨*meeting*⟩ casuale; ⟨*death*⟩ incidentale; (unintentional) involontario

accidentally /æksɪ'dentəlɪ/ *adv* per caso; (unintentionally) inavvertitamente

accident-prone *adj* soggetto a incidenti

acclaim /ə'kleɪm/ **1** *n* acclamazione *f* **2** *vt* acclamare (**as** come)

acclimatization /əklaɪmətaɪ'zeɪʃn/ *n* acclimatazione *f*

acclimatize /ə'klaɪmətaɪz/ *vt* **become ~d** acclimatarsi

accolade /'ækəleɪd/ *n* riconoscimento *m*

accommodate /ə'kɒmədeɪt/ *vt* ospitare; (oblige) favorire

accommodating /ə'kɒmədeɪtɪŋ/ *adj* accomodante

accommodation /əkɒmə'deɪʃn/ *n* (place to stay) sistemazione *f*; **look for ~** cercare una sistemazione

accompaniment /ə'kʌmpənɪmənt/ *n* accompagnamento *m*

accompanist /ə'kʌmpənɪst/ *n* Mus accompagnatore, -trice *mf*

accompany /ə'kʌmpənɪ/ *vt* (pt/pp **-ied**) accompagnare

accomplice /ə'kʌmplɪs/ *n* complice *mf*

accomplish /ə'kʌmplɪʃ/ *vt* (achieve) concludere; realizzare ⟨*aim*⟩

accomplished /ə'kʌmplɪʃt/ *adj* dotato; ⟨*fact*⟩ compiuto

accomplishment /ə'kʌmplɪʃmənt/ *n* realizzazione *f*; (achievement) risultato *m*: (talent) talento *m*

accord /ə'kɔːd/ **1** *n* (treaty) accordo *m*; **with one ~** tutti d'accordo; **of his own ~** di sua spontanea volontà **2** *vt* accordare

accordance /ə'kɔːdəns/ *n* **in ~ with** in conformità di *o* a

according /ə'kɔːdɪŋ/ *adv* **~ to** secondo

accordingly /ə'kɔːdɪŋlɪ/ *adv* di conseguenza

accordion /ə'kɔːdɪən/ *n* fisarmonica *f*

accost /ə'kɒst/ *vt* abbordare

account /ə'kaʊnt/ *n* conto *m*; (report) descrizione *f*; (of eyewitness) resoconto *m*; **~s** *pl* Comm conti *mpl*; **on ~ of** a causa di; **on no ~** per nessun motivo; **on this ~** per questo motivo; **on my ~** per causa mia; **of no ~** di nessuna importanza; **take into ~** tener conto di
■ **account for** *vt* (explain) spiegare; ⟨*person*⟩ render conto di; (constitute) costituire; (destroy) distruggere

accountability /əkaʊntə'bɪlɪtɪ/ *n* responsabilità *f*

accountable /ə'kaʊntəbl/ *adj* responsabile (**for** di)

accountancy /ə'kaʊntənsɪ/ *n* ragioneria *f*, contabilità *f*

accountant /ə'kaʊntənt/ *n* (bookkeeper) contabile *mf*; ragioniere, -a *mf* (consultant) commercialista *mf*

account book *n* libro *m* contabile

account director *n* account director *mf inv*

account holder /ə'kaʊnthəʊldə(r)/ *n* (with bank, credit company) titolare *mf* del conto

accounting /ə'kaʊntɪŋ/ *n* (field) ragioneria *f*; (auditing) contabilità *f*

accounting period *n* periodo *m* contabile

account number *n* numero *m* di conto

a

accounts department n [ufficio m] contabilità f

accounts payable npl conto m creditori diversi

accounts receivable npl conto m creditori diversi

accoutrements /əˈkuːtrəmənts/ npl equipaggiamento msg

accredited /əˈkredɪtɪd/ adj accreditato

accretion /əˈkriːʃn/ n accrescimento m

accrue /əˈkruː/ vi ⟨interest⟩ maturare

accumulate /əˈkjuːmjʊleɪt/ ① vt accumulare
② vi accumularsi

accumulation /əkjuːmjʊˈleɪʃn/ n accumulazione f

accumulator /əˈkjuːmjʊleɪtə(r)/ n Electr accumulatore m

accuracy /ˈækjʊrəsɪ/ n precisione f

accurate /ˈækjʊrət/ adj preciso

accurately /ˈækjʊrətlɪ/ adv con precisione

accusation /ækjʊˈzeɪʃn/ n accusa f

accusative /əˈkjuːzətɪv/ adj & n ~ [case] Gram accusativo m

accuse /əˈkjuːz/ vt accusare; ~ somebody of doing something accusare qualcuno di fare qualcosa

accused /əˈkjuːzd/ n the ~ l'accusato m, l'accusata f

accuser /əˈkjuːzə(r)/ n accusatore, trice mf

accusing /əˈkjuːzɪŋ/ adj accusatore

accusingly /əˈkjuːzɪŋlɪ/ adv ⟨say, point⟩ in modo accusatorio

accustom /əˈkʌstəm/ vt abituare (to a)

accustomed /əˈkʌstəmd/ adj abituato; grow or get ~ to abituarsi a

ace /eɪs/ n (in cards) asso m; Tennis ace m inv

acerbic /əˈsɜːbɪk/ adj acido

acetate /ˈæsɪteɪt/ n acetato m

ache /eɪk/ ① n dolore m
② vi dolere, far male; ~ all over essere tutto indolenzito

achieve /əˈtʃiːv/ vt ottenere ⟨success⟩; realizzare ⟨goal, ambition⟩

achievement /əˈtʃiːvmənt/ n (feat) successo m

achiever /əˈtʃiːvə(r)/ n persona f di successo

Achilles' heel /əkɪliːzˈhiːl/ n tallone m di Achille

aching /ˈeɪkɪŋ/ adj ⟨body, limbs⟩ dolorante; an ~ void un vuoto incolmabile

acid /ˈæsɪd/ ① adj acido
② n acido m

acid drop n caramella f agli agrumi

acidic /əˈsɪdɪk/ adj acido

acidity /əˈsɪdətɪ/ n acidità f

acid rain n pioggia f acida

acid stomach n Med acidità f di stomaco

acid test n fig prova f del fuoco

acknowledge /əkˈnɒlɪdʒ/ vt riconoscere; rispondere a ⟨greeting⟩; far cenno di aver notato ⟨sb's presence⟩; ~ receipt of accusare ricevuta di; ~ defeat dichiararsi vinto

acknowledgement /əkˈnɒlɪdʒmənt/ n riconoscimento m; send an ~ of a letter confermare il ricevimento di una lettera

acme /ˈækmɪ/ n the ~ of l'apice m di

acne /ˈæknɪ/ n acne f

acorn /ˈeɪkɔːn/ n ghianda f

acoustic /əˈkuːstɪk/ adj acustico

acoustically /əˈkuːstɪklɪ/ adv acusticamente

acoustic guitar n chitarra f acustica

acoustics /əˈkuːstɪks/ npl acustica fsg

acquaint /əˈkweɪnt/ vt ~ somebody with metter qualcuno al corrente di

acquaintance /əˈkweɪntəns/ n ⟨person⟩ conoscente mf; make sb's ~ fare la conoscenza di qualcuno

acquainted adj be ~ with conoscere ⟨person⟩; essere a conoscenza di ⟨fact⟩; get or become ~ with somebody fare conoscenza con qualcuno; get or become ~ with something familiarizzare con qualcosa

acquiesce /ækwɪˈes/ vi acconsentire (to, in a)

acquiescence /ækwɪˈesəns/ n acquiescenza f

acquiescent /ækwɪˈesənt/ adj arrendevole

acquire /əˈkwaɪə(r)/ vt acquisire

acquired /əˈkwaɪəd/ adj ⟨characteristic⟩ acquisito; it's an ~ taste è una cosa che si impara ad apprezzare

acquisition /ækwɪˈzɪʃn/ n acquisizione f

acquisitive /əˈkwɪzətɪv/ adj avido

acquit /əˈkwɪt/ vt (pt/pp **acquitted**) assolvere; ~ oneself well cavarsela bene

acquittal /əˈkwɪtəl/ n assoluzione f

acre /ˈeɪkə(r)/ n acro m (= 4 047 m²)

acreage /ˈeɪkərɪdʒ/ n superficie f in acri

acrid /ˈækrɪd/ adj acre

acrimonious /ækrɪˈməʊnɪəs/ adj aspro

acrimony /ˈækrɪmənɪ/ n asprezza f

acrobat /ˈækrəbæt/ n acrobata mf

acrobatic /ækrəˈbætɪk/ adj acrobatico

acrobatics /ækrəˈbætɪks/ npl acrobazie fpl

acronym /ˈækrənɪm/ n acronimo m

across /əˈkrɒs/ ① adv dall'altra parte; (wide) in larghezza; (not lengthwise) attraverso; (in crossword) orizzontale; **come ~ something** imbattersi in qualcosa; **go ~** attraversare

2 *prep* (crosswise) di traverso su; (on the other side of) dall'altra parte di

across-the-board **1** *adj* generale
2 *adv* in generale

acrylic /ə'krɪlɪk/ **1** *n* acrilico *m*
2 *attrib* ⟨garment⟩ acrilico

act /ækt/ **1** *n* atto *m*; (in variety show) numero *m*; **put on an ~** fam fare scena
2 *vi* agire; (behave) comportarsi; Theat recitare; (pretend) fingere; **~ as** fare da
3 *vt* recitare ⟨role⟩
■ **act for** *vi* agire per conto di
■ **act out** *vt* recitare ⟨part⟩; mettere in atto ⟨fantasy⟩
■ **act up** *vi* ⟨child, photocopier⟩ fare i capricci

acting /'æktɪŋ/ **1** *adj* ⟨deputy⟩ provvisorio
2 *n* Theat recitazione *f*; (profession) teatro *m*; **~ profession** professione *f* dell'attore

action /'ækʃn/ *n* azione *f*; Mil combattimento *m*; Jur azione *f* legale; **out of ~** ⟨machine⟩ fuori uso; **take ~** agire; **~!** Cinema ciac si gira!

action group *n* gruppo *m* d'azione

action-packed *adj* ⟨film⟩ d'azione

action painting *n* pittura *f* d'azione

action plan *n* piano *m* d'azione

action replay *n* replay *m inv*

activate /'æktɪveɪt/ *vt* attivare; (Chem, Phys) rendere attivo

active /'æktɪv/ *adj* attivo

active duty, **active service** *n* Mil **be on ~ ~** prestare servizio in zona di operazioni

actively /'æktɪvlɪ/ *adv* attivamente

activist /'æktɪvɪst/ *n* attivista *mf*

activity /æk'tɪvətɪ/ *n* attività *f inv*

activity holiday *n* Br vacanza *f* con attività ricreative

act of God *n* causa *f* di forza maggiore

actor /'æktə(r)/ *n* attore *m*

actress /'æktrəs/ *n* attrice *f*

actual /'æktʃʊəl/ *adj* (real) reale

actually /'æktʃʊəlɪ/ *adv* in realtà

actuary /'æktʃʊərɪ/ *n* attuario, -a *mf*

acumen /'ækjʊmən/ *n* acume *m*

acupuncture /'ækjʊpʌŋktʃə(r)/ *n* agopuntura *f*

acupuncturist /ækjʊ'pʌŋktʃərɪst/ *n* agopuntore, -trice *mf*

acute /ə'kju:t/ *adj* acuto; ⟨shortage, hardship⟩ estremo

acute accent *n* accento *m* acuto

acute angle *n* angolo *m* acuto

acutely /ə'kju:tlɪ/ *adv* acutamente; ⟨embarrassed, aware⟩ estremamente

AD *abbr* (**Anno Domini**) d.C.

ad /æd/ *n* pubblicità *f inv*; (in paper) inserzione *f*, annuncio *m*

adage /'ædɪdʒ/ *n* detto *m*, adagio *m*

adamant /'ædəmənt/ *adj* categorico (**that** sul fatto che)

Adam's apple /'ædəmz/ *n* pomo *m* di Adamo

adapt /ə'dæpt/ **1** *vt* adattare ⟨play⟩
2 *vi* adattarsi

adaptability /ədæptə'bɪlətɪ/ *n* adattabilità *f*

adaptable /ə'dæptəbl/ *adj* adattabile

adaptation /ædæp'teɪʃn/ *n* Theat adattamento *m*

adapter, **adaptor** /ə'dæptə(r)/ *n* adattatore *m*; (two-way) presa *f* multipla

add /æd/ **1** *vt* aggiungere; Math addizionare
2 *vi* addizionare
■ **add in** *vt* (include) includere
■ **add on** *vt* aggiungere
■ **add to** *vi* (fig: increase) aggravare
■ **add up** **1** *vt* addizionare ⟨figures⟩
2 *vi* addizionare; **it doesn't ~ up** fig non quadra; **~ up to** ammontare a

added /'ædɪd/ *adj* maggiore

adder /'ædə(r)/ *n* vipera *f*

addict /'ædɪkt/ *n* tossicodipendente *mf*; fig fanatico, -a *mf*

addicted /ə'dɪktɪd/ *adj* assuefatto (**to** a); **~ to drugs** tossicodipendente; **he's ~ to television** è videodipendente

addiction /ə'dɪkʃn/ *n* dipendenza *f*; (to drugs) tossicodipendenza *f*

addictive /ə'dɪktɪv/ *adj* **be ~** dare assuefazione

addition /ə'dɪʃn/ *adj* Math addizione *f*; (thing added) aggiunta *f*; **in ~** in aggiunta

additional /ə'dɪʃnəl/ *adj* supplementare

additionally /ə'dɪʃnəlɪ/ *adv* in più

additive /'ædɪtɪv/ *n* additivo *m*

addled /'ædld/ *adj* ⟨thinking⟩ confuso

add-on *adj* accessorio

address /ə'dres/ **1** *n* indirizzo *m*; (speech) discorso *m*; **form of ~** formula *f* di cortesia
2 *vt* indirizzare; (speak to) rivolgersi a ⟨person⟩; tenere un discorso a ⟨meeting⟩

address book *n* rubrica *f*

addressee /ædre'si:/ *n* destinatario, -a *mf*

adenoids /'ædənɔɪdz/ *npl* adenoidi *fpl*

adept /'ædept/ *adj* esperto, -a *mf* (**at** in)

adequate /'ædɪkwət/ *adj* adeguato

adequately /'ædɪkwətlɪ/ *adv* adeguatamente

ADHD *abbr* (**Attention Deficit and Hyperactivity Disorder**) disturbo *m* da deficit dell'attenzione con iperattività

adhere /əd'hɪə(r)/ *vi* aderire; ∼ **to** attenersi a ⟨*principles, rules*⟩

adherence /əd'hɪərəns/ *n* fedeltà *f*

adherent /əd'hɪərənt/ *n* (of doctrine) adepto, -a *mf*; (of policy) sostenitore, -trice *mf*; (of cult) seguace *mf*

adhesion /əd'hi:ʒn/ *n* adesione *f*

adhesive /əd'hi:sɪv/ ① *adj* adesivo ② *n* adesivo *m*

ad hoc /æd'hɒk/ *adj* ⟨*alliance, arrangement*⟩ ad hoc; ⟨*committee, legislation*⟩ apposito; **on an ∼ ∼ basis** secondo le esigenze del momento

adieu /ə'dju:/ *n* **bid somebody ∼** dire addio a qualcuno

ad infinitum /ædɪmfɪ'naɪtəm/ *adv* ⟨*continue*⟩ all'infinito

adjacent /ə'dʒeɪsənt/ *adj* adiacente

adjective /'ædʒɪktɪv/ *n* aggettivo *m*

adjoin /ə'dʒɔɪn/ *vt* essere adiacente a

adjoining /ə'dʒɔɪnɪŋ/ *adj* adiacente

adjourn /ə'dʒɜ:n/ *vt* aggiornare (**until** a)

adjournment /ə'dʒɜ:nmənt/ *n* aggiornamento *m*

adjudge /ə'dʒʌdʒ/ *vt* Jur (decree) giudicare; aggiudicare ⟨*costs, damages*⟩

adjudicate /ə'dʒu:dɪkeɪt/ *vi* decidere; (in competition) giudicare

adjudicator /ə'dʒu:dɪkeɪtə(r)/ *n* giudice *m*, arbitro *m*

adjunct /'ædʒʌnkt/ *n* aggiunta *f*, (hum: person) appendice *f*

adjust /ə'dʒʌst/ ① *vt* modificare; regolare ⟨*focus, sound*⟩ ② *vi* adattarsi

adjustable /ə'dʒʌstəbl/ *adj* regolabile

adjustable spanner *n* chiave *f* [inglese] a rullino

adjustment /ə'dʒʌstmənt/ *n* adattamento *m*; Techn regolamento *m*

adjutant /'ædʒʊtənt/ *n* Mil aiutante *mf*

ad lib /æd'lɪb/ ① *adj* improvvisato ② *adv* a piacere ③ *vt* (pt/pp **ad libbed**) fam improvvisare

adman /'ædmæn/ *n* fam pubblicitario *m*

admin /'ædmɪn/ *n* Br fam amministrazione *f*

administer /əd'mɪnɪstə(r)/ *vt* amministrare; somministrare ⟨*medicine*⟩

administration /ədmɪnɪ'streɪʃn/ *n* amministrazione *f*; Pol governo *m*

administration costs *n* costi *mpl* di gestione

administrative /əd'mɪnɪstrətɪv/ *adj* amministrativo

administrator /əd'mɪnɪstreɪtə(r)/ *n* amministratore, -trice *mf*

admirable /'ædmərəbl/ *adj* ammirevole

admiral /'ædmərəl/ *n* ammiraglio *m*

admiralty /'ædmɪrəltɪ/ *n* Br ministero *m* della marina militare britannica

admiration /ædmə'reɪʃn/ *n* ammirazione *f*

admire /əd'maɪə(r)/ *vt* ammirare

admirer /əd'maɪrə(r)/ *n* ammiratore, -trice *mf*

admiring /əd'maɪrɪŋ/ *adj* ⟨*person*⟩ pieno d'ammirazione; ⟨*look*⟩ ammirativo

admiringly /əd'maɪrɪŋlɪ/ *adv* ⟨*look, say*⟩ con ammirazione

admissible /əd'mɪsəbl/ *adj* ammissibile

admission /əd'mɪʃn/ *n* ammissione *f*; (to hospital) ricovero *m*; (entry) ingresso *m*

admissions office *n* Univ segreteria *f* studenti

admit /əd'mɪt/ ① *vt* (pt/pp **admitted**) (let in) far entrare; (to hospital) ricoverare; (acknowledge) ammettere ② *vi* ∼ **to something** ammettere qualcosa

admittance /əd'mɪtəns/ *n* ammissione *f*; '**no ∼**' 'vietato l'ingresso'

admittedly /əd'mɪtɪdlɪ/ *adv* bisogna riconoscerlo

admonish /əd'mɒnɪʃ/ *vt* ammonire

admonition /ædmə'nɪʃn/ *n* ammonimento *m*

ad nauseam /æd'nɔ:zɪæm/ *adv* ⟨*discuss, repeat*⟩ fino alla nausea

ado /ə'du:/ *n* **without more ∼** senza ulteriori indugi

adolescence /ædə'lesns/ *n* adolescenza *f*

adolescent /ædə'lesnt/ *adj & n* adolescente *mf*

adopt /ə'dɒpt/ *vt* adottare; Pol scegliere ⟨*candidate*⟩

adopted /ə'dɒptɪd/ *adj* ⟨*son, daughter*⟩ adottivo

adoption /ə'dɒpʃn/ *n* adozione *f*

adoption agency *n* agenzia *f* di adozioni

adoptive /ə'dɒptɪv/ *adj* adottivo

adorable /ə'dɔ:rəbl/ *adj* adorabile

adoration /ædə'reɪʃn/ *n* adorazione *f*

adore /ə'dɔ:(r)/ *vt* adorare

adoring /ə'dɔ:rɪŋ/ *adj* ⟨*fan*⟩ in adorazione; **she has an ∼ husband** ha un marito che la adora

adoringly /ə'dɔ:rɪŋlɪ/ *adv* con adorazione

adorn /ə'dɔ:n/ *vt* adornare

adornment /ə'dɔ:nmənt/ *n* ornamento *m*

adrenalin /ə'drenəlɪn/ *n* adrenalina *f*

Adriatic /eɪdrɪ'ætɪk/ *adj & n* **the ∼** [Sea] il mare Adriatico, l'Adriatico *m*

adrift /ə'drɪft/ *adj* alla deriva; **be ∼** andare alla deriva; **come ∼** staccarsi

adroit /ə'drɔɪt/ *adj* abile

adroitly /ə'drɔɪtlɪ/ *adv* abilmente

ADSL *abbr* (**Asymmetric Digital Subscriber Line**) ADSL *f*

adulation /ædjʊ'leɪʃn/ *n* adulazione *f*

adult /'ædʌlt/ *n* adulto, -a *mf*

Adult Education *n* Br ≈ corsi *mpl* serali

adulterate /ə'dʌltəreɪt/ *vt* adulterare ⟨*wine*⟩

adulterated /ə'dʌltəreɪtɪd/ *adj* ⟨*wine*⟩ adulterato

adulterous /ə'dʌltərəs/ *adj* ⟨*relationship*⟩ adulterino; ⟨*person*⟩ adultero

adultery /ə'dʌltərɪ/ *n* adulterio *m*

adulthood /'ædʌlthʊd/ *n* età *f* adulta

adult literacy classes *n* Br corso *m* di alfabetizzazione per adulti

advance /əd'vɑːns/ ① *n* avanzamento *m*; Mil avanzata *f*; (payment) anticipo *m*; **in ∼** in anticipo
② *vi* avanzare; (make progress) fare progressi
③ *vt* promuovere ⟨*cause*⟩; avanzare ⟨*theory*⟩; anticipare ⟨*money*⟩

advance booking *n* prenotazione *f* [in anticipo]

advance booking office *n* ufficio *m* prenotazioni

advanced /əd'vɑːnst/ *adj* avanzato

Advanced Level *n* Br Sch = A-LEVEL

advanced search *n* Comput ricerca *f* avanzata; **∼ option** opzione *f* ricerca avanzata

advancement /əd'vɑːnsmənt/ *n* promozione *f*

advance notice *n* preannuncio *m*

advance party *n* Mil avanguardia *f*

advance payment *n* Comm pagamento *m* anticipato

advance warning *n* preavviso *m*

advantage /əd'vɑːntɪdʒ/ *n* vantaggio *m*; **take ∼ of** approfittare di

advantageous /ædvən'teɪdʒəs/ *adj* vantaggioso

advent /'ædvent/ *n* avvento *m*; **A∼** Relig Avvento *m*

adventure /əd'ventʃə(r)/ *n* avventura *f*

adventure holiday *n* vacanza *f* avventura

adventure playground *n* Br parco *m* giochi

adventurer /əd'ventʃərə(r)/ *n* avventuriero, -a *mf*

adventuress /əd'ventʃərɪs/ *n* avventuriera *f*

adventurous /əd'ventʃərəs/ *adj* avventuroso

adverb /'ædvɜːb/ *n* avverbio *m*

adversary /'ædvəsərɪ/ *n* avversario, -a *mf*

adverse /'ædvɜːs/ *adj* avverso

adversity /əd'vɜːsətɪ/ *n* avversità *f*

advert /'ædvɜːt/ *n* fam = ADVERTISEMENT

advertise /'ædvətaɪz/ ① *vt* reclamizzare; mettere un annuncio per ⟨*job, flat*⟩
② *vi* fare pubblicità; (for job, flat) mettere un annuncio

advertisement /əd'vɜːtɪsmənt/ *n* pubblicità *f inv*; (in paper) inserzione *f*, annuncio *m*

advertiser /'ædvətaɪzə(r)/ *n* (in newspaper) inserzionista *mf*

advertising /'ædvətaɪzɪŋ/ ① *n* pubblicità *f*
② *attrib* pubblicitario

advertising agency *n* agenzia *f* pubblicitaria

advertising campaign *n* campagna *f* pubblicitaria

advertising executive *n* dirigente *mf* pubblicitario, -a

advertising industry *n* settore *m* pubblicitario

Advertising Standards Authority *n* Br organo *m* di controllo sulla pubblicità

advice /əd'vaɪs/ *n* consigli *mpl*; **piece of ∼** consiglio *m*

advice centre *n* centro *m* di consulenza

advice note *n* avviso *m*

advice slip *n* avviso *m* di accreditamento

advisability /ədvaɪzə'bɪlətɪ/ *n* opportunità *f*

advisable /əd'vaɪzəbl/ *adj* consigliabile

advise /əd'vaɪz/ *vt* consigliare; (inform) avvisare; **∼ somebody to do something** consigliare a qualcuno di fare qualcosa; **∼ somebody against something** sconsigliare qualcosa a qualcuno

advisedly /əd'vaɪzɪdlɪ/ *adv* ⟨*say*⟩ deliberatamente

adviser /əd'vaɪzə(r)/ *n* consulente *mf*

advisory /əd'vaɪzərɪ/ *adj* consultivo

advisory committee *n* comitato *m* consultivo

advisory service *n* servizio *m* di consulenza; **pensions/immigration/ pregnancy ∼** servizio di consulenza in materia di pensioni/immigrazione/ gravidanza

advocacy /'ædvəkəsɪ/ *n* appoggio *m*

advocate[1] /'ædvəkət/ *n* (supporter) fautore, -trice *mf*

advocate[2] /'ædvəkeɪt/ *vt* propugnare

Aegean /ɪ'dʒɪən/ *n* **the ∼** l'Egeo *m*

aegis /'iːdʒɪs/ *n* **under the ∼ of** sotto l'egida di

aeon /'iːən/ *n* **∼s ago** milioni *mpl* e milioni di anni fa

AER *n abbr* (**Annual Equivalence Rate**) TAN *m*

aerate /ˈeəreɪt/ *vt* aerare; addizionare anidride carbonica a ⟨*water*⟩

aerial /ˈeərɪəl/ ① *adj* aereo ② *n* antenna *f*

aerial camera *n* macchina *f* fotografica per fotografie aeree

aerial photography *n* fotografia *f* aerea

aerial warfare *n* guerra *f* aerea

aerie /ˈeərɪ/ *n* Am (eyrie) nido *m* [d'aquila]

aerobatics /eərəˈbætɪks/ *npl* (manoeuvres) acrobazie *fpl* aeree

aerobics /eəˈrəʊbɪks/ *n* aerobica *fsg*

aerodrome /ˈeərədrəʊm/ *n* aerodromo *m*

aerodynamic /eərəʊdaɪˈnæmɪk/ *adj* aerodinamico

aerodynamics /eərəʊdaɪˈnæmɪks/ *n* aerodinamica *f*

aerogram[me] /ˈeərəʊgræm/ *n* aerogramma *m*

aeronautic[al] /eərəˈnɔːtɪk[əl]/ *adj* aeronautico

aeronautic[al] engineer *n* ingegnere *m* aeronautico

aeronautic[al] engineering *n* ingegneria *f* aeronautica

aeronautics /eərəˈnɔːtɪks/ *n* aeronautica *f*

aeroplane /ˈeərəpleɪn/ *n* aeroplano *m*

aerosol /ˈeərəsɒl/ *n* bomboletta *f* spray

aerospace /ˈeərəspeɪs/ ① *n* (industry) industria *f* aerospaziale ② *attrib* ⟨*engineer, company*⟩ aerospaziale

aesthete /ˈiːsθiːt/ *n* esteta *mf*

aesthetic /iːsˈθetɪk/ *adj* estetico

aesthetically /iːsˈθetɪklɪ/ *adv* ⟨*restore*⟩ con gusto; ⟨*satisfying*⟩ esteticamente

aestheticism /iːsˈθetɪsɪzm/ *n* (taste) estetica *f*; (doctrine, quality) estetismo *m*

aesthetics /iːsˈθetɪks/ *n* estetica *f*

afar /əˈfɑː(r)/ *adv* **from ~** da lontano

affable /ˈæfəbl/ *adj* affabile

affably /ˈæfəblɪ/ *adv* affabilmente

affair /əˈfeə(r)/ *n* affare *m*; (scandal) caso *m*; (sexual) relazione *f*

affect /əˈfekt/ *vt* influire su; (emotionally) colpire; (concern) riguardare; (pretend) affettare

affectation /æfekˈteɪʃn/ *n* affettazione *f*

affected /əˈfektɪd/ *adj* affettato

affectedly /əˈfektɪdlɪ/ *adv* ⟨*talk*⟩ con affettazione

affection /əˈfekʃn/ *n* affetto *m*

affectionate /əˈfekʃnət/ *adj* affettuoso

affectionately /əˈfekʃnətlɪ/ *adv* affettuosamente

affidavit /æfɪˈdeɪvɪt/ *n* affidavit *m inv* (dichiarazione scritta e giurata davanti a un pubblico ufficiale)

affiliated /əˈfɪlɪeɪtɪd/ *adj* affiliato

affiliation /əˈfɪlɪˈeɪʃn/ *n* (process, state) affiliazione *f*; (link) legame *m*

affinity /əˈfɪnətɪ/ *n* affinità *f inv*

affinity card *n* carta *f* di credito destinata ad una causa sociale

affirm /əˈfɜːm/ *vt* affermare; Jur dichiarare solennemente

affirmative /əˈfɜːmətɪv/ ① *adj* affermativo ② *n* **in the ~** affermativamente

affix /əˈfɪks/ *vt* affiggere; apporre ⟨*signature*⟩

afflict /əˈflɪkt/ *vt* affliggere

affliction /əˈflɪkʃn/ *n* afflizione *f*

affluence /ˈæfluəns/ *n* agiatezza *f*

affluent /ˈæfluənt/ *adj* agiato

afford /əˈfɔːd/ *vt* (provide) fornire; **be able to ~ something** potersi permettere qualcosa

affordable /əˈfɔːdəbl/ *adj* abbordabile

affray /əˈfreɪ/ *n* rissa *f*

affront /əˈfrʌnt/ ① *n* affronto *m* ② *vt* fare un affronto a

Afghan /ˈæfgæn/ *n* (person) afgano, -a *mf*; (language) afgano *m*; (coat) pelliccotto *m* afgano

Afghan hound *n* levriero *m* afgano

Afghanistan /æfˈgænɪstæn/ *n* Afganistan *m*

aficionado /æfɪsjəˈnɑːdəʊ/ *n* aficionado, -a *mf*

afield /əˈfiːld/ *adv* **further ~** più lontano

aflame /əˈfleɪm/ *adj & adv* liter in fiamme, sfolgorante; **be ~** ⟨*cheek;*⟩ essere in fiamme; **be ~ with desire** ardere dal desiderio

afloat /əˈfləʊt/ *adj* a galla

afoot /əˈfʊt/ *adj* **there's something ~** si sta preparando qualcosa

aforesaid /əˈfɔːsed/ *adj* Jur suddetto

afraid /əˈfreɪd/ *adj* **be ~** aver paura; **I'm ~ not** purtroppo no; **I'm ~ so** temo di sì; **I'm ~ I can't help you** mi dispiace ma non posso esserle d'aiuto

afresh /əˈfreʃ/ *adv* da capo

Africa /ˈæfrɪkə/ *n* Africa *f*

African /ˈæfrɪkən/ *adj & n* africano, -a *mf*

African-American *n* afroamericano, -a *mf*

Afrikaans /æfrɪˈkɑːns/ *n* afrikaans *m*

Afrikaner /æfrɪˈkɑːnə(r)/ *n* boero, -a *mf*

Afro-American /æfrəʊəˈmerɪkən/ *adj & n* afroamericano, -a *mf*

Afro-Caribbean /æfrəʊkærəˈbɪən/ *adj & n* afrocaraibico, -a *mf*

aft /ɑːft/ *adv* Naut a poppa; (towards the stern) verso poppa

after /'ɑːftə(r)/ ① *adv* dopo; **the day ~** il giorno dopo; **be ~** cercare
② *prep* dopo; **~ all** dopotutto; **the day ~ tomorrow** dopodomani
③ *conj* dopo che

afterbirth *n* residui *mpl* di placenta

aftercare *n* Med ospedalizzazione *f* domiciliare

after-dinner speaker *n* persona *f* invitata a tenere un discorso dopo una cena o un ricevimento

after-effect *n* conseguenza *f*

afterlife *n* vita *f* nell'aldilà

aftermath /'ɑːftəmɑːθ/ *n* conseguenze *fpl*; **the ~ of war** il dopoguerra; **in the ~ of** nel periodo successivo a

afternoon *n* pomeriggio *m*; **good ~!** buon giorno!

afternoon tea *n* merenda *f*

afterpains *npl* dolori *mpl* post-parto

after-sales service *n* servizio *m* assistenza clienti

after-school *adj* doposcuola; **~ club/activities** club/attività doposcuola

aftershave *n* [lozione *f*] dopobarba *m inv*

aftershock *n* fig effetti *mpl*

aftersun *n & a* doposole *m inv.*

aftertaste *n* retrogusto *m*

after-tax *adj* ⟨*profits, earnings*⟩ al netto

afterthought *n* added as an **~** aggiunto in un secondo momento; **as an ~, why not...?** ripensandoci bene, perché non...?

afterwards /'ɑːftəwədz/ *adv* in seguito

again /ə'geɪn/ *adv* di nuovo; **[then] ~** (besides) inoltre; (on the other hand) d'altra parte; **~ and ~** continuamente

against /ə'geɪnst/ *prep* contro

age /eɪdʒ/ ① *n* età *f inv*; (era) era *f*; **~s** fam secoli; **~s ago** fam secoli fa; **what ~ are you?** quanti anni hai?; **be under ~** non avere l'età richiesta; **he's two years of ~** ha due anni
② *vt/i* (*pres p* ageing) invecchiare

age bracket, **age group** *n* fascia *f* d'età

aged[1] /eɪdʒd/ *adj* **~ two** di due anni

aged[2] /'eɪdʒɪd/ ① *adj* anziano
② *n* **the ~** *pl* gli anziani

aged debt *n* Fin somma *f* in scadenza

age discrimination *n* discriminazione *f* in base all'età

ageing /'eɪdʒɪŋ/ ① *n* invecchiamento *m*
② *adj* ⟨*person, population*⟩ che sta invecchiando

ageism /'eɪdʒɪzm/ *n* discriminazione *f* contro chi non è più giovane

ageless /'eɪdʒlɪs/ *adj* senza età

agency /'eɪdʒənsɪ/ *n* agenzia *f*; **have the ~ for** essere un concessionario di

agency-fee *n* commissione *f*

agency-nurse *n* infermiere, -a *mf* privato, -a

agenda /ə'dʒendə/ *n* ordine *m* del giorno; **on the ~** all'ordine del giorno; fig in programma

agent /'eɪdʒənt/ *n* agente *mf*

age-old *adj* secolare

age range *n* fascia *f* d'età

aggravate /'æɡrəveɪt/ *vt* aggravare; (annoy) esasperare

aggravating /'æɡrəveɪtɪŋ/ *adj* Jur aggravante; (fam: irritating) irritante

aggravation /æɡrə'veɪʃn/ *n* aggravamento *m*; (annoyance) esasperazione *f*

aggregate /'æɡrɪɡət/ ① *adj* totale
② *n* totale *m*; **on ~** nel complesso

aggression /ə'ɡreʃn/ *n* aggressione *f*

aggressive /ə'ɡresɪv/ *adj* aggressivo

aggressively /ə'ɡresɪvlɪ/ *adv* aggressivamente

aggressiveness /ə'ɡresɪvnɪs/ *n* aggressività *f*

aggressor /ə'ɡresə(r)/ *n* aggressore *m*

aggrieved /ə'ɡriːvd/ *adj* risentito

aggro /'æɡrəʊ/ *n* fam aggressività *f*; (problems) grane *fpl*

aghast /ə'ɡɑːst/ *adj* inorridito

agile /'ædʒaɪl/ *adj* agile

agility /ə'dʒɪlətɪ/ *n* agilità *f*

agitate /'ædʒɪteɪt/ ① *vt* mettere in agitazione; (shake) agitare
② *vi* fig **~ for** creare delle agitazioni per

agitated /'ædʒɪteɪtɪd/ *adj* agitato

agitation /ædʒɪ'teɪʃn/ *n* agitazione *f*

agitator /'ædʒɪteɪtə(r)/ *n* agitatore, -trice *mf*

AGM *n abbr* (annual general meeting) assemblea *f* generale annuale

agnostic /æɡ'nɒstɪk/ *adj & n* agnostico, -a *mf*

ago /ə'ɡəʊ/ *adv* fa; **a long time/a month ~** molto tempo/un mese fa; **how long ~ was it?** quanto tempo fa è successo?

agog /ə'ɡɒɡ/ *adj* eccitato

agonize /'æɡənaɪz/ *vi* angosciarsi (over per)

agonized /'æɡənaɪzd/ *adj* ⟨*expression, cry*⟩ angosciato

agonizing /'æɡənaɪzɪŋ/ *adj* angosciante

agony /'æɡənɪ/ *n* agonia *f*; (mental) angoscia *f*; **be in ~** avere dei dolori atroci

agony aunt *n* persona *f* chi tiene la posta del cuore in una rivista

agoraphobia /ægərə'fəʊbɪə/ n
agorafobia f

agoraphobic /ægərə'fəʊbɪk/ adj
agorafobo, -a mf

agree /ə'griː/ ① vt accordarsi su; ~ **to**
do something accettare di fare qualcosa;
~ **that** essere d'accordo [sul fatto] che
② vi essere d'accordo, ⟨figures⟩
concordare; (reach agreement) mettersi
d'accordo; (get on) andare d'accordo;
(consent) acconsentire (**to** a); **it doesn't** ~
with me mi fa male; ~ **with something**
(approve of) approvare qualcosa

agreeable /ə'griːəbl/ adj gradevole;
(willing) d'accordo

agreeably /ə'griːəblɪ/ adv (pleasantly)
piacevolmente; (amicably) in modo
amichevole

agreed /ə'griːd/ adj convenuto

agreement /ə'griːmənt/ n accordo m; **in**
~ d'accordo; **reach** ~ arrivare ad un
accordo

agricultural /ægrɪ'kʌltʃərəl/ adj
agricolo

agriculturalist /ægrɪ'kʌltʃərəlɪst/ n
agronomo, -a mf

agricultural show n fiera f agricola

agriculture /'ægrɪkʌltʃə(r)/ n
agricoltura f

agritourism /ægrɪ'tʊərɪzəm/ n
agriturismo m

agronomy /ə'grɒnəmɪ/ n agronomia f

aground /ə'graʊnd/ adv **run** ~ ⟨ship⟩
arenarsi

ah /ɑː/ int ~ **well!** (resignedly) va bene!

ahead /ə'hed/ adv avanti; **be** ~ **of** essere
davanti a; fig essere avanti rispetto a;
draw ~ passare davanti (**of** a); **go on** ~
cominciare ad andare; **get** ~ ⟨in life⟩
riuscire; **go** ~! fai pure!; **look** ~ pensare
all'avvenire; **plan** ~ fare progetti per
l'avvenire

aid /eɪd/ ① n aiuto m; **in** ~ **of** a favore di
② vt aiutare

aid agency n organizzazione f
umanitaria

aide n assistente mf

aid package n pacco m umanitario

Aids /eɪdz/ n AIDS m

Aids awareness n sensibilizzazione f
all'AIDS

aid worker n cooperante mf

ailing /'eɪlɪŋ/ adj malato

ailment /'eɪlmənt/ n disturbo m

aim /eɪm/ ① n mira f; fig scopo m; **take** ~
prendere la mira
② vt puntare ⟨gun⟩ (**at** su)
③ vi mirare; ~ **to do something** aspirare
a fare qualcosa

aimless /'eɪmlɪs/ adj senza scopo

aimlessly /'eɪmlɪslɪ/ adv senza scopo

ain't /eɪnt/ fam = am not; are not; have
not; has not

air /eə(r)/ ① n aria f; **be on the** ~
⟨programme⟩ essere in onda; **put on** ~**s**
darsi delle arie; **by** ~ in aereo; (airmail) per
via aerea
② vt arieggiare; far conoscere ⟨views⟩; pej
sfoggiare ⟨knowledge⟩

air ambulance n aereo m ambulanza;
(helicopter) eliambulanza f

air attack n attacco m aereo

air bag n Auto air bag m inv

air bed n materassino m [gonfiabile]

airborne /'eəbɔːn/ adj (plane) in volo;
⟨troops⟩ aerotrasportato m

airbrush n aerografo m

air bubble n (in liquid, plastic, wallpaper)
bolla f d'aria

air-conditioned adj con aria
condizionata

air conditioner n condizionatore m

air-conditioning n aria f condizionata

air-cooled adj ⟨engine⟩ raffreddato ad
aria

air cover n protezione f aerea

aircraft n aereo m

aircraft carrier n portaerei f inv

aircraft[s]man n Br aviere m

air crash n disastro m aereo

aircrew n equipaggio m di volo

air cushion n (inflatable cushion) cuscino
m gonfiabile; (of hovercraft) cuscino m
d'aria

air disaster n disastro m aereo

air display n esibizione f in volo

airdrop n lancio m con paracadute

air duct n condotto m dell'aria

air exclusion zone n zona f di
esclusione aerea

airfare n tariffa f aerea

airfield n campo m d'aviazione

airflow n spostamento m d'aria

air force n aviazione f

airfreight n (goods) merce f spedita via
aerea; (method of transport) trasporto m
aereo; (charge) costo m per trasporto
aereo

air-freshener n deodorante m per
ambienti

air gun n fucile m ad aria compressa

airhead n fam svampito,-a mf

air hole n sfiatatoio m

air hostess n hostess f inv

airing /'eərɪŋ/ n **give a room an** ~
arieggiare una stanza; **give an idea an** ~
fig ventilare un'idea

airing cupboard n Br sgabuzzino m del
boiler dove viene riposta la biancheria ad
asciugare

airless /'eəlɪs/ *adj* ⟨*evening*⟩ senza vento; ⟨*room*⟩ poco ventilato

air letter *n* aerogramma *m*

airlift ① *vt* trasportare con ponte aereo ② *n* ponte *m* aereo

airline *n* compagnia *f* aerea

airliner *n* aereo *m* di linea

airlock *n* bolla *f* d'aria

airmail *n* posta *f* aerea

air marshal *n* Br maresciallo *m* d'aviazione

Air Miles® *npl* Br miglia *fpl* aeree

airplane *n* Am aereo *m*

air pocket *n* vuoto *m* d'aria

airport *n* aeroporto *m*

air power *n* potenza *f* aerea

air raid *n* incursione *f* aerea

air-raid shelter *n* rifugio *m* antiaereo

air-raid siren *n* allarme *m* aereo

air-raid warning *n* allarme *m* aereo

air rifle *n* fucile *m* ad aria compressa

air-sea rescue *n* salvataggio *m* dal mare con impiego di mezzi aerei

air shaft *n* (in mine) pozzo *m* di ventilazione

airship *n* dirigibile *m*

air show *n* (trade exhibition) salone *m* dell'aviazione; (flying show) manifestazione *f* aerea

airsickness *n* mal *m* d'aereo

air sock *n* manica *f* a vento

airspeed *n* velocità *f* relativa all'aria

airspeed indicator *n* indicatore *m* di velocità (su un aereo)

air steward *n* steward *m inv*

air stewardess *n* hostess *f inv*

airstream *n* corrente *f* d'aria

airstrike *n* incursione *f* aerea

airstrip *n* pista *f* d'atterraggio

air terminal *n* (in town, terminus) [air-]terminal *m inv*

airtight *adj* ermetico

airtime *n* Radio, TV spazio *m* radiofonico/televisivo

air-to-air *adj* ⟨*missile*⟩ aria-aria; ⟨*refuelling*⟩ in volo

air traffic *n* traffico *m* aereo

air-traffic controller *n* controllore *m* di volo

air travel *n* viaggi *mpl* in aereo

air valve *n* valvola *f* pneumatica

air vent *n* presa *f* d'aria

air vice-marshal *n* Br vice-maresciallo *m* dell'aviazione

air war *n* conflitto *m* aereo

airwaves *npl* Radio, TV onde *fpl* radio

airway *n* (route) rotta *f* aerea; (airline) compagnia *f* aerea; Anat via *f* respiratoria; (ventilating passage) pozzo *m* di ventilazione

air waybill *n* polizza *f* di carico aerea

airworthiness *n* idoneità *f* di volo

airworthy *adj* idoneo al volo

airy /'eərɪ/ *adj* (**-ier, -iest**) arieggiato; ⟨*manner*⟩ noncurante

airy-fairy /eərɪ'feərɪ/ *adj* Br fam ⟨*plan, person*⟩ fuori dalla realtà

aisle /aɪl/ *n* corridoio *m*; (in supermarket) corsia *f*; (in church) navata *f*

ajar /ə'dʒɑː(r)/ *adj* socchiuso

aka *abbr* (**also known as**) alias

akin /ə'kɪn/ *adj* ∼ **to** simile a

AI *n abbr* (**artificial intelligence**) I.A. *f*

alabaster /'æləbɑːstə(r)/ *n* alabastro *m*

alacrity /ə'lækrətɪ/ *n* alacrità *f inv*

alarm /ə'lɑːm/ ① *n* allarme *m*; **set the** ∼ (of alarm clock) mettere la sveglia; **in** ∼ in stato di allarme
② *vt* allarmare; **don't be** ∼**ed!** non si allarmi!

alarm bell *n* campanello *m* d'allarme; **set the** ∼ ∼**s ringing** *n* Br fig far scattare il campanello d'allarme

alarm call *n* Teleph sveglia *f* automatica

alarm clock *n* sveglia *f*

alarmed *adj* allarmato

alarming /ə'lɑːmɪŋ/ *adj* allarmante, preoccupante

alarmist /ə'lɑːmɪst/ *adj & n* allarmista *mf*

alas /ə'læs/ *int* ahimè

Albania /æl'beɪnɪə/ *n* Albania *f*

Albanian /æl'beɪnɪən/ ① *n* (person) albanese *mf*; (language) albanese *m*
② *adj* albanese

albatross /'ælbətrɒs/ *n* (also in golf) albatro *m*

albeit /ɔːl'biːɪt/ *adv & conj* benché

albino /æl'biːnəʊ/ *adj & n* albino, -a *mf*

album /'ælbəm/ *n* album *m inv*

albumen /'ælbjʊmɪn/ *n* Biol, Bot albume *m*

alchemist /'ælkɪmɪʃt/ *n* alchimista *m*

alchemy /'ælkɪmɪ/ *n* Chem, fig alchimia *f*

alcohol /'ælkəhɒl/ *n* alcol *m*

alcoholic /ælkə'hɒlɪk/ ① *adj* alcolico
② *n* alcolizzato, -a *mf*

Alcoholics Anonymous *n* Anonima *f* Alcolisti

alcoholism /'ælkəhɒlɪzm/ *n* alcolismo *m*

alcohol-related *adj* ⟨*illness, disease*⟩ legato al consumo di alcol

alcopop /'ælkəʊpɒp/ *n* bibita *f* alcolica

alcove /'ælkəʊv/ *n* alcova *f*

alder /'ɔːldə(r)/ *n* (tree, wood) ontano *m*

ale /eɪl/ n birra f

alert /ə'lɜːt/ **1** adj attento; (watchful) vigile
2 n segnale m d'allarme; **be on the ~**
stare allerta
3 vt allertare

alertness /ə'lɜːtnɪs/ n (attentiveness)
attenzione f; (liveliness) vivacità f

A-level n Br Sch **~s** ≈ esami mpl di
maturità; **he got an ~ in history** ha
portato storia alla maturità

Alexandria /ælɪg'zændrɪə/ n
Alessandria f [d'Egitto]

alfalfa /æl'fælfə/ n erba f medicinale

alfresco /æl'freskəʊ/ adj & adv
all'aperto

algae /'ældʒiː/ npl alghe fpl

algebra /'ældʒɪbrə/ n algebra f

Algeria /æl'dʒɪərɪə/ n Algeria f

Algerian /æl'dʒɪərɪən/ adj & n algerino,
-a mf

Algiers /æl'dʒɪəz/ n Algeri f

algorithm /'ælgərɪðm/ n algoritmo m

alias /'eɪlɪəs/ **1** n pseudonimo m
2 adv alias

alibi /'ælɪbaɪ/ n alibi m inv

alien /'eɪlɪən/ **1** adj straniero; fig
estraneo
2 n straniero, -a mf; (from space) alieno, -a
mf

alienate /'eɪlɪəneɪt/ vt alienare

alienation /eɪlɪə'neɪʃn/ n alienazione f

alight¹ /ə'laɪt/ vi scendere; ⟨bird⟩ posarsi

alight² adj **be ~** essere in fiamme; **set ~**
dar fuoco a

align /ə'laɪn/ vt allineare

alignment /ə'laɪnmənt/ n allineamento
m; **out of ~** non allineato

alike /ə'laɪk/ **1** adj simile; **be ~**
rassomigliarsi
2 adv in modo simile; **look ~**
rassomigliarsi; **summer and winter ~** sia
d'estate che d'inverno

alimentary /ælɪ'mentərɪ/ adj ⟨system⟩
digerente; ⟨process⟩ digestivo

alimentary canal n tubo m digerente

alimony /'ælɪmənɪ/ n alimenti mpl

alive /ə'laɪv/ adj vivo; **~ with** brulicante
di; **~ to** sensibile a; **~ and kicking** vivo e
vegeto

alkali /'ælkəlaɪ/ n alcali m

alkaline /'ælkəlaɪn/ adj alcalino

all /ɔːl/ **1** adj tutto; **~ the children, ~**
children tutti i bambini; **~ day** tutto il
giorno; **he refused ~ help** ha rifiutato
qualsiasi aiuto; **for ~ that** (nevertheless)
perciò; **in ~ sincerity** in tutta sincerità; **be**
~ for essere favorevole a
2 pron tutto; **~ of you/them** tutti voi/
loro; **~ of it** tutto; **~ of the town** tutta la
città; **~ but one** tutti tranne uno; **in ~** in
tutto; **~ in ~** tutto sommato; **most of ~**

più di ogni altra cosa; **once and for ~** una
volta per tutte; **~ being well** salvo
complicazioni
3 adv completamente; **~ but** quasi; **~ at**
once (at the same time) tutto in una volta; **~**
at once, ~ of a sudden all'improvviso; **~**
too soon troppo presto; **~ the same**
(nevertheless) ciononostante; **~ the better**
meglio ancora; **she's not ~ that good an**
actress non è poi così brava come attrice;
~ in in tutto; fam esausto; **thirty/three ~**
(in sport) trenta/tre pari; **~ over** (finished)
tutto finito; (everywhere) dappertutto; **it's ~**
right (I don't mind) non fa niente; **I'm ~ right**
(not hurt) non ho niente; **~ right!** va bene!;
be ~ that fam esp Am essere in gamba

all-American adj ⟨record, champion⟩
americano; ⟨girl, boy, hero⟩ tipicamente
americano

all-around adj ⟨improvement⟩ generale

allay /ə'leɪ/ vt placare ⟨suspicions, anger⟩

all-clear n Mil cessato m allarme/
pericolo; (from doctor) autorizzazione f; **give**
somebody the ~ ~ fig dare il via libera a
qualcuno

all-consuming adj ⟨passion⟩ sfrenato;
⟨ambition⟩ smisurato

all-day adj ⟨event⟩ che dura tutto il
giorno

allegation /ælɪ'geɪʃn/ n accusa f

allege /ə'ledʒ/ vt dichiarare

alleged /ə'ledʒd/ adj presunto

allegedly /ə'ledʒɪdlɪ/ adv a quanto si
dice

allegiance /ə'liːdʒəns/ n fedeltà f

allegorical /ælɪ'gɒrɪkl/ adj allegorico

allegory /'ælɪgərɪ/ n allegoria f

all-embracing /-əm'breɪsɪŋ/ adj globale

allergic /ə'lɜːdʒɪk/ adj allergico

allergist /'ælədʒɪst/ n allergologo, -a mf

allergy /'ælədʒɪ/ n allergia f

allergy clinic n clinica f di allergologia

alleviate /ə'liːvɪeɪt/ vt alleviare

alleviation /əliːvɪ'eɪʃn/ n alleviamento
m, alleggerimento m

alley /'ælɪ/ n vicolo m; (for bowling) corsia f

alleyway /'ælɪweɪ/ n vicolo m

all-found adj £200 ~ 200 sterline inclusi
vitto e alloggio

alliance /ə'laɪəns/ n alleanza f

allied /'ælaɪd/ adj alleato; (fig: related)
connesso (to a)

alligator /'ælɪgeɪtə(r)/ n alligatore m

all-important adj essenziale

all in adj (Br fam: exhausted) distrutto; ⟨fee,
price⟩ tutto compreso

all-inclusive adj (fee, price) tutto
compreso

all-in-one adj ⟨garment⟩ in un pezzo
solo

all-in wresting n Sport catch m

all-night adj ⟨party, meeting⟩ che dura tutta la notte; ⟨radio station⟩ che trasmette tutta la notte; ⟨service⟩ notturno

allocate /'æləkeɪt/ vt assegnare; distribuire ⟨resources⟩

allocation /ælə'keɪʃn/ n assegnazione f; (of resources) distribuzione f

all-or-nothing adj ⟨approach, policy⟩ senza vie di mezzo

allot /ə'lɒt/ vt (pt/pp **allotted**) distribuire

allotment /ə'lɒtmənt/ n distribuzione f; (share) parte f; (land) piccolo lotto m di terreno

all-out ① adj ⟨effort⟩ estremo; ⟨attack⟩ senza esclusione di colpi.
② adv go all out to do something/for something mettercela tutta per fare qualcosa/per qualcosa

all-over adj ⟨tan⟩ integrale

all over ① prep ∼ ∼ China in/per tutta la Cina; the news is ∼ ∼ the village lo sanno tutti in paese; be ∼ ∼ somebody (fawning over) stare appiccicato a qualcuno ② adv be trembling ∼ tremare tutto; that's Mary ∼ ∼! è proprio da Mary! ③ adj when it's ∼ ∼ (finished) quando è tutto finito

allow /ə'laʊ/ vt permettere; (grant) accordare; (reckon on) contare; (agree) ammettere; ∼ somebody to do something permettere a qualcuno di fare qualcosa; you are not ∼ed to... è vietato...; how much are you ∼ed? qual è il limite? ■ allow for vt tener conto di

allowable /ə'laʊəbl/ adj permissibile; Jur lecito; ⟨tax⟩ deducibile

allowance /ə'laʊəns/ n sussidio m; (Am: pocket money) paghetta f; (for petrol etc) indennità f inv; (of luggage, duty free) limite m; (for tax purposes) deduzione f; make ∼s for essere indulgente verso ⟨somebody⟩; tener conto di ⟨something⟩

alloy /'ælɔɪ/ n lega f

alloy steel n lega f d'acciaio

alloy wheel n cerchione m in lega d'acciaio

all points bulletin n Am allarme m generale

all-powerful adj onnipotente

all-purpose adj ⟨building⟩ polivalente; ⟨utensil⟩ multiuso

all right ① adj is it ∼ ∼ if...? va bene se...?; is that ∼ ∼ with you? ti va bene?; sounds ∼ ∼ to me per me va bene; that's [quite] ∼ ∼ (it doesn't matter) non c'è problema; is my hair ∼ ∼? sono a posto i miei capelli?; it's ∼ ∼ for you per te!; she's ∼ ∼ (competent) è abbastanza brava; (attractive) non è niente male; (pleasant) è piuttosto simpatica; will you be

∼ ∼? (able to manage) te la caverai?; feel ∼ ∼ (well) sentirsi bene ② adv ⟨function, see⟩ bene; (not brilliantly) così così; can I? –∼ ∼ posso? –d'accordo; she's doing ∼ ∼ (in life) le cose le vanno bene; (in health) sta bene; (in activity) se la cava bene; she knows ∼ ∼! (without doubt) lei lo sa di sicuro!; ∼ ∼, ∼ ∼!, va bene! va bene!

all-risk adj ⟨policy, cover⟩ multirischi

all-round adj ⟨improvement⟩ generale; (athlete) completo

all-rounder /-'raʊndə(r)/ n be a good ∼ essere versatile

allspice /'ɔːlspaɪs/ n pepe m della Giamaica

all square adj be ∼ ∼ ⟨people⟩ essere pari; ⟨accounts⟩ quadrare

all-time adj ⟨record⟩ assoluto, senza precedenti; the ∼ greats (people) i grandi; ∼ high massimo m storico; be at an ∼ low ⟨person, morale⟩ essere a terra; ⟨figures, shares⟩ toccare il minimo storico

all told adv tutto sommato

allude /ə'luːd/ vi alludere

allure /æ'ljʊə(r)/ n attrattiva f

alluring /ə'ljʊrɪŋ/ adj allettante, affascinante

allusion /ə'luːʒn/ n allusione f

ally[1] /'ælaɪ/ n alleato, -a mf

ally[2] /ə'laɪ/ vt (pt/pp **-ied**) alleare; ∼ oneself with allearsi con

almighty /ɔːl'maɪtɪ/ ① adj (fam: big) mega inv ② n the A∼ l'Onnipotente m

almond /'ɑːmənd/ n mandorla f; (tree) mandorlo m

almost /'ɔːlməʊst/ adv quasi

alms /ɑːmz/ npl (liter) elemosina fsg

aloft /ə'lɒft/ adv in alto; Naut sull'alberatura; from ∼ dall'alto

alone /ə'ləʊn/ ① adj solo; leave me ∼! lasciami in pace!; let ∼ (not to mention) figurarsi ② adv da solo

along /ə'lɒŋ/ ① prep lungo ② adv ∼ with assieme a; all ∼ tutto il tempo; come ∼! (hurry up) vieni qui!; I'll bring it ∼ lo porto lì; I'll be ∼ in a minute arrivo tra un attimo; move ∼ spostarsi; move ∼! circolare!

alongside /əlɒŋ'saɪd/ ① adv lungo bordo ② prep lungo; work ∼ somebody lavorare fianco a fianco con qualcuno

aloof /ə'luːf/ adj distante

aloud /ə'laʊd/ adv ad alta voce

alpaca /æl'pækə/ n alpaca m inv

alpha /'ælfə/ n (letter) alfa f inv; Br Univ ≈ trenta m inv e lode

alphabet /'ælfəbet/ n alfabeto m

alphabetical /ælfə'betɪkl/ *adj* alfabetico

alphabetically /ælfə'betɪklɪ/ *adv* in ordine alfabetico

alpha male *n* maschio *m* dominante

alpine /'ælpaɪn/ *adj* alpino

Alps /ælps/ *npl* Alpi *fpl*

already /ɔːl'redɪ/ *adv* già

alright /ɔːl'raɪt/ = ALL RIGHT

Alsace /æl'zæs/ *n* Alsazia *f*

Alsatian /æl'seɪʃn/ *n* (dog) pastore *m* tedesco

also /'ɔːlsəʊ/ *adv* anche; ~, I need... inoltre, ho bisogno di...

altar /'ɔːltə(r)/ *n* altare *m*

altar boy *n* chierichetto *m*

altar cloth *n* tovaglia *f* da altare

altar piece *n* pala *f* d'altare

alter /'ɔːltə(r)/ ① *vt* cambiare; aggiustare ‹clothes›
② *vi* cambiare

alteration /ɔːltə'reɪʃn/ *n* modifica *f*

altercation /ɔːltə'keɪʃn/ *n* alterco *m*

alternate¹ /'ɔːltəneɪt/ ① *vi* alternarsi
② *vt* alternare

alternate² /ɔːl'tɜːnət/ *adj* alterno; **on ~ days** a giorni alterni

alternately /ɔːl'tɜːnətlɪ/ *adv* in modo alterno; (Am: alternatively) alternativamente

alternating current /'ɔːltəneɪtɪŋ/ *n* corrente *f* alternata

alternation /ɔːltə'neɪʃn/ *n* alternanza *f*

alternative /ɔːl'tɜːnətɪv/ ① *adj* alternativo
② *n* alternativa *f*

alternative energy *n* energia *f* alternativa

alternatively /ɔːl'tɜːnətɪvlɪ/ *adv* alternativamente

alternative medicine *n* medicina *f* alternativa

alternative technology *n* tecnologia *f* alternativa

alternator /'ɔːltəneɪtə(r)/ *n* Electr alternatore *m*

although /ɔːl'ðəʊ/ *conj* benché, sebbene

altimeter /'æltɪmiːtə(r)/ *n* altimetro *m*

altitude /'æltɪtjuːd/ *n* altitudine *f*

Alt key /'ælt/ *n* Comput tasto *m* Alt

alto /'æltəʊ/ *n* contralto *m*

altogether /ɔːltə'geðə(r)/ *adv* (in all) in tutto; (completely) completamente; **I'm not ~ sure** non sono del tutto sicuro

altruism /'æltruɪzm/ *n* altruismo *m*

altruistic /æltrʊ'ɪstɪk/ *adj* altruistico

aluminium /æljʊ'mɪnɪəm/ *n* Am
aluminum /ə'luːmɪnəm/ *n* alluminio *m*

aluminium foil *n* carta *f* stagnola

alumna /ə'lʌmnə/ *n* Am Sch Univ ex allieva *f*

alumnus /ə'lʌmnəs/ *n* Am Sch Univ ex allievo *m*

always /'ɔːlweɪz/ *adv* sempre

Alzheimer's disease /'æltshaɪməz/ *n* morbo *m* di Alzheimer

am /æm/ ▶ BE

a.m. *abbr* (**ante meridiem**) del mattino

amalgam /ə'mælgəm/ *n* amalgama *m*

amalgamate /ə'mælgəmeɪt/ ① *vt* fondere
② *vi* fondersi

amalgamation /əmælgə'meɪʃn/ *n* fusione *f*; (of styles) amalgama *m*

amass /ə'mæs/ *vt* accumulare

amateur /'æmətə(r)/ ① *n* non professionista *mf*; pej dilettante *mf*
② *attrib* dilettante; **~ dramatics** filodrammatica *f*

amateurish /'æmətərɪʃ/ *adj* dilettantesco

amaze /ə'meɪz/ *vt* stupire

amazed /ə'meɪzd/ *adj* stupito

amazement /ə'meɪzmənt/ *n* stupore *m*; **to her ~** con suo grande stupore; **in ~** stupito

amazing /ə'meɪzɪŋ/ *adj* incredibile

amazingly /ə'meɪzɪŋlɪ/ *adv* incredibilmente

Amazon /'æməzən/ ① *n* (in myths) Amazzone *f*; (fig: strong woman) amazzone *f*; (river) Rio *m* delle Amazzoni
② *attrib* ‹basin, forest, tribe› amazzonico

ambassador /æm'bæsədə(r)/ *n* ambasciatore, -trice *mf*

ambassador-at-large *n* Am ambasciatore, -trice *mf* a disposizione

amber /'æmbə(r)/ ① *n* ambra *f*
② *adj* (colour) ambra *inv*

ambidextrous /æmbɪ'dekstrəs/ *adj* ambidestro

ambience /'æmbɪəns/ *n* atmosfera *f*

ambient /'æmbɪənt/ *adj* ‹temperature› ambiente *inv*; (noise) circostante

ambiguity /æmbɪ'gjuːətɪ/ *n* ambiguità *f* *inv*

ambiguous /æm'bɪgjʊəs/ *adj* ambiguo

ambiguously /æm'bɪgjʊəslɪ/ *adv* in modo ambiguo

ambition /æm'bɪʃn/ *n* ambizione *f*; (aim) aspirazione *f*

ambitious /æm'bɪʃəs/ *adj* ambizioso

ambivalence /æm'bɪvələns/ *n* ambivalenza *f*

ambivalent /æm'bɪvələnt/ *adj* ambivalente

amble /'æmb(ə)l/ *vi* camminare senza fretta

ambulance /'æmbjʊləns/ *n* ambulanza *f*

ambulance man *n* guidatore *m* di ambulanze

ambush /'æmbʊʃ/ ① *n* imboscata *f* ② *vt* tendere un'imboscata a

ameba /ə'miːbə/ *n* Am ameba *f*

amen /ɑː'men/ *int* amen

amenability /əmiːnə'bɪlɪtɪ/ *n* arrendevolezza *f*

amenable /ə'miːnəbl/ *adj* conciliante; ∼ to sensibile a

amend /ə'mend/ ① *vt* modificare ② *npl* **make** ∼**s** fare ammenda (**for** di, per)

amendment /ə'mendmənt/ *n* modifica *f*

amenities /ə'miːnətɪz/ *npl* comodità *fpl*

America /ə'merɪkə/ *n* America *f*

American /ə'merɪkən/ *adj & n* americano, -a *mf*

American Civil War *n* guerra *f* di secessione [americana]

American English *n* inglese *m* americano

American Indian *n* indiano, -a *mf* d'America

Americanism /ə'merɪkənɪzm/ *n* americanismo *m*

amethyst /'æməθɪst/ *n* (gem) ametista *f*

Amex /'æmeks/ *n abbr* (**American Stock Exchange**) Borsa *f* valori americana; *abbr* American Express

amiable /'eɪmɪəbl/ *adj* amabile

amicable /'æmɪkəbl/ *adj* amichevole

amicably /'æmɪkəblɪ/ *adv* amichevolmente

amid[st] /ə'mɪd[st]/ *prep* in mezzo a

amino acid /ə'miːnəʊ/ *n* amminoacido *m*

amiss /ə'mɪs/ ① *adj* **there's something** ∼ c'è qualcosa che non va ② *adv* **take something** ∼ prendersela [a male]; **it won't come** ∼ non sarebbe sgradito

ammo /'æməʊ/ *n abbr* (**ammunition**) munizioni *fpl*

ammonia /ə'məʊnɪə/ *n* ammoniaca *f*

ammunition /æmjʊ'nɪʃn/ *n* munizioni *fpl*

amnesia /æm'niːzɪə/ *n* amnesia *f*

amnesty /'æmnəstɪ/ *n* amnistia *f*

amoeba /ə'miːbə/ *n* ameba *f*

amoebic /ə'miːbɪk/ *adj* ⟨dysentry⟩ amebico

amok /ə'mɒk/ *adv* **run** ∼ essere in preda a furore; ⟨imagination⟩ scatenarsi

among[st] /ə'mʌŋ[st]/ *prep* tra, fra; **talk** ∼ **yourselves** parlate tra [di] voi

amoral /eɪ'mɒrəl/ *adj* amorale

amorality /eɪmə'rælətɪ/ *n* amoralità *f*

amorous /'æmərəs/ *adj* amoroso

amorphous /ə'mɔːfəs/ *adj* Chem amorfo; ⟨ideas, plans⟩ confuso; ⟨shape, collection⟩ informe

amount /ə'maʊnt/ ① *n* quantità *f inv*; (sum of money) montante *m* ② *v* ∎ **amount to** *vt* ammontare a; fig equivalere a

amp /æmp/ *n* ampere *m inv*

ampere /'æmpeə(r)/ *n* ampere *m inv*

ampersand /'æmpəsænd/ *n* e *f inv* commerciale

amphetamine /æm'fetəmiːn/ *n* anfetamina *f*

amphibian /æm'fɪbɪən/ *n* anfibio *m*

amphibious /æm'fɪbɪəs/ *adj* anfibio

amphitheatre /'æmfɪθɪːətə(r)/ *n* anfiteatro *m*

ample /'æmpl/ *adj* (large) grande; ⟨proportions⟩ ampio; (enough) largamente sufficiente

amplifier /'æmplɪfaɪə(r)/ *n* amplificatore *m*

amplify /'æmplɪfaɪ/ *vt* (pt/pp **-ied**) amplificare ⟨sound⟩

amply /'æmplɪ/ *adv* largamente

amputate /'æmpjʊteɪt/ *vt* amputare

amputation /æmpjʊ'teɪʃn/ *n* amputazione *f*

amputee /æmpjʊ'tiː/ *n* mutilato, -a *mf* (in seguito ad amputazione)

amuse /ə'mjuːz/ *vt* divertire

amused /ə'mjuːzd/ *adj* divertito

amusement /ə'mjuːzmənt/ *n* divertimento *m*

amusement arcade *n* sala *f* giochi

amusement park *n* luna park *m inv*

amusing /ə'mjuːzɪŋ/ *adj* divertente

an /ən/, stressed /æn/ ▸ A

anabolic steroid /ænə'bɒlɪk/ *n* anabolizzante *m*

anachronism /ə'nækrənɪzm/ *n* **be an** ∼ ⟨object, custom⟩ essere anacronistico

anaemia /ə'niːmɪə/ *n* anemia *f*

anaemic /ə'niːmɪk/ *adj* anemico

anaerobic /æneə'rəʊbɪk/ *adj* anerobico

anaesthesia /ænəs'θiːzɪə/ *n* anestesia *f*

anaesthetic /ænəs'θetɪk/ *n* anestesia *f*; **give somebody an** ∼ somministrare a qualcuno l'anestesia

anaesthetist /ə'niːsθətɪst/ *n* anestesista *mf*

anaesthetize /ə'niːsθətaɪz/ *vt* anestetizzare

anagram /'ænəgræm/ *n* anagramma *m*

analgesic /ænəl'dʒiːzɪk/ *adj & n* analgesico *m*

analogous /ə'næləgəs/ *adj* analogo

analog[ue] /'ænəlɒg/ *adj* analogico

analogy /ə'næ*l*ədʒɪ/ *n* analogia *f*

analyse /'ænə*l*aɪz/ *vt* analizzare

analysis /ə'næləsɪs/ *n* analisi *f inv*

analyst /'ænə*l*ɪst/ *n* analista *mf*

analytical /ænə'*l*ɪtɪkl/ *adj* analitico

anaphylaxis /ænəfɪ'*l*æksɪs/,
anaphylactic shock /ænəfɪ'*l*æktɪk/
n anafilassi *f*, shock *m* anafilattico

anarchic[al] /ə'nɑːkɪk[*l*]/ *adj* anarchico

anarchist /'ænəkɪst/ *n* anarchico, -a *mf*

anarchy /'ænəkɪ/ *n* anarchia *f*

anathema /ə'næθəmə/ *n* eresia *f*

anatomical /ænə'tɒmɪkl/ *adj*
anatomico

anatomically /ænə'tɒmɪklɪ/ *adv*
anatomicamente

anatomy /ə'nætəmɪ/ *n* anatomia *f*

ANC *n abbr* (**African National
Congress**) Congresso *m* Nazionale
Africano

ancestor /'ænsestə(r)/ *n* antenato, -a *mf*

ancestral /æn'sestrəl/ *adj* ancestrale;
⟨*home*⟩ avito

ancestry /'ænsestrɪ/ *n* antenati *mpl*

anchor /'æŋkə(r)/ **①** *n* ancora *f*
② *vi* gettare l'ancora
③ *vt* ancorare

anchorage /'æŋkərɪdʒ/ *n* ancoraggio *m*

anchorman /'æŋkəmæn/ *n* Radio, TV
anchor man *m inv*; Sport staffettista *m*
dell'ultima frazione

anchorwoman /'æŋkəwʊmən/ *n* Radio
TV anchor woman *f inv*

anchovy /'æntʃəvɪ/ *n* acciuga *f*

ancient /'eɪnʃənt/ *adj* antico; fam
vecchio; ~ **Rome** l'antica Roma *f*

ancillary /æn'sɪlərɪ/ *adj* ausiliario

and /ənd/, *accentato* /ænd/ *conj* e; ~ **so
on** e così via; **two** ~ **two** due più due; **six
hundred** ~ **two** seicentodue; **more** ~ **more**
sempre più; **nice** ~ **warm** bello caldo; **try**
~ **come** cerca di venire; **go** ~ **get** vai a
prendere

Andean /'ændɪən/ *adj* andino

Andes /'ændiːz/ *npl* the ~ le Ande

Andorra /æn'dɔːrə/ *n* Andorra *f*

anecdote /'ænɪkdəʊt/ *n* aneddoto *m*

anemone /ə'nemənɪ/ *n* Bot anemone *m*

anew /ə'njuː/ *adv* di nuovo

angel /'eɪndʒl/ *n* angelo *m*

angel cake *n* dolce *m* di pan di Spagna

angelfish /'eɪndʒlfɪʃ/ *n* angelo *m* di
mare

angelic /æn'dʒelɪk/ *adj* angelico

anger /'æŋgə(r)/ **①** *n* rabbia *f*
② *vt* far arrabbiare

angina [pectoris]
/æn'dʒaɪnə('pektərɪs)/ *n* angina *f* pectoris

angle[1] /'æŋgl/ *n* angolo *m*; fig angolazione
f; **at an** ~ storto

angle[2] *vi* pescare con la lenza; ~ **for** fig
cercare di ottenere

angle bracket *n* Techn parentesi *f inv*
uncinata

Anglepoise [lamp] /'æŋglpɔɪz/ *n*
lampada *f* a braccio estensibile

angler /'æŋglə(r)/ *n* pescatore, -trice *mf*

Anglican /'æŋglɪkən/ *adj & n* anglicano,
-a *mf*

anglicism /'æŋglɪsɪzm/ *n* anglicismo *m*

anglicize /'æŋglɪsaɪz/ *vt* anglicizzare

angling /'æŋglɪŋ/ *n* pesca *f* con la lenza

Anglo+ /'æŋgləʊ/ *pref* anglo+

Anglo-American *adj & n*
angloamericano, -a *mf*

Anglophone /'æŋgləfəʊn/ *adj & n*
anglofono, -a *mf*

Anglo-Saxon /æŋgləʊ'sæksn/ *adj & n*
anglosassone *mf*

Angola /æŋ'gəʊlə/ *n* Angola *f*

angora /æŋ'gɔːrə/ *n* lana *f* d'angora

angrily /'æŋgrɪlɪ/ *adv* rabbiosamente

angry /'æŋgrɪ/ *adj* (*-ier, -iest*) arrabbiato;
get ~ arrabbiarsi; ~ **with** or **at somebody**
arrabbiato con qualcuno; ~ **at** or **about
something** arrabbiato per qualcosa

anguish /'æŋgwɪʃ/ *n* angoscia *f*; **in** ~ in
preda all'angoscia

anguished /'æŋgwɪʃt/ *adj* (suffering)
straziante; ⟨*person*⟩ angosciato

angular /'æŋgjʊlə(r)/ *adj* angolare

animal /'ænɪm(ə)l/ *adj & n* animale *m*

animal experiment *n* esperimento *m*
sugli animali

animal husbandry /'hʌzbəndrɪ/ *n*
allevamento *m*

animal kingdom *n* regno *m* animale

animal lover *n* amante *mf* degli
animali

animal product *n* prodotto *m* di
origine animale

animal rights *npl* diritti *mpl* degli
animali

animal rights activist *n* animalista
mf

animal sanctuary *n* rifugio *m* per
animali

animal testing *n* sperimentazione *f*
sugli animali

animate[1] /'ænɪmət/ *adj* animato

animate[2] /'ænɪmeɪt/ *vt* animare

animated /'ænɪmeɪtɪd/ *adj* animato;
⟨*person*⟩ vivace

animation /ænɪ'meɪʃn/ *n* animazione *f*

animator /'ænɪmeɪtə(r)/ *n* (film cartoonist)
animatore, -trice *mf*; (director) regista *mf* di
film d'animazione

animatronics /ænɪmə'trɒnɪks/ n animazione f elettronica

animosity /ænɪ'mɒsətɪ/ n animosità f inv

aniseed /'ænɪsiːd/ n anice f

ankle /'æŋk(ə)l/ n caviglia f

anklebone n astragalo m

ankle-deep adj be ∼ in mud adj essere nel fango fino alle caviglie

ankle-length adj (dress) alla caviglia

ankle sock n calzino m

annals /'ænəlz/ npl go down in the ∼ [of history] passare agli annali

annex /ə'neks/ vt annettere

annexation /ænek'seɪʃn/ n (action) annessione f; (land annexed) territorio m annesso

annex[e] /'æneks/ n annesso m

annihilate /ə'naɪəleɪt/ vt annientare

annihilation /ənaɪə'leɪʃn/ n annientamento m

anniversary /ænɪ'vɜːsərɪ/ n anniversario m

Anno Domini /ænəʊ'dɒmɪnaɪ/ adv dopo Cristo

annotate /'ænəteɪt/ vt annotare

announce /ə'naʊns/ vt annunciare

announcement /ə'naʊnsmənt/ n annuncio m

announcer /ə'naʊnsə(r)/ n annunciatore, -trice mf

annoy /ə'nɔɪ/ vt dare fastidio a

annoyance /ə'nɔɪəns/ n seccatura f; (anger) irritazione f

annoyed adj irritato; get ∼ irritarsi; ∼ with somebody irritato con qualcuno; ∼ at/about something irritato per qualcosa; ∼ that irritato che

annoying /ə'nɔɪɪŋ/ adj fastidioso

annual /'ænjʊəl/ 1 adj annuale; (income) annuo
2 n Bot pianta f annua; (children's book) almanacco m

Annual General Meeting n assemblea f generale annuale

annually /'ænjʊəlɪ/ adv annualmente; she earns £50,000∼ guadagna 50.000 sterline all'anno

annual report n resoconto m annuale

annuity /ə'njuːətɪ/ n annualità f inv

annul /ə'nʌl/ vt (pt/pp **annulled**) annullare

Annunciation /ənʌnsɪ'eɪʃn/ n Annunciazione f

anode /'ænəʊd/ n anodo m

anodyne /'ænədaɪn/ adj liter (bland) anodino; (inoffensive) innocuo

anoint /ə'nɔɪnt/ vt ungere

anomalous /ə'nɒmələs/ adj anomalo

anomaly /ə'nɒmælɪ/ n anomalia f

anon /ə'nɒn/ abbr (**anonymous**) anonimo

anonymity /ænə'nɪmətɪ/ n anonimità f

anonymous /ə'nɒnɪməs/ adj anonimo; remain ∼ mantenere l'anonimato

anonymously /ə'nɒnɪməslɪ/ adv anonimamente

anorak /'ænəræk/ n giacca f a vento

anorexia /'ænə'reksɪə/ n anoressia f

anorexic /ænə'reksɪk/ adj & n anoressico, -a mf

another /ə'nʌðə(r)/ adj & pron ∼ [one] un altro, un'altra; ∼ day un altro giorno; in ∼ way diversamente; ∼ time un'altra volta; one ∼ l'un l'altro

answer /'ɑːnsə(r)/ 1 n risposta f; (solution) soluzione f
2 vt rispondere a (person, question, letter); esaudire (prayer); ∼ the door aprire la porta; ∼ the telephone rispondere al telefono
3 vi rispondere
■ **answer back** vi ribattere
■ **answer for** vt rispondere di

answerable /'ɑːnsərəbl/ adj responsabile; be ∼ to somebody rispondere a qualcuno

answering machine n Teleph segreteria f telefonica

answering service n servizio m di segreteria telefonica

answerphone /'ɑːnsəfəʊn/ n segreteria f telefonica

ant /ænt/ n formica f

antacid /ænt'æsɪd/ adj & n antiacido m

antagonism /æn'tægənɪzm/ n antagonismo m

antagonistic /æntægə'nɪstɪk/ adj antagonistico

antagonize /æn'tægənaɪz/ vt provocare l'ostilità di

Antarctic /æn'tɑːktɪk/ 1 n Antartico m
2 adj antartico

Antarctica /æn'tɑːktɪkə/ n Antartide f

Antarctic Circle n Circolo m polare antartico

Antarctic Ocean n mare m antartico

anteater /'æntiːtə(r)/ n formichiere m

antecedent /æntɪ'siːdənt/ n (precedent) antecedente m; (ancestor) antenato, -a mf

antedate /æntɪ'deɪt/ vt (put earlier date on) retrodatare; (predate) precedere

antediluvian /æntɪdɪ'luːvɪən/ adj antidiluviano

antelope /'æntɪləʊp/ n antilope m

antenatal /æntɪ'neɪtl/ adj prenatale

antenatal class n corso m di preparazione al parto

antenatal clinic *n* Br assistenza *f* medica prenatale

antenna /æn'tenə/ *n* antenna *f*

anterior /æn'tɪərɪə/ *adj* anteriore

anteroom /'ænti-/ *n* anticamera *f*

antheap /'ænthi:p/ = ANTHILL

anthem /'ænθəm/ *n* inno *m*

anthill /'ænthɪl/ *n* formicaio *m*

anthology /æn'θɒlədʒɪ/ *n* antologia *f*

anthracite /'ænθrəsaɪt/ *n* antracite *f*

anthrax /'ænθræks/ *n* (disease) carbonchio *m*; (pustule) pustola *f* di carbonchio

anthropological /ænθrəpə'lɒdʒɪkl/ *adj* antropologico

anthropologist /ænθrə'pɒlədʒɪst/ *n* antropologo, -a *mf*

anthropology /ænθrə'pɒlədʒɪ/ *n* antropologia *f*

anti /'æntɪ/ ① *pref* anti-
② *prep* be ～ essere contro

anti-abortion *adj* antiabortista

anti-abortionist *n* antiabortista *mf*

anti-aircraft *adj* antiaereo

anti-apartheid *adj* antiapartheid *inv*

antibacterial /æntɪbæk'tɪərɪəl/ *adj* antibatterico

antiballistic missile /æntɪbəlɪstɪk'mɪsaɪl/ *n* missile *m* antimissile

antibiotic /æntɪbar'ɒtɪk/ *n* antibiotico *m*

antibody /'æntɪbɒdɪ/ *n* anticorpo *m*

anticipate /æn'tɪsɪpeɪt/ *vt* prevedere; (forestall) anticipare

anticipation /æntɪsɪ'peɪʃn/ *n* anticipo *m*; (excitement) attesa *f*; **in ～ of** in previsione di

anticlimax /æntɪ'klaɪmæks/ *n* delusione *f*

anticlockwise /æntɪ'klɒkwaɪz/ *adj* & *adv* in senso antiorario

antics /'æntɪks/ *npl* gesti *mpl* buffi

anticyclone /æntɪ'saɪkləʊn/ *n* anticiclone *m*

antidepressant /æntɪdɪ'pres(ə)nt/ *adj* & *n* antidepressivo *m*

antidote /'æntɪdəʊt/ *n* antidoto *m*

anti-establishment *adj* contestatario

antifreeze /'æntɪfri:z/ *n* antigelo *m*

antiglare /æntɪ'gleə(r)/ *adj* (screen) antiriflesso *inv*

antihistamine /æntɪ'hɪstəmi:n/ *n* antistaminico *m*

anti-inflammatory /-ɪn'flæmətrɪ/ *adj* & *n* antinfiammatorio *m*

anti-inflation *adj* anti-inflazione *inv*

anti-inflationary /-ɪn'fleɪʃnərɪ/ *adj* antinflazionistico

anti-lock *adj* antibloccaggio *inv*

antipathy /æn'tɪpəθɪ/ *n* antipatia *f*

antiperspirant /æntɪ'pɜ:spɪrənt/ *n* deodorante *m* antitraspirante

antipodean /æntɪpə'di:ən/ *adj* & *n* australiano, -a e/o neozelandese *mf*

Antipodes /æn'tɪpədi:z/ *npl* Br **the ～** gli antipodi

antiquarian /æntɪ'kweərɪən/ *adj* antiquario; **～ bookshop** negozio *m* di libri antichi

antiquated /'æntɪkweɪtɪd/ *adj* antiquato

antique /æn'ti:k/ ① *adj* antico
② *n* antichità *f inv*

antique dealer *n* antiquario, -a *mf*

antiques fair *n* fiera *f* dell'antiquariato

antique shop *n* negozio *m* d'antiquariato

antiques trade *n* antiquariato *m*

antiquity /æn'tɪkwətɪ/ *n* antichità *f*

anti-racism *n* antirazzismo *m*

anti-racist *adj* antirazzista

antiretroviral /æntɪ'retrəʊvaɪrəl/ *adj* antiretrovirale

anti-riot *adj* (police) antisommossa *inv*

anti-rust *adj* antiruggine *inv*

anti-Semitic /æntɪsɪ'mɪtɪk/ *adj* antisemita

anti-Semitism /æntɪ'semɪtɪzm/ *n* antisemitismo *m*

antiseptic /æntɪ'septɪk/ *adj* & *n* antisettico *m*

anti-skid *adj* antiscivolo *inv*

anti-smoking *adj* contro il fumo, antifumo

antisocial /æntɪ'səʊʃəl/ *adj* (behaviour) antisociale; (person) asociale

anti-terrorist *adj* antiterrorista

anti-theft *adj* (lock, device) antifurto *inv*; (camera) di sorveglianza; **～ steering lock** bloccasterzo *m*

antithesis /æn'tɪθəsɪs/ *n* antitesi *f*

antitrust /æntɪ'trʌst/ *adj* antitrust *inv*

antivirus program /æntɪ'vaɪrəs/ *n* Comput programma *m* antivirus

antivirus software *n* Comput programma *m* antivirus

antivivisectionist /æntɪvɪvɪ'sekʃənɪst/ ① *n* antivivisezionista *mf*
② *adj* antivivisezionistico

anti-war *adj* antimilitarista

antlers /'æntləz/ *npl* corna *fpl*

antonym /'æntənɪm/ *n* antonimo *m*

Antwerp /'æntwɜ:p/ *n* Anversa *f*

anus /'eɪnəs/ *n* ano *m*

anvil /'ænvɪl/ *n* incudine *f*

anxiety /æŋ'zaɪətɪ/ *n* ansia *f*

anxious /'æŋkʃəs/ *adj* ansioso

anxiously /'æŋkʃəslɪ/ *adv* con ansia

any /'enɪ/ ① *adj* (no matter which) qualsiasi, qualunque; **have we ~ wine/biscuits?** abbiamo del vino/dei biscotti?; **have we ~ jam/apples?** abbiamo della marmellata/ delle mele?; **~ colour/number you like** qualsiasi colore/numero ti piaccia; **we don't have ~ wine/biscuits** non abbiamo vino/biscotti; **I don't have ~ reason to lie** non ho nessun motivo per mentire; **for ~ reason** per qualsiasi ragione ② *pron* (some) né; (no matter which) uno qualsiasi; **I don't want ~ [of it]** non ne voglio [nessuno]; **there aren't ~** non ce ne sono; **have we ~?** ne abbiamo?; **have you read ~ of her books?** hai letto qualcuno dei suoi libri? ③ *adv* **I can't go ~ quicker** non posso andare più in fretta; **is it ~ better?** va un po' meglio?; **would you like ~ more?** ne vuoi ancora?; **I can't eat ~ more** non posso mangiare più niente

anybody /'enɪbʌdɪ/ *pron* chiunque; (after negative) nessuno; **~ can do that** chiunque può farlo; **I haven't seen ~** non ho visto nessuno

anyhow /'enɪhaʊ/ *adv* ad ogni modo, comunque; (badly) non importa come

anyone /'enɪwʌn/ *pron* = ANYBODY

anyplace /'enɪpleɪs/ *adv* Am = ANYWHERE

anything /'enɪθɪŋ/ *pron* qualche cosa, qualcosa; (no matter what) qualsiasi cosa; (after negative) niente; **take/buy ~ you like** prendi/compra quello che vuoi; **I don't remember ~** non mi ricordo niente; **he's ~ but stupid** è tutto fuorché stupido; **I'll do ~ but that** farò qualsiasi cosa, tranne quello

anytime /'enɪtaɪm/ *adv* **if at ~ you feel lonely...** se mai ti dovessi sentire solo...; **he could arrive ~ now** potrebbe arrivare da un momento all'altro; **~ after 2 pm** a qualsiasi ora dopo le due; **at ~ of the day or night** a qualsiasi ora del giorno o della notte; **~ you like** quando vuoi

anyway /'enɪweɪ/ *adv* ad ogni modo, comunque

anywhere /'enɪweə(r)/ *adv* dovunque; (after negative) da nessuna parte; **put it ~** mettilo dove vuoi; **I can't find it ~** non lo trovo da nessuna parte; **~ else** da qualche altra parte; **I don't want to go ~ else** non voglio andare da nessun'altra parte

aorta /eɪ'ɔ:tə/ *n* aorta *f*

Aosta /æ'ɒstə/ *n* Aosta *f*

apace /ə'peɪs/ *adv* liter rapidamente

apart /ə'pɑ:t/ *adv* lontano; **live ~** vivere separati; **100 miles ~** lontani 100 miglia; **born 20 minutes ~** nati a distanza di 20 minuti; **~ from** a parte; **you can't tell them ~** non si possono distinguere; **joking ~** scherzi a parte

apartheid /ə'pɑ:thaɪt/ *n* apartheid *f*

apartment /ə'pɑ:tmənt/ *n* (Am: flat) appartamento *m*; **in my ~** a casa mia

apartment block *n* stabile *m*

apartment house *n* stabile *m*

apathetic /æpə'θetɪk/ *adj* (by nature) apatico; **~ about something/towards somebody** (from illness, depression) indifferente a qualcosa/nei confronti di qualcuno

apathy /'æpəθɪ/ *n* apatia *f*

ape /eɪp/ ① *n* scimmia *f* ② *vt* scimmiottare

Apennines /'æpənaɪnz/ *npl* **the ~** gli Appennini

aperitif /ə'perəti:f/ *n* aperitivo *m*

aperture /'æpətʃə(r)/ *n* apertura *f*

apex /'eɪpeks/ *n* vertice *m*

aphid /'eɪfɪd/ *n* afide *m*

aphrodisiac /æfrə'dɪzɪæk/ *adj & n* afrodisiaco *m*

apiary /'eɪpɪərɪ/ *n* apiario *m*

apiece /ə'pi:s/ *adv* ciascuno

aplenty /ə'plentɪ/ *adv* **there were goals ~** c'è stata una valanga di gol

apocalypse /ə'pɒkəlɪps/ *n* Apocalisse *f*; (disaster, destruction) apocalisse *f*

apocalyptic /əpɒkə'lɪptɪk/ *adj* apocalittico

apocryphal /ə'pɒkrɪfəl/ *adj* apocrifo

apogee /'æpədʒi:/ *n* apogeo *m*

apolitical /eɪpə'lɪtɪkl/ *adj* apolitico

Apollo /ə'pɒləʊ/ *n* also fig Apollo *m*

apologetic /əpɒlə'dʒetɪk/ *adj* ⟨air, remark⟩ di scusa; **be ~** essere spiacente

apologetically /əpɒlə'dʒetɪklɪ/ *adv* per scusarsi

apologist /ə'pɒlədʒɪst/ *n* apologeta *mf* (for di)

apologize /ə'pɒlədʒaɪz/ *vi* scusarsi (**for** per)

apology /ə'pɒlədʒɪ/ *n* scusa *f*; fig **an ~ for a dinner** una sottospecie di cena

apoplectic /æpə'plektɪk/ *adj* (furious) furibondo; ⟨fit, attack⟩ apoplettico

apoplexy /'æpəpleksɪ/ *n* Med apoplessia *f*; (rage) rabbia *f*

apostle /ə'pɒsl/ *n* apostolo *m*

apostrophe /ə'pɒstrəfɪ/ *n* apostrofo *m*

apotheosis /əpɒθɪ'əʊsɪs/ *n* apoteosi *f* inv

appal /ə'pɔ:l/ *vt* (pt/pp **appalled**) sconvolgere

Appalachians /æpə'leɪtʃnz/ *npl* **the ~** gli Appalachi

appalling /ə'pɔ:lɪŋ/ *adj* sconvolgente; **he's an ~ teacher** fig è un disastro come professore

appallingly /ə'pɔ:lɪŋlɪ/ *adv* ⟨behave, treat⟩ orribilmente; **unemployment figures are ~ high** il tasso di disoccupazione è ⋯⟩

spaventosamente alto; **furnished in** ∼ **bad taste** arredato con pessimo gusto

apparatus /æpə'reɪtəs/ *n* apparato *m*

apparel /ə'pærəl/ *n* abbigliamento *m*

apparent /ə'pærənt/ *adj* evidente; (seeming) apparente

apparently /ə'pærəntlɪ/ *adv* apparentemente

apparition /æpə'rɪʃn/ *n* apparizione *f*

appeal /ə'pi:l/ ① *n* appello *m*; (attraction) attrattiva *f*
② *vi* fare appello; ∼ **to** (be attractive to) attrarre

appeal fund *n* raccolta *f* di fondi

appealing /ə'pi:lɪŋ/ *adj* attraente

appealingly /ə'pi:lɪŋlɪ/ *adv* (beseechingly) in modo supplichevole; (attractively) in modo attraente

appeal[s] court *n* corte *f* d'appello

appear /ə'pɪə(r)/ *vi* apparire; (seem) sembrare; ⟨*publication*⟩ uscire; Theat esibirsi; **he finally** ∼**ed at...** fam si è fatto finalmente vedere alle...; ∼ **in court** comparire in giudizio

appearance /ə'pɪərəns/ *n* apparizione *f*; (look) aspetto *m*; **to all** ∼**s** a giudicare dalle apparenze; **keep up** ∼**s** salvare le apparenze

appease /ə'pi:z/ *vt* placare

appeasement /ə'pi:zmənt/ *n* **a policy of** ∼ una politica troppo conciliante

append /ə'pend/ *vt* apporre ⟨*signature*⟩ (to a)

appendage /ə'pendɪdʒ/ *n* appendice *f*

appendicitis /əpendɪ'saɪtɪs/ *n* appendicite *f*

appendix /ə'pendɪks/ *n* (of book) (pl **-ices** /-əsi:z/) appendice *f*; (pl **-es**) Anat appendice *f*

appertain /æpə'teɪn/ *vi* ∼ **to** essere pertinente a

appetite /'æpɪtaɪt/ *n* appetito *m*

appetite suppressant *n* pillola *f* antifame

appetizer /'æpɪtaɪzə(r)/ *n* (drink) aperitivo *m*; (starter) antipasto *m*; (biscuit, olive) stuzzichino *m*

appetizing /'æpɪtaɪzɪŋ/ *adj* appetitoso

applaud /ə'plɔ:d/ *vt/i* applaudire

applause /ə'plɔ:z/ *n* applauso *m*

apple /'æpl/ *n* mela *f*; **she's the** ∼ **of his eye** è la luce dei suoi occhi

apple core *n* torsolo *m* di mela

apple orchard *n* meleto *m*

applet /'æplət/ *n* Comput applet *f*

apple tree *n* melo *m*

appliance /ə'plaɪəns/ *n* attrezzo *m*; **[electrical]** ∼ elettrodomestico *m*

applicable /'æplɪkəbl/ *adj* **be** ∼ **to** essere valido per; **not** ∼ (on form) non applicabile

applicant /'æplɪkənt/ *n* candidato, -a *mf*

application /æplɪ'keɪʃn/ *n* applicazione *f*; (request) domanda *f*; (for job) candidatura *f*; **on** ∼ su richiesta

application form *n* modulo *m* di domanda

applicator /'æplɪkeɪtə(r)/ *n* applicatore *m*

applied /ə'plaɪd/ *adj* applicato

appliqué /ə'pli:keɪ/ ① *n* applicazione *f*
② *attrib* ⟨motif, decoration⟩ applicato

apply /ə'plaɪ/ ① *vt* (pt/pp **-ied**) applicare; ∼ **oneself** applicarsi; ∼ **the brakes** frenare
② *vi* applicarsi; ⟨*law*⟩ essere applicabile; ∼ **to** (ask) rivolgersi a; ∼ **for** fare domanda per ⟨*job etc*⟩

appoint /ə'pɔɪnt/ *vt* nominare; fissare ⟨*time*⟩ **well** ∼**ed** ben equipaggiato

appointee /əpɔɪn'ti:/ *n* incaricato, -a *mf*

appointment /ə'pɔɪntmənt/ *n* appuntamento *m*; (to job) nomina *f*; (job) posto *m*

apportion /ə'pɔ:ʃn/ *vt* ripartire, attribuire

apposite /'æpəzɪt/ *adj* appropriato

apposition /æpə'zɪʃn/ *n* apposizione *f*

appraisal /ə'preɪzəl/ *n* valutazione *f*; **make an** ∼ **of something** valutare qualcosa

appraise /ə'preɪz/ *vt* valutare

appreciable /ə'pri:ʃəbl/ *adj* sensibile

appreciably /ə'pri:ʃəblɪ/ *adv* sensibilmente

appreciate /ə'pri:ʃeɪt/ ① *vt* apprezzare; (understand) comprendere
② *vi* (increase in value) aumentare di valore

appreciation /əpri:sɪ'eɪʃn/ *n* (gratitude) riconoscenza *f*; (enjoyment) apprezzamento *m*; (understanding) comprensione *f*; (in value) aumento *m*; **in** ∼ come segno di riconoscenza (**of** per)

appreciative /ə'pri:ʃətɪv/ *adj* riconoscente

apprehend /æprɪ'hend/ *vt* arrestare

apprehension /æprɪ'henʃn/ *n* arresto *m*; (fear) apprensione *f*

apprehensive /æprɪ'hensɪv/ *adj* apprensivo

apprehensively /æprɪ'hensɪvlɪ/ *adv* con apprensione

apprentice /ə'prentɪs/ *n* apprendista *mf*

apprenticeship /ə'prentɪsʃɪp/ *n* apprendistato *m*

apprise /ə'praɪz/ *vt* fml informare (**of** di)

approach /ə'prəʊtʃ/ ① *n* avvicinamento *m*; (to problem) approccio *m*; (access) accesso *m*; **make** ∼**es to** fare degli approcci con

2 *vi* avvicinarsi
3 *vt* avvicinarsi a; (with request) rivolgersi a; affrontare ⟨*problem*⟩

approachable /əˈprəʊtʃəbl/ *adj* accessibile

approach lights *npl* Aeron sentiero *m* luminoso di avvicinamento

approach path *n* Aeron rotta *f* di avvicinamento

approach road *n* strada *f* d'accesso

approbation /æprəˈbeɪʃn/ *n* approvazione *f*

appropriate[1] /əˈprəʊprɪət/ *adj* appropriato

appropriate[2] /əˈprəʊprɪeɪt/ *vt* appropriarsi di

appropriately /əˈprəʊprɪətlɪ/ *adv* (suitably) in modo appropriato; ⟨*sited*⟩ convenientemente; ⟨*designed, chosen, behave*⟩ adeguatamente

appropriation /əprəʊprɪˈeɪʃn/ *n* Am Comm stanziamento *m*; (Jur: removal) appropriazione *f*

approval /əˈpruːvl/ *n* approvazione *f*; on ∼ in prova

approve /əˈpruːv/ **1** *vt* approvare **2** *vi* ∼ of approvare ⟨*something*⟩ avere una buona opinione di ⟨*somebody*⟩

approving /əˈpruːvɪŋ/ *adj* ⟨*smile, nod*⟩ d'approvazione

approvingly /əˈpruːvɪŋlɪ/ *adv* con approvazione

approximate[1] /əˈprɒksɪmeɪt/ *vi* ∼ to avvicinarsi a

approximate[2] /əˈproksɪmət/ *adj* approssimativo

approximately /əˈprɒksɪmətlɪ/ *adv* approssimativamente

approximation /əprɒksɪˈmeɪʃn/ *n* approssimazione *f*

APR *n* (**annual percentage rate**) tasso *m* percentuale annuo

apricot /ˈeɪprɪkɒt/ *n* albicocca *f*; ∼ **tree** albicocco *m*

April /ˈeɪprəl/ *n* aprile *m*; **make an** ∼ **Fool of somebody** fare un pesce d'aprile a qualcuno

April Fools' Day *n* il primo d'aprile *m*

apron /ˈeɪprən/ *n* grembiule *m*

apropos /ˈæprəpəʊ/ *adv* ∼ **[of]** a proposito [di]

apse /æps/ *n* abside *f*

apt /æpt/ *adj* appropriato; ⟨*pupil*⟩ dotato; **be** ∼ **to do something** avere tendenza a fare qualcosa

aptitude /ˈæptɪtjuːd/ *n* disposizione *f*

aptitude test *n* test *m inv* attitudinale

aptly /ˈæptlɪ/ *adv* appropriatamente

Apulia /əˈpjuːlɪə/ *n* Puglia *f*

aqualung /ˈækwəlʌŋ/ *n* autorespiratore *m*

aquamarine /ækwəməˈriːn/ *adj & n* acquamarina *f*

aquaplane /ˈækwəpleɪn/ *vi* Sport praticare l'acquaplano; Br Auto andare in aquaplaning

aquarium /əˈkweərɪəm/ *n* acquario *m*

Aquarius /əˈkweərɪəs/ *n* Astr Acquario *m*; **be** ∼ essere dell'Acquario

aquarobics /ækwəˈrəʊbɪks/ *n* acquagym *f inv*

aquatic /əˈkwætɪk/ *adj* acquatico

aqueduct /ˈækwədʌkt/ *n* acquedotto *m*

aquiline /ˈækwɪlaɪn/ *adj* ⟨*nose, features*⟩ aquilino

Arab /ˈærəb/ *adj & n* arabo, -a *mf*

Arabia /əˈreɪbɪə/ *n* Arabia *f*

Arabian /əˈreɪbɪən/ *adj* arabo

Arabic /ˈærəbɪk/ **1** *adj* arabo; ∼ **numerals** numeri *mpl* arabi **2** *n* arabo *m*

Arab-Israeli *adj* arabo-israeliano

arable /ˈærəbl/ *adj* coltivabile

arbiter /ˈɑːbɪtə(r)/ *n* arbitro *m*

arbitrarily /ɑːbɪˈtrerɪlɪ/ *adv* arbitrariamente

arbitrary /ˈɑːbɪtrərɪ/ *adj* arbitrario

arbitrate /ˈɑːbɪtreɪt/ *vi* arbitrare

arbitration /ɑːbɪˈtreɪʃn/ *n* arbitraggio *m*

arbitrator /ˈɑːbɪtreɪtə(r)/ *n* arbitro *m*

arbour /ˈɑːbə(r)/ *n* pergolato *m*

arc /ɑːk/ *n* arco *m*

arcade /ɑːˈkeɪd/ *n* portico *m*; (shops) galleria *f*

arcane /ɑːˈkeɪn/ *adj* arcano

arch /ɑːtʃ/ **1** *n* arco *m*; (of foot) dorso *m* del piede **2** *vt* the cat ∼ed its back il gatto ha arcuato la schiena

archaeological /ɑːkɪəˈlɒdʒɪkl/ *adj* archeologico

archaeologist /ɑːkɪˈɒlədʒɪst/ *n* archeologo, -a *mf*

archaeology /ɑːkɪˈɒlədʒɪ/ *n* archeologia *f*

archaic /ɑːˈkeɪɪk/ *adj* arcaico

archbishop /ɑːtʃˈbɪʃəp/ *n* arcivescovo *m*

arched /ɑːtʃt/ *adj* (eyebrows) arcuato

arch-enemy *n* acerrimo nemico *m*

archer /ˈɑːtʃə(r)/ *n* arciere *m*

archery /ˈɑːtʃərɪ/ *n* tiro *m* con l'arco

archetypal /ɑːkɪˈtaɪpl/ *adj* the ∼ hero il prototipo dell'eroe

archetype /ˈɑːkɪtaɪp/ *n* archetipo *m*

archipelago /ɑːkɪˈpeləgəʊ/ *n* arcipelago *m*

architect /ˈɑːkɪtekt/ *n* architetto *m*

architectural /ɑːkɪˈtektʃərəl/ *adj*
architettonico

architecturally /ɑːkɪˈtektʃərəlɪ/ *adv*
architettonicamente

architecture /ˈɑːkɪˈtektʃə(r)/ *n*
architettura *f*

archive /ˈɑːkaɪv/ *vt* also Comput archiviare

archives /ˈɑːkaɪvz/ *npl* archivi *mpl*

archiving /ˈɑːkaɪvɪŋ/ *n* Comput
archiviazione *f*

archway /ˈɑːtʃweɪ/ *n* arco *m*

Arctic /ˈɑːktɪk/ ① *adj* artico
② *n* the ~ l'Artico

Arctic Circle *n* Circolo *m* polare artico

Arctic Ocean *n* mare *m* artico

ardent /ˈɑːdənt/ *adj* ardente

ardently /ˈɑːdəntlɪ/ *adv* ardentemente

ardour /ˈɑːdə(r)/ *n* ardore *m*

arduous /ˈɑːdjʊəs/ *adj* arduo

arduously /ˈɑːdjʊəslɪ/ *adv* con fatica,
con difficoltà

are /ɑː(r)/ ▶ BE

area /ˈeərɪə/ *n* area *f*; (region) zona *f*; (fig:
field) campo *m*

area code *n* prefisso *m* [telefonico]

area manager *n* direttore, -trice *mf* di
zona

arena /əˈriːnə/ *n* arena *f*

aren't /ɑːnt/ = are not ▶ BE

Argentina /ɑːdʒənˈtiːnə/ *n* Argentina *f*

Argentine /ˈɑːdʒəntaɪn/ *adj* argentino

Argentinian /ɑːdʒənˈtɪnɪən/ *adj* & *n*
argentino, -a *mf*

arguable /ˈɑːgjʊəbl/ *adj* it's ~ that... si
può sostenere che...

arguably /ˈɑːgjʊəblɪ/ *adv* he is ~... è
probabilmente...

argue /ˈɑːgjuː/ ① *vi* litigare (about su);
(debate) dibattere; don't ~! non discutere!
② *vt* (debate) dibattere; (reason) ~ that
sostenere che

argument /ˈɑːgjʊmənt/ *n* argomento *m*;
(reasoning) ragionamento *m*; have an ~
litigare

argumentative /ɑːgjʊˈmentətɪv/ *adj*
polemico

aria /ˈɑːrɪə/ *n* aria *f*

arid /ˈærɪd/ *adj* arido

aridity /əˈrɪdətɪ/ *n* also fig aridità *f*

Aries /ˈeəriːz/ *n* Astr Ariete *m*; be ~
essere dell'Ariete

arise /əˈraɪz/ *vi* (pt arose pp arisen)
⟨opportunity, need, problem;⟩ presentarsi;
(result) derivare

aristocracy /ærɪˈstɒkrəsɪ/ *n*
aristocrazia *f*

aristocrat /ˈærɪstəkræt/ *n* aristocratico,
-a *mf*

aristocratic /ærɪstəˈkrætɪk/ *adj*
aristocratico

arithmetic /əˈrɪθmətɪk/ *n* aritmetica *f*

arithmetical /ærɪθˈmetɪkl/ *adj*
aritmetico

ark /ɑːk/ *n* Noah's Ark l'Arca *f* di Noè

arm /ɑːm/ ① *n* braccio *m*; (of chair)
bracciolo *m*; ~s *pl* (weapons) armi *fpl*; ~ in
~ a braccetto; up in ~s fam furioso (about
per); fig with open ~s a braccia aperte
② *vt* armare

armadillo /ɑːməˈdɪləʊ/ *n* armadillo *m*

armaments /ˈɑːməmənts/ *npl*
armamenti *mpl*

armband /ˈɑːmbænd/ *n* (for swimmer)
bracciolo *m* (per nuotare): (for mourner)
fascia *f* al braccio

armchair /ˈɑːmtʃeə(r)/ *n* poltrona *f*

armchair traveller *n* persona *f* che si
interessa di viaggi senza viaggiare

armed /ɑːmd/ *adj* armato

armed forces /ˈfɔːsɪz/ *npl* forze *fpl*
armate

armed robbery *n* rapina *f* a mano
armata

Armenia /ɑːˈmiːnɪə/ *n* Armenia *f*

Armenian /ɑːˈmiːnɪən/ *adj* & *n* (person)
armeno, -a *mf*; (language) armeno *m*

armful /ˈɑːmfʊl/ *n* bracciata *f*

armhole /ˈɑːmhəʊl/ *n* giro *m* manica *inv*

armistice /ˈɑːmɪstɪs/ *n* armistizio *m*

Armistice Day *n* l'Anniversario *m*
dell'Armistizio (1 nov. 1918)

armour /ˈɑːmə(r)/ *n* armatura *f*

armour-clad /-ˈklæd/ *adj* ⟨vehicle⟩
blindato; ⟨ship⟩ corazzato

armoured /ˈɑːməd/ *adj* ⟨vehicle⟩ blindato

armoured car *n* autoblinda[ta] *f*

armour plate, **armour plating**
/ˈpleɪtɪŋ/ *n* corazzatura *f*

armour-plated /-ˈpleɪtɪd/ *adj* corazzato

armoury /ˈɑːmərɪ/ *n* (factory) fabbrica *f*
d'armi; (store) arsenale *m*, armeria *f*

armpit /ˈɑːmpɪt/ *n* ascella *f*

armrest /ˈɑːmrest/ *n* bracciolo *m* (di
sedia)

arms control *n* controllo *m* degli
armamenti

arms dealer *n* trafficante *mf* d'armi

arms dump *n* deposito *m* d'armi

arms embargo *n* embargo *m* sulle
armi

arms limitation *n* controllo *m* degli
armamenti

arms manufacturer *n* fabbricante *mf*
d'armi

arms race *n* corsa *f* agli armamenti

arms treaty *n* trattato *m* sul controllo
degli armamenti

arm-twisting /'ɑːmtwɪstɪŋ/ *n* pressioni *fpl*

arm-wrestling *n* braccio *m* di ferro

army /'ɑːmɪ/ *n* esercito *m*; **join the** ∼ arruolarsi

A road *n* Br [strada *f*] statale *f*

aroma /ə'rəʊmə/ *n* aroma *f*

aromatherapy /ərəʊmə'θerəpɪ/ *n* aromaterapia *f*

aromatic /ærə'mætɪk/ *adj* aromatico

arose /ə'rəʊz/ ▶ ARISE

around /ə'raʊnd/ **1** *adv* intorno; **all** ∼ tutt'intorno; **I'm not from** ∼ **here** non sono di qui; **he's not** ∼ non c'è
2 *prep* intorno a; in giro per ⟨*room, shops, world*⟩

arousal /ə'raʊzl/ *n* eccitazione *f*

arouse /ə'raʊz/ *vt* svegliare; (sexually) eccitare

arpeggio /ɑː'pedʒɪəʊ/ *n* arpeggio *m*

arrange /ə'reɪndʒ/ *vt* sistemare ⟨*furniture, books*⟩; organizzare ⟨*meeting*⟩; fissare ⟨*date, time*⟩; ∼ **to do something** combinare di fare qualcosa

arrangement /ə'reɪndʒmənt/ *n* (of furniture) sistemazione *f*; Mus arrangiamento *m*; (agreement) accordo; (of flowers) composizione *f*; **make** ∼**s** prendere disposizioni; **I've made other** ∼**s** ho preso altri impegni

array /ə'reɪ/ **1** *n* (clothes) abbigliamento *m*; (of troops, people) schieramento *m*; (of numbers) tabella *f*; (of weaponry) apparato *m*; (of goods, products) assortimento *m*; Comput matrice *f*
2 *vt* ∼**ed in ceremonial robes** abbigliato da gran cerimonia

arrears /ə'rɪəz/ *npl* arretrati *mpl*; **be in** ∼ essere in arretrato; **paid in** ∼ pagato a lavoro eseguito

arrest /ə'rest/ **1** *n* arresto *m*; **under** ∼ in stato d'arresto
2 *vt* arrestare

arresting /ə'restɪŋ/ *adj* (striking) che colpisce

arrival /ə'raɪvl/ *n* arrivo *m*; **new** ∼**s** *pl* nuovi arrivati *mpl*

arrivals board *n* tabellone *m* degli arrivi

arrival(s) lounge *n* sala *f* arrivi

arrival time *n* ora *f* d'arrivo

arrive /ə'raɪv/ *vi* arrivare; ∼ **at** fig raggiungere

arrogance /'ærəg(ə)ns/ *n* arroganza *f*

arrogant /'ærəg(ə)nt/ *adj* arrogante

arrogantly /'ærəg(ə)ntlɪ/ *adv* con arroganza

arrow /'ærəʊ/ *n* freccia *f*

arrowhead /'ærəʊhed/ *n* punta *f* di freccia

arse /ɑːs/ *n* vulg culo *m*

■ **arse about**, **arse around** *vi* vulg coglioneggiare

arsenal /'ɑːsən(ə)l/ *n* arsenale *m*

arsenic /'ɑːsənɪk/ *n* arsenico *m*

arson /'ɑːsən/ *n* incendio *m* doloso

arsonist /'ɑːsənɪst/ *n* incendiario, -a *mf*

art /ɑːt/ *n* arte *f*; **work of** ∼ opera *f* d'arte; ∼**s and crafts** *pl* artigianato *m*; **the A**∼**s** *pl* l'arte *f*; **A**∼**s degree** Univ laurea *f* in Lettere

art collection *n* collezione *f* d'arte

art collector *n* collezionista *mf* d'arte

art college *n* ≈ accademia *f* di belle arti

art dealer *n* commerciante *mf* di oggetti d'arte

art deco *n* art déco *f*

artefact /'ɑːtɪfækt/ *n* manufatto *m*

arterial /ɑː'tɪərɪəl/ *adj* Anat arterioso

arterial road *n* arteria *f* [stradale]

artery /'ɑːtərɪ/ *n* arteria *f*

art exhibition *n* mostra *f* d'arte

art form *n* forma *f* d'arte

artful /'ɑːtfl/ *adj* scaltro

artfully /'ɑːtfʊlɪ/ *adv* astutamente

art gallery *n* galleria *f* d'arte

arthritic /ɑː'θrɪtɪk/ *adj & n* artritico, -a *mf*

arthritis /ɑː'θraɪtɪs/ *n* artrite *f*

artichoke /'ɑːtɪtʃəʊk/ *n* carciofo *m*

article /'ɑːtɪkl/ *n* articolo *m*; ∼ **of clothing** capo *m* d'abbigliamento

articulate[1] /ɑː'tɪkjʊlət/ *adj* ⟨*speech*⟩ chiaro; **be** ∼ esprimersi bene

articulate[2] /ɑː'tɪkjʊleɪt/ *vt* scandire ⟨*words*⟩

articulated lorry /ɑː'tɪkjʊleɪtɪd/ *n* autotreno *m*

articulately /ɑː'tɪkjʊlətlɪ/ *adv* chiaramente

articulation /ɑːtɪkjʊ'leɪʃn/ *n* (pronunciation, Anat) articolazione *f*; (expression) espressione *f*

artifice /'ɑːtɪfɪs/ *n* artificio *m*

artificial /ɑːtɪ'fɪʃl/ *adj* artificiale

artificial insemination *n* inseminazione *f* artificiale

artificial intelligence *n* intelligenza *f* artificiale

artificiality /ɑːtɪfɪʃɪ'ælətɪ/ *n* artificiosità *f*

artificial limb *n* arto *m* artificiale

artificially /ɑːtɪ'fɪʃəlɪ/ *adv* artificialmente; ⟨*smile*⟩ artificiosamente

artificial respiration *n* respirazione *f* artificiale

artillery /ɑː'tɪlərɪ/ *n* artiglieria *f*

artisan /ɑːtɪ'zæn/ *n* artigiano, -a *mf*

artist /'ɑːtɪst/ *n* artista *mf*

artiste /ɑː'tiːst/ n Theat artista mf

artistic /ɑː'tɪstɪk/ adj artistico

artistically /ɑː'tɪstɪklɪ/ adv
artisticamente

artistry /'ɑːtɪstrɪ/ n arte f, talento m

artless /'ɑːtlɪs/ adj spontaneo

artlessly /'ɑːtlɪslɪ/ adv ‹smile›
ingenuamente

art nouveau /ɑːnuː'vəʊ/ adj & n liberty
m

art school n ≈ accademia f di belle arti

arts degree n laurea f in Lettere

arts funding n sovvenzioni fpl alle arti

arts student n studente, -essa mf di
Lettere

art student n studente, -essa mf di belle
arti

artwork /'ɑːtwɜːk/ n illustrazioni fpl

arty /'ɑːtɪ/ adj fam ‹person› intellettualoide;
‹district› degli intellettuali

AS n esame m sostenuto al termine del
primo anno del biennio di preparazione
agli A-Level

as /æz/ **1** conj come; (since) siccome,
(while) mentre; **as he grew older**
diventando vecchio; **as you get to know
her** conoscendola meglio; **young as she is**
per quanto sia giovane
2 prep come; **as a friend** come amico; **as
a child** da bambino; **as a foreigner** in
quanto straniero; **disguised as** travestito
da
3 adv as well (also) anche; **as soon as I
get home** [non] appena arrivo a casa; **as
quick as you** veloce quanto te; **as quick as
you can** più veloce che puoi; **as far as**
(distance) fino a; **as far as I'm concerned**
per quanto mi riguarda; **as long as** finché;
(provided that) purché

asap adv abbr (**as soon as possible**)
prima possibile

asbestos /æz'bestɒs/ n amianto m

ASBO /'æzbəʊ/ n Br abbr (**Antisocial
Behaviour Order**) ordinanza f
giudiziaria emessa contro chi ha
comportamenti contrari all'ordine
pubblico

ascend /ə'send/ **1** vi salire
2 vi salire a ‹throne›

ascendancy /ə'send(ə)nsɪ/ n gain the
∼ **over somebody** acquisire una posizione
dominante su qualcuno

ascendant /ə'send(ə)nt/ n be in the ∼
Astr essere in ascendente; fig ‹person›
essere in auge

Ascension /ə'senʃn/ n Relig Ascensione f

ascent /ə'sent/ n ascesa f

ascertain /æsə'teɪn/ vt accertare

ascetic /ə'setɪk/ adj & n ascetico, -a mf

asceticism /ə'setɪsɪzm/ n ascesi f

ascribe /ə'skraɪb/ vt attribuire

aseptic /eɪ'septɪk/ adj asettico

asexual /eɪ'seksjʊəl/ adj asessuale,
asessuato

ash¹ /æʃ/ n (tree) frassino m

ash² n cenere f

ashamed /ə'ʃeɪmd/ adj be/feel ∼
vergognarsi

ash blond adj biondo cenere

ashen /'æʃ(ə)n/ adj (complexion) cinereo

ashore /ə'ʃɔː(r)/ adv a terra; **go** ∼
sbarcare

ashtray n portacenere m

ash tree n frassino m

Ash Wednesday n mercoledì m inv
delle Ceneri

Asia /'eɪʒə/ n Asia f

Asia Minor n Asia f Minore

Asian /'eɪʒ(ə)n/ adj & n asiatico, -a mf;
(Br: Indian, Pakistani) indiano, -a mf

Asiatic /eɪʒɪ'ætɪk/ adj asiatico

aside /ə'saɪd/ **1** adv take somebody ∼
prendere qualcuno a parte; **put something**
∼ mettere qualcosa da parte; ∼ **from you**
Am a parte te; ∼ **from his injuries** Am a
parte le sue ferite
2 n in an ∼ tra parentesi

ask /ɑːsk/ **1** vt fare ‹question›; (invite)
invitare; ∼ **somebody something**
domandare or chiedere qualcosa a
qualcuno; ∼ **somebody to do something**
domandare or chiedere a qualcuno di fare
qualcosa
2 vi ∼ **about something** informarsi su
qualcosa;
■ **ask after** vt chiedere [notizie] di
‹somebody›
■ **ask for** vt chiedere ‹something›;
chiedere di ‹somebody›; ∼ **for trouble** fam
andare in cerca di guai
■ **ask in** vt ∼ **somebody in** invitare
qualcuno ad entrare
■ **ask out** vt ∼ **somebody out** chiedere a
qualcuno di uscire

askance /ə'skɑːns/ adv look ∼ at
somebody/something guardare qualcuno/
qualcosa di traverso

askew /ə'skjuː/ adj & adv di traverso

asking price /'ɑːskɪŋ/ n prezzo m
trattabile

asleep /ə'sliːp/ adj be ∼ dormire; fall ∼
addormentarsi

asparagus /ə'spærəgəs/ n asparagi mpl

aspect /'æspekt/ n aspetto m

aspen /'æspən/ n pioppo m tremulo

aspersions /ə'spɜːʃnz/ npl cast ∼ on
diffamare

asphalt /'æsfælt/ n asfalto m

asphyxia /əs'fɪksɪə/ n asfissia f

asphyxiate /əs'fɪksɪeɪt/ vt asfissiare

asphyxiation /əsfɪksɪ'eɪʃn/ n asfissia f

aspic /'æspɪk/ n aspic m inv

aspirate[1] /ˈæspəreɪt/ *vt* aspirare

aspirate[2] /ˈæspɪrət/ *adj* aspirato

aspirations /æspəˈreɪʃnz/ *npl* aspirazioni *fpl*

aspire /əˈspaɪə(r)/ *vi* ∼ **to** aspirare a

aspirin /ˈæsprɪn/ *n* aspirina® *f*

aspiring /əˈspaɪərɪŋ/ *adj* ∼ **authors/ journalists** aspiranti scrittori/giornalisti

ass /æs/ *n* asino *m*

assailant /əˈseɪlənt/ *n* assalitore, -trice *mf*

assassin /əˈsæsɪn/ *n* assassino, -a *mf*

assassinate /əˈsæsɪneɪt/ *vt* assassinare

assassination /əsæsɪˈneɪʃn/ *n* assassinio *m*

assault /əˈsɔːlt/ **①** *n* Mil assalto *m*; Jur aggressione *f* **②** *vt* aggredire

assault and battery *n* Jur lesioni *fpl* personali

assault course *n* Mil percorso *m* di guerra

assemblage /əˈsemblɪdʒ/ assemblaggio *m*

assemble /əˈsembl/ **①** *vi* radunarsi **②** *vi* radunare; Techn montare

assembler /əˈsemblə(r)/ *n* (in factory) montatore, -trice *mf*; Comput [programma] *m*] assemblatore *m*

assembly /əˈsemblɪ/ *n* assemblea *f*; Sch assemblea *f* giornaliera di alunni e professori di una scuola; Techn montaggio *m*

assembly line *n* catena *f* di montaggio

assent /əˈsent/ **①** *n* assenso *m* **②** *vi* acconsentire

assert /əˈsɜːt/ *vt* asserire; far valere ⟨one's rights⟩; ∼ **oneself** farsi valere

assertion /əˈsɜːʃn/ *n* asserzione *f*

assertive /əˈsɜːtɪv/ *adj* be ∼ farsi valere

assertiveness /əˈsɜːtɪvnɪs/ *n* capacità *f* di farsi valere; **lack of** ∼ scarsa sicurezza *f* di sé

assess /əˈses/ *vt* valutare; (for tax purposes) stabilire l'imponibile di

assessment /əˈsesmənt/ *n* valutazione *f*; (of tax) accertamento *m*

assessor /əˈsesə(r)/ *n* (Jur, in insurance) perito *m*; (tax) agente *m* del fisco

asset /ˈæset/ *n* (advantage) vantaggio *m*; (person) elemento *m* prezioso. ∼s *pl* beni *mpl*; (on balance sheet) attivo *msg*

asset stripping /ˈæsetstrɪpɪŋ/ *n* rilevamento *m* di un'azienda per rivenderne le single attività fisse

assiduity /æsɪˈdjuːətɪ/ *n* assiduità *f*

assiduous /əˈsɪdjʊəs/ *adj* assiduo

assign /əˈsaɪn/ *vt* assegnare

assignation /æsɪgˈneɪʃn/ *n* hum appuntamento *m* galante

assignment /əˈsaɪnmənt/ *n* (task) incarico *m*

assimilate /əˈsɪmɪleɪt/ *vt* assimilare; integrare ⟨person⟩

assimilation /əsɪmɪˈleɪʃn/ *n* assimilazione *f*

assist /əˈsɪst/ *vt/i* assistere; ∼ **somebody to do something** assistere qualcuno nel fare qualcosa

assistance /əˈsɪstəns/ *n* assistenza *f*

assistant /əˈsɪstənt/ *n* assistente *mf*; (in shop) commesso, -a *mf*

assistant manager *n* vicedirettore, -trice *mf*

assistant professor *n* Am Univ docente *mf* universitario, -a del grado più basso

assisted suicide /əˌsɪstɪd ˈsuːɪsaɪd/ *n* suicidio *m* assistito, eutanasia *f*

associate[1] /əˈsəʊʃɪeɪt/ **①** *vt* associare (**with** a); **be** ∼**d with something** (involved in) essere coinvolto in qualcosa **②** *vi* ∼ **with** frequentare

associate[2] /əˈsəʊʃɪət/ **①** *adj* associato **②** *n* collega *mf*; (member) socio, -a *mf*

associate company *n* consociata *f*

associate director *n* Comm amministratore *m* aggiunto

associate editor *n* co-redattore, -trice *mf*

associate member *n* membro *m* associato

association /əsəʊsɪˈeɪʃn/ *n* associazione *f*

Association Football *n* [gioco *m* del] calcio *m*

assorted /əˈsɔːtɪd/ *adj* assortito

assortment /əˈsɔːtmənt/ *n* assortimento *m*

assuage /əˈsweɪdʒ/ *vt* liter alleviare

assume /əˈsjuːm/ *vt* presumere; assumere ⟨control⟩; ∼ **office** entrare in carica; **assuming that you're right,...** ammettendo che tu abbia ragione,...

assumption /əˈsʌmpʃn/ *n* supposizione *f*; **on the** ∼ **that** partendo dal presupposto che; **the A**∼ Relig l'Assunzione *f*

assurance /əˈʃʊərəns/ *n* assicurazione *f*; (confidence) sicurezza *f*

assure /əˈʃʊə(r)/ *vt* assicurare; **he** ∼**d me of his innocence** mi ha assicurato di essere innocente

assured /əˈʃʊəd/ *adj* sicuro

asterisk /ˈæstərɪsk/ *n* asterisco *m*

asteroid /ˈæstərɔɪd/ *n* asteroide *m*

asthma /ˈæsmə/ *n* asma *f*

asthmatic /æsˈmætɪk/ *adj* asmatico

astigmatism /əˈstɪgmətɪzm/ *n* astigmatismo *m*

astonish /əˈstɒnɪʃ/ *vt* stupire

astonished /ə'stɒnɪʃt/ *adj* sorpreso

astonishing /ə'stɒnɪʃɪŋ/ *adj* stupefacente

astonishingly /ə'stɒnɪʃɪŋlɪ/ *adv* sorprendentemente

astonishment /ə'stɒnɪʃmənt/ *n* stupore *m*

astound /ə'staʊnd/ *vt* stupire

astounding /ə'staʊndɪŋ/ *adj* incredible

astrakhan /æstrə'kæn/ *n* astrakan *m*

astray /ə'streɪ/ **go** ∼ smarrirsi; (morally) uscire dalla retta via; **lead** ∼ traviare

astride /ə'straɪd/ ⓘ *adv* [a] cavalcioni ② *prep* a cavalcioni di

astringent /ə'strɪndʒənt/ ⓘ *adj* astringente; fig austero ② *n* astringente *m*

astrologer /ə'strɒlədʒə(r)/ *n* astrologo, -a *mf*

astrological /æstrə'lɒdʒɪkl/ *adj* astrologico

astrology /ə'strɒlədʒɪ/ *n* astrologia *f*

astronaut /'æstrənɔːt/ *n* astronauta *mf*

astronomer /ə'strɒnəmə(r)/ *n* astronomo, -a *mf*

astronomic /æstrə'nɒmɪk/ *adj* fig astronomico

astronomical /æstrə'nɒmɪkl/ *adj* also fig astronomico

astronomically /æstrə'nɒmɪklɪ/ *adv* ∼ **expensive** dal prezzo astronomico; **prices are** ∼ **high** i prezzi sono astronomici

astronomy /ə'strɒnəmɪ/ *n* astronomia *f*

astrophysicist /æstrəʊ'fɪzɪsɪst/ *n* astrofisico, -a *mf*

astrophysics /æstrəʊ'fɪzɪks/ *n* astrofisica *f*

astute /ə'stjuːt/ *adj* astuto

astutely /ə'stjuːtlɪ/ *adv* con astuzia

astuteness /ə'stjuːtnɪs/ *n* astuzia *f*

asylum /ə'saɪləm/ *n* [political] ∼ asilo *m* politico; [lunatic] ∼ manicomio *m*

asylum-seeker /ə'saɪləmsiːkə(r)/ *n* persona *f* che chiede asilo politico

asymmetric[al] /æsɪ'metrɪk[l]/ *adj* asimmetrico

at /ət/ stressed *prep* /æt/ *adj*; at the station/the market alla stazione/al mercato; at the office/the bank in ufficio/ banca; at the beginning all'inizio; at john's da John; at the hairdresser's dal parrucchiere; at home a casa; at work al lavoro; at school a scuola; at a party/ wedding a una festa/un matrimonio; at one o'clock all'una; at 50 km an hour ai 50 all'ora; at Christmas/Easter a Natale/ Pasqua; at times talvolta; two at a time due alla volta; good at languages bravo nelle lingue; at sb's request su richiesta

di qualcuno; are you at all worried? sei preoccupato?

atavistic /ætə'vɪstɪk/ *adj* atavico

ate /et/ ▶ EAT

atheism /'eɪθɪɪzm/ *n* ateismo *m*

atheist /'eɪθɪɪst/ *n* ateo, -a *mf*

atheistic /eɪθɪ'ɪstɪk/ *adj* ⟨principle⟩ ateistico; ⟨person⟩ ateo

Athenian /ə'θiːnɪən/ *adj & n* ateniese *mf*

Athens /'æθənz/ *n* Atene *f*

athlete /'æθliːt/ *n* atleta *mf*

athlete's foot *n* micosi *f*

athletic /æθ'letɪk/ *adj* atletico

athletics /æθ'letɪks/ *n* atletica *fsg*

Atlantic /ət'læntɪk/ *adj & n* the ∼ [Ocean] l'[Oceano *m*] Atlantico *m*

atlas /'ætləs/ *n* atlante *m*

Atlas Mountains *npl* Monti *mpl* dell'Atlante

ATM *n abbr* (automatic teller machine) cassa *f* continua di prelevamento

atmosphere /'ætməsfɪə(r)/ *n* atmosfera *f*

atmospheric /ætməs'ferɪk/ *adj* atmosferico

atom /'ætəm/ *n* atomo *m*

atom bomb *n* bomba *f* atomica

atomic /ə'tɒmɪk/ *adj* atomico

atomic physics *n* fisica *f* atomica

atomic power station *n* centrale *f* atomica

atomic reactor *n* reattore *m* nucleare

atomic scientist *n* fisico, -a *mf* nucleare

atomize /'ætəmaɪz/ *vt* atomizzare

atomizer /'ætəmaɪzə(r)/ *n* atomizzatore *m*

atone /ə'təʊn/ *vi* ∼ **for** pagare per

atonement /ə'təʊnmənt/ *n* espiazione *f*

at-risk *adj* a rischio; the ∼ register l'elenco dei soggetti a rischio

atrocious /ə'trəʊʃəs/ *adj* atroce; fam ⟨meal, weather⟩ abominevole

atrociously /ə'trəʊʃəslɪ/ *adv* atrocemente; ⟨rude etc⟩ terribilmente

atrocity /ə'trɒsətɪ/ *n* atrocità *f inv*

atrophy /'ætrəfɪ/ ⓘ *n* Med atrofia *f* ② *vi* Med, fig atrofizzarsi

at sign *n* Comput chiocciola *f*

attach /ə'tætʃ/ *vt* attaccare; attribuire ⟨importance⟩; be ∼ed to fig essere attaccato a

attaché /ə'tæʃeɪ/ *n* addetto *m*

attaché case *n* ventiquattrore *f inv*

attached *adj* ⟨document⟩ allegato; (fond) ∼ to affezionato a

attachment /ə'tætʃmənt/ n (affection) attaccamento m; (accessory) accessorio m; Comput allegato m

attack /ə'tæk/ ① n attacco m; (physical) aggressione f
② vt attaccare; (physically) aggredire

attacker /ə'tækə(r)/ n assalitore, -trice mf; (critic) detrattore, -trice mf

attain /ə'teɪn/ vt realizzare ⟨ambition⟩; raggiungere ⟨success, age, goal⟩

attainable /ə'teɪnəbl/ adj ⟨ambition⟩ realizzabile; ⟨success⟩ raggiungibile

attainment /ə'teɪnmənt/ n (of knowledge) acquisizione f; (of goal) realizzazione f, raggiungimento m; (success) risultato m

attempt /ə'tempt/ ① n tentativo m
② vt tentare

attend /ə'tend/ ① vt essere presente a; (go regularly to) frequentare; (accompany) accompagnare; ⟨doctor⟩ avere in cura
② vi essere presente; (pay attention) prestare attenzione
■ **attend to** vt occuparsi di; (in shop) servire

attendance /ə'tendəns/ n presenza f

attendance record n (of MP, committee member, schoolchild) tasso m di presenza

attendance register n Sch registro m

attendant /ə'tendənt/ n guardiano, -a mf

attention /ə'tenʃn/ n attenzione f; ∼! Mil attenti!; **pay** ∼ prestare attenzione; **need** ∼ aver bisogno di attenzioni; ⟨skin, hair, plant⟩ dover essere curato; ⟨car, tyres⟩ dover essere riparato; **for the** ∼ **of** all'attenzione di

attention deficit disorder n Med disturbo m da deficit dell'attenzione

attention-seeking /ə'tenʃnsiːkɪŋ/
① n bisogno m di attirare l'attenzione
② adj ⟨person⟩ che cerca di attirare l'attenzione.

attention span n he has a very short ∼ ∼ non è capace di mantenere a lungo la concentrazione

attentive /ə'tentɪv/ adj ⟨pupil, audience⟩ attento; ⟨son⟩ premuroso

attentively /ə'tentɪvlɪ/ adv attentamente

attentiveness /ə'tentɪvnɪs/ n (concentration) attenzione f; (solicitude) sollecitudine f

attenuate /ə'tenjʊeɪt/ vt attenuare

attest /ə'test/ vt/i attestare

attic /'ætɪk/ n soffitta f

attic room n mansarda f

attic window n lucernario m

attire /ə'taɪə(r)/ ① n abiti mpl
② vt vestire (in con)

attitude /'ætɪtjuːd/ n atteggiamento m

attn. abbr (**attention**) c.a.

attorney /ə'tɜːnɪ/ n (Am: lawyer) avvocato m; **power of** ∼ delega f

Attorney General n Br ≈ Procuratore m Generale; Am ≈ Ministro m di Grazia e Giustizia

attract /ə'trækt/ vt attirare

attraction /ə'trækʃn/ n attrazione f; (feature) attrattiva f

attractive /ə'træktɪv/ adj ⟨person⟩ attraente; ⟨proposal, price⟩ allettante

attractiveness /ə'træktɪvnɪs/ n (of person, place) fascino m; (of proposal) carattere m allettante; (of investment) covenienza f

attributable /ə'trɪbjʊtəbl/ adj (error, fall, loss) attribuibile; **be** ∼ **to** ⟨change, profit, success⟩ essere dovuto a

attribute[1] /'ætrɪbjuːt/ n attributo m

attribute[2] /ə'trɪbjuːt/ vt attribuire

attribution /ætrɪ'bjuːʃn/ n attribuzione f

attributive /ə'trɪbjʊtɪv/ adj attributivo

attrition /ə'trɪʃn/ n **war of** ∼ guerra f di logoramento

attune /ə'tjuːn/ vt **be** ∼**d to** (in harmony with) essere sintonizzato con; (accustomed to) essere abituato a

aubergine /'əʊbəʒiːn/ n melanzana f

auburn /'ɔːbən/ adj castano ramato

auction /'ɔːkʃn/ ① n asta f
② vt vendere all'asta

auctioneer /ɔːkʃə'nɪə(r)/ n banditore m

auction house n casa f d'aste

auction rooms npl sala f d'aste

auction sale n vendita f all'asta

audacious /ɔː'deɪʃəs/ adj sfacciato; (daring) audace

audaciously /ɔː'deɪʃəslɪ/ adv sfacciatamente; (daringly) con audacia

audacity /ɔː'dæsətɪ/ n sfacciataggine f; (daring) audacia f

audible /'ɔːdəbl/ adj udibile

audience /'ɔːdɪəns/ n Theat pubblico m; TV telespettatori mpl; Radio ascoltatori mpl; (meeting) udienza f

audience participation n partecipazione f del pubblico

audience ratings npl indici mpl di ascolto.

audience research n sondaggio m tra il pubblico

audio /'ɔːdɪəʊ/ pref audio

audiobook n audiolibro m

audio cassette n audiocassetta f

audio system n impianto m stereo

audiotape n audiocassetta f

audiotyping n trascrizione f da audiocassetta

audio typist n dattilografo, -a mf (che trascrive registrazioni)

audiovisual adj audiovisivo

audit /'ɔ:dɪt/ **1** n verifica f del bilancio **2** vt verificare

auditing /'ɔ:dɪtɪŋ/ n auditing m inv

audition /ɔ:'dɪʃn/ **1** n audizione f **2** vi fare un'audizione

auditor /'ɔ:dɪtə(r)/ n revisore m di conti

auditorium /ɔ:dɪ'tɔ:rɪəm/ n sala f

auditory /'ɔ:dɪt(ə)rɪ/ adj acustico, uditivo

augment /ɔ:g'ment/ vt aumentare

augur /'ɔ:gə(r)/ vi ~ **well/ill** essere di buon/cattivo augurio

August /'ɔ:gəst/ n agosto m

august /ɔ:'gʌst/ adj augusto

Augustinian /ɔ:gə'stɪnɪən/ adj agostiniano

aunt /ɑːnt/ n zia f

auntie, **aunty** /'ɑːntɪ/ n fam zietta f

au pair /əʊ'peə(r)/ n ~ **[girl]** ragazza f alla pari

aura /'ɔ:rə/ n aura f

aural /'ɔ:rəl/ **1** adj uditivo; Sch ‹comprehension, test› orale; ‹Med: test› audiometrico **2** n Sch esercizio m di comprensione ed espressione orale; Mus ≈ dettato m musicale

aurora australis/borealis /ɔ:'rɔ:rəɒ'strɑ:lɪs///bɔ:rɪ'ɑ:lɪs/ n aurora f australe/boreale

auspices /'ɔ:spɪsɪz/ npl under the ~ of sotto l'egida di

auspicious /ɔ:'spɪʃəs/ adj di buon augurio

Aussie /'ɒzɪ/ adj & n fam australiano, -a mf

austere /ɒ'stɪə(r)/ adj austero

austerity /ɒ'sterətɪ/ n austerità f

Australasia /ɒstrə'leɪʒə/ n Australasia f

Australia /ɒ'streɪlɪə/ n Australia f

Australian /ɒ'streɪlɪən/ adj & n australiano, -a mf

Austria /'ɒstrɪə/ n Austria f

Austrian /'ɒstrɪən/ adj & n austriaco, -a mf

Austro-Hungarian /ɒstrəʊhʌŋ'geərɪən/ adj austroungarico

autarchy /'ɔ:tɑ:kɪ/ n autarchia f

authentic /ɔ:'θentɪk/ adj autentico

authenticate /ɔ:'θentɪkeɪt/ vt autenticare

authenticity /ɔ:θen'tɪsətɪ/ n autenticità f

author /'ɔ:θə(r)/ n autore m

authoritarian /ɔ:θɒrɪ'teərɪən/ adj autoritario

authoritative /ɔ:'θɒrɪtətɪv/ adj autorevole; ‹manner› autoritario

authority /ɔ:'θɒrətɪ/ n autorità f; (permission) autorizzazione f; **who's in ~ here?** chi è il responsabile qui?; **be in ~ over** avere autorità su; **be an ~ on** essere un'autorità in materia di

authorization /ɔ:θəraɪ'zeɪʃn/ n autorizzazione f

authorize /'ɔ:θəraɪz/ vt autorizzare

authorized dealer /'ɔ:θəraɪzd/ rivenditore m autorizzato

autism /'ɔ:tɪzm/ n autismo m

autistic /ɔ:'tɪstɪk/ adj autistico

auto /'ɔ:təʊ/ **1** n Am fam auto f **2** attrib ‹industry› automobilistico; ‹workers› dell'industria automobilistica

autobiographical /ɔ:təbaɪə'græfɪkl/ adj autobiografico

autobiography /ɔ:təbaɪ'ɒgrəfɪ/ n autobiografia f

autocrat /'ɔ:təkræt/ n autocrate m

autocratic /ɔ:tə'krætɪk/ adj autocratico

autocue /'ɔ:təʊkju:/ n TV gobbo m

auto-destruct vi ‹spacecraft, missile› autodistruggersi

autograph /'ɔ:təgrɑ:f/ **1** n autografo m **2** vt autografare

autoimmune /ɔ:təʊɪ'mju:n/ adj ‹disease, system› autoimmune

automate /'ɔ:təmeɪt/ vt automatizzare

automatic /ɔ:tə'mætɪk/ **1** adj automatico **2** n (car) macchina f col cambio automatico; (washing machine) lavatrice f automatica

automatically /ɔ:tə'mætɪklɪ/ adv automaticamente

automatic pilot n (device) pilota m automatico; **be on ~ ~** also fig viaggiare con il pilota automatico inserito

automatic teller machine /'telə/ n cassa f continua di prelevamento

automation /ɔ:tə'meɪʃn/ n automazione f

automaton /ɔ:'tɒmətən/ n automa m

automobile /'ɔ:təməbi:l/ n automobile f

automotive /ɔ:tə'məʊtɪv/ adj (self-propelling) autopropulso; ‹design, industry› automobilistico

autonomous /ɔ:'tɒnəməs/ adj autonomo

autonomously /ɔ:'tɒnəməslɪ/ adv autonomamente

autonomy /ɔ:'tɒnəmɪ/ n autonomia f

autopilot /'ɔ:təʊpaɪlət/ n Aeron, fig pilota m automatico

autopsy /'ɔ:tɒpsɪ/ n autopsia f

auto-suggestion /ɔ:təʊsə'dʒestʃən/ n autosuggestione f

autumn /'ɔ:təm/ *n* autunno *m*

autumnal /ɔ:'tʌmnl/ *adj* autunnale

auxiliary /ɔ:g'zɪlɪərɪ/ ① *adj* ausiliario
② *n* ausiliare *m*

auxiliary nurse *n* infermiere, -a *mf*
ausiliario, -a

auxiliary verb *n* ausiliare *m*

avail /ə'veɪl/ ① *n* **to no ~** invano
② *vi* **~ oneself of** approfittare di

availability /əveɪlə'bɪlətɪ/ *n* (option,
service) disponibilità *f*; (of drugs) reperibilità
f, disponibilità *f*; **subject to ~** fino ad
esaurimento

available /ə'veɪləbl/ *adj* disponibile;
‹book, record etc› in vendita

avalanche /'ævəlɑ:nʃ/ *n* valanga *f*

avant-garde /ævɑ̃'gɑ:d/ ① *n*
avanguardia *f*
② *adj* d'avanguardia

avarice /'ævərɪs/ *n* avidità *f*

avaricious /ævə'rɪʃəs/ *adj* avido

Ave *abbr* (**Avenue**) V.le

avenge /ə'vendʒ/ *vt* vendicare

avenger /ə'vendʒə(r)/ *n* vendicatore,
-trice *mf*

avenging /ə'vendʒɪŋ/ *adj* vendicatore

avenue /'ævənju:/ *n* viale *m*; fig strada *f*

average /'ævərɪdʒ/ ① *adj* medio;
(mediocre) mediocre
② *n* media *f*; **on ~** in media; **above ~**
superiore al normale
③ *vt* ‹sales, attendance etc› raggiungere
una media di
∎ **average out at** *vt* risultare in media

averse /ə'vɜ:s/ *adj* **not be ~ to**
something non essere contro qualcosa

aversion /ə'vɜ:ʃn/ *n* avversione *f* (**to** per)

avert /ə'vɜ:t/ *vt* evitare ‹crisis›;
distogliere ‹eyes›

aviary /'eɪvɪərɪ/ *n* uccelliera *f*

aviation /eɪvɪ'eɪʃn/ *n* aviazione *f*

aviation fuel *n* benzina *f* avio

aviation industry *n* industria *f*
aeronautica

aviator /'eɪvɪeɪtə(r)/ *n* aviatore, -trice *mf*

avid /'ævɪd/ *adj* avido (**for** di); ‹reader›
appassionato

avidity /ə'vɪdətɪ/ *n* avidità

avidly /'ævɪdlɪ/ *adv* ‹read, collect›
avidamente; ‹support› con entusiasmo

avocado /ævə'kɑ:dəʊ/ *n* avocado *m*

avoid /ə'vɔɪd/ *vt* evitare

avoidable /ə'vɔɪdəbl/ *adj* evitabile

avoidance /ə'vɔɪdəns/ *n* **~ of one's
duty** astensione *f* dal proprio dovere

avowed /ə'vaʊd/ *adj* dichiarato

avuncular /ə'vʌŋkʊlə(r)/ *adj* benevolo

await /ə'weɪt/ *vt* attendere

awake /ə'weɪk/ ① *adj* sveglio; **wide ~**
completamente sveglio
② *vi* (pt **awoke**, pp **awoken**) svegliarsi

awaken /ə'weɪkn/ ① *vt* svegliare
② *vi* svegliarsi

awakening /ə'weɪknɪŋ/ *n* risveglio *m*

award /ə'wɔ:d/ ① *n* premio *m*; (medal)
riconoscimento *m*; (of prize) assegnazione *f*
② *vt* assegnare; ‹hand over› consegnare

award ceremony *n* cerimonia *f* di
premiazione

award winner *n* vincitore, -trice *mf* di
un premio

award-winning *adj* ‹book, film, design›
premiato

aware /ə'weə(r)/ *adj* **be ~ of** (sense)
percepire; (know) essere conscio di;
become ~ of accorgersi di; (learn) venire a
sapere di; **be ~ that** rendersi conto che

awareness /ə'weənɪs/ *n* percezione *f*;
(knowledge) consapevolezza *f*

awash /ə'wɒʃ/ *adj* inondato (**with** di)

away /ə'weɪ/ *adv* via; **go/stay ~** andare/
stare via; **he's ~ from his desk/the office**
non è alla sua scrivania/in ufficio; **far ~**
lontano; **four kilometres ~** a quattro
chilometri; **play ~** Sport giocare fuori casa

away game *n* partita *f* fuori casa

awe /ɔ:/ *n* soggezione *f*; **stand in ~ of**
somebody avere soggezione di qualcuno

awe-inspiring *adj* maestoso

awesome /'ɔ:səm/ *adj* imponente

awful /'ɔ:f(ə)l/ ① *adj* terribile; **that's an**
~ pity è un gran peccato
② *adv* fam estremamente

awfully /'ɔ:f(ʊ)lɪ/ *adv* terribilmente;
‹pretty› estremamente; **that's ~ nice of**
you è veramente gentile da parte tua;
thanks ~ grazie mille

awhile /ə'waɪl/ *adv* per un po'

awkward /'ɔ:kwəd/ *adj* ‹movement›
goffo; ‹moment, situation› imbarazzante;
‹time› scomodo

awkwardly /'ɔ:kwədlɪ/ *adv* ‹move›
goffamente; ‹say› con imbarazzo; **the**
meeting is ~ timed la riunione è ad un
orario scomodo

awkwardness /'ɔ:kwədnɪs/ *n*
‹clumsiness› goffaggine *f*; (inconvenience)
scomodità *f*; (embarrassment) imbarazzo *m*;
(delicacy of situation) delicatezza *f*

awl /ɔ:l/ *n* (for wood etc) punteruolo *m*

awning /'ɔ:nɪŋ/ *n* tendone *m*

awoke(n) /ə'wəʊk(ən)/ ▸ AWAKE

AWOL /'eɪwɒl/ *adj* & *adv* abbr (**absent**
without leave) **be/go ~** Mil assentarsi
senza permesso; hum volatilizzarsi

awry /ə'raɪ/ *adv* storto

axe /æks/ ① *n* scure *f*; **have an ~ to**
grind fig avere il proprio tornaconto

a
b

2 *vt* (pres p **axing**) fare dei tagli a ⟨*budget*⟩; sopprimere ⟨*jobs*⟩; annullare ⟨*project*⟩

axiom /'æksɪəm/ *n* assioma *m*

axiomatic /æksɪə'mætɪk/ *adj* **it is ∼ that...** è indiscutibile che...

axis /'æksɪs/ *n* (pl **axes** /-siːz/) asse *m*

axle /'æksl/ *n* Techn asse *m*

ay[e] /aɪ/ **1** *adv* sì
2 *n* sì *m inv*

Azerbaijan /æzəbaɪ'dʒɑːn/ *n* Azerbaigiano *m*

Azerbaijani /æzəbaɪ'dʒɑːnɪ/ *adj & n* (person) azerbaigiano, -a *mf*; (language) azerbaigiano *m*

Azores /ə'zɔːz/ *npl* **the ∼** le Azzorre

Aztec /'æztek/ *adj & n* (person) azteco, -a *mf*; (language) azteco *m*

azure /'eɪʒə(r)/ *adj & n* azzurro *m*

Bb

b¹, B /biː/ *n* (letter) b, B *f inv*; Mus si *m inv*

b² *abbr* **born**

b. & b. *abbr* **bed and breakfast**

BA *abbr* **Bachelor of Arts**

BAA *n abbr* (**British Airports Authority**) ente *m* che gestisce gli aeroporti britannici

baa /bɑː/ **1** *vi* belare
2 *int* bee

babble /'bæbl/ *vi* farfugliare; ⟨*stream*⟩ gorgogliare

babe /beɪb/ *n* liter bimbo, -a *mf*; (fam: woman) ragazza *f*; (fam: form of address) bella *f*; **a ∼ in arms** un bimbo in fasce; fig uno sprovveduto

baboon /bə'buːn/ *n* babbuino *m*

baby /'beɪbɪ/ *n* bambino, -a *mf*; (fam: darling) tesoro *m*

baby bird *n* uccellino *m*

baby boom *n* baby boom *m inv*

baby boomer *n* persona *f* nata durante il baby boom

baby buggy *n* Br carrozzina *f*

baby carriage *n* Am carrozzina *f*

baby carrier *n* zaino *m* portabimbo *inv*

baby-faced *adj* ⟨*person*⟩ con la faccia da bambino

babyish /'beɪbɪɪʃ/ *adj* bambinesco

baby shower *n* Am festa *f* in cui si portano regali a una mamma in attesa

baby-sit *vi* fare da baby-sitter

baby-sitter *n* baby-sitter *mf*

baby-sitting *n* **do ∼** fare il/la baby-sitter

baby talk *n* linguaggio *m* infantile

baby tooth *n* dente *m* di latte

baby walker *n* girello *m*

babywear *n* abbigliamento *m* per bambini

bachelor /'bætʃələ(r)/ *n* scapolo *m*; **B∼ of Arts/Science** laureato, -a *mf* in lettere/ in scienze

bachelor apartment, bachelor flat Br *n* appartamento *m* da scapolo

bachelorhood /'bætʃələhʊd/ *n* celibato *m*

bacillus /bə'sɪləs/ *n* (pl **-lli**) bacillo *m*

back /bæk/ **1** *n* schiena *f*; (of horse, hand) dorso *m*; (of chair) schienale *m*; (of house, cheque, page) retro *m*; (in football) difesa *f*; **at the ∼** in fondo; **in the ∼** Auto dietro; **stand ∼ to ∼** stare in piedi schiena contro schiena; **∼ to front** (sweater) il davanti di dietro; **you've got it all ∼ to front** fig hai capito tutto all'incontrario; **at the ∼ of beyond** in un posto sperduto
2 *adj* posteriore; ⟨*taxes, payments*⟩ arretrato
3 *adv* indietro; (returned) di ritorno; **turn/ move ∼** tornare/spostarsi indietro; **put it ∼ here/there** rimettilo qui/là; **∼ at home** di ritorno a casa; **I'll be ∼ in five minutes** torno fra cinque minuti; **I'm just ∼** sono appena tornato; **when do you want the book ∼?** quando rivuoi il libro?; **pay ∼** ripagare ⟨*somebody*⟩; restituire ⟨*money*⟩; **∼ in power** di nuovo al potere
4 *vt* (support) sostenere; (with money) finanziare; puntare su ⟨*horse*⟩; (cover the back of) rivestire il retro di
5 *vi* Auto fare retromarcia

■ **back away** *vi* tirarsi indietro

■ **back down** *vi* battere in ritirata

■ **back in** *vi* Auto entrare in retromarcia; ⟨*person*⟩; entrare camminando all'indietro

■ **back out** *vi* Auto uscire in retromarcia; ⟨*person*⟩ uscire camminando all'indietro; fig tirarsi indietro (**of** da)

■ **back up** **1** *vt* sostenere; confermare ⟨*person's alibi*⟩; Comput fare una copia di salvataggio di; **be ∼ed up** ⟨*traffic*⟩ essere congestionato
2 *vi* Auto fare retromarcia

backache *n* mal *m* di schiena

backbench n Br Pol scanni mpl del Parlamento dove siedono i parlamentari ordinari

backbencher n Br Pol parlamentare mf ordinario, -a

backbiting n maldicenza f

backboard n (in basketball) tabellone m

back boiler n caldaia f (posta dietro un caminetto)

backbone n spina f dorsale

back-breaking adj massacrante

back burner n put something on the ~ ~ rimandare qualcosa

backchat n risposta f impertinente

backcloth n Theat fondale m; fig sfondo m

back comb vt cotonare

back copy n numero m arretrato

back cover n retro m di copertina

backdate vt retrodatare ⟨cheque⟩; ~d to valido a partire da

back door n porta f di servizio

backdrop n Theat fondale m; fig sfondo m

back-end n (rear) fondo m

backer /'bækə(r)/ n sostenitore, -trice mf; (with money) finanziatore, -trice mf

backfire vi Auto avere un ritorno di fiamma; fig ⟨plan⟩ fallire; the joke ~d on him lo scherzo si è ritorto contro di lui

backgammon n backgammon m

background n sfondo m; (environment) ambiente m

background noise n rumore m di sottofondo

background reading n letture fpl generali

backhand n Tennis rovescio m

backhanded adj ⟨compliment⟩ implicito

backhander n (fam: bribe) bustarella f

backing /'bækɪŋ/ n (support) supporto m; (material used) fondo m; Mus accompagnamento m; ~ singer/vocals/group cantante/voci/gruppo d'accompagnamento

back issue n numero m arretrato

backlash /'bæklæʃ/ n fig reazione f opposta

backless /'bæklɪs/ adj ⟨dress⟩ scollato dietro

backlist n opere fpl pubblicate

backlog n ~ of work lavoro m arretrato

back marker n Sport ultimo, -a mf

back number n numero m arretrato

backpack n zaino m

backpacker n saccopelista mf

backpacking n go ~ viaggiare con zaino e sacco a pelo

back passage n Anat retto m

back pay n arretrato m di stipendio

back-pedal vi pedalare all'indietro; fig fare marcia indietro

back pocket n tasca f di dietro

backrest n schienale m

back room n stanza f sul retro

back room boys npl esperti mpl che lavorano dietro le quinte

back-scratcher n manina f grattaschiena inv

back seat n sedile m posteriore

back-seat driver n persona f che dà consigli non richiesti

backside n fam fondoschiena m inv

backslash n Typ backslash nm inv

back-space n Comput backspace m

back-stage adj & adv dietro le quinte

backstairs npl scale f di servizio

backstitch n impuntura f vi impunturare

backstop n Sport ricevitore m

backstory n vicende fpl passate

back straight n Sport rettilineo m

backstreet n vicolo m; attrib ⟨abortionist⟩ clandestino

backstroke n dorso m

backtalk n Am = backchat

backtrack vi tornare indietro; fig fare marcia indietro

back translation n traduzione f di una traduzione

backup n rinforzi mpl; Comput riserva f, backup m inv; do a ~ realizzare un backup

backup copy n copia f di riserva

backup light n Am luce f di retromarcia

backward /'bækwəd/ adj ⟨step⟩ indietro; ⟨child⟩ lento nell'apprendimento; ⟨country⟩ arretrato

backward-looking /'bækwədlʊkɪŋ/ adj retrogrado

backwards /'bækwədz/ adv (also Am: **backward**) indietro; ⟨fall, walk⟩ all'indietro; ~ and forwards avanti e indietro

backwater /'bækwɔːtə(r)/ n fig luogo m arretrato

backyard /bæk'jɑːd/ n cortile m; not in my ~ yard fam non a casa mia

bacon /'beɪk(ə)n/ n ≈ pancetta f

bacon-slicer /'beɪkənslaɪsə(r)/ n affettatrice f

bacteria /bæk'tɪərɪə/ npl batteri mpl

bacterial /bæk'tɪərɪəl/ adj batterico

bacteriology /bæktɪərɪ'ɒlədʒɪ/ n batteriologia f

bad /bæd/ adj (**worse, worst**) cattivo; ⟨weather, habit, news, accident⟩ brutto; ⟨apple etc⟩ marcio; the light is ~ non c'è ···›

una buona luce; **my eyesight is** ∼ non ho una buona vista; **use** ∼ **language** dire delle parolacce; **she's going through a** ∼ **patch** sta attraversando un brutto periodo; **feel** ∼ sentirsi male; (feel guilty) sentirsi in colpa; **have a** ∼ **back** avere dei problemi alla schiena; **smoking is** ∼ **for you** fumare fa male; **go** ∼ andare a male; **that's just too** ∼! pazienza!; **not** ∼ niente male; **things have gone from** ∼ **to worse** le cose sono andate di male in peggio

bad blood *n* there is ∼ ∼ **between them** tra loro non corre buon sangue

bad boy *n* ragazzaccio *m*

bad breath *n* alito *m* cattivo

bad cheque *n* assegno *m* a vuoto

bad debt *n* credito *m* inesigibile

baddie, **baddy** /'bædɪ/ *n* fam cattivo, -a *mf*

bade /bæd/ ▶ BID[1]

bad faith *n* malafede *f*

badge /bædʒ/ *n* distintivo *m*

badger /'bædʒə(r)/ [1] *n* tasso *m* [2] *vt* tormentare

badly /'bædlɪ/ *adv* male; ⟨hurt⟩ gravemente; ∼ **off** povero; ∼ **behaved** maleducato; **need** ∼ aver estremamente bisogno di

bad-mannered /-'mænəd/ *adj* maleducato

badminton /'bædmɪntən/ *n* badminton *m*

bad-tempered /-'tempəd/ *adj* irascibile

baffle /'bæfl/ *vt* confondere

baffled /'bæfld/ *adj* sconcertato

baffling /'bæflɪŋ/ *adj* sconcertante

BAFTA, **Bafta** /'bæftə/ *n abbr* (**British Academy of Film and Television Arts**) società *f* britannica delle arti cinematografiche e televisive

bag /bæg/ [1] *n* borsa *f*; (of paper) sacchetto *m*; **old** ∼ sl megera *f*; ∼**s under the eyes** occhiaie *fpl*; ∼**s of** fam un sacco di; **it's in the** ∼ fig è fatta [2] *vt* (pt/pp **bagged**) (fam: take) accaparrarsi; ∼ **somebody a seat** tenere un posto a qualcuno

bagel /'beɪgəl/ *n* panino *m* a forma di ciambella

baggage /'bægɪdʒ/ *n* bagagli *mpl*

baggage allowance *n* franchigia *f* bagaglio

baggage car *n* Rail bagagliaio *m*

baggage carousel *n* nastro *m* trasportatore per ritiro bagagli

baggage check *n* controllo *m* bagagli

baggage handler *n* addetto, -a *mf* ai bagagli

baggage locker *n* armadietto *m* per deposito bagagli

baggage reclaim *n* ritiro *m* bagagli

baggy /'bægɪ/ *adj* ⟨clothes⟩ ampio

Baghdad /bæg'dæd/ *n* Baghdad *f*

bag lady *n* fam barbona *f*

bag person *n* fam barbone, -a *mf*

bagpipes *npl* cornamusa *fsg*

bag snatcher *n* scippatore, -trice *mf*

baguette /bæg'et/ *n* baguette *f inv*

Bahamas /bə'hɑːməz/ *npl* **the** ∼ le Bahamas

Bahrain, **Bahrein** /bɑː'reɪn/ *n* Bahrein *m*

bail /beɪl/ *n* cauzione *f*; **on** ∼ su cauzione ■ **bail out** [1] *vt* Naut aggottare; ∼ **somebody out** Jur pagare la cauzione per qualcuno; fig trarre qualcuno d'impaccio [2] *vi* Aeron paracadutarsi

bail bond *n* Am Jur cauzione *f*

bailiff /'beɪlɪf/ *n* ufficiale *m* giudiziario; (of estate) fattore *m*

bait /beɪt/ [1] *n* esca *f*; **rise to the** ∼ abboccare [all'amo] [2] *vt* innescare; (fig: torment) tormentare

baize /beɪz/ *n* panno *m* (di tavolo da gioco e da biliardo)

bake /beɪk/ [1] *vt* cuocere al forno; (make) fare [2] *vi* cuocersi al forno

baked beans /beɪkt'biːnz/ *n* Culin fagioli *mpl* al pomodoro

baked potato *n* patata *f* cotta al forno (con la buccia)

baker /'beɪkə(r)/ *n* fornaio, -a *mf*, panettiere, -a *mf*

baker's [shop] /'beɪkəz/ *n* panetteria *f*

bakery /'beɪkərɪ/ *n* panificio *m*, forno *m*

baking /'beɪkɪŋ/ *n* cottura *f* al forno

baking powder *n* lievito *m* in polvere

baking soda *n* Culin bicarbonato *m* di sodio

baking tin *n* teglia *f*

balaclava /bælə'klɑːvə/ *n* passamontagna *m inv*

balance /'bæləns/ [1] *n* (equilibrium) equilibrio *m*; Comm bilancio *m*; (outstanding sum) saldo *m*; **[bank]** ∼ saldo *m*; **be** or **hang in the** ∼ fig essere in sospeso; **on** ∼ tutto sommato [2] *vt* bilanciare; equilibrare ⟨budget⟩; Comm fare il bilancio di ⟨books⟩ [3] *vi* bilanciarsi; Comm essere in pareggio

balanced /'bælənst/ *adj* equilibrato

balance of payments *n* bilancia *f* dei pagamenti

balance of power *n* Pol equilibrio *m* delle forze

balance of trade *n* bilancia *f* commerciale

balance sheet *n* bilancio *m* patrimoniale

balancing act /'bælənsɪŋ/ *n* fig **do a** ∼
∼ fare equilibrismo

balcony /'bælkənɪ/ *n* balcone *m*

bald /bɔ:ld/ *adj* ⟨person⟩ calvo; ⟨tyre⟩
liscio; ⟨statement⟩ nudo e crudo; **go** ∼
perdere i capelli

balderdash /'bɔ:ldədæʃ/ *n* sciocchezze
fpl

balding /'bɔ:ldɪŋ/ *adj* **be** ∼ stare
perdendo i capelli

baldly /'bɔ:ldlɪ/ *adv* ⟨state⟩ in modo nudo
e crudo

baldness /'bɔ:ldnɪs/ *n* calvizie *f*

bale /beɪl/ *n* balla *f*

Balearic Islands /bæler'ærɪk/ *npl*
isole *fpl* Baleari

baleful /'beɪlfl/ *adj* malvagio; (sad) triste

balefully /'beɪlfʊlɪ/ *adv* con malvagità

balk /bɔ:lk/ **①** *vt* ostacolare
② *vi* ∼ **at** ⟨horse⟩ impennarsi davanti a;
fig tirarsi indietro davanti a

Balkan /'bɔ:lkn/ *adj* dei Balcani

Balkans /'bɔ:lknz/ *npl* Balcani *mpl*

ball¹ /bɔ:l/ *n* palla *f*; (football) pallone *m*; (of
yarn) gomitolo *m*; **on the** ∼ fam sveglio

ball² *n* (dance) ballo *m*)

ballad /'bæləd/ *n* ballata *f*

ball and chain *n* palla *f* al piede

ball-and-socket joint *n* giunto *m*
sferico

ballast /'bæləst/ *n* zavorra *f*

ball-bearing *n* cuscinetto *m* a sfera

ballboy *n* Tennis raccattapalle *m inv*

ballcock *n* Techn galleggiante *m* (in
serbatoio)

ball control *n* controllo *m* della palla

ball dress *n* abito *m* da sera

ballerina /bælə'ri:nə/ *n* ballerina *f*
[classica]

ballet /'bæleɪ/ *n* balletto *m*; (art form)
danza *f*

ballet dancer *n* ballerino, -a *mf*
[classico, -a]

ballet dress *n* tutù *m inv*

ballet shoes *npl* scarpe *fpl* da danza

ballgame *n* gioco *m* con la palla; Am
partita *f* di baseball; **that's a whole
different** ∼ fig è tutto un altro paio di
maniche

ballgirl *n* Tennis raccattapalle *f inv*

ball gown *n* abito *m* da sera

ballistic /bə'lɪstɪk/ *adj* balistico

ballistics *n* balistica *fsg*

balloon /bə'lu:n/ *n* pallone *m*; Aeron
mongolfiera *f*

balloonist /bə'lu:nɪst/ *n* aeronauta *mf*

ballot /'bælət/ *n* votazione *f*

ballot box *n* urna *f*

ballot paper *n* scheda *f* di votazione

ballpark *n* Am stadio *m* di baseball

ballpark figure *n* fam cifra *f*
approssimativa

ball-point [pen] *n* penna *f* a sfera

ballroom *n* sala *f* da ballo

ballroom dancing *n* ballo *m* liscio

balls up vulg **①** *vi* incasinarsi
② *vt* incasinare

ballyhoo /bælɪ'hu:/ *n* (publicity) battage *m
inv* pubblicitario; (uproar) baccano *m*

balm /bɑ:m/ *n* balsamo *m*

balmy /'bɑ:mɪ/ *adj* (**-ier, -iest**) mite;
(fam: crazy) strampalato

balsam /'bɒlsəm/ *n* (oily) balsamo *m*

Baltic /'bɔ:ltɪk/ *adj & n* **the** ∼ **[Sea]** il
[mar] Baltico

balustrade /bælə'streɪd/ *n* balaustra *f*

bamboo /bæm'bu:/ *n* bambù *m*

bamboozle /bæm'bu:zl/ *vt* (fam: mystify)
confondere

ban /bæn/ **①** *n* proibizione *f*
② *vt* (pt/pp **banned**) proibire; ∼ **from**
espellere da ⟨club⟩; **she was** ∼ned **from
driving** le hanno ritirato la patente

banal /bə'nɑ:l/ *adj* banale

banality /bə'nælətɪ/ *n* banalità *f inv*

banana /bə'nɑ:nə/ *n* banana *f*

banana republic *n* pej repubblica *f*
delle banane

banana skin *n* buccia *f* di banana

band /bænd/ *n* banda *f*; (stripe) nastro *m*;
(Mus: pop group) complesso *m*; (Mus: brass ∼)
banda *f*; Mil fanfara *f*
■ **band together** *vi* riunirsi

bandage /'bændɪdʒ/ **①** *n* benda *f*
② *vt* fasciare
■ **bandage up** *vt* fasciare

Band-Aid® *n* Med cerotto *m*

bandanna, **bandana** /bæn'dænə/ *n*
bandana *f*

bandit /'bændɪt/ *n* bandito *m*

band leader *n* leader *mf* di un
complesso

bandmaster *n* capobanda *m* (di banda
musicale)

band saw *n* segatrice *f* a nastro

bandsman *n* bandista *m*

bandstand *n* palco *m* coperto
[dell'orchestra]

bandwagon *n* **jump on the** ∼ fig seguire
la corrente

bandy¹ /'bændɪ/ *vt* (pt/pp **-ied**)
scambiarsi ⟨words⟩
■ **bandy about** *vt* far circolare

bandy² *adj* (**-ier, -iest**) **be** ∼ avere le
gambe storte

bandy-legged /-'legd/ *adj* con le gambe
storte

bane /beɪn/ *n* **she/it is the** ∼ **of my life!** è
la mia rovina!

b

bang /bæŋ/ ① *n* (noise) fragore *m*; (of gun, firework) scoppio *m*; (blow) colpo *m*; **go with a ∼** fam essere una cannonata
② *adv* **∼ in the middle of** fam proprio nel mezzo di; **go ∼** ⟨*gun*⟩ sparare; ⟨*balloon*⟩ esplodere
③ *int* bum!
④ *vt* battere ⟨*fist*⟩; battere su ⟨*table*⟩; sbattere ⟨*door, head*⟩
⑤ *vi* scoppiare; ⟨*door*⟩ sbattere
■ **bang about**, **bang around** *vi* far rumore
■ **bang into** *vt* sbattere contro

banger /'bæŋə(r)/ *n* (firework) petardo *m*; (fam: sausage) salsiccia f: **old ∼** (fam: car) macinino *m*

Bangladesh /bæŋglə'deʃ/ *n* Bangladesh *m*

Bangladeshi /bæŋglə'deʃɪ/ ① *adj* del Bangladesh
② *n* persona f del Bangladesh

bangle /'bæŋgl/ *n* braccialetto *m*

banish /'bænɪʃ/ *vt* bandire

banishment /'bænɪʃmənt/ *n* bando *m*

banister /'bænɪstə/ *n* ringhiera f

banjo /'bænʤəʊ/ *n* banjo *m inv*

bank¹ /bæŋk/ ① *n* (of river) sponda f; (slope) scarpata f
② *vi* Aeron inclinarsi in virata

bank² ① *n* banca f
② *vt* depositare in banca
③ *vi* **∼ with** avere un conto [bancario] presso
■ **bank on** *vt* contare su

bank account *n* conto *m* in banca

bank balance *n* saldo *m*

bank-book *n* libretto *m* di risparmio

bank borrowings *npl* prestiti *mpl* bancari

bank card *n* carta f assegni

bank charges *npl* spese *fpl* bancarie, commissioni *fpl*

bank clerk *n* bancario, -a *mf*

bank details *npl* coordinate *fpl* bancarie

banker /'bæŋkə(r)/ *n* banchiere *m*

banker's draft *n* tratta f bancaria

banker's order *n* ordine *m* di pagamento

Bank Giro Credit *n* Br accreditamento *m* tramite bancogiro

bank holiday *n* giorno *m* festivo

banking /'bæŋkɪŋ/ *n* bancario *m*

banking hours *npl* orario *m* di sportello (in banca)

bank manager *n* direttore, -trice *mf* di banca

banknote *n* banconota f

bank raid *n* rapina f in banca

bank robber *n* rapinatore, -trice *mf* di banca

bank robbery *n* rapina f in banca

bankroll ① *n* finanziamento *m*
② *vt* finanziare ⟨*person, party*⟩

bankrupt /'bæŋkrʌpt/ ① *adj* fallito; **go ∼** fallire
② *n* persona f che ha fatto fallimento
③ *vt* far fallire

bankruptcy /'bæŋkrʌptsɪ/ *n* bancarotta f

bankruptcy court *n* tribunale *m* fallimentare

bankruptcy proceedings *npl* procedura f fallimentare

bank statement *n* estratto *m* conto

bank transfer *n* bonifico *m* bancario

banner /'bænə(r)/ *n* stendardo *m*; (of demonstrators) striscione *m*

banner headline *n* titolo *m* a tutta pagina

banns /bænz/ *npl* Relig pubblicazioni *fpl* [di matrimonio]

banquet /'bæŋkwɪt/ *n* banchetto *m*

bantam /'bæntəm/ *n* gallo *m* bantam

banter /'bæntə(r)/ *n* battute *fpl* di spirito

baptism /'bæptɪzm/ *n* battesimo *m*; **∼ of fire** fig battesimo *m* del fuoco

Baptist /'bæptɪst/ *adj & n* battista *mf*

baptize /bæp'taɪz/ *vt* battezzare

bar /bɑː(r)/ ① *n* sbarra f; Jur ordine *m* degli avvocati; (of chocolate) tavoletta f; (café) bar *m inv*; (counter) banco *m*; Mus battuta f, (fig: obstacle) ostacolo *m*; **∼ of soap/gold** saponetta f/lingotto *m*; **be called to the ∼** Jur entrare a far parte dell'ordine degli avvocati; **behind ∼s** fam dietro le sbarre
② *vt* (pt/pp **barred**) sbarrare ⟨*way*⟩; sprangare ⟨*door*⟩; escludere ⟨*person*⟩
③ *prep* tranne; **∼ none** in assoluto

barb /bɑːb/ *n* barbiglio *m*; (fig: remark) frecciata f

Barbados /bɑː'beɪdɒs/ *n* Barbados *fsg*

barbarian /bɑː'beərɪən/ *n* barbaro, -a *mf*

barbaric /bɑː'bærɪk/ *adj* barbarico

barbarism /'bɑːbərɪzm/ *n* (brutality, primitiveness) barbarie f inv; (error of style) barbarismo *m*

barbarity /bɑː'bærətɪ/ *n* barbarie f inv

barbarous /'bɑːbərəs/ *adj* barbaro

barbecue /'bɑːbɪkjuː/ ① *n* barbecue *m inv*; (party) grigliata f, barbecue *m inv*
② *vt* arrostire sul barbecue

barbed /bɑːbd/ *adj* **∼ wire** filo *m* spinato

barber /'bɑːbə(r)/ *n* barbiere *m*

barber's shop *n* barbiere *m*

barbiturate /bɑː'bɪtjʊrət/ *n* barbiturico *m*

bar chart *n* istogramma *m*

bar code *n* codice *m* a barre

bar-coded *adj* con codice a barre

bar code reader *n* lettore *m* di codice a barre

bard /bɑːd/ *n* liter bardo *m*

bare /beə(r)/ **①** *adj* nudo; ‹tree, room› spoglio; ‹floor› senza moquette; **the ~ bones** l'essenziale *m*
② *vt* scoprire; mostrare ‹teeth›

bareback *adv* senza sella

barefaced *adj* sfacciato

barefoot *adv* scalzo

bare-headed *adj* a capo scoperto

barely /'beəlɪ/ *adv* appena

bareness /'beənɪs/ *n* nudità *f*

bargain /'bɑːgɪn/ **①** *n* (agreement) patto *m*; (good buy) affare *m*; **into the ~** per di più
② *vi* contrattare; (haggle) trattare
■ **bargain for** *vt* (expect) aspettarsi

bargain basement *n* reparto *m* occasioni

bargaining /'bɑːgɪnɪŋ/ **①** *n* (over pay) contrattazione *f*
② *attrib* ‹power, rights› contrattuale; ‹position› di negoziato

barge /bɑːdʒ/ *n* barcone *m*
■ **barge** *vi* fam (to room) piombare dentro; (into conversation) interrompere bruscamente; **~ into** piombare dentro a ‹room›; venire addosso a ‹person›

bargepole /'bɑːdʒpəʊl/ *n* **I wouldn't touch him/it with a ~** non lo toccherei nemmeno con un dito

barista /bə'rɪstə/ *n* esp Am barista *mf*

baritone /'bærɪtəʊn/ *n* baritono *m*

bark[1] /bɑːk/ *n* (of tree) corteccia *f*

bark[2] **①** *n* abbaio *m*
② *vi* abbaiare

barking /'bɑːkɪŋ/ **①** *n* abbaio *m*
② *adj* ‹dog› che abbaia; ‹cough, laugh› convulso
③ *adv* **be ~ mad** Br fam essere matto da legare

barley /'bɑːlɪ/ *n* orzo *m*

barleycorn *n* orzo *m*; (grain) chicco *m* d'orzo

barley sugar *n* caramella *f* d'orzo

barley water *n* Br orzata *f*

barley wine *n* Br birra *f* molto forte

barmaid /'bɑːmeɪd/ *n* barista *f*

barman /'bɑːmən/ *n* barista *m*

barmy /'bɑːmɪ/ *adj* fam strampalato

barn /bɑːn/ *n* granaio *m*

barnacle /'bɑːnəkl/ *n* cirripede *m*

barn dance *n* ballo *m* tradizionale statunitense; (social gathering) festa *f* negli USA in cui si fanno balli tradizionali

barn owl *n* barbagianni *m inv*

barnstorming *adj* sensazionale

barnyard *n* aia *f*

barometer /bə'rɒmɪtə(r)/ *n* barometro *m*

baron /'bærən/ *n* barone *m*

baroness /'bærənɪs/ *n* baronessa *f*

baronial /bə'rəʊnɪəl/ *adj* baronale

baroque /bə'rɒk/ *adj* & *n* barocco *m*

barracking /'bærəkɪŋ/ *n* fischi *mpl* e insulti *mpl*

barrack room **①** *n* camerata *f*
② *attrib* pej ‹language› da caserma

barracks /'bærəks/ *npl* caserma *fsg*

barrage /'bærɑːʒ/ *n* (in river) [opera *f* di] sbarramento *m*; Mil sbarramento *m*; (fig: of criticism, abuse) sfilza *f*

barrage balloon *n* pallone *m* di sbarramento

barrel /'bærəl/ *n* barile *m*, botte *f*; (of gun) canna *f*

barrel organ *n* organetto *m* [a cilindro]

barren /'bærən/ *adj* sterile; ‹landscape› brullo

barrette /bæ'ret/ *n* Am (for hair) molletta *f*

barricade /bærɪ'keɪd/ **①** *n* barricata *f*
② *vt* barricare

barrier /'bærɪə(r)/ *n* barriera *f*; Rail cancello *m*; fig ostacolo *m*

barrier cream *n* crema *f* protettiva

barrier method *n* Med metodo *m* anticoncezionale meccanico

barrier reef *n* barriera *f* corallina

barring /'bɑːrɪŋ/ *prep* **~ accidents** salvo imprevisti

barrister /'bærɪstə(r)/ *n* avvocato *m*

barrow /'bærəʊ/ *n* carretto *m*; (wheel~) carriola *f*

bar stool *n* sgabello *m* da bar

bartender /'bɑːtendə(r)/ *n* barista *mf*

barter /'bɑːtə(r)/ *vi* barattare (**for** con)

base /beɪs/ **①** *n* base *f*
② *adj* vile
③ *vt* basare; **be ~d on** basarsi su

baseball /'beɪsbɔːl/ *n* baseball *m*

baseball cap *n* berretto *m* da baseball

base camp *n* campo *m* base *inv*

base form *n* (of verb) forma *f* non coniugata di un verbo

base lending rate *n* tasso *m* base *inv* di interesse

baseless /'beɪslɪs/ *adj* infondato

baseline /'beɪslaɪn/ *n* Tennis linea *f* di fondo; fig riferimento *m*

basement /'beɪsmənt/ *n* seminterrato *m*

basement flat *n* appartamento *m* nel seminterrato

base metal *n* metallo *m* vile *inv*

base rate *n* tasso *m* base *inv*

bash /bæʃ/ **①** *n* colpo *m* violento; **have a ~!** fam provaci!
② *vt* colpire [violentemente]; (dent) ammaccare; **~ed in** ammaccato
■ **bash down** *vt* sfondare ‹door›

■ **bash into** vt imbattersi in ⟨person⟩; sbattere contro ⟨wall, tree⟩

bashful /'bæʃfl/ adj timido

bashfully /'bæʃfʊlɪ/ adv timidamente

bashing /'bæʃɪŋ/ n fam (beating) pestaggio m; (criticism) critica f feroce; (defeat) batosta f; **take a ~** prendere una batosta

basic /'beɪsɪk/ adj di base; ⟨condition, requirement⟩ basilare; ⟨living conditions⟩ povero; **my Italian is pretty ~** il mio italiano è abbastanza rudimentale; **the ~s** (of language, science) i rudimenti; (essentials) l'essenziale m

basically /'beɪsɪklɪ/ adv fondamentalmente

basic rate n tariffa f minima; (in tax) aliquota f minima

basil /'bæzɪl/ n basilico m

basilica /bə'zɪlɪkə/ n basilica f

basin /'beɪsn/ n bacinella f; (wash-hand ~) lavabo m; (for food) recipiente m; Geog bacino m

basinful /'beɪsɪnfʊl/ n bacinella f (contenuto)

basis /'beɪsɪs/ n (pl **-ses** /'beɪsiːz/) base f

bask /bɑːsk/ vi crogiolarsi

basket /'bɑːskɪt/ n cestino m

basketball n pallacanestro f

basket chair n sedia m di vimini

basketwork n (objects) oggetti mpl in vimini; (craft) lavoro m artigianale di oggetti in vimini

Basle /bɑːl/ n Basilea f

Basque /bæsk/ adj & n (person) basco, -a mf; (language) basco m

bass /beɪs/ ① adj basso; **~ voice** voce f di basso
② n basso m

bass-baritone n baritono m basso

bass clef n chiave f di basso

bass drum n grancassa f

basset hound /'bæsɪt/ n basset hound m inv

bass guitar n (chitarra f) basso m

bassist /'beɪsɪst/ n bassista mf

bassoon /bə'suːn/ n fagotto m

bastard /'bɑːstəd/ n (illegitimate child) bastardo, -a mf; sl figlio m di puttana

baste¹ /beɪst/ vt (sew) imbastire

baste² vt Culin ungere con grasso

bastion /'bæstɪən/ n bastione m

bat¹ /bæt/ ① n mazza f; (for table tennis) racchetta f; **off one's own ~** fam tutto da solo
② vt (pt/pp **batted**) battere; **she didn't ~ an eyelid** fig non ha battuto ciglio

bat² n Zool pipistrello m

batch /bætʃ/ n gruppo m; (of goods) partita f; (of bread) infornata f

batch file n Comput batch file m inv

batch processing /'prəʊsesɪŋ/ n Comput elaborazione f a gruppi

bated /'beɪtɪd/ adj **with ~ breath** col fiato sospeso

bath /bɑːθ/ ① n (pl **~s** /bɑːðz/) bagno m; (tub) vasca f da bagno; **~s** pl piscina f; **have a ~** fare un bagno
② vt fare il bagno a
③ vi fare il bagno

bathe /beɪð/ ① n bagno m
② vi fare il bagno
③ vt lavare ⟨wound⟩

bather /'beɪðə(r)/ n bagnante mf

bathing /'beɪðɪŋ/ n bagni mpl

bathing cap n cuffia f

bathing costume n costume m da bagno

bathing hut n cabina f (al mare)

bathing suit n costume m da bagno

bathing trunks n calzoncini mpl da bagno

bath mat n tappetino m da bagno

bathrobe /'bæθrəʊb/ n accappatoio m

bathroom /'bæθruːm/ n (also: toilet) bagno m

bathroom cabinet n armadietto m del bagno

bathroom fittings npl accessori mpl per il bagno

bathroom scales npl bilancia f pesapersone

bath salts npl sali mpl da bagno

bath-towel n asciugamano m da bagno

bathtub n vasca f da bagno

baton /'bæt(ə)n/ n Mus bacchetta f

baton charge n Br carica f con lo sfollagente

baton round n Br proiettile m di gomma

batsman /'bætsmən/ n Sport battitore m

battalion /bə'tælɪən/ n battaglione m

batten /'bætn/ n assicella f

batter /'bætə(r)/ n Culin pastella f

battered /'bætəd/ adj ⟨car⟩ malandato; ⟨wife, baby⟩ maltrattato

battering /'bæt(ə)rɪŋ/ n **take a ~** (from bombs, storm, waves) essere colpito; (from other team) prendersi una batosta; (from other boxer) prenderle

battering ram n ariete m

battery /'bætərɪ/ n batteria f; (of torch, radio) pila f

battery charger n caricabatterie m inv

battery chicken n pollo m di allevamento in batteria

battery controlled adj a pile

battery farming n allevamento m in batteria

battery hen n gallina f d'allevamento in batteria

battery life n autonomia f

battery operated, **battery powered** adj a pile

battery pack n battery pack m inv

battle /'bæt(ə)l/ **1** n battaglia f; fig lotta f **2** vi fig lottare

battleaxe n fam virago f inv

battle cry n also fig grido m di battaglia

battle dress n uniforme f da combattimento

battlefield n, **battleground** n campo m di battaglia; fig terreno m di scontro

battle lines npl Mil schieramenti mpl

battlements /'bætlmənts/ npl bordo m merlato; (crenellations) merlatura f

battle order n also fig ordine m di battaglia

battle-scarred adj agguerrito; fig segnato dalla vita

battleship n corazzata f

batty /'bætɪ/ adj fam strampalato

bauble /'bɔ:b(ə)l/ n (ornament) gingillo m; (jewellery) ninnolo m

bawdiness /'bɔ:dɪnɪs/ n oscenità f

bawdy /'bɔ:dɪ/ adj (-ier, -iest) piccante

bawl /bɔ:l/ vt/i urlare
■ **bawl out** vt fam urlare ⟨name, order⟩; fare una sfuriata a ⟨somebody⟩

bay[1] /beɪ/ n Geog baia f

bay[2] n keep at ~ tenere a bada

bay[3] n Bot alloro m

bay[4] n (horse) baio m

bay leaf n foglia f d'alloro

bay window n bay window f inv (grande finestra sporgente)

bazaar /bə'zɑ:(r)/ n bazar m inv

bazooka /bə'zu:kə/ n bazooka m inv

BBC n abbr (**British Broadcasting Corporation**) BBC f

BBQ abbr (**barbecue**) barbecue m inv

BC abbr (**before Christ**) a.C.

Bcc n abbr (**blind carbon copy**) ccn f

BE abbr (**bill of exchange**) cambiale f

be /bi:/ **1** vi (pres **am, are, is, are**; pt **was, were**; pp **been**) essere; **he is a teacher** è insegnante, fa l'insegnante; **what do you want to be?** cosa vuoi fare?; **be quiet!** sta'zitto!; **I am cold/hot** ho freddo/caldo; **it's cold/hot, isn't it?** fa freddo/caldo, vero?; **how are you?** come stai?; **I am well** sto bene; **there is** c'è; **there are** ci sono; **I have been to Venice** sono stato a Venezia; **has the postman been?** è passato il postino?; **you're coming too, aren't you?** vieni anche tu, no?; **it's yours, is it?** è tuo, vero?; **was John there? – yes, he was** c'era John? – sì; **John wasn't there – yes he was!** John non c'era – sì che c'era!; **three and three are six** tre più tre fanno sei; **he is five** ha cinque anni; **that will be £10, please** fanno 10 sterline, per favore; **how much is it?** quanto costa?; **that's £5 you owe me** mi devi 5 sterline
2 v aux **I am coming/reading** sto venendo/leggendo; **I'm staying** (not leaving) resto; **I am being lazy** sono pigro; **I was thinking of you** stavo pensando a te; **you are not to tell him** non devi dirglielo; **you are to do that immediately** devi farlo subito
3 passive essere; **I have been robbed** sono stato derubato

beach /bi:tʃ/ n spiaggia f

beach ball n pallone m da spiaggia

beach buggy n dune buggy f inv

beach-comber /-kəʊmə(r)/ n persona f che vive rivendendo gli oggetti trovati sulla spiaggia

beachhead n testa f di sbarco

beach hut n cabina f [da spiaggia]

beachrobe n accappatoio m

beachwear n abbigliamento m da spiaggia

beacon /'bi:k(ə)n/ n faro m; Naut, Aeron fanale m

bead /bi:d/ n perlina f

beady-eyed /bi:dr'aɪd/ adj (sharp-eyed) a cui non sfugge niente

beagle /'bi:g(ə)l/ n beagle m inv, bracchetto m

beak /bi:k/ n becco m

beaker /'bi:kə(r)/ n coppa f; (in laboratory) becher m inv

beam /bi:m/ **1** n trave f; (of light) raggio m **2** vi irradiare; ⟨person⟩ essere raggiante; ~ **at somebody** fare un gran sorriso a qualcuno

beaming /'bi:mɪŋ/ adj raggiante

bean /bi:n/ n fagiolo m; (of coffee) chicco m; **spill the ~s** fam spiattellare tutto

bean bag n (seat) poltrona f imbottita di pallini di polistirolo

beanfeast n fam festa f

beanie /'bi:nɪ/ n zucchetto m

beanpole n (fig fam: tall thin person) spilungone, -a mf

beansprout n germoglio m di soia

bear[1] /beə(r)/ n orso m

bear[2] v (pt **bore** pp **borne**) **1** vt (endure) sopportare; mettere al mondo ⟨child⟩; (carry) portare; ~ **in mind** tenere presente; ~ **fruit** ⟨tree⟩ produrre; fig dare frutto **2** vi ~ **left/right** andare a sinistra/a destra
■ **bear out** vt confermare ⟨story, statement⟩
■ **bear with** vt aver pazienza con
■ **bear up** vi tirare avanti

bearable /'beərəbl/ *adj* sopportabile

bear cub *n* cucciolo *m* di orso

beard /bɪəd/ *n* barba *f*; **have a ~** avere la barba

bearded /'bɪədɪd/ *adj* barbuto

bearer /'beərə(r)/ *n* portatore, -trice *mf*; (of passport) titolare *mf*

bearing /'beərɪŋ/ *n* portamento *m*; Techn cuscinetto *m* [a sfera]; **have a ~ on** avere attinenza con; **get one's ~s** orientarsi; **lose one's ~s** perdere l'orientamento

bear market *n* Fin mercato *m* al ribasso

bearskin *n* (pelt) pelle *f* d'orso; (hat) colbacco *m* militare

beast /bi:st/ *n* bestia *f*; (fam: person) animale *m*

beastly /'bi:stlɪ/ *adj* (**-ier**, **-iest**) fam orribile

beat /bi:t/ **1** *n* battito *m*; (rhythm) battuta *f*; (of policeman) giro *m* d'ispezione
2 *vt* (pt **beat** pp **beaten**) battere; picchiare ⟨person⟩; **~ a retreat** Mil battere in ritirata; **~ it!** fam darsela a gambe!; **it ~s me why...** fam non capisco proprio perché...
■ **beat back** *vt* respingere ⟨flames, crowd⟩
■ **beat down** **1** *vt* buttare giù ⟨door⟩
2 *vi* ⟨sun⟩ battere a picco
■ **beat off** *vt* respingere ⟨attacker⟩
■ **beat out** *vt* domare ⟨flames⟩
■ **beat up** *vt* picchiare

beaten /'bi:tn/ *adj* **off the ~ track** fuori mano

beatify /bɪ'ætɪfaɪ/ *vt* beatificare

beating /'bi:tɪŋ/ *n* bastonata *f*; **get a ~** (with fists) essere preso a pugni; ⟨team, player⟩ prendere una batosta

beating-up *n* fam pestaggio *m*

beat-up *adj* fam ⟨car⟩ sfasciato

beau /bəʊ/ *n* liter, hum spasimante *m*

Beaufort scale /'bəʊfət/ *n* scala *f* Beaufort

beautician /bju:'tɪʃn/ *n* estetista *mf*

beautiful /'bju:tɪfl/ *adj* bello; **the ~ people** il bel mondo

beautifully /'bju:tɪfʊlɪ/ *adv* splendidamente

beautify /'bju:tɪfaɪ/ *vt* (pt/pp **-ied**) abbellire

beauty /'bju:tɪ/ *n* bellezza *f*

beauty contest *n* concorso *m* di bellezza

beauty editor *n* redattore, -trice *mf* di articoli di bellezza

beauty parlour *n* istituto *m* di bellezza

beauty queen *n* reginetta *f* di bellezza

beauty salon *n* istituto *m* di bellezza

beauty sleep *n* hum **need one's ~ ~** aver bisogno delle proprie ore di sonno

beauty spot *n* neo *m*; (place) luogo *m* pittoresco

beaver /'bi:və(r)/ *n* castoro *m*
■ **beaver away** *vi* (fam: work hard) sgobbare

becalmed /bɪ'kɑ:md/ *adj* in bonaccia

became /bɪ'keɪm/ ▶ BECOME

because /bɪ'kɒz/ **1** *conj* perché; (at start of sentence) poiché
2 *adv* **~ of** a causa di

beck /bek/ *n* **be at sb's ~ and call** dover essere a completa disposizione di qualcuno

beckon /'bekn/ *vt/i* **~ [to]** chiamare con un cenno

become /bɪ'kʌm/ *v* (pt **became**, pp **become**) **1** *vt* diventare
2 *vi* diventare; **what has ~ of her?** che ne è di lei?

becoming /bɪ'kʌmɪŋ/ *adj* ⟨clothes⟩ bello

bed /bed/ *n* letto *m*; (of sea, lake) fondo *m*; (layer) strato *m*; (of flowers) aiuola *f*; **in ~** a letto; **go to ~** andare a letto

BEd *n abbr* (**bachelor of Education**) ≈ laurea *f* in magistero

bed and board *n* vitto e alloggio *m*

bed and breakfast *n* bed and breakfast *m*

bed base *n* fondo *m* del letto

bed bath *n* **give somebody a ~ ~** lavare qualcuno a letto

bedbug *n* cimice *f*

bedchamber *n* camera *f* da letto

bedclothes *npl* lenzuola e coperte *fpl*

bedding /'bedɪŋ/ *n* biancheria *f* per il letto, materasso e guanciali

bed down *vi* coricarsi

bedeck /bɪ'dek/ *vt* ornare

bedevil /bɪ'devl/ *vt* tormentare ⟨person⟩; intralciare ⟨plans⟩

bedfellow *n* **make strange ~s** fig fare una strana coppia

bedhead *n* testata *f* del letto

bed jacket *n* liseuse *f inv*

bedlam /'bedləm/ *n* baraonda *f*

bed linen *n* biancheria *f* per il letto

bedpan /'bedpæn/ *n* padella *f*

bedraggled /bɪ'drægld/ *adj* inzaccherato

bedridden /'bedrɪdən/ *adj* allettato

bedrock /'bedrɒk/ *n* basamento *m*; fig fondamento *m*

bedroom /'bedru:m/ *n* camera *f* da letto

bedroom farce *n* Theat pochade *f inv*

bedroom slipper *n* pantofola *f*

bedroom suburb *n* Am città *f inv* dormitorio

bed-settee *n* divano *m* letto

bedside /'bedsaɪd/ n **at his ~** al suo capezzale

bedside lamp n abat-jour m inv

bedside manner n modo m di trattare i pazienti; **have a good ~ ~** saperci fare con i pazienti

bedside rug n scendiletto m

bedside table n comodino m

bed sit n, **bed-sitter** n, **bedsitting-room** n camera f ammobiliata [fornita di cucina]

bedsock n calzino m da notte

bedsore n piaga f da decubito

bedspread n copriletto m

bedstead n fusto m del letto

bedtime n l'ora f di andare a letto

bedwetting n il bagnare il letto

bee /biː/ n ape f

beech /biːtʃ/ n faggio m

beef /biːf/ n manzo m

beefburger n hamburger m inv

beefeater n guardia f della Torre di Londra

beefsteak n bistecca f

beefsteak tomato n grosso pomodoro m

beef stew n stufato m di manzo

beef tea n brodo m di manzo

beefy /'biːfɪ/ adj ⟨flavour⟩ di manzo; fam ⟨man⟩ grande e grosso

beehive /'biːhaɪv/ n alveare m

bee-keeper n apicoltore, -trice mf

bee-keeping n apicoltura f

bee-line n **make a ~ for** fam precipitarsi verso

been /biːn/ ▶ BE

beep /biːp/ **1** n (of car) suono m di clacson; (of telephone) segnale m acustico; (of electronic device, radio) bip m inv
2 vi ⟨car, driver⟩ clacsonare; ⟨device⟩ fare bip
3 vt (with beeper) chiamare con il cercapersone; **~ the horn** clacsonare

beeper /'biːpə(r)/ n cercapersone m inv

beer /bɪə(r)/ n birra f

beer belly n pancia f da beone

beer bottle n bottiglia f da birra

beer garden n giardino m di un pub

beer mat n sottobicchiere m

beer money n fam quattro soldi mpl

beerswilling adj pej ubriacone

beer tent n spazio m per incontri con mescita di birra

bee sting n puntura f d'ape

beeswax /'biːzwæks/ n cera f d'api

beet /biːt/ n (Am: beetroot) barbabietola f; [sugar] ~ barbabietola f da zucchero

beetle /'biːtl/ n scarafaggio m

■ **beetle off** vi (fam: hurry away) scappare

beetroot /'biːtruːt/ n barbabietola f

befall /bɪ'fɔːl/ vt liter accadere a

befit /bɪ'fɪt/ vt liter addirsi a

befitting /bɪ'fɪtɪŋ/ adj ⟨modesty, honesty⟩ opportuno

before /bɪ'fɔː(r)/ **1** prep prima di; **the day ~ yesterday** ieri l'altro; **~ long** fra poco
2 adv prima; **never ~ have I seen...** non ho mai visto prima... **~ that** prima; **~ going** prima di andare
3 conj (time) prima che; **~ you go** prima che tu vada

beforehand /bɪ'fɔːhænd/ adv in anticipo

before tax adj ⟨profit, income⟩ lordo, al lordo di imposte

befriend /bɪ'frend/ vt trattare da amico

befuddle /bɪ'fʌdl/ vt confondere ⟨mind⟩

beg /beg/ **1** v (pt/pp **begged**) vi mendicare
2 vt pregare; chiedere ⟨favour, forgiveness⟩

began /bɪ'gæn/ ▶ BEGIN

beggar /'begə(r)/ n mendicante mf; **you lucky ~!** che fortuna sfacciata!; **poor ~!** povero cristo!; **you little ~!** monellaccio!

beggarly /'begəlɪ/ adj ⟨existence, meal⟩ miserabile; ⟨wage⟩ da fame

begging bowl /'begɪŋ/ n ciotola f del mendicante

begging letter n lettera f che sollecita offerte in denaro

begin /bɪ'gɪn/ vt/i (pt **began** pp **begun**, pres p **beginning**) cominciare; **well, to ~ with** dunque, per cominciare

beginner /bɪ'gɪnə(r)/ n principiante mf

beginning /bɪ'gɪnɪŋ/ n principio m

begonia /bɪ'gəʊnɪə/ n begonia f

begrudge /bɪ'grʌdʒ/ vt (envy) essere invidioso di; dare malvolentieri ⟨money⟩

beguile /bɪ'gaɪl/ vt (charm) affascinare; (cheat) ingannare

beguiling /bɪ'gaɪlɪŋ/ adj accattivante

begun /bɪ'gʌn/ ▶ BEGIN

behalf /bɪ'hɑːf/ n **on ~ of** a nome di; **on my ~** a nome mio; **say hello on my ~** salutalo da parte mia

behave /bɪ'heɪv/ vi comportarsi; **~ [oneself]** comportarsi bene

behaviour /bɪ'heɪvjə(r)/ n comportamento m; (of prisoner, soldier) condotta f

behavioural /bɪ'heɪvjərəl/ adj comportamentale

behaviourist /bɪ'heɪvjərɪst/ adj & n comportamentista mf

behaviour pattern n modello m comportamentale

behead /bɪ'hed/ vt decapitare

beheld /bɪ'held/ ▶ BEHOLD

behind /bɪ'haɪnd/ **1** prep dietro; (with pronoun) dietro di; **be ~ something** fig stare dietro qualcosa
2 adv dietro, indietro; (late) in ritardo; **a long way ~** molto indietro; **in the car ~** nella macchina dietro
3 n fam didietro m

behindhand /bɪ'haɪndhænd/ adv indietro

behold /bɪ'həʊld/ vt (pt/pp **beheld**) liter vedere

beholden /bɪ'həʊldn/ adj obbligato (**to** verso)

beholder /bɪ'həʊldə(r)/ n **beauty is in the eye of the ~** è bello ciò che piace

beige /beɪʒ/ adj & n beige m inv

Beijing /beɪ'dʒɪŋ/ n Pechino f

being /'biːɪŋ/ n essere m; **come into ~** nascere

Beirut /beɪ'ruːt/ n Beirut f

bejewelled /bɪ'dʒuːəld/ adj ingioiellato

Belarus /belə'ruːs/ n Bielorussia f

belated /bɪ'leɪtɪd/ adj tardivo

belatedly /bɪ'leɪtɪdlɪ/ adv tardi

belch /beltʃ/ **1** vi ruttare
2 vt ~ **[out]** eruttare ⟨smoke⟩

beleaguered /bɪ'liːgəd/ adj ⟨city⟩ assediato; ⟨troops⟩ accerchiato; fig ⟨person⟩ tormentato; fig ⟨company⟩ in difficoltà

Belfast /bel'faːst/ n Belfast f

belfry /'belfrɪ/ n campanile m

Belgian /'beldʒən/ adj & n belga mf

Belgium /'beldʒəm/ n Belgio m

Belgrade /bel'greɪd/ n Belgrado f

belie /bɪ'laɪ/ vt (give false impression of) dissimulare; (disprove) smentire

belief /bɪ'liːf/ n fede f; (opinion) convinzione f

believable /bɪ'liːvəbl/ adj credibile

believe /bɪ'liːv/ vt/i credere
■ **believe in** vt avere fiducia in ⟨person⟩; credere a ⟨ghosts⟩

believer /bɪ'liːvə(r)/ n Relig credente mf; **be a great ~ in** credere fermamente in

belittle /bɪ'lɪtl/ vt sminuire ⟨person, achievements⟩

belittling /bɪ'lɪtlɪŋ/ adj ⟨comment⟩ che sminuisce

Belize /be'liːz/ n Belize m

bell /bel/ n campana f; (on door) campanello m; **that rings a ~** fig mi dice qualcosa

bell-bottoms npl pantaloni mpl a zampa d'elefante

bellboy /'belbɔɪ/ n Am fattorino m d'albergo

belle /bel/ n bella f

bellhop /'belhɒp/ n Am fattorino m d'albergo

belligerence /bɪ'lɪdʒərəns/ n bellicosità f; Pol belligeranza f

belligerent /bɪ'lɪdʒərənt/ adj belligerante; (aggressive) bellicoso

bell-jar n campana f di vetro

bellow /'beləʊ/ vi gridare a squarciagola; ⟨animal⟩ muggire
■ **bellow out** vt urlare ⟨name, order⟩

bellows /'beləʊz/ npl (for fire) soffietto m

bell-pull n (rope) cordone m di campanello

bell-push n pulsante m di campanello

bell-ringer n campanaro m

bell-shaped adj a campana

bell-tower n campanile m

belly /'belɪ/ n pancia f

bellyache **1** n fam mal m di pancia
2 vi fam lamentarsi

belly button n fam ombelico m

belly dancer n danzatrice f del ventre

belly flop n (in swimming) spanciata f

bellyful /'belɪfʊl/ n fam **have had a ~ of something** avere le tasche piene di qualcosa

belong /bɪ'lɒŋ/ vi appartenere (**to** a); (be member) essere socio (**to** di)

belongings /bɪ'lɒŋɪŋz/ npl cose fpl

beloved /bɪ'lʌvɪd/ adj & n amato, -a mf

below /bɪ'ləʊ/ **1** prep sotto; (with numbers) al di sotto di
2 adv sotto, di sotto; Naut sotto coperta; **see ~** vedi qui di seguito

belt /belt/ **1** n cintura f; (area) zona f; Techn cinghia f
2 vi (fam: rush) ~ **along** filare velocemente
3 vt (fam: hit) picchiare
■ **belt out** vt cantare a squarciagola ⟨song⟩
■ **belt up** vi (in car) mettersi la cintura [di sicurezza]; ~ **up!** (sl: be quiet) stai zitto!

bemoan /bɪ'məʊn/ vt lamentare

bemused /bɪ'mjuːzd/ adj confuso

bench /bentʃ/ n panchina f; (work~) piano m da lavoro; **the B~** Jur la magistratura

benchmark /'bentʃmɑːk/ n punto m di riferimento; Comput paragone m con un campione; (fin: price) prezzo m di riferimento

bench-test vt Comput testare

bend /bend/ **1** n curva f; (of river) ansa f; **round the ~** fam fuori di testa
2 vt (pt/pp **bent**) piegare
3 vi piegarsi; ⟨road⟩ curvare; ~ **[down]** chinarsi
■ **bend over** vi inchinarsi

beneath /bɪ'niːθ/ **1** prep sotto, al di sotto di; **he thinks it's ~ him** fig pensa che sia sotto al suo livello; ~ **contempt** indegno

2 *adv* giù

Benedictine /benɪˈdɪktiːn/ *adj & n* Relig benedettino *m*

benediction /benɪˈdɪkʃn/ *n* Relig benedizione *f*

benefactor /ˈbenɪfæktə(r)/ *n* benefattore, -trice *mf*

beneficial /benɪˈfɪʃl/ *adj* benefico

beneficiary /benɪˈfɪʃərɪ/ *n* beneficiario, -a *mf*

benefit /ˈbenɪfɪt/ **1** *n* vantaggio *m*; (allowance) indennità *f inv*
2 *vt* (pt/pp **-fited**, pres p **-fiting**) giovare a
3 *vi* trarre vantaggio (**from** da)

Benelux /ˈbenɪlʌks/ **1** *n* Benelux *m*
2 *attrib* ⟨countries, organization⟩ del Benelux

benevolence /bɪˈnevələns/ *n* benevolenza *f*

benevolent /bɪˈnevələnt/ *adj* benevolo

benevolently /bɪˈnevələntlɪ/ *adv* con benevolenza

Bengal /beŋˈɡɔːl/ *n* Bengala *m*

benign /bɪˈnaɪn/ *adj* benevolo; Med benigno

benignly /bɪˈnaɪnlɪ/ *adv* con benevolenza

Benin /beˈniːn/ *n* Benin *m*

bent /bent/ **1** ▶ BEND
2 *adj* ⟨person⟩ ricurvo; (distorted) curvato; (fam: dishonest) corrotto; **be ~ on doing something** essere ben deciso a fare qualcosa
3 *n* predisposizione *f*

benzene /ˈbenziːn/ *n* benzene *m*

benzine /ˈbenziːn/ *n* benzina *f*

bequeath /bɪˈkwiːð/ *vt* lasciare in eredità

bequest /bɪˈkwest/ *n* lascito *m*

berate /bɪˈreɪt/ *vt* fml redarguire

bereaved /bɪˈriːvd/ *n* **the ~** *pl* i familiari del defunto

bereavement /bɪˈriːvmənt/ *n* lutto *m*

bereft /bɪˈreft/ *adj* **~ of** privo di

beret /ˈbereɪ/ *n* berretto *m*

Berlin /bɜːˈlɪn/ *n* Berlino *f*

Berliner /bɜːˈlɪnə(r)/ *n* berlinese *mf*

Bermuda /bəˈmjuːdə/ *n* le Bermuda

Bermuda shorts *npl* bermuda *m inv*

Berne /bɜːn/ *n* Berna *f*

berry /ˈberɪ/ *n* bacca *f*

berserk /bəˈsɜːk/ *adj* **go ~** diventare una belva

berth /bɜːθ/ **1** *n* (bed) cuccetta *f*; (anchorage) ormeggio *m*; **give a wide ~ to** fam stare alla larga da
2 *vi* ormeggiare

beseech /bɪˈsiːtʃ/ *vt* (pt/pp **beseeched** or **besought**) supplicare

beseeching /bɪˈsiːtʃɪŋ/ *adj* implorante

beset /bɪˈset/ *adj* **a country ~ by strikes** un paese vessato dagli scioperi

beside /bɪˈsaɪd/ *prep* accanto a; **~ oneself** fuori di sé

besides /bɪˈsaɪdz/ **1** *prep* oltre a
2 *adv* inoltre

besiege /bɪˈsiːdʒ/ *vt* assediare

besotted /bɪˈsɒtɪd/ *adj* infatuato (**with** di)

besought /bɪˈsɔːt/ ▶ BESEECH

bespatter /bɪˈspætə(r)/ *vt* schizzare

bespectacled /bɪˈspektək(ə)ld/ *adj* con gli occhiali

bespoke /bɪˈspəʊk/ *adj* ⟨suit⟩ su misura; ⟨tailor⟩ che lavora su ordinazione

best /best/ **1** *adj* migliore; **the ~ part of a year** la maggior parte dell'anno; **~ before** Comm preferibilmente prima di; **~ wishes** migliori auguri
2 *n* **the ~** il meglio; (person) il/la migliore; **at ~** tutt'al più; **all the ~!** tanti auguri!; **do one's ~** fare del proprio meglio; **to the ~ of my knowledge** per quel che ne so; **make the ~ of it** cogliere il lato buono della cosa
3 *adv* meglio, nel modo migliore; **as ~ I could** come meglio ho potuto; **like ~** preferire

best before date *n* data *f* di scadenza

best friend *n* migliore amico, -a *mf*

bestial /ˈbestɪəl/ *adj* also fig bestiale

bestiality /bestɪˈælətɪ/ *n* bestialità *f*

best man *n* testimone *m*

bestow /bɪˈstəʊ/ *vt* conferire (**on** a)

best-seller /-ˈselə(r)/ *n* bestseller *m inv*

best-selling /-ˈselɪŋ/ *adj* ⟨novelist⟩ più venduto

bet /bet/ **1** *n* scommessa *f*
2 *vt/i* (pt/pp **bet** or **betted**) scommettere

beta blocker /ˈbiːtəblɒkə(r)/ *n* betabloccante *m*

beta-test /ˈbiːtətest/ *vt* Comput testare la versione beta di

Bethlehem /ˈbeθlɪhem/ *n* Betlemme *f*

betray /bɪˈtreɪ/ *vt* tradire

betrayal /bɪˈtreɪəl/ *n* tradimento *m*

betrothal /bɪˈtrəʊðl/ *n* fidanzamento *m*

betrothed /bɪˈtrəʊðd/ *n* liter, hum promesso sposo *m*; promessa sposa *f*; **be ~** essere fidanzato

better /ˈbetə(r)/ **1** *adj* migliore, meglio; **get ~** migliorare; (after illness) rimettersi; **I waited the ~ part of a week** ho aspettato buona parte della settimana
2 *adv* meglio; **~ off** meglio; (wealthier) più ricco; **all the ~** tanto meglio; **the sooner the ~** prima è meglio è; **I've thought ~ of** ⋯

it ci ho ripensato; **you'd ~ stay** faresti meglio a restare; **I'd ~ not** è meglio che non lo faccia

③ *vt* migliorare; **~ oneself** migliorare le proprie condizioni

betting /'betɪŋ/ *n* (activity) scommesse *fpl*; **what's the ~ that...?** quanto scommettiamo che...?

betting shop *n* ricevitoria *f* (dell'allibratore)

between /bɪ'twiːn/ ① *prep* fra, tra; **~ you and me** detto fra di noi; **~ us** (together) tra me e te

② *adv* [in] **~** in mezzo; (time) frattempo

betwixt /bɪ'twɪkst/ *adv* **be ~ and between** essere una via di mezzo

bevel /'bevl/ ① *n* (edge) spigolo *m* smussato; (tool) squadra *f* falsa

② *vt* smussare ⟨*mirror, edge*⟩

beverage /'bevərɪdʒ/ *n* bevanda *f*

bevy /'bevɪ/ *n* frotta *f*

beware /bɪ'weə(r)/ *vi* guardarsi (of da); **~ of the dog!** attenti al cane!

bewilder /bɪ'wɪldə(r)/ *vt* disorientare

bewildered /bɪ'wɪldəd/ *adj* ⟨*look, person*⟩ perplesso, sconcertato

bewildering /bɪ'wɪldərɪŋ/ *adj* sconcertante

bewilderment /bɪ'wɪldəmənt/ *n* perplessità *f*

bewitch /bɪ'wɪtʃ/ *vt* stregare; fig affascinare completamente

beyond /bɪ'jɒnd/ ① *prep* oltre; **~ reach** irraggiungibile; **~ doubt** senza alcun dubbio; **~ belief** da non credere; **it's ~ me** fam non riesco proprio a capire

② *adv* più in là

B film *n* film *m inv* di serie B

Bhutan /buː'tɑːn/ *n* Bhutan *m*

bias /'baɪəs/ ① *n* (preference) preferenza *f*; pej pregiudizio *m*

② *vt* (pt/pp **biased**) (influence) influenzare

bias binding, bias tape /'baɪndɪŋ/ *n* (in sewing) fettuccia *f* in sbieco

biased /'baɪəst/ *adj* parziale

bib /bɪb/ *n* bavaglino *m*

Bible /'baɪbl/ *n* Bibbia *f*

Bible Belt *n* zona *f* del sud degli USA, dove predomina il fondamentalismo protestante

biblical /'bɪblɪkl/ *adj* biblico

bibliographic[al] /bɪblɪə'græfɪk[l]/ *adj* bibliografico

bibliography /bɪblɪ'ɒgrəfɪ/ *n* bibliografia *f*

bicarbonate /baɪ'kɑːbəneɪt/ *n* **~ of soda** bicarbonato *m* di sodio

bicentenary /baɪsen'tiːnərɪ/ ① *n* bicentenario *m*

② *attrib* ⟨*celebration, year*⟩ bicentenario

biceps /'baɪseps/ *n* bicipite *m*

bicker /'bɪkə(r)/ *vi* litigare

bickering /'bɪkərɪŋ/ *n* bisticci *mpl*

bicycle /'baɪsɪkl/ ① *n* bicicletta *f*

② *vi* andare in bicicletta

bicycle clip *n* molletta *f* (per pantaloni)

bicycle lane *n* pista *f* ciclabile

bicycle rack *n* (in yard) rastrelliera *f* per biciclette; (on car) portabiciclette *m inv*

bid¹ /bɪd/ ① *n* offerta *f*; (attempt) tentativo *m*

② *vt/i* (pt/pp **bid**, pres p **bidding**) offrire; (in cards) dichiarare

bid² *vt* (pt **bade** or **bid**, pp **bidden** or **bid**, pres p **bidding**) liter (command) comandare; **~ somebody welcome** dare il benvenuto a qualcuno

bidder /'bɪdə(r)/ *n* offerente *mf*

bidding /'bɪdɪŋ/ *n* offerte *fpl* (durante un'asta)

bide /baɪd/ *vt* **~ one's time** aspettare il momento buono

bidet /'biːdeɪ/ *n* bidè *m inv*

biennial /baɪ'enɪəl/ *adj* biennale

bier /bɪə(r)/ *n* catafalco *m*

bifocals /baɪ'fəʊklz/ *npl* occhiali *mpl* bifocali

big /bɪg/ ① *adj* (**bigger, biggest**) grande; ⟨*brother, sister*⟩ più grande; (fam: generous) generoso; **make ~ money** fare i soldi

② *adv* **talk ~** fam sparlarle grosse

bigamist /'bɪgəmɪst/ *n* bigamo, -a *mf*

bigamous /'bɪgəməs/ *adj* bigamo

bigamy /'bɪgəmɪ/ *n* bigamia *f*

big bang *n* (in astronomy) big bang *m*

big business *n* le grandi imprese; **be ~ ~** essere un grosso affare

big cat *n* grosso felino *m*

big deal *n* fam **~ ~!** bella forza!

big dipper *n* (Br: at fair) montagne *fpl* russe

big game hunting *n* caccia *f* grossa

bighead *n* fam montato, -a *mf*, gasato, -a *mf*

big-headed *adj* fam montato, gasato

big-hearted *adj* generoso

bigmouth *n* fam pej chiacchierone, -a *mf*; **he's such a ~!** (indiscreet) ha una lingua lunga!

big name *n* (in film, art) grosso nome *m*

big noise *n* fam pezzo *m* grosso

bigot /'bɪgət/ *n* fanatico, -a *mf*

bigoted /'bɪgətɪd/ *adj* di mentalità ristretta

bigotry /'bɪgətrɪ/ *n* mentalità *f* ristretta

big screen *n* grande schermo *m*

big shot *n* fam pezzo *m* grosso

Big Smoke *n* Br hum Londra *f*

big time ① *n* **make** or **hit the ~ ~** fam raggiungere il successo

b

2 attrib **big-time** ⟨crook⟩ di alto livello

big toe n alluce m

big top n ⟨tent⟩ tendone m del circo; (fig: circus) circo m

bigwig n fam pezzo m grosso

bike /baɪk/ **1** n fam bici f inv **2** vi andare in bici **3** vt mandare per corriere

biker /'baɪkə(r)/ n motociclista mf

bikini /bɪ'kiːnɪ/ n bikini m inv

bilateral /baɪ'lætrəl/ adj bilaterale

bilberry /'bɪlbərɪ/ n mirtillo m

bile /baɪl/ n bile f

bilge /bɪldʒ/ n Naut (place) carena f; (substance) sentina f; (fam: nonsense) idiozie fpl

bilingual /baɪ'lɪŋgwəl/ adj bilingue

bilingual secretary n segretario, -a mf bilingue

bilious /'bɪljəs/ adj Med ∼ **attack** attacco m di bile

bill¹ /bɪl/ **1** n fattura f; (in restaurant etc) conto m; (poster) manifesto m; Pol progetto m di legge; (Am: note) biglietto m di banca; Theat **be top of the** ∼ essere in testa al cartellone **2** vt fatturare

bill² n (beak) becco m

billboard /'bɪlbɔːd/ n cartellone m pubblicitario

billet /'bɪlɪt/ **1** n Mil alloggio m **2** vt (pt/pp **billeted**) alloggiare (**on** presso)

billfold n Am portafoglio m

billiard ball n palla f da biliardo

billiards /'bɪljədz/ n biliardo m

billiard table /'bɪljəd/ tavolo m da biliardo

billing /'bɪlɪŋ/ n Comm fatturazione f; **get top** ∼ Theat comparire in testa al cartellone

billion /'bɪljən/ n (thousand million) miliardo m; (old-fashioned Br: million million) mille miliardi mpl

billionaire /bɪljə'neə(r)/ n miliardario, -a mf

bill of exchange n cambiale f

bill of fare n menù m inv

bill of rights n dichiarazione f dei diritti

bill of sale n atto m di vendita

billow /'bɪləʊ/ **1** n (of smoke) nube f **2** vi alzarsi in volute ■ **billow out** vi (skirt, sail) gonfiarsi; (smoke, cloud) levarsi in volute

billy /'bɪlɪ/ n (Am: truncheon) sfollagente m inv

billycan /'bɪlɪkæn/ n gamella f

billy goat n caprone m

bimbo /'bɪmbəʊ/ n pej fam bambolona f; **his latest** ∼ la sua ultima amichetta

bin /bɪn/ n bidone m

binary /'baɪnərɪ/ adj binario

bin bag n sacco m per l'immondizia

bind /baɪnd/ vt (pt/pp **bound**) legare (**to** a); (bandage) fasciare; Jur obbligare

binder /'baɪndə(r)/ n (for papers) raccoglitore m; (for cement, paint) agglomerante m

binding /'baɪndɪŋ/ **1** adj ⟨promise, contract⟩ vincolante **2** n (of book) rilegatura f; (on ski) attacco m

binge /bɪndʒ/ **1** n fam **have a** ∼ fare baldoria; (eat a lot) abbuffarsi **2** vi abbuffarsi (**on** di)

binge-drinking n il bere smodatamente in particolari occasioni, specialmente nelle sere del week-end

bingo /'bɪngəʊ/ n ≈ tombola f

bin liner n Br sacchetto m per la spazzatura

binoculars /bɪ'nɒkjʊləz/ npl [pair of] ∼ binocolo msg

biochemist /baɪəʊ'kemɪst/ n biochimico, -a mf

biochemistry /baɪəʊ'kemɪstrɪ/ n biochimica f

biodegradable /baɪəʊdɪ'greɪdəbl/ adj biodegradabile

biodiversity /baɪəʊdaɪ'vɜːsətɪ/ n biodiversità f

bioengineering /baɪəʊendʒɪ'nɪərɪŋ/ n bioingegneria f

biographer /baɪ'ɒgrəfə(r)/ n biografo, -a mf

biographical /baɪə'græfɪkl/ adj biografico

biography /baɪ'ɒgrəfɪ/ n biografia f

biological /baɪə'lɒdʒɪkl/ adj biologico

biological clock n orologio m biologico

biologically /baɪə'lɒdʒɪklɪ/ adv biologicamente

biological powder n detersivo m biologico

biological warfare n guerra f biologica

biologist /baɪ'ɒlədʒɪst/ n biologo, -a mf

biology /baɪ'ɒlədʒɪ/ n biologia f

bionic /baɪ'ɒnɪk/ adj bionico

biopic /'baɪəʊpɪk/ n Cin film m basato su una biografia

biopsy /'baɪɒpsɪ/ n biopsia f

biorhythm /'baɪəʊrɪðəm/ n bioritmo m

biosphere /'baɪəʊsfɪə(r)/ n biosfera f

biotechnology /baɪəʊtek'nɒlədʒɪ/ n biotecnologia f

bioterrorism /baɪəʊ'terərɪzm/ n bioterrorismo m

bipartisan /baɪpɑːtɪˈzæn/ *adj* Pol bipartitico

bipartite /baɪˈpɑːtaɪt/ *adj* bipartito

birch /bɜːtʃ/ *n* (tree) betulla *f*

bird /bɜːd/ *n* uccello *m*; (fam: girl) ragazza *f*; **kill two ~s with one stone** prendere due piccioni con una fava

birdbrain /ˈbɜːdbreɪn/ *n* fam **he's such a ~** ha un cervello da gallina

bird call *n* cinguettio *m*

bird flu *n* influenza *f* aviaria, influenza *f* dei polli

birdie /ˈbɜːdɪ/ *n* (in golf) birdie *m*

birdlike /ˈbɜːdlaɪk/ *adj* come un uccello

bird of paradise *n* uccello *m* del paradiso

bird of prey *n* [uccello *m*] rapace *m*

bird sanctuary *n* riserva *f* per uccelli

birdseed *n* becchime *m*

bird's eye view *n* veduta *f* panoramica dall'alto

bird's nest *n* nido *m* di uccello

bird's nest soup *n* zuppa *f* di nido di rondine

birdsong *n* canto *m* degli uccelli

birdwatcher *n* persona *f* che pratica il bird-watching

bird-watching *n* go ~ fare del bird-watching

Biro® /ˈbaɪrəʊ/ *n* biro® *f inv*

birth /bɜːθ/ *n* nascita *f*; **give ~** partorire; **give ~ to** partorire

birth certificate *n* certificato *m* di nascita

birth-control *n* controllo *m* delle nascite

birthday *n* compleanno *m*

birthday party *n* festa *f* di compleanno

birthing pool *n* piccola piscina *f* per il parto

birthmark *n* voglia *f*

birth mother *n* madre *f* biologica

birthplace *n* luogo *m* di nascita

birth-rate *n* natalità *f*

birthright *n* diritto *m* di nascita

births, marriages, and deaths *npl* annunci *mpl* di nascite, di matrimonio, mortuari (sul giornale)

births column *n* annunci *mpl* delle nascite (sul giornale)

birth sign *n* segno *m* zodiacale

biscuit /ˈbɪskɪt/ *n* biscotto *m*

biscuit barrel, **biscuit tin** *n* biscottiera *f*

bisect /baɪˈsekt/ *vt* dividere in due [parti]

bisexual /baɪˈseksjʊəl/ *adj & n* bisessuale *mf*

bishop /ˈbɪʃəp/ *n* vescovo *m*; Chess alfiere *m*

bistro /ˈbiːstrəʊ/ *n* bistrò *m inv*

bit¹ /bɪt/ *n* pezzo *m*; (smaller) pezzetto *m*; (for horse) morso *m*; Comput bit *m inv*; **a ~ of** un pezzo di ‹*cheese, paper*›; un po' di ‹*time, rain, silence*›; **~ by** ~ poco a poco; **do one's** ~ fare la propria parte

bit² ▶ BITE

bitch /bɪtʃ/ *n* cagna *f*; sl arpia *f*

bitchy /ˈbɪtʃɪ/ *adj* velenoso

bite /baɪt/ ① *n* morso *m*; (insect) ~ puntura *f*; (mouthful) boccone *m* ② *vt* (pt **bit**, pp **bitten**) mordere; ‹*insect*› pungere; ~ **one's nails** mangiarsi le unghie ③ *vi* mordere; ‹*insect*› pungere ■ **bite off** *vt* staccare (con un morso)

biting /ˈbaɪtɪŋ/ *adj* ‹*wind, criticism*› pungente; ‹*remark*› mordace

bit part *n* Theat particina *f*

bitter /ˈbɪtə(r)/ ① *adj* amaro ② *n* Br birra *f* amara

bitter almond *n* mandorla *f* amara

bitter lemon *n* limonata *f* amara

bitterly /ˈbɪtəlɪ/ *adv* amaramente; **it's ~ cold** c'è un freddo pungente

bitterness /ˈbɪtənɪs/ *n* amarezza *f*

bittersweet /bɪtəˈswiːt/ *adj* liter agrodolce

bitty /ˈbɪtɪ/ *adj* Br fam frammentario

bitumen /ˈbɪtjʊmɪn/ *n* bitume *m*

bivouac /ˈbɪvʊæk/ ① *n* bivacco *m* ② *vi* bivaccare

bizarre /bɪˈzɑː(r)/ *adj* bizzarro

blab /blæb/ *vi* (pt/pp **blabbed**) cianciare

black /blæk/ ① *adj* nero; **be ~ and blue** essere coperto di lividi ② *n* nero *m* ③ *vt* boicottare ‹*goods*› ■ **black out** ① *vt* cancellare ② *vi* (lose consciousness) perdere coscienza

Black Africa *n* Africa *f* nera

Black American *n* negro, -a americano, -a *mf*

blackball *vt* dare voto contrario a

black belt *n* cintura *f* nera

blackberry *n* mora *f*

blackberry bush *n* rovo *m*

blackbird *n* merlo *m*

blackboard *n* Sch lavagna *f*

black box *n* Aeron scatola *f* nera

black bread *n* pane *m* nero

blackcurrant *n* ribes *m inv* nero

blacken /ˈblækən/ *vt* annerire

black eye *n* occhio *m* nero

Black Forest gateau *n* dolce *m* a base di cioccolato, panna e ciliegie

blackguard /ˈblægəd/ *n* hum brigante *m*

blackhead *n* Med punto *m* nero

black-headed gull *n* gabbiano *m* comune

black humour umorismo *m* nero

black ice *n* ghiaccio *m* (sulla strada)

blacking /'blækɪŋ/ (Br: boycotting) boicottaggio *m*; (polish) lucido *m* nero (per scarpe)

blackish /'blækɪʃ/ *adj* nerastro

blackjack *n* blackjack *m*

blackleg *n* Br crumiro *m*

blacklist *vt* mettere sulla lista nera

blackmail *n* ricatto *m* *vt* ricattare

blackmailer *n* ricattatore, -trice *mf*

black mark *n* fig neo *m*

black market *n* borsa *f* nera

black marketeer *n* borsanerista *mf*

black mass *n* messa *f* nera

blackness /'blæknɪs/ *n* nero *m*; (evilness) cattiveria *f*; (of moods) scontrosità *f*

black-out *n* blackout *m inv*; **have a ~** Med perdere coscienza

black pepper *n* pepe *m* nero

black pudding *n* ≈ sanguinaccio *m*

Black Sea *n* Mar *m* Nero

black sheep *n* fig pecora *f* nera

Blackshirt *n* camicia *f* nera

blacksmith *n* fabbro *m*

black spot *n* fig luogo *m* conosciuto per gli incidenti stradali

black swan *n* cigno *m* nero

black tie *n* (on invitation) abito scuro

black widow [spider] *n* vedova *f* nera

bladder /'blædə(r)/ *n* Anat vescica *f*

blade /bleɪd/ *n* lama *f*; (of grass) filo *m*

blame /bleɪm/ ① *n* colpa *f*
② *vt* dare la colpa a; **~ somebody for doing something** dare la colpa a qualcuno per aver fatto qualcosa; **no one is to ~** non è colpa di nessuno

blameless /'bleɪmlɪs/ *adj* innocente

blameworthy /'bleɪmwɜːðɪ/ *adj* biasimevole

blanch /blɑːntʃ/ ① *vi* sbiancare
② *vt* Culin sbollentare

blancmange /blə'mɒnʒ/ *n* biancomangiare *m*

bland /blænd/ *adj* ⟨food⟩ insipido; ⟨person⟩ insulso

blandly /'blændlɪ/ *adv* ⟨say⟩ in modo piatto

blank /blæŋk/ ① *adj* bianco; ⟨look⟩ vuoto
② *n* spazio *m* vuoto; ⟨cartridge⟩ cartuccia *f* a salve
③ *vt* ignorare; **she completely ~ed me** mi ha completamente ignorato
■ **blank out** *vt* cancellare dalla memoria ⟨memory⟩

blank cheque *n* assegno *m* in bianco

blanket /'blæŋkɪt/ *n* coperta *f*; **wet ~** fam guastafeste *mf inv*

blanket box, **blanket chest** *n* Br cassapanca *f*

blanket cover *n* (in insurance) assicurazione *f* che copre tutti i rischi

blanket stitch *n* punto *m* di rinforzo

blankly /'blæŋklɪ/ *adv* (uncomprehendingly) con espressione attonita; (without expression) senza espressione

blank verse *n* versi *mpl* sciolti

blare /bleə(r)/ *vi* suonare a tutto volume
■ **blare out** *vt* strombazzare rumorosamente

blarney /'blɑːnɪ/ *n* fam lusinga *f*

blasé /'blɑːzeɪ/ *adj* blasé *inv*

blaspheme /blæs'fiːm/ *vi* bestemmiare

blasphemous /'blæsfəməs/ *adj* blasfemo

blasphemy /'blæsfəmɪ/ *n* bestemmia *f*

blast /blɑːst/ ① *n* (gust) raffica *f*; (sound) scoppio *m*
② *vt* (with explosive) far saltare
③ *int* sl maledizione!
■ **blast off** *vi* ⟨rocket⟩ decollare

blasted /'blɑːstɪd/ *adj* sl maledetto

blast furnace *n* altoforno *m*

blasting /'blɑːstɪŋ/ *n* brillamento *m*

blast-off *n* (of missile) lancio *m*

blatant /'bleɪtənt/ *adj* sfacciato

blatantly /'bleɪtəntlɪ/ *adv* ⟨copy, disregard⟩ sfacciatamente; **it's ~ obvious** è lampante

blather /'blæðə(r)/ *vi* fam blaterare

blaze /bleɪz/ ① *n* incendio *m*; **a ~ of colour** un'esplosione *f* di colori
② *vi* ardere
■ **blaze down** *vi* ⟨sun⟩ essere cocente

blazer /'bleɪzə(r)/ *n* blazer *m inv*

blazing *adj* ⟨row⟩ acceso; ⟨fire⟩ violento; ⟨building⟩ in fiamme

bleach /bliːtʃ/ ① *n* decolorante *m*: (for cleaning) candeggina *f*, varecchina *f*
② *vt* sbiancare; ossigenare ⟨hair⟩

bleak /bliːk/ *adj* desolato; fig ⟨prospects, future⟩ tetro

bleakly /'bliːklɪ/ *adv* ⟨stare, say⟩ in modo tetro

bleakness /'bliːknɪs/ *n* (of weather) tetraggine *f*; (of surroundings, future) desolazione *f*

bleary-eyed /blɪərɪ'aɪd/ *adj* **be ~** avere gli occhi gonfi

bleat /bliːt/ ① *vi* belare
② *n* belato *m*

bleed /bliːd/ ① *v* (pt/pp **bled**) *vi* sanguinare
② *vt* spurgare ⟨brakes, radiator⟩

bleeding /'bli:dɪŋ/ **1** *n* perdita di sangue *f*; (heavy) emorragia *f*; (deliberate) salasso *m*
2 *adj* ‹wound, hand› sanguinante; sl = BLOODY

bleeding heart *n* fig pej cuore *m* troppo tenero

bleep /bli:p/ **1** *n* bip *m*
2 *vi* suonare
3 *vt* chiamare col cercapersone

bleeper /'bli:pə(r)/ *n* cercapersone *m inv*

blemish /'blemɪʃ/ *n* macchia *f*

blend /blend/ **1** *n* (of tea, coffee, whisky) miscela *f*; (of colours) insieme *m*
2 *vt* mescolare
3 *vi* ‹colours, sounds› fondersi (with con)
■ **blend in 1** *vi* ‹person› passare inosservato; ∼ **in with** mescolarsi con
2 *vt* ∼ **something in** mescolare qualcosa

blender /'blendə(r)/ *n* Culin frullatore *m*

blending /'blendɪŋ/ *n* (of coffees, whiskies) miscela *f*

bless /bles/ *vt* benedire

blessed /'blesɪd/ *adj* also sl benedetto

blessing /'blesɪŋ/ *n* benedizione *f*

blew /blu:/ ▶ BLOW²

blight /blaɪt/ **1** *n* Bot ruggine *f*
2 *vt* far avvizzire ‹plants›

blighter /'blaɪtə(r)/ (Br fam: annoying person) idiota *mf*; **you lucky** ∼ hai una fortuna sfacciata!; **poor** ∼ povero diavolo *m*

blimey /'blaɪmɪ/ *int* Br fam accidenti!

blind /blaɪnd/ **1** *adj* cieco; ∼ **man/ woman** cieco/cieca
2 *npl* **the** ∼ i ciechi
3 *vt* accecare
4 *n* [roller] ∼ avvolgibile *m*; [Venetian] ∼ veneziana *f*

blind alley *n* vicolo *m* cieco

blind date *n* appuntamento *m* galante con una persona sconosciuta

blindfold 1 *adv* con gli occhi bendati
2 *adj* **be** ∼ avere gli occhi bendati
3 *n* benda *f*
4 *vt* bendare gli occhi a

blinding /'blaɪndɪŋ/ *adj* ‹light› accecante; ‹headache› da impazzire, tremendo

blindingly /'blaɪndɪŋlɪ/ *adv* ‹shine› in modo accecante; **be** ∼ **obvious** essere così lampante

blindly /'blaɪndlɪ/ *adv* ciecamente

blind-man's buff *n* moscacieca *f*

blindness /'blaɪndnɪs/ *n* cecità *f*

blind spot *n* (in car, on hill) punto *m* privo di visibilità; (in eye) punto *m* cieco; (fig: point of ignorance) punto *m* debole

blind trust *n* blind trust *m*

bling bling /ˌblɪŋ'blɪŋ/ *n* sl gioielli e abiti molto appariscenti, specialmente con riferimento a quelli indossati dai rapper americani

blink /blɪŋk/ *vi* sbattere le palpebre; ‹light› tremolare

blinkered /'blɪŋkəd/ *adj* ‹attitude, approach› ottuso; **be** ∼ avere i paraocchi

blinkers /'blɪŋkəz/ *npl* paraocchi *mpl*

blinking /'blɪŋkɪŋ/ *n* (of light) intermittenza *f*; (of eye) battere *m*

blip /blɪp/ *n* (on screen) segnale *m* luminoso a intermittenza; (on graph, line) piccola irregolarità *f*; (sound) ticchettio *m*; (hitch) intoppo *m*

bliss /blɪs/ *n* Rel beatitudine *f*; (happiness) felicità *f*

blissful /'blɪsfʊl/ *adj* beato; (happy) meraviglioso

blissfully /'blɪsfəlɪ/ *adv* beatamente; ∼ **ignorant** beatamente ignaro

blister /'blɪstə(r)/ **1** *n* Med vescica *f*; (in paint) bolla *f*
2 *vi* ‹paint› formare una bolla/delle bolle

blistering /'blɪst(ə)rɪŋ/ **1** *n* (of skin) vescica *f*; (of paint) bolle *fpl*
2 *adj* ‹sun› scottante; ‹heat› soffocante; ‹attack, criticism› feroce

blister pack *n* blister *m inv*

blithe /blaɪð/ *adj* (cheerful) gioioso; (nonchalant) spensierato

blithely /'blaɪðlɪ/ *adv* (nonchalantly) spensieratamente

blitz /blɪts/ *n* bombardamento *m* aereo; **have a** ∼ **on something** fig darci sotto con qualcosa

blizzard /'blɪzəd/ *n* tormenta *f*

bloated /'bləʊtɪd/ *adj* gonfio

blob /blɒb/ *n* goccia *f*

bloc /blɒk/ *n* Pol blocco *m*

block /blɒk/ **1** *n* blocco *m*; (building) isolato *m*; (building ∼) cubo *m* (per giochi di costruzione); ∼ **of flats** palazzo *m*
2 *vt* bloccare
■ **block out** *vt* coprire ‹light, sun›
■ **block up** *vt* bloccare

blockade /blɒ'keɪd/ **1** *n* blocco *m*
2 *vt* bloccare

blockage /'blɒkɪdʒ/ *n* ostruzione *f*

block book *vt* prenotare in blocco

block booking *n* prenotazione *f* in blocco

block-buster *n* (fam: book, film) successone *m*; Mil bomba *f* potente

block capital *n* in ∼s in stampatello

blockhead *n* fam testone, -a *mf*

blockhouse *n* Mil fortino *m*

block letters *npl* stampatello *m*

block vote *n* voto *m* per delega

block voting *n* votazione *f* per delega

blog /blɒg/ *n* Comput blog *m*

blogger /'blɒgə(r)/ *n* Comput blogger *m*

bloke /bləʊk/ *n* fam tizio *m*
blonde /blɒnd/ ① *adj* biondo
② *n* bionda *f*
blood /blʌd/ *n* sangue *m*
blood-and-thunder *adj* ⟨novel, film⟩
pieno di sangue
blood bank *n* banca *f* del sangue
blood bath *n* bagno *m* di sangue
blood blister *n* vescica *f* di sangue
blood brother *n* fratello *m* di sangue
blood cell, **blood corpuscle** *n*
globulo *m*
blood count *n* esame *m*
emocromocitometrico
blood-curdling *adj* raccapricciante
blood donor *n* donatore, -trice *mf* di
sangue
blood group *n* gruppo *m* sanguigno
bloodhound *n* segugio *m*
bloodless /ˈblʌdlɪs/ *adj* (pale) esangue;
(revolution, coup) senza spargimento di
sangue
blood-letting *n* Med salasso *m*; (killing)
spargimento *m* di sangue
blood lust *n* sete *f* di sangue
blood money *n* compenso versato ad
un killer o delatore
blood orange *n* arancia *f* sanguigna
blood poisoning *n* setticemia *f*
blood pressure *n* pressione *f* del sangue
blood-red *adj* rosso sangue *inv*
blood relative *n* parente *mf*
consanguineo, -a
bloodshed *n* spargimento *m* di sangue
bloodshot *adj* iniettato di sangue
blood sports *npl* sport *mpl* cruenti
bloodstained *adj* macchiato di sangue
bloodstream *n* sangue *m*
bloodsucker *n* also fig sanguisuga *f*
blood test *n* analisi *f inv* del sangue
bloodthirsty *adj* assetato di sangue
blood transfusion *n* trasfusione *f* del
sangue
blood type *n* gruppo *m* sanguigno
blood vessel *n* vaso *m* sanguigno
bloody /ˈblʌdɪ/ ① *adj* (-ier, -iest)
insanguinato; sl maledetto
② *adv* sl ∼ **easy/difficult** facile/difficile da
matti; ∼ **tired/funny** stanco/divertente da
morire; **you ∼ well will!** e, accidenti, lo
farai!
bloody-minded /blʌdɪˈmaɪndɪd/ *adj*
scorbutico
bloom /bluːm/ ① *n* fiore *m*; **in** ∼ (of flower)
sbocciato; (of tree) in fiore
② *vi* fiorire; fig essere in forma smagliante
bloomer /ˈbluːmə(r)/ *n* fam papera *f*
bloomers /ˈbluːməz/ *npl* mutandoni *mpl*
da donna

blooming /ˈbluːmɪŋ/ *adj* fam maledetto
blossom /ˈblɒsəm/ ① *n* fiori *mpl*
(d'albero); (single one) fiore *m*
② *vi* sbocciare
■ **blossom out** *vi* fig trasformarsi
blot /blɒt/ *n* also fig macchia *f*
■ **blot out** *vt* (pt/pp **blotted**) fig cancellare
blotch /blɒtʃ/ *n* macchia *f*
blotchy /ˈblɒtʃɪ/ *adj* chiazzato
blotter /ˈblɒtə(r)/ *n* tampone *m* di carta
assorbente; (Am: police) registro *m* di polizia
blotting paper /ˈblɒtɪŋ/ *n* carta *f*
assorbente
blotto /ˈblɒtəʊ/ *adj* fam ubriaco fradicio
blouse /blaʊz/ *n* camicetta *f*
blow¹ /bləʊ/ *n* colpo *m*
blow² *v* (pt **blew**, pp **blown**) ① *vi*
⟨wind⟩ soffiare; ⟨fuse⟩ saltare
② *vt* (fam: squander) sperperare; ∼ **one's
nose** soffiarsi il naso; ∼ **one's top** fam
andare in bestia
■ **blow away** ① *vt* far volar via
⟨papers⟩
② *vi* ⟨papers⟩ volare via
■ **blow down** ① *vt* abbattere
② *vi* abbattersi al suolo
■ **blow off** ① *vt* ⟨wind⟩ portar via
② *vi* ⟨hat, roof⟩ volare via
■ **blow out** ① *vt* (extinguish) soffiare
② *vi* ⟨candle⟩ spegnersi
■ **blow over** ① *vt* ⟨wind⟩ buttare giù
② *vi* ⟨storm⟩ passare; fig ⟨fuss, trouble⟩
dissiparsi
■ **blow up** ① *vt* (inflate) gonfiare; (enlarge)
ingrandire ⟨photograph⟩; (shatter by
explosion) far esplodere
② *vi* esplodere
blow-by-blow *adj* ⟨account⟩
particolareggiato
blow-dry *vt* asciugare con
l'asciugacapelli
blowfly *n* moscone *m* (della carne)
blowhole *n* (of whale) sfiatatoio *m*
blowlamp *n* fiamma *f* ossidrica
blown /bləʊn/ ▶ BLOW²
blowout *n* Elec corto circuito *m*; (in oil or
gas well) fuga *f*; (of tyre) scoppio *m*; (fam:
meal) abbuffata *f*
blowpipe *n* cerbottana *f*
blowtorch *n* cannello *m* ossidrico
blow-up ① *n* Phot ingrandimento *m*
② *adj* ⟨doll, toy, dinghy⟩ gonfiabile
blowy /ˈbləʊɪ/ *adj* ventoso
blowzy /ˈblaʊzɪ/ *adj* pej ⟨woman⟩
volgarmente appariscente
BLT *n abbr* (**bacon, lettuce, and
tomato**) sandwich *m* con bacon, lattuga e
pomodoro
blubber /ˈblʌbə(r)/ ① *n* (of whale) grasso
m di balena; (fam: of person) ciccia *f*
② *vi* fam piagnucolare

bludgeon /'blʌdʒən/ vt manganellare

blue /bluː/ **1** adj (pale) celeste; (navy) blu inv; (royal) azzurro; **feel ~** essere giù di corda; **~ with cold** livido per il freddo; **once in a ~ moon** una volta ogni morte di papa
2 n blu m inv; **the ~s** Music il blues; **have the ~s** essere giù di corda; **out of the ~** inaspettatamente; **a bolt from the ~** un fulmine a ciel sereno

bluebell n giacinto m di bosco

Blue Berets npl Mil Caschi blu mpl

blueberry n mirtillo m

blue blood n sangue m blu

blue-blooded adj di sangue blu

bluebottle n moscone m

blue cheese n formaggio m erborinato

blue chip adj ⟨company⟩ di altissimo livello; ⟨investment⟩ sicuro

blue-collar job n lavoro m manuale

blue-collar worker n operaio m

blue-eyed adj con gli occhi azzurri

blue-eyed boy n Br fig fam prediletto m

blue film n film m a luci rosse

blue jeans npl blue jeans mpl inv

blue light n (on emergency vehicles) luce f delle auto della polizia

blueness /'bluːnɪs/ n azzurro m

blue pencil n **go through something with the ~ ~** (censor) censurare qualcosa; (edit) fare una revisione di qualcosa

blueprint n fig progetto m

blue rinse n **she's had a ~ ~** si è tinta i capelli color grigio argentato

blue-stocking n pej [donna] intellettualoide f

blue tit n cinciarella f

Bluetooth® n Bluetooth® m

blue whale n balenottera f azzurra

bluff /blʌf/ **1** n bluff m inv
2 vi bluffare

bluish /'bluːɪʃ/ adj bluastro, azzurrognolo

blunder /'blʌndə(r)/ **1** n gaffe f inv
2 vi fare una/delle gaffe

blundering /'blʌnd(ə)rɪŋ/ adj **~ idiot** rimbecillito m

blunt /blʌnt/ adj spuntato; ⟨person⟩ reciso

bluntly /'blʌntlɪ/ adv schiettamente

bluntness /'blʌntnɪs/ n (of manner) rudezza f; (of person) brutale schiettezza f

blur /blɜː(r)/ **1** n **It's all a ~** fig è tutto confuso
2 vt (pt/pp **blurred**) rendere confuso

blurb /blɜːb/ n soffietto m editoriale

blurred /blɜːd/ adj ⟨vision, photo⟩ sfocato

blurt /blɜːt/ v
■ **blurt out** vt spifferare

blush /blʌʃ/ **1** n rossore m
2 vi arrossire

blusher /'blʌʃə(r)/ n fard m inv

bluster /'blʌstə(r)/ n (showing off) sbruffonata f

blustering /'blʌst(ə)rɪŋ/ **1** n (rage) sfuriata f; (boasting) spacconata f
2 adj (angry) infuriato; (boastful) sbruffone

blustery /'blʌst(ə)rɪ/ adj ⟨wind⟩ furioso; ⟨day, weather⟩ molto ventoso

blu-tak® /'bluːtæk/ n blu-tak® m

B movie n film m inv di serie B

BO n fam puzza f di sudore

boa /'bəʊə/ n boa m inv

boa constrictor /kən'strɪktə(r)/ boa inv

boar /bɔː(r)/ n cinghiale m

board /bɔːd/ **1** n tavola f; (for notices) tabellone m; (committee) assemblea f; **~ (of directors)** consiglio m (di amministrazione); **full ~** Br pensione f completa; **half ~** Br mezza pensione f; **~ and lodging** vitto e alloggio m; **go by the ~** fam andare a monte
2 vt Naut, Aeron salire a bordo di
3 vi ⟨passengers⟩ salire a bordo; **~ with** stare a pensione da
■ **board up** vt sbarrare con delle assi

boarder /'bɔːdə(r)/ n pensionante mf; Sch convittore, -trice mf

board game n gioco m da tavolo

boarding /'bɔːdɪŋ/ n Aeron, Naut imbarco m; (by customs officer) ispezione f; Mil abbordaggio m

boarding card n carta f di imbarco

boarding house n pensione f

boarding party n squadra f d'ispezione

boarding school n collegio m

board meeting n riunione f del consiglio di amministrazione

boardroom n sala f consiglio, sala f riunioni del consiglio di amministrazione

boardwalk n Am (by sea) lungomare m

boast /bəʊst/ **1** vi vantarsi (**about** di)
2 vt vantare

boaster /'bəʊstə(r)/ n sbruffone, -a mf

boastful /'bəʊstfʊl/ adj vanaglorioso

boat /bəʊt/ n barca f; (ship) nave f

boater /'bəʊtə(r)/ n (hat) paglietta f

boat-hook n gaffa f

boathouse /'bəʊthaʊs/ n rimessa f [per imbarcazioni]

boating /'bəʊtɪŋ/ **1** n canottaggio m
2 adj ⟨accident⟩ di navigazione

boating trip n traversata f per mare

boatload n carico m; **~s of tourists** navi fpl cariche di turisti

boatswain /'bəʊs(ə)n/ n nostromo m

boatyard n cantiere m per imbarcazioni

bob /bɒb/ **1** n (hairstyle) caschetto m

2 *vi* (pt/pp **bobbed**) (also ~ **up and down**) andare su e giù

bobbin /'bɒbɪn/ *n* bobina *f*

bobble hat /'bɒblhæt/ *n* berretto *m* a pompon

bobby /'bɒbɪ/ *n* Br fam poliziotto *m*

bobcat /'bɒbkæt/ *n* lince *f*

bobsleigh /'bɒbsleɪ/, **bobsled** /'bɒbsled/ **1** *n* bob *m inv* **2** *vi* andare sul bob

bode /bəʊd/ *vi* ~ **well/ill** essere di buono/cattivo augurio

bodge /bɒdʒ/ Br = BOTCH

bodice /'bɒdɪs/ *n* corpetto *m*

bodily /'bɒdɪlɪ/ **1** *adj* fisico **2** *adv* (forcibly) fisicamente

body /'bɒdɪ/ *n* corpo *m*; (organization) ente *m*; (amount: of poems etc) quantità *f*; **over my dead** ~! fam devi passare prima sul mio corpo!

body blow *n* deal a ~ ~ to fig assestare un duro colpo a

bodyboarding *n* bodyboarding *m inv*

bodybuilder *n* culturista *mf*

body-building *n* culturismo *m*

bodyguard *n* guardia *f* del corpo

body heat *n* calore *m* del corpo

body language *n* linguaggio *m* del corpo

body odour *n* fam puzza *f* di sudore

body piercing *n* piercing *m inv*

body politic *n* corpo *m* sociale

body shop *n* autocarrozzeria *f*

body snatching *n* furto *m* dei cadaveri

body stocking, **body suit** *n* body *m inv*

body warmer *n* gilet *m inv* imbottito

bodywork *n* Auto carrozzeria *f*

boffin /'bɒfɪn/ *n* Br fam scienziato *m*

bog /bɒg/ *n* palude *f* ■ **bog down** *vt* (pt/pp **bogged**) get ~ged down impantanarsi

bogey /'bəʊgɪ/ *n* (evil spirit) spirito *m* malvagio; (to frighten people) spauracchio *m*

boggle /'bɒg(ə)l/ *vi* the mind ~s non posso neanche immaginarlo

boggy /'bɒgɪ/ *adj* (swampy) paludoso; (muddy) fangoso

bog-standard *adj* fam ordinario

bogus /'bəʊgəs/ *adj* falso

bohemian /bəʊ'hiːmɪən/ *adj* ⟨lifestyle, person⟩ bohémien

boil[1] /bɔɪl/ *n* Med foruncolo *m*

boil[2] **1** *n* bring/come to the ~ portare/arrivare ad ebollizione **2** *vi* [far] bollire **3** *vi* bollire; (fig: with anger) ribollire; **the water** or **kettle's** ~**ing** l'acqua bolle

■ **boil away** *vi* ⟨water⟩ evaporare
■ **boil down to** *vi* fig ridursi a
■ **boil over** *vi* straboccare (bollendo)
■ **boil up** *vt* far bollire

boiler /'bɔɪlə(r)/ *n* caldaia *f*

boiler house *n* caldaia *f*

boiler room *n* locale *m* per la caldaia

boiler suit *n* tuta *f*

boiling /'bɔɪlɪŋ/ *adj* ⟨water⟩ bollente; **it's** ~ **in here!** qui si bolle!

boiling hot *adj* fam ⟨liquid⟩ bollente; ⟨day⟩ torrido

boiling point *n* punto *m* di ebollizione

boisterous /'bɔɪstərəs/ *adj* chiassoso

bold /bəʊld/ **1** *adj* audace **2** *n* Typ neretto *m*

boldly /'bəʊldlɪ/ *adv* audacemente

boldness /'bəʊldnɪs/ *n* audacia *f*

Bolivia /bə'lɪvɪə/ *n* Bolivia *f*

bollard /'bɒlɑːd/ *n* colonnina *m* di sbarramento al traffico

Bolognese /bɒlə'neɪz/ *n* ragù *m*

boloney /bə'ləʊnɪ/ *n* fam idiozie *fpl*

bolshy /'bɒlʃɪ/ *adj* Br fam (on one occasion) brontolone; **he's/she's** ~ (by temperament) è un/una piantagrane; **get** ~ fare [delle] storie

bolster /'bəʊlstə(r)/ **1** *n* cuscino *m* (cilindrico) **2** *vt* ~ [up] sostenere

bolt /bəʊlt/ **1** *n* (for door) catenaccio *m*; (for fixing) bullone *m* **2** *vt* fissare [con bulloni] (to a); chiudere col chiavistello ⟨door⟩; ingurgitare ⟨food⟩ **3** *vt* svignarsela; ⟨horse⟩ scappar via **4** *adv* ~ **upright** diritto come un fuso

bolt-hole *n* Br rifugio *m*

bomb /bɒm/ **1** *n* bomba *f* **2** *vt* bombardare ■ **bomb along** *vi* (fam: move quickly) sfrecciare

bombard /bɒm'bɑːd/ *vt* also fig bombardare

bombardment /bɒm'bɑːdmənt/ *n* bombardamento *m*

bombastic /bɒm'bæstɪk/ *adj* ampolloso

bomb attack *n* bombardamento *m*

bomb blast *n* esplosione *f*

bomb disposal *n* disinnesco *m*

bomb disposal expert *n* artificiere *m*

bomb disposal squad *n* squadra *f* artificieri

bomber /'bɒmə(r)/ *n* Aviat bombardiere *m*; (person) dinamitardo *m*

bomber jacket *n* bomber *m inv*

bombing /'bɒmɪŋ/ *n* Mil bombardamento *m*; (by terrorists) attentato *m* dinamitardo

bombproof *adj* a prova di bomba

bombscare n stato m di allarme per la presunta presenza di una bomba

bombshell n (fig: news) bomba f; **blonde ~** bionda f esplosiva

bomb shelter n rifugio m antiaereo

bombsite n zona f bombardata; (fig: mess) campo f di battaglia

Bomb Squad n squadra f artificieri

bona fide /bəʊnə'faɪdɪ/ adj ‹member, refugee› autentico; ‹attempt› genuino; ‹offer› serio

bonanza /bə'nænzə/ n (windfall) momento m di prosperità; (in mining) filone m d'oro/d'argento

bond /bɒnd/ ① n fig legame m; Comm obbligazione f
② vt ‹glue› attaccare

bondage /'bɒndɪdʒ/ n schiavitù f

bonded warehouse /'bɒndɪd/ n magazzino m doganale

bonding /'bɒndɪŋ/ n (between mother and baby) legame m madre-figlio; **male ~** solidarietà f maschile

bone /bəʊn/ ① n osso m; (of fish) spina f
② vt disossare ‹meat›; togliere le spine da ‹fish›

bone china n porcellana f fine

boned /bəʊnd/ adj ‹joint, leg, chicken› disossato; ‹fish› senza lische; ‹corset, bodice› con le stecche

bone-dry adj secco

bonehead n fam cretino, -a mf

bone idle adj fam fannullone

boneless /'bəʊnlɪs/ adj ‹chicken› disossato; ‹chicken breast› senz'osso; ‹fish› senza lische

bone marrow n midollo m osseo

bone-marrow transplant n trapianto m di midollo osseo

bonemeal n farina f d'ossa

bonfire /'bɒnfaɪə(r)/ n falò m inv

Bonfire Night n Br sera f del 5 novembre festeggiata con falò e fuochi d'artificio

bonk /bɒŋk/ vt sl scopare

bonkers /'bɒŋkəz/ adj fam suonato

bonnet /'bɒnɪt/ n cuffia f; (of car) cofano m

bonus /'bəʊnəs/ n (individual) gratifica f; (production **~**) premio m; (life insurance) dividendo m; **a ~** fig qualcosa in più

bonus point n five **~ ~s** un bonus di cinque punti

bony /'bəʊnɪ/ adj (-ier, -iest) ossuto; ‹fish› pieno di spine

boo /buː/ ① interj (to surprise or frighten) bu!
② vt/i fischiare

boob /buːb/ ① n (fam: mistake) gaffe f inv; (breast) tetta f
② vi fam fare una gaffe

booboo /'buːbuː/ n fam gaffe f inv

booby prize /'buːbɪ/ n premio m di consolazione per il peggior contendente

booby trap ① n Mil ordigno m che esplode al contatto; (joke) trabocchetto m
② vt Mil mettere un ordigno esplosivo in

boogie /'buːgɪ/ n fam boogie m

booing /'buːɪŋ/ n fischi mpl

book /bʊk/ ① n libro m; (of tickets) blocchetto m; **keep the ~s** Comm tenere la contabilità; **be in sb's bad/good ~s** essere nel libro nero/nelle grazie di qualcuno; **do something by the ~** seguire strettamente le regole
② vt (reserve) prenotare; (for offence) multare
③ vi (reserve) prenotare

bookable /'bʊkəbl/ adj ‹event, ticket› che si può prenotare; ‹offence› che può essere multato

bookbinder n rilegatore, -trice mf

bookbinding n rilegatura f

bookcase n libreria f

book club n club m inv del libro

book-ends npl reggilibri mpl

book fair n fiera f del libro

bookie /'bʊkɪ/ n fam bookmaker m inv, allibratore m

booking /'bʊkɪŋ/ n (Br: reservation) prenotazione f; **make a ~** fare una prenotazione; **get a ~** (Br: from referee) ricevere un'ammonizione

booking clerk n Br impiegato, -a mf in un ufficio prenotazioni

booking form n Br modulo m di prenotazione

booking office n biglietteria f

bookish /'bʊkɪʃ/ adj ‹person› secchione

book jacket n sopraccoperta f

bookkeeper n contabile mf

bookkeeping n contabilità f

booklet /'bʊklɪt/ n opuscolo m

book lover n amante mf della lettura

bookmaker n allibratore m

bookmark n segnalibro m

bookplate n ex libris m inv

bookrest n leggio m

bookseller n libraio, -a mf

bookshelf n (single) scaffale f; (bookcase) libreria f

bookshop n libreria f

bookstall n edicola f

bookstore n Am libreria f

book token n Br buono m acquisto per libri

bookworm n topo m di biblioteca

boom /buːm/ ① n Comm boom m inv: (upturn) impennata f; (of thunder, gun) rimbombo m

2 *vi* ⟨*thunder, gun*⟩ rimbombare; fig
prosperare

boomerang /'bu:məræŋ/ **1** *n*
boomerang *m inv*
2 *vi* ∼ **on somebody** ⟨*plan*⟩ ritorcersi
contro qualcuno

boomerang effect *n* effetto *m*
boomerang

booming /'bu:mɪŋ/ *adj* ⟨*sound*⟩ sonoro;
⟨*voice*⟩ tonante; ⟨*economy*⟩ fiorente;
⟨*demand, exports, sales*⟩ in crescita

boom microphone *n* microfono *m* a
stelo

boon /bu:n/ *n* benedizione *f*

boor /buə(r)/ *n* zoticone *m*

boorish /'buərɪʃ/ *adj* maleducato

boost /bu:st/ **1** *n* spinta *f*
2 *vt* stimolare ⟨*sales*⟩; sollevare ⟨*morale*⟩;
far crescere ⟨*hopes*⟩

booster /'bu:stə(r)/ *n* Med dose *f*
supplementare

boot /bu:t/ **1** *n* stivale *m*; (up to ankle)
stivaletto *m*; (football) scarpetta *f*; (climbing)
scarpone *m*; Auto portabagagli *m inv*
2 *vt* Comput mettere in funzione
∎ **boot out** *vt* fam cacciare
∎ **boot up** Comput **1** *vi* caricarsi
2 *vt* caricare

boot black *n* lustrascarpe *mf inv*

boot drive *n* Comput unità *f inv* di
inizializzazione

bootee /bu:'ti:/ *n* (knitted) babbuccia *f* di
lana; (leather) stivaletto *m*

booth /bu:ð/ *n* (for phoning, voting) cabina *f*;
(at market) bancarella *f*

bootlace *n* laccio *m*, stringa *f*

bootlegger *n* Am contrabbandiere *m* di
alcolici

bootlicker *n* leccapiedi *mf inv*

bootmaker *n* calzolaio *m*

boot polish *n* lucido *m* da scarpe

boot scraper *n* puliscipiedi *m inv*

bootstrap *n* (on boot) linguetta *f*
calzastivali; Comput lancio *m*; **pull oneself
up by one's** ∼**s** riuscire con le proprie
forze

boot-up *n* Comput boot *m inv*

booty /'bu:tɪ/ *n* bottino *m*

booze /bu:z/ *n* fam alcolici *mpl*

boozer /'bu:zə(r)/ *n* fam (person) beone, -a
mf;(Br: pub) bar *m inv*

booze-up *n* bella bevuta *f*

boozy /'bu:zɪ/ *adj* fam ⟨*laughter*⟩ da
ubriaco; ⟨*meal*⟩ in cui si beve molto

bop /bɒp/ fam **1** *n* (blow) colpo *m*
2 *vt* dare un colpo a
3 *vi* Br (dance) ballare

border /'bɔ:də(r)/ **1** *n* bordo *m*; (frontier)
frontiera *f*; (in garden) bordura *f*
2 *vt* confinare con; fig essere ai confini di

∎ **border on** *vt* confinare con ⟨*country,
land*⟩; essere al limite di ⟨*madness,
hysteria*⟩

border dispute *n* (fight) conflitto *m* al
confine; (disagreement) contesa *f* sul confine

border guard *n* guardia *f* di frontiera

borderline *n* linea *f* di demarcazione; ∼
case caso *m* dubbio

border raid *n* incursione *f*

bore[1] /bɔ:(r)/ ▶ BEAR[2]

bore[2] *vt* Techn forare

bore[3] **1** *n* (of gun) calibro *m*; (person)
seccatore, -trice *mf*; (thing) seccatura *f*
2 *vt* annoiare

bored /bɔ:d/ *adj* annoiato, stufo; **be** ∼ **(to
tears** or **to death)** annoiarsi (da morire)

boredom /'bɔ:dəm/ *n* noia *f*

boring /'bɔ:rɪŋ/ *adj* noioso

born /bɔ:n/ **1** *pp* **be** ∼ nascere; **I was** ∼
in 1963 sono nato nel 1963
2 *adj* nato; **a** ∼ **liar/actor** un bugiardo/un
attore nato

born-again *adj* convertito alla chiesa
evangelica

borne /bɔ:n/ ▶ BEAR[2]

Borneo /'bɔ:nɪəʊ/ *n* Borneo *m*

borough /'bʌrə/ *n* municipalità *f inv*

borough council *n* Br ≈ comune *m*

borrow /'bɒrəʊ/ *vt* prendere in prestito
(**from** da); **can I** ∼ **your pen?** mi presti la
tua penna?

borrower /'bɒrəʊə(r)/ *n* debitore, -trice
mf

borrowing /'bɒrəʊɪŋ/ *n* prestito *m*;
increase in ∼ Fin aumento *m*
dell'indebitamento

borrowing costs *n* Fin costo *m* del
denaro

borstal /'bɔ:stəl/ *n* Br riformatorio *m*

Bosnia /'bɒznɪə/ *n* Bosnia *f*

Bosnia-Herzegovina
/-hɜ:tsəgəʊ'vi:nə/ *n* Bosnia-Erzegovina *f*

Bosnian /'bɒznɪən/ *adj* & *n* bosniaco, -a
mf

bosom /'bʊzm/ *n* seno *m*

bosom buddy, bosom friend *n* fam
amico, -a *mf* del cuore

boss /bɒs/ **1** *n* direttore, -trice *mf*
2 *vt* (also ∼ **about**) comandare a
bacchetta

bossy /'bɒsɪ/ *adj* autoritario

bosun /'bəʊsən/ *n* nostromo *m*

botanical /bə'tænɪkl/ *adj* botanico

botanist /'bɒtənɪst/ *n* botanico, -a *mf*

botany /'bɒtənɪ/ *n* botanica *f*

botch /bɒtʃ/ *vt* fare un pasticcio con

both /bəʊθ/ **1** *adj* & *pron* tutti e due,
entrambi
2 *adv* ∼ **men and women** sia uomini che
donne; ∼ **[of] the children** tutti e due i ⋯▷

bambini; **they are** ~ **dead** sono morti
entrambi; ~ **of them** tutti e due

bother /'bɒðə(r)/ **❶** n preoccupazione f;
(minor trouble) fastidio m; **it's no** ~ non c'è
problema
❷ int fam che seccatura!
❸ vt (annoy) dare fastidio a; (disturb)
disturbare
❹ vi preoccuparsi (**about** di); **don't** ~
lascia perdere

Botswana /bɒt'swɑːnə/ n Botswana m

bottle /'bɒt(ə)l/ **❶** n bottiglia f; (baby's)
biberon m inv
❷ vt imbottigliare
■ **bottle up** vt fig reprimere

bottle bank n contenitore m per la
raccolta del vetro

bottle-feed vt allattare col biberon

bottle-feeding n allattamento m col
biberon

bottle green adj & n verde m bottiglia
inv

bottleneck n fig ingorgo m

bottle-opener n apribottiglie m inv

bottle top n tappo m di bottiglia

bottle-washer n hum **chief cook and** ~
tuttofare mf inv

bottom /'bɒtm/ **❶** adj ultimo; **the** ~
shelf l'ultimo scaffale in basso
❷ n (of container) fondo m; (of river) fondale
m; (of hill) piedi mpl; (buttocks) sedere m; **at
the** ~ in fondo; **at the** ~ **of the page** in
fondo alla pagina; **get to the** ~ **of** fig
vedere cosa c'è sotto
■ **bottom out** vi ⟨inflation,
unemployment etc⟩ assestarsi

bottom drawer n fig corredo m

bottom gear n Br Auto prima f

bottomless /'bɒtəmlɪs/ adj senza fondo

bottom line n Fin utile m; **that's the** ~
(decisive factor) la questione è tutta qui

botulism /'bɒtjʊlɪzm/ n botulismo m

bouffant /'buːfã/ adj ⟨hair, hairstyle⟩
cotonato; ⟨sleeve⟩ a sbuffo

bough /baʊ/ n ramoscello m

bought /bɔːt/ ▶ BUY

boulder /'bəʊldə(r)/ n masso m

bounce /baʊns/ **❶** vi rimbalzare; fam
⟨cheque⟩ essere respinto
❷ vt far rimbalzare ⟨ball⟩
■ **bounce back** vi fig riprendersi;
⟨email⟩ tornare indietro

bouncer /'baʊnsə(r)/ n fam buttafuori m
inv

bouncy /'baʊnsɪ/ adj ⟨ball⟩ che rimbalza
bene; ⟨mattress, walk⟩ molleggiato; fig
⟨person⟩ esuberante

bound¹ /baʊnd/ **❶** n balzo m
❷ vi balzare

bound² **❶** ▶ BIND

❷ adj ~ **for** ⟨ship⟩ diretto a; **be** ~ **to do**
(likely) dovere fare per forza; (obliged) essere
costretto a fare

boundary /'baʊndərɪ/ n limite m

boundless /'baʊndlɪs/ adj illimitato

bounds /baʊndz/ npl fig limiti mpl; **out of**
~ fuori dai limiti

bounty /'baʊntɪ/ n (gift) dono m;
(generosity) munificenza f

bounty hunter n cacciatore m di taglie

bouquet /bʊ'keɪ/ n mazzo m di fiori; (of
wine) bouquet m

bourbon /'bʊəbən/ n bourbon m inv

bourgeois /'bʊəʒwɑː/ adj pej borghese

bourgeoisie /bʊəʒwɑː'ziː/ n borghesia f

bout /baʊt/ n Med attacco m; Sport
incontro m

boutique /buː'tiːk/ n negozio m; **fashion**
~ negozio m di abbigliamento

bovine /'bəʊvaɪn/ adj bovino

bow¹ /bəʊ/ n (weapon) arco m; Mus
archetto m; (knot) nodo m

bow² /baʊ/ **❶** n inchino m
❷ vi inchinarsi
❸ vt piegare ⟨head⟩

bow³ /baʊ/ n Naut prua f
■ **bow out** vi (withdraw) ritirarsi (**of** da)

bowel /'baʊəl/ n intestino m; **have a** ~
movement andare di corpo; ~**s** pl
intestini mpl

bower /'baʊə(r)/ n (in garden) pergolato m;
(liter: chamber) salottino m

bowl¹ /bəʊl/ n (for soup, cereal) scodella f;
(of pipe) fornello m

bowl² **❶** n (ball) boccia f
❷ vt lanciare
❸ vi Cricket servire; (in bowls) lanciare
■ **bowl along** vi (in car etc) andare
spedito
■ **bowl over** vt buttar giù; (fig: leave
speechless) lasciare senza parole

bow-legged /bəʊ'legd/ adj dalle gambe
storte

bowler¹ /'bəʊlə(r)/ n Cricket lanciatore m;
Bowls giocatore m di bocce

bowler² n ~ [**hat**] bombetta f

bowling /'bəʊlɪŋ/ n gioco m delle bocce

bowling alley /'bəʊlɪŋælɪ/ n pista f da
bowling

bowling green n prato m da bocce

bowls /bəʊlz/ n gioco m delle bocce

bowstring n corda f d'arco

bow tie n cravatta f a farfalla

bow window n bow window f inv

box¹ /bɒks/ n scatola f; Theat palco m

box² **❶** vi Sport fare il pugile
❷ vt ~ **sb's ears** dare uno scapaccione a
qualcuno

boxer /'bɒksə(r)/ n pugile m

boxer shorts npl boxer mpl

boxing /'bɒksɪŋ/ n pugilato m

Boxing Day n Br [giorno m di] Santo Stefano m

box number n casella f

box office n Theat botteghino m

boxroom n Br sgabuzzino m

boxwood n bosso m

boy /bɔɪ/ n ragazzo m; (younger) bambino m

boy band n boy band f inv

boycott /'bɔɪkɒt/ ① n boicottaggio m ② vt boicottare

boyfriend /'bɔɪfrend/ n ragazzo m

boyhood /'bɔɪhʊd/ n (childhood) infanzia f; (adolescence) adolescenza f

boyish /'bɔɪɪʃ/ adj da ragazzino

boy scout n boy scout m inv

bpm abbr (**beats per minute**) bpm mpl

bps abbr (**bits per second**) Comput bps mpl

BR abbr (**British Rail**) ente m ferroviario britannico, ≈ FS

bra /brɑ:/ n reggiseno m

brace /breɪs/ ① n sostegno m; (dental) apparecchio m ② vt ∼ **oneself** fig farsi forza (**for** per affrontare)

bracelet /'breɪslɪt/ n braccialetto m

braces /'breɪsɪz/ npl bretelle fpl

bracing /'breɪsɪŋ/ adj tonificante

bracken /'bræken/ n felce f

bracket /'brækɪt/ ① n mensola f; (group) categoria f; Typ parentesi f inv ② vt mettere fra parentesi

brackish /'brækɪʃ/ adj salmastro

bradawl /'brædɔ:l/ n punteruolo m

brag /bræg/ vi (pt/pp **bragged**) vantarsi (**about** di)

bragging /'brægɪŋ/ n vanterie fpl

Brahmin /'brɑːmɪn/ n Relig bramino m

braid /breɪd/ n (edging) passamano m

braille /breɪl/ n braille m

brain /breɪn/ n cervello m; ∼s pl fig testa fsg

brainbox n fam capoccione m

brainchild n invenzione f personale

brain damage n lesione f cerebrale

brain-dead adj Med cerebralmente morto; fig senza cervello

brain death n morte f cerebrale

brain drain n fuga f di cervelli

brainless /'breɪnlɪs/ adj senza cervello

brain scan n scansione m inv del cervello

brain scanner n scanner m inv (per il cervello)

brainstorm n Med, fig eccesso m di pazzia; (Am: brainwave) lampo m di genio

brainstorming session n brainstorming m inv

brains trust n brain trust m inv, gruppo m di esperti

brain surgeon n neurochirurgo m

brain surgery n neurochirurgia f

brain teaser n fam rompicapo m

brainwash vt fare il lavaggio del cervello a

brainwashing n lavaggio m del cervello

brainwave n lampo m di genio

brainy /'breɪnɪ/ adj (-ier, -iest) intelligente

braise /breɪz/ vt brasare

brake /breɪk/ ① n freno m ② vi frenare

brake block n pastiglia f

brake disc n disco m dei freni

brake drum n tamburo m del freno

brake fluid n liquido m dei freni

brake-light n stop m inv

brake lining n guarnizione f del freno

brake pad n ganascia f del freno

brake pedal n pedale m del freno

bramble /'bræmb(ə)l/ n rovo m; (fruit) mora f

bran /bræn/ n crusca f

branch /brɑːntʃ/ ① n also fig ramo m; Comm succursale f; filiale f; (of bank) agenzia f; our Oxford St ∼ (of store) il negozio di Oxford St ② vi ⟨road⟩ biforcarsi
■ **branch off** vi biforcarsi
■ **branch out** vi ∼ **out into** allargare le proprie attività nel ramo di

branch line n linea f secondaria

branch manager n (of bank) direttore, -trice mf di agenzia; (of company) direttore, -trice mf di filiale; (of shop) direttore, -trice mf di succursale

branch office n filiale f; (of bank) agenzia f

brand /brænd/ ① n marca f; (on animal) marchio m ② vt marcare ⟨animal⟩; fig tacciare (**as** di)

branded /'brændɪd/ adj ⟨goods⟩ di marca

brand image n brand image f

brandish /'brændɪʃ/ vt brandire

brand leader n marca f leader inv

brand name n marca f

brand-new adj nuovo fiammante

brandy /'brændɪ/ n brandy m inv

brash /bræʃ/ adj sfrontato

brass /brɑːs/ n ottone m; **the** ∼ Mus gli ottoni mpl; **top** ∼ fam pezzi mpl grossi

brass band n banda f (di soli ottoni)

brassiere /'bræzɪə(r)/ *n* fml, Am reggiseno *m*

brass instrument *n* Mus ottone *m*

brass neck *n* Br fam faccia *f* tosta

brass rubbing *n* ricalco *m* di iscrizione tombale o commemorativa

brassy /'brɑːsɪ/ *adj* (**-ier, -iest**) fam volgare

brat /bræt/ *n* pej marmocchio, -a *mf*

bravado /brə'vɑːdəʊ/ *n* bravata *f*

brave /breɪv/ ① *adj* coraggioso ② *vt* affrontare

bravely /'breɪvlɪ/ *adv* con coraggio

bravery /'breɪvərɪ/ *n* coraggio *m*

bravo /brɑː'vəʊ/ *int* bravo!

bravura /brə'vjʊərə/ *n* virtuosismo *m*

brawl /brɔːl/ ① *n* rissa *f* ② *vi* azzuffarsi

brawn /brɔːn/ *n* Culin ≈ soppressata *f*

brawny /'brɔːnɪ/ *adj* muscoloso

bray *vi* ⟨donkey⟩ ragliare

brazen /'breɪzn/ *adj* sfrontato
■ **brazen out** *vt* affrontare con piglio sicuro

brazier /'breɪzɪə(r)/ *n* braciere *m*

Brazil /brə'zɪl/ *n* Brasile *m*

Brazilian /brə'zɪlɪən/ *adj & n* brasiliano, -a *mf*

Brazil [nut] *n* noce *f* del Brasile

breach /briːtʃ/ ① *n* (of law) violazione *f*; (gap) breccia *f*; (fig: in party) frattura *f* ② *vt* recedere ⟨contract⟩

breach of contract *n* Jur inadempienza *f* contrattuale

breach of promise *n* Jur inadempienza *f* a una promessa di matrimonio

breach of the peace *n* Jur violazione *f* dell'ordine pubblico

breach of trust *n* Jur abuso *m* di fiducia

bread /bred/ *n* pane *m*; **a slice of ~ and butter** una fetta di pane imburrato

bread and butter *n* fig fonte *f* di guadagno principale

breadbasket *n* cestino *m* per il pane; fig granaio *m*

breadbin *n* Br cassetta *f* portapane *inv*

breadboard *n* tagliere *m* per il pane

breadcrumbs *npl* briciole *fpl*; Culin pangrattato *m*

breadfruit *n* frutto *m* dell'albero del pane

breadknife *n* coltello *m* per il pane

breadline *n* be on the ~ essere povero in canna

bread roll *n* panino *m*

breadstick *n* filoncino *m*

breadth /bredθ/ *n* larghezza *f*

breadwinner /'bredwɪnə(r)/ *n* quello, -a *mf* che porta i soldi a casa

break /breɪk/ ① *n* rottura *f*; (interval) intervallo *m*; (interruption) interruzione *f*; (fam: chance) opportunità *f inv* ② *vt* (pt **broke**, pp **broken**) rompere; (interrupt) interrompere; ~ **one's arm** rompersi un braccio ③ *vi* rompersi; ⟨day⟩ spuntare; ⟨storm⟩ scoppiare; ⟨news⟩ diffondersi; ⟨boy's voice⟩ cambiare
■ **break away** *vi* scappare; fig chiudere (**from** con)
■ **break down** ① *vi* ⟨machine, car⟩ guastarsi; ⟨negotiations⟩ interrompersi; (in tears) scoppiare in lacrime ② *vt* sfondare ⟨door⟩; ripartire ⟨figures⟩
■ **break in** *vi* ⟨burglar⟩ introdursi
■ **break into** *vt* introdursi con la forza in; forzare ⟨car⟩
■ **break off** ① *vt* rompere ⟨engagement⟩ ② *vi* ⟨part of whole⟩ rompersi; (when speaking) interrompersi
■ **break out** *vi* ⟨argument, war⟩ scoppiare
■ **break through** *vi* ⟨sun⟩ spuntare
■ **break up** ① *vt* far cessare ⟨fight⟩; disperdere ⟨crowd⟩ ② *vi* ⟨crowd⟩ disperdersi; ⟨marriage⟩ naufragare; ⟨couple⟩ separarsi; Sch iniziare le vacanze

breakable /'breɪkəbl/ *adj* fragile

breakage /'breɪkɪdʒ/ *n* rottura *f*

breakaway /'breɪkəweɪ/ ① *n* (from person) separazione *f*, allontanamento *m*; (from organization) scissione *f*; Sport contropiede *m* ② *attrib* ⟨faction, group, state⟩ separatista

breakdown /'breɪkdaʊn/ *n* (of car, machine) guasto *m*; Med esaurimento *m* nervoso; (of figures) analisi *f inv*

breaker /'breɪkə(r)/ *n* (wave) frangente *m*

breaker's yard *n* Auto cimitero *m* delle macchine

break even *vi* andare in pareggio

break-even point *n* punto *m* di pareggio, punto *m* di equilibrio

breakfast /'brekfəst/ *n* [prima] colazione *f*

breakfast bar *n* tavolo *m* a penisola

breakfast bowl *n* scodella *f* per i cereali

breakfast cereals *npl* cereali *mpl* per la colazione

breakfast television, breakfast TV *n* programmi *mpl* televisivi del mattino

break free *vi* fuggire

break-in *n* irruzione *f*

breaking /'breɪkɪŋ/ *n* (of glass, seal, contract) rottura *f*; (of bone) frattura *f*; (of law, treaty) violazione *f*; (of voice) cambiamento *m*; (of promise) venuta *f* meno; (of horse) domatura *f*; (of link, sequence, tie) interruzione *f*

breaking and entering /ˈbreɪkɪŋənd ˈentərɪŋ/ *n* Jur effrazione *f* con scasso

breaking point *n* Techn punto *m* di rottura; fig limite *m* di sopportazione

breakneck *adj* ⟨pace, speed⟩ a rotta di collo

break-out *n* (from prison) evasione *f*

breakpoint *n* Tennis breakpoint *m inv*

breakthrough *n* (discovery) scoperta *f*; (in negotiations) passo *m* avanti

break-up *n* (of family, company) disgregazione *f*; (of alliance, relationship) rottura *f*; (of marriage) dissoluzione *f*

breakwater *n* frangiflutti *m inv*

breast /brest/ *n* seno *m*

breastbone *n* sterno *m*

breastfeed *vt* allattare al seno

breast pocket *n* taschino *m*

breast-stroke *n* nuoto *m* a rana

breath /breθ/ *n* respiro *m*, fiato *m*; out of ∼ senza fiato; under one's ∼ sottovoce; a ∼ of air un filo d'aria

breathalyse /ˈbreθəlaɪz/ *vt* sottoporre alla prova del palloncino

breathalyser® Br, **breathalyzer**® /ˈbreθəlaɪzə(r)/ *n* alcoltest *m inv*

breathe /briːð/ *vt/i* respirare; ∼ a sigh of relief tirare un sospiro di sollievo
■ **breathe in** ① *vi* inspirare
② *vt* respirare ⟨scent, air⟩
■ **breathe out** *vt/i* espirare

breather /ˈbriːðə(r)/ *n* pausa *f*

breathing /ˈbriːðɪŋ/ *n* respirazione *f*

breathing apparatus *n* respiratore *m*

breathing space *n* (respite) tregua *f*; give oneself a ∼ ∼ riprendere fiato

breathless /ˈbreθlɪs/ *adj* senza fiato

breathlessly /ˈbreθlɪslɪ/ *adv* senza fiato

breathtaking /ˈbreθteɪkɪŋ/ *adj* mozzafiato

breathtakingly /ˈbreθteɪkɪŋlɪ/ *adv* ∼ audacious di un'audacia stupefacente; ∼ beautiful di una bellezza mozzafiato

breath test *n* prova *f* del palloncino

bred /bred/ ▸ BREED

breech /briːtʃ/ *n* Med natiche *fpl*; (of gun) culatta *f*

breed /briːd/ ① *n* razza *f*
② *vt* (pt/pp **bred**) allevare; (give rise to) generare
③ *vi* riprodursi

breeder /ˈbriːdə(r)/ *n* allevatore, -trice *mf*

breeding /ˈbriːdɪŋ/ *n* allevamento *m*; fig educazione *f*

breeding ground *n* zona *f* di riproduzione; fig terreno *m* fertile

breeding period, **breeding season** *n* stagione *f* di riproduzione

breeze /briːz/ *n* brezza *f*

breeze block *n* Br mattone *m* fatto con scorie di coke

breezily /ˈbriːzɪlɪ/ *adv* (confidently) con sicurezza; (casually) con disinvoltura; (cheerfully) allegramente

breezy /ˈbriːzɪ/ *adj* ventoso

brevity /ˈbrevətɪ/ *n* brevità *f*

brew /bruː/ ① *n* infuso *m*
② *vt* mettere in infusione ⟨tea⟩; produrre ⟨beer⟩
③ *vi* fig ⟨trouble⟩ essere nell'aria

brewer /ˈbruːə(r)/ *n* birraio *m*

brewery /ˈbruːərɪ/ *n* fabbrica *f* di birra

brew-up *n* Br fam tè *m inv*

briar /ˈbraɪə(r)/ *n* rosa *f* selvatica; (heather) erica *f*; (thorns) rovo *m*; (pipe) pipa *f* in radica

bribe /braɪb/ ① *n* (money) bustarella *f*; (large sum of money) tangente *f*
② *vt* corrompere

bribery /ˈbraɪbərɪ/ *n* corruzione *f*

brick /brɪk/ *n* mattone *m*
■ **brick up** *vt* murare

brickbat *n* fig critica *f* spietata

brick-built *adj* di mattoni

bricklayer *n* muratore *m*

bricklaying *n* muratura *f*

brick red *adj* rosso mattone *inv*

bricks-and-mortar *adj* ⟨company, business⟩ di tipo tradizionale

brickwork *n* muratura *f* di mattoni

brickworks *n* fabbrica *f* di mattoni

bridal /ˈbraɪdl/ *adj* nuziale

bridal party *n* corteo *m* nuziale

bridal suite *n* camera *f* nuziale

bridal wear *n* confezioni *fpl* da sposa

bride /braɪd/ *n* sposa *f*

bridegroom /ˈbraɪdɡruːm/ *n* sposo *m*

bridesmaid /ˈbraɪdzmeɪd/ *n* damigella *f* d'onore

bridge¹ /brɪdʒ/ ① *n* ponte *m*; (of nose) setto *m* nasale; (of spectacles) ponticello *m*
② *vt* fig colmare ⟨gap⟩

bridge² *n* Cards bridge *m*

bridge-building *n* costruzione *f* di ponti provvisori; fig mediazione *f*

bridging loan /ˈbrɪdʒɪŋ/ *n* Br Fin pre-finanziamento *m*, credito *m* provvisorio

bridle /ˈbraɪd(ə)l/ *n* briglia *f*

bridle path, **bridleway** /ˈbraɪd(ə)lweɪ/ *n* sentiero *m* per cavalli

brief¹ /briːf/ *adj* breve; in ∼ in breve

brief² ① *n* istruzioni *fpl*; (Jur: case) causa *f*
② *vt* dare istruzioni a; Jur affidare la causa a

briefcase /'briːfkeɪs/ n cartella f

briefing /'briːfɪŋ/ n briefing m inv

briefly /'briːflɪ/ adv brevemente; **briefly,...** in breve,...

briefness /'briːfnɪs/ n brevità f

briefs /briːfs/ npl slip m inv

brigade /brɪ'ɡeɪd/ n brigata f

brigadier /brɪɡə'dɪə(r)/ n generale m di brigata

bright /braɪt/ adj ⟨metal, idea⟩ brillante; ⟨day, room, future⟩ luminoso; (clever) intelligente; ∼ **red** rosso m acceso

brighten /'braɪt(ə)n/ v ∼ **[up]** ① vt ravvivare; rallegrare ⟨person⟩ ② vi ⟨weather⟩ schiarirsi; ⟨face⟩ illuminarsi; ⟨person⟩ rallegrarsi

brightly /'braɪtlɪ/ adv ⟨shine⟩ intensamente; ⟨smile⟩ allegramente

brightness /'braɪtnɪs/ n luminosità f; (intelligence) intelligenza f

bright spark n Br fam genio m

bright young things npl Br i giovani di belle speranze

brill /brɪl/ ① n Zool rombo m liscio ② adj Br fam fantastico

brilliance /'brɪljəns/ n luminosità f; (of person) genialità f

brilliant /'brɪljənt/ adj (very good) eccezionale; (very intelligent) brillante; ⟨sunshine⟩ splendente

brilliantly /'brɪljəntlɪ/ adv ⟨shine⟩ intensamente; ⟨perform⟩ in modo eccezionale

Brillo pad® /'brɪləʊ/ n paglietta f d'acciaio

brim /brɪm/ n bordo m; (of hat) tesa f
■ **brim over** vi (pt/pp **brimmed**) traboccare

brine /braɪn/ n salamoia f

bring /brɪŋ/ vt (pt/pp **brought**) portare ⟨person, object⟩
■ **bring about** vt causare
■ **bring along** vt portare [con sé]
■ **bring back** vt restituire ⟨something borrowed⟩; reintrodurre ⟨hanging⟩; fare ritornare in mente ⟨memories⟩
■ **bring down** vt portare giù; fare cadere ⟨government⟩; fare abbassare ⟨price⟩
■ **bring forward** vt anticipare ⟨meeting, date⟩; **the meeting has been brought forward to this afternoon** la riunione è stata anticipata al pomeriggio
■ **bring in** vt introdurre ⟨legislation⟩; **his job** ∼**s in £30,000 a year** guadagna 30.000 sterline all'anno
■ **bring off** vt ∼ **something off** riuscire a fare qualcosa
■ **bring on** vt (cause) provocare
■ **bring out** vt (emphasize) mettere in evidenza; pubblicare ⟨book⟩

■ **bring round** vt portare; (persuade) convincere; far rinvenire ⟨unconscious person⟩
■ **bring up** vt (vomit) rimettere; allevare ⟨children⟩; tirare fuori ⟨question, subject⟩

bring and buy sale n Br vendita f di beneficenza

brink /brɪŋk/ n orlo m; **on the** ∼ **of disaster** sull'orlo del disastro

brinkmanship /'brɪŋkmənʃɪp/ n strategia f del rischio calcolato

brisk /brɪsk/ adj svelto; ⟨person⟩ sbrigativo; ⟨trade, business⟩ redditizio; ⟨walk⟩ a passo spedito

brisket /'brɪskɪt/ n Culin punta f di petto

briskly /'brɪsklɪ/ adv velocemente; ⟨say⟩ frettolosamente; ⟨walk⟩ di buon passo

bristle /'brɪsl/ ① n setola f ② vi **bristling with** pieno di

bristly /'brɪslɪ/ adj ⟨chin⟩ ispido

Britain /'brɪtn/ n Gran Bretagna f

British /'brɪtɪʃ/ ① adj britannico; ⟨ambassador⟩ della Gran Bretagna ② npl **the** ∼ il popolo britannico

British Airports Authority n ente m che gestisce gli aeroporti britannici

British Broadcasting Corporation n ente m radio-televisivo nazionale britannico

British Columbia n Columbia f Britannica

Britisher /'brɪtɪʃə(r)/ n Am britannico, -a mf

British Gas n Br società f del gas britannica

British Isles npl Isole fpl Britanniche

British Rail n ente m ferroviario britannico

British Telecom n Br società f britannica di telecomunicazioni

Briton /'brɪtən/ n cittadino, -a britannico, -a mf

Brittany /'brɪtənɪ/ n Bretagna f

brittle /'brɪtl/ adj fragile

brittle-bone disease n decalcificazione f ossea, osteoporosi f

broach /brəʊtʃ/ vt toccare ⟨subject⟩

B road n Br ≈ strada f provinciale

broad /brɔːd/ adj ampio; ⟨hint⟩ chiaro; ⟨accent⟩ marcato. **two metres** ∼ largo due metri; **in** ∼ **daylight** in pieno giorno

broadband n Comput banda f larga; **on** ∼ a banda larga; ∼ **connection** connessione f a banda larga

broad-based /'beɪst/ adj ⟨coalition, education⟩ diversificato; ⟨approach, campaign⟩ su larga scala; ⟨consensus⟩ generale

broad bean n fava f

broadcast /'brɔːdkæst/ ① n trasmissione f

2 *vt/i* (pt/pp **-cast**) trasmettere

broadcaster /'brɔːdkæstə(r)/ *n* giornalista *mf* radiotelevisivo, -a

broadcasting /'brɔːdkæstɪŋ/ *n* diffusione *f* radiotelevisiva; **be in** ∼ lavorare per la televisione/radio

broad-chested *adj* con il torace robusto

broaden /'brɔːdn/ **1** *vt* allargare; ∼ **one's horizons** allargare i propri orizzonti **2** *vi* allargarsi

broadly /'brɔːdlɪ/ *adv* largamente; ∼ **[speaking]** generalmente

broad-minded /-'maɪndɪd/ *adj* di larghe vedute

broadness /'brɔːdnɪs/ *n* larghezza *f*

broadsheet *n* quotidiano *m* di grande formato

broad-shouldered *adj* con le spalle larghe

broadside *n* (Naut: of ship) fiancata *f*; (enemy fire) bordata *f*; *n* (criticism) attacco *m*; **deliver a** ∼ lanciare un attacco *adv* di fianco

brocade /brə'keɪd/ *n* broccato *m*

broccoli /'brɒkəlɪ/ *n inv* broccoli *mpl*

brochure /'brəʊʃə(r)/ *n* opuscolo *m*; (travel ∼) dépliant *m inv*

brogue /'brəʊg/ *n* (shoe) scarpa *m* da passeggio; (accent) cadenza *f* dialettale

broil /brɔɪl/ **1** *vt* Culin cuocere alla griglia ‹meat› **2** *vi* cuocere alla griglia; fig arrostire

broiler /'brɔɪlə(r)/ *n* (chicken) pollastro *m*; (Am: grill) griglia *f*

broke /brəʊk/ **1** ▶ BREAK **2** *adj* fam al verde

broken /'brəʊk(ə)n/ **1** ▶ BREAK **2** *adj* rotto; ∼ **English** inglese *m* stentato

broken-down *adj* ‹machine› guasto; ‹wall› pericolante

broken heart *n* cuore *m* infranto; **die of a** ∼ essere distrutto da una delusione amorosa

broken-hearted /-'hɑːtɪd/ *adj* affranto

broken home *n* he comes from a ∼ ∼ i suoi sono divisi

broken marriage *n* matrimonio *m* fallito

broker /'brəʊkə(r)/ *n* broker *m inv*

brokerage /'brəʊkərɪdʒ/ *n* (fee, business) intermediazione *f*

broking /'brəʊkɪŋ/ *n* attività *f* di intermediazione

brolly /'brɒlɪ/ *n* fam ombrello *m*

bromide /'brəʊmaɪd/ *n* (in pharmacy printing) bromuro *m*; (fig: comment) banalità *f inv*

bronchial /'brɒŋkɪəl/ *adj* ‹infection› bronchiale; ‹wheeze, cough› di petto

bronchitis /brɒŋ'kaɪtɪs/ *n* bronchite *f*

bronze /brɒnz/ **1** *n* bronzo *m* **2** *attrib* di bronzo

Bronze Age *n* età *f* del Bronzo

brooch /brəʊtʃ/ *n* spilla *f*

brood /bruːd/ **1** *n* covata *f*; (hum: children) prole *f* **2** *vi* covare; fig rimuginare

brooding /'bruːdɪŋ/ *adj* ‹person, face› pensieroso; ‹landscape› sinistro

broody /'bruːdɪ/ *adj* (depressed) pensieroso; **feel** ∼ Br fam ‹woman› desiderare un figlio

broody hen *n* chioccia *f*

brook[1] /brʊk/ *n* ruscello *m*

brook[2] *vt* sopportare

broom /bruːm/ *n* scopa *f*; Bot ginestra *f*

broom cupboard *n* ripostiglio *m*

broom handle *n* Br manico *m* di scopa

broomstick *n* manico *m* di scopa

Bros. *abbr* (**brothers**) F.lli

broth /brɒθ/ *n* brodo *m*

brothel /'brɒθ(ə)l/ *n* bordello *m*

brother /'brʌðə(r)/ *n* fratello *m*

brotherhood /'brʌðəhʊd/ *n* (bond) fratellanza *f*; (of monks) confraternita *f*

brother-in-law *n* (pl **brothers-in-law**) cognato *m*

brotherly /'brʌðəlɪ/ *adj* fraterno

brought /brɔːt/ ▶ BRING

brow /braʊ/ *n* fronte *f*; (eyebrow) sopracciglio *m*; (of hill) cima *f*

browbeat /'braʊbiːt/ *vt* (pt **-beat**, pp **-beaten**) intimidire

brown /braʊn/ **1** *adj* marrone; castano ‹hair› **2** *n* marrone *m* **3** *vt* rosolare ‹meat› **4** *vi* ‹meat› rosolarsi

brown ale *n* Br birra *f* scura

brown bear *n* orso *m* bruno

brown bread *n* pane *m* integrale

browned-off /braʊnd'ɒf/ *adj* Br fam stufo (with di)

brown envelope *n* busta *f* di carta da pacchi

Brownie /'braʊnɪ/ *n* coccinella *f* (negli scout)

brownie point *n* fam punto *m* di merito

brownish /'braʊnɪʃ/ *adj* sul marrone

brownout *n* Am oscuramento *m* parziale

brown owl *n* allocco *m*

brown paper *n* carta *f* da pacchi

brown rice *n* riso *m* integrale

brown-skinned /-'skɪnd/ *adj* scuro di pelle

brownstone *n* (Am: house) palazzo *m* in arenaria

brown sugar n Culin zucchero m greggio

browse /brauz/ ① v vi (read) leggicchiare; (in shop) curiosare; (on Internet) navigare
② vt visitare ⟨Internet, web site⟩

browser /'brauzə(r)/ n (Comput: program) browser m inv; (in shop) persona f che curiosa

bruise /bru:z/ ① n livido m; (on fruit) ammaccatura f
② vt ammaccare ⟨fruit⟩; ~ one's arm farsi un livido sul braccio

bruised /bru:zd/ adj (physically) contuso; ⟨eye⟩ pesto; ⟨fruit⟩ ammaccato; ⟨ego, spirit⟩ ferito

bruiser /'bru:zə(r)/ n fam omaccione m

bruising /'bru:zɪŋ/ ① n livido m, contusione f
② adj ⟨game⟩ violento; (emotionally) ⟨remark⟩ pesante; ⟨campaign, encounter⟩ traumatizzante; ⟨defeat⟩ cocente

brunch /brʌntʃ/ n brunch m inv

Brunei /bru:'naɪ/ n Brunei m

brunette /bru:'net/ n bruna f

brunt /brʌnt/ n bear the ~ of something subire maggiormente qualcosa

brush /brʌʃ/ ① n spazzola f; (with long handle) spazzolone m; (for paint) pennello m; (bushes) boscaglia f; (fig: conflict) breve scontro m
② vt spazzolare ⟨hair⟩; lavarsi ⟨teeth⟩; scopare ⟨stairs, floor⟩
■ **brush against** vt sfiorare
■ **brush aside** vt fig ignorare
■ **brush off** vt spazzolare; (with hands) togliere; ignorare ⟨criticism⟩
■ **brush up** vt/i fig ~ up [on] rinfrescare

brush-off n fam give somebody the ~ mandare qualcuno a quel paese

brushstroke n pennellata f

brushup n Br have a [wash and] brushup darsi una ripulita

brushwood n sterpaglie fpl

brushwork n tocco m

brusque /brusk/ adj brusco

brusquely /'bruskli/ adv bruscamente

Brussels /'brʌsəlz/ n Bruxelles f

Brussels sprouts npl cavolini mpl di Bruxelles

brutal /'bru:t(ə)l/ adj brutale

brutality /bru:'tæləti/ n brutalità f inv

brutalize /'bru:tələɪz/ vt brutalizzare

brutally /'bru:təli/ adv brutalmente

brute /bru:t/ n bruto m; ~ force forza f bruta

brutish /'bru:tɪʃ/ adj da bruto

BS abbr Am Bachelor of Science

BSc abbr Bachelor of Science

BSE n abbr (**bovine spongiform encephalitis**) encefalite f bovina spongiforme

B side n (of record) lato m B

BST abbr (**British Summer Time**) ora f legale in Gran Bretagna

B2B /bi:tə'bi:/ abbr (**business to business**) ⟨trade, directory⟩ B2B

bubble /'bʌbl/ n bolla f; (in drink) bollicina f

bubble bath n bagnoschiuma m inv

bubble car n Br fam auto f monoposto a tre ruote

bubblegum n gomma f da masticare

bubble pack n Br (for pills) blister m inv; (for small item) involucro m di plastica

bubble wrap n plastica f a bolle

bubbling /'bʌblɪŋ/ ① n (sound) gorgoglio m
② adj che ribolle

bubbly /'bʌbli/ ① n fam champagne m inv, spumante m
② adj ⟨liquid⟩ effervescente; ⟨personality⟩ spumeggiante

bubonic plague /bjuːbɒnɪk'pleɪg/ n peste f bubbonica

buccaneer /bʌkə'nɪə(r)/ n bucaniere m

Bucharest /bju:kə'rest/ n Bucarest f

buck[1] /bʌk/ ① n maschio m del cervo; (rabbit) maschio m del coniglio
② vi ⟨horse⟩ saltare a quattro zampe

buck[2] n Am fam dollaro m

buck[3] n pass the ~ scaricare la responsabilità
■ **buck up** ① vi fam tirarsi su; (hurry) sbrigarsi
② vt you'll have to ~ your ideas up fam dovresti darti una regolata

bucket /'bʌkɪt/ ① n secchio m; kick the ~ (fam: die) crepare
② vi it's ~ing down fam piove a catinelle

bucketful /'bʌkɪtfʊl/ n secchio m

bucket seat n Auto, Aeron sedile m anatomico

bucket shop n Br fam agenzia f di viaggi che vende biglietti a prezzi scontati

bucking bronco /bʌkɪŋ'brɒŋkəʊ/ n cavallo m da rodeo

buckle /'bʌkl/ ① n fibbia f
② vt allacciare
③ vi ⟨shelf⟩ piegarsi; ⟨wheel⟩ storcersi
■ **buckle down** vi (to work) mettersi sotto
■ **buckle in** vt legare

buckram n tela f rigida

buckshot n pallettoni mpl

buckskin n pelle f di daino

buck teeth npl denti mpl da coniglio

buckwheat n grano m saraceno

bucolic /bju:'kɒlɪk/ adj & n bucolico m

bud /bʌd/ n bocciolo m

Buddha /'bʊdə/ n Budda m inv

Buddhism /'bʊdɪzm/ n buddismo m

Buddhist /'bʊdɪst/ adj & n buddista mf

budding /'bʌdɪŋ/ adj Bot (into leaf) in germoglio; (into flower) in boccio; ⟨athlete, champion, artist⟩ in erba; ⟨talent, romance⟩ nascente; ⟨career⟩ promettente

buddy /'bʌdɪ/ n fam amico, -a mf

budge /bʌdʒ/ **1** vt spostare
2 vi spostarsi
■ **budge over**, **budge up** vi fam farsi più in là

budgerigar /'bʌdʒərɪgɑ:(r)/ n cocorita f

budget /'bʌdʒɪt/ **1** n bilancio m; (allotted to specific activity) budget m inv; **I'm on a** ∼ cerco di limitare le spese
2 vi (pt/pp **budgeted**) prevedere le spese; ∼ **for something** includere qualcosa nelle spese previste

budgetary /'bʌdʒɪt(ə)rɪ/ adj budgetario; ∼ **year** esercizio m finanziario

budget day n Br Pol giorno m della presentazione del bilancio dello Stato

budgie /'bʌdʒɪ/ n fam = BUDGERIGAR

buff /bʌf/ **1** adj (colour) [color] camoscio
2 n [color m] camoscio m; fam fanatico, -a mf
3 vt lucidare

buffalo /'bʌfələʊ/ n (inv or pl **-es**) bufalo m

buffer /'bʌfə(r)/ n Rail respingente m; Comput buffer m inv; **old** ∼ fam vecchio bacucco m

buffer state n stato m cuscinetto inv

buffer zone n zona f cuscinetto inv

buffet¹ /'bʊfeɪ/ n (meal, in station) buffet m inv

buffet² /'bʌfɪt/ vt (pt/pp **buffeted**) sferzare

buffet car n Br Rail carrozza f ristorante

buffoon /bə'fu:n/ n buffone, -a mf

bug /bʌg/ **1** n (insect) insetto m; Comput bug m inv; (fam: device) cimice f
2 vt (pt/pp **bugged**) fam installare delle microspie in ⟨room⟩; mettere sotto controllo ⟨telephone⟩; (fam: annoy) scocciare

bugbear /'bʌgbeə(r)/ n (problem, annoyance) spauracchio m

bugger /'bʌgə(r)/ fam **1** n bastardo m
2 int merda!
■ **bugger about**, **bugger around** fam **1** vi (behave stupidly) fare il cretino
2 vt ∼ **somebody about** creare problemi a qualcuno
■ **bugger off** vi (fam: go away) andarsene; ∼ **off!** vai a farti friggere!

bugging device /'bʌgɪŋ/ n microfono m spia

buggy /'bʌgɪ/ n [baby] ∼ passeggino m

bugle /'bju:g(ə)l/ n tromba f

bugler /'bju:glə(r)/ n trombettiere m

build /bɪld/ **1** n (of person) corporatura f
2 vt/i (pt/pp **built**) costruire
■ **build on** vt aggiungere ⟨extra storey⟩; sviluppare ⟨previous work⟩
■ **build up** **1** vt ∼ **up one's strength** rimettersi in forza
2 vi ⟨pressure, traffic⟩ aumentare; ⟨excitement, tension⟩ crescere

builder /'bɪldə(r)/ n (company) costruttore m; (worker) muratore m

builder's labourer n muratore m

builder's merchant n fornitore m di materiale da costruzione

building /'bɪldɪŋ/ n edificio m

building block n (child's toy) pezzo m delle costruzioni; (basic element) componente m

building contractor n imprenditore m edile

building land n terreno m edificabile

building materials npl materiali mpl da costruzione

building permit n licenza f edilizia

building plot n terreno m edificabile

building site n cantiere m [di costruzione]

building society n istituto m di credito immobiliare

building trade n edilizia f

building worker n Br muratore m

build-up n (increase) aumento m; (in tension, of gas, in weapons) accumulo m; (publicity) battage m inv pubblicitario; **give something a good** ∼ (publicity) fare buona pubblicità a qualcosa

built /bɪlt/ ▶ BUILD

built-in adj ⟨unit⟩ a muro; fig ⟨feature⟩ incorporato

built-up adj region urbanizzato; ∼ **area** centro m abitato

bulb /bʌlb/ n bulbo m; Electr lampadina f

bulbous /'bʌlbəs/ adj grassoccio

Bulgaria /bʌl'geərɪə/ n Bulgaria f

Bulgarian /bʌl'geərɪən/ adj & n bulgaro, -a mf

bulge /bʌldʒ/ **1** n rigonfiamento m; **it shows all my** ∼**s** mette in evidenza tutti i miei cuscinetti [di grasso]
2 vi esser gonfio (with di); ⟨stomach, wall⟩ sporgere; ⟨eyes, with surprise⟩ uscire dalle orbite

bulging /'bʌldʒɪŋ/ adj gonfio; ⟨eyes⟩ sporgente

bulimia [nervosa] /bʊ'lɪmɪə(nɜ:'vəʊsə)/ n bulimia f

bulimic /bʊ'lɪmɪk/ adj & n bulimico, -a mf

bulk /bʌlk/ n volume m; (greater part) grosso m; **in** ∼ in grande quantità; (loose) sfuso

b

bulk-buy *vt/i* comprare in grandi quantità

bulk-buying *n* acquisto *m* in grande quantità

bulk carrier *n* mezzo *m* per il trasporto di rinfuse

bulkhead *n* Naut, Aeron paratia *f*

bulky /'bʌlkɪ/ *adj* voluminoso

bull /bʊl/ *n* toro *m*; **take the ~ by the horns** fig prendere il toro per le corna

bull bars *npl* Auto paraurti *mpl* tubolari rigidi

bulldog *n* bulldog *m inv*

bulldog clip *n* fermafogli *m inv*

bulldoze *vt* (knock down) demolire [con bulldozer]; (clear) spianare [con bulldozer]; (fig: force) costringere

bulldozer /'bʊldəʊzə(r)/ *n* bulldozer *m inv*

bullet /'bʊlɪt/ *n* pallottola *f*

bulletin /'bʊlɪtɪn/ *n* bollettino *m*

bulletin board *n* Comput bacheca *f* elettronica

bulletproof /'bʊlɪtpruːf/ *adj* antiproiettile *inv*; ⟨vehicle⟩ blindato

bulletproof vest giubbotto *m* antiproiettile

bullfight /'bʊlfaɪt/ *n* corrida *f*

bullfighter /'bʊlfaɪtə(r)/ *n* torero *m*

bullfighting /'bʊlfaɪtɪŋ/ *n* corride *fpl*

bullion /'bʊlɪən/ *n* **gold ~** oro *m* in lingotti

bullish /'bʊlɪʃ/ *adj* (optimistic) ottimistico; ⟨market, shares, stocks⟩ al rialzo

bull market *n* Fin mercato *m* al rialzo

bullock /'bʊlək/ *n* manzo *m*

bullring /'bʊlrɪŋ/ *n* arena *f*

bull's-eye /'bʊlzaɪ/ *n* centro *m* del bersaglio; **score a ~** fare centro

bully /'bʊlɪ/ ① *n* prepotente *mf* ② *vt* fare il/la prepotente con

bullying /'bʊlɪŋ/ *n* prepotenze *fpl*

bulrush /'bʊlrʌʃ/ *n* giunco *m* di palude

bulwark /'bʊlwək/ *n* Mil, fig baluardo *m*; Naut parapetto *m*; (breakwater) frangiflutti *m inv*

bum¹ /bʌm/ *n* sl sedere *m*

bum² *n* Am fam vagabondo, -a *mf*
■ **bum around** *vi* fam vagabondare

bumbag /'bʌmbæg/ *n* Br fam marsupio *m*

bumble-bee /'bʌmblbiː/ *n* calabrone *m*

bumbling /'bʌmblɪŋ/ *adj* ⟨attempt⟩ maldestro; ⟨person⟩ inconcludente

bumf /bʌmf/ *n* (Br: toilet paper) carta *f* igienica; (fam: documents) scartoffie *fpl*

bump /bʌmp/ ① *n* botta *f*; (swelling) bozzo *m*, gonfiore *m*; (in road) protuberanza *f* ② *vt* sbattere

■ **bump into** *vt* sbattere contro; (meet) imbattersi in

■ **bump off** *vt* fam far fuori

■ **bump up** *vt* fam [far] aumentare ⟨prices, salaries⟩

bumper /'bʌmpə(r)/ ① *n* Auto paraurti *m inv* ② *adj* abbondante

bumper car *n* autoscontro *m*

bumph /bʌmf/ *n* = BUMF

bumpkin /'bʌmpkɪn/ *n* **country ~** zoticone, -a *mf*

bumptious /'bʌmpʃəs/ *adj* presuntuoso

bumpy /'bʌmpɪ/ *adj* ⟨road⟩ accidentato; ⟨flight⟩ turbolento

bun /bʌn/ *n* focaccina *f* (dolce); (hair) chignon *m inv*

bunch /bʌntʃ/ *n* (of flowers, keys) mazzo *m*; (of bananas) casco *m*; (of people) gruppo *m*; **~ of grapes** grappolo *m* d'uva

bundle /'bʌndl/ ① *n* fascio *m*; (of money) mazzetta *f*; **a ~ of nerves** fam un fascio di nervi ② *vt* **~ [up]** affastellare

bundled software /'bʌndld-/ *n* Comput software *m inv* in bundle

bung /bʌŋ/ *vt* fam (throw) buttare
■ **bung up** *vt* (block) otturare

bungalow /'bʌŋɡələʊ/ *n* bungalow *m inv*

bungee jump /'bʌndʒɪdʒʌmp/ *n* salto *m* con l'elastico

bungee jumping /'bʌndʒɪdʒʌmpɪŋ/ *n* salto *m* da ponti, grattacieli, ecc. con un cavo elastico attaccato alla caviglia

bungle /'bʌŋɡl/ *vt* fare un pasticcio di

bunion /'bʌnjən/ *n* Med callo *m* all'alluce

bunk /bʌŋk/ ① *n* cuccetta *f*; **do a ~** fam svignarsela ② *vi* **~ off/~ off school** fam marinare la scuola

bunk beds *npl* letti *mpl* a castello

bunker /'bʌŋkə(r)/ *n* (for coal) carbonaia *f*; (golf) ostacolo *m*; Mil bunker *m inv*

bunkum /'bʌŋkəm/ *n* fandonie *fpl*

bunny /'bʌnɪ/ *n* fam coniglietto *m*

Bunsen [burner] /'bʌnsən['bɜːnə(r)]/ *n* becco *m* Bunsen

bunting /'bʌntɪŋ/ *n* (flags on ship) gran pavese *m*; Zool zigolo *m*

buoy /bɔɪ/ *n* boa *f*
■ **buoy up** *vt* fig sostenere ⟨prices⟩; tirare su ⟨people⟩

buoyancy /'bɔɪənsɪ/ *n* galleggiabilità *f*

buoyancy aid *n* salvagente *m*

buoyant /'bɔɪənt/ *adj* ⟨boat⟩ galleggiante; ⟨water⟩ che aiuta a galleggiare; fig ⟨person⟩ allegro; ⟨prices⟩ in aumento

burble /'bɜːb(ə)l/ ① *n* (of stream) gorgoglio *m*; (of voices) borbottio *m*

2 vi ⟨stream⟩ gorgogliare; ~ **on about something** ⟨person⟩ blaterare di qualcosa

burbling /'bɜ:blɪŋ/ **1** n (of stream) gorgoglio m; (rambling talk) borbottio m
2 adj ⟨stream⟩ gorgogliante; ⟨voice⟩ che borbotta

burden /'bɜ:dn/ **1** n carico m
2 vt caricare

burdensome /'bɜ:dnsəm/ adj gravoso

bureau /'bjʊərəʊ/ n (pl **-x** /'bjʊərəʊz/ or ~**s**) (desk) scrivania f; (office) ufficio m

bureaucracy /bjʊə'rɒkrəsɪ/ n burocrazia f

bureaucrat /'bjʊərəkræt/ n burocrate mf

bureaucratic /bjʊrə'krætɪk/ adj burocratico

burgeon /'bɜ:dʒən/ vi ⟨plant⟩ germogliare; (fig: flourish) fiorire; (fig: multiply) moltiplicarsi rapidamente, crescere rapidamente

burgeoning /'bɜ:dʒənɪŋ/ adj fiorente

burger /'bɜ:gə(r)/ n hamburger m inv

burger bar n fast-food m inv

burglar /'bɜ:glə(r)/ n svaligiatore, -trice mf

burglar alarm n antifurto m inv

burglarize /'bɜ:gləraɪz/ vt Am svaligiare

burglar-proof adj a prova di ladro

burglary /'bɜ:glərɪ/ n furto m con scasso

burgle /'bɜ:gl/ vt svaligiare; **they have been ~d** sono stati svaligiati

Burgundy /'bɜ:gəndɪ/ **1** n Borgogna f; **burgundy** (wine) borgogna m inv
2 adj (colour) rosso scuro

burial /'berɪəl/ n sepoltura f

burial ground n cimitero m

Burkina [Faso] /bɜ:kinə ('fæsəʊ)/ n Burkina Faso m

burlesque /bɜ:'lesk/ n parodia f

burly /'bɜ:lɪ/ adj (**-ier**, **-iest**) corpulento

Burma /'bɜ:mə/ n Birmania f

Burmese /bɜ:'mi:z/ adj & n birmano, -a mf

burn /bɜ:n/ **1** n bruciatura f
2 vt (pt/pp **burnt** or **burned**) bruciare; ~ **one's boats** or **bridges** fig tagliarsi i ponti alle spalle; Comput masterizzare ⟨CD, DVD⟩
3 vi bruciare
■ **burn down** vt/i bruciare
■ **burn out** vi fig esaurirsi
■ **burn up** vt fig bruciare ⟨calories, energy⟩

burned-out adj = BURNT-OUT

burner /'bɜ:nə(r)/ n (on stove) bruciatore m

burning /'bɜ:nɪŋ/ **1** n (setting on fire) incendio m; **I can smell ~!** sento odore di bruciato!

2 adj ⟨ember, coal⟩ acceso; (on fire) in fiamme; fig ⟨fever, desire⟩ bruciante; **a ~ sensation** una sensazione di bruciore; **a ~ question** una questione scottante

burnish /'bɜ:nɪʃ/ vt lucidare

burns unit n Med reparto m grandi ustionati

burnt /bɜ:nt/ ▶ BURN

burnt-out adj ⟨building, car⟩ distrutto dalle fiamme; fig ⟨person⟩ sfinito

burp /bɜ:p/ **1** n fam rutto m
2 vi fam ruttare

burr /bɜ:(r)/ n Bot lappa f; (in language) erre f moscia

burrow /'bʌrəʊ/ **1** n tana f
2 vt scavare ⟨hole⟩

bursar /'bɜ:sə(r)/ n economo, -a mf

bursary /'bɜ:sərɪ/ n borsa f di studio

burst /bɜ:st/ **1** n (of gunfire, energy, laughter) scoppio m; (of speed) scatto m
2 vt (pt/pp **burst**) far scoppiare; ~ **its banks** ⟨river⟩ rompere gli argini
3 vi scoppiare; ~ **into tears** scoppiare in lacrime; ~ **into flames** andare in fiamme; **she ~ into the room** ha fatto irruzione nella stanza; **be ~ing at the seams** ⟨room⟩ scoppiare
■ **burst in** vi (enter suddenly) fare irruzione
■ **burst out** vi ~ **out laughing/crying** scoppiare a ridere/piangere

Burundi /bʊ'rʊndɪ/ n Burundi m

bury /'berɪ/ vt (pt/pp **-ied**) seppellire; (hide) nascondere

bus /bʌs/ **1** n autobus m inv, pullman m inv; (long distance) pullman m inv, corriera f
2 vt (pt/pp **bussed**) trasportare in autobus

busby /'bʌzbɪ/ n colbacco m militare

bus conductor n ≈ bigliettaio m

bus conductress n ≈ bigliettaia f

bus driver n conducente mf di autobus

bush /bʊʃ/ n cespuglio m; (land) boscaglia f

bushed /bʊʃt/ adj (fam: tired) distrutto

bushel /'bʊʃ(ə)l/ n **hide one's light under a ~** essere troppo modesto; Am fam ~**s of** un sacco di

bushfighting n Mil guerriglia f

bushfire n incendio m in aperta campagna

bush telegraph n fig hum tamtam m inv

bushy /'bʊʃɪ/ adj (**-ier**, **-iest**) folto

busily /'bɪzɪlɪ/ adv con grande impegno

business /'bɪznɪs/ n affare m; Comm affari mpl; (establishment) attività f di commercio; **on ~** per affari; **he has no ~ to** non ha alcun diritto di; **mind one's own ~** farsi gli affari propri; **that's none of your ~** non sono affari tuoi

business activity n attività f inv economica; (of single company) attività f inv aziendale

business analyst n analista mf finanziario, -a

business associate n socio, -a mf

business call n (phone call) telefonata f di lavoro; (visit) appuntamento m di lavoro

business card n biglietto m da visita

business centre n centro m affari

business class n Aeron business class f inv

business college n scuola f di amministrazione aziendale

business contact n contatto m di lavoro

business cycle n ciclo m economico

business deal n operazione f commerciale

business expenses npl spese fpl di lavoro

business failures npl chiusura f di aziende

business hours npl (in office) orario m d'ufficio; (of shop) orario m d'apertura

business-like adj efficiente

business lunch n pranzo m di lavoro or d'affari

businessman /'bɪznɪsmən/ n uomo m d'affari

business management n amministrazione f aziendale

business park n centro m affari

business plan n piano m economico; (of single company) programma m aziendale

business premises npl sede f di un'azienda

business proposition n proposta f d'affari

business reply envelope n busta f affrancata

business school n scuola f di amministrazione aziendale

business software n software m per l'ufficio

business studies npl economia f e commercio

business suit n (for man) abito m scuro

business trip n viaggio m di lavoro

businesswoman /'bɪznɪswʊmən/ n donna f d'affari

busk /bʌsk/ vi Br ⟨singer⟩ cantare per strada; ⟨musician⟩ suonare per strada

busker /'bʌskə(r)/ n suonatore, -trice mf ambulante

bus lane n corsia f autobus

busload /'bʌsləʊd/ n **a ~ of tourists** una comitiva di turisti; **by the ~** in massa

busman's holiday /bʌsmənz'hɒlɪdeɪ/ n Br vacanze fpl passate a fare quello che si fa normalmente

bus pass n abbonamento m all'autobus

bus route n percorso m dell'autobus

bus shelter n pensilina f alla fermata dell'autobus

bus station n stazione f degli autobus

bus stop n fermata f d'autobus

bust¹ /bʌst/ n busto m; (chest) petto m

bust² /bʌst/ **1** adj fam rotto; **go ~** fallire
2 vt (pt/pp **busted** or **bust**) fam far scoppiare
3 vi scoppiare

bustle /'bʌsl/ n (activity) trambusto m
■ **bustle about** vi affannarsi

bustling /'bʌslɪŋ/ adj animato

bust size n circonferenza f del torace

bust-up n fam lite f

busy /'bɪzɪ/ **1** adj (**-ier**, **-iest**) occupato; ⟨day, time⟩ intenso; ⟨street⟩ affollato; (with traffic) pieno di traffico; **be ~ doing** essere occupato a fare
2 vt **~ oneself** darsi da fare

busybody /'bɪzɪbɒdɪ/ n ficcanaso m f inv

but /bʌt/, **1** atono /bət/ conj ma
2 prep eccetto, tranne; **nobody ~ you** nessuno tranne te; **~ for** (without) se non fosse stato per; **the last ~ one** il penultimo; **the next ~ one** il secondo
3 adv soltanto; **there were ~ two** ce n'erano soltanto due

butane /'bju:teɪn/ n butano m

butch /bʊtʃ/ adj fam ⟨man⟩ macho inv; ⟨woman⟩ mascolino

butcher /'bʊtʃə(r)/ **1** n macellaio m
2 vt macellare; (fig) massacrare

butcher's [shop] /'bʊtʃəz[ʃɒp]/ n macelleria f

butchery /'bʊtʃərɪ/ n (trade) macelleria f; (slaughter) massacro m

butler /'bʌtlə(r)/ n maggiordomo m

butt /bʌt/ **1** n (of gun) calcio m; (of cigarette) mozzicone m; (for water) barile m; (fig: target) bersaglio m
2 vt dare una testata a; ⟨goat⟩ dare un'incornata a
■ **butt in** vi interrompere

butter /'bʌtə(r)/ **1** n burro m
2 vt imburrare
■ **butter up** vt fam arruffianarsi

butter-bean n fagiolo m bianco

buttercup n ranuncolo m

butter dish n portaburro m inv

butter-fingered adj con le mani di pasta frolla

butter-fingers n fam mani fpl di pasta frolla

butterfly /'bʌtəflaɪ/ n farfalla f

butterfly nut n dado m ad alette

butterfly stroke *n* nuoto *m* a farfalla

buttermilk /'bʌtəmɪlk/ *n* latticello *m*

butterscotch /'bʌtəskɒtʃ/ *n* caramella *f* dura a base di burro e zucchero

buttocks /'bʌtəks/ *npl* natiche *fpl*

button /'bʌtn/ **①** *n* bottone *m*; (on mouse, of status bar) pulsante *m*
② *vt* ~ **[up]** abbottonare
③ *vi* ~ **[up]** abbottonarsi

button battery *n* batteria *f* a bottone

button-down *adj* ⟨collar⟩ button down, coi bottoni; ⟨shirt⟩ con il colletto coi bottoni, button down

buttonhole *n* occhiello *m*, asola *f*

button mushroom *n* piccolo champignon *m inv*

buttress /'bʌtrɪs/ **①** *n* contrafforte *m*
② *vt* fig sostenere

buxom /'bʌksəm/ *adj* formosa

buy /baɪ/ **①** *n* good/bad ~ buon/cattivo acquisto *m*
② *vt* (pt/pp **bought**) comprare; ~ **somebody a drink** pagare da bere a qualcuno; **I'll ~ this one** (drink) questo lo offro io
■ **buy into** *vt* (accept) accettare
■ **buy off** *vt* (bribe) comprare
■ **buy out** *vt* rilevare la quota di ⟨one's partner⟩
■ **buy up** *vt* (buy all of) accaparrarsi

buyer /'baɪə(r)/ *n* compratore, -trice *mf*

buyout /'baɪaʊt/ *n* Comm rilevamento *m*

buzz /bʌz/ **①** *n* ronzio *m*; **give somebody a ~** fam (on phone) dare un colpo di telefono a qualcuno; (excite) mettere in fermento qualcuno
② *vi* ronzare
③ *vt* ~ **somebody** chiamare qualcuno col cicalino
■ **buzz off** *vi* fam levarsi di torno

buzzard /'bʌzəd/ *n* poiana *f*

buzzer /'bʌzə(r)/ *n* cicalino *m*

buzzing /'bʌzɪŋ/ **①** *n* (of buzzer) trillo *m*; (of insects) ronzio *m*
② *adj* ⟨party, atmosphere, town⟩ molto animato

buzzword /'bʌzwɜːd/ *n* fam parola *f* di moda

by /baɪ/ **①** *prep* (near, next to) vicino a; (at

the latest) per; **by Mozart** di Mozart; **he was run over by a bus** è stato investito da un autobus; **by oneself** da solo; **by the sea** al mare; **by sea** via mare; **by car/bus** in macchina/autobus; **by day/night** di giorno/notte; **by the hour/metre** a ore/metri; **six metres by four** sei metri per quattro;; **he won by six metres** ha vinto di sei metri; **I missed the train by a minute** ho perso il treno per un minuto; **I'll be home by six** sarò a casa per le sei; **by this time next week** a quest'ora tra una settimana; **he rushed by me** mi è passato accanto di corsa
② *adv* **she'll be here by and by** sarà qui fra poco; **by and by the police arrived** poco dopo è arrivata la polizia; **by and large** nel complesso; **put by** mettere da parte; **go/pass by** passare

bye /baɪ/ *int* fam ciao!

bye-bye /baɪ'baɪ/ *int* fam ciao, arrivederci; **go ~s** Br (baby talk) andare a fare la nanna

by-election *n* elezione *f* straordinaria indetta per coprire una carica rimasta vacante in Parlamento

Byelorussia /bjeləʊ'rʌʃə/ *n* Bielorussia *f*

Byelorussian /bjeləʊ'rʌʃn/ *adj & n* bielorusso

bygone *adj* passato

by-law *n* legge *f* locale

by-line *n* (in newspaper) nome *m* dell'autore; Sport linea *f* laterale

BYO, BYOB *adj abbr* (**bring your own bottle**) di ristorante o festa, in cui ciascuno si porta le proprie bevande, specialmente alcoliche

bypass **①** *n* circonvallazione *f*; Med by-pass *m inv*
② *vt* evitare

by-product *n* sottoprodotto *m*

by-road *n* strada *f* secondaria

bystander *n* spettatore, -trice *mf*

byte /baɪt/ *n* Comput byte *m inv*

byway *n* strada *f* secondaria

byword *n* be a ~ for essere sinonimo di

by-your-leave *n* without so much as a ~ senza neanche chiedere il permesso

Cc

c¹, C /siː/ *n* (letter) c, C *f inv*; (Br Sch: grade) voto *m* scolastico corrispondente alla sufficienza; Mus do *m inv*

c², C *abbr* (**Celsius, centigrade**) C; *abbr* (**cent(s)**) c; *abbr* (**circa**) ca

C4 /siːˈfɔːr/ *abbr* Br (**channel four**) rete *f* televisiva britannica

CA Br *abbr* (**Chartered Accountant**) [dottore *m*] commercialista *m*; Am *abbr* (**California**) Cal; *abbr* (**Central America**) America *f* centrale

CAA *n* Br *abbr* (**Civil Aviation Authority**) organismo *m* di controllo dell'aviazione civile

CAB *n* Br *abbr* (**Citizens' Advice Bureau**) ufficio *m* di consulenza legale gratuita per i cittadini

cab /kæb/ *n* taxi *m inv*; (of lorry, train) cabina *f*

cabana /kəˈbɑːnə/ *n* (Am: hut) cabina *f* da spiaggia

cabaret /ˈkæbəreɪ/ *n* cabaret *m inv*

cabbage /ˈkæbɪdʒ/ *n* cavolo *m*

cabby /ˈkæbɪ/ *n* fam tassista *mf*

cab driver *n* tassista *mf*

cabin /ˈkæbɪn/ *n* (of plane, ship) cabina *f*; (hut) capanna *f*

cabin boy *n* mozzo *m*

cabin crew *n* Aeron equipaggio *m*

cabin cruiser *n* cabinato *m*

cabinet /ˈkæbɪnɪt/ *n* armadietto *m*; [display] ∼ vetrina *f*; C∼ Pol consiglio *m* dei ministri

cabinet-maker *n* ebanista *mf*

cabinet meeting *n* Br riunione *f* del governo

cabinet minister *n* Br ministro *m*

cabinet reshuffle *n* Br rimpasto *m* ministeriale

cable /ˈkeɪb(ə)l/ *n* cavo *m*; (TV) TV *f* via cavo; **this channel is only available on** ∼ questo canale è disponibile solo sulla TV via cavo

cable car *n* cabina *f* (della funivia)

cable company *n* rete *f* televisiva via cavo

cablegram *n* cablogramma *m*

cable-knit *adj* ‹sweater› a trecce

cable railway *n* funicolare *f*

cable-ready *adj* predisposto per la TV via cavo

cable television *n* televisione *f* via cavo

cable TV *n* TV *f inv* via cavo

cableway *n* (for people) funivia *f*

caboodle /kəˈbuːdl/ *n* fam **the whole** ∼ baracca e burattini

cab rank, **cab stand** *n* posteggio *m* dei taxi

cache /kæʃ/ *n* nascondiglio *m*; ∼ **of arms** deposito *m* segreto di armi

cache memory *n* Comput memoria *f* cache

cachet /ˈkæʃeɪ/ *n* prestigio *m*

cackle /ˈkækl/ *vi* ridacchiare

cacophony /kəˈkɒfənɪ/ *n* cacofonia *f*

cactus /ˈkæktəs/ *n* (pl **-ti** /ˈkæktaɪ/ or **-tuses**) cactus *m inv*

CAD /kæd/ *n abbr* (**computer-aided design**) CAD *m inv*

cadaver /kəˈdɑːvə(r)/ *n* cadavere *m*

cadaverous /kəˈdævərəs/ *adj* cadaverico

CADCAM /ˈkædkæm/ *n abbr* (**computer-aided design and computer-aided manufacture**) CADCAM *m inv*

caddie /ˈkædɪ/ *n* portabastoni *m inv*

caddy /ˈkædɪ/ *n* **[tea-]** ∼ barattolo *m* del tè

cadence /ˈkeɪdəns/ *n* cadenza *f*

cadet /kəˈdet/ *n* cadetto *m*

cadet corps *n* Mil corpo *m* dei cadetti

cadet school *n* scuola *f* allievi ufficiali

cadge /kædʒ/ *vt/i* fam scroccare

cadre /ˈkɑːdr(ə)/ *n* Admin, Pol quadri *mpl*

CAE *n abbr* (**computer-aided engineering**) CAE *m inv*

Caesarean, **Caesarian** /sɪˈzeərɪən/ *n* parto *m* cesareo

café /ˈkæfeɪ/ *n* caffè *m inv*

cafeteria /kæfəˈtɪərɪə/ *n* tavola *f* calda

cafetière /kæfəˈtjeə(r)/ *n* caffettiera *f* a stantuffo

caffeine /ˈkæfiːn/ *n* caffeina *f*

cage /keɪdʒ/ *n* gabbia *f*

cage bird *n* uccello *m* da gabbia

cagey /ˈkeɪdʒɪ/ *adj* fam riservato (**about** su)

cagoule /kəˈguːl/ *n* Br K-way® *m inv*

cahoots /kəˈhuːts/ *npl* fam **be in** ∼ essere in combutta

cairn /keən/ *n* (of stones) tumulo *m* di pietre

Cairo /ˈkaɪrəʊ/ *n* il Cairo

cajole /kəˈdʒəʊl/ *vt* persuadere con le lusinghe

cake /keɪk/ *n* torta *f*; (small) pasticcino *m*; ∼ **of soap** saponetta *f*; **it was a piece of** ∼ fam è stato un gioco da ragazzi; **you can't have your** ∼ **and eat it** fig non si può avere la botte piena e la moglie ubriaca; **sell like hot** ∼**s** andare a ruba

caked /keɪkt/ *adj* incrostato (**with** di)

cake mix *n* miscela *f* per torte

cake shop *n* pasticceria *f*

cake tin *n* (for baking) tortiera *f*; (for storing) scatola *f* di latta (per torte)

CAL *abbr* (**computer-assisted learning**) CAL *m inv*

Calabria /kəˈlæbrɪə/ *n* Calabria *f*

Calabrian /kəˈlæbrɪən/ *adj & n* calabrese

calamine lotion /ˈkæləmaɪn/ *n* lozione *f* alla calamina

calamitous /kə'læmɪtəs/ *adj* disastroso

calamity /kə'læmətɪ/ *n* calamità *f inv*

calcify /'kælsɪfaɪ/ *vi* calcificarsi

calcium /'kælsɪəm/ *n* calcio *m*

calculate /'kælkjʊleɪt/ *vt* calcolare

calculated /'kælkjʊleɪtɪd/ *adj* ‹risk, insult, decision› calcolato; ‹crime› premeditato

calculating /'kælkjʊleɪtɪŋ/ *adj* fig calcolatore

calculating machine *n* calcolatrice *f*

calculation /kælkjʊ'leɪʃn/ *n* calcolo *m*

calculator /'kælkjʊleɪtə(r)/ *n* calcolatrice *f*

calculus /'kælkjʊləs/ *n* Math, Med calcolo *m*

calendar /'kælɪndə(r)/ *n* calendario *m*

calendar month *n* mese *m* civile

calendar year *n* anno *m* civile

calf[1] /kɑːf/ *n* (pl **calves**) vitello *m*

calf[2] *n* (pl **calves**) Anat polpaccio *m*

calfskin /'kɑːfskɪn/ *n* [pelle *f* di] vitello *m*

calibrate /'kælɪbreɪt/ *vt* calibrare ‹instrument›; tarare ‹scales›

calibre /'kælɪbə(r)/ *n* calibro *m*

calico /'kælɪkəʊ/ *n* cotone *m* grezzo

California /kælɪ'fɔːnɪə/ *n* California *f*

Californian /kælɪ'fɔːnɪən/ *adj & n* californiano, -a *mf*

CALL *n abbr* (**computer-assisted language learning**) CALL *m inv*

call /kɔːl/ **①** *n* grido *m*; Teleph telefonata *f*; (visit) visita *f*; **be on ~** ‹doctor› essere di guardia; **good/bad ~** fam buona/pessima idea

② *vt* chiamare; indire ‹strike›; **be ~ed** chiamarsi

③ *vi* chiamare; **~ [in or round]** passare

■ **call back** *vt/i* richiamare

■ **call by** *vi* (make brief visit) passare

■ **call for** *vt* (ask for) chiedere; (require) richiedere; (fetch) passare a prendere

■ **call in** **①** *vi* (make brief visit) passare **②** *vt* chiamare ‹patient, client›; interpellare ‹expert›

■ **call off** *vt* richiamare ‹dog›; disdire ‹meeting›; revocare ‹strike›

■ **call on** *vt* chiamare; (appeal to) fare un appello a; (visit) visitare

■ **call out** *vt/i* chiamare ad alta voce

■ **call together** *vt* riunire

■ **call up** *vt* Mil chiamare alle armi; Teleph chiamare

callback facility /'kɔːlbæk/ *n* Teleph servizio *m* telefonico che permette di individuare il numero che ha chiamato

call barring *n* blocco *m* chiamate

call box *n* cabina *f* telefonica

call centre Br, **call center** Am *n* call center *m inv*

caller /'kɔːlə(r)/ *n* visitatore, -trice *mf*; Teleph persona *f* che telefona

caller identification *n* identificativo *m* del chiamante

call-girl *n* call-girl *f inv*, [ragazza *f*] squillo *f inv*

calligrapher /kə'lɪɡrəfə(r)/ *n* calligrafo, -a *mf*

calligraphy /kə'lɪɡrəfɪ/ *n* calligrafia *f*

calling /'kɔːlɪŋ/ *n* vocazione *f*

calliper /'kælɪpə(r)/ (for measuring) calibro *m*; (leg support) tutore *m*

callisthenics /kælɪs'θenɪks/ *n* ginnastica *f*

callous /'kæləs/ *adj* insensibile

callousness /'kæləsnɪs/ *n* insensibilità *f*

call-out *n* (doctor) visita *f* a domicilio; (plumber, electrician) chiamata *f*

call-out charge *n* costo *m* della chiamata

callow /'kæləʊ/ *adj* immaturo

call screening *n* filtro *m* chiamate

call sign *n* Radio segnale *m* di chiamata

call-up *n* Mil chiamata *f* alle armi

call-up papers *npl* cartolina *f* precetto

call waiting *n* avviso *m* di chiamata in linea

calm /kɑːm/ **①** *adj* calmo **②** *n* calma *f*
■ **calm down** **①** *vt* calmare **②** *vi* calmarsi

calmly /'kɑːmlɪ/ *adv* con calma

calmness /'kɑːmnɪs/ *n* calma *f*

Calor gas® /'kælə/ *n* Br liquigas® *m inv*

calorie /'kælərɪ/ *n* caloria *f*

calorific /kælə'rɪfɪk/ *adj* calorico

calve /kɑːv/ *vi* figliare

calves /kɑːvz/ *npl* ▶ CALF[1] & CALF[2]

cam /kæm/ *n* Techn camma *f*

camaraderie /kæmə'rædərɪ/ *n* cameratismo *m*

camber /'kæmbə(r)/ *n* curvatura *f*

Cambodia /kæm'bəʊdɪə/ *n* Cambogia *f*

Cambodian /kæm'bəʊdɪən/ *adj & n* cambogiano, -a *mf*

camcorder /'kæmkɔːdə(r)/ *n* videocamera *f*

came /keɪm/ ▶ COME

camel /'kæml/ *n* cammello *m*

camel hair *n* cammello *m*

camellia /kə'miːlɪə/ *n* camelia *f*

cameo /'kæmɪəʊ/ *n* cammeo *m*

cameo role *n* Theat, Cinema breve apparizione *f*

camera /'kæmərə/ *n* macchina *f* fotografica; TV telecamera *f*

camera crew *n* troupe *f inv* televisiva

cameraman /'kæmərəmæn/ n operatore m [televisivo], cameraman m inv

camera phone n telefono m con fotocamera, telefono m con videocamera

Cameroon /'kæməru:n/ n il Camerun

camisole /'kæmɪsəʊl/ n canotta f

camomile /'kæməmaɪl/ n camomilla f

camouflage /'kæməflɑ:ʒ/ ① n mimetizzazione f
② vt mimetizzare

camp¹ /kæmp/ ① n campeggio f; Mil campo m
② vi campeggiare; Mil accamparsi

camp² adj (affected) affettato

campaign /kæm'peɪn/ ① n campagna f
② vi fare una campagna

campaigner /kæm'peɪnə(r)/ n partecipante mf a una campagna

campaign trail n be on the ∼ ∼ fare la campagna elettorale

campaign worker n Br Pol membro m dello staff di una campagna elettorale

camp bed n letto m da campo

camper /'kæmpə(r)/ n campeggiatore, -trice mf; Auto camper m inv

campfire /'kæmpfaɪə(r)/ n fuoco m di bivacco

camphor /'kæmfə(r)/ n canfora f

camping /'kæmpɪŋ/ n campeggio m

camping equipment n attrezzatura f da campeggio

camping gas n gas m inv da campeggio

camping holiday n vacanza f in tenda

camping site n campeggio m

camping stool n Br sgabello m pieghevole

camping stove n fornello m da campeggio

campsite /'kæmpsaɪt/ n campeggio m

campus /'kæmpəs/ n (pl **-puses**) Univ città f universitaria, campus m inv

camshaft /'kæmʃɑ:ft/ n albero m a camme

can¹ /kæn/ ① n (for petrol) latta f; (tin) scatola f; ∼ **of beer** lattina f di birra
② vt mettere in scatola

can² /kæn/, unstressed /kən/ v aux (pres **can**; pt **could**) (be able to) potere; (know how to) sapere; **I cannot** or **can't go** non posso andare; **he could not** or **couldn't go** non poteva andare; **she can't swim** non sa nuotare; **I ∼ smell something burning** sento odor di bruciato

Canada /'kænədə/ n Canada m

Canadian /kə'neɪdɪən/ adj & n canadese mf

canal /kə'næl/ n canale m

canal boat, **canal barge** n chiatta f

canapé /'kænəpeɪ/ n canapè m inv

Canaries /kə'neərɪz/ npl Canarie fpl

canary /kə'neərɪ/ n canarino m

cancel /'kænsl/ ① v (pt/pp **cancelled**) vt disdire ⟨meeting, newspaper⟩; revocare ⟨contract, order⟩; annullare ⟨reservation, appointment, stamp⟩
② vi ⟨guest, host⟩ annullare

cancellation /kænsə'leɪʃn/ n (of meeting, contract) revoca f; (in hotel, restaurant, for flight) cancellazione f

cancer /'kænsə(r)/ n cancro m; **C**∼ Astr Cancro m

cancerous /'kænsərəs/ adj canceroso

cancer patient n malato,-a mf di cancro

cancer research n ricerca f sul cancro

candelabra /kændə'lɑ:brə/ n candelabro m

candid /'kændɪd/ adj franco

candidacy /'kændɪdəsɪ/ n Pol candidatura f

candidate /'kændɪdət/ n candidato, -a mf

candidly /'kændɪdlɪ/ adv francamente

candied /'kændɪd/ adj candito

candle /'kænd(ə)l/ n candela f

candlelight /'kænd(ə)llaɪt/ n by ∼ a lume di candela

candlelit dinner /'kænd(ə)llɪt/ n cena f a lume di candela

candlestick /'kænd(ə)lstɪk/ n portacandele m inv

candour /'kændə(r)/ n franchezza f

candy /'kændɪ/ n Am caramella f; **a [piece of]** ∼ una caramella

candyfloss /'kændɪflɒs/ n zucchero m filato

candy-striped /straɪpt/ adj (blue) a righe bianche e celesti; (pink) a righe bianche e rosa

cane /keɪn/ ① n (stick) bastone m; Sch bacchetta f
② vt prendere a bacchettate ⟨pupil⟩

cane sugar n zucchero m di canna

canine /'keɪnaɪn/ adj canino

canine tooth n canino m

canister /'kænɪstə(r)/ n barattolo m

cannabis /'kænəbɪs/ n cannabis f

canned /kænd/ adj in scatola; ∼ **music** fam musica f registrata

cannibal /'kænɪbl/ n cannibale mf

cannibalism /'kænɪbəlɪzm/ n cannibalismo m

cannibalize /'kænɪbəlaɪz/ vt riciclare parti di

cannon /'kænən/ n inv cannone m

cannon ball n palla f di cannone

cannon fodder n carne f da cannone, carne f da macello

cannot /'kænɒt/ ▶CAN²

canny /'kænɪ/ adj astuto

canoe /kə'nu:/ ① n canoa f
② vi andare in canoa

canoeing /kə'nu:ɪŋ/ n canoismo m

canon /'kænən/ n (rule) canone m; (person) canonico m

canonization /kænənaɪz'zeɪʃn/ n canonizzazione f

canonize /'kænənaɪz/ vt canonizzare

canoodle /kə'nu:dl/ vi fam sbaciucchiarsi

can-opener n apriscatole m inv

canopy /'kænəpɪ/ n baldacchino f; (of parachute) calotta f

cant /kænt/ n (hypocrisy) ipocrisia f; (jargon) gergo m

can't /kɑ:nt/ = CANNOT ▶CAN²

cantankerous /kæn'tæŋkərəs/ adj stizzoso

cantata /kæn'tɑ:tə/ n Mus cantata f

canteen /kæn'ti:n/ n mensa f; ∼ of cutlery servizio m di posate

canter /'kæntə(r)/ ① n piccolo galoppo m
② vi andare a piccolo galoppo

cantilever /'kæntɪli:və(r)/ n cantilever m inv, trave f a sbalzo

cantonal /'kæntənəl/ adj cantonale

canvas /'kænvəs/ n tela f; (painting) dipinto m su tela

canvass /'kænvəs/ vi Pol fare propaganda elettorale

canvasser /'kænvəsə(r)/ n propagandista mf elettorale (porta a porta)

canvassing /'kænvəsɪŋ/ n (door to door for votes) propaganda f porta a porta; (door to door for sales) vendita f porta a porta

canyon /'kænjən/ n canyon m inv

canyoning /'kænjənɪŋ/ n canyoning m inv

cap /kæp/ ① n berretto m; (nurse's) cuffia f; (top, lid) tappo m
② vt (pt/pp **capped**) (fig: do better than) superare

capability /keɪpə'bɪlətɪ/ n capacità f

capable /'keɪpəbl/ adj capace; (skilful) abile; be ∼ of doing something essere capace di fare qualcosa

capably /'keɪpəblɪ/ adv con abilità

capacious /kə'peɪʃəs/ adj ⟨pocket, car boot⟩ capace

capacity /kə'pæsətɪ/ n capacità f; (function) qualità f; in my ∼ as in qualità di

cape¹ /keɪp/ n (cloak) cappa f

cape² n Geog capo m

Cape of Good Hope n Capo m di Buona Speranza

caper¹ /'keɪpə(r)/ ① vi saltellare
② n fam birichinata f

caper² n Culin cappero m

Cape Town n Città f del Capo

Cape Verde /vɜ:d/ n Capo Verde m

capful /'kæpfʊl/ n tappo m

cap gun n pistola f a capsule

capillary /kə'pɪlərɪ/ adj & n capillare m

capital /'kæpɪtl/ n (town) capitale f; (money) capitale m; (letter) lettera f maiuscola

capital allowances npl detrazioni mpl per ammortamento

capital city n capitale f

capital expenditure n spese fpl in conto capitale; (personal) spese fpl di capitale

capital gains tax n imposta f sui redditi di capitale

capital goods npl beni mpl strumentali

capital-intensive adj ad uso intensivo di capitale

capital investment n investimento m di capitale

capitalism /'kæpɪtəlɪzm/ n capitalismo m

capitalist /'kæpɪtəlɪst/ adj & n capitalista mf

capitalize /'kæpɪtəlaɪz/ vi ∼ on fig trarre vantaggio da

capital letter n lettera f maiuscola

capital punishment n pena f capitale

capital spending n spese fpl in conto capitale

capital transfer tax n imposta f sui trasferimenti di capitale

capitulate /kə'pɪtjʊleɪt/ vi capitolare

capitulation /kəpɪtjʊ'leɪʃn/ n capitolazione f

capon /'keɪpɒn/ n cappone m

caprice /kə'pri:s/ n (whim) capriccio m

capricious /kə'prɪʃəs/ adj capriccioso

Capricorn /'kæprɪkɔ:n/ n Astr Capricorno m

caps /kæps/ npl abbr (**capital letters**) maius. fpl

capsicum /'kæpsɪkəm/ n peperone m

capsize /kæp'saɪz/ ① vi capovolgersi
② vt capovolgere

caps lock n Comput bloccamaiuscole m inv

capstan /'kæpstən/ n argano m

capsule /'kæpsju:l/ n capsula f

captain /'kæptɪn/ ① n capitano m
② vt comandare ⟨team⟩

caption /'kæpʃn/ *n* intestazione *f*; (of illustration) didascalia *f*

captious /'kæpʃəs/ *adj* ⟨remark⟩ ipercritico

captivate /'kæptɪveɪt/ *vt* incantare

captive /'kæptɪv/ **1** *adj* prigioniero; hold/take ∼ tenere/fare prigioniero **2** *n* prigioniero, -a *mf*

captivity /kæp'tɪvətɪ/ *n* prigionia *f*; (animals) cattività *f*

captor /'kæptə(r)/ *n* (of person) persona *f* che tiene prigioniero qualcuno; (of person for ransom) rapitore, -trice *mf*

capture /'kæptʃə(r)/ **1** *n* cattura *f* **2** *vt* catturare; attirare ⟨attention⟩

car /kɑː(r)/ *n* macchina *f*; **by** ∼ in macchina

carafe /kə'ræf/ *n* caraffa *f*

car alarm *n* antifurto *m* della macchina

caramel /'kærəməl/ *n* (sweet) caramella *f* al mou; Culin caramello *m*

carat /'kærət/ *n* carato *m*

caravan /'kærəvæn/ *n* roulotte *f inv*; (horsedrawn) carovana *f*

caravan site *n* area *f* per roulotte

caraway /'kærəweɪ/ *n* (plant) cumino *m* dei prati

carbohydrate /kɑːbə'haɪdreɪt/ *n* carboidrato *m*

carbolic /kɑː'bɒlɪk/ *adj* (soap) al fenolo

car bomb *n* autobomba *f*

carbon /'kɑːbən/ *n* carbonio *m*: (paper) carta *f* carbone; (copy) copia *f* in carta carbone

carbon copy *n* copia *f* in carta carbone; (fig: person) ritratto *m*

carbon-date *vt* datare con il carbonio 14

carbon dating *n* datazione *f* con il carbonio 14

carbon dioxide *n* anidride *f* carbonica

carbon filter *n* filtro *m* al carbone

carbon monoxide *n* monossido *m* di carbonio

carbon paper *n* carta *f* carbone

car boot sale *n* Br mercatino *m* di oggetti usati, esposti nei bagagliai delle macchine

carbuncle /'kɑːbʌŋk(ə)l/ *n* Med foruncolo *m*

carburettor /kɑːbjʊ'retə(r)/ *n* carburatore *m*

carcass /'kɑːkəs/ *n* carcassa *f*

carcinogen /kɑː'sɪnədʒən/ *n* cancerogeno *m*

carcinogenic /kɑːsɪnə'dʒenɪk/ *adj* cancerogeno

car crash *n* scontro *m* automobilistico

card /kɑːd/ *n* (for birthday, Christmas etc) biglietto *m* di auguri; (playing ∼) carta *f* [da gioco]; (membership ∼) tessera *f*; (business ∼) biglietto *m* da visita; (credit ∼) carta *f* di credito; Comput scheda *f*

cardboard /'kɑːdbɔːd/ *n* cartone *m*

cardboard box *n* scatola *f* di cartone; (large) scatolone *m*

cardboard city *n* fam zona *f* in cui vivono i senzatetto

car deck *n* (on ferry) ponte *m* auto

card game *n* gioco *m* di carte

cardiac /'kɑːdɪæk/ *adj* cardiaco

cardiac arrest *n* arresto *m* cardiaco

cardigan /'kɑːdɪgən/ *n* cardigan *m inv*

cardinal /'kɑːdɪnl/ **1** *adj* cardinale; ∼ **number** numero *m* cardinale **2** *n* Relig cardinale *m*

card index *n* schedario *m*

cardiologist /kɑːdɪ'ɒlədʒɪst/ *n* cardiologo, -a *mf*

cardiology /kɑːdɪ'ɒlədʒɪ/ *n* cardiologia *f*

cardiovascular /kɑːdɪə'væskjʊlə(r)/ *adj* cardiovascolare

card key *n* scheda *f* magnetica

cardphone *n* telefono *m* a scheda

card table *n* tappeto *m* verde

card trick *n* trucco *m* con le carte

care /keə(r)/ *n* cura *f*; (caution) attenzione *f*; (worry) preoccupazione *f*; ∼ **of** (on letter abbr **c/o**) presso; **take** ∼ (be cautious) fare attenzione; **bye, take** ∼ ciao, stammi bene; **take** ∼ **of** occuparsi di; **be taken into** ∼ essere preso in custodia da un ente assistenziale; **'[handle] with** ∼**'** 'fragile' **2** *vi* ∼ **about** interessarsi di; ∼ **for** (feel affection for) volere bene a; (look after) aver cura di; **I don't** ∼ **for chocolate** non mi piace il cioccolato; **I don't** ∼ non me ne importa; **who** ∼**s?** chi se ne frega?; **for all I** ∼ per quello che me ne importa

care assistant *n* Br Med assistente *mf* a domicilio

career /kə'rɪə(r)/ **1** *n* carriera *f*; (profession) professione *f*; ∼ **woman** *n* donna in carriera **2** *vi* andare a tutta velocità

career break *n* pausa *f* nella carriera

career move *n* passo *m* utile per un avanzamento di carriera

careers adviser *n* consulente *mf* di orientamento professionale

careers office *n* centro *m* di orientamento professionale

careers service *n* servizio *m* di orientamento professionale

carefree /'keəfriː/ *adj* spensierato

careful /'keəfʊl/ *adj* attento; ⟨driver⟩ prudente

carefully /'keəfʊlɪ/ *adv* con attenzione

care home *n* casa *f* famiglia

careless /'keəlɪs/ *adj* irresponsabile; (in work) trascurato; ⟨work⟩ fatto con poca cura; ⟨driver⟩ distratto

carelessly /'keəlɪslɪ/ *adv* negligentemente

carelessness /'keəlɪsnɪs/ *n* trascuratezza *f*

carer /'keərə(r)/ *n* Br (relative) familiare *m* che assiste un anziano o un handicappato; (professional) assistente *mf* a domicilio

caress /kə'res/ ① *n* carezza *f* ② *vt* accarezzare

caretaker /'keəteɪkə(r)/ *n* custode *mf*; (in school) bidello *m*

care worker *n* assistente *mf* sociosanitario

careworn /'keəwɔ:n/ *adj* ⟨face⟩ segnato dalle preoccupazioni

car ferry *n* traghetto *m* (per il trasporto di auto)

car-free *adj* ⟨environment⟩ senza macchine

cargo /'kɑ:gəʊ/ *n* (pl **-es**) carico *m*

cargo plane *n* aereo *m* da carico

cargo ship *n* nave *f* da carico

car hire *n* autonoleggio *m*

Caribbean /kærɪ'bi:ən/ ① *n* the ∼ (sea) il Mar *m* dei Caraibi ② *adj* caraibico

caricature /'kærɪkətjʊə(r)/ ① *n* caricatura *f* ② *vt* fare una caricatura di

caricaturist /'kærɪkətjʊərɪst/ *n* caricaturista *mf*

caring /'keərɪŋ/ *adj* ⟨parent⟩ premuroso; ⟨attitude⟩ altruista; **the ∼ professions** le attività assistenziali

carjack /'kɑ:dʒæk/ *vt* furto *m* d'auto con minaccia o violenza al conducente

carjacker /'kɑ:dʒækə(r)/ *n* chi effettua un furto d'auto con minaccia o violenza al conducente

carjacking /'kɑ:dʒækɪŋ/ *n* furto *m* d'auto con aggressione al conducente

carload /'kɑ:ləʊd/ *n* **a ∼ of people** un'automobile *f* piena di persone

carnage /'kɑ:nɪdʒ/ *n* carneficina *f*

carnal /'kɑ:n(ə)l/ *adj* carnale

carnation /kɑ:'neɪʃn/ *n* garofano *m*

carnival /'kɑ:nɪvl/ *n* carnevale *m*

carnivore /'kɑ:nɪvɔ:(r)/ *n* carnivoro *m*

carnivorous /kɑ:'nɪvərəs/ *adj* carnivoro

carob /'kærəb/ *n* (pod) carruba *f*; (tree) carrubo *m*

carol /'kærəl/ *n* **[Christmas]** ∼ canto *m* natalizio; ∼ **concert** concerto *m* natalizio; **go ∼ singing** andare a cantare le canzoni natalizie per le strade

carousel /kærʊ'sel/ *n* (merry-go-round) giostra *f*; (for luggage) nastro *m* trasportatore; (for slides) caricatore *m* circolare

carp¹ /kɑ:p/ *n inv* carpa *f*

carp² *vi* lamentarsi; ∼ **at** trovare da ridire su

car park *n* parcheggio *m*

carpenter /'kɑ:pəntə(r)/ *n* falegname *m*

carpentry /'kɑ:pəntrɪ/ *n* falegnameria *f*

carpet /'kɑ:pɪt/ ① *n* tappeto *m*; (wall-to-wall) moquette *f inv*; **be on the ∼** fig essere ammonito ② *vt* mettere la moquette in ⟨room⟩

carpet-bomb *vt* bombardare a tappeto

carpet fitter *n* artigiano *m* che mette in opera la moquette

carpet slipper *n* pantofola *f*

carpet sweeper *n* battitappeto *m inv*

carpet tile *n* riquadro *m* di moquette

car phone *n* telefono *m* in macchina

car radio *n* autoradio *f inv*

carriage /'kærɪdʒ/ *n* carrozza *f*; (of typewriter) carrello *m*; (of goods) trasporto *m*; (cost) spese *fpl* di trasporto; (bearing) portamento *m*; ∼ **paid** Comm franco di porto

carriage clock *n* orologio *m* da tavolo

carriageway /'kærɪdʒweɪ/ *n* strada *f* carrozzabile; **north-bound** ∼ carreggiata *f* nord

carrier /'kærɪə(r)/ *n* (company) impresa *f* di trasporti; Aeron compagnia *f* di trasporto aereo; (of disease) portatore *m*

carrier [bag] *n* borsa *f* [per la spesa]

carrier pigeon *n* piccione *m* viaggiatore

carrot /'kærət/ *n* carota *f*

carry /'kærɪ/ *v* (pt/pp **-ied**) ① *vt* portare; (transport) trasportare; Math riportare; **get carried away** fam lasciarsi prender la mano ② *vi* ⟨sound⟩ trasmettersi ▪ **carry forward** *vt* riportare ⟨balance, figure⟩ ▪ **carry off** *vt* portare via; vincere ⟨prize⟩ ▪ **carry on** ① *vi* continuare; (fam: make scene) fare delle storie; ∼ **on with something** continuare qualcosa; ∼ **on with somebody** fam intendersela con qcno ② *vt* mantenere ⟨business⟩; ∼ **on doing something** continuare a fare qualcosa ▪ **carry out** *vt* portare fuori; eseguire ⟨instructions, task⟩; mettere in atto threat; effettuare ⟨experiment, survey⟩

carryall *n* Am borsone *m*

carrycot /'kærɪkɒt/ *n* porte-enfant *m inv*

carry-on *n* fam (complicated procedure) impresa *f*; (bad behaviour) storie *fpl*

carryout *n* Am piatti *mpl* da asporto

car seat *n* (for baby or child) seggiolino *m* per auto

carsick /'kɑːsɪk/ *adj* **be** ∼ avere il mal d'auto

cart /kɑːt/ **①** *n* carretto *m*; **put the** ∼ **before the horse** fig mettere il carro davanti ai buoi
② *vt* (fam: carry) portare

cartel /kɑː'tel/ *n* cartello *m*

car theft *n* furto *m* d'auto

carthorse /'kɑːthɔːs/ *n* cavallo *m* da tiro

cartilage /'kɑːtɪlɪdʒ/ *n* Anat cartilagine *f*

cartographer /kɑː'tɒgrəfə(r)/ *n* cartografo, -a *mf*

cartography /kɑː'tɒgrəfɪ/ *n* cartografia *f*

carton /'kɑːt(ə)n/ *n* scatola *f* di cartone; (for drink) cartone *m*; (of cream, yoghurt) vasetto *m*; (of cigarettes) stecca *f*

cartoon /kɑː'tuːn/ *n* vignetta *f*; (strip) vignette *fpl*; (film) cartone *m* animato; (in art) bozzetto *m*

cartoonist /kɑː'tuːnɪst/ *n* vignettista *mf*; (for films) disegnatore, -trice *mf* di cartoni animati

cartridge /'kɑːtrɪdʒ/ *n* cartuccia *f*; (for film) bobina *f*; (of record player) testina *f*

cartwheel /'kɑːtwiːl/ *n* (of cart) ruota *f* di carro; (in gymnastics) ruota *f*; **do a** ∼ (in gymnastics) fare la ruota

carve /kɑːv/ *vt* scolpire; tagliare ⟨*meat*⟩
■ **carve out** *vt* crearsi ⟨*name, reputation, market*⟩
■ **carve up** *vt* spartire ⟨*estate, territory, proceeds*⟩

carving /'kɑːvɪŋ/ *n* scultura *f*

carving knife *n* trinciante *m*

car wash *n* autolavaggio *m inv*

car worker *n* operaio, -a *mf* dell'industria automobilistica

Casanova /'kæsənəʊvə/ *n* Casanova *m inv*

cascade /kæs'keɪd/ **①** *vi* scendere a cascata
② *n* cascata *f*

case¹ /keɪs/ *n* caso *m*; **in any** ∼ in ogni caso; **in that** ∼ in questo caso; **just in** ∼ per sicurezza; **in** ∼ **he comes** nel caso in cui venisse; **in** ∼ **of emergency** in caso d'emergenza

case² *n* (container) scatola *f*; (crate) cassa *f*; (for spectacles) astuccio *m*; (suitcase) valigia *f*; (for display) vetrina *f*

case history *n* Med cartella *f* clinica

casement window /'keɪsmənt/ *n* finestra *f* a battenti

casenotes *npl* pratica *f*

case study *n* analisi *f inv*

casework *n* **do** ∼ occuparsi di assistenza sociale

cash /kæʃ/ **①** *n* denaro *m* contante; (fam: money) contanti *mpl*; **pay [in]** ∼ pagare in contanti; ∼ **on delivery** pagamento alla consegna
② *vt* incassare ⟨*cheque*⟩
■ **cash in** *vt* riscuotere ⟨*bond, policy*⟩; Am incassare ⟨*check*⟩
■ **cash in on** *vt* fam approfittarsi di

cash-and-carry *n* cash and carry *m inv*

cashback *n* contanti *mpl* che si possono richiedere alla cassa di un negozio quando si effettua un pagamento con carta di debito

cash box *n* cassetta *f* portavalori

cash card *n* bancomat® *m inv*

cash desk *n* cassa *f*

cash dispenser *n* sportello *m* automatico, cassa *f* automatica

cashew [nut] /kə'ʃuː/ *n* anacardio *m*

cash flow *n* flusso *m* di cassa; ∼ ∼ **difficulties** difficoltà *fpl* di flusso di cassa; ∼ ∼ **management** gestione *f* del flusso di cassa

cashier /kæ'ʃɪə(r)/ *n* cassiere, -a *mf*

cashless /'kæʃlɪs/ *adj* ⟨*society, transaction*⟩ basato sull'uso di carte di credito, assegni ecc. anziché sul contante

cash machine *n* (sportello) bancomat® *m inv*

cashmere /'kæʃmɪə(r)/ *n* cachemire *m inv*

cash on delivery *n* pagamento *m* alla consegna

cashpoint *n* (sportello) bancomat® *m inv*

cash register *n* registratore *m* di cassa

casing /'keɪsɪŋ/ *n* (of machinery) rivestimento *m*; (of gearbox) scatola *f*; (of tyre) copertone *m*

casino /kə'siːnəʊ/ *n* casinò *m inv*

cask /kɑːsk/ *n* barile *m*

casket /'kɑːskɪt/ *n* scrigno *m*; (Am: coffin) bara *f*

casserole /'kæsərəʊl/ *n* casseruola *f*; (stew) stufato *m*

cassette /kə'set/ *n* cassetta *f*

cassette deck *n* piastra *f* di registrazione

cassette player *n* mangiacassette *m inv*

cassette recorder *n* registratore *m* (a cassette)

cassette tape *n* cassetta *f*

cassock /'kæsək/ *n* tonaca *f*

cast /kɑːst/ **①** *n* (throw) lancio *m*; (mould) forma *f*; Theat cast *m inv*; **[plaster]** ∼ Med ingessatura *f*
② *vt* (pt/pp **cast**) dare ⟨*vote*⟩; Theat assegnare le parti di ⟨*play*⟩; fondere ⟨*metal*⟩; (throw) gettare; (shed) sbarazzarsi di; ∼ **an actor as** dare ad un attore il

ruolo di; ~ **a glance at** lanciare uno sguardo a
■ **cast off** ① *vi* Naut sganciare gli ormeggi
② *vt* (in knitting) diminuire
■ **cast on** *vt* (in knitting) avviare

castanets /kæstə'nets/ *npl* nacchere *fpl*

castaway /'kɑːstəweɪ/ *n* naufrago, -a *mf*

caste /kɑːst/ *n* casta *f*

caster /'kɑːstə(r)/ *n* (wheel) rotella *f*

caster sugar *n* zucchero *m* raffinato

casting /'kɑːstɪŋ/ *n* casting *m inv*

casting director *n* direttore *m* del casting

casting vote *n* voto *m* decisivo

cast iron ① *n* ghisa *f*
② *adj* **cast-iron** di ghisa; fig solido

castle /'kɑːsl/ *n* castello *m*; (in chess) torre *f*

cast-offs *npl* abiti *mpl* smessi

castor /'kɑːstə(r)/ *n* (wheel) rotella *f*

castor oil *n* olio *m* di ricino

castor sugar *n* zucchero *m* raffinato

castrate /kæ'streɪt/ *vt* castrare

castration /kæ'streɪʃn/ *n* castrazione *f*

castrato /kæs'trɑːtəʊ/ *n* castrato *m*

casual /'kæʒʊəl/ *adj* (chance) casuale; remark senza importanza; ⟨glance⟩ di sfuggita; ⟨attitude, approach⟩ disinvolto; ⟨chat⟩ informale; ⟨clothes⟩ casual *inv*; ⟨work⟩ saltuario; ~ **wear** abbigliamento *m* casual

casualize /'kæʒʊəlaɪz/ *vt* impiegare con contratto a termine ⟨labour⟩

casually /'kæʒʊəlɪ/ *adv* ⟨dress⟩ casual; ⟨meet⟩ casualmente

casualty /'kæʒʊəltɪ/ *n* (injured person) ferito *m*; (killed) vittima *f*

casualty [department] *n* pronto soccorso *m*

cat /kæt/ *n* gatto *m*; pej arpia *f*

catacombs /'kætəkuːmz/ *npl* catacombe *fpl*

catalogue /'kætəlɒg/ ① *n* catalogo *m*
② *vt* catalogare

catalyst /'kætəlɪst/ *n* Chem & fig catalizzatore *m*

catalytic converter /kætə'lɪtɪk/ *n* Auto marmitta *f* catalitica

catamaran /kætəmə'ræn/ *n* catamarano *m*

catapult /'kætəpʌlt/ ① *n* catapulta *f*; (child's) fionda *f*
② *vt* fig catapultare

cataract /'kætərækt/ *n* Med cataratta *f*

catarrh /kə'tɑː(r)/ *n* catarro *m*

catastrophe /kə'tæstrəfɪ/ *n* catastrofe *f*

catastrophic /kætə'strɒfɪk/ *adj* catastrofico

cat burglar *n* Br scassinatore, -trice *mf* acrobata

catch /kætʃ/ ① *n* (of fish) pesca *f*; (fastener) fermaglio *m*; (on door) fermo *m*; (on window) gancio *m*; (fam: snag) tranello *m*
② *vt* (pt/pp **caught**) acchiappare ⟨ball⟩; (grab) afferrare; prendere ⟨illness, fugitive, train⟩; ~ **a cold** prendersi un raffreddore; ~ **sight of** scorgere; **I caught him stealing** l'ho sorpreso mentre rubava; ~ **one's finger in the door** chiudersi il dito nella porta; ~ **sb's eye** or **attention** attirare l'attenzione di qualcuno
③ *vi* ⟨fire⟩ prendere; (get stuck) impigliarsi
■ **catch on** *vi* fam (understand) afferrare; (become popular) diventare popolare
■ **catch out** *vt* (show to be wrong) prendere in castagna
■ **catch up** ① *vt* raggiungere
② *vi* recuperare; ⟨runner⟩ riguadagnare terreno; ~ **up with** raggiungere ⟨somebody⟩; mettersi in pari con ⟨work⟩

catch-all *adj* ⟨term⟩ polivalente; ⟨clause⟩ che comprende tutte le possibilità

catching /'kætʃɪŋ/ *adj* contagioso

catchment area /'kætʃmənt/ *n* bacino *m* d'utenza

catchphrase /'kætʃfreɪz/ *n* tormentone *m*

catch-22 situation /kætʃtwentɪ'tuː/ *n* situazione *f* senza uscita

catchword /'kætʃwɜːd/ *n* slogan *m inv*

catchy /'kætʃɪ/ *adj* (-ier, -iest) orecchiabile

catechism /'kætɪkɪzm/ *n* catechismo *m*

categorical /kætɪ'gɒrɪkl/ *adj* categorico

categorically /kætə'gɒrɪlkɪ/ *adv* categoricamente

categorize /'kætɪgəraɪz/ *vt* categorizzare

category /'kætɪgərɪ/ *n* categoria *f*

cater /'keɪtə(r)/ ① *vi* ~ **for** provvedere a ⟨needs⟩; fig venire incontro alle esigenze di
② *vt* occuparsi del rinfresco di ⟨party⟩

caterer /'keɪtərə(r)/ *n* persona *f* che si occupa di ristorazione

catering /'keɪtərɪŋ/ *n* (trade) ristorazione *f*; (food) rinfresco *m*

caterpillar /'kætəpɪlə(r)/ *n* bruco *m*

caterwaul /'kætəwɔːl/ *vi* miagolare

catfish *n* pesce *m* gatto

catflap *n* gattaiola *f*

catgut *n* catgut *m inv*

cathedral /kə'θiːdrl/ *n* cattedrale *f*

Catherine wheel /'kæθ(ə)rɪn/ *n* girandola *f*

catheter /'kæθɪtə(r)/ *n* catetere *m*

cathode-ray tube /kæθəʊd'reɪ/ *n* tubo *m* a raggi catodici

Catholic /'kæθəlɪk/ *adj* & *n* cattolico, -a *mf*

Catholicism /kə'θɒlɪsɪzm/ n cattolicesimo m

catkin /'kætkɪn/ n Bot amento m

cat litter n lettiera f del gatto

catnap vi ① fare un pisolino
② n pisolino m

cat-o'-nine-tails n gatto m a nove code

CAT scan n TAC f

cat's-eye n Br catarifrangente m (inserito nell'asfalto)

catsuit n tuta f

cattery /'kætərɪ/ n pensione f per gatti

cattle /'kæt(ə)l/ npl bestiame msg

cattle grid n recinto m metallico che impedisce al bestiame di accedere a una strada

cattle market n mercato m del bestiame; fig fam ⟨for sexual encounters⟩ locale m dove la gente va per rimorchiare

cattle shed n stalla f

catty /'kætɪ/ adj (-ier, -iest) dispettoso

catwalk /'kætwɔːk/ n passerella f

Caucasian /kɔː'keɪʒ(ə)n/ ① n (Geog: inhabitant) caucasico, -a mf; (white person) bianco, -a mf
② Geog caucasico; ⟨race, man⟩ bianco

caught /kɔːt/ ▶ CATCH

cauldron /'kɔːldrən/ n calderone m

cauliflower /'kɒlɪflaʊə(r)/ n cavolfiore m

cauliflower cheese n cavolfiori mpl gratinati

causal /'kɔːzəl/ adj causale

cause /kɔːz/ ① n causa f; (reason) motivo m; good ∼ buona causa
② vt causare; ∼ somebody to do something far fare qualcosa a qualcuno

causeway /'kɔːzweɪ/ n strada f sopraelevata

caustic /'kɔːstɪk/ adj caustico

cauterize /'kɔːtəraɪz/ vt cauterizzare

caution /'kɔːʃn/ ① n cautela f; (warning) ammonizione f
② vt mettere in guardia; Jur ammonire

cautionary /'kɔːʃ(ə)nərɪ/ adj ⟨tale⟩ di ammonimento

cautious /'kɔːʃəs/ adj cauto

cautiously /'kɔːʃəslɪ/ adv cautamente

cavalcade /kævəl'keɪd/ n sfilata f

cavalier /kævə'lɪə(r)/ ① adj noncurante
② n C∼ sostenitore, -trice mf di Carlo I durante la guerra civile inglese

cavalry /'kævəlrɪ/ n cavalleria f

cave /keɪv/ n caverna f
■ **cave in** vi ⟨roof⟩ crollare; (fig: give in) capitolare

caveat /'kævɪæt/ n avvertimento m

cave dweller n cavernicolo, -a mf

caveman n cavernicolo m

cave painting n pittura f rupestre

caver /'keɪvə(r)/ n speleologo, -a mf

cavern /'kævən/ n caverna f

caviare /'kævɪɑː(r)/ n caviale m

caving /'keɪvɪŋ/ n speleologia f

cavity /'kævətɪ/ n cavità f inv; (in tooth) carie f inv

cavity wall insulation n isolamento m per muri a intercapedine

cavort /kə'vɔːt/ vi saltellare

caw /kɔː/ ① n (noise) gracchio m
② vi gracchiare

cayenne pepper /'kaɪen/ n pepe m di Caienna

cayman /'keɪmən/ n caimano m

CB ① n abbr (**Citizens' Band**) CB f inv
② attrib ⟨equipment, radio, wavelength⟩ CB

CBI n abbr Br (**Confederation of British Industry**) ≈ Confindustria f

cc abbr (**cubic centimetre**) cc m; (**carbon copy**) cc

CCJ n abbr Br (**County Court Judgement**) sentenza f del tribunale di contea

CCTV abbr (**closed-circuit television**) televisione f a circuito chiuso

CD n abbr (**Civil Defence**) difesa f civile; abbr (**compact disc**) CD m inv; Am abbr (**Congressional District**) circoscrizione f del Congresso; abbr (**corps diplomatique**) CD m inv

CD burner, **CD writer** n masterizzatore m di CD

CD-I abbr (**compact disc interactive**) CD-I m

CD player n lettore m [di] compact, lettore m di CD

CD-R abbr (**compact disc recordable**) CD-R m

CD-Rom /siːdiːˈrɒm/ n CD-Rom m inv

CD-Rom drive n lettore m CD-Rom

CD-RW abbr (**compact disc rewritable**) CD-RW m

cease /siːs/ ① n without ∼ incessantemente
② vt/i cessare

ceasefire /'siːsfaɪə(r)/ n cessate il fuoco m inv

ceaseless /'siːslɪs/ adj incessante

ceaselessly /'siːslɪslɪ/ adv incessantemente

cedar /'siːdə(r)/ n cedro m

cede /siːd/ vt cedere

cedilla /sə'dɪlə/ n cedilla f

ceiling /'siːlɪŋ/ n soffitto m; fig tetto m [massimo]

celebrate /'selɪbreɪt/ ① vt festeggiare ⟨birthday, victory⟩

2 *vi* far festa

celebrated /'selɪbreɪtɪd/ *adj* celebre (**for** per)

celebration /selɪ'breɪʃn/ *n* celebrazione *f*

celebrity /sɪ'lebrətɪ/ *n* celebrità *f inv*

celeriac /sɪ'lerɪæk/ *n* sedano *m* rapa

celery /'selərɪ/ *n* sedano *m*

celestial /sɪ'lestɪəl/ *adj* celestiale

celibacy /'selɪbəsɪ/ *n* celibato *m*

celibate /'selɪbət/ *adj* ⟨man⟩ celibe; ⟨woman⟩ nubile

cell /sel/ *n* cella *f*; Biol cellula *f*

cellar /'selə(r)/ *n* scantinato *m*; (for wine) cantina *f*

cellist /'tʃelɪst/ *n* violoncellista *mf*

cello /'tʃeləʊ/ *n* violoncello *m*

Cellophane® /'seləfeɪn/ *n* cellophane® *m inv*

cellphone /'selfəʊn/ *n* [telefono *m*] cellulare *m*

cellular phone /seljʊlə'fəʊn/ *n* [telefono *m*] cellulare *m*

cellulite /'seljʊlaɪt/ *n* cellulite *f*

celluloid /'seljʊlɔɪd/ *n* celluloide *f*

Celsius /'selsɪəs/ *adj* Celsius

Celt /kelt/ *n* celta *mf*

Celtic /'keltɪk/ *adj* celtico

cement /sɪ'ment/ **1** *n* cemento *m*; (adhesive) mastice *m*
2 *vt* cementare; (stick) attaccare col mastice; fig consolidare

cement mixer *n* betoniera *f*

cemetery /'semətrɪ/ *n* cimitero *m*

cenotaph /'senətæf/ *n* cenotafio *m*

censor /'sensə(r)/ **1** *n* censore *m*
2 *vt* censurare

censorship /'sensəʃɪp/ *n* censura *f*

censure /'senʃə(r)/ **1** *n* biasimo *m*
2 *vt* biasimare

census /'sensəs/ *n* censimento *m*

cent /sent/ *n* (coin) centesimo *m*

centenary /sen'tiːnərɪ/ *n*, Am
centennial /sen'tenɪəl/ *n* centenario *m*

center /'sentə(r)/ *n* Am = CENTRE

centigrade /'sentɪgreɪd/ *adj* centigrado

centilitre /'sentɪliːtə(r)/ *n* centilitro *m*

centimetre /'sentɪmiːtə(r)/ *n* centimetro *m*

centipede /'sentɪpiːd/ *n* centopiedi *m inv*

central /'sentrəl/ *adj* centrale

Central African Republic *n* Repubblica *f* Centrafricana

Central America *n* America *f* centrale

central heating *n* riscaldamento *m* autonomo

centralize /'sentrəlaɪz/ *vt* centralizzare

central locking *n* Auto chiusura *f* centralizzata

centrally /'sentrəlɪ/ *adv* al centro; ∼ **heated** con riscaldamento autonomo

central nervous system *n* sistema *m* nervoso centrale

central processing unit *n* Comput unità *f inv* centrale di elaborazione

central reservation *n* Auto banchina *f* spartitraffico *inv*

centre Br, **center** Am /'sentə(r)/ **1** *n* centro *m*
2 *vt* (pt/pp **centred**) centrare
■ **centre on**, **centre around** *vt* ⟨activities, life⟩ impermiarsi su; ⟨industry, people⟩ incentrarsi su; ⟨thoughts⟩ concentrarsi su

centrefold *n* (pin-up picture) paginone *m*; (model) pin-up *f inv*

centre forward *n* centravanti *m inv*

centre ground Br, **center ground** Am *n* fig centro *m*

centre half *n* Sport centromediano *m*

centre of gravity *n* centro *m* di gravità

centrepiece *n* (of table) centrotavola *m*; (fig: of exhibition) pezzo *m* forte

centre spread *n* paginone *m*

centre stage *n* Theat centro *m* della scena; **stand** ∼ ∼ tenersi al centro della scena; **take/occupy** ∼ ∼ fig essere/ mettersi in primo piano

centrifugal /sentrɪ'fjuːgl/ *adj* ∼ **force** forza *f* centrifuga

century /'sentʃərɪ/ *n* secolo *m*

CEO *n abbr* (**Chief Executive Officer**) direttore, -trice *mf* generale

ceramic /sɪ'ræmɪk/ *adj* ceramico

ceramics /sɪ'ræmɪks/ *n* (art) ceramica *fsg*; (objects) ceramiche *fpl*

cereal /'sɪərɪəl/ *n* cereale *m*

cerebral /'serɪbrl/ *adj* cerebrale

cerebral palsy /'pɔːlzɪ/ *n* paralisi *f* cerebrale

ceremonial /serɪ'məʊnɪəl/ **1** *adj* da cerimonia
2 *n* cerimoniale *m*

ceremonially /serɪ'məʊnɪəlɪ/ *adv* secondo il rituale

ceremonious /serɪ'məʊnɪəs/ *adj* cerimonioso

ceremoniously /serɪ'məʊnɪəslɪ/ *adv* in modo cerimonioso

ceremony /'serɪmənɪ/ *n* cerimonia *f*; **without** ∼ senza cerimonie

cert /sɜːt/ *n* Br fam **it's a [dead]** ∼**!** ci puoi scommettere!

certain /'sɜːtn/ *adj* certo; **for** ∼ di sicuro; **make** ∼ accertarsi; **he is** ∼ **to win** è certo di vincere; **it's not** ∼ **whether he'll come** non è sicuro che venga

certainly /'sɜ:tnlɪ/ adv certamente; ~ not! no di certo!

certainty /'sɜ:tntɪ/ n certezza f; it's a ~ è una cosa certa

certifiable /'sɜ:tɪfaɪəbl/ adj ⟨verifiable statement, evidence⟩ dimostrabile; (mad) pazzo

certificate /sə'tɪfɪkət/ n certificato m

certified /'sɜ:tɪfaɪd/ adj autenticato

certified mail n Am (lettera) raccomandata f

certified public accountant n Am ≈ commercialista mf

certify /'sɜ:tɪfaɪ/ vt (pt/pp -ied) certificare; (declare insane) dichiarare malato di mente

certitude /'sɜ:tɪtju:d/ n certezza f

cervical /'sɜ:vɪkl/ adj cervicale

cervical cancer n tumore m del collo dell'utero

cervical smear n Pap test m inv, striscio m

cervix /'sɜ:vɪks/ n cervice f uterina, collo m dell'utero

cessation /se'seɪʃn/ n cessazione f.

cesspool /'sespu:l/ n pozzo m nero

cf. abbr (**compare**) cf, cfr

CFC n abbr (**chlorofluorocarbon**) CFC m inv

CFC-free adj ⟨product, spray⟩ senza CFC

CFE abbr **College of Further Education**

CGI abbr Comput (**common graphical interface**) CGI f

Chad /tʃæd/ n Chad m

chafe /tʃeɪf/ vt irritare

chaff /tʃɑ:f/ n pula f

chaffinch /'tʃæfɪntʃ/ n fringuello m

chagrin /'ʃægrɪn/ n much to his ~ con suo grande dispiacere

chain /tʃeɪn/ ① n catena f
② vt incatenare ⟨prisoner⟩; attaccare con la catena ⟨dog⟩ (to a)
■ **chain up** vt legare alla catena ⟨dog⟩

chain gang n gruppo m di prigionieri incatenati

chain letter n lettera f della catena di Sant'Antonio

chain mail n cotta f di maglia

chain reaction n reazione f a catena

chain saw n motosega f

chain-smoke vi fumare una sigaretta dopo l'altra

chain-smoker n fumatore, -trice mf accanito, -a

chain store n negozio m appartenente ad una catena

chair /tʃeə(r)/ ① n sedia f; Univ cattedra f
② vt presiedere

chairlift /'tʃeəlɪft/ n seggiovia f

chairman /'tʃeəmən/ n presidente m; ~ and managing director presidente m direttore generale

chairperson /'tʃeəpɜ:s(ə)n/ n presidente m, -essa f

chairwoman /'tʃeəwʊmən/ n presidentessa f

chalet /'ʃæleɪ/ n chalet m inv; (in holiday camp) bungalow m inv

chalice /'tʃælɪs/ n Relig calice m

chalk /tʃɔ:k/ n gesso m

chalky /'tʃɔ:kɪ/ adj gessoso

challenge /'tʃælɪndʒ/ ① n sfida f; Mil intimazione f
② vt sfidare; Mil intimare il chi va là a; fig mettere in dubbio ⟨statement⟩

challenger /'tʃælɪndʒə(r)/ n sfidante mf

challenging /'tʃælɪndʒɪŋ/ adj ⟨job⟩ impegnativo

chamber /'tʃeɪmbə(r)/ n C~ of Commerce Camera f di commercio

chambermaid n cameriera f ai piani

chamber music n musica f da camera

chamber orchestra n orchestra f da camera

chamber pot n vaso m da notte

chambers /'tʃeɪmbəz/ n pl Jur studio m [legale]

chameleon /kə'mi:lɪən/ n also fig camaleonte m

chamois[1] /'ʃæmwɑ:/ n inv (animal) camoscio m

chamois[2] /'ʃæmɪ/ n ~[-leather] [pelle f di] camoscio m

champagne /ʃæm'peɪn/ n champagne m inv

champion /'tʃæmpɪən/ ① n Sport campione m; (of cause) difensore m, difenditrice f
② vt (defend) difendere; (fight for) lottare per

championship /'tʃæmpɪənʃɪp/ n Sport campionato m

chance /tʃɑ:ns/ ① n caso m; (possibility) possibilità f inv; (opportunity) occasione f; by ~ per caso; take a ~ provarci; give somebody a second ~ dare un'altra possibilità a qualcuno
② attrib fortuito
③ vt if you ~ to see him se ti capita di vederlo; I'll ~ it fam corro il rischio

chancel /'tʃɑ:nsəl/ n Archit coro m

chancellor /'tʃɑ:nsələ(r)/ n cancelliere m; Univ rettore m; C~ of the Exchequer ≈ ministro m del tesoro

chancy /'tʃɑ:nsɪ/ adj rischioso

chandelier /ʃændə'lɪə(r)/ n lampadario m

chandler /'tʃɑ:ndlə(r)/ n fornitore m navale

change /tʃeɪndʒ/ **1** n cambiamento m; (money) resto m; (small coins) spiccioli mpl; **for a ~** tanto per cambiare; **have a ~ of heart** cambiare idea; **a ~ of clothes** un cambio di vestiti; **~ of address** cambiamento m d'indirizzo; **a ~ of scene** also fig un cambiamento di scena; **the ~ [of life]** la menopausa
2 vt cambiare; (substitute) scambiare (for con); **~ one's clothes** cambiarsi [i vestiti]; **~ trains** cambiare treno
3 vi cambiare; (~ clothes) cambiarsi; **all ~!** stazione terminale!
■ **change down** vi Auto passare alla marcia inferiore
■ **change up** vi Auto passare alla marcia superiore

changeability /tʃeɪndʒəˈbɪlɪtɪ/ n (of weather) instabilità f

changeable /ˈtʃeɪndʒəbl/ adj mutevole; (weather) variable

changeless /ˈtʃeɪndʒlɪs/ adj (appearance) inalterabile; (character) costante; (law, routine) immutabile

change machine n distributore m di monete

changeover /ˈtʃeɪndʒəʊvə(r)/ n (time period) periodo m di transizione; (transition) passaggio m; (of leaders) subentro m; (of employees, guards) cambio m; (Sport: in relay) passaggio m del testimone; (Sport: of ends) cambiamento m

changing /ˈtʃeɪndʒɪŋ/ adj in mutamento

changing-room n camerino m; (for sports) spogliatoio m

channel /ˈtʃænl/ **1** n canale m; **the [English] C~** la Manica
2 vt (pt/pp **channelled**) **~ one's energies into something** convogliare le proprie energie in qualcosa

channel ferry n traghetto m attraverso la Manica

channel-hop vi Br fare lo zapping

channel-hopping n Br zapping m inv

Channel Islands npl Isole fpl del Canale

channel-surf vi Am fare lo zapping

channel-surfing n Am zapping m inv

Channel Tunnel n tunnel m inv sotto la Manica

chant /tʃɑːnt/ **1** n cantilena f; (of demonstrators) slogan m inv di protesta
2 vt cantare; (demonstrators) gridare
3 vi (demonstrators) gridare slogan di protesta

chaos /ˈkeɪɒs/ n caos m

chaotic /keɪˈɒtɪk/ adj caotico

chap /tʃæp/ n fam tipo m

chapel /ˈtʃæpl/ n cappella f

chaperone, chaperon /ˈʃæpərəʊn/
1 n chaperon m inv
2 vt fare da chaperon a (somebody)

chaplain /ˈtʃæplɪn/ n cappellano m

chapped /tʃæpt/ adj (skin, lips) screpolato

chapter /ˈtʃæptə(r)/ n capitolo m

char[1] /tʃɑː(r)/ n fam donna f delle pulizie

char[2] vt (pt/pp **charred**) (burn) carbonizzare

character /ˈkærɪktə(r)/ n carattere m; (in novel, play) personaggio m; **that's out of ~** non è da te/lui; **quite a ~** fam un tipo particolare

character actor n caratterista mf

character assassination n denigrazione f

characteristic /kærəktəˈrɪstɪk/ **1** adj caratteristico
2 n caratteristica f

characteristically /kærəktəˈrɪstɪklɪ/ adv tipicamente

characterization /kærɪktəraɪˈzeɪʃn/ n caratterizzazione f

characterize /ˈkærɪktəraɪz/ vt caratterizzare

character reference n referenze fpl (relative al carattere)

charade /ʃəˈrɑːd/ n farsa f; **~s** sciarada fsg

charcoal /ˈtʃɑːkəʊl/ n carbonella f

charge /tʃɑːdʒ/ **1** n (cost) prezzo m; Electr, Mil carica f; Jur accusa f; **free of ~** gratuito; **be in ~** essere responsabile (**of** di); **take ~** assumersi la responsabilità; **take ~ of** occuparsi di
2 vt far pagare (free); far pagare a (person); Electr; Mil caricare; Jur accusare (**with** di); **~ somebody for something** far pagare qualcosa a qualcuno; **what do you ~?** quanto prende?; **~ it to my account** lo addebiti sul mio conto
3 vi (attack) caricare

charge account n (in store) apertura m di credito presso un negozio

charge card n (credit card) carta f di addebito; (store card) carta f di credito [di un negozio]

charged /tʃɑːdʒd/ adj Phys carico; **emotionally ~** (atmosphere) carico di emozione

chargé d'affaires /ʃɑːʒeɪdæˈfeə(r)/ n incaricato m d'affari

charge hand n caposquadra mf

charge nurse n caposala mf

char-grilled /-ˈɡrɪld/ adj alla brace

chariot /ˈtʃærɪət/ n cocchio m

charisma /kəˈrɪzmə/ n carisma m

charismatic /kærɪzˈmætɪk/ adj carismatico

charitable /ˈtʃærɪtəbl/ adj caritatevole; (kind) indulgente

charity /ˈtʃærɪtɪ/ n carità f; (organization) associazione f di beneficenza; **concert ···>**

given for ∼ concerto *m* di beneficenza;
live on ∼ vivere di elemosina

charity box *n* (in church) cassetta *f* delle
offerte

charity shop *n* negozio *m* dell'usato a
scopo di beneficenza

charity work *n* lavoro *m* volontario
(per beneficenza)

charlady /'tʃɑːleɪdɪ/ *n* Br donna *f* delle
pulizie

charlatan /'ʃɑːlətən/ *n* ciarlatano, -a *mf*

charm /tʃɑːm/ **1** *n* fascino *m*; (object)
ciondolo *m*
2 *vt* affascinare

charmer /'tʃɑːmə(r)/ *n* he's a real ∼ è
un vero seduttore

charming /'tʃɑːmɪŋ/ *adj* affascinante

charmingly /'tʃɑːmɪŋlɪ/ *adv* in modo
affascinante

charred /tʃɑːd/ *adj* carbonizzato

chart /tʃɑːt/ *n* carta *f* nautica; (table)
tabella *f*

charter /'tʃɑːtə(r)/ **1** *n* ∼ [flight] [volo
m] charter *m inv*
2 *vt* noleggiare

chartered accountant *n*
commercialista *mf*

chartered flight *n* Br volo *m* charter
inv

chartered surveyor *n* Br perito *m*
edile

charter plane *n* Br charter *m inv*

charwoman /'tʃɑːwʊmən/ *n* donna *f*
delle pulizie

chase /tʃeɪs/ **1** *n* inseguimento *m*; give
∼ mettersi all'inseguimento
2 *vt* inseguire
■ **chase away**, **chase off** *vt* cacciare
via
■ **chase up** *vt* fam cercare

chaser /'tʃeɪsə(r)/ *n* (fam: drink) liquore *m*
bevuto dopo la birra

chasm /'kæz(ə)m/ *n* abisso *m*

chassis /'ʃæsɪ/ *n* (pl **chassis** /'ʃæsɪz/)
telaio *m*

chaste /tʃeɪst/ *adj* casto

chasten /'tʃeɪs(ə)n/ *vt* castigare; they
looked suitably ∼ed avevano l'aria
mortificata

chastise /tʃæ'staɪz/ *vt* castigare

chastity /'tʃæstɪtɪ/ *n* castità *f*

chat /tʃæt/ **1** *n* chiacchierata *f*; have a
∼ with fare quattro chiacchiere con;
Comput chat *f inv*
2 *vi* (pt/pp **chatted**) chiacchierare;
Comput chattare
■ **chat up** *vt* abbordare

chatline *n* Teleph chat line *f inv*

chatroom *n* Comput chat room *f inv*

chat show *n* talk show *m inv*

chatshow host *n* presentatore, -trice
mf di talk show

chattel /'tʃæt(ə)l/ *n* Jur goods and ∼s
beni *mpl* mobili

chatter /'tʃætə(r)/ **1** *n* chiacchiere *fpl*
2 *vi* chiacchierare; ⟨teeth⟩ battere

chatterbox /'tʃætəbɒks/ *n* fam
chiacchierone, -a *mf*

chatty /'tʃætɪ/ *adj* (**-ier, -iest**)
chiacchierone; ⟨style⟩ familiare

chauffeur /'ʃəʊfə(r)/ *n* autista *mf*

chauvinism /'ʃəʊvɪnɪzm/ *n* sciovinismo
m

chauvinist /'ʃəʊvɪnɪst/ *n* sciovinista *mf*;
male ∼ fam maschilista *m*

cheap /tʃiːp/ **1** *adj* a buon mercato;
⟨rate⟩ economico; (vulgar) grossolano; (of
poor quality) scadente
2 *adv* a buon mercato

cheapen /'tʃiːp(ə)n/ *vt* ∼ oneself
screditarsi

cheaply /'tʃiːplɪ/ *adv* a buon mercato

cheap rate *adj* & *adv* Teleph a tariffa
ridotta

cheat /tʃiːt/ **1** *n* imbroglione, -a *mf*; (at
cards) baro *m*
2 *vt* imbrogliare; ∼ somebody out of
something sottrarre qualcosa a qualcuno
con l'inganno
3 *vi* imbrogliare; (at cards) barare
■ **cheat on** *vt* fam tradire ⟨wife⟩

Chechnya /tʃetʃ'njɑː/ *n* Cecenia *f*

check¹ /tʃek/ **1** *adj* ⟨pattern⟩ a quadri
2 *n* disegno *m* a quadri

check² **1** *n* verifica *f*; (of tickets) controllo
m; (in chess) scacco *m*; (Am: bill) conto *m*;
(Am: cheque) assegno *m*; (Am: tick) segnetto
m; keep a ∼ on controllare; keep in ∼
tenere sotto controllo
2 *vt* verificare; controllare ⟨tickets⟩;
(restrain) contenere; (stop) bloccare
3 *vi* controllare; ∼ on something
controllare qualcosa
■ **check in** **1** *vi* registrarsi all'arrivo
(in albergo); Aeron fare il check-in
2 *vt* registrare all'arrivo (in albergo)
■ **check off** *vt* spuntare ⟨item on list⟩
■ **check out** **1** *vi* (of hotel) saldare il
conto
2 *vt* (fam: investigate) controllare
■ **check up** *vi* accertarsi
■ **check up on** *vt* prendere
informazioni su

checked /tʃekt/ *adj* a quadri

checkbook *n* Am libretto *m* d'assegni

checkered /'tʃekəd/ *adj* Am ⟨cloth,
pattern⟩ a quadretti; ⟨career⟩ con alti e
bassi

checkers /'tʃekəz/ *n* Am dama *f*

check-in *n* accettazione *f*, check-in *m*
inv

check-in desk *n* banco *m* dell'accettazione, banco *m* del check-in

checking account /'tʃekɪŋ/ *n* Am conto *m* corrente

check-in time *n* check-in *m inv*

checklist *n* lista *f* di controllo

check mark *n* Am segnetto *m*

checkmate *int* scacco matto!

checkout *n* (in supermarket) cassa *f*

checkout assistant, **checkout operator** *n* Br cassiere, -a *mf*

checkpoint *n* posto *m* di blocco

checkroom *n* Am deposito *m* bagagli

check-up *n* Med visita *f* di controllo, check-up *m inv*

cheddar /'tʃedə(r)/ *n* formaggio *m* semi-stagionato

cheek /tʃiːk/ *n* guancia *f*; (impudence) sfacciataggine *f*

cheekbone /'tʃiːkbəʊn/ *n* zigomo *m*

cheekily /'tʃiːkɪlɪ/ *adv* sfacciatamente

cheeky /'tʃiːkɪ/ *adj* sfacciato

cheep /tʃiːp/ *vi* pigolare

cheer /tʃɪə(r)/ **①** *n* evviva *m inv*; **three ~s** tre urrà; **~s!** salute!; (goodbye) arrivederci; (thanks) grazie **②** *vt/i* acclamare ∎ **cheer up ①** *vt* tirare su [di morale] **②** *vi* tirarsi su [di morale]; **~ up!** su con la vita!

cheerful /'tʃɪəfʊl/ *adj* allegro

cheerfully /'tʃɪəfʊlɪ/ *adv* allegramente; **I could ~ strangle him!** lo strangolerei volentieri!

cheerfulness /'tʃɪəfʊlnɪs/ *n* allegria *f*

cheerily /'tʃɪərɪlɪ/ *adv* allegramente

cheering /'tʃɪərɪŋ/ *n* acclamazione *f*

cheerio /tʃɪərɪ'əʊ/ *int* fam arrivederci

cheerleader /'tʃɪəliːdə(r)/ *n* leader *mf* dei tifosi

cheerless /'tʃɪəlɪs/ *adj* triste, tetro

cheery /'tʃɪərɪ/ *adj* allegro

cheese /tʃiːz/ *n* formaggio *m* ∎ **cheese off** *vt* fam **be ~d off with one's job** essere stufo del proprio lavoro; **I'm really ~d off about it** ne ho le scatole piene

cheeseboard *n* (object) vassoio *m* dei formaggi; (selection) piatto *m* di formaggi

cheeseburger *n* cheeseburger *m inv*

cheesecake *n* dolce *m* al formaggio

cheesecloth *n* mussola *f*, tela *f* indiana

cheese counter *n* banco *m* dei formaggi

cheesy /'tʃiːzɪ/ *adj* (smell) di formaggio; (grin) smagliante

cheetah /'tʃiːtə/ *n* ghepardo *m*

chef /ʃef/ **①** *n* cuoco, -a *mf*, chef *m inv* **②** *vi* (pt/pp **cheffed**) fam fare lo chef

chemical /'kemɪkl/ **①** *adj* chimico **②** *n* prodotto *m* chimico

chemically /'kemɪklɪ/ *adv* chimicamente

chemise /ʃə'miːz/ *n* (undergarment) sottoveste *f inv*; (dress) chemisier *m inv*

chemist /'kemɪst/ *n* (pharmacist) farmacista *mf*; (scientist) chimico, -a *mf*

chemistry /'kemɪstrɪ/ *n* chimica *f*

chemist's [shop] *n* farmacia *f*

chemotherapy /kiːməʊ'θerəpɪ/ *n* chemioterapia *f*

cheque /tʃek/ *n* assegno *m*

chequebook /'tʃekbʊk/ *n* libretto *m* degli assegni

cheque card *n* carta *f* assegni

chequer /'tʃekə(r)/ *n* (square) scacco *m*; (pattern) motivo *m* a scacchi; (in game) pedina *f*

chequered /'tʃekəd/ *adj* (patterned) a scacchi; fig (career, history) movimentato

chequers /'tʃekəz/ *n* dama *f*

cherish /'tʃerɪʃ/ *vt* curare teneramente; (love) avere caro; nutrire (hope)

cherry /'tʃerɪ/ *n* ciliegia *f*; (tree) ciliegio *m*

cherry brandy *n* cherry-brandy *m inv*

cherry-pick *vt* scegliere accuratamente

cherry tree *n* ciliegio *m*

cherub /'tʃerəb/ *n* cherubino *m*

chervil /'tʃɜːvɪl/ *n* cerfoglio *m*

chess /tʃes/ *n* scacchi *mpl*

chessboard *n* scacchiera *f*

chessman *n* pezzo *m* degli scacchi

chessplayer *n* scacchista *mf*

chess set *n* scacchi *mpl*

chest /tʃest/ *n* petto *m*; (box) cassapanca *f*; **get something off one's ~** fig levarsi un peso [dallo stomaco]

chest freezer *n* freezer *m inv* orizzontale, congelatore *m* orizzontale

chestnut /'tʃesnʌt/ *n* castagna *f*; (tree) castagno *m*

chest of drawers *n* cassettone *m*, comò *m inv*

chesty /'tʃestɪ/ *adj* (person) che soffre di bronchite; (cough) bronchitico

chew /tʃuː/ *vt* masticare ∎ **chew over** *vt* (fam: think about carefully) rimuginare su

chewing gum /'tʃuːɪŋ/ *n* gomma *f* da masticare

chewy /'tʃuːɪ/ *adj* (meat) legnoso; (toffee) gommoso

chic /ʃiːk/ *adj* chic *inv*

chick /tʃɪk/ *n* pulcino *m*; (fam: girl) ragazza *f*

chicken /'tʃɪkn/ **①** *n* pollo *m* **②** *attrib* (soup, casserole) di pollo

3 *adj fam* fifone
■ **chicken out** *vi fam* he ∼ed out gli è venuta fifa

chicken breast *n* petto *m* di pollo

chicken curry *n* pollo *m* al curry

chicken feed *n* mangime *m* per i polli; (fam: paltry sum) miseria *f*

chicken livers *npl* fegatini *mpl* di pollo

chicken noodle soup *n* vermicelli *mpl* in brodo di pollo

chickenpox *n* varicella *f*

chicken wire *n* rete *f* metallica (a maglia esagonale)

chick flick *n fam* film *m inv* mirato ad un pubblico femminile

chick lit *n fam* romanzi *mpl* mirati ad un pubblico femminile

chickpea /'tʃɪkpiː/ *n* cece *m*

chicory /'tʃɪkərɪ/ *n* cicoria *f*

chief /tʃiːf/ **1** *adj* principale
2 *n* capo *m*

chief executive *n* direttore, -trice *mf* generale

chief executive officer *n* direttore, -trice *mf* generale

chief inspector *n* (Br: of police) ispettore *m* capo

chiefly /'tʃiːflɪ/ *adv* principalmente

chief of police *n* capo *m* della polizia

Chief of Staff *n* Mil capo *m* di stato maggiore; (of the White House) segretario *m* generale

chief superintendent *n* (Br: of police) commissario *m* capo

chiffon /'ʃɪfɒn/ **1** *n* chiffon *m*
2 *adj* ⟨dress, scarf⟩ di chiffon

chilblain /'tʃɪlbleɪn/ *n* gelone *m*

child /tʃaɪld/ *n* (pl ∼ren) bambino, -a *mf*; (son/daughter) figlio, -a *mf*

child abuse *n* violenza *f* sui minori; (sexual) violenza *f* sessuale sui minori

childbearing *n* gravidanza *f*; **of** ∼ **age** in età feconda

child benefit *n* Br assegni *mpl* familiari

childbirth *n* parto *m*

childcare *n* (bringing up children) educazione *f* dei bambini; (nurseries etc) strutture *fpl* di assistenza ai bambini

childhood /'tʃaɪldhʊd/ *n* infanzia *f*

childish /'tʃaɪldɪʃ/ *adj* infantile

childishness /'tʃaɪldɪʃnɪs/ *n* puerilità *f*

childless /'tʃaɪldlɪs/ *adj* senza figli

childlike /'tʃaɪldlaɪk/ *adj* ingenuo

child-minder *n* baby-sitter *mf inv*

child molester *n* molestatore, -trice *mf* di bambini

child prodigy *n* bambino prodigio

child-proof *adj* ⟨container⟩ a prova di bambino; ∼ **lock** sicura *f* a prova di bambino

children /'tʃɪldrən/ *npl* ▶ CHILD

children's home *n* istituto *m* per l'infanzia

child seat *n* seggiolino *m* per bambini

Chile /'tʃɪlɪ/ *n* Cile *m*

Chilean /'tʃɪlɪən/ *adj & n* cileno, -a *mf*

chill /tʃɪl/ **1** *n* freddo *m*; (illness) infreddatura *f*
2 *vt* raffreddare
■ **chill out** *vi* (relax) rilassarsi

chilli /'tʃɪlɪ/ *n* (pl -es) ∼ **[pepper]** peperoncino *m*

chilly /'tʃɪlɪ/ *adj* freddo

chime /tʃaɪm/ *vi* suonare

chimney /'tʃɪmnɪ/ *n* camino *m*

chimneybreast *n* bocca *f* del camino

chimney-pot *n* comignolo *m*

chimney-sweep *n* spazzacamino *m*

chimp /tʃɪmp/ *n fam* scimpanzé *m*

chimpanzee /'tʃɪmpæn'ziː/ *n* scimpanzé *m inv*

chin /tʃɪn/ *n* mento *m*

China /'tʃaɪnə/ *n* Cina *f*

china *n* porcellana *f*

China Sea *n* Mar *m* Cinese

Chinatown *n* quartiere *m* cinese

Chinese /tʃaɪ'niːz/ *adj & n* cinese *mf*; (language) cinese *m*; **the** ∼ *pl* i cinesi

Chinese lantern *n* lanterna *f* cinese

chink[1] /tʃɪŋk/ *n* (slit) fessura *f*

chink[2] **1** *n* (noise) tintinnio *m*
2 *vi* tintinnare

chinos /'tʃiːnəʊz/ *npl* pantaloni *mpl* cachi di cotone

chintz /tʃɪnts/ *n* chintz *m inv*

chip /tʃɪp/ **1** *n* (fragment) scheggia *f*; (in china, paintwork) scheggiatura *f*; Comput chip *m inv*; (in gambling) fiche *f inv*; ∼**s** *pl* Br Culin patatine *fpl* fritte; Am Culin patatine *fpl*; **have a** ∼ **on one's shoulder** avere un complesso di inferiorità
2 *vt* (pt/pp **chipped**) (damage) scheggiare
■ **chip in** *fam vi* intromettersi; (with money) contribuire

chip and PIN *n* sistema *m* di pagamento con carta di credito in cui il possessore della carta deve digitare il proprio PIN invece che apporre una firma

chipboard /'tʃɪpbɔːd/ *n* truciolato *m*

chipmunk /'tʃɪpmʌŋk/ *n* tamia *m inv*

chip pan *n* friggitrice *f*

chipped /tʃɪpt/ *adj* (damaged) scheggiato

chippings /'tʃɪpɪŋz/ *npl* (on road) breccia *f*; 'loose ∼' 'attenzione: breccia'

chippy /'tʃɪpɪ/ *n* (Br fam: chip shop) negozio *m* di fish and chips

chip shop *n* Br negozio *m* di fish and chips

chiropodist /kɪˈrɒpədɪst/ *n* podiatra *mf inv*

chiropody /kɪˈrɒpədɪ/ *n* podiatria *f*

chiropractor /ˈkaɪərəʊpræktə(r)/ *n* chiropratico, -a *mf*

chirp /tʃɜːp/ *vi* cinguettare; ‹cricket› fare cri cri

chirpy /ˈtʃɜːpɪ/ *adj* fam pimpante

chisel /ˈtʃɪzl/ ➊ *n* scalpello *m*
➋ *vt* (pt/pp **chiselled**) scalpellare

chit /tʃɪt/ *n* bigliettino *m*

chitchat /ˈtʃɪ(t)tʃæt/ *n* fam chiacchiere *fpl*; **spend one's time in idle ∼** fam perdere tempo in chiacchiere

chivalrous /ˈʃɪvlrəs/ *adj* cavalleresco

chivalrously /ˈʃɪvlrəslɪ/ *adv* con cavalleria

chivalry /ˈʃɪvlrɪ/ *n* cavalleria *f*

chives /tʃaɪvz/ *npl* erba *f* cipollina

chlorine /ˈklɔːriːn/ *n* cloro *m*

chlorofluorocarbon /klɔːrəʊfluərəʊˈkɑːb(ə)n/ *n* clorofluorocarburo *m*

chloroform /ˈklɒrəfɔːm/ *n* cloroformio *m*

chlorophyll /ˈklɒrəfɪl/ *n* clorofilla *f*

choc ice /ˈtʃɒk aɪs/ *n* Br gelato *m* ricoperto di cioccolato

chock /tʃɒk/ *n* zeppa *f*

chock-a-block /tʃɒkəˈblɒk/, **chock-full** /tʃɒkˈfʊl/ *adj* pieno zeppo

chocolate /ˈtʃɒkələt/ *n* cioccolato *m*; (drink) cioccolata *f*; **a ∼** un cioccolatino

choice /tʃɔɪs/ ➊ *n* scelta *f*
➋ *adj* scelto

choir /ˈkwaɪə(r)/ *n* coro *m*

choirboy /ˈkwaɪəbɔɪ/ *n* corista *m*

choirgirl /ˈkwaɪəgɜːl/ *n* corista *f*

choke /tʃəʊk/ ➊ *n* Auto aria *f*
➋ *vt/i* soffocare; **I ∼d on a fishbone** mi è rimasta in gola una lisca
■ **choke back** *vt* soffocare ‹tears, sob›

choker /ˈtʃəʊkə(r)/ *n* girocollo *m*

cholera /ˈkɒlərə/ *n* colera *m*

cholesterol /kəˈlestərɒl/ *n* colesterolo *m*

chomp /tʃɒmp/ *v*
■ **chomp on** *vt* fam masticare rumorosamente

choose /tʃuːz/ *vt/i* (pt **chose**, pp **chosen**) scegliere; **∼ to do something** scegliere di fare qualcosa; **as you ∼** come vuoi

choos[e]y /ˈtʃuːzɪ/ *adj* fam difficile

chop /tʃɒp/ ➊ *n* (blow) colpo *m* (d'ascia); Culin costata *f*; **get the ∼** fam ‹employee› essere licenziato; ‹project› essere bocciato
➋ *vt* (pt/pp **chopped**) tagliare

■ **chop down** *vt* abbattere ‹tree›
■ **chop off** *vt* spaccare

chopper /ˈtʃɒpə(r)/ *n* accetta *f*; fam elicottero *m*

chopping block *n* ceppo *m*; **put one's head on the ∼ ∼** fig esporsi a rischi

chopping board *n* tagliere *m*

chopping knife *n* coltello *m*

choppy /ˈtʃɒpɪ/ *adj* increspato

chopsticks /ˈtʃɒpstɪks/ *npl* bastoncini *mpl* cinesi

choral /ˈkɔːrəl/ *adj* corale; **∼ society** coro *m*

chord /kɔːd/ *n* Mus corda *f*

chore /tʃɔː(r)/ *n* corvè *f inv*; [household] **∼s** faccende *fpl* domestiche

choreograph /ˈkɒrɪəɡrɑːf/ *vt* coreografare

choreographer /kɒrɪˈɒɡrəfə(r)/ *n* coreografo, -a *mf*

choreography /kɒrɪˈɒɡrəfɪ/ *n* coreografia *f*

chorister /ˈkɒrɪstə(r)/ *n* corista *mf*

chortle /ˈtʃɔːtl/ *vi* ridacchiare

chorus /ˈkɔːrəs/ *n* coro *m*; (of song) ritornello *m*

chorus girl *n* ballerina *f* di varietà

chose, chosen /tʃəʊz/, /ˈtʃəʊzn/
▶ CHOOSE

chowder /ˈtʃaʊdə(r)/ *n* zuppa *m* di pesce

chow mein /tʃaʊˈmeɪn/ *n* piatto *m* cinese di spaghettini fritti con gamberetti, ecc. e verdure

Christ /kraɪst/ *n* Cristo *m*; **∼ Almighty!** fam porca miseria!

christen /ˈkrɪs(ə)n/ *vt* battezzare

christening /ˈkrɪsnɪŋ/ *n* battesimo *m*

Christian /ˈkrɪstʃən/ *adj* & *n* cristiano, -a *mf*

Christianity /krɪstɪˈænətɪ/ *n* cristianesimo *m*

Christian name *n* nome *m* di battesimo

Christmas /ˈkrɪsməs/ ➊ *n* Natale *m*
➋ *attrib* di Natale

Christmas box *n* Br mancia *f* natalizia

Christmas card *n* biglietto *m* d'auguri di Natale

Christmas carol *n* canto *m* natalizio, canto *m* di Natale

Christmas cracker *n* tubo *m* di cartone colorato contenente una sorpresa

Christmas Day *n* il giorno di Natale

Christmas Eve *n* la vigilia di Natale

Christmas present *n* regalo *m* di Natale

Christmas stocking *n* calza *f* (per i doni di Babbo Natale)

Christmas tree *n* albero *m* di Natale

chrome /krəʊm/ *n*, **chromium** /'krəʊmɪəm/ *n* cromo *m*

chromium-plated /-'pleɪtɪd/ *adj* cromato

chromosome /'krəʊməsəʊm/ *n* cromosoma *m*

chronic /'krɒnɪk/ *adj* cronico

chronicle /'krɒnɪkl/ *n* cronaca *f*

chronological /krɒnə'lɒdʒɪkl/ *adj* cronologico

chronologically /krɒnə'lɒdʒɪklɪ/ *adv* ⟨ordered⟩ in ordine cronologico

chrysalis /'krɪsəlɪs/ *n* crisalide *f*

chrysanthemum /krɪ'sænθəməm/ *n* crisantemo *m*

chubby /'tʃʌbɪ/ *adj* (**-ier, -iest**) paffuto

chuck /tʃʌk/ *vt* fam buttare
■ **chuck in** *vt* fam mollare ⟨job, boyfriend⟩
■ **chuck out** *vt* fam buttare via ⟨object⟩; buttare fuori ⟨person⟩
■ **chuck up** *vt* fam = CHUCK in

chuckle /'tʃʌk(ə)l/ *vi* ridacchiare

chuffed /tʃʌft/ *adj* fam felice come una Pasqua

chug /tʃʌg/ *vi* **the train ~ged into/out of the station** il treno è entrato nella/uscito dalla stazione sbuffando

chum /tʃʌm/ *n* fam amico, -a *mf*

chummy /'tʃʌmɪ/ *adj* fam **be ~ with** essere amico di

chump /tʃʌmp/ *n* fam zuccone *m*, -a *f*; Culin braciola *f*

chunk /tʃʌŋk/ *n* grosso pezzo *m*

chunky /'tʃʌŋkɪ/ *adj* ⟨sweater⟩ di lana grossa; ⟨jewellery⟩ massiccio; fam ⟨person⟩ tarchiato

Chunnel /'tʃʌnl/ *n* Br fam tunnel *m inv* sotto la Manica

church /tʃɜːtʃ/ *n* chiesa *f*

churchgoer *n* praticante *mf*

church hall *n* sala *f* parrocchiale

churchyard /'tʃɜːtʃjɑːd/ *n* cimitero *m*

churlish /'tʃɜːlɪʃ/ *adj* sgarbato

churn /tʃɜːn/ ① *n* zangola *f*; (for milk) bidone *m*
② *vt* fare ⟨butter⟩; far rivoltare ⟨stomach⟩
■ **churn out** *vt* sfornare ⟨novels, products⟩
■ **churn up** *vt* agitare ⟨water⟩

chute /ʃuːt/ *n* scivolo *m*; (for rubbish) canale *m* di scarico

chutney /'tʃʌtnɪ/ *n* salsa *f* piccante a base di frutti e spezie

CIA *n abbr* Am (**Central Intelligence Agency**) CIA *f*

cicada /sɪ'kɑːdə/ *n* cicala *f*

CID *abbr* **Criminal Investigation Department**

cider /'saɪdə(r)/ *n* sidro *m*

cigar /sɪ'gɑː(r)/ *n* sigaro *m*

cigarette /sɪgə'ret/ *n* sigaretta *f*

cigarette butt, **cigarette end** *n* cicca *f*, mozzicone *m* di sigaretta

cigarette lighter *n* accendino *m*

cinch /sɪntʃ/ *n* fam **it's a ~** è un gioco da ragazzi

cinder /'sɪndə(r)/ *n* (glowing) brace *f*; **burn something to a ~** carbonizzare qualcosa

Cinderella /sɪndə'relə/ *n* Cenerentola *f*

cinder track *n* pista *f* di cenere

cine-camera /'sɪnɪ-/ *n* cinepresa *f*

cine-film *n* filmino *m* a passo ridotto

cinema /'sɪnɪmə/ *n* cinema *m inv*

cinema complex *n* cinema *m inv* multisale

cinemagoer /'sɪnɪməgəʊə(r)/ *n* (spectator) spettatore, -trice *mf*; (regular) cinefilo, -a *mf*

cinematography /sɪnəmə'tɒgrəfɪ/ *n* cinematografia *f*

cinnamon /'sɪnəmən/ *n* cannella *f*

cipher /'saɪfə(r)/ *n* (code) cifre *fpl*; fig nullità *f inv*

circa /'sɜːkə/ *prep* circa

circle /'sɜːkl/ ① *n* cerchio *m*; Theat galleria *f*; **in a ~** in cerchio
② *vt* girare intorno a; cerchiare ⟨mistake⟩
③ *vi* descrivere dei cerchi

circuit /'sɜːkɪt/ *n* circuito *m*; (lap) giro *m*

circuit board *n* circuito *m* stampato

circuit breaker *n* salvavita *m*

circuitous /sə'kjuːɪtəs/ *adj* **~ route** percorso *m* lungo e indiretto

circular /'sɜːkjʊlə(r)/ *adj* & *n* circolare *f*; **~ letter** *n* circolare *f*

circular saw *n* sega *f* circolare

circulate /'sɜːkjʊleɪt/ ① *vt* far circolare
② *vi* circolare

circulation /sɜːkjʊ'leɪʃn/ *n* circolazione *f*; (of newspaper) tiratura *f*

circulatory /sɜːkjʊ'leɪtərɪ/ *adj* Med circolatorio

circumcise /'sɜːkəmsaɪz/ *vt* circoncidere

circumcision /sɜːkəm'sɪʒn/ *n* circoncisione *f*

circumference /sə'kʌmfərəns/ *n* circonferenza *f*

circumflex /'sɜːkəmfleks/ *n* accento *m* circonflesso

circumnavigate /sɜːkəm'nævɪgeɪt/ *vt* doppiare ⟨cape⟩; circumnavigare ⟨world⟩

circumnavigation /sɜːkəmnævɪ'geɪʃn/ *n* circumnavigazione *f*

circumspect /'sɜːkəmspekt/ *adj* circospetto

circumspectly /'sɜːkəmspektlɪ/ *adv* in modo circospetto

circumstance /'sɜːkəmstəns/ n
circostanza f; ~s pl (financial) condizioni
fpl finanziarie

circumstantial /sɜːkəm'stænʃl/ adj Jur
⟨evidence⟩ indiziario; (detailed)
circostanziato

circus /'sɜːkəs/ n circo m

cirrhosis /sɪ'rəʊsɪs/ n cirrosi f inv

CIS abbr (**Commonwealth of
Independent States**) CSI f

cistern /'sɪstən/ n (tank) cisterna f; (of WC)
serbatoio m

citadel /'sɪtədel/ n cittadella f

cite /saɪt/ vt citare

citizen /'sɪtɪzn/ n cittadino, -a mf; (of
town) abitante mf

Citizens' Advice Bureau n ufficio m
di consulenza legale gratuita per i
cittadini

citizen's arrest n arresto m effettuato
da un privato cittadino

citizens' band n Radio banda f
cittadina

citizenship /'sɪtɪznʃɪp/ n cittadinanza f

citric acid /sɪtrɪk'æsɪd/ acido m citrico

citrus /'sɪtrəs/ n ~ **[fruit]** agrume m

city /'sɪtɪ/ n città f inv; **the C~** la City [di
Londra]

city centre n Br centro m [della città]

city slicker n fam cittadino m
sofisticato

civic /'sɪvɪk/ ① adj civico
② ~s npl educazione fsg civica

civic centre n centro m municipale

civil /'ʃɪvl/ a civile

civil engineer n ingegnere m civile

civil engineering n ingegneria f civile

civilian /sɪ'vɪljən/ ① adj civile; **in ~
clothes** in borghese
② n civile mf

civility /sɪ'vɪlətɪ/ n cortesia f

civilization /sɪvɪlaɪ'zeɪʃn/ n civiltà f inv

civilize /'sɪvɪlaɪz/ vt civilizzare

civilized /'sɪvɪlaɪzd/ adj ⟨country⟩
civilizzato; ⟨person, behaviour⟩ civile;
become ~ civilizzarsi

civil law n diritto m civile

civil liability n Jur responsabilità f inv
civile

civil liberty n libertà f inv civile

civilly /'sɪvɪlɪ/ adv civilmente

civil rights npl ① diritti mpl civili
② attrib ⟨march, activist⟩ per i diritti
civili

civil servant n impiegato, -a mf statale

Civil Service n pubblica
amministrazione f

civil war n guerra f civile

civil wedding n matrimonio m civile

civvies /'sɪvɪz/ npl fam **in ~** in borghese

CJD n abbr (**Creutzfeldt-Jakob
disease**) morbo m di Creutzfeldt Jakob

cl abbr (**centilitre(s)**) cl

clad /klæd/ adj vestito (**in** di)

cladding /'klædɪŋ/ n rivestimento m

claim /kleɪm/ ① n richiesta f; (right)
diritto m; (assertion) dichiarazione f; **lay ~
to something** rivendicare qualcosa
② vt richiedere; reclamare ⟨lost property⟩;
rivendicare ⟨ownership⟩; ~ **that** sostenere
che
■ **claim back** vt reclamare ⟨money⟩

claimant /'kleɪmənt/ n richiedente mf;
(to throne) pretendente mf

claim form n modulo m di richiesta

clairvoyant /kleə'vɔɪənt/ n
chiaroveggente mf

clam /klæm/ n Culin vongola f
■ **clam up** vi zittirsi

clamber /'klæmbə(r)/ vi arrampicarsi

clammy /'klæmɪ/ adj (-ier, -iest)
appiccicaticcio

clamour /'klæmə(r)/ ① n (noise) clamore
m; (protest) rimostranza f
② vi ~ **for** chiedere a gran voce

clamp /klæmp/ ① n morsa f
② vt ammorsare; Auto mettere i ceppi
bloccaruote a
■ **clamp down** vi fam essere duro
■ **clamp down on** vt reprimere

clampdown n fig giro m di vite

clan /klæn/ n clan m inv

clandestine /klæn'destɪn/ adj
clandestino

clang /klæŋ/ n suono m metallico

clanger /'klæŋə(r)/ n fam gaffe f inv

clank /klæŋk/ ① n rumore m metallico
② vi fare un rumore metallico

clannish /'klænɪʃ/ adj pej ⟨family,
profession⟩ chiuso

clap /klæp/ ① n **give somebody a ~**
applaudire qualcuno; ~ **of thunder** tuono
m
② vt/i (pt/pp **clapped**) applaudire; ~
one's hands applaudire

clapboard /'klæpbɔːd/ ① n Am
rivestimento m di legno
② attrib Am rivestito di legno

clapped out /klæpt/ adj fam (past it)
sfinito; (exhausted) stanco morto; ⟨car,
machine⟩ scassato

clapping /'klæpɪŋ/ n applausi mpl

claptrap /'klæptræp/ n fam sciocchezze
fpl

claret /'klærət/ n claret m inv

clarification /klærɪfɪ'keɪʃn/ n
chiarimento m

clarify /'klærɪfaɪ/ vt/i (pt/pp **-ied**)
chiarire

clarinet /klærɪ'net/ n clarinetto m

clarinettist /klærɪ'netɪst/ n
clarinettista mf

clarity /'klærətɪ/ n chiarezza f

clash /klæʃ/ ① n scontro m; (noise)
fragore m
② vi scontrarsi; ⟨colours⟩ stonare;
⟨events⟩ coincidere

clasp /klɑːsp/ ① n chiusura f
② vt agganciare; (hold) stringere

class /klɑːs/ ① n classe f; (lesson) corso m
② vt classificare

class-conscious adj classista

class-consciousness n classismo m

classic /'klæsɪk/ ① adj classico
② n classico m; ~s pl Univ lettere fpl
classiche

classical /'klæsɪk(ə)l/ adj classico

classification /klæsɪfɪ'keɪʃn/ n
classificazione f

classified adj (secret) riservato

classified ad /klæsɪfaɪd'æd/ n
annuncio m

classified section n pagina f degli
annunci

classify /'klæsɪfaɪ/ vt (pt/pp -led)
classificare

classmate n compagno, -a mf di classe

classroom n aula f

class system n sistema m classista

classy /'klɑːsɪ/ adj (-ier, -iest) fam d'alta
classe

clatter /'klætə(r)/ ① n fracasso m
② vi far fracasso

clause /klɔːz/ n clausola f; Gram
proposizione f

claustrophobia /klɒstrə'fəʊbɪə/ n
claustrofobia f

claustrophobic /klɒstrə'fəʊbɪk/ adj
claustrofobico

clavichord /klævɪkɔːd/ n clavicordo m

clavicle /'klævɪkl/ n clavicola f

claw /klɔː/ ① n artiglio m; (of crab, lobster
& Techn) tenaglia f
② vt ⟨cat⟩ graffiare

clay /kleɪ/ n argilla f

clayey /'kleɪɪ/ adj ⟨soil⟩ argilloso

clay pigeon shooting n tiro m al
piattello

clean /kliːn/ ① adj pulito, lindo
② adv completamente
③ vt pulire ⟨shoes, windows⟩; ~ one's
teeth lavarsi i denti; have a coat ~ed
portare un cappotto in lavanderia
■ **clean out** vt ripulire ⟨room⟩; be ~ed
out (fig: have no money) essere senza un
soldo
■ **clean up** ① vt pulire
② vi far pulizia

clean-cut adj ⟨image, person⟩
rispettabile

cleaner /'kliːnə(r)/ n uomo m, donna f
delle pulizie; (substance) detersivo m; **[dry]**
~'s lavanderia f, tintoria f

cleaning /'kliːnɪŋ/ n pulizia f; **do the** ~
fare le pulizie

cleaning lady n donna f delle pulizie

cleaning product n detergente m

cleanliness /'klenlɪnɪs/ n pulizia f

clean-living /-'lɪvɪŋ/ ① n vita f integra
② adj ⟨person⟩ integro

cleanse /klenz/ vt pulire

cleanser /'klenzə(r)/ n detergente m

clean-shaven /-'ʃeɪvən/ adj sbarbato

clean sheet n start with a ~ ~ fig
voltare pagina

cleansing cream /'klenzɪŋ/ n latte m
detergente

clear /klɪə(r)/ ① adj chiaro; ⟨conscience⟩
pulito; ⟨road⟩ libero; ⟨profit, advantage,
majority⟩ netto; ⟨sky⟩ sereno; ⟨water⟩
limpido; ⟨glass⟩ trasparente; **make
something** ~ mettere qualcosa in chiaro;
have I made myself ~? mi sono fatto
capire?; **I'm not** ~ about what I have to do
non mi è ben chiaro quello che devo fare;
five ~ **days** cinque giorni buoni; **be in the**
~ essere a posto
② adv stand ~ of allontanarsi da; keep ~
of tenersi alla larga da
③ vt sgombrare ⟨room, street⟩;
sparecchiare ⟨table⟩; (acquit) scagionare;
(authorize) autorizzare; scavalcare senza
toccare ⟨fence, wall⟩; guadagnare ⟨sum of
money⟩; passare ⟨Customs⟩; ~ one's throat
schiarirsi la gola
④ vi ⟨face, sky⟩ rasserenarsi; ⟨fog⟩
dissiparsi
■ **clear away** vt metter via
■ **clear off** vi fam filar via
■ **clear out** ① vt sgombrare
② vi fam filar via
■ **clear up** ① vt (tidy) mettere a posto;
chiarire ⟨mystery⟩
② vi ⟨weather⟩ schiarirsi

clearance /'klɪərəns/ n (space) spazio m
libero; (authorization) autorizzazione f;
(Customs) sdoganamento m

clearance sale n liquidazione f

clear-cut adj ⟨plan, division⟩ ben
definito; ⟨problem, rule⟩ chiaro;
⟨difference, outline⟩ netto; **the matter is not
so** ~ la faccenda non è così semplice

clear-headed /-'hedɪd/ adj lucido

clearing /'klɪərɪŋ/ n radura f

clearly /'klɪəlɪ/ adv chiaramente

clear-out n ripulita f

clear-sighted /-'saɪtɪd/ adj perspicace

clearway /'klɪəweɪ/ n Auto strada f con
divieto di sosta

cleavage /'kliːvɪdʒ/ n (woman's) décolleté
m inv

cleave /kliːv/ vt spaccare

cleaver /'kliːvə(r)/ *n* mannaia *f*

clef /klef/ *n* Mus chiave *f*

cleft /kleft/ *n* fenditura *f*

clemency /'klemənsɪ/ *n* clemenza *f*

clement /'klemənt/ *adj* clemente

clench /klentʃ/ *vt* serrare

clergy /'klɜːdʒɪ/ *npl* clero *m*

clergyman /'klɜːdʒɪmən/ *n* ecclesiastico *m*

cleric /'klerɪk/ *n* ecclesiastico *m*

clerical /'klerɪkl/ *adj* impiegatizio; Relig clericale

clerical assistant *n* impiegato, -a *mf*

clerk /klɑːk/, Am /klɜːk/ *n* impiegato, -a *mf*; (Am: shop assistant) commesso, -a *mf*

clever /'klevə(r)/ *adj* intelligente; (skilful) abile

cleverly /'klevəlɪ/ *adv* intelligentemente; (skilfully) abilmente

cliché /'kliːʃeɪ/ *n* cliché *m inv*

clichéd /'kliːʃeɪd/ *adj* (idea, technique) convenzionale; (art, music) stereotipato; ~ **expression** frase *f* fatta

click /klɪk/ **1** *vi* scattare; (Comput: with mouse) cliccare
2 *n* (Comput: with mouse) clic *m inv*
■ **click on** *vt* Comput cliccare su

client /'klaɪənt/ *n* cliente *mf*

clientele /kliːɒn'tel/ *n* clientela *f*

cliff /klɪf/ *n* scogliera *f*

cliffhanger /'klɪfhæŋə(r)/ *n* **it was a real** ~ ci ha lasciato in sospeso

climate /'klaɪmət/ *n* clima *f*

climate change *n* cambiamento *m* climatico

climatic /klaɪ'mætɪk/ *adj* climatico

climax /'klaɪmæks/ *n* punto *m* culminante

climb /klaɪm/ **1** *n* salita *f*
2 *vt* scalare (mountain); arrampicarsi su (ladder, tree)
3 *vi* arrampicarsi; (rise) salire; (road) salire
■ **climb down** *vi* scendere; (from ladder, tree) scendere; fig tornare sui propri passi
■ **climb over** *vt* scavalcare (fence, wall)
■ **climb up** *vt* salire su (hill)

climber /'klaɪmə(r)/ *n* alpinista *mf*; (plant) rampicante *m*

climbing /'klaɪmɪŋ/ *adj* rampicante

climbing boot *n* scarpone *m* da alpinismo

climbing frame *n* struttura *f* su cui possono arrampicarsi i bambini

clinch /klɪntʃ/ **1** *vt* fam concludere (deal)
2 *n* (in boxing) clinch *m inv*

clincher /'klɪntʃə(r)/ *n* (fam: act, remark) fattore *m* decisivo; (argument) argomento *m* decisivo

cling /klɪŋ/ *vi* (pt/pp **clung**) aggrapparsi; (stick) aderire

cling film *n* pellicola *f* trasparente

clingy /'klɪŋɪ/ *adj* (dress) attillato; (person) appiccicoso

clinic /'klɪnɪk/ *n* ambulatorio *m*

clinical /'klɪnɪkl/ *adj* clinico

clinically /'klɪnɪklɪ/ *adv* clinicamente

clink /klɪŋk/ **1** *n* tintinnio *m*; (fam: prison) galera *f*
2 *vi* tintinnare

clip[1] /klɪp/ **1** *n* fermaglio *m*; (jewellery) spilla *f*
2 *vt* (pt/pp **clipped**) attaccare

clip[2] **1** *n* (extract) taglio *m*
2 *vt* obliterare (ticket)

clipart *n* clip art *f inv*

clipboard *n* fermablocco *m*

clip-clop /'klɪpklɒp/ *n* rumore *m* fatto dagli zoccoli dei cavalli

clip-on *adj* (bow tie) con la clip

clip-on microphone *n* microfono *m* con la clip

clip-ons *npl* (earrings) orecchini *mpl* con le clip

clippers /'klɪpəz/ *npl* (for hair) rasoio *m*; (for hedge) tosasiepi *m inv*; (for nails) tronchesina *f*

clipping /'klɪpɪŋ/ *n* (from newspaper) ritaglio *m*

clique /kliːk/ *n* cricca *f*

cliquey, **cliquish** /'kliːkɪ/, /'kliːkɪʃ/ *adj* (atmosphere) esclusivo; (profession, group) chiuso

cloak /kləʊk/ *n* mantello *m*

cloak-and-dagger *adj* (film) d'avventura; (surreptitious) clandestino

cloakroom *n* guardaroba *m inv*; (toilet) bagno *m*

cloakroom attendant *n* (Br: at toilets) addetto, -a *mf* ai bagni; (in hotel) guardarobiere, -a *mf*

cloakroom ticket *n* scontrino *m* del guardaroba

clobber /'klɒbə(r)/ **1** *n* fam armamentario *m*
2 *vt* (fam: hit) colpire; (defeat) stracciare

cloche /klɒʃ/ *n* (in garden) campana *f* di vetro

cloche hat *n* cloche *f inv*

clock /klɒk/ *n* orologio *m*; (fam: speedometer) tachimetro *m*
■ **clock in**, **clock on** *vi* attaccare
■ **clock out**, **clock off** *vi* staccare

clock face *n* quadrante *m*

clockmaker *n* orologiaio, -a *mf*

clock radio *n* radiosveglia *f*

clock speed *n* Comput velocità *f* di clock

clock tower *n* torre *f* dell'orologio

clock-watch vi guardare
continuamente l'orologio

clockwise adj & adv in senso orario

clockwork n ① meccanismo m; like ~
fam alla perfezione
② attrib a molla

clod /klɒd/ n zolla f

clog /klɒg/ ① n zoccolo m
② vt (pt/pp **clogged**) ~ [up] intasare
⟨drain⟩; inceppare ⟨mechanism⟩
③ vi ⟨drain⟩ intasarsi

cloister /'klɔɪstə(r)/ n chiostro m

clone /kləʊn/ ① n Biol, Comput, fig clone m
② vt clonare

cloning /'kləʊnɪŋ/ n clonazione f

close¹ /kləʊs/ ① adj vicino; ⟨friend⟩
intimo; ⟨weather⟩ afoso; have a ~ shave
fam scamparla bella; be ~ to somebody
essere unito a qualcuno
② adv vicino; ~ by vicino; it's ~ on five
o'clock sono quasi le cinque

close² /kləʊz/ ① n fine f; draw to a ~
concludere
② vt chiudere
③ vi chiudersi; ⟨shop⟩ chiudere
■ **close down** ① vt chiudere
② vi ⟨TV station⟩ interrompere la
trasmissione; ⟨factory⟩ chiudere
■ **close in** vi ⟨mist⟩ calare; ⟨enemy⟩
avvicinarsi da ogni lato
■ **close up** ① vi (come closer together)
stringersi; ⟨shop⟩ chiudere
② vt (bring closer together) avvicinare;
chiudere ⟨shop⟩

close combat n corpo a corpo m inv

close-cropped /-'krɒpt/ adj ⟨hair⟩
rasato

closed-circuit television
/kləʊzdsɜːkɪt-telɪ'vɪʒən/ n televisione f a
circuito chiuso

closed shop /kləʊzd'ʃɒp/ n azienda f
che assume solo personale aderente ad un
dato sindacato

close-fitting /kləʊs'fɪtɪŋ/ adj ⟨garment⟩
attillato

close-knit /kləʊs'nɪt/ adj fig ⟨family,
group⟩ affiatato

closely /'kləʊslɪ/ adv da vicino; ⟨watch,
listen⟩ attentamente

close-run adj ⟨race, competition⟩
combattutissimo

close season /kləʊs/ n stagione f di
chiusura della caccia e della pesca

closet /'klɒzɪt/ n Am armadio m

close-up /'kləʊs-/ n primo piano m

closing /'kləʊzɪŋ/ adj ⟨stages, minutes,
words, scene⟩ ultimo

closing date n data f di scadenza

closing-down sale n liquidazione f
totale [per cessata attività]

closing time n orario m di chiusura

closure /'kləʊʒə(r)/ n chiusura f

clot /klɒt/ ① n grumo m; (fam: idiot) tonto,
-a mf
② vi (pt/pp **clotted**) ⟨blood⟩ coagularsi

cloth /klɒθ/ n (fabric) tessuto m; (duster etc)
straccio m

clothe /kləʊð/ vt vestire

clothes /kləʊðz/ npl vestiti mpl, abiti
mpl

clothes-brush n spazzola f per abiti

clotheshanger n gruccia f
appendiabiti

clothes horse n stendibiancheria m
inv

clothes-line n corda f stendibiancheria

clothes peg n molletta f per bucato

clothes shop n negozio m di
abbigliamento

clothing /'kləʊðɪŋ/ n abbigliamento m

clotted cream /'klɒtɪd/ n Br panna f
rappresa (ottenuta scaldando il latte)

cloud /klaʊd/ n nuvola f
■ **cloud over** vi rannuvolarsi

cloudburst /'klaʊdbɜːst/ n acquazzone
m

cloudy /'klaʊdɪ/ adj (-ier, -iest)
nuvoloso; ⟨liquid⟩ torbido

clout /klaʊt/ ① n fam colpo m; (influence)
impatto m (with su)
② vt fam colpire

clove /kləʊv/ n chiodo m di garofano; ~
of garlic spicchio m d'aglio

cloven foot, cloven hoof /'kləʊvən/
n (of animal) zoccolo m fesso; (of devil) piede
m biforcuto

clover /'kləʊvə(r)/ n trifoglio m

clover leaf n raccordo m di due
autostrade

clown /klaʊn/ ① n pagliaccio m
② vi ~ [about/around] fare il pagliaccio

club /klʌb/ ① n club m inv; (weapon)
clava f; Sport mazza f; ~s pl (Cards) fiori
mpl
② vt (pt/pp **clubbed**) vt bastonare
■ **club together** vi unirsi

club car n Am carrozza f ferroviaria con
sala bar

club class n business class f inv

club foot n piede m deformato

clubhouse n (for socializing) circolo m;
(Am: for changing) spogliatoio m

club sandwich n club-sandwich m inv

cluck /klʌk/ vi chiocciare

clue /kluː/ n indizio m; (in crossword)
definizione f; I haven't a ~ fam non ne ho
idea

clued-up /kluːd'ʌp/ adj Br fam ben
informato

clueless /'kluːlɪs/ adj Br fam incapace

clump /klʌmp/ n gruppo m

■ **clump about**, **clump around** *vi* (walk noisily) camminare con passo pesante

clumsily /ˈklʌmzɪlɪ/ *adv* in modo maldestro; ⟨*remark*⟩ senza tatto

clumsiness /ˈklʌmzɪnɪs/ *n* goffaggine *f*

clumsy /ˈklʌmzɪ/ *adj* (**-ier**, **-iest**) maldestro; ⟨*tool*⟩ scomodo; ⟨*remark*⟩ senza tatto

clung /klʌŋ/ ▸ CLING

cluster /ˈklʌstə(r)/ ❶ *n* gruppo *m*
❷ *vi* raggrupparsi (**round** intorno a)

clutch /klʌtʃ/ ❶ *n* stretta *f*; Auto frizione *f*; **be in sb's ∼es** essere in balìa di qualcuno
❷ *vt* stringere; (grab) afferrare
❸ *vi* ∼ **at** afferrare

clutch bag *n* pochette *f inv*

clutch cable *n* cavo *m* della frizione

clutter /ˈklʌtə(r)/ ❶ *n* caos *m*
❷ *vt* ∼ **[up]** ingombrare

cm *abbr* (**centimetre**) cm

CND *n abbr* (**Campaign for Nuclear Disarmament**) campagna *f* per il disarmo nucleare

Co. *abbr* (**company**) C., C.ia; **and ∼** hum e compagnia; *abbr* (**county**) contea *f*

c/o *abbr* (**care of**) c/o, presso

coach /kəʊtʃ/ ❶ *n* pullman *m inv*; Rail vagone *m*; (horse-drawn) carrozza *f*; Sport allenatore, -trice *mf*
❷ *vt* far esercitare; Sport allenare

coach party *n* Br gruppo *m* di gitanti (in pullman)

coach station *n* Br stazione *f* dei pullman

coach trip *n* viaggio *m* in pullman

coachwork *n* Br carrozzeria *f*

coagulate /kəʊˈægjʊleɪt/ *vi* coagularsi

coagulation /kəʊægjʊˈleɪʃn/ *n* coagulazione *f*

coal /kəʊl/ *n* carbone *m*

coalfield *n* bacino *m* carbonifero

coal fire *n* caminetto *m* alimentato a carbone

coalition /kəʊəˈlɪʃn/ *n* coalizione *f*

coal-mine *n* miniera *f* di carbone

coalminer *n* minatore *m*

coal scuttle *n* secchio *m* del carbone

coal seam *n* giacimento *m* di carbone

coarse /kɔːs/ *adj* grossolano; ⟨*joke*⟩ spinto

coarse-grained /-ˈɡreɪnd/ *adj* ⟨*texture*⟩ a grana grossa

coarsely /ˈkɔːslɪ/ *adv* ⟨*ground*⟩ grossolanamente; ⟨*joke*⟩ in modo spinto

coast /kəʊst/ ❶ *n* costa *f*
❷ *vi* (freewheel) scendere a ruota libera; Auto scendere in folle

coastal /ˈkəʊstəl/ *adj* costiero

coaster /ˈkəʊstə(r)/ *n* (mat) sottobicchiere *m inv*

coastguard /ˈkəʊs(t)ɡɑːd/ *n* guardia *f* costiera

coastline /ˈkəʊstlaɪn/ *n* litorale *m*

coat /kəʊt/ ❶ *n* cappotto *m*; (of animal) manto *m*; (of paint) mano *f*; ∼ **of arms** stemma *f*
❷ *vt* coprire; (with paint) ricoprire

coat-hanger *n* gruccia *f*

coat-hook *n* gancio *m* [appendiabiti]

coating /ˈkəʊtɪŋ/ *n* rivestimento *m*; (of paint) stato *m*

coat rack *n* attaccapanni *m* a muro

coat-tails *npl* falde *fpl*; **be always hanging on sb's ∼** attaccarsi sempre alle falde di qualcuno

coax /kəʊks/ *vt* convincere con le moine

cob /kɒb/ *n* (of corn) pannocchia *f*

cobble /ˈkɒbl/ *vt* ∼ **together** raffazzonare

cobbler /ˈkɒblə(r)/ *n* ciabattino *m*

cobblestones /ˈkɒbəlstəʊnz/ *npl* acciottolato *msg*

cobra /ˈkəʊbrə/ *n* cobra *m inv*

cobweb /ˈkɒbweb/ *n* ragnatela *f*

cocaine /kəˈkeɪn/ *n* cocaina *f*

coccyx /ˈkɒksɪks/ *n* coccige *m*

cock /kɒk/ ❶ *n* gallo *m*; (any male bird) maschio *m*; vulg cazzo *m*
❷ *vt* sollevare il grilletto di ⟨*gun*⟩; ∼ **its ears** ⟨*animal*⟩ drizzare le orecchie
■ **cock up** fam ❶ *vt* incasinare
❷ *vi* incasinarsi

cock-a-doodle-doo /kɒkəduːd(ə)lˈduː/ *int* chicchirichì!

cock-a-hoop *adj* fam al settimo cielo

cock-and-bull story *n* fam panzana *f*

cockatoo /kɒkəˈtuː/ *n* cacatoa *m inv*

cockcrow /ˈkɒkkrəʊ/ *n* **at ∼** al primo canto del gallo

cocked hat /kɒktˈhæt/ *n* fam **knock somebody/something into a ∼ ∼** schiacciare qualcuno/qualcosa

cockerel /ˈkɒkərəl/ *n* galletto *m*

cocker spaniel /ˈkɒkə(r)/ *n* cocker *m inv* [spaniel]

cock-eyed /-ˈaɪd/ *adj* fam storto; (absurd) assurdo

cockfighting /ˈkɒkfaɪtɪŋ/ *n* combattimenti *mpl* di galli

cockle /ˈkɒkl/ *n* cardio *m*

cockney /ˈkɒknɪ/ *n* (dialect) dialetto *m* londinese; (person) abitante *mf* dell'est di Londra

cockpit /ˈkɒkpɪt/ *n* Aeron cabina *f*

cockroach /ˈkɒkrəʊtʃ/ *n* scarafaggio *m*

cocksure /kɒkˈʃʊə(r)/ *adj* ⟨*person, manner, attitude*⟩ presuntuoso

cocktail /ˈkɒkteɪl/ *n* cocktail *m inv*

cocktail bar *n* [cocktail] bar *m inv*

cocktail dress *n* abito *m* da cocktail *m inv*

cocktail party *n* cocktail-party *m inv*

cocktail shaker *n* shaker *m inv*

cocktail stick *n* stecchino *m*

cock-up *n* sl **make a** ~ fare un casino (of con)

cocky /'kɒkɪ/ *adj* (**-ier, -iest**) fam presuntuoso

cocoa /'kəʊkəʊ/ *n* cacao *m*

coconut /'kəʊkənʌt/ *n* noce *f* di cocco

coconut palm *n* palma *f* di cocco

coconut shy *n* Br tiro *m* al bersaglio in cui si devono abbattere noci di cocco

cocoon /kə'ku:n/ *n* bozzolo *m*

COD *abbr* (**cash on delivery**) pagamento *m* alla consegna

cod /kɒd/ *n inv* merluzzo *m*

coddle /'kɒd(ə)l/ *vt* coccolare

code /kəʊd/ *n* codice *m*

coded /'kəʊdɪd/ *adj* codificato

codeine /'kəʊdi:n/ *n* codeina *f*

code name *n* nome *m* in codice

codeword *n* parola *f* d'ordine

coding /'kəʊdɪŋ/ *n* Comput codifica *f*

cod-liver oil *n* olio *m* di fegato di merluzzo

coeducational /kəʊedjʊ'keɪʃənəl/ *adj* misto

coefficient /kəʊɪ'fɪʃənt/ *n* coefficiente *m*

coerce /kəʊ'ɜ:s/ *vt* costringere

coercion /kəʊ'ɜ:ʃn/ *n* coercizione *f*

coexist /kəʊɪg'zɪst/ *vi* coesistere

coexistence /kəʊɪg'zɪstəns/ *n* coesistenza *f*

C of E *abbr* (**Church of England**) Chiesa *f* anglicana

coffee /'kɒfɪ/ *n* caffè *m inv*

coffee bar *n* caffè *m inv*, bar *m inv*

coffee bean *n* chicco *m* di caffè

coffee break *n* pausa *f* per il caffè

coffee grinder *n* macinacaffè *m inv*

coffee machine *n* (in café) macchina *f* per l'espresso

coffee-maker *n* (on stove) caffettiera *f*; (electric) macchina *f* per il caffè (con il filtro)

coffee morning *n* Br riunione *m* mattutina in cui viene servito il caffè

coffee percolator *n* (on stove) caffettiera *f*; (electric) macchina *f* per il caffè (con il filtro)

coffee-pot *n* caffettiera *f*

coffee shop *n* torrefazione *f*; (café) caffè *m inv*, bar *m inv*

coffee table *n* tavolino *m*

coffer /'kɒfə(r)/ *n* forziere *m*

coffin /'kɒfɪn/ *n* bara *f*

cog /kɒg/ *n* Techn dente *m*

cogent /'kəʊdʒənt/ *adj* convincente

cogitate /'kɒdʒɪteɪt/ *vi* cogitare

cognac /'kɒnjæk/ *n* Cognac *m*

cognoscenti /kɒnə'ʃentɪ/ *npl* intenditori *mpl*

cogwheel /'kɒgwi:l/ *n* ruota *f* dentata

cohabit /kəʊ'hæbɪt/ *vi* Jur convivere

coherent /kəʊ'hɪərənt/ *adj* coerente; (when speaking) logico

cohesion /kəʊ'hi:ʒən/ *n* coesione *f*

cohort /'kəʊhɔ:t/ *n* fig seguito *m*

coil /kɔɪl/ **1** *n* rotolo *m*; Electr bobina *f*; ~s *pl* spire *fpl* **2** *vt* ~ **[up]** avvolgere

coin /kɔɪn/ **1** *n* moneta *f* **2** *vt* coniare ‹word›

coinage /'kɔɪnɪdʒ/ *n* (of coins, currency) coniatura *f*; (word, phrase) neologismo *m*

coin box *n* (pay phone) telefono *m* a monete; (on pay phone, in laundromat) gettoniera *f*

coincide /kəʊɪn'saɪd/ *vi* coincidere

coincidence /kəʊ'ɪnsɪdəns/ *n* coincidenza *f*

coincidental /kəʊɪnsɪ'dentl/ *adj* casuale

coincidentally /kəʊɪnsɪ'dentlɪ/ *adv* casualmente

coin operated *adj* a gettone

Coke® /kəʊk/ *n* Coca® *f*

coke *n* [carbone] coke *m*

Col. *abbr* (**Colonel**) Col. *m*

colander /'kʌləndə(r)/ *n* Culin colapasta *m inv*

cold /kəʊld/ **1** *adj* freddo; **I'm** ~ ho freddo; **get** ~ **feet** farsi prendere dalla fifa **2** *n* freddo *m*; Med raffreddore *m*

cold-blooded /-'blʌdɪd/ *adj* spietato

cold calling *n* Comm visita *f* senza preavviso

cold comfort *n* magra consolazione *f*

cold frame *n* telaio *m* coperto di vetro per proteggere le piante dal gelo

cold-hearted /-'hɑ:tɪd/ *adj* insensibile

coldly /'kəʊldlɪ/ *adv* fig freddamente

cold meat *n* salumi *mpl*

coldness /'kəʊldnɪs/ *n* freddezza *f*

cold shoulder *n* **1** **give somebody the** ~ ~ snobbare qualcuno **2** *vt* trattare freddamente

cold snap *n* ondata *f* di freddo

cold sore *n* herpes *m inv*

cold store *n* cella *f* frigorifera

cold sweat *n* sudore *m* freddo; **bring somebody out in a** ~ far sudare freddo qualcuno

cold turkey n (reaction) crisi f inv di astinenza; **be ~ ~** avere una crisi di astinenza; **quit ~ ~** smettere di colpo di drogarsi

Cold War n guerra f fredda

coleslaw /'kəʊlslɔ:/ n insalata f di cavolo crudo, cipolle e carote in maionese

colic /'kɒlɪk/ n colica f

collaborate /kə'læbəreɪt/ vi collaborare; **~ on something** collaborare a qualcosa

collaboration /kəlæbə'reɪʃn/ n collaborazione f; (with enemy) collaborazionismo m

collaborator /kə'læbəreɪtə(r)/ n collaboratore, -trice mf; (with enemy) collaborazionista mf

collage /kɒ'lɑːʒ/ n collage m inv; (film) montaggio m

collapse /kə'læps/ ① n crollo m ② vi (person) svenire; (roof, building) crollare

collapsible /kə'læpsəbl/ adj pieghevole

collar /'kɒlə(r)/ n colletto m; (for animal) collare m

collarbone /'kɒləbəʊn/ n clavicola f

collar size n taglia f di camicia

collate /kə'leɪt/ vt collazionare

collateral /kə'lætərəl/ n garanzia f collaterale; **put up ~** offrire una garanzia collaterale

collateral damage n danni mpl collaterali

collateral loan adj Fin prestito m con garanzia collaterale

colleague /'kɒli:g/ n collega mf

collect /kə'lekt/ ① vt andare a prendere (person); ritirare (parcel, tickets); riscuotere (taxes); raccogliere (rubbish); (as hobby) collezionare ② vi riunirsi ③ adv **call ~** Am telefonare a carico del destinatario

collected /kə'lektɪd/ adj controllato

collection /kə'lekʃn/ n collezione f; (in church) questua f; (of rubbish) raccolta f; (of post) levata f

collective /kə'lektɪv/ adj collettivo

collective bargaining n contrattazione f collettiva

collective noun n nome m collettivo

collective ownership n comproprietà f

collector /kə'lektə(r)/ n (of stamps etc) collezionista mf

collector's item n pezzo m da collezionista

college /'kɒlɪdʒ/ n istituto m parauniversitario; **C~ of ...** Scuola f di ...

college of education n Br ≈ facoltà f inv di magistero

college of further education n Br istituto m parauniversitario

collide /kə'laɪd/ vi scontrarsi

collie /'kɒlɪ/ n pastore m scozzese, collie m inv

colliery /'kɒlɪərɪ/ n miniera f di carbone

collision /kə'lɪʒn/ n scontro m; **be on a ~ course** essere in rotta di collisione

colloquial /kə'ləʊkwɪəl/ adj colloquiale

colloquialism /kə'ləʊkwɪəlɪzm/ n espressione f colloquiale

colloquially /kə'ləʊkwɪəlɪ/ adv colloquialmente

colloquium /kə'ləʊkwɪəm/ n colloquio m

collude /kə'l(j)u:d/ vi complottare

collusion /kə'l(j)u:ʒn/ n collusione f; **in ~ with** in accordo con

cologne /kə'ləʊn/ n colonia f

Colombia /kə'lɒmbɪə/ n Colombia f

Colombian /kə'lɒmbɪən/ adj & n colombiano, -a mf

colon /'kəʊlən/ n due punti mpl; Anat colon m inv

colonel /'kɜ:nl/ n colonnello m

colonial /kə'ləʊnɪəl/ adj coloniale

colonialist /kə'ləʊnɪəlɪst/ adj & n colonialista mf

colonization /kɒlənaɪ'zeɪʃn/ n colonizzazione f

colonize /'kɒlənaɪz/ vt colonizzare

colonizer /'kɒlənaɪzə(r)/ n colonizzatore, -trice mf

colonnade /kɒlə'neɪd/ n colonnato m

colony /'kɒlənɪ/ n colonia f

Colorado beetle /kɒlə'rɑːdəʊ/ n dorifora f

colossal /kə'lɒsl/ adj colossale

colour /'kʌlə(r)/ ① n colore m; (complexion) colorito m; **~s** pl (flag) bandiera fsg; **show one's true ~s** fig buttare giù la maschera; **in ~** a colori; **off ~** fam giù di tono ② vt colorare; **~ [in]** colorare ③ vi (blush) arrossire

colour bar n discriminazione f razziale

colour-blind adj daltonico

colour code vt distinguere per mezzo di colori diversi

coloured /'kʌləd/ ① adj colorato; (person) di colore ② n (person) persona f di colore

colour fast adj dai colori resistenti

colour film n film m inv a colori

colourful /'kʌləfʊl/ adj pieno di colore

colouring /'kʌlərɪŋ/ n (of plant, animal) colorazione f; (complexion) colorito m; (dye: for hair) tinta f; (for food) colorante m

colouring book n album m inv da colorare

colourless /'kʌlələs/ adj incolore

colour photo[graph] n fotografia f a colori

colour scheme n [combinazione f di] colori mpl

colour sense n senso m del colore

colour supplement n supplemento m illustrato a colori

colour television n televisione f a colori

colt /kəʊlt/ n puledro m

column /'kɒləm/ n colonna f

columnist /'kɒləmnɪst/ n giornalista mf che cura una rubrica

coma /'kəʊmə/ n coma m inv

comatose /'kəʊmətəʊz/ adj Med in stato comatoso

comb /kəʊm/ ① n pettine m; (for wearing) pettinino m
② vt pettinare; (fig: search) setacciare; ~ one's hair pettinarsi i capelli
■ **comb through** vt setacciare ⟨files, desk⟩

combat /'kɒmbæt/ ① n combattimento m
② vt (pt/pp **combated**) combattere

combat jacket n giubba f da combattimento

combination /kɒmbɪ'neɪʃn/ n combinazione f

combine¹ /kəm'baɪn/ ① vt unire; ~ a job with being a mother conciliare il lavoro con il ruolo di madre
② vi ⟨chemical elements⟩ combinarsi

combine² /'kɒmbaɪn/ n Comm associazione f

combined /kəm'baɪnd/ adj combinato

combine [harvester] n mietitrebbia f

combustible /kəm'bʌstəbl/ adj combustibile

combustion /kəm'bʌstʃn/ n combustione f

come /kʌm/ vi (pt **came**, pp **come**) venire; after coming all this way dopo tutta questa strada; where do you ~ from? da dove vieni?; ~ to (reach) arrivare a; that ~s to £10 fanno 10 sterline; I've ~ to appreciate her ho finito per apprezzarla; I don't know what the world is coming to mi chiedo dove andremo a finire; ~ into money ricevere dei soldi; that's what comes of being ... ecco cosa significa essere... ~ true/open verificarsi/ aprirsi; ~ first arrivare primo; fig venire prima di tutto; in two sizes esistere in due misure; the years to ~ gli anni a venire; how ~? fam come mai?
■ **come about** vi succedere
■ **come across** ① vi ~ across as being fam dare l'impressione di essere
② vt (find) imbattersi in

■ **come after** vt (follow) venire dopo; (chase, pursue) inseguire
■ **come along** vi venire; ⟨job, opportunity⟩ presentarsi; (progress) andare bene
■ **come apart** vi smontarsi; (break) rompersi
■ **come at** vt (attack) avventarsi su
■ **come away** vi venir via; ⟨button, fastener⟩ staccarsi
■ **come back** vi ritornare
■ **come before** vt (precede) precedere; (be more important than) venire prima di
■ **come by** ① vi passare
② vt (obtain) avere
■ **come down** vi scendere; ~ down to (reach) arrivare a; the situation comes down to... la situazione si riduce a...; don't ~ down too hard on her vacci piano con lei; ~ down with flu prendersi l'influenza
■ **come forward** vi farsi avanti
■ **come in** vi entrare; (in race) arrivare; ⟨tide⟩ salire; ~ in with somebody (in an undertaking) associarsi a qualcuno
■ **come in for** vt ~ in for criticism essere criticato
■ **come into** vt (inherit) ereditare ⟨money, inheritance⟩
■ **come off** ① vi staccarsi; (take place) esserci; (succeed) riuscire
② vt ~ off it! non farmi ridere!
■ **come on** vi (make progress) migliorare; ~ on! (hurry) dai!; (indicating disbelief) ma va là!
■ **come out** vi venir fuori; ⟨book, sun⟩ uscire; ⟨stain⟩ andar via; ⟨homosexual⟩ rivelare la propria omosessualità; ~ out [on strike] scioperare
■ **come out with** vt venir fuori con ⟨joke, suggestion⟩
■ **come over** vi venire; what's ~ over you? cosa ti prende?
■ **come round**, **come around** vi venire; (after fainting) riaversi; (change one's mind) farsi convincere
■ **come through** ① vi ⟨news⟩ arrivare
② vt attraversare ⟨operation⟩
■ **come to** vi (after fainting) riaversi.
■ **come under** vi trovarsi sotto
■ **come up** vi salire; ⟨sun⟩ sorgere; ⟨plant⟩ crescere; ⟨name, subject⟩ venir fuori; ⟨job, opportunity⟩ presentarsi; something came up (I was prevented) ho avuto un imprevisto
■ **come up against** vt incontrare
■ **come up to** vt (reach) arrivare a; essere all'altezza di ⟨expectations⟩
■ **come up with** vt tirar fuori

come-back n ritorno m

comedian /kə'mi:dɪən/ n [attore m] comico m

comedienne /kəmi:dɪ'en/ n attrice f comica

come-down n passo m indietro

comedy /'kɒmədɪ/ n commedia f

comer /'kʌmə(r)/ n open to all ~s aperto a tutti; **take on all** ~s battersi contro tutti gli sfidanti

comet /'kɒmɪt/ n cometa f

come-uppance /kʌm'ʌpəns/ n **get one's** ~ fam avere quel che si merita

comfort /'kʌmfət/ ① n benessere m; (consolation) conforto m; **all the** ~s tutti i comfort
② vt confortare

comfortable /'kʌmfətəbl/ adj comodo; **be** ~ ⟨person⟩ stare comodo; fig (in situation) essere a proprio agio; (financially) star bene

comfortably /'kʌmfətəblɪ/ adv comodamente

comforting /'kʌmfətɪŋ/ adj confortante

comfort station n Am bagno m pubblico

comfy /'kʌmfɪ/ adj fam comodo

comic /'kɒmɪk/ ① adj comico
② n comico, -a mf; (periodical) fumetto m

comical /'kɒmɪk(ə)l/ adj comico

comically /'kɒmɪk(ə)lɪ/ adv comicamente

comic book n giornalino m [a fumetti]

comic relief n provide some ~ ~ Theat fare una parentesi comica; fig sdrammatizzare

comic strip n striscia f di fumetti

coming /'kʌmɪŋ/ ① adj promettente
② n venuta f; ~s and goings viavai m

comma /'kɒmə/ n virgola f

command /kə'mɑːnd/ ① n also Comput comando m; (order) ordine m; (mastery) padronanza f; **in** ~ al comando
② vt ordinare; comandare ⟨army⟩

commandant /'kɒməndænt/ n Mil comandante m

commandeer /kɒmən'dɪə(r)/ vt requisire

commander /kə'mɑːndə(r)/ n comandante m

commanding /kə'mɑːndɪŋ/ adj ⟨view⟩ imponente; ⟨lead⟩ dominante

commanding officer n comandante m

commandment /kə'mɑːndmənt/ n comandamento m

commando /kə'mɑːndəʊ/ n commando m inv

command performance n Br Theat serata f di gala (su richiesta del capo di stato)

commemorate /kə'meməreɪt/ vt commemorare

commemoration /kəmemə'reɪʃn/ n commemorazione f

commemorative /kə'memərətɪv/ adj commemorativo

commence /kə'mens/ vt/i cominciare

commencement /kə'mensmənt/ n inizio m

commend /kə'mend/ vt complimentarsi con (on per); (recommend) raccomandare (to a)

commendable /kə'mendəbl/ adj lodevole

commendation /kɒmen'deɪʃn/ n elogio m; (for bravery) riconoscimento m

commensurate /kə'menʃərət/ adj proporzionato (with a)

comment /'kɒment/ ① n commento m; **no** ~! no comment!
② vi fare commenti (on su)

commentary /'kɒməntrɪ/ n commento m; **[running]** ~ (on radio, TV) cronaca f diretta

commentate /'kɒmənteɪt/ vt ~ **on** TV, Radio fare la cronaca di
■ **commentate on** vt fare la radiocronaca/telecronaca di ⟨sporting event⟩

commentator /'kɒmənteɪtə(r)/ n cronista mf

commerce /'kɒmɜːs/ n commercio m

commercial /kə'mɜːʃl/ ① adj commerciale
② n TV pubblicità f inv

commercial break n spot m inv [pubblicitario], interruzione f pubblicitaria

commercialism /kə'mɜːʃ(ə)lɪzm/ n pej affarismo m

commercialize /kə'mɜːʃ(ə)laɪz/ vt commercializzare

commercial law n diritto m commerciale

commercially /kə'mɜːʃ(ə)lɪ/ adv commercialmente

command centre Br, **command center** Am n centro m di comando

commercial traveller n commesso m viaggiatore

commiserate /kə'mɪzəreɪt/ vi esprimere il proprio rincrescimento (with a)

commissar /kɒmɪ'sɑː(r)/ n commissario m

commission /kə'mɪʃn/ ① n commissione f; **receive one's** ~ Mil essere promosso ufficiale; **out of** ~ fuori uso
② vt commissionare; Mil promuovere ufficiale; ~ **a painting from somebody**, ~ **somebody to do a painting** commissionare un dipinto a qualcuno

commissionaire /kəmɪʃə'neə(r)/ n portiere m

commissioner /kə'mɪʃənə(r)/ n commissario m; **C~ for Oaths** ≈ notaio m

commit /kə'mɪt/ vt (pt/pp **committed**) commettere; (to prison, hospital) affidare (to a); impegnare ⟨funds⟩; ~ **oneself** ···⊳

impegnarsi; **~ something to memory** imparare qualcosa a memoria

commitment /kə'mɪtmənt/ n impegno m; (involvement) compromissione f

committed /kə'mɪtɪd/ adj impegnato

committee /kə'mɪtɪ/ n comitato m

commodity /kə'mɒdətɪ/ n prodotto m

commodore /'kɒmədɔː(r)/ n commodoro m

common /'kɒmən/ **①** adj comune; (vulgar) volgare
② n prato m pubblico; **have in ~** avere in comune; **House of C~s** Camera f dei Comuni

common cold n raffreddore m

commoner /'kɒmənə(r)/ n persona f non nobile

common ground n fig terreno m d'intesa

common-law n diritto m consuetudinario

common-law husband n convivente m (more uxorio)

common-law marriage n matrimonio m di fatto

common-law wife n convivente f (more uxorio)

commonly /'kɒmənlɪ/ adv comunemente

Common Market n Mercato m Comune

common-or-garden adj ordinario

commonplace adj banale

common-room n sala f dei professori/ degli studenti

commonsense n buon senso m

Commonwealth n **①** Br Commonwealth m inv
② attrib ⟨country, Games⟩ del Commonwealth

Commonwealth of Independent States n Comunità f degli stati indipendenti

commotion /kə'məʊʃn/ n confusione f

communal /'kɒmjʊnəl/ adj comune

commune /'kɒmjuːn/ **①** n comune f
② /kə'mjuːn/ vi **~ with** essere in comunione con ⟨nature⟩; comunicare con person

communicable /kə'mjuːnɪkəbl/ adj ⟨disease⟩ trasmissibile

communicate /kə'mjuːnɪkeɪt/ vt/i comunicare

communication /kəmjuːnɪ'keɪʃn/ n comunicazione f; (of disease) trasmissione f; **be in ~ with somebody** essere in contatto con qualcuno; **~s** pl (technology) telecomunicazioni fpl

communication cord n fermata f d'emergenza

communications company n società f di telecomunicazioni

communications satellite n satellite m per telecomunicazioni

communications software n software m di comunicazione

communication studies /'stʌdɪz/ n studi mpl di comunicazione

communicative /kə'mjuːnɪkətɪv/ adj comunicativo

Communion /kə'mjuːnɪən/ n [Holy] **~** comunione f

communiqué /kə'mjuːnɪkeɪ/ n comunicato m stampa

Communism /'kɒmjʊnɪzm/ n comunismo m

Communist /'kɒmjʊnɪst/ adj & n comunista mf

Communist Party n partito m comunista

community /kə'mjuːnətɪ/ n comunità f

community care n cura f fuori dell'ambito ospedaliero

community centre n centro m sociale

community policing n polizia f di quartiere

community service n servizio m civile (in sostituzione di pene per reati minori)

community spirit n spirito m civico

commute /kə'mjuːt/ **①** vi fare il pendolare
② vt Jur commutare

commuter /kə'mjuːtə(r)/ n pendolare mf

commuter belt n zona f suburbana abitata dai pendolari

commuter train n treno m dei pendolari

Comoros /'kɒmərəʊz/ npl **the ~ (Islands)** le (isole) Comore fpl

compact[1] /kəm'pækt/ adj compatto

compact[2] /'kɒmpækt/ n portacipria m inv

compact disc n compact disc m inv

compact disc player n lettore m di compact disc

companion /kəm'pænjən/ n compagno, -a mf

companionable /kəm'pænjənəbl/ adj ⟨person⟩ socievole; ⟨silence⟩ non pesante

companionship /kəm'pænjənʃɪp/ n compagnia f

company /'kʌmpənɪ/ n compagnia f; (guests) ospiti mpl; **I didn't know you had ~** pensavo che fossi solo

company brochure n opuscolo m dell'azienda

company car n macchina f della ditta

company director n dirigente mf d'azienda

company letterhead n carta f intestata dell'azienda

company pension scheme n piano m di pensionamento aziendale

company policy n politica f aziendale

company secretary n direttore, -trice mf amministrativo, -a

comparable /'kɒmpərəbl/ adj paragonabile

comparative /kəm'pærətɪv/ 1 adj comparativo; (relative) relativo 2 n Gram comparativo m

comparatively /kəm'pærətɪvlɪ/ adv relativamente

compare /kəm'peə(r)/ 1 vt paragonare (with/to a) 2 vi it can't ∼ non ha paragoni

comparison /kəm'pærɪsn/ n paragone m

compartment /kəm'pɑ:tmənt/ n compartimento m; Rail scompartimento m

compass /'kʌmpəs/ n bussola f

compasses /'kʌmpəsɪz/ npl pair of ∼ compasso msg

compassion /kəm'pæʃn/ n compassione f

compassionate /kəm'pæʃənət/ adj compassionevole

compatible /kəm'pætəbl/ adj compatibile; be ∼ ⟨people⟩ avere caratteri compatibili

compatriot /kəm'pætrɪət/ n compatriota mf

compel /kəm'pel/ vt (pt/pp **compelled**) costringere

compelling /kəm'pelɪŋ/ adj ⟨reason, argument⟩ convincente; ⟨performance, film, speaker⟩ avvincente

compendium /kəm'pendɪəm/ n (handbook) compendio m; (Br: box of games) scatola f di giochi

compensate /'kɒmpənseɪt/ 1 vt risarcire 2 vi ∼ for fig compensare di

compensation /kɒmpən'seɪʃn/ n risarcimento m; (fig: comfort) consolazione f

compère /'kɒmpeə(r)/ n presentatore, -trice mf

compete /kəm'pi:t/ vi competere; (take part) gareggiare

competence /'kɒmpɪtəns/ n competenza f

competent /'kɒmpɪtənt/ adj competente

competition /kɒmpə'tɪʃn/ n concorrenza f; (contest) gara f

competitive /kəm'petɪtɪv/ adj competitivo; ∼ prices prezzi mpl concorrenziali

competitor /kəm'petɪtə(r)/ n concorrente mf

compilation /kɒmpɪ'leɪʃn/ n compilazione f; (collection) raccolta f

compile /kəm'paɪl/ vt compilare

complacency /kəm'pleɪsənsɪ/ n compiacimento m

complacent /kəm'pleɪsənt/ adj compiaciuto

complacently /kəm'pleɪsəntlɪ/ adv con compiacimento

complain /kəm'pleɪn/ vi lamentarsi (about di); (formally) reclamare; ∼ of Med accusare

complaint /kəm'pleɪnt/ n lamentela f; (formal) reclamo m; Med disturbo m

complement[1] /'kɒmplɪmənt/ n complemento m; with a full ∼ of 25 con un effettivo al completo di 25

complement[2] /'kɒmplɪment/ vt complementare; ∼ each other complementarsi a vicenda

complementary /kɒmplɪ'mentərɪ/ adj complementare

complementary medicine n medicina f alternativa

complete /kəm'pli:t/ 1 adj completo; (utter) finito 2 vt completare; compilare ⟨form⟩

completely /kəm'pli:tlɪ/ adv completamente

completion /kəm'pli:ʃn/ n fine f

complex /'kɒmpleks/ adj & n complesso m

complexion /kəm'plekʃn/ n carnagione f; that puts a different ∼ on the matter questo mette la questione in una luce nuova

complexity /kəm'pleksətɪ/ n complessità f inv

compliance /kəm'plaɪəns/ n accettazione f; (with rules) osservanza f; in ∼ with in osservanza a ⟨law⟩; conformemente a ⟨request⟩

compliant /kəm'plaɪənt/ adj accondiscendente; Comput conforme; ∼ with conforme a

complicate /'kɒmplɪkeɪt/ vt complicare

complicated /'kɒmplɪkeɪtɪd/ adj complicato

complication /kɒmplɪ'keɪʃn/ n complicazione f

complicity /kəm'plɪsətɪ/ n complicità f

compliment /'kɒmplɪmənt/ 1 n complimento m; ∼s pl omaggi mpl 2 vt complimentare

complimentary /kɒmplɪ'mentərɪ/ adj complimentoso; (given free) in omaggio

comply /kəm'plaɪ/ vi (pt/pp **-ied**) ∼ with conformarsi a

component /kəm'pəʊnənt/ adj & n ~ [part] componente m

compose /kəm'pəʊz/ vt comporre; ~ oneself ricomporsi; be ~d of essere composto da

composed /kəm'pəʊzd/ adj (calm) composto

composer /kəm'pəʊzə(r)/ n compositore, -trice mf

composite /'kɒmpəzɪt/ adj composto; ⟨style⟩ composito

composition /kɒmpə'zɪʃn/ n composizione f; (essay) tema m

compos mentis /kɒmpɒs'mentɪs/ adj nel pieno possesso delle proprie facoltà

compost /'kɒmpɒst/ n composta f

composure /kəm'pəʊʒə(r)/ n calma f

compound[1] /kəm'paʊnd/ vt (make worse) aggravare

compound[2] /'kɒmpaʊnd/ **1** adj composto
2 n Chem composto m; Gram parola f composta; (enclosure) recinto m

compound fracture n frattura f esposta

compound interest n interesse m composto

comprehend /kɒmprɪ'hend/ vt comprendere

comprehensible /kɒmprɪ'hensəbl/ adj comprensibile

comprehensibly /kɒmprɪ'hensəblɪ/ adv comprensibilmente

comprehension /kɒmprɪ'henʃn/ n comprensione f

comprehensive /kɒmprɪ'hensɪv/ adj & n comprensivo; ~ [school] scuola f media in cui gli allievi hanno capacità d'apprendimento diverse

comprehensive insurance n Auto polizza f casco

compress[1] /'kɒmpres/ n compressa f

compress[2] /kəm'pres/ vt also Comput comprimere

compressed air /kəm'prest/ n aria f compressa

compression /kəm'preʃn/ n compressione f

comprise /kəm'praɪz/ vt comprendere; (form) costituire

compromise /'kɒmprəmaɪz/ **1** n compromesso m
2 vt compromettere
3 vi fare un compromesso

compromising /'kɒmprəmaɪzɪŋ/ adj ⟨situation⟩ compromettente

compulsion /kəm'pʌlʃn/ n desiderio m irresistibile

compulsive /kəm'pʌlsɪv/ adj Psych patologico; ~ eating voglia f ossessiva di mangiare

compulsory /kəm'pʌlsərɪ/ adj obbligatorio; ~ subject materia f obbligatoria

compulsory purchase n Br espropriazione f (per pubblica utilità)

compunction /kəm'pʌŋkʃn/ n liter scrupolo m

computation /kɒmpjuː'teɪʃn/ n calcolo m

computer /kəm'pjuːtə(r)/ n computer m inv

computer-aided adj assistito da computer

computer-aided design n progettazione f assistita da computer

computer-aided learning n apprendimento m assistito dal computer

computer-assisted language learning n apprendimento m della lingua assistito da computer

computer crime n reati mpl informatici

computer dating n possibilità f di incontrare l'anima gemella tramite agenzie in rete

computer dating service n servizio m di ricerca dell'anima gemella in rete

computer engineer n tecnico m informatico

computer error n errore m informatico

computer game n gioco m su computer; ~ ~s intelligiochi mpl

computer graphics n grafica f computerizzata

computer hacker n pirata m informatico

computerization /kəmpjuːtəraɪ'zeɪʃn/ n computerizzazione f

computerize /kəm'pjuːtəraɪz/ vt computerizzare

computer-literate adj che sa usare il computer

computer operator n terminalista mf

computer program n programma m [informatico]

computer programmer n programmatore, -trice mf di computer

computer science n informatica f

computer scientist n esperto, -a mf di informatica

computer virus n virus m inv [su computer]

computing /kəm'pjuːtɪŋ/ n informatica f

comrade /'kɒmreɪd/ n camerata m; Pol compagno, -a mf

comradeship /'kɒmreɪdʃɪp/ n cameratismo m

con[1] /kɒn/ ▶ PRO

con² ① *n* fam fregatura *f*
  ② *vt* (pt/pp **conned**) fam fregare

concave /'kɒnkeɪv/ *adj* concavo

conceal /kən'siːl/ *vt* nascondere

concealment /kən'siːlmənt/ *n*
  dissimulazione *f*

concede /kən'siːd/ *vt* (admit) ammettere;
  (give up) rinunciare a; lasciar fare ⟨goal⟩

conceit /kən'siːt/ *n* presunzione *f*

conceited /kən'siːtɪd/ *adj* presuntuoso

conceivable /kən'siːvəbl/ *adj*
  concepibile

conceive /kən'siːv/ ① *vt* Biol concepire
  ② *vi* aver figli; ~ **of** fig concepire

concentrate /'kɒnsəntreɪt/ ① *vt*
  concentrare
  ② *vi* concentrarsi
  ③ *n* concentrato *m*

concentration /kɒnsən'treɪʃn/ *n*
  concentrazione *f*

concentration camp *n* campo *m* di
  concentramento

concentric /kən'sentrɪk/ *adj*
  concentrico

concept /'kɒnsept/ *n* concetto *m*

conception /kən'sepʃn/ *n* concezione *f*;
  (idea) idea *f*

conceptual /kən'septjʊəl/ *adj*
  concettuale

concern /kən'sɜːn/ ① *n* preoccupazione
  f; Comm attività *f inv*
  ② *vt* (be about, affect) riguardare; (worry)
  preoccupare; ~ **oneself with** preoccuparsi
  di; **as far as I am** ~**ed** per quanto mi
  riguarda

concerned /kən'sɜːnd/ *adj* (worried)
  preoccupato; **be** ~ **about** essere
  preoccupato per; (involved) interessato; **all
  (those)** ~ tutti gli interessati

concerning /kən'sɜːnɪŋ/ *prep* riguardo
  a

concert /'kɒnsət/ *n* concerto *m*

concerted /kən'sɜːtɪd/ *adj* collettivo

concert hall *n* sala *f* da concerti

concertina /kɒnsə'tiːnə/ *n* piccola
  fisarmonica *f*

concert master *n* Am primo violino *m*

concerto /kən'tʃeətəʊ/ *n* concerto *m*

concession /kən'seʃn/ *n* concessione *f*;
  (reduction) sconto *m*

concessionary /kən'seʃənrɪ/ *adj*
  (reduced) scontato

conciliate /kən'sɪlɪeɪt/ *vt* blandire

conciliation /kənsɪlɪ'eɪʃn/ *n*
  conciliazione *f*

conciliator /kən'sɪlɪeɪtə(r)/ *n*
  mediatore, -trice *mf*

conciliatory /kən'sɪlɪətrɪ/ *adj*
  conciliatorio

concise /kən'saɪs/ *adj* conciso

concisely /kən'saɪslɪ/ *adv* in modo
  conciso

conciseness /kən'saɪsnɪs/ *n* concisione
  f

conclude /kən'kluːd/ ① *vt* concludere
  ② *vi* concludersi

concluding /kən'kluːdɪŋ/ *adj* finale,
  conclusivo

conclusion /kən'kluːʒn/ *n* conclusione
  f; **in** ~ per concludere

conclusive /kən'kluːsɪv/ *adj* definitivo

conclusively /kən'kluːsɪvlɪ/ *adv* in
  modo definitivo

concoct /kən'kɒkt/ *vt* confezionare; fig
  inventare

concoction /kən'kɒkʃn/ *n* mistura *f*;
  (drink) intruglio *m*

concord /'kɒŋkɔːd/ *n* concordia *f*

concordance /kən'kɔːdəns/ *n* accordo
  m; (index) concordanze *fpl*; **be in** ~ **with**
  essere in accordo con

concourse /'kɒŋkɔːs/ *n* atrio *m*

concrete /'kɒŋkriːt/ ① *adj* concreto
  ② *n* calcestruzzo *m*
  ③ *vt* ricoprire di calcestruzzo

concrete jungle *n* giungla *f* d'asfalto

concrete mixer *n* betoniera *f*

concur /kən'kɜː(r)/ *vi* (pt/pp
  concurred) essere d'accordo

concurrently /kən'kʌrəntlɪ/ *adv*
  contemporaneamente

concuss /kən'kʌs/ *vt* **be** ~**ed** avere una
  commozione cerebrale

concussion /kən'kʌʃn/ *n* commozione *f*
  cerebrale

condemn /kən'dem/ *vt* condannare;
  dichiarare inagibile ⟨building⟩

condemnation /kɒndem'neɪʃn/ *n*
  condanna *f*

condensation /kɒnden'seɪʃn/ *n*
  condensazione *f*

condense /kən'dens/ ① *vt* condensare;
  Phys condensare
  ② *vi* condensarsi

condensed milk /kəndenst'mɪlk/ *n*
  latte *m* condensato

condescend /kɒndɪ'send/ *vi* degnarsi

condescending /kɒndɪ'sendɪŋ/ *adj*
  condiscendente

condescendingly /kɒndɪ'sendɪŋlɪ/
  adv in modo condiscendente

condiment /'kɒndɪmənt/ *n* condimento
  m

condition /kən'dɪʃn/ ① *n* condizione *f*;
  on ~ **that** a condizione che
  ② *vt* Psych condizionare

conditional /kən'dɪʃənəl/ ① *adj*
  ⟨acceptance⟩ condizionato; Gram
  condizionale; **be** ~ **on** essere condizionato
  da
  ② *n* Gram condizionale

conditionally /kən'dɪʃənəlɪ/ *adv* condizionatamente

conditioner /kən'dɪʃənə(r)/ *n* balsamo *m*; (for fabrics) ammorbidente *m*

conditioning /kən'dɪʃənɪŋ/ ① *n* (of hair) balsamo *m*; Psych condizionamento *m* ② *adj* ⟨shampoo, lotion etc⟩ trattante

condole /kən'dəʊl/ *vi* fare le condoglianze (**with** a)

condolences /kən'dəʊlənsɪz/ *npl* condoglianze *fpl*

condom /'kɒndəm/ *n* preservativo *m*

condo[minium] /'kɒndəʊ/, /kɒndə'mɪnɪəm/ *n* Am condominio *m*

condone /kən'dəʊn/ *vt* passare sopra a

conducive /kən'dju:sɪv/ *adj* be ∼ to contribuire a

conduct¹ /'kɒndʌkt/ *n* condotta *f*

conduct² /kən'dʌkt/ *vt* condurre; dirigere ⟨orchestra⟩

conduction /kən'dʌkʃn/ *n* conduzione *f*

conductor /kən'dʌktə(r)/ *n* direttore *m* d'orchestra; (of bus) bigliettaio *m*; Phys conduttore *m*

conductress /kən'dʌktrɪs/ *n* bigliettaia *f*

cone /kəʊn/ *n* cono *m*; Bot pigna *f*; Auto birillo *m*
■ **cone off** *vt* be ∼d off Auto essere chiuso da birilli

confection /kən'fekʃn/ *n* (cake, dessert) dolce *m*; a ∼ of (combination) una combinazione di

confectioner /kən'fekʃənə(r)/ *n* pasticciere, -a *mf*

confectionery /kən'fekʃənərɪ/ *n* pasticceria *f*

confederation /kənfedə'reɪʃn/ *n* confederazione *f*

confer /kən'fɜ:(r)/ ① *v* (pt/pp **conferred**) *vt* conferire (**on** a) ② *vi* (discuss) conferire

conference /'kɒnfərəns/ *n* conferenza *f*

conference room *n* sala *f* riunioni

confess /kən'fes/ ① *vt* confessare ② *vi* confessare; Relig confessarsi

confession /kən'feʃn/ *n* confessione *f*

confessional /kən'feʃənəl/ *n* confessionale *m*

confessor /kən'fesə(r)/ *n* confessore *m*

confetti /kən'fetɪ/ *n* coriandoli *mpl*

confide /kən'faɪd/ *vt* confidare
■ **confide in** *vt* ∼ in somebody fidarsi di qualcuno

confidence /'kɒnfɪdəns/ *n* (trust) fiducia *f*; (self-assurance) sicurezza *f* di sé; (secret) confidenza *f*; in ∼ in confidenza

confidence trick *n* truffa *f*

confidence trickster /'kɒnfɪdənstrɪkstə(r)/ *n* imbroglione, -a *mf*

confident /'kɒnfɪdənt/ *adj* fiducioso; (self-assured) sicuro di sé

confidential /kɒnfɪ'denʃl/ *adj* confidenziale

confidentiality /kɒnfɪdenʃɪ'ælɪtɪ/ *n* riservatezza *f*

confidentially /kɒnfɪ'denʃəlɪ/ *adv* confidenzialmente

confidently /'kɒnfɪdəntlɪ/ *adv* con aria fiduciosa; we ∼ expect to win siamo fiduciosi nella vittoria

confine /kən'faɪn/ *vt* rinchiudere; (limit) limitare; be ∼d to bed essere confinato a letto

confined /kən'faɪnd/ *adj* ⟨space⟩ limitato

confinement /kən'faɪnmənt/ *n* detenzione *f*; Med parto *m*

confines /'kɒnfaɪnz/ *npl* confini *mpl*

confirm /kən'fɜ:m/ *vt* confermare; Relig cresimare

confirmation /kɒnfə'meɪʃn/ *n* conferma *f*; Relig cresima *f*

confirmed /kən'fɜ:md/ *adj* incallito; ∼ bachelor scapolo *m* impenitente

confiscate /'kɒnfɪskeɪt/ *vt* confiscare

confiscation /kɒnfɪs'keɪʃn/ *n* confisca *f*

conflagration /kɒnflə'greɪʃn/ *n* conflagrazione *f*

conflate /kən'fleɪt/ *vt* fondere

conflict¹ /'kɒnflɪkt/ *n* conflitto *m*

conflict² /kən'flɪkt/ *vi* essere in contraddizione

conflicting /kən'flɪktɪŋ/ *adj* contraddittorio

confluence /'kɒnfluəns/ *n* (of rivers) confluenza *f*; fig convergenza *f*

conform /kən'fɔ:m/ *vi* ⟨person⟩ conformarsi; ⟨thing⟩ essere conforme (**to** a)

conformist /kən'fɔ:mɪst/ *n* conformista *mf*

conformity /kən'fɔ:mɪtɪ/ *n* conformità *f*; Relig ortodossia *f*; in ∼ with in conformità a

confound /kən'faʊnd/ *vt* (perplex) confondere; (show to be wrong) confutare

confounded /kən'faʊndɪd/ *adj* fam maledetto

confront /kən'frʌnt/ *vt* affrontare; the problems ∼ing us i problemi che dobbiamo affrontare

confrontation /kɒnfrʌn'teɪʃn/ *n* confronto *m*

confrontational /kɒnfrʌn'teɪʃənl/ *adj* provocatorio

confuse /kən'fju:z/ *vt* confondere

confused /kən'fju:zd/ *adj* ⟨presentation, idea⟩ ingarbugliato

confusing /kənˈfjuːzɪŋ/ *adj* che confonde

confusion /kənˈfjuːʒn/ *n* confusione *f*

congeal /kənˈdʒiːl/ *vi* ⟨blood⟩ coagularsi

congenial /kənˈdʒiːnɪəl/ *adj* congeniale

congenital /kənˈdʒenɪtl/ *adj* congenito

congested /kənˈdʒestɪd/ *adj* congestionato

congestion /kənˈdʒestʃn/ *n* congestione *f*

congestion charge *n* pedaggio *m* per circolare nelle strade del centro di Londra

conglomerate /kənˈɡlɒmərət/ *n* conglomerato *m*

Congo /ˈkɒŋɡəʊ/ *n* Congo *m*

Congolese /kɒŋɡəˈliːz/ *adj* & *n* congolese *mf*

congratulate /kənˈɡrætjʊleɪt/ *vt* congratularsi con (**on** per)

congratulations /kənɡrætjʊˈleɪʃnz/ *npl* congratulazioni *fpl*

congregate /ˈkɒŋɡrɪɡeɪt/ *vi* radunarsi

congregation /kɒŋɡrɪˈɡeɪʃn/ *n* Relig assemblea *f*

congress /ˈkɒŋɡres/ *n* congresso *m*

congressman /ˈkɒŋɡresmən/ *n* Am Pol membro *m* del congresso

conical /ˈkɒnɪkl/ *adj* conico

conifer /ˈkɒnɪfə(r)/ *n* conifera *f*

conjecture /kənˈdʒektʃə(r)/ **1** *n* congettura *f* **2** *vt* congetturare **3** *vi* fare congetture

conjugal /ˈkɒndʒʊɡl/ *adj* coniugale

conjugate /ˈkɒndʒʊɡeɪt/ *vt* coniugare

conjugation /kɒndʒʊˈɡeɪʃn/ *n* coniugazione *f*

conjunction /kənˈdʒʌŋkʃn/ *n* congiunzione *f*; **in ∼ with** insieme a

conjunctivitis /kəndʒʌŋktɪˈvaɪtɪs/ *n* congiuntivite *f*

conjure up /ˈkʌndʒə(r)/ *vt* evocare ⟨image⟩; tirar fuori dal nulla ⟨meal⟩

conjuring /ˈkʌndʒərɪŋ/ *n* giochi *mpl* di prestigio

conjuring trick /ˈkʌndʒərɪŋ/ *n* gioco *m* di prestigio

conjuror, conjurer /ˈkʌndʒərə(r)/ *n* prestigiatore, -trice *mf*

conk /kɒŋk/ *vi* ∼ **out** fam ⟨machine⟩ guastarsi; ⟨person⟩ crollare

conker /ˈkɒŋkə(r)/ *n* fam castagna *f* (d'ippocastano)

conman /ˈkɒnmæn/ *n* fam truffatore *m*

connect /kəˈnekt/ **1** *vt* collegare; **be ∼ed with** avere legami con; (be related to) essere imparentato con; **be well ∼ed** aver conoscenze influenti **2** *vi* essere collegato (**with** a); ⟨train⟩ fare coincidenza

connecting /kəˈnektɪŋ/ *adj* ⟨room⟩ di comunicazione

connecting flight *n* coincidenza *f*

connection /kəˈnekʃn/ *n* (between ideas) nesso *m*; (in travel) coincidenza *f*; Electr, Comput collegamento *m*; **in ∼ with** con riferimento a; **∼s** (people) conoscenze *fpl*

connector /kəˈnektə(r)/ *n* Comput connettore *m*

connivance /kəˈnaɪvəns/ *n* connivenza *f*

connive /kəˈnaɪv/ *vi* ∼ **at** essere connivente in

connoisseur /kɒnəˈsɜː(r)/ *n* intenditore, -trice *mf*

connotation /kɒnəˈteɪʃn/ *n* connotazione *f*

connote /kəˈnəʊt/ *vt* evocare; (in linguistics) connotare

conquer /ˈkɒŋkə(r)/ *vt* conquistare; fig superare ⟨fear⟩

conqueror /ˈkɒŋkərə(r)/ *n* conquistatore *m*

conquest /ˈkɒŋkwest/ *n* conquista *f*

conscience /ˈkɒnʃəns/ *n* coscienza *f*

conscientious /kɒnʃɪˈenʃəs/ *adj* coscienzioso

conscientiously /kɒnʃɪˈenʃəslɪ/ *adv* coscienziosamente

conscientious objector /əbˈdʒektə(r)/ *n* obiettore *m* di coscienza

conscious /ˈkɒnʃəs/ *adj* conscio; ⟨decision⟩ meditato; **[fully] ∼** cosciente; **be/become ∼ of something** rendersi conto di qualcosa

consciously /ˈkɒnʃəslɪ/ *adv* consapevolmente

consciousness /ˈkɒnʃəsnɪs/ *n* consapevolezza *f*; Med conoscenza *f*

conscript[1] /ˈkɒnskrɪpt/ *n* coscritto *m*

conscript[2] /kənˈskrɪpt/ *vt* Mil chiamare alle armi; ∼ **somebody to do something** fig reclutare qualcuno per fare qualcosa

conscription /kənˈskrɪpʃn/ *n* coscrizione *f*, leva *f*

consecrate /ˈkɒnsɪkreɪt/ *vt* consacrare

consecration /kɒnsɪˈkreɪʃn/ *n* consacrazione *f*

consecutive /kənˈsekjʊtɪv/ *adj* consecutivo

consecutively /kənˈsekjʊtɪvlɪ/ *adv* consecutivamente

consensus /kənˈsensəs/ *n* consenso *m*

consent /kənˈsent/ **1** *n* consenso *m* **2** *vi* acconsentire

consequence /ˈkɒnsɪkwəns/ *n* consequenza *f*; (importance) importanza *f*

consequent /ˈkɒnsɪkwənt/ *adj* conseguente

consequently /'kɒnsɪkwəntlɪ/ *adv* di conseguenza

conservation /kɒnsə'veɪʃn/ *n* conservazione *f*

conservation area *n* area *f* soggetta a vincoli ambientali

conservationist /kɒnsə'veɪʃənɪst/ *n* fautore, -trice *mf* della tutela ambientale

conservatism /kən'sɜːvətɪzm/ *n* conservatorismo *m*

conservative /kən'sɜːvətɪv/ ① *adj* conservativo; ⟨*estimate*⟩ ottimistico; C~ Pol *adj* conservatore
② *n* conservatore, -trice *mf*

Conservative Party *n* partito *m* conservatore

conservatory /kən'sɜːvətrɪ/ *n* spazio *m* chiuso da vetrate adiacente alla casa

conserve /kən'sɜːv/ *vt* conservare

consider /kən'sɪdə(r)/ *vt* considerare; ~ **doing something** considerare la possibilità di fare qualcosa

considerable /kən'sɪdərəbl/ *adj* considerevole

considerably /kən'sɪdərəblɪ/ *adv* considerevolmente

considerate /kən'sɪdərət/ *adj* pieno di riguardo

considerately /kən'sɪdərətlɪ/ *adv* con riguardo

consideration /kənsɪdə'reɪʃn/ *n* considerazione *f*; (thoughtfulness) attenzione *f*; (respect) riguardo *m*; (payment) compenso *m*; **take into** ~ prendere in considerazione

considering /kən'sɪdərɪŋ/ *prep* considerando; ~ **that** considerando che

consign /kən'saɪn/ *vt* affidare

consignment /kən'saɪnmənt/ *n* consegna *f*

consist /kən'sɪst/ *vi* ~ **of** consistere di

consistency /kən'sɪstənsɪ/ *n* coerenza *f*; (density) consistenza *f*

consistent /kən'sɪstənt/ *adj* coerente; ⟨*loyalty*⟩ costante; **be** ~ **with** far pensare a

consistently /kən'sɪstəntlɪ/ *adv* coerentemente; ⟨*late, loyal*⟩ costantemente

consolation /kɒnsə'leɪʃn/ *n* consolazione *f*

consolation prize *n* premio *m* di consolazione

console /kən'səʊl/ *vt* consolare

consolidate /kən'sɒlɪdeɪt/ *vt* consolidare

consolidation /kənsɒlɪ'deɪʃn/ *n* (of knowledge, position) consolidamento *m*

consoling /kən'səʊlɪŋ/ *adj* consolante

consonant /'kɒnsənənt/ *n* consonante *f*

consort[1] /'kɒnsɔːt/ *n* consorte *mf*

consort[2] /kən'sɔːt/ *vi* ~ **with** frequentare

consortium /kən'sɔːtɪəm/ *n* consorzio *m*

conspicuous /kən'spɪkjʊəs/ *adj* facilmente distinguibile; **be** ~ **by one's absence** brillare per la propria assenza

conspicuously /kən'spɪkjʊəslɪ/ *adv* ⟨*dressed*⟩ vistosamente; ⟨*placed*⟩ in evidenza; ⟨*silent, empty*⟩ in modo evidente

conspiracy /kən'spɪrəsɪ/ *n* cospirazione *f*

conspirator /kən'spɪrətə(r)/ *n* cospiratore, -trice *mf*

conspire /kən'spaɪə(r)/ *vi* cospirare

constable /'kʌnstəbl/ *n* agente *m* [di polizia]

constabulary /kən'stæbjʊlərɪ/ *n* Br polizia *f*

constancy /'kɒnstənsɪ/ *n* costanza *f*

constant /'kɒnstənt/ *adj* costante

constantly /'kɒnstəntlɪ/ *adv* costantemente

constellation /kɒnstə'leɪʃn/ *n* costellazione *f*

consternation /kɒnstə'neɪʃn/ *n* costernazione *f*

constipated /'kɒnstɪpeɪtɪd/ *adj* stitico

constipation /kɒnstɪ'peɪʃn/ *n* stitichezza *f*

constituency /kən'stɪtjʊənsɪ/ *n* collegio *m* elettorale di un deputato nel Regno Unito

constituent /kən'stɪtjʊənt/ *n* costituente *m*; Pol elettore, -trice *mf*

constitute /'kɒnstɪtjuːt/ *vt* costituire

constitution /kɒnstɪ'tjuːʃn/ *n* costituzione *f*

constitutional /kɒnstɪ'tjuːʃənl/ ① *adj* costituzionale
② *n* passeggiata *f* salutare

constitutionally /kɒnstɪ'tjuːʃənəlɪ/ *adv* Pol costituzionalmente; (innately) di costituzione

constrain /kən'streɪn/ *vt* costringere

constraint /kən'streɪnt/ *n* costrizione *f*; (restriction) restrizione *f*; (strained manner) disagio *m*

constrict /kən'strɪkt/ *vt* ⟨*tight jacket*⟩ stringere

constriction /kən'strɪkʃn/ *n* (of chest, throat) senso *m* di oppressione; (constraint) costrizione *f*; (of blood vessel) restrizione *f*

construct /kən'strʌkt/ *vt* costruire

construction /kən'strʌkʃn/ *n* costruzione *f*; (interpretation) interpretazione *f*; **under** ~ in costruzione

construction engineer *n* ingegnere *m* edile

construction paper *n* Am cartoncino *m*

construction site *n* cantiere *m*

construction worker *n* [operaio *m*] edile *m*

constructive /kən'strʌktɪv/ *adj*
costruttivo

constructively /kən'strʌktɪvlɪ/ *adv* in
modo costruttivo

construe /kən'stru:/ *vt* interpretare

consul /'kɒnsl/ *n* console *m*

consular /'kɒnsjʊlə(r)/ *adj* consolare

consulate /'kɒnsjʊlət/ *n* consolato *m*

consult /kən'sʌlt/ *vt* consultare

consultancy /kən'sʌltənsɪ/ ❶ *n* (advice)
consulenza *f*; (firm) ufficio *m* di consulenza;
Br Med posto *m* di specialista; **do ~** fare
il/la consulente
❷ *attrib* ⟨fees, service, work⟩ di
consulenza

consultant /kən'sʌltənt/ *n* consulente
mf; Med specialista *mf*

consultation /kɒnsl'teɪʃn/ *n*
consultazione *f*; Med consulto *m*

consultative /kən'sʌltətɪv/ *adj* di
consulenza

consulting hours /kən'sʌltɪŋ/ *npl* Med
orario *m* di visita

consulting room *n* Med ambulatorio *m*

consumable /kən'sju:məbl/ *n* bene *m*
di consumo

consume /kən'sju:m/ *vt* consumare

consumer /kən'sju:mə(r)/ *n*
consumatore, -trice *mf*

consumer advice *n* consigli *mpl* ai
consumatori

consumer confidence *n* fiducia *f* del
consumatore

consumer goods *npl* beni *mpl* di
consumo

consumerism /kən'sju:mərɪzm/ *n*
consumismo *m*

consumer organization *n*
organizzazione *f* per la tutela dei
consumatori

consumer products *npl* beni *mpl* di
consumo

consumer protection *n* tutela *f* dei
consumatori

consumer society *n* società *f inv*
consumista, società *f inv* dei consumi

consuming /kən'sju:mɪŋ/ *adj* ⟨passion⟩
struggente; ⟨urge⟩ pressante; ⟨hatred⟩
insaziabile

consummate /'kɒnsjʊmeɪt/ *vt*
consumare

consummation /kɒnsjʊ'meɪʃn/ *n*
consumazione *f*

consumption /kən'sʌmpʃn/ *n* consumo
m

cont. /kɒnt/ *abbr* (**continued**) segue

contact /'kɒntækt/ ❶ *n* contatto *m*;
(person) conoscenza *f*
❷ *vt* mettersi in contatto con

contactable /'kɒntæktəbl/ *adj* ⟨person⟩
reperibile

contact lenses *npl* lenti *fpl* a contatto

contagious /kən'teɪdʒəs/ *adj* contagioso

contain /kən'teɪn/ *vt* contenere; **~**
oneself controllarsi

container /kən'teɪnə(r)/ *n* recipiente *m*;
(for transport) container *m inv*

container port *n* porto *m* container

container ship *n* [nave *f*] portacontainer *f inv*

container truck *n* [autocarro *m*]
portacontainer *m inv*

contaminate /kən'tæmɪneɪt/ *vt*
contaminare

contamination /kəntæmɪ'neɪʃn/ *n*
contaminazione *f*

contd *abbr* (**continued**) segue

contemplate /'kɒntəmpleɪt/ *vt*
contemplare; (consider) considerare; **~**
doing something considerare di fare
qualcosa

contemplation /kɒntəm'pleɪʃn/ *n*
contemplazione *f*

contemplative /kən'templətɪv/ *adj*
contemplativo

contemporaneous
/kəntempə'reɪnɪəs/ *adj* contemporaneo
(**with** a)

contemporaneously
/kəntempə'reɪnɪəslɪ/ *adv*
contemporaneamente (**with** a)

contemporary /kən'tempərərɪ/ *adj & n*
contemporaneo, -a *mf*

contempt /kən'tempt/ *n* disprezzo *m*;
beneath ~ più che vergognoso; **~ of court**
oltraggio *m* alla Corte

contemptible /kən'tem(p)təbl/ *adj*
spregevole

contemptuous /kən'tem(p)tjʊəs/ *adj*
sprezzante

contemptuously /kən'tem(p)tjʊəslɪ/
adv sprezzantemente

contend /kən'tend/ ❶ *vi* **~ with**
occuparsi di
❷ *vt* (assert) sostenere

contender /kən'tendə(r)/ *n* concorrente
mf

content[1] /'kɒntent/ *n* contenuto *m*

content[2] /kən'tent/ ❶ *adj* soddisfatto
❷ *n* **to one's heart's ~** finché se ne ha
voglia
❸ *vt* **~ oneself** accontentarsi (**with** di)

contented /kən'tentɪd/ *adj* soddisfatto

contentedly /kən'tentɪdlɪ/ *adv* con aria
soddisfatta

contention /kən'tenʃn/ *n* (assertion)
opinione *f*

contentious /kən'tenʃəs/ *adj* ⟨subject⟩
controverso; ⟨view⟩ discutibile; ⟨person,
group⟩ polemico

contentment /kən'tentmənt/ *n*
soddisfazione *f*

contents /'kɒntents/ *npl* contenuto *m*

contest[1] /'kɒntest/ *n* gara *f*

contest[2] /kən'test/ *vt* contestare
⟨statement⟩; impugnare ⟨will⟩; Pol
⟨candidates⟩ contendersi; ⟨one candidate⟩
aspirare a

contestant /kən'testənt/ *n* concorrente
mf

context /'kɒntekst/ *n* contesto *m*

continent /'kɒntɪmənt/ *n* continente *m*;
the C∼ l'Europa *f* continentale

continental /kɒntɪ'nentl/ *adj*
continentale

continental breakfast *n* prima
colazione *f* a base di pane, burro,
marmellata, croissant ecc

continental quilt *n* piumone *m*

contingency /kən'tɪndʒənsɪ/ *n*
eventualità *f inv*

contingency fund *n* fondo *m*
sopravvenienze passive

contingency plan *n* piano *m*
d'emergenza

contingent /kən'tɪndʒənt/ ① *adj* be ∼
on dipendere da
② *n* Mil contingente *m*

continual /kən'tɪnjʊəl/ *adj* continuo

continually /kən'tɪnjʊəlɪ/ *adv*
continuamente

continuation /kəntɪnjʊ'eɪʃn/ *n*
continuazione *f*

continue /kən'tɪnjuː/ ① *vt* continuare;
∼ doing or to do something continuare a
fare qualcosa; to be ∼d continua
② *vi* continuare

continued /kən'tɪnjuːd/ *adj* continuo

continuity /kɒntɪ'njuːətɪ/ *n* continuità *f*

continuity announcer *n*
annunciatore, -trice *mf*

continuity girl *n* segretaria *f* di
produzione

continuous /kən'tɪnjʊəs/ *adj* continuo

continuously /kən'tɪnjʊəslɪ/ *adv*
continuamente

continuum /kən'tɪnjʊəm/ *n* continuum
m inv

contort /kən'tɔːt/ *vt* contorcere

contortion /kən'tɔːʃn/ *n* contorsione *f*

contortionist /kən'tɔːʃənɪst/ *n*
contorsionista *mf*

contour /'kɒntʊə(r)/ *n* contorno *m*; (line)
curva *f* di livello

contraband /'kɒntrəbænd/ *n*
contrabbando *m*

contraception /kɒntrə'sepʃn/ *n*
contraccezione *f*; use ∼ ricorrere alla
contraccezione

contraceptive /kɒntrə'septɪv/ *adj & n*
contraccettivo *m*

contract[1] /'kɒntrækt/ *n* contratto *m*

contract[2] /kən'trækt/ ① *vi* (get smaller)
contrarsi
② *vt* contrarre ⟨illness⟩

contraction /kən'trækʃn/ *n*
contrazione *f*

contract killer *n* sicario *m*

contractor /kən'træktə(r)/ *n*
imprenditore, -trice *mf*

contractual /kən'træktjʊəl/ *adj*
contrattuale

contract work *n* lavoro *m* su
commissione

contract worker *n* lavoratore, -trice
mf con contratto a termine

contradict /kɒntrə'dɪkt/ *vt* contraddire

contradiction /kɒntrə'dɪkʃn/ *n*
contraddizione *f*

contradictory /kɒntrə'dɪktərɪ/ *adj*
contraddittorio

contraflow /'kɒntrəfləʊ/ *n* utilizzazione
f di una corsia nei due sensi di marcia
durante lavori stradali

contraindication /kɒntrəɪndɪ'keɪʃn/ *n*
controindicazione *f*

contralto /kən'træltəʊ/ *n* contralto *m*

contraption /kən'træpʃn/ *n* fam
aggeggio *m*

contrariness /kən'treərɪnɪs/ *n* spirito
m di contraddizione

contrariwise /kən'treərɪwaɪz/ *adv*
(conversely) d'altra parte, d'altro canto; (in
the opposite direction) in direzione opposta

contrary[1] /'kɒntrərɪ/ ① *adj* contrario
② *adv* ∼ to contrariamente a
③ *n* contrario *m*; on the ∼ al contrario

contrary[2] /kən'treərɪ/ *adj* disobbediente

contrast[1] /'kɒntrɑːst/ *n* contrasto *m*

contrast[2] /kən'trɑːst/ ① *vt* confrontare
② *vi* contrastare

contrasting /kən'trɑːstɪŋ/ *adj*
contrastante

contravene /kɒntrə'viːn/ *vt* trasgredire

contravention /kɒntrə'venʃn/ *n*
trasgressione *f*

contribute /kən'trɪbjuːt/ *vt/i*
contribuire

contribution /kɒntrɪ'bjuːʃn/ *n*
contribuzione *f*; (what is contributed)
contributo *m*

contributor /kən'trɪbjʊtə(r)/ *n*
contributore, -trice *mf*

contributory /kən'trɪbjʊtərɪ/ *adj*
⟨factor⟩ concomitante; be ∼ to
contribuire a

con trick *n* raggiro *m*, truffa *f*

contrite /kən'traɪt/ *adj* contrito

contrive /kən'traɪv/ *vt* escogitare; ~ **to do something** riuscire a fare qualcosa

contrived /kən'traɪvd/ *adj* ⟨style, effect⟩ artificioso; ⟨plot, ending⟩ forzato; ⟨incident, meeting⟩ non fortuito

control /kən'trəʊl/ **①** *n* controllo *m*; ~**s** *pl* (of car, plane) comandi *mpl*; **get out of** ~ sfuggire al controllo **②** *vt* (*pt/pp* **controlled**) controllare; ~ **oneself** controllarsi

control column *n* Aeron cloche *f inv*

control key *n* Comput tasto *m* di controllo

controlled /kən'trəʊld/ *adj* ⟨explosion, performance, person⟩ controllato; **Labour-** ~ dominato dai laburisti

controller /kən'trəʊlə(r)/ *n* controllore *m*; Fin controllore *m* [della gestione]; Radio, TV direttore, -trice *mf*

control panel *n* (on machine) quadro *m* dei comandi; (for plane) quadro *m* di comando

control room *n* sala *f* di comando; Radio, TV sala *f* di regia

control tower *n* torre *f* di controllo

controversial /kɒntrə'vɜːʃl/ *adj* controverso

controversy /'kɒntrəvɜːsɪ/ *n* controversia *f*

conundrum /kə'nʌndrəm/ *n* enigma *m*

conurbation /kɒnɜː'beɪʃn/ *n* conturbazione *f*

convalesce /kɒnvə'les/ *vi* essere in convalescenza

convalescence /kɒnvə'lesəns/ *n* convalescenza *f*

convalescent /kɒnvə'lesənt/ *adj* convalescente

convalescent home *n* convalescenziario *m*

convection /kən'vekʃn/ *n* convezione *f*

convector /kən'vektə(r)/ *n* ~ **[heater]** convettore *m*

convene /kən'viːn/ **①** *vt* convocare **②** *vi* riunirsi

convener /kən'viːnə(r)/ *n* (organizer) organizzatore, -trice *mf*; (chair) presidente *m*

convenience /kən'viːnɪəns/ *n* convenienza *f*; **[public]** ~ gabinetti *mpl* pubblici; **with all modern** ~**s** con tutti i comfort

convenience foods *npl* cibi *mpl* precotti

convenience store *n* negozio *m* aperto fino a tardi

convenient /kən'viːnɪənt/ *adj* comodo; **be** ~ **for somebody** andar bene per qualcuno; **if it is** ~ **[for you]** se ti va bene

conveniently /kən'viːnɪəntlɪ/ *adv* comodamente; ~ **located** in una posizione comoda

convent /'kɒnvənt/ *n* convento *m*

convention /kən'venʃn/ *n* convenzione *f*; (assembly) convegno *m*

conventional /kən'venʃnəl/ *adj* convenzionale

conventionally /kən'venʃnəlɪ/ *adv* convenzionalmente

convention centre *n* palazzo *m* dei congressi

convent school *n* scuola *f* retta da religiose

converge /kən'vɜːdʒ/ *vi* convergere

conversant /kən'vɜːsənt/ *adj* ~ **with** pratico di

conversation /kɒnvə'seɪʃn/ *n* conversazione *f*

conversational /kɒnvə'seɪʃnəl/ *adj* di conversazione

conversationalist /kɒnvə'seɪʃnəlɪst/ *n* conversatore, -trice *mf*

converse¹ /kən'vɜːs/ *vi* conversare

converse² /'kɒnvɜːs/ *n* inverso *m*

conversely /'kɒnvɜːslɪ/ *adv* viceversa

conversion /kən'vɜːʃn/ *n* conversione *f*

conversion rate *n* [tasso *m* di] cambio *m*

conversion table *n* tabella *f* di conversione

convert¹ /'kɒnvɜːt/ *n* convertito, -a *mf*

convert² /kən'vɜːt/ *vt* convertire (**into** in); sconsacrare ⟨church⟩

converter /kən'vɜːtə(r)/ *n* Electr convertitore *m*

convertible /kən'vɜːtəbl/ **①** *adj* convertibile **②** *n* Auto macchina *f* decappottabile

convex /'kɒnveks/ *adj* convesso

convey /kən'veɪ/ *vt* portare; trasmettere ⟨idea, message⟩

conveyance /kən'veɪəns/ *n* trasporto *m*; (vehicle) mezzo *m* di trasporto

conveyancing /kən'veɪənsɪŋ/ *n* Jur passaggio *m* di proprietà

conveyor /kən'veɪə(r)/ *n* (of goods, persons) trasportatore *m*

conveyor belt *n* nastro *m* trasportatore

convict¹ /'kɒnvɪkt/ *n* condannato, -a *mf*

convict² /kən'vɪkt/ *vt* guidicare colpevole

conviction /kən'vɪkʃn/ *n* condanna *f*; (belief) convinzione *f*; **previous** ~ precedente *m* penale

convince /kən'vɪns/ *vt* convincere

convincing /kən'vɪnsɪŋ/ *adj* convincente

convincingly /kən'vɪnsɪŋlɪ/ *adv* in modo convincente

convivial /kən'vɪvɪəl/ *adj* conviviale

convoluted /'kɒnvəlu:tɪd/ *adj* contorto

convoy /'kɒnvɔɪ/ *n* convoglio *m*

convulse /kən'vʌls/ *vt* sconvolgere; be ~d with laughter contorcersi dalle risa

convulsion /kən'vʌlʃn/ *n* convulsione *f*

convulsive /kən'vʌlsɪv/ *adj* convulso; Med convulsivo

convulsively /kən'vʌlsɪvlɪ/ *adv* convulsamente

coo /ku:/ *vi* tubare

cooing /'ku:ɪŋ/ *n* (of bird, lovers) tubare *m inv*

cook /kʊk/ ① *n* cuoco, -a *mf*
② *vt* cucinare; **is it ~ed?** è cotto? ~ **the books** fam truccare i libri contabili
③ *vi* ⟨*food*⟩ cuocere; ⟨*person*⟩ cucinare
■ **cook up** *vt* (fam) inventare ⟨*excuse, story etc*⟩

cookbook /'kʊkbʊk/ *n* libro *m* di cucina

cook-chill *adj* ⟨*foods, products*⟩ precotto e surgelato

cooked meats /kʊkt'mi:ts/ *npl* salumi *mpl*

cooker /'kʊkə(r)/ *n* cucina *f*; (apple) mela *f* da cuocere

cookery /'kʊkərɪ/ *n* cucina *f*

cookery book *n* libro *m* di cucina

cookie /'kʊkɪ/ *n* Am biscotto *m*

cooking /'kʊkɪŋ/ *n* cucina *f*; **be good at ~** saper cucinare bene; **do the ~** cucinare

cooking apple *n* mela *f* da cuocere

cooking chocolate *n* cioccolato *m* da pasticceria

cooking foil *n* carta *f* stagnola

cooking salt *n* sale *m* da cucina

cooking time *n* tempo *m* di cottura

cool /ku:l/ ① *adj* fresco; (calm) calmo; (unfriendly) freddo; (fam: excellent or attractive) fantastico; **a ~ T-shirt** una maglietta fantastica; **'I won!' '~!'** 'ho vinto!' 'fantastico!'
② *n* fresco *m*; **keep/lose one's ~** mantenere/perdere la calma
③ *vt* rinfrescare
④ *vi* rinfrescarsi
■ **cool down** ① *vi* ⟨*soup, tea etc*⟩ raffreddarsi; (fig: become calm) calmarsi
② *vt* raffreddare ⟨*soup, tea etc*⟩; (fig) calmare

cool bag *n* Br borsa *f* frigo

cool-box *n* borsa *f* termica

cool-headed *adj* equilibrato

cooling /'ku:lɪŋ/ ① *n* raffreddamento *m*
② *adj* ⟨*agent*⟩ refrigerante; ⟨*system, tower*⟩ di raffreddamento; ⟨*drink, swim*⟩ rinfrescante

cooling-off period *n* (in industrial relations) periodo *m* di tregua [sindacale]; Comm fase *f* di riflessione

coolly /'ku:llɪ/ *adv* freddamente

coolness /'ku:lnɪs/ *n* freddezza *f*

coop /ku:p/ ① *n* stia *f*
② *vt* ~ **up** rinchiudere

co-op /'kəʊɒp/ *n abbr* (**cooperative**) cooperativa *f*

cooperate /kəʊ'ɒpəreɪt/ *vi* cooperare

cooperation /kəʊɒpə'reɪʃn/ *n* cooperazione *f*

cooperative /kəʊ'ɒpərətɪv/ *adj & n* cooperativa *f*

co-opt /kəʊ'ɒpt/ *vt* eleggere

coordinate /kəʊ'ɔ:dɪneɪt/ *vt* coordinare

coordinated /kəʊ'ɔ:dɪneɪtɪd/ *adj* coordinato

coordinates *npl* (clothes) coordinato *m sg*

coordination /kəʊɔ:dɪ'neɪʃn/ *n* coordinazione *f*

coordinator /kəʊ'ɔ:dɪneɪtə(r)/ *n* coordinatore, -trice *mf*

co-owner /kəʊ'əʊnə(r)/ *n* comproprietario, -a *mf*

cop /kɒp/ *n* fam poliziotto *m*

co-parent /kəʊ'peərənt/ *vt* condividere la responsabilità dell'educazione dei figli

co-parenting /kəʊ'peərəntɪŋ/ *n* condivisione *f* della responsabilità dell'educazione dei figli

cope /kəʊp/ *vi* fam farcela; **can she ~ by herself?** ce la fa da sola?; ~ **with** farcela con; **I couldn't ~ with five kids** non ce la farei con cinque bambini

Copenhagen /kəʊpən'heɪgən/ *n* Copenhagen *f*

copier /'kɒpɪə(r)/ *n* fotocopiatrice *f*

co-pilot /'kəʊpaɪlət/ *n* copilota *m*

copious /'kəʊpɪəs/ *adj* abbondante

copiously /'kəʊpɪəslɪ/ *adv* abbondantemente

cop-out *n* fam (evasive act) bidone *m*; (excuse) scappatoia *f*

copper[1] /'kɒpə(r)/ ① *n* rame *m*: ~s *pl* monete fpl da uno o due penny
② *attrib* di rame

copper[2] *n* fam poliziotto *m*

copper beech *n* faggio *m* rosso

copper-coloured *adj* [color] rame *inv*; ⟨*hair*⟩ ramato

copperplate *n* calligrafia *f* ornata

coppice /'kɒpɪs/ *n*, **copse** /kɒps/ *n* boschetto *m*

co-property /'kəʊprɒpətɪ/ *n* comproprietà *f inv*

copulate /'kɒpjʊleɪt/ *vi* accoppiarsi

copulation /kɒpjʊ'leɪʃn/ *n* copulazione *f*

copy /'kɒpɪ/ ① *n* copia *f*

2 *vt* (pt/pp **-ied**) copiare
■ **copy down** *vt* = COPY
■ **copy out** *vt* = COPY

copybook *n* blot one's ~ rovinarsi la reputazione

copycat **1** *n* pej fam copione, -a *mf*
2 *adj* ⟨*crime, murder*⟩ ispirato da un altro

copy editor *n* segretario, -a *mf* di redazione

copyright *n* diritti *mpl* d'autore

copy-typist *n* dattilografo, -a *mf*

copywriter *n* copywriter *mf inv*

coquetry /'kɒkɪtrɪ/ *n* civetteria *f*

coquettish /kɒ'ketɪʃ/ *adj* civettuolo

coral /'kɒrəl/ *n* corallo *m*

coral island *n* isola *f* di corallo

coral pink *adj* & *n* rosa *m inv* corallo

coral reef *n* barriera *f* corallina

cord /kɔːd/ *n* corda *f*; (thinner) cordoncino *m*; (fabric) velluto *m* a coste; ~**s** *pl* pantaloni *mpl* di velluto a coste

cordial /'kɔːdɪəl/ **1** *adj* cordiale
2 *n* analcolico *m*

cordially /'kɔːdɪəlɪ/ *adv* con tutto il cuore

cordless /'kɒːdlɪs/ *adj* ⟨*phone, kettle*⟩ cordless

cordless telephone *adj* telefono *m* cordless

cordon /'kɔːdn/ *n* cordone *m* (di persone)
■ **cordon off** *vt* bloccare

corduroy /'kɔːdərɔɪ/ *n* velluto *m* a coste

core /kɔː(r)/ *n* (of apple, pear) torsolo *m*; (fig: of organization) cuore *m*; (of problem, theory) nocciolo *m*

core curriculum *n* materie *fpl* fondamentali (del programma scolastico)

co-respondent /kəʊrɪ'spɒndənt/ *n* Jur correo, -a *mf* in adulterio

Corfu /kɔː'fuː/ *n* Corfù *f*

coriander /kɒrɪ'ændə(r)/ *n* coriandolo *m*

cork /kɔːk/ *n* sughero *m*; (for bottle) turacciolo *m*

corkage /'kɔːkɪdʒ/ *n* somma *f* pagata a un ristorante per servire una bottiglia di vino portata da fuori

corker /'kɔːkə(r)/ *n* Br fam (story) storia *f* strabiliante; (stroke, shot) tiro *m* da maestro

corkscrew /'kɔːkskruː/ *n* cavatappi *m inv*

corkscrew curls *npl* boccoli *mpl*

corn¹ /kɔːn/ *n* grano *m*; (Am: maize) granturco *m*

corn² *n* Med callo *m*

corncob /'kɔːnkɒb/ *n* pannocchia *f* [di mais]

cornea /'kɔːnɪə/ *n* cornea *f*

corned beef /kɔːnd'biːf/ *n* manzo *m* sotto sale

corner /'kɔːnə(r)/ **1** *n* angolo *m*; (football) calcio *m* d'angolo, corner *m inv*
2 *vt* fig bloccare; Comm accaparrarsi ⟨*market*⟩

corner shop *n* negozio *m* di quartiere

cornerstone /'kɔːnəstəʊn/ *n* pietra *f* angolare

cornet /'kɔːnɪt/ *n* Mus cornetta *f*; (for ice-cream) cono *m*

cornfield /'kɔːnfiːld/ *n* campo *m* di grano; (sweetcorn) campo *m* di mais

cornflour /'kɔːnflaʊə(r)/ *n* farina *f* finissima di mais

cornflower /'kɔːnflaʊə(r)/ *n* fiordaliso *m*

cornice /'kɔːnɪs/ *n* (inside) cornice *f*; (outside) cornicione *m*

Cornish pasty /kɔːnɪʃ'pæstɪ/ *n* fagottino *m* di pasta sfoglia ripieno di carne e verdura

corn oil *n* olio *m* di mais

corn on the cob *n* pannocchia *f* cotta

corn plaster *n* [cerotto *m*] callifugo *m*

cornstarch *n* Am fecola *f* di mais

cornucopia /kɔːnjʊ'kəʊpɪə/ *n* cornucopia *f*; fig abbondanza *f*

Cornwall /'kɔːnwɔːl/ *n* Cornovaglia *f*

corny /'kɔːnɪ/ *adj* (**-ier, -iest**) fam ⟨*joke, film*⟩ scontato; ⟨*person*⟩ banale; (sentimental) sdolcinato

corollary /kə'rɒlərɪ/ *n* corollario *m*

coronary /'kɒrənərɪ/ **1** *adj* coronario
2 *n* ~ **[thrombosis]** trombosi *f* coronarica

coronation /kɒrə'neɪʃn/ *n* incoronazione *f*

coroner /'kɒrənə(r)/ *n* coroner *m inv* (nel diritto britannico, ufficiale incaricato delle indagini su morti sospette)

coronet /'kɒrənet/ *n* coroncina *f*

corporal¹ /'kɔːpərəl/ *n* Mil caporale *m*

corporal² *adj* corporale; ~ **punishment** punizione *f* corporale

corporate /'kɔːpərət/ *adj* ⟨*decision, policy, image*⟩ aziendale; ~ **life** la vita in un'azienda

corporate hospitality *n* omaggi *mpl* offerti dalla ditta ai clienti importanti

corporate identity *n* logo *m* dell'azienda

corporate image *n* immagine *f* aziendale

corporate lawyer *n* legale *mf* specializzato, -a in diritto aziendale

corporate planning *n* pianificazione *f* aziendale

corporate raider *n* finanziere *m* d'assalto

corporation /ˌkɔːpəˈreɪʃn/ n ente m; (of town) ≈ consiglio m comunale

corporation tax n Br imposta f sul reddito delle aziende

corps /kɔː(r)/ n (pl **corps** /kɔːz/) corpo m

corps de ballet /kɔːdəˈbæleɪ/ n corpo m di ballo

corpse /kɔːps/ n cadavere m

corpulent /ˈkɔːpjʊlənt/ adj corpulento

corpus /ˈkɔːpəs/ n (of words) corpus m inv

corpuscle /ˈkɔːpʌsl/ n globulo m

correct /kəˈrekt/ ① adj corretto; be ∼ ⟨person⟩ aver ragione; ∼! esatto! ② vt correggere

correcting fluid n bianchetto m

correction /kəˈrekʃn/ n correzione f

corrective /kəˈrektɪv/ n correttivo m

correctly /kəˈrektlɪ/ adv correttamente

correlate /ˈkɒrəleɪt/ ① vt correlare ② vi essere correlato

correlation /kɒrəˈleɪʃn/ n correlazione f

correspond /kɒrɪˈspɒnd/ vi corrispondere (to a); ⟨two things⟩ corrispondere; (write) scriversi

correspondence /kɒrɪˈspɒndəns/ n corrispondenza f

correspondence course n corso m per corrispondenza

correspondent /kɒrɪˈspɒndənt/ n corrispondente mf

corresponding /kɒrɪˈspɒndɪŋ/ adj corrispondente

correspondingly /kɒrɪˈspɒndɪŋlɪ/ adv in modo corrispondente

corridor /ˈkɒrɪdɔː(r)/ n corridoio m

corroborate /kəˈrɒbəreɪt/ vt corroborare

corrode /kəˈrəʊd/ ① vt corrodere ② vi corrodersi

corrosion /kəˈrəʊʒn/ n corrosione f

corrugated /ˈkɒrəgeɪtɪd/ adj ondulato

corrugated iron n lamiera f ondulata

corrupt /kəˈrʌpt/ ① adj corrotto ② vt corrompere

corruption /kəˈrʌpʃn/ n corruzione f

corset /ˈkɔːsɪt/ n & s pl busto m

Corsica /ˈkɔːsɪkə/ n Corsica f

Corsican /ˈkɔːsɪkən/ adj & n corso, -a mf

cortège /kɔːˈteɪʒ/ n [funeral] ∼ corteo m funebre

cosh /kɒʃ/ n randello m

co-signatory /kəʊˈsɪgnətrɪ/ n cofirmatario, -a mf

cosily /ˈkəʊzɪlɪ/ adv ⟨sit, lie⟩ in modo confortevole

cosiness /ˈkəʊzɪnɪs/ n (of room) comodità f; (intimacy) intimità f

cos lettuce /kɒs/ n lattuga f romana

cosmetic /kɒzˈmetɪk/ ① adj cosmetico ② n ∼s pl cosmetici mpl

cosmetic surgery n chirurgia f estetica

cosmic /ˈkɒzmɪk/ adj cosmico

cosmonaut /ˈkɒzmənɔːt/ n cosmonauta mf

cosmopolitan /kɒzməˈpɒlɪtən/ adj cosmopolita

cosmos /ˈkɒzmɒs/ n cosmo m

Cossack /ˈkɒsæk/ adj & n cosacco, -a mf

cosset /ˈkɒsɪt/ vt coccolare

cost /kɒst/ ① n costo m; ∼s pl Jur spese fpl processuali; at all ∼s a tutti i costi; I learnt to my ∼ ho imparato a mie spese ② vt (pt/pp **cost**) costare; it ∼ me £20 mi è costato 20 sterline ③ vt (pt/pp **costed**) ∼ [out] stabilire il prezzo di

co-star /ˈkəʊstɑː/ ① n Cinema, Theat co-protagonista mf ② vi/t film ∼ring X and Y un film con X e Y come protagonisti

Costa Rica /kɒstəˈriːkə/ n Costa Rica m

cost centre n centro m di costi

cost-cutting n tagli mpl sulle spese; as a ∼ exercise [come misura] per ridurre le spese

cost-effective adj conveniente

cost-effectiveness n convenienza f

costing /ˈkɒstɪŋ/ n (process) determinazione f dei costi; (discipline) costing m inv

costly /ˈkɒstlɪ/ adj -ier, -iest costoso

cost of living n costo m della vita

cost-of-living index n indice m del costo della vita

cost price n prezzo m di costo

costume /ˈkɒstjuːm/ n costume m

costume drama n dramma m storico

costume jewellery n bigiotteria f

cosy /ˈkəʊzɪ/ ① adj -ier, -iest ⟨pub, chat⟩ intimo; it's nice and ∼ in here si sta bene qui ② n tea ∼ copriteiera m inv

cot /kɒt/ n lettino m; (Am: camp bed) branda f

cot death n Br morte f inspiegabile di un neonato nel sonno

Côte d'Azur /kəʊtdæˈzʊə(r)/ n Costa f Azzurra

cottage /ˈkɒtɪdʒ/ n casetta f

cottage cheese n fiocchi mpl di latte

cottage hospital n Br piccolo ospedale m (in zona rurale)

cottage industry n attività f inv artigianale basata sul lavoro a domicilio

cottage loaf n pagnotta f casereccia

cottage pie n Br pasticcio m di patate e carne macinata

cotton /'kɒtn/ **1** n cotone m
2 attrib di cotone
■ **cotton on** vi fam capire

cotton bud n cotton fioc® m inv

cotton mill n cotonificio m

cotton reel n rocchetto m, spagnoletta f

cotton wool n Br cotone m idrofilo

couch /kaʊtʃ/ n divano m

couchette /ku:'ʃet/ n cuccetta f

couch potato n pantofolaio, -a mf

cougar /'ku:gə(r)/ n coguaro m

cough /kɒf/ **1** n tosse f
2 vi tossire
■ **cough up** vt/i sputare; (fam: pay) sborsare

cough mixture n sciroppo m per la tosse

could /kʊd/ atono, /kəd/ v aux (▶ also CAN[2]) ~ I have a glass of water? potrei avere un bicchier d'acqua?; I ~n't do it even if I wanted to non potrei farlo nemmeno se lo volessi; I ~n't care less non potrebbe importarmene di meno; he ~n't have done it without help non avrebbe potuto farlo senza aiuto; you ~ have phoned avresti potuto telefonare

council /'kaʊnsl/ n consiglio m

council estate n Br complesso m di case popolari

council house n casa f popolare

council housing n Br case fpl popolari

councillor /'kaʊnsələ(r)/ n consigliere, -a mf

council tax n imposta f locale sugli immobili

counsel /'kaʊnsl/ **1** n consigli mpl; Jur avvocato m
2 vt (pt/pp **counselled**) consigliare a ⟨person⟩

counselling /'kaʊnsəlɪŋ/ **1** n (psychological) terapia f [psichiatrica]; Sch orientamento m scolastico; careers ~ orientamento m professionale
2 attrib ⟨group, centre, service⟩ di assistenza

counsellor /'kaʊnsələ(r)/ n consigliere, -a mf

count[1] /kaʊnt/ n (nobleman) conte m

count[2] **1** n conto m; keep ~ tenere il conto
2 vt/i contare
■ **count against** vt ⟨inexperience, police record⟩ deporre a sfavore di
■ **count among** vt ~ somebody among one's friends annoverare qualcuno tra i propri amici
■ **count in** vt (include) includere; ~ me in! io ci sto!
■ **count on** vt contare su

■ **count out** vt contare ⟨money⟩; ~ me out! fate senza di me!
■ **count up** **1** vt contare
2 vi ~ to ten contare fino a dieci

countable /'kaʊntəbl/ adj ⟨noun⟩ numerabile

countdown /'kaʊntdaʊn/ n conto m alla rovescia

countenance /'kaʊntənəns/ **1** n espressione f
2 vt approvare

counter[1] /'kaʊntə(r)/ n banco m; (in games) gettone m

counter[2] **1** adv ~ to contro, in contrasto a; go ~ to something andare contro qualcosa
2 vt/i opporre ⟨measure, effect⟩; parare ⟨blow⟩

counteract /kaʊntər'ækt/ vt neutralizzare

counter-attack n contrattacco m

counterbalance /'kaʊntəbæləns/ **1** n contrappeso m
2 vt controbilanciare

counter-claim n replica f

counter-clockwise Am **1** adj antiorario
2 adv in senso antiorario

counter-culture /'kaʊntəkʌltʃə(r)/ n controcultura f

counter-espionage n controspionaggio m

counterfeit /'kaʊntəfɪt/ **1** adj contraffatto
2 n contraffazione f
3 vt contraffare

counterfoil /'kaʊntəfɔɪl/ n matrice f

counter-inflationary /-ɪn'fleɪʃənərɪ/ adj antinflazionistico

counter-insurgency /-ɪn'sɜ:dʒənsɪ/ attrib per reprimere un'insurrezione

counter-intelligence n controspionaggio m

countermeasure /'kaʊntəmeʒə(r)/ n contromisura f

counter-offensive n controffensiva f

counterpane /'kaʊntəpeɪn/ n copriletto m

counterpart /'kaʊntəpɑ:t/ n equivalente mf

counterpoint /'kaʊntəpɔɪnt/ n contrappunto mf

counter-productive adj controproduttivo

countersign /'kaʊntəsaɪn/ vt controfirmare

countersignature n controfirma f

counter staff n commessi mpl

counter-terrorism n antiterrorismo m

countess /'kaʊntɪs/ n contessa f

countless /'kaʊntlɪs/ *adj* innumerevole

countrified /'kʌntrɪfaɪd/ *adj* ⟨person⟩ campagnolo

country /'kʌntrɪ/ *n* nazione *f*, paese *m*; (native land) patria *f*; (countryside) campagna *f*; **in the** ∼ in campagna; **go to the** ∼ andare in campagna; Pol indire le elezioni politiche

country and western *n* country *m* inv

country bumpkin *n* pej buzzurro, -a *mf*

country club *n* club *m* inv sportivo e ricreativo in campagna

country cousin *n* pej provinciale *mf*

country dancing *n* danza *f* folcloristica

country house *n* villa *f* di campagna

countryman *n* uomo *m* di campagna; (fellow ∼) compatriota *m*

country music *n* country *m* inv

countryside *n* campagna *f*

countrywide *adj & adv* in tutto il paese

county /'kaʊntɪ/ *n* contea *f* (unità amministrativa britannica)

county council *n* Br Pol consiglio *m* di contea

county court *n* Br Jur tribunale *m* di contea

coup /kuː/ *n* Pol colpo *m* di stato

couple /'kʌpl/ *n* coppia *f*; **a** ∼ **of** un paio di

coupon /'kuːpɒn/ *n* tagliando *m*; (for discount) buono *m* sconto

courage /'kʌrɪdʒ/ *n* coraggio *m*

courageous /kə'reɪdʒəs/ *adj* coraggioso

courageously /kə'reɪdʒəslɪ/ *adv* coraggiosamente

courgette /kʊə'ʒet/ *n* zucchino *m*

courier /'kʊrɪə(r)/ *n* corriere *m*; (for tourists) guida *f*

course /kɔːs/ *n* Sch corso *m*; Naut rotta *f*; Culin portata *f*; (for golf) campo *m*; ∼ **of treatment** Med serie *f* inv di cure; **of** ∼ naturalmente; **in the** ∼ **of** durante; **in due** ∼ a tempo debito; ∼ **of action** linea *f* d'azione

course book *n* libro *m* di testo

coursework /'kɔːswɜːk/ *n* Sch, Univ esercitazioni *fpl* scritte che contano per la media

court /kɔːt/ **①** *n* tribunale *m*; Sport campo *m*; **take somebody to** ∼ citare qualcuno in giudizio
② *vt* fare la corte a ⟨woman⟩; sfidare ⟨danger⟩; ∼**ing couples** coppiette *fpl*

court case *n* caso *m* giudiziario

court circular *n* bollettino quotidiano *f* di corte

courteous /'kɜːtɪəs/ *adj* cortese

courteously /'kɜːtɪəslɪ/ *adv* cortesemente

courtesy /'kɜːtəsɪ/ *n* cortesia *f*

courtesy bus *n* servizio *m* bus navetta

courtesy car *n* vettura *f* di cortesia

courthouse /'kɔːthaʊs/ *n* Jur palazzo *m* di giustizia, tribunale *m*

courtier /'kɔːtɪə(r)/ *n* cortigiano, -a *mf*

court martial **①** *n* (*pl* ∼**s martial**) corte *f* marziale
② **court-martial** *vt* (*pt* ∼**led**) portare davanti alla corte marziale

court of inquiry *n* commissione *f* d'inchiesta

court of law *n* Jur corte *f* di giustizia

court order *n* Jur ingiunzione *f*

courtroom *n* Jur aula *f* [di tribunale]

courtship /'kɔːtʃɪp/ *n* corteggiamento *m*

courtyard /'kɔːtjɑːd/ *n* cortile *m*

cousin /'kʌzn/ *n* cugino, -a *mf*

cove /kəʊv/ *n* insenatura *f*

covenant /'kʌvənənt/ *n* (agreement) accordo *m*; (payment agreement) impegno *m* scritto a pagare

cover /'kʌvə(r)/ **①** *n* copertura *f*; (of cushion, to protect something) fodera *f*; (of book, magazine) copertina *f*; **take** ∼ mettersi al riparo; **under separate** ∼ a parte
② *vt* coprire; foderare ⟨cushion⟩; Journ fare un servizio su

■ **cover for** *vt* (replace) sostituire ⟨somebody⟩

■ **cover up** *vt* coprire; fig soffocare ⟨scandal⟩

■ **cover up for** *vt* fare da copertura a ⟨somebody⟩

coverage /'kʌvərɪdʒ/ *n* Journ **it got a lot of** ∼ i media gli hanno dedicato molto spazio

cover charge *n* coperto *m*

covered market /'kʌvəd/ *n* mercato *m* coperto

covered wagon *n* carro *m* coperto

cover girl *n* ragazza *f* copertina

covering /'kʌv(ə)rɪŋ/ *n* copertura *f*; (for floor) rivestimento *m*; ∼ **of snow** strato *m* di neve

covering fire *n* fuoco *m* di copertura

covering letter *n* lettera *f* d'accompagnamento

cover note *n* (from insurance company) polizza *f* provvisoria

cover story *n* (in paper) articolo *m* di prima pagina

covert /'kəʊvɜːt/ *adj* ⟨threat⟩ velato; ⟨operation⟩ segreto; ⟨glance⟩ furtivo

covertly /'kəʊvɜːtlɪ/ *adv* furtivamente; ⟨operate⟩ in segreto

cover-up *n* messa *f* a tacere

cover version n Mus versione f non originale

covet /'kʌvɪt/ vt bramare

covetous /'kʌvətəs/ adj avido

covetously /'kʌvətəslɪ/ adv avidamente

cow /kaʊ/ n vacca f, mucca f

coward /'kaʊəd/ n vigliacco, -a mf

cowardice /'kaʊədɪs/ n vigliaccheria f

cowardly /'kaʊədlɪ/ adj da vigliacco

cowbell /'kaʊbel/ n campanaccio m

cowboy /'kaʊbɔɪ/ n cowboy m inv; fig fam buffone m

cower /'kaʊə(r)/ vi acquattarsi

cowherd /'kaʊhɜːd/ n vaccaro m

cowhide /'kaʊhaɪd/ n (leather) vacchetta f

cowl /kaʊl/ n cappuccio m

cowlick /'kaʊlɪk/ n fam ciocca f ribelle

cowl neck n collo m ad anello

cowpat /'kaʊpæt/ n sterco m di vacca

cowshed /'kaʊʃed/ n stalla f

cox /kɒks/ n **coxswain** /'kɒks(ə)n/ n timoniere, -a mf

coy /kɔɪ/ adj falsamente timido; (flirtatiously) civettuolo; **be ~ about something** essere evasivo su qualcosa

coyly /'kɔɪlɪ/ adv con falsa modestia; ⟨flirtatiously⟩ con civetteria

cozy /'kəʊzɪ/ adj Am = cosy

CPU n abbr (**central processing unit**) CPU f inv

crab /kræb/ n granchio m

crab apple n mela f selvatica

crack /kræk/ ①❭ n (in wall) crepa f; (in china, glass, bone) incrinatura f; (in noise) scoppio m; (fam: joke) battuta f; **have a ~** (try) fare un tentativo

②❭ adj (fam: best) di prim'ordine

③❭ vt incrinare ⟨china, glass⟩; schiacciare ⟨nut⟩; decifrare ⟨code⟩ fam risolvere ⟨problem⟩; **~ a joke** fam fare una battuta

④❭ vt ⟨china, glass⟩ incrinarsi; ⟨whip⟩ schioccare

■ **crack down** vi fam prendere seri provvedimenti

■ **crack down on** vt fam prendere seri provvedimenti contro

■ **crack up** vi crollare

crackdown /'krækdaʊn/ n misure fpl (on contro)

cracked /krækt/ adj ⟨plaster⟩ crepato; ⟨skin⟩ screpolato; ⟨rib⟩ incrinato; (fam: crazy) svitato

cracker /'krækə(r)/ n (biscuit) cracker m inv; (firework) petardo m; [**Christmas**] ~ cilindro m di cartone contenente una sorpresa che produce una piccola esplosione quando viene aperto

crackers /'krækəz/ adj fam matto

cracking /'krækɪŋ/ adj Br fam eccellente; **at a ~ pace** a ritmo incalzante

crackle /'krækl/ vi crepitare

crackling /'kræklɪŋ/ n (on radio) disturbo m; (of foil, cellophane) sfregamento m; (of fire) crepitio m; (crisp pork) cotenna f arrostita

crackpot /'krækpɒt/ fam ①❭ n pazzo, -a mf

②❭ adj da pazzi

cradle /'kreɪdl/ n culla f

cradle-snatcher n fam **he's/she's a ~** se la intende con i ragazzini/le ragazzine

craft¹ /krɑːft/ n inv (boat) imbarcazione f

craft² n mestiere m; (technique) arte f

craft fair n mostra f dell'artigianato

craftily /'krɑːftɪlɪ/ adv con astuzia

craftsman /'krɑːftsmən/ n artigiano m

craftsmanship /'krɑːftsmənʃɪp/ n maestria f

crafty /'krɑːftɪ/ adj (**-ier, -iest**) astuto

crag /kræg/ n rupe f

craggy /'krægɪ/ adj scosceso; ⟨face⟩ dai lineamenti marcati

cram /kræm/ ①❭ v (pt/pp **crammed**) vt stipare (**into** in)

②❭ vi (for exams) sgobbare

crammer /'kræmə(r)/ n (Br fam: school) ≈ istituto m di recupero

cramp /kræmp/ n crampo m

cramped /kræmpt/ adj ⟨room⟩ stretto; ⟨handwriting⟩ appiccicato; **it's a bit ~ in here** si sta un po' stretti qui

crampon /'kræmpən/ n rampone m

cranberry /'krænbərɪ/ n Culin mirtillo m rosso

crane /kreɪn/ ①❭ n (at docks, bird) gru f inv

②❭ vt **~ one's neck** allungare il collo

cranium /'kreɪnɪəm/ n cranio m

crank¹ /kræŋk/ n tipo, -a mf strampalato, -a

crank² n Techn manovella f

crankshaft /'kræŋkʃɑːft/ n albero m a gomiti

cranky /'kræŋkɪ/ adj strampalato; (Am: irritable) irritabile

cranny /'krænɪ/ n fessura f

crap /kræp/ n sl (faeces) merda f; (film, book etc) schifezza f; (nonsense) stronzate fpl; **have a ~** cacare

crappy /'kræpɪ/ adj sl di merda

crash /kræʃ/ ①❭ n (noise) fragore m; Auto, Aeron incidente m; Comm crollo m; Comput crash m inv

②❭ vi schiantarsi (**into** contro); ⟨plane⟩ precipitare

③❭ vt schiantare ⟨car⟩

■ **crash out** vi (sl: go to sleep) crollare; (on sofa etc) dormire

crash barrier n guardrail m inv

crash course n corso m intensivo

crash diet n dieta f drastica

crash-helmet n casco m

crash-land *vi* fare un atterraggio di fortuna

crash-landing *n* atterraggio *m* di fortuna

crass /kræs/ *adj* ⟨*ignorance*⟩ crasso

crate /kreɪt/ *n* (for packing) cassa *f*

crater /ˈkreɪtə(r)/ *n* cratere *m*

cravat /krəˈvæt/ *n* foulard *m inv*

crave /kreɪv/ *vt* morire dalla voglia di

craving /ˈkreɪvɪŋ/ *n* voglia *f* smodata

crawl /krɔːl/ ① *n* (swimming) stile *m* libero; **do the ~** nuotare a stile libero; **at a ~** a passo di lumaca
② *vi* andare carponi; **~ with** brulicare di

crawler lane /ˈkrɔːlə/ *n* Auto corsia *f* riservata al traffico lento

crayfish /ˈkreɪfɪʃ/ *n* gambero *m* d'acqua dolce

crayon /ˈkreɪən/ *n* pastello *m* a cera; (pencil) matita *f* colorata

craze /kreɪz/ *n* mania *f*

crazed /kreɪzd/ *adj* ⟨*china, glaze*⟩ screpolato; ⟨*animal, person*⟩ impazzito; **power-~** ubriaco di potere

crazy /ˈkreɪzɪ/ *adj* (**-ier**, **-iest**) matto; **be ~ about** andar matto per

crazy golf *n* Br minigolf *m inv*

crazy paving *n* Br pavimentazione *f* a mosaico irregolare

creak /kriːk/ ① *n* scricchiolio *m*
② *vi* scricchiolare

creaky /ˈkriːkɪ/ *adj* ⟨*leather*⟩ che cigola; ⟨*door, hinge*⟩ cigolante; ⟨*joint, bone, floorboard*⟩ scricchiolante; fig fam ⟨*alibi, policy*⟩ traballante

cream /kriːm/ ① *n* crema *f*; (fresh) panna *f*
② *adj* ⟨*colour*⟩ [bianco] panna *inv*
③ *vt* Culin sbattere
■ **cream off** *vt* accaparrarsi ⟨*top pupils, scientists etc*⟩

cream cheese *n* formaggio *m* cremoso

cream cracker *n* Br cracker *m inv*

cream puff *n* sfogliatina *f* alla panna *inv*

cream soda *n* soda *f* aromatizzata alla vaniglia

cream tea *n* Br tè *m inv* servito con pasticcini da mangiare con marmellata e panna

creamy /ˈkriːmɪ/ *adj* (**-ier**, **-iest**) cremoso

crease /kriːs/ ① *n* piega *f*
② *vt* stropicciare
③ *vi* stropicciarsi

crease-resistant *adj* che non si stropiccia

create /kriːˈeɪt/ *vt* creare

creation /kriːˈeɪʃn/ *n* creazione *f*

creative /kriːˈeɪtɪv/ *adj* creativo

creative director *n* direttore, -trice *mf* creativo, -a

creative writing *n* (school subject) composizione *f*

creativity /kriːeɪˈtɪvətɪ/ *n* creatività *f*

creator /kriːˈeɪtə(r)/ *n* creatore, -trice *mf*

creature /ˈkriːtʃə(r)/ *n* creatura *f*

creature comforts *npl* comodità *fpl*; **like one's ~ ~** amare le proprie comodità

crèche /kreʃ/ *n* asilo *m* nido *inv*

credence /ˈkriːdəns/ *n* credito *m*; **give ~ to something** (believe) dare credito a qualcosa

credentials /krɪˈdenʃlz/ *npl* credenziali *fpl*

credibility /kredəˈbɪlətɪ/ *n* credibilità *f*

credible /ˈkredəbl/ *adj* credibile

credit /ˈkredɪt/ ① *n* credito *m*; (honour) merito *m*; **take the ~ for** prendersi il merito di
② *vt* accreditare; **~ somebody with something** Comm accreditare qualcosa a qualcuno; fig attribuire qualcosa a qualcuno

creditable /ˈkredɪtəbl/ *adj* lodevole

credit balance *n* saldo *m* attivo

credit card *n* carta *f* di credito

credit control *n* controllo *m* del credito

credit facilities *npl* facilitazioni *fpl* creditizie

credit limit *n* limite *m* di credito

credit note *n* Comm nota *f* di accredito

creditor /ˈkredɪtə(r)/ *n* creditore, -trice *mf*

credits /ˈkredɪts/ *npl* titoli *mpl* di coda

credit side *n* on the **~ ~** tra i lati positivi

credit squeeze *n* stretta *f* creditizia

credit terms *npl* condizioni *fpl* di credito

credit transfer *n* bonifico *m*

creditworthiness /ˈkredɪ(t)wɜːðɪnɪs/ *n* capacità *f* di credito

creditworthy /ˈkredɪ(t)wɜːðɪ/ *adj* meritevole di credito

credulity /krɪˈdjuːlətɪ/ *n* credulità *f*; **strain sb's ~** essere ai limiti della credibilità

credulous /ˈkredjʊləs/ *adj* credulo

creed /kriːd/ *n* credo *m inv*

creek /kriːk/ *n* insenatura *f*; (Am: stream) torrente *m*; **up the ~** (fam: in trouble) nei guai

creep /kriːp/ ① *vi* (pt/pp **crept**) muoversi furtivamente
② *n* fam tipo *m* viscido; **it gives me the ~s** mi fa venire i brividi

creeper /ˈkriːpə(r)/ *n* pianta *f* rampicante

creepy /'kri:pɪ/ *adj* che fa venire i brividi

creepy-crawly /-'krɔːlɪ/ *n* fam insetto

cremate /krɪ'meɪt/ *vt* cremare

cremation /krɪ'meɪʃn/ *n* cremazione *f*

crematorium /kremə'tɔːrɪəm/ *n* crematorio *m*

crepe /kreɪp/ *n* (fabric) crespo *m*

crepe bandage *n* fascia *f* elastica

crepe paper *n* carta *f* crespata

crepe soles *npl* suole *fpl* di para

crept /krept/ ▶ CREEP

crescendo /krɪ'ʃendəʊ/ *n* Mus crescendo *m*; **reach a ∼** fig *(noise, protests)* raggiungere il picco; *(campaign)* raggiungere il culmine

crescent /'kresənt/ *n* mezzaluna *f*

crescent moon *n* mezzaluna *f*

cress /kres/ *n* crescione *m*

crest /krest/ *n* cresta *f*; (coat of arms) cimiero *m*; **be on the ∼ of a wave** essere sulla cresta dell'onda

crestfallen /'krestfɔːlən/ *adj* mogio

Crete /kriːt/ *n* Creta *f*

Creutzfeldt-Jakob disease /krɔɪtsfelt'jækɒb/ *n* morbo *m* di Creutzfeldt Jakob

crevasse /krɪ'væs/ *n* crepaccio *m*

crevice /'krevɪs/ *n* crepa *f*

crew /kruː/ *n* equipaggio *m*; (gang) équipe *f inv*

crew cut *n* capelli *mpl* a spazzola

crew neck *n* girocollo *m*

crew neck sweater *n* maglione *m* a girocollo

crib[1] /krɪb/ *n* (for baby) culla *f*

crib[2] *vt/i* (pt/pp **cribbed**) fam copiare

cribbage /'krɪbɪdʒ/ *n* gioco *m* di carte

crick /krɪk/ *n* **∼ in the neck** torcicollo *m*

cricket[1] /'krɪkɪt/ *n* (insect) grillo *m*

cricket[2] *n* cricket *m*

cricketer /'krɪkɪtə(r)/ *n* giocatore *m* di cricket

crime /kraɪm/ *n* crimine *m*; (criminality) criminalità *f*; **it's a ∼** fig è un delitto

crime of passion *n* delitto *m* passionale

crime prevention *n* prevenzione *f* della criminalità

criminal /'krɪmɪnl/ **1** *adj* criminale; *(law, court)* penale **2** *n* criminale *mf*

criminal charges *npl* **face ∼ ∼** essere imputato

criminal investigation *n* inchiesta *f* giudiziaria

Criminal Investigation Department *n* Br ≈ polizia *f* giudiziaria

criminal justice *n* sistema *m* penale

criminal law *n* diritto *m* penale

criminally insane /'krɪmɪnəlɪ/ *adj* pazzo criminale

criminal offence *n* reato *m*

criminal record *n* **have a/no ∼ ∼** avere la fedina penale sporca/pulita

criminology /krɪmɪ'nɒlədʒɪ/ *n* criminologia *f*

crimp /krɪmp/ *vt* pieghettare *(fabric)*; increspare *(pastry)*; arricciare *(hair)*

crimson /'krɪmz(ə)n/ *adj* cremisi *inv*

cringe /krɪndʒ/ *vi* (cower) acquattarsi; (at bad joke etc) fare una smorfia

crinkle /'krɪŋk(ə)l/ **1** *vt* spiegazzare **2** *vi* spiegazzarsi

crinkly /'krɪŋklɪ/ *adj* *(paper, material)* crespato; *(hair)* crespo

cripple /'krɪpl/ **1** *n* storpio, -a *mf* **2** *vt* storpiare; fig danneggiare

crippled /'krɪpld/ *adj* *(person)* storpio; *(ship)* danneggiato

crippling /'krɪplɪŋ/ *adj* *(taxes, debts)* esorbitante; *(disease)* devastante; *(strike, effect)* paralizzante

crisis /'kraɪsɪs/ *n* (pl **-ses** /'kraɪsiːz/) crisi *f inv*

crisp /krɪsp/ *adj* croccante; *(air)* frizzante; *(style)* incisivo

crispbread /'krɪs(p)bred/ *n* crostini *mpl* di pane

crisps /krɪsps/ *npl* patatine *fpl*

crispy /'krɪspɪ/ *adj* croccante

criss-cross /'krɪs-/ *adj* a linee incrociate

criterion /kraɪ'tɪərɪən/ *n* (pl **-ria** /kraɪ'tɪərɪə/) criterio *m*

critic /'krɪtɪk/ *n* critico, -a *mf*

critical /'krɪtɪkl/ *adj* critico

critically /'krɪtɪklɪ/ *adv* in modo critico; **∼ ill** gravemente malato

critical path analysis *n* analisi *f inv* del percorso critico

criticism /'krɪtɪsɪzm/ *n* critica *f*; **he doesn't like ∼** non ama le critiche

criticize /'krɪtɪsaɪz/ *vt* criticare

croak /krəʊk/ *vi* gracchiare; *(frog)* gracidare

Croatia /krəʊ'eɪʃə/ *n* Croazia *f*

crochet /'krəʊʃeɪ/ **1** *n* lavoro *m* all'uncinetto **2** *vt* fare all'uncinetto

crochet-hook *n* uncinetto *m*

crock /krɒk/ *n* fam **old ∼** (person) rudere *m*; (car) macinino *m*

crockery /'krɒkərɪ/ *n* terrecotte *fpl*

crocodile /'krɒkədaɪl/ *n* coccodrillo *m*

crocodile tears *npl* lacrime *fpl* di coccodrillo

crocus /ˈkrəʊkəs/ n (pl **-es**) croco m

croft /krɒft/ n piccola fattoria f

croissant /ˈkrwæsã/ n cornetto m, croissant m inv

crone /krəʊn/ n pej vecchiaccia f

crony /ˈkrəʊnɪ/ n compare m

crook /krʊk/ n (fam: criminal) truffatore, -trice mf

crooked /ˈkrʊkɪd/ adj storto; ⟨limb⟩ storpiato; (fam: dishonest) disonesto; ∼ **deal** fregatura f

croon /kruːn/ vt/i canticchiare

crop /krɒp/ **1** n raccolto m; fig quantità f inv
2 v (pt/pp **cropped**)
3 vt coltivare
■ **crop up** vi fam presentarsi

crop rotation n rotazione f delle colture

crop spraying /ˈkrɒpspreɪŋ/ n irrorazione f

croquet /ˈkrəʊkeɪ/ n croquet m

croquette /krəʊˈket/ n crocchetta f

cross /krɒs/ **1** adj (annoyed) arrabbiato; **talk at** ∼ **purposes** fraintendersi
2 n croce f; Bot, Zool incrocio m
3 vt sbarrare ⟨cheque⟩; incrociare ⟨road, animals⟩; ∼ **oneself** farsi il segno della croce; ∼ **one's arms** incrociare le braccia; ∼ **one's legs** accavallare le gambe; **keep one's fingers** ∼**ed for somebody** tenere le dita incrociate per qualcuno; **it** ∼**ed my mind** mi è venuto in mente
4 vi (go across) attraversare; ⟨lines⟩ incrociarsi
■ **cross off** vt (from list) depennare
■ **cross out** vt sbarrare; (from list) depennare

crossbar n (of goal) traversa f; (on bicycle) canna f

cross-border adj oltreconfine

crossbow n balestra f

crossbred adj ibrido

crossbreed vt ibridare, incrociare ⟨animals, plants⟩ n (animal) incrocio m, ibrido m

cross-Channel adj attraverso la Manica; ⟨ferry⟩ che attraversa la Manica

cross-check n controprova f vt fare la controprova di

cross-contamination n contaminazione f incrociata

cross-country n Sport corsa f campestre

cross-country skiing n sci m di fondo

cross-court adj ⟨shot, volley⟩ diagonale

cross-cultural adj multiculturale

crosscurrent n corrente f trasversale

cross-dressing n travestitismo m

cross-examination n controinterrogatorio m

cross-examine vt sottoporre a controinterrogatorio

cross-eyed /ˈkrɒsaɪd/ adj strabico

crossfire n fuoco m incrociato

crossing /ˈkrɒsɪŋ/ n (for pedestrians) passaggio m pedonale; (sea journey) traversata f

cross-legged /krɒsˈlegd/ adj & adv con le gambe incrociate

crossly /ˈkrɒslɪ/ adv con rabbia

crossover adj ⟨straps⟩ incrociato

cross-party adj ⟨talks, committee⟩ interpartitico

cross-purposes npl we are at ∼ non ci siamo capiti

cross-question vt interrogare ⟨person⟩

cross-reference n rimando m

crossroads n incrocio m; **reach a** ∼ fig arrivare a un bivio

cross-section n sezione f; (of community) campione m

cross-stitch n punto m croce

crosswalk n Am attraversamento m pedonale

crosswind n vento m di traverso

crosswise adv in diagonale

crossword n ∼ **[puzzle]** parole fpl crociate

crotch /krɒtʃ/ n Anat inforcatura f; (in trousers) cavallo m

crotchet /ˈkrɒtʃɪt/ n Mus semiminima f

crotchety /ˈkrɒtʃətɪ/ adj irritabile

crouch /kraʊtʃ/ vi accovacciarsi

croupier /ˈkruːpɪə(r)/ n croupier m inv

crouton /ˈkruːtɒn/ n crostino m

crow /krəʊ/ **1** n corvo m; **as the** ∼ **flies** in linea d'aria
2 vi cantare

crowbar /ˈkrəʊbɑː/ n piede m di porco

crowd /kraʊd/ **1** n folla f
2 vt affollare
3 vi affollarsi

crowd control n controllo m della folla

crowded /ˈkraʊdɪd/ adj affollato

crowd-puller /ˈkraʊdpʊlə(r)/ n (event) grande attrazione f

crowd scene n Cinema, Theat scena f di massa

crown /kraʊn/ **1** n corona f
2 vt incoronare; incapsulare ⟨tooth⟩

Crown court n Br Jur ≈ corte f d'Assise

crowning glory /ˈkraʊnɪŋ/ n culmine m; **her hair is her** ∼ ∼ i capelli sono il suo punto forte

crown jewels npl gioielli mpl della corona

crown prince n principe m ereditario

crow's feet /ˈkrəʊzˈfiːt/ npl (on face) zampe fpl di gallina

crow's nest /ˈkrəʊzˈnest/ n coffa f

crucial /ˈkruːʃl/ adj cruciale

crucially /ˈkruːʃəlɪ/ adv ~ **important** di vitale importanza

crucifix /ˈkruːsɪfɪks/ n crocifisso m

crucifixion /kruːsɪˈfɪkʃn/ n crocifissione f

crucify /ˈkruːsɪfaɪ/ vt (pt/pp **-ied**) crocifiggere

crude /kruːd/ adj ⟨oil⟩ greggio; ⟨language⟩ crudo; ⟨person⟩ rozzo

crudely /ˈkruːdlɪ/ adv (vulgarly) in modo crudo; (simply) schematicamente; (roughly: assembled) sommariamente; ⟨painted, made⟩ rozzamente; ~ **speaking** in parole povere

crudity /ˈkruːdətɪ/ n (vulgarity) volgarità f

cruel /ˈkruːəl/ adj (**-ler**, **-lest**) crudele (**to** verso)

cruelly /ˈkruːəlɪ/ adv con crudeltà

cruelty /ˈkruːəltɪ/ n crudeltà f

cruelty-free adj ⟨cosmetics⟩ non testato sugli animali

cruise /kruːz/ ❶ n crociera f
❷ vi fare una crociera; ⟨car⟩ andare a velocità di crociera

cruise liner n nave f da crociera

cruise missile n missile m cruise inv

cruiser /ˈkruːzə(r)/ n Mil incrociatore m; (motor boat) motoscafo m

cruising speed /ˈkruːzɪŋ/ n velocità m inv di crociera

crumb /krʌm/ n briciola f

crumble /ˈkrʌmbl/ ❶ vt sbriciolare
❷ vi sbriciolarsi; ⟨building, society⟩ sgretolarsi

crumbling /ˈkrʌmblɪŋ/ adj fatiscente

crumbly /ˈkrʌmblɪ/ adj friabile

crummy /ˈkrʌmɪ/ adj fam (substandard) scadente; (Am: unwell) malato

crumpet /ˈkrʌmpɪt/ n Culin focaccina f da tostare e mangiare con burro e marmellata

crumple /ˈkrʌmpl/ ❶ vt spiegazzare
❷ vi spiegazzarsi

crunch /krʌntʃ/ ❶ n fam **when it comes to the** ~ quando si viene al dunque
❷ vt sgranocchiare
❸ vi ⟨snow⟩ scricchiolare

crunchy /ˈkrʌntʃɪ/ adj ⟨vegetables, biscuits⟩ croccante

crusade /kruːˈseɪd/ n crociata f

crusader /kruːˈseɪdə(r)/ n crociato m

crush /krʌʃ/ ❶ n (crowd) calca f; **have a** ~ **on somebody** essersi preso una cotta per qualcuno
❷ vt schiacciare; sgualcire ⟨clothes⟩

crushed ice /krʌʃtˈaɪs/ n ghiaccio m tritato

crushed velvet n velluto m stazzonato

crushing /ˈkrʌʃɪŋ/ adj ⟨defeat, weight, blow⟩ schiacciante; ⟨blow⟩ tremendo

crust /krʌst/ n crosta f

crustacean /krʌˈsteɪʃn/ n crostaceo m

crusty /ˈkrʌstɪ/ adj ⟨bread⟩ croccante; (irritable) scontroso

crutch /krʌtʃ/ n gruccia f; Anat inforcatura f

crux /krʌks/ n fig punto m cruciale; ~ **of the matter** nodo m della questione

cry /kraɪ/ ❶ n grido m; ~ **for help** grido d'aiuto; **have a** ~ farsi un pianto; **a far** ~ **from** fig tutta un'altra cosa rispetto a
❷ vi (pt/pp **cried**) (weep) piangere; (call) gridare
■ **cry off** vi (Br: cancel) disdire
■ **cry out** vi (shout) urlare

cryogenics /kraɪəˈdʒenɪks/ n criogenia f

crypt /krɪpt/ n cripta f

cryptic /ˈkrɪptɪk/ adj criptico

cryptically /ˈkrɪptɪklɪ/ adv ⟨say, speak⟩ in modo enigmatico; ~ **worded** espresso in maniera sibillina

crystal /ˈkrɪstl/ n cristallo m; (glassware) cristalli mpl

crystal ball n sfera f di cristallo

crystal clear adj ⟨water, sound⟩ cristallino; **let me make it** ~ ~ lasciatemelo spiegare chiaramente

crystal-gazing /ˈkrɪstlgeɪzɪŋ/ n predizione f del futuro (con la sfera di cristallo)

crystallize /ˈkrɪstəlaɪz/ vi (become clear) concretizzarsi

CS gas n Br gas m inv lacrimogeno

CST abbr Am (**Central Standard Time**) ora f solare della zona centrale dell'America settentrionale

C2C /siːtəˈsiː/ abbr (**consumer to consumer**) C2C

cub /kʌb/ n (animal) cucciolo m; **C**~ [Scout] lupetto m

Cuba /ˈkjuːbə/ n Cuba f

Cuban /ˈkjuːbən/ adj & n cubano -a, mf

cubby-hole /ˈkʌbɪ-/ n (compartment) scomparto m; (room) ripostiglio m

cube /kjuːb/ n cubo m

cubic /ˈkjuːbɪk/ adj cubico

cubicle /ˈkjuːbɪkl/ n cabina f

cubism /ˈkjuːbɪzm/ n cubismo m

cubist /ˈkjuːbɪst/ adj & n cubista mf

cub reporter n cronista mf alle prime armi

cuckoo /ˈkʊkuː/ n cuculo m

cuckoo clock n orologio m a cucù

cucumber /ˈkjuːkʌmbə(r)/ n cetriolo m

cud /kʌd/ n also fig **chew the** ~ ruminare

cuddle /'kʌd(ə)l/ ① vt coccolare
② vi ~ **up to** starsene accoccolato insieme a
③ n **have a** ~ ⟨child⟩ farsi coccolare; ⟨lovers⟩ abbracciarsi

cuddly /'kʌd(ə)lɪ/ adj tenerone; (wanting cuddles) coccolone

cuddly toy n peluche m inv

cudgel /'kʌdʒl/ n randello m

cue¹ /kju:/ n segnale m; Theat battuta f d'entrata

cue² n (in billiards) stecca f

cue ball n pallino m

cuff /kʌf/ ① n polsino m; (Am: turn-up) orlo m; (blow) scapaccione m; **off the** ~ improvvisando
② vt dare una pacca a

cuff link n gemello m

cuisine /kwɪ'zi:n/ n cucina f; **haute** ~ /əʊt/ haute cuisine f

cul-de-sac /'kʌldəsæk/ n vicolo m cieco

culinary /'kʌlɪnərɪ/ adj culinario

cull /kʌl/ vt scegliere ⟨flowers⟩ (kill) selezionare e uccidere

culminate /'kʌlmɪneɪt/ vi culminare

culmination /kʌlmɪ'neɪʃn/ n culmine m

culottes /kju:'lɒts/ npl gonna f.sg pantalone

culpable /'kʌlpəbl/ adj colpevole

culpable homicide n Jur omicidio m colposo

culprit /'kʌlprɪt/ n colpevole mf

cult /kʌlt/ n culto m

cultivate /'kʌltɪveɪt/ vt coltivare; fig coltivarsi ⟨person⟩

cultivated /'kʌltɪveɪtɪd/ adj ⟨soil⟩ lavorato; ⟨person⟩ colto

cultural /'kʌltʃərəl/ adj culturale

cultural attaché n addetto m culturale

culture /'kʌltʃə(r)/ n cultura f

cultured /'kʌltʃəd/ adj colto

cultured pearl n perla f coltivata

culture shock n shock m inv culturale

culture vulture n fam fanatico, -a mf di cultura

culvert /'kʌlvət/ n condotto m sotterraneo

cumbersome /'kʌmbəsəm/ adj ingombrante

cumin /'kju:mɪn/ n cumino m nero

cummerbund /'kʌməbʌnd/ n fascia f (dello smoking)

cumulative /'kju:mjʊlətɪv/ adj cumulativo

cunning /'kʌnɪŋ/ ① adj astuto
② n astuzia f

cup /kʌp/ n tazza f; (prize, of bra) coppa f

cupboard /'kʌbəd/ n armadio m

cupboard love n Br hum amore m interessato

cupboard space n spazio m negli armadi

Cup Final n finale f di coppa

cupful /'kʌpfʊl/ n tazza f (contenuto)

Cupid /'kju:pɪd/ n Cupido m

cupola /'kju:pələ/ n Archit cupola f

cup tie n Br partita f eliminatoria

cur /kɜ:(r)/ n (pej: dog) cagnaccio m

curable /'kjʊərəbl/ adj curabile

curate /'kjʊərət/ n curato m

curator /kjʊə'reɪtə(r)/ n direttore, -trice mf (di museo)

curb /kɜ:b/ vt tenere a freno

curd cheese /kɜ:d/ n cagliata f

curdle /'kɜ:dl/ vi coagularsi

cure /kjʊə(r)/ ① n cura f
② vt curare; (salt) mettere sotto sale; (smoke) affumicare

cure-all n toccasana m inv, panacea f

curfew /'kɜ:fju:/ n coprifuoco m

curio /'kjʊərɪəʊ/ n curiosità f inv

curiosity /kjʊərɪ'ɒsətɪ/ n curiosità f

curious /'kjʊərɪəs/ adj curioso

curiously /'kjʊərɪəslɪ/ adv curiosamente

curl /kɜ:l/ ① n ricciolo m
② vt arricciare
③ vi arricciarsi
■ **curl up** vi raggomitolarsi

curler /'kɜ:lə(r)/ n bigodino m

curling /'kɜ:lɪŋ/ n Sport curling m

curly /'kɜ:lɪ/ adj (-ier, -iest) riccio

curly-haired, **curly-headed** /-'heəd/, /-'hedɪd/ adj (tight curls) dai capelli crespi; (loose curls) riccio

currant /'kʌrənt/ n (dried) uvetta f

currency /'kʌrənsɪ/ n valuta f; (of word) ricorrenza f; **foreign** ~ valuta f estera

current /'kʌrənt/ ① adj corrente
② n corrente f

current account n Br conto m corrente

current affairs npl attualità f

current assets npl Fin disponibilità fpl correnti

current liabilities npl Fin passività fpl correnti

currently /'kʌrəntlɪ/ adv attualmente

curriculum /kə'rɪkjʊləm/ n programma m di studi

curriculum vitae /'vi:taɪ/ n curriculum vitae m inv

curry /'kʌrɪ/ ① n curry m inv; (meal) piatto m al curry
② vt (pt/pp **-ied**) ~ **favour with somebody** cercare d'ingraziarsi qualcuno

curry powder n curry m in polvere

curse /kɜːs/ **1** *n* maledizione *f*; (oath) imprecazione *f*
2 *vt* maledire
3 *vi* imprecare

cursor /'kɜːsə(r)/ *n* cursore *m*

cursor keys *npl* tasti *mpl* cursore

cursory /'kɜːsərɪ/ *adj* sbrigativo

curt /kɜːt/ *adj* brusco

curtail /kə'teɪl/ *vt* ridurre

curtailment /kə'teɪlmənt/ *n* (of rights, freedom) limitazione *f*; (of expenditure, service) riduzione *f*; (of holiday) interruzione *f*

curtain /'kɜːtn/ *n* tenda *f*; Theat sipario *m*
■ **curtain off** *vt* separare con una tenda

curtain call *n* Theat chiamata *f* alla ribalta

curtly /'kɜːtlɪ/ *adv* bruscamente

curtsy, curtsey /'kɜːtsɪ/ **1** *n* inchino *m*
2 *vi* (pt/pp **-ied**) fare l'inchino

curvaceous /kɜː'veɪʃəs/ *adj* formoso

curve /kɜːv/ **1** *n* curva *f*
2 *vi* curvare; ~ **to the right/left** curvare a destra/sinistra

curved /kɜːvd/ *adj* curvo

curvy /'kɜːvɪ/ *adj* (**-ier, -iest**) ‹woman› formoso

cushion /'kʊʃn/ **1** *n* cuscino *m*
2 *vt* attutire; (protect) proteggere

cushy /'kʊʃɪ/ *adj* (**-ier, -iest**) fam facile

custard /'kʌstəd/ *n* (liquid) crema *f* pasticcera

custard cream *n* Br biscotto *m* farcito alla crema

custard pie *n* torta *f* alla crema (nei film comici)

custard tart *n* torta *f* alla crema

custodial sentence /kʌ'stəʊdɪəl/ *n* condanna *f* ad una pena detentiva

custodian /kʌ'stəʊdɪən/ *n* custode *mf*

custody /'kʌstədɪ/ *n* (of child) custodia *f*; (imprisonment) detenzione *f* preventiva

custom /'kʌstəm/ *n* usanza *f*; Jur consuetudine *f*; Comm clientela *f*

customary /'kʌstəmərɪ/ *adj* (habitual) abituale; **it's ~ to...** è consuetudine...

custom-built /-'bɪlt/ *adj* ‹house› ad hoc

custom car *n* vettura *f* personalizzata

customer /'kʌstəmə(r)/ *n* cliente *mf*

customer care *n* assistenza *f* alla clientela

customer feedback *n* feedback *m inv* dai clienti

customer relations *npl* rapporto *m* con i clienti

customer service *n* assistenza *f* ai clienti

customize /'kʌstəmaɪz/ *vt* personalizzare

custom-made /-'meɪd/ *adj* su misura

customs /'kʌstəmz/ *npl* dogana *f*

Customs and Excise *n* Br ufficio *m* Dazi e Dogana

customs clearance *n* sdoganamento *m*

customs declaration *n* dichiarazione *f* doganale

customs duties *npl* dazi *mpl* doganali

customs hall *n* dogana *f*

customs officer *n* doganiere *m*, guardia *f* di finanza

cut /kʌt/ **1** *n* (with knife etc, of clothes) taglio *m*; (reduction) riduzione *f*; (in public spending) taglio *m*
2 *vt/i* (pt/pp **cut**, pres p **cutting**) tagliare; (reduce) ridurre; ~ **one's finger** tagliarsi il dito; ~ **sb' hair** tagliare i capelli a qualcuno
3 *vi* (with cards) alzare
■ **cut away** *vt* tagliar via
■ **cut back** *vt* tagliare ‹hair›; potare ‹hedge›; (reduce) ridurre
■ **cut back on** *vt* (reduce) ridurre
■ **cut down** *vt* abbattere ‹tree›; (reduce) ridurre
■ **cut in 1** *vi* Auto tagliare la strada; (into conversation) interrompere
2 *vt* ~ **somebody in on a deal** dare una percentuale a qualcuno
■ **cut off** *vt* tagliar via; (disconnect) interrompere; fig isolare; **I was ~ off** Teleph la linea è caduta
■ **cut out** *vt* ritagliare; (delete) eliminare; **be ~ out for** fam essere tagliato per; ~ **it out!** fam dacci un taglio!
■ **cut short** *vt* interrompere ‹holiday, discussion›
■ **cut up** *vt* (slice) tagliare a pezzi

cut-and-dried *adj* ‹answer, solution› ovvio; **I like everything to be ~** mi piace che tutto sia ben chiaro e definito

cut and paste 1 *n* taglia e incolla *m*
2 *vt* tagliare e incollare

cut and thrust *n* **the ~ ~ ~ of debate** gli scambi *mpl* animati del dibattito

cutback /'kʌtbæk/ *n* riduzione *f*; (in government spending) taglio *m*

cute /kjuːt/ *adj* fam (in appearance) carino; (clever) acuto

cut glass *n* vetro *m* intagliato

cuticle /'kjuːtɪkl/ *n* cuticola *f*

cutlery /'kʌtlərɪ/ *n* posate *fpl*

cutlet /'kʌtlɪt/ *n* cotoletta *f*

cut-off *n* (upper limit) limite *m* [massimo]

cut-off date *n* data *f* di scadenza

cut-off point *n* limite *m*; Comm data *f* di scadenza

cut-offs *npl* (jeans) jeans *mpl* tagliati

cut-out *n* (outline) ritaglio *m*

cut-price *adj* a prezzo ridotto; ‹shop› che fa prezzi ridotti

cutter /'kʌtə(r)/ n (ship) cutter m inv; (on ship) lancia f; (for metal, glass) taglierina f

cut-throat [1] n assassino, -a mf
[2] adj ⟨competition⟩ spietato

cut-throat razor n Br rasoio m da barbiere

cutting /'kʌtɪŋ/ [1] adj ⟨remark⟩ tagliente
[2] n (from newspaper) ritaglio m; (of plant) talea f

cutting edge n (blade) filo m; **be at the ~ ~** fig essere all'avanguardia

cuttingly /'kʌtɪŋlɪ/ adv ⟨speak⟩ in maniera tagliente

cutting room n Cinema **end up on the ~ ~ floor** essere tagliato in fase di montaggio

CV n abbr (**Curriculum Vitae**) CV m

cwt abbr (**hundredweight**) Br ≈ 50 kg, Am ≈ 45 kg

cyanide /'saɪənaɪd/ n cianuro m

cybercafe /'saɪbəkæfeɪ/ n caffè m Internet

cyberculture /'saɪbəkʌltʃə(r)/ n cybercultura f

cybernetics /saɪbə'netɪks/ n cibernetica f

cyberspace /'saɪbəspeɪs/ n ciberspazio m

cyclamen /'sɪkləmən/ n ciclamino m

cycle /'saɪk(ə)l/ [1] n ciclo m; (bicycle) bicicletta f, fam bici f inv
[2] vi andare in bicicletta

cycle clip n fermacalzoni m inv

cycle lane n pista f ciclabile

cycle race n corsa f ciclistica

cycle rack n portabiciclette m inv

cycle track, **cycle path** n pista f ciclabile

cyclical /'saɪklɪkl/ adj ciclico

cycling /'saɪklɪŋ/ n ciclismo m

cycling holiday n Br vacanza f in bicicletta; **go on a ~ ~** fare una vacanza in bicicletta

cycling shorts npl pantaloncini mpl da ciclista

cyclist /'saɪklɪst/ n ciclista mf

cyclo-cross /'saɪkləʊ-/ n ciclocross m inv

cyclone /'saɪkləʊn/ n ciclone m

cygnet /'sɪgnɪt/ n cigno m giovane

cylinder /'sɪlɪndə(r)/ n cilindro m

cylindrical /sɪl'lɪndrɪkl/ adj cilindrico

cymbals /'sɪmblz/ npl Mus piatti mpl

cynic /'sɪnɪk/ n cinico, -a mf

cynical /'sɪnɪk(ə)l/ adj cinico

cynically /'sɪnɪklɪ/ adv cinicamente

cynicism /'sɪnɪsɪzm/ n cinismo m

cypress /'saɪprəs/ n cipresso m

Cypriot /'sɪprɪət/ adj & n cipriota mf

Cyprus /'saɪprəs/ n Cipro m

Cyrillic /sɪ'rɪlɪk/ adj cirillico

cyst /sɪst/ n ciste f

cystitis /sɪ'staɪtɪs/ n cistite f

Czar, czar /zɑː(r)/ n zar m inv

Czech /tʃek/ adj & n ceco, -a mf

Czechoslovak /tʃekə'sləʊvæk/ adj cecoslovacco

Czechoslovakia /tʃekəslə'vækɪə/ n Cecoslovacchia f

Czech Republic n Repubblica f Ceca

Dd

d¹, D /diː/ n (letter) d, D f inv; Mus re m inv

d² abbr (**died**) morto

dab /dæb/ [1] n colpetto m; **a ~ of un pochino di**
[2] vt (pt/pp **dabbed**) toccare leggermente ⟨eyes⟩
■ **dab on** vt mettere un po' di ⟨paint etc⟩

dabble /'dæbl/ vi **~ in something** fig occuparsi di qualcosa a tempo perso

dachshund /'dækshʊnd/ n bassotto m

dad[dy] /'dæd[ɪ]/ n fam papà m inv, babbo m

daddy-long-legs n zanzarone m [dei boschi]; (Am: spider) ragno m

daffodil /'dæfədɪl/ n giunchiglia f

daft /dɑːft/ adj sciocco

dagger /'dægə(r)/ n stiletto m; Typ croce f; **be at ~s drawn** fam essere ai ferri corti

dahlia /'deɪlɪə/ n dalia f

daily /'deɪlɪ/ [1] adj giornaliero
[2] adv giornalmente
[3] n (newspaper) quotidiano m; (fam: cleaner) donna f delle pulizie

daintily /'deɪntɪlɪ/ adv delicatamente

dainty /'deɪntɪ/ adj (**-ier, -iest**) grazioso; ⟨movement⟩ delicato

dairy /'deərɪ/ n caseificio m; (shop) latteria f

dairy cow n mucca f da latte

dairyman /'deərimən/ n (on farm) operaio m addetto all'allevamento di mucche [da latte]; (Am: farmer) allevatore m

dairy products npl latticini mpl

dais /'deɪɪs/ n pedana f

daisy /'deɪzɪ/ n margheritina f; (larger) margherita f

dale /deɪl/ n liter valle f

dally /'dælɪ/ vi (pt/pp -ied) stare a gingillarsi

dam /dæm/ ① n diga f
② vt (pt/pp **dammed**) costruire una diga su

damage /'dæmɪdʒ/ ① n danno m (to a); ~s pl Jur risarcimento msg
② vt danneggiare; fig nuocere a

damage limitation exercise n manovra f per contenere i danni

damaging /'dæmɪdʒɪŋ/ adj dannoso

damask /'dæməsk/ n damasco m

dame /deɪm/ n liter dama f; Am sl donna f

dammit /'dæmɪt/ int Br fam accidenti!

damn /dæm/ ① adj fam maledetto
② adv ⟨lucky, late⟩ maledettamente
③ n I don't care or give a ~ fam non me ne frega un accidente
④ vt dannare

damnation /dæm'neɪʃn/ ① n dannazione f
② int fam accidenti!

damnedest /'dæmdɪst/ ① n do one's ~ (to do) (fam: hardest) fare del proprio meglio (per fare)
② adj it was the ~ thing (surprising) era la cosa più straordinaria

damning /'dæmɪŋ/ adj schiacciante

damp /dæmp/ ① adj umido
② n umidità f
③ vt = DAMPEN

dampen /'dæmpən/ vt inumidire; fig raffreddare ⟨enthusiasm⟩

damper /'dæmpə(r)/ n the news put a ~ on the evening fam la notizia ha raggelato l'atmosfera della serata

dampness /'dæmpnɪs/ n umidità f

damson /'dæmzən/ n (fruit) susina f selvatica, prugna f selvatica

dance /dɑ:ns/ ① n ballo m
② vt/i ballare
∎ **dance about, dance up and down** vi saltellare qua e là

dance hall n sala f da ballo

dance music n musica f da ballo

dancer /'dɑ:nsə(r)/ n ballerino, -a mf

dancing /'dɑ:nsɪŋ/ n ballo m

dandelion /'dændɪlaɪən/ n dente m di leone

dandruff /'dændrʌf/ n forfora f

Dane /deɪn/ n danese mf; **Great ~** danese m

danger /'deɪndʒə(r)/ n pericolo m; **in/out of ~** in/fuori pericolo

danger level n livello m di guardia

danger list n on the ~ ~ in prognosi riservata; off the ~ ~ fuori pericolo

danger money n indennità f di rischio

dangerous /'deɪndʒərəs/ adj pericoloso

dangerously /'deɪndʒərəslɪ/ adv pericolosamente; ~ ill in pericolo di vita

danger signal n also fig segnale m di pericolo

dangle /'dæŋgl/ ① vi penzolare; fig **leave somebody dangling** lasciare qualcuno in sospeso
② vt far penzolare

Danish /'deɪnɪʃ/ ① adj danese
② n (language) danese m

Danish pastry n dolce m di pasta sfoglia contenente pasta di mandorle, mele ecc

dank /dæŋk/ adj umido e freddo

Danube /'dænju:b/ n Danubio m

dapper /'dæpə(r)/ adj azzimato

dappled /'dæp(ə)ld/ adj ⟨grey, horse⟩ pomellato; ⟨sky⟩ screziato; ⟨shade, surface⟩ chiazzato

dare /deə(r)/ ① vt/i osare; (challenge) sfidare (to a); ~ [to] do something osare fare qualcosa; I ~ say! molto probabilmente!
② n sfida f

daredevil /'deədevl/ n spericolato, -a mf

daring /'deərɪŋ/ ① adj audace
② n audacia f

dark /dɑ:k/ ① adj buio; ~ blue/brown blu/marrone scuro; It's getting ~ sta cominciando a fare buio; ~ horse fig (in race, contest) vincitore m imprevisto; (not much known about) misterioso m; keep something ~ fig tenere qualcosa nascosto
② n after ~ col buio; in the ~ al buio; keep somebody in the ~ fig tenere qualcuno all'oscuro

Dark Ages n alto Medioevo m

dark chocolate n cioccolato m fondente

darken /'dɑ:kn/ ① vt oscurare
② vi oscurarsi

dark-eyed /-'aɪd/ adj ⟨person⟩ dagli occhi scuri

dark glasses npl occhiali mpl scuri

darkly /'dɑ:klɪ/ adv ⟨mutter, hint⟩ cupamente

dark matter n materia f oscura

darkness /'dɑ:knɪs/ n buio m

darkroom /'dɑ:kru:m/ n camera f oscura

dark-skinned adj ⟨person⟩ dalla pelle scura

darling /'dɑːlɪŋ/ **①** adj adorabile; **my ~** Joan carissima Joan
② n tesoro m; **be a ~ and...** sii gentile e...

darn /dɑːn/ vt rammendare

darning needle /'dɑːnɪŋ/ n ago m da rammendo

dart /dɑːt/ **①** n dardo m; (in sewing) pince f inv; **~s** sg (game) freccette fpl
② vi lanciarsi

dartboard /'dɑːtbɔːd/ n bersaglio m [per freccette]

dash /dæʃ/ **①** n Typ trattino m; (in Morse) linea f; **a ~ of milk** un goccio di latte; **make a ~ for** lanciarsi verso
② vi **I must ~** devo scappare
③ vt far svanire ⟨hopes⟩; (hurl) gettare
■ **dash off ①** vi scappar via
② vt (write quickly) buttare giù
■ **dash out** vi uscire di corsa

dashboard /'dæʃbɔːd/ n cruscotto m

dashing /'dæʃɪŋ/ adj (bold) ardito; (in appearance) affascinante

DAT abbr (**digital audio tape**) DAT f inv

data /'deɪtə/ npl & sg dati mpl

databank n banca f di dati

database n banca f dati, database m inv

database management system n sistema m di gestione di data base

data capture n registrazione f di dati

data communications npl comunicazione f dati, telematica f

data compression n compressione f dati

data disk n dischetto m di dati

data entry n immissione f [di] dati

data file n file m inv dati

data handling n manipolazione f [di] dati

data input n input m dati

data link n collegamento m dati

data processing n elaborazione f [di] dati

data protection n protezione f dati

data protection act n Jur legge f britannica per la salvaguardia delle informazioni personali

data retrieval n recupero m dati

data security n sicurezza f dei dati

data storage n archiviazione f dati

data storage device n unità f archivio dati

data transmission n trasmissione f dati

date¹ /deɪt/ n (fruit) dattero m

date² **①** n data f; (meeting) appuntamento m; **to ~** fino ad oggi; **out of ~** (not fashionable) fuori moda; (expired) scaduto; ⟨information⟩ non aggiornato; **make a ~ with somebody** dare un appuntamento a qualcuno; **be up to ~** essere aggiornato
② vt/i datare; (go out with) uscire con
■ **date back to** vt risalire a

dated /'deɪtɪd/ adj fuori moda; ⟨language⟩ antiquato

date line n linea f [del cambiamento] di data

date of issue n data f di emissione

date rape n stupro m perpetrato da persona nota alla vittima

date stamp n (mark) timbro m con la data

dating agency /'deɪtɪŋ/ n agenzia f matrimoniale

dative /'deɪtɪv/ n dativo m

daub /dɔːb/ vt imbrattare ⟨walls⟩

daughter /'dɔːtə(r)/ n figlia f

daughter-in-law n (pl **daughters-in-law**) nuora f

daunt /dɔːnt/ vt scoraggiare; **nothing ~ed** per niente scoraggiato

daunting /'dɔːntɪŋ/ adj ⟨task, prospect⟩ poco allettante; ⟨person⟩ che intimidisce; **I'm faced with a ~ amount of work** mi aspetta una quantità di lavoro preoccupante; **it can be (quite) ~** può essere (piuttosto) allarmante

dauntless /'dɔːntlɪs/ adj intrepido

dawdle /'dɔːdl/ vi bighellonare; (over work) cincischiarsi

dawn /dɔːn/ **①** n alba f; **at ~** all'alba
② vi albeggiare; **it ~ed on me** fig mi è apparso chiaro

dawn raid n (police) raid m della polizia all'alba; (stock market) dawn raid m inv

day /deɪ/ n giorno m; (whole day) giornata f; (period) epoca f; **~ by ~** giorno per giorno; **~ after ~** giorno dopo giorno; **these ~s** oggigiorno; **in those ~s** a quei tempi; **it's had its ~** fam ha fatto il suo tempo

day-boy n Br Sch alunno m esterno

daybreak n **at ~** allo spuntar del giorno

day-care n (for young children) scuola f materna

day centre n centro m di accoglienza

day-dream **①** n sogno m ad occhi aperti
② vi sognare ad occhi aperti

day-girl n Sch alunna f esterna

daylight n luce del giorno f

daylight robbery n fam **it's ~ ~** è un furto!

daylight saving time n ora f legale

day nursery n (0–3 years) asilo m nido; (3–6 years) scuola f materna

day off n giorno m di riposo

day pass n biglietto m giornaliero

day release n giorno m di congedo settimanale dal lavoro da dedicare a corsi di formazione

day return n (ticket) biglietto m di andata e ritorno con validità giornaliera

day school n scuola f che non fornisce alloggio

daytime n giorno m; **in the** ∼ di giorno

daytime TV n programmi mpl televisivi trasmessi durante il giorno

day-to-day adj quotidiano; **on a** ∼ **basis** giorno per giorno

day trader n day trader m inv

day trading n day trading m inv

day trip n gita f (di un giorno)

day tripper n gitante mf

daze /deɪz/ n **in a** ∼ stordito; fig sbalordito

dazed /deɪzd/ adj stordito; fig sbalordito

dazzle /ˈdæzl/ vt abbagliare

dazzling /ˈdæzlɪŋ/ adj abbagliante

DBMS n abbr (**database management system**) DBMS m

D-day n Mil D-day m inv; (important day) giorno m fatidico

deacon /ˈdiːk(ə)n/ n diacono m

dead /ded/ ① adj morto; (numb) intorpidito; ∼ **and buried** morto e sepolto ∼ **body** morto m; ∼ **centre** pieno centro m
② adv ∼ **tired** stanco morto; ∼ **slow/easy** lentissimo/facilissimo; **you're** ∼ **right** hai perfettamente ragione; **stop** ∼ fermarsi di colpo; **be** ∼ **on time** essere in perfetto orario
③ n **the** ∼ pl i morti; **in the** ∼ **of night** nel cuore della notte

deaden /ˈded(ə)n/ vt attutire ⟨sound⟩; calmare ⟨pain⟩

dead end ① n vicolo m cieco
② attrib dead-end ⟨job⟩ senza prospettive

dead heat n **it was a** ∼ ∼ è finita a pari merito

deadline n scadenza f

deadlock n **reach** ∼ fig giungere ad un punto morto

dead loss n fam (person) buono, -a mf a nulla; (thing) oggetto m inutile

deadly /ˈdedlɪ/ adj (**-ier**, **-iest**) mortale; (fam: dreary) barboso; ∼ **sins** peccati mpl capitali

dead on arrival adj Med deceduto durante il trasporto

deadpan adj impassibile; ⟨humour⟩ all'inglese

dead ringer n fam **be a** ∼ ∼ **for somebody** essere la copia spiccicata di qualcuno

Dead Sea n Mar m Morto

dead weight n (fig: burden) peso m morto

dead wood n Br fig zavorra f

deaf /def/ adj sordo; ∼ **and dumb** sordomuto

deaf aid n apparecchio m acustico

deafen /ˈdef(ə)n/ vt assordare; (permanently) render sordo

deafening /ˈdefənɪŋ/ adj assordante

deaf mute adj & n sordomuto, -a mf

deafness /ˈdefnɪs/ n sordità f

deaf without speech adj sordomuto, -a mf

deal /diːl/ ① n (agreement) patto m; (in business) accordo m; **whose** ∼? (Cards) a chi tocca dare le carte?; **a good** or **great** ∼ molto; **get a raw** ∼ fam ricevere un trattamento ingiusto
② vt (pt/pp **dealt** /delt/) (in cards) dare; ∼ **somebody a blow** dare un colpo a qualcuno
■ **deal in** vt trattare in
■ **deal out** vt ⟨hand out⟩ distribuire
■ **deal with** vt (handle) occuparsi di; trattare con ⟨company⟩; (be about) trattare di; **that's been** ∼t **with** è stato risolto

dealer /ˈdiːlə(r)/ n commerciante mf; (in drugs) spacciatore, -trice mf

dealership /ˈdiːləʃɪp/ n Comm concessione f

dealing /ˈdiːlɪŋ/ n (in drugs) traffico m, spaccio m

dealing room n Fin borsino m

dealings /ˈdiːlɪŋz/ npl **have** ∼ **with** avere a che fare con

dean /diːn/ n decano m; Univ preside mf di facoltà

dear /dɪə(r)/ ① adj caro; (in letter) Caro; (formal) Gentile
② n caro, -a mf
③ int oh ∼! Dio mio!

dearly /ˈdɪəlɪ/ adv ⟨love⟩ profondamente; ⟨pay⟩ profumatamente

dearth /dɜːθ/ n penuria f

death /deθ/ n morte f

deathbed n letto m di morte

death camp n campo m di sterminio

death certificate n certificato m di morte

death duty n tassa f di successione

death knell n campane fpl a morto; fig tramonto m

death list n lista f dei bersagli (di un assassino)

deathly /ˈdeθlɪ/ ① adj ∼ **silence** silenzio m di tomba
② adv ∼ **pale** di un pallore cadaverico

death mask n maschera f mortuaria

death penalty n pena f di morte

death rate n tasso m di mortalità

death ray n raggio m mortale

death row /rəʊ/ n Am braccio m della morte

death sentence n also fig condanna f a morte

death threat n minaccia f di morte

death throes npl also fig agonia f

death toll n bilancio m delle vittime

death trap n trappola f mortale

death warrant n ordine m di esecuzione di una condanna a morte

death wish n desiderio m di morire

debacle /deɪˈbɑːk(ə)l/ n sfacelo m

debar /dɪˈbɑː(r)/ vt (pt/pp **debarred**) escludere

debase /dɪˈbeɪs/ vt degradare

debatable /dɪˈbeɪtəbl/ adj discutibile

debate /dɪˈbeɪt/ ① n dibattito m
② vt discutere; (in formal debate) dibattere
③ vi ~ whether to... considerare se...

debauchery /dɪˈbɔːtʃərɪ/ n dissolutezza f

debenture bond /dɪˈbentʃə(r)/ n obbligazione f non garantita

debilitating /dɪˈbɪlɪteɪtɪŋ/ adj ‹disease› debilitante

debility /dɪˈbɪlətɪ/ n debilitazione f

debit /ˈdebɪt/ ① n debito m
② vt (pt/pp **debited**) Comm addebitare ‹sum, account›

debit card n carta f di debito

debonair /debəˈneə(r)/ adj ‹person› elegante e cortese

debrief /diːˈbriːf/ vt chiamare a rapporto; **be ~ed** ‹defector, freed hostage› essere interrogato; ‹diplomat, agent› essere chiamato a rapporto

debriefing /diːˈbriːfɪŋ/ n (of hostage, defector) interrogatorio m

debris /ˈdebriː/ n macerie fpl

debt /det/ n debito m; **be in ~** avere dei debiti

debt collection n esazione f crediti

debt collection agency n agenzia f di recupero crediti

debt collector n esattore m dei crediti

debtor /ˈdetə(r)/ n debitore, -trice mf

debt relief n cancellazione f del debito

debug /diːˈbʌg/ vt (pt/pp **debugged**) Comput correggere gli errori di; togliere i microfoni spia da ‹room›

debunk /dɪˈbʌŋk/ vt ridicolizzare ‹theory, myth›

début /ˈdeɪbuː/ n debutto m

decade /ˈdekeɪd/ n decennio m

decadence /ˈdekədəns/ n decadenza f

decadent /ˈdekədənt/ adj decadente

decaffeinated /diːˈkæfɪneɪtɪd/ adj decaffeinato

decalitre /ˈdekəliːtə(r)/ n decalitro m

decametre /ˈdekəmiːtə(r)/ n decametro m

decamp /dɪˈkæmp/ vi sgattaiolare via; ~ **with something** (steal) squagliarsela con qualcosa

decant /dɪˈkænt/ vt travasare

decanter /dɪˈkæntə(r)/ n caraffa f (di cristallo)

decapitate /dɪˈkæpɪteɪt/ vt decapitare

decathlon /dɪˈkæθlɒn/ n decathlon m inv

decay /dɪˈkeɪ/ ① n (also fig) decadenza f; (rot) decomposizione f; (of tooth) carie f inv
② vi imputridire; (rot) decomporsi; ‹tooth› cariarsi

deceased /dɪˈsiːst/ ① adj defunto
② n **the ~** il defunto; la defunta

deceit /dɪˈsiːt/ n inganno m

deceitful /dɪˈsiːtfʊl/ adj falso

deceitfully /dɪˈsiːtfʊlɪ/ adv falsamente

deceive /dɪˈsiːv/ vt ingannare

decelerate /diːˈseləreɪt/ vi decelerare

deceleration /diːseləˈreɪʃn/ n decelerazione f

December /dɪˈsembə(r)/ n Dicembre m

decency /ˈdiːsənsɪ/ n decenza f

decent /ˈdiːsənt/ adj decente; (respectable) rispettabile; **very ~ of you** molto gentile da parte tua

decently /ˈdiːsəntlɪ/ adv decentemente; (kindly) gentilmente

decentralization /diːsentrəlaɪˈzeɪʃn/ n decentramento m

decentralize /diːˈsentrəlaɪz/ vt decentrare

deception /dɪˈsepʃn/ n inganno m

deceptive /dɪˈseptɪv/ adj ingannevole

deceptively /dɪˈseptɪvlɪ/ adv ingannevolmente; **it looks ~ easy** sembra facile ma non lo è

decibel /ˈdesɪbel/ n decibel m inv

decide /dɪˈsaɪd/ ① vt decidere; **that's ~d then** siamo d'accordo, allora
② vi decidere (**on** di)
■ **decide on** vt scegliere ‹date, outfit, course of action›

decided /dɪˈsaɪdɪd/ adj risoluto

decidedly /dɪˈsaɪdɪdlɪ/ adv risolutamente; (without doubt) senza dubbio

decider /dɪˈsaɪdə(r)/ n (point) punto m decisivo; (goal) goal m inv decisivo; (game) spareggio m

deciduous /dɪˈsɪdjʊəs/ adj a foglie decidue

decigram[me] /ˈdesɪgræm/ n decigrammo m

decilitre /ˈdesɪliːtə(r)/ n decilitro m

decimal /ˈdesɪml/ ① adj decimale
② n numero m decimale

decimal point n virgola f

decimal system *n* sistema *m* decimale

decimate /'desɪmeɪt/ *vt* decimare

decimetre /'desɪmiːtə(r)/ *n* decimetro *m*

decipher /dɪˈsaɪfə(r)/ *vt* decifrare

decision /dɪˈsɪʒn/ *n* decisione *f*

decision-maker /dɪˈsɪʒnmeɪkə(r)/ *n* persona *f* che ama o ha il potere di prendere decisioni

decision-making /dɪˈsɪʒnmeɪkɪŋ/ *n* be good/bad at ∼ saper/non saper prendere decisioni; ∼ **process** *n* processo *m* decisionale

decisive /dɪˈsaɪsɪv/ *adj* decisivo

decisively /dɪˈsaɪsɪvlɪ/ *adv* con decisione

deck¹ /dek/ *vt* abbigliare

deck² *n* Naut ponte *m*; **on** ∼ in coperta; **top** ∼ (of bus) piano *m* di sopra; ∼ **of cards** mazzo *m*

deckchair /'dektʃeə(r)/ *n* [sedia *f* a] sdraio *f inv*

declaration /deklə'reɪʃn/ *n* dichiarazione *f*

declare /dɪˈkleə(r)/ *vt* dichiarare; **anything to** ∼? niente da dichiarare?; ∼ **one's love** dichiararsi

declassify /diːˈklæsɪfaɪ/ *vt* rimuovere dai vincoli di segretezza ⟨*document, information*⟩

declension /dɪˈklenʃn/ *n* declinazione *f*

decline /dɪˈklaɪn/ **①** *n* declino *m* **②** *vt* also Gram declinare **③** *vi* (decrease) diminuire; ⟨*health*⟩ deperire; (say no) rifiutare

declutch /diːˈklʌtʃ/ *vi* Br lasciare la frizione

decode /diːˈkəʊd/ *vt* decifrare; Comput decodificare

decoding /diːˈkəʊdɪŋ/ *n* decodifica *f*, decodificazione *f*

décolleté /deɪˈkɒlteɪ/ *adj* décolleté *inv*, scollato

decompose /diːkəmˈpəʊz/ *vi* decomporsi

decomposition /diːkɒmpəˈzɪʃn/ *n* scomposizione *f*

decompress /diːkəmˈpres/ *vt* decomprimere

decompression /diːkəmˈpreʃn/ *n* decompressione *f*

decontaminate /diːkənˈtæmɪneɪt/ *vt* decontaminare

décor /'deɪkɔː(r)/ *n* decorazione *f*; (including furniture) arredamento *m*

decorate /'dekəreɪt/ *vt* decorare; (paint) pitturare; (wallpaper) tappezzare

decoration /dekəˈreɪʃn/ *n* decorazione *f*

decorative /'dekərətɪv/ *adj* decorativo

decorator /'dekəreɪtə(r)/ *n* painter and ∼ imbianchino *m*

decorous /'dekərəs/ *adj* decoroso

decorously /'dekərəslɪ/ *adv* decorosamente

decorum /dɪˈkɔːrəm/ *n* decoro *m*

decoy¹ /'diːkɔɪ/ *n* esca *f*

decoy² /dɪˈkɔɪ/ *vt* adescare

decrease¹ /'diːkriːs/ *n* diminuzione *f*; **be on the** ∼ essere in diminuzione

decrease² /dɪˈkriːs/ *vt/i* diminuire

decreasing /dɪˈkriːsɪŋ/ *adj* in diminuzione

decreasingly /dɪˈkriːsɪŋlɪ/ *adv* sempre meno

decree /dɪˈkriː/ **①** *n* decreto *m* **②** *vt* decretare

decrepit /dɪˈkrepɪt/ *adj* decrepito

decriminalization /diːkrɪmɪnəlaɪˈzeɪʃn/ *n* depenalizzazione *f*

decriminalize /diːˈkrɪmɪnəlaɪz/ *vt* depenalizzare

dedicate /'dedɪkeɪt/ *vt* dedicare

dedicated /'dedɪkeɪtɪd/ *adj* ⟨*person*⟩ scrupoloso

dedication /dedɪˈkeɪʃn/ *n* dedizione *f*; (in book) dedica *f*

deduce /dɪˈdjuːs/ *vt* dedurre (from da)

deduct /dɪˈdʌkt/ *vt* dedurre

deduction /dɪˈdʌkʃn/ *n* deduzione *f*

deed /diːd/ *n* azione *f*; Jur atto *m* di proprietà

deed of covenant *n* Jur accordo *m* accessorio ad un contratto immobiliare

deed poll *n* change one's name by ∼ ∼ cambiare nome con un atto unilaterale

deem /diːm/ *vt* ritenere

deep /diːp/ *adj* profondo; **go off the** ∼ **end** fam arrabbiarsi

deepen /'diːpn/ **①** *vt* approfondire; scavare più profondamente ⟨*trench*⟩ **②** *vi* approfondirsi; fig ⟨*mystery*⟩ infittirsi

deep-fat-fryer *n* friggitrice *f*

deepfelt *adj* profondo

deep-freeze *n* congelatore *m*

deep-fried *adj* fritto (in molto olio)

deep-frozen *adj* surgelato

deep-fry *vt* friggere (in molto olio)

deeply *adv* profondamente

deep-rooted *adj* ⟨*habit, prejudice*⟩ radicato

deep-sea *adj* ⟨*exploration, diving*⟩ in profondità; ⟨*fisherman, fishing*⟩ d'alto mare

deep-sea diver *n* palombaro *m*

deep-seated *adj* radicato

deep-set *adj* ⟨*eyes*⟩ infossato

deep South *n* Am il profondo Sud

deep-vein thrombosis *n* trombosi *f* venosa profonda

deer /dɪə(r)/ *n inv* cervo *m*

de-escalate /diːˈeskəleɪt/ *vt* ridurre ⟨crisis, violence⟩

deface /dɪˈfeɪs/ *vt* sfigurare ⟨picture⟩; deturpare ⟨monument⟩

defamation /defəˈmeɪʃn/ *n* diffamazione *f*

defamatory /dɪˈfæmətərɪ/ *adj* diffamatorio

default /dɪˈfɔːlt/ **①** *n* (Jur: non-payment) morosità *f*; (failure to appear) contumacia *f*; Comput default *m inv*; **win by** ∼ Sport vincere per abbandono dell'avversario; **in** ∼ **of** per mancanza di **②** *adj* ∼ **drive** Comput lettore *m* di default **③** *vi* (not pay) venir meno ad un pagamento; Comput ∼ **to something** ritornare all'impostazione di default

defeat /dɪˈfiːt/ **①** *n* sconfitta *f* **②** *vt* sconfiggere; (frustrate) vanificare ⟨attempts⟩; **that** ∼**s the object** questo fa fallire l'obiettivo

defeatist /dɪˈfiːtɪst/ *adj & n* disfattista *mf*

defecate /ˈdefəkeɪt/ *vi* defecare

defect¹ /dɪˈfekt/ *vi* Pol fare defezione

defect² /ˈdiːfekt/ *n* difetto *m*

defective /dɪˈfektɪv/ *adj* difettoso

defector /dɪˈfektə(r)/ *n* (from party) defezionista *mf*; (from country) fuor[i]uscito, -a *mf*

defence /dɪˈfens/ *n* difesa *f*

defenceless /dɪˈfenslɪs/ *adj* indifeso

Defence Minister *n* ministro *m* della difesa

defend /dɪˈfend/ *vt* difendere; (justify) giustificare

defendant /dɪˈfendənt/ *n* Jur imputato, -a *mf*

defender /dɪˈfendə(r)/ *n* difensore *m*, -ditrice *f*

defensive /dɪˈfensɪv/ **①** *adj* difensivo **②** *n* difensiva *f*; **on the** ∼ sulla difensiva

defer /dɪˈfɜː(r)/ **①** *vt* (pt/pp **deferred**) (postpone) rinviare **②** *vi* ∼ **to somebody** rimettersi a qualcuno

deference /ˈdefərəns/ *n* deferenza *f*

deferential /defəˈrenʃl/ *adj* deferente

deferentially /defəˈrenʃəlɪ/ *adv* con deferenza

deferment, **deferral** /dɪˈfɜːmənt/, /dɪˈfɜːrəl/ *n* (postponement) rinvio *m*

defiance /dɪˈfaɪəns/ *n* sfida *f*; **in** ∼ **of** sfidando

defiant /dɪˈfaɪənt/ *adj* ⟨person⟩ ribelle; ⟨gesture, attitude⟩ di sfida

defiantly /dɪˈfaɪəntlɪ/ *adv* con aria di sfida

deficiency /dɪˈfɪʃənsɪ/ *n* insufficienza *f*

deficient /dɪˈfɪʃənt/ *adj* insufficiente; **be** ∼ **in** mancare di

deficit /ˈdefɪsɪt/ *n* deficit *m inv*

defile /dɪˈfaɪl/ *vt* fig contaminare

define /dɪˈfaɪn/ *vt* definire

defined *adj* ⟨role⟩ definito

definite /ˈdefɪnɪt/ *adj* definito; (certain) ⟨answer, yes⟩ definitivo; ⟨improvement, difference⟩ netto; **he was** ∼ **about it** è stato chiaro in proposito

definite article *n* (grammatical) articolo *m* determinativo

definitely /ˈdefɪnɪtlɪ/ *adv* sicuramente

definition /defɪˈnɪʃn/ *n* definizione *f*

definitive /dɪˈfɪnətɪv/ *adj* definitivo

deflate /dɪˈfleɪt/ *vt* sgonfiare

deflation /dɪˈfleɪʃn/ *n* Comm deflazione *f*

deflationary /dɪˈfleɪʃənrɪ/ *adj* deflazionistico

deflect /dɪˈflekt/ *vt* deflettere

deformed /dɪˈfɔːmd/ *adj* deforme

deformity /dɪˈfɔːmətɪ/ *n* deformità *f inv*

DEFRA *abbr* Br (**Department for Environment, Food, and Rural Affairs**) ≈ Ministero *m* per le Politiche Agricole e Forestali

defrag /ˈdiːfræg/ *vt* fam deframmentare

defragment /ˈdiːfrægˈment/ *vt* Comput deframmentare

defraud /dɪˈfrɔːd/ *vt* defraudare

defray /dɪˈfreɪ/ *vt* fml sostenere

defrost /diːˈfrɒst/ *vt* sbrinare ⟨fridge⟩; scongelare ⟨food⟩

deft /deft/ *adj* abile

deftly /ˈdeftlɪ/ *adv* con destrezza

deftness /ˈdeftnɪs/ *n* destrezza *f*

defunct /dɪˈfʌŋkt/ *adj* morto e sepolto; ⟨law⟩ caduto in disuso

defuse /diːˈfjuːz/ *vt* disinnescare; calmare ⟨situation⟩

defy /dɪˈfaɪ/ *vt* (pt/pp **-ied**) (challenge) sfidare; resistere a ⟨attempt⟩; (not obey) disobbedire a

degenerate¹ /dɪˈdʒenəreɪt/ *vi* degenerare; ∼ **into** fig degenerare in

degenerate² /dɪˈdʒenərət/ *adj* degenerato

degeneration /dɪdʒenəˈreɪʃn/ *n* degenerazione *f*

degenerative /dɪˈdʒenərətɪv/ *adj* degenerativo

degradation /degrəˈdeɪʃn/ *n* (debasement) degradazione *f*; (of culture) deterioramento *m*; (squalor) desolazione *f*

degrade /dɪˈgreɪd/ *vt* (humiliate) degradare ⟨person⟩; (damage) deteriorare ⟨environment⟩

degrading /dɪˈgreɪdɪŋ/ *adj* degradante

degree /dɪˈɡriː/ n grado m; Univ laurea f; **20 ~s** 20 gradi; **not to the same ~** non allo stesso livello

degree ceremony n Br Univ cerimonia f di consegna delle lauree

degree course n Br Univ corso m di laurea

dehydrate /diːhaɪˈdreɪt/ vt disidratare

dehydrated /diːhaɪˈdreɪtɪd/ adj disidratato

dehydration /diːhaɪˈdreɪʃn/ n disidratazione f

de-ice /diːˈaɪs/ vt togliere il ghiaccio da

de-icer /diːˈaɪsə(r)/ n (mechanical) sbrinatore m; (chemical) liquido m scongelante

deign /deɪn/ vi **~ to do something** degnarsi di fare qualcosa

deity /ˈdiːətɪ/ n divinità f inv

déjà vu /deɪʒɑːˈvuː/ n déjà vu m inv

dejected /dɪˈdʒektɪd/ adj demoralizzato

dejectedly /dɪˈdʒektɪdlɪ/ adv con aria demoralizzata

dejection /dɪˈdʒekʃn/ n abbacchiamento m

delay /dɪˈleɪ/ **①** n ritardo m **without ~** senza indugio
② vt ritardare **be ~ed** ⟨person⟩ essere trattenuto; ⟨train, aircraft⟩ essere in ritardo
③ vi indugiare

delayed action /dɪˈleɪd/ adj ad azione ritardata; ⟨bomb⟩ a scoppio ritardato

delegate[1] /ˈdelɪɡət/ n delegato, -a mf

delegate[2] /ˈdelɪɡeɪt/ vt delegare

delegation /delɪˈɡeɪʃn/ n delegazione f

delete /dɪˈliːt/ vt cancellare

delete [key] n tasto m di cancellazione

deletion /dɪˈliːʃn/ n cancellatura f

deliberate[1] /dɪˈlɪbərət/ adj deliberato; (slow) posato

deliberate[2] /dɪˈlɪbəreɪt/ vi/i deliberare

deliberately /dɪˈlɪbərətlɪ/ adv deliberatamente; (slowly) in modo posato

deliberation /dɪlɪbəˈreɪʃn/ n deliberazione f; **with ~** in modo posato

delicacy /ˈdelɪkəsɪ/ n delicatezza f; (food) prelibatezza f

delicate /ˈdelɪkət/ adj delicato

delicately /ˈdelɪkətlɪ/ adv ⟨handle, phrase⟩ con delicatezza; ⟨crafted, flavoured⟩ con raffinatezza

delicatessen /delɪkəˈtesn/ n negozio m di specialità gastronomiche

delicious /dɪˈlɪʃəs/ adj delizioso

delight /dɪˈlaɪt/ **①** n piacere m
② vt deliziare
③ vi **~ in** dilettarsi con

delighted /dɪˈlaɪtɪd/ adj lieto

delightful /dɪˈlaɪtfʊl/ adj delizioso

delineate /dɪˈlɪnɪeɪt/ vt also fig delineare

delineation /dɪlɪnɪˈeɪʃn/ n delineazione f

delinquency /dɪˈlɪŋkwənsɪ/ n delinquenza f

delinquent /dɪˈlɪŋkwənt/ **①** adj delinquente
② n delinquente mf

delirious /dɪˈlɪrɪəs/ adj **be ~** delirare; (fig: very happy) essere pazzo di gioia

delirium /dɪˈlɪrɪəm/ n delirio m

deliver /dɪˈlɪvə(r)/ vt consegnare; recapitare ⟨post, newspaper⟩; tenere ⟨speech⟩; dare ⟨message⟩; tirare ⟨blow⟩; (set free) liberare; **~ a baby** far nascere un bambino

deliverance /dɪˈlɪv(ə)rəns/ n liberazione f

delivery /dɪˈlɪvərɪ/ n consegna f; (of post) distribuzione f; Med parto m; **cash on ~** pagamento m alla consegna

delivery address n indirizzo m del destinatario

delivery man n fattorino m

delivery room n Med sala f parto

delta /ˈdeltə/ n delta m inv

delude /dɪˈluːd/ vt ingannare; **~ oneself** illudersi

deluge /ˈdeljuːdʒ/ **①** n diluvio m
② vt (fig: with requests etc) inondare

delusion /dɪˈluːʒn/ n illusione f; **~s of grandeur** mania f di grandezza

de luxe /dəˈlʌks/ adj di lusso

delve /delv/ vi **~ into** (into pocket etc) frugare in; (into notes, the past) fare ricerche in

demagnetize /diːˈmæɡnətaɪz/ vt smagnetizzare

demand /dɪˈmɑːnd/ **①** n richiesta f; Comm domanda f; **in ~** richiesto; **on ~** a richiesta
② vt esigere (of/from da)

demanding /dɪˈmɑːndɪŋ/ adj esigente

demanning /diːˈmænɪŋ/ n Br taglio m di personale

demarcation /diːmɑːˈkeɪʃn/ n demarcazione f

demean /dɪˈmiːn/ vt **~ oneself** abbassarsi (to a)

demeaning /dɪˈmiːnɪŋ/ adj degradante

demeanour /dɪˈmiːnə(r)/ n comportamento m

demented /dɪˈmentɪd/ adj demente

dementia /dɪˈmenʃə/ n demenza f

demerara [sugar] /deməˈreərə/ n zucchero m grezzo di canna

demilitarization /diːmɪlɪtəraɪˈzeɪʃn/ n demilitarizzazione f

demilitarize /diːˈmɪlɪtəraɪz/ vt smilitarizzare

demise /dɪ'maɪz/ n decesso m

demister /diː'mɪstə(r)/ n Auto sbrinatore m

demo /'deməʊ/ n (pl ~s) fam manifestazione f

demobilize /diː'məʊbəlaɪz/ vt Mil smobilitare

democracy /dɪ'mɒkrəsɪ/ n democrazia f

democrat /'deməkræt/ n democratico, -a mf

democratic /demə'krætɪk/ adj democratico

democratically /demə'krætɪklɪ/ adv democraticamente

demo disk n Comput demo disk m inv

demographic /demə'græfɪk/ adj demografico

demolish /dɪ'mɒlɪʃ/ vt demolire

demolition /demə'lɪʃn/ n demolizione f

demon /'diːmən/ n demonio m

demonic /dɪ'mɒnɪk/ adj ⟨aspect, power⟩ demoniaco

demonize /'diːmənaɪz/ vt demonizzare

demonstrable /'demənstrəbl/ adj dimostrabile

demonstrably /'demənstrəblɪ/ adv ⟨false, untrue⟩ manifestamente

demonstrate /'demənstreɪt/ ① vt dimostrare; dare una dimostrazione dell'uso di ⟨appliance⟩ ② vi Pol manifestare

demonstration /demən'streɪʃn/ n dimostrazione f; Pol manifestazione f

demonstrative /dɪ'mɒnstrətɪv/ adj Gram dimostrativo; **be** ~ essere espansivo

demonstrator /'demənstreɪtə(r)/ n Pol manifestante mf; (for product) dimostratore, -trice mf

demoralize /dɪ'mɒrəlaɪz/ vt demoralizzare

demoralizing /dɪ'mɒrəlaɪzɪŋ/ adj demoralizzante, avvilente

demote /dɪ'məʊt/ vt retrocedere di grado; Mil degradare

demur /dɪ'mɜː/ ① vi (pt/pp **demurred**) (complain) protestare; (disagree) obiettare ② n without ~ senza obiezioni

demure /dɪ'mjʊə(r)/ adj schivo

demurely /dɪ'mjʊəlɪ/ adv in modo schivo

den /den/ n tana f; (room) rifugio m

denationalize /diː'næʃ(ə)nəlaɪz/ vt denazionalizzare

denial /dɪ'naɪəl/ n smentita f

denier /'denɪə(r)/ n denaro m

denigrate /'denɪgreɪt/ vt denigrare

denigrating /'denɪgreɪtɪŋ/ adj denigratore

denim /'denɪm/ n [tessuto m] jeans m; ~s pl [blue-]jeans mpl

Denmark /'denmɑːk/ n Danimarca f

denomination /dɪnɒmɪ'neɪʃn/ n Relig confessione f; (money) valore f

denote /dɪ'nəʊt/ vt denotare

denounce /dɪ'naʊns/ vt denunciare

dense /dens/ adj denso; ⟨crowd, forest⟩ fitto; (stupid) ottuso

densely /'denslɪ/ adv ⟨populated⟩ densamente; ~ **wooded** fittamente ricoperto di alberi

density /'densətɪ/ n densità f inv; (of forest) fittezza f

dent /dent/ ① n ammaccatura f ② vt ammaccare

dental /'dentl/ adj dei denti; ⟨treatment⟩ dentistico; ⟨hygiene⟩ dentale

dental appointment n appuntamento m dal dentista

dental clinic n (hospital) clinica f odontoiatrica; (part of hospital) reparto m odontoiatrico

dental floss n filo m interdentale

dental plate n dentiera f

dental surgeon n odontoiatra mf, medico m dentista

dental surgery n Br (premises) studio m dentistico; (treatment) visita f dentistica

dented /'dentɪd/ adj ammaccato; ~ **pride** orgoglio m ferito

dentist /'dentɪst/ n dentista mf

dentistry /'dentɪstrɪ/ n odontoiatria f

dentures /'dentʃəz/ npl dentiera fsg

denude /dɪ'njuːd/ vt denudare

denunciation /dɪnʌnsɪ'eɪʃn/ n denuncia f

Denver boot /'denvə/ n Am = WHEEL CLAMP

deny /dɪ'naɪ/ vt (pt/pp **-ied**) negare; (officially) smentire; ~ **somebody something** negare qualcosa a qualcuno; **I can't** ~**it** non posso negarlo

deodorant /diː'əʊdərənt/ n deodorante m

deodorize /diː'əʊdəraɪz/ vt deodorare

depart /dɪ'pɑːt/ vi ⟨plane, train⟩ partire; liter ⟨person⟩ andare via; (deviate) allontanarsi (**from** da)

departed /dɪ'pɑːtɪd/ adj (euph: dead) scomparso

department /dɪ'pɑːtmənt/ n reparto m; Pol ministero m; (of company) sezione f; Univ dipartimento m

departmental /diː'pɑːt'mentl/ adj ⟨Pol: colleague, meeting⟩ di sezione; (in business) di reparto

department head n caporeparto mf; Univ direttore, -trice mf d'istituto

department manager n (of business) direttore, -trice mf di reparto; (of store) caporeparto mf inv

Department of Defense n Am ministero m della Difesa

Department of Energy n Am ≈ ministero m dell'Industria

Department of Health n ministero m della Sanità

Department of Homeland Security n Am Dipartimento m per la sicurezza nazionale

Department of Social Security n Br ≈ Istituto m Nazionale della Previdenza Sociale

Department of the Environment n Br ministero m dell'Ambiente

Department of Trade and Industry n Br ministero m del Commercio e dell'Industria

department store n grande magazzino m

departure /dɪ'pɑ:tʃə(r)/ n partenza f; (from rule) allontanamento m; **new ∼** svolta f

departure gate n (at airport) uscita f

departure lounge n (at airport) sala f d'attesa

departure platform n Rail binario m

departures board n tabellone m delle partenze

depend /dɪ'pend/ vi dipendere (on da); (rely) contare (on su); **it all ∼s** dipende; **∼ing on what he says** a seconda di quello che dice

dependability /dɪpendə'bɪlətɪ/ n affidabilità f

dependable /dɪ'pendəbl/ adj fidato

dependant /dɪ'pendənt/ n persona f a carico

dependence /dɪ'pendəns/ n dipendenza f

dependent /dɪ'pendənt/ adj dipendente (on da)

depict /dɪ'pɪkt/ vt (in writing) dipingere; (with picture) rappresentare

depiction /dɪ'pɪkʃn/ n rappresentazione f

depilatory /dɪ'pɪlətərɪ/ n (cream) crema f depilatoria

deplete /dɪ'pli:t/ vt ridurre; **totally ∼d** completamente esaurito

depletion /dɪ'pli:ʃn/ n (of resources, funds) impoverimento m

deplorable /dɪ'plɔ:rəbl/ adj deplorevole

deplore /dɪ'plɔ:(r)/ vt deplorare

deploy /dɪ'plɔɪ/ ① vt Mil spiegare ② vi schierarsi

deployment /dɪ'plɔɪmənt/ n schieramento m

depoliticize /di:pə'lɪtɪsaɪz/ vt depoliticizzare

depopulate /di:'pɒpjʊleɪt/ vt spopolare

depopulation /di:pɒpjʊ'leɪʃn/ n spopolamento m

deport /dɪ'pɔ:t/ vt deportare

deportation /di:pɔ:'teɪʃn/ n deportazione f

deportee /di:pɔ:'ti:/ n deportato, -a mf

deportment /dɪ'pɔ:tmənt/ n portamento m

depose /dɪ'pəʊz/ vt deporre

deposit /dɪ'pɒzɪt/ ① n deposito m; (against damage) cauzione f; (first instalment) acconto m ② vt depositare

deposit account n libretto m di risparmio; (without instant access) conto m vincolato

depositor /dɪ'pɒzɪtə(r)/ n Fin depositante mf

depot /'depəʊ/ n deposito m; Am Rail stazione f ferroviaria

deprave /dɪ'preɪv/ vt depravare

depraved /dɪ'preɪvd/ adj depravato

depravity /dɪ'prævətɪ/ n depravazione f

deprecate /'deprəkeɪt/ vt disapprovare

deprecatory /deprɪ'keɪtərɪ/ adj (disapproving) di disapprovazione; (apologetic) di scusa

depreciate /dɪ'pri:ʃɪeɪt/ vi deprezzarsi

depreciation /dɪpri:sɪ'eɪʃn/ n deprezzameto m

depress /dɪ'pres/ vt deprimere; (press down) premere

depressed /dɪ'prest/ adj depresso; **∼ area** zona f depressa

depressing /dɪ'presɪŋ/ adj deprimente

depression /dɪ'preʃn/ n depressione f

depressive /dɪ'presɪv/ ① adj depressivo ② n depresso, -a mf

depressurize /di:'preʃəraɪz/ vi depressurizzare

deprivation /deprɪ'veɪʃn/ n privazione f

deprive /dɪ'praɪv/ vt **∼ somebody of something** privare qualcuno di qualcosa

deprived /dɪ'praɪvd/ adj ⟨area, childhood⟩ disagiato

dept abbr **department**

depth /depθ/ n profondità f inv: **in ∼** ⟨study, analyse⟩ in modo approfondito; **in the ∼s of winter** in pieno inverno; **in the ∼s of despair** nella più profonda disperazione; **be out of one's ∼** (in water) non toccare il fondo; fig sentirsi in alto mare

deputation /depjʊ'teɪʃn/ n deputazione f

deputize /'depjʊtaɪz/ vi **∼ for** fare le veci di

deputy /'depjʊtɪ/ n vice mf; (temporary) sostituto, -a mf

deputy chairman n vicepresidente m

deputy leader *n* Br Pol sottosegretario *m*

deputy president *n* vicepresidente *mf*

deputy premier, **deputy prime minister** *n* Pol vice primo ministro *m*

derail /dɪ'reɪl/ *vt* **be** ∼**ed** ⟨*train*⟩ essere deragliato

derailleur gears /dɪ'reɪljə/ *npl* deragliatore *msg*

derailment /dɪ'reɪlmənt/ *n* deragliamento *m*

deranged /dɪ'reɪndʒd/ *adj* squilibrato

deregulate /di:'regjʊleɪt/ *vt* deregolamentare ⟨*market*⟩

deregulation /di:regjʊ'leɪʃn/ *n* deregolamentazione *f*

derelict /'derəlɪkt/ *adj* abbandonato

deride /dɪ'raɪd/ *vt* deridere

derision /dɪ'rɪʒn/ *n* derisione *f*

derisive /dɪ'raɪsɪv/ *adj* derisorio

derisory /dɪ'raɪsərɪ/ *adj* ⟨*laughter*⟩ derisorio; ⟨*offer*⟩ irrisorio

derivation /derɪ'veɪʃn/ *n* derivazione *f*

derivative /dɪ'rɪvətɪv/ **1** *adj* derivato **2** *n* derivato *m*

derive /dɪ'raɪv/ **1** *vt* (obtain) derivare; **be** ∼**d from** ⟨*word*⟩ derivare da **2** *vi* ∼ **from** derivare da

dermatitis /dɜ:mə'taɪtɪs/ *n* dermatite *f*

dermatologist /dɜ:mə'tɒlədʒɪst/ *n* dermatologo, -a *mf*

derogatory /dɪ'rɒgətrɪ/ *adj* ⟨*comments*⟩ peggiorativo

derrick /'derɪk/ *n* derrick *m inv*

derv /dɜ:v/ *n* Br gasolio *m*

descaler /di:'skeɪlə(r)/ *n* Br disincrostante *m*

descend /dɪ'send/ **1** *vi* scendere; **be** ∼**ed from** discendere da **2** *vt* scendere da
■ **descend on** *vt* (attack) piombare su; (visit) capitare [all'improvviso]

descendant /dɪ'sendənt/ *n* discendente *mf*

descent /dɪ'sent/ *n* discesa *f*; (lineage) origine *f*

descrambler /di:'skræmblə(r)/ *n* Teleph, TV decodificatore *m*

describe /dɪ'skraɪb/ *vt* descrivere

description /dɪ'skrɪpʃn/ *n* descrizione *f*; **they had no help of any** ∼ non hanno avuto proprio nessun aiuto

descriptive /dɪ'skrɪptɪv/ *adj* descrittivo; (vivid) vivido

desecrate /'desɪkreɪt/ *vt* profanare

desecration /desɪ'kreɪʃn/ *n* profanazione *f*

desegregate /di:'segrɪgeɪt/ *vt* abolire la segregazione razziale in ⟨*school*⟩

deselect /di:sɪ'lekt/ *vt* Br **be** ∼**ed** non avere riconferma della candidatura alle elezioni da parte del proprio partito

desensitize /di:'sensɪtaɪz/ *vt* desensibilizzare

desert[1] /'dezət/ **1** *n* deserto *m* **2** *adj* deserto; ∼ **island** isola *f* deserta

desert[2] /dɪ'zɜ:t/ **1** *vt* abbandonare **2** *vi* disertare

desert boot *n* scarponcino *m* Clark®

deserted /dɪ'zɜ:tɪd/ *adj* deserto

deserter /dɪ'zɜ:tə(r)/ *n* Mil disertore *m*

desertion /dɪ'zɜ:ʃn/ *n* Mil diserzione *f*; (of family) abbandono *m*

deserts /dɪ'zɜ:ts/ *npl* **get one's just** ∼ ottenere ciò che ci si merita

deserve /dɪ'zɜ:v/ *vt* meritare

deservedly /dɪ'zɜ:vədlɪ/ *adv* meritatamente

deserving /dɪ'zɜ:vɪŋ/ *adj* meritevole; ∼ **cause** opera *f* meritoria

desiccated /'desɪkeɪtɪd/ *adj* essiccato; (pej: dried up) secco

design /dɪ'zaɪn/ **1** *n* progettazione *f*; (fashion ∼, appearance) design *m inv*; (pattern) modello *m*; (aim) proposito *m*; **have** ∼**s on** aver mire su **2** *vt* progettare; disegnare ⟨*clothes, furniture, model*⟩; **be** ∼**ed for** essere fatto per

designate /'dezɪgneɪt/ *vt* designare

designation /dezɪg'neɪʃn/ *n* designazione *f*

design consultant *n* progettista *mf*

designer /dɪ'zaɪnə(r)/ *n* progettista *mf*; (of clothes) stilista *mf*; (Theat: of set) scenografo, -a *mf*

design fault *n* difetto *m* di concezione

design feature *n* prestazione *f*

designing /dɪ'zaɪnɪŋ/ *adj* pej calcolatore

desirable /dɪ'zaɪərəbl/ *adj* desiderabile

desire /dɪ'zaɪə(r)/ **1** *n* desiderio *m* **2** *vt* desiderare

desist /dɪ'zɪst/ *vi* desistere (**from** da)

desk /desk/ *n* scrivania *f*; (in school) banco *m*; (in hotel) reception *f inv*; (cash ∼) cassa *f*; (check-in ∼) check-in *m inv*

deskbound *adj* ⟨*job*⟩ sedentario

desk diary *n* agenda da tavolo

desk pad *n* (blotter) tampone *m*; (notebook) block-notes *m inv*

desktop *n* piano *m* della scrivania; (computer) [computer *m inv*] desktop *m inv*

desktop publishing *n* desktop publishing *m inv*, editoria *f* da tavolo

desolate /'desələt/ *adj* desolato

desolation /desə'leɪʃn/ *n* desolazione *f*

despair /dɪ'speə(r)/ **1** *n* disperazione *f*; **in** ∼ disperato; ⟨*say*⟩ per disperazione

2 *vi* I ~ **of that boy** quel ragazzo mi fa disperare

desperate /'despərət/ *adj* disperato; **be** ~ ⟨*criminal*⟩ essere un disperato; **be** ~ **for something** morire dalla voglia di

desperately /'despərətlı/ *adv* disperatamente; **he said** ~ ha detto, disperato

desperation /despə'reɪʃn/ *n* disperazione *f*; **in** ~ per disperazione

despicable /dɪ'spɪkəbl/ *adj* disprezzevole

despise /dɪ'spaɪz/ *vt* disprezzare

despite /dɪ'spaɪt/ *prep* malgrado

despondency /dɪ'spɒndənsɪ/ *n* abbattimento *m*

despondent /dɪ'spɒndənt/ *adj* abbattuto

despot /'despɒt/ *n* despota *m*

despotism /'despətɪzm/ *n* dispotismo *m*

des res /dez'rez/ *n abbr* fam (**desirable residence**) abitazione *f* desiderabile

dessert /dɪ'zɜːt/ *n* dolce *m*

dessert spoon *n* cucchiaio *m* da dolce

dessert wine *n* vino *m* da dessert

destabilize /diː'steɪbɪlaɪz/ *vt* destabilizzare

destination /destɪ'neɪʃn/ *n* destinazione *f*

destine /'destɪn/ *vt* destinare; **be ~d for something** essere destinato a qualcosa; **~d for each other** fatti l'uno per l'altra

destined /'destɪnd/ *adj* ~ **for Paris** ⟨*train, package*⟩ con destinazione Parigi; **it was** ~ **to happen** era destino che succedesse

destiny /'destɪnɪ/ *n* destino *m*

destitute /'destɪtjuːt/ *adj* bisognoso

destitution /destɪ'tjuːʃn/ *n* indigenza *f*

destroy /dɪ'strɔɪ/ *vt* distruggere

destroyer /dɪ'strɔɪə(r)/ *n* Naut cacciatorpediniere *m*

destruct /dɪ'strʌkt/ *vi* distruggersi

destruction /dɪ'strʌkʃn/ *n* distruzione *f*

destructive /dɪ'strʌktɪv/ *adj* distruttivo; fig ⟨*criticism*⟩ negativo

destructiveness /dɪ'strʌktɪvnɪs/ *n* distruttività *f*

desultory /'desəltrɪ/ *adj* ⟨*conversation*⟩ sconnesso; ⟨*friendship*⟩ incostante; ⟨*attempt*⟩ poco convinto

detach /dɪ'tætʃ/ *vt* staccare

detachable /dɪ'tætʃəbl/ *adj* separabile

detached /dɪ'tætʃt/ *adj* fig distaccato; ~ **house** villetta *f*

detached retina *n* Med retina *f* distaccata

detachment /dɪ'tætʃmənt/ *n* distacco *m*; Mil distaccamento *m*

detail /'diːteɪl/ **1** *n* particolare *m*, dettaglio *m*; **in** ~ particolareggiatamente **2** *vt* esporre con tutti i particolari; Mil assegnare

detail drawing *n* disegno *m* dettagliato

detailed /'diːteɪld/ *adj* particolareggiato, dettagliato

detain /dɪ'teɪn/ *vt* ⟨*police*⟩ trattenere; (delay) far ritardare

detainee /diːteɪ'niː/ *n* detenuto, -a *mf*

detect /dɪ'tekt/ *vt* individuare; (perceive) percepire

detectable /dɪ'tektəbl/ *adj* individuabile

detection /dɪ'tekʃn/ *n* scoperta *f*

detective /dɪ'tektɪv/ *n* investigatore, -trice *mf*

detective constable *n* Br agente *mf* della polizia giudiziaria

detective inspector *n* Br ispettore, -trice *mf* della polizia giudiziaria

detective story *n* racconto *m* poliziesco

detective work *n* indagini *fpl*

detector /dɪ'tektə(r)/ *n* (for metal) cercametalli *m inv*, metal detector *m inv*

detention /dɪ'tenʃn/ *n* detenzione *f*; Sch punizione *f*

detention centre *n* centro *m* di accoglienza

deter /dɪ'tɜː(r)/ *vt* (pt/pp **deterred**) impedire; ~ **somebody from doing something** impedire a qualcuno di fare qualcosa

detergent /dɪ'tɜːdʒənt/ *n* detersivo *m*

deteriorate /dɪ'tɪərɪəreɪt/ *vi* deteriorarsi

deterioration /dɪtɪərɪə'reɪʃn/ *n* deterioramento *m*

determination /dɪtɜːmɪ'neɪʃn/ *n* determinazione *f*

determine /dɪ'tɜːmɪn/ *vt* (ascertain) determinare; ~ **to** (resolve) decidere di

determined /dɪ'tɜːmɪnd/ *adj* deciso

determining /dɪ'tɜːmɪnɪŋ/ *adj* determinante

deterrent /dɪ'terənt/ *n* deterrente *m*

detest /dɪ'test/ *vt* detestare

detestable /dɪ'testəbl/ *adj* detestabile

detonate /'detəneɪt/ **1** *vt* far detonare **2** *vi* detonare

detonation /detə'neɪʃn/ *n* detonazione *f*

detonator /'detəneɪtə(r)/ *n* detonatore *m*

detour /'diːtʊə(r)/ *n* deviazione *f*

detox[1] /'diːtɒks/ *n* disintossicazione *f*

detox[2] /diː'tɒks/ **1** *vi* disintossicarsi **2** *vt* disintossicare

detoxify /diː'tɒksɪfaɪ/ *vt* disintossicare

d

detract /dɪ'trækt/ *vi* ~ **from** sminuire ⟨*merit*⟩; rovinare ⟨*pleasure, beauty*⟩

detractor /dɪ'træktə(r)/ *n* detrattore, -trice *mf*

detriment /'detrɪmənt/ *n* **to the** ~ **of** a danno di

detrimental /detrɪ'mentl/ *adj* dannoso

detritus /dɪ'traɪtəs/ *n* detriti *mpl*

deuce /dju:s/ *n* Tennis deuce *m inv*

devaluation /di:væljʊ'eɪʃn/ *n* svalutazione *f*

devalue /di:'vælju:/ *vt* svalutare ⟨*currency*⟩

devastate /'devəsteɪt/ *vt* devastare

devastated /'devəsteɪtɪd/ *adj* fam sconvolto

devastating /'devəsteɪtɪŋ/ *adj* devastante; ⟨*news*⟩ sconvolgente

devastation /devə'steɪʃn/ *n* devastazione *f*

develop /dɪ'veləp/ ① *vt* sviluppare; contrarre ⟨*illness*⟩; (add to value of) valorizzare ⟨*area*⟩
② *vi* svilupparsi; ~ **into** divenire

developer /dɪ'veləpə(r)/ *n* [property] ~ imprenditore, -trice *mf* edile

developing bath *n* Phot bagno *m* di sviluppo, bagno *m* rivelatore

developing country *n* paese *m* in via di sviluppo

developing tank *n* Phot vasca *f* di sviluppo

development /dɪ'veləpmənt/ *n* sviluppo *m*; (of vaccine etc) messa *f* a punto

development company *n* (for property) impresa *f* edile

deviant /'di:vɪənt/ *adj* deviato

deviate /'di:vɪeɪt/ *vi* deviare

deviation /di:vɪ'eɪʃn/ *n* deviazione *f*

device /dɪ'vaɪs/ *n* dispositivo *m*; **leave somebody to his own** ~**s** lasciare qualcuno per conto suo

devil /'devl/ *n* diavolo *m*

devilish /'dev(ə)lɪʃ/ *adj* diabolico

devilishly /'dev(ə)lɪʃlɪ/ *adv* fig fam terribilmente

devil-may-care *adj* menefreghista

devilment /'dev(ə)lmənt/ *n* Br cattiveria *f*

devil's advocate *n* avvocato *m* del diavolo

devil worship *n* culto *m* satanico

devious /'di:vɪəs/ *adj* ⟨*person*⟩ subdolo; ⟨*route*⟩ tortuoso

deviously /'di:vɪəslɪ/ *adv* subdolamente

devise /dɪ'vaɪz/ *vt* escogitare

devoid /dɪ'vɔɪd/ *adj* ~ **of** privo di

devolution /di:və'lu:ʃn/ *n* (of power) decentramento *m*

devote /dɪ'vəʊt/ *vt* dedicare

devoted /dɪ'vəʊtɪd/ *adj* ⟨*daughter etc*⟩ affezionato; **be** ~ **to something** consacrarsi a qualcosa

devotedly /dɪ'vəʊtɪdlɪ/ *adv* con dedizione

devotee /devə'ti:/ *n* appassionato, -a *mf*

devotion /dɪ'vəʊʃn/ *n* dedizione *f*; ~**s** *pl* Relig devozione *fsg*

devour /dɪ'vaʊə(r)/ *vt* divorare

devout /dɪ'vaʊt/ *adj* devoto

devoutly /dɪ'vaʊtlɪ/ *adv* Relig devotamente; (sincerely) fervidamente

dew /dju:/ *n* rugiada *f*

dewy /'dju:ɪ/ *adj* rugiadoso

dewy-eyed /-'aɪd/ *adj* (moved) con gli occhi lucidi; (naive) ingenuo

dexterity /dek'sterətɪ/ *n* destrezza *f*

dexterous /'dekstrəs/ *adj* ⟨*person, movement*⟩ agile, destro; ⟨*hand*⟩ abile; ⟨*mind*⟩ acuto

dexterously /'dekstrəslɪ/ *adv* ⟨*move*⟩ agilmente; ⟨*manage*⟩ abilmente

DfES *abbr* Br (**Department for Education and Skills**) ≈ Ministero *m* dell'Istruzione

dg *abbr* (**decigram**) dg *m*

diabetes /daɪə'bi:ti:z/ *n* diabete *m*

diabetic /daɪə'betɪk/ *adj & n* diabetico, -a *mf*

diabolical /daɪə'bɒlɪkl/ *adj* diabolico

diabolically /daɪə'bɒlɪklɪ/ *adv* (wickedly) diabolicamente; (fam: badly) orribilmente

diacritic /daɪə'krɪtrɪk/ *adj* (accent, mark) diacritico

diaeresis /daɪ'erɪsɪs/ *n* dieresi *f inv*

diagnose /'daɪəgnəʊz/ *vt* diagnosticare

diagnosis /daɪəg'nəʊsɪs/ *n* (pl **-oses** /daɪəg'nəʊsi:z/) diagnosi *f inv*

diagnostic /daɪəg'nɒstɪk/ *adj* diagnostico

diagnostics /daɪəg'nɒstɪks/ *n* Med diagnostica *f*

diagonal /daɪ'ægənl/ *adj & n* diagonale *f*

diagonally /daɪ'ægənlɪ/ *adv* diagonalmente

diagram /'daɪəgræm/ *n* diagramma *m*

dial /'daɪəl/ ① *n* (of clock, machine) quadrante *m*; Teleph disco *m* combinatore
② *vi* (pt/pp **dialled**) Teleph fare il numero; ~ **direct** chiamare in teleselezione
③ *vt* fare ⟨*number*⟩

dialect /'daɪəlekt/ *n* dialetto *m*

dialectic /daɪə'lektɪk/ ① *n* dialettica *f*
② *adj* dialettico

dialectics /daɪə'lektɪks/ *n* dialettica *f*

dialling code /'daɪəlɪŋ/ *n* prefisso *m*

dialling tone *n* segnale *m* di linea libera

dialogue /'daɪəlɒg/ n dialogo m

dialogue box n Comput finestra f di dialogo

dial tone n Am Teleph segnale m di linea libera

dial-up adj ⟨connection, access⟩ dial-up

dialysis /daɪˈælɪsɪs/ n dialisi f

dialysis machine n rene m artificiale

diameter /daɪˈæmɪtə(r)/ n diametro m

diametrically /daɪəˈmetrɪklɪ/ adv ~ opposed diametralmente opposto

diamond /'daɪəmənd/ n diamante m, brillante m; (shape) losanga f; ~s pl (in cards) quadri mpl

diamond jubilee n sessantesimo anniversario m

diamond-shaped adj romboidale

diamond wedding [anniversary] n nozze fpl di diamante

diaper /'daɪəpə(r)/ n Am pannolino m

diaphragm /'daɪəfræm/ n diaframma m

diarist /'daɪərɪst/ n (author) diarista mf; (journalist) giornalista mf di piccola cronaca

diarrhoea /daɪəˈriːə/ n diarrea f

diary /'daɪərɪ/ n (for appointments) agenda f; (for writing in) diario m

diatribe /'daɪətraɪb/ n diatriba f

dice /daɪs/ ① n inv dadi mpl
② vt Culin tagliare a dadini

dicey /'daɪsɪ/ adj fam rischioso

dichotomy /daɪˈkɒtəmɪ/ n dicotomia f

dicky /'dɪkɪ/ ① n (shirt front) pettino m, sparato m
② adj Br fam ⟨heart⟩ malandato

dictate /dɪkˈteɪt/ vt/i dettare

dictation /dɪkˈteɪʃn/ n dettato m

dictator /dɪkˈteɪtə(r)/ n dittatore m

dictatorial /dɪktəˈtɔːrɪəl/ adj dittatoriale

dictatorship /dɪkˈteɪtəʃɪp/ n dittatura f

diction /'dɪkʃn/ n dizione f

dictionary /'dɪkʃənrɪ/ n dizionario m

dictum /'dɪktəm/ n (maxim) massima f; (statement) affermazione f

did /dɪd/ ▶ DO

didactic /dɪˈdæktɪk/ adj didattico

diddle /'dɪdl/ vt fam gabbare

didn't /'dɪdnt/ = DID NOT

die¹ /daɪ/ n Techn (metal mould) stampo m; (for cutting) matrice f

die² vi (pres p **dying**) morire (of di); be dying to do something fam morire dalla voglia di fare qualcosa; be dying for a drink fam morire dalla voglia di bere qualcosa
■ **die away** vi ⟨noise, applause⟩ smorzarsi
■ **die down** vi calmarsi; ⟨fire, flames⟩ spegnersi
■ **die off** vi morire uno dopo l'altro

■ **die out** vi estinguersi; ⟨custom⟩ morire

diehard /'daɪhɑːd/ n (Pol: in party) fanatico, -a mf; (stubborn person) ultraconservatore mf

diesel /'diːzl/ n diesel m

diesel engine n motore m diesel

diesel train n treno m con locomotiva diesel

diet /'daɪət/ ① n regime m alimentare; (restricted) dieta f; be on a ~ essere a dieta
② vi essere a dieta

dietary /'daɪətrɪ/ adj ⟨habit⟩ alimentare

dietary fibre n fibre fpl alimentari

dietary supplement n integratore m dietetico

dietician /daɪəˈtɪʃn/ n dietologo, -a mf

differ /'dɪfə(r)/ vi differire; (disagree) non essere d'accordo

difference /'dɪfrəns/ n differenza f; (disagreement) divergenza f

different /'dɪfrənt/ adj diverso, differente; (various) diversi; be ~ from essere diverso da

differential /dɪfəˈrenʃl/ ① adj differenziale
② n differenziale m

differentiate /dɪfəˈrenʃɪeɪt/ vt distinguere (**between** fra); (discriminate) discriminare (**between** fra); (make different) differenziare

differentiation /dɪfərenʃɪˈeɪʃn/ n differenziazione f

differently /'dɪfrəntlɪ/ adv in modo diverso; ~ from diversamente da

differently abled /'eɪbld/ adj diversamente abile

difficult /'dɪfɪkəlt/ adj difficile

difficulty /'dɪfɪkəltɪ/ n difficoltà f inv; with ~ con difficoltà

diffidence /'dɪfɪdəns/ n mancanza f di sicurezza

diffident /'dɪfɪdənt/ adj senza fiducia in se stesso

diffidently /'dɪfɪdəntlɪ/ adv senza fiducia in se stesso

diffuse¹ /dɪˈfjuːs/ adj diffuso; (wordy) prolisso

diffuse² /dɪˈfjuːz/ vt Phys diffondere

diffuseness /dɪˈfjuːsnɪs/ n (of organization) estensione f; (of argument) prolissità f

dig /dɪg/ ① n (poke) spinta f; (remark) frecciata f; Archaeol scavo m; ~s pl fam camera fsg ammobiliata
② vt/i (pp/pp **dug**, pres p **digging**) scavare ⟨hole⟩; vangare ⟨garden⟩; (thrust) conficcare; ~ somebody in the ribs dare una gomitata a qualcuno
■ **dig out** vt fig tirar fuori
■ **dig up** vt scavare ⟨garden, object⟩; sradicare ⟨tree⟩; (fig: find) scovare

digest¹ /'daɪdʒest/ n compendio m

digest² /daɪ'dʒest/ *vt* digerire

digestible /daɪ'dʒestəbl/ *adj* digeribile

digestion /daɪ'dʒestʃn/ *n* digestione *f*

digestive /daɪ'dʒestɪv/ *adj* digestivo

digestive [biscuit] *n* Br biscotto *m* di farina integrale

digestive system *n* apparato *m* digerente

digestive tract *n* apparato *m* digerente

digger /'dɪgə(r)/ *n* Techn scavatrice *f*

diggings /'dɪgɪŋz/ *npl* (in archaeology) scavi *mpl*

digicam /'dɪdʒɪkæm/ *n* fam fotocamera *f* digitale

digit /'dɪdʒɪt/ *n* cifra *f*; (finger) dito *m*

digital /'dɪdʒɪtl/ *adj* digitale

digital [television] *n* TV *f* digitale

digital audio tape *n* audiocassetta *f* digitale

digital camera *n* fotocamera *f* digitale

digital clock *n* orologio *m* digitale

digital computer *n* computer *m* digitale

digitalize /'dɪdʒɪtəlaɪz/ *vt* digitalizzare

digitizer /'dɪdʒɪtaɪzə(r)/ *n* Comput tavoletta *f* grafica

dignified /'dɪgnɪfaɪd/ *adj* dignitoso

dignify /'dɪgnɪfaɪ/ *vt* nobilitare ‹occasion, building›

dignitary /'dɪgnɪtərɪ/ *n* dignitario *m*

dignity /'dɪgnətɪ/ *n* dignità *f*

digress /daɪ'gres/ *vi* divagare

digression /daɪ'greʃn/ *n* digressione *f*

dike /daɪk/ *n* diga *f*

dilapidated /dɪ'læpɪdeɪtɪd/ *adj* cadente

dilapidation /dɪlæpɪ'deɪʃn/ *n* rovina *f*

dilate /daɪ'leɪt/ ① *vt* dilatare ② *vi* dilatarsi

dilation /daɪ'leɪʃn/ *n* dilatazione *f*

dilatory /'dɪlətərɪ/ *adj* dilatorio

dilemma /dɪ'lemə/ *n* dilemma *m*

dilettante /dɪlɪ'tæntɪ/ *n* dilettante *mf*

diligence /'dɪlɪdʒəns/ *n* diligenza *f*

diligent /'dɪlɪdʒənt/ *adj* diligente

dill /dɪl/ *n* aneto *m*

dilly-dally /'dɪlɪdælɪ/ *vi* (pt/pp **-ied**) fam tentennare

dilute /daɪ'lju:t/ *vt* diluire

dilution /daɪ'lju:ʃn/ *n* also fig diluizione *f*

dim /dɪm/ ① *adj* (dimmer, dimmest) ‹light› debole; (dark) scuro; ‹prospect, chance› scarso; (indistinct) impreciso; (fam: stupid) tonto ② *vt/i* (pt/pp **dimmed**) affievolire

dime /daɪm/ *n* Am moneta *f* da dieci centesimi

dimension /daɪ'menʃn/ *n* dimensione *f*

dime store *n* Am grande magazzino *m* con prezzi molto bassi

diminish /dɪ'mɪnɪʃ/ *vt/i* diminuire

diminished /dɪ'mɪnɪʃt/ *adj* ridotto; Mus diminuito; **on grounds of ~ responsibility** Jur per seminfermità mentale

diminutive /dɪ'mɪnjʊtɪv/ *adj & n* diminutivo *m*

dimly /'dɪmlɪ/ *adv* ‹see, remember› indistintamente; ‹shine› debolmente

dimmer /'dɪmə(r)/ *n* interruttore *m* a reostato

dimple /'dɪmpl/ *n* fossetta *f*

dimwit /'dɪmwɪt/ *n* fam stupido *m*

dim-witted /-'wɪtɪd/ *adj* fam stupido

din /dɪn/ *n* baccano *m* ■ **din into** *vt* ~ **something into somebody** ficcare qualcosa in testa a qualcuno

dine /daɪn/ *vi* pranzare

diner /'daɪnə(r)/ *n* (Am: restaurant) tavola *f* calda; **the last ~ in the restaurant** l'ultimo cliente nel ristorante

dingdong /'dɪŋdɒŋ/ *n* dindon *m*

dingdong battle *n* Br battibecco *m*

dinghy /'dɪŋgɪ/ *n* dinghy *m*; (inflatable) canotto *m* pneumatico

dingy /'dɪndʒɪ/ *adj* (-ier, -iest) squallido e tetro

dining car *n* carrozza *f* ristorante

dining hall *n* refettorio *m*

dining room *n* sala *f* da pranzo

dining table *n* tavolo *m* da pranzo

dinky /'dɪŋkɪ/ *adj* Br fam carino

dinner /'dɪnə(r)/ *n* cena *f*; (at midday) pranzo *m*

dinner dance *n* cena *f* danzante

dinner fork *n* forchetta *f*

dinner hour *n* Br Sch pausa *f* del pranzo

dinner jacket *n* smoking *m inv*

dinner knife *n* coltello *m*

dinner money *n* Br Sch soldi *mpl* dati dai genitori agli scolari per il pranzo

dinner party *n* cena *f* (con invitati)

dinner plate *n* piatto *m* piano

dinner service, dinner set *n* servizio *m* da tavola

dinner time *n* (evening) ora *f* di cena; (midday) ora *f* di pranzo

dinnerware /'dɪnəweə(r)/ *n* Am servizio *m* da tavola

dinosaur /'daɪnəsɔ:(r)/ *n* dinosauro *m*

dint /dɪnt/ *n* **by ~ of** a forza di

diocese /'daɪəsɪs/ *n* diocesi *f inv*

diode /'daɪəʊd/ *n* diodo *m*

dioxide /daɪ'ɒksaɪd/ *n* biossido *m*

dip /dɪp/ ① *n* (in ground) inclinazione *f*; Culin salsina *f*; **go for a ~** andare a fare una nuotata

2 vt (pt/pp **dipped**) (in liquid) immergere; abbassare ⟨head, headlights⟩
3 vi ⟨land⟩ formare un avvallamento
■ **dip into** vt scorrere ⟨book⟩

diphtheria /dɪfˈθɪərɪə/ n difterite f

diphthong /ˈdɪfθɒŋ/ n dittongo m

diploma /dɪˈpləʊmə/ n diploma m

diplomacy /dɪˈpləʊməsɪ/ n diplomazia f

diplomat /ˈdɪpləmæt/ n diplomatico, -a mf

diplomatic /dɪpləˈmætɪk/ adj diplomatico

diplomatically /dɪpləˈmætɪklɪ/ adv con diplomazia

diplomatic bag n valigia f diplomatica

diplomatic immunity n immunità f diplomatica

dippy /ˈdɪpɪ/ adj (fam: crazy, weird) pazzo

dipstick /ˈdɪpstɪk/ n Auto astina f dell'olio

dire /ˈdaɪə(r)/ adj ⟨situation, consequences⟩ terribile

direct /daɪˈrekt/ **1** adj diretto
2 adv direttamente
3 vt (aim) rivolgere ⟨attention, criticism⟩; (control) dirigere; fare la regia di ⟨film, play⟩; ~ **somebody** (show the way) indicare la strada a qualcuno; ~ **somebody to do something** ordinare a qualcuno di fare qualcosa

direct access n Comput accesso m diretto

direct current n corrente m continua

direct debit n addebitamento m diretto

direct dialling n teleselezione f

direct hit n Mil colpo m diretto

direction /dɪˈrekʃn/ n direzione f; (of play, film) regia f; ~**s** pl indicazioni fpl; ~**s for use** istruzioni fpl per l'uso

directional /daɪˈrekʃənəl/ adj direzionale

directive /daɪˈrektɪv/ n direttiva f

direct line n linea f diretta

directly /daɪˈrektlɪ/ **1** adv direttamente; (at once) immediatamente
2 conj [non] appena

direct mail n mailing m inv

directness /daɪˈrektnɪs/ n (of person, attitude) franchezza f; (of play, work, writing) chiarezza f

direct object n complemento m oggetto

director /dɪˈrektə(r)/ n Comm direttore, -trice mf; (of play, film) regista mf

directorate /daɪˈrektərət/ n (board) consiglio m d'amministrazione

director general n presidente mf

Director of Public Prosecutions n Br ≈ Procuratore m della Repubblica

directorship /dɪˈrektəʃɪp/ n posto m di direttore

directory /dɪˈrektərɪ/ n elenco m; Teleph elenco m [telefonico]; (of streets) stradario m

directory assistance n Am servizio m informazioni abbonati

directory enquiries npl Br servizio m informazioni abbonati

direct rule n Pol sottomissione f al governo centrale

direct speech n discorso m diretto

direct transfer n trasferimento m automatico

dirt /dɜːt/ n sporco m; ~ **cheap** fam ad [un] prezzo stracciato

dirtiness /ˈdɜːtɪnɪs/ n (of person etc) sporcizia f

dirt track n (road) strada f sterrata; Sport pista f sterrata

dirty /ˈdɜːtɪ/ **1** adj (**-ier, -iest**) sporco
2 vt sporcare

dirty bomb n bomba f sporca

dirty-minded /-ˈmaɪndɪd/ adj fissato sul sesso

dirty trick n brutto scherzo m

dirty tricks npl Pol faccende fpl sporche

dirty weekend n fam weekend m inv clandestino con l'amante

dirty word n parolaccia f

disability /dɪsəˈbɪlətɪ/ n infermità f inv

disable /dɪˈseɪbl/ vt (make useless) mettere fuori uso ⟨machine⟩; (in accident) rendere invalido; Comput disabilitare; **be ~d by arthritis** essere menomato dall'artrite

disabled /dɪˈseɪbld/ adj invalido

disabled access n (to public building etc) accesso m per gli invalidi

disabled driver n guidatore, -trice mf invalido, -a

disabled person n invalido, -a mf

disabuse /dɪsəˈbjuːz/ vt disingannare

disadvantage /dɪsədˈvɑːntɪdʒ/ n svantaggio m; **at a ~** in una posizione di svantaggio

disadvantaged /dɪsədˈvɑːntɪdʒd/ adj svantaggiato

disadvantageous /dɪsædvənˈteɪdʒəs/ adj svantaggioso

disaffected /dɪsəˈfektɪd/ adj disilluso

disagree /dɪsəˈɡriː/ vi non essere d'accordo; ~ **with** ⟨food⟩ far male a

disagreeable /dɪsəˈɡriːəbl/ adj sgradevole

disagreement /dɪsəˈɡriːmənt/ n disaccordo m; (quarrel) dissidio m

disallow /dɪsəˈlaʊ/ vt respingere; Sport annullare

disappear /dɪsəˈpɪə(r)/ vi scomparire

disappearance /dɪsə'pɪərəns/ n
scomparsa f

disappoint /dɪsə'pɔɪnt/ vt deludere

disappointed /dɪsə'pɔɪntɪd/ adj deluso;
I am ~ in you mi hai deluso

disappointing /dɪsə'pɔɪntɪŋ/ adj
deludente

disappointment /dɪsə'pɔɪntmənt/ n
delusione f

disapproval /dɪsə'pruːvəl/ n
disapprovazione f

disapprove /dɪsə'pruːv/ vi
disapprovare; ~ of somebody/something
disapprovare qualcuno/qcsa

disapproving /dɪsə'pruːvɪŋ/ adj ⟨look,
gesture⟩ di disapprovazione

disarm /dɪs'ɑːm/ ① vt disarmare
② vi Mil disarmarsi

disarmament /dɪs'ɑːməmənt/ n
disarmo m

disarming /dɪs'ɑːmɪŋ/ adj ⟨frankness
etc⟩ disarmante

disarrange /dɪsə'reɪndʒ/ vt
scompigliare

disarray /dɪsə'reɪ/ n in ~ in disordine

disaster /dɪ'zɑːstə(r)/ n disastro m

disaster area n zona f disastrata; (fig:
person) disastro m

disaster fund n fondi mpl a favore dei
disastrati

disaster movie n film m inv
catastrofico

disaster relief n soccorso m disastri

disaster victim n disastrato, -a mf

disastrous /dɪ'zɑːstrəs/ adj disastroso

disastrously /dɪ'zɑːstrəslɪ/ adv ⟨fail⟩
disastrosamente; ⟨end, turn out⟩ in modo
catastrofico; go ~ wrong essere un
disastro

disband /dɪs'bænd/ ① vt sciogliere;
smobilitare ⟨troops⟩
② vi sciogliersi; ⟨regiment⟩ essere
smobilitato

disbelief /dɪsbɪ'liːf/ n incredulità f; in ~
con incredulità

disbelieve /dɪsbɪ'liːv/ vt non credere

disc /dɪsk/ n disco m; (CD) compact disc
m inv

discard /dɪ'skɑːd/ vt scartare; (throw away)
eliminare; scaricare ⟨boyfriend⟩

disc brakes npl Auto freni mpl a disco

discern /dɪ'sɜːn/ vt discernere

discernible /dɪ'sɜːnəbl/ adj discernibile

discerning /dɪ'sɜːnɪŋ/ adj perspicace

discharge¹ /'dɪstʃɑːdʒ/ n Electr scarica f;
(dismissal) licenziamento m; Mil congedo m;
(Med: of blood) emissione f; (of cargo) scarico
m

discharge² /dɪs'tʃɑːdʒ/ ① vt scaricare
⟨battery, cargo⟩; (dismiss) licenziare; Mil

congedare; Jur assolvere ⟨accused⟩;
dimettere ⟨patient⟩; ~ one's duty esaurire
il proprio compito
② vi Electr scaricarsi

disciple /dɪ'saɪpl/ n discepolo m

disciplinarian /dɪsɪplɪ'neərɪən/ n
persona f autoritaria

disciplinary /'dɪsɪplɪnərɪ/ adj
disciplinare

discipline /'dɪsɪplɪn/ ① n disciplina f
② vt disciplinare; (punish) punire

disciplined /'dɪsɪplɪnd/ adj ⟨person,
approach⟩ sistematico

disc jockey n disc jockey m inv

disclaim /dɪs'kleɪm/ vt negare

disclaimer /dɪs'kleɪmə(r)/ n rifiuto m

disclose /dɪs'kləʊz/ vt svelare

disclosure /dɪs'kləʊʒə(r)/ n rivelazione
f

disco /'dɪskəʊ/ n discoteca f

discoloration /dɪskʌlə'reɪʃn/ n (process)
scolorimento m; (spot) macchia f scolorita

discolour /dɪs'kʌlə(r)/ ① vt scolorire
② vi scolorirsi

discomfort /dɪs'kʌmfət/ n scomodità f;
fig disagio m

disconcert /dɪskən'sɜːt/ vt sconcertare

disconcerting /dɪskən'sɜːtɪŋ/ adj
sconcertante

disconnect /dɪskə'nekt/ vt
disconnettere

disconsolate /dɪs'kɒnsələt/ adj
sconsolato

discontent /dɪskən'tent/ n scontentezza
f

discontented /dɪskən'tentɪd/ adj
scontento

discontinue /dɪskən'tɪnjuː/ vt cessare,
smettere; Comm sospendere la produzione
di; ~d line fine f serie

discontinuity /dɪskɒntɪ'njuːɪtɪ/ n
discontinuità f

discord /'dɪskɔːd/ n discordia f; Mus
dissonanza f

discordant /dɪ'skɔːdənt/ adj ~ note
nota f discordante

discothèque /'dɪskətek/ n discoteca f

discount¹ /'dɪskaʊnt/ n sconto m

discount² /dɪs'kaʊnt/ vt (not believe) non
credere a; (leave out of consideration) non
tener conto di

discount card n tessera f di sconto

discount flight n volo m a prezzo
ridotto

discount store n discount m inv

discourage /dɪs'kʌrɪdʒ/ vt scoraggiare;
(dissuade) dissuadere

discouragement /dɪs'kʌrɪdʒmənt/ n
(despondency) scoraggiamento m;
(disincentive) disincentivo m

discourse /'dɪskɔ:s/ n discorso m
discourteous /dɪs'kɜ:tɪəs/ adj scortese
discourteously /dɪs'kɜ:tɪəslɪ/ adv
scortesemente
discover /dɪ'skʌvə(r)/ vt scoprire
discovery /dɪs'kʌvərɪ/ n scoperta f
discredit /dɪs'kredɪt/ 1 n discredito m
2 vt screditare
discreet /dɪ'skri:t/ adj discreto
discreetly /dɪ'skri:tlɪ/ adv
discretamente
discrepancy /dɪ'skrepənsɪ/ n
discrepanza f
discretion /dɪ'skreʃn/ n discrezione f
discriminate /dɪ'skrɪmɪneɪt/ vi
discriminare (**against** contro); ~ **between**
distinguere tra
discriminating /dɪ'skrɪmɪneɪtɪŋ/ adj
esigente
discrimination /dɪskrɪmɪ'neɪʃn/ n
discriminazione f; (quality) discernimento
m
discriminatory /dɪs'krɪmɪnətərɪ/ adj
discriminatorio, discriminativo
discus /'dɪskəs/ n disco m
discuss /dɪ'skʌs/ vt discutere; (examine
critically) esaminare
discussion /dɪ'skʌʃn/ n discussione f
discussion document,
discussion paper n documento m in
abbozzo
disdain /dɪs'deɪn/ 1 n sdegno f
2 vt sdegnare
disdainful /dɪs'deɪnfʊl/ adj sdegnoso
disease /dɪ'zi:z/ n malattia f
diseased /dɪ'zi:zd/ adj malato
disembark /dɪsem'bɑ:k/ vi sbarcare
disembodied /dɪsem'bɒdɪd/ adj ⟨voices⟩
evanescente; ⟨head⟩ senza corpo; ⟨soul⟩
disincarnato
disenchant /dɪsen'tʃɑ:nt/ vt
disincantare
disenchanted /dɪsen'tʃɑ:ntɪd/ adj
disincantato
disenchantment /dɪsen'tʃɑ:ntmənt/ n
disincanto m
disenfranchise /dɪsen'fræntʃaɪz/ vt
privare del diritto di voto
disengage /dɪsen'geɪdʒ/ vt
disimpegnare; disinnestare ⟨clutch⟩
disentangle /dɪsen'tæŋgəl/ vt
districare
disfavour /dɪs'feɪvə(r)/ n sfavore m; **fall
into** ~ perdere il favore
disfigure /dɪs'fɪgə(r)/ vt deformare
disgorge /dɪs'gɔ:dʒ/ vt rigettare
disgrace /dɪz'greɪs/ 1 n vergogna f; **fail
into** ~ cadere in disgrazia; **I am in** ~ sono
caduto in disgrazia; **it's a** ~ è una
vergogna

2 vt disonorare
disgraceful /dɪz'greɪsfʊl/ adj
vergognoso
disgruntled /dɪs'grʌntld/ adj
malcontento
disguise /dɪs'gaɪz/ 1 n travestimento
m; **in** ~ travestito
2 vt contraffare ⟨voice⟩; dissimulare
⟨emotions⟩; ~**d as** travestito da
disgust /dɪs'gʌst/ 1 n disgusto m: **in** ~
con aria disgustata
2 vt disgustare
disgusting /dɪs'gʌstɪŋ/ adj disgustoso
dish /dɪʃ/ n piatto m; **do the** ~**es** lavare i
piatti
■ **dish out** vt (serve) servire; (distribute)
distribuire
■ **dish up** vt servire
dishcloth /'dɪʃklɒθ/ n strofinaccio m
dishearten /dɪs'hɑ:t(ə)n/ vt scoraggiare
disheartening /dɪs'hɑ:t(ə)nɪŋ/ adj
scoraggiante
dishevelled /dɪ'ʃevld/ adj scompigliato
dishonest /dɪs'ɒnɪst/ adj disonesto
dishonestly /dɪs'ɒnɪstlɪ/ adv
disonestamente
dishonesty /dɪs'ɒnɪstɪ/ n disonestà f
dishonour /dɪs'ɒnə(r)/ 1 n disonore m
2 vt disonorare ⟨family⟩; non onorare
⟨cheque⟩
dishonourable /dɪs'ɒnərəbl/ adj
disonorevole
dishonourably /dɪs'ɒnərəblɪ/ adv in
modo disonorevole
dishtowel n strofinaccio m per i piatti
dishwasher /'dɪʃwɒʃə(r)/ n lavapiatti f
inv
dishwasher-safe adj lavabile in
lavastoviglie
dishy /'dɪʃɪ/ adj (-**ier**, **est**) Br fam ⟨man,
woman⟩ fico, figo
disillusion /dɪsɪ'lu:ʒn/ vt disilludere
disillusioned /dɪsɪ'lu:ʒnd/ adj deluso
(with di)
disillusionment /dɪsɪ'lu:ʒnmənt/ n
disillusione f
disincentive /dɪsɪn'sentɪv/ n
disincentivo m
disinclined /dɪsɪn'klaɪnd/ adj riluttante
disinfect /dɪsɪn'fekt/ vt disinfettare
disinfectant /dɪsɪn'fektənt/ n
disinfettante m
disingenuous /dɪsɪn'dʒenjʊəs/ adj
⟨comment⟩ insincero; ⟨smile⟩ falso
disinherit /dɪsɪn'herɪt/ vt diseredare
disintegrate /dɪs'ɪntəgreɪt/ vi
disintegrarsi
disintegration /dɪsɪntɪ'greɪʃn/ n
disgregazione f

d

disinterested /dɪsˈɪntərestɪd/ *adj* disinteressato

disjointed /dɪsˈdʒɔɪntɪd/ *adj* sconnesso

disk /dɪsk/ *n* Comput disco *m*; (diskette) dischetto *m*

disk drive *n* lettore *m* [di disco]

disk operating system /ˈdɪskɒpəreɪtɪŋ/ *n* sistema *m* operativo su disco

dislike /dɪsˈlaɪk/ **1** *n* avversione *f*; **your likes and ~s** i tuoi gusti **2** *vt* **I ~ him/it** non mi piace; **I don't ~ him/it** non mi dispiace

dislocate /ˈdɪsləkeɪt/ *vt* slogare; **~ one's shoulder** slogarsi una spalla

dislocation /dɪslə'keɪʃn/ *n* (of hip, knee) lussazione *f*

dislodge /dɪsˈlɒdʒ/ *vt* sloggiare

disloyal /dɪsˈlɔɪəl/ *adj* sleale

disloyally /dɪsˈlɔɪəlɪ/ *adv* slealmente

disloyalty /dɪsˈlɔɪəltɪ/ *n* slealtà *f*

dismal /ˈdɪzməl/ *adj* ⟨person⟩ abbacchiato; ⟨news, weather⟩ deprimente; ⟨performance⟩ mediocre

dismantle /dɪsˈmæntl/ *vt* smontare ⟨tent, machine⟩; fig smantellare

dismay /dɪsˈmeɪ/ *n* sgomento *m*; **much to my ~** con mio grande sgomento

dismayed /dɪsˈmeɪd/ *adj* sgomento

dismember /dɪsˈmembə(r)/ *vt* also fig smembrare

dismiss /dɪsˈmɪs/ *vt* licenziare ⟨employee⟩; (reject) scartare ⟨idea, suggestion⟩

dismissal /dɪsˈmɪsəl/ *n* licenziamento *m*

dismissive /dɪsˈmɪsɪv/ *adj* ⟨person, attitude⟩ sprezzante; **be ~ of** essere sprezzante verso

dismount /dɪsˈmaʊnt/ *vi* smontare

disobedience /dɪsəˈbiːdɪəns/ *n* disubbidienza *f*

disobedient /dɪsəˈbiːdɪənt/ *adj* disubbidiente

disobey /dɪsəˈbeɪ/ **1** *vt* disubbidire a ⟨rule⟩ **2** *vi* disubbidire

disorder /dɪsˈɔːdə(r)/ *n* disordine *m*; Med disturbo *m*

disordered /dɪsˈɔːdəd/ *adj* ⟨life⟩ disordinato; ⟨mind⟩ disturbato

disorderly /dɪsˈɔːdəlɪ/ *adj* disordinato; ⟨crowd⟩ turbolento; **~ conduct** turbamento *m* della quiete pubblica

disorganization /dɪsɔːgənaɪˈzeɪʃn/ *n* disorganizzazione *f*

disorganized /dɪsˈɔːgənaɪzd/ *adj* disorganizzato

disorientate /dɪsˈɔːrɪənteɪt/ *vt* disorientare

disorientation /dɪsɔːrɪenˈteɪʃn/ *n* disorientamento *m*

disown /dɪsˈəʊn/ *vt* disconoscere; **I'll ~ you** fam faccio finta di non conoscerti

disparaging /dɪˈspærɪdʒɪŋ/ *adj* sprezzante

disparagingly /dɪˈspærɪdʒɪŋlɪ/ *adv* sprezzantemente

disparate /ˈdɪspərət/ *adj* (different) eterogeneo; ⟨incompatible⟩ disparato

disparity /dɪˈspærətɪ/ *n* disparità *f inv*

dispassionate /dɪˈspæʃənət/ *adj* spassionato

dispassionately /dɪsˈpæʃənətlɪ/ *adv* spassionatamente

dispatch /dɪˈspætʃ/ **1** *n* Comm spedizione *f*; (Mil, report) dispaccio *m*; **with ~** con prontezza **2** *vt* spedire; (kill) spedire al creatore

Dispatch Box *n* Br Pol postazione *f* da cui parlano i ministri nel Parlamento britannico

dispatch box *n* valigia *f* diplomatica

dispatch rider *n* staffetta *f*

dispel /dɪˈspel/ *vt* (pt/pp **dispelled**) dissipare

dispensable /dɪˈspensəbl/ *adj* dispensabile

dispensary /dɪˈspensərɪ/ *n* farmacia *f*

dispense /dɪˈspens/ *vt* distribuire; **~ with** fare a meno di

dispenser /dɪˈspensə(r)/ *n* (device) distributore *m*

dispensing chemist /dɪˈspensɪŋ/ *n* farmacista *mf*; (shop) farmacia *f*

dispensing optician *n* Br ottico *m*

dispersal /dɪˈspɜːsl/ *n* dispersione *f*

disperse /dɪˈspɜːs/ **1** *vt* disperdere **2** *vi* disperdersi

dispersion /dɪˈspɜːʃn/ *n* dispersione *f*

dispirited /dɪˈspɪrɪtɪd/ *adj* scoraggiato

displace /dɪsˈpleɪs/ *vt* spostare

displaced person *n* profugo, -a *mf*

displacement /dɪsˈpleɪsmənt/ *n* spostamento *m*

display /dɪˈspleɪ/ **1** *n* mostra *f*; Comm esposizione *f*; (of feelings) manifestazione *f*; pej ostentazione *f*; Comput display *m inv* **2** *vt* mostrare; esporre ⟨goods⟩; manifestare ⟨feelings⟩; Comput visualizzare

display advertisement *n* annuncio *m* pubblicitario di grande formato

display cabinet, **display case** *n* vetrina *f*

display rack *n* espositore *m*

display window *n* vetrina *f*

displease /dɪsˈpliːz/ *vt* non piacere a; **be ~d with** essere scontento di

displeasure /dɪs'pleʒə(r)/ *n*
malcontento *m*; **incur sb's ~** scontentare
qualcuno

disposable /dɪ'spəʊzəbl/ *adj* (throwaway)
usa e getta; ⟨*income*⟩ disponibile

disposal /dɪ'spəʊzl/ *n* (getting rid of)
eliminazione *f*; **be at sb's ~** essere a
disposizione di qualcuno

dispose /dɪ'spəʊz/ *vi* **~ of** (get rid of)
disfarsi di; **be well ~d** essere ben disposto
(to verso)

disposition /dɪspə'zɪʃn/ *n* disposizione
f; (nature) indole *f*

dispossessed /dɪspə'zest/ *adj* ⟨*family*⟩
spossessato; ⟨*son*⟩ diseredato

disproportionate /dɪsprə'pɔːʃənət/ *adj*
sproporzionato

disproportionately /dɪsprə'pɔːʃənətlɪ/
adv in modo sproporzionato

disprove /dɪs'pruːv/ *vt* confutare

dispute /dɪ'spjuːt/ **①** *n* disputa *f*;
(industrial) contestazione *f*
② *vt* contestare ⟨*statement*⟩

disqualification /dɪskwɒlɪfɪ'keɪʃn/ *n*
squalifica *f*; (from driving) ritiro *m* della
patente

disqualify /dɪs'kwɒlɪfaɪ/ *vt* escludere;
Sport squalificare; **~ somebody from
driving** ritirare la patente a qualcuno

disquiet /dɪs'kwaɪət/ *n* inquietudine *f*

disquieting /dɪs'kwaɪətɪŋ/ *adj*
allarmante

disregard /dɪsrɪ'gɑːd/ **①** *n* mancanza *f*
di considerazione
② *vt* ignorare

disrepair /dɪsrɪ'peə(r)/ *n* **fall into ~**
deteriorarsi; **in a state of ~** in cattivo
stato

disreputable /dɪs'repjʊtəbl/ *adj*
malfamato

disrepute /dɪsrɪ'pjuːt/ *n* discredito *m*;
bring somebody into ~ rovinare la
reputazione a qualcuno

disrespect /dɪsrɪ'spekt/ *n* mancanza *f*
di rispetto

disrespectful /dɪsrɪ'spektfʊl/ *adj*
irrispettoso

disrespectfully /dɪsrɪ'spektfʊlɪ/ *adv*
irrispettosamente

disrupt /dɪs'rʌpt/ *vt* creare scompiglio
in; sconvolgere ⟨*plans*⟩

disruption /dɪs'rʌpʃn/ *n* scompiglio *m*;
(of plans) sconvolgimento *m*

disruptive /dɪs'rʌptɪv/ *adj* ⟨*person,
behaviour*⟩ indisciplinato

dissatisfaction /dɪ(s)sætɪs'fækʃn/ *n*
malcontento *m*

dissatisfied /dɪ(s)'sætɪsfaɪd/ *adj*
scontento

dissect /dɪ'sekt/ *vt* sezionare

dissection /dɪ'sekʃn/ *n* dissezione *f*

disseminate /dɪ'semɪneɪt/ *vt* divulgare

dissemination /dɪsemɪ'neɪʃn/ *n*
divulgazione *f*

dissension /dɪ'senʃn/ *n* (discord)
dissenso *m*

dissent /dɪ'sent/ **①** *n* dissenso *m*
② *vi* dissentire

dissertation /dɪsə'teɪʃn/ *n* tesi *f inv*

disservice /dɪ(s)'sɜːvɪs/ *n* **do
somebody/oneself a ~** rendere un cattivo
servizio a qualcuno/se stesso

dissidence /'dɪsɪdəns/ *n* dissidenza *f*

dissident /'dɪsɪdənt/ *n* dissidente *mf*

dissimilar /dɪ(s)'sɪmɪlə(r)/ *adj* dissimile
(to da)

dissimilarity /dɪs(s)ɪmɪ'lærətɪ/ *n*
diversità *f inv*

dissipate /'dɪsɪpeɪt/ *vt* dissipare ⟨*hope,
enthusiasm*⟩

dissipated /'dɪsɪpeɪtɪd/ *adj* dissipato

dissipation *n* dissipatezza *f*,
sregolatezza *f*

dissociate /dɪ'səʊʃɪeɪt/ *vt* dissociare; **~
oneself from** dissociarsi da

dissolute /'dɪsəluːt/ *adj* dissoluto

dissolution /dɪsə'luːʃn/ *n* scioglimento
m

dissolve /dɪ'zɒlv/ **①** *vt* dissolvere
② *vi* dissolversi

dissonance /'dɪsənəns/ *n* dissonanza *f*

dissonant /'dɪsənənt/ *adj* Mus
dissonante

dissuade /dɪ'sweɪd/ *vt* dissuadere

distance /'dɪstəns/ *n* distanza *f*; **it's a
short ~ from here to the station** la
stazione non è lontana da qui; **in the ~** in
lontananza; **from a ~** da lontano

distance learning *n* corsi *mpl* di
studio a distanza

distant /'dɪstənt/ *adj* distante; ⟨*relative*⟩
lontano

distantly /'dɪstəntlɪ/ *adv* ⟨*reply*⟩ con
distacco

distaste /dɪs'teɪst/ *n* avversione *f*

distasteful /dɪs'teɪstfʊl/ *adj* spiacevole

distemper /dɪ'stempə(r)/ *n* (paint)
tempera *f*; (in horses, dogs) cimurro *m*

distend /dɪ'stend/ *vi* dilatarsi

distil /dɪ'stɪl/ *vt* (pt/pp **distilled**)
distillare

distillation /dɪstɪ'leɪʃn/ *n* distillazione *f*

distillery /dɪ'stɪlərɪ/ *n* distilleria *f*

distinct /dɪ'stɪŋkt/ *adj* chiaro; (different)
distinto

distinction /dɪ'stɪŋkʃn/ *n* distinzione *f*;
Sch massimo *m* dei voti

distinctive /dɪ'stɪŋktɪv/ *adj*
caratteristico

distinctly /dɪ'stɪŋktlɪ/ *adv* chiaramente

distinguish /dɪˈstɪŋgwɪʃ/ *vt/i*
distinguere; ~ **oneself** distinguersi

distinguishable /dɪˈstɪŋgwɪʃəbl/ *adj*
distinguibile

distinguished /dɪˈstɪŋgwɪʃt/ *adj*
rinomato; ⟨appearance⟩ distinto; ⟨career⟩
brillante

distinguishing /dɪˈstɪŋgwɪʃɪŋ/ *adj*
⟨feature⟩ distintivo

distort /dɪˈstɔːt/ *vt* distorcere

distortion /dɪˈstɔːʃn/ *n* distorsione *f*

distract /dɪˈstrækt/ *vt* distrarre

distracted /dɪˈstræktɪd/ *adj* assente;
(fam: worried) preoccupato

distracting /dɪˈstræktɪŋ/ *adj* che
distrae; **I found the noise too** ~ il rumore
mi disturbava troppo

distraction /dɪˈstrækʃn/ *n* distrazione *f*;
(despair) disperazione *f*; **drive somebody to**
~ portare qualcuno alla disperazione

distraught /dɪˈstrɔːt/ *adj* sconvolto

distress /dɪˈstres/ ① *n* angoscia *f*; (pain)
sofferenza *f*; (danger) difficoltà *f*
② *vt* sconvolgere; (sadden) affliggere

distressed /dɪˈstrest/ *adj* (upset) turbato;
(stronger) afflitto

distressing /dɪˈstresɪŋ/ *adj* penoso;
(shocking) sconvolgente

distress signal *n* segnale *m* di
richiesta di soccorso

distribute /dɪˈstrɪbjuːt/ *vt* distribuire

distribution /dɪstrɪˈbjuːʃn/ *n*
distribuzione *f*

distribution network *n* rete *f* di
distribuzione

distributor /dɪˈstrɪbjʊtə(r)/ *n*
distributore *m*

district /ˈdɪstrɪkt/ *n* regione *f*; Admin
distretto *m*

district attorney *n* Am procuratore *m*
distrettuale

district council *n* Br consiglio *m*
distrettuale

district court *n* Am corte *f* distrettuale
federale

district manager *n* direttore, -trice *mf*
di zona

district nurse *n* infermiere, -a *mf* che
fa visite a domicilio

distrust /dɪsˈtrʌst/ ① *n* sfiducia *f*
② *vt* non fidarsi di

distrustful /dɪsˈtrʌstfʊl/ *adj* diffidente

disturb /dɪˈstɜːb/ *vt* disturbare;
(emotionally) turbare; spostare ⟨papers⟩

disturbance /dɪˈstɜːbəns/ *n* disturbo *m*;
~**s** *pl* (rioting etc) disordini *mpl*

disturbed /dɪˈstɜːbd/ *adj* turbato;
[mentally] ~ malato di mente

disturbing /dɪˈstɜːbɪŋ/ *adj* inquietante

disuse /dɪsˈjuːs/ *n* **fall into** ~ cadere in
disuso

disused /dɪsˈjuːzd/ *adj* non utilizzato

ditch /dɪtʃ/ ① *n* fosso *m*
② *vt* (fam: abandon) abbandonare ⟨plan,
car⟩; piantare ⟨lover⟩

ditchwater /ˈdɪtʃwɔːtə(r)/ *n* **as dull as**
~ una barba

dither /ˈdɪðə(r)/ *vi* titubare

ditto /ˈdɪtəʊ/ *adv* idem; (in list) idem come
sopra

ditto marks *npl* virgolette *fpl*

divan /dɪˈvæn/ *n* divano *m*

dive /daɪv/ ① *n* tuffo *m*; Aeron picchiata *f*;
(fam: place) bettola *f*
② *vi* tuffarsi; (when in water) immergersi;
Aeron scendere in picchiata; (fam: rush)
precipitarsi

dive-bomb *vt* Mil bombardare in
picchiata

diver /ˈdaɪvə(r)/ *n* (from board) tuffatore,
-trice *mf*; (scuba) sommozzatore, -trice *mf*;
(deep sea) palombaro *m*

diverge /daɪˈvɜːdʒ/ *vi* divergere

divergent /daɪˈvɜːdʒənt/ *adj* divergente

diverse /daɪˈvɜːs/ *adj* vario

diversify /daɪˈvɜːsɪfaɪ/ *vt/i* (pt/pp -**ied**)
Comm diversificare

diversion /daɪˈvɜːʃn/ *n* deviazione *f*;
(distraction) diversivo *m*

diversionary /daɪˈvɜːʃənərɪ/ *adj* ⟨tactic,
attack⟩ diversivo

diversity /daɪˈvɜːsətɪ/ *n* varietà *f*

divert /daɪˈvɜːt/ *vt* deviare ⟨traffic⟩;
distogliere ⟨attention⟩

divest /daɪˈvest/ *vt* privare (of di)

divide /dɪˈvaɪd/ ① *vt* dividere (by per);
six ~**d by two** sei diviso due
② *vi* dividersi
■ **divide out** *vt* = DIVIDE
■ **divide up** *vt* = DIVIDE

dividend /ˈdɪvɪdend/ *n* dividendo *m*; **pay**
~**s** fig ripagare

divider /dɪˈvaɪdə(r)/ *n* (in room) divisorio
m; (in file) cartoncino *m* separatore

dividers /dɪˈvaɪdəz/ *npl* compasso *m* a
punte fisse

dividing /dɪˈvaɪdɪŋ/ *adj* ⟨wall, fence⟩
divisorio

dividing line *n* linea *f* di demarcazione

divine /dɪˈvaɪn/ *adj* divino

divinely /dɪˈvaɪnlɪ/ *adv* also fam
divinamente

diving /ˈdaɪvɪŋ/ *n* (from board) tuffi *mpl*;
(scuba) immersione *f*

diving board *n* trampolino *m*

diving mask *n* maschera *f* [subacquea]

diving suit *n* muta *f*; (deep sea)
scafandro *m*

divinity /dɪˈvɪnəti/ n divinità f inv; (subject) teologia f; (at school) religione f

divisible /dɪˈvɪzəbl/ adj divisibile (**by** per)

division /dɪˈvɪʒn/ n divisione f; (in sports league) serie f

divisional /dɪˈvɪʒənəl/ adj ⟨commander, officer⟩ di divisione

divisive /dɪˈvaɪsɪv/ adj ⟨policy⟩ che crea discordia; **be socially** ∼ creare delle divisioni sociali

divorce /dɪˈvɔːs/ ①️ n divorzio m ②️ vt divorziare da

divorced /dɪˈvɔːst/ adj divorziato; **get** ∼ divorziare

divorcee /dɪvɔːˈsiː/ n divorziato, -a mf

divulge /daɪˈvʌldʒ/ vt rendere pubblico
■ **divvy up** vt fam = DIVIDE up

DIY abbr **do-it-yourself**

dizziness /ˈdɪzɪnɪs/ n giramenti mpl di testa

dizzy /ˈdɪzi/ adj (**-ier, -iest**) vertiginoso; **I feel** ∼ mi gira la testa

DJ n abbr (**disc jockey**) DJ m inv; Br abbr (**dinner jacket**) smoking m inv

Djibouti /dʒɪˈbuːti/ n Gibuti f

DNA ①️ n abbr (**deoxyribonucleic acid**) DNA m inv ②️ attrib ⟨testing⟩ del DNA

DNR abbr Am (**Department of Natural Resources**) ≈ Ministero m dell'Ambiente e della Tutela del Territorio; (**do not resuscitate**) non rianimare

do /duː/ ①️ n (pl **dos** or **do's**) fam festa f ②️ vt (3 sg pres tense **does**; pt **did**; pp **done**) fare; (fam: cheat) fregare; **do somebody out of something** (money) fregare qualcosa a qualcuno; (opportunity) defraudare qualcuno di qualcosa; **be done** Culin essere cotto; **well done** bravo; Culin ben cotto; **do the flowers** sistemare i fiori; **do the washing up** lavare i piatti; **do one's hair** farsi i capelli ③️ vi (be suitable) andare; (be enough) bastare; **this will do** questo va bene; **that will do!** basta così!; **do well/badly** cavarsela bene/male; **how is he doing?** come sta? ④️ v aux **do you speak Italian?** parli italiano?; **you don't like him, do you?** non ti piace, vero?; (expressing astonishment) non dirmi che ti piace!; **yes, I do** sì; (emphatic) invece sì; **no, I don't** no; **I don't smoke** non fumo; **don't you/doesn't he?** vero?; **so do I** anch'io; **do come in, John** entra, John; **how do you do?** piacere
■ **do away with** vt abolire ⟨rule⟩
■ **do for** vt (ruin) rovinare
■ **do in** vt (fam: kill) uccidere; farsi male a ⟨back⟩; **done in** fam esausto
■ **do up** vt (fasten) abbottonare; (renovate) rimettere a nuovo; (wrap) avvolgere

■ **do with** vt **I could do with a spanner** mi ci vorrebbe una chiave inglese
■ **do without** vt fare a meno di

d.o.b. abbr (**date of birth**) data f di nascita

docile /ˈdəʊsaɪl/ adj docile

dock¹ /dɒk/ n Jur banco m degli imputati

dock² ①️ n Naut bacino m ②️ vi entrare in porto; ⟨spaceship⟩ congiungersi

docker /ˈdɒkə(r)/ n portuale m

docket /ˈdɒkɪt/ ①️ n (Comm: label) etichetta f; (customs certificate) ricevuta f doganale ②️ vt Comm etichettare ⟨parcel, package⟩

docking /ˈdɒkɪŋ/ n Naut ormeggio m; (of spaceshuttle) aggancio m

docks /dɒks/ npl porto m

dockworker /ˈdɒkwɜːkə(r)/ n portuale m

dockyard /ˈdɒkjɑːd/ n cantiere m navale

doctor /ˈdɒktə(r)/ ①️ n dottore m, dottoressa f ②️ vt alterare ⟨drink⟩; castrare ⟨cat⟩

doctorate /ˈdɒktərət/ n dottorato m

Doctor of Philosophy n titolare mf di un dottorato di ricerca

doctor's note /ˈdɒktəz/ n certificato m medico

doctrine /ˈdɒktrɪn/ n dottrina f

docudrama /ˈdɒkjʊdrɑːmə/ n film m inv verità

document /ˈdɒkjʊmənt/ n documento m

documentary /dɒkjʊˈmentəri/ adj & n documentario m

documentation /dɒkjʊmenˈteɪʃn/ n documentazione f

document holder n (for keyboarder) leggio m

document wallet n (folder) cartellina f

doddery /ˈdɒdəri/ adj fam barcollante

doddle /ˈdɒd(ə)l/ n Br fam **it's a** ∼ è un gioco da ragazzi

dodge /dɒdʒ/ ①️ n fam trucco m ②️ vt schivare ⟨blow⟩; evitare ⟨person⟩ ③️ vi scansarsi; ∼ **out of the way** scansarsi

dodgems /ˈdɒdʒəmz/ npl autoscontro msg

dodgy /ˈdɒdʒi/ adj (**-ier, -iest**) (fam: dubious) sospetto

DOE n Br abbr (**Department of the Environment**) ministero m dell'Ambiente; Am abbr (**Department of Energy**) ≈ ministero m dell'Industria

doe /dəʊ/ n femmina f (di daino, renna, lepre); (rabbit) coniglia f

does /dʌz/ ▶ DO

doesn't /ˈdʌznt/ = DOES NOT

dog /dɒg/ ①️ n cane m

2 vt (pt/pp **dogged**) ⟨illness, bad luck⟩ perseguitare

dog biscuit n biscotto m per cani

dog breeder n allevatore, -trice mf di cani

dog collar n collare m (per cani); Relig fam collare m del prete

dog-eared /-ɪəd/ adj con le orecchie

dog-end n fam cicca f

dogfight n combattimento m di cani; Aeron combattimento m aereo

dogged /'dɒgɪd/ adj ostinato

doggedly /'dɒgɪdlɪ/ adv ostinatamente

doggy bag /'dɒgɪ/ n sacchetto m per portarsi a casa gli avanzi di un pasto al ristorante

doggy-paddle n fam nuoto m a cagnolino

dog handler n addestratore, -trice mf di cani

doghouse /'dɒghaʊs/ n Am canile m; **in the** ~ Br & Am fam in disgrazia

dogma /'dɒgmə/ n dogma m

dogmatic /dɒg'mætɪk/ adj dogmatico

do-gooder /duː'gʊdə(r)/ n pej pseudo benefattore, -trice mf

dog-paddle n nuoto m a cagnolino

dogsbody n fam tirapiedi mf inv

dog tag n Am Mil fam piastrina f di riconoscimento

doh /dəʊ/ n Mus do m

doily /'dɔɪlɪ/ n centrino m

doing /'duːɪŋ/ n **it's none of my** ~ non sono stato io; **this is her** ~ questa è opera sua; **it takes some** ~! ce ne vuole!

do-it-yourself /duːɪtjə'self/ n fai da te m, bricolage m

do-it-yourself shop n negozio m di bricolage

doldrums /'dɒldrəmz/ npl **be in the** ~ essere giù di corda; ⟨business⟩ essere in fase di stasi

dole /dəʊl/ n sussidio m di disoccupazione; **be on the** ~ essere disoccupato

■ **dole out** vt distribuire

doleful /'dəʊlfl/ adj triste

dolefully /'dəʊlfʊlɪ/ adv tristemente

dole queue n Br coda f per riscuotere il sussidio di disoccupazione; (fig: number of unemployed) numero m dei disoccupati

doll /dɒl/ n bambola f

■ **doll up** vt fam ~ **oneself up** mettersi in ghingheri

dollar /'dɒlə(r)/ n dollaro m

dollar bill n banconota f da un dollaro

dollar diplomacy n politica f di investimenti all'estero

dollar sign n simbolo m del dollaro

dollop /'dɒləp/ n fam cucchiaiata f

dolly /'dɒlɪ/ n (fam: doll) bambola f; Cinema, TV dolly m inv

Dolomites /'dɒləmaɪts/ npl Dolomiti mpl

dolphin /'dɒlfɪn/ n delfino m

domain /də'meɪn/ n dominio m

domain name n Comput nome m di dominio

dome /dəʊm/ n cupola f

domed /dəʊmd/ adj ⟨skyline, city⟩ ricco di cupole; ⟨roof, ceiling⟩ a cupola; ⟨forehead, helmet⟩ bombato

domestic /də'mestɪk/ adj domestico; Pol interno; Comm nazionale.

domestic animal n animale m domestico

domestic appliance n elettrodomestico m

domesticate /də'mestɪkeɪt/ vt addomesticare

domesticated /də'mestɪkeɪtɪd/ adj ⟨animal⟩ addomesticato

domestic flight n volo m nazionale

domestic help n collaboratore, -trice mf familiare

domesticity /dɒme'stɪsətɪ/ n ⟨home life⟩ vita f di famiglia; ⟨household duties⟩ faccende fpl domestiche

domestic servant n domestico, -a mf

domiciliary /dɒmɪ'sɪlɪərɪ/ adj ⟨visit, care⟩ a domicilio

dominance /'dɒmɪnəns/ n Biol, Zool dominanza f; (domination) predominio m; (numerical strength) preponderanza f

dominant /'dɒmɪnənt/ adj dominante

dominate /'dɒmɪneɪt/ vt/i dominare

domination /dɒmɪ'neɪʃn/ n dominio m

domineering /dɒmɪ'nɪərɪŋ/ adj autoritario

Dominica /də'mɪnɪkə/ n Dominica f

Dominican Republic /də'mɪnɪkən/ n Repubblica f Dominicana

dominion /də'mɪnjən/ n Br Pol dominio m inv

domino /'dɒmɪnəʊ/ n (pl **-es**) tessera f del domino; ~**es** sg (game) domino m

don[1] /dɒn/ vt (pt/pp **donned**) liter indossare

don[2] n docente mf universitario, -a

donate /dəʊ'neɪt/ vt donare

donation /dəʊ'neɪʃn/ n donazione f

done /dʌn/ ▶ DO

donkey /'dɒŋkɪ/ n asino m

donkey jacket n giacca f pesante

donkey's years fam **not for** ~ ~ non da secoli

donkey-work n sgobbata f

donor /'dəʊnə(r)/ n donatore, -trice mf

donor card n tessera f del donatore di organi

don't /dəʊnt/ = DO NOT

doodle /'duːdl/ vi scarabocchiare

doom /duːm/ **1** n fato m; (ruin) rovina f **2** vt be ∼ed to failure essere destinato al fallimento

doomed /duːmd/ adj ⟨vessel⟩ destinato ad affondare

doomsday /'duːmzdeɪ/ n giorno m del giudizio

doomwatch /'duːmwɒtʃ/ n catastrofismo m

door /dɔː(r)/ n porta f; (of car) portiera f; out of ∼s all'aperto

door bell n campanello m

doorman n portiere m

doormat n zerbino m

door plate n (of doctor etc) targa f

doorstep n gradino m della porta

doorstop n fermaporta m inv

door-to-door **1** adj ⟨canvassing, selling⟩ porta a porta **2** adv ⟨sell⟩ porta a porta

doorway n vano m della porta

dope /dəʊp/ **1** n fam (drug) droga f leggera; (information) indiscrezioni fpl; (idiot) idiota mf **2** vt drogare; Sport dopare

dope test n Sport antidoping m inv

dopey /'dəʊpɪ/ adj fam addormentato

dormant /'dɔːmənt/ adj latente; ⟨volcano⟩ inattivo

dormer /'dɔːmə(r)/ n ∼ [window] abbaino m

dormitory /'dɔːmɪtərɪ/ n dormitorio m

dormitory town n città f inv dormitorio

dormouse /'dɔːmaʊs/ n (pl **dormice** /'dɔːmaɪs/) ghiro m

dosage /'dəʊsɪdʒ/ n dosaggio m

dose /dəʊs/ n dose f

doss /dɒs/ vi sl accamparsi ■ **doss down** vi sistemarsi [a dormire]

dosser /'dɒsə(r)/ n barbone, -a mf

doss-house n dormitorio m pubblico

dot /dɒt/ n punto m; at 8 o'clock on the ∼ alle 8 in punto

dotage /'dəʊtɪdʒ/ n be in one's ∼ essere un vecchio rimbambito

dot-com /dɒt'kɒm/ **1** adj ⟨company⟩ che opera in Internet; ⟨millionaire⟩ arricchito grazie a Internet **2** n azienda f che opera in Internet

dote /dəʊt/ vi ∼ on stravedere per

dot matrix [printer] n stampante f a matrice di punti

dotted /'dɒtɪd/ adj ∼ line linea f punteggiata; sign on the ∼ line firmare

nell'apposito spazio; be ∼ with essere punteggiato di

dotty /'dɒtɪ/ adj (-ier, -iest) fam tocco; ⟨idea⟩ folle

double /'dʌbl/ **1** adj doppio **2** adv cost ∼ costare il doppio; see ∼ vedere doppio; ∼ the amount la quantità doppia **3** n doppio m; (person) sosia m inv; ∼s pl Tennis doppio m; at the ∼ di corsa **4** vt raddoppiare; (fold) piegare in due **5** vi raddoppiare ■ **double back** vi (go back) fare dietro front ■ **double up** vi (bend over) piegarsi in due (with per); (share) dividere una stanza

double act n Theat, fig numero m eseguito da due attori

double-barrelled /-'bærəld/ adj ⟨gun⟩ a doppia canna

double-barrelled surname n cognome m doppio

double-bass n contrabbasso m

double bed n letto m matrimoniale

double bend n Auto doppia curva f

double bill n Theat rappresentazione f di due spettacoli

double bluff n atto m del dire la verità facendola sembrare una menzogna

double-book **1** vi ⟨hotel, airline, company⟩ fare prenotazioni doppie **2** vt ∼ a room/seat etc riservare la stessa camera/lo stesso posto a due persone

double-breasted adj a doppio petto

double-check **1** vt/i ricontrollare **2** n double check ulteriore controllo m

double chin n doppio mento m

double-click vi Comput fare doppio click; ∼ on fare doppio click su

double cream n Br ≈ panna f densa

double-cross vt ingannare

double cuff n polsino m con risvolto

double-dealing **1** n doppio gioco m **2** adj doppio

double-decker n autobus m inv a due piani

double door[s] n [pl] porta f a due battenti

double Dutch n fam ostrogoto m

double-edged /-'edʒd/ adj also fig a doppio taglio

double entendre /duːblɑ̃'tɑ̃dr(ə)/ n doppio senso m

double entry book-keeping n contabilità f in partita doppia

double exposure n Phot sovrimpressione f

double fault n Tennis doppio fallo m

double feature n Cinema proiezione f di due film con biglietto unico

double-fronted /-'frʌntɪd/ adj ⟨house⟩ con due finestre ai lati della porta principale

double glazing n doppio vetro m

double-jointed adj ⟨person, limb⟩ snodato

double knitting [wool] n lana f grossa

double lock vt chiudere a doppia mandata

double-park vt/i parcheggiare in doppia fila

double-quick adv rapidissimamente adj in ∼ time in un baleno

double room n camera f doppia

double saucepan n Br bagnomaria m inv

double spacing n Typ interlinea f doppia

double spread n Journ articolo m/ pubblicità f su due pagine

double standard n have ∼ ∼s usare metri diversi

double take n do a ∼ ∼ reagire a scoppio ritardato

double talk n pej discorso m ambiguo

double time n Am Mil marcia f forzata; be paid ∼ ∼ ricevere doppia paga per lo straordinario

double vision n have ∼ ∼ vederci doppio

double whammy n (fam: two bits of bad luck) sfortuna f doppia

double yellow line[s] n[pl] Br Aut due linee fpl gialle continue indicanti divieto di fermata e di sosta

doubly /'dʌblɪ/ adv doppiamente

doubt /daʊt/ **1** n dubbio m
2 vt dubitare di

doubtful /'daʊtfʊl/ adj dubbio; (having doubts) in dubbio

doubtfully /'daʊtfʊlɪ/ adv con aria dubbiosa

doubtless /'daʊtlɪs/ adv indubbiamente

douche /duːʃ/ n (Med: vaginal) irrigazione f

dough /dəʊ/ n pasta f; (for bread) impasto m; (fam: money) quattrini mpl

doughnut /'dəʊnʌt/ n bombolone m, krapfen m inv

dour /'dʊə(r)/ adj ⟨mood, landscape⟩ cupo; ⟨person, expression⟩ arcigno; ⟨building⟩ austero

douse /daʊs/ vt spegnere

dove /dʌv/ n colomba f

dovecot[e] /'dʌvkɒt/ n colombaia f

dovetail /'dʌvteɪl/ n Techn incastro m a coda di rondine

dowdy /'daʊdɪ/ adj (-ier, -iest) trasandato

down[1] /daʊn/ n (feathers) piumino m

down[2] /daʊn/ **1** adv giù; **go/come** ∼ scendere; ∼ **there** laggiù; **sales are** ∼ le vendite sono diminuite; **£50** ∼ 50 sterline d'acconto; ∼ **10%** ridotto del 10% ∼ **with...!** abbasso...!
2 prep **walk** ∼ **the road** comminare per strada; ∼ **the stairs** giù per le scale; **fall** ∼ **the stairs** cadere giù dalle scale; **get that** ∼ **you!** fam butta giù!; **be** ∼ **the pub** fam essere al pub
3 vt bere tutto d'un fiato ⟨drink⟩; ∼ **tools** staccare; (in protest) interrompere il lavoro per protesta

down-and-out n spiantato, -a mf

downbeat adj (pessimistic) pessimistico; (laidback) distaccato

downcast adj abbattuto

downfall n caduta f; (of person) rovina f

downgrade vt (in seniority) degradare

down-hearted /-'hɑːtɪd/ adj scoraggiato

downhill adv in discesa; **go** ∼ fig essere in declino

downhill skiing n sci m di fondo

down-in-the-mouth adj fam abbattuto

download vt Comput scaricare

down-market adj ⟨newspaper, programme⟩ rivolto al pubblico delle fasce basse; ⟨products⟩ dozzinale; ⟨area⟩ popolare; ⟨hotel, restaurant⟩ economico

down payment n deposito m

downpipe n Br tubo m di scolo

downplay vt minimizzare

downpour n acquazzone m

downright **1** adj (absolute) totale; ⟨lie⟩ bell'e buono; (idiot) perfetto
2 adv (completely) completamente

downs /daʊnz/ npl Br (hills) colline fpl di gesso nell'Inghilterra meridionale

downside /'daʊnsaɪd/ n svantaggio m

downside up adj & adv Am sottosopra

downsize /'daʊnsaɪz/ **1** vt ⟨company⟩ ridurre l'organico di
2 vi ridurre l'organico

Down's syndrome /'daʊnz/ n sindrome f di Down

downstairs adv al piano di sotto adj del piano di sotto

downstream adv a valle

down-to-earth adj (person) con i piedi per terra

downtown adv Am in centro

downtrodden /'daʊntrɒd(ə)n/ adj oppresso

downturn n (in economy) fase f discendente; (in career) svolta f negativa

down under *adv* fam in Australia e/o Nuova Zelanda

downward[s] /'daʊnwəd[z]/ **1** *adj* verso il basso; ‹*slope*› in discesa **2** *adv* verso il basso

downwind /daʊn'wɪnd/ *adv* sottovento

downy /'daʊnɪ/ *adj* (**-ier**, **-iest**) coperto di peluria

dowry /'daʊrɪ/ *n* dote *f*

doz *abbr* (**dozen**) dozzina *f*

doze /dəʊz/ **1** *n* sonnellino *m* **2** *vi* sonnecchiare
■ **doze off** *vi* assopirsi

dozen /'dʌzn/ *n* dozzina *f*; ~s of books libri a dozzine

DPhil *n abbr* (**Doctor of Philosophy**) titolare *mf* di un dottorato di ricerca

DPP *n* Br *abbr* (**Director of Public Prosecutions**) ≈ Procuratore *m* della Repubblica

Dr *abbr* (**doctor**) Dott. *m*, Dott.essa *f*; *abbr* (**drive**) ≈ via *f*

drab /dræb/ *adj* ‹*colour*› spento; ‹*building*› tetro; ‹*life*› scialbo

draft¹ /drɑ:ft/ **1** *n* abbozzo *m*; Comm cambiale *f*; Am Mil leva *f* **2** *vt* abbozzare; Am Mil arruolare
■ **draft in** *vt* chiamare ‹*reinforcements, police*›

draft² *n* Am = DRAUGHT

draft dodger /'dɒdʒə(r)/ *n* renitente *mf* alla leva

draftsman /'drɑ:ftsmən/ *n* Am = DRAUGHTSMAN

drag /dræg/ **1** *n* fam scocciatura *f*; in ~ fam ‹*man*› travestito da donna **2** *vt* (pt/pp **dragged**) trascinare; dragare ‹*river*›
■ **drag on** *vi* ‹*time, meeting*› trascinarsi
■ **drag out** *vt* tirare per le lunghe ‹*discussion*›; ~ something out of somebody tirar fuori qualcosa a qualcuno con le pinze
■ **drag up** *vt* (mention unnecessarily) tirare in ballo

drag and drop *vt* Comput trascinare e rilasciare

dragon /'drægən/ *n* drago *m*

dragonfly /'drægənflaɪ/ *n* libellula *f*

drag show *n* spettacolo *m* di travestiti

drain /dreɪn/ **1** *n* tubo *m* di scarico; (grid) tombino *m*; the ~s le fognature; be a ~ on sb's finances prosciugare le finanze di qualcuno **2** *vt* drenare ‹*land, wound*›; scolare ‹*liquid, vegetables*›; svuotare ‹*tank glass, person*› **3** *vi* ~ [away] andar via; leave something to ~ lasciare qualcosa a scolare

drainage /'dreɪnɪdʒ/ *n* (system) drenaggio *m*; (of land) scolo *m*

draining board /'dreɪnɪŋ/ *n* scolapiatti *m inv*

drainpipe /'dreɪnpaɪp/ *n* tubo *m* di scarico

drainpipe trousers *npl* pantaloni *mpl* a tubo

drake /dreɪk/ *n* maschio *m* dell'anatra

drama /'drɑ:mə/ *n* arte *f* drammatica; (play) opera *f* teatrale; (event) dramma *m*

dramatic /drə'mætɪk/ *adj* drammatico

dramatically /drə'mætɪklɪ/ *adv* in modo drammatico

dramatics /drə'mætɪks/ *npl* arte *f* drammatica; pej atteggiamento *m* teatrale

dramatist /'dræmətɪst/ *n* drammaturgo, -a *mf*

dramatization /dræmətaɪ'zeɪʃn/ *n* (for cinema) adattamento *m* cinematografico; (for stage) adattamento *m* teatrale; (for TV) adattamento *m* televisivo; (exaggeration) drammatizzazione *f*

dramatize /'dræmətaɪz/ *vt* adattare per il teatro; fig drammatizzare

drank /dræŋk/ ▶ DRINK

drape /dreɪp/ **1** *n* Am tenda *f* **2** *vt* appoggiare (**over** su)

drastic /'dræstɪk/ *adj* drastico

drastically /'dræstɪklɪ/ *adv* drasticamente

draught /drɑ:ft/ *n* corrente *f* [d'aria]

draught beer *n* birra *f* alla spina

draught-proof **1** *adj* a tenuta d'aria **2** *vt* tappare le fessure di

draughts /drɑ:fts/ *n sg* (game) [gioco *m* della] dama *fsg*

draughtsman /'drɑ:ftsmən/ *n* disegnatore, -trice *mf*

draughty /'drɑ:ftɪ/ *adj* pieno di correnti d'aria; it's ~ c'è corrente

draw /drɔ:/ **1** *n* (attraction) attrazione *f*; Sport pareggio *m*; (in lottery) sorteggio *m* **2** *vt* (pt **drew**, pp **drawn**) tirare; (attract) attirare; disegnare ‹*picture*›; tracciare ‹*line*›; ritirare ‹*money*›; attingere ‹*water*›; ~ lots tirare a sorte **3** *vi* ‹*tea*› essere in infusione; Sport pareggiare; ~ near avvicinarsi
■ **draw away** *vi* (go ahead) distanziarsi; (move off) allontanarsi
■ **draw back** **1** *vt* tirare indietro; ritirare ‹*hand*›; tirare ‹*curtains*› **2** *vi* (recoil) tirarsi indietro
■ **draw in** **1** *vt* ritrarre ‹*claws etc*› **2** *vi* ‹*train*› arrivare; ‹*days*› accorciarsi
■ **draw on** *vt* attingere a ‹*savings, sb's experience*›
■ **draw out** **1** *vt* (pull out) tirar fuori; ritirare ‹*money*› **2** *vi* ‹*train*› partire; ‹*days*› allungarsi
■ **draw up** **1** *vt* redigere ‹*document*›; accostare ‹*chair*›; ~ oneself up [to one's full height] drizzarsi

② *vi* (stop) fermarsi

drawback /'drɔːbæk/ *n* inconveniente *m*

drawbridge /'drɔːbrɪdʒ/ *n* ponte *m* levatoio

drawee /drɔː'iː/ *n* trattario *m*

drawer /drɔː(r)/ *n* cassetto *m*; Fin traente *mf*

drawing /'drɔːɪŋ/ *n* disegno *m*

drawing board *n* tavolo *m* da disegno; fig go back to the ∼ ∼ ricominciare da capo

drawing pin *n* puntina *f*

drawing rights *npl* Fin diritti *mf* di prelievo

drawing room *n* salotto *m*

drawl /drɔːl/ *n* pronuncia *f* strascicata

drawn /drɔːn/ ▶ DRAW

dread /dred/ ① *n* terrore *m*
② *vt* aver il terrore di

dreadful /'dredfʊl/ *adj* terribile

dreadfully /'dredfʊlɪ/ *adv* terribilmente

dream /driːm/ ① *n* sogno *m*
② *attrib* di sogno
③ *vt/i* (pt/pp **dreamt** /dremt/ or **dreamed**) sognare (**about/of** di)
■ **dream up** *vt* escogitare ⟨*plan, idea*⟩

dreamer /'driːmə(r)/ *n* (idealist) sognatore, -trice *mf*; (inattentive) persona *f* con la testa fra le nuvole

dream-world *n* live in a ∼ vivere tra le nuvole

dreamy /'driːmɪ/ *adj* fam ⟨*house etc*⟩ di sogno; ⟨*person*⟩ che è un sogno; (distracted) distratto; ⟨*sound, music*⟩ dolce

dreary /'drɪərɪ/ *adj* (**-ier**, **-iest**) tetro; (boring) monotono

dredge /dredʒ/ *vt/i* dragare
■ **dredge up** *vt* riesumare ⟨*the past*⟩

dredger /'dredʒə(r)/ *n* draga *f*

dregs /dregz/ *npl* feccia *fsg*

drench /drentʃ/ *vt* get ∼ed inzupparsi

drenched /drentʃt/ *adj* zuppo

dress /dres/ ① *n* (woman's) vestito *m*; (clothing) abbigliamento *m*
② *vt* vestire; (decorate) adornare; Culin condire; Med fasciare; ∼ oneself, get ∼ed vestirsi
③ *vi* vestirsi
■ **dress up** *vi* mettersi elegante; (in disguise) travestirsi (**as** da)

dress circle *n* Theat prima galleria *f*

dress designer *n* stilista *mf*

dresser /'dresə(r)/ *n* (furniture) credenza *f*; (Am: dressing table) toilette *f inv*

dressing /'dresɪŋ/ *n* Culin condimento *m*; Med fasciatura *f*

dressing down *n* fam sgridata *f*

dressing gown *n* vestaglia *f*

dressing room *n* (in gym) spogliatoio *m*; Theat camerino *m*

dressing table *n* toilette *f inv*

dressmaker *n* sarta *f*

dressmaking *n* confezioni *fpl* (per donna)

dress rehearsal *n* prova *f* generale

dress sense *n* have ∼ ∼ saper abbinare i capi d'abbigliamento

dressy /'dresɪ/ *adj* (**-ier**, **-iest**) elegante

drew /druː/ ▶ DRAW

dribble /'drɪbl/ *vi* gocciolare; ⟨*baby*⟩ sbavare; Sport dribblare

dribs and drabs /'drɪbzən'dræbz/ *npl* in ∼ alla spicciolata

dried /draɪd/ *adj* ⟨*food*⟩ essiccato

drier /'draɪə(r)/ *n* asciugabiancheria *m inv*

drift /drɪft/ ① *n* movimento *m* lento; ⟨*of snow*⟩ cumulo *m*; (meaning) senso *m*
② *vi* (off course) andare alla deriva; ⟨*snow*⟩ accumularsi; fig ⟨*person*⟩ procedere senza meta
■ **drift apart** *vi* ⟨*people*⟩ allontanarsi l'uno dall'altro

drifter /'drɪftə(r)/ *n* persona *f* senza meta

driftwood /'drɪftwʊd/ *n* pezzi *mpl* di legno galleggianti

drill /drɪl/ ① *n* trapano *m*; Mil esercitazione *f*
② *vt* trapanare; Mil fare esercitare
③ *vi* Mil esercitarsi; ∼ for oil trivellare in cerca di petrolio

drily /'draɪlɪ/ *adv* seccamente

drink /drɪŋk/ ① *n* bevanda *f*; (alcoholic) bicchierino *m*; have a ∼ bere qualcosa; a ∼ of water un po' d'acqua
② *vt/i* (pt **drank**, pp **drunk**) bere
■ **drink to** *vt* (toast) brindare a
■ **drink up** ① *vt* finire
② *vi* finire il bicchiere

drinkable /'drɪŋkəbl/ *adj* potabile

drink-driving *n* Br guida *f* in stato di ebbrezza

drinker /'drɪŋkə(r)/ *n* bevitore, -trice *mf*

drinking chocolate /'drɪŋkɪŋ/ *n* Br cioccolata *f* in polvere

drinking water *n* acqua *f* potabile

drink problem *n* Br he has a ∼ ∼ beve

drinks cupboard *n* Br mobile *m* bar

drinks dispenser *n* Br distributore *m* di bevande

drinks machine *n* Br distributore *m* di bevande

drinks party *n* Br cocktail *m inv*

drip /drɪp/ ① *n* gocciolamento *m*; (drop) goccia *f*; Med flebo *f inv*; (fam: person) mollaccione, -a *mf*
② *vi* (pt/pp **dripped**) gocciolare

drip-dry *adj* che non si stira

drip-feed *n* flebo [clisi] *f inv*

dripping /'drɪpɪŋ/ **1** n (from meat) grasso m d'arrosto

2 adj ~ **[wet]** fradicio

drive /draɪv/ **1** n (in car) giro m; (entrance) viale m; (energy) grinta f; Psych pulsione f; (organized effort) operazione f; Techn motore m; Comput lettore m, unità f inv

2 vt (pt **drove** pp **driven**) portare ⟨person by car⟩; guidare ⟨car⟩; (Sport: hit) mandare; Techn far funzionare; ~ **somebody mad** far diventare matto qualcuno

3 vi guidare

■ **drive at** vt what are you driving at? dove vuoi arrivare?

■ **drive away** **1** vt portare via in macchina; (chase) cacciare

2 vi andare via in macchina

■ **drive back** **1** vt respingere ⟨people, animals⟩; (in car) riportare

2 vi ritornare in macchina

■ **drive in** **1** vt piantare ⟨nail⟩

2 vi arrivare [in macchina]

■ **drive off** **1** vt portare via in macchina; (chase) cacciare

2 vi andare via in macchina

■ **drive on** vi proseguire; ~ **on!** avanti!

■ **drive up** vi arrivare (in macchina)

drive-by shooting n sparatoria f da auto in corsa

drive-in adj ~ **cinema** cinema m inv drive-in

drivel /'drɪvl/ n fam sciocchezze fpl

driven /'drɪvn/ ▶ DRIVE

driver /'draɪvə(r)/ n guidatore, -trice mf; (of train) conducente mf

driver's license n Am patente f di guida

drive-through n Am drive-in m inv

driveway /'draɪvweɪ/ n strada f d'accesso

driving /'draɪvɪŋ/ **1** adj ⟨rain⟩ violento; ⟨force⟩ motore

2 n guida f

driving force n spinta f; (person behind) forza f trainante

driving instructor n istruttore, -trice mf di guida

driving lesson n lezione f di guida

driving licence n patente f di guida

driving mirror n (rearview) specchietto m retrovisore

driving school n scuola f guida

driving seat n be in the ~ ~ essere alla guida

driving test n esame m di guida; take one's ~ ~ fare l'esame di guida

drizzle /'drɪzl/ **1** n pioggerella f

2 vi piovigginare

droll /drəʊl/ adj divertente

drone /drəʊn/ n (bee) fuco m: (sound) ronzio m

■ **drone on** vi (talk boringly) tirarla per le lunghe

drool /druːl/ vi sbavare; ~ **over something/somebody** fig fam sbavare per qualcosa/qualcuno

droop /druːp/ vi abbassarsi; ⟨flowers⟩ afflosciarsi

drop /drɒp/ **1** n (of liquid) goccia f; (fall) caduta f; (in price, temperature) calo m

2 vt (pt/pp **dropped**) far cadere; sganciare ⟨bomb⟩; (omit) omettere; (give up) abbandonare; ~ **the subject** cambiare discorso

3 vi cadere; ⟨price, temperature, wind⟩ calare; ⟨ground⟩ essere in pendenza

■ **drop behind** vi rimanere indietro

■ **drop by** vi = drop in

■ **drop in** vi passare

■ **drop off** **1** vt depositare ⟨person⟩

2 vi cadere; (fall asleep) assopirsi

■ **drop out** vi cadere; (from race, society) ritirarsi; ~ **out of school** lasciare la scuola

drop-dead adv fam ~ **gorgeous** stupendo

drop-down menu n Comput menu m inv a tendina

drop handlebars npl manubrio m ricurvo

drop-out n persona f contro il sistema sociale

droppings /'drɒpɪŋz/ npl sterco m

drop shot n Sport drop shot m inv, smorzata f

drop zone n (for supplies etc) zona f di lancio

drought /draʊt/ n siccità f

drove /drəʊv/ ▶ DRIVE

droves /drəʊvz/ npl in ~ in massa

drown /draʊn/ **1** vi annegare

2 vt annegare; coprire ⟨noise⟩; he was ~ed è annegato

drowning /draʊnɪŋ/ n annegamento m

drowse /draʊz/ vi sonnecchiare; (be very sleepy) essere sonnolento

drowsiness /'draʊzɪnɪs/ n sonnolenza f

drowsy /'draʊzɪ/ adj sonnolento

drudgery /'drʌdʒərɪ/ n lavoro m pesante e noioso

drug /drʌg/ **1** n droga f; Med farmaco m; take ~s drogarsi

2 vt (pt/pp **drugged**) drogare

drug abuse n abuso m di stupefacenti

drug addict n tossicomane, -a mf

drug addiction n tossicodipendenza f

drug dealer n spacciatore, -trice mf [di droga]

drugged /drʌgd/ adj drogato

druggist /'drʌgɪst/ n Am farmacista mf

drug habit n tossicodipendenza f

drug mule n corriere m della droga

Drug Squad n Br [squadra f] narcotici f

drugs raid n operazione f antidroga

drugs ring n rete f di narcotrafficanti

drugstore /'drʌgstɔː(r)/ n Am negozio m di generi vari, inclusi medicinali, che funge anche da bar; (dispensing) farmacia f

drug-taking n consumo m di stupefacenti; Sport doping m inv

drug test n Sport antidoping m inv

drug user n tossicomane, -a mf

drum /drʌm/ ⓵ n tamburo m; (for oil) bidone m; ~s pl (in pop group) batteria f ⓶ vi (pt/pp **drummed**) suonare il tamburo; (in pop group) suonare la batteria ⓷ vt ~ **something into somebody** fam ripetere qualcosa a qualcuno cento volte; ~ **one's fingers on the table** tamburellare con le dita sul tavolo
■ **drum up** vt ottenere ⟨business, customers, support⟩

drum kit n batteria f

drummer /'drʌmə(r)/ n percussionista mf; (in pop group) batterista mf

drumstick /'drʌmstɪk/ n bacchetta f; (of chicken, turkey) coscia f

drunk /drʌŋk/ ⓵ ▶ DRINK ⓶ adj ubriaco; **get** ~ ubriacarsi ⓷ n ubriaco, -a mf

drunkard /'drʌŋkəd/ n ubriacone, -a mf

drunken /'drʌŋkən/ adj ubriaco

drunken driving n guida f in stato di ebbrezza

dry /draɪ/ ⓵ adj (**drier**, **driest**) asciutto; ⟨climate, country⟩ secco ⓶ vt/i asciugare; ~ **one's eyes** asciugarsi le lacrime
■ **dry out** vi ⟨clothes⟩ asciugarsi; ⟨alcoholic⟩ disintossicarsi
■ **dry up** vi seccarsi; fig ⟨source⟩ prosciugarsi; (fam; be quiet) stare zitto; (do dishes) asciugare i piatti

dry cell n cella f a secco

dry-clean vt pulire a secco

dry-cleaner's n (shop) tintoria f

dryer /'draɪə/ n = DRIER

dry ice n ghiaccio m secco

drying-up /draɪɪŋ-/ n Br **do the** ~ asciugare i piatti

dryness /'draɪnɪs/ n secchezza f

dry rot n carie f del legno

DSS n Br abbr (**Department of Social Security**) (local office) ≈ Ufficio m della Previdenza Sociale; (ministry) ≈ Istituto m Nazionale della Previdenza Sociale

DTI n Br abbr (**Department of Trade and Industry**) ≈ ministero m del Commercio e dell'Industria

DTP n abbr (**desktop publishing**) DTP m

dual /'djuːəl/ adj doppio

dual carriageway n strada f a due carreggiate

dual nationality n doppia nazionalità f

dual-purpose adj a doppio uso

dub /dʌb/ vt (pt/pp **dubbed**) doppiare ⟨film⟩; (name) soprannominare

dubbing /'dʌbɪŋ/ n doppiaggio m

dubious /'djuːbɪəs/ adj dubbio; **be** ~ **about** avere dei dubbi riguardo

dubiously /'djuːbɪəslɪ/ adv ⟨look at⟩ con aria dubbiosa; (say) con esitazione

Dublin /'dʌblɪn/ n Dublino f

duchess /'dʌtʃɪs/ n duchessa f

duck /dʌk/ ⓵ n anatra f ⓶ vt (in water) immergere; ~ **one's head** abbassare la testa ⓷ vi abbassarsi
■ **duck out of** vt sottrarsi a ⟨task⟩

duckling /'dʌklɪŋ/ n anatroccolo m

duct /dʌkt/ n condotto m; Anat dotto m

dud /dʌd/ ⓵ adj Mil fam disattivato; ⟨coin⟩ falso; ⟨cheque⟩ a vuoto ⓶ n fam (banknote) banconota f falsa; (Mil: shell) granata f disattivata

due /djuː/ ⓵ adj dovuto; **be** ~ ⟨train⟩ essere previsto; **the baby is** ~ **next week** il bambino dovrebbe nascere la settimana prossima; ~ **to** (owing to) a causa di; **be** ~ **to** (causally) essere dovuto a; **I'm** ~ **to...** dovrei...; **in** ~ **course** a tempo debito ⓶ adv ~ **north** direttamente a nord

duel /'djuːəl/ n duello m

dues /djuːz/ npl quota f [di iscrizione]

duet /djuː'et/ n duetto m

duffel bag /dʌf(ə)l/ n sacca f da viaggio

duffel coat n montgomery m inv

dug /dʌg/ ▶ DIG

duke /djuːk/ n duca m

dull /dʌl/ ⓵ adj (overcast, not bright) cupo; (not shiny) opaco; ⟨sound⟩ soffocato; (boring) monotono; (stupid) ottuso ⓶ vt intorpidire ⟨mind⟩; attenuare ⟨pain⟩

dullness /'dʌlnɪs/ n (of life) monotonia f; (of company, conversation) noia f; (no shine) opacità f

dully /'dʌllɪ/ adv ⟨say, repeat⟩ monotonamente

duly /'djuːlɪ/ adv debitamente

dumb /dʌm/ adj muto; (fam: stupid) ottuso
■ **dumb down** vt abbassare il livello intellettuale di ⟨course, programme⟩

dumbfounded /dʌm'faʊndɪd/ adj sbigottito

dummy /'dʌmɪ/ n (tailor's) manichino m; (for baby) succhiotto m; (model) riproduzione f

dummy run n (trial) prova f

dump /dʌmp/ ⓵ n (for refuse) scarico m; (fam: town) mortorio m; **be down in the** ~s fam essere depresso

2 *vt* scaricare; (fam: put down) lasciare; (fam: get rid of) liberarsi di

dumping /'dʌmpɪŋ/ *n* Fin dumping *m inv*, esportazione *f* sottocosto; **no** ~ divieto *m* di scarico

dumpling /'dʌmplɪŋ/ *n* gnocco *m*

dumpy /'dʌmpɪ/ *adj* (plump) tracagnotto

dunce /dʌns/ *n* zuccone, -a *mf*

dune /dju:n/ *n* duna *f*

dung /dʌŋ/ *n* sterco *m*

dungarees /dʌŋgə'ri:z/ *npl* tuta *fsg*

dungeon /'dʌndʒən/ *n* prigione *f* sotterranea

dunk /dʌŋk/ *vt* inzuppare

dunno /də'nəʊ/ fam (I don't know) boh

duo /'dju:əʊ/ *n* duo *m inv*; Mus duetto *m*

dupe /dju:p/ **1** *n* zimbello *m*
2 *vt* gabbare

duplicate¹ /'dju:plɪkət/ **1** *adj* doppio
2 *n* duplicato *m*; (document) copia *f*; **in** ~ in duplicato

duplicate² /'dju:plɪkeɪt/ *vt* fare un duplicato di; ⟨research⟩ essere una ripetizione di ⟨work⟩

duplicator /'dju:plɪkeɪtə(r)/ *n* duplicatore *m*

duplicity /dju'plɪsətɪ/ *n* duplicità *f*, doppiezza *f*

durable /'djʊərəbl/ *adj* resistente; ⟨basis, institution⟩ durevole

duration /djʊə'reɪʃn/ *n* durata *f*

duress /djʊə'res/ *n* costrizione *f*; **under** ~ sotto minaccia

during /'djʊərɪŋ/ *prep* durante

dusk /dʌsk/ *n* crepuscolo *m*

dusky /'dʌskɪ/ *adj* ⟨complexion⟩ scuro

dust /dʌst/ **1** *n* polvere *f*
2 *vt* spolverare; (sprinkle) cospargere ⟨cake⟩ (with di)
3 *vi* spolverare

dustbin *n* pattumiera *f*

dustbin man *n* Br netturbino *m*

dust-cart *n* camion *m* della nettezza urbana

dust cover *n* (on book) sopraccoperta *f*; (on furniture) telo *m* di protezione

duster /'dʌstə(r)/ *n* strofinaccio *m*

dustman *n* spazzino *m*

dustpan *n* paletta *f* per la spazzatura

dust sheet *n* (on furniture) telo *m* di protezione

dusty /'dʌstɪ/ *adj* (-ier, -iest) polveroso

Dutch /dʌtʃ/ **1** *adj* olandese; **go** ~ fam fare alla romana
2 *n* (language) olandese *m*; **the** ~ *pl* gli olandesi

Dutch courage *n* spavalderia *f* ispirata dall'alcool

Dutchman /'dʌtʃmən/ *n* olandese *m*

dutiable /'dju:tɪəbl/ *adj* soggetto a imposta

dutiful /'dju:tɪfl/ *adj* rispettoso

dutifully /'dju:tɪfʊlɪ/ *adv* a dovere

duty /'dju:tɪ/ *n* dovere *m*; (task) compito *m*; (tax) dogana *f*; **be on** ~ essere di servizio

duty chemist *n* farmacia *f* di turno

duty-free **1** *adj* esente da dogana
2 *n* duty-free *m inv*

duty-free allowance *n* limite *m* d'acquisto di merci esenti da dogana

duty roster, **duty rota** *n* tabella *f* dei turni

duvet /'du:veɪ/ *n* piumone *m*

duvet cover *n* Br copripiumone *m*

DVD *n abbr* (**digital video disc**) DVD *m*

DVD player *n* lettore *m* DVD

DVT *abbr* (**deep-vein thrombosis**) TVP *f*

dwarf /dwɔ:f/ **1** *n* (*pl* **-s** *or* **dwarves**) nano, -a *mf*
2 *vt* rimpicciolire

dweeb /dwi:b/ *n* esp Am: fam secchione, -a *mf*

dwell /dwel/ *vi* (pt/pp **dwelt**) liter dimorare
■ **dwell on** *vt* fig soffermarsi su

dweller /'dwelə(r)/ *n* city/town ~ cittadino, -a *mf*

dwelling /'dwelɪŋ/ *n* abitazione *f*

dwindle /'dwɪndl/ *vi* diminuire

dwindling /'dwɪndlɪŋ/ *adj* (strength, health) in calo; ⟨resources, audience, interest⟩ in diminuzione

DWP *abbr* Br (**Department for Work and Pensions**) ≈ Ministero *m* del Lavoro e delle Politiche Sociali

dye /daɪ/ **1** *n* tintura *f*
2 *vt* (pres p **dyeing**) tingere

dyed-in-the-wool /daɪdɪnðə'wʊl/ *adj* inveterato

dying /'daɪɪŋ/ ▶ DIE²

dyke /daɪk/ *n* (to prevent flooding) diga *f*; (beside ditch) argine *m*; (Br: ditch) canale *m* di scolo

dynamic /daɪ'næmɪk/ *adj* dinamico

dynamics /daɪ'næmɪks/ *n* dinamica *fsg*

dynamism /'daɪnə'mɪzm/ *n* dinamismo *m*

dynamite /'daɪnəmaɪt/ *n* dinamite *f*

dynamo /'daɪnəməʊ/ *n* dinamo *f inv*

dynasty /'dɪnəstɪ/ *n* dinastia *f*

dysentery /'dɪsəntrɪ/ *n* dissenteria *f*

dysfunctional /dɪs:fʌnkʃ(ə)nəl/ *adj* disfunzionale

dyslexia /dɪs'leksɪə/ *n* dislessia *f*

dyslexic /dɪs'leksɪk/ *adj* dislessico

Ee

e¹, **E** /iː/ *n* (letter) e, E *f inv*; Mus mi *m*

e² *abbr* (**euro**) EUR *m*

E *abbr* (**east**) E

each /iːtʃ/ ① *adj* ogni
② *pron* ognuno; **£1** ~ una sterlina ciascuno; **they love/hate** ~ **other** si amano/odiano; **we lend** ~ **other money** ci prestiamo i soldi; **bet on a horse** ~ **way** puntare su un cavallo piazzato e vincente

eager /'iːgə(r)/ *adj* ansioso (**to do** di fare); ⟨*pupil*⟩ avido di sapere

eager beaver *n* fam be an ~ ~ essere pieno di zelo

eagerly /'iːgəlɪ/ *adv* ⟨*wait*⟩ ansiosamente; ⟨*offer*⟩ premurosamente

eagerness /'iːgənɪs/ *n* premura *f*

eagle /'iːgl/ *n* aquila *f*

eagle-eyed /'-aɪd/ *adj* (sharp-eyed) che ha un occhio di falco

ear /'ɪə(r)/ *n* orecchio *m*; (of corn) spiga *f*

earache /'ɪəreɪk/ *n* mal *m* d'orecchi

eardrum /'ɪədrʌm/ *n* timpano *m*

earl /ɜːl/ *n* conte *m*

ear lobe *n* lobo *m* dell'orecchio

early /'ɜːlɪ/ ① *adj* (**-ier**, **-iest**) (before expected time) in anticipo; ⟨*spring*⟩ prematuro; ⟨*reply*⟩ pronto; ⟨*works, writings*⟩ primo; **be here** ~! sii puntuale!; **you're** ~! sei in anticipo!; ~ **morning walk** passeggiata *f* mattutina; **in the** ~ **morning** la mattina presto; **in the** ~ **spring** all'inizio della primavera
② *adv* presto; (ahead of time) in anticipo; ~ **in the morning** la mattina presto

early retirement *n* prepensionamento *m*; **take** ~ andare in prepensionamento

early warning *n* **come as an** ~ ~ **of something** essere il segno premonitore di qualcosa

early warning system *n* Mil sistema *m* d'allarme avanzato

earmark /'ɪəmɑːk/ *vt* riservare (**for** a)

earmuffs /'ɪəmʌfs/ *npl* paraorecchie *m inv*

earn /ɜːn/ *vt* guadagnare; (deserve) meritare

earned income /ɜːnd/ *n* reddito *m* da lavoro

earner /'ɜːnə(r)/ *n* (person) persona *f* che guadagna; **the main [revenue]** ~ la principale fonte di sostentamento; **a nice little** ~ fam un'ottima fonte di guadagno

earnest /'ɜːnɪst/ ① *adj* serio
② *n* **in** ~ sul serio

earnestly /'ɜːnɪstlɪ/ *adv* con aria seria

earning power /'ɜːnɪŋ/ *n* (of person) capacità *f* di guadagno; (of company) redditività *f inv*

earnings /'ɜːnɪŋz/ *npl* guadagni *mpl*; (salary) stipendio *m*

ear, nose, and throat department *n* reparto *m* otorinolaringoiatrico

earphones *npl* cuffia *fsg*

earplug *n* (for noise) tappo *m* per le orecchie

ear-ring *n* orecchino *m*

earshot *n* **within** ~ a portata d'orecchio; **he is out of** ~ non può sentire

ear-splitting /'ɪəsplɪtɪŋ/ *adj* ⟨*scream, shout*⟩ lacerante

earth /ɜːθ/ ① *n* terra *f*; (of fox) tana *f*; **where/what on** ~? dove/che diavolo?
② *vt* Electr mettere a terra

earthenware /'ɜːθnweə/ *n* terraglia *f*

earthly /'ɜːθlɪ/ *adj* terrestre; **be no** ~ **use** fam essere perfettamente inutile

earthquake *n* terremoto *m*

earth sciences *npl* scienze *fpl* della terra

earthshaking *adj* fam ⟨*news*⟩ sconvolgente; ⟨*experience*⟩ travolgente

earth tremor *n* scossa *f* sismica

earthwork *n* (embankment) terrapieno *m*; (excavation work) lavori *mpl* di scavo

earthworm *n* lombrico *m*

earthy /'ɜːθɪ/ *adj* terroso; (coarse) grossolano

earwax /'ɪəwæks/ *n* cerume *m*

earwig /'ɪəwɪg/ *n* forbicina *f*

ease /iːz/ ① *n* **at** ~ a proprio agio; **at** ~! Mil riposo!; **ill at** ~ a disagio; **with** ~ con facilità
② *vt* calmare ⟨*pain*⟩; alleviare ⟨*tension, shortage*⟩; (slow down) rallentare; (loosen) allentare
③ *vi* ⟨*pain, situation, wind*⟩ calmarsi
■ **ease off** ① *vi* ⟨*pain, pressure, tension*⟩ attenuarsi
② *vt* (remove gently) togliere con delicatezza
■ **ease up** *vi* = ease off

easel /'iːzl/ *n* cavalletto *m*

easily /'iːzɪlɪ/ *adv* con facilità ~ **the best** certamente il meglio

east /iːst/ ① *n* est *m*; **to the** ~ **of** a est di
② *adj* dell'est
③ *adv* verso est

East Africa *n* Africa *f* orientale

East Berlin n Berlino f Est

eastbound adj ⟨carriageway, traffic⟩ diretto a est

East End n quartiere m nella zona est di Londra

Easter /'i:stə(r)/ n Pasqua f

easterly /'i:stəlɪ/ adj da levante

Easter egg n uovo m di Pasqua

Easter Monday n lunedì m dell'Angelo, Pasquetta f

eastern /'i:stən/ adj orientale

Eastern bloc n paesi mpl dell'est

Easter Sunday n [domenica f di] Pasqua f

East German n Pol tedesco, -a mf dell'est

East Germany n Pol Germania f est

East Indies npl Indie fpl orientali

East Timor /'ti:mɔ:(r)/ n Timor Est m

eastward[s] /'i:stwəd[z]/ adv verso est

easy /'i:zɪ/ adj (-ier, -iest) facile; take it or things ∼ prendersela con calma; take it ∼! (don't get excited) calma!; go ∼ with andarci piano con

easy-care adj facilmente lavabile

easy chair n poltrona f

easy-going adj conciliante; too ∼ troppo accomodante

easy terms npl facilitazioni fpl di pagamento

eat /i:t/ vt/i (pt **ate**, pp **eaten**) mangiare
■ **eat into** vt intaccare
■ **eat out** vi mangiar fuori
■ **eat up** vt mangiare tutto ⟨food⟩; fig inghiottire ⟨profits⟩

eatable /'i:təbl/ adj mangiabile

eater /'i:tə(r)/ n (apple) mela f da tavola; be a big ∼ ⟨person⟩ essere una buona forchetta; he's a fast ∼ mangia sempre in fretta

eatery /'i:tərɪ/ n fam tavola f calda

eating disorder n disoressia f

eating habits npl abitudini fpl alimentari

eau-de-Cologne /əʊdəkə'ləʊn/ n acqua f di colonia

eaves /i:vz/ npl cornicione msg

eavesdrop /'i:vzdrɒp/ vi (pt/pp **-dropped**) origliare; ∼ on ascoltare di nascosto

e-banking /'i:bæŋkɪŋ/ n e-banking m

ebb /eb/ ① n (tide) riflusso m; at a low ∼ fig a terra
② vi rifluire; fig declinare

ebony /'ebənɪ/ n ebano m

EBRD n abbr (**European Bank for Reconstruction and Development**) BERS f

ebullient /ɪ'bʌlɪənt/ adj esuberante

e-business /'i:bɪznɪs/ n e-business m inv

EC n abbr (**European Community**) CE f

e-cash /'i:kæʃ/ n denaro m virtuale

eccentric /ek'sentrɪk/ adj & n eccentrico, -a mf

eccentricity /eksen'trɪsətɪ/ n eccentricità f inv

ecclesiastical /ɪkli:zɪ'æstɪkl/ adj ecclesiastico

ECG n abbr (**electrocardiogram**) ECG m

echo /'ekəʊ/ ① n (pl **-es**) eco f or m
② vt (pt/pp **echoed**, pres p **echoing**) echeggiare; ripetere ⟨words⟩
③ vi risuonare (**with** di)

eclectic /ɪ'klektɪk/ n eclettico

eclipse /ɪ'klɪps/ ① n Astr eclissi f inv
② vt fig eclissare

eco-friendly adj che rispetta l'ambiente

ecological /i:kə'lɒdʒɪkl/ adj ecologico

ecologist /ɪ'kɒlədʒɪst/ ① n ecologo, -a mf
② adj ecologico

ecology /ɪ'kɒlədʒɪ/ n ecologia f

e-commerce /'i:kɒmɜ:s/ n e-commerce m inv

economic /i:kə'nɒmɪk/ adj economico

economical /i:kə'nɒmɪkl/ adj economico

economically /i:kə'nɒmɪklɪ/ adv economicamente; ⟨thriftily⟩ in economia; ∼ priced a prezzo economico

economic analyst n analista mf economico, -a

economic migrant n chi emigra per motivi esclusivamente economici, in contrapposizione a chi cerca asilo politico

economics /i:kə'nɒmɪks/ n economia f

economist /ɪ'kɒnəmɪst/ n economista mf

economize /ɪ'kɒnəmaɪz/ vi economizzare (**on** su)

economy /ɪ'kɒnəmɪ/ n economia f

economy class n Aeron classe f turistica

economy drive n campagna f di risparmio

economy pack, economy size n confezione f economica inv

ecosystem /'i:kəʊsɪstəm/ n ecosistema m

ecoterrorism n ecoterrorismo m

eco-warrior n eco-guerriliero, -a mf

ecstasy /'ekstəsɪ/ n estasi f inv; (drug) ecstasy f

ecstatic /ɪk'stætɪk/ adj estatico

ecstatically /ɪk'stætɪklɪ/ adv estaticamente

ectopic pregnancy /ek'tɒpɪk/ n
gravidanza f extrauterina

Ecuador /'ekwədɔː(r)/ n Ecuador m

ecumenical /iːkjʊ'menɪkl/ adj
ecumenico

eczema /'eksɪmə/ n eczema m

eddy /'edɪ/ n vortice m

Eden /'iːd(ə)n/ n eden m, paradiso m
terrestre

edge /edʒ/ ① n bordo m; (of knife) filo m;
(of road) ciglio m; **on** ~ con i nervi tesi;
have the ~ **on** fam avere un vantaggio su
② vt bordare
■ **edge forward** vi avanzare lentamente

edgeways /'edʒweɪz/ adv di fianco; **I
couldn't get a word in** ~ non ho potuto
infilare neanche mezza parola nel
discorso

edging /'edʒɪŋ/ n bordo m

edgy /'edʒɪ/ adj (nervous) nervoso; (fam:
modern) all'avanguardia

edible /'edəbl/ adj commestibile; **this
pizza's not** ~ questa pizza è immangiabile

edict /'iːdɪkt/ n editto m

edifice /'edɪfɪs/ n edificio m

edify /'edɪfaɪ/ vt (pt/pp **-ied**) edificare

edifying /'edɪfaɪɪŋ/ adj edificante

Edinburgh /'edɪmb(ə)rə/ n Edimburgo f

edit /'edɪt/ vt (pt/pp **edited**) far la
revisione di ⟨text⟩; curare l'edizione di
⟨anthology, dictionary⟩; dirigere
⟨newspaper⟩; montare ⟨film⟩; editare
⟨tape⟩; ~**ed by** ⟨book⟩ a cura di
■ **edit out** vt tagliare

edition /ɪ'dɪʃn/ n edizione f

editor /'edɪtə(r)/ n (of anthology, dictionary)
curatore, -trice mf; (of newspaper) redattore,
-trice mf; (of film) responsabile mf del
montaggio

editorial /edɪ'tɔːrɪəl/ ① adj redazionale
② n Journ editoriale m

EDP n abbr (**electronic data
processing**) EDP m, EED f

EDT abbr Am (**Eastern Daylight Time**)
ora f legale degli stati orientali
dell'America settentrionale

educate /'edjʊkeɪt/ vt istruire; educare
⟨public, mind⟩; **be** ~**d at Eton** essere
educato a Eton

educated /'edjʊkeɪtɪd/ adj istruito

education /edjʊ'keɪʃn/ n istruzione f;
(culture) cultura f, educazione f

educational /edjʊ'keɪʃnəl/ adj
istruttivo; ⟨visit⟩ educativo; ⟨publishing⟩
didattico

educationalist /edjʊ'keɪʃnəlɪst/ n
studioso, -a mf di pedagogia

educationally /edjʊ'keɪʃnəlɪ/ adv
⟨disadvantaged, privileged⟩ dal punto di
vista degli studi; ⟨useless, useful⟩ dal
punto di vista didattico

educational psychology n
psicopedagogia f, psicologia f
dell'educazione

educational television n televisione
f scolastica

education authority n Br autorità fpl
scolastiche

education committee n Br consiglio
m scolastico

education department n Br
ministero m della pubblica istruzione; (in
local government) provveditorato m agli
studi; (in university) istituto m di pedagogia

educative /'edjʊkətɪv/ adj educativo,
istruttivo

educator /'edjʊkeɪtə(r)/ n educatore,
-trice mf

Edwardian /ed'wɔːdɪən/ n del regno di
Edoardo VII

EEA abbr (**European Economic Area**)
EEA f

EEC ① n abbr (**European Economic
Community**) CEE f
② attrib ⟨policy, directive⟩ della CEE

eel /iːl/ n anguilla f

eerie /'ɪərɪ/ adj (**-ier**, **-iest**) inquietante

efface /ɪ'feɪs/ vt cancellare

effect /ɪ'fekt/ ① n effetto m; **in** ~ in
effetti; **take** ~ ⟨law⟩ entrare in vigore;
⟨medicine⟩ fare effetto
② vt effettuare

effective /ɪ'fektɪv/ adj efficace; (striking)
che colpisce; (actual) di fatto; ~ **from** in
vigore a partire da

effectively /ɪ'fektɪvlɪ/ adv
efficacemente; (actually) di fatto

effectiveness /ɪ'fektɪvnɪs/ n efficacia f

effeminate /ɪ'femɪnət/ adj effeminato

effervescent /efə'vesnt/ adj
effervescente

effete /ɪ'fiːt/ adj ⟨person⟩ senza nerbo;
⟨civilization⟩ che ha fatto il suo tempo

efficacious /efɪ'keɪʃəs/ adj efficace

efficacy /'efɪkəsɪ/ n efficacia f

efficiency /ɪ'fɪʃənsɪ/ n efficienza f; (of
machine) rendimento m

efficient /ɪ'fɪʃənt/ adj efficiente

efficiently /ɪ'fɪʃəntlɪ/ adv
efficientemente

effigy /'efɪdʒɪ/ n effigie f

effluent /'eflʊənt/ ① n (waste) refluo m;
(river) emissario m
② attrib ⟨treatment, management⟩ dei
reflui

effort /'efət/ n sforzo m; **make an** ~
sforzarsi

effortless /'efətlɪs/ adj facile

effortlessly /'efətlɪslɪ/ adv con facilità

effrontery /ɪ'frʌntərɪ/ n sfrontatezza f

effusion /ɪ'fjuːʒn/ n (emotional) effusione f

effusive /ɪˈfjuːsɪv/ *adj* espansivo; ⟨*speech*⟩ caloroso

e-fit /ˈiːfɪt/ *n* identikit *m inv* elettronico

EFL ① *n abbr* (**English as a Foreign Language**) EFL *m*
② *attrib* ⟨*teacher, course*⟩ di inglese come lingua straniera

EFT *n abbr* **electronic funds transfer**

EFTA /ˈeftə/ *n abbr* (**European Free Trade Association**) EFTA *f*

e.g. *abbr* (**exempli gratia**) per es.

egalitarian /ɪɡælɪˈteərɪən/ *adj* egalitario

egg /eɡ/ *n* uovo *m*
■ **egg on** *vt* fam incitare

egg box *n* cartone *m* di uova

eggcup *n* portauovo *m inv*

egg custard *n* crema *f* pasticcera

egghead *n* pej fam intellettuale *mf*

eggplant *n* Am melanzana *f*

eggshaped /ˈeɡʃeɪpt/ *adj* ovale

eggshell *n* guscio *m* d'uovo

egg-timer *n* clessidra *f* per misurare il tempo di cottura delle uova

egg whisk *n* frusta *f*

egg white *n* albume *m*, bianco *m* d'uovo

egg yolk *n* tuorlo *m*, rosso *m*

ego /ˈiːɡəʊ/ *n* ego *m*

egocentric /iːɡəʊˈsentrɪk/ *adj* egocentrico

egoism /ˈeɡəʊɪzm/ *n* egoismo *m*

egoist /ˈeɡəʊɪst/ *n* egoista *mf*

egotism /ˈeɡəʊtɪzm/ *n* egotismo *m*

egotist /ˈeɡəʊtɪst/ *n* egotista *mf*

Egypt /ˈiːdʒɪpt/ *n* Egitto *m*

Egyptian /ɪˈdʒɪpʃn/ *adj & n* egiziano, -a *mf*

eiderdown /ˈaɪdədaʊn/ *n* (quilt) piumino *m*

eight /eɪt/ *adj & n* otto *m*

eighteen /eɪˈtiːn/ *adj & n* diciotto *m*

eighteenth /eɪˈtiːnθ/ *adj & n* diciottesimo, -a *mf*

eighth /eɪtθ/ *adj & n* ottavo, -a *mf*

eighties /ˈeɪtɪz/ *npl* (period) the ~ gli anni Ottanta *mpl*; (age) ottant'anni *mpl*;
▶ also FORTIES

eightieth /ˈeɪtɪθ/ *adj & n* ottantesimo, -a *mf*

eighty /ˈeɪtɪ/ *adj & n* ottanta *m*

Eire /ˈeərə/ *n* Repubblica *f* d'Irlanda

either /ˈaɪðə(r)/ ① *adj & pron* ~ [of them] l'uno o l'altro; I don't like ~ [of them] non mi piace né l'uno né l'altro; on ~ side da tutte e due le parti
② *adv* I don't ~ nemmeno io; I don't like John or his brother ~ non mi piace John e nemmeno suo fratello

③ *conj* ~ John or his brother will be there ci saranno o John o suo fratello; I don't like ~ John or his brother non mi piacciono né John né suo fratello; ~ you go to bed or [else]... o vai a letto o [altrimenti]...

ejaculate /ɪˈdʒækjʊleɪt/ ① *vi* eiaculare
② *vt* (exclaim) prorompere

ejaculation /ɪˈdʒækjʊleɪʃn/ *n* eiaculazione *f*; (exclamation) esclamazione *f*

eject /ɪˈdʒekt/ *vt* eiettare ⟨*pilot*⟩; espellere ⟨*tape, drunk*⟩

eject button *n* tasto *m* eject

ejection /ɪˈdʒekʃn/ *n* (of gases, waste, troublemaker) espulsione *f*; (of lava) emissione *f*; Aeron eiezione *f*

eke /iːk/ *vt* ~ out far bastare; (increase) arrotondare; ~ out a living arrangiarsi

elaborate¹ /ɪˈlæbərət/ *adj* elaborato

elaborate² /ɪˈlæbəreɪt/ *vi* entrare nei particolari (on di)

elaborately /ɪˈlæbərətlɪ/ *adv* in modo elaborato

elaboration /ɪlæbəˈreɪʃn/ *n* (of plan, theory) elaborazione *f*

elapse /ɪˈlæps/ *vi* trascorrere

elastic /ɪˈlæstɪk/ ① *adj* elastico
② *n* elastico *m*

elasticated /ɪˈlæstɪkeɪtɪd/ *adj* ⟨*waistband, bandage*⟩ elastico; ⟨*material*⟩ elasticizzato

elastic band *n* elastico *m*

elasticity /ɪlæsˈtɪsətɪ/ *n* elasticità *f*

elated /ɪˈleɪtɪd/ *adj* esultante

elation /ɪˈleɪʃn/ *n* euforia *f*

elbow /ˈelbəʊ/ *n* gomito *m*

elbow grease *n* fam olio *m* di gomito

elbow room *n* (room to move) spazio *m* vitale; there isn't much ~ in this kitchen si è un po' allo stretto in questa cucina

elder¹ /ˈeldə(r)/ *n* (tree) sambuco *m*

elder² ① *adj* maggiore
② *n* the ~ il/la maggiore

elderberry /ˈeldəbərɪ/ *n* bacca *f* di sambuco

elderly /ˈeldəlɪ/ *adj* anziano

elder statesman *n* decano *m* della politica

eldest /ˈeldɪst/ ① *adj* maggiore
② *n* the ~ il/la maggiore

e-learning /ˈiːlɜːnɪŋ/ *n* Comput formazione *f* in rete

elect /ɪˈlekt/ ① *adj* the president ~ il futuro presidente
② *vt* eleggere; ~ to do something decidere di fare qualcosa

election /ɪˈlekʃn/ *n* elezione *f*

election campaign *n* campagna *f* elettorale

electioneering /ɪˈlekʃənɪərɪŋ/ n (campaigning) propaganda f elettorale; pej elettoralismo m

elective /ɪˈlektɪv/ adj ⟨office, official⟩ elettivo, eletto; (empowered to elect) elettorale; Sch, Univ facoltativo; ~ **surgery** interventi mpl chirurgici facoltativi

elector /ɪˈlektə(r)/ n elettore, -trice mf

electoral /ɪˈlektərəl/ adj elettorale

electoral roll n liste fpl elettorali

electorate /ɪˈlektərət/ n elettorato m

electric /ɪˈlektrɪk/ adj elettrico

electrical /ɪˈlektrɪkl/ adj elettrico

electrical engineer n elettrotecnico m

electrical engineering n elettrotecnica f

electrically /ɪˈlektrɪk(ə)lɪ/ adv ~ **driven** [a motore] elettrico

electric blanket n termocoperta f

electric fire n stufa f elettrica

electrician /ɪlekˈtrɪʃn/ n elettricista m

electricity /ɪlekˈtrɪsətɪ/ n elettricità f

electricity board n Br azienda f elettrica

electricity supply n alimentazione f elettrica

electric shock n **get an** ~ ~ prendere la scossa

electric storm n temporale m

electrify /ɪˈlektrɪfaɪ/ vt (pt/pp **-ied**) elettrificare; fig elettrizzare

electrifying /ɪˈlektrɪfaɪɪŋ/ adj fig elettrizzante

electrocute /ɪˈlektrəkjuːt/ vt fulminare; (execute) giustiziare sulla sedia elettrica

electrocution /ɪlektrəˈkjuːʃn/ n elettrocuzione f

electrode /ɪˈlektrəʊd/ n elettrodo m

electrolysis /ɪlekˈtrɒlɪsɪs/ n Chem elettrolisi f; (hair removal) depilazione f diatermica

electron /ɪˈlektrɒn/ n elettrone m

electronic /ɪlekˈtrɒnɪk/ adj elettronico

electronic banking n servizi mpl bancari telematici

electronic engineer n tecnico m elettronico; (with diploma) perito m elettronico; (with degree) ingegnere m elettronico

electronic engineering n ingegneria f elettronica

electronic eye n cellula f fotoelettrica

electronic funds transfer n sistemi mpl telematici di trasferimento fondi

electronic mail n posta f elettronica

electronic organizer n Comput agenda f elettronica

electronic publishing n editoria f elettronica

electronics /ɪlekˈtrɒnɪks/ n elettronica f

electronic tagging n sorveglianza f tramite braccialetto elettronico

electro-shock therapy, **electroshock treatment** /ɪˈlektrəʊ-/ n terapia f elettroshock

elegance /ˈelɪgəns/ n eleganza f

elegant /ˈelɪgənt/ adj elegante

elegantly /ˈelɪgəntlɪ/ adv elegantemente

elegy /ˈelədʒɪ/ n elegia f

element /ˈelɪmənt/ n elemento m

elementary /elɪˈmentərɪ/ adj elementare

elephant /ˈelɪfənt/ n elefante m

elephantine /elɪˈfæntaɪn/ adj ⟨person⟩ mastodontico

elevate /ˈelɪveɪt/ vt elevare

elevated adj ⟨language, rank⟩ elevato; ⟨walkway, railway⟩ sopraelevato

elevation /elɪˈveɪʃn/ n elevazione f; (height) altitudine f; (angle) alzo m

elevator /ˈelɪveɪtə(r)/ n Am ascensore m

eleven /ɪˈlevn/ adj & n undici m

eleven plus n (formerly) esame m di ammissione alla scuola secondaria inglese

elevenses /ɪˈlevənzɪz/ n Br fam pausa f per il caffè (a metà mattina)

eleventh /ɪˈlevənθ/ adj & n undicesimo, -a mf; **at the** ~ **hour** fam all'ultimo momento

elf /elf/ n (pl **elves**) elfo m

elicit /ɪˈlɪsɪt/ vt ottenere

eligible /ˈelɪdʒəbl/ adj eleggibile; ~ **young man** buon partito; **be** ~ **for** aver diritto a

eliminate /ɪˈlɪmɪneɪt/ vt eliminare

elimination /ɪlɪmɪˈneɪʃn/ n eliminazione f; **by a process of** ~ procedendo per eliminazione

élite /erˈliːt/ n fior fiore m

élitist /ɪˈliːtɪst/ adj elitista

ellipse /ɪˈlɪps/ n ellisse f

elliptical /ɪˈlɪptɪk(ə)l/ adj also fig ellittico

elm /elm/ n olmo m

elocution /eləˈkjuːʃn/ n elocuzione f

elongate /ˈiːlɒŋgeɪt/ vt allungare

elongated /ˈiːlɒŋgeɪtɪd/ adj allungato

elope /ɪˈləʊp/ vi fuggire [per sposarsi]

elopement /ɪˈləʊpmənt/ n fuga f romantica

eloquence /ˈeləkwəns/ n eloquenza f

eloquent /ˈeləkwənt/ adj eloquente

eloquently /ˈeləkwəntlɪ/ adv con eloquenza

El Salvador /elˈsælvədɔː(r)/ n El Salvador m; **in** ~ ~ nel Salvador

else /els/ adv altro; who ∼? e chi altro?; he did of course, who ∼? l'ha fatto lui e chi, se no?; **nothing** ∼ nient'altro; **or** ∼ altrimenti; **someone** ∼ qualcun altro; **somewhere** ∼ da qualche altra parte; **anyone** ∼ chiunque altro; (as question) nessun'altro?; **anything** ∼ qualunque altra cosa; (as question) altro?

elsewhere /els'weə(r)/ adv altrove

elucidate /ɪ'lu:sɪdeɪt/ vt delucidare

elude /ɪ'lu:d/ vt eludere; (avoid) evitare; **the name** ∼**s me** il nome mi sfugge

elusive /ɪ'lu:sɪv/ adj elusivo

emaciated /ɪ'meɪsɪeɪtɪd/ adj emaciato

e-mail ① n e-mail f, posta f elettronica ② vt spedire per e-mail

e-mail account n account m inv di posta elettronica

e-mail address n indirizzo m di posta elettronica

emanate /'eməneɪt/ vi emanare

emancipate vt emancipare

emancipated /ɪ'mænsɪpeɪtɪd/ adj emancipato

emancipation /ɪmænsɪ'peɪʃn/ n emancipazione f; (of slaves) liberazione f

e-marketing /'i:mɑ:kɪtɪŋ/ n e-marketing m inv

emasculate /ɪ'mæskjʊleɪt/ vt evirare; fig svigorire

embalm /ɪm'bɑ:m/ vt imbalsamare

embankment /ɪm'bæŋkmənt/ n argine m; Rail massicciata f

embargo /em'bɑ:gəʊ/ n (pl **-es**) embargo m

embark /ɪm'bɑ:k/ vi imbarcarsi; ∼ **on** intraprendere

embarkation /embɑ:'keɪʃn/ n imbarco m

embarrass /em'bærəs/ vt imbarazzare

embarrassed /em'bærəst/ adj imbarazzato

embarrassing /em'bærəsɪŋ/ adj imbarazzante

embarrassment /em'bærəsmənt/ n imbarazzo m

embassy /'embəsɪ/ n ambasciata f

embed /ɪm'bed/ vt Comput integrare ‹command›; ∼**ded in** ‹gem› incastonato in; ‹plant› piantato in; ‹sharp object› conficcato in; ‹rock› incluso in; ∼**ded** ‹traditions, feelings› radicato; ‹journalist› aggregato (a un'unità militare); **be** ∼**ded in** fig radicarsi in

embellish /ɪm'belɪʃ/ vt abbellire

embers /'embəz/ npl braci fpl

embezzle /ɪm'bezl/ vt appropriarsi indebitamente di

embezzlement /ɪm'bez(ə)lmənt/ n appropriazione f indebita

emblem /'embləm/ n emblema m

emblematic /emblə'mætɪk/ adj emblematico

embodiment /ɪm'bɒdɪmənt/ n incarnazione f

embody /ɪm'bɒdɪ/ vt (pt/pp **-ied**) incorporare; ∼ **what is best in...** rappresentare quanto c'è di meglio di...

embolism /'embəlɪzm/ n Med embolia f

emboss /ɪm'bɒs/ vt sbalzare ‹metal›; stampare in rilievo ‹paper›

embossed /ɪm'bɒst/ adj in rilievo

embrace /ɪm'breɪs/ ① n abbraccio m ② vt abbracciare ③ vi abbracciarsi

embroider /ɪm'brɔɪdə(r)/ vt ricamare ‹design›; fig abbellire

embroidery /ɪm'brɔɪdərɪ/ n ricamo m

embroil /ɪm'brɔɪl/ vt **become** ∼**ed in something** rimanere invischiato in qualcosa

embryo /'embrɪəʊ/ n embrione m

embryonic /embrɪ'ɒnɪk/ adj Biol. fig embrionale

emend /ɪ'mend/ vt emendare

emerald /'emərəld/ n smeraldo m

emerge /ɪ'mɜ:dʒ/ vi emergere; (come into being: nation) nascere; ‹sun, flowers› spuntare fuori

emergence /ɪ'mɜ:dʒəns/ n emergere m; (of new country) nascita f

emergency /ɪ'mɜ:dʒənsɪ/ n emergenza f; **in an** ∼ in caso di emergenza

emergency ambulance service n pronto soccorso m autoambulanze

emergency case n Med caso m di emergenza

emergency centre n (for refugees etc) centro m di accoglienza; Med centro m di soccorso mobile

emergency exit n uscita f di sicurezza

emergency landing n Aeron atterraggio m di fortuna

emergency laws npl Pol leggi fpl straordinarie

emergency number n numero m di emergenza

emergency powers npl Pol poteri mpl straordinari

emergency rations npl viveri mpl di sopravvivenza

emergency service n Med servizio m di pronto soccorso

emergency services npl servizi mpl di pronto intervento

emergency surgery n undergo ∼ ∼ essere operato d'urgenza

emergency ward n [reparto m di] pronto soccorso m

emergency worker n addetto m a operazioni di soccorso

emergent /ɪˈmɜːdʒənt/ adj ⟨industry, nation⟩ emergente

emery board /ˈeməri/ n limetta f per le unghie di carta.

emery paper n carta f vetrata

emigrant /ˈemɪɡrənt/ n emigrante mf

emigrate /ˈemɪɡreɪt/ vi emigrare

emigration /emɪˈɡreɪʃn/ n emigrazione f

eminence /ˈemɪnəns/ n (fame) eminenza f, gloria f; (honour) distinzione f; (hill) altura f

eminent /ˈemɪnənt/ adj eminente

eminently /ˈemɪnəntlɪ/ adv eminentemente

emirate /ˈemɪərət/ n emirato m

emissary /ˈemɪsərɪ/ n emissario m (to di)

emission /ɪˈmɪʃn/ n emissione f; (of fumes) esalazione f

emit /ɪˈmɪt/ vt (pt/pp **emitted**) emettere; esalare ⟨fumes⟩

Emmy /ˈemɪ/ n Emmy m, Oscar m inv televisivo americano

emoticon /ɪˈməʊtɪkɒn/ n Comput emoticon m inv

emotion /ɪˈməʊʃn/ n emozione f

emotional /ɪˈməʊʃənəl/ adj denso di emozione; ⟨person, reaction⟩ emotivo; **become ∼** avere una reazione emotiva; **don't get so ∼** non lasciarti prendere dalle emozioni

emotionally /ɪˈməʊʃənəlɪ/ adv ⟨speak⟩ emotivamente; **∼ disturbed** con turbe emotive

emotionless /ɪˈməʊʃənlɪs/ adj impassibile

emotive /ɪˈməʊtɪv/ adj emotivo

empathize /ˈempəθaɪz/ vi **∼ with somebody** immedesimarsi nei problemi di qualcuno

empathy /ˈempəθɪ/ n comprensione f

emperor /ˈempərə(r)/ n imperatore m

emphasis /ˈemfəsɪs/ n enfasi f; **put the ∼ on something** accentuare qualcosa

emphasize /ˈemfəsaɪz/ vt accentuare ⟨word, syllable⟩; sottolineare ⟨need⟩

emphatic /ɪmˈfætɪk/ adj categorico

emphatically /ɪmˈfætɪklɪ/ adv categoricamente

empire /ˈempaɪə(r)/ n impero m

empirical /emˈpɪrɪkl/ adj empirico

empiricism /emˈpɪrɪsɪzm/ n empirismo m

employ /emˈplɔɪ/ vt impiegare; fig usare ⟨tact⟩

employable /emˈplɔɪəbl/ adj ⟨person⟩ che ha i requisiti per svolgere un lavoro

employee /emplɔɪˈiː/ n impiegato, -a mf

employee buyout n rilevamento m dipendenti

employer /emˈplɔɪə(r)/ n datore m di lavoro

employment /emˈplɔɪmənt/ n occupazione f; (work) lavoro m

employment agency n ufficio m di collocamento

employment contract n contratto m di lavoro

employment exchange n agenzia f di collocamento

employment figures npl dati mpl sull'occupazione

Employment Minister, Employment Secretary n ministro m del lavoro

emporium /emˈpɔːrɪəm/ n hum emporio m

empower /ɪmˈpaʊə(r)/ vt autorizzare; (enable) mettere in grado

empowerment /ɪmˈpaʊəmənt/ n empowerment m inv

empress /ˈemprɪs/ n imperatrice f

empties /ˈemptɪz/ npl vuoti mpl

emptiness /ˈemptɪnɪs/ n vuoto m

empty /ˈemptɪ/ **❶** adj vuoto; ⟨promise, threat⟩ vano
❷ vt (pt/pp **-ied**) vuotare ⟨container⟩
❸ vi vuotarsi
■ **empty out** vt/i = EMPTY

empty-handed /-ˈhændɪd/ adj ⟨arrive, leave⟩ a mani vuote

empty-headed /-ˈhedɪd/ adj scriteriato

EMS n abbr (**European Monetary System**) SME m

EMU abbr (**European Monetary Union**) UME f

emulate /ˈemjʊleɪt/ vt emulare

emulsify /ɪˈmʌlsɪfaɪ/ **❶** v (pt/pp **-ied**) vt emulsionare
❷ vi emulsionarsi

emulsion /ɪˈmʌlʃn/ n emulsione f

enable /ɪˈneɪbl/ vt **∼ somebody to** mettere qualcuno in grado di

enact /ɪˈnækt/ vt Theat rappresentare; decretare ⟨law⟩

enamel /ɪˈnæml/ **❶** n smalto m
❷ vt (pt/pp **enamelled**) smaltare

enamelling /ɪˈnæməlɪŋ/ n (process) smaltatura f; (art) decorazione f a smalto

enamoured /ɪˈnæməd/ adj **be ∼ of** essere innamorato di

enc. abbr (**enclosures**) alleg.

encampment /ɪnˈkæmpmənt/ n accampamento m

encapsulate /enˈkæpsjʊleɪt/ vt (include) incapsulare; (summarize) sintetizzare

encase /enˈkeɪs/ vt rivestire (**in** di)

encash /en'kæʃ/ *vt* Br incassare

encephalogram /en'kefələgræm/ *n* encefalogramma *m*

enchant /ɪn'tʃɑːnt/ *vt* incantare

enchanting /ɪn'tʃɑːntɪŋ/ *adj* incantevole

enchantment /ɪn'tʃɑːntmənt/ *n* incanto *m*

encircle /ɪn'sɜːkl/ *vt* circondare

encl *abbr* (**enclosed; enclosure**) all.

enclave /'enkleɪv/ *n* enclave *f inv*; fig territorio *m*

enclose /ɪn'kləʊz/ *vt* circondare ‹land›; (in letter) allegare (**with** a)

enclosed /ɪn'kləʊzd/ *adj* ‹space› chiuso; (in letter) allegato

enclosure /ɪn'kləʊzə(r)/ *n* (at zoo) recinto *m*; (in letter) allegato *m*

encode /ɪn'kəʊd/ *vt* codificare

encoder /ɪn'kəʊdə(r)/ *n* codificatore, -trice *mf*

encompass /ɪn'kʌmpəs/ *vt* (include) comprendere

encore /'ɒŋkɔː(r)/ *n & int* bis *m inv*

encounter /ɪn'kaʊntə(r)/ ① *n* incontro *m*; (battle) scontro *m*
② *vt* incontrare

encourage /ɪn'kʌrɪdʒ/ *vt* incoraggiare; promuovere ‹the arts, independence›

encouragement /ɪn'kʌrɪdʒmənt/ *n* incoraggiamento *m*; (of the arts) promozione *f*

encouraging /ɪn'kʌrɪdʒɪŋ/ *adj* incoraggiante; ‹smile› di incoraggiamento

encroach /ɪn'krəʊtʃ/ *vt* ~ **on** invadere ‹land, privacy›; abusare di ‹time›; interferire con ‹rights›

encrust /en'krʌst/ *vt* be ~ed **with** ‹ice› essere incrostato di; ‹jewels› essere tempestato di

encrypt /en'krɪpt/ *vt* criptare

encumber /ɪn'kʌmbə(r)/ *vt* be ~ed **with** essere carico di ‹children, suitcases›; essere ingombro di ‹furniture›

encumbrance /ɪn'kʌmbrəns/ *n* peso *m*

encyclop[a]edia /ɪnsaɪklə'piːdɪə/ *n* enciclopedia *f*

encyclop[a]edic /ɪnsaɪklə'piːdɪk/ *adj* enciclopedico

end /end/ ① *n* fine *f*; (of box, table, piece of string) estremità *f*; (of town, room) parte *f*; (purpose) fine *m*; **in the** ~ alla fine; **at the** ~ **of May** alla fine di maggio; **at the** ~ **of the street/garden** in fondo alla strada/al giardino; **on** ~ (upright) in piedi; **for days on** ~ per giorni e giorni; **for six days on** ~ per sei giorni di fila; **put an** ~ **to something** mettere fine a qualcosa; **make** ~**s meet** fam sbarcare il lunario; **no** ~ **of** fam un sacco di
② *vt/i* finire

■ **end in** *vt* ‹word› terminare in; finire in ‹failure, argument›

■ **end off** *vt* concludere ‹meal, speech›

■ **end up** *vi* finire; ~ **up doing something** finire col fare qualcosa

endanger /ɪn'deɪndʒə(r)/ *vt* rischiare ‹one's life›; mettere a repentaglio ‹somebody else, success of something›

endangered species /ɪn'deɪndʒəd/ *n* specie *f* a rischio

endear /ɪn'dɪə(r)/ *vt* ~ **oneself to somebody** conquistarsi la simpatia di qualcuno; ~ **somebody to** conquistare a qualcuno la simpatia di

endearing /ɪn'dɪərɪŋ/ *adj* accattivante

endearingly /ɪn'dɪərɪŋlɪ/ *adv* ‹smile› in modo accattivante; ~ **honest** di un'onestà disarmante

endearment /ɪn'dɪəmənt/ *n* **term of** ~ vezzeggiativo *m*

endeavour /ɪn'devə(r)/ ① *n* tentativo *m*
② *vi* sforzarsi (**to** di)

endemic /en'demɪk/ ① *adj* endemico
② *n* (situation) endemia *f*

ending /'endɪŋ/ *n* fine *f*; Gram desinenza *f*

endive /'endaɪv/ *n* indivia *f*

endless /'endlɪs/ *adj* interminabile; ‹patience› infinito

endlessly /'endlɪslɪ/ *adv* continuamente; ‹patient› infinitamente

endocrinology /endəʊkrɪ'nɒlədʒɪ/ *n* endocrinologia *f*

endorse /en'dɔːs/ *vt* girare ‹cheque›; ‹sports personality› fare pubblicità a ‹product›; approvare ‹plan›

endorsement /en'dɔːsmənt/ *n* (of cheque) girata *f*; (of plan) conferma *f*; (on driving licence) registrazione *f* su patente di un'infrazione

endow /ɪn'daʊ/ *vt* dotare

endowment insurance /ɪn'daʊmənt/ *n* assicurazione *f* sulla vita che fornisce un reddito in caso di sopravvivenza

endpaper *n* risguardo *m*

end product *n* prodotto *m* finito

end result *n* risultato *m* finale

endurable /ɪn'djʊərəbl/ *adj* sopportabile

endurance /ɪn'djʊərəns/ *n* resistenza *f*; **it is beyond** ~ è insopportabile

endurance test *n* prova *f* di resistenza

endure /ɪn'djʊə(r)/ ① *vt* sopportare
② *vi* durare

enduring /ɪn'djʊərɪŋ/ *adj* duraturo

end user *n* utente *m* finale

enema /'enɪmə/ *n* Med clistere *m*

enemy /'enəmɪ/ ① *n* nemico, -a *mf*
② *attrib* nemico

energetic /enə'dʒetɪk/ *adj* energico

energetically /enə'dʒetɪklɪ/ *adv* ‹speak, promote, publicize› vigorosamente; ‹work, ⋯▸

exercise⟩ con energia; ⟨*deny*⟩ risolutamente

energize /'enədʒaɪz/ *vt* stimolare; Electr alimentare [elettricamente]

energizing /'enədʒaɪzɪŋ/ *adj* ⟨*influence*⟩ stimolante

energy /'enədʒɪ/ *n* energia *f*

energy efficiency *n* razionalizzazione *f* del consumo energetico

energy-efficient *adj* a consumo ottimale di energia

energy policy *n* politica *f* energetica

energy resources *npl* risorse *fpl* energetiche

energy saving *n* risparmio *m* energetico

energy-saving *adj* ⟨*device*⟩ che fa risparmiare energia; ⟨*measure*⟩ per risparmiare energia

enervate /'enəveɪt/ *vt* snervare

enfold /en'fəʊld/ *vt* avvolgere

enforce /ɪn'fɔːs/ *vt* far rispettare ⟨*law*⟩

enforced /ɪn'fɔːst/ *adj* forzato

enforcement /ɪn'fɔːsmənt/ *n* applicazione *f*; (of discipline) imposizione *f*

ENG *abbr* (**electronic news gathering**) ENG *m*

engage /ɪn'geɪdʒ/ ① *vt* assumere ⟨*staff*⟩; Theat ingaggiare; Auto ingranare ⟨*gear*⟩; ∼ **somebody in conversation** fare conversazione con qualcuno
② *vi* Techn ingranare; ∼ **in** impegnarsi in

engaged /ɪn'geɪdʒd/ *adj* (in use, busy) occupato; ⟨*person*⟩ impegnato; (to be married) fidanzato; **get** ∼ fidanzarsi (**to** con)

engaged tone *n* Br segnale *m* di occupato

engagement /ɪn'geɪdʒmənt/ *n* fidanzamento *m*; (appointment) appuntamento *m*; Mil combattimento *m*

engagement ring *n* anello *m* di fidanzamento

engagements book *n* agenda *f*

engaging /ɪn'geɪdʒɪŋ/ *adj* attraente

engender /ɪn'dʒendə(r)/ *vt* fig generare

engine /'endʒɪn/ *n* motore *m*; Rail locomotrice *f*

engine drive *n* macchinista *m*

engineer /endʒɪ'nɪə(r)/ ① *n* ingegnere *m*; (service, installation) tecnico *m*; Naut, Am Rail macchinista *m*
② *vt* fig architettare

engineering /endʒɪ'nɪərɪŋ/ *n* ingegneria *f*

engine failure *n* guasto *m* [al motore]; (in jet) avaria *f*

engine oil *n* olio *m* [del] motore

engine room *n* sala *f* macchine

engine shed *n* Rail deposito *m*

England /'ɪŋglənd/ *n* Inghilterra *f*

English /'ɪŋglɪʃ/ ① *adj* inglese; **the** ∼ **Channel** la Manica
② *n* (language) inglese *m*; **the** ∼ *pl* gli inglesi

English as a Foreign Language *n* inglese *m* come lingua straniera

English as a Second Language *n* inglese *m* come seconda lingua

Englishman *n* inglese *m*

English rose *n* donna *f* dalla bellezza tipicamente inglese

English speaker *n* anglofono, -a *mf*

English-speaking *adj* anglofono

Englishwoman *n* inglese *f*

engrave /ɪn'greɪv/ *vt* incidere

engraving /ɪn'greɪvɪŋ/ *n* incisione *f*

engross /ɪn'grəʊs/ *vt* ∼**ed in** assorto in

engrossing /ɪn'grəʊsɪŋ/ *adj* avvincente

engulf /ɪn'gʌlf/ *vt* ⟨*fire, waves*⟩ inghiottire

enhance /ɪn'hɑːns/ *vt* accrescere ⟨*beauty, reputation*⟩; migliorare ⟨*performance*⟩

enigma /ɪ'nɪgmə/ *n* enigma *m*

enigmatic /enɪg'mætɪk/ *adj* enigmatico

enjoy /ɪn'dʒɔɪ/ *vt* godere di ⟨*good health*⟩; ∼ **oneself** divertirsi; **I** ∼ **cooking/painting** mi piace cucinare/dipingere; **I** ∼**ed the meal/film** mi è piaciuto il pranzo/il film; ∼ **your meal** buon appetito

enjoyable /ɪn'dʒɔɪəbl/ *adj* piacevole

enjoyment /ɪn'dʒɔɪmənt/ *n* piacere *m*

enlarge /ɪn'lɑːdʒ/ ① *vt* ingrandire
② *vi* ∼ **upon** dilungarsi su

enlargement /ɪn'lɑːdʒmənt/ *n* ingrandimento *m*

enlarger /ɪn'lɑːdʒə(r)/ *n* Phot ingranditore *m*

enlighten /ɪn'laɪtn/ *vt* illuminare

enlightened /ɪn'laɪtənd/ *adj* progressista

enlightening /ɪn'laɪtnɪŋ/ *adj* istruttivo

enlightenment /ɪn'laɪtənmənt/ *n* **The E**∼ l'Illuminismo *m*

enlist /ɪn'lɪst/ ① *vt* Mil reclutare; ∼ **sb's help** farsi aiutare da qualcuno
② *vi* Mil arruolarsi

enliven /ɪn'laɪvn/ *vt* animare

enmesh /en'meʃ/ *vt* **become** ∼**ed in** fig impegolarsi in

enmity /'enmətɪ/ *n* inimicizia *f*

ennoble /en'nəʊbl/ *vt* nobilitare

enormity /ɪ'nɔːmətɪ/ *n* enormità *f*

enormous /ɪ'nɔːməs/ *adj* enorme

enormously /ɪ'nɔːməslɪ/ *adv* estremamente; ⟨*grateful*⟩ infinitamente

enough /ɪ'nʌf/ ① *adj* & *n* abbastanza; **I didn't bring** ∼ **clothes** non ho portato abbastanza vestiti; **have you had** ∼**?** (to eat/drink) hai mangiato/bevuto abbastanza?; **I've had** ~! fam ne ho abbastanza!; **is that** ~? basta?; **that's** ~! basta così!; **£50 isn't** ~ 50 sterline non sono sufficienti

② *adv* abbastanza; **you're not working fast** ~ non lavori abbastanza in fretta; **funnily** ~ stranamente

enquire /ɪn'kwaɪə(r)/ *vi* domandare; ~ **about** chiedere informazioni su

enquiring /ɪn'kwaɪərɪŋ/ *adj* ⟨look⟩ indagatore; ⟨mind⟩ avido di sapere

enquiry /ɪn'kwaɪərɪ/ *n* domanda *f*; (investigation) inchiesta *f*

enrage /ɪn'reɪdʒ/ *vt* fare arrabbiare

enrich /ɪn'rɪtʃ/ *vt* arricchire; (improve) migliorare ⟨vocabulary⟩

enrol /ɪn'rəʊl/ *vt* (pt/pp **-rolled**) (for exam, in club) iscriversi (**for, in** a)

enrolment /ɪn'rəʊlmənt/ *n* iscrizione *f*

ensconced /ɪn'skɒnst/ *adj* comodamente sistemato (**in** in)

ensemble /ɒn'sɒmbl/ *n* (clothing & Mus) complesso *m*

ensign /'ensaɪn/ *n* insegna *f*

enslave /ɪn'sleɪv/ *vt* render schiavo

ensue /ɪn'sju:/ *vi* seguire; ~ **from** sorgere da; **the ensuing discussion** la discussione che ne è seguita

en suite /ɑ̃'swi:t/ **①** *n* (bathroom) camera *f* con bagno annesso

② *adj* ⟨bathroom⟩ annesso; ⟨room⟩ con bagno

ensure /ɪn'ʃʊə(r)/ *vt* assicurare; ~ **that** ⟨person⟩ assicurarsi che; ⟨measure⟩ garantire che

ENT *n abbr* (**Ear Nose and Throat**) otorino *m*

entail /ɪn'teɪl/ *vt* comportare; **what does it** ~? in che cosa consiste?

entangle /ɪn'tæŋgl/ *vt* **get** ~**d in** rimanere impigliato in; fig rimanere coinvolto in

entanglement /ɪn'tæŋg(ə)lmənt/ *n* (emotional) legame *m* sentimentale; (complicated situation) pasticcio *m*

enter /'entə(r)/ **①** *vt* entrare in; iscrivere ⟨horse, runner in race⟩; cominciare ⟨university⟩; partecipare a ⟨competition⟩; Comput immettere ⟨data⟩; (write down) scrivere

② *vi* entrare; Theat entrare in scena; (register as competitor) iscriversi; (take part) partecipare (**in** a)

③ *n* Comput invio *m*

■ **enter into** *vt* (begin) intavolare ⟨negotiations, an argument⟩

enteritis /entə'raɪtɪs/ *n* enterite *f*

enterprise /'entəpraɪz/ *n* impresa *f*; (quality) iniziativa *f*

enterprising /'entəpraɪzɪŋ/ *adj* intraprendente

entertain /entə'teɪn/ **①** *vt* intrattenere; (invite) ricevere; nutrire ⟨ideas, hopes⟩; prendere in considerazione ⟨possibility⟩

② *vi* intrattenersi; (have guests) ricevere

entertainer /entə'teɪnə(r)/ *n* artista *mf*

entertaining /entə'teɪnɪŋ/ *adj* ⟨person⟩ di gradevole compagnia; ⟨evening, film, play⟩ divertente

entertainment /entə'teɪnmənt/ *n* (amusement) intrattenimento *m*

entertainment industry *n* l'industria *f* dello spettacolo

enthral /ɪn'θrɔ:l/ *vt* (pt/pp **enthralled**) **be** ~**led** essere affascinato (**by** da)

enthralling /ɪn'θrɔ:lɪŋ/ *adj* ⟨novel, performance⟩ affascinante

enthuse /ɪn'θju:z/ *vi* ~ **over** entusiasmarsi per

enthusiasm /ɪn'θju:zɪæzm/ *n* entusiasmo *m*

enthusiast /ɪn'θju:zɪæst/ *n* entusiasta *mf*

enthusiastic /ɪnθju:zɪ'æstɪk/ *adj* entusiastico

enthusiastically /ɪnθju:zɪ'æstɪklɪ/ *adv* entusiasticamente

entice /ɪn'taɪs/ *vt* attirare

enticement /ɪn'taɪsmənt/ *n* (incentive) incentivo *m*

enticing /ɪn'taɪsɪŋ/ *adj* ⟨prospect, offer⟩ allettante; ⟨person⟩ seducente; ⟨food, smell⟩ invitante

entire /ɪn'taɪə(r)/ *adj* intero

entirely /ɪn'taɪəlɪ/ *adv* del tutto; **I'm not** ~ **satisfied** non sono completamente soddisfatto

entirety /ɪn'taɪərətɪ/ *n* **in its** ~ nell'insieme

entitle /ɪn'taɪtl/ *vt* dare diritto a; ~ **somebody to something** dare a qualcuno il diritto di qualcosa

entitled /ɪn'taɪtld/ *adj* ⟨book⟩ intitolato; **be** ~ **to something** aver diritto a qualcosa

entitlement /ɪn'taɪtlmənt/ *n* diritto *m*

entity /'entɪtɪ/ *n* entità *f*

entomology /entə'mɒlədʒɪ/ *n* entomologia *f*

entourage /'ɒntʊrɑ:ʒ/ *n* entourage *m inv*

entrails /'entreɪlz/ *npl* intestini *mpl*

entrance[1] /'entrəns/ *n* entrata *f*; Theat entrata *f* in scena; (right to enter) ammissione *f*; **'no** ~**'** 'ingresso vietato'

entrance[2] /ɪn'trɑ:ns/ *vt* estasiare

entrance examination *n* esame *m* di ammissione

entrance fee *n* **how much is the** ~ ~? quanto costa il biglietto di ingresso?

entrance hall *n* (in house) ingresso *m*

entrance requirements *npl* requisiti *mpl* di ammissione

entrance ticket *n* biglietto *m* d'ingresso

entrancing /ɪnˈtrɑːnsɪŋ/ *adj* incantevole

entrant /ˈentrənt/ *n* concorrente *mf*

entreat /ɪnˈtriːt/ *vt* supplicare

entreatingly /ɪnˈtriːtɪŋlɪ/ *adv* ‹*beg, ask*› in tono implorante

entreaty /ɪnˈtriːtɪ/ *n* supplica *f*

entrée /ˈɑ̃treɪ/ *n* Br (starter) primo *m*; (Am: main course) secondo *m*; **her wealth gave her an ∼ into high society** il denaro le ha aperto le porte dell'alta società

entrenched /ɪnˈtrentʃt/ *adj* ‹*ideas, views*› radicato

entrepreneur /ɒntrəprəˈnɜː(r)/ *n* imprenditore, -trice *mf*

entrepreneurial /ɒntrəprəˈnɜːrɪəl/ *adj* imprenditoriale; **have ∼ skills** avere il senso degli affari

entrust /ɪnˈtrʌst/ *vt* ∼ **somebody with something**, ∼ **something to somebody** affidare qualcosa a qualcuno

entry /ˈentrɪ/ *n* ingresso *m*; (way in) entrata *f*; (in directory etc) voce *f*; (in appointment diary) appuntamento *m*; '**no ∼**' 'ingresso vietato'; Auto 'accesso vietato'

entry fee *n* quota *f* di iscrizione

entry form *n* modulo *m* di ammissione

entry permit *n* visto *m* di entrata

entryphone *n* citofono *m*

entry requirements *npl* requisiti *mpl* di ammissione

entry visa *n* visto *m* di ingresso

entwine /ɪnˈtwaɪn/ *vt* also fig intrecciare

E-number *n* Br sigla *f* degli additivi

enumerate /ɪˈnjuːməreɪt/ *vt* enumerare

enumeration /ɪnjuːməˈreɪʃn/ *n* (list) enumerazione *f*; (counting) conto *m*

enunciate /ɪˈnʌnsɪeɪt/ *vt* enunciare

enunciation /ɪnʌnsɪˈeɪʃn/ *n* (of principle, facts) enunciazione *f*; (of word) articolazione *f*

envelop /ɪnˈveləp/ *vt* (pt/pp **enveloped**) avviluppare

envelope /ˈenvələʊp/ *n* busta *f*

enviable /ˈenvɪəbl/ *adj* invidiabile

envious /ˈenvɪəs/ *adj* invidioso

enviously /ˈenvɪəslɪ/ *adv* con invidia

environment /ɪnˈvaɪrənmənt/ *n* ambiente *m*

environmental /ɪnvaɪrənˈmentl/ *adj* ambientale

environmental health *n* salute *f* pubblica

environmentalist /ɪnvaɪrənˈmentəlɪst/ *n* ambientalista *mf*

environmentally /ɪnvaɪrənˈmentəlɪ/ *adv* ∼ **friendly** che rispetta l'ambiente

environmental scientist *n* studioso, -a *mf* di ecologia applicata

Environmental Studies *npl* Br Sch ecogeografia *f* e ecobiologia *f*

envisage /ɪnˈvɪzɪdʒ/ *vt* prevedere

envoy /ˈenvɔɪ/ *n* inviato, -a *mf*

envy /ˈenvɪ/ **①** *n* invidia *f* **②** *vt* (pt/pp **-ied**) ∼ **somebody something** invidiare qualcuno per qualcosa

enzyme /ˈenzaɪm/ *n* enzima *m*

EOF *abbr* Comput (**end of file**) EOF *m*

ephemeral /ɪˈfemərəl/ *adj* effimero

epic /ˈepɪk/ **①** *adj* epico **②** *n* epopea *f*

epicentre /ˈepɪsentə(r)/ *n* epicentro *m*

epidemic /epɪˈdemɪk/ *n* epidemia *f*

epidermis /epɪˈdɜːmɪs/ *n* epidermide *f*

epidural /epɪˈdjʊərəl/ *n* Med anestesia *f* epidurale

epigram /ˈepɪgræm/ *n* epigramma *m*

epilepsy /ˈepɪlepsɪ/ *n* epilessia *f*

epileptic /epɪˈleptɪk/ *adj & n* epilettico, -a *mf*

epilogue /ˈepɪlɒg/ *n* epilogo *m*

Epiphany /ɪˈpɪfənɪ/ *n* Epifania *f*

episode /ˈepɪsəʊd/ *n* episodio *m*

episodic /epɪˈsɒdɪk/ *adj* episodico

epistle /ɪˈpɪsl/ *n* liter epistola *f*

epitaph /ˈepɪtɑːf/ *n* epitaffio *m*

epithet /ˈepɪθet/ *n* epiteto *m*

epitome /ɪˈpɪtəmɪ/ *n* epitome *f*

epitomize /ɪˈpɪtəmaɪz/ *vt* essere il classico esempio di

epoch /ˈiːpɒk/ *n* epoca *f*

epoch-making *adj* che fa epoca

eponymous /ɪˈpɒnɪməs/ *adj* eponimo

EQ *abbr* (**graphic equalizer**) EQ *m*

equable /ˈekwəbl/ *adj* ‹*climate*› temperato; ‹*temperament*› equilibrato

equably /ˈekwəblɪ/ *adv* con serenità

equal /ˈiːkwl/ **①** *adj* ‹*parts, amounts*› uguale; **of ∼ height** della stessa altezza; **be ∼ to the task** essere all'altezza del compito **②** *n* pari *m inv*; **treat somebody as an ∼** trattare qualcuno da pari a pari **③** *vt* (pt/pp **equalled**) (be same in quantity as) essere pari a; (rival) uguagliare; **5 plus 5 ∼s 10** 5 più 5 [è] uguale a 10

equality /ɪˈkwɒlətɪ/ *n* uguaglianza *f*

equalize /ˈiːkwəlaɪz/ *vi* Sport pareggiare

equalizer /ˈiːkwəlaɪzə(r)/ *n* Sport pareggio *m*; **get the ∼** pareggiare

equally /ˈiːkwəlɪ/ *adv* ‹*divide*› in parti uguali; ∼ **intelligent** della stessa intelligenza; ∼,... allo stesso tempo ...

equal opportunities *npl* uguaglianza *f* dei diritti

Equal Opportunities Commission n Br commissione f per l'uguaglianza dei diritti nei rapporti di lavoro

equal opportunity attrib ⟨legislation⟩ per l'uguaglianza dei diritti nei rapporti di lavoro; ⟨employer⟩ che applica l'uguaglianza dei diritti

equal rights npl parità f dei diritti

equals sign n segno m uguale

equanimity /ekwə'nɪmətɪ/ n equanimità f

equate /ɪ'kweɪt/ vt ∼ something with something equiparare qualcosa a qualcosa

equation /ɪ'kweɪʒn/ n Math equazione f

equator /ɪ'kweɪtə(r)/ n equatore m

equatorial /ekwə'tɔːrɪəl/ adj equatoriale

Equatorial Guinea n Guinea Equatoriale f

equestrian /ɪ'kwestrɪən/ adj equestre

equidistant /i:kwɪ'dɪstənt/ adj equidistante

equilateral /i:kwɪ'lætərəl/ adj equilatero

equilibrium /i:kwɪ'lɪbrɪəm/ n equilibrio m

equine /'ekwaɪn/ adj ⟨disease, species⟩ equino; ⟨features⟩ cavallino

equinox /'i:kwɪnɒks/ n equinozio m

equip /ɪ'kwɪp/ vt (pt/pp equipped) equipaggiare; attrezzare ⟨kitchen, office⟩

equipment /ɪ'kwɪpmənt/ n attrezzatura f

equitable /'ekwɪtəbl/ adj giusto

equity /'ekwətɪ/ n (justness) equità f; Comm azioni fpl

equity capital n Fin capitale m azionario

equity financing n Fin finaziamento m attraverso l'emissione di azioni

equity market n Fin mercato m azionario

equivalent /ɪ'kwɪvələnt/ ① adj equivalente; be ∼ to equivalere a ② n equivalente m

equivocal /ɪ'kwɪvəkl/ adj equivoco

equivocate /ɪ'kwɪvəkeɪt/ vi parlare in modo equivoco, giocare sull'equivoco

equivocation /ɪkwɪvə'keɪʃn/ n affermazione f equivoca; too much ∼ troppi equivoci

era /'ɪərə/ n età f; (geological) era f

eradicate /ɪ'rædɪkeɪt/ vt eradicare

erase /ɪ'reɪz/ vt cancellare

erase head n Comput testina f di cancellazione

eraser /ɪ'reɪzə(r)/ n gomma f [da cancellare]; (for blackboard) cancellino m

erasure /ɪ'reɪʒə(r)/ n (act) cancellazione f; (on paper) cancellatura f

erect /ɪ'rekt/ ① adj eretto ② vt erigere

erection /ɪ'rekʃn/ n erezione f

ergonomic /ɜːgə'nɒmɪk/ adj ergonomico; ⟨seat⟩ anatomico

ergonomics /ɜːgə'nɒmɪks/ n ergonomia f

Erie /'ɪərɪ/ n Lake E∼ il lago Erie

Eritrea /errɪ'treɪə/ n Eritrea f

ERM n abbr **Exchange Rate Mechanism**

ermine /'ɜːmɪn/ n ermellino m

erode /ɪ'rəʊd/ vt ⟨water⟩ erodere; ⟨acid⟩ corrodere

erogenous /ɪ'rɒdʒɪnəs/ adj erogeno

erosion /ɪ'rəʊʒn/ n erosione f; (by acid) corrosione f

erotic /ɪ'rɒtɪk/ adj erotico

erotica /ɪ'rɒtɪkə/ npl (art) arte f erotica; (literature) letteratura f erotica; Cinema film mpl erotici

eroticism /ɪ'rɒtɪsɪzm/ n erotismo m

err /ɜː(r)/ vi errare; (sin) peccare

errand /'erənd/ n commissione f

errant /'erənt/ adj ⟨husband, wife⟩ infedele

erratic /ɪ'rætɪk/ adj irregolare; ⟨person, moods⟩ imprevedibile; ⟨exchange rate⟩ incostante

erroneous /ɪ'rəʊnɪəs/ adj erroneo

erroneously /ɪ'rəʊnɪəslɪ/ adv erroneamente

error /'erə(r)/ n errore m; in ∼ per errore

error message n Comput messaggio m di errore

ersatz /'ɜːsæts/ n surrogato m; ∼ tobacco surrogato del tabacco

erudite /'erʊdaɪt/ adj erudito

erudition /erʊ'dɪʃn/ n erudizione f

erupt /ɪ'rʌpt/ vi eruttare; ⟨spots⟩ spuntare; (fig: in anger) dare in escandescenze

eruption /ɪ'rʌpʃn/ n eruzione f; fig scoppio m

escalate /'eskəleɪt/ ① vi intensificarsi ② vt intensificare

escalation /eskə'leɪʃn/ n escalation f inv

escalator /'eskəleɪtə(r)/ n scala f mobile

escapade /'eskəpeɪd/ n scappatella f

escape /ɪ'skeɪp/ ① n fuga f; (from prison) evasione f; have a narrow ∼ cavarsela per un pelo ② vi ⟨prisoner⟩ evadere (from da); sfuggire (from somebody alla sorveglianza di qualcuno); ⟨animal⟩ scappare; ⟨gas⟩ fuoriuscire ③ vt ∼ notice passare inosservato; the name ∼s me mi sfugge il nome

escape [key] n (tasto) escape m inv

escape chute n Aeron scivolo m

escape clause n clausola f di recesso

escapee /ɪskeɪ'pi:/ n evaso m

escape hatch n Naut portello m di sicurezza

escape route n (for fugitives) itinerario m di fuga; (in case of fire etc) percorso m di emergenza

escapism /ɪ'skeɪpɪzm/ n evasione f dalla realtà

escapologist /eskə'pɒlədʒɪst/ n illusionista mf capace di liberarsi dalle catene

escarpment /es'kɑ:pmənt/ n scarpata f

eschew /ɪs'tʃu:/ vt evitare ⟨discussion⟩; rifuggire ⟨temptation⟩; rifuggire da ⟨violence⟩

escort[1] /'eskɔ:t/ n (of person) accompagnatore, -trice mf; Mil etc scorta f

escort[2] /ɪ'skɔ:t/ vt accompagnare; Mil etc scortare

Eskimo /'eskɪməʊ/ n esquimese mf

esophagus /ɪ'sɒfəgəs/ n Am esofago m

esoteric /esə'terɪk/ adj esoterico

ESP n abbr (**extrasensory perception**) ESP f; n abbr **English for Special Purposes**

esp abbr **especially**

especial /ɪ'speʃl/ adj speciale

especially /ɪ'speʃəlɪ/ adv specialmente; ⟨kind⟩ particolarmente

espionage /'espɪənɑ:ʒ/ n spionaggio m

espouse /ɪ'spaʊz/ vt abbracciare ⟨cause⟩

espresso /e'spresəʊ/ n (coffee) espresso m

Esq Br abbr (**esquire**) James McBride, ∼ Egr. Sig. James McBride

essay /'eseɪ/ n saggio m; Sch tema f

essence /'esns/ n essenza f; **in** ∼ in sostanza

essential /ɪ'senʃl/ ① adj essenziale ② n the ∼s pl l'essenziale m

essentially /ɪ'senʃəlɪ/ adv essenzialmente

essential oil n olio m essenziale

est abbr (**established**) fondato nel

EST abbr Am (**Eastern Standard Time**) ora f solare degli stati orientali dell'America settentrionale

establish /ɪ'stæblɪʃ/ vt stabilire ⟨contact, lead⟩; fondare ⟨firm⟩; (prove) accertare; ∼ **oneself as** affermarsi come

established /ɪ'stæblɪʃt/ adj ⟨way of doing something, view⟩ generalmente accettato; ⟨company⟩ affidabile; ⟨brand⟩ riconosciuto; **a well** ∼ **fact** un dato di fatto; **the** ∼ **church** la religione di Stato

establishment /ɪ'stæblɪʃmənt/ n (firm) azienda f; **the E**∼ l'establishment m

estate /ɪ'steɪt/ n tenuta f; (possessions) patrimonio m; (housing) quartiere m residenziale

estate agency n agenzia f immobiliare

estate agent n agente m immobiliare

estate car n giardiniera f

estate duty n Br imposta f di successione

esteem /ɪ'sti:m/ ① n stima f ② vt stimare; (consider) giudicare

ester /'estə(r)/ n estere m

estimate[1] /'estɪmət/ n valutazione f; Comm preventivo m; **at a rough** ∼ a occhio e croce

estimate[2] /'estɪmeɪt/ vt stimare

estimated time of arrival /'estɪmeɪtɪd/ n ora f prevista di arrivo

estimation /estɪ'meɪʃn/ n (esteem) stima f; **in my** ∼ (judgement) a mio giudizio

Estonia /ɪ'stəʊnɪə/ n Estonia f

estrange /ɪ'streɪndʒ/ vt estraniare; ∼**d from somebody** separato da qualcuno; **her** ∼**d husband** il marito da cui è separata

estrangement /ɪ'streɪndʒmənt/ n disamoramento m

estuary /'estjʊərɪ/ n estuario m

ETA n abbr **estimated time of arrival**

et al /et'æl/ abbr (**et alii**) e altri

etc /et'setərə/ abbr (**et cetera**) ecc

et cetera, etcetera /et'setərə/ adv eccetera

etch /etʃ/ vt incidere all'acquaforte; ∼**ed on her memory** fig impresso nella sua memoria

etching /'etʃɪŋ/ n acquaforte f

eternal /ɪ'tɜ:nl/ adj eterno

eternal life n vita f eterna

eternally /ɪ'tɜ:nəlɪ/ adv eternamente

eternity /ɪ'tɜ:nətɪ/ n eternità f

ether /'i:θə(r)/ n etere m

ethereal /ɪ'θɪərɪəl/ adj etereo

ethic /'eθɪk/ n etica f

ethical /'eθɪkl/ adj etico

ethical bank n banca f etica

ethics /'eθɪks/ n etica f

Ethiopia /i:θɪ'əʊpɪə/ n Etiopia f

ethnic /'eθnɪk/ adj etnico

ethnically /'eθnɪklɪ/ adv etnicamente

ethnic cleansing n epurazione f etnica

ethnic minority n minoranza f etnica

ethnology /eθ'nɒlədʒɪ/ n etnologia f

ethos /'i:θɒs/ n **company** ∼ filosofia f dell'azienda

e-ticket /'i:tɪkɪt/ n Comput biglietto m elettronico

etiquette /'etɪket/ n etichetta f

etymology /etɪ'mɒlədʒɪ/ n etimologia f

EU n abbr (**European Union**) UE f

eucalyptus /ju:kə'lɪptəs/ n eucalipto m

eugenics /ju:'dʒenɪks/ n eugenetica f

eulogize /'ju:lədʒaɪz/ ① vt fare il panegirico di ② vi ~ over something tessere le lodi di qualcosa

eulogy /'ju:lədʒɪ/ n elogio m

eunuch /'ju:nək/ n eunuco m

euphemism /'ju:fəmɪzm/ n eufemismo m

euphemistic /ju:fə'mɪstɪk/ adj eufemistico

euphemistically /ju:fə'mɪstɪklɪ/ adv eufemisticamente

euphoria /ju:'fɔ:rɪə/ n euforia f

euphoric /ju:'fɒrɪk/ adj euforico

Eurasian /jʊ'reɪʒ(ə)n/ adj ⟨people, region⟩ eurasiatico

EURATOM /jʊr'ætəm/ n abbr (**European Atomic Energy Community**) EURATOM f

eurhythmics /jʊ'rɪðmɪks/ n ginnastica f ritmica

euro /'jʊərəʊ/ n euro m inv

eurobond n eurobbligazione f

Eurocheque n eurochèque m inv

Eurocrat /'jʊərəʊkræt/ n eurocrate mf

eurocurrency n eurovaluta f

Eurodollar n eurodollaro m

euromarket n euromercato m

Euro-MP n eurodeputato, -a mf

Europe /'jʊərəp/ n Europa f

European /jʊərə'pɪən/ adj & n europeo, -a mf

European Bank for Reconstruction and Development n Banca f Europea per la Ricostruzione e lo Sviluppo

European Commission n Commissione f Europea

European Community n Comunità f Europea

European Court of Human Rights n Corte f europea per i diritti dell'uomo

European Court of Justice n Corte f europea di giustizia

European Economic Community n Comunità f Economica Europea

European Free Trade Association n Associazione f Europea di Libero Scambio

European Monetary System n Sistema m Monetario Europeo

European Monetary Union n Unione f Monetaria Europea

European Parliament n Parlamento m Europeo

European Union n Unione f Europea

Euro-sceptic n Br euroscettico, -a mf

euthanasia /ju:θə'neɪzɪə/ n eutanasia f

evacuate /ɪ'vækjʊeɪt/ vt evacuare ⟨building, area⟩

evacuation /ɪvækjʊ'eɪʃn/ n evacuazione f

evacuee /ɪvæjʊ'i:/ n sfollato m

evade /ɪ'veɪd/ vt evadere ⟨taxes⟩; evitare ⟨the enemy, authorities⟩; ~ the issue evitare l'argomento

evaluate /ɪ'væljʊeɪt/ vt valutare

evaluation /ɪvæljʊ'eɪʃn/ n valutazione f, stima f

evangelical /i:væn'dʒelɪkl/ adj evangelico

evangelist /ɪ'vændʒəlɪst/ n evangelista m

evaporate /ɪ'væpəreɪt/ vi evaporare; fig svanire

evaporated milk /ɪ'væpəreɪtɪd/ n latte m condensato

evaporation /ɪvæpə'reɪʃn/ n evaporazione f

evasion /ɪ'veɪʒn/ n evasione f

evasive /ɪ'veɪsɪv/ adj evasivo

evasively /ɪ'veɪsɪvlɪ/ adv in modo evasivo

eve /i:v/ n liter vigilia f

even /'i:vn/ ① adj (level) piatto; (same, equal) uguale; (regular) regolare; ⟨number⟩ pari; **get ~ with** vendicarsi di; **now we're ~** adesso siamo pari ② adv anche, ancora; ~ **if** anche se; ~ **so** con tutto ciò; **not ~** nemmeno; ~ **bigger/ hotter** ancora più grande/caldo ③ vt ~ **the score** Sport pareggiare ∎ **even out** vi livellarsi ∎ **even up** vt livellare

even-handed /-'hændɪd/ adj imparziale

evening /'i:vnɪŋ/ n sera f; (whole evening) serata f; **this ~** stasera; **in the ~** la sera

evening class n corso m serale

evening dress n (man's) abito m scuro; (woman's) abito m da sera

evening performance n spettacolo m serale

evening primrose n enotera f

evening star n Venere f

evenly /'i:vnlɪ/ adv ⟨distributed⟩ uniformemente; ⟨breathe⟩ regolarmente; ⟨divided⟩ in uguali parti

event /ɪ'vent/ n avvenimento m; (function) manifestazione f; Sport gara f; **in the ~ of** nell'eventualità di; **in the ~** alla fine

even-tempered /-'tempəd/ adj pacato

eventful /ɪ'ventfʊl/ adj movimentato

eventing /ɪ'ventɪŋ/ n Br concorso m ippico completo

e

eventual /ɪ'ventjʊəl/ *adj* the ∼ **winner was...** alla fine il vincitore è stato...

eventuality /ɪventjʊ'ælətɪ/ *n* eventualità *f*

eventually /ɪ'ventjʊəlɪ/ *adv* alla fine; ∼! finalmente!

ever /'evə(r)/ *adv* mai; **I haven't** ∼... non ho mai...; **for** ∼ per sempre; **hardly** ∼ quasi mai; ∼ **since** da quando; (since that time) da allora; ∼ **so** fam veramente

evergreen /'evəgriːn/ *n* sempreverde *m*

everlasting /evə'læstɪŋ/ *adj* eterno

every /'evrɪ/ *adj* ogni; ∼ **one** ciascuno; ∼ **other day** un giorno sì un giorno no

everybody /'evrɪbɒdɪ/ *pron* tutti *pl*

everyday /'evrɪdeɪ/ *adj* quotidiano, di ogni giorno

everyone /'evrɪwʌn/ *pron* tutti *pl*; ∼ **else** tutti gli altri

everyplace /'evrɪpleɪs/ *adv* Am fam = EVERYWHERE

everything /'evrɪθɪŋ/ *pron* tutto; ∼ **else** tutto il resto

everywhere /'evrɪweə(r)/ *adv* dappertutto; (wherever) dovunque

evict /ɪ'vɪkt/ *vt* sfrattare

eviction /ɪ'vɪkʃn/ *n* sfratto *m*

evidence /'evɪdəns/ *n* evidenza *f*; Jur testimonianza *f*; **give** ∼ testimoniare

evident /'evɪdənt/ *adj* evidente

evidently /'evɪdəntlɪ/ *adv* evidentemente

evil /'iːvl/ ① *adj* cattivo
② *n* male *m*

evil-smelling /-'smelɪŋ/ *adj* puzzolente

evocative /ɪ'vɒkətɪv/ *adj* evocativo; **be** ∼ **of** evocare

evoke /ɪ'vəʊk/ *vt* evocare

evolution /iːvə'luːʃn/ *n* evoluzione *f*

evolutionary /iːvə'luːʃn(ə)rɪ/ *adj* evolutivo

evolve /ɪ'vɒlv/ ① *vt* evolvere
② *vi* evolversi

ewe /juː/ *n* pecora *f*

ex /eks/ *n* (fam: former partner) ex *mf*

ex+ *pref* ex+

exacerbate /ɪg'sæsəbeɪt/ *vt* esacerbare 〈situation〉

exact /ɪg'zækt/ ① *adj* esatto
② *vt* esigere

exacting /ɪg'zæktɪŋ/ *adj* esigente

exactitude /ɪg'zæktɪtjuːd/ *n* esattezza *f*

exactly /ɪg'zæktlɪ/ *adv* esattamente; **not** ∼ non proprio

exactness /ɪg'zæktnɪs/ *n* precisione *f*

exaggerate /ɪg'zædʒəreɪt/ *vt/i* esagerare

exaggerated /ɪg'zædʒəreɪtɪd/ *adj* esagerato; **he has an** ∼ **sense of his own importance** si crede chissà chi

exaggeration /ɪgzædʒə'reɪʃn/ *n* esagerazione *f*

exalt /ɪg'zɔːlt/ *vt* elevare; (praise) vantare

exam /ɪg'zæm/ *n* esame *m*

examination /ɪgzæmɪ'neɪʃn/ *n* esame *m*; (of patient) visita *f*; (of wreckage) ispezione *f*

examination paper *n* testo *m* d'esame

examine /ɪg'zæmɪn/ *vt* esaminare; visitare 〈patient〉

examinee /ɪgzæmɪ'niː/ *n* esaminando *m*

examiner /ɪg'zæmɪnə(r)/ *n* Sch esaminatore, -trice *mf*

example /ɪg'zɑːmpl/ *n* esempio *m*; **for** ∼ per esempio; **make an** ∼ **of somebody** punire qualcuno per dare un esempio; **be an** ∼ **to somebody** dare il buon esempio a qualcuno

exasperate /ɪg'zæspəreɪt/ *vt* esasperare

exasperation /ɪgzæspə'reɪʃn/ *n* esasperazione *f*

excavate /'ekskəveɪt/ *vt* scavare; Archaeol fare gli scavi di

excavation /ekskə'veɪʃn/ *n* scavo *m*

excavator /'ekskəveɪtə(r)/ *n* (machine) escavatrice *f*, escavatore *m*

exceed /ɪk'siːd/ *vt* eccedere

exceedingly /ɪk'siːdɪŋlɪ/ *adv* estremamente

excel /ɪk'sel/ ① *v* (pt/pp **excelled**) *vi* eccellere
② *vt* ∼ **oneself** superare se stessi

excellence /'eksələns/ *n* eccellenza *f*

Excellency /'eksələnsɪ/ *n* (title) Eccellenza *f*

excellent /'eksələnt/ *adj* eccellente

excellently /'eksələntlɪ/ *adv* in modo eccellente

except /ɪk'sept/ ① *prep* eccetto, tranne; ∼ **for** eccetto, tranne; ∼ **that...** eccetto che...
② *vt* eccettuare

excepting /ɪk'septɪŋ/ *prep* eccetto, tranne

exception /ɪk'sepʃn/ *n* eccezione *f*; **take** ∼ **to** fare obiezioni a

exceptional /ɪk'sepʃənəl/ *adj* eccezionale

exceptionally /ɪk'sepʃənəlɪ/ *adv* eccezionalmente

excerpt /'eksɜːpt/ *n* estratto *m*

excess /ɪk'ses/ *n* eccesso *m*; **in** ∼ **of** oltre

excess baggage *n* bagaglio *m* eccedente

excess fare *n* supplemento *m*

excessive /ɪk'sesɪv/ *adj* eccessivo

excessively /ɪk'sesɪvlɪ/ *adv* eccessivamente

excess postage *n* soprattassa *f* postale

excess profits *npl* sovraprofitto *m*

exchange /ɪks'tʃeɪndʒ/ **①** *n* scambio *m*; Teleph centrale *f*; Comm cambio *m*; [stock] ∼ borsa *f* valori; **in** ∼ in cambio (**for** di) **②** *vt* scambiare (**for** con): cambiare ⟨*money*⟩; ∼ **views** scambiarsi i punti di vista; ∼ **contracts** fare il rogito **③** *vi* (on house purchase) fare il rogito

exchange control *n* controllo *m* dei cambi

exchange controls *npl* misure *fpl* di controllo dei cambi

exchange rate *n* tasso *m* di cambio

Exchange Rate Mechanism *n* meccanismo *m* di cambio dello Sme

exchequer /ɪks'tʃekə(r)/ *n* Pol tesoro *m*

excise¹ /'eksaɪz/ *n* dazio *m*

excise² /ek'saɪz/ *vt* recidere

excise duty *n* dazio *m*

excitable /ɪk'saɪtəbl/ *adj* eccitabile

excite /ɪk'saɪt/ *vt* eccitare

excited /ɪk'saɪtɪd/ *adj* eccitato; **get** ∼ eccitarsi

excitedly /ɪk'saɪtɪdlɪ/ *adv* tutto eccitato

excitement /ɪk'saɪtmənt/ *n* eccitazione *f*

exciting /ɪk'saɪtɪŋ/ *adj* eccitante; ⟨*story, film*⟩ appassionante; ⟨*holiday*⟩ entusiasmante

excl *abbr* **excluding**

exclaim /ɪk'skleɪm/ *vt/i* esclamare

exclamation /eksklə'meɪʃn/ *n* esclamazione *f*

exclamation mark *n*, Am **exclamation point** *n* punto *m* esclamativo

exclude /ɪk'sklu:d/ *vt* escludere

excluding /ɪk'sklu:dɪŋ/ *pron* escluso

exclusion /ɪk'sklu:ʒn/ *n* esclusione *f*

exclusion zone *n* zona *f* proibita

exclusive /ɪk'sklu:sɪv/ *adj* ⟨*rights, club*⟩ esclusivo; ⟨*interview*⟩ in esclusiva; ∼ **of...** ...escluso

exclusively /ɪk'sklu:sɪvlɪ/ *adv* esclusivamente

excommunicate /ekskə'mjun:nɪkeɪt/ *vt* scomunicare

excrement /'ekskrɪmənt/ *n* escremento *m*

excreta /ɪk'skri:tə/ *npl* escrementi *mpl*

excrete /ɪk'skri:t/ *vt* espellere; secernere ⟨*liquid*⟩

excretion /ɪk'skri:ʃn/ *n* (of animal, human) escremento *m*

excruciating /ɪk'skru:ʃɪeɪtɪŋ/ *adj* atroce ⟨*pain*⟩; (fam: very bad) spaventoso

excursion /ɪk'skɜ:ʃn/ *n* escursione *f*

excusable /ɪk'skju:zəbl/ *adj* perdonabile

excuse¹ /ɪk'skju:s/ *n* scusa *f*

excuse² /ɪk'skju:z/ *vt* scusare; ∼ **from** esonerare da; ∼ **me!** (to get attention) scusi!; (to get past) permesso!, scusi!; (indignant) come ha detto?

ex-directory *adj* **be** ∼ non figurare sull'elenco telefonico

exec /ɪg'zek/ *n* Am *abbrev* fam **executive**

execrable /'eksɪkrəbl/ *adj* esecrabile

executable file /'eksɪkju:təbl/ *n* Comput eseguibile *m*

execute /'eksɪkju:t/ *vt* eseguire; (put to death) giustiziare; attuare ⟨*plan*⟩

execution /eksɪ'kju:ʃn/ *n* esecuzione *f*; (of plan) attuazione *f*

executioner /eksɪ'kju:ʃənə(r)/ *n* boia *m inv*

executive /ɪg'zekjʊtɪv/ **①** *adj* esecutivo **②** *n* dirigente *mf*; Pol esecutivo *m*

executive committee *n* comitato *m* esecutivo

executive director *n* direttore, -trice *mf* [esecutivo, -a]

executive jet *n* jet *m inv* privato

executive producer *n* Cinema direttore, -trice *mf* di produzione

executive secretary *n* segretario, -a *mf* di direzione

executor /ɪg'zekjʊtə(r)/ *n* Jur esecutore, -trice *mf*

exemplary /ɪg'zemplərɪ/ *adj* esemplare

exemplify /ɪg'zemplɪfaɪ/ *vt* (pt/pp **-ied**) esemplificare

exempt /ɪg'zempt/ **①** *adj* esente **②** *vt* esentare (**from** da)

exemption /ɪg'zempʃn/ *n* esenzione *f*

exercise /'eksəsaɪz/ **①** *n* esercizio *m*; Mil esercitazione *f*; **physical** ∼**s** ginnastica *f*; **take** ∼ fare del moto; **you need more** ∼ devi muoverti di più **②** *vt* esercitare ⟨*muscles, horse*⟩; portare a spasso ⟨*dog*⟩; usare ⟨*patience*⟩; mettere in pratica ⟨*skills*⟩ **③** *vi* esercitarsi; ∼ **more** fare più moto

exercise bike *n* cyclette® *f inv*

exercise book *n* quaderno *m*

exert /ɪg'zɜ:t/ *vt* esercitare; ∼ **oneself** sforzarsi

exertion /ɪg'zɜ:ʃn/ *n* sforzo *m*

ex gratia /eks'greɪʃə/ *adj* ⟨*award, payment*⟩ a titolo di favore

exhale /eks'heɪl/ *vt/i* esalare

exhaust /ɪg'zɔ:st/ *n* Auto scappamento *m*; (pipe) tubo *m* di scappamento

exhausted /ɪg'zɔ:stɪd/ *adj* esausto

exhaust fumes **①** *npl* fumi *mpl* di scarico *m* **②** *vt* esaurire

exhausting /ɪgˈzɔːstɪŋ/ adj estenuante; ⟨climate, person⟩ sfibrante

exhaustion /ɪgˈzɔːstʃn/ n esaurimento m

exhaustive /ɪgˈzɔːstɪv/ adj fig esauriente

exhibit /ɪgˈzɪbɪt/ ① n oggetto m esposto; Jur reperto m
② vt esporre; fig dimostrare

exhibition /eksɪˈbɪʃn/ n mostra f; (of strength, skill) dimostrazione f

exhibition centre n palazzo m delle esposizioni

exhibitionist /eksɪˈbɪʃənɪst/ n esibizionista mf

exhibitor /ɪgˈzɪbɪtə(r)/ n espositore, -trice mf

exhilarated /ɪgˈzɪləreɪtɪd/ adj rallegrato

exhilarating /ɪgˈzɪləreɪtɪŋ/ adj stimolante; ⟨mountain air⟩ tonificante

exhilaration /ɪgzɪləˈreɪʃn/ n allegria f

exhort /ɪgˈzɔːt/ vt esortare

exhume /ɪgˈzjuːm/ vt esumare

exile /ˈeksaɪl/ ① n esilio m; (person) esule mf
② vt esiliare

exist /ɪgˈzɪst/ vi esistere

existence /ɪgˈzɪstəns/ n esistenza f; in ~ esistente; be in ~ esistere

existential /egzɪˈstenʃ(ə)l/ adj esistenziale

existentialism /egzɪˈstenʃəlɪzm/ n esistenzialismo m

existing /ɪgˈzɪstɪŋ/ adj ⟨policy, management, leadership⟩ attuale; ⟨laws, order⟩ vigente

exit /ˈeksɪt/ ① n uscita f; Theat uscita f di scena
② vi Theat uscire di scena; Comput uscire (from da)

exit sign n cartello m di uscita

exodus /ˈeksədəs/ n esodo m

ex officio /eksəˈfɪʃɪəʊ/ adj ⟨member⟩ di diritto

exonerate /ɪgˈzɒnəreɪt/ vt esonerare

exorbitant /ɪgˈzɔːbɪtənt/ adj esorbitante

exorcism /ˈeksɔːsɪzm/ n esorcismo m

exorcist /ˈeksɔːsɪst/ n esorcista mf

exorcize /ˈeksɔːsaɪz/ vt esorcizzare

exotic /ɪgˈzɒtɪk/ adj esotico

exotica /ɪgˈzɒtɪkə/ npl oggetti mpl esotici

expand /ɪkˈspænd/ ① vt espandere; sviluppare ⟨economy⟩
② vi espandersi; Comm svilupparsi; ⟨metal⟩ dilatarsi
■ **expand on** vt (explain better) approfondire

expandable /ɪkˈspændəbl/ adj Comput ⟨memory⟩ espandibile

expanding /ɪkˈspændɪŋ/ adj ⟨file⟩ a soffietto inv; ⟨population, sector⟩ in espansione; ⟨bracelet⟩ allungabile

expanse /ɪkˈspæns/ n estensione f

expansion /ɪkˈspænʃn/ n espansione f; Comm sviluppo m; (of metal) dilatazione f

expansion board, **expansion card** n Comput scheda f di espansione

expansionist /ɪkˈspænʃənɪst/ n & a espansionista mf

expansion slot n Comput fessura f [per la scheda] di espansione, slot m di espansione

expansive /ɪkˈspænsɪv/ adj espansivo

expatriate /eksˈpætrɪət/ n espatriato, -a mf

expect /ɪkˈspekt/ vt aspettare ⟨letter, baby⟩; (suppose) pensare; (demand) esigere; I ~ so penso di sì; we ~ to arrive on Monday contiamo di arrivare lunedì; I didn't ~ that questo non me lo aspettavo; she ~s too much from him pretende troppo da lui; be ~ing essere in stato interessante

expectancy /ɪkˈspektənsɪ/ n aspettativa f

expectant /ɪkˈspektənt/ adj in attesa; ~ mother donna f incinta

expectantly /ɪkˈspektəntlɪ/ adv con impazienza

expectation /ekspekˈteɪʃn/ n aspettativa f, speranza f

expediency /ɪkˈspiːdɪənsɪ/ n (appropriateness) opportunità f; (self-interest) opportunismo m

expedient /ɪkˈspiːdɪənt/ ① adj conveniente
② n espediente m

expedite /ˈekspɪdaɪt/ vt fml accelerare

expedition /eksprɪˈdɪʃn/ n spedizione f

expeditionary /ekspɪˈdɪʃənərɪ/ adj Mil di spedizione

expeditionary force n corpo m di spedizione

expel /ɪkˈspel/ vt (pt/pp **expelled**) espellere

expend /ɪkˈspend/ vt consumare

expendable /ɪkˈspendəbl/ adj sacrificabile

expenditure /ɪkˈspendɪtʃə(r)/ n spesa f

expense /ɪkˈspens/ n spesa f; business ~s pl spese fpl; at my ~ a mie spese; at the ~ of fig a spese di

expense account n conto m spese

expensive /ɪkˈspensɪv/ adj caro, costoso

expensively /ɪkˈspensɪvlɪ/ adv costosamente

experience /ɪkˈspɪərɪəns/ ① n esperienza f
② vt provare ⟨sensation⟩; avere ⟨problem⟩

experienced /ɪkˈspɪərɪənst/ adj esperto

experiment /ɪk'sperɪmənt/ **1** n esperimento
2 /ɪk'sperɪment/ vi sperimentare

experimental /ɪksperɪ'mentl/ adj sperimentale

experimentation /ɪksperɪmen'teɪʃn/ n sperimentazione f; ~ **with drugs** esperienza f della droga

expert /'eksps:t/ adj & n esperto, -a mf

expertise /eksps:'ti:z/ n competenza f

expertly /'eksps:tlɪ/ adv abilmente

expiate /'ekspɪeɪt/ vt espiare ⟨crime, sin⟩; fare ammenda per ⟨guilt⟩

expiration /ekspɪ'reɪʃn/ n (end, exhalation) espirazione f

expire /ɪk'spaɪə(r)/ vi scadere

expiry /ɪk'spaɪərɪ/ n scadenza f

expiry date n data f di scadenza

explain /ɪk'spleɪn/ vt spiegare
■ **explain away** vt (give reasons for) trovare delle giustificazioni per

explanation /eksplə'neɪʃn/ n spiegazione f

explanatory /ɪk'splænətərɪ/ adj esplicativo

expletive /ɪk'spli:tɪv/ n imprecazione f

explicit /ɪk'splɪsɪt/ adj esplicito

explicitly /ɪk'splɪsɪtlɪ/ adv esplicitamente

explode /ɪk'spləʊd/ **1** vi esplodere
2 vt fare esplodere

exploit[1] /'eksplɔɪt/ n impresa f

exploit[2] /ɪk'splɔɪt/ vt sfruttare

exploitation /eksplɔɪ'teɪʃn/ n sfruttamento m

exploitative /ɪk'splɔɪtətɪv/ adj inteso a sfruttare gli individui; ⟨attitude, system⟩ a carattere di sfruttamento

exploration /eksplə'reɪʃn/ n esplorazione f

exploratory /ɪk'splɒrətərɪ/ adj esplorativo

explore /ɪk'splɔ:(r)/ vt esplorare; fig studiare ⟨implications⟩

explorer /ɪk'splɔ:rə(r)/ n esploratore, -trice mf

explosion /ɪk'spləʊʒn/ n esplosione f

explosive /ɪk'spləʊsɪv/ adj & n esplosivo m

exponent /ɪk'spəʊnənt/ n esponente mf

exponential /ekspə'nenʃəl/ adj esponenziale

export[1] /'ekspɔ:t/ n esportazione f

export[2] /ek'spɔ:t/ vt esportare

export agent n esportatore, -trice mf

export control n controllo m delle esportazioni

export credit n credito m all'esportazione

export drive n campagna f di esportazione

export duty n tassa f di esportazione

export earnings npl ricavato m delle esportazioni

exporter /ek'spɔ:tə(r)/ n esportatore, -trice mf

export finance n finanziamento m delle esportazioni

export-import company n azienda di import-export

export licence n licenza f di esportazione

export market n mercato m delle esportazioni

export trade n commercio m di esportazione

expose /ɪk'spəʊz/ vt esporre; ⟨reveal⟩ svelare; smascherare ⟨traitor etc⟩

exposée /ɪk'spəʊzeɪ/ n (of scandal) rivelazioni fpl

exposition /ekspə'zɪʃn/ n (of facts) esposizione f

exposure /ɪk'spəʊʒə(r)/ n esposizione f; Med esposizione f prolungata al freddo/caldo; (of crimes) smascheramento m; **24 ~s** Phot 24 pose

exposure meter n Phot esposimetro m

exposure time n Phot tempo m di esposizione

expound /ɪk'spaʊnd/ vt esporre

express /ɪk'spres/ **1** adj espresso
2 adv ⟨send⟩ per espresso
3 n (train) espresso m
4 vt esprimere; ~ **oneself** esprimersi

expression /ɪk'spreʃn/ n espressione f

expressionless /ɪk'spreʃənlɪs/ adj ⟨tone, voice⟩ distaccato; ⟨playing⟩ piatto; ⟨eyes, face⟩ inespressivo

expressive /ɪk'spresɪv/ adj espressivo

expressively /ɪk'spresɪvlɪ/ adv espressamente

expulsion /ɪk'spʌlʃn/ n espulsione f

expurgate /'ekspəgeɪt/ vt espurgare

exquisite /ek'skwɪzɪt/ adj squisito

exquisitely /ek'skwɪzɪtlɪ/ adv ⟨dressed, written⟩ in modo elegante e raffinato; ~ **beautiful** di una bellezza fine

ex-serviceman /'sɜ:vɪsmən/ n ex-combattente m

ex-servicewoman /'sɜ:vɪswʊmən/ n ex-combattente f

extant /ɪk'stænt/ adj ancora esistente

extempore /ɪk'stempərɪ/ adv ⟨speak⟩ senza preparazione

extend /ɪk'stend/ **1** vt prolungare ⟨visit, road⟩; prorogare ⟨visa, contract⟩; ampliare ⟨building, knowledge⟩; (stretch out) allungare; tendere ⟨hand⟩
2 vi ⟨garden, knowledge⟩ estendersi

extendable /ɪk'stendəbl/ adj ⟨cable⟩ allungabile; ⟨contract⟩ prorogabile

extension /ɪk'stenʃn/ n prolungamento m; (of visa, contract) proroga f; (of treaty) ampliamento m; (part of building) annesso m; (length of cable) prolunga f; Teleph interno m; ~ **226** interno 226; (hair) ~s le extension

extension ladder n scala f allungabile

extension lead n Electr prolunga f

extensive /ɪk'stensɪv/ adj ampio, vasto

extensively /ɪk'stensɪvlɪ/ adv ampiamente

extent /ɪk'stent/ n (scope) portata f; **to a certain** ~ fino a un certo punto; **to such an** ~ **that...** fino al punto che...

extenuating /ɪk'stenjʊeɪtɪŋ/ adj ~ **circumstances** attenuanti fpl

exterior /ɪk'stɪərɪə(r)/ adj & n esterno m

exterminate /ɪk'stɜ:mmeɪt/ vt sterminare

extermination /ɪkstɜ:mɪ'neɪʃn/ n sterminio m

external /ɪk'stɜ:nl/ adj esterno; **for** ~ **use only** Med per uso esterno

externalize /ɪk'stɜ:nəlaɪz/ vt esteriorizzare

externally /ɪk'stɜ:nəlɪ/ adv esternamente

externals /ɪk'stɜ:n(ə)lz/ npl apparenze fpl

extinct /ɪk'stɪŋkt/ adj estinto

extinction /ɪk'stɪŋkʃn/ n estinzione f

extinguish /ɪk'stɪŋgwɪʃ/ vt estinguere

extinguisher /ɪk'stɪŋgwɪʃə(r)/ n estintore m

extol /ɪk'stəʊl/ vt (pt/pp **extolled**) lodare

extort /ɪk'stɔ:t/ vt estorcere

extortion /ɪk'stɔ:ʃn/ n estorsione f

extortionate /ɪk'stɔ:ʃənət/ adj esorbitante

extra /'ekstrə/ ① adj in più; ⟨train⟩ straordinario; **an** ~ **£10** 10 sterline extra, 10 sterline in più
② adv in più; (especially) più; **pay** ~ pagare in più, pagare extra; ~ **strong**/ **busy** fortissimo/occupatissimo
③ n Theat comparsa f; ~s pl extra mpl

extra charge n supplemento m; **at no** ~ ~ senza ulteriori spese

extract[1] /'ekstrækt/ n estratto m

extract[2] /ɪk'strækt/ vt estrarre ⟨tooth, oil⟩; strappare ⟨secret⟩; ricavare ⟨truth⟩

extraction /ɪk'strækʃn/ n (process) estrazione f; **of French** ~ di origine francese

extractor [fan] /ɪk'stræktə(r)/ n aspiratore m

extra-curricular /-kə'rɪkjʊlə(r)/ adj extrascolastico

extradite /'ekstrədaɪt/ vt Jur estradare

extradition /ekstrə'dɪʃn/ n estradizione f

extra-dry adj ⟨sherry, wine⟩ extra dry inv

extra-fast adj ultrarapido

extra-large adj ⟨pullover, shirt⟩ extra large inv

extramarital /ekstrə'mærɪtəl/ adj extraconiugale

extramural /ekstrə'mjʊərəl/ adj Br Univ ⟨course, lecture⟩ organizzato dall'università e aperto a tutti

extraneous /ɪk'streɪnɪəs/ adj (not essential) inessenziale; ⟨issue, detail⟩ superfluo

extraordinarily /ɪk'strɔ:dɪnərɪlɪ/ adv straordinariamente

extraordinary /ɪk'strɔ:dɪnərɪ/ adj straordinario

extrapolate /ɪk'stræpəleɪt/ vt arguire; Math estrapolare

extrasensory perception /ekstrə'sensərɪ/ n percezione f extrasensoriale

extra-special adj eccezionale

extra-strong adj ⟨thread⟩ robustissimo; ⟨coffee⟩ fortissimo; ⟨disinfectant, weed killer⟩ potentissimo; ⟨paper⟩ ultraresistente inv

extraterrestrial /ekstrətɪ'restrɪəl/ n & adj extraterrestre mf

extra time n tempo m supplementare; **play** ~ giocare i tempi supplementari

extravagance /ɪk'strævəgəns/ n (with money) prodigalità f; (of behaviour) stravaganza f

extravagant /ɪk'strævəgənt/ adj spendaccione; (bizarre) stravagante; ⟨claim⟩ esagerato

extravagantly /ɪk'strævəgəntlɪ/ adv dispendiosamente

extravaganza /ɪkstrævə'gænzə/ n rappresentazione f spettacolare

extra virgin olive oil n olio m extravergine d'oliva

extreme /ɪk'stri:m/ ① adj estremo ② n estremo m; **in the** ~ al massimo

extremely /ɪk'stri:mlɪ/ adv estremamente

extreme sports npl sport mpl estremi

extremism /ɪk'stri:mɪzm/ n estremismo m

extremist /ɪk'stri:mɪst/ n estremista mf

extremity /ɪk'stremətɪ/ n (end) estremità f inv

extricate /'ekstrɪkeɪt/ vt districare

extrovert /'ekstrəvɜ:t/ n estroverso, -a mf

exuberance /ɪg'zju:bərəns/ n esuberanza f

exuberant /ɪgˈzju:bərənt/ *adj* esuberante

exude /ɪgˈzju:d/ *vt* also fig trasudare

exult /ɪgˈzʌlt/ *vi* esultare

exultant /ɪgˈzʌltənt/ *adj* esultante; ⟨cry⟩ di esultanza

exultantly /ɪgˈzʌltəntlɪ/ *adv* con esultanza

ex-works *adj* ⟨price, value⟩ franco fabbrica

eye /aɪ/ ① *n* occhio *m*; (of needle) cruna *f*; **keep an ∼ on** tener d'occhio; **see ∼ to ∼** aver le stesse idee
② *vt* (pt/pp **eyed**, pres p **ey[e]ing**) guardare
■ **eye up** *vt* adocchiare ⟨somebody⟩

eyeball *n* bulbo *m* oculare

eyebath *n* bagno *m* oculare

eyebrow *n* sopracciglio *m* (pl sopracciglia *f*)

eyebrow pencil *n* matita *f* per le sopracciglia

eye-catching /ˈaɪkætʃɪŋ/ *adj* che attira l'attenzione

eye contact *n* **avoid ∼ ∼ with somebody** evitare di incrociare lo sguardo di qualcuno; **try to make ∼ ∼ with somebody** tentare di incrociare lo sguardo di qualcuno

eyedrops *n pl* collirio *m*

eyeful /ˈaɪfʊl/ *n* **get an ∼** (of something) avere gli occhi pieni (di qualcosa); (fam: good look) lustrarsi la vista

eyeglass *n* (monocle) monocolo *m*

eyeglasses *n pl* Am occhiali *mpl* [da vista]

eyelash *n* ciglio *m* (pl ciglia *f*)

eyelet /ˈaɪlɪt/ *n* occhiello *m*

eye-level *adj* ⟨grill, shelf⟩ all'altezza degli occhi

eyelid *n* palpebra *f*

eye liner *n* eye liner *m inv*

eye make-up *n* trucco *m* per gli occhi

eye-opener *n* rivelazione *f*

eyepatch *n* benda *f* per gli occhi

eye-shade *n* visiera *f*

eyeshadow *n* ombretto *m*

eyesight *n* vista *f*

eyesore *n fam* pugno *m* nell'occhio

eye strain *n* affaticamento *m* degli occhi

eye test *n* esame *m* della vista

eyewash *n* bagno *m* oculare; (fig: nonsense) fumo *m* negli occhi

eyewitness *n* testimone *mf* oculare

eyrie /ˈɪərɪ/ *n* nido *m* d'aquila

e-zine /ˈiːziːn/ *n* Comput e-zine *f inv*

Ff

F¹ *abbr* (**Fahrenheit**) F

f², **F** /ef/ *n* (letter) f, F *f inv*; Mus fa *m inv*

FA *n* Br abbr (**Football Association**) associazione *f* calcistica britannica, ≈ FIGC *f*

façade /fəˈsɑːd/ *n* (of building, person) facciata *f*

fable /ˈfeɪbl/ *n* favola *f*

fabric /ˈfæbrɪk/ *n* also fig tessuto *m*

fabricate /ˈfæbrɪkeɪt/ *vt* fabbricare; inventare ⟨story⟩

fabrication /fæbrɪkeɪʃn/ *n* invenzione *f*; (manufacture) fabbricazione *f*

fabric softener /sɒfnə(r)/ *n* ammorbidente *m*

fabulous /ˈfæbjʊləs/ *adj fam* favoloso

face /feɪs/ ① *n* faccia *f*, viso *m*; (grimace) smorfia *f*; (surface) faccia *f*; (of clock) quadrante *m*; **pull ∼s** far boccacce; **in the ∼ of** di fronte a; **on the ∼ of it** in apparenza
② *vt* essere di fronte a; (confront) affrontare; **∼ north** ⟨house⟩ dare a nord; **∼ the fact that** arrendersi al fatto che
■ **face up to** *vt* accettare ⟨facts⟩; affrontare ⟨person⟩

face flannel *n* ≈ guanto *m* di spugna

faceless /ˈfeɪslɪs/ *adj* anonimo

facelift /ˈfeɪslɪft/ *n* plastica *f* facciale

face pack *n* maschera *f* di bellezza

face powder *n* cipria *f*

face saving *adj* ⟨plan, solution⟩ per salvare la faccia

facet /ˈfæsɪt/ *n* sfaccettatura *f*; fig aspetto *m*

facetious /fəˈsiːʃəs/ *adj* spiritoso. **∼ remarks** spiritosaggini *mpl*

face to face ① *adj* ⟨meeting⟩ a quattr'occhi
② *adv* ⟨be seated⟩ faccia a faccia; **meet somebody ∼ ∼ ∼** avere un incontro a quattr'occhi con qualcuno; **come ∼ ∼ ∼ with** trovarsi di fronte a

face value n (of money) valore m nominale; **take someone/something at ~** ~ fermarsi alle apparenze

facial /'feɪʃl/ **1** adj facciale **2** n trattamento m di bellezza al viso

facile /'fæsaɪl/ adj semplicistico

facilitate /fə'sɪlɪteɪt/ vt rendere possibile; (make easier) facilitare

facilitator /fə'sɪlɪteɪtə(r)/ n mediatore m

facility /fə'sɪlətɪ/ n facilità f; **facilities** pl (of area, in hotel etc) attrezzature fpl; **credit facilities** pl facilitazioni fpl di pagamento

facing /'feɪsɪŋ/ prep **~ the sea** ⟨house⟩ che dà sul mare; **the person ~ me** la persona di fronte a me

facsimile /fæk'sɪməlɪ/ n facsimile m

fact /fækt/ n fatto m; **in ~** infatti

fact finding adj ⟨mission⟩ di inchiesta

faction /'fækʃn/ n fazione f

factional /'fækʃnəl/ adj ⟨leader, activity⟩ di una fazione; ⟨fighting⟩ tra fazioni

factor /'fæktə(r)/ n fattore m

factory /'fæktərɪ/ n fabbrica f

factory farming n allevamento m su scala industriale

factory floor n (place) reparto m produzione; (workers) operai mpl

factory inspector n verificatore, -trice mf

factory made adj prodotto in fabbrica

factory shop n negozio m di vendita diretta dalla fabbrica al consumatore

factory unit n unità f inv di produzione

factory worker n operaio, -a mf

fact sheet n (one issue) prospetto m illustrativo; (periodical) bollettino m d'informazione

factual /'fæktʃʊəl/ adj **be ~** attenersi ai fatti

factually /'fæktʃʊəlɪ/ adv ⟨inaccurate⟩ dal punto di vista dei fatti

faculty /'fækəltɪ/ n facoltà f inv

fad /fæd/ n capriccio m

faddish /'fædɪʃ/ adj ⟨person⟩ sempre in preda a una nuova mania

fade /feɪd/ vi sbiadire; ⟨sound, light⟩ affievolirsi; ⟨flower⟩ appassire
▪ **fade away** vi ⟨sound⟩ affievolirsi; (dying person) spegnersi
▪ **fade in** vt cominciare in dissolvenza ⟨picture⟩
▪ **fade out** vt finire in dissolvenza ⟨picture⟩

faded /'feɪdɪd/ adj ⟨clothing, carpet, colour⟩ sbiadito; ⟨flower, beauty⟩ appassito; ⟨glory⟩ svanito

faeces /'fi:si:z/ npl feci fpl

fag /fæg/ n (chore) fatica f; (fam: cigarette) sigaretta f; (Am sl: homosexual) frocio m

fag end n fam mozzicone m di sigaretta, cicca f; (of day, decade, conversation) fine f; (of material) scampolo m

fagged /fægd/ adj **~ out** fam stanco morto

faggot /'fægət/ n (meatball) polpetta f di carne; (firewood) fascina f

Fahrenheit /'færənhaɪt/ adj Fahrenheit

fail /feɪl/ **1** n **without ~** senz'altro **2** vi ⟨attempt⟩ fallire; ⟨eyesight, memory⟩ indebolirsi; ⟨engine, machine⟩ guastarsi; ⟨marriage⟩ andare a rotoli; (in exam) essere bocciato; **~ to do something** non fare qualcosa; **I tried but I ~ed** ho provato ma non ci sono riuscito; **a ~ed politician** un politico fallito **3** vt non superare ⟨exam⟩; bocciare ⟨candidate⟩; (disappoint) deludere; **words ~ me** mi mancano le parole; **unless my memory ~s me** se la memoria non mi tradisce

failing /'feɪlɪŋ/ **1** n difetto m **2** prep **~ that** altrimenti

fail-safe adj ⟨device, system⟩ di sicurezza

failure /'feɪljə(r)/ n fallimento m; (mechanical) guasto m; (person) incapace mf

faint /feɪnt/ **1** adj leggero; ⟨memory⟩ vago; **feel ~** sentirsi mancare **2** n svenimento m **3** vi svenire

faint-hearted /-'hɑːtɪd/ adj timido

fainting fit /'feɪntɪŋ/ n svenimento m

faintly /'feɪntlɪ/ adv (slightly) leggermente

faintness /'feɪntnɪs/ n (physical) debolezza f

fair[1] /feə(r)/ n fiera f

fair[2] **1** adj ⟨hair, person⟩ biondo; ⟨skin⟩ chiaro; ⟨weather⟩ bello; (just) giusto; (quite good) discreto; Sch abbastanza bene; **a ~ amount** abbastanza **2** adv **play ~** fare un gioco pulito

fair copy n bella copia f

fairground /'feəgraʊnd/ n luna park m inv

fair-haired adj dai capelli chiari

fairly /'feəlɪ/ adv con giustizia; (rather) discretamente, abbastanza

fair-minded /feə'maɪndɪd/ adj equo

fairness /'feənɪs/ n giustizia f

fair play n fair play m inv

fair skinned /-'skɪnd/ adj di carnagione chiara

fair trade n commercio m equo e solidale, commercio m equosolidale

fairway n Naut via f d'acqua navigabile; (in golf) fairway m inv

fair weather friend n pej amico m finché tutto va bene

fairy /'feərɪ/ n fata f; **good ~** fata [buona]; **wicked ~** strega f

fairy godmother n fata f buona

fairy lights *npl* Br lampadine *fpl* colorate

fairy story, fairy-tale *n* fiaba *f*

faith /feɪθ/ *n* fede *f*; (trust) fiducia *f*; **in good/bad ∼** in buona/mala fede

faithful /'feɪθfl/ *adj* fedele

faithfully /'feɪθfʊlɪ/ *adv* fedelmente; **yours ∼** distinti saluti

faithfulness /'feɪθfʊlnɪs/ *n* fedeltà *f*

faith-healer /-hiːlə(r)/ *n* guaritore, -trice *mf*

faith healing /-hiːlɪŋ/ *n* guarigione *f* per fede

faithless /'feɪθlɪs/ *adj* ⟨friend, servant⟩ sleale; ⟨husband⟩ infedele

fake /feɪk/ **1** *adj* falso ▸ **2** *n* falsificazione *f*; (person) impostore *m* ▸ **3** *vt* falsificare; (pretend) fingere

falcon /'fɔːlkən/ *n* falcone *m*

Falklands /'fɔːlkləndz/ *npl* le isole Falkland, le isole Malvine

fall /fɔːl/ **1** *n* caduta *f*; (in prices) ribasso *m*; (Am: autumn) autunno *m*; **have a ∼** fare una caduta ▸ **2** *vi* (pt **fell**, pp **fallen**) cadere; ⟨night⟩ scendere; **∼ in love** innamorarsi
■ **fall about** *vi* (with laughter) morire dal ridere
■ **fall apart** *vi* ⟨table, car, house⟩ cadere a pezzi; ⟨shoes⟩ rompersi; fig ⟨person⟩ crollare
■ **fall back** *vi* indietreggiare; ⟨army⟩ ritirarsi
■ **fall back on** *vt* ritornare su
■ **fall behind** *vi* rimanere indietro; **∼ behind with** Br or **in** Am essere indietro con ⟨work, project, payments⟩
■ **fall down** *vi* cadere; ⟨building⟩ crollare
■ **fall for** *vt* fam innamorarsi di ⟨person⟩; cascarci ⟨something, trick⟩
■ **fall in** *vi* caderci dentro; (collapse) crollare; Mil mettersi in riga; **∼ in with** concordare con ⟨suggestion, plan⟩
■ **fall off** *vi* cadere; (diminish) diminuire
■ **fall open** *vi* ⟨book⟩ aprirsi (cadendo); ⟨robe⟩ aprirsi
■ **fall out** *vi* (quarrel) litigare; **his hair is ∼ing out** perde i capelli
■ **fall over** *vi* cadere
■ **fall through** *vi* ⟨plan⟩ andare a monte

fallacious /fə'leɪʃəs/ *adj* fallace

fallacy /'fæləsɪ/ *n* errore *m*

fallible /'fæləbl/ *adj* fallibile

Fallopian tube /fə'ləʊpɪən/ *n* tromba *f* di Falloppio

fallout /'fɔːlaʊt/ *n* pioggia *f* radioattiva

fallout shelter *n* rifugio *m* antiatomico

fallow /'fæləʊ/ *adj* **lie ∼** essere a maggese

false /fɔːls/ *adj* falso

false alarm *n* falso allarme *m*

false bottom *n* doppio fondo *m*

falsehood /'fɔːlshʊd/ *n* menzogna *f*

falsely /'fɔːlslɪ/ *adv* falsamente

falseness /'fɔːlsnɪs/ *n* falsità *f*

false pretences *npl* **under ∼ ∼** sotto false spoglie; Jur con la frode

false start *n* Sport falsa partenza *f*

false teeth *npl* dentiera *f*

falsetto /fɔːl'setəʊ/ **1** *n* (voice) falsetto *m* *inv* ▸ **2** *adj* in falsetto

falsification /fɔːlsɪfɪ'keɪʃn/ *n* (of document, figures) falsificazione *f*; (of truth, facts) deformazione *f*

falsify /'fɔːlsɪfaɪ/ *vt* (pt/pp **-ied**) falsificare

falsity /'fɔːlsətɪ/ *n* falsità *f*

falter /'fɔːltə(r)/ *vi* vacillare; (making speech) esitare

faltering /'fɔːltərɪŋ/ *adj* ⟨economy⟩ vacillante; ⟨voice⟩ esitante

fame /feɪm/ *n* fama *f*

famed /feɪmd/ *adj* rinomato

familiar /fə'mɪljə(r)/ *adj* familiare; **be ∼ with** (know) conoscere; **become too ∼** prendersi troppe confidenze

familiarity /fəmɪlɪ'ærətɪ/ *n* familiarità *f*

familiarize /fə'mɪlɪəraɪz/ *vt* familiarizzare; **∼ oneself with something** familiarizzarsi con qualcosa

family /'fæməlɪ/ *n* famiglia *f*

family allowance *n* assegni *mpl* familiari

family circle *n* (group) cerchia *f* familiare; Am Theat seconda galleria *f*

family doctor *n* medico *m* di famiglia

family life *n* vita *f* familiare

family name *n* cognome *m*

family planning *n* pianificazione *f* familiare

family tree *n* albero *m* genealogico

family unit *n* nucleo *m* familiare

famine /'fæmɪn/ *n* carestia *f*

famished /'fæmɪʃt/ *adj* **be ∼** fam avere una fame da lupo

famous /'feɪməs/ *adj* famoso

fan¹ /fæn/ **1** *n* ventilatore *m*; (handheld) ventaglio *m* ▸ **2** *vt* (pt/pp **fanned**) far vento a; **∼ oneself** sventagliarsi; fig **∼ the flames** soffiare sul fuoco
■ **fan out** *vi* spiegarsi a ventaglio

fan² *n* (admirer) ammiratore, -trice *mf*, fan *mf*; Sport tifoso *m*; (of Verdi etc) appassionato, -a *mf*

fanatic /fə'nætɪk/ *n* fanatico, -a *mf*

fanatical /fə'nætɪkl/ *adj* fanatico

fanatically /fə'nætɪklɪ/ *adv* con fanatismo

fanaticism /fə'nætɪsɪzm/ n fanatismo m

fan belt n cinghia f per ventilatore

fanciful /'fænsɪfl/ adj fantasioso

fancy /'fænsɪ/ ① n fantasia f; **I've taken a real ~ to him** mi è molto simpatico; **as the ~ takes you** come ti pare
② adj fantasia inv
③ vt (believe) credere; (fam: want) aver voglia di; **he fancies you** fam gli piaci; **~ that!** ma guarda un po'!

fancy dress n costume m

fancy dress party n festa f mascherata

fanfare /'fænfeə(r)/ n fanfara f

fang /fæŋ/ n zanna f; (of snake) dente m

fan heater n termoventilatore m

fanlight n lunetta f

fan mail n posta f dei fan

fantasize /'fæntəsaɪz/ vi fantasticare

fantastic /fæn'tæstɪk/ adj fantastico

fantasy /'fæntəsɪ/ n fantasia f

fanzine /'fænziːn/ n fanzine f inv

FAQ abbr (**frequently asked questions**) FAQ fpl

far /fɑː(r)/ ① adv lontano; (much) molto; **by ~** di gran lunga; **~ away** lontano; **as ~ as the church** fino alla chiesa; **how ~ is it from here?** quanto dista da qui?; **as ~ as I know** per quanto io sappia
② adj ⟨end, side⟩ altro; **the F~ East** l'Estremo Oriente m; **in the ~ distance** in lontananza

faraway /'fɑːrəweɪ/ adj ⟨land⟩ lontano; ⟨look⟩ assente

farce /fɑːs/ n farsa f

farcical /'fɑːsɪkl/ adj ridicolo

fare /feə(r)/ n tariffa f; (food) vitto m

fare-dodger /-dɒdʒə(r)/ n passeggero, -a mf senza biglietto

farewell /feə'wel/ ① int liter addio!
② n addio m; **~ dinner** cena f d'addio

far-fetched /-'fetʃt/ adj improbabile

far flung /-'flʌŋ/ adj (remote) remoto; (widely distributed) sparpagliato; ⟨network⟩ esteso

farm /fɑːm/ ① n fattoria f, azienda f agricola
② vi fare l'agricoltore
③ vt coltivare ⟨land⟩
■ **farm out** vt dare in appalto ⟨work⟩

farmer /'fɑːmə(r)/ n agricoltore m

farmers' market n vendita f diretta dal produttore agricolo al consumatore

farmhand /'fɑːmhænd/ n bracciante m

farmhouse /'fɑːmhaʊs/ n casa f colonica

farming /'fɑːmɪŋ/ n agricoltura f

farm produce n prodotto m agricolo

farmyard /'fɑːmjɑːd/ n aia f

far-off adj lontano

far-reaching /-'riːtʃɪŋ/ adj ⟨programme, plan, proposal⟩ di larga portata; ⟨effect, implication, change⟩ notevole

far-sighted /-'saɪtɪd/ adj ⟨policy⟩ lungimirante; (Am: long-sighted) presbite

fart /fɑːt/ fam ① n scoreggia f
② vi scoreggiare

farther /'fɑːðə(r)/ ① adv più lontano
② adj **at the ~ end of** all'altra estremità di

farthest adj & adv = FURTHEST

fascia /'feɪʃɪə/ n Br (dashboard) cruscotto m; (for mobile phone) guscio m

fascinate /'fæsɪneɪt/ vt affascinare

fascinating /'fæsɪneɪtɪŋ/ adj affascinante

fascination /fæsɪ'neɪʃn/ n fascino m

fascism /'fæʃɪzm/ n fascismo m

fascist /'fæʃɪst/ adj & n fascista mf

fashion /'fæʃn/ ① n moda f; (manner) maniera f; **in ~** di moda; **out of ~** non più di moda
② vt modellare

fashionable /'fæʃ(ə)nəbl/ adj di moda; **be ~** essere alla moda

fashionably /'fæʃ(ə)nəblɪ/ adv alla moda

fashion designer n stilista mf

fashion house n casa f di moda

fashion model n indossatore, -trice mf, modello, -a mf

fashion show n sfilata f di moda

fast¹ /fɑːst/ ① adj veloce; ⟨colour⟩ indelebile; **be ~** ⟨clock⟩ andare avanti
② adv velocemente; (firmly) saldamente; **~er!** più in fretta!; **be ~ asleep** dormire profondamente

fast² ① n digiuno m
② vi digiunare

fasten /'fɑːsn/ ① vt allacciare; chiudere ⟨window⟩; (stop flapping) mettere un fermo a
② vi allacciarsi

fastener /'fɑːsnə(r)/ n, **fastening** /'fɑːsnɪŋ/ n chiusura f

fast food ① n fast food m inv
② attrib ⟨chain⟩ di fast food; **~ ~ restaurant** fast food m inv

fast forward ① n avanzamento m veloce
② vt far avanzare velocemente ⟨tape⟩
③ attrib ⟨key, button⟩ di avanzamento veloce

fast growing adj in rapida espansione

fastidious /fə'stɪdɪəs/ adj esigente

fast lane n Auto corsia f di sorpasso; **life in the ~ ~** fig vita f frenetica

fast-talking adj ⟨salesperson⟩ che raggira con la sua parlantina

fast track n corsia f preferenziale

fast-track vt accelerare la carriera di ⟨somebody⟩

fat /fæt/ ① *adj* (**fatter, fattest**) ⟨*person, cheque*⟩ grasso; fam **that's a ~ lot of use** non serve a un accidente ② *n* grasso *m*

fatal /'feɪtl/ *adj* mortale; ⟨*error*⟩ fatale

fatalism /'feɪtəlɪzm/ *n* fatalismo *m*

fatalist /'feɪtəlɪst/ *n* fatalista *mf*

fatality /fə'tæləti/ *n* morte *f*

fatally /'feɪtəli/ *adv* mortalmente

fate /feɪt/ *n* destino *m*

fated /'feɪtɪd/ *adj* destinato; **it was ~** era destino

fateful /'feɪtfʊl/ *adj* fatidico

fat free *adj* magro

fat-head *n* fam zuccone, -a *mf*

father /'fɑːðə(r)/ ① *n* padre *m* ② *vt* generare ⟨*child*⟩

Father Christmas Babbo *m* Natale

father confessor *n* Relig confessore *m*

father figure *n* figura *f* paterna

fatherhood *n* paternità *f*

father-in-law *n* (pl **fathers-in-law**) suocero *m*

fatherland *n* patria *f*

fatherly /'fɑːðəli/ *adj* paterno

Father's Day /'fɑːðəz/ *n* la festa del papà

fathom /'fæðəm/ ① *n* Naut braccio *m* ② *vt* ~ **[out]** comprendere

fatigue /fə'tiːg/ ① *n* fatica *f* ② *vt* affaticare

fatness /'fætnɪs/ *n* grassezza *f*

fatten /'fætn/ *vt* ingrassare ⟨*animal*⟩

fattening /'fætnɪŋ/ *adj* **cream is ~** la panna fa ingrassare

fatty /'fæti/ ① *adj* grasso ② *n* fam ciccione, -a *mf*

fatuous /'fætjʊəs/ *adj* fatuo

faucet /'fɔːsɪt/ *n* Am rubinetto *m*

fault /fɔːlt/ ① *n* difetto *m*; Geol faglia *f*; Tennis fallo *m*; **be at ~** avere torto; **find ~ with** trovare da ridire su; **it's your ~** è colpa tua ② *vt* criticare

fault-finding /'fɔːltfaɪndɪŋ/ ① *n* (of person) atteggiamento *m* ipercritico; Techn localizzazione *f* del guasto ② *adj* ⟨*attitude*⟩ da criticone; ⟨*person*⟩ ipercritico

faultless /'fɔːltlɪs/ *adj* impeccabile

faultlessly /'fɔːltlɪsli/ *adv* impeccabilmente

faulty /'fɔːlti/ *adj* difettoso

fauna /'fɔːnə/ *n* fauna *f*

faux pas /fəʊ'pɑː/ *n* gaffe *f inv*

favour /'feɪvə(r)/ ① *n* favore *m*; **be in ~ of something** essere a favore di qualcosa; **do somebody a ~** fare un piacere a qualcuno ② *vt* (prefer) preferire

favourable /'feɪv(ə)rəbl/ *adj* favorevole

favourably /'feɪv(ə)rəbli/ *adv* favorevolmente

favourite /'feɪv(ə)rɪt/ ① *adj* preferito ② *n* preferito, -a *mf*; Sport favorito, -a *mf*

favouritism /'feɪv(ə)rɪtɪzm/ *n* favoritismo *m*

fawn /fɔːn/ ① *adj* fulvo ② *n* (animal) cerbiatto *m*

fax /fæks/ ① *n* (document, machine) fax *m inv*; **by ~** per fax ② *vt* faxare

fax machine *n* fax *m inv*

fax-modem *n* fax-modem *m inv*

fax number *n* numero *m* di fax

faze /feɪz/ *vt* fam scompaginare

FBI *n abbr* Am (**Federal Bureau of Investigation**) FBI *m*

FC *abbr* (**football club**) FC

fear /fɪə(r)/ ① *n* paura *f*; **no ~!** fam vai tranquillo! ② *vt* temere ③ *vi* ~ **for something** temere per qualcosa

fearful /'fɪəfl/ *adj* pauroso; (awful) terribile

fearless /'fɪəlɪs/ *adj* impavido

fearlessly /'fɪəlɪsli/ *adv* senza paura

fearsome /'fɪəsəm/ *adj* spaventoso

feasibility /fiːzɪ'bɪləti/ *n* praticabilità *f*

feasible /'fiːzəbl/ *adj* fattibile; (possible) probabile

feast /fiːst/ ① *n* festa *f*; (banquet) banchetto *m* ② *vi* banchettare ■ **feast on** *vt* godersi

feat /fiːt/ *n* impresa *f*

feather /'feðə(r)/ *n* piuma *f*; **you could have knocked me down with a ~** sono rimasto di sasso

feather-brained /-breɪnd/ *adj* che non ha un briciolo di cervello

feather duster *n* piumino *m* (per spolverare)

featherweight *n* peso *m* piuma *inv*

feature /'fiːtʃə(r)/ ① *n* (quality) caratteristica *f*; Journ articolo *m*; ~**s** *pl* (of face) lineamenti *mpl* ② *vt* ⟨*film*⟩ avere come protagonista ③ *vi* (on a list etc) comparire

feature film *n* lungometraggio *m*

feature length film *n* lungometraggio *m*

February /'februəri/ *n* febbraio *m*

feces /'fiːsiːz/ *npl* feci *fpl*

feckless /'feklɪs/ *adj* inetto

fecund /'fekənd/ *adj* fecondo

fed /fed/ ① ▶ FEED ② *adj* **be ~ up** fam essere stufo (**with** di)

federal /'fed(ə)rəl/ *adj* federale

federalist /'fed(ə)rəlɪst/ *n & adj* federalista *mf*

Federal Republic of Germany *n* Repubblica *f* Federale Tedesca

federate /'fed(ə)rət/ *adj* federato

federation /fedə'reɪʃn/ *n* federazione *f*

fee /fiː/ *n* tariffa *f*; (lawyer's, doctor's) onorario *m*; (for membership, school) quota *f*

feeble /'fiːbl/ *adj* debole; ⟨*excuse*⟩ fiacco

feeble minded /-'maɪndɪd/ *adj* deficiente

feebleness /'fiːblnɪs/ *n* debolezza *f*

feed /fiːd/ ① *n* mangiare *m*; (for baby) pappa *f*; **five ∼s a day** cinque pasti al giorno
② *vt* (*pt/pp* **fed**) dar da mangiare a ⟨*animal*⟩; (support) nutrire; **∼ something into something** inserire qualcosa in qualcosa; **∼ paper into the printer** alimentare la stampante con fogli
③ *vi* mangiare
■ **feed up** *vt* ingrassare ⟨*somebody*⟩

feedback /'fiːdbæk/ *n* controreazione *f*; (of information) reazione *f*, feedback *m*

feeder /'fiːdə(r)/ *n* (for printer, photocopier) mettifoglio *m inv*; (Br; bib) bavaglino *m*; (road) raccordo *m*

feeding bottle /'fiːdɪŋ/ *n* Br biberon *m inv*

feeding time *n* (in zoo) l'ora *f* del pasto degli animali

feel /fiːl/ ① *vt* (*pt/pp* **felt**) sentire; (experience) provare; (think) pensare; (touch: searching) tastare; (touch: for texture) toccare
② *vi* **∼ soft/hard** essere duro/morbido al tatto; **∼ hot/hungry** aver caldo/fame; **∼ ill** sentirsi male; **I don't ∼ like it** non ne ho voglia; **how do you ∼ about it?** (opinion) che te ne pare?; **it doesn't ∼ right** non mi sembra giusto
■ **feel for** *vt* (feel sympathy for) dispiacersi per
■ **feel up to** *vt* **∼ up to doing something** sentirsi in grado di fare qualcosa; **I don't ∼ up to it** non me la sento

feeler /'fiːlə(r)/ *n* (of animal) antenna *f*; **put out ∼s** fig tastare il terreno

feel-good factor *n* sensazione *f* di benessere

feeling /'fiːlɪŋ/ *n* sentimento *m*; (awareness) sensazione *f*

fee paying *adj* ⟨*school*⟩ a pagamento, privato; ⟨*parent, pupil*⟩ che paga l'iscrizione (a una scuola privata)

feet /fiːt/ ▶ FOOT

feign /feɪn/ *vt* simulare

feint /feɪnt/ *n* finta *f*

feisty /'faɪstɪ/ *adj* Am (quarrelsome) stizzoso; (fam: lively) esuberante

felicitous /fə'lɪsɪtəs/ *adj* felice

feline /'fiːlaɪn/ *adj* felino

fell¹ /fel/ *vt* (knock down) abbattere

fell² ▶ FALL

fellow /'feləʊ/ *n* (of society) socio *m*; (fam: man) tipo *m*

fellow citizen *n* concittadino, -a *mf*

fellow countryman *n* compatriota *m*

fellow men *npl* prossimi *mpl*

fellowship /'feləʊʃɪp/ *n* cameratismo *m*; (group) associazione *f*; Univ incarico *m* di ricercatore, -trice *mf*

fellow traveller *n* compagno, -a *mf* di viaggio; Pol, fig compagno, -a *mf* di strada

felon /'felən/ *n* Jur criminale *mf*

felony /'felənɪ/ *n* delitto *m*

felt¹ /felt/ ▶ FEEL

felt² *n* feltro *m*

felt-tipped pen /-tɪpt'pen/ *n* pennarello *m*

female /'fiːmeɪl/ ① *adj* femminile; **the ∼ antelope** l'antilope femmina
② *n* femmina *f*

feminine /'femɪnɪn/ ① *adj* femminile
② *n* Gram femminile *m*

femininity /femɪ'nɪnətɪ/ *n* femminilità *f*

feminist /'femɪnɪst/ *adj & n* femminista *mf*

fen /fen/ *n* zona *f* paludosa

fence /fens/ ① *n* recinto *m*; (fam: person) ricettatore *m*
② *vi* Sport tirar di scherma
■ **fence in** *vt* chiudere in un recinto

fencer /'fensə(r)/ *n* schermidore *m*

fencing /'fensɪŋ/ *n* steccato *m*; Sport scherma *f*

fend /fend/ *vi* **∼ for oneself** badare a se stesso
■ **fend off** *vt* parare; difendersi da ⟨*criticisms*⟩

fender /'fendə(r)/ *n* parafuoco *m inv*; Naut parabordo *m*; (Am: on car) parafango *m*

fennel /'fenl/ *n* finocchio *m*

ferment¹ /'fɜːment/ *n* fermento *m*

ferment² /fə'ment/ ① *vi* fermentare
② *vt* far fermentare

fermentation /fɜːmen'teɪʃn/ *n* fermentazione *f*

fern /fɜːn/ *n* felce *f*

ferocious /fə'rəʊʃəs/ *adj* feroce

ferocity /fə'rɒsətɪ/ *n* ferocia *f*

ferret /'ferɪt/ *n* furetto *m*
■ **ferret about** *vi* curiosare; **∼ about in** curiosare in
■ **ferret out** *vt* scovare

ferrous /'ferəs/ *adj* ferroso

ferry /'ferɪ/ ① *n* traghetto *m*
② *vt* (*pt/pp* **-ied**) traghettare

ferryman /'ferɪmən/ *n* traghettatore *m*

fertile /'fɜːtaɪl/ *adj* fertile

fertility /fɜː'tɪlətɪ/ *n* fertilità *f*

fertility drug *n* farmaco *m* contro la sterilità

fertility treatment *n* cura *f* della fertilità

fertilize /'fɜːtɪlaɪz/ *vt* fertilizzare ⟨land, ovum⟩

fertilizer /'fɜːtɪlaɪzə(r)/ *n* fertilizzante *m*

fervent /'fɜːvənt/ *adj* fervente

fervour /'fɜːvə(r)/ *n* fervore *m*

fester /'festə(r)/ *vi* suppurare

festival /'festɪvl/ *n* Mus, Theat festival *m*; Relig festa *f*

festive /'festɪv/ *adj* festivo; ~ **season** periodo *m* delle feste natalizie

festivities /fe'stɪvətɪz/ *npl* festeggiamenti *mpl*

festoon /fe'stuːn/ *vt* ~ **with** ornare di

fetch /fetʃ/ *vt* andare/venire a prendere; (be sold for) raggiungere [il prezzo di]

fetching /'fetʃɪŋ/ *adj* attraente

fête /feɪt/ **1** *n* festa *f*
2 *vt* festeggiare

fetid /'fetɪd/ *adj* fetido

fetish /'fetɪʃ/ *n* feticcio *m*

fetter /'fetə(r)/ *vt* incatenare

fettle /'fetl/ *n* **in fine** ~ in buona forma

fetus /'fiːtəs/ *n* (pl **-tuses**) feto *m*

feud /fjuːd/ *n* faida *f*

feudal /'fjuːdl/ *adj* feudale

fever /'fiːvə(r)/ *n* febbre *f*

fevered /'fiːvəd/ *adj* ⟨brow⟩ febbricitante; ⟨imagination⟩ febbrile

feverish /'fiːvərɪʃ/ *adj* febbricitante; fig febbrile

fever pitch *n* **bring a crowd to** ~ ~ esaltare la folla

few /fjuː/ **1** *adj* pochi; **every** ~ **days** ogni due o tre giorni; **a** ~ **people** alcuni; ~ **people know that** poche persone lo sanno; ~**er reservations** meno prenotazioni; **the** ~**est number** il numero più basso
2 *pron* pochi; ~ **of us** pochi di noi; **a** ~ alcuni; **quite a** ~ parecchi; ~**er than last year** meno dell'anno scorso

fez /fez/ *n* fez *m inv*

fiancé /fi'ɒnseɪ/ *n* fidanzato *m*

fiancée /fi'ɒnseɪ/ *n* fidanzata *f*

fiasco /fi'æskəʊ/ *n* fiasco *m*

fib /fɪb/ *n* storia *f*; **tell a** ~ raccontare una storia

fibber /'fɪbə(r)/ *n* fam contaballe *mf inv*

fibre /'faɪbə(r)/ *n* fibra *f*

fibreglass **1** *n* fibra *f* di vetro
2 *attrib* in fibra di vetro

fibre optic *adj* ⟨cable⟩ a fibre ottiche

fibre optics *n* fibra *f* ottica

fibroid /'faɪbrɔɪd/ **1** *n* fibroma *m*
2 *adj* fibroso

fibula /'fɪbjʊlə/ *n* Anat perone *m*

fiche /fiːʃ/ *n* microscheda *f*

fickle /'fɪkl/ *adj* incostante

fiction /'fɪkʃn/ *n* **[works of]** ~ narrativa *f*: (fabrication) finzione *f*

fictional /'fɪkʃənəl/ *adj* immaginario

fictionalize /'fɪkʃənəlaɪz/ *vt* romanzare

fictitious /fɪk'tɪʃəs/ *adj* fittizio

fiddle /'fɪdl/ **1** *n* fam violino *m*; (cheating) imbroglio *m*
2 *vi* gingillarsi (**with** con)
3 *vt* fam truccare ⟨accounts⟩

fiddly /'fɪdlɪ/ *adj* intricato

fidelity /fɪ'delətɪ/ *n* fedeltà *f*

fidget /'fɪdʒɪt/ *vi* agitarsi

fidgety /'fɪdʒətɪ/ *adj* agitato

field /fiːld/ *n* campo *m*

field day *n* **have a** ~ ~ ⟨press, critics⟩ godersela; (make money) fare affari d'oro

fielder /'fiːldə(r)/ *n* Sport esterno *m*

field events *npl* atletica *fsg* leggera

field glasses *npl* binocolo *msg*

Field Marshal *n* feldmaresciallo *m*

field mouse *n* topo *m* campagnolo

field trip *n* gita *f* didattica

fieldwork *n* ricerche *fpl* sul terreno

fiend /fiːnd/ *n* demonio *m*

fiendish /'fiːndɪʃ/ *adj* diabolico

fierce /fɪəs/ *adj* feroce

fiercely /'fɪəslɪ/ *adv* ferocemente

fierceness /'fɪəsnɪs/ *n* ferocia *f*

fiery /'faɪərɪ/ *adj* (**-ier, -iest**) focoso

fiesta /fɪ'estə/ *n* sagra *f*

fife /faɪf/ *n* piffero *m*

fifteen /fɪf'tiːn/ *adj* & *n* quindici *m*

fifteenth /fɪf'tiːnθ/ *adj* & *n* quindicesimo, -a *mf*

fifth /fɪfθ/ *adj* & *n* quinto, -a *mf*

fifties /'fɪftɪz/ *npl* (period) **the** ~ gli anni Cinquanta *mpl*; (age) cinquant'anni *mpl*; ▶ also FORTIES

fiftieth /'fɪftɪɪθ/ *adj* & *n* cinquantesimo, -a *mf*

fifty /'fɪftɪ/ *adj* & *n* cinquanta *m*

fifty-fifty **1** *adj* **have a** ~ **chance** avere una probabilità su due
2 *adv* **go** ~ fare [a] metà e metà; **split something** ~ dividersi qualcosa a metà

fig /fɪg/ *n* fico *m*

fig. *abbr* (**figure**) fig.

fight /faɪt/ **1** *n* lotta *f*; (brawl) zuffa *f*; (argument) litigio *m*; (boxing) incontro *m*
2 *vt* (pt/pp **fought**) also fig combattere
3 *vi* combattere; (brawl) azzuffarsi; (argue) litigare
■ **fight back** **1** *vi* reagire
2 *vt* frenare ⟨tears⟩
■ **fight for** *vt* lottare per ⟨freedom, independence⟩
■ **fight off** *vt* combattere ⟨cold⟩

fighter /'faɪtə(r)/ n combattente mf; Aeron caccia m inv; **he's a ~** ha uno spirito combattivo

fighter-bomber n cacciabombardiere m

fighter pilot n pilota m di cacciabombardiere

fighting /'faɪtɪŋ/ n combattimento m

fighting chance n have a ~ ~ avere buone probabilità

fighting fit adj in piena forma

figment /'fɪgmənt/ n it's a ~ of your imagination questo è tutta una tua invenzione

fig tree n fico m

figurative /'fɪgərətɪv/ adj ‹sense› figurato; ‹art› figurativo

figuratively /'fɪgərətɪvlɪ/ adv ‹use› in senso figurato

figure /'fɪgə(r)/ ① n (digit) cifra f; (carving, sculpture, illustration, form) figura f; (body shape) linea f; ~ **of speech** modo m di dire
② vi (appear) figurare
③ vt (Am: think) pensare
■ **figure out** vt dedurre; capire ‹person›

figurehead n figura f simbolica

figure of speech n modo m di dire; (literary device) figura f retorica

figure skating n pattinaggio m artistico

figurine /'fɪgəriːn/ n statuetta f

Fiji /'fiːdʒiː/ n Figi fpl

filament /'fɪləmənt/ n filamento m

filch /fɪltʃ/ vt fam rubacchiare

file¹ /faɪl/ ① n scheda f; (set of documents) incartamento m; (folder) cartellina f; Comput file m inv
② vt archiviare ‹documents›

file² n (line) fila f; **in single ~** in fila

file³ ① n Techn lima f
② vt limare

file cabinet n Am = FILING CABINET

file extension n Comput estensione f del file

file manager n Comput file manager m inv

filename n Comput nome m del file

file transfer protocol n Comput protocollo m per il trasferimento di file

filial /'fɪlɪəl/ adj filiale

filibuster /'fɪlɪbʌstə(r)/ n ostruzionismo m parlamentare

filigree /'fɪlɪgriː/ n filigrana f

filing /'faɪlɪŋ/ n archiviazione f

filing cabinet n schedario m, classificatore m

filing card n scheda f

filing clerk n archivista mf

filings /'faɪlɪŋz/ npl limatura fsg

filing system n sistema m di classificazione, sistema m di archivio

fill /fɪl/ ① n eat one's ~ mangiare a sazietà
② vt riempire; otturare ‹tooth›
③ vi riempirsi
■ **fill in** vt compilare ‹form›
■ **fill in for** vt rimpiazzare someone
■ **fill in on** vt ~ **somebody in on something** mettere qualcuno al corrente di qualcosa
■ **fill out** vt compilare ‹form›
■ **fill up** ① vi ‹room, tank› riempirsi; Auto far il pieno
② vt riempire

filler /'fɪlə(r)/ n mastice m

fillet /'fɪlɪt/ ① n filetto m
② vt (pt/pp **filleted**) disossare

fillet steak n bistecca f di filetto

fill in n (fam: replacement) rimpiazzo m

filling /'fɪlɪŋ/ n Culin ripieno m; (of tooth) piombatura f

filling station n stazione f di rifornimento

filly /'fɪlɪ/ n puledra f

film /fɪlm/ ① n Cinema film m inv; Phot pellicola f; **[cling] ~** pellicola f per alimenti
② vt/i filmare

film buff n cinefilo, -a mf

film festival n festival m cinematografico

film-goer /'fɪlmgəʊə(r)/ n frequentatore, -trice mf di cinema

film industry n industria f cinematografica

filming /'fɪlmɪŋ/ n riprese fpl

filmset n allestimento m scenico

film star n star f inv, divo, -a mf

film studio n studio m cinematografico

filmy /'fɪlmɪ/ adj (thin: fabric, screen) trasparente; (thin) sottilissimo

filter /'fɪltə(r)/ ① n filtro m
② vt filtrare
■ **filter through** vi ‹news› trapelare

filter cigarette n sigaretta f con filtro

filter coffee n (ground coffee) caffè m macinato per filtro; (cup of coffee) caffè m inv fatto con il filtro

filter-paper n carta f da filtro

filter tip n filtro m; (cigarette) sigaretta f col filtro

filth /fɪlθ/ n sudiciume m

filthy /'fɪlθɪ/ adj (-ier, -iest) sudicio; ‹language› sconcio

filthy rich adj fam ricco sfondato

fin /fɪn/ n pinna f

final /'faɪnl/ ① adj finale; (conclusive) decisivo
② n Sport finale f; ~**s** pl Univ esami mpl finali

finale /fɪˈnɑːlɪ/ n finale m

finalist /ˈfaɪnəlɪst/ n finalista mf

finality /faɪˈnælətɪ/ n finalità f

finalize /ˈfaɪnəlaɪz/ vt mettere a punto ⟨text⟩; definire ⟨agreement⟩

finally /ˈfaɪnəlɪ/ adv (at last) finalmente; (at the end) alla fine; (to conclude) per finire

finance /ˈfaɪnæns/ ① n finanza f ② vt finanziare

finance company, finance house n società f finanziaria

finance director n direttore, -trice mf finanziario, -a

finances npl finanze fpl

financial /faɪˈnænʃl/ adj finanziario

financially /faɪˈnænʃəlɪ/ adv finanziariamente

financial year n Br esercizio m [finanziario]

finch /fɪntʃ/ n fringuello m

find /faɪnd/ ① n scoperta f ② vt (pt/pp **found**) trovare; (establish) scoprire; ∼ **somebody guilty** Jur dichiarare qualcuno colpevole ■ **find out** ① vt scoprire ② vi (enquire) informarsi

findings /ˈfaɪndɪŋz/ npl conclusioni fpl

fine¹ /faɪn/ ① n (penalty) multa f ② vt multare

fine² ① adj bello; (slender) fine; **he's** ∼ (in health) sta bene ② adv bene; **that's cutting it** ∼ non ci lascia molto tempo. ③ int [va] bene

fine art, fine arts npl belle arti fpl

finely /ˈfaɪnlɪ/ adv ⟨cut⟩ finemente

finery /ˈfaɪnərɪ/ n splendore m

finesse /fɪˈnes/ n finezza f

fine-tooth[ed] comb /-tuːθ[t]/ n **go over something with a** ∼ ∼ passare qualcosa al setaccio

fine-tune vt mettere a punto

fine tuning n messa f a punto

finger /ˈfɪŋgə(r)/ ① n dito m (pl dita f) ② vt tastare

finger bowl n lavadita m inv

finger hole n Mus foro m

fingermark n ditata f

fingernail n unghia f

finger-paint vi dipingere con le dita

fingerprint n impronta f digitale

fingertip n punta f del dito; **have something at one's** ∼**s** sapere qualcosa a menadito; (close at hand) avere qualcosa a portata di mano

finicky /ˈfɪnɪkɪ/ adj (person) pignolo; ⟨task⟩ intricato

finish /ˈfɪnɪʃ/ ① n fine f; (finishing line) traguardo m; (of product) finitura f; **have a good** ∼ ⟨runner⟩ avere un buon finale

② vt finire; ∼ **reading** finire di leggere ③ vi finire ■ **finish off** vt finire ⟨something⟩; (fam: exhaust) sfinire ■ **finish with** vt (no longer be using) finire (di adoperare); (end relationship with) lasciare ■ **finish up** vt finire ⟨drink, meal⟩

finishing line /ˈfɪnɪʃɪŋlaɪn/ n traguardo m

finishing touches /ˈtʌtʃɪz/ npl ritocchi mpl

finite /ˈfaɪnaɪt/ adj limitato

Finland /ˈfɪnlənd/ n Finlandia f

Finn /fɪn/ n finlandese mf

Finnish /ˈfɪnɪʃ/ ① adj finlandese ② n (language) finnico m

fiord /fjɔːd/ n fiordo m

fir /fɜː(r)/ n abete m

fir cone n pigna f (di abete)

fire /ˈfaɪə(r)/ ① n fuoco m; (forest, house) incendio m; **be on** ∼ bruciare; **catch** ∼ prendere fuoco; **set** ∼ **to** dar fuoco a; **under** ∼ sotto il fuoco ② vt cuocere ⟨pottery⟩; sparare ⟨shot⟩; tirare ⟨gun⟩; (fam: dismiss) buttar fuori ③ vi sparare (**at** a)

fire alarm n allarme m antincendio inv

firearm n arma f da fuoco

firebomb ① n ordigno m incendiario ② vt lanciare ordigni incendiari contro ⟨building⟩

fire brigade n vigili mpl del fuoco

fire door n porta f antincendio

fire drill n esercitazione f per l'evacuazione in caso di incendio

fire engine n autopompa f

fire escape n uscita f di sicurezza

fire exit n uscita f di sicurezza

fire extinguisher n estintore m

firefighter n vigile m del fuoco

fireguard n parafuoco m inv

fireman n pompiere m, vigile m del fuoco

fireplace n caminetto m

fireproof adj ⟨door⟩ antincendio, ⟨clothing⟩ ignifugo

fire-retardant /rɪˈtɑːdənt/ adj ⟨material⟩ ignifugo

fire service n vigili mpl del fuoco

fireside n **by** or **at the** ∼ accanto al fuoco

fire station n caserma f dei pompieri

firewall n Comput firewall m inv

firewood n legna f (da ardere)

firework n fuoco m d'artificio; ∼**s** pl (display) fuochi mpl d'artificio

firing line /ˈfaɪərɪŋ/ n **be in the** ∼ essere sulla linea di tiro

firing squad n plotone m d'esecuzione

firm¹ /fɜːm/ n ditta f, azienda f

firm[2] *adj* fermo; ⟨*soil*⟩ compatto; (stable, properly fixed) solido; (resolute) risoluto

firmly /ˈfɜːmlɪ/ *adv* ⟨*hold*⟩ stretto; ⟨*say*⟩ con fermezza

first /fɜːst/ **1** *adj & n* primo, -a *mf*; **at ~** all'inizio; **who's ~?** chi è il primo?; **from the ~** [fin] dall'inizio
2 *adv* ⟨*arrive, leave*⟩ per primo; (beforehand) prima; (in listing) prima di tutto, innanzitutto

first aid *n* pronto soccorso *m*

first-aid kit *n* cassetta *f* di pronto soccorso

first-class **1** *adj* di prim'ordine; Rail di prima classe
2 *adv* ⟨*travel*⟩ in prima classe

first cousin *n* cugino, -a *mf* di primo grado

first edition *n* prima edizione *f*

first floor *n* primo piano *m*; (Am: ground floor) pianterreno *m*

first grade *n* Am prima *f* elementare

firsthand *adj & adv* di prima mano

firstly /ˈfɜːstlɪ/ *adv* in primo luogo

first name *n* nome *m* di battesimo

first night *n* Theat prima *f*

first-rate *adj* ottimo

first time buyer *n* acquirente *mf* della prima casa

firth /fɜːθ/ *n* foce *f*

fiscal /ˈfɪskəl/ *adj* fiscale

fiscal year *n* Am esercizio *m* finanziario

fish /fɪʃ/ **1** *n* pesce *m*
2 *vt/i* pescare
■ **fish out** *vt* tirar fuori

fish and chips *n* pesce *m* fritto e patatine

fish and chip shop *n* friggitoria *f* dove si vende pesce fritto e patatine

fishbone /ˈfɪʃbəʊn/ *n* lisca *f*

fishbowl *n* boccia *f* dei pesci rossi

fisherman /ˈfɪʃəmən/ *n* pescatore *m*

fish farm *n* vivaio *m*

fish finger *n* bastoncino *m* di pesce

fishing /ˈfɪʃɪŋ/ *n* pesca *f*

fishing boat *n* peschereccio *m*

fishing rod *n* canna *f* da pesca

fish market *n* mercato *m* del pesce

fishmonger /ˈfɪʃmʌŋgə(r)/ *n* pescivendolo *m*

fishnet /ˈfɪʃnet/ *adj* ⟨*stockings*⟩ a rete

fish slice *n* paletta *f* per fritti

fish tank *n* acquario *m*

fishy /ˈfɪʃɪ/ *adj* (fam: suspicious) sospetto

fission /ˈfɪʃn/ *n* Phys fissione *f*

fist /fɪst/ *n* pugno *m*

fistful /ˈfɪstfʊl/ *n* manciata *f*, pugno *m*

fit[1] /fɪt/ *n* (attack) attacco *m*; (of rage) accesso *m*; (of generosity) slancio *m*

fit[2] *adj* (**fitter, fittest**) (suitable) adatto; (healthy) in buona salute; Sport in forma; **be ~ to do something** essere in grado di fare qualcosa; **~ to eat** buono da mangiare; **keep ~** tenersi in forma; **do as you see ~** fai come ritieni meglio

fit[3] **1** *n* (of clothes) taglio *m*; **it's a good ~** ⟨*coat etc*⟩ ti/le sta bene
2 *vi* (pt/pp **fitted**) (be the right size) andare bene; **it won't ~** (no room) non ci sta
3 *vt* (fix) applicare (**to** a); (install) installare; **it doesn't ~ me** ⟨*coat etc*⟩ non mi va bene; **~ with** fornire di
■ **fit in** **1** *vi* ⟨*person*⟩ adattarsi; **it won't ~ in** (no room) non ci sta
2 *vt* (in schedule, vehicle) trovare un buco per

fitful /ˈfɪtfl/ *adj* irregolare

fitfully /ˈfɪtfʊlɪ/ *adv* ⟨*sleep*⟩ a sprazzi

fitment /ˈfɪtmənt/ *n* ~**s** (in house) impianti *mpl* fissi

fitness /ˈfɪtnɪs/ *n* (suitability) capacità *f*; [physical] ~ forma *f*, fitness *m*

fitness programme *n* programma *m* di fitness

fitness video *n* video *m* di fitness

fitted /ˈfɪtɪd/ *adj* ⟨*wardrobe*⟩ a muro; ⟨*kitchen, bedroom*⟩ componibile; ⟨*jacket*⟩ attillato

fitted carpet *n* moquette *f inv*

fitted cupboard *n* armadio *m* a muro; (smaller) armadietto *m* a muro

fitted kitchen *n* cucina *f* componibile

fitted sheet *n* lenzuolo *m* con angoli

fitter /ˈfɪtə(r)/ *n* installatore, -trice *mf*

fitting /ˈfɪtɪŋ/ **1** *adj* appropriato
2 *n* (of clothes) prova *f*; Techn montaggio *m*; ~**s** *pl* accessori *mpl*

fitting room *n* camerino *m*

five /faɪv/ *adj & n* cinque *m*

five-a-side *n* Br (football) calcio *m* a cinque

fiver /ˈfaɪvə(r)/ *n* fam biglietto *m* da cinque sterline

fix /fɪks/ **1** *n* (sl: drugs) pera *f*; **be in a ~** fam essere nei guai
2 *vt* fissare; (repair) aggiustare; preparare ⟨*meal*⟩
■ **fix up** *vt* fissare ⟨*meeting*⟩

fixation /fɪkˈseɪʃn/ *n* fissazione *f*

fixative /ˈfɪksətɪv/ *n* fissativo *m*

fixed /ˈfɪkst/ *adj* fisso

fixed assets *npl* attività *fpl* fisse, immobilizzazioni *fpl*

fixed price *n* prezzo *m* a forfait

fixed-term contract *n* contratto *m* a tempo determinato

fixer /ˈfɪksə(r)/ *n* Phot fissatore *m*; (fam: person) trafficone, -a *mf*

fixture /ˈfɪkstʃə(r)/ *n* Sport incontro *m*; ~**s and fittings** impianti *mpl* fissi

fizz /fɪz/ *vi* frizzare

fizzle /'fɪzl/ *vi* ∼ **out** finire in nulla

fizzy /'fɪzɪ/ *adj* gassoso

fizzy drink *n* bibita *f* gassata

fjord /fjɔːd/ *n* fiordo *m*

flab /flæb/ *n* fam ciccia *f* cascante

flabbergasted /'flæbəgɑːstɪd/ *adj* be ∼ rimanere a bocca aperta

flabby /'flæbɪ/ *adj* floscio

flag[1] /flæg/ *n* bandiera *f*

flag[2] *vi* (pt/pp **flagged**) cedere
■ **flag down** *vt* (pt/pp **flagged**) far segno di fermarsi a ‹*taxi*›

flagellation /flædʒə'leɪʃn/ *n* flagellazione *f*

flagon /'flægən/ *n* bottiglione *m*

flagpole /'flægpəʊl/ *n* asta *f* della bandiera

flagrant /'fleɪgrənt/ *adj* flagrante

flagship /'flægʃɪp/ *n* Naut nave *f* ammiraglia; fig fiore *m* all'occhiello

flagstone /'flægstəʊn/ *n* pietra *f* per lastricato

flail /fleɪl/ ① *n* (for threshing corn etc) correggiato *m*
② *vt* battere ‹*corn*›
■ **flail about**, **flail around** *vi* ‹*arms, legs*› agitare

flair /fleə(r)/ *n* (skill) talento *m*; (style) stile *m*

flak /flæk/ *n* Mil artiglieria *f* antiaerea; (fig fam: criticism) valanga *f* di critiche; **take a lot of** ∼ subire molte critiche

flake /fleɪk/ ① *n* fiocco *m*
② *vi* ∼ [**off**] cadere in fiocchi

flaky /'fleɪkɪ/ *adj* a scaglie

flaky pastry *n* pasta *f* sfoglia

flamboyant /flæm'bɔɪənt/ *adj* ‹*personality*› brillante; ‹*tie*› sgargiante

flame /fleɪm/ *n* fiamma *f*

flamenco /flə'meŋkəʊ/ *n* flamenco *m*

flamer /'fleɪmə(r)/ *n* Comput flamer *m*, utente *mf* email che manda messaggi offensivi

flame retardant /rɪtɑːdənt/ *adj* ‹*substance, chemical*› ignifugo; ‹*furniture, fabric*› ignifugato

flame-thrower /-θrəʊə(r)/ *n* Mil lanciafiamme *m inv*

flaming /'fleɪmɪŋ/ ① *adj* ‹*row*› acceso: ‹*building*› in fiamme
② *n* Comput flaming *m inv*, invio *m* di messaggi offensivi

flamingo /flə'mɪŋgəʊ/ *n* fenicottero *m*

flammable /'flæməbl/ *adj* infiammabile

flan /flæn/ *n* [fruit] ∼ crostata *f*

flange /flændʒ/ *n* (on pipe etc) flangia *f*

flank /flæŋk/ ① *n* fianco *m*
② *vt* fiancheggiare

flannel /'flæn(ə)l/ *n* flanella *f*; (for washing) ≈ guanto *m* di spugna

flannelette /flænə'let/ *n* flanella *f* di cotone

flannels /'flæn(ə)lz/ *npl* (trousers) pantaloni *mpl* di flanella

flap /flæp/ ① *n* (of pocket, envelope) risvolto *m*; (of table) ribalta *f*; **in a** ∼ fam in grande agitazione
② *vi* (pt/pp **flapped**) sbattere; fam agitarsi
③ *vt* ∼ **its wings** battere le ali

flapjack /'flæpdʒæk/ *n* Br dolcetto *m* di fiocchi d'avena; Am frittella *f*

flare /fleə(r)/ *n* fiammata *f*; (device) razzo *m*
■ **flare up** *vi* ‹*rash*› venire fuori; ‹*fire*› fare una fiammata; ‹*person, situation*› esplodere

flared /fleəd/ *adj* ‹*garment*› svasato

flares /fleəz/ *npl* (trousers) pantaloni *mpl* a zampa d'elefante

flash /flæʃ/ ① *n* lampo *m*; **in a** ∼ fam in un attimo
② *vi* lampeggiare; ∼ **past** passare come un bolide
③ *vt* lanciare ‹*smile*›; ∼ **one's headlights** lampeggiare; ∼ **a torch at** puntare una torcia su
■ **flash by** *vi* ‹*person, years, landscape*› passare come un lampo

flashback *n* scena *f* retrospettiva

flashbulb *n* Phot flash *m inv*

flashcard *n* Sch scheda *f* didattica

flasher /'flæʃə(r)/ *n* Auto lampeggiatore *m*

flash flood *n* alluvione *f* improvvisa

flashgun *n* Phot flash *m inv*

flashing /'flæʃɪŋ/ *adj* ‹*light*› lampeggiante

flashlight *n* Phot flash *m inv*; (Am: torch) torcia *f* [elettrica]

flashpoint *n* (trouble spot) punto *m* caldo; Chem punto *m* di infiammabilità

flashy /'flæʃɪ/ *adj* vistoso

flask /flɑːsk/ *n* fiasco *m*; (vacuum ∼) termos *m inv*

flat /flæt/ ① *adj* (**flatter**, **flattest**) piatto; ‹*refusal*› reciso; ‹*beer*› sgassato; ‹*battery*› scarico; ‹*tyre*› a terra; **A** ∼ Mus la bemolle
② *n* appartamento *m*; Mus bemolle *m*; (puncture) gomma *f* a terra

flat broke *adj* fam completamente al verde

flat feet *npl* piedi *mpl* piatti

flatfish *n* pesce *m* piatto

flat-footed /-'fʊtɪd/ *adj* be ∼ ∼ avere i piedi piatti

flat hunting *n* Br go ∼ ∼ andare in cerca di un appartamento

flatly /'flætlɪ/ adv ⟨refuse⟩ categoricamente

flatmate n Br persona f con cui si divide un appartamento

flat out adv ⟨drive, work⟩ a tutto gas; **it only does 120 kph ~ ~** arriva a 120 km all'ora andando a tutta manetta; **go ~ ~ for something** mettercela tutta per fare qualcosa

flat racing n corse fpl piane

flat rate ⟦1⟧ n forfait m inv; (unitary rate) tariffa f unica
⟦2⟧ attrib ⟨fee, tax⟩ forfettario

flat spin n Aeron virata f piatta; **be in a ~ ~** fam essere in fibrillazione

flatten /'flætn/ vt appiattire

flatter /'flætə(r)/ vt adulare

flattering /'flætərɪŋ/ adj ⟨comments⟩ lusinghiero; ⟨colour, dress⟩ che fa sembrare più bello

flattery /'flætərɪ/ n adulazione f

flat tyre n gomma f a terra

flatulence /'flætjʊləns/ n flatulenza f

flaunt /flɔːnt/ vt ostentare

flautist /'flɔːtɪst/ n flautista mf

flavour /'fleɪvə(r)/ ⟦1⟧ n sapore m
⟦2⟧ vt condire; **chocolate ~ed** al sapore di cioccolato

flavour-enhancer /-ɪnhɑːnsə(r)/ n esaltatore m dell'aroma

flavouring /'fleɪvərɪŋ/ n condimento m

flavourless /'fleɪvəlɪs/ adj insipido

flaw /flɔː/ n difetto m

flawed /flɔːd/ adj difettoso

flawless /'flɔːlɪs/ adj perfetto

flax /flæks/ n lino m

flaxen /'flæksən/ adj ⟨hair⟩ biondo platino

flea /fliː/ n pulce f

flea-bitten /'fliːbɪtən/ adj infestato dalle pulci; fig pidocchioso

flea market n mercato m delle pulci

fleapit n Br fam pej pidocchietto m

fleck /flek/ n macchiolina f

fled /fled/ ▶ FLEE

fledg[e]ling /'fledʒlɪŋ/ ⟦1⟧ n uccellino m (che ha appena messo le ali)
⟦2⟧ attrib fig ⟨democracy, enterprise⟩ giovane; ⟨party, group⟩ alle prime armi

flee /fliː/ vt/i (pt/pp **fled**) fuggire (**from** da)

fleece /fliːs/ ⟦1⟧ n pelliccia f
⟦2⟧ vt fam spennare

fleecy /'fliːsɪ/ adj ⟨lining⟩ felpato

fleet /fliːt/ n flotta f; (of cars) parco m

fleeting /'fliːtɪŋ/ adj **catch a ~ glance of something** intravedere qualcosa; **for a ~ moment** per un attimo

Flemish /'flemɪʃ/ adj fiammingo

flesh /fleʃ/ n carne f; **in the ~** in persona; **one's own ~ and blood** il proprio sangue
■ **flesh out** vt dare più consistenza a ⟨essay etc⟩

flesh eating /-iːtɪŋ/ adj carnivoro

flesh wound n ferita f superficiale

fleshy /'fleʃɪ/ adj carnoso

flew /fluː/ ▶ FLY²

flex¹ /fleks/ vt flettere ⟨muscle⟩

flex² n Electr filo m

flexibility /fleksə'bɪlətɪ/ n flessibilità f

flexible /'fleksəbl/ adj flessibile

flexitime /'fleksɪtaɪm/ n orario m flessibile

flick /flɪk/ vt dare un buffetto a; **~ something off something** togliere qualcosa da qualcosa con un colpetto
■ **flick through** vt sfogliare

flicker /'flɪkə(r)/ vi tremolare

flick knife n Br coltello m a scatto

flier /'flaɪə(r)/ n = FLYER

flight¹ /flaɪt/ n (fleeing) fuga f; **take ~** darsi alla fuga

flight² n (flying) volo m; **~ of stairs** rampa f

flight attendant n assistente mf di volo

flight bag n bagaglio m a mano

flight deck n Aeron cabina f di pilotaggio; Naut ponte m di volo

flight engineer n motorista mf di bordo

flight lieutenant n Mil capitano m

flight path n traiettoria f di volo

flight recorder n registratore m di volo

flighty /'flaɪtɪ/ adj (-ier, -iest) frivolo

flimsy /'flɪmzɪ/ adj (-ier, -iest) ⟨material⟩ leggero; ⟨shelves⟩ poco robusto; ⟨excuse⟩ debole

flinch /flɪntʃ/ vi (wince) sussultare; (draw back) ritirarsi; **~ from a task** fig sottrarsi a un compito

fling /flɪŋ/ ⟦1⟧ n **have a ~** (fam: affair) avere un'avventura
⟦2⟧ vt (pt/pp **flung**) gettare
■ **fling away** vt gettar via
■ **fling open** vt spalancare ⟨door, window⟩

flint /flɪnt/ n pietra f focaia; (for lighter) pietrina f

flip /flɪp/ ⟦1⟧ vt (pt/pp **flipped**) dare un colpetto a; buttare in aria ⟨coin⟩
⟦2⟧ vi fam uscire dai gangheri; (go mad) impazzire
■ **flip through** vt sfogliare

flip chart n lavagna f a fogli mobili

flip-flop n (sandal) infradito m inv; (Comput: device) flip-flop m inv,

multivibratore *m* bistabile; (Am: about face) voltafaccia *m inv*

flippant /'flɪpənt/ *adj* irriverente

flipper /'flɪpə(r)/ *n* pinna *f*

flipping /'flɪpɪŋ/ Br fam **1** *adj* maledetto **2** *adv* ⟨*stupid, painful, cold*⟩ maledettamente

flip side *n* (of record) retro *m*; (fig: other side) rovescio *m*

flirt /flɜːt/ **1** *n* civetta *f* **2** *vi* flirtare

flirtation /flɜː'teɪʃn/ *n* flirt *m inv*

flirtatious /flɜː'teɪʃəs/ *adj* civettuolo

flit /flɪt/ *vi* (pt/pp **flitted**) volteggiare

float /fləʊt/ **1** *n* galleggiante *m*; (in procession) carro *m*; (money) riserva *f* di cassa **2** *vi* galleggiare; Fin fluttuare **∎ float off** *vi* ⟨*boat*⟩ andare alla deriva: ⟨*balloon*⟩ volare via

floating /'fləʊtɪŋ/ *adj* ⟨*bridge*⟩ galleggiante; ⟨*population*⟩ fluttuante

floating rate interest *n* Fin interesse *m* a tasso variabile

floating voter *n* Pol elettore, -trice *mf* indeciso, -a

flock /flɒk/ **1** *n* gregge *m*; (of birds) stormo *m* **2** *vi* affollarsi

floe /fləʊ/ *n* banchisa *f*

flog /flɒg/ *vt* (pt/pp **flogged**) bastonare; (fam: sell) vendere

flood /flʌd/ **1** *n* alluvione *f*; (of river) straripamento *m*; (fig: of replies, letters, tears) diluvio *m*: be in ∼ ⟨*river*⟩ essere straripato **2** *vt* allagare **3** *vi* ⟨*river*⟩ straripare

flood control *n* prevenzione *f* delle inondazioni

flood damage *n* danno *m* provocato da un'inondazione

floodgate *n* chiusa *f*; open the ∼s fig spalancare le porte

floodlight **1** *n* riflettore *m* **2** *vt* (pt/pp **floodlit**) illuminare con riflettori

floodplain *n* pianura *f* alluvionale

flood tide *n* marea *f* montante

flood waters *npl* acque *fpl* alluvionali

floor /flɔː(r)/ **1** *n* pavimento *m*; (storey) piano *m*; (for dancing) pista *f* **2** *vt* (baffle) confondere; (knock down) stendere ⟨*person*⟩

floorboard *n* asse *f* del pavimento

floorcloth *n* straccio *m* per lavare il pavimento

floor exercises *npl* esercizi *mpl* a terra

floor manager *n* TV direttore, -trice *mf* di studio; Comm gerente *mf* di un negozio

floor polish *n* cera *f* per il pavimento

floor show *n* spettacolo *m* di varietà

floor space *n* superficie *f*; we don't have the ∼ ∼ non abbiamo lo spazio

flop /flɒp/ **1** *n* fam (failure) tonfo *m*; Theat fiasco *m* **2** *vi* (pt/pp **flopped**) (fam: fail) far fiasco **∎ flop down** *vi* accasciarsi

floppy /'flɒpɪ/ *adj* floscio

floppy disk *n* floppy disk *m inv*

floppy [disk] drive *n* lettore *m* di floppy

flora /'flɔːrə/ *n* flora *f*

floral /'flɔːrəl/ *adj* floreale

Florence /'flɒrəns/ *n* Firenze *f*

Florentine /'flɒrəntaɪn/ *adj* fiorentino

florid /'flɒrɪd/ *adj* ⟨*complexion*⟩ florido; ⟨*style*⟩ troppo ricercato

florist /'flɒrɪst/ *n* fioraio, -a *mf*

floss /flɒs/ **1** *n* filo *m* interdentale **2** *vt* ∼ one's teeth usare il filo interdentale **3** *vi* usare il filo interdentale

flotsam /'flɒtsəm/ *n* relitti *mpl* alla deriva

flounce /flaʊns/ **1** *n* balza *f* **2** *vi* ∼ out uscire con aria melodrammatica

flounder[1] /'flaʊndə(r)/ *vi* dibattersi; ⟨*speaker*⟩ impappinarsi

flounder[2] *n* (fish) passera *f* di mare

flour /'flaʊə(r)/ *n* farina *f*

flourish /'flʌrɪʃ/ **1** *n* gesto *m* drammatico; (scroll) ghirigoro *m* **2** *vi* prosperare **3** *vt* brandire

flourishing /'flʌrɪʃɪŋ/ *adj* ⟨*industry, business*⟩ fiorente; ⟨*garden*⟩ rigoglioso

floury /'flaʊərɪ/ *adj* farinoso

flout /flaʊt/ *vt* fregarsene di ⟨*rules*⟩

flow /fləʊ/ **1** *n* flusso *m* **2** *vi* scorrere; (hang loosely) ricadere

flow chart *n* diagramma *m* di flusso

flower /'flaʊə(r)/ **1** *n* fiore *m* **2** *vi* fiorire

flower arrangement *n* composizione *f* floreale

flower arranging *n* composizione *f* floreale

flower bed *n* aiuola *f*

flowered /'flaʊəd/ *adj* a fiori

flower garden *n* giardino *m* fiorito

flowering /'flaʊərɪŋ/ **1** *n* Bot fioritura *f*; (fig: development) espansione *f* **2** *adj* ⟨*shrub, tree*⟩ in fiore; early/late ∼ a fioritura precoce/tardiva

flowerpot *n* vaso *m* [per i fiori]

flower shop *n* fiorista *m*

flower show *n* mostra *f* floreale

flowery /'flaʊərɪ/ adj fiorito

flown /fləʊn/ ▶ FLY²

fl oz abbr **fluid ounces**

flu /fluː/ n influenza f

fluctuate /'flʌktjʊeɪt/ vi fluttuare

fluctuation /flʌktjʊ'eɪʃn/ n fluttuazione f

flue /fluː/ n (of chimney, stove) canna f fumaria

fluency /'fluːənsɪ/ n (in speaking) competenza f; (in writing) speditezza f

fluent /'fluːənt/ adj spedito; **speak ~ Italian** parlare correntemente l'italiano

fluently /'fluːəntlɪ/ adv speditamente

fluff /flʌf/ n peluria f

fluffy /'flʌfɪ/ adj (**-ier, -iest**) vaporoso; ⟨toy⟩ di peluche

fluid /'fluːɪd/ ❶ adj fluido
❷ n fluido m

fluid ounce n oncia f fluida

fluke /fluːk/ n colpo m di fortuna

flummox /'flʌməks/ vt fam sbalestrare

flung /flʌŋ/ ▶ FLING

flunk /flʌŋk/ vt Am fam essere bocciato in

fluorescent /flʊə'resnt/ adj fluorescente

fluorescent lighting n luce f fluorescente

fluoride /'flʊəraɪd/ n fluoruro m

flurry /'flʌrɪ/ n (snow) raffica f: fig agitazione f

flush /flʌʃ/ ❶ n (blush) [vampata f di] rossore m
❷ vi arrossire
❸ vt lavare con un getto d'acqua; **~ the toilet** tirare l'acqua
❹ adj a livello (**with** di); (fam: affluent) pieno di soldi
■ **flush out** vt snidare ⟨spy⟩

flushed /flʌʃt/ adj (cheeks) rosso; **~ with** eccitato da ⟨success⟩; raggiante di ⟨pride⟩

fluster /'flʌstə(r)/ vt agitare

flustered /'flʌstəd/ adj in agitazione; **get ~** mettersi in agitazione

flute /fluːt/ n flauto m

flutter /'flʌtə(r)/ ❶ n battito m
❷ vi svolazzare

flux /flʌks/ n **in a state of ~** in uno stato di flusso

fly¹ /flaɪ/ n (pl **flies**) mosca f

fly² ❶ vi (pt **flew**, pp **flown**) volare; (go by plane) andare in aereo; ⟨flag⟩ sventolare; (rush) precipitarsi; **~ open** spalancarsi
❷ vt pilotare ⟨plane⟩; trasportare [in aereo] ⟨troops, supplies⟩; volare con ⟨Alitalia etc⟩
■ **fly away** vi volare via

fly³ n & **flies** pl (on trousers) patta f

flyaway /'flaɪəweɪ/ adj ⟨hair⟩ che non stanno a posto

fly-by-night adj ⟨person⟩ irresponsabile; ⟨company⟩ non affidabile

flycatcher /'flaɪkætʃə(r)/ n pigliamosche m inv

fly-drive adj con la formula aereo più auto

flyer /'flaɪə(r)/ n aviatore m; (leaflet) volantino m

fly-fishing n pesca f con la mosca

flying /'flaɪɪŋ/ n aviazione f

flying buttress n arco m rampante

flying colours: with **~ ~** a pieni voti

flying saucer n disco m volante

flying start n ottima partenza f: **get off to a ~ ~** partire benissimo

flying visit n visita f lampo inv

flyleaf n risguardo m

fly on the wall adj ⟨documentary⟩ con telecamera nascosta

flyover n cavalcavia m inv

fly-past n Br Aeron parata f aerea

flysheet n (handbill) volantino m; (of tent) soprattenda m inv

fly spray n moschicida m

FM abbr (**Frequency Modulation**) FM

foal /fəʊl/ n puledro m

foam /fəʊm/ ❶ n schiuma f; (synthetic) gommapiuma® f
❷ vi spumare; **~ at the mouth** far la bava alla bocca

foam bath n bagnoschiuma m

foam rubber n gommapiuma® f

fob /fɒb/ vt (pt/pp **fobbed**) **~ something off** affibbiare qualcosa (**on somebody** a qualcuno); **~ somebody off** liquidare qualcuno

focal /'fəʊkl/ adj focale

focal point n (of village, building) centro m di attrazione; (main concern) punto m centrale; (in optics) fuoco m; **the room lacks a ~ ~** nella stanza manca un punto che focalizzi l'attenzione

focus /'fəʊkəs/ ❶ n fuoco m; **in ~** a fuoco; **out of ~** sfocato
❷ vt (pt/pp **focused** or **focussed**) fig concentrare (**on** su)
❸ vi **~ on** something Phot mettere a fuoco qualcosa; fig concentrarsi su qualcosa

fodder /'fɒdə(r)/ n foraggio m

foe /fəʊ/ n nemico, -a mf

foetal /'fiːtl/ adj fetale

foetid /'fetɪd/ adj fetido

foetus /'fiːtəs/ n (pl **-tuses**) feto m

fog /fɒg/ n nebbia f

fog bank n banco m di nebbia

fogey /'fəʊgɪ/ n old **~** persona f antiquata

foggy /'fɒgɪ/ adj (**foggier, foggiest**) nebbioso; **it's ~** c'è nebbia; **I haven't got**

the foggiest [idea] fam non ne ho la più pallida idea

foghorn /'fɒɡhɔːn/ n sirena f da nebbia

fog lamp, foglight /'fɒɡlaɪt/ n Auto [faro m] antinebbia m inv

foible /'fɔɪbl/ n punto m debole

foil[1] /fɔɪl/ n lamina f di metallo

foil[2] vt (thwart) frustrare

foil[3] n (sword) fioretto m

foist /fɔɪst/ vt appioppare (**on somebody** a qualcuno)

fold[1] /fəʊld/ n (for sheep) ovile m

fold[2] ① n piega f
② vt piegare; ~ **one's arms** incrociare le braccia
③ vi piegarsi; (fail) crollare
■ **fold back** vt ripiegare ⟨sheets⟩; aprire ⟨shutters⟩
■ **fold in** vt incorporare ⟨flour, eggs⟩
■ **fold up** ① vt ripiegare ⟨chair⟩
② vi essere pieghevole; fam ⟨business⟩ collassare

foldaway /'fəʊldəweɪ/ adj ⟨bed⟩ pieghevole; ⟨table⟩ estraibile

folder /'fəʊldə(r)/ n cartella f

folding /'fəʊldɪŋ/ adj pieghevole

folding seat n strapuntino m, sedile m pieghevole

folding stool n sgabello m pieghevole

fold-out n (in magazine) pieghevole m

foliage /'fəʊlɪdʒ/ n fogliame m

folk /fəʊk/ npl gente f; **my ~s** (family) i miei; **hello there ~s** ciao a tutti

folk dance n danza f popolare

folklore n folclore m

folk medicine n rimedio m della nonna

folk memory n memoria f collettiva

folk music n musica f folk

folk song n canto m popolare

folk wisdom n saggezza f popolare

follow /'fɒləʊ/ vt/i seguire; **it doesn't ~** non è necessariamente così; ~ **suit** fig fare lo stesso; **as ~s** come segue
■ **follow through** vt portare avanti ⟨project, idea⟩
■ **follow up** vt fare seguito a ⟨letter⟩

follower /'fɒləʊə(r)/ n seguace mf

following /'fɒləʊɪŋ/ ① adj seguente
② n seguito m; (supporters) seguaci mpl
③ prep in seguito a

follow-on n seguito m

follow-up ① n (of social work case) controllo m; (of patient, ex inmate) visita f di controllo; (film, record, single, programme) seguito m
② attrib ⟨survey, work, interview⟩ successivo; ~ **letter** lettera f che fa seguito

folly /'fɒlɪ/ n follia f

foment /fə'ment/ vt fig fomentare

fond /fɒnd/ adj affezionato; ⟨hope⟩ vivo; **be ~ of** essere appassionato di ⟨music⟩ **I'm ~ of...** ⟨food, person⟩ mi piace moltissimo...

fondle /'fɒndl/ vt coccolare

fondly /'fɒndlɪ/ adv ⟨hope⟩ ingenuamente

fondness /'fɒndnɪs/ n affetto m; (for things) amore m

font /fɒnt/ n fonte f battesimale; Typ carattere m di stampa

food /fuːd/ n cibo m; (for animals, groceries) mangiare m; **let's buy some ~** compriamo qualcosa da mangiare

food aid n aiuti mpl alimentari

foodie /'fuːdɪ/ n fam buongustaio, -a mf

food mixer n frullatore m

food poisoning n intossicazione f alimentare

food processor n tritatutto m inv elettrico

foodstuffs npl generi mpl alimentari

fool[1] /fuːl/ ① n sciocco, -a mf; **she's no ~** non è una stupida; **make a ~ of oneself** rendersi ridicolo
② vt prendere in giro
③ vi ~ **around** giocare; ⟨husband, wife⟩ avere l'amante

fool[2] n Culin crema f

foolhardy /'fuːlhɑːdɪ/ adj temerario

foolish /'fuːlɪʃ/ adj stolto

foolishly /'fuːlɪʃlɪ/ adv scioccamente

foolishness /'fuːlɪʃnɪs/ n sciocchezza f

foolproof /'fuːlpruːf/ adj facilissimo

foolscap /'fuːlskæp/ n (Br: paper) carta f protocollo

foot /fʊt/ n (pl **feet**) piede m; (of animal) zampa f; (measure) piede (= 30,48 cm); **on ~** a piedi; **on one's feet** in piedi; **put one's ~ in it** fam fare una gaffe

footage /'fʊtɪdʒ/ n (piece of film) spezzone m; **news ~** servizio m [filmato]

foot-and-mouth disease n afta f epizootica

football n calcio m; (ball) pallone m

footballer n giocatore m di calcio

football pools npl totocalcio m

footbrake n freno m a pedale

footbridge n passerella f

foothills npl colline fpl pedemontane

foothold n punto m d'appoggio

footing n **lose one's ~** perdere l'appiglio; **on an equal ~** in condizioni di parità

footlights npl luci nfpl della ribalta

footloose and fancy-free adj libero come l'aria

footman n valletto m

footnote n nota f a piè di pagina

foot passenger n (on boat) passeggero, -a mf

footpath n sentiero m

footprint n orma f; (of machine) ingombro m

footrest n poggiapiedi m inv

footsore adj be ∼ avere male ai piedi

footstep n passo m; **follow in somebody's ∼s** fig seguire l'esempio di qualcuno

footstool n sgabellino m

footwear n calzature fpl

for /fə(r)/, accentato/fɔː(r)/ **①** prep per; ∼ **this reason** per questa ragione; **I have lived here ∼ ten years** vivo qui da dieci anni; ∼ **supper** per cena; ∼ **all that** nonostante questo; **what ∼?** a che scopo?; **send ∼ a doctor** chiamare un dottore; **fight ∼ a cause** lottare per una causa; **go ∼ a walk** andare a fare una passeggiata; **there's no need ∼ you to go** non c'è bisogno che tu vada; **it's not ∼ me to say** non sta a me dirlo; **now you're ∼ it** ora sei nei pasticci **②** conj poiché, perché

forage /'fɒrɪdʒ/ **①** n foraggio m **②** vi ∼ **for** cercare

foray /'fɒreɪ/ n Mil incursione f, **make a ∼ into** (politics, acting) tentare la strada di

forbade /fə'bæd/ ▶ FORBID

forbearance /fɔː'beərəns/ n pazienza f

forbearing /fɔː'beərɪŋ/ adj tollerante

forbid /fə'bɪd/ vt (pt **forbade**, pp **forbidden**) proibire

forbidden /fə'bɪd(ə)n/ adj ⟨fruit, place⟩ proibito

forbidding /fə'bɪdɪŋ/ adj ⟨prospect⟩ che spaventa; ⟨stem⟩ severo

force /fɔːs/ **①** n forza f; **in ∼** in vigore; (in large numbers) in massa; **come into ∼** entrare in vigore; **the [armed] ∼s** pl le forze armate **②** vt forzare; ∼ **something on somebody** ⟨decision⟩ imporre qualcosa a qualcuno; ⟨drink⟩ costringere qualcuno a fare qualcosa

■ **force back** vt trattenere ⟨tears⟩

■ **force down** vt buttar giù (controvoglia) ⟨food, drink⟩

forced /fɔːst/ adj forzato

forced landing n atterraggio m forzato

force-feed vt (pt/pp **-fed**) nutrire a forza

forceful /'fɔːsfʊl/ adj energico

forcefully /'fɔːsfʊlɪ/ adv ⟨say, argue⟩ con forza

forceps /'fɔːseps/ npl forcipe m

forcible /'fɔːsəbl/ adj forzato

forcibly /'fɔːsəblɪ/ adv forzatamente

ford /fɔːd/ **①** n guado m **②** vt guadare

fore /fɔː(r)/ n **to the ∼** in vista; **come to the ∼** salire alla ribalta

forearm /'fɔːrɑːm/ n avambraccio m

forebears /'fɔːbeəz/ npl antenati mpl

foreboding /fɔː'bəʊdɪŋ/ n presentimento m

forecast /'fɔːkɑːst/ **①** n previsione f **②** vt (pt/pp **forecast**) prevedere

forecaster /'fɔːkɑːstə(r)/ n pronosticatore, -trice mf; (economic) analista mf della congiuntura; (of weather) meteorologo, -a mf

forecourt n (of garage) spiazzo m [antistante]

forefathers npl antenati mpl

forefinger n [dito m] indice m

forefront n **be in the ∼** essere all'avanguardia

foregone adj **be a ∼ conclusion** essere una cosa scontata

foreground n primo piano m

forehand n Tennis diritto m

forehead /'fɔːhed/, /'fɒrɪd/ n fronte f

foreign /'fɒrən/ adj straniero; estero; (not belonging) estraneo; **he is ∼** è uno straniero

foreign affairs npl affari mpl esteri

foreign body n corpo m estraneo

foreign correspondent n corrispondente mf estero

foreign currency n valuta f estera

foreigner /'fɒrənə(r)/ n straniero, -a mf

foreign exchange n (currency) valuta f estera

foreign exchange market n mercato m dei cambi

foreign language n lingua f straniera

foreign minister n ministro m degli Esteri

Foreign Office n Br ministero m degli [affari] Esteri

Foreign Secretary n Br Ministro m degli Esteri

foreleg /'fɔːleg/ n zampa f anteriore

foreman /'fɔːmən/ n caporeparto m

foremost /'fɔːməʊst/ **①** adj principale **②** adv **first and ∼** in primo luogo

forename /'fɔːneɪm/ n nome m di battesimo

forensic /fə'rensɪk/ adj ∼ **medicine** medicina legale

forensic evidence n prova f medicolegale

forensic science n medicina f legale

forensic scientist n medico m legale

forensic tests npl perizia f sg medicolegale

forerunner /'fɔːrʌnə(r)/ n precursore m

foresee /fɔː'siː/ *vt* (pt **-saw**, pp **-seen**) prevedere

foreseeable /fɔː'siːəbl/ *adj* in the ~ future nel futuro immediato

foreshadow *vt* prevedere

foresight /'fɔːsaɪt/ *n* previdenza *f*

foreskin /'fɔːskɪn/ *n* Anat prepuzio *m*

forest /'fɒrɪst/ *n* foresta *f*

forestall /fɔː'stɔːl/ *vt* prevenire

forester /'fɒrɪstə(r)/ *n* guardia *f* forestale

forest fire *n* incendio *m* nei boschi

forest ranger /'reɪndʒə(r)/ *n* Am guardia *f* forestale

forestry /'fɒrɪstrɪ/ *n* silvicoltura *f*

foretaste /'fɔːteɪst/ *n* pregustazione *f*

foretell /fɔː'tel/ *vt* (pt/pp **-told**) predire

forethought /'fɔːθɔːt/ *n* accortezza *f*, previdenza *f*

forever /fə'revə(r)/ *adv* per sempre; he's ~ complaining si lamenta sempre

forewarn /fɔː'wɔːn/ *vt* avvertire

foreword /'fɔːwɜːd/ *n* prefazione *f*

forfeit /'fɔːfɪt/ **1** *n* (in game) pegno *m*; Jur penalità *f*
2 *vt* perdere

forfeiture /'fɔːfɪtʃə(r)/ *n* (of right) perdita *f*; (of property) confisca *f*

forgave /fə'geɪv/ ▸ FORGIVE

forge[1] /fɔːdʒ/ *vi* ~ ahead ⟨runner⟩ lasciarsi indietro gli altri; fig farsi strada

forge[2] **1** *n* fucina *f*
2 *vt* fucinare; (counterfeit) contraffare

forger /'fɔːdʒə(r)/ *n* contraffattore *m*

forgery /'fɔːdʒərɪ/ *n* contraffazione *f*

forget /fə'get/ *vt/i* (pt **-got**, pp **-gotten**) dimenticare; dimenticarsi di ⟨language, skill⟩; ~ oneself perdere la padronanza di sé

■ **forget about** *vt* dimenticarsi di

forgetful /fə'getfʊl/ *adj* smemorato

forgetfulness /fə'getfʊlnɪs/ *n* smemoratezza *f*

forget-me-not *n* non-ti-scordar-di-mè *m inv*

forgettable /fə'getəbl/ *adj* ⟨day, fact, film⟩ da dimenticare

forgive /fə'gɪv/ *vt* (pt **-gave**, pp **-given**) ~ somebody for something perdonare qualcuno per qualcosa

forgiveness /fə'gɪvnɪs/ *n* perdono *m*

forgiving /fə'gɪvɪŋ/ *adj* ⟨person⟩ indulgente

forgo /fɔː'gəʊ/ *vt* (pt **-went**, pp **-gone**) rinunciare a

forgot(ten) /fə'gɒt(n)/ ▸ FORGET

fork /fɔːk/ **1** *n* forchetta *f*; (for digging) forca *f*; (in road) bivio *m*
2 *vi* ⟨road⟩ biforcarsi; ~ right prendere a destra

■ **fork out** **1** *vt* fam sborsare
2 *vi* sborsare soldi

forked lightning /fɔːkt/ *n* fulmine *m* ramificato

fork-lift truck *n* elevatore *m*

forlorn /fə'lɔːn/ *adj* ⟨look⟩ perduto; ⟨place⟩ derelitto; ~ hope speranza *f* vana

form /fɔːm/ **1** *n* forma *f*; (document) modulo *m*; Sch classe *f*
2 *vt* formare; formulare ⟨opinion⟩
3 *vi* formarsi

formal /'fɔːml/ *adj* formale

formal dress *n* abito *m* da cerimonia

formalin /'fɔːməlɪn/ *n* formalina *f*

formality /fɔː'mælətɪ/ *n* formalità *f inv*

formally /'fɔːmælɪ/ *adv* in modo formale; (officially) ufficialmente

format /'fɔːmæt/ **1** *n* formato *m*
2 *vt* formattare ⟨disk, page⟩

formation /fɔː'meɪʃn/ *n* formazione *f*

formative /'fɔːmətɪv/ *adj* ~ years anni formativi

former /'fɔːmə(r)/ *adj* precedente; ⟨PM, colleague⟩ ex; the ~, the latter il primo, l'ultimo

formerly /'fɔːməlɪ/ *adv* precedentemente; (in olden times) in altri tempi

formidable /'fɔːmɪdəbl/ *adj* formidabile

formless /'fɔːmlɪs/ *adj* ⟨mass⟩ informe; ⟨novel⟩ che manca di struttura

form teacher *n* Br Sch ≈ coordinatore, -trice *mf* del consiglio di classe

formula /'fɔːjʊlə/ *n* (pl **-ae** /'fɔːmjʊliː/ or **-s**) formula *f*

formulate /'fɔːmjʊleɪt/ *vt* formulare

formulation /fɔːmjʊ'leɪʃn/ *n* formulazione *f*

fornication /fɔːnɪ'keɪʃn/ *n* fornicazione *f*

forsake /fə'seɪk/ *vt* (pt **-sook** /fə'sʊk/, pp **-saken**) abbandonare

forseeable /fə'siːəbl/ *adj* in the ~ future in futuro per quanto si possa prevedere

forswear /fɔː'sweə(r)/ *vt* (renounce) abiurare

fort /fɔːt/ *n* Mil forte *m*

forte /'fɔːteɪ/ *n* [pezzo *m*] forte *m*

forth /fɔːθ/ *adv* back and ~ avanti e indietro; and so ~ e così via

forthcoming /fɔːθ'kʌmɪŋ/ *adj* prossimo; (communicative) comunicativo; no response was ~ non arrivava nessuna risposta

forthright /'fɔːθraɪt/ *adj* schietto

forthwith /fɔːθ'wɪθ/ *adv* immediatamente

forties /'fɔːtɪz/ *npl* (period) the ~ gli anni Quaranta *mpl*; (age) quarant'anni *mpl*; a man in his ~ un quarantenne

fortieth /'fɔːtɪɪθ/ *adj & n* quarantesimo, -a *mf*

fortification /fɔːtɪfɪ'keɪʃn/ *n* fortificazione *f*

fortified /'fɔːtɪfaɪd/ *adj* fortificato; ~ **wine** vino liquoroso; ~ **with vitamins** arricchito con vitamine

fortify /'fɔːtɪfaɪ/ *vt* (pt/pp -**ied**) fortificare; fig rendere forte

fortitude /'fɔːtɪtjuːd/ *n* coraggio *m*

fortnight /'fɔːtnaɪt/ *n* Br quindicina *f*

fortnightly /'fɔːtnaɪtlɪ/ ① *adj* bimensile ② *adv* ogni due settimane

fortress /'fɔːtrɪs/ *n* fortezza *f*

fortuitous /fɔː'tjuːɪtəs/ *adj* fortuito

fortunate /'fɔːtʃənət/ *adj* fortunato; **that's** ~! meno male!

fortunately /'fɔːtʃənətlɪ/ *adv* fortunatamente

fortune /'fɔːtʃuːn/ *n* fortuna *f*

fortune cookie *n* Am biscottino *m* che racchiude un foglietto con una predizione

fortune-teller *n* indovino, -a *mf*

forty /'fɔːtɪ/ *adj & n* quaranta *m*; **have** ~ **winks** fam fare un pisolino

forum /'fɔːrəm/ *n* foro *m*

forward /'fɔːwəd/ ① *adv* avanti; (towards the front) **move** ~ andare avanti ② *adj* in avanti; (presumptuous) sfacciato ③ *n* Sport attaccante *m* ④ *vt* inoltrare ⟨letter⟩; spedire ⟨goods⟩

forward buying *n* Fin acquisto *m* a termine

forwarding address *n* indirizzo *m* a cui inoltrare la corrispondenza

forward-looking *adj* ⟨company, person⟩ lungimirante

forward planning *n* pianificazione *f* a lungo termine

forwards /'fɔːwədz/ *adv* avanti

forward slash *n* slash *m inv*

fossil /'fɒs(ə)l/ *n* fossile *m*

fossil fuel *n* combustibile *m* fossile

fossilized /'fɒsɪlaɪzd/ *adj* fossile; ⟨ideas⟩ fossilizzato

foster /'fɒstə(r)/ *vt* allevare ⟨child⟩

foster child *n* figlio, -a *mf* in affidamento

foster family *n* famiglia *f* affidataria

foster home *n* famiglia *f* affidataria

foster mother *n* madre *f* affidataria

fought /fɔːt/ ▶ FIGHT

foul /faʊl/ ① *adj* ⟨smell, taste⟩ cattivo; ⟨air⟩ viziato; ⟨language⟩ osceno; ⟨mood, weather⟩ orrendo ② *vt* inquinare ⟨water⟩; Sport commettere un fallo contro; ⟨nets, rope⟩ impigliarsi in ■ **foul up** *vt* (fam: spoil) mandare in malora

foul-mouthed /-'maʊðd/ *adj* sboccato

foul play ① *n* Jur delitto *m* ② *n* Sport fallo *m*

foul-smelling /-'smelɪŋ/ *adj* puzzo.

foul-up *n* pasticcio *m*

found[1] /faʊnd/ ▶ FIND

found[2] *vt* fondare

foundation /faʊn'deɪʃn/ *n* (basis) fondamento *m*; (charitable) fondazione *f*; ~**s** *pl* (of building) fondamenta *fpl*; **lay the** ~-**stone** porre la prima pietra

foundation course *n* Br Univ corso *m* propedeutico

founder[1] /'faʊndə(r)/ *n* fondatore, trice *mf*

founder[2] *vi* ⟨ship⟩ affondare

foundry /'faʊndrɪ/ *n* fonderia *f*

fount /faʊnt/ *n* Typ carattere *m* [stampa]

fountain /'faʊntɪn/ *n* fontana *f*

fountain pen *n* penna *f* stilografica

four /fɔː(r)/ *adj & n* quattro *m*

four-by-four *n* (vehicle) quattro per quattro *f*

four four time *n* Mus quattro quarti

four-letter word *n* parolaccia *f*

four-poster [bed] *n* letto *m* a baldacchino

foursome /'fɔːsəm/ *n* quartetto *m*

four-star ① *adj* ⟨hotel, restaurant⟩ a quattro stelle ② *n* (petrol) super *f*

four-stroke *adj* ⟨engine⟩ a quattro tempi

fourteen /fɔː'tiːn/ *adj & n* quattordici *m*

fourteenth /fɔː'tiːnθ/ *adj & n* quattordicesimo, -a *mf*

fourth /fɔːθ/ *adj & n* quarto, -a *mf*

fourthly /'fɔːθlɪ/ *adv* in quarto luogo

fourth rate *adj* ⟨job, hotel, film⟩ di terz'ordine

four-wheel drive [vehicle] *n* quattro per quattro *m inv*

fowl /faʊl/ *n* pollame *m*

fox /fɒks/ ① *n* volpe *f* ② *vt* (puzzle) ingannare

fox cub *n* volpacchiotto *m*

fox fur *n* pelliccia *f* di volpe

foxglove *n* digitale *f*

foxhound *n* foxhound *m inv*

fox-hunt *n* caccia *f* alla volpe

fox hunting *n* caccia *f* alla volpe

fox terrier *n* fox-terrier *m inv*

foxtrot *n* fox-trot *m inv*

foxy /'fɒksɪ/ *adj* (-**ier**, -**iest**) (fam: sexy) sexy *inv*; (crafty) scaltro

foyer /'fɔɪeɪ/ *n* Theat ridotto *m*; (in hotel) salone *m* d'ingresso

fracas /'frækɑː/ *n* baruffa *f*

fraction /'frækʃn/ *n* frazione *f*

fractionally /'frækʃənəlɪ/ *adv* (slightly) leggermente

fracture /'fræktʃə(r)/ ❶ *n* frattura *f*
❷ *vt* fratturare
❸ *vi* fratturarsi

fragile /'frædʒaɪl/ *adj* fragile

fragment /'frægmənt/ *n* frammento *m*

fragmentary /'frægm(ə)ntərɪ/ *adj* frammentario

fragrance /'freɪgrəns/ *n* fragranza *f*

fragrant /'freɪgrənt/ *adj* fragrante

frail /freɪl/ *adj* gracile

frailty /'freɪltɪ/ *n* (imperfection) debolezza *f* (of person: moral) fragilità *f inv*; (of person: physical) gracilità *f*; (of health, state) precarietà *f inv*

frame /freɪm/ ❶ *n* (of picture, door, window) cornice *f*; (of spectacles) montatura *f*; Anat ossatura *f*; (structure, of bike) telaio *m*
❷ *vt* incorniciare ‹picture›; fig formulare; (sl: incriminate) montare

frame of mind *n* stato *m* d'animo

framework /'freɪmwɜːk/ *n* struttura *f*; within the ~ of the law nell'ambito della legge

franc /fræŋk/ *n* franco *m*

France /frɑːns/ *n* Francia *f*

franchise /'fræntʃaɪz/ *n* Pol diritto *m* di voto; Comm franchigia *f*

Franciscan /fræn'sɪskən/ *n* francescano *m*

frank[1] /fræŋk/ *vt* affrancare ‹letter›

frank[2] *adj* franco

Frankfurt /'fræŋkfɜːt/ *n* Francoforte *f*

frankfurter /'fræŋkfɜːtə(r)/ *n* würstel *m inv*

frankincense /'fræŋkɪnsens/ *n* incenso *m*

franking machine /'fræŋkɪŋ/ *n* affrancatrice *f*

frankly /'fræŋklɪ/ *adv* francamente

frantic /'fræntɪk/ *adj* frenetico; be ~ with worry essere agitatissimo

frantically /'fræntɪklɪ/ *adv* freneticamente

fraternal /frə'tɜːnl/ *adj* fraterno

fraternity /frə'tɜːnətɪ/ *n* (club) associazione *f*; (spirit, brotherhood) fratellanza *f*

fraud /frɔːd/ *n* frode *f*; (person) impostore *m*

fraudulent /'frɔːdjʊlənt/ *adj* fraudolento

fraught /frɔːt/ *adj* ~ with pieno di

fray[1] /freɪ/ *n* mischia *f*

fray[2] *vi* sfilacciarsi

frayed /freɪd/ *adj* ‹cuffs› sfilacciato; ‹nerves› a pezzi

frazzle /'fræz(ə)l/ *n* be worn to a ~ essere ridotto uno straccio; burn something to a ~ carbonizzare qualcosa

freak /friːk/ ❶ *n* fenomeno *m*; (person) scherzo *m* di natura; (fam: weird person) tipo *m* strambo
❷ *adj* anormale
■ **freak out** *vi* (fam: lose control, go crazy) andar fuori di testa

freakish /'friːkɪʃ/ *adj* strambo

freckle /'frekl/ *n* lentiggine *f*

freckled /'frekld/ *adj* lentigginoso

free /friː/ ❶ *adj* (**freer, freest**) libero; ‹ticket, copy› gratuito; (lavish) generoso; ~ of charge gratuito; set ~ liberare; ~ with... Comm in omaggio per...
❷ *vt* (pt/pp **freed**) liberare

free agent *n* persona *f* libera di agire come vuole

free and easy *adj* disinvolto

freebee, freebie /'friːbɪ/ *n* fam (free gift) omaggio *m*; (trip) viaggio *m* gratuito; (newspaper) giornale *m* gratuito

freedom /'friːdəm/ *n* libertà *f*

freedom fighter *n* combattente *mf* per la libertà

free enterprise *n* liberalismo *m* economico

free fall *n* caduta *f* libera

Freefone®, Freephone *n* numero *m* verde

free-for-all *n* (disorganized situation, fight) baraonda *f*

free gift *n* omaggio *m*

freehand *adv* a mano libera

freehold *n* proprietà *f* [fondiaria] assoluta

free house *n* Br pub *m inv* che non è legato a nessun produttore di birra

free-kick *n* calcio *m* di punizione

freelance *adj* & *adv* indipendente

freeloader *n* fam scroccone *m*

freely /'friːlɪ/ *adv* liberamente; (generously) generosamente; I ~ admit that... devo ammettere che...

free market *n* economia *f* di libero mercato

Freemason *n* massone *m*

Freemasonry *n* massoneria *f*

Freephone *n* = FREEFONE

freephone number *n* numero *m* verde

freepost *n* Br affrancatura *f* a carico del destinatario

free-range *adj* ‹eggs› di allevamento a terra; ‹hens› allevato a terra

free-range egg *n* uovo *m* di gallina ruspante

free sample *n* campione *m* gratuito

free speech *n* libertà *f* di parola

free spirit *n* persona *f* che ama la sua indipendenza

free-standing adj ⟨heater⟩ non incassato; ⟨statue⟩ a tutto tondo; ⟨lamp⟩ a stelo

freestyle n stile m libero

free trade n libero scambio m

free trial period n periodo m di prova gratuito

freeware /ˈfriːweə/ n Comput freeware m inv

freeway n Am autostrada f

freewheel vi ⟨car⟩ (in neutral) andare in folle; (with engine switched off) andare a motore spento; ⟨bicycle⟩ andare a ruota libera

free will n of one's own ∼ di spontanea volontà

freeze /friːz/ ① vt (pt **froze**, pp **frozen**) gelare; bloccare ⟨wages⟩
② vi ⟨water⟩ gelare; **it's freezing** si gela; **my hands are freezing** ho le mani congelate

freeze-dried adj liofilizzato

freeze-frame n (video) fermo m immagine

freezer /ˈfriːzə(r)/ n freezer m inv, congelatore m

freezer compartment n scomparto m freezer

freezing /ˈfriːzɪŋ/ ① adj gelido
② n below ∼ sotto zero

freezing cold adj gelido

freezing fog n nebbia f ghiacciata

freezing point n punto m di congelamento

freight /freɪt/ n carico m

freight charges npl costi mpl di spedizione

freighter /ˈfreɪtə(r)/ n nave f da carico

freight forwarder n spedizioniere m

freight train n Am treno m merci

French /frentʃ/ ① adj francese
② n (language) francese m; the ∼ pl i francesi

French beans npl fagiolini mpl [verdi]

French bread n filone m (di pane)

French Canadian ① n canadese mf francofono, -a
② adj del Canada francofono

French doors npl porta-finestra f inv

French dressing n Br vinaigrette f inv

French fries npl patate fpl fritte

French horn n corno m da caccia

French kiss n bacio m profondo

French knickers npl culottes fpl

Frenchman n francese m

French polish n vernice f a olio e gommalacca

French-speaking adj francofono

French toast n pane m immerso nell'uovo sbattuto e fritto

French window n porta-finestra f

Frenchwoman n francese f

frenetic /frəˈnetɪk/ adj ⟨activity⟩ frenetico

frenzied /ˈfrenzɪd/ adj frenetico

frenzy /ˈfrenzɪ/ n frenesia f

frequency /ˈfriːkwənsɪ/ n frequenza f

frequent¹ /ˈfriːkwənt/ adj frequente

frequent² /frɪˈkwent/ vt frequentare

frequent-flyer miles npl Am miglia fpl aeree

frequently /ˈfriːkwəntlɪ/ adv frequentemente

fresco /ˈfreskəʊ/ n affresco m

fresh /freʃ/ adj fresco; (new) nuovo; (Am: cheeky) sfacciato

fresh air n aria f fresca; **get some** ∼ prendere una boccata d'aria

freshen /ˈfreʃn/ vi ⟨wind⟩ rinfrescare
■ **freshen up** ① vt dare una rinfrescata a
② vi rinfrescarsi

fresh-faced /-ˈfeɪst/ adj dalla faccia giovanile

freshly /ˈfreʃlɪ/ adv di recente

freshman /ˈfreʃmən/ n Am matricola f; (fig: in congress, in firm) nuovo arrivato m

freshness /ˈfreʃnɪs/ n freschezza f

freshwater /ˈfreʃwɔːtə(r)/ adj di acqua dolce

fret /fret/ vi (pt/pp **fretted**) inquietarsi

fretful /ˈfretfʊl/ adj irritabile

fretsaw /ˈfretsɔː/ n seghetto m da traforo

fretwork /ˈfretwɜːk/ n [lavoro m di] traforo m

Freudian slip /ˈfrɔɪdɪən/ n lapsus m inv freudiano

friar /ˈfraɪə(r)/ n frate m

friction /ˈfrɪkʃn/ n frizione f

Friday /ˈfraɪdeɪ/ n venerdì m inv

fridge /frɪdʒ/ n frigo m

fridge-freezer n frigocongelatore m

fried /fraɪd/ ① ▶ FRY¹
② adj fritto; ∼ **egg** uovo m fritto

friend /frend/ n amico, -a mf

friendly /ˈfrendlɪ/ adj (**-ier**, **-iest**) ⟨relations, meeting, match⟩ amichevole; ⟨neighbourhood, smile⟩ piacevole; ⟨software⟩ di facile uso; **be** ∼ **with** essere amico di

friendly fire n fuoco m amico

friendship /ˈfrendʃɪp/ n amicizia f

frieze /friːz/ n fregio m

frigate /ˈfrɪgət/ n fregata f

fright /fraɪt/ n paura f; **take** ∼ spaventarsi

frighten /ˈfraɪt(ə)n/ vt spaventare

■ **frighten away** *vt* far scappare ⟨*bird, intruder*⟩

frightened /'fraɪtənd/ *adj* spaventato; **be** ~ aver paura (**of** di)

frightening /'fraɪt(ə)nɪŋ/ *adj* spaventoso

frightful /'fraɪtfl/ *adj* terribile

frightfully /'fraɪtfʊlɪ/ *adv* terribilmente

frigid /'frɪdʒɪd/ *adj* frigido

frigidity /frɪ'dʒɪdətɪ/ *n* freddezza *f*; Psych frigidità *f*

frill /frɪl/ *n* volant *m inv*

frilly /'frɪlɪ/ *adj* ⟨*dress*⟩ con tanti volant

fringe /frɪndʒ/ *n* frangia *f*; (of hair) frangetta *f*; (fig: edge) margine *m*

fringe benefits *npl* benefici *mpl* supplementari

frisk /frɪsk/ *vt* (search) perquisire

frisky /'frɪskɪ/ *adj* (**-ier**, **-iest**) vispo

fritter /'frɪtə(r)/ *n* frittella *f*
■ **fritter away** *vt* sprecare

frivolity /frɪ'vɒlətɪ/ *n* frivolezza *f*

frivolous /'frɪvələs/ *adj* frivolo

frizzy /'frɪzɪ/ *adj* (**-ier**, **-iest**) crespo

fro /frəʊ/ ▶ TO

frock /frɒk/ *n* abito *m*

frog /frɒg/ *n* rana *f*

frogman *n* uomo *m* rana *inv*

frogmarch *vt* Br portare via a forza

frogs' legs *npl* cosce *fpl* di rana

frogspawn *n* uova *fpl* di rana

frolic /'frɒlɪk/ *vi* (pt/pp **frolicked**) ⟨*lambs*⟩ sgambettare; fam ⟨*people*⟩ folleggiare

from /frɒm/ *prep* da; ~ **Monday** da lunedì; ~ **that day** da quel giorno; **he's** ~ **London** è di Londra; **this is a letter** ~ **my brother** questa è una lettera di mio fratello; **documents** ~ **the 16th century** documenti del XVI secolo; **made** ~ fatto con; **she felt ill** ~ **fatigue** si sentiva male dalla stanchezza; ~ **now on** d'ora in poi

front /frʌnt/ ① *n* parte *f* anteriore; (fig: organization etc) facciata *f*; (of garment) davanti *m*; **sea** ~ lungomare *m*; Mil, Pol, Meteorol fronte *m*; **in** ~ **of** davanti a; **in** *or* **at the** ~ davanti; **to the** ~ avanti; ② *adj* davanti; ⟨*page, row, wheel*⟩ anteriore

frontage /'frʌntɪdʒ/ *n* (of house) facciata *f*; **with ocean/river** ~ (access) prospiciente l'oceano/il fiume

frontal /'frʌntl/ *adj* frontale

front bench *n* Br Pol parlamentari *mpl* di maggiore importanza

front door *n* porta *f* d'entrata

front garden *n* giardino *m* sul davanti

frontier /'frʌntɪə(r)/ *n* frontiera *f*

front line *n* Mil prima linea *f*; **be in the** ~ ~ fig essere in prima linea

front of house *n* Br Theat foyer *m inv*

front page ① *n* prima pagina *f* ② *adj* ⟨*picture, spread*⟩ in prima pagina

front runner *n* Sport concorrente *mf* in testa; (favourite) favorito, -a *mf*

front-wheel drive *n* trazione *f* anteriore

frost /frɒst/ *n* gelo *m*; **hoar** ~ brina *f*

frostbite /'frɒs(t)baɪt/ *n* congelamento *m*

frostbitten /'frɒs(t)bɪtən/ *adj* congelato

frosted /'frɒstɪd/ *adj* ~ **glass** vetro *m* smerigliato

frostily /'frɒstɪlɪ/ *adv* gelidamente

frosting /'frɒstɪŋ/ *n* Am Culin glassa *f*

frosty /'frɒstɪ/ *adj* (**-ier**, **-iest**) also fig gelido

froth /frɒθ/ ① *n* schiuma *f* ② *vi* far schiuma

frothy /'frɒθɪ/ *adj* (**-ier**, **-iest**) schiumoso

frown /fraʊn/ ① *n* cipiglio *m* ② *vi* aggrottare le sopracciglia
■ **frown on** *vt* disapprovare

froze /frəʊz/ ▶ FREEZE

frozen /'frəʊzn/ ① ▶ FREEZE ② *adj* ⟨*corpse, hand*⟩ congelato; ⟨*wastes*⟩ gelido; Culin surgelato; **I'm** ~ sono gelato

frozen food *n* surgelati *mpl*

frugal /'fruːgl/ *adj* frugale

frugally /'fruːgəlɪ/ *adv* frugalmente

fruit /fruːt/ *n* frutto *m*; (collectively) frutta *f*; **eat more** ~ mangia più frutta

fruit bowl *n* fruttiera *f*

fruit cake *n* dolce *m* con frutta candita

fruit cocktail *n* macedonia *f* [di frutta]

fruit drop *n* drop *m inv* alla frutta

fruiterer /'fruːtərə(r)/ *n* fruttivendolo, -a *mf*

fruit farmer *n* frutticoltore *m*

fruit fly *n* moscerino *m* della frutta

fruitful /'fruːtfʊl/ *adj* fig fruttuoso

fruit gum *n* caramella *f* alla frutta

fruition /fruː'ɪʃn/ *n* **come to** ~ dare dei frutti

fruit juice *n* succo *m* di frutta

fruitless /'fruːtlɪs/ *adj* infruttuoso

fruitlessly /'fruːtlɪslɪ/ *adv* senza risultato

fruit machine *n* macchinetta *f* mangiasoldi

fruit salad *n* macedonia *f* [di frutta]

fruity /'fruːtɪ/ *adj* ⟨*wine*⟩ fruttato

frump /frʌmp/ *n* donna *f* scialba

frumpy /'frʌmpɪ/ *adj* scialbo

frustrate /frʌ'streɪt/ *vt* frustrare; rovinare ⟨*plans*⟩

frustrated /frʌ'streɪtɪd/ *adj* frustrato

frustrating /frʌ'streɪtɪŋ/ *adj* frustrante

frustration /frʌ'streɪʃn/ *n* frustrazione *f*

fry[1] /fraɪ/ *n inv* **small ~** fig pesce *m* piccolo

fry[2] *vt/i* (pt/pp **fried**) friggere

frying pan /'fraɪɪŋ/ *n* padella *f*

ft. *abbr* (**foot** or **feet**) piede, piedi

ftp *abbr* (**file transfer protocol**) Comput FTP *m*

fuchsia /'fjuːʃə/ *n* fucsia *f*

fuck /fʌk/ vulg 1 *vt/i* scopare
2 *n* I don't give a ~ me ne sbatto; **what the ~ are you doing?** che cazzo fai?
3 *int* cazzo!
■ **fuck off** *vi* (vulg) ~ **off!** vaffanculo!
■ **fuck up** *vt* (vulg: ruin) mandare a puttane

fucking /'fʌkɪŋ/ *adj* vulg del cazzo

fuddled /'fʌd(ə)ld/ *adj* (confused) confuso; (slightly drunk) brillo

fuddy-duddy /'fʌdɪdʌdɪ/ *n* fam matusa *mf inv*

fudge /fʌdʒ/ *n* caramella *f* a base di zucchero, burro e latte

fuel /'fjuːəl/ 1 *n* carburante *m*; fig nutrimento *m*
2 *vt* fig alimentare

fuel consumption *n* consumo *m* di carburante

fuel efficient *adj* economico

fuel injection *n* iniezione *f*

fuel injection engine *n* motore *m* a iniezione

fuel oil *n* nafta *f*

fuel pump *n* pompa *f* della benzina

fuel tank *n* serbatoio *m*

fuggy /'fʌgɪ/ *adj* (Br: smoky) fumoso

fugitive /'fjuːdʒɪtɪv/ *n* fuggiasco, -a *mf*

fugue /fjuːg/ *n* Mus fuga *f*

fulcrum /'fʊlkrəm/ *n* fulcro *m*

fulfil /fʊl'fɪl/ *vt* (pt/pp **-filled**) soddisfare ⟨conditions, need⟩; adempiere a ⟨promise⟩; realizzare ⟨dream, desire⟩; ~ **oneself** realizzarsi

fulfilling /fʊl'fɪlɪŋ/ *adj* soddisfacente

fulfilment /fʊl'fɪlmənt/ *n* **sense of ~** senso *m* di appagamento

full /fʊl/ 1 *adj* pieno (**of** di); (detailed) esauriente; ⟨bus, hotel⟩ completo; ⟨skirt⟩ ampio; **at ~ speed** a tutta velocità; **in ~ swing** in pieno fervore
2 *adv* in pieno; **you know ~ well that** sai benissimo che
3 *n* **in ~** per intero

full-back *n* difensore *m*

full beam *n* Auto [fari *mpl*] abbaglianti *mpl*

full blast *adv* fam the TV was on ~ ~ c'era la TV a manetta

full-blown /-'bləʊn/ *adj* ⟨epidemic⟩ vero a e proprio; ⟨disease⟩ conclamato

full board *n* pensione *f* completa

full-bodied /-'bɒdɪd/ *adj* ⟨wine⟩ corposo

full-cream milk *n* latte *m* intero

full-frontal *adj* ⟨photograph⟩ di nudo frontale

full house *n* Theat tutto esaurito *m inv*; (in poker) full *m inv*

full-length *adj* ⟨dress⟩ lungo; ⟨curtain⟩ lungo fino a terra; ⟨portrait⟩ intero; ~ **film** lungometraggio *m*

full moon *n* luna *f* piena

full name *n* nome *m* per esteso

full price *n* prezzo *m* intero

full-scale *adj* ⟨model⟩ in scala reale; ⟨alert⟩ di massima gravità

full stop *n* punto *m*

full-time *adj & adv* a tempo pieno

fully /'fʊlɪ/ *adv* completamente; (in detail) dettagliatamente; ~ **booked** ⟨hotel, restaurant⟩ tutto prenotato

fully fledged /-'fledʒd/ *adj* ⟨bird⟩ che ha messo tutte le penne; ⟨lawyer⟩ con tutte le qualifiche; ⟨member⟩ a tutti gli effetti

fulsome /'fʊlsəm/ *adj* esagerato

fumble /'fʌmbl/ *vi* ~ **in** rovistare in; ~ **with** armeggiare con; ~ **for one's keys** rovistare alla ricerca delle chiavi
■ **fumble about** *vi* (in dark) andare a tentoni; ~ **in** rovistare in ⟨bag⟩

fume /fjuːm/ *vi* (be angry) essere furioso

fumes /fjuːmz/ *npl* fumi *mpl*; (from car) gas *mpl* di scarico

fumigate /'fjuːmɪgeɪt/ *vt* suffumicare

fun /fʌn/ *n* divertimento *m*; **for** ~ per ridere; **make ~ of** prendere in giro; **have** ~ divertirsi

function /'fʌŋkʃn/ 1 *n* funzione *f*; (event) cerimonia *f*
2 *vi* funzionare; ~ **as** (serve as) funzionare da

functional /'fʌŋkʃ(ə)nəl/ *adj* funzionale

function key *n* Comput tasto *m* [di] funzioni

function room *n* sala *f* di ricevimento

fund /fʌnd/ 1 *n* fondo *m*; fig pozzo *m*; ~**s** *pl* fondi *mpl*
2 *vt* finanziare

fundamental /fʌndə'mentl/ *adj* fondamentale

fundamentalist /fʌndə'mentəlɪst/ *n* fondamentalista *mf*

funding /'fʌndɪŋ/ *n* (financial aid) finanziamento *m*; (of debt) consolidamento *m*

fund-raiser /-reɪzə(r)/ *n* (person) promotore, -trice *mf* di raccolte di fondi; (event) manifestazione *f* per la raccolta di fondi

fund-raising /-reɪzɪŋ/ *n* raccolta *f* di fondi

funeral /'fjuːnərəl/ *n* funerale *m*

funeral directors *n* impresa *f* di pompe funebri

funeral home, funeral parlour Am *n* camera *f* ardente

funeral march *n* marcia *f* funebre

funeral service *n* rito *m* funebre

funereal /fju:'nɪərɪəl/ *adj* lugubre

funfair /'fʌnfeə(r)/ *n* luna park *m inv*

fungal /'fʌŋgəl/ *adj* ⟨infection⟩ micotico

fungus /'fʌŋgəs/ *n* (pl **-gi** /'fʌŋgaɪ/) fungo *m*

funicular /fju:'nɪkjʊlə(r)/ *n* funicolare *f*

fun loving /'fʌnlʌvɪŋ/ *adj* ⟨person⟩ amante del divertimento

funnel /'fʌnl/ *n* imbuto *m*; (on ship) ciminiera *f*

funnily /'fʌnɪlɪ/ *adv* comicamente; (oddly) stranamente; **~ enough** strano a dirsi

funny /'fʌnɪ/ *adj* (**-ier, -iest**) buffo; (odd) strano

funny bone *n* osso *m* del gomito

funny business *n* fam affare *m* losco

fur /fɜ:(r)/ *n* pelo *m*; (for clothing) pelliccia *f*; (in kettle) deposito *m*

fur coat *n* pelliccia *f*

furious /'fjʊərɪəs/ *adj* furioso

furiously /'fjʊərɪəslɪ/ *adv* furiosamente

furl /fɜ:l/ *vt* serrare ⟨sail⟩

furnace /'fɜ:nɪs/ *n* fornace *f*

furnish /'fɜ:nɪʃ/ *vt* ammobiliare ⟨flat⟩; fornire ⟨supplies⟩

furnished /'fɜ:nɪʃt/ *adj* **~ room** stanza *f* ammobiliata

furnishings /'fɜ:nɪʃɪŋz/ *npl* mobili *mpl*

furniture /'fɜ:nɪtʃə(r)/ *n* mobili *mpl*

furniture remover /rɪmu:və(r)/ *n* Br impresa *f* di traslochi

furniture van *n* furgone *m* per i traslochi

furore /fjʊ'rɔ:rɪ/ *n* (outrage, criticism) scalpore *m*; (acclaim) entusiasmo *m*

furred /fɜ:d/ *adj* ⟨tongue⟩ impastato

furrow /'fʌrəʊ/ *n* solco *m*

furry /'fɜ:rɪ/ *adj* ⟨animal⟩ peloso; ⟨toy⟩ di peluche

further /'fɜ:ðə(r)/ 1 *adj* (additional) ulteriore; **at the ~ end** all'altra estremità;

until ~ notice fino a nuovo avviso 2 *adv* più lontano; **~,...** inoltre,... **~ off** più lontano 3 *vt* promuovere

further education *n* istruzione *f* parauniversitaria

furthermore /fɜ:ðə'mɔ:(r)/ *adv* per di più

furthest /'fɜ:ðɪst/ 1 *adj* più lontano 2 *adv* più lontano; **the ~ advanced of the students** lo studente più avanti

furtive /'fɜ:tɪv/ *adj* furtivo

furtively /'fɜ:tɪvlɪ/ *adv* furtivamente

fury /'fjʊərɪ/ *n* furore *m*

fuse¹ /fju:z/ *n* (of bomb) detonatore *m*; (cord) miccia *f*

fuse² 1 *n* Electr fusibile *m* 2 *vt* fondere; Electr far saltare 3 *vi* fondersi; Electr saltare; **the lights have~d** sono saltate le luci

fuse box *n* scatola *f* dei fusibili

fuselage /'fju:zəlɑ:ʒ/ *n* Aeron fusoliera *f*

fuse wire *n* [filo *m* di] fusibile *m*

fusillade /fju:zɪl'ɑ:d/ *n* Mil scarica *f*; fig raffica *f*

fusion /'fju:ʒn/ *n* fusione *f*

fuss /fʌs/ 1 *n* storie *fpl*; **make a ~** fare storie; **make a ~ of** colmare di attenzioni 2 *vi* fare storie

fussy /'fʌsɪ/ *adj* (**-ier, -iest**) ⟨person⟩ difficile da accontentare; ⟨clothes etc⟩ pieno di fronzoli

fusty /'fʌstɪ/ *adj* che odora di stantio; ⟨smell⟩ di stantio

futile /'fju:taɪl/ *adj* inutile

futility /fjʊ'tɪlətɪ/ *n* futilità *f*

future /'fju:tʃə(r)/ *adj* & *n* futuro; **in ~** in futuro

future perfect *n* futuro *m* anteriore

futures *npl* Fin contratti *mpl* a termine

futuristic /fju:tʃə'rɪstɪk/ *adj* futuristico

fuze /fju:z/ *n* & *v* Am = FUSE

fuzz /fʌz/ *n* **the ~** (sl: police) la pula

fuzzy /'fʌzɪ/ *adj* (**-ier, -iest**) ⟨hair⟩ crespo; ⟨photo⟩ sfuocato

FYI *abbr* (**for your information**) per vostra informazione

- -

Gg

- -

g¹, G /dʒi:/ *n* (letter) g, G *f inv*; Mus sol *m inv*

g² *abbr* (**gram(s)**) g

G8 *n abbr* (**group of 8**) G8 *mpl*

gab /gæb/ *n* fam **have the gift of the ~** avere la parlantina

gabardine /ˈgæbəˈdiːn/ n gabardine f

gabble /ˈgæb(ə)l/ vi parlare troppo in fretta

gable /ˈgeɪb(ə)l/ n frontone m

Gabon /gəˈbɒn/ n Gabon m

gad /gæd/ vi (pt/pp **gadded**) ~ **about** andarsene in giro

gadget /ˈgædʒɪt/ n aggeggio m

Gaelic /ˈgeɪlɪk/ adj & n gaelico m

gaff /gæf/ n Br fam **blow the** ~ spifferare un segreto; **blow the** ~ **on something** svelare la verità su qualcosa

gaffe /gæf/ n gaffe f inv

gaffer /ˈgæfə(r)/ n (Br: foreman) caposquadra m; (Br: boss) capo m; Cinema, TV tecnico m delle luci

gag /gæg/ ❶ n bavaglio m; (joke) battuta f ❷ vt (pt/pp **gagged**) imbavagliare

gaga /ˈɡɑːɡɑː/ adj fam rimbambito

gage /geɪdʒ/ n & vt Am = GAUGE

gaiety /ˈgeɪətɪ/ n allegria f

gaily /ˈgeɪlɪ/ adv allegramente

gain /geɪn/ ❶ n guadagno m; (increase) aumento m
❷ vt acquisire; ~ **weight** aumentare di peso; ~ **access** accedere
❸ vi ‹clock› andare avanti
■ **gain on** vt guadagnare terreno su ‹runner, car›

gainful /ˈgeɪnfʊl/ adj ~ **employment** lavoro m remunerativo

gainsay /geɪnˈseɪ/ vt contraddire ‹person›; contestare ‹argument›

gait /geɪt/ n andatura f

gala /ˈgɑːlə/ ❶ n gala f; **swimming** ~ manifestazione f di nuoto
❷ attrib di gala

galaxy /ˈgæləksɪ/ n galassia f

gale /geɪl/ n bufera f

gale warning n avviso m di imminente bufera

gall /gɔːl/ n (impudence) impudenza f

gallant /ˈgælənt/ adj coraggioso; (chivalrous) galante

gallantly /ˈgæləntlɪ/ adv galantemente

gallantry /ˈgæləntrɪ/ n coraggio m

gall bladder n cistifellea f

gallery /ˈgælərɪ/ n galleria f

galley /ˈgælɪ/ n (ship's kitchen) cambusa f

galley [proof] n bozza f in colonna

Gallic /ˈgælɪk/ adj francese

galling /ˈgɔːlɪŋ/ adj irritante

gallivant /ˈgælɪvænt/ vi fam andare in giro

gallon /ˈgælən/ n gallone m (Br = 4,5 l; Am = 3,7 l)

gallop /ˈgæləp/ ❶ n galoppo m
❷ vi galoppare

gallows /ˈgæləʊz/ n forca f

gallstone /ˈgɔːlstəʊn/ n calcolo m biliare

galore /gəˈlɔː(r)/ adv a bizzeffe

galvanize /ˈgælvənaɪz/ vt Techn galvanizzare; fig stimolare (**into** a)

Gambia /ˈgæmbɪə/ n Gambia m

gambit /ˈgæmbɪt/ n prima mossa f

gamble /ˈgæmbl/ ❶ n (risk) azzardo m
❷ vi giocare; (on Stock Exchange) speculare; ~ **on** (rely) contare su

gambler /ˈgæmblə(r)/ n giocatore, -trice mf [d'azzardo]

gambling /ˈgæmblɪŋ/ n gioco m [d'azzardo]

gambol /ˈgæmb(ə)l/ vi saltellare

game /geɪm/ ❶ n gioco m; (match) partita f; (animals, birds) selvaggina f; ~**s** pl Sch ≈ ginnastica f
❷ adj (brave) coraggioso; **are you** ~? ti va?; **be** ~ **for** essere pronto per

game bird n uccello m da cacciagione

gamekeeper n guardacaccia m inv

game park n = game reserve

game plan n tattica f

game point n Tennis game point m inv

game reserve n (for hunting) riserva f di caccia; (for preservation) parco m naturale [faunistico]

games console n console f per videogiochi

game show n ≈ quiz m inv televisivo

gamesmanship /ˈgeɪmzmənʃɪp/ n stratagemmi mpl

games room n sala f giochi

games software n computer game m inv

game warden n guardacaccia m inv

gaming /ˈgeɪmɪŋ/ n **on-line** ~ giochi online

gaming laws npl leggi fpl che regolano il gioco d'azzardo

gaming machine n slot machine f inv

gaming zone n sito m su cui giocare online

gammon /ˈgæmən/ n coscia f di maiale affumicata

gamut /ˈgæmət/ n fig gamma f

gander /ˈgændə(r)/ n oca f maschio; **take a** ~ **at something** fam dare un'occhiata a qualcosa

gang /gæŋ/ n banda f; (of workmen) squadra f
■ **gang up** vi far comunella (**on** contro)

gangland /ˈgæŋlænd/ n malavita f

gangleader /ˈgæŋliːdə(r)/ n capobanda mf inv

gangling /ˈgæŋglɪŋ/ adj spilungone

gangplank /ˈgæŋplæŋk/ n passerella f

gang rape n stupro m collettivo

gangrene /ˈgæŋgriːn/ n cancrena f

gangrenous /'gæŋgrɪnəs/ *adj* cancrenoso

gangster /'gæŋstə(r)/ *n* gangster *m inv*

gangway /'gæŋweɪ/ *n* passaggio *m*; Naut, Aeron passerella *f*

gaol /dʒeɪl/ **①** *n* carcere *m* **②** *vt* incarcerare

gaoler /'dʒeɪlə(r)/ *n* carceriere *m*

gap /gæp/ *n* spazio *m*; (in ages, between teeth) scarto *m*; (in memory) vuoto *m*; (in story) punto *m* oscuro

gape /geɪp/ *vi* stare a bocca aperta; (be wide open) spalancarsi; ∼ **at** guardare a bocca aperta

gaping /'geɪpɪŋ/ *adj* aperto

gap year *n* anno *m* sabbatico tra la fine della scuola superiore e l'inizio dell'università

garage /'gærɑːʒ/ *n* garage *m inv*; (for repairs) meccanico *m*; (for petrol) stazione *f* di servizio

garage mechanic *n* meccanico *m*

garage sale *n* vendita *f* di articoli usati a casa propria

garb /gɑːb/ *n* tenuta *f*

garbage /'gɑːbɪdʒ/ *n* immondizia *f*; (nonsense) idiozie *fpl*

garbage can *n* Am bidone *m* dell'immondizia

garbage truck *n* Am camion *m* della nettezza urbana

garbled /'gɑːbld/ *adj* confuso

garden /'gɑːdn/ **①** *n* giardino *m*; [public] ∼**s** *pl* giardini *mpl* pubblici **②** *vi* fare giardinaggio

garden centre *n* Br vivaio *m* (che vende anche articoli da giardinaggio)

garden city *n* città *f inv* giardino

gardener /'gɑːdnə(r)/ *n* giardiniere, -a *mf*

garden flat *n* appartamento *m* al pianterreno o seminterrato che dà sul giardino

gardening /'gɑːdnɪŋ/ *n* giardinaggio *m*

garden shears *npl* cesoie *fpl*

garden suburb *n* periferia *f* verde

garden-variety *adj* Am ⟨writer, book⟩ insignificante

gargle /'gɑːgl/ **①** *n* gargarismo *m* **②** *vi* fare gargarismi

gargoyle /'gɑːgɔɪl/ *n* gargouille *f inv*

garish /'geərɪʃ/ *adj* sgargiante

garland /'gɑːlənd/ *n* ghirlanda *f*

garlic /'gɑːlɪk/ *n* aglio *m*

garlic bread *n* pane *m* condito con aglio

garlic press *n* spremiaglio *m inv*

garment /'gɑːmənt/ *n* indumento *m*

garnet /'gɑːnɪt/ *n* granato *m*

garnish /'gɑːnɪʃ/ **①** *n* guarnizione *f* **②** *vt* guarnire

garret /'gærɪt/ *n* soffitta *f*

garrison /'gærɪsn/ *n* guarnigione *f*

garrotte /gə'rɒt/ **①** *n* Br garrotta *f* **②** *vt* (strangle) strangolare

garrulous /'gærʊləs/ *adj* chiacchierone

garter /'gɑːtə(r)/ *n* giarrettiera *f*; (Am: for man's socks) reggicalze *m inv* da uomo

gas /gæs/ **①** *n* gas *m inv*; (Am fam: petrol) benzina *f* **②** *vt* (pt/pp **gassed**) asfissiare **③** *vi* fam blaterare

gas burner *n* becco *m* a gas

gas chamber *n* camera *f* a gas

gas cooker *n* cucina *f* a gas

gaseous /'gæsɪəs/ *adj* gassoso

gas fire *n* stufa *f* a gas

gas-fired /-faɪəd/ *adj* ⟨boiler, water heater⟩ a gas

gash /gæʃ/ **①** *n* taglio *m* **②** *vt* tagliare; ∼ **one's arm** farsi un taglio nel braccio

gasket /'gæskɪt/ *n* Techn guarnizione *f*

gas main *n* conduttura *f* del gas

gas mask *n* maschera *f* antigas

gas meter *n* contatore *m* del gas

gasoline /'gæsəliːn/ *n* Am benzina *f*

gas oven *n* forno *m* a gas

gasp /gɑːsp/ *vi* avere il fiato mozzato

gas pedal *n* Am pedale *m* dell'acceleratore

gas ring *n* Br (fixed) bruciatore *m*; (portable) fornelletto *m* [portatile]

gas station *n* Am distributore *m* di benzina

gastric /'gæstrɪk/ *adj* gastrico

gastric flu *n* influenza *f* gastro-intestinale

gastric ulcer *n* ulcera *f* gastrica

gastritis /gæ'straɪtɪs/ *n* gastrite *f*

gastroenteritis /gæstrəʊentə'raɪtɪs/ *n* gastroenterite *f*

gastronomy /gæ'strɒnəmɪ/ *n* gastronomia *f*

gate /geɪt/ *n* cancello *m*; (at airport) uscita *f*

gâteau /'gætəʊ/ *n* torta *f*

gatecrash **①** *vt* entrare senza invito a **②** *vi* entrare senza invito

gatecrasher *n* intruso, -a *mf*

gatehouse *n* (to castle) corpo *m* di guardia; (to park) casa *f* del custode

gatekeeper *n* custode *mf*

gatepost *n* palo *m* del cancello

gateway *n* ingresso *m*

gateway drug *n* droga *f* di passaggio

gather /'gæðə(r)/ **①** *vt* raccogliere; (conclude) dedurre; (in sewing) arricciare; ∼ **speed** acquistare velocità; ∼ **together** ⋯⟶

radunare ⟨*people, belongings*⟩; (obtain gradually) acquistare

2 *vi* ⟨*people*⟩ radunarsi; **a storm is ~ing** si sta preparando un acquazzone

gathering /'gæðərɪŋ/ *n* **family ~** ritrovo *m* di famiglia

GATT /gæt/ *abbr* (**General Agreement on Tariffs and Trade**) GATT *m*

gauche /gəʊʃ/ *adj* ⟨*person, attitude*⟩ impacciato; ⟨*remark*⟩ inopportuno

gaudy /'gɔːdɪ/ *adj* (**-ier, -iest**) pacchiano

gauge /geɪdʒ/ **1** *n* calibro *m*; Rail scartamento *m*; (device) indicatore *m* **2** *vt* misurare; fig stimare

gaunt /gɔːnt/ *adj* (thin) smunto

gauntlet /'gɔːntlɪt/ *n* **throw down the ~** lanciare il guanto della sfida

gauze /gɔːz/ *n* garza *f*

gave /geɪv/ ▶ GIVE

gawky /'gɔːkɪ/ *adj* (**-ier, -iest**) sgraziato

gawp /gɔːp/ *vi* **~ (at)** fam guardare con aria da ebete

gay /geɪ/ *adj* gaio; (homosexual) omosessuale; ⟨*bar, club*⟩ gay

Gaza strip /'gɑːzə/ *n* la striscia *f* di Gaza

gaze /geɪz/ **1** *n* sguardo *m* fisso **2** *vi* guardare; **~ at** fissare; **~ into space** avere lo sguardo perso nel vuoto

gazelle /gə'zel/ *n* gazzella *f*

gazette /gə'zet/ *n* (official journal) bollettino *m* ufficiale; (newspaper title) gazzetta *f*

gazetteer /gæzɪ'tɪə(r)/ *n* (book) dizionario *m* geografico; (part of book) indice *m* dei nomi geografici

gazump /gə'zʌmp/ *vt* Comm sl **we've been ~ed** il proprietario della casa ha optato per un'offerta migliore dopo avere accettato la nostra

GB *abbr* (**Great Britain**) GB

GBH *n abbr* (**grievous bodily harm**) lesioni *fpl* personali gravi

GCSE *n* Br *abbr* (**General Certificate of Secondary Education**) esami *mpl* conclusivi della scuola dell'obbligo

GDP *n abbr* (**gross domestic product**) PIL *m*

gear /gɪə(r)/ **1** *n* equipaggiamento *m*; Techn ingranaggio *m*; Auto marcia *f*; **in ~** con la marcia innestata; **change ~** cambiare marcia **2** *vt* finalizzare (**to** a) **3** *vi* **~ up for** prepararsi per ⟨*election*⟩; **~ up to do something** prepararsi per fare qualcosa

gearbox /'gɪəbɒks/ *n* Auto scatola *f* del cambio

gear lever, gearstick, Am **gear shift** *n* leva *f* del cambio

gear wheel *n* moltiplica *f*

geese /giːs/ ▶ GOOSE

geezer /'giːzə(r)/ *n* sl tipo *m*

gel /dʒel/ *n* gel *m inv*

gelatine /'dʒelətɪn/ *n* gelatina *f*

gelatinous /dʒɪ'lætɪnəs/ *adj* gelatinoso

gelding /'geldɪŋ/ *n* (horse) castrone *m*; (castration) castrazione *f*

gelignite /'dʒelɪgnaɪt/ *n* gelatina *f* esplosiva

gem /dʒem/ *n* gemma *f*

Gemini /'dʒemɪnaɪ/ *n* Astr Gemelli *mpl*

gen /dʒen/ *n* Br fam informazioni *fpl*; **what's the ~ on this?** cosa c'è da sapere su questo?

gender /'dʒendə(r)/ *n* Gram genere *m*

gene /dʒiːn/ *n* gene *m*

genealogy /dʒiːnɪ'ælədʒɪ/ *n* genealogia *f*

gene library *n* genoteca *f*

gene pool *n* pool *m* genetico

general /'dʒenrəl/ **1** *adj* generale **2** *n* generale *m*; **in ~** in generale

general election *n* elezioni *fpl* politiche

generalization /dʒenrəlaɪ'zeɪʃn/ *n* generalizzazione *f*

generalize /'dʒenrəlaɪz/ *vi* generalizzare

general knowledge *n* cultura *f* generale

generally /'dʒenrəlɪ/ *adv* generalmente

general practitioner *n* medico *m* generico

general public *n* [grande] pubblico *m*

general-purpose *adj* multiuso *inv*

general strike *n* sciopero *m* generale

generate /'dʒenəreɪt/ *vt* generare

generation /dʒenə'reɪʃn/ *n* generazione *f*

generation gap *n* gap *m inv* generazionale

generator /'dʒenəreɪtə(r)/ *n* generatore *m*

generic /dʒɪ'nerɪk/ *adj* **~ term** termine *m* generico

generosity /dʒenə'rɒsətɪ/ *n* generosità *f*

generous /'dʒenərəs/ *adj* generoso

generously /'dʒenərəslɪ/ *adv* generosamente

genesis /'dʒenəsɪs/ *n* fig genesi *f inv*

gene therapy *n* terapia *f* genica

genetic /dʒɪ'netɪk/ *adj* genetico

genetically modified /dʒɪ'netɪklɪ 'mɒdɪfaɪd/ *adj* ⟨*crops*⟩ modificato geneticamente

genetic engineering *n* ingegneria *f* genetica

genetic fingerprinting /'fɪŋgəprɪntɪŋ/ *n* impronte *fpl* genetiche

geneticist /dʒɪ'netɪsɪst/ *n* genetista *mf*

genetics /dʒɪ'netɪks/ n genetica f
genetic testing n test mpl genetici
Geneva /dʒɪ'niːvə/ n Ginevra f
genial /'dʒiːnɪəl/ adj gioviale
genially /'dʒiːnɪəlɪ/ adv con giovialità
genie /'dʒiːnɪ/ n genio m
genitals /'dʒenɪtlz/ npl genitali mpl
genitive /'dʒenɪtɪv/ adj & n ~ [case] genitivo m
genius /'dʒiːnɪəs/ n (pl **-uses**) genio m
Genoa /'dʒenəʊə/ n Genova f
genocide /'dʒenəsaɪd/ n genocidio m
genome /'dʒiːnəʊm/ n genoma m
genre /'ʒɑ̃rə/ n genere m [letterario]
gent /dʒent/ n fam signore m; **the ~s** sg il bagno per uomini
genteel /dʒen'tiːl/ adj raffinato
gentle /'dʒentl/ adj delicato; ⟨breeze, tap, slope⟩ leggero
gentleman /'dʒentlmən/ n signore m; (well-mannered) gentiluomo m
gentleness /'dʒentlnɪs/ n delicatezza f
gently /'dʒentlɪ/ adv delicatamente
gentry /'dʒentrɪ/ n alta borghesia f
genuine /'dʒenjʊɪn/ adj genuino
genuinely /'dʒenjʊɪnlɪ/ adv ⟨sorry⟩ sinceramente
genus /'dʒiːnəs/ n Biol genere m
geographer /dʒɪ'ɒɡrəfə(r)/ n geografo m
geographical /dʒɪə'ɡræfɪkl/ adj geografico
geographically /dʒɪə'ɡræfɪklɪ/ adv geograficamente
geography /dʒɪ'ɒɡrəfɪ/ n geografia f
geological /dʒɪə'lɒdʒɪkl/ adj geologico
geologist /dʒɪ'ɒlədʒɪst/ n geologo, -a mf
geology /dʒɪ'ɒlədʒɪ/ n geologia f
geometric[al] /dʒɪə'metrɪk[l]/ adj geometrico
geometry /dʒɪ'ɒmətrɪ/ n geometria f
geophysics /dʒɪəʊ'fɪzɪks/ n geofisica f
geopolitical /dʒiː'əʊpə'lɪtɪkl/ adj geopolitico
Georgia /'dʒɔːdʒə/ n Georgia f
Georgian /'dʒɔːdʒən/ n & adj georgiano, -a mf; (language) georgiano m
geranium /dʒə'reɪnɪəm/ n geranio m
gerbil /'dʒɜːbəl/ n gerbillo m
geriatric /dʒerɪ'ætrɪk/ adj geriatrico
geriatrics /dʒerɪ'ætrɪks/ n geriatria f
geriatric ward n reparto m geriatria
germ /dʒɜːm/ n germe m; **~s** pl microbi mpl
German /'dʒɜːmən/ n & adj tedesco, -a mf; (language) tedesco m
germane /dʒə'meɪn/ adj ⟨point, remark⟩ pertinente

Germanic /dʒə'mænɪk/ adj germanico f
German measles n rosolia f
German shepherd n pastore m tedesco
Germany /'dʒɜːmənɪ/ n Germania f
germinate /'dʒɜːmɪneɪt/ vi germogliare
germ warfare n guerra f batteriologica
gerrymandering /'dʒerɪmænd(ə)rɪŋ/ n manipolazione f dei confini di una circoscrizione elettorale
gerund /'dʒerənd/ n gerundio m
gestate /dʒe'steɪt/ vi Biol essere incinta; fig maturare
gestation /dʒe'steɪʃən/ n gestazione f
gesticulate /dʒe'stɪkjʊleɪt/ vi gesticolare
gesture /'dʒestʃə(r)/ n gesto m
get /get/ **①** vt (pt/pp **got** pp Am also **gotten**, pres p **getting**) (receive) ricevere; (obtain) ottenere; trovare ⟨job⟩; (buy, catch, fetch) prendere; (transport, deliver to airport etc) portare; (reach on telephone) trovare; (fam: understand) comprendere; preparare ⟨meal⟩; ~ **somebody to do something** far fare qualcosa a qualcuno
② vi (become) ~ **tired/bored/angry** stancarsi/annoiarsi/arrabbiarsi; **I'm ~ting hungry** mi sta venendo fame; ~ **real!** fatti furbo!; ~ **dressed/married** vestirsi/sposarsi; ~ **something ready** preparare qualcosa; ~ **nowhere** non concludere nulla; **this is ~ting us nowhere** questo non ci è di nessun aiuto; ~ **to** (reach) arrivare a
■ **get about** vi ⟨person⟩ muoversi; ⟨rumour⟩ circolare
■ **get across** vt far capire ⟨message, meaning⟩; ~ **something across to somebody** far capire qualcosa a qualcuno
■ **get ahead** vi (progress) fare progressi
■ **get along** vi = **get on**
■ **get along with** vt andare d'accordo con ⟨somebody⟩
■ **get around** vi = **get about**
■ **get at** vi (criticize) criticare; **I see what you're ~ting at** ho capito cosa vuoi dire; **what are you ~ting at?** dove vuoi andare a parare?
■ **get away** vi (leave) andarsene; (escape) scappare
■ **get away with** vt restare impunito per
■ **get behind with** vt rimanere indietro con
■ **get by** vi passare; (manage) cavarsela
■ **get down** **①** vi scendere; ~ **down to work** mettersi al lavoro
② vt (depress) buttare giù
■ **get in** **①** vi entrare
② vt mettere dentro ⟨washing⟩; far venire ⟨plumber⟩
■ **get into** vt penetrare in ⟨building⟩; mettersi in ⟨trouble⟩; (squeeze into) entrare in ⟨dress⟩

■ **get off** ① *vi* scendere; (from work) andarsene; Jur essere assolto; ~ **off the bus/one's bike** scendere dal pullman/dalla bici

② *vt* (remove) togliere

■ **get on** *vi* salire; (be on good terms) andare d'accordo; (make progress) andare avanti; (in life) riuscire; ~ **on the bus/one's bike** salire sul pullman/sulla bici; **how are you ~ting on?** come va?

■ **get on with** *vt* andare d'accordo con ⟨*person*⟩; andare avanti in ⟨*work*⟩

■ **get out** ① *vi* uscire; (of car) scendere; ~ **out!** fuori!

② *vt* togliere ⟨*cork, stain*⟩

■ **get out of** *vt* (avoid doing) evitare

■ **get over** ① *vi* andare al di là

② *vt* fig riprendersi da ⟨*illness*⟩

■ **get round** ① *vt* aggirare ⟨*rule*⟩; rigirare ⟨*person*⟩

② *vi* **I never ~ round to it** non mi sono mai deciso a farlo

■ **get through** *vi* (on telephone) prendere la linea

■ **get together** ① *vi* (meet) incontrarsi

② *vt* mettere insieme ⟨*people, money, report*⟩

■ **get up** ① *vi* alzarsi; (climb) salire

② *vt* salire su; ~ **up a hill** salire su una collina

■ **get up to** *vt* combinare ⟨*mischief*⟩

getaway *n* fuga *f*

get-together *n* incontro *m* fra amici

get-up *n* tenuta *f*

get-up-and-go *n* dinamismo *m*

geyser /ˈgiːzə(r)/ *n* scaldabagno *m*; Geol geyser *m inv*

G-force *n* forza *f* di gravità

Ghana /ˈgɑːnə/ *n* Ghana *m*

ghastly /ˈgɑːstlɪ/ *adj* (-ier, -iest) terribile; **feel ~** sentirsi da cani

gherkin /ˈgɜːkɪn/ *n* cetriolino *m*

ghetto /ˈgetəʊ/ *n* ghetto *m*

ghetto blaster /blɑːstə(r)/ *n* fam radioregistratore *m* stereo portatile

ghost /ɡəʊst/ *n* fantasma *m*

ghostly /ˈɡəʊstlɪ/ *adj* spettrale

ghost town *n* città *f inv* fantasma

ghost writer *n* negro *m*

ghoulish /ˈɡuːlɪʃ/ *adj* macabro

giant /ˈdʒaɪənt/ ① *n* gigante *m*

② *adj* gigante

gibberish /ˈdʒɪbərɪʃ/ *n* stupidaggini *fpl*

gibe /dʒaɪb/ ① *n* malignità *f inv*

② *vi* beffarsi (**at** di)

giblets /ˈdʒɪblɪts/ *npl* frattaglie *fpl*

giddiness /ˈɡɪdɪnɪs/ *n* vertigini *fpl*

giddy /ˈɡɪdɪ/ *adj* (-ier, -iest) vertiginoso; **feel ~** avere le vertigini

giddy spell *n* giramento *m* di testa

gift /ɡɪft/ *n* dono *m*; (made to charity) donazione *f*

gifted /ˈɡɪftɪd/ *adj* dotato

gift shop *n* negozio *m* di souvenir

gift token *n* Br buono *m* acquisto

gift voucher *n* Br buono *m* acquisto

gift-wrap *vt* impacchettare in carta da regalo

gig /ɡɪɡ/ *n* Mus fam concerto *m*

gigantic /dʒaɪˈɡæntɪk/ *adj* gigantesco

giggle /ˈɡɪɡ(ə)l/ ① *n* risatina *f*

② *vi* ridacchiare

giggly /ˈɡɪɡlɪ/ *adj* ⟨*person*⟩ che ha la ridarella

gild /ɡɪld/ *vt* dorare

gilding /ˈɡɪldɪŋ/ *n* doratura *f*

gill /dʒɪl/ *n* (measure) quarto *m* di pinta

gills /ɡɪlz/ *npl* branchia *fsg*

gilt /ɡɪlt/ ① *adj* dorato

② *n* doratura *f*

gilt-edged stock /-edʒd/ *n* Fin investimento *m* sicuro

gimlet /ˈɡɪmlɪt/ *n* succhiello *m*

gimmick /ˈɡɪmɪk/ *n* trovata *f*

gimmicky /ˈɡɪmɪkɪ/ *adj* ⟨*production*⟩ pieno di trovate a effetto

gin /dʒɪn/ *n* gin *m inv*

ginger /ˈdʒɪndʒə(r)/ ① *adj* rosso fuoco *inv*; ⟨*cat*⟩ rosso

② *n* zenzero *m*

ginger ale *n* bibita *f* gassata allo zenzero

ginger beer *n* bibita *f* allo zenzero

gingerbread *n* panpepato *m*

ginger-haired /-ˈheəd/ *adj* con i capelli rossi

gingerly /ˈdʒɪndʒəlɪ/ *adv* con precauzione

ginger nut, ginger snap *n* biscotto *m* allo zenzero

gingham /ˈɡɪŋəm/ *n* tessuto *m* vichy

gin rummy *n* variante *f* del gioco del ramino

gipsy /ˈdʒɪpsɪ/ *n* = GYPSY

giraffe /dʒɪˈrɑːf/ *n* giraffa *f*

girder /ˈɡɜːdə(r)/ *n* Techn trave *f*

girdle /ˈɡɜːdl/ *n* cintura *f*; (corset) busto *m*

girl /ɡɜːl/ *n* ragazza *f*; (female child) femmina *f*

girl Friday *n* segretaria *f* tuttofare *inv*

girlfriend *n* amica *f*; (of boy) ragazza *f*

girl guide *n* Br giovane esploratrice *f*

girlish /ˈɡɜːlɪʃ/ *adj* da ragazza

giro /ˈdʒaɪərəʊ/ *n* bancogiro *m*; (cheque) sussidio *m* di disoccupazione

girth /ɡɜːθ/ *n* circonferenza *f*

gist /dʒɪst/ *n* **the ~** la sostanza

give /ɡɪv/ ① *n* elasticità *f*

② *vt* (pt **gave**, pp **given**) dare; (as present) regalare (**to** a); fare ⟨*lecture,* *present, shriek*⟩; donare ⟨*blood*⟩; ~ **birth** partorire

3 *vi* (to charity) fare delle donazioni; (yield) cedere

■ **give away** *vt* dar via; (betray) tradire; (distribute) assegnare; ~ **away the bride** portare la sposa all'altare

■ **give back** *vt* restituire

■ **give in** **1** *vt* consegnare

2 *vi* (yield) arrendersi

■ **give off** *vt* emanare

■ **give out** **1** *vi* ⟨*supplies, patience*⟩ esaurirsi; ⟨*engine, heart*⟩ fermarsi

2 *vt* (distribute) distribuire; diffondere ⟨*heat*⟩

■ **give over** *vi* ~ over! piantala!

■ **give up** **1** *vt* rinunciare a; ~ **oneself up** arrendersi

2 *vi* rinunciare

■ **give way** *vi* cedere; Auto dare la precedenza; (collapse) crollare

give-and-take *n* concessioni *fpl* reciproche

giveaway *n* **to be a dead** ~ essere un indizio ovvio

given /'gɪvn/ ▶ GIVE

given name *n* nome *m* di battesimo

GLA *n* Br *abbr* (**Greater London Authority**) organismo *m* di governo di Londra

glacier /'glæsɪə(r)/ *n* ghiacciaio *m*

glad /glæd/ *adj* contento (of di)

gladden /'glædn/ *vt* rallegrare

glade /gleɪd/ *n* radura *f*

gladiator /'glædɪeɪtə(r)/ *n* gladiatore *m*

gladiolus /glædɪ'əʊləs/ *n* gladiolo *m*

gladly /'glædlɪ/ *adv* volentieri

glamorize /'glæməraɪz/ *vt* rendere affascinante

glamorous /'glæmərəs/ *adj* affascinante

glamour /'glæmə(r)/ *n* fascino *m*

glance /glɑːns/ **1** *n* sguardo *m*

2 *vi* ~ **at** dare un'occhiata a

■ **glance off** *vt* ⟨*bullet, stone*⟩ rimbalzare contro

■ **glance up** *vi* alzare gli occhi

gland /glænd/ *n* ghiandola *f*

glandular /'glændjʊlə(r)/ *adj* ghiandolare

glandular fever *n* mononucleosi *f*

glare /gleə(r)/ **1** *n* bagliore *m*; (look) occhiataccia *f*

2 *vi* ~ **at** dare un'occhiataccia a

glaring /'gleərɪŋ/ *adj* sfolgorante; ⟨*mistake*⟩ madornale

glass /glɑːs/ *n* vetro *m*; (for drinking) bicchiere *m*

glass ceiling *n* barriera *f* invisibile che impedisce alle donne di avanzare nella carriera

glasses /'glɑːsɪz/ *npl* (spectacles) occhiali *mpl*

glasshouse /'glɑːshaʊs/ *n* serra *f*

glassy /'glɑːsɪ/ *adj* vitreo

glassy-eyed /-'aɪd/ *adj* (from drink, illness) che ha gli occhi vitrei

glaucoma /glɔː'kəʊmə/ *n* glaucoma *m*

glaze /gleɪz/ **1** *n* smalto *m*

2 *vt* mettere i vetri a ⟨*door, window*⟩; smaltare ⟨*pottery*⟩; Culin spennellare

glazed /gleɪzd/ *adj* ⟨*eyes*⟩ vitreo

glazier /'gleɪzɪə(r)/ *n* vetraio *m*

gleam /gliːm/ **1** *n* luccichio *m*

2 *vi* luccicare

gleaming /'gliːmɪŋ/ *adj* (clean) splendente; ~ **white teeth** denti bianchi splendenti

glean /gliːn/ *vt* racimolare ⟨*information*⟩

glee /gliː/ *n* gioia *f*

gleeful /'gliːfʊl/ *adj* gioioso

gleefully /'gliːfʊlɪ/ *adv* gioiosamente

glen /glen/ *n* vallone *m*

glib /glɪb/ *adj* pej insincero

glibly /'glɪblɪ/ *adv* pej senza sincerità

glide /glaɪd/ *vi* scorrere; (through the air) planare

glider /'glaɪdə(r)/ *n* aliante *m*

gliding /'glaɪdɪŋ/ *n* volo *m* a vela

glimmer /'glɪmə(r)/ **1** *n* barlume *m*

2 *vi* emettere un barlume

glimpse /glɪmps/ **1** *n* occhiata *f*; **catch a** ~ **of** intravedere

2 *vt* intravedere

glint /glɪnt/ **1** *n* luccichio *m*

2 *vi* luccicare

glisten /'glɪsn/ *vi* luccicare

glitch /glɪtʃ/ *n* Comput problema *m* tecnico

glitter /'glɪtə(r)/ *vi* brillare

gloat /gləʊt/ *vi* gongolare (over su)

global /'gləʊbl/ *adj* mondiale

globalization *n* globalizzazione *f*

global warming *n* riscaldamento *m* dell'atmosfera terrestre

globe /gləʊb/ *n* globo *m*; (as a map) mappamondo *m*

globe-trotting /-trɒtɪŋ/ **1** *n* viaggi *mpl* intorno al mondo

2 *adj* ⟨*life*⟩ da giramondo; ⟨*person*⟩ giramondo

globule /'glɒbjuːl/ *n* globulo *m*

gloom /gluːm/ *n* oscurità *f*; (sadness) tristezza *f*

gloomily /'gluːmɪlɪ/ *adv* (sadly) con aria cupa

gloomy /'gluːmɪ/ *adj* (**-ier, -iest**) cupo

glorify /'glɔːrɪfaɪ/ *vt* (pt/pp **-ied**) glorificare; **a glorified waitress** niente più che una cameriera

glorious /'glɔːrɪəs/ *adj* splendido; ⟨*deed, hero*⟩ glorioso

g

glory /'glɔːrɪ/ ① *n* gloria *f*; (splendour) splendore *m*; (cause for pride) vanto *m* ② *vi* ~ in vantarsi di

glory-hole *n* fam ripostiglio *m*

gloss /glɒs/ *n* lucentezza *f*
■ **gloss over** *vt* sorvolare su

glossary /'glɒsərɪ/ *n* glossario *m*

gloss paint *n* vernice *f* lucida

glossy /'glɒsɪ/ *adj* (**-ier**, **-iest**) lucido; ⟨paper⟩ patinato

glossy magazine *n* rivista *f* patinata

glottal stop /'glɒt(ə)l/ *n* occlusiva *f* glottale

glove /glʌv/ *n* guanto *m*

glove compartment *n* Auto cruscotto *m*

glove puppet *n* burattino *m*

glow /gləʊ/ ① *n* splendore *m*; (in cheeks) rossore *m*; (of candle) luce *f* soffusa ② *vi* risplendere; ⟨candle⟩ brillare; ⟨person⟩ avvampare

glower /'glaʊə(r)/ *vi* ~ (at) guardare in cagnesco

glowing /'gləʊɪŋ/ *adj* ardente; ⟨account⟩ entusiastico

glow-worm *n* lucciola *f*

glucose /'gluːkəʊs/ *n* glucosio *m*

glue /gluː/ ① *n* colla *f* ② *vt* incollare

glue sniffer *n* persona *f* che sniffa colla

glue-sniffing /-snɪfɪŋ/ *n* sniffare *m* la colla

glum /glʌm/ *adj* (**glummer**, **glummest**) tetro

glumly /'glʌmlɪ/ *adv* con aria tetra

glut /glʌt/ *n* eccesso *m*

glutinous /'gluːtɪnəs/ *adj* colloso

glutton /'glʌtən/ *n* ghiottone, -a *mf*

gluttonous /'glʌtənəs/ *adj* ghiotto

gluttony /'glʌtənɪ/ *n* ghiottoneria *f*

glycerine /'glɪsəriːn/ *n* glicerina *f*

GM *abbr* (**genetically modified**) MG

gm *abbr* (**gram**) g

GMO *abbr* (**genetically modified organism**) OGM *m inv*

GMT *abbr* (**Greenwich mean time**) GMT

gnarled /nɑːld/ *adj* nodoso

gnash /næʃ/ *vt* ~ one's teeth digrignare i denti

gnat /næt/ *n* moscerino *m*

gnaw /nɔː/ *vt* rosicchiare

gnome /nəʊm/ *n* gnomo *m*

GNP *abbr* (**gross national product**) PNL *m*

GNVQ *n abbr* Br (**General National Vocational Qualification**) diploma *m* di istituto tecnico

go /gəʊ/ ① *n* (pl **goes**) energia *f*; (attempt) tentativo *m*; **on the go** in movimento; **at one go** in una sola volta; **it's your go** tocca a te; **make a go of it** riuscire ② *vi* (pt **went**, pp **gone**) andare; (leave) andar via; (vanish) sparire; (become) diventare; (be sold) vendersi; **go and see** andare a vedere; **go swimming/shopping** andare a nuotare/fare spese; **where's the time gone?** come ha fatto il tempo a volare cosi?; **it's all gone** è finito; **be going to do** stare per fare; **I'm not going to** non ne ho nessuna intenzione; **to go** Am ⟨hamburgers etc⟩ da asporto; **a coffee to go** un caffè da portar via
■ **go about** ① *vi* andare in giro ② *vt* affrontare ⟨task⟩
■ **go after** *vt* (chase, pursue) correr dietro a
■ **go ahead** *vi* (event) aver luogo; **go ahead with** mandare avanti ⟨plans, wedding⟩
■ **go along** *vi* make something up as you go along inventare qualcosa mentre si va avanti
■ **go along with** *vt* concordare con ⟨person, view, plan⟩
■ **go around** *vi* ⟨rumour⟩ girare; **go around with** (person) andare in giro con
■ **go around together** *vi* ⟨people⟩ andare in giro insieme
■ **go away** *vi* andarsene
■ **go back** *vi* ritornare
■ **go back on** *vt* rimangiarsi ⟨promise⟩; tornare su ⟨decision⟩
■ **go by** *vi* passare
■ **go down** *vi* scendere; ⟨sun⟩ tramontare; ⟨ship⟩ affondare; ⟨swelling⟩ diminuire
■ **go for** *vt* andare a prendere; andare a cercare ⟨doctor⟩; (choose) optare per; (fam: attack) aggredire; **he's not the kind I go for** non è il genere che mi attira
■ **go in** *vi* entrare
■ **go in for** *vt* partecipare a ⟨competition⟩; darsi a ⟨tennis⟩
■ **go into** *vt* entrare in ⟨building⟩; (discuss) discutere
■ **go off** *vi* andarsene; ⟨alarm⟩ scattare; ⟨gun, bomb⟩ esplodere; ⟨food, milk⟩ andare a male; **go off well** riuscire
■ **go on** *vi* andare avanti; **what's going on?** cosa succede?
■ **go on at** *vt* fam scocciare
■ **go on with** *vt* (continue) andare avanti con
■ **go out** *vi* uscire; ⟨light, fire⟩ spegnersi
■ **go out with** *vt* uscire con somebody
■ **go over** ① *vi* andare ② *vt* (check) controllare
■ **go round** *vi* andare in giro; (visit) andare; (turn) girare; **is there enough to go round?** ce n'è abbastanza per tutti?
■ **go through** ① *vi* ⟨bill, proposal⟩ passare

2 *vt* (suffer) subire; (check) controllare; (read) leggere
■ **go through with** *vt* portare a termine ⟨*plan*⟩
■ **go under** *vi* passare sotto; ⟨*ship, swimmer*⟩ andare sott'acqua; (fail) fallire
■ **go up** *vi* salire; ⟨*Theat: curtain*⟩ aprirsi
■ **go with** *vt* accompagnare
■ **go without 1** *vt* fare a meno di ⟨*supper; sleep*⟩
2 *vi* fare senza

goad /gəʊd/ *vt* spingere (**into** a); (taunt) spronare

go-ahead 1 *adj* ⟨*person, company*⟩ intraprendente
2 *n* okay *m*

goal /gəʊl/ *n* porta *f*; (point scored) gol *m inv*; (in life) obiettivo *m*; **score a** ∼ segnare

goalie /'gəʊlɪ/ *fam*, **goalkeeper** /'gəʊlkiːpə(r)/ *n* portiere *m*

goalpost /'gəʊlpəʊst/ *n* palo *m*

goat /gəʊt/ *n* capra *f*

goatee /gəʊ'tiː/ *n* pizzetto *m*

gobble /'gɒbl/ *vi* ⟨*turkey*⟩ fare glu glu
■ **gobble up** *vt* trangugiare

gobbledygook /'gɒb(ə)ldɪguːk/ *n* ostrogoto *m*

go-between *n* intermediario, -a *mf*

goblet /'gɒblɪt/ *n* calice *m*

goblin /'gɒblɪn/ *n* folletto *m*

gobsmacked /'gɒbsmækt/ *adj* Br fam **I was** ∼ sono rimasto a bocca aperta

God, **god** /gɒd/ *n* Dio *m*, dio *m*

godchild *n* figlioccio, -a *mf*

goddamn *adj* maledetto

god-daughter *n* figlioccia *f*

goddess /'gɒdes/ *n* dea *f*

godfather *n* padrino *m*

god-fearing /-fɪərɪŋ/ *adj* timorato di Dio

god-forsaken /-fəseɪkən/ *adj* dimenticato da Dio

godless /'gɒdlɪs/ *adj* empio

godlike /'gɒdlaɪk/ *adj* divino

godly /'gɒdlɪ/ *adj* (**-ier**, **-iest**) pio

godmother *n* madrina *f*

godparents *npl* padrino *m* e madrina *f*

godsend *n* manna *f*

godson *n* figlioccio *m*

goer /'gəʊə(r)/ *n* Br **be a** ∼ ⟨*car*⟩ essere una bomba

go-getter /'gəʊgetə(r)/ *n* persona *f* intraprendente

go-getting /-getɪŋ/ *adj* intraprendente

goggle /'gɒgl/ *vi* fam ∼ **at** fissare con gli occhi sgranati

goggles *npl* occhiali *mpl*; (of swimmer) occhialini *mpl* [da piscina]: (of worker) occhiali *mpl* protettivi

going /'gəʊɪŋ/ **1** *adj* ⟨*price, rate*⟩ corrente; ∼ **concern** azienda *f* florida
2 *n* **it's hard** ∼ è una faticaccia; **while the** ∼ **is good** finché si può

going-over *n* (cleaning) pulizia *f* da cima a fondo; (examination) revisione *f*; **the doctor gave me a thorough** ∼ il dottore mi ha fatto una visita completa; **give somebody a** ∼ (beat up) dare una manica di botte a qualcuno

goings-on *npl* avvenimenti *mpl*

go-kart /-kɑːt/ *n* go-kart *m inv*

go-karting /-kɑːtɪŋ/ *n* kartismo *m*; **go** ∼ fare del kartismo

gold /gəʊld/ **1** *n* oro *m*
2 *adj* d'oro

gold-digger *n* fig cacciatore, -trice *mf* di dote

gold dust *n* polvere *f* d'oro; fig cosa *f* rara

golden /'gəʊldn/ *adj* dorato

golden handshake *n* Br buonuscita *f* (al termine di un rapporto di lavoro)

golden rule *n* regola *f* fondamentale

golden wedding *n* nozze *fpl* d'oro

goldfish *n inv* pesce *m* rosso

gold medal *n* medaglia *f* d'oro

gold medallist *n* (vincitore, -trice *mf* della) medaglia *f* d'oro

gold mine *n* miniera *f* d'oro

gold-plated /'pleɪtɪd/ *adj* placcato d'oro

gold rush *n* corsa *f* all'oro

goldsmith *n* orefice *m*

golf /gɒlf/ *n* golf *m*

golf club *n* circolo *m* di golf; (implement) mazza *f* da golf

golf course *n* campo *m* di golf

golfer /'gɒlfə(r)/ *n* giocatore, -trice *mf* di golf

golliwog /'gɒlɪwɒg/ *n* bambolotto *m* negro

gondola /'gɒndələ/ *n* gondola *f*

gondolier /gɒndə'lɪə(r)/ *n* gondoliere *m*

gone /gɒn/ ▸ GO

goner /'gɒnə(r)/ *n* fam **be a** ∼ essere spacciato

gong /gɒŋ/ *n* gong *m inv*

gonorrh[o]ea /gɒnə'rɪə/ *n* gonorrea *f*

good /gʊd/ **1** *adj* (**better**, **best**) buono; ⟨*child, footballer, singer*⟩ bravo; ⟨*holiday, film*⟩ bello; ∼ **at** bravo in; **a** ∼ **deal of anger** molta rabbia; **as** ∼ **as** (almost) quasi; ∼ **morning**, ∼ **afternoon** buon giorno; ∼ **evening** buona sera; ∼ **night** buona notte; **have a** ∼ **time** divertirsi
2 *n* bene *m*; **for** ∼ per sempre; **do** ∼ far del bene; **do somebody** ∼ far bene a qualcuno; **it's no** ∼ è inutile; **be up to no** ∼ combinare qualcosa

goodbye /gʊd'baɪ/ *int* arrivederci

good-for-nothing ① *n* buono, -a *mf* a nulla
② *adj* her ~ son quel buono a nulla di suo figlio

Good Friday *n* Venerdì *m* Santo

good-humoured /-ˈhjuːməd/ *adj* amichevole; ⟨remark, smile⟩ bonario

goodies /ˈgʊdɪz/ *npl* (fam: to eat) bontà *fpl*

good-looking /-ˈlʊkɪŋ/ *adj* bello

good-natured /-ˈneɪtʃəd/ *adj* be ~ avere un buon carattere

goodness /ˈgʊdnɪs/ *n* bontà *f*; my ~! santo cielo!; thank ~! grazie al cielo!

goods /gʊdz/ *npl* prodotti *mpl*

goods train *n* treno *m* merci

good-time girl *n* (fun-loving) ragazza *f* allegra; (euph: prostitute) donnina *f* allegra

goodwill /gʊdˈwɪl/ *n* buona *f* volontà; Comm avviamento *m*

goody /ˈgʊdɪ/ *n* (fam: person) buono *m*

goody bag *n* omaggi *mpl* consegnati ai visitatori di una fiera dalle aziende espositrici

goody-goody *n* santarellino, -a *mf*

gooey /ˈguːɪ/ *adj* fam appiccicaticcio; fig sdolcinato

goof /guːf/ *vi* fam cannare

goofy /ˈguːfɪ/ *adj* fam sciocco

google /ˈguːgl/ *vi* usare Google

goon /guːn/ *n* (clown) svitato *m*; (thug) picchiatore *m*

goose /guːs/ *n* (pl **geese**) oca *f*

gooseberry /ˈgʊzbərɪ/ *n* uva *f* spina

goose-flesh *n*, **goose-pimples** *npl* pelle *fsg* d'oca

goose-step *n* passo *m* dell'oca

gore¹ /gɔː(r)/ *n* sangue *m*

gore² *vt* incornare

gorge /gɔːdʒ/ ① *n* Geog gola *f*
② *vt* ~ oneself ingozzarsi

gorgeous /ˈgɔːdʒəs/ *adj* stupendo

gorilla /gəˈrɪlə/ *n* gorilla *m inv*

gormless /ˈgɔːmlɪs/ *adj* fam stupido

gorse /gɔːs/ *n* ginestrone *m*

gory /ˈgɔːrɪ/ *adj* (**-ier, -iest**) cruento

gosh /gɒʃ/ *int* fam caspita

gosling /ˈgɒzlɪŋ/ *n* ochetta *f*

go-slow *n* forma *f* di protesta che consiste in un rallentamento del ritmo di lavoro

gospel /ˈgɒspl/ *n* vangelo *m*

gospel music *n* musica *f* gospel

gospel truth *n* sacrosanta verità *f*

gossamer /ˈgɒsəmə(r)/ *n* (fabric) mussola *f*; (cobweb) fili *mpl* di ragnatela

gossip /ˈgɒsɪp/ ① *n* pettegolezzi *mpl*; (person) pettegolo, -a *mf*
② *vi* pettegolare

gossip column *n* cronaca *f* mondana

gossipy /ˈgɒsɪpɪ/ *adj* pettegolo

got /gɒt/ ▶ GET; have ~ avere; have ~ to do something dover fare qualcosa

Gothic /ˈgɒθɪk/ *adj* gotico

gotten /ˈgɒtn/ Am ▶ GET

gouge /gaʊdʒ/ *vt* ~ out cavare

goulash /ˈguːlæʃ/ *n* gulash *m inv*

gourd /gʊəd/ *n* (fruit) zucca *f*

gourmet /ˈgʊəmeɪ/ *n* buongustaio, -a *mf*

gout /gaʊt/ *n* gotta *f*

govern /ˈgʌv(ə)n/ *vt/i* governare; (determine) determinare

governess /ˈgʌvənɪs/ *n* istitutrice *f*

governing *adj* ⟨party⟩ al potere; ⟨class⟩ dirigente; the ~ body (school governors) il consiglio d'istituto

government /ˈgʌvnmənt/ *n* governo *m*

governmental /gʌvnˈmentl/ *adj* governativo

government health warning *n* avviso *m* a cura del ministero della salute

government stocks *npl* titoli *mpl* di stato

governor /ˈgʌvənə(r)/ *n* governatore *m*; (of school) amministratore, -trice *mf*; (of prison) direttore, -trice *mf*; (fam: boss) capo *m*

gown /gaʊn/ *n* vestito *m*; Univ, Jur toga *f*

GP *abbr* **general practitioner**

GPA *n abbr* Am (**grade point average**) media *f* scolastica

grab /græb/ *vt* (pt/pp **grabbed**) ~ [hold of] afferrare

Grace *n* his/your ~ (duke) il signor duca; (archbishop) Sua Eccellenza; her/your ~ (duchess) la signora duchessa

grace /greɪs/ *n* grazia *f*; (before meal) benedicite *m inv*; with good ~ volentieri; say ~ dire il benedicite; three days' ~ tre giorni di proroga

graceful /ˈgreɪsfʊl/ *adj* aggraziato

gracefully /ˈgreɪsfʊlɪ/ *adv* con grazia

gracious /ˈgreɪʃəs/ *adj* cortese; (elegant) lussuoso

gradation /grəˈdeɪʃn/ *n* gradazione *f*

grade /greɪd/ ① *n* livello *m*; Comm qualità *f*; Sch voto *m*; (Am Sch: class) classe *f*; Am = GRADIENT
② *vt* Comm classificare; Sch dare il voto a

grade crossing *n* Am passaggio *m* a livello

grade school *n* Am scuola *f* elementare

gradient /ˈgreɪdɪənt/ *n* pendenza *f*

gradual /ˈgrædʒʊəl/ *adj* graduale

gradually /ˈgrædʒʊəlɪ/ *adv* gradualmente

graduate¹ /ˈgrædʒʊət/ *n* laureato, -a *mf*

graduate² /ˈgrædʒʊeɪt/ *vi* Univ laurearsi

graduated /'grædʒʊeɪtɪd/ *adj*
〈*container*〉 graduato

graduate training scheme *n*
formazione *f* professionale postlaurea

graduation /grædʒʊ'eɪʃn/ *n* laurea *f*;
(calibration) graduazione *f*

graduation ceremony *n* cerimonia *f*
di consegna dei diplomi di laurea

graffiti /grə'fi:tɪ/ *npl* graffiti *mpl*

graffiti artist *n* pittore, -trice *mf* di
graffiti

graft /grɑːft/ ① *n* Bot, Med innesto *m*;
(Med: organ) trapianto *m*; (fam: hard work)
duro lavoro *m*; (fam: corruption) corruzione *f*
② *vt* innestare; trapiantare 〈*organ*〉

grain /greɪn/ *n* (of sand, salt) granello *m*; (of
rice) chicco *m*; (cereals) cereali *mpl*; (in wood)
venatura *f*; **it goes against the ~** fig è
contro la mia/sua natura

grainy /'greɪnɪ/ *adj* 〈*photograph*〉
sgranato; 〈*paintwork*〉 granulato

gram /græm/ *n* grammo *m*

grammar /'græmə(r)/ *n* grammatica *f*

grammarian /grə'meərɪən/ *n*
grammatico, -a *mf*

grammar school *n* ≈ liceo *m*

grammatical /grə'mætɪkl/ *adj*
grammaticale

grammatically /grə'mætɪklɪ/ *adv*
grammaticalmente

gran /græn/ *n* fam nonna *f*

granary /'grænərɪ/ *n* granaio *m*

granary bread *n* pane *m* integrale

grand /grænd/ *adj* grandioso; fam
eccellente

grandad /'grændæd/ *n* fam nonno *m*

grandchild *n* nipote *mf*

granddaughter *n* nipote *f*

grandeur /'grændʒə(r)/ *n* grandiosità *f*

grandfather *n* nonno *m*

grandfather clock *n* pendolo *m* (che
poggia a terra)

grandiose /'grændɪəʊs/ *adj* grandioso

grandma /'grændmɑː/ *n* nonna *f*

grandmother *n* nonna *f*

grandpa /'grændpɑː/ *n* nonno *m*

grandparents *npl* nonni *mpl*

grand piano *n* pianoforte *m* a coda

grand slam *n* vittoria *f* di tutte le fasi
di una gara

grandson *n* nipote *m*

grandstand *n* tribuna *f*

grand total *n* totale *m* complessivo

granite /'grænɪt/ *n* granito *m*

granny /'grænɪ/ *n* fam nonna *f*

granny flat *n* Br appartamentino *m*
indipendente per genitori anziani annesso
all'abitazione principale

grant /grɑːnt/ ① *n* (money) sussidio *m*;
Univ borsa *f* di studio
② *vt* accordare; (admit) ammettere; **take
something for ~ed** dare per scontato
qualcosa; **take somebody for ~ed**
considerare quello che qualcuno fa come
dovuto

granular /'grænjʊlə(r)/ *adj* granulare

granulated /'grænjʊleɪtɪd/ *adj* **~ sugar**
zucchero *m* semolato

granule /'grænjuːl/ *n* granello *m*

grape /greɪp/ *n* acino *m*; **~s** *pl* uva *fsg*

grapefruit /'greɪpfruːt/ *n inv* pompelmo
m

grapeseed oil /'greɪpsiːd/ *n* olio *m* di
vinaccioli

grapevine /'greɪpvaɪn/ *n* vite *f*; **hear
something on the ~** sentir dire in giro
qualcosa

graph /grɑːf/ *n* grafico *m*

graphic /'græfɪk/ *adj* grafico; (vivid)
vivido

graphically /'græfɪklɪ/ *adv*
graficamente; (vividly) vividamente

graphic design *n* grafica *f*

graphic designer *n* grafico, -a *mf*

graphics /'græfɪks/ *n* grafica *f*

graphics card *n* Comput scheda *f*
grafica

graphics interface *n* Comput
interfaccia *f* grafica

graphite /'græfaɪt/ *n* grafite *f*

graphologist /græ'fɒlədʒɪst/ *n*
grafologo, -a *mf*

graph paper *n* carta *f* millimetrata

grapple /'græpl/ *vi* **~ with** also fig essere
alle prese con

grasp /grɑːsp/ ① *n* stretta *f*; (understanding)
comprensione *f*
② *vt* afferrare

grasping /'grɑːspɪŋ/ *adj* avido

grass /grɑːs/ *n* erba *f*

grass court *n* campo *m* in erba

grasshopper *n* cavalletta *f*

grassland *n* prateria *f*

grassroots *npl* base *f*; **at the ~** alla
base

grass snake *n* biscia *f*

grassy /'grɑːsɪ/ *adj* erboso

grate[1] /greɪt/ *n* grata *f*

grate[2] ① *vt* Culin grattugiare; **~ one's
teeth** far stridere i denti
② *vi* stridere

grateful /'greɪtfl/ *adj* grato

gratefully /'greɪtfʊlɪ/ *adv* con
gratitudine

grater /'greɪtə(r)/ *n* Culin grattugia *f*

gratification /grætɪfɪ'keɪʃn/ *n*
soddisfazione *f*

gratified /ˈgrætɪfaɪd/ *adj* appagato

gratify /ˈgrætɪfaɪ/ *vt* (*pt/pp* **-ied**) appagare

gratifying /ˈgrætɪfaɪɪŋ/ *adj* appagante

grating /ˈgreɪtɪŋ/ *n* grata *f*

gratis /ˈgrɑːtɪs/ *adv* gratis

gratitude /ˈgrætɪtjuːd/ *n* gratitudine *f*

gratuitous /grəˈtjuːɪtəs/ *adj* gratuito

gratuity /grəˈtjuːətɪ/ *n* gratifica *f*

grave¹ /greɪv/ *adj* grave

grave² *n* tomba *f*

gravedigger /ˈgreɪvdɪgə(r)/ *n* becchino *m*

gravel /ˈgrævl/ *n* ghiaia *f*

gravelly /ˈgrævəlɪ/ *adj* ⟨voice⟩ rauco

gravely /ˈgreɪvlɪ/ *adv* gravemente

graven image /ˈgreɪvən/ *n* idolo *m*

gravestone /ˈgreɪvstəʊn/ *n* lapide *f*

graveyard /ˈgreɪvjɑːd/ *n* cimitero *m*

gravitate /ˈgrævɪteɪt/ *vi* gravitare

gravity /ˈgrævətɪ/ *n* gravità *f*

gravy /ˈgreɪvɪ/ *n* sugo *m* della carne

gravy boat *n* salsiera *f*

gray /greɪ/ *adj* Am = GREY

graze¹ /greɪz/ *vi* ⟨animal⟩ pascolare

graze² ① *n* escoriazione *f*
② *vt* (touch lightly) sfiorare; (scrape) escoriare; sbucciarsi ⟨knee⟩

grease /griːs/ ① *n* grasso *m*
② *vt* ungere

greasepaint /ˈgriːspeɪnt/ *n* cerone *m*

greaseproof paper
/griːspruːˈfpeɪpə(r)/ *n* carta *f* oleata

greaser /ˈgriːsə(r)/ *n* (motorcyclist) componente *m* di una banda giovanile di motociclisti

greasy /ˈgriːsɪ/ *adj* (**-ier, -iest**) untuoso; ⟨hair, skin⟩ grasso

great /greɪt/ *adj* grande; (fam: marvellous) eccezionale

great-aunt *n* prozia *f*

great big *adj* enorme

Great Britain *n* Gran Bretagna *f*

Great Dane *n* danese *m*

great-grandchildren *npl* pronipoti *mpl*

great-grandfather *n* bisnonno *m*

great-grandmother *n* bisnonna *f*

great-great-grandchildren *npl* pronipoti *mpl*

greatly /ˈgreɪtlɪ/ *adv* enormemente

greatness /ˈgreɪtnɪs/ *n* grandezza *f*

great-uncle *n* prozio *m*

Grecian /ˈgriːʃ(ə)n/ *adj* greco

Greece /griːs/ *n* Grecia *f*

greed /griːd/ *n* avidità *f*; (for food) ingordigia *f*

greedily /ˈgriːdɪlɪ/ *adv* avidamente; ⟨eat⟩ con ingordigia

greedy /ˈgriːdɪ/ *adj* (**-ier, -iest**) avido; (for food) ingordo

Greek /griːk/ *adj* & *n* greco, -a *mf*; (language) greco *m*

green /griːn/ ① *adj* verde; (fig: inexperienced) immaturo
② *n* verde *m*; (grass) prato *m*; (in golf) green *m inv*; **~s** *pl* verdura *f*; **the G~s** *pl* Pol i verdi

green beans *n* fagiolini *mpl*

green belt *n* zona *f* verde intorno a una città

green card *n* carta *f* verde; Am permesso *m* di soggiorno

greenery /ˈgriːnərɪ/ *n* verde *m*

green-eyed monster /-aɪdˈmɒnstə(r)/ *n* gelosia *f*

greenfield site /ˈgriːnfiːld/ *n* terreno *m* su cui non sono mai esistiti insediamenti urbani

greenfinch *n* verdone *m*

green fingers *npl* have **~ ~** avere il pollice verde

greenfly *n* afide *m*

greengage *n* susina *f* verde

greengrocer *n* fruttivendolo, -a *mf*

greenhorn *n* (new) novellino *m*; (gullible) pivello *m*

greenhouse *n* serra *f*

greenhouse effect *n* effetto *m* serra

Greenland *n* Groenlandia *f*

green light *n* fam verde *m*

green onion *n* Am cipollotto *m*

green salad *n* insalata *f* verde

greet /griːt/ *vt* salutare; (welcome) accogliere

greeting /ˈgriːtɪŋ/ *n* saluto *m*; (welcome) accoglienza *f*

greetings card /ˈgriːtɪŋz/ *n* biglietto *m* d'auguri

gregarious /grɪˈgeərɪəs/ *adj* gregario; (person) socievole

gremlin /ˈgremlɪn/ *n* hum spirito *m* maligno

Grenada /grɪˈneɪdə/ *n* Grenada *f*

grenade /grɪˈneɪd/ *n* granata *f*

grenadier /grenəˈdɪə(r)/ *n* Mil guardia *f* reale inglese

grew /gruː/ ▸ GROW

grey Br, **gray** Am /greɪ/ ① *adj* grigio; ⟨hair⟩ bianco
② *n* grigio *m*
③ *vi* diventare bianco
■ **grey out** *vt* Comput visualizzare con sfondo azzurro ombreggiato

grey area *n* zona *f* oscura

grey-haired /heəd/ *adj* dai capelli grigi

greyhound *n* levriero *m*

grey matter n (brain) materia f grigia

grey squirrel n scoiattolo m grigio

grid /grɪd/ n griglia f; (on map) reticolato m; Electr rete f.

griddle /'grɪd(ə)l/ n (for meat) piastra f

gridiron n griglia f; Am campo m di football americano

gridlock n (fig: deadlock) situazione f di stallo; (in traffic) imbottigliamento m

grid reference n coordinate fpl

grief /gri:f/ n dolore m; **come to ~** ⟨plans⟩ naufragare

grief-stricken /-strɪkən/ adj affranto dal dolore

grievance /'gri:vəns/ n lamentela f

grieve /gri:v/ ① vt addolorare
② vi essere addolorato

grievous /'gri:vəs/ adj doloroso

grievous bodily harm n lesioni fpl personali gravi

grievously /'gri:vəslɪ/ adv tristemente

grill /grɪl/ ① n graticola f; (for grilling) griglia f; **mixed ~** grigliata f mista
② vt cuocere alla griglia; (interrogate) sottoporre al terzo grado
③ vi cuocere alla griglia

grille /grɪl/ n grata f

grim /grɪm/ adj (**grimmer, grimmest**) arcigno; ⟨determination⟩ accanito

grimace /'grɪməs/ ① n smorfia f
② vi fare una smorfia

grime /graɪm/ n sudiciume m

grimly /'grɪmlɪ/ adv accanitamente

Grim Reaper n Morte f

grimy /'graɪmɪ/ adj (**-ier, -iest**) sudicio

grin /grɪn/ ① n sorriso m
② vi (pt/pp **grinned**) fare un gran sorriso

grind /graɪnd/ ① n (fam: hard work) sfacchinata f
② vt (pt/pp **ground**) macinare; affilare ⟨knife⟩; (Am: mince) tritare; **~ one's teeth** digrignare i denti

grindstone /'graɪndstəʊn/ n mola f; **keep one's nose to the ~** lavorare indefessamente

grip /grɪp/ ① n presa f; fig controllo m; (bag) borsone m; **be in the ~ of** essere in preda a; **get a ~ of oneself** controllarsi
② vt (pt/pp **gripped**) afferrare; ⟨tyres⟩ far presa su; tenere avvinto ⟨attention⟩

gripe /graɪp/ vi (fam: grumble) lagnarsi

gripping /'grɪpɪŋ/ adj avvincente

grisly /'grɪzlɪ/ adj (**-ier, -iest**) raccapricciante

gristle /'grɪsl/ n cartilagine f

grit /grɪt/ ① n graniglia f; (for roads) sabbia f; (courage) coraggio m
② vt (pt/pp **gritted**) spargere sabbia su ⟨road⟩; **~ one's teeth** serrare i denti

gritter /'grɪtə(r)/ n Br Auto spandighiaia m inv

gritty /'grɪtɪ/ adj (sandy) pieno di terra; (gravelly) ghiaioso; (hard, determined) grintoso; novel, film crudo

grizzle /'grɪzl/ vi piagnucolare

grizzly /'grɪzlɪ/ n (bear) grizzly m inv

groan /grəʊn/ ① n gemito m
② vi gemere

grocer /'grəʊsə(r)/ n droghiere, -a mf

groceries /'grəʊsərɪz/ npl generi mpl alimentari

grocer's [shop] n drogheria f

groggy /'grɒgɪ/ adj (**-ier, -iest**) stordito; (unsteady) barcollante

groin /grɔɪn/ n Anat inguine m

groom /gru:m/ ① n sposo m; (for horse) stalliere m
② vt strigliare ⟨horse⟩; fig preparare; **well-~ed** ben curato

groove /gru:v/ n scanalatura f

grope /grəʊp/ vi brancolare; **~ for** cercare a tastoni

gross /grəʊs/ ① adj obeso; (coarse) volgare; (glaring) grossolano; ⟨salary, weight⟩ lordo
② n inv grossa f

gross domestic product n prodotto m interno lordo

gross indecency n Jur oltraggio m al pudore

grossly /'grəʊslɪ/ adv (very) enormemente

gross national product n prodotto m nazionale lordo

grotesque /grəʊ'tesk/ adj grottesco

grotesquely /grəʊ'tesklɪ/ adv in modo grottesco

grotto /'grɒtəʊ/ n (pl **-es**) grotta f

grotty /'grɒtɪ/ adj (**-ier, -iest**) fam ⟨flat, street⟩ squallido

grouch /graʊtʃ/ vi brontolare (**about** contro)

grouchy /'graʊtʃɪ/ adj brontolone

ground¹ /graʊnd/ ▶ GRIND

ground² ① n terra f; Sport terreno m; (reason) ragione f; **~s** pl (park) giardini mpl; (of coffee) fondi mpl
② vi ⟨ship⟩ arenarsi
③ vt bloccare a terra ⟨aircraft⟩; Am Electr mettere a terra

ground control n base f di controllo

ground crew n personale m di terra

ground floor n pianterreno m

grounding /'graʊndɪŋ/ n base f

groundless /'graʊndlɪs/ adj infondato

groundnut oil n olio m d'arachidi

ground rules npl principi mpl fondamentali

groundsheet n telone m impermeabile

ground troops npl truppe fpl di terra

groundwork n lavoro m di preparazione

group /gru:p/ **1** n gruppo m
2 vt raggruppare
3 vi raggrupparsi

groupage /'gru:pɪdʒ/ n Comm raggruppamento m

group booking n prenotazione f di gruppo

group leader n capogruppo m

group therapy n terapia f di gruppo

group work n lavoro m di gruppo

grouse[1] /graʊs/ n inv gallo m cedrone

grouse[2] vi fam brontolare

grove /grəʊv/ n boschetto m

grovel /'grɒvl/ vi (pt/pp **grovelled**) strisciare

grovelling /'grɒv(ə)lɪŋ/ adj leccapiedi inv

grow /grəʊ/ **1** vi (pt **grew**, pp **grown**) crescere; (become) diventare; ⟨unemployment, fear⟩ aumentare; ⟨town⟩ ingrandirsi
2 vt coltivare; ~ one's hair farsi crescere i capelli
■ **grow apart** vi ⟨friends, couple⟩ disamorarsi
■ **grow on** vt (fam: become pleasing to) **it'll ~ on you** finirà per piacerti
■ **grow out of** vt he's ~n out of his jumper il golf gli è diventato troppo piccolo
■ **grow up** vi crescere; ⟨town⟩ svilupparsi

growbag /'grəʊbæg/ n sacco m di terriccio dentro cui si coltivano piante

grower /'grəʊə(r)/ n coltivatore, -trice mf

growing pains /'grəʊɪŋ/ npl (of child) dolori mpl della crescita; (fig: of firm, project) difficoltà fpl iniziali nello sviluppo

growl /graʊl/ **1** n grugnito m
2 vi ringhiare

grown /grəʊn/ **1** ▶ GROW
2 adj adulto

grown-up adj & n adulto, -a mf

growth /grəʊθ/ n crescita f; (increase) aumento m; Med tumore m

growth area n area f di sviluppo

growth industry n industria f in rapida crescita

growth rate n tasso m di crescita

groyne /grɔɪn/ n Br pennello m (per difendere le spiagge dall'erosione)

grub /grʌb/ n larva f; (fam: food) mangiare m

grubby /'grʌbɪ/ adj (-ier, -iest) sporco

grudge /grʌdʒ/ **1** n rancore m; **bear somebody a ~** portare rancore a qualcuno
2 vt dare a malincuore

grudging /'grʌdʒɪŋ/ adj riluttante

grudgingly /'grʌdʒɪŋlɪ/ adv a malincuore

gruelling /'gru:əlɪŋ/ adj estenuante

gruesome /'gru:səm/ adj macabro

gruff /grʌf/ adj burbero

gruffly /'grʌflɪ/ adv in modo burbero

grumble /'grʌmbl/ vi brontolare (**at** contro)

grumpy /'grʌmpɪ/ adj (-ier, -iest) scorbutico

grunge /grʌndʒ/ n (dirt) lerciume m; (style) grunge m inv

grunt /grʌnt/ **1** n grugnito m
2 vi fare un grugnito

G-string n (garment) tanga m inv

guarantee /gærən'ti:/ **1** n garanzia f
2 vt garantire

guarantor /gærən'tɔ:(r)/ n garante mf

guard /gɑ:d/ **1** n guardia f; (security) guardiano m; (on train) capotreno m; Techn schermo m protettivo; **be on ~** essere di guardia; **on one's ~** in guardia
2 vt sorvegliare; (protect) proteggere
■ **guard against** vt guardarsi da

guard-dog n cane m da guardia

guarded /'gɑ:dɪd/ adj guardingo

guardian /'gɑ:dɪən/ n (of minor) tutore, -trice mf

guardian angel n also fig angelo m custode

guard of honour n guardia f d'onore

guardroom n corpo m di guardia

guard's van n Br Rail carrozza f bagagliaio

Guatemala /gwætə'mɑ:lə/ n Guatemala m

guava /'gwɑ:və/ n (fruit) guava f; (tree) albero m di guava

Guernsey /'gɜ:nzɪ/ n Guernsey f

guerrilla /gə'rɪlə/ n guerrigliero, -a mf

guerrilla warfare n guerriglia f

guess /ges/ **1** n supposizione f
2 vt indovinare
3 vi indovinare; (Am: suppose) supporre

guesstimate /'gestɪmət/ n calcolo m approssimativo

guesswork /'gesw3:k/ n supposizione f

guest /gest/ n ospite mf; (in hotel) cliente mf

guest house n pensione f

guest room n camera f degli ospiti

guest worker n lavoratore m immigrato; lavoratrice f immigrata

guff /gʌf/ n (nonsense) stupidaggini fpl

guffaw /gʌ'fɔ:/ **1** n sghignazzata f
2 vi sghignazzare

guidance /'gaɪdəns/ n guida f; (advice) consigli mpl

guide /gaɪd/ ① *n* guida *f*; [Girl] G∼ giovane esploratrice *f*
② *vt* guidare

guidebook /'gaɪdbʊk/ *n* guida *f* turistica

guided missile /'gaɪdɪd/ *n* missile *m* teleguidato

guide dog *n* cane *m* per ciechi

guided tour *n* giro *m* guidato

guidelines /'gaɪdlaɪnz/ *npl* direttive *fpl*

guiding principle /gaɪdɪŋ'prɪnsɪp(ə)l/ *n* direttrice *f*

guild /gɪld/ *n* corporazione *f*

guile /gaɪl/ *n* astuzia *f*

guileless /'gaɪllɪs/ *adj* senza malizia

guillotine /'gɪləti:n/ *n* ghigliottina *f*; (for paper) taglierina *f*

guilt /gɪlt/ *n* colpa *f*

guiltily /'gɪltɪlɪ/ *adv* con aria colpevole

guilty /'gɪltɪ/ *adj* (**-ier, -iest**) colpevole; **have a ∼ conscience** avere la coscienza sporca

Guinea /'gɪnɪ/ *n* Guinea *f*

guinea /'gɪnɪ/ *n* ghinea *f*

Guinea-Bissau /-bɪ'saʊ/ *n* Guinea-Bissau *f*

guinea fowl faraona *f*

guinea pig *n* porcellino *m* d'India; (in experiments) cavia *f*

guise /gaɪz/ *n* **in the ∼ of** sotto le spoglie di

guitar /gɪ'tɑ:(r)/ *n* chitarra *f*

guitarist /gɪ'tɑ:rɪst/ *n* chitarrista *mf*

Gulag /'gu:læg/ *n* gulag *m inv*

gulch /gʌltʃ/ *n* Am burrone *m*

gulf /gʌlf/ *n* Geog golfo *m*; fig abisso *m*

Gulf States *npl* gli stati *mpl* del Golfo

Gulf War *n* la guerra *f* del Golfo

gull /gʌl/ *n* gabbiano *m*

gullet /'gʌlɪt/ *n* esofago *m*; (throat) gola *f*

gullible /'gʌləbl/ *adj* credulone

gully /'gʌlɪ/ *n* burrone *m*; (drain) canale *m* di scolo

gulp /gʌlp/ ① *n* azione *f* di deglutire; (of food) boccone *m*; (of liquid) sorso *m*
② *vi* deglutire

■ **gulp down** *vt* tranguiare ⟨food⟩; scolarsi ⟨liquid⟩

gum[1] /gʌm/ *n* Anat gengiva *f*

gum[2] ① *n* gomma *f*; (chewing-gum) gomma *f* da masticare, chewing-gum *m inv*
② *vt* (pt/pp **gummed**) ingommare (**to** a)

gumboot /'gʌmbu:t/ *n* stivale *m* di gomma

gummed /gʌmd/ ① ▸ GUM[2]
② *adj* ⟨label⟩ adesivo

gumption /'gʌmpʃn/ *n* fam buon senso *m*

gumshoe /'gʌmʃu:/ *n* (fam: private investigator) investigatore *m* privato

gum tree *n* fam **be up a ∼ ∼** essere in difficoltà

gun /gʌn/ *n* pistola *f*; (rifle) fucile *m*; (cannon) cannone *m*; **he had a ∼** era armato

■ **gun down** *vt* (pt/pp **gunned**) freddare

gun barrel *n* canna *f* di fucile

gunboat *n* cannoniera *f*

gun dog *n* cane *m* da caccia

gunfire *n* spari *mpl*; (of cannon) colpi *mpl* [di cannone]

gunge /gʌndʒ/ *n* Br poltiglia *f* [disgustosa]

gung-ho /gʌŋ'həʊ/ *adj* hum (eager for war) guerrafondaio; (overzealous) esaltato

gun laws *npl* leggi *fpl* sulle armi

gun licence *n* porto *m* d'armi

gunman /'gʌnmən/ *n* uomo *m* armato

gunner /'gʌnə(r)/ *n* artigliere *m*

gunpoint *n* **hold somebody up at ∼** assalire qualcuno a mano armata

gunpowder *n* polvere *f* da sparo

gunshot *n* colpo *m* [di pistola]

gunshot wound *n* ferita *f* d'arma da fuoco

gunslinger *n* pistolero *m*

gurgle /'gɜ:gl/ *vi* gorgogliare; ⟨baby⟩ fare degli urletti

guru /'guru:/ *n* guru *m inv*

gush /gʌʃ/ *vi* sgorgare; (enthuse) parlare con troppo entusiasmo (**over** di)

■ **gush out** *vi* sgorgare

gushing /'gʌʃɪŋ/ *adj* eccessivamente entusiastico

gusset /'gʌsɪt/ *n* gherone *m*

gust /gʌst/ *n* (of wind) raffica *f*

gusto /'gʌstəʊ/ *n* **with ∼** con trasporto

gusty /'gʌstɪ/ *adj* ventoso

gut /gʌt/ ① *n* intestino *m*; ∼**s** *pl* pancia *f*; (fam: courage) fegato *m*
② *vt* (pt/pp **gutted**) Culin svuotare delle interiora; ∼**ted by fire** sventrato da un incendio

gutsy /'gʌtsɪ/ *adj* (brave) coraggioso; (spirited) gagliardo

gutter /'gʌtə(r)/ *n* canale *m* di scolo; (on roof) grondaia *f*; fig bassifondi *mpl*

guttering /'gʌtərɪŋ/ *n* grondaie *fpl*

gutter press *n* stampa *f* scandalistica

guttersnipe /'gʌtəsnaɪp/ *n* ragazzo, -a *mf* di strada

guttural /'gʌtərəl/ *adj* gutturale

guv, guvnor /gʌv/, /'gʌvnə(r)/ *n* (Br fam: boss) capo *m*

guy /gaɪ/ *n* fam tipo *m*, tizio *m*

Guyana /gaɪ'ɑ:nə/ *n* Guyana *f*

Guy Fawkes Day /fɔ:ks/ *n* Br anniversario *m* del fallimento della Congiura delle Polveri (5 novembre)

guzzle /'gʌzl/ *vt* ingozzarsi con ⟨*food*⟩; he's ~d the lot si è sbafato tutto

gym /dʒɪm/ *n* fam palestra *f*; (gymnastics) ginnastica *f*

gymkhana /dʒɪm'kɑːnə/ *n* manifestazione *f* equestre

gymnasium /dʒɪm'neɪzɪəm/ *n* palestra *f*

gymnast /'dʒɪmnæst/ *n* ginnasta *mf*

gymnastics /dʒɪm'næstɪks/ *n* ginnastica *f*

gym shoes *npl* scarpe *fpl* da ginnastica

gym-slip *n* Sch ≈ grembiule *m* (da bambina)

gynaecologist /gaɪnɪ'kɒlədʒɪst/ *n* ginecologo, -a *mf*

gynaecology /gaɪnɪ'kɒlədʒɪ/ *n* ginecologia *f*

gyp /dʒɪp/ *n* Br my back is giving me ~ ho un terribile mal di schiena

gypsum /'dʒɪpsəm/ *n* gesso *m*

gypsy /'dʒɪpsɪ/ *n* zingaro, -a *mf*

gyrate /dʒaɪ'reɪt/ *vi* roteare

Hh

h, H /eɪtʃ/ *n* h, H *f inv*

ha! ha! /hɑː'hɑː/ *int* ah! ah!

haberdashery /hæbə'dæʃərɪ/ *n* merceria *f*; Am negozio *m* d'abbigliamento da uomo

habit /'hæbɪt/ *n* abitudine *f*; (Relig: costume) tonaca *f*; be in the ~ of doing something avere l'abitudine di fare qualcosa

habitable /'hæbɪtəbl/ *adj* abitabile

habitat /'hæbɪtæt/ *n* habitat *m inv*

habitation /hæbɪ'teɪʃn/ *n* unfit for human ~ inagibile

habit-forming /-fɔːmɪŋ/ *adj* be ~ creare assuefazione

habitual /hə'bɪtjʊəl/ *adj* abituale; ⟨*smoker, liar*⟩ inveterato

habitually /hə'bɪtjʊəlɪ/ *adv* regolarmente

habitual offender *n* delinquente *mf* recidivo

hack¹ /hæk/ *n* (writer) scribacchino, -a *mf*

hack² *vt* tagliare; ~ to pieces tagliare a pezzi

hacker /'hækə(r)/ *n* Comput pirata *m* informatico

hacking /'hækɪŋ/ *n* Comput pirateria *f* informatica

hacking cough *n* brutta tosse *f*

hackles /'hæk(ə)lz/ *npl* (on animal) pelo *m* del collo; (on bird) piumaggio *m* del collo; make sb's ~ rise fig far imbestialire qualcuno

hackney cab /'hæknɪ/ *n* fml taxi *m inv*

hackneyed /'hæknɪd/ *adj* trito [e ritrito]

hacksaw /'hæksɔː/ *n* seghetto *m*

had /hæd/ ▶ HAVE

haddock /'hædək/ *n inv* eglefino *m*

haematoma /hiːmə'təʊmə/ *n* ematoma *m*

haemoglobin /hiːmə'gləʊbɪn/ *n* emoglobina *f*

haemophilia /hiːmə'fɪlɪə/ *n* emofilia *f*

haemophiliac /hiːmə'fɪlɪæk/ *n* emofiliaco, -a *mf*

haemorrhage /'hemərɪdʒ/ *n* emorragia *f*

haemorrhoids /'hemərɔɪdz/ *npl* emorroidi *fpl*

hag /hæg/ *n* old ~ vecchia befana *f*

haggard /'hægəd/ *adj* sfatto

haggis /'hægɪs/ *n* piatto *m* scozzese a base di frattaglie di pecora e avena

haggle /'hægl/ *vi* contrattare (over per)

Hague /heɪg/ *n* the ~ l'Aia *f*

hail¹ /heɪl/ ① *vt* salutare; far segno a ⟨*taxi*⟩
② *vi* ~ from provenire da

hail² ① *n* grandine *f*
② *vi* grandinare

hailstone /'heɪlstəʊn/ *n* chicco *m* di grandine

hailstorm /'heɪlstɔːm/ *n* grandinata *f*

hair /heə(r)/ *n* capelli *mpl*; (on body, of animal) pelo *m*; wash one's ~ lavarsi i capelli

hairband *n* (rigid) cerchietto *m*; (elastic) fascia *f* [per capelli]

hairbrush *n* spazzola *f* per capelli

hair curler *n* arricciacapelli *m inv*

haircut *n* taglio *m* di capelli; have a ~ farsi tagliare i capelli

hairdo *n* fam pettinatura *f*

hairdresser *n* parrucchiere, -a *mf*

hairdryer, hairdrier *n* fon *m inv*; (with hood) casco *m* (asciugacapelli)

hair gel *n* gel *m inv* [per capelli]

hairgrip *n* molletta *f*

hairless /'heəlɪs/ *adj* ⟨*animal*⟩ senza peli; ⟨*body*⟩, chin) glabro

hairline *n* (on head) attaccatura *f* dei capelli

hairline crack *n* incrinatura *f* sottilissima

hairline fracture *n* Med frattura *f* capillare

hairnet *n* retina *f* per capelli

hairpiece *n* toupet *m inv*

hairpin *n* forcina *f*

hairpin bend *n* tornante *m*, curva *f* a gomito

hair-raising /'heəreɪzɪŋ/ *adj* terrificante

hair remover *n* crema *f* depilatoria

hairslide *n* Br fermacapelli *m inv*

hair-splitting /'heəsplɪtɪŋ/ *n* pedanteria *f*

hairspray *n* lacca *f* [per capelli]

hairstyle *n* acconciatura *f*

hairstylist *n* parrucchiere, -a *mf*

hair transplant *n* trapianto *m* di capelli

hairy /'heərɪ/ *adj* (**-ier, -iest**) peloso; (fam: frightening) spaventoso

Haiti /'heɪtɪ/ *n* Haiti *m*

Haitian /'heɪʃ(ə)n/ *n & adj* haitiano, -a *mf*; (language) haitiano *m*

hake /heɪk/ *n inv* nasello *m*

halal /hæ'læl/ *adj* ⟨*meat, butcher*⟩ halal

halcyon days /'hælsɪən/ *npl* bei tempi *mpl* andati

hale /heɪl/ *adj* ∼ **and hearty** in piena forma

half /hɑːf/ ① *n* (pl **halves**) metà *f inv*; **cut in** ∼ tagliare a metà; **one and a** ∼ uno e mezzo; ∼ **a dozen** mezza dozzina; ∼ **an hour** mezz'ora
② *adj* mezzo; [at] ∼ **price** [a] metà prezzo
③ *adv* a metà; ∼ **past two** le due e mezza

half-and-half ① *adj* mezzo e mezzo
② *adv* a metà; **go** ∼ fare a metà

half-back *n* mediano *m*

half-baked *adj* fam che non sta in piedi

half board *n* mezza pensione *f*

half-breed *n & adj* mezzosangue *mf inv*

half-brother *n* fratellastro *m*

half-caste *n* meticcio, -a *mf*

half-century *n* mezzo secolo *m*

half cock *n* **go off at** ∼ ∼ partire col piede sbagliato

half-conscious *adj* semicosciente

halfcrown, half a crown *n* Br mezza corona *f*

half-cut *adj* (fam: drunk) ciucco

half day *n* mezza giornata *f*

half-dead *adj* also fig mezzo morto

half-dozen *n* mezza dozzina *f*

half fare *n* metà tariffa *f*

half-hearted /-'hɑːtɪd/ *adj* esitante

half-heartedly /-'hɑːtɪdlɪ/ *adv* senza entusiasmo

half hour *n* mezz'ora *f*

halfhourly *adj & adv* ogni mezz'ora

half-length *adj* ⟨*portrait*⟩ a mezzo busto

half-light *n* penombra *f*

half mast *n* **at** ∼ a mezz'asta

half measures *npl* mezze misure *fpl*

half-moon ① *n* mezzaluna *f*; (of fingernail) lunula *f*
② *attrib* ⟨*spectacles*⟩ a mezzaluna

half pay *n* metà stipendio *m*

halfpenny /'heɪpnɪ/ *n* Br mezzo penny *m inv*

half-pint *n* mezza pinta *f* (Br = 0,28 l, Am = 0,24 l); (beer) piccola *f*; fig mezza calzetta *f*

half price ① *adj* a metà prezzo
② *adv* [a] metà prezzo

half-sister *n* sorellastra *f*

half size ① *n* (of shoe) mezzo numero *m*
② *adj* ⟨*copy*⟩ ridotto della metà

half smile *n* mezzo sorriso *m*

half-starved *adj* mezzo morto di fame

half-term *n* vacanza *f* di metà trimestre

half-time *n* Sport intervallo *m*

half-truth *n* mezza verità *f inv*

halfway ① *adj* **the** ∼ **mark/stage** il livello intermedio
② *adv* a metà strada; **get** ∼ fig arrivare a metà

halfway house *n* (compromise) via *f* di mezzo; (rehabilitation centre) centro *m* di riabilitazione per ex detenuti

halfway line *n* Sport linea *f* mediana

halfwit *n* idiota *mf*

half-year ① *n* Fin, Comm semestre *m*
② *attrib* ⟨*profit, results*⟩ semestrale

half-yearly *adj* ⟨*meeting, payment*⟩ semestrale

halibut /'hælɪbət/ *n inv* ippoglosso *m*

halitosis /hælɪ'təʊsɪs/ *n* alitosi *f inv*

hall /hɔːl/ *n* (entrance) ingresso *m*; (room) sala *f*; (mansion) residenza *f* the room

hallelujah /(h)ælɪ'luːjə/ *int* alleluia!

hallmark /'hɔːlmɑːk/ *n* marchio *m* di garanzia; fig marchio *m*

hallo /hə'ləʊ/ *int* ciao!; (on telephone) pronto!; **say** ∼ **to** salutare

hall of residence *n* residenza *f* universitaria

hallowed /'hæləʊd/ *adj* ⟨*ground*⟩ consacrato; ⟨*tradition*⟩ sacro

Halloween /hæləʊ'iːn/ *n* vigilia *f* d'Ognissanti e notte delle streghe, celebrata soprattutto dai bambini

hallucinate /hə'luːsɪneɪt/ *vi* avere le allucinazioni

hallucination /həlu:sɪ'neɪʃn/ *n*
allucinazione *f*

hallucinatory /hə'lu:sɪnət(ə)rɪ/ *adj*
⟨*drug*⟩ allucinogeno

hallucinogen /hə'lu:sɪnədʒən/ *n*
sostanza *f* allucinante

hallucinogenic /həlu:sɪnə'dʒenɪk/ *adj*
allucinogeno

hallway /'hɔ:lweɪ/ *n* ingresso *m*

halo /'heɪləʊ/ *n* (pl **-es**) aureola *f*; Astr
alone *m*

halogen /'hælədʒən/ *n* alogeno *m*

halt /hɔ:lt/ **1** *n* alt *m inv*; **come to a** ∼
fermarsi; ⟨*traffic*⟩ bloccarsi
2 *vi* fermarsi; ∼! alt!
3 *vt* fermare

halter /'hɔ:ltə(r)/ *n* (for horse) cavezza *f*

halter-neck *n* modello *m* con
allacciatura dietro il collo che lascia la
schiena scoperta

halting /'hɔ:ltɪŋ/ *adj* esitante

haltingly /'hɔ:ltɪŋlɪ/ *adv* con esitazione

halve /hɑːv/ *vt* dividere a metà; (reduce)
dimezzare

ham /hæm/ *n* prosciutto *m*; Theat attore,
-trice *mf* da strapazzo

hamburger /'hæmbɜːgə(r)/ *n*
hamburger *m inv*

ham-fisted /-'fɪstɪd/ *adj* Br fam maldestro

hamlet /'hæmlɪt/ *n* paesino *m*

hammer /'hæmə(r)/ **1** *n* martello *m*
2 *vt* martellare
3 *vi* ∼ **at/on** picchiare a
■ **hammer in** *vt* piantare ⟨*nail*⟩
■ **hammer out** *vt* definire con grandi
sforzi ⟨*agreement, policy*⟩

hammer and sickle *n* falce *f* e
martello *m*

hammered /'hæməd/ *adj* (fam: drunk)
sbronzo

hammock /'hæmək/ *n* amaca *f*

hamper[1] /'hæmpə(r)/ *n* cesto *m*; [gift] ∼
cestino *m*

hamper[2] *vt* ostacolare

hamster /'hæmstə(r)/ *n* criceto *m*

hamstring /'hæmstrɪŋ/ **1** *n* (of horse)
tendine *m* del garretto; (of human) tendine
m del ginocchio
2 *vt* fig rendere impotente

hand /hænd/ **1** *n* mano *f*; (of clock)
lancetta *f*; (writing) scrittura *f*; (worker)
manovale *m*; **all** ∼**s** Naut l'equipaggio al
completo; **at** ∼, **to** ∼ a portata di mano;
by ∼ a mano; **on the one** ∼ da un lato; **on
the other** ∼ d'altra parte; **out of** ∼
incontrollabile; (summarily) su due piedi; **in**
∼ in corso; ⟨*situation*⟩ sotto controllo;
(available) disponibile; **give somebody a** ∼
dare una mano a qualcuno; ∼ **in** ⟨*run,
walk*⟩ mano nella mano; **go** ∼ **in** ∼ fig
andare di pari passo (**with** con)

2 *vt* porgere
■ **hand back** *vt* restituire ⟨*something*⟩
■ **hand down** *vt* tramandare
■ **hand in** *vt* consegnare
■ **hand on** *vt* passare
■ **hand out** *vt* distribuire
■ **hand over** *vt* passare; (to police)
consegnare

handbag *n* borsa *f* (da signora)

hand baggage *n* bagaglio *m* a mano

handball *n* pallamano *f*; (fault in football)
fallo *m* di mano; ∼! mano!

handbasin *n* lavandino *m*

handbook *n* manuale *m*

handbrake *n* freno *m* a mano

handcart *n* carretto *m*

hand cream *n* crema *f* per le mani

handcuffs *npl* manette *fpl*

hand-dryer, hand-drier *n*
asciugamani *m inv* ad aria

hand-eye coordination *n*
coordinazione *f* occhio-mano

handful /'hændfʊl/ *n* manciata *f*; **be
[quite] a** ∼ fam essere difficile da tenere a
freno

hand grenade *n* bomba *f* a mano

handgun *n* pistola *f*

hand-held *adj* a mano

handicap /'hændɪkæp/ *n* handicap *m
inv*

handicapped /'hændɪkæpt/ *adj*
mentally/physically ∼ mentalmente/
fisicamente handicappato

handicraft /'hændɪkrɑːft/ *n* artigianato
m

handiwork /'hændɪwɜːk/ *n* opera *f*

handkerchief /'hæŋkətʃɪf/ *n* (pl **-s** &
-chieves) fazzoletto *m*

handle /'hændl/ **1** *n* manico *m*; (of door)
maniglia *f*; **fly off the** ∼ fam perdere le
staffe
2 *vt* maneggiare; occuparsi di ⟨*problem,
customer*⟩; prendere ⟨*difficult person*⟩;
trattare ⟨*subject*⟩; **be good at handling
somebody** saperci fare con qualcuno

handlebar moustache
/hændlbɑːmə'stɑːʃ/ *n* baffi *mpl* a
manubrio

handlebars /'hændlbɑːz/ *npl* manubrio
m

handler /'hændlə(r)/ *n* (of dog)
addestratore, -trice *mf*

handling /'hændlɪŋ/ *n* (touching, holding)
manipolazione *f*; (of weapon) maneggio *m*;
(dealing with) gestione *f*

handling charge *n* (for goods) spese *fpl*
di movimentazione; (administrative) spese *fpl*
di amministrazione

hand lotion *n* lozione *f* per le mani

hand-luggage *n* bagaglio *m* a mano

handmade *adj* fatto a mano

handout *n* (at lecture) foglio *m* informativo; (fam: money) elemosina *f*

handover *n* (of prisoner, ransom) consegna *f*; (of property, territory) cessione *f*; ~ **of power** passaggio *m* delle consegne

hand-pick *vt* scegliere ‹produce›; selezionare con cura ‹staff›

handrail *n* corrimano *m*

hand-reared /-'rɪəd/ *adj* ‹animal› allattato con il biberon

handset *n* Teleph ricevitore *m*

handshake *n* stretta *f* di mano

hand signal *n* Auto segnalazione *f* con la mano

hands-off *adj* ‹policy› di non intervento; ‹manager› che delega le responsabilità

handsome /'hænsəm/ *adj* bello; (fig: generous) generoso; ‹salary› considerevole

hands-on *adj* ‹experience› pratico; ‹approach› pragmatico; ‹control› diretto; ‹manager› che segue direttamente le varie attività

handspring *n* salto *m* sulle mani

handstand *n* verticale *f*

hand-to-hand *adj & adv* ‹fight› corpo a corpo

hand-to-mouth *adj* ‹existence› precario

hand towel *n* asciugamano *m*

hand-woven /-'wəʊvən/ *adj* tessuto a mano

handwriting *n* calligrafia *f*

handwritten *adj* scritto a mano

handy /'hændɪ/ *adj* (**-ier**, **-iest**) pratico; ‹person› abile; **have/keep** ~ avere/tenere a portata di mano

handyman /'hændɪmæn/ *n* tuttofare *m* *inv*

hang /hæŋ/ ① *vt* (pt/pp **hung**) appendere ‹picture›; (pt/pp **hanged**) impiccare ‹criminal›; ~ **oneself** impiccarsi; ~ **wallpaper** tappezzare ② *vi* (pt/pp **hung**) pendere; ‹hair› scendere ③ *n* **get the** ~ **of it** fam afferrare
■ **hang about** *vi* gironzolare
■ **hang around** *vi* = HANG ABOUT
■ **hang back** *vi* (hesitate) esitare
■ **hang down** *vi* ‹hem› pendere
■ **hang on** *vi* tenersi stretto; (fam: wait) aspettare; Teleph restare in linea
■ **hang on to** *vt* tenersi stretto a; (keep) tenere
■ **hang out** ① *vi* spuntare; **where does he usually** ~ **out?** fam dove bazzica di solito? ② *vt* stendere ‹washing›
■ **hang up** ① *vt* appendere; Teleph riattaccare ② *vi* essere appeso; Teleph riattaccare

hangar /'hæŋə(r)/ *n* hangar *m* *inv*

hanger /'hæŋə(r)/ *n* gruccia *f*

hanger-on *n* leccapiedi *mf* *inv*

hang-glider *n* deltaplano *m*

hang-gliding *n* deltaplano *m*

hanging /'hæŋɪŋ/ *n* (of person) impiccagione *f*; (curtain) tendaggio *m*; (on wall) arazzo *m*

hangman *n* boia *m*

hangover *n* postumi *mpl* della sbornia

hang-up *n* fam complesso *m*

hank /hæŋk/ *n* (of hair) ciocca *f*; (of wool etc) matassa *f*

hanker /'hæŋkə(r)/ *vi* ~ **after something** smaniare per qualcosa

hanky, **hankie** /'hæŋkɪ/ *n* fam fazzoletto *m*

hanky-panky /hæŋkɪ'pæŋkɪ/ *n* fam qualcosa *m* di losco

ha'penny /'heɪpnɪ/ *n* Br *abbr* (**halfpenny**) mezzo penny *m* *inv*

haphazard /hæp'hæzəd/ *adj* a casaccio; **in a** ~ **fashion** a casaccio

haphazardly /hæp'hæzədlɪ/ *adv* a casaccio

hapless /'hæplɪs/ *adj* sventurato

happen /'hæpn/ *vi* capitare, succedere; **as it** ~**s** per caso; **I** ~**ed to meet him** mi è capitato di incontrarlo; **what has** ~**ed to him?** cosa gli è capitato?; (become of) che fine ha fatto?

happening /'hæp(ə)nɪŋ/ *n* avvenimento *m*

happily /'hæpɪlɪ/ *adv* felicemente; (fortunately) fortunatamente

happiness /'hæpɪnɪs/ *n* felicità *f*

happy /'hæpɪ/ *adj* (**-ier**, **-iest**) contento, felice

happy ending *n* lieto fine *m*

happy-go-lucky *adj* spensierato

happy hour *n* ora *f* in cui nei pub le bevande vengono vendute a prezzi scontati

happy medium *n* giusto mezzo *m*

harangue /hə'ræŋ/ *vt* ‹morally› fare un sermone a; ‹politically› arringare

harass /'hærəs/ *vt* perseguitare

harassed /'hærəst/ *adj* stressato

harassment /'hærəsmənt/ *n* persecuzione *f*; **sexual** ~ molestie *fpl* sessuali

harbinger /'hɑːbɪndʒə(r)/ *n* liter segnale *m*; (person) precursore *m*; precorritrice *f*

harbour /'hɑːbə(r)/ ① *n* porto *m* ② *vt* dare asilo a; nutrire ‹grudge›

hard /hɑːd/ ① *adj* duro; ‹question, problem› difficile; **be** ~ **on somebody** ‹person› essere duro con qualcuno ② *adv* ‹work› duramente; ‹pull, hit, rain, snow› forte; ~ **hit by unemployment** duramente colpito dalla disoccupazione; **take something** ~ non accettare qualcosa; **think** ~**!** pensaci bene!; **try** ~ mettercela ⋯

tutta; **try ~er** metterci più impegno; **~ done by** fam trattato ingiustamente

hard and fast adj ⟨rule, distinction⟩ preciso

hardback n edizione f rilegata

hardboard n truciolato m

hard-boiled /-'bɔɪld/ adj ⟨egg⟩ sodo

hard cash n contante m

hard copy n copia f stampata

hard core ① n (in construction) massicciata f; (of group, demonstrators) zoccolo m duro
② adj ⟨pornography, video⟩ hard-core; ⟨supporter, opponent⟩ irriducibile

hard court n campo m in superficie dura

hard disk n hard disk m inv, disco m rigido

hard drive n Comput hard drive m

hard drug n droga f pesante

hard-earned /-'ɜnd/ adj ⟨cash⟩ sudato

harden /'hɑːdn/ vi indurirsi

hardened adj ⟨criminal⟩ inveterato; ⟨drinker⟩ cronico

hard-faced /-'feɪst/ adj ⟨person⟩ dai tratti duri

hard-fought adj ⟨battle⟩ accanito

hard hat n casco m

hard-headed /-'hedɪd/ adj pratico; ⟨businessman⟩ dal sangue freddo

hardhearted /-'hɑːtɪd/ adj dal cuore duro

hard-hitting /-'hɪtɪŋ/ adj ⟨report, speech⟩ incisivo

hard labour n Br lavori mpl forzati

hard lens n lente f a contatto rigida

hardline ① adj ⟨policy, regime⟩ duro
② n linea f dura; **~ lines!** che sfortuna!

hardliner n Pol fautore, -trice mf della linea dura

hard luck n sfortuna f

hard-luck story n **give somebody a ~ ~** raccontare a qualcuno le proprie disgrazie

hardly /'hɑːdlɪ/ adv appena; **~ ever** quasi mai

hardness /'hɑːdnɪs/ n durezza f

hard-nosed /-'nəʊzd/ adj ⟨attitude, businessman, government⟩ duro

hard of hearing adj duro d'orecchio

hard-on n fam erezione f

hard porn n pornografia f hard-core

hard-pressed /-'prest/ adj in difficoltà; (for time) a corto di tempo

hard-pushed /-'pʊʃt/ adj (having problems) in difficoltà

hard rock n Mus hard rock m

hard sell n tecnica f di vendita aggressiva

hardship /'hɑːdʃɪp/ n avversità f inv

hard shoulder n Auto corsia f d'emergenza

hard up adj fam a corto di soldi; **~ ~ for something** a corto di qualcosa

hardware n ferramenta fpl; Comput hardware m inv

hardware shop n negozio m di ferramenta

hard-wearing /-'weərɪŋ/ adj resistente

hardwood n legno m duro

hard-working /-'wɜːkɪŋ/ adj **be ~** essere un gran lavoratore

hardy /'hɑːdɪ/ adj (**-ier, -iest**) dal fisico resistente; ⟨plant⟩ che sopporta il gelo

hare /heə(r)/ n lepre f

hare-brained /'heəbreɪnd/ adj ⟨scheme⟩ da scervellati; ⟨person⟩ scervellato

harelip /heə'lɪp/ n labbro m leporino

harem /hɑːriːm/ n serraglio m

hark /hɑːk/ v
■ **hark back** vt fig **~ back to** ritornare su

haricot [bean] /'hærɪkəʊ/ n fagiolo m bianco

harm /hɑːm/ ① n male m; (damage) danni mpl; **out of ~'s way** in un posto sicuro; **it won't do any ~** non farà certo male
② vt far male a; (damage) danneggiare

harmful /'hɑːmfʊl/ adj dannoso

harmless /'hɑːmlɪs/ adj innocuo

harmonica /hɑː'mɒnɪkə/ n armonica f [a bocca]

harmonious /hɑː'məʊnɪəs/ adj armonioso

harmoniously /hɑː'məʊnɪəslɪ/ adv in armonia

harmonize /'hɑːmənaɪz/ vi fig armonizzare

harmony /'hɑːmənɪ/ n armonia f

harness /'hɑːnɪs/ ① n finimenti mpl; (of parachute) imbracatura f
② vt bardare ⟨horse⟩; sfruttare ⟨resources⟩

harp /hɑːp/ n arpa f
■ **harp on** vi fam insistere (**about** su)

harpist /'hɑːpɪst/ n arpista mf

harpoon /hɑː'puːn/ n arpione m

harpsichord /'hɑːpsɪkɔːd/ n clavicembalo m

harrow /'hærəʊ/ n erpice m

harrowing /'hærəʊɪŋ/ adj straziante

harry /'hærɪ/ vt (pursue, harass) assillare

harsh /hɑːʃ/ adj duro; ⟨light⟩ abbagliante

harshly /'hɑːʃlɪ/ adv duramente

harshness /'hɑːʃnɪs/ n durezza f

harvest /'hɑːvɪst/ ① n raccolta f; (of grapes) vendemmia f; (crop) raccolto m
② vt raccogliere

harvester /'hɑːvɪstə(r)/ *n* (person) mietitore, -trice *mf*; (machine) mietitrice *f*

harvest festival *n* festa *f* del raccolto

has /hæz/ ▶HAVE

has-been /-biːn/ *n* fam (person) persona *f* che ha fatto il suo tempo; (thing) anticaglia *f*

hash /hæʃ/ *n* **make a** ∼ **of** fam fare un casino con

hash [sign] *n* cancelletto *m*

hashish /'hæʃɪʃ/ *n* hashish *m*

hassle /'hæsl/ 1 *n* fam rottura *f*
2 *vt* rompere le scatole a

hassock /'hæsək/ *n* cuscino *m* di inginocchiatoio

haste /heɪst/ *n* fretta *f*; **make** ∼ affrettarsi

hasten /'heɪsn/ 1 *vi* affrettarsi
2 *vt* affrettare

hastily /'heɪstɪlɪ/ *adv* frettolosamente

hasty /'heɪstɪ/ *adj* (**-ier, -iest**) frettoloso; ⟨*decision*⟩ affrettato

hat /hæt/ *n* cappello *m*

hatbox /'hætbɒks/ *n* cappelliera *f*

hatch[1] /hætʃ/ *n* (for food) sportello *m* passavivande *inv*; Naut boccaporto *m*

hatch[2] 1 *vi* ∼ **[out]** rompere il guscio; ⟨*egg*⟩ schiudersi
2 *vt* covare; tramare ⟨*plot*⟩
■ **hatch up** *vt* tramare ⟨*plot*⟩

hatchback /'hætʃbæk/ *n* Auto (car) tre/ cinque porte *m inv*; (door) porta *f* del bagagliaio

hatchet /'hætʃɪt/ *n* ascia *f*

hate /heɪt/ 1 *n* odio *m*
2 *vt* odiare

hateful /'heɪtfʊl/ *adj* odioso

hate mail *n* lettere *fpl* offensive o minatorie

hatpin /'hætpɪn/ *n* spillone *m*

hatred /'heɪtrɪd/ *n* odio *m*

hat-trick *n* tripletta *f*

haughtily /'hɔːtɪlɪ/ *adv* altezzosamente

haughty /'hɔːtɪ/ *adj* (**-ier, -iest**) altezzoso

haul /hɔːl/ 1 *n* (fish) pescata *f*; (loot) bottino *m*; (pull) tirata *f*
2 *vt* tirare; trasportare ⟨*goods*⟩
3 *vi* ∼ **on** tirare

haulage /'hɔːlɪdʒ/ *n* trasporto *m*

haulier /'hɔːlɪə(r)/ *n* autotrasportatore *m*

haunch /hɔːntʃ/ *n* anca *f*

haunt /hɔːnt/ 1 *n* ritrovo *m*
2 *vt* frequentare; (linger in the mind) perseguitare; **this house is** ∼**ed** questa casa è abitata dai fantasmi

haunted /'hɔːntɪd/ *adj* ⟨*house*⟩ infestato dai fantasmi; ⟨*look*⟩ tormentato

haunting /'hɔːntɪŋ/ *adj* ⟨*memory, melody*⟩ ossessionante

have /hæv/ 1 *vt* (3 sg pres tense **has**; pt/pp **had**) avere; fare ⟨*breakfast, bath, walk etc*⟩; ∼ **a drink** bere qualcosa; ∼ **lunch/dinner** pranzare/cenare; ∼ **a rest** riposarsi; **I had my hair cut** mi sono tagliata i capelli; **we had the flat painted** abbiamo fatto tinteggiare la casa; **I had it made** l'ho fatto fare; ∼ **to do something** dover fare qualcosa; ∼ **him telephone me tomorrow** digli di telefonarmi domani; **he has** *or* **he's got two houses** ha due case; **you've got the money,** ∼**n't you?** hai i soldi, no?
2 *v aux* avere; (with verbs of motion & some others) essere; **I** ∼ **seen him** l'ho visto; **he has never been there** non ci è mai stato;
3 *npl* **the** ∼**s and the** ∼**-nots** i ricchi e i poveri
■ **have in** *vt* avere in casa/ufficio etc ⟨*builders etc*⟩
■ **have off** *vt* fam **he's having it off with his secretary** si fa la segretaria
■ **have on** *vt* (be wearing) portare; (dupe) prendere in giro; **I've got something on tonight** ho un impegno stasera; **you're having me on!** tu mi stai prendendo in giro!
■ **have out** *vt* ∼ **it out with somebody** chiarire le cose con qualcuno; ∼ **a tooth out** farsi togliere un dente

haven /'heɪvn/ *n* fig rifugio *m*

haver /'heɪvə(r)/ *vi* (dither) titubare

haversack /'hævəsæk/ *n* zaino *m*

havoc /'hævək/ *n* strage *f*; **play** ∼ **with** fig scombussolare

haw /hɔː/ ▶HUM

Hawaii /hə'waɪɪ/ *n* le Hawaii

Hawaiian /hə'waɪən/ *n* & *adj* hawaiano, -a *mf*; (language) hawaiano *m*

hawk[1] /hɔːk/ *n* falco *m*

hawk[2] *vt* vendere in giro

hawker /'hɔːkə(r)/ *n* venditore, -trice *mf* ambulante

hawkish /'hɔːkɪʃ/ *adj* Pol intransigente

hawthorn /'hɔːθɔːn/ *n* biancospino *m*

hay /heɪ/ *n* fieno *m*

hay fever *n* raffreddore *m* da fieno

hayloft *n* fienile *m*

haymaking *n* fienagione *f*

haystack *n* pagliaio *m*

haywire *adj* fam **go** ∼ dare i numeri; ⟨*plans*⟩ andare all'aria

hazard /'hæzəd/ 1 *n* (risk) rischio *m*
2 *vt* rischiare; ∼ **a guess** azzardare un'ipotesi

hazardous /'hæzədəs/ *adj* rischioso

hazard [warning] lights *npl* Auto luci *fpl* d'emergenza

haze /'heɪz/ *n* foschia *f*

hazel /'heɪz(ə)l/ *n* nocciolo *m*; (colour) [color] *m* nocciola *m*

hazelnut /'heɪz(ə)lnʌt/ n nocciola f

hazy /'heɪzɪ/ adj (**-ier**, **-iest**) nebbioso; fig ⟨person⟩ confuso; ⟨memories⟩ vago

HDTV abbr (**high-definition television**) HDTV f

he /hiː/ pron lui; **he's tired** è stanco; **I'm going but he's not** io vengo, ma lui no

head /hed/ ① n testa f; (of firm) capo m; (of primary school) direttore, -trice mf; (of secondary school) preside mf; (on beer) schiuma f; **use your ~!** usa la testa!; **be off one's ~** essere fuori di testa; **have a good ~ for business** avere il senso degli affari; **have a good ~ for heights** non soffrire di vertigini; **10 pounds a ~** 10 sterline a testa; **20 ~ of cattle** 20 capi di bestiame; **~ first** a capofitto; **~ over heels in love** innamorato pazzo; **~s or tails?** testa o croce?
② vt essere a capo di; essere in testa a ⟨list⟩; colpire di testa ⟨ball⟩
③ vi **~ for** dirigersi verso

headache n mal m di testa

headband n fascia f per capelli

head boy n Br Sch alunno m che rappresenta la scuola nelle manifestazioni ufficiali e che ha responsabilità speciali

head-butt vt dare una testàta a

head case n fam **be a ~ ~** essere matto da legare

head cold n raffreddore m di testa

headcount n **do a ~** contare i presenti

headdress n acconciatura f

header /'hedə(r)/ n colpo m di testa; (dive) tuffo m di testa; (on document) intestazione f

headfirst adv ⟨dive, fall⟩ di testa; ⟨rush into⟩ a testa bassa

headgear n copricapo m

head girl n Br Sch alunna f che rappresenta la scuola nelle manifestazioni ufficiali e che ha responsabilità speciali

headhunt vt cercare per assumere

headhunter n also Comm cacciatore, -trice mf di teste

headhunting n Comm ricerca f ad hoc di personale

heading n (in list etc) titolo m

headlamp n Auto fanale m

headland n promontorio m

headlight n Auto fanale m

headline n titolo m

headlong adj & adv a capofitto

head louse n pidocchio m

headmaster n (of primary school) direttore m; (of secondary school) preside m

headmistress n (of primary school) direttrice f; (of secondary school) preside f

head of department n capo mf reparto

head office n sede f centrale

head-on ① adj ⟨collision⟩ frontale ② adv frontalmente

headphones npl cuffie fpl

headquarters npl sede fsg; Mil quartier msg generale

headrest n poggiatesta m inv

headroom n sottotetto m; (of bridge) altezza f libera di passaggio

headscarf n foulard m inv, fazzoletto m

headset n cuffia f con microfono

headstand n **do a ~** fare la verticale

head start n **have a ~ ~** partire avvantaggiato

headstone n (of grave) lapide f

headstrong adj testardo

head teacher n (of primary school) direttore, -trice mf; (of secondary school) preside mf

head-to-head n confronto m diretto adj diretto

head waiter n capocameriere m

headway n progresso m

headwind n vento m di prua

heady /'hedɪ/ adj che dà alla testa

heal /hiːl/ vt/i guarire

healer /'hiːlə(r)/ n guaritore, -trice mf; **time is a great ~** il tempo guarisce tutti i mali

healing /'hiːlɪŋ/ adj ⟨power, effect⟩ curativo; **the ~ process** il processo di guarigione

health /helθ/ n salute f

health care n assistenza f sanitaria

health centre n Br ambulatorio m

health check n controllo m

health club n club m ginnico

health farm n centro m di rimessa in forma

health foods npl alimenti mpl macrobiotici

health-food shop n negozio m di macrobiotica

health hazard n pericolo m per la salute

healthily /'helθɪlɪ/ adv in modo sano

health insurance n assicurazione f contro malattie

health officer n ufficiale m sanitario

health resort n (in mountains, by sea) stazione f climatica; (spa town) stazione f termale

Health Service n (Br: for public) servizio m sanitario; (Am: Univ) infermeria f

health visitor n Br infermiere, -a mf che fa visite a domicilio

health warning n avviso m del ministero della sanità

healthy /'helθɪ/ adj (**-ier**, **-iest**) sano

heap /hiːp/ ① *n* mucchio *m*; ~s of fam un sacco di
② *vt* ~ [up] ammucchiare

heaped /hiːpt/ *adj* a ~ spoonful un cucchiaio colmo

hear /hɪə(r)/ *vt/i* (pt/pp **heard**) sentire; ~, ~! bravo!
■ **hear about** *vt* (learn of) sentir parlare di
■ **hear from** *vi* aver notizie di
■ **hear of** *vi* sentir parlare di; **he would not** ~ **of it** non ne ha voluto sentir parlare

hearing /'hɪərɪŋ/ *n* udito *m*; Jur udienza *f*

hearing aid *n* apparecchio *m* acustico

hearing-impaired /-ɪm'peəd/ *adj* audioleso

hearsay /'hɪəseɪ/ *n* from ~ per sentito dire

hearse /hɜːs/ *n* carro *m* funebre

heart /hɑːt/ *n* cuore *m*; ~s *pl* (Cards) cuori *mpl*; **at** ~ di natura; **by** ~ a memoria

heartache *n* pena *f*

heart attack *n* infarto *m*

heartbeat *n* battito *m* cardiaco

heartbreak *n* afflizione *f*

heartbreaking *adj* straziante

heart-broken *adj* be ~ avere il cuore spezzato

heartburn *n* mal *m* di stomaco

heart disease *n* malattia *f* cardiaca

hearten /'hɑːt(ə)n/ *vt* rincuorare

heartening /'hɑːt(ə)nɪŋ/ *adj* rincuorante

heart failure *n* arresto *m* cardiaco

heartfelt /'hɑːtfelt/ *adj* di cuore

hearth /hɑːθ/ *n* focolare *m*

hearthrug /'hɑːθrʌg/ *n* tappeto *m* davanti al camino

heartily /'hɑːtɪlɪ/ *adv* di cuore; ⟨eat⟩ con appetito; **be** ~ **sick of something** non poterne più di qualcosa

heartland /'hɑːtlænd/ *n* (industrial, rural) cuore *m*; Pol roccaforte *f*

heartless /'hɑːtlɪs/ *adj* spietato

heartlessly /'hɑːtlɪslɪ/ *adv* in modo spietato

heart-lung machine *n* polmone *m* artificiale

heart rate *n* battito *m* cardiaco

heart-rending /-rendɪŋ/ *adj* ⟨sigh, story⟩ straziante

heart-searching *n* esame *m* di coscienza

heart surgeon *n* cardiochirurgo, -a *mf*

heartthrob *n* fam rubacuori *m inv*

heart-to-heart ① *n* conversazione *f* a cuore aperto
② *adj* a cuore aperto

heart transplant *n* trapianto *m* di cuore

heart-warming *adj* toccante

hearty /'hɑːtɪ/ *adj* caloroso; ⟨meal⟩ copioso; ⟨person⟩ gioviale

heat /hiːt/ ① *n* calore *m*; Sport prova *f* eliminatoria
② *vt* scaldare
③ *vi* scaldarsi
■ **heat up** *vt* scaldare ⟨food, drink⟩; riscaldare ⟨room⟩

heated /'hiːtɪd/ *adj* ⟨swimming pool⟩ riscaldato; ⟨discussion⟩ animato

heater /'hiːtə(r)/ *n* (for room) stufa *f*; (for water) boiler *m inv*; Auto riscaldamento *m*

heath /hiːθ/ *n* brughiera *f*

heat haze *n* foschia *f* (dovuta all'afa)

heathen /'hiːðn/ *adj* & *n* pagano, -a *mf*

heather /'heðə(r)/ *n* erica *f*

heating /'hiːtɪŋ/ *n* riscaldamento *m*

heat loss *n* perdita *f* di calore

heat-resistant *adj* resistente al calore

heat sink *n* dissipatore *m* termico

heatstroke *n* colpo *m* di sole

heat treatment *n* Med termoterapia *f*

heatwave *n* ondata *f* di calore

heave /hiːv/ ① *vt* tirare; (lift) tirare su; (fam: throw) gettare; emettere ⟨sigh⟩
② *vi* tirare; **my stomach** ~d avevo la nausea

heaven /'hev(ə)n/ *n* paradiso *m*; ~ **help you if...** Dio vi scampi se... **raise one's eyes to** ~ alzare gli occhi al cielo; **H**~s! santo cielo!

heavenly /'hev(ə)nlɪ/ *adj* celeste; fam delizioso

heaven-sent /-'sent/ *adj* ⟨opportunity⟩ provvidenziale

heavily /'hevɪlɪ/ *adv* pesantemente; ⟨smoke, drink etc⟩ molto

heaviness /'hevɪnɪs/ *n* pesantezza *f*

heavy /'hevɪ/ *adj* (**-ier**, **-iest**) pesante; ⟨traffic⟩ intenso; ⟨rain, cold⟩ forte; **be a** ~ **smoker/drinker** essere un gran fumatore/ bevitore

heavy-duty *adj* ⟨equipment, shoes⟩ molto resistente

heavy goods vehicle *n* veicolo *m* pesante da trasporto

heavy-handed /-'hændɪd/ *adj* (severe) severo; (clumsy) maldestro

heavy industry *n* industria *f* pesante

heavy metal *n* Mus heavy metal *m*

heavyweight *n* peso *m* massimo

Hebrew /'hiːbruː/ *adj* & *n* ebreo

heck /hek/ fam ① *int* cavolo
② *n* a ~ of a lot of un sacco di; **what the** ~**!** chi se ne frega!; **what the** ~ **is going on?** che cavolo succede?

heckle /'hekl/ vt interrompere di
continuo

heckler /'heklə(r)/ n disturbatore, -trice
mf

hectare /'hekteə(r)/ n ettaro m

hectic /'hektɪk/ adj frenetico

hectoring /'hektərɪŋ/ adj prepotente

hedge /hedʒ/ ① n siepe f
② vi fig essere evasivo

hedge-clippers npl cesoie fpl

hedgehog n riccio m

hedgerow n siepe f

hedonism /'hiːdənɪzm/ n edonismo m

hedonistic /hiːdə'nɪstɪk/ adj edonistico

heebie-jeebies /hiːbɪ'dʒiːbɪz/ npl fam
give somebody the ∼ far venire i brividi
a qualcuno

heed /hiːd/ ① n pay ∼ to prestare
ascolto a
② vt prestare ascolto a

heedless /'hiːdlɪs/ adj noncurante

heel[1] /hiːl/ n tallone m; (of shoe) tacco m;
down at ∼ fig trasandato; **take to one's** ∼s
fam darsela a gambe

heel[2] vi ∼ **over** Naut inclinarsi

heel bar n calzolaio m

hefty /'heftɪ/ adj (-ier, -iest) massiccio

heifer /'hefə(r)/ n giovenca f

height /haɪt/ n altezza f; (of plane)
altitudine f; (of season, fame) culmine m

heighten /'haɪt(ə)n/ vt fig accrescere

heinous /'hiːnəs/ adj abominevole

heir /eə(r)/ n erede mf

heiress /eə'res/ n ereditiera f

heirloom /'eəluːm/ n cimelio m di
famiglia

heist /haɪst/ adj Am fam furto m; (armed)
rapina f

held /held/ ▶ HOLD[2]

helicopter /'helɪkɒptə(r)/ n elicottero m

heliport /'helɪpɔːt/ n eliporto m

helium /'hiːlɪəm/ n elio m

helix /'hiːlɪks/ n elica f

hell /hel/ ① n inferno m; **go to** ∼! sì va'
al diavolo!; **make sb's life** ∼ rendere la
vita infernale a qualcuno
② int porca miseria!

hell-bent adj ∼ **on doing something**
deciso a tutti i costi a fare qualcosa

Hellenic /hɪ'lenɪk/ adj ellenico

hellfire /'helfaɪə(r)/ n pene fpl dell'
inferno

hell-for-leather adv fam **go** ∼ andare a
spron battuto

hello /hə'ləʊ/ int & n = HALLO

Hell's angel n Hell's angel m inv

helm /helm/ n timone m; **at the** ∼ fig al
timone

helmet /'helmɪt/ n casco m

help /help/ ① n aiuto m; (employee) aiuto
m domestico; **that's no** ∼ non è d'aiuto
② vt aiutare; ∼ **oneself to something**
servirsi di qualcosa; ∼ **yourself** (at table)
serviti pure; **I could not** ∼ **laughing** non
ho potuto trattenermi dal ridere; **it cannot
be** ∼**ed** non c'è niente da fare; **I can't** ∼ **it**
non ci posso far niente
③ vi aiutare
■ **help out** ① vt dare una mano a
② vi dare una mano

help desk n help desk m inv

helper /'helpə(r)/ n aiutante mf

helpful /'helpfʊl/ adj ⟨person⟩ di aiuto;
⟨advice⟩ utile

helping /'helpɪŋ/ n porzione f

helping hand n give somebody a ∼ ∼
dare una mano a qualcuno

helpless /'helplɪs/ adj (unable to manage)
incapace; (powerless) impotente

helplessly /'helplɪslɪ/ adv con
impotenza; ⟨laugh⟩ incontrollatamente

helpline n assistenza f telefonica

help window n Comput finestrella f di
aiuto

helter-skelter /heltə'skeltə(r)/ ① adv
in fretta e furia
② n scivolo m a spirale nei luna park

hem /hem/ ① n orlo m
② vt (pt/pp **hemmed**) orlare
■ **hem in** vt intrappolare

hemisphere /'hemɪsfɪə(r)/ n emisfero m

hemline /'hemlaɪn/ n orlo m

hemlock /'hemlɒk/ n cicuta f

hemophilia n Am = HAEMOPHILIA

hemp /hemp/ n canapa f

hen /hen/ n gallina f; (any female bird)
femmina f

hence /hens/ adv (for this reason) quindi;
(from now on) a partire da ora; (from here) da
qui

henceforth /hens'fɔːθ/ adv fml (from that
time on) da allora in poi; (from now on) d'ora
in poi

henchman /'hentʃmən/ n pej tirapiedi m
inv

hen-coop n stia f

hen house n pollaio m

henna /'henə/ n hennè m

hen night n fam addio m al nubilato

hen party n fam festa f di addio al
nubilato

henpecked /'henpekt/ adj
tiranneggiato dalla moglie

hepatitis /hepə'taɪtɪs/ n epatite f

her /hɜː(r)/ ① poss adj suo m, sua f, suoi
mpl, sue fpl; ∼ **job/house** il suo lavoro/la
sua casa; **her mother/father** sua madre/suo
padre
② pers pron (direct object) la; (indirect object)
le; (after prep) lei; **I know** ∼ la conosco; **give**

~ **the money** dalle i soldi; **give it to** ~ daglielo; **I came with** ~ sono venuto con lei; **it's** ~ è lei; **I've seen** ~ l'ho vista; **I've seen** ~, **but not him** ho visto lei, ma non lui

herald /'herəld/ *vt* annunciare

heraldic /he'rældɪk/ *adj* araldico

heraldry /'herəldrɪ/ *n* araldica *f*

herb /hɜ:b/ *n* erba *f*

herbaceous /hɜ:'beɪʃəs/ *adj* erbaceo; ~ **border** aiuola *f*

herbal /'hɜ:b(ə)l/ *adj* alle erbe

herbalist /'hɜ:bəlɪst/ *n* erborista *mf*

herbal tea *n* tisana *f*

herb garden *n* aromatario *m*

herbs /hɜ:bz/ *npl* (for cooking) aromi *mpl* [da cucina]; (medicinal) erbe *fpl*

herb tea *n* tisana *f*

herculean /hɜ:kjʊ'li:ən/ *adj* ⟨task⟩ erculeo

herd /hɜ:d/ **①** *n* gregge *m* **②** *vt* (tend) sorvegliare; (drive) far muovere; fig ammassare
■ **herd together** **①** *vi* raggrupparsi **②** *vt* raggruppare

here /hɪə(r)/ *adv* qui qua; **in** ~ qui dentro; **come/bring** ~ vieni/porta qui; ~ **is...**, ~ **are...** ecco...; ~ **you are!** ecco qua!

hereabouts /hɪərə'baʊts/ Br, **hereabout** Am *adv* da queste parti

hereafter *adv* in futuro

here and now *adv* seduta stante *n* **the** ~ ~ ~ il presente

hereby *adv* con la presente

hereditary /hɪ'redɪtərɪ/ *adj* ereditario

heredity /hɪ'redətɪ/ *n* ereditarietà *f*

heresy /'herəsɪ/ *n* eresia *f*

heretic /'herətɪk/ *n* eretico, -a *mf*

herewith /hɪə'wɪð/ *adv* Comm con la presente

heritage /'herɪtɪdʒ/ *n* eredità *f*

hermetic /hɜ:'metɪk/ *adj* ermetico

hermetically /hɜ:'metɪklɪ/ *adv* ermeticamente

hermit /'hɜ:mɪt/ *n* eremita *mf*

hernia /'hɜ:nɪə/ *n* ernia *f*

hero /'hɪərəʊ/ *n* (pl **-es**) eroe *m*

heroic /hɪ'rəʊɪk/ *adj* eroico

heroically /hɪ'rəʊɪklɪ/ *adv* eroicamente

heroin /'herəʊɪn/ *n* eroina *f* (droga)

heroin addict *n* eroinomane *mf*

heroine /'herəʊɪn/ *n* eroina *f*

heroism /'herəʊɪzm/ *n* eroismo *m*

heron /'herən/ *n* airone *m*

hero-worship **①** *n* culto *m* degli eroi **②** *vt* venerare

herpes /'hɜ:pi:z/ *n* herpes *m*

herring /'herɪŋ/ *n* aringa *f*

herringbone /'herɪŋbəʊn/ *adj* ⟨pattern⟩ spigato

hers /hɜ:z/ *poss pron* il suo *m*, la sua *f*, i suoi *mpl*, le sue *fpl*; **a friend of** ~ un suo amico; **friends of** ~ dei suoi amici; **that is** ~ quello è suo; (as opposed to mine) quello è il suo

herself /hə'self/ *pers pron* (reflexive) si; (emphatic) lei stessa; (after prep) sé, se stessa; **she poured** ~ **a drink** si è versata da bere; **she told me so** ~ me lo ha detto lei stessa; **she's proud of** ~ è fiera di sé; **by** ~ da sola

hesitant /'hezɪtənt/ *adj* esitante

hesitantly /'hezɪtəntlɪ/ *adv* con esitazione

hesitate /'hezɪteɪt/ *vi* esitare

hesitation /hezɪ'teɪʃn/ *n* esitazione *f*

hessian /'hesɪən/ *n* tela *f* di iuta

heterogeneous /hetərə'dʒi:nɪəs/ *adj* eterogeneo

heterosexual /hetərəʊ'sekʃʊəl/ *adj* eterosessuale

het up /het/ *adj* fam agitato

hew /hju:/ *vt* (pt **hewed**, pp **hewed** or **hewn**) spaccare

hexagon /'heksəgən/ *n* esagono *m*

hexagonal /hek'sægənl/ *adj* esagonale

hey /heɪ/ *int* ehi!

heyday /'heɪdeɪ/ *n* tempi *mpl* d'oro

hey presto /heɪ'prestəʊ/ *int* (magic) e voilà!

HGV *abbr* **heavy goods vehicle**

hi /haɪ/ *int* ciao!

hiatus /haɪ'eɪtəs/ *n* (pl **-tuses**) iato *m*

hibernate /'haɪbəneɪt/ *vi* andare in letargo

hibernation /haɪbə'neɪʃn/ *n* letargo *m*

hiccup /'hɪkʌp/ **①** *n* singhiozzo *m*; (fam: hitch) intoppo *m*; **have the** ~**s** avere il singhiozzo **②** *vi* fare un singhiozzo

hick /hɪk/ *n* Am fam buzzurro, -a *mf*

hick town *n* Am fam città *f inv* provinciale

hid /hɪd/, **hidden** /'hɪdn/ ▶ HIDE²

hide¹ /haɪd/ *n* (leather) pelle *f* (di animale)

hide² **①** *vt* (pt **hid**, pp **hidden**) nascondere **②** *vi* nascondersi

hide-and-seek *n* play ~ giocare a nascondino

hideaway /'haɪdəweɪ/ *n* (secluded place) rifugio *m*; (hiding place) nascondiglio *m*

hidebound /'haɪdbaʊnd/ *adj* (conventional) limitato

hideous /'hɪdɪəs/ *adj* orribile

hideously /'hɪdɪəslɪ/ *adv* orribilmente

hideout /'haɪdaʊt/ *n* nascondiglio *m*

h

hiding[1] /'haɪdɪŋ/ n (fam: beating) bastonata; (defeat) batosta f

hiding[2] n go into ～ sparire dalla circolazione

hiding place n nascondiglio m

hierarchic[al] /haɪə'rɑːkɪk[l]/ adj gerarchico

hierarchy /'haɪərɑːkɪ/ n gerarchia f

hieroglyphics /haɪərə'glɪfɪks/, **hieroglyphs** npl geroglifici mpl

hi-fi /'haɪfaɪ/ n abbr (**high fidelity**) hi-fi m inv; (set of equipment) impianto m hi-fi, stereo m inv

higgledy-piggledy /hɪgldɪ'pɪgldɪ/ adv alla rinfusa

high /haɪ/ **1** adj alto; ⟨meat⟩ che comincia ad andare a male; ⟨wind⟩ forte; (on drugs) fatto; **it's ～ time we did something about it** è ora di fare qualcosa in proposito
2 adv in alto; ～ **and low** in lungo e in largo
3 n massimo m; (temperature) massima f; **from on ～** dall'alto; **be on a ～** fam essere fatto

high and dry adj fig **leave somebody ～ ～ ～** piantare in asso qualcuno

high-beam n Am abbagliante m

high-born adj nobile

highbrow adj & n intellettuale mf

high chair n seggiolone m

high-class adj ⟨hotel, shop, car⟩ d'alta classe; ⟨prostitute⟩ di alto bordo

high command n stato m maggiore

High Commission n alto commissariato m

High Commissioner n alto commissario m

High Court n ≈ Corte f Suprema

high-definition adj ad alta definizione

high-definition television n televisione f ad alta definizione

high diving n tuffo m

high-end adj ⟨product, model⟩ della fascia più alta

higher education /haɪəredjʊ'keɪʃn/ n istruzione f universitaria

higher mathematics n matematica f avanzata

highfaluting /haɪfə'luːtɪŋ/ adj fam ⟨ideas⟩ pretenzioso; ⟨language⟩ pomposo

high fashion n alta moda f

high-fibre adj ⟨diet⟩ ricco di fibre

high-fidelity **1** n alta fedeltà f
2 adj ad alta fedeltà

high finance n alta finanza f

high-flier n (person) persona f che mira alto

high-flown adj ⟨phrases⟩ ampolloso

high-flying adj ⟨aircraft⟩ da alta quota; ⟨career⟩ ambizioso; ⟨person⟩ che mira alto

high-frequency adj alta frequenza f

High German n alto tedesco m

high-grade adj ⟨oil, mineral, product⟩ di prima qualità

high ground n collina f; **take the moral ～ ～** assumere un atteggiamento moralistico

high-handed /-'hændɪd/ adj dispotico

high-handedly /-'hændɪdlɪ/ adv dispoticamente

highheeled /-hiːld/ adj coi tacchi alti

high heels npl tacchi mpl alti

high jinks /dʒɪŋks/ npl baldoria f

high jump n salto m in alto

Highland games /haɪlənd/ n manifestazione f tradizionale scozzese con gare sportive e musicali

Highlands /'haɪləndz/ npl Highlands fpl (regione della Scozia del nord)

high-level adj ⟨talks⟩ ad alto livello; ⟨official⟩ di alto livello

high life n bella vita f

highlight /'haɪlaɪt/ **1** vt (emphasize, with pen) evidenziare
2 n (in art) luce f; (in hair) riflesso m, colpo m di sole; (of exhibition) parte f saliente; (of week, year) avvenimento m saliente; (of match, show) momento m clou

highlighter /'haɪlaɪtə(r)/ n (marker) evidenziatore m

highly /'haɪlɪ/ adv molto; **speak ～ of** lodare; **think ～ of** avere un'alta opinione di

highly-paid /-'peɪd/ adj ben pagato

highlystrung /-'strʌŋ/ adj nervoso

High Mass n messa f solenne

high-minded /-'maɪndɪd/ adj ⟨person⟩ di animo nobile

high-necked /-'nekt/ adj a collo alto

Highness /'haɪnɪs/ n altezza f; **Your ～** Sua Altezza

high noon n mezzogiorno m in punto

high-performance adj ad alta prestazione

high-pitched /-'pɪtʃt/ adj ⟨voice, sound⟩ acuto

high point n momento m culminante

high-powered adj ⟨car, engine⟩ molto potente; ⟨job⟩ di alta responsabilità; ⟨person⟩ dinamico

high pressure **1** n Meteorol alta pressione f
2 attrib Techn ad alta pressione; ⟨job⟩ stressante

high priest n Relig gran sacerdote m; fig guru m inv

high priestess n Relig, fig gran sacerdotessa f

high-principled *adj* ⟨person⟩ di alti principi

high-profile *adj* ⟨politician, group⟩ di spicco; ⟨visit⟩ di grande risonanza

high-ranking *adj* di alto rango

high-rise ① *adj* ⟨building⟩ molto alto ② *n* edificio *m* molto alto

high road *n* strada *f* principale

high school *n* Am ≈ scuola *f* superiore; Br ≈ scuola *f* media e superiore

high sea *n* on the ∼ ∼s in alto mare

high season *n* alta stagione *f*

high society *n* alta società *f*

high-sounding /-'saʊndɪŋ/ *adj* ⟨title⟩ altisonante

high-speed *adj* ⟨train, film⟩ rapido

high-spirited *adj* pieno di brio

high spirits *npl* brio *m*

high spot *n* momento *m* culminante

high street *n* strada *f* principale

high-street shop *n* negozio *m* popolare

high-street spending *n* acquisto *m* di beni di consumo

high tea *n* pasto *m* pomeridiano servito insieme al tè

high tech /'tek/ *n* high tech *f*

high tide *n* alta marea *f*

high treason *n* alto tradimento *m*

high voltage *n* alta tensione *f*

highway /'haɪweɪ/ *n* public ∼ strada *f* pubblica

Highway Code *n* Br Codice *m* stradale

highwayman *n* brigante *m*

highway robbery *n* brigantaggio *m*

high wire *n* filo *m* (per acrobati)

hijack /'haɪdʒæk/ ① *vt* dirottare ② *n* dirottamento *m*

hijacker /'haɪdʒækə(r)/ *n* dirottatore, -trice *mf*

hijacking /'haɪdʒækɪŋ/ *n* dirottamento *m*

hike /haɪk/ ① *n* escursione *f* a piedi; (in price) aumento *m* ② *vi* fare un'escursione a piedi

hiker /'haɪkə(r)/ *n* escursionista *mf*

hiking /'haɪkɪŋ/ *n* escursionismo *m*

hiking boots *npl* pedule *fpl*

hilarious /hɪ'leərɪəs/ *adj* da morir dal ridere

hilarity /hɪ'lærətɪ/ *n* ilarità *f*

hill /hɪl/ *n* collina *f*; (mound) collinetta *f*; (slope) altura *f*

hill-billy /-bɪlɪ/ *n* Am montanaro *m* degli Stati Uniti sudorientali

hillock /'hɪlək/ *n* poggio *m*

hillside /'hɪlsaɪd/ *n* pendio *m*

hilltop /'hɪltɒp/ *n* sommità *f inv* di una collina

hilly /'hɪlɪ/ *adj* collinoso

hilt /hɪlt/ *n* impugnatura *f*; to the ∼ fam ⟨support⟩ fino in fondo; ⟨mortgaged⟩ fino al collo

him /hɪm/ *pers pron* (direct object) lo; (indirect object) gli; (with prep) lui; **I know** ∼ lo conosco; **give** ∼ **the money** dagli i soldi; **give it to** ∼ daglielo; **I spoke to** ∼ gli ho parlato; **it's** ∼ è lui; **she loves** ∼ lo ama; **she loves** ∼, **not you** ama lui, non te

Himalayas /hɪmə'leɪəz/ *npl* Himalaia *msg*

himself /hɪm'self/ *pers pron (reflexive)* si; (emphatic) lui stesso; (after prep) sé, se stesso; **he poured** ∼ **out a drink** si è versato da bere; **he told me so** ∼ me lo ha detto lui stesso; **he's proud of** ∼ è fiero di sé; **by** ∼ da solo

hind /haɪnd/ *adj* posteriore

hinder /'hɪndə(r)/ *vt* intralciare

hind legs *npl* zampe *fpl* posteriori

hindquarters /'haɪn(d)kwɔːtəz/ *npl* didietro *m*

hindrance /'hɪndrəns/ *n* intralcio *m*

hindsight /'haɪndsaɪt/ *n* with ∼ con il senno del poi

Hindu /'hɪnduː/ *adj & n* indù *mf inv*

Hinduism /'hɪnduɪzm/ *n* induismo *m*

hinge /hɪndʒ/ ① *n* cardine *m* ② *vi* ∼ **on** fig dipendere da

hint /hɪnt/ ① *n* (clue) accenno *m*; (advice) suggerimento *m*; (indirect suggestion) allusione *f*; (trace) tocco *m* ② *vt* ∼ **that...** far capire che... ③ *vi* ∼ **at** alludere a

hinterland /'hɪntəlænd/ *n* entroterra *m inv*, hinterland *m inv*

hip /hɪp/ *n* fianco *m*

hip bone *n* ileo *m*

hip flask *n* fiaschetta *f*

hippie /'hɪpɪ/ *n* hippy *mf inv*

hippo /'hɪpəʊ/ *n* fam ippopotamo *m*

hip pocket *n* tasca *f* posteriore

Hippocratic oath /hɪpə'krætɪk/ *adj* giuramento *m* d'Ippocrate

hippopotamus /hɪpə'pɒtəməs/ *n* (pl **-muses** or **-mi** /hɪpə'pɒtəmaɪ/) ippopotamo *m*

hip replacement *n* protesi *f inv* all'anca

hire /'haɪə(r)/ ① *vt* affittare; assumere ⟨person⟩; ∼ **[out]** affittare ② *n* noleggio *m*; **'for** ∼**'** 'affittasi'

hire car *n* macchina *f* a noleggio

hire purchase *n* Br acquisto *m* rateale; on ∼ ∼ a rate

his /hɪz/ ① *poss adj* suo *m*, sua *f*, suoi *mpl*, sue *fpl*; ∼ **job/house** il suo lavoro/la ⋯⟶

sua casa; ~ **mother/father** sua madre/suo padre
2 *poss pron* il suo *m*, la sua *f*, i suoi *mpl*, le sue *fpl*; **a friend of** ~ un suo amico; **friends of** ~ dei suoi amici; **that is** ~ questo è suo; (as opposed to mine) questo è il suo

Hispanic /hɪ'spænɪk/ *adj* ispanico

hiss /hɪs/ **1** *n* sibilo *m*; (of disapproval) fischio *m*
2 *vt* fischiare
3 *vi* sibilare; (in disapproval) fischiare

historian /hɪ'stɔːrɪən/ *n* storico, -a *mf*

historic /hɪ'stɒrɪk/ *adj* storico

historical /hɪ'stɒrɪkl/ *adj* storico

historically /hɪ'stɒrɪklɪ/ *adv* storicamente

history /'hɪstərɪ/ *n* storia *f*; **make** ~ passare alla storia

histrionic /hɪstrɪ'ɒnɪk/ *adj* istrionico

histrionics /hɪstrɪ'ɒnɪks/ *npl* scene *fpl*

hit /hɪt/ **1** *n* (blow) colpo *m*; (fam: success) successo *m*; **score a direct** ~ ⟨*missile*⟩ colpire in pieno
2 *vt* (pt/pp **hit**, pres p **hitting**) colpire; ~ **one's head on the table** battere la testa contro il tavolo; **the car** ~ **the wall** la macchina ha sbattuto contro il muro; ~ **the target** colpire il bersaglio; ~ **the nail on the head** fare centro; ~ **the roof** fam perdere le staffe
■ **hit back** *vi* ⟨*retaliate*⟩ ribattere
■ **hit off** *vt* ~ **it off** andare d'accordo
■ **hit on** *vt* fig trovare

hit-and-miss *adj* ⟨*affair, undertaking*⟩ imprevedibile; ⟨*method*⟩ a casaccio

hit-and-run *adj* ⟨*raid, attack*⟩ lampo *inv*; ⟨*accident*⟩ causato da un pirata della strada

hit-and-run driver *adj* pirata *m* della strada

hitch /hɪtʃ/ **1** *n* intoppo *m*; **technical** ~ problema *m* tecnico
2 *vt* attaccare; ~ **a lift** chiedere un passaggio
■ **hitch up** *vt* tirarsi su ⟨*trousers*⟩

hitch-hike *vi* fare l'autostop

hitchhiker *n* autostoppista *mf*

hitch-hiking *n* autostop *m*

hi-tech *adj* ▶ HIGH TECH

hither /'hɪðə(r)/ *adv* ~ **and thither** di qua e di là

hitherto /hɪðə'tuː/ *adv* finora

hit list *n* lista *f* degli obiettivi

hit man *n* sicario *m*

hit-or-miss *adj* **on a very** ~ **basis** all'improvvisata

hit parade *n* hit parade *f inv*, classifica *f*

hit single *n* singolo *m* di successo

HIV *n abbr* (**human immunodeficiency virus**) HIV; ~ **positive** sieropositivo; ~ **negative** sieronegativo

hive /haɪv/ *n* alveare *m*; ~ **of industry** fucina *f* di lavoro
■ **hive off** *vt* Comm separare

HM *abbr* (**Her Majesty** *or* **His Majesty**) SM

HMS *abbr* **His/Her Majesty's Ship**

hoard /hɔːd/ **1** *n* provvista *f*; (of money) gruzzolo *m*
2 *vt* accumulare

hoarding /'hɔːdɪŋ/ *n* palizzata *f*; (with advertisements) tabellone *m* per manifesti pubblicitari

hoar frost /'hɔː(r)/ *n* brina *f*

hoarse /hɔːs/ *adj* rauco

hoarsely /'hɔːslɪ/ *adv* con voce rauca

hoarseness /'hɔːsnɪs/ *n* raucedine *f*

hoary /'hɔːrɪ/ *adj* ⟨*person*⟩ con i capelli bianchi; ~ **old joke** barzelletta *f* vecchia

hoax /həʊks/ *n* scherzo *m*; (false alarm) falso allarme *m*

hoaxer /'həʊksə(r)/ *n* burlone, -a *mf*

hob /hɒb/ *n* piano *m* di cottura

hobble /'hɒbl/ *vi* zoppicare

hobby /'hɒbɪ/ *n* hobby *m inv*

hobby horse *n* fig fissazione *f*

hobnailed /'hɒbneɪld/ *adj* ~ **boots** *pl* scarponi *mpl* chiodati

hobnob /'hɒbnɒb/ *v*
■ **hobnob with** *vt* (pt/pp **hobnobbed**) frequentare

hobo /'həʊbəʊ/ *n* Am vagabondo, -a *mf*

hock /hɒk/ *n* vino *m* bianco del Reno

hockey /'hɒkɪ/ *n* hockey *m*

hocus-pocus /həʊkəs'pəʊkəs/ *n* (trickery) trucco *m*

hod /hɒd/ *n* (for coal) secchio *m* del carbone; (for bricks) cassetta *f* (per trasportare mattoni)

hoe /həʊ/ **1** *n* zappa *f*
2 *vt* (pres p **hoeing**) zappare

hog /hɒg/ **1** *n* maiale *m*
2 *vt* (pt/pp **hogged**) fam monopolizzare

hog-tie /'hɒgtaɪ/ *vt* legare le quattro zampe di ⟨*pig, cow*⟩; Am fig ostacolare ⟨*person*⟩

hogwash /'hɒgwɒʃ/ *n* fam cretinate *fpl*

hoi polloi /hɔɪpɒ'lɔɪ/ *npl* plebaglia *fsg*

hoist /hɔɪst/ **1** *n* montacarichi *m inv*; (fam: push) spinta *f* in su
2 *vt* sollevare; innalzare ⟨*flag*⟩; levare ⟨*anchor*⟩

hoity-toity /hɔɪtɪ'tɔɪtɪ/ *adj* fam altezzoso

hokum /'həʊkəm/ *n* Am fam (sentimentality) polpettone *m* sentimentale; (nonsense) cretinate *fpl*

hold¹ /həʊld/ *n* Naut, Aeron stiva *f*

hold² **1** *n* presa *f*; (fig: influence) ascendente *m*; **get ∼ of** trovare; procurarsi ‹*information*›
2 *vt* (pt/pp **held**) tenere; ‹*container*› contenere; essere titolare di ‹*licence, passport*›; trattenere ‹*breath, suspect*›; mantenere vivo ‹*interest*›; ‹*civil servant etc*› occupare ‹*position*›; (retain) mantenere; **∼ sb's hand** tenere qualcuno per mano; **∼ one's tongue** tenere la bocca chiusa; **∼ somebody responsible** considerare qualcuno responsabile; **∼ that** (believe) ritenere che
3 *vi* tenere; ‹*weather, luck*› durare; ‹*offer*› essere valido; Teleph restare in linea; **I don't ∼ with the idea that...** fam non sono d'accordo sul fatto che...
■ **hold against** *vt* **∼ something against somebody** avercela con qualcuno per qualcosa
■ **hold back** **1** *vt* rallentare
2 *vi* esitare
■ **hold down** *vt* tenere a bada ‹*somebody*›
■ **hold on** *vi* (wait) attendere; Teleph restare in linea
■ **hold on to** *vt* aggrapparsi a; (keep) tenersi
■ **hold out** **1** *vt* porgere ‹*hand*›; fig offrire ‹*possibility*›
2 *vi* (resist) resistere
■ **hold to** *vt* **∼ somebody to something** far mantenere qualcosa a qualcuno
■ **hold up** *vt* tenere su; (delay) rallentare; (rob) assalire; **∼ one's head up** fig tenere la testa alta

holdall /'həʊldɔːl/ *n* borsone *m*

holder /'həʊldə(r)/ *n* titolare *mf*; (of record) detentore, -trice *mf*; (container) astuccio *m*

holding /'həʊldɪŋ/ *n* (land) terreno *m* in affitto; Comm azioni *fpl*

holding company *n* società *f inv* finanziaria

hold-up *n* ritardo *m*; (attack) rapina *f* a mano armata

hole /həʊl/ *n* buco *m*

hole-in-the-wall *n* fam sportello *m* del Bancomat®

holiday /'hɒlɪdeɪ/ **1** *n* vacanza *f*; (public) giorno *m* festivo; (day off) giorno *m* di ferie; **go on ∼** andare in vacanza
2 *vi* andare in vacanza

holiday home *n* casa *f* per le vacanze

holiday job *n* (Br: in summer) lavoretto *m* estivo

holiday-maker *n* vacanziere *mf*

holiday resort *n* luogo *m* di villeggiatura

holier-than-thou /həʊlɪəðən'ðaʊ/ *adj* ‹*attitude*› da santerellino

holiness /'həʊlɪnɪs/ *n* santità *f*; **Your H∼** Sua Santità

Holland /'hɒlənd/ *n* Olanda *f*

holler /'hɒlə(r)/ *vi* urlare (**at** contro)

hollow /'hɒləʊ/ **1** *adj* cavo; ‹*promise*› a vuoto; ‹*voice*› assente; ‹*cheeks*› infossato
2 *n* cavità *f inv*; (in ground) affossamento *m*
■ **hollow out** *vt* scavare

holly /'hɒlɪ/ *n* agrifoglio *m*

hollyhock /'hɒlɪhɒk/ *n* malvone *m*

holocaust /'hɒləkɔːst/ *n* olocausto *m*

hologram /'hɒləgræm/ *n* ologramma *m*

holograph /'hɒləgrɑːf/ *n* documento *m* olografo

hols /hɒlz/ *n* Br fam *abbr* (**holidays**) vacanze *fpl*

holster /'həʊlstə(r)/ *n* fondina *f*

holy /'həʊlɪ/ *adj* (**-ier, -est**) santo; ‹*water*› benedetto

Holy Bible *n* Sacra Bibbia *f*

Holy Land *n* Terra *f* Santa

Holy Scriptures sacre scritture *fpl*

Holy Ghost, **Holy Spirit** *n* Spirito *m* Santo

Holy Week *n* settimana *f* santa

homage /'hɒmɪdʒ/ *n* omaggio *m*; **pay ∼ to** rendere omaggio a

homburg /'hɒmbɜːg/ *n* cappello *m* di feltro

home /həʊm/ **1** *n* casa *f*; (for children) istituto *m*; (for old people) casa *f* di riposo; (native land) patria *f*
2 *adv* **at ∼** a casa; (football) in casa; **feel at ∼** sentirsi a casa propria; **come/go ∼** venire/andare a casa; **drive a nail ∼** piantare un chiodo a fondo.
3 *adj* domestico; ‹*movie, video*› casalingo; ‹*team*› ospitante; Pol nazionale

home address *n* indirizzo *m* di casa

home brew *n* (beer) birra *f* fatta in casa

home cinema [system], **home entertainment system** *n* (sistema di) home cinema *m*

homecoming *n* (return home) ritorno *m* a casa

home computer *n* computer *m inv* da casa

home cooking *n* cucina *f* casalinga

Home Counties *npl* contee *fpl* intorno a Londra

home economics *n* Sch economia *f* domestica

home front *n* (during war) fronte *m* interno; (in politics) politica *f* interna

home game *n* partita *f* in casa

home ground *n* **play on one's ∼ ∼** giocare in casa

home-grown /-'grəʊn/ *adj* ‹*produce*› del proprio orto; fig nostrano

home help *n* aiuto *m* domestico (per persone non autosufficienti)

h

homeland *n* patria *f*

homeless /'həʊmlɪs/ *adj* senza tetto

home loan *n* mutuo *m* per la casa

homeloving /'həʊmlʌvɪŋ/ *adj* casalingo

homely /'həʊmlɪ/ *adj* (**-ier, -iest**) *adj* semplice; ⟨atmosphere⟩ familiare; (Am; ugly) bruttino

home-made *adj* fatto in casa

home market *n* mercato *m* interno

Home Office *n* Br ministero *m* degli interni

homeopathic /həʊmɪə'pæθɪk/ *adj* omeopatico

homeopathy /həʊmɪ'ɒpəθɪ/ *n* omeopatia *f*

homeowner *n* proprietario, -a *mf* immobiliare

home page *n* Comput home page *f inv*

home rule *n* autogoverno *m*

Home Secretary *n* Br ≈ ministro *m* degli interni

home shopping *n* acquisti *mpl* attraverso la televisione

homesick *adj* be ∼ avere nostalgia (**for** di)

homesickness *n* nostalgia *f* di casa

homestead *n* fattoria *f*

home town *n* città *f inv* natia

home truth *n* tell somebody a few ∼ ∼s dirne quattro a qualcuno

home video *n* filmato *m* di videoamatore

homeward /'həʊmwəd/ **1** *adj* di ritorno
2 *adv* ∼[s] verso casa; ∼ **bound** sulla strada del ritorno; **travel** ∼[s] tornare a casa

homework /'həʊmwɜ:k/ *n* Sch compiti *mpl*

homeworker /'həʊmwɜ:kə(r)/ *n* lavoratore, -trice *mf* a domicilio

homeworking /'həʊmwɜ:kɪŋ/ *n* lavoro *m* a domicilio

homey /'həʊmɪ/ *adj* (home-loving) casalingo; (cosy) accogliente

homicidal /hɒmɪ'saɪdəl/ *adj* omicida

homicide /'hɒmɪsaɪd/ *n* (crime) omicidio *m*

homily /'hɒmɪlɪ/ *n* omelia *f*

homing /'həʊmɪŋ/ *adj* ⟨missile, device⟩ autoguidato

homing pigeon piccione *f* homing

homoeopathic /həʊmɪə'pæθɪk/ *adj* omeopatico

homoeopathy /həʊmɪ'ɒpəθɪ/ *n* omeopatia *f*

homogeneous /hɒmə'dʒi:nɪəs/ *adj* omogeneo

homogenize /hə'mɒdʒənaɪz/ *vt* omogeneizzare

homogenous /hə'mɒdʒənəs/ *adj* omogeneo

homograph /'hɒməgrɑːf/ *n* omografo *m*

homonym /'hɒmənɪm/ *n* omonimo *m*

homophobia /həʊmə'fəʊbɪə/ *n* omofobia *f*

homosexual /həʊmə'sekʃʊəl/ *adj & n* omosessuale *mf*

homosexuality /həʊməsekʃʊ'ælɪtɪ/ *n* omosessualità *f*

Hon. *abbr* (**Honourable**) On.

Honduras /hɒn'djʊərəs/ *n* Honduras *m*

hone /həʊn/ *vt* (sharpen) affilare; (perfect) affinare

honest /'ɒnɪst/ *adj* onesto; ⟨frank⟩ sincero

honestly /'ɒnɪstlɪ/ *adv* onestamente; (frankly) sinceramente; ∼! ma insomma!

honesty /'ɒnɪstɪ/ *n* onestà *f*; ⟨frankness⟩ sincerità *f*

honey /'hʌnɪ/ *n* miele *m*; (fam: darling) tesoro *m*

honeycomb /'hʌnɪkəʊm/ *n* favo *m*

honeydew melon /'hʌnɪdjuː/ *n* melone *m* (dalla buccia gialla)

honeymoon /'hʌnɪmuːn/ *n* luna *f* di miele

honeysuckle /'hʌnɪsʌkl/ *n* caprifoglio *m*

honey trap *n* trappola *f* tesa a qualcuno servendosi di una collaboratrice graziosa

Hong Kong /hɒŋ'kɒŋ/ *n* Hong Kong *f*

honk /hɒŋk/ *vi* Auto clacsonare

honky-tonk /'hɒŋkɪtɒŋk/ *adj* ⟨piano⟩ honkytonky *inv*

honor /'ɒnə(r)/ *n* Am = HONOUR

honorary /'ɒnərərɪ/ *adj* onorario

honorific /ɒnə'rɪfɪk/ *adj* onorifico

honour /'ɒnə(r)/ **1** *n* onore *m* **2** *vt* onorare

honourable /'ɒnərəbl/ *adj* onorevole

honourably /'ɒnərəblɪ/ *adv* con onore

honours degree /'ɒnəz/ *n* ≈ diploma *m* di laurea

hood /hʊd/ *n* cappuccio *m*; (of pram) tettuccio *m*; (over cooker) cappa *f*; Am Auto cofano *m*

hoodlum /'huːdləm/ *n* teppista *m*

hoodwink /'hʊdwɪŋk/ *vt* fam infinocchiare

hoody, hoodie /'hʊdɪ/ *n* fam maglia *f* con cappuccio

hoof /huːf/ *n* (pl ∼s or **hooves**) zoccolo *m*

hoo-ha /'huːhɑː/ *n* fam **cause a** ∼ fare scalpore

hook /hʊk/ **1** *n* gancio *m*; (for crochet) uncinetto *m*; (for fishing) amo *m*; **off the** ∼ Teleph staccato; fig fuori pericolo; **by** ∼ **or by crook** in un modo o nell' altro

② *vt* agganciare
③ *vi* agganciarsi

hookah /'hʊkə/ *n* narghilè *m inv*

hook and eye *n* gancino *m*

hooked /hʊkt/ *adj* ⟨nose⟩ adunco; ∼ **on** (fam: drugs) dedito a; **be** ∼ **on skiing** essere un fanatico dello sci

hooker /'hʊkə(r)/ *n* Am sl battona *f*

hookey /'hʊkɪ/ *n* **play** ∼ Am fam marinare la scuola

hooligan /'hu:lɪgən/ *n* teppista *f*

hooliganism /'hu:lɪgənɪzm/ *n* teppismo *m*

hoop /hu:p/ *n* cerchio *m*

hoopla /'hu:plɑ:/ *n* (Br: at fair) lancio *m* degli anelli (nei luna park); (Am: fuss) trambusto *m*

hooray /hʊ'reɪ/ *int* & *n* = HURRAH

hoot /hu:t/ **①** *n* colpo *m* di clacson; (of siren) ululato *m*; (of owl) grido *m*; ∼s **of laughter** risate *fpl*
② *vi* ⟨owl⟩ gridare; ⟨car⟩ clacsonare; ⟨siren⟩ ululare; (jeer) fischiare

hooter /'hu:tə(r)/ *n* (siren) sirena *f*; Auto clacson *m inv*; (Br fam: nose) nasone *m*

hoover® /'hu:və(r)/ **①** *n* aspirapolvere *m inv*
② *vt* passare l'aspirapolvere su ⟨carpet⟩; passare l'aspirapolvere in ⟨room⟩
③ *vi* passare l'aspirapolvere

hop¹ /hɒp/ *n* luppolo *m*

hop² **①** *n* saltello *m*: **catch somebody on the** ∼ fam prendere qualcuno alla sprovvista
② *vi* (pt/pp **hopped**) saltellare; ∼ **it!** fam tela!
■ **hop in** *vi* fam saltar su
■ **hop out** *vi* fam saltar giù; ∼ **out to the shops** fare un salto ai negozi

hope /həʊp/ **①** *n* speranza *f*; **there's no** ∼ **of that happening** non c'è nessuna speranza che succeda
② *vi* sperare (**for** in); **I** ∼ **so/not** spero di sì/no
③ *vt* ∼ **that** sperare che

hopeful /'həʊpfʊl/ *adj* pieno di speranza; (promising) promettente; **be** ∼ **that** avere buone speranze che

hopefully /'həʊpfʊlɪ/ *adv* con speranza; (it is hoped) se tutto va bene

hopeless /'həʊplɪs/ *adj* senza speranze; (useless) impossibile; (incompetent) incapace

hopelessly /'həʊplɪslɪ/ *adv* disperatamente; ⟨inefficient, lost⟩ completamente

hopelessness /'həʊplɪsnɪs/ *n* disperazione *f*

hopscotch /'hɒpskɒtʃ/ *n* campana *f* (gioco)

horde /hɔ:d/ *n* orda *f*

horizon /hə'raɪzn/ *n* orizzonte *m*; **on the** ∼ all'orizzonte

horizontal /hɒrɪ'zɒntl/ *adj* orizzontale

horizontal bar *n* sbarra *f* orizzontale

horizontally /hɒrɪ'zɒntəlɪ/ *adv* orizzontalmente

hormonal /hɔ:'məʊnəl/ *adj* ormonale; (moody) lunatico

hormone /'hɔ:məʊn/ *n* ormone *m*

hormone replacement therapy *n* terapia *f* ormonale sostitutiva

horn /hɔ:n/ *n* corno *m*; Auto clacson *m inv*

hornet /'hɔ:nɪt/ *n* calabrone *m*

horn-rimmed /-rɪmd/ *adj* ⟨spectacles⟩ con la montatura di tartaruga

horny /'hɔ:nɪ/ *adj* calloso; (fam: sexually) arrapato

horoscope /'hɒrəskəʊp/ *n* oroscopo *m*

horrendous /hə'rendəs/ *adj* spaventoso

horrible /'hɒrəbl/ *adj* orribile

horribly /'hɒrəblɪ/ *adv* orribilmente

horrid /'hɒrɪd/ *adj* orrendo

horrific /hə'rɪfɪk/ *adj* raccapricciante; fam ⟨accident, prices, story⟩ terrificante

horrify /'hɒrɪfaɪ/ *vt* (pt/pp **-ied**) far inorridire; **I was horrified** ero inorridito

horrifying /'hɒrɪfaɪɪŋ/ *adj* terrificante

horror /'hɒrə(r)/ *n* orrore *m*

horror film *n* film *m inv* dell'orrore

horror story *n* racconto *m* dell'orrore

hors-d'œuvre /ɔ:'dɜ:vr/ *n* antipasto *m*

horse /hɔ:s/ *n* cavallo *m*
■ **horse around** *vi* fare il pagliaccio

horseback *n* **on** ∼ a cavallo

horseback riding *n* Am equitazione *f*

horsebox *n* furgone *m* per il trasporto dei cavalli

horse chestnut *n* ippocastano *m*

horsefly *n* tafano *m*

horsehair *n* crine *m* di cavallo

horseman *n* cavaliere *m*

horse manure *n* concime *m*

horseplay *n* gioco *m* pesante

horsepower *n* cavallo *m* [vapore]

horse race *n* corsa *f* ippica

horse racing *n* corse *fpl* di cavalli

horseradish *n* rafano *m*

horseradish sauce *n* salsa *f* di rafano

horseriding *n* equitazione *f*

horseshoe *n* ferro *m* di cavallo

horseshow *n* concorso *m* ippico

hors[e]y /'hɔ:sɪ/ *adj* ⟨person⟩ che adora i cavalli; ⟨face⟩ cavallino

horticultural /hɔ:tɪ'kʌltʃʊrəl/ *adj* di orticoltura

horticulture /'hɔ:tɪkʌltʃə(r)/ *n* orticoltura *f*

hose /həʊz/ *n* (pipe) manichetta *f*
■ **hose down** *vt* lavare con la manichetta

hosepipe /'həʊzpaɪp/ n manichetta f

hosiery /'həʊʒərɪ/ n maglieria f

hospice /'hɒspɪs/ n (for the terminally ill) ospedale m per i malati in fase terminale

hospitable /hɒ'spɪtəbl/ adj ospitale

hospitably /hɒ'spɪtəblɪ/ adv con ospitalità

hospital /'hɒspɪtl/ n ospedale m

hospitality /hɒspɪ'tælətɪ/ n ospitalità f

hospitalize /'hɒspɪtəlaɪz/ vt ricoverare [in ospedale]

host¹ /həʊst/ n **a ∼ of** una moltitudine di

host² n ospite m

host³ n Relig ostia f

hostage /'hɒstɪdʒ/ n ostaggio m; **hold somebody ∼** tenere qualcuno in ostaggio

host country n paese m ospitante

hostel /'hɒstl/ n ostello m

hostess /'həʊstɪs/ n padrona f di casa; Aeron hostess f inv

hostile /'hɒstaɪl/ adj ostile

hostility /hɒ'stɪlətɪ/ n ostilità f; **hostilities** pl ostilità fpl

hot /hɒt/ adj (**hotter, hottest**) caldo; (spicy) piccante; **I am** or **feel ∼** ho caldo; **it is ∼** fa caldo; **in ∼ water** fig nei guai

hot-air balloon n mongolfiera f

hotbed n fig focolaio m

hot-blooded /-'blʌdɪd/ adj ⟨person⟩ focoso; ⟨reaction⟩ passionale

hot cake n **sell like ∼ ∼s** andare a ruba

hotchpotch /'hɒtʃpɒtʃ/ n miscuglio m

hot cross bun n panino m dolce con spezie e uvette, tipicamente pasquale

hot dog n hot dog m inv

hotdogging n sci m acrobatico

hotel /həʊ'tel/ n hotel m inv, albergo m

hotelier /həʊ'telɪə(r)/ n albergatore, -trice mf

hotfoot adv hum ⟨go⟩ di gran carriera

hothead n persona f impetuosa

hot-headed /-'hedɪd/ adj impetuoso

hothouse n serra f

hotline n linea f diretta; Mil, Pol telefono m rosso

hotly /'hɒtlɪ/ adv fig accanitamente

hotplate n piastra f riscaldante

hot seat n **be in the ∼** essere in una posizione difficile

hotshot n fam persona di successo; pej carrierista mf

hot spot n (trouble zone) zona f calda; (sunny place) luogo m assolato

hot tap n rubinetto m dell'acqua calda

hot-tempered /-'tempəd/ adj irascibile

hot-water bottle n borsa f dell'acqua calda

hound /haʊnd/ ① n cane da caccia m

② vt fig perseguire

hour /'aʊə(r)/ n ora f

hourglass /'aʊəɡlɑːs/ n clessidra f

hourly /'aʊəlɪ/ ① adj ad ogni ora; ⟨pay, rate⟩ a ora

② adv ogni ora

house¹ /haʊs/ n casa f; Pol Camera f; Theat sala f; **at my ∼** a casa mia, da me

house² /haʊz/ vt alloggiare ⟨person⟩; incastrare ⟨machine⟩

houseboat n casa f galleggiante

housebound adj costretto in casa

housebreaking n furto m con scasso

house call n visita f a domicilio

household n casa f, famiglia f

household appliance n elettrodomestico m

householder n capo m di famiglia

household name n noto m

house husband n casalingo m

housekeeper n governante f di casa

housekeeping n governo m della casa; (money) soldi mpl per le spese di casa

House of Commons n Camera f dei Comuni

House of Lords n Camera f dei Lord

House of Representatives n Camera f dei Rappresentanti

house plant n pianta f da appartamento

house-proud adj orgoglioso della propria casa

Houses of Parliament npl Parlamento m

house-to-house adj ⟨search⟩ casa per casa

house-trained /-treɪnd/ adj che non sporca in casa

house-warming [party] n festa f di inaugurazione della nuova casa

housewife n casalinga f

housework n lavori mpl domestici

housing /'haʊzɪŋ/ n alloggio m; Techn alloggiamento m

housing estate n zona f residenziale

hovel /'hɒvl/ n tugurio m

hover /'hɒvə(r)/ vi librarsi; (linger) indugiare; **∼ on the brink of doing something** essere sul punto di fare qualcosa

hovercraft /'hɒvəkrɑːft/ n hovercraft m inv

how /haʊ/ adv come; **∼ are you?** come stai?; **∼ about a coffee/going on holiday?** che ne diresti di un caffè/di andare in vacanza?; **∼ do you do?** molto lieto!; **∼ old are you?** quanti anni hai?; **∼ long** quanto tempo; **∼ many** quanti; **∼ much** quanto; **∼ often** ogni quanto; **and ∼!** eccome!; **∼ odd!** che strano!

however /haʊ'evə(r)/ *adv* (nevertheless)
comunque; ~ **small** per quanto piccolo
howl /haʊl/ **1** *n* ululato *m*
2 *vi* ululare; (cry with laughter) singhiozzare
howler /'haʊlə(r)/ *n* fam strafalcione *m*
HP *abbr* **hire purchase**; *abbr* (**horse power**) C. V.
HQ *n* Mil *abbr* (**headquarters**) Q.G.
HR *abbr* (**human resources**) RU
HRT *abbr* (**hormone replacement therapy**) TOS *f*
HTML *abbr* (**hypertext markup language**) Comput HTML *m*
HTTP *abbr* (**hypertext transfer protocol**) Comput HTTP *m*
hub /hʌb/ *n* mozzo *m*; fig centro *m*
hubbub /'hʌbʌb/ *n* baccano *m*
hubcap /'hʌbkæp/ *n* coprimozzo *m*
huckleberry /'hʌklbərɪ/ *n* Am mirtillo *m* americano
huddle /'hʌdl/ *vi* ~ **together** rannicchiarsi l'uno contro l'altro
hue¹ /hju:/ *n* colore *m*
hue² *n* ~ **and cry** clamore *m*
huff /hʌf/ *n* **be in a/go into a** ~ fare il broncio
hug /hʌg/ **1** *n* abbraccio *m*; **give somebody a** ~ abbracciare qualcuno **2** *vt* (pt/pp **hugged**) abbracciare; (keep close to) tenersi vicino a; aggrapparsi a ⟨*wall*⟩
huge /hju:dʒ/ *adj* enorme
hugely /'hju:dʒlɪ/ *adv* enormemente
huh /hʌ/ *int* (inquiry) eh?; (in surprise) oh!
hulk /hʌlk/ *n* (of ship, tank etc) carcassa *f*
hulking /'hʌlkɪŋ/ *adj* fam grosso
hull /hʌl/ *n* Naut scafo *m*
hullabaloo /hʌləbə'lu:/ *n* fam (noise) trambusto *m*; (outcry) fracasso *m*
hullo /hə'ləʊ/ *int* = HALLO
hum /hʌm/ **1** *n* ronzio *m* **2** *vt* (pt/pp **hummed**) canticchiare **3** *vi* ⟨*motor*⟩ ronzare; fig fervere di attività; ~ **and haw** esitare
human /'hju:mən/ **1** *adj* umano **2** *n* essere *m* umano
human being *n* essere *m* umano
humane /hju:'meɪn/ *adj* umano
humanely /hju:'meɪnlɪ/ *adv* umanamente
human interest story *n* storia *f* di vita vissuta
humanitarian /hju:mænɪ'teərɪən/ *adj* & *n* umanitario, -a *mf*
humanities /hju:'mænɪtɪz/ *pl* Univ dottrine *fpl* umanistiche
humanity /hju:'mænətɪ/ *n* umanità *f*
human nature *n* natura *f* umana

human resources *npl* risorse *fpl* umane
human resources manager *n* responsabile *mf* delle risorse umane
humble /'hʌmbl/ **1** *adj* umile **2** *vt* umiliare
humbly /'hʌmblɪ/ *adv* umilmente
humbug /'hʌmbʌg/ *n* (nonsense) sciocchezze *fpl*; (dishonesty) falsità *f*; (Br: sweet) caramella *f* alla menta
humdrum /'hʌmdrʌm/ *adj* noioso
humid /'hju:mɪd/ *adj* umido
humidifier /hju:'mɪdɪfaɪə(r)/ *n* umidificatore *m*
humidity /hju:'mɪdətɪ/ *n* umidità *f*
humiliate /hju:'mɪlɪeɪt/ *vt* umiliare
humiliating /hju:'mɪlɪeɪtɪŋ/ *adj* avvilente
humiliation /hju:mɪlɪ'eɪʃn/ *n* umiliazione *f*
humility /hju:'mɪlətɪ/ *n* umiltà *f*
hummingbird /'hʌmɪŋbɜ:d/ *n* colibrì *m inv*
hummock /'hʌmək/ *n* (of earth) poggio *m*
hummus /'hʊməs/ *n* hummus *m*, purè *m* di ceci
humorist /'hju:mərɪst/ *n* umorista *mf*
humorous /'hju:mərəs/ *adj* umoristico
humorously /'hju:mərəslɪ/ *adv* con spirito
humour /'hju:mə(r)/ **1** *n* umorismo *m*; (mood) umore *m*; **have a sense of** ~ avere il senso dell'umorismo **2** *vt* compiacere
hump /hʌmp/ *n* protuberanza *f*; (of camel, hunchback) gobba *f*; **he's got the** ~ sl è di malumore
humpback[ed] bridge /'hʌm(p)bæk[t]/ *n* ponte *m* a schiena d'asino
humus /'hju:məs/ *n* humus *m*
hunch /hʌntʃ/ *n* (idea) intuizione *f*
hunchback /'hʌntʃbæk/ *n* gobbo, -a *mf*
hunched /hʌntʃt/ *adj* ~ **up** incurvato
hundred /'hʌndrəd/ **1** *adj* **one/a** ~ cento **2** *n* cento *m inv*; ~**s of** centinaia di
hundredfold /'hʌndrədfəʊld/ *adv* **increase a** ~ centuplicare
hundredth /'hʌndrədθ/ *adj* & *n* centesimo *m*
hundredweight /'hʌndrədweɪt/ *n* cinquanta chili *m*
hung /hʌŋ/ ▶ HANG
Hungarian /hʌŋ'geərɪən/ *n* & *adj* ungherese *mf*; (language) ungherese *m*
Hungary /'hʌŋgərɪ/ *n* Ungheria *f*
hunger /'hʌŋgə(r)/ *n* fame *f*
■ **hunger for** *vt* aver fame di
hunger strike *n* sciopero *m* della fame

hung-over *adj* be ~ avere i postumi della sbornia

hungrily /'hʌŋgrɪlɪ/ *adv* con appetito

hungry /'hʌŋgrɪ/ *adj* (**-ier**, **-iest**) affamato; be ~ aver fame

hung-up *adj* fam (tense) complessato; be ~ **on** somebody/something (obsessed) essere fissato con qualcuno/qualcosa

hunk /hʌŋk/ *n* grosso pezzo *m*; (fam: man) figo *m*

hunky-dory /hʌŋkɪ'dɔːrɪ/ *adj* fam perfetto

hunt /hʌnt/ ❶ *n* caccia *f*
❷ *vt* andare a caccia di ⟨animal⟩; dare la caccia a ⟨criminal⟩
❸ *vi* andare a caccia; ~ **for** cercare

hunter /'hʌntə(r)/ *n* cacciatore *m*

hunting /'hʌntɪŋ/ *n* caccia *f*

hunt saboteur *n* Br sabotatore, -trice *mf* della caccia

huntsman /'hʌntsmən/ *n* (hunter) cacciatore *m*; (fox-hunter) cacciatore *m* di volpe

hurdle /'hɜːdl/ *n* Sport & fig ostacolo *m*

hurdler /'hɜːdlə(r)/ *n* ostacolista *mf*

hurdy-gurdy /hɜːdɪ'gɜːdɪ/ *n* organino *m*

hurl /hɜːl/ *vt* scagliare

hurly-burly /hɜːlɪ'bɜːlɪ/ *n* chiasso *m*

hurrah /hʊ'rɑː/, **hurray** /hʊ'reɪ/ ❶ *int* urrà!
❷ *n* urrà *m*

hurricane /'hʌrɪkən/ *n* uragano *m*

hurried /'hʌrɪd/ *adj* affrettato; ⟨job⟩ fatto in fretta

hurriedly /'hʌrɪdlɪ/ *adv* in fretta

hurry /'hʌrɪ/ ❶ *n* fretta *f*; be in a ~ aver fretta
❷ *vi* (pt/pp **-ied**) affrettarsi
■ **hurry up** ❶ *vi* sbrigarsi
❷ *vt* mettere fretta a ⟨person⟩; accelerare ⟨things⟩

hurt /hɜːt/ ❶ *n* male *m*
❷ *vt* (pt/pp **hurt**) far male a; (offend) ferire
❸ *vi* far male; my leg ~s mi fa male la gamba

hurtful /'hɜːtfʊl/ *adj* fig offensivo

hurtle /'hɜːtl/ *vi* ~ **along** andare a tutta velocità

husband /'hʌzbənd/ *n* marito *m*

hush /hʌʃ/ *n* silenzio *m*
■ **hush up** *vt* mettere a tacere

hushed /hʌʃt/ *adj* ⟨voice⟩ sommesso

hush-hush *adj* fam segretissimo

husky /'hʌskɪ/ *adj* (**-ier**, **-iest**) ⟨voice⟩ rauco

hussar /hʊ'zɑː(r)/ *n* ussaro *m*

hustings /'hʌstɪŋz/ *n* on the ~ in campagna elettorale

hustle /'hʌsl/ ❶ *vt* affrettare

❷ *n* attività *f* incessante; ~ **and bustle** trambusto *m*

hut /hʌt/ *n* capanna *f*

hutch /hʌtʃ/ *n* conigliera *f*

hyacinth /'haɪəsɪnθ/ *n* giacinto *m*

hybrid /'haɪbrɪd/ ❶ *adj* ibrido
❷ *n* ibrido *m*

hydrangea /haɪ'dreɪndʒə/ *n* ortensia *f*

hydrant /'haɪdrənt/ *n* [fire] ~ idrante *m*

hydraulic /haɪ'drɔːlɪk/ *adj* idraulico

hydrocarbon /haɪdrəʊ'kɑːbən/ *n* idrocarburo *m*

hydrochloric /haɪdrə'klɔːrɪk/ *adj* ~ **acid** acido *m* cloridrico

hydroelectric /haɪdrəʊɪ'lektrɪk/ *adj* idroelettrico

hydroelectricity /haɪdrəʊɪlek'trɪsɪtɪ/ *n* energia *f* idroelettrica

hydroelectric power station *n* centrale *f* idroelettrica

hydrofoil /'haɪdrəfɔɪl/ *n* aliscafo *m*

hydrogen /'haɪdrədʒən/ *n* idrogeno *m*

hydrolysis /haɪ'drɒləsɪs/ *n* idrolisi *f*

hydrophobia /haɪdrə'fəʊbɪə/ *n* idrofobia *f*

hydroplane /'haɪdrəpleɪn/ *n* (boat) aliscafo *m*; (Am: seaplane) idrovolante *m*

hydrotherapy /haɪdrəʊ'θerəpɪ/ *n* idroterapia *f*

hyena /haɪ'iːnə/ *n* iena *f*

hygiene /'haɪdʒiːn/ *n* igiene *m*

hygienic /haɪ'dʒiːnɪk/ *adj* igienico

hygienically /haɪ'dʒiːnɪklɪ/ *adv* igienicamente

hymn /hɪm/ *n* inno *m*

hymn book *n* libro *m* dei canti

hype /haɪp/ *n* fam grande pubblicità *f*; media ~ battage *m* pubblicitario
■ **hype up** *vt* fam fare grande pubblicità a ⟨film, star, book⟩; (exaggerate) gonfiare

hyper /'haɪpə(r)/ *adj* fam eccitato

hyperactive /haɪpər'æktɪv/ *adj* iperattivo

hyperactivity /haɪpəræk'tɪvɪtɪ/ *n* iperattività *f*

hyperbole /haɪ'pɜːbəlɪ/ *n* iperbole *f*

hypercritical /haɪpə'krɪtɪkl/ *adj* ipercritico

hyperlink *n* Comput hyperlink *m inv*, collegamento *m* ipertestuale

hypermarket /'haɪpəmɑːkɪt/ *n* ipermercato *m*

hypersensitive /haɪpə'sensɪtɪv/ *adj* pej permaloso; (physically) ipersensibile

hypertension /haɪpə'tenʃn/ *n* ipertensione *f*

hypertext /'haɪpətekst/ *n* Comput ipertesto *m*

hypertext markup language n
Comput linguaggio m per la marcatura di
ipertesti

hypertext transfer protocol n
Comput protocollo m per il trasferimento di
ipertesti

hyperventilate /haɪpə'ventɪleɪt/ vi
iperventilare

hyphen /'haɪfn/ n trattino m

hyphenate /'haɪfəneɪt/ vt unire con
trattino

hypnosis /hɪp'nəʊsɪs/ n ipnosi f

hypnotherapy /hɪpnəʊ'θerəpɪ/ n
ipnoterapia f

hypnotic /hɪp'nɒtɪk/ adj ipnotico

hypnotism /'hɪpnətɪzm/ n ipnotismo m

hypnotist /'hɪpnətɪst/ n ipnotizzatore,
-trice mf

hypnotize /'hɪpnətaɪz/ vt ipnotizzare

hypoallergenic /haɪpəʊælə'dʒenɪk/ adj
anallergico

hypochondria /haɪpə'kɒndrɪə/ n
ipocondria f

hypochondriac /haɪpə'kɒndrɪæk/ adj
& n ipocondriaco, -a mf

hypocrisy /hɪ'pɒkrəsɪ/ n ipocrisia f

hypocrite /'hɪpəkrɪt/ n ipocrita mf

hypocritical /hɪpə'krɪtɪkl/ adj ipocrita

hypocritically /hɪpə'krɪtɪklɪ/ adv
ipocriticamente

hypodermic /haɪpə'dɜːmɪk/ adj & n ∼
[syringe] siringa f ipodermica

hypotenuse /haɪ'pɒtənjuːz/ n ipotenusa
f

hypothermia /haɪpəʊ'θɜːmɪə/ n
ipotermia f

hypothesis /haɪ'pɒθəsɪs/ n ipotesi f inv

hypothetical /haɪpə'θetɪkl/ adj
ipotetico

hypothetically /haɪpə'θetɪklɪ/ adv in
teoria; ⟨speak⟩ per ipotesi

hysterectomy /hɪstə'rektəmɪ/ n
isterectomia f

hysteria /hɪ'stɪərɪə/ n isterismo m

hysterical /hɪ'sterɪkl/ adj isterico

hysterically /hɪ'sterɪklɪ/ adv
istericamente; ∼ **funny** da morir dal
ridere

hysterics /hɪ'sterɪks/ npl attacco m
isterico

Ii

i[1], **I** /aɪ/ n (letter) i, I f inv

I[2] /aɪ/ pron io; **I'm tired** sono stanco; **he's
going, but I'm not** lui va, ma io no

IAP n abbr (**internet access
provider**) Comput IAP m

IBA n abbr (**Independent
Broadcasting Authority**) organismo m
indipendente di vigilanza sulla
radiotelevisione

ibex /'aɪbeks/ n stambecco m

ICC n abbr (**International Criminal
Court**) TPI m

ice /aɪs/ ① n ghiaccio m
② vt glassare ⟨cake⟩
■ **ice over**, **ice up** vi ghiacciarsi

ice age n era f glaciale

ice axe n piccozza f per il ghiaccio

iceberg n iceberg m inv

icebox n Am frigorifero m

ice-breaker n Naut rompighiaccio m inv

ice bucket n secchiello m del ghiaccio

ice cap n calotta f glaciale

ice-cold adj ghiacciato

ice cream n gelato m

ice-cream parlour n gelateria f

ice-cream sundae n coppa f [di]
gelato guarnita

ice cube n cubetto m di ghiaccio

ice dancer n ballerino, -a mf sul
ghiaccio

ice floe n banco m di ghiaccio

ice hockey hockey m su ghiaccio

Iceland /'aɪslənd/ n Islanda f

Icelander /'aɪsləndə(r)/ n islandese mf

Icelandic /aɪs'lændɪk/ adj & n islandese
m

ice lolly n ghiacciolo m

ice pack n impacco m di ghiaccio

ice pick n piccone m da ghiaccio

ice rink n pista f di pattinaggio

ice-skate n pattino m da ghiaccio

ice-skater pattinatore, -trice mf sul
ghiaccio

ice-skating pattinaggio m sul ghiaccio

ice-tray n vaschetta f per il ghiaccio

icicle /'aɪsɪkl/ n ghiacciolo m

icily /'aɪsɪlɪ/ adv gelidamente

icing /'aɪsɪŋ/ n glassa f

icing sugar n zucchero m a velo

icon /'aɪkɒn/ n icona f

iconize /'aɪkənaɪz/ vt Comput iconizzare

ICT n abbr (**information and communication technology**) ICT f

icy /'aɪsɪ/ adj (**-ier, -iest**) ghiacciato; fig gelido

id /ɪd/ n the ∼ l'Es m

ID n abbr (**identification, identity**) documento m d'identità; ∼ **card** n carta f d'identità

idea /aɪ'dɪə/ n idea f; **I've no** ∼! non ne ho idea!

ideal /aɪ'dɪəl/ ① adj ideale
② n ideale m

idealism /aɪ'dɪəlɪzm/ n idealismo m

idealist /aɪ'dɪəlɪst/ n idealista mf

idealistic /aɪdɪə'lɪstɪk/ adj idealistico

idealize /aɪ'dɪəlaɪz/ vt idealizzare

ideally /aɪ'dɪəlɪ/ adv idealmente

identical /aɪ'dentɪkl/ adj identico

identical twin n gemello, -a mf monozigote

identifiable /aɪdentɪ'faɪəbl/ adj identificabile

identification /aɪdentɪfɪ'keɪʃn/ n identificazione f; (proof of identity) documento m di riconoscimento

identify /aɪ'dentɪfaɪ/ ① vt (pt/pp **-ied**) identificare
② vi ∼ **with** identificarsi con

identikit® /aɪ'dentɪkɪt/ n identikit m inv

identity /aɪ'dentətɪ/ n identità f inv

identity bracelet n braccialetto m identificativo

identity card n carta f d'identità

identity parade n confronto m all'americana

identity theft n l'utilizzare il nome e i dati personali di qualcuno allo scopo di ottenere carte di credito, prelevare denaro da conti bancari ecc.

ideological /aɪdɪə'lɒdʒɪkl/ adj ideologico

ideology /aɪdɪ'ɒlədʒɪ/ n ideologia f

idiocy /'ɪdɪəsɪ/ n idiozia f

idiom /'ɪdɪəm/ n idioma f

idiomatic /ɪdɪə'mætɪk/ adj idiomatico

idiomatically /ɪdɪə'mætɪklɪ/ adv in modo idiomatico

idiosyncrasy /ɪdɪə'sɪŋkrəsɪ/ n idiosincrasia f

idiosyncratic /ɪdɪəsɪŋ'krætɪk/ adj particolare

idiot /'ɪdɪət/ n idiota mf

idiotic /ɪdɪ'ɒtɪk/ adj idiota

idle /'aɪd(ə)l/ ① adj (lazy) pigro, ozioso; (empty) vano; ⟨machine⟩ fermo
② vi oziare; ⟨engine⟩ girare a vuoto
■ **idle away** vt passare nell'ozio ⟨day⟩

idleness /'aɪd(ə)lnɪs/ n ozio m

idly /'aɪdlɪ/ adv oziosamente

idol /'aɪd(ə)l/ n idolo m

idolize /'aɪdəlaɪz/ vt idolatrare

idyll /'ɪdɪl/ n idillio m

idyllic /ɪ'dɪlɪk/ adj idillico

i.e. abbr (**id est**) cioè

if /ɪf/ conj se; **as if** come se

iffy /'ɪfɪ/ adj incerto

igloo /'ɪglu:/ n igloo m inv

ignite /ɪg'naɪt/ ① vt dar fuoco a
② vi prender fuoco

ignition /ɪg'nɪʃn/ n Auto accensione f

ignition key n chiave f d'accensione

ignoramus /ɪgnə'reɪməs/ n ignorante mf

ignorance /'ɪgnərəns/ n ignoranza f

ignorant /'ɪgnərənt/ adj (lacking knowledge) ignaro; (rude) ignorantè

ignore /ɪg'nɔ:(r)/ vt ignorare

ill /ɪl/ ① adj ammalato; **feel** ∼ **at ease** sentirsi a disagio
② adv male
③ n male m

ill-advised /-əd'vaɪzd/ adj avventato

ill-bred /-'bred/ adj maleducato

ill-considered /-kən'sɪdəd/ adj ⟨measure, remark⟩ avventato

ill effect n effetto m negativo

illegal /ɪ'li:gl/ adj illegale

illegality /ɪlɪ'gælətɪ/ n illegalità f

illegally /ɪ'li:gəlɪ/ adv illegalmente

illegible /ɪ'ledʒəbl/ adj illeggibile

illegibly /ɪ'ledʒəblɪ/ adv in modo illeggibile

illegitimacy /ɪlɪ'dʒɪtɪməsɪ/ n illegittimità f

illegitimate /ɪlɪ'dʒɪtɪmət/ adj illegittimo

ill-equipped /-ɪ'kwɪpt/ adj non equipaggiato

ill-fated /-'feɪtɪd/ adj sfortunato

ill feeling n rancore m

ill-fitting adj ⟨garment⟩ che non va bene

ill-founded /-'faʊndɪd/ adj ⟨argument, gossip⟩ infondato

ill-gotten gains /ɪlgɒ(t)n'geɪnz/ adj guadagni mpl illeciti

ill health n problemi mpl di salute

illicit /ɪ'lɪsɪt/ adj illecito

illicitly /ɪ'lɪsɪtlɪ/ adv illecitamente

ill-informed /-ɪn'fɔ:md/ adj ⟨person⟩ male informato

illiteracy /ɪ'lɪtərəsɪ/ n analfabetismo m

illiterate /ɪ'lɪtərət/ adj & n analfabeta mf

ill-mannered /-'mænəd/ adj maleducato

illness /'ɪlnɪs/ n malattia f

illogical /ɪ'lɒdʒɪkl/ adj illogico

illogically /ɪ'lɒdʒɪklɪ/ adv illogicamente

ill-prepared /-prɪ'peəd/ adj impreparato

ill-timed /-'taɪmd/ *adj* ⟨*arrival*⟩ inopportuno; ⟨*campaign*⟩ fatto al momento sbagliato

ill-treat *vt* maltrattare

ill-treatment *n* maltrattamento *m*

illuminate /ɪ'lu:mɪneɪt/ *vt* illuminare

illuminated /ɪ'lu:mɪnеɪtɪd/ *adj* ⟨*sign*⟩ luminoso

illuminating /ɪ'lu:mɪneɪtɪŋ/ *adj* chiarificatore

illumination /ɪlu:mɪ'neɪʃn/ *n* illuminazione *f*

illuminations *npl* Br luminarie *fpl*

illusion /ɪ'lu:ʒn/ *n* illusione *f*; **be under the ~ that** avere l'illusione che

illusory /ɪ'lu:sərɪ/ *adj* illusorio

illustrate /'ɪləstreɪt/ *vt* illustrare

illustration /ɪlə'streɪʃn/ *n* illustrazione *f*

illustrative /'ɪləstrətɪv/ *adj* illustrativo

illustrator /'ɪləstreɪtə(r)/ *n* illustratore, -trice *mf*

illustrious /ɪ'lʌstrɪəs/ *adj* illustre

ill will *n* malanimo *m*

image /'ɪmɪdʒ/ *n* immagine *f*; (exact likeness) ritratto *m*

image-conscious *adj* attento all'immagine

image maker *n* persona *f* che cura l'immagine

image processing *n* trattamento *m* dell'immagine

imagery /'ɪmɪdʒərɪ/ *n* immagini *fpl*

imaginable /ɪ'mædʒɪnəbl/ *adj* immaginabile

imaginary /ɪ'mædʒɪnərɪ/ *adj* immaginario

imagination /ɪmædʒɪ'neɪʃn/ *n* immaginazione *f*, fantasia *f*; **it's your ~** è solo una tua idea

imaginative /ɪ'mædʒɪnətɪv/ *adj* fantasioso

imaginatively /ɪ'mædʒɪnətɪvlɪ/ *adv* con fantasia or immaginazione

imagine /ɪ'mædʒɪn/ *vt* immaginare; (wrongly) inventare

IMAP *abbr* (**Internet mail access protocol**) Comput protocollo *m* di gestione remota della posta elettronica

imbalance /ɪm'bæləns/ *n* squilibrio *m*

imbecile /'ɪmbəsi:l/ *n* imbecille *mf*

imbibe /ɪm'baɪb/ ① *vt* ingerire; fig assorbire ② *vi* hum bere

imbue /ɪm'bju:/ *vt* **~d with** impregnato di

IMF *n abbr* (**International Monetary Fund**) FMI *m*

imitate /'ɪmɪteɪt/ *vt* imitare

imitation /ɪmɪ'teɪʃn/ *n* imitazione *f*

imitative /'ɪmɪtətɪv/ *adj* imitativo

imitator /'ɪmɪteɪtə(r)/ *n* imitatore, -trice *mf*

immaculate /ɪ'mækjʊlət/ *adj* immacolato

immaculately /ɪ'mækjʊlətlɪ/ *adv* immacolatamente

immaterial /ɪmə'tɪərɪəl/ *adj* (unimportant) irrilevante

immature /ɪmə'tʃʊə(r)/ *adj* immaturo

immeasurable /ɪ'meʒərəbl/ *adj* incommensurabile

immediacy /ɪ'mi:dɪəsɪ/ *n* immediatezza *f*

immediate /ɪ'mi:dɪət/ *adj* immediato; ⟨*relative*⟩ stretto; **in the ~ vicinity** nelle immediate vicinanze

immediately /ɪ'mi:dɪətlɪ/ ① *adv* immediatamente; **~ next to** subito accanto a ② *conj* [non] appena

immemorial /ɪmɪ'mɔ:rɪəl/ *adj* **from time ~** da tempo immemorabile

immense /ɪ'mens/ *adj* immenso

immensely /ɪ'menslɪ/ *adv* immensamente

immensity /ɪ'mensətɪ/ *n* immensità *f*

immerse /ɪ'mɜ:s/ *vt* immergere; **be ~d in** fig essere immerso in

immersion /ɪ'mɜ:ʃn/ *n* immersione *f*

immersion course *n* Br corso *m* full immersion

immersion heater *n* scaldabagno *m* elettrico

immigrant /'ɪmɪgrənt/ *n* immigrante *mf*

immigrate /'ɪmɪgreɪt/ *vi* immigrare

immigration /ɪmɪ'greɪʃn/ *n* immigrazione *f*

immigration control *n* controllo *m* dell'immigrazione

imminence /'ɪmɪnəns/ *n* imminenza *f*

imminent /'ɪmɪnənt/ *adj* imminente

immobile /ɪ'məʊbaɪl/ *adj* immobile

immobilize /ɪ'məʊbɪlaɪz/ *vt* immobilizzare

immobilizer /ɪ'məʊbɪlaɪzə(r)/ *n* Auto immobilizzatore *m* elettronico

immoderate /ɪ'mɒdərət/ *adj* smodato

immodest /ɪ'mɒdɪst/ *adj* immodesto

immoral /ɪ'mɒrəl/ *adj* immorale

immorality /ɪmə'rælətɪ/ *n* immoralità *f*

immortal /ɪ'mɔ:tl/ *adj* immortale

immortality /ɪmɔ:'tælətɪ/ *n* immortalità *f*

immortalize /ɪ'mɔ:təlaɪz/ *vt* immortalare

immovable /ɪ'mu:vəbl/ *adj* fig irremovibile

immune /ɪˈmjuːn/ adj immune (to/from da)

immune system n sistema m immunitario

immunity /ɪˈmjuːnətɪ/ n immunità f

immunization /ɪmjʊnaɪˈzeɪʃn/ n immunizzazione f

immunize /ˈɪmjʊnaɪz/ vt immunizzare

immunodeficiency /ɪmjʊnəʊdɪˈfɪʃənsɪ/ n immunodeficienza f

immunodepressant /ɪmjʊnəʊdɪˈpres(ə)nt/ ① adj immunodepressivo
② n immunodepressivo m

immunology /ɪmjʊˈnɒlədʒɪ/ n immunologia f

immutable /ɪˈmjuːtəbl/ adj immutabile

imp /ɪmp/ n diavoletto m

impact /ˈɪmpækt/ n impatto m

impacted /ɪmˈpæktɪd/ adj ⟨tooth⟩ incluso; ⟨fracture⟩ incuneato

impair /ɪmˈpeə(r)/ vt danneggiare

impaired /ɪmˈpeəd/ adj hearing ∼ audioleso: **visually** ∼ videoleso

impale /ɪmˈpeɪl/ vt impalare

impalpable /ɪmˈpælpəbl/ adj (intangible) impalpabile

impart /ɪmˈpɑːt/ vt impartire

impartial /ɪmˈpɑːʃəl/ adj imparziale

impartiality /ɪmpɑːʃɪˈælətɪ/ n imparzialità f

impassable /ɪmˈpɑːsəbl/ adj impraticabile

impasse /æmˈpɑːs/ n fig impasse f inv

impassioned /ɪmˈpæʃnd/ adj appassionato

impassive /ɪmˈpæsɪv/ adj impassibile

impassively /ɪmˈpæsɪvlɪ/ adv impassibilmente

impatience /ɪmˈpeɪʃns/ n impazienza f

impatient /ɪmˈpeɪʃnt/ adj impaziente

impatiently /ɪmˈpeɪʃntlɪ/ adv impazientemente

impeach /ɪmˈpiːtʃ/ vt accusare

impeccable /ɪmˈpekəbl/ adj impeccabile

impeccably /ɪmˈpekəblɪ/ adv in modo impeccabile

impede /ɪmˈpiːd/ vt impedire

impediment /ɪmˈpedɪmənt/ n impedimento m; (in speech) difetto m

impel /ɪmˈpel/ vt (pt/pp **impelled**) costringere; feel ∼led to sentire l'obbligo di

impending /ɪmˈpendɪŋ/ adj imminente

impenetrable /ɪmˈpenɪtrəbl/ adj impenetrabile

imperative /ɪmˈperətɪv/ ① adj imperativo
② n Gram imperativo m

imperceptible /ɪmpəˈseptəbl/ adj impercettibile

imperfect /ɪmˈpɜːfɪkt/ ① adj imperfetto; (faulty) difettoso
② n Gram imperfetto m

imperfection /ɪmpəˈfekʃn/ n imperfezione f

imperial /ɪmˈpɪərɪəl/ adj imperiale

imperialism /ɪmˈpɪərɪəlɪzm/ n imperialismo m

imperialist /ɪmˈpɪərɪəlɪst/ n imperialista mf

imperil /ɪmˈperəl/ vt (pt/pp **imperilled**) mettere in pericolo

imperious /ɪmˈpɪərɪəs/ adj imperioso

imperiously /ɪmˈpɪərɪəslɪ/ adv in modo imperioso

impermeable /ɪmˈpɜːmɪəbl/ adj impermeabile

impersonal /ɪmˈpɜːsənəl/ adj impersonale

impersonate /ɪmˈpɜːsəneɪt/ vt impersonare

impersonation /ɪmpɜːsəˈneɪʃn/ n imitazione f

impersonator /ɪmˈpɜːsəneɪtə(r)/ n imitatore, -trice mf

impertinence /ɪmˈpɜːtɪnəns/ n impertinenza f

impertinent /ɪmˈpɜːtɪnənt/ adj impertinente

imperturbable /ɪmpəˈtɜːbəbl/ adj imperturbabile

impervious /ɪmˈpɜːvɪəs/ adj ∼ to fig indifferente a

impetuous /ɪmˈpetjʊəs/ adj impetuoso

impetuously /ɪmˈpetjʊəslɪ/ adv impetuosamente

impetus /ˈɪmpɪtəs/ n impeto m

impiety /ɪmˈpaɪətɪ/ n Relig empietà f

impinge /ɪmˈpɪndʒ/ v
■ **impinge on** vt (affect) influire su; (restrict) condizionare

impious /ˈɪmpɪəs/ adj Relig empio

impish /ˈɪmpɪʃ/ adj birichino

implacable /ɪmˈplækəbl/ adj implacabile

implant¹ /ɪmˈplɑːnt/ vt trapiantare; fig inculcare

implant² /ˈɪmplɑːnt/ n trapianto m

implausible /ɪmˈplɔːzəbl/ adj poco plausibile

implement¹ /ˈɪmplɪmənt/ n attrezzo m

implement² /ˈɪmplɪment/ vt mettere in atto

implementation /ɪmplɪmənˈteɪʃn/ n (of law, policy, idea) attuazione f; Comput implementazione f

implicate /ˈɪmplɪkeɪt/ vt implicare

implication /ɪmplɪˈkeɪʃn/ *n*
implicazione *f*; **by** ∼ implicitamente

implicit /ɪmˈplɪsɪt/ *adj* implicito;
(absolute) assoluto

implicitly /ɪmˈplɪsɪtlɪ/ *adv*
implicitamente; (absolutely) completamente

implied /ɪmˈplaɪd/ *adj* implicito,
sottinteso

implore /ɪmˈplɔː(r)/ *vt* implorare

imploring /ɪmˈplɔːrɪŋ/ *adj* implorante

implosion /ɪmˈpləʊʒn/ *n* implosione *f*

imply /ɪmˈplaɪ/ *vt* (pt/pp **-ied**) implicare;
what are you ∼**ing?** che cosa vorresti
insinuare?

impolite /ɪmpəˈlaɪt/ *adj* sgarbato

impolitely /ɪmpəˈlaɪtlɪ/ *adv*
sgarbatamente

import[1] /ˈɪmpɔːt/ *n* Comm importazione *f*;
(importance) importanza *f*; (meaning)
rilevanza *f*

import[2] /ɪmˈpɔːt/ *vt* importare

importance /ɪmˈpɔːtəns/ *n* importanza *f*

important /ɪmˈpɔːtənt/ *adj* importante

importation /ɪmpɔːˈteɪʃn/ *n* Comm
importazione *f*

import duty /ˈɪmpɔːt/ *n* dazio *m*
d'importazione

importer /ɪmˈpɔːtə(r)/ *n* importatore,
-trice *mf*

import-export /ˈɪmpɔːtˈekspɔːt/ *n*
import-export *m*

importing country /ɪmˈpɔːtɪŋ/ *n* paese
m di importazione

impose /ɪmˈpəʊz/ ① *vt* imporre (on a)
② *vi* imporsi; ∼ **on** abusare di

imposing /ɪmˈpəʊzɪŋ/ *adj* imponente

imposition /ɪmpəˈzɪʃn/ *n* imposizione *f*

impossibility /ɪmˈpɒsɪbɪlətɪ/ *n*
impossibilità *f*

impossible /ɪmˈpɒsəbl/ *adj* impossibile

impossibly /ɪmˈpɒsəblɪ/ *adv*
impossibilmente

impostor /ɪmˈpɒstə(r)/ *n* impostore, -a
mf

impotence /ˈɪmpətəns/ *n* impotenza *f*

impotent /ˈɪmpətənt/ *adj* impotente

impound /ɪmˈpaʊnd/ *vt* confiscare

impoverished /ɪmˈpɒvərɪʃt/ *adj*
impoverito

impracticable /ɪmˈpræktɪkəbl/ *adj*
impraticabile

impractical /ɪmˈpræktɪkl/ *adj* non
pratico

imprecise /ɪmprɪˈsaɪs/ *adj* impreciso

impregnable /ɪmˈpregnəbl/ *adj*
imprendibile

impregnate /ˈɪmpregneɪt/ *vt*
impregnare (with di); Biol fecondare

impresario /ɪmprɪˈsɑːrɪəʊ/ *n* (pl **-os**)
impresario *m* (di spettacoli)

impress /ɪmˈpres/ *vt* imprimere; fig
colpire (positivamente); ∼ **something
[up]on somebody** fare capire qualcosa a
qualcuno

impression /ɪmˈpreʃn/ *n* impressione *f*;
(imitation) imitazione *f*

impressionable /ɪmˈpreʃənəbl/ *adj*
⟨child, mind⟩ influenzabile

impressionism /ɪmˈpreʃənɪzm/ *n*
impressionismo *m*

impressionist /ɪmˈpreʃənɪst/ *n*
imitatore, -trice *mf*; (artist) impressionista
mf

impressionistic /ɪmpreʃəˈnɪstɪk/ *adj*
impressionista; ⟨account⟩ approssimativo

impressive /ɪmˈpresɪv/ *adj* imponente

imprint[1] /ˈɪmprɪnt/ *n* impressione *f*

imprint[2] /ɪmˈprɪnt/ *vt* imprimere; ∼**ed
on my mind** impresso nella mia memoria

imprison /ɪmˈprɪzən/ *vt* incarcerare

imprisonment /ɪmˈprɪzənmənt/ *n*
reclusione *f*

improbable /ɪmˈprɒbəbl/ *adj*
improbabile

impromptu /ɪmˈprɒmptjuː/ ① *adj*
improvvisato
② *adv* in modo improvvisato

improper /ɪmˈprɒpə(r)/ *adj* ⟨use⟩
improprio; ⟨behaviour⟩ scorretto

improperly /ɪmˈprɒpəlɪ/ *adv*
scorrettamente

impropriety /ɪmprəˈpraɪətɪ/ *n*
scorrettezza *f*

improve /ɪmˈpruːv/ *vt/i* migliorare
■ **improve [up]on** *vt* perfezionare

improvement /ɪmˈpruːvmənt/ *n*
miglioramento *m*

improvident /ɪmˈprɒvɪdənt/ *adj*
(heedless of the future) imprevidente

improvisation /ɪmprəvaɪˈzeɪʃn/ *n*
improvvisazione *f*

improvise /ˈɪmprəvaɪz/ *vt/i*
improvvisare

imprudent /ɪmˈpruːdənt/ *adj*
imprudente

impudence /ˈɪmpjʊdəns/ *n* sfrontatezza
f

impudent /ˈɪmpjʊdənt/ *adj* sfrontato

impudently /ˈɪmpjʊdəntlɪ/ *adv*
sfrontatamente

impulse /ˈɪmpʌls/ *n* impulso *m*; **on [an]**
∼ impulsivamente

impulse buy *n* acquisto *m* d'impulso

impulse buying *n* acquisti *mpl* fatti
d'impulso

impulsive /ɪmˈpʌlsɪv/ *adj* impulsivo

impulsively /ɪmˈpʌlsɪvlɪ/ *adv*
impulsivamente

impunity /ɪmˈpjuːnətɪ/ n with ~ impunemente

impure /ɪmˈpjʊə(r)/ adj impuro

impurity /ɪmˈpjʊərətɪ/ n impurità f inv; **impurities** pl impurità fpl

impute /ɪmˈpjuːt/ vt imputare (**to** a)

in /ɪn/ ① prep in; (with names of towns) a; **in the garden** in giardino; **in the street** in or per strada; **in bed/hospital** a letto/all'ospedale; **in the world** nel mondo; **in the rain** sotto la pioggia; **in the sun** al sole; **in this heat** con questo caldo; **in summer/winter** in estate/inverno; **in 1995** nel 1995; **in the evening** la sera; **he's arriving in two hours' time** arriva fra due ore; **deaf in one ear** sordo da un orecchio; **in the army** nell'esercito; **in English/Italian** in inglese/italiano; **in ink/pencil** a penna/matita; **in red** ⟨dressed, circled⟩ di rosso; **the man in the raincoat** l'uomo con l'impermeabile; **in a soft/loud voice** a voce bassa/alta; **one in ten people** una persona su dieci; **in doing this, he...** nel far questo,...; **in itself** in sé; **in that** in quanto
② adv (at home) a casa; (indoors) dentro; **he's not in yet** non è ancora arrivato; **in there/here** lì/qui dentro; **ten in all** dieci in tutto; **day in, day out** giorno dopo giorno; **have it in for somebody** fam avercela con qualcuno; **send him in** fallo entrare; **come in** entrare; **bring in the washing** portare dentro i panni
③ adj (fam: in fashion) di moda
④ n **the ins and outs** i dettagli

in. abbr (**inch**) pollice m

inability /ɪnəˈbɪlətɪ/ n incapacità f

inaccessible /ɪnækˈsesəbl/ adj inaccessibile

inaccuracy /ɪnˈækjʊrəsɪ/ n inesattezza f

inaccurate /ɪnˈækjʊrət/ adj inesatto

inaccurately /ɪnˈækjʊrətlɪ/ adv in modo inesatto

inaction /ɪnˈækʃn/ n (not being active) inazione f; (failure to act) inerzia f

inactive /ɪnˈæktɪv/ adj inattivo

inactivity /ɪnækˈtɪvətɪ/ n inattività f

inadequacy /ɪnˈædɪkwəsɪ/ n inadeguatezza f

inadequate /ɪnˈædɪkwət/ adj inadeguato

inadequately /ɪnˈædɪkwətlɪ/ adv inadeguatamente

inadmissible /ɪnædˈmɪsəbl/ adj inammissibile

inadvertent /ɪnədˈvɜːtənt/ adj involontario

inadvertently /ɪnədˈvɜːtəntlɪ/ adv inavvertitamente

inadvisable /ɪnædˈvaɪzəbl/ adj sconsigliabile

inalienable /ɪnˈeɪlɪənəbl/ adj inalienabile

inane /ɪˈneɪn/ adj futile

inanely /ɪˈneɪnlɪ/ adv in modo vacuo

inanimate /ɪnˈænɪmət/ adj esanime

inanity /ɪˈnænətɪ/ n stupidità f inv

inapplicable /məˈplɪkəbl/ adj inapplicabile

inappropriate /ɪnəˈprəʊprɪət/ adj inadatto

inapt /ɪnˈæpt/ adj (inappropriate) inappropriato

inarticulate /ɪnɑːˈtɪkjʊlət/ adj inarticolato

inasmuch /ɪnəzˈmʌtʃ/ conj ~ **as** (insofar as) in quanto; (seeing that) poiché

inattention /ɪnəˈtenʃn/ n disattenzione f

inattentive /ɪnəˈtentɪv/ adj disattento

inaudible /ɪnˈɔːdəbl/ adj impercettibile

inaudibly /ɪnˈɔːdəblɪ/ adv in modo impercettibile

inaugural /ɪˈnɔːgjʊrəl/ adj inaugurale

inaugurate /ɪˈnɔːgjʊreɪt/ vt inaugurare

inauguration /ɪnɔːgjʊˈreɪʃn/ n inaugurazione f

inauspicious /ɪnɔːˈspɪʃəs/ adj infausto

in-between adj intermedio

inborn /ˈɪnbɔːn/ adj innato

inbox /ˈɪnbɒks/ n posta f in arrivo

inbred /ɪnˈbred/ adj congenito

inbreeding /ɪnˈbriːdɪŋ/ n (in animals) inbreeding m; (in humans) unioni mpl fra consanguinei

inbuilt /ɪnˈbɪlt/ adj ⟨feeling⟩ innato

Inc. abbr (**Incorporated**) Spa f

incalculable /ɪnˈkælkjʊləbl/ adj incalcolabile

incandescence /ɪnkænˈdesəns/ n liter incandescenza f

incandescent /ɪnkænˈdesənt/ adj liter incandescente

incapable /ɪnˈkeɪpəbl/ adj incapace

incapacitate /ɪnkəˈpæsɪteɪt/ vt rendere incapace

incapacity /ɪnkəˈpæsətɪ/ n also Jur incapacità f

incarcerate /ɪnˈkɑːsəreɪt/ vt incarcerare

incarnate /ɪnˈkɑːnət/ adj **the devil** ~ il diavolo in carne e ossa

incarnation /ɪnkɑːˈneɪʃn/ n incarnazione f

incendiary /ɪnˈsendɪərɪ/ ① adj incendiario
② n ~ **[bomb]** bomba f incendiaria

incendiary device n ordigno m incendiario

incense[1] /ˈɪnsens/ n incenso m-

incense[2] /ɪnˈsens/ vt esasperare

incensed /ɪn'senst/ *adj* furibondo

incentive /ɪn'sentɪv/ *n* incentivo *m*

incentive scheme *n* piano *m* di incentivi

inception /ɪn'sepʃn/ *n* inizio *m*

incessant /ɪn'sesənt/ *adj* incessante

incessantly /ɪn'sesəntlɪ/ *adv* incessantemente

incest /'ɪnsest/ *n* incesto *m*

incestuous /ɪn'sestjʊəs/ *adj* incestuoso

inch /ɪntʃ/ ① *n* pollice *m* (= 2,54 cm)
② *vi* ~ **forward** avanzare gradatamente

incidence /'ɪnsɪdəns/ *n* incidenza *f*

incident /'ɪnsɪdənt/ *n* incidente *m*

incidental /ɪnsɪ'dentl/ *adj* incidentale; ~ **expenses** spese *fpl* accessorie

incidentally /ɪnsɪ'dent(ə)lɪ/ *adv* incidentalmente; (by the way) a proposito

incident room *n* (for criminal investigation) centrale *f* operativa

incinerate /ɪn'sɪnəreɪt/ *vt* incenerire

incinerator /ɪn'sɪnəreɪtə(r)/ *n* inceneritore *m*

incipient /ɪn'sɪpɪənt/ *adj* incipiente

incision /ɪn'sɪʒn/ *n* incisione *f*

incisive /ɪn'saɪsɪv/ *adj* incisivo

incisor /ɪn'saɪzə(r)/ *n* incisivo *m*

incite /ɪn'saɪt/ *vt* incitare

incitement /ɪn'saɪtmənt/ *n* incitamento *m*

incivility /ɪnsɪ'vɪlətɪ/ *n* scortesia *f*

incl *abbr* **inclusive**; *abbr* **including**

inclement /ɪn'klemənt/ *adj* inclemente

inclination /ɪnklɪ'neɪʃn/ *n* inclinazione *f*

incline¹ /ɪn'klaɪn/ ① *vt* inclinare; **be** ~**d to do something** essere propenso a fare qualcosa
② *vi* inclinarsi

incline² /'ɪnklaɪn/ *n* pendio *m*

include /ɪn'kluːd/ *vt* includere

including /ɪn'kluːdɪŋ/ *prep* incluso

inclusion /ɪn'kluːʒn/ *n* inclusione *f*

inclusive /ɪn'kluːsɪv/ ① *adj* incluso; ~ **of** comprendente; **be** ~ **of** comprendere. ② *adv* incluso

incognito /ɪnkɒg'niːtəʊ/ *adv* incognito

incoherent /ɪnkə'hɪərənt/ *adj* incoerente; (because drunk etc) incomprensibile

incoherently /ɪnkə'hɪərəntlɪ/ *adv* incoerentemente; (because drunk etc) incomprensibilmente

income /'ɪnkəm/ *n* reddito *m*

income bracket *n* fascia *f* di reddito

income tax *n* imposta *f* sul reddito

income tax return *n* dichiarazione *f* dei redditi

incoming /'ɪnkʌmɪŋ/ *adj* in arrivo; ~ **tide** marea *f* montante

incommunicado /ɪnkəmjuːnɪ'kɑːdəʊ/ *adj* (involuntarily) segregato; **he's** ~ (in meeting) non vuole essere disturbato

incomparable /ɪn'kɒmp(ə)rəbl/ *adj* incomparabile

incompatibility /ɪnkəmpætɪ'bɪlətɪ/ *n* incompatibilità *f*

incompatible /ɪnkəm'pætəbl/ *adj* incompatibile

incompetence /ɪn'kɒmpɪtəns/ *n* incompetenza *f*

incompetent /ɪn'kɒmpɪtənt/ *adj* incompetente

incomplete /ɪnkəm'pliːt/ *adj* incompleto

incomprehensible /ɪnkɒmprɪ'hensəbl/ *adj* incomprensibile

inconceivable /ɪnkən'siːvəbl/ *adj* inconcepibile

inconclusive /ɪnkən'kluːsɪv/ *adj* inconcludente

incongruity /ɪnkɒn'gruːətɪ/ *n* (of appearance) contrasto *m*; (of situation) assurdità *f inv*

incongruous /ɪn'kɒŋgrʊəs/ *adj* contrastante

inconsequential /ɪnkɒnsɪ'kwenʃl/ *adj* senza importanza

inconsiderate /ɪnkən'sɪdərət/ *adj* trascurabile

inconsistency /ɪnkən'sɪstənsɪ/ *n* incoerenza *f*

inconsistent /ɪnkən'sɪstənt/ *adj* incoerente; **be** ~ **with** non essere coerente con

inconsistently /ɪnkən'sɪstəntlɪ/ *adv* in modo incoerente

inconsolable /ɪnkən'səʊləbl/ *adj* inconsolabile

inconspicuous /ɪnkən'spɪkjʊəs/ *adj* non appariscente

inconspicuously /ɪnkən'spɪkjʊəslɪ/ *adv* modestamente

inconstancy /ɪn'kɒnstənsɪ/ *n* incostanza *f*

inconstant /ɪn'kɒnstənt/ *adj* ‹conditions› variabile; ‹lover› volubile

incontestable /ɪnkən'testəbl/ *adj* incontestabile

incontinence /ɪn'kɒntɪnəns/ *n* incontinenza *f*

incontinent /ɪn'kɒntɪnənt/ *adj* incontinente

inconvenience /ɪnkən'viːnɪəns/ *n* scomodità *f*; (drawback) inconveniente *m*; **put somebody to** ~ dare disturbo a qualcuno

inconvenient /ɪnkən'viːnɪənt/ *adj* scomodo; ‹time, place› inopportuno

inconveniently /ɪnkən'viːnɪəntlɪ/ *adv* in modo inopportuno

incorporate /ɪn'kɔːpəreɪt/ *vt* incorporare; (contain) comprendere

incorrect /ɪnkə'rekt/ *adj* incorretto

incorrectly /ɪnkə'rektlɪ/ *adv* scorrettamente

incorrigible /ɪn'kɒrɪdʒəbl/ *adj* incorreggibile

incorruptible /ɪnkə'rʌptəbl/ *adj* incorruttibile

increase¹ /'ɪnkriːs/ *n* aumento *m*; **on the ∼** in aumento

increase² /ɪn'kriːs/ *vt/i* aumentare

increased *adj* ⟨demand, risk⟩ maggiore

increasing /ɪn'kriːsɪŋ/ *adj* ⟨impatience etc⟩ crescente; ⟨numbers⟩ in aumento

increasingly /ɪn'kriːsɪŋlɪ/ *adv* sempre più

incredible /ɪn'kredəbl/ *adj* incredibile

incredibly /ɪn'kredəblɪ/ *adv* incredibilmente

incredulity /ɪnkrə'djuːlətɪ/ *n* incredulità *f*

incredulous /ɪn'kredjʊləs/ *adj* incredulo

increment /'ɪnkrɪmənt/ *n* incremento *m*

incremental /ɪnkrɪ'mentəl/ *adj* Comput, Math incrementale; ⟨effect, measures⟩ progressivo

incriminate /ɪn'krɪmɪneɪt/ *vt* Jur incriminare

incriminating /ɪn'krɪmɪneɪtɪŋ/ *adj* ⟨evidence⟩ incriminante

in-crowd *n* be in with the ∼ frequentare gente alla moda

incubate /'ɪŋkjʊbeɪt/ *vt* incubare

incubation /ɪŋkjʊ'beɪʃn/ *n* incubazione *f*

incubation period *n* Med periodo *m* di incubazione

incubator /'ɪŋkjʊbeɪtə(r)/ *n* (for baby) incubatrice *f*

inculcate /'ɪnkʌlkeɪt/ *vt* inculcare

incumbent /ɪn'kʌmbənt/ *adj* be ∼ on somebody incombere a qualcuno

incur /ɪn'kɜː(r)/ *vt* (pt/pp **incurred**) incorrere; contrarre ⟨debts⟩

incurable /ɪn'kjʊərəbl/ *adj* incurabile

incurably /ɪn'kjʊərəblɪ/ *adv* incurabilmente

incursion /ɪn'kɜːʃn/ *n* incursione *f*

indebted /ɪn'detɪd/ *adj* obbligato (to verso)

indecency /ɪn'diːsənsɪ/ *n* oscenità *f*; (offence) atti *mpl* osceni; **gross ∼** atti *mpl* osceni

indecent /ɪn'diːsənt/ *adj* indecente

indecent assault *n* atti *mpl* di libidine violenta

indecent exposure *n* esibizionismo *m* (dei genitali)

indecipherable /ɪndɪ'saɪfərəbl/ *adj* indecifrabile

indecision /ɪndɪ'sɪʒn/ *n* indecisione *f*

indecisive /ɪndɪ'saɪsɪv/ *adj* indeciso

indecisiveness /ɪndɪ'saɪsɪvnɪs/ *n* indecisione *f*

indeed /ɪn'diːd/ *adv* (in fact) difatti; **yes ∼!** sì, certamente!; **∼ I am/do** veramente!; **very much ∼** moltissimo; **thank you very much ∼** grazie infinite; **∼?** davvero?

indefatigable /ɪndɪ'fætɪgəbl/ *adj* instancabile

indefensible /ɪndɪ'fensəbl/ *adj* Mil indifendibile; (morally) ingiustificabile; (logically) insostenibile

indefinable /ɪndɪ'faɪnəbl/ *adj* indefinibile

indefinite /ɪn'defɪnɪt/ *adj* indefinito

indefinitely /ɪn'defɪnɪtlɪ/ *adv* indefinitamente; ⟨postpone⟩ a tempo indeterminato

indelible /ɪn'deləbl/ *adj* indelebile

indelibly /ɪn'deləblɪ/ *adv* in modo indelebile

indelicacy /ɪn'delɪkəsɪ/ *n* (tactlessness) mancanza *f* di tatto; (coarseness) rozzezza *f*

indelicate /ɪn'delɪkət/ *adj* (tactless) privo di tatto; (coarse) rozzo

indemnity /ɪn'demnətɪ/ *n* indennità *f inv*

indent¹ /'ɪndent/ *n* Typ rientranza *f* dal margine

indent² /ɪn'dent/ *vt* Typ fare rientrare dal margine

indentation /ɪnden'teɪʃn/ *n* (notch) intaccatura *f*

independence /ɪndɪ'pendəns/ *n* indipendenza *f*

Independence Day *n* Am = anniversario *m* dell'Indipendenza degli USA (4 luglio)

independent /ɪndɪ'pendənt/ *adj* indipendente

independently /ɪndɪ'pendəntlɪ/ *adv* indipendentemente

in-depth *adj* ⟨analysis, study, knowledge⟩ approfondito

indescribable /ɪndɪ'skraɪbəbl/ *adj* indescrivibile

indescribably /ɪndɪ'skraɪbəblɪ/ *adv* indescrivibilmente

indestructible /ɪndɪ'strʌktəbl/ *adj* indistruttibile

indeterminate /ɪndɪ'tɜːmɪnət/ *adj* indeterminato

index /'ɪndeks/ *n* indice *m*

indexation /ɪndek'seɪʃn/ *n* indicizzazione *f*

index card n scheda f

index finger n dito m indice

index-linked adj ⟨pension⟩ legato al costo della vita

India /ˈɪndɪə/ n India f

Indian /ˈɪndɪən/ **1** adj indiano; (American) indiano [d'America]
2 n indiano, -a mf; (American) indiano [d'America]

Indian elephant n elefante m indiano

Indian ink n inchiostro m di china

Indian Ocean n oceano m Indiano

Indian summer n estate f di San Martino

indicate /ˈɪndɪkeɪt/ **1** vt indicare; (register) segnare
2 vi Auto mettere la freccia; ∼ **left** mettere la freccia a sinistra

indication /ɪndɪˈkeɪʃn/ n indicazione f

indicative /ɪnˈdɪkətɪv/ **1** adj be ∼ of essere indicativo di
2 n Gram indicativo m

indicator /ˈɪndɪkeɪtə(r)/ n Auto freccia f

indict /ɪnˈdaɪt/ vt accusare

indictment /ɪnˈdaɪtmənt/ n Jur imputazione f

indie /ˈɪndɪ/ **1** adj fam Cinema, Mus indipendente
2 n (band) gruppo m musicale legato a una casa discografica indipendente; (film) film m prodotto da una casa di produzione indipendente

indifference /ɪnˈdɪf(ə)rəns/ n indifferenza f

indifferent /ɪnˈdɪf(ə)rənt/ adj indifferente; (not good) mediocre

indifferently /ɪnˈdɪf(ə)rəntlɪ/ adv in modo indifferente; (not well) in modo mediocre

indigenous /ɪnˈdɪdʒɪnəs/ adj indigeno

indigestible /ɪndɪˈdʒestəbl/ adj indigesto

indigestion /ɪndɪˈdʒestʃn/ n indigestione f

indignant /ɪnˈdɪɡnənt/ adj indignato

indignantly /ɪnˈdɪɡnəntlɪ/ adv con indignazione

indignation /ɪndɪɡˈneɪʃn/ n indignazione f

indignity /ɪnˈdɪɡnətɪ/ n umiliazione f

indigo /ˈɪndɪɡəʊ/ n indaco m

indirect /ɪndaɪˈrekt/ adj indiretto

indirectly /ɪndaɪˈrektlɪ/ adv indirettamente

indirect speech n discorso m indiretto

indiscernible /ɪndɪˈsɜːnəbl/ adj indistinguibile

indiscreet /ɪndɪˈskriːt/ adj indiscreto

indiscretion /ɪndɪˈskreʃn/ n indiscrezione f

indiscriminate /ɪndɪˈskrɪmɪnət/ adj indiscriminato

indiscriminately /ɪndɪˈskrɪmɪnətlɪ/ adv senza distinzione

indispensable /ɪndɪˈspensəbl/ adj indispensabile

indisposed /ɪndɪˈspəʊzd/ adj indisposto

indisputable /ɪndɪˈspjuːtəbl/ adj indisputabile

indisputably /ɪndɪˈspjuːtəblɪ/ adv indisputabilmente

indistinct /ɪndɪˈstɪŋkt/ adj indistinto

indistinctly /ɪndɪˈstɪŋktlɪ/ adv indistintamente

indistinguishable /ɪndɪˈstɪŋgwɪʃəbl/ adj indistinguibile

individual /ɪndɪˈvɪdjʊəl/ **1** adj individuale
2 n individuo m

individualist /ɪndɪˈvɪdjʊəlɪst/ n individualista mf

individualistic /ɪndɪvɪdjʊəˈlɪstɪk/ adj individualistico

individuality /ɪndɪvɪdjʊˈælətɪ/ n individualità f

individually /ɪndɪˈvɪdjʊəlɪ/ adv individualmente

indivisible /ɪndɪˈvɪzəbl/ adj indivisibile

Indochina /ɪndəʊˈtʃaɪnə/ n Indocina f

indoctrinate /ɪnˈdɒktrɪneɪt/ vt indottrinare

Indo-European /ɪndəʊjʊərəˈpɪən/ adj indoeuropeo

indolence /ˈɪndələns/ n indolenza

indolent /ˈɪndələnt/ adj indolente

indomitable /ɪnˈdɒmɪtəbl/ adj indomito

Indonesia /ɪndəˈniːzjə/ n Indonesia f

Indonesian /ɪndəˈniːzjən/ adj & n (person) indonesiano, -a mf; (language) indonesiano m

indoor /ˈɪndɔː(r)/ adj interno; ⟨shoes⟩ per casa; ⟨plant⟩ da appartamento; ⟨swimming pool etc⟩ coperto

indoors /ɪnˈdɔːz/ adv dentro; **go** ∼ andare dentro

indubitable /ɪnˈdjuːbɪtəbl/ adj indubitabile

indubitably /ɪnˈdjuːbɪtəblɪ/ adv indubitabilmente

induce /ɪnˈdjuːs/ vt indurre (**to** a); (produce) causare

inducement /ɪnˈdjuːsmənt/ n (incentive) incentivo m

induction /ɪnˈdʌkʃn/ n (inauguration) introduzione f; (of labour) parto m indotto; Electr induzione f

induction ceremony n cerimonia f inaugurale

induction course n corso m introduttivo

induction loop n sistema m di amplificazione sonora

indulge /ɪn'dʌldʒ/ **1** vt soddisfare; viziare ⟨child⟩
2 vi ~ in concedersi

indulgence /ɪn'dʌldʒəns/ n lusso m; (leniency) indulgenza f

indulgent /ɪn'dʌldʒənt/ adj indulgente

industrial /ɪn'dʌstrɪəl/ adj industriale

industrial accident n infortunio m sul lavoro

industrial action n sciopero m; **take** ~ ~ scioperare

industrial dispute n vertenza f sindacale

industrial espionage n spionaggio m industriale

industrial estate n zona f industriale

industrialist /ɪn'dʌstrɪəlɪst/ n industriale mf

industrialized /ɪn'dʌstrɪələaɪzd/ adj industrializzato

industrial relations npl relazioni fpl industriali

industrial tribunal n tribunale m competente per i conflitti di lavoro

industrial waste n rifiuti mpl industriali

industrious /ɪn'dʌstrɪəs/ adj industrioso

industriously /ɪn'dʌstrɪəslɪ/ adv in modo industrioso

industry /'ɪndəstrɪ/ n industria f; (zeal) operosità f

inebriated /ɪ'niːbrɪeɪtɪd/ adj ebbro

inedible /ɪn'edəbl/ adj immangiabile

ineffective /ɪnɪ'fektɪv/ adj inefficace

ineffectively /ɪnɪ'fektɪvlɪ/ adv inutilmente, invano

ineffectual /ɪnɪ'fektʃʊəl/ adj inutile; ⟨person⟩ inconcludente

inefficiency /ɪnɪ'fɪʃənsɪ/ n inefficienza f

inefficient /ɪnɪ'fɪʃnt/ adj inefficiente

ineligible /ɪn'elɪdʒəbl/ adj inadatto

inept /ɪ'nept/ adj inetto

ineptitude /ɪ'neptɪtjuːd/ n inettitudine f

inequality /ɪnɪ'kwɒlətɪ/ n ineguaglianza f

inert /ɪ'nɜːt/ adj inerte

inertia /ɪ'nɜːʃə/ n inerzia f

inescapable /ɪnɪ'skeɪpəbl/ adj inevitabile

inestimable /ɪn'estɪməbl/ adj inestimabile

inevitable /ɪn'evɪtəbl/ adj inevitabile

inevitably /ɪn'evɪtəblɪ/ adv inevitabilmente

inexact /ɪnɪg'zækt/ adj inesatto

inexcusable /ɪnɪk'skjuːzəbl/ adj imperdonabile

inexhaustible /ɪnɪg'zɔːstəbl/ adj inesauribile

inexorable /ɪn'eksərəbl/ adj inesorabile

inexorably /ɪn'egzərəblɪ/ adv inesorabilmente

inexpensive /ɪnɪk'spensɪv/ adj poco costoso

inexpensively /ɪnɪk'spensɪvlɪ/ adv a buon mercato

inexperience /ɪnɪk'spɪərɪəns/ n inesperienza f

inexperienced /ɪnɪk'spɪərɪənst/ adj inesperto

inexplicable /ɪnɪk'splɪkəbl/ adj inesplicabile

inexplicably /ɪnɪk'splɪkəblɪ/ adv inesplicabilmente, inspiegabilmente

inextricable /ɪnɪk'strɪkəbl/ adj inestricabile

inextricably /ɪnɪk'strɪkəblɪ/ adv inestricabilmente

infallibility /ɪnfælɪ'bɪlətɪ/ n infallibilità f

infallible /ɪn'fæləbl/ adj infallibile

infamous /'ɪnfəməs/ adj infame; ⟨person⟩ famigerato

infamy /'ɪnfəmɪ/ n infamia f

infancy /'ɪnfənsɪ/ n infanzia f; **in its** ~ fig agli inizi

infant /'ɪnfənt/ n bambino, -a mf piccolo, -a

infanticide /ɪn'fæntɪsaɪd/ n infanticidio m

infantile /'ɪnfəntaɪl/ adj infantile

infantry /'ɪnfəntrɪ/ n fanteria f

infant school n scuola f elementare per bambini dai 5 ai 7 anni

infatuated /ɪn'fætʃʊeɪtɪd/ adj infatuato (**with** di)

infatuation /ɪnfætʃʊ'eɪʃn/ n infatuazione f

infect /ɪn'fekt/ vt infettare; **become** ~**ed** ⟨wound⟩ infettarsi

infection /ɪn'fekʃn/ n infezione f

infectious /ɪn'fekʃəs/ adj infettivo

infer /ɪn'fɜː(r)/ vt (pt/pp **inferred**) dedurre (**from** da); (imply) implicare

inference /'ɪnfərəns/ n deduzione f

inferior /ɪn'fɪərɪə(r)/ **1** adj inferiore; ⟨goods⟩ scadente; (in rank) subalterno **2** n inferiore mf; (in rank) subalterno, -a mf

inferiority /ɪnfɪərɪ'ɒrətɪ/ n inferiorità f

inferiority complex n complesso m di inferiorità

infernal /ɪn'fɜːnl/ adj infernale

inferno /ɪn'fɜːnəʊ/ n inferno m

infertile /ɪnˈfɜːtaɪl/ *adj* sterile

infertility /ɪnfəˈtɪlətɪ/ *n* sterilità *f*

infest /ɪnˈfest/ *vt* be ~ed with essere infestato di

infestation /ɪnfeˈsteɪʃn/ *n* infestazione *f*

infidelity /ɪnfɪˈdelətɪ/ *n* infedeltà *f inv*

infighting /ˈɪnfaɪtɪŋ/ *n* fig lotta *f* per il potere

infiltrate /ˈɪnfɪltreɪt/ *vt* infiltrare; Pol infiltrarsi in

infiltration /ɪnfɪlˈtreɪʃn/ *n* infiltrazione *f*

infinite /ˈɪnfɪnɪt/ *adj* infinito

infinitely /ˈɪnfɪnɪtlɪ/ *adv* infinitamente

infinitesimal /ɪnfɪnɪˈtesɪml/ *adj* infinitesimo

infinitive /ɪnˈfɪnətɪv/ *n* Gram infinito *m*

infinity /ɪnˈfɪnətɪ/ *n* infinità *f*

infirm /ɪnˈfɜːm/ *adj* debole

infirmary /ɪnˈfɜːm(ə)rɪ/ *n* infermeria *f*

infirmity /ɪnˈfɜːmətɪ/ *n* debolezza *f*

in flagrante delicto /ɪnfləˈgræntɪdɪˈlɪktəʊ/ *adv* in flagrante

inflame /ɪnˈfleɪm/ *vt* infiammare

inflamed /ɪnˈfleɪmd/ *adj* infiammato; become ~ infiammarsi

inflammable /ɪnˈflæməbl/ *adj* infiammabile

inflammation /ɪnfləˈmeɪʃn/ *n* infiammazione *f*

inflammatory /ɪnˈflæmətrɪ/ *adj* incendiario

inflatable /ɪnˈfleɪtəbl/ *adj* gonfiabile

inflate /ɪnˈfleɪt/ *vt* gonfiare

inflated /ɪnˈfleɪtɪd/ *adj* ‹price, fee, claim› eccessivo; ‹style› ampolloso; ‹tyre› gonfio; an ~ ego un'alta opinione di sé

inflation /ɪnˈfleɪʃn/ *n* inflazione *f*

inflationary /ɪnˈfleɪʃənərɪ/ *adj* inflazionario

inflect /ɪnˈflekt/ *vt* flettere ‹noun, adjective›; modulare ‹voice›

inflected /ɪnˈflektɪd/ *adj* ‹language› flessivo; ‹form› flesso

inflection /ɪnˈflekʃn/ *n* (of voice) modulazione *f*

inflexible /ɪnˈfleksəbl/ *adj* inflessibile

inflexion /ɪnˈflekʃn/ *n* inflessione *f*

inflict /ɪnˈflɪkt/ *vt* infliggere (on a)

in-flight *adj* a bordo

influence /ˈɪnflʊəns/ **1** *n* influenza *f*; use one's ~ esercitare la propria influenza **2** *vt* influenzare

influential /ɪnflʊˈenʃl/ *adj* influente

influenza /ɪnflʊˈenzə/ *n* influenza *f*

influx /ˈɪnflʌks/ *n* affluenza *f*

info /ˈɪnfəʊ/ *n* fam informazione *f*

inform /ɪnˈfɔːm/ **1** *vt* informare; keep somebody ~ed tenere qualcuno al corrente
2 *vi* ~ against denunziare

informal /ɪnˈfɔːml/ *adj* informale; ‹agreement› ufficioso

informality /ɪnfəˈmælətɪ/ *n* informalità *f inv*

informally /ɪnˈfɔːməlɪ/ *adv* in modo informale

informant /ɪnˈfɔːmənt/ *n* informatore, -trice *mf*

information /ɪnfəˈmeɪʃn/ *n* informazioni *fpl*; a piece of ~ un'informazione

information desk *n* banco *m* informazioni

information highway *n* autostrada *f* telematica

information officer *n* addetto, -a *mf* stampa

information pack *n* pacchetto *m* informativo

information processing *n* elaborazione *f* dati

information superhighway *n* Comput autostrada *f* dell'informazione

information system *n* sistema *m* informativo

information technology *n* informatica *f*

informative /ɪnˈfɔːmətɪv/ *adj* informativo; ‹film, book› istruttivo

informer /ɪnˈfɔːmə(r)/ *n* informatore, -trice *mf*; Pol delatore, -trice *mf*

infra-red /ɪnfrəˈred/ *adj* infrarosso

infrastructure /ˈɪnfrəstrʌktʃə(r)/ *n* infrastruttura *f*

infrequent /ɪnˈfriːkwənt/ *adj* infrequente

infrequently /ɪnˈfriːkwəntlɪ/ *adv* raramente

infringe /ɪnˈfrɪndʒ/ *vt* ~ on usurpare

infringement /ɪnˈfrɪndʒmənt/ *n* violazione *f*

infuriate /ɪnˈfjʊərɪeɪt/ *vt* infuriare

infuriating /ɪnˈfjʊərɪeɪtɪŋ/ *adj* esasperante

infuse /ɪnˈfjuːz/ *vi* ‹tea› restare in infusione

infusion /ɪnˈfjuːʒn/ *n* (drink) infusione *f*; (of capital, new blood) afflusso *m*

ingenious /ɪnˈdʒiːnɪəs/ *adj* ingegnoso

ingenuity /ɪndʒɪˈnjuːətɪ/ *n* ingegnosità *f*

ingenuous /ɪnˈdʒenjʊəs/ *adj* ingenuo

ingest /ɪnˈdʒest/ *vt* ingerire ‹food›; assimilare ‹fact›

ingot /ˈɪŋɡət/ *n* lingotto *m*

ingrained /ɪnˈɡreɪnd/ *adj* (in person) radicato; ‹dirt› incrostato

ingratiate /ɪnˈɡreɪʃɪeɪt/ vt ~ oneself with somebody ingraziarsi qualcuno

ingratitude /ɪnˈɡrætɪtjuːd/ n ingratitudine f

ingredient /ɪnˈɡriːdɪənt/ n ingrediente m

ingrowing /ˈɪnɡrəʊɪŋ/ adj ⟨nail⟩ incarnito

inhabit /ɪnˈhæbɪt/ vt abitare

inhabitable /ɪnˈhæbɪtəbl/ adj abitabile

inhabitant /ɪnˈhæbɪtənt/ n abitante mf

inhale /ɪnˈheɪl/ ① vt aspirare; Med inalare
② vi inspirare; (when smoking) aspirare

inhaler /ɪnˈheɪlə(r)/ n (device) inalatore ms

inherent /ɪnˈhɪərənt/ adj inerente

inherit /ɪnˈherɪt/ vt ereditare

inheritance /ɪnˈherɪtəns/ n eredità f inv

inhibit /ɪnˈhɪbɪt/ vt inibire

inhibited /ɪnˈhɪbɪtɪd/ adj inibito

inhibition /ɪnhɪˈbɪʃn/ n inibizione f

inhospitable /ɪnhɒˈspɪtəbl/ adj inospitale

in-house adj ⟨training⟩ interno all'azienda; ⟨magazine⟩ aziendale

inhuman /ɪnˈhjuːmən/ adj disumano

inhumanity /ɪnhjʊˈmænɪtɪ/ n disumanità f

inimitable /ɪˈnɪmɪtəbl/ adj inimitabile

iniquitous /ɪˈnɪkwɪtəs/ adj iniquo

initial /ɪˈnɪʃl/ ① adj iniziale
② n iniziale f
③ vt (pt/pp **initialled**) siglare

initially /ɪˈnɪʃəlɪ/ adv all'inizio

initiate /ɪˈnɪʃɪeɪt/ vt iniziare

initiation /ɪnɪʃɪˈeɪʃn/ n iniziazione f

initiative /ɪˈnɪʃɪətɪv/ n iniziativa f; take the ~ prendere l'iniziativa

inject /ɪnˈdʒekt/ vt iniettare

injection /ɪnˈdʒekʃn/ n iniezione f

in-joke n it's an ~ è una battuta tra di noi/loro

injunction /ɪnˈdʒʌŋkʃn/ n ingiunzione f

injure /ˈɪndʒə(r)/ vt ferire; (wrong) nuocere

injured /ˈɪndʒəd/ ① adj ferito; Jur the ~ party la parte lesa
② npl the ~ i feriti

injury /ˈɪndʒərɪ/ n ferita f; (wrong) torto m

injury time n Sport recupero m

injustice /ɪnˈdʒʌstɪs/ n ingiustizia f; do somebody an ~ giudicare qualcuno in modo sbagliato

ink /ɪŋk/ n inchiostro m

ink-jet printer n stampante f a getto d'inchiostro

inkling /ˈɪŋklɪŋ/ n sentore m

inky /ˈɪŋkɪ/ adj macchiato d'inchiostro

inlaid /ɪnˈleɪd/ adj intarsiato

inland /ˈɪnlənd/ ① adj interno
② adv all'interno

Inland Revenue n fisco m

in-laws /ˈɪnlɔːz/ npl fam parenti mpl acquisiti

inlay /ˈɪnleɪ/ n intarsio m

inlet /ˈɪnlet/ n insenatura f; Techn entrata f

inmate /ˈɪnmeɪt/ n (of hospital) degente mf; (of prison) detenuto, -a mf

inn /ɪn/ n locanda f

innards /ˈɪnədz/ npl fam frattaglie fpl

innate /ɪˈneɪt/ adj innato

inner /ˈɪnə(r)/ adj interno

inner city ① n quartieri mpl nel centro di una città caratterizzati da problemi sociali
② attrib ⟨problems⟩ dell'area urbana con problemi sociali

inner ear n orecchio m interno

innermost /ˈɪnəməʊst/ adj il più profondo

inner tube n camera f d'aria

innings /ˈɪnɪŋz/ nsg (in cricket) turno m di battuta; **have had a good ~** (Br fig: when leaving job etc) aver avuto una carriera lunga e gratificante; (when dead) aver avuto una vita lunga e piena di soddisfazioni

innkeeper /ˈɪnkiːpə(r)/ n locandiere, -a mf

innocence /ˈɪnəsəns/ n innocenza f

innocent /ˈɪnəsənt/ adj innocente

innocently /ˈɪnəsəntlɪ/ adv innocentemente

innocuous /ɪˈnɒkjʊəs/ adj innocuo

innovate /ˈɪnəveɪt/ vi innovare

innovation /ɪnəˈveɪʃn/ n innovazione f

innovative /ˈɪnəvətɪv/ adj innovativo

innovator /ˈɪnəveɪtə(r)/ n innovatore, -trice mf

innuendo /ɪnjʊˈendəʊ/ n (pl **-es**) insinuazione f

innumerable /ɪˈnjuːmərəbl/ adj innumerevole

inoculate /ɪˈnɒkjʊleɪt/ vt vaccinare

inoculation /ɪnɒkjʊˈleɪʃn/ n vaccinazione f

inoffensive /ɪnəˈfensɪv/ adj inoffensivo

inoperable /ɪnˈɒpərəbl/ adj inoperabile

inopportune /ɪnˈɒpətjuːn/ adj inopportuno

inordinate /ɪˈnɔːdɪnət/ adj smodato

inordinately /ɪˈnɔːdɪnətlɪ/ adv smodatamente

inorganic /ɪnɔːˈɡænɪk/ adj inorganico

in-patient n degente mf

input /ˈɪnpʊt/ n input m inv, ingresso m

inquest /ˈɪnkwest/ n inchiesta f

inquire /ɪnˈkwaɪə(r)/ **1** vi informarsi (**about** su); ~ **into** far indagini su **2** vt domandare

inquiring /ɪnˈkwaɪərɪŋ/ adj ⟨mind⟩ curioso; ⟨look, voice⟩ interrogativo

inquiry /ɪnˈkwaɪərɪ/ n domanda f; (investigation) inchiesta f

inquisitive /ɪnˈkwɪzətɪv/ adj curioso

inquisitively /ɪnˈkwɪzɪtɪvlɪ/ adv con molta curiosità

inroad /ˈɪnrəʊd/ n make ~s **into** intaccare ⟨savings⟩; cominciare a risolvere ⟨problem⟩

INS n abbr Am (**Immigration and Naturalization Service**) ufficio m immigrazione e naturalizzazione

insalubrious /ɪnsəˈluːbrɪəs/ adj (dirty) insalubre; (sleazy) sordido

insane /ɪnˈseɪn/ adj pazzo; fig insensato

insanitary /ɪnˈsænɪt(ə)rɪ/ adj malsano

insanity /ɪnˈsænətɪ/ n pazzia f

insatiable /ɪnˈseɪʃəbl/ adj insaziabile

inscribe /ɪnˈskraɪb/ vt iscrivere

inscription /ɪnˈskrɪpʃn/ n iscrizione f

inscrutable /ɪnˈskruːtəbl/ adj impenetrabile

insect /ˈɪnsekt/ n insetto m

insecticide /ɪnˈsektɪsaɪd/ n insetticida m

insect repellent n insettifugo m

insecure /ɪnsɪˈkjʊə(r)/ adj malsicuro; fig ⟨person⟩ insicuro

insecurity /ɪnsɪˈkjʊərətɪ/ n mancanza f di sicurezza

insemination /ɪnsemɪˈneɪʃn/ n inseminazione f

insensitive /ɪnˈsensɪtɪv/ adj insensibile

inseparable /ɪnˈsep(ə)rəbl/ adj inseparabile

insert[1] /ˈɪnsɜːt/ n inserto m

insert[2] /ɪnˈsɜːt/ vt inserire

insertion /ɪnˈsɜːʃn/ n inserzione f

inset /ˈɪnset/ **1** n (map, photo) dettaglio m **2** adj ~ **with** ⟨necklace⟩ incastonato di; ⟨table⟩ intarsiato di

inshore /ˈɪnʃɔː(r)/ **1** adj ⟨current⟩ diretta a riva; ⟨fishing, waters, current⟩ costiero; ⟨wind⟩ dal mare **2** adv ⟨fish⟩ sotto costa

inside /ɪnˈsaɪd/ **1** n interno m; ~**s** pl fam pancia f **2** adv dentro; ~ **out** a rovescio; (thoroughly) a fondo **3** prep dentro; (of time) entro

inside lane n Auto corsia f interna

inside leg n interno m della gamba

insider /ɪnˈsaɪdə(r)/ n persona f all'interno

insider dealer, **insider trader** n Fin persona f che pratica l'insider trading

insider dealing, **insider trading** /ˈdiːlɪŋ/, /ˈtreɪdɪŋ/ n Fin insider trading m

insidious /ɪnˈsɪdɪəs/ adj insidioso

insidiously /ɪnˈsɪdɪəslɪ/ adv insidiosamente

insight /ˈɪnsaɪt/ n intuito m (**into** per); an ~ **into** un quadro di

insignia /ɪnˈsɪgnɪə/ npl insegne fpl

insignificant /ɪnsɪgˈnɪfɪkənt/ adj insignificante

insincere /ɪnsɪnˈsɪə(r)/ adj poco sincero

insincerity /ɪnsɪnˈserətɪ/ n mancanza f di sincerità

insinuate /ɪnˈsɪnjʊeɪt/ vt insinuare

insinuation /ɪnsɪnjʊˈeɪʃn/ n insinuazione f

insipid /ɪnˈsɪpɪd/ adj insipido

insist /ɪnˈsɪst/ **1** vi insistere (**on** per) **2** vt ~ **that** insistere che

insistence /ɪnˈsɪstəns/ n insistenza f

insistent /ɪnˈsɪstənt/ adj insistente

insistently /ɪnˈsɪstəntlɪ/ adv insistentemente

insofar /ɪnsəˈfɑː(r)/ conj ~ **as** (to the extent that) nella misura in cui; (seeing that) in quanto; ~ **as I know** per quanto ne sappia

insole /ˈɪnsəʊl/ n soletta f

insolence /ˈɪnsələns/ n insolenza f

insolent /ˈɪnsələnt/ adj insolente

insolently /ˈɪnsələntlɪ/ adv con insolenza

insoluble /ɪnˈsɒljʊbl/ adj insolubile

insolvency /ɪnˈsɒlvənsɪ/ n insolvenza f

insolvent /ɪnˈsɒlvənt/ adj insolvente

insomnia /ɪnˈsɒmnɪə/ n insonnia f

insomniac /ɪnˈsɒmnɪæk/ n persona f che soffre di insonnia

insomuch /ɪnsəˈmʌtʃ/ conj ~ **as** (to the extent that) nella misura in cui; (seeing that) in quanto

inspect /ɪnˈspekt/ vt ispezionare; controllare ⟨ticket⟩

inspection /ɪnˈspekʃn/ n ispezione f; (of ticket) controllo m

inspector /ɪnˈspektə(r)/ n ispettore, -trice mf; (of tickets) controllore m

inspiration /ɪnspəˈreɪʃn/ n ispirazione f

inspire /ɪnˈspaɪə(r)/ vt ispirare

inspired /ɪnˈspaɪəd/ adj ⟨person, performance⟩ ispirato; ⟨idea⟩ luminosa

inspiring /ɪnˈspaɪərɪŋ/ adj ⟨person, speech⟩ entusiasmante

instability /ɪnstəˈbɪlətɪ/ n instabilità f

install /ɪnˈstɔːl/ vt installare; insediare ⟨person⟩

installation /ɪnstəˈleɪʃn/ n installazione f

instalment /ɪn'stɔːlmənt/ n Comm rata f; (of serial) puntata f; (of publication) fascicolo m

instance /'ɪnstəns/ n (case) caso m; (example) esempio m; **in the first ~** in primo luogo; **for ~** per esempio

instant /'ɪnstənt/ **①** adj immediato; Culin espresso
② n istante m

instantaneous /ɪnstən'teɪnɪəs/ adj istantaneo

instant camera n polaroid® f inv

instant coffee n caffè m inv solubile

instantly /'ɪnstəntlɪ/ adv immediatamente

instant messaging n instant messaging m, messaggistica f instantanea

instant replay n Sport replay m inv

instead /ɪn'sted/ adv invece; **~ of doing** anziché fare; **~ of me** al mio posto; **~ of going** invece di andare

instep /'ɪnstep/ n collo m del piede

instigate /'ɪnstɪɡeɪt/ vt istigare

instigation /ɪnstɪ'ɡeɪʃn/ n istigazione f; **at his ~** dietro suo suggerimento

instigator /'ɪnstɪɡeɪtə(r)/ n istigatore, -trice mf

instil /ɪn'stɪl/ vt (pt/pp **instilled**) inculcare (**into** in)

instinct /'ɪnstɪŋkt/ n istinto m

instinctive /ɪn'stɪŋktɪv/ adj istintivo

instinctively /ɪn'stɪŋktɪvlɪ/ adv istintivamente

institute /'ɪnstɪtjuːt/ **①** n istituto m
② vt istituire ⟨scheme⟩; iniziare ⟨search⟩; intentare ⟨legal action⟩

institution /ɪnstɪ'tjuːʃn/ n istituzione f; (home for elderly) istituto m per anziani; (for mentally ill) istituto m per malati di mente

institutionalize /ɪnstɪ'tjuːʃənəlaɪz/ vt istituzionalizzare

institutionalized /ɪnstɪ'tjuːʃənəlaɪzd/ adj ⟨racism, violence⟩ istituzionalizzato; **become ~** (officially established) essere istituzionalizzato; **be ~d** ⟨person⟩ non essere autonomo a causa di un lungo soggiorno in ospedale psichiatrico

instruct /ɪn'strʌkt/ vt istruire; (order) ordinare

instruction /ɪn'strʌkʃn/ n istruzione f; **~s** pl (orders) ordini mpl

instruction book n libretto m di istruzioni

instructive /ɪn'strʌktɪv/ adj istruttivo

instructor /ɪn'strʌktə(r)/ n istruttore, -trice mf

instrument /'ɪnstrʊmənt/ n strumento m

instrumental /ɪnstrʊ'ment(ə)l/ adj strumentale; **be ~ in** contribuire a

instrumentalist /ɪnstrʊ'mentəlɪst/ n strumentista mf

insubordinate /ɪnsə'bɔːdɪnət/ adj insubordinato

insubordination /ɪnsəbɔːdɪ'neɪʃn/ n insubordinazione f

insubstantial /ɪnsəb'stænʃəl/ adj (unreal) irreale; ⟨evidence⟩ inconsistente; ⟨flimsy, building⟩ poco solido; ⟨meal⟩ poco sostanzioso

insufferable /ɪn'sʌf(ə)rəbl/ adj insopportabile

insufficient /ɪnsə'fɪʃənt/ adj insufficiente

insufficiently /ɪnsə'fɪʃəntlɪ/ adv insufficientemente

insular /'ɪnsjʊlə(r)/ adj fig gretto

insulate /'ɪnsjʊleɪt/ vt isolare

insulating tape /'ɪnsjʊleɪtɪŋ/ n nastro m isolante

insulation /ɪnsjʊ'leɪʃn/ n isolamento m

insulator /'ɪnsjʊleɪtə(r)/ n isolante m

insulin /'ɪnsjʊlɪn/ n insulina f

insult[1] /'ɪnsʌlt/ n insulto m

insult[2] /ɪn'sʌlt/ vt insultare

insuperable /ɪn'suːpərəbl/ adj insuperabile

insurable value /ɪn'ʃʊərəbl/ n valore m assicurabile

insurance /ɪn'ʃʊərəns/ n assicurazione f

insurance broker n broker mf inv d'assicurazioni

insurance claim n richiesta f di indennizzo (ad assicurazione)

insurance policy n polizza f d'assicurazione

insurance premium n premio m assicurativo

insure /ɪn'ʃʊə(r)/ vt assicurare

insurgent /ɪn'sɜːdʒənt/ n rivoltoso, -a mf

insurmountable /ɪnsə'maʊntəbl/ adj insormontabile

insurrection /ɪnsə'rekʃn/ n insurrezione f

intact /ɪn'tækt/ adj intatto

intake /'ɪnteɪk/ n immissione f; (of food) consumo m

intangible /ɪn'tændʒəbl/ adj intangibile

integral /'ɪntɪɡrəl/ adj integrale

integrate /'ɪntɪɡreɪt/ **①** vt integrare
② vi integrarsi

integration /ɪntɪ'ɡreɪʃn/ n integrazione f

integrity /ɪn'teɡrətɪ/ n integrità f

intellect /'ɪntəlekt/ n intelletto m

intellectual /ɪntə'lektjʊəl/ adj & n intellettuale mf

intelligence /ɪnˈtelɪdʒəns/ n
intelligenza f; Mil informazioni fpl

intelligent /ɪnˈtelɪdʒənt/ adj intelligente

intelligently /ɪnˈtelɪdʒəntlɪ/ adv
intelligentemente

intelligentsia /ɪntelɪˈdʒentsɪə/ n
intellighenzia f

intelligible /ɪnˈtelɪdʒəbl/ adj
intelligibile

intemperate /ɪnˈtemp(ə)rət/ adj
⟨language, person⟩ intemperante;
⟨weather⟩ rigido; ⟨attack⟩ violento

intend /ɪnˈtend/ vt destinare; (have in mind)
aver intenzione di; **be ~ed for** essere
destinato a

intended /ɪnˈtendɪd/ **①** adj ⟨visit,
purchase⟩ programmato; ⟨result⟩ voluto,
desiderato
② n her ~ hum il suo fidanzato; his ~ hum
la sua fidanzata

intense /ɪnˈtens/ adj intenso; ⟨person⟩
dai sentimenti intensi

intensely /ɪnˈtenslɪ/ adv intensamente;
(very) estremamente

intensification /ɪntensɪfɪˈkeɪʃn/ n
intensificazione f

intensify /ɪnˈtensɪfaɪ/ **①** v (pt/pp -ied)
vt intensificare
② vi intensificarsi

intensity /ɪnˈtensətɪ/ n intensità f

intensive /ɪnˈtensɪv/ adj intensivo; ~
care terapia f intensiva

intensive care [unit] n [reparto m]
rianimazione f

intensively /ɪnˈtensɪvlɪ/ adv
intensivamente

intent /ɪnˈtent/ **①** adj intento; ~ **on**
(absorbed in) preso da; **be ~ on doing
something** essere intento a fare qualcosa
② n intenzione f; **to all ~s and purposes**
a tutti gli effetti

intention /ɪnˈtenʃn/ n intenzione f

intentional /ɪnˈtenʃənəl/ adj
intenzionale

intentionally /ɪnˈtenʃənəlɪ/ adv
intenzionalmente

intently /ɪnˈtentlɪ/ adv attentamente

inter /ɪnˈtɜː(r)/ vt (pt/pp **interred**) fml
interrare

interact /ɪntərˈækt/ vi ⟨two factors,
people⟩ interagire; Comput dialogare

interaction /ɪntərˈækʃn/ n
cooperazione f

interactive /ɪntərˈæktɪv/ adj interattivo

interactive television n televisione f
interattiva

interactive video n video m
interattivo

interbreed /ɪntəˈbriːd/ **①** vt ibridare
② vi incrociarsi

interbreeding /ɪntəˈbriːdɪŋ/ n
ibridazione f

intercede /ɪntəˈsiːd/ vi intercedere (**on
behalf of** a favore di)

intercept /ɪntəˈsept/ vt intercettare

interchange /ˈɪntətʃeɪndʒ/ n scambio
m; Auto raccordo m [autostradale]

interchangeable /ɪntəˈtʃeɪndʒəbl/ adj
interscambiabile

intercity /ɪntəˈsɪtɪ/ **①** n (Br: train)
intercity m inv
② adj intercity

intercom /ˈɪntəkɒm/ n citofono m

interconnecting /ɪntəkəˈnektɪŋ/ adj
⟨rooms⟩ comunicante

intercontinental /ɪntəkɒntɪˈnentəl/
adj intercontinentale

intercourse /ˈɪntəkɔːs/ n (sexual)
rapporti mpl [sessuali]

interdepartmental
/ɪntədiːpɑːtˈment(ə)l/ adj Univ, Comm
interdipartimentale; Pol interministeriale

interdependent /ɪntədɪˈpendənt/ adj
interdipendente

interdisciplinary /ɪntədɪsɪˈplɪnərɪ/ adj
interdisciplinare

interest /ˈɪntrəst/ **①** n interesse m; **have
an ~ in** Comm essere cointeressato in; **be
of ~** essere interessante
② vt interessare
③ adj interessato

interest-bearing adj fruttifero

interested /ˈɪntrəstɪd/ adj interessato

interest-free adj senza interessi

interest-free loan n prestito m senza
interessi

interesting /ˈɪnt(ə)rəstɪŋ/ adj
interessante

interest rate n tasso m di interesse

interface /ˈɪntəfeɪs/ **①** n Comput, fig
interfaccia f
② vi interfacciarsi
③ vt interfacciare

interfere /ɪntəˈfɪə(r)/ vi interferire; ~
with interferire con

interference /ɪntəˈfɪərəns/ n
interferenza f

interfering /ɪntəˈfɪərɪŋ/ adj ⟨person⟩
impiccione

interim /ˈɪntərɪm/ **①** adj temporaneo; ~
payment acconto m
② n **in the ~** nel frattempo

interior /ɪnˈtɪərɪə(r)/ **①** adj interiore
② n interno m

interior decorator n arredatore, -trice
mf

interior designer n (of colours, fabrics
etc) arredatore, -trice mf; (of walls, space)
architetto m d'interni

interject /ɪntəˈdʒekt/ vt intervenire

interjection /ɪntəˈdʒekʃn/ n Gram interiezione f; (remark) intervento m

interlink /ɪntəˈlɪŋk/ vt connettere; **be ~ed with** essere connesso con

interlock /ɪntəˈlɒk/ vi ⟨parts⟩ incastrarsi

interlocking /ˈɪntəlɒkɪŋ/ adj a incastro

interloper /ˈɪntələʊpə(r)/ n intruso, -a mf

interlude /ˈɪntəluːd/ n intervallo m

intermarry /ɪntəˈmæri/ vi sposarsi tra parenti; ⟨different groups⟩ contrarre matrimoni misti

intermediary /ɪntəˈmiːdɪərɪ/ n intermediario, -a mf

intermediate /ɪntəˈmiːdɪət/ adj intermedio

interminable /ɪnˈtɜːmɪnəbl/ adj interminabile

intermission /ɪntəˈmɪʃn/ n intervallo m

intermittent /ɪntəˈmɪtənt/ adj intermittente

intermittently /ɪntəˈmɪtəntlɪ/ adv a intermittenza

intern /ɪnˈtɜːn/ vt internare

internal /ɪnˈtɜːnl/ adj interno

internal combustion engine n motore m a scoppio

internally /ɪnˈtɜːnəlɪ/ adv internamente; ⟨deal with⟩ all'interno

international /ɪntəˈnæʃ(ə)nəl/ ❶ adj internazionale
❷ n (game) incontro m internazionale; (player) competitore, -trice mf in gare internazionali

internationally /ɪntəˈnæʃ(ə)nəlɪ/ adv internazionalmente; **it applies ~** ha validità internazionale

international money order n vaglia m inv postale internazionale

International Phonetic Alphabet n Alfabeto m Fonetico Internazionale

international reply coupon n tagliando m di risposta internazionale

internee /ɪntɜːˈniː/ n internato, -a mf

internet /ˈɪntənet/ n Internet m

Internet access n Comput accesso m Internet

Internet access provider n Comput fornitore m di accesso ai servizi Internet

Internet café n caffè m Internet

Internet kiosk n Internet point m inv

Internet protocol n Comput protocollo m Internet

Internet service provider n Comput fornitore m di servizi Internet

Internet user n utente mf di Internet

internist /ɪnˈtɜːnɪst/ n Am internista mf

internment /ɪnˈtɜːnmənt/ n internamento m

interplay /ˈɪntəpleɪ/ n azione f reciproca

interpolate /ɪnˈtɜːpəleɪt/ vt interpolare

interpose /ɪntəˈpəʊz/ vt (insert) frapporre; interrompere con ⟨comment, remark⟩

interpret /ɪnˈtɜːprɪt/ ❶ vt interpretare ❷ vi fare l'interprete.

interpretation /ɪntɜːprɪˈteɪʃn/ n interpretazione f

interpreter /ɪnˈtɜːprɪtə(r)/ n interprete mf

interpreting /ɪnˈtɜːprɪtɪŋ/ n interpretariato m

interrelated /ɪntərɪˈleɪtɪd/ adj ⟨facts⟩ in correlazione

interrogate /ɪnˈterəgeɪt/ vt interrogare

interrogation /ɪnterəˈgeɪʃn/ n interrogazione f; (by police) interrogatorio m

interrogative /ɪntəˈrɒgətɪv/ adj & n ~ [pronoun] interrogativo m

interrupt /ɪntəˈrʌpt/ vt/i interrompere

interruption /ɪntəˈrʌpʃn/ n interruzione f

intersect /ɪntəˈsekt/ ❶ vi intersecarsi ❷ vt intersecare

intersection /ɪntəˈsekʃn/ n intersezione f; (of street) incrocio m

interspersed /ɪntəˈspɜːst/ adj ~ **with** inframmezzato di

interstate /ˈɪntəsteɪt/ Am ❶ n superstrada f fra stati
❷ adj ⟨commerce, links⟩ fra stati

intertwine /ɪntəˈtwaɪn/ vi attorcigliarsi

interval /ˈɪntəvl/ n intervallo m; **bright ~s** pl schiarite fpl

intervene /ɪntəˈviːn/ vi intervenire

intervention /ɪntəˈvenʃn/ n intervento m

interview /ˈɪntəvjuː/ ❶ n Journ intervista f; (for job) colloquio m [di lavoro] ❷ vt intervistare

interviewee /ɪntəvjuːˈiː/ n (on TV, radio, in survey) intervistato, -a mf; (for job) persona f sottoposta a un colloquio di lavoro

interviewer /ˈɪntəvjuːə(r)/ n intervistatore, -trice mf

interwar adj **the ~ years** gli anni tra le due guerre

interweave /ɪntəˈwiːv/ vt intrecciare ⟨themes, threads⟩; mischiare ⟨rhythms⟩

intestinal /ɪnteˈstaɪnəl/ adj intestinale

intestine /ɪnˈtestɪn/ n intestino m

intimacy /ˈɪntɪməsɪ/ n intimità f

intimate[1] /ˈɪntɪmət/ adj intimo; **be ~ with** (sexually) avere relazioni intime con

intimate[2] /ˈɪntɪmeɪt/ vt far capire; (imply) suggerire

intimately /ˈɪntɪmətlɪ/ adv intimamente

intimidate /ɪnˈtɪmɪdeɪt/ vt intimidire

intimidating *adj* ‹behaviour, person› intimidatorio; ‹prospect› impressionante

intimidation /ɪntɪmɪ'deɪʃn/ *n* intimidazione *f*

into /'ɪntə/, *di fronte a una vocale* /'ɪntʊ/ *prep* dentro, in; **go ∼ the house** andare dentro [casa] *or* in casa; **be ∼** (fam: like) essere appassionato di; **I'm not ∼ that** questo non mi piace; **7 ∼ 21 goes 3** il 7 nel 21 ci sta 3 volte; **translate ∼ French** tradurre in francese; **get ∼ trouble** mettersi nei guai

intolerable /ɪn'tɒlərəbl/ *adj* intollerabile

intolerance /ɪn'tɒlərəns/ *n* intolleranza *f*

intolerant /ɪn'tɒlərənt/ *adj* intollerante

intonation /ɪntə'neɪʃn/ *n* intonazione *f*

intone /ɪn'təʊn/ *vt* recitare ‹prayer›

intoxicated /ɪn'tɒksɪkeɪtɪd/ *adj* inebriato

intoxicating /ɪn'tɒksɪkeɪtɪŋ/ *adj* ‹drink› alcolico; ‹smell, sight› inebriante

intoxication /ɪntɒksɪ'keɪʃn/ *n* ebbrezza *f*

intractable /ɪn'træktəbl/ *adj* intrattabile; ‹problem› insolubile

intramural /ɪntrə'mjʊərəl/ *adj* ‹studies› tenuto in sede

intranet /'ɪntrənet/ *n* Comput intranet *f*

intransìgence /ɪn'trænzɪdʒəns/ *n* intransigenza *f*

intransigent /ɪn'trænzɪdʒənt/ *adj* intransigente

intransitive /ɪn'trænzɪtɪv/ *adj* intransitivo

intransitively /ɪn'trænzɪtɪvlɪ/ *adv* intransitivamente

intrauterine device /ɪntrəju:tərəɪndɪ'vaɪs/ *n* Med spirale *f*, dispositivo *m* anticoncezionale intrauterino

intravenous /ɪntrə'vi:nəs/ *adj* endovenoso

intravenous drip *n* flebo[clisi] *f inv*

intravenous drug user *n* tossicomane *mf* che si inietta in vena

intravenously /ɪntrə'vi:nəslɪ/ *adv* per via endovenosa

in-tray *n* vassoio *m* per pratiche e corrispondenza da evadere

intrepid /ɪn'trepɪd/ *adj* intrepido

intricacy /'ɪntrɪkəsɪ/ *n* complessità *f*

intricate /'ɪntrɪkət/ *adj* complesso

intrigue /ɪn'tri:g/ ① *n* intrigo *m* ② *vt* intrigare ③ *vi* tramare

intriguing /ɪn'tri:gɪŋ/ *adj* intrigante

intrinsic /ɪn'trɪnsɪk/ *adj* intrinseco

introduce /ɪntrə'dju:s/ *vt* presentare; (bring in, insert) introdurre

introduction /ɪntrə'dʌkʃn/ *n* introduzione *f*; (to person) presentazione *f*; (to book) prefazione *f*

introductory /ɪntrə'dʌktərɪ/ *adj* introduttivo

introspective /ɪntrə'spektɪv/ *adj* introspettivo

introvert /'ɪntrəvɜ:t/ *n* introverso, -a *mf*

introverted /'ɪntrəvɜ:tɪd/ *adj* introverso

intrude /ɪn'tru:d/ *vi* intromettersi

intruder /ɪn'tru:də(r)/ *n* intruso, -a *mf*

intrusion /ɪn'tru:ʒn/ *n* intrusione *f*

intrusive *adj* ‹camera, question› indiscreto

intuition /ɪntjʊ'ɪʃn/ *n* intuito *m*

intuitive /ɪn'tju:ɪtɪv/ *adj* intuitivo

intuitively /ɪn'tju:ɪtɪvlɪ/ *adv* intuitivamente

inundate /'ɪnəndeɪt/ *vt* fig inondare (**with** di)

inure /ɪn'jʊə(r)/ *vt* **become ∼d to something** assuefarsi a qualcosa

invade /ɪn'veɪd/ *vt* invadere

invader /ɪn'veɪdə(r)/ *n* invasore *m*

invalid¹ /'ɪnvəlɪd/ *n* invalido, -a *mf*

invalid² /ɪn'vælɪd/ *adj* non valido

invalidate /ɪn'vælɪdeɪt/ *vt* invalidare

invaluable /ɪn'væljʊ(ə)bl/ *adj* prezioso; (priceless) inestimabile

invariable /ɪn'veərɪəbl/ *adj* invariabile

invariably /ɪn'veərɪəblɪ/ *adv* invariabilmente

invasion /ɪn'veɪʒn/ *n* invasione *f*

invective /ɪn'vektɪv/ *n* invettiva *f*

invent /ɪnvent/ *vt* inventare

invention /ɪn'venʃn/ *n* invenzione *f*

inventive /ɪn'ventɪv/ *adj* inventivo

inventor /ɪn'ventə(r)/ *n* inventore, -trice *mf*

inventory /'ɪnvəntrɪ/ *n* inventario *m*

inverse /ɪn'vɜ:s/ ① *adj* inverso ② *n* inverso *m*

inversely /ɪn'vɜ:slɪ/ *adv* inversamente

invert /ɪn'vɜ:t/ *vt* invertire; **in ∼ed commas** tra virgolette

invertebrate /ɪn'vɜ:tɪbrət/ *adj & n* invertebrato *m*

invest /ɪn'vest/ ① *vt* investire ② *vi* fare investimenti; **∼ in** (fam: buy) comprarsi

investigate /ɪn'vestɪgeɪt/ *vt* investigare

investigation /ɪnvestɪ'geɪʃn/ *n* investigazione *f*

investigative journalism /ɪn'vestɪgətɪv/ *n* dietrologia *f*

investiture /ɪn'vestɪtʃə(r)/ *n* investitura *f*

investment /ɪn'vestmənt/ n
investimento m

investment capital n capitale m di
investimento

investment income n reddito m da
investimenti

investment manager n responsabile
mf della gestione del portafoglio fondi di
investimento

investment trust n fondo m comune
di investimento

investor /ɪn'vestə(r)/ n investitore, -trice
mf

inveterate /ɪn'vetərət/ adj inveterato

invidious /ɪn'vɪdɪəs/ adj ingiusto;
⟨position⟩ antipatico

invigilate /ɪn'vɪdʒɪleɪt/ vi Sch
sorvegliare lo svolgimento di un esame

invigilator /ɪn'vɪdʒɪleɪtə(r)/ n persona f
che sorveglia lo svolgimento di un esame

invigorate /ɪn'vɪgəreɪt/ vt rinvigorire

invigorating /ɪn'vɪgəreɪtɪŋ/ adj
tonificante

invincible /ɪn'vɪnsəbl/ adj invincibile

inviolable /ɪn'vaɪələbl/ adj inviolabile

invisible /ɪn'vɪzəbl/ adj invisibile

invisible ink n inchiostro m simpatico

invitation /ɪnvɪ'teɪʃn/ n invito m

invitation card n biglietto m d'invito

invite /ɪn'vaɪt/ vt invitare; (attract) attirare
■ **invite in** vt invitare a entrare
■ **invite round** vt invitare a casa

inviting /ɪn'vaɪtɪŋ/ adj invitante

in vitro fertilization
/ɪnvi:trəʊfɜ:tɪlaɪ'zeɪʃn/ n fecondazione f in
vitro

invoice /'ɪnvɔɪs/ ① n fattura f
② vt ~ **somebody** emettere una fattura a
qualcuno

invoke /ɪn'vəʊk/ vt invocare

involuntarily /ɪn'vɒlʌntərɪlɪ/ adv
involontariamente

involuntary /ɪn'vɒləntrɪ/ adj
involontario

involve /ɪn'vɒlv/ vt comportare; (affect,
include) coinvolgere; (entail) implicare; **get
~d with somebody** legarsi a qualcuno;
(romantically) legarsi sentimentalmente a
qualcuno

involved /ɪn'vɒlvd/ adj complesso

involvement /ɪn'vɒlvmənt/ n
coinvolgimento m

invulnerable /ɪn'vʌln(ə)rəbl/ adj
invulnerabile; ⟨position⟩ inattaccabile

inward /'ɪnwəd/ adj interno; ⟨thoughts
etc⟩ interiore

inward investment n Comm
investimento m di capitali stranieri

inward-looking /'ɪnwədlʊkɪŋ/ adj
⟨person⟩ egocentrico; ⟨society, policy⟩
chiuso

inwardly /'ɪnwədlɪ/ adv interiormente

inward[s] /'ɪnwəd[z]/ adv verso
l'interno

in-your-face adj fam aggressivo

iodine /'aɪədi:n/ n iodio m

Ionian Sea /aɪəʊnɪən/ n mar m Ionio

iota /aɪ'əʊtə/ n briciolo m

IOU abbr (**I owe you**) pagherò m inv

IPA n abbr (**International Phonetic
Alphabet**) AFI m

IQ abbr (**intelligence quotient**) Q.I. m

IRA abbr (**Irish Republican Army**)
I.R.A. f

Iran /ɪ'rɑ:n/ n Iran m

Iranian /ɪ'reɪnɪən/ adj & n iraniano, -a
mf

Iraq /ɪ'rɑ:k/ n Iraq m

Iraqi /ɪ'rɑ:kɪ/ adj & n iracheno, -a mf

irascible /ɪ'ræsəbl/ adj irascibile

irate /aɪ'reɪt/ adj adirato

Ireland /'aɪələnd/ n Irlanda f

iris /'aɪrɪs/ n Anat iride f; Bot iris f inv

Irish /'aɪrɪʃ/ ① adj irlandese
② n the l~ pl gli irlandesi

Irishman /'aɪrɪʃmən/ n irlandese m

Irish Republic n Repubblica f
d'Irlanda

Irish sea n mare m d'Irlanda

Irishwoman /'aɪrɪʃwʊmən/ n irlandese
f

irk /ɜ:k/ vt infastidire

irksome /'ɜ:ksəm/ adj fastidioso

iron /'aɪən/ ① adj di ferro
② n ferro m; (appliance) ferro m [da stiro]
③ vt/i stirare
■ **iron out** vt eliminare stirando; fig
appianare

Iron Curtain n cortina f di ferro

iron fist n fig pugno m di ferro

ironic[al] /aɪ'rɒnɪk[l]/ adj ironico

ironing /'aɪənɪŋ/ n stirare m; (articles)
roba f da stirare; **do the ~** stirare

ironing board n asse f da stiro

iron lung n polmone m d'acciaio

ironmonger /'aɪənmʌŋgə(r)/ n ~'s
[shop] negozio m di ferramenta

irony /'aɪərənɪ/ n ironia f

irradiate /ɪ'reɪdɪeɪt/ vt irradiare

irrational /ɪ'ræʃənl/ adj irrazionale

irreconcilable /ɪ'rekənsaɪləbl/ adj
irreconciliabile

irrecoverable /ɪrɪ'kʌv(ə)rəbl/ adj
⟨debt, object⟩ irrecuperabile; ⟨loss⟩
irreparabile

irredeemable /ɪrɪ'di:məbl/ adj Fin
⟨shares, loan⟩ irredimibile; ⟨loss⟩

irreparabile; Relig ⟨*sinner*⟩ che non è redimibile

irrefutable /ɪrɪ'fjuːtəbl/ *adj* irrefutabile

irregular /ɪ'regʊlə(r)/ *adj* irregolare

irregularity /ɪregjʊ'lærətɪ/ *n* irregolarità *f inv*

irregularly /ɪ'regjʊləlɪ/ *adv* in modo irregolare

irrelevant /ɪ'reləvənt/ *adj* non pertinente

irreligious /ɪrɪ'lɪdʒəs/ *adj* irreligioso

irreparable /ɪ'repərəbl/ *adj* irreparabile

irreparably /ɪ'rep(ə)rəblɪ/ *adv* irreparabilmente

irreplaceable /ɪrɪ'pleɪsəbl/ *adj* insostituibile

irrepressible /ɪrɪ'presəbl/ *adj* irrefrenabile; ⟨*person*⟩ incontenibile

irreproachable /ɪrɪ'prəʊtʃəbl/ *adj* irreprensibile

irresistible /ɪrɪ'zɪstəbl/ *adj* irresistibile

irresolute /ɪ'rezəluːt/ *adj* irresoluto

irrespective /ɪrɪ'spektɪv/ *adj* ∼ of senza riguardo per

irresponsible /ɪrɪ'spɒnsəbl/ *adj* irresponsabile

irresponsibly /ɪrɪ'spɒnsəblɪ/ *adv* irresponsabilmente

irretrievable /ɪrɪ'triːvəbl/ *adj* ⟨*loss, harm*⟩ irreparabile

irreverence /ɪ'revərəns/ *n* irriverenza *f*

irreverent /ɪ'revərənt/ *adj* irriverente

irreverently /ɪ'revərəntlɪ/ *adv* in modo irriverente

irreversible /ɪrɪ'vɜːsəbl/ *adj* irreversibile

irreversibly /ɪrɪ'vɜːsɪblɪ/ *adv* irreversibilmente

irrevocable /ɪ'revəkəbl/ *adj* irrevocabile

irrevocably /ɪ'revəkəblɪ/ *adv* irrevocabilmente

irrigate /'ɪrɪgeɪt/ *vt* irrigare

irrigation /ɪrɪ'geɪʃn/ *n* irrigazione *f*

irritability /ɪrɪtə'bɪlətɪ/ *n* irritabilità *f*

irritable /'ɪrɪtəbl/ *adj* irritabile

irritable bowel syndrome *n* sindrome *f* da colon irritabile

irritant /'ɪrɪtənt/ *n* sostanza *f* irritante; (fig: person) persona *f* irritante

irritate /'ɪrɪteɪt/ *vt* irritare

irritated /'ɪrɪteɪtɪd/ *adj* irritato, stizzito

irritating /'ɪrɪteɪtɪŋ/ *adj* irritante

irritation /ɪrɪ'teɪʃn/ *n* irritazione *f*

IRS *n abbr* Am (**Internal Revenue Service**) fisco *m*

is /ɪz/ ▶ BE

Islam /'ɪzlɑːm/ *n* Islam *m*

Islamic /ɪz'læmɪk/ *adj* islamico

Islamist /'ɪzləmɪst/ *n* (fundamentalist) estremista *mf* islamico (-a); (scholar) islamista *mf*

island /'aɪlənd/ *n* isola *f*; (in road) isola *f* spartitraffico

islander /'aɪləndə(r)/ *n* isolano, -a *mf*

island hopping /'aɪləndhɒpɪŋ/ *n* go ∼ ∼ andare di isola in isola

isle /aɪl/ *n* liter isola *f*

Isle of Man *n* l'isola *f* di Man

isobar /'aɪsəbɑː(r)/ *n* isobara *f*

isolate /'aɪsəleɪt/ *vt* isolare

isolated /'aɪsəleɪtɪd/ *adj* isolato

isolation /aɪsə'leɪʃn/ *n* isolamento *m*

isosceles /aɪ'sɒsəliːz/ *adj* isoscele

ISP *n abbr* (**Internet service provider**) Comput ISP *m*

Israel /'ɪzreɪl/ *n* Israele *m*

Israeli /ɪz'reɪlɪ/ *adj & n* israeliano, -a *mf*

issue /'ɪʃuː/ **1** *n* (outcome) risultato *m*; (of magazine) numero *m*; (of stamps etc) emissione *f*; (offspring) figli *mpl*; (matter, question) questione *f*; **at** ∼ in questione; **take** ∼ **with somebody** prendere posizione contro qualcuno **2** *vt* distribuire ⟨*supplies*⟩; rilasciare ⟨*passport*⟩; emettere ⟨*stamps, order*⟩; pubblicare ⟨*book*⟩; **be** ∼**d with something** ricevere qualcosa **3** *vi* ∼ **from** uscire da

isthmus /'ɪsməs/ *n* (pl **-muses**) istmo *m*

it /ɪt/ *pron* (direct object) lo *m*, la *f*; (indirect object) gli *m*, le *f*; **it's broken** è rotto/rotta; **will it be enough?** basterà?; **it's hot** fa caldo; **it's raining** piove; **it's me** sono io; **who is it?** chi è?; **it's two o'clock** sono le due; **I doubt it** ne dubito; **take it with you** prendilo con te; **give it a wipe** dagli una pulita

IT *n abbr* (**information technology**) informatica *f*

Italian /ɪ'tæljən/ *adj & n* italiano, -a *mf*; (language) italiano *m*

italic /ɪ'tælɪk/ *adj* in corsivo

italics /ɪ'tælɪks/ *npl* corsivo *msg*; **in** ∼ in corsivo

Italy /'ɪtəlɪ/ *n* Italia *f*

itch /ɪtʃ/ **1** *n* prurito *m* **2** *vi* avere prurito, prudere; **be** ∼**ing to** fam avere una voglia matta di

itchy /'ɪtʃɪ/ *adj* che prude; **my foot is** ∼ ho prurito al piede; **have** ∼ **feet** fig avere la terra che scotta sotto i piedi

item /'aɪtəm/ *n* articolo *m*; (on agenda, programme) punto *m*; (on invoice) voce *f*; ∼ [**of news**] notizia *f*

itemize /'aɪtəmaɪz/ *vt* dettagliare ⟨*bill*⟩

itinerant /aɪ'tɪnərənt/ *adj* itinerante

itinerary /aɪ'tɪnərərɪ/ *n* itinerario *m*

ITN *n abbr* Br (**independent television**) rete *f* televisiva britannica

its /ɪts/ *poss pron* suo *m*, sua *f*, suoi *mpl*, sue *fpl*; ∼ **mother/cage** sua madre/la sua gabbia

it's = it is, it has

itself /ɪt'self/ *pron* (reflexive) si; (emphatic) essa stessa; **the baby looked at** ∼ **in the mirror** il bambino si è guardato nello specchio; **by** ∼ **alone**, da solo; **the machine in** ∼ **is simple** la macchina di per sé è semplice

ITV *abbr* (**Independent Television**)

stazione *f* televisiva privata

IUD *n abbr* (**intrauterine device**) spirale *f*

IVF *n abbr* (**in vitro fertilization**) FIV *f*

ivory /'aɪvərɪ/ **1** *n* avorio *m*
2 *attrib* d'avorio

Ivory Coast *n* Costa *f* d'Avorio

ivory tower *n* fig torre *f* d'avorio

ivy /'aɪvɪ/ *n* edera *f*

Jj

j, J /dʒeɪ/ *n* (letter) j, J *f inv*

jab /dʒæb/ **1** *n* colpo *m* secco; (fam: injection) puntura *f*
2 *vt* (pt/pp **jabbed**) punzecchiare

jabber /'dʒæbə(r)/ *vi* borbottare

jack /dʒæk/ *n* Auto cric *m inv*; Teleph jack *m inv*; (in cards) fante *m*, jack *m inv*
■ **jack in** *vt* sl piantare ⟨job⟩
■ **jack up** *vt* Auto sollevare [con il cric]; fam aumentare di molto ⟨salary etc⟩

jackal /'dʒæk(ə)l/ *n* sciacallo *m*

jackboot /'dʒækbuːt/ *n* stivale *m* militare

jackdaw /'dʒækdɔː/ *n* taccola *f*

jacket /'dʒækɪt/ *n* giacca *f*; (of book) sopraccopertina *f*

jacket potato *n* patata *f* cotta al forno con la buccia

jack-in-the-box *n* scatola *f* a sorpresa contenente un pupazzo a molla

jackknife /'dʒæknaɪf/ **1** *n* coltello *m* a serramanico
2 *vi* sbandare finendo di traverso rispetto al rimorchio

jackpot /'dʒækpɒt/ *n* premio *m* (di una lotteria); **win the** ∼ vincere alla lotteria; **hit the** ∼ fig fare un colpo grosso

jackrabbit /'dʒækræbɪt/ *n* lepre *f* americana

jade /dʒeɪd/ **1** *n* giada *f*
2 *attrib* di giada

jaded /'dʒeɪdɪd/ *adj* spossato

jagged /'dʒægɪd/ *adj* dentellato

jail /dʒeɪl/ = GAOL

jailbird *n* avanzo *m* di galera

jailbreak *n* evasione *f*

jail sentence *n* condanna *f* al carcere

jalopy /dʒə'lɒpɪ/ *n* fam vecchia carretta *f*

jam¹ /dʒæm/ *n* marmellata *f*

jam² **1** *n* Auto ingorgo *m*; (fam: difficulty) guaio *m*

2 *vt* (pt/pp **jammed**) (cram) pigiare; disturbare ⟨broadcast⟩; inceppare ⟨mechanism, drawer etc⟩; **be** ∼**med** ⟨roads⟩ essere congestionato
3 *vi* ⟨mechanism⟩ incepparsi; ⟨window, drawer⟩ incastrarsi
■ **jam on** *vt* ∼ **on the brakes** inchiodare

Jamaica /dʒə'meɪkə/ *n* Giamaica *f*

Jamaican /dʒə'meɪkən/ *adj & n* giamaicano, -a *mf*

jam jar *n* barattolo *m* per la marmellata

jam-packed *adj* fam pieno zeppo

jampot *n* vasetto *m* per la marmellata

jangle /'dʒæŋgl/ **1** *vt* far squillare
2 *vi* squillare

janitor /'dʒænɪtə(r)/ *n* (caretaker) custode *m*; (in school) bidello, -a *mf*

January /'dʒænjʊərɪ/ *n* gennaio *m*

Japan /dʒə'pæn/ *n* Giappone *m*

Japanese /dʒæpə'niːz/ *adj & n* giapponese *mf*; (language) giapponese *m*

jar¹ /dʒɑː(r)/ *n* (glass) barattolo *m*

jar² *vi* (pt/pp **jarred**) ⟨sound⟩ stridere

jargon /'dʒɑːgən/ *n* gergo *m*

jarring /'dʒɑːrɪŋ/ *adj* stridente

jasmine /'dʒæsmɪn/ *n* gelsomino *m*

jaundice /'dʒɔːndɪs/ *n* itterizia *f*

jaundiced /'dʒɔːndɪst/ *adj* fig inacidito

jaunt /dʒɔːnt/ *n* gita *f*

jaunty /'dʒɔːntɪ/ *adj* (**-ier**, **-iest**) sbarazzino

javelin /'dʒævlɪn/ *n* giavellotto *m*

jaw /dʒɔː/ **1** *n* mascella *f*; (bone) mandibola *f*
2 *vi* fam ciarlare

jawbone /'dʒɔːbəʊn/ *n* Anat osso *m* mascellare

jawline *n* mento *m*

jay /dʒeɪ/ *n* ghiandaia *f*

jaywalker /'dʒeɪwɔːkə(r)/ *n* pedone *m* indisciplinato

jazz /dʒæz/ n jazz m
■ **jazz up** vt ravvivare
jazz band n complesso m di jazz
jazzy /'dʒæzɪ/ adj vistoso
jealous /'dʒeləs/ adj geloso
jealously /'dʒeləslɪ/ adv gelosamente
jealousy /'dʒeləsɪ/ n gelosia f
jeans /dʒiːnz/ npl [blue] jeans mpl
jeep /dʒiːp/ n jeep f inv
jeer /dʒɪə(r)/ ① n scherno m
② vi schernire; ∼ **at** prendersi gioco di
③ vt (boo) fischiare
jeering /'dʒɪərɪŋ/ n fischi mpl
jell /dʒel/ vi concretarsi
jellied /'dʒelɪd/ adj ⟨eels⟩ in gelatina
Jell-o® /'dʒel-ʊ/ n Am dolce m di gelatina
di frutta
jelly /'dʒelɪ/ n gelatina f
jelly baby n caramella f gommosa a
forma di pupazzetto
jelly bean n caramella f di gelatina di
frutta
jellyfish n medusa f
jemmy /'dʒemɪ/ n piede m di porco
jeopardize /'dʒepədaɪz/ vt mettere in
pericolo
jeopardy /'dʒepədɪ/ n **in** ∼ in pericolo
jerk /dʒɜːk/ ① n scatto m, scossa f
② vt scattare
③ vi sobbalzare; ⟨limb, muscle⟩ muoversi
a scatti
jerkily /'dʒɜːkɪlɪ/ adv a scatti
jerkin /'dʒɜːkɪn/ n gilè m inv
jerky /'dʒɜːkɪ/ adj traballante
jerry-built /'dʒerɪbɪlt/ adj pej costruito
alla bell'e meglio
jersey /'dʒɜːzɪ/ n maglia f; Sport maglietta
f; (fabric) jersey m
Jerusalem /dʒəˈruːsələm/ n
Gerusalemme f
jest /dʒest/ ① n scherzo m; **in** ∼ per
scherzo
② vi scherzare
jester /'dʒestə(r)/ n buffone m
Jesuit /'dʒezjʊɪt/ ① n gesuita m
② adj gesuitico
Jesus /'dʒiːzəs/ n Gesù m
jet¹ /dʒet/ n (stone) giaietto m
jet² n (of water) getto m; (nozzle) becco m;
(plane) aviogetto m, jet m inv
jet-black adj nero ebano
jet engine n motore m a reazione
jet fighter n caccia m inv a reazione
jetfoil n aliscafo m
jet lag n scombussolamento m da fuso
orario
jet-lagged adj be ∼ soffrire di jet lag
jet-propelled adj a reazione

jet propulsion n propulsione f a getto
jet setter n be a ∼ appartenere al jet
set
jet ski n moto m d'acqua
jet-skier n persona m che fa moto
d'acqua
jet-skiing n moto m d'acqua
jettison /'dʒetɪsn/ vt gettare a mare; fig
abbandonare
jetty /'dʒetɪ/ n molo m
Jew /dʒuː/ n ebreo m
jewel /'dʒuːəl/ n gioiello m
jewelled /'dʒuːəld/ adj ornato di pietre
preziose
jeweller /'dʒuːələ(r)/ n gioielliere m; ∼'s
[shop] gioielleria f
jewellery /'dʒuːəlrɪ/ n gioielli mpl
Jewess /'dʒuːɪs/ n ebrea f
Jewish /'dʒuːɪʃ/ adj ebreo
Jew's harp n Mus scacciapensieri m inv
jib /dʒɪb/ vi (pt/pp **jibbed**) fig mostrarsi
riluttante (**at** a)
jibe /dʒaɪb/ n ▸ GIBE
jiffy /'dʒɪfɪ/ n fam **in a** ∼ in un batter
d'occhio
Jiffy bag® n busta f imbottita
jig /dʒɪg/ n Mus giga f (danza popolare)
jiggle /'dʒɪg(ə)l/ vt scuotere
jigsaw /'dʒɪgsɔː/ n ∼ **[puzzle]** puzzle m
inv
jilt /dʒɪlt/ vt piantare
jingle /'dʒɪŋgl/ ① n (rhyme) canzoncina f
pubblicitaria
② vi tintinnare
③ vt far tintinnare
jingoist /'dʒɪŋgəʊɪst/ n Pol sciovinista mf
jingoistic /dʒɪŋgəʊˈɪstɪk/ adj Pol
sciovinistico
jinx /dʒɪŋks/ n fam (person) iettatore, -trice
mf; it's got a ∼ on it è iellato
jinxed /dʒɪŋkst/ adj be ∼ essere iellato
jitters /'dʒɪtəz/ npl fam have the ∼ aver
una gran fifa
jittery /'dʒɪtərɪ/ adj fam in preda alla fifa
jive /dʒaɪv/ n (Am fam: talk) storie fpl
Jnr abbr **junior**
job /dʒɒb/ n lavoro m; this is going to be
quite a ∼ fam [questa] non sarà
un'impresa facile; it's a good ∼ that...
meno male che...
jobcentre n ufficio m statale di
collocamento
job creation scheme n Br
programma m di creazione di posti di
lavoro
job description n mansionario m
job-hunting n ricerca f impiego
jobless /'dʒɒblɪs/ adj senza lavoro

job lot n (at auction) insieme m di oggetti disparati

job satisfaction n soddisfazione f nel lavoro

job security n sicurezza f di impiego

job seeker n persona f che cerca lavoro

job seeker's allowance n Br indennità f di disoccupazione

job-share ① n (position) posto m condiviso
② attrib ‹scheme› di condivisione del posto di lavoro

job-sharing n job sharing m inv

jockey /'dʒɒkɪ/ n fantino m

jockey shorts npl boxer mpl

jockstrap n sospensorio m

jocular /'dʒɒkjʊlə(r)/ adj scherzoso

jocularly /'dʒɒkjʊləlɪ/ adv scherzosamente

jodhpurs /'dʒɒdpəz/ npl calzoni mpl alla cavallerizza

Joe Bloggs /dʒəʊ'blɒgz/ n l'uomo qualunque

jog /dʒɒg/ ① n colpetto m; **at a ∼** in un balzo; Sport **go for a ∼** andare a fare jogging
② vt (pt/pp **jogged**) (hit) urtare; **∼ sb's memory** farlo ritornare in mente a qualcuno
③ vi Sport fare jogging
■ **jog along** vi fig tirare avanti

jogger /dʒɒgə(r)/ n persona f che fa jogging

jogging /'dʒɒgɪŋ/ n jogging m

john /dʒɒn/ n (Am fam: toilet) gabinetto m

John Bull n il tipico inglese

John Doe n Am uomo m non identificato

join /dʒɔɪn/ ① n giuntura f
② vt raggiungere, unire; raggiungere ‹person›; (become member of) iscriversi a; entrare in ‹firm›
③ vi ‹roads› congiungersi
■ **join in** vi partecipare
■ **join up** ① vi Mil arruolarsi
② vt unire
■ **join up with** vt (meet) raggiungere ‹friends›; congiungersi a ‹road; river›

joiner /'dʒɔɪnə(r)/ n falegname m

joint /dʒɔɪnt/ ① adj comune
② n articolazione f; (in wood, brickwork) giuntura f; Culin arrosto m; (fam: bar) bettola f; (sl: drug) spinello m

joint account n conto m [corrente] comune

joint agreement n accordo m collettivo

jointed /'dʒɔɪntɪd/ adj Culin ‹chicken› tagliato a pezzi; ‹doll, puppet› snodabile; ‹rod, pole› smontabile

joint effort n collaborazione f

joint honours npl Br Univ laurea f in due discipline

jointly /'dʒɔɪntlɪ/ adv unitamente

joint owner n comproprietario, -a mf

joint venture n joint venture f inv

joist /dʒɔɪst/ n travetto m

joke /dʒəʊk/ ① n (trick) scherzo m; (funny story) barzelletta f
② vi scherzare

joker /'dʒəʊkə(r)/ n burlone, -a mf; (in cards) jolly m inv

joking /'dʒəʊkɪŋ/ n ∼ **apart** scherzi a parte

jokingly /'dʒəʊkɪŋlɪ/ adv per scherzo

jollity /'dʒɒlətɪ/ n allegria f

jolly /'dʒɒlɪ/ ① adj (-ier, -iest) allegro
② adv fam molto

Jolly Roger /'rɒdʒə(r)/ n bandiera f dei pirati

jolt /dʒəʊlt/ ① n scossa f, sobbalzo m
② vt far sobbalzare
③ vi sobbalzare

Jordan /'dʒɔːdn/ n Giordania f; (river) Giordano m

Jordanian /dʒɔː'deɪnɪən/ adj & n giordano, -a mf

joss stick /'dʒɒs/ n bastoncino m d'incenso

jostle /'dʒɒsl/ vt spingere

jot /dʒɒt/ n nulla f
■ **jot down** vt (pt/pp **jotted**) annotare

jotter /'dʒɒtə(r)/ n taccuino m; (with a spine) quaderno m

jottings /'dʒɒtɪŋz/ npl annotazioni fpl

journal /'dʒɜːnl/ n giornale m; (diary) diario m

journalese /dʒɜːnə'liːz/ n gergo m giornalistico

journalism /'dʒɜːnəlɪzm/ n giornalismo m

journalist /'dʒɜːnəlɪst/ n giornalista mf

journey /'dʒɜːnɪ/ ① n viaggio m
② vi viaggiare

jovial /'dʒəʊvɪəl/ adj gioviale

jowl /dʒaʊl/ n (jaw) mascella f; (fleshy fold) guancia f; **cheek by ∼ with somebody** fianco a fianco con qualcuno

joy /dʒɔɪ/ n gioia f

joyful /'dʒɔɪfʊl/ adj gioioso

joyfully /'dʒɔɪfʊlɪ/ adv con gioia

joyless /'dʒɔɪlɪs/ adj ‹occasion› triste; ‹marriage› infelice

joypad n Comput joypad m

joyride n fam giro m con una macchina rubata

joyrider n fam persona f che ruba una macchina per andare a fare un giro

joyriding n giri mpl su una macchina rubata

joystick *n* Comput joystick *m inv*

JP *n abbr* Br (**Justice of the Peace**) giudice *m* di pace

Jr *abbr* **junior**

jubilant /'dʒu:bɪlənt/ *adj* giubilante

jubilation /dʒu:bɪ'leɪʃn/ *n* giubilo *m*

jubilee /'dʒu:bɪli:/ *n* giubileo *m*

Judaism /'dʒu:deɪɪzm/ *n* giudaismo *m*

judder /'dʒʌdə(r)/ *vi* vibrare violentemente

judge /dʒʌdʒ/ **1** *n* giudice *m*
2 *vt* giudicare; (estimate) valutare; (consider) ritenere
3 *vi* giudicare (**by** da)

judgement, judgment /'dʒʌdʒmənt/ *n* giudizio *m*; Jur sentenza *f*

judicial /dʒu:'dɪʃl/ *adj* giudiziario

judiciary /dʒu:'dɪʃərɪ/ *n* magistratura *f*

judicious /dʒu:'dɪʃəs/ *adj* giudizioso

judo /'dʒu:dəʊ/ *n* judo *m*

jug /dʒʌg/ *n* brocca *f*; (small) bricco *m*

juggernaut /'dʒʌgənɔ:t/ *n* fam grosso autotreno *m*

juggle /'dʒʌgl/ *vi* fare giochi di destrezza

juggler /'dʒʌglə(r)/ *n* giocoliere, -a *mf*

jugular /'dʒʌgjʊlə(r)/ *n* giugulare *f*; **go straight for the ~** fig colpire nel punto debole

juice /dʒu:s/ *n* succo *m*; **~ extractor** *n* spremiagrumi *m inv* elettrico

juicy /'dʒu:sɪ/ *adj* (**-ier, -iest**) succoso; fam ‹story› piccante

ju-jitsu /dʒju:'dʒɪtsu:/ *n* jujitsu *m*

jukebox /'dʒu:kbɒks/ *n* juke-box *m inv*

July /dʒʊ'laɪ/ *n* luglio *m*

jumble /'dʒʌmbl/ **1** *n* accozzaglia *f*
2 *vt* ~ **[up]** mischiare

jumble sale *n* vendita *f* di beneficenza

jumbo /'dʒʌmbəʊ/ *n* ~ **[jet]** jumbo jet *m inv*

jump /dʒʌmp/ **1** *n* salto *m*; (in prices) balzo *m*; (in horse racing) ostacolo *m*
2 *vi* saltare; (with fright) sussultare; ‹prices› salire rapidamente; ~ **to conclusions** saltare alle conclusioni
3 *vt* saltare; ~ **the gun** fig precipitarsi; ~ **the queue** non rispettare la fila
■ **jump at** *vt* fig accettare con entusiasmo ‹offer›
■ **jump back** *vi* fare un salto indietro
■ **jump down** *vt* ~ **down sb's throat** saltare addosso a qualcuno
■ **jump in** *vi* (to vehicle) saltar su
■ **jump on** *vt* saltare su ‹bus, train, bike, horse›; (attack) aggredire ‹somebody›
■ **jump out** *vi* saltare fuori; ~ **out of something** saltare giù da qualcosa ‹window, train, bed›
■ **jump up** *vi* rizzarsi in piedi

jumped-up /dʒʌmpt'ʌp/ *adj* montato

jumper /'dʒʌmpə(r)/ *n* (sweater) golf *m inv*

jump jet *n* aeroplano *m* a decollo e atterraggio verticali

jump leads *npl* cavi *mpl* per batteria

jump-start *vt* far partire con i cavi da batteria

jumpsuit *n* tuta *f*

jumpy /'dʒʌmpɪ/ *adj* nervoso

junction /'dʒʌŋkʃn/ *n* (of roads) incrocio *m*; Rail nodo *m* ferroviario

juncture /'dʒʌŋktʃə(r)/ *n* **at this ~** a questo punto

June /dʒu:n/ *n* giugno *m*

Jungian /'jʊŋɪən/ *adj* junghiano

jungle /'dʒʌŋgl/ *n* giungla *f*

junior /'dʒu:nɪə(r)/ **1** *adj* giovane; (in rank) subalterno; Sport junior *inv*
2 *n* the ~**s** *pl* Sch i più giovani

junior doctor *n* assistente *mf* ospedaliero, -a

junior high school *n* Am scuola *f* media inferiore

junior minister *n* sottosegretario *m*

junior school *n* scuola *f* elementare

juniper /'dʒu:nɪpə(r)/ *n* ginepro *m*

junk /dʒʌŋk/ *n* cianfrusaglie *fpl*

junk food *n* fam cibo *m* poco sano, porcherie *fpl*

junkie /'dʒʌŋkɪ/ *n* sl tossico, -a *mf*

junk mail *n* posta *f* spazzatura

junk shop *n* negozio *m* di rigattiere

junkyard *n* (for scrap) rottamaio *m*; (for old cars) cimitero *m* delle macchine

junta /'dʒʌntə/ *n* giunta *f* militare

Jupiter /'dʒu:pɪtə(r)/ *n* Giove *m*

jurisdiction /dʒʊərɪs'dɪkʃn/ *n* giurisdizione *f*

jurisprudence /dʒʊrɪs'pru:dəns/ *n* giurisprudenza *f*

jurist /'dʒʊərɪst/ *n* giurista *mf*

juror /'dʒʊərə(r)/ *n* giurato, -a *mf*

jury /'dʒʊərɪ/ *n* giuria *f*

jury box *n* banco *m* dei giurati

jury duty *n* esp. Am = JURY SERVICE

jury service *n* **do ~ ~** far parte di una giuria popolare

just /dʒʌst/ **1** *adj* giusto
2 *adv* (barely) appena; (simply) solo; (exactly) esattamente; ~ **as tall** altrettanto alto; ~ **as I was leaving** proprio quando stavo andando via; **I've ~ seen her** l'ho appena vista; **it's ~ as well** meno male; ~ **at that moment** proprio in quel momento; ~ **listen!** almeno ascolta!; **I'm ~ going** sto andando proprio ora

justice /'dʒʌstɪs/ *n* giustizia *f*; **do ~ to** rendere giustizia a

Justice Department *n* Am ministero *m* di Grazia e Giustizia

Justice of the Peace *n* giudice *m* di pace

justifiable /dʒʌstɪ'faɪəbl/ *adj* giustificabile

justifiably /dʒʌstɪ'faɪəblɪ/ *adv* in modo giustificato

justification /dʒʌstɪfɪ'keɪʃn/ *n* giustificazione *f*

justified /'dʒʌstɪfaɪd/ *adj* ⟨action⟩ motivato

justify /'dʒʌstɪfaɪ/ *vt* (*pt/pp* **-ied**) giustificare

justly /'dʒʌstlɪ/ *adv* giustamente

justness /'dʒʌstnɪs/ *n* (of decision) giustezza *f*; (of claim, request) legittimità *f*

jut /dʒʌt/ *vi* (*pt/pp* **jutted**) ~ **out** sporgere

jute /dʒuːt/ *n* iuta *f*

juvenile /'dʒuːvənaɪl/ ① *adj* giovanile; (childish) infantile; (for the young) per i giovani
② *n* giovane *mf*

juvenile crime *n* delinquenza *f* minorile

juvenile delinquency *n* delinquenza *f* minorile

juvenile delinquent *n* delinquente *mf* minorile

juvenile offender *n* Jur imputato, -a *mf* minorenne

juxtapose /dʒʌkstə'pəʊz/ *vt* giustapporre

Kk

k¹, **K** /keɪ/ *n* (letter) k, K *f inv*

K² *abbr* (**kilo**) k; *abbr* (**kilobyte**) KB, Kbyte *m inv*; *abbr* **thousand pounds**; **he earns £50 K** guadagna 50 mila sterline

kale /keɪl/, **curly kale** *n* cavolo *m* riccio

kaleidoscope /kə'laɪdəskəʊp/ *n* caleidoscopio *m*

kangaroo /kæŋgə'ruː/ *n* canguro *m*

kaput /kə'pʊt/ *adj* fam kaputt *inv*

karaoke /kærɪ'əʊkɪ/ *n* karaoke *m inv*

karaoke machine *n* apparecchio *m* per il karaoke

karate /kə'rɑːtɪ/ *n* karatè *m*

kart /kɑːt/ *n* kart *m inv*

Kashmir /kæʃ'mɪə(r)/ *n* Kashmir *m*

Kashmiri /kæʃ'mɪərɪ/ ① *adj* del Kashmir
② *n* nativo, -a *mf* del Kashmir

kayak /'kaɪæk/ *n* kayak *m inv*

Kazakhstan /kæzək'stɑːn/ *n* Kazakistan *m*

KB *n abbr* (**kilobyte**) KB, Kbyte *m inv*

kebab /kɪ'bæb/ *n* Culin spiedino *m* di carne

kedgeree /'kedʒəriː/ *n* Br piatto *m* indiano a base di pesce, riso e uova

keel /kiːl/ *n* chiglia *f*
■ **keel over** *vi* capovolgersi

keen /kiːn/ *adj* (intense) acuto; ⟨interest⟩ vivo; ⟨eager⟩ entusiastico; ⟨competition⟩ feroce; ⟨wind, knife⟩ tagliente; ~ **on** entusiasta di; **she's** ~ **on him** le piace molto; **be** ~ **to do something** avere voglia di fare qualcosa

keenly /'kiːnlɪ/ *adv* intensamente

keenness /'kiːnnɪs/ *n* entusiasmo *m*

keep /kiːp/ ① *n* (maintenance) mantenimento *m*; (of castle) maschio *m*; **for** ~**s** per sempre
② *vt* (*pt/pp* **kept**) tenere; (not throw away) conservare; (detain) trattenere; mantenere ⟨family, promise⟩; tenere ⟨shop⟩; allevare ⟨animals⟩; rispettare ⟨law, rules⟩; ~ **something hot** tenere qualcosa in caldo; ~ **somebody waiting** far aspettare qualcuno; ~ **something to oneself** tenere qualcosa per sé;
③ *vi* (remain) rimanere; ⟨food⟩ conservarsi; ~ **calm** rimanere calmo; ~ **left/right** tenere la sinistra/la destra; ~ **[on] doing something** continuare a fare qualcosa
■ **keep at** *vt* (persevere with) ~ **at it!** non mollare!
■ **keep away** ① *vi* non avvicinarsi, stare alla larga
② *vt* tenere lontano
■ **keep away from** *vt* non avvicinarsi a ⟨fire⟩; stare alla larga da ⟨somebody⟩; ~ **somebody away from something** tener qualcuno lontano da qualcosa
■ **keep back** ① *vt* trattenere ⟨person⟩; ~ **something back from somebody** tenere nascosto qualcosa a qualcuno
② *vi* tenersi indietro
■ **keep down** ① *vi* star giù
② *vt* mandar giù ⟨food⟩; mantenere basso ⟨prices, inflation etc⟩; ~ **one's voice down** non alzare la voce
■ **keep from** *vt* ~ **somebody from doing something** impedire a qualcuno di fare qualcosa; ~ **somebody from** impedire a qualcuno di ⟨falling⟩; ~ **somebody from their work** distogliere qualcuno dal lavoro;

$\sim$ **something from somebody** tenere nascosto qualcosa a qualcuno; $\sim$ **the truth from somebody** nascondere la verità a qualcuno

■ **keep in** *vt* (in school) trattenere oltre l'orario per punizione; reprimere ⟨*indignation, anger etc*⟩

■ **keep in with** *vt* mantenersi in buoni rapporti con

■ **keep off** *vt* (avoid) astenersi da ⟨*cigarettes, chocolate etc*⟩; evitare ⟨*delicate subject*⟩

■ **keep on** ① *vi* (continue one's journey) proseguire; fam assillare (**at somebody** qualcuno)

② *vt* non togliersi ⟨*coat, hat*⟩; tenere ⟨*employee*⟩

■ **keep out** ① *vt* tenere fuori; $\sim$ **out!** alla larga!

② *vt* non far entrare ⟨*person, animal*⟩

■ **keep out of** *vt* ⟨*person*⟩ non entrare in ⟨*place*⟩; tenersi fuori da ⟨*argument*⟩; $\sim$ **somebody out of** tenere qualcuno alla larga da ⟨*place*⟩; $\sim$ **me out of this!** lasciamene fuori!

■ **keep to** *vt* non deviare da ⟨*path, subject*⟩; $\sim$ **something to oneself** tenere qualcosa per sé

■ **keep up** ① *vi* ⟨*remain level*⟩ stare al passo; ⟨*rain, good weather*⟩ mantenersi

② *vt* (continue) continuare; (prevent from going to bed) tenere alzato; mantenere alto ⟨*prices*⟩; tener su ⟨*trousers*⟩

■ **keep up with** *vt* (in race) stare al passo con ⟨*person, fashion*⟩; ⟨*wages*⟩ seguire il corso di ⟨*inflation*⟩

keeper /'ki:pə(r)/ *n* custode *mf*

keep-fit *n* ginnastica *f*

keeping /'ki:pɪŋ/ *n* custodia *f*; **be in** $\sim$ **with** essere in armonia con

keepsake /'ki:pseɪk/ *n* ricordo *m*

keg /keg/ *n* barilotto *m*

kelp /kelp/ *n* laminaria *f*, fuco *m*

kennel /'kenl/ *n* canile *m*; $\sim$**s** *pl* (boarding) canile *m*; (breeding) allevamento *m* di cani

Kenya /'kenjə/ *n* Kenya *m*

Kenyan /'kenjən/ *adj & n* keniota *mf*

kept /kept/ ▶ KEEP

kerb /kɜ:b/ *n* bordo *m* del marciapiede

kernel /'kɜ:nl/ *n* nocciolo *m*

kerosene /'kerəsi:n/ *n* Am cherosene *m*

kestrel /'kestrəl/ *n* gheppio *m*

ketchup /'ketʃʌp/ *n* ketchup *m*

kettle /'ket(ə)l/ *n* bollitore *m*; **put the** $\sim$ **on** mettere l'acqua a bollire

kettledrum /'ket(ə)ldrʌm/ *n* timpano *m*

key /ki:/ ① *n* also Mus chiave *f*; (of piano, typewriter) tasto *m*

② *vt* $\sim$ **[in]** digitare ⟨*character*⟩; **could you** $\sim$ **this?** puoi battere questo?

keyboard *n* Comput, Mus tastiera *f*

keyboarder *n* tastierista *mf*

keyboard player *n* tastierista *mf*

keyboards *npl* Mus tastiere *fpl*

keyed-up /ki:d'ʌp/ *adj* (excited) teso; (anxious) estremamente agitato; (ready to act) psicologicamente preparato

keyhole *n* buco *m* della serratura

keyhole surgery *n* chirurgia *f* endoscopica

keynote *n* Mus tonica *f*; (main theme) tema *m* principale

keynote speech *n* discorso *m* programmatico

keypad *n* Comput tastierino *m* numerico

keyring *n* portachiavi *m inv*

key signature *n* Mus armatura *f* di chiave

keystroke *n* Comput keystroke *m inv*

keyword *n* parola *f* chiave

key worker *n* chi lavora in settori, come l'insegnamento, la sanità, la sicurezza, ritenuti essenziali per la vita di una comunità

kg *abbr* (**kilogram**) kg

khaki /'kɑ:kɪ/ ① *adj* cachi *inv*

② *n* cachi *m*

kibbutz /ki'bʊts/ *n* (pl **-es** or **-im**) kibbutz *m inv*

kibosh /'kaɪbɒʃ/ *n* fam **put the** $\sim$ **on something** mandare all'aria qualcosa

kick /kɪk/ ① *n* calcio *m*; (fam: thrill) piacere *m*; **for** $\sim$**s** fam per spasso; **get a** $\sim$ **out of something** trovare un piacere incredibile in qualcosa

② *vt* dar calci a; $\sim$ **the bucket** fam crepare

③ *vi* ⟨*animal*⟩; scalciare; ⟨*person*⟩ dare calci

■ **kick around** *vi* fam ① essere in giro

② *vt* buttar giù ⟨*idea*⟩

■ **kick in** *vt* sfondare a calci ⟨*door*⟩

■ **kick off** *vi* Sport dare il calcio d'inizio; fam iniziare

■ **kick out** *vt* (fam: of school, club etc) sbatter fuori

■ **kick up** *vt* $\sim$ **up a row** fare una scenata

kickback /'kɪkbæk/ *n* fam tangente *f*

kick-off *n* Sport calcio *m* d'inizio; **for a** $\sim$ fam tanto per cominciare

kick-start *vt* mettere in moto ⟨*motorbike*⟩; rilanciare ⟨*economy*⟩

kid /kɪd/ ① *n* capretto *m*; (fam; child) ragazzino, -a *mf*

② *vt* (pt/pp **kidded**) fam prendere in giro.

③ *vi* fam scherzare

kid gloves *npl* guanti *mpl* di capretto; **handle somebody with** $\sim$ $\sim$ trattare qualcuno con i guanti

kidnap /'kɪdnæp/ *vt* (pt/pp **-napped**) rapire, sequestrare

kidnapper /'kɪdnæpə(r)/ *n* sequestratore, -trice *mf*, rapitore, -trice *mf*

k

kidnapping /'kɪdnæpɪŋ/ n rapimento m, sequestro m [di persona]

kidney /'kɪdnɪ/ n rene m; Culin rognone m

kidney bean n fagiolo m comune

kidney dialysis n dialisi f

kidney failure n collasso m renale

kidney machine n rene m artificiale

kidney-shaped /'kɪdnɪʃeɪpt/ adj a forma di fagiolo

kidney stone n calcolo m renale

kill /kɪl/ vt uccidere; fig metter fine a; ammazzare ⟨time⟩
∎ **kill off** vt eliminare ⟨people⟩; distruggere ⟨plants, insects⟩

killer /'kɪlə(r)/ n assassino, -a mf; **it was a real ~** fig è stato micidiale

killer instinct n istinto m di uccidere; fig spietatezza f

killer whale n orca f

killing /'kɪlɪŋ/ n uccisione f; (murder) omicidio m

killjoy /'kɪldʒɔɪ/ n guastafeste mf inv

kiln /kɪln/ n fornace f

kilo /'kiːləʊ/ n chilo m

kilobyte n kilobyte m inv

kilogram n chilogrammo m

kilohertz n chilohertz m inv

kilometre n chilometro m

kilowatt n chilowatt m inv

kilt /kɪlt/ n kilt m inv (gonnellino degli scozzesi)

kimono /kɪ'məʊnəʊ/ n kimono m inv, chimono m inv

kin /kɪn/ n congiunti mpl; **next of ~** parente m stretto

kind¹ /kaɪnd/ n genere m, specie f; (brand, type) tipo m; **what ~ of car?** che tipo di macchina?; **~ of** fam alquanto; **two of a ~** due della stessa specie

kind² adj gentile, buono; **~ to animals** amante degli animali; **~ regards** cordiali saluti

kindergarten /'kɪndəgɑːtn/ n asilo m infantile

kind-hearted /-'hɑːtɪd/ adj ⟨person⟩ di [buon] cuore

kindle /'kɪndl/ vt accendere

kindly /'kaɪndlɪ/ **1** adj -ier, -iest benevolo
2 adv gentilmente; (if you please) per favore

kindness /'kaɪndnɪs/ n gentilezza f

kindred /'kɪndrɪd/ adj **she's a ~ spirit** è la mia/sua/tua anima gemella

kinetic /kɪ'netɪk/ adj cinetico

kinetics /kɪ'netɪks/ n cinetica f

king /kɪŋ/ n re m inv

kingdom /'kɪŋdəm/ n regno m

kingfisher /'kɪŋfɪʃə(r)/ n martin m inv pescatore

kingly /'kɪŋlɪ/ adj also fig regale

king-sized /'kɪŋsaɪzd/ adj ⟨cigarette⟩ king-size inv, lungo; ⟨bed⟩ matrimoniale grande

kink /kɪŋk/ n attorcigliamento m

kinky /'kɪŋkɪ/ adj fam bizzarro

kinship /'kɪnʃɪp/ n (blood relationship) parentela f; (empathy) affinità f

kiosk /'kiːɒsk/ n chiosco m; Teleph cabina f telefonica

kip /kɪp/ **1** n fam pisolino m; **have a ~** schiacciare un pisolino
2 vi (pt/pp **kipped**) fam dormire

kipper /'kɪpə(r)/ n aringa f affumicata

kirk /kɜːk/ n (Scottish) chiesa f

kiss /kɪs/ **1** n bacio m
2 vt baciare
3 vi baciarsi

kiss of death n colpo m di grazia

kiss of life n respirazione f bocca a bocca; **give somebody the ~** fare la respirazione bocca a bocca a qualcuno

kissogram /'kɪsəgræm/ n servizio m commerciale in cui un messaggio di auguri viene scherzosamente recapitato con un bacio da una ragazza in abiti succinti

kit /kɪt/ **1** n equipaggiamento m, kit m inv; (tools) attrezzi mpl; (construction kit) pezzi mpl da montare, kit m inv
2 vt (pt/pp **kitted**) **~ out** equipaggiare

kitbag /'kɪtbæg/ n sacco m a spalla

kitchen /'kɪtʃɪn/ **1** n cucina f
2 attrib di cucina

kitchenette /kɪtʃɪ'net/ n cucinino m

kitchen foil n carta f di alluminio

kitchen garden n orto m

kitchen paper n carta f da cucina

kitchen roll n Scottex® m inv

kitchen scales npl bilancia f da cucina

kitchen sink n lavello m; **everything bar the ~** fig proprio tutto quanto

kitchen-sink drama n teatro m neorealista

kitchen towel n Scottex® m inv

kitchen unit n elemento m componibile da cucina

kitchenware n (crockery) stoviglie fpl; (implements) utensili mpl da cucina

kite /kaɪt/ n aquilone m

kitemark /'kaɪtmɑːk/ n Br marchio m di conformità alle norme britanniche

kith /kɪθ/ n **~ and kin** amici e parenti mpl

kitsch /kɪtʃ/ n kitsch m inv

kitten /'kɪtn/ n gattino m

kitty /'kɪtɪ/ n (money) cassa f comune

kiwi /'ki:wi:/ n Zool kiwi m inv
kiwi fruit n kiwi m inv
kleptomania /kleptə'meɪnɪə/ n cleptomania f
kleptomaniac /kleptə'meɪnɪæk/ n cleptomane mf
km abbr (**kilometre**) km
kmh abbr (**kilometres per hour**) km/h
knack /næk/ n tecnica f; **have the ~ for doing something** avere la capacità di fare qualcosa
knapsack /'næpsæk/ n sacco m da montagna
knave /neɪv/ n (in cards) fante m; (rogue) furfante m
knead /ni:d/ vt impastare
knee /ni:/ n ginocchio m; **go down on one's ~s to somebody** inginocchiarsi davanti qualcuno
kneecap /'ni:kæp/ n rotula f
knee-deep adj **the water was ~** l'acqua arrivava alle ginocchia
kneel /ni:l/ vi (pt/pp **knelt**) **~ [down]** inginocchiarsi; **be ~ing** essere inginocchiato
knee-length adj ⟨boots⟩ alto; ⟨skirt⟩ al ginocchio; ⟨socks⟩ lungo
knee-pad n ginocchiera f
knees-up /'ni:zʌp/ n Br fam festa f
knell /nel/ n campana f a morto; **sound the death ~ for something** segnare la fine di qualcosa
knelt /nelt/ ▶ KNEEL
knew /nju:/ ▶ KNOW
knickerbocker glory /nɪkəbɒkə'glɔːrɪ/ n coppa f [gelato] gigante
knickers /'nɪkəz/ npl mutandine fpl
knick-knacks /'nɪknæks/ npl ninnoli mpl
knife /naɪf/ **1** n (pl **knives**) coltello m **2** vt fam accoltellare
knife-edge n **be on a ~** ⟨person⟩ trovarsi sul filo del rasoio; ⟨negotiations⟩ essere appeso a un filo
knifepoint n **at ~** sotto la minaccia di un coltello
knife sharpener n affilacoltelli m inv
knight /naɪt/ **1** n cavaliere m; (in chess) cavallo m **2** vt nominare cavaliere
knighthood /'naɪthʊd/ n **receive a ~** ricevere il titolo di cavaliere
knit /nɪt/ vt/i (pt/pp **knitted**) lavorare a maglia; **~ one, purl one** un diritto, un rovescio; **~ one's brow** aggrottare le sopracciglia
knitted /'nɪtɪd/ adj lavorato a maglia
knitting /'nɪtɪŋ/ n lavorare m a maglia; (product) lavoro m a maglia
knitting needle n ferro m da calza

knitwear /'nɪtweə(r)/ n maglieria f
knives /naɪvz/ npl ▶ KNIFE
knob /nɒb/ n pomello m; (of stick) pomo m; (of butter) noce f
knobbly /'nɒblɪ/ adj nodoso; (bony) spigoloso
knock /nɒk/ **1** n colpo m; **there was a ~ at the door** hanno bussato alla porta **2** vt bussare a ⟨door⟩; (fam: criticize) denigrare; **~ a hole in something** fare un buco in qualcosa; **~ one's head** battere la testa (**on** contro) **3** vi (at door) bussare
■ **knock about 1** vt malmenare **2** vi fam girovagare
■ **knock back** vt (fam: drink quickly) buttar giù tutto d'un fiato
■ **knock down** vt far cadere; (with fist) stendere con un pugno; (in car) investire; (demolish) abbattere; (fam: reduce) ribassare ⟨price⟩
■ **knock off 1** vt (fam: steal) fregare; (fam: complete quickly) fare alla bell'e meglio **2** vi (fam: cease work) staccare
■ **knock out** vt eliminare; (make unconscious) mettere K.O.; (fam: anaesthetize) addormentare
■ **knock over** vt rovesciare; (in car) investire
■ **knock up** vt fam (prepare quickly) buttare giù; (sl: make pregnant) mettere incinta
knockabout n Sport **have a ~** palleggiare
knock-down furniture n mobili mpl scomponibili
knock-down price n prezzo m stracciato
knocker /'nɒkə(r)/ n battente m; (critic) denigratore, -trice mf
knocking /'nɒkɪŋ/ n (on door) colpi mpl; Auto battito m in testa
knocking-off time /nɒkɪŋ'ɒf/ n **~ ~ is five o'clock** si stacca alle cinque
knock-kneed /-'ni:d/ adj con gambe storte
knock-on effect n implicazioni fpl
knock-out n knock-out m inv; **be a ~** fig essere uno schianto
knoll /nəʊl/ n collinetta f
knot /nɒt/ **1** n nodo m; **to tie the ~** fam convolare a giuste nozze **2** vt (pt/pp **knotted**) annodare; Br fam **get ~ted!** vai a farti friggere!
knotty /'nɒtɪ/ adj (**-ier**, **-iest**) fam spinoso
know /nəʊ/ **1** vt (pt **knew**, pp **known**) sapere; conoscere ⟨person, place⟩; (recognize) riconoscere; **get to ~ somebody** conoscere qualcuno; **~ how to swim** sapere nuotare; **~ right from wrong** saper distinguere il bene dal male **2** vi sapere; **did you ~ about this?** lo sapevi?

3 *n* **in the** ∼ fam al corrente
■ **know of** *vt* conoscere; **not that I** ∼ **of** non che io sappia
know-all *n* fam sapientone, -a *mf*
know-how *n* know-how *m inv*
knowing /'nəʊɪŋ/ *adj* d'intesa
knowingly /'nəʊɪŋlɪ/ *adv* (intentionally) consapevolmente; ⟨*smile etc*⟩ con un aria d'intesa
knowledge /'nɒlɪdʒ/ *n* conoscenza *f*
knowledgeable, **knowledgable** /'nɒlɪdʒəbl/ *adj* ben informato
known /nəʊn/ **1** ▶ KNOW
2 *adj* noto
knuckle /'nʌkl/ *n* nocca *f*
■ **knuckle down** *vi* darci sotto (**to** con)
■ **knuckle under** *vi* sottomettersi
knuckle-duster *n* tirapugni *m inv*
koala [bear] /kəʊ'ɑːlə/ *n* koala *m inv*
Koran /kə'rɑːn/ *n* Corano *m*
Korea /kə'rɪə/ *n* Corea *f*
Korean /kə'rɪən/ *adj* & *n* coreano, -a *mf*;

(language) coreano *m*
kosher /'kəʊʃə(r)/ *adj* kasher *inv*
Kosovan /'kɒsəvn/ **1** *adj* kosovaro
2 *n* kosovaro, -a *mf*
Kosovo /'kɒsəvəʊ/ *n* Kosovo *m*
kowtow /kaʊ'taʊ/ *vi* piegarsi
kph *abbr* (**kilometres per hour**) km/h
kudos /'kjuːdɒs/ *n* fam gloria *f*
Kurd /'kɜːd/ **1** *n* curdo, -a *mf*
2 *adj* curdo
Kurdish /'kɜːdɪʃ/ *adj* & *n* (language) curdo *m*
Kurdistan /kɜːdɪ'stɑːn/ *n* Kurdistan *m*
Kuwait /kʊ'weɪt/ *n* Kuwait *m*
Kuwaiti /kʊ'weɪtɪ/ *adj* & *n* kuwaitiano, -a *mf*
kW *abbr* (**kilowatt**) kW
kWh *abbr* (**kilowatt-hour**) kWh
Kyrgyzstan /kɪəgɪ'stɑːn/ *n* Kirghizistan *m*

Ll

l, **L** /el/ *n* (letter) l, L *f inv*
L *abbr* (**lake**) L; *abbr* (**large**) L; *abbr* (**learner**) P; *abbr* (**left**) sinistra *f*; *abbr* (**line**) v; *abbr* (**litre(s)**) l
lab /læb/ *n* fam laboratorio *m*
lab assistant *n* assistente *mf* di laboratorio
lab coat *n* camice *m*
label /'leɪbl/ **1** *n* etichetta *f*
2 *vt* (pt/pp **labelled**) mettere un'etichetta a; fig etichettare ⟨*person*⟩
labelling /'leɪbəlɪŋ/ *n* (act) etichettatura *f*
labor /'leɪbə(r)/ *n* & *v* Am = LABOUR
laboratory /lə'bɒrətrɪ/ *n* laboratorio *m*
laborer /'leɪbərə(r)/ *n* Am = LABOURER
laborious /lə'bɔːrɪəs/ *adj* laborioso
laboriously /lə'bɔːrɪəslɪ/ *adv* in modo laborioso
labor union /'leɪbə/ *n* Am sindacato *m*
labour /'leɪbə(r)/ **1** *n* lavoro *m*; (workers) manodopera *f*; Med doglie *fpl*; **be in** ∼ avere le doglie; **L**∼ Pol partito *m* laburista
2 *attrib* Pol laburista
3 *vi* lavorare
4 *vt* ∼ **the point** fig ribadire il concetto
labour camp *n* campo *m* di lavoro
laboured /'leɪbəd/ *adj* ⟨*breathing*⟩ affannato
labourer /'leɪbərə(r)/ *n* manovale *m*

labour exchange *n* old ufficio *m* di collocamento
labour force *n* manodopera *f*
labouring /'leɪbərɪŋ/ *n* lavoro *m* manuale
labour-intensive *adj* ad uso intensivo di lavoro; **be** ∼ richiedere molta manodopera
labour market *n* mercato *m* del lavoro
Labour Party *n* Partito *m* laburista
labour relations *npl* relazioni *fpl* industriali
labour-saving /'leɪbəseɪvɪŋ/ *adj* che fa risparmiare lavoro e fatica
labour ward *n* reparto *m* maternità
labrador /'læbrədɔː(r)/ *n* (dog) labrador *m inv*
lab technician *n* tecnico, -a *mf* di laboratorio
laburnum /lə'bɜːnəm/ *n* maggiociondolo *m*
labyrinth /'læbərɪnθ/ *n* labirinto *m*
lace /leɪs/ **1** *n* pizzo *m*; (of shoe) laccio *m*
2 *attrib* di pizzo
3 *vt* allacciare ⟨*shoes*⟩; correggere ⟨*drink*⟩
lacerate /'læsəreɪt/ *vt* lacerare
laceration /læsə'reɪʃn/ *n* lacerazione *f*
lace-up [shoe] *n* scarpa *f* stringata

lack /læk/ ① *n* mancanza *f*; ∼ **of interest** disinteressamento *m*; ∼ **of evidence** insufficienza *f* di prove
② *vt* **the programme** ∼**s originality** il programma manca di originalità; **I** ∼ **the time** mi manca il tempo
③ *vi* **be** ∼**ing** mancare; **be** ∼**ing in something** mancare di qualcosa

lackadaisical /lækə'deɪzɪkl/ *adj* senza entusiasmo

lackey /'lækɪ/ *n* lacchè *m inv*

lackluster /'læklʌstə(r)/ *adj* Am = LACKLUSTRE

lacklustre /'læklʌstə(r)/ *adj* scialbo

laconic /lə'kɒnɪk/ *adj* laconico

laconically /lə'kɒnɪklɪ/ *adv* laconicamente

lacquer /'lækə(r)/ *n* lacca *f*

lactate /læk'teɪt/ *vi* produrre latte

lactation /læk'teɪʃn/ *n* lattazione *f*

lacy /'leɪsɪ/ *adj* di pizzo

lad /læd/ *n* ragazzo *m*

ladder /'lædə(r)/ ① *n* scala *f*; (in tights) smagliatura *f*
② *vi* smagliarsi

ladderproof /'lædəpru:f/ *adj* ⟨stockings⟩ indemagliabile

laddish /'lædɪʃ/ *adj* fam da ragazzacci

laden /'leɪdn/ *adj* carico (**with** di)

la-di-da /lɑːdɪ'dɑː/ *adj* affettato

ladle /'leɪdl/ ① *n* mestolo *m*
② *vt* ∼ [**out**] versare (col mestolo)

lady /'leɪdɪ/ *n* signora *f*; (title) Lady *f*; **ladies [room]** *n* bagno *m* per donne

ladybird *n*, Am **ladybug** *n* coccinella *f*

lady-in-waiting /-weɪtɪŋ/ *n* dama *f* di corte

ladykiller *n* fam dongiovanni *m inv*

ladylike /'leɪdɪlaɪk/ *adj* signorile

lady mayoress *n* moglie *f* del Lord Mayor

Ladyship *n* **her/your L**∼ (to aristocrat) ≈ Signora Contessa

lady's maid *n* cameriera *f* personale

lag¹ /læg/ *vi* (pt/pp **lagged**) ∼ **behind** restare indietro

lag² *vt* (pt/pp **lagged**) isolare ⟨pipes⟩

lager /'lɑːgə(r)/ *n* birra *f* chiara

lager lout *n* Br pej giovinastro *m* ubriaco

lagging /'lægɪŋ/ *n* (for pipes) materiale *m* isolante

lagoon /lə'gu:n/ *n* laguna *f*

laid /leɪd/ ▶ LAY³; sl **get** ∼ scopare

laid-back *adj* fam rilassato

laid up *adj* **be** ∼ essere allettato

lain /leɪn/ ▶ LIE²

lair /leə(r)/ *n* tana *f*

laird /leəd/ *n* (in Scotland) proprietario *m* terriero

laity /'leɪətɪ/ *n* laicato *m*

lake /leɪk/ *n* lago *m*; **L**∼ **Garda** lago di Garda

lakeside /'leɪksaɪd/ ① *n* riva *f* del lago
② *attrib* ⟨café, scenery⟩ della/sulla riva del lago

lama /'lɑːmə/ *n* lama *m inv*

lamb /læm/ *n* agnello *m*

lambast[e] /læm'beɪst/ *vt* biasimare ⟨person, organization⟩

lamb chop *n* cotoletta *f* d'agnello

lambskin *n* pelle *f* d'agnello

lambswool *n* lana *f* d'agnello, lambswool *m inv*

lame /leɪm/ *adj* zoppo; fig ⟨argument⟩ zoppicante; ⟨excuse⟩ traballante

lamé /'lɑːmeɪ/ *n* lamé *m*

lame duck *n* (person) inetto, -a *mf*; (firm) azienda *f* in cattive acque

lament /lə'ment/ ① *n* lamento *m*
② *vt* lamentare
③ *vi* lamentarsi

lamentable /'læməntəbl/ *adj* deplorevole

laminated /'læmɪneɪtɪd/ *adj* laminato

lamp /læmp/ *n* lampada *f*; (in street) lampione *m*

lampoon /læm'pu:n/ ① *n* satira *f*
② *vt* fare oggetto di satira

lamp-post *n* lampione *m*

lampshade /'læmpʃeɪd/ *n* paralume *m*

lance /lɑːns/ ① *n* lancia *f*
② *vt* Med incidere

lance corporal *n* appuntato *m*

lancet /'lɑːnsɪt/ *n* Med bisturi *m inv*

land /lænd/ ① *n* terreno *m*; (country) paese *m*; (as opposed to sea) terra *f*; **plot of** ∼ pezzo *m* di terreno
② *vt* Naut sbarcare; fam ⟨obtain⟩ assicurarsi; **be** ∼**ed with something** fam ritrovarsi fra capo e collo qualcosa
③ *vi* Aeron atterrare; (fall) cadere; ∼ **on one's feet** fig cadere in piedi
■ **land up** *vi* fam finire

land agent *n* (on estate) fattore *m*

land army *n* gruppo *m* di lavoratrici agricole durante la seconda guerra mondiale

landfall *n* Naut approdo *m*; **make** ∼ (reach) approdare; (sight) avvistare terra

landfill site *n* discarica *f* in cui i rifiuti vengono interrati

landing /'lændɪŋ/ *n* Naut sbarco *m*; Aeron atterraggio *m*; (top of stairs) pianerottolo *m*

landing card *n* Aeron, Naut carta *f* di sbarco

landing craft *n* mezzo *m* da sbarco

landing gear *n* Aeron carrello *m* d'atterraggio

landing lights *npl* luci *fpl* d'atterraggio

landing party *n* Mil reparto *m* da sbarco

landing-stage *n* pontile *m* da sbarco

landing strip *n* pista *f* d'atterraggio

landlady *n* proprietaria *f*; (of flat) padrona *f* di casa

landlocked *adj* privo di sbocco sul mare

landlord *n* proprietario *m*; (of flat) padrone *m* di casa

landlubber /'lændlʌbə(r)/ *n* marinaio *m* d'acqua dolce

landmark *n* punto *m* di riferimento; fig pietra *f* miliare

land mass *n* continente *m*

landmine *n* Mil mina *f* terrestre

landowner *n* proprietario, -a *mf* terriero, -a

landscape *n* paesaggio *m*

landscape architect *n* paesaggista *mf*

landscape gardener *n* paesaggista *mf*

landslide *n* frana *f*; Pol valanga *f* di voti

landslip *n* smottamento *m*

lane /leɪn/ *n* sentiero *m*; Auto, Sport corsia *f*

lane closure *n* (on motorway) chiusura *f* di corsia

lane markings *n* (on road) [strisce *fpl* di] mezzeria *f*

langoustine /'lɒŋɡʊstiːn/ *n* scampo *m*

language /'læŋɡwɪdʒ/ *n* lingua *f*; (speech, style, Comput) linguaggio *m*

language barrier *n* barriera *f* linguistica

language laboratory *n* laboratorio *m* linguistico

languid /'læŋɡwɪd/ *adj* languido

languidly /'læŋɡwɪdlɪ/ *adv* languidamente

languish /'læŋɡwɪʃ/ *vi* languire

languor /'læŋɡə(r)/ *n* languore *m*

lank /læŋk/ *adj* ⟨hair⟩ liscio

lanky /'læŋkɪ/ *adj* (**-ier**, **-iest**) allampanato

lanolin /'lænəlɪn/ *n* lanolina *f*

lantern /'læntən/ *n* lanterna *f*

lanyard /'lænjəd/ *n* (Naut: rope) cima *f*

Laos /laʊs/ *n* Laos *m*

lap¹ /læp/ *n* grembo *m*

lap² ① *n* (Sport, of journey) tappa *f*; ~ **of honour** giro *m* d'onore
② *vi* (pt/pp **lapped**) ⟨water⟩ ~ **against** lambire
③ *vt* Sport doppiare

lap³ *vt* (pt/pp **lapped**) ~ **up** bere avidamente; bersi completamente ⟨lies⟩; credere ciecamente a ⟨praise⟩

lap and shoulder belt *n* Auto, Aeron cintura *f* di sicurezza

laparoscope /'læpərəskəʊp/ *n* laparoscopio *m*

laparoscopy /læpə'rɒskəpɪ/ *n* laparoscopia *f*

lap belt *n* Auto, Aeron cintura *f* di sicurezza addominale

lapdog /'læpdɒɡ/ *n* cane *m* da salotto; **he's her** ~ è il suo cagnolino

lapel /lə'pel/ *n* bavero *m*

Lapland /'læplænd/ *n* Lapponia *f*

lapse /læps/ ① *n* sbaglio *m*; (moral) sbandamento *m* [morale]; (of time) intervallo *m*
② *vi* (expire) scadere; (morally) scivolare; ~ **into** cadere in

laptop /'læptɒp/ *n* ~ [**computer**] computer *m inv* portatile, laptop *m inv*

larceny /'lɑːsənɪ/ *n* furto *m*

larch /lɑːtʃ/ *n* larice *m*

lard /lɑːd/ *n* strutto *m*

larder /'lɑːdə(r)/ *n* dispensa *f*

large /lɑːdʒ/ *adj & adv* grande; ⟨number, amount⟩ grande, grosso; **by and** ~ in complesso; **at** ~ in libertà; (in general) ampiamente

large intestine *n* intestino *m* crasso

largely /'lɑːdʒlɪ/ *adv* ~ **because of** in gran parte a causa di

largeness /'lɑːdʒnɪs/ *n* grandezza *f*

large-scale *adj* ⟨map⟩ a grande scala; ⟨operation⟩ su larga scala

largesse /lɑː'ʒes/ *n* generosità *f*

lark¹ /lɑːk/ *n* (bird) allodola *f*

lark² *n* (joke) burla *f*
■ **lark about** *vi* giocherellare

larva /'lɑːvə/ *n* (pl **-vae** /'lɑːviː/) larva *f*

laryngitis /lærɪn'dʒaɪtɪs/ *n* laringite *f*

larynx /'lærɪŋks/ *n* laringe *f*

lasagne /lə'zænjə/ *n* lasagne *fpi*

lascivious /lə'sɪvɪəs/ *adj* lascivo

laser /'leɪzə(r)/ *n* laser *m inv*

laser disc *n* disco *m* laser

laser printer *n* stampante *f* laser

laser treatment *n* laserterapia *f*

lash /læʃ/ ① *n* frustata *f*; (eyelash) ciglio *m*
② *vt* (whip) frustare; (tie) legare fermamente
■ **lash out** *vi* attaccare; (spend) sperperare (**on** in)

lashings /'læʃɪŋz/ *npl* ~ **of** fam una marea di

lass /læs/ *n* ragazzina *f*

lasso /lə'suː/ *n* lazo *m*

last /lɑːst/ ① *adj* (final) ultimo; (recent) scorso; ~ **year** l'anno scorso; ~ **night** ieri sera; **at** ~ alla fine; **at** ~! finalmente!;

last-ditch ⋯▸ lavatorial

that's the ∼ straw fam questa è l'ultima
goccia
2) n ultimo, -a mf; **the ∼ but one** il
penultimo
3) adv per ultimo; (last time) l'ultima volta;
∼ **but not least** per ultimo ma non il
meno importante
4) vi durare
last-ditch adj ⟨attempt⟩ disperato
lasting /'lɑːstɪŋ/ adj durevole
lastly /'lɑːstlɪ/ adv infine
last-minute adj all'ultimo minuto
last name n (surname) cognome m
last rites npl Relig estrema unzione f
Last Supper n Ultima Cena f
latch /lætʃ/ n chiavistello m; (on gate)
saliscendi m inv; **leave the door on the ∼**
chiudere la porta senza far scattare la
serratura
■ **latch on to** vt fissarsi con ⟨person,
idea⟩
latchkey /lætʃki:/ n chiave f di casa
latchkey child n bambino m che ha le
chiavi di casa in quanto i genitori
lavorano
late /leɪt/ **1)** adj (delayed) in ritardo; (at a
late hour) tardo; (deceased) defunto; **it's ∼** (at
night) è tardi; **in ∼ November** alla fine di
novembre; **of ∼** recentemente; **be a ∼
developer** ⟨child⟩ essere lento
nell'apprendimento
2) adv tardi; **stay up ∼** stare alzati fino a
tardi
latecomer /'leɪtkʌmə(r)/ n ritardatario,
-a mf; (to political party etc) nuovo, -a
arrivato, -a mf
late developer n (child) **be a ∼** essere
tardivo
lately /'leɪtlɪ/ adv recentemente
lateness /'leɪtnɪs/ n ora f tarda; (delay)
ritardo m
late-night adj ⟨film⟩ ultimo; **it's ∼
shopping on Thursdays** i negozi
rimangono aperti fino a tardi il giovedì
latent /'leɪtnt/ adj latente
later /'leɪtə(r)/ **1)** adj ⟨train⟩ che parte
più tardi; ⟨edition⟩ più recente
2) adv più tardi; ∼ **on** più tardi, dopo
lateral /'lætərəl/ adj laterale
late riser /'raɪzə(r)/ n dormiglione, -a
mf
latest /'leɪtɪst/ **1)** adj ultimo; (most recent)
più recente; **the ∼ [news]** le ultime
notizie
2) n **six o'clock at the ∼** alle sei al più
tardi
latex /leɪteks/ n la[t]tice m
lath /læθ/ n assicella f
lathe /leɪð/ n tornio m
lather /'lɑːðə(r)/ **1)** n schiuma f
2) vt insaponare

3) vi far schiuma
Latin /'lætɪn/ **1)** adj latino
2) n latino m
Latin America n America f Latina
Latin American n & adj latino-
americano mf
Latino /lə'tiːnəʊ/ n Am latino-americano,
-a mf
latitude /'lætɪtjuːd/ n Geog latitudine f;
fig libertà f d'azione
latrine /lə'triːn/ n latrina f
latter /'lætə(r)/ **1)** adj ultimo
2) n **the ∼** quest'ultimo
latter-day adj moderno
latterly /'lætəlɪ/ adv ultimamente
lattice /'lætɪs/ n traliccio m
lattice window n finestra f con vetri a
losanghe
lattice-work n intelaiatura f a traliccio
Latvia /'lætvɪə/ n Lettonia f
Latvian /'lætvɪən/ adj & n lettone mf;
(language) lettone m
laudable /'lɔːdəbl/ adj lodevole
laudatory /'lɔːdətrɪ/ adj elogiativo
laugh /lɑːf/ **1)** n risata f
2) vi ridere (**at/about** di); ∼ **at somebody**
(mock) prendere in giro qualcuno
■ **laugh off** vt ridere di ⟨criticism⟩
laughable /'lɑːfəbl/ adj ridicolo
laughing gas /'lɑːfɪŋ/ n gas m inv
esilarante
laughing stock n zimbello m
laughter /'lɑːftə(r)/ n risata f
launch¹ /lɔːntʃ/ n (boat) lancia f
launch² **1)** n lancio m; (of ship) varo m
2) vt lanciare ⟨rocket, product⟩; varare
⟨ship⟩; sferrare ⟨attack⟩
■ **launch into** vt intraprendere ⟨career⟩;
imbarcarsi in ⟨speech⟩
launcher /'lɔːntʃə(r)/ n lanciamissili m
inv
launch[ing] pad /'lɔːntʃ[ɪŋ]/ n
piattaforma f di lancio; fig trampolino m
di lancio
launch pad n piattaforma f di lancio
launder /'lɔːndə(r)/ vt lavare e stirare; ∼
money fig riciclare denaro sporco
launderette /lɔːndə'ret/ n lavanderia f
automatica
laundry /'lɔːndrɪ/ n lavanderia f; (clothes)
bucato m
laureate /'lɒrɪət/ adj poet ∼ poeta m di
corte; **Nobel ∼** vincitore, -trice mf del
Nobel
laurel /'lɒrəl/ n alloro m; **rest on one's
∼s** fig dormire sugli allori
lav /læv/ n Br fam gabinetto m
lava /'lɑːvə/ n lava f
lavatorial /lævə'tɔːrɪəl/ adj ⟨humour⟩
scatologico

lavatory /'lævətrɪ/ *n* gabinetto *m*

lavender /'lævəndə(r)/ *n* lavanda *f*

lavender blue *adj* color lavanda

lavish /'lævɪʃ/ **1** *adj* copioso; (wasteful) prodigo; **on a ~ scale** su vasta scala **2** *vt* ~ **something on somebody** ricoprire qualcuno di qualcosa

lavishly /'lævɪʃlɪ/ *adv* copiosamente

law /lɔː/ *n* legge *f*; **study ~** studiare giurisprudenza, studiare legge; **take the ~ into one's own hands** farsi giustizia da sé; **~ of the jungle** legge della giungla

law-abiding /'lɔːəbaɪdɪŋ/ *adj* che rispetta la legge

law and order *n* ordine *m* pubblico

lawbreaker /'lɔːbreɪkə(r)/ *n* persona *f* che infrange la legge

law court *n* tribunale *m*

lawful /'lɔːfʊl/ *adj* legittimo

lawfully /'lɔːfʊlɪ/ *adv* legittimamente

lawfulness /'lɔːfʊlnɪs/ *n* legalità *f*

lawless /'lɔːlɪs/ *adj* senza legge

lawmaker /'lɔːmeɪkə(r)/ *n* legislatore *m*

lawn /lɔːn/ *n* prato *m* [all'inglese]

lawnmower /'lɔːnməʊə(r)/ *n* tosaerba *m inv*

law school *n* facoltà *f* di giurisprudenza

lawsuit /'lɔːsuːt/ *n* causa *f*

lawyer /'lɔːjə(r)/ *n* avvocato *m*

lax /læks/ *adj* negligente; ⟨morals etc⟩ lassista

laxative /'læksətɪv/ *n* lassativo *m*

laxity /'læksətɪ/ *n* lassismo *m*

lay[1] /leɪ/ *adj* laico; *fig* profano

lay[2] ▶ LIE[2]

lay[3] **1** *vt* (pt/pp **laid**) porre, mettere; apparecchiare ⟨table⟩ **2** *vi* ⟨hen⟩ fare le uova
■ **lay aside** *vt* mettere da parte
■ **lay down** *vt* posare; stabilire ⟨rules, conditions⟩
■ **lay in** *vt* farsi una scorta di ⟨coal, supplies etc⟩
■ **lay into** *vt* sl picchiare
■ **lay off** **1** *vt* licenziare ⟨workers⟩ **2** *vi* (fam: stop) ~ **off!** smettila!
■ **lay on** *vt* (organize) organizzare
■ **lay out** *vt* (display, set forth) esporre; (plan) pianificare ⟨garden⟩; (spend) sborsare; Typ impaginare
■ **lay up** *vt* **I was laid up in bed for a week** sono stato costretto a letto per una settimana

layabout /'leɪəbaʊt/ *n* fannullone, -a *mf*

lay-by *n* piazzola *f* di sosta

layer /'leɪə(r)/ *n* strato *m*

layette /leɪ'et/ *n* corredino *m*

layman /'leɪmən/ *n* profano *m*

lay-off *n* (permanent) licenziamento *m*; (temporary) sospensione *f*

layout /'leɪaʊt/ *n* disposizione *f*; Typ impaginazione *f*, layout *m inv*

lay preacher *n* predicatore *m* laico

laze /leɪz/ *vi* ~ **[about]** oziare

lazily /'leɪzɪlɪ/ *adv* ⟨move, wander etc⟩ pigramente

laziness /'leɪzɪnɪs/ *n* pigrizia *f*

lazy /'leɪzɪ/ *adj* (**-ier, -iest**) pigro

lazybones /'leɪzɪbəʊnz/ *n* poltrone, -a *mf*

lazy eye *n* ambliopia *f*

lb *abbr* (**pound**) libbra

LCD *n abbr* (**liquid crystal display**) LCD *m*

lead[1] /led/ *n* piombo *m*; (of pencil) mina *f*

lead[2] /liːd/ **1** *n* guida *f*; (leash) guinzaglio *m*; (flex) filo *m*; (clue) indizio *m*; Theat parte *f* principale; (distance ahead) distanza *f* (over su); **in the ~** in testa; **follow sb's ~** seguire l'esempio di qualcuno **2** *vt* (pt/pp **led**) condurre; dirigere ⟨expedition, party etc⟩; (induce) indurre; ~ **the way** mettersi in testa; ~ **into temptation** indurre in tentazione **3** *vi* (be in front) condurre; (in race, competition) essere in testa
■ **lead astray** *vt* sviare
■ **lead away** *vt* portar via
■ **lead on** *vt* ingannare
■ **lead off** **1** *vi* (begin) cominciare **2** *vt* (take away) portare via
■ **lead to** *vt* portare a
■ **lead up to** *vt* preludere; **the period ~ing up to the election** il periodo precedente le elezioni; **what's this ~ing up to?** dove porta questo?

leaded /'ledɪd/ *adj* con piombo

leaded petrol Br, **leaded gasoline** Am *n* benzina *f* con piombo

leaden /'ledən/ *adj* di piombo

leader /'liːdə(r)/ *n* capo *m*; (of orchestra) primo violino *m*; (in newspaper) articolo *m* di fondo

leadership /'liːdəʃɪp/ *n* direzione *f*, leadership *f inv*; **show ~** mostrare capacità di comando

leadership contest *n* elezione *f* alla direzione del partito

lead-free /'ledfriː/ *adj* senza piombo

lead-in /'liːdɪn/ *n* presentazione *f*

leading[1] /'liːdɪŋ/ *adj* principale

leading[2] /'ledɪŋ/ *n* Typ interlinea *f*

leading article *n* articolo *m* di fondo

leading edge *n* Aeron bordo *m* d'attacco; **at the ~ ~ of** (technology) all'avanguardia in

leading lady attrice *f* principale

leading light *n* personaggio *m* di spicco

leading man attore *m* principale

leading question *n* domanda *f* che influenza la risposta

lead poisoning *n* saturnismo *m*

lead story *n* articolo *f* principale

leaf /liːf/ *n* (pl **leaves**) foglia *f*; (of table) asse *f*; fig **take a ~ out of sb's book** imparare la lezione di qualcuno; **turn over a new ~** voltare pagina
■ **leaf through** *vt* sfogliare

leaflet /'liːflɪt/ *n* dépliant *m inv*; (advertising) dépliant *m inv* pubblicitario; (political) manifestino *m*

leafy /'liːfɪ/ *adj* ⟨tree⟩ ricco di foglie; ⟨wood⟩ molto verde; ⟨suburb, area⟩ ricco di verde

league /liːg/ *n* lega *f*; Sport campionato *m*; **be in ~ with** essere in combutta con

league table *n* classifica *f* del campionato

leak /liːk/ ① *n* (hole) fessura *f*; Naut falla *f*; (of gas & fig) fuga *f*
② *vi* colare; ⟨ship⟩ fare acqua; ⟨liquid, gas⟩ fuoriuscire
③ *vt* ~ **something to somebody** fig far trapelare qualcosa a qualcuno

leakage /'liːkɪdʒ/ *n* perdita *f*; (of gas & fig) fuga *f*

leaky /'liːkɪ/ *adj* che perde; Naut che fa acqua

lean¹ /liːn/ *adj* magro

lean² ① *vt* (pt/pp **leaned** or **leant** /lent/) appoggiare (**against/on** contro/su); ~ **one's elbows on the table** appoggiare i gomiti sul tavolo
② *vi* appoggiarsi (**against/on** contro/su); (not be straight) pendere; **be ~ing against** essere appoggiato contro; ~ **on somebody** (depend on) appoggiarsi a qualcuno; (fam: exert pressure on) stare alle calcagna di qualcuno
■ **lean back** *vi* sporgersi indietro
■ **lean forward** *vi* piegarsi in avanti
■ **lean out** *vi* sporgersi
■ **lean over** *vi* piegarsi
■ **lean towards** *vt* (favour) propendere per

leaning /'liːnɪŋ/ ① *adj* pendente; **the L~ Tower of Pisa** la torre di Pisa, la torre pendente
② *n* tendenza *f*

leanness /'liːnnɪs/ *n* magrezza *f*

lean-to *n* garage *m inv* adiacente alla casa

leap /liːp/ ① *n* salto *m*
② *vi* (pt/pp **leapt** /lept/ or **leaped**) saltare; **he leapt at it** fam l'ha preso al volo

leapfrog /'liːpfrɒg/ *n* cavallina *f*

leap year *n* anno *m* bisestile

learn /lɜːn/ ① *vt* (pt/pp **learnt** or **learned**) imparare; ~ **to swim** imparare a nuotare; **I have ~ed that...** (heard) sono venuto a sapere che...; fig **he's ~t his lesson** ha imparato la lezione

② *vi* imparare; **as I've ~t to my cost** come ho imparato a mie spese

learned /'lɜːnɪd/ *adj* colto

learner /'lɜːnə(r)/ *n* also Auto principiante *mf*

learning /'lɜːnɪŋ/ *n* cultura *f*

learning curve *n* curva *f* di apprendimento

learning difficulties *npl* (of schoolchildren) difficoltà *fpl* d'apprendimento

learning disability *n* difficoltà *fpl* d'apprendimento

lease /liːs/ ① *n* contratto *m* d'affitto; (rental) affitto *m*; **the job has given him a new ~ of life** grazie al lavoro ha ripreso gusto alla vita
② *vt* affittare

leasehold /'liːshəʊld/ *n* proprietà *f* in affitto

leaseholder /'liːshəʊldə(r)/ *n* titolare *mf* di un contratto d'affitto

leash /liːʃ/ *n* guinzaglio *m*

leasing /'liːsɪŋ/ *n* (by company) leasing *m*; ~ **scheme** piano di leasing

least /liːst/ ① *adj* più piccolo; (smallest amount) meno; **you've got ~ luggage** hai meno bagagli di tutti
② *n* **the ~** il meno; **that's the ~ of my worries** questa è la cosa che mi preoccupa di meno; **at ~** almeno; **not in the ~** niente affatto
③ *adv* meno; **the ~ expensive wine** il vino meno caro

leather /'leðə(r)/ ① *n* pelle *f*; (of soles) cuoio *m*
② *attrib* di pelle/cuoio; ~ **jacket** giubbotto *m* di pelle

leathery /'leðərɪ/ *adj* (meat, skin) duro

leave /liːv/ ① *n* (holiday) congedo *m*; Mil licenza *f*; **on ~** in congedo/licenza; **take one's ~** accomiatarsi; ~ **of absence** aspettativa *f*
② *vt* (pt/pp **left**) lasciare; uscire da ⟨house, office⟩; (forget) dimenticare; **there is nothing left** non è rimasto niente; ~ **somebody in peace** lasciare in pace qualcuno
③ *vi* andare via; ⟨train, bus⟩ partire
■ **leave aside** *vt* (disregard) lasciare da parte
■ **leave behind** *vt* lasciare; (forget) dimenticare
■ **leave out** *vt* omettere; (not put away) lasciare fuori

leaves /liːvz/ ▸ LEAF

leaving /'liːvɪŋ/ *adj* ⟨party, present⟩ d'addio

Lebanese /lebə'niːz/ *adj & n* libanese *mf*

Lebanon /'lebənən/ *n* Libano *m*

lecher /'letʃə(r)/ *n* libertino *m*

lecherous /'letʃərəs/ *adj* lascivo

lechery /'letʃərɪ/ n lascivia f

lectern /'lektɜːn/ n leggio m, scannello m

lecture /'lektʃə(r)/ ① n conferenza f; Univ lezione f; (reproof) ramanzina f ② vi fare una conferenza (**on** su); Univ insegnare (**on something** qualcosa) ③ vt ~ **somebody** rimproverare qualcuno

lecturer /'lektʃərə(r)/ n conferenziere, -a mf; Univ docente mf universitario, -a

lecture room n Br Univ aula f magna

lectureship /'lektʃəʃɪp/ n Br Univ docenza f universitaria

lecture theatre n Br Univ aula f magna

LED abbr (**light-emitting diode**) LED m inv

led /led/ ▶ LEAD²

ledge /ledʒ/ n cornice f; (of window) davanzale m

ledger /'ledʒə(r)/ n libro m mastro

leech /liːtʃ/ n sanguisuga f

leek /liːk/ n porro m

leer /lɪə(r)/ ① n sguardo m libidinoso ② vi ~ (**at**) guardare in modo libidinoso

lees /liːz/ npl (wine sediment) fondi mpl

leeway /'liːweɪ/ n fig libertà f di azione

left¹ /left/ ▶ LEAVE

left² ① adj sinistro ② adv a sinistra ③ n also Pol sinistra f: **on the** ~ a sinistra

left-hand adj di sinistra; **on the** ~ **side** sulla sinistra

left-hand drive adj ⟨car⟩ con la guida a sinistra

left-handed /-'hændɪd/ adj mancino; ⟨scissors etc⟩ per mancini

leftie /'leftɪ/ n sinistrorso, -a mf

leftist /'leftɪst/ adj & n sinistrorso, -a mf

left-luggage lockers npl deposito m bagagli automatico

left luggage [office] n deposito m bagagli

leftovers npl rimasugli mpl

left wing n Pol sinistra f; Sport ala f sinistra

left-wing adj Pol di sinistra

left-winger n Pol persona f di sinistra; Sport ala f sinistra

leg /leg/ ① n gamba f; (of animal) zampa f; (of journey) tappa f; Culin (of chicken) coscia f; (of lamb) cosciotto m; **be on one's last** ~**s** ⟨machine⟩ funzionare per miracolo; **not have a** ~ **to stand on** non avere una ragione che regga ② vt ~ **it** fam darsela a gambe

legacy /'legəsɪ/ n lascito m

legal /'liːgl/ adj legale; **take** ~ **action** intentare un'azione legale

legal adviser n consulente mf legale

legal aid n gratuito patrocinio m

legal eagle n hum principe m del foro

legal holiday n Am festa f nazionale

legality /lɪ'gæfətɪ/ n legalità f

legalization /liːgəlaɪ'zeɪʃn/ n legalizzazione f

legalize /'liːgəlaɪz/ vt legalizzare

legally /'liːgəlɪ/ adv legalmente

legal proceedings npl procedimento m sg giudiziario

legal tender n valuta f a corso legale

legend /'ledʒənd/ n leggenda f

legendary /'ledʒəndərɪ/ adj leggendario

leggings /'legɪŋz/ npl (for baby) ghette fpl; (for woman) pantacollant mpl; (for man) gambali mpl

leggy /'legɪ/ adj ⟨person⟩ con le gambe lunghe

Leghorn /'leghɔːn/ n Livorno f

legibility /ledʒə'bɪlətɪ/ n leggibilità f

legible /'ledʒəbl/ adj leggibile

legibly /'ledʒəblɪ/ adv in modo leggibile

legion /'liːdʒn/ n legione f

legionnaire /liːdʒə'neə(r)/ n Mil legionario m

legionnaire's disease n legionellosi f

legislate /'ledʒɪsleɪt/ vi legiferare

legislation /ledʒɪs'leɪʃn/ n legislazione f

legislative /'ledʒɪslətɪv/ adj legislativo

legislator /'ledʒɪsleɪtə(r)/ n legislatore m

legislature /'ledʒɪsleɪtʃə(r)/ n legislatura f

legitimacy /lɪ'dʒɪtɪməsɪ/ n (lawfulness) legittimità f; (of argument) validità f

legitimate /lɪ'dʒɪtɪmət/ adj legittimo; ⟨excuse⟩ valido

legitimately /lɪ'dʒɪtɪmətlɪ/ adv legittimamente

legitimize /lɪdʒɪtɪ'maɪz/ vt rendere legittimo

legless /'leglɪs/ adj senza gambe; (Br: drunk) ubriaco fradicio

leg-pulling n presa f in giro

legroom n spazio m per le gambe

leg warmer n scaldamuscoli m inv

legwork n fatica f; **do the** ~ fare da galoppino

leisure /'leʒə(r)/ n tempo m libero; **at your** ~ con comodo

leisure centre n centro m sportivo e ricreativo

leisurely /'leʒəlɪ/ adj senza fretta

leisure time n tempo m libero

leisurewear /'leʒəweə(r)/ n abbigliamento m per il tempo libero

lemming /'lemɪŋ/ n lemming m inv

lemon /'lemən/ n limone m

lemonade /lemə'neɪd/ n limonata f
lemon curd n crema f al limone
lemon juice n (drink) succo m di limone
lemon sole n sogliola f limanda
lemon squash n sciroppo m di limone
lemon tea n tè m inv al limone
lemon tree n limone m
lemon yellow ① n giallo m limone
② adj giallo limone
lend /lend/ vt (pt/pp **lent**) prestare; ~ **a hand** fig dare una mano; ~ **an ear** prestare ascolto; ~ **itself to** prestarsi a
lender /'lendə(r)/ n prestatore, -trice mf
lending library /'lendɪn/ n biblioteca f per il prestito
length /leŋθ/ n lunghezza f; (piece) pezzo m; (of wallpaper) parte f; (of visit) durata f; **at** ~ **a** lungo; (at last) alla fine
lengthen /'leŋθən/ ① vt allungare
② vi allungarsi
lengthways /'leŋθweɪz/ adv per lungo
lengthwise /'leŋθwaɪz/ adv longitudinale
lengthy /'leŋθɪ/ adj (-ier, -iest) lungo
lenience /'liːnɪəns/ n indulgenza f
lenient /'liːnɪənt/ adj indulgente
leniently /'liːnɪəntlɪ/ adv con indulgenza
lens /lenz/ n lente f; Phot obiettivo m; (of eye) cristallino m
lens cap n copriobiettivo m
Lent /lent/ n Quaresima f
lent ▶ LEND
lentil /'lentl/ n Bot lenticchia f
Leo /'liːəʊ/ n Astr Leone m
leopard /'lepəd/ n leopardo m
leopardskin /'lepədskɪn/ ① n pelle f di leopardo
② attrib di [pelle di] leopardo
leotard /'liːətaːd/ n body m inv
leper /'lepə(r)/ n lebbroso, -a mf; fig appestato, -a mf
leprosy /'leprəsɪ/ n lebbra f
lesbian /'lezbɪən/ ① adj lesbico
② n lesbica f
lesbianism /'lezbɪənɪzm/ n lesbismo m
lesion /'liːʒn/ n lesione f
Lesotho /lə'suːtuː/ n Lesotho m
less /les/ ① adj meno di; ~ **and** ~ sempre meno;
② adv & prep meno
③ n meno m
lessee /le'siː/ n Jur affittuario, -a mf
lessen /'lesn/ vt/i diminuire
lesser /'lesə(r)/ adj minore; **the** ~ **of two evils** il minore fra i due mali
lesson /'lesn/ n lezione f; **teach somebody a** ~ fig dare una lezione a qualcuno
lessor /le'sɔː/ n Jur locatore, -trice mf

lest /lest/ conj liter per timore che
let /let/ ① vt (pt/pp **let**, pres p **letting**) lasciare, permettere; (rent) affittare; ~ **alone** (not to mention) tanto meno; '**to** ~' 'affittasi'; ~ **us go** andiamo; ~ **somebody do something** lasciare fare qualcosa a qualcuno, permettere a qualcuno di fare qualcosa; ~ **me know** fammi sapere; **just** ~ **him try!** che ci provi solamente!; ~ **onself in for something** fam impelagarsi in qualcosa
② n Tennis colpo m nullo; (Br: lease) contratto m d'affitto
③ vi ~ **fly at somebody** aggredire qualcuno
■ **let down** vt sciogliersi ⟨hair⟩; abbassare ⟨blinds⟩; (lengthen) allungare; (disappoint) deludere; **don't** ~ **me down** conto su di te
■ **let go** ① vi mollare; ~ **go of** lasciare andare
② vt mollare ⟨rope, person⟩; ~ **somebody go** rilasciare ⟨prisoner⟩; licenziare ⟨employee⟩; ~ **oneself go** lasciarsi andare
■ **let in** vt far entrare
■ **let off** vt far partire; (not punish) perdonare; ~ **somebody off doing something** abbonare qualcosa a qualcuno; ~ **off steam** fig scaricarsi
■ **let on** vi sl **don't** ~ **on** non spifferare niente
■ **let out** vt far uscire; (make larger) allargare; emettere ⟨scream, groan⟩
■ **let through** vt far passare
■ **let up** vi fam diminuire
let-down n delusione f
lethal /'liːθl/ adj letale; ~ **dose** n dose f letale
lethargic /lɪ'θaːdʒɪk/ adj apatico
lethargy /'leθədʒɪ/ n apatia f
let-out n fam via f d'uscita
letter /'letə(r)/ n lettera f
letter bomb n lettera f esplosiva
letter box n buca f per le lettere
letterhead n (heading) intestazione f; (paper) carta f intestata
lettering /'letərɪn/ n caratteri mpl
letter of apology n lettera f di scuse
letter of credit n Comm lettera f di credito
letter of introduction n lettera f di presentazione
lettuce /'letɪs/ n lattuga f
let-up n fam pausa f
leukaemia /luːˈkiːmɪə/ n leucemia f
level /'levl/ ① adj piano; (in height, competition) allo stesso livello; ⟨spoonful⟩ raso; **draw** ~ **with somebody** affiancare qualcuno; **do one's** ~ **best** fare del proprio meglio
② n livello m; **on the** ~ fam giusto
③ vt (pt/pp **levelled**) livellare; (aim) puntare (**at** su)

■ **level off** *vi* ‹*inflation, unemployment*› stabilizzarsi

■ **level out** *vi* ‹*surface*› diventare pianeggiante; ‹*aircraft*› mettersi in orizzontale

■ **level with** *vt* (fam: be honest with) essere franco con

level crossing *n* passaggio *m* a livello

level-headed /-'hedɪd/ *adj* posato

level pegging *n* it's ~ ~ so far finora sono alla pari

lever /'li:və(r)/ *n* leva *f*

■ **lever off**, **lever up** *vt* sollevare (con una leva)

leverage /'li:vərɪdʒ/ *n* azione *f* di una leva; fig influenza *f*

leveret /'levərət/ *n* leprotto *m*

levitate /'levɪteɪt/ *vi* levitare

levity /'levɪtɪ/ *n* leggerezza *f*

levy /'levɪ/ *vt* (pt/pp **levied**) imporre ‹*tax*›

lewd /lju:d/ *adj* osceno

lexical /'leksɪkəl/ *adj* lessicale

lexicographer /leksɪ'kɒɡrəfə(r)/ *n* lessicografo, -a *mf*

lexicographic /leksɪkə'ɡræfɪk/ *adj* lessicografico

lexicography /leksɪ'kɒɡrəfɪ/ *n* lessicografia *f*

lexicon /'leksɪkən/ *n* lessico *m*

liability /laɪə'bɪlətɪ/ *n* responsabilità *f*; (fam: burden) peso *m*; **liabilities** *pl* passività *fpl*

liable /'laɪəbl/ *adj* responsabile (**for** di); **be ~ to** ‹*rain, break etc*› rischiare di; (tend to) tendere a

liaise /lɪ'eɪz/ *vi* fam essere in contatto

liaison /lɪ'eɪzɒn/ *n* contatti *mpl*; Mil collegamento *m*; (affair) relazione *f*

liar /'laɪə(r)/ *n* bugiardo, -a *mf*

Lib Dem /lɪb'dem/ Br Pol *abbr* Liberal Democrat

libel /'laɪbl/ ① *n* diffamazione *f*
② *vt* (pt/pp **libelled**) diffamare

libellous Br, **libelous** Am *adj* diffamatorio

liberal /'lɪb(ə)rəl/ ① *adj* (tolerant) di larghe vedute; (generous) generoso. **L~** *adj* Pol liberale
② *n* liberale *mf*

Liberal Democrat *n* Br Pol liberal-democratico, -a *mf*

liberalism /'lɪb(ə)rəlɪzm/ *n* liberalismo *m*

liberalization /lɪbərəlaɪ'zeɪʃn/ *n* (of trade) liberalizzazione *f*

liberalize /'lɪbərəlaɪz/ *vt* liberalizzare

liberally /'lɪbrəlɪ/ *adv* liberalmente

liberate /'lɪbəreɪt/ *vt* liberare

liberated /'lɪbəreɪtɪd/ *adj* ‹*woman*› emancipata

liberating /'lɪbəreɪtɪŋ/ *adj* liberatorio

liberation /lɪbə'reɪʃn/ *n* liberazione *f*; (of women) emancipazione *f*

liberator /'lɪbəreɪtə(r)/ *n* liberatore, -trice *mf*

Liberia /laɪ'bɪərɪə/ *n* Liberia *f*

libertarian /lɪbə'teərɪən/ *adj* & *n* liberale *mf*

libertarianism /lɪbə'teərɪənɪzm/ *n* liberalismo *m*

liberty /'lɪbətɪ/ *n* libertà *f*; **take the ~ of doing something** prendersi la libertà di fare qualcosa; **take liberties** prendersi delle libertà; **be at ~ to do something** essere libero di fare qualcosa

libido /lɪ'bi:dəʊ/ *n* libido *f inv*

Libra /'li:brə/ *n* Astr Bilancia *f*

librarian /laɪ'breərɪən/ *n* bibliotecario, -a *mf*

library /'laɪbrərɪ/ *n* biblioteca *f*

libretto /lɪ'bretəʊ/ *n* (pl **-tti** or **-ttos**) libretto *m* di opera

Libya /'lɪbɪə/ *n* Libia *f*

Libyan /'lɪbɪən/ *adj* & *n* libico, -a *mf*

lice /laɪs/ ▶ LOUSE

licence /'laɪsns/ *n* licenza *f*; (for TV) canone *m* televisivo; (for driving) patente *f*; (freedom) sregolatezza *f*

licence number *n* numero *m* di targa

licence plate *n* targa *f*

license /'laɪsns/ *vt* autorizzare; **be ~d** ‹*car*› avere il bollo; ‹*restaurant*› essere autorizzato alla vendita di alcolici

licensee /laɪsən'si:/ *n* titolare *mf* di licenza (per la vendita di alcolici)

licensing hours /'laɪsənsɪŋ/ *npl* Br orario *m* in cui è permessa la vendita di alcolici

licensing laws *npl* Br normativa *f sg* sulla vendita di alcolici

licentious /laɪ'senʃəs/ *adj* licenzioso

licentiousness /laɪ'senʃəsnɪs/ *n* licenziosità *f*

lichen /'laɪkən/ *n* Bot lichene *m*

lick /lɪk/ ① *n* leccata *f*; **a ~ of paint** una passata leggera di pittura
② *vt* leccare; (fam: defeat) battere; leccarsi ‹*lips*›; fam ~ **somebody into shape** rendere qualcuno efficiente

licorice /'lɪkərɪs/ *n* Am = LIQUORICE

lid /lɪd/ *n* coperchio *m*; (of eye) palpebra *f*; **keep the ~ on something** fam non lasciare trapelare qualcosa

lido /'li:dəʊ/ *n* (beach) lido *m*; ‹*Br: pool*› piscina *f* scoperta

lie[1] /laɪ/ ① *n* bugia *f*; **tell a ~** mentire
② *vi* (pt/pp **lied**, pres p **lying**) mentire

lie² *vi* (pt **lay**, pp **lain**, pres p **lying**)
⟨*person*⟩ sdraiarsi; ⟨*object*⟩ stare; (remain)
rimanere; **leave something lying about** *or*
around lasciare qualcosa in giro; **here**
∼**s...** qui giace...; ∼ **low** tenersi nascosto
■ **lie around** ①*vi* ⟨*person*⟩ girellare
②*vt* girellare in ⟨*house*⟩
■ **lie back** *vi* (relax) rilassarsi
■ **lie down** *vi* sdraiarsi
■ **lie in** *vi* (stay in bed) rimanere a letto
Liechtenstein /'lɪktənstaɪn/ *n*
Liechtenstein *m*
lie detector *n* macchina *f* della verità
lie-down *n* have a ∼ fare un riposino
lie-in *n* fam have a ∼ restare a letto fino a
tardi
lieu /lju:/ *n* in ∼ of in luogo di
lieutenant /leftenant/ *n* tenente *m*
life /laɪf/ *n* (pl **lives**) vita *f*; **give one's** ∼
for somebody/one's country dare la vita
per qualcuno/la patria; **give one's** ∼ **to**
(devote oneself to) dedicare la propria vita a;
lose one's ∼ perdere la vita; **for dear** ∼
per salvare la pelle; **not on your** ∼! fam
neanche morto!
life-and-death *adj* ⟨*struggle*⟩ disperato
lifebelt *n* salvagente *m*
lifeblood *n* fig linfa *f* vitale
lifeboat *n* lancia *f* di salvataggio; (on
ship) scialuppa *f* di salvataggio
lifebuoy *n* salvagente *m*
life coach *n* life coach *mf inv*
life drawing *n* disegno *m* dal vero
life expectancy *n* vita *f* media
life form *n* forma *f* di vita
lifeguard *n* (on beach etc) bagnino, -a *mf*
life-imprisonment *n* ergastolo *m*
life insurance *n* assicurazione *f* sulla
vita
life jacket *n* giubbotto *m* di salvataggio
lifeless /'laɪflɪs/ *adj* inanimato
lifelike *adj* realistico
lifeline *n* sagola *f* di salvataggio
lifelong *adj* di tutta la vita
lifer /'laɪfə(r)/ *n* fam ergastolano, -a *mf*
lifesaving /'laɪfseɪvɪŋ/ *n* salvataggio *m*
life sentence *n* condanna *f*
all'ergastolo
life-size[d] /'laɪfsaɪz[d]/ *adj* a grandezza
naturale
lifespan *n* durata *f* della vita
life story *n* biografia *f*
lifestyle *n* stile *m* di vita
lifestyle drug *n* medicinale *m* che
migliora la qualità della vita
life support *n* Med respirazione *f*
assistita; **on** ∼ attaccato al respiratore
artificiale; ∼ **machine** respiratore
artificiale

lifetime *n* vita *f*; **the chance of a** ∼
un'occasione unica; ∼ **guarantee** garanzia
f a vita
lift /lɪft/ ① *n* ascensore *m*; Auto passaggio
m; **give somebody a** ∼ dare un passaggio
a qualcuno; **I got a** ∼ mi hanno dato un
passaggio
② *vt* sollevare; revocare ⟨*restrictions*⟩;
(fam: steal) rubare
③ *vi* ⟨*fog*⟩ alzarsi
■ **lift off** *vi* ⟨*rocket*⟩ partire
■ **lift up** *vt* sollevare
liftboy *n* Br lift *m inv*
lift-off *n* decollo *m* (di razzo)
ligament /'lɪgəmənt/ *n* Anat legamento *m*
light¹ /laɪt/ ① *adj* (not dark) luminoso; ∼
green verde chiaro
② *n* luce *f*; (lamp) lampada *f*; **in the** ∼ of fig
alla luce di; **have you got a** ∼? ha da
accendere?; **come to** ∼ essere rivelato
③ *vt* (pt/pp **lit** or **lighted**) accendere;
(illuminate) illuminare
■ **light up** ① *vt* accendere ⟨*pipe,*
cigarette⟩; illuminare ⟨*face*⟩; rischiarare
⟨*sky*⟩
② *vi* ⟨*face*⟩ illuminarsi
light² ① *adj* (not heavy) leggero; **make** ∼
of non dare peso a
② *adv* **travel** ∼ viaggiare con poco
bagaglio
light bulb *n* lampadina *f*
lighten¹ /'laɪtn/ *vt* illuminare
lighten² *vt* alleggerire ⟨*load*⟩
light entertainment *n* varietà *m inv*
lighter /'laɪtə(r)/ *n* accendino *m*
lighter fuel *n* (liquid) gas *m inv* da
accendino
light-fingered /-'fɪŋgəd/ *adj* svelto di
mano
light-headed /-'hedɪd/ *adj* sventato
light-hearted /-'hɑtɪd/ *adj* spensierato
lighthouse *n* faro *m*
light industry *n* industria *f* leggera
lighting /'laɪtɪŋ/ *n* illuminazione *f*
lightly /'laɪtlɪ/ *adv* leggermente; ⟨*accuse*⟩
con leggerezza; ⟨*take something*⟩ alla
leggera; (without concern) senza dare
importanza alla cosa; **get off** ∼ cavarsela
a buon mercato
lightness /'laɪtnɪs/ *n* leggerezza *f*
lightning /'laɪtnɪŋ/ *n* lampo *m*, fulmine
m
lightning conductor *n* parafulmine
m
lightning strike *n* sciopero *m* a
sorpresa
light-pen *n* (for computer screen) penna *f*
ottica
lightweight *adj* leggero *n* (in boxing) peso
m leggero

light year *n* anno *m* luce; **it was ~ ~s ago** è stato secoli fa

like¹ /laɪk/ **①** *adj* simile
② *prep* come; **~ this/that** così; **what's he ~?** com'è?
③ *conj* (fam: as) come; (Am: as if) come se

like² **①** *vt* piacere, gradire; **I should** *or* **would ~** vorrei, gradirei; **I ~ him** mi piace; **I ~ this car** mi piace questa macchina; **I ~ dancing** mi piace ballare; **I ~ that!** fam questa mi è piaciuta!; **~ it or lump it!** abbozzala!
② *n* **~s and dislikes** *pl* gusti *mpl*

likeable /'laɪkəbl/ *adj* simpatico

likelihood /'laɪklɪhʊd/ *n* probabilità *f*

likely /'laɪklɪ/ **①** *adj* (**-ier, -iest**) probabile
② *adv* probabilmente; **not ~!** fam neanche per sogno!

like-minded /laɪk'maɪndɪd/ *adj* con gusti affini

liken /'laɪkən/ *vt* paragonare (**to** a)

likeness /'laɪknɪs/ *n* somiglianza *f*

likewise /'laɪkwaɪz/ *adv* lo stesso

liking /'laɪkɪŋ/ *n* gusto *m*; **is it to your ~?** è di suo gusto?; **take a ~ to somebody** prendere qualcuno in simpatia

lilac /'laɪlək/ **①** *n* lillà *m*
② *adj* lilla

Lilo® /'laɪləʊ/ *n* materassino *m* gonfiabile

lilting /'lɪltɪŋ/ *adj* cadenzato

lily /'lɪlɪ/ *n* giglio *m*

lily of the valley *n* mughetto *m*

lily pond *n* stagno *m* con ninfee

limb /lɪm/ *n* arto *m*

limber /'lɪmbə(r)/ *vi* **~ up** sciogliersi i muscoli

limbo /'lɪmbəʊ/ *n* (Relig, fig, dance) limbo *m*; **be in ~** ⟨*person*⟩ essere nel limbo del dubbio; ⟨*future of something*⟩ essere in sospeso

lime¹ /laɪm/ *n* (fruit) limetta *f*; (tree) tiglio *m*

lime² *n* calce *f*

lime-green *adj* & *n* verde *m* limone

limelight /'laɪmlaɪt/ *n* **be in the ~** essere molto in vista

limestone /'laɪmstəʊn/ *n* calcare *m*

limit /'lɪmɪt/ **①** *n* limite *m*; **be the ~** essere il colmo; **that's the ~!** fam questo è troppo!
② *vt* limitare (**to** a)

limitation /lɪmɪ'teɪʃn/ *n* limite *m*

limited /'lɪmɪtɪd/ *adj* ristretto

limited company *n* società *f inv* a responsabilità limitata

limited edition *n* (book, lithograph) edizione *f* limitata

limited liability *n* responsabilità *f* limitata

limitless /'lɪmɪtlɪs/ *adj* infinito

limousine /'lɪməzi:n/ *n* limousine *f inv*

limp¹ /lɪmp/ **①** *n* andatura *f* zoppicante; **have a ~** zoppicare
② *vi* zoppicare

limp² *adj* floscio

limpet /'lɪmpɪt/ *n* **be like a ~** fig essere attaccaticcio

limpid /'lɪmpɪd/ *adj* limpido

limp-wristed /-'rɪstɪd/ *adj* pej effeminato

linchpin /'lɪntʃpɪn/ *n* (fig: essential element) perno *m*

line¹ /laɪn/ **①** *n* linea *f*; (length of rope, cord) filo *m*; (of writing) riga *f*; (of poem) verso *m*; (row) fila *f*; (wrinkle) ruga *f*; (of business) settore *m*; (Am: queue) coda *f*; **in ~ with** in conformità con; **bring into ~** mettere al passo ⟨*structure, law*⟩; **in the ~ of duty** (of policeman) nell'esercizio delle proprie funzioni; **~ of fire** linea *f* di tiro; **stand in ~** (Am: queue) fare la coda; **in ~ for** ⟨*promotion etc*⟩ in lista per; **on the ~** ⟨*job, career*⟩ in serio pericolo; **read between the ~s** fig leggere tra le righe
② *vt* segnare; fiancheggiare ⟨*street*⟩; foderare ⟨*garment*⟩
■ **line up** **①** *vi* allinearsi
② *vt* allineare

lineage /'lɪnɪɪdʒ/ *n* lignaggio *m*

linear /'lɪnɪə(r)/ *adj* lineare

lined¹ /laɪnd/ *adj* ⟨*face*⟩ rugoso; ⟨*paper*⟩ a righe

lined² *adj* ⟨*garment*⟩ foderato

line manager *n* line manager *m inv*

linen /'lɪnɪn/ **①** *n* lino *m*; (articles) biancheria *f*
② *attrib* di lino

linen basket *n* cesto *m* della biancheria

liner /'laɪnə(r)/ *n* nave *f* di linea

linesman /'laɪnzmən/ *n* Sport guardalinee *m inv*

line-up *n* (personnel, Sport) formazione *f*; (identification) confronto *m* all'americana

linger /'lɪŋgə(r)/ *vi* indugiare

lingerie /'lãʒərɪ/ *n* biancheria *f* intima (da donna)

lingering /'lɪŋgərɪŋ/ *adj* ⟨*illness*⟩ lento; ⟨*look*⟩ prolungato; ⟨*doubt*⟩ persistente

linguist /'lɪŋgwɪst/ *n* linguista *mf*

linguistic /lɪŋ'gwɪstɪk/ *adj* linguistico

linguistically /lɪŋ'gwɪstɪklɪ/ *adv* linguisticamente

linguistics /lɪŋ'gwɪstɪks/ *n* linguistica *fsg*

lining /'laɪnɪŋ/ *n* (of garment) fodera *f*; (of brakes) guarnizione *f*

link /lɪŋk/ **①** *n* (of chain) anello *m*; fig legame *m*

2 vt collegare; ~ **arms** prendersi sottobraccio; Comput ⟨web pages⟩ linkare
■ **link up** vi unirsi (with a); TV collegarsi
linkage /'lɪŋkɪdʒ/ n (connection) connessione f; (in genetics) associazione f
link road n bretella f
links /lɪŋks/ n or npl campo msg da golf
link-up n collegamento m
lino /'laɪnəʊ/ n, **linoleum** /lɪ'nəʊlɪəm/ n linoleum m
linseed oil /'lɪnsiːdɔɪl/ n olio m [di semi] di lino
lint /lɪnt/ n garza f
lintel /'lɪntəl/ n architrave m
lion /'laɪən/ n leone m; **get the ~'s share** fig prendersi la fetta più grossa
lion cub n leoncino m
lioness /'laɪənɪs/ n leonessa f
lip /lɪp/ n labbro m (pl labbra f); (edge) bordo m
lip gloss n lucidalabbra m inv
liposuction /'laɪpəʊsʌkʃn/ n liposuzione f
lip-read vi leggere le labbra
lip-reading n lettura f delle labbra
lipsalve n burro m [di] cacao
lip-service n pay ~ **to** approvare soltanto a parole
lipstick n rossetto m
liquefy /'lɪkwɪfaɪ/ **1** v (pt/pp **-ied**) vt liquefare
2 vi liquefarsi
liqueur /lɪ'kjʊə(r)/ n liquore m
liquid /'lɪkwɪd/ **1** n liquido m
2 adj liquido
liquidate /'lɪkwɪdeɪt/ vt liquidare
liquidation /lɪkwɪ'deɪʃn/ n liquidazione f; go into ~ Comm andare in liquidazione
liquidator /'lɪkwɪdeɪtə(r)/ n liquidatore, -trice mf
liquid crystal display n visualizzatore m a cristalli liquidi
liquidize /'lɪkwɪdaɪz/ vt rendere liquido
liquidizer /'lɪkwɪdaɪzə(r)/ n Culin frullatore m
liquor /'lɪkə(r)/ n bevanda f alcolica
liquorice /'lɪkərɪs/ n liquirizia f
liquor store n Am negozio m di alcolici
lira /'lɪərə/ n old lira f; **50,000 lire** 50.000 lire
lisp /lɪsp/ **1** n pronuncia f con la lisca; **have a ~** parlare con la lisca
2 vi parlare con la lisca
list¹ /lɪst/ **1** n lista f
2 vt elencare
list² vi ⟨ship⟩ inclinarsi
listen /'lɪsn/ vi ascoltare; ~ **to** ascoltare
■ **listen in** vi (secretly) origliare; ~ **in on** ascoltare di nascosto ⟨conversation⟩

listener /'lɪs(ə)nə(r)/ n ascoltatore, -trice mf
listeria /lɪ'stɪərɪə/ n (illness) listeriosi f; (bacteria) listeria f
listings /'lɪstɪŋz/ npl rubrica f degli spettacoli
listless /'lɪstlɪs/ adj svogliato
listlessly /'lɪstlɪslɪ/ adv in modo svogliato
list price n prezzo m di listino
lit /lɪt/ ▸ LIGHT¹
litany /'lɪtənɪ/ n litania f
literacy /'lɪtərəsɪ/ n alfabetizzazione f
literal /'lɪtərəl/ adj letterale
literally /'lɪt(ə)rəlɪ/ adv letteralmente
literary /'lɪtərərɪ/ adj letterario
literary critic n critico, -a mf letterario, -a
literary criticism n critica f letteraria
literate /'lɪtərət/ adj be ~ saper leggere e scrivere
literati /'lɪtə'rɑːtiː/ npl letterati mpl
literature /'lɪtrətʃə(r)/ n letteratura f
lithe /laɪð/ adj flessuoso
lithographer /lɪ'θɒɡrəfə(r)/ n litografo, -a mf
lithography /lɪ'θɒɡrəfɪ/ n litografia f
Lithuania /lɪθjʊ'eɪnɪə/ n Lituania f
Lithuanian /lɪθjʊ'eɪnɪən/ adj & n lituano, -a mf; (language) lituano m
litigation /lɪtɪ'ɡeɪʃn/ n causa f [giudiziaria]
litmus paper /'lɪtməs/ n cartina f di tornasole
litmus test n Chem test m inv con cartina di tornasole; fig prova f del nove
litre /'liːtə(r)/ n litro m
litter /'lɪtə(r)/ **1** n immondizie fpl; Zool figliata f
2 vt be ~ed **with something** essere ingombrato di qualcosa
litter-bin n bidone m della spazzatura
litterbug /'lɪtəbʌɡ/ n persona f che butta per terra cartacce e rifiuti
little /'lɪtl/ **1** adj piccolo; (not much) poco
2 adv & n poco m; a ~ un po'; a ~ **water** un po' d'acqua; a ~ **better** un po' meglio; ~ **by** ~ a poco a poco
little finger n mignolo m (della mano)
little-known adj poco noto
liturgical /lɪ'tɜːdʒɪkl/ adj liturgico
liturgy /'lɪtədʒɪ/ n liturgia f
live¹ /laɪv/ **1** adj vivo; ⟨ammunition⟩ carico; ~ **broadcast** trasmissione f in diretta; be ~ Electr essere sotto tensione
2 adv ⟨broadcast⟩ in diretta
live² /lɪv/ vi vivere; (reside) abitare
■ **live down** vt far dimenticare

■ **live for** *vt* vivere solo per ⟨*one's work, family*⟩

■ **live in** *vi* ⟨*nanny, au-pair*⟩ abitare sul posto di lavoro

■ **live off** *vt* vivere alle spalle di

■ **live on** ① *vt* vivere di
② *vi* sopravvivere

■ **live through** *vt* vivere

■ **live together** *vi* ⟨*friends*⟩ vivere insieme; ⟨*lovers*⟩ convivere

■ **live up** *vt* ~ **it up** far la bella vita

■ **live up to** *vt* essere all'altezza di

■ **live with** *vt* convivere con ⟨*lover, situation*⟩; vivere con ⟨*mother etc*⟩

lived-in /'lɪvdɪn/ *adj* **have that** ~ **look** ⟨*room, flat*⟩ avere un'aria vissuta

live-in *adj* ⟨*maid, nanny*⟩ che vive in casa

livelihood /'laɪvlɪhʊd/ *n* mezzi *mpl* di sostentamento

liveliness /'laɪvlɪnɪs/ *n* vivacità *f*

lively /'laɪvlɪ/ *adj* (**-ier**, **-iest**) vivace

liven /'laɪvn/ *v*
■ **liven up** /'laɪvn/ ① *vt* vivacizzare
② *vi* vivacizzarsi

liver /'lɪvə(r)/ *n* fegato *m*

liver pâté *n* pâté *m inv* di fegato

Liverpudlian /lɪvə'pʌdlɪən/ *n* ⟨*born there*⟩ originario, -a *mf* di Liverpool; ⟨*living there*⟩ abitante *mf* di Liverpool

livery /'lɪvərɪ/ *n* (uniform) livrea *f*

lives /laɪvz/ ▶ LIFE

livestock /'laɪvstɒk/ *n* bestiame *m*

live wire *n* fig **be a** ~ essere superdinamico

livid /'lɪvɪd/ *adj* fam livido

living /'lɪvɪŋ/ ① *adj* vivo
② *n* **earn one's** ~ guadagnarsi da vivere; **the** ~ *pl* i vivi

living room *n* soggiorno *m*

living will *n* testamento *m* biologico

lizard /'lɪzəd/ *n* lucertola *f*

llama /'lɑːmə/ *n* lama *m*

LLB *abbr* (**Bachelor of Laws**) laureato, -a *mf* in legge

load /ləʊd/ ① *n* carico *m*; ~**s of** fam un sacco di; **that's a** ~ **off my mind** mi sono tolto un peso [dallo stomaco]
② *vt* ~ **[up]** caricare

loaded /'ləʊdɪd/ *adj* carico; (fam: rich) ricchissimo; ~ **question** domanda *f* esplosiva *f*

loading bay /'ləʊdɪŋ/ *n* piazzola *f* di carico e scarico

loaf¹ /ləʊf/ *n* (pl **loaves**) pane *m*; (round) pagnotta *f*; **use one's** ~ (fam) pensare con il proprio cervello

loaf², ~ **about** or **around** *vi* oziare

loafer /'ləʊfə(r)/ *n* (idler) scansafatiche *mf inv*; (shoe) mocassino *m*

loan /ləʊn/ ① *n* prestito *m*; **on** ~ in prestito
② *vt* prestare

loan shark *n* fam strozzino, -a *mf*

loath /ləʊθ/ *adj* **be** ~ **to do something** essere restio a fare qualcosa

loathe /ləʊð/ *vt* detestare

loathing /'ləʊðɪŋ/ *n* disgusto *m*

loathsome /'ləʊðsəm/ *adj* disgustoso

loaves /ləʊvz/ ▶ LOAF¹

lob /lɒb/ ① *vt* (pres p etc **-bb-**) lanciare in alto; Sport respingere a pallonetto
② *n* Sport pallonetto *m*

lobby /'lɒbɪ/ ① *n* atrio *m*; Pol gruppo *m* di pressione, lobby *f inv*
② *v* ~ **for something** fare pressioni per qualcosa

lobbying /'lɒbɪɪŋ/ *n* lobbismo *m*

lobbyist /'lɒbɪɪst/ *n* lobbista *mf*

lobe /ləʊb/ *n* (of ear) lobo *m*

lobelia /lə'biːlɪə/ *n* lobelia *f*

lobster /'lɒbstə(r)/ *n* aragosta *f*

lobster pot *n* nassa *f* per aragoste

local /'ləʊkl/ ① *adj* locale; **under** ~ **anaesthetic** sotto anestesia locale; **I'm not** ~ non sono del posto
② *n* abitante *mf* del luogo; (fam: public house) pub *m inv* locale

local authority *n* autorità *f* locale

local bus *n* bus *m* locale

local call *n* Teleph telefonata *f* urbana

local election *n* elezioni *fpl* amministrative

local government *n* autorità *f inv* locale

locality /ləʊ'kælətɪ/ *n* zona *f*

localized /'ləʊkəlaɪzd/ *adj* localizzato

locally /'ləʊkəlɪ/ *adv* localmente; ⟨*live, work*⟩ nei paraggi

local network *n* Comput rete *f* locale

locate /ləʊ'keɪt/ *vt* situare; trovare ⟨*person*⟩; **be** ~**d** essere situato

location /ləʊ'keɪʃn/ *n* posizione *f*; **filmed on** ~ girato in esterni

loch /lɒx/ *n* lago *m*

lock¹ /lɒk/ *n* (of hair) ciocca *f*

lock² ① *n* (on door) serratura *f*: (on canal) chiusa *f*
② *vt* chiudere a chiave; bloccare ⟨*wheels*⟩
③ *vi* chiudersi
■ **lock in** *vt* chiudere dentro
■ **lock out** *vt* chiudere fuori
■ **lock together** *vi* ⟨*pieces*⟩ incastrarsi
■ **lock up** ① *vt* (in prison) mettere dentro
② *vi* chiudere

locker /'lɒkə(r)/ *n* armadietto *m*

locker room *n* spogliatoio *m*

locket /'lɒkɪt/ *n* medaglione *m*

lockout n serrata f
locksmith n fabbro m
lock-up n (prison) guardina f
loco /'ləʊkəʊ/ adj (Br: crazy) toccato
locomotion /ləʊkə'məʊʃn/ n locomozione f
locomotive /ləʊkə'məʊtɪv/ n locomotiva f
locum /'ləʊkəm/ n sostituto, -a mf
locust /'ləʊkəst/ n locusta f
lodge /lɒdʒ/ ① n (porter's) portineria f; (masonic) loggia f ② vt presentare ⟨claim, complaint⟩; (with bank, solicitor) depositare; **be ~d** essersi conficcato ③ vi essere a pensione (**with** da); (become fixed) conficcarsi
lodger /'lɒdʒə(r)/ n inquilino, -a mf
lodgings /'lɒdʒɪŋ/ npl camere fpl in affitto
loft /lɒft/ n soffitta f
loft conversion n soppalco f abitabile
lofty /'lɒftɪ/ adj (-ier, -iest) alto; (haughty) altezzoso
log /lɒg/ ① n ceppo m; Auto libretto m di circolazione; Naut giornale m di bordo; **sleep like a ~** fam dormire come un ghiro ② vt (pt/pp **logged**) registrare
■ **log in** vi aprire una sessione
■ **log off** vi disconnettersi
■ **log on** vi connettersi (**to** a)
■ **log out** vi chiudere una sessione
logarithm /'lɒgərɪðm/ n logaritmo m
logbook /'lɒgbʊk/ n Naut giornale m di bordo; Auto libretto m di circolazione
log cabin n capanna f di tronchi
logger /'lɒgə(r)/ n boscaiolo m
loggerheads /'lɒgəhedz/ npl **be at ~** fam essere in totale disaccordo
logic /'lɒdʒɪk/ n logica f
logical /'lɒdʒɪkl/ adj logico
logically /'lɒdʒɪklɪ/ adv logicamente
logistics /lə'dʒɪstɪks/ npl logistica f
logo /'ləʊgəʊ/ n logo m inv
loin /lɔɪn/ n Culin lombata f
loin chop n lombatina f
loincloth /'lɔɪnklɒθ/ n perizoma m
loiter /'lɔɪtə(r)/ vi gironzolare
loll /lɒl/ vi **~ about** (posture) stravaccarsi; (do nothing) starsene in panciolle
lollipop /'lɒlɪpɒp/ n lecca-lecca m inv
lollop /'lɒləp/ vi ⟨rabbit, person⟩ avanzare a balzi
lolly /'lɒlɪ/ n lecca-lecca m inv; (fam: money) quattrini mpl
Lombardy /'lɒmbədɪ/ n Lombardia f
London /'lʌndən/ ① n Londra f ② attrib londinese, di Londra
Londoner /'lʌndənə(r)/ n londinese mf

lone /ləʊn/ adj solitario
loneliness /'ləʊnlɪnɪs/ n solitudine f
lonely /'ləʊnlɪ/ adj (-ier, -iest) solitario; ⟨person⟩ solo
lonely hearts' column n rubrica f dei cuori solitari
loner /'ləʊnə(r)/ n persona f solitaria
lonesome /'ləʊnsəm/ adj solo
long[1] /lɒŋ/ ① adj (-er /'lɒŋgə(r)/, -est /'lɒŋgɪst/) (lungo; **a ~ time** molto tempo; **a ~ way** distante; **in the ~ run** a lungo andare; (in the end) alla fin fine ② adv a lungo, lungamente; **how ~ is it?** quanto è lungo?; ⟨in time⟩ quanto dura?; **all day ~** tutto il giorno; **not ~ ago** non molto tempo fa; **before ~** fra breve; **he's no ~er here** non è più qui; **as** or **so~ as** finché; (provided that) purché; **so ~!** fam ciao!; **will you be ~?** ti ci vuole molto?
long[2] vi **~ for** desiderare ardentemente
long-awaited adj tanto atteso
long-distance adj a grande distanza; Sport di fondo; ⟨call⟩ interurbano
long division n divisione f
longevity /lɒn'dʒevətɪ/ n longevità f
long face n muso m lungo
longhand /'lɒŋhænd/ n **in ~** in scrittura ordinaria
long-haul attrib su lunga distanza; ⟨plane⟩ per lunghi tragitti
longing /'lɒŋɪŋ/ ① adj desideroso ② n brama f
longingly /'lɒŋɪŋlɪ/ adv con desiderio
longitude /'lɒŋgɪtjuːd/ n Geog longitudine f
long jump n salto m in lungo
long-life milk n latte m a lunga conservazione
long-lived /-'lɪvd/ adj longevo
long-playing record n 33 giri m inv
long-range adj Mil, Aeron a lunga portata; ⟨forecast⟩ a lungo termine
long-sighted /-saɪtɪd/ adj presbite
long-sleeved /-'sliːvd/ adj a maniche lunghe
long-standing adj di vecchia data
long-suffering adj infinitamente paziente
long-term adj a lunga scadenza
long-time adj ⟨partner⟩ di lunga data
long wave n onde fpl lunghe
long-winded /-'wɪndɪd/ adj prolisso
loo /luː/ n fam gabinetto m
look /lʊk/ ① n occhiata f; (appearance) aspetto m; **[good] ~s** pl bellezza f; **have a ~ at** dare un'occhiata a ② vi guardare. (seem) sembrare; **~ here!** mi ascolti bene!; **~ at** guardare; **~ for** cercare; **~ somebody in the eye** guardare negli occhi qualcuno; **~ somebody up and** ⋯▸

down guardare qualcuno dall'alto in basso; ∼ **a fool** fare la figura del cretino; ∼ **young/old for one's age** portarsi bene/male gli anni; ∼ **like** (resemble) assomigliare a; **it** ∼**s as if it's going to rain** sembra che stia per piovere; ∼ **sharp** (fam: hurry up) darsi una mossa

■ **look after** vt badare a

■ **look ahead** vi (think of the future) guardare al futuro

■ **look back** vi girarsi; (think of the past) guardare indietro

■ **look down** vi guardare in basso; ∼ **down on somebody** fig guardare dall'alto in basso qualcuno

■ **look forward to** vt essere impaziente di

■ **look in on** vt passare da

■ **look into** vt (examine) esaminare

■ **look on** ① vi (watch) guardare ② vt ∼ **on somebody/something as** (consider to be) considerare qualcuno/qualcosa come

■ **look on to** vt ⟨room⟩ dare su

■ **look out** ① vi guardare fuori; (take care) fare attenzione; ∼ **out!** attento! ② vt cercare ⟨something for somebody⟩

■ **look out for** vt cercare

■ **look over** vt riguardare ⟨notes⟩; ispezionare ⟨house⟩

■ **look round** vi girarsi; (in shop, town etc) dare un'occhiata

■ **look through** vt dare un'occhiata a ⟨script, notes⟩

■ **look to** vt (rely on) contare su

■ **look up** ① vi guardare in alto ② vt cercare [nel dizionario] ⟨word⟩; (visit) andare a trovare

■ **look up to** vt fig rispettare

look-alike n sosia mf inv

looker-on /lʊkər'ɒn/ n (pl **lookers-on**) spettatore, -trice mf

look-in n Br fam **give somebody a** ∼ dare una chance a qualcuno; **get a** ∼ avere una chance

lookout /'lʊkaʊt/ n guardia f; (prospect) prospettiva f; **be on the** ∼ **for** tenere gli occhi aperti per

loom¹ /luːm/ n telaio m

loom² vi apparire; fig profilarsi

loony /'luːnɪ/ adj & n fam matto, -a mf; ∼ **bin** manicomio m

loop /luːp/ n cappio m; (on garment) passante m

loophole /'luːphəʊl/ n (in the law) scappatoia f

loopy /'luːpɪ/ adj fam matto

loose /luːs/ adj libero; ⟨knot⟩ allentato; ⟨page⟩ staccato; ⟨clothes⟩ largo; ⟨morals⟩ dissoluto; (inexact) vago; **be at a** ∼ **end** non sapere cosa fare; **come** ∼ ⟨knot⟩ sciogliersi; **set** ∼ liberare

loose change n spiccioli mpl

loose chippings npl ghiaino m

loose-leaf notebook n raccoglitore m di fogli

loosely /'luːslɪ/ adv scorrevolmente; ⟨defined⟩ vagamente

loosely knit adj ⟨group⟩ poco unito

loosen /'luːsn/ vt sciogliere

■ **loosen up** ① vt sciogliere ⟨muscles⟩ ② vi (fam: relax) rilassarsi

loot /luːt/ ① n bottino m ② vt/i depredare

looter /luːtə(r)/ n saccheggiatore, -trice mf

looting /'luːtɪŋ/ n saccheggio m

lop /lɒp/ vt ∼ **off** (pt/pp **lopped**) potare

lope /ləʊp/ vi ∼ **off** andarsene a passi lunghi

lop-eared /lɒpɪəd/ adj con le orecchie [a] penzoloni

lopsided /lɒp'saɪdɪd/ adj sbilenco

loquacious /lə'kweɪʃəs/ adj loquace

lord /lɔːd/ n signore m; (title) Lord m; **House of L**∼**s** Camera f dei Lord; **the L**∼**'s Prayer** il Padrenostro; **good L**∼! Dio Mio!

Lord Mayor n sindaco m della City di Londra

Lordship /'lɔːdʃɪp/ n **your/his L**∼ (of noble) Sua Signoria; **your L**∼ (to judge) Signor Giudice

lore /lɔː(r)/ n tradizioni fpl

lorry /'lɒrɪ/ n camion m inv

lorry driver n camionista mf

lose /luːz/ ① vt (pt/pp **lost**) perdere; ∼ **heart** perdersi d'animo; ∼ **one's inhibitions** disinibirsi; ∼ **one's nerve** farsi prendere dalla paura; ∼ **sight of** perdere di vista, perdere d' occhio; ∼ **touch with** perdere di vista; ∼ **track of time** perdere la nozione del tempo; ∼ **weight** calare di peso ② vi perdere; ⟨clock⟩ essere indietro

■ **lose out** vi rimetterci

loser /'luːzə(r)/ n perdente mf

losing battle /'luːzɪŋ/ n battaglia f persa

loss /lɒs/ n perdita f; ∼**es** pl Comm perdite fpl; **be at a** ∼ essere perplesso; **be at a** ∼ **for words** non trovare le parole; **make a** ∼ Comm subire una perdita

loss adjuster /'lɒsədʒʌstə(r)/ n Comm perito m di assicurazione

loss-leader n articolo m civetta

loss-making /'lɒsmeɪkɪŋ/ adj ⟨company⟩ in passivo; ⟨product⟩ che non vende

lost /lɒst/ ① ▶ LOSE ② adj perduto; **get** ∼ perdersi; **get** ∼! fam va' a quel paese!

lost and found n Am oggetti mpl smarriti

lost property n Br oggetti mpl smarriti

lost property office *n* ufficio *m* oggetti smarriti

lot[1] /lɒt/ (at auction) lotto *m*; (piece of land) lotto *m*; **draw ~s** tirare a sorte

lot[2] *n* **the ~** il tutto; **a ~ of, ~s of** molti; **the ~ of you** tutti voi; **it has changed a ~** è cambiato molto

lotion *n* lozione *f*

lottery /'lɒtərɪ/ *n* lotteria *f*

lottery ticket *n* biglietto *m* della lotteria

loud /laʊd/ 1 *adj* sonoro, alto; ‹colours› sgargiante
2 *adv* forte; **out ~** ad alta voce

loud hailer /'heɪlə(r)/ *n* megafono *m*

loudly /'laʊdlɪ/ *adv* forte

loudspeaker /laʊd'spi:kə(r)/ *n* altoparlante *m*

lounge /laʊndʒ/ 1 *n* salotto *m*; (in hotel) salone *m*
2 *vi* poltrire
■ **lounge about** *vi* stare in panciolle

lounge suit *n* vestito *m* da uomo (formale)

louse /laʊs/ *n* (pl **lice**) pidocchio *m*
■ **louse up** *vt* (fam: ruin) guastare

lousy /'laʊzɪ/ *adj* (-**ier**, -**iest**) fam schifoso

lout /laʊt/ *n* zoticone *m*

loutish /'laʊtɪʃ/ *adj* rozzo

louvred /'lu:vəd/ *adj* ‹door, blinds› con le gelosie

lovable /'lʌvəbl/ *adj* adorabile

love /lʌv/ 1 *n* amore *m*; (Tennis) zero *m*; **in ~** innamorato (**with** di)
2 *vt* amare ‹person, country›; **I ~ watching tennis** mi piace molto guardare il tennis

love affair *n* relazione *f* [sentimentale]

lovebite *n* succhiotto *m*

love letter *n* lettera *f* d'amore

love life *n* vita *f* sentimentale

lovely /'lʌvlɪ/ *adj* (-**ier**, -**iest**) bello; (in looks) bello, attraente; (in character) piacevole; ‹meal› delizioso; **have a ~ time** divertirsi molto

lovemaking *n* il fare l'amore

lover /'lʌvə(r)/ *n* amante *mf*

love song *n* canzone *f* d'amore

love story *n* storia *f* d'amore

lovey-dovey /lʌvɪ'dʌvɪ/ *adj* Br fam **get all ~** fare i piccioncini

loving /'lʌvɪŋ/ *adj* affettuoso

lovingly /'lʌvɪŋlɪ/ *adv* affettuosamente

low /ləʊ/ 1 *adj* basso; (depressed) giù *inv*
2 *adv* basso; **feel ~** sentirsi giù
3 *n* minimo *m*; Meteorol depressione *f*; **at an all-time ~** ‹prices etc› al livello minimo

low-alcohol *adj* ‹beer› a bassa gradazione alcolica

lowbrow /'ləʊbraʊ/ *adj* di scarsa cultura

low-budget *adj* ‹flight, airline› low-cost *inv*

low-calorie *adj* ipocalorico

low-cost *adj* low-cost *inv*

low-cut *adj* ‹dress› scollato

low-down 1 *adj* fam ‹trick› mancino
2 *n* (details) informazioni *fpl*

lower /'ləʊə(r)/ 1 *adj & adv* ▶ LOW
2 *vt* abbassare; **~ oneself** abbassarsi

lower class 1 *adj* del ceto basso
2 *n* ceto *m* basso

lowest common denominator /'ləʊɪst/.../di'nɒmɪneɪtə(r)/ *n* minimo denominatore *m* comune

low-fat *adj* ‹diet› a basso contenuto di grassi; ‹cheese, milk› magro

low gear *n* Auto marcia *f* bassa

low-grade *adj* di qualità inferiore

low-income *adj* ‹families› a basso reddito

low-key *adj* fig moderato

lowlands *npl* pianure *fpl*

low-level *adj* ‹talks› informale; ‹radiation› debole; ‹bombing› a bassa quota

lowly /'ləʊlɪ/ *adj* (-**ier**, -**iest**) umile

low-lying *adj* ‹land› a bassa quota

low-maintenance *adj* **a ~ garden** un giardino che richiede poca manutenzione

low-paid *adj* ‹job, worker› mal pagato

low-priced *adj* a basso prezzo

low profile *n* **keep a ~** mantenere un profilo basso

low-profile *adj* ‹campaign› di basso profilo

low-quality *adj* scadente

low-risk *adj* a basso rischio

low season *n* bassa stagione *f*

low-tech *adj* a bassa tecnologia

low tide *n* bassa marea *f*

loyal /'lɔɪəl/ *adj* leale

loyally /'lɔɪəlɪ/ *adv* lealmente

loyalty /'lɔɪəltɪ/ *n* lealtà *f*

loyalty card *n* carta *f* fedeltà

lozenge /'lɒzɪndʒ/ *n* losanga *f*; (tablet) pastiglia

LP *n abbr* (**long-playing record**) LP *m inv*

L-plate *n* Br Auto cartello *m* che indica che il conducente non ha ancora preso la patente

LSD *n* LSD *m*

LST *abbr* (**local standard time**) ora *f* locale

Ltd *abbr* (**Limited**) s.r.l.

lubricant /'lu:brɪkənt/ *n* lubrificante *m*

lubricate /'lu:brɪkeɪt/ *vt* lubrificare

lubrication /luːbrɪˈkeɪʃn/ n
lubrificazione f

lucid /ˈluːsɪd/ adj ⟨explanation⟩ chiaro;
(sane) lucido

lucidity /luːˈsɪdətɪ/ n lucidità f; (of
explanation) chiarezza f

luck /lʌk/ n fortuna f; **bad** ∼ sfortuna f;
good ∼! buona fortuna!

luckily /ˈlʌkɪlɪ/ adv fortunatamente

lucky /ˈlʌkɪ/ adj (-ier, -iest) fortunato;
be ∼ essere fortunato; ⟨thing⟩ portare
fortuna

lucky charm n portafortuna m inv

lucky dip n pesca f di beneficenza

lucrative /ˈluːkrətɪv/ adj lucrativo

lucre /ˈluːkə(r)/ n (fam: money) soldi mpl

ludicrous /ˈluːdɪkrəs/ adj ridicolo

ludicrously /ˈluːdɪkrəslɪ/ adv ⟨expensive,
complex⟩ eccessivamente

ludo /ˈluːdəʊ/ n Br gioco m da tavolo

lug /lʌg/ vt (pt/pp **lugged**) fam trascinare

luggage /ˈlʌgɪdʒ/ n bagaglio

luggage-rack n portabagagli m inv

luggage trolley n carrello m
portabagagli

luggage van n bagagliaio m

lughole /ˈlʌghəʊl/ n (Br fam: ear) orecchio
m

lugubrious /lʊˈguːbrɪəs/ adj lugubre

lukewarm /ˈluːkwɔːm/ adj tiepido; fig
poco entusiasta

lull /lʌl/ ① n pausa f
② vt ∼ **to sleep** cullare

lullaby /ˈlʌləbaɪ/ n ninnananna f

lumbago /lʌmˈbeɪgəʊ/ n lombaggine f

lumbar /ˈlʌmbə(r)/ adj lombare

lumber /ˈlʌmbə(r)/ ① n cianfrusaglie fpl:
(Am: timber) legname m
② vt fam ∼ **somebody with something**
affibbiare qualcosa a qualcuno

lumberjack /ˈlʌmbədʒæk/ n
tagliaboschi m inv

luminary /ˈluːmɪnərɪ/ n (fig: person)
luminare mf

luminous /ˈluːmɪnəs/ adj luminoso

lump[1] /lʌmp/ ① n (of sugar) zolletta f;
(swelling) gonfiore m; (in breast) nodulo m; (in
sauce) grumo m; **a** ∼ **in one's throat** un
groppo alla gola
② vt ∼ **together** ammucchiare

lump[2] vt ∼ **it** fam **you'll just have to** ∼ **it**
che ti piaccia o no è così

lump sugar n zucchero m in zollette

lump sum n somma f globale

lumpy /ˈlʌmpɪ/ adj (-ier, -iest) grumoso

lunacy /ˈluːnəsɪ/ n follia f

lunar /ˈluːnə(r)/ adj lunare

lunatic /ˈluːnətɪk/ n pazzo, -a mf

lunch /lʌntʃ/ ① n pranzo m; **she's gone
to** ∼ è andata a pranzo; **let's have** ∼
together sometime pranziamo qualche
volta insieme
② vi pranzare

lunch box n cestino m del pranzo

lunchbreak n pausa f pranzo

luncheon /ˈlʌntʃn/ n (formal) pranzo m

luncheon meat n carne f in scatola

luncheon voucher n buono m pasto

lunch hour n pausa f pranzo

lunchtime /ˈlʌntʃtaɪm/ n ora f di pranzo

lung /lʌŋ/ n polmone m

lung cancer n cancro m al polmone

lunge /lʌndʒ/ vi lanciarsi (**at** su)

lurch[1] /lɜːtʃ/ n **leave in the** ∼ fam lasciare
nei guai

lurch[2] vi barcollare

lure /lʊə(r)/ ① n esca f; fig lusinga f
② vt adescare

lurid /ˈlʊərɪd/ adj (gaudy) sgargiante;
(sensational) sensazionalistico

lurk /lɜːk/ vi appostarsi

luscious /ˈlʌʃəs/ adj saporito; fig sexy
inv

lush /lʌʃ/ adj lussureggiante

lust /lʌst/ ① n lussuria f
② vi ∼ **after** desiderare [fortemente]

lustful /ˈlʌstfʊl/ adj lussurioso

lustre /ˈlʌstə(r)/ n lustro m

lusty /ˈlʌstɪ/ adj (-ier, -iest) vigoroso

lute /luːt/ n liuto m

luvvy, luvvie /ˈlʌvɪ/ n fam attore, -trice
mf pretenzioso

Luxembourg /ˈlʌksəmbɜːg/ n (city)
Lussemburgo f; (state) Lussemburgo m

luxuriant /lʌgˈʒʊərɪənt/ adj
lussureggiante, rigoglioso

luxuriantly /lʌgˈʒjʊərɪəntlɪ/ adv
rigogliosamente

luxurious /lʌgˈʒʊərɪəs/ adj lussuoso

luxuriously /lʌgˈʒʊərɪəslɪ/ adv
lussuosamente

luxury /ˈlʌkʃərɪ/ ① n lusso m; **live in** ∼
vivere nel lusso
② attrib di lusso

LV abbr **luncheon voucher**

LW abbr (**long wave**) OL

lychee /ˈlaɪtʃiː/ n litchi m inv

lych-gate /ˈlɪtʃ-/ n entrata f coperta di
un cimitero

lycra® /ˈlaɪkrə/ n lycra f

lying /ˈlaɪɪŋ/ ① ▶ LIE[1], ▶ LIE[2]
② n mentire m

lymph gland /ˈlɪmf/ n linfoghiandola f

lymph node n linfonodo m

lynch /lɪntʃ/ vt linciare

lynch mob n linciatori mpl

lynchpin /'lɪntʃpɪn/ n fig pilastro m
lynx /lɪŋks/ n lince f
lyric /'lɪrɪk/ adj lirico
lyrical /'lɪrɪkl/ adj lirico; (fam: enthusiastic)
entusiasta; ~ **poetry** n poesia f lirica
lyricism /'lɪrɪsɪzm/ n lirismo m
lyricist /'lɪrɪsɪst/ n paroliere, -a mf
lyrics /'lɪrɪks/ npl parole fpl

m¹, **M** /em/ n (letter) m, M f inv
m² abbr (**metre(s)**) m; abbr (**million**)
milione m; abbr (**mile(s)**) miglio
MA n abbr (**Master of Arts**) (diploma)
laurea f in lettere; (person) laureato, -a mf
in lettere; Am abbr **Massachusetts**
ma'am /mɑːm/ int signora; (to queen) Sua
Altezza
mac /mæk/ n fam impermeabile m
macabre /məˈkɑːbr/ adj macabro
macaroni /mækəˈrəʊnɪ/ n maccheroni
mpl
macaroni cheese n maccheroni mpl
gratinati al formaggio
macaroon /mækəˈruːn/ n ≈ amaretto m
mace¹ /meɪs/ n (staff) mazza f
mace² n (spice) macis mf
Macedonia /mæsəˈdəʊnɪə/ n Macedonia
f
machete /məˈʃetɪ/ n machete m inv
Machiavellian /mækɪəˈvelɪən/ adj
machiavellico
machinations /mækɪˈneɪʃnz/
macchinazioni fpl
machine /məˈʃiːn/ ① n macchina f
② vt (sew) cucire a macchina; Techn
lavorare a macchina
machine-gun n mitragliatrice f
machine operator n addetto, -a mf
alle macchine
machine-readable adj ⟨data, text⟩
leggibile dalla macchina
machinery /məˈʃiːnərɪ/ n macchinario
m; fig meccanismo m
machine-stitch vt cucire a macchina
machine tool n macchina f utensile
machine translation n traduzione f
elettronica
machinist /məˈʃiːnɪst/ n macchinista
mf; (on sewing machine) lavorante mf adetto,
-a alla macchina da cucire
machismo /məˈkɪzməʊ/ n machismo m
macho /ˈmætʃəʊ/ adj macho inv
mackerel /ˈmækr(ə)l/ n inv sgombro m
mackintosh /ˈmækɪntɒʃ/ n
impermeabile m

macro /ˈmækrəʊ/ n Comput macro f inv
macrocosm /ˈmækrəʊkɒzm/ n
macrocosmo m
mad /mæd/ adj (**madder**, **maddest**)
pazzo, matto; (fam: angry) furioso (**at** con);
like ~ fam come un pazzo; **be** ~ **about**
somebody/something (fam: keen on) andare
matto per qualcuno/qualcosa
Madagascar /mædəˈgæskə(r)/ n
Madagascar m
madam /ˈmædəm/ n signora f
mad cow disease n fam = BSE
madden /ˈmædən/ vt (make angry) far
diventare matto
maddening /ˈmæd(ə)nɪŋ/ adj ⟨delay,
person⟩ esasperante
made /meɪd/ ▶ MAKE
Madeira cake /məˈdɪərə/ n pan m di
Spagna
made to measure adj [fatto] su
misura
made-up adj (wearing make-up) truccato;
⟨road⟩ asfaltata; ⟨story⟩ inventato
madhouse /ˈmædhaʊs/ n fam
manicomio m; **it's like a** ~ **in here!**
sembra di essere in un manicomio
madly /ˈmædlɪ/ adv fam follemente; ~ **in**
love innamorato follemente
madman /ˈmædmən/ n pazzo m
madness /ˈmædnɪs/ n pazzia f
madonna /məˈdɒnə/ n madonna f
madwoman /ˈmædwʊmən/ n pazza f
mafia /ˈmæfɪə/ n also fig mafia f
mag /mæg/ n abbr **magazine**
magazine /mægəˈziːn/ n rivista f; Mil,
Phot magazzino m
maggot /ˈmægət/ n verme m
maggoty /ˈmægətɪ/ adj coi vermi
Magi /ˈmeɪdʒaɪ/ npl the **M**~ i Re Magi
magic /ˈmædʒɪk/ ① n magia f; (tricks)
giochi mpl di prestigio
② adj magico; ⟨trick⟩ di prestigio
magical /ˈmædʒɪkl/ adj magico
magic carpet n tappeto m volante
magician /məˈdʒɪʃn/ n mago, -a mf;
(entertainer) prestigiatore, -trice mf

magistrate /'mædʒɪstreɪt/ n magistrato
m

magistrate's court n ≈ pretura f

magnanimity /mægnə'nɪmətɪ/ n
magnanimità f

magnanimous /mæg'nænɪməs/ adj
magnanimo

magnate /'mægneɪt/ n magnate m

magnesia /mæg'ni:ʃə/ n magnesia f

magnesium /mæg'ni:zɪəm/ n magnesio
m

magnet /'mægnɪt/ n magnete m,
calamita f

magnetic /mæg'netɪk/ adj magnetico

magnetic resonance imaging n
Med risonanza f magnetica

magnetic tape n nastro m magnetico

magnetism /'mægnətɪzm/ n
magnetismo m

magnetize /'mægnətaɪz/ vt
magnetizzare

magnification /mægnɪfɪ'keɪʃn/ n
ingrandimento m

magnificence /mæg'nɪfɪsəns/ n
magnificenza f

magnificent /mæg'nɪfɪsənt/ adj
magnifico

magnificently /mæg'nɪfɪsəntlɪ/ adv
magnificamente

magnify /'mægnɪfaɪ/ vt (pt/pp **-ied**)
ingrandire; (exaggerate) ingigantire

magnifying glass /'mægnɪfaɪɪŋ/ n
lente f d'ingrandimento

magnitude /'mægnɪtju:d/ n grandezza f;
(importance) importanza f; **a project of this**
~ un progetto di tale portata

magnolia /mæg'nəʊlɪə/ n (tree) magnolia
f; (colour) crema m

magnum opus /mægnəm'ɒpəs/ n opera
f principale

magpie /'mægpaɪ/ n gazza f

mahogany /mə'hɒgənɪ/ ① n mogano m
② attrib di mogano

maid /meɪd/ n cameriera f; **old** ~ pej
zitella f

maiden /'meɪdn/ ① n liter fanciulla f
② adj ‹speech, voyage› inaugurale

maiden aunt n zia f zitella

maiden name n nome m da ragazza

mail /meɪl/ ① n posta f
② vt impostare

mailbag n sacco m postale

mail bomb n pacco m esplosivo
(arrivato per posta)

mailbox n Am cassetta f delle lettere; (e-
mail) casella f postale

mail coach n Rail vagone m postale

mail delivery n consegna f della posta

mailing /'meɪlɪŋ/ n (action) mailing m inv;
(document) pubblicità f

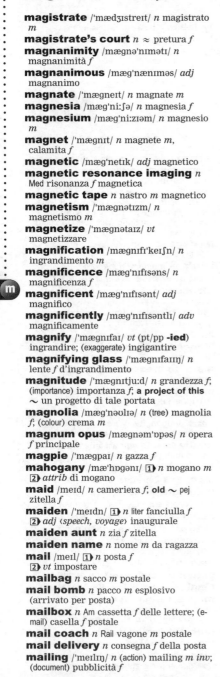

mailing address n recapito m postale

mailing list n elenco m d'indirizzi per
un mailing

mailman /'meɪlmən/ n Am postino m

mail order ① n vendita f per
corrispondenza
② attrib ‹business› di vendita per
corrispondenza; ‹goods› comprati per
corrispondenza

mail-order catalogue n catalogo m
di vendita per corrispondenza

mail-order firm n ditta f di vendita per
corrispondenza

mail room n reparto m spedizioni

mail server n Comput server m inv di
posta

mailshot n mailing m inv

mail train n treno m postale

mail van n (delivery vehicle) furgone m
postale; (in train) vagone m postale

maim /meɪm/ vt menomare

main¹ /meɪn/ n (water; gas, electricity)
conduttura f principale

main² ① adj principale; **the** ~ **thing is**
to... la cosa essenziale è di...
② n **in the** ~ in complesso

main course n secondo m

main deck n ponte m di coperta

mainframe n Comput mainframe m inv

mainland n continente m

main line ① n Rail linea f principale
② attrib ‹station, terminus, train› della
linea principale

mainly /'meɪnlɪ/ adv principalmente

main memory n Comput memoria f
principale

main office n (of company) sede f centrale

main road n strada f principale

mainsail n randa f, vela f di taglio

mainstay n fig pilastro m

mainstream ① adj (conventional)
tradizionale
② n corrente f principale

main street n via f principale

maintain /meɪn'teɪn/ vt mantenere; (keep
in repair) curare la manutenzione di; (claim)
sostenere

maintenance /'meɪntənəns/ n
mantenimento m; (care) manutenzione f;
(allowance) alimenti mpl

maintenance grant n (for student)
presalario m

maintenance order n Br obbligo m
degli alimenti

maisonette /meɪzə'net/ n appartamento
m a due piani

maize /meɪz/ n granoturco m

Maj abbr (**Major**) Mag

majestic /mə'dʒestɪk/ adj maestoso

majestically /məˈdʒəestɪklɪ/ adv
maestosamente

majesty /ˈmædʒəstɪ/ n maestà f inv;
His/Her M~ Sua Maestà

major /ˈmeɪdʒə(r)/ **①** adj maggiore; **~
road** strada f con diritto di precedenza
② n Mil, Mus maggiore m
③ vi Am **~ in** specializzarsi in

Majorca /məˈjɔːkə/ n Maiorca f

major general n generale m di
divisione

majority /məˈdʒɒrətɪ/ n maggioranza f;
be in the ~ avere la maggioranza

make /meɪk/ **①** n (brand) marca f
② vt (pt/pp **made**) fare; (earn)
guadagnare; rendere ⟨happy, clear⟩;
prendere ⟨decision⟩; **~ somebody laugh**
far ridere qualcuno; **~ somebody do**
something far fare qualcosa a qualcuno;
~ it (to party, top of hill etc) farcela; **what time
do you ~ it?** che ore fai?
③ vi **~ as if to** fare per
■ **make after** vt (chase) inseguire
■ **make do** vi arrangiarsi
■ **make for** vt dirigersi verso
■ **make good** **①** vi riuscire
② vt compensare ⟨loss⟩; risarcire
⟨damage⟩
■ **make off** vi fuggire
■ **make off with** vt (steal) sgraffignare
■ **make out** vt (distinguish) distinguere;
(write out) rilasciare ⟨cheque⟩; compilare
⟨list⟩; (claim) far credere
■ **make over** vt cedere
■ **make up** **①** vt (constitute) comporre;
(complete) completare; (invent) inventare;
(apply cosmetics to) truccare; fare ⟨parcel⟩; **~
up one's mind** decidersi; **~ it up** (after
quarrel) riconciliarsi
② vi (after quarrel) fare la pace
■ **make up for** vt compensare; **~ up for
lost time** recuperare il tempo perso
■ **make up to** vt arruffianarsi

make-believe **①** adj finto
② n finzione f

make-do-and-mend vi arrangiarsi col
poco che si ha

make-over n trasformazione f

maker /ˈmeɪkə(r)/ n fabbricante mf; **M~**
Relig Creatore m; **send somebody to meet
his/her ~** spedire qualcuno all'altro
mondo

makeshift **①** adj di fortuna
② n espediente m

make-up n trucco m; (character) natura f

make-up artist n truccatore, -trice mf

make-up bag n astuccio m per il
trucco

make-up remover n struccante m

making /ˈmeɪkɪŋ/ n (manufacture)
fabbricazione f; **be the ~ of** essere la
causa del successo di; **have the ~s of** aver
la stoffa di; **in the ~** in formazione

maladjusted /mæləˈdʒʌstɪd/ adj
disadattato

maladjustment /mæləˈdʒʌstmənt/ n
disadattamento m

Malagasy /mæləˈgæzɪ/ n (native of
Madagascar) malgascio, -a mf; (language)
malgascio m

malaise /məˈleɪz/ n fig malessere m

malaria /məˈleərɪə/ n malaria f

Malawi /məˈlɑːwɪ/ n Malawi m

Malaysia /məˈleɪʒə/ n Malesia f

Malaysian /məˈleɪʒən/ n & adj malese
mf

Maldives /ˈmɔːldiːvz/ npl the **~** le
Maldive

male /meɪl/ **①** adj maschile
② n maschio m

male chauvinism n maschilismo m

male chauvinist [pig] n [sporco m]
maschilista m

male menopause n andropausa f

male model n indossatore m

male nurse n infermiere m

male voice choir n coro m maschile

malevolence /məˈlevələns/ n
malevolenza f

malevolent /məˈlevələnt/ adj malevolo

malformation /mælfɔːˈmeɪʃn/ n
malformazione f

malformed /mælˈfɔːmd/ adj malformato

malfunction /mælˈfʌŋkʃn/ **①** n
funzionamento m imperfetto
② vi funzionare male

Mali /ˈmɑːlɪ/ n Mali m

malice /ˈmælɪs/ n malignità f; **bear
somebody ~** voler del male a qualcuno

malicious /məˈlɪʃəs/ adj maligno

maliciously /məˈlɪʃəslɪ/ adv con
malignità

malign /məˈlaɪn/ vt malignare su

malignancy /məˈlɪgnənsɪ/ n malignità f

malignant /məˈlɪgnənt/ adj maligno

malinger /məˈlɪŋgə(r)/ vi fingersi malato

malingerer /məˈlɪŋgərə(r)/ n
scansafatiche mf inv

mall /mæl/ n (shopping arcade, in suburb)
centro m commerciale; (Am: street) strada f
pedonale

mallard /ˈmælɑːd/ n germano m reale

malleable /ˈmælɪəbl/ adj malleabile

mallet /ˈmælɪt/ n martello m di legno

malnourished /mælˈnʌrɪʃt/ adj
malnutrito

malnutrition /mælnjʊˈtrɪʃn/ n
malnutrizione f

malpractice /mælˈpræktɪs/ n
negligenza f

malt /mɔːlt/ n malto m

Malta /ˈmɔːltə/ n Malta f

Maltese /mɔːlˈtiːz/ adj & n maltese mf

maltreat /mælˈtriːt/ vt maltrattare

maltreatment /mælˈtriːtmənt/ n maltrattamento m

malt whisky n whisky m inv di malto

mammal /ˈmæml/ n mammifero m

mammary /ˈmæməri/ adj mammario

mammograph /ˈmæməgrɑːf/ n mammografia f

mammoth /ˈmæməθ/ ① adj mastodontico
② n mammut m inv

man /mæn/ ① n (pl **men**) uomo m; (chess, draughts) pedina f; **the ~ in the street** l'uomo della strada; **~ to ~** da uomo a uomo
② vt (pt/pp **manned**) equipaggiare; far funzionare ⟨pump⟩; essere di servizio a ⟨counter, telephones⟩

manacle /ˈmænəkl/ vt ammanettare

manage /ˈmænɪdʒ/ ① vt dirigere; gestire ⟨shop, affairs⟩; (cope with) farcela; **~ to do something** riuscire a fare qualcosa
② vi riuscire; (cope) farcela (**on** con)

manageable /ˈmænɪdʒəbl/ adj ⟨hair⟩ docile; ⟨size⟩ maneggevole

management /ˈmænɪdʒmənt/ n gestione f; **the ~** la direzione

management accounting n contabilità f di gestione

management buyout n buyout m inv da parte dei manager, rilevamento m dirigenti

management consultancy n (firm) consulente m aziendale; (activity) consulenza f aziendale

management consultant n consulente mf aziendale

manager /ˈmænɪdʒə(r)/ n direttore m; (of shop, bar) gestore m; Sport manager m inv

manageress /mænɪdʒəˈres/ n direttrice f

managerial /mænɪˈdʒɪərɪəl/ adj **~ staff** personale m direttivo

managing director /ˈmænɪdʒɪŋ/ n direttore, -trice mf generale

mandarin /ˈmændərɪn/ n **~ [orange]** mandarino m

mandate /ˈmændeɪt/ n mandato m

mandatory /ˈmændətrɪ/ adj obbligatorio

mandolin /ˈmændəlɪn/ n mandolino m

mandrake /ˈmændreɪk/ n mandragola f

mane /meɪn/ n criniera f

manful /ˈmænfl/ adj coraggioso

manfully /ˈmænfʊlɪ/ adv coraggiosamente

manger /ˈmeɪndʒə(r)/ n mangiatoia f

mangle /ˈmæŋgl/ vt (damage) maciullare

mango /ˈmæŋgəʊ/ n (pl **-es**) mango m

mangrove /ˈmæŋgrəʊv/ n mangrovia f

mangy /ˈmeɪndʒɪ/ adj ⟨dog⟩ rognoso

manhandle /ˈmænhændl/ vt malmenare

manhole /ˈmænhəʊl/ n botola f

manhole cover n tombino m

manhood /ˈmænhʊd/ n età f adulta; (quality) virilità f

man-hour n ora f lavorativa

manhunt /ˈmænhʌnt/ n caccia f all'uomo

mania /ˈmeɪnɪə/ n mania f

maniac /ˈmeɪnɪæk/ n maniaco, -a mf

manic /ˈmænɪk/ adj (obsessive) maniacale; (frenetic) frenetico

manic depression n psicosi f inv maniaco-depressiva

manic-depressive adj maniaco-depressivo

manicure /ˈmænɪkjʊə(r)/ ① n manicure f inv
② vt fare la manicure a

manicurist /ˈmænɪkjʊərɪst/ n manicure f inv

manifest /ˈmænɪfest/ ① adj manifesto
② n Comm manifesto m
③ vt manifestare; **~ itself** manifestarsi

manifestation /mænɪfeˈsteɪʃn/ n manifestazione f

manifestly /ˈmænɪfestlɪ/ adv palesemente

manifesto /mænɪˈfestəʊ/ n manifesto m

manifold /ˈmænɪfəʊld/ adj molteplice

manipulate /məˈnɪpjuleɪt/ vt manipolare

manipulation /mənɪpjʊˈleɪʃn/ n manipolazione f

manipulative /məˈnɪpjʊlətɪv/ adj manipolatore

mankind /mænˈkaɪnd/ n genere m umano

manly /ˈmænlɪ/ adj virile

man-made adj artificiale; **~ fibre** n fibra f sintetica

manna /ˈmænə/ n manna f: **~ from heaven** fig manna f dal cielo

mannequin /ˈmænɪkɪn/ n manichino m

manner /ˈmænə(r)/ n maniera f: **in this ~** in questo modo; **have no ~s** avere dei pessimi modi; **good/bad ~s** buone/cattive maniere

mannered /ˈmænəd/ adj pej manierato

mannerism /ˈmænərɪzm/ n affettazione f

mannish /ˈmænɪʃ/ adj mascolino

manoeuvrable /məˈnuːvrəbl/ adj manovrabile

manoeuvre /məˈnuːvə(r)/ ① n manovra f

2 *vt* fare manovra con ⟨*vehicle*⟩; manovrare ⟨*person*⟩

manor /'mænə(r)/ *n* maniero *m*

manpower /'mænpaʊə(r)/ *n* manodopera *f*

manse /mæns/ *n* canonica *f*

mansion /'mænʃn/ *n* palazzo *m*

manslaughter /'mænslɔːtə(r)/ *n* omicidio *m* colposo

mantelpiece /'mæntlpiːs/ *n* mensola *f* di caminetto

mantis /'mæntɪs/ *n* mantide *f*

Mantua /'mæntjʊə/ *n* Mantova *f*

manual /'mænjʊəl/ **1** *adj* manuale **2** *n* manuale *m*

manufacture /mænjʊ'fæktʃə(r)/ **1** *vt* fabbricare **2** *n* manifattura *f*

manufacturer /mænjʊ'fæktʃərə(r)/ *n* fabbricante *m*

manure /mə'njʊə(r)/ *n* concime *m*

manuscript /'mænjʊskrɪpt/ *n* manoscritto *m*

Manx /mæŋks/ *n* (language) lingua *f* parlata nell'isola di Man; **the M∼** *pl* (people) gli abitanti dell'isola di Man

many /'menɪ/ *adj & pron* molti; **there are as ∼ boys as girls** ci sono tanti ragazzi quante ragazze; **as ∼ as 500** ben 500; **as ∼ as that** così tanti; **as ∼** altrettanti; **very ∼, a good/great ∼** moltissimi; **∼ a time** molte volte

many-sided /-'saɪdɪd/ *adj* ⟨*personality, phenomenon*⟩ sfaccettato

map /mæp/ *n* carta *f* geografica; (of town) mappa *f*
■ **map out** *vt* (*pt/pp* **mapped**) fig programmare

maple /'meɪpl/ *n* acero *m*

mar /mɑː(r)/ *vt* (*pt/pp* **marred**) rovinare

marathon /'mærəθən/ *n* maratona *f*

marauder /mə'rɔːdə(r)/ *n* predone *m*

marble /'mɑːbl/ **1** *n* marmo *m*; (for game) pallina *f* **2** *attrib* di marmo

March /mɑːtʃ/ *n* marzo *m*

march **1** *n* marcia *f*; (protest) dimostrazione *f* **2** *vi* marciare **3** *vt* far marciare; **∼ somebody off** scortare qualcuno fuori

marcher /'mɑːtʃə(r)/ *n* (in procession, band) persona *f* che marcia in una processione, in un corteo ecc; (in demonstration) dimostrante *mf*

marchioness /mɑːʃə'nes/ *n* marchesa *f*

march past *n* sfilata *f*

mare /'meə(r)/ *n* giumenta *f*

margarine /mɑdʒə'riːn/ *n* margarina *f*

marge /mɑdʒ/ *n* (Br fam: margarine) margarina *f*

margin /'mɑdʒɪn/ *n* margine *m*

marginal /'mɑdʒɪnəl/ *adj* marginale

marginalize /'mɑːdʒɪnəlaɪz/ *vt* marginalizzare

marginally /'mɑdʒɪnəlɪ/ *adv* marginalmente

marigold /'mærɪgəʊld/ *n* calendula *f*

marijuana /mærʊ'wɑːnə/ *n* marijuana *f*

marina /mə'riːnə/ *n* porticciolo *m*

marinade /mærɪ'neɪd/ **1** *n* marinata *f* **2** *vt* marinare

marine /mə'riːn/ **1** *adj* marino **2** *n* (sailor) soldato *m* di fanteria marina

Marine Corps *n* i Marine

marine engineer *n* ingegnere *m* navale; (works in engine room) macchinista *m*

marionette /mærɪə'net/ *n* marionetta *f*

marital /'mærɪtl/ *adj* coniugale; **∼ status** stato *m* civile

maritime /'mærɪtaɪm/ *adj* marittimo

marjoram /'mɑːdʒərəm/ *n* maggiorana *f*

mark¹ /mɑːk/ *n* (currency) marco *m*

mark² **1** *n* (stain) macchia *f*; (sign, indication) segno *m*; Sch voto *m*; **be the ∼ of** designare **2** *vt* segnare; (stain) macchiare; Sch correggere; Sport marcare; **∼ time** Mil segnare il passo; fig non far progressi; **∼ my words** ricordati quello che dico
■ **mark down** *vt* (reduce the price of) ribassare
■ **mark out** *vt* delimitare; fig designare
■ **mark up** *vt* (increase the price of) aumentare

marked /mɑːkt/ *adj* marcato

markedly /'mɑːkɪdlɪ/ *adv* notevolmente

marker /'mɑːkə(r)/ *n* (for highlighting) evidenziatore *m*; Sport marcatore *m* (of exam) esaminatore, -trice *mf*

marker pen *n* evidenziatore *m*

market /'mɑːkɪt/ **1** *n* mercato *m* **2** *vt* vendere al mercato; (launch) commercializzare; **on the ∼** sul mercato

market analyst *n* analista *mf* di mercato

market day *n* giorno *m* di mercato

market economy *n* economia *f* di mercato

market forces *npl* forze *fpl* di mercato

market garden *n* orto *m*

market gardener *n* ortofrutticoltore, -trice *mf*

market gardening *n* ortofrutticoltura *f*

marketing /'mɑːkɪtɪŋ/ *n* marketing *m*

marketing campaign *n* campagna *f* promozionale *or* pubblicitaria

marketing department *n* ufficio *m* marketing

marketing man *n* addetto, -a *mf* al marketing

marketing mix *n* mix *m inv* del marketing

marketing strategy *n* strategia *f* di marketing

market leader *n* (company, product) leader *m inv* del mercato

market place *n* (square, Fin) mercato *m.*

market price *n* prezzo *m* di mercato

market research *n* ricerca *f* di mercato

market square *n* piazza *f* del mercato

market stall *n* banco *m* del mercato

market survey *n* indagine *f* di mercato

market town *n* cittadina *f* dove si tiene il mercato

market trader *n* venditore, -trice *mf* al mercato

market value *n* valore *m* di mercato

markings /'mɑːkɪŋz/ *npl* (on animal) colori *mpl*

marksman /'mɑːksmən/ *n* tiratore *m* scelto

marksmanship /'mɑːksmənʃɪp/ *n* abilità *f* nel tiro

mark-up *n* (margin) margine *m* di vendita; (price increase) aumento *m*

marmalade /'mɑːməleɪd/ *n* marmellata *f* d'arance

maroon /mə'ruːn/ *adj* marrone rossastro

marooned /mə'ruːnd/ *adj* abbandonato

marquee /mɑː'kiː/ *n* tendone *m*; (Am: awning) pensilina *f* con pubblicità

marquess /'mɑːkwɪs/ *n* marchese *m*

marquetry /'mɑːkɪtrɪ/ *n* intarsio *m*

marquis /'mɑːkwɪs/ *n* marchese *m*

marriage /'mærɪdʒ/ *n* matrimonio *m*

marriage ceremony *n* cerimonia *f* nuziale

marriage certificate *n* certificato *m* di matrimonio

marriage guidance counsellor *n* consulente *mf* matrimoniale

marriage of convenience *n* matrimonio *m* di convenienza

married /'mærɪd/ *adj* sposato; ⟨life⟩ coniugale

marrow /'mærəʊ/ *n* Anat midollo *m*; (vegetable) zucca *f*

marrowbone /'mærəʊbəʊn/ *n* midollo *m* osseo

marry /'mærɪ/ ① *vt* (pt/pp **-led**) sposare; **get married** sposarsi ② *vi* sposarsi

Mars /mɑːz/ *n* Marte *m*

marsh /mɑːʃ/ *n* palude *f*

marshal /'mɑːʃl/ ① *n* (steward) cerimoniere *m* ② *vt* (pt/pp **marshalled**) fig organizzare ⟨arguments⟩

Marshall Islands /'mɑːʃl/ *npl* **the** ∼ le isole Marshall

marshmallow /mɑːʃ'mæləʊ/ *n* caramella *f* gommosa e pastosa

marshy /'mɑːʃɪ/ *adj* paludoso

marsupial /mɑː'suːpɪəl/ *n* marsupiale *m*

marten /'mɑːtɪn/ *n* martora *f*

martial /'mɑːʃl/ *adj* marziale

Martian /'mɑːʃn/ *adj & n* marziano, -a *mf*

martinet /mɑːtɪ'net/ *n* fanatico, -a *mf* della disciplina

martyr /'mɑːtə(r)/ ① *n* martire *mf* ② *vt* martirizzare

martyrdom /'mɑːtədəm/ *n* martirio *m*

martyred /'mɑːtəd/ *adj* fam da martire

marvel /'mɑːvl/ ① *n* meraviglia *f* ② *vi* (pt/pp **marvelled**) meravigliarsi (**at** di)

marvellous /'mɑːvələs/ *adj* meraviglioso

marvellously /'mɑːvələslɪ/ *adv* meravigliosamente

Marxism /'mɑːksɪzm/ *n* marxismo *m*

Marxist /'mɑːksɪst/ *adj & n* marxista *mf*

marzipan /'mɑːzɪpæn/ *n* marzapane *m*

mascara /mæ'skɑːrə/ *n* mascara *m inv*

mascot /'mæskət/ *n* mascotte *f inv*

masculine /'mæskjʊlɪn/ ① *adj* maschile ② *n* Gram maschile *m*

masculinity /mæskjʊ'lɪnətɪ/ *n* mascolinità *f*

mash /mæʃ/ ① *n* Culin fam purè *m inv* ② *vt* impastare

mashed potatoes /mæʃt/ *npl* purè *m inv* di patate

mask /mɑːsk/ ① *n* maschera *f* ② *vt* mascherare

masked ball /mɑːskt'bɔːl/ *n* ballo *m* in maschera

masking tape /'mɑːskɪŋ/ *n* nastro *m* di carta adesiva

masochism /'mæsəkɪzm/ *n* masochismo *m*

masochist /'mæsəkɪst/ *n* masochista *mf*

Mason /'meɪsn/ *n* massone *m*

mason *n* muratore *m*

Masonic /mə'sɒnɪk/ *adj* massonico

masonry /'meɪsnrɪ/ *n* muratura *f*; **two tons of** ∼ due tonnellate di pietre

masquerade /mæskə'reɪd/ ① *n* fig mascherata *f* ② *vi* ∼ **as** (pose) farsi passare per

mass¹ /mæs/ *n* Relig messa *f*

mass² ① n massa f; ~**es of** fam un sacco di
② vi ammassarsi

massacre /'mæsəkə(r)/ ① n massacro m
② vt massacrare

massage /'mæsɑːʒ/ ① n massaggio m
② vt massaggiare; fig manipolare
⟨statistics⟩

masseur /mæ'sɜː(r)/ n massaggiatore m

masseuse /mæ'sɜːz/ n massaggiatrice f

mass grave n fossa f comune

mass hysteria n isterismo m di massa

massive /'mæsɪv/ adj enorme

massively /'mæsɪvlɪ/ adv estremamente

mass market ① n mercato m di massa
② attrib del mercato di massa

mass-marketing n
commercializzazione f di massa

mass media npl mezzi mpl di
comunicazione di massa, mass media mpl

mass murder n omicidio m di massa

mass murderer n omicida mf di
massa

mass-produce vt produrre in serie

mass production n produzione f in
serie

mass screening n Med controllo m su
larga scala

mast /mɑːst/ n Naut albero m; (for radio)
antenna f

master /'mɑːstə(r)/ ① n maestro m,
padrone m; (teacher) professore m; (of ship)
capitano m; **M~** (boy) signorino m
② vt imparare perfettamente; avere
padronanza di ⟨language⟩

master bedroom n camera f da letto
principale

master builder n capomastro m

master copy n originale m

master disk n Comput disco m master

master key n passe-partout m inv

masterly /'mɑːstəlɪ/ adj magistrale

mastermind ① n cervello m
② vt ideare e dirigere

Master of Arts n (diploma) laurea f in
lettere; (person) laureato, -a mf in lettere

master of ceremonies n (presenting
entertainment) presentatore m; (of formal
occasion) maestro m di cerimonie

Master of Science n (diploma) laurea f
in discipline scientifiche; (person) laureato,
-a mf in discipline scientifiche

masterpiece n capolavoro m

master plan n piano m generale

master race n razza f superiore

master stroke n colpo m da maestro

master tape n nastro m matrice

mastery /'mæstərɪ/ n (of subject)
padronanza f

masticate /'mæstɪkeɪt/ vi masticare

masturbate /'mæstəbeɪt/ vi
masturbarsi

masturbation /mæstə'beɪʃn/ n
masturbazione f

mat /mæt/ n stuoia f; (on table) sottopiatto
m

match¹ /mætʃ/ ① n Sport partita f; (equal)
uguale mf; (marriage) matrimonio m; (person
to marry) partito m; **be a good ~** ⟨colours⟩)
intonarsi bene; **be no ~ for** non essere
dello stesso livello di
② vt (equal) uguagliare; (be like) andare
bene con
③ vi intonarsi

match² n fiammifero m

matchbox /'mætʃbɒks/ n scatola f di
fiammiferi

matching /'mætʃɪŋ/ adj intonato

matchmaker n he's a successful ~ (for
couples) è stato l'artefice di molti
matrimoni

match point n Tennis match point m inv

matchstick n fiammifero m

mate¹ /meɪt/ ① n compagno, -a mf;
(assistant) aiuto m; Naut secondo m; (fam:
friend) amico, -a mf
② vi accoppiarsi
③ vt accoppiare

mate² n (in chess) scacco m matto

material /mə'tɪərɪəl/ ① n materiale m;
(fabric) stoffa f; **raw ~s** pl materie fpl
prime
② adj materiale

materialism /mə'tɪərɪəlɪzm/ n
materialismo m

materialistic /mətɪərɪə'lɪstɪk/ adj
materialistico

materialize /mə'tɪərɪəlaɪz/ vi
materializzarsi

maternal /mə'tɜːnl/ adj materno

maternity /mə'tɜːnətɪ/ n maternità f

maternity clothes npl abiti mpl pre-
maman

maternity department n (in store)
reparto m pre-maman

maternity hospital n maternità f inv

maternity leave n congedo m per
maternità

maternity unit n reparto m maternità

maternity ward n maternità f inv

matey /'meɪtɪ/ adj fam amichevole

math /mæθ/ n Am matematica f

mathematical /mæθə'mætɪkl/ adj
matematico

mathematically /mæθə'mætɪklɪ/ adv
matematicamente

mathematician /mæθəmə'tɪʃn/ n
matematico, -a mf

mathematics /mæθ'mætɪks/ *n* matematica *fsg*

maths /mæθs/ *n* fam matematica *fsg*

matinée /'mætɪneɪ/ *n* Theat matinée *f inv*

mating /'meɪtɪŋ/ *n* accoppiamento *m*

mating call *n* richiamo *m* [per l'accoppiamento]

mating season *n* stagione *f* degli amori

matriarchal /meɪtrɪ'ɑːkl/ *adj* matriarcale

matriarchy /'meɪtrɪɑːkɪ/ *n* matriarchia *f*

matrices /'meɪtrɪsiːz/ ▶ MATRIX

matriculate /mə'trɪkjʊleɪt/ *vi* immatricolarsi

matriculation /mətrɪkjʊ'leɪʃn/ *n* immatricolazione *f*

matrimonial /mætrɪ'məʊnɪəl/ *adj* matrimoniale

matrimony /'mætrɪmənɪ/ *n* matrimonio *m*

matrix /'meɪtrɪks/ *n pl* **matrices** /'meɪtrɪsiːz/ matrice *f*

matron /'meɪtrən/ *n* (of hospital) capoinfermiera *f*: (of school) governante *f*

matronly /'meɪtrənlɪ/ *adj* matronale

matron of honour *n* Br damigella *f* d'onore (sposata)

matt /mæt/ *adj* opaco

matted /'mætɪd/ *adj* ~ **hair** capelli *mpl* tutti appiccicati tra loro

matter /'mætə(r)/ **1** *n* (affair) faccenda *f*; (question) questione *f*; (pus) pus *m*; (Phys: substance) materia *f*; **money** ~**s** questioni *fpl* di soldi; **as a** ~ **of fact** a dire la verità; **what is the** ~? che cosa c'è?
2 *vi* importare; ~ **to somebody** essere importante per qualcuno; **it doesn't** ~ non importa

matter-of-fact *adj* pratico

matting /'mætɪŋ/ *n* materiale *m* per stuoie

mattress /'mætrɪs/ *n* materasso *m*

maturation /mætʃʊ'reɪʃn/ *n* (of tree, body) sviluppo *m*: (of whisky, wine) invecchiamento *m*; (of cheese) stagionatura *f*

mature /mə'tʃʊə(r)/ **1** *adj* maturo; Comm in scadenza
2 *vi* maturare
3 *vt* far maturare

mature student *n* Br persona *f* che riprende gli studi universitari dopo i 25 anni

maturity /mə'tʃʊərətɪ/ *n* maturità *f*; Comm maturazione *f*

maudlin /'mɔːdlɪn/ *adj* ⟨song⟩ sdolcinato; ⟨person⟩ piagnucoloso

maul /mɔːl/ *vt* malmenare

Maundy /'mɔːndɪ/ *n* ~ **Thursday** giovedì *m* santo

Mauritania /mɒrɪ'teɪnɪə/ *n* Mauritania *f*

Mauritius /mə'rɪʃəs/ *n* [isola *f* di] Maurizio *f*

mausoleum /mɔːsə'lɪəm/ *n* mausoleo *m*

mauve /məʊv/ *adj* malva

maverick /'mævərɪk/ *n, adj* anticonformista *mf*

mawkish /'mɔːkɪʃ/ *adj* sdolcinato

max. *abbr* (**maximum**) max. *m*

maxi /'mæksɪ/ *n* (dress) vestito *m* alla caviglia; (skirt) gonna *f* alla caviglia

maxim /'mæksɪm/ *n* massima *f*

maximization /mæksɪmaɪ'zeɪʃn/ *n* massimizzazione *f*

maximize /'mæksɪmaɪz/ *vt* massimizzare ⟨profits, sales⟩; Comput ingrandire ⟨window⟩

maximum /'mæksɪməm/ **1** *adj* massimo; **ten minutes** ~ dieci minuti al massimo
2 *n* (pl **-ima**) massimo *m*

maximum security prison *n* carcere *m* di massima sicurezza

May /meɪ/ *n* maggio *m*

may *v aux* (only in present) potere; ~ **I come in?** posso entrare?; **if I** ~ **say so** se mi posso permettere; ~ **you both be very happy** siate felici; **I** ~ **as well stay** potrei anche rimanere; **it** ~ **be true** potrebbe esser vero; **she** ~ **be old, but...** sarà anche vecchia, ma...

maybe /'meɪbiː/ *adv* forse, può darsi

May-bug *n* maggiolino *m*

Mayday *n* Radio mayday *m inv*

May Day *n* il primo maggio

mayhem /'meɪhem/ *n* **create** ~ creare scompiglio

mayonnaise /meɪə'neɪz/ *n* maionese *f*

mayor /'meə(r)/ *n* sindaco *m*

mayoress /meə'res/ *n* sindaco *m*; (wife of mayor) moglie *f* del sindaco

maypole /'meɪpəʊl/ *n* palo *m* intorno al quale si balla durante la celebrazione del primo maggio

May queen *n* reginetta *f* di calendimaggio

maze /meɪz/ *n* labirinto *m*

Mb *abbr* (**megabyte**) MB *m inv*

MBA *n abbr* (**Master of Business Administration**) laurea *f inv* in economia e commercio

MBE *n* Br *abbr* (**Member of the Order of the British Empire**) onorificenza *f* britannica

MBO *n abbr* **management buyout**

MC *n abbr* (**Master of Ceremonies**) (in cabaret) presentatore *m*; (at banquet) maestro *m* delle cerimonie; Am *abbr* (**Member of Congress**) membro *m* del Congresso

McCoy /mə'kɔɪ/ *n* **this whisky is the real** ∼ questo è un vero whisky

MD *abbr* (**Managing Director**) direttore, -trice *mf* generale; *abbr* (**Doctor of Medicine**) dottore *m* in medicina; Am *abbr* **Maryland**

ME *n abbr* (**myalgic encephalomyelitis**) encefalomelite *f* mialgica; Am *abbr* **Maine**

me /miː/ *pers pron* (object) mi; (with preposition) me; **he knows me** mi conosce; **she called me, not you** ha chiamato me, non te; **give me the money** dammi i soldi; **give it to me** dammelo; **he explained it to me** me lo ha spiegato; **it's me** sono io

mead /miːd/ *n* idromele *m*

meadow /'medəʊ/ *n* prato *m*

meagre /'miːgə(r)/ *adj* scarso

meal¹ /miːl/ *n* pasto *m*; **did you enjoy your** ∼? ha mangiato bene?

meal² *n* (grain) farina *f*

meal ticket *n* (fig: quality, qualification) fonte *f* di guadagno; **she's only a** ∼ ∼ **to her** le interessano solo i suoi soldi

mealy-mouthed /miːlɪ'maʊðd/ *adj* ambiguo

mean¹ /miːn/ *adj* avaro; (unkind) meschino; (low in rank) basso; (accommodation) misero

mean² ① *adj* medio ② *n* (average) media *f*; **Greenwich** ∼ **time** ora *f* media di Greenwich

mean³ *vt* (pt/pp **meant**) voler dire; (signify) significare; (intend) intendere; **I** ∼ **it** lo dico seriamente; ∼ **well** avere buone intenzioni; **be** ∼**t for** ⟨present⟩ essere destinato a; ⟨remark⟩ essere riferito a

meander /mɪ'ændə(r)/ *vi* vagare

meaning /'miːnɪŋ/ *n* significato *m*

meaningful /'miːnɪŋfʊl/ *adj* significativo

meaningless /'miːnɪŋlɪs/ *adj* senza senso

meanness /'miːnnɪs/ *n* (with money) avarizia *f*; (unkindness) meschinità *f*

means /miːnz/ ① *n* mezzo *m*; ∼ **of transport** mezzo *m* di trasporto; **by** ∼ **of** per mezzo di; **by all** ∼! certamente!; **by no** ∼ niente affatto ② *npl* (resources) mezzi *mpl*; ∼ **test** *n* accertamento *m* patrimoniale

meant /ment/ ▶ MEAN³

meantime /'miːntaɪm/ ① *n* **in the** ∼ nel frattempo ② *adv* intanto

meanwhile /'miːnwaɪl/ *adv* intanto

measles /'miːzlz/ *nsg* morbillo *m*

measly /'miːzlɪ/ *adj* fam misero

measurable /'meʒərəbl/ *adj* misurabile

measure /'meʒə(r)/ ① *n* misura *f* ② *vt/i* misurare
■ **measure out** *vt* dosare ⟨amount⟩
■ **measure up** *vi* fig avere i requisiti richiesti
■ **measure up to** *vt* fig essere all'altezza di

measured /'meʒəd/ *adj* misurato

measurement /'meʒəmənt/ *n* misura *f*

measuring jug /'meʒərɪŋ/ *n* dosatore *m*

measuring spoon *n* misurino *m*

meat /miːt/ *n* carne *f*

meatball *n* Culin polpetta *f* di carne

meat-eater *n* (animal) carnivoro *m*; **I'm not a** ∼ non mangio carne

meat hook *n* gancio *m* da macellaio

meat loaf *n* polpettone *m*

meat pie *n* tortino *m* di carne

meaty /'miːtɪ/ *adj* (**-ier**, **-iest**) di carne; fig sostanzioso

Mecca /'mekə/ *n* La Mecca

mechanic /mɪ'kænɪk/ *n* meccanico *m*

mechanical /mɪ'kænɪkl/ *adj* meccanico

mechanical engineering *n* ingegneria *f* meccanica

mechanically /mɪ'kænɪklɪ/ *adv* meccanicamente

mechanics /mɪ'kænɪks/ ① *n* meccanica *f* ② *npl* meccanismo *msg*

mechanism /'mekənɪzm/ *n* meccanismo *m*

mechanization /mekənaɪ'zeɪʃn/ *n* meccanizzazione *f*

mechanize /'mekənaɪz/ *vt* meccanizzare

medal /'medl/ *n* medaglia *f*

medallion /mɪ'dælɪən/ *n* medaglione *m*

medallist /'medəlɪst/ *n* vincitore, -trice *mf* di una medaglia

meddle /'medl/ *vi* immischiarsi (**in** in); (tinker) armeggiare (**with** con)

media /'miːdɪə/ ① *n* ▶ MEDIUM ② *npl* **the** ∼ i mass media

median /'miːdɪən/ *adj* ∼ **strip** Am banchina *f* spartitraffico

media studies *npl* scienze *fpl* delle comunicazioni

mediate /'miːdɪeɪt/ *vi* fare da mediatore

mediation /miːdɪ'eɪʃn/ *n* mediazione *f*

mediator /'miːdɪeɪtə(r)/ *n* mediatore, -trice *mf*

medic /'medɪk/ *n* (fam: doctor) medico *m*; (fam: student) studente, -essa *mf* di medicina; Mil fam infermiere, -a *mf* militare

medical /'medɪkl/ ① *adj* medico ② *n* visita *f* medica

medical care *n* assistenza *f* medica

medical check-up n controllo m
medico

medical examiner n Am =
PATHOLOGIST

medical history n anamnesi f inv

medical insurance n assicurazione f
sanitaria

medically /'medɪklɪ/ adv ~ **qualified**
con qualifiche di medico; ~ **fit** in buona
salute

medical officer n Mil ufficiale m
medico

medical profession n (occupation)
professione f del medico; (doctors collectively)
categoria f medica

medical student n studente, -essa mf
di medicina

medicated /'medɪkeɪtɪd/ adj medicato

medication /medɪ'keɪʃn/ n (drugs)
medicinali mpl; **are you on any** ~? sta
prendendo delle medicine?

medicinal /mɪ'dɪsɪnl/ adj medicinale

medicine /'medsən/ n medicina f

medicine ball n palla f medica

medicine bottle n flacone m

medicine cabinet n armadietto m dei
medicinali

medicine man n stregone m

medieval /medɪ'i:vl/ adj medievale

mediocre /mi:dɪ'əʊkə(r)/ adj mediocre

mediocrity /mi:dɪ:'ɒkrətɪ/ n mediocrità
f

meditate /'medɪteɪt/ vi meditare (**on** su)

meditative /'medɪtətɪv/ adj (music,
person) meditativo; (mood, expression)
meditabondo

Mediterranean /medɪtə'reɪnɪən/ ① n
the ~ [Sea] il [mare] Mediterraneo
② adj mediterraneo

medium /'mi:dɪəm/ ① adj medio; Culin di
media cottura
② n mezzo m; (pl **-s**) (person) medium mf
inv

medium dry adj (drink) semisecco

medium-length adj (book, film, hair)
di media lunghezza

medium-range adj (missile) di media
portata

medium-rare adj (meat) appena al
sangue

medium-sized /'mi:dɪəmsaɪzd/ adj di
taglia media

medium wave n onde fpl medie

medley /'medlɪ/ n miscuglio m; Mus
miscellanea f

meek /mi:k/ adj mite, mansueto

meekly /'mi:klɪ/ adv docilmente

meet /mi:t/ ① vt (pt/pp **met**) incontrare;
(at station, airport) andare incontro a; (for first
time) far la conoscenza di; pagare (bill);
soddisfare (requirements)
② vi incontrarsi; (committee) riunirsi; ~
with incontrare (problem); incontrarsi con
(person)
③ n raduno m (sportivo)
■ **meet up** vi (people) incontrarsi; ~ **up**
with somebody incontrare qualcuno

meeting /'mi:tɪŋ/ n riunione f, meeting
m inv; (large) assemblea f; (by chance)
incontro m; **be in a** ~ essere in riunione

meeting-place n luogo m d'incontro

meeting-point n punto m d'incontro

mega+ /'megə/ pref mega+

megabyte /'megəbaɪt/ n Comput
megabyte m inv

megalith /'megəlɪθ/ n megalite m

megalomania /megələ'meɪnɪə/ n
megalomania f

megalomaniac /megələ'meɪnɪæk/ adj
& n megalomane mf

megaphone /'megəfəʊn/ n megafono m

melancholy /'melənkəlɪ/ ① adj
malinconico
② n malinconia f

mellow /'meləʊ/ ① adj (wine) generoso;
(sound, colour) caldo; (person) dolce
② vi (person) addolcirsi

melodic /mɪ'lɒdɪk/ adj melodico

melodious /mɪ'ləʊdɪəs/ adj melodioso

melodrama /'melədrɑːmə/ n
melodramma m

melodramatic /melədrə'mætɪk/ adj
melodrammatico

melodramatically /melədrə'mætɪklɪ/
adv in modo melodrammatico

melody /'melədɪ/ n melodia f

melon /'melən/ n melone m

melt /melt/ ① vt sciogliere
② vi sciogliersi
■ **melt away** vi (snow) sciogliersi;
(crowd) disperdersi; (support) venir meno
■ **melt down** vt fondere

meltdown /'meltdaʊn/ n (in nuclear
reactor) fusione f del nocciolo

melting point /'meltɪŋ/ n punto m di
fusione

melting pot n fig crogiuolo m

member /'membə(r)/ n membro m; **be a**
~ **of the family** far parte della famiglia

member countries paesi mpl membri

Member of Congress n Am membro
m del Congresso

Member of Parliament deputato, -a
mf

**Member of the European
Parliament** n eurodeputato, -a mf

membership /'membəʃɪp/ n iscrizione
f; (members) soci mpl

membrane /'membreɪn/ n membrana f

memento /mɪˈmentəʊ/ n ricordo m
memo /ˈmeməʊ/ n promemoria m inv
memoirs /ˈmemwɑːz/ npl ricordi mpl
memo pad n blocchetto m
memorabilia /memərəˈbɪlɪə/ npl cimeli mpl
memorable /ˈmemərəbl/ adj memorabile
memorandum /meməˈrændəm/ n promemoria m inv
memorial /mɪˈmɔːrɪəl/ n monumento m
memorial service n funzione f commemorativa
memorize /ˈmeməraɪz/ vt memorizzare
memory /ˈmemərɪ/ n also Comput memoria f; (thing remembered) ricordo m; from ∼ a memoria; in ∼ of in ricordo di
men /men/ ▶ MAN
menace /ˈmenəs/ ① n minaccia f; (nuisance) piaga f ② vt minacciare
menacing /ˈmenəsɪŋ/ adj minaccioso
menacingly /ˈmenəsɪŋlɪ/ adv minacciosamente
mend /mend/ ① vt riparare; (darn) rammendare ② n on the ∼ in via di guarigione
menfolk /ˈmenfəʊk/ n uomini mpl
menial /ˈmiːnɪəl/ adj umile
meningitis /menɪnˈdʒaɪtɪs/ n meningite f
menopause /ˈmenəpɔːz/ n menopausa f
Menorca /mɪˈnɔːkə/ n Minorca f
men's room n toilette f inv degli uomini
menstruate /ˈmenstrʊeɪt/ vi mestruare
menstruation /menstrʊˈeɪʃn/ n mestruazione f
menswear /ˈmenzweə(r)/ n abbigliamento m per uomo
mental /ˈmentl/ adj mentale; (fam: mad) pazzo
mental arithmetic n calcolo m mentale
mental block n blocco m psicologico
mental health n (of person) salute f mentale
mental health care n assistenza f psichiatrica
mental home n clinica f psichiatrica
mental illness n malattia f mentale
mentality /menˈtælətɪ/ n mentalità f inv
mentally /ˈmentəlɪ/ adv mentalmente; ∼ ill malato di mente
mentholated /ˈmenθəleɪtɪd/ adj al mentolo
mention /ˈmenʃn/ ① n menzione f ② vt menzionare; don't ∼ it non c'è di che

mentor /ˈmentɔː(r)/ n mentore m
menu /ˈmenjuː/ n menu m inv
menu bar n Comput barra f dei menu
MEP n abbr (**Member of the European parliament**) eurodeputato, -a mf
mercantile /ˈmɜːkəntaɪl/ adj mercantile
mercenary /ˈmɜːsɪnərɪ/ ① adj mercenario ② n mercenario m
merchandise /ˈmɜːtʃəndaɪz/ n merce f
merchant /ˈmɜːtʃənt/ n commerciante mf
merchant bank n Br banca f d'affari
merchant banker n (owner) proprietario, -a mf di una banca d'affari; (executive) dirigente mf di banca d'affari
merchant navy n marina f mercantile
merciful /ˈmɜːsɪfl/ adj misericordioso
mercifully /ˈmɜːsɪfʊlɪ/ adv fam grazie a Dio
merciless /ˈmɜːsɪlɪs/ adj spietato
mercilessly /ˈmɜːsɪlɪslɪ/ adv senza pietà
mercurial /mɜːˈkjʊərɪəl/ adj fig volubile
mercury /ˈmɜːkjʊrɪ/ n mercurio m
mercy /ˈmɜːsɪ/ n misericordia f; be at sb's ∼ essere alla mercé or in balia di qualcuno
mercy killing n eutanasia f
mere /mɪə(r)/ adj solo
merely /ˈmɪəlɪ/ adv solamente
merest /ˈmɪərɪst/ adj minimo
merge /mɜːdʒ/ ① vi fondersi ② vt Comm fondere
merger /ˈmɜːdʒə(r)/ n fusione f
meridian /məˈrɪdɪən/ n meridiano m
meringue /məˈræŋ/ n meringa f
merit /ˈmerɪt/ ① n merito m; (advantage) qualità f inv ② vt meritare
mermaid /ˈmɜːmeɪd/ n sirena f
merrily /ˈmerɪlɪ/ adv allegramente
merriment /ˈmerɪmənt/ n baldoria f
merry /ˈmerɪ/ adj (**-ier, -iest**) allegro; M∼ Christmas! Buon Natale!; make ∼ far festa
merry-go-round n giostra f
merry-making /ˈmerɪmeɪkɪŋ/ n festa f
mesh /meʃ/ n maglia f
mesmerize /ˈmezməraɪz/ vt ipnotizzare
mesmerized /ˈmezməraɪzd/ adj fig ipnotizzato
mess /mes/ n disordine m, casino m fam; (trouble) guaio m; (something spilt) sporco m: Mil mensa f; make a ∼ of (botch) fare un pasticcio di
■ **mess about** ① vi perder tempo; ∼ about with armeggiare con ② vt prendere in giro ⟨person⟩

■ **mess up** *vt* mettere in disordine, incasinare fam; (botch) mandare all'aria

■ **mess with** *vt* (fam: interfere with) trafficare con ⟨*computer, radio etc*⟩; contrariare ⟨*person*⟩

message /'mesɪdʒ/ *n* messaggio *m*

message window *n* Comput finestra *f* di messaggio

messaging /'mesɪdʒɪŋ/ *n* messaggeria *f* elettronica

mess dress *n* Mil uniforme *f* di gala

messenger /'mesɪndʒə(r)/ *n* messaggero *m*

messenger boy *n* fattorino *m*

Messiah /mɪ'saɪə/ *n* Messia *m*

Messrs /'mesəz/ *npl* (on letter) ∼ Smith Spett. ditta Smith

messy /'mesɪ/ *adj* (**-ier**, **-iest**) disordinato; (in dress) sciatto

met /met/ ▸ MEET

metabolism /mɪ'tæbəlɪzm/ *n* metabolismo *m*

metal /'metl/ **1** *n* metallo *m* **2** *adj* di metallo

metal detector *n* metal detector *m inv*

metal fatigue *n* fatica *f* del metallo

metallic /mɪ'tælɪk/ *adj* metallico

metallurgy /mɪ'tælədʒɪ/ *n* metallurgia *f*

metal polish *n* lucido *m* per metalli

metalwork /'metlwɜːk/ *n* lavorazione *f* del metallo

metamorphose /metə'mɔːfəʊz/ **1** *vt* trasformare **2** *vi* trasformarsi (**into** in)

metamorphosis /metə'mɔːfəsɪs/ *n* (pl **-phoses** /metə'mɔːfəsiːz/) metamorfosi *f inv*

metaphor /'metəfə(r)/ *n* metafora *f*

metaphorical /metə'fɒrɪkl/ *adj* metaforico

metaphorically /metə'fɒrɪklɪ/ *adv* metaforicamente

metaphysical /metə'fɪzɪkl/ *adj* metafisico; (abstract) astruso

mete /miːt/ *v*

■ **mete out** *vt* dispensare ⟨*punishment, justice*⟩

meteor /'miːtɪə(r)/ *n* meteora *f*

meteoric /miːtɪ'ɒrɪk/ *adj* fig fulmineo

meteorite /'miːtɪəraɪt/ *n* meteorite *m*

meteorological /miːtɪərə'lɒdʒɪkl/ *adj* meteorologico

Meteorological Office *n* Ufficio *m* meteorologico

meteorologist /miːtɪə'rɒlədʒɪst/ *n* meteorologo, -a *mf*

meteorology /miːtɪə'rɒlədʒɪ/ *n* meteorologia *f*

meter[1] /'miːtə(r)/ *n* contatore *m*

meter[2] *n* Am = METRE

meter reader *n* persona *f* incaricata di leggere il contatore (di gas, elettricità)

methane /'miːθeɪn/ *n* metano *m*

method /'meθəd/ *n* metodo *m*

method acting *n* metodo *m* dell'Actors' Studio

method actor *n* attore *m* che segue il metodo dell'Actors' Studio

methodical /mɪ'θɒdɪkl/ *adj* metodico

methodically /mɪ'θɒdɪklɪ/ *adv* metodicamente

Methodist /'meθədɪst/ *n* metodista *mf*

methodology /meθə'dɒlədʒɪ/ *n* metodologia *f*

meths /meθs/ *n* fam alcol *m* denaturato

methyl /'miːθaɪl/ *n* metile *m*

methylated /'meθɪleɪtɪd/ *adj* ∼ **spirit(s)** alcol *m* denaturato

meticulous /mɪ'tɪkjʊləs/ *adj* meticoloso

meticulously /mɪ'tɪkjʊləslɪ/ *adv* meticolosamente

metre /'miːtə(r)/ *n* metro *m*

metric /'metrɪk/ *adj* metrico

metrication /metrɪ'keɪʃn/ *n* conversione *f* al sistema metrico

metronome /'metrənəʊm/ *n* metronomo *m*

metropolis /mɪ'trɒpəlɪs/ *n* metropoli *f inv*

metropolitan /metrə'pɒlɪtən/ *adj* metropolitano

metropolitan district *n* Br circoscrizione *f* amministrativa urbana

Metropolitan police *n* Br polizia *f* di Londra

mettle /'metl/ *n* coraggio *m*; **show one's** ∼ mostrare di che stoffa si è fatti

mew /mjuː/ **1** *n* miao *m* **2** *vi* miagolare

mews /mjuːz/ *n* Br (stables) scuderie *fpl*; (street) stradina *f*; (yard) cortile *m*

mews flat *n* Br piccolo appartamento *m* ricavato da vecchie scuderie

Mexican /'meksɪkən/ *adj* & *n* messicano, -a *mf*

Mexican wave *n* ola *f inv*

Mexico /'meksɪkəʊ/ *n* Messico *m*

mezzanine /'metsəniːn/ *n* mezzanino *m*

miaow /mɪ'aʊ/ **1** *n* miao *m* **2** *vi* miagolare

mice /maɪs/ ▸ MOUSE

Michaelmas /'mɪkəlməs/ *n* festa *f* di San Michele (29 settembre)

Michaelmas daisy *n* Br margherita *f* settembrina

Michaelmas Term *n* Br Univ primo trimestre *m*

mickey /'mɪkɪ/ *n* **take the** ∼ **out of** prendere in giro

Mickey Mouse *n* Topolino *m*

microbe /'maɪkrəʊb/ *n* microbo *m*

microchip /'maɪkrəʊtʃɪp/ *n* microchip *m inv*

microcomputer /'maɪkrəʊkəmpju:tə(r)/ *n* microcomputer *m inv*

microcosm /'maɪkrəkɒzm/ *n* microcosmo *m*

microfilm *n* microfilm *m inv*

microlight *n* ultraleggero *m*

microlighting *n* volo *m* con l'ultraleggero

micromesh tights *npl* collant *mpl* velati

microphone *n* microfono *m*

microphysics *n* microfisica *f*

microprocessor *n* microprocessore *m*

microscope *n* microscopio *m*

microscopic *adj* microscopico

microsurgery *n* microchirurgia *f*

microwave *n* microonda *f*; (oven) forno *m* a microonde

mid /mɪd/ *adj* ~ May metà maggio; in ~ air a mezz'aria

midday /mɪd'deɪ/ *n* mezzogiorno *m*

middle /'mɪdl/ ① *adj* di centro; **the M~ Ages** il medioevo; **the ~ class(es)** la classe media; **the M~ East** il Medio Oriente
② *n* mezzo *m*; **in the ~ of** ⟨room, floor etc⟩ in mezzo a; **in the ~ of the night** nel pieno della notte, a notte piena

middle-aged /-'eɪdʒd/ *adj* di mezza età

middle-age spread *n* pancetta *f* di mezza età

Middle America *n* (social group) ceto *m* medio americano a tendenza conservatrice

middlebrow *adj* ⟨book⟩ per il lettore medio; ⟨person⟩ con interessi culturali convenzionali

middle-class *adj* borghese

middle distance *n* Phot, Cinema secondo piano *m*; **gaze into the ~ ~** avere lo sguardo perso nel vuoto

middle-eastern *adj* mediorientale

Middle English *n* medio inglese *m*

middle finger *n* dito *m* medio

middle ground *n* Pol centro *m*; **occupy the ~ ~** adottare una posizione intermedia

middle-income *adj* ⟨person, family, country⟩ dal reddito medio

middleman /'mɪdlmæn/ *n* Comm intermediario *m*

middle manager *n* quadro *m* intermedio

middle-of-the-road *adj* (ordinary) ordinario; ⟨policy⟩ moderato

middle-size[d] /-saɪz[d]/ *adj* di misura media

middleweight *n* peso *m* medio

middling /'mɪdlɪŋ/ *adj* discreto

midfield /'mɪd'fi:ld/ *n* centrocampo *m*

midfield player *n* centrocampista *m*

midge /mɪdʒ/ *n* moscerino *m*

midget /'mɪdʒɪt/ *n* nano, -a *mf*

Midlands /'mɪdləndz/ *npl* **the M~** l'Inghilterra *fsg* centrale

mid-life *n* mezza età *f*

mid-life crisis *n* crisi *f inv* di mezza età

midnight /'mɪdnaɪt/ *n* mezzanotte *f*

mid-range *attrib* ⟨car⟩ (in price) di prezzo medio; (in power) di media cilindrata; ⟨hotel⟩ intermedio

midriff /'mɪdrɪf/ *n* diaframma *m*

mid-season *adj* di metà stagione

midshipman /'mɪdʃɪpmən/ *n* Br cadetto *m* di marina; Am allievo *m* dell'Accademia Navale

midst /mɪdst/ *n* **in the ~ of** in mezzo a; **in our ~** fra di noi, in mezzo a noi

midstream /mɪd'stri:m/ *adv* **in ~** (in river) nel mezzo della corrente; (fig: in speech) nel mezzo del discorso

midsummer /'mɪdsʌmə(r)/ *n* mezza estate *f*

Midsummer's Day *n* festa *f* di San Giovanni (24 giugno)

mid-term *attrib* Sch di metà trimestre; Pol a metà del mandato del governo

midtown *n* Am centro *m* (cittadino); **a ~ apartment** un appartamento in centro

midway /'mɪdweɪ/ *adv* a metà strada

midweek /mɪd'wi:k/ ① *adj* di metà settimana
② *adv* a metà settimana

midwife /'mɪdwaɪf/ *n* ostetrica *f*

midwifery /'mɪdwɪfrɪ/ *n* ostetricia *f*

midwinter /mɪd'wɪntə(r)/ *n* pieno inverno *m*

miffed /mɪft/ *adj* fam seccato

might[1] /maɪt/ *v aux* **I ~** potrei; **will you come? – I ~** vieni? – può darsi; **it ~ be true** potrebbe essere vero; **I ~ as well stay** potrei anche restare; **he asked if he ~ go** ha chiesto se poteva andare; **you ~ have drowned** avresti potuto affogare; **you ~ have said so!** avresti potuto dirlo!

might[2] *n* potere *m*

mighty /'maɪtɪ/ ① *adj* (**-ier, -iest**) potente
② *adv* fam molto

migraine /'mi:greɪn/ *n* emicrania *f*

migrant /'maɪgrənt/ ① *adj* migratore
② *n* (bird) migratore, -trice *mf*; (person: for work) emigrante *mf*

migrate /maɪ'greɪt/ *vi* migrare

m

migration /maɪˈɡreɪʃn/ n migrazione f

migratory /maɪˈɡreɪtərɪ/ adj ⟨animal⟩ migratore

mike /maɪk/ n fam microfono f

Milan /mɪˈlæn/ n Milano f

Milanese /mɪləˈniːz/ adj milanese

mild /maɪld/ adj ⟨weather⟩ mite; ⟨person⟩ dolce; ⟨flavour⟩ delicato; ⟨illness⟩ leggero

mildew /ˈmɪldjuː/ n muffa f

mildly /ˈmaɪldlɪ/ adv moderatamente; ⟨say⟩ dolcemente; **to put it ∼** a dir poco, senza esagerazione

mildness /ˈmaɪldnɪs/ n (of person, words) dolcezza f; (of weather) mitezza f

mile /maɪl/ n miglio m (= 1,6 km); ∼**s nicer** fam molto più bello; ∼**s too big** fam eccessivamente grande

mileage /ˈmaɪlɪdʒ/ n chilometraggio m

mileage allowance n indennità f inv di trasferta per chilometro

milestone /ˈmaɪlstəʊn/ n pietra f miliare

milieu /mɪˈljɜː/ n ambiente m

militant /ˈmɪlɪtənt/ adj & n militante mf

militarism /ˈmɪlɪtərɪzm/ n militarismo m

militarize /ˈmɪlɪtəraɪz/ vt militarizzare

military /ˈmɪlɪtrɪ/ adj militare

military academy n accademia f militare

military policeman n agente m di polizia militare

military service n servizio m militare

militate /ˈmɪlɪteɪt/ vi ∼ **against** opporsi a

militia /mɪˈlɪʃə/ n milizia f

milk /mɪlk/ ① n latte m ② vt mungere

milk chocolate n cioccolato m al latte

milk float n Br furgone m del lattaio

milk jug n bricco m del latte

milkman n lattaio m

milk pudding n budino m a base di latte

milk shake n frappé m inv

milk train n primo treno m del mattino

milky /ˈmɪlkɪ/ adj (-**ier**, -**iest**) latteo; ⟨tea etc⟩ con molto latte

Milky Way n Astr Via f Lattea

mill /mɪl/ ① n mulino m; (factory) fabbrica f; (for coffee etc) macinino m ② vt macinare ⟨grain⟩ ■ **mill around, mill around** vi brulicare

millennium /mɪˈlenɪəm/ n millennio m

miller /ˈmɪlə(r)/ n mugnaio m

millet /ˈmɪlɪt/ n miglio m

milligram /ˈmɪlɪɡræm/ n milligrammo m

millimetre /ˈmɪlɪmiːtə(r)/ n millimetro m

million /ˈmɪljən/ adj & n milione m; **a ∼ pounds** un milione di sterline

millionaire /mɪljəˈneə(r)/ n miliardario, -a mf

millipede /ˈmɪlɪpiːd/ n millepiedi m inv

millpond n **like a ∼** calmo come una tavola

millstone n **a ∼ round one's neck** fig un peso

mill-wheel n ruota f di mulino

milometer /maɪˈlɒmɪtə(r)/ n Br ≈ contachilometri m inv

mime /maɪm/ ① n mimo m ② vt mimare

mime artist n mimo, a mf

mimic /ˈmɪmɪk/ ① n imitatore, -trice mf ② vt (pt/pp **mimicked**) imitare

mimicry /ˈmɪmɪkrɪ/ n mimetismo m

mimosa /mɪˈməʊzə/ n mimosa f

min. abbr (**minute**) min.; abbr **minimum**

minaret /mɪnəˈret/ n minareto m

mince /mɪns/ ① n carne f tritata ② vt Culin tritare; **not ∼ words** parlare senza mezzi termini

mincemeat /ˈmɪnsmiːt/ n miscuglio m di frutta secca; **make ∼ of** fig demolire

mince pie n pasticcino m a base di frutta secca

mincer /ˈmɪnsə(r)/ n tritacarne m inv

mind /maɪnd/ ① n mente f; (sanity) ragione f; **to my ∼** a mio parere; **give somebody a piece of one's ∼** dire chiaro e tondo a qualcuno quello che si pensa; **make up one's ∼** decidersi; **have something in ∼** avere qualcosa in mente; **bear something in ∼** tenere presente qualcosa; **have something on one's ∼** essere preoccupato; **have a good ∼ to** avere una grande voglia di; **I have changed my ∼** ho cambiato idea; **be out of one's ∼** essere fuori di sé ② vt (look after) occuparsi di; **I don't ∼ the noise** il rumore non dà fastidio; **I don't ∼ what we do** non mi importa quello che facciamo; **∼ the step!** attenzione al gradino! ③ vi **I don't ∼** non mi importa; **never ∼!** non importa!; **do you ∼ if...?** ti dispiace se...? ■ **mind out** vi ∼ **out!** [fai] attenzione!

mind-bending /-bendɪŋ/ adj ⟨problem⟩ complicatissimo; ∼ **drugs** psicofarmaci mpl

mind-blowing /-bləʊɪŋ/ adj fam sconvolgente

mind-boggling /-bɒɡlɪŋ/ adj fam incredibile

minded /ˈmaɪndɪd/ adj **if you're so ∼** se vuole

minder /ˈmaɪndə(r)/ n (Br: bodyguard) gorilla m inv; (for child) baby-sitter mf inv

mindful /ˈmaɪndfʊl/ adj ∼ **of** attento a

mindless /'maɪndlɪs/ *adj* noncurante

mind-reader *n* persona *f* che legge nel pensiero; **I'm not a** ∼ non leggo nel pensiero

mine¹ /maɪn/ *poss pron* il mio *m*, la mia *f*, i miei *mpl*, le mie *fpl*; **a friend of** ∼ un mio amico; **friends of** ∼ dei miei amici; **that is** ∼ questo è mio; (as opposed to yours) questo è il mio

mine² **1** *n* miniera *f*; (explosive) mina *f* **2** *vt* estrarre; Mil minare

mine-detector *n* rivelatore *m* di mine

minefield /'maɪnfiːld/ *n* also fig campo *m* minato

miner /'maɪnə(r)/ *n* minatore *m*

mineral /'mɪnərəl/ **1** *n* minerale *m* **2** *adj* minerale

mineral oil *n* (Am: paraffin) olio *m* minerale

mineral rights *npl* concessioni *fpl* minerarie

mineral water *n* acqua *f* minerale

minesweeper /'maɪnswiːpə(r)/ *n* dragamine *m inv*

mingle /'mɪŋgl/ *vi* ∼ **with** mescolarsi a

mini /'mɪnɪ/ *n* ▶ MINISKIRT

mini+ *pref* mini+

miniature /'mɪnɪtʃə(r)/ **1** *adj* in miniatura **2** *n* miniatura *f*

miniature golf *n* minigolf *m inv*

miniature railway *n* trenino *m*

mini-budget *n* Br Pol budget *m inv* provvisorio

minibus *n* minibus *m inv*, pulmino *m*

minicab *n* taxi *m inv*

minidisc *n* minidisc *m inv*

minidisc player *n* lettore *m* di minidisc

minim /'mɪnɪm/ *n* Mus minima *f*

minimal /'mɪnɪməl/ *adj* minimo

minimalist *adj* minimalista

minimally /'mɪnɪməlɪ/ *adv* (very slightly) minimamente

minimarket /'mɪnɪmɑːkɪt/ *n* minimarket *m inv*

minimize /'mɪnɪmaɪz/ *vt* minimizzare

minimum /'mɪnɪməm/ **1** *n* (pl **-ima**) minimo *m* **2** *adj* minimo; **ten minutes** ∼ minimo dieci minuti

mining /'maɪnɪŋ/ **1** *n* estrazione *f* **2** *attrib* estrattivo

mining engineer *n* ingegnere *m* minerario

miniskirt /'mɪnɪskɜːt/ *n* minigonna *f*

minister /'mɪnɪstə(r)/ *n* ministro *m*; Relig pastore *m*

ministerial /mɪnɪ'stɪərɪəl/ *adj* ministeriale

minister of state *n* Br Pol titolo *m* di un parlamentare con competenze specifiche in seno a un ministero

ministry /'mɪnɪstrɪ/ *n* Pol ministero *m*; **the** ∼ Relig il ministero sacerdotale

mink /mɪŋk/ *n* visone *m*

minnow /'mɪnəʊ/ *n* (fish) pesciolino *m* d'acqua dolce

minor /'maɪnə(r)/ **1** *adj* minore **2** *n* minorenne *mf*

Minorca /mɪ'nɔːkə/ *n* Minorca *f*

minority /maɪ'nɒrətɪ/ *n* minoranza *f*; (age) minore età *f*

minority leader *n* Am Pol leader *mf inv* dell'opposizione

minority rule *n* governo *m* di minoranza

minor offence *n* Br reato *m* minore

minor road *n* strada *f* secondaria

minster /'mɪnstə(r)/ *n* (cathedral) cattedrale *f*

minstrel /'mɪnstrəl/ *n* menestrello *m*

mint¹ /mɪnt/ **1** *n* zecca *f*; fam patrimonio *m* **2** *adj* in ∼ **condition** in condizione perfetta **3** *vt* coniare

mint² *n* (herb) menta *f*

mint-flavoured /-fleɪvəd/ *adj* al gusto di menta

minuet /mɪnjʊ'et/ *n* minuetto *m*

minus /'maɪnəs/ **1** *prep* meno; (fam: without) senza **2** *n* ∼ **[sign]** meno *m*

minuscule /'mɪnəskjuːl/ *adj* minuscolo

minute¹ /'mɪnɪt/ *n* minuto *m*; **in a** ∼ (shortly) tra un minuto; ∼**s** *pl* (of meeting) verbale *msg*

minute² /maɪ'njuːt/ *adj* minuto; (precise) minuzioso

minute hand /'mɪnɪt/ *n* lancetta *f* dei minuti

minutely /maɪ'njuːtlɪ/ *adv* ⟨vary, differ⟩ di poco; ⟨describe, examine⟩ minuziosamente

minutiae /maɪ'njuːʃɪaɪ/ *npl* minuzie *fpl*

miracle /'mɪrəkl/ *n* miracolo *m*

miraculous /mɪ'rækjʊləs/ *adj* miracoloso

mirage /'mɪrɑːʒ/ *n* miraggio *m*

mire /'maɪə(r)/ *n* pantano *m*

mirror /'mɪrə(r)/ **1** *n* specchio *m* **2** *vt* rispecchiare

mirror image *n* (exact replica) copia *f* esatta; (inverse) immagine *f* speculare

mirth /mɜːθ/ *n* ilarità *f*

misadventure /mɪsæd'ventʃə(r)/ *n* disavventura *f*

misanthropist /mɪ'zænθrəpɪst/ *n* misantropo, -a *mf*

misapprehension /mɪsæprɪ'henʃn/ *n* malinteso *m*; **be under a** ∼ avere frainteso

misappropriate /mɪsə'prəʊprɪeɪt/ *vt* appropriarsi indebitamente di ⟨*funds*⟩

misbehave /mɪsbɪ'heɪv/ *vi* comportarsi male

misbehaviour /mɪsbɪ'heɪvjə(r)/ *n* comportamento *m* scorretto

miscalculate /mɪs'kælkjʊleɪt/ *vt/i* calcolare male

miscalculation /mɪskælkjʊ'leɪʃn/ *n* calcolo *m* sbagliato

miscarriage /'mɪskærɪdʒ/ *n* aborto *m* spontaneo; ∼ **of justice** errore *m* giudiziario

miscarry /mɪs'kærɪ/ *vi* abortire

miscellaneous /mɪsə'leɪnɪəs/ *adj* assortito

miscellany /mɪ'selənɪ/ *n* (of people, things) misto *m*; (anthology) miscellanea *f*

mischief /'mɪstʃɪf/ *n* malefatta *f*; (harm) danno *m*

mischievous /'mɪstʃɪvəs/ *adj* (naughty) birichino; (malicious) dannoso

mischievously /'mɪstʃɪvəslɪ/ *adv* in modo birichino

misconceived /mɪskən'siːvd/ *adj* ⟨*argument, project*⟩ sbagliato

misconception /mɪskən'sepʃn/ *n* concetto *m* erroneo

misconduct /mɪs'kɒndʌkt/ *n* cattiva condotta *f*

misconstrue /mɪskən'struː/ *vt* fraintendere

miscount /mɪs'kaʊnt/ *vt/i* contare male

misdeed /mɪs'diːd/ *n* misfatto *m*

misdemeanour /mɪsdɪ'miːnə(r)/ *n* reato *m*

misdirect /mɪsdaɪ'rekt/ *vt* mettere l'indirizzo sbagliato su ⟨*letter, parcel*⟩; dare istruzioni sbagliate a ⟨*jury*⟩; **the letter was** ∼**ed to our old address** la lettera ci è stata erroneamente spedita al vecchio indirizzo

miser /'maɪzə(r)/ *n* avaro *m*

miserable /'mɪzrəbl/ *adj* (unhappy) infelice; (wretched) miserabile; fig ⟨*weather*⟩ deprimente

miserably /'mɪzrəbl/ *adv* ⟨*live, fail*⟩ miseramente; ⟨*say*⟩ tristemente

miserly /'maɪzəlɪ/ *adj* avaro; ⟨*amount*⟩ ridicolo

misery /'mɪzərɪ/ *n* miseria *f*; (fam: person) piagnone, -a *mf*

misfire /mɪs'faɪə(r)/ *vi* ⟨*gun*⟩ far cilecca; ⟨*plan etc*⟩ non riuscire

misfit /'mɪsfɪt/ *n* disadattato, -a *mf*

misfortune /mɪs'fɔːtʃuːn/ *n* sfortuna *f*

misgivings /mɪs'gɪvɪŋz/ *npl* dubbi *mpl*

misguided /mɪs'gaɪdɪd/ *adj* fuorviato

mishandle /mɪs'hændl/ *vt* gestire male ⟨*operation, meeting*⟩; non prendere per il verso giusto ⟨*person*⟩; (roughly) maneggiare senza precauzioni ⟨*object*⟩; maltrattare ⟨*person, animal*⟩

mishap /'mɪshæp/ *n* disavventura *f*

mishear /mɪs'hɪə(r)/ *vt* sentire male

mishmash /'mɪʃmæʃ/ *n* fam guazzabuglio *m*

misinform /mɪsɪn'fɔːm/ *vt* informar male

misinformation /mɪsɪnfə'meɪʃn/ *n* informazioni *fpl* sbagliate

misinterpret /mɪsɪn'tɜːprɪt/ *vt* fraintendere

misinterpretation /mɪsɪntɜːprɪ'teɪʃn/ *n* interpretazione *f* sbagliata

misjudge /mɪs'dʒʌdʒ/ *vt* giudicar male; (estimate wrongly) valutare male

mislay /mɪs'leɪ/ *vt* (pt/pp **-laid**) smarrire

mislead /mɪs'liːd/ *vt* (pt/pp **-led**) fuorviare

misleading /mɪs'liːdɪŋ/ *adj* fuorviante

mismanage /mɪs'mænɪdʒ/ *vt* amministrare male

mismanagement /mɪs'mænɪdʒmənt/ *n* cattiva amministrazione *f*

mismatch /'mɪsmætʃ/ *n* discordanza *f*

misname /mɪs'neɪm/ *vt* dare il nome sbagliato a

misnomer /mɪs'nəʊmə(r)/ *n* termine *m* improprio

misogynist /mɪs'ɒdʒənɪst/ *n* misogino *m*

misplace /mɪs'pleɪs/ *vt* mettere in un posto sbagliato; ∼ **one's trust** riporre male la propria fiducia

misprint /'mɪsprɪnt/ *n* errore *m* di stampa

mispronounce /mɪsprə'naʊns/ *vt* pronunciare male

mispronunciation /mɪsprənʌnsɪeɪʃn/ *n* (act) pronuncia *f* sbagliata; (instance) errore *m* di pronuncia

misquote /mɪs'kwəʊt/ *vt* citare erroneamente

misread /mɪs'riːd/ *vt* leggere male ⟨*sentence, meter*⟩; (misinterpret) fraintendere ⟨*actions*⟩

misrepresent /mɪsreprɪ'zent/ *vt* rappresentare male

misrepresentation /mɪsreprɪzen'teɪʃn/ *n* (of facts, opinions) travisamento *m*

Miss /mɪs/ *n* (pl **-es**) signorina *f*

miss ① *n* colpo *m* mancato ② *vt* (fail to hit or find) mancare; perdere ⟨*train, bus, class*⟩; (feel the loss of) sentire la mancanza di; **I** ∼**ed that part** (failed to notice) mi è sfuggita quella parte; ~ **the point** non afferrare il punto

3 *vi* but he ~ed (failed to hit) ma l'ha mancato

■ **miss out** *vt* saltare, omettere

misshapen /mɪsˈʃeɪpən/ *adj* malformato

missile /ˈmɪsaɪl/ *n* missile *m*

missing /ˈmɪsɪŋ/ *adj* mancante; ‹*person*› scomparso; Mil disperso; **be ~** essere introvabile; **~ in action** Mil disperso

mission /ˈmɪʃn/ *n* missione *f*

missionary /ˈmɪʃənrɪ/ *n* missionario, -a *mf*

missive /ˈmɪsɪv/ *n* missiva *f*

misspell /mɪsˈspel/ *vt* (pt/pp **-spelt**, **-spelled**) sbagliare l'ortografia di

misspent /mɪsˈspent/ *adj* a ~ **youth** una gioventù sprecata

mist /mɪst/ *n* (fog) foschia *f*; **because of the ~ on the windows** a causa dei vetri appannati

■ **mist over** *vi* ‹*eyes*› velarsi

■ **mist up** *vi* appannarsi, annebbiarsi

mistake /mɪˈsteɪk/ **1** *n* sbaglio *m*; **by ~** per sbaglio

2 *vt* (pt **mistook**, pp **mistaken**) sbagliare ‹*road, house*›; fraintendere ‹*meaning, words*›; **~ for** prendere per

mistaken /mɪˈsteɪkən/ *adj* sbagliato; **be ~** sbagliarsi; **~ identity** errore *m* di persona

mistakenly /mɪˈsteɪkənlɪ/ *adv* erroneamente

mister /ˈmɪstə(r)/ *n* signore *m*

mistletoe /ˈmɪsltəʊ/ *n* vischio *m*

mistranslate /mɪstrænzˈleɪt/ *vt* tradurre in modo sbagliato

mistranslation /mɪstrænzˈleɪʃn/ *n* traduzione *f* sbagliata

mistreat /mɪsˈtriːt/ *vt* maltrattare

mistreatment /mɪsˈtriːtmənt/ *n* maltrattamento *m*

mistress /ˈmɪstrɪs/ *n* padrona *f*; (teacher) maestra *f*; (lover) amante *f*

mistrust /mɪsˈtrʌst/ **1** *n* sfiducia *f*

2 *vt* non aver fiducia in

misty /ˈmɪstɪ/ *adj* (**-ier**, **-iest**) nebbioso; fig indistinto

misty-eyed /-ˈaɪd/ *adj* ‹*look*› commosso; **he goes all ~ about it** a parlarne si commuove

misunderstand /mɪsʌndəˈstænd/ *vt* (pt/pp **-stood**) fraintendere

misunderstanding /mɪsʌndəˈstændɪŋ/ *n* malinteso *m*

misuse¹ /mɪsˈjuːz/ *vt* usare male

misuse² /mɪsˈjuːs/ *n* cattivo uso *m*

mite /maɪt/ *n* Zool acaro *m*; (child) piccino, -a *mf*

mitigate /ˈmɪtɪgeɪt/ *vt* attenuare

mitigating /ˈmɪtɪgeɪtɪŋ/ *adj* attenuante

mitre Br, **miter** Am /ˈmaɪtə(r)/ *n* mitra *f*

mitt /mɪt/ *n* (no separate fingers) muffola *f*; (cut-off fingers) mezzo guanto *m*; (in baseball) guantone *m*; (fam: hand) mano *f*

mitten /ˈmɪtn/ *n* manopola *f*, muffola *f*

mix /mɪks/ **1** *n* (combination) mescolanza *f*; Culin miscuglio *m*; (ready-made) preparato *m*

2 *vt* mischiare

3 *vi* mischiarsi; ‹*person*› inserirsi; **~ with** (associate with) frequentare

■ **mix in** *vt* incorporare ‹*eggs, flour etc*›

■ **mix up** *vt* mescolare ‹*papers*›; (confuse, mistake for) confondere

mixed /mɪkst/ *adj* misto

mixed ability *adj* ‹*class, teaching*› per alunni di capacità diverse

mixed bag *n* **it was a very ~ ~** fig c'era un po' di tutto

mixed blessing *n* **be a ~ ~** avere vantaggi e svantaggi

mixed doubles *npl* Tennis doppio *m* misto

mixed economy *n* economia *f* mista

mixed grill *n* grigliata *f* di carne mista

mixed marriage *n* matrimonio *m* misto

mixed-media *adj* multimediale

mixed metaphor *n* abbinamento *m* di parte di due o più metafore diverse con effetto comico

mixed race **1** *adj* ‹*children*› con genitori di razze diverse

2 *n* **she's of ~** i suoi genitori sono di razze diverse

mixed-up *adj* ‹*person, emotions*› confuso

mixed vegetables *npl* verdure *fpl* miste

mixer /ˈmɪksə(r)/ *n* Culin frullatore *m*, mixer *m inv*; **he's a good ~** è un tipo socievole

mixing /ˈmɪksɪŋ/ *n* (of people, objects, ingredients) mescolamento *m*: Mus mixaggio *m*

mixture /ˈmɪkstʃə(r)/ *n* mescolanza *f*; (medicine) sciroppo *m*; Culin miscela *f*

mix-up *n* (confusion) confusione *f*; (mistake) pasticcio *m*

mm *abbr* (**millimetre(s)**) mm

MMS *abbr* (**multimedia messaging service**) MMS *m*

MO *abbr* (**medical officer**) ufficiale *m* medico; *abbr* (**money order**) vaglia *m inv* postale; Am *abbr* **Missouri**

moan /məʊn/ **1** *n* lamento *m*

2 *vi* lamentarsi; (complain) lagnarsi

moat /məʊt/ *n* fossato *m*

mob /mɒb/ **1** *n* folla *f*; (rabble) gentaglia *f*; (fam: gang) banda *f*

2 *vt* (pt/pp **mobbed**) assalire

mobile /ˈməʊbaɪl/ **1** *adj* mobile

m

② n composizione f mobile; (phone) [telefono m] cellulare m

mobile home n casa f roulotte

mobile library n Br biblioteca f itinerante

mobile phone n (telefono m) cellulare m, telefonino m

mobile shop n furgone m attrezzato per la vendita

mobility /mə'bɪlətɪ/ n mobilità f

mobility allowance n Br indennità f inv di accompagnamento

mobilization /məʊbɪlaɪ'zeɪʃn/ n mobilitazione f

mobilize /'məʊbɪlaɪz/ vt mobilitare

mocha /'mɒkə/ n moca m inv

mock /mɒk/ **①** adj finto **②** vt canzonare

mockery /'mɒkərɪ/ n derisione f; a ∼ of una parodia di

mock-up n modello m in scala

MoD n abbr (**Ministry of Defence**) Br Ministero m della Difesa

modal /'məʊdl/ adj ∼ auxiliary verbo m modale

mod con /mɒd'kɒn/ Br abbr (**modern convenience**) all ∼ ∼s tutti i comfort

mode /məʊd/ n modo m; Comput modalità f

model /'mɒdl/ **①** n modello m; [fashion] ∼ indossatore, -trice mf, modello, -a mf **②** adj ⟨yacht, plane⟩ in miniatura; ⟨pupil, husband⟩ esemplare, modello **③** vt (pt/pp **modelled**) indossare ⟨clothes⟩ **④** vi fare l'indossatore, -trice mf: (for artist) posare

modelling /'mɒd(ə)lɪŋ/ n (with clay etc) modellare m con la creta; (of clothes) professione f di indossatore; **do some** ∼ (for artist) fare il modello

modelling clay n creta f per modellare

modem /'məʊdem/ **①** n modem m inv **②** vt mandare per modem

moderate¹ /'mɒdəreɪt/ **①** vt moderare **②** vi moderarsi

moderate² /'mɒdərət/ **①** adj moderato **②** n Pol moderato, -a mf

moderately /'mɒdərətlɪ/ adv ⟨drink, speak etc⟩ moderatamente; ⟨good, bad etc⟩ relativamente

moderation /mɒdə'reɪʃn/ n moderazione f; in ∼ con moderazione

modern /'mɒdn/ adj moderno

modern-day adj attuale

modernism /'mɒdənɪzm/ n modernismo m

modernity /mə'dɜːnətɪ/ n modernità f

modernization /mɒdənaɪ'zeɪʃn/ n modernizzazione f

modernize /'mɒdənaɪz/ vt modernizzare

modern languages npl lingue fpl moderne

modest /'mɒdɪst/ adj modesto

modesty /'mɒdɪstɪ/ n modestia f

modicum /'mɒdɪkəm/ n **a** ∼ **of** un po' di

modification /mɒdɪfɪ'keɪʃn/ n modificazione f

modifier /'mɒdɪfaɪə(r)/ n (in linguistics) modificatore m

modify /'mɒdɪfaɪ/ vt (pt/pp **-fied**) modificare

modular /'mɒdjʊlə(r)/ adj ⟨course⟩ a moduli; ⟨construction, furniture⟩ modulare

modulate /'mɒdjʊleɪt/ vt/i modulare

module /'mɒdjuːl/ n modulo m

modus operandi /məʊdəsɒpə'rændi:/ n modus operandi m inv

mogul /məʊgl/ n magnate m

Mohammed /məhæmɪd/ n Maometto m

mohican /məʊ'hiːkən/ n (hairstyle) taglio m [di capelli] alla moicana

moist /mɔɪst/ adj umido

moisten /'mɔɪsn/ vt inumidire

moisture /'mɔɪstʃə(r)/ n umidità f

moisturizer /'mɔɪstʃəraɪzə(r)/ n [crema f] idratante m

molar /'məʊlə(r)/ n molare m

molasses /mə'læsɪz/ n Am melassa f

mold /məʊld/ Am = MOULD

Moldavia /mɒl'deɪvɪə/ n Moldavia f

mole¹ /məʊl/ n (on face etc) neo m

mole² n Zool talpa f

mole³ n (breakwater) molo m

molecular /mə'lekjʊlə(r)/ adj molecolare

molecule /'mɒlɪkjuːl/ n molecola f

molehill /'məʊlhɪl/ n monticello m

moleskin /'məʊlskɪn/ n (fur) pelliccia f di talpa

molest /mə'lest/ vt molestare

mollify /'mɒlɪfaɪ/ vt (pt/pp **-ied**) placare

mollusc /'mɒləsk/ n mollusco m

mollycoddle /'mɒlɪkɒdl/ vt tenere nella bambagia

molt /məʊlt/ Am = MOULT

molten /'məʊltən/ adj fuso

mom /mɒm/ n Am fam mamma f

moment /'məʊmənt/ n momento m; **at the** ∼ in questo momento

momentarily /məʊmən'terɪlɪ/ adv (for an instant) per un momento; (Am: at any moment) da un momento all'altro; (Am; very soon) tra un momento

momentary /'məʊməntrɪ/ adj momentaneo

momentous /mə'mentəs/ adj molto importante

momentum /mə'mentəm/ n impeto m

Monaco /'mɒnəkəʊ/ n Principato m di Monaco

monarch /'mɒnək/ n monarca m

monarchist /'mɒnəkɪst/ n monarchico, -a mf

monarchy /'mɒnəkɪ/ n monarchia f

monastery /'mɒnəstrɪ/ n monastero m

monastic /mə'næstɪk/ adj monastico

Monday /'mʌndeɪ/ n lunedì m inv

monetary /'mʌnətrɪ/ adj monetario

money /'mʌnɪ/ n denaro m

money box n salvadanaio m

moneylender n usuraio m

moneymaker n (business) attività f redditizia; (product) prodotto m che rende bene

money order n vaglia m inv postale

Mongolia /mɒŋ'gəʊlɪə/ n Mongolia f

mongrel /'mʌŋgrəl/ n bastardino m

monitor /'mɒnɪtə(r)/ **1** n Techn monitor m inv
2 vt controllare

monk /mʌŋk/ n monaco m

monkey /'mʌŋkɪ/ n scimmia f
■ **monkey about with** vt (fam: interfere with) armeggiare con

monkey business n fam (fooling) scherzi mpl; (cheating) imbrogli mpl

monkey-nut n nocciolina f americana

monkey wrench n chiave f inglese a rullino

monkfish /'mʌŋkfɪʃ/ n bottatrice f

mono /'mɒnəʊ/ n mono m

monochrome /'mɒnəkrəʊm/ adj monocromatico; Cinema, TV in bianco e nero

monocle /'mɒnəkl/ n monocolo m

monogamous /mə'nɒgəməs/ adj monogamo

monogamy /mə'nɒgəmɪ/ n monogamia f

monogram /'mɒnəgræm/ n monogramma m

monograph /'mɒnəgrɑːf/ n monografia f

monolith /'mɒnəlɪθ/ n monolito m

monologue /'mɒnəlɒg/ n monologo m

monomania /mɒnə'meɪnɪə/ n monomania f

monoplane /'mɒnəpleɪn/ n monoplano m

monopolize /mə'nɒpəlaɪz/ vt monopolizzare

monopoly /mə'nɒpəlɪ/ n monopolio m

monoski /'mɒnəʊskiː/ **1** n monoscì m inv
2 vi praticare il monoscì

monosodium glutamate /mɒnəsəʊdɪəm'gluːtəmeɪt/ n glutammato m di sodio

monosyllabic /mɒnəsɪ'læbɪk/ adj monosillabico

monosyllable /'mɒnəsɪləbl/ n monosillabo m

monotone /'mɒnətəʊn/ n speak in a ~ parlare con tono monotono

monotonous /mə'nɒtənəs/ adj monotono

monotonously /mə'nɒtənəslɪ/ adv in modo monotono

monotony /mə'nɒtənɪ/ n monotonia f

monsoon /mɒn'suːn/ n monsone m

monster /'mɒnstə(r)/ n mostro m

monstrosity /mɒn'strɒsətɪ/ n mostruosità f

monstrous /'mɒnstrəs/ adj mostruoso

montage /mɒn'tɑːʒ/ n montaggio m

Mont Blanc /mɒn'blɑ̃/ n Monte m Bianco

Montenegro /mɒntɪ'niːgrəʊ/ n Montenegro m

month /mʌnθ/ n mese m

monthly /'mʌnθlɪ/ **1** adj mensile
2 adv mensilmente
3 n (periodical) mensile m

monument /'mɒnjʊmənt/ n monumento m

monumental /mɒnjʊ'mentl/ adj fig monumentale

monumentally /mɒnjʊ'mentəlɪ/ adv ⟨boring, ignorant⟩ enormemente

moo /muː/ **1** n muggito m
2 vi (pt/pp **mooed**) muggire

mooch /muːtʃ/ vi ~ **about** fam gironzolare; ~ **about the house** gironzolare per casa

mood /muːd/ n umore m; **be in a good/ bad** ~ essere di buon/cattivo umore; **be in the** ~ **for** essere in vena di

moody /'muːdɪ/ adj (**-ier, -iest**) (variable) lunatico; (bad-tempered) di malumore

moon /muːn/ n luna f: **over the** ~ fam al settimo cielo
■ **moon about, moon around** vi (fam: wander aimlessly) gironzolare
■ **moon over** vt fam sospirare d'amore per ⟨somebody⟩

moonbeam n raggio m di luna

moon buggy n veicolo m lunare

moonlight **1** n chiaro m di luna
2 vi fam lavorare in nero

moonlighting n fam lavoro m nero

moonlit adj illuminato dalla luna

moonshine n (nonsense) fantasie fpl; (Am: liquor) liquore m di contrabbando

moor[1] /mʊə(r)/ n brughiera f

moor[2] vt Naut ormeggiare

moorhen /'mʊəhen/ n gallinella f d'acqua

mooring /'mʊərɪŋ/ n (place) ormeggio m; ∼s pl (chains) ormeggi mpl

Moorish /'mʊərɪʃ/ adj moresco

moorland /'mʊələnd/ n brughiera f

moose /muːs/ n (pl **moose**) alce m

moot /muːt/ adj it's a ∼ point è un punto controverso

mop /mɒp/ ① n mocio® m inv; ∼ of hair zazzera f
② vt (pt/pp **mopped**) lavare con il mocio®
■ **mop up** vt (dry) asciugare con il mocio®; (clean) pulire con il mocio®

mope /məʊp/ vi essere depresso
■ **mope about**, **mope around** vi trascinarsi

moped /'məʊped/ n ciclomotore m

moral /'mɒrəl/ ① adj morale
② n morale f

morale /mə'rɑːl/ n morale m; be a ∼ booster tirare su di morale

moral fibre n forza f morale

moralistic /mɒrə'lɪstɪk/ adj moralistico

morality /mə'rælətɪ/ n moralità f

moralize /'mɒrəlaɪz/ vi moraleggiare

morally /'mɒrəlɪ/ adv moralmente

morals /'mɒrəlz/ npl moralità f

moratorium /mɒrə'tɔːrɪəm/ n moratoria f

morbid /'mɔːbɪd/ adj morboso

more /mɔː(r)/ ① adj più; a few ∼ books un po' più di libri; some ∼ tea? ancora un po' di tè?; there's no ∼ bread non c'è più pane; there are no ∼ apples non ci sono più mele; one ∼ word and... ancora una parola e...
② pron di più; would you like some ∼? ne vuoi ancora?; no ∼, thank you non ne voglio più, grazie
③ adv più; ∼ interesting più interessante; ∼ (and ∼) quickly (sempre) più veloce; ∼ than più di; I don't love him any ∼ non lo amo più; once ∼ ancora una volta; ∼ or less più o meno; the ∼ I see him, the ∼ I like him più lo vedo, più mi piace

moreish /'mɔːrɪʃ/ adj fam be ∼ tirare per la gola

moreover /mɔː'rəʊvə(r)/ adv inoltre

morgue /mɔːg/ n obitorio m

MORI /'mɔːrɪ/ n abbr (**Market Opinion Research Institute**) istituto m di sondaggio e ricerche di mercato

moribund /'mɒrɪbʌnd/ adj moribondo

morning /'mɔːnɪŋ/ n mattino m, mattina f; spend the ∼ doing something passare la mattinata facendo qualcosa; in the ∼ del mattino; (tomorrow) domani mattina

morning-after pill n pillola f del giorno dopo

morning coffee n caffè m inv del mattino

morning dress n tight m inv

morning sickness n nausea f mattutina

Moroccan /mə'rɒk(ə)n/ adj & n marocchino, -a mf

Morocco /mə'rɒkəʊ/ n Marocco m

morocco leather n marocchino m

moron /'mɔːrɒn/ n fam deficiente mf

morose /mə'rəʊs/ adj scontroso

morosely /mə'rəʊslɪ/ adv in modo scontroso

morphine /'mɔːfiːn/ n morfina f

morris dance /'mɒrɪs/ n danza f tradizionale inglese

Morse /mɔːs/ n ∼ [code] [codice m] Morse m

morsel /'mɔːsl/ n (food) boccone m

mortal /'mɔːtl/ adj & n mortale mf

mortal combat n duello m mortale

mortality /mɔː'tælətɪ/ n mortalità f

mortally /'mɔːtəlɪ/ adv (wounded, offended) a morte; (afraid) da morire

mortar /'mɔːtə(r)/ n mortaio m

mortgage /'mɔːgɪdʒ/ ① n mutuo m; (money raised on collateral of property) ipoteca f
② vt ipotecare

mortgage rate n tasso m d'interesse sui mutui

mortgage relief n sgravio m fiscale sul mutuo

mortgage repayment n rata f del mutuo

mortician /mɔː'tɪʃn/ n Am impresario, -a mf di pompe funebri

mortification /mɔːtɪfɪ'keɪʃn/ n (of the flesh, embarrassment) mortificazione f

mortify /'mɔːtɪfaɪ/ vt (pt/pp -ied) mortificare

mortuary /'mɔːtjʊərɪ/ n camera f mortuaria

mosaic /məʊ'zeɪɪk/ n mosaico m

Moscow /'mɒskəʊ/ n Mosca f

Moselle /məʊ'zel/ n (wine) vino m della Mosella

Moses /'məʊzɪz/ n Mosè

Moslem /'mʊzlɪm/ adj & n musulmano, -a mf

mosque /mɒsk/ n moschea f

mosquito /mɒs'kiːtəʊ/ n (pl -es) zanzara f

mosquito bite n puntura m di zanzara

mosquito net n zanzariera f

mosquito repellent n antizanzare m inv

moss /mɒs/ n muschio m

mossy /'mɒsɪ/ adj muschioso

most /məʊst/ **1** *adj* (majority) la maggior parte di; **for the ~ part** per lo più **2** *adv* più, maggiormente; (very) estremamente, molto; **the ~ interesting day** la giornata più interessante; **a ~ interesting day** una giornata estremamente interessante; **the ~ beautiful woman in the world** la donna più bella del mondo; **~ unlikely** veramente improbabile
3 *pron* **~ of them** la maggior parte di loro; **at [the] ~** al massimo; **make the ~ of** sfruttare al massimo; **~ of the time** la maggior parte del tempo

mostly /'məʊs(t)lɪ/ *adv* per lo più

MOT *n* Br revisione *f* obbligatoria di autoveicoli

motel /məʊ'tel/ *n* motel *m inv*

moth /mɒθ/ *n* falena *f*: [clothes-] ~ tarma *f*

mothball /'mɒθbɔ:l/ *n* pallina *f* di naftalina

moth-eaten /-i:tən/ *adj* tarmato

mother /'mʌðə(r)/ **1** *n* madre *f*
2 *vt* fare da madre a

motherboard /'mʌðəbɔ:d/ *n* scheda *f* madre

motherhood /'mʌðəhʊd/ *n* maternità *f*

Mothering Sunday /mʌðərɪŋ'sʌndeɪ/ *n* la festa della mamma

mother-in-law *n* (pl **mothers-in-law**) suocera *f*

motherland /'mʌðəlænd/ *n* patria *f*

motherless /'mʌðəlɪs/ *adj* orfano, -a *mf* di madre

motherly /'mʌðəlɪ/ *adj* materno

mother-of-pearl *n* madreperla *f*

mother's boy *n* mammone *m*

Mother's Day *n* la festa della mamma

mother's help *n* Br aiuto *m* domestico

mother-to-be *n* futura mamma *f*

mother tongue *n* madrelingua *f*

mothproof /'mɒθpru:f/ *adj* antitarmico

motif /məʊ'ti:f/ *n* motivo *m*

motion /'məʊʃn/ **1** *n* moto *m*; (proposal) mozione *f*; (gesture) gesto *m*
2 *vt/i* ~ [to] **somebody to come in** fare segno a qualcuno di entrare

motionless /'məʊʃ(ə)nlɪs/ *adj* immobile

motionlessly /'məʊʃənlɪslɪ/ *adv* senza alcun movimento

motion picture **1** *n* film *m inv* [per il cinema]
2 *attrib* ⟨industry⟩ cinematografico

motivate /'məʊtɪveɪt/ *vt* motivare

motivated /'məʊtɪveɪtɪd/ *adj* ⟨person, student⟩ motivato; **politically/racially ~** ⟨act⟩ a sfondo politico/razziale

motivation /məʊtɪ'veɪʃn/ *n* motivazione *f*

motive /'məʊtɪv/ *n* motivo *m*

motley /'mɒtlɪ/ *adj* disparato

motor /'məʊtə(r)/ **1** *n* motore *m*; (car) macchina *f*
2 *adj* a motore; Anat motore
3 *vi* andare in macchina

Motorail /'məʊtəreɪl/ *n* treno *m* per trasporto auto

motorbike /'məʊtəbaɪk/ *n* fam moto *f inv*

motor boat *n* motoscafo *m*

motorcade /'məʊtəkeɪd/ *n* Am corteo *m* di auto

motor car *n* automobile *f*

motorcycle *n* motocicletta *f*

motorcycle escort *n* scorta *f* di motociclette

motorcycle messenger *n* corriere *m* in moto

motorcyclist *n* motociclista *mf*

motorhome *n* camper *m inv*; (towed) roulotte *f inv*

motoring /'məʊtərɪŋ/ *n* automobilismo *m*

motorist /'məʊtərɪst/ *n* automobilista *mf*

motor launch *n* motolancia *f*

motor mechanic *n* meccanico *m*

motormouth *n* fam chiacchierone, -a *mf*

motor oil *n* olio *m* lubrificante

motor racing *n* corse *fpl* automobilistiche

motor scooter *n* motorino *m*

motor vehicle *n* autoveicolo *m*

motorway *n* autostrada *f*

mottled /'mɒtld/ *adj* chiazzato

motto /'mɒtəʊ/ *n* (pl **-es**) motto *m*

mould[1] /'məʊld/ *n* (fungus) muffa *f*

mould[2] **1** *n* stampo *m*
2 *vt* foggiare; fig formare

moulder /'məʊldə(r)/ *vi* ⟨corpse, refuse⟩ andare in decomposizione

moulding /'məʊldɪŋ/ *n* Archit cornice *f*

mouldy /'məʊldɪ/ *adj* ammuffito; (fam: worthless) ridicolo

moult /məʊlt/ *vi* ⟨bird⟩ fare la muta; ⟨animal⟩ perdere il pelo

mound /maʊnd/ *n* mucchio *m*; (hill) collinetta *f*

mount /maʊnt/ **1** *n* (horse) cavalcatura *f*; (of jewel, photo, picture) montatura *f*
2 *vt* montare a ⟨horse⟩; salire su ⟨bicycle⟩; incastonare ⟨jewel⟩; incorniciare ⟨photo, picture⟩
3 *vi* aumentare
■ **mount up** *vi* aumentare

mountain /'maʊntɪn/ *n* montagna *f*: **make a ~ out of a molehill** fare di una mosca un elefante

mountain bike *n* mountain bike *f inv*

mountain climbing *n* alpinismo *m*

m

mountaineer /maʊntɪˈnɪə(r)/ n
alpinista mf

mountaineering /maʊntɪˈnɪərɪŋ/ n
alpinismo m

mountainous /ˈmaʊntɪnəs/ adj
montagnoso

mountain range n catena f montuosa

mounted police /maʊntɪdpəˈliːs/ n
polizia f a cavallo

mourn /mɔːn/ ❶ vt lamentare
❷ vi ∼ **for** piangere la morte di

mourner /ˈmɔːnə(r)/ n persona f che
participa a un funerale

mournful /ˈmɔːnfʊl/ adj triste

mournfully /ˈmɔːnfʊlɪ/ adv tristemente

mourning /ˈmɔːnɪŋ/ n **in** ∼ in lutto

mouse /maʊs/ n (pl **mice**) topo m;
Comput mouse m inv

mousehole n tana f di topi/di un topo

mouse mat n Comput tappetino m

mousetrap n trappola f [per topi]

mousse /muːs/ n Culin mousse f inv

moustache /məˈstɑːʃ/ n baffi mpl

mousy /ˈmaʊsɪ/ adj ⟨colour⟩ grigio topo

mouth¹ /maʊð/ vt ∼ **something** dire
qualcosa silenziosamente muovendo
solamente le labbra

mouth² /maʊθ/ n bocca f; (of river) foce f

mouthful /ˈmaʊθfʊl/ n boccone m

mouth organ n armonica f [a bocca]

mouthpiece n imboccatura f; (fig:
person) portavoce m inv

mouth-to-mouth resuscitation n
respirazione f bocca a bocca

mouthwash n colluttorio m

mouthwatering /-wɔːtərɪŋ/ adj che fa
venire l'acquolina in bocca

movable /ˈmuːvəbl/ adj movibile

move /muːv/ ❶ n mossa f; (moving house)
trasloco m; **on the** ∼ in movimento; **get a**
∼ **on** fam darsi una mossa
❷ vt muovere; (emotionally) commuovere;
spostare ⟨car⟩; (transfer) trasferire; (propose)
proporre; ∼ **house** traslocare
❸ vi muoversi; (move house) traslocare;
don't ∼! non muoverti!
■ **move about**, **move around** vi (in
house) muoversi; (in country) spostarsi
■ **move along** ❶ vi andare avanti
❷ vt muovere in avanti
■ **move away** ❶ vi allontanarsi; (move
house) trasferirsi
❷ vt allontanare
■ **move forward** ❶ vi avanzare
❷ vt spostare avanti
■ **move in** vi (to a house) trasferirsi
■ **move off** vi ⟨vehicle⟩ muoversi
■ **move on** ❶ vi (move to another place)
muoversi
❷ vt ⟨police⟩ far circolare
■ **move on to** vt passare a ⟨new topic⟩

■ **move out** vi (of house) andare via
■ **move over** ❶ vi spostarsi
❷ vt spostare
■ **move up** vi muoversi; (advance, increase)
avanzare

movement /ˈmuːvmənt/ n movimento
m; (of clock) meccanismo m

movie /ˈmuːvɪ/ n film m inv; **go to the** ∼s
andare al cinema

movie camera n cinepresa f

movie director n regista mf
cinematografico, -a

movie-goer n persona f che va al
cinema

movie star n stella f del cinema, star f
inv del cinema

movie theater n Am cinema m

moving /ˈmuːvɪŋ/ adj mobile; (touching)
commovente

mow /məʊ/ vt (pt **mowed**, pp **mown** or
mowed) tagliare ⟨lawn⟩
■ **mow down** vt (destroy) sterminare

mower /ˈməʊə(r)/ n tosaerba m inv

Mozambique /məʊzæmˈbiːk/ n
Mozambico m

MP abbr (**Member of Parliament**)
deputato, -a mf

MP3 player n lettore m di MP3

mpg abbr (**miles per gallon**) miglia al
gallone

mph abbr (**miles per hour**) miglia
all'ora

MPV n abbr (**multi-purpose vehicle**)
MPV m

Mr /ˈmɪstə(r)/ n (pl **Messrs**) Signor m

MRI n abbr (**magnetic resonance
imaging**) RM f

Mrs /ˈmɪsɪz/ n Signora f

MRSA n abbr (**methicillin-resistant
Staphylococcus aureus**) MRSA m

Ms /mɪz/ n Signora f (modo m formale di
rivolgersi ad una donna quando non si
vuole indicarla come sposata o nubile)

MS n abbr (**multiple sclerosis**) sclerosi
f a placche or multipla; abbr
(**manuscript**) ms; Am abbr **Mississippi**

MSc n abbr (**Master of Science**)
(diploma) laurea f in discipline scientifiche;
(person) laureato, -a mf in discipline
scientifiche

MST abbr Am (**Mountain Standard
Time**) tempo f medio della zona delle
Montagne Rocciose

Mt. abbr (**mount**) (in place names) M.

much /mʌtʃ/ adj, adv & pron molto; ∼
as per quanto; **I love you just as** ∼ **as
before/him** ti amo quanto prima/lui; **as** ∼
as £5 million ben cinque milioni di
sterline; **as** ∼ **as that** così tanto; **very** ∼
tantissimo, moltissimo; ∼ **the same** quasi
uguale

muck /mʌk/ *n* (dirt) sporcizia *f*; (farming) letame *m*; (fam: filth) porcheria *f*
 ■ **muck about** *vi* fam perder tempo; ∼ **about with** trafficare con
 ■ **muck in** *vi* fam dare una mano
 ■ **muck up** *vt* fam rovinare; (make dirty) sporcare

muckraking /'mʌkreɪkɪŋ/ *n* scandalismo *m*

mucky /'mʌkɪ/ *adj* (**-ier**, **-iest**) sudicio

mucus /'mjuːkəs/ *n* muco *m*

mud /mʌd/ *n* fango *m*

muddle /'mʌdl/ ① *n* disordine *m*; (mix-up) confusione *f*
 ② *vt* ∼ [up] confondere ⟨dates⟩
 ■ **muddle through** *vi* farcela alla bell'e meglio

muddle-headed /-'hedɪd/ *adj* ⟨plan⟩ confuso; ⟨person⟩ confusionario

muddy /'mʌdɪ/ *adj* (**-ier**, **-iest**) ⟨path⟩ fangoso; ⟨shoes⟩ infangato

mudflat *n* distesa *f* di fango

mudguard *n* parafango *m*

mud hut *n* capanna *f* di fango

mudpack *n* (for beauty treatment) maschera *f* di fango

mud pie *n* formina *f* di fango

mudslide *n* colata *f* di fango

mud-slinging /-slɪŋɪŋ/ *n* diffamazione *f*

muesli /'mjuːzlɪ/ *n* muesli *m inv*

muffle /'mʌfl/ *vt* smorzare ⟨sound⟩
 ■ **muffle up** *vi* (for warmth) imbacuccarsi

muffler /'mʌflə(r)/ *n* sciarpa *f*; Am Auto marmitta *f*

mug¹ /mʌg/ *n* tazza *f*; (for beer) boccale *m*; (fam: face) muso *m*; (fam: simpleton) pollo *m*

mug² *vt* (pt/pp **mugged**) aggredire e derubare
 ■ **mug up** *vt* (fam: learn) imparare alla bell'e meglio

mugger /'mʌgə(r)/ *n* assalitore, -trice *mf*

mugging /'mʌgɪŋ/ *n* aggressione *f* per furto

muggy /'mʌgɪ/ *adj* (**-ier**, **-iest**) afoso

Muhammad /mə'hæmɪd/ *n* Maometto *m*

mulatto /mjuː'lætəʊ/ *adj & n* Am mulatto, -a *mf*

mulberry /'mʌlb(ə)rɪ/ *n* Am (fruit) mora *f* di gelso; (tree) gelso *m*

mule¹ /mjuːl/ *n* mulo *m*

mule² *n* (slipper) ciabatta *f*

mulish /'mjuːlɪʃ/ *adj* testardo

mull /mʌl/ *vt* ∼ **over** rimuginare su

mulled /mʌld/ *adj* ∼ **wine** vin brûlé *m inv*

multi+ /'mʌltɪ/ *pref* multi+

multi-access *n* Comput accesso *m* multiplo

multichannel /mʌltɪ'tʃænəl/ *adj* ⟨television⟩ con molti canali

multicoloured /'mʌltɪkʌləd/ *adj* variopinto

multicultural /mʌltɪ'kʌltʃərəl/ *adj* multiculturale

multidisciplinary /mʌltɪdɪsɪ'plɪnərɪ/ *adj* Sch, Univ pluridisciplinare

multi-ethnic *adj* multietnico

multifaceted /mʌltɪ'fæsɪtɪd/ *adj* ⟨gemstone⟩ sfaccettato; ⟨career⟩ variegato; ⟨personality⟩ sfaccettato

multifunction /mʌltɪ'fʌŋkʃn/ *adj* multifunzionale

multigym /'mʌltɪdʒɪm/ *n* attrezzo *m* multiuso

multilateral /mʌltɪ'læt(ə)rəl/ *adj* Pol multilaterale

multilevel /'mʌltɪlevəl/ *adj* ⟨parking, access⟩ a più piani; ⟨analysis⟩ a più livelli

multilingual /mʌltɪ'lɪŋgwəl/ *adj* multilingue *inv*

multimedia /mʌltɪ'miːdɪə/ ① *n* multimedia *mpl*
 ② *adj* multimediale

multinational /mʌltɪ'næʃnəl/ ① *adj* multinazionale
 ② *n* multinazionale *f*

multipack *n* confezione *f* multipla

multi-party /'mʌltɪpɑːtɪ/ *adj* ⟨government, system⟩ pluripartitico

multiplayer *adj* Comput ⟨game⟩ in multiplayer

multiple /'mʌltɪpl/ *adj & n* multiplo *m*

multiple choice *adj* scelta *f* multipla

multiple choice question *n* Sch test *m inv* a scelta multipla

multiple ownership *n* comproprietà *f*

multiple pileup *n* tamponamento *m* a catena

multiple sclerosis *n* sclerosi *f* a placche *or* multipla

multiple store *n* Br negozio *m* appartenente a una catena

multiplex /'mʌltɪpleks/ ① *n* Teleph multiplex *m inv*; Cinema cinema *m inv* multisale
 ② *adj* Teleph in multiplex

multiplication /mʌltɪplɪ'keɪʃn/ *n* moltiplicazione *f*

multiply /'mʌltɪplaɪ/ ① *vt* (pt/pp **-ied**) moltiplicare (**by** per)
 ② *vi* moltiplicarsi

multi-purpose *adj* ⟨tool, gadget⟩ multiuso *inv*; ⟨organization⟩ con più scopi

multi-purpose vehicle *n* monovolume *f*

multi-racial *adj* multirazziale

multi-storey *adj* ∼ **car park** parcheggio *m* a più piani

multitask *vi* ⟨person⟩ eseguire varie mansioni; ⟨computer⟩ eseguire il multitasking

multi-track *adj* ⟨*sound system*⟩ a più piste

multitude /'mʌltɪtjuːd/ *n* moltitudine *f*; **hide a ~ of sins** ⟨*rug etc*⟩ nascondere un sacco di magagne

multi-user *adj* ⟨*system, installation*⟩ multiutente

mum¹ /mʌm/ *adj* **keep ~** fam non aprire bocca

mum² *n* fam mamma *f*

mumble /'mʌmbl/ *vt/i* borbottare

mumbo-jumbo /mʌmbəʊ'dʒʌmbəʊ/ *n* (fam: speech, writing) paroloni *mpl*

mummy¹ /'mʌmɪ/ *n* fam mamma *f*

mummy² *n* Archaeol mummia *f*

mummy's boy *n* Br pej mammone *m*

mumps /mʌmps/ *n* orecchioni *mpl*

munch /mʌntʃ/ *vt/i* sgranocchiare

mundane /mʌn'deɪn/ *adj* (everyday) banale

municipal /mjʊ'nɪsɪpl/ *adj* municipale

munitions /mjʊ'nɪʃnz/ *npl* munizioni *fpl*

mural /'mjʊərəl/ *n* dipinto *m* murale

murder /'mɜːdə(r)/ ❶ *n* assassinio *m* ❷ *vt* assassinare; (fam: ruin) massacrare

murder case *n* caso *m* di omicidio

murder charge *n* imputazione *f* di omicidio

murderer /'mɜːdərə(r)/ *n* assassino, -a *mf*

murderess /'mɜːdəres/ *n* assassina *f*

murderous /'mɜːdərəs/ *adj* omicida

murky /'mɜːkɪ/ *adj* (-ier, -iest) oscuro

murmur /'mɜːmə(r)/ ❶ *n* mormorio *m* ❷ *vt/i* mormorare

murmuring /'mɜːmərɪŋ/ *n* mormorio *m*; **~s** *pl* (of discontent) segnali *mpl* di malcontento

muscle /'mʌsl/ *n* muscolo *m*
■ **muscle in** *vi* sl intromettersi (**to** in)

muscle strain *n* strappo *m* muscolare

muscular /'mʌskjʊlə(r)/ *adj* muscolare; (strong) muscoloso

muscular dystrophy /'dɪstrəfɪ/ *n* distrofia *f* muscolare

muse /mjuːz/ *vi* meditare (**on** su)

museum /mjuː'zɪəm/ *n* museo *m*

mushroom /'mʌʃrʊm/ ❶ *n* fungo *m* ❷ *vi* fig spuntare come funghi

mushroom cloud *n* fungo *m* atomico

mushy /'mʌʃɪ/ *adj* fig sdolcinato

music /'mjuːzɪk/ *n* musica *f*; (written) spartito *m*; **set to ~** musicare

musical /'mjuːzɪkl/ ❶ *adj* musicale; ⟨*person*⟩ dotato di senso musicale ❷ *n* commedia *f* musicale

musical box *n* carillon *m inv*

musical instrument *n* strumento *m* musicale

music box *n* carillon *m inv*

music centre *n* impianto *m* stereo

music hall *n* teatro *m* di varietà

musician /mjuː'zɪʃn/ *n* musicista *mf*

music lover *n* amante *mf* della musica

musicology /mjuːzɪ'kɒlədʒɪ/ *n* musicologia *f*

music stand *n* leggio *m*

music stool *n* sgabello *m* per pianoforte

music video *n* video clip *m inv*

musings /'mjuːzɪŋz/ *npl* riflessioni *fpl*

musk /mʌsk/ *n* muschio *m*

musket /'mʌskɪt/ *n* moschetto *m*

musketeer /mʌskə'tɪə(r)/ *n* moschettiere *m*

musky /'mʌskɪ/ *adj* muschiato

Muslim /'mʌzlɪm/ *adj* & *n* musulmano, -a *mf*

mussel /'mʌsl/ *n* cozza *f*

must /mʌst/ ❶ *v aux* (only in present) dovere; **you ~ not be late** non devi essere in ritardo; **she ~ have finished by now** (probability) deve aver finito ormai ❷ *n a* ~ fam una cosa da non perdere

mustache /mə'stɑːʃ/ *n* Am = MOUSTACHE

mustard /'mʌstəd/ *n* senape *f*

muster /'mʌstə(r)/ *vt* radunare ⟨*troops*⟩; fare appello a ⟨*strength*⟩

musty /'mʌstɪ/ *adj* (-ier, -iest) stantio

mutant /'mjuːtənt/ *n* & *adj* mutante *mf*

mutate /mjuː'teɪt/ ❶ *vi* ⟨*cell, organism*⟩ subire una mutazione; **~ into** ⟨*alien, monster*⟩ trasformarsi in ❷ *vt* far subire una mutazione

mutation /mjuː'teɪʃn/ *n* Biol mutazione *f*

mute /mjuːt/ *adj* muto

muted /'mjuːtɪd/ *adj* smorzato

mutilate /'mjuːtɪleɪt/ *vt* mutilare

mutilation /mjuːtɪ'leɪʃn/ *n* mutilazione *f*

mutinous /'mjuːtɪnəs/ *adj* ammutinato

mutiny /'mjuːtɪnɪ/ ❶ *n* ammutinamento *m* ❷ *vi* (pt/pp **-ied**) ammutinarsi

mutter /'mʌtə(r)/ ❶ *n* borbottio *m* ❷ *vt/i* borbottare

mutton /'mʌtn/ *n* carne *f* di montone

mutual /'mjuːtjʊəl/ *adj* reciproco; (fam: common) comune

mutually /'mjuːtjʊəlɪ/ *adv* reciprocamente

Muzak® /'mjuːzæk/ *n* musica *f* di sottofondo

muzzle /'mʌzl/ ❶ *n* (of animal) muso *m*; (of firearm) bocca *f*; (for dog) museruola *f* ❷ *vt* fig mettere il bavaglio a

MW *abbr* (**medium wave**) OM

my /maɪ/ *poss adj* mio *m*, mia *f*, miei *mpl*, mie *fpl*; **my job/house** il mio lavoro/la mia casa; **my mother/father** mia madre/ mio padre

myalgic encephalomyelitis /maɪˌældʒɪkensefələʊmaɪəˈlaɪtɪs/ *n* encefalomelite *f* mialgica

Myanmar /maɪænˈmɑːr/ *n* Myanmar *f*

myopic /maɪˈɒpɪk/ *adj* miope

myself /maɪˈself/ *pers pron* (reflexive) mi; (emphatic) me stesso; (after prep) me; **I've seen it ~** l'ho visto io stesso; **by ~** da solo; **I thought to ~** ho pensato tra me e me; **I'm proud of ~** sono fiero di me

mysterious /mɪˈstɪərɪəs/ *adj* misterioso

mysteriously /mɪˈstɪərɪəslɪ/ *adv* misteriosamente

mystery /ˈmɪstərɪ/ *n* mistero *m*; **~ [story]** racconto *m* del mistero

mystery play *n* mistero *m* (teatrale)

mystery tour *n* viaggio *m* con destinazione a sorpresa

mystic[al] /ˈmɪstɪk[l]/ *adj* mistico

mysticism /ˈmɪstɪsɪzm/ *n* misticismo *m*

mystification /mɪstɪfɪˈkeɪʃn/ *n* disorientamento *m*

mystified /ˈmɪstɪfaɪd/ *adj* disorientato

mystify /ˈmɪstɪfaɪ/ *vt* disorientare

mystique /mɪˈstiːk/ *n* mistica *f*

myth /mɪθ/ *n* mito *m*

mythical /ˈmɪθɪkl/ *adj* mitico

mythological /mɪθəˈlɒdʒɪkl/ *adj* mitologico

mythology /mɪˈθɒlədʒɪ/ *n* mitologia *f*

Nn

n¹, **N** /en/ *n* (letter) n, N *f inv*

N² *abbr* (**north**) N

n/a, **N/A** *abbr* (**not applicable**) non pertinente

nab /næb/ *vt* (pt/pp **nabbed**) fam beccare

nadir /ˈneɪdə(r)/ *n* nadir *m*; fig punto *m* più basso, fondo *m*

naff /næf/ *adj* Br fam banale

nag¹ /næg/ *n* (horse) ronzino *m*

nag² ① *vt* (pt/pp **nagged**) assillare ② *vi* essere insistente ③ *n* (person) brontolone, -a *mf*

nagging /ˈnægɪŋ/ *adj* ⟨pain⟩ persistente

nail /neɪl/ *n* chiodo *m*; (of finger, toe) unghia *f*; **on the ~** fam sull'unghia ■ **nail down** *vt* inchiodare; **~ somebody down to a time/price** far fissare a qualcuno un'ora/un prezzo

nail-biting /-baɪtɪŋ/ ① *n* abitudine *f* di mangiarsi le unghie ② *adj* ⟨match, finish⟩ mozzafiato *inv*; ⟨wait⟩ esasperante

nail brush *n* spazzolino *m* da unghie

nail clippers *npl* tronchesina *m*

nail file *n* limetta *f* da unghie

nail polish *n* smalto *m* [per unghie]

nail polish remover *n* acetone *m*, solvente *m* per unghie

nail scissors *npl* forbicine *fpl* da unghie

nail varnish *n* smalto *m* [per unghie]

nail varnish remover *n* solvente *m* per smalto

naïve /naɪˈiːv/ *adj* ingenuo

naïvely /naɪˈvlɪ/ *adv* ingenuamente

naïvety /naɪˈiːvtɪ/ *n* ingenuità *f*

naked /ˈneɪkɪd/ *adj* nudo; **with the ~ eye** a occhio nudo

nakedness /ˈneɪkɪdnɪs/ *n* nudità *f*

name /neɪm/ ① *n* nome *m*; **what's your ~?** come ti chiami?; **my ~ is Matthew** mi chiamo Matthew; **I know her by ~** la conosco di nome; **by the ~ of Bates** di nome Bates; **make a ~ for oneself** farsi un nome; **call somebody ~s** fam insultare qualcuno ② *vt* (to position) nominare; chiamare ⟨baby⟩; (identify) citare; **be ~d after** essere chiamato col nome di

name day *n* Relig onomastico *m*

name-drop *vi* **he's always ~ping** si vanta sempre di conoscere persone famose

nameless /ˈneɪmlɪs/ *adj* senza nome

namely /ˈneɪmlɪ/ *adv* cioè

nameplate *n* targhetta *f*

namesake *n* omonimo, -a *mf*

name tag *n* targhetta *f* attaccata ad un oggetto con il nome del proprietario

name tape *n* fettuccia *f* attaccata ad un oggetto con il nome del proprietario

Namibia /nəˈmɪbɪə/ *n* Namibia *f*

nanny /ˈnænɪ/ *n* bambinaia *f*

nanny goat *n* capra *f*

nanosecond /ˈnænəʊsekənd/ *n* fam nanosecondo *m*

nap /næp/ ① *n* pisolino *m*; **have a ~** fare un pisolino

2 *vi* catch somebody ∼ping cogliere qualcuno alla sprovvista

napalm /'neɪpɑːm/ *n* napalm *m*

nape /neɪp/ *n* ∼ [of the neck] nuca *f*

napkin /'næpkɪn/ *n* tovagliolo *m*

Naples /'neɪp(ə)lz/ *n* Napoli *f*

nappy /'næpɪ/ *n* pannolino *m*

nappy liner *n* filtrante *m*

nappy rash *n* Br eritema *m* da pannolini

narcotic /nɑːˈkɒtɪk/ *adj & n* narcotico *m*

narcotics agent *n* Am agente *m* della squadra antidroga

narked /nɑːkt/ *adj* fam scocciato

narrate /nəˈreɪt/ *vt* narrare

narration /nəˈreɪʃn/ *n* narrazione *f*

narrative /'nærətɪv/ **1** *adj* narrativo **2** *n* narrazione *f*

narrator /nəˈreɪtə(r)/ *n* narratore, -trice *mf*

narrow /'nærəʊ/ **1** *adj* stretto; fig ⟨*views*⟩ ristretto; ⟨*margin, majority*⟩ scarso; **have a ∼ escape** scamparla per un pelo **2** *vi* restringersi
■ **narrow down** *vt* (reduce) restringere

narrowly /'nærəʊlɪ/ *adv* ∼ **escape death** evitare la morte per un pelo

narrow-minded /-ˈmaɪndɪd/ *adj* di idee ristrette

nasal /'neɪzl/ *adj* nasale

nasal spray *n* spray *m inv* nasale

nastily /'nɑːstɪlɪ/ *adv* (spitefully) con cattiveria

nasty /'nɑːstɪ/ *adj* (-**ier**, -**iest**) ⟨*smell, person, remark*⟩ cattivo; ⟨*injury, situation, weather*⟩ brutto; **turn ∼** ⟨*person*⟩ diventare cattivo; ⟨*situation*⟩ mettersi male; ⟨*weather*⟩ volgere al brutto

nation /'neɪʃn/ *n* nazione *f*

national /'næʃən(ə)l/ **1** *adj* nazionale **2** *n* cittadino, -a *mf*

national anthem *n* inno *m* nazionale

National Curriculum *n* Br programma *m* scolastico ministeriale per il Galles e l'Inghilterra

national debt *n* debito *m* pubblico

National Front *n* Br partito *m* britannico di estrema destra

national grid *n* Electr rete *f* elettrica nazionale

National Health *n* Br servizio *m* nazionale di assistenza sanitaria

National Health Service *n* servizio *m* sanitario britannico

National Insurance *n* ≈ Previdenza *f* sociale

National Insurance number *n* numero *m* di Previdenza sociale

Nationalism /'næʃənəlɪzm/ *n* nazionalismo *m*

nationality /næʃəˈnælətɪ/ *n* nazionalità *f inv*

nationalization /næʃənəlaɪˈzeɪʃn/ *n* nazionalizzazione

nationalize /'næʃənəlaɪz/ *vt* nazionalizzare

National Lottery *n* Lotteria *f* di Stato

nationally /'næʃənəlɪ/ *adv* a livello nazionale

national monument *n* monumento *m* nazionale

National Savings Bank *n* Br Cassa *f* di risparmio

national service *n* Br servizio *m* militare

National Trust *n* Br associazione *f* per la tutela del patrimonio culturale e ambientale in Gran Bretagna

nation state *n* stato-nazione *m*

nationwide /'neɪʃnwaɪd/ *adj* su scala nazionale

native /'neɪtɪv/ **1** *adj* nativo; (innate) innato **2** *n* nativo, -a *mf*; (local inhabitant) abitante *mf* del posto; (outside Europe) indigeno, -a *mf* **she's a ∼ of Venice** è originaria di Venezia

Native American *adj & n* amerindio, -a *mf*

native land *n* paese *m* nativo

native language *n* lingua *f* madre

native speaker *n* persona *f* di madrelingua; **Italian ∼ ∼s** italiani madrelingua

Nativity /nəˈtɪvətɪ/ *n* **the ∼** la Natività

Nativity play *n* rappresentazione sulla nascita di Gesù

Nato, NATO /'neɪtəʊ/ *n abbr* (**North Atlantic Treaty Organization**) NATO *f*

natter /'nætə(r)/ **1** *n* have a ∼ fam fare quattro chiacchiere **2** *vi* fam chiacchierare

natty /'nætɪ/ *adj* fam (smart) chic *inv*; (clever) geniale

natural /'nætʃ(ə)rəl/ *adj* naturale

natural childbirth *n* parto *m* indolore

natural gas *n* metano *m*

natural history *n* storia *f* naturale

naturalist /'nætʃ(ə)rəlɪst/ *n* naturalista *mf*

naturalization /nætʃ(ə)rəlaɪˈzeɪʃn/ *n* naturalizzazione *f*

naturalize /'nætʃ(ə)rəlaɪz/ *vt* naturalizzare

naturally /'nætʃ(ə)rəlɪ/ *adv* (of course) naturalmente; (by nature) per natura

nature /'neɪtʃə(r)/ *n* natura *f*; **by ∼** per natura

nature conservancy *n* protezione *f* della natura

nature reserve *n* riserva *f* naturale

nature trail *n* percorso *m* ecologico

naturism /'neɪtʃərɪzm/ *n* nudismo *m*

naturist /'neɪʃərɪst/ ① *n* naturista *mf* ② *adj* naturistico

naught /nɔːt/ *n* = NOUGHT

naughtily /'nɔːtɪlɪ/ *adv* male

naughtiness /'nɔːtɪnɪs/ *n* (of child, pet) birbanteria *f*; (of joke, suggestion) maliziosità *f inv*

naughty /'nɔːtɪ/ *adj* (**-ier, -iest**) monello; (slightly indecent) spinto

nausea /'nɔːzɪə/ *n* nausea *f*

nauseate /'nɔːzɪeɪt/ *vt* nauseare

nauseating /'nɔːzɪeɪtɪŋ/ *adj* nauseante

nauseatingly /'nɔːzɪeɪtɪŋlɪ/ *adv* ‹rich, sweet› disgustosamente

nauseous /'nɔːzɪəs/ *adj* I feel ∼ ho la nausea

nautical /'nɔːtɪkl/ *adj* nautico

nautical mile *n* miglio *m* marino

naval /'neɪvl/ *adj* navale

naval base *n* base *f* navale

naval dockyard *n* cantiere *m* navale militare

naval officer *n* ufficiale *m* di marina

naval station *n* base *f* navale

naval stores *npl* (depot) magazzini *mpl* della marina militare

nave /neɪv/ *n* navata *f* centrale

navel /'neɪvl/ *n* ombelico *m*

navel ring *n* piercing *m inv* all'ombelico

navigable /'nævɪgəbl/ *adj* navigabile

navigate /'nævɪgeɪt/ ① *vi* navigare; Auto fare da navigatore ② *vt* navigare su ‹river›

navigation /nævɪ'geɪʃn/ *n* navigazione *f*

navigational /nævɪ'geɪʃənəl/ *adj* ‹instruments› di navigazione; ‹science› della navigazione

navigator /'nævɪgeɪtə(r)/ *n* navigatore *m*

navvy /'nævɪ/ *n* manovale *m*

navy /'neɪvɪ/ ① *n* marina *f* ② ∼ [blue] *adj* blu scuro *inv* ③ *n* blu *m inv* scuro

nay /neɪ/ ① *adv* anzi ② *n* (negative vote) no *m*

Nazi /'nɑːtsɪ/ *n & adj* nazista *mf*

NB *abbr* (**nota bene = please note**) n.b. *m*

NBC *n abbr* (**National Broadcasting Company**) NBC *f* (rete nazionale televisiva statunitense)

NC Am *abbr* **North Carolina**

NCO *n abbr* (**non-commissioned officer**) sottufficiale *m*

ND Am *abbr* **North Dakota**

NE *abbr* (**north-east**) NE

Ne Am *abbr* **Nebraska**

Neapolitan /nɪə'pɒlɪtən/ *adj & n* napoletano, -a *mf*

near /nɪə(r)/ ① *adj* vicino; ‹future› prossimo; the ∼est bank la banca più vicina ② *adv* vicino; draw ∼ avvicinarsi; ∼ at hand a portata di mano ③ *prep* vicino a; he was ∼ to tears aveva le lacrime agli occhi ④ *vt* avvicinarsi a

nearby /nɪə'baɪ/ *adj & adv* vicino

near-death experience *n* esperienza *f* ultraterrena

Near East *n* Medio Oriente *m*

nearly /'nɪəlɪ/ *adv* quasi; it's not ∼ enough non è per niente sufficiente

near miss *n* have a ∼ ∼ ‹planes, cars› evitare per poco uno scontro

nearness /'nɪənɪs/ *n* vicinanza *f*

nearside *n* Auto (in Britain) lato *m* sinistro; (in America, rest of Europe) lato *m* destro

near-sighted /-'saɪtɪd/ *adj* Am miope

near-sightedness *n* miopia *f*

neat /niːt/ *adj* (tidy) ordinato; (clever) efficace; (undiluted) liscio

neaten /'niːtən/ *vt* riordinare ‹pile of paper›; dare un'aggiustatina a ‹tie, skirt›

neatly /'niːtlɪ/ *adv* ordinatamente; (cleverly) efficacemente

neatness /'niːtnɪs/ *n* (tidiness) ordine *m*

necessarily /nesə'serɪlɪ/ *adv* necessariamente

necessary /'nesəsərɪ/ *adj* necessario

necessitate /nɪ'sesɪteɪt/ *vt* rendere necessario

necessity /nɪ'sesətɪ/ *n* necessità *f inv*

neck /nek/ *n* collo *m*; (of dress) colletto *m*; ∼ and ∼ testa a testa

necking /'nekɪŋ/ *n* fam pomiciata *f*

necklace /'neklɪs/ *n* collana *f*

neckline *n* scollatura *f*

necktie *n* cravatta *f*

nectar /'nektə(r)/ *n* nettare *m*

nectarine /'nektərɪn/ *n* nettarina *f*

neé /neɪ/ *adj* ∼ Brett nata Brett

need /niːd/ ① *n* bisogno *m*; be in ∼ essere bisognoso; be in ∼ of avere bisogno di; if ∼ be se ce ne fosse bisogno; there is a ∼ for c'è bisogno di; there is no ∼ for that non ce n'è bisogno; there is no ∼ for you to go non c'è bisogno che tu vada ② *vt* aver bisogno di; I ∼ to know devo saperlo; it ∼s to be done bisogna farlo ③ *v aux* you ∼ not go non c'è bisogno che tu vada; ∼ I come? devo venire?

needful /'niːdfʊl/ ① *adj* necessario

② *n* do the ∼ fare il necessario

needle /'niːdl/ **①** *n* ago *m*; (for knitting) uncinetto *m*; (of record player) puntina *f*
② *vt* (fam: annoy) punzecchiare

needless /'niːdlɪs/ *adj* inutile

needlessly /'niːdlɪslɪ/ *adv* inutilmente

needlework /'niːdlwɜːk/ *n* cucito *m*

needs /niːdz/ *adv* ∼ must il dovere chiama

need-to-know *adj* we have a ∼ policy la nostra politica consiste nel tenere informati solo i diretti interessati

needy /'niːdɪ/ *adj* (-ier,-iest) bisognoso

negate /nɪ'geɪt/ *vt* (cancel out) annullare; mettere in forma negativa ‹*sentence*›; (contradict) contraddire; (deny) negare

negation /nɪ'geɪʃn/ *n* negazione *f*

negative /'negətɪv/ **①** *adj* negativo
② *n* negazione *f*; Phot negativo *m*; in the ∼ Gram alla forma negativa

neglect /nɪ'glekt/ **①** *n* trascuratezza *f*; state of ∼ stato di abbandono
② *vt* trascurare; he ∼ed to write non si è curato di scrivere

neglected /nɪ'glektɪd/ *adj* trascurato

neglectful /nɪ'glektfʊl/ *adj* negligente; be ∼ of trascurare

negligée /'neglɪʒeɪ/ *n* négligé *m inv*

negligence /'neglɪdʒəns/ *n* negligenza *f*

negligent /'neglɪdʒənt/ *adj* negligente

negligently /'neglɪdʒəntlɪ/ *adv* con negligenza

negligible /'neglɪdʒɪbl/ *adj* trascurabile

negotiable /nɪ'gəʊʃəbl/ *adj* ‹*road*› transitabile; Comm negoziabile; not ∼ ‹*cheque*› non trasferibile

negotiate /nɪ'gəʊʃɪeɪt/ **①** *vt* negoziare; Auto prendere ‹*bend*›
② *vi* negoziare

negotiating /nɪ'gəʊʃɪeɪtɪŋ/ *adj* ‹*rights*› al negoziato; ‹*team, committee*› che conduce le trattative; ‹*ploy, position*› di negoziato; the ∼ table il tavolo delle trattative

negotiation /nɪgəʊʃɪ'eɪʃn/ *n* negoziato *m*

negotiator /nɪ'gəʊʃɪeɪtə(r)/ *n* negoziatore, -a *mf*

Negro /'niːgrəʊ/ *adj & n* (*pl* -es) negro, -a *mf*

neigh /neɪ/ *vi* nitrire

neighbour /'neɪbə(r)/ *n* vicino, -a *mf*

neighbourhood /'neɪbəhʊd/ *n* vicinato *m*; in the ∼ of nei dintorni di; fig circa

neighbourhood watch scheme *n* vigilanza *f* da parte della gente del quartiere

neighbouring /'neɪbərɪŋ/ *adj* vicino

neighbourly /'neɪbəlɪ/ *adj* amichevole

neither /'naɪðə(r)/ **①** *adj & pron* nessuno dei due, né l'uno né l'altro
② *adv* ∼... nor né... né
③ *conj* nemmeno, neanche; ∼ do/did I nemmeno io

neo+ /'niːəʊ/ *pref* neo+

neologism /nɪ'ɒlədʒɪzm/ *n* neologismo *m*

neon /'niːɒn/ *n* neon *m*

neon light *n* luce *f* al neon

Nepal /nɪ'pɔːl/ *n* Nepal *m*

nephew /'nevjuː/ *n* nipote *m*

nephritis /nɪ'fraɪtəs/ *n* nefrite *f*

nepotism /'nepətɪzm/ *n* nepotismo *m*

Neptune /'neptjuːn/ *n* Nettuno *m*

nerve /nɜːv/ *n* nervo *m*; (fam: courage) coraggio *m*; (fam: impudence) faccia *f* tosta; lose one's ∼ perdersi d'animo; you've got a ∼ hai una bella faccia tosta!; live on one's ∼s vivere con i nervi a fior di pelle; be a bag of ∼s avere i nervi a fior di pelle

nerve-racking /'nɜːvrækɪŋ/ *adj* logorante

nerviness /'nɜːvɪnɪs/ *n* Br nervosismo *m*; Am grinta *f*

nervous /'nɜːvəs/ *adj* nervoso; he makes me ∼ mi mette in agitazione

nervous breakdown *n* esaurimento *m* nervoso

nervous energy *n* energia *f* in eccesso

nervously /'nɜːvəslɪ/ *adv* nervosamente

nervousness /'nɜːvəsnɪs/ *n* nervosismo *m*; (before important event) tensione *f*

nervous system *n* sistema *m* nervoso

nervous wreck *n* fascio *m* di nervi

nervy /'nɜːvɪ/ *adj* (-ier, -iest) nervoso; (Am: impudent) sfacciato

nest /nest/ **①** *n* nido *m*
② *vi* fare il nido

nested /'nestɪd/ *adj* Comput nidificato

nest egg *n* gruzzolo *m*

nesting /'nestɪŋ/ **①** *n* Zool nidificazione *f*; Comput nesting *m inv*, nidificazione *f*
② *attrib* ‹*habit*› di nidificare; ‹*place*› per nidificare; ‹*season*› della nidificazione

nestle /'nesl/ *vi* accoccolarsi
■ **nestle up to** *vt* accoccolarsi accanto a ‹*somebody*›

nestling /'nes(t)lɪŋ/ *n* nidiace *m*

net¹ /net/ **①** *n* rete *f*
② *vt* (pt/pp **netted**) (catch) prendere (con la rete)

net² **①** *adj* netto; ∼ of VAT al netto dell'IVA
② *vt* (pt/pp **netted**) incassare un utile netto di

netball /'netbɔːl/ *n* sport *m inv* femminile simile alla pallacanestro

Netherlands /'neðələndz/ *npl* the ∼ i Paesi Bassi

netiquette /'netɪket/ *n* Comput netiquette *f inv*

netspeak *n* Comput linguaggio *m* del net

netting /'netɪŋ/ *n* [wire] ∼ reticolato *m*

nettle /'netl/ *n* ortica *f*

net ton *n* Am tonnellata *f* corta americana

network /'netwɜ:k/ *n* rete *f*

networkable /'netwɜ:kəbl/ *adj* Comput installabile in rete

network card *n* Comput scheda *f* di rete

networked /'netwɜ:kt/ *adj* Comput collegato in rete

networking /'netwɜ:kɪŋ/ *n* (establishing contacts) stabilmento *m* di una rete di contatti; Comput collegamento *m* in rete

network television *n* Am network *m inv* televisivo

neuralgia /njʊə'rældʒə/ *n* nevralgia *f*

neuritis /njʊə'raɪtɪs/ *n* nevrite *f*

neurologist /njʊə'rɒlədʒɪst/ *n* neurologo, -a *mf*

neurology /njʊə'rɒlədʒɪ/ *n* neurologia *f*

neurosis /njʊə'rəʊsɪs/ *n* (pl **-oses** /njʊə'rəʊsi:z/) nevrosi *f inv*

neurosurgeon /'njʊərəsɜ:dʒən/ *n* neurochirurgo *m*

neurotic /njʊə'rɒtɪk/ *adj* nevrotico

neurotically /njʊə'rɒtɪklɪ/ *adv* in modo ossessivo

neuter /'nju:tə(r)/ **1** *adj gram* neutro **2** *n* gram neutro *m* **3** *vt* sterilizzare

neutral /'nju:trəl/ **1** *adj* neutro; (country, person) neutrale **2** *n* in ∼ Auto in folle

neutrality /nju:'trælətɪ/ *n* neutralità *f*

neutralize /'nju:trəlaɪz/ *vt* neutralizzare

never /'nevə(r)/ *adv* [non...] mai; (fam: expressing disbelief) ma va'; ∼ **again** mai più; **well I** ∼! chi l'avrebbe detto!

never-ending *adj* interminabile

nevermore /nevə'mɔ:(r)/ *adv* mai più

never-never *n* fam **buy something on the** ∼ comprare qualcosa a rate

never-never land *n* mondo *m* dei sogni

nevertheless /nevəðə'les/ *adv* tuttavia

new /nju:/ *adj* nuovo

New Age **1** *n* New Age *f inv* **2** *attrib* (music, ideas, sect) New Age *inv*

new blood *n* nuove leve *fpl*

newborn *adj* neonato

New Caledonia *n* Nuova Caledonia *f*

newcomer *n* nuovo, -a arrivato, -a *mf*

newfangled *adj* pej modernizzante

newfound *adj* nuovo

Newfoundland /'nju:fən(d)lənd/ *n* Terranova *f*

New Guinea *n* Nuova Guinea *f*

newish /'nju:ɪʃ/ *adj* abbastanza nuovo

new-laid /'nju:leɪd/ *adj* fresco

new look **1** *adj* (car, team) nuovo; (edition, show) rinnovato; (product) dall'aspetto nuovo **2** *n* they have given the shop a completely ∼ ∼ hanno completamente rinnovato il negozio

newly /'nju:lɪ/ *adv* (recently) di recente

newly-built *adj* costruito di recente

newly-weds /'nju:lɪwedz/ *npl* sposini *mpl*

new moon *n* luna *f* nuova

newness /'nju:nɪs/ *n* novità *f*

news /nju:z/ *n* notizie *fpl*; TV telegiornale *m*; Radio giornale *m* radio; **piece of** ∼ notizia *f*

news agency *n* agenzia *f* di stampa

newsagent's *n* Br giornalaio *m* (che vende anche tabacchi, caramelle ecc)

news bulletin *n* notiziario *m*

newscast *n* Am notiziario *m*

newscaster *n* giornalista *mf* televisivo, -a/radiofonico, -a

news conference *n* conferenza *f* stampa *inv*

newsdealer *n* Am giornalaio, -a *mf*

news desk *n* (at newspaper) redazione *f*

news editor *n* caporedattore, -trice *mf* di servizi di cronaca

newsflash *n* notizia *f* flash

newsgroup *n* newsgroup *m inv*

news headlines *npl* TV titoli *mpl* delle principali notizie

news item *n* notizia *f* di attualità

newsletter *n* bollettino *m* d'informazione

newspaper /'nju:zpeɪpə(r)/ *n* giornale *m*; (material) carta *f* di giornale

newspaperman *n* giornalista *m*

newspaper office *n* ufficio *m* della redazione

newspaperwoman *n* giornalista *f*

newspeak /'nju:spi:k/ *n* Am giornalese *m*

newsprint *n* (paper) carta *f* da giornale; (ink) inchiostro *m* di stampa

newsreader *n* giornalista *mf* televisivo, -a/radiofonico, -a

newsreel *n* cinegiornale *m*

newsroom *n* redazione *f*

news sheet *n* bollettino *m*

newsstand *n* edicola *f*

news value *n* interesse *m* mediatico

newsworthy *adj* che merita di essere pubblicato

n

newsy /'nju:zɪ/ *adj* ⟨letter⟩ pieno di notizie

newt /nju:t/ *n* tritone *m*

new technology *n* nuova tecnologia *f*

New Testament *n* Nuovo Testamento *m*

new wave *n* & *adj* new wave *f inv*

New Year *n* (January 1st) Capodanno *m*; (next year) l'anno *m* nuovo; **Happy ~ ~!** buon anno!; **closed for ~ ~** chiuso per le feste di Capodanno; **see in the ~ ~** festeggiare il Capodanno

New Year Honours list *n* Br lista *f* delle persone che ricevono decorazioni il 1 gennaio

New Year's Day *n* Capodanno *m*

New Year's Eve *n* vigilia *f* di Capodanno

New Year's resolution *n* proposito *m* per l'anno nuovo

New Zealand /'zi:lənd/ *n* Nuova Zelanda *f*

New Zealander /'zi:ləndə(r)/ *n* neozelandese *mf*

next /nekst/ ❶ *adj* prossimo; (adjoining) vicino; **who's ~?** a chi tocca?; **the ~ best thing would be to...** alternativamente la cosa migliore sarebbe di...; **~ to nothing** quasi niente; **the ~ day** il giorno dopo; **~ week** la settimana prossima; **the week after ~** fra due settimane; **the ~ thing I knew** la sola cosa che ho saputo dopo ❷ *adv* dopo; **when will you see him ~?** quando lo rivedi la prossima volta?; **~ to** accanto a ❸ *n* seguente *mf*; **~ of kin** parente *m* prossimo

next door ❶ *adj* ⟨dog, bell⟩ dei vicini; ⟨office⟩ accanto *inv*; **the girl ~** also fig la ragazza della porta accanto ❷ *adv* ⟨live, move in⟩ nella casa accanto

next-door neighbour *n* vicino *m* di casa

nexus /'neksəs/ *n* (network) rete *f*

NF *n* Br Pol *abbr* **National Front**

NH Am *abbr* **New Hampshire**

NHS *n abbr* **National Health Service**

NI *n* Br *abbr* **National Insurance**) previdenza *f* sociale; *abbr* (**Northern Ireland**) Irlanda *f* del Nord

nib /nɪb/ *n* pennino *m*

nibble /'nɪbl/ *vt/i* mordicchiare
■ **nibble at, nibble on** *vt* = NIBBLE

Nicaragua /nɪkə'rægjʊə/ *n* Nicaragua *m*

nice /naɪs/ *adj* ⟨day, weather, holiday⟩ bello; ⟨person⟩ gentile, simpatico; ⟨food⟩ buono; **it was ~ meeting you** è stato un piacere conoscerla

nice-looking *adj* carino

nicely /'naɪslɪ/ *adv* gentilmente; (well) bene

niceties /'naɪsətɪz/ *npl* finezze *fpl*

niche /ni:ʃ/ *n* nicchia *f*

niche market *n* mercato *m* specializzato

nick /nɪk/ ❶ *n* tacca *f*; (on chin etc) taglietto *m*; (fam: prison) galera *f*; (fam: police station) centrale *f* [di polizia]; **in the ~ of the time** fam appena in tempo; **in good ~** fam in buono stato ❷ *vt* intaccare; (fam: steal) fregare; (fam: arrest) beccare; **~ one's chin** farsi un taglietto nel mento

nickel /'nɪkl/ *n* nichel *m*; Am moneta *f* da cinque centesimi

nickel-and-dime *adj* Am fam da quattro soldi

nickelodeon /nɪkəl'əʊdɪən/ *n* (Am: juke box) juke box *m inv*

nickname /'nɪkneɪm/ ❶ *n* soprannome *m* ❷ *vt* soprannominare

nicotine /'nɪkəti:n/ *n* nicotina *f*

nicotine patch *n* cerotto *m* (transdermico) alla nicotina

niece /ni:s/ *n* nipote *f*

nifty /'nɪftɪ/ *adj* fam (skilful) geniale; (attractive) sfizioso

Niger /'naɪdʒə(r)/ *n* Niger *m*

Nigeria /naɪ'dʒɪərɪə/ *n* Nigeria *f*

Nigerian /naɪ'dʒɪərɪən/ *adj* & *n* nigeriano, -a *mf*

niggardly /'nɪgədlɪ/ *adj* ⟨person⟩ tirchio; ⟨salary⟩ misero

niggle /'nɪgl/ fam ❶ *n* (complaint) cosetta *f* da ridire ❷ *vi* (complain) lamentarsi in continuazione ❸ *vt* (irritate) dar fastidio a

niggling /'nɪglɪŋ/ *adj* ⟨detail⟩ insignificante; ⟨pain⟩ fastidioso; ⟨doubt⟩ persistente

night /naɪt/ ❶ *n* notte *f*; (evening) sera *f*; **at ~** la notte, di notte; (in the evening) la sera, di sera; **Monday ~** lunedì notte/sera; **work ~s** lavorare la notte ❷ *adj* di notte

nightcap *n* papalina *f*; (drink) bicchierino *m* bevuto prima di andare a letto

nightclub *n* locale *m* notturno, night[club] *m inv*

nightclubbing *n* **go ~** andare nei night [club]

nightdress *n* camicia *f* da notte

nightfall *n* crepuscolo *m*

nightgown, fam **nightie** *n* camicia *f* da notte

nightingale /'naɪtɪŋgeɪl/ *n* usignolo *m*

nightlife *n* vita *f* notturna

night light *n* lumino *m* da notte

nightly /'naɪtlɪ/ ① adj di notte, di sera ② adv ogni notte, ogni sera

nightmare /'naɪtmeə(r)/ n also fig incubo m

nightmarish /'naɪtmeərɪʃ/ adj da incubo

night owl n nottambulo, -a mf

night porter n portiere m di notte

night school n scuola f serale

nightshade n Bot deadly ∼ belladonna f

night shelter n dormitorio m pubblico

nightshift n (workers) turno m di notte; be on the ∼ fare il turno di notte

nightshirt n camicia f da notte (da uomo)

nightspot n night club m inv

nightstand n Am comodino m

nightstick n (Am: truncheon) manganello m

night-time n at ∼ di notte, la notte

night vision n visione f notturna

nightwatchman n guardiano m notturno

nightwear n indumenti mpl da notte

nil /nɪl/ n nulla m; Sport zero m

Nile /naɪl/ n Nilo m

nimble /'nɪmbl/ adj agile

nimbly /'nɪmblɪ/ adv agilmente

nincompoop /'nɪŋkəmpuːp/ n fam scemo m

nine /naɪn/ adj & n nove m

ninepin /'naɪnpɪn/ n birillo m; be falling like ∼s ⟨troops, guards, candidates⟩ cadere come le mosche

nineteen /naɪn'tiːn/ adj & n diciannove m

nineteenth /naɪn'tiːnθ/ adj & n diciannovesimo, -a mf

nineties /'naɪntɪz/ npl (period) the ∼ gli anni Novanta mpl; (age) novant'anni mpl; ▶ also FORTIES

ninetieth /'naɪntɪɪθ/ adj & n novantesimo, -a mf

nine-to-five ① adj ⟨job⟩ in un ufficio; ⟨routine⟩ dell'ufficio ② adv ⟨work⟩ dalle nove alle cinque

ninety /'naɪntɪ/ adj & n novanta m

ninth /naɪnθ/ adj & n nono, -a mf

nip /nɪp/ ① n pizzicotto m; (bite) morso m ② vt pizzicare; (bite) mordere; ∼ in the bud fig stroncare sul nascere ③ vi (fam: run) fare un salto

nipper /'nɪpə(r)/ n fam ragazzino, -a mf

nipple /'nɪpl/ n capezzolo m; (Am: on bottle) tettarella f

nippy /'nɪpɪ/ adj (-ier,-iest) fam (cold) pungente; (quick) svelto

nit /nɪt/ n (egg) lendine m; (larva) larva f di pidocchio

nit-pick vi cercare il pelo nell'uovo

nitrate /'naɪtreɪt/ n nitrato m

nitric /'naɪtrɪk/ adj nitrico

nitrogen /'naɪtrədʒn/ n azoto m

nitty-gritty /nɪtɪ'grɪtɪ/ n fam the ∼ il nocciolo [della questione]; **get down to the** ∼ arrivare al dunque

nitwit /'nɪtwɪt/ n fam imbecille mf

NJ Am abbr **New Jersey**

NM Am abbr **New Mexico**

no /nəʊ/ ① adv no ② n (pl **noes**) no m invar ③ adj nessuno; **I have no time** non ho tempo; **in no time** in un baleno; **'no parking'** 'sosta vietata'; **'no smoking'** 'vietato fumare'; **it's no go** è inutile

no., **No.** abbr (**number**) No.

Noah /'nəʊə/ n Noè m; ∼'s Ark l'arca f di Noè

nobility /nəʊ'bɪlətɪ/ n nobiltà f

noble /'nəʊbl/ adj nobile

nobleman /'nəʊblmən/ n nobile m

noble-minded /-'maɪndɪd/ adj di animo nobile

noble savage n buon selvaggio m

nobly /'nəʊblɪ/ adv (selflessly) generosamente; ∼ **born** di nobili natali

nobody /'nəʊbədɪ/ ① pron nessuno; **he knows** ∼ non conosce nessuno; **he's** ∼ **important** non è nessuno d'importante ② n he's a ∼ non è nessuno

no claims bonus n abbuono m in assenza di sinistri

nocturnal /nɒk'tɜːnl/ adj notturno

nod /nɒd/ ① n cenno m del capo; **give a** ∼ fare un cenno col capo ② vt (pt/pp **nodded**) fare un cenno col capo; (in agreement) fare di sì col capo ③ vi ∼ **one's head** fare di sì col capo ■ **nod off** vi assopirsi

node /nəʊd/ n nodo m

nodule /'nɒdjuːl/ n nodulo m

no-go adj fam **it's** ∼ non è possibile

no-go area n zona f calda a cui la polizia può accedere solo con la forza

no-hoper /nəʊ'həʊpə(r)/ n persona f senza prospettive

noise /nɔɪz/ n rumore m; (loud) rumore m, chiasso m

noiseless /'nɔɪzlɪs/ adj silenzioso

noiselessly /'nɔɪzlɪslɪ/ adv silenziosamente

noise level n intensità f inv del rumore

noise pollution n inquinamento m acustico

noisily /'nɔɪzɪlɪ/ adv rumorosamente

noisy /'nɔɪzɪ/ adj (-ier, -iest) rumoroso

nomad /'nəʊmæd/ n nomade mf

nomadic /nəʊ'mædɪk/ adj nomade

n

nominal /'nɒmɪnl/ *adj* nominale

nominally /'nɒmɪnəlɪ/ *adv* nominalmente

nominate /'nɒmɪneɪt/ *vt* proporre come candidato; (appoint) designare

nomination /nɒmɪ'neɪʃn/ *n* nomina *f*; (person nominated) candidato, -a *mf*

nominative /'nɒmɪnətɪv/ *adj & n gram* ~ **[case]** nominativo *m*

nominee /nɒmɪ'niː/ *n* persona *f* nominata

non+ /nɒn/ *pref* non+, in+

non-academic *adj* ⟨course⟩ pratico; ⟨staff⟩ non insegnante

non-addictive *adj* che non dà assuefazione

non-alcoholic *adj* analcolico

non-attendance *n* mancata presenza *f*

non-believer *n* non credente *mf*

nonchalant /'nɒnʃələnt/ *adj* disinvolto

nonchalantly /'nɒnʃələntlɪ/ *adv* in modo disinvolto

non-classified *adj* ⟨information⟩ non confidenziale

non-combustible *adj* incombustibile

non-commercial *adj* ⟨event, activity⟩ senza fini di lucro

non-commissioned /-kə'mɪʃnd/ *adj* ~ **officer** sottufficiale *m*

non-committal /-kə'mɪtəl/ *adj* che non si sbilancia

non-compliance *n* (with standards) non conformità *f* (**with** a); (with orders) inadempienza *f* (**with** a)

nonconformist /nɒnkən'fɔːmɪst/ *adj & n* anticonformista *mf*

non-cooperation *n* non cooperazione *f*

non-denominational /-dɪnɒmɪ'neɪʃənəl/ *adj* ⟨church⟩ ecumenico; ⟨school⟩ laico

nondescript /'nɒndɪskrɪpt/ *adj* qualunque

none /nʌn/ **1** *pron* (person) nessuno; (thing) niente; ~ **of us** nessuno di noi; ~ **of this** niente di questo; **there's** ~ **left** non ce n'è più **2** *adv* **she's** ~ **too pleased** non è per niente soddisfatta; **I'm** ~ **the wiser** non ne so più di prima

non-EC *adj* ⟨national⟩ extracomunitario; ⟨country⟩ che non appartiene alla Comunità Europea

nonentity /nɒ'nentətɪ/ *n* nullità *f inv*

non-essentials /-ɪ'senʃlz/ *npl* (details) dettagli *mpl*; (objects) cose *fpl* accessorie

nonetheless /nʌnðə'les/ *adv* = NEVERTHELESS

non-event *n* delusione *f*

non-existent *adj* inesistente

non-family *adj* al di fuori della famiglia

non-fat *adj* magro; ⟨diet⟩ senza grassi

non-fiction *n* saggistica *f*

non-flammable *adj* non infiammabile

non-fulfilment *n* (of contract, obligation) inadempienza *f* (**of** a); (of desire) inappagamento *m*

non-infectious *adj* non infettivo

non-iron *adj* che non si stira

non-judgmental *adj* imparziale

non-league *adj* Sport fuori campionato

no-no *n* fam cosa *f* proibita; **that's a** ~ è un argomento tabù

no-nonsense *adj* ⟨manner, attitude⟩ diretto; ⟨tone⟩ spiccio; ⟨look, policy⟩ pratico; ⟨person⟩ franco

non-partisan *adj* imparziale

non-party *adj* ⟨issue, decision⟩ apartitico; ⟨person⟩ indipendente

non-person *n* (insignificant person) nullità *f inv*; **officially, he is a** ~ Pol ufficialmente non è mai esistito

nonplussed /nɒn'plʌst/ *adj* perplesso

non-professional *adj* dilettante

non-profit-making /-'prɒfɪtmeɪkɪŋ/ *adj* ⟨organization⟩ senza fini di lucro

non-redeemable *adj* Fin vincolato

non-refillable *adj* ⟨lighter, pen⟩ non ricaricabile; ⟨can, bottle⟩ non riutilizzabile

non-religious *adj* laico

non-resident **1** *adj* ⟨job, course⟩ non residenziale; Comput che non risiede in permanenza nella memoria centrale **2** *n* non residente *mf*

non-residential *adj* ⟨guest⟩ di passaggio; ⟨student, visitor⟩ non residente; ⟨caretaker⟩ che non alloggia sul posto; ⟨area⟩ non residenziale

non-returnable *adj* ⟨bottle⟩ a perdere

non-segregated *adj* ⟨area⟩ non segregato; ⟨society⟩ non segregazionista

nonsense /'nɒnsəns/ *n* sciocchezze *fpl*

nonsensical /nɒn'sensɪkl/ *adj* assurdo

non sequitur /nɒn'sekwɪtə(r)/ *n* affermazione *f* senza legame con quanto detto prima

non-skid *adj* antiscivolo *inv*

non-smoker *n* non fumatore, -trice *mf*; (compartment) scompartimento *m* non fumatori

non-smoking *adj* non fumatori *inv*

non-specialized *adj* non specializzato

non-starter *n* **be a** ~ ⟨person⟩ non avere nessuna probabilità di riuscita; ⟨plan, idea⟩ essere destinato al fallimento

non-stick *adj* antiaderente

non-stop **1** *adj* ⟨talk, work, pressure, noise⟩ continuo; ⟨train⟩ diretto; ⟨journey⟩ senza fermate; ⟨flight⟩ senza scalo

2 adv ⟨work, talk⟩ senza sosta; ⟨travel, fly⟩ senza scalo

non-swimmer n persona f che non sa nuotare

non-taxable adj non imponibile

non-union adj ⟨person⟩ non iscritto ad un sindacato; ⟨company⟩ non sindacalizzato

non-violent adj non violento

non-white, non-White n persona f di colore

noodles /ˈnuːdlz/ npl taglierini mpl

nook /nʊk/ n cantuccio m

noon /nuːn/ n mezzogiorno m; **at ~** a mezzogiorno

no one pron nessuno

noose /nuːs/ n nodo m scorsoio

nor /nɔː(r)/ adv & conj né; **~ do I** neppure io

Nordic /ˈnɔːdɪk/ adj nordico

norm /nɔːm/ n norma f

normal /ˈnɔːml/ adj normale

normality /nɔːˈmæləti/ n normalità f

normally /ˈnɔːməli/ adv (usually) normalmente

Norman /ˈnɔːmən/ **1** adj normanno; ⟨landscape village⟩ della Normandia **2** n normanno m

Norse /nɔːs/ adj ⟨mythology, saga⟩ norreno

north /nɔːθ/ **1** n nord m; **to the ~ of a** nord di **2** adj del nord, settentrionale **3** adv a nord

North Africa n Africa f del Nord

North African adj & n nordafricano, -a mf

North America n America f del Nord

North American adj & n nordamericano, -a mf

Northants /nɔːˈθænts/ Br abbr **Northamptonshire**

northbound /ˈnɔːθbaʊnd/ adj ⟨traffic, carriageway⟩ in direzione nord

Northd Br abbr **Northumberland**

north-east **1** adj di nord-est, nordorientale **2** n nord-est m **3** adv a nord-est; ⟨travel⟩ verso nord-est

north-easterly **1** adj ⟨point⟩ a nord-est; ⟨wind⟩ di nord-est **2** n vento m di nord-est

northeastern /nɔːˈθiːstən/ adj nordorientale

northerly /ˈnɔːðəli/ adj ⟨direction⟩ nord; ⟨wind⟩ del nord

northern /ˈnɔːðən/ adj del nord, settentrionale

Northern Ireland n Irlanda f del Nord

Northern Lights npl aurora f boreale

North Korea n Corea f del Nord

North Pole n polo m nord

North Sea n Mare m del Nord

North Star n stella f polare

northward[s] /ˈnɔːθwəd[z]/ adv verso nord

north-west **1** adj di nord-ovest, nordoccidentale **2** n nord-ovest m **3** adv a nord-ovest; ⟨travel⟩ verso nord-ovest

north-westerly **1** adj ⟨point⟩ a nord-ovest; ⟨wind⟩ di nord-ovest **2** n vento m di nord-ovest

north-western adj nordoccidentale

Norway /ˈnɔːweɪ/ n Norvegia f

Norwegian /nɔːˈwiːdʒən/ adj & n norvegese mf

nose /nəʊz/ n naso m
■ **nose about** vi curiosare

nosebleed /ˈnəʊzbliːd/ n emorragia f nasale

nosedive /ˈnəʊzdaɪv/ n Aeron picchiata f; **take a ~** fig ⟨prices;⟩ scendere vertiginosamente

nosey /ˈnəʊzi/ adj = NOSY

no-show n persona f che non si è presentata

nosily /ˈnəʊzɪli/ adv in modo indiscreto

nostalgia /nɒˈstældʒɪə/ n nostalgia f

nostalgic /nɒˈstældʒɪk/ adj nostalgico

nostril /ˈnɒstrəl/ n narice f

nosy /ˈnəʊzi/ adj (-ier, -iest) fam ficcanaso inv

not /nɒt/ adv non; **he is ~ Italian** non è italiano; **I hope ~** spero di no; **~ all of us have been invited** non siamo stati tutti invitati; **if ~** se no; **~ at all** niente affatto; **~ a bit** per niente; **~ even** neanche; **~ yet** non ancora; **in the ~ too distant future** in un futuro non troppo lontano; **~ only... but also...** non solo... ma anche...

notable /ˈnəʊtəbl/ adj (remarkable) notevole

notably /ˈnəʊtəbli/ adv (in particular) in particolare

notary /ˈnəʊtəri/ n notaio m; **~ public** notaio m

notation /nəʊˈteɪʃn/ n notazione f

notch /nɒtʃ/ n tacca f
■ **notch up** vt (score) segnare

note /nəʊt/ **1** n nota f; (short letter, banknote) biglietto m; (memo, written comment etc) appunto m; **of ~** ⟨person⟩ di spicco; ⟨comments, event⟩ degno di nota; **make a ~ of** prendere nota di; **take ~ of** (notice) prendere nota di **2** vt (notice) notare; (write) annotare
■ **note down** vt annotare

notebook /ˈnəʊtbʊk/ n taccuino m

notebook [PC] n notebook m inv

n

noted /'nəʊtɪd/ *adj* noto, celebre (**for** per)

notepad *n* blocco *m* per appunti

notepaper *n* carta *f* da lettere

noteworthy *adj* degno di nota

nothing /'nʌθɪŋ/ ① *pron* niente, nulla ② *adv* niente affatto; **for** ∼ (free, in vain) per niente; (with no reason) senza motivo; ∼ **but** nient'altro che; ∼ **much** poco o nulla; ∼ **interesting** niente di interessante; **it's** ∼ **to do with you** non ti riguarda

notice /'nəʊtɪs/ ① *n* (on board) avviso *m*; (review) recensione *f*; (termination of employment) licenziamento *m*; **[advance]** ∼ preavviso *m*; **two months'** ∼ due mesi di preavviso; **at short** ∼ con breve preavviso; **until further** ∼ fino nuovo avviso; **give [in one's]** ∼ ‹*employee*› dare le dimissioni; **give an employee** ∼ dare il preavviso ad un impiegato; **take no** ∼ **of** non fare caso a; **take no** ∼! non farci caso!
② *vt* notare

noticeable /'nəʊtɪsəbl/ *adj* evidente

noticeably /'nəʊtɪsəblɪ/ *adv* sensibilmente

noticeboard /'nəʊtɪsbɔːd/ *n* bacheca *f*

notification /nəʊtɪfɪ'keɪʃn/ *n* notifica *f*

notify /'nəʊtɪfaɪ/ *vt* (pt/pp **-ied**) notificare

notion /'nəʊʃn/ *n* idea *f*, nozione *f*; **he hasn't the slightest** ∼ **of time** gli manca completamente la nozione del tempo; ∼**s** *pl* (Am: haberdashery) merceria *f*

notoriety /nəʊtə'raɪətɪ/ *n* notorietà *f*

notorious /nəʊ'tɔːrɪəs/ *adj* famigerato; **be** ∼ **for** essere tristemente famoso per

notoriously /nəʊ'tɔːrɪəslɪ/ *adv* **they're** ∼ **unreliable** tutti sanno che su di loro non si può mai fare affidamento

Notts /nɒts/ Br *abbr* **Nottinghamshire**

notwithstanding /nɒtwɪð'stændɪŋ/ ① *prep* malgrado ② *adv* ciononostante

nougat /'nʌgət/ *n* torrone *m*

nought /nɔːt/ *n* zero *m*

noughts and crosses *n* tris *m*

noun /naʊn/ *n* nome *m*, sostantivo *m*

nourish /'nʌrɪʃ/ *vt* nutrire

nourishing /'nʌrɪʃɪŋ/ *adj* nutriente

nourishment /'nʌrɪʃmənt/ *n* nutrimento *m*

novel /'nɒvl/ ① *adj* insolito ② *n* romanzo *m*

novelette /nɒvə'let/ *n* (oversentimental) romanzetto *m* rosa

novelist /'nɒvəlɪst/ *n* romanziere, -a *mf*

novelty /'nɒvltɪ/ *n* novità *f*; **novelties** *pl* (objects) oggettini *mpl*

November /nəʊ'vembə(r)/ *n* novembre *m*

novice /'nɒvɪs/ *n* novizio, -a *mf*

now /naʊ/ ① *adv* ora, adesso; **by** ∼ ormai; **just** ∼ proprio ora; **right** ∼ subito; ∼ **and again**, ∼ **and then** ogni tanto; ∼, ∼! su! ② *conj* ∼ **[that]** ora che, adesso che

nowadays /'naʊədeɪz/ *adv* oggigiorno

nowhere /'nəʊweə(r)/ *adv* in nessun posto, da nessuna parte

noxious /'nɒkʃəs/ *adj* nocivo

nozzle /'nɒzl/ *n* bocchetta *f*

nr *abbr* **near**

NSPCC *n* Br *abbr* (**National Society for the Prevention of Cruelty to Children**) Società *f* nazionale per la protezione dell'infanzia

NT *abbr* **New Testament**

nth /enθ/ *adj* Math, fig **to the** ∼ **power/ degree** all'ennesima potenza; **for the** ∼ **time** per l'ennesima volta

nuance /'njuːɑ̃s/ *n* sfumatura *f*

nub /nʌb/ *n* **the** ∼ **of the matter** il nocciolo della questione

nubile /'njuːbaɪl/ *adj* ‹*attractive*› desiderabile

nuclear /'njuːklɪə(r)/ *adj* nucleare

nuclear bomb *n* bomba *f* atomica

nuclear deterrent *n* deterrente *m* nucleare

nuclear energy *n* energia *f* nucleare

nuclear-free zone *n* Br zona *f* denuclearizzata

nuclear physics *n* fisica *f* nucleare

nuclear power *n* (energy) energia *f* nucleare; (country) potenza *f* nucleare

nuclear power station *n* centrale *f* nucleare

nuclear shelter *n* rifugio *m* antiatomico

nuclear waste *n* scorie *fpl* nucleari

nucleus /'njuːklɪəs/ *n* (pl **-lei** /'njuːklɪaɪ/) nucleo *m*

nude /njuːd/ ① *adj* nudo ② *n* nudo *m*; **in the** ∼ nudo

nudge /nʌdʒ/ ① *n* colpetto *m* di gomito ② *vt* dare un colpetto col gomito a

nudism /'njuːdɪzm/ *n* nudismo *m*

nudist /'njuːdɪst/ *n* nudista *mf*

nudity /'njuːdətɪ/ *n* nudità *f*

nugget /'nʌgɪt/ *n* pepita *f*

nuisance /'njuːsəns/ *n* seccatura *f*; (person) piaga *f*; **what a** ∼! che seccatura!

nuisance call *n* Teleph telefonata *f* anonima

null /nʌl/ *adj* ∼ **and void** nullo

nullify /'nʌlɪfaɪ/ *vt* (pt/pp **-ied**) annullare

numb /nʌm/ ① *adj* intorpidito; ∼ **with cold** intirizzito dal freddo ② *vt* intorpidire

number /'nʌmbə(r)/ ① *n* numero *m*; **a** ∼ **of people** un certo numero di persone

2 *vt* numerare; (include) annoverare

numbering /'nʌmbərɪŋ/ *n* numerazione *f*

number one *n* (most important) numero uno *m*; **look after** ∼ ∼ (oneself) pensare prima di tutto a se stessi

number plate *n* targa *f*

numeracy /'nju:mərəsɪ/ *n* **improve standards of** ∼ migliorare il livello nel calcolo

numeral /'nju:mərəl/ *n* numero *m*, cifra *f*

numerate /'nju:mərət/ *adj* **be** ∼ sapere far di calcolo

numerical /nju:'merɪkl/ *adj* numerico; **in** ∼ **order** in ordine numerico

numerically /nju:'merɪklɪ/ *adv* numericamente

numeric keypad /nju:'merɪk/ *n* Comput tastierino *m* numerico

numerous /'nju:mərəs/ *adj* numeroso

nun /nʌn/ *n* suora *f*

nuptial /'ʌpʃl/ **1** *adj* nuziale
2 ∼**s** *npl* nozze *fpl*

nurse /nɜ:s/ **1** *n* infermiere, -a *mf*; **children's** ∼ bambinaia *f*
2 *vt* curare

nursemaid *n* bambinaia *f*

nursery /'nɜ:sərɪ/ *n* stanza *f* dei bambini; (for plants) vivaio *m*; **[day]** ∼ asilo *m*

nursery rhyme *n* filastrocca *f*

nursery school *n* scuola *f* materna

nursery slope *n* Br pista *f* per principianti

nurse's aid *n* Am aiuto infermiere, -a *mf*

nursing /'nɜ:sɪŋ/ *n* professione *f* d'infermiere

nursing auxiliary *n* Br aiuto infermiere, -a *mf*

nursing home *n* casa *f* di cura per anziani

nurture /'nɜ:tə(r)/ *vt* allevare; fig coltivare

nut /nʌt/ *n* noce *f*; Techn dado *m*; (fam: head) zucca *f*

nutcrackers /'nʌtkrækəz/ *npl* schiaccianoci *m inv*

nutmeg /'nʌtmeg/ *n* noce *f* moscata

nutrient /'nju:trɪənt/ *n* sostanza *f* nutritiva

nutrition /nju:'trɪʃn/ *n* nutrizione *f*

nutritional /nju:'trɪʃnəl/ *adj* nutritivo

nutritionist /nju:'trɪʃənɪst/ *n* nutrizionista *mf*

nutritious /nju:'trɪʃəs/ *adj* nutriente

nuts /nʌts/ *npl* frutta *f* secca; **be** ∼ fam essere svitato

nutshell /'nʌtʃel/ *n* guscio *m* di noce; **in a** ∼ fig in parole povere

nuzzle /'nʌzl/ *vt* ⟨horse, dog⟩ strofinare il muso contro
■ **nuzzle up** *vi* ∼ **up against** or **to somebody** rannicchiarsi contro qualcuno

NV Am *abbr* **Nevada**

NVQ *n abbr* Br (**national vocational qualification**) diploma conseguito presso un istituto tecnico o professionale

NW *abbr* (**north-west**) NO

NY Am *abbr* **New York**

NYC Am *abbr* **New York City**

nylon /'naɪlɒn/ **1** *n* nailon *m*: ∼**s** *pl* calze *fpl* di nailon
2 *attrib* di nailon

nymph /nɪmf/ *n* ninfa *f*

nymphomaniac /nɪmfə'meɪnɪæk/ **1** *n* ninfomane *f*
2 *adj* da ninfomane

NZ *abbr* **New Zealand**

Oo

o,¹ O /əʊ/ *n* (letter) o, O *f inv*

O² /əʊ/ *n* Teleph zero *m*

oaf /əʊf/ *n* (pl **oafs**) zoticone, -a *mf*

oak /əʊk/ **1** *n* quercia *f*
2 *attrib* di quercia

OAP *abbr* (**old-age pensioner**) pensionato, -a *mf*

oar /ɔ:(r)/ *n* remo *m*

oarsman /'ɔ:zmən/ *n* vogatore *m*

oasis /əʊ'eɪsɪs/ *n* (pl **oases** /əʊ'eɪsi:z/) oasi *f inv*

oatcake /'əʊtkeɪk/ *n* galletta *f* di avena

oath /əʊθ/ *n* giuramento *m*; (swear-word) bestemmia *f*

oatmeal /'əʊtmi:l/ *n* farina *f* d'avena

oats /əʊts/ *npl* avena *fsg*; Culin **[rolled]** ∼ fiocchi *mpl* d'avena

obdurate /'ɒbdjʊrət/ *adj* (stubborn) irremovibile; (hardhearted) insensibile

OBE *n* Br *abbr* (**Officer of the (Order of the) British Empire**) onorificenza *f* britannica

obedience /ə'bi:dɪəns/ *n* ubbidienza *f*

obedient /ə'bi:dɪənt/ *adj* ubbidiente

n
o

obediently /ə'bi:dɪəntlɪ/ *adv*
ubbidientemente

obelisk /'ɒbəlɪsk/ *n* obelisco *m*

obese /ə'bi:s/ *adj* obeso

obesity /ə'bi:sətɪ/ *n* obesità *f*

obey /ə'beɪ/ ❶ *vt* ubbidire a; osservare
⟨*instructions, rules*⟩
❷ *vi* ubbidire

obituary /ə'bɪtjʊərɪ/ *n* necrologio *m*

object[1] /'ɒbdʒɪkt/ *n* oggetto *m*; Gram
complemento *m* oggetto; **money is no** ~ i
soldi non sono un problema

object[2] /əb'dʒekt/ *vi* (be against) opporsi
(to a); ~ **that...** obiettare che...

objection /əb'dʒekʃn/ *n* obiezione *f*;
have no ~ non avere niente in contrario

objectionable /əb'dʒekʃ(ə)nəbl/ *adj*
discutibile; ⟨*person*⟩ sgradevole

objective /əb'dʒektɪv/ ❶ *adj* oggettivo
❷ *n* obiettivo *m*

objectively /əb'dʒektɪvlɪ/ *adv*
obiettivamente

objectivity /ɒbdʒek'təvətɪ/ *n* oggettività
f

objector /əb'dʒektə(r)/ *n* oppositore,
-trice *mf*

obligation /ɒblɪ'geɪʃn/ *n* obbligo *m*; **be
under an** ~ avere un obbligo; **without** ~
senza impegno

obligatory /ə'blɪgətrɪ/ *adj* obbligatorio

oblige /ə'blaɪdʒ/ *vt* (compel) obbligare; (do
a small service for) fare una cortesia a; **much
~d** grazie mille

obliging /ə'blaɪdʒɪŋ/ *adj* disponibile

oblique /ə'bli:k/ *adj* obliquo; fig indiretto;
~ **[stroke]** *n* barra *f*

obliterate /ə'blɪtəreɪt/ *vt* obliterare

obliteration /əblɪtə'reɪʃn/ *n* (of mark,
memory) rimozione *f*; (of city) annientamento
m

oblivion /ə'blɪvɪən/ *n* oblio *m*

oblivious /ə'blɪvɪəs/ *adj* **be** ~ essere
dimentico (**of, to** di)

oblong /'ɒblɒŋ/ ❶ *adj* oblungo
❷ *n* rettangolo *m*

obnoxious /əb'nɒkʃəs/ *adj* detestabile

oboe /'əʊbəʊ/ *n* oboe *m inv*

obscene /əb'si:n/ *adj* osceno; ⟨*profits,
wealth*⟩ vergognoso

obscenity /əb'senətɪ/ *n* oscenità *f inv*

obscure /əb'skjʊə(r)/ ❶ *adj* oscuro
❷ *vt* oscurare; (confuse) mettere in ombra

obscurity /əb'skjʊərətɪ/ *n* oscurità *f*

obsequious /əb'si:kwɪəs/ *adj*
ossequioso

observable /əb'zɜ:vəbl/ *adj* (discernible)
percettibile

observance /əb'zɜ:vəns/ *n* (of custom)
osservanza *f*

observant /əb'zɜ:vənt/ *adj* attento

observation /ɒbzə'veɪʃn/ *n*
osservazione *f*

observation car *n* carrozza *f*
belvedere

observation tower *n* torre *f* di
osservazione

observatory /əb'zɜ:vətrɪ/ *n* osservatorio
m

observe /əb'zɜ:v/ *vt* osservare; (notice)
notare; (keep, celebrate) celebrare

observer /əb'zɜ:və(r)/ *n* osservatore,
-trice *mf*

obsess /əb'ses/ *vt* **be** ~**ed by** essere
fissato con

obsession /əb'seʃn/ *n* fissazione *f*

obsessive /əb'sesɪv/ *adj* ossessivo

obsessively /əb'sesɪvlɪ/ *adv*
ossessivamente

obsolescence /ɒbsə'lesəns/ *n*
obsolescenza *f*; **built-in** ~ obsolescenza *f*
programmata

obsolete /'ɒbsəli:t/ *adj* obsoleto; ⟨*word*⟩
desueto; ⟨*idea*⟩ sorpassato

obstacle /'ɒbstəkl/ *n* ostacolo *m*

obstacle course *n* Mil, fig percorso *m*
ad ostacoli

obstacle race *n* corsa *f* ad ostacoli

obstetrician /ɒbstə'trɪʃn/ *n* ostetrico,
-a *mf*

obstetrics /ɒb'stetrɪks/ *n* ostetricia *f*

obstinacy /'ɒbstɪnɪsɪ/ *n* ostinazione *f*

obstinate /'ɒbstɪnət/ *adj* ostinato

obstinately /'ɒbstɪnɪtlɪ/ *adv*
ostinatamente

obstreperous /əb'strepərəs/ *adj*
turbolento

obstruct /əb'strʌkt/ *vt* ostruire; (hinder)
ostacolare

obstruction /əb'strʌkʃn/ *n* ostruzione *f*;
(obstacle) ostacolo *m*

obstructive /əb'strʌktɪv/ *adj* **be** ~
⟨*person*⟩ creare dei problemi

obtain /əb'teɪn/ ❶ *vt* ottenere
❷ *vi* prevalere

obtainable /əb'teɪnəbl/ *adj* ottenibile

obtrusive /əb'tru:sɪv/ *adj* ⟨*object*⟩
stonato

obtuse /əb'tju:s/ *adj* ottuso

obverse /'ɒbvɜ:s/ *adj* **the** ~ **side/face** (of
coin) l'altra faccia *f*

obviate /'ɒbvɪeɪt/ *vt* fml ovviare a

obvious /'ɒbvɪəs/ *adj* ovvio

obviously /'ɒbvɪəslɪ/ *adv* ovviamente

occasion /ə'keɪʒn/ ❶ *n* occasione *f*;
(event) evento *m*; **on** ~ talvolta; **on the** ~
of in occasione di
❷ *vt* cagionare

occasional /ə'keɪʒənl/ *adj* saltuario; **he
has the** ~ **glass of wine** ogni tanto beve
un bicchiere di vino

occasionally /ə'keɪʒənəlɪ/ *adv* ogni tanto

occult /ɒ'kʌlt/ *adj* occulto

occupancy /'ɒkjʊpənsɪ/ *n* available for immediate ∼ libero immediatamente; change of ∼ cambio *m* di inquilino

occupant /'ɒkjʊpənt/ *n* occupante *mf*; (of vehicle) persona *f* a bordo

occupation /ɒkjʊ'peɪʃn/ *n* occupazione *f*; (job) professione *f*

occupational /ɒkjʊ'peɪʃənəl/ *adj* professionale

occupational hazard *n* rischio *m* professionale

occupational health *n* medicina *f* del lavoro

occupational pension *n* Br pensione *f* di lavoro

occupational psychologist *n* psicologo, -a *mf* del lavoro

occupational therapist *n* ergoterapista *mf*

occupational therapy *n* ergoterapia *f*

occupier /'ɒkjʊpaɪə(r)/ *n* residente *mf*

occupy /'ɒkjʊpaɪ/ *vt* (pt/pp **occupied**) occupare; (keep busy) tenere occupato

occur /ə'kɜ:(r)/ *vi* (pt/pp **occurred**) accadere; (exist) trovarsi; it ∼ red to me that mi è venuto in mente che

occurrence /ə'kʌrəns/ *n* (event) fatto *m*

ocean /'əʊʃn/ *n* oceano *m*

ocean-going /'əʊʃəngəʊɪŋ/ *adj* ⟨ship⟩ d'alto mare

ochre /'əʊkə(r)/ *n & adj* (colour) ocra *f*

o'clock /ə'klɒk/ *adv* it's 7 ∼ sono le sette; at 7 ∼ alle sette

octagon /'ɒktəgən/ *n* ottagono *m*

octagonal /ɒk'tægənl/ *adj* ottagonale

octave /'ɒktɪv/ *n* Mus ottava *f*

octet /ɒk'tet/ *n* Mus ottetto *m*

October /ɒk'təʊbə(r)/ *n* ottobre *m*

octogenarian /ɒktədʒɪ'neərɪən/ *n & adj* ottantenne *mf*

octopus /'ɒktəpəs/ *n* (pl **-puses**) polpo *m*

oculist /'ɒkjʊlɪst/ *n* oculista *mf*

OD *n abbr* (**overdose**) overdose *f inv*

odd /ɒd/ *adj* ⟨number⟩ dispari; (not of set) scompagnato; (strange) strano; forty ∼ quaranta e rotti; ∼ jobs lavoretti *mpl*; the ∼ one out l'eccezione *f*; at ∼ moments a tempo perso; have the ∼ glass of wine bere un bicchiere di vino ogni tanto

oddball /'ɒdbɔ:l/ *n* fam eccentrico, -a *mf*

odd bod /'ɒdbɒd/ *n* Br fam tipo, -a *mf* strano, -a

oddity /'ɒdətɪ/ *n* stranezza *f*

odd-job man *n* tuttofare *m inv*

odd jobs *npl* lavoretti *mpl*

oddly /'ɒdlɪ/ *adv* stranamente; ∼ enough stranamente

oddment /'ɒdmənt/ *n* (of fabric) scampolo *m*

odds /ɒdz/ *npl* (chances) probabilità *fpl*; at ∼ in disaccordo; ∼ and ends cianfrusaglie *fpl*; it makes no ∼ non fa alcuna differenza

odds-on *adj* be the ∼ favourite (in betting) essere il gran favorito; she has an ∼ chance of... ha molte probabilità di...; it is ∼ that è molto probabile che

ode /əʊd/ *n* ode *f*

odious /'əʊdɪəs/ *adj* odioso

odium /'əʊdɪəm/ *n* odio *m*

odometer /əʊ'dɒmɪtə(r)/ *n* Am contachilometri *m inv*, odometro *m*

odour /'əʊdə(r)/ *n* odore *m*

odourless /'əʊdəlɪs/ *adj* inodore

odyssey /'ɒdɪsɪ/ *n* odissea *f*

OECD *n abbr* (**Organization for Economic Cooperation and Development**) OCSE *f*

oedema /ɪ'di:mə/ *n* edema *m*

oesophagus /ɪ'sɒfəgəs/ *n* esofago *m*

oestrogen /'i:strədʒən/ *n* estrogeno *m*

of /ɒv/ *prep* di; a cup of tea/coffee una tazza di tè/caffè; the hem of my skirt l'orlo della mia gonna; the summer of 1989 l'estate del 1989; the two of us noi due; made of di; that's very kind of you è molto gentile da parte tua; a friend of mine un mio amico; a child of three un bambino di tre anni; the fourth of January il quattro gennaio; within a year of their divorce a circa un anno dal loro divorzio; half of it la metà; the whole of the room tutta la stanza

off /ɒf/ ① *prep* da; (distant from) lontano da; take £10 ∼ the price ridurre il prezzo di 10 sterline; ∼ the coast presso la costa; a street ∼ the main road una traversa della via principale; (near) una strada vicina alla via principale; get ∼ the ladder scendere dalla scala; get ∼ the bus scendere dall'autobus; leave the lid ∼ the saucepan lasciare la pentola senza il coperchio

② *adv* ⟨button, handle⟩ staccato; ⟨light, machine⟩ spento; ⟨brake⟩ disinserito; ⟨tap⟩ chiuso; 'off' (on appliance) 'off'; 2 kilometres ∼ a due chilometri di distanza; a long way ∼ molto distante; (time) lontano; ∼ and on di tanto in tanto; with his hat/coat ∼ senza il cappotto/cappello; with the light ∼ a luce spenta; 20% ∼ 20% di sconto; be ∼ (leave) essere partito; Sport essere partito; ⟨food⟩ essere andato a male; (all gone) essere finito; ⟨wedding, engagement⟩ essere cancellato; I'm ∼ drugs/alcohol ho smesso di drogarmi/bere; be ∼ one's food non avere appetito; she's ∼ today (on holiday) è in ferie oggi; (ill) è malata oggi; ⋯▷

I'm ~ home vado a casa; you'd be better ~ doing... faresti meglio a fare...; have a day ~ avere un giorno di vacanza; drive/ sail ~ andare via

offal /'ɒfl/ n Culin frattaglie fpl

offbeat /'ɒfbiːt/ adj insolito

off-centre adj Br fuori centro

off chance n there's an ~ that c'è una remota possibilità che; just on the ~ ~ that nella remota possibilità che

off colour adj (not well) giù di forma; ⟨joke, story⟩ sporco

offence /ə'fens/ n (illegal act) reato m; give ~ offendere; take ~ offendersi (at per)

offend /ə'fend/ vt offendere

offender /ə'fendə(r)/ n Jur colpevole mf

offensive /ə'fensɪv/ ① adj offensivo ② n offensiva f; go on the ~ passare all'offensiva

offer /'ɒfə(r)/ ① n offerta f; on special ~ in offerta speciale ② vt offrire; opporre ⟨resistance⟩; ~ somebody something offrire qualcosa a qualcuno; ~ to do something offrirsi di fare qualcosa

offering /'ɒfərɪŋ/ n offerta f

offer price n Comm prezzo m d'offerta

offertory /'ɒfətrɪ/ n Relig offertorio m

offhand /ɒf'hænd/ ① adj (casual) spiccio ② adv su due piedi

office /'ɒfɪs/ n ufficio m; (post, job) carica f

office automation n burotica f

office block n Br complesso m di uffici

office building n Br complesso m di uffici

office hours npl orario m di ufficio

office junior n fattorino, -a mf

office politics n intrighi mpl di ufficio

officer /'ɒfɪsə(r)/ n ufficiale m; (police) agente m [di polizia]

office worker n impiegato, -a mf

official /ə'fɪʃl/ ① adj ufficiale ② n funzionario, -a mf; Sport dirigente m

officialdom /ə'fɪʃəldəm/ n burocrazia f

officially /ə'fɪʃəlɪ/ adv ufficialmente

officiate /ə'fɪʃɪeɪt/ vi officiare

officious /ə'fɪʃəs/ adj autoritario

officiously /ə'fɪʃəslɪ/ adv in modo autoritario

offing /'ɒfɪŋ/ n in the ~ in vista

off-key adj Mus stonato

off-licence n negozio m per la vendita di alcolici

off-limits adj off-limits inv

off-line adj Comput fuori linea inv, off-line inv

offload /ɒf'ləʊd/ vt scaricare

off-message adj Pol be ~ non essere in linea con la politica del governo

off-peak adj ⟨travel⟩ fuori dagli orari di punta; ⟨electricity⟩ a tariffa notturna ridotta; ~ call Teleph telefonata f a tariffa ridotta

offprint /'ɒfprɪnt/ n estratto m

off-putting /-pʊtɪŋ/ adj fam scoraggiante

off-road vi viaggiare in fuoristrada

off-roader /'ɒfrəʊdə(r)/, **off-road vehicle** n fuoristrada

off-screen ① adj ⟨voice, action⟩ fuoricampo inv; ⟨relationship⟩ nella vita privata ② adv nella vita privata

off-season adj ⟨losses⟩ di bassa stagione; ⟨cruise⟩ in bassa stagione

offset /'ɒfset/ vt (pt/pp -set, pres p -setting) controbilanciare

offset printing n offset m inv

offshoot /'ɒfʃuːt/ n ramo m; fig diramazione f

offshore /'ɒfʃɔː(r)/ adj ⟨wind⟩ di terra; ⟨company, investment⟩ offshore inv

offside /ɒf'saɪd/ adj Sport [in] fuori gioco; ⟨wheel etc⟩ (left) sinistro; (right) destro

offspring /'ɒfsprɪŋ/ n prole f

off-stage adv dietro le quinte

off-the-cuff adj ⟨remark⟩ spontaneo; ⟨speech⟩ improvvisato

off-the-peg adj ⟨garment⟩ prêt-à-porter inv, confezionato

off-the-record adj ⟨comment, statement⟩ ufficioso

off-the-shelf adj Comm standard inv

off-the-shoulder adj ⟨dress⟩ senza bretelle

off-the-wall adj fam ⟨sense of humour⟩ strano

off-white adj bianco sporco

often /'ɒfn/ adv spesso; how ~ ogni quanto; every so ~ una volta ogni tanto

ogle /'əʊgl/ vt mangiarsi con gli occhi

ogre /'əʊgə(r)/ n orco m

oh /əʊ/ int oh!; **oh dear** oh Dio!

OHMS Br abbr (**On Her/His Majesty's Service**) abbreviazione f apposta su corrispondenza ufficiale del governo britannico

OHP n abbr (**overhead projector**) lavagna f luminosa

oil /ɔɪl/ ① n olio m; (petroleum) petrolio m; (for heating) nafta f ② vt oliare

oil-burning adj ⟨stove, boiler⟩ a nafta

oil can n (applicator) oliatore m

oil change n cambio m dell'olio

oilcloth n tela f cerata

oilfield n giacimento m di petrolio

oil filter n filtro m dell'olio

oil-fired /-faɪəd/ adj ⟨furnace, heating⟩ a nafta

oil gauge *n* indicatore *m* [del livello] dell'olio

oil heater *n* stufa *f* a nafta

oil lamp *n* lampada *f* a olio

oil paint *n* colore *m* a olio

oil painting *n* pittura *f* a olio

oil pipeline *n* oleodotto *m*

oil pressure *n* pressione *f* dell'olio

oil producing /-prədju:sɪŋ/ *adj* ⟨country⟩ produttore di petrolio

oil refinery *n* raffineria *f* di petrolio

oil rig *n* piattaforma *f* petrolifera, offshore *m inv*

oilseed rape /'ɔɪlsi:d/ *n* colza *f*

oilskins *npl* indumenti *mpl* di tela cerata

oil slick *n* chiazza *f* di petrolio

oil spill *n* fuoriuscita *f* di petrolio

oil stove *n* stufa *f* a nafta

oil tank *n* (domestic) serbatoio *m* della nafta; (industrial) cisterna *f* della nafta

oil tanker *n* petroliera *f*

oil well *n* pozzo *m* petrolifero

oily /'ɔɪlɪ/ *adj* (**-ier, -iest**) unto; fig untuoso

ointment /'ɔɪntmənt/ *n* pomata *f*

OK, okay /əʊ'keɪ/ **1** *int* va bene, o.k. **2** *adj* **if that's OK with you** se ti va bene; **she's OK** (well) sta bene; **is the milk still OK?** il latte è ancora buono? **3** *adv* (well) bene **4** *vt* (*pt/pp* **OK'd, okayed**) dare l'o.k. a

old /əʊld/ *adj* vecchio; ⟨girlfriend⟩ ex; **how ~ is she?** quanti anni ha?; **she is ten years ~** ha dieci anni

old age *n* vecchiaia *f*

old-age pension *n* Br pensione *f* di vecchiaia

old-age pensioner *n* pensionato, -a *mf*

old boy *n* Sch ex-allievo *m*

old country *n* paese *m* d'origine

olden /'əʊldən/ *adj* **the ~ days** i tempi andati

old-established /-ɪ'stæblɪʃt/ *adj* di lunga data

olde-worlde /əʊldɪ'wɜːldɪ/ *adj* hum dall'aria falsamente antica

old-fashioned /-'fæʃ(ə)nd/ *adj* antiquato

old favourite *n* (book, play) classico *m*; (song, film) vecchio successo *m*

old flame *n* fam vecchia fiamma *f*

old girl *n* ex-allieva *f*

Old Glory *n* bandiera *f* statunitense

old hand *n* **be an ~ ~ at something/at doing something** saperci fare con qualcosa/a fare qualcosa

old hat *adj* fam **be ~ ~** essere roba vecchia

oldie /'əʊldɪ/ *n* (person) vecchio, -a *mf*; (film, song) vecchio successo *m*

old lady *n* (elderly woman) signora *f* anziana; **my ~ ~** (mother) la mia vecchia; (wife) la mia signora

old maid *n* zitella *f*

old man *n* (elderly man) uomo *m* anziano; (old: dear chap) vecchio *m* mio; **my ~ ~** (father) il mio vecchio; (husband) mio marito *m*; **the ~ ~** (boss) il capo

old master *n* (work) dipinto *m* antico (specialmente di un pittore europeo del XIII-XVII secolo)

old people's home *n* casa *f* di riposo

old soldier *n* (former soldier) veterano *m*

Old Testament *n* Antico Testamento *m*

old-time *adj* di un tempo; **~ dancing** ballo *m* liscio

old-timer *n* veterano, -a *mf*

old wives' tale *n* superstizione *f*

old woman *n* (elderly lady) donna *f* anziana; **my ~ ~** (mother) mia madre *f*; (wife) la mia signora; **be an ~ ~** pej: man essere una donnicciola

olive /'ɒlɪv/ **1** *n* (fruit, colour) oliva *f*; (tree) olivo *m* **2** *adj* d'oliva; (colour) olivastro

olive branch *n* fig ramoscello *m* d'olivo

olive green *adj & n* verde *m* oliva *inv*

olive grove *n* oliveto *m*

olive oil *n* olio *m* di oliva

olive-skinned /-'skɪnd/ *adj* olivastro

Olympic /ə'lɪmpɪk/ *adj* olimpico

Olympic Games, Olympics *npl* Olimpiadi *fpl*

Oman /əʊ'mɑːn/ *n* Oman *m*

ombudsman /'ɒmbʊdzmən/ *n* difensore *m* civico

omelette /'ɒmlɪt/ *n* omelette *f inv*

omen /'əʊmən/ *n* presagio *m*

ominous /'ɒmɪnəs/ *adj* sinistro

omission /'əmɪʃn/ *n* omissione *f*

omit /ə'mɪt/ *vt* (*pt/pp* **omitted**) omettere; **~ to do something** tralasciare di fare qualcosa

omnibus /'ɒmnɪbəs/ *n* (bus) omnibus *m inv*

omnibus edition *n* Br TV replica *f* delle puntate precedenti

omnipotent /ɒm'nɪpətənt/ *adj* onnipotente

omnipresent /ɒmnɪ'prez(ə)nt/ *adj* onnipresente

on /ɒn/ **1** *prep* su; (on horizontal surface) su, sopra; **on Monday** lunedì; **on Mondays** di lunedì; **on the first of May** il primo maggio; **on arriving** all'arrivo; **on one's** ···❯

o

finger nel dito; **on foot** a piedi; **on the right/left** a destra/sinistra; **on the Rhine/Thames** sul Reno/Tamigi; **on the radio/television** alla radio/televisione; **on the bus/train** in autobus/treno; **go on the bus/train** andare in autobus/treno; **get on the bus/train** salire sull'autobus/sul treno; **on me** (with me) con me; **it's on me** fam tocca a me

2 *adv* (further on) dopo; (switched on) acceso; ⟨*brake*⟩ inserito; (in operation) in funzione; **'on'** (on machine) 'on'; **he had his hat/coat on** portava il cappello/cappotto; **without his hat/coat on** senza cappello/capotto; **with/without the lid on** con/senza coperchio; **be on** ⟨*film, programme, event*⟩ esserci; **it's not on** fam non è giusto; **be on at** fam tormentare (to per); **on and on** senza sosta; **on and off** a intervalli; **and so on** e così via; **go on** continuare; **stick on** attaccare; **sew on** cucire

on-board *adj* di bordo

once /wʌns/ **1** *adv* una volta; (formerly) un tempo; **~ upon a time there was** c'era una volta; **at ~** subito; (at the same time) contemporaneamente; **~ and for all** una volta per tutte
2 *conj* [non] appena

once-over *n* fam **give somebody/something the ~** (look, check) dare un'occhiata veloce a qualcuno/qualcosa

oncoming /ˈɒnkʌmɪŋ/ *adj* che si avvicina dalla direzione opposta

one /wʌn/ **1** *adj* uno, una; **not ~ person** nemmeno una persona
2 *n* uno *m*
3 *pron* uno; (impersonal) si; **~ another** l'un l'altro; **~ by ~** [a] uno a uno; **~ never knows** non si sa mai

one-armed bandit /wʌnɑːmdˈbændɪt/ *n* slot-machine *f inv*

one-dimensional /-daɪˈmenʃənəl/ *adj* unidimensionale; **be ~** fig ⟨*character*⟩ mancare di spessore

one-eyed /-ˈaɪd/ *adj* con un occhio solo

one-for-one *adj* = ONE-TO-ONE

one-handed /-ˈhændɪd/ *adv* ⟨*catch, hold*⟩ con una sola mano

one-horse town *n* fam cittadina *f* di provincia

one-legged /-ˈlegɪd/ *adj* con una sola gamba

one-liner *n* battuta *f* d'effetto

one-man *adj* ⟨*bobsled*⟩ monoposto *inv*; ⟨*for one person*⟩ per una sola persona; **she's a ~ woman** è una donna fedele; **it's a ~ outfit/operation** manda avanti tutto da solo

one-man band *n* musicista *m* che suona più strumenti contemporaneamente; **be a ~ ~** fig mandare avanti tutto da solo

one-off *adj* Br ⟨*experiment, order, deal*⟩ unico e irripetibile; ⟨*event, decision, offer, payment*⟩ eccezionale; ⟨*example, design*⟩ unico; ⟨*issue, magazine*⟩ speciale

one-parent family *n* famiglia *f* con un solo genitore

one-piece *adj* **~ swimsuit** costume intero

one-room flat, one-room apartment *n* monolocale *m*

one's /wʌnz/ *poss adj* **one has to look after ~ health** ci si deve preoccupare della propria salute

oneself /wʌnˈself/ *pron* (reflexive) si; (emphatic) sé, se stesso; **by ~** da solo; **be proud of ~** essere fieri di sé

one-shot *adj* Am = ONE-OFF

one-sided /-ˈsaɪdɪd/ *adj* unilaterale

one-time *adj* ex *inv*

one-to-one *adj* ⟨*personal relationship*⟩ fra due persone; ⟨*private lesson*⟩ individuale; ⟨*correspondence*⟩ di uno a uno

one-upmanship /-ˈʌpmənʃɪp/ *n* arte *f* di primeggiare

one-way *adj* ⟨*street*⟩ a senso unico; ⟨*ticket*⟩ di sola andata

one-woman *adj* **it's a ~ outfit** manda avanti tutto da sola; **he's a ~ man** è un uomo fedele

ongoing /ˈɒnɡəʊɪŋ/ *adj* ⟨*process*⟩ continuo; ⟨*battle, saga*⟩ in corso

onion /ˈʌnjən/ *n* cipolla *f*

on-line *adj* Comput in linea, on-line *inv*: **go ~ to...** connettersi a...; **~ time** durata *f* del collegamento

onlooker /ˈɒnlʊkə(r)/ *n* spettatore, -trice *mf*

only /ˈəʊnlɪ/ **1** *adj* solo; **~ child** figlio, -a *mf* unico, -a
2 *adv & conj* solo, solamente; **~ just** appena

on-message *adj* Pol **be ~** essere in linea con la politica del governo

o.n.o. Br *abbr* (**or nearest offer**) trattabile

on-off *adj* ⟨*button, control*⟩ di accensione

onrush /ˈɒnrʌʃ/ *n* (of people, water) ondata *f*

on-screen *adj* sullo schermo

onset /ˈɒnset/ *n* (beginning) inizio *m*

onshore /ˈɒnʃɔː(r)/ *adj* ⟨*wind*⟩ di mare; ⟨*work*⟩ a terra

onside /ɒnˈsaɪd/ *adj & adv* Sport non in fuorigioco

on-site *adj* sul posto

onslaught /ˈɒnslɔːt/ *n* attacco *m*

on-stage *adj & adv* in scena

on-target earnings *npl* guadagni *mpl* previsti incluse commissioni

on-the-job *adj* ‹*training*› in sede
on-the-spot *adj* ‹*advice, quotation*› immediato
onto /'ɒntu:/ *prep* (also **on to**) su
onus /'əʊnəs/ *n* the ~ **is on me** spetta a me la responsabilità (**to** di)
onward[s] /'ɒnwəd[z]/ *adv* in avanti; **from then** ~ da allora [in poi]
oodles /'u:dlz/ *n fam* un sacco
ooh /u:/ *int* oh!
oomph /u:mf/ *n fam* verve *f inv*
oops /u:ps/ *int* ops!
ooze /u:z/ *vi* fluire
op /ɒp/ *n* = OPERATION
opal /'əʊpl/ *n* opale *f*
opaque /ər'peɪk/ *adj* opaco
Opec, OPEC /'əʊpek/ *n abbr* (**Organization of petroleum Exporting Countries**) OPEC *f*
open /'əʊpən/ **①** *adj* aperto; (free to all) pubblico; ‹*job*› vacante; **in the** ~ **air** all'aperto
② *n* **in the** ~ all'aperto; *fig* alla luce del sole
③ *vt* aprire
④ *vi* aprirsi; ‹*shop*› aprire; ‹*flower*› sbocciare
■ **open onto** *vt* ‹*door, window;*› dare su
■ **open out** **①** *vi* ‹*road*› allargarsi; ‹*flower*› aprisi
② *vt* aprire ‹*map, newspaper*›
■ **open up** **①** *vt* aprire
② *vi* aprirsi
■ **open with** *vi* (start with) iniziare con
open-air *adj* ‹*pool, market, stage*› all'aperto
opencast mining *n* Br miniera *f* a cielo aperto
open competition *n* concorso *m*
open day *n* giorno *m* di apertura al pubblico
open-ended /-'endɪd/ *adj* ‹*relationship, question, contract*› aperto; ‹*stay*› a tempo indeterminato; ‹*period*› indeterminato; ‹*strategy*› flessibile
opener /'əʊpənə(r)/ *n* (for tins) apriscatole *m inv*; (for bottles) apribottiglie *m inv*
open government *n* politica *f* di trasparenza
open-handed /-'hændɪd/ *adj* generoso
open-heart surgery *n* intervento *m* a cuore aperto
open house *n* (Am: open day) giornata *f* di apertura al pubblico; **it's always** ~ ~ **at the Batemans'** i Bateman sono sempre molto ospitali
opening /'əʊpənɪŋ/ *n* apertura *f*; (beginning) inizio *m*; (job) posto *m* libero
opening balance *n* Fin saldo *m* iniziale

opening ceremony *n* cerimonia *f* inaugurale
opening hours *npl* orario *m* d'apertura
open learning *n* open learning *m inv*
openly /'əʊpənlɪ/ *adv* apertamente
open market *n* Econ mercato *m* aperto
open minded /-'maɪndɪd/ *adj* aperto; (broad-minded) di vedute larghe
open-mouthed /-'maʊðd/ *adj* bocca aperta
open-necked /-'nekt/ *adj* ‹*shirt*› col colletto sbottonato
openness /'əʊpənnɪs/ *n* (of government, atmosphere) trasparenza *f*: (candour) franchezza *f*; (receptiveness) apertura *f* mentale
open-plan *adj* a pianta aperta
open sandwich *n* tartina *f*
open scholarship *n* Univ borsa *f* di studio assegnata per concorso
open season *n* (in hunting) stagione *f* della caccia
open secret *n* segreto *m* di Pulcinella
open ticket *n* biglietto *m* aperto
Open University *n* Br Univ corsi *mpl* universitari per corrispondenza
open verdict *n* Jur verdetto *m* che dichiara non accertabili le cause della morte
opera /'ɒpərə/ *n* opera *f*
operable /'ɒpərəbl/ *adj* operabile
opera glasses *npl* binocolo *msg* da teatro
opera house *n* teatro *m* lirico
opera singer *n* cantante *mf* lirico, -a
operate /'ɒpəreɪt/ **①** *vt* far funzionare ‹*machine, lift*›; azionare ‹*lever, brake*›; mandare avanti ‹*business*›
② *vi* Techn funzionare; (be in action) essere in funzione; Mil, *fig* operare
■ **operate on** *vt* Med operare
operatic /ɒpə'rætɪk/ *adj* lirico, operistico
operating costs /'ɒpəreɪtɪŋ/ *npl* spese *fpl* di esercizio
operating instructions *npl* istruzioni *fpl* per l'uso
operating room *n* Am sala *f* operatoria
operating system *n* Comput sistema *m* operativo
operating table *n* Med tavolo *m* operatorio
operating theatre *n* Br sala *f* operatoria
operation /ɒpə'reɪʃn/ *n* operazione *f*; Tech funzionamento *m*: **in** ~ Techn in funzione; **come into** ~ *fig* entrare in funzione; ‹*law*› entrare in vigore; **have an** ~ Med subire un'operazione

operational /ɒpə'reɪʃənəl/ *adj* operativo; ⟨*law etc*⟩ in vigore

operations room *n* Mil centro *m* operativo; (police) centrale *f* operativa

operative /'ɒpərətɪv/ *adj* operativo

operator /'ɒpəreɪtə(r)/ *n* (user) operatore, -trice *mf*; Teleph centralinista *mf*

operetta /ɒpə'retə/ *n* operetta *f*

ophthalmic /ɒf'θælmɪk/ *adj* oftalmico

opinion /ə'pɪnjən/ *n* opinione *f*; **in my ~** secondo me

opinionated /ə'pɪnɪəneɪtɪd/ *adj* dogmatico

opinion poll *n* sondaggio *m* di opinione

opium /'əʊpɪəm/ *n* oppio *m*

opponent /ə'pəʊnənt/ *n* avversario, -a *mf*

opportune /'ɒpətjuːn/ *adj* opportuno

opportunist /ɒpə'tjuːnɪst/ *n* opportunista *mf*

opportunistic /ɒpətjʊ'nɪstɪk/ *adj* opportunistico

opportunity /ɒpə'tjuːnətɪ/ *n* opportunità *f inv*

oppose /ə'pəʊz/ *vt* opporsi a; **be ~d to something** essere contrario a qualcosa; **as ~d to** al contrario di

opposing /ə'pəʊzɪŋ/ *adj* avversario; (opposite) opposto

opposite /'ɒpəzɪt/ **1** *adj* opposto; ⟨*house*⟩ di fronte; **~ number** fig controparte *f*; **the ~ sex** l'altro sesso **2** *n* contrario *m* **3** *adv* di fronte **4** *prep* di fronte a

opposition /ɒpə'zɪʃn/ *n* opposizione *f*

oppress /ə'pres/ *vt* opprimere

oppression /ə'preʃn/ *n* oppressione *f*

oppressive /ə'presɪv/ *adj* oppressivo; ⟨*heat*⟩ opprimente

oppressor /ə'presə(r)/ *n* oppressore *m*

opt /ɒpt/ *v*
■ **opt for** *vt* optare per
■ **opt out** *vi* dissociarsi (**of** da)

optic /'ɒptɪk/ *adj* ⟨*nerve, disc, fibre*⟩ ottico

optical /'ɒptɪkl/ *adj* ottico; **~ illusion** illusione *f* ottica

optician /ɒp'tɪʃn/ *n* ottico, -a *mf*

optics /'ɒptɪks/ *n* ottica *f*

optimism /'ɒptɪmɪzm/ *n* ottimismo *m*

optimist /'ɒptɪmɪst/ *n* ottimista *mf*

optimistic /ɒptɪ'mɪstɪk/ *adj* ottimistico

optimistically /ɒptɪ'mɪstɪklɪ/ *adv* ottimisticamente

optimize /'ɒptɪmaɪz/ *vt* ottimizzare

optimum /'ɒptɪməm/ **1** *adj* ottimale **2** *n* (pl **-ima**) optimum *m*

option /'ɒpʃn/ *n* scelta *f*; Comm opzione *f*

optional /'ɒpʃənəl/ *adj* facoltativo; **~ extras** optional *m inv*

opulence /'ɒpjʊləns/ *n* opulenza *f*

opulent /'ɒpjʊlənt/ *adj* opulento

opus /'əʊpəs/ *n* (pl **opuses** or **opera**) opera *f*

or /ɔː(r)/ *conj* o, oppure; (after negative) né; **or [else]** se no; **in a year or two** fra un anno o due

oracle /'ɒrəkl/ *n* oracolo *m*

oral /'ɔːrəl/ **1** *adj* orale **2** *n* fam esame *m* orale

orally /'ɔːrəlɪ/ *adv* oralmente

orange /'ɒrɪndʒ/ **1** *n* arancia *f*; (colour) arancione *m* **2** *adj* arancione

orangeade /ɒrɪndʒ'eɪd/ *n* aranciata *f*

orange blossom *n* fiori *mpl* d'arancio

orange juice *n* succo *m* d'arancia

orange peel *n* scorza *f* d'arancia

orange squash *n* Br succo *m* d'arancia (diluito in acqua)

orange tree *n* arancio *m*

oration /ə'reɪʃn/ *n* orazione *f*

orator /'ɒrətə(r)/ *n* oratore, -trice *mf*

oratorio /ɒrə'tɔːrɪəʊ/ *n* oratorio *m*

oratory /'ɒrətrɪ/ *n* oratorio *m*

orbit /'ɔːbɪt/ **1** *n* orbita *f* **2** *vt* orbitare

orbital /'ɔːbɪtl/ *adj* **~ road** tangenziale *f*

orchard /'ɔːtʃəd/ *n* frutteto *m*

orchestra /'ɔːkɪstrə/ *n* orchestra *f*

orchestral /ɔː'kestrəl/ *adj* orchestrale

orchestra pit *n* [fossa *f* dell']orchestra *f*

orchestrate /'ɔːkɪstreɪt/ *vt* orchestrare

orchid /'ɔːkɪd/ *n* orchidea *f*

ordain /ɔː'deɪn/ *vt* decretare; Relig ordinare

ordeal /ɔː'diːl/ *n* fig terribile esperienza *f*

order /'ɔːdə(r)/ **1** *n* ordine *m*; Comm ordinazione *f*; **out of ~** ⟨*machine*⟩ fuori servizio; **in ~ that** affinché; **in ~ to** per; **take holy ~s** prendere i voti **2** *vt* ordinare
■ **order about**, **order around** *vt* (give orders to) impartire ordini a

order book *n* registro *m* degli ordini

order form *n* modulo *m* di ordinazione

orderly /'ɔːdəlɪ/ **1** *adj* ordinato **2** *n* Mil attendente *m*; Med inserviente *m*

orderly officer *n* Mil attendente *m*

order number *n* numero *m* d'ordine

ordinal /'ɔːdɪnəl/ *n* & *adj* ordinale *m*

ordinarily /ɔːdɪ'nerɪlɪ/ *adv* (normally) normalmente

ordinary /'ɔːdɪnərɪ/ *adj* ordinario

ordination /ɔːdɪ'neɪʃn/ *n* Relig ordinazione *f*

ordnance /'ɔːdnəns/ n Mil materiale m militare

Ordnance Survey n Br istituto m cartografico; ~ ~ **Map** carta f topografica dell'istituto cartografico

ore /ɔː(r)/ n minerale m grezzo

oregano /ɒrɪ'gɑːnəʊ/ n origano m

organ /'ɔːgən/ n Anat Mus organo m

organ donor n Med donatore, -trice mf di organi

organic /ɔː'gænɪk/ adj organico; (without chemicals) biologico

organically /ɔː'gænɪklɪ/ adv organicamente; ~ **grown** coltivato biologicamente

organic chemistry n chimica f organica

organic farm n azienda f agricola specializzata in prodotti biologici

organic farming n agricoltura f biologica

organism /'ɔːgənɪzm/ n organismo m

organist /'ɔːgənɪst/ n organista mf

organization /ɔːgənaɪ'zeɪʃn/ n organizzazione f

organizational /ɔːgənaɪ'zeɪʃənəl/ adj ⟨ability, role⟩ organizzativo

organize /'ɔːgənaɪz/ vt organizzare

organized crime /ɔːgənaɪzd'kraɪm/ n criminalità f organizzata

organized labour n manodopera f organizzata

organizer /'ɔːgənaɪzə(r)/ n organizzatore, -trice mf

organ transplant n Med trapianto m di organi

orgasm /'ɔːgæzm/ n orgasmo m

orgy /'ɔːdʒɪ/ n orgia f

Orient /'ɔːrɪənt/ n Oriente m

oriental /ɔːrɪ'entl/ ① adj orientale; ~ **carpet** tappeto m persiano ② n orientale mf

orientate /'ɔːrɪənteɪt/ vt ~ **oneself** orientarsi

orientation /ɔːrɪən'teɪʃn/ n orientamento m

orienteering /ɔːrɪen'tɪərɪŋ/ n orientamento m

orifice /'ɒrɪfɪs/ n orifizio m

origin /'ɒrɪdʒɪn/ n origine f

original /ə'rɪdʒɪnl/ ① adj originario; (not copied, new) originale; ② n originale m; **in the** ~ in versione originale

originality /ərɪdʒɪ'nælətɪ/ n originalità f

originally /ə'rɪdʒɪnəlɪ/ adv originariamente

originate /ə'rɪdʒɪneɪt/ vi ~ **in** avere origine in

originator /ə'rɪdʒɪneɪtə(r)/ n ideatore, -trice mf

Orkney /'ɔːknɪ/ n (also Orkney Islands) Orcadi fpl

ornament /'ɔːnəmənt/ n ornamento m; (on mantelpiece etc) soprammobile m

ornamental /ɔːnə'mentl/ adj ornamentale

ornamentation /ɔːnəmen'teɪʃn/ n decorazione f

ornate /ɔː'neɪt/ adj ornato

ornithologist /ɔːnɪ'θɒlədʒɪst/ n ornitologo, -a mf

ornithology /ɔːnɪ'θɒlədʒɪ/ n ornitologia f

orphan /'ɔːfn/ ① n orfano, -a mf ② vt rendere orfano; **be** ~**ed** rimanere orfano; **be** ~**ed by**... essere reso orfano da...

orphanage /'ɔːfənɪdʒ/ n orfanotrofio m

orphaned /'ɔːfənd/ adj rimasto orfano

orthodox /'ɔːθədɒks/ adj ortodosso

orthopaedic /ɔːθə'piːdɪk/ adj ortopedico

orthopaedics /ɔːθə'piːdɪks/ n ortopedia f

OS abbr (**outsize**) per taglie forti

oscillate /'ɒsɪleɪt/ vi oscillare

osmosis /ɒz'məʊsɪs/ n osmosi f inv; **by** ~ per osmosi

ostensible /ɒ'stensəbl/ adj apparente

ostensibly /ɒ'stensəblɪ/ adv apparentemente

ostentation /ɒsten'teɪʃn/ n ostentazione f

ostentatious /ɒsten'teɪʃəs/ adj ostentato

ostentatiously /ɒsten'teɪʃəslɪ/ adv ostentatamente

osteopath /'ɒstɪəpæθ/ n osteopata mf

osteoporosis /ɒstɪəɪpə'rəʊsɪs/ n osteoporosi f

ostracism /'ɒstrəsɪzm/ n ostracismo m

ostracize /'ɒstrəsaɪz/ vt ostracizzare

ostrich /'ɒstrɪtʃ/ n struzzo m

OTE abbr (**on-target earnings**) guadagni mpl previsti incluse commissioni

other /'ʌðə(r)/ ① adj, pron & n altro, -a mf; **the** ~ [**one**] l'altro, -a mf; **the** ~ **two** gli altri due; **two** ~**s** altri due; ~ **people** gli altri; **any** ~ **questions?** altre domande?; **every** ~ **day** (alternate days) a giorni alterni; **the** ~ **day** l'altro giorno; **the** ~ **evening** l'altra sera; **someone/ something or** ~ qualcuno/qualcosa ② adv ~ **than him** tranne lui; **somehow or** ~ in qualche modo; **somewhere or** ~ da qualche parte

otherwise /'ʌðəwaɪz/ adv altrimenti; (differently) diversamente

other-worldly /ʌðə'wɜːldlɪ/ *adj* disinteressato alle cose materiali

OTT *abbr fam* (**over-the-top**) esagerato

otter /'ɒtə(r)/ *n* lontra *f*

OU *n Br abbr* (**Open University**) corsi *mpl* universitari per corrispondenza

ouch /aʊtʃ/ *int* ahi!

ought /ɔːt/ *v aux* I/we ∼ to stay dovrei/ dovremmo rimanere; he ∼ not to have done it non avrebbe dovuto farlo; that ∼ to be enough questo dovrebbe bastare

ounce /aʊns/ *n* oncia *f* (= 28,35 g)

our /'aʊə(r)/ *poss adj* il nostro *m*, la nostra *f*, i nostri *mpl*, le nostre *fpl*; ∼ mother/father nostra madre/nostro padre

ours /'aʊəz/ *poss pron* il nostro *m*, la nostra *f*, i nostri *mpl*, le nostre *fpl*; a friend of ∼ un nostro amico; friends of ∼ dei nostri amici; that is ∼ quello è nostro; (as opposed to yours) quello è il nostro

ourselves /aʊə'selvz/ *pers pron* (reflexive) ci; (emphatic) noi, noi stessi; we poured ∼ a drink ci siamo versati da bere; we heard it ∼ l'abbiamo sentito noi stessi; we are proud of ∼ siamo fieri di noi; by ∼ da soli

oust /aʊst/ *vt* rimuovere

out /aʊt/ **①** *adv* fuori; (not alight) spento; be ∼ ⟨flower⟩ essere sbocciato; ⟨workers⟩ essere in sciopero; ⟨calculation⟩ essere sbagliato; Sport essere fuori; (unconscious) aver perso i sensi; (fig: not feasible) essere fuori questione; the sun is ∼ è uscito il sole; ∼ and about in piedi; get ∼! fam fuori!; you should get ∼ more dovresti uscire più spesso; ∼ with it! fam sputa il rospo!; be ∼ to avere l'intenzione di; **②** *prep* ∼ of fuori da; ∼ of date non aggiornato; ⟨passport⟩ scaduto; ∼ of order guasto; ∼ of print/stock esaurito; ∼ of sorts indisposto; ∼ of tune (singer) stonato; (instrument) scordato; be ∼ of bed/the room fuori dal letto/dalla stanza; ∼ of breath senza fiato; ∼ of danger fuori pericolo; ∼ of work disoccupato; nine ∼ of ten nove su dieci; be ∼ of sugar/bread rimanere senza zucchero/pane; go ∼ of the room uscire dalla stanza

out-and-out *adj* ⟨success, failure⟩ totale; ⟨villain, liar⟩ vero e proprio

outback /'aʊtbæk/ *n* entroterra *m inv* australiano

outbid /aʊt'bɪd/ *vt* (pt/pp **-bid**. pres p **-bidding**) ∼ somebody rilanciare l'offerta di qualcuno

outboard /'aʊtbɔːd/ *adj* ∼ motor fuoribordo *m inv*

outbreak /'aʊtbreɪk/ *n* (of war) scoppio *m*; (of disease) insorgenza *f*

outbuilding /'aʊtbɪldɪŋ/ *n* costruzione *f* annessa

outburst /'aʊtbɜːst/ *n* esplosione *f*

outcast /'aʊtkɑːst/ *n* esule *mf*; (social) escluso *m*

outclass /aʊt'klɑːs/ *vt* surclassare

outcome /'aʊtkʌm/ *n* risultato *m*

outcrop /'aʊtkrɒp/ *n* affioramento *m*

outcry /'aʊtkraɪ/ *n* protesta *f*

outdated /aʊt'deɪtɪd/ *adj* sorpassato

outdo /aʊt'duː/ *vt* (pt **-did**, pp **-done**) superare

outdoor /'aʊtdɔː(r)/ *adj* ⟨life, sports⟩ all'aperto; ∼ swimming pool piscina *f* scoperta

outdoors /aʊt'dɔːz/ *adv* all'aria aperta; go ∼ uscire all'aria aperta

outer /'aʊtə(r)/ *adj* esterno

outer space *n* spazio *m* cosmico

outfit /'aʊtfɪt/ *n* equipaggiamento *m*; (clothes) completo *m*; (fam: organization) organizzazione *f*

outfitter /'aʊtfɪtə(r)/ *n* men's ∼ 's negozio *m* di abbigliamento maschile

outflow /'aʊtfləʊ/ *n* (of money) uscite *fpl*

outgoing /'aʊtgəʊɪŋ/ **①** *adj* (president) uscente; ⟨mail⟩ in partenza; (sociable) estroverso **②** *npl* ∼s uscite *fpl*

outgrow /aʊt'grəʊ/ *vi* (pt **-grew**, pp **-grown**) diventare troppo grande per

outhouse /'aʊthaʊs/ *n* costruzione *f* annessa

outing /'aʊtɪŋ/ *n* gita *f*

outlandish /aʊt'lændɪʃ/ *adj* stravagante

outlast /aʊt'lɑːst/ *vt* durare più a lungo di

outlaw /'aʊtlɔː/ **①** *n* fuorilegge *mf inv* **②** *vt* dichiarare illegale

outlay /'aʊtleɪ/ *n* spesa *f*

outlet /'aʊtlet/ *n* sbocco *m*; fig sfogo *m*; Comm punto *m* [di] vendita

outline /'aʊtlaɪn/ **①** *n* contorno *m*; (summary) sommario *m* **②** *vt* tracciare il contorno di; (describe) descrivere

outline agreement *n* abbozzo *m* di accordo

outlive /aʊt'lɪv/ *vt* sopravvivere a

outlook /'aʊtlʊk/ *n* vista *f*; (future prospect) prospettiva *f*; (attitude) visione *f*

outlying /'aʊtlaɪɪŋ/ *adj* ∼ areas zone *fpl* periferiche

outmanoeuvre /aʊtmə'nuːvə(r)/ *vt* ∼ somebody passare in vantaggio su qualcuno con un'abile manovra

outmoded /aʊt'məʊdɪd/ *adj* fuori moda

outnumber /aʊt'nʌmbə(r)/ *vt* superare in numero

out-of-body experience *n* esperienza *f* extracorporea

out of bounds *adj & adv* ⟨area⟩ vietato l'accesso

out-of-date *adj* ⟨*theory, concept*⟩ sorpassato; ⟨*ticket, passport*⟩ scaduto

out-of-pocket *adj* **be out of pocket** essere in perdita; **~ expenses** spese *fpl* extra

out-of-the-way *adj* ⟨*places*⟩ fuori mano

outpatient /ˈaʊtpeɪʃnt/ *n* paziente *mf* esterno, -a; **~s' department** ambulatorio *m*

outpost /ˈaʊtpəʊst/ *n* avamposto *m*

output /ˈaʊtpʊt/ *n* produzione *f*

outrage /ˈaʊtreɪdʒ/ **1** *n* oltraggio *m*
2 *vt* oltraggiare

outrageous /aʊtˈreɪdʒəs/ *adj* oltraggioso; ⟨*price*⟩ scandaloso

outrider /ˈaʊtraɪdə(r)/ *n* battistrada *m inv*

outright[1] /ˈaʊtraɪt/ *adj* completo; ⟨*refusal*⟩ netto

outright[2] /aʊtˈraɪt/ *adv* completamente; (at once) immediatamente; (frankly) francamente

outrun /aʊtˈrʌn/ *vt* superare

outsell /aʊtˈsel/ *vt* vendere meglio di ⟨*product*⟩

outset /ˈaʊtset/ *n* inizio *m*; **from the ~** fin dall'inizio

outside[1] /ˈaʊtsaɪd/ **1** *adj* esterno
2 *n* esterno *m*; **from the ~** dall'esterno; **at the ~** al massimo

outside[2] /aʊtˈsaɪd/ **1** *adv* all'esterno, fuori; (out of doors) fuori; **go ~** andare fuori
2 *prep* fuori da; (in front of) davanti a

outsider /aʊtˈsaɪdə(r)/ *n* estraneo, -a *mf*

outsize /ˈaʊtsaɪz/ *adj* smisurato; ⟨*clothes*⟩ per taglie forti

outskirts /ˈaʊtskɜːts/ *npl* sobborghi *mpl*

outsmart /aʊtˈsmɑːt/ *vt* essere più furbo di

outsource /ˈaʊtsɔːs/ *vt* appaltare a imprese esterne

outsourcing /ˈaʊtsɔːsɪŋ/ *n* appalto *m* a imprese esterne

outspoken /aʊtˈspəʊkn/ *adj* schietto

outspread /ˈaʊtspred/ *adj* ⟨*wings*⟩ spiegato; ⟨*arms, fingers*⟩ disteso

outstanding /aʊtˈstændɪŋ/ *adj* eccezionale; ⟨*landmark*⟩ prominente; (not settled) in sospeso

outstandingly /aʊtˈstændɪŋlɪ/ *adv* eccezionalmente; **~ good** eccezionale

outstay /aʊtˈsteɪ/ *vt* **~ one's s welcome** abusare dell'ospitalità di qualcuno

outstretched /ˈaʊtstretʃt/ *adj* allungato

outstrip /aʊtˈstrɪp/ *vt* (pt/pp **-stripped**) superare

out-tray *n* vassoio *m* per corrispondenza e pratiche evase

outvote /aʊtˈvəʊt/ *vt* mettere in minoranza

outward /ˈaʊtwəd/ **1** *adj* esterno; (journey) di andata
2 *adv* verso l'esterno

outwardly /ˈaʊtwədlɪ/ *adv* esternamente

outwards /ˈaʊtwədz/ *adv* verso l'esterno

outweigh /aʊtˈweɪ/ *vt* aver maggior peso di

outwit /aʊtˈwɪt/ *vt* (pt/pp **-witted**) battere in astuzia

outworker /ˈaʊtwɜːkə(r)/ *n* Br lavoratore, -trice *mf* a domicilio

outworn /aʊtˈwɔːn/ *adj* ⟨*outmoded*⟩ sorpassato

oval /ˈəʊvl/ **1** *adj* ovale
2 *n* ovale *m*

ovary /ˈəʊvərɪ/ *n* Anat ovaia *f*

ovation /əʊˈveɪʃn/ *n* ovazione *f*

oven /ˈʌvn/ *n* forno *m*

oven cleaner *n* detergente *m* per il forno

oven glove *n* guanto *m* da forno

ovenproof *adj* da forno

oven-ready *adj* pronto da mettere in forno

over /ˈəʊvə(r)/ **1** *prep* sopra; (across) al di là di; (during) durante; (more than) più di; **~ the phone** al telefono; **~ the page** alla pagina seguente; **all ~ Italy** in tutta [l']Italia; ⟨*travel*⟩ per l'Italia
2 *adv* Math col resto di; (ended) finito; **~ again** un'altra volta; **~ and ~** più volte; **~ and above** oltre a; **~ here/there** qui/là; **all ~** (everywhere) dappertutto; **it's all ~** è tutto finito; **I ache all ~** ho male dappertutto; **come/bring ~** venire/ portare; **turn ~** girare

over+ *pref* (too) troppo

overact /əʊvərˈækt/ *vi* strafare

overactive /əʊvərˈæktɪv/ *adj* ⟨*imagination*⟩ sbrigliato

overall[1] /ˈəʊvərɔːl/ *n* grembiule *m*

overall[2] /əʊvərˈɔːl/ **1** *adj* complessivo; (general) generale
2 *adv* complessivamente

overalls /ˈəʊvərɔːlz/ *npl* tuta *fsg* [da lavoro]

overarm /ˈəʊvərɑːm/ *adj & adv* ⟨*throw*⟩ col braccio al di sopra della spalla

overawe /əʊvərˈɔː/ *vt* fig intimidire

overbalance /əʊvəˈbæləns/ *vi* perdere l'equilibrio

overbearing /əʊvəˈbeərɪŋ/ *adj* prepotente

overblown /əʊvəˈbləʊn/ *adj* ⟨*style*⟩ ampolloso

overboard /ˈəʊvəbɔːd/ *adv* Naut in mare

overbook /əʊvəˈbʊk/ *vt* accettare un numero di prenotazioni superiore ai posti disponibili

overburden /əʊvə'bɜːdən/ vt
sovraccaricare (**with** di)

overcapacity /əʊvəkə'pæsəti/ n
eccesso m di capacità produttiva

overcast /'əʊvəkɑːst/ adj coperto

overcharge /əʊvə'tʃɑːdʒ/ ① vt ~
somebody far pagare più del dovuto a
② vi far pagare più del dovuto

overcoat /'əʊvəkəʊt/ n cappotto m

overcome /əʊvə'kʌm/ vt (pt -**came**, pp
-**come**) vincere; **be ~ by** essere
sopraffatto da

overcompensate /əʊvə'kɒmpənseɪt/
vi compensare eccessivamente

overconfident /əʊvə'kɒnfɪdənt/ adj
troppo sicuro di sé

overcook /əʊvə'kʊk/ vt cuocere troppo

overcrowded /əʊvə'kraʊdɪd/ adj
sovraffollato

overcrowding /əʊvə'kraʊdɪŋ/ n (in
transport) calca f; (in city, institution)
sovraffollamento m

overdo /əʊvə'duː/ vt (pt -**did**, pp -**done**)
esagerare; (cook too long) stracuocere; ~ **it**
(fam: do too much) strafare

overdose /'əʊvədəʊs/ n overdose f inv

overdraft /'əʊvədrɑːft/ n scoperto m;
have an ~ avere il conto scoperto

overdraw /əʊvə'drɔː/ vt (pt -**drew**, pp
-**drawn**) ~ **one's account** andare allo
scoperto; **be ~n by...** ⟨account⟩ essere
scoperto di...

overdressed /əʊvə'drest/ adj troppo
elegante

overdrive /'əʊvədraɪv/ n Auto overdrive
m inv

overdue /əʊvə'djuː/ adj in ritardo

overeat /əʊvər'iːt/ vi mangiare troppo

overemphasize /əʊvər'emfəsaɪz/ vt
esagerare ⟨importance⟩; dare troppo
rilievo a ⟨aspect, fact⟩

overenthusiastic
/əʊvərɪnθjuːzɪ'æstɪk/ adj troppo
entusiasta

overestimate /əʊvər'estɪmeɪt/ vt
sopravvalutare

overexcited /əʊvərɪk'saɪtɪd/ adj
sovreccitato; **get ~** sovreccitarsi

overexert /əʊvərɪg'zɜːt/ vt ~ **oneself**
sovraffaticarsi

overexposure /əʊvərek'spəʊʒə(r)/ n
Phot sovresposizione f; (in the media)
attenzione f eccessiva da parte dei media

overfeed /əʊvə'fiːd/ vt sovralimentare
⟨child, pet⟩; concimare troppo ⟨plant⟩

overflow[1] /'əʊvəfləʊ/ n (water) acqua f
che deborda; (people) pubblico m in
eccesso; (outlet) scarico m

overflow[2] /əʊvə'fləʊ/ vi debordare

overgenerous /əʊvə'dʒenərəs/ adj
⟨amount⟩ troppo generoso

overgrown /əʊvə'grəʊn/ adj ⟨garden⟩
coperto di erbacce

overhang[1] /'əʊvəhæŋ/ n sporgenza f

overhang[2] /əʊvə'hæŋ/ ① vi (pt/pp
-**hung**) sporgere
② vt sovrastare

overhanging /əʊvə'hæŋɪŋ/ adj ⟨ledge,
cliff⟩ sporgente

overhaul[1] /'əʊvəhɔːl/ n revisione f

overhaul[2] /əʊvə'hɔːl/ vt Techn
revisionare

overhead[1] /əʊvə'hed/ adv in alto

overhead[2] /'əʊvəhed/ ① adj aereo;
⟨railway⟩ sopraelevato; ⟨lights⟩ da soffitto
② npl ~s spese fpl generali

overhead light n lampada f da soffitto

overhead locker n Aeron armadietto m
[per il bagaglio a mano]

overhead projector n lavagna f
luminosa

overhear /əʊvə'hɪə(r)/ vt (pt/pp -**heard**)
sentire per caso ⟨conversation⟩; **I ~d him
saying it** l'ho sentito per caso mentre lo
diceva

overheat /əʊvə'hiːt/ ① vi Auto
surriscaldarsi
② vt surriscaldare

over-indulge ① vi eccedere
② vt viziare ⟨child⟩

over-indulgence n (excess) eccesso m;
(laxity towards) indulgenza f eccessiva

overjoyed /əʊvə'dʒɔɪd/ adj felicissimo

overkill /'əʊvəkɪl/ n (exaggerated treatment)
esagerazione f

overland /'əʊvəlænd/ adj & adv via
terra; ~ **route** via f terrestre

overlap /əʊvə'læp/ ① vi (pt/pp -**lapped**)
sovrapporsi
② vt sovrapporre

overlay /əʊvə'leɪ/ vt ricoprire

overleaf /əʊvə'liːf/ adv sul retro

overload[1] /əʊvə'ləʊd/ vt sovraccaricare

overload[2] /'əʊvələʊd/ n Electr
sovratensioni fpl

overlook /əʊvə'lʊk/ vt dominare; (fail to
see, ignore) lasciarsi sfuggire

overly /'əʊvəli/ adv eccessivamente

overmanned /əʊvə'mænd/ adj con
un'eccedenza di personale

overmanning /əʊvə'mænɪŋ/ n eccesso
m di personale

overmuch /əʊvə'mʌtʃ/ adv troppo

overnight[1] /'əʊvənaɪt/ adj notturno

overnight[2] /əʊvə'naɪt/ vt inviare
tramite sistemi di spedizione notturna
con consegna il mattino seguente ⟨goods⟩

overnight bag n piccola borsa f da
viaggio

overnight stay n sosta f per la notte

overpass /'əʊvəpɑːs/ n cavalcavia m inv

overpay /əʊvə'peɪ/ *vt* (pt/pp **-paid**)
strapagare

overplay /əɪvə'pleɪ/ *vt* (exaggerate)
esagerare

overpopulated /əʊvə'pɒpjʊleɪtɪd/ *adj*
sovrappopolato

overpower /əʊvə'paʊə(r)/ *vt* sopraffare

overpowering /əʊvə'paʊərɪŋ/ *adj*
insostenibile

overpriced /əʊvə'praɪst/ *adj* troppo
caro

overproduce /əʊvəprə'djuːs/ *vt*
produrre in eccesso

overqualified /əʊvə'kwɒlɪfaɪd/ *adj*
troppo qualificato

overrate /əʊvə'reɪt/ *vt* sopravvalutare

overrated /əʊvə'reɪtɪd/ *adj*
sopravvalutato

overreach /əʊvə'riːtʃ/ *vt* ~ oneself
puntare troppo in alto

overreact /əʊvərɪ'ækt/ *vi* avere una
reazione eccessiva

overreaction /əʊvərɪ'ækʃn/ *n* reazione
f eccessiva

override /əʊvə'raɪd/ *vt* (pt **-rode**, pp
-ridden) passare sopra a

overriding /əʊvə'raɪdɪŋ/ *adj* prevalente

overrule /əʊvə'ruːl/ *vt* annullare
⟨*decision*⟩; **we were ~d by the chairman** il
direttore ha prevalso su di noi

overrun /əʊvə'rʌn/ *vt* (pt **-ran**, pp **-run**,
pres p **-running**) invadere; oltrepassare
⟨*time*⟩; **be ~ with** essere invaso da

overseas[1] /əʊvə'siːz/ *adv* oltremare

overseas[2] /'əʊvəsiːz/ *adj* d'oltremare

oversee /əʊvə'siː/ *vt* (pt **-saw**, pp
-seen) sorvegliare

oversell /əʊvə'sel/ *vt* lodare
esageratamente ⟨*idea, plan*⟩

oversensitive /əʊvə'sensɪtɪv/ *adj*
⟨*person*⟩ ipersensibile

oversexed /əʊvə'sekst/ *adj* fam **be ~**
essere un maniaco/una maniaca del sesso

overshadow /əʊvə'ʃædəʊ/ *vt*
adombrare

overshoot /əʊvə'ʃuːt/ *vt* (pt/pp **-shot**)
oltrepassare

oversight /'əʊvəsaɪt/ *n* disattenzione *f*;
an ~ una svista

oversimplification
/əʊvəsɪmplɪfɪ'keɪʃn/ *n* semplificazione *f*
eccessiva

oversimplified /əʊvə'sɪmplɪfaɪd/ *adj*
semplicistico

oversimplify /əʊvə'sɪmplɪfaɪ/ *vt*
semplificare eccessivamente

oversize[d] /əʊvə'saɪz[d]/ *adj* più
grande del normale

oversleep /əʊvə'sliːp/ *vi* (pt/pp **-slept**)
svegliarsi troppo tardi

overspend /əʊvə'spend/ *vi* spendere
troppo

overspending /əʊvə'spendɪŋ/ *n* spese
fpl eccessive; Fin spese *fpl* superiori al
bilancio di previsione

overspill /'əʊvəspɪl/ **1** *n* (excess amount)
eccedenza *f*
2 *attrib* ~ **housing development** città *f*
inv satellite; ~ **population** popolazione *f*
in eccesso

overstaffed /əʊvə'stɑːft/ *adj* **be ~**
avere personale in eccedenza

overstaffing /əʊvə'stɑːfɪŋ/ *n* eccedenza
f di personale

overstate /əʊvə'steɪt/ *vt* esagerare; **its
importance cannot be ~d** la sua
importanza non sarà mai sottolineata a
sufficienza; ~ **the case** esagerare le cose

overstatement /əʊvə'steɪtmənt/ *n*
esagerazione *f*

overstay /əʊvə'steɪ/ *vt* ~ **one's time**
trattenersi troppo a lungo; ~ **one's visa**
trattenersi oltre la scadenza del visto

overstep /əʊvə'step/ *vt* (pt/pp
-stepped) ~ **the mark** oltrepassare ogni
limite

overstretched /əʊvə'stretʃt/ *adj*
⟨*person*⟩ sovraccarico [di lavoro]; ⟨*budget,
resources*⟩ sfruttato fino al limite

oversubscribed /əʊvəsəb'skraɪbd/ *adj*
⟨*share issue*⟩ sottoscritto in eccesso; ⟨*offer,
tickets*⟩ richiesto oltre la disponibilità

overt /əʊ'vɜːt/ *adj* palese

overtake /əʊvə'teɪk/ *vt/i* (pt **-took**, pp
-taken) sorpassare

overtaking /əʊvə'teɪkɪŋ/ *n* sorpasso *m*;
no ~ divieto di sorpasso

overtax /əʊvə'tæks/ *vt* fig abusare di

over-the-counter *adj* ⟨*medicines*⟩
venduto senza ricetta

over-the-top *adj* fam esagerato; **go over
the top** esagerare

overthrow[1] /'əʊvəθrəʊ/ *n* Pol
rovesciamento *m*

overthrow[2] /əʊvə'θrəʊ/ *vt* (pt **-threw**,
pp **-thrown**) Pol rovesciare

overtime /'əʊvətaɪm/ **1** *n* lavoro
straordinario *m*
2 *adv* **work ~** fare lo straordinario

overtired /əʊvə'taɪəd/ *adj* sovraffaticato

overtly /əʊ'vɜːtlɪ/ *adv* apertamente

overtone /'əʊvətəʊn/ *n* fig sfumatura *f*

overture /'əʊvətjʊə(r)/ *n* Mus preludio *m*;
~**s** *pl* fig approccio *msg*; **make ~s to**
mostrare un atteggiamento di apertura
verso

overturn /əʊvə'tɜːn/ **1** *vt* ribaltare
2 *vi* ribaltarsi

overvalue /əʊvə'væljuː/ *vt*
sopravvalutare ⟨*currency, property*⟩

overview /'əʊvəvjuː/ n visione f d'insieme

overweight /əʊvə'weɪt/ adj sovrappeso

overwhelm /əʊvə'welm/ vt sommergere (with di); (with emotion) confondere

overwhelming /əʊvə'welmɪŋ/ adj travolgente; ⟨victory, majority⟩ schiacciante

overwhelmingly /əʊvə'welmɪŋlɪ/ adv ⟨vote, accept, reject⟩ con una maggioranza schiacciante; ⟨generous⟩ straordinariamente

overwork /əʊvə'wɜːk/ **1** n lavoro m eccessivo
2 vt far lavorare eccessivamente
3 vi lavorare eccessivamente

overworked /əʊvə'wɜːkt/ adj affaticato dal troppo lavoro

overwrite /əʊvə'raɪt/ vt Comput registrare sopra a

overwrought /əʊvə'rɔːt/ adj in stato di agitazione

ovulation /ɒvjʊ'leɪʃn/ n ovulazione f

ow /aʊ/ int ahi!

owe /əʊ/ vt also fig dovere ([to] somebody a qualcuno); ∼ somebody something dovere qualcosa a qualcuno

owing /'əʊɪŋ/ **1** adj be ∼ ⟨money⟩ essere da pagare
2 prep ∼ to a causa di

owl /aʊl/ n gufo m

own¹ /əʊn/ **1** adj proprio
2 pron a car of my ∼ una macchina per

conto mio; **on one's ∼** da solo; **hold one's ∼ with** tener testa a; **get one's ∼ back** fam prendersi una rivincita

own² vt possedere; (confess) ammettere; **I don't ∼ it** non mi appartiene
■ **own up** vi confessare (**to something** qualcosa)

owner /'əʊnə(r)/ n proprietario, -a mf

owner-driver n persona f che guida un'auto di sua proprietà

owner-occupied /-'ɒkjʊpaɪd/ adj abitato dal proprietario

owner-occupier n persona f che abita in una casa di sua proprietà

ownership /'əʊnəʃɪp/ n proprietà f

ox /ɒks/ n (pl **oxen**) bue m (pl buoi)

Oxbridge /'ɒksbrɪdʒ/ n le università di Oxford e Cambridge

oxide /'ɒksaɪd/ n ossido m

oxidize /'ɒksɪdaɪz/ **1** vt ossidare
2 vi ossidarsi

oxygen /'ɒksɪdʒən/ n ossigeno m

oxygen mask n maschera f ad ossigeno

oyster /'ɔɪstə(r)/ n ostrica f

oz abbr (**ounce(s)**) oncia f

ozone /'əʊzəʊn/ n ozono m

ozone depletion n distruzione f dell'ozonosfera

ozone-friendly adj che non danneggia l'ozono

ozone layer n fascia f d'ozono

Pp

p, P /piː/ n (letter) p, P f inv; Br abbr **penny, pence**

p & p n abbr (**postage and packing**) spese fpl di spedizione

P45 n Br (form) ≈ modello CUD m

PA abbr (**personal assistant**) segretario, -a mf personale; Am abbr (**Pennsylvania**) Pennsylvania f

p.a. abbr (**per annum**) all'anno

pace /peɪs/ **1** n passo m; (speed) ritmo m; **keep ∼ with** camminare di pari passo con
2 vi ∼ **up and down** camminare avanti e indietro

pacemaker /'peɪsmeɪkə(r)/ n Med pacemaker m inv; (runner) battistrada m inv

pace-setter n (athlete) battistrada m inv

Pacific /pə'sɪfɪk/ adj & n **the ∼ [Ocean]** l'oceano m Pacifico, il Pacifico

pacifier /'pæsɪfaɪə(r)/ n Am ciuccio m, succhiotto m

pacifism /'pæsɪfɪzm/ n pacifismo m

pacifist /'pæsɪfɪst/ n pacifista mf

pacify /'pæsɪfaɪ/ vt (pt/pp **-led**) placare ⟨person⟩; pacificare ⟨country⟩

pack /pæk/ **1** n (of cards) mazzo m; (of hounds) muta f; (of wolves, thieves) branco m; (of cigarettes etc) pacchetto m; **a ∼ of lies** un mucchio di bugie
2 vt impacchettare ⟨article⟩; fare ⟨suitcase⟩; mettere in valigia ⟨swimsuit etc⟩; (press down) comprimere; ∼**ed** (crowded) strapieno, pieno zeppo
3 vi fare i bagagli; **send somebody ∼ing** fam mandare qualcuno a quel paese
■ **pack in** vt fam mollare ⟨job⟩; ∼ **it in!** (stop it) piantala!
■ **pack off** vt (send) spedire

■ **pack out** *vt* be ~ed out ⟨*cinema, shops*⟩ essere strapieno, essere pieno zeppo

■ **pack up** ① *vt* impacchettare ② *vi* fam ⟨*machine*⟩ guastarsi

package /'pækɪdʒ/ ① *n* pacco *m* ② *vt* impacchettare

package deal *n* offerta *f* tutto compreso

package holiday *n* vacanza *f* organizzata

package tour *n* viaggio *m* organizzato

packaging /'pækɪdʒɪŋ/ *n* (materials) confezione *f*; (promotion: of product) presentazione *f* pubblicitaria

packed /pækt/ *adj* pieno zeppo; ~ **with** pieno zeppo di

packed lunch *n* pranzo *m* al sacco

packer /'pækə(r)/ *n* (in factory) imballatore, -trice *mf*

packet /'pækɪt/ *n* pacchetto *m*; **cost a** ~ fam costare un sacco

pack ice *n* banchisa *f*

packing /'pækɪŋ/ *n* imballaggio *m*

pact /pækt/ *n* patto *m*

pad[1] /pæd/ ① *n* imbottitura *f*; (for writing) bloc-notes *m inv*, taccuino *m*; (fam: home) casa *f* ② *vt* (pt/pp **padded**) imbottire

pad[2] *vi* (pt/pp **padded**) camminare con passo felpato

■ **pad out** *vt* gonfiare

padded bra *n* reggiseno *m* imbottito

padded cell *n* cella *f* con le pareti imbottite

padded envelope *n* busta *f* imbottita

padded shoulders *npl* spalline *fpl* imbottite

padding /'pædɪŋ/ *n* imbottitura *f*; (in written work) fronzoli *mpl*

paddle /'pædl/ ① *n* pagaia *f*; **go for a** ~ sguazzare ② *vt* (row) spingere remando ③ *vi* (wade) sguazzare

paddling pool *n* (public) piscina *f* per bambini; (inflatable) piscina *f* gonfiabile

paddock /'pædək/ *n* recinto *m*

padlock /'pædlɒk/ ① *n* lucchetto *m* ② *vt* chiudere con lucchetto

padre /'pɑːdreɪ/ *n* padre *m*

Padua /'pædjʊə/ *n* Padova *f*

paediatric /piːdɪ'ætrɪk/ *adj* pediatrico

paediatrician /piːdɪə'trɪʃn/ *n* pediatra *mf*

paediatrics /piːdɪ'ætrɪks/ *n* pediatria *f*

paedophile /'piːdəfaɪl/ *n* pedofilo, -a *mf*

paedophilia /piːdəʊ'fɪlɪə/ *n* pedofilia *f*

pagan /'peɪɡən/ *adj & n* pagano, -a *mf*

paganism /'peɪɡənɪzm/ *n* paganesimo *m*

page[1] /peɪdʒ/ *n* pagina *f*

page[2] ① *n* (boy) paggetto *m*; (in hotel) fattorino *m* ② *vt* far chiamare ⟨*person*⟩

pageant /'pædʒənt/ *n* parata *f*

pageantry /'pædʒəntrɪ/ *n* cerimoniale *m*

pageboy *n* (at wedding) paggio *m*

page proof *n* bozza *f* definitiva

pager /'peɪdʒə(r)/ *n* cercapersone *m inv*

page three *n* Br terza pagina *f* di quotidiano scandalistico inglese con una pin-up

page three girl *n* Br pin-up *f inv*

paid /peɪd/ ① ▶ PAY ② *adj* ~ **employment** lavoro *m* remunerato; **put** ~ **to** mettere fine a

paid-up *adj* Br ⟨*member*⟩ che ha pagato la sua quota; ⟨*instalment*⟩ versato

pail /peɪl/ *n* secchio *m*

pain /peɪn/ ① *n* dolore *m*; **be in** ~ soffrire; **take** ~**s to do something** fare il possibile per fare qualcosa; ~ **in the neck** fam rottura *f* di scatole; ⟨*person*⟩ rompiscatole *mf inv* ② *vt* fig addolorare

pained /peɪnd/ *adj* addolorato

painful /'peɪnfʊl/ *adj* doloroso; (laborious) penoso

painfully /'peɪnfʊlɪ/ *adv* ~ **shy** incredibilmente timido

painkiller /'peɪnkɪlə(r)/ *n* calmante *m*

painkilling /'peɪnkɪlɪŋ/ *adj* antinevralgico

painless /'peɪnlɪs/ *adj* indolore

painlessly /'peɪnlɪslɪ/ *adv* in modo indolore

painstaking /'peɪnzteɪkɪŋ/ *adj* minuzioso

paint /peɪnt/ ① *n* pittura *f*; ~**s** *pl* colori *mpl* ② *vt/i* pitturare; ⟨*artist*⟩ dipingere; ~ **the town red** folleggiare

■ **paint over** *vt* (cover with paint) coprire di vernice

paintbox /'peɪntbɒks/ *n* scatola *f* di colori

paintbrush /'peɪntbrʌʃ/ *n* pennello *m*

painter /'peɪntə(r)/ *n* pittore, -trice *mf*; (decorator) imbianchino *m*

pain threshold *n* soglia *f* del dolore

painting /'peɪntɪŋ/ *n* pittura *f*; (picture) dipinto *m*

paintpot *n* latta *f* di pittura

paint remover *n* sverniciante *m*

paint roller *n* rullo *m*

paint spray *n* pistola *f* a spruzzo

paint stripper *n* (tool) macchina *f* sverniciante; (chemical) sverniciante *m*

paintwork *n* pittura *f*

pair /peə(r)/ n paio m; (of people) coppia f:
a ~ of trousers/scissors un paio di
pantaloni/forbici
■ **pair off** vi mettersi in coppia
■ **pair up** vi ‹dancers› fare coppia; (for
game) formare una coppia

paisley /'peɪzlɪ/ n motivo m cachemire
inv

pajamas /pə'dʒɑːməz/ npl Am pigiama
msg

Pakistan /pɑːkɪ'stɑːn/ n Pakistan m

Pakistani /pɑːkɪ'stɑːnɪ/ adj & n
pakistano, -a mf

pal /pæl/ n fam amico, -a mf
■ **pal up** vi (fam: become friends) fare
amicizia (with con)

palace /'pælɪs/ n palazzo m

palaentology /pælɪən'tɒlədʒɪ/ n
paleontologia f

palaeontologist /pælɪən'tɒlədʒɪst/ n
paleontologo, -a mf

palatable /'pælətəbl/ adj gradevole al
gusto

palate /'pælət/ n palato m

palatial /pə'leɪʃl/ adj sontuoso

palaver /pə'lɑːvə(r)/ n (fam: fuss) storie
fpl

pale[1] /peɪl/ n (stake) palo m; **beyond the ~**
fig inaccettabile

pale[2] [1] adj pallido
[2] vi impallidire; ~ **into insignificance**
diventare insignificante

paleness /'peɪlnɪs/ n pallore m

Palestine /'pælɪstaɪn/ n Palestina f

Palestinian /pælə'stɪnɪən/ adj & n
palestinese mf

palette /'pælɪt/ n tavolozza f

palette knife n spatola f

paling /'peɪlɪŋ/ n (stake) palo m; (fence)
palizzata f

palisade /pælɪ'seɪd/ n (fence) palizzata f

pall /pɔːl/ [1] n drappo m funebre; fig velo
m di tristezza; (of smoke) cappa f
[2] vi stufare

pallet /'pælɪt/ n pallet m inv

palliative /'pælɪətɪv/ n palliativo m

pallid /'pælɪd/ adj pallido

pallor /'pælə(r)/ n pallore m

palm /pɑːm/ n palmo m; (tree) palma f
■ **palm off** vt ~ **something off on
somebody** rifilare qualcosa a qualcuno

palmist /'pɑːmɪst/ n chiromante mf

palmistry /'pɑːmɪstrɪ/ n chiromanzia f

Palm Sunday n Domenica f delle
Palme

palmtop [computer] n Comput
palmtop m inv

palpable /'pælpəbl/ adj palpabile;
(perceptible) tangibile

palpate /pæl'peɪt/ vi palpare

palpitate /'pælpɪteɪt/ vi palpitare

palpitations /pælpɪ'teɪʃnz/ npl
palpitazioni fpl

paltry /'pɔːltrɪ/ adj (-ler, -lest)
insignificante

pampas /'pæmpəs/ n pampas fpl

pamper /'pæmpə(r)/ vt viziare

pamphlet /'pæmflɪt/ n opuscolo m

pan /pæn/ [1] n tegame m, pentola f; (for
frying) padella f; (of scales) piatto m
[2] vt (pt/pp **panned**) (fam: criticize)
stroncare
■ **pan out** vi (fam: develop) mettersi

panacea /pænə'siːə/ n panacea f

panache /pə'næʃ/ n stile m

Panama /'pænəmɑː/ n Panama m; **the ~
Canal** il canale di Panama

pancake /'pænkeɪk/ n crêpe f inv,
frittella f

Pancake Day n martedì m inv grasso

pancreas /'pæŋkrɪəs/ n pancreas m inv

panda /'pændə/ n panda m inv

panda car n macchina f della polizia

pandemonium /pændɪ'məʊnɪəm/ n
pandemonio m

pander /'pændə(r)/ vi ~ **to somebody**
compiacere qualcuno

pane /peɪn/ n ~ **[of glass]** vetro m

panel /'pænl/ n pannello m; (group of
people) giuria f; ~ **of experts** gruppo m di
esperti; ~ **of judges** giuria f

panelling /'pænəlɪŋ/ n pannelli mpl

panellist /'pænəlɪst/ n Radio, TV
partecipante mf

pan-fry vt friggere

pang /pæŋ/ n ~**s of hunger** morsi mpl
della fame; ~**s of conscience** rimorsi mpl
di coscienza

panhandler /'pænhændlə(r)/ n Am: fam
mendicante mf

panic /'pænɪk/ [1] n panico m
[2] vi (pt/pp **panicked**) lasciarsi
prendere dal panico

panic button n fam **hit the ~** ~ farsi
prendere dal panico

panic buying n accaparramento m

panicky /'pænɪkɪ/ adj che si lascia
prendere dal panico facilmente

panic-stricken /'pænɪkstrɪkən/ adj in
preda al panico

pannier /'pænɪə(r)/ n (on bike) borsa f; (on
mule) bisaccia f

panorama /pænə'rɑːmə/ n panorama m

panoramic /pænə'ræmɪk/ adj
panoramico

pan scourer n paglietta f

pansy /'pænzɪ/ n viola f del pensiero;
(fam: effeminate man) finocchio m

pant /pænt/ vi ansimare

pantechnicon /pæn'teknɪkən/ *n* furgone *m* per traslochi

panther /'pænθə(r)/ *n* pantera *f*

panties /'pæntɪz/ *npl* mutandine *fpl*

panting /'pæntɪŋ/ *adj* ansante

pantomime /'pæntəmaɪm/ *n* pantomima *f*

pantry /'pæntrɪ/ *n* dispensa *f*

pants /pænts/ *npl* (underwear) mutande *fpl*; (woman's) mutandine *fpl*; (trousers) pantaloni *mpl*

panty girdle /'pæntɪ/ *n* guaina *f*

pantyhose *n* Am collant *m inv*

panty-liner *n* salvaslip *m inv*

papal /'peɪpl/ *adj* papale

paparazzi /pæpə'rætzɪ/ *npl* paparazzi *mpl*

paper /'peɪpə(r)/ **1** *n* carta *f*; (wallpaper) carta *f* da parati; (newspaper) giornale *m*; (exam) esame *m* scritto; (treatise) saggio *m*: ∼s *pl* (documents) documenti *mpl*; (for identification) documento *msg* [d'identità]; **on** ∼ in teoria; **put down on** ∼ mettere per iscritto
2 *attrib* di carta; (version) su carta
3 *vt* tappezzare
■ **paper over** *vt* ∼ **over the cracks** dissimulare le divergenze

paperback *n* edizione *f* economica

paper bank *n* contenitore *m* per la raccolta della carta

paper boy *n* ragazzo *m* che recapita i giornali a domicilio

paper chain *n* festone *m* di carta

paper chase *n* corsa *f* campestre in cui i partecipanti seguono una scia di pezzetti di carta

paper clip *n* graffetta *f*

paper currency *n* banconote *fpl*

paper feed tray *n* Comput vassoio *m* della carta

paperknife *n* tagliacarte *m inv*

paper mill *n* cartiera *f*

paper money *n* cartamoneta *f*

paper napkin *n* tovagliolo *m* di carta

paper round *n* he does a ∼ ∼ recapita i giornali a domicilio

paper shop *n* edicola *f*

paper shredder *n* distruttore *m* di documenti

paper-thin *adj* sottilissimo

paper towel *n* (toilet) asciugamano *m* di carta; (kitchen) carta *f* asciugatutto

paper-weight *n* fermacarte *m inv*

paperwork *n* lavoro *m* d'ufficio

papery /'peɪpərɪ/ *adj* ⟨texture, leaves⟩ cartaceo

paprika /pə'priːkə/ *n* paprica *f*

Papua New Guinea /'pæpjʊə/ *n* Papua Nuova Guinea *f*

par /pɑː(r)/ *n* (in golf) par *m inv*; **on a** ∼ **with** alla pari con; **feel below** ∼ essere un po' giù di tono

para¹ /'pærə/ *n* (paragraph) paragrafo *m*

para² *n* Br Mil para *m inv*

parable /'pærəbl/ *n* parabola *f*

parachute /'pærəʃuːt/ **1** *n* paracadute *m inv*
2 *vi* lanciarsi col paracadute

parachute drop *n* (of supplies) lancio *m* col paracadute

parachute jump *n* lancio *m* col paracadute

parachuting /'pærəʃuːtɪŋ/ *n* paracadutismo *m*

parachutist /'pærəʃuːtɪst/ *n* paracadutista *mf*

parade /pə'reɪd/ **1** *n* (military) parata *f* militare; (display) sfoggio *m*
2 *vi* sfilare
3 *vt* (show off) far sfoggio di

paradigm /'pærədaɪm/ *n* paradigma *m*

paradise /'pærədaɪs/ *n* paradiso *m*

paradox /'pærədɒks/ *n* paradosso *m*

paradoxical /pærə'dɒksɪkl/ *adj* paradossale

paradoxically /pærə'dɒksɪklɪ/ *adv* paradossalmente

paraffin /'pærəfɪn/ *n* paraffina *f*; (oil) cherosene *m*

paragliding /'pærəglaɪdɪŋ/ *n* parapendio *m*

paragon /'pærəgən/ *n* ∼ **of virtue** modello *m* di virtù

paragraph /'pærəgrɑːf/ *n* paragrafo *m*

Paraguay /'pærəgwaɪ/ *n* Paraguay *m*

parallel /'pærəlel/ **1** *adj & adv* parallelo
2 *n* Geog, fig parallelo *m*; (line) parallelo *f*
3 *vt* essere paragonabile a

parallel bars *npl* parallele *fpl*

parallelogram /pærə'leləʊgræm/ *n* Math parallelogramma *m*

parallel port *n* Comput porta *f* parallela

Paralympics *npl* Paraolimpiadi *fpl*

paralyse /'pærəlaɪz/ *vt* paralizzare

paralysis /pə'ræləsɪs/ *n* (pl **-ses**) /pə'ræləsiːz/ paralisi *f inv*

paralytic /pærə'lɪtɪk/ *adj* ⟨person⟩ paralitico; ⟨arm, leg⟩ paralizzato; (Br fam; drunk) ubriaco fradicio

paramedic /pærə'medɪk/ *n* paramedico *m*

parameter /pə'ræmɪtə(r)/ *n* parametro *m*

paramilitary /pærə'mɪlɪtrɪ/ **1** *n* appartenente *mf* ad un gruppo paramilitare
2 *adj* paramilitare

paramount /'pærəmaʊnt/ *adj* supremo; **be** ∼ essere essenziale

paranoia /pærə'nɔɪə/ n paranoia f

paranoid /'pærənɔɪd/ adj paranoico

paranormal /pærə'nɔːməl/ adj & n paranormale m

parapet /'pærəpɪt/ n parapetto m

paraphernalia /pærəfə'neɪlɪə/ n armamentario m

paraphrase /'pærəfreɪz/ ① n parafrasi f inv
② vt parafrasare

paraplegic /pærə'pliːdʒɪk/ adj & n paraplegico, -a mf

parascending /'pærəsendɪŋ/ n Br paracadutismo m ascensionale

parasite /'pærəsaɪt/ n parassita mf

parasitic /pærə'sɪtɪk/ adj parassitario

parasol /'pærəsɒl/ n parasole m

paratrooper /'pærətruːpə(r)/ n paracadutista m

parboil /'pɑːbɔɪl/ vt scottare

parcel /'pɑːsl/ n pacco m
■ **parcel up** vt impacchettare ‹clothes etc›

parcel bomb n pacco m bomba inv

parch /pɑːtʃ/ vt dissecare

parched /'pɑːtʃt/ adj ‹land› riarso; (thirsty) I'm ~ sto morendo di sete

parchment /'pɑːtʃmənt/ n pergamena f

pardon /'pɑːdn/ ① n perdono m; Jur grazia f; ~? prego?; I beg your ~? fml chiedo scusa? I do beg your ~ (sorry) chiedo scusa!
② vt perdonare; Jur graziare

pare /peə(r)/ vt (peel) pelare

parent /'peərənt/ n genitore m

parentage /'peərəntɪdʒ/ n natali mpl

parental /pə'rentl/ adj dei genitori

parent company n casa f madre

parenthesis /pə'renθəsɪs/ n (pl **-ses** /pə'renθəsiːz/) parentesi f inv

parenthood /'peərənthʊd/ n (fatherhood) paternità f; (motherhood) maternità f

parenting /'peərəntɪŋ/ n educazione f dei figli; ~ classes corsi di sostegno pratico e psicologico per nuovi genitori

parents' evening n riunione f dei genitori degli alunni

parer /'peərə(r)/ n sbucciatore m

pariah /pə'raɪə/ n paria m

parings /'peərɪŋz/ npl (of fruit) bucce fpl; (of nails) ritagli mpl di unghie

Paris /'pærɪs/ n Parigi f

parish /'pærɪʃ/ n parrocchia f

parishioner /pə'rɪʃənə(r)/ n parrocchiano, -a mf

parish priest n (Catholic) parroco m; (Protestant) pastore m

Parisian /pə'rɪzɪən/ adj & n parigino, -a mf

parity /'pærɪtɪ/ n parità f

park /pɑːk/ ① n parco m
② vt Auto posteggiare, parcheggiare; ~ oneself fam installarsi
③ vi posteggiare, parcheggiare

parka /'pɑːkə/ n parka m inv

park-and-ride n parcheggio m collegato al centro di una città da mezzi pubblici

parking /'pɑːkɪŋ/ n parcheggio m, posteggio m; 'no ~' 'divieto di sosta'

parking attendant n parcheggiatore, -trice mf, posteggiatore, -trice mf

parking lot n Am posteggio m, parcheggio m

parking meter n parchimetro m

parking space n posteggio m, parcheggio m

parkland n parco m

park ranger, **park warden** n guardaparco m inv

parliament /'pɑːləmənt/ n parlamento m

parliamentary /pɑːlə'mentərɪ/ adj parlamentare

parlour /'pɑːlə(r)/ n salotto m

parochial /pə'rəʊkɪəl/ adj parrocchiale; fig ristretto

parochialism /pə'rəʊkɪəlɪzm/ n campanilismo m

parody /'pærədɪ/ ① n parodia f
② vt (pt/pp **-ied**) parodiare

parole /pə'rəʊl/ ① n on ~ sulla parola; eligible for ~ suscettibile di essere liberato sulla parola
② vt mettere in libertà sulla parola

paroxysm /'pærəksɪzm/ n accesso m

parquet floor /'pɑːkeɪ/ n parquet m

parquet flooring /'flɔːrɪŋ/ n parquet m inv

parrot /'pærət/ n pappagallo m

parry /'pærɪ/ vt (pt/pp **-ied**) parare ‹blow›; (in fencing) eludere

parse /pɑːz/ vt fare l'analisi grammaticale di ‹sentence›; Comput analizzare la sintassi di

parsimonious /pɑːsɪ'məʊnɪəs/ adj parsimonioso

parsing /'pɑːzɪŋ/ n analisi f grammaticale; Comput analisi f sintattica

parsley /'pɑːslɪ/ n prezzemolo m

parsnip /'pɑːsnɪp/ n pastinaca f

parson /'pɑːsn/ n pastore m

part /pɑːt/ ① n parte f; (of machine) pezzo m; for my ~ per quanto mi riguarda; on the ~ of da parte di; take sb's ~ prendere le parti di qualcuno; take ~ in prendere parte a
② adv in parte
③ vt ~ one's hair farsi la riga
④ vi ‹people› separarsi; ~ with separarsi da

part exchange *n* take in ∼ ∼ prendere indietro come pagamento parziale

partial /'pɑːʃl/ *adj* parziale; be ∼ to aver un debole per

partiality /pɑːʃɪ'ælətɪ/ *n* (liking) predilezione *f*

partially /'pɑːʃəlɪ/ *adv* parzialmente; ∼ **sighted** parzialmente cieco

participant /pɑː'tɪsɪpənt/ *n* partecipante *mf*

participate /pɑː'tɪsɪpeɪt/ *vi* partecipare (in a)

participation /pɑːtɪsɪ'peɪʃn/ *n* partecipazione *f*

participatory /pɑːtɪsɪ'peɪtərɪ/ *adj* partecipativo

participle /'pɑːtɪsɪpl/ *n* participio *m*; **present/past** ∼ participio presente/passato

particle /'pɑːtɪkl/ *n* Phys, Gram particella *f*

particular /pə'tɪkjʊlə(r)/ *adj* particolare; (precise) meticoloso; pej difficile; **in** ∼ in particolare

particularly /pə'tɪkjʊləlɪ/ *adv* particolarmente

particulars /pə'tɪkjʊləz/ *npl* particolari *mpl*

parting /'pɑːtɪŋ/ **1** *n* separazione *f*; (in hair) scriminatura *f* **2** *attrib* di commiato

partisan /pɑːtɪ'zæn/ *n* partigiano, -a *mf*

partition /pɑː'tɪʃn/ **1** *n* (wall) parete *f* divisoria; Pol divisione *f* **2** *vt* dividere

■ **partition off** *vt* separare

partly /'pɑːtlɪ/ *adv* in parte

partner /'pɑːtnə(r)/ *n* Comm socio, -a *mf*; (sport, in relationship) compagno, -a *mf*

partnership /'pɑːtnəʃɪp/ *n* Comm società *f inv*

part of speech *n* categoria *f* grammaticale

part owner *n* comproprietario, -a *mf*

part payment *n* acconto *m*

partridge /'pɑːtrɪdʒ/ *n* pernice *f*

part-time *adj & adv* part time; **be** or **work** ∼ lavorare part time

part-way *adv* ∼ **through the evening** a metà serata

party /'pɑːtɪ/ *n* ricevimento *m*, festa *f*; (group) gruppo *m*; Pol partito *m*; Jur parte *f*; **be** ∼ to essere parte attiva in

party animal *n* festaiolo, -a *mf*

party dress *n* abito *m* da sera

party-goer *n* festaiolo, -a *mf*

party hat *n* cappellino *m* di carta

party leader *n* dirigente *m* di partito

party line *n* Teleph duplex *m inv*; Pol linea *f* del partito

party piece *n* pezzo *m* forte; **do one's** ∼ ∼ esibirsi nel proprio pezzo forte

party political broadcast *n* comunicato *m* di partito (trasmesso per radio o per televisione)

party politics *n* politica *f* di partito

party wall *n* muro *m* divisorio

pass /pɑːs/ **1** *n* lasciapassare *m inv*; (in mountains) passo *m*; Sport passaggio *m*; (Sch: mark) [voto *m*] sufficiente *m*; **get a** ∼ Sch ottenere la sufficienza; **make a** ∼ **at** fam fare delle avances a **2** *vt* passare; (overtake) sorpassare; (approve) far passare; (exceed) oltrepassare; fare ⟨remark⟩; esprimere ⟨judgement⟩; Jur pronunciare ⟨sentence⟩; ∼ **water** orinare; ∼ **the time** passare il tempo **3** *vi* passare; (in exam) essere promosso; **let something** ∼ fig lasciar correre qualcosa; ∼**!** (in game) passo!

■ **pass as** *vt* = PASS FOR

■ **pass away** *vi* mancare

■ **pass by** *vi* (go past) passare

■ **pass down** *vt* passare; fig trasmettere

■ **pass for** *vt* (be accepted as) passare per

■ **pass off** **1** *vi* (disappear) passare; (take place) svolgersi **2** *vt* ∼ **somebody/something off as** far passare qualcuno/qualcosa per

■ **pass on** *vt* passare ⟨message, information⟩

■ **pass on to** *vt* passare a ⟨new subject, next question⟩

■ **pass out** *vi* fam svenire

■ **pass over** **1** *vt* (not mention) passare sopra a; ∼ **somebody over for promotion** non prendere in considerazione qualcuno per una promozione **2** *vi* (die) spirare

■ **pass round** *vt* far passare

■ **pass through** *vt* attraversare

■ **pass up** *vt* passare; (fam: miss) lasciarsi scappare

passable /'pɑːsəbl/ *adj* ⟨road⟩ praticabile; (satisfactory) passabile

passage /'pæsɪdʒ/ *n* passaggio *m*; (corridor) corridoio *m*; (voyage) traversata *f*

pass book *n* Fin libretto *m* di risparmio

passé /pæ'seɪ/ *adj* pej sorpassato

passenger /'pæsɪndʒə(r)/ *n* passeggero, -a *mf*

passenger compartment *n* Br Auto abitacolo *m*

passenger ferry *n* traghetto *m*

passenger plane *n* aereo *m* passeggeri

passenger seat *n* posto *m* accanto al guidatore

passenger train *n* treno *m* passeggeri

passepartout /pæspɑː'tuː/ *n* (key, frame) passe-partout *m inv*

passer-by /pɑːsə'baɪ/ *n* (pl **-s-by**) passante *mf*

passing /'pɑːsɪŋ/ *adj* ‹motorist› di passaggio; ‹thought› di sfuggita; ‹reference› en passant; ‹resemblance› vago

passing place /'pɑːsɪŋ/ *n* piazzola *f* di sosta per consentire il transito dei veicoli nei due sensi

passing shot *n* Tennis passante *m*

passion /'pæʃn/ *n* passione *f*

passionate /'pæʃənət/ *adj* appassionato

passionately /'pæʃənətlɪ/ *adv* appassionatamente

passion fruit *n* frutto *m* della passione

passive /'pæsɪv/ *adj & n* passivo *m*

passively /'pæsɪvlɪ/ *adv* passivamente

passiveness /'pæsɪvnɪs/ *n* passività *f*

passive resistance *n* resistenza *f* passiva

passive smoking *n* fumo *m* passivo

pass-key *n* (master-key) passe-partout *m* inv; (for access) chiave *f*

pass mark *n* Sch [voto *m*] sufficiente *m*

Passover *n* Pasqua *f* ebraica

passport *n* passaporto *m*

password *n* parola *f* d'ordine

password-protected *adj* Comput ‹file, site› protetto da password

past /pɑːst/ ① *adj* passato; (former) ex; that's all ∼ tutto questo è passato; in the ∼ few days nei giorni scorsi; the ∼ week la settimana scorsa
② *n* passato *m*
③ *prep* oltre; at ten ∼ two alle due e dieci
④ *adv* oltre; go/come ∼ passare

pasta /'pæstə/ *n* pasta [asciutta] *f*

paste /peɪst/ ① *n* pasta *f*; (dough) impasto *m*; (adhesive) colla *f*
② *vt* incollare
▪ **paste down** *vt* incollare
▪ **paste in** *vt* incollare
▪ **paste up** *vt* affiggere ‹notice, poster›

paste jewellery *n* bigiotteria *f*

pastel /'pæstl/ ① *n* pastello *m*
② *attrib* pastello

pasteurization /pɑːstʃəraɪ'zeɪʃn/ *n* pastorizzazione *f*

pasteurize /'pɑːstʃəraɪz/ *vt* pastorizzare

pasteurized /'pɑːstʃəraɪzd/ *adj* pastorizzato

pastille /'pæstɪl/ *n* pastiglia *f*

pastime /'pɑːstaɪm/ *n* passatempo *m*

pasting /'peɪstɪŋ/ *n* (fam: defeat, criticism) batosta *f*

past master *n* esperto, -a *mf*

pastor /'pɑːstə(r)/ *n* pastore *m*

pastoral /'pɑːstərəl/ *adj* pastorale

past participle *n* participio *m* passato

pastrami /pæ'strɑːmɪ/ *n* carne di manzo affumicata

pastry /'peɪstrɪ/ *n* pasta *f*; **pastries** *pl* pasticcini *mpl*

past tense *n* passato *m*

pasture /'pɑːstʃə/ *n* pascolo *m*

pasty¹ /'pæstɪ/ *n* ≈ pasticcio *m*

pasty² /'peɪstɪ/ *adj* smorto

pat /pæt/ ① *n* buffetto *m*; (of butter) pezzetto *m*
② *adv* have something off ∼ conoscere qualcosa a menadito
③ *vt* (pt/pp **patted**) dare un buffetto a; ∼ somebody on the back fig congratularsi con qualcuno

patch /pætʃ/ ① *n* toppa *f*; (spot) chiazza; *f*; (period) periodo *m*: not a ∼ on fam molto inferiore a
② *vt* mettere una toppa su
▪ **patch up** *vt* riparare alla bell'e meglio; appianare ‹quarrel›

patchwork /'pætʃwɜːk/ *n* patchwork *m* inv; fig mosaico *m*

patchy /'pætʃɪ/ *adj* incostante

pâté /'pæteɪ/ *n* pâté *m* inv

patent /'peɪtnt/ ① *adj* palese
② *n* brevetto *m*
③ *vt* brevettare

patent leather *n* vernice *m*

patently /'peɪtntlɪ/ *adv* in modo palese

paternal /pə'tɜːnl/ *adj* paterno

paternalism /pə'tɜːnəlɪzm/ *n* paternalismo *m*

paternalistic /pətɜːnə'lɪstɪk/ *adj* paternalistico

paternity /pə'tɜːnɪtɪ/ *n* paternità *f*

paternity leave *n* congedo *m* di paternità

paternity suit *n* causa *f* per il riconoscimento di paternità

path /pɑːθ/ *n* (pl ∼s /pɑːðz/) sentiero *m*; (orbit) traiettoria *f*; fig strada *f*

pathetic /pə'θetɪk/ *adj* patetico; (fam: very bad) penoso

pathological /pæθə'lɒdʒɪkl/ *adj* patologico

pathologist /pə'θɒlədʒɪst/ *n* patologo, -a *mf*

pathology /pə'θɒlədʒɪ/ *n* patologia *f*

pathos /'peɪθɒs/ *n* pathos *m*

patience /'peɪʃns/ *n* pazienza *f*; (game) solitario *m*

patient /'peɪʃnt/ *adj & n* paziente *mf*

patiently /'peɪʃntlɪ/ *adv* pazientemente

patio /'pætɪəʊ/ *n* terrazza *f*

patio doors *npl* portafinestra *f*

patio garden *n* cortile *m*

patriarch /'peɪtrɪɑːk/ *n* patriarca *m*

patriarchal /peɪtrɪ'ɑːkəl/ *adj* patriarcale

patriarchy /'peɪtrɪɑːkɪ/ *n* patriarcato *m*

patriot /'pætrɪət/ *n* patriota *mf*

patriotic /pætrɪ'ɒtɪk/ *adj* patriottico

patriotism /'pætrɪətɪzm/ n patriottismo m

patrol /pə'trəʊl/ ① n pattuglia f ② vt/i pattugliare

patrol boat n motovedetta f

patrol car n autopattuglia f

patron /'peɪtrən/ n patrono m; (of charity) benefattore, -trice mf; (of the arts) mecenate mf; (customer) cliente mf

patronage /'pætrənɪdʒ/ n patrocinio m; (of shop etc) frequentazione f

patronize /'pætrənaɪz/ vt frequentare abitualmente; fig trattare con condiscendenza

patronizing /'pætrənaɪzɪŋ/ adj condiscendente

patronizingly /'pætrənaɪzɪŋlɪ/ adv con condiscendenza

patron saint n [santo, -a mf] patrono, -a mf

patter¹ /'pætə(r)/ ① n picchiettio m ② vi picchiettare

patter² n (of salesman) chiacchiere fpl

pattern /'pætn/ n motivo m; (for knitting, sewing, in behaviour) modello m

patterned /'pætənd/ adj ⟨material⟩ fantasia

paunch /pɔːntʃ/ n pancia f

pauper /'pɔːpə(r)/ n povero, -a mf

pause /pɔːz/ ① n pausa f ② vi fare una pausa

pave /peɪv/ vt pavimentare; ∼ the way preparare la strada (for a)

pavement /'peɪvmənt/ n marciapiede m

pavement café n caffè m con tavolini all'aperto

pavilion /pə'vɪljən/ n padiglione m; (Cricket) costruzione f annessa al campo da gioco con gli spogliatoi

paving /'peɪvɪŋ/ n lastricato m

paving slab, paving stone n lastra f di pietra

paw /pɔː/ ① n zampa f ② vt fam mettere le zampe addosso a

pawn¹ /pɔːn/ n (in chess) pedone m; fig pedina f

pawn² ① vt impegnare ② n in ∼ in pegno

pawnbroker /'pɔːnbrəʊkə(r)/ n prestatore, -trice mf su pegno

pawnshop /'pɔːnʃɒp/ n monte m di pietà

pawpaw /'pɔːpɔː/ n papaia f

pay /peɪ/ ① n paga f; in the ∼ of al soldo di
② vt (pt/pp **paid**) pagare; prestare ⟨attention⟩; fare ⟨compliment, visit⟩; ∼ cash pagare in contanti
③ vi pagare; (be profitable) rendere; it doesn't ∼ to... fig è fatica sprecata...; ∼ in instalments pagare a rate; ∼ through the nose fam pagare profumatamente
■ **pay back** vt ripagare
■ **pay for** vt pagare per
■ **pay in** vt versare
■ **pay off** ① vt saldare ⟨debt⟩ ② vi fig dare dei frutti
■ **pay out** vt (spend) pagare
■ **pay up** vi pagare

payable /'peɪəbl/ adj pagabile; make ∼ to intestare a

pay-as-you-go adj ⟨tariff⟩ a consumo

pay cheque Br, **pay check** Am n assegno m della paga

payday n giorno m di paga

PAYE Br abbr (**pay-as-you-earn**) trattenute fpl fiscali alla fonte

payee /peɪ'iː/ n beneficiario m

payer /'peɪə(r)/ n pagante mf

paying-in slip /peɪɪŋ'ɪn/ n distinta f di versamento

payload /'peɪləʊd/ n (of bomb) carica f esplosiva; (of aircraft, ship) carico m utile

payment /'peɪmənt/ n pagamento m; ∼ by instalments pagamento m rateale

pay-packet n busta f paga inv

pay-per-view n pay per view f; ∼ programme/film un film/programma pay per view

payphone n telefono m pubblico

payroll n (list) libro m paga; (sum of money) paga f del personale; (employees collectively) personale m

payslip n busta f paga inv

pay television n pay tv f

PC abbr (**personal computer**) PC m inv; abbr (**police constable**) agente m di polizia

pc abbr (**per cent**) per cento; abbr (**politically correct**) politicamente corretto; abbr (**postcard**) cartolina f postale

pd Am abbr (**police department**) reparto m di polizia

PDF abbr (**portable document format**) Comput PDF m; a ∼ file un file PDF

PE n abbr (**physical education**) educazione f fisica

pea /piː/ n pisello m

peace /piːs/ n pace f; ∼ of mind tranquillità f

peaceable /'piːsəbl/ adj pacifico

peaceful /'piːsfʊl/ adj calmo, sereno

peacefully /'piːsfʊlɪ/ adv in pace

peacekeeping ① n Mil Pol mantenimento m della pace ② attrib ⟨force, troops⟩ di mantenimento della pace

peacemaker n mediatore, -trice mf

peace process n processo m di pace

peacetime ① n tempo m di pace ② attrib ⟨planning, government⟩ del tempo di pace; ⟨army, alliance, training⟩ in tempo di pace

peace treaty n trattato m di pace

peach /piːtʃ/ n pesca f; (tree) pesco m

peacock /'piːkɒk/ n pavone m

pea green adj verde pisello

peak /piːk/ n picco m; fig culmine m

peaked cap /piːkt/ n berretto m a punta

peak hours npl ore fpl di punta

peak period n ora f di punta

peak rate n tariffa f ore di punta; ∼ **calls** Teleph chiamate a tariffa ore di punta

peak season n alta stagione f

peak time n = PRIME TIME

peaky /'piːkɪ/ adj malaticcio

peal /piːl/ n (of bells) scampanio m; ∼**s of laughter** fragore msg di risate

peanut /'piːnʌt/ n nocciolina f [americana]; ∼**s** pl fam miseria fsg

peanut butter n burro m di arachidi

pear /peə(r)/ n pera f; (tree) pero m

pearl /pɜːl/ n perla f

pearl barley n orzo m perlato

pearl-diver n pescatore, -trice mf di perle

pearl grey ① n grigio m perla inv ② adj grigio perla inv

Pearly Gates /pɜːlɪ/ npl hum porte fpl del paradiso

peasant /'peznt/ n contadino, -a mf

peat /piːt/ n torba f

pebble /'pebl/ n ciottolo m

pebble-dash n intonaco m a pinocchino

pecan /'piːkən/ n (tree) pecan m inv; (nut) noce f pecan inv

peck /pek/ ① n beccata f; (kiss) bacetto m
② vt beccare; (kiss) dare un bacetto a
■ **peck at** vi beccare

pecking order /'pekɪŋ/ n gerarchia f

peckish /'pekɪʃ/ adj be ∼ fam avere un languorino allo stomaco

pecs /peks/ fam, **pectorals** /'pektərəlz/ npl pettorali mpl

pectoral /'pektərəl/ adj & n pettorale m

peculiar /pɪ'kjuːlɪə(r)/ adj strano; (special) particolare; ∼ **to** tipico di

peculiarity /pɪkjuːlɪ'ærətɪ/ n stranezza f; (feature) particolarità f inv

peculiarly /pɪ'kjuːlɪəlɪ/ adv singolarmente

pecuniary /pə'kjuːnɪərɪ/ adj pecuniario

pedagogical /pedə'gɒdʒɪkl/ adj pedagogico

pedagogy /'pedəgɒdʒɪ/ n pedagogia f

pedal /'pedl/ ① n pedale m
② vi pedalare

pedal bin n pattumiera f a pedale

pedant /'pedənt/ n pedante m

pedantic /pɪ'dæntɪk/ adj pedante

pedantically /pɪ'dæntɪklɪ/ adv in modo pedante

pedantry /'pedəntrɪ/ n pedanteria f

peddle /'pedl/ vt vendere porta a porta

pedestal /'pedɪstl/ n piedistallo m

pedestrian /pɪ'destrɪən/ ① n pedone m
② adj fig scadente

pedestrian crossing n passaggio m pedonale

pedestrian precinct n zona f pedonale

pediatrician /piːdɪə'trɪʃn/ n Am = PAEDIATRICIAN

pedicure /'pedɪkjʊə(r)/ n pedicure f inv

pedigree /'pedɪgriː/ ① n pedigree m inv; (of person) lignaggio m
② attrib ⟨animal⟩ di razza, con pedigree

pedlar, peddler /'pedlə(r)/ n old venditore, -trice mf ambulante; **drug** ∼ spacciatore, -trice mf di droga

pedophile /'piːdəfaɪl/ n Am = PAEDOPHILE

pee /piː/ fam ① vi (pt/pp **peed**) fare la pipì
② n go for a ∼ andare a fare la pipì

peek /piːk/ fam ① vi sbirciare
② n take a ∼ at something dare una sbirciata a qualcosa

peekaboo /piːkə'buː/ int cucù

peel /piːl/ ① n buccia f
② vt sbucciare
③ vi ⟨nose etc⟩ spellarsi; ⟨paint⟩ staccarsi
■ **peel off** ① vt togliersi ⟨item of clothing⟩
② vi ⟨wallpaper⟩ staccarsi; ⟨skin⟩ squamarsi

peeler /'piːlə(r)/ n sbucciatore m

peelings /'piːlɪŋz/ npl bucce fpl

peep /piːp/ ① n sbirciata f
② vi sbirciare

peephole /'piːphəʊl/ n spioncino m

Peeping Tom /'piːpɪŋ/ n fam guardone m

peer[1] /pɪə(r)/ vi ∼ **at** scrutare

peer[2] n nobile m; his ∼**s** pl (in rank) i suoi pari; (in age) i suoi coetanei

peerage /'pɪərɪdʒ/ n Br Pol nobiltà f; (book) almanacco m nobiliare; **be given a** ∼ essere elevato al rango di pari

peer group n (of same status) pari mpl; (of same age) coetanei mpl; ∼ ∼ **pressure** pressione f esercitata dal gruppo cui si appartiene

peerless /'pɪəlɪs/ adj impareggiabile

peeved /piːvd/ adj fam irritato

peevish /'piːvɪʃ/ adj fam irritabile

peg /peg/ ① n (hook) piolo m; (for tent) picchetto m; (for clothes) molletta f; **off the ~** fam prêt-a-porter
② vt (pt/pp **pegged**) fissare ⟨prices⟩; stendere con le mollette ⟨washing⟩

pegboard /'pegbɔːd/ n segnapunti m inv

pejorative /pɪ'dʒɒrətɪv/ adj peggiorativo

pejoratively /pɪ'dʒɒrətɪvlɪ/ adv in modo peggiorativo

peke /piːk/ n fam (dog) pechinese m

Peking /piːkɪŋ/ n Pechino f

pekin[g]ese /piːkɪ'niːz/ n pechinese m

pelican /'pelɪkən/ n pellicano m

pelican crossing n passaggio m pedonale con semaforo

pellet /'pelɪt/ n pallottola f

pell-mell /pel'mel/ adv alla rinfusa

pelmet /'pelmɪt/ n mantovana f

pelt[1] /pelt/ n (skin) pelliccia f

pelt[2] ① vt bombardare
② vi (fam: run fast) catapultarsi; (rain heavily) venir giù a fiotti
■ **pelt along** vi (move quickly) precipitarsi lungo
■ **pelt down** vi ⟨rain⟩ venir giù a fiotti

pelvis /'pelvɪs/ n Anat bacino m

pen[1] /pen/ n (for animals) recinto m

pen[2] n penna f; (ball-point) penna f a sfera

penal /'piːnl/ adj penale

penal code n codice m penale

penalize /'piːnəlaɪz/ vt penalizzare

penalty /'penltɪ/ n sanzione f; (fine) multa f; (in football) [calcio m di] rigore m

penalty area, penalty box n area f di rigore

penalty clause n Comm, Jur clausola f penale

penalty kick n [calcio m di] rigore m

penalty shoot-out n rigori mpl

penance /'penəns/ n penitenza f

pence /pens/ ▶ PENNY

penchant /'pãʃã/ n debole m

pencil ① n /'pensl/ matita f
② vt (pt/pp **pencilled**) scrivere a matita
■ **pencil in** vt annotare provvisoriamente ⟨date⟩

pencil case n [astuccio m] portamatite m inv

pencil sharpener n temperamatite m inv

pendant /'pendənt/ n ciondolo m

pending /'pendɪŋ/ ① adj in sospeso
② prep in attesa di

pendulum /'pendjʊləm/ n pendolo m

penetrate /'penɪtreɪt/ vt/i penetrare

penetrating /'penɪtreɪtɪŋ/ adj ⟨sound, stare⟩ penetrante; ⟨remark⟩ acuto

penetration /penɪ'treɪʃn/ n penetrazione f

penfriend /'penfrend/ n amico, -a mf di penna

penguin /'peŋgwɪn/ n pinguino m

penicillin /penɪ'sɪlɪn/ n penicillina f

peninsula /pɪ'nɪmsjʊlə/ n penisola f

penis /'piːnɪs/ n pene m

penitence /'penɪtəns/ n penitenza f

penitent /penɪtənt/ adj & n penitente mf

penitentiary /penɪ'tenʃərɪ/ n Am penitenziario m

penknife /'pennaɪf/ n temperino m

pen-name n pseudonimo m

pennant /'penənt/ n bandiera f

penniless /'penɪlɪs/ adj senza un soldo

penny /'penɪ/ n (pl **pence**; single coins **pennies**) penny m; Am centesimo m; **spend a ~** fam andare in bagno; **the ~'s dropped!** fam ci è arrivato!

penny-farthing n velocipede m

penny-pinching /'penɪpɪntʃɪŋ/ ① adj taccagno
② n taccagneria f

penny whistle n zufolo m

pen-pusher n fam scribacchino, -a mf

pension /'penʃn/ n pensione f
■ **pension off** vt (force to retire) mandare in pensione

pensioner /'penʃənə(r)/ n pensionato, -a mf

pension fund n fondo m pensioni; (of an individual) fondo m pensione

pension scheme n piano m di pensionamento

pensive /'pensəv/ adj pensoso

pentagon /'pentəgən/ n pentagono m; Am Pol **the P~** il Pentagono

pentagonal /pen'tægənəl/ adj pentagonale

pentathlete /pen'tæθliːt/ n pentatleta mf

pentathlon /pen'tæθlɒn/ n pentathlon m inv

Pentecost /'pentɪkɒst/ n Pentecoste f

penthouse /'penthaʊs/ n attico m

pent-up /'pentʌp/ adj represso

penultimate /pɪ'nʌltɪmət/ adj penultimo

penury /'penjʊrɪ/ n miseria f

peony /'pɪənɪ/ n peonia f

people /'piːpl/ ① npl persone fpl, gente fsg; (citizens) popolo msg; **a lot of ~** una marea di gente; **the ~** la gente; **English ~** gli inglesi; **~ say** si dice; **for four ~** per quattro
② vt popolare

people carrier n monovolume f

pep /pep/

p

■ **pep up** vt vivacizzare ⟨party, conversation⟩; tirare su ⟨person⟩

PEP /pep/ abbr Br (**personal equity plan**) piano m di investimento azionario personale

pepper /'pepə(r)/ ① n pepe m; (vegetable) peperone m
② vt (season) pepare

peppercorn n grano m di pepe

peppercorn rent affitto m nominale

pepper mill n macinapepe m inv

peppermint n menta f piperita; (sweet) caramella f alla menta

pepper pot n pepiera f

pep pill /'peppɪl/ n fam stimolante m

pep talk n discorso m d'incoraggiamento

peptic /'peptɪk/ adj peptico

peptic ulcer n ulcera f peptica

per /pɜː(r)/ prep per

per annum /pər'ænəm/ adv all'anno

per capita /pə'kæpɪtə/ adj & adv pro capite

perceive /pə'siːv/ vt percepire; (interpret) interpretare

per cent adv per cento

percentage /pə'sentɪdʒ/ n percentuale f

perceptible /pə'septəbl/ adj percettibile; fig sensibile

perceptibly /pə'septɪblɪ/ adv percettibilmente; fig sensibilmente

perception /pə'sepʃn/ n percezione f

perceptive /pə'septɪv/ adj perspicace

perch[1] /pɜːtʃ/ ① n pertica f
② vi ⟨bird⟩ appollaiarsi

perch[2] n inv (fish) pesce m persico

percolate /'pɜːkəleɪt/ vi infiltrarsi; ⟨coffee⟩ passare

percolator /'pɜːkəleɪtə(r)/ n caffettiera f a filtro

percussion /pə'kʌʃn/ n percussione f

percussion instrument n strumento m a percussione

percussionist /pə'kʌʃ(ə)nɪst/ n percussionista mf

peremptory /pə'remptərɪ/ adj perentorio

perennial /pə'renɪəl/ ① adj perenne
② n pianta f perenne

perfect[1] /'pɜːfɪkt/ ① adj perfetto
② n Gram passato m prossimo

perfect[2] /pə'fekt/ vt perfezionare

perfection /pə'fekʃn/ n perfezione f; to ∼ alla perfezione

perfectionism /pə'fekʃənɪzm/ n perfezionismo m

perfectionist /pə'fekʃ(ə)nɪst/ adj & n perfezionista mf

perfectly /'pɜːfɪktlɪ/ adv perfettamente

perfidious /pə'fɪdɪəs/ adj perfido

perforate /'pɜːfəreɪt/ vt perforare

perforated /'pɜːfəreɪtɪd/ adj perforato; ⟨ulcer⟩ perforante

perforation /pɜːfə'reɪʃn/ n perforazione f

perform /pə'fɔːm/ ① vt compiere, fare; eseguire ⟨operation, sonata⟩; recitare ⟨role⟩; mettere in scena ⟨play⟩
② vi Theat recitare; Techn funzionare

performance /pə'fɔːməns/ n esecuzione f; (at theatre, cinema) rappresentazione f; Techn rendimento m

performance artist n performance artist mf

performance bonus n premio m di produttività

performance indicators npl indicatori mpl di performance

performance-related adj commensurato alla produttività

performer /pə'fɔːmə(r)/ n artista mf

performing arts /pə'fɔːmɪŋ/ npl arti fpl dello spettacolo

perfume /'pɜːfjuːm/ n profumo m

perfumed /'pɜːfjuːmd/ adj profumato

perfunctory /pə'fʌŋktərɪ/ adj superficiale

perhaps /pə'hæps/ adv forse

peril /'perɪl/ n pericolo m

perilous /'perɪləs/ adj pericoloso

perilously /'perɪləslɪ/ adv pericolosamente

perimeter /pə'rɪmɪtə(r)/ n perimetro m

period /'pɪərɪəd/ ① n periodo m; (menstruation) mestruazioni fpl; Sch ora f di lezione; (full stop) punto m fermo
② attrib (costume) d'epoca; ⟨furniture⟩ in stile

periodic /pɪərɪ'ɒdɪk/ adj periodico

periodical /pɪərɪ'ɒdɪkl/ n periodico m, rivista f

periodically /pɪərɪ'ɒdɪklɪ/ adv periodicamente

period of notice n periodo m di preavviso

peripheral /pə'rɪfərəl/ ① adj periferico
② n Comput periferica f

periphery /pə'rɪfərɪ/ n periferia f

periscope /'perɪskəup/ n periscopio m

perish /'perɪʃ/ vi (rot) deteriorarsi; (die) perire

perishable /'perɪʃəbl/ ① adj deteriorabile
② ∼s npl merce f deperibile

perished /'perɪʃt/ adj (fam: freezing cold) be ∼ essere intirizzito

perishing /'perɪʃɪŋ/ adj fam it's ∼ fa freddo da morire

peritonitis /perɪtə'naɪtɪs/ n peritonite f

perjure /'pɜːdʒə(r)/ *vt* ~ **oneself**
spergiurare

perjury /'pɜːdʒərɪ/ *n* spergiuro *m*

perk[1] /pɜːk/ *n* fam vantaggio *m*

perk[2] *vi* Am ⟨*coffee*⟩ passare
■ **perk up** ① *vt* tirare su
② *vi* tirarsi su

perky /'pɜːkɪ/ *adj* allegro

perm /pɜːm/ ① *n* permanente *f*
② *vt* ~ **sb's hair** fare la permanente a
qno

permanent /'pɜːmənənt/ ① *adj*
permanente; ⟨*job, address*⟩ stabile
② *n* Am = PERM

permanently /'pɜːmənəntlɪ/ *adv*
stabilmente

permeable /'pɜːmɪəbl/ *adj* permeabile

permeate /'pɜːmɪeɪt/ *vt* impregnare

permissible /pə'mɪsəbl/ *adj*
ammissibile

permission /pə'mɪʃn/ *n* permesso *m*

permissive /pə'mɪsɪv/ *adj* permissivo

permit[1] /pə'mɪt/ *vt* (pt/pp **-mitted**)
permettere; ~ **somebody to do something**
permettere a qualcuno di fare qualcosa

permit[2] /'pɜːmɪt/ *n* autorizzazione *f*

pernicious /pə'nɪʃəs/ *adj* pernicioso

pernickety /pə'nɪkətɪ/ *adj* Br fam
puntiglioso, pignolo; (about food) difficile

peroxide blonde /pə'rɒksaɪd/ *n*
bionda *f* ossigenata

perpendicular /pɜːpən'dɪkjʊlə(r)/ *adj*
& *n* perpendicolare *f*

perpetrate /'pɜːpɪtreɪt/ *vt* perpetrare

perpetrator /'pɜːpɪtreɪtə(r)/ *n* autore,
-trice *mf*

perpetual /pə'petjʊəl/ *adj* perenne

perpetually /pə'petjʊəlɪ/ *adv*
perennemente

perpetuate /pə'petjʊeɪt/ *vt* perpetuare

perplex /pə'pleks/ *vt* lasciare perplesso

perplexed /pə'plekst/ *adj* perplesso

perplexity /pə'pleksɪtɪ/ *n* perplessità *f*
inv

perquisite /'pɜːsɪkjuːt/ *n* fringe benefit
m inv, beneficio *m* accessorio

per se /pɜː'seɪ/ *adv* in sé

persecute /'pɜːsɪkjuːt/ *vt* perseguitare

persecution /pɜːsɪ'kjuːʃn/ *n*
persecuzione *f*

persecutor /'pɜːsɪkjuːtə(r)/ *n*
persecutore, -trice *mf*

perseverance /pɜːsɪ'vɪərəns/ *n*
perseveranza *f*

persevere /pɜːsɪ'vɪə(r)/ *vi* perseverare

persevering /pɜːsɪ'vɪərɪŋ/ *adj* assiduo

Persian /'pɜːʃn/ *adj* persiano

persist /pə'sɪst/ *vi* persistere; ~ **in doing
something** persistere nel fare qualcosa

persistence /pə'sɪstəns/ *n* persistenza *f*

persistent /pə'sɪsənt/ *adj* persistente

persistently /pə'sɪstəntlɪ/ *adv*
persistentemente

persistent offender *n* recidivo, -a *mf*

person /'pɜːsn/ *n* persona *f*; **in** ~ di
persona

persona /pə'səʊnə/ *n* Psych individuo *m*;
Theat personaggio *m*

personable /'pɜːsənəbl/ *adj* di bella
presenza

personage /'pɜːsənɪdʒ/ *n* personaggio *m*

personal /'pɜːsənl/ *adj* personale

personal ad *n* annuncio *m* personale

personal allowance *n* (in taxation)
quota *f* non imponibile

personal assistant *n* segretario, -a
mf personale

personal belongings *npl* effetti *mpl*
personali

personal column *n* rubrica *f* degli
annunci personali

personal computer *n* personal
computer *m inv*

personal hygiene *n* igiene *f* personale

personality /pɜːsə'nælətɪ/ *n* personalità
f inv; (on TV) personaggio *m*

personalize /'pɜːsənəlaɪz/ *vt*
personalizzare ⟨*stationery, clothing*⟩;
mettere sul piano personale ⟨*issue,
dispute*⟩

personal loan *n* prestito *m* a privato

personally /'pɜːsənəlɪ/ *adv*
personalmente

personal organizer *n* Comput agenda *f*
elettronica

personal stereo *n* walkman® *m inv*

personification /pəsɒnɪfɪ'keɪʃn/ *n* the
~ **of** la personificazione di

personify /pə'sɒnɪfaɪ/ *vt* (pt/pp **-ied**)
personificare

personnel /pɜːsə'nel/ *n* personale *m*

personnel director *n* direttore, -trice
mf del personale

personnel management *n* gestione
f del personale

perspective /pə'spektɪv/ *n* prospettiva
f

perspex® /'pɜːspeks/ *n* plexiglas® *m*

perspicacious /pɜːspɪ'keɪʃəs/ *adj*
perspicace

perspiration /pɜːspɪ'reɪʃn/ *n* sudore *m*

perspire /pə'spaɪə(r)/ *vi* sudare

persuade /pə'sweɪd/ *vt* persuadere

persuasion /pə'sweɪʒn/ *n* persuasione *f*;
(belief) convinzione *f*

persuasive /pə'sweɪsɪv/ *adj* persuasivo

persuasively /pə'sweɪsɪvlɪ/ *adv* in
modo persuasivo

p

pert /pɜːt/ *adj* (lively) esuberante

pertinent /'pɜːtɪnənt/ *adj* pertinente (**to** a)

perturb /pə'tɜːb/ *vt* perturbare

perturbing /pə'tɜːbɪŋ/ *adj* conturbante

Peru /pə'ruː/ *n* Perù *m*

peruse /pə'ruːz/ *vt* leggere

Peruvian /pə'ruːvɪən/ *adj & n* peruviano, -a *mf*

pervade /pə'veɪd/ *vt* pervadere

pervasive /pə'veɪsɪv/ *adj* pervasivo

perverse /pə'vɜːs/ *adj* perverso; (illogical) irragionevole

perversely /pə'vɜːslɪ/ *adv* in modo perverso

perversion /pə'vɜːʃn/ *n* perversione *f*

perversity /pə'vɜːsɪtɪ/ *n* perversità *f*

pervert[1] /pə'vɜːt/ *vt* deviare ⟨*course of justice*⟩

pervert[2] /'pɜːvɜːt/ *n* pervertito, -a *mf*

perverted /pə'vɜːtɪd/ *adj* perverso

pessary /'pesərɪ/ *n* candeletta *f*

pessimism /'pesɪmɪzm/ *n* pessimismo *m*

pessimist /'pesɪmɪst/ *n* pessimista *mf*

pessimistic /pesɪ'mɪstɪk/ *adj* pessimistico

pessimistically /pesɪ'mɪstɪklɪ/ *adv* in modo pessimistico

pest /pest/ *n* piaga *f*; (fam: person) peste *f*

pester /'pestə(r)/ *vt* molestare

pesticide /'pestɪsaɪd/ *n* pesticida *m*

pestilential /pestɪ'lenʃəl/ *adj* (hum: annoying) fastidiosissimo

pestle /'pesl/ *n* pestello *m*

pet /pet/ ① *n* animale *m* domestico; (favourite) cocco, -a *mf* ② *adj* (favourite) prediletto ③ *vt* (pt/pp **petted**) coccolare ④ *vi* ⟨*couple*⟩ praticare il petting

petal /'petl/ *n* petalo *m*

peter /'piːtə(r)/ *vi* ~ **out** finire

pet food *n* cibo *m* per animali

pet hate *n* Br bestia *f* nera

petite /pə'tiːt/ *adj* minuto

petition /pə'tɪʃn/ *n* petizione *f*

pet name *n* vezzeggiativo *m*

petrified /'petrɪfaɪd/ *adj* (frightened) pietrificato

petrify /'petrɪfaɪ/ *vt* (pt/pp **-ied**) pietrificare

petrochemical /petrəʊ'kemɪkl/ *n* petrolchimico *m*

petrodollar /'petrəʊdɒlə(r)/ *n* petroldollaro *m*

petrol /'petrəl/ *n* Br benzina *f*

petrol bomb *n* Br [bomba *f*] molotov *f* inv

petrol can *n* tanica *f* di benzina

petroleum /pɪ'trəʊlɪəm/ *n* petrolio *m*

petroleum jelly *n* vaselina *f*

petrol-pump *n* Br pompa *f* di benzina

petrol station n Br stazione *f* di servizio

petrol tank *n* Br serbatoio *m* della benzina

pet shop *n* negozio *m* di animali

petticoat /'petɪkəʊt/ *n* sottoveste *f*

pettifogging /'petɪfɒgɪŋ/ *adj* pej cavilloso

petty /'petɪ/ *adj* (**-ier**, **-iest**) insignificante; (mean) meschino

petty cash *n* cassa *f* per piccole spese

petty crime *n* piccola criminalità *f*

petty minded /-'maɪndɪd/ *adj* meschino

petty officer *n* sottufficiale *m*

petty theft *n* furto *m* di minore entità

petulance /'petjʊləns/ *n* petulanza *f*

petulant /'petjʊlənt/ *adj* petulante

pew /pjuː/ *n* banco *m* (di chiesa)

pewter /'pjuːtə(r)/ *n* peltro *m*

PGCE *n abbr* Br (**postgraduate certificate in education**) diploma *m* di specializzazione nell'insegnamento

phallic /'fælɪk/ *adj* fallico

phallic symbol *n* simbolo *m* fallico

phallus /'fæləs/ *n* fallo *m*

phantom /'fæntəm/ *n* fantasma *m*

pharaoh /'feərəʊ/ *n* faraone *m*

pharmaceutical /fɑːmə'sjuːtɪkl/ *adj* farmaceutico

pharmacist /'fɑːməsɪst/ *n* farmacista *mf*

pharmacy /'fɑːməsɪ/ *n* farmacia *f*

phase /feɪz/ ① *n* fase *f* ② *vt* ~ **in/out** introdurre/eliminare gradualmente

PhD *abbr* (**Doctor of Philosophy**) ≈ dottorato *m* di ricerca

pheasant /'feznt/ *n* fagiano *m*

phenomenal /fɪ'nɒmɪnl/ *adj* fenomenale; (incredible) incredibile

phenomenally /fɪ'nɒmɪnəlɪ/ *adv* incredibilmente

phenomenon /fɪ'nɒmɪnən/ *n* (pl **-na**) fenomeno *m*

phew /fjuː/ *int* (when too hot, in relief) uff!; (in surprise) oh!

philanderer /fɪ'lændərə(r)/ *n* donnaiolo *m*

philanthropic /fɪlən'θrɒpɪk/ *adj* filantropico

philanthropist /fɪ'lænθrəpɪst/ *adj* filantropo, -a *mf*

philatelist /fɪ'lætəlɪst/ *n* filatelico, -a *mf*

philately /fɪ'lætəlɪ/ *n* filatelia *f*

philharmonic /fɪhɑː'mɒnɪk/ **①** n (orchestra) orchestra f filarmonica **②** adj filarmonico

Philippines /'fɪlɪpiːnz/ npl Filippine fpl

philistine /'fɪlɪstaɪn/ adj & n filisteo, -a mf

philology /fɪ'lɒlədʒɪ/ n filologia f

philosopher /fɪ'lɒsəfə(r)/ n filosofo, -a. mf

philosophical /fɪlə'sɒfɪkl/ adj filosofico

philosophically /fɪlə'sɒfɪklɪ/ adv con filosofia

philosophy /fɪ'lɒsəfɪ/ n filosofia f

phishing /'fɪʃɪŋ/ n forma di frode telematica consistente nell'inviare finte e-mail di banche o altre ditte allo scopo di entrare in possesso dei dati personali del destinatario

phlebitis /flɪ'baɪtɪs/ n flebite f

phlegm /flem/ n Med flemma f

phlegmatic /fleg'mætɪk/ adj flemmatico

phobia /'fəʊbɪə/ n fobia f

phobic /'fəʊbɪk/ adj fobico

phoenix /'fiːnɪks/ n fenice f

phone /fəʊn/ **①** n telefono m; **be on the** ∼ avere il telefono; (be phoning) essere al telefono **②** vt telefonare a ■ **phone back** vt richiamare ■ **phone in** vi telefonare al lavoro; **he** ∼**d in sick** ha telefonato [al lavoro] per dire che è ammalato ■ **phone up** **①** vi telefonare **②** vt dare un colpo di telefono a

phone book n guida f del telefono

phone booth n cabina f telefonica

phone box n cabina f telefonica

phone call n telefonata f

phonecard n scheda f telefonica

phone-in n trasmissione f con chiamate in diretta

phone link n phone link m inv

phoneme /'fəʊniːm/ n fonema m

phone number n numero m telefonico

phonetic /fə'netɪk/ adj fonetico

phonetics /fə'netɪks/ n fonetica f

phoney /'fəʊnɪ/ **①** adj (**-ler, -lest**) fasullo **②** n ciarlatano, -a mf

phonology /fə'nɒlədʒɪ/ n fonologia f

phosphate /'fɒsfeɪt/ n fosfato m

phosphorus /'fɒsfərəs/ n fosforo m

photo /'fəʊtəʊ/ n foto f

photo album n album m inv di fotografie

photo booth n macchina f fototessere inv

photocall n photo opportunity f

photocell n fotocellula f

photocopier n fotocopiatrice f

photocopy **①** n fotocopia f **②** vt fotocopiare

photoengraving n fotoincisione f

photofit® n Br fotofit m inv

photogenic /fəʊtəʊ'dʒenɪk/ adj fotogenico

photograph /'fəʊtəɡrɑːf/ **①** n fotografia f **②** vt fotografare

photographer /fə'tɒɡrəfə(r)/ n fotografo, -a mf

photographic /fəʊtə'ɡræfɪk/ adj fotografico

photography /fə'tɒɡrəfɪ/ n fotografia f

photojournalism n fotoreportage m

photojournalist n fotogiornalista mf

photo opportunity n photo opportunity f

photosynthesis n fotosintesi f

phrase /freɪz/ **①** n espressione f **②** vt esprimere

phrase book n libro m di fraseologia

phut /fʌt/ adv fam **go** ∼ ⟨car, etc⟩ scassarsi; ⟨plan⟩ andare in fumo

physical /'fɪkl/ adj fisico

physical education n educazione f fisica

physical fitness n forma f fisica

physically /'fɪzɪklɪ/ adv fisicamente

physically handicapped adj handicappato fisicamente

physician /fɪ'zɪʃn/ n medico m

physicist /'fɪzɪsɪst/ n fisico, -a mf

physics /'fɪzɪks/ n fisica f

physio /'fɪzɪəʊ/ n Br fam (physiotherapist) fisioterapista mf; (physiotherapy) fisioterapia f

physiology /fɪzɪ'ɒlədʒɪ/ n fisiologia f

physiotherapist /fɪzɪəʊ'θerəpɪst/ n fisioterapista mf

physiotherapy /fɪzɪəʊ'θerəpɪ/ n fisioterapia f

physique /fɪ'ziːk/ n fisico m

pianist /'pɪənɪst/ n pianista mf

piano /pɪ'ænəʊ/ n piano m

pianola® /pɪə'nəʊlə/ n pianola® f

piazza /pɪ'ætsə/ n (public square) piazza f; (Am: veranda) veranda f

pick¹ /pɪk/ n (tool) piccone m

pick² **①** n scelta f; **take your** ∼ prendi quello che vuoi **②** vt (select) scegliere; cogliere ⟨flowers⟩; scassinare ⟨lock⟩; borseggiare ⟨pockets⟩; ∼ **one's nose** mettersi le dita nel naso; ∼ **a quarrel** attaccar briga; ∼ **holes in something** (fam: criticize) criticare qualcosa **③** vi ∼ **and choose** fare il difficile ■ **pick at** vt piluccare ⟨food⟩; stuzzicare ⟨scab⟩

■ **pick off** *vt* (remove) togliere

■ **pick on** *vt* (fam: nag) assillare; **he always** ∼**s on me** ce l'ha con me

■ **pick out** *vt* (identify) individuare

■ **pick up** ① *vt* sollevare; raccogliere ⟨*fallen object, information*⟩; prendere in braccio ⟨*baby*⟩; prendere ⟨*passengers, habit*⟩; ⟨*police*⟩ arrestare ⟨*criminal*⟩; fam rimorchiare ⟨*girl*⟩; prendersi ⟨*illness*⟩; captare ⟨*signal*⟩; (buy) comprare; (learn) imparare; (collect) andare/venire a prendere; ∼ **oneself up** riprendersi ② *vi* (improve) recuperare; ⟨*weather*⟩ rimettersi

pickaxe /'pɪkæks/ *n* piccone *m*

picker /'pɪkə(r)/ *n* raccoglitore, -trice *mf*

picket /'pɪkɪt/ ① *n* picchettista *mf* ② *vt* picchettare

picket line *n* picchetto *m*

pickings /'pɪkɪŋz/ *npl* rich ∼ grossi guadagni

pickle /'pɪkl/ ① *n* ∼s *pl* sottaceti *mpl*; **in a** ∼ fig nei pasticci ② *vt* mettere sottaceto

pick-me-up *n* (alcohol) cicchetto *m*; (medicine) tonico *m*

pickpocket /'pɪkpɒkɪt/ *n* borsaiolo *m*

pick-up *n* (truck) furgone *m*; (on record-player) pickup *m inv*

picky /'pɪkɪ/ *adj* (fam: choosy, fussy) difficile

picnic /'pɪknɪk/ ① *n* picnic *m* ② *vi* (pt/pp **-nicked**) fare un picnic

pictogram /'pɪktəgræm/ *n* (symbol) pittogramma *m*; (chart) tabella *f*

pictorial /pɪk'tɔːrɪəl/ *adj* illustrato

picture /'pɪktʃə(r)/ ① *n* (painting) quadro *m*; (photo) fotografia *f*; (drawing) disegno *m*; (film) film *m inv*: **as pretty as a** ∼ ⟨*girl*⟩ bella come una madonna; **put somebody in the** ∼ fig mettere qualcuno al corrente; **the** ∼**s** Br fam il cinema ② *vt* (imagine) immaginare

picture [card] *n* (in pack of cards) figura *f*

picture messaging *n* Teleph picture messaging *m inv*

picturesque /pɪktʃə'resk/ *adj* pittoresco

piddle /'pɪdl/ *vi* fam fare pipì

pie /paɪ/ *n* torta *f*

piece /piːs/ *n* pezzo *m*; (in game) pedina *f*; **a** ∼ **of bread/paper** un pezzo di pane/carta; **a** ∼ **of news/advice/junk** una notizia/un consiglio/una patacca; **take to** ∼**s** smontare

■ **piece together** *vt* montare; fig ricostruire

piecemeal /'piːsmiːl/ *adv* un po' alla volta

piecework /'piːswɜːk/ *n* lavoro *m* a cottimo ·

pie chart *n* grafico *f* a torta

Piedmont /'piːdmɒnt/ *n* Piemonte *m*

pier /pɪə(r)/ molo *m*; (pillar) pilastro *m*

pierce /pɪəs/ *vt* perforare; ∼ **a hole in something** fare un buco in qualcosa

piercing /'pɪəsɪŋ/ ① *adj* penetrante ② *n* (in body) piercing *m inv*

pig /pɪg/ *n* maiale *m*

■ **pig out** *vi* fam abbuffarsi; ∼ **out on** abbuffarsi di

pigeon /'pɪdʒɪn/ *n* piccione *m*

pigeon-hole ① *n* casella *f* ② *vt* incasellare

pigeon-toed /-təʊd/ *adj* be ∼ camminare con i piedi in dentro

piggery /'pɪgərɪ/ *n* (pigsty) porcile *m*; (fam: overeating) ingordigia *f*

piggyback /'pɪgɪbæk/ *n* **give somebody a** ∼ portare qualcuno sulle spalle

piggy bank /'pɪgɪ/ *n* salvadanaio *m*

pig-headed /-'hedɪd/ *adj* fam cocciuto

piglet /'pɪglət/ *n* maialino *m*, porcellino *m*

pigment /'pɪgmənt/ *n* pigmento *m*

pigmentation /pɪgmən'teɪʃn/ *n* pigmentazione *f*

pigpen *n* Am = PIGSTY

pigskin /'pɪgskɪn/ *n* pelle *f* di cinghiale

pigsty *n* Br porcile *m*

pigtail /'pɪgteɪl/ *n* (plait) treccina *f*

pike /paɪk/ *n inv* (fish) luccio *m*

pilchard /'pɪltʃəd/ *n* sardina *f*

pile /paɪl/ ① *n* (heap) pila *f* ② *vt* ∼ **something on to something** impilare qualcosa su qualcosa

■ **pile in** *vi* (enter, get on) entrare disordinatamente

■ **pile up** ① *vt* accatastare ② *vi* ammucchiarsi

piles /paɪlz/ *npl* emorroidi *fpl*

pile-up *n* tamponamento *m* a catena

pilfer /'pɪlfə(r)/ *vi/t* rubacchiare

pilfering /'pɪlfərɪŋ/ *n* piccoli furti *mpl*

pilgrim /'pɪlgrɪm/ *n* pellegrino, -a *mf*

pilgrimage /'pɪlgrɪmɪdʒ/ *n* pellegrinaggio *m*

pill /pɪl/ *n* pillola *f*

pillage /'pɪlɪdʒ/ *vt* saccheggiare

pillar /'pɪlə(r)/ *n* pilastro *m*

pillar box *n* buca *f* delle lettere

pillion /'pɪljən/ *n* sellino *m* posteriore; **ride** ∼ viaggiare dietro

pillory /'pɪlərɪ/ *vt* (pt/pp **-ied**) fig mettere alla berlina

pillow /'pɪləʊ/ *n* guanciale *m*

pillowcase /'pɪləʊkeɪs/ *n* federa *f*

pilot /'paɪlət/ ① *n* pilota *mf* ② *vt* pilotare

pilot light *n* fiamma *f* di sicurezza

pilot scheme *n* progetto *m* pilota *inv*

pimp /pɪmp/ *n* protettore *m*

pimple /'pɪmpl/ *n* foruncolo *m*

pimply /'pɪmplɪ/ *adj* brufoloso

PIN /pɪn/ *n abbr* (**personal identification number**) [numero *m* di] codice *m* segreto

pin /pɪn/ **①** *n* spillo *m*; electr spinotto *m*; Med chiodo *m*; **I have ~s and needles in my leg** fam mi formicola una gamba **②** *vt* (pt/pp **pinned**) appuntare (**to/on** su); (sewing) fissare con gli spilli; (hold down) immobilizzare; **~ something on somebody** fam addossare a qualcuno la colpa di qualcosa
■ **pin down** *vt* (physically) immobilizzare; (to date) far fissare una data a ⟨*somebody*⟩; (identify) definire ⟨*feeling, cause*⟩
■ **pin up** *vt* appuntare; (on wall) affiggere

pinafore /'pɪnəfɔ:(r)/ *n* grembiule *m*

pinafore dress *n* scamiciato *m*

pinball /'pɪnbɔ:l/ *n* flipper *m inv*

pinball machine *n* flipper *m inv*

pincers /'pɪnsəz/ *npl* tenaglie *fpl*

pinch /pɪntʃ/ **①** *n* pizzicotto *m*; (of salt) presa *f*; **at a ~** fam in caso di bisogno **②** *vt* pizzicare; (fam: steal) fregare **③** *vi* ⟨*shoe*⟩ stringere

pincushion /'pɪnkʊʃən/ *n* puntaspilli *m inv*

pine¹ /paɪn/ *n* (tree) pino *m*

pine² *vi* **she is pining for you** le manchi molto
■ **pine away** *vi* deperire

pineapple *n* ananas *m inv*

pine cone *n* pigna *f*

pine-needle *n* ago *m* di pino

pine nut *n* pinolo *m*

ping /pɪŋ/ *n* rumore *m* metallico

ping-pong *n* ping-pong *m*

pinhead /'pɪnhed/ *n* capocchia *f* di spillo; fam, pej testa *f* di rapa

pink /pɪŋk/ *adj* rosa *inv*

pinking shears, pinking scissors /'pɪŋkɪŋ/ *npl* forbici *fpl* a zigzag

pinnacle /'pɪnəkl/ *n* guglia *f*

PIN number *n* codice *m* segreto

pinpoint /'pɪnpɔɪnt/ *vt* definire con precisione

pinprick /'pɪnprɪk/ *n* puntura *f* di spillo; (fig: of jealousy, remorse) punta *f*

pinstripe /'pɪnstraɪp/ *adj* gessato

pint /'pɪntə/ *n* pinta *f* (Br = 0,57 l, Am = 0,47 l); **a ~** fam una birra media

pin-up *n* ragazza *f* da copertina, pin-up *f inv*

pioneer /paɪə'nɪə(r)/ **①** *n* pioniere, -a *mf* **②** *vt* essere un pioniere di

pious /'paɪəs/ *adj* pio

pip¹ /pɪp/ *n* (seed) seme *m*

pip² *n* **the ~s** il segnale orario; (telephone) il segnale telefonico

pip³ *vt* (pt/pp **pipped**) **be ~ped at the post** essere battuto all'ultimo minuto

pipe /paɪp/ **①** *n* tubo *m*; (for smoking) pipa *f*; **the ~s** *pl* Mus la cornamusa **②** *vt* far arrivare con tubature ⟨*water, gas etc*⟩; Culin mettere
■ **pipe down** *vi* fam abbassare la voce; (shut up) stare zitto
■ **pipe up** *vi* **~ with a suggestion** venir fuori con una proposta

pipe-cleaner *n* scovolino *m*

piped music /paɪpt/ *n* musichetta *f* di sottofondo

pipe dream *n* illusione *f*

pipeline /'paɪplaɪn/ *n* conduttura *f*: **in the ~** fam in cantiere

piper /'paɪpə(r)/ *n* suonatore *m* di cornamusa

piping /'paɪpɪŋ/ *adj* **~ hot** bollente

pique /pi:k/ *n* **in a fit of ~** risentito

piracy /'paɪrəsɪ/ *n* pirateria *f*

piranha /pɪ'rɑ:nə/ *n* piranha *m*

pirate /'paɪrət/ **①** *n* pirata *m* **②** *vt* pirateggiare

pirate copy *n* copia *f* pirata

pirated *adj* /'paɪrətɪd/ pirateggiato

pirate radio *n* radio *f* pirata

pirouette /pɪru:'et/ **①** *n* piroetta *f* **②** *vi* piroettare

Pisces /'paɪsi:z/ *n* Astr Pesci *mpl*

piss /pɪs/ *sl* **①** *n* piscia *f* **②** *vi* pisciare
■ **piss about, piss around** **①** *vi* (waste time, play the fool) cazzeggiare **②** *vt* **~ somebody about** rompere le palle a qualcuno
■ **piss down** *vi* **it's ~ing down** (raining heavily) piove a dirotto
■ **piss off** **①** *vt* fare incacchiare; **that type of behaviour ~es me off** questi comportamenti mi stanno sulle palle **②** *vi* (leave) filarsela; **~ off!** levati dalle palle!, va' a cagare!

pissed /pɪst/ *adj* sl sbronzo; **~ as a newt** sbronzo come una cocuzza

pissed off *adj* sl scoglionato

pistachio [nut] /pɪ'stæʃɪəʊ/ *n* pistacchio *m*

pistol /'pɪstl/ *n* pistola *f*

piston /'pɪstn/ *n* Techn pistone *m*

pit /pɪt/ **①** *n* fossa *f*; (mine) miniera *f*; (for orchestra) orchestra *f*; (of stomach) bocca *f* **②** *vt* (pt/pp **pitted**) fig opporre (**against** a)

pit-a-pat /'pɪtəpæt/ *n* **go ~** ⟨*heart*⟩ palpitare

pitbull [terrier] *n* pitbull *m inv*

pitch¹ /pɪtʃ/ **①** *n* (tone) tono *m*; (level) altezza *f*; (in sport) campo *m*; (fig: degree) grado *m* **②** *vt* montare ⟨*tent*⟩

pitch² *n* (substance) pece *f*

p

■ **pitch in** *vi* fam mettersi sotto

pitch-black *adj* nero come la pece; ‹*night*› buio pesto

pitch-dark *adj* buio pesto

pitcher /'pɪtʃə(r)/ *n* brocca *f*

pitchfork /'pɪtʃfɔːk/ *n* forca *f*

piteous /'pɪtɪəs/ *adj* pietoso

pitfall /'pɪtfɔːl/ *n* fig trabocchetto *m*

pith /pɪθ/ *n* (of lemon, orange) interno *m* della buccia; fig essenza *f*

pithy /'pɪθɪ/ *adj* (**-ier**, **-iest**) fig conciso

pitiable /'pɪtɪəbl/ *adj* pietoso

pitiful /'pɪtɪfl/ *adj* pietoso

pitifully /'pɪtɪfʊlɪ/ *adv* da far pietà

pitiless /'pɪtɪlɪs/ *adj* spietato

pitilessly /'pɪtɪlɪslɪ/ *adv* senza pietà

pittance /'pɪtns/ *n* miseria *f*

pitted /'pɪtɪd/ *adj* ‹*surface*› bucherellato; ‹*face, skin*› butterato; ‹*olive*› snocciolato

pituitary /prɪ'tjuːɪt(ə)rɪ/ *adj* pituitario

pituitary gland *n* ghiandola *f* pituitaria, ipofisi *f*

pity /'pɪtɪ/ ① *n* pietà *f*; **[what a]** ~! che peccato!; **take** ~ **on** avere compassione di ② *vt* aver pietà di

pivot /'pɪvət/ ① *n* perno *m*; fig fulcro *m* ② *vi* imperniarsi (**on** su)

pivotal /'pɪvətl/ *adj* ‹*role*› centrale; ‹*decision*› cruciale

pixel /'pɪksəl/ *n* pixel *m inv*

pixie /'pɪksɪ/ *n* folletto *m*

pizza /'piːtsə/ *n* pizza *f*

placard /'plækɑːd/ *n* cartellone *m*

placate /plə'keɪt/ *vt* placare

place /pleɪs/ ① *n* posto *m*; (fam: house) casa *f*; (in book) segno *m*; **feel out of** ~ sentirsi fuori posto; **take** ~ aver luogo; **all over the** ~ dappertutto ② *vt* collocare; (remember) identificare; ~ **an order** fare un'ordinazione; **be** ~**d** (in race) piazzarsi

placebo /plə'siːbəʊ/ *n* Med placebo *m inv*; fig contentino *m*

place mat *n* sottopiatto *m*

placement /'pleɪsmənt/ *n* (act: in accommodation) collocamento *m*; (Br: job) stage *m inv*

place name *n* toponimo *m*

placenta /plə'sentə/ *n* placenta *f*

placid /'plæsɪd/ *adj* placido

plagiarism /'pleɪdʒərɪzm/ *n* plagio *m*

plagiarist /'pleɪdʒərɪst/ *n* plagiario, -a *mf*

plagiarize /'pleɪdʒəraɪz/ *vt* plagiare

plague /pleɪg/ *n* peste *f*

plaice /pleɪs/ *n inv* platessa *f*

plaid /plæd/ ① *n* (fabric) plaid *m inv*; (pattern) motivo *m* scozzese ② *attrib* ‹*scarf, shirt*› scozzese

plain /pleɪn/ ① *adj* chiaro; (simple) semplice; (not pretty) scialbo; (not patterned) in tinta unita; ‹*chocolate*› fondente; **in** ~ **clothes** in borghese ② *adv* (simply) semplicemente ③ *n* pianura *f*

plain-clothes *adj* ‹*policeman etc*› in borghese

plainly /'pleɪnlɪ/ *adv* francamente; (simply) semplicemente; (obviously) chiaramente

plain-spoken *adj* franco

plaintiff /'pleɪntɪf/ *n* Jur parte *f* lesa

plaintive /'pleɪntɪv/ *adj* lamentoso

plaintively /'pleɪntɪvlɪ/ *adv* con aria lamentosa

plait /plæt/ ① *n* treccia *f* ② *vt* intrecciare

plan /plæn/ ① *n* progetto *m*, piano *m* ② *vt* (pt/pp **planned**) progettare; (intend) prevedere

■ **plan ahead** *vi* pianificare

plane[1] /pleɪn/ *n* (tree) platano *m*

plane[2] *n* aeroplano *m*; (in geometry) piano *m*

plane[3] ① *n* (tool) pialla *f* ② *vt* piallare

plane crash *n* incidente *m* aereo

planet /'plænɪt/ *n* pianeta *m*

plank /plæŋk/ *n* asse *f*

■ **plank down** *vt* (fam: put down) mollare

plankton /'plæŋktən/ *n* plancton *m*

planner /'plænə(r)/ *n* progettista *mf*; (in town planning) urbanista *mf*

planning /'plænɪŋ/ *n* pianificazione *f*

planning permission *n* licenza *f* edilizia

plant /plɑːnt/ ① *n* pianta *f*; (machinery) impianto *m*; (factory) stabilimento *m* ② *vt* piantare; ~ **oneself in front of somebody** piantarsi davanti a qualcuno

plantation /plæn'teɪʃn/ *n* piantagione *f*

planter /'plɑːntə(r)/ *n* (person) piantatore, -trice *mf*; (machine) piantatrice *f*

plant life *n* flora *f*

plaque /plɑːk/ *n* placca *f*

plasma /'plæzmə/ *n* plasma *m*

plasma screen *n* schermo *m* al plasma

plaster /'plɑːstə(r)/ ① *n* intonaco *m*; Med gesso *m*; (sticking ~) cerotto *m*; **in** ~ ingessato ② *vt* intonacare ‹*wall*›; (cover) ricoprire

plaster cast *n* ingessatura *f*

plastered /'plɑːstəd/ *adj* (sl: drunk) sbronzo

plasterer /'plɑːstərə(r)/ *n* intonacatore *m*

plaster of Paris *n* gesso *m*

plastic /'plæstɪk/ ① *n* plastica *f* ② *adj* plastico

Plasticine® /'plæstɪsiːn/ *n* Plastilina® *f*

plastic surgeon ⋯⟩ plight ⋯

plastic surgeon *n* chirurgo *m* plastico

plastic surgery *n* chirurgia *f* plastica

plate /pleɪt/ **1** *n* piatto *m*; (flat sheet) placca *f*; (gold and silverware) argenteria *f*; (in book) tavola *f* fuori testo
2 *vt* (cover with metal) placcare

plateau /'plætəʊ/ **1** *n* (pl ~x /'plætəʊz/) altopiano *m*
2 *vi* fig livellarsi

plate glass *n* lastra *f* di vetro

platform /'plætfɔːm/ *n* (stage) palco *m*; Rail marciapiede *m*; Pol piattaforma *f*; ~ **5** binario 5

platform shoes *npl* scarpe *fpl* con la zeppa

platinum /'plætɪnəm/ **1** *n* platino *m*
2 *attrib* di platino

platinum blonde *n* bionda *f* platinata

platitude /'plætɪtjuːd/ *n* luogo *m* comune

platonic /plə'tɒnɪk/ *adj* platonico

platoon /plə'tuːn/ *n* Mil plotone *m*

platter /'plætə(r)/ *n* piatto *m* da portata

platypus /'plætɪpəs/ *n* ornitorinco *m*

plausibility /plɔːzɪ'bɪlɪtɪ/ *n* plausibilità *f*

plausible /'plɔːzəbl/ *adj* plausibile

play /pleɪ/ **1** *n* gioco *m*; Theat, TV dramma *m*, opera *f* teatrale; (performance) rappresentazione *f*; Radio sceneggiato *m* radiofonico; ~ **on words** gioco *m* di parole
2 *vt* giocare a; (act) recitare; suonare ⟨*instrument*⟩; giocare ⟨*card*⟩
3 *vi* giocare; Mus suonare; ~ **by the rules** stare alle regole; ~ **with fire** scherzare col fuoco; ~ **dumb** fare lo gnorri; ~ **safe** non prendere rischi
■ **play along** *vi* ~ **along with somebody** (fam: cooperate) fare il gioco di qualcuno
■ **play around with** *vt* (meddle with) cincischiarsi con
■ **play back** *vt* riascoltare ⟨*recording*⟩
■ **play down** *vt* minimizzare
■ **play on 1** *vi* (continue to play) continuare a giocare
2 *vt* (exploit) giocare su
■ **play out** *vt* vivere ⟨*drama, fantasy*⟩
■ **play up** *vi* fam fare i capricci

play-acting *n* commedia *f*

playboy /'pleɪbɔɪ/ *n* playboy *m inv*

player /'pleɪə(r)/ *n* giocatore, -trice *mf*

playful /'pleɪfʊl/ *adj* scherzoso

playfully /'pleɪfʊlɪ/ *adv* in modo scherzoso

playground /'pleɪgraʊnd/ *n* Sch cortile *m* (per la ricreazione)

playgroup /'pleɪgruːp/ *n* asilo *m*

playhouse *n* casetta *f* per i giochi

playing card /'pleɪɪŋ/ *n* carta *f* da gioco

playing field *n* campo *m* da gioco

playmate *n* compagno, -a *mf* di gioco

playpen *n* box *m inv*

play-off *n* play off *m inv*

playroom /'pleɪruːm/ *n* ludoteca *f*

plaything *n* giocattolo *m*

playtime *n* ricreazione *f*

playwright /'pleɪraɪt/ *n* drammaturgo, -a *mf*

plaza /'plɑːzə/ *n* (public square) piazza *f*; (shopping ~) centro *m* commerciale; (Am: services point) area *f* di servizio; (Am: toll point) casello *m*

plc *abbr* (**public limited company**) s.r.l.

plea /pliː/ *n* richiesta *f*; **enter a ~ of not guilty** Jur dichiararsi non colpevole; **make a ~ for** fare un appello a

plead /pliːd/ **1** *vi* fare appello (for a); ~ **guilty** dichiararsi colpevole; ~ **with somebody** implorare qualcuno
2 *vt* Jur perorare ⟨*case*⟩

pleasant /'pleznt/ *adj* piacevole

pleasantly /'plezntlɪ/ *adv* piacevolmente; ⟨say, smile⟩ cordialmente

pleasantry /'plezntrɪ/ *n* (joke) battuta *f*; **pleasantries** (*pl*: polite remarks) convenevoli *mpl*

please /pliːz/ **1** *adv* per favore; ~ **do** prego
2 *vt* far contento; ~ **oneself** fare il proprio comodo; ~ **yourself!** come vuoi!; pej fai pure!

pleased /pliːzd/ *adj* lieto; ~ **with/about** contento di

pleasing /'pliːzɪŋ/ *adj* gradevole

pleasurable /'pleʒərəbl/ *adj* gradevole

pleasure /'pleʒə(r)/ *n* piacere *m*; **with ~** con piacere, volentieri

pleat /pliːt/ **1** *n* piega *f*
2 *vt* pieghettare

pleated /'pliːtɪd/ *adj* a pieghe

pleb /pleb/ *n* fam plebeo, -a *mf*

plebby /'plebɪ/ *adj* fam plebeo

plebeian /plɪ'biːən/ pej **1** *n* plebeo, -a *mf*
2 *adj* plebeo

plebiscite /'plebɪsaɪt/ *n* plebiscito *m*

pledge /pledʒ/ **1** *n* pegno *m*; (promise) promessa *f*
2 *vt* (pawn) impegnare; ~ **to do something** impegnarsi a fare qualcosa

plenary /'pliːnərɪ/ *adj* ⟨session⟩ plenario; ⟨powers⟩ pieno; ⟨authority⟩ assoluto

plentiful /'plentɪfl/ *adj* abbondante

plenty /'plentɪ/ *n* abbondanza *f*; ~ **of money** molti soldi; ~ **of people** molta gente; **I've got ~** ne ho in abbondanza

pleurisy /'plʊərəsɪ/ *n* pleurite *f*

pliability /plaɪə'bɪlɪtɪ/ *n* flessibilità *f*

pliable /'plaɪəbl/ *adj* flessibile

pliers /'plaɪəz/ *npl* pinze *fpl*

plight /plaɪt/ *n* triste condizione *f*

p

plimsolls /'plɪmsɒlz/ npl scarpe fpl da ginnastica

plinth /plɪnθ/ n plinto m

plod /plɒd/ vi (pt/pp **plodded**) trascinarsi; (work hard) sgobbare
■ **plod away** vi (work hard) sgobbare; ~ away at sgobbare su

plodder /'plɒdə(r)/ n sgobbone, -a mf

plonk[1] /plɒŋk/ n fam vino m; (poor wine) vinaccio m

plonk[2] vt (fam: put) sbattere

plop /plɒp/ ① n plop m inv
② vi (pt/pp **plopped**) fare plop

plot /plɒt/ ① n complotto m; (of novel) trama f; ~ **of land** appezzamento m [di terreno]
② vt/i (pt/pp **plotted**) complottare

plotter /'plɒtə(r)/ n (schemer) cospiratore, -trice mf; Comput plotter m inv, tracciatore m

plough /plaʊ/ ① n aratro m
② vt/i arare
■ **plough back** vt Comm reinvestire
■ **plough into** vt (crash into) schiantarsi contro
■ **plough through** vt procedere a fatica in

ploughman /'plaʊmən/ n aratore m

ploughman's lunch n Br piatto m freddo a base di pane, formaggio e sottaceti

plow /plaʊ/ Am ① n aratro m
② vt/i arare

ploy /plɔɪ/ n fam manovra f

pluck /plʌk/ ① n fegato m
② vt strappare; depilare ⟨eyebrows⟩; spennare ⟨bird⟩; cogliere ⟨flower⟩
■ **pluck up** vt ~ **up courage** farsi coraggio

plucky /'plʌkɪ/ adj (**-ier, -iest**) coraggioso

plug /plʌg/ ① n tappo m; Electr spina f; Auto candela f; (fam: advertisement) pubblicità f inv
② vt (pt/pp **plugged**) tappare; (fam: advertise) pubblicizzare
■ **plug away** vi (work hard) lavorare sodo
■ **plug in** vt Electr inserire la spina di

plug and play n Comput plug and play m inv

plughole /'plʌghəʊl/ n Br scarico m

plug-in adj con la spina

plum /plʌm/ n susina f; (tree) susino m

plumage /'pluːmɪdʒ/ n piumaggio m

plumb /plʌm/ ① adj verticale
② adv esattamente
■ **plumb in** vt collegare

plumber /'plʌmə(r)/ n idraulico m

plumbing /'plʌmɪŋ/ n impianto m idraulico

plumb line n filo m a piombo

plume /pluːm/ n piuma f

plummet /'plʌmɪt/ vi precipitare; ⟨prices⟩ crollare

plump /plʌmp/ adj paffuto
■ **plump down** vt (put down) lasciare cadere
■ **plump for** vt scegliere

plumpness /'plʌmpnɪs/ n rotondità f

plunder /'plʌndə(r)/ ① n (booty) bottino m
② vt saccheggiare

plunge /plʌndʒ/ ① n tuffo m; **take the** ~ fam buttarsi
② vt tuffare; fig sprofondare; ~ **somebody into despair** piombare qualcuno nella disperazione
③ vi tuffarsi

plunger /'plʌndʒə(r)/ n (tool) sturalavandini m inv; (handle) stantuffo m

plunging /'plʌndʒɪŋ/ adj ~ **neckline** scollatura f profonda

pluperfect /pluː'pɜːfɪkt/ n trapassato m prossimo

plural /'plʊərəl/ adj & n plurale m

plus /plʌs/ ① prep più
② adj in più; **500** ~ più di 500
③ n più m; (advantage) extra m inv

plush /plʌʃ/ adj ⟨hotel etc⟩ lussuoso

plus sign n (segno m) più m inv

Pluto /'pluːtəʊ/ n Plutone m

plutonium /pluː'təʊnɪəm/ n plutonio m

ply /plaɪ/ vt (pt/pp **plied**) esercitare ⟨trade⟩; ~ **somebody with drink** continuare ad offrire da bere a qualcuno

plywood /'plaɪwʊd/ n compensato m

PM abbr **Prime Minister**

p.m. abbr (**post meridiem**) del pomeriggio

PMS n abbr (**premenstrual syndrome**) sindrome f premestruale

PMT n abbr (**premenstrual tension**) tensione f premestruale

pneumatic /njuː'mætɪk/ adj pneumatico

pneumatic drill n martello m pneumatico

pneumonia /njuː'məʊnɪə/ n polmonite f

PO abbr (**Post Office**) ≈ P.T.; abbr (**postal order**) vaglia m inv postale

poach /pəʊtʃ/ vt Culin bollire; cacciare di frodo ⟨deer⟩; pescare di frodo ⟨salmon⟩; ~**ed egg** uovo m in camicia

poacher /'pəʊtʃə(r)/ n bracconiere m

PO Box n abbr (**Post Office Box**) C.P. f

pocket /'pɒkɪt/ ① n tasca f; ~ **of resistance** sacca f di resistenza; **be out of** ~ rimetterci
② vt intascare

pocket-book n taccuino m; (wallet) portafoglio m

pocket-money *n* denaro *m* per le piccole spese

pock-marked /'pɒkmɑːkt/ *adj* butterato

pod /pɒd/ *n* baccello *m*

podgy /'pɒdʒɪ/ *adj* (**-ier**, **-iest**) grassoccio

podiatrist /pə'daɪətrɪst/ *n* Am pedicure *mf inv*

podium /'pəʊdɪəm/ *n* podio *m*

poem /'pəʊɪm/ *n* poesia *f*

poet /'pəʊɪt/ *n* poeta *m*

poetic /pəʊ'etɪk/ *adj* poetico

poetic licence *n* licenza *f* poetica

Poet Laureate /'lɔːrɪət/ *n* poeta *m* laureato

poetry /'pəʊɪtrɪ/ *n* poesia *f*

po-faced /pəʊ'feɪst/ *adj* Br fam **look/be** ∼ avere un'aria di disapprovazione

poignancy /'pɔɪmjənsɪ/ *n* pregnanza *f*

poignant /'pɔɪmjənt/ *adj* pregnante

point /pɔɪnt/ ① *n* punto *m*; (sharp end) punta *f*; (meaning, purpose) senso *m*; Electr presa *f*; **what is the** ∼**?** a che scopo?; **the** ∼ **is** il fatto è; **I don't see the** ∼ non vedo il senso; **up to a** ∼ fino ad un certo punto; **be on the** ∼ **of doing something** essere sul punto di fare qualcosa; ∼**s** *pl* Rail scambio *m*; **good/bad** ∼**s** aspetti *mpl* positivi/ negativi

② *vt* puntare (**at** verso)

③ *vi* (with finger) puntare il dito; ∼ **at/to** ⟨person⟩ mostrare col dito; ⟨indicator⟩ indicare; ∼ **and click** Comput punta e clicca

■ **point out** *vt* far notare ⟨fact⟩; ∼ **something out to somebody** far notare qualcosa a qualcuno

point-blank *adj* a bruciapelo

pointed /'pɔɪntɪd/ *adj* appuntito; ⟨question⟩ diretto

pointer /'pɔɪntə(r)/ *n* (piece of advice) consiglio *m*

pointillism /'pwæntɪlɪzm/ *n* divisionismo *m*

pointillist /'pwæntɪlɪst/ *n* divisionista *mf*

pointing /'pɔɪntɪŋ/ *n* Constr rifinitura *f* con la malta

pointing device *n* Comput dispositivo *m* di puntamento

pointless /'pɔɪntlɪs/ *adj* inutile

point of order *n* mozione *f* d'ordine

point of sale *n* (place) punto *m* di vendita; (promotional material) materiale *m* pubblicitario

point-of-sale promotion *n* promozione *f* punto vendita

point of view *n* punto *m* di vista

poise /pɔʊz/ *n* padronanza *f*

poised /pɔɪzd/ *adj* in equilibrio; (composed) padrone di sé; ∼ **to** sul punto di

poison /'pɔɪzn/ ① *n* veleno *m*
② *vt* avvelenare

poisoned /'pɔɪz(ə)nd/ *adj* avvelenato

poisoner /'pɔɪzənə(r)/ *n* avvelenatore, -trice *mf*

poisonous /'pɔɪzənəs/ *adj* velenoso

poison-pen letter *n* lettera *f* anonima diffamatoria

poke /pəʊk/ ① *n* spintarella *f*
② *vt* spingere; ⟨fire⟩ attizzare; (put) ficcare; ∼ **fun at** prendere in giro

■ **poke about**, **poke around** *vi* frugare

■ **poke out** *vi* (protrude) spuntare

poker[1] /'pəʊkə(r)/ *n* attizzatoio *m*

poker[2] *n* (Cards) poker *m*

poker-faced /-'feɪst/ *adj* ⟨person⟩ impassibile

poky /'pəʊkɪ/ *adj* (**-ier**, **-iest**) angusto

Poland /'pəʊlənd/ *n* Polonia *f*

polar /'pəʊlə(r)/ *adj* polare

polar bear *n* orso *m* bianco

polarity /pə'lærətɪ/ *n* Electr, Phys, fig polarità *f inv*

polarize /'pəʊləraɪz/ *vt* polarizzare

polarized *adj* polarizzato

Pole /pəʊl/ *n* polacco, -a *mf*

pole[1] *n* palo *m*

pole[2] *n* Geog, Electr polo *m*

polemic /pə'lemɪk/ *n* polemica *f*

polemical /pə'lemɪkl/ *adj* polemico

pole star *n* stella *f* polare

pole vault *n* salto *m* con l'asta

police /pə'liːs/ ① *npl* polizia *f*
② *vt* pattugliare ⟨area⟩; sorvegliare ⟨behaviour⟩

police car *n* gazzella *f*

police constable *n* agente *mf* di polizia

Police Department *n* Am dipartimento *m* di polizia

police force *n* polizia *f*

policeman *n* poliziotto *m*

police officer *n* agente *mf* di polizia

police state *n* stato *m* militarista

police station *n* commissariato *m*

policewoman *n* donna *f* poliziotto

policing /pə'liːsɪŋ/ *n* (maintaining law and order) mantenimento *m* dell'ordine pubblico; (of demonstrarion, match) organizzazione *f* del servizio d'ordine

policy[1] /'pɒlɪsɪ/ *n* politica *f*

policy[2] *n* (insurance) polizza *f*

policyholder *n* titolare *mf* della polizza

policy unit *n* Pol comitato *m* responsabile della linea politica

polio /'pəʊlɪəʊ/ *n* polio *f*

p

Polish /ˈpəʊlɪʃ/ *adj & n* polacco *m*

polish /ˈpɒlɪʃ/ **1** *n* (shine) lucentezza *f*; (substance) lucido *m*; (for nails) smalto *m*; fig raffinatezza *f*
2 *vt* lucidare; fig smussare
■ **polish off** *vt* fam finire; far fuori ⟨food⟩
■ **polish up** *vt* rispolverare ⟨Italian⟩

polished /ˈpɒlɪʃt/ *adj* ⟨manner⟩ raffinato; ⟨performance⟩ senza sbavature

polisher /ˈpɒləʃə(r)/ *n* (machine) lucidatrice *f*

polite /pəˈlaɪt/ *adj* cortese

politely /pəˈlaɪtlɪ/ *adv* cortesemente

politeness /pəˈlaɪtnɪs/ *n* cortesia *f*

politic /ˈpɒlɪtɪk/ *adj* prudente

political /pəˈlɪtɪkl/ *adj* politico

politically /pəˈlɪtɪklɪ/ *adv* dal punto di vista politico; ∼ **correct** politicamente corretto

political prisoner *n* prigioniero, -a *mf* politico

politician /pɒlɪˈtɪʃn/ *n* politico *m*

politicize /pəˈlɪtɪsaɪz/ *vt* politicizzare

politics /ˈpɒlɪtɪks/ *n* politica *f*

polka /ˈpɒlkə/ *n* polka *f*

polka dot **1** *n* pois *m inv*, pallino *m*
2 *attrib* a pois

poll /pəʊl/ **1** *n* votazione *f*; (election) elezioni *fpl*; [opinion] ∼ sondaggio *m* d'opinione; **go to the** ∼**s** andare alle urne
2 *vt* ottenere ⟨votes⟩

pollen /ˈpɒlən/ *n* polline *m*

polling booth /ˈpəʊlɪŋ/ *n* cabina *f* elettorale

polling day *n* giorno *m* delle elezioni

polling station *n* seggio *m* elettorale

pollster /ˈpəʊlstə(r)/ *n* (person) persona *f* che esegue un sondaggio d'opinione

poll tax *n* imposta *f* locale sulle persone fisiche

pollutant /pəˈluːtənt/ *n* sostanza *f* inquinante

pollute /pəˈluːt/ *vt* inquinare

polluted /pəˈluːtɪd/ *adj* inquinato

polluter /pəˈluːtə(r)/ *n* inquinatore, -trice *mf*

pollution /pəˈluːʃn/ *n* inquinamento *m*

polo /ˈpəʊləʊ/ *n* polo *m*

polo neck *n* collo *m* alto

polo shirt *n* dolcevita *f*

poltergeist /ˈpɒltəgaɪst/ *n* poltergeist *m inv*

poly /ˈpɒlɪ/ *n* (Br fam: polytechnic) politecnico *m*

poly bag *n* sacchetto *m* di plastica

polyester /pɒlɪˈestə(r)/ *n* poliestere *m*

polygamous /pəˈlɪgəməs/ *adj* poligamico

polygamy /pəˈlɪgəmɪ/ *n* poligamia *f*

polymath /ˈpɒlɪmæθ/ *n* erudito, -a *mf*

polymer /ˈpɒlɪmə(r)/ *n* polimero *m*

polystyrene® /pɒlɪˈstaɪriːn/ *n* polistirolo *m*

polytechnic /pɒlɪˈteknɪk/ *n* politecnico *m*

polythene /ˈpɒlɪθiːn/ *n* politene *m*

polythene bag *n* sacchetto *m* di plastica

polyunsaturates /pɒlɪʌnˈsætjʊreɪts/ *npl* grassi *mpl* polinsaturi

pomade /pəˈmeɪd/ *n* pomata *f*

pomegranate /ˈpɒmɪgrænɪt/ *n* melagrana *f*

pomp /pɒmp/ *n* pompa *f*

pompom /ˈpɒmpɒm/, **pompon** /ˈpɒmpɒn/ *n* pompon *m*

pomposity /pɒmˈpɒsətɪ/ *n* pomposità *f*

pompous /ˈpɒmpəs/ *adj* pomposo

pompously /ˈpɒmpəslɪ/ *adv* pomposamente

poncy /ˈpɒnsɪ/ *adj* fam da finocchio; ⟨person⟩ finocchio

pond /pɒnd/ *n* stagno *m*

ponder /ˈpɒndə(r)/ *vt/i* ponderare

ponderous /ˈpɒndərəs/ *adj* ponderoso; fig pesante

pong /pɒŋ/ **1** *n* fam puzza *f*
2 *vi* puzzare

pontiff /ˈpɒntɪf/ *n* pontefice *m*

pontificate /pɒnˈtɪfɪkeɪt/ *vi* pontificare

pontoon /pɒnˈtuːn/ *n* (float) galleggiante *m*; (pier) pontile *m*; (Br: game) ventuno *m*

pony /ˈpəʊnɪ/ *n* pony *m inv*

ponytail /ˈpəʊnɪteɪl/ *n* coda *f* di cavallo

pony-trekking /ˈpəʊnɪtrekɪŋ/ *n* escursioni *fpl* col pony

pooch /puːtʃ/ *n* (fam: dog) cagnetto *m*

poodle /ˈpuːdl/ *n* barboncino *m*

poof /pʊf/, **poofter** /ˈpʊftə(r)/ *n* (Br fam: homosexual) finocchio *m*

pooh /puː/ **1** *int* (scorn, disgust) puah!
2 *n* (Br: baby talk) popò *f inv*

pooh-pooh /puːˈpuː/ *vt* fam ridere di ⟨suggestion⟩

pool[1] /puːl/ *n* (of water, blood) pozza *f*; [swimming] ∼ piscina *f*

pool[2] **1** *n* (common fund) cassa *f* comune; (in cards) piatto *m*; (game) biliardo *m* a buca; ∼**s** *pl* ≈ totocalcio *msg*
2 *vt* mettere insieme

pool table *n* tavolo *m* da biliardo

pooped /puːpt/ *adj* fam **be** ∼ **[out]** essere stanco morto

poor /pʊə(r)/ **1** *adj* povero; (not good) scadente; **in** ∼ **health** in cattiva salute
2 *npl* **the** ∼ i poveri

poorly /ˈpʊəlɪ/ **1** *adj* **be** ∼ non stare bene

2 *adv* male

pop¹ /pɒp/ **1** *n* botto *m*; (drink) bibita *f* gasata
2 *vt* (pt/pp **popped**) (fam: put) mettere; (burst) far scoppiare
3 *vi* (burst) scoppiare
■ **pop in** *vi* fam fare un salto
■ **pop out** *vi* fam uscire; ∼ **out to the shop** fare un salto al negozio
■ **pop round** *vi* fam passare; ∼ **round to Ann's** passare da Ann
■ **pop up** *vi* (fam: appear unexpectedly) saltare fuori

pop² **1** *n* fam musica *f* pop
2 *attrib* pop *inv*

popcorn /'pɒpkɔːn/ *n* popcorn *m inv*

pope /pəʊp/ *n* papa *m*

poplar /'pɒplə(r)/ *n* pioppo *m*

poppy /'pɒpɪ/ *n* papavero *m*

pop sock *n* gambaletto *m*

populace /'pɒpjʊləs/ *n* popolo *m*

popular /'pɒpjʊlə(r)/ *adj* popolare; ⟨*belief*⟩ diffuso

popularity /pɒpjʊ'lærətɪ/ *n* popolarità *f*

popularize /'pɒpjʊləraɪz/ *vt* divulgare

populate /'pɒpjʊleɪt/ *vt* popolare

population /pɒpjʊ'leɪʃn/ *n* popolazione *f*

populist /'pɒpjʊlɪst/ *adj & n* populista *mf*

populous /'pɒpjʊləs/ *adj* popoloso

pop-up book *n* libro *m* con immagini tridimensionali

pop-up menu *n* Comput menu *m* a tendina

pop-up toaster *n* tostapane *m inv* a espulsione automatica

porcelain /'pɔːsəlɪn/ *n* porcellana *f*

porch /pɔːtʃ/ *n* portico *m*; Am veranda *f*

porcupine /'pɔːkjʊpaɪn/ *n* porcospino *m*

pore¹ /pɔː(r)/ *n* poro *m*

pore² *vi* ∼ **over** immergersi in

pork /pɔːk/ *n* carne *f* di maiale

porn /pɔːn/ *n* fam porno *m*

porno /'pɔːnəʊ/ *adj* fam porno *inv*

pornographic /pɔːnə'ɡræfɪk/ *adj* pornografico

pornography /pɔː'nɒɡrəfɪ/ *n* pornografia *f*

porous /'pɔːrəs/ *adj* poroso

porpoise /'pɔːpəs/ *n* focena *f*

porridge /'pɒrɪdʒ/ *n* farinata *f* di fiocchi d'avena

port¹ /pɔːt/ *n* porto *m*

port² *n* (Naut: side) babordo *m*

port³ *n* (wine) porto *m*

portable /'pɔːtəbl/ *adj & n* portatile *m*

Portakabin® /'pɔːtəkæbɪn/ *n* casotto *m* prefabbricato

portcullis /pɔːt'kʌlɪs/ *n* saracinesca *f*

portentous /pɔː'tentəs/ *adj* (significant) solenne; (ominous) infausto

porter /'pɔːtə(r)/ *n* portiere *m*; (for luggage) facchino *m*

portfolio /pɔːt'fəʊlɪəʊ/ *n* cartella *f*; Comm portafoglio *m*

porthole /'pɔːthəʊl/ *n* oblò *m inv*

portion /'pɔːʃn/ *n* parte *f*; (of food) porzione *f*

portly /'pɔːtlɪ/ *adj* (**-ier, -iest**) corpulento

portrait /'pɔːtrɪt/ *n* ritratto *m*

portrait painter *n* ritrattista *mf*

portray /pɔː'treɪ/ *vt* ritrarre; (represent) descrivere; ⟨*actor*⟩ impersonare

portrayal /pɔː'treɪəl/ *n* ritratto *m*; (by actor) caratterizzazione *f*

Portugal /'pɔːtjʊɡl/ *n* Portogallo *m*

Portuguese /pɔːtjʊ'ɡiːz/ *adj & n* portoghese *mf*; (language) portoghese *m*

pose /pəʊz/ **1** *n* posa *f*
2 *vt* porre ⟨*problem, question*⟩
3 *vi* (for painter) posare; ∼ **as** atteggiarsi a

poser /'pəʊzə(r)/ *n* fam (puzzle) rompicapo *m inv*; (person) montato, -a *mf*

posh /pɒʃ/ *adj* fam lussuoso; ⟨*people*⟩ danaroso

position /pə'zɪʃn/ **1** *n* posizione *f*; (job) posto *m*; (status) ceto *m* [sociale]
2 *vt* posizionare

positive /'pɒzɪtɪv/ **1** *adj* positivo; (certain) sicuro; (progress) concreto
2 *n* positivo *m*

positive discrimination *n* misure *fpl* antidiscriminatorie

positively /'pɒzɪtɪvlɪ/ *adv* positivamente; (decidedly) decisamente

posse /'pɒsɪ/ *n* gruppo *m* di volontari armati

possess /pə'zes/ *vt* possedere

possession /pə'zeʃn/ *n* possesso *m*; ∼**s** *pl* beni *mpl*

possessive /pə'zesɪv/ *adj* possessivo

possessiveness /pə'zesɪvnɪs/ *n* carattere *m* possessivo

possessor /pə'zesə(r)/ *n* possessore, -ditrice *mf*

possibility /pɒsə'bɪlətɪ/ *n* possibilità *f inv*

possible /'pɒsəbl/ *adj* possibile

possibly /'pɒsəblɪ/ *adv* possibilmente; I couldn't ∼ accept non mi è possibile accettare; he can't ∼ be right non è possibile che abbia ragione; could you ∼...? potrebbe per favore...?

possum /'pɒsəm/ *n* fam opossum *m inv*; play ∼ far finta di dormire; (pretend to be dead) fare il morto

post¹ /pəʊst/ **1** *n* (pole) palo *m*
2 *vt* affiggere ⟨*notice*⟩

post² **1** *n* (place of duty) posto *m*

2 *vt* appostare; (transfer) assegnare

post³ **1** *n* (mail) posta *f*; by ∼ per posta **2** *vt* spedire; (put in letter box) imbucare; (as opposed to fax) mandare per posta; **keep somebody ∼ed** tenere qualcuno al corrente

post+ *pref* post+

postage /'pəustɪdʒ/ *n* affrancatura *f*; ∼ **and packaging** spese *fpl* di posta

postage stamp *n* francobollo *m*

postal /'pəustl/ *adj* postale

postal order *n* vaglia *m inv* postale

postbox *n* cassetta *f* delle lettere

postcard *n* cartolina *f*

postcode *n* codice *m* postale

post-date *vt* postdatare

poster /'pəustə(r)/ *n* poster *m inv*; (advertising, election) cartellone *m*

posterior /pɒ'stɪərɪə(r)/ *n fam* posteriore *m*

posterity /pɒ'sterətɪ/ *n* posterità *f*

poster paint *n* pittura *f* a guazzo

postgraduate /pəus(t)'grædjuət/ **1** *n* laureato, -a *mf* che continua gli studi **2** *adj* successivo alla laurea

posthumous /'pɒstjuməs/ *adj* postumo

posthumously /'pɒstjuməslɪ/ *adv* dopo la morte

posting /'pəustɪŋ/ *n* (job) incarico *m*; (Br: in mail) spedizione *f*; Comput posting *m inv*

postman /'pəustmən/ *n* postino *m*

postmark /'pəustmɑːk/ *n* timbro *m* postale

postmodern *adj* postmoderno

post-mortem /-'mɔːtəm/ *n* autopsia *f*

post-natal /-'neɪtl/ *adj* postnatale

post office *n* ufficio *m* postale

post office box *n* casella *f* postale

postpone /pəus(t)'pəun/ *vt* rimandare

postponement /pəus(t)'pəunmənt/ *n* rinvio *m*

postscript /'pəus(t)skrɪpt/ *n* post scriptum *m inv*

posture /'pɒstʃə(r)/ *n* posizione *f*

post-war *adj* del dopoguerra

pot /pɒt/ *n* vaso *m*; (for tea) teiera *f*; (for coffee) caffettiera *f*; (for cooking) pentola *f*; (sl: marijuana) erba *f*; ∼**s of money** *fam* un sacco di soldi; **go to** ∼ *fam* andare in malora

potash /'pɒtæʃ/ *n* potassa *f*

potassium /pə'tæsɪəm/ *n* potassio *m*

potato /pə'teɪtəu/ *n* (pl **-es**) patata *f*

potato chips Am, **potato crisps** Br *npl* patatine *fpl*

potato-peeler /-'piːlə(r)/ *n* pelapatate *m inv*

pot-bellied /'pɒtbelɪd/ *adj* panciuto

pot-belly /'pɒtbelɪ/ *n fam* pancione *m*

potent /'pəutənt/ *adj* potente

potentate /'pəutənteɪt/ *n* potentato *m*

potential /pə'tenʃl/ **1** *adj* potenziale **2** *n* potenziale *m*

potentially /pə'tenʃəlɪ/ *adv* potenzialmente

pothole *n* cavità *f inv*; (in road) buca *f*

potholer *n* speleologo, -a *mf*

potholing /'pɒthəulɪŋ/ *n* speleologia *f*

pot-luck *n* take ∼ affidarsi alla sorte

pot plant *n* pianta *f* da appartamento

pot-shot *n* take a ∼ at sparare a casaccio a

potted /'pɒtɪd/ *adj* conservato; (shortened) condensato

potted plant *n* pianta *f* da appartamento

potter¹ /'pɒtə(r)/ *vi* ∼ **[about]** gingillarsi

potter² *n* vasaio, -a *mf*

pottery /'pɒtərɪ/ *n* lavorazione *f* della ceramica; (articles) ceramiche *fpl*; (workshop) laboratorio *m* di ceramiche

potting compost /'pɒtɪŋ/ *n* terriccio *m*

potty /'pɒtɪ/ **1** *adj* (**-ier**, **-iest**) *fam* matto **2** *n* vasino *m*

pouch /pautʃ/ *n* marsupio *m*

pouffe /puːf/ *n* pouf *m inv*

poultry /'pəultrɪ/ *n* pollame *m*

pounce /pauns/ *vi* balzare; ∼ **on** saltare su

pound¹ /paund/ *n* libbra *f* (= 0,454 kg); (money) sterlina *f*

pound² **1** *vt* battere **2** *vi* ⟨heart⟩ battere forte; (run heavily) correre pesantemente

pound³ *n* (for cars) deposito *m* auto

pounding /'paundɪŋ/ **1** *n* martellio *m* **2** *adj* martellante

pour /pɔː(r)/ **1** *vt* versare **2** *vi* riversarsi; (with rain) piovere a dirotto
∎ **pour away** *vi* svuotare
∎ **pour in** *vi* ⟨people⟩ arrivare in massa; ⟨letters, money⟩ arrivare a valanghe; ⟨water⟩ entrare a fiotti
∎ **pour out** **1** *vi* riversarsi fuori **2** *vt* versare ⟨drink⟩; sfogare ⟨troubles⟩

pout /paut/ **1** *vi* fare il broncio **2** *n* broncio

poverty /'pɒvətɪ/ *n* povertà *f*

poverty line *n* soglia *f* di povertà

poverty-stricken *adj* indigente

POW *n abbr* ⟨**prisoner of war**⟩ prigioniero, -a *mf* di guerra

powder /'paudə(r)/ **1** *n* polvere *f*; (cosmetic) cipria *f* **2** *vt* polverizzare; (face) incipriare

powdered /'paudəd/ *adj* ⟨milk⟩ in polvere

powder room *n euph* toilette *f inv* per signore

powdery /'paʊdərɪ/ *adj* polveroso

power /'paʊə(r)/ *n* potere *m*; Electr corrente *f* [elettrica]; Math potenza *f*

powerboat *n* fuoribordo *m*

power cut *n* interruzione *f* di corrente

powered /'paʊəd/ *adj* ∼ **by electricity** alimentato da corrente elettrica

powerful /'paʊəfʊl/ *adj* potente

powerhouse /'paʊəhaʊs/ *n* (fig: person) persona *f* dinamica ed energica; **a ∼ of ideas** un vulcano di idee

powerless /'paʊəlɪs/ *adj* impotente

power line *n* linea *f* elettrica

power of attorney *n* procura *f*

power-on light *n* spia *f* di accensione

power plant *n* centrale *f* elettrica

power sharing *n* condivisione *f* del potere

power station *n* centrale *f* elettrica

power steering *n* Auto servosterzo *m*

power switch *n* pulsante *m* di alimentazione

power unit *n* (of computer etc) alimentatore *m*

power-walk **1** *n* camminata *f* a passo sostenuto
2 *vi* camminare a passo sostenuto

power-walker *n* persona *f* che fa camminate a passo sostenuto

power-walking *n* camminate *fpl* a passo sostenuto (come esercizio fisico)

pow-wow /'paʊwaʊ/ *n* (of American Indians) raduno *m* tribale; (fam: discussion) discussione *f*

pp *abbr* (**pages**) pp.; *abbr* (**per procurationem**) pp.

PPP *abbr* (**public-private partnership**) partnership *f* tra un ente pubblico e un'impresa privata

PR *n abbr* (**proportional representation**) proporzionale *f*; *abbr* (**public relations**) pubbliche relazioni *fpl*

practicable /'præktɪkəbl/ *adj* praticabile

practical /'præktɪkl/ *adj* pratico

practicality /præktɪ'kælɪtɪ/ *n* praticità *f*

practical joke *n* scherzo *m* pratico

practically /'præktɪklɪ/ *adv* praticamente

practice /'præktɪs/ *n* pratica *f*; (custom) usanza *f*; (habit) abitudine *f*; (exercise) esercizio *m*; Sport allenamento *m*; **in ∼** (in reality) in pratica; **out of ∼** fuori esercizio; **put into ∼** mettere in pratica

practicing /'præktɪsɪŋ/ *adj* Am = PRACTISING

practise /'præktɪs/ **1** *vt* fare pratica in; (carry out) mettere in pratica; esercitare ⟨*profession*⟩
2 *vi* esercitarsi; ⟨*doctor*⟩ praticare

practised /'præktɪst/ *adj* esperto

practising /'præktɪsɪŋ/ *adj* Br praticante; **a ∼ lawyer** un avvocato che esercita

pragmatic /præg'mætɪk/ *adj* pragmatico

pragmatism /'prægmətɪzm/ *n* pragmatismo *m*

pragmatist /'prægmətɪst/ *n* pragmatico, -a *mf*

prairie /'preərɪ/ *n* prateria *f*

praise /preɪz/ **1** *n* lode *f*
2 *vt* lodare

praiseworthy /'preɪzwɜːðɪ/ *adj* lodevole

pram /præm/ *n* carrozzella *f*

prance /prɑːns/ *vi* saltellare

prank /præŋk/ *n* tiro *m*

prattle /'prætl/ *vi* parlottare

prawn /prɔːn/ *n* gambero *m*

prawn cocktail *n* cocktail *m inv* di gamberetti

pray /preɪ/ *vi* pregare

prayer /preə(r)/ *n* preghiera *f*

preach /priːtʃ/ *vt/i* predicare

preacher /'priːtʃə(r)/ *n* predicatore, -trice *mf*

preamble /priː'æmbl/ *n* preambolo *m*

pre-arrange /priː-/ *vt* predisporre

precarious /prɪ'keərɪəs/ *adj* precario

precariously /prɪ'keərɪəslɪ/ *adv* in modo precario

precast /'priːkɑːst/ *adj* ⟨*concrete*⟩ prefabbricato

precaution /prɪ'kɔːʃn/ *n* precauzione *f*; **as a ∼** per precauzione

precautionary /prɪ'kɔːʃnərɪ/ *adj* preventivo

precede /prɪ'siːd/ *vt* precedere

precedence /'presɪdəns/ *n* precedenza *f*

precedent /'presɪdənt/ *n* precedente *m*

preceding /prɪ'siːdɪŋ/ *adj* precedente

preceptor /prɪ'septə(r)/ *n* Am Univ precettore *m*

precinct /'priːsɪŋkt/ *n* (traffic-free) zona *f* pedonale; (Am: district) circoscrizione *f*

precious /'preʃəs/ **1** *adj* prezioso; ⟨*style*⟩ ricercato
2 *adv* fam ∼ **little** ben poco

precipice /'presɪpɪs/ *n* precipizio *m*

precipitate¹ /prɪ'sɪpɪtət/ *adj* precipitoso

precipitate² /prɪ'sɪpɪteɪt/ *vt* precipitare

precipitation /prɪsɪpɪ'teɪʃn/ *n* precipitazione *f*

précis /'preɪsiː/ *n* (pl **précis** /'preɪsiːz/) sunto *m*

precise /prɪ'saɪs/ *adj* preciso

precisely /prɪ'saɪslɪ/ *adv* precisamente

P

precision /prɪˈsɪʒn/ *n* precisione *f*

preclude /prɪˈkluːd/ *vt* precludere

precocious /prɪˈkəʊʃəs/ *adj* precoce

precociousness /prɪˈkəʊʃsnɪs/ *n* precocità *f*

preconceived /priːkənˈsiːvd/ *adj* preconcetto

preconception /priːkənˈsepʃn/ *n* preconcetto *m*

precondition /priːkənˈdɪʃn/ ① *n* presupposto *m*
② *vt* Psych condizionare

precook /priːˈkʊk/ *vt* cuocere in anticipo

precursor /priːˈkɜːsə(r)/ *n* precursore *m*

predate /priːˈdeɪt/ *vt* retrodatare ⟨cheque⟩; ⟨building, painting⟩ essere antecedente a

predator /ˈpredətə(r)/ *n* predatore, -trice *mf*

predatory /ˈpredət(ə)rɪ/ *adj* rapace

predecessor /ˈpriːdɪsesə(r)/ *n* predecessore, -a *mf*

predetermine /priːdɪˈtɜːmɪn/ *vt* predeterminare

predicament /prɪˈdɪkəmənt/ *n* situazione *f* difficile

predicate /ˈpredɪkət/ *n* Gram predicato *m*

predicative /prɪˈdɪkətɪv/ *adj* predicativo

predict /prɪˈdɪkt/ *vt* predire

predictable /prɪˈdɪktəbl/ *adj* prevedibile

prediction /prɪˈdɪkʃn/ *n* previsione *f*

predigested /priːdaɪˈdʒestɪd/ *adj* predigerito

predispose /priːdɪˈspəʊz/ *vt* predisporre

predisposition /priːdɪspəˈzɪʃn/ *n* predisposizione *f*

predominant /prɪˈdɒmɪnənt/ *adj* predominante

predominantly /prɪˈdɒmɪnəntlɪ/ *adv* prevalentemente

predominate /prɪˈdɒmɪneɪt/ *vi* predominare

pre-eminent /priːˈemɪnənt/ *adj* preminente

pre-empt /priːˈempt/ *vt* (prevent) prevenire

pre-emptive /priːˈemptɪv/ *adj* preventivo

preen /priːn/ *vt* lisciarsi; ∼ oneself *fig* farsi bello

prefab /ˈpriːfæb/ *n* fam casa *f* prefabbricata

prefabricated /priːˈfæbrɪkeɪtɪd/ *adj* prefabbricato

preface /ˈprefɪs/ *n* prefazione *f*

prefatory /ˈprefət(ə)rɪ/ *adj* ⟨comments⟩ preliminare; ⟨pages, notes⟩ introduttivo

prefect /ˈpriːfekt/ *n* Schol studente, -tessa *mf* della scuola superiore con responsabilità disciplinari ecc

prefer /prɪˈfɜː(r)/ *vt* (pt/pp **preferred**) preferire; I ∼ to walk preferisco camminare

preferable /ˈprefərəbl/ *adj* preferibile (**to** a)

preferably /ˈprefərəblɪ/ *adv* preferibilmente

preference /ˈprefərəns/ *n* preferenza *f*

preferential /prefəˈrenʃl/ *adj* preferenziale

prefigure /priːˈfɪgə(r)/ *vt* preannunciare

prefix /ˈpriːfɪks/ *n* prefisso *m*

pregnancy /ˈpregnənsɪ/ *n* gravidanza *f*

pregnant /ˈpregnənt/ *adj* incinta

preheat /priːˈhiːt/ *vt* preriscaldare ⟨oven⟩

prehensile /priːˈhensaɪl/ *adj* prensile

prehistoric /priːhɪsˈtɒrɪk/ *adj* preistorico

pre-ignition /priːɪgˈnɪʃn/ *n* preaccensione *f*

pre-installed /priːɪnˈstɔːld/ *adj* preinstallato

prejudge /priːˈdʒʌdʒ/ *vt* giudicare prematuramente ⟨issue⟩

prejudice /ˈpredʒʊdɪs/ ① *n* pregiudizio *m*
② *vt* influenzare (**against** contro); (harm) danneggiare

prejudiced /ˈpredʒʊdɪst/ *adj* prevenuto

preliminary /prɪˈlɪmɪnərɪ/ *adj* preliminare

preloaded /priːˈləʊdɪd/ *adj* precaricato

prelude /ˈpreljuːd/ *n* preludio *m*

premarital /priːˈmærɪtl/ *adj* prematrimoniale

premarital sex *n* rapporti *mpl* prematrimoniali

premature /ˈpremətjʊə(r)/ *adj* prematuro

premature birth *n* parto *m* prematuro

prematurely /ˈpremətjʊəlɪ/ *adv* prematuramente

premeditated /priːˈmedɪteɪtɪd/ *adj* premeditato

premeditation /priːmedɪˈteɪʃn/ *n* premeditazione *f*

premenstrual syndrome /priːˈmenstrʊəl/ *n* sindrome *f* premestruale

premenstrual tension *n* tensione *f* premestruale

premier /ˈpremɪə(r)/ ① *adj* primario
② *n* Pol primo ministro *m*, premier *m* *inv*

première /ˈpremɪeə(r)/ *n* prima *f*

premiership /'premɪəʃɪp/ n Pol carica f di primo ministro nel Regno Unito; ≈ presidenza f del consiglio

premises /'premɪsɪz/ npl locali mpl; **on the ∼** sul posto

premium /'priːmɪəm/ n premio m; **be at a ∼** essere una cosa rara

premium bond n obbligazione f a premio

premonition /premə'nɪʃn/ n presentimento m

prenatal /priː'neɪtl/ adj esp Am prenatale

prenuptial agreement /priːˌnʌpʃl ə'griːmənt/ n accordo m prematrimoniale

preoccupation /priːɒkjʊ'peɪʃn/ n preoccupazione f

preoccupied /priː'ɒkjʊpaɪd/ adj preoccupato

preoperative /priː'ɒp(ə)rətɪv/ adj preoperatorio

preordained /priːɔː'deɪnd/ adj prestabilito; ⟨outcome⟩ predestinato

pre-owned /priː'əʊnd/ adj ⟨video, game⟩ di seconda mano

prep /prep/ n Sch compiti mpl

pre-packed /priː'pækt/ adj preconfezionato

prepaid /priː'peɪd/ adj pagato in anticipo; ⟨envelope⟩ già affrancato

preparation /prepə'reɪʃn/ n preparazione f; **∼s** pl preparativi mpl

preparatory /prɪ'pærətrɪ/ adj preparatorio; **∼ to** come preparazione per

preparatory school n Br = PREP SCHOOL

prepare /prɪ'peə(r)/ ① vt preparare ② vi prepararsi (**for** per); **∼d to** disposto a

prepay /priː'peɪ/ vt (pt/pp **-paid**) pagare in anticipo

preponderance /prɪ'pɒndərəns/ n preponderanza f

preponderantly /prɪ'pɒndərəntlɪ/ adv in modo preponderante

preponderate /prɪ'pɒndəreɪt/ vi predominare

preposition /prepə'zɪʃn/ n preposizione f

prepossessing /priːpə'zesɪŋ/ adj attraente

preposterous /prɪ'pɒstərəs/ adj assurdo

pre-programmed /priː'prəʊɡræmd/ adj programmato; Comput preprogrammato

prep school n scuola f elementare privata

pre-recorded /-rɪ'kɔː:dɪd/ adj in differita

prerequisite /priː'rekwɪzɪt/ n condizione f sine qua non

prerogative /prɪ'rɒɡətɪv/ n prerogativa f

Pres. abbr (**President**) Pres.

Presbyterian /prezbɪ'tɪərɪən/ adj & n presbiteriano, -a mf

pre-school /'priːskuːl/ ① n Am scuola f materna, asilo m ② adj ⟨child⟩ in età prescolastica; ⟨years⟩ prescolastico

prescribe /prɪ'skraɪb/ vt prescrivere

prescription /prɪ'skrɪpʃn/ n Med ricetta f

prescription charges npl Br ≈ ticket m inv sui medicinali

prescriptive /prɪ'skrɪptɪv/ adj normativo

presence /'prezns/ n presenza f

presence of mind n presenza f di spirito

present¹ /'preznt/ ① adj presente ② n presente m; **at ∼** attualmente

present² n (gift) regalo m; **give somebody something as a ∼** regalare qualcosa a qualcuno

present³ /prɪ'zent/ vt presentare; **∼ somebody with an award** consegnare un premio a qualcuno

presentable /prɪ'zentəbl/ adj **be ∼** essere presentabile

presentation /prezn'teɪʃn/ n presentazione f

present-day adj attuale

presenter /prɪ'zentə(r)/ n TV, Radio presentatore, -trice mf

presently /'prezntlɪ/ adv fra poco; (Am: now) attualmente

present perfect n passato m prossimo

preservation /prezə'veɪʃn/ n conservazione f

preservative /prɪ'zɜːvətɪv/ n conservante m

preserve /prɪ'zɜːv/ ① vt preservare; (maintain & Culin) conservare ② n (in hunting & fig) riserva f; (jam) marmellata f

pre-set /priː'set/ vt programmare

pre-shrunk /priː'ʃrʌŋk/ adj ⟨fabric⟩ irrestringibile

preside /prɪ'zaɪd/ vi presiedere (**over** a)

presidency /'prezɪdənsɪ/ n presidenza f

president /'prezɪdənt/ n presidente m

presidential /prezɪ'denʃl/ adj presidenziale

press /pres/ ① n (machine) pressa f; (newspapers) stampa f ② vt premere; pressare ⟨flower⟩; (iron) stirare; (squeeze) stringere ③ vi (urge) incalzare
■ **press ahead** vi (continue) proseguire
■ **press for** vi fare pressione per; **be ∼ed for** (short of) essere a corto di

■ **press on** *vi* andare avanti

press agency *n* agenzia *f* di stampa

press conference *n* conferenza *f* stampa

press cutting *n* ritaglio *m* di giornale

press-gang *vt* forzare

pressing /'presɪŋ/ *adj* urgente

press release *n* comunicato *m* stampa

press stud *n* [bottone *m*] automatico *m*

press-up *n* flessione *f*

pressure /'preʃɪŋ/ ① *n* pressione *f* ② *vt* = PRESSURIZE

pressure-cooker *n* pentola *f* a pressione

pressure group *n* gruppo *m* di pressione

pressurize /'preʃə(r)/ *vt* far pressione su

pressurized /'preʃəraɪzd/ *adj* ⟨cabin⟩ pressurizzato

prestige /pre'sti:ʒ/ *n* prestigio *m*

prestigious /pre'stɪdʒəs/ *adj* prestigioso

presumably /prɪ'zju:məblɪ/ *adv* presumibilmente

presume /prɪ'zju:m/ ① *vt* presumere; ~ to do something permettersi di fare qualcosa ② *vi* ~ on approfittare di

presumption /prɪ'zʌmpʃn/ *n* presunzione *f*; (boldness) impertinenza *f*

presumptuous /prɪ'zʌmptjʊəs/ *adj* impertinente

presuppose /pri:sə'pəʊz/ *vt* presupporre

presupposition /pri:sʌpə'zɪʃn/ *n* presupposizione *f*

pre-tax /'pri:tæks/ *adj* al lordo d'imposta

pretence /prɪ'tens/ *n* finzione *f*; (pretext) pretesto *m*; it's all ~ è tutta una scena

pretend /prɪ'tend/ ① *vt* fingere; (claim) pretendere ② *vi* fare finta

pretender /prɪ'tendə(r)/ *n* pretendente *mf*

pretension /pri:'tenʃn/ *n* pretesa *f*

pretentious /prɪ'tenʃəs/ *adj* pretenzioso

preterite /'pretərɪt/ *n* preterito *m*

pretext /'pri:tekst/ *n* pretesto *m*

pretty /'prɪtɪ/ ① *adj* (-ier, -iest) carino ② *adv* (fam: fairly) abbastanza

prevail /prɪ'veɪl/ *vi* prevalere; ~ upon somebody to do something convincere qualcuno a fare qualcosa

prevailing /prɪ'veɪlɪŋ/ *adj* prevalente

prevalence /'prevələns/ *n* diffusione *f*

prevalent /'prevələnt/ *adj* diffuso

prevaricate /prɪ'værɪkeɪt/ *vi* tergiversare

prevent /prɪ'vent/ *vt* impedire; ~ somebody [from] doing something impedire a qualcuno di fare qualcosa

preventable /prɪ'venʃn/ *adj* evitabile

prevention /prɪ'venʃn/ *n* prevenzione *f*

preventive /prɪ'ventɪv/ *adj* preventivo

preview /'pri:vju:/ *n* anteprima *f*

previous /'pri:vɪəs/ *adj* precedente

previously /'pri:vɪəslɪ/ *adv* precedentemente

pre-war /pri:'wɔ:(r)/ *adj* anteguerra

pre-wash /'pri:wɒʃ/ *n* prelavaggio *m*

prey /preɪ/ ① *n* preda *f*; bird of ~ uccello *m* rapace ② *vi* ~ on far preda di; ~ on sb's mind attanagliare qualcuno

price /praɪs/ ① *n* prezzo *m* ② *vt* Comm fissare il prezzo di

price-conscious *adj* consapevole dell'andamento dei prezzi

price cut *n* riduzione *f* di prezzo

price cutting *n* taglio *m* dei prezzi

price freeze *n* congelamento *m* dei prezzi

price increase *n* aumento *m* di prezzo

priceless /'praɪslɪs/ *adj* inestimabile; (fam: amusing) spassosissimo

price list *n* listino *m* prezzi

price/performance ratio *n* rapporto *m* prezzo/prestazioni

price range *n* gamma *f* di prezzi

price rise *n* rialzo *m* dei prezzi

price tag *n* talloncino *m* del prezzo

price war *n* guerra *f* dei prezzi

pricey /'praɪsɪ/ *adj* fam caro

pricing policy /'praɪsɪŋ/ *n* politica *f* di determinazione dei prezzi

prick /prɪk/ ① *n* puntura *f*; vulg (penis) cazzo *m*; (person) stronzo *m* ② *vt* pungere

■ **prick up** *vt* ~ up one's ears rizzare le orecchie

prickle /'prɪkl/ *n* spina *f*; (sensation) formicolio *m*

prickly /'prɪklɪ/ *adj* pungente; ⟨person⟩ irritabile

pride /praɪd/ ① *n* orgoglio *m*; (of lions) branco *m*; ~ of place posizione *f* d'onore ② *vt* ~ oneself on vantarsi di

priest /pri:st/ *n* prete *m*

priesthood /'pri:sthʊd/ *n* (clergy) clero *m*; (calling) sacerdozio *m*; enter the ~ farsi prete

prig /prɪg/ *n* presuntuoso *m*

priggish /'prɪgɪʃ/ *adj* presuntuoso

prim /prɪm/ *adj* (primmer, primmest) perbenino

primacy /'praɪməsɪ/ *n* primato *m*; (of party, power) supremazia *f*; Relig carica *f* di primate

prima facie /praɪmə'feɪʃi/ **1** *adv* (at first) a prima vista
2 *adj* a prima vista legittimo

primal /'praɪməl/ *adj* ⟨quality, myth, feeling⟩ primitivo

primarily /'praɪmərɪlɪ/ *adv* in primo luogo

primary /'praɪmərɪ/ *adj* primario; (chief) principale

primary colour *n* colore *m* primario

primary school *n* scuola *f* elementare

primate /'praɪmeɪt/ *n* Zool, Relig primate *m*

prime[1] /praɪm/ **1** *adj* principale, primo; (first-rate) eccellente
2 *n* **be in one's ~** essere nel fiore degli anni

prime[2] *vt* preparare ⟨surface, person⟩

Prime Minister *n* Primo Ministro *m*

prime mover *n* promotore, -trice *mf*

primer /'praɪmə(r)/ *n* (paint) base *f*; (for detonating) innesco *m*

prime time **1** *n* prime time *m inv*, fascia *f* di massimo ascolto
2 *attrib* ⟨advertising, programme⟩ nella fascia di massimo ascolto

primeval /praɪ'miːvl/ *adj* primitivo

primitive /'prɪmɪtɪv/ *adj* primitivo

primordial /praɪ'mɔːdɪəl/ *adj* primordiale

primrose /'prɪmrəʊz/ *n* primula *f*

prince /prɪns/ *n* principe *m*

princely /'prɪnslɪ/ *adj* ⟨life, role⟩ da principe; ⟨amount, style⟩ principesco

princess /prɪn'ses/ *n* principessa *f*

principal /'prɪnsɪpl/ **1** *adj* principale
2 *n* Sch preside *m*

principality /prɪnsɪ'pælɪtɪ/ *n* principato *m*

principally /'prɪnsəplɪ/ *adv* principalmente

principle /'prɪnsəpl/ *n* principio *m*; **in ~** in teoria; **on ~** per principio; **~s** *pl* (fundamentals) fondamenti *mpl*

print /prɪnt/ **1** *n* (mark, trace) impronta *f*; Phot copia *f*; (letters) stampatello *m*; (picture) stampa *f*; **in ~** (printed out) stampato; ⟨book⟩ in commercio; **out of ~** esaurito
2 *vt/i* stampare; (write in capitals) scrivere in stampatello
■ **print off** *vt* stampare ⟨copies⟩
■ **print out** *vt/i* Comput stampare

printed matter /'prɪntɪd/ *n* stampe *fpl*

printer /'prɪntə(r)/ *n* stampante *f*; (person) tipografo, -a *mf*

printer port *n* porta *f* per la stampante

printing /'prɪntɪŋ/ *n* tipografia *f*

printout /'prɪntaʊt/ *n* Comput stampa *f*

print-preview *vt* Comput fare l'anteprima di stampa di

print speed *n* velocità *f* di stampa

prior /'praɪə(r)/ **1** *adj* precedente
2 *prep* **~ to** prima di

priority /praɪ'ɒrətɪ/ *n* precedenza *f*; (matter) priorità *f inv*

priory /'praɪərɪ/ *n* monastero *m*

prise /praɪz/ *vt* **~ open/up** forzare
■ **prise off** *vt* togliere facendo leva ⟨lid⟩

prism /'prɪzm/ *n* prisma *m*

prison /'prɪzn/ *n* prigione *f*

prison camp *n* campo *m* di prigionia

prisoner /'prɪz(ə)nə(r)/ *n* prigioniero, -a *mf*

prison officer *n* guardia *f* carceraria

prison sentence *n* pena *f* detentiva

prissy /'prɪsɪ/ *adj* ⟨person⟩ perbenista

pristine /'prɪstiːn/ *adj* originario; (unspoilt) intatto

privacy /'prɪvəsɪ/ *n* privacy *f*

private /'praɪvət/ **1** *adj* privato; ⟨car, secretary, letter⟩ personale
2 *n* Mil soldato *m* semplice; **in ~** in privato

private enterprise *n* iniziativa *f* privata

private eye *n* fam investigatore, -trice *mf* privato, -a

privately /'praɪvətlɪ/ *adv* ⟨funded, educated etc⟩ privatamente; (in secret) in segreto; (confidentially) in privato; (inwardly) interiormente

private property *n* proprietà *f* privata

privation /praɪ'veɪʃn/ *n* privazione *f*; **~s** *pl* stenti *mpl*

privatization /praɪvətaɪ'zeɪʃn/ *n* privatizzazione *f*

privatize /'praɪvətaɪz/ *vt* privatizzare

privilege /'prɪvəlɪdʒ/ *n* privilegio *m*

privileged /'prɪvəlɪdʒd/ *adj* privilegiato

privy /'prɪvɪ/ *adj* **be ~ to** essere al corrente di

prize /praɪz/ **1** *n* premio *m*
2 *adj* (idiot etc) perfetto
3 *vt* apprezzare

prize draw *n* estrazione *f* a premi

prize-giving /'praɪzɡɪvɪŋ/ *n* premiazione *f*

prize money *n* montepremi *m*

prizewinner *n* vincitore, -trice *mf*

prize-winning *adj* vincente

pro /prəʊ/ *n* (fam: professional) professionista *mf*; **the ~s and cons** il pro e il contro

proactive /'prəʊ'æktɪv/ *adj* ⟨approach⟩ proattivo

probability /prɒbə'bɪlətɪ/ *n* probabilità *f inv*

probable /'prɒbəbl/ *adj* probabile

probably /'prɒbəblɪ/ *adv* probabilmente

p

probate /'prəʊbeɪt/ n Jur omologazione f

probation /prə'beɪʃn/ n prova f; Jur libertà f vigilata

probationary /prə'beɪʃnəri/ adj in prova; ~ **period** periodo m di prova

probationer /prə'beɪʃnə(r)/ n (employee on trial) impiegato, -a mf in prova; (trainee) apprendista mf

probation officer n agente m addetto alla sorveglianza di chi si trova in regime di libertà vigilata

probe /prəʊb/ ❶ n sonda f; (fig: investigation) indagine f
❷ vt sondare; (investigate) esaminare a fondo

probing /'prəʊbɪŋ/ adj ⟨question⟩ penetrante

problem /'prɒbləm/ ❶ n problema m
❷ attrib difficile

problematic /prɒblə'mætɪk/ adj problematico

problem page n posta f del cuore

procedural /prə'siːdʒərəl/ adj ⟨detail, error⟩ procedurale

procedure /prə'siːdʒe(r)/ n procedimento m

proceed /prə'siːd/ ❶ vi procedere
❷ vt ~ to do something proseguire facendo qualcosa

proceedings /prə'siːdɪŋz/ npl (report) atti mpl; Jur azione fsg legale

proceeds /'prəʊsiːdz/ npl ricavato msg

process /'prəʊses/ ❶ n processo m; (procedure) procedimento m; in the ~ nel far ciò
❷ vt trattare; Admin occuparsi di; Phot sviluppare

processing /'prəʊsesɪŋ/ n trattamento m; food ~ l'industria alimentare

procession /prə'seʃn/ n processione f

processor /'prəʊsesə(r)/ n Comput processore m; (for food) tritatutto m inv

pro-choice /prəʊ'tʃɔɪs/ adj abortista

proclaim /prə'kleɪm/ vt proclamare

proclamation /prɒklə'meɪʃn/ n proclamazione f

proclivity /prə'klɪvəti/ n tendenza f

procrastinate /prə'kræstɪneɪt/ vi procrastinare

procrastination /prəkræstɪ'neɪʃn/ n procrastinazione f

procreate /'prəʊkrɪeɪt/ vi procreare

procreation /prəʊkrɪ'eɪʃn/ n procreazione f

procure /prə'kjʊə(r)/ vt ottenere

prod /prɒd/ ❶ n colpetto m
❷ vt (pt/pp **prodded**) punzecchiare; fig incitare

prodigal /'prɒdɪgl/ adj prodigo

prodigal son n figliol m prodigo

prodigious /prə'dɪdʒəs/ adj prodigioso

prodigy /'prɒdɪdʒɪ/ n **[infant]** ~ bambino m prodigio

produce[1] /'prɒdjuːs/ n prodotti mpl; ~ **of Italy** prodotto in Italia

produce[2] /prə'djuːs/ vt produrre; (bring out) tirar fuori; (cause) causare; (fam: give birth to) fare

producer /prə'djuːsə(r)/ n produttore m

product /'prɒdʌkt/ n prodotto m

production /prə'dʌkʃn/ n produzione f; Theat spettacolo m

production control n controllo m della produzione

production director n direttore, -trice mf della produzione

production line n catena f di montaggio

production management n gestione f della produzione

production manager n direttore, -trice mf della produzione

productive /prə'dʌktɪv/ adj produttivo

productivity /prɒdʌk'tɪvəti/ n produttività f

product range n gamma f di prodotti

Prof. /prɒf/ abbr (**Professor**) Prof.

profane /prə'feɪn/ adj profano; (blasphemous) blasfemo

profanity /prə'fænəti/ n (oath) bestemmia f

profess /prə'fes/ vt (claim) dichiarare

professed /prə'fest/ adj (claiming to be) sedicente

profession /prə'feʃn/ n professione f

professional /prə'feʃnəl/ ❶ adj professionale; (not amateur) professionista; (piece of work) da professionista; ⟨man⟩ di professione
❷ n professionista mf

professionalism /prə'feʃnəlɪzm/ n (of person, organization, work) professionalità f; Sport professionismo m

professionally /prə'feʃnəlɪ/ adv professionalmente

professor /prə'fesə(r)/ n professore m [universitario]

professorial /prɒfə'sɔːrɪəl/ adj ⟨duties, post, salary⟩ professorale

proffer /'prɒfə(r)/ vt (hold out) porgere; (fig: offer) offrire

proficiency /prə'fɪʃnsɪ/ n competenza f

proficient /prə'fɪʃnt/ adj competente (in in)

profile /'prəʊfaɪl/ n profilo m

profiling /'prəʊfaɪlɪŋ/ n profilo m; genetic ~ profilo genetico

profit /'prɒfɪt/ ❶ n profitto m
❷ vi ~ from trarre profitto da

profitable /'prɒfɪtəbl/ adj proficuo

profitably /'prɒfɪtəblɪ/ *adv* in modo proficuo

profit and loss account *n* conto *m* profitti e perdite

profiteer /prɒfɪ'tɪə(r)/ *n* profittatore, -trice *mf*

profiterole /prə'fɪtərəʊl/ *n* profiterole *m inv*

profit margin *n* margine *m* di profitto

profit-sharing *n* partecipazione *f* agli utili

profligate /'prɒflɪgət/ *adj* (extravagant) spendaccione; (dissolute) dissoluto; (spending) eccessivo

pro forma invoice /'fɔːmə/ *n* fattura *f* proforma

profound /prə'faʊnd/ *adj* profondo

profoundly /prə'faʊndlɪ/ *adv* profondamente

profuse /prə'fjuːs/ *adj* ~ apologies una profusione di scuse

profusely /prə'fjuːslɪ/ *adv* profusamente

profusion /prə'fjuːʒn/ *n* profusione *f*; in ~ in abbondanza

progeny /'prɒdʒənɪ/ *n* progenie *f inv*

prognosis /prɒg'nəʊsɪs/ *n* (pl **-oses**) (prediction) previsione *f*; Med prognosi *f inv*

prognosticate /prɒg'nɒstɪkeɪt/ *vt* pronosticare

program /'prəʊgræm/ ① *n* Comput programma *m*
② *vt* (pt/pp **programmed**) programmare

programme /'prəʊgræm/ *n* Br programma *m*

programmer /'prəʊgræmə(r)/ *n* Comput programmatore, -trice *mf*

programming /'prəʊgræmɪŋ/ *n* programmazione *f*

progress¹ /'prəʊgres/ *n* progresso *m*; in ~ in corso; **make** ~ *fig* fare progressi

progress² /prə'gres/ *vi* progredire; *fig* fare progressi

progression /prə'greʃn/ *n* (development) progresso *m*; (improvement) evoluzione *f*; (series) serie *f*

progressive /prə'gresɪv/ *adj* progressivo; (reforming) progressista

progressively /prə'gresɪvlɪ/ *adv* progressivamente

progress report *n* (on project) resoconto sull'andamento del progetto; (on patient) cartella *f* clinica

prohibit /prə'hɪbɪt/ *vt* proibire

prohibition /prəʊhɪ'bɪʃn/ *n* proibizione; P~ Am proibizionismo *m*

prohibitive /prə'hɪbɪtɪv/ *adj* proibitivo

prohibitively /prə'hɪbɪtɪvlɪ/ *adv* ⟨expensive⟩ in modo proibitivo

project¹ /'prɒdʒekt/ *n* progetto *m*; Sch ricerca *f*

project² /prə'dʒekt/ ① *vt* proiettare ⟨film, image⟩
② *vi* (jut out) sporgere

projectile /prə'dʒektaɪl/ *n* proiettile *m*

projection /prə'dʒekʃn/ *n* (of figures) proiezione *f*

project manager *n* project manager *mf inv*

projector /prə'dʒektə(r)/ *n* proiettore *m*

proletarian /prəʊlə'teərɪən/ *adj & n* proletario, -a *mf*

proletariat /prəʊlɪ'teərɪət/ *n* proletariato *m*

pro-life /prəʊ'laɪf/ *adj* antiabortista

proliferate /prə'lɪfəreɪt/ *vi* proliferare

proliferation /prəlɪfə'reɪʃn/ *n* proliferazione *f*

prolific /prə'lɪfɪk/ *adj* prolifico

prologue /'prəʊlɒg/ *n* prologo *m*

prolong /prə'lɒŋ/ *vt* prolungare

prom /prɒm/ *n* (Br fam: at seaside) lungomare *m inv*; (Am fam: at high school) ballo *m* studentesco

promenade /prɒmə'nɑːd/ *n* lungomare *m inv*

prominence /'prɒmɪnəns/ *n* (of person, issue) importanza *f*; (of object) sporgenza *f*; (hill) rilievo *m*

prominent /'prɒmɪnənt/ *adj* prominente; (conspicuous) di rilievo

promiscuity /prɒmɪ'skjuːətɪ/ *n* promiscuità *f*

promiscuous /prə'mɪskjʊəs/ *adj* promiscuo

promise /'prɒmɪs/ ① *n* promessa *f*
② *vt* promettere; ~ somebody that promettere a qualcuno che; **I** ~**d to** l'ho promesso

Promised Land /prɒmɪst'lænd/ *n* Terra *f* Promessa

promising /'prɒmɪsɪŋ/ *adj* promettente

promo /'prəʊməʊ/ *n* (fam: of product) campagna *f* promozionale; (video) video *m inv* promozionale

promontory /'prɒmənt(ə)rɪ/ *n* promontorio *m*

promote /prə'məʊt/ *vt* promuovere; **be** ~**d** essere promosso

promoter /prə'məʊtə(r)/ *n* promotore, -trice *mf*

promotion /prə'məʊʃn/ *n* promozione *f*

promotional /prə'məʊʃnəl/ *adj* Comm promozionale

promotional video *n* video *m* promozionale

prompt /prɒmpt/ ① *adj* immediato; (punctual) puntuale
② *adv* in punto
③ *vt* incitare (**to** a); Theat suggerire a
④ *vi* suggerire
⑤ *n* Comput prompt *m inv*

prompter /'prɒmptə(r)/ n suggeritore, -trice mf

promptly /'prɒmptlɪ/ adv puntualmente

Proms /prɒmz/ npl rassegna f di concerti estivi di musica classica presso l'Albert Hall a Londra

prone /prəʊn/ adj prono; **be ∼ to do something** essere incline a fare qualcosa

prong /prɒŋ/ n dente m

pronoun /'prəʊnaʊn/ n pronome m

pronounce /prə'naʊns/ vt pronunciare; (declare) dichiarare
■ **pronounce on** vt pronunciarsi su ⟨case, subject⟩

pronounced /prə'naʊnst/ adj (noticeable) pronunciato

pronouncement /prə'naʊnsmənt/ n dichiarazione f

pronunciation /prənʌnsɪ'eɪʃn/ n pronuncia f

proof /pruːf/ ① n prova f; Typ bozza f, prova f; **12% ∼** 12° ② adj **∼ against** a prova di

proof of purchase n ricevuta f d'acquisto

proof-read vt correggere le bozze di

proof-reader n correttore, -trice mf di bozze

proof-reading n revisione f di bozze

prop¹ /prɒp/ ① n puntello m ② vt (pt/pp **propped**) **∼ open** tenere aperto; **∼ against** (lean) appoggiare a
■ **prop up** vt sostenere

prop² n Theat, fam accessorio m di scena

propaganda /prɒpə'gændə/ n propaganda f

propagate /'prɒpəgeɪt/ vt propagare

propagator /'prɒpəgeɪtə(r)/ n propagatore m

propane /'prəʊpeɪn/ n propano m

propel /prə'pel/ vt (pt/pp **propelled**) spingere

propellant /prə'pelənt/ n (in aerosol) gas m inv propellente; (in rocket) propellente m

propeller /prə'pelə(r)/ n elica f

propelling pencil /prə'pelɪŋ/ n portamina m inv

propensity /prə'pensəti/ n tendenza f

proper /'prɒpə(r)/ adj corretto; (suitable) adatto; (fam: real) vero [e proprio]

properly /'prɒpəlɪ/ adv correttamente

proper name, **proper noun** n nome m proprio

property /'prɒpəti/ n proprietà f inv

property developer n impresa f edile; (person) impresario m edile

property market n mercato m immobiliare

prophecy /'prɒfəsi/ n profezia f

prophesy /'prɒfɪsaɪ/ vt (pt/pp **-ied**) profetizzare

prophet /'prɒfɪt/ n profeta m

prophetic /prə'fetɪk/ adj profetico

prophylactic /prɒfɪ'læktɪk/ ① n (condom) profilattico m, preservativo m; (Med: treatment) misura f profilattica ② adj profilattico

proponent /prə'pəʊnənt/ n fautore, -trice mf

proportion /prə'pɔːʃn/ n proporzione f; (share) parte f; **be in ∼** essere proporzionato (to a); **be out of ∼** essere sproporzionato; **∼s** pl (dimensions) proporzioni fpl

proportional /prə'pɔːʃnəl/ adj proporzionale

proportionally /prə'pɔːʃnəlɪ/ adv in proporzione

proportional representation n rappresentanza f proporzionale

proposal /prə'pəʊzl/ n proposta f; (of marriage) proposta f di matrimonio

propose /prə'pəʊz/ ① vt proporre; (intend) proporsi ② vi fare una proposta di matrimonio

proposition /prɒpə'zɪʃn/ n proposta f; (fam: task) impresa f

proprietor /prə'praɪətə(r)/ n proprietario, -a mf

propriety /prə'praɪəti/ n correttezza f; **the proprieties** pl l'etichetta f

propulsion /prə'pʌlʃn/ n propulsione f

pro rata /'rɑːtə/ adj **on a ∼ ∼ basis** in proporzione

prosaic /prə'zeɪɪk/ adj prosaico

proscribe vt (exile) esiliare; (ban) bandire

prose /prəʊz/ n prosa f

prosecute /'prɒsɪkjuːt/ vt intentare azione contro

prosecution /prɒsɪ'kjuːʃn/ n azione f giudiziaria; **the ∼** l'accusa f

prosecutor /'prɒsɪkjuːtə(r)/ n [Public] **P∼** Pubblico Ministero m

prospect¹ /'prɒspekt/ n (expectation) prospettiva f; (view) vista f

prospect² /prə'spekt/ vi **∼ for** cercare

prospective /prə'spektɪv/ adj (future) futuro; (possible) potenziale

prospector /prə'spektə(r)/ n cercatore m

prospectus /prə'spektəs/ n prospetto m

prosper /'prɒspə(r)/ vi prosperare; ⟨person⟩ stare bene finanziariamente

prosperity /prɒ'sperəti/ n prosperità f

prosperous /'prɒspərəs/ adj prospero

prostate /'prɒsteɪt/ n prostata f

prosthesis /prɒs'θiːsɪs/ n protesi f

prostitute /'prɒstɪtjuːt/ ① n prostituta f ② vt fig prostituire

prostitution /prɒstɪˈtjuːʃn/ *n*
prostituzione *f*

prostrate /ˈprɒstreɪt/ *adj* prostrato; ∼
with grief *fig* prostrato dal dolore

protagonist /prəˈtægənɪst/ *n*
protagonista *mf*

protect /prəˈtekt/ *vt* proteggere (**from** da)

protection /prəˈtekʃn/ *n* protezione *f*

protection factor *n* (of suntan lotion)
fattore *m* di protezione

protection racket *n* racket *m inv* di
protezione

protective /prəˈtektɪv/ *adj* protettivo

protector /prəˈtektə(r)/ *n* protettore,
-trice *mf*

protégé /ˈprɒtɪʒeɪ/ *n* protetto *m*

protein /ˈprəʊtiːn/ *n* proteina *f*

protest[1] /ˈprəʊtest/ *n* protesta *f*

protest[2] /prəˈtest/ *vt/i* protestare

Protestant /ˈprɒtɪstənt/ *adj & n*
protestante *mf*

Protestantism /ˈprɒtɪstəntɪzm/ *n*
protestantesimo *m*

protestation /prɒtɪˈsteɪʃn/ *n* protesta *f*

protester /prəˈtestə(r)/ *n* contestatore,
-trice *mf*; (at demonstration) dimostrante *mf*

protocol /ˈprəʊtəkɒl/ *n* protocollo *m*

prototype /ˈprəʊtətaɪp/ *n* prototipo *m*

protract /prəˈtrækt/ *vt* protrarre

protracted /prəˈtræktɪd/ *adj* prolungato

protractor /prəˈtræktə(r)/ *n* goniometro
m

protrude /prəˈtruːd/ *vi* sporgere

protruding /prəˈtruːdɪŋ/ *adj* ‹teeth, chin,
ledge› sporgente

protuberance /prəˈtuːbərəns/ *n*
protuberanza *f*

proud /praʊd/ *adj* fiero (**of** di)

proudly /ˈpraʊdlɪ/ *adv* fieramente

prove /pruːv/ ① *vt* provare
② *vi* ∼ to be a lie rivelarsi una bugia

proven /ˈpruːvən/ *adj* dimostrato

proverb /ˈprɒvɜːb/ *n* proverbio *m*

proverbial /prəˈvɜːbɪəl/ *adj* proverbiale

provide /prəˈvaɪd/ ① *vt* fornire; ∼
somebody with something fornire
qualcosa a qualcuno
② *vi* ∼ for (allow for) tenere conto di; ‹law›
prevedere

provided /prəˈvaɪdɪd/ *conj* ∼ [that]
purché

providence /ˈprɒvɪdəns/ *n* provvidenza
f

provident /ˈprɒvɪdənt/ *adj* previdenziale

providential /prɒvɪˈdenʃl/ *adj*
provvidenziale

provider /prəˈvaɪdə(r)/ *n* (in family)
persona *f* che mantiene la famiglia

providing /prəˈvaɪdɪŋ/ *conj* = PROVIDED

province /ˈprɒvɪns/ *n* provincia *f*; fig
campo *m*

provincial /prəˈvɪnʃl/ *adj* provinciale

provincialism /prəˈvɪnʃəlɪzm/ *n*
provincialismo *m*

provision /prəˈvɪʒn/ *n* (of food, water)
approvvigionamento *m* (of di); (of law)
disposizione *f*; make ∼ for ‹law›
prevedere; ∼s *pl* provviste *fpl*

provisional /prəˈvɪʒ(ə)nəl/ *adj*
provvisorio

provisionally /prəˈvɪʒ(ə)nəlɪ/ *adv*
provvisoriamente

proviso /prəˈvaɪzəʊ/ *n* condizione *f*

provocation /prɒvəˈkeɪʃn/ *n*
provocazione *f*

provocative /prəˈvɒkətɪv/ *adj*
provocatorio; (sexually) provocante

provocatively /prəˈvɒkətɪvlɪ/ *adv* in
modo provocatorio; ‹smile, be dressed› in
modo provocante

provoke /prəˈvəʊk/ *vt* provocare

provost /ˈprɒvəst/ *n* Am Univ decano *m*; Br
Univ, Sch rettore *m*; (in Scotland) sindaco *m*

prow /praʊ/ *n* prua *f*

prowess /ˈpraʊɪs/ *n* abilità *f inv*

prowl /praʊl/ ① *vi* aggirarsi
② *n* on the ∼ in cerca di preda

prowler /ˈpraʊlə(r)/ *n* tipo *m* sospetto

proximity /prɒkˈsɪmətɪ/ *n* prossimità *f*

proxy /ˈprɒksɪ/ *n* procura *f*; (person)
persona *f* che agisce per procura

prude /pruːd/ *n* be a ∼ essere
eccessivamente pudico

prudence /ˈpruːdəns/ *n* prudenza *f*

prudent /ˈpruːdənt/ *adj* prudente; (wise)
oculato *f*

prudently /ˈpruːdəntlɪ/ *adv* con
prudenza

prudish /ˈpruːdɪʃ/ *adj* eccessivamente
pudico

prudishness /ˈpruːdɪʃnɪs/ *n* eccessivo
pudore *m*

prune[1] /pruːn/ *n* prugna *f* secca

prune[2] *vt* potare

pry /praɪ/ *vi* (pt/pp **pried**) ficcare il naso

prying /ˈpraɪɪŋ/ *adj* curioso

PS *n abbr* (**postscriptum**) PS *m inv*

psalm /sɑːm/ *n* salmo *m*

pseud /sjuːd/ *n fam* intellettualoide *mf*

pseudonym /ˈsjuːdənɪm/ *n* pseudonimo
m

PSHE *n abbr* Br (**personal social and
health education**) (school subject) studio
m degli aspetti personali, sociali e
sanitari dell'individuo in relazione alla
collettività

PST *abbr* Am (**Pacific Standard Time**)
tempo *m* medio della zona del Pacifico

psych /saɪk/ vt ~ **out** (fam: unnerve)
snervare ~ **up** vt (fam: prepare mentally)
preparare psicologicamente

psychedelic /saɪkə'delɪk/ adj
psichedelico

psychiatric /saɪkɪ'ætrɪk/ adj
psichiatrico

psychiatrist /saɪ'kaɪətrɪst/ n psichiatra
mf

psychiatry /saɪkaɪətrɪ/ n psichiatria f

psychic /'saɪkɪk/ ① n sensitivo, -a mf
② adj psichico; I'm not ~ non sono un
indovino

psychoanalyse /saɪkəʊ'ænəlaɪz/ vt
psicanalizzare

psychoanalysis /saɪkəʊə'nælɪsɪs/ n
psicanalisi f

psychoanalyst /saɪkəʊ'ænəlɪst/ n
psicanalista mf

psychological /saɪkə'lɒdʒɪkl/ adj
psicologico

psychologically /saɪkə'lɒdʒɪklɪ/ adv
psicologicamente

psychologist /saɪ'kɒlədʒɪst/ n
psicologo, -a mf

psychology /saɪ'kɒlədʒɪ/ n psicologia f

psychopath /'saɪkəpæθ/ n psicopatico,
-a mf

psychopathic /saɪkə'pæθɪk/ adj
psicopatico

psychosis /saɪ'kəʊsɪs/ n psicosi f inv

psychosomatic /saɪkəʊsə'mætɪk/ adj
psicosomatico

psychotherapist n psicoterapista mf,
psicoterapeuta mf

psychotic /saɪ'kɒtɪk/ adj & n psicotico,
-a mf

PT n abbr (**physical training**)
educazione f fisica

PTA n abbr (**Parent-Teacher
Association**) ≈ consiglio m d'istituto

PTO abbr (**please turn over**) vedi retro

pub /pʌb/ n fam pub m inv

puberty /'pju:bətɪ/ n pubertà f

pubic hair /'pju:bɪk/ n peli mpl del pube

public /'pʌblɪk/ ① adj pubblico; make ~
rendere pubblico
② n the ~ il pubblico; in ~ in pubblico

public address system n impianto
m di amplificazione

publican /'pʌblɪkən/ n gestore, -trice mf/
proprietario, -a mf di un pub

public assistance n Am assistenza f
pubblica

publication /pʌblɪ'keɪʃn/ n
pubblicazione f

public company n società f per azioni

public convenience n gabinetti mpl
pubblici

public holiday n festa f nazionale

public house n pub m inv

publicist /'pʌblɪsɪst/ n (press agent) press
agent mf inv, addetto, -a mf stampa

publicity /pʌb'lɪsəti/ n pubblicità f

publicity campaign n campagna f
pubblicitaria

publicity department n settore m
pubblicità

publicity director n direttore, -trice
mf della pubblicità

publicity stunt n trovata f
pubblicitaria

publicize /'pʌblɪsaɪz/ vt pubblicizzare

public library n biblioteca f pubblica

public limited company /'lɪmɪtɪd/ n
società f inv per azioni

publicly /'pʌblɪklɪ/ adv pubblicamente

public opinion n opinione f pubblica

public prosecutor n Pubblico
Ministero m

public relations npl pubbliche
relazioni fpl

public relations department n
ufficio m pubbliche relazioni

public relations officer n addetto, -a
mf alle pubbliche relazioni

public school n scuola f privata; Am
scuola f pubblica

public sector n settore m pubblico

public-spirited adj be ~ essere dotato
di senso civico

public transport n mezzi mpl pubblici

publish /'pʌblɪʃ/ vt pubblicare

publisher /'pʌblɪʃə(r)/ n editore m; (firm)
editore m, casa f editrice

publishing /'pʌblɪʃɪŋ/ n editoria f

puce /pju:s/ adj color bruno rossastro

puck /pʌk/ n (in ice-hockey) disco m; (sprite)
folletto m

pucker /'pʌkə(r)/ vi ⟨material⟩
arricciarsi

pudding /'pʊdɪŋ/ n dolce m cotto al
vapore; (course) dolce m

puddle /'pʌdl/ n pozzanghera f

pudgy /'pʌdʒɪ/ adj (**-ier, -iest**)
grassoccio

puerile /'pjʊəraɪl/ adj puerile

puff /pʌf/ ① n (of wind) soffio m; (of smoke)
tirata f; (for powder) piumino m
② vt sbuffare
■ **puff at** vt tirare boccate da ⟨pipe⟩
■ **puff out** vt lasciare senza fiato
⟨person⟩; spegnere ⟨candle⟩
■ **puff up** ① vi ⟨feathers⟩ arruffarsi; ⟨eye,
rice⟩ gonfiarsi
② vt arruffare ⟨feathers, fur⟩; ~**ed up
with pride** gonfio d'orgoglio

puffed /pʌft/ adj (out of breath) senza fiato

puff pastry n pasta f sfoglia

puff sleeve n manica f a palloncino

puffy /'pʌfɪ/ *adj* gonfio

pug /pʌg/ *n* (dog) carlino *m*

pugnacious /pʌg'neɪʃəs/ *adj* aggressivo

pull /pʊl/ ❶ *n* trazione *f*; (fig: attraction) attrazione *f*; (fam: influence) influenza *f*
❷ *vt* tirare; estrarre ⟨*tooth*⟩; stirarsi ⟨*muscle*⟩; ∼ **a fast one** fam giocare un brutto tiro; ∼ **faces** far boccacce; ∼ **oneself together** ricomporsi; ∼ **one's weight** mettercela tutta; ∼ **sb's leg** fam prendere in giro qualcuno
■ **pull ahead** *vi* (move in front) passare davanti
■ **pull apart** *vt* (dismantle) smontare; (destroy) fare a pezzi
■ **pull away** *vi* (increase one's lead) distanziarsi
■ **pull back** ❶ *vi* ⟨*soldiers*⟩ ritirarsi; (not act) tirarsi indietro
❷ *vt* far ritirare ⟨*soldiers*⟩
■ **pull down** *vt* (demolish) demolire
■ **pull in** *vi* Auto accostare
■ **pull off** *vt* togliere; fam azzeccare
■ **pull out** ❶ *vt* tirar fuori
❷ *vi* Auto spostarsi; (of competition) ritirarsi
■ **pull over** *vi* Aut accostare
■ **pull through** *vi* (recover) farcela
■ **pull together** *vi* (co-operate) sommare le forze
■ **pull up** ❶ *vt* sradicare ⟨*plant*⟩; (reprimand) rimproverare
❷ *vi* Auto fermarsi

pull-down menu *n* Comput menu *m inv* a discesa

pulley /'pʊlɪ/ *n* Techn puleggia *f*

pull-in *n* Br (lay-by) piazzuola *f* di sosta; (cafe) bar *m inv* sul bordo della strada

pullover /'pʊləʊvə(r)/ *n* pullover *m inv*

pulmonary /'pʌlmənərɪ/ *adj* polmonare

pulp /pʌlp/ *n* poltiglia *f*; (of fruit) polpa *f*; (for paper) pasta *f*

pulp fiction *n* letteratura *f* pulp

pulpit /'pʌlpɪt/ *n* pulpito *m*

pulsar /'pʌlsɑː(r)/ *n* pulsar *m inv*

pulsate /pʌl'seɪt/ *vi* pulsare

pulse /pʌls/ *n* polso *m*

pulse rate *n* polso *m*

pulses /'pʌlsɪz/ *npl* legumi *mpl* secchi

pulverize /'pʌlvəraɪz/ *vt* polverizzare

puma /'pjuːmə/ *n* puma *m inv*

pumice /'pʌmɪs/ *n* pomice *f*

pummel /'pʌml/ *vt* (pt/pp **pummelled**) prendere a pugni

pump /pʌmp/ ❶ *n* pompa *f*
❷ *vt* pompare; fam cercare di estorcere informazioni da
■ **pump up** *vt* (inflate) gonfiare

pumpkin /'pʌmpkɪn/ *n* zucca *f*

pun /pʌn/ *n* gioco *m* di parole

punch¹ /pʌntʃ/ ❶ *n* pugno *m*; (device) pinza *f* per forare
❷ *vt* dare un pugno a; forare ⟨*ticket*⟩; perforare ⟨*hole*⟩

punch² *n* (drink) punch *m inv*

Punch-and-Judy show *n* spettacolo *m* di burattini

punchbag *n* punching bag *f inv*

punch-drunk *adj* (in boxing) groggy *inv*; fig stordito

punchline *n* battuta *f* finale

punch-up *n* rissa *f*

punctual /'pʌŋktjʊəl/ *adj* puntuale

punctuality /pʌŋktjʊ'ælətɪ/ *n* puntualità *f*

punctually /'pʌŋktjʊəlɪ/ *adv* puntualmente

punctuate /'pʌŋktjʊeɪt/ *vt* punteggiare

punctuation /pʌŋktjʊ'eɪʃn/ *n* punteggiatura *f*

punctuation mark *n* segno *m* di interpunzione

puncture /'pʌŋktʃə(r)/ ❶ *n* foro *m*: (tyre) foratura *f*
❷ *vt* forare

pundit /'pʌndɪt/ *n* esperto *m*

pungency /'pʌndʒənsɪ/ *n* asprezza *f*

pungent /'pʌndʒənt/ *adj* acre

punish /'pʌnɪʃ/ *vt* punire

punishable /'pʌnɪʃəbl/ *adj* punibile

punishment /'pʌnɪʃmənt/ *n* punizione *f*

punitive /'pjuːnɪtɪv/ *adj* punitivo

punk /pʌŋk/ *n* punk *m inv*

punk rock *n* punk rock *m inv*

punk rocker /'rɒkə(r)/ *n* punk *mf inv*

punnet /'pʌnɪt/ *n* cestello *m*

punt /pʌnt/ *n* (boat) barchino *m*

punter /'pʌntə(r)/ *n* (gambler) scommettitore, -trice *mf*; (fam: client) consumatore, -trice *mf*

puny /'pjuːnɪ/ *adj* (**-ier**, **-iest**) striminzito

pup /pʌp/ *n* = PUPPY

pupil /'pjuːpl/ *n* alunno, -a *mf*; (of eye) pupilla *f*

puppet /'pʌpɪt/ *n* marionetta *f*; (glove, fig) burattino *m*

puppy /'pʌpɪ/ *n* cucciolo *m*

purchase /'pɜːtʃəs/ ❶ *n* acquisto *m*; (leverage) presa *f*
❷ *vt* acquistare

purchase invoice *n* fattura *f* di acquisto

purchase ledger *n* libro *m* mastro degli acquisti

purchase order *n* ordine *m* di acquisto

purchase price *n* prezzo *m* di acquisto

purchaser /'pɜːtʃəsə(r)/ *n* acquirente *mf*

purchasing [department] /'pɜːtʃəsɪŋ/ *n* ufficio *m* acquisti

purchasing power n potere m
d'acquisto

purdah /'pɜːdə/ n reclusione f delle
donne in alcune società musulmane e
indù

pure /pjʊə(r)/ adj puro

pure-bred /-bred/ ① n (horse)
purosangue m inv
② adj purosangue inv

purée /pjʊəreɪ/ ① n purè m inv
② vt passare

purely /'pjʊəlɪ/ adv puramente

purgatory /'pɜːgətrɪ/ n purgatorio m

purge /pɜːdʒ/ Pol ① n epurazione f
② vt epurare

purification /pjʊərɪfɪ'keɪʃn/ n
purificazione f

purify /'pjʊərɪfaɪ/ vt (pt/pp **-ied**)
purificare

purist /'pjʊərɪst/ adj & n purista mf

puritan /'pjʊərɪtən/ ① n puritano, -a mf
② adj fig puritano

puritanical /pjʊərɪ'tænɪkl/ adj puritano

purity /'pjʊərɪtɪ/ n purità f

purl /pɜːl/ ① n (Knitting) maglia f rovescia
② vt/i lavorare a rovescio

purple /'pɜːpl/ adj viola inv

purport /pə'pɔːt/ vt ~ **to be** farsi passare
per

purpose /'pɜːpəs/ n scopo m;
(determination) fermezza f; **on** ~ apposta

purpose-built /-'bɪlt/ adj costruito ad
hoc

purposeful /'pɜːpəsfʊl/ adj deciso

purposefully /'pɜːpəsfʊlɪ/ adv con
decisione

purposely /'pɜːpəslɪ/ adv apposta

purpose-made adj Br fatto
appositamente

purr /pɜː(r)/ vi (cat) fare le fusa

purse /pɜːs/ ① n borsellino m; (Am:
handbag) borsa f
② vt increspare (lips)

purser /'pɜːsə(r)/ n commissario m di
bordo

pursue /pə'sjuː/ vt inseguire; fig
proseguire

pursuer /pə'sjuːə(r)/ n inseguitore, -trice
mf

pursuit /pə'sjuːt/ n inseguimento m; (fig:
of happiness) ricerca f; (pastime) attività f
inv; **in** ~ all'inseguimento

pus /pʌs/ n pus m

push /pʊʃ/ ① n spinta f; (fig: effort) sforzo
m; (drive) iniziativa f; **at a** ~ in caso di
bisogno; **get the** ~ fam essere licenziato
② vt spingere; premere (button);
(pressurize) far pressione su; **be** ~**ed for
time** fam non avere tempo
③ vi spingere

■ **push around** vt (bully) fare il
prepotente con

■ **push aside** vt scostare

■ **push back** vt respingere

■ **push for** vt fare pressione per ottenere
(reform)

■ **push in** ① vi (in queue) farsi largo
spingendo
② vt spingere (button)

■ **push off** ① vt togliere
② vi (fam: leave) levarsi dai piedi

■ **push on** vi (continue) continuare

■ **push over** vt (cause to fall) far cadere

■ **push through** vt (have accepted quickly)
fare accettare

■ **push up** vt alzare (price)

push-button n pulsante m

pushchair /'pʊʃtʃeə(r)/ n passeggino m

pusher /'pʊʃə(r)/ n (fam: of drugs)
spacciatore, -trice mf [di droga]

pushover n fam bazzecola f

push start ① vt spingere (per far
partire) (vehicle)
② n **give something a** ~ ~ dare una
spinta a qualcosa

push-up n flessione f

pushy /'pʊʃɪ/ adj fam troppo
intraprendente

puss /pʊs/, **pussy** /'pʊsɪ/ n micio m

pussyfoot around /'pʊsɪfʊt/ vi fam
tergiversare

pussyfooting /'pʊsɪfʊtɪŋ/ ① n fam
tentennamento m
② adj fam (attitude, behaviour)
tergiversante

put /pʊt/ ① vt (pt/pp **put**, pres p
putting) ~ mettere; **the cost of
something at £50** valutare il costo di
qualcosa 50 sterline; ~ **an end to** porre
fine o termine a; ~ **in writing** mettere per
iscritto; ~ **into effect** mettere in opera
② vi ~ **to sea** salpare
③ adj **stay** ~! rimani lì!

■ **put about** vt mettere in giro (rumour)

■ **put across** vt raccontare (joke);
esprimere (message)

■ **put aside** vt mettere da parte

■ **put away** vt mettere via

■ **put back** vt rimettere; mettere
indietro (clock)

■ **put by** vt mettere da parte

■ **put down** vt mettere giù; (suppress)
reprimere; (kill) sopprimere; (write)
annotare; (criticize unfairly) sminuire; ~
one's foot down fam essere fermo; Auto
dare un'accelerata; ~ **down to** (attribute)
attribuire

■ **put forward** vt avanzare; mettere
avanti (clock)

■ **put in** ① vt (insert) introdurre; (submit)
presentare
② vi ~ **in for** far domanda di

■ **put off** vt spegnere (light); (postpone)
rimandare; ~ **somebody off** tenere a bada

qualcuno; (deter) smontare qualcuno; (disconcert) distrarre qualcuno; ~ **somebody off something** (disgust) disgustare qualcuno di qualcosa
■ **put on** *vt* mettersi ⟨*clothes*⟩; mettere ⟨*brake*⟩; Culin mettere su; accendere ⟨*light*⟩ mettere in scena ⟨*play*⟩; prendere ⟨*accent*⟩; ~ **on weight** mettere su qualche chilo; **he's just ~ting it on** è solo una messa in scena
■ **put on to** *vt* (help find) indicare ⟨*doctor, restaurant etc*⟩
■ **put out** *vt* spegnere ⟨*fire, light*⟩; tendere ⟨*hand*⟩; (inconvenience) creare degli inconvenienti a
■ **put through** *vt* far passare; Teleph **I'll ~ you through to him** glielo passo
■ **put to** *vt* ~ **somebody to trouble** scomodare qualcuno; **I ~ it to you that...** ritengo che...
■ **put together** *vt* montare ⟨*machine*⟩; fare ⟨*model, jigsaw*⟩
■ **put up** ① *vt* alzare; erigere ⟨*building*⟩; montare ⟨*tent*⟩; aprire ⟨*umbrella*⟩; affiggere ⟨*notice*⟩; aumentare ⟨*price*⟩; ospitare ⟨*guest*⟩; ~ **somebody up to something** mettere qualcosa in testa a qualcuno
② *vi* (at hotel) stare; ~ **up with** sopportare
put-down *n* commento *m* umiliante
putrefaction /pjuːtrɪˈfækʃn/ *n* putrefazione *f*

putrefy /ˈpjuːtrɪfaɪ/ *vi* (pt/pp **-ied**) putrefarsi
putrid /ˈpjuːtrɪd/ *adj* putrido
putt /pʌt/ ① *n* putt *m inv*
② *vi* colpire leggermente
putty /ˈpʌtɪ/ *n* mastice *m*
put-up job *n* fam truffa *f*
puzzle /ˈpʌzl/ ① *n* enigma *m*; (jigsaw) puzzle *m inv*
② *vt* lasciare perplesso
③ *vi* ~ **over** scervellarsi su
■ **puzzle out** *vt* trovare ⟨*solution*⟩
puzzled /ˈpʌzld/ *adj* perplesso
puzzling /ˈpʌzlɪŋ/ *adj* inspiegabile
PVC ① *n* PVC *m*
② *attrib* di PVC
pygmy /ˈpɪgmɪ/ *n* pigmeo, -a *mf*
pyjamas /pəˈdʒɑːməz/ *npl* pigiama *msg*
pylon /ˈpaɪlən/ *n* pilone *m*
pyramid /ˈpɪrəmɪd/ *n* piramide *f*
pyre /paɪə(r)/ *n* pira *f*
Pyrex® /ˈpaɪreks/ *n* Pyrex *m*
pyromaniac /paɪrəˈmeɪnɪæk/ *n* piromane *mf*
pyrotechnics /paɪrəˈtekniks/ *n* (display) fuochi *mpl* pirotecnici
python /ˈpaɪθn/ *n* pitone *m*

Qq

q, **Q** /kjuː/ *n* (letter) q, Q *f inv*
Qatar /ˈkætɑ(r)/ *n* Qatar *m*
QC *n* Br Jur avvocato *m* di rango superiore
QED *abbr* (**quod erat demonstrandum**) qed
quack[1] /kwæk/ ① *n* qua qua *m inv*
② *vi* fare qua qua
quack[2] *n* (doctor) ciarlatano *m*
quad /kwɒd/ *n* (fam: court) = QUADRANGLE; ~**s** *pl* fam = QUADRUPLETS
quadrangle /ˈkwɒdræŋgl/ *n* quadrangolo *m*; (court) cortile *m* quadrangolare
quadratic equation /kwɒˈdrætɪk/ *n* equazione *f* di secondo grado
quadriplegic /kwɒdrɪˈpliːdʒɪk/ *adj* quadriplegico
quadruped /ˈkwɒdrʊped/ *n* quadrupede *m*
quadruple /ˈkwɒdrʊpl/ ① *adj* quadruplo
② *vt* quadruplicare

③ *vi* quadruplicarsi
quadruplets /kwɒdˈruːplɪts/ *npl* quattro gemelli *mpl*
quadruplicate /kwɒdˈruːplɪkət/ *n* **in ~** in quattro copie
quagmire /ˈkwɒgmaɪə(r)/ *n* pantano *m*
quail /kweɪl/ *vi* farsi prendere dalla paura
quaint /kweɪnt/ *adj* pittoresco; (odd) bizzarro
quake /kweɪk/ ① *n* fam terremoto *m*
② *vi* tremare
Quaker /ˈkweɪkə(r)/ *n* quacchero, -a *mf*
qualification /kwɒlɪfɪˈkeɪʃn/ *n* qualifica *f*; (reservation) riserva *f*
qualified /ˈkwɒlɪfaɪd/ *adj* qualificato; (limited) con riserva
qualifier /ˈkwɒlɪfaɪə(r)/ *n* Sport concorrente *mf* qualificato, -a
qualify /ˈkwɒlɪfaɪ/ ① *vt* (pt/pp **-ied**) ⟨*course*⟩ dare la qualifica a (**as** di); ⟨*entitle*⟩ dare diritto a; ⟨*limit*⟩ precisare

2 *vi* ottenere la qualifica; Sport qualificarsi

qualitative /'kwɒlɪtətɪv/ *adj* qualitativo

quality /'kwɒlətɪ/ *n* qualità *f inv*

quality assurance *n* verifica *f* qualità

quality control *n* controllo *m* [di] qualità

quality controller *n* addetto, -a *mf* al controllo di qualità

qualm /kwɑːm/ *n* scrupolo *m*

quandary /'kwɒndərɪ/ *n* dilemma *m*

quango /'kwæŋgəʊ/ *n* Br organismo *m* autonomo ma finanziato dal governo

quantifiable /'kwɒntɪfaɪəbl/ *adj* quantificabile

quantify /'kwɒntɪfaɪ/ *vt* quantificare

quantitative /'kwɒntɪtətɪv/ *adj* quantitativo

quantity /'kwɒntətɪ/ *n* quantità *f inv*; **in** ~ in grande quantità

quantity surveyor *n* geometra *mf* che calcola quantità e costo di materiali da costruzione

quantum leap /kwɒntəm'liːp/ *n* fig balzo *m* in avanti

quantum mechanics *n* meccanica *f* quantistica

quarantine /'kwɒrəntiːn/ *n* quarantena *f*

quarrel /'kwɒrəl/ **1** *n* lite *f*
2 *vi* (pt/pp **quarrelled**) litigare

quarrelsome /'kwɒrəlsəm/ *adj* litigioso

quarry¹ /'kwɒrɪ/ *n* (prey) preda *f*

quarry² *n* cava *f*

quarry tile *n* mattonella *f* grezza

quart /kwɔːt/ *n* = 1,14 litre

quarter /'kwɔːtə(r)/ **1** *n* quarto *m*; (of year) trimestre *m*; Am 25 centesimi *mpl*; ~**s** *pl* Mil quartiere *msg*; **at [a]** ~ **to six** alle sei meno un quarto; **from all** ~**s** da tutti i lati
2 *vt* dividere in quattro

quarterdeck /'kwɔːtədek/ *n* Naut cassero *m*

quarter-final *n* quarto *m* di finale

quarterly /'kwɔːtəlɪ/ **1** *adj* trimestrale
2 *adv* trimestralmente

quartermaster /'kwɔːtəmɑːstə(r)/ *n* ‹in navy› timoniere *m*; ‹in army› furiere *m*

quartet /kwɔː'tet/ *n* quartetto *m*

quartz /kwɔːts/ *n* quarzo *m*; ~ **watch** orologio *m* al quarzo

quash /kwɒʃ/ *vt* annullare; soffocare ‹rebellion›

quasi+ /'kweɪzaɪ/ *pref* semi+

quaver /'kweɪvə(r)/ **1** *n* Mus croma *f*
2 *vi* tremolare

quay /kiː/ *n* banchina *f*

quayside *n* banchina *f*

queasiness /'kwiːzɪnɪs/ *n* nausea *f*

queasy /'kwiːzɪ/ *adj* **I feel** ~ ho la nausea

Quebec /kwɪ'bek/ *n* (province) Quebec *m*; (town) Quebec *f*

queen /kwiːn/ *n* regina *f*

queen bee *n* ape *f* regina; **she thinks she's the** ~ ~ fig si crede chissà chi

queenly /'kwiːnlɪ/ *adj* da regina

queen mother *n* regina *f* madre

Queen's Counsel *n* Br Jur avvocato *m* di rango superiore

Queen's English *n* Br **speak the** ~ ~ parlare un inglese corretto e senza accento

Queen's evidence *n* Br Jur **turn** ~ ~ deporre contro i propri complici

Queen's Regulations *npl* Br Mil codice *m* militare

queer /kwɪə(r)/ **1** *adj* strano; (dubious) sospetto; (fam: homosexual) finocchio
2 *n* fam finocchio *m*

quell /kwel/ *vt* reprimere

quench /kwentʃ/ *vt* ~ **one's thirst** dissetarsi

querulous /'kwerələs/ *adj* lamentoso

query /'kwɪərɪ/ **1** *n* domanda *f*; (question mark) punto *m* interrogativo
2 *vt* (pt/pp **-ied**) interrogare; (doubt) mettere in dubbio

quest /kwest/ *n* ricerca *f* (**for** di)

question /'kwestʃən/ **1** *n* domanda *f*; (for discussion) questione *f*; **out of the** ~ fuori discussione; **without** ~ senza dubbio; **in** ~ in questione
2 *vt* interrogare; (doubt) mettere in dubbio

questionable /'kwestʃ(ə)nəbl/ *adj* discutibile

questioner /'kwestʃ(ə)nə(r)/ *n* interrogante *mf*

questioning /'kwestʃ(ə)nɪŋ/ **1** *n* (of person) interrogatorio *m*; (of criteria) messa *f* in discussione
2 *adj* ‹look, tone› inquisitorio

question mark *n* punto *m* interrogativo

question master *n* presentatore, -trice *mf* di quiz

questionnaire /kwestʃə'neə(r)/ *n* questionario *m*

question tag *n* domanda *f* di conferma

queue /kjuː/ **1** *n* coda *f*, fila *f*
2 *vi* ~ **[up]** mettersi in coda (**for** per)

queue-jump *vi* Br passare davanti alle altre persone in coda

quibble /'kwɪbl/ *vi* cavillare

quick /kwɪk/ **1** *adj* veloce; **be** ~ sbrigati!; **have a** ~ **meal** fare uno spuntino
2 *adv* in fretta

3 *n* be cut to the ∼ fig essere punto sul vivo

quick-assembly *adj* facile da montare

quicken /'kwɪkən/ **1** *vt* accelerare ⟨*pace*⟩
2 *vi* ⟨*pace*⟩ accelerarsi; ⟨*interest*⟩ intensificarsi

quick-fire *adj* ⟨*questions*⟩ a mitraglia

quick-freeze *vt* surgelare

quickie /'kwɪkɪ/ *n* fam (question) domanda *f* rapida; (drink) bicchierino *m* rapido; (film) cortometraggio *m*

quicklime /'kwɪklaɪm/ *n* calce *f* viva

quickly /'kwɪklɪ/ *adv* in fretta

quick march *n* Mil passo *m* di marcia veloce

quicksand *n* sabbie *fpl* mobili

quick-setting /-'setɪŋ/ *adj* a presa rapida

quicksilver *n* Chem argento *m* vivo, mercurio *m*

quick-tempered /-'tempəd/ *adj* collerico

quick time *n* Am marcia *f* veloce

quick-witted /-'wɪtɪd/ *adj* ⟨*reaction*⟩ pronto; ⟨*person*⟩ sveglio

quid /kwɪd/ *n inv* fam sterlina *f*

quid pro quo /kwɪdprəʊ'kwəʊ/ *n* contraccambio *m*

quiet /'kwaɪət/ **1** *adj* (calm) tranquillo; (silent) silenzioso; (voice, music) basso; **keep** ∼ **about** fam non raccontare a nessuno **2** *n* quiete *f*; **on the** ∼ di nascosto

quieten /'kwaɪətn/ *vt* calmare
■ **quieten down 1** *vt* calmare
2 *vi* calmarsi

quietly /'kwaɪətlɪ/ *adv* (peacefully) tranquillamente; ⟨*say*⟩ a bassa voce

quietness /'kwaɪətnɪs/ *n* quiete *f*

quiff /kwɪf/ *n* (Br: hair) ciuffo *m*

quill /kwɪl/ *n* penna *f* d'uccello; (spine) spina *f*

quilt /kwɪlt/ *n* piumino *m*

quilted /'kwɪltɪd/ *adj* trapuntato

quilting /'kwɪltɪŋ/ *n* (fabric) matelassé *m inv*

quince /kwɪns/ *n* cotogna *f*; (tree) melo *m* cotogno

quinine /'kwɪniːn/ *n* chinino *m*

quins /kwɪnz/ *npl* fam = QUINTUPLETS

quintessential /kwɪntɪ'senʃl/ *adj* ⟨*quality*⟩ fondamentale

quintet /kwɪn'tet/ *n* quintetto *m*

quintuple /'kwɪntjʊpl/ **1** *vt* quintuplicare
2 *adj* quintuplo

quintuplets /'kwɪntjʊplɪts/ *npl* cinque gemelli *mpl*

quip /kwɪp/ **1** *n* battuta *f*
2 *vt* (pt/pp **quipped**) dire scherzando

quirk /kwɜːk/ *n* stranezza *f*

quisling /'kwɪzlɪŋ/ *n* pej collaborazionista *mf*

quit /kwɪt/ **1** *v* (pt/pp **-tted** or **quit**) *vt* lasciare; (give up) smettere (**doing** di fare); Comput uscire da
2 *vi* (fam: resign) andarsene; Comput uscire; **give somebody notice to** ∼ dare a qualcuno preavviso di sfratto

quite /kwaɪt/ *adv* (fairly) abbastanza; (completely) completamente; (really) veramente; ∼ **[so]!** proprio così!; ∼ **a few** parecchi

quits /kwɪts/ *adj* pari

quiver /'kwɪvə(r)/ *vi* tremare

quiz /kwɪz/ **1** *n* (game) quiz *m inv*
2 *vt* (pt/pp **quizzed**) interrogare

quiz game, **quiz show** *n* quiz *m inv*

quizzical /'kwɪzɪkl/ *adj* sardonico

quoit /kwɔɪt/ *n* anello *m* (del gioco)

quoits *n* (game) gioco *m* degli anelli

quorum /'kwɔːrəm/ *n* quorum *m inv*; **have a** ∼ avere il quorum

quota /'kwəʊtə/ *n* quota *f*

quotation /kwəʊ'teɪʃn/ *n* citazione *f*; (price) preventivo *m*; (of shares) quota *f*

quotation marks *npl* virgolette *fpl*

quote /kwəʊt/ **1** *n* fam = QUOTATION; **in** ∼**s** tra virgolette
2 *vt* citare; quotare ⟨*price*⟩; ∼**d on the Stock Exchange** quotato in Borsa

Rr

r¹, R /ɑː(r)/ *n* (letter) r, R *f inv*; **the three Rs** leggere, scrivere e contare

R² Br abbr (**regina**) regina *f*

R & B *n* rhythm and blues *m*

R & D *n* ricerca *f* e sviluppo *m*

rabbi /'ræbaɪ/ *n* rabbino *m*; (title) rabbi

rabbit /'ræbɪt/ *n* coniglio *m*
■ **rabbit on** *vi* fam what's he ∼ting on about now? cosa sta blaterando?

rabbit hutch *n* conigliera *f*

rabble /'ræbl/ n the ~ la plebaglia

rabble rouser /'rauzə(r)/ n agitatore, -trice nmf

rabble rousing n incitazione f alla violenza

rabid /'ræbɪd/ adj fig rabbioso

rabies /'reɪbiːz/ n rabbia f

RAC n abbr Br (**Royal Automobile Club**) ≈ ACI f

raccoon /rə'kuːn/ n procione m, orsetto m lavatore

race[1] /reɪs/ n (people) razza f

race[2] ① n corsa ⟨f⟩
② vi correre
③ vt gareggiare con; fare correre ⟨horse⟩

racecourse /'reɪskɔːs/ n ippodromo m

racehorse /'reɪshɔːs/ n cavallo m da corsa

racer /'reɪsə(r)/ n (bike) bicicletta f da corsa; (motorbike) motocicletta f da corsa; (car) automobile f da corsa; (runner, cyclist etc) corridore, -trice mf

race relations npl rapporti mpl tra le razze

race riots npl scontri mpl razziali

racetrack /'reɪstræk/ n pista f

racial /'reɪʃl/ adj razziale

racialism /'reɪʃəlɪzm/ n razzismo m

racially /'reɪʃ(ə)lɪ/ adv razzialmente

racing /'reɪsɪŋ/ n corse fpl; (horse-~) corse fpl dei cavalli

racing car n macchina f da corsa

racing driver n corridore m automobilistico

racism /'reɪsɪzm/ n razzismo m

racist /'reɪsɪst/ adj & n razzista mf

rack[1] /ræk/ ① n (for bikes) rastrelliera f; (for luggage) portabagagli m inv; (for plates) scolapiatti m inv
② vt ~ one's brains scervellarsi

rack[2] n go to ~ and ruin andare in rovina

racket[1] /'rækɪt/ n Sport racchetta f

racket[2] n (din) chiasso m; (swindle) truffa f; (crime) racket m inv, giro m

racketeer /rækɪ'tɪə(r)/ n trafficante m

racketeering /rækɪ'tɪərɪŋ/ n traffici mpl illeciti

racking /'rækɪŋ/ adj ⟨pain⟩ atroce

raconteur /rækɒnt3ː(r)/ n bravo narratore m, brava narratrice f

racquetball /'rækɪtbɔːl/ n Am = SQUASH

racy /'reɪsɪ/ adj (**-ier**, **-iest**) vivace; (risqué) osé inv, spinto

radar /'reɪdɑː(r)/ n radar m

radar trap n Auto tratto m di strada sul quale la polizia controlla la velocità dei veicoli

radial /'reɪdɪəl/ ① n (tyre) [pneumatico m] radiale m
② adj ⟨lines, roads⟩ radiale

radiance /'reɪdɪəns/ n radiosità f

radiant /'reɪdɪənt/ adj raggiante

radiate /'reɪdɪeɪt/ ① vt irradiare
② vi ⟨heat⟩ irradiarsi; ⟨roads⟩ partire

radiation /reɪdɪ'eɪʃn/ n radiazione f

radiation exposure n esposizione f a radiazioni

radiation sickness n patologia f da radiazioni

radiator /'reɪdɪeɪtə(r)/ n radiatore m

radical /'rædɪkl/ adj & n radicale mf

radicalism /'rædɪkəlɪzm/ n radicalismo m

radically /'rædɪklɪ/ adv radicalmente

radio /'reɪdɪəʊ/ ① n radio f inv
② vt mandare via radio ⟨message⟩

radioactive /reɪdɪəʊ'æktɪv/ adj radioattivo

radioactive waste n scorie fpl radioattive

radioactivity /reɪdɪəʊæk'tɪvətɪ/ n radioattività f

radio alarm n radiosveglia f

radio cassette player n radioregistratore m

radio-controlled adj radiocomandato

radiographer /reɪdɪ'ɒgrəfə(r)/ n radiologo, -a mf

radiography /reɪdɪ'ɒgrəfɪ/ n radiografia f

radio ham n radioamatore, -trice mf

radiologist /reɪdɪ'ɒlədʒɪst/ n radiologo, -a mf

radiology /reɪdɪ'ɒlədʒɪ/ n radiologia f

radio station n stazione f radiofonica

radiotherapy /reɪdɪəʊ'θerəpɪ/ n radioterapia f

radish /'rædɪʃ/ n ravanello m

radius /'reɪdɪəs/ n (pl **-dii** /'reɪdɪaɪ/) raggio m

RAF n abbr Br (**Royal Air Force**) aviazione f militare inglese

raffle /'ræfl/ ① n lotteria f
② vt mettere in palio

raft /rɑːft/ n zattera f

rafter /'rɑːftə(r)/ n trave f

rag[1] /ræg/ n straccio m; (pej: newspaper) giornalaccio m; in ~s stracciato

rag[2] ① vt (pt/pp **ragged**) fam fare scherzi a
② n Univ festa f di beneficenza organizzata da studenti universitari

ragamuffin /'rægəmʌfɪn/ n monellaccio m

rag-and-bone man n Br rigattiere m, straccivendolo m

ragbag /'rægbæg/ n fig accozzaglia f

rage /reidʒ/ **①** n rabbia f; **all the ~** fam all'ultima moda
② vi infuriarsi; ⟨storm⟩ infuriare; ⟨epidemic⟩ imperversare

ragged /'rægid/ adj logoro; ⟨edge⟩ frastagliato

raging /'reidʒiŋ/ adj ⟨blizzard, sea⟩ furioso; ⟨thirst, pain⟩ atroce; ⟨passion, argument⟩ acceso

raglan /'ræglən/ **①** adj raglan inv
② n manica f raglan

rag trade n fam settore m dell'abbigliamento

rag week n Br Univ settimana f di manifestazioni a scopo benefico organizzata dagli studenti

raid /reid/ **①** n (by thieves) rapina f; Mil incursione f, raid m inv; (by police) irruzione f
② vt Mil fare un'incursione in; ⟨police, thieves⟩ fare irruzione in

raider /'reidə(r)/ n (of bank) rapinatore, -trice mf

rail¹ /reil/ n ringhiera f; ⟨Rail⟩ rotaia f; Naut parapetto m; **by ~** per ferrovia

rail² vi **~ against** or **at** inveire contro

railcard /'reilkɑːd/ n tessera f di riduzione ferroviaria

railings /'reiliŋz/ npl ringhiera f

railroad /'reilrəud/ **①** n Am = RAILWAY
② vt **~ somebody into doing something** spingere qualcuno a fare qualcosa

railroad car n Am vagone m ferroviario

railroad schedule n Am orario m ferroviario

rail traffic n traffico m ferroviario

railway /'reilwei/ n ferrovia f

railway carriage n Br vagone m ferroviario

railwayman /'reilweimən/ n ferroviere m

railway station n stazione f ferroviaria

rain /rein/ **①** n pioggia f
② vi piovere; **~ down on somebody** fig piovere addosso a qualcuno
③ vt **~ blows on somebody** tempestare qualcuno di colpi
■ **rain off** vt be **~ed** off essere annullato a causa della pioggia

rainbow n arcobaleno m

raincheck n Am **can I take a ~?** facciamo un'altra volta

raincoat n impermeabile m

raindrop n goccia f di pioggia

rainfall n precipitazione f [atmosferica]

rainforest n foresta f pluviale, foresta f equatoriale

rainstorm n temporale m

rain water n acqua f piovana

rainy /'reini/ adj (**-ier,-iest**) piovoso

rainy day n save something for a **~ ~** fig mettere qualcosa in serbo per i tempi di magra

rainy season n stagione f delle piogge

raise /reiz/ **①** n Am aumento m
② vt alzare; levarsi ⟨hat⟩; allevare ⟨children, animals⟩; sollevare ⟨question⟩; ottenere ⟨money⟩; **~ hell** indiavolarsi; **~ a laugh** ⟨joke, remark⟩ far ridere; **~ the stakes** rilanciare; **~ one's voice** alzare la voce

raised /reizd/ adj ⟨flowerbed, platform⟩ soprelevato; **~ voices** urla

raisin /'reizn/ n uvetta f; **~s** pl uvetta f, uva f passa

Raj /rɑːʒ/ n governo m britannico in India

rake /reik/ **①** n rastrello m
② vt rastrellare
■ **rake in** vt fam farsi ⟨profits, money⟩; **he's raking it in** sta facendo un sacco di soldi
■ **rake together** vt fig racimolare ⟨money⟩
■ **rake up** vt raccogliere col rastrello; fam rivangare

rake-off n fam parte f

rakish /'reikiʃ/ adj (dissolute) dissoluto; (jaunty) disinvolto

rally /'ræli/ **①** n raduno m; Auto rally m inv; (Tennis) scambio m; (recovery) ripresa f
② vt (pt/pp **-ied**) radunare
③ vi radunarsi; (recover strength) riprendersi

rallying cry /'ræliiŋ/, **rallying call** n slogan m inv

RAM /ræm/ n memoria f RAM

ram /ræm/ **①** n montone m; Astr Ariete m
② vt (pt/pp **rammed**) cozzare contro

ramble /'ræmbl/ **①** n escursione f
② vi gironzolare; (in speech) divagare
■ **ramble on** vi fam parlare/scrivere a ruota libera

rambler /'ræmblə(r)/ n escursionista mf; (rose) rosa f rampicante

rambling /'ræmbliŋ/ adj (in speech) sconnesso; ⟨club⟩ escursionistico

ramification /ræmifi'keiʃən/ n ramificazione f

ramify /'ræmifai/ vi (pt/pp **-ied**) ramificarsi

ramp /ræmp/ n rampa f; Auto dosso m

rampage /'ræmpeidʒ/ **①** n be/go on the **~** scatenarsi
② vi **~ through the streets** scatenarsi per le strade

rampant /'ræmpənt/ adj dilagante; (in heraldry) rampante

rampart /'ræmpɑːt/ n bastione f

ram raid n rapina f in un negozio con scasso della vetrina effettuato con un'auto

r

ram raider *n* rapinatore *m* che scassa la vetrina di un negozio con un'auto

ramshackle /'ræmʃækl/ *adj* sgangherato

ran /ræn/ ▶RUN

ranch /rɑːntʃ/ *n* ranch *m inv*

rancher /'rɑːntʃə(r)/ *n* (worker) cow-boy *m inv*; (owner) proprietario *m* di ranch

rancid /'rænsɪd/ *adj* rancido

rancour /'ræŋkə(r)/ *n* rancore *m*

random /'rændəm/ ① *adj* casuale; ~ **sample** campione *m* a caso
② *n* **at** ~ a casaccio

random-access *adj* ad accesso casuale

random-access memory *n* memoria *f* viva

randy /'rændɪ/ *adj* (**-ier**, **-iest**) fam eccitato

rang /ræŋ/ ▶RING²

range /reɪndʒ/ ① *n* serie *f*; Comm, Mus gamma *f*; (of mountains) catena *f*; (distance) raggio *m*; (for shooting) portata *f*; (stove) cucina *f* economica; **at a** ~ **of** ad una distanza di
② *vi* estendersi; ~ **from...to...** andare da...a...

ranger /'reɪndʒə(r)/ *n* guardia *f* forestale

rank¹ /ræŋk/ ① *n* (row) riga *f*; Mil grado *m*; (social position) rango *m*; **the** ~ **and file** la base; **the** ~**s** *pl* Mil i soldati *mpl* semplici
② *vt* (place) annoverare (**among** tra)
③ *vi* (be placed) collocarsi

rank² *adj* ‹smell› puzzolente; ‹plants› rigoglioso; fig vero e proprio

ranking /'ræŋkɪŋ/ *n* classificazione *f*

rankle /'ræŋkl/ *vi* fig bruciare; **it still** ~**s with him** gli brucia ancora

ransack /'rænsæk/ *vt* rovistare; (pillage) saccheggiare

ransom /'rænsəm/ *n* riscatto *m*; **hold somebody to** ~ tenere qualcuno in ostaggio per il riscatto

rant /rænt/ *vi* ~ **[and rave]** inveire; **what's he** ~**ing on about?** cosa sta blaterando?

rap /ræp/ ① *n* colpo *m* secco; Mus rap *m*
② *vt* (pt/pp **rapped**) dare colpetti a; ~ **somebody over the knuckles** fig dare una tirata d'orecchie a qualcuno
③ *vi* ~ **at** bussare a

rape¹ /reɪp/ *n* Bot colza *f*

rape² ① *n* (sexual) stupro *m*
② *vt* violentare, stuprare

rape[seed] oil /'reɪp[siːd]/ *n* olio *m* [di semi] di colza

rapid /'ræpɪd/ *adj* rapido

rapidity /rə'pɪdətɪ/ *n* rapidità *f*

rapidly /'ræpɪdlɪ/ *adv* rapidamente

rapids /'ræpɪdz/ *npl* rapida *fsg*

rapist /'reɪpɪst/ *n* violentatore *m*

rapper /'ræpə(r)/ *n* (Br: door-knocker) battiporta *m inv*; Mus rapper *mf inv*

rapport /ræ'pɔː(r)/ *n* rapporto *m* di intesa

rapt /ræpt/ *adj* ‹look› rapito; ~ **in** assorto in

rapture /'ræptʃə(r)/ *n* estasi *f*

rapturous /'ræptʃərəs/ *adj* entusiastico

rapturously /'ræptʃərəslɪ/ *adv* entusiasticamente

rare¹ /reə(r)/ *adj* raro

rare² *adj* Culin al sangue

rarefied /'reərɪfaɪd/ *adj* rarefatto

rarely /'reəlɪ/ *adv* raramente

raring /'reərɪŋ/ *adj* fam **be** ~ **to** non vedere l'ora di

rarity /'reərətɪ/ *n* rarità *f inv*

rascal /'rɑːskl/ *n* mascalzone *m*

rash¹ /ræʃ/ *n* Med eruzione *f*

rash² *adj* avventato

rasher /'ræʃə(r)/ *n* fetta *f* di pancetta

rashly /'ræʃlɪ/ *adv* avventatamente

rashness /'ræʃnɪs/ *n* avventatezza *f*

rasp /rɑːsp/ *n* (noise) stridio *m*

raspberry /'rɑːzbərɪ/ *n* lampone *m*

rasping /'rɑːspɪŋ/ *adj* stridente

rat /ræt/ ① *n* topo *m*; (fam: person) carogna *f*; **smell a** ~ fam sentire puzzo di bruciato
② *vi* (pt/pp **ratted**) fam ~ **on** far la spia a

rat-a-tat-tat /rætətæ(t) 'tæt/ *n* toc toc *m inv*

rat-catcher *n* addetto, -a *mf* alla derattizzazione

ratchet /'rætʃɪt/ *n* (toothed rack) cremagliera *f*

rate /reɪt/ ① *n* (speed) velocità *f inv*; (of payment) tariffa *f*; (of exchange) tasso *m*; ~**s** *pl* (taxes) imposte *fpl* comunali sui beni immobili; **at any** ~ in ogni caso; **at this** ~ di questo passo
② *vt* stimare; ~ **among** annoverare tra
③ *vt* ~ **as** essere considerato

ratepayer /'reɪtpeɪə(r)/ *n* contribuente *mf*

rather /'rɑːðə(r)/ *adv* piuttosto; ~**!** eccome!; ~ **too... un po' troppo...

ratification /rætɪfɪ'keɪʃn/ *n* ratifica *f*

ratify /'rætɪfaɪ/ *vt* (pt/pp **-ied**) ratificare

rating /'reɪtɪŋ/ *n* valutazione *f*; (class) livello *m*; (sailor) marinaio *m* semplice; ~**s** *pl* Radio, TV indice *m* d'ascolto, audience *f inv*

ratio /'reɪʃɪəʊ/ *n* rapporto *m*; **in a** ~ **of two to one** in [un] rapporto di due a uno

ration /'ræʃn/ ① *n* razione *f*
② *vt* razionare

rational /'ræʃənl/ *adj* razionale

rationale /ræʃə'nɑːl/ *n* (logic) base *f* logica; (reasons) ragioni *fpl*

rationalize /ˈræʃ(ə)nəlaɪz/ *vt/i* razionalizzare

rationally /ˈræʃ(ə)nəlɪ/ *adv* razionalmente

rationing /ˈræʃ(ə)nɪŋ/ *n* razionamento *m*

rat race *n* fam corsa *f* al successo

rat run *n* scorciatoia *f* usata dagli automobilisti in zone residenziali

rattan /rəˈtæn/ *n* (tree, material) malacca *f*

rattle /ˈrætl/ ① *n* tintinnio *m*; (toy) sonaglio *m*
② *vi* tintinnare
③ *vt* (shake) scuotere; fam innervosire
■ **rattle off** *vt* fam sciorinare
■ **rattle on** *vi* (talk at length) parlare ininterrottamente
■ **rattle through** *vt* (say quickly) dire velocemente; (do quickly) fare velocemente

rattlesnake /ˈrætlsneɪk/ *n* serpente *m* a sonagli

ratty /ˈrætɪ/ *adj* (Br fam: grumpy) irascibile; Am ⟨hair⟩ sudicio

raucous /ˈrɔːkəs/ *adj* rauco

raunchy /ˈrɔːntʃɪ/ *adj* fam ⟨performer, voice, song⟩ sexy *inv*; (bawdy) spinto

ravage /ˈrævɪdʒ/ *vt* devastare

ravages /ˈrævɪdʒɪz/ *npl* danni *mpl*

rave /reɪv/ *vi* vaneggiare; ~ **about** andare in estasi per

raven /ˈreɪvn/ *n* corvo *m* imperiale

ravenous /ˈrævənəs/ *adj* ⟨person⟩ affamato

rave-up *n* Br fam festa *f* animata

ravine /rəˈviːn/ *n* gola *f*

raving /ˈreɪvɪŋ/ *adj* ~ **mad** fam matto da legare

ravings /ˈreɪvɪŋz/ *npl* vaneggiamenti *mpl*

ravioli /rævɪˈəʊlɪ/ *n* ravioli *mpl*

ravishing /ˈrævɪʃɪŋ/ *adj* incantevole

raw /rɔː/ *adj* crudo; (not processed) grezzo; ⟨weather⟩ gelido; (inexperienced) inesperto

raw deal *n* get a ~ ~ fam farsi fregare

rawhide *n* (leather) cuoio *m* grezzo

Rawlplug ® /ˈrɔːlplʌg/ *n* tassello *m*

raw materials *npl* materie *fpl* prime

ray /reɪ/ *n* raggio *m*; ~ **of hope** barlume *m* di speranza

rayon® /ˈreɪɒn/ *n* raion® *m*

raze /reɪz/ *vt* ~ **to the ground** radere al suolo

razor /ˈreɪzə(r)/ *n* rasoio *m*

razor blade *n* lametta *f* da barba

razor-sharp *adj* affilatissimo

razzle /ˈræzl/ *n* Br fam go on the ~ andare a fare baldoria

razzle-dazzle *n* fam baldoria *f*

razzmatazz /ræzməˈtæz/ *n* fam clamore *m*

RC ① *n* (Roman Catholic) cattolico, -a *mf*
② *adj* cattolico

Rd. *abbr* (**Road**) Via

re /riː/ *prep* con riferimento a

reach /riːtʃ/ ① *n* portata *f*; (of river) tratto *m*; **within** ~ a portata di mano; **out of** ~ **of** fuori dalla portata di; **within easy** ~ facilmente raggiungibile
② *vt* arrivare a ⟨place, decision⟩; (contact) contattare; (pass) passare; **I can't** ~ **it** non ci arrivo
③ *vi* arrivare (**to** a); **I can't** ~ non ci arrivo; ~ **for** allungare la mano per prendere

reaches /ˈriːtʃɪz/ *npl* (of river) **the upper/ lower** ~ la parte superiore/inferiore

react /rɪˈækt/ *vi* reagire

reaction /rɪˈækʃn/ *n* reazione *f*

reactionary /rɪˈækʃ(ə)nərɪ/ *adj & n* reazionario, -a *mf*

reactor /rɪˈæktə(r)/ *n* reattore *m*

read /riːd/ ① *vt* (pt/pp **read** /red/) leggere; Univ studiare
② *vi* leggere; ⟨instrument⟩ indicare
■ **read back** *vt* (say aloud) rileggere
■ **read on** *vi* (continue reading) continuare a leggere
■ **read out** *vt* leggere ad alta voce
■ **read up on** *vt* studiare a fondo

readable /ˈriːdəbl/ *adj* piacevole a leggersi; (legible) leggibile

reader /ˈriːdə(r)/ *n* lettore, -trice *mf*; (book) antologia *f*

readership /ˈriːdəʃɪp/ *n* numero *m* di lettori

read head *n* Comput testina *f* di lettura

readily /ˈredɪlɪ/ *adv* volentieri; (easily) facilmente

readiness /ˈredɪnɪs/ *n* disponibilità; *f*; **in** ~ pronto

reading /ˈriːdɪŋ/ *n* lettura *f*

readjust /riːəˈdʒʌst/ ① *vt* regolare di nuovo
② *vi* riabituarsi (**to** a)

readjustment /riːəˈdʒʌstmənt/ *n* riadattamento *m*

read-only memory *n* Comput memoria *f* di sola lettura

readvertise /ˈriːædvətaɪz/ *vt* far ripubblicare un'inserzione per ⟨position, item⟩

ready /ˈredɪ/ *adj* (**-ier**, **-iest**) pronto; (quick) veloce; **get** ~ prepararsi

ready-made *adj* confezionato

ready-mixed *adj* già miscelato

ready money *n* contanti *mpl*

ready-to-wear *adj* prêt-à-porter

reaffirm /riːəˈfɜːm/ *vt* riaffermare

reafforestation /riːəfɒrɪˈsteɪʃn/ *n* rimboschimento *m*

real /riːl/ ① *adj* vero; ⟨increase⟩ reale

2 *adv* Am fam veramente

real estate *n* beni *mpl* immobili

realign /riːəˈlaɪn/ **1** *vt* riallineare
2 *vi* fig formare nuove alleanze

realignment /riːəˈlaɪnmənt/ *n* Pol
formazione *f* di nuove alleanze; Fin
riallineamento *m*

realism /ˈrɪəlɪzm/ *n* realismo *m*

realist /ˈrɪəlɪst/ *n* realista *mf*

realistic /rɪəˈlɪstɪk/ *adj* realistico

realistically /rɪəˈlɪstɪklɪ/ *adv*
realisticamente

reality /rɪˈælətɪ/ *n* realtà *f inv*

reality TV *n* reality TV *f*, reality *m*,
reality show *mpl*

realization /rɪəlaɪˈzeɪʃn/ *n* realizzazione
f

realize /ˈrɪəlaɪz/ *vt* realizzare

real life *n* realtà *f*: in ~ life nella realtà

real-life *attrib* autentico

reallocate /riːˈæləkeɪt/ *vt* riassegnare

reallocation /riːæləˈkeɪʃn/ *n*
riassegnazione *f*

really /ˈrɪəlɪ/ *adv* davvero

realm /relm/ *n* regno *m*

real time **1** *n* tempo *m* reale; in ~ ~ in
tempo reale
2 *adj* in tempo reale

realtor /ˈrɪəltə(r)/ *n* Am agente *mf*
immobiliare

realty /ˈrɪəltɪ/ *n* Am beni *mpl* immobili

reanimate /riːˈænɪmeɪt/ *vt* rianimare

reap /riːp/ *vt* mietere

reappear /riːəˈpɪə(r)/ *vi* riapparire

reappearance /riːəˈpɪərəns/ *n*
ricomparsa *f*

reapply /riːəˈplaɪ/ *vi* (pt/pp **-ied**)
ripresentare domanda

reappoint /riːəˈpɔɪnt/ *vt* riconfermare

reappraisal /riːəˈpreɪzl/ *n*
riconsiderazione *f*

reappraise /riːəˈpreɪz/ *vt* riesaminare
‹question, policy›; rivalutare ‹writer, work›

rear[1] /rɪə(r)/ *adj* posteriore; Auto di dietro

rear[2] **1** *vt* allevare
2 *vi* ~ [up] ‹horse› impennarsi
3 *n* the ~ (of building) il retro; (of bus, plane)
la parte posteriore; from the ~ da dietro

rear end *n* fam di dietro *m*

rearguard /ˈrɪəɡɑːd/ *n* Mil, fig
retroguardia *f*

rear light *n* luce *f* posteriore

rearm /riːˈɑːm/ **1** *vt* riarmare
2 *vi* riarmarsi

rearmament /riːˈɑːməmənt/ *n* riarmo
m

rearmost /ˈrɪəməʊst/ *adj* ultimo;
‹carriage› di coda

rearrange /riːəˈreɪndʒ/ *vt* cambiare la
disposizione di

rear-view mirror *n* Auto specchietto *m*
retrovisore

reason /ˈriːzn/ **1** *n* ragione *f*; within ~
nei limiti del ragionevole; listen to ~
ascoltare la ragione
2 *vi* ragionare; ~ with cercare di far
ragionare

reasonable /ˈriːznəbl/ *adj* ragionevole

reasonably /ˈriːznəblɪ/ *adv* (in reasonable
way, fairly) ragionevolmente

reasoning /ˈriːznɪŋ/ *n* ragionamento *m*

reassemble /riːəˈsemb(ə)l/ *vt*
riassemblare

reassembly /riːəˈsemblɪ/ *n*
riassemblaggio *m*

reassert /riːəˈsɜːt/ *vt* riaffermare
‹authority›

reassess /riːəˈses/ *vt* riesaminare
‹situation›; riaccertare ‹tax liability›

reassessment /riːəˈsesmənt/ *n* (of
situation) riesame *m*; (of tax) nuovo
accertamento *m*

reassurance /riːəˈʃʊərəns/ *n*
rassicurazione *f*

reassure /riːəˈʃʊə(r)/ *vt* rassicurare; ~
somebody of something rassicurare
qualcuno su qualcosa

reassuring /riːəˈʃʊərɪŋ/ *adj*
rassicurante

reawaken /riːəˈweɪkn/ *vt* fig risvegliare
‹interest›

rebate /ˈriːbeɪt/ *n* rimborso *m*; (discount)
deduzione *f*

rebel[1] /ˈrebl/ *n* ribelle *mf*

rebel[2] /rɪˈbel/ *vi* (pt/pp **rebelled**)
ribellarsi

rebellion /rɪˈbeljən/ *n* ribellione *f*

rebellious /rɪˈbeljəs/ *adj* ribelle

rebelliousness /rɪˈbeljəsnɪs/ *n* spirito
m di ribellione

rebirth "/riːbɜːθ/ *n* rinascita *f*

reboot /riːˈbuːt/ *vt* Comput reinizializzare

reborn /riːˈbɔːn/ *adj* Relig be ~ rinascere;
be ~ as something rinascere come
qualcosa

rebound[1] /rɪˈbaʊnd/ *vi* rimbalzare; fig
ricadere

rebound[2] /ˈriːbaʊnd/ *n* rimbalzo *m*

rebuff /rɪˈbʌf/ **1** *n* rifiuto *m*
2 *vt* respingere

rebuild /riːˈbɪld/ *vt* (pt/pp **-built**)
ricostruire

rebuke /rɪˈbjuːk/ **1** *n* rimprovero *m*
2 *vt* rimproverare

rebut /rɪˈbʌt/ *vt* confutare

rebuttal /rɪˈbʌtl/ *n* rifiuto *m*

recalcitrant /rɪˈkælsɪtrənt/ *adj* fml
ricalcitrante

recalculate /ri:'kælkjʊleɪt/ vt
ricalcolare

recall /rɪ'kɔ:l/ 1 n richiamo m; **beyond**
~ irrevocabile
2 vt richiamare; riconvocare ⟨diplomat,
parliament⟩; (remember) rievocare

recant /rɪ'kænt/ vi abiurare

recap /'ri:kæp/ 1 vt/i fam =
RECAPITULATE
2 n ricapitolazione f

recapitulate /ri:kə'pɪtjʊleɪt/ vt/i
ricapitolare

recapture /ri:'kæptʃə(r)/ vt
riconquistare; ricatturare ⟨person,
animal⟩

recast /ri:'kɑ:st/ vt rimaneggiare ⟨text,
plan⟩; riformulare ⟨sentence⟩

recede /rɪ'si:d/ vt allontanarsi

receding /rɪ'si:dɪŋ/ adj ⟨forehead, chin⟩
sfuggente; **have** ~ **hair** essere stempiato

receipt /rɪ'si:t/ n ricevuta f; (receiving)
ricezione f; ~s pl Comm entrate fpl

receive /rɪ'si:v/ vt ricevere

receiver /rɪ'si:və(r)/ n Teleph ricevitore
m; Radio, TV, apparecchio m ricevente; (of
stolen goods) ricettatore, -trice mf

receivership /rɪ'si:vəʃɪp/ n Br **go into** ~
essere sottomesso all'amministrazione
controllata

receiving /rɪ'si:vɪŋ/ n (stolen goods)
ricettazione f

receiving end n be on the ~ essere
dall'altro lato della barricata

recent /'ri:snt/ adj recente

recently /'ri:səntlɪ/ adv recentemente

receptacle /rɪ'septəkl/ n recipiente m

reception /rɪ'sepʃn/ n ricevimento m;
(welcome) accoglienza f; Radio ricezione f; ~
[**desk**] (in hotel) reception f inv

receptionist /rɪ'sepʃənɪst/ n persona f
alla reception

receptive /rɪ'septɪv/ adj ricettivo

recess /rɪ'ses/ n rientranza f; (holiday)
vacanza f; Am Sch intervallo m

recession /rɪ'seʃn/ n recessione f

recharge /ri:'tʃɑ:dʒ/ vt ricaricare

rechargeable /ri:'tʃɑ:dʒəbl/ adj
⟨battery⟩ ricaricabile; ⟨costs⟩ addebitabile

recidivism /rɪ'sɪdɪvɪzm/ n recidività f

recidivist /rɪ'sɪdɪvɪst/ n recidivo, -a mf

recipe /'resəpɪ/ n ricetta f

recipe book n libro m di ricette

recipient /rɪ'sɪpɪənt/ n (of letter, parcel)
destinatario, -a mf; (of money) beneficiario,
-a mf

reciprocal /rɪ'sɪprəkl/ adj reciproco

reciprocate /rɪ'sɪprəkeɪt/ vt ricambiare

recital /rɪ'saɪtl/ n recital m inv

recitation /resɪ'teɪʃn/ n recitazione f

recite /rɪ'saɪt/ vt recitare; (list) elencare

reckless /'reklɪs/ adj ⟨action, decision⟩
sconsiderato; **be a** ~ **driver** guidare in
modo spericolato

recklessly /'reklɪslɪ/ adv in modo
sconsiderato

recklessness /'reklɪsnɪs/ n
sconsideratezza f

reckon /'rekən/ vt calcolare; (consider)
pensare; **be** ~ed essere considerato
■ **reckon on**, **reckon with** vt fare i
conti con
■ **reckon without** vt fare i conti senza

reckoning /'rekənɪŋ/ n stima f, calcoli
mpl; **by my/your etc** ~ secondo i miei/
tuoi ecc. calcoli

reclaim /rɪ'kleɪm/ vt reclamare;
bonificare ⟨land⟩

reclaimable /rɪ'kleɪməbl/ adj
⟨expenses⟩ rimborsabile

recline /rɪ'klaɪn/ vi sdraiarsi

reclining /rɪ'klaɪnɪŋ/ adj ⟨seat⟩
reclinabile

recluse /rɪ'klu:s/ n recluso, -a mf

reclusive /rɪ'klu:sɪv/ adj solitario

recognition /rekəg'nɪʃn/ n
riconoscimento m; **in** ~ come
riconoscimento (**of** per); **beyond** ~
irriconoscibile

recognizable /'rekəgnaɪzəbl/ adj
riconoscibile

recognize /'rekəgnaɪz/ vt riconoscere

recoil[1] /'ri:kɔɪl/ n (of gun) rinculo m

recoil[2] /rɪ'kɔɪl/ vi (in fear) indietreggiare

recollect /rekə'lekt/ vt ricordare

recollection /rekə'lekʃn/ n ricordo m

recommence /ri:kə'mens/ vt/i
ricominciare

recommend /rekə'mend/ vt
raccomandare

recommendation /rekəmen'deɪʃn/ n
raccomandazione f

recommended retail price
/rekə'mendɪd/ n Comm prezzo m di vendita
raccomandato

recompense /'rekəmpens/ 1 n
ricompensa f
2 vt ricompensare

reconcile /'rekənsaɪl/ vt riconciliare;
conciliare ⟨facts⟩; far quadrare ⟨bank
statement⟩; ~ **oneself to** rassegnarsi a

reconciliation /rekənsɪlɪ'eɪʃn/ n
riconciliazione f

recondition /ri:kən'dɪʃn/ vt
ripristinare; ~ed **engine** motore m che ha
subito riparazioni

reconnaissance /rɪ'kɒnɪsns/ n Mil
ricognizione f; **on** ~ in ricognizione

reconnoitre /rekə'nɔɪtə(r)/ 1 vi (pres p
-tring) fare una ricognizione
2 vt fare una ricognizione di

r

reconsider /ri:kən'sɪdə(r)/ vt
riconsiderare

reconstruct /ri:kən'strʌkt/ vt
ricostruire

reconstruction /ri:kən'strʌkʃn/ n
ricostruzione f

reconvene /ri:kən'vi:n/ vi riunirsi
nuovamente

record¹ /rɪ'kɔ:d/ vt registrare; (make a
note of) annotare

record² /'rekɔd/ n (file) documentazione f;
Mus disco m; Sport record m inv; ∼s pl
(files) schedario m; **keep a** ∼ **of** tener
nota di; **off the** ∼ in via ufficiosa; **have a
[criminal]** ∼ avere la fedina penale sporca

record book n libro m dei record

record-breaker /'rekɔ:dbreɪkə(r)/ n **be
a** ∼ battere un record

recorded /rɪ'kɔ:dɪd/ adj (on tape)
⟨message⟩ registrato; (in document)
⟨sighting, case⟩ documentato

recorded delivery n raccomandata f

recorder /rɪ'kɔ:də(r)/ n Mus flauto m
dolce

record-holder n primatista mf

recording /rɪ'kɔ:dɪŋ/ n registrazione f

recording studio n sala f di
registrazione

record player n giradischi m inv

recount /rɪ'kaʊnt/ vt raccontare

re-count¹ /ri:'kaʊnt/ vt ricontare

re-count² /'ri:kaʊnt/ n Pol nuovo
conteggio m

recoup /rɪ'ku:p/ vt rifarsi di ⟨losses⟩

recourse /rɪ'kɔ:s/ n **have** ∼ **to** ricorrere
a

recover /rɪ'kʌvə(r)/ vt/i recuperare

re-cover /ri:'kʌvə(r)/ vt rifoderare

recovery /rɪ'kʌvəri/ n recupero m; (of
health) guarigione f

recovery vehicle n autogrù f

recreate /ri:krɪ'eɪt/ vt ricreare

recreation /rekrɪ'eɪʃn/ n ricreazione f

recreational /rekrɪ'eɪʃənəl/ adj
ricreativo

recreational drug n sostanza f
stupefacente che si assume
occasionalmente

recrimination /rɪkrɪmɪ'neɪʃn/ n
recriminazione f

recruit /rɪ'kru:t/ ① n Mil recluta f; **new** ∼
(member) nuovo, -a adepto, -a mf; (worker)
neoassunto, -a mf
② vt assumere ⟨staff⟩

recruitment /rɪ'kru:tmənt/ n
assunzione f

rectangle /'rektæŋgl/ n rettangolo m

rectangular /rek'tæŋgjʊlə(r)/ adj
rettangolare

rectify /'rektɪfaɪ/ vt (pt/pp **-ied**)
rettificare

rector /'rektə(r)/ n Univ rettore m

rectory /'rektəri/ n presbiterio m

rectum /'rektəm/ n retto m

recuperate /rɪ'kju:pəreit/ vi ristabilirsi

recur /rɪ'kɜ:(r)/ vi (pt/pp **recurred**)
ricorrere; ⟨illness⟩ ripresentarsi

recurrence /rɪ'kʌrəns/ n ricorrenza f
(of illness) ricomparsa f

recurrent /rɪ'kʌrənt/ adj ricorrente

recyclable /ri:'saɪkləbl/ adj riciclabile

recycle /ri:'saɪkl/ vt riciclare; ∼**d paper**
carta f riciclata

recycling /ri:'saɪklɪŋ/ n riciclaggio m

red /red/ ① adj (**redder, reddest**) rosso
② n rosso m; **be in the** ∼ ⟨account⟩ essere
scoperto; ⟨person⟩ avere il conto scoperto

red alert n allarme m rosso; **be on** ∼
essere in stato di massima allerta

redbrick adj Univ di recente fondazione

Red Cross n Croce f Rossa

redcurrant n ribes m rosso

redden /'redn/ ① vt arrossare
② vi arrossire

reddish /'redɪʃ/ adj rossastro

redecorate /ri:'dekəreit/ vt ⟨paint⟩
ridipingere; (wallpaper) ritappezzare

redeem /rɪ'di:m/ vt (Relig, from pawnshop)
riscattare; ∼**ing quality** unico aspetto m
positivo

redefine /ri:dɪ'faɪn/ vt ridefinire

redemption /rɪ'dempʃn/ n riscatto m

redeploy /ri:dɪ'plɔɪ/ vt ridistribuire

redevelop /ri:dɪ'veləp/ vt risanare
⟨area, site⟩

red-faced adj also fig paonazzo

red-haired /-'heəd/ adj con i capelli
rossi

red-handed /-'hændɪd/ adj **catch
somebody** ∼ cogliere qualcuno con le
mani nel sacco

redhead n rosso, -a mf (di capelli)

red herring n diversione f

red-hot adj rovente

redial /ri:'daɪəl/ Teleph ① vt ricomporre
② vi ricomporre il numero

redial facility n Teleph funzione f di
ricomposizione automatica dell'ultimo
numero

redirect /ri:daɪ'rekt/ vt mandare al
nuovo indirizzo ⟨letter⟩

rediscover /ri:dɪ'skʌvə(r)/ vt riscoprire

redistribute /ri:dɪs'trɪbju:t/ vt
ridistribuire

redistribution /ri:dɪstrɪ'bju:ʃn/ n
ridistribuzione f

red-letter day n giorno m memorabile

red light n Auto semaforo m rosso; **go through a ~ ~** passare col rosso.

red light area, **red light district** n quartiere m a luci rosse

red meat n carne f rossa

redness /'rednɪs/ n rossore m

redo /riː'duː/ vt (pt **-did**, pp **-done**) rifare

redolent /'redələnt/ adj profumato (**of** di)

redouble /riː'dʌbl/ vt raddoppiare

red pepper n peperone m rosso

redraft /riː'drɑːft/ vt stendere nuovamente

redress /rɪ'dres/ ① n riparazione f
② vt ristabilire ⟨balance⟩

red tape n fam burocrazia f

reduce /rɪ'djuːs/ vt ridurre; Culin far consumare

reductio ad absurdum /rɪdʌktɪəʊædəb'sɜːdəm/ n ragionamento m per assurdo

reduction /rɪ'dʌkʃn/ n riduzione f

redundancy /rɪ'dʌndənsɪ/ n licenziamento m; (payment) cassa f integrazione

redundant /rɪ'dʌndənt/ adj superfluo; **make ~** licenziare; **be made ~** essere licenziato

reed /riːd/ n Bot canna f

reedy /'riːdɪ/ adj ⟨voice, tone⟩ acuto

reef /riːf/ n scogliera f

reefer /'riːfə(r)/ n (jacket) giubbotto m a doppio petto; (fam: dope) spinello m

reef knot n nodo m piano

reek /riːk/ vi puzzare (**of** di)

reel /riːl/ ① n bobina f
② vi (stagger) vacillare

re-elect vt rieleggere

re-election n rielezione f

reel off vt fig snocciolare

re-emerge vi riemergere

re-emergence n ricomparsa f

re-enact /riːɪ'nækt/ vt ricostruire ⟨crime⟩; Jur rimettere in vigore; recitare nuovamente ⟨role⟩

re-enter /riː'entə(r)/ vt rientrare in

re-entry n (of spacecraft) rientro m

re-establish vt ristabilire, ripristinare

re-establishment n ripristino m

re-examination n riesame m

re-examine vt riesaminare

ref /ref/ n abbr Br: fam (**referee**) arbitro m

refectory /rɪ'fektərɪ/ n refettorio m; Univ mensa f universitaria

refer /rɪ'fɜː(r)/ ① vt (pt/pp **referred**) rinviare ⟨matter⟩; indirizzare ⟨person⟩

② vi **~ to** fare allusione a; (consult) rivolgersi a ⟨book⟩; **are you ~ ring to me?** alludi a me?

referee /refə'riː/ ① n arbitro m; (for job) garante mf
② vt/i (pt/pp **refereed**) arbitrare

reference /'ref(ə)rəns/ n riferimento m; (in book) nota f bibliografica; (for job) referenza f; Comm '**your ~**' 'riferimento'; **with ~ to** con riferimento a; **make [a] ~ to** fare riferimento a

reference book n libro m di consultazione

reference library n biblioteca f per la consultazione

reference number n numero m di riferimento

referendum /refə'rendəm/ n referendum m inv

referral /rɪ'fɜːrəl/ n (of matter, problem) deferimento m; Med (act) invio m di un paziente a un altro medico; (person) paziente mf mandato da un medico a un altro

refill¹ /riː'fɪl/ vt riempire di nuovo; ricaricare ⟨pen, lighter⟩

refill² /'riːfɪl/ n (for pen) ricambio m

refine /rɪ'faɪn/ vt raffinare

refined /rɪ'faɪnd/ adj raffinato

refinement /rɪ'faɪnmənt/ n raffinatezza f

refinery /rɪ'faɪnərɪ/ n raffineria f

refining /rɪ'faɪnɪŋ/ n Techn raffinazione f

refit¹ /'riːfɪt/ n Naut raddobbo m; (of shop, factory etc) rinnovo m

refit² /riː'fɪt/ vt raddobbare ⟨ship⟩ rinnovare ⟨shop, factory etc⟩

reflate /riː'fleɪt/ vt reflazionare ⟨economy⟩

reflect /rɪ'flekt/ ① vt riflettere; **be ~ed in** essere riflesso in
② vt (think) riflettere (**on** su); **~ badly on somebody** fig mettere in cattiva luce qualcuno

reflection /rɪ'flekʃn/ n riflessione f; ⟨image⟩ riflesso m; **on ~** dopo riflessione

reflective /rɪ'flektɪv/ adj riflessivo

reflectively /rɪ'flektɪvlɪ/ adv in modo riflessivo

reflector /rɪ'flektə(r)/ n riflettore m

reflex /'riːfleks/ ① n riflesso m
② attrib di riflesso

reflexive /rɪ'fleksɪv/ adj riflessivo

reflexive verb n verbo m riflessivo

refloat /riː'fləʊt/ vt Naut, Comm rimettere a galla

reforestation /riːfɒrɪ'steɪʃn/ n rimboschimento m

reform /rɪ'fɔːm/ ① n riforma f
② vt riformare
③ vi correggersi.

r

reformat /ri:'fɔ:mæt/ vt riformattare

Reformation /refə'meɪʃn/ n Relig Riforma f

reformer /rɪ'fɔ:mə(r)/ n riformatore, -trice mf

refrain[1] /rɪ'freɪn/ n ritornello m

refrain[2] vi astenersi (**from** da)

refresh /rɪ'freʃ/ vt rinfrescare; Comput aggiornare

refresher course /rɪ'freʃə(r)/ n corso m d'aggiornamento

refreshing /rɪ'freʃɪŋ/ adj rinfrescante

refreshments /rɪ'freʃmənts/ npl rinfreschi mpl

refrigerate /rɪ'frɪdʒəreɪt/ vt conservare in frigo; Ind refrigerare

refrigerated lorry /rɪ'frɪdʒəreɪtɪd/ n camion m inv frigorifero

refrigeration /rɪfrɪdʒə'reɪʃn/ n Ind refrigerazione f

refrigerator /rɪ'frɪdʒəreɪtə(r)/ n frigorifero m

refuel /ri:'fjʊəl/ 1 vt (pt/pp **-fuelled**) rifornire di carburante
2 vi fare rifornimento

refuge /'refju:dʒ/ n rifugio m; **take ~** rifugiarsi

refugee /refjʊ'dʒi:/ n rifugiato, -a mf

refugee camp n campo m profughi

refund[1] /'ri:fʌnd/ n rimborso m

refund[2] /rɪ'fʌnd/ vt rimborsare

refurbish /ri:'fɜ:bɪʃ/ vt rimettere a nuovo

refurbishment /ri:'fɜ:bɪʃmənt/ n rinnovo m

refusal /rɪ'fju:zl/ n rifiuto m

refuse[1] /rɪ'fju:z/ vt/i rifiutare; **~ to do something** rifiutare di fare qualcosa

refuse[2] /'refju:s/ n rifiuti mpl

refuse collection n raccolta f dei rifiuti

refuse collector n Br spazzino, -a mf

refute /rɪ'fju:t/ vt confutare

regain /rɪ'geɪn/ vt riconquistare

regal /'ri:gl/ adj regale

regale /rɪ'geɪl/ vt **~ somebody with something** deliziare qualcuno con qualcosa

regalia /rɪ'geɪlɪə/ npl insegne fpl reali

regard /rɪ'gɑ:d/ 1 n (heed) riguardo m; (respect) considerazione f; **~s** pl; saluti mpl; **send/give my ~s to your brother** salutami tuo fratello; **with ~ to** riguardo a
2 vt (consider) considerare (**as** come); **as ~s** riguardo a

regarding /rɪ'gɑ:dɪŋ/ prep riguardo a

regardless /rɪ'gɑ:dlɪs/ adv lo stesso; **~ of** senza badare a

regatta /rɪ'gætə/ n regata f

regency /'ri:dʒənsɪ/ n reggenza f

regenerate /rɪ'dʒenəreɪt/ 1 vt rigenerare
2 vi rigenerarsi

regent /'ri:dʒənt/ n reggente mf

reggae /'regeɪ/ n reggae m

regime /reɪ'ʒi:m/ n regime m

regiment[1] /'redʒɪmənt/ n reggimento m

regiment[2] /'redʒɪment/ vt irreggimentare

regimental /redʒɪ'mentl/ adj reggimentale

regimentation /redʒɪmən'teɪʃn/ n irreggimentazione f

regimented /'redʒɪmentɪd/ adj irreggimentato

region /'ri:dʒən/ n regione f; **in the ~ of** fig approssimativamente

regional /'ri:dʒənl/ adj regionale

register /'redʒɪstə(r)/ 1 n registro m
2 vt registrare; mandare tramite assicurata ⟨letter, package⟩; assicurare ⟨luggage⟩; immatricolare ⟨motor vehicle⟩; mostrare ⟨feeling⟩
3 vi ⟨instrument⟩ funzionare; ⟨student⟩ iscriversi (**for** a); **it didn't ~ with me** fig non ci ho fatto attenzione; **~ with** iscriversi nella lista di ⟨doctor⟩

registered /'redʒɪstəd/ adj ⟨voter, student⟩ iscritto; ⟨vehicle⟩ immatricolato

registered letter n lettera f assicurata

registered trademark n marchio m depositato

registrar /redʒɪ'strɑ:(r)/ n ufficiale m di stato civile

registration /redʒɪ'streɪʃn/ n (of vehicle) immatricolazione f; (of letter, luggage) assicurazione f; (for course) iscrizione f

registration fee n tassa f d'iscrizione

registration number n Auto [numero m di] targa f

registry office /'redʒɪstrɪ/ n anagrafe f

regress /rɪ'gres/ vi Biol, Psych, fig regredire

regression /rɪ'greʃən/ n regressione f

regressive /rɪ'gresɪv/ adj Biol, Psych regressivo

regret /rɪ'gret/ 1 n rammarico m
2 vt (pt/pp **regretted**) rimpiangere; **I ~ that** mi rincresce che

regretfully /rɪ'gretfʊlɪ/ adv con rammarico

regrettable /rɪ'gretəbl/ adj spiacevole

regrettably /rɪ'gretəblɪ/ adv spiacevolmente; (before adjective) deplorevolmente

regroup /ri:'gru:p/ vi riorganizzarsi

regular /'regjʊlə(r)/ 1 adj regolare; (usual) abituale
2 n cliente mf abituale

regularity /regjʊˈlærətɪ/ *n* regolarità *f*

regularly /ˈregjʊləlɪ/ *adv* regolarmente

regulate /ˈregʊleɪt/ *vt* regolare

regulation /regjʊˈleɪʃn/ *n* (rule) regolamento *m*

regulator /ˈregʊleɪtə(r)/ *n* (person) regolatore, -trice *mf*; (device) regolatore *m*

regurgitate /rɪˈgɜːdʒɪteɪt/ *vt* rigurgitare; fig pej ripetere meccanicamente

rehabilitate /riːhəˈbɪlɪteɪt/ *vt* riabilitare

rehabilitation /riːhəbɪlɪˈteɪʃn/ *n* riabilitazione *f*

rehabilitation centre Br, **rehabilitation center** Am *n* (after drug addiction, illness, prison) comunità *f* terapeutica

rehash[1] /riːˈhæʃ/ *vt* rimaneggiare

rehash[2] /ˈriːhæʃ/ *n* rimaneggiamento *m*

rehearsal /rɪˈhɜːsl/ *n* Theat prova *f*

rehearse /rɪˈhɜːs/ *vt/i* provare

reheat /riːˈhiːt/ *vt* scaldare di nuovo

rehouse /riːˈhaʊz/ *vt* rialloggiare

reign /reɪn/ [1] *n* regno *m* [2] *vi* regnare

reimburse /riːɪmˈbɜːs/ *vt* ~ somebody for something rimborsare qualcosa a qualcuno

reimbursement /riːɪmˈbɜːsmənt/ *n* rimborso *m*

rein /reɪn/ *n* redine *f*

reincarnate /riːɪnˈkɑːneɪt/ *vt* be ~d reincarnarsi

reincarnation /riːɪnkɑːˈneɪʃn/ *n* reincarnazione *f*

reindeer /ˈreɪndɪə(r)/ *n inv* renna *f*

reinforce /riːɪnˈfɔːs/ *vt* rinforzare

reinforced concrete *n* cemento *m* armato

reinforcement /riːɪnˈfɔːsmənt/ *n* rinforzo *m*; ~s *pl* Mil rinforzi *mpl*

reinstall /ˈriːɪnstɔl/ *vt* Comput reinstallare ‹software, program›

reinstate /riːɪnˈsteɪt/ *vt* reintegrare

reinstatement /riːɪnˈsteɪtmənt/ *n* reintegrazione *f*

reinterpret /riːɪntˈtɜːprɪt/ *vt* reinterpretare

reinterpretation /riːɪntɜːprɪˈteɪʃn/ *n* reinterpretazione *f*

reintroduce /riːɪntrəˈdjuːs/ *vt* reintrodurre

reintroduction /riːɪntrəˈdʌkʃn/ *n* reintroduzione *f*

reiterate /riːˈɪtəreɪt/ *vt* reiterare

reiteration /riːɪtəˈreɪʃn/ *n* reiterazione *f*

reject /rɪˈdʒekt/ *vt* rifiutare

rejection /rɪˈdʒekʃn/ *n* rifiuto *m*; Med rigetto *m*

rejects /ˈriːdʒekts/ *npl* Comm scarti *mpl*

rejig /riːˈdʒɪg/ *vt* (pt/pp **rejigged**) Br riorganizzare

rejoice /rɪˈdʒɔɪs/ *vi* liter rallegrarsi

rejoicing /rɪˈdʒɔɪsɪŋ/ *n* gioia *f*

rejoin /rɪˈdʒɔɪn/ *vt* riassociarsi a ‹club, party›; Mil reintegrarsi in ‹regiment›; (answer) replicare

rejuvenate /rɪˈdʒuːvəneɪt/ *vt* rinnovare; ringiovanire ‹person›

rejuvenation /rɪˈdʒuːvəneɪʃn/ *n* rinnovamento *m*; (of person) ringiovanimento *m*

rekindle /riːˈkɪndl/ *vt* riattizzare

relapse /rɪˈlæps/ [1] *n* ricaduta *f* [2] *vi* ricadere

relate /rɪˈleɪt/ *vt* (tell) riportare; (connect) collegare

■ **relate to** *vt* riferirsi a; identificarsi con ‹person›

related /rɪˈleɪtɪd/ *adj* imparentato (**to** a); ‹ideas etc› affine

relation /rɪˈleɪʃn/ *n* rapporto *m*; (person) parente *mf*

relationship /rɪˈleɪʃnʃɪp/ *n* rapporto *m*; (blood tie) parentela *f*; (affair) relazione *f*

relative /ˈrelətɪv/ [1] *n* parente *mf* [2] *adj* relativo

relatively /ˈrelətɪvlɪ/ *adv* relativamente

relativity /reləˈtɪvətɪ/ *n* relatività *f*

relativity theory *n* Phys teoria *f* della relatività

relaunch[1] /ˈriːlɔːntʃ/ *n* rilancio *m*

relaunch[2] /riːˈlɔːntʃ/ *vt* rilanciare

relax /rɪˈlæks/ [1] *vt* rilassare; allentare ‹pace grip› [2] *vi* rilassarsi

relaxation /riːlækˈseɪʃn/ *n* rilassamento *m*, relax *m*; (recreation) svago *m*

relaxed /rɪˈlækst/ *adj* rilassato

relaxing /rɪˈlæksɪŋ/ *adj* rilassante

relay[1] /riːˈleɪ/ *vt* (pt/pp **-layed**) trasmettere

relay[2] /ˈriːleɪ/ *n* Electr relais *m inv*; work in ~s fare i turni

relay [race] /ˈriːleɪ/ *n* [corsa *f* a] staffetta *f*

release /rɪˈliːs/ [1] *n* rilascio *m*; (of film) distribuzione *f* [2] *vt* liberare; lasciare ‹hand›; togliere ‹brake›; distribuire ‹film›; rilasciare ‹information etc›

relegate /ˈrelɪgeɪt/ *vt* relegare; be ~d Br Sport essere retrocesso

relegation /relɪˈgeɪʃn/ *n* relegazione *f*; Br Sport retrocessione *f*

relent /rɪˈlent/ *vi* cedere

relentless /rɪˈlentlɪs/ *adj* inflessibile; (unceasing) incessante

relentlessly /rɪˈlentlɪslɪ/ *adv* incessantemente

relevance /'reləvəns/ n pertinenza f

relevant /'reləvənt/ adj pertinente (**to** a)

reliability /rɪlaɪə'bɪlətɪ/ n affidabilità f

reliable /rɪ'laɪəbl/ adj affidabile

reliably /rɪ'laɪəblɪ/ adv in modo affidabile; **be ~ informed** sapere da fonte certa

reliance /rɪ'laɪəns/ n fiducia f (**on** in)

reliant /rɪ'laɪənt/ adj fiducioso (**on** in)

relic /'relɪk/ n Relig reliquia f; **~s** pl resti mpl

relief /rɪ'liːf/ n sollievo m; (assistance) soccorso m; (distraction) diversivo m; (replacement) cambio m; (in art) rilievo m; **in ~** in rilievo

relief agency n organizzazione f umanitaria

relief map n carta f in rilievo

relief supplies npl soccorsi mpl, aiuti mpl umanitari

relief train n treno m supplementare

relief work n lavoro m presso un'organizzazione umanitaria

relief worker n persona f che lavora per un'organizzazione umanitaria

relieve /rɪ'liːv/ vt alleviare; (take over from) dare il cambio a; **~ of** liberare da ⟨burden⟩

religion /rɪ'lɪdʒən/ n religione f

religious /rɪ'lɪdʒəs/ adj religioso

religiously /rɪ'lɪdʒəslɪ/ adv (conscientiously) scrupolosamente

relinquish /rɪ'lɪŋkwɪʃ/ vt abbandonare; **~ something to somebody** rinunciare a qualcosa in favore di qualcuno

relish /'relɪʃ/ ❶ n gusto m; Culin salsa f ❷ vt fig apprezzare

relive /riː'lɪv/ vt rivivere

reload /riː'ləʊd/ vt ricaricare

relocate /riːlə'keɪt/ ❶ vt trasferire ❷ vi trasferirsi

relocation /riːlə'keɪʃn/ n (of employee, company) trasferimento m

relocation allowance n indennità f inv di trasferimento

reluctance /rɪ'lʌktəns/ n riluttanza f

reluctant /rɪ'lʌktənt/ adj riluttante

reluctantly /rɪ'lʌktəntlɪ/ adv con riluttanza, a malincuore

rely /rɪ'laɪ/ vi (pt/pp **-ied**) **~ on** dipendere da; (trust) contare su

remain /rɪ'meɪn/ vi restare

remainder /rɪ'meɪndə(r)/ ❶ n resto m; Comm rimanenza f ❷ vt Comm svendere

remaining /rɪ'meɪnɪŋ/ adj restante

remains /rɪ'meɪnz/ npl resti mpl; (dead body) spoglie fpl

remake /'riːmeɪk/ n (of film, recording) remake m inv

remand /rɪ'mɑːnd/ ❶ n **on ~** in custodia cautelare ❷ vt **~ in custody** rinviare con detenzione provvisoria

remand centre n Br istituto m di carcerazione preventiva

remark /rɪ'mɑːk/ ❶ n osservazione f ❷ vt osservare

remarkable /rɪ'mɑːkəbl/ adj notevole

remarkably /rɪ'mɑːkəblɪ/ adv notevolmente

remarry /riː'mærɪ/ vi (pt/pp **-ied**) risposarsi

remaster /riː'mɑːstə(r)/ vt incidere di nuovo ⟨recording⟩

rematch /'riːmætʃ/ n Sport partita f di ritorno; (in boxing) secondo incontro m

remedial /rɪ'miːdɪəl/ adj correttivo; Med curativo

remedy /'remədɪ/ ❶ n rimedio m (**for** contro) ❷ vt (pt/pp **-ied**) rimediare a

remember /rɪ'membə(r)/ ❶ vt ricordare, ricordarsi; **~ to do something** ricordarsi di fare qualcosa; **~ me to him** salutamelo ❷ vi ricordarsi

Remembrance Day /rɪ'membrəns/ n commemorazione f dei caduti (11 novembre)

remind /rɪ'maɪnd/ vt **~ somebody of something** ricordare qualcosa a qualcuno

reminder /rɪ'maɪndə(r)/ n ricordo m; (memo) promemoria m inv; (letter) lettera f di sollecito; (to pay) sollecitazione f di pagamento

reminisce /remɪ'nɪs/ vi rievocare il passato

reminiscences /remɪ'nɪsənsɪz/ npl reminiscenze fpl

reminiscent /remɪ'nɪsənt/ adj **be ~ of** richiamare alla memoria

remiss /rɪ'mɪs/ adj negligente

remission /rɪ'mɪʃn/ n remissione f; (of sentence) condono m

remit /rɪ'mɪt/ vt (pt/pp **remitted**) rimettere ⟨money⟩

remittance /rɪ'mɪtəns/ n rimessa f

remix¹ /riː'mɪks/ vt Mus rimixare

remix² /'riːmɪks/ n Mus rimixaggio m

remnant /'remnənt/ n resto m; (of material) scampolo m; (trace) traccia f

remonstrate /'remənstreɪt/ vi fare rimostranze (**with somebody** a qualcuno)

remorse /rɪ'mɔːs/ n rimorso m

remorseful /rɪ'mɔːsfʊl/ adj pieno di rimorso

remorsefully /rɪ'mɔːsfʊlɪ/ adv con rimorso

remorseless /rɪ'mɔːslɪs/ adj spietato

remorselessly /rɪˈmɔslɪslɪ/ *adv* senza pietà

remote /rɪˈməʊt/ *adj* remoto; (slight) minimo

remote access *n* Comput accesso *m* remoto

remote control *n* telecomando *m*

remote-controlled *adj* telecomandato

remotely /rɪˈməʊtlɪ/ *adv* lontanamente; be not ∼... non essere lontanamente...

remoteness /rɪˈməʊtnɪs/ *n* lontananza *f*

remould /ˈriːməʊld/ *n* pneumatico *m* ricostruito

remount /riːˈmaʊnt/ *vt* rimontare in sella a ⟨bike, horse⟩

removable /rɪˈmuːvəbl/ *adj* rimovibile

removal /rɪˈmuːvl/ *n* rimozione *f*; (from house) trasloco *m*

removal man *n* addetto *m* ai traslochi

removal van *n* camion *m inv* da trasloco

remove /rɪˈmuːv/ *vt* togliere; togliersi ⟨clothes⟩; eliminare ⟨stain, doubts⟩

removers /rɪˈmuːvəz/ *npl* fam traslocatori *mpl*

remuneration /rɪmjuːnəˈreɪʃn/ *n* rimunerazione *f*

remunerative /rɪˈmjuːnərətɪv/ *adj* rimunerativo

renaissance /rɪˈneɪsãs/ *n* rinascita *f*; R∼ Rinascimento *m*

renal /ˈriːnəl/ *adj* renale

render /ˈrendə(r)/ *vt* rendere ⟨service⟩

rendering /ˈrend(ə)rɪŋ/ *n* Mus interpretazione *f*

rendezvous /ˈrɒndeɪvuː/ *vi esp* Mil incontrarsi

rendition /renˈdɪʃn/ *n* interpretazione *f*

renegade /ˈrenɪgeɪd/ *n* rinnegato, -a *mf*

renege /rɪˈneɪg/ *vi* venire meno (on a)

renegotiate /riːnɪˈgəʊʃɪeɪt/ *vt* rinegoziare

renegotiation /riːnɪgəʊʃɪˈeɪʃn/ *n* rinegoziato *m*

renew /rɪˈnjuː/ *vt* rinnovare ⟨contract⟩

renewable /rɪˈnjuːəbl/ *adj* rinnovabile

renewal /rɪˈnjuːəl/ *n* rinnovo *m*

renewed *adj* ⟨strength, interest⟩ rinnovato; ⟨attack⟩ nuovo

renounce /rɪˈnaʊns/ *vt* rinunciare a

renovate /ˈrenəveɪt/ *vt* rinnovare

renovation /renəˈveɪʃn/ *n* rinnovo *m*

renown /rɪˈnaʊn/ *n* fama *f*

renowned /rɪˈnaʊnd/ *adj* rinomato

rent /rent/ ① *n* affitto *m* ② *vt* affittare; ∼ [out] dare in affitto

rental /ˈrentl/ *n* affitto *m*

rent boy *n* ragazzo *m* di vita

rent-free ① *adj* ⟨accommodation⟩ gratuito ② *adv* ⟨live, use⟩ senza pagare l'affitto

renunciation /rɪnʌnsɪˈeɪʃn/ *n* rinuncia *f*

reoffend /riːəˈfend/ *vi* recidivare

reopen /riːˈəʊpən/ *vt/i* riaprire

reorganization /riːɔːgənəˈzeɪʃn/ *n* riorganizzazione *f*

reorganize /riːˈɔːgənaɪz/ *vt* riorganizzare

rep /rep/ *n* Comm fam rappresentante *mf*; Theat ≈ teatro *m* stabile

repackage /riːˈpækɪdʒ/ *vt* Comm cambiare la confezione di; (fig: change public image of) cambiare l'immagine pubblica di; cambiare i termini di ⟨proposal⟩

repaint /riːˈpeɪnt/ *vt* ridipingere

repair /rɪˈpeə(r)/ ① *n* riparazione *f*; In good/bad ∼ in buone/cattive condizioni ② *vt* riparare

repairman *n* tecnico *m* (delle riparazioni)

reparation /repəˈreɪʃn/ *n* make ∼s for something risarcire qualcosa

repartee /repɑːˈtiː/ *n* botta e risposta *m inv*; piece of ∼ risposta *f* pronta

repatriate /riːˈpætrɪeɪt/ *vt* rimpatriare

repatriation /riːpætrɪˈeɪʃn/ *n* rimpatrio *m*

repay /riːˈpeɪ/ *vt* (pt/pp **-paid**) ripagare

repayment /riːˈpeɪmənt/ *n* rimborso *m*

repeal /rɪˈpiːl/ ① *n* abrogazione *f* ② *vt* abrogare

repeat /rɪˈpiːt/ ① *n* TV replica *f* ② *vt/i* ripetere; ∼ oneself ripetersi

repeated /rɪˈpiːtɪd/ *adj* ripetuto

repeatedly /rɪˈpiːtɪdlɪ/ *adv* ripetutamente

repel /rɪˈpel/ *vt* (pt/pp **repelled**) respingere; fig ripugnare

repellent /rɪˈpelənt/ *adj* ripulsivo

repent /rɪˈpent/ *vi* pentirsi

repentance /rɪˈpentəns/ *n* pentimento *m*

repentant /rɪˈpentənt/ *adj* pentito

repercussions /riːpəˈkʌʃnz/ *npl* ripercussioni *fbl*

repertoire /ˈrepətwɑː(r)/ *n* repertorio *m*

repertory /ˈrepətrɪ/ *n* ≈ teatro *m* stabile

repertory company *n* compagnia *f* di un teatro stabile

repetition /repɪˈtɪʃn/ *n* ripetizione *f*

repetitious /repɪˈtɪʃəs/, **repetitive** /rɪˈpetɪtɪv/ *adj* ripetitivo

repetitive strain injury *n* patologia *f* da sforzo ripetuto

replace /rɪˈpleɪs/ *vt* (put back) rimettere a posto; (take the place of) sostituire; ∼ ⋯⟩

r

something with something sostituire
qualcosa con qualcosa

replacement /rɪ'pleɪsmənt/ n
sostituzione f; (person) sostituto, -a mf

replacement part n pezzo m di
ricambio

replant /ri:'plɑ:nt/ vt ripiantare

replay /'ri:pleɪ/ n Sport partita f ripetuta;
[action] ~ replay m inv

replenish /rɪ'plenɪʃ/ vt rifornire
⟨stocks⟩; (refill) riempire di nuovo

replete /rɪ'pli:t/ adj ~ with riempito di

replica /'replɪkə/ n copia f

replicate /'replɪkeɪt/ vt ripetere
⟨experiment⟩

reply /rɪ'plaɪ/ ① n risposta f (to a)
② vt (pt/pp **replied**) rispondere

reply-paid envelope n busta f
affrancata per rispondere

report /rɪ'pɔ:t/ ① n rapporto m; TV, Radio
servizio m; Journ cronaca f; Sch pagella f;
(rumour) diceria f
② vt riportare; ~ somebody to the police
denunciare qualcuno alla polizia
③ vi riportare; (present oneself) presentarsi
(to a)

report card n Am scheda f di
valutazione scolastica

reportedly /rɪ'pɔ:tɪdlɪ/ adv secondo
quanto si dice

reporter /rɪ'pɔ:tə(r)/ n cronista mf,
reporter mf inv

repose /rɪ'pəʊz/ n riposo m

repository /rɪ'pɒzɪt(ə)rɪ/ n (place)
deposito, m; (of secret, authority) depositario,
-a mf

repossess /ri:pə'zes/ vt riprendere
possesso di

repossession /ri:pə'zeʃn/ n esproprio
m

repot /ri:'pɒt/ vt rinvasare ⟨plant⟩

reprehensible /reprɪ'hensəbl/ adj
riprovevole

represent /reprɪ'zent/ vt rappresentare

representation /reprɪzen'teɪʃn/ n
rappresentazione f; **make ~s to** fare delle
rimostranze a

representative /reprɪ'zentətɪv/ ① adj
rappresentativo
② n rappresentante mf

repress /rɪ'pres/ vt reprimere

repression /rɪ'preʃn/ n repressione f

repressive /rɪ'presɪv/ adj repressivo

reprieve /rɪ'pri:v/ ① n commutazione f
della pena capitale; (postponement)
sospensione f della pena capitale; fig
tregua f
② vt sospendere la sentenza a; fig
risparmiare

reprimand /'reprɪmɑ:nd/ ① n
rimprovero m

② vt rimproverare

reprint¹ /'ri:prɪnt/ n ristampa f

reprint² /ri:'prɪnt/ vt ristampare

reprisal /rɪ'praɪzl/ n rappresaglia f; **in ~
for** per rappresaglia contro

reproach /rɪ'prəʊtʃ/ ① n rimprovero m
② vt rimproverare a (**for doing something**
di fare qualcosa)

reproachful /rɪ'prəʊtʃfʊl/ adj
riprovevole

reproachfully /rɪ'prəʊtʃfʊlɪ/ adv con
aria di rimprovero

reprocess /ri:'prəʊses/ vt trattare di
nuovo

reprocessing plant /ri:'prəʊsesɪŋ/ n
impianto m di rilavorazione (di scorie
nucleari)

reproduce /ri:prə'dju:s/ ① vt
riprodurre
② vi riprodursi

reproduction /ri:prə'dʌkʃn/ n
riproduzione f

reproduction furniture n
riproduzioni fpl di mobili antichi

reproductive /ri:prə'dʌktɪv/ adj
riproduttivo

reproof /rɪ'pru:f/ n rimprovero m

reprove /rɪ'pru:v/ vt rimproverare

reptile /'reptaɪl/ n rettile m

republic /rɪ'pʌblɪk/ n repubblica f

republican /rɪ'pʌblɪkn/ adj & n
repubblicano, -a mf

republish /ri:'pʌblɪʃ/ vt ripubblicare

repudiate /rɪ'pju:dɪeɪt/ vt ripudiare;
respingere ⟨view, suggestion⟩

repugnance /rɪ'pʌgnəns/ n ripugnanza
f

repugnant /rɪ'pʌgnənt/ adj ripugnante

repulse /rɪ'pʌls/ vt fml respingere
⟨attack⟩; rifiutare ⟨assistance⟩

repulsion /rɪ'pʌlʃn/ n repulsione f

repulsive /rɪ'pʌlsɪv/ adj ripugnante

reputable /'repjʊtəbl/ adj affidabile

reputation /repjʊ'teɪʃn/ n reputazione f

repute /rɪ'pju:t/ n reputazione f

reputed /rɪ'pju:tɪd/ adj presunto; **he is
~ to be** si presume che sia

reputedly /rɪ'pju:tɪdlɪ/ adv
presumibilmente

request /rɪ'kwest/ ① n richiesta f
② vt richiedere

request stop n fermata f a richiesta

requiem /'rekwɪəm/ n requiem m inv

require /rɪ'kwaɪə(r)/ vt (need) necessitare
di; (demand) esigere

required /rɪ'kwaɪəd/ adj richiesto

requirement /rɪ'kwaɪəmənt/ n esigenza
f; (condition) requisito m

requisite /'rekwɪzɪt/ ① adj necessario

2 n toilet/travel ~s pl articoli mpl da toilette/viaggio

requisition /rekwɪ'zɪʃn/ **1** n ~ [order] [domanda f di] requisizione f
2 vt requisire

reread /ri:'ri:d/ vt rileggere

re-release /ri:rɪ'li:s/ **1** n (of film) nuova distribuzione f
2 vt ridistribuire ⟨film⟩

reroof /ri:'ru:f/ vt rifare il tetto di ⟨building⟩

reroute /ri:'ru:t/ vt dirottare ⟨flight, traffic⟩

rerun /'ri:rʌn/ n (of film, play) replica f; (fig: repeat) ripetizione f

resale /ri:'seɪl/ n rivendita f

reschedule /ri:'ʃedju:l/ vt (change date of) cambiare la data di; (change time of) cambiare l'orario di; rinegoziare ⟨debt⟩

rescind /rɪ'sɪnd/ vt rescindere

rescue /'reskju:/ **1** n salvataggio m
2 vt salvare

rescuer /'reskjʊə(r)/ n salvatore, -trice mf

rescue worker n soccorritore, -trice mf

research /rɪ'sɜ:tʃ/ **1** n ricerca f
2 vt fare ricerche su; Journ fare un'inchiesta su
3 vi ~ into fare ricerche su

research and development n ricerca f e sviluppo m

researcher /rɪ'sɜ:tʃə(r)/ n ricercatore, -trice mf

research fellow n Br Univ ricercatore, -trice mf

resell /ri:'sel/ vt (pt/pp resold) rivendere

resemblance /rɪ'zembləns/ n rassomiglianza f

resemble /rɪ'zembl/ vt rassomigliare a

resent /rɪ'zent/ vt risentirsi per

resentful /rɪ'zentfʊl/ adj pieno di risentimento

resentfully /rɪ'zentfʊlɪ/ adv con risentimento

resentment /rɪ'zentmənt/ n risentimento m

reservation /rezə'veɪʃn/ n (booking) prenotazione f; (doubt, enclosure) riserva f

reserve /rɪ'zɜ:v/ **1** n riserva f; (shyness) riserbo m
2 vt riservare; riservarsi ⟨right⟩

reserved /rɪ'zɜ:vd/ adj riservato

reservoir /'rezəvwɑ:(r)/ n bacino m idrico

reset /ri:'set/ vt riprogrammare ⟨clock⟩; (zero) azzerare

reshape /ri:'ʃeɪp/ vt ristrutturare

reshuffle /ri:'ʃʌfl/ **1** Pol n rimpasto m

2 vt rimpastare

reside /rɪ'zaɪd/ vi risiedere

residence /'rezɪdəns/ n residenza f; (stay) soggiorno m

residence permit n permesso m di soggiorno

resident /'rezɪdənt/ adj & n residente mf

residential /rezɪ'denʃl/ adj residenziale

residential area n quartiere m residenziale

residual /rɪ'zɪdjʊəl/ adj residuo

residue /'rezɪdju:/ n residuo m

resign /rɪ'zaɪn/ **1** vt dimettersi da; ~ oneself to rassegnarsi a
2 vt dare le dimissioni

resignation /rezɪg'neɪʃn/ n rassegnazione f; (from job) dimissioni fpl

resigned /rɪ'zaɪnd/ adj rassegnato

resignedly /rɪ'zaɪnɪdlɪ/ adv con rassegnazione

resilient /rɪ'zɪlɪənt/ adj elastico; fig con buone capacità di ripresa

resin /'rezɪn/ n resina f

resist /rɪ'zɪst/ **1** vt resistere a
2 vi resistere

resistance /rɪ'zɪstəns/ n resistenza f

resistance fighter n combattente mf delle forze di resistenza

resistant /rɪ'zɪstənt/ adj resistente

resit /ri:'sɪt/ Br **1** vt (pt/pp resat) ridare ⟨exam⟩
2 n esame m di recupero

resize /ri:'saɪz/ vt ridimensionare

reskill /ri:'skɪl/ vt riqualificare ⟨workers⟩

resolute /'rezəlu:t/ adj risoluto

resolutely /'rezəlu:tlɪ/ adv con risolutezza

resolution /rezə'lu:ʃn/ n risolutezza f

resolve /rɪ'zɒlv/ **1** n risolutezza f; (decision) risoluzione f
2 vt (solve) risolvere; ~ to do decidere di fare

resolved /rɪ'zɒlvd/ adj risoluto

resonance /'rezənəns/ n risonanza f

resonant /'rezmənt/ adj risonante

resonate /'rezəneɪt/ vi risuonare

resort /rɪ'zɔ:t/ **1** n (place) luogo m di villeggiatura; as a last ~ come ultima risorsa
2 vi ~ to ricorrere a

resound /rɪ'zaʊnd/ vi risonare (with di)

resounding /rɪ'zaʊndɪŋ/ adj ⟨success⟩ risonante

resoundingly /rɪ'zaʊndɪŋlɪ/ adv in modo risonante

resource /rɪ'sɔ:s/ n ~s pl risorse fpl

resourceful /rɪ'sɔ:sfʊl/ adj pieno di risorse; ⟨solution⟩ ingegnoso

resourcefulness /rɪˈsɔːsfʊlnɪs/ *n* ingegnosità *f*

respect /rɪˈspekt/ ① *n* rispetto *m*; (aspect) aspetto *m*; **with ~ to** per quanto riguarda
② *vt* rispettare

respectability /rɪspektəˈbɪlətɪ/ *n* rispettabilità *f*

respectable /rɪˈspektəbl/ rispettabile

respectably /rɪˈspektəblɪ/ *adv* rispettabilmente

respectful /rɪˈspektfʊl/ *adj* rispettoso

respectfully /rɪˈspektfʊlɪ/ *adv* rispettosamente

respective /rɪˈspektɪv/ *adj* rispettivo

respectively /rɪˈspektɪvlɪ/ *adv* rispettivamente

respiration /respɪˈreɪʃn/ *n* respirazione *f*

respirator /ˈrespɪreɪtə(r)/ *n* (apparatus) respiratore *m*

respiratory /rɪˈspɪrətrɪ/ *adj* respiratorio

respite /ˈrespaɪt/ *n* respiro *m*

resplendent /rɪˈsplendənt/ *adj* risplendente

respond /rɪˈspɒnd/ *vi* rispondere; (react) reagire (to a); ⟨patient⟩ rispondere (to a)

respondent /rɪˈspɒndənt/ *n* Jur convenuto, -a *mf*; (to questionnaire) interrogato, -a *mf*

response /rɪˈspɒns/ *n* risposta *f*; (reaction) reazione *f*

responsibility /rɪspɒnsɪˈbɪlətɪ/ *n* responsabilità *f inv*

responsible /rɪˈspɒnsəbl/ *adj* responsabile; (trustworthy) responsabile; (job) impegnativo

responsibly /rɪˈspɒnsəblɪ/ *adv* in modo responsabile

responsive /rɪˈspɒnsɪv/ *adj* **be ~** ⟨audience etc⟩ reagire; ⟨brakes⟩ essere sensibile; **she wasn't very ~** non era molto cooperativa

respray¹ /riːˈspreɪ/ *vt* riverniciare ⟨vehicle⟩

respray² /ˈriːspreɪ/ *n* riverniciatura *f*; **it's had a ~** è stato riverniciato

rest¹ /rest/ ① *n* riposo *m*; Mus pausa *f*; **have a ~** riposarsi
② *vt* riposare; (lean, place) appoggiare (on su)
③ *vi* riposarsi; ⟨elbows⟩ appoggiarsi; ⟨hopes⟩ riposare; **it ~s with you** sta a te
■ **rest up** *vi* riposarsi

rest² *n* **the ~** il resto; (people) gli altri

restart /riːˈstɑːt/ *vt* rimettere in moto ⟨engine⟩; riprendere ⟨talks⟩; Comput riavviare

restate /riːˈsteɪt/ *vt* (say differently) riformulare; (say again) ribadire

restaurant /ˈrestərɒnt/ *n* ristorante *m*

restaurant car *n* vagone *m* ristorante

restful /ˈrestfl/ *adj* riposante

rest home *n* casa *f* di riposo

restitution /restɪˈtjuːʃn/ *n* restituzione *f*

restive /ˈrestɪv/ *adj* irrequieto

restless /ˈrestlɪs/ *adj* nervoso

restlessly /ˈrestlɪslɪ/ *adv* nervosamente

restlessness /ˈrestlɪsnɪs/ agitazione *f*

restock /riːˈstɒk/ ① *vt* rifornire ⟨shelf, shop⟩
② *vi* rifornirsi

restoration /restəˈreɪʃn/ *n* ristabilimento *m*; (of building) restauro *m*; (of stolen property etc) restituzione *f*

restore /rɪˈstɔː(r)/ *vt* ristabilire; restaurare ⟨building⟩; (give back) restituire

restorer /rɪˈstɔːrə(r)/ *n* (person) restauratore, -trice *mf*

restrain /rɪˈstreɪn/ *vt* trattenere; **~ oneself** controllarsi

restrained /rɪˈstreɪnd/ *adj* controllato

restraint /rɪˈstreɪnt/ *n* restrizione *f*; (moderation) ritegno *m*

restrict /rɪˈstrɪkt/ *vt* limitare (to a)

restricted /rɪˈstrɪktɪd/ *adj* ⟨access, parking⟩ riservato; ⟨growth, movement⟩ limitato; ⟨document, information⟩ confidenziale

restriction /rɪˈstrɪkʃn/ *n* limite *m*; (restraint) restrizione *f*

restrictive /rɪˈstrɪktɪv/ *adj* limitativo

restring /riːˈstrɪŋ/ *vt* rinfilare ⟨necklace, beads⟩; sostituire le corde di ⟨instrument, racket⟩

restroom /ˈrestruːm/ *n* Am toilette *f inv*

restructure /riːˈstrʌktʃə(r)/ *vt* ristrutturare

restructuring /riːˈstrʌktʃərɪŋ/ *n* ristrutturazione *f*

restyle /riːˈstaɪl/ *vt* cambiare il taglio di ⟨hair⟩; cambiare la linea di ⟨car⟩; rimodernare ⟨shop⟩

resubmit /riːsʌbˈmɪt/ *vt* ripresentare

result /rɪˈzʌlt/ ① *n* risultato *m*; **as a ~** di conseguenza; **as a ~ of** a causa di
② *vi* **~ from** risultare da; **~ in** portare a

resume /rɪˈzjuːm/ *vt/i* riprendere

résumé /ˈrezjʊmeɪ/ *n* riassunto *m*; Am curriculum *m inv* vitae

resumption /rɪˈzʌmpʃn/ *n* ripresa *f*

resurface /riːˈsɜːfɪs/ ① *vi* ⟨sub, person, rumour⟩ riemergere
② *vt* rifare la copertura di ⟨road⟩

resurgence /rɪˈsɜːdʒəns/ *n* rinascita *f*

resurrect /rezəˈrekt/ *vt* fig risuscitare

resurrection /rezəˈrekʃn/ *n* **the R~** Relig la Risurrezione

resuscitate /rɪˈsʌsɪteɪt/ *vt* rianimare

resuscitation /rɪsʌsɪˈteɪʃn/ *n* rianimazione *f*

retail /'ri:teɪl/ **①** *n* vendita *f* al minuto *o* al dettaglio
② *adj & adv* al minuto
③ *vt* vendere al minuto
④ *vi* ∼ **at** essere venduto al pubblico al prezzo di

retailer /'ri:teɪlə(r)/ *n* dettagliante *mf*

retail price *n* prezzo *m* al minuto

retail sales *npl* vendite *fpl* al dettaglio

retail trade *n* commercio *m* al dettaglio

retain /rɪ'teɪn/ *vt* conservare; (hold back) trattenere

retainer /rɪ'teɪnə(r)/ *n* (fee) anticipo *m*; (old: servant) servitore, -trice *mf*

retake¹ /ri:'teɪk/ *vt* Cinema girare di nuovo; Sch, Univ ridare; Mil riconquistare

retake² /'ri:teɪk/ *n* Cinema ulteriore ripresa *f*

retaliate /rɪ'tælɪeɪt/ *vi* vendicarsi

retaliation /rɪtælɪ'eɪʃn/ *n* rappresaglia *f*; in ∼ **for** per rappresaglia contro

retarded /rɪ'tɑ:dɪd/ *adj* ritardato

retch /retʃ/ *vi* avere conati di vomito

retention /rɪ'tenʃn/ *n* conservazione *f*; (of information) memorizzazione *f*; (of fluid) ritenzione *f*

retentive /rɪ'tentɪv/ *adj* ⟨memory⟩ buono

retentiveness /rɪ'tentɪvnɪs/ *n* capacità *f* di memorizzazione

rethink /ri:'θɪŋk/ **①** *vt* (pt/pp **rethought**) riconsiderare
② *n* have a ∼ riconsiderare la cosa

reticence /'retɪsəns/ *n* reticenza *f*

reticent /'retɪsənt/ *adj* reticente

retina /'retɪnə/ *n* retina *f*

retinue /'retɪnju:/ *n* seguito *m*

retire /rɪ'taɪə(r)/ **①** *vi* andare in pensione; (withdraw) ritirarsi
② *vt* mandare in pensione ⟨employee⟩

retired /rɪ'taɪəd/ *adj* in pensione

retirement /rɪ'taɪəmənt/ *n* pensione *f*; since my ∼ da quando sono andato in pensione

retirement age *n* età *f* della pensione

retirement home *n* casa *f* di riposo

retiring /rɪ'taɪərɪŋ/ *adj* riservato

retort /rɪ'tɔ:t/ **①** *n* replica *f*; Chem storta *f*
② *vt* ribattere

retouch /ri:'tʌtʃ/ *vt* Phot ritoccare

retouching /ri:'tʌtʃɪŋ/ *n* Phot ritocco *m*

retrace /rɪ'treɪs/ *vt* ripercorrere; ∼ one's steps ritornare sui propri passi

retract /rɪ'trækt/ **①** *vt* ritirare; ritrattare ⟨statement, accusation⟩
② *vi* ritrarsi

retractable /rɪ'træktəbl/ *adj* ⟨landing gear⟩ retrattile; ⟨pen⟩ con la punta retrattile

retraction /rɪ'trækʃn/ *n* ritiro *m*; (of statement, accusation) ritrattazione *f*

retrain /ri:'treɪn/ **①** *vt* riqualificare
② *vi* riqualificarsi

retraining /ri:'treɪnɪŋ/ *n* riqualificazione *f*

retread /'ri:tred/ *n* pneumatico *m* ricostruito

retreat /rɪ'tri:t/ **①** *n* ritirata *f*; (place) ritiro *m*
② *vi* ritirarsi; Mil battere in ritirata

retrench /rɪ'trentʃ/ *vi* ridurre le spese

retrenchment /rɪ'trentʃmənt/ *n* riduzione *f* delle spese

retrial /ri:'traɪəl/ *n* nuovo processo *m*

retribution /retrɪ'bju:ʃn/ *n* castigo *m*

retrievable /rɪ'tri:vəbl/ *adj* recuperabile

retrieval /rɪ'tri:vəl/ *n* recupero *m*

retrieve /rɪ'tri:v/ *vt* recuperare

retroactive /retrəʊ'æktɪv/ *adj* retroattivo

retroactively /retrəʊ'æktɪvlɪ/ *adv* retroattivamente

retrograde /'retrəgreɪd/ *adj* retrogrado

retrospect /'retrəspekt/ *n* in ∼ guardando indietro

retrospective /retrə'spektɪv/ **①** *adj* ⟨exhibit⟩ retrospettivo; ⟨legislation⟩ retroattivo
② *n* retrospettiva *f*

retrospectively /retrə'spektɪvlɪ/ *adv* retrospettivamente

retrovirus /'retrəʊvaɪrəs/ *n* retrovirus *m inv*

retry /ri:'traɪ/ *vt* Jur riprocessare; Comput riprovare

return /rɪ'tɜ:n/ **①** *n* ritorno *m*; (giving back) restituzione *f*; Comm profitto *m*; (ticket) biglietto *m* di andata e ritorno; **by** ∼ **[of post]** a stretto giro di posta; **in** ∼ in cambio (**for** di); **many happy** ∼**s!** cento di questi giorni!; ∼ **on investment** utile *m* sul capitale investito
② *vi* ritornare
③ *vt* (give back) restituire; ricambiare ⟨affection, invitation⟩; (put back) rimettere; (send back) mandare indietro; (elect) eleggere

returnable /rɪ'tɜ:nəbl/ *adj* restituibile

return flight *n* volo *m* di andata e ritorno

return match *n* rivincita *f*

return ticket *n* biglietto *m* di andata e ritorno

reunification /ri:ju:nɪfɪ'keɪʃn/ *n* riunificazione *f*

reunify /ri:'ju:nɪfaɪ/ *vt* riunificare

reunion /ri:'ju:njən/ *n* riunione *f*

reunite /ri:jʊ'naɪt/ *vt* riunire

reusable /ri:'ju:zəbl/ *adj* riutilizzabile

reuse /ri:'ju:z/ *vt* riutilizzare

rev /rev/ **1** n Auto giro; **∼s per minute** regime m di giri
2 vt ∼ **[up]** far andare su di giri
3 vi andare su di giri

revaluation /ri:'vælju'eɪʃn/ n rivalutazione f

revalue /ri:'vælju:/ vt Comm rivalutare

revamp /ri:'væmp/ vt riorganizzare ⟨company⟩; rimodernare ⟨building, clothing⟩

rev counter n contagiri m

Rev[d] abbr (**Reverend**) Reverendo

reveal /rɪ'vi:l/ vt rivelare; ⟨dress⟩ scoprire

revealing /rɪ'vi:lɪŋ/ adj rivelatore; ⟨dress⟩ osé inv

revel /'revl/ vi (pt/pp **revelled**) ∼ **in something** godere di qualcosa

revelation /revə'leɪʃn/ n rivelazione f

reveller /'rev(ə)lə(r)/ n festaiolo -a mf

revelry /'rev(ə)lrɪ/ n baldoria f

revenge /rɪ'vendʒ/ **1** n vendetta f; Sport rivincita f; **take** ∼ vendicarsi (**on somebody for something** di qualcuno per qualcosa)
 2 vt vendicare

revenue /'revənju:/ n reddito m

reverberate /rɪ'vɜ:bəreɪt/ vi riverberare

reverberations /rɪvɜ:bə'reɪʃnz/ npl fig ripercussione f

revere /rɪ'vɪə(r)/ vt riverire

reverence /'revərəns/ n riverenza f

Reverend /'revərənd/ adj Reverendo

reverent /'revərənt/ adj riverente

reverential /revə'renʃ(ə)l/ adj riverente

reverently /'revərəntlɪ/ adv rispettosamente

reverie /'revərɪ/ n sogno m ad occhi aperti

reversal /rɪ'vɜ:sl/ n inversione f

reverse /rɪ'vɜ:s/ **1** adj opposto; **in** ∼ **order** in ordine inverso
 2 n contrario m; (back) rovescio m; Auto marcia m indietro
 3 vt invertire; ∼ **the car into the garage** entrare in garage a marcia indietro; ∼ **the charges** Teleph fare una telefonata a carico del destinatario
 4 vi Auto fare marcia indietro

reverse charge [phone-]call n telefonata f a carico del destinatario

reversible /rɪ'vɜ:sɪbl/ adj ⟨jacket⟩ double-face; ⟨procedure⟩ reversibile

reversing lights /rɪ'vɜ:sɪŋ/ npl luci fpl di retromarcia

revert /rɪ'vɜ:t/ vi ∼ **to** tornare a

review /rɪ'vju:/ **1** n (survey) rassegna f; (reexamination) riconsiderazione f; Mil rivista f; (of book, play) recensione f
 2 vt riesaminare ⟨situation⟩; Mil passare in rivista; recensire ⟨book, play⟩

reviewer /rɪ'vju:ə(r)/ n critico, -a mf

revile /rɪ'vaɪl/ vt ingiuriare

revise /rɪ'vaɪz/ vt rivedere; (for exam) ripassare

revision /rɪ'vɪʒn/ n revisione f; (for exam) ripasso m

revisionism /rɪ'vɪʒənɪzm/ n revisionismo m

revisionist /rɪ'vɪʒənɪst/ adj & n revisionista mf

revisit /ri:'vɪzɪt/ vt rivisitare ⟨person, museum etc⟩

revitalization /ri:vaɪtəlaɪ'zeɪʃn/ n rivitalizzazione f

revitalize /ri:'vaɪtəlaɪz/ vt rivitalizzare

revival /rɪ'vaɪvl/ n ritorno m; (of patient) recupero m; (from coma) risveglio m

revivalist /rɪ'vaɪvəlɪst/ adj Relig revivalista

revive /rɪ'vaɪv/ **1** vt resuscitare; rianimare ⟨person⟩
 2 vi riprendersi; ⟨person⟩ rianimarsi

revocation /revə'keɪʃn/ n (of decision, order) revoca f; (of law) abrogazione f; (of will) annullamento m

revoke /rɪ'vəʊk/ vt revocare ⟨decision, order⟩; abrogare ⟨law⟩; annullare ⟨will⟩

revolt /rɪ'vəʊlt/ **1** n rivolta f
 2 vi ribellarsi
 3 vt rivoltare

revolting /rɪ'vəʊltɪŋ/ adj rivoltante

revolution /revə'lu:ʃn/ n rivoluzione f; **∼s per minute** Auto giri mpl al minuto

revolutionary /revə'lu:ʃənərɪ/ adj & n rivoluzionario, -a mf

revolutionize /revə'lu:ʃənaɪz/ vt rivoluzionare

revolve /rɪ'vɒlv/ vi ruotare; ∼ **around** girare intorno a

revolver /rɪ'vɒlvə(r)/ n rivoltella f, revolver m inv

revolving /rɪ'vɒlvɪŋ/ adj ruotante

revolving doors npl porta f girevole

revue /rɪ'vju:/ n rivista f

revulsion /rɪ'vʌlʃn/ n ripulsione f

reward /rɪ'wɔ:d/ **1** n ricompensa f
 2 vt ricompensare

reward card n = LOYALTY CARD

rewarding /rɪ'wɔ:dɪŋ/ adj gratificante

rewind /ri:'waɪnd/ vt riavvolgere ⟨tape, film⟩

rewind button /'ri:waɪnd/ n tasto m di riavvolgimento

rewire /ri:'waɪə(r)/ vt rifare l'impianto elettrico di

reword /ri:'wɜ:d/ vt esprimere con parole diverse

rework /ri:'wɜ:k/ vt modificare

rewritable /riːˈraɪtəbl/ *adj* Comput ‹CD-Rom› riscrivibile

rewrite /riːˈraɪt/ *vt* (pt **rewrote**, pp **rewritten**) riscrivere

rhapsody /ˈræpsədɪ/ *n* rapsodia *f*

rhesus /ˈriːsəs/ *n* reso *m*

rhesus-negative *adj* Rh-negativo

rhesus-positive *adj* Rh-positivo

rhetoric /ˈretərɪk/ *n* retorica *f*

rhetorical /rɪˈtɒrɪkl/ *adj* retorico

rhetorically /rɪˈtɒrɪklɪ/ *adv* retoricamente

rhetorical question *n* domanda *f* retorica

rheumatic /rʊˈmætɪk/ *adj* reumatico

rheumatism /ˈruːmətɪzm/ *n* reumatismo *m*

rheumatoid arthritis /ˈruːmətɔɪd/ *n* periartrite *f*

Rhine /raɪn/ *n* Reno *m*

rhino /ˈraɪnəʊ/ *n* fam rinoceronte *m*

rhinoceros /raɪˈnɒsərəs/ *n* rinoceronte *m*

rhombus /ˈrɒmbəs/ *n* rombo *m*

rhubarb /ˈruːbɑːb/ *n* rabarbaro *m*

rhyme /raɪm/ ① *n* rima *f*; (poem) filastrocca *f*
② *vi* rimare; ~ **with something** far rima con qualcosa

rhythm /ˈrɪðm/ *n* ritmo *m*

rhythmic[al] /ˈrɪðmɪk[l]/ *adj* ritmico

rhythmically /ˈrɪðmɪklɪ/ *adv* con ritmo

rhythm method *n* (of contraception) metodo *m* Ogino-Knauss

rib /rɪb/ ① *n* costola *f*; ~s *pl* Culin costata *f*
② *vt* (pt/pp **ribbed**) fam punzecchiare

ribald /ˈrɪbld/ *adj* spinto

ribbon /ˈrɪbən/ *n* nastro *m*; **in** ~s a brandelli

ribcage /ˈrɪbkeɪdʒ/ *n* gabbia *f* toracica, cassa *f* toracica

rice /raɪs/ *n* riso *m*

ricefield /ˈraɪsfiːld/ *n* risaia *f*

rice-paper *n* Culin carta *f* di riso

rich /rɪtʃ/ ① *adj* ricco; ‹food› pesante
② *n* **the** ~ *pl* i ricchi; ~**es** *pl* ricchezze *fpl*

richly /ˈrɪtʃlɪ/ *adv* riccamente; ‹deserve› largamente

richness /ˈrɪtʃnɪs/ *n* (of food) pesantezza *f*; (of furnishings) sfarzosità *f*; (of person, company) ricchezza *f*

Richter scale /ˈrɪktə(r)/ *n* scala *f* Richter

rick /rɪk/ *vt* Br ~ **one's ankle** prendere una storta alla caviglia

rickets /ˈrɪkɪts/ *n* rachitismo *m*

rickety /ˈrɪkətɪ/ *adj* malfermo

rickshaw /ˈrɪkʃɔː/ *n* risciò *m inv*

ricochet /ˈrɪkəʃeɪ/ ① *vi* rimbalzare
② *n* rimbalzo *m*

rid /rɪd/ *vt* (pt/pp **rid**, pres p **ridding**) sbarazzare (**of** di); **get** ~ **of** sbarazzarsi di

riddance /ˈrɪdns/ *n* **good** ~! che liberazione!

ridden /ˈrɪdn/ ▶ RIDE

riddle /ˈrɪdl/ *n* enigma *m*

riddled /ˈrɪdld/ *adj* ~ **with** crivellato di

ride /raɪd/ ① *n* (on horse) cavalcata *f*; (in vehicle) giro *m*; (journey) viaggio *m*; **take somebody for a** ~ fam prendere qualcuno in giro
② *vt* (pt **rode**, pp **ridden**) montare ‹horse›; andare su ‹bicycle›
③ *vi* andare a cavallo; ‹jockey, showjumper› cavalcare; ‹cyclist› andare in bicicletta; (in vehicle) viaggiare
∎ **ride out** *vt* superare ‹storm, crisis›
∎ **ride up** *vi* ‹rider› arrivare; ‹skirt› salire

rider /ˈraɪdə(r)/ *n* cavallerizzo, -a *mf*; (in race) fantino *m*; (on bicycle) ciclista *mf*; (in document) postilla *f*

ridge /rɪdʒ/ *n* spigolo *m*; (on roof) punta *f*; (of mountain) cresta *f*; (of high pressure) zona *f* ad alta pressione [atmosferica]

ridicule /ˈrɪdɪkjuːl/ ① *n* ridicolo *m*
② *vt* mettere in ridicolo

ridiculous /rɪˈdɪkjʊləs/ *adj* ridicolo

ridiculously /rɪˈdɪkjʊləslɪ/ *adv* in modo ridicolo; ~ **expensive/easy** carissimo/facilissimo

riding /ˈraɪdɪŋ/ ① *n* equitazione *f*
② *attrib* d'equitazione

rife /raɪf/ *adj* **be** ~ essere diffuso; ~ **with** pieno di

riff-raff /ˈrɪfræf/ *n* marmaglia *f*

rifle /ˈraɪfl/ ① *n* fucile *m*
② *vt* ~ **[through]** mettere a soqquadro

rifle-range *n* tiro *m* al bersaglio

rift /rɪft/ *n* fessura *f*; fig frattura *f*

rig[1] /rɪg/ *n* equipaggiamento *m*; (at sea) piattaforma *f* per trivellazioni subacquee

rig[2] *vt* (pt/pp **rigged**) manovrare ‹election›
∎ **rig out** *vt* equipaggiare; (with clothes) parare
∎ **rig up** *vt* allestire

rigging /ˈrɪgɪŋ/ *n* Naut sartiame *m*; (of election, competition) broglio *m*

right /raɪt/ ① *adj* giusto; (not left) destro; **be** ~ ‹person› aver ragione; ‹clock› essere giusto; **put** ~ mettere all'ora ‹clock›; correggere ‹person›; rimediare a ‹situation›; **that's** ~! proprio così! **do you have the** ~ **time?** ha l'ora esatta?
② *adv* (correctly) bene; (not left) a destra; (directly) proprio; (completely) completamente; **too** ~! altroché!

3 n giusto m; (not left) destra f; (what is due) diritto m; **the R~** Pol la destra; **on/to the ~** a destra; **be in the ~** essere nel giusto; **by ~s** secondo giustizia; **be within one's ~s** avere tutti i diritti (**in doing something** di fare qualcosa)
4 vt raddrizzare; **~ a wrong** fig riparare ad un torto

right angle n angolo m retto

right away adv subito

righteous /'raɪtʃəs/ adj virtuoso; (cause) giusto

rightful /'raɪtfl/ adj legittimo

rightfully /'raɪtfʊlɪ/ adv legittimamente

right-hand adj di destra; **on the ~ side** sulla destra

right-hand drive n (vehicle) guida f a destra

right-handed /-'hændɪd/ adj che usa la mano destra

right-hand man n fig braccio m destro

rightly /'raɪtlɪ/ adv giustamente

right-minded /-'maɪndɪd/ adj sensato

right-of-centre adj Pol di centrodestra

right of way n diritto m di transito; (path) passaggio m; Auto precedenza f

right-on 1 int fam bene!
2 adj fam **they're very ~** sono molto impegnati

rights issue n emissione f riservata agli azionisti

right-thinking adj sensato

right turn n svolta f a destra

right wing n Pol destra; Sport ala f destra

right-wing adj Pol di destra

right-winger n Pol persona f di destra; Sport ala f destra

rigid /'rɪdʒɪd/ adj rigido

rigidity /rɪ'dʒɪdətɪ/ n rigidità f

rigidly adv (apply) rigorosamente; (oppose) fermamente

rigmarole /'rɪgmərəʊl/ n trafila f; (story) tiritera f

rigor mortis /rɪgə'mɔːtɪs/ n rigidità f cadaverica

rigorous /'rɪgərəs/ adj rigoroso

rigorously /'rɪgərəslɪ/ adv rigorosamente

rigour /'rɪgə(r)/ n rigore m

rig-out n (fam: clothes) tenuta f

rile /raɪl/ vt fam irritare

rim /rɪm/ n bordo m; (of wheel) cerchione m

rind /raɪnd/ n (on cheese) crosta f; (on bacon) cotenna f

ring¹ /rɪŋ/ **1** n (circle) cerchio m; (on finger) anello m; (boxing) ring m inv; (for circus) pista f; **stand in a ~** essere in cerchio
2 vt accerchiare; **~ in red** fare un cerchio rosso intorno a

ring² **1** n suono m; **give somebody a ~** Teleph dare un colpo di telefono a qualcuno
2 vt (pt **rang**, pp **rung**) suonare; Teleph telefonare a; **it ~s a bell** fig mi dice qualcosa; **~ the changes** fig cambiare
3 vi suonare; Teleph telefonare; **~ true** aver l'aria di essere vero
■ **ring back** vt/i richiamare
■ **ring off** vi Teleph riattaccare
■ **ring out** vi (voice, shot etc) risuonare chiaramente
■ **ring round** vi Teleph fare un giro di telefonate
■ **ring up** Teleph **1** vt telefonare a
2 vi telefonare

ring-binder /'rɪŋbaɪndə(r)/ n raccoglitore m ad anelli

ring finger n anulare m

ringing /'rɪŋɪŋ/ n (noise of bell, alarm) suono m; (in ears) fischio m

ringleader /'rɪŋliːdə(r)/ n capobanda m

ringlet /'rɪŋlɪt/ n boccolo m

ringmaster n direttore m di circo

ring-pull n linguetta f; **~ can** n lattina f con linguetta

ring road n circonvallazione f

ringside n **at the ~** in prima fila; **have a ~ seat** fig essere in prima fila

ringtone n suoneria f

rink /rɪŋk/ n pista f di pattinaggio

rinse /rɪns/ **1** n risciacquo m; (hair colour) cachet m inv
2 vt sciacquare
■ **rinse off** vt sciacquare via
■ **rinse out** vt sciacquare (cup, glass); sciacquare via (shampoo, soap)

riot /'raɪət/ **1** n rissa f; (of colour) accozzaglia f; **~s** pl disordini mpl; **run ~** impazzare
2 vi creare disordini

riot act n read the **~ ~** to somebody fig dare una lavata di capo a qualcuno

rioter /'raɪətə(r)/ n dimostrante mf

riot gear n tenuta f antisommossa

riotous /'raɪətəs/ adj sfrenato

riotously /'raɪətəslɪ/ adv **~ funny** divertente da morire

riot police n DIGOS f, Divisione f Investigazioni Generali e Operazioni Speciali

RIP abbr (**rest in peace**) R.I.P.

rip /rɪp/ **1** n strappo m
2 vt (pt/pp **ripped**) strappare; **~ open** aprire con uno strappo
3 vi strapparsi; **let ~** scatenarsi
■ **rip off** vt (remove) togliere; (fam: cheat) fregare
■ **rip through** vt (blast) squaciare (building)
■ **rip up** vt stracciare (letter)

ripcord /'rɪpkɔːd/ n cavo m di spiegamento

ripe /raɪp/ adj maturo; ‹cheese› stagionato

ripen /'raɪpn/ ① vi maturare; ‹cheese› stagionarsi
② vt far maturare; stagionare ‹cheese›

ripeness /'raɪpnɪs/ n maturazione f

rip-off n fam frode f; these prices are a ~! questi prezzi sono un furto!

riposte /rɪ'pɒst/ n replica f

ripple /'rɪpl/ ① n increspatura f; ‹sound› mormorio m
② vt increspare
③ vi incresparsi

rip-roaring /'rɪprɔːrɪŋ/ adj ‹fam: success› travolgente

rise /raɪz/ ① n (of sun) levata f; (fig: to fame, power) ascesa f; (increase) aumento m; give ~ to dare adito a
② vi (pt **rose**, pp **risen**) alzarsi; ‹sun› sorgere; ‹dough› lievitare; ‹prices, water level› aumentare; (to power, position) arrivare (**to** a); (rebel) sollevarsi; ‹Parliament, court› aggiornare la seduta; (for holidays) sospendere i lavori
■ **rise above** vt superare ‹difficulty›

riser /'raɪzə(r)/ n early ~ persona f mattiniera

rising /'raɪzɪŋ/ ① adj ‹sun› levante; ~ generation nuova generazione f
② n (revolt) sollevazione f

risk /rɪsk/ ① n rischio m; run the ~ of correre il rischio di; at ~ in pericolo; at one's own ~ a proprio rischio e pericolo; at the ~ of doing something a costo di fare qualcosa
② vt rischiare

risky /'rɪskɪ/ adj (-ier, -iest) rischioso

risotto /rɪ'zɒtəʊ/ n risotto m

risqué /'rɪskeɪ/ adj spinto

rissole /'rɪsəʊl/ n crocchetta f

rite /raɪt/ n rito m; last ~s pl estrema unzione fsg

ritual /'rɪtjʊəl/ adj & n rituale m

ritzy /'rɪtsɪ/ adj (fam: hotel, style, decoration) lussuoso

rival /'raɪvl/ ① adj rivale
② n rivale mf; ~s pl Comm concorrenti mpl
③ vt (pt/pp **rivalled**) rivaleggiare con

rivalry /'raɪv(ə)lrɪ/ n rivalità f inv; Comm concorrenza f

river /'rɪvə(r)/ n fiume m

riverbank n riva f di fiume

river-bed n letto m del fiume

riverside ① n lungofiume m
② attrib sul fiume

rivet /'rɪvɪt/ ① n rivetto m
② vt rivettare; be ~ed by fig essere avvinto da

riveting /'rɪvɪtɪŋ/ adj fig avvincente

Riviera /rɪvɪ'eərə/ n the French ~ la Costa Azzurra; the Italian ~ la riviera ligure

roach /rəʊtʃ/ n (fish) lasca f; (Am fam: insect) scarafaggio m

road /rəʊd/ n strada f, via f; be on the ~ viaggiare

roadblock n blocco m stradale

road haulage n trasporto m su strada

road hog n fam pirata m della strada

road hump n dosso m di rallentamento

roadie /'rəʊdɪ/ n roadie m inv

road map n fig a ~ to peace la roadmap per la pace

road safety n sicurezza f sulle strade

road sense n prudenza f (per strada)

roadshow n (play, show) spettacolo m di tournée; (publicity tour) giro m promozionale

roadside n bordo m della strada

road sign n cartello m stradale

road surface n fondo m stradale

road sweeper n (person) spazzino, -a nmf; (machine) autospazzatrice f

road tax n tassa f di circolazione

roadway n carreggiata f, corsia f

roadworks npl lavori mpl stradali

roadworthy adj sicuro

roam /rəʊm/ vt/i girovagare
■ **roam around** vi girovagare

roar /rɔː(r)/ ① n ruggito m; ~s of laughter scroscio msg di risa
② vi ruggire; ‹lorry, thunder› rombare; ~ with laughter ridere fragorosamente
■ **roar out** vt gridare
■ **roar past** vi ‹move noisily› passare rombando

roaring /'rɔːrɪŋ/ ① adj do a ~ trade fam fare affari d'oro
② adv ~ drunk fam ubriaco fradicio

roast /rəʊst/ ① adj arrosto; ~ pork arrosto m di maiale
② n arrosto m
③ vt arrostire ‹meat›
④ vi arrostirsi

roasting [hot] /'rəʊstɪŋ/ adj fam caldissimo

roasting pan n teglia f per arrosti

rob /rɒb/ vt (pt/pp **robbed**) derubare (**of** di); svaligiare ‹bank›

robber /'rɒbə(r)/ n rapinatore, -trice mf

robbery /'rɒbərɪ/ n rapina f

robe /rəʊb/ n tunica f; (Am: bathrobe) accappatoio m

robin /'rɒbɪn/ n pettirosso m

robot /'rəʊbɒt/ n robot m inv

robotic /rəʊ'bɒtɪk/ adj ‹movement, voice› robotico; ‹tool, device, machine› robotizzato

robotics n robotica f

robust /rəʊ'bʌst/ adj robusto

r

rock[1] /rɒk/ n roccia f; (in sea) scoglio m; (sweet) zucchero m candito; **on the ~s** ⟨ship⟩ incagliato; ⟨marriage⟩ finito; ⟨drink⟩ con ghiaccio

rock[2] [1] vt cullare ⟨baby⟩; (shake) far traballare; (shock) scuotere
[2] vi dondolarsi

rock[3] n Mus rock m

rock and roll n rock and roll m

rock-bottom [1] adj bassissimo
[2] n livello m più basso; **hit ~** toccare il fondo

rock-climber n scalatore, -trice mf

rock-climbing n roccia f

rockery /'rɒkərɪ/ n giardino m roccioso

rocket /'rɒkɪt/ [1] n razzo m; **give somebody a ~** fam fare un cicchetto a qualcuno
[2] vi salire alle stelle

rocket launcher /'lɔːntʃə(r)/ n lanciarazzi m inv

rocket science n fam **it's not ~** non ci vuole la laurea!

rock face n parete f rocciosa

rocking chair /'rɒkɪŋ/ n sedia f a dondolo

rocking horse n cavallo m a dondolo

rock star n rock star mf inv

rocky /'rɒkɪ/ adj (-ier, -iest) roccioso; fig traballante

Rocky Mountains npl le Montagne fpl Rocciose

rod /rɒd/ n bacchetta f; (for fishing) canna f

rode /rəʊd/ ▶ RIDE

rodent /'rəʊdnt/ n roditore m

roe[1] /rəʊ/ n uova fpl di pesce; (soft) latte m di pesce

roe[2] n (pl **roe** or **roes**) ~ [deer] capriolo m

roebuck /'rəʊbʌk/ n capriolo m maschio

roger /'rɒdʒə(r)/ int Teleph ricevuto

rogue /rəʊg/ n farabutto m

rogue state n stato m canaglia

role /rəʊl/ n ruolo m

role model n Psych modello m comportamentale

role-play, **role-playing** /'rəʊlpleɪŋ/ n Psych role playing m inv

roll /rəʊl/ [1] n rotolo m; ⟨bread⟩ panino m: (list) lista f; ⟨of ship, drum⟩ rullio m
[2] vi rotolare; **be ~ing in money** fam nuotare nell'oro
[3] vt spianare ⟨lawn, pastry⟩;~ed into one allo stesso tempo
■ **roll around**, **roll about** vi ⟨person, puppy⟩ rotolarsi; ⟨ball, marbles⟩ rotolare
■ **roll back** vt ridurre ⟨prices⟩
■ **roll by** vi ⟨time⟩ passare
■ **roll down** vt srotolare ⟨blind, sleeves⟩
■ **roll in** vi (fam: arrive in large quantities) arrivare a valanghe; (arrive) arrivare

■ **roll on** vi ~ **on Friday!** non vedo l'ora che sia venerdì!
■ **roll over** vi rigirarsi; (fam: capitulate) arrendersi
■ **roll up** [1] vt arrotolare; rimboccarsi ⟨sleeves⟩
[2] vi fam arrivare

roll-call n appello m

roller /'rəʊlə(r)/ n rullo m; (for hair) bigodino m

rollerblade [1] n pattino m a rotelle in linea
[2] vi pattinare (con pattini in linea)

roller blind n tapparella f

roller coaster n montagne fpl russe

roller skate n pattino m a rotelle

roller-skating n pattinaggio m a rotelle

rollicking /'rɒlɪkɪŋ/ adj **have a ~ time** divertirsi da pazzi

rolling pin n mattarello m

rolling stock n materiale m rotabile

rolling stone n fig vagabondo, -a mf

rollneck n collo m alto; (whole sweater) dolcevita f

roll-on n (deodorant) deodorante m a sfera

roll-on roll-off ferry n traghetto m roll-on roll-off

ROM /rɒm/ n Comput Rom f inv

Roma /'rəʊmə/ npl i rom mpl

Roman /'rəʊmən/ [1] adj (also print) romano
[2] n romano, -a mf

Roman Catholic adj & n cattolico, -a mf

romance /rəʊ'mæns/ n (love affair) storia f d'amore; (book) romanzo m rosa

Romania /rəʊ'meɪnɪə/ n Romania f

Romanian /rəʊ'meɪnɪən/ adj & n rumeno, -a mf; (language) rumeno m

roman numeral n numero m romano

romantic /rəʊ'mæntɪk/ adj romantico

romantically /rəʊ'mæntɪklɪ/ adv romanticamente

romanticism /rəʊ'mæntɪsɪzm/ n romanticismo m

romanticize /rəʊ'mæntɪsaɪz/ vt romantizzare

romanticized /rəʊ'mæntɪsaɪzd/ adj romanzato

Romany /'rəʊmənɪ/ n rom mf inv

Rome /rəʊm/ n Roma f

Romeo /'rəʊmɪəʊ/ n (fam: ladykiller) dongiovanni m inv

romp /rɒmp/ [1] n gioco m rumoroso
[2] vi giocare rumorosamente
■ **romp home** vi (win easily) vincere senza difficoltà
■ **romp through** vt [1] passare senza difficoltà ⟨exam⟩
[2] vi riuscire senza difficoltà

rompers /'rɒmpəz/ *npl* pagliaccetto *msg*

roof /ru:f/ ① *n* tetto *m*; (of mouth) palato *m*; **live under one** ∼ vivere sotto lo stesso tetto; **go through the** ∼ (fam: increase) andare alle stelle; (be very angry) andare su tutte le furie
② *vt* mettere un tetto su

roof-rack *n* portabagagli *m inv*

rooftop /'ru:ftɒp/ *n* tetto *m*; **shout it from the** ∼**s** fig gridarlo ai quattro venti

rook /rʊk/ ① *n* corvo *m*; (in chess) torre *f*
② *vt* (fam: swindle) fregare

rookie /'rʊkɪ/ *n* Am fam novellino, -a *mf*

room /'ru:m/ *n* stanza *f*; (bedroom) camera *f*; (for functions) sala *f*; (space) spazio *m*

room-mate *n* (Am: flatmate) compagno, -a *mf* di appartamento; (in same room) compagno, -a *mf* di stanza

room service *n* servizio *m* in camera

room temperature *n* temperatura *f* ambiente

roomy /'ru:mɪ/ *adj* spazioso; (clothes) ampio

roost /ru:st/ ① *n* posatoio *m*
② *vi* appollaiarsi

rooster /'ru:stə(r)/ *n* gallo *m*

root[1] /ru:t/ ① *n* radice *f*; **take** ∼ metter radici; **put down** ∼**s** fig metter radici
② *vi* metter radici

root[2] /ru:t/ *vi* ∼ **for somebody** fam fare il tifo per qualcuno
■ **root about, root around** *vi* grufolare; ∼ **about for something** rovistare alla ricerca di qualcosa
■ **root out** *vt* fig scovare

rope /rəʊp/ *n* corda *f*; **know the** ∼**s** fam conoscere i trucchi del mestiere
■ **rope in** *vt* fam coinvolgere

rope ladder *n* scala *f* di corda

ropey /'rəʊpɪ/ *adj* Br fam scadente; **feel** ∼ sentirsi poco bene

rosary /'rəʊzərɪ/ *n* rosario *m*

rosé /'rəʊzeɪ/ *n* [vino *m*] rosé *m inv*

rose[1] /rəʊz/ *n* rosa *f*; (of watering-can) bocchetta *f*

rose[2] ▶ RISE

rosebud /'rəʊzbʌd/ *n* bocciolo *m* di rosa

rosehip /'rəʊzhɪp/ *n* frutto *m* della rosa canina

rosemary /'rəʊzmərɪ/ *n* rosmarino *m*

rose-tinted spectacles /'rəʊztɪntɪd/ *npl* wear ∼ ∼ vedere tutto rosa

rosette /rəʊ'zet/ *n* coccarda *f*

roster /'rɒstə(r)/ *n* tabella *f* dei turni

rostrum/'rɒstrəm/ *n* podio *m*

rosy /'rəʊzɪ/ *adj* (**-ier, -iest**) roseo

rot /rɒt/ ① *n* marciume *m*; (fam: nonsense) sciocchezze *fpl*
② *vi* (pt/pp **rotted**) marcire

rota /'rəʊtə/ *n* tabella *f* dei turni

rotary /'rəʊtərɪ/ *adj* rotante

rotate /rəʊ'teɪt/ ① *vt* far ruotare; avvicendare (crops)
② *vi* ruotare

rotation /rəʊ'teɪʃn/ *n* rotazione *f*; **in** ∼ a turno

rote /rəʊt/ *n* by ∼ meccanicamente

rotten /'rɒn/ *adj* marcio; fam schifoso; (person) penoso

rotund /rəʊ'tʌnd/ *adj* paffuto

rotunda /rəʊ'tʌndə/ *n* rotonda *f*

rouble /'ru:bl/ *n* rublo *m*

rough /rʌf/ ① *adj* (not smooth) ruvido; (ground) accidentato; (behaviour) rozzo; (sport) violento; (area) malfamato; (crossing, time) brutto; (estimate) approssimativo
② *adv* (play) grossolanamente; **sleep** ∼ dormire sotto i ponti
③ *n* do something in ∼ far qualcosa alla bell'e meglio
④ *vi* ∼ **it** vivere senza confort
■ **rough out** *vt* abbozzare
■ **rough up** *vt* fam malmenare (person)

roughage /'rʌfɪdʒ/ *n* fibre *fpl*

rough-and-ready *adj* (person, manner) sbrigativo; (conditions, method) rudimentale

rough-and-tumble *n* (rough play) zuffa *f*

rough copy *n* brutta copia *f*

rough draft *n* abbozzo *m*

roughen /'rʌfən/ *vt* rendere ruvido (surface)

roughly /'rʌflɪ/ *adv* rozzamente; (more or less) pressappoco

roughness /'rʌfnɪs/ *n* ruvidità *f*; (of behaviour) rozzezza *f*

rough paper *n* carta *f* da brutta

roughshod /'rʌfʃɒd/ *adv* ride ∼ over infischiarsi di (person, objection); calpestare (feelings)

roulette /ru:'let/ *n* roulette *f*

round /raʊnd/ ① *adj* rotondo
② *n* tondo *m*; (slice) fetta *f*; (of visits, drinks) giro *m*; (of competition) partita *f*; (boxing) ripresa *f*, round *m inv*; **do one's** ∼**s** (doctor) fare il giro delle visite
③ *prep* intorno a; **open** ∼ **the clock** aperto ventiquattr'ore
④ *adv* **all** ∼ tutt'intorno; **ask somebody** ∼ invitare qualcuno; **go/come** ∼ **to** (a friend etc) andare da; **turn/look** ∼ girarsi; ∼ **about** (approximately) intorno a
⑤ *vt* arrotondare; girare (corner)
■ **round down** *vt* arrotondare (per difetto)
■ **round off** *vt* (end) terminare
■ **round on** *vt* aggredire
■ **round up** *vt* radunare; arrotondare (prices)

roundabout /'raʊndəbaʊt/ ① *adj* indiretto

⟨2⟩ *n* giostra *f*; (for traffic) rotonda *f*

round bracket *n* parentesi *f* tonda

rounders /'raʊndəz/ *n* Br Sport gioco *m* simile al baseball

round figure *n* cifra *f* tonda

round robin *n* petizione *f*

round-shouldered /-'ʃəʊldəd/ *adj* con le spalle curve

round table *n* tavola *f* rotonda

round the clock *adv* 24 ore su 24

round-the-clock *adj* ⟨Br: care, surveillance⟩ ventiquattr'ore su ventiquattro

round-the-world *adj* ⟨trip⟩ intorno al mondo

round trip *n* viaggio *m* di andata e ritorno

round-up *n* (of suspects) retata *f*; (of cattle) raduno *m*; (summary) riepilogo *m*

rouse /raʊz/ *vt* svegliare; risvegliare ⟨suspicion, interest⟩

rousing /'raʊzɪŋ/ *adj* ⟨speech⟩ che solleva il morale; ⟨music⟩ trionfale

rout /raʊt/ ⟨1⟩ *vt* Mil, fig sbaragliare
⟨2⟩ *n* disfatta *f*

route /ruːt/ *n* itinerario *m*; Naut, Aeron rotta *f*; (of bus) percorso *m*

routine /ruːˈtiːn/ ⟨1⟩ *adj* di routine
⟨2⟩ *n* routine *f* inv; Theat numero *m*

routinely /ruːˈtiːnlɪ/ *adv* d'ufficio

rove /rəʊv/ *vi* girovagare

roving /'rəʊvɪŋ/ *adj* ⟨reporter, ambassador⟩ itinerante

roving eye *n* have a ∼ essere sempre in cerca di avventure amorose

row[1] /rəʊ/ *n* (line) fila *f*; **three years in a** ∼ tre anni di fila

row[2] ⟨1⟩ *vi* (in boat) remare
⟨2⟩ *vt* ∼ **a boat** remare

row[3] /raʊ/ ⟨1⟩ *n* fam (quarrel) litigata *f*; (noise) baccano *m*; **we've had a** ∼ abbiamo litigato
⟨2⟩ *vi* fam litigare

rowboat /'rəʊbəʊt/ *n* Am barca *f* a remi

rowdy /'raʊdɪ/ ⟨1⟩ *adj* (-ier, -iest) chiassoso
⟨2⟩ *n* attaccabrighe *m* inv

rower /'rəʊə(r)/ *n* rematore, -trice *mf*

rowing /'rəʊɪŋ/ *n* (sport) canottaggio *m*

rowing boat *n* barca *f* a remi

rowing machine *n* vogatore *m*

rowlock /'rɒlək/ *n* Br scalmo *m*

royal /'rɔɪəl/ ⟨1⟩ *adj* reale
⟨2⟩ *n* membro *m* della famiglia reale

royal blue *n* & *adj* blu *m* scuro

Royal Highness *n* His/Her ∼ Sua Altezza reale; **Your** ∼ Vostra Altezza

royally /'rɔɪəlɪ/ *adv* regalmente

royalties /'rɔɪəltɪz/ *npl* (payments) diritti *mpl* d'autore

royalty /'rɔɪəltɪ/ *n* appartenenza *f* alla famiglia reale; (persons) i membri della famiglia reale

rpm *abbr* (**revolutions per minute**) giri *mpl* al minuto

RSI *abbr* (**repetitive strain injury**) patologia *f* da sforzo ripetuto

RSVP *abbr* (**répondez s'il vous plaît = please reply**) SPR, si prega rispondere

rub /rʌb/ ⟨1⟩ *n* sfregata *f*
⟨2⟩ *vt* (pt/pp **rubbed**) sfregare; ∼ **one's hands** fregarsi le mani
■ **rub along** *vi* sopportarsi [a vicenda]
■ **rub down** *vt* frizionare ⟨person, body⟩; levigare ⟨wood⟩
■ **rub in** *vt* far assorbire (massaggiando) ⟨cream⟩; **don't** ∼ **it in** fam non rigirare il coltello nella piaga
■ **rub off** ⟨1⟩ *vt* mandar via sfregando ⟨stain⟩; (from blackboard) cancellare
⟨2⟩ *vi* andar via; ∼ **off on** essere trasmesso a
■ **rub out** *vt* cancellare
■ **rub up** *vt* ∼ **somebody up the wrong way** prendere qualcuno per il verso sbagliato

rubber /'rʌbə(r)/ *n* gomma *f*; (eraser) gomma *f* [da cancellare]

rubber band *n* elastico *m*

rubber bullet *n* proiettile *m* di gomma

rubberneck *n* fam (onlooker) curioso, -a *mf*; (tourist) turista *mf*

rubber plant *n* ficus *m* inv

rubberstamp *vt* fig approvare senza discutere

rubber tree *n* albero *m* della gomma

rubbery /'rʌbərɪ/ *adj* gommoso

rubbish /'rʌbɪʃ/ ⟨1⟩ *n* immondizie *fpl*; (fam: nonsense) idiozie *fpl*; (fam: junk) robaccia *f*
⟨2⟩ *vt* fam fare a pezzi

rubbish bin *n* pattumiera *f*

rubbish dump *n* discarica *f*; (official) discarica *f* comunale

rubbishy /'rʌbɪʃɪ/ *adj* fam schifoso

rubble /'rʌbl/ *n* macerie *fpl*

rub-down *n* strofinata *f*

rubella /rʊ'belə/ *n* rosolia *f*

rubric /'ruːbrɪk/ *n* rubrica *f*

ruby /'ruːbɪ/ ⟨1⟩ *n* rubino *m*
⟨2⟩ *attrib* di rubini; ⟨lips⟩ scarlatto

rucksack /'rʌksæk/ *n* zaino *m*

ructions /'rʌkʃ(ə)nz/ *npl* fam finimondo *msg*; **there'll be** ∼ **if he finds out** se lo scopre succede il finimondo

rudder /'rʌdə(r)/ *n* timone *m*

ruddy /'rʌdɪ/ *adj* (-ier, -iest) rubicondo; fam maledetto

rude /ru:d/ *adj* scortese; (improper) spinto

rudely /'ru:dlɪ/ *adv* scortesemente

rudeness /'ru:dnɪs/ *n* scortesia *f*

rudimentary /ru:dɪ'mentərɪ/ *adj* rudimentale

rudiments /'ru:dɪmənts/ *npl* rudimenti *mpl*

rue[1] /ru:/ *vt* pentirsi di ⟨*decision*⟩; ~ **the day** maledire il giorno

rue[2] *n* Bot ruta *f*

rueful /'ru:fl/ *adj* rassegnato

ruefully /'ru:fʊlɪ/ *adv* con rassegnazione

ruff /rʌf/ *n* (of lace) colletto *m*; (of fur, feathers) collare *m*

ruffian /'rʌfɪən/ *n* farabutto *m*

ruffle /'rʌfl/ ⓵ *n* gala *f*
 ⓶ *vt* scompigliare ⟨*hair*⟩

rug /rʌg/ *n* tappeto *m*; (blanket) coperta *f*

rugby /'rʌgbɪ/ *n* ~ **[football]** rugby *m*

rugby league *n* rugby *m* a tredici

rugby union *n* rugby *m* a quindici

rugged /'rʌgɪd/ *adj* ⟨*coastline*⟩ roccioso; ⟨*face, personality*⟩ duro

ruin /'ru:ɪn/ ⓵ *n* rovina *f*; **in** ~**s** in rovina
 ⓶ *vt* rovinare

ruined /'ru:ɪnd/ *adj* ⟨*building, clothes*⟩ rovinato

ruinous /'ru:məs/ *adj* estremamente costoso

rule /ru:l/ ⓵ *n* regola *f*; (control) ordinamento *m*; (for measuring) metro *m*; ~**s** *pl* regolamento *msg*; **as a** ~ generalmente; **make it a** ~ **to do something** fare qualcosa sistematicamente
 ⓶ *vt* governare; dominare ⟨*colony, behaviour*⟩; ~ **that** stabilire che
 ⓷ *vi* governare
 ■ **rule out** *vt* escludere

ruled /ru:ld/ *adj* ⟨*paper*⟩ a righe

rule of thumb *n* principio *m* empirico

ruler /'ru:lə(r)/ *n* capo *m* di Stato; (sovereign) sovrano, -a *mf*; (measure) righello *m*, regolo *m*

ruling /'ru:lɪŋ/ ⓵ *adj* ⟨*class*⟩ dirigente; ⟨*party*⟩ di governo
 ⓶ *n* decisione *f*

rum[1] /rʌm/ *n* rum *m inv*

rum[2] *adj* (fam: peculiar) curioso

rumble /'rʌmbl/ ⓵ *n* rombo *m*; (of stomach) brontolio *m*
 ⓶ *vi* rombare; ⟨*stomach*⟩ brontolare

rumble strip *n* banda *f* rumorosa

rumbustious /rʌm'bʌstʃəs/ *adj* (noisy, very lively) chiassoso

ruminant /'ru:mɪnənt/ *n* ruminante *m*

ruminate /'ru:mɪneɪt/ *vi* ⟨*animals*⟩ ruminare; (think) rimuginare

rummage /'rʌmɪdʒ/ *vi* rovistare (**in**/ **through** in)

rummy /'rʌmɪ/ *n* ramino *m*

rumour /'ru:mə(r)/ ⓵ *n* diceria *f*
 ⓶ *vt* **it is** ~**ed that** si dice che

rumour-monger /'ru:məmʌŋgə(r)/ *n* persona *f* che sparge pettegolezzi

rump /rʌmp/ *n* natiche *fpl*

rumple /'rʌmpl/ *vt* sgualcire ⟨*clothes, sheets, papers*⟩; scompigliare ⟨*hair*⟩

rump steak *n* bistecca *f* di girello

rumpus /'rʌmpəs/ *n fam* baccano *m*

run /rʌn/ ⓵ *n* (on foot) corsa *f*; (distance to be covered) tragitto *m*; (outing) giro *m*; Theat rappresentazioni *fpl*; (in skiing) pista *f*; (Am: ladder) smagliatura *f* (in calze); **at a** ~ di corsa; ~ **of bad luck** periodo *m* sfortunato; **on the** ~ in fuga; **have the** ~ **of** avere a disposizione; **in the long** ~ a lungo termine
 ⓶ *vi* (*pt* **ran**, *pp* **run**, *pres p* **running**) correre; ⟨*river*⟩ scorrere; ⟨*nose, makeup*⟩ colare; ⟨*bus*⟩ fare servizio; ⟨*play*⟩ essere in cartellone; ⟨*colours*⟩ sbiadire; (in election) presentarsi [come candidato]; ⟨*software*⟩ girare; ~ **aground** insabbiarsi; ~ **low on,** ~ **short of** essere a corto di
 ⓷ *vt* (manage) dirigere; tenere ⟨*house*⟩; (drive) dare un passaggio a; correre ⟨*risk*⟩; Comput lanciare; Journ pubblicare ⟨*article*⟩; (pass) far scorrere ⟨*eyes, hand*⟩; ~ **a temperature** avere la febbre; ~ **a bath** far scorrere l'acqua per il bagno
 ■ **run about** *vi* ⟨*children*⟩ correre di qua e di là; (be busy) correre
 ■ **run across** *vt* imbattersi in
 ■ **run after** *vt* (chase) rincorrere; (romantically) andare dietro a
 ■ **run along** *vi* (go away) andare via
 ■ **run away** *vi* scappare [via], andare via di corsa; (from home) scappare di casa
 ■ **run away with** *vt* scappare con ⟨*lover, money*⟩; **she let her enthusiasm** ~ **away with her** si è lasciata trasportare dall'entusiasmo
 ■ **run back** ⓵ *vi* correre indietro
 ⓶ *vt* (transport by car) riaccompagnare
 ■ **run back over** *vt* (review) rivedere
 ■ **run down** ⓵ *vi* ⟨*clock*⟩ scaricarsi; ⟨*stocks*⟩ esaurirsi
 ⓶ *vt* Auto investire; (reduce) esaurire; (fam: criticize) denigrare
 ■ **run in** *vi* entrare di corsa
 ■ **run into** *vi* (meet) imbattersi in; (knock against) urtare
 ■ **run off** ⓵ *vi* scappare [via], andare via di corsa; (from home) scappare di casa
 ⓶ *vt* stampare ⟨*copies*⟩
 ■ **run off with** *vt* = RUN AWAY WITH
 ■ **run on** *vi* ⟨*meeting*⟩ protrarsi; ⟨*person*⟩ chiacchierare senza sosta
 ■ **run out** *vi* uscire di corsa; ⟨*supplies, money*⟩ esaurirsi; ~ **out of** rimanere senza
 ■ **run over** ⓵ *vi* correre; (overflow) traboccare
 ⓶ *vt* (review) dare una scorsa a; Auto investire

■ **run through** *vt* (use up) fare fuori; (be present in) pervadere; (review) dare una scorsa a

■ **run to** *vt* (be enough for) essere sufficiente per; (have enough money for) potersi permettere

■ **run up** ① *vi* salire di corsa; (towards) arrivare di corsa

② *vt* accumulare ⟨debts, bill⟩; (sew) cucire

■ **run up against** *vt* incontrare ⟨difficulties⟩

runabout *n* (vehicle) utilitaria *f*

run-around *n* he's giving me/her the ~ mi/la sta menando per il naso

runaway ① *n* fuggitivo, -a *mf*, fuggiasco, -a *mf*; (child) ragazzo, -a *mf* scappato, -a di casa

② *adj* ⟨person⟩ in fuga; ⟨child⟩ scappato di casa; ⟨inflation⟩ galoppante; ⟨success⟩ eclatante

run-down ① *adj* ⟨area⟩ in abbandono; ⟨person⟩ esaurito

② *n* analisi *f inv*

rung[1] /rʌŋ/ *n* (of ladder) piolo *m*

rung[2] ▶ RING[2]

run-in *n* (fam: argument) lite *f*

runner /'rʌnə(r)/ *n* podista *mf*; (in race) corridore, -trice *mf*; (on sledge) pattino *f*; (carpet) guida *f*

runner bean *n* fagiolino *m*

runner-up *n* secondo, -a classificato, -a *mf*

running /'rʌnɪŋ/ ① *adj* in corsa; ⟨water⟩ corrente; **four times ~** quattro volte di seguito

② *n* corsa *f*; (management) direzione *f*; **be in the ~** essere in lizza

running battle *n* lotta *f* continua

running commentary *n* cronaca *f*

running total *n* totale *m* aggiornato

runny /'rʌnɪ/ *adj* semiliquido; **~ nose** naso *m* che cola

run-of-the-mill *adj* ordinario

runs /rʌnz/ *npl* **the ~** (fam: diarrhoea) la sciolta

runt /rʌnt/ *n* (of litter) cucciolo *m* più piccolo e debole di una figliata; (pej: weakling) mezza cartuccia *f*

run-through *n* prova *f* generale

run-up *n* Sport rincorsa *f*; **the ~ to** il periodo precedente

runway /'rʌnweɪ/ *n* pista *f*

rupee /ru:'pi:/ *n* rupia *f*

rupture /'rʌptʃə(r)/ ① *n* rottura *f*; Med ernia *f*

② *vt* rompere; **~ oneself** farsi venire l'ernia

③ *vi* rompersi

rural /'rʊərəl/ *adj* rurale

ruse /ru:z/ *n* astuzia *f*

rush[1] /rʌʃ/ *n* Bot giunco *m*

rush[2] ① *n* fretta *f*; **in a ~** di fretta

② *vi* precipitarsi

③ *vt* far premura a; **~ somebody to hospital** trasportare qualcuno di corsa all'ospedale

■ **rush away**, **rush off** *vi* andar via in fretta

■ **rush into** *vt* **~ into marriage** sposarsi senza riflettere; **~ into doing something** lanciarsi a fare qualcosa senza riflettere; **~ somebody into doing something** spingere qualcuno a fare qualcosa

■ **rush out** *vi* uscire di corsa

■ **rush through** *vt* svolgere in fretta ⟨task⟩; **~ something through** fare approvare qualcosa in fretta ⟨legislation, order⟩

rush hour ① *n* ora *f* di punta

② *attrib* delle ore di punta

rusk /rʌsk/ *n* biscotto *m*

russet /'rʌsɪt/ *adj* rossastro

Russia /'rʌʃə/ *n* Russia *f*

Russian /'rʌʃən/ *adj & n* russo, -a *mf*; (language) russo *m*

Russian roulette *n* roulette *f* russa

rust /rʌst/ ① *n* ruggine *f*

② *vi* arrugginirsi

③ *vt* arrugginire

rustic /'rʌstɪk/ *adj* rustico

rustle /'rʌsl/ ① *vi* frusciare

② *vt* far frusciare; Am rubare ⟨cattle⟩

■ **rustle up** *vt* fam fare ⟨meal, cup of coffee⟩

rustler /'rʌslə(r)/ *n* ladro *m* di bestiame

rustproof /'rʌstpru:f/ *adj* a prova di ruggine

rusty /'rʌstɪ/ *adj* (**-ier**, **-iest**) arrugginito

rut /rʌt/ *n* solco *m*; **in a ~** fam nella routine

ruthless /'ru:θlɪs/ *adj* spietato

ruthlessly /'ru:θlɪslɪ/ *adv* spietatamente

ruthlessness /'ru:θlɪsnɪs/ *n* spietatezza *f*

rutting /'rʌtɪŋ/ *n* accoppiamento *m*

rutting season *n* stagione *f* degli amori

RV *n abbr* Am (**recreational vehicle**) camper *m*

Rwanda /ru:'ændə/ *n* Rwanda *m*

rye /raɪ/ *n* segale *f*

rye bread *n* pane *m* di segale

Ss

s¹, S /es/ *n* (letter) s, S *f inv*

S² *abbr* **small**; *abbr* **(south)** S

sabbath /'sæbəθ/ *n* domenica *f*; (Jewish) sabato *m*

sabbatical /sə'bætɪkl/ *n* Univ anno *m* sabbatico

sable /'seɪbl/ *n* (animal, fur) zibellino *m*

sabotage /'sæbətɑːʒ/ ① *n* sabotaggio *m* ② *vt* sabotare

saboteur /sæbə'tɜː(r)/ *n* sabotatore, -trice *mf*

sabre /'seɪbə(r)/ *n* sciabola *f*

sac /sæk/ *n* Anat, Zool sacco *m*; Bot sacca *f*; **honey ∼** cestella *f*

saccharin /'sækərɪn/ *n* saccarina *f*

sachet /'sæʃeɪ/ *n* bustina *f*; (scented) sacchetto *m* profumato

sack¹ /sæk/ *vt* (plunder) saccheggiare

sack² ① *n* sacco *m*; **get the ∼** fam essere licenziato; **give somebody the ∼** licenziare qualcuno
② *vt* fam licenziare

sackcloth /'sækklɒθ/ *n* tela *f* di sacco; **wear ∼ and ashes** cospargersi il capo di cenere

sackful /'sækfʊl/ *n* sacco *m* (contenuto)

sacking /'sækɪŋ/ *n* tela *f* per sacchi; (fam: dismissal) licenziamento *m*

sackload /'sæklaʊd/ *n* sacco *m* (contenuto)

sacrament /'sækrəmənt/ *n* sacramento *m*

sacred /'seɪkrɪd/ *adj* sacro

sacred cow /kaʊ/ *n* (institution) istituzione *f* intoccabile; (principle) principio *m* inderogabile; (person) mostro *m* sacro

sacrifice /'sækrɪfaɪs/ ① *n* sacrificio *m* ② *vt* sacrificare; **∼ oneself** immolarsi

sacrificial /sækrɪ'fɪʃəl/ *adj* ‹victim› sacrificale

sacrilege /'sækrɪlɪdʒ/ *n* sacrilegio *m*

sacrilegious /sækrɪ'lɪdʒəs/ *adj* sacrilego

sacristy /'sækrɪstɪ/ *n* sagrestia *f*

sacrosanct /'sækrəʊsæŋkt/ *adj* sacrosanto

sacrum /'sækrʌm/ *n* Anat osso *m* sacro

SAD *n abbr* **(seasonal affective disorder)** Med disturbi *mpl* affettivi stagionali

sad /sæd/ *adj* **(sadder, saddest)** triste

sadden /'sædn/ *vt* rattristare

saddle /'sædl/ ① *n* sella *f*; **be in the ∼** fig tenere le redini
② *vt* sellare; **I've been ∼d with...** fig mi hanno affibbiato...

sadism /'seɪdɪzm/ *n* sadismo *m*

sadist /'seɪdɪst/ *n* sadico, -a *mf*

sadistic /sə'dɪstɪk/ *adj* sadico

sadistically /sə'dɪstɪklɪ/ *adv* sadicamente

sadly /'sædlɪ/ *adv* tristemente; (unfortunately) sfortunatamente

sadness /'sædnɪs/ *n* tristezza *f*

sadomasochism /seɪdəʊ'mæsəkɪzm/ *n* sadomasochismo *m*

sadomasochist /seɪdəʊ'mæsəkɪst/ *n* sadomasochista *m*

sadomasochistic /seɪdəʊ'mæsəkɪstɪk/ *adj* sadomasochistico

sae *abbr* **stamped addressed envelope**

safari /sə'fɑːrɪ/ *n* safari *m inv*

safari park *n* zoosafari *m inv*

safe /seɪf/ ① *adj* sicuro; (out of danger) salvo; ‹object› al sicuro; **∼ and sound** sano e salvo
② *n* cassaforte *f*

safe bet *n* **it's a ∼ ∼ that he will come** è certo che verrà

safe-breaker *n* scassinatore, -trice *mf*

safe-conduct *n* salvacondotto *m*

safe-deposit box safety-deposit box *n* cassetta *f* di sicurezza

safeguard /'seɪfgɑːd/ ① *n* protezione *f* ② *vt* proteggere

safe house *n* rifugio *m*

safe keeping *n* custodia *f*; **for ∼ ∼** in custodia

safely /'seɪflɪ/ *adv* in modo sicuro; ‹arrive› senza incidenti; ‹assume› con certezza

safe sex *n* sesso *m* sicuro

safety /'seɪftɪ/ *n* sicurezza *f*

safety belt *n* cintura *f* di sicurezza

safety catch *n* sicura *f*

safety curtain *n* tagliafuoco *m*

safety-deposit box *n* = SAFE-DEPOSIT BOX

safety glass *n* vetro *m* di sicurezza

safety net *n* (for acrobat) rete *f* di protezione; fig protezione

safety pin *n* spilla *f* di sicurezza o da balia

safety razor *n* rasoio *m* di sicurezza

safety valve *n* valvola *f* di sicurezza; fig valvola *f* di sfogo

saffron /'sæfrən/ *n* zafferano *m*

sag /sæg/ *vi* (pt/pp **sagged**) abbassarsi

saga /'sɑːgə/ *n* saga *f*

sagacity /sə'gæsətɪ/ *n* sagacia *f*

sage¹ /seɪdʒ/ *n* (herb) salvia *f*

sage² *adj* & *n* saggio, -a *mf*

sagely /'seɪdʒlɪ/ *adv* ⟨reply, nod⟩ saggiamente

Sagittarius /sædʒɪ'teərɪəs/ *n* Sagittario *m*

sago /'seɪgəʊ/ *n* sagù *m*

Sahara /sə'hɑːrə/ *n* Sahara *m*

said /sed/ ▶ SAY

sail /seɪl/ **1** *n* vela *f*; (trip) giro *m* in barca a vela
2 *vi* navigare; Sport praticare la vela; (leave) salpare
3 *vt* pilotare
■ **sail through** *vt* superare senza problemi ⟨exam⟩

sailboard /'seɪlbɔːd/ *n* tavola *f* da windsurf

sailboarder /'seɪlbɔːdə(r)/ *n* windsurfista *mf*

sailboarding /'seɪlbɔːdɪŋ/ *n* windsurf *m inv*

sailboat /'seɪlbəʊt/ *n* Am barca *f* a vela

sailing /'seɪlɪŋ/ *n* vela *f*

sailing boat *n* barca *f* a vela

sailing ship *n* veliero *m*

sailor /'seɪlə(r)/ *n* marinaio *m*

saint /seɪnt/ *n* santo, -a *mf*

sainthood /'seɪnthʊd/ *n* santità *f*

saintly /'seɪntlɪ/ *adj* da santo

sake /seɪk/ *n* for the ∼ of ⟨person⟩ per il bene di; ⟨peace⟩ per amor di; for the ∼ of it per il gusto di farlo

salacious /sə'leɪʃəs/ *adj* ⟨joke⟩ salace; ⟨book⟩ licenzioso; ⟨look⟩ lascivo

salad /'sæləd/ *n* insalata *f*

salad bar *n* tavola *f* fredda

salad bowl *n* insalatiera *f*

salad cream *n* salsa *f* per condire l'insalata

salad days *npl* anni *mpl* verdi

salad dressing *n* condimento *m* per insalata

salami /sə'lɑːmɪ/ *n* salame *m*

salaried /'sælərɪd/ *adj* stipendiato

salary /'sælərɪ/ *n* stipendio *m*

salary review *n* revisione *f* dello stipendio

salary scale *n* tabella *f* retributiva

sale /seɪl/ *n* vendita *f*; (at reduced prices) svendita *f*; for/on ∼ in vendita; 'for ∼' 'vendesi'

sale price *n* prezzo *m* scontato

sales and marketing *n* vendite *fpl* e marketing

sales and marketing department *n* ufficio *m* vendite e marketing

sales assistant *n* commesso, -a *mf*

sales director *n* capo *mf* dell'ufficio vendite

sales engineer *n* tecnico *m* commerciale

sales executive *n* direttore, -trice *mf* commerciale

sales figures *npl* volumi *mpl* d'affari

sales force *n* rappresentanti *mpl*

sales invoice *n* fattura *f* di vendita

sales ledger *n* partitario *m* vendite

salesman *n* venditore *m*; (traveller) rappresentante *m*

sales pitch *n* discorso *m* imbonitore

sales rep, **sales representative** *n* rappresentante *mf* di commercio

salesroom *n* (for auctions) sala *f* d'aste

sales team *n* team *m inv* vendite

saleswoman *n* venditrice *f*

salient /'seɪlɪənt/ *adj* saliente

saline /'seɪlaɪn/ *adj* salino

saliva /sə'laɪvə/ *n* saliva *f*

salivary glands /sə'laɪvərɪ/ *npl* ghiandole *fpl* salivari

salivate /'sælɪveɪt/ *vi* salivare; **the smell of chicken roasting makes me** ∼ l'odore di pollo arrosto mi fa venire l'acquolina in bocca

sallow /'sæləʊ/ *adj* giallastro

sally /'sælɪ/ **1** *n* (witty remark) battuta *f*; Mil sortita *f*
2 *vi* saltar fuori

salmon /'sæmən/ *n* salmone *m*

salmonella /sælmə'nelə/ *n* salmonella *f*

salmon-pink *adj* [rosa *inv*] salmone *inv*

salmon trout *n* trota *f* salmonata

salon /'sælɒn/ *n* salone *m*

saloon /sə'luːn/ *n* Auto berlina *f*; (Am: bar) bar *m*

salsa /'sælsə/ *n* salsa *f*

salt /sɔːlt/ **1** *n* sale *m*
2 *adj* salato; ⟨fish, meat⟩ sotto sale
3 *vt* salare; ⟨cure⟩ mettere sotto sale

salt cellar *n* saliera *f*

saltiness /'sɔːltɪnɪs/ *n* salinità *f*

salt water *n* acqua *f* di mare

salt-water fish *n* pesce *m* d'acqua salata

salty /'sɔːltɪ/ *adj* salato

salubrious /sə'luːbrɪəs/ *adj* ⟨neighbourhood⟩ raccomandabile; **it's not a very** ∼ **area** è una zona poco raccomandabile

salutary /'sæljʊtərɪ/ *adj* salutare

salute /sə'lu:t/ Mil **1** *n* saluto *m*
2 *vt* salutare
3 *vi* fare il saluto

salvage /'sælvɪdʒ/ **1** *n* Naut recupero *m*
2 *vt* recuperare

salvation /sæl'veɪʃn/ *n* salvezza *f*

Salvation Army *n* Esercito *m* della
Salvezza

salve /sælv/ *vt* ∼ **one's conscience**
mettersi la coscienza a posto

salver /'sælvə(r)/ *n* vassoio *m* (di
metallo)

salvo /'sælvəʊ/ *n* salva *f*

Samaritan /səm'ærɪtən/ *n* **a good** ∼ un
buon samaritano; **the** ∼**s** ≈ telefono *m*
amico

samba /'sæmbə/ *n* samba *f*

same /seɪm/ **1** *adj* stesso (**as** di)
2 *pron* **the** ∼ lo stesso; **be all the** ∼
essere tutti uguali
3 *adv* **the** ∼ nello stesso modo; **all the** ∼
(however) lo stesso; **the** ∼ **to you** altrettanto

same-day *adj* ⟨*service*⟩ in giornata

same-day delivery *n* consegna *f* in
giornata

same-sex *adj* ⟨*couple, marriage*⟩
omosessuale

sample /'sɑ:mpl/ **1** *n* campione *m*
2 *vt* testare

sanatorium /sænə'tɔ:rɪəm/ *n* casa *f* di
cura

sanctify /'sæŋktɪfaɪ/ *vt* (pt/pp **-fied**)
santificare

sanctimonious /sæŋktɪ'məʊnɪəs/ *adj*
moraleggiante

sanction /'sæŋkʃn/ **1** *n* (approval)
autorizzazione *f*; (penalty) sanzione *f*
2 *vt* autorizzare

sanctity /'sæŋktətɪ/ *n* santità *f*

sanctuary /'sæŋktjʊərɪ/ *n* Relig
santuario *m*; (refuge) asilo *m*; (for wildlife)
riserva *f*

sanctum /'sæŋktəm/ *n* (holy place)
santuario *m*; (private place) rifugio *m*; **the
inner** ∼ Relig il Sancta Sanctorum

sand /sænd/ **1** *n* sabbia *f*
2 *vt* ∼ **[down]** carteggiare

sandal /'sændl/ *n* sandalo *m*

sandbag *n* sacchetto *m* di sabbia

sandbank *n* banco *m* di sabbia

sandblast *vt* sabbiare

sandblasting *n* sabbiatura *f*

sandcastle *n* castello *m* di sabbia

sand dune *n* duna *f*

sander /'sændə(r)/ *n* (machine) levigatrice
f

sandpaper **1** *n* carta *f* vetrata
2 *vt* cartavetrare

sandpit *n* recinto *m* contenente sabbia
dove giocano i bambini

sandstone *n* arenaria *f*

sandstorm *n* tempesta *f* di sabbia

sandwich /'sænwɪdʒ/ **1** *n* tramezzino
m
2 *vt* ∼**ed between** schiacciato tra

sandwich bar *n* locale *m* in cui si
comprano sandwich e panini pronti o su
ordinazione

sandwich course *n* corso *m* che
comprende dei periodi di tirocinio

sandwich-man *n* uomo *m* sandwich

sandy /'sændɪ/ *adj* (**-ier, -iest**) ⟨*beach,
soil*⟩ sabbioso; ⟨*hair*⟩ biondiccio

sane /seɪn/ *adj* (not mad) sano di mente;
(sensible) sensato

sang /sæŋ/ ▶ SING

sangria /sæŋ'griə/ *n* sangria *f*

sanguine /'sæŋgwɪn/ *adj* ottimistico

sanitary /'sænɪtərɪ/ *adj* igienico;
⟨*system*⟩ sanitario

sanitary napkin *n* Am, **sanitary
towel** assorbente *m* igienico

sanitation /sænɪ'teɪʃn/ *n* impianti *mpl*
igienici

sanity /'sænətɪ/ *n* sanità *f* di mente;
(sensibleness) buon senso *m*

sank /sæŋk/ ▶ SINK

Santa [Claus] /'sæntə[klɔːz]/ *n* Babbo
m Natale

sap /sæp/ **1** *n* Bot linfa *f*
2 *vt* (pt/pp **sapped**) indebolire

sapling /'sæplɪŋ/ *n* alberello *m*

sapper /'sæpə(r)/ *n* Br Mil geniere *m*

sapphire /'sæfaɪə(r)/ **1** *n* zaffiro *m*
2 *attrib* blu zaffiro *inv*

sarcasm /'sɑ:kæzm/ *n* sarcasmo *m*

sarcastic /sɑ:'kæstɪk/ *adj* sarcastico

sarcastically /sɑ:'kæstɪklɪ/ *adv*
sarcasticamente

sarcophagus /sɑ:'kɒfəgəs/ *n* sarcofago
m

sardine /sɑ:'di:n/ *n* sardina *f*

Sardinia /sɑ:'dɪnɪə/ *n* Sardegna *f*

Sardinian /sɑ:'dɪnɪən/ *adj & n* sardo, -a
mf

sardonic /sɑ:'dɒnɪk/ *adj* sardonico

sardonically /sɑ:'dɒnɪklɪ/ *adv*
sardonicamente

sari /'sɑ:rɪ/ *n* sari *m inv*

sarong /sə'rɒŋ/ *n* pareo *m*

SARS /sɑ:z/ *n abbr* (**severe acute
respiratory syndrome**) SARS *f*

SAS *n* Br abbr (**Special Air Service**)
commando *mpl* britannico per operazioni
speciali

sash /sæʃ/ *n* fascia *f*; (for dress) fusciacca *f*

sashay /'sæʃeɪ/ *vi* fam (casually)
camminare in modo disinvolto; (seductively)
camminare in modo provocante

S

sassy /'sæsɪ/ adj Am fam (cheeky) sfacciato; (smart) chic inv

sat /sæt/ ▶ SIT

Satan /'seɪtən/ n Satana m

satanic /sə'tænɪk/ adj satanico

satchel /'sætʃl/ n cartella f

sated /'seɪtɪd/ adj ⟨person⟩ sazio; ⟨desire⟩ appagato; ⟨appetite⟩ soddisfatto

satellite /'sætəlaɪt/ n satellite m

satellite channel n rete f televisiva satellitare

satellite dish n antenna f parabolica

satellite television n televisione f satellitare

satiate /'seɪʃɪeɪt/ vt saziare ⟨person⟩; appagare ⟨desire⟩; soddisfare ⟨appetite⟩

satin /'sætɪn/ ① n raso m
② attrib di raso

satire /'sætaɪə(r)/ n satira f

satirical /sə'tɪrɪkl/ adj satirico

satirically /sə'tɪrɪklɪ/ adv satiricamente

satirist /'sætərɪst/ n scrittore, -trice mf satirico, -a; (comedian) comico, -a mf satirico, -a

satirize /'sætɪraɪz/ vt satireggiare

satisfaction /sætɪs'fækʃn/ n soddisfazione f; be to sb's ~ soddisfare qualcuno

satisfactorily /sætɪs'fækt(ə)rɪlɪ/ adv in modo soddisfacente

satisfactory /sætɪs'fæktərɪ/ adj soddisfacente

satisfied /'sætɪsfaɪd/ adj (pleased) soddisfatto; ~ with soddisfatto di; (convinced) convinto; ~ that convinto che

satisfy /'sætɪsfaɪ/ vt (pt/pp -ied) soddisfare; (convince) convincere

satisfying /'sætɪsfaɪɪŋ/ adj soddisfacente

SATs /sæts/ npl abbr Br (standard assessment tasks) esami mpl sostenuti per tranche d'età allo scopo di testare la preparazione degli alunni

saturate /'sætʃəreɪt/ vt inzuppare (with di); Chem, fig saturare (with di)

saturated /'sætʃəreɪtɪd/ adj saturo

saturation /sætʃə'reɪʃn/ n reach ~ point raggiungere il punto di saturazione

Saturday /'sætədeɪ/ n sabato m

Saturn /'sætən/ n Saturno m

sauce /sɔːs/ n salsa f; (cheek) impertinenza f

saucepan /'sɔːspən/ n pentola f

saucer /'sɔːsə(r)/ n piattino m

saucy /'sɔːsɪ/ adj (-ier, -iest) impertinente

Saudi /'saʊdɪ/ ① adj saudita
② n (person) saudita mf; (country) Arabia f Saudita

Saudi Arabia /ə'reɪbɪə/ n Arabia f Saudita

Saudi Arabian adj & n saudita mf

sauerkraut /'saʊəkraʊt/ n crauti mpl

sauna /'sɔːnə/ n sauna f

saunter /'sɔːntə(r)/ vi andare a spasso

sausage /'sɒsɪdʒ/ n salsiccia f; (dried) salame m

sausage dog /'sɒsɪdʒdɒg/ n fam bassotto m

sausage roll n involtino m di pasta sfoglia con salsiccia

sauté /'səʊteɪ/ ① vt rosolare
② adj rosolato

savage /'sævɪdʒ/ ① adj feroce; ⟨tribe, custom⟩ selvaggio
② n selvaggio, -a mf
③ vt fare a pezzi

savagely /'sævɪdʒlɪ/ adv ⟨attack⟩ selvaggiamente; ⟨criticize⟩ ferocemente

savagery /'sævɪdʒrɪ/ n ferocia f

save /seɪv/ ① n Sport parata f
② vt salvare (from da); (keep, collect) tenere; risparmiare ⟨time, money⟩; (avoid) evitare; Sport parare ⟨goal⟩; Comput salvare, memorizzare; ~ face salvar la faccia
③ vi ~ [up] risparmiare
④ prep salvo

saver /'seɪvə(r)/ n risparmiatore, -trice mf

saving grace /seɪvɪŋ'greɪs/ n that's his one ~ ~ si salva grazie a questo

savings /'seɪvɪŋz/ npl (money) risparmi mpl

savings account n libretto m di risparmio

savings and loan association n Am associazione f mutua di risparmi e prestiti

savings bank n cassa f di risparmio

saviour /'seɪvjə(r)/ n salvatore m

savoir faire /sævwɑː'feə(r)/ n (social) savoir-faire m

savory /'seɪvərɪ/ n Bot santoreggia f

savour /'seɪvə(r)/ ① n sapore m
② vt assaporare

savoury /'seɪvərɪ/ adj salato; fig rispettabile

saw¹ /sɔː/ ▶ SEE¹

saw² ① n sega f
② vt (pt **sawed**, pp **sawn** or **sawed**) segare

sawdust /'sɔːdʌst/ n segatura f

sawmill /'sɔːmɪl/ n segheria f

sawn-off shotgun /'sɔːn/ n fucile m a canne mozze

Saxon /'sæksən/ adj & n sassone mf; (language) sassone m

saxophone /'sæksəfəʊn/ n sassofono m

saxophonist /sæk'sɒfənɪst/ n sassofonista mf

say /seɪ/ **1** n have one's ~ dire la propria; have a ~ avere voce in capitolo **2** vt/i (pt/pp **said**) dire; that is to ~ cioè; that goes without ~ing questo è ovvio; when all is said and done alla fine dei conti; ~ yes/no dire di sì/no; just ~ the word and I'll come tu chiama e io vengo; what more can I ~? che altro dire?; some time next week ~? la prossima settimana, diciamo?; the clock ~s ten to six la sveglia fa le sei meno dieci; you can ~ that again! puoi dirlo forte!; the tree is said to be very old a quanto pare l'albero è vecchissimo; he said you were to bring the car ha detto che dovevi portare la macchina; it ~s a lot for him that... il fatto che... la dice lunga sul suo conto; what have you got to ~ for yourself? che scusa hai?; to ~ nothing of... per non parlare di..., what would you ~ to a new car? cosa ne diresti di una macchina nuova?

saying /'seɪɪŋ/ n proverbio m

scab /skæb/ n crosta f; pej crumiro m

scabby /'skæbɪ/ adj ⟨plant⟩ coperto di galle; ⟨skin⟩ coperto di croste; ⟨animal⟩ rognoso; (fam: nasty) schifoso

scaffold /'skæfəld/ n patibolo m

scaffolding /'skæfəldɪŋ/ n impalcatura f

scalar /'skeɪlə(r)/ adj scalare

scald /skɔːld/ **1** vt scottare; (milk) scaldare **2** n scottatura f

scalding /'skɔːldɪŋ/ adj bollente

scale¹ /skeɪl/ n (of fish) scaglia f

scale² **1** n scala f; on a grand ~ su vasta scala; to ~ in scala; ~ of values scala f di valori **2** vt (climb) scalare ∎ **scale down** vt diminuire

scale drawing n disegno m in scala

scale model n modello m in scala

scales /skeɪlz/ npl (for weighing) bilancia fsg

scallop /'skɒləp/ **1** n (in sewing) smerlo m, festone m; Zool pettine m; Culin cappasanta f **2** vt (in sewing) smerlare; ~ed potatoes patate fpl gratinate

scalp /skælp/ **1** n cuoio m capelluto **2** vt scalpare

scalpel /'skælpl/ n bisturi m inv

scaly /'skeɪlɪ/ adj ⟨wing, fish⟩ squamoso; ⟨plaster, wall⟩ scrostato

scam /skæm/ n fam fregatura f

scamper /'skæmpə(r)/ vi ~ away sgattaiolare via

scampi /'skæmpɪ/ npl scampi mpl

scan /skæn/ **1** n Med scanning m inv, scansioscintigrafia f **2** vt (pt/pp **scanned**) scrutare; (quickly) dare una scorsa a; Med fare uno scanning di; Comput scannerizzare **3** vi ⟨poetry⟩ scandire

scandal /'skændl/ n scandalo m; (gossip) pettegolezzi mpl

scandalize /'skændəlaɪz/ vt scandalizzare

scandalmonger /'skænd(ə)lmʌŋgə(r)/ n malalingua f

scandalous /'skændələs/ adj scandaloso

Scandinavia /skændɪ'neɪvɪə/ n Scandinavia f

Scandinavian /skændɪ'neɪvɪən/ adj & n scandinavo, -a mf

scanner /'skænə(r)/ n Med, Comput scanner m inv; (radar) antenna f radar; (for bar codes) lettore m di codice a barre

scanning /'skænɪŋ/ n Comput scannerizzazione f

scant /skænt/ adj scarso

scantily /'skæntɪlɪ/ adv scarsamente; ⟨clothed⟩ succintamente

scanty /'skæntɪ/ adj (-ier, -iest) scarso; ⟨clothing⟩ succinto

scapegoat /'skeɪpgəʊt/ n capro m espiatorio

scar /skɑː(r)/ **1** n cicatrice f **2** vt (pt/pp **scarred**) lasciare una cicatrice a

scarce /skeəs/ adj scarso; fig raro; make oneself ~ fam svignarsela

scarcely /'skeəslɪ/ adv appena; ~ anything quasi niente

scarcity /'skeəsətɪ/ n scarsezza f

scare /skeə(r)/ **1** n spavento m; (panic) panico m **2** vt spaventare; be ~d aver paura (of di) ∎ **scare away** vt far scappare

scarecrow /'skeəkrəʊ/ n spaventapasseri m inv

scaremonger /'skeəmʌŋgə(r)/ n allarmista mf

scaremongering /'skeəmʌŋgərɪŋ/ n allarmismo m

scarf /skɑːf/ n (pl **scarves**) sciarpa f; (square) foulard m inv

scarlet /'skɑːlət/ adj scarlatto

scarlet fever n scarlattina f

scarper /'skɑːpə(r)/ vi Br fam squagliarsela

scart connector /skɑːt/ n presa f scart inv

scar tissue n tessuto m di cicatrizzazione

scary /'skeərɪ/ adj be ~ far paura

scathing /'skeɪðɪŋ/ adj mordace

scatter /'skætə(r)/ **1** vt spargere; (disperse) disperdere **2** vi disperdersi

S

scatterbrained /'skætəbreɪnd/ adj fam scervellato

scattered /'skætəd/ adj sparso

scatty /'skætɪ/ adj (-ier, -iest) fam svitato

scavenge /'skævɪndʒ/ vi frugare nella spazzatura

scavenger /'skævɪndʒə(r)/ n persona f che fruga nella spazzatura

scenario /sɪ'nɑːrɪəʊ/ n scenario m

scene /siːn/ n scena f; (quarrel) scenata f; **behind the** ∼**s** dietro le quinte

scene-of-crime adj ⟨officer, team, investigation⟩ della polizia scientifica

scenery /'siːnərɪ/ n scenario m

scenic /'siːnɪk/ adj panoramico

scent /sent/ n odore m; (trail) scia f; (perfume) profumo m

scented /'sentɪd/ adj profumato (**with** di)

sceptic /'skeptɪk/ n scettico, -a mf

sceptical /'skeptɪkl/ adj scettico

sceptically /'skeptɪklɪ/ adv in modo scettico

scepticism /'skeptɪsɪzm/ n scetticismo m

schedule /'ʃedjuːl/ ① n piano m, programma m; (of work) programma m; (Am: timetable) orario m; **behind** ∼ indietro; **on** ∼ nei tempi previsti; **according to** ∼ secondo i tempi previsti
② vt prevedere

scheduled flight /ʃedjuːld'flaɪt/ n volo m di linea

schematic /skɪ'mætɪk/ adj schematico

scheme /skiːm/ ① n (plan) piano m; (plot) macchinazione f
② vi pej macchinare

scheming /'skiːmɪŋ/ ① n pej macchinazioni fpl, intrighi mpl
② adj ⟨person⟩ intrigante

schism /'skɪzm/ n scisma m

schizophrenia /skɪtsə'friːnɪə/ n schizofrenia f

schizophrenic adj schizofrenico

schmaltzy /'ʃmɒltsɪ/ adj sdolcinato

scholar /'skɒlə(r)/ n studioso, -a mf

scholarly /'skɒləlɪ/ adj erudito

scholarship /'skɒləʃɪp/ n erudizione f; (grant) borsa f di studio

scholastic /skə'læstɪk/ adj scolastico

school /skuːl/ ① n scuola f; (in university) facoltà f; (of fish) banco m
② vt addestrare ⟨animal⟩

school age n **of** ∼ ∼ in età scolare

schoolbag n cartella f di scuola

schoolboy n scolaro m

schoolchild n scolaro, -a mf

schooldays npl tempi mpl della scuola

school fees npl tasse fpl scolastiche

schoolfriend n compagno, -a mf di scuola

schoolgirl n scolara f

schooling /'skuːlɪŋ/ n istruzione f

school leaver n ≈ neo diplomato, -a mf

school-leaving age n età f della scuola dell'obbligo

school lunch n pranzo m della mensa scolastica

schoolmaster n maestro m; (secondary) insegnante m

schoolmistress n maestra f; (secondary) insegnante f

school report n scheda f di valutazione scolastica

schoolteacher n insegnante mf

schoolwork n lavoro m scolastico

schooner /'skuːnə(r)/ n (Am: glass) boccale m da birra; (Br: glass) grande bicchiere m da sherry; (boat) goletta f

sciatica /saɪ'ætɪkə/ n sciatica f

science /'saɪəns/ n scienza f

science fiction n fantascienza f

scientific /saɪən'tɪfɪk/ adj scientifico

scientifically /saɪən'tɪfɪklɪ/ adv scientificamente

scientist /'saɪəntɪst/ n scienziato, -a mf

sci-fi /'saɪfaɪ/ n fam fantascienza f

scintillate /'sɪntɪleɪt/ vi fig brillare

scintillating /'sɪntɪleɪtɪŋ/ adj brillante

scissors /'sɪzəz/ npl forbici fpl

scoff[1] /skɒf/ vi ∼ **at** schernire

scoff[2] vt fam divorare

scold /skəʊld/ vt sgridare

scolding /'skəʊldɪŋ/ n sgridata f

scollop /'skɒləp/ = SCALLOP

scone /skɒn/ n pasticcino m da tè

scoop /skuːp/ n paletta f; Journ scoop m inv
■ **scoop out** vt svuotare
■ **scoop up** vt tirar su

scoot /skuːt/ vi fam filare

scooter /'skuːtə(r)/ n motoretta f

scope /skəʊp/ n portata f; (opportunity) opportunità f inv

scorch /skɔːtʃ/ vt bruciare

scorcher /'skɔːtʃə(r)/ n fam giornata f torrida

scorching /'skɔːtʃɪŋ/ adj caldissimo

score /skɔː(r)/ ① n punteggio m; Mus partitura f; (for film, play) musica f; **a** ∼ **[of]** (twenty) una ventina [di]; **keep [the]** ∼ tenere il punteggio; **on that** ∼ a questo proposito
② vt segnare ⟨goal⟩; (cut) incidere
③ vi far punti; (in football etc) segnare; (keep score) tenere il punteggio
■ **score out** vt cancellare

scoreboard *n* /'skɔːbɔːd/ tabellone *m* segnapunti

scorer /'skɔːrə(r)/ *n* segnapunti *m inv*; (of goals) giocatore, -trice *mf* che segna; **top** ∼ cannoniere *m*

scorn /skɔːn/ ① *n* disprezzo *m*
② *vt* disprezzare

scornful /'skɔːnfʊl/ *adj* sprezzante

scornfully /'skɔːnfʊlɪ/ *adv* sdegnosamente

Scorpio /'skɔːpɪəʊ/ *n* Astr Scorpione *m*

scorpion /'skɔːpɪən/ *n* scorpione *m*

Scot /skɒt/ *n* scozzese *mf*

Scotch /skɒtʃ/ ① *adj* scozzese
② *n* (whisky) whisky *m* [scozzese]

scotch /skɒtʃ/ *vt* far cessare

Scotch egg *n* Br polpetta *f* di salsiccia che racchiude un uovo sodo

Scotch tape *n* Am scotch® *m inv*

scot-free *adj* **get off** ∼ cavarsela impunemente

Scotland /'skɒtlənd/ *n* Scozia *f*

Scots, Scottish /skɒts/, /'skɒtɪʃ/ *adj* scozzese

scoundrel /'skaʊndrəl/ *n* mascalzone *m*

scour¹ /'skaʊə(r)/ *vt* (search) perlustrare

scour² *vt* (clean) strofinare

scourer /'skaʊərə(r)/ *n* (pad) paglietta *f*

scourge /skɜːdʒ/ *n* flagello *m*

scouring pad /'skaʊərɪŋ/ *n* paglietta *f* in lana d'acciaio

Scout *n* **[Boy]** ∼ **[boy]scout** *m inv*

scout /skaʊt/ ① *n* Mil esploratore *m*
② *vi or* **scout around for** andare in cerca di

scowl /skaʊl/ ① *n* sguardo *m* torvo
② *vi* guardare storto

Scrabble® /'skræbl/ *n* Scarabeo® *m*
■ **scrabble around** *vi* (search) cercare a tastoni

scraggy /'skrægrɪ/ *adj* (**-ier, -iest**) pej scarno

scram /skræm/ *vi* fam levarsi dai piedi

scramble /'skræmbl/ ① *n* (climb) arrampicata *f*
② *vi* (clamber) arrampicarsi; ∼ **for** azzuffarsi per
③ *vt* Teleph creare delle interferenze in; (eggs) strapazzare

scrambled eggs /'skræmbəld/ *npl* uova *fpl* strapazzate

scrambler /'skræmblə(r)/ *n* (Br: motorcyclist) [moto]crossista *mf*

scrambling /'skræmblɪŋ/ *n* (sport) motocross *m*

scrap¹ /skræp/ *n* (fam: fight) litigio *m*

scrap² ① *n* pezzetto *m*; (metal) ferraglia *f*; ∼**s** *pl* (of food) avanzi *mpl*
② *vt* (pt/pp **scrapped**) buttare via

scrapbook /'skræpbʊk/ *n* album *m inv*

scrape /skreɪp/ *vt* raschiare; (damage) graffiare
■ **scrape by** *vi* (financially) sbarcare il lunario
■ **scrape in** *vi* (to university, school) entrare per il rotto della cuffia
■ **scrape out** *vt* (empty) svuotare (bowl); (clean) scrostare (pan)
■ **scrape through** *vi* passare per un pelo
■ **scrape together** *vt* racimolare

scraper /'skreɪpə(r)/ *n* raschietto *m*

scrap heap *n* be on the ∼ ∼ fig essere inutile

scrap iron *n* ferraglia *f*

scrap merchant *n* ferrovecchio *m*

scrap paper *n* carta *f* qualsiasi

scrappy /'skræpɪ/ *adj* frammentario

scrapyard /'skræpjɑːd/ *n* deposito *m* di ferraglia; (for cars) cimitero *m* delle macchine

scratch /skrætʃ/ ① *n* graffio *m*; (to relieve itch) grattata *f*; **start from** ∼ partire da zero; **up to** ∼ (work) all'altezza
② *vt* graffiare; (to relieve itch) grattare
③ *vi* grattarsi

scratch card *n* gratta e vinci *m inv*

scratchy /'skrætʃɪ/ *adj* (recording) pieno di fruscii

scrawl /skrɔːl/ ① *n* scarabocchio *m*
② *vt/i* scarabocchiare

scrawny /'skrɔːnɪ/ *adj* (**-ier, -iest**) pej magro

scream /skriːm/ ① *n* strillo *m*; **be a** ∼ fam (situation, film, person) essere uno spasso
② *vt/i* strillare

scree /skriː/ *n* ghiaione *m*

screech /skriːtʃ/ ① *n* stridore *m*; ∼ **of** tyres sgommata *f*
② *vi* stridere
③ *vt* strillare

screen /skriːn/ ① *n* paravento *m*; Cinema, TV, Comput schermo *m*
② *vt* proteggere; (conceal) riparare; proiettare (film); passare al setaccio (candidates); Med sottoporre a visita medica

screening /'skriːnɪŋ/ *n* Med visita *f* medica; (of film) proiezione *f*

screenplay *n* sceneggiatura *f*

screen saver *n* Comput salvaschermo *m*

screen test *n* Cinema provino *m*

screen-writer *n* Cinema sceneggiatore, -trice *mf*

screw /skruː/ ① *n* vite *f*
② *vt* avvitare; vulg trombare; ∼ something to something avvitare qualcosa a qualcosa
■ **screw up** *vt* (crumple) accartocciare; strizzare (eyes); storcere (face); (sl: bungle) ··⟶

mandare all'aria; ∼ **up one's courage** prendere il coraggio a due mani

screwdriver /'skruːdraɪvə(r)/ n cacciavite m inv

screwed up /skruːd/ adj fam incasinato

screw top n tappo m a vite

screwy /'skruːɪ/ adj (**-ier, -iest**) fam svitato

scribble /'skrɪbl/ ① n scarabocchio m ② vt/i scarabocchiare

scrimmage /'skrɪmɪdʒ/ n (struggle) zuffa f; (Am: in football) mischia f

scrimp /skrɪmp/ vi risparmiare; ∼ **and save** risparmiare fino all'osso; ∼ **on something** risparmiare su qualcosa

script /skrɪpt/ n scrittura f; (of film etc) sceneggiatura f

Scriptures /'skrɪptʃəz/ npl Sacre Scritture fpl

scriptwriter /'skrɪptraɪtə(r)/ n sceneggiatore, -trice mf

scroll /skrəʊl/ ① n rotolo m (di pergamena); (decoration) voluta f ② vi Comput far scorrere
■ **scroll down** Comput vi scorrere in giù
■ **scroll up** Comput vi scorrere in su

scroll bar n Comput barra f di scorrimento

Scrooge /skruːdʒ/ n fam tirchio, -a mf

scrotum /'skrəʊtəm/ n scroto m

scrounge /skraʊndʒ/ vt/i scroccare

scrounger /'skraʊndʒə(r)/ n scroccone, -a mf

scrub¹ /skrʌb/ n (land) boscaglia f

scrub² vt/i (pt/pp **scrubbed**) strofinare; (fam: cancel) cancellare ⟨plan⟩
■ **scrub up** vi ⟨doctor⟩ lavarsi; fam ∼ **up well** fare un figurone

scrubbing brush /'skrʌbɪŋ/ n spazzolone m

scruff /skrʌf/ n **by the** ∼ **of the neck** per la collottola

scruffy /'skrʌfɪ/ adj (**-ier, -iest**) trasandato

scrum /skrʌm/ n (in rugby) mischia f

scrum half n mediano m di mischia

scrunch /skrʌntʃ/ ① vi ⟨footsteps in snow, tyres⟩ scricchiolare ② n scricchiolio m
■ **scrunch up** vt accartocciare

scrunchie /'skrʌntʃɪ/ n fermacoda m inv di stoffa

scruple /'skruːpl/ n scrupolo m; **have no** ∼**s** essere senza scrupoli

scrupulous /'skruːpjʊləs/ adj scrupoloso

scrupulously /'skruːpjʊləslɪ/ adv scrupolosamente

scrutinize /'skruːtɪnaɪz/ vt scrutinare

scrutiny /'skruːtɪnɪ/ n (look) esame m minuzioso

scuba diver /'skuːbə/ n sommozzatore, -trice mf

scuba diving n immersione f subacquea

scud /skʌd/ vi (pt/pp **scudded**) ⟨clouds⟩ muoversi velocemente

scuff /skʌf/ vt strascicare ⟨one's feet⟩

scuffle /'skʌfl/ n tafferuglio m

scull /skʌl/ ① vi (with two oars) vogare di coppia; (with one oar) vogare a bratto ② n (boat) imbarcazione f da regata con un vogatore

scullery /'skʌlərɪ/ n retrocucina m inv

sculpt /skʌlpt/ vt/i scolpire

sculptor /'skʌlptə(r)/ n scultore m

sculpture /'skʌlptʃə(r)/ n scultura f

scum /skʌm/ n schiuma f; (people) feccia f

scurrilous /'skʌrɪləs/ adj scurrile

scurry /'skʌrɪ/ vi (pt/pp **-ied**) affrettare il passo

scuttle¹ /'skʌtl/ n secchio m per il carbone

scuttle² vt affondare ⟨ship⟩

scuttle³ vi (hurry) ∼ **away** correre via

scythe /saɪð/ n falce f

SE abbr (**south-east**) SE

sea /siː/ n mare m; **at** ∼ in mare; fig confuso; **by** ∼ via mare; **by the** ∼ sul mare

seabed n fondale m marino

seabird n uccello m marino

seaboard n costiera f

seafaring adj ⟨nation⟩ marinaro

seafood n frutti mpl di mare

seafront n lungomare m

seagull n gabbiano m

sea horse n cavalluccio m marino

SEAL /siːl/ n abbr Am (**sea, air, land**) reparti mpl speciali delle forze armate

seal¹ /siːl/ n Zool foca f

seal² ① n sigillo m; Techn chiusura f ermetica ② vt sigillare; Techn chiudere ermeticamente
■ **seal off** vt bloccare ⟨area⟩

sea level n livello m del mare; **above** ∼ ∼ sopra il livello del mare

sealing wax /'siːlɪŋ/ n ceralacca f

sea lion n leone m marino

seam /siːm/ n cucitura f; (of coal) strato m

seaman /'siːmən/ n marinaio m

seamless /'siːmlɪs/ adj senza cucitura

seamy /'siːmɪ/ adj ⟨scandal⟩ sordido; ⟨area⟩ malfamato

seance /'seɪɑːns/ n seduta f spiritica

seaplane /'siːpleɪn/ n idrovolante m

s

seaport /'si:pɔ:t/ *n* porto *m* di mare

sear /sɪə(r)/ *vt* cauterizzare ⟨*wound*⟩; rosolare [a fuoco vivo] ⟨*meat*⟩; (scorch) bruciacchiare

search /sɜ:tʃ/ **1** *n* ricerca *f*; (official) perquisizione *f*; **in** ∼ **of** alla ricerca di **2** *vt* frugare (**for** alla ricerca di); perlustrare ⟨*area*⟩; (officially) perquisire **3** *vi* ∼ **for** cercare

search and replace *n* Comput ricerca *f* e sostituzione

search engine *n* Comput motore *m* di ricerca

searching /'sɜ:tʃɪŋ/ *adj* penetrante

searchlight *n* riflettore *m*

search party *n* squadra *f* di ricerca

search warrant *n* mandato *m* di perquisizione

searing /'sɪərɪŋ/ *adj* bruciante; ⟨*pace*⟩ travolgente; ⟨*pain*⟩ lancinante

sea salt *n* sale *m* marino

seascape *n* paesaggio *m* marino

seashell *n* conchiglia *f*

seashore *n* spiaggia *f*

seasick *adj* be/get ∼ avere il mal di mare

seaside *n* at/to the ∼ al mare

seaside resort *n* stazione *f* balneare

seaside town *n* città *f* di mare

season /'si:zn/ **1** *n* stagione *f*; **in** ∼ ⟨*fruit*⟩ di stagione; ⟨*animal*⟩ in calore **2** *vt* (flavour) condire

seasonal /'si:zənəl/ *adj* stagionale

seasoned /'si:znd/ *adj* Culin ⟨*dish*⟩ condito; ⟨*timber*⟩ stagionato; ⟨*actor, politician*⟩ consumato; ⟨*leader*⟩ di provata capacità; ∼ **traveller** persona *f* che ha viaggiato molto; ∼ **soldier** veterano *m*

seasoning /'si:z(ə)nɪŋ/ *n* condimento *m*

season ticket *n* abbonamento *m*

seat /si:t/ **1** *n* (chair) sedia *f*; (in car) sedile *m*; (place to sit) posto *m* [a sedere]; (bottom) didietro *m*; (of government) sede *f*; **take a** ∼ sedersi **2** *vt* mettere a sedere; (have seats for) aver posti [a sedere] per; **remain** ∼**ed** mantenere il proprio posto

seat belt *n* cintura *f* di sicurezza; **fasten one's** ∼ ∼ allacciare la cintura di sicurezza

seating /'si:tɪŋ/ *n* (places) posti *mpl* a sedere; (arrangement) disposizione *f* dei posti a sedere

seating capacity *n* numero *m* dei posti a sedere

sea urchin *n* riccio *m* di mare

sea view *n* vista *f* sul mare

seaweed *n* alga *f* marina

seaworthy *adj* in stato di navigare

sec /sek/ *n* (fam: short instant) attimo *m*, secondo *m*; abbr (**second**) s

secateurs /sekə'tɜ:z/ *npl* cesoie *fpl*

secede /sɪ'si:d/ *vi* staccarsi

secession /sɪ'seʃn/ *n* secessione *f*

secluded /sɪ'klu:dɪd/ *adj* appartato

seclusion /sɪ'klu:ʒn/ *n* isolamento *m*

second¹ /sɪ'kɒnd/ *vt* (transfer) distaccare

second² /'sekənd/ **1** *adj* secondo; **in** ∼ **gear** Auto in seconda; **on** ∼ **thoughts** ripensandoci meglio; **be having** ∼ **thoughts** ripensarci; **2** *n* secondo *m*; ∼**s** *pl* (goods) merce *fsg* di seconda scelta; **have** ∼**s** (at meal) fare il bis; **John the S**∼ Giovanni Secondo **3** *adv* (in race) al secondo posto **4** *vt* assistere; appoggiare ⟨*proposal*⟩

secondary /'sekəndrɪ/ *adj* secondario

secondary school *n* ≈ scuola *f* media (inferiore e superiore)

second-best *adj* secondo dopo il migliore; **be** ∼ pej essere un ripiego

second-class *adj* di seconda classe

second class *adv* ⟨*travel, send*⟩ in seconda classe

seconder /'sekəndə(r)/ *n* (of motion) persona *f* che appoggia una mozione

second-guess *vt* anticipare

second hand *n* (on watch, clock) lancetta *f* dei secondi

second-hand **1** *adj* ⟨*car, goods, news, information*⟩ di seconda mano; ⟨*clothes*⟩ usato; ⟨*market*⟩ dell'usato; ⟨*opinion*⟩ preso a prestito **2** *adv* ⟨*sell*⟩ di seconda mano

second in command *n* vice *mf inv*; Mil vicecomandante *m*

secondly /'sekəndlɪ/ *adv* in secondo luogo

secondment /sɪ'kɒndmənt/ *n* **on** ∼ in trasferta

second name *n* (surname) cognome *m*; (middle name) secondo nome *m*

second-rate *adj* di second'ordine

secrecy /'si:krəsɪ/ *n* segretezza *f*; **in** ∼ in segreto

secret /'si:krɪt/ **1** *adj* segreto **2** *n* segreto *m*; **make no** ∼ **of something** non fare mistero di qualcosa

secret agent *n* agente *m* segreto

secretarial /sekrə'teərɪəl/ *adj* ⟨*work, staff*⟩ di segreteria

secretariat /sekrə'teərɪət/ *n* segretariato *m*

secretary /'sekrətərɪ/ *n* segretario, -a *mf*

Secretary of State *n* Segretario *m* di Stato; Am Pol ministro *m* degli Esteri

secret ballot *n* scrutinio *m* segreto, votazione *f* a scrutinio segreto

s

secrete /sɪˈkriːt/ *vt* secernere ⟨*poison*⟩

secretion /sɪˈkriːʃn/ *n* secrezione *f*

secretive /ˈsiːkrətɪv/ *adj* riservato

secretly /ˈsiːkrɪtlɪ/ *adv* segretamente

secretness /ˈsiːkrɪtnɪs/ *n* riserbo *m*

secret police *n* polizia *f* segreta

secret service *n* servizi *mpl* segreti

secret society *n* società *f* segreta

secret weapon *n* arma *f* segreta

sect /sekt/ *n* setta *f*

sectarian /sekˈteərɪən/ *n & adj* settario, -a *mf*

section /ˈsekʃn/ *n* sezione *f*

sector /ˈsektə(r)/ *n* settore *m*

secular /ˈsekjʊlə(r)/ *adj* secolare; ⟨*education*⟩ laico

secure /sɪˈkjʊə(r)/ ① *adj* sicuro ② *vt* proteggere; chiudere bene ⟨*door*⟩; rendere stabile ⟨*ladder*⟩; (obtain) assicurarsi

securely /sɪˈkjʊəlɪ/ *adv* saldamente

secure unit *n* (in psychiatric hospital, prison) reparto *m* di massima sicurezza

security /sɪˈkjʊərətɪ/ *n* sicurezza *f*; (for loan) garanzia *f*; **securities** *pl* titoli *mpl*

Security Council *n* (of the UN) Consiglio *m* di Sicurezza

security guard *n* guardia *f* giurata

security leak *n* fuga *f* di notizie

security risk *n* be a ~ ~ costituire un pericolo per la sicurezza

sedan /sɪˈdæn/ *n* Am berlina *f*

sedate[1] /sɪˈdeɪt/ *adj* posato

sedate[2] *vt* somministrare sedativi a

sedately /sɪˈdeɪtlɪ/ *adv* in modo posato

sedation /sɪˈdeɪʃn/ *n* somministrazione *f* di sedativi; **be under** ~ essere sotto l'effetto di sedativi

sedative /ˈsedətɪv/ ① *adj* sedativo ② *n* sedativo *m*

sedentary /ˈsedəntərɪ/ *adj* sedentario

sediment /ˈsedɪmənt/ *n* sedimento *m*

seduce /sɪˈdjuːs/ *vt* sedurre

seduction /sɪˈdʌkʃn/ *n* seduzione *f*

seductive /sɪˈdʌktɪv/ *adj* seducente

seductively /sɪˈdʌktɪvlɪ/ *adv* con aria seducente

see[1] /siː/ ① *vt* (pt **saw**, pp **seen**) vedere; (understand) capire; (escort) accompagnare; **go and** ~ andare a vedere; (visit) andare a trovare; ~ **you!** ci vediamo!; ~ **you later!** a più tardi!; ~**ing that** visto che; ~ **somebody to the door** accompagnare qualcuno alla porta; **I can't** ~ **myself doing this forever** non mi ci vedo a farlo per sempre; **I can't think what she** ~**s in him** non capisco cosa trovi in lui; ~ **reason** ragionare; **you're** ~**ing things** hai le traveggole

② *vi* vedere; (understand) capire; ~ **that** (make sure) assicurarsi che; **let me** ~ (think) fammi pensare; **I** ~ (understand) ho capito
■ **see about** *vt* occuparsi di
■ **see off** *vt* salutare alla partenza; (chase away) mandar via
■ **see out** *vt* ~ **somebody out** accompagnare qualcuno alla porta
■ **see through** ① *vi* vedere attraverso; fig non farsi ingannare da ② *vt* portare a buon fine
■ **see to** *vi* occuparsi di

see[2] *n* Relig diocesi *f inv*

seed /siːd/ *n* seme *m*; Tennis testa *f* di serie; **go to** ~ fare seme; fig lasciarsi andare

seeded player /ˈsiːdɪd/ *n* Tennis testa *f* di serie

seedless /ˈsiːdlɪs/ *adj* senza semi

seedling /ˈsiːdlɪŋ/ *n* pianticella *f*

seedy /ˈsiːdɪ/ *adj* (**-ier**, **-iest**) squallido; **feel** ~ fam sentirsi poco bene

seek /siːk/ *vt* (pt/pp **sought**) cercare
■ **seek out** *vt* scovare

seeker /ˈsiːkə(r)/ *n* ~ **after** or **for something** persona *f* che è alla ricerca di qualcosa; **gold** ~ cercatore, -trice *mf* d'oro

seem /siːm/ *vi* sembrare

seeming /ˈsiːmɪŋ/ *adj* apparente

seemingly /ˈsiːmɪŋlɪ/ *adv* apparentemente

seemly /ˈsiːmlɪ/ *adj* decoroso

seen /siːn/ ▶ SEE[1]

seep /siːp/ *vi* filtrare

seepage /ˈsiːpɪdʒ/ *n* (leak: from container) perdita *f*; Geol trasudamento *m* superficiale; (trickle) lenta fuoriuscita *f*; (into structure, soil) infiltrazione *f*

see-saw /ˈsiːsɔː/ *n* altalena *f*

seethe /siːð/ *vi* ~ **with anger** ribollire di rabbia

see-through *adj* trasparente

segment /ˈsegmənt/ *n* segmento *m*; (of orange) spicchio *m*

segregate /ˈsegrɪgeɪt/ *vt* segregare

segregated /ˈsegrɪgeɪtɪd/ *adj* segregazionistico

segregation /segrɪˈgeɪʃn/ *n* segregazione *f*

seismic /ˈsaɪzmɪk/ *adj* sismico

seismograph /ˈsaɪzməgrɑːf/ *n* sismografo *m*

seismology /saɪzˈmɒlədʒɪ/ *n* sismologia *f*

seize /siːz/ *vt* afferrare; Jur confiscare; ~ **the opportunity** prendere la palla al balzo
■ **seize up** *vi* Techn bloccarsi

seizure /ˈsiːʒə(r)/ *n* Jur confisca *f*; Med colpo *m* [apoplettico]

seldom /ˈseldəm/ *adv* raramente

select /sɪˈlekt/ **1** *adj* scelto; (exclusive) esclusivo
2 *vt* scegliere; selezionare ⟨*team*⟩
selection /sɪˈlekʃn/ *n* selezione *f*
selective /sɪˈlektɪv/ *adj* selettivo
selectively /sɪˈlektɪvlɪ/ *adv* con criterio
selector /sɪˈlektə(r)/ *n* Sport selezionatore, -trice *mf*
self /self/ *n* io *m*
self-addressed *adj* con il proprio indirizzo
self-addressed envelope *n* busta *f* affrancata con il proprio indirizzo
self-adhesive *adj* autoadesivo
self-analysis *n* autoanalisi *f*
self-assembly *adj* da montare
self-assurance *n* sicurezza *f* di sé
self-assured *adj* sicuro di sé
self-catering *adj* in appartamento attrezzato di cucina
self-centred *adj* egocentrico
self-cleaning *adj* ⟨*oven*⟩ autopulente
self-confessed *adj* dichiarato
self-confidence *n* fiducia *f* in se stesso
self-confident *adj* sicuro di sé
self-conscious *adj* impacciato
self-contained *adj* ⟨*flat*⟩ con ingresso indipendente
self-control *n* autocontrollo *m*
self-defence *n* autodifesa *f*; Jur legittima difesa *f*
self-denial *n* abnegazione *f*
self-destruct *vi* ⟨*missile, spacecraft*⟩ autodistruggersi
self-destruction *n* autodistruzione *f*; fig autolesionismo *m*
self-destructive *adj* autodistruttivo
self-determination *n* autodeterminazione *f*
self-discipline *n* autodisciplina *f*
self-disciplined *adj* disciplinato
self-effacing /-ɪˈfeɪsɪŋ/ *adj* modesto, schivo
self-employed *adj* che lavora in proprio; the ∼ i lavoratori autonomi
self-esteem *n* stima *f* di sé
self-evident *adj* ovvio
self-explanatory *adj* be ∼ parlare da sé
self-expression *n* espressione *f* della propria personalità
self-financing /-faɪˈnænsɪŋ/ *n* autofinanziamento *m*
self-governing /-ˈɡʌvənɪŋ/ *adj* autonomo
self-government *n* autogoverno *m*
self-harm *n* autolesionismo *m*
self-help *n* iniziativa *f* personale

self-image *n* immagine *f* di sé
self-important *adj* borioso
self-imposed /-ɪmˈpəʊzd/ *adj* autoimposto
self-improvement *n* crescita *f* personale
self-induced /ɪnˈdjuːsd/ *adj* autoindotto
self-indulgent *adj* indulgente con se stesso
self-inflicted *adj* Anna's problems are ∼ sono problemi che Anna si è creata da sé; ∼ wound autolesione *f*
self-interest *n* interesse *m* personale
self-interested *adj* interessato
selfish /ˈselfɪʃ/ *adj* egoista
selfishly /ˈselfɪʃlɪ/ *adv* egoisticamente
selfishness /ˈselfɪʃnɪs/ *n* egoismo *m*
selfless /ˈselflɪs/ *adj* disinteressato
selflessly /ˈselflɪslɪ/ *adv* disinteressatamente
selflessness /ˈselflɪsnɪs/ *n* disinteresse *m*
self-locking /-ˈlɒkɪŋ/ *adj* ⟨*door*⟩ a chiusura automatica
self-made *adj* che si è fatto da sé
self-pity *n* autocommiserazione *f*
self-portrait *n* autoritratto *m*
self-possessed /-pəˈzest/ *adj* padrone di sé
self-preservation *n* istinto *m* di conservazione
self-raising flour Br, **self-rising flour** Am /ˈreɪzɪŋ/, /ˈraɪzɪŋ/ *n* farina *f* contenente lievito
self-reliant *adj* autosufficiente
self-respect *n* amor *m* proprio
self-respecting *adj* di rispetto
self-righteous *adj* presuntuoso
self-rising flour Am = SELF-RAISING FLOUR
self-rule *n* autogoverno *m*
self-sacrifice *n* abnegazione *f*
selfsame *adj* stesso
self-satisfied *adj* compiaciuto di sé
self-service **1** *n* self-service *m inv*
2 *attrib* self-service
self-styled *adj* sedicente
self-sufficiency *n* autosufficienza *f*
self-sufficient *adj* autosufficiente
self-supporting *adj* ⟨*person*⟩ indipendente (economicamente)
self-tan *n* autoabbronzante *m*
self-tanning /-ˈtænɪŋ/ *adj* autoabbronzante
self-taught /-ˈtɔːt/ *adj* ⟨*person*⟩ autodidatta
self-willed /-ˈwɪld/ *adj* ostinato

S

sell /sel/ ① *vt* (*pt/pp* **sold**) vendere; **be sold out** essere esaurito; **~ somebody on the idea of...** fam convincere qualcuno di... ② *vi* vendersi
■ **sell off** *vt* liquidare
■ **sell out** *vi* (of tickets, goods) andare esaurito; **'sold out'** 'tutto esaurito'; **~ out of something** esaurire qualcosa; (on one's principles) vendersi
■ **sell up** *vi* liquidare i propri beni

sell-by date *n* data *f* di scadenza per la vendita

seller /'selə(r)/ *n* venditore, -trice *mf*

sellers' market /'seləzma:kɪt/ *n* mercato *m* al rialzo

selling /'selɪŋ/ ① *adj* ⟨price⟩ di vendita ② *n* vendita *f*

selling price *n* prezzo *m* di vendita

Sellotape® /'seləʊteɪp/ *n* nastro *m* adesivo, scotch® *m*

sell-out *n* (fam: betrayal) tradimento *m*; **be a ~** ⟨concert⟩ fare il tutto esaurito

selvage, selvedge /'selvɪdʒ/ *n* cimosa *f*

selves /selvz/ *pl of* self

semantic /sɪ'mæntɪk/ *adj* semantico

semantics /sɪ'mæntɪks/ *n* (subject) semantica *f*; **that's just ~** sono solo sfumature di significato

semblance /'sembləns/ *n* parvenza *f*

semen /'si:mən/ *n* Anat liquido *m* seminale

semester /sɪ'mestə(r)/ *n* Am semestre *m*

semi /'semɪ/ *n* (Br: house) villetta *f* bifamiliare; Am Auto autoarticolato *m*

semi+ *pref* semi+

semi-automatic *adj* semiautomatico

semibreve *n* Mus semibreve *f*

semicircle *n* semicerchio *m*

semicircular *adj* semicircolare

semicolon *n* punto e virgola *m*

semiconscious *adj* semiincosciente

semi-darkness *n* semioscurità *f*

semi-detached ① *adj* gemella ② *n* casa *f* gemella

semi-final *n* semifinale *f*

semifinalist *n* semifinalista *mf*

seminal /'semɪnəl/ *adj* (major) determinante

seminar /'semɪnɑ:(r)/ *n* seminario *m*

seminary /'semɪnərɪ/ *n* seminario *m*

semi-precious *adj* semiprezioso; **~ stone** pietra *f* dura

semi-skilled /-'skɪld/ *adj* qualificato

semi-skimmed /-'skɪmd/ *adj* parzialmente scremato

semitone *n* Mus semitono *m*

semolina /semə'li:nə/ *n* semolino *m*

senate /'senət/ *n* senato *m*

senator /'senətə(r)/ *n* senatore *m*

send /send/ *vt/i* (*pt/pp* **sent**) mandare; (by mail) spedire
■ **send away for** *vt* farsi spedire ⟨information etc⟩
■ **send down** *vt* (send to prison) mandare in galera
■ **send for** *vt* mandare a chiamare ⟨person⟩; far venire ⟨thing⟩
■ **send in** *vt* presentare ⟨application⟩; far entrare ⟨person⟩
■ **send off** *vt* spedire ⟨letter, parcel⟩; espellere ⟨footballer⟩
■ **send on** *vt* spedire ⟨luggage, letter, parcel⟩
■ **send out** *vt* emettere ⟨light, heat⟩; mandare fuori dalla porta ⟨pupil⟩
■ **send up** *vt* fam parodiare

sender /'sendə(r)/ *n* mittente *mf*; **return to ~** (on letter) rispedire al mittente

send-off *n* commiato *m*

send-up *n* Br: fam parodia *f*

Senegal /senɪ'gɔ:l/ *n* Senegal *m*

senile /'si:naɪl/ *adj* arteriosclerotico

senile dementia /dɪ'menʃə/ *n* demenza *f* senile

senility /sɪ'nɪlətɪ/ *n* senilismo *m*

senior /'si:nɪə(r)/ ① *adj* più vecchio; (in rank) superiore ② *n* (in rank) superiore *mf*; (in sport) senior *mf*; **she's two years my ~** è più vecchia di me di due anni

senior citizen *n* anziano, -a *mf*

senior high school *n* Am ≈ scuola superiore

seniority /si:nɪ'ɒrɪtɪ/ *n* anzianità *f* di servizio

senior management *n* alta dirigenza *f*

sensation /sen'seɪʃn/ *n* sensazione *f*; **cause a ~** fare scalpore

sensational /sen'seɪʃənəl/ *adj* sensazionale

sensationalist /sen'seɪʃənəlɪst/ *adj* ⟨headline, report⟩ sensazionalistico

sensationalize /sen'seɪʃənəlaɪz/ *vt* pej dare un tono scandalistico a

sensationally /sen'seɪʃənəlɪ/ *adv* in modo sensazionale

sense /sens/ ① *n* senso *m*; (common ~) buon senso *m*; **in a ~** in un certo senso; **make ~** aver senso ② *vt* sentire

senseless /'senslɪs/ *adj* insensato; (unconscious) privo di sensi

senselessly /'senslɪslɪ/ *adv* insensatamente

sensible /'sensəbl/ *adj* sensato; (suitable) appropriato

sensibly /'sensəblɪ/ *adv* in modo appropriato

sensitive /'sensətɪv/ *adj* sensibile; (touchy) suscettibile

sensitive data *n* dati *mpl* sensibili

sensitively /'sensətɪvlɪ/ *adv* con sensibilità

sensitivity /sensə'tɪvətɪ/ *n* sensibilità *f inv*

sensitize /'sensɪtaɪz/ *vt* **become ∼d to** (allergic to) diventare ipersensibile a

sensor /'sensə(r)/ *n* sensore *m*

sensory /'sensərɪ/ *adj* sensoriale

sensual /'sensjʊəl/ *adj* sensuale

sensuality /sensjʊ'ælətɪ/ *n* sensualità *f inv*

sensuous /'sensjʊəs/ *adj* voluttuoso

sent /sent/ ▶ SEND

sentence /'sentəns/ **1** *n* frase *f*; Jur sentenza *f*; (punishment) condanna *f* **2** *vt* ∼ **to** condannare a

sentiment /'sentɪmənt/ *n* sentimento *m*; (opinion) opinione *f*; (sentimentality) sentimentalismo *m*

sentimental /sentɪ'mentl/ *adj* sentimentale; pej sentimentalista

sentimentality /sentɪmen'tælətɪ/ *n* sentimentalità *f inv*

sentinel /'sentɪnəl/ *n* sentinella *f*

sentry /'sentrɪ/ *n* sentinella *f*

separable /'sepərəbl/ *adj* separabile

separate[1] /'sepərət/ *adj* separato

separate[2] /'sepəreɪt/ **1** *vt* separare **2** *vi* separarsi

separately /'sepərətlɪ/ *adv* separatamente

separates /'sepərəts/ *npl* [indumenti *npl*] coordinati *npl*

separation /sepə'reɪʃn/ *n* separazione *f*

separatist /'sepərətɪst/ *n & adj* separatista *mf*

sepia /'si:pɪə/ *n* (colour) seppia *m*

September /sep'tembə(r)/ *n* settembre *m*

septic /'septɪk/ *adj* settico; **go ∼** infettarsi

septicaemia /septɪ'si:mɪə/ *n* setticemia *f*

septic tank *n* fossa *f* biologica

sequel /'si:kwəl/ *n* seguito *m*

sequence /'si:kwəns/ *n* sequenza *f*; **in ∼** nell'ordine giusto

sequential /sɪ'kwenʃəl/ *adj* sequenziale

sequin /'si:kwɪn/ *n* lustrino *m*, paillette *f inv*

Serb /sɜ:b/ *adj & n* serbo, -a *mf*

Serbia /'sɜ:bɪə/ *n* Serbia *f*

Serbian /'sɜ:bɪən/ **1** *n* serbo, -a *mf*; (language) serbo *m* **2** *adj* serbo

Serbo-Croat[ian] /sɜ:bəʊ'krəʊæt/, /sɜ:bəʊkrəʊ'eɪʃən/ **1** *n* (language) serbo-croato *m* **2** *adj* serbo-croato

serenade /serə'neɪd/ **1** *n* serenata *f* **2** *vt* fare una serenata a

serene /sɪ'ri:n/ *adj* sereno

serenely /sɪ'ri:nlɪ/ *adv* serenamente

serenity /sɪ'renətɪ/ *n* serenità *inv*

sergeant /'sɑ:dʒənt/ *n* sergente *m*

sergeant major *n* sergente *m* maggiore

serial /'sɪərɪəl/ **1** *n* racconto *m* a puntate; TV sceneggiato *m* a puntate; Radio commedia *f* radiofonica a puntate **2** *adj* Comput seriale

serialize /'sɪərɪəlaɪz/ *vt* pubblicare a puntate; Radio, TV trasmettere a puntate

serial killer *n* serial killer *mf inv*

serial number *n* numero *m* di serie

serial port *n* Comput porta *f* seriale

series /'sɪəri:z/ *n* serie *f inv*

serious /'sɪərɪəs/ *adj* serio; ⟨illness, error⟩ grave

seriously /'sɪərɪəslɪ/ *adv* seriamente; ⟨ill⟩ gravemente; **take ∼** prendere sul serio

seriousness /'sɪərɪəsnɪs/ *n* serietà *f*; (of situation) gravità *f*

sermon /'sɜ:mən/ *n* predica *f*

seropositive /sɪərəʊ'pɒzɪtɪv/ *adj* sieropositivo

serotonin /serə'təʊnɪn/ *n* serotonina *f*

serpent /'sɜ:pənt/ *n* serpente *m*

serrated /se'reɪtɪd/ *adj* dentellato

serum /'sɪərəm/ *n* siero *m*

servant /'sɜ:vənt/ *n* domestico, -a *mf*

serve /sɜ:v/ **1** *n* Tennis servizio *m* **2** *vt* servire; Jur notificare ⟨writ⟩ (**on somebody** a qualcuno); scontare ⟨sentence⟩; ∼ **its purpose** servire al proprio scopo; **it ∼s you right!** ben ti sta!; ∼**s two** per due persone **3** *vi* prestare servizio; Tennis servire; ∼ **as** servire da

server /'sɜ:və(r)/ *n* (piece of cutlery) posata *f* da portata; (plate) piatto *m* da portata; (tray) vassoio *m* da portata; Sport giocatore, -trice *mf* che effettua il servizio; Comput server *m inv*

service /'sɜ:vɪs/ **1** *n* servizio *m*; Relig funzione *f*; (maintenance) revisione *f*; ∼**s** *pl* forze *fpl* armate; (on motorway) area *f* di servizio; **in the ∼s** sotto le armi; **of ∼ to** utile a; **out of ∼** ⟨machine⟩ guasto **2** *vt* Techn revisionare

serviceable /'sɜ:vɪsəbl/ *adj* utilizzabile; (hard-wearing) resistente; (practical) pratico

service area *n* area *f* di servizio

S

service centre Br, **service center** Am n (garage) officina f; (in shop) centro m di assistenza tecnica

service charge n servizio m

service company n compagnia f del settore terziario

service industry n industria f terziaria

serviceman n militare m

service provider n Comput fornitore m di servizi Internet

service road n strada f d'accesso

service station n stazione f di servizio

servicewoman n soldatessa f

serviette /sɜːvɪ'et/ n tovagliolo m

servile /'sɜːvaɪl/ adj servile

servility /sə'vɪlɪtɪ/ n servilismo m

serving /'sɜːvɪŋ/ 1 adj ⟨officer⟩ di carriera
2 n (helping) porzione f

serving dish n piatto m da portata

serving spoon n cucchiaio m da servizio

session /'seʃn/ n seduta f; Jur sessione f; Univ anno m accademico

set /set/ 1 n serie f inv, set m inv; (of crockery, cutlery) servizio m; TV, Radio apparecchio m; Math insieme m; Theat scenario m; Cinema, Tennis set m inv; (of people) circolo m; (of hair) messa f in piega
2 adj (ready) pronto; (rigid) fisso; ⟨book⟩ in programma; **be ∼ on doing something** essere risoluto a fare qualcosa; **be ∼ in one's ways** essere abitudinario
3 vt (pt/pp **set**, pres p **setting**) mettere, porre; mettere ⟨alarm clock⟩; assegnare ⟨task, homework⟩; fissare ⟨date, limit⟩; chiedere ⟨questions⟩; montare ⟨gem⟩; assestare ⟨bone⟩; apparecchiare ⟨table⟩; Typ comporre; **∼ fire to** dare fuoco a; **∼ free** liberare; **∼ a good example** dare il buon esempio; **∼ sail for** far vela per; **∼ in motion** dare inizio a; **∼ to music** musicare; **the film is ∼ in Rome/the 18th century** il film è ambientato a Roma/nel XVIII secolo; **∼ to music** musicare; **∼ about doing something** mettersi a fare qualcosa
4 vi ⟨sun⟩ tramontare; ⟨jelly, concrete⟩ solidificarsi; **∼ to work (on something)** mettersi al lavoro (su qualcosa)
■ **set apart** vt (distinguish) distinguere; **∼ somebody or something apart from** distinguere qualcuno o qualcosa da
■ **set aside** vt mettere da parte ⟨money, time⟩; riservare ⟨room, area⟩
■ **set back** vt mettere indietro; (hold up) ritardare; (fam: cost) costare a
■ **set down** vt (establish) stabilire ⟨rules, conditions⟩; (write down) scrivere ⟨facts⟩
■ **set in** vi ⟨rain, infection, recession⟩ prendere piede
■ **set off** 1 vi partire
2 vt avviare; mettere ⟨alarm⟩; fare esplodere ⟨bomb⟩
■ **set on** vt **∼ on somebody** (attack) aggredire qualcuno; **∼ the dogs on somebody** aizzare i cani contro qualcuno
■ **set out** 1 vi partire; **∼ out to do something** proporsi di fare qualcosa
2 vt disporre; (state) esporre
■ **set to** vi mettersi all'opera
■ **set up** vt fondare ⟨company⟩; istituire ⟨committee⟩

setback /'setbæk/ n (hitch) contrattempo m; Mil sconfitta f, scacco m; Fin tracollo m; (in health) ricaduta f

set design n scenografia f

set designer n scenografo, -a mf

set meal n menù m inv fisso

settee /se'tiː/ n divano m

setter /'setə(r)/ n (dog) setter m inv

setting /'setɪŋ/ n scenario m; (position) posizione f; (of sun) tramonto m; (of jewel) montatura f

setting-up n (of project, business) creazione f

settle /'setl/ 1 vt (decide) definire; risolvere ⟨argument⟩; fissare ⟨date⟩; calmare ⟨nerves⟩; saldare ⟨bill⟩; **that's ∼d then** allora è deciso
2 vi (live) stabilirsi; ⟨snow, dust, bird⟩ posarsi; (subside) assestarsi; ⟨sediment⟩ depositarsi
■ **settle down** vi sistemarsi; (stop making noise) calmarsi
■ **settle for** vt accontentarsi di
■ **settle in** vi (in new house, job) ambientarsi
■ **settle up** vi regolare i conti

settlement /'setlmənt/ n (agreement) accordo m; (of bill) saldo m; Comm liquidazione f; (colony) insediamento m

settler /'setlə(r)/ n colonizzatore, -trice mf

set-to n fam zuffa f; (verbal) battibecco m

set-top box n decoder m inv

set-up n situazione f

seven /'sevn/ adj & n sette m

seventeen /sevən'tiːn/ adj & n diciassette m

seventeenth /sevən'tiːn/ adj & n diciasettesimo, -a mf

seventh /'sevnθ/ adj & n settimo, -a mf

seventies /'sevntɪz/ npl (period) **the ∼** gli anni Settanta mpl; (age) settant'anni mpl; ▶ also FORTIES

seventieth /'sevntɪɪθ/ adj & n settantesimo, -a mf

seventy /'sevntɪ/ adj & n settanta m

seven-year itch n fam crisi f inv del settimo anno

sever /'sevə(r)/ vt troncare ⟨relations⟩

several /'sevrəl/ adj & pron parecchi

severance /'sev(ə)rəns/ n ~ **pay** trattamento m di fine rapporto

severe /sɪ'vɪə(r)/ adj severo; ⟨pain⟩ violento; ⟨illness⟩ grave; ⟨winter⟩ rigido

severe acute respiratory syndrome n Med sindrome f respiratoria acuta severa

severely /sɪ'vɪəlɪ/ adv severamente; ⟨ill⟩ gravemente

severity /sɪ'verətɪ/ n severità f; (of pain) violenza f; (of illness) gravità f; (of winter) rigore m

sew /səʊ/ vt/i (pt **sewed**, pp **sewn** or **sewed**) cucire
∎ **sew up** vt ricucire

sewage /'suːɪdʒ/ n acque fpl di scolo

sewer /'suːə(r)/ n fogna f

sewing /'səʊɪŋ/ n cucito m; (work) lavoro m di cucito

sewing machine n macchina f da cucire

sewn /səʊn/ ▶ SEW

sex /seks/ n sesso m; **have** ~ avere rapporti sessuali, fare l'amore

sex appeal n sex appeal m

sex change n **have a** ~ cambiare sesso

sex change operation n intervento m per il cambiamento di sesso

sex discrimination n discriminazione f sessuale

sex education n educazione f sessuale

sexism /'seksɪzm/ n sessismo m

sexist /'seksɪst/ adj sessista mf

sex life n vita f sessuale

sex maniac n maniaco m sessuale

sex object n oggetto m sessuale

sex offender n colpevole mf di delitti a sfondo sessuale

sextet /seks'tet/ n sestetto m

sex tourism n turismo m a scopo sessuale

sexual /'seksjʊəl/ adj sessuale

sexual abuse n abusi mpl sessuali

sexual assault n atti mpl di libidine violenta

sexual equality n parità f dei sessi

sexual harassment n molestie fpl sessuali

sexual intercourse n rapporti mpl sessuali

sexuality /seksjʊ'ælətɪ/ n sessualità f

sexually /'seksjʊəlɪ/ adv sessualmente; **be** ~ **assaulted** subire atti di libidine violenta

sexually transmitted disease /trænz'mɪtɪd/ n malattia f trasmissibile per via sessuale

sexy /'seksɪ/ adj (-ier, -iest) sexy inv

Seychelles /seɪ'ʃelz/ npl **the** ~ le Seychelles

sh /ʃ/ int silenzio!, sst!

shabbily /'ʃæbɪlɪ/ adv in modo scialbo; ⟨treat⟩ in modo meschino

shabbiness /'ʃæbɪnɪs/ n trasandatezza f; (of treatment) meschinità f

shabby /'ʃæbɪ/ adj (-ier, -iest) scialbo; ⟨treatment⟩ meschino

shack /ʃæk/ n catapecchia f

shackles /'ʃæklz/ npl catene fpl

shade /ʃeɪd/ ❶ n ombra f; (of colour) sfumatura f; (for lamp) paralume m; (Am: for window) tapparella f; **a** ~ **better** un tantino meglio
❷ vt riparare dalla luce; (draw lines on) ombreggiare

shades /ʃeɪdz/ npl fam occhiali mpl da sole

shading /'ʃeɪdɪŋ/ n (slight variation in colour) tonalità f inv; (to give effect of darkness) ombreggiature fpl

shadow /'ʃædəʊ/ ❶ n ombra f
❷ vt (follow) pedinare

shadow boxing n allenamento m di boxe con l'ombra

Shadow Cabinet n governo m ombra

shadowy /'ʃædəʊɪ/ adj (indistinct) confuso

shady /'ʃeɪdɪ/ adj (-ier, -iest) ombroso; (fam: disreputable) losco

shaft /ʃɑːft/ n Techn albero m; (of light) raggio m; (of lift, mine) pozzo m; ~**s** pl (of cart) stanghe fpl

shaggy /'ʃægɪ/ adj (-ier, -iest) irsuto; ⟨animal⟩ dal pelo arruffato

shaggy dog story n fam barzelletta f interminabile dal finale deludente

shake /ʃeɪk/ ❶ n scrollata f
❷ vt (pt **shook**, pp **shaken**) scuotere; agitare ⟨bottle⟩; far tremare ⟨building⟩; ~ **hands with** stringere la mano a; ~ **one's head** scuotere la testa
❸ vi tremare
∎ **shake off** vt scrollarsi di dosso
∎ **shake up** vt agitare ⟨bottle⟩; ⟨news, experience⟩ scuotere ⟨person⟩

shaken [up] /'ʃeɪkən/ adj (after accident etc) scosso

shaker /'ʃeɪkə(r)/ n (for salad) centrifuga f [asciugaverdure]; (for dice) bicchiere m; (for cocktails) shaker m inv; (for pepper) pepaiola f; (for salt) saliera f

shake-up n Pol rimpasto m; Comm ristrutturazione f

shakily /'ʃeɪkɪlɪ/ adv ⟨say something⟩ con voce tremante; ⟨walk⟩ con passo esitante

shaky /'ʃeɪkɪ/ adj (-ier, -iest) tremante; ⟨table etc⟩ traballante; (unreliable) vacillante

shall /ʃæl/ v aux **I** ~ **go** andrò; **we** ~ **see** vedremo; **what** ~ **I do?** cosa faccio?; **I'll come too,** ~ **I?** vengo anch'io, no?; **thou shalt not kill** liter non uccidere; **passengers** ⋯⋗

~ **remain seated** i passeggeri devono rimanere seduti

shallot /ʃə'lɒt/ n scalogno m

shallow /'ʃæləʊ/ adj basso, poco profondo; ⟨dish⟩ poco profondo; fig superficiale

shallows /'ʃæləʊz/ npl secche fpl

sham /ʃæm/ ① adj falso
② n finzione f; (person) spaccone, -a mf
③ vt (pt/pp **shammed**) simulare

shambles /'ʃæmblz/ n caos msg

shame /ʃeɪm/ n vergogna f; **it's a ~ that** è un peccato che; **what a ~!** che peccato!; **~ on you!** vergognati!; **put somebody/ something to ~** far sfigurare qualcuno/ qualcosa

shamefaced /ʃeɪm'feɪst/ adj vergognoso

shameful /'ʃeɪmfl/ adj vergognoso

shamefully /'ʃeɪmfʊlɪ/ adv vergognosamente

shameless /'ʃeɪmlɪs/ adj spudorato

shamelessly /'ʃeɪmlɪslɪ/ adv spudoratamente

shampoo /ʃæm'pu:/ ① n shampoo m inv; ~ **and set** shampoo m inv e messa in piega
② vt fare uno shampoo a ⟨carpet, person's hair etc⟩

shamrock /'ʃæmrɒk/ n trifoglio m (simbolo dell'Irlanda)

shandy /'ʃændɪ/ n bevanda f a base di birra e gassosa

shank /ʃæŋk/ n garretto m; (of knife) manico m; (of gold club) impugnatura f; (of screw) gambo m; (of anchor) fuso m; (of person) gamba f (dal ginocchio in giù)

shan't /ʃɑ:nt/ = shall not

shanty /'ʃæntɪ/ n (hut) baracca f; (song) marinaro

shanty town /'ʃæntɪtaʊn/ n bidonville f inv, baraccopoli f inv

shape /ʃeɪp/ ① n forma f; (figure) ombra f; **take ~** prendere forma; **get back in ~** ritornare in forma; **be out of ~** non essere in forma
② vt dare forma a (**into** di)
③ vi ~ **[up]** mettere la testa a posto; ~ **up nicely** mettersi bene

shapeless /'ʃeɪplɪs/ adj informe

shapely /'ʃeɪplɪ/ adj (-ier, -iest) ben fatto

shard /ʃɑ:d/ n frammento m; (of clay) coccio m

share /ʃeə(r)/ ① n porzione f; Comm azione f
② vt dividere; condividere ⟨views⟩
③ vi dividere; ~ **in** partecipare a
■ **share out** vt spartire; (including oneself) spartirsi

share capital n capitale m azionario

shared /ʃeəd/ adj ⟨house⟩ condiviso; ⟨bathroom⟩ in comune

share dealing n contrattazione f di azioni

shareholder n azionista mf

shareholding n titoli mpl azionari

share index n indice m azionario

share option scheme n partecipazione f agli utili dell'azienda tramite acquisto di azioni

shareware /'ʃeəweə/ n Comput shareware m inv

shark /ʃɑ:k/ n squalo m, pescecane m; fig truffatore, -trice mf

sharp /ʃɑ:p/ ① adj ⟨knife etc⟩ tagliente; ⟨pencil⟩ appuntito; ⟨drop⟩ a picco; ⟨reprimand⟩ severo; ⟨outline⟩ marcato; (alert) acuto; (unscrupulous) senza scrupoli; ~ **pain** fitta f
② adv **at three o'clock ~** alle tre in punto; **look ~!** sbrigati!
③ n Mus diesis m inv

sharpen /'ʃɑ:pn/ vt affilare ⟨knife⟩; appuntire ⟨pencil⟩

sharpener /'ʃɑ:pnə(r)/ n (for pencils) temperamatite m inv; (for knife) affilacoltelli m inv

sharply /'ʃɑ:plɪ/ adv ⟨turn, rise, fall⟩ bruscamente; ⟨speak⟩ in tono brusco

shatter /'ʃætə(r)/ vt frantumare; fig mandare in frantumi

shattered /'ʃætəd/ ① adj (fam: exhausted) a pezzi
② vi frantumarsi

shave /ʃeɪv/ ① n rasatura f; **have a ~** farsi la barba
② vt radere
③ vi radersi

shaver /'ʃeɪvə(r)/ n rasoio m elettrico

shaving brush /'ʃeɪvɪŋ/ n pennello m da barba

shaving foam n schiuma f da barba

shavings /'ʃeɪvɪŋz/ npl (of wood, metal) trucioli mpl

shaving soap n sapone m da barba

shawl /ʃɔ:l/ n scialle m

she /ʃi:/ pers pron lei; ~ **is tired** è stanca; **I'm going, but ~ is not** io vado, ma lei no

sheaf /ʃi:f/ n (pl **sheaves**) fascio m

shear /ʃɪə(r)/ vt (pt **sheared**, pp **shorn** or **sheared**) tosare

shears /ʃɪəz/ npl (for hedge) cesoie fpl

sheath /ʃi:θ/ n (pl ~**s** /ʃi:ðz/) guaina f

sheathe /ʃi:ð/ vt rifoderare; rivestire ⟨cable⟩

sheaves /ʃi:vz/ ▶ SHEAF

shed[1] /ʃed/ n baracca f; (for cattle) stalla f

shed[2] vt (pt/pp **shed**, pres p **shedding**) perdere; versare ⟨blood, tears⟩; ~ **light on** far luce su

shedload n Br: fam ~s of money un sacco di soldi

sheen /ʃiːn/ n lucentezza f

sheep /ʃiːp/ n inv pecora f

sheepdog /'ʃiːpdɒg/ n cane m da pastore

sheepish /'ʃiːpɪʃ/ adj imbarazzato

sheepishly /'ʃiːpɪʃlɪ/ adv con aria imbarazzata

sheepskin /'ʃiːpskɪn/ n [pelle f di] montone m

sheer /ʃɪə(r)/ ⓵ adj puro; (steep) a picco; (transparent) trasparente
⓶ adv a picco

sheet /ʃiːt/ n lenzuolo m; (of paper) foglio m; (of glass, metal) lastra f

sheet lightning n bagliore m diffuso dei lampi; (without a storm) lampi mpl di calore

sheet metal n lamiera f

sheet music n spartiti mpl

sheikh /ʃeɪk/, **sheik** n sceicco m

shelf /ʃelf/ n (pl shelves) ripiano m; (set of shelves) scaffale m

shelf-life n (of product) durata f di conservazione; (fig: of technology, pop music) durata f di vita; (fig: of politician, star) periodo m di gloria

shell /ʃel/ ⓵ n conchiglia f; (of egg, snail, tortoise) guscio m; (of crab) corazza f; (of unfinished building) ossatura f; Mil granata f
⓶ vt sgusciare ⟨peas⟩; Mil bombardare
■ **shell out** vi fam sborsare

shellfish n inv mollusco m; Culin frutti mpl di mare

shell-shocked /'ʃelʃɒkt/ adj ⟨soldier⟩ traumatizzato da un bombardamento; fig in stato di shock

shell suit n tuta f di acetato

shelter /'ʃeltə(r)/ ⓵ n rifugio m; (air raid ~) rifugio m antiaereo; **take** ~ rifugiarsi
⓶ vt riparare (**from** da); fig mettere al riparo; (give lodging to) dare asilo a
⓷ vi rifugiarsi

sheltered /'ʃeltəd/ adj ⟨spot⟩ riparato; ⟨life⟩ ritirato

sheltered accommodation n residenza f protetta

shelve /ʃelv/ ⓵ vt accantonare ⟨project⟩
⓶ vi ⟨slope⟩ scendere

shelves /ʃelvz/ ▶ SHELF

shelving /'ʃelvɪŋ/ n (shelves) ripiani mpl

shepherd /'ʃepəd/ ⓵ n pastore m
⓶ vt guidare

shepherdess /'ʃepədes/ n pastora f

shepherd's pie /ʃepədz'paɪ/ n pasticcio m di carne tritata e patate

sherbet /'sɜːbət/ n (Br: powder) polverina f effervescente al gusto di frutta; (Am: sorbet) sorbetto m

sheriff /'ʃerɪf/ n sceriffo m

Sherpa /'ʃɜːpə/ n scerpa m

sherry /'ʃerɪ/ n sherry m inv

shield /ʃiːld/ ⓵ n scudo m; (for eyes) maschera f; Techn schermo m
⓶ vt proteggere (**from** da)

shift /ʃɪft/ ⓵ n cambiamento m; (in position) spostamento m; (at work) turno m
⓶ vt spostare; (take away) togliere; riversare ⟨blame⟩
⓷ vi spostarsi; ⟨wind⟩ cambiare; (fam: move quickly) darsi una mossa

shift key n tasto m delle maiuscole

shiftless /'ʃɪftlɪs/ adj privo di risorse

shift work n turni mpl

shift worker n turnista mf

shifty /'ʃɪftɪ/ adj (-ier, -iest) pej losco; ⟨eyes⟩ sfuggente

Shiite /'ʃiːaɪt/ adj & n sciita mf

shilling /'ʃɪlɪŋ/ n scellino m

shilly-shally /'ʃɪlɪʃælɪ/ vi titubare

shimmer /'ʃɪmə(r)/ ⓵ n luccichio m
⓶ vi luccicare

shin /ʃɪn/ ⓵ n stinco m
⓶ vi ~ up/down something (climb) arrampicarsi su/scendere giù da qualcosa

shindig /'ʃɪndɪg/ n fam (party) baldoria f; (disturbance) pandemonio m

shindy /'ʃɪndɪ/ n fam (disturbance) pandemonio m; (party) baldoria f

shine /ʃaɪn/ ⓵ n lucentezza f; **give something a** ~ dare una lucidata a qualcosa
⓶ vi (pt/pp **shone**) splendere; (reflect light) brillare; ⟨hair, shoes⟩ essere lucido
⓷ vt ~ **a light on** puntare una luce su
■ **shine through** vi ⟨talent, ability⟩ trasparire

shingle /'ʃɪŋgl/ n (pebbles) ghiaia f

shingles /'ʃɪŋglz/ n Med fuoco m di Sant'Antonio

shin-guard n parastinchi m inv

shining /'ʃaɪnɪŋ/ adj ⟨eyes, jewel⟩ splendente; ⟨hair⟩ lucente **a** ~ **example** un fulgido esempio

shiny /'ʃaɪnɪ/ adj (-ier, -iest) lucido

ship /ʃɪp/ ⓵ n nave f
⓶ vt (pt, pp **-pped**) spedire; (by sea) spedire via mare

shipbuilder /'ʃɪpbɪldə(r)/ n costruttore m navale

shipbuilding /'ʃɪpbɪldɪŋ/ n costruzione f di navi

shipment /'ʃɪpmənt/ n spedizione f; (consignment) carico m

shipowner /'ʃɪpəʊnə(r)/ n armatore m

shipper /'ʃɪpə(r)/ n spedizioniere m

shipping /'ʃɪpɪŋ/ n trasporto m; (traffic) imbarcazioni fpl

shipping agent n spedizioniere m

shipping company n compagnia f di spedizione

shipshape adj & adv in perfetto ordine

shipwreck n naufragio m

shipwrecked naufragato

shipyard n cantiere m navale

shire /ʃaɪə(r)/ n Br contea f

shire-horse n cavallo m da tiro

shirk /ʃɜːk/ vt scansare

shirker /ˈʃɜːkə(r)/ n scansafatiche mf inv

shirt /ʃɜːt/ n camicia f; **in ∼-sleeves** in maniche di camicia

shirty /ˈʃɜːtɪ/ adj Br fam incavolato; **get ∼ with somebody** incavolarsi con qualcuno

shish kebab /ʃɪʃkɪˈbæb/ n spiedino m di carne e verdure

shit /ʃɪt/ vulg ① n & int merda f
② vi (pt/pp **shit**) cagare

shit-scared adj vulg **be ∼** farsela sotto

shiver /ˈʃɪvə(r)/ ① n brivido m
② vi rabbrividire

shoal /ʃəʊl/ n (of fish) banco m

shock /ʃɒk/ ① n (impact) urto m; Electr scossa f [elettrica]; fig colpo m, shock m inv; Med shock m inv; **get a ∼** Electr prendere la scossa; **in ∼** Med in stato di shock
② vt scioccare

shock absorber n Auto ammortizzatore m

shocking /ˈʃɒkɪŋ/ adj scioccante; fam ⟨weather, handwriting etc⟩ tremendo

shockingly /ˈʃɒkɪŋlɪ/ adv ⟨behave⟩ in modo pessimo; ⟨expensive⟩ eccessivamente

shocking pink n rosa m shocking

shockproof adj antiurto

shock treatment n terapia f d'urto

shock wave n onda f d'urto

shod /ʃɒd/ ▸ SHOE

shoddily /ˈʃɒdɪlɪ/ adv in modo scadente

shoddy /ˈʃɒdɪ/ adj (-ier, -iest) scadente

shoe /ʃuː/ ① n scarpa f; (of horse) ferro m
② vt (pt/pp **shod**, pres p **shoeing**) ferrare ⟨horse⟩

shoehorn n calzante m

shoelace n laccio m da scarpa

shoemaker n calzolaio m

shoe rack n scarpiera f

shoe-shop n calzoleria f

shoestring n **on a ∼** fam con una miseria

shoe-tree n forma f da scarpa

shone /ʃɒn/ ▸ SHINE

shoo /ʃuː/ ① vt **∼ away** cacciar via
② int sciò!

shook /ʃʊk/ ▸ SHAKE

shoot /ʃuːt/ ① n Bot germoglio m; (hunt) battuta f di caccia

② vt (pt/pp **shot**) sparare, girare ⟨film⟩; **∼ oneself in the foot** fig darsi la zappa sui piedi
③ vi (hunt) andare a caccia
■ **shoot down** vt abbattere
■ **shoot out** vi (rush) precipitarsi fuori
■ **shoot up** vi (grow) crescere in fretta; ⟨prices⟩ salire di colpo

shooting /ˈʃuːtɪŋ/ ① n (pastime) caccia f; (killing) uccisione f
② adj ⟨pain⟩ lancinante

shooting range n poligono m di tiro

shooting star n stella f cadente

shoot-out n fam sparatoria f

shop /ʃɒp/ ① n negozio m; (workshop) officina f; **talk ∼** fam parlare di lavoro
② vi (pt/pp **shopped**, pres p **shopping**) far compere; **go ∼ping** andare a fare compere
■ **shop around** vi confrontare i prezzi

shopaholic /ʃɒpəˈhɒlɪk/ n fanatico, -a mf dello shopping

shop assistant n commesso, -a mf

shop floor n **problems on the ∼ ∼** problemi tra gli operai

shopkeeper n negoziante mf

shoplifter n taccheggiatore, -trice mf

shoplifting n taccheggio m

shopper /ˈʃɒpə(r)/ n compratore, -trice mf

shopping /ˈʃɒpɪŋ/ n compere fpl; (articles) acquisti mpl; **do the ∼** fare la spesa

shopping bag n borsa f per la spesa

shopping basket n (Comput: on web site) carrello m della spesa

shopping centre n centro m commerciale

shopping list n lista f della spesa

shopping mall n centro m commerciale

shopping trolley n carrello m

shop-soiled adj ⟨garment⟩ sporco (per lunga permanenza in negozio)

shop steward n rappresentante mf sindacale

shop window n vetrina f

shore /ʃɔː(r)/ n riva f
■ **shore up** vt puntellare ⟨building, wall⟩

shorn /ʃɔːn/ ▸ SHEAR

short /ʃɔːt/ ① adj corto; (not lasting) breve; ⟨person⟩ basso; (curt) brusco; **a ∼ time ago** poco tempo fa; **be ∼ of** essere a corto di; **be in ∼ supply** essere scarso; fig essere raro; **Mick is ∼ for Michael** Mick è il diminutivo di Michael; **cut ∼** interrompere ⟨holiday⟩; **to cut a long story ∼**... per farla breve...; **in the ∼ term** nell'immediato futuro, a breve termine
② adv bruscamente; **in ∼** in breve; **∼ of doing** a meno di fare; **go ∼** essere privato (of di); **stop ∼ of doing something** non

arrivare fino a fare qualcosa; **you're 10p** **~ mancano 10 pence**
3 *n* (Cinema) cortometraggio *m*

shortage /'ʃɔːtɪdʒ/ *n* scarsità *f inv*

shortbread *n* biscotto *m* di pasta frolla

short-change *vt* dare meno resto del dovuto a; (deliberately) imbrogliare sul resto; fig imbrogliare

short circuit 1 *n* corto *m* circuito
2 *vt* mandare in cortocircuito
3 *vi* causare un cortocircuito

shortcoming *n* difetto *m*

shortcrust pastry *n* pasta *f* frolla

short cut *n* scorciatoia *f*

shorten /'ʃɔːtn/ *vt* abbreviare; accorciare ⟨garment⟩

shortfall *n* (in budget, accounts) deficit *m inv*

shorthand *n* stenografia *f*

short-handed /-'hændɪd/ *adj* a corto di personale

shorthand typist *n* stenodattilografo, -a *mf*

short list *n* lista *f* dei candidati selezionati per un lavoro

short-lived /-'lɪvd/ *adj* di breve durata

shortly /'ʃɔːtlɪ/ *adv* presto; **~ before/after** poco prima/dopo

shortness /'ʃɔːtnɪs/ *n* brevità *f inv*; (of person) bassa statura *f*

short notice *n* **at ~ ~** con poco preavviso

short-range *adj* di breve portata

shorts /ʃɔːts/ *npl* calzoncini *mpl* corti

short-sighted /-'saɪtɪd/ *adj* miope

short-sleeved /-'sliːvd/ *adj* a maniche corte

short-staffed /-'stɑːft/ *adj* a corto di personale

short story *n* racconto *m*, novella *f*

short-tempered /-'tempəd/ *adj* irascibile

short-term *adj* a breve termine

short time *n* **be on ~ ~** ⟨worker⟩ fare orario ridotto

short wave *n* onde *fpl* corte

short wave radio *n* radio *f inv* a onde corte

shot /ʃɒt/ **1** ▶ SHOOT
2 *n* colpo *m*; (pellets) piombini *mpl*; (person) tiratore *m*; Phot foto *f inv*; (injection) puntura *f*; (fam: attempt) prova *f*; **like a ~** fam come un razzo

shotgun *n* fucile *m* da caccia

shot put *n* (event) lancio *m* del peso

shot-putter *n* pesista *mf*

shot-putting *n* Sport lancio *m* del peso

should /ʃʊd/ *v aux* **I ~ go** dovrei andare; **I ~ have seen him** avrei dovuto vederlo; **you ~n't have said that** non avresti

dovuto dire questo; **I ~ like** mi piacerebbe; **this ~ be enough** questo dovrebbe bastare; **if he ~ come** se dovesse venire, se venisse

shoulder /'ʃəʊldə(r)/ **1** *n* spalla *f*; **~ to ~** gomito a gomito
2 *vt* mettersi in spalla; fig accollarsi

shoulder bag *n* borsa *f* a tracolla

shoulder blade *n* scapola *f*

shoulder-length *adj* ⟨hair⟩ lungo fino alle spalle

shoulder pad *n* spallina *f*

shoulder strap *n* spallina *f*; (of bag) tracolla *f*

shout /ʃaʊt/ **1** *n* grido *m*
2 *vt/i* gridare
■ **shout at** *vi* alzar la voce con
■ **shout down** *vt* azzittire gridando

shouting /'ʃaʊtɪŋ/ *n* grida *fpl*

shove /ʃʌv/ **1** *n* spintone *m*
2 *vt* spingere; (fam: put) ficcare
3 *vi* spingere
■ **shove off** *vi* fam togliersi di torno
■ **shove up** *vi* (fam: make room) farsi più in là

shovel /'ʃʌvl/ **1** *n* pala *f*
2 *vt* (pt/pp **shovelled**) spalare

show /ʃəʊ/ **1** *n* (display) manifestazione *f*; (exhibition) mostra *f*; (ostentation) ostentazione *f*; Theat, TV spettacolo *m*; (programme) programma *m*; **on ~** esposto
2 *vt* (pt **showed**, pp **shown**) mostrare; (put on display) esporre; proiettare ⟨film⟩; **~ somebody to the door** accompagnare qualcuno alla porta; **~ somebody the door** mettere alla porta qualcuno
3 *vi* ⟨film⟩ essere proiettato; **your slip is ~ing** ti si vede la sottoveste
■ **show in** *vt* fare accomodare
■ **show off 1** *vi* fam mettersi in mostra
2 *vt* mettere in mostra
■ **show out** *vt* **~ somebody out** fare uscire qualcuno
■ **show round** *vt* **~ somebody round** far visitare a qualcuno ⟨house, town⟩
■ **show up 1** *vi* risaltare; (fam: arrive) farsi vedere
2 *vt* (fam: embarrass) far fare una brutta figura a

showbiz /'ʃəʊbɪz/ *n* fam mondo *m* dello spettacolo

show business *n* mondo *m* dello spettacolo

showcase 1 *n* also fig vetrina *f*
2 *attrib* ⟨village, prison⟩ modello

show-down *n* regolamento *m* dei conti

shower /'ʃaʊə(r)/ **1** *n* doccia *f*; (of rain) acquazzone *m*; **have a ~** fare la doccia
2 *vt* **~ with** coprire di
3 *vi* fare la doccia

shower-cap *n* cuffia *f* da doccia

shower-curtain *n* tenda *f* della doccia

shower-head *n* bocchetta *f*

showerproof adj impermeabile

showery /'ʃaʊərɪ/ adj it was ∼ ci sono stati diversi acquazzoni

show house n casa f di nuova costruzione arredata per essere mostrata ad eventuali acquirenti

showjumper /'ʃəʊdʒʌmpə(r)/ n cavaliere m/cavallerizza f di salto ad ostacoli

showjumping /'ʃəʊdʒʌmpɪŋ/ n concorso m ippico

shown /ʃəʊn/ ▶ SHOW

show-off n esibizionista mf

show of hands n voto m per alzata di mano

showpiece n pezzo m forte

showplace n attrazione f

showroom n salone m [per] esposizioni

showy /'ʃəʊɪ/ adj appariscente

shrank /ʃræŋk/ ▶ SHRINK

shrapnel /'ʃræpnl/ n schegge fpl di granata, shrapnel m

shred /ʃred/ ① n brandello m; fig briciolo m
② vt (pt/pp **shredded**) fare a brandelli; Culin tagliuzzare

shredder /'ʃredə(r)/ n distruttore m di documenti

shrew /ʃru:/ n Zool toporagno m; (pej: woman) bisbetica f

shrewd /ʃru:d/ adj accorto

shrewdly /'ʃru:dlɪ/ adv con accortezza

shrewdness /'ʃru:dnɪs/ n accortezza f

shriek /ʃri:k/ ① n strillo m
② vt/i strillare

shrift /ʃrɪft/ n give somebody short ∼ liquidare qualcuno rapidamente

shrill /ʃrɪl/ adj penetrante

shrillness /'ʃrɪlnɪs/ n acutezza f

shrilly /'ʃrɪlɪ/ adv in modo penetrante

shrimp /ʃrɪmp/ n gamberetto m

shrine /ʃraɪn/ n (place) santuario m

shrink /ʃrɪŋk/ ① vi (pt **shrank**, pp **shrunk**) restringersi; (draw back) ritrarsi (from da)
② n fam strizzacervelli mf inv

shrinkage /'ʃrɪŋkɪdʒ/ n (of fabric) restringimento m; (of area, company) rimpicciolimento m; (in a shop) perdite fpl; (of resources) diminuzione f

shrinking violet /ʃrɪŋkɪŋ'vaɪələt/ n hum mammoletta f

shrink-proof adj irrestringibile

shrink-resistant adj irrestringibile

shrink-wrap ① vt avvolgere nella pellicola trasparente
② n pellicola f trasparente

shrivel /'ʃrɪvl/ vi (pt/pp **shrivelled**) raggrinzare

shroud /ʃraʊd/ ① n sudario m; fig manto m
② vt ∼ed in fig avvolto in

Shrove /ʃrəʊv/ n ∼ **Tuesday** martedì m grasso

shrub /ʃrʌb/ n arbusto m

shrubbery /'ʃrʌbərɪ/ n (in garden) zona f piantata ad arbusti

shrug /ʃrʌg/ ① n scrollata f di spalle
② vt/i (pt/pp **shrugged**) ∼ [one's shoulders] scrollare le spalle
■ **shrug off** vt ignorare

shrunk /ʃrʌŋk/ ▶ SHRINK.

shudder /'ʃʌdə(r)/ ① n fremito m
② vi fremere

shuffle /'ʃʌfl/ ① vi strascicare i piedi
② vt mescolare ⟨cards⟩
③ n strascicamento m; (at cards) mescolata f

shufty /'ʃʊftɪ/ n Br fam have a ∼ at something dare un'occhiata a qualcosa

shun /ʃʌn/ vt (pt/pp **shunned**) rifuggire

shunt /ʃʌnt/ vt smistare

shush /ʃʊʃ/ int zitto!

shut /ʃʌt/ ① vt (pt/pp **shut**, pres p **shutting**) chiudere
② vi chiudersi; ⟨shop⟩ chiudere
■ **shut down** vt/i chiudere
■ **shut in** vt rinchiudere ⟨person, animal⟩
■ **shut off** vt chiudere ⟨water, gas⟩
■ **shut out** vt bloccare ⟨light⟩; impedire ⟨view⟩; scacciare ⟨memory⟩
■ **shut up** ① vt chiudere; fam far tacere
② vi fam stare zitto; ∼ up! stai zitto!

shutdown /'ʃʌtdaʊn/ n chiusura f

shut-eye n (fam: short sleep) get some ∼ fare un pisolino

shutter /'ʃʌtə(r)/ n serranda f; Phot otturatore m

shuttle /'ʃʌtl/ ① n navetta f
② vi far la spola

shuttlecock /'ʃʌtlkɒk/ n volano m

shuttle service n servizio m pendolare

shy /ʃaɪ/ ① adj (timid) timido
② vi (pt/pp **shied**) ⟨horse⟩ fare uno scarto
■ **shy away from** vt rifuggire da

shyly /'ʃaɪlɪ/ adv timidamente

shyness /'ʃaɪnɪs/ n timidezza f

Siamese /saɪə'mi:z/ adj siamese

Siamese twins npl fratelli mpl/sorelle fpl siamesi

Siberia /saɪ'bɪərɪə/ n Siberia f

sibling /'sɪblɪŋ/ n (brother) fratello m; (sister) sorella f; ∼s pl fratelli mpl

sibling rivalry n rivalità f tra fratelli

sibylline /'sɪbɪlaɪn/ adj sibillino

Sicilian /sɪ'sɪlɪən/ adj & n siciliano, -a mf

Sicily /'sɪsɪlɪ/ n Sicilia f

sick /sɪk/ *adj* ammalato; ⟨*humour*⟩ macabro; **be ~** (vomit) vomitare; **be ~ of something** fam essere stufo di qualcosa; **feel ~** aver la nausea

sick bay *n* (in school) infermeria *f*

sick building syndrome *n* sindrome *f* da edifici malsani

sicken /'sɪkn/ ① *vt* disgustare ② *vi* be ~ing for something covare qualche malanno

sickening /'sɪkənɪŋ/ *adj* disgustoso

sick leave *n* congedo *m* per malattia

sickly /'sɪklɪ/ *adj* (-ier, -iest) malaticcio

sickness /'sɪknɪs/ *n* malattia *f*; (vomiting) nausea *f*

sickness benefit *n* sussidio *m* di malattia

sick note *n* (from doctor) certificato *m* medico

sickpay *n* indennità *f* di malattia

sickroom /'sɪkruːm/ *n* camera *f* dell'ammalato

side /saɪd/ ① *n* lato *m*; (of person, mountain) fianco *m*; (of road) bordo *m*; **on the ~** (as sideline) come attività secondaria; **~ by ~** fianco a fianco; **take ~s** immischiarsi; **take sb's ~** prendere le parti di qualcuno; **be on the safe ~** andare sul sicuro ② *attrib* laterale ③ *vi* ~ **with** parteggiare per

sideboard *n* credenza *f*

sideboards /'saɪdbɔːdz/ *npl* Br = SIDEBURNS

sideburns *npl* basette *fpl*

side effect *n* effetto *m* collaterale

side impact bars *npl* Auto barre *fpl* laterali antintrusione

sidekick *n* fam (companion) compare *mf*; (assistant) braccio *m* destro

sidelights *npl* luci *fpl* di posizione

sideline *n* attività *f inv* complementare

sidelong *adj* ~ **glance** sguincio *m*

side plate *n* piattino *m*

side road *n* strada *f* secondaria

side-saddle *adv* all'amazzone

sideshow *n* attrazione *f*

sidestep *vt* schivare

side street *n* strada *f* laterale

sidetrack *vt* sviare

sidewalk *n* Am marciapiede *m*

sideways *adv* obliquamente

siding /'saɪdɪŋ/ *n* binario *m* di raccordo

sidle /'saɪdl/ *vi* camminare furtivamente (up to verso)

siege /siːdʒ/ *n* assedio *m*

Sierra Leone /sɪeərəlɪ'əʊn/ *n* Sierra Leone *f*

siesta /sɪ'estə/ *n* siesta *f*; **take a ~** fare una siesta

sieve /sɪv/ ① *n* setaccio *m* ② *vt* setacciare

sift /sɪft/ *vt* setacciare; ~ **[through]** fig passare al setaccio

sigh /saɪ/ ① *n* sospiro *m*; **give a ~** sospirare ② *vi* sospirare

sight /saɪt/ ① *n* vista *f*; (on gun) mirino *m*; **the ~s** *pl* le cose da vedere; **at first ~** a prima vista; **be within/out of ~** essere/ non essere in vista; **within ~ of** vicino a; **lose ~ of** perdere di vista; **know by ~** conoscere di vista; **have bad ~** vederci male ② *vt* avvistare

sightseeing /'saɪtsiːɪŋ/ *n* **go ~** andare a visitare posti

sightseer /'saɪtsiːə(r)/ *n* turista *mf*

sign /saɪn/ ① *n* segno *m*; (notice) insegna *f* ② *vt/i* firmare ■ **sign for** *vt* firmare la ricevuta di ⟨*letter, parcel*⟩; firmare un contratto con ⟨*football club*⟩ ■ **sign in** *vi* ⟨*hotel guest*⟩ firmare il registro ■ **sign on** *vi* (as unemployed) presentarsi all'ufficio di collocamento; Mil arruolarsi ■ **sign up** *vi* Mil arruolarsi; ~ **up for a course** iscriversi a un corso

signal /'sɪgnl/ ① *n* segnale *m* ② *vt* (pt/pp **signalled**) segnalare ③ *vi* fare segnali; ~ **to somebody** far segno a qualcuno (**to** di)

signal box *n* cabina *f* di segnalazione

signalman /'sɪgnəlmən/ *n* casellante *m*

signatory /'sɪgnət(ə)rɪ/ *n* firmatario, -a *mf*

signature /'sɪgnətʃə(r)/ *n* firma *f*

signature tune *n* sigla *f* [musicale]

signet ring /'sɪgnɪt/ *n* anello *m* con sigillo

significance /sɪg'nɪfɪkəns/ *n* significato *m*

significant /sɪg'nɪfɪkənt/ *adj* significativo

significantly /sɪg'nɪfɪkəntlɪ/ *adv* in modo significativo

signify /'sɪgnɪfaɪ/ *vt* (pt/pp **-ied**) indicare

signing /'saɪnɪŋ/ *n* (of treaty) firma *f*; (of footballer) ingaggio *m*; (footballer) nuovo acquisto *m*; (sign language) linguaggio *m* dei segni

sign language *n* linguaggio *m* dei segni

signpost /'saɪnpəʊst/ *n* segnalazione *f* stradale

Sikh /siːk/ ① *n* sikh *mf inv* ② *adj* sikh *inv*

silage /'saɪlɪdʒ/ *n* foraggio *m* conservato in silo

silence /'saɪləns/ ① *n* silenzio *m*; **in ~** in silenzio

S

2 *vt* far tacere

silencer /'saɪlənsə(r)/ *n* (on gun) silenziatore *m*; Auto marmitta *f*

silent /'saɪlənt/ *adj* silenzioso; ⟨film⟩ muto; **remain ∼** rimanere in silenzio; **the ∼ majority** la maggioranza silenziosa

silently /'saɪləntlɪ/ *adv* silenziosamente

silhouette /sɪlʊ'et/ **1** *n* sagoma *f*, silhouette *f inv*
2 *vt* be ∼d profilarsi

silica gel /'sɪlɪkə/ *n* gel *m inv* di silice

silicon /'sɪlɪkən/ *n* silicio *m*

silicon chip *n* Comput chip *m inv* di silicio, piastrina *f* di silicio

silicone /'sɪlɪkəʊn/ *n* Chem silicone *m*

silicone varnish *n* vernice *f* siliconica

silk /sɪlk/ **1** *n* seta *f*
2 *attrib* di seta

silkworm /'sɪlkwɜːm/ *n* baco *m* da seta

silky /'sɪlkɪ/ *adj* (-ier, -iest) come la seta

sill /ʃɪl/ *n* davanzale *m*

silly /'ʃɪlɪ/ *adj* (-ier, -iest) sciocco

silo /'saɪləʊ/ *n* silo *m*

silt /sɪlt/ *n* melma *f*

silver /'sɪlvə(r)/ **1** *adj* d'argento; ⟨paper⟩ argentato
2 *n* argento *m*; (silverware) argenteria *f*

silver birch *n* betulla *f* bianca

silver foil *n* carta *f* stagnola, foglio *m* d'alluminio

silver-plated *adj* placcato d'argento

silver service *n* servizio *m* a tavola in cui il cameriere fa il giro dei commensali

silversmith *n* argentiere *m*

silverware *n* argenteria *f*

silver wedding *n* nozze *fpl* d'argento

silvery /'sɪlvərɪ/ *adj* argentino

SIM card /sɪm/ *n* carta *f* SIM

similar /'sɪmɪlə(r)/ *adj* simile

similarity /sɪmɪ'lærətɪ/ *n* somiglianza *f*

similarly /'sɪmɪləlɪ/ *adv* in modo simile

simile /'sɪmɪlɪ/ *n* similitudine *f*

simmer /'sɪmə(r)/ **1** *vi* bollire lentamente
2 *vt* far bollire lentamente
■ **simmer down** *vi* calmarsi

simper /'sɪmpə(r)/ *vi* ostentare un sorriso

simpering /'sɪmp(ə)rɪŋ/ *adj* ⟨smile⟩ affettato; ⟨person⟩ smanceroso

simple /'sɪmpl/ *adj* semplice; ⟨person⟩ sempliciotto

simple-minded /-'maɪndɪd/ *adj* sempliciotto

simpleton /'sɪmpltən/ *n* sempliciotto, -a *mf*

simplicity /sɪm'plɪsətɪ/ *n* semplicità *f*

simplification /sɪmplɪfɪ'keɪʃn/ *n* semplificazione *f*

simplify /'sɪmplɪfaɪ/ *vt* (pt/pp **-ied**) semplificare

simplistic /sɪm'plɪstɪk/ *adj* semplicistico

simply /'sɪmplɪ/ *adv* semplicemente

simulate /'sɪmjʊleɪt/ *vt* simulare

simulation /sɪmjʊ'leɪʃn/ *n* simulazione *f*

simulator /'sɪmjʊleɪtə(r)/ *n* simulatore *m*

simulcast /'sɪmʊlkɑːst/ *vt* teleradiotrasmettere

simultaneous /sɪml'teɪnɪəs/ *adj* simultaneo

simultaneously /sɪməl'teɪnɪəslɪ/ *adv* simultaneamente

sin /sɪn/ **1** *n* peccato *m*
2 *vi* (pt/pp **sinned**) peccare

since /sɪns/ *prep* **1** da; **∼ when?** da quando in qua?
2 *adv* da allora
3 *conj* da quando; (because) siccome

sincere /sɪn'sɪə(r)/ *adj* sincero

sincerely /sɪn'sɪəlɪ/ *adv* sinceramente; **Yours ∼** Distinti saluti

sincerity /sɪn'serətɪ/ *n* sincerità *f*

sine /saɪn/ *n* Math seno *m*

sinew /'sɪnjuː/ *n* tendine *m*

sinful /'sɪnfl/ *adj* peccaminoso

sing /sɪŋ/ *vt/i* (pt **sang**, pp **sung**) cantare

singalong /'sɪŋəlɒŋ/ *n* have a ∼ cantare [tutti] insieme

Singapore /sɪŋə'pɔː(r)/ *n* Singapore *f*

singe /sɪndʒ/ *vt* (pres p **-geing**) bruciacchiare

singer /'sɪŋə(r)/ *n* cantante *mf*

singer-songwriter /-'sɒŋraɪtə(r)/ *n* cantautore, -trice *mf*

singing /'sɪŋɪŋ/ *n* canto *m*

single /'sɪŋgl/ **1** *adj* solo; (not double) semplice; (unmarried) celibe; ⟨woman⟩ nubile; ⟨room⟩ singolo; ⟨bed⟩ a una piazza; **I haven't spoken to a ∼ person** non ho parlato con nessuno
2 *n* (ticket) biglietto *m* di sola andata; (record) singolo *m*
■ **single out** *vt* scegliere; (distinguish) distinguere

single-breasted /-'brestɪd/ *adj* ad un petto

single cream *n* panna *f* da cucina liquida

single currency *n* (in Europe) moneta *f* unica

single-decker /-'dekə(r)/ *n* autobus *m inv* (a un piano solo)

single file *adv* in fila indiana

single-handed /-'hændɪd/ *adj & adv* da solo

single-handedly /-'hændıdlı/ *adv* da solo

single market *n* mercato *m* unico

single-minded /-'maındıd/ *adj* risoluto

single mother *n* madre *f* single *inv*

single-parent *adj* ⟨family⟩ monoparentale

singles /'sıŋglz/ *npl* Tennis singolo *m*; (people) single *mpl*; **the women's ∼** il singolo femminile

singles bar *n* bar ritrovo *m* *inv* per single

singles charts *npl* classifica *f inv* dei singoli

single-sex *adj* (for boys) maschile; (for girls) femminile

single-storey *adj* ⟨house⟩ ad un piano

singlet /'sıŋlıt/ *n* Br canottiera *f*

singly /'sıŋglı/ *adv* singolarmente

sing-song Br ① *adj* ⟨voice, dialect⟩ che ha una sua particolare cadenza ② *n* **have a ∼** cantare [tutti] insieme

singular /'sıŋgjʊlə(r)/ ① *adj* Gram singolare; (uncommon) eccezionale ② *n* singolare *m*

singularly /'sıŋgjʊləlı/ *adv* singolarmente

sinister /'sınıstə(r)/ *adj* sinistro

sink /sıŋk/ ① *n* lavandino *m* ② *vi* (pt **sank**, pp **sunk**) affondare ③ *vt* affondare ⟨ship⟩; scavare ⟨shaft⟩; investire ⟨money⟩ ■ **sink in** *vi* penetrare; **it took a while to ∼ in** (fam: be understood) c'è voluto un po' a capirlo

sinker /'sıŋkə(r)/ *n* (in fishing) piombo *m*; Am Culin ≈ bombolone *m*

sinking /'sıŋkıŋ/ *n* affondamento *m*

sink unit *n* mobile *m* di cucina comprendente il lavandino

sinner /'sınə(r)/ *n* peccatore, -trice *mf*

sinuous /'sınjʊəs/ *adj* sinuoso

sinus /'saınəs/ *n* seno *m* paranasale

sinusitis /saınə'saıtıs/ *n* sinusite *f*

sip /sıp/ ① *n* sorso *m* ② *vt* (pt/pp **sipped**) sorseggiare

siphon /'saıfn/ *n* (bottle) sifone *m* ■ **siphon off** *vt* travasare (con sifone)

sir /sɜː(r)/ *n* signore *m*; **S∼** (title) Sir *m*; **Dear S∼** Egregio Signore; **Dear S∼s** Spettabile Ditta

sire /saıə(r)/ *vt* generare

siren /'saırən/ *n* sirena *f*

sirloin /'sɜːlɔın/ *n* (of beef) controfiletto *m*

sirloin steak *n* bistecca *f* di controfiletto

sissy /'sısı/ *n* femminuccia *f*

sister /'sıstə(r)/ *n* sorella *f*; (nurse) [infermiera *f*] caposala *f*

sisterhood /'sıstəhʊd/ *n* Relig congregazione *f* religiosa femminile; (in feminism) solidarietà *f inv* femminile

sister-in-law *n* (*pl* ∼s-in-law) cognata *f*

sisterly /'sıstəlı/ *adj* da sorella

Sistine Chapel /'sıstiːn/ *n* Cappella *f* Sistina

sit /sıt/ ① *vi* (pt/pp **sat**, pres p **sitting**) essere seduto; (sit down) sedersi; ⟨committee⟩ riunirsi ② *vt* sostenere ⟨exam⟩ ■ **sit about**, **sit around** *vi* stare senza far niente ■ **sit back** *vi* fig starsene con le mani in mano ■ **sit by** *vi* starsene a guardare ■ **sit down** *vi* mettersi a sedere; **please ∼ down** si accomodi; **∼ down!** siediti! ■ **sit for** *vi* posare per ⟨portrait⟩ ■ **sit in** *vi* (observe) assistere; **∼ in on a class** assistere (da osservatore) a una lezione ■ **sit on** *vt* far parte di ⟨committee⟩ ■ **sit up** *vi* mettersi seduto; (not slouch) star seduto diritto; (stay up) stare alzato

sitcom /'sıtkɒm/ *n* fam situation comedy *f inv*

sit-down *n* Br **have a ∼** sedersi un momento

site /saıt/ ① *n* posto *m*; Archaeol sito *m*; (building ∼) cantiere *m* ② *vt* collocare

sit-in /'sıtın/ *n* occupazione *f* (di fabbrica ecc), sit-in *m inv*

sitter /'sıtə(r)/ *n* (babysitter) baby-sitter *mf inv*; (for artist) modello *m*

sitting /'sıtıŋ/ *n* seduta *f*; (for meals) turno *m*

sitting duck *n* fam facile bersaglio *m*

sitting room *n* salotto *m*

sitting target *n* facile bersaglio *m*

sitting tenant *n* locatario *m* residente

situate /'sıtjʊeıt/ *vt* situare

situated /'sıtjʊeıtıd/ *adj* situato

situation /sıtjʊ'eıʃn/ *n* situazione *f*; (location) posizione *f*; (job) posto *m*; '∼s vacant' 'offerte di lavoro'

situation report *n* quadro *m* della situazione

sit-ups *npl* addominali *mpl*

six /sıks/ *adj* & *n* sei *m*

six-pack *n* confezione *f* da sei (di bottiglie o lattine)

sixteen /sıks'tiːn/ *adj* & *n* sedici *m*

sixteenth /sıks'tiːnθ/ *adj* & *n* sedicesimo, -a *mf*

sixteenth-century *adj* cinquecentesco

sixth /sıksθ/ *adj* & *n* sesto, -a *mf*

sixth form *n* Sch ultimo biennio *m* facoltativo della scuola superiore

S

sixth form college n Br istituto m che prepara studenti dai 16 ai 18 anni agli esami di maturità

sixth sense n sesto senso m

sixties /'sɪkstɪz/ npl (period) the ~ gli anni Sessanta mpl; (age) sessant'anni mpl; ▶ also FORTIES

sixtieth /'sɪkstɪɪθ/ adj & n sessantesimo, -a mf

sixty /'sɪkstɪ/ adj & n sessanta m

size /saɪz/ n dimensioni fpl; (of clothes) taglia f. misura f; (of shoes) numero m; what ~ is the room? che dimensioni ha la stanza?
■ **size up** vt fam valutare

sizeable /'saɪzəbl/ adj piuttosto grande

sizzle /'sɪzl/ vi sfrigolare

skate[1] /skeɪt/ n inv (fish) razza f

skate[2] [1] n pattino m
[2] vi pattinare
■ **skate over** vt fig glissare su

skateboard /'skeɪtbɔːd/ n skateboard m inv

skateboarder /'skeɪtbɔːdə(r)/ n persona f che va in skateboard

skateboarding /'skeɪtbɔːdɪŋ/ n skateboard m

skater /skeɪt/ n pattinatore, -trice mf

skating /'skeɪtɪŋ/ n pattinaggio m

skating rink n pista f di pattinaggio

skeletal /'skelɪtl/ adj also fig scheletrico; ⟨disease⟩ dello scheletro

skeleton /'skelɪtn/ n scheletro m

skeleton key n passe-partout m inv

skeleton staff n personale m ridotto

skeptic /'skeptɪk/ n Am = SCEPTIC

skeptical /'skeptɪkl/ adj Am = SCEPTICAL

skepticism /'skeptɪsɪzm/ n Am = SCEPTICISM

sketch /sketʃ/ [1] n schizzo m; Theat sketch m inv
[2] vt fare uno schizzo di
■ **sketch out** vt delineare

sketchbook /'sketʃbʊk/ n (for sketching) album m inv per schizzi; (book of sketches) album m inv di schizzi

sketchily /'sketʃɪlɪ/ adv in modo abbozzato

sketchpad /'sketʃpæd/ n blocco m per schizzi

sketchy /'sketʃɪ/ adj (-ier, -iest) abbozzato

skew /skjuː/ vt alterare ⟨figures⟩

skewer /'skjʊə(r)/ n spiedo m

ski /skiː/ [1] n sci m inv
[2] vi (pt/pp **skied**, pres p **skiing**) sciare; go ~ing andare a sciare

ski boot n scarpone m da sci

skid /skɪd/ [1] n slittata f; go into a ~ slittare
[2] vi (pt/pp **skidded**) slittare

skid mark n segno m di frenata

skier /'skiːə(r)/ n sciatore, -trice mf

skiing /'skiːɪŋ/ n sci m

ski instructor n maestro, -a mf di sci

ski jump n (competition) salto m con gli sci; (slope) trampolino m

ski jumping n salto m dal trampolino

skilful /'skɪlfl/ adj abile

skilfully /'skɪlfʊlɪ/ adv abilmente

ski lift n impianto m di risalita

skill /skɪl/ n abilità f inv

skilled /skɪld/ adj dotato; ⟨worker⟩ specializzato

skillet /'skɪlət/ n Am padella f

skim /skɪm/ vt (pt/pp **skimmed**) schiumare; scremare ⟨milk⟩
■ **skim off** vt togliere
■ **skim over** vt sfiorare ⟨surface, subject⟩
■ **skim through** vt scorrere

skimmed milk /skɪmd/ n latte m scremato

skimp /skɪmp/ vi ~ on lesinare su

skimpy /'skɪmpɪ/ adj (-ier, -iest) succinto

skin /skɪn/ [1] n pelle f; (on fruit) buccia f; soaked to the ~ fradicio fino all'osso
[2] vt (pt/pp **skinned**) spellare

skin cancer n cancro m alla pelle

skincare n cura f della pelle

skin cream n crema f per la pelle

skin-deep adj superficiale

skin diver n sub mf inv

skin diving n nuoto m subacqueo

skinflint /'skɪnflɪnt/ n miserabile mf

skin graft n innesto m epidermico

skinhead /'skɪnhed/ n skinhead m inv

skinny /'skɪnɪ/ adj (-ier, -iest) molto magro

skint /skɪnt/ adj fam al verde

skintight /skɪn'taɪt/ adj aderente

skip[1] /skɪp/ n (container) benna f

skip[2] [1] n salto m
[2] vi (pt/pp **skipped**) saltellare; (with rope) saltare la corda
[3] vt omettere

ski pants npl pantaloni mpl da sci

ski pass n ski-pass m inv

ski pole n bastone m da sci

skipper /'skɪpə(r)/ n skipper m inv

skipping /'skɪpɪŋ/ n salto m della corda

skipping rope n corda f per saltare

ski rack n portasci m inv

ski resort n stazione f sciistica

skirmish /'skɜːmɪʃ/ n scaramuccia f

skirt /skɜːt/ [1] n gonna f
[2] vt costeggiare

skirting board /'skɜ:tɪŋ/ *n* battiscopa *m inv*, zoccolo *m*

ski run *n* pista *f* da sci

ski slope *n* pista *f* da sci

ski stick *n* bastone *m* da sci

ski suit *n* tuta *f* da sci

skit /skɪt/ *n* bozzetto *m* comico

skittish /'skɪtɪʃ/ *adj* (difficult to handle) ombroso; (playful) giocherellone

skittle /'skɪtl/ *n* birillo *m*

skive /skaɪv/ *vi* fam fare lo scansafatiche

skivvy /'skɪvɪ/ *n* Br fam sguattera *f*

ski wax *n* sciolina *f*

skulduggery /skʌl'dʌgərɪ/ *n* fam imbrogli *mpl*

skulk /skʌlk/ *vi* aggirarsi furtivamente

skull /skʌl/ *n* cranio *m*

skunk /skʌŋk/ *n* moffetta *f*; (person) farabutto *m*

sky /skaɪ/ *n* cielo *m*

skydiving *n* paracadutismo *m* in caduta libera

sky-high ① *adj* ⟨prices⟩ alle stelle; ⟨rates⟩ esorbitante
② *adv* rise ∼ salire alle stelle

skyjacker /'skaɪdʒækə(r)/ *n* dirottatore, -trice *mf* aereo

skylight *n* lucernario *m*

skyline *n* (of city) profilo *m*

skyrocket *vi* ⟨prices⟩ andare alle stelle

skyscraper *n* grattacielo *m*

slab /slæb/ *n* lastra *f*; (slice) fetta *f*; (of chocolate) tavoletta *f*

slack /slæk/ ① *adj* lento; ⟨person⟩ fiacco
② *vi* fare lo scansafatiche
■ **slack off** *vi* rilassarsi

slacken /'slækn/ ① *vi* allentare; ∼ [off] ⟨trade⟩ rallentare; ⟨speed, rain⟩ diminuire
② *vt* allentare; diminuire ⟨speed⟩

slacker /'slækə(r)/ *n* lazzarone *m*

slacks /slæks/ *npl* pantaloni *mpl* sportivi

slag /slæg/ *n* scorie *fpl*
■ **slag off** *vt* (*pt/pp* **slagged**) Br fam sparlare di

slain /sleɪn/ ▶ SLAY

slalom /'slɑːləm/ *n* slalom *m inv*

slam /slæm/ ① *vt* (*pt/pp* **slammed**) sbattere; (fam: criticize) stroncare
② *vi* sbattere

slammer /'slæmə(r)/ *n* (fam: prison) galera *f*

slander /'slɑːndə(r)/ ① *n* diffamazione *f*
② *vt* diffamare

slanderer /'slɑːndərə(r)/ *n* diffamatore, -trice *mf*

slanderous /'slɑːnd(ə)rəs/ *adj* diffamatorio

slang /slæŋ/ *n* gergo *m*

slangy /'slæŋɪ/ *adj* gergale

slant /slɑːnt/ ① *n* pendenza *f*; (point of view) angolazione *f*; on the ∼ in pendenza
② *vt* pendere; fig distorcere ⟨report⟩
③ *vi* pendere

slanted /'slɑːntɪd/ *adj* fig ⟨report⟩ tendenzioso

slap /slæp/ ① *n* schiaffo *m*
② *vt* (*pt/pp* **slapped**) schiaffeggiare; (put) schiaffare
③ *adv* in pieno

slap bang *adv* fam he went ∼ ∼ into the wall è andato a sbattere in pieno contro il muro

slapdash *adj* fam frettoloso

slapstick *n* farsa *f* da torte in faccia

slap-up *adj* fam di prim'ordine

slash /slæʃ/ ① *n* taglio *m*; Typ barra *f*; Comput slash *m inv*
② *vt* tagliare; ridurre drasticamente ⟨prices⟩; ∼ one's wrists svenarsi

slat /slæt/ *n* stecca *f*

slate /sleɪt/ ① *n* ardesia *f*
② *vt* fam fare a pezzi

slater /'sleɪtə(r)/ *n* (roofer) addetto *m* alla ricopertura dei tetti con tegole di ardesia; Zool onisco *m*

slatted /'slætɪd/ *adj* ⟨shutter⟩ a stecche

slaughter /'slɔːtə(r)/ ① *n* macello *m*; (of people) massacro *m*
② *vt* macellare; massacrare ⟨people⟩

slaughterhouse /'slɔːtəhaʊs/ *n* macello *m*

Slav /slɑːv/ ① *adj* slavo
② *n* slavo, -a *mf*

slave /sleɪv/ ① *n* schiavo, -a *mf*
② *vi* ∼ [away] lavorare come un negro

slave-driver *n* schiavista *mf*

slavery /'sleɪvərɪ/ *n* schiavitù *f*

Slavic /'slɑːvɪk/ *adj* slavo

slavish /'sleɪvɪʃ/ *adj* servile

slavishly /'sleɪvɪʃlɪ/ *adv* in modo servile

Slavonic /slə'vɒnɪk/ *adj* slavo

slaw /slɔː/ *n* Am = COLESLAW

slay /sleɪ/ *vt* (*pt* **slew**, *pp* **slain**) ammazzare

sleaze /sliːz/ *n* fam (pornography) pornografia *f*; (corruption) corruzione *f*

sleazy /'sliːzɪ/ *adj* (-ier, -iest) sordido

sled /sled/ ① *n* slitta *f*
② *vi* andare in slitta

sledge /sledʒ/ *n* slitta *f*

sledgehammer /'sledʒhæmə(r)/ *n* martello *m*

sleek /sliːk/ *adj* liscio, lucente; (well-fed) pasciuto

sleep /sliːp/ ① *n* sonno *m*; go to ∼ addormentarsi; put to ∼ far addormentare; in my ∼ nel sonno; a good night's ∼ una bella dormita

S

[2] *vi* (*pt/pp* **slept**) dormire; ∼ **like a log** dormire come un ghiro; ∼ **on it** dormirci sopra; ∼ **with somebody** andare a letto con qualcuno

[3] *vt* ∼**s six** ha sei posti letto

■ **sleep around** *vi* andare a letto con tutti

■ **sleep in** *vi* dormire più a lungo

sleeper /'sli:pə(r)/ *n* Rail treno *m* con vagoni letto; (compartment) vagone *m* letto; (on track) traversina *f*; **be a light/heavy** ∼ avere il sonno leggero/pesante

sleepily /'sli:pɪlɪ/ *adv* con aria assonnata

sleeping bag *n* sacco *m* a pelo

sleeping car *n* vagone *m* letto

sleeping partner *n* Br Comm socio *m* accomodante

sleeping pill *n* sonnifero *m*

sleeping policeman *n* dosso *m* di rallentamento

sleepless /'sli:plɪs/ *adj* insonne; **have a** ∼ **night** passare una notte insonne

sleeplessness /'sli:plɪsnɪs/ *n* insonnia *f*

sleepover /'sli:pəʊvə(r)/ *n* **the kids are having a** ∼ i bambini hanno invitato degli amichetti a dormire a casa

sleepsuit *n* tutina *f*

sleepwalk *vi* essere sonnambulo

sleepwalker *n* sonnambulo, -a *mf*

sleepwalking *n* sonnambulismo *m*

sleepy /'sli:pɪ/ *adj* (**-ier, -iest**) assonnato; **be** ∼ aver sonno

sleet /sli:t/ [1] *n* nevischio *m*

[2] *vi* **it is** ∼**ing** nevischia

sleeve /sli:v/ *n* manica *f*; (for record) copertina *f*

sleeveless /'sli:vlɪs/ *adj* senza maniche

sleigh /sleɪ/ *n* slitta *f*

sleight /slaɪt/ *n* ∼ **of hand** gioco *m* di prestigio

slender /'slendə(r)/ *adj* snello; (fingers, stem) affusolato; fig scarso; (chance) magro

slept /slept/ ▶ SLEEP

sleuth /slu:θ/ *n* investigatore *m*, detective *m inv*

slew[1] /slu:/ *vi* girare

slew[2] ▶ SLAY

slice /slaɪs/ [1] *n* fetta *f*

[2] *vt* affettare; ∼**d bread** pane *m* a cassetta

slick /slɪk/ [1] *adj* liscio; (cunning) astuto

[2] *n* (of oil) chiazza *f* di petrolio

slide /slaɪd/ [1] *n* scivolata *f*; (in playground) scivolo *m*; (for hair) fermaglio *m* [per capelli]; Phot diapositiva *f*

[2] *vi* (*pt/pp* **slid**) scivolare

[3] *vt* far scivolare

slide projector *n* proiettore *m* per diapositive

slide rule *n* regolo *m* calcolatore

slide show *n* proiezione *f* di diapositive

sliding /'slaɪdɪŋ/ *adj* (door, seat) scorrevole

sliding scale *n* scala *f* mobile

slight /slaɪt/ [1] *adj* leggero; (importance) poco; (slender) esile; ∼**est** minimo; **not in the** ∼**est** niente affatto

[2] *vt* offendere

[3] *n* offesa *f*

slightly /'slaɪtlɪ/ *adv* leggermente

slim /slɪm/ [1] *adj* (**slimmer, slimmest**) snello; fig scarso; (chance) magro

[2] *vi* dimagrire

slime /slaɪm/ *n* melma *f*

slimy /'slaɪmɪ/ *adj* melmoso; fig viscido

sling /slɪŋ/ [1] *n* Med benda *f* al collo

[2] *vt* (*pt/pp* **slung**) fam lanciare

sling-back *n* sandalo *m* (chiuso davanti)

slingshot /'slɪŋʃɒt/ *n* fionda *f*

slink /slɪŋk/ *vi* (*pt/pp* **slunk**) entrare furtivamente

slinky /'slɪŋkɪ/ *adj* fam (dress) sexy *inv*, attillato

slip /slɪp/ [1] *n* scivolata *f*; (mistake) lieve errore *m*; (petticoat) sottoveste *f*; (for pillow) federa *f*; (paper) scontrino *m*; **give somebody the** ∼ fam sbarazzarsi di qualcuno; ∼ **of the tongue** lapsus *m inv*

[2] *vi* (*pt/pp* **slipped**) scivolare; (go quickly) sgattaiolare; (decline) retrocedere; **let something** ∼ (reveal) lasciarsi sfuggire qualcosa

[3] *vt* **he** ∼**ped it into his pocket** se l'è infilato in tasca; ∼ **sb's mind** sfuggire di mente a qualcuno

■ **slip away** *vi* sgusciar via; (time) sfuggire

■ **slip into** *vi* infilarsi (clothes)

■ **slip on** *vt* infilarsi (jacket etc)

■ **slip up** *vi* fam sbagliare

slip-knot *n* nodo *m* scorsoio

slip-on [shoe] *n* mocassino *m*

slipped disc /slɪpt'dɪsk/ *n* Med ernia *f* del disco

slipper /'slɪpə(r)/ *n* pantofola *f*

slippery /'slɪpərɪ/ *adj* scivoloso

slip road *n* bretella *f*

slipshod /'slɪpʃɒd/ *adj* trascurato

slip-up *n* fam sbaglio *m*

slit /slɪt/ [1] *n* spacco *m*; (tear) strappo *m*; (hole) fessura *f*

[2] *vt* (*pt/pp* **slit**) tagliare

slither /'slɪðə(r)/ *vi* scivolare

sliver /'slɪvə(r)/ *n* scheggia *f*

slob /slɒb/ *n* fam (messy) maiale *m*; (lazy) pelandrone *m*

slobber /'slɒbə(r)/ *vi* sbavare

sloe /sləʊ/ *n* (fruit) prugnola *f*; (bush) prugnolo *m*

slog /slɒg/ ① n [hard] ∼ sgobbata f
② vi (pt/pp **slogged**) (work) sgobbare

slogan /'sləʊgən/ n slogan m inv

slop /slɒp/ vt (pt/pp **slopped**) versare
■ **slop over** vi versarsi

slope /sləʊp/ ① n pendenza f; (ski ∼)
pista f
② vi essere inclinato, inclinarsi
■ **slope off** vi scantonare

sloping /'sləʊpɪŋ/ adj in pendenza

sloppiness /'slɒpɪnɪs/ n (of work)
trascuratezza f

sloppy /'slɒpɪ/ adj (**-ier**, **-iest**) ⟨work⟩
trascurato; ⟨worker⟩ negligente; (in dress)
sciatto; (sentimental) sdolcinato

slosh /slɒʃ/ ① vi fam ⟨person, feet⟩
sguazzare; ⟨water⟩ scrosciare
② vt (fam: hit) colpire

sloshed /slɒʃt/ adj fam sbronzo

slot /slɒt/ ① n fessura f; (time- ∼) spazio
m
② vt (pt/pp **slotted**) infilare
■ **slot in** vi incastrarsi
■ **slot together** vi ⟨pieces⟩ incastrarsi

sloth /sləʊθ/ n accidia f

slot machine n distributore m
automatico; (for gambling) slot-machine f inv

slouch /slaʊtʃ/ vi (in chair) stare
scomposto

Slovak /'sləʊvæk/ adj & n slovacco, -a
mf

Slovakia /sləʊ'vækɪə/ n Slovacchia f

Slovene /'sləʊviːn/ adj & n sloveno, -a
mf

Slovenia /sləʊ'viːnɪə/ n Slovenia f

slovenliness /'slʌvənlɪnɪs/ n sciatteria
f

slovenly /'slʌvnlɪ/ adj sciatto

low /sləʊ/ ① adj lento; **be** ∼ ⟨clock⟩
essere indietro; **in** ∼ **motion** al
rallentatore
② adv lentamente
■ **slow down** vt/i rallentare
■ **slow up** vt/i rallentare

slowcoach /'sləʊkəʊtʃ/ n fam tartaruga
f

slowly /'sləʊlɪ/ adv lentamente

slow-moving adj ⟨film, river⟩ lento

slowness /'sləʊnɪs/ n lentezza f

slow puncture n foratura f

sludge /slʌdʒ/ n fanghiglia f

slug /slʌg/ n lumacone m; (bullet)
pallottola f

sluggish /'slʌgɪʃ/ adj lento

sluggishly /'slʌgɪʃnɪs/ adv lentamente

sluice /sluːs/ n chiusa f

sluice gate n saracinesca f (di chiusa)

slum /slʌm/ n (house) tugurio m; ∼s pl
bassifondi mpl

slumber /'slʌmbə(r)/ ① n sonno m
② vi dormire

slump /slʌmp/ ① n crollo m; (economic)
depressione f
② vi crollare

slung /slʌŋ/ ▶ SLING

slunk /slʌŋk/ ▶ SLINK

slur /slɜː(r)/ ① n (discredit) calunnia f
② vt (pt/pp **slurred**) biascicare

slurp /slɜːp/ vt/i bere rumorosamente

slurry /'slʌrɪ/ n (waste from animals)
liquame m; (waste from factory) fanghiglia f
semiliquida; (of cement) impasto m
semiliquido

slush /slʌʃ/ n pantano m nevoso; fig
sdolcinatezza f

slush fund n fondi mpl neri

slushy /'slʌʃɪ/ adj fangoso; (sentimental)
sdolcinato

slut /slʌt/ n sgualdrina f

sly /slaɪ/ ① adj (**-ier**, **-iest**) scaltro
② n **on the** ∼ di nascosto

slyly /'slaɪlɪ/ adv scaltramente

SM n abbr **sadomasochism**

smack¹ /smæk/ ① n (on face) schiaffo m;
(on bottom) sculaccione m
② vt (on face) schiaffeggiare; (on bottom)
sculacciare; ∼ **one's lips** far schioccare le
labbra
③ adv fam in pieno

smack² vi ∼ **of** fig sapere di

smacker /'smækə(r)/ n (fam: kiss) bacio
m; **500** ∼**s** (£500) 500 sterline

small /smɔːl/ ① adj piccolo; **be out/work
until the** ∼ **hours** fare le ore piccole
② adv **chop up** ∼ fare a pezzettini
③ n **the** ∼ **of the back** le reni

small ads npl annunci mpl
[commerciali]

small business n piccola impresa f

small change n spiccioli mpl

small-holding n piccola tenuta f

small hours npl ore fpl piccole

small letter n lettera f minuscola

small-minded /-'maɪndɪd/ adj
meschino

smallpox n vaiolo m

small print n caratteri mpl piccoli; **read
the** ∼ fig leggere tutto fin nei minimi
particolari

small talk n chiacchiere fpl; **make** ∼ ∼
fare conversazione

smarmy /'smɑːmɪ/ adj (**-ier**, **-iest**) fam
untuoso

smart /smɑːt/ ① adj elegante; (clever)
intelligente; (brisk) svelto; **be** ∼ (fam:
cheeky) fare il furbo
② vi (hurt) bruciare

smart alec[k] /'smɑːtælɪk/ n fam
sapientone m

smart bomb n bomba f intelligente

smart card *n* carta *f* intelligente

smarten /'smɑːt(ə)n/ *vt* ~ **oneself up** farsi bello

smartly /'smɑːtlɪ/ *adv* elegantemente; (cleverly) intelligentemente; (briskly) velocemente; (cheekily) sfacciatamente

smart money *n* fam **the** ~ ~ **was on Desert Orchid** gli esperti hanno puntato su Desert Orchid

smartphone *n* smartphone *m inv*

smash /smæʃ/ ① *n* fragore *m*; (collision) scontro *m*; Tennis schiacciata *f*
② *vt* spaccare; Tennis schiacciare
③ *vi* spaccarsi; (crash) schiantarsi (**into** contro)
■ **smash up** *vt* distruggere ⟨car, bar⟩

smash-and-grab *n* Br rapina *f* ad un negozio (con sfascio di vetrina)

smashed /smæʃt/ *adj* ⟨window⟩ in frantumi; ⟨vehicle⟩ sfasciato; ⟨limb⟩ fracassato; (fam: on drugs) fatto; (fam: on alcohol) ubriaco fradicio

smash [hit] *n* successo *m*

smashing /'smæʃɪŋ/ *adj* fam fantastico

smattering /'smætərɪŋ/ *n* infarinatura *f*

smear /smɪə(r)/ ① *n* macchia *f*; Med striscio *m*
② *vt* imbrattare; (coat) spalmare (**with** di); fig calunniare
③ *vi* sbavare

smear campaign *n* campagna *f* diffamatoria

smear test *n* Med striscio *m*, Pap test *m inv*

smell /smel/ ① *n* odore *m*; (sense) odorato *m*
② *vt* (pt/pp **smelt** or **smelled**) odorare (**of** di); **that** ~**s good** ha un buon odore

smelling salts /'smelɪŋ/ *npl* Med sali *mpl*

smelly /'smelɪ/ *adj* (**-ier, -iest**) puzzolente

smelt¹ /smelt/ ▶ SMELL

smelt² *vt* fondere

smidgeon /'smɪdʒɪn/ *n* (of something to eat) pizzico *m*; (of something to drink) goccio *m*

smile /smaɪl/ ① *n* sorriso *m*
② *vi* sorridere; ~ **at** sorridere a ⟨somebody⟩; sorridere di ⟨something⟩
■ **smile on** *vt* ⟨weather, fortune⟩ sorridere a ⟨person⟩

smiley /'smaɪlɪ/ *n* fam smiley *m inv*, faccina *f* sorridente

smirk /smɜːk/ ① *n* sorriso *m* compiaciuto
② *vi* sorridere con aria compiaciuta

smithereens /smɪðə'riːnz/ *npl* **to/in** ~ in mille pezzi

smithy /'smɪðɪ/ *n* fucina *f*

smitten /'smɪtn/ *adj* ~ **with** tutto preso da

smock /smɒk/ *n* grembiule *m*

smog /smɒg/ *n* smog *m inv*

smoke /sməʊk/ ① *n* fumo *m*
② *vt/i* fumare

smoke alarm *n* allarme *m* antifumo *inv*

smoked /sməʊkt/ *adj* affumicato

smoke-free zone *n* zona *f* non-fumatori; '~ ~' 'vietato fumare'

smokeless /'sməʊklɪs/ *adj* senza fumo; ⟨fuel⟩ che non fa fumo

smoker /'sməʊkə(r)/ *n* fumatore, -trice *mf*; Rail vagone *m* fumatori

smokescreen /'sməʊkskriːn/ *n* also fig cortina *f* di fumo

smoking /'sməʊkɪŋ/ *n* fumo *m*; '**no** ~' 'vietato fumare'; '~ **or non-**~?' 'fumatori o non fumatori?'

smoking-related *adj* ⟨illness⟩ legato al fumo

smoky /'sməʊkɪ/ *adj* (**-ier, -iest**) fumoso; ⟨taste⟩ di fumo

smooch /smuːtʃ/ *vi* fam pomiciare

smooth /smuːð/ ① *adj* liscio; ⟨movement⟩ scorrevole; ⟨sea⟩ calmo; ⟨manners⟩ mellifluo
② *vt* lisciare; ~ **things over** sistemare le cose
■ **smooth out** *vt* lisciare

smoothly /'smuːðlɪ/ *adv* in modo scorrevole; **go** ~ andare liscio

smooth-running *adj* ⟨event, service⟩ ben organizzato

smooth-tongued /-'tʌŋd/ *adj* pej mellifluo

smother /'smʌðə(r)/ *vt* soffocare

smoulder /'sməʊldə(r)/ *vi* fumare; (with rage) consumarsi

SMS *n abbr* (**short message service**) SMS *m*

SMS message *n* sms *m inv*

smudge /smʌdʒ/ ① *n* macchia *f*
② *vt/i* imbrattare

smug /smʌg/ *adj* (**smugger, smuggest**) compiaciuto

smuggle /'smʌgl/ *vt* contrabbandare

smuggler /'smʌglə(r)/ *n* contrabbandiere, -a *mf*

smuggling /'smʌglɪŋ/ *n* contrabbando *m*

smugly /'smʌglɪ/ *adv* con aria compiaciuta

smugness /'smʌgnɪs/ *n* compiacimento *m*

smut /smʌt/ *n* macchia *f* di fuliggine; fig sconcezza *f*

smutty /'smʌtɪ/ *adj* (**-ier, -iest**) fuligginoso; fig sconcio

snack /snæk/ *n* spuntino *m*

snack-bar *n* snack bar *m inv*

snag[1] /snæg/ n (problem) intoppo m

snag[2] vt smagliarsi ‹tights› (on con)

snail /sneɪl/ n lumaca f; at a ~'s pace a passo di lumaca

snail mail n fam posta f tradizionale, così chiamata dagli utenti di email

snake /sneɪk/ n serpente m

snakebite n morso m di serpente

snake charmer n incantatore, -trice mf di serpenti

snakes and ladders n Br gioco m dell'oca

snap /snæp/ ① n colpo m secco; (photo) istantanea f
② attrib ‹decision› istantaneo
③ vi (pt/pp **snapped**) (break) spezzarsi
④ vt (break) spezzare; (say) dire seccamente; Phot fare un'istantanea di; schioccare ‹fingers›
■ **snap at** ‹dog› cercare di azzannare; ‹person› parlare seccamente a
■ **snap off** vt ~ sb's head off fam aggredire qualcuno
■ **snap out** vi ~ out of it venirne fuori
■ **snap up** vt afferrare

snappy /'snæpɪ/ adj (-ier, -iest) scorbutico; (smart) elegante; make it ~! sbrigati!

snapshot /'snæpʃɒt/ n istantanea f

snare /sneə(r)/ n trappola f

snarl /snɑːl/ ① n ringhio m
② vi ringhiare

snarled-up /snɑːld'ʌp/ adj ‹traffic› bloccato

snarl-up n (in traffic, network) ingorgo m

snatch /snætʃ/ ① n strappo m; (fragment) brano m; (theft) scippo m; make a ~ at something cercare di afferrare qualcosa
② vt strappare [di mano] (from a); (steal) scippare; rapire ‹child›

snazzy /'snæzɪ/ adj fam sciccoso

sneak /sniːk/ ① n (fam: devious person) tipo, -a mf subdolo, -a; (Br fam: telltale) spia f
② vt (fam: steal) fregare; rubare ‹kiss›; ~ a glance at dare una sbirciatina a
③ vi (Br fam: tell tales) fare la spia
④ attrib ‹visit› furtivo; have a ~ preview of something vedere qualcosa in anteprima
■ **sneak away** vi sgattaiolare via
■ **sneak in** vi sgattaiolare dentro
■ **sneak out** vi sgattaiolare fuori

sneakers /'sniːkəz/ npl Am scarpe fpl da ginnastica

sneaking /'sniːkɪŋ/ adj furtivo; ‹suspicion› vago

sneaky /'sniːkɪ/ adj sornione

sneer /snɪə(r)/ ① n ghigno m
② vi sogghignare; ~ at (mock) ridere di

sneeze /sniːz/ ① n starnuto m
② vi starnutire; it's not to be ~d at non ci sputerei sopra

snide /snaɪd/ adj fam insinuante

sniff /snɪf/ ① n (of dog) annusata f; give a ~ ‹person› tirare su col naso
② vi tirare su col naso
③ vt odorare ‹flower›; sniffare ‹glue›; ‹dog› annusare

sniffer dog /'snɪfə/ n cane m poliziotto (antidroga, antiterrorismo)

sniffle /'snɪfl/ ① n have a ~ or the ~s (slight cold) avere un po' di raffreddore; give a ~ tirar su col naso
② vi tirar su col naso

sniffy /'snɪfɪ/ adj (fam: haughty) con la puzza sotto il naso

snigger /'snɪgə(r)/ ① n risatina f soffocata
② vi ridacchiare

snip /snɪp/ ① n taglio m; (fam: bargain) affare m
② vt/t ~ [at] tagliare
■ **snip off** vt tagliare via ‹corner, end›

snipe /snaɪp/ vi ~ at tirare su; fig sparare a zero su

sniper /'snaɪpə(r)/ n cecchino m

snippet /'snɪpɪt/ n a ~ of information/ news una breve notizia/informazione

snivel /'snɪvl/ vi (pt/pp **snivelled**) piagnucolare

snivelling /'snɪv(ə)lɪŋ/ adj piagnucoloso

snob /snɒb/ n snob mf inv

snobbery /'snɒbərɪ/ n snobismo m

snobbish /'snɒbɪʃ/ adj da snob; be ~ ‹person› essere uno/una snob; ‹club etc› essere molto snob

snobbishness /'snɒbɪʃnɪs/ n snobismo m

snog /snɒg/ vi Br sl pomiciare

snooker /'snuːkə(r)/ ① n (game) snooker m; (shot) impallatura f
② vt Sport impallare; fig mettere in difficoltà

snoop /snuːp/ ① n spia f
② vi fam curiosare

snooper /'snuːpə(r)/ n ficcanaso mf

snooty /'snuːtɪ/ adj fam sdegnoso

snooze /snuːz/ ① n sonnellino m
② vi fare un sonnellino

snore /snɔː(r)/ vi russare

snoring /'snɔːrɪŋ/ n il russare

snorkel /'snɔːkl/ n respiratore m

snorkelling /'snɔːklɪŋ/ Br, **snorkeling** Am n snorkelling m inv

snort /snɔːt/ ① n sbuffo m
② vi sbuffare
③ vt fiutare ‹cocaine›

snot /snɒt/ n (fam: mucus) moccolo m

snotty /'snɒtɪ/ adj fam ‹nose› moccioso; (disagreeable) sgradevole

snotty-nosed kid /-nəʊzd/ n moccioso, -a mf

snout /snaʊt/ n grugno m

snow /snəʊ/ **①** n neve f
② vi nevicare; ~**ed under with** fig sommerso di

snowball ① n palla f di neve
② vi fig fare a palle di neve

snowboard ① n snowboard m inv
② vi fare snowboard

snowboarding /'snəʊ'bɔːdɪŋ/ n snowboard m inv

snowdrift n cumulo m di neve

snowdrop n bucaneve m inv

snowfall n nevicata f

snowflake n fiocco m di neve

snowman n pupazzo m di neve

snowmobile /'snəʊməbiːl/ n gatto m delle nevi

snowplough n spazzaneve m inv

snowshoe n racchetta f da neve

snowstorm n tormenta f

snow tyres npl pneumatici mpl chiodati

snowy /'snəʊɪ/ adj nevoso

Snr abbr Senior

snub /snʌb/ **①** n sgarbo m
② vt (pt/pp **snubbed**) snobbare

snub-nosed /'snʌbnəʊzd/ adj dal naso all'insù

snuff[1] /snʌf/ n tabacco m da fiuto

snuff[2] vt ~ **[out]** spegnere ⟨candle⟩; ~ **it** fam tirare le cuoia

snug /snʌg/ adj (**snugger**, **snuggest**) comodo; (tight) aderente

snuggle /'snʌgl/ vi rannicchiarsi (**up to** accanto a)

so /səʊ/ **①** adv così; **so far** finora; **so am I** anch'io; **so I see** così pare; **you've left the door open –so I have!** hai lasciato la porta aperta –è vero!; **that is so** è così; **so much** così tanto; **so much the better** tanto meglio; **so it is** proprio così; **if so** se è così; **so as to** in modo da; **so long!** fam a presto!
② pron **I hope/think/am afraid so** spero/ penso/temo di sì; **I told you so** te l'ho detto; **because I say so** perché lo dico io; **I did so!** l'ho fatto!; **so saying/doing,...** così dicendo/facendo,...; **or so** circa; **very much so** sì, molto; **and so forth** or **on** e così via
③ conj (therefore) perciò; (in order that) così; **so that** affinché; **so there!** ecco!; **so what?** e allora?; **so where have you been?** allora, dove sei stato?

soak /səʊk/ **①** vt mettere a bagno
② vi stare a bagno
■ **soak in** vi penetrare
■ **soak into** vt ⟨liquid⟩ penetrare
■ **soak up** vt assorbire

soaked /səʊkt/ adj fradicio; ~ **in something** impregnato di qualcosa

soaking /'səʊkɪŋ/ **①** n ammollo m

② adj & adv ~ **[wet]** fam inzuppato

so-and-so n tal dei tali mf; (euphemism) specie f di imbecille

soap /səʊp/ n sapone m

soap opera n telenovela f, soap opera f inv

soap powder n detersivo m in polvere

soapy /'səʊpɪ/ adj (**-ier**, **-iest**) insaponato

soar /sɔː(r)/ vi elevarsi; ⟨prices⟩ salire alle stelle

soaring /'sɔːrɪŋ/ adj ⟨costs, temperatures, inflation⟩ in forte aumento

S.O.B. n Am abbr son of a bitch

sob /sɒb/ **①** n singhiozzo m
② vi (pt/pp **sobbed**) singhiozzare

sobbing /'sɒbɪŋ/ n singhiozzi mpl

sober /'səʊbə(r)/ adj sobrio; (serious) serio
■ **sober up** vi ritornare sobrio

soberly /'səʊbəlɪ/ adv sobriamente; (seriously) con aria seria

sobriety /sə'braɪətɪ/ n (not drinking) sobrietà f; (seriousness) serietà f

sob story n storia f lacrimevole

so-called /'səʊkɔːld/ adj cosiddetto

soccer /'sɒkə(r)/ n calcio m

soccer pitch n campo m di calcio

soccer player n giocatore m di calcio

sociable /'səʊʃəbl/ adj socievole

social /'səʊʃl/ adj sociale; (sociable) socievole

social climber n arrampicatore, -trice mf sociale

social climbing n arrivismo m sociale

social club n circolo m sociale

socialism /'səʊʃəlɪzm/ n socialismo m

socialist /'səʊʃəlɪst/ **①** adj socialista
② n socialista mf

socialite /'səʊʃəlaɪt/ n persona f che fa vita mondana

socialize /'səʊʃəlaɪz/ vi socializzare

socially /'səʊʃəlɪ/ adv socialmente; **know somebody** ~ frequentare qualcuno

social science n scienze fpl sociali

social security n previdenza f sociale

social services npl servizi mpl sociali

social work n assistenza f sociale

social worker n assistente mf sociale

society /sə'saɪətɪ/ n società f inv

socio-economic /səʊsɪəʊiːkə'nɒmɪk/ adj socioeconomico

sociological /səʊsɪə'lɒdʒɪkl/ adj sociologico

sociologist /səʊsɪ'ɒlədʒɪst/ n sociologo, -a mf

sociology /səʊsɪ'ɒlədʒɪ/ n sociologia f

sock[1] /sɒk/ n calzino m; (kneelength) calzettone m

sock² fam ① n pugno m
② vt dare un pugno a

socket /'sɒkɪt/ n (of eye) orbita f; (wall plug) presa f [di corrente]; (for bulb) portalampada m inv

sod /sɒd/ n fam stronzo m; **you lucky ∼**! che fortuna sfacciata!
■ **sod off** vi fam togliersi dai piedi

soda /'səʊdə/ n soda f; Am gazzosa f

soda water n seltz m inv

sodden /'sɒdn/ adj inzuppato

sodium /'səʊdɪəm/ n sodio m

sodium bicarbonate n bicarbonato m di sodio

Sod's Law /sɒdz/ n fam hum regola f per cui, se qualcosa può andare storto, va storto

sofa /'səʊfə/ n divano m

sofa bed n divano m letto

soft /sɒft/ adj morbido, soffice; ⟨voice⟩ sommesso; ⟨light, colour⟩ tenue; (not strict) indulgente; (fam: silly) stupido

soft-boiled /-'bɔɪld/ adj ⟨egg⟩ bazzotto

soft contact lenses npl lenti fpl a contatto morbide

soft drink n bibita f analcolica

soft drug n droga f leggera

soften /'sɒfn/ ① vt ammorbidire; fig attenuare
② vi ammorbidirsi
■ **soften up** vi ammorbidirsi vt ∼ somebody up ammorbidire qualcuno ⟨opponent, enemy, customer⟩

softener /'sɒf(ə)nə(r)/ n (for water) dolcificatore m; (substance) anti-calcare m inv; (for fabrics) ammorbidente m

soft furnishings npl tappeti mpl e tessuti mpl da arredamento

soft-hearted adj dal cuore tenero

soft ice-cream n mantecato m

softie /'sɒftɪ/ n fam = SOFTY

softly /'sɒftlɪ/ adv (say) sottovoce; ⟨treat⟩ con indulgenza; ⟨play music⟩ in sottofondo

soft option n take the ∼ ∼ scegliere la soluzione più semplice

soft-pedal vt fig minimizzare

soft porn n fam pornografia f soft[-core]

soft sell n metodo m di vendita basato sulla persuasione

soft soap n fig lusinghe fpl

soft-soap vt fig lusingare

soft-spoken adj dalla voce dolce

soft spot n have a ∼ ∼ for somebody fam avere un debole per qualcuno

soft-top n Auto decappottabile f

soft touch n be a ∼ ∼ lasciarsi spremere

soft toy n pupazzo m di peluche

software /'sɒftweə(r)/ n software m

software engineer n softwarista mf

software house n software house f

software package n pacchetto m software

software piracy n pirateria f informatica

software writer n scrittore, -trice mf di programmi

softy /'sɒftɪ/ n fam (weak person) pappamolle mf inv; (indulgent person) bonaccione, -a mf

soggy /'sɒgɪ/ adj (-ier, -iest) zuppo

soil¹ /sɔɪl/ n suolo m

soil² vt sporcare

soiled /sɔɪld/ adj sporco

solace /'sɒləs/ n sollievo m

solar /'səʊlə(r)/ adj solare

solar eclipse n eclissi f inv di sole

solar energy n energia f solare,

solar panel n pannello m solare

solar power n energia f solare

solar system n sistema m solare

sold /səʊld/ ▶ SELL

solder /'səʊldə(r)/ ① n lega f da saldatura
② vt saldare

soldier /'səʊldʒə(r)/ n soldato m
■ **soldier on** vi perseverare

sole¹ /səʊl/ n (of foot) pianta f; (of shoe) suola f

sole² n (fish) sogliola f

sole³ adj unico, solo

sole agency n rappresentanza f esclusiva

solecism /'sɒlɪsɪzm/ n (social) scorrettezza f; (linguistic) solecismo m

solely /'səʊllɪ/ adv unicamente

solemn /'sɒləm/ adj solenne

solemnity /sə'lemnətɪ/ n solennità f inv

solemnly /'sɒləmlɪ/ adv solennemente

sol-fa /'sɒlfɑ:/ n solfeggio m

solicit /sə'lɪsɪt/ ① vt sollecitare
② vi ⟨prostitute⟩ adescare

soliciting /sə'lɪsɪtɪŋ/ n Jur adescamento m

solicitor /sə'lɪsɪtə(r)/ n avvocato m

solicitous /sə'lɪsɪtəs/ adj premuroso

solicitously /sə'lɪsɪtəslɪ/ adv premurosamente

solid /'sɒlɪd/ ① adj solido; ⟨oak, gold⟩ massiccio; **it took a ∼ hour** ci è voluta ben un'ora
② n (figure) solido m; **∼s** pl (food) cibi mpl solidi

solidarity /sɒlɪ'dærətɪ/ n solidarietà f inv

solidify /sə'lɪdɪfaɪ/ vi (pt/pp -ied) solidificarsi

soliloquy /sə'lɪləkwɪ/ n soliloquio m

S

solitaire /sɒlɪˈteə(r)/ n solitario m

solitary /ˈsɒlɪtərɪ/ adj solitario; (sole) solo

solitary confinement n cella f di isolamento

solitude /ˈsɒlɪtjuːd/ n solitudine f

solo /ˈsəʊləʊ/ ① n Mus assolo m
② adj ⟨flight⟩ in solitario
③ adv in solitario

soloist /ˈsəʊləʊɪst/ n solista mf

solstice /ˈsɒlstɪs/ n solstizio m

soluble /ˈsɒljʊbl/ adj solubile

solution /səˈluːʃn/ n soluzione f

solvable /ˈsɒlvəbl/ adj risolvibile

solve /sɒlv/ vt risolvere

solvency /ˈsɒlvənsɪ/ n Fin solvibilità f

solvent /ˈsɒlvənt/ adj & n solvente m

solvent abuse n uso m di solventi come stupefacenti

Somali /səˈmɑːlɪ/ adj & n somalo, -a mf

Somalia /səˈmɑːlɪə/ n Somalia f

sombre /ˈsɒmbə(r)/ adj tetro; ⟨clothes⟩ scuro

some /sʌm/ ① adj (a certain amount of) del; (a certain number of) alcuni, dei; ~ **bread/ water** del pane/dell'acqua; ~ **books/ oranges** dei libri/delle arance; **I need** ~ **money/books** ho bisogno di soldi/libri; **do** ~ **shopping** fare qualche acquisto; ~ **day** un giorno o l'altro
② pron (a certain amount) un po'; (a certain number) alcuni; **I want** ~ ne voglio; **would you like** ~? ne vuoi?; ~ **of the butter** una parte del burro; ~ **of the apples/women** alcune delle mele/donne

somebody /ˈsʌmbədɪ/ ① pron qualcuno m; ~ **else will bring it** la porterà un altro
② n **he thinks he's** ~ si crede chissà chi

somehow /ˈsʌmhaʊ/ adv in qualche modo; ~ **or other** in un modo o nell'altro

someone /ˈsʌmwʌn/ pron & n = SOMEBODY

somersault /ˈsʌməsɔːlt/ ① n capriola f; **turn a** ~ fare una capriola
② vi fare una capriola

something /ˈsʌmθɪŋ/ pron qualche cosa, qualcosa; ~ **different** qualcosa di diverso; ~ **like** un po' come; (approximately) qualcosa come; **see** ~ **of somebody** vedere qualcuno ogni tanto; **she is** ~ **of an expert** è un'esperta

sometime /ˈsʌmtaɪm/ ① adv un giorno o l'altro; ~ **last summer** durante l'estate scorsa
② adj ex

sometimes /ˈsʌmtaɪmz/ adv qualche volta

somewhat /ˈsʌmwɒt/ adv piuttosto

somewhere /ˈsʌmweə(r)/ ① adv da qualche parte

② pron ~ **to eat** un posto in cui mangiare

son /sʌn/ n figlio m

sonar /ˈsəʊnɑː(r)/ n sonar m

sonata /səˈnɑːtə/ n sonata f

song /sɒŋ/ n canzone f

song and dance n **make a** ~ ~ ~ **about something** (fuss) far tante storie per qualcosa

songbird n uccello m canoro

songwriter n compositore, -trice mf di canzoni

sonic /ˈsɒnɪk/ adj sonico

sonic boom n bang m inv sonico

son-in-law n (pl ~s-in-law) genero m

sonnet /ˈsɒnɪt/ n sonetto m

son of a bitch n fam figlio m di un cane

sonorous /ˈsɒnərəs/ adj sonoro; ⟨name⟩ altisonante

soon /suːn/ adv presto; (in a short time) tra poco; **as** ~ **as** [non] appena; **as** ~ **as possible** il più presto possibile; ~**er or later** prima o poi; **the** ~**er the better** prima è meglio è; **no** ~**er had I arrived than...** ero appena arrivato quando...; **I would** ~**er go** preferirei andare; ~ **after** subito dopo

soot /sʊt/ n fuliggine f

soothe /suːð/ vt calmare

soothing /ˈsuːðɪŋ/ adj calmante

sooty /ˈsʊtɪ/ adj fuligginoso

sop /sɒp/ n **throw a** ~ **to** dare un contentino a

sophisticated /səˈfɪstɪkeɪtɪd/ adj sofisticato; (complex) complesso

sophistication /səfɪstɪˈkeɪʃn/ n (elegance) sofisticatezza f, raffinatezza f; (complexity) complessità f

soporific /sɒpəˈrɪfɪk/ adj soporifero

soppiness /ˈsɒpɪnɪs/ n fam svenevolezza f

sopping /ˈsɒpɪŋ/ adj & adv **be** ~ **[wet]** essere bagnato fradicio

soppy /ˈsɒpɪ/ adj (-ier, -iest) fam svenevole

soprano /səˈprɑːnəʊ/ n soprano m

sorcerer /ˈsɔːsərə(r)/ n stregone m

sorceress /ˈsɔːsərɪs/ n strega f, maga f

sorcery /ˈsɔːsərɪ/ n (witchcraft) stregoneria f

sordid /ˈsɔːdɪd/ adj sordido

sordidness /ˈsɔːdɪdnɪs/ n sordidezza f

sore /sɔː(r)/ ① adj dolorante; (Am: vexed) arrabbiato; **it's** ~ fa male; **have a** ~ **throat** avere mal di gola; **it's a** ~ **point with her** un punto delicato per lei
② n piaga f

sorely /ˈsɔːlɪ/ adv ⟨tempted⟩ seriamente

soreness /ˈsɔːnɪs/ n dolore m

sorrel /ˈsɒrəl/ n Bot acetosa f

sorrow /'sɒrəʊ/ *n* tristezza *f*

sorrowful /'sɒrəʊfʊl/ *adj* triste

sorrowfully /'sɒrəʊfʊlɪ/ *adv* tristemente

sorry /'sɒrɪ/ *adj* (**-ier**, **-iest**) (sad) spiacente; (wretched) pietoso; **you'll be ~!** te ne pentirai!; **I am ~** mi dispiace; **be** or **feel ~ for** provare compassione per; **~!** scusa!; (more polite) scusi!

sort /'sɔːt/ **①** *n* tipo *m*; **it's a ~ of fish** è un tipo di pesce; **be out of ~s** (fam: unwell) stare poco bene
② *vt* classificare; fam sistemare ⟨*problem, person*⟩
■ **sort out** *vt* selezionare ⟨*papers*⟩; fig risolvere ⟨*problem*⟩; occuparsi di ⟨*person*⟩

sort code *n* Fin coordinate *fpl* bancarie

sorter /'sɔːtə(r)/ *n* (on photocopier) fascicolatrice *f*, fascicolatore *m*

SOS *n* SOS *m*; fig segnale *m* di soccorso

so-so *adj & adv* così così

sotto voce /sɒtəʊ'vəʊtʃeɪ/ *adv* ⟨*say, add*⟩ sottovoce

soufflé /'suːfleɪ/ *n* soufflé *m*

sought /sɔːt/ ▶ SEEK

sought-after *adj* ⟨*job, brand, person*⟩ richiesto

soul /'səʊl/ *n* anima *f*; **poor ~** poveretto; **there was not a ~ in sight** non c'era anima viva

soul-destroying /-dɪstrɔɪɪŋ/ *adj* ⟨*job*⟩ che abbruttisce

soulful /'səʊlfʊl/ *adj* sentimentale

soulmate *n* anima *f* gemella

soulsearching /-sɜːtʃɪŋ/ *n* esame *m* di coscienza

soul-stirring /-stɜːrɪŋ/ *adj* molto commovente

sound¹ /saʊnd/ **①** *adj* sano; (sensible) saggio; (secure) solido; ⟨*thrashing*⟩ clamoroso
② *adv* **~ asleep** profondamente addormentato

sound² **①** *n* suono *m*; (noise) rumore *m*; **I don't like the ~ of it** fam non mi suona bene
② *vi* suonare; (seem) aver l'aria; **it ~s to me as if...** mi sa che...
③ *vt* (pronounce) pronunciare; Med auscultare ⟨*chest*⟩
■ **sound off** *vi* fare grandi discorsi
■ **sound out** *vt* fig sondare

sound barrier *n* muro *m* del suono

sound bite *n* breve frase *f* dal forte impatto mediatico

sound card *n* Comput scheda *f* audio

sound effect *n* effetto *m* sonoro

sound engineer *n* tecnico *m* del suono

soundless /'saʊndlɪs/ *adj* silenzioso

soundlessly /'saʊndlɪslɪ/ *adv* silenziosamente

soundly /'saʊndlɪ/ *adv* ⟨*sleep*⟩ profondamente; ⟨*defeat*⟩ clamorosamente

soundproof **①** *adj* impenetrabile al suono
② *vt* insonorizzare

sound system *n* (hifi) stereo *m*; (for disco etc) impianto *m* audio

soundtrack *n* colonna *f* sonora

soup /suːp/ *n* minestra *f*; **in the ~** fam nei pasticci

souped-up /suːpt'ʌp/ *adj* fam ⟨*engine*⟩ truccato

soup kitchen *n* mensa *f* dei poveri

soup plate *n* piatto *m* fondo

soup spoon *n* cucchiaio *m* da minestra

sour /'saʊə(r)/ *adj* agro; (not fresh & fig) acido

source /sɔːs/ *n* fonte *f*; **at ~** ⟨*deducted*⟩ alla fonte

source language *n* lingua *f* di partenza

sour cream *n* panna *f* acida

sourdough *n* lievito *m*

sour-faced /saʊə'feɪst/ *adj* ⟨*person*⟩ dall'espressione dura

sour grapes *npl* fam **it's just ~ ~ [on his part]** fa come la volpe con l'uva

south /saʊθ/ **①** *n* sud *m*; **to the ~ of** a sud di
② *adj* del sud, meridionale
③ *adv* a sud

South Africa *n* Sudafrica *f*

South African *adj & n* sudafricano, -a *mf*

South America *n* America *f* del Sud

South American *adj & n* sudamericano, -a *mf*

southbound *adj* ⟨*traffic*⟩ diretto a sud; ⟨*carriageway*⟩ sud

south-east /saʊθ'iːst/ *n* sud-est *m*

southerly /'sʌðəlɪ/ *adj* del sud

southern /'sʌðən/ *adj* del sud, meridionale; **~ Italy** il Mezzogiorno

southerner /'sʌðənə(r)/ *n* meridionale *mf*

South Korea *n* Corea *f* del Sud

southpaw /'saʊθpɔː/ *n* (in boxing) pugile *m* mancino

South Pole *n* polo *m* sud

southward[s] /'saʊθwəd[z]/ *adv* verso sud

south-west /saʊθ'west/ *n* sud-ovest *m*

south-western /saʊθ'westən/ *adj* sudoccidentale

souvenir /suːvə'nɪə(r)/ *n* ricordo *m*, souvenir *m inv*

sovereign /'sɒvrɪn/ *adj & n* sovrano, -a *mf*

sovereignty /'sɒvrɪntɪ/ *n* sovranità *f inv*

Soviet /ˈsəʊvɪət/ *adj* sovietico

Soviet Union *n* Unione *f* Sovietica

sow[1] /saʊ/ *n* scrofa *f*

sow[2] /səʊ/ *vt* (pt **sowed**, pp **sown** or **sowed**) seminare

soya /ˈsɔɪə/ *n* soya *f*

soya bean *n* soia *f*

soy sauce /sɔɪ/, **soya sauce** *n* salsa *f* di soia

sozzled /ˈsɒzld/ *adj* fam sbronzo

spa /spɑː/ *n* stazione *f* termale

space /speɪs/ [1] *n* spazio *m*
[2] *adj* ⟨research etc⟩ spaziale
[3] *vt* ~ [out] distanziare

space age [1] *n* era *f* spaziale
[2] *attrib* dell'era spaziale

space bar *n* barra *f* spaziatrice

space cadet *n* fig fam allucinato, -a *mf*

space capsule *n* capsula *f* spaziale

spacecraft *n* navetta *f* spaziale

spaced out /speɪstˈaʊt/ *adj* fam **he's completely** ~ ~ è completamente fuori di testa

space-saving *adj* poco ingombrante

spaceship *n* astronave *f*

space shuttle *n* shuttle *m inv*

space station *n* stazione *f* spaziale

spacesuit *n* tuta *f* spaziale

space travel *n* viaggi *mpl* nello spazio

space walk *n* passeggiata *f* nello spazio

spacing /ˈspeɪsɪŋ/ *n* distanziamento *m*; **single/double** ~ interlinea *m* semplice/doppia

spacious /ˈspeɪʃəs/ *adj* spazioso

spade /speɪd/ *n* vanga *f*; (for child) paletta *f*; ~s *pl* (Cards) picche *fpl*; **call a** ~ **a** ~ dire pane al pane e vino al vino

spadework /ˈspeɪdwɜːk/ *n* fig lavoro *m* preparatorio

spaghetti /spəˈɡetɪ/ *n* spaghetti *mpl*

spaghetti bolognese /bɒləˈneɪz/ *n* spaghetti *mpl* al ragù

spaghetti junction *n* fam intricato raccordo *m* autostradale

Spain /speɪn/ *n* Spagna *f*

spam /spæm/ *n* Comput spam *m inv*

spamming /ˈspæmɪŋ/ *n* Comput invio *m* di spam

span[1] /spæn/ [1] *n* spanna *f*; (of arch) luce *f*; (of time) arco *m*; (of wings) apertura *f*
[2] *vt* (pt/pp **spanned**) estendersi su

span[2] ▶ SPICK

Spaniard /ˈspænjəd/ *n* spagnolo, -a *mf*

spaniel /ˈspænjəl/ *n* spaniel *m inv*

Spanish /ˈspænɪʃ/ [1] *adj* spagnolo
[2] *n* (language) spagnolo *m*; **the** ~ *pl* gli spagnoli

spank /spæŋk/ *vt* sculacciare

spanking /ˈspæŋkɪŋ/ [1] *n* sculacciata *f*
[2] *adj* fam **at a** ~ **pace** con passo spedito
[3] *adv* fam **a** ~ **new car** una macchina nuova di zecca

spanner /ˈspænə(r)/ *n* chiave *f* inglese

spar /spɑː(r)/ *vi* (pt/pp **sparred**) (boxing) allenarsi; (argue) litigare

spare /speə(r)/ [1] *adj* (surplus) in più; (additional) di riserva; **go** ~ (Br fam: be very angry) andare su tutte le furie
[2] *n* (part) ricambio *m*
[3] *vt* risparmiare; (do without) fare a meno di; **can you** ~ **five minutes?** avresti cinque minuti?; **no expense was** ~**d** non si è badato a spese; **to** ~ (surplus) in eccedenza

spare part *n* pezzo *m* di ricambio

spare ribs *npl* costine *fpl*

spare room *n* stanza *f* degli ospiti

spare time *n* tempo *m* libero

spare tyre Br, **spare tire** Am *n* Auto gomma *f* di scorta; (fam: fat) trippa *f*

spare wheel *n* ruota *f* di scorta

sparing /ˈspeərɪŋ/ *adj* parco (**with** di)

sparingly /ˈspeərɪŋlɪ/ *adv* con parsimonia

spark /spɑːk/ *n* scintilla *f*
■ **spark off** *vt* far scoppiare

sparkle /ˈspɑːkl/ [1] *n* scintillio *m*
[2] *vi* scintillare

sparkler /ˈspɑːklə(r)/ *n* candela *f* magica

sparkling /ˈspɑːklɪŋ/ *adj* frizzante; ⟨wine⟩ spumante

spark-plug *n* Auto candela *f*

sparrow /ˈspærəʊ/ *n* passero *m*

sparse /spɑːs/ *adj* rado

sparsely /ˈspɑːslɪ/ *adv* scarsamente; ~ **populated** ⟨area⟩ a bassa densità di popolazione

sparseness /ˈspɑːsnɪs/ *n* (of vegetation) radezza *f*

spartan /ˈspɑːtn/ *adj* spartano

spasm /ˈspæzm/ *n* spasmo *m*

spasmodic /spæzˈmɒdɪk/ *adj* spasmodico

spasmodically /spæzˈmɒdɪklɪ/ *adv* spasmodicamente

spastic /ˈspæstɪk/ [1] *adj* spastico
[2] *n* spastico, -a *mf*

spat /spæt/ ▶ SPIT[1]

spate /speɪt/ *n* (series) successione *f*; **be in full** ~ essere in piena

spatial /ˈspeɪʃl/ *adj* spaziale

spatio-temporal /speɪʃɪəˈtempərəl/ *adj* spazio-temporale

spatter /ˈspætə(r)/ *vt/i* schizzare

spatula /ˈspætjʊlə/ *n* spatola *f*

spawn /spɔːn/ [1] *n* uova *fpl* (di pesci, rane ecc)
[2] *vi* deporre le uova
[3] *vt* fig generare

spay /speɪ/ *vt* sterilizzare

speak /spiːk/ ① *vi* (pt **spoke**, pp **spoken**) parlare (**to** a); ~**ing!** Teleph sono io!
② *vt* dire; ~ **one's mind** dire quello che si pensa
■ **speak for** *vt* parlare a nome di; ~ **for yourself!** parla per te!
■ **speak of** *vt* ~ **well/ill of somebody** parlare bene/male di qualcuno; **nothing to** ~ **of** niente di speciale; (quantity) non un granché; ~**ing of holidays...** a proposito di vacanze...
■ **speak out** *vi* (protest) parlare
■ **speak up** *vi* parlare più forte; ~ **up for oneself** farsi valere

speaker /'spiːkə(r)/ *n* parlante *mf*; (in public) oratore, -trice *mf*; (of stereo) cassa *f*

speaking terms /'spiːkɪŋ/ *npl* **we are not on** ~ ~ non ci parliamo

spear /'spɪə(r)/ ① *n* lancia *f*
② *vt* trafiggere

spearhead /'spɪəhed/ *vt* fig essere l'iniziatore di

spearmint /'spɪəmɪnt/ *n* menta *f* verde

spec /spek/ *n* **on** ~ fam ⟨take, use⟩ in prova; ⟨go somewhere⟩ per ispezione

special /'speʃl/ *adj* speciale

special correspondent *n* inviato, -a *mf* speciale

special delivery *n* espresso *m*

special effect ① *n* Cinema, TV effetto *m* speciale
② *attrib* ~**s** ⟨specialist, team⟩ degli effetti speciali

special envoy *n* inviato, -a *mf* speciale

specialist /'speʃəlɪst/ *n* specialista *mf*

speciality /speʃɪ'ælətɪ/ *n* specialità *f inv*

specialize /'speʃəlaɪz/ *vi* specializzarsi

specially /'speʃəlɪ/ *adv* specialmente; (particularly) particolarmente

special measures *n* Br insieme di provvedimenti migliorativi di natura didattica, organizzativa, finanziaria o strutturale che una scuola deve adottare qualora non raggiunga gli standard educativi stabiliti dall'Ofsted

special needs *npl* difficoltà *f* d'apprendimento; **children with** ~ ~ bambini con difficoltà d'apprendimento

special offer *n* vendita *f* promozionale

special school *n* scuola *f* per bambini con difficoltà d'apprendimento

special treatment *n* trattamento *m* di riguardo

species /'spiːʃiːz/ *n* specie *f inv*

specific /spə'sɪfɪk/ *adj* specifico

specifically /spə'sɪfɪklɪ/ *adv* in modo specifico

specifications /spesɪfɪ'keɪʃnz/ *npl* descrizione *f*

specify /'spesɪfaɪ/ *vt* (pt/pp **-ied**) specificare

specimen /'spesɪmən/ *n* campione *m*

specious /'spiːʃəs/ *adj* ⟨argument, reasoning⟩ specioso

speck /spek/ *n* macchiolina *f*; (particle) granello *m*

speckled /'spekld/ *adj* picchiettato

spectacle /'spektəkl/ *n* (show) spettacolo *m*

spectacles /'spektəklz/ *npl* occhiali *mpl*

spectacular /spek'tækjʊlə(r)/ *adj* spettacolare

spectacularly /spek'tækjʊlətɪ/ *adv* in modo spettacolare

spectator /spek'teɪtə(r)/ *n* spettatore, -trice *mf*

spectator sport *n* sport *m inv* di intrattenimento

spectre /'spektə(r)/ *n* spettro *m*

spectrum /'spektrəm/ *n* (pl **-tra**) spettro *m*; fig gamma *f*

speculate /'spekjʊleɪt/ *vi* speculare

speculation /spekjʊ'leɪʃn/ *n* speculazione *f*

speculative /'spekjʊlətɪv/ *adj* speculativo

speculator /'spekjʊleɪtə(r)/ *n* speculatore, -trice *mf*

sped /sped/ ▶ SPEED

speech /spiːtʃ/ *n* linguaggio *m*; (address) discorso *m*; **make/give a** ~ fare un discorso

speech impediment *n* difetto *m* di pronuncia

speechless /'spiːtʃlɪs/ *adj* senza parole

speech therapist *n* logoterapista *mf*

speech therapy *n* logoterapia *f*

speech-writer *n* persona *f* che scrive i discorsi di personaggi pubblici

speed /spiːd/ ① *n* velocità *f inv*; (gear) marcia *f*; **at** ~ a tutta velocità
② *vi* (pt/pp **sped**) andare veloce
③ *vi* (pt/pp **speeded**) (go too fast) andare a velocità eccessiva
■ **speed up** (pt/pp **speeded up**) *vt/i* accelerare

speedboat *n* motoscafo *m*

speed bump *n* rallentatore *m*

speed camera *n* autovelox® *m inv*

speed hump *n* dosso *m* di rallentamento

speedily /'spiːdɪlɪ/ *adv* rapidamente

speeding /'spiːdɪŋ/ *n* eccesso *m* di velocità

speeding fine *n* multa *f* per eccesso di velocità

speed limit *n* limite *m* di velocità

s

speedometer /spiːˈdɒmɪtə(r)/ n
tachimetro m

speed skating n pattinaggio m di
velocità

speed trap n Auto tratto m di strada sul
quale la polizia controlla la velocità dei
veicoli

speedy /ˈspiːdɪ/ adj (**-ier**, **-iest**) rapido

speleologist /spiːlɪˈɒlədʒɪst/ n
speleologo, -a mf

speleology /spiːlɪˈɒlədʒɪ/ n speleologia f

spell[1] /spel/ n (turn) turno m; (of weather)
periodo m

spell[2] [1] vt (pt/pp **spelled** or **spelt**)
how do you ~...? come si scrive...?; **could
you ~ that for me?** me lo può compitare?;
~ disaster fig essere disastroso
[2] vi **he can't ~** fa molti errori
d'ortografia
■ **spell out** vt compitare; fig spiegare

spell[3] n (magic) incantesimo m

spellbound /ˈspelbaʊnd/ adj affascinato

spellcheck vt Comput fare il controllo
ortografico di ⟨document⟩

spellchecker /ˈspeltʃekə(r)/ n Comput
correttore m ortografico

spelling /ˈspelɪŋ/ n ortografia f

spelt /spelt/ ► SPELL[2]

spend /spend/ vt/i (pt/pp **spent**)
spendere; passare ⟨time⟩

spending cut n taglio m alla spesa

spending money /ˈspendɪŋ/ n soldi
mpl per le piccole spese

spending power n potere m
d'acquisto

spending spree n spese fpl folli

spendthrift /ˈspendθrɪft/ [1] adj
spendaccione; ⟨habit, policy⟩ dispendioso
[2] n spendaccione, -a mf

spent /spent/ ► SPEND

sperm /spɜːm/ n spermatozoo m; (semen)
sperma m

sperm bank n banca f dello sperma

sperm count n conteggio m di
spermatozoi

sperm donor n donatore m del seme

spermicidal /spɜːmɪˈsaɪdl/ adj
spermicida inv

spermicide /ˈspɜːmɪsaɪd/ n spermicida
m

spew /spjuː/ vt/i vomitare

sphere /sfɪə(r)/ n sfera f

sphere of influence n sfera f di
influenza

spherical /ˈsferɪkl/ adj sferico

spice /spaɪs/ n spezia f; fig pepe m

spick /spɪk/ adj **~ and span** lindo

spicy /ˈspaɪsɪ/ adj piccante

spider /ˈspaɪdə(r)/ n ragno m

spiderweb n Am = WEB

spiel /ʃpiːl/ n fam (sales pitch)
imbonimento m; (long repetitive speech)
tiritera f; **he gave me some ~ about...** mi
ha raccontato un sacco di storie su...

spike /spaɪk/ n punta f; Bot, Zool spina f;
(on shoe) chiodo m

spikes npl (shoes) scarpe fpl chiodate

spiky /ˈspaɪkɪ/ adj ⟨plant⟩ spinoso

spill /spɪl/ [1] vt (pt/pp **spilt** or **spilled**)
versare ⟨blood⟩; **~ the beans** fam vuotare
il sacco
[2] vi rovesciarsi
■ **spill over** vi ⟨water⟩ traboccare; **~
over into** degenerare in ⟨violence, rioting⟩

spillage /ˈspɪlɪdʒ/ n (of oil, chemical)
perdita f

spin /spɪn/ [1] vt (pt/pp **spun**, pres p
spinning) far girare; filare ⟨wool⟩;
centrifugare ⟨washing⟩
[2] vi girare; ⟨washing machine⟩
centrifugare
[3] n rotazione f; (short drive) giretto m
■ **spin out** vt far durare
■ **spin round** [1] vi (turn quickly) girare
vorticosamente; ⟨dancer, skater⟩
volteggiare; ⟨car⟩ fare un testa coda
[2] vt **~ somebody** or **something round** far
girare qualcuno o qualcosa

spinach /ˈspɪnɪdʒ/ n spinaci mpl

spinal /ˈspaɪnl/ adj spinale

spinal column n colonna f vertebrale

spinal cord n midollo m spinale

spindle /ˈspɪndl/ n fuso m

spindly /ˈspɪndlɪ/ adj affusolato

spin doctor n persona f incaricata di
presentare le scelte di un partito politico
sotto una luce favorevole

spin-drier n centrifuga f

spine /spaɪn/ n spina f dorsale; (of book)
dorso m; Bot, Zool spina f

spineless /ˈspaɪnlɪs/ adj fig smidollato

spinning /ˈspɪnɪŋ/ n filatura f

spinning wheel n filatoio m

spin-off n ricaduta f

spinster /ˈspɪnstə(r)/ n donna f nubile;
(old maid, fam) zitella f

spiny /ˈspaɪnɪ/ adj ⟨plant, animal⟩
spinoso

spiral /ˈspaɪrəl/ [1] adj a spirale
[2] n spirale f
[3] vi (pt/pp **spiralled**) formare una
spirale

spiral staircase n scala f a chiocciola

spire /spaɪə(r)/ n guglia f

spirit /ˈspɪrɪt/ n spirito m; (courage) ardore
m; **~s** pl (alcohol) liquori mpl; **in good ~s**
di buon umore; **in low ~s** abbattuto
■ **spirit away** vt far sparire

spirited /ˈspɪrɪtɪd/ adj vivace; (courageous)
pieno d'ardore

spirit level *n* livella *f* a bolla d'aria

spirit stove *n* fornellino *m* [da campeggio]

spiritual /'spɪrɪtjʊəl/ **1** *adj* spirituale **2** *n* spiritual *m*

spiritualism /'spɪrɪtjʊəlɪzm/ *n* spiritismo *m*

spiritualist /'spɪrɪtjʊəlɪst/ *n* spiritista *mf*

spit¹ /spɪt/ *n* (for roasting) spiedo *m*

spit² **1** *n* sputo *m*
2 *vt/i* (pt/pp **spat**, pres p **spitting**) sputare; ⟨cat⟩ soffiare; ⟨fat⟩ sfrigolare; **it's ~ting [with rain]** pioviggina; **the ~ting image of** il ritratto spiccicato di

spite /spaɪt/ **1** *n* dispetto *m*; **in ~ of** malgrado
2 *vt* far dispetto a

spiteful /'spaɪtfʊl/ *adj* indispettito

spitefully /'spaɪtfʊlɪ/ *adv* con aria indispettita

spit out *vt* sputare ⟨food⟩; **~ it out!** fam sputa l'osso!

spittle /'spɪtl/ *n* saliva *f*

splash /splæʃ/ **1** *n* schizzo *m*; (of colour) macchia *f*; (fam: drop) goccio *m*
2 *vt* schizzare; **~ somebody with something** schizzare qualcuno di qualcosa
3 *vi* schizzare
■ **splash about** *vi* schizzarsi
■ **splash down** *vi* ⟨spacecraft⟩ ammarare
■ **splash out** *vi* (spend freely) darsi alle spese folli

splashdown /'splæʃdaʊn/ *n* ammaraggio *m*

splatter /'splætə(r)/ **1** *vt* schizzare; **~ somebody/something with something** schizzare qualcuno/qualcosa di qualcosa
2 *vi* **~ onto/over something** ⟨ink, paint⟩ schizzare su qualcosa

splay /spleɪ/ *vt* divaricare ⟨legs, feet, fingers⟩; svasare ⟨end of pipe etc⟩; strombare ⟨side of window, door⟩; **~ed** ⟨feet, fingers, legs⟩ scartato

spleen /spliːn/ *n* Anat milza *f*

splendid /'splendɪd/ *adj* splendido

splendidly /'splendɪdlɪ/ *adv* splendidamente

splendour /'splendə(r)/ *n* splendore *m*

splice /splaɪs/ *vt* aggiuntare ⟨tape, film⟩

splint /splɪnt/ *n* Med stecca *f*

splinter /'splɪntə(r)/ **1** *n* scheggia *f*
2 *vi* scheggiarsi

splinter group *n* gruppo *m* scissionista

split /splɪt/ **1** *n* fessura *f*; (quarrel) rottura *f*; (division) scissione *f*; (tear) strappo *m*
2 *vt* (pt/pp **split**, pres p **splitting**) spaccare; (share, divide) dividere; (tear) strappare; **~ hairs** spaccare il capello in quattro; **~ one's sides** sbellicarsi dalle risa

3 *vi* spaccarsi; (tear) strapparsi; (divide) dividersi; **~ on somebody** fam denunciare qualcuno
4 *adj* **a ~ second** una frazione di secondo
■ **split up** **1** *vt* dividersi
2 *vi* ⟨couple⟩ separarsi

split ends *npl* (in hair) doppie punte *fpl*

split personality *n* sdoppiamento *m* della personalità

split screen *n* schermo *m* diviso

splitting /'splɪtɪŋ/ *adj* **have a ~ headache** avere un tremendo mal di testa

splutter /'splʌtə(r)/ *vi* farfugliare

spoil /spɔɪl/ **1** *n* **~s** *pl* bottino *msg*
2 *vt* (pt/pp **spoilt** or **spoiled**) rovinare; viziare ⟨person⟩
3 *vi* andare a male

spoiler /'spɔɪlə(r)/ *n* Auto, Aeron spoiler *m inv*

spoilsport /'spɔɪlspɔːt/ *n* guastafeste *mf inv*

spoilt /spɔɪlt/ *adj* ⟨child⟩ viziato; **be ~ for choice** non avere che l'imbarazzo della scelta

spoke¹ /spəʊk/ *n* raggio *m*

spoke² ▶ SPEAK

spoken /'spəʊkən/ **1** ▶ SPEAK
2 *adj* ⟨language⟩ parlato; **be ~ for** essere messo da parte per qualcuno

spokesman /'spəʊksmən/ *n* portavoce *m inv*

spokesperson /'spəʊkspɜːsn/ *n* portavoce *mf*

spokeswoman /'spəʊkswʊmən/ *n* portavoce *f*

sponge /spʌndʒ/ **1** *n* spugna *f*
2 *vt* pulire con la spugna
3 *vi* **~ on** fam scroccare da

sponge bag *n* nécessaire *m inv*

sponge cake *n* pan *m* di Spagna

sponger /'spʌndʒə(r)/ *n* scroccone, -a *mf*

spongy /'spʌndʒɪ/ *adj* spugnoso

sponsor /'spɒnsə(r)/ **1** *n* garante *mf*; Radio, TV sponsor *m inv*; (god-parent) padrino *m*, madrina *f*; (for membership) socio, -a *mf* garante
2 *vt* sponsorizzare

sponsorship /'spɒnsəʃɪp/ *n* sponsorizzazione *f*

sponsorship deal *n* accordo *m* con uno sponsor

spontaneity /spɒntə'neɪətɪ/ *n* spontaneità *f*

spontaneous /spɒn'teɪnɪəs/ *adj* spontaneo

spontaneously /spɒn'teɪnɪəslɪ/ *adv* spontaneamente

spoof /spuːf/ *n* fam parodia *f*

spook /spuːk/ fam ① vt (haunt)
perseguitare; (frighten) spaventare
② n (ghost) fantasma m; (Am: spy) spia f

spooky /'spuːkɪ/ adj (-ier, -iest) fam
sinistro

spool /spuːl/ n bobina f

spooling /'spuːlɪŋ/ n Comput spooling m

spoon /spuːn/ ① n cucchiaio m
② vt mettere col cucchiaio

spoonerism /'spuːnərɪzm/ n scambio m
delle iniziali di due parole con effetto
umoristico

spoon-feed vt (pt/pp -fed) fig imboccare

spoonful /'spuːnfʊl/ n cucchiaiata f

sporadic /spə'rædɪk/ adj sporadico

sporadically /spə'rædɪklɪ/ adv
sporadicamente

spore /spɔː(r)/ n spora f

sporran /'spɒrən/ n borsa f di cuoio o
pelo portata alla cintura dagli scozzesi
insieme al kilt

sport /spɔːt/ ① n sport m inv; **be a
[good]** ∼**!** sii sportivo!
② vt sfoggiare

sporting /'spɔːtɪŋ/ adj sportivo

sporting calendar n calendario m
sportivo

sporting chance n possibilità f inv

sports car n automobile f sportiva

sports centre Br, **sports center** Am
n centro m polisportivo

sports club n club m sportivo

sports coat n, **sports jacket** n
giacca f sportiva

sports ground n (large) stadio m; (in
school) campo m sportivo

sports jacket n = SPORTS COAT

sportsman n sportivo m

sports star n star f inv dello sport

sportswear n abbigliamento m
sportivo

sportswoman n sportiva f

sports writer n giornalista mf
sportivo, -a

sporty /'spɔːtɪ/ adj (-ier, -iest) sportivo

spot /spɒt/ ① n macchia f; (pimple)
brufolo m; (place) posto m; (in pattern) pois
m inv; (of rain) goccia f; (of water) goccio m;
∼**s** pl (rash) sfogo msg; **a** ∼ **of** fam un po'
di; **a** ∼ **of bother** qualche problema; **on
the** ∼ sul luogo; (immediately)
immediatamente; **in a [tight]** ∼ fam in
difficoltà
② vt (pt/pp **spotted**) macchiare; (fam:
notice) individuare

spot check n (without warning) controllo
m a sorpresa; **do a** ∼ ∼ **on something**
dare una controllata a qualcosa

spotless /'spɒtlɪs/ adj immacolato

spotlight n riflettore m; fig riflettori mpl

spot-on adj Br esatto

spot rate n Fin tasso m di cambio a vista

spotted /'spɒtɪd/ adj ⟨material⟩ a pois

spotty /'spɒtɪ/ adj (-ier, -iest) (pimply)
brufoloso

spot-weld vt saldare a punti

spouse /spaʊz/ n consorte mf

spout /spaʊt/ ① n becco m; **up the** ∼
(fam: ruined) all'aria
② vi zampillare (**from** da)

sprain /spreɪn/ ① n slogatura f
② vt slogare; ∼ **one's ankle** slogarsi la
caviglia

sprang /spræŋ/ ▶ SPRING²

sprat /spræt/ n spratto m

sprawl /sprɔːl/ vi (in chair) stravaccarsi;
⟨city etc⟩ estendersi; **go** ∼**ing** (fall) cadere
disteso

sprawling /'sprɔːlɪŋ/ adj ⟨suburb, city⟩
che si propaga disordinatamente;
⟨handwriting⟩ che occupa tutta la pagina

spray¹ /spreɪ/ n (of flowers) rametto m;
(bouquet) mazzolino m

spray² ① n spruzzo m; (from sea) spruzzo
m; (preparation) spray m inv; (container)
spruzzatore m
② vt spruzzare

spray can n bomboletta f spray inv

spray-gun n pistola f a spruzzo

spray-on adj ⟨conditioner, glitter⟩ spray
inv

spread /spred/ ① n estensione f; (of
disease) diffusione f; (paste) crema f; (fam:
feast) banchetto m
② vt (pt/pp **spread**) spargere; spalmare
⟨butter, jam⟩; stendere ⟨cloth, arms⟩;
diffondere ⟨news, disease⟩; dilazionare
⟨payments⟩; ∼ **something with** spalmare
qualcosa di
③ vi spargersi; ⟨butter⟩ spalmarsi;
⟨disease⟩ diffondersi
■ **spread out** ① vt sparpagliare
② vi sparpagliarsi

spread-eagled /-'iːgld/ adj a gambe e
braccia aperte

spreadsheet /'spredʃiːt/ n Comput foglio
m elettronico

spree /spriː/ n fam **go on a** ∼ far
baldoria; **go on a shopping** ∼ fare spese
folli

sprig /sprɪg/ n rametto m

sprightly /'spraɪtlɪ/ adj (-ier, -iest)
vivace

spring¹ /sprɪŋ/ ① n primavera f; **in** ∼, **in
the** ∼ in primavera
② attrib primaverile

spring² ① n (jump) balzo m; (water)
sorgente f; (device) molla f; (elasticity)
elasticità f
② vi (pt **sprang**, pp **sprung**) balzare;
(arise) provenire (**from** da); ∼ **to mind**
saltare in mente

3 *vt* **he just sprang it on me** me l'ha detto a cose fatte

■ **spring up** *vi* balzare; fig spuntare

springboard *n* trampolino *m*

spring chicken *n* Culin pollastrello *m*, pollastrella *f*; **she's no ~ ~** fam non è una giovincella

spring-clean *vt* pulire a fondo

spring-cleaning *n* pulizie *fpl* di Pasqua

spring onion *n* cipollotto *m*

springtime *n* primavera *f*

springy /'sprɪŋɪ/ *adj* ‹mattress, sofa› molleggiato

sprinkle /'sprɪŋkl/ *vt* (scatter) spruzzare ‹liquid›; spargere ‹flour, cocoa›; **~ something with** spruzzare qualcosa di ‹liquid›; cospargere qualcosa di ‹flour, cocoa›

sprinkler /'sprɪŋklə(r)/ *n* sprinkler *m inv*; (for garden) irrigatore *m*

sprinkling /'sprɪŋklɪŋ/ *n* (of liquid) spruzzatina *f*; (of pepper, salt) pizzico *m*; (of flour, sugar) spolveratina *f*; (of knowledge) infarinatura *f*; (of people) pugno *m*

sprint /sprɪnt/ **1** *n* sprint *m inv* **2** *vi* fare uno sprint; Sport sprintare

sprinter /'sprɪntə(r)/ *n* sprinter *mf inv*

sprite /spraɪt/ *n* folletto *m*

spritzer /'sprɪtsə(r)/ *n* spritz *m inv*, spritzer *m inv*

sprout /spraʊt/ **1** *n* germoglio *m*; **[Brussels] ~s** *pl* cavolini *mpl* di Bruxelles **2** *vi* germogliare

spruce /spru:s/ **1** *adj* elegante **2** *n* abete *m*

■ **spruce up** *vt* dare una ripulita a

sprung /sprʌŋ/ **1** ▶ SPRING² **2** *adj* molleggiato

spry /spraɪ/ *adj* (**-er, -est**) arzillo

spud /spʌd/ *n* fam patata *f*

spun /spʌn/ ▶ SPIN

spur /spɜ:(r)/ **1** *n* sperone *m*; (stimulus) stimolo *m*; (road) svincolo *m*; **on the ~ of the moment** su due piedi **2** *vt* (pt/pp **spurred**) **~ [on]** fig spronare

spurious /'spjʊərɪəs/ *adj* falso

spuriously /'spjʊərɪəslɪ/ *adv* falsamente

spurn /spɜ:n/ *vt* sdegnare

spurt /spɜ:t/ **1** *n* getto *m*; Sport scatto *m*; **put on a ~** fare uno scatto **2** *vi* sprizzare; (increase speed) scattare

sputter /'spʌtə(r)/ **1** *vi* ‹engine› scoppiettare **2** *n* colpi *mpl* irregolari del motore

spy /spaɪ/ **1** *n* spia *f* **2** *vi* spiare **3** *vt* (fam: see) spiare

■ **spy on** *vt* spiare

■ **spy out** *vt* esplorare

spying /'spaɪɪŋ/ *n* spionaggio *m*

squabble /'skwɒbl/ **1** *n* bisticcio *m* **2** *vi* bisticciare

squabbling /'skwɒblɪŋ/ *n* bisticci *mpl*

squad /skwɒd/ *n* squadra *f*

squad car *n* macchina *f* della volante

squaddie /'skwɒdɪ/ *n* Br fam soldato *m* semplice

squadron /'skwɒdrən/ *n* Mil squadrone *m*; Aeron, Naut squadriglia *f*

squalid /'skwɒlɪd/ *adj* squallido

squalidly /'skwɒlɪdlɪ/ *adv* squallidamente

squall /skwɔ:l/ **1** *n* (howl) strillo *m*; (storm) bufera *f* **2** *vi* strillare

squally /'skwɔ:lɪ/ *adj* burrascoso

squalor /'skwɒlə(r)/ *n* squallore *m*

squander /'skwɒndə(r)/ *vt* sprecare

square /skweə(r)/ **1** *adj* quadrato; ‹meal› sostanzioso; (fam: old-fashioned) vecchio stampo; **all ~** fam pari **2** *n* quadrato *m*; (in city) piazza *f*; (on chessboard) riquadro *m*; **be back to ~ one** riessere al punto di partenza **3** *vt* (settle) far quadrare; Math elevare al quadrato **4** *vi* (agree) armonizzare

■ **square up** *vi* (settle accounts) saldare

■ **square up to** *vt* affrontare

square bracket *n* parentesi *f inv* quadra; **in ~ ~s** tra parentesi quadre

square dance *n* quadriglia *f*

squarely /'skweəlɪ/ *adv* direttamente

square root *n* radice *f* quadrata

squash /skwɒʃ/ **1** *n* calca *f*; (drink) spremuta *f*; (sport) squash *m*; (vegetable) zucca *f* **2** *vt* schiacciare; soffocare ‹rebellion› ■ **squash up** *vi* (move closer together) stringersi

squashy /'skwɒʃɪ/ *adj* floscio

squat /skwɒt/ **1** *adj* tarchiato **2** *n* fam edificio *m* occupato abusivamente **3** *vi* (pt/pp **squatted**) accovacciarsi; **~ in** occupare abusivamente

squatter /'skwɒtə(r)/ *n* occupante *mf* abusivo, -a

squaw /skwɔ:/ *n* squaw *f inv*

squawk /skwɔ:k/ **1** *n* gracchio *m* **2** *vi* gracchiare

squeak /skwi:k/ **1** *n* squittio *m*; (of hinge, brakes) cigolio *m* **2** *vi* squittire; ‹hinge, brakes› cigolare

squeaking /'skwi:kɪŋ/ *n* (of door, hinge) cigolio *m*

squeaky /'skwi:kɪ/ *adj* ‹door, hinge› cigolante

squeaky-clean *adj* fam ‹glass, hair› lucente; ‹floor› tirato a specchio; fig ····>

S

⟨*person*⟩ senza vizi; ⟨*company*⟩ al di sopra di ogni sospetto

squeal /skwiːl/ ① *n* strillo *m*; (of brakes) cigolio *m*
② *vi* strillare; sl spifferare

squeamish /'skwiːmɪʃ/ *adj* dallo stomaco delicato; (scrupulous) troppo scrupoloso

squeegee /'skwiːdʒiː/ *n* Phot rullo *m* asciugatore; (for glasses) lavavetri *m inv*

squeeze /skwiːz/ ① *n* stretta *f*; (crush) pigia pigia *m inv*; **give sb's hand a ~** dare a qualcuno una stretta di mano
② *vt* premere; (to get juice) spremere; stringere ⟨*hand*⟩; (force) stringere a forza; (fam: extort) estorcere (**out of** da)
■ **squeeze in/out** *vi* sgusciare dentro/ fuori
■ **squeeze past** *vi* ⟨*person, car*⟩ passare
■ **squeeze up** *vi* stringersi

squelch /skweltʃ/ *vi* sguazzare

squib /skwɪb/ *n* petardo *m*

squid /skwɪd/ *n* calamaro *m*

squidgy /'skwɪdʒɪ/ *adj* (Br fam: squashy) molliccio

squiggle /'skwɪɡl/ *n* scarabocchio *m*

squint /skwɪnt/ ① *n* strabismo *m*
② *vi* essere strabico

squire /'skwaɪə(r)/ *n* signorotto *m* di campagna

squirm /skwɜːm/ *vi* contorcersi; (feel embarrassed) sentirsi imbarazzato

squirrel /'skwɪrəl/ *n* scoiattolo *m*

squirt /skwɜːt/ ① *n* spruzzo *m*; (fam: person) presuntuoso *m*
② *vt/i* spruzzare

Sri Lanka /srɪ'læŋkə/ *n* Sri Lanka *m*

St abbr (**Saint**) S; abbr **Street**

stab /stæb/ ① *n* pugnalata *f*, coltellata *f*; (sensation) fitta *f*; (fam: attempt) tentativo *m*
② *vt* (pt/pp **stabbed**) pugnalare, accoltellare

stability /stə'bɪlətɪ/ *n* stabilità *f inv*

stabilization /steɪbɪlaɪ'zeɪʃn/ *n* stabilizzazione *f*

stabilize /'steɪbɪlaɪz/ ① *vt* stabilizzare
② *vi* stabilizzarsi

stabilizer /'steɪbɪlaɪzə(r)/ *n* stabilizzatore *m*; (on bike) rotella *f*; (in food) stabilizzante *m*

stable¹ /'steɪbl/ *adj* stabile

stable² *n* stalla *f*; (establishment) scuderia *f*

staccato /stə'kɑːtəʊ/ ① *adj* Mus staccato; ⟨*gasps, shots*⟩ intermittente
② *adv* ⟨*play*⟩ staccatamente

stack /stæk/ ① *n* catasta *f*; (of chimney) comignolo *m*; (chimney) ciminiera *f*; (fam: large quantity) montagna *f*; **~s of** ⟨*money, time, work*⟩ un sacco di
② *vt* accatastare

stadium /'steɪdɪəm/ *n* stadio *m*

staff /stɑːf/ ① *n* (stick) bastone *m*; (employees) personale *m*; (teachers) corpo *m* insegnante; Mil Stato *m* Maggiore
② *vt* fornire di personale

staff meeting *n* riunione *f* del corpo insegnante

staffroom /'stɑːfruːm/ *n* Sch sala *f* insegnanti

stag /stæɡ/ *n* cervo *m*

stage /steɪdʒ/ ① *n* palcoscenico *m*; (profession) teatro *m*; (in journey) tappa *f*; (in process) stadio *m*; **go on the ~** darsi al teatro; **by** or **in ~s** a tappe
② *vt* mettere in scena; (arrange) organizzare

stagecoach *n* diligenza *f*

stage door *n* ingresso *m* degli artisti

stage fright *n* panico *m* da palcoscenico

stage-manage *vt* fig orchestrare

stage manager *n* direttore, -trice *mf* di scena

stage-struck /-strʌk/ *adj* appassionatissimo di teatro

stagger /'stæɡə(r)/ ① *vi* barcollare
② *vt* sbalordire; scaglionare ⟨*holidays, payments etc*⟩; **I was ~ed** sono rimasto sbalordito
③ *n* vacillamento *m*

staggering /'stæɡərɪŋ/ *adj* sbalorditivo

stagnant /'stæɡnənt/ *adj* stagnante

stagnate /stæɡ'neɪt/ *vi* fig [ri]stagnare

stagnation /stæɡ'neɪʃn/ *n* fig inattività *f*

stag night, **stag party** *n* addio *m* al celibato

staid /steɪd/ *adj* posato

stain /steɪn/ ① *n* macchia *f*; (for wood) mordente *m*
② *vt* macchiare; ⟨*wood*⟩ dare il mordente a

stained glass /steɪnd'ɡlɑːs/ *n* vetro *m* colorato

stained-glass window *n* vetrata *f* colorata

stainless /'steɪnlɪs/ *adj* senza macchia

stainless steel *n* acciaio *m* inossidabile

stain remover *n* smacchiatore *m*

stair /steə(r)/ *n* gradino *m*; **~s** *pl* scale *fpl*

staircase /'steəkeɪs/ *n* scale *fpl*

stairlift *n* montascale *m inv*

stake /steɪk/ ① *n* palo *m*; (wager) posta *f*; Comm partecipazione *f*; **at ~** in gioco
② *vt* puntellare; (wager) scommettere; **~ a claim to something** rivendicare qualcosa
■ **stake out** *vt* mettere sotto sorveglianza ⟨*building*⟩

stake-out *n* fam sorveglianza *f*

stalactite /'stæləktaɪt/ *n* stalattite *f*

stalagmite /'stæləgmaɪt/ n stalagmite f

stale /steɪl/ adj stantio; ⟨air⟩ viziato; (uninteresting) trito [e ritrito]

stalemate /'steɪlmeɪt/ n (in chess) stallo m; (deadlock) situazione f di stallo

stalk[1] /stɔːk/ n gambo m

stalk[2] [1] vt inseguire
[2] vi camminare impettito

stalker /'stɔːkə(r)/ n (of person) persona f che perseguita qualcuno per cui ha una fissazione maniacale

stalking /'stɔːkɪŋ/ n (of person) persecuzione f di una persona per cui si ha una fissazione maniacale

stall /stɔːl/ [1] n box m inv; (in market) bancarella f; ~s pl Theat platea f
[2] vi ⟨engine⟩ spegnersi; fig temporeggiare
[3] vt far spegnere ⟨engine⟩; tenere a bada ⟨person⟩

stallholder /'stɔːlhəʊldə(r)/ n bancarellista mf

stallion /'stæljən/ n stallone m

stalwart /'stɔːlwət/ [1] adj fedele
[2] n sostenitore m fedele

stamina /'stæmɪnə/ n [capacità f di] resistenza f

stammer /'stæmə(r)/ [1] n balbettio m
[2] vt/i balbettare

stamp /stæmp/ [1] n (postage ~) francobollo m; (instrument) timbro m; fig impronta f
[2] vt affrancare ⟨letter⟩; timbrare ⟨bill⟩; battere ⟨feet⟩
■ **stamp out** vt spegnere; fig soffocare

stamp collecting n filatelia f

stamp collector n collezionista mf di francobolli

stamped addressed envelope busta f affrancata per la risposta

stampede /stæm'piːd/ [1] n fuga f precipitosa; fam fuggifuggi m inv
[2] vi fuggire precipitosamente

stance /stɑːns/ n posizione f

stand /stænd/ [1] n (for bikes) rastrelliera f; (at exhibition) stand m inv; (in market) bancarella f; (in stadium) gradinata f; fig posizione f
[2] vi (pt/pp **stood**) stare in piedi; (rise) alzarsi [in piedi]; (be) trovarsi; (be candidate) essere candidato (**for** a); (stay valid) rimanere valido; **I don't know where I** ~ non so qual è la mia posizione; ~ **still** non muoversi; ~ **firm** fig tener duro; ~ **on ceremony** formalizzarsi; ~ **together** essere solidali; ~ **to lose/gain** rischiare di perdere/vincere; ~ **to reason** essere logico
[3] vt (withstand) resistere a; (endure) sopportare; (place) mettere; ~ **a chance** avere una possibilità; ~ **one's ground** tener duro; ~ **the test of time** superare la prova del tempo; ~ **somebody a beer** offrire una birra a qualcuno

■ **stand back** vi (withdraw) farsi da parte
■ **stand by** [1] vi stare a guardare; (be ready) essere pronto
[2] vt (support) appoggiare
■ **stand down** vi (retire) ritirarsi
■ **stand for** vt (mean) significare; (tolerate) tollerare
■ **stand in for** vt sostituire
■ **stand out** vi spiccare
■ **stand up** vi alzarsi [in piedi]
■ **stand up for** vt prendere le difese di; ~ **up for oneself** farsi valere
■ **stand up to** vt affrontare

stand-alone adj Comput stand-alone

standard /'stændəd/ [1] adj standard; **be** ~ **practice** essere pratica corrente
[2] n standard m inv; Techn norma f; (level) livello m; (quality) qualità f inv; (flag) stendardo m; ~s pl (morals) valori mpl

Standard Assessment Tasks n Br esami mpl sostenuti per tranche d'età allo scopo di testare la preparazione degli alunni

standardization /stændədar'zeɪʃn/ n standardizzazione f

standardize /'stændədaɪz/ vt standardizzare

standard lamp n lampada f a stelo

standard of living n tenore m di vita

standby /'stændbaɪ/ [1] n (person) riserva f
[2] attrib ⟨circuit, battery⟩ di emergenza; ⟨passenger⟩ in lista di attesa; ⟨ticket⟩ stand-by inv
[3] adv ⟨fly⟩ con biglietto stand-by

stand-in n controfigura f

standing /'stændɪŋ/ [1] adj (erect) in piedi; (permanent) permanente
[2] n posizione f; (duration) durata f

standing charge n canone m

standing order n ordine m permanente

standing ovation n **give somebody a** ~ ~ alzarsi per applaudire qualcuno

standing room n posti mpl in piedi

stand-off n punto m morto

stand-offish /stænd'ɒfɪʃ/ adj scostante

standpoint n punto m di vista

standstill n **come to a** ~ fermarsi; **at a** ~ in un periodo di stasi

stand-up [1] adj ⟨buffet⟩ in piedi; ⟨argument⟩ accanito
[2] n (comedy) recital m inv di un comico

stand-up comedian comico m che intrattiene il pubblico con barzellette

stank /stæŋk/ ▶ STINK

Stanley knife® /'stænlɪ/ n cutter m inv

stanza /'stænzə/ n strofa f

staple[1] /'steɪpl/ n (product) prodotto m principale

staple[2] [1] n graffa f, pinzatrice f

2 *vt* pinzare

staple diet *n* a ~ ~ of una dieta basata principalmente su

staple gun *n* pistola *f* sparachiodi

stapler /'steɪplə(r)/ *n* pinzatrice *f*, cucitrice *f*

staple remover *n* levapunti *m inv*

star /stɑː(r)/ **1** *n* stella *f*; (asterisk) asterisco *m*; Theat, Cinema, Sport divo, -a *mf*, stella *f*
2 *vi* (pt/pp **starred**) essere l'interprete principale (**in** di)

starboard /'stɑːbəd/ *n* tribordo *m*

starch /stɑːtʃ/ **1** *n* amido *m*
2 *vt* inamidare

starchy /'stɑːtʃɪ/ *adj* ricco di amido; fig compito

stardom /'stɑːdəm/ *n* celebrità *f*

stare /steə(r)/ **1** *n* sguardo *m* fisso
2 *vi* it's rude to ~ è da maleducati fissare la gente; ~ at fissare; ~ into space guardare nel vuoto

starfish /'stɑːfɪʃ/ *n* stella *f* di mare

stark /stɑːk/ **1** *adj* austero; ⟨contrast⟩ forte
2 *adv* completamente; ~ **naked** completamente nudo

starlet /'stɑːlɪt/ *n* stellina *f*

starling /'stɑːlɪŋ/ *n* storno *m*

starlit /'stɑːlɪt/ *adj* stellato

starry /'stɑːrɪ/ *adj* stellato

starry-eyed /-'aɪd/ *adj* fam ingenuo

star sign *n* segno *m* zodiacale

star-struck /-strʌk/ *adj* ossessionato dalle celebrità

star-studded /-stʌdɪd/ *adj* ⟨cast, line-up⟩ con molti interpreti famosi; ⟨sky⟩ stellato

start /stɑːt/ **1** *n* inizio *m*; (departure) partenza *f*; (jump) sobbalzo *m*; **from the ~** [fin] dall'inizio; **for a ~** tanto per cominciare; **give somebody a ~** Sport dare un vantaggio a qualcuno
2 *vi* [in]cominciare; (set out) avviarsi; ⟨engine, car⟩ partire; (jump) trasalire; **to ~ with,...** tanto per cominciare,...
3 *vt* [in]cominciare; (cause) dare inizio a; (found) mettere su; mettere in moto ⟨car⟩; mettere in giro ⟨rumour⟩
■ **start off** *vi* (begin) cominciare
■ **start on** *vt* fam (attack) criticare; (nag) punzecchiare
■ **start out** *vi* (on journey) partire
■ **start over** *vt* Am (with task) ricominciare
■ **start up** *vt* mettere in funzione ⟨engine⟩; avviare ⟨business⟩

starter /'stɑːtə(r)/ *n* Culin primo *m* [piatto *m*]; (in race: giving signal) starter *m inv*; (participant) concorrente *mf*; Auto motorino *m* d'avviamento

starting point /'stɑːtɪŋ/ *n* punto *m* di partenza

starting salary *n* stipendio *m* iniziale

startle /'stɑːtl/ *vt* far trasalire; ⟨news⟩ sconvolgere

startling /'stɑːtlɪŋ/ *adj* sconvolgente

start-up capital *n* capitale *m* di avviamento

starvation /stɑː'veɪʃn/ *n* fame *f*

starve /stɑːv/ **1** *vi* morire di fame
2 *vt* far morire di fame

starving /'stɑːvɪŋ/ *adj* be ~ (dying of hunger) soffrire la fame; (fam: very hungry) morire di fame

stash /stæʃ/ *vt* fam ~ **[away]** nascondere

state /steɪt/ **1** *n* stato *m*; Pol Stato *m*; (grand style) pompa *f*; **be in a ~** ⟨person⟩ essere agitato; **lie in ~** essere esposto
2 *attrib* di Stato; Sch pubblico; (with ceremony) di gala
3 *vt* dichiarare; (specify) precisare

state-aided /-'eɪdɪd/ *adj* sovvenzionato dallo Stato

State Department *n* Am Pol ministero *m* degli [affari] esteri

state-funded *adj* sovvenzionato dallo Stato

stateless /'steɪtlɪs/ *adj* apolide

stately /'steɪtlɪ/ *adj* (**-ier, -iest**) maestoso

stately home *n* dimora *f* signorile

statement /'steɪtmənt/ *n* dichiarazione *f*; Jur deposizione *f*; (from bank) estratto *m* conto; (account) rapporto *m*

state of emergency *n* stato *m* di emergenza

state of play *n* punteggio *m*

state of the art *adj* ⟨technology⟩ il più avanzato

stateside /'steɪtsaɪd/ **1** *adj* degli Stati Uniti
2 *adv* negli Stati Uniti

statesman /'steɪtsmən/ *n* statista *m*

static /'stætɪk/ *adj* statico

static electricity *n* elettricità *f* statica

station /'steɪʃn/ **1** *n* stazione *f*; (police) commissariato *m*
2 *vt* appostare ⟨guard⟩; **be ~ed in** Germany essere di stanza in Germania

stationary /'steɪʃənərɪ/ *adj* immobile

stationer /'steɪʃənə(r)/ *n* ~'s **[shop]** cartoleria *f*

stationery /'steɪʃənərɪ/ *n* cartoleria *f*

station wagon *n* Am station-wagon *f inv*

statistical /stə'tɪstɪkl/ *adj* statistico

statistically /stə'tɪstɪklɪ/ *adv* statisticamente

statistician /stætɪs'tɪʃn/ *n* esperto *m* di statistica

statistics /stə'tɪstɪks/ *n* (subject) statistica *f*; (pl: figures) statistiche *fpl*

statue /'stætju:/ *n* statua *f*

statuesque /stætju'esk/ *adj* statuario

stature /'stætʃə(r)/ *n* statura *f*

status /'steɪtəs/ *n* condizione *f*; (high rank) alto rango *m*

status bar *n* Comput barra *f* di stato

status quo /kwəʊ/ *n* statu quo *m inv*

status symbol *n* status symbol *m inv*

statute /'stætju:t/ *n* statuto *m*

statutory /'stætjʊtərɪ/ *adj* statutario

staunch /stɔ:ntʃ/ *adj* fedele

staunchly /'stɔ:ntʃlɪ/ *adv* fedelmente

stave /steɪv/ *vt* ∼ **off** tenere lontano

stay /steɪ/ ① *n* soggiorno *m*
② *vi* restare, rimanere; (reside) alloggiare; ∼ **the night** passare la notte; ∼ **put** non muoversi
③ *vt* ∼ **the course** resistere fino alla fine
■ **stay away** *vi* stare lontano
■ **stay behind** *vi* non andare con gli altri
■ **stay in** *vi* (at home) stare in casa; Sch restare a scuola dopo le lezioni
■ **stay on** *vi* (remain) rimanere; ∼ **on at school** continuare gli studi
■ **stay up** *vi* stare su; (person) stare alzato

staying power /'steɪɪŋ/ *n* capacità *f* di resistenza

STD *abbr* **sexually transmitted disease**

STD [area] code *n* Br prefisso *m* [di teleselezione]

stead /sted/ *n* **in his** ∼ in sua vece; **stand somebody in good** ∼ tornare utile a qualcuno

steadfast /'stedfɑ:st/ *adj* fedele; (refusal) fermo

steadily /'stedɪlɪ/ *adv* (continually) continuamente

steady /'stedɪ/ ① *adj* (**-ier, -iest**) saldo, fermo; (breathing) regolare; (job, boyfriend) fisso; (dependable) serio
② *adv* **be going** ∼ (couple) fare coppia fissa

steak /steɪk/ *n* (for stew) spezzatino *m*; (for grilling, frying) bistecca *f*

steal /sti:l/ *vt* (*pt* **stole**, *pp* **stolen**) rubare (**from** da); ∼ **the show** essere al centro dell'attenzione
■ **steal in/out** *vi* entrare/uscire furtivamente

stealth /stelθ/ *n* **by** ∼ di nascosto

stealthily /'stelθɪlɪ/ *adv* furtivamente

stealthy /'stelθɪ/ *adj* furtivo

steam /sti:m/ ① *n* vapore *m*; **under one's own** ∼ fam da solo; **let off** ∼ fig sfogarsi
② *vt* Culin cucinare a vapore
③ *vi* fumare
■ **steam up** *vi* (window) appannarsi

steamed up /sti:md'ʌp/ *adj* **get** ∼ **up** (angry) andare su tutte le furie

steam engine *n* locomotiva *f*

steamer /'sti:mə(r)/ *n* piroscafo *m*; (saucepan) pentola *f* a vapore

steam iron *n* ferro *m* [da stiro] a vapore

steamroller /'sti:mrəʊlə(r)/ *n* rullo *m* compressore

steamy /'sti:mɪ/ *adj* appannato; fig (scene) spinto

steel /sti:l/ ① *n* acciaio *m*
② *vt* ∼ **oneself** temprarsi

steel wool *n* lana *f* d'acciaio

steelworks *n* acciaieria *f*

steely /'sti:lɪ/ *adj* d'acciaio

steep¹ /sti:p/ *vt* (soak) lasciare a bagno; ∼**ed in** fig immerso in

steep² *adj* ripido; fam (price) esorbitante

steeple /'sti:pl/ *n* campanile *m*

steeplechase /'sti:pltʃeɪs/ *n* corsa *f* ippica a ostacoli

steeplejack /'sti:pldʒæk/ *n* persona *f* che ripara campanili e ciminiere

steeply /'sti:plɪ/ *adv* ripidamente

steer /stɪə(r)/ *vt/i* guidare; ∼ **clear of** stare alla larga da

steering /'stɪərɪŋ/ *n* Auto sterzo *m*

steering column *n* Auto piantone *m* dello sterzo

steering committee *n* comitato *m* direttivo

steering lock *n* Auto bloccasterzo *m*; (turning circle) angolo *m* di massima sterzata

steering wheel *n* volante *m*

stem¹ /stem/ ① *n* stelo *m*; (of glass) gambo *m*; (of word) radice *f*
② *vi* (*pt/pp* **stemmed**) ∼ **from** derivare da

stem² *vt* (*pt/pp* **stemmed**) contenere

stem ginger *n* zenzero *m* sciroppato

stench /stentʃ/ *n* fetore *m*

stencil /'stensl/ ① *n* stampino *m*; (decoration) stampo *m*
② *vt* (*pt/pp* **stencilled**) stampinare

stenographer /stɪ'nɒgrəfə(r)/ *n* stenografo, -a *mf*

stenography /stɪ'nɒgrəfɪ/ *n* stenografia *f*

step /step/ ① *n* passo *m*; (stair) gradino *m*; ∼**s** *pl* (ladder) scaleo *m*; **in** ∼ al passo; **be out of** ∼ non stare al passo; ∼ **by** ∼ un passo alla volta
② *vi* (*pt/pp* **stepped**) ∼ **into** entrare in; ∼ **into sb's shoes** succedere a qualcuno; ∼ **out of** uscire da; ∼ **out of line** sgarrare
■ **step back** *vi* fare un passo indietro; ∼ **back from something** fig prendere le distanze da qualcosa
■ **step down** *vi* fig dimettersi
■ **step forward** *vi* farsi avanti

S

■ **step in** *vi* fig intervenire
■ **step up** *vt* (increase) aumentare
step aerobics *n* step *m inv*
stepbrother *n* fratellastro *m*
stepchild *n* figliastro, -a *mf*
stepdaughter *n* figliastra *f*
stepfather *n* patrigno *m*
stepladder *n* scaleo *m*
stepmother *n* matrigna *f*
stepping stone /'stepɪŋ/ *n* pietra *f* per guadare; fig trampolino *m*
stepsister /'stepsɪstə(r)/ *n* sorellastra *f*
stepson /'stepsʌn/ *n* figliastro *m*
stereo /'sterɪəʊ/ *n* stereo *m*; **in ~** in stereofonia
stereophonic /sterɪəʊ'fɒnɪk/ *adj* stereofonico
stereoscopic /sterɪəʊ'skɒɪk/ *adj* stereoscopico
stereotype /'sterɪətaɪp/ *n* stereotipo *m*
stereotyped /'sterɪətaɪpt/ *adj* stereotipato
sterile /'steraɪl/ *adj* sterile
sterility /stə'rɪlətɪ/ *n* sterilità *f*
sterilization /sterəlaɪ'zeɪʃn/ *n* sterilizzazione *f*
sterilize /'sterɪlaɪz/ *vt* sterilizzare
sterling /'stɜːlɪŋ/ ① *adj* fig apprezzabile ② *n* sterlina *f*
sterling silver *n* argento *m* pregiato
stern¹ /stɜːn/ *adj* severo
stern² *n* (of boat) poppa *f*
sternly /'stɜːnlɪ/ *adv* severamente
steroid /'sterɔɪd/ *n* steroide *m*
stet /stet/ (in proofreading) vive
stethoscope /'steθəskəʊp/ *n* stetoscopio *m*
stetson /'stetsən/ *n* cappello *m* da cowboy
stew /stjuː/ ① *n* stufato *m*; **in a ~** fam agitato ② *vt/i* cuocere in umido; **~ed fruit** frutta *f* cotta
steward /'stjuːəd/ *n* (at meeting) organizzatore, -trice *mf*; (on ship, aircraft) steward *m inv*
stewardess /stjuːə'des/ *n* hostess *f inv*
stick¹ /stɪk/ *n* bastone *m*; (of celery, rhubarb) gambo *m*; Sport mazza *f*
stick² ① *vt* (pt/pp **stuck**) (stab) conficcare; (glue) attaccare; (fam: put) mettere; (fam: endure) sopportare; **be stuck** (vehicle, person) essere bloccato; (drawer) essere incastrato; **stuck in a traffic jam** bloccato nel traffico; **be stuck for an answer** non saper cosa rispondere; **stuck on** fam attratto da; **be stuck with something** fam farsi incastrare con qualcosa

② *vi* (adhere) attaccarsi (**to** a); (jam) bloccarsi
■ **stick around** *vi* (fam: stay) rimanere
■ **stick at** *vt* **~ at it** fam tener duro; **~ at nothing** fam non fermarsi di fronte a niente
■ **stick by** *vt* (be faithful to) rimanere al fianco di (somebody)
■ **stick down** *vt* incollare (flap); (fam: write down, put down) mettere
■ **stick out** ① *vi* (project) sporgere; (fam: catch the eye) risaltare ② *vt* fam fare (tongue); **~ it out** (endure) tener duro; **~ one's neck out** sbilanciarsi
■ **stick to** *vt* (keep to) attenersi a (rules, facts); mantenere (story); perseverare in (task); **I'll ~ to beer** continuo con la birra
■ **stick together** *vi* (pages) incollarsi; (be loyal) aiutarsi a vicenda; (not split up) rimanere uniti
■ **stick up** *vi* (project) sporgere
■ **stick up for** *vt* fam difendere
■ **stick with** *vt* (remain with) rimanere con (somebody)
sticker /'stɪkə(r)/ *n* autoadesivo *m*
sticking plaster /'stɪkɪʃ/ *n* cerotto *m*
stick insect *n* insetto stecco *m*
stick-in-the-mud *n* retrogrado *m*
stickler /'stɪklə(r)/ *n* **be a ~ for** tenere molto a
stick-up *n* fam rapina *f* a mano armata
sticky /'stɪkɪ/ ① *adj* (**-ier**, **-iest**) appiccicoso; (adhesive) adesivo; (fig: difficult) difficile ② *n* fam post-it® *m inv*
sticky tape *n* fam nastro *m* adesivo
stiff /stɪf/ *adj* rigido; (brush, task) duro; (person) controllato; (drink) forte; (penalty) severo; (price) alto; **bored ~** fam annoiato a morte; **~ neck** torcicollo *m*
stiffen /'stɪfn/ ① *vt* irrigidire ② *vi* irrigidirsi
stiffly /'stɪflɪ/ *adv* rigidamente; (smile, answer) in modo controllato
stiffness /'stɪfnɪs/ *n* rigidità *f*
stifle /'staɪfl/ *vt* soffocare
stifling /'staɪflɪŋ/ *adj* soffocante
stigma /'stɪgmə/ *n* marchio *m*
stigmatize /'stɪgmətaɪz/ *vt* bollare
stile /staɪl/ *n* scaletta *f*
stiletto /stɪ'letəʊ/ *n* stiletto *m*; **~ heels** tacchi *mpl* a spillo; **~s** (pl: shoes) scarpe *fpl* coi tacchi a spillo
still¹ /stɪl/ *n* distilleria *f*
still² ① *adj* fermo; (drink) non gasato; **keep/stand ~** stare fermo ② *n* quiete *f*; (photo) posa *f* ③ *adv* ancora; (nevertheless) nondimeno, comunque; **I'm ~ not sure** non sono ancora sicuro
stillborn /'stɪlbɔːn/ *adj* nato morto
still life *n* natura *f* morta

stilted /'stɪltɪd/ *adj* artificioso

stilts /stɪlts/ *npl* trampoli *mpl*

stimulant /'stɪmjʊlənt/ *n* eccitante *m*

stimulate /'stɪmjʊleɪt/ *vt* stimolare

stimulating /'stɪmjʊleɪtɪŋ/ *adj* stimolante

stimulation /stɪmjʊ'leɪʃn/ *n* stimolo *m*

stimulus /'stɪmjʊləs/ *n* (pl **-li** /'stɪmjʊlaɪ/) stimolo *m*

sting /stɪŋ/ ① *n* puntura *f*; (organ) pungiglione *m*
② *vt* (pt/pp **stung**) pungere; ⟨jellyfish⟩ pizzicare
③ *vi* ⟨insect⟩ pungere

stinging nettle /'stɪŋɪŋ/ *n* ortica *f*

stingy /'stɪndʒɪ/ *adj* (**-ier, -iest**) tirchio

stink /stɪŋk/ ① *n* puzza *f*
② *vi* (pt **stank**, pp **stunk**) puzzare

stink bomb *n* fialetta *f* puzzolente

stinker /'stɪŋkə(r)/ *n* (fam: difficult problem etc) rompicapo *m*

stinking /'stɪŋkɪŋ/ *adv* be ~ rich fam essere ricco sfondato

stint /stɪnt/ ① *n* lavoro *m*; do one's ~ fare la propria parte
② *vt* ~ on lesinare su

stipend /'staɪpend/ *n* congrua *f*

stipulate /'stɪpjʊleɪt/ *vt* porre come condizione

stipulation /stɪpjʊ'leɪʃn/ *n* condizione *f*

stir /stɜː(r)/ ① *n* mescolata *f*; (commotion) trambusto *m*
② *vt* (pt/pp **stirred**) muovere; (mix) mescolare
③ *vi* muoversi
■ **stir up** *vt* fomentare ⟨hatred⟩

stir-fry ① *vt* saltare in padella
② *n* pietanza *f* saltata in padella

stirring /'stɜːrɪŋ/ *adj* ⟨speech, music⟩ commovente

stirrup /'stɪrəp/ *n* staffa *f*

stitch /stɪtʃ/ ① *n* punto *m*; (Knitting) maglia *f*; (pain) fitta *f*; have somebody in ~es fam far ridere qualcuno a crepapelle
② *vt* cucire
■ **stitch up** *vt* ricucire ⟨wound⟩; the deal's ~ed up l'affare è concluso

stoat /stəʊt/ *n* ermellino *m*

stock /stɒk/ ① *n* (for use or selling) scorta *f*, stock *m inv*; (livestock) bestiame *m*; (lineage) stirpe *f*; Fin titoli *mpl*; Culin brodo *m*; in ~ disponibile; out of ~ esaurito; take ~ fig fare il punto
② *adj* solito
③ *vt* ⟨shop⟩ vendere; approvvigionare ⟨shelves⟩
■ **stock up** *vi* far scorta (with di)

stockbroker *n* agente *m* di cambio

stock car *n* (for racing) stock-car *m inv*

stock-car racing *n* corsa *f* di stock-car

stock cube *n* dado *m* [da brodo]

Stock Exchange *n* Borsa *f* Valori

Stockholm /'stɒkhəʊm/ *n* Stoccolma *f*

stocking /'stɒkɪŋ/ *n* calza *f*

stockist /'stɒkɪst/ *n* rivenditore *m*

stockmarket *n* mercato *m* azionario

stockpile ① *vt* fare scorta di
② *n* riserva *f*

stockroom *n* magazzino *m*

stock-still *adj* immobile

stocktaking *n* Comm inventario *m*

stocky /'stɒkɪ/ *adj* (**-ier, -iest**) tarchiato

stodge /stɒdʒ/ *n* (Br fam: food) ammazzafame *m inv*

stodgy /'stɒdʒɪ/ *adj* indigesto

stoic /'stəʊɪk/ *n* stoico, -a *mf*

stoical /'stəʊɪkl/ *adj* stoico

stoically /'stəʊɪklɪ/ *adv* stoicamente

stoicism /'stəʊɪsɪzm/ *n* stoicismo *m*

stoke /stəʊk/ *vt* alimentare

stole¹ /stəʊl/ *n* stola *f*

stole², stolen /'stəʊlən/ ▸ STEAL

stolid /'stɒlɪd/ *adj* apatico

stolidly /'stɒlɪdlɪ/ *adv* apaticamente

stomach /'stʌmək/ ① *n* pancia *f*; Anat stomaco *m*
② *vt* fam reggere

stomach-ache *n* mal *m* di pancia

stomp /stɒmp/ *vi* (walk heavily) camminare con passo pesante

stone /stəʊn/ ① *n* pietra *f*; (in fruit) nocciolo *m*; Med calcolo *m*; (weight) 6,348 kg; within a ~'s throw of a un tiro di schioppo da
② *adj* di pietra
③ *vt* snocciolare ⟨fruit⟩

Stone Age *n* età *f* della pietra

stone circle *n* cromlech *m inv*

stone-cold *adj* gelido

stone-cold sober *adj* perfettamente sobrio

stoned /stəʊnd/ *adj* (fam: on drugs, drink) fatto

stone-deaf *adj* fam sordo come una campana

stonemason *n* scalpellino *m*

stonewall *vi* fare muro di gomma

stone-washed *adj* ⟨jeans, denim⟩ scolorito, stone-washed

stonework *n* lavoro *m* in muratura

stony /'stəʊnɪ/ *adj* pietroso; ⟨glare⟩ glaciale

stony-broke *adj* Br fam al verde

stood /stʊd/ ▸ STAND

stooge /stuːdʒ/ *n* Theat spalla *f*; (underling) tirapiedi *mf inv*

stool /stuːl/ *n* sgabello *m*

stool-pigeon *n* fam informatore, -trice *mf*

stoop /stuːp/ **①** *n* curvatura *f*; **walk with a ~** camminare con la schiena curva **②** *vi* stare curvo; (bend down) chinarsi; fig abbassarsi

stop /stɒp/ **①** *n* (break) sosta *f*; (for bus, train) fermata *f*; Gram punto *m*; **come to a ~** fermarsi; **put a ~ to something** mettere fine a qualcosa **②** *vt* (pt/pp **stopped**) fermare; arrestare ⟨machine⟩; (prevent) impedire; **~ somebody doing something** impedire a qualcuno di fare qualcosa; **~ doing something** smettere di fare qualcosa; **~ that!** smettila!; **~ a cheque** bloccare un assegno **③** *vi* fermarsi; ⟨rain⟩ smettere **④** *int* fermo! ■ **stop by** *vi* (make a brief visit) passare ■ **stop off** *vi* fare una sosta ■ **stop up** *vt* otturare ⟨sink⟩; tappare ⟨hole⟩ ■ **stop with** *vi* (fam: stay with) fermarsi da

stopcock *n* rubinetto *m* di arresto

stopgap *n* palliativo *m*; (person) tappabuchi *m inv*

stop lights *npl* luci *fpl* di arresto

stop-off *n* sosta *f*

stopover *n* sosta *f*; Aeron scalo *m*

stoppage /'stɒpɪdʒ/ *n* ostruzione *f*; (strike) interruzione *f*; (deduction) trattenute *fpl*

stopper /'stɒpə(r)/ *n* tappo *m*

stop press *n* ultimissime *fpl*

stop sign *n* (segnale *m* di) stop *m inv*

stopwatch /'stɒpwɒtʃ/ *n* cronometro *m*

storage /'stɔːrɪdʒ/ *n* deposito *m*; (in warehouse) immagazzinaggio *m*; Comput memoria *f*

storage heater *n* caldaia *f* ad accumulo

store /stɔː(r)/ **①** *n* (stock) riserva *f*; (shop) grande magazzino *m*; (depot) deposito *m*; **in ~** in deposito; **there's trouble in ~ for him** ci sono guai in vista per lui; **what the future has in ~ for me** cosa mi riserva il futuro; **set great ~ by** tenere in gran conto **②** *vt* tenere; (in warehouse, Comput) immagazzinare ■ **store up** *vt* (accumulate) far scorte di

store card *n* carta *f* di credito di grandi magazzini

storekeeper *n* Am = SHOPKEEPER

storeroom /'stɔːruːm/ *n* magazzino *m*

storey /'stɔːrɪ/ *n* piano *m*

stork /stɔːk/ *n* cicogna *f*

storm /stɔːm/ **①** *n* temporale *m*; (with thunder) tempesta *f* **②** *vt* prendere d'assalto

stormy /'stɔːmɪ/ *adj* tempestoso

story /'stɔːrɪ/ *n* storia *f*; (in newspaper) articolo *m*

storybook /'stɔːrɪbʊk/ *n* libro *m* di racconti

storyteller /'stɔːrɪtelə(r)/ *n* (writer) narratore, -trice *mf*; (liar) contaballe *mf inv*

stout /staʊt/ **①** *adj* ⟨shoes⟩ resistente; (fat) robusto; ⟨defence⟩ strenuo **②** *n* birra *f* scura

stoutly /'staʊtlɪ/ *adv* strenuamente

stove /stəʊv/ *n* cucina *f* [economica]; (for heating) stufa *f*

stow /stəʊ/ *vt* metter via ■ **stow away** *vi* Naut imbarcarsi clandestinamente

stowaway /'stəʊəweɪ/ *n* passeggero, -a *mf* clandestino, -a

straddle /'strædl/ *vt* stare a cavalcioni su; (standing) essere a cavallo su

strafe /streɪf/ *vt* mitragliare da bassa quota

straggle /'strægl/ *vi* crescere disordinatamente; (dawdle) rimanere indietro

straggler /'stræglə(r)/ *n* persona *f* che rimane indietro

straggly /'stræglɪ/ *adj* **have ~ hair** avere pochi capelli sottili

straight /streɪt/ **①** *adj* diritto, dritto; ⟨answer, question, person⟩ diretto; (tidy) in ordine; ⟨drink, hair⟩ liscio; **three ~ wins** tre vittorie di seguito **②** *adv* diritto, dritto; (directly) direttamente; **~ away** immediatamente; **~ on** or **ahead** diritto; **~ out** fig apertamente; **go ~** fam rigare diritto; **put something ~** mettere qualcosa in ordine; **sit/stand up ~** stare diritto; **let's get something ~** mettiamo una cosa in chiaro

straighten /'streɪtn/ **①** *vt* raddrizzare **②** *vi* raddrizzarsi; **~ [up]** ⟨person⟩ mettersi diritto ■ **straighten out** *vt* fig chiarire ⟨situation⟩

straight face *n* **keep a ~ ~** restare serio

straight-faced /-'feɪst/ *adj* con l'aria seria

straightforward *adj* franco; (simple) semplice

straight man *n* Theat spalla *f*

strain¹ /streɪn/ *n* (streak) vena *f*; Bot varietà *f inv*; (of virus) forma *f*

strain² **①** *n* tensione *f*; (injury) stiramento *m*; **~s** *pl* (of music) note *fpl*; **put a ~ on** fig introdurre delle tensioni in; **under a lot of ~** estremamente sotto pressione **②** *vt* tirare; sforzare ⟨eyes, voice⟩; stirarsi ⟨muscle⟩; Culin scolare **③** *vi* sforzarsi

strained /streɪnd/ *adj* ⟨relations⟩ teso

strainer /'streɪnə(r)/ n colino m

strait /streɪt/ n stretto m; **in dire ∼s** in serie difficoltà

straitjacket /'streɪtdʒækɪt/ n camicia f di forza

strait-laced /-'leɪst/ adj puritano

strand¹ /strænd/ n (of thread) gugliata f; (of beads) filo m; (of hair) capello m

strand² vt be ∼ed rimanere bloccato

strange /streɪndʒ/ adj strano; (not known) sconosciuto; (unaccustomed) estraneo

strangely /'streɪndʒlɪ/ adv stranamente; ∼ **enough** curiosamente

strangeness /'streɪndʒnəs/ n stranezza f

stranger /'streɪndʒə(r)/ n estraneo, -a mf

strangle /'stræŋgl/ vt strangolare; fig reprimere

stranglehold /'stræŋglhəʊld/ n (physical grip) presa f alla gola; (fig: powerful control) stretta f mortale; **have a ∼ on something** fig avere in pugno qualcosa

strangulation /stræŋgjʊ'leɪʃn/ n strangolamento m

strap /stræp/ ① n cinghia f; (to grasp in vehicle) maniglia f; (of watch) cinturino m; (shoulder ∼) bretella f, spallina f ② vt (pt/pp **strapped**) legare; ∼ **in**/**down** assicurare

strapless /'stræplɪs/ adj ⟨bra, dress⟩ senza spalline

strapped /stræpt/ adj fam be ∼ **for** essere a corto di

strapping /'stræpɪŋ/ adj robusto

strata /'strɑːtə/ ▶ STRATUM

stratagem /'strætədʒəm/ n stratagemma m

strategic /strə'tiːdʒɪk/ adj strategico

strategically /strə'tiːdʒɪklɪ/ adv strategicamente

strategist /'strætədʒɪst/ n stratega mf

strategy /'strætədʒɪ/ n strategia f

stratosphere /'strætəsfɪə(r)/ n stratosfera f

stratum /'strɑːtəm/ n (pl strata) strato m

straw /strɔː/ n paglia f; (single piece) fuscello m; (for drinking) cannuccia f; **the last ∼** l'ultima goccia

strawberry /'strɔːbərɪ/ n fragola f

straw poll n Pol sondaggio m d'opinione non ufficiale

stray /streɪ/ ① adj (animal) randagio ② n randagio m ③ vi andarsene per conto proprio; (deviate) deviare (**from** da)

streak /striːk/ ① n striatura f; (fig: trait) vena f; ∼**s** (pl: in hair) mèche fpl ② vi (move fast) sfrecciare

streaky /'striːkɪ/ adj striato; ⟨bacon⟩ grasso

stream /striːm/ ① n ruscello m; (current) corrente f; (of blood, people) flusso m; Sch classe f; **come on ∼** (start operating) entrare in attività; ⟨oil⟩ cominciare a scorrere ② vi scorrere
■ **stream in** vi entrare a fiotti
■ **stream out** vi uscire a fiotti

streamer /'striːmə(r)/ n (paper) stella f filante; (flag) pennone m

streaming /'striːmɪŋ/ ① adj a ∼ **cold** raffreddore con naso che cola; Comput ⟨media, video⟩ in streaming ② n (in school) divisione f degli studenti in base alle loro capacità

streamline /'striːmlaɪn/ vt rendere aerodinamico; (simplify) snellire

streamlined /'striːmlaɪnd/ adj aerodinamico; (simplified) snellito

street /striːt/ n strada f

streetcar n Am tram m inv

street cred n fam immagine f pubblica

street lamp n lampione m

street market n mercato m all'aperto

street plan n stradario m

street value n (of drugs) valore m di mercato

streetwalker n passeggiatrice f

streetwise adj fam ⟨person⟩ che conosce tutti i trucchi per sopravvivere in una metropoli

strength /streŋθ/ n forza f; (of wall, bridge etc) solidità f; ∼**s** pl punti mpl forti; **on the ∼ of** grazie a

strengthen /'streŋθən/ vt rinforzare

strenuous /'strenjʊəs/ adj faticoso; ⟨attempt, denial⟩ energico

strenuously /'strenjʊəslɪ/ adv energicamente

stress /stres/ ① n (emphasis) insistenza f; Gram accento m tonico; (mental) stress m inv; Mech spinta f ② vt (emphasize) insistere su; Gram mettere l'accento (tonico) su
■ **stress out** vt ∼ **somebody out** stressare qualcuno

stressed /strest/ adj (mentally) ∼ **[out]** stressato

stressful /'stresfʊl/ adj stressante

stretch /stretʃ/ ① n stiramento m; (period) periodo m di tempo; (of road) tratto m; (elasticity) elasticità f; **at a ∼** di fila; **have a ∼** stirarsi ② vt tirare; allargare ⟨shoes, sweater, etc⟩; ∼ **one's legs** stendere le gambe; ∼ **a point** fare uno strappo alla regola ③ vi (become wider) allargarsi; (extend) estendersi; ⟨person⟩ stirarsi
■ **stretch out** ① vt allungare ⟨one's hand, legs⟩; allargare ⟨arms⟩ ② vi ⟨person⟩ sdraiarsi; ⟨land⟩ estendersi

stretcher /'stretʃə(r)/ n barella f

stretchy /'stretʃɪ/ adj elastico

strew /stru:/ vt (pt/pp **strewn** or **strewed**) sparpagliare; ~n with coperto di

stricken /'strikn/ adj prostrato; ~ with affetto da ⟨illness⟩

strict /strikt/ adj severo; (precise) preciso

strictly /'striktli/ adv severamente; ~ speaking in senso stretto

strictness /'striktnis/ n severità f

stricture /'striktʃə(r)/ n critica f; (constriction) restringimento m

stride /straid/ ① n [lungo] passo m; make great ~s fig fare passi da gigante; take something in one's ~ accettare qualcosa con facilità
② vi (pt **strode**, pp **stridden**) andare a gran passi

strident /'straidənt/ adj stridente; ⟨colour⟩ vistoso

stridently /'straidəntli/ adv con voce stridente

strife /straif/ n conflitto m

strike /straik/ ① n sciopero m; Mil attacco m; on ~ in sciopero
② vt (pt/pp **struck**) colpire; accendere ⟨match⟩; trovare ⟨oil, gold⟩; (delete) depennare; (occur to) venire in mente a; Mil attaccare; ~ somebody a blow colpire qualcuno
③ vi ⟨lightning⟩ cadere; ⟨clock⟩ suonare; Mil attaccare; ⟨workers⟩ scioperare; ~ lucky azzeccarla
■ **strike back** vi fare rappresaglia; (at critics) reagire
■ **strike off** vt eliminare; be struck off [the register] ⟨doctor⟩ essere radiato [dall'albo]
■ **strike out** vt eliminare
■ **strike up** vt fare ⟨friendship⟩; attaccare ⟨conversation⟩

strike-breaker n persona f che non aderisce a uno sciopero

strike-breaking n crumiraggio m

strike force n forze fpl d'intervento

striker /'straikə(r)/ n scioperante mf

striking /'straikiŋ/ adj impressionante; (attractive) affascinante

string /striŋ/ ① n spago m; (of musical instrument, racket) corda f; (of pearls) filo m; (of lies) serie f; the ~s pl Mus gli archi; pull ~s fam usare le proprie conoscenze
② vt (pt/pp **strung**) (thread) infilare ⟨beads⟩
■ **string along** ① vt (fam: deceive) prendere in giro
② vi I'll ~ along (come too) vengo anch'io; ~ along with somebody andare/venire con qcno
■ **string out** ① vi (spread out) allinearsi
② vt disporre in fila; be strung out (sl: on drugs) essere fatto
■ **string together** vt mettere insieme ⟨words, remarks⟩

string bean n fagiolino m

stringed /striŋd/ adj ⟨instrument⟩ a corda

stringent /'strindʒnt/ adj rigido

stringy /'striŋi/ adj ⟨person, build⟩ asciutto; ⟨hair⟩ come spaghetti; Culin filaccioso

strip /strip/ ① n striscia f
② vt (pt/pp **stripped**) spogliare; togliere le lenzuola da ⟨bed⟩; scrostare ⟨wood, furniture⟩; smontare ⟨machine⟩; (deprive) privare (of di)
③ vi (undress) spogliarsi
■ **strip down** vt smontare ⟨engine⟩

strip cartoon n striscia f

strip club n locale m di strip-tease

stripe /straip/ n striscia f; Mil gallone m

striped /straipt/ adj a strisce

stripey /'straipi/ adj a strisce, a righe

strip light n tubo m al neon

strip lighting n illuminazione f al neon

stripper /'stripə(r)/ n spogliarellista mf; (solvent) sverniciatore m

strip-search ① n perquisizione f (facendo spogliare qualcuno)
② vt perquisire (facendo spogliare)

striptease /'stripti:z/ n spogliarello m, strip-tease m inv

strive /straiv/ vi (pt **strove**, pp **striven**) sforzarsi (to di); ~ for sforzarsi di ottenere

strobe /strəub/ n luce f stroboscopica

strode /strəud/ ▶ STRIDE

stroke¹ /strəuk/ n colpo m; (of pen) tratto m; (in swimming) bracciata f; Med ictus m inv; ~ of luck colpo m di fortuna; put somebody off his ~ far perdere il filo a qualcuno

stroke² ① vt accarezzare
② n carezza f

stroll /strəul/ ① n passeggiata f; go for a ~ andare a far due passi
② vi passeggiare

stroller /'strəulə(r)/ n (Am: push-chair) passeggino m

strong /strɒŋ/ adj (-er /'strɒŋgə(r)/, -est /'strɒŋgist/) forte; ⟨argument⟩ valido

strongbox /'strɒŋbɒks/ n cassaforte f

stronghold /'strɒŋhəuld/ n roccaforte f

strong language n (forceful terms) linguaggio m incisivo; (swearing) linguaggio m offensivo

strongly /'strɒŋli/ adv fortemente; feel ~ about something avere molto a cuore qualcosa

strong-minded /-'maindid/ adj risoluto

strong point n punto m di forza

strongroom n camera f blindata

strong stomach n stomaco m di ferro

strong-willed /-'wild/ adj tenace

stroppiness /'strɒpɪnɪs/ n scontrosità f

stroppy /'strɒpɪ/ adj fam scorbutico, scontroso

strove /strəʊv/ ▶ STRIVE

struck /strʌk/ ▶ STRIKE; ~ **on** adj fam entusiasta di

structural /'strʌktʃərəl/ adj strutturale

structural damage n danni mpl alla struttura portante

structurally /'strʌktʃərəlɪ/ adv strutturalmente

structure /'strʌktʃə(r)/ ① n struttura f ② vt strutturare

struggle /'strʌgl/ ① n lotta f; **with a** ~ con difficoltà
② vi lottare; ~ **for breath** respirare con fatica; ~ **to do something** fare fatica a fare qualcosa; ~ **to one's feet** alzarsi con fatica

struggling /'strʌglɪŋ/ adj **a** ~ **artist/ writer** un artista/uno scrittore che fatica ad affermarsi

strum /strʌm/ vt/i (pt/pp **strummed**) strimpellare

strung /strʌŋ/ ▶ STRING

strung out adj **be** ~ (from drugs) essere fatto; **be** ~ **on** essere dipendente da ⟨drugs⟩

strut[1] /strʌt/ n (component) puntello m

strut[2] vi (pt/pp **strutted**) camminare impettito

stub /stʌb/ ① n mozzicone m; (counterfoil) matrice f
② vt (pt/pp **stubbed**) ~ **one's toe** sbattere il dito del piede (**on** contro)
■ **stub out** vt spegnere ⟨cigarette⟩

stubble /'stʌbl/ n (on face) barba f ispida

stubbly /'stʌblɪ/ adj ispido

stubborn /'stʌbən/ adj testardo; ⟨refusal⟩ ostinato

stubbornly /'stʌbənlɪ/ adv testardamente; ⟨refuse⟩ ostinatamente

stubbornness /'stʌbənnɪs/ n (of person) testardaggine f

stubby /'stʌbɪ/ adj (**-ier, -iest**) tozzo

stucco /'stʌkəʊ/ n stucco m

stuck /stʌk/ ▶ STICK[2]

stuck-up adj fam snob inv

stud[1] /stʌd/ n (on boot) tacchetto m; (on jacket) borchia f; (for ear) orecchino m [a bottone]

stud[2] n (of horses) scuderia f

studded with /'stʌdɪd/ adj fig tempestato di

student /'stjuːdənt/ n studente m, studentessa f; (school child) scolaro, -a mf

student grant n borsa f di studio

student nurse n studente, -tessa mf infermiere, -a

student teacher n insegnante mf tirocinante

student union n (organization) organizzazione f studentesca; (building) casa f dello studente

stud-horse n stallone m [da monta]

studied /'stʌdɪd/ adj intenzionale; ⟨politeness⟩ studiato

studio /'stjuːdɪəʊ/ n studio m

studio apartment n Am monolocale m

studio flat n monolocale m

studious /'stjuːdɪəs/ adj studioso; ⟨attention⟩ studiato

studiously /'stjuːdɪəslɪ/ adv studiosamente; (carefully) attentamente

stud mare n giumenta f fattrice

study /'stʌdɪ/ ① n studio m
② vt/i (pt/pp **-ied**) studiare; ~ **for an exam** preparare un esame

study aid n sussidio m didattico

stuff /stʌf/ ① n materiale m; (fam: things) roba f
② vt riempire; (with padding) imbottire; Culin farcire; ~ **something into a drawer/one's pocket** ficcare qualcosa alla rinfusa in un cassetto/in tasca; ~ **oneself** ingozzarsi (**with** di); **get** ~**ed!** fam va' a quel paese!

stuffing /'stʌfɪŋ/ n (padding) imbottitura f; Culin ripieno m

stuffy /'stʌfɪ/ adj che sa di chiuso; (old-fashioned) antiquato

stultifying /'stʌltɪfaɪɪŋ/ adj che abbruttisce

stumble /'stʌmbl/ vi inciampare; ~ **across** or **on** imbattersi in

stumbling block /'stʌmblɪŋ/ n ostacolo m

stump /stʌmp/ n ceppo m; (of limb) moncone m
■ **stump up** vt/i fam sganciare

stumped /stʌmpt/ adj fam perplesso

stumpy /'stʌmpɪ/ adj (**-ier, -iest**) ⟨person, legs⟩ tozzo

stun /stʌn/ vt (pt/pp **stunned**) stordire; (astonish) sbalordire

stung /stʌŋ/ ▶ STING

stunk /stʌŋk/ ▶ STINK

stunned /stʌnd/ adj ⟨expression⟩ sbalordito

stunning /'stʌnɪŋ/ adj fam favoloso; ⟨blow, victory⟩ sbalorditivo

stunt[1] /stʌnt/ n fam trovata f pubblicitaria

stunt[2] vt arrestare lo sviluppo di

stunted /'stʌntɪd/ adj stentato

stuntman /'stʌntmən/ n stuntman m inv, cascatore m

stuntwoman /'stʌntwʊmən/ n stuntwoman f inv

stupefaction /stjuːpɪ'fækʃn/ n stupore m

stupefy /'stju:pɪfaɪ/ *vt* (pt/pp **-ied**) (astonish) stupire

stupefying /'stju:pɪfaɪɪŋ/ *adj* stupefacente

stupendous /stju:'pendəs/ *adj* stupendo

stupendously /stju:'pendəslɪ/ *adv* stupendamente

stupid /'stju:pɪd/ *adj* stupido

stupidity /stju:'pɪdətɪ/ *n* stupidità *f*

stupidly /'stju:pɪdlɪ/ *adv* stupidamente

stupor /'stju:pə(r)/ *n* torpore *m*

sturdy /'stɜ:dɪ/ *adj* (**-ier**, **-iest**) robusto; ⟨*furniture*⟩ solido

stutter /'stʌtə(r)/ **①** *n* balbuzie *f*; **have a ∼** balbettare
② *vt/i* balbettare

St Valentine's Day /'væləntaɪnz/ *n* san Valentino *m*

sty[1] /staɪ/ *n* (*pl* **sties**) porcile *m*

sty[2], **stye** *n* (*pl* **styes**) Med orzaiolo *m*

style /staɪl/ *n* stile *m*; (fashion) moda *f*; (sort) tipo *m*; (hair ∼) pettinatura *f*; **in ∼** in grande stile

styling /'staɪlɪŋ/ **①** *adj* ⟨*gel, mousse*⟩ modellante
② *n* (design) styling *m*; (in hairdressing) acconciatura *f*

stylish /'staɪlɪʃ/ *adj* elegante

stylishly /'staɪlɪʃlɪ/ *adv* con eleganza

stylist /'staɪlɪst/ *n* stilista *mf*; (hair ∼) *n* parrucchiere, -a *mf*

stylistic /staɪ'lɪstɪk/ *adj* stilistico

stylistically /staɪ'lɪstɪklɪ/ *adv* stilisticamente

stylized /'staɪlaɪzd/ *adj* stilizzato

stylus /'staɪləs/ *n* (on record player) puntina *f*

styptic pencil /'stɪptɪk/ *n* matita *f* emostatica

suave /swɑ:v/ *adj* dai modi garbati

sub-aqua /sʌb'ækwə/ *adj* ⟨*club*⟩ di sport subacquei

subcommittee /'sʌbkəmɪtɪ/ *n* sottocommissione *f*

subconscious /sʌb'kɒnʃəs/ **①** *adj* subcosciente
② *n* subcosciente *m*

subconsciously /sʌb'kɒnʃəslɪ/ *adv* in modo inconscio

subcontinent /sʌb'kɒntɪnənt/ *n* subcontinente *m*

subcontract /sʌbkən'trækt/ *vt* subappaltare (**to** a)

subcontractor /'sʌbkəntræktə(r)/ *n* subappaltatore, -trice *mf*

subdirectory /'sʌbdaɪrektərɪ/ *n* Comput sottodirectory *f inv*

subdivide /sʌbdɪ'vaɪd/ *vt* suddividere

subdivision /'sʌbdɪvɪʒn/ *n* suddivisione *f*

subdue /səb'dju:/ *vt* sottomettere; (make quieter) attenuare

subdued /səb'dju:d/ *adj* ⟨*light*⟩ attenuato; ⟨*person, voice*⟩ pacato

subheading /'sʌbhedɪŋ/ *n* sottotitolo *m*

subhuman /sʌb'hju:mən/ *adj* (cruel, not fit for humans) disumano; fam ⟨*appearance*⟩ da paleolitico

subject[1] /'sʌbdʒekt/ **①** *adj* **∼ to** soggetto a; (depending on) subordinato a; **∼ to availability** nei limiti della disponibilità
② *n* soggetto *m*; (of ruler) suddito, -a *mf*; Sch materia *f*; **change the ∼** parlare di qualcos'altro

subject[2] /səb'dʒekt/ *vt* (to attack, abuse) sottoporre; assoggettare ⟨*country*⟩

subjective /səb'dʒektɪv/ *adj* soggettivo

subjectively /səb'dʒektɪvlɪ/ *adv* soggettivamente

subjectiveness /səb'dʒektɪvnɪs/ *n* soggetività *f*

subjugate /'sʌbdʒʊgeɪt/ *vt* soggiogare, sottomettere

subjugation /sʌbdʒə'geɪʃn/ *n* sottomissione *f*

subjunctive /səb'dʒʌŋktɪv/ *adj* & *n* congiuntivo *m*

sub-let /sʌb'let/ *vt* (pt/pp **-let**, pres p **-letting**) subaffittare

sublime /sə'blaɪm/ *adj* sublime

sublimely /sə'blaɪmlɪ/ *adv* sublimamente

subliminal /sə'blɪmɪnl/ *adj* subliminale

sub-machine gun *n* mitraglietta *f*

submarine /'sʌbməri:n/ *n* sommergibile *m*

submerge /səb'mɜ:dʒ/ **①** *vt* immergere; **be ∼d** essere sommerso
② *vi* immergersi

submission /səb'mɪʃn/ *n* sottomissione *f*

submissive /səb'mɪsɪv/ *adj* sottomesso

submissively /səb'mɪsɪvlɪ/ *adv* remissivamente

submissiveness /səb'mɪsɪvnɪs/ *n* remissività *f*

submit /səb'mɪt/ **①** *vt* (pt/pp **-mitted**, pres p **-mitting**) sottoporre
② *vi* sottomettersi

subnormal /sʌb'nɔ:ml/ *adj* ⟨*temperature*⟩ al di sotto della norma; ⟨*person*⟩ subnormale

subordinate[1] /sə'bɔ:dɪnɪt/ *adj* & *n* subordinato, -a *mf*

subordinate[2] /sə'bɔ:dɪneɪt/ *vt* subordinare (**to** a)

subpoena /səb'pi:nə/ **①** *n* mandato *m* di comparizione
② *vt* citare

subroutine /'sʌbru:ti:n/ *n* Comput subroutine *f*

subscribe /səb'skraɪb/ *vi* contribuire; ∼ **to** abbonarsi a ⟨*newspaper*⟩; sottoscrivere ⟨*fund*⟩; fig aderire a ⟨*theory*⟩

subscriber /səb'skraɪbə(r)/ *n* abbonato, -a *mf*

subscription /səb'skrɪpʃn/ *n* (to club) sottoscrizione *f*; (to newspaper) abbonamento *m*

subsequent /'sʌbsɪkwənt/ *adj* susseguente

subsequently /'sʌbsɪkwəntlɪ/ *adv* in seguito

subservience /səb'sɜ:vɪəns/ *n* asservimento *m*

subservient /səb'sɜ:vɪənt/ *adj* subordinato; (servile) servile

subserviently /səb'sɜ:vɪəntlɪ/ *adv* servilmente

subset /'sʌbset/ *n* Math sottoinsieme *m*

subside /səb'saɪd/ *vi* sprofondare; ⟨*ground*⟩ avvallarsi; ⟨*storm*⟩ placarsi

subsidence /'sʌbsɪdəns/ *n* (of land) cedimento *m*

subsidiary /səb'sɪdɪərɪ/ **①** *adj* secondario
② *n* ∼ **[company]** filiale *f*

subsidize /'sʌbsɪdaɪz/ *vt* sovvenzionare

subsidy /'sʌbsɪdɪ/ *n* sovvenzione *f*

subsist /səb'sɪst/ *vi* vivere (**on** di)

subsistence /səb'sɪstəns/ *n* sussistenza *f*

subsistence level *n* livello *m* di sussistenza

substance /'sʌbstəns/ *n* sostanza *f*

sub-standard /sʌb'stændəd/ *adj* di qualità inferiore

substantial /səb'stænʃl/ *adj* sostanziale; ⟨*meal*⟩ sostanzioso; (strong) solido

substantially /səb'stænʃəlɪ/ *adv* sostanzialmente; ⟨*built*⟩ solidamente

substantiate /səb'stænʃɪeɪt/ *vt* comprovare

substitute /'sʌbstɪtju:t/ **①** *n* sostituto *m*
② *vt* ∼ **A for B** sostituire B con A
③ *vi* ∼ **for somebody** sostituire qualcuno

substitution /sʌbstɪ'tju:ʃn/ *n* sostituzione *f*

subterfuge /'sʌbtəfju:dʒ/ *n* sotterfugio *m*

subterranean /sʌbtə'reɪnɪən/ *adj* sotterraneo

subtext /'sʌbtekst/ *n* storia *f* secondaria; fig messaggio *m* implicito

subtitle /'sʌbtaɪtl/ **①** *n* sottotitolo *m*
② *vt* sottotitolare

subtitled /'sʌbtaɪtld/ *adj* sottotitolato

subtle /'sʌtl/ *adj* sottile; ⟨*taste, perfume*⟩ delicato

subtlety /'sʌtltɪ/ *n* sottigliezza *f*

subtly /'sʌtlɪ/ *adv* sottilmente

subtotal /'sʌbtəʊtl/ *n* totale *m* parziale

subtract /səb'trækt/ *vt* sottrarre

subtraction /səb'trækʃn/ *n* sottrazione *f*

suburb /'sʌbɜ:b/ *n* sobborgo *m*; **in the** ∼**s** in periferia

suburban /sə'bɜ:bən/ *adj* suburbano

suburbia /sə'bɜ:bɪə/ *n* sobborghi *mpl*

subversive /səb'vɜ:sɪv/ *adj* sovversivo

subway /'sʌbweɪ/ *n* sottopassaggio *m*; (Am: railway) metropolitana *f*, metrò *m inv*

sub-zero /sʌb'zɪərəʊ/ *adj* sottozero *inv*

succeed /sək'si:d/ **①** *vi* riuscire (**in doing something** a fare qualcosa); (follow) succedere (**to** a)
② *vt* succedere a ⟨*king*⟩

succeeding /sək'si:dɪŋ/ *adj* successivo

success /sək'ses/ *n* successo *m*; **be a** ∼ (in life) aver successo

successful /sək'sesfʊl/ *adj* riuscito; ⟨*businessman, artist etc*⟩ di successo

successfully /sək'sesfʊlɪ/ *adv* con successo

succession /sək'seʃn/ *n* successione *f*; **in** ∼ di seguito

successive /sək'sesɪv/ *adj* successivo

successively /sə'sesɪvlɪ/ *adv* successivamente

successor /sək'sesə(r)/ *n* successore *m*

success rate *n* percentuale *f* di promozioni

success story *n* successo *m*

succinct /sək'sɪŋkt/ *adj* succinto

succinctly /sək'sɪŋktlɪ/ *adv* succintamente

succour /'sʌkə(r)/ **①** *vt* soccorrere
② *n* soccorso *m*

succulence /'sʌkjʊləns/ *n* succulenza *f*

succulent /'ʃʌkjʊlənt/ *adj* succulento

succumb /sə'kʌm/ *vi* soccombere (**to** a)

such /sʌtʃ/ **①** *adj* tale; ∼ **a book** un libro così; ∼ **a thing** una cosa del genere; ∼ **a long time ago** talmente tanto tempo fa; **there is no** ∼ **thing/person** non c'è una cosa/persona così
② *pron* **as** ∼ in quanto tale; ∼ **as** come; **and** ∼ e simili; ∼ **as it is** per quel che vale; **if** ∼ **is the case** se questo è il caso

such and such *adj* tale; **for** ∼ ∼ **an amount** per un tot; **go on** ∼ ∼ **a day at** ∼ ∼ **a time** vai il tal giorno alla tal ora

suchlike /'sʌtʃlaɪk/ *pron* fam di tal genere

suck /sʌk/ *vt* succhiare
■ **suck up** *vt* assorbire
■ **suck up to** *vt* fam fare il lecchino con

sucker /'ʃʌkə(r)/ *n* Bot pollone *m*; (fam: person) credulone, -a *mf*

suckle /'ʃʌkl/ *vt* allattare

suction /'sʌkʃn/ n aspirazione f

suction pad n ventosa f

Sudan /sʊ'dæn/ n Sudan m

Sudanese /sʊdən'iːz/ adj & n sudanese mf

sudden /'sʌdn/ **1** adj improvviso **2** n all of a ~ all'improvviso

sudden death n (football) sudden death f

suddenly /'sʌdənlı/ adv improvvisamente

suds /sʌdz/ npl (foam) schiuma f; (soapy water) acqua f saponata

sue /suː/ **1** vt (pres p **suing**) fare causa a (for per) **2** vi fare causa

suede /sweɪd/ n pelle f scamosciata

suet /'suːɪt/ n grasso m di rognone

suffer /'sʌfə(r)/ **1** vi soffrire (from per) **2** vt soffrire di ⟨pain⟩; subire ⟨loss etc⟩

sufferance /'sʌf(ə)rəns/ n you're here on ~ qui tu sei appena tollerato

sufferer /'sʌfərə(r)/ n malato, -a mf; Aids ~s malati di Aids

suffering /'sʌf(ə)rɪŋ/ n sofferenza f

suffice /sə'faɪs/ vi bastare

sufficient /sə'fʃənt/ adj sufficiente

sufficiently /sə'fɪʃəntlı/ adv sufficientemente

suffix /'sʌfɪks/ n suffisso m

suffocate /'sʌfəkeɪt/ vt/i soffocare

suffocating /'sʌfəkeɪtɪŋ/ adj ⟨heat⟩ soffocante

suffocation /sʌfə'keɪʃn/ n soffocamento m

suffrage /'sʌfrɪdʒ/ n (right) diritto m di voto; (system) suffragio m

suffragette /sʌfrə'dʒet/ n suffragetta f

sugar /'ʃʊgə(r)/ **1** n zucchero m **2** vt zuccherare; ~ **the pill** fig addolcire la pillola

sugar basin, sugar bowl n zuccheriera f

sugar beet n barbabietola f da zucchero

sugar cane n canna f da zucchero

sugar-coated /-'kəʊtɪd/ adj ricoperto di zucchero

sugar cube n zolletta f

sugar daddy n fam vecchio amante m danaroso

sugar-free adj senza zucchero

sugar lump n zolletta f

sugary /'ʃʊgərɪ/ adj zuccheroso; fig sdolcinato

suggest /sə'dʒest/ vt suggerire; (indicate, insinuate) fare pensare a

suggestible /sə'dʒestəbl/ adj suggestionabile

suggestion /sə'dʒestʃən/ n suggerimento m; (trace) traccia f

suggestive /sə'dʒestɪv/ adj allusivo; be ~ of fare pensare a

suggestively /sə'dʒestɪvlı/ adv in modo allusivo

suicidal /suːɪ'saɪdl/ adj suicida

suicide /'suːɪsaɪd/ n suicidio m; (person) suicida mf; **commit** ~ suicidarsi

suicide attempt n tentato suicidio m

suicide pact n patto m suicida

suit /suːt/ **1** n vestito m; (woman's) tailleur m inv; (Cards) seme m; Jur causa f; **follow** ~ fig fare lo stesso **2** vt andar bene a; (adapt) adattare (to a); (be convenient for) andare bene per; **be ~ed to** or **for** essere adatto a; ~ **yourself!** fa' come vuoi!

suitability /suːtə'bɪlıtı/ n adeguatezza f

suitable /'suːtəbl/ adj adatto

suitably /'suːtəblı/ adv convenientemente

suitcase /'suːtkeɪs/ n valigia f

suite /swiːt/ n suite f inv; (of furniture) divano m e poltrone fpl assortiti

sulk /sʌlk/ vi fare il broncio

sulkily /'sʌlkılı/ adv con aria imbronciata

sulky /'sʌlkı/ adj imbronciato

sullen /'sʌlən/ adj svogliato

sullenly /'sʌlənlı/ adv svogliatamente

sulphur /'sʌlfə(r)/ n zolfo m

sulphur dioxide /daɪ'ɒksaɪd/ n anidride f solforosa

sulphuric acid /sʌl'fjʊərɪk/ n acido m solforico

sultana /sʌl'tɑːnə/ n uva f sultanina

sultry /'sʌltrı/ adj (-ier, -iest) ⟨weather⟩ afoso; fig sensuale

sum /sʌm/ n somma f; Sch addizione f ■ **sum up** vi (pt/pp summed) **1** riassumere **2** vt valutare

summarily /sʌ'merɪlı/ adv sommariamente; ⟨dismissed⟩ sbrigativamente

summarize /'sʌməraɪz/ vt riassumere

summary /'sʌmərı/ **1** n sommario m **2** adj sommario; ⟨dismissal⟩ sbrigativo

summer /'sʌmə(r)/ n estate f; in ~, in the ~ in estate

summer camp n ≈ colonia f

summer holiday n vacanze fpl estive

summer house n padiglione m

summer school n corso m estivo

summertime n (season) estate f

summer time n (clock change) ora f legale

summery /'sʌmərı/ adj estivo

summing-up /ˌsʌmɪŋˈʌp/ n riepilogo m; Jur ricapitolazione f del processo

summit /ˈsʌmɪt/ n cima f

summit conference n vertice m

summon /ˈsʌmən/ vt convocare; Jur citare
■ **summon up** vt raccogliere ⟨strength⟩; rievocare ⟨memory⟩

summons /ˈsʌmənz/ **1** n Jur citazione f **2** vt citare in giudizio

sump /sʌmp/ n Auto coppa f dell'olio

sumptuous /ˈsʌmptjʊəs/ adj sontuoso

sumptuously /ˈsʌmptjʊəslɪ/ adv sontuosamente

sum total n totale m

sun /sʌn/ **1** n sole m **2** vt (pt/pp **sunned**) ∼ **oneself** prendere il sole

sunbathe vi prendere il sole

sunbed n lettino m solare

sunblock n prodotto m solare a protezione totale

sunburn n scottatura f (solare)

sunburnt adj scottato (dal sole)

sun cream n crema f solare

sundae /ˈsʌndeɪ/ n gelato m guarnito

Sunday /ˈsʌndeɪ/ n domenica f

Sunday best n in one's ∼ con l'abito della festa

Sunday trading n apertura f domenicale (dei negozi)

sundial /ˈsʌndaɪəl/ n meridiana f

sundress n prendisole m

sun-dried tomatoes /ˈsʌndraɪd/ npl pomodori mpl secchi

sundries /ˈsʌndrɪz/ npl articoli mpl vari

sundry /ˈsʌndrɪ/ adj svariati; **all and** ∼ tutti quanti

sunflower /ˈsʌnflaʊə(r)/ n girasole m

sung /sʌŋ/ ▸ SING

sunglasses /ˈsʌnglɑːsɪz/ npl occhiali mpl da sole

sun hat n cappello m da sole

sunk /sʌŋk/ ▸ SINK

sunken /ˈsʌŋkn/ adj incavato

sunlamp /ˈsʌnlæmp/ n lampada f abbronzante

sunlight /ˈsʌnlaɪt/ n [luce f del] sole m

sunny /ˈsʌnɪ/ adj (**-ier, -iest**) assolato

sunrise n alba f

sunroof n Auto tettuccio m apribile

sunscreen n (to prevent sunburn) crema f solare protettiva

sunset n tramonto m

sunshade n parasole m

sunshine n [luce f del] sole m

sunshine roof n tettuccio m apribile

sunstroke n insolazione f

suntan n abbronzatura f

suntan lotion n lozione f solare

sun-tanned adj abbronzato

suntan oil n olio m solare

super /ˈsuːpə(r)/ adj fam fantastico

superannuated /suːpərˈænjʊeɪtɪd/ adj fig che ha fatto il suo tempo

superannuation /suːpərænjʊˈeɪʃn/ n (contributions) contributi mpl pensionistici; (pension) pensione f

superannuation fund n fondo m pensione

superb /sʊˈpɜːb/ adj splendido

superbly /sʊˈpɜːblɪ/ adv splendidamente

supercilious /suːpəˈsɪlɪəs/ adj altezzoso

superciliously /suːpəˈsɪlɪəslɪ/ adv in modo altezzoso

superficial /suːpəˈfɪʃl/ adj superficiale

superficiality /suːpəfɪʃɪˈælɪtɪ/ n superficialità f

superficially /suːpəˈfɪʃəlɪ/ adv superficialmente

superfluous /sʊˈpɜːflʊəs/ adj superfluo

superhighway /ˈsuːpəhaɪweɪ/ n [information] ∼ Comput autostrada f telematica

superhuman /suːpəˈhjuːmən/ adj sovrumano

superimpose /suːpərɪmˈpəʊz/ vt sovrapporre ⟨picture, soundtrack⟩ (on a); ∼d title titolo m in sovrimpressione

superintendent /suːpərɪnˈtendənt/ n (of police) commissario m di polizia

superior /suːˈpɪərɪə(r)/ adj & n superiore mf

superiority /suːpɪərɪˈɒrətɪ/ n superiorità f

superlative /suːˈpɜːlətɪv/ **1** adj eccellente **2** n superlativo m

superlatively /suːˈpɜːlətɪvlɪ/ adv ⟨perform⟩ in modo eccezionale; ⟨good⟩ estremamente

superman /ˈsuːpəmæn/ n superuomo m

supermarket /ˈsuːpəmɑːkɪt/ n supermercato m

supermodel /ˈsuːpəmɒdl/ n top model f inv

supernatural /suːpəˈnætʃrəl/ adj soprannaturale

superpower /ˈsuːpəpaʊə(r)/ n superpotenza f

superscript /ˈsuːpəskrɪpt/ adj ⟨number, letter⟩ all'esponente

supersede /suːpəˈsiːd/ vt rimpiazzare

supersonic /suːpəˈsɒnɪk/ adj supersonico

superstar n superstar mf

superstition /suːpəˈstɪʃn/ n superstizione f

superstitious /suːpəˈstɪʃəs/ *adj* superstizioso

superstitiously /suːpəˈstɪʃəslɪ/ *adv* in modo superstizioso

superstore /ˈsuːpəstɔː(r)/ *n* ipermercato *m*

superstructure /ˈsuːpəstrʌktʃə(r)/ *n* sovrastruttura *f*

supertax /ˈsuːpətæks/ *n* Fin soprattassa *f*

supervise /ˈsuːpəvaɪz/ *vt* supervisionare

supervision /suːpəˈvɪʒn/ *n* supervisione *f*

supervisor /ˈsuːpəvaɪzə(r)/ *n* supervisore *m*

supervisory /suːpəˈvaɪzərɪ/ *adj* di supervisione

superwoman /ˈsuːpəwʊmən/ *n* superdonna *f*

supper /ˈsʌpə(r)/ *n* cena *f*; **have ∼** cenare

supple /ˈsʌpl/ *adj* slogato

supplement /ˈsʌplɪmənt/ ① *n* supplemento *m* ② *vt* integrare

supplementary /sʌplɪˈmentərɪ/ *adj* supplementare

supplier /səˈplaɪə(r)/ *n* fornitore, -trice *mf*

supply /səˈplaɪ/ ① *n* fornitura *f*; Econ offerta *f*; **be in short ∼** scarseggiare; **∼ and demand** domanda *f* e offerta *f*; **supplies** *pl* Mil approvvigionamenti *mpl* ② *vt* (pt/pp **-ied**) fornire; **∼ somebody with something** fornire qualcosa a qualcuno

supply teacher *n* supplente *mf*

support /səˈpɔːt/ ① *n* sostegno *m*; (base) supporto *m*; (keep) sostentamento *m* ② *vt* sostenere; mantenere ‹family›; (give money to) mantenere finanziariamente; Sport fare il tifo per; Comput supportare

supporter /səˈpɔːtə(r)/ *n* sostenitore, -trice *mf*; Sport tifoso, -a *mf*

support group *n* gruppo *m* di sostegno

supporting actor /səˈpɔːtɪŋ/ *n* attore *m* non protagonista

supporting actress *n* attrice *f* non protagonista

supportive /səˈpɔːtɪv/ *adj* incoraggiante; **be ∼ of somebody** dare tutto il proprio appoggio a qualcuno

support stockings *npl* calze *fpl* elastiche

suppose /səˈpəʊz/ *vt* (presume) supporre; (imagine) pensare; **be ∼d to do** dover fare; **not be ∼d to** non avere il permesso di; **I ∼ so** suppongo di sì

supposedly /səˈpəʊzɪdlɪ/ *adv* presumibilmente

supposing /səˈpəʊzɪŋ/ *conj* **∼ (that) he agrees** supponiamo che accetti

supposition /sʌpəˈzɪʃn/ *n* supposizione *f*

suppository /səˈpɒzɪtrɪ/ *n* supposta *f*

suppress /səˈpres/ *vt* sopprimere

suppressant /səˈpresənt/ *n* Med inibitore *m*

suppression /səˈpreʃn/ *n* soppressione *f*

suppurate /ˈsʌpjʊreɪt/ *vi* suppurare

supremacy /suːˈpreməsɪ/ *n* supremazia *f*

supreme /suːˈpriːm/ *adj* supremo

supremo /suːˈpriːməʊ/ *n* massima autorità *f inv*

Supt. *abbr* (**Superintendent**) commissario *m* di polizia

surcharge /ˈsɜːtʃɑːdʒ/ *n* supplemento *m*

sure /ʃʊə(r)/ ① *adj* sicuro, certo; **make ∼** accertarsi; **be ∼ to do it** accertati di farlo ② *adv* Am fam certamente; **∼ enough** infatti

sure-fire *adj* fam garantito

sure-footed /-ˈfʊtɪd/ *adj* agile

surely /ˈʃʊəlɪ/ *adv* certamente; (Am: gladly) volentieri

surety /ˈʃʊərətɪ/ *n* garanzia *f*; **stand ∼ for somebody/something** fare da garante a qualcuno/per qualcosa

surf /sɜːf/ ① *n* schiuma *f* ② *vt* **∼ the Net** navigare in Internet

surface /ˈsɜːfɪs/ ① *n* superficie *f*; **on the ∼** fig in apparenza ② *vi* (emerge) emergere

surface mail *n* **by ∼ ∼** per posta ordinaria

surface-to-air missile *n* missile *m* terra-aria

surfboard /ˈsɜːfbɔːd/ *n* tavola *f* da surf

surfeit /ˈsɜːfɪt/ *n* eccesso *m*

surfer /ˈsɜːfə(r)/ *n* surfista *mf*

surfing /ˈsɜːfɪŋ/ *n* surf *m*

surge /sɜːdʒ/ ① *n* (of sea) ondata *f*; (of interest) aumento *m*; (in demand) impennata *f*; (of anger, pity) impeto *m* ② *vi* riversarsi; **∼ forward** buttarsi in avanti

surgeon /ˈsɜːdʒən/ *n* chirurgo *m*

surgery /ˈsɜːdʒərɪ/ *n* chirurgia *f*; (place, consulting room) ambulatorio *m*; (hours) ore *fpl* di visita; **have ∼** subire un intervento [chirurgico]

surgical /ˈsɜːdʒɪkl/ *adj* chirurgico

surgically /ˈsɜːdʒɪklɪ/ *adv* chirurgicamente

surgical spirit *n* alcol *m* denaturato

Surinam /sʊərɪˈnæm/ *n* Suriname *m*

surliness /ˈsɜːlɪnɪs/ *n* scontrosità *f*

surly /ˈsɜːlɪ/ *adj* (**-ier**, **-iest**) scontroso

surmise /səˈmaɪz/ *vt* supporre

surmount /səˈmaʊnt/ *vt* sormontare

surname /'sɜːneɪm/ n cognome m

surpass /sə'pɑːs/ vt superare

surplus /'sɜːpləs/ **1** adj d'avanzo; **be ~ to requirements** essere in eccedenza rispetto alle necessità **2** n sovrappiù m

surprise /sə'praɪz/ **1** n sorpreso f **2** vt sorprendere; **be ~d** essere sorpreso (**at** da)

surprising /sə'praɪzɪŋ/ adj sorprendente

surprisingly /sə'praɪzɪŋlɪ/ adv sorprendentemente; **~ enough** stranamente

surreal /sə'rɪəl/ adj surreale

surrealism /sə'rɪəlɪzm/ n surrealismo m

surrealist /sə'rɪəlɪst/ **1** n surrealista mf **2** adj surrealistico

surrender /sə'rendə(r)/ **1** n resa f **2** vi arrendersi **3** vt cedere

surreptitious /sʌrəp'tɪʃəs/ adj furtivo

surreptitiously /sʌrəp'tɪʃəslɪ/ adv furtivamente

surrogate /'sʌrəgət/ n surrogato m

surrogate mother n madre f surrogata

surround /sə'raʊnd/ vt circondare; **~ed by** circondato da

surrounding /sə'raʊndɪŋ/ adj circostante

surroundings /sə'raʊndɪŋz/ npl dintorni mpl

surtax /'sɜːtæks/ n soprattassa f; (on income) imposta f supplementare

surveillance /sə'veɪləns/ n sorveglianza f; **under ~** sotto sorveglianza

survey¹ /'sɜːveɪ/ n sguardo m; (poll) sondaggio m; (investigation) indagine f; (of land) rilevamento m; (of house) perizia f

survey² /sə'veɪ/ vt esaminare; fare un rilevamento di ⟨land⟩; fare una perizia di ⟨building⟩

surveyor /sə'veɪə(r)/ n perito m; (of land) topografo, -a mf

survival /sə'vaɪvl/ n sopravvivenza f; (relic) resto m

survive /sə'vaɪv/ **1** vt sopravvivere a **2** vi sopravvivere

surviving /sə'vaɪvɪŋ/ adj ⟨relative⟩ sopravvissuto

survivor /sə'vaɪvə(r)/ n superstite mf; **be a ~** fam riuscire sempre a cavarsela

susceptible /sə'septəbl/ adj influenzabile; **~ to** sensibile a

suspect¹ /sə'spekt/ vt sospettare; (assume) supporre

suspect² /'sʌspekt/ adj & n sospetto, -a mf

suspend /sə'spend/ vt appendere; (stop, from duty) sospendere

suspended sentence /sə'spendɪd/ n (sospensione f) condizionale f (della pena)

suspender belt /sə'spendə/ n reggicalze m inv

suspenders /sə'spendəz/ npl giarrettiere fpl; (Am: braces) bretelle fpl

suspense /sə'spens/ n tensione f; (in book etc) suspense f

suspension /sə'spenʃn/ n Auto sospensione f

suspension bridge n ponte m sospeso

suspicion /sə'spɪʃn/ n sospetto m; (trace) pizzico m; **under ~** sospettato

suspicious /sə'spɪʃəs/ adj sospettoso; (arousing suspicion) sospetto

suspiciously /sə'spɪʃəslɪ/ adv sospettosamente; (arousing suspicion) in modo sospetto

suss vt **~ out** Br fam intuire ⟨person⟩; capire ⟨software, technique⟩; **I've got you ~ed [out]** ho scoperto il tuo piano

sustain /sə'steɪn/ vt sostenere; mantenere ⟨life⟩; subire ⟨injury⟩

sustainable /sə'steɪnəbl/ adj ⟨development, growth⟩ sostenibile; ⟨resource, forest⟩ rinnovabile

sustained /sə'steɪnd/ adj ⟨effort⟩ prolungato

sustenance /'sʌstɪnəns/ n nutrimento m

suture n /'suːtʃə(r)/ sutura f

SUV n abbr Am (**sports utility vehicle**) SUV f inv

SW abbr (**south-west**) SO

swab /swɒb/ n Med tampone m

swagger /'swægə(r)/ vi pavoneggiarsi

swallow¹ /'swɒləʊ/ vt/i inghiottire ■ **swallow up** vt divorare; ⟨earth, crowd⟩ inghiottire

swallow² n (bird) rondine f

swam /swæm/ ▶ SWIM

swamp /swɒmp/ **1** n palude f **2** vt fig sommergere

swampy /'swɒmpɪ/ adj paludoso

swan /swɒn/ n cigno m

swank /swæŋk/ vi fam darsi delle arie

swanky /'swæŋkɪ/ adj (fam: posh) snob inv

swap /swɒp/ **1** n fam scambio m **2** vt (pt/pp **swapped**) fam scambiare (**for** con) **3** vi fare cambio

swarm /swɔːm/ **1** n sciame m **2** vi sciamare; **be ~ing with** fig brulicare di

swarthy /'swɔːðɪ/ adj (**-ier**, **-iest**) di carnagione scura

swashbuckling /'swɒʃbʌklɪŋ/ adj ⟨hero, appearance⟩ spericolato; ⟨adventure, tale⟩ di cappa e spada

swastika /'swɒstɪkə/ n svastica f

swat /swɒt/ vt (pt/pp **swatted**) schiacciare

swathe /sweɪð/ [1] n (of grass, corn) falciata f; (land) larga striscia f
[2] vt (in bandages, silk) avvolgere

sway /sweɪ/ [1] n fig influenza f
[2] vi oscillare; ⟨person⟩ ondeggiare
[3] vt (influence) influenzare

Swaziland /'swɑːzɪlænd/ n Swaziland m

swear /sweə(r)/ [1] vt (pt **swore**, pp **sworn**) giurare; **I could have sworn that...** avrei giurato che...
[2] vi giurare; (curse) dire parolacce; **I'd ~ to it!** ci potrei giurare!; **~ at somebody** imprecare contro qualcuno; **~ by** (believe in) credere ciecamente in
■ **swear in** vt prestare giuramento ⟨president⟩
■ **swear off** vt (fam: give up) smettere di

swear word n parolaccia f

sweat /swet/ [1] n sudore m
[2] vi sudare
[3] vt **~ blood** sudare sangue
■ **sweat out** vt **~ it out** (endure to the end) tener duro fino alla fine

sweatband /'swetbænd/ n fascia f per il sudore; (for wrist) polsino m

sweater /'swetə(r)/ n golf m inv

sweat pants npl Am pantaloni mpl della tuta

sweatshirt /'swetʃɜːt/ n felpa f

sweatshop n Br manifattura f in cui il personale viene sfruttato

sweaty /'swetɪ/ adj sudato

Swede /swiːd/ n svedese mf

swede n rapa f svedese

Sweden /'swiːdn/ n Svezia f

Swedish /'swiːdɪʃ/ adj & n svedese m

sweep /swiːp/ [1] n scopata f, spazzata f; (curve) curva f; (movement) movimento m ampio; **make a clean ~** fig fare piazza pulita
[2] vt (pt/pp **swept**) scopare, spazzare; ⟨wind⟩ spazzare; **~ the board** fare piazza pulita
[3] vi (go swiftly) andare rapidamente; ⟨wind⟩ soffiare
■ **sweep aside** vt ignorare ⟨objection⟩
■ **sweep away** vt fig spazzare via
■ **sweep up** vt spazzare

sweeper /'swiːpə(r)/ n (machine) spazzatrice f; (person) spazzino m; (in football) libero m

sweeping /'swiːpɪʃ/ adj ⟨gesture⟩ ampio; ⟨statement⟩ generico; ⟨changes⟩ radicale

sweet /swiːt/ [1] adj dolce; **have a ~ tooth** essere goloso
[2] n caramella f; (dessert) dolce m

sweet and sour adj agrodolce

sweetbread n (veal) animella f di vitello; (lamb) animella di agnello

sweetcorn n mais m, granturco m

sweeten /'swiːtn/ vt addolcire
■ **sweeten up** vt raddolcire ⟨person⟩

sweetener /'swiːtnə(r)/ n dolcificante m; (fam: incentive) incentivo m; (fam: bribe) bustarella f

sweetheart /'swiːthɑːt/ n innamorato, -a mf; **hi, ~** ciao, tesoro

sweetly /'swiːtlɪ/ adv dolcemente

sweetness /'swiːtnɪs/ n dolcezza f

sweet pea n pisello m odoroso

sweet potato n patata f americana

sweetshop n negozio m di dolciumi

sweet-talk vt **~ somebody into doing something** convincere qualcuno a fare qualcosa con tante belle parole

swell /swel/ [1] n (of sea) mare m lungo
[2] vi (pt **swelled**, pp **swollen** or **swelled**) gonfiarsi; (increase) aumentare
[3] vt gonfiare; (increase) far salire
[4] adj fam eccellente

swelling /'swelɪʃ/ n gonfiore m

swelter /'sweltə(r)/ vi soffocare [dal caldo]

sweltering /'sweltərɪʃ/ adj torrido

swept /swept/ ▶ SWEEP

swerve /swɜːv/ vi deviare bruscamente

swift /swɪft/ adj rapido

swiftly /'swɪftlɪ/ adv rapidamente

swiftness /'swɪftnɪs/ n rapidità f

swig /swɪg/ fam [1] n sorso m
[2] vt (pt/pp **swigged**) scolarsi

swill /swɪl/ [1] n (for pigs) brodaglia f
[2] vt **~ [out]** risciacquare

swim /swɪm/ [1] n **have a ~** fare una nuotata
[2] vi (pt **swam**, pp **swum**) nuotare; ⟨room⟩ girare; **go ~ming** andare a nuotare; **my head is ~ming** mi gira la testa
[3] vt percorrere a nuoto ⟨distance⟩

swimmer /'swɪmə(r)/ n nuotatore, -trice mf

swimming /'swɪmɪʃ/ n nuoto m

swimming baths npl piscina fsg

swimming costume n costume m da bagno

swimmingly /'swɪmɪʃlɪ/ adv **go ~** andar liscio

swimming pool n piscina f

swimming trunks npl calzoncini mpl da bagno

swimsuit /'swɪmsuːt/ n costume m da bagno

swindle /'swɪndl/ [1] n truffa f
[2] vt truffare

swindler /'swɪndlə(r)/ n truffatore, -trice mf

swine /swaɪn/ n fam porco m

swing /swɪʃ/ **1** n oscillazione f; (shift) cambiamento m; (seat) altalena f; Mus swing m; **in full ~** in piena attività
2 vi (pt/pp **swung**) oscillare; (on swing, sway) dondolare; (dangle) penzolare; (turn) girare
3 vt oscillare; far deviare ⟨vote⟩

swing-door n porta f a vento

swingeing /'swɪndʒɪŋ/ adj ⟨increase⟩ drastico

swingometer /swɪŋ'ɒmɪtə(r)/ n strumento m che permette di seguire l'andamento delle votazioni

swipe /swaɪp/ **1** n fam botta f
2 vt fam colpire; (fam: steal) rubare; far passare nella macchinetta ⟨credit card⟩

swipe card n tessera f magnetica

swirl /swɜːl/ **1** n (of smoke, dust) turbine m
2 vt far girare
3 vi ⟨water⟩ fare mulinello

swish[1] /swɪʃ/ adj fam chic

swish[2] vi schioccare

Swiss /swɪs/ adj & n svizzero, -a mf; **the ~ pl** gli svizzeri

Swiss roll n rotolo m di pan di Spagna ripieno di marmellata

switch /swɪtʃ/ **1** n interruttore m; (change) mutamento m
2 vt cambiare; (exchange) scambiare
3 vi cambiare; **~ to** passare a
■ **switch off** vt spegnere
■ **switch on** vt accendere
■ **switch over** vi TV cambiare [canale]; **~ over to** passare a
■ **switch round** vt (change one for the other) scambiare

switchback n montagne fpl russe

switchblade n coltello m a scatto

switchboard n centralino m

switchboard operator n centralinista mf

switched line /swɪtʃt/ n Teleph linea f commutata

swither /'swɪðə(r)/ vi (fam: hesitate) tentennare

Switzerland /'swɪtsələnd/ n Svizzera f

swivel /'swɪvl/ **1** vt (pt/pp **swivelled**) girare
2 vi girarsi

swivel chair n sedia f girevole

swizz /swɪz/ n (fam: swindle) fregatura f

swollen /'swəʊlən/ **1** ▶ SWELL
2 adj gonfio

swollen-headed /-'hedɪd/ adj presuntuoso

swoon /swuːn/ vi svenire

swoop /swuːp/ **1** n (by police) incursione f
2 vi **~ [down]** ⟨bird⟩ piombare; fig fare un'incursione

sword /sɔːd/ n spada f

swordfish /'sɔːdfɪʃ/ n pesce m spada inv

swore /swɔː(r)/ ▶ SWEAR

sworn /swɔːn/ ▶ SWEAR

sworn enemy n nemico m giurato

swot /swɒt/ **1** n fam sgobbone, -a mf
2 vt (pt/pp **swotted**) fam sgobbare (**for an exam** per un esame)

swum /swʌm/ ▶ SWIM

swung /swʌŋ/ ▶ SWING

sycamore /'sɪkəmɔː(r)/ n sicomoro m

sycophant /'sɪkəfænt/ n adulatore, -trice mf

sycophantic /sɪkə'fæntɪk/ adj adulatorio

syllable /'sɪləbl/ n sillaba f

syllabus /'sɪləbəs/ n programma m [dei corsi]

syllogism /'sɪlədʒɪzm/ n sillogismo m

sylph /sɪlf/ n silfide f

symbiosis /sɪmbaɪ'əʊsɪs/ n simbiosi f inv

symbiotic /sɪmbaɪ'ɒtɪk/ adj simbiotico

symbol /'sɪmbl/ n simbolo m (**of** di)

symbolic /sɪm'bɒlɪk/ adj simbolico

symbolically /sɪm'bɒlɪklɪ/ adv simbolicamente

symbolism /'sɪmbəlɪzm/ n simbolismo m

symbolist /'sɪmbəlɪst/ n simbolista mf

symbolize /'sɪmbəlaɪz/ vt simboleggiare

symmetrical /sɪ'metrɪkl/ adj simmetrico

symmetrically /sɪ'metrɪklɪ/ adv simmetricamente

symmetry /'sɪmətrɪ/ n simmetria f

sympathetic /sɪmpə'θetɪk/ adj (understanding) comprensivo; (showing pity) compassionevole

sympathetically /sɪmpə'θetɪklɪ/ adv con comprensione/compassione

sympathize /'sɪmpəθaɪz/ vi capire; (in grief) solidarizzare; **~ with somebody** capire qualcuno/solidarizzare con qualcuno

sympathizer /'sɪmpəθaɪzə(r)/ n Pol simpatizzante mf

sympathy /'sɪmpəθɪ/ n comprensione f; (pity) compassione f; (condolences) condoglianze fpl; **in ~ with** ⟨strike⟩ per solidarietà con

symphonic /sɪm'fɒnɪk/ adj sinfonico

symphony /'sɪmfənɪ/ n sinfonia f

symphony orchestra n orchestra f sinfonica

symptom /'sɪmptəm/ n sintomo m

symptomatic /sɪmptə'mætɪk/ adj sintomatico (**of** di)

synagogue /'sɪnəgɒg/ n sinagoga f

S

sync[h] /sɪŋk/ *n* sincronia *f*; **be out of ~** essere sfasato; **be in ~** essere in sincronia; **be in ~ with/out of ~ with** essere sincronizzato/sfasato rispetto a

synchronize /'sɪŋkrənaɪz/ *vt* sincronizzare

synchronous /'sɪŋkrənəs/ *adj* sincrono

syndicate /'sɪndɪkət/ *n* gruppo *m*

syndrome /'sɪndrəʊm/ *n* sindrome *f*

synonym /'sɪnənɪm/ *n* sinonimo *m*

synonymous /sɪ'nɒnɪməs/ *adj* sinonimo

synopsis /sɪ'nɒpsɪs/ *n* (pl **-opses** /sɪ'nɒpsi:z/) (of opera, ballet) trama *f*; (of book) riassunto *m*

syntactic[al] /sɪn'tæktɪk[l]/ *adj* sintattico

syntax /'sɪntæks/ *n* sintassi *f inv*

synthesis /'sɪnθəsɪs/ *n* (pl **-theses** /'sɪnθəsi:z/) sintesi *f inv*

synthesize /'sɪnθəsaɪz/ *vt* sintetizzare

synthesizer /'sɪnθəsaɪzə(r)/ *n* Mus sintetizzatore *m*

synthetic /sɪn'θetɪk/ ①*adj* sintetico ②*n* fibra *f* sintetica

syphilis /'sɪfɪlɪs/ *n* sifilide *f*

Syria /'sɪrɪə/ *n* Siria *f*

Syrian /'sɪrɪən/ *adj & n* siriano, -a *mf*

syringe /sɪ'rɪndʒ/ ①*n* siringa *f* ②*vt* siringare

syrup /'sɪrəp/ *n* sciroppo *m*; Br tipo *m* di melassa

syrupy /'sɪrəpɪ/ *adj* sciropposo

system /'sɪstəm/ *n* sistema *m*

systematic /sɪstə'mætɪk/ *adj* sistematico

systematically /sɪstə'mætɪklɪ/ *adv* sistematicamente

systems analysis *n* analisi *f* dei sistemi

systems analyst *n* analista *mf* programmatore, -trice *mf*

systems design *n* progettazione *f* di sistemi

systems engineer *n* sistemista *mf*

Tt

t, T /ti:/ *n* (letter) t, T *f inv*

tab /tæb/ *n* linguetta *f*; (with name) etichetta *f*; **keep ~s on** fam sorvegliare; **pick up the ~** fam pagare il conto

tabby /'tæbɪ/ *n* gatto *m* tigrato

tab key *n* tasto *m* tabulatore

table /'teɪbɪ/ ①*n* tavolo *m*; (list) tavola *f*; **at [the] ~** a tavola ②*vt* proporre

table-cloth *n* tovaglia *f*

table lamp *n* lampada *f* da tavolo

table mat *n* sottopiatto *m*

table of contents tavola *f* delle materie

table salt *n* sale *m* fine

tablespoon *n* cucchiaio *m* da tavola

tablespoonful *n* cucchiaiata *f*

tablet /'tæblɪt/ *n* pastiglia *f*; (slab) lastra *f*; **~ of soap** saponetta *f*

table tennis *n* tennis *m* da tavolo; (everyday level) ping pong *m*

tabloid /'tæblɔɪd/ *n* tabloid *m inv*; pej giornale *m* scandalistico

taboo /tə'bu:/ ①*adj* tabù *inv* ②*n* tabù *m inv*

tabulate /'tæbjʊleɪt/ *vt* tabulare

tabulation /tæbjʊ'leɪʃn/ *n* (of data, results) tabulazione *f*

tabulator /'tæbjʊleɪtə(r)/ *n* tabulatore *m*

tachograph /'tækəgrɑ:f/ *n* tachigrafo *m*

tachometer /tæ'kɒmɪtə(r)/ *n* tachimetro *m*

tacit /'tæsɪt/ *adj* tacito

tacitly /'tæsɪtlɪ/ *adv* tacitamente

taciturn /'tæsɪtɜ:n/ *adj* taciturno

tack /tæk/ ①*n* (nail) chiodino *m*; (stitch) imbastitura *f*; Naut virata *f*; fig linea *f* di condotta ②*vt* inchiodare; (sew) imbastire ③*vi* Naut virare ■ **tack on** (add later) *vt* aggiungere ⟨ending, paragraph⟩

tackle /'tækl/ ①*n* (equipment) attrezzatura *f*; (football etc) contrasto *m*, tackle *m inv* ②*vt* affrontare

tacky /'tækɪ/ *adj* ⟨paint⟩ non ancora asciutto; ⟨glue⟩ appiccicoso; fig pacchiano

tact /tækt/ *n* tatto *m*

tactful /'tæktfʊl/ *adj* pieno di tatto; ⟨remark⟩ delicato

tactfully /'tæktfʊlɪ/ *adv* con tatto

tactical /'tæktɪkl/ *adj* tattico

tactically /'tæktɪklɪ/ *adv* tatticamente

tactician /tæk'tɪʃn/ *n* stratega *mf*

tactics /'tæktɪks/ *npl* tattica *fsg*

tactile /'tæktaɪl/ *adj* tattile

tactless /'tæktlɪs/ *adj* privo di tatto

tactlessly /'tæktlɪslɪ/ *adv* senza tatto

tactlessness /'tæktlɪsnɪs/ *n* mancanza *f* di tatto; (of remark) indelicatezza *f*

tadpole /'tædpəʊl/ *n* girino *m*

tae kwon do /taɪ'kwɒndəʊ/ *n* tae-kwon-do *m*

taffeta /'tæfɪtə/ *n* taffettà *m*

tag[1] /tæg/ ①*n* (label) etichetta *f* ② *vt* (pt/pp **tagged**) attaccare l'etichetta a

tag[2] *n* (game) acchiapparello *m*
■ **tag along** *vi* seguire passo passo
■ **tag on** *vt* (attach) aggiungere

tail /teɪl/ ①*n* coda *f*; **~s** *pl* (tailcoat) frac *m inv*
② *vt* (fam: follow) pedinare
■ **tail off** *vi* diminuire

tailback *n* coda *f*

tail-end *n* parte *f* finale; (of train) coda *f*

tailgate *n* sponda *f* posteriore ribaltabile

tail light *n* fanalino *m* di coda

tail-off *n* diminuzione *f*

tailor /'teɪlə(r)/ ①*n* sarto *m*
② *vt* **~ something to someone's needs** adattare qualcosa alle esigenze di qualcuno

tailor-made *adj* fatto su misura

tailspin /'teɪlspɪn/ *n* Aeron vite *f* di coda

tailwind /'teɪlwɪnd/ *n* vento *m* di coda

taint /teɪnt/ *vt* contaminare

Taiwan /taɪ'wɑːn/ *n* Taiwan *f*

Tajikistan /tədʒiːkɪr'stɑːn/ *n* Tajikistan *m*

take /teɪk/ ①*n* (Cinema) ripresa *f*
② *vt* (pt **took**, pp **taken**) prendere; (to a place) portare ⟨*person, object*⟩; (contain) contenere ⟨*passengers etc*⟩; (endure) sopportare; (require) occorrere; (teach) insegnare; (study) studiare ⟨*subject*⟩; fare ⟨*exam, holiday, photograph, walk, bath*⟩; sentire ⟨*pulse*⟩; misurare ⟨*sb's temperature*⟩; **~ something to the cleaner's** portare qualcosa in lavanderia; **~ somebody home** (by car) portare qualcuno a casa; **~ somebody prisoner** fare prigioniero qualcuno; **be ~n ill** ammalarsi; **~ something calmly** prendere con calma qualcosa; **~ the dog for a walk** portare a spasso il cane; **~ one's time doing something** fare qualcosa con calma; **this will only ~ a minute** ci vuole solo un minuto; **I ~ it that...** (assume) presumo che... **~ it from me!** (believe me) dai retta a me!; **~ hold** ⟨*idea, disease*⟩ prendere piede; **~ part** prendere parte; **~ part in** prendere parte a; **~ place** svolgersi
③ *vi* ⟨*plant*⟩ attecchire
■ **take aback** *vt* (surprise) cogliere di sorpresa
■ **take after** *vt* assomigliare a

■ **take against** *vt* (turn against) prendere in antipatia
■ **take apart** *vt* (dismantle) smontare
■ **take away** *vt* (with one) portare via; (remove) togliere; (subtract) sottrarre; **'to ~ away'** 'da asporto'
■ **take back** *vt* riprendere; ritirare ⟨*statement*⟩; (return) riportare [indietro]; **she took him back** (as husband, boyfriend) lo ha perdonato
■ **take down** *vt* portare giù; (remove) tirare giù; (write down) prendere nota di
■ **take in** *vt* (bring indoors) portare dentro; (to one's home) ospitare; (understand) capire; (deceive) ingannare; riprendere ⟨*garment*⟩; (include) includere; vedere ⟨*film etc*⟩
■ **take off** ①*vt* togliersi ⟨*clothes*⟩; (deduct) togliere; (mimic) imitare; **~ time off** prendere delle vacanze; **~ oneself off** andarsene
② *vi* Aeron decollare; (fam: leave) andarsene; (become successful) decollare
■ **take on** *vt* farsi carico di; assumere ⟨*employee*⟩; (as opponent) prendersela con; **~ it on oneself to do something** arrogarsi il diritto di fare qualcosa
■ **take out** *vt* portare fuori; togliere ⟨*word, stain*⟩; (withdraw) ritirare ⟨*money, books*⟩; **~ out a subscription to something** abbonarsi a qualcosa; **she took a pen out of her pocket** ha preso una penna dalla tasca; **I'm taking my wife out tonight** esco con mia moglie stasera; **~ somebody out to dinner** portare a cena fuori qualcuno; **it'll ~ you out of yourself** (take your mind off things) servirà a distrarti; **~ it out on somebody** fam prendersela con qualcuno
■ **take over** ①*vt* assumere il controllo di ⟨*firm*⟩
② *vi* **~ over from somebody** sostituire qualcuno; (permanently) succedere a qualcuno
■ **take to** *vt* (as a habit) darsi a; **I took to her** (liked) mi è piaciuta
■ **take up** ①*vt* portare su; accettare ⟨*offer*⟩; intraprendere ⟨*profession*⟩; dedicarsi a ⟨*hobby*⟩; prendere ⟨*time*⟩; occupare ⟨*space*⟩; tirare su ⟨*floor-boards*⟩; accorciare ⟨*dress*⟩; **~ something up with somebody** discutere qualcosa con qualcuno; **~ somebody up on something** (question further) chiedere ulteriori chiarimenti a qualcuno su qualcosa; **I'll ~ you up on your offer** (accept) accetto la tua offerta
② *vi* **~ up with somebody** legarsi a qualcuno

takeaway /'teɪkəweɪ/ *n* (meal) piatto *m* da asporto; (restaurant) ristorante *m* che prepara piatti da asporto

take-home pay *n* stipendio *m* netto

taken /'teɪkən/ *adj* ⟨*room etc*⟩ occupato; **be very ~ with somebody/something** essere conquistato da qualcuno/qualcosa

take-off *n* Aeron decollo *m*

take-out n Am = TAKEAWAY
takeover n rilevamento m
takeover bid n offerta f pubblica di acquisto
takings /'teɪkɪŋz/ npl incassi mpl
talc /tælk/ n (boro)talco m
talcum /'tælkəm/ n ∼ **[powder]** talco m
tale /teɪl/ n storia f; pej fandonia f; **tell ∼s** fare la spia
talent /'tælənt/ n talento m
talent contest n concorso m per giovani talenti
talented /'tæləntɪd/ adj [ricco] di talento
talent scout n talent scout mf inv
Taliban /'tælɪbæn/ n talebani mpl
talisman /'tælɪzmən/ n talismano m
talk /tɔːk/ ① n conversazione f; (lecture) conferenza f; (gossip) chiacchiere fpl; **make small ∼** parlare del più e del meno
② vi parlare
③ vt parlare di ⟨politics etc⟩; ∼ **somebody into something** convincere qualcuno di qualcosa
■ **talk about** vt parlare di; ∼ **about bad luck!** e quando si dice la sfortuna!
■ **talk back** vi (reply defiantly) rispondere
■ **talk down to** vt (patronize) parlare con condiscendenza a
■ **talk of** vt parlare di; ∼ **ing of food...** a proposito di mangiare...
■ **talk over** vt discutere
■ **talk to** vt parlare con; (reprimand) fare un discorsetto a; ∼ **to oneself** parlare da solo
talkative /'tɔːkətɪv/ adj loquace
talking /'tɔːkɪŋ/ adj ⟨doll, parrot⟩ parlante
talking book n audiolibro m
talking head n mezzobusto m
talking-to n sgridata f
talk show n talk show m inv
tall /tɔːl/ adj alto; **how ∼ are you?** quanto sei alto?
tallboy n cassettone m
tall order n impresa f difficile
tall story n frottola f
tally /'tælɪ/ ① n conteggio m; **keep a ∼ of** tenere il conto di
② vi coincidere
talon /'tælən/ n artiglio m
tambourine /tæmbə'riːn/ n tamburello m
tame /teɪm/ ① adj ⟨animal⟩ domestico; (dull) insulso
② vt domare
tamely /'teɪmlɪ/ adv docilmente
tamer /'teɪmə(r)/ n domatore, -trice mf
tamper /'tæmpə(r)/ vi ∼ **with** manomettere
tampon /'tæmpɒn/ n tampone m

tan /tæn/ ① adj marrone rossiccio inv
② n marrone m rossiccio; (from sun) abbronzatura f
③ vt (pt/pp **tanned**) conciare ⟨hide⟩
④ vi abbronzarsi
tandem /'tændəm/ n tandem m inv; **in ∼** in tandem
tang /tæŋ/ n sapore m forte; (smell) odore m penetrante
tangent /'tændʒənt/ n tangente f; **go off at a ∼** fam partire per la tangente
tangerine /tændʒə'riːn/ ① n (fruit) tipo m di mandarino; (colour) arancione m
② adj arancione
tangible /'tændʒɪbl/ adj tangibile
tangibly /'tændʒɪblɪ/ adv tangibilmente
tangle /'tæŋgl/ ① n groviglio m; (in hair) nodo m
② vt ∼ **[up]** aggrovigliare
③ vi aggrovigliarsi
tango /'tæŋgəʊ/ n tango m
tangy /'tæŋɪ/ adj forte; ⟨smell⟩ penetrante
tank /tæŋk/ n contenitore m; (for petrol) serbatoio m; (fish ∼) acquario m; Mil carro m armato
tankard /'tæŋkəd/ n boccale m
tanker /'tæŋkə(r)/ n nave f cisterna; (lorry) autobotte f
tank top n canottiera f
tanned /tænd/ adj abbronzato
tannin /'tænɪn/ n tannino m
Tannoy® /'tænɔɪ/ n Br sistema m di altoparlanti
tantalize /'tæntəlaɪz/ vt tormentare
tantalizing /'tæntəlaɪzɪŋ/ adj allettante; ⟨smell⟩ stuzzicante
tantamount /'tæntəmaʊnt/ adj ∼ **to** equivalente a
tantrum /'tæntrəm/ n scoppio m d'ira; **throw a ∼** fare i capricci
Tanzania /tænzə'nɪə/ n Tanzania f
tap /tæp/ ① n rubinetto m; (knock) colpo m; **on ∼** a disposizione
② vt (pt/pp **tapped**) dare un colpetto a; sfruttare ⟨resources⟩; mettere sotto controllo ⟨telephone⟩
③ vi picchiettare
tap-dance ① n tip tap m
② vi ballare il tip tap
tap-dancer n ballerino, -a mf di tip tap
tape /teɪp/ ① n nastro m; (recording) cassetta f
② vt legare con nastro; (record) registrare
tape backup drive n Comput unità f di backup a nastro
tape deck n piastra f
tape-measure n metro m [a nastro]
taper /'teɪpə(r)/ ① n candela f sottile
② vi assottigliarsi

■ **taper off** *vi* assottigliarsi

tape-record *vt* registrare su nastro

tape recorder *n* registratore *m*

tape recording *n* registrazione *f*

tapered /'teɪpəd/ *adj* ⟨trousers⟩ affusolato

tape streamer *n* Comput unità *f* a nastro magnetico

tapestry /'tæpɪstrɪ/ *n* arazzo *m*

tapeworm /'teɪpwɜ:m/ *n* verme *m* solitario, tenia *f*

tapping /'tæpɪŋ/ *n* (noise) picchiettio *m*

tap water *n* acqua *f* del rubinetto

tar /tɑ:(r)/ **①** *n* catrame *m*
② *vt* (pt/pp **tarred**) incatramare

tardy /'tɑ:dɪ/ *adj* (-**ier**, -**iest**) tardivo

target /'tɑ:gɪt/ **①** *n* bersaglio *m*; fig obiettivo *m*
② *vt* stabilire come obiettivo ⟨market⟩

target language *n* lingua *f* d'arrivo

target market *n* mercato *m* obiettivo

target practice *n* tiro *m* al bersaglio

tariff /'tærɪf/ **①** *n* (price) tariffa *f*; (duty) dazio *m*
② *adj* tariffario

Tarmac® /'tɑ:mæk/ *n* macadam *m* al catrame

tarmac **①** *n* asfalto *m*; (Br: of airfield) pista *f*
② *attrib* ⟨road, footpath⟩ asfaltato
③ *vt* asfaltare

tarnish /'tɑ:nɪʃ/ **①** *vi* ossidarsi
② *vt* ossidare; fig macchiare

tarpaulin /tɑ:'pɔ:lɪn/ *n* telone *m* impermeabile

tarragon /'tærəgən/ *n* dragoncello *m*

tart¹ /tɑ:t/ *adj* aspro; fig acido

tart² *n* crostata *f*; (individual) crostatina *f*; (sl: prostitute) donnaccia *f*
■ **tart up** *vt* fam ∼ **oneself up** agghindarsi

tartan /'tɑ:tn/ **①** *n* tessuto *m* scozzese, tartan *m inv*
② *attrib* di tessuto scozzese

tartar /'tɑ:tə(r)/ *n* (on teeth) tartaro *m*

tartar sauce *n* salsa *f* tartara

task /tɑ:sk/ *n* compito *m*; **take somebody to** ∼ riprendere qualcuno

task bar *n* Comput barra *f* delle applicazioni

task force *n* Pol commissione *f*; Mil taskforce *f inv*

taskmaster *n* tiranno *m*; **be a hard** ∼ essere molto esigente

tassel /'tæsl/ *n* nappa *f*

taste /teɪst/ **①** *n* gusto *m*; (sample) assaggio *m*; **get a** ∼ **of something** fig assaporare il gusto di qualcosa; **in good/bad** ∼ di buongusto/di cattivo gusto

② *vt* sentire il sapore di; (sample) assaggiare
③ *vi* sapere (**of** di); **it** ∼**s lovely** è ottimo; ∼ **like something** sapere di qualcosa

taste buds *npl* papille *fpl* gustative

tasteful /'teɪs(t)fʊl/ *adj* di [buon] gusto

tastefully /'teɪs(t)fʊlɪ/ *adv* con gusto

tasteless /'teɪs(t)lɪs/ *adj* senza gusto

tastelessly /'teɪs(t)lɪslɪ/ *adv* con cattivo gusto

taster /'teɪstə(r)/ *n* (foretaste) assaggio *m*; (person) assaggiatore, -trice *mf*

tasty /'teɪstɪ/ *adj* (-**ier**, -**iest**) saporito

tat /tæt/ ▶ TIT²

tattered /'tætəd/ *adj* cencioso; ⟨pages⟩ stracciato

tatters /'tætəz/ *npl* in ∼ a brandelli

tattle /'tætl/ **①** *vi* spettegolare
② *n* pettegolezzo *m*

tattoo¹ /tæ'tu:/ **①** *n* tatuaggio *m*
② *vt* tatuare

tattoo² *n* Mil parata *f* militare

tatty /'tætɪ/ *adj* (-**ier**, -**iest**) ⟨clothes, person⟩ trasandato; ⟨book⟩ malandato

taught /tɔ:t/ ▶ TEACH

taunt /tɔ:nt/ **①** *n* scherno *m*
② *vt* schernire

Taurus /'tɔ:rəs/ *n* Astr Toro *m*

taut /tɔ:t/ *adj* teso

tauten /'tɔ:tən/ **①** *vt* tendere
② *vi* tendersi

tautology /tɔ:'tɒlədʒɪ/ *n* tautologia *f*

tavern /'tævən/ *n* liter taverna *f*

tawdry /'tɔ:drɪ/ *adj* (-**ier**, -**iest**) pacchiano

tawny /'tɔ:nɪ/ *adj* fulvo

tax /tæks/ **①** *n* tassa *f*; (on income) imposte *fpl*; **before** ∼ ⟨price⟩ tasse escluse; ⟨salary⟩ lordo
② *vt* tassare; fig mettere alla prova; ∼ **with** accusare di

taxable /'tæksəbl/ *adj* tassabile; ∼ **income** reddito *m* imponibile

tax allowance *n* detrazione *f* di imposta

taxation /tæk'seɪʃn/ *n* tasse *fpl*; ∼ **at source** ritenuta *f* alla fonte

tax avoidance *n* elusione *f* fiscale

tax bracket *n* scaglione *m* d'imposta

tax break *n* agevolazione *f* fiscale

tax burden *n* aggravio *m* fiscale

tax code *n* codice *m* fiscale

tax consultant *n* fiscalista *m*

tax-deductible *adj* detraibile

tax disc *n* Auto bollo *m*

tax evader *n* evasore *m* fiscale

tax evasion *n* evasione *f* fiscale

tax exile *n* (person) espatriato, -a *mf* per motivi fiscali

tax-free *adj* esentasse

tax haven *n* paradiso *m* fiscale

taxi /'tæksɪ/ ① *n* taxi *m inv*
② *vi* (pt/pp **taxied**, pres p **taxiing**) ⟨*aircraft*⟩ rullare

taxi driver *n* tassista *mf*

tax incentive *n* incentivo *m* fiscale

taxing /'tæksɪŋ/ *adj* (exhausting) sfiancante

tax inspector *n* ispettore *m* delle tasse

taxi rank *n* posteggio *m* per taxi

taxman /'tæksmæn/ *n* **the** ~ il fisco

tax office *n* ufficio *m* delle imposte

taxpayer *n* contribuente *mf*

tax rebate *n* rimborso *m* d'imposta

tax return *n* dichiarazione *f* dei redditi

tax shelter *n* paradiso *m* fiscale

tax system *n* regime *m* fiscale

TB *n abbr* (**tuberculosis**) TBC *f*

tbsp *abbr* (**tablespoon**)

tea /tiː/ *n* tè *m inv*

tea-bag *n* bustina *f* di tè

tea-break *n* intervallo *m* per il tè

teach /tiːtʃ/ *vt/i* (pt/pp **taught**) insegnare; ~ **somebody something** insegnare qualcosa a qualcuno; ~ **somebody a lesson** fig dare una lezione a qualcuno

teacher /'tiːtʃə(r)/ *n* insegnante *mf*; (primary) maestro, -a *mf*

teacher training *n* formazione *f* professionale per insegnanti

teaching /'tiːtʃɪŋ/ *n* insegnamento *m*

teaching hospital *n* ≈ ospedale *m* universitario

teacloth *n* (for drying) asciugapiatti *m inv*

tea cosy *n* copriteiera *f*

teacup *n* tazza *f* da tè

teak /tiːk/ *n* tek *m*

tea leaves *npl* tè *m inv* sfuso; (when infused) fondi *mpl* di tè

team /tiːm/ *n* squadra *f*; fig équipe *f inv*
■ **team up** *vi* unirsi

team captain *n* caposquadra *mf*

team manager *n* direttore *m* sportivo

team-mate *n* compagno *m* di squadra

team player *n* persona *f* che dimostra spirito di squadra

team spirit *n* spirito *m* di squadra

teamwork *n* lavoro *m* di squadra; fig lavoro *m* d'équipe

teapot /'tiːpɒt/ *n* teiera *f*

tear[1] /teə(r)/ ① *n* strappo *m*
② *vt* (pt **tore**, pp **torn**) strappare; ~ **to pieces** or **shreds** fare a pezzi; stroncare ⟨*book, film*⟩
③ *vi* strappare; ⟨*material*⟩ strapparsi; (run) precipitarsi
■ **tear apart** *vt* (fig: criticize) fare a pezzi; (separate) dividere

■ **tear away** *vt* ~ **oneself away from** staccarsi da ⟨*television*⟩; abbandonare a malincuore ⟨*party*⟩

■ **tear into** *vt* fam (reprimand) attaccare duramente; (make a vigorous start on) dare dentro a

■ **tear off** *vt* (carefully) staccare; (violently) strappare

■ **tear open** *vt* aprire strappando

■ **tear out** *vt* staccare; ~ **one's hair out** mettersi le mani nei capelli

■ **tear up** *vt* strappare; rompere ⟨*agreement*⟩

tear[2] /tɪə(r)/ *n* lacrima *f*

tearaway /'teərəweɪ/ *n* giovane teppista *mf*

tearful /'tɪəfʊl/ *adj* ⟨*person*⟩ in lacrime; ⟨*farewell*⟩ lacrimevole

tearfully /'tɪəfʊlɪ/ *adv* in lacrime

tear gas /'tɪə/ *n* gas *m* lacrimogeno

tearing /'teərɪŋ/ *adj* **be in a** ~ **hurry** avere una gran fretta

tear-jerker /'tɪədʒɜːkə(r)/ *n* fam **this film is a real** ~ è davvero un film strappalacrime

tease /tiːz/ *vt* prendere in giro ⟨*person*⟩; tormentare ⟨*animal*⟩

teasel /'tiːzl/ *n* Bot cardo *m*

teaset /'tiːset/ *n* servizio *m* da tè

tea shop *n* sala *f* da tè

teasing /'tiːzɪŋ/ *adj* canzonatorio

teaspoon *n* cucchiaino *m* [da tè]

teaspoon[ful] *n* cucchiaino *m*

tea-strainer *n* colino *m* per il tè

teat /tiːt/ *n* capezzolo *m*; (on bottle) tettarella *f*

teatime *n* ora *f* del tè

tea towel *n* strofinaccio *m* [per i piatti]

technical /'teknɪkl/ *adj* tecnico

technical college *n* istituto *m* tecnico professionale

technical drawing *n* (skill or process, plan) disegno *m* tecnico

technical hitch *n* contrattempo *m* tecnico

technicality /teknɪ'kælətɪ/ *n* tecnicismo *m*; Jur cavillo *m* giuridico

technically /'teknɪklɪ/ *adv* tecnicamente; (strictly) strettamente

technician /tek'nɪʃn/ *n* tecnico, -a *mf*

technique /tek'niːk/ *n* tecnica *f*

techno /'teknəʊ/ *n* techno *f*

technocrat /'teknəkræt/ *n* tecnocrate *m*

technological /teknə'lɒdʒɪkl/ *adj* tecnologico

technologically /teknə'lɒdʒɪklɪ/ *adv* tecnologicamente

technology /tek'nɒlədʒɪ/ *n* tecnologia *f*

technophobe /'teknəfəʊb/ *n* tecnofobo, -a *mf*

teddy /'tedɪ/ *n* ~ **[bear]** orsacchiotto *m*

tedious /'tiːdɪəs/ *adj* noioso

tedium /'tiːdɪəm/ *n* tedio *m*

tee /tiː/ *n* (Golf) tee *m inv*

teem /tiːm/ *vi* (rain) piovere a dirotto; **be ~ing with** (full of) pullulare di

teen /tiːn/ *adj* ⟨fashion, idol⟩ degli adolescenti

teenage /'tiːneɪdʒ/ *adj* per ragazzi; ~ **boy/girl** adolescente *mf*

teenager /'tiːneɪdʒə(r)/ *n* adolescente *mf*

teens /tiːnz/ *npl* **the ~** l'adolescenza *fsg*; **be in one's ~** essere adolescente

teeny /'tiːnɪ/ *adj* fam (**-ier**, **-iest**) piccolissimo

teeny-weeny /tiːnɪ'wiːnɪ/ *adj* fam minuscolo

tee-shirt *n* T-shirt *f inv*, maglietta *f* [a maniche corte]

teeter /'tiːtə(r)/ *vi* barcollare

teeth /tiːθ/ ▸ TOOTH

teethe /tiːð/ *vi* mettere i primi denti

teething troubles /'tiːðɪŋ/ *npl* fig difficoltà *fpl* iniziali

teetotal /tiː'təʊtl/ *adj* astemio

teetotaller /tiː'təʊt(ə)lə(r)/ *n* astemio, -a *mf*

TEFL /'tefl/ *n* insegnamento *m* dell'inglese come lingua straniera

tel. *abbr* (**telephone**) tel.

telebanking /'telɪbæŋkɪŋ/ *n* servizi *mpl* bancari telematici

telecast /'telɪkɑːst/ ① *n* trasmissione *f* televisiva
② *vt* far vedere in televisione

telecomms /'telɪkɒmz/ *npl* telecomunicazioni *fpl*

telecommunications /telɪkəmjuːnɪ'keɪʃnz/ *npl* telecomunicazioni *fpl*

telecommuter /telɪkə'mjuːtə(r)/ *n* persona *f* che lavora da casa con computer

telecommuting /telɪkə'mjuːtɪŋ/ *n* lavoro *m* su computer da casa

teleconference /'telɪkɒnf(ə)r(ə)ns/ *n* videoconferenza *f*

telegenic /telɪ'dʒenɪk/ *adj* telegenico

telegram /'telɪgræm/ *n* telegramma *m*

telegraph /'telɪgrɑːf/ *n* telegrafo *m*

telegraphic /telɪ'græfɪk/ *adj* telegrafico

telegraph pole *n* palo *m* del telegrafo

telemarketing /'telɪmɑːkətɪŋ/ *n* telemarketing *m*

telematics /telɪ'mætɪks/ *n* telematica *f*

telemessage /'telɪmesɪdʒ/ *n* Br telegramma *m*

telepathic /telɪ'pæθɪk/ *adj* telepatico

telepathy /tɪ'lepəθɪ/ *n* telepatia *f*; **by ~** per telepatia

telephone /'telɪfəʊn/ ① *n* telefono *m*; **be on the ~** avere il telefono; (be telephoning) essere al telefono
② *vt* telefonare a
③ *vi* telefonare

telephone answering service *n* segreteria *f* telefonica

telephone banking *n* servizi *mpl* bancari via telefono

telephone book *n* elenco *m* telefonico

telephone booking *n* prenotazione *f* telefonica

telephone booth *n*, **telephone box** *n* cabina *f* telefonica

telephone call *n* telefonata *f*

telephone conversation *n* conversazione *f* telefonica

telephone directory *n* elenco *m* telefonico

telephone helpline *n* servizio *m* telefonico

telephone message *n* messaggio *m* telefonico

telephone number *n* numero *m* di telefono

telephone operator *n* centralinista *mf*

telephone tapping *n* intercettazione *f* telefonica

telephonist /tɪ'lefənɪst/ *n* telefonista *mf*

telephoto /telɪ'fəʊtəʊ/ *adj* ~ **lens** teleobiettivo *m*

teleprinter /'telɪprɪntə(r)/ *n* telescrivente *f*

telerecording /'telɪkrɪkɔːdɪŋ/ *n* programma *m* [televisivo] registrato

telesales /'telɪseɪlz/ *n* vendita *f* per telefono

telescope /'telɪskəʊp/ *n* telescopio *m*

telescopic /telɪ'skɒpɪk/ *adj* telescopico

teleshopping /'telɪʃɒpɪŋ/ *n* acquisti *mpl* per telefono

teletext /'telɪtekst/ *n* televideo *m*

telethon /'telɪθɒn/ *n* telethon *m inv*

televise /'telɪvaɪz/ *vt* trasmettere per televisione

television /'telɪvɪʒn/ *n* televisione *f*; **watch ~** guardare la televisione; **on ~** alla televisione

television channel *n* rete *f* televisiva

television licence *n* abbonamento *m* alla televisione

television licence fee *n* costo *m* dell'abbonamento alla televisione

television programme *n* programma *m* televisivo

television screen *n* teleschermo *m*

television serial *n* sceneggiato *m*

television set *n* televisore *m*

televisual /telɪ'vɪʒʊəl/ *adj* televisivo

t

teleworking /'telıwɜ:kıŋ/ n telelavoro m

telex /'teleks/ ① n telex m inv
② vt mandare via telex ‹message›; mandare un telex a ‹person›

tell /tel/ ① vt (pt/pp **told**) dire; raccontare ‹story›; (distinguish) distinguere (from da); ~ **somebody something** dire qualcosa a qualcuno; ~ **somebody to do something** dire a qualcuno di fare qualcosa; ~ **the time** dire l'ora; **I couldn't** ~ **why...** non sapevo perché...; **you're** ~**ing me!** a chi lo dici!
② vi (produce an effect) avere effetto; **time will** ~ il tempo ce lo dirà; **his age is beginning to** ~ l'età comincia a farsi sentire [per lui]; **don't** ~ **me** non dirmelo; **you mustn't** ~ non devi dire niente
■ **tell apart** vt distinguere
■ **tell off** vt sgridare
■ **tell on** vt (Sch: inform against) fare la spia a

teller /'telə(r)/ n (in bank) cassiere, -a mf

telling /'telıŋ/ adj significativo; (argument) efficace

telling-off n cicchetto m

tell-tale ① n spione, -a mf
② adj rivelatore

telly /'telı/ n fam tv f inv, tele f inv

temerity /tı'merətı/ n audacia f

temp /temp/ fam ① n impiegato, -a mf temporaneo, -a
② vi lavorare come impiegato, -a temporaneo, -a

temper /'tempə(r)/ ① n (disposition) carattere m; (mood) umore m; (anger) collera f; **lose one's** ~ arrabbiarsi; **be in a** ~ essere arrabbiato; **keep one's** ~ mantenere la calma
② vt fig temperare

temperament /'temprəmənt/ n temperamento m

temperamental /temprə'mentl/ adj (moody) capriccioso

temperamentally /temprə'mentəlı/ adv **they are** ~ **unsuited** tra loro c'è incompatibilità di carattere

temperance /'tempərəns/ n (abstinence) astinenza f dal bere

temperate /'tempərət/ adj ‹climate› temperato

temperature /'temprətʃə(r)/ n temperatura f; **have** or **run a** ~ avere la febbre

tempest /'tempıst/ n tempesta f

tempestuous /tem'pestjʊəs/ adj tempestoso

template /'templıt/ n sagoma f

temple[1] /'templ/ n tempio m

temple[2] n Anat tempia f

tempo /'tempəʊ/ n ritmo m; Mus tempo m

temporal /'tempər(ə)l/ adj temporale

temporarily /tempə'rerılı/ adv temporaneamente; ‹introduced, erected› provvisoriamente

temporary /'tempərərı/ adj temporaneo; ‹measure, building› provvisorio

tempt /tempt/ vt tentare; sfidare ‹fate›; ~ **somebody to** indurre qualcuno a; **be** ~**ed** essere tentato (**to** di); **I am** ~**ed by the offer** l'offerta mi tenta

temptation /temp'teıʃn/ n tentazione f

tempting /'temptıŋ/ adj allettante; ‹food, drink› invitante

temptress /'temptrıs/ n seduttrice f

ten /ten/ adj & n dieci m; **the T**~ **Commandments** i Dieci Comandamenti

tenable /'tenəbl/ adj fig sostenibile

tenacious /tı'neıʃəs/ adj tenace

tenacity /tı'næsətı/ n tenacia f

tenancy /'tenənsı/ n locazione f

tenant /'tenənt/ n inquilino, -a mf; Comm locatario, -a mf

tend[1] /tend/ vt (look after) prendersi cura di

tend[2] vi ~ **to do something** tendere a far qualcosa

tendency /'tendənsı/ n tendenza f

tendentious /ten'denʃəs/ adj tendenzioso

tender[1] /'tendə(r)/ ① n Comm offerta f; **put out to** ~ dare in appalto; **be legal** ~ avere corso legale
② vt offrire; presentare ‹resignation›

tender[2] adj tenero; (painful) dolorante

tender-hearted /-ha:tıd/ adj dal cuore tenero

tenderize /'tendəraız/ vt rendere tenero ‹meat›

tenderly /'tendəlı/ adv teneramente

tenderness /'tendənıs/ n tenerezza f; (painfulness) dolore m

tendon /'tendən/ n tendine m

tendril /'tendrıl/ n (of plant) viticcio m

tenement /'tenəmənt/ n casamento m

tenet /'tenıt/ n principio m

tenner /'tenə(r)/ n fam biglietto m da dieci sterline

tennis /'tenıs/ n tennis m

tennis ball n palla f da tennis

tennis-court n campo m da tennis

tennis match n partita f di tennis

tennis player n tennista mf

tennis racket n racchetta f da tennis

tennis shoes npl scarpe fpl da tennis

tenor /'tenə(r)/ n tenore m

tenpin bowling Br, **tenpins** Am n bowling m

tense[1] /tens/ n Gram tempo m

tense[2] ① adj teso
② vt tendere ‹muscle›

■ **tense up** *vi* tendersi

tension /'tenʃn/ *n* tensione *f*

tent /tent/ *n* tenda *f*

tentacle /'tentəkl/ *n* tentacolo *m*

tentative /'tentətɪv/ *adj* provvisorio; ⟨smile, gesture⟩ esitante

tentatively /'tentətɪvlɪ/ *adv* timidamente; ⟨accept⟩ provvisoriamente

tent city *n* tendopoli *f inv*

tenterhooks /'tentəhʊks/ *npl* be on ∼ essere sulle spine

tenth /tenθ/ *adj & n* decimo, -a *mf*

tenuous /'tenjʊəs/ *adj* fig debole

tenure /'tenjə(r)/ *n* (period of office) permanenza *f* in carica; (Univ: job security) ruolo *m*; (of land, property) possesso *m*; **security of** ∼ (of land, property) diritto *m* di possesso

tepid /'tepɪd/ *adj* tiepido

tercentenary /tɜ:sen'ti:nərɪ/ *n* terzo centenario *m*

term /tɜ:m/ *n* periodo *m*; Sch Univ trimestre *m*; (in Italy) Sch quadrimestre *m*; Univ semestre *m*; (expression) termine *m*; ∼s *pl* (conditions) condizioni *fpl*; ∼ **of office** carica *f*; **in the short/long** ∼ a breve/lungo termine; **be on good/bad** ∼s essere in buoni/cattivi rapporti; **come to** ∼s **with** accettare ⟨past, fact⟩; **easy** ∼s facilità *fpl* di pagamento; ∼s **of reference** *pl* (of committee) competenze *fpl*

terminal /'tɜ:mɪnl/ **①** *adj* finale; Med terminale
② *n* Aeron terminal *m inv*; Rail stazione *f* di testa; (of bus) capolinea *m*; (on battery) morsetto *m*; Comput terminale *m*

terminally /'tɜ:mɪnəlɪ/ *adv* be ∼ ill essere in fase terminale

terminate /'tɜ:mɪneɪt/ **①** *vt* terminare; rescindere ⟨contract⟩; interrompere ⟨pregnancy⟩
② *vi* terminare; ∼ **in** finire in

termination /tɜ:mɪ'neɪʃn/ *n* termine *m*; Med interruzione *f* di gravidanza

terminologist /tɜ:mɪ'nɒlədʒɪst/ *n* linguista *mf* specializzato, -a in terminologia

terminology /tɜ:mɪ'nɒlədʒɪ/ *n* terminologia *f*

terminus /'tɜ:mɪnəs/ *n* (pl **-ni** /'tɜ:mɪnaɪ/) (for bus) capolinea *m*; (for train) stazione *f* di testa

term-time *n* during ∼ durante il trimestre

terrace /'terəs/ *n* terrazza *f*; (houses) fila *f* di case a schiera; **the** ∼s *pl* Sport le gradinate

terraced house /'terəsd/ *n* casa *f* a schiera

terracotta /terə'kɒtə/ *n* (earthenware) terracotta *f*; (colour) color *m* terracotta

terrain /te'reɪn/ *n* terreno *m*

terrestrial /tɪ'restrɪəl/ **①** *n* terrestre *mf*
② *adj* terrestre; ∼ **television** televisione *f* terrestre

terrible /'terəbl/ *adj* terribile

terribly /'terəblɪ/ *adv* terribilmente; **I'm** ∼ **sorry** sono infinitamente spiacente

terrier /'terɪə(r)/ *n* terrier *m inv*

terrific /tə'rɪfɪk/ *adj* fam (excellent) fantastico; (huge) enorme

terrifically /tə'rɪfɪklɪ/ *adv* fam terribilmente

terrify /'terɪfaɪ/ *vt* (pt/pp **-ied**) atterrire; **be terrified** essere terrorizzato

terrifying /'terɪfaɪɪŋ/ *adj* terrificante

territorial /terɪ'tɔːrɪəl/ *adj* territoriale

territorial waters /wɔːtəz/ *npl* acque *fpl* territoriali

territory /'terɪtərɪ/ *n* territorio *m*

terror /'terə(r)/ *n* terrore *m*

terrorism /'terərɪzm/ *n* terrorismo *m*

terrorist /'terərɪst/ *n* terrorista *mf*

terrorize /'terəraɪz/ *vt* terrorizzare

terror-stricken *adj* terrorizzato

terry towelling /terɪ'taʊəlɪŋ/ Br, **terry cloth** Am *n* tessuto *m* di spugna

terse /tɜ:s/ *adj* conciso

tersely /'tɜ:slɪ/ *adv* concisamente

tertiary /'tɜ:ʃ(ə)rɪ/ *adj* ⟨era, industry, sector⟩ terziario; ⟨education, college⟩ superiore

Terylene® /'terɪli:n/ *n* terilene® *m*

test /test/ **①** *n* esame *m*; (in laboratory) esperimento *m*; (of friendship, machine) prova *f*; (of intelligence, aptitude) test *m inv*; **put to the** ∼ mettere alla prova; **pass one's** ∼ Auto passare l'esame di guida
② *vt* esaminare; provare ⟨machine⟩

testament /'testəmənt/ *n* testamento *m*; **Old/New T**∼ Antico/Nuovo Testamento *m*

test ban *n* divieto *m* di test nucleari

test case *n* caso *m* giudiziario che fa giurisprudenza

test-drive **①** *vt* ⟨manufacturer⟩ collaudare; ⟨buyer⟩ provare
② *n* collaudo *m*; prova *f*

tester /'testə(r)/ *n* (person) collaudatore, -trice *mf*; (device) tester *m inv*; (sample: of make-up, perfume) campione *m*

testicle /'testɪkl/ *n* testicolo *m*

testify /'testɪfaɪ/ *vt/i* (pt/pp **-ied**) testimoniare

testily /'testɪlɪ/ *adv* ⟨say, reply⟩ in modo scontroso

testimonial /testɪ'məʊnɪəl/ *n* lettera *f* di referenze

testimony /'testɪmənɪ/ *n* testimonianza *f*

t

testing /'testɪŋ/ *n* (of drug) test *mpl*; (of blood, water) analisi *fpl*; (of children) esami *mpl*

test market *n* mercato *m* di prova

test match *n* partita *f* internazionale

testosterone /tes'tɒstərəun/ *n* testosterone *m*

test pilot *n* pilota *mf* collaudatore, -trice

test tube *n* provetta *f*

test tube baby *n* fam bambino, -a *mf* in provetta

testy /'testɪ/ *adj* irascibile

tetanus /'tetənəs/ *n* tetano *m*

tetanus injection *n* antitetanica *f*

tetchy /'tetʃɪ/ *adj* facilmente irritabile

tether /'teðə(r)/ **1** *n* be at the end of one's ∼ non poterne più
2 *vt* legare

Teutonic /tju:'tɒnɪk/ *adj* teutonico

text /tekst/ **1** *n* testo *m*; (on mobile phone) sms *m inv*
2 *vi* (on mobile phone) mandare sms
3 *vt* mandare sms a ⟨*somebody*⟩

textbook /'tekstbʊk/ *n* manuale *m*

textile /'tekstaɪl/ **1** *adj* tessile
2 *n* stoffa *f*

texting /'tekstɪŋ/ *n* fam scambio *m* di sms

text message *n* sms *m inv*, messaggio *m* di testo

text messaging /'mesɪdʒɪŋ/ *n* scambio *m* di sms

textual /'tekstjʊəl/ *adj* testuale

texture /'tekstʊə(r)/ *n* (of skin) grana *f*; (of food) consistenza *f*; of a smooth ∼ (to the touch) soffice al tatto

Thai /taɪ/ *adj & n* tailandese *mf*; (language) tailandese *m*

Thailand /'taɪlænd/ *n* Tailandia *f*

Thames /temz/ *n* Tamigi *m*

than /ðən/ stressed /ðæn/ *conj* che; (with numbers, names) di; older ∼ me più vecchio di me

thank /θæŋk/ *vt* ringraziare; ∼ you [very much] grazie [mille]

thankful /'θæŋkfʊl/ *adj* grato

thankfully /'θæŋkfʊlɪ/ *adv* con gratitudine; (happily) fortunatamente

thankless /'θæŋklɪs/ *adj* ingrato

thanks /θæŋks/ *npl* ringraziamenti *mpl*; ∼! fam grazie!; ∼ to grazie a; no ∼ to you! non certo grazie a te!

thank-you letter *n* lettera *f* di ringraziamento

that /ðæt/ **1** *adj & pron* (*pl* those) quel, quei *pl*; (before s + consonant, gn, ps, z) quello, quegli *pl*; (before vowel) quell' *mf*, quegli *mpl*, quelle *fpl*; ∼ shop quel negozio; those shops quei negozi; ∼ mirror quello specchio; ∼ man/woman quell'uomo/

quella donna; those men/women quegli uomini/quelle donne; ∼ one quello; I don't like those quelli non mi piacciono; ∼ is cioè; is ∼ you? sei tu?; who is ∼? chi è?; what did you do after ∼? cosa hai fatto dopo?; like ∼ in questo modo, così; a man like ∼ un uomo così; ∼ is why ecco perché; ∼ is the reason she gave me questa è la ragione che mi ha dato; ∼ is the easiest thing to do è la cosa più facile da fare; ∼'s it! (you've understood) ecco!; (I've finished) ecco fatto!; (I've had enough) basta così!; (there's nothing more) tutto qui!; ∼'s ∼! (with job) ecco fatto!; (with relationship) è tutto finito!; and ∼'s ∼! punto e basta!
2 *adv* così; it wasn't ∼ good non era poi così buono
3 *rel pron* che; the man ∼ I spoke to l'uomo con cui ho parlato; the day ∼ I saw him il giorno in cui l'ho visto; all ∼ I know tutto quello che so
4 *conj* che; I think ∼... penso che...

thatch /θætʃ/ *n* tetto *m* di paglia

thatched /θætʃt/ *adj* coperto di paglia

thaw /θɔ:/ **1** *n* disgelo *m*
2 *vt* fare scongelare ⟨*food*⟩
3 *vi* ⟨*food*⟩ scongelarsi; it's ∼ing sta sgelando

the /ðə/ **1** before a vowel /ðɪ/ *def art* il *m*, la *f*; i *mpl*, le *fpl*; (before s + consonant, gn, ps, z) lo *m*, gli *mpl*; (before vowel) l' *mf*, gli *mpl*, le *fpl*; at ∼ cinema/station al cinema/alla stazione; from ∼ cinema/station dal cinema/dalla stazione
2 *adv* ∼ more ∼ better più ce n'è meglio è; (with reference to pl) più ce ne sono meglio è; all ∼ better tanto meglio

theatre /'θɪətə(r)/ *n* teatro *m*; Med sala *f* operatoria

theatregoer /'θi:ətəgəuə(r)/ *n* persona *f* che va a teatro

theatregoing /'θi:ətəgəuɪŋ/ *n* l'andare *m* a teatro

theatrical /θɪ'ætrɪkl/ *adj* teatrale; (showy) melodrammatico

theft /θeft/ *n* furto *m*

theft-proof *adj* antiscippo

their /ðeə(r)/ *poss adj* il loro *m*, la loro *f*, i loro *mpl*, le loro *fpl*; ∼ mother/father la loro madre/il loro padre

theirs /ðeəz/ *poss pron* il loro *m*, la loro *f*, i loro *mpl*, le loro *fpl*; a friend of ∼ un loro amico; friends of ∼ dei loro amici; those are ∼ quelli sono loro; (as opposed to ours) quelli sono i loro

them /ðem/ *pers pron* (direct object) li *m*, le *f*; (indirect object) gli, loro *fml*; (after prep: with people) loro; (after preposition: with things) essi; we haven't seen ∼ non li/le abbiamo visti/viste; give ∼ the money dai loro *o* dagli i soldi; give it to ∼ dateglielo; I've spoken to ∼ ho parlato con loro; it's ∼ sono loro

theme /θi:m/ *n* tema *m*

theme park *n* parco *m* a tema

theme song *n* motivo *m* conduttore

themselves /ðem'selvz/ *pron* (reflexive) si; (emphatic) se stessi; **they poured ~ a drink** si sono versati da bere; **they said so ~** lo hanno detto loro stessi; **they kept it to ~** se lo sono tenuti per sé; **by ~** da soli

then /ðen/ ① *adv* allora; (next) poi; **by ~** (in the past) ormai; (in the future) per allora; **since ~** sin da allora; **before ~** prima di allora; **from ~ on** da allora in poi; **now and ~** ogni tanto; **there and ~** all'istante ② *adj* di allora

thence /ðens/ *adv* (from there) di là; (therefore) perciò

theologian /θɪə'ləʊdʒɪən/ *n* teologo, -a *mf*

theological /θɪə'lɒdʒɪkl/ *adj* teologico

theology /θɪ'ɒlədʒɪ/ *n* teologia *f*

theorem /'θɪərəm/ *n* teorema *m*

theoretical /θɪə'retɪkl/ *adj* teorico

theoretically /θɪə'retɪklɪ/ *adv* teoricamente

theorist /'θɪərɪst/ *n* teorico *m*

theorize /'θɪəraɪz/ *vi* teorizzare

theory /'θɪərɪ/ *n* teoria *f*; **in ~** in teoria

therapeutic /θerə'pjuːtɪk/ *adj* terapeutico

therapist /'θerəpɪst/ *n* terapista *mf*

therapy /'θerəpɪ/ *n* terapia *f*

there /ðeə(r)/ ① *adv* là, li; **down/up ~** laggiù/lassù; **~ is/are** c'è/ci sono; **~ he/ she is** eccolo/eccola ② *int* **~**, **~!** dai, su!

thereabouts /ðeərə'baʊts/ *adv* (roughly) all'incirca

thereafter *adv* dopo di che

thereby *adv* in tal modo

therefore /'ðeəfɔː(r)/ *adv* perciò

therein *adv* **~ lies...** in ciò risiede...; **contained ~** (Jur: in contract) contenuto nello stesso

thermal /'θɜːml/ *adj* termico; ⟨treatment⟩ termale

thermal imaging *n* termografia *f*

thermal paper *n* carta *f* termica

thermal printer *n* stampante *f* termica

thermal underwear *n* biancheria *f* che mantiene la temperatura corporea

thermometer /θə'mɒmɪtə(r)/ *n* termometro *m*

Thermos® /'θɜːməs/ *n* ~ **[flask]** termos *m inv*

thermostat /'θɜːməstæt/ *n* termostato *m*

thesaurus /θɪ'sɔːrəs/ *n* (of particular field) dizionario *m* specialistico; (of synonyms) dizionario *m* dei sinonimi

these /ðiːz/ ▶ THIS

thesis /'θiːsɪs/ *n* (pl **-ses** /-siːz/) tesi *f inv*

they /ðeɪ/ *pers pron* loro; **~ are tired** sono stanchi; **we're going, but ~ are not** noi andiamo, ma loro no; **~ say** (generalizing) si dice; **~ are building a new road** stanno costruendo una nuova strada

thick /θɪk/ ① *adj* spesso; ⟨forest⟩ fitto; ⟨liquid⟩ denso; ⟨hair⟩ folto; (fam: stupid) ottuso; (fam: close) molto unito; **be 5 mm ~** essere 5 mm di spessore; **give somebody a ~ ear** fam dare uno schiaffone a qualcuno ② *adv* densamente ③ *n* **in the ~ of** nel mezzo di

thicken /'θɪkn/ ① *vt* ispessire ⟨sauce⟩ ② *vi* ispessirsi; ⟨fog⟩ infittirsi

thicket /'θɪkɪt/ *n* boscaglia *f*

thickhead /'θɪkhed/ *n* fam zuccone *mf*

thickie /'θɪkɪ/ *n* fam zucca *f* vuota

thickly /'θɪklɪ/ *adv* densamente; ⟨cut⟩ a fette spesse

thickness /'θɪknɪs/ *n* spessore *m*

thicko /'θɪkəʊ/ *n* fam zucca *f* vuota

thickset /'θɪkset/ *adj* tozzo

thick-skinned /-'skɪnd/ *adj* fam insensibile

thief /θiːf/ *n* (pl **thieves**) ladro, -a *mf*

thieving /'θiːvɪŋ/ ① *adj* ladro ② *n* furti *mpl*

thigh /θaɪ/ *n* coscia *f*

thimble /'θɪmbl/ *n* ditale *m*

thimbleful /'θɪmbəlfʊl/ *n* (of wine etc) goccino *m*

thin /θɪn/ ① *adj* (**thinner**, **thinnest**) sottile; ⟨shoes, sweater⟩ leggero; ⟨liquid⟩ liquido; ⟨person⟩ magro; fig ⟨excuse, plot⟩ inconsistente; **be [going] ~ on top** (be going bald) perdere i capelli; **vanish into ~ air** volatilizzarsi ② *adv* ≈ **thinly** ③ *vt* (pt/pp **thinned**) diluire ⟨liquid⟩ ④ *vi* diradarsi ■ **thin down** ① *vt* diluire ⟨paint etc⟩ ② *vi* (become slimmer) dimagrire ■ **thin out** *vi* diradarsi

thing /θɪŋ/ *n* cosa *f*; **~s** *pl* (belongings) roba *fsg*; **for one ~** in primo luogo; **the right ~** la cosa giusta; **just the ~!** proprio quel che ci vuole!; **how are ~s?** come vanno le cose?; **the latest ~** fam l'ultima cosa; **the best ~ would be** la cosa migliore sarebbe; **poor ~!** poveretto!; **have a ~ about** (be frightened of) aver la fobia di; (be attracted to) avere un debole per

thingumabob /'θɪŋəməbɒb/ *n* fam coso *m*

thingumajig /'θɪŋəmədʒɪg/ *n* fam coso *m*

think /θɪŋk/ *vt/i* (pt/pp **thought**) pensare; (believe) credere; **I ~ so** credo di sì; **what do you ~?** (what is your opinion?) cosa ne pensi?; **~ of/about** pensare a; **what do you ~ of it?** cosa ne pensi di questo?; **~ of doing something** pensare di ⋯⟶

t

fare qualcosa; ∼ **better of it** ripensarci; ∼ **for oneself** pensare con la propria testa
■ **think again** *vi* pensarci su; **you can** ∼ **again!** sei matto!
■ **think ahead** *vi* pensare al futuro; ∼ **ahead to something** pensare in anticipo a qualcosa
■ **think back** *vi* ∼ **back to something** ripensare a qualcosa
■ **think out** *vt* mettere a punto ⟨*strategy*⟩
■ **think over** *vt* riflettere su
■ **think through** *vt* riflettere bene su ⟨*problem*⟩
■ **think up** *vt* escogitare; trovare ⟨*name*⟩
thinker /'θɪŋkə(r)/ *n* pensatore, -trice *mf*
thinking /'θɪŋkɪŋ/ *n* (opinion) opinione *f*
think-tank *n* gruppo *m* d'esperti
thinly /'θɪnlɪ/ *adv* ⟨*populated*⟩ scarsamente; ⟨*disguised*⟩ leggermente; ⟨*cut*⟩ a fette sottili
thinner /'θɪnə(r)/ *n* diluente *m*
thinness /'θɪnnɪs/ *n* (of person) magrezza *f*; (of material) finezza *f*
thin-skinned /-'skɪnd/ *adj* (sensitive) permaloso
third /θɜːd/ *adj & n* terzo, -a *mf*
third age *n* terza età *f*
third degree *n* give somebody the ∼ ∼ fare il terzo grado a qualcuno
third-degree burns *npl* ustioni *fpl* di terzo grado
thirdly /'θɜːdlɪ/ *adv* terzo
third party *n* (in insurance, law) terzi *mpl*
third-party insurance *n* assicurazione *f* contro terzi
third person *n* terzo *m*
third-rate *adj* scadente
third sector *n* terzo settore *m*
Third World *n* Terzo Mondo *m*
thirst /θɜːst/ *n* sete *f*
thirstily /'θɜːstɪlɪ/ *adv* con sete
thirsty /'θɜːstɪ/ *adj* assetato; **be** ∼ aver sete
thirteen /θɜː'tiːn/ *adj & n* tredici *m*
thirteenth /θɜː'tiːnθ/ *adj & n* tredicesimo, -a *mf*
thirties /'θɜːtɪz/ *npl* (period) **the** ∼ gli anni Trenta *mpl*; (age) trent'anni *mpl*; ▶ *also* FORTIES
thirtieth /'θɜːtɪɪθ/ *adj & n* trentesimo, -a *mf*
thirty /'θɜːtɪ/ *adj & n* trenta *m*
thirty-something *n* trentenne *mf*
this /ðɪs/ ①️ *adj* (*pl* these) questo; ∼ **man/woman** quest'uomo/questa donna; **these men/women** questi uomini/queste donne; ∼ **one** questo; ∼ **evening/morning** stamattina/stasera
②️ *pron* (*pl* **these**) questo; **we talked about** ∼ **and that** abbiamo parlato del più e del meno; **like** ∼ così; ∼ **is Peter** questo

è Peter; Teleph sono Peter; **who is** ∼**?** chi è?; Teleph chi parla?; ∼ **is the happiest day of my life** è il giorno più felice della mia vita
③️ *adv* così; ∼ **big** così grande
thistle /'θɪsl/ *n* cardo *m*
thong /θɒŋ/ *n* (on whip) cinghia *f*; (on shoe, garment) laccetto *m*; (underwear) cache-sexe *m inv*; ∼**s** (*pl*: sandals) infradito *mpl or fpl*
thorn /θɔːn/ *n* spina *f*
thorny /'θɔːnɪ/ *adj* spinoso
thorough /'θʌrə/ *adj* completo; ⟨*knowledge*⟩ profondo; ⟨*clean, search, training*⟩ a fondo; ⟨*person*⟩ scrupoloso
thoroughbred *n* purosangue *m inv*
thoroughfare *n* via *f* principale; **'no** ∼**'** 'strada non transitabile'
thoroughly /'θʌrəlɪ/ *adv* ⟨*clean, search*⟩ a fondo; (extremely) estremamente
thoroughness /'θʌrənɪs/ *n* completezza *f*
those /ðəʊz/ ▶ THAT
though /ðəʊ/ ①️ *conj* sebbene; **as** ∼ come se
②️ *adv* fam tuttavia
thought /θɔːt/ ①️ ▶ THINK
②️ *n* pensiero *m*; (idea) idea *f*; **I've given this some** ∼ ci ho pensato su
thoughtful /'θɔːtfʊl/ *adj* pensieroso; (considerate) premuroso
thoughtfully /'θɔːtfʊlɪ/ *adv* pensierosamente; (considerately) premurosamente
thoughtfulness /'θɔːtfʊlnɪs/ *n* (kindness) considerazione *f*
thoughtless /'θɔːtlɪs/ *adj* (inconsiderate) sconsiderato
thoughtlessly /'θɔːtlɪslɪ/ *adv* con noncuranza
thoughtlessness /'θɔːtlɪsnɪs/ *n* sconsideratezza *f*
thought-out *adj* well/badly ∼ ben/male progettato
thought-provoking *adj* ⟨*book, film etc*⟩ che fa riflettere
thousand /'θaʊznd/ ①️ *adj* one/a ∼ mille *m inv*
②️ *n* mille *m inv*; ∼**s of** migliaia *fpl* di
thousandth /'θaʊzndθ/ *adj & n* millesimo
thrash /θræʃ/ *vt* picchiare; (defeat) sconfiggere
■ **thrash about** *vi* dibattersi
■ **thrash out** *vt* mettere a punto
thrashing /'θræʃɪŋ/ *n* (defeat) sconfitta *f*; **give somebody a** ∼ (beating) picchiare qualcuno
thread /θred/ ①️ *n* filo *m*; (of screw) filetto *m*
②️ *vt* infilare ⟨*beads*⟩; ∼ **one's way through** farsi strada fra

threadbare /'θredbeə(r)/ *adj* logoro

threat /θret/ *n* minaccia *f*

threaten /'θretn/ **1** *vt* minacciare (**to do** di fare)
2 *vi* fig incalzare

threatening /'θretnɪŋ/ *adj* minaccioso; ‹*sky, atmosphere*› sinistro

threateningly /'θretnɪŋlɪ/ *adv* minacciosamente

three /θriː/ *adj* & *n* tre *m*

three-dimensional /-daɪ'menʃ(ə)nəl/ *adj* tridimensionale

threefold/'θriːfəʊld/ *adj* & *adv* triplo

3G *adj abbr* (**third generation**) ‹*technology, phone*› di terza generazione

three-legged /-'legɪd/ *adj* con tre gambe

three-piece suit *n* vestito *m* da uomo con panciotto

three-piece suite *n* insieme *m* di divano e due poltrone coordinati

three-quarter length *adj* ‹*portrait*› di tre quarti; ‹*sleeve*› a tre quarti

three-quarters *adv* ‹*empty, full, done*› per tre quarti

threesome /'θriːsəm/ *n* trio *m*

three-wheeler/-'wiːlə(r)/ *n* (car) auto *f inv* a tre ruote

thresh /θreʃ/ *vt* trebbiare

threshold /'θreʃəʊld/ *n* soglia *f*

threw /θruː/ ▶ THROW

thrift /θrɪft/ *n* economia *f*

thrifty /'θrɪftɪ/ *adj* parsimonioso

thrill /θrɪl/ **1** *n* emozione *f*; (of fear) brivido *m*
2 *vt* entusiasmare; **be ~ed with** essere entusiasta di

thriller /'θrɪlə(r)/ *n* (book) [romanzo *m*] giallo *m*; (film) [film *m inv*] giallo *m*

thrilling /'θrɪlɪŋ/ *adj* eccitante

thrive /θraɪv/ *vi* (pt **thrived or throve**, pp **thrived**) ‹*business*› prosperare; ‹*child, plant*› crescere bene; **I ~ on pressure** mi piace essere sotto tensione

thriving /'θraɪvɪŋ/ *adj* fiorente

throat /θrəʊt/ *n* gola *f*; **sore ~** mal *m* di gola

throaty /'θrəʊtɪ/ *adj* (husky) roco; (fam: with sore throat) rauco

throb /θrɒb/ **1** *n* pulsazione *f*; (of heart) battito *m*
2 *vi* (pt/pp **throbbed**) (vibrate) pulsare; ‹*heart*› battere

throbbing /'θrɒbɪŋ/ *adj* ‹*pain*› lancinante; ‹*music*› martellante

throes /θrəʊz/ *npl* **in the ~ of** fig alle prese con

thrombosis /θrɒm'bəʊsɪs/ *n* trombosi *f*

throne /θrəʊn/ *n* trono *m*

throng /θrɒŋ/ *n* calca *f*

throttle /'θrɒtl/ **1** *n* (on motorbike) manopola *f* di accelerazione
2 *vt* strozzare

through /θruː/ **1** *prep* attraverso; (during) durante; (by means of) tramite; (thanks to) grazie a; **Saturday ~ Tuesday** Am da sabato a martedì incluso
2 *adv* attraverso; **~ and ~** fino in fondo; **wet ~** completamente bagnato; **read something ~** dare una lettura a qualcosa; **let ~** lasciar passare ‹*somebody*›
3 *adj* ‹*train*› diretto; **be ~** (finished) aver finito; Teleph avere la comunicazione

throughout /θruː'aʊt/ **1** *prep* per tutto
2 *adv* completamente; (time) per tutto il tempo

throughway *n* Am superstrada *f*

throve /θrəʊv/ ▶ THRIVE

throw /θrəʊ/ **1** *n* tiro *m*
2 *vt* (pt **threw**, pp **thrown**) lanciare; (throw away) gettare; azionare ‹*switch*›; disarcionare ‹*rider*›; (fam: disconcert) disorientare; fam dare ‹*party*›
■ **throw about** *vt* spargere; **~ one's money about** sbandierare i propri soldi
■ **throw away** *vt* gettare via
■ **throw back** *vt* ributtare in acqua ‹*fish*›; rilanciare ‹*ball*›
■ **throw in** *vt* (include at no extra cost) aggiungere [gratuitamente]; (in football) rimettere in gioco; **~ in the towel** *or* **the sponge** fig abbandonare il campo
■ **throw off** *vt* seminare ‹*pursuers*›; liberarsi di ‹*cold, infection etc*›
■ **throw together** *vt* (assemble hastily) mettere insieme; improvvisare ‹*meal*›; (bring into contact) fare incontrare
■ **throw out** *vt* gettare via; rigettare ‹*plan*›; buttare fuori ‹*person*›
■ **throw up** **1** *vt* alzare
2 *vi* (vomit) vomitare

throwaway *adj* ‹*remark*› buttato lì; ‹*paper cup*› usa e getta *inv*

throwback *n* Biol atavismo *m*; fig regressione *f*

throw-in *n* Sport rimessa *f* laterale

thrush /θrʌʃ/ *n* tordo *m*; Med mughetto *m*; (in woman) candida *f*

thrust /θrʌst/ **1** *n* spinta *f*
2 *vt* (pt/pp **thrust**) (push) spingere; (insert) conficcare; **~ [up] on** imporre a

thud /θʌd/ *n* tonfo *m*

thug /θʌg/ *n* delinquente *m*

thuggish /'θʌgɪʃ/ *adj* violento

thumb /θʌm/ **1** *n* pollice *m*; **as a rule of ~** come regola generale; **under sb's ~** succube di qualcuno
2 *vt* **~ a lift** fare l'autostop
■ **thumb through** *vt* sfogliare

thumb-index *n* indice *m* a rubrica

thumbnail sketch *n* breve descrizione *f*

thumbs down n fam get the ~ ~ non ottenere l'ok; **give somebody/something the ~ ~** non dare l'ok a qualcuno/qualcosa

thumbs up n fam get the ~ ~ ricevere l'ok; **give somebody/something the ~ ~** dare l'ok a qualcuno/qualcosa

thumbtack n Am cimice f, puntina f [da disegno]

thump /θʌmp/ **①** n colpo m; (noise) tonfo m
② vt battere su ⟨table, door⟩; battere ⟨fist⟩; colpire ⟨person⟩
③ vi battere (on su); ⟨heart⟩ battere forte
■ **thump about** vi camminare pesantemente

thumping /'θʌmpɪŋ/ adj (fam: very large) enorme; **a ~ headache** un mal di testa martellante

thunder /'θʌndə(r)/ **①** n tuono m; (loud noise) rimbombo m
② vi tuonare; (make loud noise) rimbombare

thunderbolt /'θʌndəbəʊlt/ n folgore f

thunderclap /'θʌndəklæp/ n rombo m di tuono

thundering /'θʌndərɪŋ/ adj (fam: very big or great) tremendo

thunderous /'θʌndərəs/ adj ⟨applause⟩ scrosciante

thunderstorm /'θʌndəstɔːm/ n temporale m

thunderstruck /'θʌndəstrʌk/ adj sbigottito

thundery /'θʌndərɪ/ adj temporalesco

Thursday /'θɜːzdeɪ/ n giovedì m inv

thus /ðʌs/ adv così

thwack /θwæk/ **①** vt colpire
② n colpo m

thwart /θwɔːt/ vt ostacolare

thyme /taɪm/ n timo m

thyroid /'θaɪrɔɪd/ n tiroide f

tiara /tɪ'ɑːrə/ n diadema m

Tiber /'taɪbə(r)/ n Tevere m

Tibet /tɪ'bet/ n Tibet m

tick¹ /tɪk/ n on ~ fam a credito

tick² **①** n (sound) ticchettio m; (mark) segno m; (fam: instant) attimo m
② vi ticchettare
■ **tick off** vt spuntare; fam sgridare
■ **tick over** vi ⟨engine⟩ andare al minimo

ticket /'tɪkɪt/ n biglietto m; (for item deposited, library) tagliando m; (label) cartellino m; (fine) multa f

ticket barrier n cancelletto m di entrata e uscita

ticket-collector n controllore m

ticket-holder n persona f munita di biglietto

ticket-office n biglietteria f

ticket tout n Br bagarino m

ticket window n sportello m della biglietteria

tickle /'tɪkl/ **①** n solletico m
② vt fare il solletico a; (amuse) divertire
③ vi fare prurito

ticklish /'tɪklɪʃ/ adj che soffre il solletico; ⟨problem⟩ delicato

tidal /'taɪdl/ adj ⟨river, harbour⟩ di marea

tidal wave n onda f di marea

tiddly /'tɪdlɪ/ adj (Br fam: drunk) brillo

tiddlywinks /'tɪdlɪwɪŋks/ n gioco m delle pulci

tide /taɪd/ n marea f; (of events) corso m; **the ~ is in/out** c'è alta/bassa marea
■ **tide over** vt ~ **somebody over** aiutare qualcuno ad andare avanti

tidemark /'taɪdmɑːk/ n linea f di marea; (Br fig: line of dirt) tracce fpl di sporco (nella vasca da bagno)

tidily /'taɪdɪlɪ/ adv in modo ordinato

tidiness /'taɪdɪnɪs/ n ordine m

tidy /'taɪdɪ/ **①** adj (-ier, -iest) ordinato; fam ⟨amount⟩ bello
② vt ordinare
■ **tidy away** vt mettere a posto ⟨toys, books⟩
■ **tidy out** vt mettere in ordine ⟨drawer, cupboard⟩
■ **tidy up** vt ordinare; ~ **oneself up** mettersi in ordine

tie /taɪ/ **①** n cravatta f; (cord) legaccio m; (fig: bond) legame m; (restriction) impedimento m; Sport pareggio m
② vt (pres p **tying**) legare; fare ⟨knot⟩ **be ~d** (in competition) essere in parità
③ vi pareggiare
■ **tie back** vt legare [dietro la nuca] ⟨hair⟩
■ **tie down** vt anche fig legare
■ **tie in with** vi corrispondere a
■ **tie on** vt attaccare
■ **tie up** vt legare; vincolare ⟨capital⟩ **be ~d up** (busy) essere occupato

tie-break[er] n Tennis tie-break m inv; (in quiz) spareggio m

tie-dye vt tingere annodando

tie-on adj ⟨label⟩ volante

tiepin n fermacravatta m

tier /tɪə(r)/ n fila f; (of cake) piano m; (in stadium) gradinata f

tiff /tɪf/ n battibecco m

tiger /'taɪgə(r)/ n tigre f

tiger's-eye /'taɪgəz/ n occhio m di tigre

tight /taɪt/ **①** adj stretto; (taut) teso; (fam: drunk) sbronzo; (fam: mean) spilorcio; ~ **corner** fam brutta situazione f
② adv strettamente; ⟨hold⟩ forte; ⟨closed⟩ bene

tighten /'taɪtn/ **①** vt stringere; avvitare ⟨screw⟩; intensificare ⟨control⟩; ~ **one's belt** fig tirare la cinghia
② vi stringersi

■ **tighten up** *vt* stringere ‹*screw*›; rendere più severo ‹*security*› *vi* (become stricter) diventare più severo

tight-fisted /-'fɪstɪd/ *adj* tirchio

tight-fitting /-'fɪtɪŋ/ *adj* attillato

tight-knit *adj* fig ‹*community, group*› unito

tight-lipped /-'lɪpt/ *adj* **they are remaining** ∼ **about events** mantengono il riserbo sull'accaduto

tightly /'taɪtlɪ/ *adv* strettamente; ‹*hold*› forte; ‹*closed*› bene

tightrope /'taɪtrəʊp/ *n* fune *f* (da funamboli)

tightrope walker *n* equilibrista *mf*

tights /taɪts/ *npl* collant *m inv*

tigress /'taɪgrɪs/ *n* tigre *f* femmina

tile /taɪl/ **1** *n* mattonella *f*; (on roof) tegola *f*
  2 *vt* rivestire di mattonelle ‹*wall*›; coprire con tegole ‹*roof*›; Comput affiancare

till[1] /tɪl/ *prep & conj* ≈ **until**

till[2] *n* cassa *f*

tiller /'tɪlə(r)/ *n* barra *f* del timone

tilt /tɪlt/ **1** *n* inclinazione *f*; **at full** ∼ **a** tutta velocità
  2 *vt* inclinare
  3 *vi* inclinarsi

timber /'tɪmbə(r)/ *n* legname *m*

time /taɪm/ **1** *n* tempo *m*; (occasion) volta *f*; (by clock) ora *f*; **two** ∼**s four** due volte quattro; **at any** ∼ in qualsiasi momento; **this** ∼ questa volta; **at** ∼**s, from** ∼ **to** ∼ ogni tanto; ∼ **and again** cento volte; **two at a** ∼ due alla volta; **on** ∼ in orario; **in** ∼ in tempo; (eventually) col tempo; **in no** ∼ **at all** velocemente; **in a year's** ∼ fra un anno; **behind** ∼ in ritardo; **behind the** ∼**s** antiquato; **for the** ∼ **being** per il momento; **what is the** ∼? che ora è?; **by the** ∼ **we arrive** quando arriviamo; **do you have the** ∼? (what ∼ is it?) hai l'ora?; **did you have a nice** ∼? ti sei divertito?; **have a good** ∼! divertiti!
  2 *vt* scegliere il momento per; cronometrare ‹*race*›; **be well** ∼**d** essere ben calcolato

time bomb *n* bomba *f* a orologeria

time-consuming *adj* che porta via molto tempo

time difference *n* differenza *f* di fuso orario

time-frame *n* arco *m* temporale

time-honoured /-ɒnəd/ *adj* venerando

timekeeper *n* Sport cronometrista *mf*; **be a good** ∼ (be punctual) essere sempre puntuale

time lag *n* intervallo *m* [di tempo]

timeless /'taɪmlɪs/ *adj* eterno

time limit *n* limite *m* di tempo

timely /'taɪmlɪ/ *adj* opportuno

time off *n* (leave) permesso *m*; **take some** ∼ ∼ prendere delle ferie

time-out *n* (break) pausa *f*; Sport time out *m inv*

timer /'taɪmə(r)/ *n* timer *m inv*

timescale *n* periodo *m*

timeshare *n* (apartment) appartamento *m* in multiproprietà; (house) casa *f* in multiproprietà

time sheet *n* foglio *m* di presenza

time signal *n* segnale *m* orario

time span *n* arco *m* di tempo

time switch *n* interruttore *m* a tempo

timetable *n* orario *m*

time zone *n* fuso *m* orario

timid /'tɪmɪd/ *adj* (shy) timido; (fearful) timoroso

timidly /'tɪmɪdlɪ/ *adv* timidamente

timidness /'tɪmɪdnɪs/ *n* (shyness) timidezza *f*; (fear) paura *f*

timing /'taɪmɪŋ/ *n* Sport, Techn cronometraggio *m*; **the** ∼ **of the election** il momento scelto per le elezioni; **have no sense of** ∼ non saper scegliere il momento opportuno

timorous /'tɪm(ə)rəs/ *adj* timoroso

timpani /'tɪmpənɪ/ *npl* timpani *mpl*

tin /tɪn/ **1** *n* stagno *m*; (container) barattolo *m*
  2 *vt* (pt/pp **tinned**) inscatolare

tin can *n* lattina *f*, scatoletta *f*

tin foil *n* [carta *f*] stagnola *f*

tinge /tɪndʒ/ **1** *n* sfumatura *f*
  2 *vt* ∼**d with** fig misto a

tingle /'tɪŋgl/ *vi* pizzicare

tinker /'tɪŋkə(r)/ *vi* armeggiare

tinkle /'tɪŋkl/ **1** *n* tintinnio *m*; (fam: phone call) colpo *m* di telefono
  2 *vi* tintinnare

tinned /tɪnd/ *adj* in scatola

tinnitus /'tɪnɪtəs/ *n* Med ronzio *m* auricolare

tinny /'tɪnɪ/ *adj* ‹*sound, music*› metallico; (badly made) che sembra fatta di latta

tin-opener /-əʊpnə(r)/ *n* apriscatole *m inv*

tinpot /'tɪnpɒt/ *adj* pej ‹*firm*› da due soldi

tinsel /'tɪnsl/ *n* filo *m* d'argento

tint /tɪnt/ **1** *n* tinta *f*
  2 *vt* tingersi ‹*hair*›; ∼**ed glasses** occhiali *mpl* colorati

tiny /'taɪnɪ/ *adj* (**-ier, -iest**) minuscolo

tip[1] /tɪp/ *n* (point, top) punta *f*

tip[2] **1** *n* (money) mancia *f*; (advice) consiglio *m*; (for rubbish) discarica *f*
  2 *vt* (pt/pp **tipped**) (tilt) inclinare; (overturn) capovolgere; (pour) versare; (reward) dare una mancia a
  3 *vi* inclinarsi; (overturn) capovolgersi

t

■ **tip off** *vt* ∼ **somebody off** (inform) fare una soffiata a qualcuno

■ **tip off** *vt* rovesciare

■ **tip over** *vt* capovolgere *vi* capovolgersi

■ **tip up** *vt* sollevare ⟨*seat*⟩; (overturn) rovesciare

tip-off *n* soffiata *f*

tipped /tɪpt/ *adj* ⟨*cigarette*⟩ col filtro

tipple /'tɪpl/ **1** *vi* bere [alcool]
2 *n* have a ∼ prendere un bicchierino; my favourite ∼ il mio liquore preferito

tipster /'tɪpstə(r)/ *n* esperto *m* che dà suggerimenti su cavalli da corsa, azioni ecc

tipsy /'tɪpsɪ/ *adj* fam brillo

tiptoe /'tɪptəʊ/ *n* on ∼ in punta di piedi

tip-top *adj* fam in condizioni perfette

tirade /taɪ'reɪd/ *n* filippica *f*

tire /'taɪə(r)/ **1** *vt* stancare
2 *vi* stancarsi

■ **tire out** *vt* (exhaust) sfinire

tired /'taɪəd/ *adj* stanco; ∼ **of** stanco di; ∼ **out** stanco morto

tiredness /'taɪədnɪs/ *n* stanchezza *f*

tireless /'taɪəlɪs/ *adj* instancabile

tirelessly /'taɪəlɪslɪ/ *adv* instancabilmente

tiresome /'taɪəsəm/ *adj* fastidioso

tiring /'taɪərɪŋ/ *adj* stancante

tissue /'tɪʃuː/ *n* tessuto *m*; (handkerchief) fazzolettino *m* di carta

tissue-paper *n* carta *f* velina

tit[1] /tɪt/ *n* (bird) cincia *f*

tit[2] *n* ∼ **for tat** pan per focaccia

tit[3] *n* fam (breast) tetta *f*; (fool) stupido *m*

titbit /'tɪtbɪt/ *n* ghiottoneria *f*; (fig: of news) notizia *f* appetitosa

titillate /'tɪtɪleɪt/ *vt* titillare

titivate /'tɪtɪveɪt/ *vt* agghindare; ∼ **oneself** agghindarsi

title /'taɪtl/ *n* titolo *m*

title bar *n* Comput barra *f* di titolo

title deed *n* atto *m* di proprietà

title-holder *n* detentore, -trice *mf* del titolo

title-page *n* frontespizio *m*

title role *n* ruolo *m* principale

titter /'tɪtə(r)/ **1** *vi* ridere nervosamente
2 *n* risatina *f* nervosa

tittle-tattle /'tɪtltætl/ *n* pettegolezzi *mpl*

titular /'tɪtjʊlə(r)/ *adj* nominale

tizzy /'tɪzɪ/ *n* fam **in a** ∼ in grande agitazione

TLC *n abbr* fam (**tender loving care**) cura e gentilezza *f*

TM *abbr* (**trademark**) marchio *m* di fabbrica

to /tuː/, unstressed /tə/ **1** *prep* a; (to countries) in; (towards) verso; (up to, until) fino a; **I'm going to John's/the butcher's** vado da John/dal macellaio; **come/go to somebody** venire/andare da qualcuno; **to Italy/Switzerland** in Italia/Svizzera; **I've never been to Rome** non sono mai stato a Roma; **go to the market** andare al mercato; **to the toilet/my room** in bagno/camera mia; **to an exhibition** ad una mostra; **to university** all'università; **twenty/quarter to eight** le otto meno venti/un quarto; **5 to 6 kilos** da 5 a 6 chili; **to the end** alla fine; **to this day** fino a oggi; **to the best of my recollection** per quanto mi possa ricordare; **give/say something to somebody** dare/dire qualcosa a qualcuno; **give it to me** dammelo; **there's nothing to it** è una cosa da niente
2 verbal constructions **to go** andare; **learn to swim** imparare a nuotare; **I want to/have to go** voglio/devo andare; **it's easy to forget** è facile da dimenticare; **too ill/tired to go** troppo malato/stanco per andare; **you have to** devi; **I don't want to** non voglio; **he wants to be a teacher** vuole diventare un insegnante; **live to be 90** vivere fino a 90 anni; **he was the last to arrive** è stato l'ultimo ad arrivare; **to be honest,...** per essere sincero,...
3 *adv* **pull to** chiudere; **to and fro** avanti e indietro

toad /təʊd/ *n* rospo *m*

toadstool /'təʊdstuːl/ *n* fungo *m* velenoso

toady /'təʊdɪ/ *v*
■ **toady to** *vi* fare da leccapiedi a

toast /təʊst/ **1** *n* pane *m* tostato; (drink) brindisi *m inv*; **be** ∼ fam essere fritto; **if he finds out, we're** ∼ se lo scopre siamo fritti
2 *vt* tostare ⟨*bread*⟩; (drink a ∼ to) brindare a

toaster /'təʊstə(r)/ *n* tostapane *m inv*

toast rack /'təʊstræk/ *n* portatoast *m inv*

tobacco /tə'bækəʊ/ *n* tabacco *m*

tobacconist's [shop] /tə'bækənɪsts [ʃɒp]/ *n* tabaccheria *f*

toboggan /tə'bɒɡən/ **1** *n* toboga *m inv*
2 *vi* andare in toboga

today /tə'deɪ/ *adj & adv* oggi *m*; **a week** ∼ una settimana ad oggi; ∼**'s paper** il giornale di oggi

toddle /'tɒdl/ *vi* ⟨*child*⟩ cominciare a camminare; ∼ **into town** fam fare una passeggiata in centro; **I must be toddling** fam devo scappare

toddler /'tɒdlə(r)/ *n* bambino, -a *mf* piccolo, -a

toddy /'tɒdɪ/ *n* grog *m inv*

to-do /tə'duː/ *n* fam baccano *m*

toe /təʊ/ **1** *n* dito *m* del piede; (of footwear) punta *f*; **on one's** ∼**s** fig pronto ad agire; **big** ∼ alluce *m*; **little** ∼ mignolo *m* [del piede]

2 vt ~ **the line** rigar diritto

toe-curling adj imbarazzante

toe-hold n punto m d'appoggio

toenail n unghia f del piede

toff /tɒf/ n fam elegantone, -a mf

toffee /'tɒfɪ/ n caramella f al mou

toffee apple n mela f caramellata

toffee-nosed adj Br fam con la puzza sotto il naso

together /tə'geðə(r)/ adv insieme; (at the same time) allo stesso tempo; ~ **with** insieme a

togetherness /tə'geðənɪs/ n intimità f

toggle /'tɒgl/ n (fastening) olivetta f

Togo /'təʊgəʊ/ n Togo m

toil /tɔɪl/ **1** n duro lavoro m
2 vi lavorare duramente

toilet /'tɔɪlɪt/ n (lavatory) gabinetto m

toilet bag n nécessaire m inv

toilet paper n carta f igienica

toiletries /'tɔɪlɪtrɪz/ npl articoli mpl da toilette

toilet roll n rotolo m di carta igienica

toilet soap n sapone m

toilet tissue n carta f igienica

toilet-train vt ~ **a child** insegnare ad un bambino ad usare il vasino

toilet water n acqua f di colonia

token /'təʊkən/ **1** n segno m; (counter) gettone m; (voucher) buono m
2 attrib simbolico

told /təʊld/ **1** ▶ TELL
2 adj all ~ in tutto

tolerable /'tɒl(ə)rəbl/ adj tollerabile; (not bad) discreto

tolerably /'tɒl(ə)rəblɪ/ adv discretamente

tolerance /'tɒl(ə)r(ə)ns/ n tolleranza f

tolerant /'tɒl(ə)r(ə)nt/ adj tollerante

tolerantly /'tɒl(ə)r(ə)ntlɪ/ adv con tolleranza

tolerate /'tɒləreɪt/ vt tollerare

toll¹ /təʊl/ n pedaggio m; **death** ~ numero m di morti; **take a heavy** ~ costare gravi perdite

toll² vi suonare a morto

toll-booth n casello m

toll call n Am chiamata f in teleselezione

toll-free number n Am Teleph numero m verde

toll motorway n autostrada f con pedaggio

tom /tɒm/ n (cat) gatto m maschio

tomato /tə'mɑːtəʊ/ n (pl -es) pomodoro m

tomato ketchup n ketchup m

tomato purée n concentrato m di pomodoro

tomato sauce n salsa f di pomodoro

tomb /tuːm/ n tomba f

tomboy /'tɒmbɔɪ/ n maschiaccio m

tombstone /'tuːmstəʊn/ n pietra f tombale

tom-cat n gatto m maschio

tome /təʊm/ n tomo m

tomfoolery /tɒm'fuːlərɪ/ n stupidaggini fpl

tomorrow /tə'mɒrəʊ/ adj & adv domani; ~ **morning** domani mattina; **the day after** ~ dopodomani; **see you** ~! a domani!

tom-tom n tamtam m inv

ton /tʌn/ n tonnellata f (= 1, 016 kg); ~**s of** fam un sacco di

tonal /'təʊnl/ adj tonale

tonality /təʊ'nælətɪ/ n tonalità f inv

tone /təʊn/ n tono m; (colour) tonalità f inv
■ **tone down** vt attenuare
■ **tone in** vi intonarsi
■ **tone up** vt tonificare ⟨muscles⟩

tone-deaf adj be ~ non avere orecchio

toneless /'təʊnlɪs/ adj (unmusical) piatto

toner /'təʊnə(r)/ n toner m

Tonga /'tɒŋgə/ n Tonga f

tongs /tɒŋz/ npl pinze fpl

tongue /tʌŋ/ n lingua f; ~ **in cheek** fam ⟨say⟩ ironicamente

tongue-lashing n (severe reprimand) strigliata f

tongue stud n piercing m inv nella lingua

tongue-tied adj senza parole

tongue-twister n scioglilingua m inv

tonic /'tɒnɪk/ n tonico m; (for hair) lozione f per i capelli; fig toccasana m inv; ~ [water] acqua f tonica

tonight /tə'naɪt/ **1** adv stanotte; (evening) stasera
2 n questa notte f; (evening) questa sera f

tonnage /'tʌnɪdʒ/ n stazza f

tonne /tʌn/ n tonnellata f metrica

tonsil /'tɒnsl/ n Anat tonsilla f; **have one's** ~**s out** operarsi di tonsille

tonsillitis /tɒnsə'laɪtɪs/ n tonsillite f; **have** ~ avere la tonsillite

too /tuː/ adv troppo; (also) anche; ~ **many** troppi; ~ **much** troppo; ~ **little** troppo poco

took /tʊk/ ▶ TAKE

tool /tuːl/ n attrezzo m

tool-bag n borsa f degli attrezzi

toolbar n Comput barra f degli strumenti

toolbox n cassetta f degli attrezzi

tool kit n astuccio m di attrezzi

toot /tuːt/ **1** n suono m di clacson
2 vi Auto clacsonare

tooth /tuːθ/ n (pl **teeth**) dente m

tooth ache /'tu:θeɪk/ n mal m di denti; **have ∼** avere mal di denti

toothbrush /'tu:θbrʌʃ/ n spazzolino m da denti

toothless /'tu:θlɪs/ adj sdentato

toothpaste /'tu:θpeɪst/ n dentifricio m

toothpick /'tu:θpɪk/ n stuzzicadenti m inv

toothy /'tu:θɪ/ adj give a ∼ grin fare un sorriso a trentadue denti

top¹ /tɒp/ n (toy) trottola f

top² **①** n cima f; Sch primo, -a mf; (upper part or half) parte f superiore; (of page, list, street) inizio m; (upper surface) superficie f; (lid) coperchio m; (of bottle) tappo m; (garment) maglia f; (blouse) camicia f; Auto marcia f più alta; **at the ∼** fig al vertice; **at the ∼ of one's voice** a squarciagola; **on ∼/on ∼ of** sopra; **on ∼ of that** (besides) per di più; **from ∼ to bottom** da cima a fondo; **blow one's ∼** fam perdere le staffe; **over the ∼** (fam: exaggerated, too much) eccessivo **②** adj in alto; ⟨official, floor of building⟩ superiore; ⟨pupil, musician etc⟩ migliore; ⟨speed⟩ massimo **③** vt (pt/pp **topped**) essere in testa a ⟨list⟩; (exceed) sorpassare; **∼ped with ice-cream** ricoperto di gelato; **∼ oneself** sl suicidarsi
  ■ **top up** vt riempire

topaz /'təʊpæz/ n topazio m

top brass n fam pezzi mpl grossi

topcoat n (of paint) strato m finale

top-end adj ⟨computer, model⟩ della fascia più alta

top floor n ultimo piano m

top gear n Auto marcia f più alta

top hat n cilindro m

top-heavy adj con la parte superiore sovraccarica

topic /'tɒpɪk/ n soggetto m; (of conversation) argomento m

topical /'tɒpɪkl/ adj d'attualità; **very ∼** di grande attualità

topless /'tɒplɪs/ adj & adv topless

top-level adj ad alto livello

top management n dirigenza f

topmost /'tɒpməʊst/ adj più alto

top-notch adj fam eccellente

top-of-the-range adj ⟨model⟩ della fascia più alta

topping /'tɒpɪŋ/ n **with a chocolate ∼** ricoperto di cioccolato; **pizza with a ham and mushroom ∼** pizza al prosciutto e funghi

topple /'tɒpl/ **①** vt rovesciare **②** vi rovesciarsi
  ■ **topple off** vi cadere

top-ranking adj ⟨official⟩ di massimo grado

top secret adj segretissimo, top secret inv

top security adj di massima sicurezza

top-shelf adj ⟨magazine⟩ pornografico

topsoil n strato m superficiale del terreno

topspin n topspin m inv

topsy-turvy /tɒpsɪ'tɜ:vɪ/ adj & adv sottosopra

top ten npl primi dieci mpl in classifica

top-up **①** n would you like a ∼? ti riempio il bicchiere/la tazza? **②** vt ⟨phone⟩ ricaricare

top-up card n ricarica f

torch /tɔ:tʃ/ n torcia f [elettrica]; (flaming) fiaccola f

tore /tɔ:(r)/ ▶TEAR¹

torment¹ /'tɔ:ment/ n tormento m

torment² /tɔ:'ment/ vt tormentare

tormentor /tɔ:'mentə(r)/ n tormentatore, -trice mf

torn /tɔ:n/ **①** ▶TEAR¹ **②** adj bucato

tornado /tɔ:'neɪdəʊ/ n (pl -es) tornado m inv

torpedo /tɔ:'pi:dəʊ/ **①** n (pl -es) siluro m **②** vt silurare

torpid /'tɔ:pɪd/ adj intorpidito

torrent /'tɒrənt/ n torrente m

torrential /tə'renʃl/ adj ⟨rain⟩ torrenziale

torrid /'tɒrɪd/ adj torrido

torso /'tɔ:səʊ/ n torso m; (in art) busto m

tortoise /'tɔ:təs/ n tartaruga f

tortoiseshell /'tɔ:təsʃel/ n tartaruga f

tortuous /'tɔ:tʃʊəs/ adj tortuoso

tortuously /'tɔ:tʃʊəslɪ/ adv tortuosamente

torture /'tɔ:tʃə(r)/ **①** n tortura f **②** vt torturare

Tory /'tɔ:rɪ/ Br **①** n conservatore, -trice mf (appartenente al partito britannico conservatore) **②** adj del partito conservatore

toss /tɒs/ **①** vt gettare; (into the air) lanciare in aria; (shake) scrollare; ⟨horse⟩ disarcionare; mescolare ⟨salad⟩; rivoltare facendo saltare in aria ⟨pancake⟩; **∼ a coin** fare testa o croce **②** vi **∼ and turn** (in bed) rigirarsi; **let's ∼ for it** facciamo testa o croce
  ■ **toss out** vt buttare via ⟨newspaper, rubbish⟩; **toss somebody out** buttare fuori qualcuno

toss-up n fam **let's have a ∼ to decide** facciamo testa o croce

tot¹ /tɒt/ n bimbetto, -a mf; (fam: of liquor) goccio m

tot[2] *vt* (pt/pp **totted**) ∼ **up** fam fare la somma di

total /'təʊtl/ **1** *adj* totale
2 *n* totale *m*
3 *vt* (pt/pp **totalled**) ammontare a; (add up) sommare

totalitarian /təʊtælɪ'teərɪən/ *adj* totalitario

totally /'təʊtəlɪ/ *adv* totalmente

tote bag /təʊt/ *n* sporta *f*

totem /'təʊtəm/ *n* totem *m inv*

totem pole *n* totem *m inv*

totter /'tɒtə(r)/ *vi* barcollare; ⟨*government*⟩ vacillare

touch /tʌtʃ/ **1** *n* tocco *m*; (sense) tatto *m*; (contact) contatto *m*; (trace) traccia *f*; (of irony, humour) tocco *m*; **get/be in** ∼ mettersi/ essere in contatto
2 *vt* toccare; (lightly) sfiorare; (equal) eguagliare; (fig: move) commuovere
3 *vi* toccarsi
■ **touch down** *vi* Aeron atterrare
■ **touch off** *vi* fig scatenare
■ **touch on** *vt* fig accennare a
■ **touch up** *vt* ritoccare ⟨*painting*⟩; ∼ **somebody up** (sexually) allungare le mani su qualcuno

touch-and-go *adj* incerto

touchdown /'tʌtʃdaʊn/ *n* Aeron atterraggio *m*; Sport meta *f*

touché /tuː'ʃeɪ/ *int* fig touché!

touched /tʌtʃt/ *adj* (crazy) toccato

touching /'tʌtʃɪŋ/ *adj* commovente

touchingly /'tʌtʃɪŋlɪ/ *adv* in modo commovente

touchline *n* (in football) linea *f* laterale; (in rugby) touche *nf inv*

touchpad *n* Comput touchpad *m inv*

touch screen *n* Comput touch screen *m inv*, schermo *m* a sfioramento

touch[-sensitive] screen *n* Comput schermo *m* a sfioramento

touch-tone *adj* ⟨*telephone*⟩ a tastiera

touch-type *vi* dattilografare a tastiera cieca

touch-typing *n* dattilografia *f* a tastiera cieca

touch-up *n* (of paintwork) ritocco *m*

touchy /'tʌtʃɪ/ *adj* permaloso; ⟨*subject*⟩ delicato

tough /tʌf/ *adj* duro; (severe, harsh) severo; (durable) resistente; (resilient) forte; ∼! (fam: too bad) peggio per te/lui!

toughen /'tʌfn/ *vt* rinforzare
■ **toughen up** *vt* rendere più forte ⟨*person*⟩

toupee /'tuːpeɪ/ *n* toupet *m inv*

tour /tʊə(r)/ **1** *n* giro *m*; (of building, town) visita *f*; Theat, Sport tournée *f inv*; (of duty) servizio *m*
2 *vt* visitare

3 *vi* fare un giro turistico; Theat essere in tournée

tour guide *n* guida *f* turistica

tourism /'tʊərɪzm/ *n* turismo *m*

tourist /'tʊərɪst/ **1** *n* turista *mf*
2 *attrib* turistico

tourist class *n* classe *f* turistica

tourist office *n* ufficio *m* turistico

tourist resort *n* località *f* turistica

tourist route *n* itinerario *m* turistico

tourist trap *n* locale *o* località per turisti dove i prezzi sono molto alti

touristy /'tʊərɪstɪ/ *adj* fam pej da turisti; it's too ∼ here è troppo turistico qui

tournament /'tʊənəmənt/ *n* torneo *m*

tourniquet /'tʊənɪkeɪ/ *n* laccio *m* emostatico

tour operator *n* tour operator *mf inv*, operatore, -trice *mf* turistico, -a

tousle /'taʊzl/ *vt* spettinare

tousled /'taʊzld/ *adj* ⟨*hair*⟩ arruffato; appearance scarmigliato

tout /taʊt/ **1** *n* (ticket ∼) bagarino *m*; (horseracing) informatore *m*
2 *vi* ∼ **for** sollecitare

tow /təʊ/ **1** *n* rimorchio *m*; 'on ∼' 'a rimorchio'; **in** ∼ fam al seguito
2 *vt* rimorchiare
■ **tow away** *vt* portare via col carro attrezzi

toward[s] /tə'wɔːd(z)/ *prep* verso; (with respect to) nei riguardi di

tow bar *n* barra *f* di rimorchio

towel /'taʊəl/ *n* asciugamano *m*
■ **towel down** *vt* asciugare

towelling /'taʊəlɪŋ/ *n* spugna *f*

towelling robe *n* accappatoio *m*

towel rail *n* portasciugamano *m*

tower /'taʊə(r)/ **1** *n* torre *f*; **be a** ∼ **of strength to somebody** essere di grande conforto per qualcuno
2 *vi* ∼ **above** dominare

tower block *n* palazzone *m*

towering /'taʊərɪŋ/ *adj* torreggiante; ⟨*rage*⟩ violento

tow line *n* cavo *m* da rimorchio

town /taʊn/ *n* città *f inv*; **in** ∼ nel centro

town-and-country planning *n* pianificazione *f* territoriale

town centre *n* centro *m* della città

town council *n* municipalità *f inv*

town hall *n* municipio *m*

town house *n* casa *f* a schiera a tre o più piani

town planner *n* urbanista *mf*

town planning *n* urbanistica *f*

township *n* comune *m*; (in South Africa) township *f inv*

towpath /'təʊpɑːθ/ *n* strada *f* alzaia

tow rope n cavo m da rimorchio

tow truck n carro m attrezzi inv

toxic /'tɒksɪk/ adj tossico

toxicity /tɒk'sɪsɪtɪ/ n tossicità f

toxicologist /tɒksɪ'kɒlədʒɪst/ n tossicologo, -a mf

toxicology /tɒksɪ'kɒlədʒɪ/ n tossicologia f

toxic waste n rifiuti mpl tossici

toxin /'tɒksɪn/ n tossina f

toy /tɔɪ/ n giocattolo m
- **toy with** vt giocherellare con

toyboy /'tɔɪbɔɪ/ n Br fam uomo-oggetto m

toyshop /'tɔɪʃɒp/ n negozio m di giocattoli

trace /treɪs/ ① n traccia f
② vt seguire le tracce di; (find) rintracciare; (draw) tracciare; (with tracing-paper) ricalcare
- **trace back** vt trovare tracce di ⟨family⟩
- **trace out** vt tracciare

tracer /'treɪsə(r)/ n Mil proiettile m tracciante

tracing /'treɪsɪŋ/ n ricalco m

tracing-paper n carta f da ricalco

track /træk/ ① n traccia f; (path, Sport) pista f; Rail binario m; **keep ~ of** tenere d'occhio
② vt seguire le tracce di
- **track down** vt scovare

trackball, tracker ball n Comput trackball f inv

tracker /'trækə(r)/ n (dog) segugio m

track record n fig background m inv

tracksuit /'træksuːt/ n tuta f da ginnastica

tract /trækt/ n (pamphlet) opuscolo m

tractable /'træktəbl/ adj trattabile; (docile) maneggevole

traction /'trækʃn/ n (of wheel) trazione f

traction engine n trattore m

tractor /'træktə(r)/ n trattore m

trade /treɪd/ ① n commercio m; (line of business) settore m; (craft) mestiere m; **by ~** di mestiere
② vt commerciare; **~ something for something** scambiare qualcosa per qualcosa
③ vi commerciare
- **trade in** vt (give in part exchange) dare in pagamento parziale
- **trade off** vt scambiare
- **trade on** vt approfittarsi di

trade deficit n bilancio m commerciale in deficit

trade discount n sconto m commerciale

trade fair n fiera f commerciale

trade-in n permuta f come pagamento parziale

trade mark n marchio m di fabbrica

trade-name n nome m despositato

trade-off n compromesso m

trade price n prezzo m all'ingrosso

trader /'treɪdə(r)/ n commerciante mf

trade secret n segreto m commerciale

tradesman /'treɪdzmən/ n (joiner etc) operaio m

tradesman's entrance n entrata f di servizio

Trades Union Congress n confederazione f dei sindacati britannici

trade union n sindacato m

trade unionist n sindacalista mf

trade union representative n rappresentante mf sindacale

trading /'treɪdɪŋ/ n commercio m

trading estate n zona f industriale

trading floor n Fin sala f delle contrattazioni

trading stamp n bollino m premio

tradition /trə'dɪʃn/ n tradizione f

traditional /trə'dɪʃnl/ adj tradizionale

traditionalist /trə'dɪʃn(ə)lɪst/ n tradizionalista mf

traditionally /trə'dɪʃn(ə)lɪ/ adv tradizionalmente

traffic /'træfɪk/ ① n traffico m
② vi trafficare

traffic calming n misure fpl per rallentare la circolazione

traffic calming measures npl misure fpl per rallentare il traffico in città

traffic circle n Am isola f rotatoria

traffic cone n birillo m

traffic island n isola f spartitraffico

traffic jam n ingorgo m

trafficker /'træfɪkə(r)/ n trafficante mf

traffic lights npl semaforo msg

traffic offence n infrazione f al codice della strada

traffic warden n vigile m [urbano]; (woman) vigilessa f

tragedy /'trædʒədɪ/ n tragedia f

tragic /'trædʒɪk/ adj tragico

tragically /'trædʒɪklɪ/ adv tragicamente

trail /treɪl/ ① n traccia f; (path) sentiero m
② vi strisciare; ⟨plant⟩ arrampicarsi; **~ [behind]** rimanere indietro; (in competition) essere in svantaggio
③ vt trascinare

trail bike n moto f fuoristrada

trailblazer /'treɪlbleɪzə(r)/ n pioniere, -a mf

trailblazing /'treɪlbleɪzɪŋ/ adj innovatore

trailer /'treɪlə(r)/ *n* Auto rimorchio *m*; (Am: caravan) roulotte *f inv*; (film) presentazione *f* (di un film)

trailer park *n* Am area *f* di sosta per roulotte

train /treɪn/ **①** *n* treno *m*; (of dress) strascico *m*; **by** ~ in treno; ~ **of thought** filo *m* dei pensieri
② *vt* formare professionalmente; Sport allenare; (aim) puntare; educare ‹child›; addestrare ‹animal, soldier›; far crescere ‹plant›
③ *vi* fare il tirocinio; Sport allenarsi

trained /treɪnd/ *adj* ‹animal› addestrato (**to do** a fare)

trainee /treɪ'niː/ *n* apprendista *mf*

trainer /'treɪnə(r)/ *n* Sport allenatore, -trice *mf*; (in circus) domatore, -trice *mf*; (of dog, race-horse) addestratore, -trice *mf*; ~**s** (*pl*: shoes) scarpe *fpl* da ginnastica

training /'treɪnɪŋ/ *n* tirocinio *m*; Sport allenamento *m*; (of animal, soldier) addestramento *m*

training college *n* istituto *m* professionale

training course *n* corso *m* di formazione

train set *n* trenino *m*

train spotter /spɒtə(r)/ *n* appassionato, -a *mf* di treni

traipse /treɪps/ *vi* ~ **around** fam andare in giro

trait /treɪt/ *n* caratteristica *f*

traitor /'treɪtə(r)/ *n* traditore, -trice *mf*

trajectory /trə'dʒekt(ə)rɪ/ *n* traiettoria *f*

tram /træm/ *n* tram *m inv*

tram-lines *npl* rotaie *fpl* del tram

tramp /træmp/ **①** *n* (hike) camminata *f*; (vagrant) barbone, -a *mf*; (of feet) calpestio *m*
② *vi* camminare con passo pesante; (hike) percorrere a piedi

trample /'træmpl/ *v*
■ **trample on** *vt* calpestare

trampoline /'træmpəliːn/ *n* trampolino *m*

trance /trɑːns/ *n* trance *f inv*

tranquil /'træŋkwɪl/ *adj* tranquillo

tranquillity /træŋ'kwɪlətɪ/ *n* tranquillità *f*

tranquillizer /'træŋkwɪlaɪzə(r)/ *n* tranquillante *m*

transact /træn'zækt/ *vt* trattare

transaction /træn'zækʃn/ *n* transazione *f*

transatlantic /trænzət'læntɪk/ *adj* ‹flight› transatlantico; ‹accent› americano

transceiver /træn'siːvə(r)/ *n* ricetrasmittente *f*

transcend /træn'send/ *vt* trascendere

transcontinental /trænzkɒntɪ'nent(ə)l/ *adj* transcontinentale

transcribe /træn'skraɪb/ *vt* trascrivere

transcript /'trænskrɪpt/ *n* trascrizione *f*

transcription /træn'skrɪpʃn/ *n* trascrizione *f*

transept /'trænsept/ *n* transetto *m*

transfer[1] /'trænsfɜː(r)/ *n* trasferimento *m*; Sport cessione *f*; (design) decalcomania *f*

transfer[2] /træns'fɜː(r)/ **①** *vt* (pt/pp **transferred**) trasferire; Sport cedere; Comput trasferire
② *vi* trasferirsi; (when travelling) cambiare

transferable /træns'fɜːrəbl/ *adj* trasferibile

transfer fee *n* (for footballer) prezzo *m* d'acquisto

transfer list *n* (in football) lista *f* di giocatori da cedere

transferred charge call /træns'fɜːd/ *n* chiamata *f* a carico del destinatario

transfigure /træns'fɪgə(r)/ *vt* trasfigurare

transfix /træns'fɪks/ *vt* trafiggere; fig immobilizzare

transfixed /træns'fɪkst/ *adj* (with fascination) folgorato; (with horror) paralizzato

transform /træns'fɔːm/ *vt* trasformare

transformation /trænsfə'meɪʃn/ *n* trasformazione *f*

transformer /træns'fɔːmə(r)/ *n* trasformatore *m*

transfusion /træns'fjuːʒn/ *n* trasfusione *f*

transgender /trænz'dʒendə(r)/ *adj* trans, dei trans

transgression /træns'greʃn/ *n* Jur trasgressione *f*; Relig peccato *m*

transient /'trænzɪənt/ *adj* passeggero

transistor /træn'zɪstə(r)/ *n* transistor *m inv*; (radio) radiolina *f* a transistor

transit /'trænzɪt/ *n* transito *m*; **in** ~ (goods) in transito

transition /træn'zɪʃn/ *n* transizione *f*

transitional /træn'zɪʃənl/ *adj* di transizione

transitive /'trænzɪtɪv/ *adj* transitivo

transitively /'trænzɪtɪvlɪ/ *adv* transitivamente

transit lounge *n* sala *f* d'attesa transiti

transitory /'trænzɪtərɪ/ *adj* transitorio

transit passenger *n* passeggero *m* in transito

translate /trænz'leɪt/ *vt* tradurre

translation /trænz'leɪʃn/ *n* traduzione *f*

translation agency *n* agenzia *f* di traduzioni

translator /trænz'leɪtə(r)/ *n* traduttore, -trice *mf*

t

translucent /trænz'lu:snt/ *adj* liter traslucido

transmissible /trænz'mɪsəbl/ *adj* trasmissibile

transmission /trænz'mɪʃn/ *n* trasmissione *f*

transmit /trænz'mɪt/ *vt* (pt/pp **transmitted**) trasmettere

transmitter /trænz'mɪtə(r)/ *n* trasmettitore *m*

transparency /træn'spærənsɪ/ *n* Phot diapositiva *f*

transparent /træn'spærənt/ *adj* trasparente

transpire /træn'spaɪə(r)/ *vi* emergere; (fam: happen) accadere

transplant¹ /'trænsplɑ:nt/ *n* trapianto *m*

transplant² /træns'plɑ:nt/ *vt* trapiantare

transport¹ /'trænspɔ:t/ *n* trasporto *m*; do you have ∼? hai un mezzo di trasporto?

transport² /træn'spɔ:t/ *vt* trasportare

transportation /trænspɔ:'teɪʃn/ *n* trasporto *m*

transpose /træns'pəʊz/ *vt* trasporre

transsexual /trænz'seksʃʊəl/ ⓵ *n* transessuale *mf*
⓶ *adj* transessuale

trans-shipment /trænz'ʃɪpmənt/ *n* trasbordo *m*

transverse /trænz'vɜːs/ *adj* trasversale

transvestite /trænz'vestaɪt/ *n* travestito, -a *mf*

trap /træp/ ⓵ *n* trappola *f*; (fam: mouth) boccaccia *f*; (carriage) calesse *m*
⓶ *vt* (pt/pp **trapped**) intrappolare; schiacciare ⟨finger in door⟩; be ∼ped essere intrappolato

trapdoor /'træpdɔ:(r)/ *n* botola *f*

trapeze /trə'pi:z/ *n* trapezio *m*

trappings /'træpɪŋz/ *npl* (dress) ornamenti *mpl*; the ∼ of wealth/success i segni esteriori della ricchezza/del successo

traschcan /'træʃkæn/ *n* Am pattumiera *f*, secchio *m* della spazzatura

trash /træʃ/ *n* robaccia *f*; (rubbish) spazzatura *f*; (nonsense) schiocchezze *fpl*

trashy /'træʃɪ/ *adj* scadente

trauma /'trɔ:mə/ *n* trauma *m*

traumatic /trɔ:'mætɪk/ *adj* traumatico

traumatize /'trɔ:mətaɪz/ *vt* traumatizzare

travel /'trævl/ ⓵ *n* viaggi *mpl*
⓶ *vi* (pt/pp **travelled**) viaggiare; ⟨to work⟩ andare
⓷ *vt* percorrere ⟨distance⟩

travel agency *n* agenzia *f* di viaggi

travel agent *n* agente *mf* di viaggio

travel card *n* tessera *f* dei trasporti pubblici

travel expenses *npl* spese *fpl* di viaggio

traveller /'trævələ(r)/ *n* viaggiatore, -trice *mf*; Comm commesso *m* viaggiatore; ∼s *pl* (gypsies) zingari *mpl*

traveller's cheque *n* traveller's cheque *m inv*

travelling /'trævəlɪŋ/ Br, **traveling** Am *adj* ⟨circus, theatre company⟩ itinerante; ⟨companion, conditions, expenses, allowance⟩ di viaggio

travelling salesman *n* commesso *m* viaggiatore

travel news *n* informazioni *fpl* sulla viabilità

travelogue /'trævəlɒg/ *n* (film) documentario *m* di viaggio; (talk) conferenza *f* su un viaggio

travel-sick *adj* be/get ∼ (on plane) soffrire il mal d'aria; (in car) soffrire il mal d'auto; (on boat) soffrire il mal di mare

travel-sickness ⓵ *n* (on plane) mal *m* d'aria; (in car) mal *m* d'auto; (on boat) mal *m* di mare
⓶ *attrib* ⟨pills⟩ per il mal d'aria/d'auto/di mare

traverse /trə'vɜːs/ *vt* traversare

travesty /'trævɪstɪ/ *n* (fig: farce) farsa *f*; a ∼ of justice una presa in giro della giustizia

trawler /'trɔ:lə(r)/ *n* peschereccio *m*

tray /treɪ/ *n* vassoio *m*; (for baking) teglia *f*; (for documents) vaschetta *f*; (of printer, photocopier) vassoio *m*, cassetto *m*

treacherous /'tretʃərəs/ *adj* traditore; ⟨weather, currents⟩ pericoloso

treachery /'tretʃ(ə)rɪ/ *n* tradimento *m*

treacle /'tri:kl/ *n* melassa *f*

tread /tred/ ⓵ *n* andatura *f*; (step) gradino *m*; (of tyre) battistrada *m inv*
⓶ *vi* (pt **trod**, pp **trodden**) (walk) camminare
■ **tread on** *vt* calpestare ⟨grass⟩; pestare ⟨foot⟩

treadmill /'tredmɪl/ *n* fig solito tran tran *m*

treason /'tri:zn/ *n* tradimento *m*

treasonable /'tri:z(ə)nəbl/ *adj* proditorio

treasure /'treʒə(r)/ ⓵ *n* tesoro *m*
⓶ *vt* tenere in gran conto

treasurer /'treʒərə(r)/ *n* tesoriere, -a *mf*

treasury /'treʒərɪ/ *n* the T∼ il Ministero del Tesoro

treat /tri:t/ ⓵ *n* piacere *m*; (present) regalo *m*; give somebody a ∼ fare una sorpresa a qualcuno

2 *vt* trattare; Med curare; ~ **somebody to something** offrire qualcosa a qualcuno; ~ **somebody for something** Med sottoporre qualcuno ad una cura per qualcosa

treatise /ˈtriːtɪz/ *n* trattato *m*

treatment /ˈtriːtmənt/ *n* trattamento *m*; Med cura *f*

treaty /ˈtriːtɪ/ *n* trattato *m*

treble /ˈtrebl/ 1 *adj* triplo; ~ **the amount** il triplo
2 *n* Mus (voice) voce *f* bianca
3 *vt* triplicare
4 *vi* triplicarsi

treble clef *n* chiave *f* di violino

tree /triː/ *n* albero *m*

tree house *n* capanna *f* su un albero

tree stump *n* ceppo *m*

treetop *n* cima *f* di un albero

tree trunk *n* tronco *m* d'albero

trek /trek/ 1 *n* scarpinata *f*; (as holiday) trekking *m inv*
2 *vi* (pt/pp **trekked**) farsi una scarpinata; (on holiday) fare trekking

trekking /ˈtrekɪŋ/ *n* trekking *m*

trellis /ˈtrelɪs/ *n* graticolato *m*

tremble /ˈtrembl/ *vi* tremare (**with** di)

trembling /ˈtremblɪŋ/ *adj* tremante

tremendous /trɪˈmendəs/ *adj* (huge) enorme; (fam: excellent) formidabile

tremendously /trɪˈmendəslɪ/ *adv* (very) straordinariamente; (a lot) enormemente

tremor /ˈtremə(r)/ *n* tremito *m*; [earth] ~ scossa *f* [sismica]

tremulous /ˈtremjʊləs/ *adj* tremulo

trench /trentʃ/ *n* fosso *m*; Mil trincea *f*

trenchant /ˈtrentʃənt/ *adj* ⟨comment, criticism⟩ mordace

trench coat *n* trench *m inv*

trend /trend/ *n* tendenza *f*; (fashion) moda *f*

trend-setter *n* persona *f* che detta la moda

trend-setting *adj* che detta la moda

trendy /ˈtrendɪ/ *adj* (**-ier, -iest**) fam di or alla moda

trepidation /trepɪˈdeɪʃn/ *n* trepidazione *f*

trespass /ˈtrespəs/ *vi* ~ **on** introdursi abusivamente in; fig abusare di

trespasser /ˈtrespəsə(r)/ *n* intruso, -a *mf*

trestle /ˈtresl/ *n* cavalletto *m*

trestle table *n* tavolo *m* a cavalletto

trial /ˈtraɪəl/ *n* Jur processo *m*; (test, ordeal) prova *f*; **on** ~ in prova; Jur in giudizio; **by** ~ **and error** per tentativi

trial period *n* periodo *m* di prova

trial run *n* (preliminary test) prova *f*

triangle /ˈtraɪæŋgl/ *n* triangolo *m*

triangular /traɪˈæŋgjʊlə(r)/ *adj* triangolare

tribal /ˈtraɪbl/ *adj* tribale

tribe /traɪb/ *n* tribù *f inv*

tribulation /trɪbjʊˈleɪʃn/ *n* tribolazione *f*

tribunal /traɪˈbjuːnl/ *n* tribunale *m*

tributary /ˈtrɪbjʊtərɪ/ *n* affluente *m*

tribute /ˈtrɪbjuːt/ *n* tributo *m*; **pay** ~ rendere omaggio

trice /traɪs/ *n* **in a** ~ in un attimo

tricentenary /traɪsenˈtiːnərɪ/ 1 *n* terzo centenario *m*
2 *adj* del terzo centenario

trick /trɪk/ 1 *n* trucco *m*; (joke) scherzo *m*; (Cards) presa *f*; **do the** ~ fam funzionare; **play a** ~ **on** fare uno scherzo a
2 *vt* imbrogliare; ~ **of the trade** trucco *m* del mestiere
▪ **trick into** *vt* ~ **somebody into doing something** convincere qualcuno a fare qualcosa con l'inganno
▪ **trick out** *vt* ~ **somebody out of something** fregare qualcuno a qualcosa

trick cyclist *n* (sl: psychiatrist) psichiatra *mf*

trickle /ˈtrɪkl/ *vi* colare
▪ **trickle away** *vi* ⟨water⟩ uscire lentamente; ⟨people⟩ allontanarsi lentamente
▪ **trickle in** *vi* fig entrare poco per volta
▪ **trickle out** *vi* fig uscire poco per volta

trick question *n* domanda *f* trabocchetto *inv*

trickster /ˈtrɪkstə(r)/ *n* imbroglione, -a *mf*

tricky /ˈtrɪkɪ/ *adj* (**-ier, -iest**) *adj* ⟨operation⟩ complesso; ⟨situation⟩ delicato

tricolour /ˈtrɪkələ(r)/ *n* tricolore *m*

tricycle /ˈtraɪsɪkl/ *n* triciclo *m*

tried /traɪd/ ▸ TRY

tried and tested *adj* ⟨method⟩ sperimentato

trifle /ˈtraɪfl/ *n* inezia *f*; Culin zuppa *f* inglese

trifling /ˈtraɪflɪŋ/ *adj* insignificante

trig /trɪg/ *n* (fam: trigonometry) trigonometria *f*

trigger /ˈtrɪgə(r)/ 1 *n* grilletto *m*; fig causa *f*
2 *vt* ~ [**off**] scatenare

trigger-happy *adj* fam dalla pistola facile; fig impulsivo

trigonometry /trɪgəˈnɒmɪtrɪ/ *n* trigonometria *f*

trilateral /traɪˈlætərəl/ *adj* trilaterale

trilby /ˈtrɪlbɪ/ *n* cappello *m* di feltro

trill /trɪl/ *n* Mus trillo *m*

trilogy /ˈtrɪlədʒɪ/ *n* trilogia *f*

trim /trɪm/ 1 *adj* (**trimmer, trimmest**) curato; ⟨figure⟩ snello

2 n (of hair, hedge) spuntata f; (decoration) rifinitura f; in good ∼ in buono stato; ⟨person⟩ in forma
3 vt (pt/pp **trimmed**) spuntare ⟨hair etc⟩; (decorate) ornare; Naut orientare
■ **trim off** vt tagliare via

trimming /'trɪmɪŋ/ n bordo m; ∼s pl (of pastry) ritagli mpl; (decorations) guarnizioni fpl; with all the ∼s Culin guarnito

Trinidad and Tobago /'trɪnɪdæd, tə'beɪgəʊ/ n Trinidad e Tobago m

Trinity /'trɪnɪtɪ/ n the [Holy] ∼ la [Santissima] Trinità

trinket /'trɪŋkɪt/ n ninnolo m

trio /'tri:əʊ/ n trio m

trip /trɪp/ **1** n (excursion) gita f; (journey) viaggio m; (stumble) passo m falso
2 vt (pt/pp **tripped**) far inciampare
3 vi inciampare (on/over in)
■ **trip up** vt far inciampare

tripartite /traɪ'pɑ:taɪt/ adj tripartito

tripe /traɪp/ n trippa f; (sl: nonsense) fesserie fpl

triple /'trɪpl/ **1** adj triplo
2 vt triplicare
3 vi triplicarsi

triplets /'trɪplɪts/ npl tre gemelli mpl

triplicate /'trɪplɪkət/ n in ∼ in triplice copia

tripod /'traɪpɒd/ n treppiede m inv

tripper /'trɪpə(r)/ n gitante mf

trite /traɪt/ adj banale

triteness /'traɪtnɪs/ n banalità f

triumph /'traɪʌmf/ **1** n trionfo m
2 vi trionfare (over su)

triumphant /traɪ'ʌmf(ə)nt/ adj trionfante

triumphantly /traɪ'ʌmf(ə)ntlɪ/ adv ⟨exclaim⟩ con tono trionfante

triumvirate /traɪ'ʌmvɪrət/ n triumvirato m

trivia /'trɪvɪə/ npl cose fpl secondarie

trivial /'trɪvɪəl/ adj insignificante

triviality /trɪvɪ'ælətɪ/ n banalità f inv

trivialize /'trɪvɪəlaɪz/ vt sminuire

trod, trodden /trɒd/, /'trɒdn/ ▶ TREAD

trolley /'trɒlɪ/ n carrello m; (Am: tram) tram m inv

trolley bus n filobus m inv

trombone /trɒm'bəʊn/ n trombone m

trombonist /trɒm'bəʊnɪst/ n trombonista mf

troop /tru:p/ **1** n gruppo m; ∼s pl truppe fpl
2 vi ∼ in/out entrare/uscire in gruppo

trooper /'tru:pə(r)/ n Mil soldato m di cavalleria; (Am: policeman) poliziotto m

trophy /'trəʊfɪ/ n trofeo m

tropic /'trɒpɪk/ n tropico m; ∼s pl tropici mpl

tropical /'trɒpɪkl/ adj tropicale

tropical fruit n frutta f inv esotica

trot /trɒt/ **1** n trotto m
2 vi (pt/pp **trotted**) trottare
■ **trot out** vt (fam: produce) tirar fuori

trotter /'trɒtə(r)/ n Culin piedino m di maiale

trouble /'trʌbl/ **1** n guaio m; (difficulties) problemi mpl; (inconvenience, Med) disturbo m; (conflict) conflitto m; be in ∼ essere nei guai; ⟨swimmer, climber⟩ essere in difficoltà; get into ∼ finire nei guai; get somebody into ∼ mettere qualcuno nei guai; take the ∼ to do something darsi la pena di far qualcosa; it's no ∼ nessun disturbo; the ∼ with you is... il tuo problema è...
2 vt (worry) preoccupare; (inconvenience) disturbare; ⟨conscience, old wound⟩ tormentare
3 vi don't ∼! non ti disturbare!

troubled /'trʌbld/ adj ⟨mind⟩ inquieto; ⟨person, expression⟩ preoccupato; ⟨times, area⟩ difficile; ⟨waters, sleep⟩ agitato

troublefree adj senza problemi

troublemaker /'trʌblmeɪkə(r)/ n be a ∼ seminare zizzania

troubleshooter n rilevatore e risolutore m di problemi

troublesome /'trʌblsəm/ adj fastidioso

trouble spot n zona f calda

trough /trɒf/ n trogolo m; (atmospheric) depressione f

trounce /traʊns/ vt (in competition) schiacciare

troupe /tru:p/ n troupe f inv

trouser press n stiracalzoni m inv

trousers /'traʊzəz/ npl pantaloni mpl

trouser suit n tailleur m inv pantalone

trousseau /'tru:səʊ/ n corredo m

trout /traʊt/ n inv trota f

trowel /'traʊəl/ n (for gardening) paletta f; (for builder) cazzuola f

truancy /'tru:ənsɪ/ n assenze fpl ingiustificate

truant /'tru:ənt/ n play ∼ marinare la scuola

truce /tru:s/ n tregua f

truck /trʌk/ n (lorry) camion m inv

truck driver n camionista mf

trucker /'trʌkə(r)/ n (fam: lorry driver) camionista mf

truck farmer n Am ortofrutticoltore m, ortolano m

truculent /'trʌkjʊlənt/ adj aggressivo

truculently /'trʌkjʊləntlɪ/ adv aggressivamente

trudge /trʌdʒ/ **1** n camminata f faticosa
2 vi arrancare

true /tru:/ adj vero; come ∼ avverarsi

true-life *adj* ‹*adventure, story*› vero

truffle /'trʌfl/ *n* tartufo *m*

truism /'tru:ɪzm/ *n* truismo *m*

truly /'tru:lɪ/ *adv* veramente; **Yours ~** Distinti saluti

trump /trʌmp/ ① *n* (Cards) atout *m inv* ② *vt* prendere con l'atout
∎ **trump up** *vt* fam inventare

trump card *n* fig asso *m* nella manica

trumped-up /'trʌmptʌp/ *adj* ‹*charges*› inventato

trumpet /'trʌmpɪt/ *n* tromba *f*

trumpeter /'trʌmpɪtə(r)/ *n* trombettista *mf*

truncate /'trʌŋkeɪt/ *vt* tagliare ‹*text*›; interrompere ‹*process, journey, event*›

truncheon /'trʌntʃn/ *n* manganello *m*

trundle /'trʌndl/ ① *vt* far rotolare ② *vi* rotolare

trunk /trʌŋk/ *n* (of tree, body) tronco *m*; (of elephant) proboscide *f*; (for travelling, storage) baule *m*; (Am: of car) bagagliaio *m*, portabagagli *m inv*

trunk road *n* statale *f*

trunks /trʌŋks/ *npl* calzoncini *mpl* da bagno

truss /trʌs/ *n* Med cinto *m* erniario
∎ **truss up** *vt* legare

trust /trʌst/ ① *n* fiducia *f*; (group of companies) trust *m inv*; (organization) associazione *f*; **on ~** sulla parola ② *vt* fidarsi di; (hope) augurarsi ③ *vi* **~ in** credere in; **~ to** affidarsi a

trust company *n* società *f* fiduciaria

trusted /'trʌstɪd/ *adj* fidato

trustee /trʌs'ti:/ *n* amministratore, -trice *mf* fiduciario, -a

trustful /'trʌstfʊl/ *adj* fiducioso

trustfully /'trʌstfʊlɪ/ *adv* fiduciosamente

trust fund *n* fondo *m* fiduciario

trusting /'trʌstɪŋ/ *adj* fiducioso

trustworthiness /'trʌstwɜ:ðɪnɪs/ *n* (of person) affidabilità *f*; (of source) attendibilità *f*

trustworthy /'trʌstwɜ:ðɪ/ *adj* fidato

trusty /'trʌstɪ/ *adj* fam fidato

truth /tru:θ/ *n* (pl **-s** /tru:ðz/) verità *f inv*

truthful /'tru:θfʊl/ *adj* ‹*person*› sincero; ‹*statement*› veritiero

truthfully /'tru:θfʊlɪ/ *adv* sinceramente

truthfulness /'tru:θfʊlnɪs/ *n* (of person) sincerità *f*; (of account) veridicità *f*

try /traɪ/ ① *n* tentativo *m*, prova *f*; (in rugby) meta *f*; **I'll give it a ~** faccio un tentativo ② *vt* (pt/pp **tried**) provare; (be a strain on) mettere a dura prova; Jur processare ‹*person*›; discutere ‹*case*›; **~ to do something** provare a fare qualcosa ③ *vi* provare

∎ **try for** *vi* cercare di ottenere
∎ **try on** *vt* provarsi ‹*garment*›
∎ **try out** *vt* provare

trying /'traɪɪŋ/ *adj* duro; ‹*person*› irritante

try-out *n* **give somebody a ~** mettere alla prova qualcuno

tsar /zɑ:(r)/ *n* zar *m inv*

tsarina /tsɑ:'ri:nə/ *n* zarina *f*

T-shirt *n* maglietta *f*

tsp *abbr* **teaspoonful**

tsunami *n* tsunami *m*

tub /tʌb/ *n* tinozza *f*; (carton) vaschetta *f*; (bath) vasca *f* da bagno

tuba /'tju:bə/ *n* Mus tuba *f*

tubby /'tʌbɪ/ *adj* (**-ier, -iest**) tozzo

tube /tju:b/ *n* tubo *m*; (of toothpaste) tubetto *m*; Br Rail metro *f*

tuber /'tju:bə(r)/ *n* tubero *m*

tuberculosis /tjuːbɜːkjʊ'ləʊsɪs/ *n* tubercolosi *f*

tubing /'tju:bɪŋ/ *n* tubi *mpl*

tubular /'tju:bjʊlə(r)/ *adj* tubolare

TUC *n abbr* Br (**Trades Union Congress**) confederazione *f* dei sindacati britannici

tuck /tʌk/ ① *n* piega *f* ② *vt* (put) infilare
∎ **tuck away** *vt* (put in a safe place) mettere al sicuro; (eat) spolverare
∎ **tuck in** ① *vt* rimboccare; **~ somebody in** rimboccare le coperte a qualcuno ② *vi* (fam: eat) mangiare con appetito
∎ **tuck into** *vt* mangiare di gusto ‹*meal*›; **~ something into one's pocket** infilarsi in tasca qualcosa; **~ somebody into bed** rimboccare le coperte a qualcuno
∎ **tuck up** *vt* rimboccarsi ‹*sleeves*›; (in bed) rimboccare le coperte a

Tuesday /'tju:zdeɪ/ *n* martedì *m inv*

tuft /tʌft/ *n* ciuffo *m*

tug /tʌg/ ① *n* strattone *m*; Naut rimorchiatore *m* ② *vt* (pt/pp **tugged**) tirare ③ *vi* dare uno strattone

tug-of-love *n* disputa *f* tra i genitori per l'affidamento dei figli

tug of war *n* tiro *m* alla fune

tuition /tju:'ɪʃn/ *n* lezioni *fpl*

tuition fees *npl* tasse *fpl* universitarie

tulip /'tju:lɪp/ *n* tulipano *m*

tumble /'tʌmbl/ ① *n* ruzzolone *m* ② *vi* ruzzolare; **~ to something** (fam: realize) afferrare qualcosa
∎ **tumble down** *vi* ‹*wall, building*› crollare

tumbledown /'tʌmbəldaʊn/ *adj* cadente

tumble-dry *vt* asciugare nell'asciugabiancheria

tumble-dryer, **tumble-drier** *n* asciugabiancheria *m*

t

tumbler /'tʌmblə(r)/ *n* bicchiere *m* (senza stelo)

tummy /'tʌmɪ/ *n fam* pancia *f*

tummy button *n fam* ombelico *m*

tumour /'tju:mə(r)/ *n* tumore *m*

tumult /'tju:mʌlt/ *n* tumulto *m*

tumultuous /tju:'mʌltjʊəs/ *adj* tumultuoso

tuna /'tju:nə/ *n* tonno *m*

tune /tju:n/ ① *n* motivo *m*; **out of/in ~** ⟨*instrument*⟩ scordato/accordato; ⟨*person*⟩ stonato/intonato; **to the ~ of** *fam* per la modesta somma di ② *vt* accordare ⟨*instrument*⟩; sintonizzare ⟨*radio, TV*⟩; mettere a punto ⟨*engine*⟩ ■ **tune in** ① *vt* sintonizzare ② *vi* sintonizzarsi (**to** su) ■ **tune up** *vi* ⟨*orchestra*⟩ accordare gli strumenti

tuneful /'tju:nfl/ *adj* melodioso

tuner /'tju:nə(r)/ *n* accordatore, -trice *mf*; Radio, TV sintonizzatore *m*

tune-up *n* (of engine) messa *f* a punto

tungsten /'tʌŋstən/ *n* tungsteno *m*

tunic /'tju:nɪk/ *n* tunica *f*; Mil giacca *f*; Sch ≈ grembiule *m*

tuning-fork /'tju:nɪŋ/ *n* diapason *m inv*

Tunisia /tju:'nɪzɪə/ *n* Tunisia *f*

Tunisian /tju:'nɪzɪən/ *adj & n* tunisino, -a *mf*

tunnel /'tʌnl/ ① *n* tunnel *m inv* ② *vi* (pt/pp **tunnelled**) scavare un tunnel

tunnel vision *n* Med restringimento *m* del campo visivo; fig paraocchi *m inv*

tuppence /'tʌpəns/ *n* due penny

turban /'tɜ:bən/ *n* turbante *m*

turbine /'tɜ:baɪn/ *n* turbina *f*

turbo /'tɜ:bəʊ/ *n* turbo *m inv*

turbocharged /'tɜ:bəʊtʃɑ:dʒd/ *adj* con motore turbo

turbocharger /'tɜ:bəʊtʃɑ:dʒə(r)/ *n* turbocompressore *m*

turbot /'tɜ:bət/ *n* rombo *m* gigante

turbulence /'tɜ:bjʊləns/ *n* turbolenza *f*

turbulent /'tɜ:bjʊlənt/ *adj* turbolento

turd /tɜ:d/ *n sl* (excrement) stronzo *m*; (pej: person) stronzo, -a *m*

tureen /tjʊ'ri:n/ *n* zuppiera *f*

turf /tɜ:f/ *n* erba *f*; (segment) zolla *f* erbosa ■ **turf out** *vt fam* buttar fuori

turf accountant *n* allibratore *m*

turgid /'tɜ:dʒɪd/ *adj* ⟨*style, water*⟩ turgido

Turin /tjʊ'rɪn/ *n* Torino *m*

Turk /tɜ:k/ *n* turco, -a *mf*

Turkey /'tɜ:kɪ/ *n* Turchia *f*

turkey *n* tacchino *m*

Turkish /'tɜ:kɪʃ/ *adj* turco

Turkish bath *n* bagno *m* turco

Turkish delight *n* cubetti *mpl* di gelatina ricoperti di zucchero a velo

Turkmenistan /tɜ:kmenɪ'stɑ:n/ *n* Turkmenistan *m*

turmeric /'tɜ:mərɪk/ *n* (spice) curcumina *f*; (plant) curcuma *f*

turmoil /'tɜ:mɔɪl/ *n* tumulto *m*

turn /tɜ:n/ ① *n* (rotation, short walk) giro *m*; (in road) svolta *f*, curva *f*; (development) svolta *f*; Theat numero *m*; (fam: attack) crisi *f inv*; **a ~ for the better/worse** un miglioramento/peggioramento *m*; **do somebody a good ~** rendere un servizio a qualcuno; **take ~s** fare a turno; **in ~** a turno; **out of ~** ⟨*speak*⟩ a sproposito; **It's your ~** tocca a te ② *vt* girare; voltare ⟨*back, eyes*⟩; dirigere ⟨*gun, attention*⟩ ③ *vi* girare; ⟨*person*⟩ girarsi; ⟨*leaves*⟩ ingiallire; (become) diventare; **~ right/left** girare a destra/sinistra; **~ sour** inacidirsi; **~ to somebody** girarsi verso qualcuno; fig rivolgersi a qualcuno ■ **turn against** ① *vi* diventare ostile a ② *vt* mettere contro ■ **turn around** ① *vi* ⟨*person*⟩ girarsi; ⟨*car*⟩ girare ② *vt* girare ⟨*object*⟩; risollevare ⟨*company*⟩ ■ **turn away** ① *vt* mandare via ⟨*people*⟩; girare dall'altra parte ⟨*head*⟩ ② *vi* girarsi dall'altra parte ■ **turn back** ① *vi* tornare indietro ② *vt* mandare indietro ⟨*people*⟩; ripiegare ⟨*covers, sheet etc*⟩ ■ **turn down** *vt* piegare ⟨*collar*⟩; abbassare ⟨*heat, gas, sound*⟩; respingere ⟨*person, proposal*⟩ ■ **turn in** ① *vt* ripiegare in dentro ⟨*edges*⟩; consegnare ⟨*lost object*⟩ ② *vi* (fam: go to bed) andare a letto; **~ in to the drive** entrare nel viale ■ **turn into** *vt* (become) diventare ■ **turn off** ① *vt* spegnere; chiudere ⟨*tap, water*⟩; **~ somebody off** (fam: disgust) fare schifo a qualcuno ② *vi* ⟨*car*⟩ girare ■ **turn on** ① *vt* accendere; aprire ⟨*tap, water*⟩; (fam: attract) eccitare ② *vi* (attack) attaccare ■ **turn out** ① *vt* (expel) mandar via; spegnere ⟨*light, gas*⟩; (produce) produrre; (empty) svuotare ⟨*room, cupboard*⟩ ② *vi* (transpire) risultare; (to see, do something) venire; **~ out well/badly** ⟨*cake, dress*⟩ riuscire bene/male; ⟨*situation*⟩ andare bene/male ■ **turn over** ① *vt* girare; **~ somebody over to the police** consegnare qualcuno alla polizia; **he ~ed the business over to her** le ha ceduto l'azienda ② *vi* girarsi; **please ~ over** vedi retro ■ **turn round** *vi* girarsi; ⟨*car*⟩ girare ■ **turn up** ① *vt* tirare su ⟨*collar*⟩; alzare ⟨*heat, gas, sound, radio*⟩ ② *vi* farsi vedere

turn-about n (fig: change of direction) cambiamento m

turnaround n (in attitude) dietrofront m inv; (of fortune) capovolgimento m; (for the better) ripresa f

turncoat n voltagabbana mf inv

turning /'tɜːnɪŋ/ n svolta f

turning-point n svolta f decisiva

turnip /'tɜːnɪp/ n rapa f

turn-off n strada f laterale; **it's a real ~** fam ti fa davvero passar la voglia

turn of mind n indole f

turn of phrase n espressione f

turn-on n fam **be a real ~** essere veramente eccitante

turnout n (of people) affluenza f

turnover n Comm giro m d'affari, fatturato m; (of staff) ricambio m

turnpike n Am autostrada f

turnround n (in policy etc) cambiamento m

turnstile n cancelletto m girevole

turntable n piattaforma f girevole; (on record-player) piatto m

turn-up n (of trousers) risvolto m

turpentine /'tɜːpəntaɪn/ n trementina f

turquoise /'tɜːkwɔɪz/ **①** adj (colour) turchese

② n turchese m

turret /'tʌrɪt/ n torretta f

turtle /'tɜːtl/ n tartaruga f acquatica

turtle-dove n tortora f

turtleneck /'tɜːtlnek/ n collo m a lupetto; (sweater) maglia f a lupetto

Tuscan /'tʌskən/ adj toscano

Tuscany /'tʌskənɪ/ n Toscana f

tusk /tʌsk/ n zanna f

tussle /'tʌsl/ **①** n zuffa f

② vi azzuffarsi

tussock /'tʌsək/ n ciuffo m d'erba

tut /tʌt/ **①** vi fare un'esclamazione di disapprovazione

② int ts!

tutor /'tjuːtə(r)/ n insegnante mf privato, -a; Univ insegnante mf universitario, -a che segue individualmente un ristretto numero di studenti

tutorial /tjuː'tɔːrɪəl/ n discussione f col tutor

tutorial package n Comput software m di autoapprendimento

tuxedo /tʌk'siːdəʊ/ n Am smoking m inv

TV abbr (**television**) tv f inv, tivù f inv

TV dinner n pasto m pronto

twaddle /'twɒdl/ n scemenze fpl

twain /twein/ npl **the ~** i due; **and never the ~ shall meet** e mai i due si incontreranno

twang /twæŋ/ **①** n (in voice) suono m nasale

② vt far vibrare

tweak /twiːk/ **①** vt tirare ⟨ear, nose⟩; (adjust) apportare delle modifiche a

② n (adjustment) modifica f; **give sb's ears a ~** dare una tirata d'orecchie a qualcuno

twee /twiː/ adj Br fam ⟨manner⟩ affettato

tweed /twiːd/ n tweed m inv

tweezers /'twiːzəz/ npl pinzette f

twelfth /twelfθ/ adj & n dodicesimo, -a mf

twelve /twelv/ adj & n dodici m

twenties /'twentɪz/ npl (period) **the ~** gli anni Venti mpl; (age) vent'anni mpl; ▶ also FORTIES

twentieth /'twentɪɪθ/ adj & n ventesimo, -a mf

twenty /'twentɪ/ adj & n venti m

twerp /twɜːp/ n fam stupido, -a mf

twice /twaɪs/ adv due volte; **she's done ~ as much as you** ha fatto il doppio di quanto hai fatto tu

twiddle /'twɪdl/ vt giocherellare con; **~ one's thumbs** fig girarsi i pollici

twig[1] /twɪg/ n ramoscello m

twig[2] vt/i (pt/pp **twigged**) fam intuire

twilight /'twaɪlaɪt/ n crepuscolo m

twilight zone n (mysterious place or situation) zona f d'ombra

twill /twɪl/ n spigato m

twin /twɪn/ **①** n gemello, -a mf

② attrib gemello

twin beds npl letti mpl gemelli

twine /twaɪn/ **①** n spago m

② vi intrecciarsi; ⟨plant⟩ attorcigliarsi

③ vt intrecciare

twinge /twɪndʒ/ n fitta f; **~ of conscience** rimorso m di coscienza

twinkle /'twɪŋkl/ **①** n scintillio m

② vi scintillare

twinning /'twɪnɪŋ/ n (of companies) gemellaggio m

twin town n città f inv gemellata

twirl /twɜːl/ **①** vt far roteare

② vi volteggiare

③ n piroetta f

twist /twɪst/ **①** n torsione f; (curve) curva f; (in rope) attorcigliata f; (in book, plot) colpo m di scena; **round the ~** (fam: crazy) ammattito

② vt attorcigliare ⟨rope⟩; torcere ⟨metal⟩; girare ⟨knob, cap⟩; (distort) distorcere; **~ one's ankle** storcersi la caviglia

③ vi attorcigliarsi; ⟨road⟩ essere pieno di curve

twisted /'twɪstɪd/ adj ⟨wire, rope⟩ ritorto; ⟨ankle, wrist⟩ slogato; ⟨sense of humour, mind⟩ perverso

twister /'twɪstə(r)/ n fam imbroglione, -a mf; (tornado) tornado m inv

t

twit /twɪt/ n fam cretino, -a mf
twitch /twɪtʃ/ ① n tic m inv; (jerk) strattone m
② vi contrarsi
twitchy /'twɪtʃɪ/ adj (fam: nervous) nervosetto
twitter /'twɪtə(r)/ ① n cinguettio m; in a ~ fam agitato
② vi cinguettare; ⟨person⟩ cianciare
■ **twitter on about** vt parlare incessantemente di
two /tu:/ adj & n due m; put ~ and ~ together fare due più due
two-faced /-'feɪst/ adj falso
twofold ① adj a ~ increase un raddoppio
② adv to increase ~ raddoppiare
two-piece adj (swimsuit) due pezzi m inv; (suit) completo m
two-seater /-'si:tə(r)/ n biposto m inv
twosome /'tu:səm/ n coppia f
two-tier adj ⟨system, health service⟩ a due velocità
two-time vt fam fare le corna a
two-tone adj (in colour) bicolore; (in sound) bitonale
two-way adj ⟨traffic⟩ a doppio senso di marcia
two-way mirror n specchio m unidirezionale
two-way radio n (radio f) ricetrasmittente f
tycoon /taɪ'ku:n/ n magnate m
tying /'taɪɪŋ/ ▶ TIE
type /taɪp/ ① n tipo m; (printing) carattere m [tipografico]
② vt/i scrivere a macchina
typecast ① vt Theat, fig far fare sempre la stessa parte a ⟨person⟩
② adj a ruolo fisso
typeface n carattere m tipografico
typeset vt comporre
typesetter n compositore m
typewriter n macchina f da scrivere
typewritten adj dattiloscritto
typhoid /'taɪfɔɪd/ n febbre f tifoidea
typhoon /taɪ'fu:n/ n tifone m
typical /'tɪpɪkl/ adj tipico
typically /'tɪpɪklɪ/ adv tipicamente; (as usual) come al solito
typify /'tɪpɪfaɪ/ vt (pt/pp -ied) essere tipico di
typing /'taɪpɪŋ/ n dattilografia f
typist /'taɪpɪst/ n dattilografo, -a mf
typo /'taɪpəʊ/ n errore m di stampa; (keying error) errore m di battitura
typography /taɪ'pɒɡrəfɪ/ n tipografia f
tyrannical /tɪ'rænɪkl/ adj tirannico
tyrannize /'tɪrənaɪz/ vt tiranneggiare
tyranny /'tɪrənɪ/ n tirannia f
tyrant /'taɪrənt/ n tiranno, -a mf
tyre /'taɪə(r)/ n gomma f, pneumatico m
tyre pressure n pressione f delle gomme
Tyrrhenian Sea /tɪ'ri:nɪən/ n mar m Tirreno
tzar /zɑ:(r)/ n zar m
tzarina /tsɑ:'ri:nə/ n zarina f

Uu

u¹, U /ju:/ n (letter) u, U f inv
u² abbr Cinema (**universal**) per tutti
U-bend n (in pipe) gomito m; (in road) curva f a gomito
ubiquitous /ju:'bɪkwɪtəs/ adj onnipresente
UCAS /'ju:kæs/ abbr Br (**Universities and Colleges Admissions Service**) organismo m di valutazione delle ammissioni all'università
udder /'ʌdə(r)/ n mammella f (di vacca, capra ecc)
UEFA /ju:'i:fə, -'eɪfə/ n abbr (**Union of European Football Associations**) UEFA f
UFO abbr (**unidentified flying object**) ufo m inv

Uganda /ju:'gændə/ n Uganda f
Ugandan /ju:'gændən/ adj & n ugandese mf
ugliness /'ʌɡlɪnɪs/ n bruttezza f
ugly /'ʌɡlɪ/ adj (-ier, -iest) brutto
UHF abbr (**ultra-high frequency**) UHF
UHT abbr (**ultra-heat-treated**) ⟨milk⟩ UHT
UK abbr **United Kingdom**
Ukraine /ju:'kreɪn/ n Ucraina f
Ukrainian /ju:'kreɪnɪən/ adj & n ucraino, -a mf; (language) ucraino m
ulcer /'ʌlsə(r)/ n ulcera f
ulterior /ʌl'tɪərɪə(r)/ adj ~ motive secondo fine m

ultimate /'ʌltɪmət/ *adj* definitivo; (final) finale; (fundamental) fondamentale

ultimately /'ʌltɪmətlɪ/ *adv* alla fine

ultimatum /ʌltɪ'meɪtəm/ *n* ultimatum *m inv*

ultramarine /ʌltrəmə'ri:n/ ① *adj* oltremarino
② *n* azzurro *m* oltremarino

ultrasound /'ʌltrəsaʊnd/ *n* Med ecografia *f*

ultrasound scan *n* ecografia *m*

ultrasound scanner *n* scanner *m inv* per ecografia

ultraviolet /ʌltrə'vaɪələt/ *adj* ultravioletto

umbilical /ʌm'bɪlɪkl/ *adj* ∼ **cord** cordone *m* ombelicale

umbrage /'ʌmbrɪdʒ/ *n* take ∼ offendersi

umbrella /ʌm'brelə/ *n* ombrello *m*

umbrella stand *n* portaombrelli *m inv*

umpire /'ʌmpaɪə(r)/ ① *n* arbitro *m*
② *vt/i* arbitrare

umpteen /ʌmp'ti:n/ *adj* fam innumerevole

umpteenth /ʌmp'ti:nθ/ *adj* fam ennesimo; **for the** ∼ **time** per l'ennesima volta

UN *abbr* (**United Nations**) ONU *f*

unabashed /ʌnə'bæʃt/ *adj* spudorato

unabated /ʌnə'beɪtɪd/ *adj* ⟨enthusiasm⟩ inalterato; **continue** ∼ ⟨gales⟩ continuare con la stessa intensità

unable /ʌn'eɪbl/ *adj* **be** ∼ **to do something** non potere fare qualcosa; (not know how) non sapere fare qualcosa

unabridged /ʌnə'brɪdʒd/ *adj* integrale

unacceptable /ʌnək'septəbl/ *adj* ⟨proposal, suggestion⟩ inaccettabile

unaccompanied /ʌnə'kʌmpnɪd/ *adj* non accompagnato; ⟨luggage⟩ incustodito

unaccountable /ʌnə'kaʊntəbl/ *adj* inspiegabile

unaccountably /ʌnə'kaʊntəblɪ/ *adv* inspiegabilmente

unaccounted /ʌnə'kaʊntɪd/ *adj* **be** ∼ **for** (not explained) non avere spiegazione; (not found) mancare

unaccustomed /ʌnə'kʌstəmd/ *adj* insolito; **be** ∼ **to** non essere abituato a

unadorned /ʌnə'dɔ:nd/ *adj* ⟨walls⟩ disadorno

unadulterated /ʌnə'dʌltəreɪtɪd/ *adj* ⟨water⟩ puro; ⟨wine⟩ non sofisticato; fig assoluto

unadventurous /ʌnəd'ventʃ(ə)rəs/ *adj* ⟨person, production⟩ poco avventuroso; ⟨meal⟩ poco fantasioso

unaffected /ʌnə'fektɪd/ *adj* (natural) semplice ; **be** ∼ **by** non essere interessato da

unafraid /ʌnə'freɪd/ *adj* senza paura

unaided /ʌn'eɪdɪd/ *adj* senza aiuto

unalloyed /ʌnə'lɔɪd/ *adj* fig puro

unambiguous /ʌnæm'bɪgjʊəs/ *adj* inequivocabile

unanimity /ju:nə'nɪmətɪ/ *n* unanimità *f*

unanimous /ju:'nænɪməs/ *adj* unanime

unanimously /ju:'nænɪməslɪ/ *adv* all'unanimità

unannounced /ʌnə'naʊnst/ *adj* inaspettato

unanswerable /ʌn'ɑ:ns(ə)rəbl/ *adj* ⟨remark, case⟩ irrefutabile; ⟨question⟩ senza risposta

unanswered /ʌn'ɑ:nsəd/ *adj* ⟨question, letter⟩ senza risposta

unappealing /ʌnə'pi:lɪŋ/ *adj* poco attraente

unappetizing /ʌn'æpetaɪzɪŋ/ *adj* poco appetitoso

unappreciated /ʌnə'pri:ʃɪeɪtɪd/ *adj* ⟨work of art⟩ incompreso

unappreciative /ʌnə'pri:ʃ(ɪ)ətɪv/ *adj* ⟨audience⟩ indifferente; ⟨person⟩ ingrato

unapproachable /ʌnə'prəʊtʃəbl/ *adj* ⟨person⟩ inavvicinabile

unarmed /ʌn'ɑ:md/ *adj* disarmato

unarmed combat *n* lotta *f* senza armi

unashamedly /ʌnə'ʃeɪmd/ *adv* sfacciatamente

unasked /ʌn'ɑ:skt/ *adv* **he came** ∼ è venuto senza che nessuno glielo chiedesse

unassuming /ʌnə'sju:mɪŋ/ *adj* senza pretese

unattached /ʌnə'tætʃd/ *adj* staccato; ⟨person⟩ senza legami

unattainable /ʌnə'teɪnəbl/ *adj* irraggiungibile

unattended /ʌnə'tendɪd/ *adj* incustodito

unattractive /ʌnə'træktɪv/ *adj* ⟨person⟩ poco attraente; ⟨proposition⟩ poco allettante; ⟨characteristic⟩ sgradevole; ⟨building, furniture⟩ brutto

unauthorized /ʌn'ɔ:θəraɪzd/ *adj* non autorizzato

unavailable /ʌnə'veɪləbl/ *adj* non disponibile

unavoidable /ʌnə'vɔɪdəbl/ *adj* inevitabile

unavoidably /ʌnə'vɔɪdəblɪ/ *adv* inevitabilmente; **I was** ∼ **detained** sono stato trattenuto da cause di forza maggiore

unaware /ʌnə'weə(r)/ *adj* **be** ∼ **of something** non rendersi conto di qualcosa

unawares /ʌnə'weəz/ *adv* **catch somebody** ∼ prendere qualcuno alla sprovvista

u

unbalanced /ʌnˈbælənst/ *adj* non equilibrato; (mentally) squilibrato

unbearable /ʌnˈbeərəbl/ *adj* insopportabile

unbearably /ʌnˈbeərəblɪ/ *adv* insopportabilmente

unbeatable /ʌnˈbiːtəbl/ *adj* imbattibile

unbeaten /ʌnˈbiːtən/ *adj* imbattuto

unbecoming /ʌnbɪˈkʌmɪŋ/ *adj* ⟨garment⟩ che non dona

unbeknown /ʌnbɪˈnəʊn/ *adj* fam ∼ **to me** a mia insaputa

unbelievable /ʌnbɪˈliːvəbl/ *adj* incredibile

unbend /ʌnˈbend/ *vi* (pt/pp **-bent**) (relax) distendersi

unbending /ʌnˈbendɪŋ/ *adj* (insistent) inflessibile

unbiased /ʌnˈbaɪəst/ *adj* obiettivo

unblock /ʌnˈblɒk/ *vt* sbloccare

unbolt /ʌnˈbəʊlt/ *vt* togliere il chiavistello di

unborn /ʌnˈbɔːn/ *adj* non ancora nato

unbreakable /ʌnˈbreɪkəbl/ *adj* infrangibile

unbridled /ʌnˈbraɪdld/ *adj* sfrenato

unbroken /ʌnˈbrəʊk(ə)n/ *adj* ⟨sequence, sleep, silence⟩ ininterrotto

unbuckle /ʌnˈbʌkl/ *vt* slacciare ⟨belt⟩

unburden /ʌnˈbɜːdən/ *vt* ∼ **oneself** fig sfogarsi (**to** con)

unbutton /ʌnˈbʌtən/ *vt* sbottonare

uncalled-for /ʌnˈkɔːldfɔː(r)/ *adj* fuori luogo

uncannily /ʌnˈkænɪlɪ/ *adv* incredibilmente

uncanny /ʌnˈkænɪ/ *adj* sorprendente; ⟨silence, feeling⟩ inquietante

uncared-for /ʌnˈkeədfɔː(r)/ *adj* ⟨house, pet⟩ trascurato

uncaring /ʌnˈkeərɪŋ/ *adj* ⟨world⟩ indifferente

unceasing /ʌnˈsiːsɪŋ/ *adj* incessante

uncensored /ʌnˈsensəd/ *adj* ⟨film, book⟩ non censurato

unceremonious /ʌnserɪˈməʊnɪəs/ *adj* (abrupt) brusco

unceremoniously /ʌnserɪˈməʊnɪəslɪ/ *adv* senza tante cerimonie

uncertain /ʌnˈsɜːtən/ *adj* incerto; ⟨weather⟩ instabile; **in no** ∼ **terms** senza mezzi termini

uncertainty /ʌnˈsɜːtəntɪ/ *n* incertezza *f*

unchallenged /ʌnˈtʃæləndʒd/ *adj* ⟨statement, decision⟩ incontestato; **I can't let that go** ∼ non posso non contestarlo

unchanged /ʌnˈtʃeɪndʒd/ *adj* invariato

uncharacteristic /ʌnkærəktəˈrɪstɪk/ *adj* ⟨generosity⟩ insolito

uncharitable /ʌnˈtʃærɪtəbl/ *adj* duro

unchecked /ʌnˈtʃekt/ *adv* incontrollato; **go** ∼ dilagare

uncivilized /ʌnˈsɪvɪlaɪzd/ *adj* ⟨people, nation⟩ non civilizzato; ⟨treatment, conditions⟩ incivile

unclassified /ʌnˈklæsɪfaɪd/ *adj* ⟨document, information⟩ non riservato; ⟨road⟩ non classificato

uncle /ˈʌŋkl/ *n* zio *m*

unclear /ʌnˈklɪːr/ *adj* ⟨instructions, reason, voice, writing⟩ non chiaro; ⟨future⟩ incerto; **be** ∼ **about something** ⟨person⟩ non aver ben chiaro qualcosa

unclog /ʌnˈklɒg/ *vt* sturare ⟨pipe⟩

uncoil /ʌnˈkɔɪl/ *vt* srotolare

uncomfortable /ʌnˈkʌmftəbl/ *adj* scomodo; imbarazzante ⟨silence, situation⟩; **feel** ∼ fig sentirsi a disagio

uncomfortably /ʌnˈkʌmftəblɪ/ *adv* ⟨sit⟩ scomodamente; (causing alarm etc) spaventosamente

uncommon /ʌnˈkʌmʌn/ *adj* insolito

uncommunicative /ʌnkəˈmjuːnɪkətɪv/ *adj* poco comunicativo

uncomplimentary /ʌnkʌmplɪˈmentərɪ/ *adj* poco complimentoso

uncompromising /ʌnˈkʌmprəmaɪzɪŋ/ *adj* intransigente

unconcerned /ʌnkənˈsɜːnd/ *adj* indifferente

unconditional /ʌnkənˈdɪʃ(ə)nl/ *adj* incondizionato

unconditionally /ʌnkənˈdɪʃnəlɪ/ *adv* incondizionatamente

unconfirmed /ʌnkənˈfɜːmd/ *adj* ⟨report, sighting⟩ non confermato

unconnected /ʌnkəˈnektɪd/ *adj* ⟨incidents, facts⟩ senza alcun legame tra loro

unconscious /ʌnˈkɒnʃəs/ *adj* privo di sensi; (unaware) inconsapevole; **be** ∼ **of something** non rendersi conto di qualcosa

unconsciously /ʌnˈkɒnʃəslɪ/ *adv* inconsapevolmente

unconstitutional /ʌnkɒnstɪˈtjuːʃənl/ *adj* incostituzionale

uncontested /ʌnkʌnˈtestɪd/ *adj* Pol ⟨seat⟩ non disputato

uncontrollable /ʌnkənˈtrəʊləbl/ *adj* incontrollabile; ⟨sobbing⟩ irrefrenabile

uncontrollably /ʌnkənˈtrəʊləblɪ/ *adv* ⟨increase⟩ incontrollatamente; ⟨laugh, sob⟩ senza potersi controllare

unconventional /ʌnkənˈvenʃnəl/ *adj* poco convenzionale

unconvincing /ʌnkənˈvɪnsɪŋ/ *adj* poco convincente

uncooked /ʌnˈkʊkt/ *adj* crudo

uncooperative /ʌnkəʊˈɒpr(ə)tɪv/ *adj* poco cooperativo

uncoordinated /ʌnkəʊˈɔːdɪneɪtɪd/ *adj* ⟨*action, efforts*⟩ non coordinato; **be ~** (person) essere scoordinato

uncork /ʌnˈkɔːk/ *vt* sturare

uncorroborated /ʌnkəˈrɒbəreɪtɪd/ *adj* non convalidato

uncouth /ʌnˈkuːθ/ *adj* zotico

uncover /ʌnˈkʌvə(r)/ *vt* scoprire; portare alla luce ⟨*buried object*⟩

uncritical /ʌnˈkrɪtɪkl/ *adj* poco critico

uncross /ʌnˈkrɒs/ *vt* disincrociare ⟨*legs, arms*⟩

unctuous /ˈʌŋktjʊəs/ *adj* untuoso

uncultivated /ʌnˈkʌltɪveɪtɪd/ *adj* incolto

uncut /ʌnˈkʌt/ *adj* ⟨*film*⟩ in versione integrale; ⟨*diamond*⟩ non tagliato

undamaged /ʌnˈdæmɪdʒd/ *adj* intatto

undaunted /ʌnˈdɔːntɪd/ *adj* imperterrito; **~ by something** per nulla intimidito da qualcosa

undecided /ʌndɪˈsaɪdɪd/ *adj* indeciso; (not settled) incerto

undefined /ʌndɪˈfaɪnd/ *adj* ⟨*objective, nature*⟩ indeterminato

undelivered /ʌndɪˈlɪvəd/ *adj* ⟨*mail*⟩ non recapitato

undemanding /ʌndɪˈmɑːndɪŋ/ *adj* ⟨*job, course*⟩ poco impegnativo

undemocratic /ʌndeməˈkrætɪk/ *adj* antidemocratico

undemonstrative /ʌndɪˈmɒnstrətɪv/ *adj* poco espansivo

undeniable /ʌndɪˈnaɪəbl/ *adj* innegabile

undeniably /ʌndɪˈnaɪəblɪ/ *adv* innegabilmente

under /ˈʌndə(r)/ **①** *prep* sotto; (less than) al di sotto di; **~ there** li sotto; **~ repair/construction** in riparazione/costruzione; **~ way** fig in corso; **②** *adv* (**~ water**) sott'acqua; (unconscious) sotto anestesia

underachieve /ʌndərəˈtʃiːv/ *vi* Sch restare al di sotto delle proprie possibilità

underachiever /ʌndərəˈtʃiːvə(r)/ *n* **be an ~** non dare il meglio

underage /ʌndərˈeɪdʒ/ *adj* **~ drinking** consumo di alcolici da parte dei minorenni; **be ~** essere minorenne

underarm /ˈʌndərɑːm/ *adj* ⟨*deodorant*⟩ per le ascelle; ⟨*hair*⟩ sotto le ascelle; ⟨*service, throw*⟩ dal basso verso l'alto

undercarriage /ˈʌndəkærɪdʒ/ *n* Aeron carrello *m*

undercharge /ʌndəˈtʃɑːdʒ/ *vt* far pagare meno del dovuto a

underclass /ˈʌndəklɑːs/ *n* sottoproletariato *m*

underclothes /ˈʌndəkləʊðz/ *npl* biancheria *fsg* intima

undercoat /ˈʌndəkəʊt/ *n* prima mano *f*

undercook /ʌndəˈkʊk/ *vt* non cuocere abbastanza

undercover /ʌndəˈkʌvə(r)/ *adj* clandestino

undercurrent /ˈʌndəkʌrənt/ *n* corrente *f* sottomarina; fig sottofondo *m*

undercut /ʌndəˈkʌt/ *vt* (pt/pp **-cut**) Comm vendere a minor prezzo di

underdeveloped /ʌndərɪˈveləpt/ *adj* ⟨*country*⟩ sottosviluppato; Phot non completamente sviluppato

underdog /ˈʌndədɒg/ *n* perdente *m*

underdone /ʌndəˈdʌn/ *adj* ⟨*meat*⟩ al sangue

underemployed /ʌndərɪmˈplɔɪd/ *adj* ⟨*person*⟩ sottoccupato; ⟨*resources, equipment etc*⟩ non sfruttato completamente

underequipped /ʌndərɪˈkwɪpt/ *adj* ⟨*army, person*⟩ insufficientemente equipaggiato; ⟨*schools, gym*⟩ insufficientemente attrezzato

underestimate /ʌndərˈestɪmeɪt/ *vt* sottovalutare

underexpose /ʌndərɪksˈpəʊz/ *vt* Phot sottoesporre

underfed /ʌndəˈfed/ *adj* denutrito

underfloor /ˈʌndəflɔː(r)/ *adj* ⟨*pipes, wiring*⟩ sotto il pavimento

underfoot /ʌndəˈfʊt/ *adv* sotto i piedi; **trample ~** calpestare

underfunded /ʌndəˈfʌndɪd/ *adj* insufficientemente finanziato

underfunding /ʌndəˈfʌndɪŋ/ *n* finanziamento *m* insufficiente

undergo /ʌndəˈgəʊ/ *vt* (pt **-went**, pp **-gone**) subire ⟨*operation, treatment*⟩; **~ repair** essere in riparazione

undergraduate /ʌndəˈgrædʒʊət/ *n* studente, -tessa *mf* universitario, -a

underground¹ /ʌndəˈgraʊnd/ *adv* sottoterra

underground² /ˈʌndəgraʊnd/ **①** *adj* sotterraneo; (secret) clandestino **②** *n* (railway) metropolitana *f*

u

underground car park *n* parcheggio *m* sotterraneo

undergrowth /ˈʌndəgrəʊθ/ *n* sottobosco *m*

underhand /ʌndəˈhænd/ *adj* subdolo

underlay /ˈʌndəleɪ/ *n* strato *m* di gomma o feltro posto sotto la moquette

underlie /ʌndəˈlaɪ/ *vt* (pt **-lay**, pp **-lain**, pres p **-lying**) fig essere alla base di

underline /ʌndəˈlaɪn/ *vt* sottolineare

underling /ˈʌndəlɪŋ/ *n* pej subalterno, -a *mf*

underlying /ʌndəˈlaɪɪŋ/ *adj* fig fondamentale

undermanned /ʌndəˈmænd/ *adj* ⟨*factory*⟩ a corto di mano d'opera

undermentioned /ˌʌndə'menʃnd/ *adj* sottoindicato

undermine /ˌʌndə'maɪn/ *vt* fig minare

underneath /ˌʌndə'niːθ/ ① *prep* sotto; ~ it sotto
② *adv* sotto

undernourished /ˌʌndə'nʌrɪʃt/ *adj* denutrito

underpaid /ˌʌndə'peɪd/ *adj* mal pagato

underpants /'ʌndəpænts/ *npl* mutande *fpl*

underpass /'ʌndəpɑːs/ *n* sottopassaggio *m*

underpay /ˌʌndə'peɪ/ *vt* sottopagare ⟨*employee*⟩

underpin /ˌʌndə'pɪn/ *vt* puntellare ⟨*wall*⟩; rafforzare ⟨*currency, power, theory*⟩; essere alla base di ⟨*religion, society*⟩

underpopulated /ˌʌndə'pɒpjʊleɪtɪd/ *adj* sottopopolato

underprivileged /ˌʌndə'prɪvɪlɪdʒd/ *adj* non abbiente

underrate /ˌʌndə'reɪt/ *vt* sottovalutare

underscore /ˌʌndə'skɔː(r)/ ① *n* segno *m* di sottolineatura
② *vt* sottolineare

underseal /'ʌndəsiːl/ *n* Auto antiruggine *m inv*

under-secretary /ˌʌndə'sekrət(ə)rɪ/ *n* Br Pol sottosegretario *m*

undersell /ˌʌndə'sel/ *vt* vendere a prezzo inferiore rispetto a ⟨*competitor*⟩; pubblicizzare poco ⟨*product*⟩

undersexed /ˌʌndə'sekst/ *adj* con scarsa libido

undershirt /'ʌndəʃɜːt/ *n* Am maglia *f* della salute

undersigned /ˌʌndə'saɪnd/ *adj* sottoscritto

undersized /ˌʌndə'saɪzd/ *adj* ⟨*portion*⟩ scarso; ⟨*animal*⟩ troppo piccolo; ⟨*person*⟩ di statura inferiore alla media

understaffed /ˌʌndə'stɑːft/ *adj* a corto di personale

understand /ˌʌndə'stænd/ ① *vt* (pt/pp **-stood**) capire; I ~ that... (have heard) mi risulta che...
② *vi* capire

understandable /ˌʌndə'stændəbl/ *adj* comprensibile

understandably /ˌʌndə'stændəblɪ/ *adv* comprensibilmente

understanding /ˌʌndə'stændɪŋ/ ① *adj* comprensivo
② *n* comprensione *f*; (agreement) accordo *m*; reach an ~ trovare un accordo; on the ~ that a condizione che

understatement /'ʌndəsteɪtmʌnt/ *n* that's an ~ non è dire abbastanza

understudy /'ʌndəstʌdɪ/ *n* Theat sostituto, a *mf*

undertake /ˌʌndə'teɪk/ *vt* (pt **-took**, pp **-taken**) intraprendere; ~ to do something impegnarsi a fare qualcosa

undertaker /'ʌndəteɪkə(r)/ *n* impresario *m* di pompe funebri; [firm of] ~s *n* impresa *f* di pompe funebri

undertaking /ˌʌndə'teɪkɪŋ/ *n* impresa *f*; (promise) promessa *f*

under-the-counter *adj* ⟨*goods, supply, trade*⟩ comprato/venduto sottobanco

undertone /'ʌndətəʊn/ *n* fig sottofondo *m*; in an ~ sottovoce

undervalue /ˌʌndə'væljuː/ *vt* sottovalutare; the shares are ~d le azioni si sono svalutate

underwater[1] /'ʌndəwɔːtə(r)/ *adj* subacqueo

underwater[2] /ˌʌndə'wɔːtə(r)/ *adv* sott'acqua

under way *adj* be ~ ~ ⟨*vehicle*⟩ essere in corsa; ⟨*filming, talks*⟩ essere in corso; get ~ ~ ⟨*vehicle*⟩ mettersi in viaggio; ⟨*preparations, season*⟩ avere inizio

underwear /'ʌndəweə(r)/ *n* biancheria *f* intima

underweight /ˌʌndə'weɪt/ *adj* sotto peso

underworld /'ʌndəwɜːld/ *n* (criminals) malavita *f*

underwriter /'ʌndəraɪtə(r)/ *n* assicuratore *m*

undeserved /ˌʌndɪ'zɜːvd/ *adj* ⟨*praise, reward, win*⟩ immeritato; ⟨*blame, punish*⟩ ingiusto

undeservedly /ˌʌndɪ'zɜːvɪdlɪ/ *adv* ⟨*praise, reward, win*⟩ immeritatamente; ⟨*blame, punish*⟩ ingiustamente

undesirable /ˌʌndɪ'zaɪərəbl/ *adj* indesiderato; ⟨*person*⟩ poco raccomandabile

undetected /ˌʌndɪ'tektɪd/ ① *adj* ⟨*crime, cancer*⟩ non scoperto; ⟨*flaw, movement, intruder*⟩ non visto; go ~ ⟨*cancer, crime*⟩ non essere scoperto; ⟨*person*⟩ passare inosservato
② *adv* ⟨*break in, listen*⟩ senza essere scoperto

undeterred /ˌʌndɪ'tɜːd/ *adj* imperterrito

undeveloped /ˌʌndɪ'veləpt/ *adj* non sviluppato; ⟨*land*⟩ non sfruttato

undies /'ʌndɪz/ *npl* fam biancheria *f* intima (da donna)

undignified /ʌn'dɪgnɪfaɪd/ *adj* poco dignitoso

undisciplined /ʌn'dɪsɪplɪnd/ *adj* indisciplinato

undiscovered /ˌʌndɪs'kʌvəd/ *adj* ⟨*secret*⟩ non svelato; ⟨*crime, document*⟩ non scoperto; ⟨*land*⟩ inesplorato; ⟨*species*⟩ sconosciuto; ⟨*talent*⟩ non ancora scoperto

undiscriminating /ˌʌndɪs'krɪmɪneɪtɪŋ/ *adj* che non sa fare distinzioni

undisguised /ˌʌndɪs'gaɪzd/ *adj* evidente

undisputed /ʌndɪ'spjuːtɪd/ *adj* indiscusso

undisturbed /ʌndɪ'stɜːbd/ *adj* ⟨*sleep, night*⟩ indisturbato

undivided /ʌndɪ'vaɪdɪd/ *adj* ⟨*loyalty, attention*⟩ assoluto

undo /ʌn'duː/ *vt* (*pt* **-did**, *pp* **-done**) disfare; slacciare ⟨*dress, shoes*⟩; sbottonare ⟨*shirt*⟩; fig, Comput annullare

undone /ʌn'dʌn/ *adj* ⟨*shirt, button*⟩ sbottonato; ⟨*shoes, dress*⟩ slacciato; (not accomplished) non fatto; **leave ~** ⟨*job*⟩ tralasciare

undoubted /ʌn'daʊtɪd/ *adj* indubbio

undoubtedly /ʌn'daʊtɪdlɪ/ *adv* senza dubbio

undress /ʌn'dres/ ① *vt* spogliare; **get ~ed** spogliarsi ② *vi* spogliarsi

undrinkable /ʌn'drɪŋkəbl/ *adj* (unpleasant) imbevibile; (dangerous) non potabile

undue /ʌn'djuː/ *adj* eccessivo

undulating /'ʌndjʊleɪtɪŋ/ *adj* ondulato; ⟨*country*⟩ collinoso

unduly /ʌn'djuːlɪ/ *adv* eccessivamente

undying /ʌn'daɪɪŋ/ *adj* eterno

unearned /ʌn'ɜːnd/ *adj* immeritato; **~ income** rendita *f*

unearth /ʌn'ɜːθ/ *vt* dissotterrare; fig scovare; scoprire ⟨*secret*⟩

unearthly /ʌn'ɜːθlɪ/ *adj* soprannaturale; **at an ~ hour** fam ad un'ora impossibile

unease /ʌn'iːz/ *n* disagio *m*

uneasily /ʌn'iːzɪlɪ/ *adv* a disagio

uneasiness /ʌn'iːzɪnəs/ *n* disagio *m*

uneasy /ʌn'iːzɪ/ *adj* a disagio; ⟨*person*⟩ inquieto; ⟨*feeling*⟩ inquietante; (truce) precario

uneatable /ʌn'iːtəbl/ *adj* immangiabile

uneconomic /ʌniːkə'nɒmɪk/ *adj* poco remunerativo

uneconomical /ʌniːkə'nɒmɪkl/ *adj* poco economico

uneducated /ʌn'edjʊkeɪtɪd/ *adj* ⟨*person*⟩ non istruito; ⟨*tastes*⟩ non raffinato; ⟨*accent, speech*⟩ da persona non istruita

unemotional /ʌnɪ'məʊʃənəl/ *adj* distaccato

unemployed /ʌnem'plɔɪd/ ① *adj* disoccupato ② *npl* **the ~** i disoccupati

unemployment /ʌnem'plɔɪmʌnt/ *n* disoccupazione *f*

unemployment benefit *n* sussidio *m* di disoccupazione

unemployment rate *n* tasso *m* di disoccupazione

unending /ʌn'endɪŋ/ *adj* senza fine

unenthusiastic /ʌnɪnθjuːzɪ'æstɪk/ *adj* poco entusiasta

unenviable /ʌn'envɪəbl/ *adj* ⟨*position*⟩ poco invidiabile

unequal /ʌn'iːkwəl/ *adj* disuguale; ⟨*struggle*⟩ impari; **be ~ to a task** non essere all'altezza di un compito

unequalled /ʌn'iːkwəld/ *adj* ⟨*achievement, quality, record*⟩ ineguagliato

unequally /ʌn'iːkwəlɪ/ *adv* in modo disuguale

unequivocal /ʌnə'kwɪvəkl/ *adj* inequivocabile; ⟨*person*⟩ esplicito

unequivocally /ʌnə'kwɪvəklɪ/ *adv* inequivocabilmente

unerring /ʌn'ɜːrɪŋ/ *adj* infallibile

unethical /ʌn'eθɪkl/ *adj* immorale

uneven /ʌn'iːvən/ *adj* irregolare; ⟨*distribution*⟩ ineguale; ⟨*number*⟩ dispari

unevenly /ʌn'iːvənlɪ/ *adv* irregolarmente; ⟨*distributed*⟩ inegualmente

uneventful /ʌnɪ'ventfʊl/ *adj* senza avvenimenti di rilievo

unexciting /ʌnɪk'saɪtɪŋ/ *adj* poco entusiasmante

unexpected /ʌnɪk'spektɪd/ *adj* inaspettato

unexpectedly /ʌnɪk'spektɪdlɪ/ *adv* inaspettatamente

unexplored /ʌnɪk'splɔːd/ *adj* inesplorato

unfailing /ʌn'feɪlɪŋ/ *adj* infallibile

unfair /ʌn'feə(r)/ *adj* ingiusto

unfair dismissal *n* licenziamento *m* ingiustificato

unfairly /ʌn'feəlɪ/ *adv* ingiustamente

unfairness /ʌn'feənəs/ *n* ingiustizia *f*

unfaithful /ʌn'feɪθfʊl/ *adj* infedele

unfamiliar /ʌnfə'mɪljə(r)/ *adj* sconosciuto; **be ~ with** non conoscere

unfashionable /ʌn'fæʃənəbl/ *adj* fuori moda

unfasten /ʌn'fɑːsn/ *vt* slacciare; (detach) staccare

unfathomable /ʌn'fæð(ə)məbl/ *adj* imperscrutabile

unfavourable /ʌn'feɪv(ə)rəbl/ *adj* sfavorevole; ⟨*impression*⟩ negativo

unfeeling /ʌn'fiːlɪŋ/ *adj* insensibile

unfinished /ʌn'fɪnɪʃt/ *adj* da finire; ⟨*business*⟩ in sospeso

unfit /ʌn'fɪt/ *adj* inadatto; (morally) indegno; Sport fuori forma; **~ for work** non in grado di lavorare; **~ for human consumption** non commestibile

unflappable /ʌn'flæpəbl/ *adj* fam calmo

unflattering /ʌn'flæt(ə)rɪŋ/ *adj* ⟨*clothes, hairstyle*⟩ che non dona; ⟨*portrait, description*⟩ poco lusinghiero

u

unflinching /ʌnˈflɪntʃɪŋ/ *adj* risoluto

unfold /ʌnˈfəʊld/ **1** *vt* spiegare; (spread out) aprire; fig rivelare **2** *vi* ⟨view⟩ spiegarsi

unforeseeable /ʌnfɔːˈsiːəbl/ *adj* imprevedibile

unforeseen /ʌnfɔːˈsiːn/ *adj* imprevisto

unforgettable /ʌnfəˈɡetəbl/ *adj* indimenticabile

unforgivable /ʌnfəˈɡɪvəbl/ *adj* imperdonabile

unforgiving /ʌnfəˈɡɪvɪŋ/ *adj* che non perdona

unfortunate /ʌnˈfɔːtʃənət/ *adj* sfortunato; (regrettable) spiacevole; ⟨remark, choice⟩ infelice

unfortunately /ʌnˈfɔːtʃənətlɪ/ *adv* purtroppo

unfounded /ʌnˈfaʊndɪd/ *adj* infondato

unfriendly /ʌnˈfrendlɪ/ *adj* ⟨person, remark⟩ scortese, poco amichevole; ⟨place, climate, reception⟩ ostile; ⟨software⟩ difficile da usare

unfulfilled /ʌnfʊlˈfɪld/ *adj* ⟨prophecy⟩ non avverato; ⟨promise⟩ non mantenuto; ⟨ambition⟩ non realizzato; ⟨desire, need⟩ non soddisfatto; ⟨condition⟩ non rispettato; **feel** ∼ essere insoddisfatto

unfurl /ʌnˈfɜːl/ **1** *vt* spiegare **2** *vi* spiegarsi

unfurnished /ʌnˈfɜːnɪʃt/ *adj* non ammobiliato

ungainly /ʌnˈɡeɪnlɪ/ *adj* sgraziato

ungentlemanly /ʌnˈdʒentlmənlɪ/ *adj* non da gentiluomo

ungodly /ʌnˈɡɒdlɪ/ *adj* empio; ∼ **hour** fam ora f impossibile

ungracious /ʌnˈɡreɪʃəs/ *adj* sgarbato

ungrammatical /ʌnɡrəˈmætɪkl/ *adj* sgrammaticato

ungrateful /ʌnˈɡreɪtfʊl/ *adj* ingrato

ungratefully /ʌnˈɡreɪtfʊlɪ/ *adv* senza riconoscenza

unhappily /ʌnˈhæpɪlɪ/ *adv* infelicemente; (unfortunately) purtroppo

unhappiness /ʌnˈhæpɪnəs/ *n* infelicità f

unhappy /ʌnˈhæpɪ/ *adj* infelice; (not content) insoddisfatto (with di)

unharmed /ʌnˈhɑːmd/ *adj* incolume

unhealthy /ʌnˈhelθɪ/ *adj* poco sano; (insanitary) malsano

unheard-of /ʌnˈhɜːdəv/ *adj* ⟨actor, brand⟩ mai sentito; ⟨levels, price⟩ incredibile

unheated /ʌnˈhiːtɪd/ *adj* senza riscaldamento

unheeded /ʌnˈhiːdɪd/ *adj* ignorato; **go** ∼ ⟨warning, plea⟩ venir ignorato

unhelpful /ʌnˈhelpfʊl/ *adj* ⟨person, attitude⟩ poco disponibile; ⟨witness⟩ che non collabora; ⟨remark⟩ di poco aiuto

unhindered /ʌnˈhɪndəd/ *adj* senza intralci; ∼ **by** senza essere ostacolato da ⟨rules, obstacles⟩

unholy /ʌnˈhəʊlɪ/ *adj* ⟨alliance, pact⟩ paradossale; fam ⟨mess, hour⟩ indecente

unhook /ʌnˈhʊk/ *vt* sganciare; staccare ⟨picture⟩

unhurried /ʌnˈhʌrɪd/ *adj* tranquillo

unhurt /ʌnˈhɜːt/ *adj* illeso

unhygienic /ʌnhaɪˈdʒiːnɪk/ *adj* non igienico

unicorn /ˈjuːnɪkɔːn/ *n* unicorno *m*

unidentified /ʌnaɪˈdentɪfaɪd/ *adj* non identificato

unification /juːnɪfɪˈkeɪʃn/ *n* unificazione f

uniform /ˈjuːnɪfɔːm/ **1** *adj* uniforme **2** *n* uniforme f

uniformly /ˈjuːnɪfɔːmlɪ/ *adv* uniformemente

unify /ˈjuːnɪfaɪ/ *vt* (pt/pp -**ied**) unificare

unilateral /juːnɪˈlæt(ə)rəl/ *adj* unilaterale

unilaterally /juːnɪˈlæt(ə)rəlɪ/ *adv* unilateralmente

unimaginable /ʌnɪˈmædʒɪnəbl/ *adj* inimmaginabile

unimaginative /ʌnɪˈmædʒɪnətɪv/ *adj* privo di fantasia

unimpeded /ʌnɪmˈpiːdɪd/ *adj* ⟨access⟩ libero

unimportant /ʌnɪmˈpɔːtənt/ *adj* irrilevante

unimpressed /ʌnɪmˈprest/ *adj* non impressionato

uninformed /ʌnɪmˈfɔːmd/ *adj* ⟨person⟩ disinformato

uninhabitable /ʌnɪnˈhæbɪtəbl/ *adj* inabitabile

uninhabited /ʌnɪnˈhæbɪtɪd/ *adj* disabitato

uninhibited /ʌnɪnˈhɪbɪtɪd/ *adj* ⟨person, attitude⟩ disinibito; ⟨performance, remarks⟩ disinvolto; **be** ∼ **about doing something** non avere problemi a fare qualcosa

uninitiated /ʌnɪˈnɪʃɪeɪtɪd/ **1** *adj* ⟨person⟩ non iniziato **2** *npl* **the** ∼ i profani

uninjured /ʌnˈɪndʒəd/ *adj* illeso

uninspired /ʌnɪnˈspaɪəd/ *adj* privo di immaginazione; ⟨performance⟩ piatto; ⟨times⟩ banale

unintelligible /ʌnɪnˈtelɪdʒəbl/ *adj* incomprensibile

unintended /ʌnɪnˈtendɪd/ *adj* ⟨irony, consequence⟩ non voluto

unintentional /ˌʌnɪnˈtenʃənl/ *adj* involontario

unintentionally /ˌʌnɪnˈtenʃənəlɪ/ *adv* involontariamente

uninterested /ʌnˈɪntrəstɪd/ *adj* disinteressato

uninteresting /ʌnˈɪnt(ə)rəstɪŋ/ *adj* poco interessante

uninvited /ˌʌnɪnˈvaɪtɪd/ *adj* ⟨*attentions*⟩ non richiesto; ∼ **guest** ospite *mf* senza invito

uninviting /ˌʌnɪnˈvaɪtɪŋ/ *adj* ⟨*room, food*⟩ poco invitante

union /ˈjuːnɪən/ *n* unione *f*; (trade ∼) sindacato *m*

Unionist /ˈjuːnɪənɪst/ *n* unionista *mf*

Union Jack *n* bandiera *f* del Regno Unito

unique /juːˈniːk/ *adj* unico

uniquely /juːˈniːklɪ/ *adv* unicamente

unisex /ˈjuːnɪseks/ *adj* unisex *inv*

unison /ˈjuːnɪsn/ *n* in ∼ all'unisono

unit /ˈjuːnɪt/ *n* unità *f inv*; (department) reparto *m*; (of furniture) elemento *m*

unit cost *n* costo *m* unitario

unite /juːˈnaɪt/ **1** *vt* unire **2** *vi* unirsi

united /juːˈnaɪtɪd/ *adj* unito

United Arab Emirates /ˈemɪrəts/ *npl* the ∼ gli Emirati Arabi Uniti

United Kingdom *n* Regno *m* Unito

United Nations *n* [Organizzazione *f* delle] Nazioni Unite *fpl*

United States [of America] *n* Stati *mpl* Uniti [d'America]

unit trust *n* Fin fondo *m* comune di investimento aperto

unity /ˈjuːnɪtɪ/ *n* unità *f*; (agreement) accordo *m*

universal /juːnɪˈvɜːsl/ *adj* universale

universally /juːnɪˈvɜːsəlɪ/ *adv* universalmente

universe /ˈjuːnɪvɜːs/ *n* universo *m*

university /juːnɪˈvɜːsətɪ/ **1** *n* università *f inv* **2** *attrib* universitario

unjust /ʌnˈdʒʌst/ *adj* ingiusto

unjustifiable /ʌnˈdʒʌstɪfaɪəbl/ *adj* ingiustificato

unjustifiably /ʌnˈdʒʌstɪfaɪəblɪ/ *adv* ⟨*act*⟩ senza giustificazione

unjustified /ʌnˈdʒʌstɪfaɪd/ *adj* ⟨*suspicion*⟩ ingiustificato

unjustly /ʌnˈdʒʌstlɪ/ *adv* ingiustamente

unkempt /ʌnˈkempt/ *adj* trasandato; ⟨*hair*⟩ arruffato

unkind /ʌnˈkaɪnd/ *adj* scortese

unkindly /ʌnˈkaɪndlɪ/ *adv* in modo scortese

unkindness /ʌnˈkaɪndnɪs/ *n* mancanza *f* di gentilezza

unknown /ʌnˈnəʊn/ *adj* sconosciuto

unlace /ʌnˈleɪs/ *vt* slacciare ⟨*shoes*⟩

unlawful /ʌnˈlɔːfʊl/ *adj* illecito, illegale

unlawfully /ʌnˈlɔːfʊlɪ/ *adv* illegalmente

unleaded /ʌnˈledɪd/ *adj* senza piombo

unleaded petrol *n* benzina *f* senza piombo *o* verde

unleash /ʌnˈliːʃ/ *vt* fig scatenare

unleavened /ʌnˈlevnd/ *adj* ⟨*bread*⟩ non lievitato

unless /ʌnˈles/ *conj* a meno che; ∼ **I am** mistaken se non mi sbaglio

unlicensed /ʌnˈlaɪsnst/ *adj* ⟨*transmitter, activity*⟩ abusivo; ⟨*vehicle*⟩ senza bollo; ⟨*restaurant*⟩ non autorizzato a vendere alcolici

unlike /ʌnˈlaɪk/ **1** *adj* (not the same) diversi **2** *prep* diverso da; **that's** ∼ **him** non è da lui; ∼ **me, he...** diversamente da me, lui...

unlikely /ʌnˈlaɪklɪ/ *adj* improbabile

unlimited /ʌnˈlɪmɪtɪd/ *adj* illimitato

unlined /ʌnˈlaɪnd/ *adj* ⟨*face*⟩ senza rughe; ⟨*paper*⟩ senza righe; ⟨*garment, curtain*⟩ senza fodera

unlit /ʌnˈlɪt/ *adj* ⟨*cigarette, fire*⟩ spento; ⟨*room, street*⟩ non illuminato

unload /ʌnˈləʊd/ *vt* scaricare

unlock /ʌnˈlɒk/ *vt* aprire (con chiave); sbloccare ⟨*mobile phone*⟩

unloved /ʌnˈlʌvd/ *adj* feel ∼ ⟨*person*⟩ non sentirsi amato

unluckily /ʌnˈlʌkɪlɪ/ *adv* sfortunatamente

unlucky /ʌnˈlʌkɪ/ *adj* sfortunato; **it's** ∼ **to...** porta sfortuna...

unmade /ʌnˈmeɪd/ *adj* ⟨*bed*⟩ sfatto

unmade-up *adj* ⟨*road*⟩ non asfaltato

unmanageable /ʌnˈmænɪdʒəbl/ *adj* ⟨*number, company*⟩ difficile da gestire; ⟨*hair, child, animal*⟩ ribelle; ⟨*size*⟩ ingombrante

unmanly /ʌnˈmænlɪ/ *adj* poco virile

unmanned /ʌnˈmænd/ *adj* senza equipaggio

unmarked /ʌnˈmɑːkt/ *adj* Sport smarcato; ⟨*skin*⟩ senza segni; ⟨*container*⟩ non contrassegnato; ∼ **police car** [auto *f inv*] civetta *f*

unmarried /ʌnˈmærɪd/ *adj* non sposato

unmarried mother *n* ragazza *f* madre

unmask /ʌnˈmɑːsk/ *vt* fig smascherare

unmentionable /ʌnˈmenʃnəbl/ *adj* innominabile

unmistakable /ˌʌnmɪˈsteɪkəbl/ *adj* inconfondibile

unmistakably /ˌʌnmɪˈsteɪkəblɪ/ *adv* chiaramente

u

unmitigated /ʌnˈmɪtɪɡeɪtɪd/ *adj* assoluto

unmotivated /ʌnˈməʊtɪveɪtɪd/ *adj* immotivato

unmoved /ʌnˈmuːvd/ *adj* fig impassibile

unnamed /ʌnˈneɪmd/ *adj* (not having a name) senza nome; (name not divulged) di cui non si conosce il nome; **the as yet ∼ winner...** il vincitore di cui ancora non si conosce il nome...

unnatural /ʌnˈnætʃər(ə)l/ *adj* innaturale; pej anormale

unnaturally /ʌnˈnætʃər(ə)lɪ/ *adv* in modo innaturale; pej in modo anormale

unnecessarily /ʌnˈnesəs(ə)rɪlɪ/ *adv* inutilmente

unnecessary /ʌnˈnesəs(ə)rɪ/ *adj* inutile

unnerve /ʌnˈnɜːv/ *vt* scuotere

unnerving /ʌnˈnɜːvɪŋ/ *adj* inquietante

unnoticed /ʌnˈnəʊtɪst/ *adj* inosservato

unobservant /ʌnəbˈzɜːvənt/ *adj* senza spirito d'osservazione

unobserved /ʌnəbˈzɜːvd/ *adj* inosservato; **go ∼** passare inosservato

unobstructed /ʌnəbˈstrʌktɪd/ *adj* (view, path) libero

unobtainable /ʌnəbˈteɪnəbl/ *adj* (product) introvabile; (phone number) non ottenibile

unobtrusive /ʌnəbˈtruːsɪf/ *adj* discreto

unobtrusively /ʌnəbˈtruːsɪvlɪ/ *adv* in modo discreto

unoccupied /ʌnˈɒkjuːpaɪd/ *adj* (house, block, shop) vuoto; (table, seat) libero

unofficial /ʌnəˈfɪʃl/ *adj* non ufficiale

unofficially /ʌnəˈfɪʃ(ə)lɪ/ *adv* ufficiosamente

unopened /ʌnˈəʊpənd/ *adj* (bottle, packet) chiuso; (package) ancora incartato

unorthodox /ʌnˈɔːθədɒks/ *adj* poco ortodosso

unpack /ʌnˈpæk/ ⓵ *vi* disfare le valigie ⓶ *vt* svuotare (parcel); spacchettare (books); **∼ one's case** disfare la valigia

unpaid /ʌnˈpeɪd/ *adj* da pagare; (work) non retribuito

unpalatable /ʌnˈpælətəbl/ *adj* sgradevole

unparalleled /ʌnˈpærəleld/ *adj* senza pari

unpasteurized /ʌnˈpɑːstʃəraɪzd/ *adj* non pastorizzato

unperturbed /ʌnpəˈtɜːbd/ *adj* imperturbato

unpick /ʌnˈpɪk/ *vt* disfare

unplanned /ʌnˈplænd/ *adj* (stoppage, increase) imprevisto

unpleasant /ʌnˈplezənt/ *adj* sgradevole; (person) maleducato

unpleasantly /ʌnˈplezəntlɪ/ *adv* sgradevolmente; (behave) maleducatamente

unpleasantness /ʌnˈplezəntnɪs/ *n* (bad feeling) tensioni *fpl*

unplug /ʌnˈplʌɡ/ *vt* (pt/pp **-plugged**) staccare

unpolluted /ʌnpəˈluːtɪd/ *adj* (water) non inquinato; (mind) incontaminato

unpopular /ʌnˈpɒpjʊlə(r)/ *adj* impopolare

unprecedented /ʌnˈpresɪdentɪd/ *adj* senza precedenti

unpredictable /ʌnprɪˈdɪktəbl/ *adj* imprevedibile

unprejudiced /ʌnˈpredʒʊdɪst/ *adj* (person) senza pregiudizi; (opinion, judgement) imparziale

unpremeditated /ʌnpriːˈmedɪteɪtɪd/ *adj* involontario

unprepared /ʌnprɪˈpeəd/ *adj* impreparato

unprepossessing /ʌnpriːpəˈzesɪŋ/ *adj* poco attraente

unpretentious /ʌnprɪˈtenʃəs/ *adj* senza pretese

unprincipled /ʌnˈprɪnsɪpəld/ *adj* senza principi; (behaviour) scorretto

unproductive /ʌnprəˈdʌktɪv/ *adj* (discussion, meeting) poco produttivo

unprofessional /ʌnprəˈfeʃnl/ *adj* non professionale; **it's ∼** è una mancanza di professionalità

unprofitable /ʌnˈprɒfɪtəbl/ *adj* non redditizio

unprompted /ʌnˈprɒm(p)tɪd/ *adj* (offer) spontaneo; (answer) non suggerito

unpronounceable /ʌnprəˈnaʊnsəbl/ *adj* impronunciabile

unprotected /ʌnprəˈtektɪd/ *adj* (sex) non protetto; (person) indifeso

unprovoked /ʌnprəˈvəʊkt/ *adj* (attack, aggression) non provocato; **the attack was ∼** l'attacco è avvenuto senza provocazione

unqualified /ʌnˈkwɒlɪfaɪd/ *adj* non qualificato; (fig: absolute) assoluto

unquestionable /ʌnˈkwestʃənəbl/ *adj* incontestabile

unquote /ʌnˈkwəʊt/ *vi* chiudere le virgolette

unravel /ʌnˈrævl/ *vt* (pt/pp **-lled**) districare; (in knitting) disfare

unreal /ʌnˈrɪəl/ *adj* irreale; fam inverosimile

unrealistic /ʌnrɪəˈlɪstɪk/ *adj* (character, presentation) poco realistico; (expectation, aim) irrealistico; (person) poco realista

unreasonable /ʌnˈriːz(ə)nəbl/ *adj* irragionevole

unrecognizable /ʌnˈrekəgnaɪzəbl/ *adj* irriconoscibile

unrecorded /ʌnrɪˈkɔːdɪd/ *adj* non documentato; **go** ~ non essere documentato

unrefined /ʌnrɪˈfaɪnd/ *adj* ⟨*person, manners, style*⟩ rozzo; ⟨*oil*⟩ greggio; ⟨*flour, sugar*⟩ non raffinato

unrehearsed /ʌnrɪˈhɜːst/ *adj* ⟨*response, action*⟩ imprevisto; ⟨*speech*⟩ improvvisato

unrelated /ʌnrɪˈleɪtɪd/ *adj* ⟨*facts*⟩ senza rapporto (**to** con); ⟨*person*⟩ non imparentato (**to** con)

unrelenting /ʌnrɪˈlentɪŋ/ *adj* ⟨*person*⟩ ostinato; ⟨*stare*⟩ insistente; ⟨*pursuit*⟩ continuo; ⟨*heat, zeal*⟩ costante

unreliable /ʌnrɪˈlaɪəbl/ *adj* inattendibile; ⟨*person*⟩ inaffidabile, che non dà affidamento

unremitting /ʌnrɪˈmɪtɪŋ/ *adj* costante; ⟨*struggle*⟩ continuo

unrepeatable /ʌnrɪˈpiːtəbl/ *adj* ⟨*offer, bargain*⟩ unico; **his comment was** ~ il commento che ha fatto è irripetibile

unrepentant /ʌnrɪˈpentənt/ *adj* irriducibile; ⟨*sinner*⟩ impenitente

unrequited /ʌnrɪˈkwaɪtɪd/ *adj* non corrisposto

unreservedly /ʌnrɪˈzɜːvɪdlɪ/ *adv* senza riserve; (frankly) francamente

unresolved /ʌnrɪˈzɒlvd/ *adj* irrisolto

unrest /ʌnˈrest/ *n* fermenti *mpl*

unrestricted /ʌnrɪˈstrɪktɪd/ *adj* ⟨*access, view*⟩ libero

unrewarding /ʌnrɪˈwɔːdɪŋ/ *adj* ⟨*job*⟩ poco gratificante

unripe /ʌnˈraɪp/ *adj* ⟨*fruit*⟩ acerbo; ⟨*wheat*⟩ non maturo

unrivalled /ʌnˈraɪvəld/ *adj* ineguagliato

unroll /ʌnˈrəʊl/ **①** *vt* srotolare **②** *vi* srotolarsi

unruffled /ʌnˈrʌfld/ *adj* ⟨*person*⟩ imperturbato; ⟨*hair*⟩ a posto; ⟨*water*⟩ non mosso; **be** ~ ⟨*person*⟩ rimanere imperturbato; ⟨*person, hair*⟩ essere a posto

unruly /ʌnˈruːlɪ/ *adj* indisciplinato

unsafe /ʌnˈseɪf/ *adj* pericoloso

unsaid /ʌnˈsed/ *adj* inespresso

unsalaried /ʌnˈsælərɪd/ *adj* ⟨*post*⟩ non stipendiato

unsalted /ʌnˈsɔːltɪd/ *adj* non salato

unsatisfactory /ʌnsætɪsˈfækt(ə)rɪ/ *adj* poco soddisfacente

unsatisfied /ʌnˈsætɪsfaɪd/ *adj* ⟨*person, need*⟩ insoddisfatto

unsatisfying /ʌnˈsætɪsfaɪɪŋ/ *adj* poco soddisfacente

unsavoury /ʌnˈseɪvərɪ/ *adj* equivoco

unscathed /ʌnˈskeɪðd/ *adj* illeso

unscheduled /ʌnˈʃedjuːld/ *adj* ⟨*flight*⟩ supplementare; ⟨*appearance, speech*⟩ fuori programma; ⟨*stop*⟩ non programmato

unscramble /ʌnˈskræmbl/ *vt* decifrare ⟨*code, words*⟩; sbrogliare ⟨*ideas, thoughts*⟩

unscrew /ʌnˈskruː/ *vt* svitare

unscrupulous /ʌnˈskruːpjʊləs/ *adj* senza scrupoli

unseasoned /ʌnˈsiːznd/ *adj* ⟨*wood*⟩ non stagionato; ⟨*food*⟩ scondito

unseat /ʌnˈsiːt/ *vt* disarcionare ⟨*rider*⟩

unseemly /ʌnˈsiːmlɪ/ *adj* indecoroso

unseen /ʌnˈsiːn/ *adv* ⟨*escape, slip away*⟩ senza essere visto

unselfconscious /ʌnselfkɒnʃəs/ *adj* naturale

unselfish /ʌnˈselfɪʃ/ *adj* disinteressato

unsentimental /ʌnsentɪˈmentl/ *adj* poco sentimentale

unsettled /ʌnˈsetld/ *adj* in agitazione; ⟨*weather*⟩ variabile; ⟨*bill*⟩ non saldato

unsettling /ʌnˈsetlɪŋ/ *adj* ⟨*experience, novel*⟩ inquietante

unshakeable /ʌnˈʃeɪkəbl/ *adj* categorico

unshaken /ʌnˈʃeɪkən/ *adj* ⟨*belief*⟩ saldo

unshaven /ʌnˈʃeɪvn/ *adj* non rasato

unsightly /ʌnˈsaɪtlɪ/ *adj* brutto

unsinkable /ʌnˈsɪŋkəbl/ *adj* ⟨*ship, object*⟩ inaffondabile; hum ⟨*personality*⟩ che non si deprime

unskilled /ʌnˈskɪld/ *adj* non specializzato

unskilled worker *n* manovale *m*

unsmiling /ʌnˈsmaɪlɪŋ/ *adj* ⟨*person*⟩ serioso

unsociable /ʌnˈsəʊʃəbl/ *adj* scontroso

unsocial hours /ʌnˈsəʊʃl/ *npl* **to work** ~ lavorare al di fuori degli orari standard

unsolicited /ʌnsəˈlɪsɪtɪd/ *adj* ⟨*help, advice*⟩ non richiesto; ⟨*job application*⟩ spontaneo

unsophisticated /ʌnsəˈfɪstɪkeɪtɪd/ *adj* semplice

unsound /ʌnˈsaʊnd/ *adj* ⟨*building, reasoning*⟩ poco solido; ⟨*advice*⟩ poco sensato; **of** ~ **mind** malato di mente

unspeakable /ʌnˈspiːkəbl/ *adj* indicibile

unspoiled /ʌnˈspɔɪld/ *adj* ⟨*town*⟩ non deturpato; ⟨*landscape*⟩ intatto; **she was** ~ **by fame** la fama non l'ha cambiata

unspoken /ʌnˈspəʊkən/ *adj* (implicit) tacito

unstable /ʌnˈsteɪbl/ *adj* instabile; (mentally) squilibrato

unsteadily /ʌnˈstedɪlɪ/ *adv* ⟨*walk, speak*⟩ in modo malsicuro

unsteady /ʌnˈstedɪ/ *adj* malsicuro

u

unstoppable /ʌn'stɒpəbl/ *adj* ⟨force, momentum⟩ inarrestabile

unstressed /ʌn'strest/ *adj* ⟨vowel, word⟩ atono

unstuck /ʌn'stʌk/ *adj* **come ∼** staccarsi; (fam: project) andare a monte

unsubstantiated /ʌnsəb'stænʃieɪtɪd/ *adj* ⟨report⟩ non corroborato

unsuccessful /ʌnsək'sesfʊl/ *adj* fallimentare; **be ∼** (in attempt) non aver successo

unsuccessfully /ʌnsək'sesfʊlɪ/ *adv* senza successo

unsuitable /ʌn'suːtəbl/ *adj* (inappropriate) inadatto; (inconvenient) inopportuno

unsupervised /ʌn'suːpəvaɪzd/ *adj* ⟨activity⟩ non controllato

unsure /ʌn'ʃʊə(r)/ *adj* incerto; **be ∼ about** non essere sicuro di; **∼ of oneself** essere insicuro

unsuspecting /ʌnsə'spektɪŋ/ *adj* fiducioso

unsweetened /ʌn'swiːtənd/ *adj* senza zucchero

unsympathetic /ʌnsɪmpə'θetɪk/ *adj* ⟨person, attitude, manner, tone⟩ poco comprensivo; ⟨person, character⟩ antipatico; **she is ∼ to the cause** non appoggia la causa

untamed /ʌn'teɪmd/ *adj* ⟨lion⟩ non addomesticato; ⟨passion, person⟩ indomito

untangle /ʌn'tæŋgl/ *vt* sbrogliare ⟨threads⟩; risolvere ⟨difficulties, mystery⟩

untaxed /ʌn'tækst/ *adj* ⟨goods⟩ non imponibile; ⟨income⟩ esente da imposte

untenable /ʌn'tenəbl/ *adj* ⟨position, argument⟩ insostenibile

unthinkable /ʌn'θɪŋkəbl/ *adj* impensabile

unthought-of /ʌn'θɔːtəv/ *adj* impensato; **hitherto ∼** finora impensato

untidily /ʌn'taɪdɪlɪ/ *adv* disordinatamente

untidiness /ʌn'taɪdɪnɪs/ *n* disordine *m*

untidy /ʌn'taɪdɪ/ *adj* disordinato

untie /ʌn'taɪ/ *vt* slegare

until /ʌn'tɪl/ **①** *prep* fino a; **not ∼** non prima di; **∼ the evening** fino alla sera; **∼ his arrival** fino al suo arrivo **②** *conj* finché, fino a quando; **not ∼ you've seen it** non prima che tu l'abbia visto

untimely /ʌn'taɪmlɪ/ *adj* inopportuno; (premature) prematuro

untiring /ʌn'taɪərɪŋ/ *adj* instancabile

untold /ʌn'təʊld/ *adj* ⟨wealth⟩ incalcolabile; ⟨suffering⟩ indescrivibile; ⟨story⟩ inedito

untouched /ʌn'tʌtʃt/ *adj* (unchanged, undisturbed) intatto; (unscathed) incolume;

(unaffected) non toccato; **leave one's dinner/a meal ∼** non toccare cibo

untoward /ʌntə'wɔːd/ *adj* **if nothing ∼ happens** se non capita un imprevisto

untrained /ʌn'treɪnd/ *adj* ⟨voice⟩ non impostato; ⟨eye, artist, actor⟩ inesperto; **be ∼** ⟨worker⟩ non avere una formazione professionale

untranslatable /ʌntrænz'leɪtəbl/ *adj* intraducibile

untreated /ʌn'triːtɪd/ *adj* ⟨sewage, water⟩ non depurato; ⟨illness⟩ non curato

untroubled /ʌn'trʌbld/ *adj* ⟨sleep⟩ tranquillo

untrue /ʌn'truː/ *adj* falso; **that's ∼** non è vero

untrustworthy /ʌn'trʌstwɜːðɪ/ *adj* ⟨person⟩ inaffidabile

unused¹ /ʌn'juːzd/ *adj* non usato

unused² /ʌn'juːst/ *adj* **be ∼ to** non essere abituato a

unusual /ʌn'juːʒəl/ *adj* insolito

unusually /ʌn'juːʒəlɪ/ *adv* insolitamente

unveil /ʌn'veɪl/ *vt* scoprire

unversed /ʌn'vɜːst/ *adj* inesperto (**in** di)

unwanted /ʌn'wɒntɪd/ *adj* ⟨child, pet, visitor⟩ indesiderato; ⟨goods, produce⟩ che non serve; **feel ∼** sentirsi respinto

unwarranted /ʌn'wɒrəntɪd/ *adj* ingiustificato

unwelcome /ʌn'welkəm/ *adj* sgradito

unwell /ʌn'wel/ *adj* indisposto

unwieldy /ʌn'wiːldɪ/ *adj* ingombrante

unwilling /ʌn'wɪlɪŋ/ *adj* riluttante

unwillingly /ʌn'wɪlɪŋlɪ/ *adv* malvolentieri

unwillingness /ʌn'wɪlɪŋnɪs/ *n* riluttanza

unwind /ʌn'waɪnd/ **①** *vt* (pt/pp **unwound**) svolgere, srotolare **②** *vi* svolgersi, srotolarsi; (fam: relax) rilassarsi

unwise /ʌn'waɪz/ *adj* imprudente

unwisely /ʌn'waɪzlɪ/ *adv* imprudentemente

unwitting /ʌn'wɪtɪŋ/ *adj* involontario; ⟨victim⟩ inconsapevole

unwittingly /ʌn'wɪtɪŋlɪ/ *adv* involontariamente

unworldly /ʌn'wɜːldlɪ/ *adj* (not materialistic) poco materialista; (naive) ingenuo; (spiritual) non materialista

unworthy /ʌn'wɜːðɪ/ *adj* non degno

unwrap /ʌn'ræp/ *vt* (pt/pp **-wrapped**) scartare ⟨present, parcel⟩

unwritten /ʌn'rɪtn/ *adj* tacito

unyielding /ʌn'jiːldɪŋ/ *adj* rigido

unzip /ʌn'zɪp/ *vt* aprire [la cerniera di] ⟨garment, bag⟩

up /ʌp/ **①** *adv* su; (not in bed) alzato; ⟨*road*⟩ smantellato; ⟨*theatre curtain, blinds*⟩ alzato; ⟨*shelves, tent*⟩ montato; ⟨*notice*⟩ affisso; ⟨*building*⟩ costruito; **prices are up** i prezzi sono aumentati; **be up for sale** essere in vendita; **up here/there** quassù/ lassù; **time's up** tempo scaduto; **what's up?** fam cosa è successo?; **up to** (as far as) fino a; **be up to** essere all'altezza di ⟨*task*⟩; **what's he up to?** fam cosa sta facendo?; (plotting) cosa sta combinando?; **I'm up to page 100** sono arrivato a pagina 100; **feel up to it** sentirsela; **be one up on somebody** fam essere in vantaggio su qualcuno; **go up** salire; **lift up** alzare; **up against** fig alle prese con **②** *prep* su; **the cat ran/is up the tree** il gatto è salito di corsa/è sull'albero; **further up this road** più avanti su questa strada; **row up the river** risalire il fiume; **go up the stairs** salire su per le scale; **be up the pub** fam essere al pub; **be up on** or **in something** essere bene informato su qualcosa **③** *npl* **ups and downs** alti *mpl* e bassi

up-and-coming *adj* promettente

upbeat /ˈʌpbiːt/ *adj* ottimistico

upbringing /ˈʌpbrɪŋɪŋ/ *n* educazione *f*

update /ʌpˈdeɪt/ *vt* aggiornare

upfront /ʌpˈfrʌnt/ **①** *adj* fam (frank) aperto; ⟨*money*⟩ anticipato **②** *adv* ⟨*pay*⟩ in anticipo

upgrade /ʌpˈɡreɪd/ **①** *vt* promuovere ⟨*person*⟩; modernizzare ⟨*equipment*⟩ **②** *n* aggiornamento *m*

upheaval /ʌpˈhiːvl/ *n* scompiglio *m*

uphill /ʌpˈhɪl/ **①** *adj* in salita; fig arduo **②** *adv* in salita

uphold /ʌpˈhəʊld/ *vt* (pt/pp **upheld**) sostenere ⟨*principle*⟩; confermare ⟨*verdict*⟩

upholster /ʌpˈhəʊlstə(r)/ *vt* tappezzare

upholsterer /ʌpˈhəʊlstərə(r)/ *n* tappezziere, -a *mf*

upholstery /ʌpˈhəʊlstərɪ/ *n* tappezzeria *f*

upkeep /ˈʌpkiːp/ *n* mantenimento *m*

uplifting /ʌpˈlɪftɪŋ/ *adj* (morally) edificante

upload /ʌpˈləʊd/ *vt* Comput fare l'upload di

up-market *adj* di qualità

upon /əˈpɒn/ *prep* su; ~ **arriving home** una volta arrivato a casa

upper /ˈʌpə(r)/ **①** *adj* superiore **②** *n* (of shoe) tomaia *f*

upper-case *adj* maiuscolo

upper circle *n* seconda galleria *f*

upper class *n* alta borghesia *f*

upper crust *adj* hum aristocratico

upper hand *n* **have the** ~ ~ avere il sopravvento

upper middle class *n* ceto *m* medio-alto

uppermost /ˈʌpəməʊst/ *adj* più alto; **that's** ~ **in my mind** è la mia preoccupazione principale

upright /ˈʌpraɪt/ **①** *adj* dritto; ⟨*piano*⟩ verticale; (honest) retto **②** *n* montante *m*

upright freezer *n* freezer *m inv* verticale

uprising /ˈʌpraɪzɪŋ/ *n* rivolta *f*

upriver /ʌpˈrɪvə(r)/ *adv* ⟨*lie*⟩ a monte; ⟨*sail*⟩ controcorrente

uproar /ˈʌprɔː(r)/ *n* tumulto *m*; **be in an** ~ essere in trambusto

uproot /ʌpˈruːt/ *vt* sradicare

upset¹ /ʌpˈset/ *vt* (pt/pp **upset**, pres p **upsetting**) rovesciare; sconvolgere ⟨*plan*⟩; (distress) turbare; **get** ~ **about something** prendersela per qualcosa; **be very** ~ essere sconvolto; **have an** ~ **stomach** avere l'intestino disturbato

upset² /ˈʌpset/ *n* scombussolamento *m*

upsetting /ʌpˈsetɪŋ/ *adj* (distressing) sconvolgente; (annoying) fastidioso

upshot /ˈʌpʃɒt/ *n* risultato *m*

upside down *adv* sottosopra; **turn** ~ ~ capovolgere

upstage /ʌpˈsteɪdʒ/ **①** *vt* Theat, fig distogliere l'attenzione del pubblico da **②** *adv* Theat ⟨*stand*⟩ al fondo del palcoscenico; ⟨*move*⟩ verso il fondo del palcoscenico

upstairs¹ /ʌpˈsteəz/ *adv* [al piano di] sopra

upstairs² /ˈʌpsteəz/ *adj* del piano superiore

upstart /ˈʌpstɑːt/ *n* arrivato, -a *mf*

upstream /ʌpˈstriːm/ *adv* controcorrente

upsurge /ˈʌpsɜːdʒ/ *n* (in sales) aumento *m* improvviso; (of enthusiasm, crime) ondata *f*

uptake /ˈʌpteɪk/ *n* **be slow on the** ~ essere lento nel capire; **be quick on the** ~ capire le cose al volo

uptight /ʌpˈtaɪt/ *adj* teso

up-to-date *adj* moderno; ⟨*news*⟩ ultimo; ⟨*person, information, records*⟩ aggiornato

up-to-the-minute *adj* ⟨*information*⟩ dell'ultimo minuto

uptown /ˈʌptaʊn/ *adj* (Am: smart) dei quartieri alti

upturn /ˈʌptɜːn/ *n* ripresa *f*

upward /ˈʌpwəd/ **①** *adj* verso l'alto, in su; ~ **slope** salita *f* **②** *adv* ~**[s]** verso l'alto; ~**s of** oltre

upwardly mobile /ʌpwədlɪˈməʊbaɪl/ *adj* che sale nella scala sociale

uranium /jʊˈreɪnɪəm/ *n* uranio *m*

Uranus /ˈjʊərənəs/ *n* Urano *m*

urban /ˈɜːbən/ *adj* urbano

urban blight, **urban decay** *n* degrado *m* urbano

urbane /ɜː'beɪn/ adj cortese
urban planning n urbanistica f
urchin /'ɜːtʃɪn/ n riccio m di mare
Urdu /'ʊəduː/ n urdu m
urge /ɜːdʒ/ **1** n forte desiderio m
  2 vt esortare (**to** a)
  ■ **urge on** vt spronare
urgency /'ɜːdʒənsɪ/ n urgenza f
urgent /'ɜːdʒənt/ adj urgente
urgently /'ɜːdʒəntlɪ/ adv urgentemente
urinal /jʊ'raɪnl/ n (fixture) orinale m; (place)
  vespasiano m
urinate /'jʊərɪneɪt/ vi urinare
urine /'jʊərɪn/ n urina f
URL abbr (**Unified Resource
  Locator**) URL m
urn /ɜːn/ n urna f; (for tea) contenitore m
  munito di rubinetto che si trova nei self-
  service, mense ecc
Uruguay /'jʊərəgwaɪ/ n Uruguay m
US n abbr (**United States**) U.S.A. mpl
us /ʌs/ pers pron ci; (after prep) noi; **they
  know us** ci conoscono; **give us the money**
  dateci i soldi; **give it to us** datecelo; **they
  showed it to us** ce l'hanno fatto vedere;
  they meant us, not you intendevano noi,
  non voi; **it's us** siamo noi; **she hates us** ci
  odia
USA n abbr (**United States of
  America**) U.S.A. mpl
usable /'juːzəbl/ adj usabile
usage /'juːsɪdʒ/ n uso m
use¹ /juːs/ n uso m; **be of ∼** essere utile;
  be of no ∼ essere inutile; **make ∼ of**
  usare; (exploit) sfruttare; **it is no ∼** è
  inutile; **what's the ∼?** a che scopo?
use² /juːz/ vt usare
  ■ **use up** vt consumare
used¹ /juːzd/ adj usato
used² /juːst/ pt **be ∼ to something** essere
  abituato a qualcosa; **get ∼ to** abituarsi a;
  he ∼ to say diceva; **he ∼ to live here**
  viveva qui
useful /'juːsfl/ adj utile
usefulness /'juːsflnɪs/ n utilità f
useless /'juːslɪs/ adj inutile; fam ⟨person⟩
  incapace; **you're ∼!** sei un idiota!
user /'juːzə(r)/ n utente mf

user-friendliness n facilità f d'uso
user-friendly adj facile da usare
user group n Comput gruppo m di utenti
user manual n manuale m d'uso
username n nome m utente
usher /'ʌʃə(r)/ n Theat maschera f; Jur
  usciere m; (at wedding) persona f che
  accompagna gli invitati ad un
  matrimonio ai loro posti in chiesa
  ■ **usher in** vt fare entrare ⟨person⟩;
  inaugurare ⟨new age⟩
usherette /ʌʃə'ret/ n maschera f
USS abbr Am (**United States Ship**)
  nave f da guerra americana
USSR n URSS f
usual /'juːʒʊəl/ adj usuale; **as ∼** come al
  solito
usually /'juːʒʊəlɪ/ adv di solito
usurp /jʊ'zɜːp/ vt usurpare
usurper /jʊ'zɜːpə(r)/ n usurpatore, -trice
  mf
utensil /jʊ'tensl/ n utensile m
uterus /'juːtərəs/ n utero m
utilitarian /jʊtɪlɪ'teərɪən/ adj funzionale
utility /jʊ'tɪlətɪ/ n utilità f; (public) servizio
  m
utility company n servizio m pubblico
utility program n Comput [programma
  m di] utilità f
utility room n stanza f in casa privata
  per il lavaggio, la stiratura dei panni ecc
utilize /'juːtɪlaɪz/ vt utilizzare
utmost /'ʌtməʊst/ **1** adj estremo
  2 n **one's ∼** tutto il possibile
Utopia /juː'təʊpɪə/ n utopia f
Utopian /juː'təʊpɪən/ **1** n utopista mf
  2 adj utopistico
utter¹ /'ʌtə(r)/ adj totale
utter² vt emettere ⟨sigh, sound⟩; proferire
  ⟨word⟩
utterance /'ʌtərəns/ n dichiarazione f
utterly /'ʌtəlɪ/ adv completamente
U-turn n Auto inversione f a U; fig marcia
  f indietro
UV abbr (**ultraviolet**) UVA mpl
Uzbekistan /ʌzbekɪ'stɑːn/ n Uzbekistan
  m

Vv

v¹, V /viː/ n (letter) v, V f inv

v² abbr (**versus**) contro; abbr (**volt**) V m

vac /væk/ n Br abbr (**vacation**) vacanze
  fpl

vacancy /'veɪk(ə)nsɪ/ n (job) posto m

vacant ···> variation ···

vacante; (room) stanza *f* disponibile

vacant /'veɪknt/ *adj* libero; ⟨position⟩ vacante; ⟨look⟩ assente

vacant possession *n* Br Jur bene *m* immobile libero

vacate /və'keɪt/ *vt* lasciare libero

vacation /və'keɪʃn/ *n* Univ & Am vacanza *f*

vacationer /və'keɪʃənə(r)/ *n* Am vacanziere, -a *mf*

vaccinate /'væksɪmeɪt/ *vt* vaccinare

vaccination /væksɪ'neɪʃn/ *n* vaccinazione *f*

vaccine /'væksiːn/ *n* vaccino *m*

vacillate /'væsɪleɪt/ *vi* tentennare

vacuous /'vækjʊəs/ *adj* ⟨person, look, expression⟩ vacuo; ⟨person⟩ superficiale

vacuum /'vækjʊəm/ ① *n* vuoto *m* ② *vt* passare l'aspirapolvere in/su

vacuum cleaner *n* aspirapolvere *m* inv

vacuum flask *n* thermos *m* inv

vacuum-pack *vt* confezionare sotto vuoto ⟨food⟩

vacuum-packed *adj* confezionato sottovuoto

vagabond /'vægəbɒnd/ *n* vagabondo, -a *mf*

vagaries /'veɪgərɪz/ *npl* capricci *mpl*

vagina /və'dʒaɪnə/ *n* Anat vagina *f*

vagrancy /'veɪgrənsɪ/ *n* Jur vagabondaggio *m*

vagrant /'veɪgrənt/ *n* vagabondo, -a *mf*

vague /veɪg/ *adj* vago; ⟨outline⟩ impreciso; (absent-minded) distratto; **I'm still ∼ about it** non ho ancora le idee chiare in proposito

vaguely /'veɪglɪ/ *adv* vagamente

vagueness /'veɪgnɪs/ *n* (imprecision) vaghezza *f*; (of wording, proposals) indeterminatezza *f*; (of image) nebulosità *f*; (of thinking) imprecisione *f*

vain /veɪn/ *adj* vanitoso; ⟨hope, attempt⟩ vano; **in ∼** invano

vainly /'veɪnlɪ/ *adv* vanamente

valance /'væləns/ *n* (above curtains) mantovana *f*; (on bed base) balza *f*

vale /veɪl/ *n* liter valle *f*

valentine /'væləntaɪn/ *n* (card) biglietto *m* di San Valentino

Valentine's Day *n* giorno *m* di San Valentino

valet /'væleɪ/ *n* servitore *m* personale

valet parking *n* servizio *m* di parcheggio per clienti di alberghi e ristoranti

valiant /'vælɪənt/ *adj* valoroso

valiantly /'vælɪəntlɪ/ *adv* coraggiosamente

valid /'vælɪd/ *adj* valido

validate /'vælɪdeɪt/ *vt* (confirm) convalidare

validity /və'lɪdətɪ/ *n* validità *f*

valley /'vælɪ/ *n* valle *f*

valour /'vælə(r)/ *n* valore *m*

valuable /'væljʊəbl/ *adj* di valore; fig prezioso

valuables /'væljʊəblz/ *npl* oggetti *mpl* di valore

valuation /væljʊ'eɪʃn/ *n* valutazione *f*

value /'væljuː/ ① *n* valore *m*; (usefulness) utilità *f* ② *vt* valutare; (cherish) apprezzare

value added tax /'ædɪd/ *n* imposta *f* sul valore aggiunto

valued /'væljuːd/ *adj* (appreciated) apprezzato

valuer /'væljʊə(r)/ *n* stimatore, -trice *mf*

valve /vælv/ *n* valvola *f*

vamp /væmp/ *n* vamp *f* inv

vampire /'væmpaɪə(r)/ *n* vampiro *m*

van /væn/ *n* furgone *m*

vandal /'vændl/ *n* vandalo, -a *mf*

vandalism /'vænd(ə)lɪzm/ *n* vandalismo *m*

vandalize /'vænd(ə)laɪz/ *vt* vandalizzare

vane /veɪn/ *n* banderuola *f*

vanguard /'vængɑːd/ *n* avanguardia *f*; **in the ∼** all'avanguardia

vanilla /və'nɪlə/ *n* vaniglia *f*

vanish /'vænɪʃ/ *vi* svanire

vanishing cream *n* crema *f* base per il trucco

vanishing point *n* punto *m* di fuga

vanishing trick *n* trucco *m* da illusionista per far sparire un oggetto; **he's done his ∼ ∼ again** fam è sparito come al solito

vanity /'vænɪtɪ/ *n* vanità *f* inv

vanity bag, **vanity case** *n* beauty-case *m* inv

vanity mirror *n* Auto specchietto *m* di cortesia

vanquish /'væŋkwɪʃ/ *vt* sconfiggere ⟨enemy⟩

vantage point /'vɑːntɪdʒ/ *n* punto *m* d'osservazione; fig punto *m* di vista

vaporize /'veɪpəraɪz/ *vt* vaporizzare ⟨liquid⟩

vaporizer /'veɪpəraɪzə(r)/ *n* apparecchio *m* per aerosol

vapour /'veɪpə(r)/ *n* vapore *m*

vapour trail *n* scia *f*

variable /'veərɪəbl/ *adj* variabile; (adjustable) regolabile

variance /'veɪrɪəns/ *n* **be at ∼** essere in disaccordo

variant /'veɪrɪənt/ *n* variante *f*

variation /veərɪ'eɪʃn/ *n* variazione *f*

v

varicose /'værɪkəʊs/ adj ∼ **veins** vene fpl varicose

varied /'veərɪd/ adj vario; ⟨diet⟩ diversificato; ⟨life⟩ movimentato

variegated /'veərɪəgeɪtɪd/ adj variegato

variety /və'raɪətɪ/ n varietà f inv

variety show n spettacolo m di varietà

varifocal /veərɪ'fəʊkl/ adj ⟨lens⟩ multifocale

varifocals /veərɪ'fəʊklz/ npl (glasses) occhiali mpl multifocali

various /'veərɪəs/ adj vario

variously /'veərɪəslɪ/ adv variamente

varnish /'vɑːnɪʃ/ **1** n vernice f; (for nails) smalto m
2 vt verniciare; ∼ **one's nails** mettersi lo smalto

vary /'veərɪ/ vt/i (pt/pp **-ied**) variare

varying /'veərɪɪŋ/ adj variabile; (different) diverso

vascular /'væskjʊlə(r)/ adj Anat, Bot vascolare

vase /vɑːz/ n vaso m

vasectomy /və'sektəmɪ/ n vasectomia f

vast /vɑːst/ adj vasto; ⟨difference, amusement⟩ enorme

vastly /'vɑːstlɪ/ adv ⟨superior⟩ di gran lunga; ⟨different, amused⟩ enormemente

VAT /viːeɪ'tiː/, /væt/ abbr (**value added tax**) I.V.A. f

vat /væt/ n tino m

Vatican /'vætɪkən/ n the ∼ il Vaticano; ∼ **City** la città del Vaticano

vaudeville /'vɔːdəvɪl/ n Theat varietà m

vault¹ /vɔːlt/ n (roof) volta f; (in bank) caveau m inv; (tomb) cripta f

vault² **1** n salto m
2 vt/i ∼ **[over]** saltare

VCR abbr n (**video cassette recorder**) VCR m

VD abbr (**venereal disease**) malattia f venerea

VDU abbr (**visual display unit**) VDU m

veal /viːl/ **1** n carne f di vitello
2 attrib di vitello

vector /'vektə(r)/ n Biol, Math vettore m; Aeron rotta f

veer /vɪə(r)/ vi cambiare direzione; Naut, Auto virare

vegan /'viːgn/ **1** n vegetaliano, -a mf
2 adj vegetaliano

veganism /'viːgnɪzm/ n vegetalismo m

vegeburger /'vedʒɪbɜːgə(r)/ n = VEGGIE BURGER

vegetable /'vedʒtəbl/ **1** n (food) verdura f; (when growing) ortaggio m
2 attrib ⟨oil, fat⟩ vegetale

vegetarian /vedʒɪ'teərɪən/ adj & n vegetariano, -a mf

vegetarianism /vedʒɪ'teərɪənɪzm/ n vegetarianismo m

vegetate /'vedʒɪteɪt/ vi vegetare

vegetation /vedʒɪ'teɪʃn/ n vegetazione f

veggie burger /'vedʒɪbɜːgə(r)/ n hamburger m inv vegetariano

vehemence /'viːəməns/ n veemenza f

vehement /'viːəmənt/ adj veemente

vehemently /'viːəməntlɪ/ adv con veemenza

vehicle /'viːɪkl/ n veicolo m; (fig: medium) mezzo m

vehicular /vɪ'hɪkjʊlə(r)/ adj no ∼ **access**, no ∼ **traffic** circolazione vietata

veil /veɪl/ **1** n velo m
2 vt velare

veiled /veɪld/ adj ⟨woman⟩ velato, col velo; ⟨threat⟩ velato

vein /veɪn/ n vena f; (mood) umore m; (manner) tenore m

veined /veɪnd/ adj venato

Velcro® /'velkrəʊ/ n ∼ **fastening** chiusura f con velcro

vellum /'veləm/ n pergamena f

velocity /vɪ'lɒsətɪ/ n velocità f inv

velvet /'velvɪt/ n velluto m

velvety /'velvətɪ/ adj vellutato

venal /'viːnl/ adj venale

vendetta /ven'detə/ n vendetta f

vending machine /'vendɪŋ/ n distributore m automatico

vendor /'vendə(r)/ n venditore, -trice mf

veneer /və'nɪə(r)/ n impiallacciatura f; fig vernice f

veneered /və'nɪərd/ adj impiallacciato

venerable /'venərəbl/ adj venerabile

veneration /venə'reɪʃn/ n venerazione f

venereal /vɪ'nɪərɪəl/ adj ∼ **disease** malattia f venerea

Venetian /və'niːʃn/ adj & n veneziano, -a mf

Venetian blind n persiana f alla veneziana

Venezuela /venɪz'weɪlə/ n Venezuela m

Venezuelan /venɪz'weɪlən/ adj & n venezuelano, -a mf

vengeance /'vendʒəns/ n vendetta f; with a ∼ fam a più non posso

Venice /'venɪs/ n Venezia f

venison /'venɪsn/ n Culin carne f di cervo

venom /'venəm/ n veleno m

venomous /'venəməs/ adj velenoso

vent¹ /vent/ **1** n presa f d'aria; give ∼ to fig dar libero sfogo a
2 vt fig sfogare ⟨anger⟩

vent² n (in jacket) spacco m

ventilate /'ventɪleɪt/ vt ventilare

ventilation /ventɪ'leɪʃn/ n ventilazione f; (installation) sistema m di ventilazione

ventilator /'ventɪleɪtə(r)/ n ventilatore m

ventriloquist /ven'trɪləkwɪst/ n ventriloquo, -a mf

venture /'ventʃə(r)/ ① n impresa f ② vt azzardare ③ vi avventurarsi

venture capital n capitale m a rischio

venue /'venju:/ n luogo m (di convegno, concerto ecc)

Venus /'vi:nəs/ n Venere f

veracity /və'ræsətɪ/ n veridicità f

veranda /və'rændə/ n veranda f

verb /vɜ:b/ n verbo m

verbal /'vɜ:bl/ adj verbale

verbally /'vɜ:b(ə)lɪ/ adv verbalmente

verbatim /vɜ:'beɪtɪm/ ① adj letterale ② adv parola per parola

verbose /vɜ:'bəʊs/ adj prolisso

verdict /'vɜ:dɪkt/ n verdetto m; (opinion) parere m

verdigris /'vɜ:dɪgri:/ n verderame m

verge /vɜ:dʒ/ n orlo m; be on the ~ of doing something essere sul punto di fare qualcosa

■ **verge on** vt fig rasentare

verger /'vɜ:dʒə(r)/ n sagrestano m

verification /verɪfɪ'keɪʃn/ n verifica f

verify /'verɪfaɪ/ vt (pt/pp -**led**) verificare; (confirm) confermare

veritable /'verɪtəbl/ adj vero

vermicelli /vɜ:mɪ'tʃelɪ/ n (pasta) capelli mpl d'angelo; (chocolate) pezzettini mpl di cioccolato per decorazione

vermilion /və'mɪljɪn/ ① n rosso m vermiglio ② adj vermiglio

vermin /'vɜ:mɪn/ n animali mpl nocivi

vermouth /'vɜ:məθ/ n vermut m inv

vernacular /vɜ:'nækjʊlə(r)/ n vernacolo m

verruca /və'ru:kə/ n verruca f

versatile /'vɜ:sətaɪl/ adj versatile

versatility /vɜ:sə'tɪlətə/ n versatilità f

verse /vɜ:s/ n verso m; (of Bible) versetto m; (poetry) versi mpl

versed /vɜ:st/ adj ~ in versato in

versifier /'vɜ:sɪfaɪə(r)/ n pej versificatore, -trice mf

version /'vɜ:ʃn/ n versione f; (translation) traduzione f

versus /'vɜ:səs/ prep contro

vertebra /'vɜ:tɪbrə/ n (pl -**brae** /-bri:/) Anat vertebra f

vertebrate /'vɜ:tɪbrət/ ① n vertebrato m ② adj vertebrato

vertex /'vɜ:teks/ n Anat sommità f inv del capo; Math vertice m

vertical /'vɜ:tɪkl/ adj & n verticale m

vertically /'vɜ:tɪklɪ/ adv verticalmente

vertigo /'vɜ:tɪgəʊ/ n Med vertigine f

verve /vɜ:v/ n verve f

very /'verɪ/ ① adv molto; ~ **much** molto; ~ **little** pochissimo; ~ **many** moltissimi; ~ **few** pochissimi; ~ **probably** molto probabilmente; ~ **well** benissimo; at the ~ **most** tutt'al più; at the ~ **latest** al più tardi ② adj the ~ **first** il primissimo; the ~ **thing** proprio ciò che ci vuole; at the ~ **end/beginning** proprio alla fine/all'inizio; that ~ **day** proprio quel giorno; the ~ **thought** la sola idea; only a ~ **little** solo un pochino

vespers /'vespəz/ npl vespri mpl

vessel /'vesl/ n nave f; (receptacle) recipiente m; Anat vaso m

vest /vest/ ① n maglia f della salute; (Am: waistcoat) gilè m inv ② vt ~ **something in somebody** investire qualcuno di qualcosa

vested interest /vestɪd'ɪntrəst/ n interesse m personale

vestige /'vestɪdʒ/ n (of past) vestigio m

vestment /'vestmənt/ n Relig paramento m

vestry /'vestrɪ/ n sagrestia f

vet /vet/ ① n veterinario, -a mf ② vt (pt/pp **vetted**) controllare minuziosamente

veteran /'vetərən/ n veterano, -a mf

veteran car n auto f inv d'epoca (costruita prima del 1916)

veterinarian /vetərɪ'neərɪən/ n Am = VET

veterinary /'vetərɪnərɪ/ adj veterinario

veterinary surgeon n medico m veterinario

veto /'vi:təʊ/ ① n (pl -**es**) veto m ② vt proibire

vetting /'vetɪŋ/ n verifica f del passato di un individuo

vex /veks/ vt irritare

vexation /vek'seɪʃn/ n irritazione f

vexatious /vek'seɪʃəs/ adj ⟨person⟩ fastidioso; ⟨situation⟩ spiacevole

vexed /vekst/ adj irritato; ~ **question** questione f controversa

vexing /'veksɪŋ/ adj irritante

VHF abbr (**very high frequency**) VHF

via /'vaɪə/ prep via; (by means of) attraverso

viability /vaɪə'bɪlətɪ/ n probabilità f di sopravvivenza; (of proposition) attuabilità f

viable /'vaɪəbl/ adj ⟨life form, relationship, company⟩ in grado di sopravvivere; ⟨proposition⟩ attuabile

viaduct /'vaɪədʌkt/ n viadotto m

vibes /vaɪbz/ *npl fam* **I'm getting good/ bad** ∼ provo una sensazione gradevole/ sgradevole

vibrant /'vaɪbrənt/ *adj fig* che sprizza vitalità

vibrate /vaɪ'breɪt/ *vi* vibrare

vibration /vaɪ'breʃn/ *n* vibrazione *f*

vicar /'vɪkə(r)/ *n* parroco *m* (protestante)

vicarage /'vɪkərɪdʒ/ *n* casa *f* parrocchiale

vicarious /vɪ'keərɪəs/ *adj* indiretto

vice[1] /vaɪs/ *n* vizio *m*

vice[2] *n* Techn morsa *f*

vice-captain *n* Sport vicecapitano *m*

vice-chairman *n* vicepresidente *mf*

vice-chancellor *n* Br Univ vicerettore *m*; Am Jur vicecancelliere *m*

vice-president *n* vicepresidente *mf*

vice-principal *n* (of senior school) vicepreside *mf*; (of junior school, college) vicedirettore, -trice *mf*

vice squad *n* buoncostume *f*

vice versa /vaɪsə'vɜːsə/ *adv* viceversa

vicinity /vɪ'sɪnətɪ/ *n* vicinanza *f*; **in the** ∼ **of** nelle vicinanze di

vicious /'vɪʃəs/ *adj* cattivo; ⟨attack⟩ brutale; ⟨animal⟩ pericoloso

vicious circle *n* circolo *m* vizioso

viciously /'vɪʃəslɪ/ *adv* ⟨attack⟩ brutalmente

victim /'vɪktɪm/ *n* vittima *f*

victimization /vɪktɪmaɪ'zeʃn/ *n* vittimizzazione *f*

victimize /'vɪktɪmaɪz/ *vt* vittimizzare

victor /'vɪktə(r)/ *n* vincitore *m*

Victorian /vɪk'tɔːrɪən/ ❶ *n* persona *f* vissuta in epoca vittoriana
❷ *adj* ⟨writer, poverty, age⟩ vittoriano

victorious /vɪk'tɔːrɪəs/ *adj* vittorioso

victory /'vɪktərɪ/ *n* vittoria *f*

video /'vɪdɪəʊ/ ❶ *n* video *m inv*; (cassette) videocassetta *f*; (recorder) videoregistratore *m*
❷ *attrib* video
❸ *vt* registrare

video camera *n* videocamera *f*, telecamera *f*

video card *n* scheda *f* video

video cassette *n* videocassetta *f*

video clip *n* videoclip *m inv*

videoconference *n* videoconferenza *f*

videoconferencing /'kɒnfərənsɪŋ/ *n* videoconferenza *f*

videodisc *n* videodisco *m*

video game *n* videogioco *m*

video library *n* videoteca *f*

video nasty *n* film *m inv* con scene violente o pornografiche

videophone *n* videocitofono *m*

video recorder *n* videoregistratore *m*

video shop *n* negozio *m* che affitta o vende videocassette

video surveillance *n* videosorveglianza *f*

videotape *n* videocassetta *f*

vie /vaɪ/ *vi* (pres p **vying**) rivaleggiare

Vienna /vɪ'enə/ *n* Vienna *f*

Viennese /vɪə'niːz/ *adj & n* viennese

Vietnam /vɪet'næm/ *n* Vietnam *m*

Vietnamese /vɪetnæ'miːz/ *adj & n* vietnamita *mf*; (language) vietnamita *m*

view /vjuː/ ❶ *n* vista *f*; (photographed, painted) veduta *f*; (opinion) visione *f*; **look at the** ∼ guardare il panorama; **in my** ∼ secondo me; **in** ∼ **of** in considerazione di; **on** ∼ esposto; **with a** ∼ **to** con l'intenzione di
❷ *vt* visitare ⟨house⟩; consider considerare
❸ *vi* TV guardare

viewer /'vjuːə(r)/ *n* TV telespettatore, -trice *mf*; Phot visore *m*

viewfinder /'vjuːfaɪndə(r)/ *n* Phot mirino *m*

viewing /'vjuːɪŋ/ ❶ *n* TV programmi *mpl* della televisione; (of film) proiezione *f*; (of new range) presentazione *f*; (of exhibition, house) visita *f*; **it makes good** ∼ TV vale la pena di vederlo; **what's tonight's** ∼? cosa danno alla tv stasera?
❷ *attrib* ⟨habits, preferences⟩ dei telespettatori; **the** ∼ **public** i telespettatori

view phone *n* videotelefono *m*

viewpoint /'vjuːpɔɪnt/ *n* punto *m* di vista

vigil /'vɪdʒɪl/ *n* veglia *f*

vigilance /'vɪdʒɪləns/ *n* vigilanza *f*

vigilant /'vɪdʒɪlənt/ *adj* vigile

vigilante /vdʒɪ'læntɪ/ *n* membro *m* di un'organizzazione privata per la prevenzione della criminalità

vigorous /'vɪg(ə)rəs/ *adj* vigoroso

vigorously /'vɪg(ə)rəslɪ/ *adv* vigorosamente

vigour /'vɪgə(r)/ *n* vigore *m*

vile /vaɪl/ *adj* disgustoso; ⟨weather⟩ orribile; ⟨temper, mood⟩ pessimo

vilification /vɪlɪfɪ'keɪʃn/ *n* denigrazione *f*

villa /'vɪlɪ/ *n* (for holidays) casa *f* di villeggiatura

village /'vɪlɪdʒ/ *n* paese *m*

village green *n* giardino *m* pubblico nel centro di un paese

village hall *n* sala *f* utilizzata per feste e altre attività

villager /'vɪlɪdʒə(r)/ *n* paesano, -a *mf*

villain /'vɪlɪn/ *n* furfante *m*; (in story) cattivo *m*

villainous /'vɪlənəs/ *adj* infame

V

vim /vɪm/ *n* fam energia *f*

vindicate /'vɪndɪkeɪt/ *vt* (from guilt) discolpare; **you are ∼d** ti sei dimostrato nel giusto

vindictive /vɪn'dɪktɪv/ *adj* vendicativo

vine /vaɪn/ *n* vite *f*

vinegar /'vɪnɪgə(r)/ *n* aceto *m*

vinegary /'vɪnɪg(ə)rɪ/ *adj* agro

vineyard /'vɪnjɑːd/ *n* vigneto *m*

vintage /'vɪntɪdʒ/ ① *adj* ⟨wine⟩ d'annata ② *n* (year) annata *f*

vintage car *n* auto *f inv* d'epoca (costruita tra il 1917 e il 1930)

vintage year *n* also fig anno *m* memorabile

vinyl /'vaɪnɪl/ ① *n* vinile *m* ② *attrib* ⟨paint⟩ vinilico

viola /vɪ'əʊlə/ *n* Mus viola *f*

violate /'vaɪəleɪt/ *vt* violare

violation /vaɪə'leɪʃn/ *n* violazione *f*

violence /'vaɪələns/ *n* violenza *f*

violent /'vaɪələnt/ *adj* violento

violently /'vaɪələntlɪ/ *adv* violentemente

violet /'vaɪələt/ ① *adj* violetto ② *n* (flower) violetta *f*; (colour) violetto *m*

violin /vaɪə'lɪn/ *n* violino *m*

violinist /vaɪə'lɪnɪst/ *n* violinista *mf*

VIP *n abbr* (very important person) vip *mf*

viper /'vaɪpə(r)/ *n* vipera *f*

virgin /'vɜːdʒɪn/ ① *adj* vergine ② *n* vergine *f*

virginal /'vɜːdʒɪn(ə)l/ *adj* verginale

virginals /'vɜːdʒɪn(ə)lz/ *npl* Mus spinetta *f*

Virginia creeper /vədʒɪnɪə'kriːpə(r)/ *n* vite *f* del Canada

virginity /və'dʒɪnətɪ/ *n* verginità *f*

Virgo /'vɜːgəʊ/ *n* Astr Vergine *f*

virile /'vɪraɪl/ *adj* virile

virility /vɪ'rɪlətɪ/ *n* virilità *f*

virologist /vaɪ'rɒlədʒɪst/ *n* virologo *m*

virtual /'vɜːtjʊəl/ *adj* effettivo

virtually /'vɜːtjʊəlɪ/ *adv* praticamente

virtual reality *n* realtà *f* virtuale

virtue /'vɜːtjuː/ *n* virtù *f inv*; (advantage) vantaggio *m*; **by** or **in ∼ of** a causa di

virtuoso /vɜːtʊ'əʊzəʊ/ *n* (*pl* **-si** /-ziː/) virtuoso *m*

virtuous /'vɜːtjʊəs/ *adj* virtuoso

virulent /'vɪrʊlənt/ *adj* virulento

virus /'vaɪərəs/ *n* virus *m inv*

virus checker *n* Comput (programma *m*) antivirus *m inv*

virus protection *n* Comput protezione *f* antivirus

visa /'viːzə/ *n* visto *m*

vis-à-vis /viːzɑː'viː/ *prep* rispetto a

visceral /'vɪs(ə)rəl/ *adj* ⟨power, performance⟩ viscerale

viscount /'vaɪkaʊnt/ *n* visconte *m*

viscous /'vɪskəs/ *adj* vischioso

visibility /vɪzə'bɪlətɪ/ *n* visibilità *f*

visible /'vɪzəbl/ *adj* visibile

visibly /'vɪzəblɪ/ *adv* visibilmente

vision /'vɪʒn/ *n* visione *f*; (sight) vista *f*

visionary /'vɪʒn(ə)rɪ/ *adj & n* visionario, -a *mf*

vision mixer *n* (person) tecnico *m* del mixaggio video; (equipment) mixaggio *m* video

visit /'vɪzɪt/ ① *n* visita *f* ② *vt* andare a trovare ⟨person⟩; andare da ⟨doctor etc⟩; visitare ⟨town, building⟩

visiting card *n* biglietto *m* da visita

visiting hours *npl* orario *m* delle visite

visiting lecturer *n* conferenziere, -a *mf*

visiting team *n* squadra *f* ospite

visiting time *n* orario *m* delle visite

visitor /'vɪzɪtə(r)/ *n* ospite *mf*; (of town, museum) visitatore, -trice *mf*; (in hotel) cliente *mf*

visitor centre *n* centro *m* di accoglienza e di informazione per i visitatori

visitors' book *n* (in exhibition) albo *m* dei visitatori; (in hotel) registro *m* dei clienti

visor /'vaɪzə(r)/ *n* visiera *f*; Auto parasole *m*

vista /'vɪstə/ *n* (view) panorama *m*

visual /'vɪzjʊəl/ *adj* visivo

visual aids *npl* supporto *m* visivo

visual arts *npl* arti *fpl* visive

visual display unit *n* visualizzatore *m*

visualize /'vɪzjʊəlaɪz/ *vt* visualizzare

visually /'vɪzjʊəlɪ/ *adv* visualmente; **∼ handicapped** non vedente

vital /'vaɪtl/ *adj* vitale

vitality /vaɪ'tælətɪ/ *n* vitalità *f*

vitally /'vaɪtəlɪ/ *adv* estremamente

vital statistics *npl* fam misure *fpl*

vitamin /'vɪtəmɪn/ *n* vitamina *f*

vitreous /'vɪtrɪəs/ *adj* vetroso; ⟨enamel⟩ vetrificato

vitriolic /vɪtrɪ'ɒlɪk/ *adj* Chem di vetriolo; fig al vetriolo

vituperative /vɪ'tjuːp(ə)rətɪv/ *adj* ingiurioso

viva /'vaɪvə/ *n* Br Univ [esame *m*] orale *m*

vivacious /vɪ'veɪʃəs/ *adj* vivace

vivaciously /vɪ'veɪʃəslɪ/ *adv* vivacemente

vivacity /vɪ'væsətɪ/ *n* vivacità *f*

vivid /'vɪvɪd/ *adj* vivido

vividly /'vɪvɪdlɪ/ *adv* in modo vivido

vivisect /'vɪvɪsekt/ *vt* vivisezionare
vivisection /vɪvɪ'sekʃn/ *n* vivisezione *f*
vixen /'vɪksn/ *n* volpe *f* femmina
viz /vɪz/ *adv* cioè
V-neck *n* (neckline) scollo *m* a V; (sweater) maglione *m* con scollo a V
vocabulary /və'kæbjʊlərɪ/ *n* vocabolario *m*; (list) glossario *m*
vocal /'vəʊkl/ *adj* vocale; (vociferous) eloquente
vocal cords *npl* corde *fpl* vocali
vocalist /'vəʊkəlɪst/ *n* vocalista *mf*
vocalize /'vəʊkəlaɪz/ *vt* (fig: express) esprimere a parole; articolare ⟨sound⟩
vocals /'vəʊklz/ *npl* do the ∼ cantare
vocation /və'keɪʃn/ *n* vocazione *f*
vocational /və'keɪʃ(ə)nl/ *adj* di orientamento professionale
vocational course *n* corso *m* di formazione professionale
vociferous /və'sɪfərəs/ *adj* vociante
vodka /'vɒdkə/ *n* vodka *f inv*
vogue /vəʊg/ *n* moda *f*; in ∼ in voga
voice /vɔɪs/ ①- *n* voce *f*
②- *vt* esprimere
voice box *n* Anat laringe *f*
voiceless /'vɔɪslɪs/ *adj* ⟨minority⟩ silenzioso; ⟨group⟩ privo del diritto di parola
voicemail /'vɔɪsmeɪl/ *n* posta *f* elettronica vocale
voice-over *n* voce *f* fuori campo
voice recognition *n* Comput riconoscimento *m* vocale
void /vɔɪd/ ①- *adj* (not valid) nullo; ∼ of privo di
②- *n* vuoto *m*
vol /vɒl/ *abbr* (**volume**) vol.
volatile /'vɒlətaɪl/ *adj* volatile; ⟨person⟩ volubile
volcanic /vɒl'kænɪk/ *adj* vulcanico
volcano /vɒl'keɪnəʊ/ *n* vulcano *m*
volition /və'lɪʃn/ *n* of his own ∼ di sua spontanea volontà
volley /'vɒlɪ/ *n* (of gunfire) raffica *f*; (Tennis) volée *f inv*
volleyball /'vɒlɪbɔːl/ *n* pallavolo *f*
volt /vəʊlt/ *n* volt *m inv*
voltage /'vəʊltɪdə/ *n* Electr voltaggio *m*
voluble /'vɒljʊbl/ *adj* loquace
volume /'vɒljuːm/ *n* volume *m*; (of work, traffic) quantità *f inv*
volume control *n* volume *m*
voluntarily /'vɒləntərɪlɪ/ *adv* volontariamente
voluntary /'vɒləntərɪ/ *adj* volontario

voluntary redundancy *n* Br dimissioni *fpl* volontarie
voluntary work *n* volontariato *m*
volunteer /vɒlən'tɪə(r)/ ①- *n* volontario, -a *mf*
②- *vt* offrire volontariamente ⟨information⟩
③- *vi* offrirsi volontario; Mil arruolarsi come volontario
voluptuous /və'lʌptjʊəs/ *adj* voluttuoso
vomit /'vɒmɪt/ ①- *n* vomito *m*
②- *vt/i* vomitare
voodoo /'vuːduː/ *n* vudù *m inv*
voracious /və'reɪʃəs/ *adj* vorace
vortex /'vɔːteks/ *n* vortice *m*; fig turbine *m*
vote /vəʊt/ ①- *n* voto *m*; (ballot) votazione *f*; (right) diritto *m* di voto; take a ∼ on votare su
②- *vi* votare
③- *vt* ∼ somebody president eleggere qualcuno presidente
▪ **vote down** *vt* (reject by vote) bocciare ai voti
▪ **vote in** *vt* (elect) eleggere
vote of confidence *n* Pol, fig voto *m* di fiducia
vote of thanks *n* discorso *m* di ringraziamento
voter /'vəʊtə(r)/ *n* elettore, -trice *mf*
voting /'vəʊtɪŋ/ *n* votazione *f*
voting age *n* età *f inv* per votare
voting booth *n* cabina *f* elettorale
vouch /vaʊtʃ/ *vi* ∼ for garantire per
voucher /'vaʊtʃə(r)/ *n* buono *m*
vow /vaʊ/ ①- *n* voto *m*
②- *vt* giurare
vowel /'vaʊəl/ *n* vocale *f*
vox pop /vɒks'pɒp/ *n* TV, Radio opinione *f* pubblica
voyage /'vɔɪɪdʒ/ *n* viaggio *m* [marittimo]; (in space) viaggio *m* [nello spazio]
vs *abbr* (**versus**) contro
V-sign *n* (offensive gesture) gestaccio *m*; (victory sign) segno *m* di vittoria
VSO *abbr* (**Voluntary Service Overseas**) servizio *m* civile volontario nei paesi in via di sviluppo
vulgar /'vʌlgə(r)/ *adj* volgare
vulgar fraction *n* Math frazione *f* ordinaria
vulgarity /vʌl'gærətɪ/ *n* volgarità *f inv*
vulnerable /'vʌlnərəbl/ *adj* vulnerabile
vulture /'vʌltʃə(r)/ *n* avvoltoio *m*
vying /'vaɪɪŋ/ ▶ VIE

Ww

w¹, **W** /'dʌblju:/ n (letter) w, W f inv

W² abbr (West) O; abbr Electr (**watt**) w

wad /wɒd/ n batuffolo m; (bundle) rotolo m

wadding /'wɒdɪŋ/ n ovatta f

waddle /'wɒdl/ vi camminare ondeggiando

wade /weɪd/ vi guadare
■ **wade in** vi (fam: start working) mettersi al lavoro; (take part) prendere parte
■ **wade into** vt (attack) scagliarsi contro
■ **wade through** vt fam procedere faticosamente in ⟨book⟩

wader /'weɪdə(r)/ n Zool trampoliere m; ~s (pl: boots) stivaloni mpl di gomma

wafer /'weɪfə(r)/ n cialda f, wafer m inv; Relig ostia f

wafer-thin adj sottilissimo

waffle¹ /'wɒfl/ vi fam blaterare

waffle² n Culin cialda f

waft /wɒft/ ① vt trasportare ② vi diffondersi

wag /wæg/ ① vt (pt/pp **wagged**) agitare ② vi agitarsi

wage¹ /weɪdʒ/ vt dichiarare ⟨war⟩ lanciare ⟨campaign⟩

wage² n & ~s pl salario msg

wage earner n salariato, -a mf

wage packet n busta f paga

wager /'weɪdʒə(r)/ n scommessa f

wage slip n cedolino m dello stipendio

waggle /'wægl/ ① vt dimenare ② vi dimenarsi

wagon /'wægən/ n carro m; Rail vagone m merci; **be on the** ~ fam astenersi dall'alcol

waif /weɪf/ n trovatello, -a mf

wail /weɪl/ ① n piagnucolio m; (of wind) lamento m; (of baby) vagito m ② vi piagnucolare; ⟨wind⟩ lamentarsi; ⟨baby⟩ vagire

Wailing Wall /'weɪlɪŋ/ n Muro m del pianto

waist /weɪst/ n vita f

waistband n cintura f

waistcoat n gilè m inv; (of man's suit) panciotto m

waistline n vita f

waist measurement n giro m vita

wait /weɪt/ ① n attesa f; **lie in** ~ **for** appostarsi per sorprendere ② vi aspettare; ~ **at table** servire ai tavoli; ~ **for** aspettare

③ vt ~ **one's turn** aspettare il proprio turno
■ **wait about**, **wait around** vi aspettare
■ **wait behind** vi trattenersi
■ **wait in** vi rimanere a casa ad aspettare
■ **wait on** vt servire
■ **wait up** vi rimanere alzato ad aspettare; **don't** ~ **up for me** non mi aspettare alzato

waiter /'weɪtə(r)/ n cameriere m

waiter service n servizio m al tavolo

waiting game n **play a** ~ ~ n temporeggiare

waiting list n lista f d'attesa

waiting room n sala f d'aspetto

waitress /'weɪtrɪs/ n cameriera f

waive /weɪv/ vt rinunciare a ⟨claim⟩; non tener conto di ⟨rule⟩

waiver /'weɪvə(r)/ n Jur rinuncia f

wake¹ /weɪk/ ① n veglia f funebre ② vt (pt **woke**, pp **woken**) ~ **[up]** svegliare ③ vi svegliarsi
■ **wake up to** vt ~ up to the fact that... (realize) aprire gli occhi di fronte al fatto che...

wake² n Naut scia f; **in the** ~ **of** fig nella scia di

wakeful /'weɪkfʊl/ adj ⟨night⟩ insonne

waken /'weɪkn/ ① vt svegliare ② vi svegliarsi

wake-up call n sveglia f telefonica

Wales /weɪlz/ n Galles m

walk /wɔːk/ ① n passeggiata f; (gait) andatura f; (path) sentiero m; **go for a** ~ andare a fare una passeggiata; ~ **of life** livello m sociale ② vi camminare; (as opposed to drive etc) andare a piedi; (ramble) passeggiare; '~' Am (at crossing) 'avanti' ③ vt portare a spasso ⟨dog⟩; percorrere ⟨streets⟩
■ **walk away** vi (leave) allontanarsi; ~ **away from** abbandonare ⟨place, person⟩; disinteressarsi di ⟨problem⟩; (survive unscathed) uscire illeso da ⟨accident⟩
■ **walk away with** vt (win easily) vincere senza difficoltà ⟨game, election, prize⟩
■ **walk back** vi ritornare a piedi
■ **walk in** vi entrare all'improvviso
■ **walk into** vt entrare in ⟨room⟩; andare a sbattere contro ⟨door, lamp post⟩; cadere in ⟨trap⟩; trovare facilmente ⟨job⟩
■ **walk off** vi (leave) andarsene

■ **walk off with** vt (win easily) riportare senza difficoltà; (take, steal) portarsi via
■ **walk out** vi ⟨husband, employee⟩ andarsene; ⟨workers⟩ scioperare
■ **walk out of** vt uscire da ⟨room⟩; abbandonare ⟨meeting⟩
■ **walk out on** vt lasciare
■ **walk over** vt ~ all over somebody (defeat) stracciare qualcuno; (treat badly) trattare qualcuno come una pezza da piedi
■ **walk through** vt superare senza difficoltà ⟨exam, interview⟩
■ **walk up** vi (as opposed to taking the lift) salire a piedi; (approach) avvicinarsi

walkabout /'wɔːkəbaʊt/ n escursione f periodica degli aborigeni australiani nell'entroterra; (by royalty) incontro m con la folla; **go ~** ⟨queen, politician⟩ camminare tra la folla

walker /'wɔːkə(r)/ n camminatore, -trice mf; (rambler) escursionista mf

walkie-talkie /wɔːkɪ'tɔːkɪ/ n walkie-talkie m inv

walk-in adj ~ closet stanzino m

walking /'wɔːkɪŋ/ n camminare m; (rambling) fare m delle escursioni

walking boots npl scarponi mpl [da trekking]

walking distance n it's within ~ ~ ci si arriva a piedi

walking frame n Med deambulatore m

walking pace n passo m

walking shoes npl scarpe fpl da passeggio

walking-stick n bastone m da passeggio

walking wounded npl feriti mpl in grado di camminare

Walkman® /'wɔːkmən/ n Walkman® m inv

walk-on ① n Theat comparsa f
② adj ⟨role⟩ piccolo

walkout n sciopero m

walkover n fig vittoria f facile

walkway n passaggio m pedonale

wall /wɔːl/ n muro m; **go to the ~** fam andare a rotoli; **drive somebody up the ~** fam far diventare matto qualcuno
■ **wall up** vt murare

wallchart /'wɔːltʃɑːt/ n tabellone m

walled /wɔːld/ adj ⟨city⟩ fortificato

wallet /'wɒlɪt/ n portafoglio m

wallflower /'wɔːlflaʊə(r)/ n violaciocca f

wall hanging n decorazione f murale

wallop /'wɒləp/ ① n fam colpo m
② vt (pt/pp **walloped**) fam colpire

walloping /'wɒləpɪŋ/ fam ① adj enorme
② adv ~ **great** (very big) enorme
③ n **give somebody a ~** suonarle a qualcuno

wallow /'wɒləʊ/ vi sguazzare; (in self-pity, grief) crogiolarsi

wallpaper /'wɔːlpeɪpə(r)/ ① n tappezzeria f
② vt tappezzare

wall-to-wall adj che copre tutto il pavimento

walnut /'wɔːlnʌt/ n noce f

walrus /'wɔːlrəs/ n tricheco m

waltz /wɔːlts/ ① n valzer m inv
② vi ballare il valzer; **he came ~ing up and said...** fam è arrivato e ha detto con nonchalance...
■ **waltz off with** vt (fam: take, win) portarsi via
■ **waltz through** vt superare facilmente ⟨exam⟩

wan /wɒn/ adj esangue

wand /wɒnd/ n (magic ~) bacchetta f [magica]

wander /'wɒndə(r)/ vi girovagare; (fig: digress) divagare
■ **wander about** vi andare a spasso
■ **wander away** vi allontanarsi
■ **wander off** vi allontanarsi; **I'd better be ~ing off** fam è meglio che vada

wanderer /'wɒndərə(r)/ n vagabondo, -a mf

wanderlust /'wɒndəlʌst/ n smania f dei viaggi

wane /weɪn/ ① n **be on the ~** essere in fase calante
② vi calare

wangle /'wæŋgl/ vt fam rimediare ⟨invitation, holiday⟩

waning /'weɪnɪŋ/ ① n (of moon) calare m; (weakening) declino m
② adj ⟨moon⟩ calante; ⟨popularity⟩ in declino

wannabee /'wɒnəbiː/ n fam persona f che sogna di diventare famosa

want /wɒnt/ ① n (hardship) bisogno m; (lack) mancanza f
② vt volere; (need) aver bisogno di; ~ **[to have] something** volere qualcosa; ~ **to do something** voler fare qualcosa; **we ~ to stay** vogliamo rimanere; **I ~ you to go** voglio che tu vada; **it ~s painting** ha bisogno d'essere dipinto; **you ~ to learn to swim** bisogna che impari a nuotare
③ vi ~ **for** mancare di

wanted /'wɒntɪd/ adj ricercato

wanted list n lista f dei ricercati

wanting /'wɒntɪŋ/ adj **be ~** mancare; **be ~ in** mancare di

wanton /'wɒntən/ adj ⟨cruelty, neglect⟩ gratuito; (morally) debosciato

WAP /wæp/ abbr (**wireless application protocol**) WAP m; ~ **phone** telefonino WAP

WAP-enabled /ɪ'neɪbld/ adj ⟨device, system⟩ abilitato al WAP

war /wɔ:(r)/ n guerra f; fig lotta f (**on** contro); **at** ~ in guerra

warble /'wɔ:bl/ vt/i trillare; ⟨singer⟩ gorgheggiare

war cabinet n consiglio m di guerra

war cry n grido m di guerra

ward /wɔ:d/ n (in hospital) reparto m; (child) minore m sotto tutela
- **ward off** vt evitare; parare ⟨blow⟩

warden /'wɔ:dn/ n guardiano, -a mf

warder /'wɔ:də(r)/ n guardia f carceraria

wardrobe /'wɔ:drəʊb/ n guardaroba m

wardrobe assistant n costumista mf

ward round n Med giro m delle corsie

ward sister n Br Med caposala f inv

warehouse /'weəhaʊs/ n magazzino m

wares /weəz/ npl merci mpl

warfare /'wɔ:feə(r)/ n guerra f

war game n Mil simulazione f di scontro militare

warhead n testata f

warhorse n cavallo m da battaglia; (fig: campaigner) veterano m

warily /'weərɪlɪ/ adv cautamente

warlike /'wɔ:laɪk/ adj bellicoso

warm /wɔːm/ ① adj caldo; ⟨welcome⟩ caloroso; **be** ~ ⟨person⟩ aver caldo; **it is** ~ ⟨weather⟩ fa caldo
② vt scaldare
- **warm to** vt prendere in simpatia ⟨person⟩
- **warm up** vt scaldare vi scaldarsi; fig animarsi

warm-blooded /-'blʌdɪd/ adj Zool con temperatura corporea costante

war memorial n monumento m ai caduti

warm-hearted /-'hɑ:tɪd/ adj espansivo

warmly /'wɔ:mlɪ/ adv ⟨greet⟩ calorosamente; ⟨dress⟩ in modo pesante

warmongering /'wɔ:mʌŋgərɪŋ/ ① n bellicismo m
② adj ⟨article⟩ bellicistico; ⟨person⟩ guerrafondaio

warmth /wɔ:mθ/ n calore m

warm-up n Sport riscaldamento m; (of musicians) prove fpl

warn /wɔ:n/ vt avvertire
- **warn off** vt dare un avvertimento a

warning /'wɔ:nɪŋ/ n avvertimento m; (advance notice) preavviso m

warning light n spia f luminosa

warning shot n sparo m d'avvertimento

warning sign n (road sign) segnale m di pericolo; (of illness) segnale m d'allarme

warning triangle n triangolo m di segnalazione

warp /wɔ:p/ ① vt deformare; fig distorcere

② vi deformarsi

warpaint /'wɔ:peɪnt/ n Mil pitture fpl di guerra

warpath /'wɔ:pɑ:θ/ n **on the** ~ sul sentiero di guerra

warped /wɔ:pt/ adj deformato; ⟨personality⟩ contorto; ⟨sexuality⟩ deviato; ⟨view⟩ distorto

warplane /'wɔ:pleɪn/ n aereo m da guerra

warrant /'wɒrənt/ ① n (for arrest, search) mandato m
② vt (justify) giustificare; (guarantee) garantire

warranty /'wɒrəntɪ/ n garanzia f

warren /'wɒr(ə)n/ n (of rabbits) area f piena di tane di conigli; (building, maze of streets) labirinto m

warring /'wɔ:rɪŋ/ adj in guerra

warrior /'wɒrɪə(r)/ n guerriero, -a mf

Warsaw /'wɔ:sɔ:/ n Varsavia f

warship /'wɔ:ʃɪp/ n nave f da guerra

wart /wɔ:t/ n porro m

wartime /'wɔ:taɪm/ n tempo m di guerra

war-torn /'wɔ:tɔ:n/ adj logorato dalla guerra

wary /'weərɪ/ adj (-ier, -iest) (careful) cauto; (suspicious) diffidente

was /wɒz/ ▸ BE

wash /wɒʃ/ ① n lavata f; (clothes) bucato m; (in washing machine) lavaggio m; **have a** ~ darsi una lavata
② vt lavare; ⟨sea⟩ bagnare; ~ **one's hands** lavarsi le mani
③ vi lavarsi
- **wash away** vt ⟨rain⟩ portare via; ⟨sea, floodwaters⟩ spazzare via
- **wash off** ① vt lavar via ⟨stain, mud⟩
② vi andar via
- **wash out** vt sciacquare ⟨soap⟩; sciacquarsi ⟨mouth⟩
- **wash up** ① vt lavare
② vi lavare i piatti; Am lavarsi

washable /'wɒʃəbl/ adj lavabile

wash-and-wear adj che non si stira

wash bag n Br = TOILET BAG

washbasin n lavandino m

washbowl n Am = WASHBASIN

wash cloth n Am ≈ guanto m da bagno

washed out /wɒʃt'aʊt/ adj (faded) scolorito; (tired) spossato

washed up adj fam (finished) finito; (tired) distrutto

washer /'wɒʃə(r)/ n Techn guarnizione f; (machine) lavatrice f

washer-dryer /-'draɪə(r)/ n asciugabiancheria m inv

washing /'wɒʃɪŋ/ n bucato m

washing line n corda f per il bucato

washing machine n lavatrice f

washing powder n detersivo m

washing soda n soda f da bucato

washing-up n do the ~ lavare i piatti

washing-up bowl n bacinella f (per i piatti)

washing-up liquid n detersivo m per i piatti

washing-up water n rigovernatura f

wash load n carico m di lavatrice

wash-out n disastro m

washroom n bagno m

wash-stand n Am = WASHBASIN

WASP or **Wasp** /wɒsp/ n abbr Am (**White Anglo-Saxon Protestant**) WASP m

wasp /wɒsp/ n vespa f

waspish /'wɒspɪʃ/ adj pungente

wastage /'weɪstɪdʒ/ n perdita f

waste /weɪst/ ① n spreco m; (rubbish) rifiuto m; ~s pl distesa fsg desolata; ~ of time perdita f di tempo
② adj ⟨product⟩ di scarto; ⟨land⟩ desolato; lay ~ devastare
③ vt sprecare
∎ **waste away** vi deperire

wastebasket n cestino m della carta straccia

waste bin n (for paper) cestino m della carta straccia; (for rubbish) secchio m della spazzatura

wasted /'weɪstɪd/ adj ⟨energy, effort, life⟩ sprecato; ⟨limb⟩ atrofizzato; body scarnito

waste disposal n smaltimento m dei rifiuti

waste disposal unit n eliminatore m di rifiuti

wasteful /'weɪstfʊl/ adj dispendioso

wasteland n area f desolata

waste paper n carta f straccia

waste-paper basket n cestino m per la carta [straccia]

waste pipe n tubo m di scarico

watch /wɒtʃ/ ① n guardia f; (period of duty) turno m di guardia; (timepiece) orologio m; be on the ~ stare all'erta
② vt guardare ⟨film, match, television⟩; (be careful of, look after) stare attento a
③ vi guardare
∎ **watch out** vi (be careful) stare attento (for a)
∎ **watch out for** vt (look for) fare attenzione all'arrivo di ⟨person⟩
∎ **watch over** vt proteggere ⟨person⟩

watchband n Am = WATCH STRAP

watchdog /'wɒtʃdɒg/ n cane m da guardia

watchful /'wɒtʃfʊl/ adj attento

watchfully /'wɒtʃfʊlɪ/ adv attentamente

watchmaker n orologiaio, -a mf

watchman n guardiano m

watch strap n cinturino m dell'orologio

watchtower n torre f di guardia

watchword n motto m

water /'wɔːtə(r)/ ① n acqua f; ~s pl acque fpl
② vt annaffiare ⟨garden, plant⟩; (dilute) annacquare; dare da bere a ⟨horse etc⟩
③ vi ⟨eyes⟩ lacrimare; my mouth was ~ing avevo l'acquolina in bocca
∎ **water down** vt diluire; fig attenuare

water authority n ente m dell'acqua

water bed n materasso m ad acqua

waterbird n uccello m acquatico

water birth n parto m in acqua

water bottle n borraccia f

water cannon n idrante m

watercolour n acquerello m

water company n società f inv dell'acqua

watercress n crescione m

water divining n rabdomanzia f

waterfall n cascata f

water filter n brocca f con filtro per l'acqua

waterfront n (by lakeside, riverside) riva f; (on harbour) zona f portuale

water-heater n scaldacqua m inv

waterhole n pozza f d'acqua

watering can /'wɔːtərɪŋ/ n annaffiatoio m

water jump n riviera f

water lily n ninfea f

waterline n linea f di galleggiamento

waterlogged adj inzuppato

water main n conduttura f dell'acqua

watermark n filigrana f

watermeadow n marcita f

watermelon n cocomero m, anguria f

watermill n mulino m ad acqua

water polo n pallanuoto f

water-power n energia f idraulica

waterproof ① adj ⟨coat⟩ impermeabile; ⟨make-up⟩ waterproof inv
② n impermeabile m

waterproofs npl sovrapantaloni mpl e giacca impermeabili

water rates mpl Br tariffe fpl dell'acqua

water-resistant adj ⟨sun cream⟩ resistente all'acqua; ⟨garment, watch⟩ impermeabile

watershed n spartiacque m inv; fig svolta f

waterside ① n riva f
② attrib ⟨cafe, hotel⟩ sulla riva

water-ski vi fare sci nautico

waterskiing n sci m nautico

water slide n acquascivolo m

water softener *n* (equipment) addolcitore *m*; (substance) anticalcare *m inv*

water-soluble *adj* idrosolubile

water sport *n* sport *m inv* acquatico

water-table *n* Geog superficie *f* freatica

watertight *adj* stagno; fig irrefutabile

water tower *n* serbatoio *m* idrico a torre

waterway *n* canale *m* navigabile

water-wheel *n* ruota *f* idraulica

water wings *npl* braccioli *mpl*

waterworks *n* impianto *m* idrico; **turn on the ~** fam mettersi a piangere come una fontana

watery /'wɔːtərɪ/ *adj* acquoso; ⟨eyes⟩ lacrimoso

watt /wɒt/ *n* watt *m inv*

wattage /'wɒtɪdʒ/ *n* wattaggio *m*

wave /weɪv/ **①** *n* onda *f*; (gesture) cenno *m*; fig ondata *f*
② *vt* agitare; **~ one's hand** agitare la mano
③ *vi* far segno; ⟨flag⟩ sventolare
■ **wave aside** *vt* respingere ⟨criticism⟩
■ **wave down** *vt* far segno di fermarsi a ⟨vehicle⟩

waveband /'weɪvbænd/ *n* gamma *f* d'onda

wavelength /'weɪvleŋθ/ *n* lunghezza *f* d'onda; **be on the same ~** fig essere sulla stessa lunghezza d'onda

waver /'weɪvə(r)/ *vi* vacillare; (hesitate) esitare

wavy /'weɪvɪ/ *adj* ondulato

wax /wæks/ *vi* ⟨moon⟩ crescere; (fig: become) diventare

wax² **①** *n* cera *f*; (in ear) cerume *m*
② *vt* dare la cera a

waxed jacket /wækst/ *n* cerata *f*

waxwork /'wækswɔːk/ *n* statua *f* di cera

waxworks /'wækswɔːks/ *n* museo *m* delle cere

waxy /'wæksɪ/ *adj* ⟨skin, texture⟩ cereo

way /weɪ/ **①** *n* percorso *m*; (direction) direzione *f*; (manner, method) modo *m*; **~s** *pl* (customs) abitudini *fpl*; **be in the ~** essere in mezzo; **on the ~** to Rome andando a Roma; **I'll do it on the ~** lo faccio mentre vado; **it's on my ~** è sul mio percorso; **a long ~ off** lontano; **this ~** da questa parte; (like this) così; **by the ~** a proposito; **by ~ of** come; (via) via; **either ~** (whatever we do) in un modo o nell'altro; **in some ~s** sotto certi aspetti; **in a ~** in un certo senso; **in a bad ~** ⟨person⟩ molto grave; **out of the ~** fuori mano; **under ~** in corso; **lead the ~** far strada; fig aprire la strada; **make ~** far posto (**for** a); **give ~** Auto dare la precedenza; **go out of one's ~** fig scomodarsi (**to** per); **get one's [own] ~** averla vinta

② *adv* **~ behind** molto indietro

way in *n* entrata *f*

waylay /weɪ'leɪ/ *vt* (pt/pp **-laid**) aspettare al varco ⟨person⟩; intercettare ⟨letter⟩

way-out *adj* fam eccentrico

way out *n* uscita *f*; fig via *f* d'uscita

wayside /'weɪsaɪd/ *n* bordo *m*; **fall by the ~** (morally) smarrire la retta via; (fail) fallire

wayward /'weɪwəd/ *adj* capriccioso

WC *abbr* WC; **the WC** il gabinetto

we /wiː/ *pers pron* noi; **we're the last** siamo gli ultimi; **they're going, but we're not** loro vanno, ma noi no

weak /wiːk/ *adj* debole; ⟨liquid⟩ leggero; **go ~ at the knees** fam sentirsi piegare le ginocchia

weaken /'wiːkn/ **①** *vt* indebolire
② *vi* indebolirsi

weakling /'wiːklɪŋ/ *n* smidollato, -a *mf*

weakly /'wiːklɪ/ *adv* debolmente

weak-minded /-'maɪndɪd/ *adj* (indecisive) debole; (simple) poco intelligente

weakness /'wiːknɪs/ *n* debolezza *f*; (liking) debole *m*

weak-willed /-'wɪld/ *adj* debole

weal /wiːl/ *n* piaga *f*

wealth /welθ/ *n* ricchezza *f*; fig gran quantità *f*

wealthy /'welθɪ/ *adj* (**-ier**, **-iest**) ricco

wean /wiːn/ *vt* svezzare

weapon /'wepən/ *n* arma *f*

weapon of mass destruction *n* arma *f* di distruzione di massa

weaponry /'wepənrɪ/ *n* armamento *m*

wear /weə(r)/ **①** *n* (clothing) abbigliamento *m*; **for everyday ~** da portare tutti i giorni; **~ [and tear]** usura *f*
② *vt* (pt **wore**, pp **worn**) portare; (damage) consumare; **~ a hole in something** logorare qualcosa fino a fare un buco; **what shall I ~?** cosa mi metto?
③ *vi* consumarsi; (last) durare
■ **wear away** **①** *vt* consumare
② *vi* consumarsi
■ **wear down** *vt* estenuare ⟨opposition etc⟩
■ **wear off** *vi* scomparire; ⟨effect⟩ finire
■ **wear out** **①** *vt* consumare [fino in fondo]; (exhaust) estenuare
② *vi* estenuarsi
■ **wear through** *vi* ⟨elbow, knee, shoe⟩ bucarsi

wearable /'weərəbl/ *adj* portabile

wearily /'wɪərɪlɪ/ *adv* stancamente

weariness /'wɪərɪnɪs/ *n* stanchezza *f*

wearing /'weərɪŋ/ *adj* (tiring) faticoso; (irritating) fastidioso

weary /'wɪərɪ/ **①** *adj* (**-ier**, **-iest**) sfinito
② *vt* (pt/pp **wearied**) sfinire

W

3 *vi* ∼ **of** stancarsi di

weasel /'wi:zl/ *n* donnola *f*

weather /'weðə(r)/ **1** *n* tempo *m*; **in this** ∼ con questo tempo; **under the** ∼ fam giù di corda
2 *vt* sopravvivere a ⟨*storm*⟩

weather balloon *n* pallone *m* sonda

weather-beaten /-bi:tn/ *adj* ⟨*face*⟩ segnato dalle intemperie

weathercock *n* gallo *m* segnavento

weather forecast *n* previsioni *fpl* del tempo

weatherman *n* TV meteorologo *m*

weatherproof *adj* ⟨*garment, shoe*⟩ impermeabile; ⟨*shelter, door*⟩ resistente alle intemperie

weather-vane *n* banderuola *f*

weave¹ /wi:v/ *vi* (pt/pp **weaved**) (move) zigzagare

weave² **1** *n* (Tex) tessuto *m*
2 *vt* (pt **wove**, pp **woven**) tessere; intrecciare ⟨*flowers etc*⟩; intrecciare le fila di ⟨*story etc*⟩

weaver /'wi:və(r)/ *n* tessitore, -trice *mf*

weaving /'wi:vɪŋ/ *n* tessitura *f*

web /web/ *n* rete *f*; Comput web *m*, rete *f*; (of spider) ragnatela *f*

web-based /beɪst/ *adj* ⟨*learning, software*⟩ basato sul web

webbed feet /webd'fi:t/ *npl* piedi *mpl* palmati

webbing /'webɪŋ/ *n* (material) cinghie *fpl*

web cam /kæm/ *n* Comput web cam *f inv*

web developer *n* Comput sviluppatore *m* web

weblog /'weblɒg/ *n* Comput = BLOG

weblogger /'weblɒgə(r)/ *n* Comput = BLOGGER

webmaster *n* Comput webmaster *mf inv*

web page *n* Comput pagina *f* web

web presence *n* Comput presenza *f* in Internet

web server *n* Comput server *m* web

web site *n* Comput sito *m* web

web space *n* Comput spazio *m* web

wed /wed/ **1** *vt* (pt/pp **wedded**) sposare
2 *vi* sposarsi

wedding /'wedɪŋ/ *n* matrimonio *m*

wedding anniversary *n* anniversario *m* di nozze

wedding bells *npl* fig marcia *f* nuziale

wedding breakfast *n* rinfresco *m* di nozze

wedding cake *n* torta *f* nuziale

wedding day *n* giorno *m* del matrimonio

wedding dress *n* vestito *m* da sposa

wedding march *n* marcia *f* nuziale

wedding night *n* prima notte *f* di nozze

wedding reception *n* ricevimento *m* di nozze

wedding ring *n* fede *f*

wedding vows *npl* voti *mpl* nuziali

wedge /wedʒ/ **1** *n* zeppa *f*; (for splitting wood) cuneo *m*; (of cheese) fetta *f*
2 *vt* (fix) fissare

wedlock /'wedlɒk/ *n* **born out of** ∼ nato fuori dal matrimonio

Wednesday /'wenzdeɪ/ *n* mercoledì *m inv*

wee¹ /wi:/ *adj* fam piccolo

wee² **1** *n* fam **do a** ∼ fare la pipì
2 *vi* fam fare la pipì

weed /wi:d/ **1** *n* erbaccia *f*; (fam: person) mollusco *m*
2 *vt* estirpare le erbacce da
3 *vi* estirpare le erbacce
■ **weed out** *vt* fig eliminare

weedkiller /'wi:dkɪlə(r)/ *n* erbicida *m*

weedy /'wi:dɪ/ *adj* fam mingherlino

week /wi:k/ *n* settimana *f*

weekday /'wi:kdeɪ/ *n* giorno *m* feriale

weekend /'wi:kend/ *n* fine *m* settimana

weekend bag *n* piccola borsa *f* da viaggio

weekly /'wi:klɪ/ **1** *adj* settimanale
2 *n* settimanale *m*
3 *adv* settimanalmente

weep /wi:p/ *vi* (pt/pp **wept**) piangere

weeping willow /wi:pɪŋ'wɪləʊ/ *n* salice *m* piangente

weepy /'wi:pɪ/ *adj* ⟨*film*⟩ strappalacrime *inv*

weigh /weɪ/ *vt/i* pesare; ∼ **anchor** levare l'ancora
■ **weigh down** *vt* fig piegare
■ **weigh in** *vi* (fam: join in discussion) intromettersi
■ **weigh out** *vt* pesare ⟨*flour*⟩
■ **weigh up** *vt* fig soppesare; valutare ⟨*person*⟩

weighing machine /'weɪŋ/ *n* bilancia *f*

weight /weɪt/ *n* peso *m*; **put on/lose** ∼ ingrassare/dimagrire

weighting /'weɪtɪŋ/ *n* (allowance) indennità *f inv*

weightlessness /'weɪtlɪsnɪs/ *n* assenza *f* di gravità

weightlifter *n* sollevatore *m* di pesi

weightlifting *n* sollevamento *m* pesi

weight problem *n* problemi *mpl* di peso

weight training *n* **do** ∼ ∼ allenarsi con i pesi

weight-watcher *n* (in group) persona *f* che segue una dieta dimagrante

weighty /'weɪtɪ/ *adj* (**-ier, -iest**) pesante; (important) di un certo peso

weir /wɪə(r)/ *n* chiusa *f*

weird /wɪəd/ *adj* misterioso; (bizarre) bizzarro

welcome /'welkəm/ **1** *adj* benvenuto; you're ~! prego!; you're ~ to have it/to come prendilo/vieni pure
2 *n* accoglienza *f*
3 *vt* accogliere; (appreciate) gradire

welcoming /'welkəmɪŋ/ *adj* ⟨ceremony⟩ di benvenuto; ⟨committee, smile⟩ di accoglienza; ⟨house⟩ accogliente

weld /weld/ *vt* saldare

welder /'weldə(r)/ *n* saldatore *m*

welfare /'welfeə(r)/ *n* benessere *m*; (aid) assistenza *f*; Am previdenza *f* sociale

welfare services *n* servizi *mpl* sociali

Welfare State *n* Stato *m* assistenziale

welfare work *n* assistenza *m* sociale

well[1] /wel/ *n* pozzo *m*; (oil ~) pozzo *m*; (of staircase) tromba *f*

well[2] **1** *adv* (better, best) bene; as ~ anche; as ~ as (in addition) oltre a; ~ done! bravo!; very ~ benissimo
2 *adj* he is not ~ non sta bene; get ~ soon! guarisci presto!
3 *int* beh!; ~ I never! ma va'!

well-attended /-ə'tendɪd/ *adj* ben frequentato

well-balanced /'bælənst/ *adj* ⟨person, diet, meal⟩ equilibrato

well-behaved /-bɪ'heɪvd/ *adj* educato

well-being /'welbiːɪŋ/ *n* benessere *m*

well-bred /wel'bred/ *adj* beneducato

well-defined /-dɪ'faɪnd/ *adj* ⟨role, boundary⟩ ben definito; ⟨outline, image⟩ netto

well-disposed /-dɪ'spəʊzd/ *adj* benevolo; be ~ towards essere bendisposto verso ⟨person⟩; essere favorevole a ⟨idea⟩

well done /dʌn/ *adj* ⟨task⟩ ben fatto; Culin ben cotto

well-educated *adj* istruito; (cultured) colto

well-founded /-'faʊndɪd/ *adj* fondato

well-heeled /-'hiːld/ *adj* fam danaroso

well-informed /-ɪn'fɔːmd/ *adj* beninformato

wellingtons /'welɪŋtənz/ *npl* stivali *mpl* di gomma

well-judged /-'dʒʌdʒd/ *adj* ⟨performance⟩ molto intelligente; ⟨shot⟩ ben assestato; ⟨statement, phrase⟩ ponderato

well-kept /-'kept/ *adj* ⟨garden⟩ curato; ⟨secret⟩ ben custodito

well-known /-'nəʊn/ *adj* famoso

well-liked /-'laɪkt/ *adj* popolare

well-made /-'meɪd/ *adj* benfatto

well-mannered /-'mænəd/ *adj* educato

well-meaning *adj* con buone intenzioni

well-meant /-'ment/ *adj* con le migliori intenzioni

well-nigh /'welnaɪ/ *adv* quasi

well-off *adj* benestante

well-read /-'red/ *adj* colto

well-respected /rɪ'spektɪd/ *adj* molto rispettato

well-rounded /'raʊndɪd/ *adj* ⟨education, individual⟩ completo

well-spoken /-'spəʊkən/ *adj* ⟨person⟩ che parla bene

well-thought-of *adj* stimato

well-timed /'taɪmd/ *adj* tempestivo

well-to-do *adj* ricco

well-trodden /-'trɒdn/ *adj* also fig battuto

well-wisher /'welwɪʃə(r)/ *n* simpatizzante *mf*

well-worn /-'wɔːn/ *adj* ⟨steps, floorboards⟩ consunto; ⟨carpet, garment⟩ logoro; fig ⟨argument⟩ trito e ritrito

Welsh /welʃ/ *adj & n* gallese *mf*; (language) gallese *m*; the ~ *pl* i gallesi

Welshman /'welʃmən/ *n* gallese *m*

Welsh rabbit *n* toast *m* inv al formaggio

welt /welt/ *n* (on shoe) rinforzo *m*; (on skin) segno *m* di frustata

welterweight /'weltəweɪt/ *n* pesi *mpl* welter

went /went/ ▶ GO

wept /wept/ ▶ WEEP

were /wɜː(r)/ ▶ BE

west /west/ **1** *n* ovest *m*; to the ~ of a ovest di; the W~ l'Occidente *m*
2 *adj* occidentale
3 *adv* verso occidente; go ~ fam andare in malora

West Bank *n* Cisgiordania *f*

West Country *n* sud-ovest *m* dell'Inghilterra

West End *n* zona *f* di Londra con un'alta concentrazione di teatri e negozi di lusso

westerly /'westəlɪ/ *adj* verso ovest; occidentale ⟨wind⟩

western /'westən/ **1** *adj* occidentale
2 *n* western *m* inv

Westerner /'westənə(r)/ *n* occidentale *mf*

westernize /'westənaɪz/ *vt* occidentalizzare; become ~d occidentalizzarsi

Western Samoa /sə'məʊə/ *n* Samoa *fpl* Occidentali

West Germany *n* Germania *f* occidentale

West Indian *adj & n* antillese *mf*

w

West Indies /'ɪndɪz/ *npl* Antille *fpl*

westward[s] /'westwəd[z]/ *adv* verso ovest

wet /wet/ ➊ *adj* (**-tter, -test**) bagnato; fresco ⟨*paint*⟩; (rainy) piovoso; fam ⟨*person*⟩ smidollato; **get ~** bagnarsi
➋ *vt* (*pt/pp* **wet, wetted**) bagnare

wet blanket *n* guastafeste *mf inv*

wet fish *n* Br pesce *m* fresco

wet-look *adj* ⟨*plastic, leather*⟩ lucido

wetsuit *n* muta *f*

whack /wæk/ ➊ *n* fam colpo *m*
➋ *vt* fam dare un colpo a

whacked /wæk/ *adj* fam stanco morto

whacking /'wækɪŋ/ ➊ *adj* (Br fam: enormous) enorme
➋ *n* fam sculacciata *f*

whale /weɪl/ *n* balena *f*; **have a ~ of a time** fam divertirsi un sacco

whaling /'weɪlɪŋ/ *n* caccia *f* alla balena

wham /wæm/ *int* bum!

wharf /wɔːf/ *n* banchina *f*

what /wɒt/ ➊ *pron* che, [che] cosa; **~ for?** perché?; **~ is that for?** a che cosa serve?; **~ is it?** (what do you want) cosa c'è?; **~ is it like?** com'è?; **~ is your name?** come ti chiami?; **~ is the weather like?** com'è il tempo?; **~ is the film about?** di cosa parla il film?; **~ is he talking about?** di cosa sta parlando?; **he asked me ~ she had said** mi ha chiesto cosa ha detto; **~ about going to the cinema?** e se andassimo al cinema?; **~ about the children?** (what will they do) e i bambini?; **~ if it rains?** e se piove?
➋ *adj* quale, che; **take ~ books you want** prendi tutti i libri che vuoi; **~ kind of** che tipo di; **at ~ time?** a che ora?
➌ *adv* che; **~ a lovely day!** che bella giornata!
➍ *int* **~!** [che] cosa!; **~?** [che] cosa?

what-d'yer-call-it /'wɒtdʒəkɔːlɪt/ *n* fam aggeggio *m*

whatever /wɒt'evə(r)/ ➊ *adj* qualunque
➋ *pron* qualsiasi cosa; **~ is it?** cos'è?; **~ he does** qualsiasi cosa faccia; **~ happens** qualunque cosa succeda; **nothing ~** proprio niente

whatnot /'wɒtnɒt/ *n* coso *m*; (stand) scaffaletto *m*; **and ~** (and so on) e così via

what's-her-name /'wɒtzəneɪm/ *n* fam cosa *f*

what's-his-name /'wɒtsɪzneɪm/ *n*, fam, coso *m*

whatsit /'wɒtsɪt/ *n* fam aggeggio *m*, coso *m*

what's-its-name *n* fam coso, -a *mf*

whatsoever /wɒtsəʊ'evə(r)/ *adj & pron* = WHATEVER

wheat /wiːt/ *n* grano *m*, frumento *m*

wheatgerm /'wiːtdʒɜːm/ *n* germoglio *m* di grano

wheatmeal /'wiːtmiːl/ *n* farina *f* di frumento

wheedle /'wiːdl/ *vt* **~ something out of somebody** ottenere qualcosa da qualcuno con le lusinghe

wheel /wiːl/ ➊ *n* ruota *f*; (steering **~**) volante *m*; **at the ~** al volante
➋ *vt* (push) spingere
➌ *vi* (circle) ruotare; **~ round** ruotare

wheelbarrow *n* carriola *f*

wheelchair *n* sedia *f* a rotelle

wheelchair access *n* accesso *m* disabili

wheelchair-accessible *adj* accessibile alle carrozzelle, accessibile alle sedie a rotelle

wheel clamp *n* ceppo *m* bloccaruote

wheeler-dealer /wiːlə'diːlə(r)/ *n* trafficone, -a *mf*

wheelie bin /'wiːlɪ/ *n* cassonetto *m*

wheeze /wiːz/ *vi* ansimare

wheezy /'wiːzɪ/ *adj* ⟨*voice, cough*⟩ dal respiro affannoso

when /wen/ *adv & conj* quando; **the day ~** il giorno in cui; **~ swimming/reading** nuotando/leggendo

whence /wens/ *adv* liter donde

whenever /wen'evə(r)/ *adv & conj* in qualsiasi momento; (every time that) ogni volta che; **~ did it happen?** quando è successo?

where /weə(r)/ *adv & conj* dove; **the street ~ I live** la via in cui abito; **~ do you come from?** da dove vieni?

whereabouts[1] /'weərəbaʊts/ *adv* dove

whereabouts[2] /'weərəbaʊts/ *n* **nobody knows his ~** nessuno sa dove si trovi

whereas /weər'æz/ *conj* dal momento che; (in contrast) mentre

whereby /weə'baɪ/ *adv* attraverso il quale

whereupon /weərə'pɒn/ *adv* dopo di che

wherever /weər'evə(r)/ *adv & conj* dovunque; **~ is he?** dov'è mai?; **~ possible** dovunque sia possibile

wherewithal /'weəwɪðɔːl/ *n* mezzi *mpl*

whet /wet/ *vt* (*pt/pp* **whetted**) aguzzare ⟨*appetite*⟩

whether /'weðə(r)/ *conj* se; **~ you like it or not** che ti piaccia o no

whew /fjuː/ *int* (in relief) fiuu; (when hot) uff; (in surprise) wow

which /wɪtʃ/ ➊ *adj & pron* quale; **~ one?** quale?; **~ one of you?** chi di voi?; **~ way?** (direction) in che direzione?
➋ *rel pron* (object) che; **~ he does frequently** cosa che fa spesso; **after ~** dopo di che; **on/in ~** su/in cui

w

whichever /wɪtʃ'evə(r)/ *adj & pron*
qualunque; ∼ **it is** qualunque sia; ∼ **one
of you** chiunque tra voi

whiff /wɪf/ *n* zaffata *f*; **have a** ∼ **of
something** odorare qualcosa

while /waɪl/ **①** *n* **a long** ∼ un bel po'; **a
little** ∼ un po'
② *conj* mentre; (as long as) finché; (although)
sebbene; **he met her** ∼ **in exile** l'ha
incontrata mentre era in esilio
■ **while away** *vt* passare ⟨time⟩

whilst /waɪlst/ *conj* = WHILE

whim /wɪm/ *n* capriccio *m*

whimper /'wɪmpə(r)/ *vi* piagnucolare;
⟨dog⟩ mugolare

whimsical /'wɪmzɪkl/ *adj* capriccioso;
⟨story⟩ fantasioso

whine /waɪn/ **①** *n* lamento *m*; (of dog)
guaito *m*
② *vi* lamentarsi; ⟨dog⟩ guaire

whinge /wɪndʒ/ *vi* fam lagnarsi

whining /'waɪnɪŋ/ **①** *adj* ⟨voice, child⟩
lagnoso
② *n* (complaints) lagne *fpl*; (of dog) guaiti
mpl

whinny /'wɪnɪ/ **①** *n* nitrito *m*
② *vi* ⟨horse⟩ nitrire

whip /wɪp/ **①** *n* frusta *f*; (Pol: person)
parlamentare *mf* incaricato, -a di
assicurarsi della presenza dei membri del
suo partito alle votazioni
② *vt* (pt/pp **whipped**) frustare; Culin
sbattere; (snatch) afferrare; (fam: steal)
fregare
■ **whip up** *vt* (incite) stimolare; fam
improvvisare ⟨meal⟩

whiplash injury /'wɪplæʃ/ *n* Med colpo
m di frusta

whipped cream /wɪpt'kriːm/ *n* panna
f montata

whipping boy /'wɪpɪŋ/ *n* capro *m*
espiatorio

whip-round *n* fam colletta *f*; **have a** ∼
fare una colletta

whirl /wɜːl/ **①** *n* (movement) rotazione *f*;
my mind's in a ∼ ho le idee confuse
② *vi* girare rapidamente
③ *vt* far girare rapidamente

whirlpool /'wɜːlpuːl/ *n* vortice *m*

whirlpool bath *n* vasca *f* con
idromassaggio

whirlwind /'wɜːlwɪnd/ *n* turbine *m*

whirr /wɜː(r)/ *vi* ronzare

whisk /wɪsk/ **①** *n* Culin frullino *m*
② *vt* Culin frullare
■ **whisk away** *vt* portare via

whisker /'wɪskə(r)/ *n* ∼**s** *pl* (of cat) baffi
mpl; (on man's cheek) basette *fpl*; **by a** ∼ per
un pelo

whisky /'wɪskɪ/ *n* whisky *m inv*

whisper /'wɪspə(r)/ **①** *n* sussurro *m*;
(rumour) diceria *f*

② *vt/i* sussurrare

whispering gallery /'wɪspərɪŋ/ *n*
galleria *f* acustica

whistle /'wɪsl/ **①** *n* fischio *m*; (instrument)
fischietto *m*
② *vt* fischiettare
③ *vi* fischiettare; ⟨referee⟩ fischiare

whistle-stop tour *n* Pol giro *m*
elettorale

white /waɪt/ **①** *adj* bianco; **go** ∼ (pale)
sbiancare
② *n* bianco *m*; (of egg) albume *m*; (person)
bianco, -a *mf*

whitebait *n* bianchetti *npl*

white-board *n* lavagna *f* bianca

white coffee *n* caffè *m inv* macchiato

white-collar worker *n* colletto *m*
bianco

white elephant *n* (public project)
progetto *m* dispendioso e di scarsa
efficacia; (building) cattedrale *f* nel deserto;
(item, knick-knack) oggetto *m* inutile

white goods *n* (linen) biancheria *f* per
la casa; (appliances) elettrodomestici *mpl*

Whitehall *n* strada *f* di Londra sede
degli uffici del governo britannico; fig
amministrazione *f* britannica

white horses *npl* cavalloni *mpl*

white-hot *adj* ⟨metal⟩ arroventato

White House *n* **the** ∼ la Casa Bianca

white knight *n* Fin white knight *m inv*

white-knuckle ride *n* corsa *f* al
cardiopalmo

white lie *n* bugia *f* pietosa

whiten /'waɪtn/ **①** *vt* imbiancare
② *vi* sbiancare

whitener /'waɪt(ə)nə(r)/ *n* (for shoes)
bianchetto *m*; (for clothes) sbiancante *m*; (for
coffee, tea) surrogato *m* del latte

whiteness /'waɪtnɪs/ *n* bianchezza *f*

white spirit *n* acquaragia *f*

white tie *n* (tie) cravattino *m* bianco;
(formal dress) frac *m inv*

whitewash *n* intonaco *m*; fig copertura *f*
vt dare una mano d'intonaco a; fig coprire

white water *n* rapide *fpl*

white-water rafting /'rɑːftɪŋ/ *n*
discesa *f* sulle rapide

white wedding *n* matrimonio *m* in
bianco

whither /'wɪðə(r)/ *adv* liter dove

whiting /'waɪtɪŋ/ *n* (fish) merlano *m*

Whitsun /'wɪtsn/ *n* Pentecoste *f*

whittle /'wɪtl/ *v*
■ **whittle away** *vt* intaccare ⟨savings⟩;
ridurre ⟨lead in race⟩
■ **whittle down** *vt* ridurre

Whit Sunday /wit/ *n* Pentecoste *f*

whiz[z] /wɪz/ *vi* (pt/pp **whizzed**)
sibilare

w

whiz[z]-kid *n* fam giovane *m* prodigio
WHO *n abbr* (**World Health Organization**) OMS *f*
who /huː/ ① *inter pron* chi
② *rel pron* che; **the children, ∼ were all tired,...** i bambini che erano tutti stanchi,...
whodunnit /huːˈdʌnɪt/ *n* fam [romanzo *m*] giallo *m*
whoever /huːˈevə(r)/ *pron* chiunque; **∼ he is** chiunque sia; **∼ can that be?** chi può mai essere?
whole /həʊl/ ① *adj* tutto; (not broken) intatto; **the ∼ truth** tutta la verità; **the ∼ world** il mondo intero; **the ∼ lot** (everything) tutto; (*pl*) tutti; **the ∼ lot of you** tutti voi
② *n* tutto *m*; **as a ∼** nell'insieme; **on the ∼** tutto considerato; **the ∼ of Italy** tutta l'Italia
wholefood *n* cibo *m* macrobiotico
wholehearted /ˈhəʊlhɑːtɪd/ *adj* di tutto cuore
wholeheartedly /həʊlˈhɑːtɪdlɪ/ *adv* ⟨agree, support⟩ senza riserve
wholemeal *adj* integrale
whole milk *n* latte *m* intero
whole number *n* numero *m* intero
wholesale /ˈhəʊlseɪl/ *adj & adv* all'ingrosso; fig in massa
wholesaler /ˈhəʊlseɪlə(r)/ *n* grossista *mf*
wholesome /ˈhəʊlsəm/ *adj* sano
wholewheat *adj* = WHOLEMEAL
wholly /ˈhəʊlɪ/ *adv* completamente
wholly-owned subsidiary *n* consociata *f* interamente controllata
whom /huːm/ ① *rel pron* che; **the man ∼ I saw** l'uomo che ho visto; **to/with ∼** a/con cui
② *inter pron* chi; **to ∼ did you speak?** con chi hai parlato?
whoop /wuːp/ ① *n* (shout) grido *m*
② *vi* gridare
whoopee /ˈwʊpɪ/ ① *int* evviva!
② *n* hum **make ∼** (have fun) fare baldoria; (make love) fare l'amore
whooping cough /ˈhuːpɪŋ/ *n* pertosse *f*
whoosh /wʊʃ/ *int* vuum!
whopper /ˈwɒpə(r)/ *n* fam (lie) balla *f*; **what a ∼!** è veramente gigantesco!
whopping /ˈwɒpɪŋ/ *adj* fam enorme
whore /hɔː(r)/ *n* puttana *f* vulg
whorl /wɜːl/ *n* (of cream, chocolate etc) ghirigoro *m*; (of fingerprint) spirale *f*
whose /huːz/ ① *rel pron* il cui; **people ∼ name begins with D** le persone i cui nomi cominciano con la D
② *inter pron* di chi; **∼ is that?** di chi è quello?
③ *adj* **∼ car did you use?** di chi è la macchina che hai usato?

Who's Who *n* pubblicazione *f* annuale con l'elenco delle personalità di spicco
why /waɪ/ ① *adv* (inter) perché; **the reason ∼** la ragione per cui; **that's ∼** per questo
② *int* diamine!
WI *abbr* (**Women's Institute**); Am abbr **Wisconsin**
wick /wɪk/ *n* stoppino *m*
wicked /ˈwɪkɪd/ *adj* cattivo; (mischievous) malizioso
wicker /ˈwɪkə(r)/ ① *n* vimini *mpl*
② *attrib* di vimini
wicket /ˈwɪkɪt/ *n* (field gate) cancelletto *m*; Sport porta *f*; (Am: of ticket office etc) sportello *m*; **be on a sticky ∼** fam essere in una situazione difficile
wide /waɪd/ ① *adj* largo; ⟨experience, knowledge⟩ vasto; ⟨difference⟩ profondo; (far from target) lontano; **10 cm ∼** largo 10 cm; **how ∼ is it?** quanto è largo?
② *adv* (off target) lontano dal bersaglio; **∼ awake** del tutto sveglio; **∼ open** spalancato; **open ∼!** apri bene!; **far and ∼** in lungo e in largo
wide-angle lens *n* grandangolo *m*
wide-eyed /-ˈaɪd/ *adj* ⟨person, innocence⟩ ingenuo; (with fear, surprise) con gli occhi sbarrati
widely /ˈwaɪdlɪ/ *adv* largamente; ⟨known, accepted⟩ generalmente; ⟨different⟩ profondamente
widely read /red/ *adj* ⟨student⟩ colto; ⟨writer⟩ molto letto
widen /ˈwaɪdn/ ① *vt* allargare; **∼ the gap** fig accentuare il contrasto
② *vi* allargarsi
widening /ˈwaɪdnɪŋ/ *adj* ⟨gap, division⟩ sempre più grande
wide open *adj* ⟨door, window, eyes⟩ spalancato
wide-ranging /ˈreɪndʒɪŋ/ *adj* ⟨interests, reforms, discussion⟩ di ampio respiro
wide screen *n* Cinema schermo *m* panoramico
wide-screen TV *n* televisore *m* con schermo panoramico
widespread /ˈwaɪdspred/ *adj* diffuso
widow /ˈwɪdəʊ/ *n* vedova ⟨f⟩
widowed /ˈwɪdəʊd/ *adj* vedovo
widower /ˈwɪdəʊə(r)/ *n* vedovo *m*
width /wɪdθ/ *n* larghezza *f*; (of material) altezza *f*
widthways /ˈwɪdθweɪz/ *adv* trasversalmente
wield /wiːld/ *vt* maneggiare; esercitare ⟨power⟩
wife /waɪf/ *n* (pl **wives**) moglie *f*
wife battering /ˈwaɪfbæt(ə)rɪŋ/ *n* maltrattamento *m* della coniuge
wig /wɪg/ *n* parrucca *f*
wiggle /ˈwɪgl/ ① *vi* dimenarsi

w

2 *vt* dimenare

wild /waɪld/ **1** *adj* selvaggio; ⟨*animal, flower*⟩ selvatico; (furious) furibondo; ⟨*applause*⟩ fragoroso; ⟨*idea*⟩ folle; (with joy) pazzo; ⟨*guess*⟩ azzardato; **be ∼ about** (keen on) andare pazzo per

2 *adv* **run ∼** crescere senza controllo

3 *n* **in the ∼** allo stato naturale; **the ∼s** *pl* le zone sperdute

wild boar *n* cinghiale *m*

wild card *n* jolly *m inv*; Comput carattere *m* jolly

wildcat strike *n* sciopero *m* selvaggio

wild dog *n* cane *m* randagio

wilderness /'wɪldənɪs/ *n* deserto *m*; (fig: garden) giungla *f*

wild-eyed /-'aɪd/ *adj* (distressed) dall'aria angosciata; (angry) dallo sguardo minaccioso

wildfire *n* **spread like ∼** allargarsi a macchia d'olio

wild flower *n* fiore *m* di campo

wildfowl *n* (bird) uccello *m* selvatico; (birds collectively) uccelli *mpl* selvatici; (game) selvaggina *f* di penna

wild-goose chase *n* ricerca *f* di inutile

wildlife *n* animali *mpl* selvatici

wildlife park *n* parco *m* naturale

wildlife reserve *n* riserva *f* naturale

wildlife sanctuary *n* riserva *f* naturale

wildly /'waɪldlɪ/ *adv* fig ⟨*exaggerated*⟩ estremamente; ⟨*speak*⟩ senza riflettere; ⟨*applaud*⟩ fragorosamente; ⟨*hit out*⟩ all'impazzata

Wild West *n* il far west *m*

wiles /waɪlz/ *npl* astuzie *fpl*

wilful /'wɪlfʊl/ *adj* intenzionale; ⟨*person, refusal*⟩ ostinato

wilfully /'wɪlfʊlɪ/ *adv* intenzionalmente; ⟨*refuse*⟩ ostinatamente

will¹ /wɪl/ *v aux* **he ∼ arrive tomorrow** arriverà domani; **I won't tell him** non glielo dirò; **you ∼ be back soon, won't you?** tornerai presto, no?; **he ∼ be there, won't he?** sarà là, no?; **she ∼ be there by now** sarà là ormai; **∼ you go?** (do you intend to go) pensi di andare?; **∼ you go to the baker's and buy...?** puoi andare dal fornaio a comprare...?; **∼ you be quiet!** vuoi stare calmo!; **∼ you have some wine?** vuoi del vino?; **the engine won't start** la macchina non parte

will² *n* volontà *f inv*; (document) testamento *m*

willing /'wɪlɪŋ/ *adj* disposto; (eager) volonteroso

willingly /'wɪlɪŋlɪ/ *adv* volentieri

willingness /'wɪlɪŋnɪs/ *n* buona volontà *f*

willow /'wɪləʊ/ *n* salice *m*

willowy /'wɪləʊɪ/ *adj* ⟨*person, figure*⟩ slanciato

will-power *n* forza *f* di volontà

willy-nilly /wɪlɪ'nɪlɪ/ *adv* (at random) a casaccio; (wanting to or not) volente o nolente

wilt /wɪlt/ *vi* appassire

wily /'waɪlɪ/ *adj* (**-ier, -iest**) astuto

wimp /wɪmp/ *n* rammollito, -a *mf*

wimpish /'wɪmpɪʃ/ *adj* fam ⟨*behaviour*⟩ da rammollito

wimpy /'wɪmpɪ/ *adj* fam ⟨*person*⟩ rammollito

win /wɪn/ **1** *n* vittoria *f*; **have a ∼** riportare una vittoria

2 *vt* (pt/pp **won**; pres p **winning**) vincere; conquistare ⟨*fame*⟩

3 *vi* vincere

■ win back *vt* recuperare

■ win over *vt* convincere

■ win through *vi* (fam: be successful) uscire vittorioso

wince /wɪns/ *vi* contrarre il viso

winch /wɪntʃ/ *n* argano *m*

■ winch up *vt* tirare con l'argano

wind¹ /wɪnd/ **1** *n* vento *m*; (breath) fiato *m*; (fam: flatulence) aria *f*; **get/have the ∼ up** fam aver fifa; **get ∼ of** aver sentore di; **in the ∼** nell'aria

2 *vt* **∼ somebody** lasciare qualcuno senza fiato; **∼ a baby** far fare il ruttino ad un neonato

wind² /waɪnd/ **1** *vt* (pt/pp **wound**) (wrap) avvolgere; (move by turning) far girare; ⟨*clock*⟩ caricare

2 *vi* ⟨*road*⟩ serpeggiare

■ wind down *vi* (relax) rilassarsi; (gradually come to an end) diminuire *vt* (gradually bring to an end) metter fine in modo graduale a

■ wind up *vt* caricare ⟨*clock*⟩; concludere ⟨*proceedings*⟩; fam sfottere ⟨*somebody*⟩ *vi* (end up) **∼ up doing something** finire per fare qualcosa

windbreak *n* frangivento *m*

windcheater *n* Br giacca *f* a vento

windchill factor *n* fattore *m* di raffreddamento da vento

wind chimes *npl* campane *fpl* eoliche

wind energy *n* forza *f* del vento

winder /'waɪndə(r)/ *n* (for car window) manovella *f* alzacristalli; (for watch) bottone *m* di carica

windfall *n* fig fortuna *f* inaspettata; **∼s** *pl* (fruit) frutta *f* abbattuta dal vento

winding /'waɪndɪŋ/ *adj* tortuoso

wind instrument /'wɪnd/ *n* strumento *m* a fiato

windmill /'wɪn(d)mɪl/ *n* mulino *m* a vento

window /'wɪndəʊ/ *n* finestra *f*; (of car) finestrino *m*; (of shop) vetrina *f*

window box *n* cassetta *f* per i fiori

W

window cleaner n (person) lavavetri mf inv

window display n Comm esposizione f in vetrina

window dresser n vetrinista mf

window dressing n vetrinistica f; fig fumo m negli occhi

window envelope n busta f a finestra

window frame n telaio m di finestra

window ledge n davanzale m

window pane n vetro m

window seat n (in room) panca f sotto la finestra; (in plane, train) posto m accanto al finestrino

window-shopping n go ~ andare in giro a vedere le vetrine

window sill n davanzale m

windpipe n trachea f

windpower n energia f eolica

windscreen n, Am **windshield** n parabrezza m inv

windscreen washer n getto m d'acqua

windscreen-wiper n tergicristallo m

wind-sleeve n manica f a vento

wind-sock n manica f a vento

windsurf vi fare windsurf

windsurfer n (person) windsurfista mf; (board) windsurf m inv

windsurfing n windsurf m inv

windswept adj esposto al vento; ⟨person⟩ scompigliato

windy /'wɪndɪ/ adj (-ier, -iest) ventoso

wine /waɪn/ n vino m

wine bar n ≈ enoteca f

wine box n contenitore m di vino con rubinetto

wine cellar n cantina f

wine cooler n (ice bucket) secchiello m del ghiaccio; (Am: drink) bibita f leggermente alcolica

wineglass n bicchiere m da vino

wine grower /'grəʊə(r)/ n viticultore, -trice mf

wine growing /'grəʊɪŋ/ n viticultura f

wine list n carta f dei vini

wine merchant n commerciante mf di vini

wine producer n produttore, -trice mf di vini

wine rack n portabottiglie m inv

winery /'waɪnərɪ/ n Am vigneto m

wine tasting /'waɪnteɪstɪŋ/ n degustazione f di vini

wine vinegar n aceto m di vino

wine waiter n sommelier m inv

wing /wɪŋ/ n ala f; Auto parafango m; ~s pl Theat quinte fpl; under sb's ~ sotto l'ala [protettiva] di qualcuno

wing chair n poltrona f con ampio schienale

wing collar n colletto m rigido

wing commander n tenente m colonnello delle forze aeree

winger /'wɪŋə(r)/ n Sport ala f

wing-half n (in soccer) mediano m

wing mirror n Br specchietto m laterale

wing nut n dado m ad alette

wingspan n apertura f alare

wink /wɪŋk/ ① n strizzata f d'occhio; not sleep a ~ non chiudere occhio ② vi strizzare l'occhio; ⟨light⟩ lampeggiare

winner /'wɪnə(r)/ n vincitore, -trice mf

winning /'wɪnɪŋ/ adj vincente; ⟨smile⟩ accattivante

winning post n linea f d'arrivo

winnings /'wɪnɪŋz/ npl vincite fpl

winning streak n periodo m fortunato; be on a ~ essere in un periodo fortunato

winsome /'wɪnsəm/ adj accattivante

winter /'wɪntə(r)/ n inverno m

winter sports npl sport mpl invernali

wintertime /'wɪntətaɪm/ n inverno m

wintry /'wɪntrɪ/ adj invernale

wipe /waɪp/ ① n passata f; (to dry) asciugata f ② vt strofinare; (dry) asciugare ■ **wipe away** vt asciugare ⟨tears, sweat⟩; pulire ⟨dirt, mark⟩ ■ **wipe off** vt asciugare; (erase) cancellare ■ **wipe out** vt annientare; eliminare ⟨village⟩; estinguere ⟨debt⟩ ■ **wipe up** vt asciugare ⟨dishes⟩

wipe-clean adj ⟨surface, cover⟩ facile da pulire

wiper blade /'waɪpə/ n Auto bordo m gommato del tergicristallo

wire /'waɪə(r)/ n fil m di ferro; (electrical) filo m elettrico

wire brush n spazzola f metallica

wire-cutters npl tronchese msg

wire-haired /-'heəd/ adj dal pelo ispido

wireless /'waɪəlɪs/ n radio f inv

wire mesh n rete f metallica

wire netting n rete f metallica

wire wool n lana f d'acciaio

wiring /'waɪərɪŋ/ n impianto m elettrico

wiry /'waɪərɪ/ adj (-ier, -iest) ⟨person⟩ dal fisico asciutto; ⟨hair⟩ ispido

wisdom /'wɪzdəm/ n saggezza f; (of action) sensatezza f

wisdom tooth n dente m del giudizio

wise /waɪz/ adj saggio; (prudent) sensato ■ **wise up** fam ① vi (become more aware) aprire gli occhi ② vt aprire gli occhi a (**to** su)

wisecrack /'waɪzkræk/ fam ① n battuta f salace
② vi far battute salaci

wise guy n fam sapientone m

wisely /'waɪzlɪ/ adv saggiamente; ⟨act⟩ sensatamente

Wise Men npl Re Magi mpl

wish /wɪʃ/ ① n desiderio m; make a ~ esprimere un desiderio; with best ~es con i migliori auguri
② vt desiderare; ~ somebody well fare tanti auguri a qualcuno; I ~ you every success ti auguro buona fortuna; I ~ you could stay vorrei che tu potessi rimanere; ~ something on somebody fam sbolognare qualcosa a qualcuno
③ vi ~ for something desiderare qualcosa

wishbone /'wɪʃbəʊn/ n forcella f (di pollo o tacchino)

wishful /'wɪʃfʊl/ adj ~ thinking illusione f

wishy-washy /'wɪʃɪwɒʃɪ/ adj ⟨colour⟩ spento; ⟨personality⟩ insignificante

wisp /wɪsp/ n (of hair) ciocca f; (of smoke) filo m; (of grass) ciuffo m

wispy /'wɪspɪ/ adj ⟨hair, beard⟩ a ciocche; ⟨clouds⟩ vaporoso

wisteria /wɪs'tɪərɪə/ n glicine m

wistful /'wɪstfʊl/ adj malinconico

wistfully /'wɪstfʊlɪ/ adv malinconicamente

wit /wɪt/ n spirito m; (person) persona f di spirito; be at one's ~s' end non saper che pesci pigliare; scared out of one's ~s spaventato a morte

witch /wɪtʃ/ n strega f

witchcraft n magia f

witch doctor n stregone m

witch-hunt n caccia f alle streghe

with /wɪð/ prep con; (fear, cold, jealousy etc) di; I'm not ~ you fam non ti seguo; can I leave it ~ you? (task) puoi occupartene tu?; ~ no regrets/money senza rimpianti/soldi; be ~ it fam essere al passo coi tempi; (alert) essere concentrato

withdraw /wɪð'drɔː/ ① vt (pt -drew, pp -drawn) ritirare; prelevare ⟨money⟩
② vi ritirarsi

withdrawal /wɪð'drɔː(ə)l/ n ritiro m; (of money) prelevamento m; (from drugs) crisi f inv di astinenza; Psych chiusura f in se stessi

withdrawal symptoms npl sintomi mpl da crisi di astinenza

withdrawn /wɪð'drɔːn/ ① ▶ WITHDRAW
② adj ⟨person⟩ chiuso in se stesso

wither /'wɪðə(r)/ vi ⟨flower⟩ appassire

withering /'wɪðərɪŋ/ adj ⟨look⟩ fulminante

withhold /wɪð'həʊld/ vt (pt/pp -held) rifiutare ⟨consent⟩ (from a); nascondere ⟨information⟩ (from a); trattenere ⟨smile⟩

within /wɪð'ɪn/ ① prep in; (before the end of) entro; ~ the law legale
② adv all'interno

without /wɪð'aʊt/ prep senza; ~ stopping senza fermarsi; how could it have happened ~ you noticing it? come è potuto succedere senza che tu lo notassi?

withstand /wɪð'stænd/ vt (pt/pp -stood) resistere a

witness /'wɪtnɪs/ ① n testimone mf; bear ~ portare testimonianza
② vt autenticare ⟨signature⟩; essere testimone di ⟨accident⟩

witness box, Am **witness-stand** n banco m dei testimoni

witticism /'wɪtɪsɪzm/ n spiritosaggine f

wittingly /'wɪtɪŋlɪ/ adv consapevolmente

witty /'wɪtɪ/ adj (-ier, -iest) spiritoso

wives /waɪvz/ ▶ WIFE

wizard /'wɪzəd/ n mago m

wizardry /'wɪzədrɪ/ n stregoneria f

wizened /'wɪznd/ adj raggrinzito

wk abbr **week**

WMD n abbr (**weapon of mass destruction**) ADM fpl

wobble /'wɒbl/ vi traballare

wobbly /'wɒblɪ/ adj traballante

wodge /wɒdʒ/ n fam mucchio m

woe /wəʊ/ n afflizione f; ~ is me! me meschino!

woeful /'wəʊfʊl/ adj ⟨story, sight⟩ triste; ⟨lack⟩ vergognoso

woke, woken /wəʊk/, /'wəʊkn/ ▶ WAKE¹

wolf /wʊlf/ ① n (pl wolves /wʊlvz/) lupo m; (fam: womanizer) donnaiolo m
② vt ~ [down] divorare

wolf cub n cucciolo m di lupo

wolfhound n Br cane m lupo

wolf whistle ① n fischio m
② vi ~-whistle at somebody fischiare dietro a qualcuno

woman /'wʊmən/ n (pl women) donna f

womanizer /'wʊmənaɪzə(r)/ n donnaiolo m

womanly /'wʊmənlɪ/ adj femminile

womb /wuːm/ n utero m

women /'wɪmɪn/ ▶ WOMAN

Women's Institute n associazione f che si occupa dei problemi delle donne

Women's Libber /wɪmɪnz'lɪbə(r)/ n femminista f

Women's Liberation n movimento m femminista

women's movement n movimento m per l'emancipazione della donna

women's refuge n casa f rifugio inv

w

women's studies *npl* storia *f* dell'emancipazione femminile

won /wʌn/ ▸ WIN

wonder /'wʌndə(r)/ ⓵ *n* meraviglia *f*; (surprise) stupore *m*; **no ~!** non c'è da stupirsi!; **it's a ~ that...** è incredibile che... ⓶ *vi* restare in ammirazione; (be surprised) essere sorpreso; **I ~** è quello che mi chiedo; **I ~ whether she is ill** mi chiedo se è malata

wonderful /'wʌndəfʊl/ *adj* meraviglioso

wonderfully /'wʌndəfʊlɪ/ *adv* meravigliosamente

wonderland /'wʌndəlænd/ *n* paese *m* delle meraviglie

wonky /'wɒŋkɪ/ *adj* Br fam (faulty) difettoso; ⟨furniture⟩ traballante; (crooked) storto

wont /wəʊnt/ ⓵ *n* **as was his ~** come suo solito ⓶ *adj* **he was ~ to fall asleep** era solito addormentarsi

won't /wəʊnt/ = will not

woo /wuː/ *vt* corteggiare; fig cercare di accattivarsi ⟨voters⟩; cercare di ottenere ⟨fame, fortune⟩

wood /wʊd/ *n* legno *m*; (for burning) legna *f*; (forest) bosco *m*; **out of the ~** fig fuori pericolo; **touch ~!** tocca ferro!

woodcarving /'wʊdkɑːvɪŋ/ *n* scultura *f* di legno

wooded /'wʊdɪd/ *adj* boscoso

wooden /'wʊdn/ *adj* di legno; fig legnoso

wooden horse *n* cavallo *m* di Troia

wooden spoon *n* mestolo *m* di legno; fig premio *m* di consolazione

woodland *n* terreno *m* boschivo

woodlouse *n* onisco *m*

wood-pecker *n* picchio *m*

wood pigeon *n* colombaccio *m*

wood shavings *npl* trucioli *mpl*

woodshed *n* legnaia *f*

wood stove *n* stufa *f* a legna

woodwind *n* strumenti *mpl* a fiato

woodwork *n* (wooden parts) parti *fpl* in legno; (craft) falegnameria *f*

woodworm *n* tarlo *m*

woody /'wʊdɪ/ *adj* legnoso; ⟨hill⟩ boscoso

wool /wʊl/ ⓵ *n* lana *f*; **pull the ~ over sb's eyes** gettar fumo negli occhi a qualcuno ⓶ *attrib* di lana

woollen /'wʊlən/ *adj* di lana

woollens /'wʊlənz/ *npl* capi *mpl* di lana

woolly /'wʊlɪ/ *adj* (**-ier, -iest**) ⟨sweater⟩ di lana; fig confuso

woozy /'wuːzɪ/ *adj* intontito

word /wɜːd/ *n* parola *f*; (news) notizia *f*; **by ~ of mouth** a viva voce; **have a ~ with** dire due parole a; **have ~s** bisticciare; **in**

other ~s in altre parole; **go back on one's ~** rimangiarsi la parola

word-for-word ⓵ *adj* ⟨translation⟩ letterale ⓶ *adv* parola per parola

wording /'wɜːdɪŋ/ *n* parole *fpl*

word-perfect *adj* che sa a memoria

word processing *n* Comput word processing *m*, elaborazione *f* testi

word processor *n* sistema *m* di videoscrittura, word processor *m* inv

wordy /'wɜːdɪ/ *adj* prolisso

wore /wɔː(r)/ ▸ WEAR

work /wɜːk/ ⓵ *n* lavoro *m*; (of art) opera *f*; **~s** *pl* (factory) fabbrica *fsg*; (mechanism) meccanismo *msg*; **at ~** al lavoro; **out of ~** disoccupato ⓶ *vi* lavorare; ⟨machine, ruse⟩ funzionare; (study) studiare ⓷ *vt* far funzionare ⟨machine⟩; far lavorare ⟨employee⟩; far studiare ⟨student⟩; **~ one's way through something** (read) leggere attentamente

■ **work in** *vt* inserire ⟨comment, fact⟩; Culin incorporare ⟨butter⟩

■ **work off** *vt* sfogare ⟨anger⟩; lavorare per estinguere ⟨debt⟩; fare sport per smaltire ⟨weight⟩

■ **work on** *vt* lavorare a ⟨book, report⟩; occuparsi di ⟨problem, case⟩; cercare ⟨solution⟩ *vi* (continue) continuare a lavorare

■ **work out** ⓵ *vt* elaborare ⟨plan⟩; risolvere ⟨problem⟩; calcolare ⟨bill⟩ **I ~ed out how he did it** ho capito come l'ha fatto ⓶ *vi* evolvere

■ **work up** *vt* **I've ~ed up an appetite** mi è venuto appetito; **don't get ~ed up** (anxious) non farti prendere dal panico; (angry) non arrabbiarti

workable /'wɜːkəbl/ *adj* (feasible) fattibile

workaday /'wɜːkədeɪ/ *adj* ⟨clothes, life⟩ ordinario

workaholic /wɜːkə'hɒlɪk/ *n* stacanovista *mf*

workbench *n* banco *m* da lavoro

workbook *n* (blank) quaderno *m*; (with exercises) libro *m* di esercizi

workday *n* giorno *m* lavorativo

worker /'wɜːkə(r)/ *n* lavoratore, -trice *mf*; (manual) operaio, -a *mf*

work experience *n* esperienza *f* professionale; (part of training programme) stage *m* inv

workforce *n* forza *f* lavoro

workhorse *n* fig lavoratore, -trice *mf* indefesso, -a

working /'wɜːkɪŋ/ *adj* ⟨clothes etc⟩ da lavoro; ⟨day⟩ feriale; **in ~ order** funzionante

working capital *n* capitale *m* netto di esercizio

working-class *adj* operaio; **be ~** appartenere alla classe operaia

working class *n* classe *f* operaia

workings /'wɜːkɪŋz/ *npl* meccanismi *mpl*

working week *n* settimana *f* lavorativa

workload *n* carico *m* di lavoro

workman *n* operaio *m*

workmanlike *adj* fatto con competenza

workmanship *n* lavorazione *f*

workmate *n* collega *mf*

work of art *n* opera *f* d'arte

workout *n* allenamento *m*

work permit *n* permesso *m* di lavoro

workplace *n* posto *m* di lavoro

work-sharing *n* divisione *f* di un posto di lavoro tra più persone

worksheet *n* foglio *m* degli esercizi

workshop *n* officina *f*; (discussion) dibattito *m*

work-shy *adj* pigro

workstation *n* stazione *f* di lavoro

work surface *n* piano *m* di lavoro

worktop *n* piano *m* di lavoro

work-to-rule *n* sciopero *m* bianco

world /wɜːld/ *n* mondo *m*; **a ~ of difference** una differenza abissale; **out of this ~** favoloso; **think the ~ of somebody** andare matto per qualcuno

world-class *adj* di livello internazionale

World Cup *n* (in football) Mondiali *mpl*

world-famous *adj* di fama mondiale

world leader *n* (politician, company) leader *m* mondiale; (athlete) campione, -essa *mf* mondiale

worldly /'wɜːldlɪ/ *adj* materiale; ⟨person⟩ materialista

worldly-wise *adj* vissuto

world music *n* world music *f*

world power *n* potenza *f* mondiale

worldview *n* visione *f* del mondo

world war *n* guerra *f* mondiale

worldwide /'wɜːldwaɪd/ **①** *adj* mondiale
② *adv* mondialmente

World Wide Web *n* Comput World Wide Web *m*

worm /wɜːm/ **①** *n* verme *m*
② *vt* **~ one's way into sb's confidence** conquistarsi la fiducia di qualcuno in modo subdolo
■ **worm out** *vt* **~ something out of somebody** carpire qualcosa a qualcuno

worm-eaten /'wɜːmiːtən/ *adj* ⟨wood⟩ tarlato; ⟨fruit⟩ bacato

wormhole /'wɜːmhəʊl/ *n* (in wood) buco *m* di tarlo; (in fruit, plant) buco *m* del verme

worn /wɔːn/ **①** ▸ WEAR
② *adj* sciupato

worn-out *adj* consumato; ⟨person⟩ sfinito

worried /'wʌrɪd/ *adj* preoccupato

worrier /'wʌrɪə(r)/ *n* ansioso, -a *mf*; **he's a terrible ~** è ansioso da morire

worry /'wʌrɪ/ **①** *n* preoccupazione *f*
② *vt* (*pt/pp* **worried**) preoccupare; (bother) disturbare
③ *vi* preoccuparsi
■ **worry at** *vt* ⟨dog⟩ rosicchiare ⟨bone, toy⟩; ⟨person⟩ sviscerare ⟨problem⟩

worry beads *npl* rosario *m* per scaricare la tensione

worrying /'wʌrɪɪŋ/ *adj* preoccupante

worse /wɜːs/ **①** *adj* peggiore
② *adv* peggio
③ *n* peggio *m*

worsen /'wɜːsn/ *vt/i* peggiorare

worsening /'wɜːsnɪŋ/ **①** *adj* ⟨situation, problem⟩ sempre più grave
② *n* peggioramento *m*

worse off *adj* **be ~ ~ than** stare peggio di; **be £100 ~ ~** avere 100 sterline in meno

worship /'wɜːʃɪp/ **①** *n* culto *m*; (service) funzione *f*; **Your/His W~** (to judge) signor giudice/il giudice
② *vt* (*pt/pp* **-shipped**) venerare
③ *vi* andare a messa

worshipper /'wɜːʃɪpə(r)/ *n* fedele *mf*

worst /wɜːst/ **①** *adj* peggiore
② *adv* peggio
③ *n* **the ~** il peggio; **get the ~ of it** avere la peggio; **if the ~ comes to the ~** nella peggiore delle ipotesi

worsted /'wʊstɪd/ *n* lana *f* pettinata

worth /wɜːθ/ **①** *n* valore *m*; **£10 ~ of petrol** 10 sterline di benzina
② *adj* **be ~** valere; **be ~ it** fig valerne la pena; **it is ~ trying** vale la pena provare; **it's ~ my while** mi conviene; **I'll make it ~ your while** te ne ricompenserò

worthless /'wɜːθlɪs/ *adj* senza valore

worthwhile /wɜːθ'waɪl/ *adj* che vale la pena; ⟨cause⟩ lodevole

worthy /'wɜːðɪ/ *adj* degno; ⟨cause, motive⟩ lodevole

would /wʊd/ *v aux* **I ~ do it** lo farei; **~ you go?** andresti?; **~ you mind if I opened the window?** ti dispiace se apro la finestra?; **he ~ come if he could** verrebbe se potesse; **he said he ~n't** ha detto di no; **he said he ~n't have** ha detto che non lo avrebbe fatto; **~ you like a drink?** vuoi qualcosa da bere?; **what ~ you like to drink?** cosa prendi da bere?; **you ~n't, ~ you?** non lo faresti, vero?

would-be *adj* pej ⟨actor, singer⟩ sedicente; ⟨investor, buyer⟩ aspirante

wound¹ /wuːnd/ **①** *n* ferita *f*

② *vt* ferire

wound² /waʊnd/ ▶ WIND²

wove, **woven** /wəʊv/, /'wəʊvn/ ▶ WEAVE²

wow /waʊ/ ① *n* (fam: success) successone *m*; (in sound system) wow *m*
② *vt* fam entusiasmare ⟨*person*⟩
③ *int* caspita!

WP *abbr* (**word processing**) elaborazione *f* testi

wpm *abbr* (**words per minute**) parole *fpl* al minuto

wrangle /'ræŋgl/ ① *n* litigio *m*
② *vi* litigare

wrap /ræp/ ① *n* (shawl) scialle *m*
② *vt* (pt/pp **wrapped**) ~ [**up**] avvolgere; ⟨*present*⟩ incartare; **be** ~**ped up in** fig essere completamente preso da
③ *vi* ~ **up warmly** coprirsi bene

wraparound /'ræpəraʊnd/ *adj* ⟨*skirt*⟩ a pareo; ⟨*window, windscreen*⟩ panoramico

wraparound sunglasses *npl* occhiali *mpl* da sole avvolgenti

wrap-over *adj* ⟨*skirt, dress*⟩ a portafoglio

wrapper /'ræpə(r)/ *n* (for sweet) carta *f* [di caramella]

wrapping /'ræpɪŋ/ *n* materiale *m* da imballaggio

wrapping paper *n* carta *f* da pacchi; (for gift) carta *f* da regalo

wrath /rɒθ/ *n* ira *f*

wreak /riːk/ *vt* ~ **havoc with something** scombussolare qualcosa

wreath /riːθ/ *n* (*pl* ~**s** /riːðz/) corona *f*

wreathed /riːðd/ *adj* ~ **in** avvolto in ⟨*mists*⟩; **her face was** ~ **in smiles** era raggiante

wreck /rek/ ① *n* (of ship) relitto *m*; (of car) carcassa *f*; (person) rottame *m*
② *vt* far naufragare; demolire ⟨*car*⟩

wreckage /'rekɪdʒ/ *n* rottami *mpl*; fig brandelli *mpl*

wrecked /rekt/ *adj* ⟨*ship, car*⟩ distrutto; ⟨*building*⟩ demolito; (fig: exhausted) distrutto

wren /ren/ *n* scricciolo *m*

wrench /rentʃ/ ① *n* (injury) slogatura *f*; (tool) chiave *f* inglese; (pull) strattone *m*; **it was a** ~ **leaving home** fig è stato un passo difficile andarsene da casa
② *vt* (pull) strappare; slogarsi ⟨*wrist, ankle etc*⟩

wrest /rest/ *vt* strappare (**from** a)

wrestle /'resl/ *vi* lottare corpo a corpo; fig lottare

wrestler /'reslə(r)/ *n* lottatore, -trice *mf*

wrestling /'reslɪŋ/ *n* lotta *f* libera; (all-in) catch *m*

wretch /retʃ/ *n* disgraziato, -a *mf*

wretched /'retʃɪd/ *adj* odioso; ⟨*weather*⟩ orribile; **feel** ~ (unhappy) essere triste; (ill) sentirsi malissimo

wriggle /'rɪgl/ ① *n* contorsione *f*
② *vi* contorcersi; (move forward) strisciare; ~ **out of something** fam sottrarsi a qualcosa

wriggly /'rɪglɪ/ *adj* ⟨*person*⟩ che si dimena; ⟨*snake, worm*⟩ che si contorce

wring /rɪŋ/ *vt* (pt/pp **wrung**) torcere ⟨*sb's neck*⟩; strizzare ⟨*clothes*⟩; ~ **one's hands** torcersi le mani; ~ **something out of somebody** fig estorcere qualcosa a qualcuno; ~**ing wet** inzuppato

wrinkle /'rɪŋkl/ ① *n* grinza *f*; (on skin) ruga *f*
② *vt/i* raggrinzire

wrinkled /'rɪŋkld/ *adj* ⟨*skin, face*⟩ rugoso; ⟨*clothes*⟩ raggrinzito

wrist /rɪst/ *n* polso *m*

wristband /'rɪs(t)bænd/ *n* polsino *m*; (on watch) cinturino *m*

wristwatch /'rɪstwɒtʃ/ *n* orologio *m* da polso

writ /rɪt/ *n* Jur mandato *m*

write /raɪt/ *vt/i* (pt **wrote**, pp **written**, pres p **writing**) scrivere
▪ **write away for** *vt* richiedere per posta ⟨*information*⟩
▪ **write back** *vi* rispondere
▪ **write down** *vt* annotare
▪ **write in** *vi* scrivere
▪ **write off** *vt* cancellare ⟨*debt*⟩; distruggere ⟨*car*⟩
▪ **write out** *vt* fare ⟨*cheque, prescription*⟩; (copy) ricopiare
▪ **write up** *vt* redigere; aggiornare ⟨*diary*⟩; elaborare ⟨*notes*⟩

write-off *n* (car) rottame *m*

write-protect *vt* Comput proteggere da sovrascrittura

writer /'raɪtə(r)/ *n* autore, -trice *mf*; **she's a** ~ è una scrittrice

writer's block *n* blocco *m* dello scrittore

write-up *n* (review) recensione *f*

writhe /raɪð/ *vi* contorcersi; ~ **with embarrassment** vergognarsi a morte

writing /'raɪtɪŋ/ *n* (occupation) scrivere *m*; (words) scritte *fpl*; (handwriting) scrittura *f*; ~**s** *pl* scritti *mpl*; **in** ~ per iscritto

writing desk *n* scrivania *f*

writing pad *n* (for notes) bloc-notes *m inv*; (for letters) blocco *m* di carta da lettere

writing paper *n* carta *f* da lettere

written /'rɪtn/ ▶ WRITE

wrong /rɒŋ/ ① *adj* sbagliato; **be** ~ ⟨*person*⟩ sbagliare; **what's** ~? cosa c'è che non va?
② *adv* ⟨*spelt*⟩ in modo sbagliato; **go** ~ ⟨*person*⟩ sbagliare; ⟨*machine*⟩ funzionare

male; ⟨*plan*⟩ andar male; **don't get me ∼** non fraintendermi
3 *n* ingiustizia *f*; **in the ∼** dalla parte del torto; **know right from ∼** distinguere il bene dal male
4 *vt* fare torto a
wrongdoer /'rɒnduːə(r)/ *n* malfattore *m*
wrong-foot *vt* Sport, fig prendere in contropiede
wrongful /'rɒnfʊl/ *adj* ingiusto
wrongfully /'rɒnfʊlɪ/ *adv* ⟨*accuse*⟩ ingiustamente
wrongly /'rɒnlɪ/ *adv* in modo sbagliato; ⟨*accuse, imagine*⟩ a torto; ⟨*informed*⟩ male
wrote /rəʊt/ ▶ WRITE

wrought iron /rɔːt'aɪən/ **1** *n* ferro *m* battuto
2 *attrib* di ferro battuto
wrung /rʌŋ/ ▶ WRING
wry /raɪ/ *adj* (**-er, -est**) ⟨*humour, smile*⟩ beffardo
WW1 *or* **WWI** *abbr* (**World War One**) prima guerra *f* mondiale
WW2 *or* **WWII** *abbr* (**World War Two**) seconda guerra *f* mondiale
WWW *abbr* (**World Wide Web**) WWW *m*
WYSIWYG /'wɪzɪwɪg/ *abbr* Comput (**what you see is what you get**) ciò che vedi è ciò che ottieni

Xx

x¹, X /eks/ *n* (letter) x, X *f inv*; (anonymous person, place etc) X
x² *n* Math *x f inv*
X certificate *adj* Br vietato ai minori di 18 anni
xenophobia /zenə'fəʊbɪə/ *n* xenofobia *f*
xerox® /'zɪərɒks/ **1** *vt* xerocopiare
2 *n* (machine) xerocopiatrice *f*; (document) xerocopia *f*
Xmas /'krɪsməs/ *n* fam Natale *m*

XML *abbr* (**extensible markup language**) Comput XML *m*
X-rated *adj* ⟨*film*⟩ vietato ai minori
X-ray **1** *n* (picture) radiografia *f*; **have an ∼** farsi fare una radiografia
2 *vt* passare ai raggi X
X-ray machine *n* apparecchio *m* radiografico
X-ray unit *n* reparto *m* di radiologia
xxx *n* (at end of letter) baci *mpl*

Yy

y, Y /waɪ/ *n* (letter) y, Y *f inv*
yacht /jɒt/ *n* yacht *m inv*; (for racing) barca *f* a vela
yachting /'jɒtɪŋ/ *n* vela *f*
yachtsman /'jɒtsmən/ *n* diportista *m*
yak /jæk/ *n* Zool yak*m inv*
Yale® /jeɪl/ *n* (lock) serratura *f* di sicurezza
yam /jæm/ *n* (tropical) igname *m*; (Am: sweet potato) patata *f* dolce
Yank /jæŋk/ *n* fam americano, -a *mf*
yank /jæŋk/ *vt* fam tirare
Yankee /'jæŋkɪ/ *n* (pej: American) yankee *m inv*; (soldier) nordista *m*; (Am: of Northern USA) abitante *mf* degli USA settentrionali; (Am: inhabitant of New England) abitante *mf* della Nuova Inghilterra
yap /jæp/ *vi* (pt/pp **yapped**) ⟨*dog*⟩ guaire

yapping /'jæpɪŋ/ *n* (of dogs) guaiti *mpl*; (fam: of people) ciance *fpl*
yard¹ /jɑːd/ *n* cortile *m*; (for storage) deposito *m*; **the Y∼** fam Scotland Yard *f* (polizia londinese)
yard² /jɑːd/ *n* iarda *f* (= 91,44 cm)
yardstick /'jɑːdstɪk/ *n* fig pietra *f* di paragone
yarn /jɑːn/ *n* filo *m*; (fam: tale) storia *f*
yashmak /'jæʃmæk/ *n* velo *m* (delle donne musulmane)
yawn /jɔːn/ **1** *n* sbadiglio *m*
2 *vi* sbadigliare
yawning /'jɔːnɪŋ/ *adj* ∼ **gap** sbadiglio *m*
yd *abbr* **yard**
yeah /je/ *adv* fam sì; **oh ∼?** ma davvero?
year /jɪə(r)/ *n* anno *m*; (of wine) annata *f*; **for ∼s** fam da secoli

yearbook /'jɪəbʊk/ n annuario m

yearlong adj ⟨stay⟩ di un anno

yearly /'jɪəlɪ/ ① adj annuale
② adv annualmente

yearn /jɜːn/ vi struggersi

yearning /'jɜːnɪŋ/ n desiderio m struggente

year out n = GAP YEAR

year-round adj ⟨supply, source⟩ permanente

yeast /jiːst/ n lievito m

yell /jel/ ① n urlo m
② vi urlare

yelling /'jelɪŋ/ n urla fpl

yellow /'jeləʊ/ adj & n giallo m

yellow-belly n fam fifone m

yellow card n Sport cartellino m giallo

yellowish /'jeləʊɪʃ/ adj giallastro

yellow pages npl pagine fpl gialle

yellowy /'jeləʊɪ/ adj giallastro

yelp /jelp/ ① n (of dog) guaito m
② vi ⟨dog⟩ guaire

Yemen /'jemən/ n Yemen m

Yemeni /'jemənɪ/ adj & n yemenita mf

yen /jen/ n forte desiderio m (for di)

yeoman /'jəʊmən/ n Br piccolo proprietario m terriero; Y∼ of the Guard guardiano m della Torre di Londra

yep /jep/ adv fam sì

yes /jes/ ① adv sì
② n sì m inv

yes-man n fam tirapiedi m inv

yesterday /'jestədeɪ/ n & adv ieri m inv; ∼'s paper il giornale di ieri; the day before ∼ l'altroieri; ∼ afternoon ieri pomeriggio; ∼ evening ieri sera; ∼ morning ieri mattina

yesteryear /'jestəjɪə(r)/ n lit passato m; the music of ∼ la musica del passato

yet /jet/ ① adv ancora; as ∼ fino ad ora; not ∼ non ancora; the best ∼ il migliore finora
② conj eppure

yew /juː/ n tasso m (albero)

Y-fronts npl Br slip m inv da uomo con apertura

YHA Br abbr (Youth Hostels Association) associazione f degli ostelli della gioventù

Yiddish /'jɪdɪʃ/ n yiddish m

yield /jiːld/ ① n produzione f; ⟨profit⟩ reddito m
② vt produrre; fruttare ⟨profit⟩
③ vi cedere; Am Auto dare la precedenza

yielding /'jiːldɪŋ/ adj (submissive) arrendevole; ⟨ground⟩ cedevole; ⟨person⟩ flessibile

YMCA abbr (Young Men's Christian Association) Associazione f Cristiana dei Giovani

yob /jɒb/, **yobbo** n Br: fam teppista mf

yodel /'jəʊdl/ vi (pt/pp **yodelled**) cantare jodel

yoga /'jəʊgə/ n yoga m

yoghurt /'jɒgət/ n yogurt m inv

yoke /jəʊk/ n giogo m; (of garment) carré m inv

yokel /'jəʊkl/ n zotico, -a mf

yolk /jəʊk/ n tuorlo m

yonder /'jɒndə(r)/ adv liter laggiù

yonks /jɒŋks/ npl fam I haven't seen him for ∼ è un secolo che non lo vedo

yore /jɔː(r)/ n in days of ∼ un tempo

you /juː/ pers pron (subject) tu, voi pl; (formal) lei, voi pl; (direct/indirect object) ti, vi pl; (formal: direct object) la; (formal: indirect object) le; (after prep) te, voi pl; (formal: after prep) lei; ∼ are very kind (sg) sei molto gentile; (formal) è molto gentile; (pl & formal pl) siete molto gentili; ∼ can stay, but he has to go (sg) tu puoi rimanere, ma lui deve andarsene; (pl) voi potete rimanere, ma lui deve andarsene; all of ∼ tutti voi; I'll give ∼ the money (sg) ti darò i soldi; (pl) vi darò i soldi; I'll give it to ∼ (sg) te/ (pl) ve lo darò; it does ∼ good (sg) ti/(pl) vi fa bene; it was ∼! (sg) eri tu!; (pl) eravate voi!; ∼ have to be careful these days si deve fare attenzione di questi tempi; ∼ can't tell the difference non si vede la differenza

you'd /juːd/ abbr **you would**; **you had**

you-know-what pron fam sai cosa

you-know-who pron fam sai chi

you'll /juːl/ abbr **you will**

young /jʌŋ/ ① adj giovane; ∼ lady signorina f; ∼ man giovanotto m; her ∼ man (boyfriend) il suo ragazzo
② npl (animals) piccoli mpl; the ∼ (people) i giovani

young blood n nuove leve fpl

youngish /'jʌŋɪʃ/ adj abbastanza giovane

young-looking adj dall'aria giovanile

young offender n delinquente mf minorenne

youngster /'jʌŋstə(r)/ n ragazzo, -a mf; (child) bambino, -a mf

your /jɔː(r)/ poss adj tuo m, tua f; (formal) suo m, sua f, suoi mpl, tue fpl; (formal) suo m, sua f, suoi mpl, sue fpl; (pl & formal pl) vostro m, vostra f, vostri mpl, vostre fpl; ∼ task/house il tuo compito/la tua casa; (formal) il suo compito/la sua casa; (pl & formal pl) il vostro compito/la vostra casa; ∼ mother/father tua madre/tuo padre; (formal) sua madre/ suo padre; (pl & formal pl) vostra madre/ vostro padre

you're /jʊə(r)/ abbr **you are**

yours /jɔːz/ poss pron il tuo m, la tua f, i tuoi mpl, le tue fpl; (formal) il suo m, la sua f, i suoi mpl, le sue fpl; (pl & formal pl) il vostro m, la vostra f, i vostri mpl, le vostre *fpl*; **a friend of** ∼ un tuo/suo/vostro amico; **friends of** ∼ dei tuoi/vostri/suoi amici; **that is** ∼ quello è tuo/vostro/suo; (as opposed to mine) quello è il tuo/il vostro/il suo

yourself /jɔː'self/ *pers pron* (reflexive) ti; (formal) si; (emphatic) te stesso; (formal) sé, se stesso; **do pour** ∼ **a drink** versati da bere; (formal) si versi da bere; **you said so** ∼ lo hai detto tu stesso; (formal) lo ha detto lei stesso; **you can be proud of** ∼ puoi essere fiero di te; (formal) può essere fiero di sé; **by** ∼ da solo

yourselves /jɔː'selvz/ *pers pron* (reflexive) vi; (emphatic) voi stessi; **do pour** ∼ **a drink** versatevi da bere; **you said so** ∼ lo avete detto voi stessi; **you can be proud of** ∼ potete essere fieri di voi; **by** ∼ da soli

youth /juːθ/ *n* (pl **youths** /juːðz/) gioventù *f inv*; (boy) giovanetto *m*; **the** ∼ (young people) i giovani

youth club *n* club *m* per i giovani

youthful /'juːθfʊl/ *adj* giovanile

youth hostel *n* ostello *m* [della gioventù]

youth hostelling n viaggiare *m* pernottando in ostelli della gioventù

youth work *n* lavoro *m* di educatore

youth worker *n* educatore, -trice *mf*

you've /juːv/ *abbr* **you have**

yowl /jaʊl/ *vi* ‹*dog*› ululare; ‹*cat*› miagolare; ‹*baby*› frignare

yo-yo® /'jəʊjəʊ/ **1** *n* yo-yo *m inv* **2** *vi* (prices, inflation) andare su e giù

yr *abbr* **year**

yuck /jʌk/ *int* Br: fam bleah

yucky /'jʌkɪ/ *adj* Br: fam schifoso

Yugoslav /'juːɡəslɑːv/ *adj & n* jugoslavo, -a *mf*

Yugoslavia /juːɡə'slɑːvɪə/ *n* Jugoslavia *f*

Yule log /juːl/ *n* tronchetto *m* natalizio

yummy /'jʌmɪ/ fam **1** *adj* squisito **2** *int* gnam gnam

yup /jʌp/ *adv* fam sì

yuppie /'jʌpɪ/ *n* yuppie *mf inv*

yuppie flu *n* sindrome *f* da affaticamento cronico

YWCA *abbr* (**Young Women's Christian Association**) Associazione *f* Cristiana delle Giovani

Zz

z, Z /zed/ *n* (letter) z, Z *f inv*

Zaire /zɑː'ɪə(r)/ *n* Zaire *m*

Zambia /'zæmbɪə/ *n* Zambia *m*

zany /'zeɪnɪ/ *adj* (**-ier**, **-iest**) demenziale

zap /zæp/ **1** *n* (fam: energy) energia *f* **2** *vt* (pt/pp **zapped**) fam (destroy) distruggere ‹*town*›; far fuori ‹*person, animal*›; (fire at) fulminare; (Comput: delete) cancellare

zapper /'zæpə(r)/ *n* (fam: for TV) telecomando *m*

zeal /ziːl/ *n* zelo *m*

zealot /'zelət/ *n* fig fanatico *m*

zealous /'zeləs/ *adj* zelante

zealously /'zeləslɪ/ *adv* con zelo

zebra /'zebrə/ *n* zebra *f*

zebra crossing *n* passaggio *m* pedonale, zebre *fpl*

zenith /'zenɪθ/ *n* zenit *m inv*; fig apogeo *m*

zero /'zɪərəʊ/ *n* zero *m*
■ **zero in on** *vt* concentrarsi su ‹*problem, person*›; localizzare ‹*place*›; Mil mirare ‹*target*›

zero gravity *n* assenza *f* di gravità

zero hour *n* Mil, fig ora *f* zero

zero-rated /-'reɪtɪd/ *adj* Br esente [da] IVA

zest /zest/ *n* gusto *m*; (peel) scorza *f* (di agrumi)

zigzag /'zɪɡzæɡ/ **1** *n* zigzag *m inv* **2** *vi* (pt/pp **-zagged**) zigzagare

zilch /zɪltʃ/ *n* fam un tubo; **I understood** ∼ non ho capito un tubo

Zimbabwe /zɪm'bæbweɪ/ *n* Zimbabwe *m*

Zimmer® /'zɪmə(r)/ *n* Br deambulatore *m*

zinc /zɪŋk/ *n* zinco *m*

zinc oxide *n* ossido *m* di zinco

zing /zɪŋ/ **1** *n* fam (energy) brio *m*; (sound) sibilo *m* **2** *vt* (Am: criticize) stroncare

Zionism /'zaɪənɪzm/ *n* sionismo *m*

zip /zɪp/ **1** *n* ∼ **[fastener]** cerniera *f* [lampo] **2** *vt* (pt/pp **zipped**) ∼ **[up]** chiudere con la cerniera [lampo]
■ **zip along** *vi* (move quickly) procedere velocemente
■ **zip through** *vt* (do quickly) svolgere velocemente ‹*work*›; (read quickly) leggere velocemente ‹*book*›

■ **zip up** *vt* chiudere la cerniera di
⟨*jacket, bag*⟩ *vi* chiudersi con la cerniera
zip code *n* Am codice *m* [di avviamento]
postale, C.A.P. *m inv*
zipper /'zɪpə(r)/ *n* Am cerniera *f* [lampo]
zippy /'zɪpɪ/ *adj* fam ⟨*vehicle*⟩ scattante
zither /'zɪðə(r)/ *n* cetra *f*
zodiac /'zəʊdɪæk/ *n* zodiaco *m*
zombie /'zɒmbɪ/ *n* fam zombi *mf inv*
zone /zəʊn/ *n* zona *f*
zoning /'zəʊnɪŋ/ *n* zonazione *f*

zonked /zɒŋkt/ *adj* (fam: on drugs, drunk,
tired) fatto
zoo /zu:/ *n* zoo *m inv*
zoo keeper *n* guardiano, -a *mf* dello zoo
zoological /zəʊə'lɒdʒɪkl/ *adj* zoologico
zoologist /zəʊ'ɒlədʒɪst/ *n* zoologo, -a *mf*
zoology /zəʊ'ɒlədʒɪ/ *n* zoologia *f*
zoom /zu:m/ *vi* sfrecciare
zoom lens *n* zoom *m inv*
zucchini /zʊ'ki:nɪ/ *n* zucchino *m*,
zucchina *f*

z

Summary of Italian grammar

Nouns

Gender

All Italian nouns are either masculine or feminine. As a general rule, nouns ending in **-o** are usually masculine.

il ragazzo boy **l'amico** friend
lo sbaglio mistake **un albero** tree
un treno train **uno specchio** mirror

Nouns ending in **-a** are usually feminine.

la ragazza girl **la scuola** school
l'arancia orange **un'amica** friend
una sorella sister **una zia** aunt

Nouns ending in **-e** can be either masculine or feminine.

il nome name **la stazione** station
una ragione reason **un giornale** newspaper

Plural forms

Masculine nouns ending in **-o** change to **-i** in the plural:

i ragazzi boys **gli amici** friends
gli sbagli mistakes

Feminine nouns ending in **-a** change to **-e**:

le ragazze girls **le scuole** schools
le amiche friends

All nouns ending in **-e** change to **-i**:

i genitori parents **le stazioni** stations

Nouns ending in accented vowels do not change in the plural.

il caffè coffee **i caffè** coffees
la città city **le città** cities
la virtù virtue **le virtù** virtues

Nouns ending in a consonant (imported from other languages) do not change in the plural.

il computer **i computer**
lo sport **gli sport**
l'autobus **gli autobus**

The definite article

Masculine forms before:

	singular	plural	
most consonants	il	i	il treno, i treni
a, e, i, o, u	l'	gli	l'albero, gli alberi
gn, ps, z, s+ consonant	lo	gli	lo studente, gli studenti

Feminine forms before:

	singular	plural	
any consonant	la	le	la camera, le camere
a, e, i, o, u	l'	le	l'arancia, le arance

The indefinite article

Masculine forms before:

	singular	
vowel or most consonants	un	un ombrello, un caffè
gn, ps, z, s+consonant	uno	uno zoo

Feminine forms before:

	singular	
any consonant	una	una stanza
a, e, i, o, u	un'	un'aspirina

Adjectives

Adjectives agree in number and gender with the noun to which they refer.
Italian adjectives end in either **-o** or **-e**.

	singular	plural	
masculine	pigro	pigri	lazy
	felice	felici	happy
	singular	plural	
feminine	pigra	pigre	lazy
	felice	felici	happy

When you have a mixture of masculine and feminine nouns, the adjective ending is masculine.

Max e Anna sono **pigri**/**gentili**.
Max and Anna are lazy/kind.

Position

Adjectives are usually placed after the noun they describe.

Ho letto **un libro interessante**.
I've read an interesting book.

There are, however, a few common adjectives, such as **bello**, **brutto**, **buono**, **cattivo**, **piccolo**, **grande**, **giovane**, **vecchio**, **nuovo**, which can be placed before the noun.

Ho visto **un bel film**.
I have seen a lovely film.

Possessive adjectives

In Italian, the possessive adjective agrees in gender and number with what is possessed and not with the possessor. The possessive adjective is generally preceded by the definite article: **il mio ufficio**.

	singular	
	masculine	*feminine*
my	**il mio**	**la mia**
your [*informal*]	**il tuo**	**la tua**
his/her; your [*formal*]	**il suo**	**la sua**
our	**il nostro**	**la nostra**
your [*plural*]	**il vostro**	**la vostra**
their	**il loro**	**la loro**

	plural	
	masculine	*feminine*
my	**i miei**	**le mie**
your [*informal*]	**i tuoi**	**le tue**
his/her; your [*formal*]	**i suoi**	**le sue**
our	**i nostri**	**le nostre**
your [*plural*]	**i vostri**	**le vostre**
their	**i loro**	**le loro**

Except with **loro**, the definite article is dropped when the noun refers to single immediate family members – **mia sorella**, **tuo fratello**, but **le mie sorelle**, **i tuoi fratelli**; **la loro sorella**, **i loro fratelli**.

Questo and *quello*

Questo and **quello** can be used both as adjectives ('this'/'that') and pronouns ('this one'/'that one'). **Questo** takes the usual adjective endings (**-o/-a/-i/-e**) whether it is used as an adjective or a pronoun. **Quello** also takes these endings when used as a pronoun;

however, when it comes before a noun, it takes the same endings as the definite article.

singular	**quel, quello, quell', quella**	**quella casa** **quell'amico**
plural	**quei, quegli, quelle**	**quegli amici** **quelle case**

Subject pronouns

In Italian, subject pronouns are generally omitted (unless you want to place emphasis on them): the subject is shown in the verb ending.

io	I	**noi**	we
tu	you [*informal*]	**voi**	you [*plural*]
lui	he	**loro**	they
lei	she		
lei	you [*formal*]		

The **tu** form is used when speaking to a child or someone you know well;
the **lei** form when speaking to an adult you don't know well.

Object pronouns

Direct object pronouns

mi	me	**ci**	us
ti	you	**vi**	you
lo	him/it [*m*]	**li**	them [*m*]
la	her/it [*f*]	**le**	them [*f*]
la	you [*formal*]		

Indirect object pronouns

mi	to (etc.) me	**ci**	to us
ti	to you	**vi**	to you
gli	to him/to it [*m*]	**gli**	to them [*m/f*]
le	to her/to it [*f*]		
le	to you [*formal*]		

Indirect object pronouns are used with verbs which are normally followed by a preposition, such as **telefonare a** ('to telephone') and **dare a** ('to give to').

Anna telefona a Maria. Anna **le** telefona.
Anna telefona a Mario. Anna **gli** telefona.

The position of direct and indirect object pronouns

Both direct and indirect object pronouns come before the verb (or before **avere**/**essere** in the perfect tense). When both appear in a sentence, the indirect comes before the direct pronoun: the indirect pronoun may also change form (see below).

Ti offro un caffè.
I'll buy you a coffee.

Le scrivo domani.
I'll write to her tomorrow.

Mi piacciono quegli stivali. **Li** compro!
I like those boots. I'll buy them!

Me lo avete comprato.
You bought it for me.

When there are two verbs, and the second is an infinitive, the pronoun comes either before the first verb or combines with the infinitive.

Ti vorrei incontrare.
I'd like to meet you.

Vorrei incontrar**ti**.
I'd like to meet you.

Before a direct object pronoun, the indirect object pronouns **mi**, **ti**, **ci**, and **vi** change respectively to **me**, **te**, **ce**, and **ve**.

Ti abbiamo già dato il libro.
We have already given the book to you.

Te lo abbiamo già dato.
We have already given it to you.

Vi mando la lettera domani.
I'll send the letter to you tomorrow.

Ve la mando domani.
I'll send it to you tomorrow.

The third person indirect pronouns – **le** and **gli** – change to **glie-** and combine with **lo**, **la**, **li**, and **le** to form one word.

Mando un biglietto d'auguri ai nonni. **Glielo** mando.
I'll send a card to our grandparents.
I'll send it to them.

These forms come before the verb or can be joined to an infinitive.

Glielo dovrei dare.
I should give it to him/her/them.

Dovrei dar**glielo**.
I should give it to him/her/them.

Disjunctive pronouns

me	me	**noi**	us
te	you [*informal*]	**voi**	you [*plural*]
lui	him	**loro**	them
lei	her		
lei	you [*formal*]		

Disjunctive pronouns are used for emphasis and after prepositions, such as **di**, **a**, **da**, **con**, etc.:

Conosco **lui**.
I know him.

Mario gioca con **noi**.
Mario plays with us.

Lo fa per **me**.
He does it for me.

Viene con **te**?
Is he coming with you?

Possessive pronouns

These have the same form as the possessive adjectives.

Questa è la mia bicicletta.
That's my bike.

E quella è **la mia**.
And that's mine.

The definite article is used with family members in the singular.

Mia nonna abita a Roma.
My grandmother lives in Rome.

La mia abita a Napoli.
Mine lives in Naples.

ci

ci is used to refer to location. It is used to mean 'here' or 'there', although in some instances its meaning in English is understood rather than translated. It usually comes before the verb.

Siete mai stati a Parigi? Sì, **ci** siamo andati molte volte.
Have you ever been to Paris? Yes, we've been there many times.

Quando andate a Roma? **Ci** andiamo venerdì.
When are you going to Rome? We're going (there) on Friday.

ne

ne can mean 'of it/him/her', 'about it/him/her', etc., or 'of them', 'about them', etc. In some instances it isn't translated, but it must be included.

Vorrei delle banane.
I would like some bananas.

Quante **ne** vuole?
How many (of them) do you want?

Maria parlerà delle sue vacanze.
Maria will talk about her holidays.

Maria **ne** parlerà.
Maria will talk about them.

Prepositions

In addition to the general meanings of the prepositions the following uses are particularly worth noting.

a   with cities

> Abito **a** Parma.
> I live in Parma.

> Vado **a** Parigi.
> I am going to Paris.

in   with countries and regions

> Vivono **in** Italia – **in** Toscana.
> They live in Italy – in Tuscany.

di   to express possession

> la mamma **di** Federica.
> Federica's mum

da   + name of a person means 'to or at their house, shop, etc.'

> Vai **da** Paola?
> Are you going to Paola's?

> Andate **dal** giornalaio?
> Are you going to the newsagent's?

> Sei già stato **dal** dentista?
> Have you already been to the dentist's?

da   + present tense to describe an action which began in the past and which continues in the present ('for', 'since')

> **È** malato **da** due giorni.
> He has been ill for two days.

> **Lavorano** qui **dal** 1975.
> They have worked here since 1975.

Prepositions and articles

When the prepositions **a** ('to'), **da** ('from'), **di** ('of'), **in** ('in'), and **su** ('on') are followed by the definite article, the words combine as follows.

	singular				*plural*		
	il	lo	l'	la	i	gli	le
a	al	allo	all'	alla	ai	agli	alle
da	dal	dallo	dall'	dalla	dai	dagli	dalle
di	del	dello	dell'	della	dei	degli	delle
in	nel	nello	nell'	nella	nei	negli	nelle
su	sul	sullo	sull'	sulla	sui	sugli	sulle

La sveglia è **sul** comodino.
The alarm clock is on the bedside cabinet.

I pantaloni sono **nell'**armadio.
The trousers are in the wardrobe.

Adverbs

Regular adverbs

Most adverbs are formed by adding **-mente** to the feminine form of the adjective.

| **lento** slow | **lenta*mente*** slowly |
| **vero** true | **vera*mente*** truly |

Adjectives ending in **–e** in the singular simply add **-mente**.

| **triste** sad | **triste*mente*** sadly |
| **semplice** simple | **semplice*mente*** simply |

However, if the adjective ends in **-re** or **-le**, the **-e** is dropped:

| **normale** normal | **normal*mente*** normally |
| **regolare** regular | **regolar*mente*** regularly |

The comparative and superlative

Comparative

più ... di	Lui è **più** giovane **di** lei.
	He is younger than she is.
meno ... di	Lui è **meno** vivace **di** lei.
	He is less lively than she is.
(tanto) ...	Lui è alto **quanto** lei.
quanto/come	He's as tall as she is.

Superlative

To say 'the most ...' in Italian is **il / la / i / le più**; 'the least ...' is **il / la / i / le meno**.

Mara è **la più** giovane.
Mara is the youngest.

Franco è **il più** alto.
Franco is the tallest.

After a superlative 'in' is translated by **di**.

È **la ragazza** più intelligente **della** classe.
She is the cleverest girl in her class.

È **l'albergo** più costoso **di** Venezia.
It is the most expensive hotel in Venice.

Irregular forms

Some adjectives have two different forms of the comparative and superlative. The distinctions in meaning are slight and best learnt in context.

	singular	*plural*
buono (good)	più buono / migliore	il/la più buono/a il/la migliore
cattivo (bad)	più cattivo / peggiore	il/la più cattivo/a il/la peggiore

Summary of Italian grammar

Expressing quantities

di + *article*

Ordino **del** vino?
Shall I order some wine?

Preferisco **dell'**acqua.
I'd prefer some water.

Compra **dei** pomodori.
Buy some tomatoes.

Hai **delle** aspirine?
Do you have any aspirins®?

qualche

qualche is always followed by a singular noun.

Ho **qualche amico** a Roma.
I have some friends in Rome.

Asking questions

There are two ways of asking questions: (a) you keep the same wording as the sentence, but use a rising intonation; (b) you use a question word – then the verb and the subject change places.

È inglese?
Are you English?

Dove lavora Roberta?
Where does Roberta work?

Negatives

To make a sentence negative, you simply put **non** in front of the verb.

Sono americano.
I'm American.

Non sono americano.
I'm not American.

Numbers

1	uno	16	sedici
2	due	17	diciassette
3	tre	18	diciotto
4	quattro	19	diciannove
5	cinque	20	venti
6	sei	21	ventuno
7	sette	22	ventidue
8	otto	23	ventitré
9	nove	30	trenta
10	dieci	40	quaranta
11	undici	50	cinquanta
12	dodici	60	sessanta
13	tredici	70	settanta
14	quattordici	71	settantuno
15	quindici	72	settantadue

73	settantatré	101	centouno
74	settantaquattro, etc.	102	centodue
80	ottanta	200	duecento
81	ottantuno	202	duecentodue
82	ottantadue, etc.	999	novecentonovantanove
90	novanta		
91	novantuno	1000	mille
92	novantadue, etc.	2000	duemila
100	cento	2001	duemilauno

Verbs

The infinitive

Dictionaries and glossaries usually list verbs in the infinitive form, which in Italian has three different endings: **-are**, **-ere**, or **-ire** (apart from a few irregular forms in **-rre**). Regular verbs within each group take the same endings.

Reflexive verbs

Reflexive verbs can easily be identified by the additional **si** which appears at the end of the infinitive (**chiamarsi**): they end in **-arsi**, **-ersi**, or **-irsi**, taking the endings for **-are**, **-ere**, and **-ire** verbs respectively. They just add the reflexive pronouns **mi**, **ti**, **si**, **ci**, **vi**, and **si** in front of the verb.

	alzarsi – to get up	**divertirsi** – to enjoy oneself
(io)	*mi* alzo	*mi* diverto
(tu)	*ti* alzi	*ti* diverti
(lui/lei)	*si* alza	*si* diverte
(noi)	*ci* alziamo	*ci* divertiamo
(voi)	*vi* alzate	*vi* divertite
(loro)	*si* alzano	*si* divertono

Non **si alzano** mai prima delle otto.
They never get up before eight.

Si divertirà senz'altro.
He will definitely enjoy himself.

The imperative

The imperative is used to give orders, instructions, and advice. Irregular imperative forms are covered in the verb tables on pages 954–962.

The **tu** form of the imperative is used to address children or people you know well. The **voi** form is used to address a group of people. Except for the **tu** form of the **-are** verbs, the other forms are the same as the **tu** form of the present tense.

	parlare	credere	sentire	finire
(tu)	parla	credi	senti	finisci
(voi)	parlate	credete	sentite	finite

The imperative also has a *noi* form, translated 'let's …'. This is the same as the *noi* form of the present tense.

	parlare	credere	sentire	finire
(noi)	parliamo	crediamo	sentiamo	finiamo

The *lei* form of the imperative is used with adults you don't know.

	parlare	credere	sentire	finire
(lei)	parli	creda	senta	finisca

The imperative and object pronouns

Direct and indirect object pronouns come *before the lei imperative*.

La guardi meglio. È tutta sporca!
Look at it more closely. It's all dirty!

Non **lo ascolti**! Scherza.
Don't listen to him. He's joking.

However, they are added to the *end of the tu, voi,* and *noi imperatives*.

Telefonate**gli** al più presto.
Ring him very soon.

Alziamoci alle sette.
Let's get up at seven o'clock.

Non parliamo**ne** più.
Let's not speak about it any more.

When you add a pronoun to the *tu* imperative forms of **andare, fare, dare, dire,** and **stare,** the first letter of the pronoun is doubled. The only exception to this is **gli**.

D**imm**i la verità!
Tell me the truth!

Da**ll**e questo.
Give her this.

Digli che arrivo domani.
Tell him I'll be arriving tomorrow.

The negative imperative

tu form	non + infinitive	**Non fumare**, per favore. Please don't smoke.
other forms	non + imperative	**Non fumate**, per favore. Please don't smoke.

In the negative, object pronouns come *before the lei imperative*.

Non **lo** dica!
Don't say it!

They can either come before the *tu, voi,* and *noi* imperatives or be added on to the end of

it. In the negative *tu* form, the final **-e** of the infinitive is dropped when an object pronoun is added on.

Non **dirlo**!/Non **lo dire**!
Don't say it!

The present tense

The single present tense in Italian has a wider use than its English equivalent: **io lavoro** can be translated as either 'I work' or 'I am working', according to context. Besides expressing actions which relate to the immediate present, it can also be used to express:

– actions which are done regularly

Ogni mattina **faccio** una passeggiata.
Every morning I go for a walk.

– actions which relate to a future intention.

Fra un mese **andiamo** in Spagna.
In a month we're going to Spain.

For the forms of the present tense, see the verb tables on pages 954–962.

The progressive forms

The progressive forms are used to say what is or was happening at the moment of speaking. These forms are less common in Italian than in English, because it is perfectly normal to use the simple present tense to convey the same idea.

The progressives are formed by combining the verb **stare** with the gerund, the form of the verb which ends with **-ando** or **-endo**. The present tense and the imperfect tense of **stare** are used respectively to talk about the present and the past.

parlare	prendere	dormire
sto/ stavo parlando	sto/ stavo prendendo	sto/ stavo dormendo
stai/ stavi parlando	stai/ stavi prendendo	stai/ stavi dormendo
sta/ stava parlando	sta/ stava prendendo	sta/ stava dormendo
stiamo/ stavamo parlando	stiamo/ stavamo prendendo	stiamo/ stavamo dormendo
state/ stavate parlando	state/ stavate prendendo	state/ stavate dormendo

parlare	prendere	dormire
stanno/ stavano parlando	stanno/ stavano prendendo	stanno/ stavano dormendo

Sta piovendo.
It is raining.

Che **stavi facendo**?
What were you doing?

The perfect tense

The perfect tense is used to describe a single completed event or action which took place in the past. It can be translated in one of two ways, depending on the context: for example, **ho parlato** can mean either 'I spoke' or 'I have spoken'. It is formed with the present tense of **avere** or **essere** + the past participle of the verb required. For regular verbs this is formed as follows: **-are** verbs → **-ato**, **-ere** verbs → **-uto**, and **-ire** verbs → **-ito**.

parl*ato* cred*uto* sent*ito*

With avere

Most transitive verbs form the perfect tense with **avere**.

Ho mangiato troppo.
I've eaten too much.

Non **ha avuto** molta fortuna.
She didn't have much luck.

When **avere** is used, the past participle must agree with any direct object which comes before the verb. Note that **lo** and **la** shorten to **l'**; **li** and **le** don't.

Ho comprato una macchina. **L'ho comprata** ieri.
I bought a car. I bought it yesterday.

Hai visto Maria e Carla? Sì, **le ho viste** ieri.
Did you see Maria and Carla? Yes, I saw them yesterday.

With essere

Most intransitive verbs, all reflexive verbs, and a few others (such as **essere**, **piacere**, **sembrare**, etc.) form the perfect tense with **essere**. When this happens, the past participle acts like an adjective: it agrees with the subject in gender and number.

Maria **è andata** a Roma molte volte.
Maria has been to Rome many times.

Ci siamo annoiati molto.
We got really bored.

La serata **è stata** veramente piacevole.
The evening was very pleasant.

Irregular past participles

* indicates a verb forming the perfect with **essere**

infinitive	past participle
aprire (to open)	**aperto**
bere (to drink)	**bevuto**
chiedere (to ask)	**chiesto**
chiudere (to close)	**chiuso**
crescere* (to grow)	**cresciuto**
decidere (to decide)	**deciso**
dire (to say)	**detto**
essere* (to be)	**stato**
fare (to do)	**fatto**
leggere (to read)	**letto**
mettere (to put)	**messo**
morire* (to die)	**morto**
nascere* (to be born)	**nato**
perdere (to lose)	**perso**
piacere* (to please)	**piaciuto**
prendere (to take)	**preso**
rimanere* (to stay)	**rimasto**
scegliere (to choose)	**scelto**
scrivere (to write)	**scritto**
stare* (to stay, to be situated)	**stato**
succedere* (to happen)	**successo**
trascorrere (to spend)	**trascorso**
vedere (to see)	**visto**
venire* (to come)	**venuto**
vincere* (to win)	**vinto**
vivere* (to live)	**vissuto**

The imperfect tense

The imperfect tense is used:

1 to describe something which used to happen frequently or regularly in the past.

   Andavamo a scuola a piedi.
   We walked/We used to walk to school.

2 to describe what was happening or what the situation was when something else happened.

   Dormivo quando Sergio **è arrivato**.
   I was sleeping when Sergio arrived.

   Aveva sei anni quando **è nata** Carla.
   He was six when Carla was born.

3 to express an emotional or physical state in the past and to refer to time, age, or the weather.

   Ieri sera Beatrice **era** stanca.
   Beatrice was tired.

   Aveva i capelli biondi.
   She had blonde hair.

Erano le sette.
It was seven o'clock.

Quando **eravamo** piccoli, ci piaceva andare al mare.
When we were little, we used to like going to the seaside.

Era una bella giornata.
It was a lovely day.

The imperfect tense is formed by adding the following endings to the stem.

	parlare	credere	sentire
(io)	parlavo	credevo	sentivo
(tu)	parlavi	credevi	sentivi
(lui/lei; lei)	parlava	credeva	sentiva
(noi)	parlavamo	credevamo	sentivamo
(voi)	parlavate	credevate	sentivate
(loro)	parlavano	credevano	sentivano

See the verb tables for details of verbs which are irregular in the imperfect.

Use of the perfect and the imperfect

The perfect is used to describe a completed or single action in the past; the imperfect describes a continuing, repeated, or habitual action. When they are used together, the imperfect is the tense that sets the scene, while the perfect is used to move the action forward.

Ho visto Marco giovedì.
I saw Marco on Thursday.

Andavo in piscina il giovedì.
I used to go swimming on Thursdays.

Poiché **faceva** caldo, **siamo andati** tutti al mare.
Because it was hot, we all went to the seaside.

The past historic tense

The past historic is a tense that refers to something that happened in the past, generally in the relatively distant past. It is formed by adding a set of endings to the verb. Before adding the endings, the infinitive ending (-are, -ere, or –ire) is dropped. For some –ere verbs there is a choice of endings for some forms; both sets of endings are commonly used. A large number of verbs form their past historic in irregular ways.

parlare	vendere	dormire	
(io)	parlai	vendei or vendetti	dormii
(tu)	parlasti	vendesti	dormisti

(lui/lei; lei)	parlò	vendé or vendette	dormì
(noi)	parlammo	vendemmo	dormimmo
(voi)	parlaste	vendeste	dormiste
(loro)	parlarono	venderono or vendettero	dormirono

Pagò il conto e se ne andò.
He paid the bill and left.

La città **fu fondata** nel 500 a.C.
The city was founded in 500 BC.

The pluperfect tense

The pluperfect tense is used to talk about events that happened *before* the event that is the main focus of attention. Like the perfect tense, it uses a form of **avere** or **essere** with the past participle: the past tense of **avere** (or **essere** if the verb forms its compound tenses with **essere**) is followed by the past participle. If the verb uses **essere** as an auxiliary, the past participle agrees with the subject (see the section on the perfect tense).

Li **avevo visti** l'estate prima.
I had seen them the summer before.

Ci **eravamo** già **conosciuti**.
We had already met.

The future tense

In Italian, the future can be expressed in different ways.

1 You can use the present tense with an appropriate time expression when talking about plans (as in English):

   Non **sono** libero domani.
   I'm not/I won't be available tomorrow.

   Partiamo per le vacanze lunedì prossimo.
   We're going on holiday next Monday.

2 You can use the future tense – especially when making predictions (as in weather forecasts or horoscopes) or stating a fact about the future.

   Avrete molto successo.
   You will have great success.

   Balleranno tutta la notte.
   They'll dance all night.

   Domani **nevicherà**.
   Tomorrow it will snow.

The future tense is formed by dropping the final **-e** of the infinitive and adding the future endings. In -are verbs, the **a** in the infinitive changes to **e**.

Summary of Italian grammar

	parlare	prendere	dormire
(io)	parlerò	prenderò	dormirò
(tu)	parlerai	prenderai	dormirai
(lui)	parlerà	prenderà	dormirà
(noi)	parleremo	prenderemo	dormiremo
(voi)	parlerete	prenderete	dormirete
(loro)	parleranno	prenderanno	dormiranno

Stasera Elio **parlerà** con il padre.
Tonight Elio will talk to his father.

Non lo **lascerà** mai.
She'll never leave him.

Verbs ending in **-care** and **-gare** add an **h** before the endings to keep the hard sound of the stem.

Gli spie**gheremo** tutto noi.
We will explain everything to him.

Cer**cherete** subito lavoro?
Will you be looking for work straight away?

For irregular future forms, see the verb tables on pages 954–962.

The conditional

In Italian the conditional is used for polite requests and suggestions, and to express a wish or a probable action. The endings are the same for all conjugations and, like the future tense, are added to the infinitive minus the final **-e** (or, if irregular, to the same stem used for the future tense). As with the future, the **a** in **-are** verbs changes to **e**. The rules affecting the spelling of **cercare**, **spiegare**, etc. also apply: see above.

	parlare	prendere	dormire
(io)	parlerei	prenderei	dormirei
(tu)	parleresti	prenderesti	dormiresti
(lui/lei; lei)	parlerebbe	prenderebbe	dormirebbe
(noi)	parleremmo	prenderemmo	dormiremmo
(voi)	parlereste	prendereste	dormireste
(loro)	parlerebbero	prenderebbero	dormirebbero

Potremmo venire con te.
We could come with you.

Dovresti andare a letto presto.
You should go to bed early.

Vorrebbe fare una partita a tennis?
Would you like to have a game of tennis?

Non **vivrebbero** mai all'estero.
They'd never live abroad.

Saresti il primo a saperlo.
You'd be the first to know.

The subjunctive

The subjunctive is a special form of the verb that expresses doubt, unlikelihood, or desire. The subjunctive is not very common in modern English, and often forms with *let*, *should*, etc. do the same job. In Italian the subjunctive is very common, and is obligatory in certain circumstances. The subjunctive is commonly used to show that what is being said is not a concrete fact, for example to indicate doubt or necessity, or after verbs of ordering, requiring, or persuasion. It contrasts with the *indicative*, the normal form of the verb, which always implies a greater degree of certainty. The subjunctive is sometimes translated by an infinitive in English.

The present subjunctive is generally used when the main verb in the sentence is in the present; the past subjunctive is used when the main verb is in the past, or in order to talk about hypothetical situations.

For the forms of the subjunctive, see the verb tables on pages 954–962.

Credo che tu abbia ragione.
I think you're right.

Spero che questo problema si risolva.
I hope this problem is solved.

Bisogna che tu legga tutto.
It's necessary for you to read it all.

Voglio che tu mi aiuti.
I want you to help me.

Volevo che mi aiutassi.
I wanted you to help me.

Regular verbs -are

parlare – to speak (past participle **parlato**)

	present	future	conditional	perfect	imperfect
io	parlo	parlerò	parlerei	ho parlato	parlavo
tu	parli	parlerai	parleresti	hai parlato	parlavi
lui/lei; lei	parla	parlerà	parlerebbe	ha parlato	parlava
noi	parliamo	parleremo	parleremmo	abbiamo parlato	parlavamo
voi	parlate	parlerete	parlereste	avete parlato	parlavate
loro	parlano	parleranno	parlerebbero	hanno parlato	parlavano

	pluperfect	past historic	present subjunctive	past subjunctive	imperative
io	avevo parlato	parlai	parli	parlassi	
tu	avevi parlato	parlasti	parli	parlassi	parla
lui/lei; lei	aveva parlato	parlò	parli	parlasse	parli
noi	avevamo parlato	parlammo	parliamo	parlassimo	parliamo
voi	avevate parlato	parlaste	parliate	parlaste	parlate
loro	avevano parlato	parlarono	parlino	parlassero	

Verbs ending in **-care** and **-gare**, such as **cercare**, ('to look for') or **spiegare** ('to explain'), add an **h** before **i** or **e**.

Cherchiamo un posto tranquillo. We're looking for a quiet place.
Ti spieghiamo tutto domani. We'll explain everything tomorrow.

Regular verbs -ere

credere – to believe (past participle **creduto**)

	present	future	conditional	perfect	imperfect
io	credo	crederò	crederei	ho creduto	credevo
tu	credi	crederai	crederesti	hai creduto	credevi
lui/lei; lei	crede	crederà	crederebbe	ha creduto	credeva
noi	crediamo	crederemo	crederemmo	abbiamo creduto	credevamo
voi	credete	crederete	credereste	avete creduto	credevate
loro	credono	crederanno	crederebbero	hanno creduto	credevano

	pluperfect	past historic	present subjunctive	past subjunctive	imperative
io	avevo creduto	credei or credetti	creda	credessi	
tu	avevi creduto	credesti	creda	credessi	credi
lui/lei; lei	aveva creduto	credé or credette	creda	credesse	creda
noi	avevamo creduto	credemmo	crediamo	credessimo	crediamo
voi	avevate creduto	credeste	crediate	credeste	credete
loro	avevano creduto	crederono or credettero	credano	credessero	

Summary of Italian grammar

Regular verbs -ire (1)

sentire – to hear (past participle **sentito**)

	present	future	conditional	perfect	imperfect
io	sento	sentirò	sentirei	ho sentito	sentivo
tu	senti	sentirai	sentiresti	hai sentito	sentivi
lui/lei; lei	sente	sentirà	sentirebbe	ha sentito	sentiva
noi	sentiamo	sentiremo	sentiremmo	abbiamo sentito	sentivamo
voi	sentite	sentirete	sentireste	avete sentito	sentivate
loro	sentono	sentiranno	sentirebbero	hanno sentito	sentivano

	pluperfect	past historic	present subjunctive	past subjunctive	imperative
io	avevo sentito	sentii	senta	sentissi	
tu	avevi sentito	sentisti	senta	sentissi	senti
lui/lei; lei	aveva sentito	sentì	senta	sentisse	senta
noi	avevamo sentito	sentimmo	sentiamo	sentissimo	sentiamo
voi	avevate sentito	sentiste	sentiate	sentiste	sentite
loro	avevano sentito	sentirono	sentano	sentissero	

Regular verbs -ire (2)

Some verbs ending in **-ire** insert **-isc-** between the stem and the ending in the three singular forms and in the 3rd person plural form of the present tense.

finire – to finish (past participle **finito**)

	present	future	conditional	perfect	imperfect
io	finisco	finirò	finirei	ho finito	finivo
tu	finisci	finirai	finiresti	hai finito	finivi
lui/lei; lei	finisce	finirà	finirebbe	ha finito	finiva
noi	finiamo	finiremo	finiremmo	abbiamo finito	finivamo
voi	finite	finirete	finireste	avete finito	finivate
loro	finiscono	finiranno	finirebbero	hanno finito	finivano

	pluperfect	past historic	present subjunctive	past subjunctive	imperative
io	avevo finito	finii	finisca	finissi	
tu	avevi finito	finisti	finisca	finissi	finisci
lui/lei; lei	aveva finito	finì	finisca	finisse	finisca
noi	avevamo finito	finimmo	finiamo	finissimo	finiamo
voi	avevate finito	finiste	finiate	finiste	finite
loro	avevano finito	finirono	finiscano	finissero	

. . . .

Irregular verbs

avere – to have (past participle avuto)

	present	future	conditional	perfect	imperfect
io	ho	avrò	avrei	ho avuto	avevo
tu	hai	avrai	avresti	hai avuto	avevi
lui/lei; lei	ha	avrà	avrebbe	ha avuto	aveva
noi	abbiamo	avremo	avremmo	abbiamo avuto	avevamo
voi	avete	avrete	avreste	avete avuto	avevate
loro	hanno	avranno	avrebbero	hanno avuto	avevano

	pluperfect	past historic	present subjunctive	past subjunctive	imperative
io	avevo avuto	ebbi	abbia	avessi	
tu	avevi avuto	avesti	abbia	avessi	abbi
lui/lei; lei	aveva avuto	ebbe	abbia	avesse	abbia
noi	avevamo avuto	avemmo	abbiamo	avessimo	abbiamo
voi	avevate avuto	aveste	abbiate	aveste	abbiate
loro	avevano avuto	ebbero	abbiano	avessero	

essere* – to be (past participle stato)

	present	future	conditional	perfect	imperfect
io	sono	sarò	sarei	sono stato/stata	ero
tu	sei	sarai	saresti	sei stato/stata	eri
lui/lei; lei	è	sarà	sarebbe	è stato/stata	era
noi	siamo	saremo	saremmo	siamo stati/state	eravamo
voi	siete	sarete	sareste	siete stati/state	eravate
loro	sono	saranno	sarebbero	sono stati/state	erano

	pluperfect	past historic	present subjunctive	past subjunctive	imperative
io	ero stato/stata	fui	sia	fossi	
tu	eri stato/stata	fosti	sia	fossi	sii
lui/lei; lei	era stato/stata	fu	sia	fosse	sia
noi	eravamo stati/state	fummo	siamo	fossimo	siamo
voi	eravate stati/state	foste	siate	foste	siate
loro	erano stati/state	furono	siano	fossero	

• •

Irregular verbs cont.

andare* – to go (past participle **andato**)

	present	future	conditional	perfect	imperfect
io	vado	andrò	andrei	sono andato/andata	andavo
tu	vai	andrai	andresti	sei andato/andata	andavi
lui/lei; lei	va	andrà	andrebbe	è andato/andata	andava
noi	andiamo	andremo	andremmo	siamo andati/andate	andavamo
voi	andate	andrete	andreste	siete andati/andate	andavate
loro	vanno	andranno	andrebbero	sono andati/andate	andavano

	pluperfect	past historic	present subjunctive	past subjunctive	imperative
io	ero andato/andata	andai	vada	andassi	
tu	eri andato/andata	andasti	vada	andassi	va'
lui/lei; lei	era andato/andata	andò	vada	andasse	vada
noi	eravamo andati/andate	andammo	andiamo	andassimo	andiamo
voi	eravate andati/andate	andaste	andiate	andaste	andate
loro	erano andati/andate	andarono	vadano	andassero	

bere – to drink (past participle **bevuto**)

	present	future	conditional	perfect	imperfect
io	bevo	berrò	berrei	ho bevuto	bevevo
tu	bevi	berrai	berresti	hai bevuto	bevevi
lui/lei; lei	beve	berrà	berrebbe	ha bevuto	beveva
noi	beviamo	berremo	berremmo	abbiamo bevuto	bevevamo
voi	bevete	berrete	berreste	avete bevuto	bevevate
loro	bevono	berranno	berrebbero	hanno bevuto	bevevano

	pluperfect	past historic	present subjunctive	past subjunctive	imperative
io	avevo bevuto	bevvi *or* bevetti	beva	bevessi	
tu	avevi bevuto	bevesti	beva	bevessi	bevi
lui/lei; lei	aveva bevuto	bevve *or* bevette	beva	bevesse	beva
noi	avevamo bevuto	bevemmo	beviamo	bevessimo	beviamo
voi	avevate bevuto	beveste	beviate	beveste	bevete
loro	avevano bevuto	bevvero *or* bevettero	bevano	bevessero	

Irregular verbs cont.

dare – to give (past participle dato)

	present	future	conditional	perfect	imperfect
io	do	darò	darei	ho dato	davo
tu	dai	darai	daresti	hai dato	davi
lui/lei; lei	dà	darà	darebbe	ha dato	dava
noi	diamo	daremo	daremmo	abbiamo dato	davamo
voi	date	darete	dareste	avete dato	davate
loro	danno	daranno	darebbero	hanno dato	davano

	pluperfect	past historic	present subjunctive	past subjunctive	imperative
io	avevo dato	diedi or detti	dia	dessi	
tu	avevi dato	desti	dia	dessi	da'
lui/lei; lei	aveva dato	diede or dette	dia	desse	dia
noi	avevamo dato	demmo	diamo	dessimo	diamo
voi	avevate dato	deste	diate	deste	date
loro	avevano dato	diedero or dettero	diano	dessero	

dire – to say (past participle detto)

	present	future	conditional	perfect	imperfect
io	dico	dirò	direi	ho detto	dicevo
tu	dici	dirai	diresti	hai detto	dicevi
lui/lei; lei	dice	dirà	direbbe	ha detto	diceva
noi	diciamo	diremo	diremmo	abbiamo detto	dicevamo
voi	dite	direte	direste	avete detto	dicevate
loro	dicono	diranno	direbbero	hanno detto	dicevano

	pluperfect	past historic	present subjunctive	past subjunctive	imperative
io	avevo detto	dissi	dica	dicessi	
tu	avevi detto	dicesti	dica	dicessi	di'
lui/lei; lei	aveva detto	disse	dica	dicesse	dica
noi	avevamo detto	dicemmo	diciamo	dicessimo	diciamo
voi	avevate detto	diceste	diciate	diceste	dite
loro	avevano detto	dissero	dicano	dicessero	

Irregular verbs cont.

dovere – to have to (past participle dovuto)

	present	future	conditional	perfect	imperfect
io	devo	dovrò	dovrei	ho dovuto	dovevo
tu	devi	dovrai	dovresti	hai dovuto	dovevi
lui/lei; lei	deve	dovrà	dovrebbe	ha dovuto	doveva
noi	dobbiamo	dovremo	dovremmo	abbiamo dovuto	dovevamo
voi	dovete	dovrete	dovreste	avete dovuto	dovevate
loro	devono	dovranno	dovrebbero	hanno dovuto	dovevano

	pluperfect	past historic	present subjunctive	past subjunctive
io	avevo dovuto	dovetti	deva	dovessi
tu	avevi dovuto	dovesti	deva	dovessi
lui/lei; lei	aveva dovuto	dovette	deva	dovesse
noi	avevamo dovuto	dovemmo	dobbiamo	dovessimo
voi	avevate dovuto	doveste	dobbiate	doveste
loro	avevano dovuto	dovettero	devano	dovessero

fare – to do, to make (past participle fatto)

	present	future	conditional	perfect	imperfect
io	faccio	farò	farei	ho fatto	facevo
tu	fai	farai	faresti	hai fatto	facevi
lui/lei; lei	fa	farà	farebbe	ha fatto	faceva
noi	facciamo	faremo	faremmo	abbiamo fatto	facevamo
voi	fate	farete	fareste	avete fatto	facevate
loro	fanno	faranno	farebbero	hanno fatto	facevano

	pluperfect	past historic	present subjunctive	past subjunctive	imperative
io	avevo fatto	feci	faccia	facessi	
tu	avevi fatto	facesti	faccia	facessi	fa'
lui/lei; lei	aveva fatto	fece	faccia	facesse	faccia
noi	avevamo fatto	facemmo	facciamo	facessimo	facciamo
voi	avevate fatto	faceste	facciate	faceste	fate
loro	avevano fatto	fecero	facciano	facessero	

. . . .

Irregular verbs cont.

potere – to be able to (past participle **potuto**)

	present	future	conditional	perfect	imperfect
io	posso	potrò	potrei	ho potuto	potevo
tu	puoi	potrai	potresti	hai potuto	potevi
lui/lei; lei	può	potrà	potrebbe	ha potuto	poteva
noi	possiamo	potremo	potremmo	abbiamo potuto	potevamo
voi	potete	potrete	potreste	avete potuto	potevate
loro	possono	potranno	potrebbero	hanno potuto	potevano

	pluperfect	past historic	present subjunctive	past subjunctive
io	avevo potuto	potei	possa	potessi
tu	avevi potuto	potesti	possa	potessi
lui/lei; lei	aveva potuto	poté	possa	potesse
noi	avevamo potuto	potemmo	possiamo	potessimo
voi	avevate potuto	poteste	possiate	poteste
loro	avevano potuto	poterono	possano	potessero

sapere – to know (a fact, how to do something) (past participle **saputo**)

	present	future	conditional	perfect	imperfect
io	so	saprò	saprei	ho saputo	sapevo
tu	sai	saprai	sapresti	hai saputo	sapevi
lui/lei; lei	sa	saprà	saprebbe	ha saputo	sapeva
noi	sappiamo	sapremo	sapremmo	abbiamo saputo	sapevamo
voi	sapete	saprete	sapreste	avete saputo	sapevate
loro	sanno	sapranno	saprebbero	hanno saputo	sapevano

	pluperfect	past historic	present subjunctive	past subjunctive	imperative
io	avevo saputo	seppi	sappia	sapessi	
tu	avevi saputo	sapesti	sappia	sapessi	sappi
lui/lei; lei	aveva saputo	seppe	sappia	sapesse	sappia
noi	avevamo saputo	sapemmo	sappiamo	sapessimo	sappiamo
voi	avevate saputo	sapeste	sappiate	sapeste	sappiate
loro	avevano saputo	seppero	sappiano	sapessero	

Irregular verbs cont.

stare* – to stay (past participle **stato**)

	present	future	conditional	perfect	imperfect
io	sto	starò	starei	sono stato/stata	stavo
tu	stai	starai	staresti	sei stato/stata	stavi
lui/lei; lei	sta	starà	starebbe	è stato/stata	stava
noi	stiamo	staremo	staremmo	siamo stati/state	stavamo
voi	state	starete	stareste	siete stati/state	stavate
loro	stanno	staranno	starebbero	sono stati/state	stavano

	pluperfect	past historic	present subjunctive	past subjunctive	imperative
io	ero stato/stata	stetti	stia	stessi	
tu	eri stato/stata	stesti	stia	stessi	sta'
lui/lei; lei	era stato/stata	stette	stia	stesse	stia
noi	eravamo stati/state	stemmo	stiamo	stessimo	stiamo
voi	eravate stati/state	steste	stiate	steste	state
loro	erano stati/state	stettero	stiano	stessero	

uscire* – to go out (past participle **uscito**)

	present	future	conditional	perfect	imperfect
io	esco	uscirò	uscirei	sono uscito/uscita	uscivo
tu	esci	uscirai	usciresti	sei uscito/uscita	uscivi
lui/lei; lei	esce	uscirà	uscirebbe	è uscito/uscita	usciva
noi	usciamo	usciremo	usciremmo	siamo usciti/uscite	uscivamo
voi	uscite	uscirete	uscireste	siete usciti/uscite	uscivate
loro	escono	usciranno	uscirebbero	sono usciti/uscite	uscivano

	pluperfect	past historic	present subjunctive	past subjunctive	imperative
io	ero uscito/uscita	uscii	esca	uscissi	
tu	eri uscito/uscita	uscisti	esca	uscissi	esci
lui/lei; lei	era uscito/uscita	uscì	esca	uscisse	esca
noi	eravamo usciti/uscite	uscimmo	usciamo	uscissimo	usciamo
voi	eravate usciti/uscite	usciste	usciate	usciste	uscite
loro	erano usciti/uscite	uscirono	escano	uscissero	

· ·

Irregular verbs cont.

venire* – to come (past participle **venuto**)

	present	*future*	*conditional*	*perfect*	*imperfect*
io	vengo	verrò	verrei	sono venuto/venuta	venivo
tu	vieni	verrai	verresti	sei venuto/venuta	venivi
lui/lei; lei	viene	verrà	verrebbe	è venuto/venuta	veniva
noi	veniamo	verremo	verremmo	siamo venuti/venute	venivamo
voi	venite	verrete	verreste	siete venuti/venute	venivate
loro	vengono	verranno	verrebbero	sono venuti/venute	venivano

	pluperfect	*past historic*	*present subjunctive*	*past subjunctive*	*imperative*
io	ero venuto/venuta	venni	venga	venissi	
tu	eri venuto/venuta	venisti	venga	venissi	vieni
lui/lei; lei	era venuto/venuta	venne	venga	venisse	venga
noi	eravamo venuti/venute	venimmo	veniamo	venissimo	veniamo
voi	eravate venuti/venute	veniste	veniate	veniste	venite
loro	erano venuti/venute	vennero	vengano	venissero	

volere – to want (past participle **voluto**)

	present	*future*	*conditional*	*perfect*	*imperfect*
io	voglio	vorrò	vorrei	ho voluto	volevo
tu	vuoi	vorrai	vorresti	hai voluto	volevi
lui/lei; lei	vuole	vorrà	vorrebbe	ha voluto	voleva
noi	vogliamo	vorremo	vorremmo	abbiamo voluto	volevamo
voi	volete	vorrete	vorreste	avete voluto	volevate
loro	vogliono	vorranno	vorrebbero	hanno voluto	volevano

	pluperfect	*past historic*	*present subjunctive*	*past subjunctive*
io	avevo voluto	volli	voglia	volessi
tu	avevi voluto	volesti	voglia	volessi
lui/lei; lei	aveva voluto	volle	voglia	volesse
noi	avevamo voluto	volemmo	vogliamo	volessimo
voi	avevate voluto	voleste	vogliate	voleste
loro	avevano voluto	vollero	vogliano	volessero

Note sulla grammatica inglese

Gli articoli

l'articolo indeterminativo

L'articolo indeterminativo è **a** davanti a una parola che comincia con consonante o con il suono 'i + vocal' (/j/):

a ball	**a girl**	**a union**
una palla	una ragazza	un'unione

È **an** davanti a vocale o h muta:

an apple	**an hour**
una mela	un'ora

L'uso dell'articolo indeterminativo è generalmente limitato ai nomi numerabili. Da notare i seguenti usi:

* con professione

She is a doctor.
È medico.

He is an engineer.
È ingegnere.

* dopo una preposizione

She works as a tour guide.
Fa la guida turistica.

Anna has gone out without an umbrella.
Anna è uscita senza ombrello.

* con senso generico

A whale is larger than a frog.
La balena è più grande della rana.

l'articolo determinativo

L'articolo determinativo è **the**, sia per i nomi singolari che per i plurali:

the cat	**the owls**
il gatto	le civette

L'articolo determinativo *non* viene generalmente usato con le parole che designano:

* istituzioni

I don't go to church.
Non vado in chiesa.

He's starting school next week.
Comincia la scuola la settimana prossima.

Quando ci si riferisce all'edificio, il nome viene invece accompagnato dall'articolo:
Turn right at the school (Alla scuola, gira a destra).

* pasti

Breakfast is at 8.30.
La colazione è alle 8.30.

Dinner is ready!
La cena è pronta!

* periodi del giorno, dopo una preposizione (eccetto **in** o **during**)

I'm never out at night.
Non esco mai di sera.

They left in the morning.
Sono partiti di mattina.

* cose astratte

Hatred is a destructive force.
L'odio è una forza distruttrice.

The book is on English grammar.
Il libro è sulla grammatica inglese.

* malattie

She's got tonsillitis.
Ha la tonsillite.

* stagioni

Spring is here!
È arrivata la primavera!

It's like winter today.
Oggi, sembra inverno.

* nazioni

France la Francia
England l'Inghilterra

* vie, parchi, ecc.

a concert in Central Park
un concerto a Central Park

I work on Bath Street.
Lavoro in Bath Street.

L'articolo è tuttavia utilizzato nei seguenti tipi di frasi:

The breakfast he served was awful.
La colazione che ha servito era orribile.

Le seguenti categorie di nomi prendono generalmente l'articolo determinativo:

* nomi geografici plurali

the Netherlands i Paesi Bassi
the United States gli Stati Uniti
the Alps le Alpi

• •

• nomi di fiumi e oceani

the Thames il Tamigi
the Pacific il Pacifico

• nomi di hotel, pub, teatri, musei, ecc.

the Hilton
the Fox and Hounds
the Odeon

Il plurale

Il plurale di un nome è di solito formato aggiungendo **-s** in fine di parola:

dog, dogs cane, cani
tape, tapes cassetta, cassette

-es viene aggiunto a parole che terminano in **-s, -ss, -sh, -ch, -x** o **-zz**:

dress, dresses vestito, vestiti
box, boxes scatola, scatole

Nomi che terminano in consonante + y:

baby, babies bambino, bambini

Nomi che terminano in vocale + y:

valley, valleys valle, valli

I nomi che terminano in **-o** talvolta prendono **-s**, talvolta **-es**:

potato, potatoes patata, patate
tomato, tomatoes pomodoro, pomodori
solo, solos assolo, assoli
zero, zeros zero, zeri

I plurali dei nomi terminanti in **-f(e)** sono di tre tipi:

life, lives vita, vite
dwarf, dwarfs/dwarves nano, nani
roof, roofs tetto, tetti

I plurali irregolari più frequenti includono:

child, children bambino, bambini
foot, feet piede, piedi
man, men uomo, uomini
mouse, mice topo, topi
tooth, teeth dente, denti
woman, women donna, donne

I nomi composti

I nomi composti possono avere diverse forme.

nome + nome:

summer dress abito estivo
tennis shoes scarpe da tennis
record collection collezione di dischi

nome + gerundio:

disco dancing ballo da discoteca
dressmaking cucito

gerundio + nome:

parking meter parchimetro
writing course corso di scrittura
boarding card carta di imbarco

Da notare la forma di composti quali **record collection**: a record collection (senza la **s** del plurale in record), ma **a collection of records** [una collezione di dischi]; **a photo album**, ma **an album of photos** [un album di fotografie].

Nel caso di nomi numerabili, la **s** del plurale va aggiunta al secondo elemento del composto: **summer dresses** [abiti estivi], **boarding cards** [carte di imbarco].

Il femminile

L'inglese ha un numero relativamente basso di forme femminili di parole. Pertanto, **cousin** = cugino o cugina; **friend** = amico o amica; **doctor** = dottore o dottoressa.

Dovendo specificare il sesso della persona alla quale ci si riferisce, si dirà, ad esempio, **a male student** (uno studente), **a woman doctor** (una dottoressa).

Il genitivo

Le regole sull'uso del genitivo – **s** preceduto dall'apostrofo (**'s**) o **s** seguito dall'apostrofo (**s'**) – sono le seguenti:

-'s viene aggiunto a nomi singolari:

the boy's book (il libro del ragazzo)

il solo apostrofo (**'**) viene aggiunto a nomi plurali terminanti in **-s**:

the boys' room (la camera dei ragazzi)
the boys' books (i libri dei ragazzi)

Se un nome plurale non termina in **-s** il genitivo si forma aggiungendo **-'s**:

the children's toys (i giocattoli dei bambini)

Con nomi propri terminanti in **-s** si possono trovare entrambe le forme **'s** e **s'**, benché **s'** sia più frequente: **Keats's poetry** o **Keats' poetry** [le poesie di Keats]. I nomi greci e romani terminanti in **s**, tuttavia, prendono in genere solo l'apostrofo: **Socrates' death** [la morte di Socrate], **Catullus' poetry** [le poesie di Catullo].

Il genitivo viene usato soprattutto con persone, animali (in particolare domestici) e paesi: **Andrew's house** [la casa di Andrew], **the lion's den** [la tana del leone], **America's foreign policy** [la politica estera dell'America].

Da notare i seguenti usi del genitivo:

We're going to Anne's.
Andiamo a casa di Anne.

We're going to Peter and Anne's.
Andiamo a casa di Peter e Anne. (Non, per lo più, **Peter's and Anne's** se Peter e Anne sono una coppia.)

Jane Austen's and George Orwell's novels
i romanzi di Jane Austen e quelli di George Orwell (Jane Austen e George Orwell sono ben distinti l'una dall'altro.)

I got it at the baker's/the chemist's.
L'ho preso dal panettiere/in farmacia. (Letteralmente, nel negozio del panettiere/del farmacista.)

Nell'inglese colloquiale il 'doppio genitivo' è frequente:

He's a friend of my brother's.
È un amico di mio fratello.

It was an idea of Anne's.
È stata un'idea di Anne.

Gli aggettivi

Gli aggettivi in inglese hanno un'unica forma, non concordano, cioè, né nel genere, né nel numero:

an old man
un uomo vecchio

three old women
tre donne vecchie

posizione dell'aggettivo

L'aggettivo può precedere il nome: **a long story** [una storia lunga] o seguire il verbo: **this story is long** [questa storia è lunga].

Alcuni aggettivi non possono essere usati davanti al nome: **The girl is upset.** [La ragazza è sconvolta.]; non si può dire **the upset girl.**

gradi comparativi

Ci sono tre gradi comparativi: la forma assoluta, il comparativo e il superlativo.

Gli aggettivi composti da una sola sillaba

formano il comparativo e il superlativo con l'aggiunta di **-(e)r** e **-(e)st**:

   dull noioso
   duller più noioso
   dullest il più noioso

   big grande
   bigger
   biggest

(Da notare che una consonante semplice in fine di parola viene raddoppiata.)

   nice bello
   nicer
   nicest

Gli aggettivi di tre sillabe, per lo più, formano il comparativo e il superlativo con **more** e **most**:

   generous generoso
   more generous
   most generous

Lo stesso vale per alcuni aggettivi di due sillabe, ad esempio **useful** [utile].

Non esistono tuttavia regole assolute per gli aggettivi bisillabici, benché **-er/-est** siano particolarmente frequenti con aggettivi terminanti in **-y, -le, -ow, -er**. Esempi:

   pretty carino (da notare che **-y** diventa **-ie**)
   prettier
   prettiest

   narrow stretto
   narrower
   narrowest

   curious curioso
   more curious
   most curious

Per i participi presenti e passati si usa la forma con **more/most**:

   boring noioso
   more boring
   most boring

   bored annoiato
   more bored
   most bored

Most può essere inoltre usato come sinonimo di 'estremamente' o 'molto':
That was a most interesting story (Quella era una storia molto interessante).

alcuni aggettivi irregolari frequenti

   bad cattivo
   worse peggiore

worst il peggiore

good buono

better migliore

best il migliore

little poco

less meno

least il meno

many/much molti/molto

more più

most il più

far lontano

further

furthest (con riferimento a spazio, tempo, quantità, numero)

far lontano

farther

farthest (solo per distanza nello spazio)

old (1) vecchio

elder

eldest (usato solo per persone)

(1) Le forme regolari (**old, older, oldest** vecchio, più vecchio, il più vecchio) sono usate sia per persone che per cose.

Le comparazioni negative possono essere espresse dall'uso di **less/least**:

far lontano

less far meno lontano

least far il meno lontano

Gli aggettivi possono svolgere la funzione di nomi, in particolare quando si riferiscono a gruppi di persone: **the young** i giovani; **the old** i vecchi; **the unemployed** i disoccupati.

Gli aggettivi possessivi

Gli aggettivi possessivi sono:

my mio, mia, miei, mie
our nostro, nostra, nostri, nostre

your tuo, tua, tuoi, tue; suo,
your vostro, vostra, vostri, sua, suoi, sue vostre

his, her, its suo, sua, suoi, sue

their loro

Concordano con il possessore e non con la cosa posseduta:

his mother sua madre (la madre del ragazzo, ad esempio)

her mother sua madre (la madre della ragazza, ad esempio)

their mother la loro madre (la madre delle ragazze, o dei ragazzi, o dei ragazzi e delle ragazze)

Mantengono la stessa forma con nomi singolari e plurali:

my cat il mio gatto
my boots i miei stivali

Gli avverbi

Gli avverbi possono qualificare aggettivi:

The job was extremely dangerous.
Il lavoro era estremamente pericoloso.

verbi:

He finished quickly.
Ha finito in fretta.

altri avverbi:

very quickly
molto in fretta

Extremely, quickly e **very** sono avverbi.

Molti avverbi sono formati con il suffisso **-ly** aggiunto all'aggettivo: **sad, sadly** triste, tristemente; **brave, bravely** coraggioso, coraggiosamente; **beautiful, beautifully** bello, molto bene.

Possono tuttavia intervenire dei cambiamenti nell'ortografia: **true, truly** vero, veramente; **due, duly** dovuto, debitamente; **whole, wholly** intero, interamente.

Altri mutamenti fonetici regolari riguardano:

y in fine di parola: **ready, readily** pronto, prontamente

consonante in fine di parola + **le**: **gentle, gently** dolce, dolcemente.

Alcuni avverbi hanno forma identica all'aggettivo corrispondente; tra questi **back** dietro, **early** presto, **far** lontano, **fast** velocemente, **left** a sinistra, **little** poco, **long** a lungo, **more** più, **much** molto, **only** solo, **right** a destra, giustamente, **still** tranquillamente, **straight** dritto, **well** bene, **wrong** in modo sbagliato. Esempi:

a wrong answer (aggettivo)
una risposta sbagliata

He did it wrong. (avverbio)
L'ha fatto in modo sbagliato.

• •

an early summer
un'estate precoce

Summer arrived early.
L'estate è arrivata in anticipo.

a straight road
una strada dritta

He came straight to the point.
È andato dritto al punto.

I pronomi

pronomi personali

soggetto	*complemento*
I io	me me, mi
you tu; lei	you te, ti; la, le
he egli, lui	him lo, gli
she essa, lei	her la, le
it esso, essa	it lo, la, gli, le
we noi	us ci
you voi	you vi
they essi, loro	them li, loro

Il soggetto di un verbo in inglese non è espresso dalla forma del verbo stesso; pertanto, la traduzione dell'italiano **vado**, ad esempio, è **I go** e non **go**.

I pronomi complemento sono usati come complemento oggetto:

Mary loves him.
Mary lo ama.

come complemento di termine:

John gave me a lift.
John mi ha dato un passaggio.

e dopo una preposizione:

The book is from her.
Il libro è da parte sua.

altri usi dei pronomi personali

he e she

Questi pronomi sono talvolta usati per indicare degli animali, specialmente domestici:

Poor Whiskers, we had to take him to the vet's.
Povero Whiskers, abbiamo dovuto portarlo dal veterinario.

it

• è usato in costruzioni impersonali:

It's sunny.
C'è il sole.

It's hard to know what to do.
È difficile sapere cosa fare.

It looks as though they were right.
Parrebbe che avessero ragione.

• in espressioni temporali e spaziali:

It's five o'clock.
Sono le cinque.

It's January the sixth.
È il sei gennaio.

How far is it to Edinburgh?
Quanto dista Edimburgo?

Va notato che **it's** è la forma contratta di **it is**, da non confondersi con il pronome possessivo **its**.

you

Rivolgendosi ad una persona, l'inglese non distingue l'uso del pronome **tu** dal pronome **lei** che vengono entrambi tradotti con **you**.

You è spesso usato in senso generico, per indicare la gente in generale:

You never know; it might be sunny this afternoon.
Non si sa mai; potrebbe esserci il sole oggi pomeriggio.

You can't buy cars like that any more.
Non si possono più comprare macchine così.

they

• è impiegato per riferirsi a un gruppo di persone sconosciute, specialmente se dotate di un qualche potere, autorità o abilità:

They don't make cars like that any more.
Non ne fanno più di macchine così.

They will have to find the murderer first.
Dovranno prima trovare l'assassino.

You'll have to get them to repair it.
Dovrai farglielo riparare.

• al posto di **he or she** (lui o lei)

The person appointed will be answerable to the director. They will be responsible for ...
La persona prescelta dovrà rispondere al direttore. Sarà responsabile di ...

A personal secretary will assist them. (= him/her)
Una segretaria personale lo/la assisterà.

• per rimandare ai pronomi indefiniti **somebody, someone** qualcuno; **anybody, anyone** chiunque; **everybody, everyone** tutti; **nobody, no one** nessuno:

If anyone has seen my pen, will they please tell me.
Se qualcuno ha visto la mia penna, per favore, me lo dica.

one

One è equivalente al pronome generico **you**, ma è più formale:

One needs to get a clearer picture of what one wants.
Bisogna avere un'idea più chiara di quello che si vuole.

L'uso ripetuto di **one** viene di solito evitato.

pronomi riflessivi

myself mi	**ourselves** ci
yourself ti; si	**yourselves** vi
himself, herself, itself, oneself si	**themselves** si

Esempi dell'uso:

He burned himself badly. (complemento oggetto)
Si è bruciato seriamente.

I always buy myself a Christmas present. (complemento di termine)
Mi compro sempre un regalo di Natale.

She talks to herself. (dopo preposizione)
Parla da sola.

Do it yourself. (enfatico)
Fallo da te.

pronomi possessivi

mine il mio, la mia, i miei, le mie
yours il tuo, la tua, i tuoi, le tue
his, hers il suo, la sua, i suoi, le sue
ours il nostro, la nostra, i nostri, le nostre
yours il vostro, la vostra, i vostri, le vostre
theirs il loro, la loro, i loro, le loro

I pronomi possessivi concordano con il possessore e non con la cosa posseduta:

Whose book is this? – It's hers.
Di chi è questo libro? – È suo.

Whose shoes are these? – They're hers.
Di chi sono queste scarpe? – Sono le sue.

Whose car is that? – It's theirs.
Di chi è questa macchina? – È la loro.

Gli aggettivi e i pronomi interrogativi

who chi
whom chi
whose di chi
which quale, quali
what quale, quali, che

Who è usato per persona con funzione di soggetto:

Who is it? Chi è?

Whom è usato per persona con funzione di complemento:

To whom did you send the letter?
A chi hai spedito la lettera?

Whom did you see?
Chi hai visto?

Whom è considerato piuttosto formale e tende ad essere sostituito da **who**:

Who did you send the letter to?
A chi hai spedito la lettera?

Who did you see?
Chi hai visto?

Whose è la forma genitiva di **who**:

Whose are these?
Di chi sono questi?

Whose socks are these?
Di chi sono queste calze?

Which può designare sia persone che cose. È usato con funzione di soggetto:

Which of you are going?
Chi di voi va?

Which is bigger?
Qual è più grande?

Which box is bigger?
Quale scatola è più grande?

e di complemento:

Which of the singers/pictures do you prefer?
Quale cantante/quadro preferisci?

Which dress should I wear?
Che vestito mi metto?

What è usato esclusivamente per cose. Può avere funzione di soggetto:

What is this?
Cos'è questo?

What type of bird is that?
Che tipo di uccello è quello?

e di complemento:

What are you going to do?
Cosa farai?

What sort of books do you like?
Che tipo di libri ti piacciono?

What implica una gamma di possibilità più estesa o meno definita rispetto a **which**.

I pronomi relativi

who, whom che   which che
that chi, che   whose il cui

I pronomi relativi rimandano normalmente ad un antecedente (cioè qualcosa che è già stato menzionato). In **She phoned the man who had contacted her** (Ha telefonato all'uomo che l'aveva contattata), il pronome relativo **who** (che) si riferisce a **the man** (l'uomo).

antecedente	soggetto	complemento
persone	who/that	whom/who/that
cose	which/that	which/that

persone: soggetto

Who è il pronome relativo generalmente usato in questo caso; anche **that** viene però usato:

> **There is a prize for the student who/that gets the highest mark.**
> C'è un premio per lo studente che ottiene il voto più alto.

persone: complemento

> **The man whom/who/that she met that night was a spy.**
> L'uomo che ha incontrato quella notte era una spia.

Whom viene considerato piuttosto formale ed è generalmente sostituito da **who** o **that**.

Il pronome relativo può anche essere omesso:

> **The man she met last night was a spy.**
> L'uomo che ha incontrato la notte scorsa era una spia.

cose: soggetto

> **The book, which is on the table, was a present.**
> Il libro che è sul tavolo è un regalo.

> **John gave me the book which/that is on the table.**
> John mi ha dato il libro che è sul tavolo.

cose: complemento

> **His latest film, which we went to see last week, was excellent.**
> Il suo ultimo film, che siamo andati a vedere la settimana scorsa, era ottimo.

> **The film which/that we went to see last week was excellent.**
> Il film che siamo andati a vedere la settimana scorsa era ottimo.

Nell'ultimo esempio, il pronome relativo può anche essere omesso:

> **The film we went to see last week was excellent.**
> Il film che siamo andati a vedere la settimana scorsa era ottimo.

Whose è la forma genitiva:

> **This is the boy whose dog has been killed.**
> Questo è il ragazzo il cui cane è stato ucciso.

La forma **of which** (il cui) è usata nel linguaggio più formale o tecnico per riferirsi a cose:

> **Water, the boiling point of which is 100°C, is a colourless liquid.**
> L'acqua, il cui punto di ebollizione è a 100°C, è un liquido incolore.

Si noti che **who's** è la forma contratta di **who is** (chi è), da non confondersi con il pronome relativo **whose** (il cui).

Gli aggettivi e i pronomi indefiniti

some/any

Come aggettivi, vengono usati con nomi plurali o non numerabili:

> **Take some biscuits.**
> Prendi dei biscotti.

> **Take some jam.**
> Prendi della marmellata.

> **Have you got any biscuits?**
> Hai dei biscotti?

> **Have you any jam?**
> Hai della marmellata?

Come pronomi, sostituiscono nomi plurali o non numerabili:

> **We haven't got any.**
> Non ne abbiamo.

Some (aggettivo e pronome) si usa in:

- frasi affermative

> **He bought some.**
> Ne ha comprato.

> **He bought some jam.**
> Ha comprato della marmellata.

> **He bought some biscuits.**
> Ha comprato dei biscotti.

- domande alle quali ci si aspetta una risposta affermativa

Can you lend me some money?
Mi puoi prestare dei soldi?

• offerte e richieste

Would you like some?
Ne vuoi?

Could you buy some onions for me?
Mi puoi comprare delle cipolle?

Any (aggettivo e pronome) si usa in:

• frasi negative

I haven't got any brothers or sisters.
Non ho né fratelli, né sorelle.

• domande

Have you got any bananas?
Hai delle banane?

I composti di **some** e **any** vengono usati in modo simile. Esempi:

I saw something really strange today.
Ho visto qualcosa di veramente strano oggi.

Did you meet anyone you knew?
Hai incontrato qualcuno che conoscevi?

We didn't see anything interesting.
Non abbiamo visto niente di interessante.

I verbi

L'infinito costituisce la radice o forma di base. La forma intera dell'infinito comprende **to**: **to live** vivere, **to die** morire, ecc.

Per una lista di verbi irregolari vedi p.980.

I verbi regolari vengono coniugati come segue:

infinito

want	love(1)	stop(2)	prefer(3)

participio presente/gerundio

wanting	loving	stopping	preferring

passato semplice/participio passato

wanted	loved	stopped	preferred

(1) infinito terminante in **-e**
(2) infinito monosillabico terminante in vocale + consonante semplice
(3) infinito terminante in vocale accentata + consonante semplice

Il gerundio è usato con funzione nominale:

I don't like swimming.
Non mi piace nuotare.

Dancing is fun.
Ballare è divertente.

I tempi

presente

to be essere	to have avere
I am sono	I have ho
you are sei	you have hai
he/she/it is è	he/she/it has ha
we are siamo	we have abbiamo
you are siete	you have avete
they are sono	they have hanno

Per gli altri verbi, la forma è la stessa della radice, con l'eccezione della terza persona singolare, che prende la desinenza **-s**:

to want (volere): I want, you want, he/she/it wants, we want, you want, they want

to love (amare): I love, you love, he/she/it loves, we love, you love, they love

La terza persona singolare dei verbi terminanti in **-s, -ss, -sh, -ch, -x** o **-zz** è formata con la desinenza **-es**:

to watch guardare: he/she/it watches
to kiss baciare: he/she/it kisses

Il presente esprime:

• azioni abituali, verità generalmente accettate ed enunciazioni di fatti:

He takes the 8 o'clock train to work.
Prende il treno delle 8 per andare al lavoro.

I work in publishing.
Lavoro nell'editoria.

• gusti e opinioni

I hate Monday mornings.
Odio i lunedì mattina.

He doesn't believe in God.
Non crede in Dio.

• percezioni sensoriali

It tastes delicious.
È squisito.

passato semplice

La forma è la stessa per tutte le persone, sia singolari che plurali:

I/you/he/she/it/we/you/they wanted

È impiegato per descrivere azioni compiute o avvenimenti del passato:

He flew to America last week.
Ha preso l'aereo per l'America la settimana scorsa.

passato composto

È composto dal presente di **have** (avere) e il participio passato:

I/you have loved, he/she/it has loved, we/you/they have loved

Descrive azioni passate o avvenimenti che hanno una qualche rilevanza per il presente.

Si può osservare la differenza tra il passato composto e il passato semplice confrontando le seguenti frasi:

Have you seen Peter this morning?
Hai visto Peter stamattina? (è sempre mattina)

Did you see Peter this morning?
Hai visto Peter stamattina? (è ora pomeriggio o sera)

Va notato il seguente uso del present perfect:

I have lived in Glasgow for three years.
Vivo a Glasgow da tre anni.

trapassato

È composto dal tempo passato di **have** (avere) e il participio passato:

I/you/he/she/it/we/you/they had wanted

Descrive azioni o avvenimenti passati precedenti rispetto ad altre azioni o avvenimenti anch'essi passati:

She had already left home when I arrived.
Era già uscita di casa quando sono arrivato.

Le forme perifrastiche

Le forme perifrastiche sono formate dal verbo **be** (essere), nel tempo e persona richiesti, e dal participio presente.

presente progressivo

I am singing sto cantando, **you are singing**, ecc.

Descrive eventi, di solito temporanei, ancora in corso:

What are you doing? – I'm trying to fix the television.
Cosa stai facendo? – Sto cercando di riparare la televisione.

He always interrupts when I'm reading to the children.
Mi interrompe sempre mentre sto leggendo per i bambini.

passato progressivo

I was singing stavo cantando, **you were singing**, ecc.

Descrive avvenimenti passati ancora in corso nel momento in cui un altro avvenimento passato ha luogo:

He rushed into my office while I was talking to the director.
Si è precipitato nel mio ufficio mentre stavo parlando al direttore.

Anche gli altri tempi verbali hanno una forma progressiva: **I have been living; I had been living; I will be living.**

Da notare il seguente uso del passato composto nella forma progressiva:

I have been living in Glasgow for three years.
Vivo a Glasgow da tre anni.

Il futuro

In inglese ci sono diversi modi per parlare del futuro.

• will/shall

Will può essere usato con tutte le persone; **shall** è usato esclusivamente con la prima persona singolare e plurale.

I will/shall go andrò
we will/shall go andremo

you will go andrai
you will go andrete

he/she/it will go andrà
they will go andranno

Will e le forme negative **will not** e **shall not** possono essere contratte:

You'll be angry.
Ti arrabbierai.

We won't/shan't stay long.
Non staremo a lungo.

• going to

Questa forma viene spesso usata per esprimere un'intenzione o per predire qualcosa che accadrà:

I'm going to go to London tomorrow.
Vado a Londra domani.

The boss is going to be furious when he hears.
Il capo si infurierà quando lo verrà a sapere.

Going to è spesso intercambiabile con will:

The boss will be furious when he hears.
Il capo si infurierà quando lo verrà a sapere.

I wonder whether the car is going to/will start.
Mi chiedo se la macchina partirà.

- il presente

Può essere usato per esprimere qualcosa che accadrà in un momento determinato, specialmente con riferimento ad un orario:

When does term finish?
Quando finisce il trimestre?

There is a train for London at 10 o'clock.
C'è un treno per Londra alle 10.

- il presente progressivo

Viene usato in modo simile a **going to** per esprimere un'intenzione:

I'm spending Christmas in Paris.
Passerò il Natale a Parigi.

Where are you going for your holidays?
Dove vai in vacanza?

L'imperativo

La radice del verbo è usata per impartire ordini:

Be quiet!
Fai silenzio!

Shut the door!
Chiudi la porta!

L'imperativo negativo viene formato con **don't**:

Don't forget to phone Alan!
Non dimenticarti di telefonare ad Alan!

Let's viene usato per la prima persona plurale per fare delle proposte:

Let's go.
Andiamo.

Don't let's go.
Non andiamo.

Let's not go.
Non andiamo.

La forma interrogativa

La forma interrogativa di frasi contenenti il presente e il passato semplice prevede l'uso del verbo **do**, accordato con il soggetto della frase:

Do you live here?
Vivi qui?

Did you live here?
Vivevi qui?

Se la frase contiene un verbo ausiliare (**have**, **be**) o modale, la forma interrogativa è realizzata invertendo il verbo e il soggetto:

Are they going to get married?
Si sposano?

Have they seen us?
Ci hanno visti?

Can John come at eight?
Può venire alle otto John?

Con i pronomi interrogativi, i modelli sono i seguenti:

Who came?
Chi è venuto?

Who fed the cat?
Chi ha dato da mangiare al gatto?

What have they done to you?
Che cosa ti hanno fatto?

What shall we write about?
Di cosa scriviamo?

In frasi negative **not** segue il soggetto, a meno che sia utilizzata la forma contratta:

Did they not say they would come?/
Didn't they say they would come?
Non avevano detto che sarebbero venuti?

Will the director not be there?/
Won't the director be there?
Non ci sarà il direttore?

Nell'inglese parlato, l'ordine delle parole nelle domande è spesso lo stesso che nelle affermazioni, ma l'intonazione è crescente:

He told you to leave?
Ti ha detto di andartene?

He left without saying a word?
Se ne è andato senza dire una parola?

Le domande di conferma

Si tratta di domande brevi, aggiunte alla fine di una frase, per chiedere una conferma di quanto si è detto.

Una frase affermativa è di solito seguita da una domanda negativa:

You smoke, don't you?
Fumi, no?

Da notare l'ausiliare **don't** che sostituisce nella domanda il verbo **smoke**.

Una frase negativa è invece generalmente seguita da una domanda in forma affermativa:

> **You don't smoke, do you?**
> Non fumi, vero?

Se la frase contiene un verbo ausiliare o modale, questo è ripetuto nella domanda:

> **You aren't going, are you?**
> Non ci vai, vero?

> **You will come, won't you?**
> Vieni, no?

> **You shouldn't say that, should you?**
> Non dovresti dire questo, vero?

Va notata la forma della domanda quando il verbo nell'affermazione è **am**:

> **I am lucky, aren't I?**
> Sono fortunato, no?

Il tempo verbale nella domanda è lo stesso che nella frase da cui dipende:

> **You wanted to go home, didn't you?**
> Volevi andare a casa, no?

Le risposte brevi

Nelle risposte non è necessario ripetere la forma intera del verbo; si può infatti semplicemente ripetere il verbo ausiliare (**be, have, do**) o modale contenuto nella domanda.

> **Is it raining? – Yes, it is./No, it isn't.**
> Piove? – Sì./No.

> **Do you like fish? – Yes, I do./No, I don't.**
> Ti piace il pesce? – Sì./No.

> **Can you drive? – Yes, I can./No, I can't.**
> Guidi? – Sì./No.

Le frasi negative

Le proposizioni negative sono formate con l'ausiliare **do** concordato con il soggetto + **not**. Le forme contratte sono **don't** e **doesn't** per il presente e **didn't** per il passato.

> **They do not/don't understand English.**
> Non capiscono l'inglese.

> **We did not/didn't go anywhere yesterday.**
> Non siamo andati da nessuna parte ieri.

Quando il verbo è impiegato con tono enfatico, viene utilizzata la forma non contratta:

> **I do not approve!**
> Non approvo!

I verbi modali

can, could; may, might; shall, should; will, would; must; ought

I verbi modali sono invariabili: **I can, you can, he can**, ecc.

La forma interrogativa si ottiene con l'inversione del soggetto e del verbo: **Can I go now?** (Posso andare ora?)

È facile trovare i modali nella forma contratta. **Will** e **shall** si contraggono in **'ll: I'll be going** (Andrò).

Would si contrae in **'d: I'd like a cup of tea** (Vorrei una tazza di tè).

La forma negativa dei verbi modali prevede l'uso di **not** (**would not, might not**, ecc.) È particolare la forma negativa di **can: cannot** (cioè un'unica parola nell'inglese britannico).

Le forme negative contratte sono: **can't, couldn't, mightn't, shan't, shouldn't, won't, wouldn't, mustn't, oughtn't**. (**Mayn't** non è frequente.)

can

- autorizzazione

> **Can I leave the table, please?**
> Posso alzarmi da tavola, per favore?

> **I can have another sweet, daddy said so.**
> Posso avere un'altra caramella, lo ha detto papà.

- capacità

> **He can count to a hundred.**
> Sa contare fino a cento.

> **Can he drive?**
> Sa guidare?

- possibilità

> **Accidents can happen.**
> Gli incidenti possono capitare.

- richieste

> **Can you open the door for me, please?**
> Mi puoi aprire la porta, per favore?

Note sulla grammatica inglese

could

Could è la forma passata di **can**. I suoi significati comprendono:

- autorizzazione, capacità, possibilità, richiesta, espresse nel passato

  Daddy said I could have another sweet.
  Papà ha detto che potevo avere un'altra caramella.

  By the time he was three, he could count to a hundred.
  A tre anni sapeva contare fino a cento.

  She asked if he could open the door for her.
  Gli ha chiesto se poteva aprirle la porta.

- richiesta formale

  Could I leave a message, please?
  Potrei lasciare un messaggio, per favore?

- possibilità

  I don't know where John is; I suppose he could be at Anne's.
  Non so dov'è John; forse potrebbe essere da Anne.

- indignazione

  You could have warned me!
  Avresti potuto avvertirmi!

may

- autorizzazione e richiesta formale

  May I use your phone, please?
  Potrei usare il suo telefono, per favore?

  You may not leave the examination hall until I give the sign.
  Non potete allontanarvi dalla sala d'esame prima che io abbia dato il segnale.

- possibilità

  We may get an extra day's holiday.
  Potremmo avere un giorno di vacanza in più.

  They may have left.
  Potrebbero essere andati via.

might

- possibilità

Might si differenzia da **may** in quanto spesso suggerisce che si tratta di una possibilità poco probabile:

  We might get a pay rise.
  Magari avremo un aumento di stipendio.
  (= è improbabile)

Viene usato anche nel passato:

  He was afraid he might have missed the train.
  Aveva paura di aver perso il treno.

- autorizzazione e richiesta formale

  Do you think I might have another whisky?
  Pensa che potrei avere un altro whisky?

- indignazione

  You might have phoned!
  Avresti potuto telefonare!

shall

Per l'uso di **shall** per esprimere il futuro vedi p. 971. **Shall** può essere inoltre usato per indicare:

- richieste di ordini o consigli

  Where shall we put the shopping?
  Dove mettiamo la spesa?

  What time shall I set the alarm for?
  Per che ora devo mettere la sveglia?

- offerte o suggerimenti

  Shall I make you a cup of tea?
  Ti preparo una tazza di tè?

  Shall we meet outside the station?
  Ci vediamo fuori dalla stazione?

should

Should è la forma passata di **shall** e viene inoltre impiegato per esprimere:

- convenienza o obbligo

  You shouldn't tell lies.
  Non dovresti dire le bugie.

  What do you think we should do?
  Cosa pensi che dovremmo fare?

- probabilità

  Once this job is finished, we should have more spare time.
  Una volta finito questo lavoro, dovremmo avere più tempo libero.

  They should be here by now.
  Dovrebbero essere qui ormai.

  The keys should be in that drawer. That's where I left them.
  Le chiavi dovrebbero essere in quel cassetto. È lì che le ho lasciate.

will

Per l'uso di **will** per esprimere il futuro, vedi p. 971. Per **will** in proposizioni condizionali, vedi p. 975.

· ·

Will può essere anche impiegato per
esprimere:

- un comportamento tipico o una
caratteristica innata

  The stadium will seat 4,000 people.
  Lo stadio ha 4 000 posti a sedere.

  Hot air will rise.
  L'aria calda sale verso l'alto.

- la volontà, un desiderio, il consenso

  Will you see to the post for me?
  Puoi occuparti della posta per me?

  I'll do what I can to help him.
  Farò quello che posso per aiutarlo.

- un'offerta

  Will you have another slice of cake?
  Prendi un'altra fetta di dolce?

- una forte probabilità o una deduzione

  **There's someone at the door. That will be
  Kenneth.**
  C'è qualcuno alla porta, sarà Kenneth.

- un ordine

  You will go and wash your hands immediately.
  Vai subito a lavarti le mani.

would

Per l'uso di **would** in frasi condizionali, vedi
Sotto. **Would** è la forma passata di **will**. Può
esprimere anche:

- il 'futuro nel passato', o un'intenzione
passata

  He told me he would do it immediately.
  Mi ha detto che l'avrebbe fatto
  immediatamente.

  They said they wouldn't wait for me.
  Hanno detto che non mi avrebbero
  aspettato.

- abitudini nel passato

  He would always get up at 6 a.m.
  Si alzava sempre alle 6.

must

- obbligo

  You must make sure you lock up.
  Devi assicurarti di chiudere a chiave.

  I must check whether my neighbour is all right.
  Devo controllare se il mio vicino sta bene.

Da notare che **mustn't** significa che non si è
autorizzati a fare qualcosa:

You mustn't park there.
Non puoi parcheggiare qui. (= è vietato)

Se si vuole dire che non è necessario fare
qualcosa, si può usare **don't have to** o **needn't** o
don't need to.

**You don't have to eat that./You needn't eat that./
You don't need to eat that.**
Non sei obbligato a mangiarlo.

- probabilità

  They must be there by now.
  Devono essere là ormai.

  You must have been annoyed by the decision.
  La decisione deve averti seccato.

ought

- obbligo

  You ought to be leaving.
  Dovresti andare via.

  They ought to send him away.
  Lo dovrebbero mandare via.

- probabilità/attesa

  They ought to be there by now.
  Dovrebbero essere là ormai.

  Two kilos of potatoes. That ought to be enough.
  Due chili di patate. Dovrebbero bastare.

Le frasi ipotetiche con *if* (se)

I modelli di base sono:

if + presente, proposizione principale con
will:

  **If we hurry, we'll catch the train./We'll catch the
  train if we hurry.**
  Se ci sbrighiamo, prenderemo il treno.

if + passato semplice, proposizione
principale con **would**:

  **If I won the lottery, I would buy a new house./I
  would buy a new house if I won the lottery.**
  Se vincessi la lotteria, mi comprerei una
  casa nuova.

if + trapassato, proposizione principale con
would have:

  **If Paolo hadn't lost the tickets, we would have
  arrived on time./We would have arrived on time if
  Paolo hadn't lost the tickets.**
  Se Paolo non avesse perso i biglietti,
  saremmo arrivati in orario.

I verbi frasali

Numerosi verbi possono combinarsi con una preposizione per formare i cosiddetti verbi frasali. La preposizione può cambiare il significato del verbo:

to take (prendere):

John took a book.
John ha preso un libro.

to take off:

He took off his boots./He took his boots off.
Si è tolto gli stivali.

The plane took off.
L'aereo ha decollato.

to take after:

He takes after his mother.
Assomiglia a sua madre.

Da notare che il complemento oggetto, nel primo esempio di **take off**, può trovarsi in due posizioni diverse: dopo la preposizione o tra il verbo e la preposizione.

Quando il complemento oggetto è un pronome, però, la sola posizione possibile è tra il verbo e la preposizione:

He looked it up in the dictionary.
Lo ha cercato nel dizionario.

They have put it off.
Lo hanno rimandato.

Italian verb tables

Regular verbs:

1. in **-are** (*eg* **compr**|**are**)

> **Present** ~o, ~i, ~a, ~iamo, ~ate, ~ano
> **Imperfect** ~avo, ~avi, ~ava, ~avamo, ~avate, ~avano
> **Past historic** ~ai, ~asti, ~ò, ~ammo, ~aste, ~arono
> **Future** ~erò, ~erai, ~erà, ~eremo, ~erete, ~eranno
> **Present subjunctive** ~i, ~i, ~i, ~iamo, ~iate, ~ino
> **Past subjunctive** ~assi, ~assi, ~asse, ~assimo, ~aste, ~assero
> **Present participle** ~ando
> **Past participle** ~ato
> **Imperative** ~a (*fml* ~i), ~iamo, ~ate
> **Conditional** ~erei, ~eresti, ~erebbe, ~eremmo, ~ereste, ~erebbero

2. in **-ere** (*eg* **vend**|**ere**)

> **Pres** ~o, ~i, ~e, ~iamo, ~ete, ~ono
> **Impf** ~evo, ~evi, ~eva, ~evamo, ~evate, ~evano
> **Past hist** ~ei *or* ~etti, ~esti, ~è *or* ~ette, ~emmo, ~este, ~erono *or* ~ettero
> **Fut** ~erò, ~erai, ~erà, ~eremo, ~erete, ~eranno
> **Pres sub** ~a, ~a, ~a, ~iamo, ~iate, ~ano
> **Past sub** ~essi, ~essi, ~esse, ~essimo, ~este, ~essero
> **Pres part** ~endo
> **Past part** ~uto
> **Imp** ~i (*fml* ~a), ~iamo, ~ete
> **Cond** ~erei, ~eresti, ~erebbe, ~eremmo, ~ereste, ~erebbero

3. in **-ire** (*eg* **dorm**|**ire**)

> **Pres** ~o, ~i, ~e, ~iamo, ~ite, ~ono
> **Impf** ~ivo, ~ivi, ~iva, ~ivamo, ~ivate, ~ivano
> **Past hist** ~ii, ~isti, ~ì, ~immo, ~iste, ~irono
> **Fut** ~irò, ~irai, ~irà, ~iremo, ~irete, ~iranno
> **Pres sub** ~a, ~a, ~a, ~iamo, ~iate, ~ano
> **Past sub** ~issi, ~issi, ~isse, ~issimo, ~iste, ~issero
> **Pres part** ~endo
> **Past part** ~ito
> **Imp** ~i (*fml* ~a), ~iamo, ~ite
> **Cond** ~irei, ~iresti, ~irebbe, ~iremmo, ~ireste, ~irebbero

Notes

- Many verbs in the third conjugation take *isc* between the stem and the ending in the first, second, and third person singular and in the third person plural of the present, the present subjunctive, and the imperative: fin|ire **Pres** ~isco, ~isci, ~isce, ~iscono. **Pres sub** ~isca, ~iscano **Imp** ~isci.

- The three forms of the imperative are the same as the corresponding forms of the present for the second and third conjugation. In the first conjugation the forms are also the same except for the second person singular: present *compri*, imperative *compra*. The negative form of the second person singular is formed by putting *non* before the infinitive for all conjugations: *non comprare*. In polite forms the third person of the present subjunctive is used instead for all conjugations: *compri*.

Italian verb tables

. . . .

Irregular verbs:

Certain forms of all irregular verbs are regular (except for *essere*). These are: the second person plural of the present, the past subjunctive, and the present participle. Forms not listed below can be derived from the parts given. Only those irregular verbs considered to be the most useful are shown in the tables.

accadere *as* cadere

accendere • **Past hist** accesi, accendesti • **Past part** acceso

affliggere • **Past hist** afflissi, affliggesti • **Past part** afflitto

ammettere *as* mettere

andare • **Pres** vado, vai, va, andiamo, andate, vanno • **Fut** andrò *etc* • **Pres sub** vada, vadano • **Imp** va', vada, vadano

apparire • **Pres** appaio *or* apparisco, appari *or* apparisci, appare *or* apparisce, appaiono *or* appariscono • **Past hist** apparvi *or* apparsi, apparisti, apparve *or* apparì *or* apparse, apparvero *or* apparirono *or* apparsero • **Pres sub** appaia *or* apparisca

aprire • **Pres** apro • **Past hist** aprii, apristi • **Pres sub** apra • **Past part** aperto

avere • **Pres** ho, hai, ha, abbiamo, hanno • **Past hist** ebbi, avesti, ebbe, avemmo, aveste, ebbero • **Fut** avrò *etc* • **Pres sub** abbia *etc* • **Imp** abbi, abbia, abbiate, abbiano

bere • **Pres** bevo *etc* • **Impf** bevevo *etc* • **Past hist** bevvi *or* bevetti, bevesti • **Fut** berrò *etc* • **Pres sub** beva *etc* • **Past sub** bevessi *etc* • **Pres part** bevendo • **Cond** berrei *etc*

cadere • **Past hist** caddi, cadesti • **Fut** cadrò *etc*

chiedere • **Past hist** chiesi, chiedesti • **Pres sub** chieda *etc* • **Past part** chiesto *etc*

chiudere • **Past hist** chiusi, chiudesti • **Past part** chiuso

cogliere • **Pres** colgo, colgono • **Past hist** colsi, cogliesti • **Pres sub** colga • **Past part** colto

correre • **Past hist** corsi, corresti • **Past part** corso

crescere • **Past hist** crebbi • **Past part** cresciuto

cuocere • **Pres** cuocio, cuociamo, cuociono • **Past hist** cossi, cocesti • **Past part** cotto

dare • **Pres** do, dai, da, diamo, danno • **Past hist** diedi *or* detti, desti • **Fut** darò *etc* • **Pres sub** dia *etc* • **Past sub** dessi *etc* • **Imp** da' (*fml* dia)

dire • **Pres** dico, dici, dice, diciamo, dicono • **Impf** dicevo *etc* • **Past hist** dissi, dicesti • **Fut** dirò *etc* • **Pres sub** dica, diciamo, diciate, dicano • **Past sub** dicessi *etc* • **Pres part** dicendo • **Past part** detto • **Imp** di' (*fml* dica)

dovere • **Pres** devo *or* debbo, devi, deve, dobbiamo, devono *or* debbono • **Fut** dovrò *etc* • **Pres sub** deva *or* debba, dobbiamo, dobbiate, devano *or* debbano • **Cond** dovrei *etc*

essere • **Pres** sono, sei, è, siamo, siete, sono • **Impf** ero, eri, era, eravamo, eravate, erano • **Past hist** fui, fosti, fu, fummo, foste, furono • **Fut** sarò *etc* • **Pres sub** sia *etc* • **Past sub** fossi, fossi, fosse, fossimo, foste, fossero • **Past part** stato • **Imp** sii (*fml* sia), siate • **Cond** sarei *etc*

fare • **Pres** faccio, fai, fa, facciamo, fanno • **Impf** facevo *etc* • **Past hist** feci, facesti • **Fut** farò *etc* • **Pres sub** faccia *etc* • **Past sub** facessi *etc* • **Pres part** facendo • **Past part** fatto • **Imp** fa' (*fml* faccia) • **Cond** farei *etc*

fingere • **Past hist** finsi, fingesti, finsero • **Past part** finto

giungere • **Past hist** giunsi, giungesti, giunsero • **Past part** giunto

leggere • **Past hist** lessi, leggesti • **Past part** letto

mettere • **Past hist** misi, mettesti • **Past part** messo

morire • **Pres** muoio, muori, muore, muoiono • **Fut** morirò *or* morrò *etc* • **Pres sub** muoia • **Past part** morto

muovere • **Past hist** mossi, movesti • **Past part** mosso

nascere • **Past hist** nacqui, nascesti • **Past part** nato

offrire • **Past hist** offersi *or* offrii, offristi • **Pres sub** offra • **Past part** offerto

parere • **Pres** paio, pari, pare, pariamo, paiono • **Past hist** parvi *or* parsi, paresti • **Fut** parrò *etc* • **Pres sub** paia, paiamo *or* pariamo, pariate, paiano • **Past part** parso

piacere • **Pres** piaccio, piaci, piace, piacciamo, piacciono • **Past hist** piacqui,

Italian verb tables

• •

piacesti, piacque, piacemmo, piaceste, piacquero • **Pres sub** piaccia *etc* • **Past part** piaciuto

porre • **Pres** pongo, poni, pone, poniamo, ponete, pongono • **Impf** ponevo *etc* • **Past hist** posi, ponesti • **Fut** porrò *etc* • **Pres sub** ponga, poniamo, poniate, pongano • **Past sub** ponessi *etc*

potere • **Pres** posso, puoi, può, possiamo, possono • **Fut** potrò *etc* • **Pres sub** possa, possiamo, possiate, possano • **Cond** potrei *etc*

prendere • **Past hist** presi, prendesti • **Past part** preso

ridere • **Past hist** risi, ridesti • **Past part** riso

rimanere • **Pres** rimango, rimani, rimane, rimaniamo, rimangono • **Past hist** rimasi, rimanesti • **Fut** rimarrò *etc* • **Pres sub** rimanga • **Past part** rimasto • **Cond** rimarrei

salire • **Pres** salgo, sali, sale, saliamo, salgono • **Pres sub** salga, saliate, salgano

sapere • **Pres** so, sai, sa, sappiamo, sanno • **Past hist** seppi, sapesti • **Fut** saprò *etc* • **Pres sub** sappia *etc* • **Imp** sappi (*fml* sappia), sappiate • **Cond** saprei *etc*

scegliere • **Pres** scelgo, scegli, sceglie, scegliamo, scelgono • **Past hist** scelsi, scegliesti *etc* • **Past part** scelto

scrivere • **Past hist** scrissi, scrivesti *etc* • **Past part** scritto

sedere • **Pres** siedo *or* seggo, siedi, siede, siedono • **Pres sub** sieda *or* segga

spegnere • **Pres** spengo, spengono • **Past**

hist spensi, spegnesti • **Past part** spento

stare • **Pres** sto, stai, sta, stiamo, stanno • **Past hist** stetti, stesti • **Fut** starò *etc* • **Pres sub** stia *etc* • **Past sub** stessi *etc* • **Past part** stato • **Imp** sta' (*fml* stia)

tacere • **Pres** taccio, tacciono • **Past hist** tacqui, tacque, tacquero • **Pres sub** taccia

tendere • **Past hist** tesi • **Past part** teso

tenere • **Pres** tengo, tieni, tiene, tengono • **Past hist** tenni, tenesti • **Fut** terrò *etc* • **Pres sub** tenga

togliere • **Pres** tolgo, tolgono • **Past hist** tolsi, tolse, tolsero • **Pres sub** tolga, tolgano • **Past part** tolto • **Imp** *fml* tolga

trarre • **Pres** traggo, trai, trae, traiamo, traete, traggono • **Past hist** trassi, traesti • **Fut** trarrò *etc* • **Pres sub** tragga • **Past sub** traessi *etc* • **Past part** tratto

uscire • **Pres** esco, esci, esce, escono • **Pres sub** esca • **Imp** esci (*fml* esca)

valere • **Pres** valgo, valgono • **Past hist** valsi, valesti • **Fut** varrò *etc* • **Pres sub** valga, valgano • **Past part** valso • **Cond** varrei *etc*

vedere • **Past hist** vidi, vedesti • **Fut** vedrò *etc* • **Past part** visto *or* veduto • **Cond** vedrei *etc*

venire • **Pres** vengo, vieni, viene, vengono • **Past hist** venni, venisti • **Fut** verrò *etc*

vivere • **Past hist** vissi, vivesti • **Fut** vivrò *etc* • **Past part** vissuto • **Cond** vivrei *etc*

volere • **Pres** voglio, vuoi, vuole, vogliamo, volete, vogliono • **Past hist** volli, volesti • **Fut** vorrò *etc* • **Pres sub** voglia *etc* • **Imp** vogliate • **Cond** vorrei *etc*

Verbi inglesi

Infinitive	Past Tense	Past Participle	Infinitive	Past Tense	Past Participle
Infinito	*Passato*	*Participio passato*	*Infinito*	*Passato*	*Participio passato*
arise	arose	arisen	**fall**	fell	fallen
awake	awoke	awoken	**feed**	fed	fed
be	was	been	**feel**	felt	felt
bear	bore	borne	**fight**	fought	fought
beat	beat	beaten	**find**	found	found
become	became	become	**flee**	fled	fled
begin	began	begun	**fling**	flung	flung
behold	beheld	beheld	**fly**	flew	flown
bend	bent	bent	**forbid**	forbade	forbidden
beseech	beseeched	beseeched	**forget**	forgot	forgotten
	besought	besought	**forgive**	forgave	forgiven
bet	bet,	bet,	**forsake**	forsook	forsaken
	betted	betted	**freeze**	froze	frozen
bid	bade,	bidden,	**get**	got	got,
	bid	bid			gotten *Am*
bind	bound	bound	**give**	gave	given
bite	bit	bitten	**go**	went	gone
bleed	bled	bled	**grind**	ground	ground
blow	blew	blown	**grow**	grew	grown
break	broke	broken	**hang**	hung,	hung,
breed	bred	bred		hanged (*vt*)	hanged
bring	brought	brought	**have**	had	had
build	built	built	**hear**	heard	heard
burn	burnt,	burnt,	**hew**	hewed	hewed,
	burned	burned			hewn
burst	burst	burst	**hide**	hid	hidden
bust	busted,	busted,	**hit**	hit	hit
	bust	bust	**hold**	held	held
buy	bought	bought	**hurt**	hurt	hurt
cast	cast	cast	**keep**	kept	kept
catch	caught	caught	**kneel**	knelt	knelt
choose	chose	chosen	**know**	knew	known
cling	clung	clung	**lay**	laid	laid
come	came	come	**lead**	led	led
cost	cost,	cost,	**lean**	leaned,	leaned,
	costed (*vt*)	costed		leant	leant
creep	crept	crept	**leap**	leapt,	leapt,
cut	cut	cut		leaped	leaped
deal	dealt	dealt	**learn**	learnt,	learnt,
dig	dug	dug		learned	learned
do	did	done	**leave**	left	left
draw	drew	drawn	**lend**	lent	lent
dream	dreamt,	dreamt,	**let**	let	let
	dreamed	dreamed	**lie**	lay	lain
drink	drank	drunk	**light**	lit,	lit,
drive	drove	driven		lighted	lighted
dwell	dwelt	dwelt	**lose**	lost	lost
eat	ate	eaten	**make**	made	made

Infinitive	Past Tense	Past Participle	Infinitive	Past Tense	Past Participle
Infinito	*Passato*	*Participio passato*	*Infinito*	*Passato*	*Participio passato*
mean	meant	meant	**spell**	spelled, spelt	spelled, spelt
meet	met	met			
mow	mowed	mown, mowed	**spend**	spent	spent
			spill	spilt, spilled	spilt, spilled
overhang	overhung	overhung			
pay	paid	paid	**spin**	spun	spun
put	put	put	**spit**	spat	spat
quit	quitted, quit	quitted, quit	**split**	split	split
			spoil	spoilt, spoiled	spoilt, spoiled
read	read /red/	read /red/			
rid	rid	rid	**spread**	spread	spread
ride	rode	ridden	**spring**	sprang	sprung
ring	rang	rung	**stand**	stood	stood
rise	rose	risen	**steal**	stole	stolen
run	ran	run	**stick**	stuck	stuck
saw	sawed	sawn, sawed	**sting**	stung	stung
			stink	stank	stunk
say	said	said	**strew**	strewed	strewn, strewed
see	saw	seen			
seek	sought	sought	**stride**	strode	stridden
sell	sold	sold	**strike**	struck	struck
send	sent	sent	**string**	strung	strung
set	set	set	**strive**	strove	striven
sew	sewed	sewn, sewed	**swear**	swore	sworn
			sweep	swept	swept
shake	shook	shaken	**swell**	swelled	swollen, swelled
shear	sheared	shorn, sheared			
			swim	swam	swum
shed	shed	shed	**swing**	swung	swung
shine	shone	shone	**take**	took	taken
shit	shit	shit	**teach**	taught	taught
shoe	shod	shod	**tear**	tore	torn
shoot	shot	shot	**tell**	told	told
show	showed	shown	**think**	thought	thought
shrink	shrank	shrunk	**thrive**	thrived, throve	thrived, thriven
shut	shut	shut			
sing	sang	sung	**throw**	threw	thrown
sink	sank	sunk	**thrust**	thrust	thrust
sit	sat	sat	**tread**	trod	trodden
slay	slew	slain	**understand**	understood	understood
sleep	slept	slept	**undo**	undid	undone
slide	slid	slid	**wake**	woke	woken
sling	slung	slung	**wear**	wore	worn
slit	slit	slit	**weave**	wove	woven
smell	smelt, smelled	smelt, smelled	**weep**	wept	wept
			wet	wet, wetted	wet, wetted
sow	sowed	sown, sowed			
			win	won	won
speak	spoke	spoken	**wind**	wound	wound
speed	sped, speeded	sped, speeded	**wring**	wrung	wrung
			write	wrote	written